FIRST SIGHT.

FIRST STRIRE.

PILKINGTON
OPTRONICS

Barr & Stroud Limited
1 Linthouse Road, Govan, Glasgow G51 4BZ
Telephone: 041-440 4000
Fax: 041-440 4001

Dusk. The constant surveillance of a nation's maritime frontiers goes on. Watches change, but the equipment remains on continuous alert.

The watchful eyes of the nation.

A supreme responsibility that demands the supreme vision of Pilkington Optronics – manufacturers of the most advanced submarine periscope and mast systems – from midget to nuclear – to 14 of today's navies.

Pilkington Optronics non-hull penetrating sensor systems keep them at the leading edge of technology.

The far-seeing naval forces of tomorrow.

First choice!

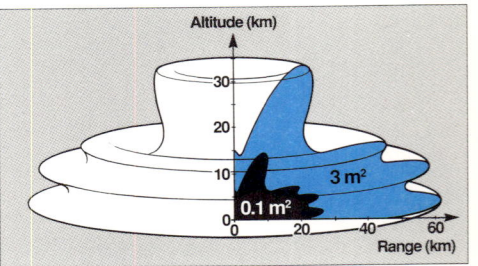

Sea GIRAFFE has been chosen for a large number of new ships up to and including frigate size.

Chosen for its performance and cost effectiveness.

You can detect and designate air and surface targets at full combat ranges – no matter how small, fast, sea skimming or high-diving – also in heavily jammed and cluttered environment.

You get proven high performance, growth potential, low life-cycle costs and complete logistic support.

Your ships survival depends on first class surveillance.

Fit Sea GIRAFFE – first choice for the nineties and beyond.

Ericsson Radar Electronics AB
S-431 84 Mölndal, Sweden
Phone: +46 31 671000. Fax: +46 31 671703

JANE'S FIGHTING SHIPS

FOUNDED IN 1897 BY FRED T JANE

EDITED BY

Captain RICHARD SHARPE OBE RN

1993-94

ISBN 0 7106 1065 3
JANE'S DATA DIVISION
"Jane's" is a registered trade mark

Copyright © 1993 by Jane's Information Group Limited, Sentinel House, 163 Brighton Road, Coulsdon, Surrey CR5 2NH, UK

In the USA and its dependencies
Jane's Information Group Inc, 1340 Braddock Place, Suite 300, Alexandria, VA 22314-1651, USA

All rights reserved. No part of this publication may be reproduced, stored in retrieval systems or transmitted in any form or by any means, electronic, mechanical, photocopying, recording or otherwise, without the prior written permission of the Publishers.
Licences, particularly for use of the data in databases or local area networks are available on application to the Publishers.
Infringements of any of the above rights will be liable to prosecution under UK or US civil or criminal law.
Whilst every care has been taken in the compilation of this publication to ensure its accuracy at the time of going to press, the Publishers cannot be held responsible for any errors or omissions or any loss arising therefrom.

British Library Cataloguing-in-Publication Data.
A catalogue record for this book is available from the British Library.

Printed and bound in Great Britain by Butler and Tanner Limited, Frome and London.

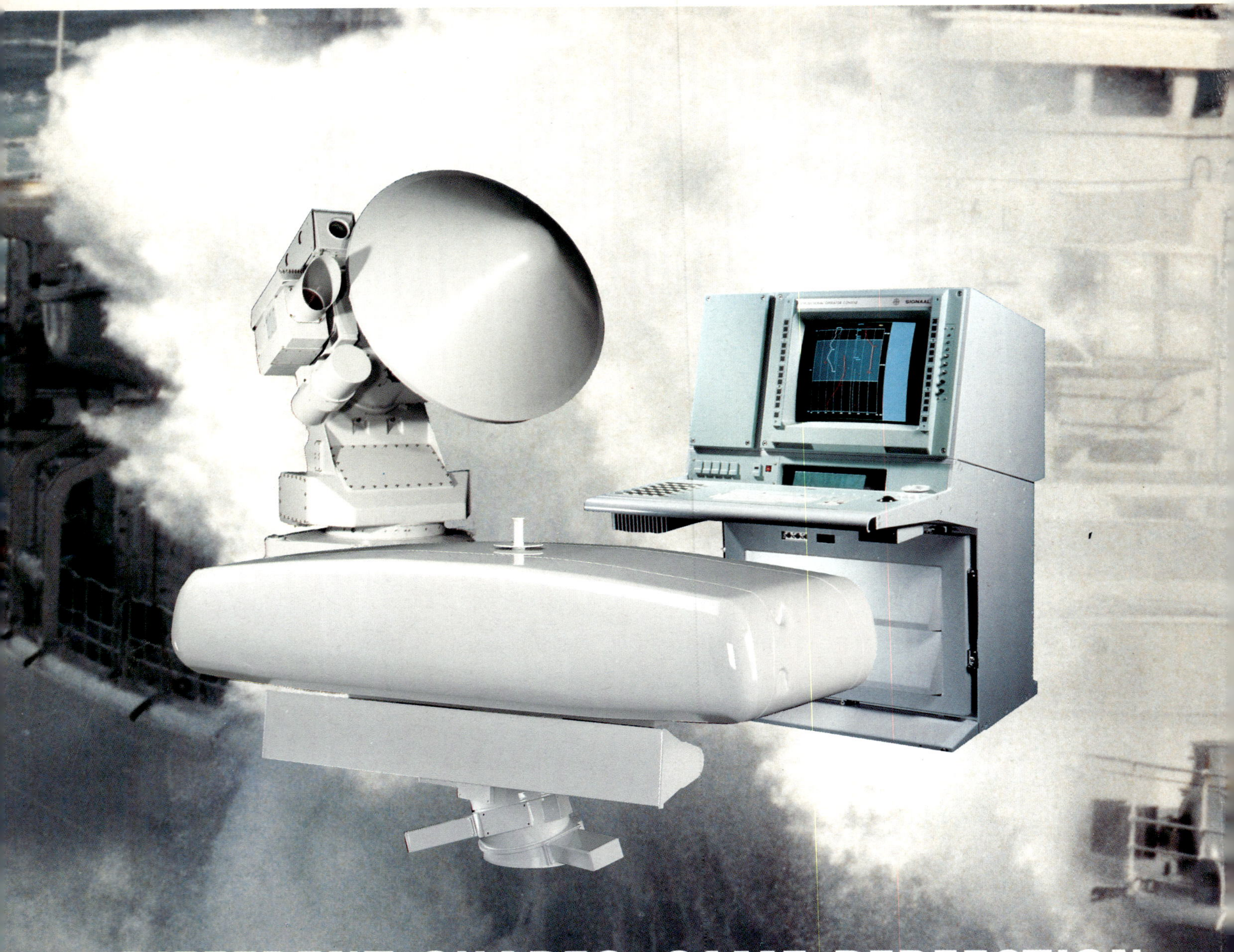

DIFFERENT SHAPES, SAME PERFECTION
An unparalleled combination for small to medium patrol craft

Developed from the same high tech designs as SIGNAAL's blue water fleet versions, compact, lightweight, state-of-the-art systems such as TACTICOS, STING and VARIANT are perfectly suited to guard Exclusive Economic Zones (EEZ's) and to protect valuable sea lanes.

Integrated into a Fully Distributed architecture, SIGNAAL's latest SEWACO FD configuration provides a technical solution today for the requirements of tomorrow. Reduced manpower, commonality of components and corresponding low cost make this integrated system as impressive as some ocean waves.

The core of the SEWACO FD system is the TACTICOS Command & Control system. A variable number of Multifunction Operator Consoles (MOC) with excellent high definition full-colour presentation, fabulous processing power and Ada programming, make TACTICOS a flexible system.

Using advanced processing techniques, the STING dual-band gun and missile fire control director acquires and tracks very small and fast manoeuvring targets automatically. A TV/IR camera permits passive operations.

The VARIANT surveillance and target indication radar combines a dual-band pulse doppler main radar and a single-band Low Probability of Intercept CW radar to provide Air/Surveillance target detection and tracking. Meticulous surface target tracking (TWS) provides superior gun-fire targeting accuracy.

Different shapes, same perfection and increased performance supplied by SIGNAAL.

Hollandse Signaalapparaten B.V.   P.O. Box 42   7550 GD Hengelo Ov   The Netherlands   Telephone +31.74.488111   Fax +31.74.425936

SPECIALISTS IN NAVAL COMBAT SYSTEMS

Contents

Foreword ... [39]	Faeroes ... 187	Nicaragua ... 442
	Falkland Islands ... 187	Nigeria ... 443
Acknowledgements ... [63]	Fiji ... 188	Norway ... 448
	Finland ... 189	Oman ... 456
Glossary ... [65]	France ... 199	Pakistan ... 462
	Gabon ... 229	Panama ... 471
Flags and Ensigns of the World's Navies ... [67]	Gambia ... 230	Papua New Guinea ... 473
	Georgia ... 230	Paraguay ... 474
	Germany ... 231	Peru ... 476
Ranks and Insignia of the World's Navies ... [75]	Ghana ... 251	Philippines ... 484
	Greece ... 252	Poland ... 490
	Grenada ... 265	Portugal ... 500
Pennant List of Major Surface Ships ... [97]	Guatemala ... 266	Qatar ... 508
	Guinea ... 267	Romania ... 509
	Guinea-Bissau ... 268	Russia and associated States ... 515
SHIP REFERENCE SECTION	Guyana ... 269	
Albania ... 2	Haiti ... 269	St Kitts-Nevis ... 597
Algeria ... 4	Honduras ... 270	St Lucia ... 597
Angola ... 8	Hong Kong ... 271	St Vincent and the Grenadines ... 598
Anguilla ... 9	Hungary ... 274	Saudi Arabia ... 599
Antigua and Barbuda ... 9	Iceland ... 275	Senegal ... 605
Argentina ... 10	India, Navy ... 276	Seychelles ... 607
Australia ... 22	Coast Guard ... 291	Sierra Leone ... 608
Austria ... 34	Indonesia ... 292	Singapore ... 608
Azerbaijan ... 35	Iran ... 305	Solomon Islands ... 613
Bahamas ... 36	Iraq ... 312	Somalia ... 613
Bahrain ... 37	Ireland ... 315	South Africa ... 614
Bangladesh ... 40	Israel ... 316	Spain ... 617
Barbados ... 46	Italy ... 321	Sri Lanka ... 635
Belgium ... 47	Ivory Coast ... 340	Sudan ... 638
Belize ... 51	Jamaica ... 341	Surinam ... 639
Benin ... 52	Japan, Maritime Self Defence Force ... 342	Sweden ... 640
Bermuda ... 52		Switzerland ... 656
Bolivia ... 53	Maritime Safety Agency ... 364	Syria ... 656
Brazil ... 53	Jordan ... 374	Taiwan ... 659
Brunei ... 68	Kenya ... 375	Tanzania ... 674
Bulgaria ... 70	Korea, Democratic People's Republic (North) ... 376	Thailand ... 675
Burma ... 75		Togo ... 689
Cambodia ... 80	Korea, Republic (South) ... 381	Tonga ... 689
Cameroon ... 81	Kuwait ... 391	Trinidad and Tobago ... 690
Canada, Navy ... 82	Laos ... 392	Tunisia ... 692
Coast Guard ... 93	Latvia ... 392	Turkey ... 694
Cape Verde ... 102	Lebanon ... 393	Turks and Caicos ... 713
Chile ... 103	Liberia ... 394	Uganda ... 713
China, People's Republic ... 114	Libya ... 395	Ukraine ... 714
Colombia ... 138	Lithuania ... 400	United Arab Emirates ... 714
Comoro Islands ... 145	Madagascar ... 401	United Kingdom ... 717
Congo ... 145	Malawi ... 402	United States of America, Navy ... 753
Cook Islands ... 146	Malaysia ... 402	Coast Guard ... 823
Costa Rica ... 146	Maldives ... 410	Uruguay ... 833
Croatia ... 147	Malta ... 411	Vanuatu ... 837
Cuba ... 151	Marshall Islands ... 412	Venezuela ... 837
Cyprus, Republic ... 154	Mauritania ... 413	Vietnam ... 842
Denmark ... 155	Mauritius ... 414	Virgin Islands ... 846
Djibouti ... 166	Mexico ... 415	Western Samoa ... 846
Dominica ... 166	Micronesia ... 423	Yemen ... 847
Dominican Republic ... 167	Montserrat ... 423	Yugoslavia ... 849
Ecuador ... 170	Morocco ... 424	Zaire ... 856
Egypt ... 175	Mozambique ... 427	
El Salvador ... 183	Namibia ... 427	**Indexes**
Equatorial Guinea ... 184	NATO ... 428	Named Ships ... 857
Estonia ... 184	Netherlands ... 428	Classes ... 872
Ethiopia ... 185	New Zealand ... 438	Aircraft ... 875

ADMINISTRATION

Publishing Director: Robert Hutchinson

Managing Editor: Keith Faulkner

Publishing Supervisor: Ruth Simmance

Publishing Assistant: Diana Burns

Product Group (Marketing) Manager: Aine Molloy

EDITORIAL OFFICES

Jane's Information Group Limited, Sentinel House,
163 Brighton Road, Coulsdon, Surrey CR5 2NH, United Kingdom

Tel: 081 763 1030 International +44 81 763 1030
Telex: 916907 Janes G
Fax: 081 763 1006 International +44 81 763 1006

SALES OFFICES

Send enquiries to:
Peter McSherry, Sales Manager,
Jane's Information Group Limited, UK address as above

Send USA enquiries to:
Joe McHale, Senior Vice-President Product Sales,
Jane's Information Group Inc, 1340 Braddock Place, Suite 300,
Alexandria, VA 22314-1651

Tel: +1 703 683 3700
Telex: 6819193
Fax: +1 703 836 0029

ADVERTISEMENT SALES OFFICES

Advertisement Sales Manager: Barbara Urry

Australia: Brendan Gullifer, Havre & Gullifer (PTY) Ltd, 253 Richardson Street, Middle Park, Victoria 3206, Australia

Tel: +61 (3) 6960288
Fax: +61 (3) 6966951

Benelux: Barbara Urry, Jane's Information Group (see United Kingdom)

Brazil: L Bilyk, Brazmedia International S/C Ltda, Alameda Gabriel Monteiro da Silva, 366 CEP, 01442, São Paulo

Tel: +55 11 853 4133
Telex: 32836 BMED BR
Fax: +55 11 852 6485

France: Patrice Février, Jane's Information Group – France, 35 avenue Mac Mahon, F-75017 Paris, France

Tel: +33 1 45 72 3311
Fax: +33 1 45 72 1795

Germany and Austria: Rainer Vogel, Media Services International, Schwabenbergstrasse 12, D-8089 Emmering.

Tel: +49 (8141) 42534
Fax: +49 (8141) 6706

Greece: Anwar Aswad, A&M Advertising & Marketing Consultants, Zaimi 7-9, Apt 1, Palaio-Faliron

Tel: +30 1 982 2577
Telex: 218947 GNM
Fax: +30 1 723 2990

Hong Kong: Jeremy Miller, Major Media Ltd, Room 142, 14F Capitol Centre, 5-19 Jardine's Bazaar, Causeway Bay

Tel: +852 5 890 3110
Fax: +852 5 576 3397

Israel: Oreet Ben-Yaacov, Oreet International Media, 15 Kineret Street 51201 Bene Berak

Tel: +972 3 570 6527
Fax: +972 3 570 6526

Italy and Switzerland: Ediconsult Internazionale Srl, Piazza Fontane Marose 3, I-16123 Genoa

Tel: +39 10 583520, 583684
Telex: 281197 EDINT I
Fax: +39 10 566578

Korea: Young Seoh Chinn, JES Media International, KPO Box 576, Seoul

Tel: +82 2 545 8001/2
Fax: +82 2 549 8861

Singapore, Indonesia, Malaysia, Philippines, Taiwan and Thailand: Hoo Siew Sai, Major Media (Singapore) Pte Ltd, 6th Floor, 52 Chin Swee Road, Singapore 0316

Tel: +65 738 0122
Telex: RS 43370 AMPLS
Fax: +65 738 2108

Spain: Jesus Moran Iglesias, Varex SA, Modesto Lafuente 4, E-28010 Madrid

Tel: +34 1 448 7622
Fax: +34 1 446 0198

USA and Canada: Kimberly S. Hanson, Director of Advertising Sales and Marketing, Jane's Information Group Inc, 1340 Braddock Place, Suite 300, Alexandria, VA 22314-1651

Tel: +1 703 683 3700
Telex: 6819193
Fax: +1 703 836 0029

USA South Eastern Region: Kristin Schulze, Regional Advertising Manager
(see United States and Canada)

USA North Eastern Region and Canada: Melissa C Gunning, Regional Advertising Manager

USA Western Region and Canada: Anne Marie St. John-Brooks, Regional Advertising Manager, Jane's Information Group, 1523 Rollins Road, Burlingame, CA 94010

Tel: (415) 259 9982
Fax: (415) 259 9751

United Kingdom/Rest of World: Barbara Urry, Jane's Information Group, Sentinel House, 163 Brighton Road, Coulsdon, Surrey CR5 2NH

Tel: 081 763 1030 International +44 81 763 1030
Telex: 916907 Janes G
Fax: 081 763 1006 International +44 81 763 1006

Administration: Tara Betts, Jane's Information Group
(see United Kingdom)

Alphabetical list of advertisers

A

acbLIPS S. A
F-44040 Nantes Cedex 1,
France .... [5]

Alenia Elsag Sistemi Navali
28/30 Via di S. Alessandro,
I-00131 Rome, Italy .... [13]

B

Barr & Stroud
1 Linthouse Road, Govan,
Glasgow, G51 4B7
Scotland .... *Facing Inside Front Cover*

Bofors Weapon Systems
S-691 80 Karlskoga,
Sweden .... [15]

C

Castoldi SpA
Viale Mazzini 161,
I-20081 Abbiategrasso, Milan, Italy .... [25]

Chantiers de l'Atlantique (GEC Alsthom)
38 avenue Kleber, F-75116 Paris,
France .... *Facing Inside Back Cover*

C. I. S. DEG
Via GB Morgagni 30/E,
I-00161 Rome, Italy .... [31]

Consorzio SMIN SpA
Via Panama 52, I-00198 Rome,
Italy .... [23]

Crestitalia SpA
Via Armezzone 1, I-19031 Ameglia (SP),
Italy .... [21]

CRM SpA
41 Via Marnate, I-21053 Castellanza,
Italy .... [29]

D

Daewoo Shipbuilding & Heavy Machinery Ltd
541 Namdaemun ro 5-GA,
Chung-Gu, Seoul, Korea .... [11]

Danyard Aalborg A/S
PO Box 660, DK-9100,
Aalborg, Denmark .... [9]

DCN International
19-21 rue du Colonel Pierre Avia,
F-75015 Paris, France .... [19]

E

Elbit Ltd
PO Box 539, Haifa 31053,
Israel .... [66]

Elettronica SpA
Via Tiburtina Km 13.700,
Rome, Italy .... [33]

Empresa Nacional Bazan
55 Castellana, E-28046 Madrid 1,
Spain .... [62]

Etienne Lacroix Défense
BP 213, F-31601 Muret,
Cedex France .... *Back Index*

Ericsson Radar Electronics AB
S-431 84 Mölndal, Sweden .... *Facing Page* [1]

Eurocorvette
38 avenue Kléber,
F-75116 Paris, France .... [56]

F

Fincantieri Cantieri Navali Italiani SpA
Via Cipro 11, I-16129 Genoa, Italy .... [27]

FR Lürssen Werft (GmbH & Co)
PO Box 75 06 62, D-28020 Bremen-Vegesack,
Germany .... [46]

Yarrow Shipbuilders Limited

LEAD SHIPBUILDER FOR THE TYPE 23 FRIGATE SETTING NEW STANDARDS FOR THE 21ST CENTURY

DESIGN · CONSTRUCTION · WEAPON ENGINEERING · SUPPORT

CORVETTE   **GRP MCMV**   **WEAPON ENGINEERING**

SOUTH STREET · SCOTSTOUN · GLASGOW G14 0XN
Tel: 041-959 1207   Telex: 77357   Fax: 041-958 0642

A Member Company of GEC

ALPHABETICAL LIST OF ADVERTISERS

France Helices
Z. I. de la Frayère,
F-06150 Cannes la Bocca,
France .... [25]

H

HDW
PO Box 14 63 09, D-2300 Kiel 14,
Germany .... [52]

Hollandse Signaalapparaten BV
PO Box 42, Hengelo 7550 GD,
The Netherlands .... [2]

Hyundai Heavy Industries Company Ltd
Special & Naval Shipbuilding Division,
1 Cheonha-don, Ulsan, Republic of Korea ...... [32]

I

Ingalls Shipbuilding
PO Box 149, Pascagoula, Mississippi 39568-0149,
USA .... [74]

K

Kelvin Hughes Limited
New North Road, Hainault, Ilford,
Essex IG6 2UR, UK .... [35]

Korea Tacoma Marine Industries Ltd
PO Box 339, Masan, Korea .... [17]

L

Loral Hycor
10 Gill Street, Woburn
MA 01801,USA .... [30]

Loral Librascope
833 Sonora Avenue,
Glendale, CA 91201-0279,
USA .... [42]

M

MacTaggart Scott & Company Ltd
PO Box 1, Hunter Avenue, Loanhead,
Midlothian EH20 9SP, Scotland .... [66]

MagneTek
901E Ball Road,
Anaheim, CA 92805
USA .... [40]

Mathiesen's Baadebyggeri A/S
Baadebyggervej 7, Vestre Badehavn,
DK-9000 Aalborg, Denmark .... [16]

Matra Défense
37 avenue Louis Bréguet
F-78140 Vélizy-Villacoublay Cedex
France .... [96]

N

The Netherlands Naval Industries Group
PO Box 16350, 2500 BJ The Hague,
The Netherlands .... [50]

NEVESBU
PO Box 16350, 2500 BJ The Hague,
The Netherlands .... [60]

P

Pilkington Optronics
1 Linthouse Road, Govan,
Glasgow G51 4BZ, Scotland .... *Facing Inside Front Cover*

R

Riva Calzoni SpA
Via Emilia Ponente 72,
I-40133 Bologna, Italy .... *Inside Front Cover*

Royal Schelde
PO Box 16, 4380 AA, Vlissingen,
Holland .... [38]

OFFSHORE AND COASTAL PATROL VESSELS

STANDARD FLEX FAMILY

- 400 to 1500 t displacement
- Proven designs derived from Danish Niels Juel-class corvettes and Flyvefisken class (Standard Flex 300)
- Multi-role capability
- Helicopter operation capability

OSPREY FAMILY

- 150, 250 and 450 t displacement types available
- Proven design
- Based on experience from Osprey-class ships in service in 3 continents
- Naval, coast guard and customs craft

Purpose-designed for EEZ patrols

Based on Naval Team Denmark accumulated experience from ROYAL DANISH NAVY Beskytteren-class and Thetis-class EEZ operations, and Flyvefisken-class multi-role operations.

DANYARD

member of

DANYARD AALBORG A/S · P.O.Box 660 · DK-9100 Aalborg · Fax +45 99373702

ALPHABETICAL LIST OF ADVERTISERS

S

Safare-Crouzet SA
98 avenue Saint-Lambert,
F-06105 Nice Cedex 2, France .... [35]

SEMT Pielstick
2 quai de Seine, F-93202 Saint-Denis,
France .... [58]

Société Française Materials d'Armement (SOFMA)
17 blvd Malesherbes, F-75008 Paris,
France .... [48]

Sperry Marine Inc
1070 Seminole Trail,
Charlottesville, VA-22901,
USA .... [44]

Sulzer Escher Wyss
D-7980 Ravensburg,
Germany .... [58]

T

The Cincinnati Gear Company
5657 Wooster Pike, Cincinnati,
Ohio 45227, USA .... [54]

Thyssen Nordseewerke GmbH
PO Box 2351, 2361 D-2970 Emden,
Federal Republic of Germany .... [34]

W

Wartsila Diesel Group
40 rue du Moulin des Bruyères,
F-92400 Courbevoie, France .... [64]

Y

Yarrow (Shipbuilders) Ltd
South Street, Scotstoun, Glasgow G14 0XN,
Scotland .... [7]

New Horizon Of Naval Shipbuilding-DAEWOO

As a leading shipbuilder for existing classes of proven major warships for the ROK Navy, we're setting a new pace for the future in warship technology.
- Destroyers, Frigates, Corvettes
- OPVs, Patrol boats,
- Landing ships, Various support ships
- Submarines

DAEWOO
DAEWOO SHIPBUILDING & HEAVY MACHINERY LTD.
NAVAL AND SPECIAL SHIP DIVISION

BUSINESS OFFICE
541 NAMDAEMUN RO 5-GA,
CHUNG-GU, SEOUL, KOREA
C.P.O. BOX 6208, SEOUL, KOREA
TELEX: K24698, 22213 DWOKPO
TEL: (02) 779-0761 FAX: (02) 756-4390

OKPO SHIPYARD
1, AJOO-DONG, CHANSUNG PO,
KYONGSANGNAM-DO, KOREA
TELEX: K52131-5, DWOKPO
TEL: (0558) 680-2114
FAX: (0558) 681-4030

Classified list of advertisers

The companies advertising in this publication have informed us that they are involved in the fields of manufacture indicated below:

Accelerometers
MagneTek Defense

AC Generators for electric systems, ships
MagneTek Defense
Netherlands Naval Industries Group
Wartsila Diesel

Acoustic range equipment
Safare-Crouzet

Acoustic transducers
Safare-Crouzet

Action information systems
Elbit Computers

Action speed tactical trainers (ASTT)
Elbit Computers

Action information systems
Hollandse Signaalapparaten

Air cushion vehicles
DCN
Hyundai Heavy Industries
Korea Tacoma Marine

Aircraft arresting gear
MacTaggart Scott

Aircraft carriers
DCN
Ingalls Shipbuilding
Sperry Marine
Swan Hunter

Air-sea rescue launches
Castoldi
FR Lürssen Werft

Ammunition
Bofors
Empresa Nacional Bazan
Etienne Lacroix

Ammunition fuzes
Bofors
DCN
Etienne Lacroix
Matra Défense

Ammunition hoists
DCN
MacTaggart Scott

Amphibious ships
Chantiers de l'Atlantique
Hyundai Heavy Industries
Ingalls Shipbuilding
Korea Tacoma Marine
Royal Schelde
Swan Hunter
Yarrow Shipbuilders

Antennas
Elbit Computers
Elettronica
Hollandse Signaalapparaten
Sperry Marine

Anti-aircraft missiles
Matra Défense

Anti-aircraft missiles (ship-launched)
Bofors
Matra Défense

Anti-ship missiles
Matra Défense

Anti-ship missile defence systems
Bofors
Breda Meccanica Bresciana
Empresa Nacional Bazan
Hollandse Signaalapparaten
Matra Défense

Anti-ship missile (ship-launched)
DCN
Matra Défense

Anti-submarine launchers
DCN
Loral Librascope
Matra Défense

Anti-submarine rocket launchers
DCN
Matra Défense

Anti-submarine systems
Bofors
Matra Défense
Loral Librascope
Safare-Crouzet

Anti-submarine systems integration
Safare-Crouzet

Anti-submarine weapon systems, long-range
Loral Librascope
Matra Défense
Safare-Crouzet

Anti-tank missiles
Bofors
Matra Défense

Armoured vehicles
Bofors
SOFMA

Artificial intelligence
DCN
Elbit Computers
NEVESBU

Artillery
Bofors
Empresa Nacional Bazan

Assault craft
Crestitalia
Daewoo Shipbuilding & Heavy Machinery
FR Lürssen Werft
Hyundai Heavy Industries

Assault ships
Chantiers de l'Atlantique
Crestitalia
Daewoo Shipbuilding & Heavy Machinery
DCN
FR Lürssen Werft
Ingalls Shipbuilding
SOFMA
Yarrow Shipbuilders

ASW helicopter mission simulators
DCN

ASW weapon control systems
DCN
Hollandse Signaalapparaten
Safare-Crouzet

Automatic control systems
Riva Calzoni
Safare-Crouzet

Auxiliary machinery
DCN
Empresa Nacional Bazan
Wartsila Diesel

Auxiliary propulsion systems
Empresa Nacional Bazan
France Helics
MacTaggart Scott
MagneTek Defense
Riva Calzoni
Wartsila Diesel

Auxiliary vessels
Chantiers de l'Atlantique
Daewoo Shipbuilding & Heavy Machinery
DCN
Empresa Nacional Bazan
Fincantieri
FR Lürssen Werft
Hyundai Heavy Industries
Ingalls Shipbuilding
Yarrow Shipbuilders

Boilers
Empresa Nacional Bazan
Daewoo Shipbuilding & Heavy Machinery
DCN
Hyundai Heavy Industries

Bulk carriers
Chantiers de l'Atlantique
Daewoo Shipbuilding & Heavy Machinery
Fincantieri
Hyundai Heavy Industries
Sperry Marine

Cable-laying vessels
Daewoo Shipbuilding & Heavy Machinery
Fincantieri
Hyundai Heavy Industries

Cable looms
DCN

Capstans and windlasses
MacTaggart Scott
Riva Calzoni

Car ferries
Chantiers de l'Atlantique
Daewoo Shipbuilding & Heavy Machinery
DCN
Fincantieri
Hyundai Heavy Industries
Sperry Marine

Cargo handling equipment
Hyundai Heavy Industries
MacTaggart Scott

Cargo ships
Chantiers de l'Atlantique
Daewoo Shipbuilding & Heavy Machinery
Fincantieri
Sperry Marine

Castings, aluminium-bronze
DCN
France Helics
Netherlands Naval Industries Group

Castings, high-duty iron
DCN
Netherlands Naval Industries Group

Castings, non-ferrous
DCN
Netherlands Naval Industries Group

ALENIA ELSAG SISTEMI NAVALI. ADVANCED ELECTRONICS FOR SAILING IN SAFE WATERS.

Alenia Elsag Sistemi Navali has specialized for more than 30 years in advanced electronic systems. The Company, which is coordinated by Alenia, operates producing search radars, command and control systems, surface-to-air missile systems, radar and electro-optical tracking systems, sonar systems for surface and underwater units, all operational with the Italian Navy and with those of many other countries. These reliable high technology systems guarantee the safety and defense of those who work at sea. Alenia Elsag Sistemi Navali makes sailing in safe waters a reality.

Alenia Elsag Sistemi Navali

A F I N M E C C A N I C A C O M P A N Y

CLASSIFIED LIST OF ADVERTISERS

Castings, shell-moulded
DCN
Netherlands Naval Industries Group

Castings, SG iron
DCN
Netherlands Naval Industries Group

Castings, steel
DCN
Netherlands Naval Industries Group

Catamarans, multi-role, high-speed and workboats
Daewoo Shipbuilding & Heavy Machinery
DCN
Fincantieri
Hyundai Heavy Industries
Sperry Marine

Centralised & automatic control
Riva Calzoni
Safare-Crouzet

Chaff
Bofors
Etienne Lacroix

Chaff dispensers
Elbit Computers
Etienne Lacroix
Matra Défense

Chaff launchers
Bofors
Etienne Lacroix

Coast guard
Fincantieri

Coast guard/patrol ships
Chantiers de l'Atlantique
Crestitalia
Daewoo Shipbuilding & Heavy Machinery
DCN
Empresa Nacional Bazan
Hyundai Heavy Industries
Korea Tacoma Marine
Netherlands Naval Industries Group
SOFMA
Sperry Marine
Yarrow Shipbuilders

Coast guard systems
FR Lürssen Werft
Safare-Crouzet

Coastal and inshore minesweepers
Crestitalia
DCN
FR Lürssen Werft
Netherlands Naval Industries Group
SOFMA
Yarrow Shipbuilders

Combat support boats
Crestitalia
Daewoo Shipbuilding & Heavy Machinery
FR Lürssen Werft
Hyundai Heavy Industries
Netherlands Naval Industries Group

Combat systems engineering
C. I. S. DEG
DCN
Empresa Nacional Bazan
Hollandse Signaalapparaten
Loral Librascope
Safare-Crouzet
Yarrow Shipbuilders

Command/control/communications systems
Elbit Computers
Elettronica
Empresa Nacional Bazan
Hollandse Signaalapparaten
Loral Librascope
Safare-Crouzet
Sperry Marine

Command/control real-time displays
Elbit Computers
Hollandse Signaalapparaten
Loral Librascope
Sperry Marine

Communications systems
Elbit Computers
Loral Librascope
Safare-Crouzet
Sperry Marine

Computer-assisted communications systems
Elbit Computers
Safare-Crouzet
Sperry Marine

Computer guidance
Sperry Marine

Computers
Hollandse Signaalapparaten
Netherlands Naval Industries Group

Computer services
NEVESBU

Construction, extension and modernisation
C. I. S. DEG
Empresa Nacional Bazan
Hyundai Heavy Industries

Container ships
Chantiers de l'Atlantique
Daewoo Shipbuilding & Heavy Machinery
Fincantieri
Hyundai Heavy Industries
Sperry Marine

Control desks, electric
Netherlands Naval Industries Group

Corvettes
Chantiers de l'Atlantique
Daewoo Shipbuilding & Heavy Machinery
DCN
Empresa Nacional Bazan
Eurocorvette
Fincantieri
FR Lürssen Werft
Hyundai Heavy Industries
Ingalls Shipbuilding
Korea Tacoma Marine
Netherlands Naval Industries Group
Sperry Marine
Yarrow Shipbuilding

Countermeasures
Elettronica
Loral Librascope
MacTaggart Scott
MagneTek Defense
Matra Défense
NobelTech Electronics
Safare-Crouzet
Sperry Marine

Craneships
Daewoo Shipbuilding & Heavy Machinery
Fincantieri
Hyundai Heavy Industries
Sperry Marine

Cruisers
Chantiers de L'Atlantique
Fincantieri
Ingalls Shipbuilding
Sperry Marine

Cruise liners
Chantiers de l'Atlantique
Fincantieri
Sperry Marine

Current limiting devices
MagneTek Defense

Custom craft
Daewoo Shipbuilding & Heavy Machinery

Data links
Elbit Computers
Hollandse Signaalapparaten
Signaal Special Products
Sperry Marine

Data recording systems
Hollandse Signaalapparaten
Signaal Special Products

DC power supplies
MagneTek Defense
Signaal Special Products
Wartsila Diesel

Deck machinery
DCN
Hyundai Heavy Industries
MacTaggart Scott
Riva Calzoni

Decoy systems (anti-ship missile)
Etienne Lacroix
Safare-Crouzet

Deep ocean survey
Safare-Crouzet

Defence contractors
Elbit Computers
Elettronica
Hollandse Signaalapparaten
MagneTek Defense
Safare-Crouzet

Degaussing systems
MagneTek Defense

Design of fast patrol boats/craft
Crestitalia
Daewoo Shipbuilding & Heavy Machinery
DCN
Empresa Nacional Bazan
Fincantieri
FR Lürssen Werft
Hyundai Heavy Industries
Korea Tacoma Marine
NEVESBU

Design-systems study and management services
C. I. S. DEG
Empresa Nacional Bazan
Ingalls Shipbuilding
NEVESBU
Safare-Crouzet

Destroyers
Chantiers de l'Atlantique
DCN
Empresa Nacional Bazan
Fincantieri
Hyundai Heavy Industries
Korea Tacoma Marine
Sperry Marine
Yarrow Shipbuilding

Diesel engines
CRM
Hyundai Heavy Industries
SEMT Pielstick
Wartsila Diesel

Diesel engines, auxiliary
Empresa Nacional Bazan
Fincantieri
Hyundai Heavy Industries
Netherlands Naval Industries Group
SEMT Pielstick
Wartsila Diesel

Diesel engines for locomotives
SEMT Pielstick

Success and survival

Warships are faster and more versatile than ever before. But their degree of success and their means to survive can depend ultimately on their air and surface defence capability.

Bofors 57 mm Mk2 Multi-purpose Gun is compact, easy to use in all weather conditions and utilizes the latest stealth technology to minimize its radar signature – an essential parameter in modern warfare.

Reaction time is short, dispersion is low, the gun opens up, engages a surface target, shifts immediately to a missile or aircraft, back to a surface target with splitsecond change of ammunition while still maintaining its rate of fire.

The 57 mm Mk2 together with its specially designed ammunition forms a defence system that enhances mission success and the means to survive.

Bofors Proximity-Fuzed Prefregmented High Explosive shell (PFHE) defeats any aerial target with proximity or impact function.

Bofors High Capacity Extended Range shell (HCER) with impact fuze and built-in delay penetrates the hull before devastating the interior.

Bofors Weapon Systems
S-691 80 KARLSKOGA, Sweden
Telephone +46 586 810 00
Telefax +46 586 581 45. Telex 73210 bofors s

CLASSIFIED LIST OF ADVERTISERS

Diesel engines, main propulsion
Empresa Nacional Bazan
Fincantieri
Hyundai Heavy Industries
Netherlands Naval Industries Group
SEMT Pielstick
Wartsila Diesel

Diesel engine spare parts
Empresa Nacional Bazan
Fincantieri
Netherlands Naval Industries Group
SEMT Pielstick
Wartsila Diesel

Digital databus systems, shipborne
Alenia Elsag Sistemi Navali
Elbit Computers
Hollandse Signaalapparaten

Display systems
Elbit Computers
Hollandse Signaalapparaten
Sperry Marine

Distress beacon-submariner
Safare-Crouzet

Diver communications
Safare-Crouzet

Diving equipment
DCN
Safare-Crouzet

Diving systems
DCN
MacTaggart Scott
Safare-Crouzet

Diving vessels
Crestitalia
Daewoo Shipbuilding & Heavy Machinery
DCN
Hyundai Heavy Industries
Korea Tacoma Marine

Dock gates
DCN
MacTaggart Scott

Dredgers
Chantiers de l'Atlantique
Daewoo Shipbuilding & Heavy Machinery
DCN
Hyundai Heavy Industries
Sperry Marine

Dry cargo vessel
Chantiers de l'Atlantique
Daewoo Shipbuilding & Heavy Machinery
Fincantieri
Hyundai Heavy Industries
Sperry Marine

Dry dock proprietors
DCN
Empresa Nacional Bazan

Dynamic positioning
Riva Calzoni

Early warning systems
Elettronica
Hollandse Signaalapparaten
Safare-Crouzet

Early warning systems, infa-red
Elettronica
Hollandse Signaalapparaten

Echo sounders
Safare-Crouzet

Electric-propulsion control panel on submarines
MagneTek Defense

Electrical auxiliaries
MagneTek Defense
Wartsila Diesel

Electrical equipment
MagneTek Defense
Wartsila Diesel

Electrical installations and repairs
DCN
Netherlands Naval Industries Group
Wartsila Diesel

Electrical switchgear
Netherlands Naval Industries Group

Electro-hydraulic auxiliaries
DCN
Hyundai Heavy Industries
MacTaggart Scott
Riva Calzoni

Electro-optics for airborne naval and ground defence
Barr & Stroud
Elettronica
Hollandse Signaalapparaten
Pilkington Optronics

Electronic countermeasures
Barr & Stroud
Elettronica
Loral Librascope
MagneTek Defense
Matra Défense
Pilkington Optronics
Safare-Crouzet
Sperry Marine

A well earned reputation of fastmoving composite structures makes us feel confident in offering you our services.
New vessels and repair jobs up to 85'0" L.O.A.
Pilot boats & Launches

May we serve you?

MATHIESEN'S BAADEBYGGERI A/S
BAADEBYGGERVEJ 7
DK-9000 AALBORG
DENMARK   Phone 08 120550
             Fax   081 28198

Jane's
INFORMATION GROUP

Leading suppliers of impartial, factual, professional information to the defence, aerospace and transport industries.

The Group's unique capabilities for research and analysis enables it to provide the most comprehensive information from a single source.

JANE'S INFORMATION GROUP
the unique answer to your intelligence requirements

Sentinel House
163 Brighton Road
Coulsdon
Surrey CR5 2NH
United Kingdom
Tel: (081) 763 1030

1340 Braddock Place
Suite 300
Alexandria
VA 22314-1651
United States
Tel: (703) 683 3700

Our Specialty Helps Build Up Your Navy

If you wish to add to your naval defence, it can better come true with us on our long experience.

- HOVERCRAFT
- FAST PATROL BOAT
- OFFSHORE PATROL VESSEL
- CORVETTE
- FRIGATE
- LANDING SHIP TANK

KOREA TACOMA MARINE INDUSTRIES, LTD.

MAIN OFFICE/SHIPYARD
- PO BOX 339, MASAN, KOREA
- TEL: (551) 55-1181-8
- TLX: K53662, KOTAMAN
- FAX: (551) 94-9449

MARKETING DIVISION, SEOUL
- CPO BOX 4296, SEOUL, KOREA
- TEL: (2) 728-5446-8, 754-2410
- TLX: K27526, KALHO
- FAX: (2) 757-0884

CLASSIFIED LIST OF ADVERTISERS

Electronic engine room telegraph
Safare-Crouzet

Electronic equipment
DCN
Matra Défense
MagneTek Defense
Riva Calzoni
Safare-Crouzet
Sperry Marine

Electronic equipment refits
DCN
MagneTek Defense
Safare-Crouzet

Electronic power systems
MagneTek Defense
Safare-Crouzet

Electronic warfare (communications)
Elettronica
Safare-Crouzet

Electronic warfare evaluation systems
Elettronica
Safare-Crouzet
Sperry Marine

Engine monitors and data loggers
SEMT Pielstick

Engine parts, diesel
CRM
Empresa Nacional Bazan
Netherlands Naval Industries Group
SEMT Pielstick
Wartsila Diesel

Engine speed controls
MagneTek Defense

Engine start and shut-down controls
DCN
Hyundai Heavy Industries

Engines, diesel
Empresa Nacional Bazan
Fincantieri
Hyundai Heavy Industries
Netherlands Naval Industries Group
SEMT Pielstick
Wartsila Diesel

Engines, gas turbine
Empresa Nacional Bazan
Hyundai Heavy Industries

Engines, steam turbine
Empresa Nacional Bazan

Equipment for helicopters
DCN
Elbit Computers

Equipment protection
Signaal Special Products

Exhibition organisers
DCN

Fast attack craft
Crestitalia
Daewoo Shipbuilding & Heavy Machinery
DCN
Fincantieri
FR Lürssen Werft
Hyundai Heavy Industries
Yarrow Shipbuilders

Fast patrol craft
Crestitalia
Daewoo Shipbuilding & Heavy Machinery
DCN
Empresa Nacional Bazan
Fincantieri
Hyundai Heavy Industries
Korea Tacoma Marine
Sperry Marine
Yarrow Shipbuilders

Fast strike craft
Crestitalia
Daewoo Shipbuilding & Heavy Machinery
DCN
FR Lürssen Werft
Yarrow Shipbuilders

Fast offshore patrol and attack craft
Crestitalia
Daewoo Shipbuilding & Heavy Machinery
DCN
Empresa Nacional Bazan
Fincantieri
FR Lürssen Werft
Korea Tacoma Marine
Netherlands Naval Industries Group
Royal Schelde
Yarrow Shipbuilders

Fast warship design service
Daewoo Shipbuilding & Heavy Machinery
DCN
Empresa Nacional Bazan
FR Lürssen Werft
Ingalls Shipbuilding
Korea Tacoma Marine
Yarrow Shipbuilders

Ferries
Chantiers de l'Atlantique
Daewoo Shipbuilding & Heavy Machinery
DCN
Fincantieri
FR Lürssen Werft
Korea Tacoma Marine
Sperry Marine

Fibreglass vessels and other products
Crestitalia
Empresa Nacional Bazan

Fibre optics
Hollandse Signaalapparaten
Safare-Crouzet
Sperry Marine

Fire control systems
Barr & Stroud
Elbit Computers
Hollandse Signaalapparaten
Loral Librascope
Pilkington Optronics

Fire control and gunnery equipment
Barr & Stroud
Hollandse Signaalapparaten
Pilkington Optronics

Firefighting ships
Crestitalia
Daewoo Shipbuilding & Heavy Machinery
Empresa Nacional Bazan
FR Lürssen Werft
Korea Tacoma Marine

Fishery protection
Chantiers de l'Atlantique
Crestitalia
Empresa Nacional Bazan
FR Lürssen Werft

Fittings, ships
Empresa Nacional Bazan
Netherlands Naval Industries Group

Flares
Etienne Lacroix

Forgings, steel
Empresa Nacional Bazan

Frequency converters
MagneTek Defense

Frigates
Chantiers de l'Atlantique
Daewoo Shipbuilding & Heavy Machinery
DCN
Empresa Nacional Bazan

Eurocorvette
Fincantieri
Hyundai Heavy Industries
Korea Tacoma Marine
Netherlands Naval Industries Group
Royal Schelde
Sperry Marine
Yarrow Shipbuilding

Frigates (light)
Chantiers de l'Atlantique
Daewoo Shipbuilding & Heavy Machinery
DCN
Empresa Nacional Bazan
Eurocorvette
FR Lürssen Werft
Hyundai Heavy Industries
Ingalls Shipbuilding
Netherlands Naval Industries Group
Royal Schelde
Yarrow Shipbuilding

Gas turbine boats
Empresa Nacional Bazan
FR Lürssen Werft

Gas turbines
Empresa Nacional Bazan

Generators, diesel
Netherlands Naval Industries Group
SEMT Pielstick
Wartsila Diesel

Generators, electric
MagneTek Defense
Netherlands Naval Industries Group

Glassfibre vessels and other products
DCN
Empresa Nacional Bazan
FR Lürssen Werft
Yarrow Shipbuilders

Guided missile launcher systems
FR Lürssen Werft
Matra Défense

Guided missiles
Matra Défense

Guided missile ships
Chantiers de l'Atlantique
Daewoo Shipbuilding & Heavy Machinery
DCN
Ingalls Shipbuilding
Matra Défense

Gunnery equipment
Empresa Nacional Bazan

Guns and mountings
DCN
Empresa Nacional Bazan

Harbour defence vessels
Daewoo Shipbuilding & Heavy Machinery
Crestitalia
FR Lürssen Werft

Heat exchangers
Empresa Nacional Bazan

Heavy-duty mooring motorboats
Crestitalia
Mathiesen's Badebyggeri

Helicopter handling systems
MacTaggart Scott
Riva Calzoni
SOFMA

Helicopter, maritime reconnaissance
Aerospace

High energy laser systems
Barr & Stroud
Pilkington Optronics

CLASSIFIED LIST OF ADVERTISERS

Hydraulic equipment
DCN
MacTaggart Scott
Riva Calzoni

Hydraulic Machinery
DCN
MacTaggart Scott
Riva Calzoni

Hydraulic plant
DCN
Riva Calzoni
Wartsila Diesel

Hydrofoils
DCN
Fincantieri
Hyundai Heavy Industries
Safare-Crouzet
Sperry Marine

Hydraulic survey equipment/vessels
Daewoo Shipbuilding & Heavy Machinery
FR Lürssen Werft
Hyundai Heavy Industries

Hydrographic survey equipment/vessels
Chantiers de l'Atlantique
Crestitalia
Daewoo Shipbuilding & Heavy Machinery
DCN
Empresa Nacional Bazan
MacTaggart Scott
NEVESBU
Yarrow Shipbuilders

Icebreakers
Chantiers de l'Atlantique
Ingalls Shipbuilding
Sperry Marine

IFF radar
Hollandse Signaalapparaten

Infra-red countermeasure systems
Etienne Lacroix
Matra Défense

Infra-red materials
Barr & Stroud
Pilkington Optronics

Infra-red search & tracking systems
Barr & Stroud
Elettronica
Hollandse Signaalapparaten
Pilkington Optronics

Infra-red systems
Barr & Stroud
Elettronica
Hollandse Signaalapparaten
Pilkington Optronics

Instruments, electronic
Safare-Crouzet
Sperry Marine

Instruments, test equipment
Hollandse Signaalapparaten
Safare-Crouzet

Integrated communications systems
Safare-Crouzet
Sperry Marine

Integrated logistic support
Barr & Stroud
Elbit Computers
Elettronica
Hollandse Signaalapparaten
MagneTek Defense
Pilkington Optronics
Royal Schelde
Safare-Crouzet
Sperry Marine

Intercommunications systems
Safare-Crouzet
Sperry Marine

Interior design and furnishing for ships
DCN
Empresa Nacional Bazan

Inverters and battery chargers
MagneTek Defense

Landing craft
Crestitalia
Daewoo Shipbuilding & Heavy Machinery
DCN
Empresa Nacional Bazan
Fincantieri
FR Lürssen Werft
Hyundai Heavy Industries
Korea Tacoma Marine

Landing craft, logistics
Daewoo Shipbuilding & Heavy Machinery
Empresa Nacional Bazan
Fincantieri
FR Lürssen Werft
Hyundai Heavy Industries
Korea Tacoma Marine
Sperry Marine
Yarrow Shipbuilders

Landing ship tank
Chantiers de l'Atlantique
Daewoo Shipbuilding & Heavy Machinery
FR Lürssen Werft
Hyundai Heavy Industries
Korea Tacoma Marine
Yarrow Shipbuilders

Laser rangefinders
Barr & Stroud
Pilkington Optronics

Laser systems
Barr & Stroud
Pilkington Optronics

Launches, rescue
Crestitalia

Lifeboats/rescue
Crestitalia
Fincantieri

Lifts, hydraulic
MacTaggart Scott

Logistics management services
C. I. S. DEG
Empresa Nacional Bazan
Hollandse Signaalapparaten
MagneTek Defense
Safare-Crouzet

Logistics support information systems
C. I. S. DEG
Empresa Nacional Bazan
MagneTek Defense
Safare-Crouzet
SOFMA
Wartsila Diesel
Yarrow Shipbuilders

Logistics support vessels
Daewoo Shipbuilding & Heavy Machinery
DCN
Empresa Nacional Bazan
Hyundai Heavy Industries
Korea Tacoma Marine
Sperry Marine
Yarrow Shipbuilding

Machined parts, ferrous
DCN
Empresa Nacional Bazan

Machined parts, non-ferrous
DCN

Magnetic measurements facilities
MagneTek Defense

Maintenance and repair ships
Chantiers de l'Atlantique
DCN
Empresa Nacional Bazan
Ingalls Shipbuilding
Netherlands Naval Industries Group

Management services
C. I. S. DEG
Hollandse Signaalapparaten

Marine architects
Daewoo Shipbuilding & Heavy Machinery
DCN
NEVESBU

Marine consultants
Daewoo Shipbuilding & Heavy Machinery
NEVESBU
Safare-Crouzet

Marine electronic equipment
Netherlands Naval Industries Group
Safare-Crouzet
Sperry Marine
Wartsila Diesel

Marine engine monitoring and data recording systems
Safare-Crouzet
Wartsila Diesel

Merchant ships
Chantiers de l'Atlantique
Daewoo Shipbuilding & Heavy Machinery
Hyundai Heavy Industries
Fincantieri
Royal Schelde
Sperry Marine

Microwave components
Elettronica
Hollandse Signaalapparaten

Microwave systems
Elettronica
Hollandse Signaalapparaten
Royal Schelde

Mines
Bofors
DCN
Etienne Lacroix

Mines (exercise)
Bofors
DCN

Mines (naval)
Bofors
DCN

Mines and countermining charges
Bofors
DCN

Mines countermeasure vessels
Crestitalia
DCN
FR Lürssen Werft
Yarrow Shipbuilders

Mine countermeasures
Consorzio SMIN
DCN
FR Lürssen Werft
MacTaggart Scott
MagneTek Defense

Minehunters
Crestitalia
DCN
Fincantieri
FR Lürssen Werft

Crestitalia S.p.A.

M/V 85' FAST PATROL BOAT

Length overall	27,00 m
Maximum beam	6,95 m
Full load displacement	80 tons
Range at economic speed	48 hours at 18 knots
Construction material	structural composite materials
Propulsion	2 x M.T.U. 16 V 396 TB 94
Developing a total of	3480 HP each
Maximum speed	45 knots

Manufacturers of Fast Patrol Boats and Rescue Crafts in the range from 7 to 40 meters, currently supplied to the Port Authority, the Coast Guard, the Navy, the Police and the Custom Force in Italy and abroad.

M/V 100' DIVERS SUPPORT BOAT

Length overall	31,35 m
Maximum beam	6,90 m
Full load displacement	100 tons
Range at economic speed	24 hours at 18 knots
Construction material	structural composite materials
Propulsion	2 x M.T.U. 12 V 396 TB 93
Developing a total of	1975 HP each
Maximum speed	27 knots

M/V 45' FAST PATROL BOAT

Length overall	14,52 m
Maximum beam	3,80 m
Full load displacement	17 tons
Range at economic speed	275 n.m.
Construction material	structural composite materials
Propulsion	2 x 635 HP
Maximum speed	plus 32 knots

Shipyard and Sales Offices
Cantiere e Sege Legale:
19031 Ameglia (SP) - Via Armezzone 1
Tel.: 39-187-65.583 / 65.746
Telefax 39-187-65.282 - Telex 283042 CRESTI I

Liason Offices:
Sedi Secondarie:
20151 Milano - Via Gallarate 34 D
Tel.: 39-02-32.71.873

00192 Roma - Via Ottaviano, 32
Tel.: 39-06-31.85.94

CLASSIFIED LIST OF ADVERTISERS

Netherlands Naval Industries Group
SOFMA
Yarrow Shipbuilders

Minehunting support and training systems
FR Lürssen Werft
Riva Calzoni

Minelayers
Fincantieri
FR Lürssen Werft
Hyundai Heavy Industries
Yarrow Shipbuilders

Minesweepers
FR Lürssen Werft
Netherlands Naval Industries Group
SOFMA
Yarrow Shipbuilders

Minesweeping equipment
MagneTek Defense
MacTaggart Scott
Safare-Crouzet
SOFMA
Wartsila Diesel

Missile control systems
Hollandse Signaalapparaten
Matra Défense

Missile installations
DCN
Hyundai Heavy Industries
Matra Défense

Missile launching systems
DCN
Loral Librascope
Matra Défense
Riva Calzoni

Missile ships
Chantiers de l'Atlantique
Crestitalia
Daewoo Shipbuilding & Heavy Machinery
DCN
FR Lürssen Werft
Hyundai Heavy Industries
Ingalls Shipbuilding
Matra Défense
Yarrow Shipbuilders

Motors, hydraulic
DCN
Hyundai Heavy Industries
MacTaggart Scott
Riva Calzoni

Motor Torpedo boats
FR Lürssen Werft

Naval architects
DCN
Hyundai Heavy Industries
Ingalls Shipbuilding
Netherlands Naval Industries Group
NEVESBU
Royal Schelde
Yarrow Shipbuilders

Naval-based design
Daewoo Shipbuilding & Heavy Machinery
FR Lürssen Werft
Ingalls Shipbuilding
NEVESBU
Wartsila Diesel

Naval guns
Bofors
Empresa Nacional Bazan

Naval patrol vessels
Crestitalia
Daewoo Shipbuilding & Heavy Machinery
DCN
Empresa Nacional Bazan
Eurocorvette
Fincantieri

FR Lürssen Werft
Hyundai Heavy Industries
Ingalls Shipbuilding
Korea Tacoma Marine
Netherlands Naval Industries Group
SOFMA
Sperry Marine
Yarrow Shipbuilders

Naval radar
Hollandse Signaalapparaten
Sperry Marine

Naval systems, installation
C. I. S. DEG
Empresa Nacional Bazan
Hollandse Signaalapparaten
Hyundai Heavy Industries
Ingalls Shipbuilding
Netherlands Naval Industries Group
NEVESBU
Safare-Crouzet
Sperry Marine

Naval systems, planning and integration
C. I. S. DEG
Elbit Computers
Ingalls Shipbuilding
NEVESBU
Riva Calzoni
Safare-Crouzet
Sperry Marine

Navigation aids
Sperry Marine

NBC protecion equipment
Elbit Computers
Etienne Lacroix
SOFMA

Night vision systems
Barr & Stroud
Elbit Computers
Elettronica
Hollandse Signaalapparaten
Pilkington Optronics
Swedish Ordnance

Non-hull penetrating masts
Barr & Stroud
MacTaggart Scott
Sperry Marine
Pilkington Optronics
Riva Calzoni

Non-magnetic minesweepers
Crestitalia
FR Lürssen Werft
MacTaggart Scott
Netherlands Naval Industries Group
Yarrow Shipbuilders

Oceanographic survey ships
Chantiers de l'Atlantique
Crestitalia
Daewoo Shipbuilding & Heavy Machinery
DCN
Empresa Nacional Bazan
FR Lürssen Werft
Hyundai Heavy Industries
Korea Tacoma Marine
Royal Schelde
Yarrow Shipbuilders

Offshore countermeasures
FR Lürssen Werft

Offshore patrol vessels
Chantiers de l'Atlantique
Crestitalia
Daewoo Shipbuilding & Heavy Machinery
DCN
Empresa Nacional Bazan
Eurocorvette
Fincantieri
FR Lürssen Werft
Hyundai Heavy Industries
Korea Tacoma Marine

Netherlands Naval Industries Group
Royal Schelde
SOFMA
Sperry Marine
Yarrow Shipbuilders

Oil drilling rigs
Daewoo Shipbuilding & Heavy Machinery
Hyundai Heavy Industries
Sperry Marine
Wartsila Diesel

Oil pollution control vessels
Daewoo Shipbuilding & Heavy Machinery
FR Lürssen Werft
Hyundai Heavy Industries
Sperry Marine

Oil rig supply vessels and work boats
Daewoo Shipbuilding & Heavy Machinery
Fincantieri
Hyundai Heavy Industries
Wartsila Diesel

Optical equipment
Hollandse Signaalapparaten

Optronics
Barr & Stroud
Hollandse Signaalapparaten
Matra Défense
Pilkington Optronics
Sperry Marine

Optronics masts
Barr & Stroud
MacTaggart Scott
Pilkington Optronics
Riva Calzoni
Sperry Marine

Ordnance
Bofors
Empresa Nacional Bazan
Netherlands Naval Industries Group

Parts for diesel engines
Empresa Nacional Bazan
Netherlands Naval Industries Group
SEMT Pielstick
Wartsila Diesel

Passenger ships
Chantiers de l'Atlantique
Crestitalia
Daewoo Shipbuilding & Heavy Machinery
DCN
Fincantieri
Korea Tacoma Marine
Sperry Marine

Patrol boats
Crestitalia
Daewoo Shipbuilding & Heavy Machinery
DCN
Empresa Nacional Bazan
Fincantieri
FR Lürssen Werft
Hyundai Heavy Industries
SOFMA
Sperry Marine
Yarrow Shipbuilders

Patrol boats, launches
Castoldi
Crestitalia
DCN
FR Lürssen Werft
Hyundai Heavy Industries
Korea Tacoma Marine

Patrol boats: launches, tenders and pinnacles
Castoldi
Crestitalia
Daewoo Shipbuilding & Heavy Machinery
DCN
FR Lürssen Werft
Hyundai Heavy Industries

MIN-MK 2
MINE IDENTIFICATION AND NEUTRALIZATION SYSTEM

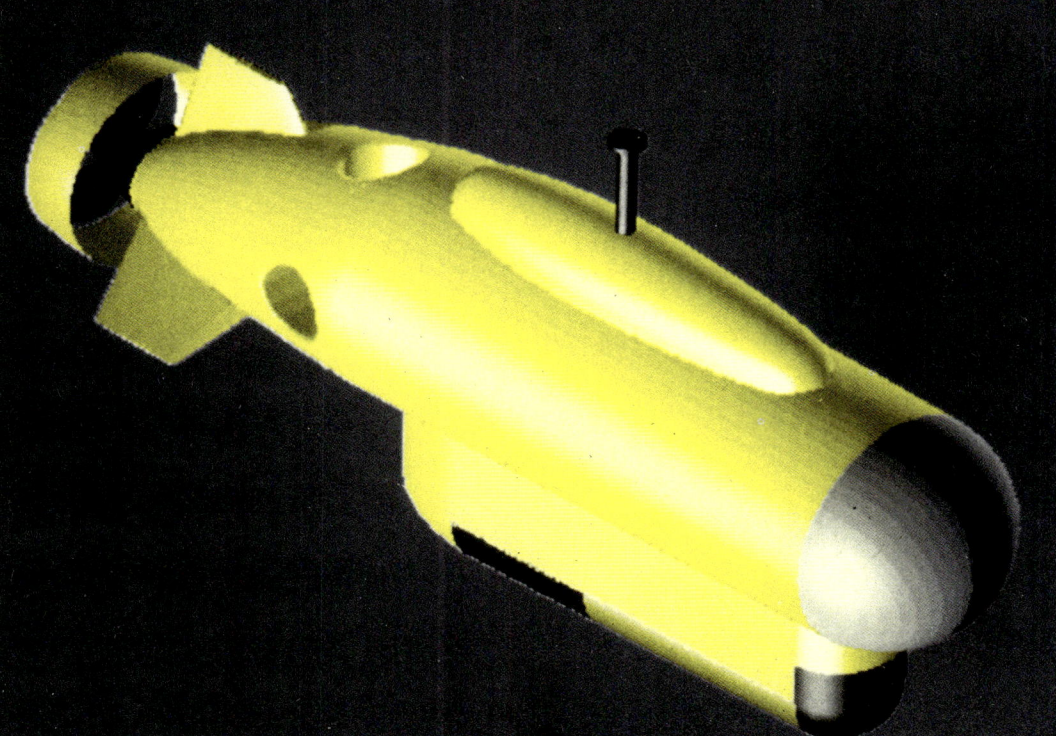

SMIN
- THE SYSTEM ADOPTED BY THE ITALIAN NAVY.
- FULLY INTEGRABLE INSIDE MINE HUNTING AND SWEEPING SUITE.
- MDS WITH NATO CHARGE AND CUTTER
- NEW HIGH DEFINITION SONAR
- TRACKING SYSTEM

CONSORZIO SMIN
52, Via Panama
00198 ROME (Italy)
Phone (06) 8541528
Telefax (06) 862582

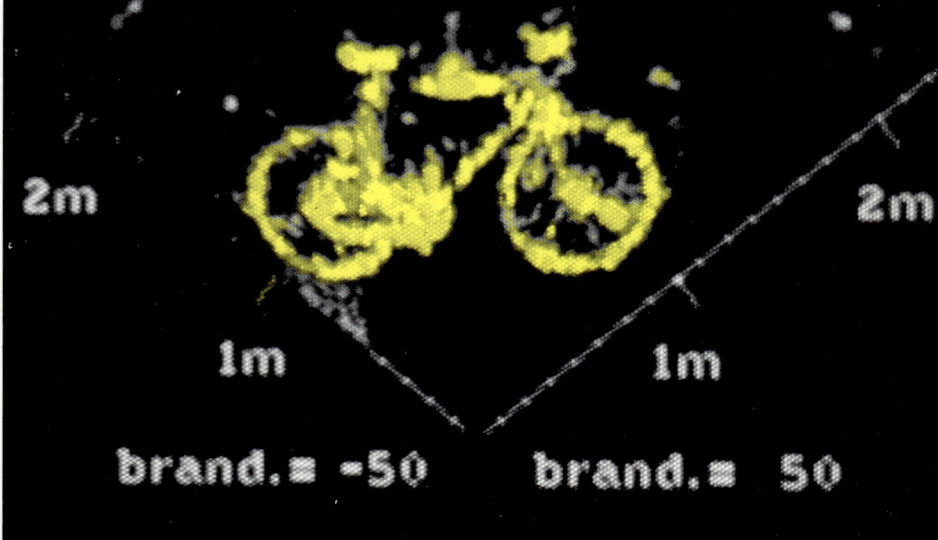

CLASSIFIED LIST OF ADVERTISERS

Periscope fairings
Riva Calzoni

Periscopes
Barr & Stroud
MacTaggart Scott
Pilkington Optronics
Sperry Marine

Periscopes search
Barr & Stroud
MacTaggart Scott
Pilkington Optronics
Sperry Marine

Periscopes attack
Barr & Stroud
MacTaggart Scott
Pilkington Optronics
Sperry Marine

Pilot boats
Crestitalia
Hyundai Heavy Industries

Plotting tables
Hollandse Signaalapparaten
Loral Librascope

Plotting and tracking systems
Hollandse Signaalapparaten
Sperry Marine

Portable and containerised equipment
Hollandse Signaalapparaten

Portable testing equipment
Hollandse Signaalapparaten

Power supplies
Hollandse Signaalapparaten
MagneTek Defense
Wartsila Diesel

Pressure vessels
Daewoo Shipbuilding & Heavy Machinery
Hyundai Heavy Industries

Project management
DCN
Hollandse Signaalapparaten
NEVESBU

Propeller shaft couplings, flexible
DCN
Wartsila Diesel

Propeller shafts
DCN
France Helics
Sulzer
Wartsila Diesel

Propeller shafts and intermediate shafts
DCN
France Helics
Sulzer
Wartsila Diesel

Propellers, ship research
DCN
France Helics
Wartsila Diesel

Propellers, ships
acbLIPS
DCN
France Helics
Hyundai Heavy Industries
Sulzer
Wartsila Diesel

Propulsion gearing
DCN
France Helics
Hyundai Heavy Industries
The Cincinnati Gear Company
Wartsila Diesel

Propulsion machinery
DCN
SEMT Pielstick
Riva Calzoni
Wartsila Diesel

Propulsion machinery control
DCN
SEMT Pielstick
Wartsila Diesel

Propulsion machinery surveillance
DCN
Empresa Nacional Bazan
SEMT Pielstick
Wartsila Diesel

Propulsion systems
DCN
Empresa Nacional Bazan
Fincantieri
France Helics
MacTaggart Scott
MagneTek Defense
SEMT Pielstick
Wartsila Diesel

Pumps
MacTaggart Scott
Netherlands Naval Industries Group

Radar antennas
Hollandse Signaalapparaten
Sperry Marine

Radar countermeasures
Elettronica
Etienne Lacroix
Sperry Marine

Radar for fire control
Hollandse Signaalapparaten

Radar subsystems units
Hollandse Signaalapparaten

Radar transponders
Hollandse Signaalapparaten
Signaal Special Products

Radar, 360 maritime patrol
Hollandse Signaalapparaten

Radio equipment
Sperry Marine

Radio transmitters and receivers
Sperry Marine

Radomes rangefinders
DCN

Railcar diesel engines
SEMT Pielstick

Re-equipment, modernisation of naval vessels
Wartsila Diesel

Remote level indicator equipment for submarine trim tanks
DCN

Remote power control systems
Wartsila Diesel

Research ships
Daewoo Shipbuilding & Heavy Machinery
DCN
Empresa Nacional Bazan
FR Lürssen Werft
Hyundai Heavy Industries
Royal Schelde
Yarrow Shipbuilders

Reverse reduction gears, oil operated
Empresa Nacional Bazan
The Cincinnati Gear Company

Rocket launchers
DCN
Matra Défense

Salvage vessels
Crestitalia
Daewoo Shipbuilding & Heavy Machinery
Korea Tacoma Marine
Hyundai Heavy Industries

Search and rescue vessels
Crestitalia
Daewoo Shipbuilding & Heavy Machinery
Empresa Nacional Bazan
Hyundai Heavy Industries
SOFMA

Ship design
Hyundai Heavy Industries
Ingalls Shipbuilding
NEVESBU
Royal Schelde

Ship and repair yard design
Daewoo Shipbuilding & Heavy Machinery
DCN
Empresa Nacional Bazan
FR Lürssen Werft
Ingalls Shipbuilding
Netherlands Naval Industries Group
NEVESBU

Ship and submarine design
Daewoo Shipbuilding & Heavy Machinery
DCN
Empresa Nacional Bazan
Ingalls Shipbuilding
Fincantieri
Netherlands Naval Industries Group
NEVESBU

Ship defence systems
Barr & Stroud
Bofors
Empresa Nacional Bazan
Hollandse Signaalapparaten
MagneTek Defense
Pilkington Optronics

Ship machinery
Empresa Nacional Bazan
MacTaggart Scott
Riva Calzoni
Wartsila Diesel

Ship repair/refit
Daewoo Shipbuilding & Heavy Machinery
DCN
Empresa Nacional Bazan
Fincantieri
Ingalls Shipbuilding
Wartsila Diesel
Yarrow Shipbuilders

Ship systems engineering
DCN
Hollandse Signaalapparaten
Ingalls Shipbuilding
MacTaggart Scott
NEVESBU
Wartsila Diesel

Simulators
DCN
Elbit Computers
Elettronica
Hollandse Signaalapparaten
Riva Calzoni

Simulators hyperbaric
DCN

Software services
DCN

Sonar decoys
Safare-Crouzet

FRANCE HELICES

6 bladed silent surface piercing propeller

HIGH SPEED PROPELLER MANUFACTURER SPECIALIZED IN CLASS S BRONZE ALUMINIUM AND STAINLESS STEEL PROPELLERS CNC MILLING MANUFACTURING AQUAP 4-ABS-BV-DNV-LRS

Z.I. DE LA FRAYÈRE - 06150 CANNES LA BOCCA - FRANCE
PHONE: 33 93 47 69 38 - FAX: 33 93 47 08 59

FROM CASTOLDI, THE COMPANY UNANIMOUSLY CONSIDERED AS THE INNOVATOR OF WATER JET PROPULSION SYSTEMS

THE MOST TECHNICALLY ADVANCED, EFFICIENT, DURABLE AND COMPLETE WATER JET UNIT FOR FAST BOATS

WITH THE FULL RELIABILITY OF THE MASS PRODUCTION

20 years of thorough research and development have enabled us to develop high class units, built to the highest possible standards. Our facilities allow us to deliver fully and perfectly equipped drives, complete with all components and fittings that we consider are necessary to get the best performance for many years. Among these, the built-in gear box, the integral disconnecting clutch, the movable debris screen rake, the special mechanical, mechanical/hydraulic or electronic/hydraulic proportional controls and the anti-corrosion protection by hard anodizing treatment. More than 20,000 units are propelling all over the world, patrol, rescue and civil work boats; assault, landing and auxiliary craft; passenger ferries; in operation with Naval forces, Coastguards, Customs, Rescue Organisations, Army, Special Corps and Private Companies.

All of these operations appreciate the superb benefits that the Castoldi jet drives grant to their vessels:
- Outstanding manoeuvrability at all speeds and braking capability
- Maximum safety
- High speed performance which regularly outperforms propeller drives in similar installations from 25 knots vp.
- Great sea-keeping characteristics
- Maximum endurance
- Longer engine life
- Minimum service requirement
- Low noise vibration level
- The maximum field of employment from shallow inshore, to rough outshore waters.

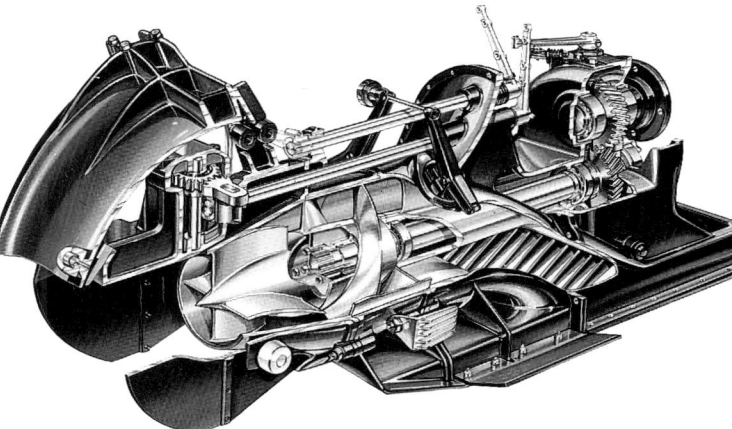

CASTOLDIJET

CASTOLDI S.p.A • Viale Mazzini 161 • 20081 Abbiategrasso • Milano • Italia • tel .+39.2.94821 (12 lin.) • Telex 330236 CAST I • Telefax + 39.2.94960800

CLASSIFIED LIST OF ADVERTISERS

Sonar calibration equipment
Safare-Crouzet

Sonar equipment
Hollandse Signaalapparaten
MagneTek Defense
Safare-Crouzet

Sonar equipment (passive active-intercept)
Safare-Crouzet

Sonar equipment hull fittings and hydraulics
MacTaggart Scott
Riva Calzoni
Safare-Crouzet

Sonar interceptor direction-finder
Safare-Crouzet

Sonar rangers (design and installation)
Safare-Crouzet

Sonobuoys
Safare-Crouzet

Spare parts for diesel engines
Empresa Nacional Bazan
Netherlands Naval Industries Group
Wartsila Diesel

Speed boats
Daewoo Shipbuilding & Heavy Machinery
Mathiesen's Badebyggeri
Hyundai Heavy Industries
Korea Tacoma Marine

Stabilising equipment
DCN
Sperry Marine

Steam-raising plant, conventional
DCN

Steam-raising plant, nuclear
DCN

Steam turbines
Hyundai Heavy Industries

Steel alloy and special steel forgings, plates and section stampings
Empresa Nacional Bazan

Steering gear
MacTaggart Scott

Submarine control systems
Loral Librascope
Safare-Crouzet
SOFMA
Riva Calzoni

Submarine fire control
Loral Librascope

Submarine forward retractable hydroplanes
MacTaggart Scott

Submarine hull equipment
MacTaggart Scott
Netherlands Naval Industries Group
Riva Calzoni

Submarine inverters
MagneTek Defense

Submarine mast actuation
MacTaggart Scott
Riva Calzoni

Submarine snorkels
Riva Calzoni

Submarine team and attack trainers
Loral Librascope

Submarine winches
MacTaggart Scott
Riva Calzoni

Submarines
Daewoo Shipbuilding & Heavy Machinery
DCN
Empresa Nacional Bazan
Fincantieri
Korea Tacoma Marine
Netherlands Naval Industries
SOFMA
Yarrow Shipbuilders

Submarines, conventional
Daewoo Shipbuilding & Heavy Machinery
DCN
Empresa Nacional Bazan
Fincantieri
Netherlands Naval Industries Group
Yarrow Shipbuilders

Submarines, external propelling systems
MacTaggart Scott
Netherlands Naval Industries Group

Submarines, unmanned submersibles
DCN
Riva Calzoni
Safare-Crouzet

Submarines, wet
DCN
Safare-Crouzet

Submersible search and recovery systems
DCN
Riva Calzoni

Supply ships
Chantiers de l'Atlantique
Daewoo Shipbuilding & Heavy Machinery
DCN
Empresa Nacional Bazan
Fincantieri
Hyundai Heavy Industries

Support services
Daewoo Shipbuilding & Heavy Machinery
DCN
Ingalls Shipbuilding
Wartsila Diesel
Yarrow Shipbuilders

Support service vessels
Chantiers de l'Atlantique
DCN
FR Lürssen Werft
Hyundai Heavy Industries

Surface effect ships
DCN
Empresa Nacional Bazan
FR Lürssen Werft
Hyundai Heavy Industries
Royal Schelde

Surveillance craft
Chantiers de l'Atlantique
Crestitalia
Daewoo Shipbuilding & Heavy Machinery
FR Lürssen Werft

Tactical training simulators
DCN
Elettronica

Tankers
Daewoo Shipbuilding & Heavy Machinery
DCN
Fincantieri
Korea Tacoma Marine
SOFMA
Sperry Marine

Tankers, small
Daewoo Shipbuilding & Heavy Machinery
DCN
Sperry Marine

Tanker, vessels
Chantiers de l'Atlantique
DCN
Fincantieri
Hyundai Heavy Industries
Sperry Marine

Technical co-operation
Daewoo Shipbuilding & Heavy Machinery
Hollandse Signaalapparaten
Wartsila Diesel

Technical publications
C. I. S. DEG
Hollandse Signaalapparaten
Ingalls Shipbuilding
Wartsila Diesel

Telecommunications equipment
Safare-Crouzet
Sperry Marine

Tender vessels
Chantiers de l'Atlantique
Crestitalia
Daewoo Shipbuilding & Heavy Machinery
FR Lürssen Werft
Hyundai Heavy Industries
Royal Schelde

Test equipment for fire control systems
Barr & Stroud
DCN
Hollandse Signaalapparaten
Pilkington Optronics

Thermal imaging systems
Barr & Stroud
Elbit Computers
Elettronica
Pilkington Optronics

Throughwater communications
Safare-Crouzet

Thrusters
MagneTek Defense

Torpedo control systems
DCN
Loral Librascope
Safare-Crouzet

Torpedo decoys
DCN
Etienne Lacroix
Loral Librascope
Safare-Crouzet

Torpedo handling systems
MacTaggart Scott
Riva Calzoni

Torpedo launching systems
DCN
Loral Librascope

Torpedo side-launchers
DCN
Korea Tacoma Marine

Torpedo-testing vessels
FR Lürssen Werft
Royal Schelde

Torpedo tubes
DCN

Torpedo workshops
DCN

Torpedoes
DCN

Towed array systems
DCN
MacTaggart Scott

Training equipment
Elbit Computers

L 9892
FINCANTIERI IS
BUILDING FOR THE SEA
FINCANTIERI
Cantieri Navali Italiani S.p.A.
NAVAL SHIPBUILDING DIVISION
16129 Genova/Italy Via Cipro 11
Tel. (0) 10 59951 Tlx 270168 FINCGE I
Fax (0) 10 5995379
IRI
GRUPPO

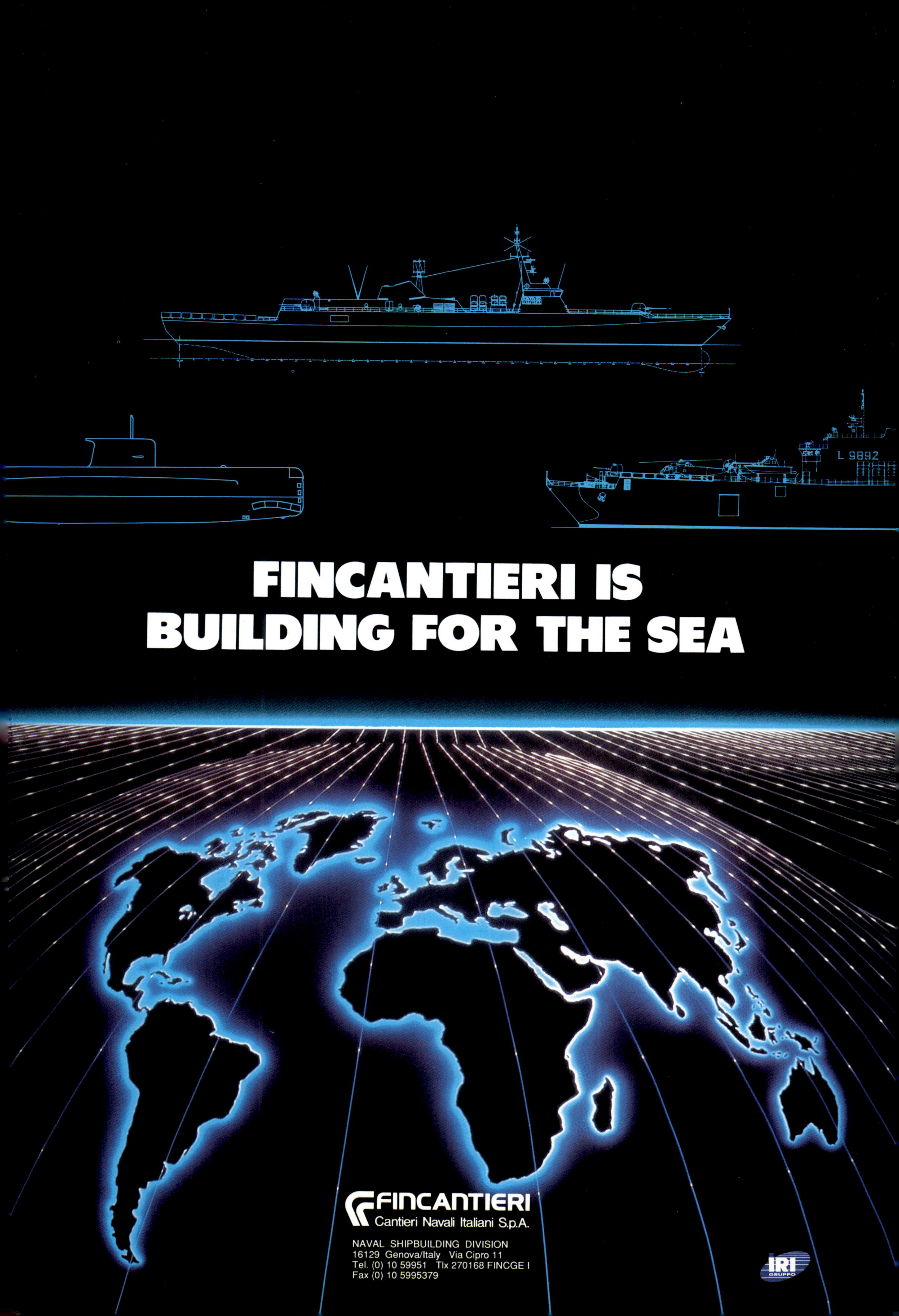

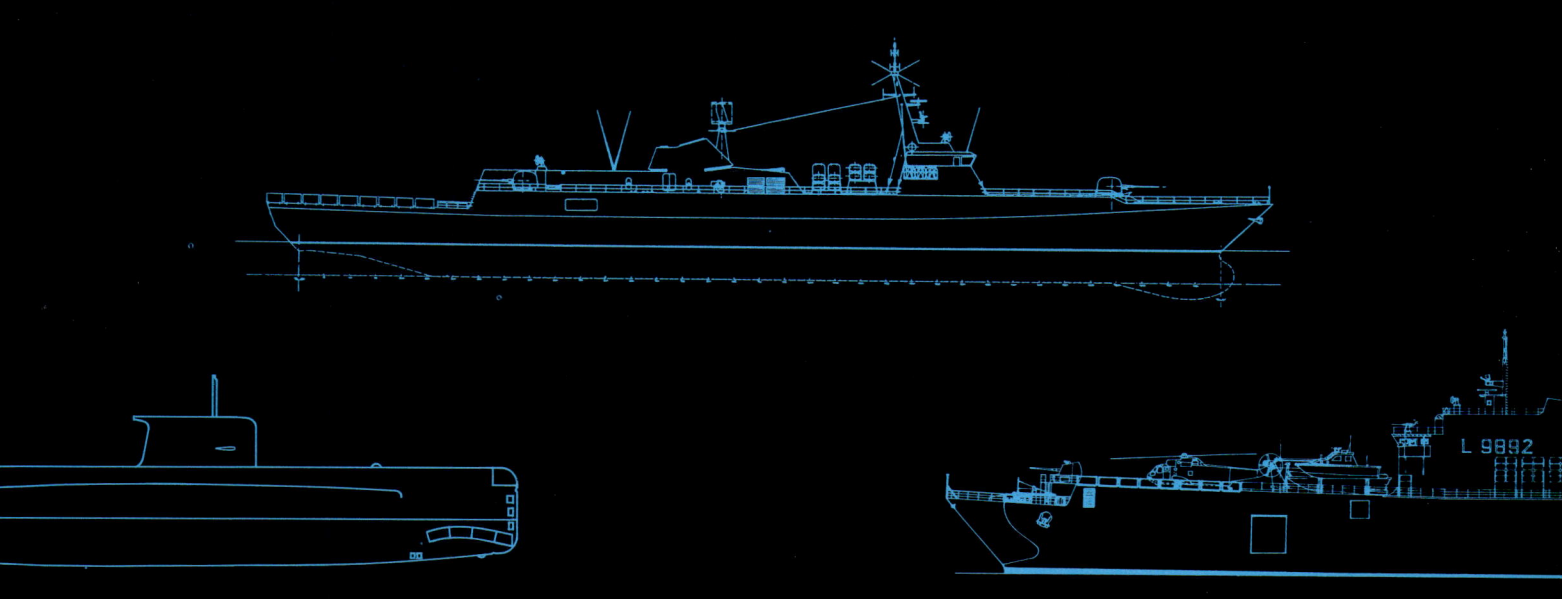

CLASSIFIED LIST OF ADVERTISERS

Etienne Lacroix
DCN
Hollandse Signaalapparaten

Training programmes
C. I. S. DEG
Empresa Nacional Bazan
Hollandse Signaalapparaten
Sperry Marine
Wartsila Diesel

Training services
C. I. S. DEG
Hollandse Signaalapparaten
Sperry Marine
Wartsila Diesel

Transducer arrays
Safare-Crouzet

Transducer calibration
Safare-Crouzet

Transducers
MagneTek Defense
Safare-Crouzet

Trawlers
Mathiesen's Badebyggeri

Troop ships
Chantiers de l'Atlantique
Ingalls Shipbuilding
Korea Tacoma Marine
Sperry Marine

Tugs
Empresa Nacional Bazan
Daewoo Shipbuilding & Heavy Machinery
DCN
Hyundai Heavy Industries
Korea Tacoma Marine
Sperry Marine

Turbine gears
DCN

Turbines
DCN
Empresa Nacional Bazan

Turbines, gas marine
Empresa Nacional Bazan
Hyundai Heavy Industries

Turbines, steam marine
Empresa Nacional Bazan
DCN
Hyundai Heavy Industries

Ultra-fast attack boats
Crestitalia
FR Lürssen Werft

Ultra-fast patrol boats
Crestitalia
FR Lürssen Werft

Underwater acoustic systems
Safare-Crouzet

Underwater communications
Safare-Crouzet
Signaal Special Products

Underwater sonar towing systems
MacTaggart Scott
Safare-Crouzet

Underwater television equipment
Safare-Crouzet

Underwater warning systems
Safare-Crouzet

Warship design
Daewoo Shipbuilding & Heavy Machinery
DCN
Empresa Nacional Bazan
Fincantieri
FR Lürssen Werft
Hyundai Heavy Industries
Ingalls Shipbuilding
Korea Tacoma Marine
Netherlands Naval Industries Group
NEVESBU
Wartsila Diesel
Yarrow Shipbuilders

Warship design (systems engineering)
DCN
FR Lürssen Werft
Ingalls Shipbuilding
Netherlands Naval Industries Group
NEVESBU
Yarrow Shipbuilders

Warship fire-fighting equipment and systems
DCN

Warship repairs
Daewoo Shipbuilding & Heavy Machinery
DCN
Empresa Nacional Bazan
Fincantieri
FR Lürssen Werft
Hyundai Heavy Industries
Ingalls Shipbuilding
Netherlands Naval Industries Group

Warships
Chantiers de l'Atlantique
Daewoo Shipbuilding & Heavy Machinery
Empresa Nacional Bazan
Eurocorvette
Fincantieri
FR Lürssen Werft
Hyundai Heavy Industries
Ingalls Shipbuilding
Royal Schelde
Yarrow Shipbuilders

Waterjet propulsion systems
Castoldi
Riva Calzoni

Watertight doors
MacTaggart Scott
Netherlands Naval Industries Group

Weapon control systems
Bofors
DCN
Empresa Nacional Bazan
Elbit Computers
Hollandse Signaalapparaten
Loral Librascope
Matra Défense
Safare-Crouzet

Weapon systems
Bofors
Empresa Nacional Bazan
Elbit Computers
Loral Librascope
Matra Défense
Safare-Crouzet

Weapon systems, engineering
DCN
Elbit Computers
Empresa Nacional Bazan
Hollandse Signaalapparaten
Loral Librascope
Matra Défense
Safare-Crouzet

Weapon systems sonar component
DCN
Safare-Crouzet
Signaal Special Products

Welding: arc, argon arc or gas
DCN

X-ray work
DCN

Yachts, powered
DCN
FR Lürssen Werft

DIESEL POWER

We build 12 - and 18-cylinder high-speed diesel engines, providing a power coverage of 900 bhp (662 KW) to 2.100 bhp (1.545 KW), reverse gears reduction gears and vee-drives

---

Head Office and Plant: 21053 Castellanza - Via Marnate, 41
Tel. (0331) 501548 - Telefax (0331) 505501 - Telex 334382

Quick Response!

The best defense often depends upon a quick response. Loral Hycor now offers a quick-response computerized control for shipboard-launched chaff/IR decoy countermeasures. Designated **ALEX** (for **A**utomatic **L**aunch of **EX**pendables), this new system is compatible with our proven RBOC II and Super RBOC decoy delivery systems.

ALEX determines the best tactical countermeasure solution—automatically selecting decoy type, launcher, and tactical firing sequence as well as recommended course to steer—and fires. The system operates in fully automatic, semi-automatic, or manual modes. In the automatic mode, the firing response to a threat is nearly instantaneous! Manual override is always available.

Advanced electronics and modular construction permit a much smaller, lighterweight system. Digital operation dramatically reduces cabling size and weight requirements. A small cable is all that's needed between stations. Software can be updated in the field.

ALEX is a product of Loral Hycor, the leading developer and supplier of expendable decoy cartridges and launch systems to the navies of the free world. Send for complete description. Loral Hycor • 10 Gill St, Woburn, MA 01801 U.S.A. • Telephone (617) 935-5950 • FAX (617) 932-3764 • TWX 710-393-6345

LORAL
Hycor

c.i.s. DEG

00161 Rome - Via Morgagni, 30/E - Telefax 4403723 - Tel.: 06/4403722 - 4403729 - 4403682 - 4403731 - 4403725

- AESN — Rome
- ALENIA — Rome
- ELETTRONICA — Rome
- ELMER — Pomezia
- OTO MELARA — La Spezia
- S.M.A. — Florence

ENGINEERING CONSORTIUM C.I.S.DEG A TOP LEVEL TECHNICAL ORGANIZATION SINCE 1974 THE MAJOR CONTRACTOR OF THE ITALIAN NAVY FOR DESIGN INTEGRATION, INSTALLATION OF COMBACT SYSTEMS ON FIGHTING UNITS

Failing ship standard compass, design by G.W. Lyth, Stockholm; end of 19th century.

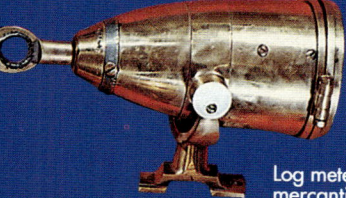

Log meter for mercantile ship, French make and design, beginning of 20th century.

Torpedo-boat Zenith clock with second and rewind indicator; beginning of 20th century.

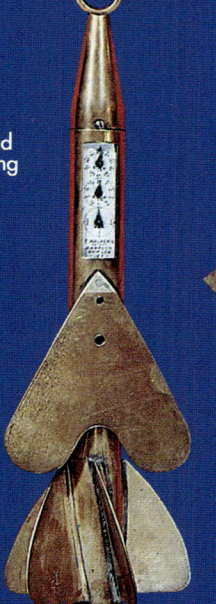

Walker three face log with incorporated meter; end of 19th century.

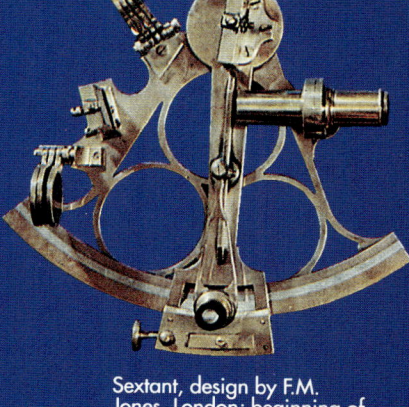

Sextant, design by F.M. Jones, London; beginning of 20th century.

C.I.S.DEG ACTIVITIES

- **ADVANCED DESIGN AND ENGINEERING**
- **INTEGRATION EQUIPMENT AND SYSTEM DESIGN**
- **INSTALLATION AND SEA ACCEPTANCE TRIALS**
- **CONFIGURATION CONTROL**
- **HIGH LEVEL QUALITY CONTROL**
- **INTEGRATED LOGISTICS SUPPORT**
- **MILITARY STANDARD HANDBOOKS**

The latest technology goes to sea

THYSSEN NORDSEEWERKE GMBH

P.O. Box 2351, 2361 · D-2970 Emden
Phone (4921) 850 · Telex 27802 · Fax (4921) 31327

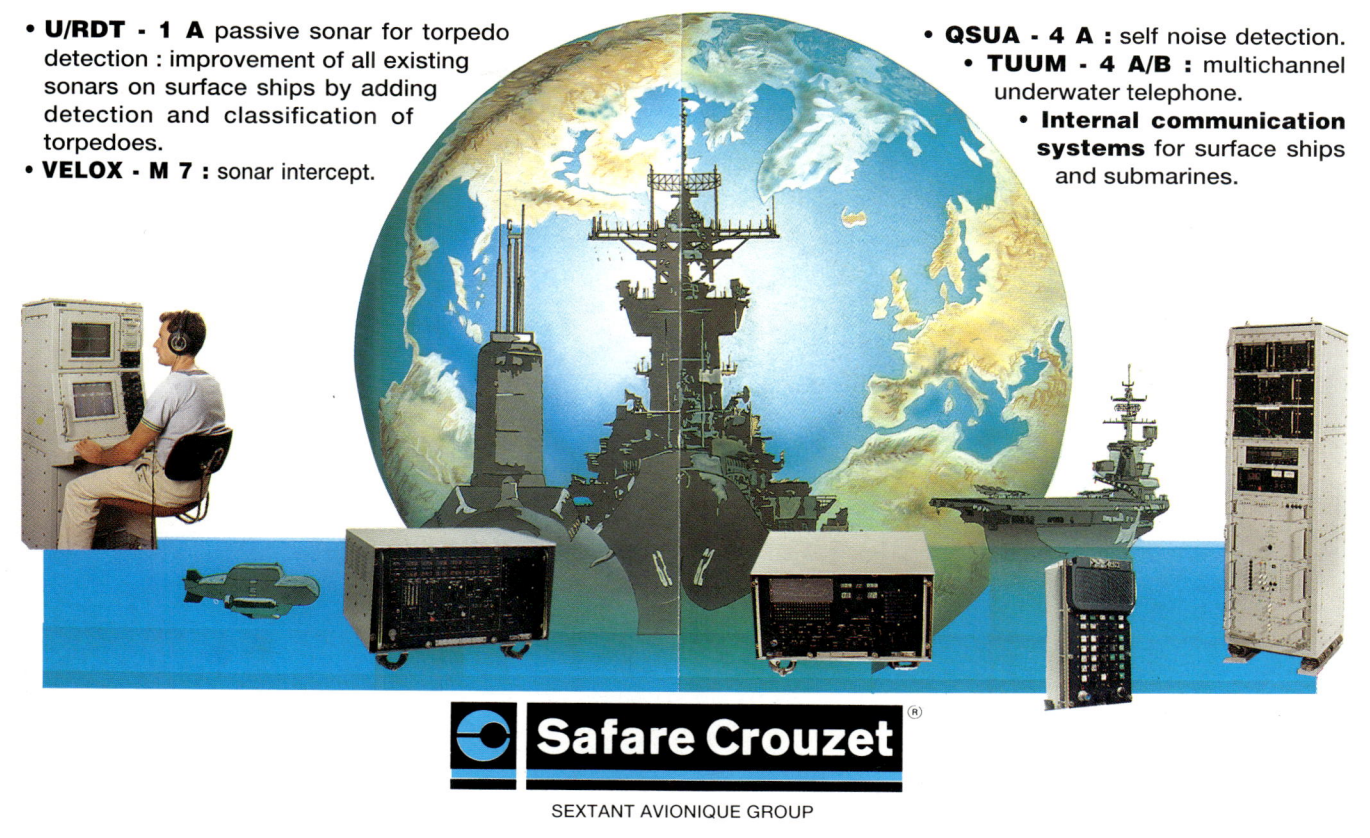

From the Sea. Littoral warfare takes priority.

JANE'S FIGHTING SHIPS 1993-94

Jane's Information Group Limited, Sentinel House, 163 Brighton Road, Coulsdon, Surrey CR5 2NH, UK
Jane's Information Group Inc, 1340 Braddock Place, Suite 300, Alexandria, VA 22314-1651, USA

SCHELDE SHIPBUILDING

"OUR KNOW-HOW TURNS IDEAS INTO PRACTICAL REALITIES"

For coastal states naval defence is of key importance. So is their selection of naval vessels, which must be reliable and technologically advanced to meet all threats. Schelde Shipbuilding, with many years of proven,

successful experience in building the most advanced naval vessels is well qualified to provide vessels designed to meet a wide range of defence criteria. Frigates, corvettes, high-speed patrol boats and fleet auxilliary support vessels: whatever the requirement, our know-how serves to fulfill your needs. Modern vessels, with compact powerful and integrated combat systems, served by a total integrated logistical support system, as required for the 21st century. When you have defined your requirements, discuss them with us. We turn your ideas into practical realities.

SCHELDE SHIPBUILDING
P.O. Box 16, 4380 AA Vlissingen, Holland.
Telephone (31) 1184 82118. Telefax (31) 1184 85010. Telex 37815 kms nl.

ROYAL SCHELDE

Foreword

"In one phase men seem to have been right. In another they seem to have been wrong. Then again, a few years later, when the perspective of time has lengthened, all stands in a different setting. There is a new proportion. There is another scale of values."

Churchill in 1940 sought to explain, in as kindly a way as possible, why his predecessor had been overtaken by events. Culling through the editorials of today's strategic and defence journals, there is a sense of incoherence and a lack of any secure framework within which to place military long-term planning. Specific threats are unfashionable, perhaps because of their proliferation and apparently minor nature or perhaps because we think we know, post-Desert Storm, that Western technology under American leadership can crush or at least contain any or all of them whenever necessary.

On the naval side there is a great imbalance between the United States Fleet and that of any other nation, assuming the continued hibernation of the Russians. In spite of Churchill's warning it is difficult to imagine that there will ever again be a decisive sea battle between opposing surface Fleets. Modern submarines, long-range missiles and shipborne aircraft and helicopters are too potent a mixture to allow surface to surface engagements other than on a small scale.

For most navies, coastal in origin and with few deep water pretensions, the local tasks remain unchanged. It is defining the blue water role which has become more difficult and, in the absence of any organised threat to merchant shipping, it is no surprise to see in the last year the emergence of joint operations against the land as the principle focus for forward planning by those few Fleets capable of operating worldwide.

Some of this change may just be presentational but, as one American Admiral put it in a recent interview: "If you don't pass the test with the six new warfare assessments, you don't get into the Navy budget. Those six areas are joint strike, joint littoral warfare, joint surveillance, space and electronic warfare, strategic sealift and strategic deterrence."

If the American Navy has come late to the concept of jointness as a first priority, others have been there for some years, driven by a number of different motives. The dismantling of elitist cells has always been a prerequisite for greater central control and nothing is more elitist than a single service with a strong sense of its own identity. The Canadians were perhaps the first to carry jointness to the point of common drab green uniforms and naval officers who answered to the rank of Major.

An imbalance between the power of the US Navy and that of other nations *Horst Dehnst*

Commonsense soon returned and some of the worst excesses were rescinded, but the purple ticket had by then been established in many headquarters around the world, and single service staffs were beginning to lose their authority and their power to influence governments.

Jointness, as in joint operations, is essential. There are few military events these days which do not have an overlap of some kind between land, sea and air. It is when you extend the concept into basic training, equipment procurement, staff intervention, or even high-level decision making, that you begin to stand into danger.

The requirements of being a successful junior officer are different for the sailor, the aviator or the infantryman. The platoon commander is a leader who fails if his troops refuse to follow. His naval equivalent needs technical competence and the ability to inspire a high level of concentration from those around him, doing mostly sedentary but skilful jobs. The airman requires the co-ordination of mind and muscle, and the highest level of short term individual competence because if he fails himself there is seldom anyone to back him up.

Equally there is little commonality in the conditions of service. The human problems associated with being at sea in a tin can for months on end are not to be compared with life in the barracks or field, or the stop/start existence of land-based airmen. Joint selection, training and experience have almost no relevance at this level.

Equipment procurement looks more promising, particularly in aviation. The exasperated civilian cry of "Why do we need three (or four) different airforces?" strikes an immediate positive response. But once you descend into the detailed specifications and operational requirements, the drive for different technical characteristics, for endurance, firepower, even of such things as landing gear and protection from the elements, all lead in divergent directions.

Army guns have been made to work in ships, but not often, and various sensors with common names such as radar, have to perform on land, at sea and in the air in conditions often as different as the lifestyle of their operators. Communications ought to be a common point of contact, but again only in limited and specific application.

An effective operational staff cannot afford to be too large. So the more joint it becomes the more specialised warfare expertise becomes diluted. Even within a single service such as a Navy, operational planning experts are needed in aviation, submarine and surface warfare, air defence, anti-submarine operations, mine countermeasures, amphibious assault, special operations, space and electronic warfare, communications–the list is endless. Joint command and control must therefore of necessity be broad brush, being prepared to delegate whenever specialist knowledge or experience is needed. Unfortunately, it is in the nature of many senior officers to assume a greater personal expertise than is often the case. Also, decisions may have to be taken without the necessary consultation with the specialist, and joint staffs are more likely to make this mistake by virtue of the spread of knowledge that in theory they possess, but in reality do not. This problem is seen at its worst when a staff officer seeks, or is told, to intervene on behalf of his Commander in an operation of which he has no first-hand expertise. An example of this was the sending of a Central Staff officer who by chance happened to be a nuclear submariner, to investigate the failings of an infantry company commander in a UN operation in a Mediterranean littoral country. An extreme case perhaps, but it illustrates the problems.

High-level decision making is merely an extension of the same difficulty facing the joint staff. However well briefed he may be, a Chief of Defence Staff pressed for an urgent opinion by a President or Prime Minister may have no 'feel' for the best answer if he has no personal experience in that type of warfare. In most circumstances he will be able to buy time by saying he has to consult further with his colleagues, but if he does, the moment may pass and an opportunity be lost. Had there been no combined arms leader, the right expert would have been present in the first place.

Another reason often put forward by advocates of a joint staff approach is that it prevents single service rivalries. As already discussed, at the technical training level there is almost no common ground and thus in no sense is rivalry a danger, although it can provide healthy competition and foster *esprit de corps*. Inevitably there are some crossover points between services, mostly in aviation and in land/air warfare by Marines, but few of even the strongest advocates of jointness are prepared, at least in public, to press for the logical abolishment of a single service air force in favour of land/air (soldiers) and sea/air (sailors).

During operations, if you are single handedly fighting the enemy, the

MagneTek. Teledyne INET. Together, the winning team.

MagneTek's recent acquisition of Teledyne INET has produced a powerful new combination. It provides the DoD, DoT and their contractors with an even more responsive ally in the field of power electronics.

MagneTek's approach to power systems solutions ranges from ruggedized commercial equipment for high reliability at low cost to totally engineered power systems for military specified applications.

Now There's Even More Power Behind The Power.

MagneTek static power sources include a complete array of power converters, power supplies, power conditioners, distribution transformers – even ruggedized lighting ballasts and adjustable speed motor drives.

MagneTek rotating systems span the gamut of AC and DC motors and generators. **Plus, MagneTek developmental engineering** incorporates extensive power system simulation and modeling, as well as thorough analyses of power system and power component cost alternatives.

Let MagneTek's expanded team of systems engineers develop the right power solution to match your requirements – and fit your budget.

To obtain a free copy of our new Power Systems Resource Guide, contact **MagneTek**, 901 E. Ball Road, Anaheim, CA 92805, (714) 956-9200, FAX: (714) 956-5397.

This artist's impression portrays the vital electrical systems and circuitry on which the ship's mission depends.

©1993 MagneTek, Inc.

colour of the reinforcements' uniforms are irrelevant as long as they are on your side. General Schwarzkopf, in his autobiography, does recount one extraordinary event in which a Marine officer tried to refuse the use of Marine helicopters to lift Army personnel during a low key operation in the Caribbean, but such an action would normally be unthinkable in wartime.

There are some crossover points between the Services   *H M Steele*

So it is only at the politico/military level, and in particular in the competition for funding new equipment, that inter-service rivalries are acute. And what is wrong with that? Surely it is better to have a red-blooded open and competitive debate, than the behind closed doors secretive compromises that are the hallmark of a defence department's joint staff? Furthermore, in the single service environment, the individual staff officer can make his point with force, based on his own convictions and expertise. Any such conduct in a central staff is likely to cause him to be labelled as a single-service fanatic unable to see the broader, well rounded compromise so favoured by his career-minded colleagues. In other words, genuine debate is stifled, and real disagreements are suppressed. To applaud such a move speaks more for the power of idiosyncratic military fashion than it does of training or tradition.

There is another form of jointness which can be even more insidious in its effects than cross dressing between services, if it spills over the boundaries of sensible application. Collaboration between nations has some of the same characteristics as collaboration between services. Like joint service operations, but for different reasons, military coalitions between nations are becoming more and more essential if armed intervention in the affairs of another country is to be judged acceptable by world public opinion. Because of the military weaknesses of nations other than the United States (and the dormant Russians), the combining of resources is also becoming necessary if a serious show of force is required. But, just as with joint staffs, there is a need to recognise the weaknesses and limitations of international collaboration.

The first requirement is rapid politico/military decision making and a clear command and control organisation under an accepted unified leadership. It was done by the Allies in the second half of World War II, in Korea in the 1950s and again in Kuwait in 1991, each time under American leadership. NATO might have achieved the most spectacular example, had the Warsaw Pact attacked western Europe. NATO certainly had the infrastructure, but the post-cold war assumption that its political backbone and politico/military decision making process would have proved adequate if put to the ultimate test, is still only an assumption. Neither do we know for certain that the Warsaw Pact would have functioned as a successful collaborative military machine in war, although such was the Soviet domination that this somehow seems more probable. Nonetheless it was an open secret that Soviet reinforcements for a ground offensive against western Europe were planned to bypass Poland.

Jointness in the form of equipment collaboration between nations is also seen at a superficial level as automatically a good thing. With increasing numbers of defence industries merging with international partners, the national provenance of some equipment is becoming as difficult to define as it is in the motor car industry. In spite of this there is a strong case that can be made against major multi-national projects, embracing such uncertainties as commitment and reliability throughout the long design and development phase, effects on national industries, the need for an initial extension of the logistic support and training base, and the danger of higher through-life costs.

Perhaps most important of all in this Gadarene rush towards jointness is the potential loss of the sense of identity with like-minded people and institutions, which causes individuals to perform in war to standards they could not normally achieve. The larger and more disparate the organisation, whether combined service or international in character, the less easy it is for the individual to establish his own position and commitment.

Fighting for unit, service and country has proved to be a sound basis for maintaining the traditional loyalties for which men and women are prepared to die. We should be careful to restrain the pursuit of jointness from expanding into areas where it has little relevance and can only weaken unit effectiveness.

United States

The behaviour of a small number of officers ashore is not something which would normally rate a mention in this annual review. However, the 1991 Tailhook incident, in which a group of US naval aviators were accused of sexual harrassment of female officers, has achieved disproportionate downstream effects, impacting badly both on the level of public support for the Navy and on the careers of many senior officers who were seen to have had some measure of responsibility.

Problems with naval pilots are not unique to the USN. When the British still had large fixed wing carriers, the Wardroom was sometimes a war zone between those 'flyboys' who believed the ship was merely a convenient temporary accommodation and landing strip to which they owed no particular allegiance, and the 'fishheads', or regular ship's company, who viewed with contempt some of the loutish self-centred youths who descended on them, literally, every time their ship put to sea.

It takes a special kind of person to be a naval aviator, flying a multimillion dollar high tech machine in all weathers by day and night from a mobile postage stamp, often with no alternative airfields as safe havens in an emergency. Many don't make it out of training, and there are regular fatalities even in peacetime operations. With such a larger than life existence, it would be surprising if behaviour ashore did not occasionally go over the top. Nonetheless, a disciplined service has to come down hard on any conduct not worthy of an officer. If a well defined line is crossed, and all professionals know where that line is, those doing the crossing must be on the receiving end of immediate and decisive disciplinary action. Any fudge or mudge inevitably brings further discredit to the service, and in this case the timing could not have been worse or the long-term effect on the Navy more unfortunate.

The ending of a war always heralds some fairly drastic cutbacks in the military establishment. It was in some ways fortuitous that the winding down of the cold war coincided with the need to drive Iraq out of Kuwait, cushioning the impending blow, but the inevitable is now well under way and it is not at all clear where the process stops. The annual Deletions columns reflect how many ships had gone by mid-1993, but unless the Russian bear again raises its ugly head it seems certain that more SSNs, aircraft carriers and non-Aegis-fitted cruisers are destined for decommissioning long before their planned service lives come to an end. SSNs surplus to operational requirements are likely to be kept in service until de-activation facilities for nuclear reactors catch up on the backlog of SSBNs. Some of the early Los Angeles class may go when they come up for refuelling and before the last of the Sturgeons. As it costs considerably more to inactivate an SSN than to keep it running, accelerating retirement would merely increase near-term budget requirements.

In a year of radical change the reorganisation of the House Armed Services committees and the subsequent loss of the dedicated Seapower subcommittee is seen as a blow to the influence which for years the Navy has been able to maintain in Congress. Far-reaching effects, not all of them good, will also stem from the dismantling of the empires of the so-called platform barons, which since 1943 have enabled Assistant Chiefs for surface, subsurface and air warfare to bring concentrated expertise to bear across the whole range of these specialised activities. Such fiefdoms, with their competing priorities and tribal loyalties, are anathema to the bureaucratic mentality, and it is symptomatic that in the civilian explanation of their demise, perjorative phrases such as 'rivalries and jealousies' were trotted out as though competition itself was to be deplored. Perhaps a more convincing explanation for downgrading the tribal chiefs was that, respectively, their handling of the Seawolf, AX, A12 and MCM projects (to name a few) was not a good advertisement for their organisations. This may be true given the revolution in the defence scene in the last few years, but major equipment projects are long term in nature and expensive to adjust in the later stages of development. With the benefit of hindsight it is easy to criticise decisions which were taken in a different budgetary and threat environment. There is a danger of throwing out the baby with the bath water.

The year has seen the final closure of the Subic Base in the Philippines and with it the start of a new relationship with the Asia Pacific region. Some administrative units previously based in the Philippines have been

Tomorrow's Technology Today
Advanced Naval Combat Systems

....from
Loral Librascope

Librascope has been designing and developing ASW weapon and combat control systems for the U.S. Navy and allied navies for more than 30 years.

Today, Librascope is the only contractor working on the two most advanced ASW submarine combat control systems in the world (U.S. and international). Librascope successfully competed for and is designing and developing (1) The combat control system and weapon subsystem for the U.S. Navy's attack class submarine SSN-21 SEAWOLF, and (2) The combat control system for the Royal Australian Navy's New Construction Type 471 Submarines.

Loral Librascope
833 Sonora Avenue
Glendale, CA 91201-0279
(818) 244-6541
TWX: 910-497-2266
TELEX: 215620

LORAL
Librascope

FOREWORD

relocated to Japan, Singapore and Thailand but the majority have either shifted to Guam or been withdrawn to the United States. Other countries in the region such as Malaysia and Indonesia are providing some ship repair facilities, but Guam has now assumed the role of supplying battle groups in the Indian Ocean and Arabian Sea. Diego Garcia remains an invaluable forward base for operations in the Gulf.

No one doubts that American influence in the China Seas and in the Eastern Pacific will remain for at least a few more years, but the signs of retrenchment are unambiguous.

If all this is not enough change for twelve calendar months, the Navy and Marine Corps strategy 'From the Sea' represents just about as big a shift in operational priorities as it is possible to imagine. Strategies, concepts, tactics and weapons evolved over decades, and most recently articulated in the Foreward Maritime Strategy of the late 1980s, have been moved to one side to change the emphasis from deep sea global warfare to regional challenges and joint operations mounted from the sea. It is as though the Navy recognises that for the time being there is nothing left to oppose in the open oceans, so its major contribution is now to support land battles and operations in unstable coastal regions, for which hitherto it has been less well equipped.

Some of this change is for home political consumption and represents commendably fast footwork, building on the foundations laid by the substantial Navy and Marines contributions to the war against Iraq and demonstrating the new policy in the landings in Somalia.

No one needs to remind the US Navy that the potential for a deep water challenge still exists, or that the continuing role of world policeman sits uneasily on the precipitous north face of a national budget deficit. Carried to extremes 'From the Sea' would have a revolutionary effect on almost every aspect of naval affairs and, on the whole, revolutions are undesirable in even the most flexible of institutions. The next few difficult years are more likely to be characterised by internal fire-fighting and damage control than by broad sweeps of alternative strategies.

One immediate effect of 'From the Sea' has been a much greater amalgamation between the Navy and Marine Corps at most staff levels. In the front line, selected USMC strike/fighter squadrons are now operating with Navy carrier air wings as regular components of the carrier battle group.

Other changes include the setting up of an Expeditionary Forces branch under the Chief of Naval Operations. This merges special warfare activities, carried out by SEALS, with mine and amphibious requirements sections, to improve mobility and stealth within the inshore zone.

Exoatmospheric projectile — *Ingalls*

Designed for operations in coastal regions — *Intermarine USA*

A surface ship defence system programme is under way to provide a quicker and more comprehensive reaction to the anti-ship missile threat, particularly at medium range, and to counter weapons fired from coastal batteries.

Developments in missiles have included the operational testing of SLAM which is now in production and represents a formidable augmentation to the improved Tomahawk in the offensive weapon inventory.

Also going ahead is the LEAP (Lightweight Exoatmospheric Projectile) scheme which aims at using the Standard Block IV SAM of the Aegis system as a carrier of LEAP, designed to intercept ballistic missiles. Engagement would either be initiated by forward deployment to catch the strategic missile ascending or alternatively as a defence against theatre systems such as Scud.

Of several unresolved equipment problems, the most pressing are the next generation long-range naval strike aircraft and the maintenance of a viable submarine building capability while the post-Seawolf construction gap is being bridged.

Some details of the helicopter carrying Arleigh Burke Flight IIA destroyer and LX amphibious designs are included in this new edition, and the conversion of the LPH *Inchon* as an MCM command and control vessel has been confirmed and should complete in 1996. The so-called silver bullet procurement strategy of buying small quantities of high technology weapon systems and placing them in less sophisticated platforms seems to be the flavour of 1993, but is an unlikely winner in the long-term stakes.

Unusually, this year there is no five year shipbuilding or aircraft plan. A bottom-up review of Defense Needs and Programmes is to be completed by late summer culminating in a Future Years Defense Programme (FYDP) which will cover the projections for FY 1995-1999.

Overall, the Navy has braced itself for a five year cut in manpower to 375 000 people and a reduction to 320 ships by the end of the decade. This latter number would include about 12 aircraft carriers, 45 SSNs and some 50 amphibious ships. As the projected building rate is inadequate even to maintain this number of ships, it seems likely that, on present trends, the Navy may decline in the long term to less than half the 600 ship goal set by the Reagan administration and nearly achieved in 1988.

Is everyone in Europe and in the rest of the developed world paying attention?

Russia and Associated States

Exactly 90 years ago the founder of Jane's, Fred T Jane, forecast that the white flag with the blue St Andrew's cross would one day rule the seas. There was no chance of that happening while the Russian Fleets flew the hammer and sickle, but since 26 July 1992 they are again sailing under their old national flag. It would be fanciful to repeat Jane's warning, given the current state of Russian disarray, but it would be irresponsible not to continue objectively to chart the movements of what is still by far the world's second most powerful Navy.

Western correspondents have been falling over themselves in reporting horror stories aimed at debunking the former Soviet military. Recent naval samples include senior officers who are seldom sober in the North,

Navigation At The Speed Of Light!

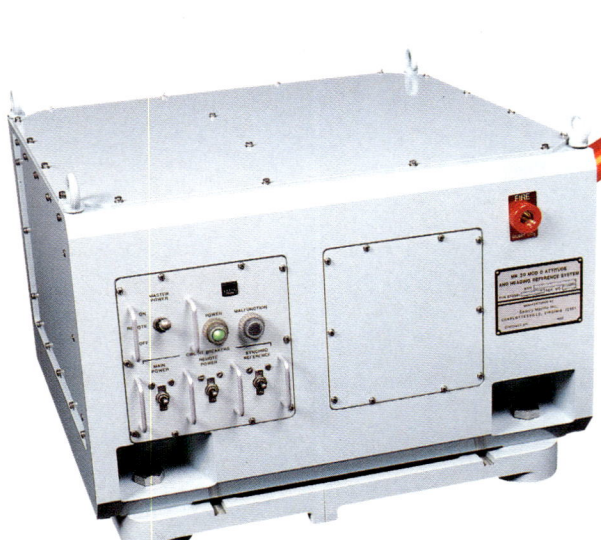

Ring Laser Gyro Attitude and Heading Reference System

Providing Performance, Reliability and Value into the 21st Century!

The MK-39 is the world's first production marine Ring Laser Gyro Attitude and Heading Reference System (RLG AHRS).

The MK-39 is the result of over 30 years of effort in RLG technology and over 10 years directed toward the application of that technology to the marine navigation environment. The MK-39 represents the future of compass and attitude systems, with a reliability and performance that is unmatched by spinning or ballistic systems available today.

MK-39 Features:
- RLG MTBF of over 200,000 hours
- Accuracies - Heading: 4 ARC mins SEC Lat RMS, Roll: 1.75 ARC mins, Pitch: 1.75 ARC mins
- Dynamic Stability - Roll/Pitch: 0.001 deg/sec, Heading: 0.003 deg/sec
- Operates in latitudes up to 85 degrees • Vessel speeds up to 60 Knots and virtually unlimited turning rates • Full BIT
- D.C. Operation • Numerous interface options • Self-Aligning, precision mounting plate • MTTR of less than 30 minutes

MK-39 Benefits:
- Low through-life cost • Extremely high reliability • No need for external cooling or noisy fans, totally enclosed
- Can be used on virtually any vessel type including surface effect and hovercraft
- Automatic fault isolation and system protection eases troubleshooting and protects unit
- Hands off operation - does not require operator intervention
- Price competitive with current technologies • Easy installation on existing as well as new platforms

For further information on all Sperry Marine products contact:

Sperry Marine Inc.
1070 Seminole Trail
Charlottesville, VA 22901
Phone: (804) 974-2000
FAX: (804) 974-2259

Subsidiary
Newport News Shipbuilding
A Tenneco Company

FOREWORD

sailors starving to death in the Pacific, indiscriminate dumping at sea of radioactive materials, conscripts not turning up for duty, all the best people leaving, equipment supply lines no longer functioning and all ships new and old up for sale. Perhaps the worst piece of misreporting was the worldwide repetition of a speech made in Seoul in November last year, indicating that President Yeltsin had pledged to stop building all submarines within two years. In fact he was talking only about the Komsomolsk Pacific yard, having ten days earlier signed a Presidential decree making Severodvinsk on the White Sea the lead yard for nuclear submarines.

The St Andrews Cross at sea again.

This last report is particularly relevant because it highlights the source of the disinformation problem, which is selective reporting of events that have a kernel of truth but are far from being the whole story. You can do this to any organisation. How about ''The United States Navy has officers that abuse females, ships that fire missiles indiscriminately at civilian airlines and friendly destroyers, and guns that are more a danger to the turret's crew than the enemy''? The British contribution would be ''Brand new submarines that are unable to fire torpedoes, naval aircraft that lob practice bombs on to the flight decks of their own aircraft carriers and officers who, when not being caught *'in flagrante'* with their female counterparts, are being court martialled for bigamy''. Not a bad point at which to stop and demand a more objective view.

It is not yet clear even to the Russians where the cutbacks in warship yards will end, but the consensus is that the major complexes at Severodvinsk and St Petersburg are to be retained, plus about three smaller yards. Indicative of current intentions is the launching in the last year of four nuclear submarines, the continuation of the Sovremenny, Udaloy II and Neustrashimy major warship programmes, the building of diesel submarines for export and the unexpected appearance at the Dubai

Nuclear submarines are being dumped at sea

military exposition in February this year of designs for a new light frigate building at Zelenodolsk, as well as detailed information on existing classes of missile boats and hovercraft, all of which are available for export. On top of that there are the Ukrainian shipyards with, amongst other warships, an uncompleted Kuznetsov class carrier. This is small beer by comparison with the building programmes of even three years

ago, and there is a danger of drift or even of collapse of the whole industry unless order is restored to the economy.

Operationally most of the Fleets have spent little time in the last year outside home waters, but weapons training continues in local exercise areas. There was one burst of activity from the Northern Fleet into the Norwegian Sea which by chance coincided with the British Trident submarine *Vanguard* starting sea trials. For a day or two the media's attempt to establish linkage between the two events was quite like old times.

Then there has been the historic co-operation between Western warships in the Gulf and a Russian Udaloy class destroyer, allocated by the Pacific Fleet for UN sanctions patrols against Iraq, starting in October last year. Many favourable comments have been made, not least about the high standard of helicopter operations.

Hydrographic and other research ships have been active to a limited extent, particularly in the Atlantic, and some have been earning hard currency through commercial activities. One example is the *Keldysh* which has been diving for treasure off the Mexican coast, an area to which it would not have had access a couple of years ago.

Overall numbers of ships continue to reduce as the older vessels are scrapped, and some newer ones are also being paid off if they have suffered bad equipment failures. The most notable in the latter category is one of the three Kiev class aircraft carriers which damaged its main engines beyond reasonable repair. A second of this class also needs new boilers if it is ever to become operational again. The Pacific Fleet is the worst affected, being at the nether end of a tenuous logistic supply line.

The Baltic Fleet units have finally left their former East German and Polish ports, and are slowly pulling out of the three Baltic republics, although the final withdrawal is expected to take until the end of 1994. In spite of its isolation from Russian territories, the Kaliningrad/Baltysk complex is being retained and expanded, because unlike the other bases at St Petersburg and Kronstadt, it remains ice-free throughout the year. This Fleet has a political and historical importance in Russian minds which probably transcends its military significance in the post-cold war era.

The Baltic Fleet is withdrawing to Russian territories *Antonio Moreno*

The same cannot be said of the Black Sea Fleet which has been making most of the headlines, and is a continuing potential flashpoint between Russia and Ukraine. The so-called Yalta Agreement, announced on 3 August last year, attempted to defuse tensions by establishing a joint command for the next three years, and this has even led to the introduction of a combined flag. However, in December the Commander of the Ukrainian Navy was making belligerent noises about his own Navy

LÜRSSEN
FR. LÜRSSEN WERFT

Fr. Lürssen Werft (GmbH & Co) · D-2820 Bremen-Vegesack · Germany
P.O.B. 750 662 · Phone (421) 66 04-0 · Fax (421) 66 04-443 · Tx 0 244 484 aflwd

Intensive training

in most modern facilities

is an integrated part of our delivery
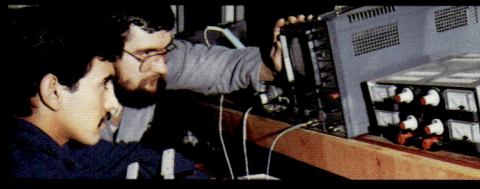

LÜRSSEN · SINCE 1875

Fr. Lürssen Werft (GmbH & Co) · D-2820 Bremen-Vegesack · Germany
P.O.B. 750 662 · Phone (421) 66 04-0 · Fax (421) 66 04-443 · Tx 0 244 484 aflwd

FOREWORD

which has plans for 40 000 sailors and tens of new ships, including the Flagship, *Slavutich*, which is the second of the Kamchatka class. The intention now is for Ukraine to have a guided missile cruiser, several diesel submarines and a number of patrol craft, auxiliaries and naval aircraft.

Georgia, too, is in the process of establishing its own coastal defence force, and Azerbaijan has control of some 30% of the old Caspian Sea Flotilla. Both the projected and actual extent of autonomy for these lesser Republics changes monthly, and any authoritative statement is almost immediately contradicted. The Black Sea Fleet, in an area of great instability, and with access to the Mediterranean, is central to Russian aspirations of retaining its traditional role of being the most influential player in the region.

Russian dependence on its submarine-launched missiles for strategic deterrence has been enhanced by uncertainties on land, and work on a new solid-fuelled ballistic missile is going ahead. The Admiral in charge of shipbuilding has said that numbers of SSBNs will be allowed to decline slowly to about 25 to meet START II limits, and then the remaining Typhoon, Delta III and Delta IV hulls will be replaced on a one for one basis in the next decade.

The next generation of attack submarine is being worked on by the Malachite design bureau and, although not expected to achieve the original schedule projected by US Navy officials as being completed in mid decade, the first of class may still appear well before the end of the century.

The fate of fixed wing carrier-borne aviation is less certain. *Kuznetsov* has been working up with fixed wing fighters embarked and is expected to deploy this year. Although frequently reported as 'sold' to almost every nation with any interest in carriers, her sister ship *Varyag* is still wanted by the Russian Navy, and is still making some progress towards completion at Nikolayev South shipyard in the Ukraine. The nuclear powered *Ulyanovsk* did not achieve her launch date and has now been broken up for scrap.

A major effort is being made by Russian industry to break into the lucrative Middle East defence markets, which are dominated by the West. The trouble is, that although the products are cheap, no one has much confidence in the logistic backup and such successes as there are, for instance submarines to Iran, are mostly to those countries which find it difficult to shop openly for Western equipment.

There are some disconcerting similarities between the present state of Russia and the German Weimar republic after the First World War. Hyperinflation, no-one apparently able to control events, and a military discomfited over the loss of its former status, all adds up to an uncomfortable and uncertain future. The Navy reflects this uncertainty, but its potential remains formidable.

United Kingdom

The past year started well with a Statement of Defence Estimates, which for the first time for very many years gave priority to the UK as a national institution, rather than as an appendage to NATO. Even the naval force levels had an air of stability although, conspicuously, there was no specific analysis of UK dependence upon the sea or its worldwide maritime interests, as opposed to wider security concerns. A key security interest is apparently to sustain the present network of Western co-operation and to avoid any reversion to nationally driven defence. This is assumed, not argued, which presumably means that alternatives were not considered. For instance, is it really in the security interests of any European nation to contribute ships simultaneously to national, NATO and Western European Union forces patrolling the Adriatic?

The bad news came with the autumn statement that there were further financial cutbacks on defence spending over and above those assumed after the ending of the Cold War in Options for Change, and as usual it is equipment projects which are to provide the quickest means of finding the money. In this kind of emergency cost cutting exercise no attempt is made to justify the contingency options in relation to existing defence policy. Alternatives are listed; political, defence and industrial considerations noted; and decisions are then made by a process more geared to political damage control than to the long-term national interests.

The result of all this is that not a single warship or major auxiliary, except Trident, has been ordered since January 1992 and although there is a design for a new SSN, no attack submarines of any kind are being built at present. New amphibious ships, to which there have been repeated statements of commitment since 1987, may still be funded but no-one can be certain until a shipyard contract is placed. Worse than that is the projected sale or lease of the last four diesel submarines, one of which is still in commission, and the possible commercialisation of the survey flotilla. Planned new frigate and minehunter orders are postponed again, existing frigates are being paid off early or placed in a state of 'reduced readiness', and action on the urgent need for new tankers is put off once more. Deployable destroyers and frigates that form the backbone of most of today's directed tasks are on course to sink in the long term to a level of nearer twenty than thirty, unless the order rate for new ships picks up fairly soon.

Other news is that a major Dockyard in Scotland is to be kept open even though the Navy says it doesn't need it, and the only future project which is politically sacrosanct is the Anglo-French new generation frigate which requires equipment compromises from both nations, while at the same time extending the training and logistic support tail to embrace weapon systems which are not at the moment part of the existing inventory in either Navy. For example, the choice of the Exocet SSM would be logical for the French, but not the British who have Harpoon embarked in their modern frigates. The competing designs released by both nations are included in this edition in their respective country sections. To achieve a common ship, large numbers of compromises are going to have to be made.

The first Vanguard class Trident SSBN has started sea trials and is planned to enter operational service in late 1994. The Trident system offers greater warhead capacity than is thought either necessary or desirable, and there is a strong case for taking up the slack by fitting non-strategic or theatre weapons. All naval tactical nuclear weapons are being scrapped.

Operationally the Navy completed a group deployment in late 1992, designed to maintain links with nations in the Indian Ocean, China Seas and on the Pacific Rim. The first of the Type 23 frigates was part of the Task Force.

A global maritime presence — H M Steele

Other global commitments include the Armilla patrol in the Gulf and standing contingency duties in Hong Kong, the South Atlantic, the West Indies and NATO's standing naval forces, of which there are now three, including the recently formed Mediterranean squadron. The UN sanctions operations against Serbia have been supported by contributions to the NATO and WEU forces in the Adriatic, and a sizeable national naval force was also despatched early this year to back up Army relief operations in Bosnia.

The defence climate has changed, but British dependence on the sea has not. The silent service in its traditional and unassuming way will continue to put up a competent performance at sea as long as it can, while hoping that the self evident case for adequate funding will eventually be apparent even to those internationalists in Whitehall who have had a long standing hostility to the Navy, the national flag merchant marine and the British fishing industry. The sea services are being damaged. Defence of national interests is the first duty of the state. A robust presentation of the long term consequences of the present failure to order new warships is overdue.

SOFMA

The value of experience

As an export agency, SOFMA markets ground weaponry, naval armament and security equipment produced by the french industry.

SOFMA also offers after-sales services and logistic support. On behalf of its foreign partners, SOFMA can undertake certain feasability studies related to particular needs : financial packages, trade-off possibilities, materiel retrofitting, industrial cooperation and technology transfer.

Its continual action throughout the world together with its knowledge of defense markets have enabled SOFMA to develop its role as an expert in this field.

SOCIETE FRANÇAISE DE MATERIELS D'ARMEMENT
17, Bd MALESHERBES 75008 PARIS TEL. : (1) 42 65 97 10
TELEX : SOFMA 280 566 F - FAX : (1) 42 65 10 06

What is happening to the Royal Navy may in future years serve as a textbook case of the effect of taking strong minded single service advocacy out of the front line of the defence decision making process. The US Navy should take note.

Europe
In the sense of a workable federal entity the Europe of the European Community continues to advance if only in the hearts and minds of its bureaucracy. Recessions dominate national political agendas, particularly in times of elections, to the exclusion of grand ideas and multinational activities. Nonetheless the fact that the Western European Union (WEU) survives at all indicates that while NATO is still seen as the only effective military coalition organisation in the continent, there is a desire for a more European identity. The trouble is that no-one wants to pay for an effective WEU infrastructure and, even if one was created, it is not possible to see how politico/military leadership could be managed with a number of nearly equal partners, at least one of which is not prepared to serve in a subordinate role.

The danger in all this is that national bureaucracies may assume (some already have) a coalition mentality in national force level planning, leaving that country or countries singularly naked should the assumptions prove to be wrong.

The Baltic region is currently least affected by this particular drift in Europe's current affairs. Sweden, Finland and Poland are all structuring their navies towards more effective autonomous coastal defences. In November Sweden laid down the world's first diesel submarine to be built from the keel up with an air independent propulsion system. Operationally, the Navy has now got political approval to extend the kill zone against intruding underwater vessels out to the limits of the 12 mile territorial zone. A Russo-Swedish group of experts has concluded that such incursions have taken place although no-one has yet named the GRU as the probable culprit.

The three Baltic States have each formed a Coast Guard. Estonia received patrol craft from Russia, Finland and Sweden, and Lithuania has acquired two Grisha III frigates, as well as patrol craft from Russia and Sweden. Latvia on the other hand has no intention of taking Russian vessels and is making do with converted fishing boats and ex-Swedish Coast Guard craft, although it is possible that Poland may provide more heavily armed ships in due course. Latvian manpower numbers are expected to quadruple from 270 in January to over 1000 by the same time next year.

In Denmark a new two year defence plan calls for reductions in spending by 4.2% this year and 7.3% in 1994. This is likely to curtail the multipurpose Flyvefisken project to a total of 14 ships, all of which can embark weapon systems modules for surveillance, combat, mine countermeasures or minelaying roles. The first of class is being used to test the first MCM module which includes control of two minesweeping drones.

NATO's Standing Naval Force Mediterranean *H M Steele*

Norway's first twin hulled minehunter has had her in-service date delayed until later in the year. More seriously, the Navy may have to lay up some major ships and reduce sea time for others. The Coast Guard is exempt from the latest round of budget cuts but the Chief of the Defence Staff complained late last year that Norway was heading towards a gradual dismantling of a balanced defence against invasion. Given what is going on in other NATO European navies, Norway may have to hope that such a threat really is a thing of the past, because amphibious reinforcement may soon not be an option for her European allies.

Contrary to popular belief the German constitution does not specifically forbid the deployment of troops in active combat roles outside the NATO countries. What has happened is that it has become 'state practice' not to do so and therefore, once this self-imposed inhibition is broken, the precedent would be set for Germany to join other international forces on a regular basis. Not surprisingly, having to stay out of harm's way is unpopular with the regular element of the armed forces, and by contributing to UN peace-keeping forces and even low level sanctions operations, such as those in the Adriatic, the non-involvement stranglehold is slowly being broken, although not without internal political opposition.

With the Baltic an area of comparative calm, at least for the time being, it is natural that the Navy would like to continue the process of widening the scope of its operations. Meanwhile defence cuts pile on defence cuts and the latest plan includes only four new frigates, one of four of a new class of submarines and two replenishment vessels between 1996 and 2005. Virtually all the ships of the former East German Navy have now either been sold or are awaiting disposal.

There has been much talk of the Netherlands losing its submarine capability altogether. This conclusion stemmed from the defence secretary's comment in early 1992 that it was not necessary to maintain a complete defence force because the country would no longer operate independently. He therefore intended to pay off the Zwaardvis class in 1994 because in his opinion "A submarine service is no longer necessary. In international operations our contribution will be frigates and minehunters, while our allies can supply the submarines." A fashionable comment if ever there was one, but there seems to have been a change of plan and more frigates are now to be paid off early and the new tripartite minehunter project may not go ahead, while the four Walrus class submarines appear to be safe. There is a suspicion here of a deal with the British to provide diesel submarines to aid training, should the Upholder class be sold or leased abroad. This is a neat agreement on paper but may in practice be found to have a few programming difficulties when priorities conflict. If the cancellation of the new minehunter is ratified, some of the Alkmaars will get a remote-controlled drone capability, based on an update of the German Troika system.

The Rafale fighter starts sea trials *Dassault/F Robineau*

There is a danger that anything written about the French Navy is going to need an early review as a result of the change of government in March. In 1992 the Naval Chief of Staff continued his public row about the state of the Navy, and in the process got much of what he wanted in Optimar 95, which is a three year plan to rationalise and restructure the organisation of the Fleet. He also managed to retain most of the major equipment programmes and, by threatening to resign in October, kept the reorganisation on track.

The new plan means the regrouping of most deployable vessels (force d'action naval) to Toulon, replacing the Mediterranean Fleet, while the Atlantic Fleet is abolished in favour of an ASW action group (group d'action sous-marine) operating from Brest, to support the strategic oceanic force and provide anti-submarine escorts. Mine warfare activity

NETHERLANDS NAVAL INDUSTRIES GROUP

The Netherlands Naval Industries Group represents a group of companies all with vast experience in their specific fields of expertise, covering all the disciplines necessary to build modern high-technology ships.

The goal of the NNIG is to offer governments, naval forces and industries throughout the world the gateway to the members of the group. Besides their specific fields of expertise to build high-technology naval ships the NNIG member companies cover also a wide range of general engineering technology with the capabilities to develop and supply advanced products and systems for civil as well as for defence markets.

Surface vessels and submarines built in The Netherlands have proved themselves on the high seas in the past and today. They will continue to do so tomorrow! For more information ask for the NNIG brochure.

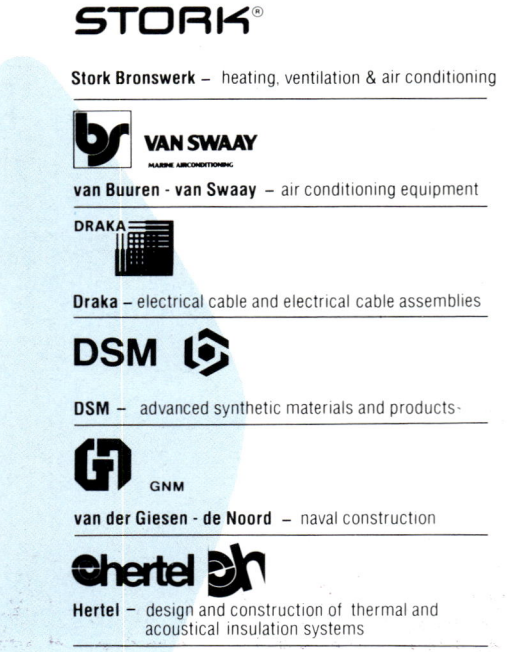

STORK

Stork Bronswerk – heating, ventilation & air conditioning

van Buuren - van Swaay – air conditioning equipment

Draka – electrical cable and electrical cable assemblies

DSM – advanced synthetic materials and products

van der Giesen - de Noord – naval construction

Hertel – design and construction of thermal and acoustical insulation systems

MARIN

Marin – maritime research institute netherlands

Nevesbu – ship designers and consultants

RDM – design and construction of submarines and defense equipment

van Rietschoten & Houwens – design, construction and installation of complete electrical and electronic equipment

Royal Schelde – design and construction of surface combatants

Stork-Wärtsilä Diesel – design and manufacture of diesel engines and complete power systems

The NNIG P.O. Box 16350 2500 BJ The Hague The NETHERLANDS Tel.: +31 (0) 70 3497 979 Fax: +31 (0) 70 3854 460 Tlx.: 31640 gnuf nl

The Netherlands Naval Industries Group is ready to serve you

is also being based at Brest although attachments will remain at Toulon. Operations at Cherbourg and Lorient are being much reduced and some naval air stations are to be run down.

Operationally the French Navy retains a global presence. Apart from standing forces in the Caribbean, Tahiti, Reunion and New Caledonia, there has been activity in the Indian Ocean and Red Sea, off Somalia and as part of the WEU force in the Adriatic. SSBN patrols have been scaled down from three to two submarines normally deployed, and in common with America and Britain, projected SSN numbers are being reduced, in this case by cutting back on the building programme.

Trials of the Rafale M fighter started in the carrier *Foch* early this year. Production deliveries are scheduled to begin in 1996 but the aircraft's full capability will have to wait for the nuclear-powered *Charles de Gaulle* to enter service with improved catapults.

Major concerns continue over the building rate of new escorts, because of the age of many of those in service. This has given impetus to the Franco-British air defence ship project which has also impacted on the normal French equipment procurement processes.

Women are being accepted in sea-going billets as a matter of course, starting this year. Numbers per ship initially are not to exceed 15% and they will not be employed in submarines.

Any suggestion that the French Navy might have to rely on other nations to provide some capabilities would be met with incredulity. Like the British, but for different reasons, France has reduced its forces to the point where any further cutbacks will force a major defence review.

Most European navies have fallen on hard times but the Spanish more than any of the others. For a time all defence procurement was placed on hold and the minister responsible resigned in protest. The only naval construction programmes making progress in 1993 are the last two Santa Maria class frigates, the new Fleet logistic tanker and, almost as an afterthought the four CME class Sandown derivative minehunters. Operational seatime has also been severely reduced.

The Spanish remain deeply concerned about terrorist activity, as well as illegal immigration and drug running from North Africa. A Support and Surveillance ship was taken up from trade into the Navy in 1992, a former East German AGI has been refurbished and enters service this year and the paramilitary Guardia Civil Del Mar, formed in 1991, is being rapidly built up into a formidable coast guard, with a number of very fast patrol craft.

The Mediterranean and Black Seas
UN-imposed sanctions on Serbia have created considerable maritime activity in the Adriatic. On 18 November 1992 the NATO Standing Naval Force Mediterranean started to enforce compliance by stopping and searching suspect vessels and, eleven days later, warships operating under the auspices of the WEU followed suit. As the relevant UN resolution was passed on 15 November it could be argued that both organisations were slower to respond than they should have been, with the WEU inevitably lagging behind NATO. To be effective, multinational Command and Control organisations have got to gear themselves to rapid responses if they are to gain the confidence of those at the sharp end of even low key operations. As an example of a worse case, a former UN commander in Bosnia is on record as saying that at weekends he could not get an answer from the New York Headquarters. WEU activities are now commanded from Brussels and in the Adriatic are controlled from the Italian headquarters at Santa Rosa, near Rome. NATO forces in this area are controlled by COMNAVSOUTH in Naples. The Italian Navy has also been particularly active in contributing forces in its own back yard.

As the STANAVFORMED and WEU forces largely comprise ships from the same navies, and use identical procedures at sea, it is reasonable to ask "Why the duplication?" Was not the WEU supposed to be the European pillar of NATO? Only those familiar with the confusion surrounding the European Community's Maastricht Treaty will know the answer to this question, and the fact that mostly it was the same Foreign and Defence Ministers who authorised the commitment of both forces needs no further comment from simple sailors.

Italy is going through a rough patch politically as the nation has grown tired of a corrupt bureaucracy. New construction plans for the Navy are inevitably confused, perhaps best exemplified by the stop-start-stop of the Artigliere class project. These are four Lupo frigates built for Iraq and left stranded with shipbuilders Fincantieri when Iraq invaded Kuwait. Whether these ships will finally see service in the Italian Navy remains to be seen.

One shipbuilding programme that is going ahead rapidly is the third San Giorgio class LPD which is earmarked as a training ship. Six more air defence destroyers are also needed and Italy has joined the Anglo-French project in 1993 with a view to having the first one in service by the end of the century.

Deprived of its former major Fleet maintenance facilities which now belong to Croatia, the Serbian and Montenegran rump of the Yugoslav Federation Navy is doing its best to remain operational while spread around ports and harbours of the Bay of Cattaro. The Federation has considerable stocks of mines and it is surprising that so far none of these has claimed a victim. Of the ships which were not taken over by Croatia, about 80% are still considered to be operational and capabilities, although in decline, should not be underestimated. Croatia on the other hand has an active building programme with missile corvettes of the Kralj class and an LCT/minelayer being commissioned.

It was disappointing to visit the Defendory defence equipment exhibition in Athens late last year and find no visible sign of Greek warships in the deep water berths alongside the exhibition hall, or of displays from the two major warship yards. From a security point of view Greece's position has markedly deteriorated in the last couple of years, with trade routes cut off through Yugoslavia, refugees pouring in from Albania and Bulgaria, and tensions with Turkey unchanged. Maybe the Navy was too busy to be able to spend time in Athens although the same cannot be said of the shipyards, which have been having severe funding problems.

The Hellenic Navy continues to benefit from basing agreements with the United States, and if the indigenous shipyards are making slow progress on new frigates, LSTs and fast attack craft, there has been no shortage of reinforcements in the form of ex-USN destroyers, frigates and maritime patrol aircraft. Germany and The Netherlands are also being generous in the provision of more frigates, corvettes, landing craft and small auxiliaries. Greece became a full member of the WEU in November last year.

The possible extension of the Yugoslav crisis into the rest of the Balkans remains a real fear, and is the principle reason for the heavy international presence in Bosnia, even if no-one has yet worked out a way to keep the warring factions apart. The security of Greece is of fundamental importance to the containment of the war in Yugoslavia.

National, NATO and WEU forces are operating in the Adriatic

In the Black Sea the Bulgarian and Romanian Navies are still restricted in the amount of time spent at sea which is often no more than two or three days per month. Bulgaria has embarked on an ambitious modernisation programme with the aim of establishing a Fleet of some 50 combatant units by the end of the decade. These are to include replacement submarines, about 20 missile craft and patrol ships, a dozen minelayers and 20 MCMVs; 12 helicopters are also required. About 36 ships of the existing Fleet are to be paid off.

Turkey now has military co-operation agreements with Albania, Bulgaria and Romania, to add to the full membership of NATO and associate membership of the WEU. This link with the WEU allows access to sensitive European technology, although such is the US involvement in Turkey's military industries that it is not thought this change will make much immediate impact.

Current naval construction programmes include modern submarines,

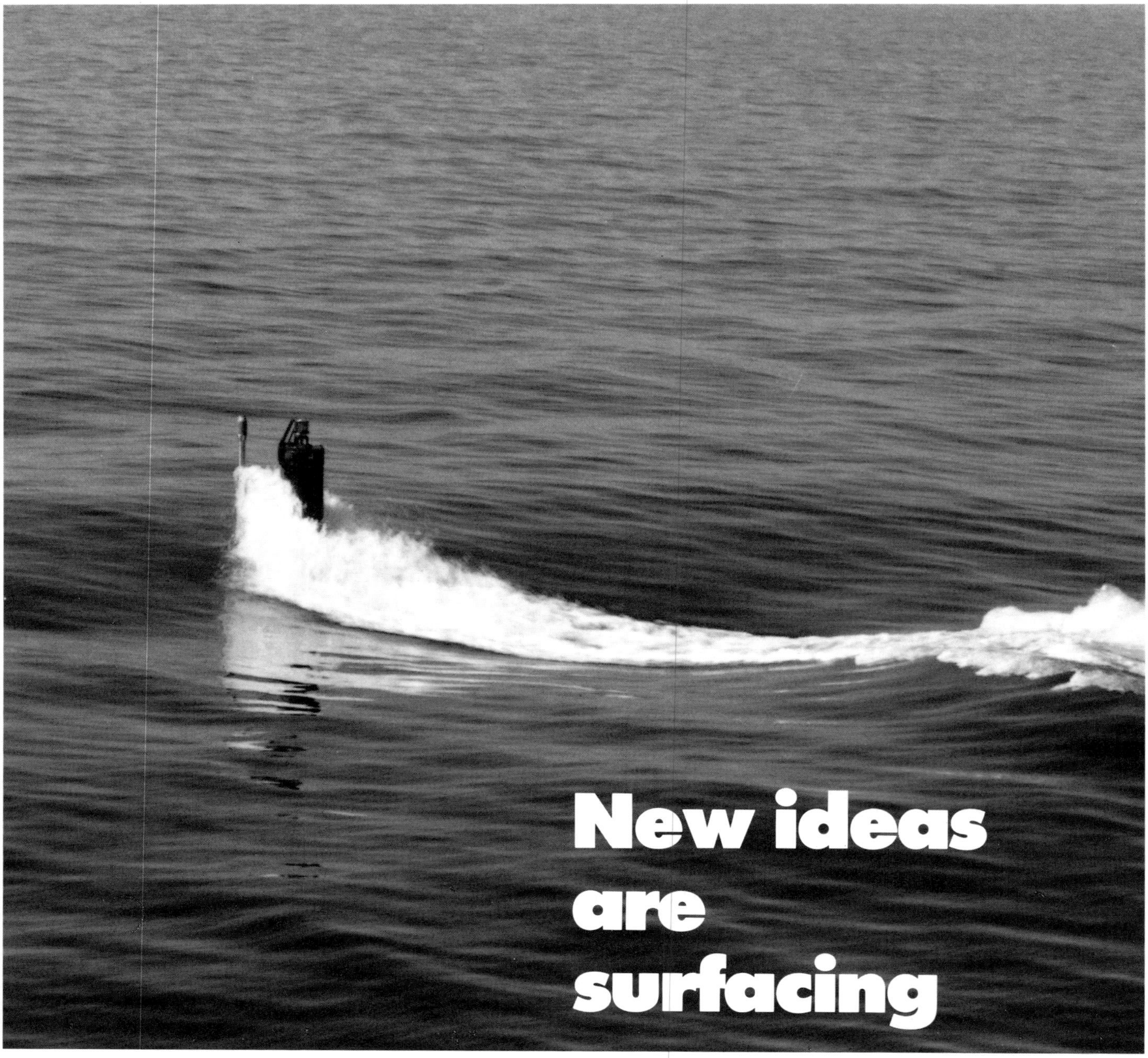

New ideas are surfacing

Fuel cell propulsion for submarines

Hydrogen and oxygen provide the power for non-nuclear air-independent silent underwater cruising. This superior propulsion system for submarines has been realized in cooperation with INGENIEURKONTOR LUEBECK GMBH, FERROSTAAL AG and SIEMENS AG.

Howaldtswerke-Deutsche Werft AG
P.O. Box 14 63 09, D-2300 Kiel 14, Phone: 04 31 / 7 00-0
Telex: 292288-0 hdw d, Telefax: 04 31 / 7 00-23 12

HOWALDTSWERKE-DEUTSCHE WERFT AG

A Member of the Preussag Group

FOREWORD

frigates and missile attack craft, and although not yet confirmed, up to four ex-US Knox class frigates are expected to transfer starting later this year. One of them is to replace the elderly destroyer *Muavenet*, taken out of service after being hit on the bridge by a Sea Sparrow missile fired in error by the aircraft carrier *Saratoga*. Orders for new minehunters have been postponed to 1993/94.

At the eastern end of the Mediterranean, Syria still owes money to Russia which probably accounts for the failure to update her ageing submarines and patrol forces. Israel has launched her first corvette, the heavily armed *Eilat*, which should be delivered at the end of the year with two more to follow in 1994. The *Eilat* is double the size of any previous Israeli warship and will be able to stay at sea for longer periods than the attack craft which hitherto have comprised the bulk of the Navy.

Egypt's concern with the activities of Iran in North Africa came to a head in March this year with a blunt warning that Egypt will attack Iranian warships if they try to establish a naval base at Port Sudan, half way up the Red Sea. There is growing evidence that Iran is financing Islamic terrorism from camps within Sudan in an attempt to destabilise the whole of North Africa.

As well as controlling the Suez canal, Egypt has the region's largest navy and is trying to update it with the assistance of the United States. Work has finally started in America on modernising the ex-Chinese Romeo class submarines and new MCMVs are also under construction. The old Soviet T43 minesweepers are to be given helicopter platforms and used as patrol vessels. The Navy may also become one more recipient of the ubiquitous Knox class frigates released by the USN and slowly finding their way into fleets around the world. There are also plans for a new series of fast attack craft to be built under licence in local shipyards.

Of the other navies on the southern shores of the Mediterranean, Morocco is almost certainly acquiring Assad class corvettes originally built in Italy for Iraq but not delivered, and Tunisia and Malta have both received ex-German Kondor class patrol craft. Tunisia is also expecting Chinese Huludao class attack craft and has bought from the USN a former Robert D Conrad class survey ship, probably to replace her elderly training frigate. Libya has already lost one submarine delivered to the Baltic for a refit which was never completed, and the departure last year of the final Russian support ship has further exacerbated maintenance problems for the rest of the Fleet.

Indian Ocean and The Gulf

The flotillas of the Arabian peninsula provide a lively market for Western technology even though the Gulf continues to be policed by the world's major navies. Because of the intense competition between warship builders, it is not always immediately clear when a statement of intention is the preface to a firm order, or merely an expression of wishful thinking by the shipyard concerned.

Most of the sought after contracts are for patrol craft of varying types but Oman is buying two Vosper missile corvettes, the UAE is expected to invite tenders for similar vessels, and Saudi Arabia is still trying to decide on whether to confirm the *accord cadre* with France to build three air defence frigates. Saudi Arabia is also in the process of taking delivery of three new Sandown class minehunters but has been slow to order more, and the former general interest of the Gulf States in MCM vessels appears to have subsided in favour of letting more experienced navies provide mine clearance capabilities.

A clearer picture has emerged in the last year of what is left of Iraq's Navy. Two corvettes remain under embargo in Italy, a tanker is still at Alexandria and a few vessels are left in the Gulf, some at the commercial port of Umm Qasr.

On the eastern shore of the Gulf, Iran's military expansion and implacable opposition to Western interests shows no sign of changing and is contained only by the country's economic difficulties. On top of Egypt's warning over the use of a Sudanese base in the Red Sea, the Gulf Co-operation Council has denounced Iranian attempts to annex three disputed islands, and commented unfavourably on growing links between Tehran and Muslim groups in the adjacent republics of the former Soviet Union.

Internationally the most photographed warship of the year was the first Iranian Kilo class submarine, which sailed from the Baltic under the Russian flag last October. Throughout its passage to Bandar Abbas, no Iranians were seen on the bridge, and there is not much doubt that some experienced Russian submariners are still assisting in bringing the ship up to an operational standard. Delivery of one or two more of the same class is expected in the next couple of years. Although these submarines could represent a real menace to merchant ships in transit through the Arabian Sea, they will be at their most vulnerable to Western technology when tied up alongside in harbour.

More Hegu class attack craft have been ordered from China but the contract has been delayed by arguments over the type of missiles to be fitted. There is also an active indigenous small craft industry which now advertises its products on the international market.

To rub salt into the wounds caused to Iraq by its ejection from Kuwait by coalition forces, the Iranian Navy has commissioned an ex-Iraqi Osa missile craft and a Bogomol patrol boat that defected to Iranian ports in early 1991. A Polnochny LST has also been retained but so far has not been taken into service.

Pakistan's five year leases on eight ex-US Brooke and Garcia class escorts have begun to expire and the ships are sequentially being taken out of service, with the last to go in early 1994, unless the US Administration changes its mind. The propulsion plant of these ships is notoriously unreliable and the Pakistan Navy wants to replace them with British Type 21 and possibly more Leander class frigates to join the two already in service.

With Pakistan keen to improve its long-term economic prospects by serving as an outlet to the sea for Afghanistan and some of the Central Asian Muslim republics, the strategic importance of Karachi is self-evident, even though there are plans to build a new naval base at Ormara. Minehunting capabilities have been enhanced by the delivery of a French Eridan class MCMV, a second is building at Lorient and a third will be shipped to Karachi as a hull for fitting out.

The elderly Gearing class destroyers are beginning to pay off and there is a pressing need for new shipborne helicopters, as well as maritime patrol aircraft to substitute for the three Orions embargoed in America. Three more Agosta submarines are to be acquired from France, as long as the money can be found to pay for them.

The last year has seen no end to the fascination with which the rest of the world continues to watch events in India. The Navy has not been exempt from this scrutiny, and the combination of a long period of secrecy, coupled with the expansion of island bases and the lease for a short time of a nuclear submarine, led many military analysts to suggest there was a risk that India wished to impose herself on the whole Indian Ocean region. You don't operate nuclear submarines for coastal defence.

Recently though, perceptions have shifted. The SSN has gone, and although an indigenous nuclear submarine project has a high priority, it is a long way from being realised. The surface ship construction programme, with its dependence on technology from the former Soviet Navy, has suffered a reverse because of the current unreliability of the logistic supply lines from the independent republics. Perhaps most important of all, the Navy has come out of its shell and, after a quarter of a century of near isolation, is now actively engaged in dialogue with ASEAN navies and with Australia. It has also carried out the first ever joint exercise with Oman, and is conducting low level exercises and restoring links with passing warships from the USA, Britain and France.

India is conducting low level exercises with other navies

Overall defence spending is up by nearly 10% for 1993/94, although the real increase is much smaller after allowing for inflation. The Navy's ambition is to improve its share from the current 13% to about 20% by the end of the decade. The third Delhi class destroyer has been laid down, improved Godavari frigates are building and the fifth Khukri class corvette was launched late last year. The progress of these and other shipbuilding projects is in part governed by the extent of dependence on Russian equipment supplies, and many of the Soviet-designed ships in service are also suffering from a lack of spares, with some being cannibalised to keep others going. Indigenous weapons programmes are seen as the long-term solution, but there is going to have to be a greater reliance on Western technology to bridge the gap, at a cost in excess of the friendly financial terms provided by the former Soviet Union.

HIGH Performance Marine Reduction Gearboxes

Cincinnati Gear sets the standard for high performance marine drives, specializing in surface hardened and precision ground epicyclic and parallel shaft gearsets for diesel and gas turbine driven marine propulsion systems.

1,000 to 50,000 HP

- The Jetfoil and PHM, by Boeing Marine Systems, both utilize gas turbine drives. The Jetfoil, currently manufactured by Kawasaki, uses the 501 and the PHM uses the LM 2500.

- American Enterprise crewboat, built by Halter Marine, Inc., has a 501 gas turbine drive and a 2-stage CGCO reduction gear.

- The LCAC, built by Textron Marine Systems, is powered by four, TF40 gas turbines and has eight, CGCO gearboxes.

- The T-AO 187 fleet oiler made by Avondale Shipyards, Inc., has the largest carburized, hardened, and precision ground gears in the U.S. Navy. It is powered by two 10PC4.2V diesels.

- AOE-6, built by NASSCO, features two Cincinnati Gear dual input locked train reduction gears incorporating a hydraulic reversing coupling. This marks the first reversing reduction gear of its size in a U.S. Navy surface ship. The AOE-6 is powered by four LM 2500 gas turbines.

- Mulder Design Mega Yacht features a TF40 gas turbine and a MA-107 CGCO reduction gear driving a water jet.

JETFOIL

PHM

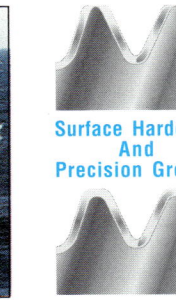
Surface Hardened And Precision Ground

CREWBOAT

Product Leadership

High power density gearing is the new standard for the U.S. Navy marine propulsion gearing, and Cincinnati Gear is leading the way. All of these programs use Cincinnati Gear surface hardened and precision ground marine propulsion gearing:

LCAC

T-AO 187

AOE-6

Facility & Equipment

- Precision gear hobbing machine cuts class 14 gears up to 200" in diameter.

- Precision gear grinder produces class 15 surface hardened gears up to 158" in diameter by 63" face.

- Internal hobbing head attachment cuts internal gears up to 220" pitch diameter.

MULDER DESIGN

...Good Gears Only, Since 1907!

The **Cincinnati Gear** Company

5657 Wooster Pike • Cincinnati, Ohio 45227, U.S.A. • 513-271-7700 • Fax 513-271-0049

Overall, the equipment picture is much less rosy than was the case a few years ago, at the same time as the Asia Pacific zone grows more unstable.

Bangladesh has replaced a couple of attack craft sunk in a typhoon in 1991 with two more delivered from China in June last year. For warship enthusiasts, it is a pleasure to report that the Salisbury and Leopard class frigates are still in excellent repair. Sri Lanka also lost an LCM which sank in October last year, but the ship has been salvaged and may be repairable.

Burma's links with China are as strong as ever. Sailors are regularly sent to China for training and more attack craft deliveries are expected in due course. China is also assisting in the construction of a new naval base at Haingyi Island in the Irawaddy delta and is updating the facilities at Great Coco Island, north of the Andaman Islands. It is not yet clear whether the Chinese Navy is seeking regular access.

Pacific Asia and The China Seas
Suddenly China looks more threatening. As little as two years ago the Soviet Pacific Fleet was the major maritime player in the region, counterbalanced by a formidable American presence in the Philippines, Japan and South Korea. The Soviet ships now fly the Russian flag and are at the furthest and most neglected end of a disorganised logistic supply line. The US Navy has left the Philippines and there are strong voices in Congress calling for further military withdrawals from the region, now that the superpower confrontation has ended and Japan is more than capable of paying for its own defence.

An American presence in Japanese waters *Hachiro Nakai*

China meanwhile is taking advantage of a buyers' market in Russian equipment and is beginning to show signs of wanting to expand into the void left by the scaled-down US presence. Last year the Chinese finally claimed all the disputed Spratley Islands as sovereign territory and are reinforcing their island garrisons, as well as basing squadrons of newly acquired Russian fighter bombers within striking range. Peking's invective towards Hong Kong grows increasingly shrill, with obvious implications for Taiwan, which remains unable to acquire much of the European technology it wants, because China threatens to stop trading with any country which provides equipment for Taiwan. Such is the potential of the Chinese market that few are prepared to take this risk.

Counting Chinese naval vessels is a particularly unrewarding task because large numbers of the older submarines and coastal patrol craft are in various states of reserve and without crews, although many of these vessels would be available if needed. In this edition the number of Chinese ships in reserve is shown for the first time.

The shipbuilding industry is beginning to take advantage of Western technology, with the improvement of hitherto almost non-existent air defences taking a high priority. French Crotale SAM is fitted in the new Luhu class destroyer and the latest version of the indigenous HQ61 appears in a sextuple launcher on the forecastle of *Anqing* and *Huainan* which are the first two Jiangwei class frigates. An improved Luda class destroyer *Zhuhai* appears to be fitted with a set of ASW missile launchers for the CY-1 air flight weapon which has been known about for some years but not seen at sea. It is possible that the Luhu class may also have this weapon in dual capability box launchers.

Rumours that China had bought the Kuznetsov class aircraft carrier *Varyag*, building at Nikolayev, proved to be inaccurate, but there is no doubt that a multi-aircraft platform is a high priority naval requirement. A helicopter carrier, possibly a merchant conversion, is a more likely first step, but as Chinese and Russian commercial links appear to be strengthening, anything is possible and transfers of second-hand ships can happen very quickly.

If China wants a foothold in the Indian Ocean, she has it in Burma, but although there have been a number of new support ships sighted in the last year, deep sea fleet replenishment does not seem to be a high priority.

An expansionist maritime policy is not an option given the current state of Fleet training and equipment. Nonetheless the Navy is a credible force in coastal regions and in support of land forces, and building a 'quality Navy' is now a stated Chinese objective.

Across the Yellow Sea the Korean peninsula looms as a loose cannon waiting to explode. A normalisation agreement signed between South Korea and China in August 1992 has left North Korea almost isolated, and its ageing Navy cut off from both its former suppliers and facing an economic cul-de-sac. There appeared to be signs of some attempts at reconciliation with the South towards the end of the year, but more recently the threat of nuclear weapons has grown, with the North refusing to allow inspections by the International Atomic Energy Authority.

South Korea builds its first submarine *Daewoo*

The South Korean Navy is rushing ahead with its submarine programme, giving unusual publicity to the launch last October of the first hull built by Daewoo, while the first of the class which was built in Germany is already in service. The Koreans are not having the problems in building advanced submarines that have plagued countries such as India and Argentina. Much less dynamic has been the KDX frigate programme which has suffered countless delays with project definition extended into 1993, and it may now be overtaken by a new operational requirement for a much larger class of air defence destroyer. As an interim measure more Ulsan class are building. More minehunters are also under construction, the first of two LSTs is to start trials at the end of this year, and two large salvage ships have recently been commissioned into the Coast Guard, while a third is being built for the Navy. It is an impressive programme and reflects the priority for defence spending being given to the Navy.

After nearly two years of tortuous debate, Japan's parliament finally passed a law in June 1992 allowing the military to be used in peace keeping operations in support of the United Nations. This was heralded abroad as a great triumph suggesting a new heavyweight status in global geopolitics. In reality, such deployments are still hedged around with so many conditions that further weighty amendments will be necessary before the new law can be described as a conventional foreign policy. Although some of Japan's neighbours still have long memories stretching back over fifty years, the principal opposition to changing the restrictions placed on the use of armed forces continues to come from within the country. Nonetheless, the naval deployment in 1992 to Cambodia followed the minesweeping operation in the Gulf a year earlier, and provides precedents on which to build for the future.

In spite of some cutbacks, defence spending is set to rise by about 2% a year to 1996 and this year, in the month of March alone, the Navy commissioned a destroyer, a frigate, a submarine, two hydrofoil attack craft, and two minehunters, and the Maritime Safety Agency commissioned a training ship and two patrol craft.

POWERFUL COMBATANT

EUROCORVETTE

A naval European venture of
Bremer Vulkan, Germany
Chantiers de l'Atlantique, France

Head Office : 38, avenue Kléber - 75116 Paris - France
Tel : (33-1) 47 55 27 70 - Fax (33-1) 47 55 28 48

Much the most interesting naval development is the inclusion in the 1993 shipbuilding programme of a helicopter-capable ship listed as an 8900 ton LST. This project was first proposed in a slightly different form in 1989 and again in 1990 but did not get the necessary approval. Although the design has a docking well for amphibious craft, it also has a flight deck which stretches over the whole length of the ship and hangar lifts for light helicopters. One flight deck spot is to be strengthened for operations by a medium lift helicopter.

In the restricted terms of the age and numbers of their front line escorts and conventional submarines the Japanese can claim to have the world's third most powerful Fleet, after the USA and Russia. It also has a powerful combination of indigenous and licensed modern technology, the latter mostly American in origin. Apart from the limitations of the force structure which by design lacks offensive capability and reach, the main problem is the Navy's inability to attract adequate numbers of recruits. Most volunteer sailors in major navies like to travel abroad and act as ambassadors for their country. To a lively 18 year old who wants to go to sea to see the world, the 1000 mile limit on deployments must be a difficult problem for the recruiters to explain away.

In terms of escorts, the world's third largest Navy   *A Sheldon Duplaix*

If Taiwan had hoped that time would eventually help heal the rift with China, current events in Hong Kong must be discouraging. Attempts in Hong Kong to increase the influence of the democratically elected element of the administrative council prior to the hand over to China in 1997, have led to a disproportionate campaign of vilification by Peking. The linkage with China's attitude to Taiwan is inescapable and fully justifies the modernisation of the ROC Navy, which is going ahead mostly with help from the United States.

Because of frequent Chinese submarine incursions, anti-submarine warfare is a top priority, and for this Taiwan badly needs more diesel submarines. The problem continues to be one of finding a shipbuilder whose government will stand up to Chinese threats to impose trade sanctions if a contract is negotiated. France is building La Fayette class light frigate hulls which will be fitted out in Taiwan, and will augment the modified Oliver Perry class ships being built with US assistance at Keelung. The first of the latter commissions this Summer.

At the same time three ex-US Knox class frigates have been transferred, with probably three more to come, which will allow some of the World War II vintage ships to be scrapped. Twelve shipborne Seasprite helicopters are being acquired in August this year. More minehunters may also be built under licence and logistic support ship numbers are being steadily reinforced. Like South Korea, it is a most impressive programme and could only be achieved by a country that believes itself to be seriously threatened from the sea.

In the South China Seas there are a number of expansionist programmes which are beginning to be described with journalistic overstatement as being part of a regional arms race. On the other hand an arms race is what it may become if China overplays her hand.

Having cancelled a contract with Bremer Vulcan for a helicopter carrier, Thailand has now ordered a Principe De Asturias type from Bazán. This ship will be STOVL-capable with a 12 degree ski jump and its main tasks are defined as EEZ surveillance and search and rescue co-ordination, with a secondary role of air support for all maritime operations. Chinese-built frigates are still being delivered and, now that the indigenous ASW corvette programme has completed, two additional modified Jianghu class with helicopter platforms are to be built in Thailand.

So concerned is the Thai Government with illegal activities in coastal waters that a Coast Guard force was officially authorised in September last year, and the Coastal Defence Command has been rapidly expanded to defend the eastern seaboard of the Gulf of Thailand. In addition there is a Marine Police Command with some 125 armed patrol craft up to the size of a 630 ton corvette.

If the lawlessness in the Gulf of Thailand is of growing concern to the Thais, the problem of piracy in the commercial shipping lanes of Southeast Asia is affecting the whole international maritime community. The worst affected area is in the Malaccan Straits between Singapore and Sumatra, and in July 1992 an accord was signed between Singapore and Indonesia to co-ordinate naval patrols. The Malaysian Navy is also alert to the need to step up its naval presence, but as this is one of the busiest waterways in the world it is not an easy task to identify the culprits, who conduct themselves with military precision and discipline. As these pirates frequently kill or immobilise key members of the crew, there is a danger of an ecological disaster, should a tanker be driven ashore while not under command. Not surprisingly there are calls from shipowners for an international standing naval force to police the area.

Apart from piracy, the region is beset by disputes over the ownership of various islands and archipelagoes. Although there are some bilateral defence accords, multilateral coalitions remain as elusive as ever.

Malaysia has ordered two more frigates, Singapore is to replace its gun-armed fast attack craft and is acquiring four Landsort class minehunters, and Indonesia is in the process of resolving its long-standing need for more patrol ships, mine countermeasures vessels and landing ships by buying 16 Parchim class, nine Kondor and 12 Frosch class from Germany. These former East German vessels also include a couple of supply ships. Apart from the Philippines and Vietnam, Indonesian warships in 1992 averaged out as the oldest in the region. Buying second hand is not going to rejuvenate the Fleet by as much as the Navy might have hoped, but in the endless argument in all navies of quantity versus quality, the nature of the Indonesian archipelago is a persuasive reason for going for quantity.

No longer under the protective umbrella of the US Navy based at Subic Bay, The Philippines are coming to terms with their inability to protect their maritime interests. Illegal fishing alone is claimed to be costing the country about one billion US dollars a year, money it can ill afford to lose. Patrol craft are being built locally to augment those recently delivered from the USA which is also constructing two Frank S Besson class LSVs for commissioning this year. Further patrol craft orders placed in Australia and Spain are awaiting adequate funds, and more support ships may be acquired from China. From 1995 it is hoped to purchase a frigate, three corvettes and a number of MCMVs. The Philippines Navy is making a determined effort to make good years of neglect, but it is going to be a long haul.

Southern Hemisphere

No one is trying harder than Australia to broaden military and economic ties within the Asia Pacific region. Whether this will eventually lead to a multilateral security framework currently seems unlikely, but much groundwork is being done should existing tensions erupt into something more serious.

Maritime co-operation with Indonesia has advanced to the point of exercising procedures for the co-ordination of combined surveillance operations on a small scale, and contacts are being reinforced as far afield as India and Japan. In May this year Australia is hosting a Fleet training period with ships from Malaysia, Singapore and Thailand, and observers from Indonesia.

The Navy is also showing skill in piloting its new equipment programmes through some fairly hostile financial conditions. So far the new Collins class submarine project is on time and within its budget, although subject to the usual barrage of selective criticism which accompanies any major defence project in countries with a free press. The ANZAC frigate programme has also advanced to the point where defence savings would be difficult to find in the short term. This means that the urgency behind the new minehunter programme may well not be enough to guarantee adherence to the scheduled timetable, and the replacement for the Fremantle class patrol craft has already receded to the end of the decade.

The selection process for a new class of minehunter is in theory due to complete later this year. Typical Australian water conditions include a coral type seabed with high sonar reverberation levels, unusually warm seawater temperatures and generally higher sea states than most MCMV forces have to cope with. There are no cheap solutions if effective minehunting is to be achieved.

Another project close to the Navy's heart is the proposed training and helicopter support ship. This has a wide measure of popular support but building (or conversion) funds have not been allocated until 1997.

New Zealand's two main priorities are replacement helicopters and the provision of a military sealift ship for disaster relief and other contingencies. The image of the south west Pacific as some sort of sub-tropical paradise dies hard despite the fall-out from French nuclear weapon testing. In fact there are destabilising and potentially violent forces at play in Papua New Guinea, East Timor and Fiji, although the latter is beginning to restore normal relations with its neighbours after

The simple diesel solution

S.E.M.T. PIELSTICK

For naval ship propulsion

FRIGATE "CASSARD" (CODAD) - FRANCE

UNDERWAY REPLENISHMENT TANKER "DURANCE" - FRANCE

NUCLEAR FLEET SUB. "CASABIANCA" - FRANCE

PATROL FRIGATE "FLOREAL" (CODAD) - FRANCE

S.E.M.T. Pielstick
2, quai de Seine — 93302 Saint-Denis — France
Tel.: 33 (1) 48 09 76 00 — Telex: SEMT 236 773
Fax: 33 (1) 42 43 81 02

Sevenbladed partially submerged C.P. propellers for a SES.

ESCHER WYSS CONTROLLABLE PITCH PROPELLERS

The versatile **ESCHER WYSS Controllable Pitch Propeller** design that fulfills the stringent hydrodynamic, hydroacoustic and mechanical requirements of today's high technology naval vessels.

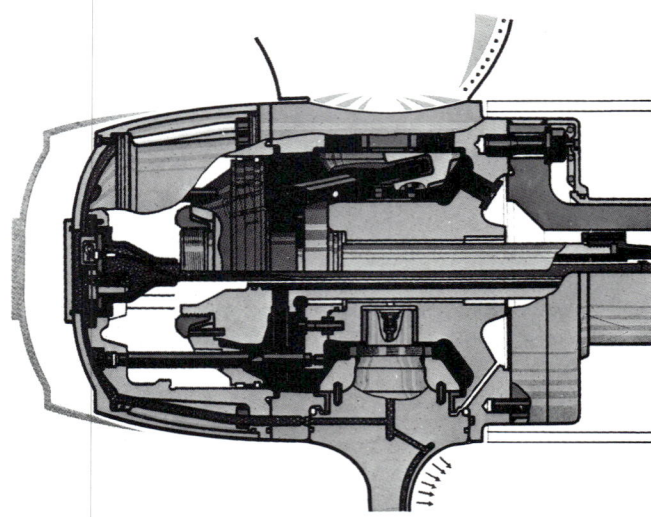

A fivebladed naval propeller with prairie air supply, additional electronic pitch measuring device and hub purging system.

A frigate propeller: 25000 HP.

SULZER ESCHER WYSS

D-7980 Ravensburg/F.R.G., Tel. (07 51) 8 30, Telex 7 32 901   VP 80

FOREWORD

two military coups in the last five years.

On the other side of the Indian Ocean the navies of central and southern Africa are mostly in steep decline as a result of the withdrawal of the competing funds which flowed during the superpower confrontation. The combination of corrupt regimes and hostile environmental conditions has proved to be too destructive in many cases, although there are still a few operational patrol craft to be found. Some others still listed in this edition are in various states of decay but could be restored if the money was available. Although not strictly in the southern hemisphere, a good example is the Nigerian corvette *Otobo* which is decaying alongside in Genoa with a refit planned but no money to pay for it.

The main exception is the South African Navy which has been steadily declining in size but has retained its high standards of operational efficiency. As a centre of disciplined excellence and regional influence the Navy is now seeking to play a role in nation building for the new South Africa. Whether it is able to retain its standards will depend on whether it is allowed to remain politically neutral, and train its people as it has done in the past. It will also need sufficient funds to modernise the ageing Fleet. The elderly support ship *Tafelberg* is being replaced with commendable speed by a merchant ship conversion, which may be an encouraging sign for the future. Warships are once again displaying pennant numbers.

Some democracies in South America are under stress as a result of structural reforms which are improving economic growth but only at the expense of greater unemployment and falling wages. With internal instability the major preoccupation, and few signs of any immediate external threats, it is not surprising that new naval equipment programmes are taking a low priority. The litany of change in naval strengths is less dramatic here than almost anywhere else in the world.

The Argentine building programme has stalled and the prospect of sales of uncompleted ships recedes each year. The aircraft carrier is still waiting for new engines and the highest priority is being given to the acquisition of ex-USN helicopters. The plan to confine the Coast Guard to territorial waters while leaving the Navy to patrol the EEZ has been withdrawn.

Brazil's aircraft carrier is in refit and may go to sea again in 1994. New frigate and patrol craft programmes proceed at slow speed, as does submarine construction which has now been limited to three of the Type 209 class followed, possibly, by two of an improved type. Plans to acquire ex-USN destroyers were not funded. Chile is hoping to order new submarines this year and is building its own patrol craft. A survey ship of the Robert D Conrad class was transferred from the USN in 1992 and the Navy is taking up some former ocean-going tugs and converting them to patrol gunboats.

At the request of the United Nations, Uruguayan naval officials have been active in assisting Cambodia. The Navy acquired four ex-German Kondor class minesweepers in late 1991. Contrary to reports at the time, these vessels have retained a minesweeping capability.

Central America and Canada

Most nations with a Caribbean seaboard are involved in one way or another with anti-narcotics activities. Colombia and Venezuela have both been recipients of ex-US patrol vessels of various types; Colombia in particular is receiving this year some 15 river patrol craft and 45 assault boats for drug interdiction patrols.

Mexico has reorganised its command system, and within the last 12 months commissioned four locally built 1300 ton gunships, and started to fit helicopter decks to some of the Admirable class patrol ships.

Canadians are not impressed by outsiders who comment on their idiosyncratic style of government, but perhaps it is in order to express relief that constitutional difficulties which seemed to be leading towards a national break up, appear to be less severe than was the case six months ago.

While committed to withdrawing forces from Europe, Canada remains a soft touch for any international peacekeeping or humanitarian relief operation that comes up, and there are a lot of them about. In fact some commentators are suggesting that an occasional 'no' would be in order, particularly in the context of overstretch of the Navy's three supply ships. Towards the end of 1992 there were Canadian servicemen in Yugoslavia, Iraq/Kuwait, Somalia, Cambodia, Cyprus, Western Sahara, Sinai, Angola and El Salvador.

The original naval goal of providing a high quality ASW contribution to NATO in the Atlantic has been overtaken by the end of the cold war. A multi-role force is now emerging, capable of a balanced input both to the preservation of national sovereignty and to whatever next takes the international community by surprise. Adequate surveillance of the Arctic region will remain an Achilles heel until the elderly Oberon class submarines are replaced. Interest has been shown in possible 'off the shelf' acquisitions of new British and Dutch diesel submarines, should they become available. The state of the art in air independent propulsion is probably far enough advanced to allow a reliable under-ice capability, although some form of nuclear power remains the best operational solution.

If the Halifax class programme completes, the last Iroquois class destroyer conversions run to time, projected new corvettes and the already ordered coastal defence vessels (MCDV) go ahead, and the contract signed last year for 35 EH 101 helicopters is allowed to stand, the Navy will have a rejuvenated and modern surface Fleet by the end of the decade.

From the sea

EXPERTISE AND EXPERIENCE

- Advanced design and engineering
- Consultancy, supervision and surveys
- System integration and automation
- Design automation
- Logistic support, transfer of technology

Nevesbu

Nederlandse Verenigde Scheepsbouw Bureaus
P.O. Box 16350, 2500 BJ The Hague
Phone: (+3170) 3497979
Fax (3170) 3854460

NAVAL SHIP DESIGNERS & CONSULTANTS

FOREWORD

In Conclusion

It is always easier to write about technology than people, about weapon systems rather than operators, about organisation as opposed to morale. Worldwide, there are well equipped armies which are not much more than a uniformed rabble, navies which can float but not move or fight, and air forces which are as much a risk to their pilots as to any potential enemy. Equally there are efficient and effective forces where none ought to exist. Between these two extremes lies the majority where competence, within a single nation or even service, ranges across the whole spectrum from excellence down to almost useless.

It is in the nature of scientists and builders of new technology to want to try and remove the unpredictable human element from the operation of their equipment. Computers work faster than people and, given benign and predictable circumstances, weapon systems are more reliable, needing no sleep and suffering no emotional distractions. No user of military equipment in circumstances which are seldom benign, needs to be reminded of the underlying weaknesses of this approach. Automation has its place and as long as the human being remains in control and understands the limits of his equipment, there is no conflict. The relationship between computer automation and people in a military environment is a long way from being resolved, but there is no shortage of effort in trying to achieve the best combinations.

Much more dangerous to military competence is too much change too quickly, undermining the self confidence and certainties which come from operating in an environment in which experience is at a premium, loyalties are assumed and successful innovation grows out of a bedrock of knowledge of what works and what does not.

Navies are not being cut back by every nation, but they are by those Western countries which faced up to the former Soviet Union. Under such circumstances naval hierarchies have enough to cope with in retaining good people and high standards during a period of retraction or drawdown. This is not the time to play political games with the emotional environment in which sailors have grown accustomed to operate.

Women are slowly being assimilated in fighting ships of many navies and as long as strict discipline is maintained, this can only lead to a more natural atmosphere and improved standards of behaviour. Even the strongest advocates recognise the risks if there is any laxity in applying a few commonsense rules about personal relationships, and the overall effect on fighting efficiency will not be known until put to the ultimate test of prolonged operations under attack.

Homosexuals have always existed in the Armed Forces. In the confines of a ship many people recognise those most likely to be that way inclined, and it creates no problems as long as any overt behaviour leads to immediate dismissal. Releasing people from fear of that sanction generates tensions that are detrimental to discipline and the maintenance of morale, which is so much more significant in achieving fighting effectiveness than all the new technology put together.

The progressive move towards greater international collaboration and joint service operations must give proper regard to essential national and single service characteristics.

The management of change, particularly on the scale we are now seeing in some navies, needs to be handled with great sensitivity and by paying as much attention to the advice of senior officers as would be the case in war. Those impatient with tradition, who see tribalism as arrogance, cultures as cults and competition as divisive, should not be allowed anywhere near the management of the armed forces.

Anyone who believes that strong and competent navies are no longer a top priority for industrialised nation states which trade by sea should reflect on Churchill's response to a similar assumption in 1912:

"Are you quite sure? It would be a pity to be wrong."

April 1993   Richard Sharpe

It would be a pity to be wrong

Acknowledgements

It is a pleasure to acknowledge that more and more navies are seeing the advantages of being accurately represented in this annual update. There are still a few nations which believe Jane's yearbook editors belong to some sort of intrusive intelligence organisation, but nothing could be further from the truth.

Most of what we publish is collated from official sources, either first or second hand, and our principle contribution is to put it all together in one place for easy access, either from the book or by data retrieval from compact disc.

Perhaps the main area in which the gifted amateur still plays a major role is in photography because so many official photographs tend to be a year or more out of date on receipt. We prefer the majority of our pictures of the major navies to have been taken during the twelve months preceding publication, in order to show progress in the constant stream of new programmes and modifications. The warship enthusiast has a particular role to play here but the picture below is not typical of the way most photographs are obtained. The cameraman is much more likely to be an invited visitor or guest.

Page composition continues to be driven by the needs of supplying comprehensive operational data to the man in a hurry for a quick answer. Much care is taken to prevent pages spilling over, or cross references being needed to answer straightforward questions.

My thanks as always to the Naval Attachés in London, government departments worldwide and the shipbuilding industry. Captain Vince Thomas, the editor of the US Navy League's Seapower Almanac, continues his major contribution, as does Ian Sturton with his uncluttered and accurate scale drawings. Many of the drawings have had significant revisions this year, most have had some changes and plan views of aircraft carriers are growing in number. My thanks also to Arthur Wilcox for his continuing work in rationalising the Main Machinery entries. New information on Flags and Ensigns has been provided by the Flag Institute, Chester, England and put together by Keith Faulkner. This now includes the bastardised ensign of the combined Russian and Ukraine forces in the Black Sea. As a result of requests received from several people we have included for the first time for some years officer rank insignia, the work for which has been done by W Maitland Thornton. James Pargiter has again done the Index and Pennant Lists. His inclusion of ship names and classes mentioned only in the Notes continues to receive favourable comment.

Amongst individuals who have sent photographs or information or both are Cdr Massimo Annati, Dr Giorgio Arra, Monsieur Guy de Bakker, Herr Ralf Bendfeldt, Señor J Bermudez, Herr Siegfried Breyer, Mr J L M van der Burg, Señor Camil Busquets i Vilanova, Señor Albert Campanera i Rovira, Mr Paul Campbell, Señor Diego Quevedo Carmona, Senhor Mario Roberto Vaz Carneiro, Herr Harald Carstens, Señor Julio Caufero, Dr Chien Chung, Senhor Sergio Baptista da Costa, Mr Gary Davies, Mr Horst Dehnst, Mr Demetrios Dervissis, Mr Henry Dodds, Herr Hartmut Ehlers, Mr Marko Enqvist, Mr Peter Felstead, Herr Bernd Fischer, Cdr Aldo Fraccaroli, Mr Keith Franks, Señor Francisco Gamez Balcazar, Signor Giorgio Ghiglione, Signor Giorgio Giorgerini, Mr Leo van Ginderen, Lt Col Werner Globke, Cdr James Goldrick, Cdr A W Grazebrook, Mr Eric Grove, Mr G Gyssels, Cdr Ian Hewitt, Mr P Humphries, Mr G Keith Jacobs, Mr Vic Jeffery, Mr Ziro Kimata, Cdr H J Klagges, Herr G Koop, Mr Per Kornefeldt, Herr Jurg Kursener, Lt P Longley, Vice Admiral Sergio Loperena Garcia, Señor Thomas Lozada, Ldg Seaman B McBride, Flight Lt I M McKenzie, Mr C Douglas Maginley, Mr Erik Matzen Laursen, Mr Julio Montes, Captain J E Moore, Señor Antonio Moreno Garcia, Mr John Mortimer, Mr Hachiro Nakai, Herr M Nitz, Mr Gunnar Olsen, Mr P O'Keeffe, Mr Robert Pabst, Mr S Poynton, Mr A J R Risseeuw, Cdr L Robbins, Monsieur J Y Robert, Mr Colin Rossiter, Mr F Sadek, Herr Jochen Sachse, Mr Selim San, Señor Juan Sanchez, Mr W Sartori, Lt J Sears, Monsieur A Sheldon Duplaix, Herr N A Sifferlinger, Mr Adam Smigielski, Señor Miguel A Soto, Mr H M Steele, Mr B Sullivan, Señor X I Taibo, C & S Taylor, Herr S Terzibaschitsh, Mr Guy Toremans, Mr Marek Twardowski, Mr Maurice Voss, Dr Milan Vego, Dr Andre Wessels, Messrs Wright & Logan, Mr Cem D Yaylali, Señor Luis Oscar Zunino.

From the Jane's catalogue, All the World's Aircraft, High-Speed Marine Craft, Strategic Weapon Systems, Naval Weapon Systems, Radar and EW Systems and Underwater Warfare Systems have all been consulted, as have the various contributors to the Jane's magazines, in particular International Defense Review, Jane's Intelligence Review and Jane's Defence Weekly. My acknowledgements are due also to other international naval reference books including Almanacco Navale (Italy), Flottes de Combat (France) and Weyers Flotten Taschenbuch (Germany).

For the first time page composition has been done in-house but with the same skilled team of Jack Brenchley and Keith Biller. A new photographic reproduction process has been used to considerable effect by Kevan Box. The translation of literally thousands of editorial hieroglyphics into sensible copy has all been taken care of with great calm and efficiency by Ruth Simmance, Diana Burns, Sarah Erskine and Chrissie Richards, and the transposition into CD-ROM by Alan Ricketts. No one who has been responsible for the production of this kind of book will have any illusions as to how much work is involved in the whole process, nor of the patience required to meet the administrative demands of the office, which are dealt with by my wife Joanna. Over 4000 letters and packages have been received or sent in the last 12 months.

Updating never stops so new information is welcome at any time, and modern technology allows changes to be made up to a few weeks before publication in May. However, because of the size of the book and the volume of change each year, major entries start to be made in October and regular contributors, particularly the countries in the first half of the book, are asked to send in their first updates by then. The Fax machine has become a universal method of bypassing slow and not always reliable international mail services, but photographs must still be sent by post. Whichever method is selected for sending material it will always be acknowledged within a few days of receipt.

My address is:

Captain Richard Sharpe
Foundry House
Kingsley
Bordon
Hampshire GU35 9LY
United Kingdom

Fax number (UK) 0420 477833

Note: No illustration from this book may be reproduced without the publisher's permission, but the Press may reproduce information and governmental photographs provided that Jane's Fighting Ships is acknowledged as the source. Photographs credited to other than official organisations must not be reproduced without permission from the originator.

Biographical note: The Editor

In 34 years in the Royal Navy the editor travelled all over the world. He has commanded nuclear and conventional submarines as well as a guided missile destroyer which was for some of the time the Flagship of NATO's Standing Naval Force Atlantic. He has also served in several appointments at the Ministry of Defence in London, including one in Naval Intelligence, and has been the Submarine Operations Officer on the staff of the UK Commander-in-Chief Fleet. In his last job before taking over as editor of Jane's Fighting Ships he was responsible for the selection of the next generation of RN officers.

Proven power

With over 1000 engines on active duty with the world's navies, the Wärtsilä Diesel Group is a leader in high and medium speed marine propulsion, auxiliary engines and propulsion systems.

Installations range from fast patrol craft through mine sweeper hunters, corvettes and multipurpose frigates to landing ships, underway replenishment ships and maritime prepositioning ships; all deliver the absolute reliability, availability and superior performance navies and coastal defence forces demand.

The Wärtsilä Diesel Group's engines offer fast load-change characteristics, shock durability, fuel economy, long overhaul intervals and ease of maintenance. Back-up is provided by a round-the-clock global service network. No matter how special the vessel, the Wärtsilä Diesel Group has the resources and experience to provide the custom-made solution.

WÄRTSILÄ DIESEL
GROUP

Navy Business
40, rue du Moulin des Bruyères, 92400 Courbevoie, France
Telephone +33-1-47 17 11 10, Telefax +33-1-43 34 93 21

Glossary

(see also Type abbreviations at head of Pennant List)

AAW	Anti-air warfare
ACV	Air cushion vehicle
AEW	Airborne early warning
AGR	Radar picket ship
AIP	Air independent propulsion
ANV	Advanced naval vehicle
ARM	Anti-radiation missile
A/S, ASW	Anti-submarine (warfare)
ASM	Air-to-surface missile
BPDMS	Base point defence missile system
Cal	Calibre — the diameter of a gun barrel; also used for measuring length of the barrel eg a 6 in gun 50 calibres long (6 in/50) would be 25 ft long
CIWS	Close in weapon system
COD	Carrier onboard delivery
CODAG, CODOG, CODLAG, COGAG, COGOG, COSAG	Descriptions of mixed propulsion systems: combined diesel and gas turbine, diesel-electric and gas turbine, diesel or gas turbine, gas turbine and gas turbine, gas turbine or gas turbine, steam and gas turbine
CONAS	Combined nuclear and steam
cp	Controllable pitch (propellers)
DC	Depth charge
DCT	Depth charge thrower
DP	Dual purpose (gun) for surface or AA use
Displacement	Basically the weight of water displaced by a ship's hull when floating: (a) Light: without fuel, water or ammunition (b) Normal: used for Japanese MSA ships. Similar to 'standard' (c) Standard: as defined by Washington Naval Conference 1922 — fully manned and stored but without fuel or reserve feed-water (d) Full load: fully laden with all stores, ammunition, fuel and water
DSRV	Deep submergence recovery vessel
dwt	Deadweight tonnage
ECM	Electronic countermeasures eg jamming
ECCM	Electronic counter-countermeasures
EEZ	Exclusive economic zone
EHF	Extreme high frequency
ELF	Extreme low frequency radio
ELINT	Electronic intelligence eg recording radar, W/T etc
ESM	Electronic support measures eg intercept
EW	Electronic warfare
FAC	Fast attack craft
FLIR	Forward looking infra-red radar
FRAM	Fleet rehabilitation and modernisation programme
GFCS	Gun fire control system
GMLS	Guided missile launch system
GPS	Geographical positioning system
grt	Gross registered tonnage
GT	Geared turbine
GWS	Guided weapon system
HF	High frequency

Horsepower (hp) or (hp(m))	Power developed or applied:
	 (a) bhp: brake horsepower = power available at the crankshaft
	 (b) shp: shaft horsepower = power delivered to the propeller shaft
	 (c) ihp: indicated horsepower = power produced by expansion of gases in the cylinders of reciprocating steam engines
	 (d) 1 kW = 1.341 hp = 1.360 metric hp
	     1 hp = 0.746 kW = 1.014 metric hp
	     1 metric hp = 0.735 kW = 0.968 hp
	 (e) Sustained horsepower may be different for similar engines in different conditions

IFF	Identification friend/foe
kT	Kiloton
kW	Kilowatt
LAMPS	Light airborne multi-purpose system
LCM	Landing craft, mechanised
LCU	Landing craft, utility
LCVP/LCP	Landing craft, vehicles/personnel
Length	Expressed in various ways: (a) oa: overall = length between extremities (b) pp: between perpendiculars = between fore side of the stem and after side of the rudderpost (c) wl: water-line = between extremities on the water-line
LF	Low frequency
LMCR	Liquid metal cooled reactor
LRMP	Long-range maritime patrol
LSM	Landing ship, medium
MAD	Magnetic Anomaly Detector — for anti-submarine detection identifying a steel body in the earth's magnetic field
MAP	US Military Assistance Programme
MCMV	Mine countermeasures vessel
MDF	Maritime defence force
Measurement	See Tonnage
MF	Medium frequency
MFCS	Missile fire control system
MG	Machine gun
MIRV	Multiple, independently targetable re-entry vehicle
MRV	Multiple re-entry vehicle
MSA	Maritime safety agency
MSC	US Military Sealift Command
MSC	Coastal minesweeper
MSH	Minehunter
MW	Megawatt
NBC	Nuclear, biological and chemical (warfare)
net	Net registered tonnage
nm	Nautical miles
NTDS	Naval tactical data system
NTU	New Threat Upgrade
oa	Overall length
OPV	Offshore patrol vessel
OTC	Officer in Tactical Command
PDMS	Point defence missile system
PUFFS	Passive underwater fire control system
PWR	Pressurised water reactor
RAM	Radar absorbent material
RAS	Replenishment at sea
RBU	Anti-submarine rocket launcher
RIB	Rigid inflatable boat
Ro-flow	A ship able to embark smaller craft in a dock
Ro-ro	Roll-on/roll-off
ROV	Remote operated vehicle
rpm	Revolutions per minute of engines, propellers, radar aerials etc
SAM	Surface-to-air missile
SAR	Search and rescue
SATCOM	Satellite communications
SES	Surface effect ship
SHF	Super high frequency
SINS	Ship's inertial navigation system
SLBM	Submarine-launched ballistic missile
SLCM	Ship-launched cruise missile
SLEP	Service Life Extension Program
SNLE	Nuclear-powered ballistic missile submarine (French)
SRBOC	Super rapid blooming offboard chaff
SS	Attack submarine
SSAN	Auxiliary nuclear-powered submarine
SSBN	Nuclear-powered ballistic missile submarine
SSDE	Submerged signal and decoy ejector
SSG	Guided missile submarine
SSGN	Nuclear-powered guided missile submarine
SSM	Surface-to-surface missile
SSN	Nuclear-powered attack submarine
STIR	Surveillance Target Indicator Radar
Subroc/Asroc	Rocket-assisted torpedo part of whose range is in the air
SURTASS	Surface Towed Array Surveillance System
SUWN-1	Surface-to-underwater missile launcher
SWATH	Small waterplane area twin hull
TACAN	Tactical air navigation beacon
TACTASS	Tactical Towed Acoustic Sensor System
TAS	Target Acquisition System
TASS	Towed Array Surveillance System
Tonnage	Measurement tons, computed on capacity of a ship's hull rather than its 'displacement' (see above): (a) Gross: the internal volume of all spaces within the hull and all permanently enclosed spaces above decks that are available for cargo, stores and accommodation. The result in cubic feet divided by 100 = gross tonnage (b) Net: gross minus all those spaces used for machinery, accommodation etc ('non-earning' spaces) (c) Deadweight (dwt): the amount of cargo, bunkers, stores etc that a ship can carry at her load draught
UHF	Ultra-high frequency
VDS	Variable depth sonar which is lowered to best listening depth. Known as dunking sonar in helicopters.
Vertrep	Vertical replenishment
VLF	Very low frequency radio
VLS	Vertical launch system
VSTOL	Vertical or short take-off/landing
VTOL	Vertical take off/landing
WIG	Wing-in-ground effect
wl	Waterline length

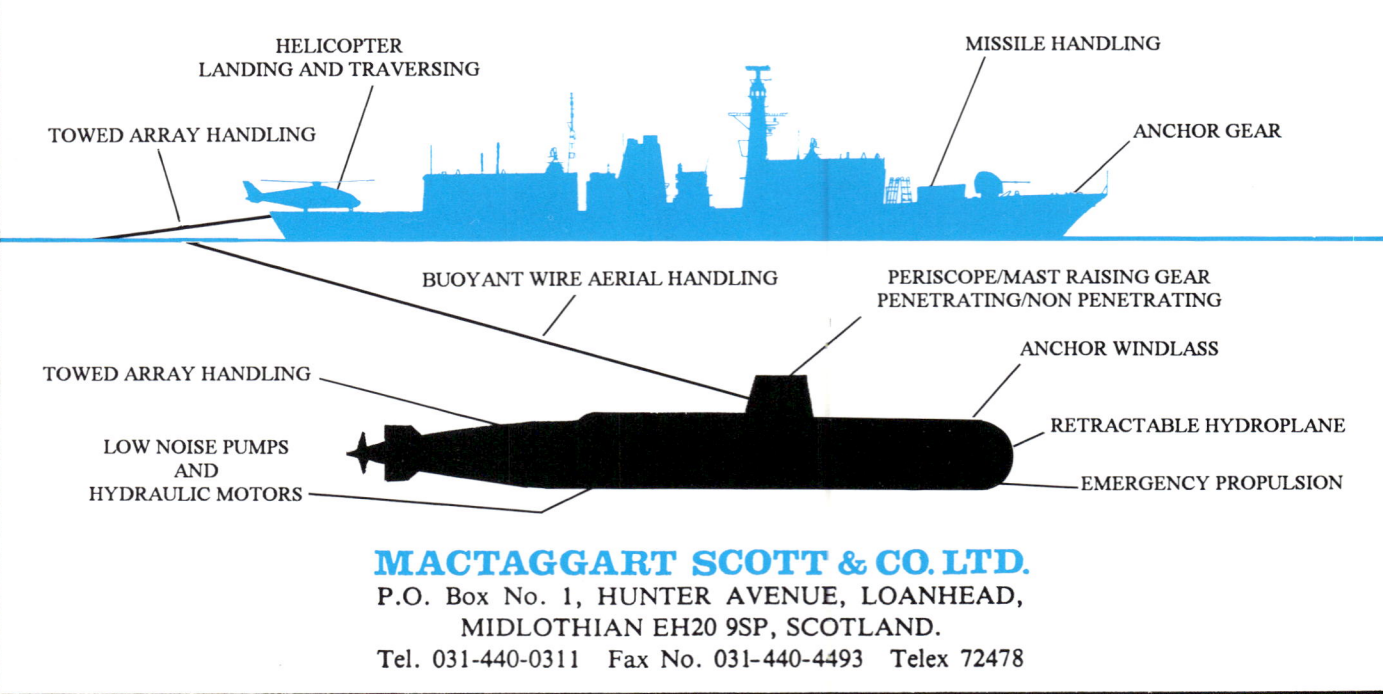

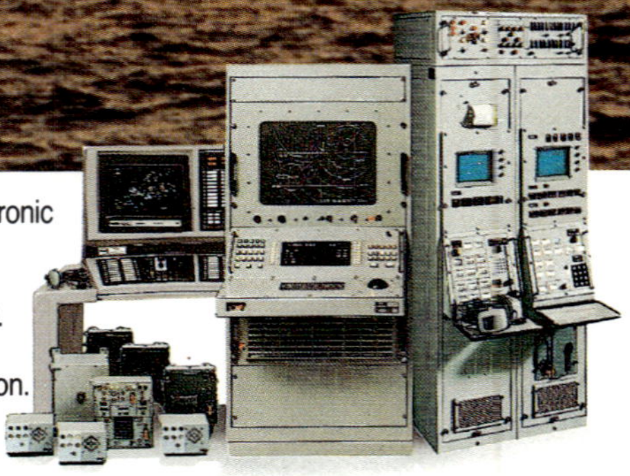

Ensigns and Flags of the World's Navies

The following pictorial representations show each country's ensign where it has one or its national flag. In cases where countries do not have ensigns their warships normally fly the national flag.

Albania
National Flag

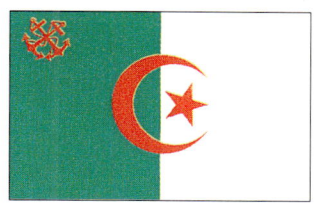

Algeria
Ensign

Angola
National Flag

Antigua
National Flag

Argentina
National Flag and Ensign

Australia
Ensign

Austria
Ensign

Azerbaijan
National Flag

Bahamas
Ensign

Bahrain
National Flag

Bangladesh
National Flag

Barbados
Ensign

Belgium
Ensign

Belize
National Flag

Benin
National Flag

Bermuda
National Flag

Bolivia
Ensign

Brazil
National Flag

Brunei
Ensign

Bulgaria
Ensign

ENSIGNS AND FLAGS OF THE WORLD'S NAVIES

Burma
National Flag

Cambodia
National Flag

Cameroon
National Flag

Canada
National Flag and Ensign

Cape Verde
National Flag

Chile
National Flag and Ensign

China, People's Republic
Ensign

Colombia
Ensign

Comoro Islands
National Flag

Congo
National Flag

Cook Islands
National Flag

Costa Rica
Ensign and Government Flag

Croatia
National Flag

Cuba
National Flag and Ensign

Cyprus, Republic
National Flag

Cyprus, Turkish Republic
(Not recognised by United Nations)
National Flag

Czechoslovakia
National Flag

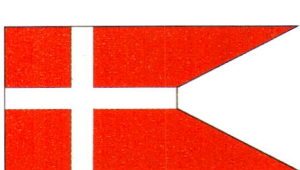
Denmark
Ensign

Djibouti
National Flag

Dominica
National Flag

Dominican Republic
Ensign

Ecuador
National Flag and Ensign

Egypt
Ensign

El Salvador
National Flag and Ensign

ENSIGNS AND FLAGS OF THE WORLD'S NAVIES

Equatorial Guinea
National Flag

Estonia
National Flag

Ethiopia
National Flag

Faroes
The Islands Flag

Falkland Islands
Falkland Islands Flag

Fiji
Ensign

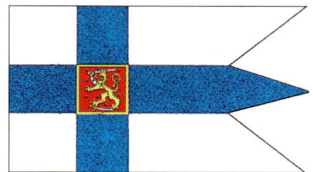
Finland
Ensign

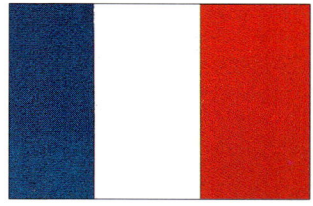
France
Ensign

Gabon
National Flag

Gambia
National Flag

Georgia
National Flag

Germany
Ensign

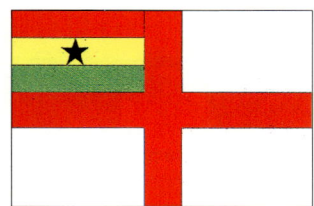
Ghana
Ensign

Greece
National Flag and Ensign

Grenada
Ensign

Guatemala
National Flag and Ensign

Guinea
National Flag

Guinea-Bissau
National Flag

Guyana
National Flag

Haiti
State Flag and Ensign

Honduras
Ensign

Hong Kong
Hong Kong Flag

Hungary
National Flag

Iceland
Ensign

[69]

ENSIGNS AND FLAGS OF THE WORLD'S NAVIES

India
Ensign

Indonesia
National Flag and Ensign

Iran
National Flag

Iraq
National Flag

Ireland
National Flag and Ensign

Israel
Ensign

Italy
Ensign

Ivory Coast
National Flag

Jamaica
Ensign

Japan
Ensign

Jordan
Ensign

Kenya
Ensign

Korea, Democratic People's Republic (North)
National Flag

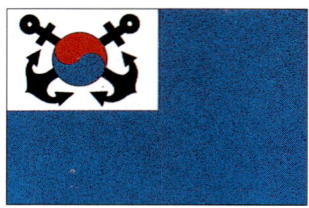
Korea, Republic (South)
Ensign

Kuwait
National Flag

Laos
National Flag

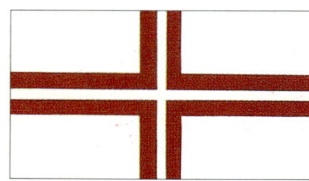
Latvia
Ensign

Lebanon
National Flag

Liberia
National Flag and Ensign

Libya
National Flag

Lithuania
National Flag

Madagascar
National Flag

Malawi
National Flag

Malaysia
Ensign

ENSIGNS AND FLAGS OF THE WORLD'S NAVIES

Maldives
National Flag

Mali
National Flag

Malta
National Flag

Mauritania
National Flag

Mauritius
Ensign

Mexico
National Flag and Ensign

Monserrat
National Flag

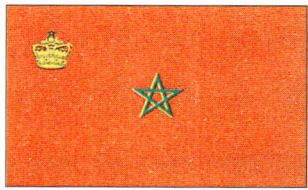
Morocco
Ensign

Mozambique
National Flag

NATO
Flag of the North Atlantic Treaty Organization

Netherlands
National Flag and Ensign

New Zealand
Ensign

Nicaragua
National Flag and Ensign

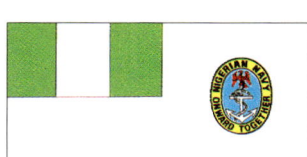
Nigeria
Ensign

Norway
Ensign

Oman
Ensign

Pakistan
Ensign

Panama
National Flag and Ensign

Papua New Guinea
Ensign

Paraguay
National Flag and Ensign

Paraguay
National Flag and Ensign (reverse)

Peru
Ensign

Philippines
National Flag

Poland
Ensign

[71]

ENSIGNS AND FLAGS OF THE WORLD'S NAVIES

Portugal
National Flag and Ensign

Qatar
National Flag

Romania
National Flag and Ensign

Russia
Ensign

Russia & Ukraine (Black Sea Fleet)
Ensign

St Kitts-Nevis
National Flag

St Lucia
National Flag

St Vincent
National Flag

Saudi Arabia
Ensign

Senegal
National Flag

Seychelles
National Flag

Sierre Leone
National Flag

Singapore
Ensign

Slovenia
National Flag

Solomon Islands
National Flag

Somalia
National Flag

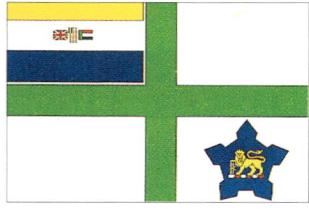
South Africa
Naval Ensign

Spain
National Flag and Ensign

Sri Lanka
Ensign

Sudan
National Flag

Surinam
National Flag

Sweden
Ensign and Jack

Switzerland
National Flag

Syria
National Flag

[72]

ENSIGNS AND FLAGS OF THE WORLD'S NAVIES

Taiwan
National Flag and Ensign

Tanzania
Ensign

Thailand
Ensign

Togo
National Flag

Tonga
Ensign

Trinidad and Tobago
Ensign

Tunisia
National Flag

Turkey
National Flag and Ensign

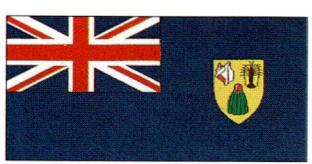
Turks and Caicos
National Flag

Uganda
National Flag

Ukraine
National Flag

Union of Soviet Socialist Republics (former)
Ensign

United Arab Emirates
National Flag

United Kingdom
Ensign

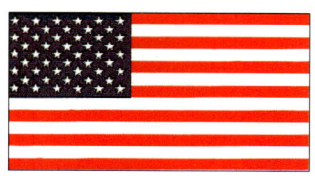
United States of America
National Flag and Ensign

Uruguay
National Flag and Ensign

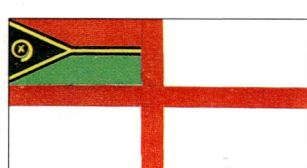
Vanuatu
Ensign

Venezuela
National Flag and Ensign

Vietnam
National Flag

Virgin Islands
National Flag

Western Samoa
National Flag

Yemen
National Flag

Yugoslavia
National Flag

Zaire
National Flag

The Systems Approach To Superiority

Ingalls Shipbuilding has long applied a systems approach in meeting the U.S. Navy's surface combatant needs.

This unique philosophy allows Ingalls to utilize its fullest capabilities from vessel concept through combat readiness, as is currently being accomplished in the construction of the TICONDEROGA (CG 47) Class Aegis guided missile cruisers, ARLEIGH BURKE (DDG 51) Class Aegis guided missile destroyers and WASP (LHD 1) Class multipurpose amphibious assault ships.

Ingalls is now applying this systems approach to the international shipbuilding marketplace with the design and construction of SA'AR 5 Class corvettes.

Building on a half-century of producing the world's most sophisticated warships, Ingalls Shipbuilding is setting new standards for innovation and excellence.

And a systems approach to superiority is the reason.

For More Information, Contact:
Director, Business Development
Ingalls Shipbuilding
P.O. Box 149
Pascagoula, Mississippi, USA 39568-0149
Telephone: 601-935-4703   FAX: 601-935-4611

Litton
Ingalls Shipbuilding

Ranks and Insignia of the World's Navies

After a gap of many years diagrammatic representations of naval ranks and insignia have been reintroduced. Instead of showing ranks at the beginning of the country, as previously, all the diagrams have been compiled together in order to make this section more easily used for research.

These diagrams cover the major, as well as many smaller navies. They will be updated each year, and added to, until all countries in the book are represented.

Where possible, the rank titles are shown in the language of the relevant country followed by the equivalent ranks in English.

The sleeves are drawn to one scale and the shoulder insignia to another allowing respective comparisons of size to be made. The exception to this is Croatia where badges worn on the right breast of the uniforms are depicted.

Algeria

a: *'Aqid*, Captain   b: *Muqaddam*, Commander   c: *Ra'id*, Lieutenant Commander
d: *Naqib*, Lieutenant   e: *Mulazim Awwal*, Sub Lieutenant   f: *Mulazim*, Acting Sub Lieutenant

Gold on navy blue.

Angola

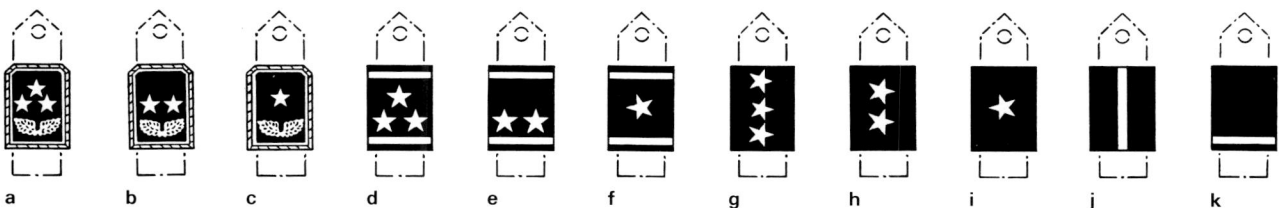

a: *Almirante*, Admiral   b: *Vice-Almirante*, Vice Admiral   c: *Contra-Almirante*, Rear Admiral   d: *Capitão-de-Mar-e-Guerra*, Captain   e: *Capitão-de-Fragata*, Commander   f: *Capitão-de-Corveta*, Lieutenant Commander   g: *Tenente-de-Navio*, Lieutenant   h: *Tenente-de-Fragata*, Sub Lieutenant   i: *Tenente-de-Corveta*, Acting Sub Lieutenant   j: *Alférez*, Midshipman   k: *Aspirante*, Cadet

Admiral to Lieutenant Commander, gold on navy blue. Lieutenant to Sub Lieutenant, silver on navy blue. Midshipman and Cadet, light blue on navy blue.

Argentina (Navy)

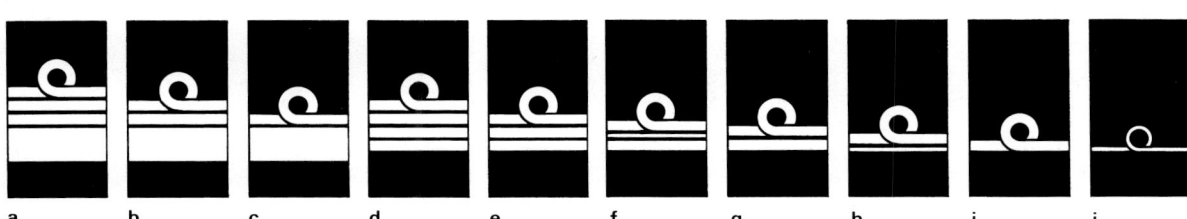

a: *Almirante*, Admiral   b: *Vicealmirante*, Vice Admiral   c: *Contraalmirante*, Rear Admiral   d: *Capitán de Navío*, Captain   e: *Capitán de Fragata*, Commander   f: *Capitán de Corbeta*, Lieutenant Commander   g: *Teniente de Navío*, Lieutenant   h: *Teniente de Fragata*, Sub Lieutenant   i: *Teniente de Corbeta*, Acting Lieutenant   j: *Guardiamarina*, Midshipman

Gold on navy blue.

RANKS AND INSIGNIA OF THE WORLD'S NAVIES

Argentina (Coast Guard)

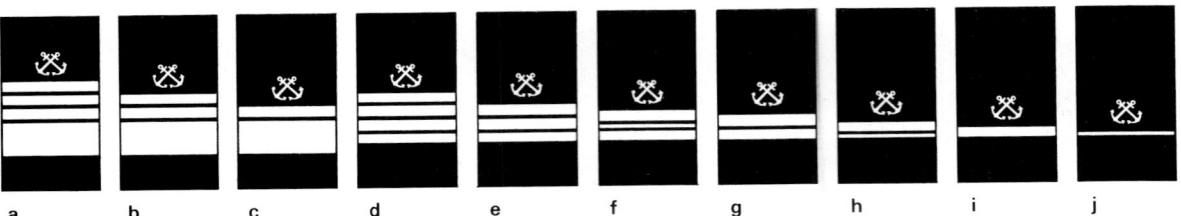

a: *Almirante*, Admiral   b: *Vicealmirante*, Vice Admiral   c: *Contraalmirante*, Rear Admiral   d: *Capitán de Navio*, Captain   e: *Capitán de Fragata*, Commander   f: *Capitán de Corbeta*, Lieutenant Commander   g: *Teniente de Navio*, Lieutenant   h: *Teniente de Fragata*, Sub Lieutenant   i: *Teniente de Corbeta*, Acting Lieutenant   j: *Guardiamarina*, Midshipman

Gold on navy blue.

Australia

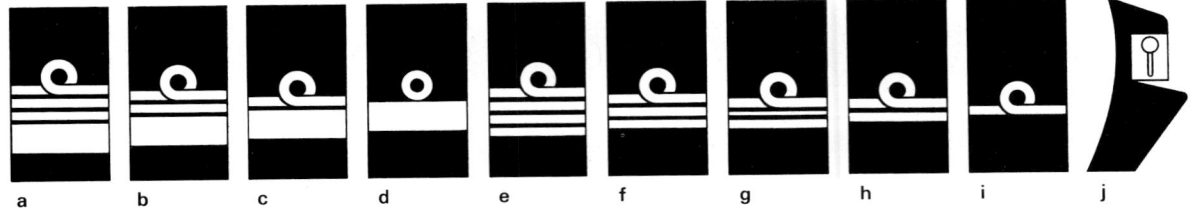

a: Admiral   b: Vice Admiral   c: Rear Admiral   d: Commodore   e: Captain   f: Commander   g: Lieutenant Commander   h: Lieutenant   i: Sub Lieutenant   j: Midshipman

Gold on navy blue.

Bahamas

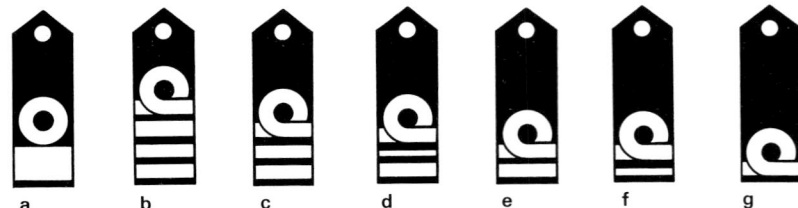

a: Commodore   b: Captain   c: Commander   d: Lieutenant Commander   e: Lieutenant   f: Junior Lieutenant   g: Sub Lieutenant

Gold on black.

Bahrain

a: *'Aqid*, Colonel   b: *Muqaddam*, Lieutenant Colonel   c: *Ra'id*, Major   d: *Naqib*, Captain   e: *Mulazim Awwal*, Lieutenant   f: *Mulazim Thani*, Second Lieutenant

Gold and red on navy blue.

Bangladesh

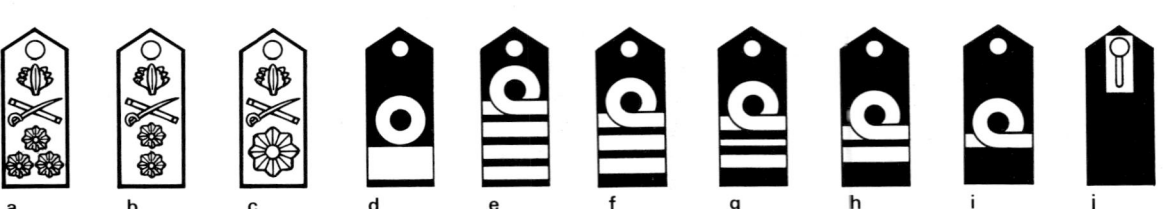

a: Admiral   b: Vice Admiral   c: Rear Admiral   d: Commodore   e: Captain   f: Commander   g: Lieutenant Commander   h: Lieutenant   i: Sub Lieutenant   j: Midshipman

Gold on navy blue. Flag ranks, gold edged blue, silver devices. White patch on midshipman's shoulder strap.

RANKS AND INSIGNIA OF THE WORLD'S NAVIES

Barbados

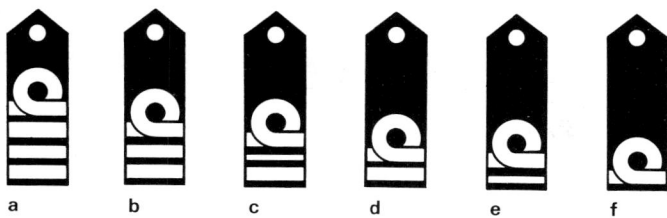

a: Captain   b: Commander   c: Lieutenant Commander   d: Lieutenant   e: Junior Lieutenant   f: Sub Lieutenant

Gold on black.

Belgium

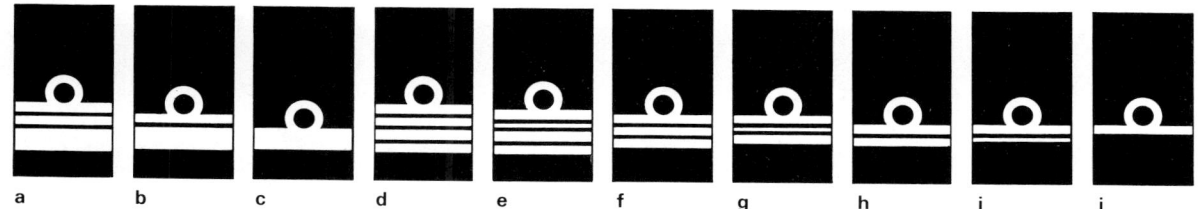

a: *Vice-Admiraal/Vice Amiral*, Vice Admiral   b: *Divisie-Admiraal/Amiral de Division*, Rear Admiral   c: *Commodore/Commodore*, Commodore   d: *Kapitein-ter-Zee/Capitaine de Vaisseau*, Captain   e: *Fregatkapitein/Capitaine de Frégate*, Commander   f: *Corvetkapitein/Capitaine de Corvette*, Lieutenant Commander   g: *Luitenant-ter-Zee 1ste Klasse/Lieutenant de Vaisseau 1re Classe*, Senior Lieutenant   h: *Luitenant-ter-Zee/Lieutenant de Vaisseau*, Lieutenant   i: *Vaandrig-ter-Zee/Enseigne de Vaisseau*, Sub Lieutenant   j: *Vaandrig-ter-Zee 2e Klasse/Enseigne de Vaisseau 2e Classe*, Acting Sub Lieutenant

Ranks given in Flemish, French and English. Gold on navy blue.

Bolivia

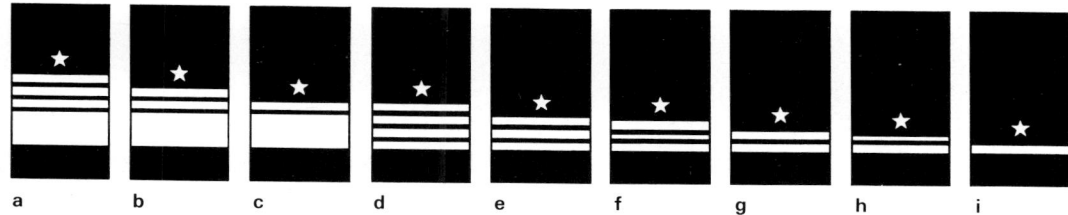

a: *Almirante*, Admiral   b: *Vicealmirante*, Vice Admiral   c: *Contraalmirante*, Rear Admiral   d: *Capitán de Navío*, Captain   e: *Capitán de Fragata*, Commander   f: *Capitán de Corbeta*, Lieutenant Commander   g: *Teniente de Navío*, Lieutenant   h: *Teniente de Fragata*, Sub Lieutenant   i: *Alférez*, Acting Sub Lieutenant

Gold on navy blue.

Brazil

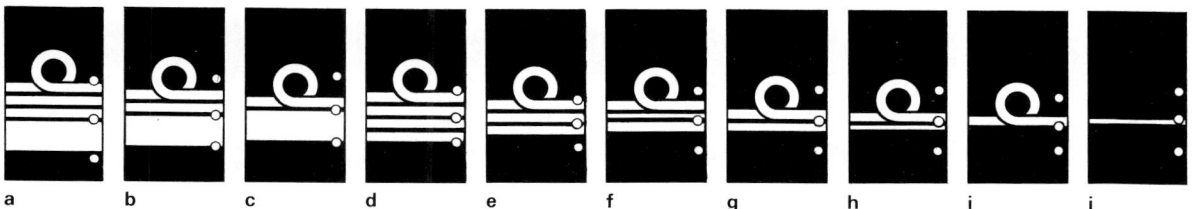

a: *Almirante*, Admiral   b: *Vice-Almirante*, Vice Admiral   c: *Contra-Almirante*, Rear Admiral   d: *Capitão-de-Mar-e-Guerra*, Captain   e: *Capitão-de-Fragata*, Commander   f: *Capitão-de-Corveta*, Lieutenant Commander   g: *Capitão-de-Tenente*, Lieutenant   h: *Primeiro-Tenente*, Sub Lieutenant   i: *Segundo-Tenente*, Acting Sub Lieutenant   j: *Guarda-Marinha*, Midshipman

Gold on dark blue.

Burma

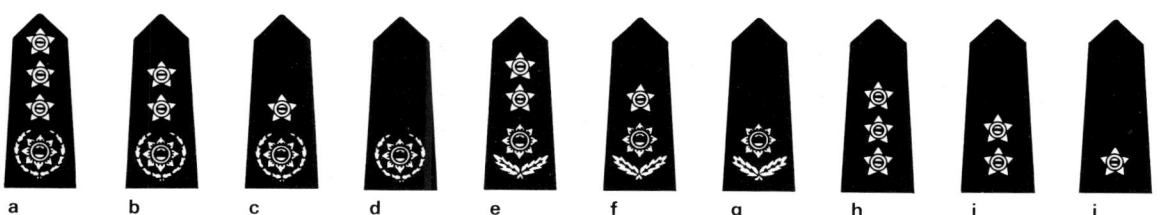

a: Admiral   b: Vice Admiral   c: Rear Admiral   d: Commodore   e: Captain   f: Commander   g: Lieutenant Commander   h: Lieutenant   i: Sub Lieutenant   j: Acting Sub Lieutenant

Gold on dark blue. All three services have same rank insignia based on the army.

RANKS AND INSIGNIA OF THE WORLD'S NAVIES

Cameroon

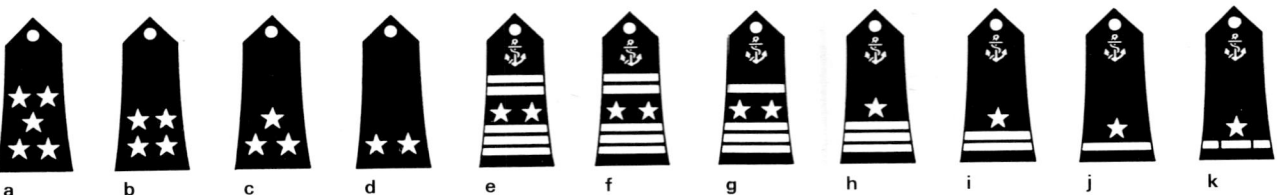

a: *Amiral d'Escadre*, Admiral of the Fleet   b: *Vice-Amiral d'Escadre*, Admiral   c: *Vice-Amiral*, Vice Admiral   d: *Contre-Amiral*, Rear Admiral   e: *Capitaine de Vaisseau*, Captain   f: *Capitaine de Frégate*, Commander   g: *Capitaine de Corvette*, Lieutenant Commander   h: *Lieutenant de Vaisseau*, Lieutenant   i: *Enseigne de Vaisseau 1re Classe*, Sub Lieutenant   j: *Enseigne de Vaisseau 2e Class*, Acting Sub Lieutenant   k: *Aspirant*, Midshipman

Gold on navy blue. Top two stripes for Commander, silver.

Canada

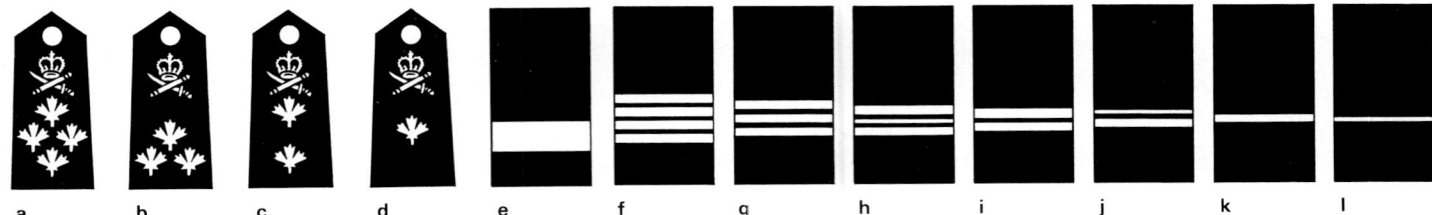

a: Admiral   b: Vice Admiral   c: Rear Admiral   d: Commodore   e: All Flag Ranks   f: Captain   g: Commander   h: Lieutenant Commander   i: Lieutenant   j: Sub Lieutenant   k: Acting Sub Lieutenant   l: Officer Cadet

Gold on black.

Chile

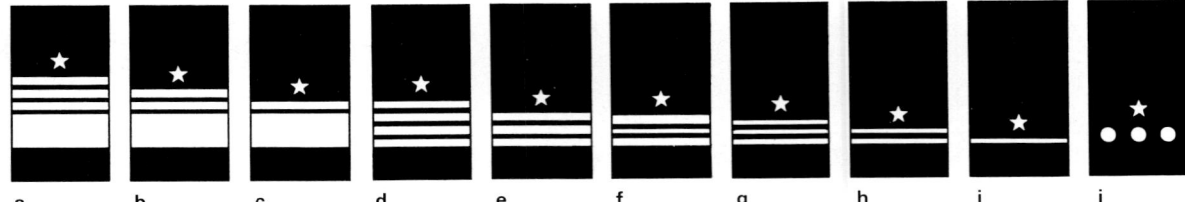

a: *Almirante*, Admiral   b: *Vicealmirante*, Vice Admiral   c: *Contraalmirante*, Rear Admiral   d: *Capitán de Navío*, Captain   e: *Capitán de Fragata*, Commander   f: *Capitán de Corbeta*, Lieutenant Commander   g: *Teniente Primero*, Lieutenant   h: *Teniente Segundo*, Junior Lieutenant   i: *Sub Teniente*, Sub Lieutenant   j: *Guardia Marina*, Midshipman

Gold on black.

China

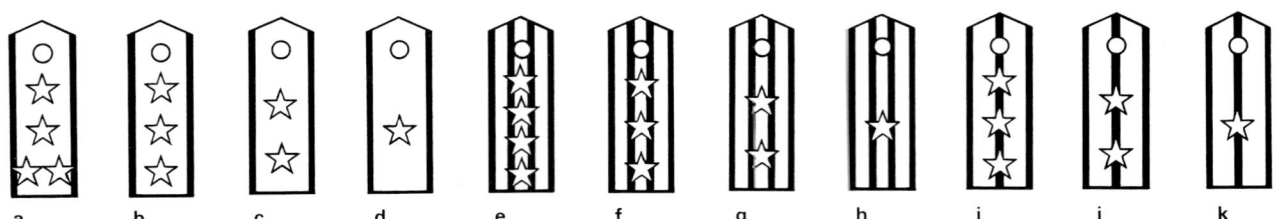

a: *Senior General*, Admiral of the Fleet   b: *General*, Admiral   c: *Lieutenant General*, Vice Admiral   d: *Major General*, Rear Admiral   e: *Senior Colonel*, Commodore   f: *Colonel*, Captain   g: *Lieutenant Colonel*, Commander   h: *Major Colonel*, Lieutenant Commander   i: *Captain*, Lieutenant   j: *Lieutenant*, Sub Lieutenant   k: *Second Lieutenant*, Acting Sub Lieutenant

Generals, gold edged dark blue. Gold button. Silver stars. Senior Colonel to Major Colonel two dark blue stripes. Captain to Lieutenant one dark blue stripe.

Colombia

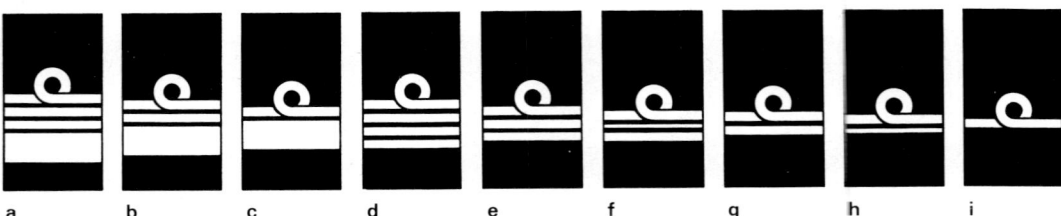

a: *Almirante*, Admiral   b: *Vicealmirante*, Vice Admiral   c: *Contraalmirante*, Rear Admiral   d: *Capitán de Navío*, Captain   e: *Capitán de Fragata*, Commander   f: *Capitán de Corbeta*, Lieutenant Commander   g: *Teniente de Navío*, Lieutenant   h: *Teniente de Fragata*, Sub Lieutenant   i: *Teniente de Corbeta*, Acting Sub Lieutenant

Gold on black.

RANKS AND INSIGNIA OF THE WORLD'S NAVIES

Congo

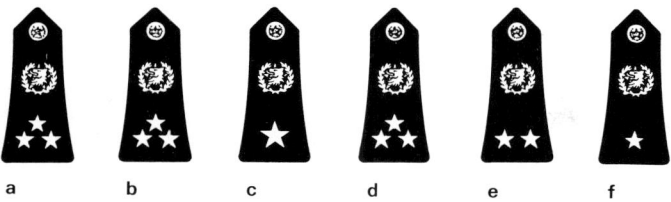

a: *Capitaine de Vaisseau*, Captain   b: *Capitaine de Frégate*, Commander
c: *Capitaine de Corvette*, Lieutenant Commander   d: *Lieutenant de Vaisseau*, Lieutenant   e: *Enseigne de Vaisseau 1re Classe*, Sub Lieutenant   f: *Enseigne de Vaisseau 2e Classe*, Acting Sub Lieutenant

Captain three red stars, Commander one gold over two red stars, Lieutenant Commander one red star, remainder gold stars, all on black.

Croatia (not to scale)

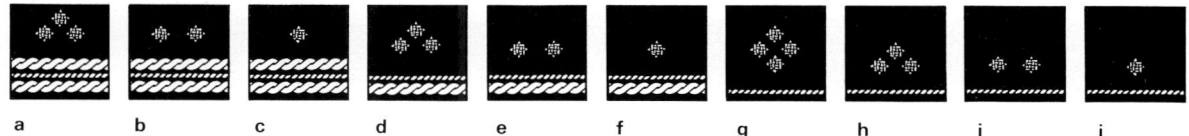

a: *Admiral*, Admiral   b: *Viceadmiral*, Vice Admiral   c: *Kontraadmiral*, Rear Admiral   d: *Kapetan Bojnog Broda*, Captain   e: *Kapetan Fregate*, Commander   f: *Kapetan Korvete*, Lieutenant Commander   g: *Porucnik Bojnog Broda*, Senior Lieutenant   h: *Porucnik Fregate*, Lieutenant   i: *Porucnik Korvete*, Sub Lieutenant   j: *Zastavnik*, Ensign

Gold on camouflage background. Device worn as patch on breast of uniform.

Cuba

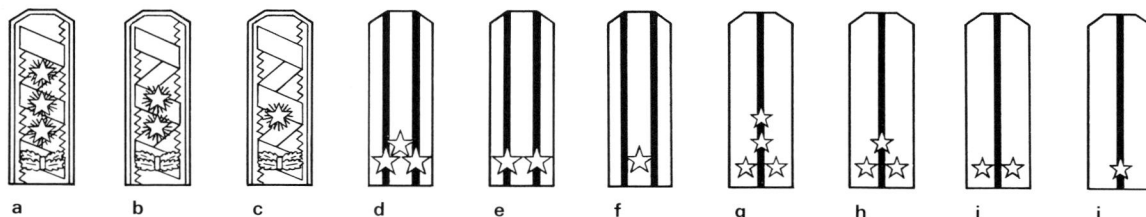

a: *Almirante*, Admiral   b: *Vicealmirante*, Vice Admiral   c: *Contraalmirante*, Rear Admiral   d: *Capitán de Navío*, Captain   e: *Capitán de Fregata*, Commander   f: *Capitán de Corbeta*, Lieutenant Commander   g: *Teniente de Navío*, Senior Lieutenant   h: *Teniente de Fregata*, Lieutenant   i: *Teniente de Corbeta*, Sub Lieutenant   j: *Alférez*, Acting Sub Lieutenant

Black stripes. Admirals, gold stars on blue design.

Denmark

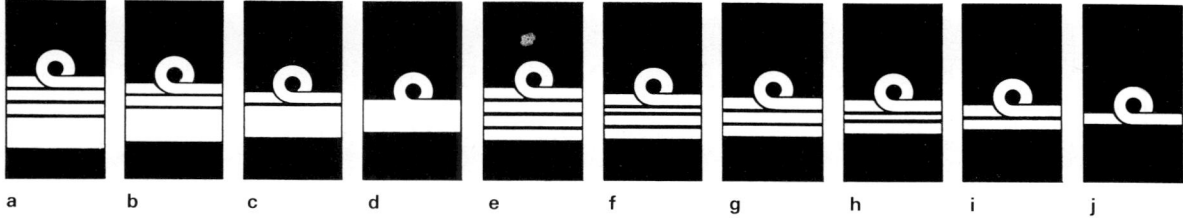

a: *Admiral*, Admiral   b: *Viceadmiral*, Vice Admiral   c: *Kontreadmiral*, Rear Admiral   d: *Flotilleadmiral*, Commodore   e: *Kommandør*, Captain   f: *Kommandørkaptajn*, Senior Commander   g: *Orlogskaptajn*, Commander   h: *Kaptajnløjtnant*, Lieutenant Commander   i: *Premierløjtnant*, Lieutenant   j: *Løjtnant*, Sub Lieutenant

Gold on black.

Dominican Republic

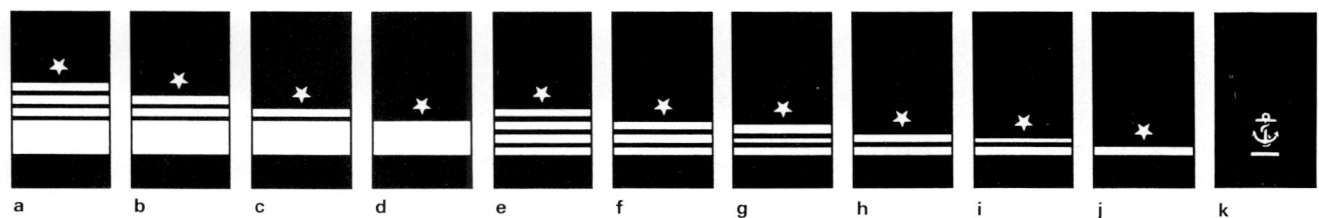

a: *Almirante*, Admiral   b: *Vicealmirante*, Vice Admiral   c: *Contraalmirante*, Rear Admiral   d: *Comodoro*, Commodore   e: *Capitán de Navío*, Captain   f: *Capitán de Fragata*, Commander   g: *Capitán de Corbeta*, Lieutenant Commander   h: *Teniente de Navío*, Lieutenant   i: *Alférez de Navío*, Sub Lieutenant   j: *Alférez de Fragata*, Acting Sub Lieutenant   k: *Guariamarina*, Midshipman

Gold on black.

RANKS AND INSIGNIA OF THE WORLD'S NAVIES

Ecuador

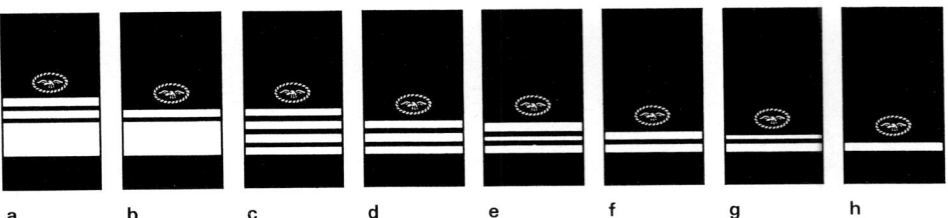

a: *Vicealmirante*, Vice Admiral   b: *Contraalmirante*, Rear Admiral   c: *Capitán de Navio*, Captain   d: *Capitán de Fragata*, Commander   e: *Capitán de Corbeta*, Lieutenant Commander   f: *Teniente de Fragata*, Lieutenant   g: *Alférez de Navio*, Sub Lieutenant   h: *Alférez de Fragata*, Acting Sub Lieutenant

Gold on black.

Egypt

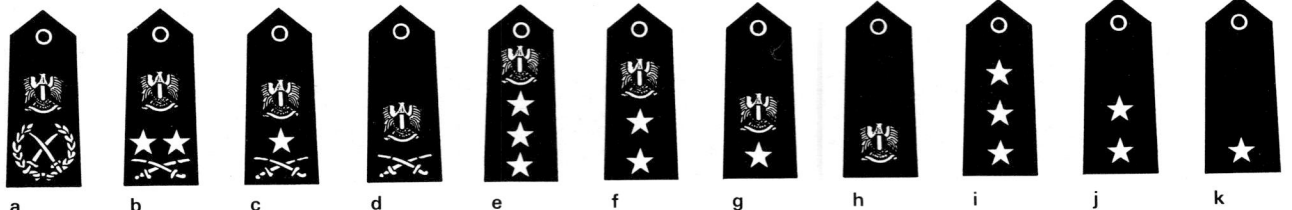

a: *Mushir*, Admiral of the Fleet   b: *Fariq Awwal*, Admiral   c: *Fariq*, Vice Admiral   d: *Liwa'*, Rear Admiral   e: *'Amid*, Commodore   f: *'Aqid*, Captain   g: *Muqaddam*, Commander   h: *Ra'id*, Lieutenant Commander   i: *Naqib*, Lieutenant   j: *Mulazim Awwal*, Sub Lieutenant   k: *Mulazim*, Acting Sub Lieutenant

Gold on black. Shield on eagle's breast black, white and red.

El Salvador

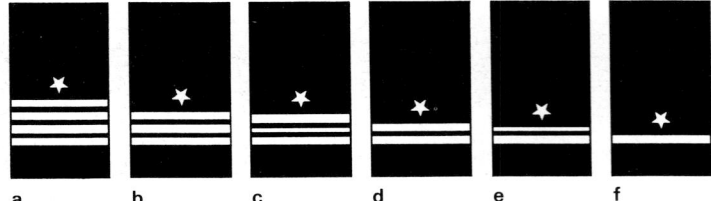

a: *Coronel*, Captain   b: *Teniente Coronel*, Commander   c: *Mayor*, Lieutenant Commander   d: *Capitán*, Lieutenant   e: *Teniente*, Sub Lieutenant   f: *Sub Teniente*, Acting Sub Lieutenant

Gold on navy blue.

Finland

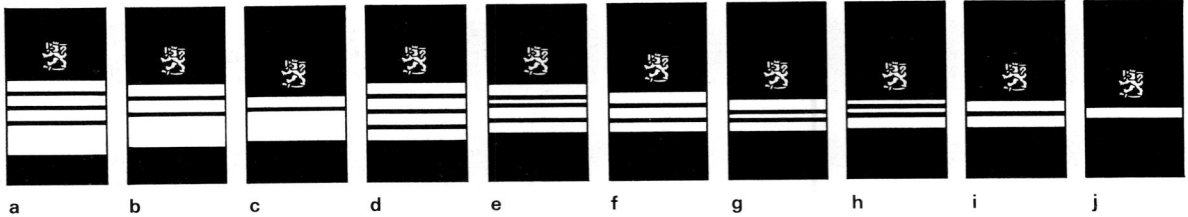

a: *Amiraali*, Admiral   b: *Vara-amiraali*, Vice Admiral   c: *Kontra-amiraali*, Rear Admiral   d: *Kommodori*, Captain   e: *Komentaja*, Commander   f: *Komentajakapteeni*, Lieutenant Commander   g: *Kapteeniluutnantti*, Senior Lieutenant   h: *Yliluutnantti*, Lieutenant   i: *Luutnantti*, Junior Lieutenant   j: *Aliluutnantti*, Sub Lieutenant

Gold on black.

France

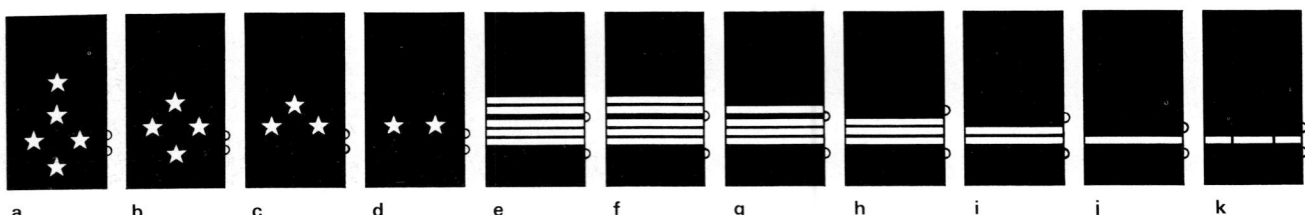

a: *Amiral*, Admiral of the Fleet   b: *Vice-Amiral d'Escadre*, Admiral   c: *Vice-Amiral*, Vice Admiral   d: *Contre-Amiral*, Rear Admiral   e: *Capitaine de Vaisseau*, Captain   f: *Capitaine de Frégate*, Commander   g: *Capitaine de Corvette*, Lieutenant Commander   h: *Lieutenant de Vaisseau*, Lieutenant   i: *Enseigne de Vaisseau de 1re Classe*, Sub Lieutenant   j: *Enseigne de Vaisseau de 2e Classe*, Acting Sub Lieutenant   k: *Aspirant*, Midshipman

Flag ranks, silver stars. Captain, gold. Commander, three gold two silver. Lieutenant Commander to Midshipman, gold. Vertical stripes on Midshipman's lace, mid blue. All on dark blue.

RANKS AND INSIGNIA OF THE WORLD'S NAVIES

Gabon

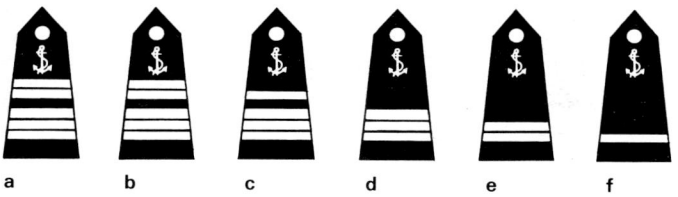

a: *Capitaine de Vaisseau*, Captain   **b**: *Capitaine de Frégate*, Commander
c: *Capitaine de Corvette*, Lieutenant Commander   **d**: *Lieutenant de Vaisseau*, Lieutenant   **e**: *Enseigne de Vaisseau 1re Classe*, Sub Lieutenant   **f**: *Enseigne de Vaisseau 2e Classe*, Acting Sub Lieutenant

Gold on black. Commander, three gold, two silver.

Germany

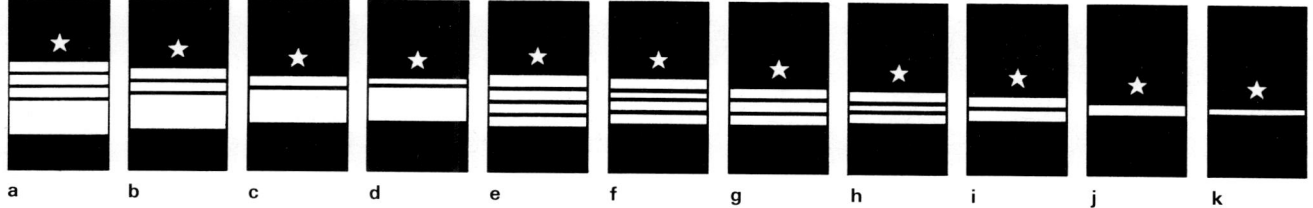

a: *Admiral*, Admiral   **b**: *Viceadmiral*, Vice Admiral   **c**: *Konteradmiral*, Rear Admiral   **d**: *Flottillenadmiral*, Commodore   **e**: *Kapitan zur See*, Captain
f: *Fregattenkapitan*, Commander   **g**: *Korvettenkapitan*, Lieutenant Commander   **h**: *Kapitanleutnant*, Lieutenant   **i**: *Oberleutnant zur See*, Sub Lieutenant
j: *Leutnant zur See*, Acting Sub Lieutenant   **k**: *Oberfahnrich zur See*, Midshipman

Gold on navy blue.

Ghana

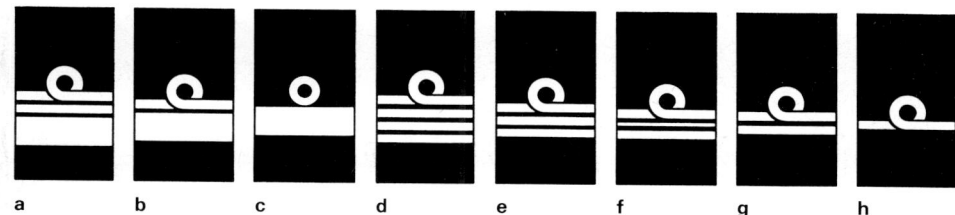

a: Vice Admiral   **b**: Rear Admiral   **c**: Commodore   **d**: Captain   **e**: Commander   **f**: Lieutenant Commander
g: Lieutenant   **h**: Sub Lieutenant

Gold on navy blue.

Greece (Navy)

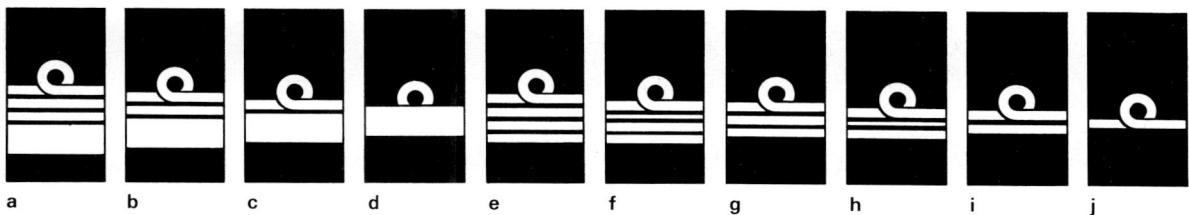

a: *Navarchos*, Admiral   **b**: *Antinavarchos*, Vice Admiral   **c**: *Yponavarchos*, Rear Admiral   **d**: *Archipiarchos*, Commodore   **e**: *Pliarchos*, Captain   **f**: *Antipliarchos*, Commander   **g**: *Plotarchos*, Lieutenant Commander   **h**: *Ypopliarchos*, Lieutenant   **i**: *Anthypopliarchos*, Sub Lieutenant   **j**: *Simaioforos*, Acting Sub Lieutenant

Gold on navy blue.

Greece (Coast Guard)

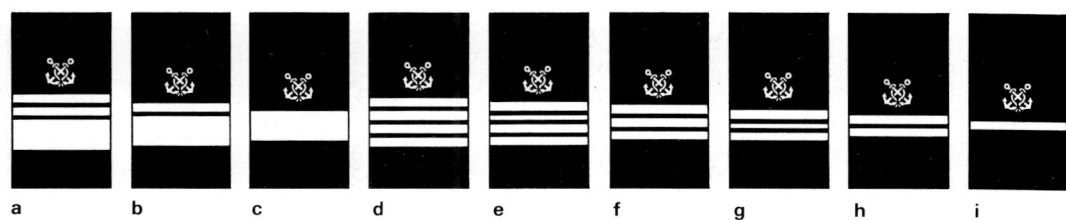

a: *Antinavarchos*, Vice Admiral   **b**: *Yponavarchos*, Rear Admiral   **c**: *Archipiarchos*, Commodore   **d**: *Pliarchos*, Captain
e: *Antipliarchos*, Commander   **f**: *Plotarchos*, Lieutenant Commander   **g**: *Ypopliarchos*, Lieutenant   **h**: *Anthypopliarchos*, Sub Lieutenant   **i**: *Simaioforos*, Acting Sub Lieutenant

Gold on navy blue.

RANKS AND INSIGNIA OF THE WORLD'S NAVIES

Guatemala

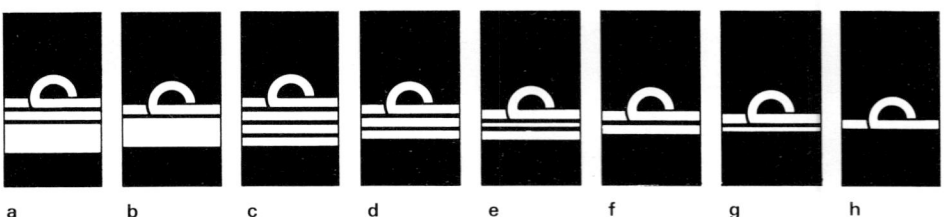

a: *Vicealmirante*, Vice Admiral   **b**: *Contraalmirante*, Rear Admiral   **c**: *Capitán de Navío*, Captain   **d**: *Capitán de Fragata*, Commander   **e**: *Capitán de Corbeta*, Lieutenant Commander   **f**: *Teniente de Navío*, Lieutenant   **g**: *Teniente de Fragata*, Sub Lieutenant   **h**: *Teniente de Corbeta*, Acting Sub Lieutenant

Gold on navy blue.

Guinea

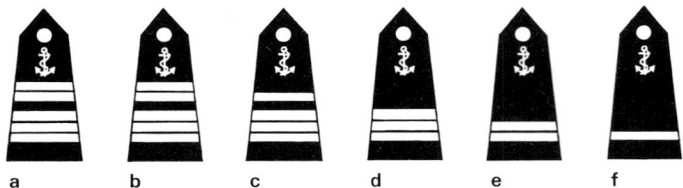

a: *Capitaine de Vaisseau*, Captain   **b**: *Capitaine de Frégate*, Commander   **c**: *Capitaine de Corvette*, Lieutenant Commander   **d**: *Lieutenant de Vaisseau*, Lieutenant   **e**: *Enseigne de Vaisseau 1re Classe*, Sub Lieutenant   **f**: *Enseigne de Vaisseau 2e Classe*, Acting Sub Lieutenant

Gold on black. Commander, three gold two silver stripes.

Haiti

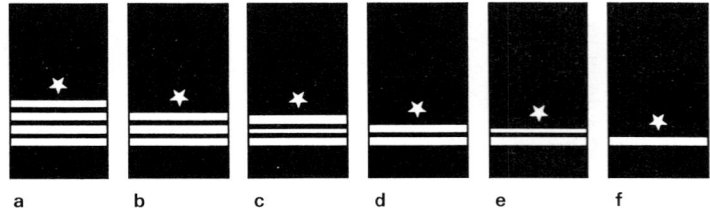

a: *Capitaine de Vaisseau*, Captain   **b**: *Commandant*, Commander   **c**: *Lieutenant Commandant*, Lieutenant Commander   **d**: *Lieutenant de Vaisseau*, Lieutenant   **e**: *Sous Lieutenant de Vaisseau*, Sub Lieutenant   **f**: *Enseigne de Vaisseau*, Acting Sub Lieutenant

Gold on navy blue.

Hondurus

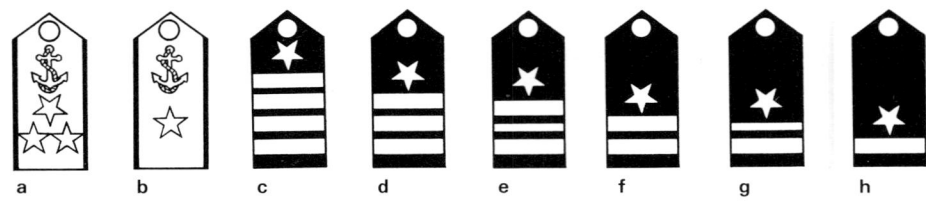

a: *Almirante*, Vice Admiral   **b**: *Contralmirante*, Rear Admiral   **c**: *Capitán de Navío*, Captain   **d**: *Capitán de Fragata*, Commander   **e**: *Capitán de Corbeta*, Lieutenant Commander   **f**: *Teniente de Navío*, Lieutenant   **g**: *Teniente de Fragata*, Sub Lieutenant   **h**: *Alférez de Fragata*, Acting Sub Lieutenant

Gold on navy blue. Flag ranks, gold shoulder boards edged blue, silver devices.

India

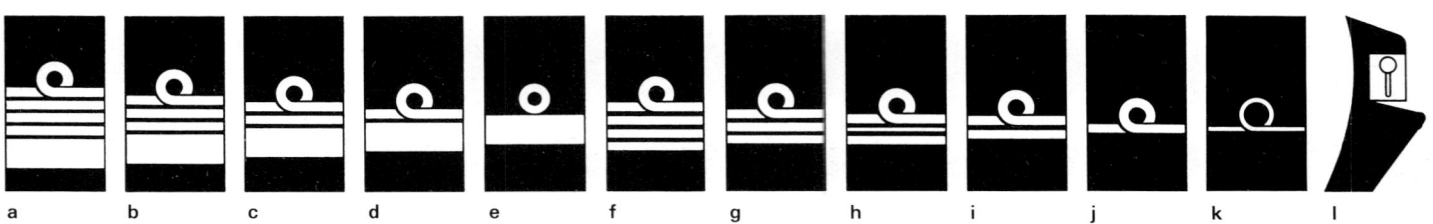

a: Admiral of the Fleet   **b**: Admiral   **c**: Vice Admiral   **d**: Rear Admiral   **e**: Commodore   **f**: Captain   **g**: Commander   **h**: Lieutenant Commander   **i**: Lieutenant   **j**: Sub Lieutenant   **k**: Commissioned Officer   **l**: Midshipman (Lapel)

Gold on navy blue.

RANKS AND INSIGNIA OF THE WORLD'S NAVIES

Iran

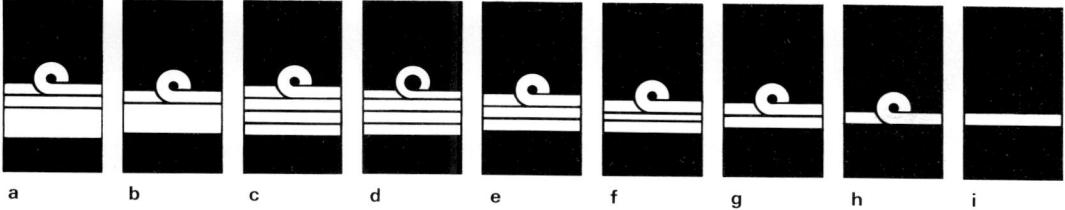

a: *Daryaban*, Vice Admiral   b: *Daryadar*, Rear Admiral   c: *Nakhoda Yekom*, Captain   d: *Nakhoda Dovom*, Commander   e: *Nakhoda Sevom*, Lieutenant Commander   f: *Navsarvan*, Lieutenant   g: *Navban Yekom*, Junior Lieutenant   h: *Navban Dovom*, Sub Lieutenant   i: *Navban Sevom*, Midshipman
Gold on navy blue.

Iraq

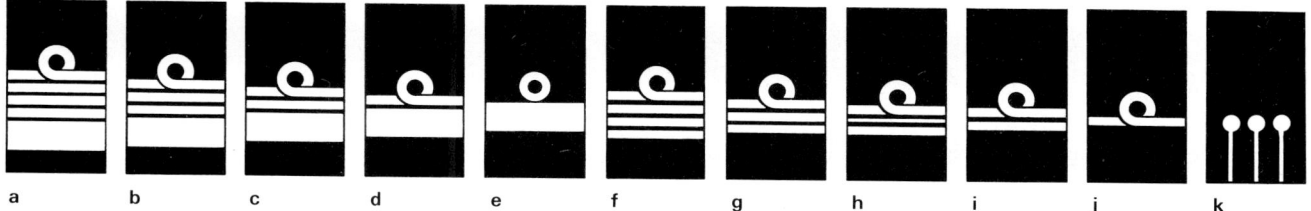

a: *Mushir*, Admiral of the Fleet   b: *Fariq Awwal*, Admiral   c: *Fariq*, Vice Admiral   d: *Liwa'*, Rear Admiral   e: *'Amid*, Commodore   f: *'Aqid*, Captain   g: *Muqaddam*, Commander   h: *Ra'id*, Lieutenant Commander   i: *Naqib*, Lieutenant   j: *Mulazim Awwal*, Sub Lieutenant   k: *Mulazim*, Midshipman
Gold on navy blue.

Ireland

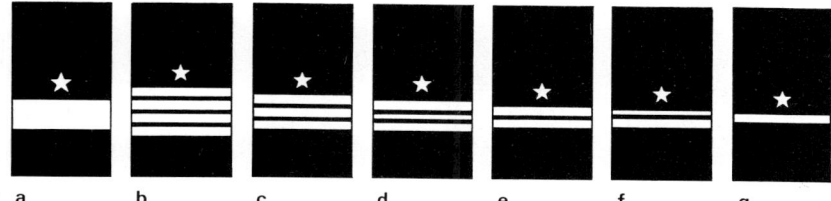

a: Commodore   b: Captain   c: Commander   d: Lieutenant Commander   e: Lieutenant   f: Sub Lieutenant   g: Ensign
Gold on navy blue.

Israel

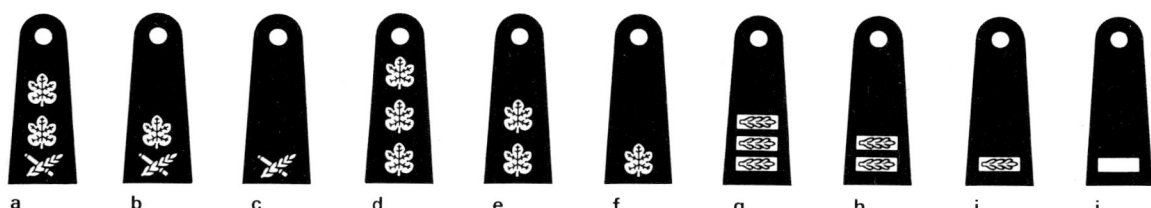

a: *General (Rav-Aluf)*, Vice Admiral   b: *Major General (Aluf)*, Rear Admiral   c: *Brigadier (Tat-Aluf)*, Commodore   d: *Colonel (Alut-Mishneh)*, Captain   e: *Lieutenant Colonel (Sgan-Aluf)*, Commander   f: *Major (Rav-Seren)*, Lieutenant Commander   g: *Captain (Seren)*, Lieutenant   h: *First Lieutenant (Segen)*, Sub Lieutenant   i: *Second Lieutenant (Segen-Mishneh)*, Acting Sub Lieutenant   j: *Officer Aspirant (Mamak)*, Officer Candidate
Bright brass or gold generally on dark blue or black. Officer Candidate, white bar.

Italy

a: *Ammiraglio di Squadra*, Admiral Commanding Navy   b: *Ammiraglio di Squadra*, Admiral   c: *Ammiraglio di Divisione*, Vice Admiral   d: *Contrammiraglio*, Rear Admiral   e: *Capitano di Vascello*, Captain   f: *Capitano di Fregata*, Commander   g: *Capitano di Corvetta*, Lieutenant Commander   h: *1° Tenente di Vascello*, First Lieutenant   i: *Tenente di Vascello*, Lieutenant   j: *Sottotenente di Vascello*, Sub Lieutenant   k: *Guardiamarina*, Midshipman   l: *Aspirante Guardiamarina*, (Officer Candidate)
Gold on dark blue.

RANKS AND INSIGNIA OF THE WORLD'S NAVIES

Jamaica

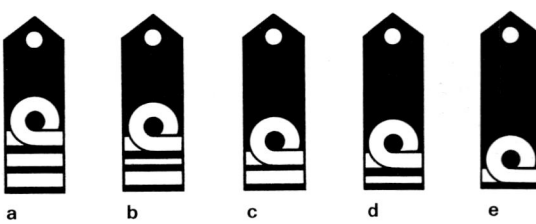

a: Commander   b: Lieutenant Commander   c: Lieutenant
d: Junior Lieutenant   e: Ensign

Gold on black.

Japan (MSA)

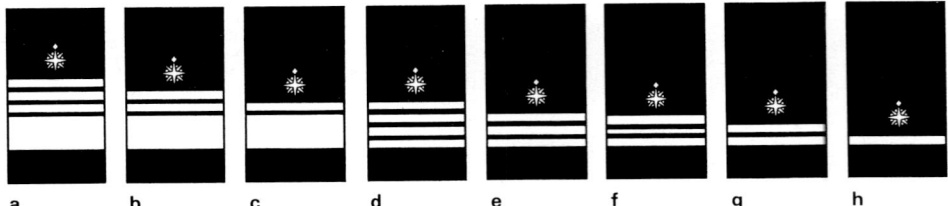

a: Commandant   b: Vice Commandant   c: Maritime Safety Superintendent First Grade   d: Maritime Safety Superintendent Second Grade   e: Maritime Safety Superintendent Third Grade   f: Maritime Safety Officer First Grade   g: Maritime Safety Officer Second Grade   h: Maritime Safety Officer Third grade

Gold on navy blue.

Japan (MSDF)

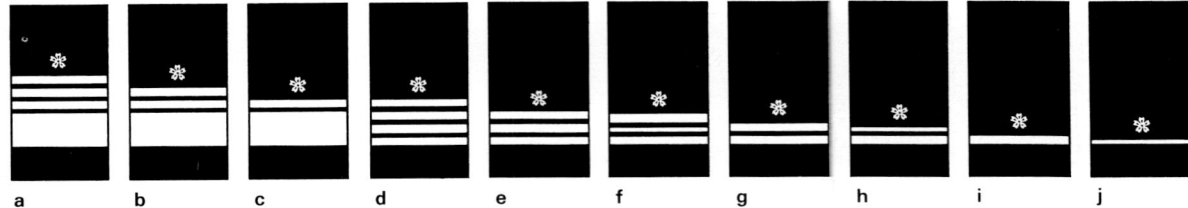

a: Admiral   b: Vice Admiral   c: Rear Admiral   d: Captain   e: Commander   f: Lieutenant Commander   g: Lieutenant   h: Sub Lieutenant   i: Acting Sub Lieutenant   j: Warrant Officer

Gold on navy blue.

Kenya

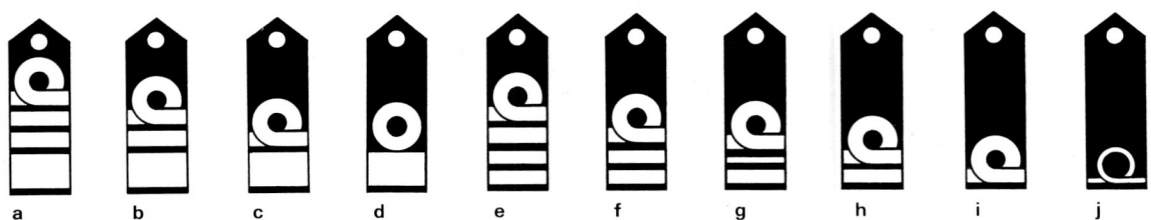

a: *General*, Admiral   b: *Lieutenant General*, Vice Admiral   c: *Major General*, Rear Admiral   d: *Brigadier*, Commodore   e: *Colonel*, Captain
f: *Lieutenant Colonel*, Commander   g: *Major*, Lieutenant Commander   h: *Captain*, Lieutenant   i: *Lieutenant*, Sub Lieutenant   j: *Second Lieutenant*, Acting Sub Lieutenant

Gold on black.

Korea, Democratic People's Republic (North)

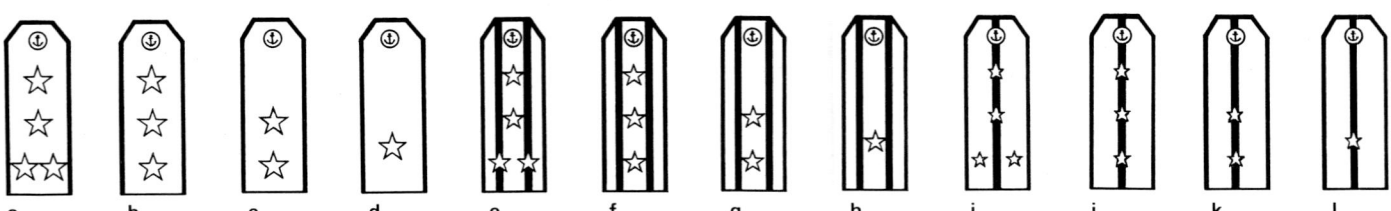

a: Admiral of the Fleet   b: Admiral   c: Vice Admiral   d: Rear Admiral   e: Commodore   f: Captain   g: Commander   h: Lieutenant Commander   i: Senior Lieutenant   j: Lieutenant   k: Sub Lieutenant   l: Acting Sub Lieutenant

Black stripes, silver stars on gold.

Korea, Republic (South)

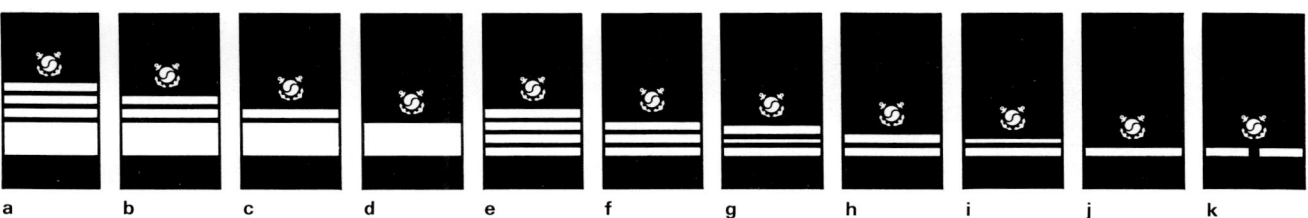

a: Admiral b: Vice Admiral c: Rear Admiral d: Commodore e: Captain f: Commander g: Lieutenant Commander h: Lieutenant i: Sub Lieutenant j: Acting Sub Lieutenant k: Warrant Officer

Gold on navy blue.

Kuwait

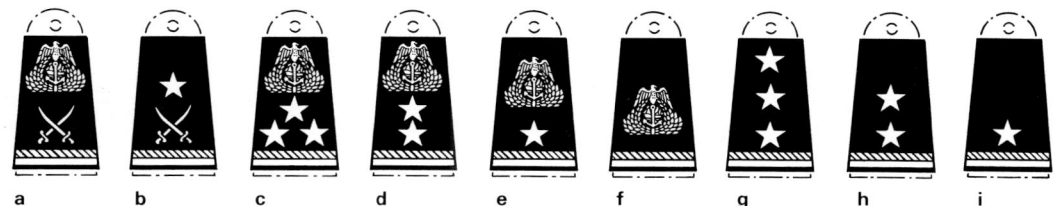

a: *Fariq*, Vice Admiral b: *Liwa'*, Rear Admiral c: *'Amid*, Commodore d: *'Aqid*, Captain e: *Muqaddam*, Commander f: *Ra'id*, Lieutenant Commander g: *Naqib*, Lieutenant h: *Mulazim Awwal*, Sub Lieutenant i: *Mulazim*, Acting Sub Lieutenant

Usually gold on tan. Can be gold on dark green or dark blue.

Laos

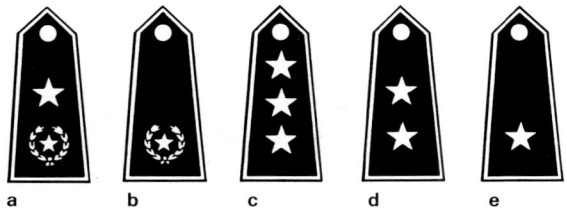

a: *Phavatho*, Commander b: *Phavatri*, Lieutenant Commander c: *Ruaek*, Lieutenant d: *Ruatho*, Sub Lieutenant e: *Ruatri*, Acting Sub Lieutenant

Gold on dark blue.

Lebanon

a: *'Imad*, Vice Admiral b: *Liwa'*, Rear Admiral c: *'Amid*, Commodore d: *'Aqid*, Captain e: *Muqaddam*, Commander f: *Ra'id*, Lieutenant Commander g: *Ra'is*, Lieutenant h: *Mulazim Awwal*, Sub Lieutenant i: *Mulazim*, Acting Sub Lieutenant

Gold on black.

Liberia

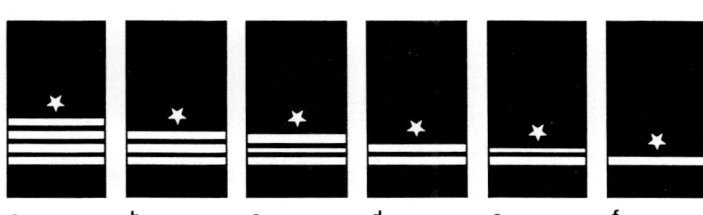

a: Captain b: Commander c: Lieutenant Commander d: Lieutenant e: Lieutenant Junior Grade f: Ensign

Gold on black.

RANKS AND INSIGNIA OF THE WORLD'S NAVIES

Libya

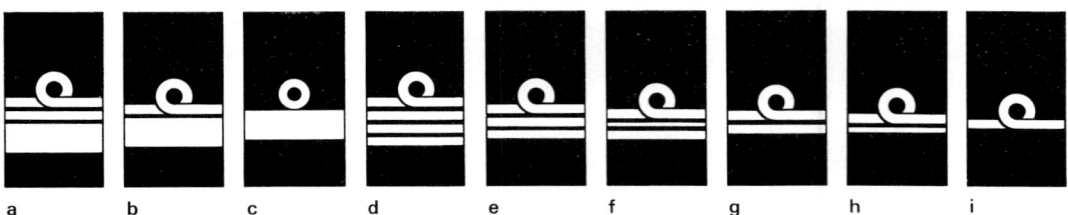

a: *Fariq*, Vice Admiral   b: *Liwa'*, Rear Admiral   c: *'Amid*, Commodore   d: *'Aqid*, Captain   e: *Muqaddam*, Commander   f: *Ra'id*, Lieutenant Commander   g: *Naqib*, Lieutenant   h: *Mulazim Awwal*, Sub Lieutenant   i: *Mulazim*, Acting Sub Lieutenant

Gold on navy blue.

Madagascar

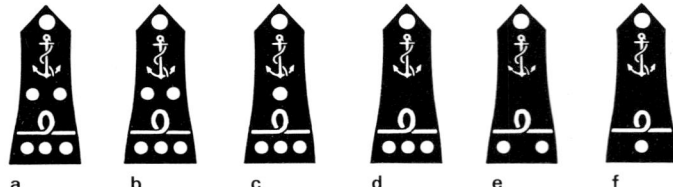

a: *Capitaine de Vaisseau*, Captain   b: *Capitaine de Frégate*, Commander   c: *Capitaine de Corvette*, Lieutenant Commander   d: *Lieutenant de Vaisseau*, Lieutenant   e: *Enseigne de Vaisseau 1re Classe*, Sub Lieutenant   f: *Enseigne de Vaisseau 2e Classe*, Acting Sub Lieutenant

Gold on black. Commander, top two discs silver.

Malaysia

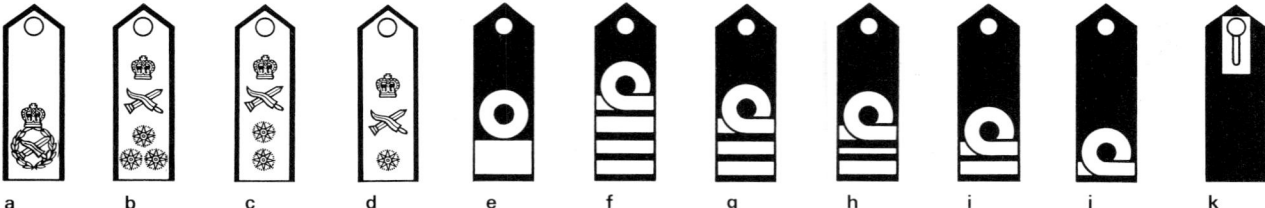

a: *Laksamana Armada*, Admiral of the Fleet   b: *Laksamana*, Admiral   c: *Laksamana Madya*, Vice Admiral   d: *Laksamana Muda*, Rear Admiral   e: *Laksamana Pertama*, Commodore   f: *Keptan*, Captain   g: *Komander*, Commander   h: *Leftenan Komander*, Lieutenant Commander   i: *Leftenan*, Lieutenant   j: *Leftenan Madya and Leftenan Muda*, Sub Lieutenant and Acting Sub Lieutenant   k: *Kadet Kanan*, Midshipman

Admiral of the Fleet to Rear Admiral, gold edged dark blue, silver devices. Remainder gold on black.

Mauritania

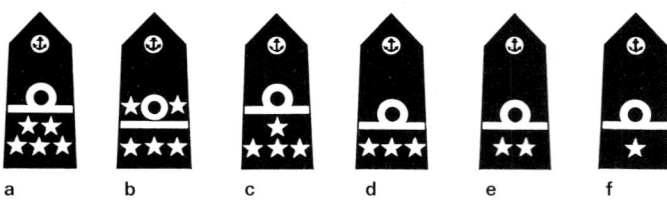

a: *Colonel*, Captain   b: *Lieutenant Colonel*, Commander   c: *Major*, Lieutenant Commander   d: *Captain*, Lieutenant   e: *Lieutenant*, Sub Lieutenant   f: *2nd Lieutenant*, Acting Sub Lieutenant

Gold on blue or green. Exception is two silver stars above lace for commander.

Mexico

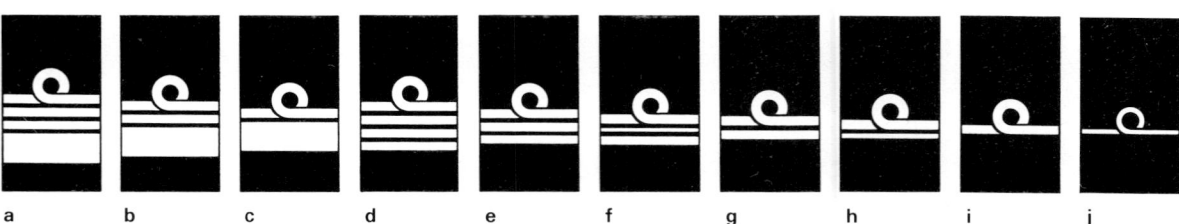

a: *Almirante*, Admiral   b: *Vicealmirante*, Vice Admiral   c: *Contraalmirante*, Rear Admiral   d: *Capitán de Navío*, Captain   e: *Capitán de Fragata*, Commander   f: *Capitán de Corbeta*, Lieutenant Commander   g: *Teniente de Navío*, Lieutenant   h: *Teniente de Fragata*, Sub Lieutenant   i: *Teniente de Corbeta*, Acting Sub Lieutenant   j: *Guardiamarina*, Midshipman

Gold on navy blue.

RANKS AND INSIGNIA OF THE WORLD'S NAVIES

Morocco

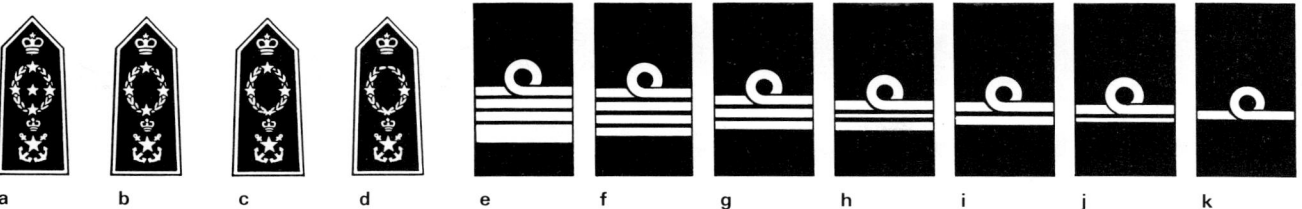

a: *Amiral*, Admiral of the Fleet   b: *Amiral D'Escadre*, Admiral   c: *Vice Amiral*, Vice Admiral   d: *Contre Amiral*, Rear Admiral   e: *Capitaine de Vaisseau Major*, Commodore   f: *Capitaine de Vaisseau*, Captain   g: *Capitaine de Frégate*, Commander   h: *Capitaine de Corvette*, Lieutenant Commander   i: *Lieutenant de Vaisseau*, Lieutenant   j: *Enseigne de Vaisseau 1re Classe*, Sub Lieutenant   k: *Enseigne de Vaisseau 2e Classe*, Acting Sub Lieutenant

Gold on black. Flag ranks silver stars.

Mozambique

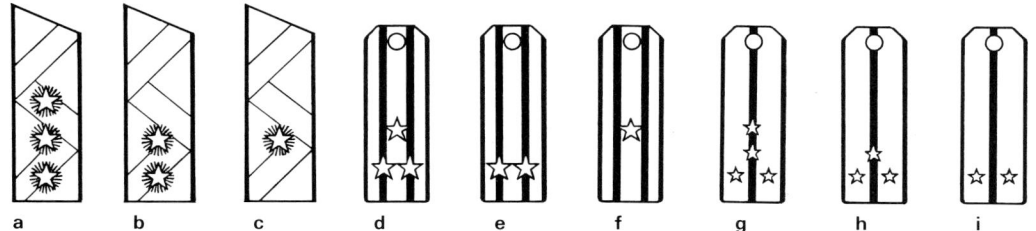

a: *Almirante*, Admiral   b: *Vice-Almirante*, Vice Admiral   c: *Contra-Almirante*, Rear Admiral   d: *Capitão-de-Mar-e-Guerra*, Captain   e: *Capitão-de-Fregate*, Commander   f: *Capitão-Tenente*, Lieutenant Commander   g: *Primerio-Tenente*, Lieutenant   h: *Segundo-Tenente*, Sub Lieutenant   i: *Guarda-Marinha*, Midshipman

Black rays, edging and stripes, silver stars. All on gold.

Netherlands

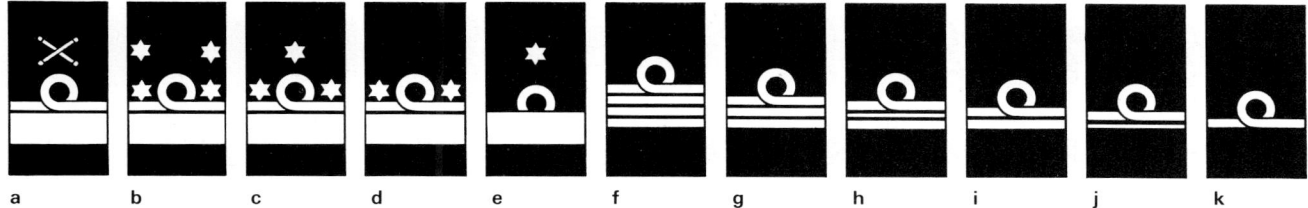

a: *Admiraal*, Admiral of the Fleet   b: *Luitenant-Admiraal*, Admiral   c: *Vice-Admiraal*, Vice Admiral   d: *Schout-bij-nacht*, Rear Admiral   e: *Commandeur*, Commodore   f: *Kapitein ter zee*, Captain   g: *Kapitein-luitenant ter zee*, Commander   h: *Luitenant ter see der eerste klasse*, Lieutenant Commander   i: *Luitenant ter zee der tweede klasse oudste categorie*, Lieutenant   j: *Luitenant ter zee der tweede klasse*, Sub Lieutenant   k: *Luitenant ter zee der derde klasse*, Acting Sub Lieutenant

Gold on navy blue. Stars and crossed batons, silver.

New Zealand

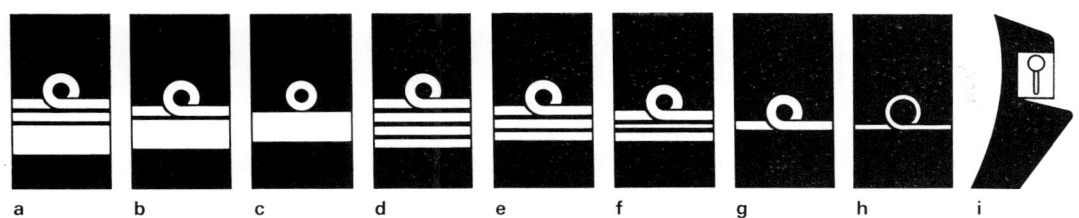

a: Vice Admiral   b: Rear Admiral   c: Commodore   d: Captain   e: Commander   f: Lieutenant Commander   g: Sub Lieutenant   h: Ensign   i: Midshipman

Gold on navy blue.

Nigeria

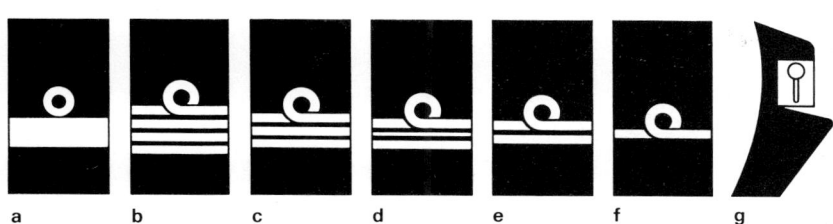

a: *Brigadier*, Commodore   b: *Colonel*, Captain   c: *Lieutenant Colonel*, Commander   d: *Major*, Lieutenant Commander   e: *Captain*, Lieutenant   f: *Lieutenant*, Sub Lieutenant   g: *Second Lieutenant*, Midshipman

Gold on navy blue.

RANKS AND INSIGNIA OF THE WORLD'S NAVIES

Norway

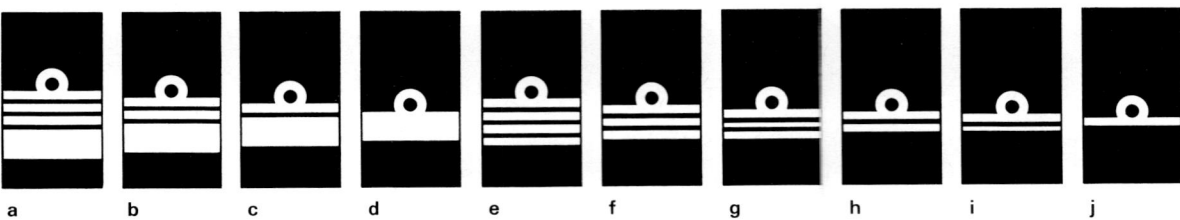

a: *Admiral*, Admiral   b: *Viseadmiral*, Vice Admiral   c: *Kontreadmiral*, Rear Admiral   d: *Kommandør*, Commodore   e: *Kommandør Kaptein*, Captain   f: *Orlogskaptein*, Commander   g: *Kapteinløytnant*, Lieutenant Commander   h: *Løytnant*, Lieutenant   i: *Fenrik*, Sub Lieutenant   j: *Ustskrevet*, Acting Sub Lieutenant

Gold on navy blue.

Oman

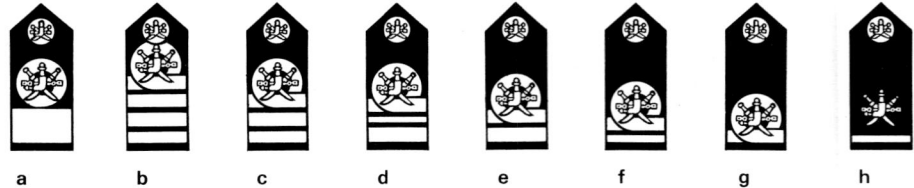

a: *'Amid Bahriyya*, Commodore   b: *'Aqid Bahriyya*, Captain   c: *Muqaddam Bahriyya*, Commander   d: *Ra'id Bahriyya*, Lieutenant Commander   e: *Naqib Bahriyya*, Lieutenant   f: *Mulazim Awwal Bahriyya*, Sub Lieutenant   g: *Mulazim Tanin Bahriyya*, Acting Sub Lieutenant   h: *Dabit Murashshah*, Midshipman

Gold on navy blue. White stripe, midshipman.

Pakistan

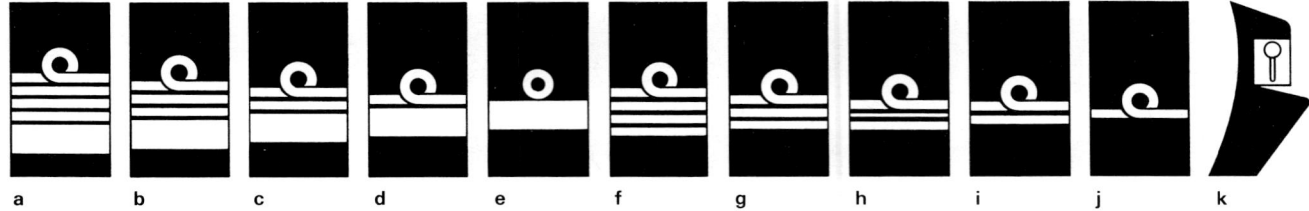

a: Admiral of the Fleet   b: Admiral   c: Vice Admiral   d: Rear Admiral   e: Commodore   f: Captain   g: Commander   h: Lieutenant Commander   i: Lieutenant   j: Sub Lieutenant   k: Midshipman

Gold on navy blue.

Paraguay

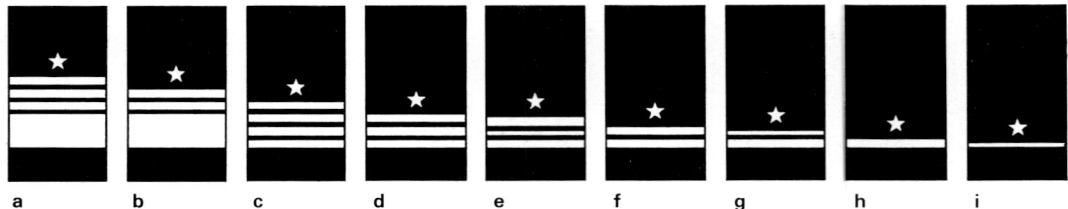

a: *Vicealmirante*, Vice Admiral   b: *Contralmirante*, Rear Admiral   c: *Capitán de Navío*, Captain   d: *Capitán de Fragata*, Commander   e: *Capitán de Corbeta*, Lieutenant Commander   f: *Teniente de Navío*, Lieutenant   g: *Teniente de Fragata*, Sub Lieutenant   h: *Teniente de Corbeta*, Acting Sub Lieutenant   i: *Guardiamarinha*, Midshipman

Gold on navy blue.

Peru

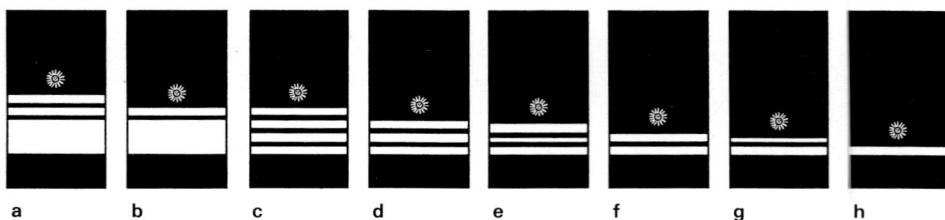

a: *Vicealmirante*, Vice Admiral   b: *Contraalmirante*, Rear Admiral   c: *Capitán de Navío*, Captain   d: *Capitán de Fragata*, Commander   e: *Capitán de Corbeta*, Lieutenant Commander   f: *Teniente Primero*, Lieutenant   g: *Teniente Segundo*, Sub Lieutenant   h: *Alférez de Fragata*, Acting Sub Lieutenant

Gold on navy blue.

RANKS AND INSIGNIA OF THE WORLD'S NAVIES

Philippines

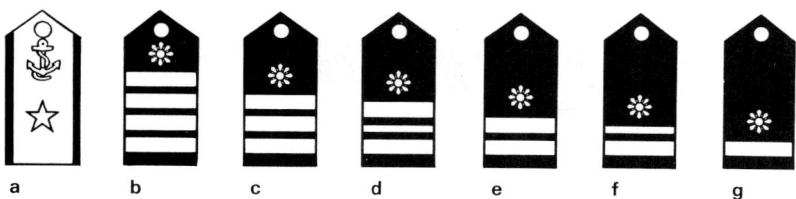

a: Commodore   b: Captain   c: Commander   d: Lieutenant Commander   e: Lieutenant
f: Lieutenant Junior Grade   g: Ensign

Gold on black. Commodore, dark blue edged, silver devices on gold.

Poland

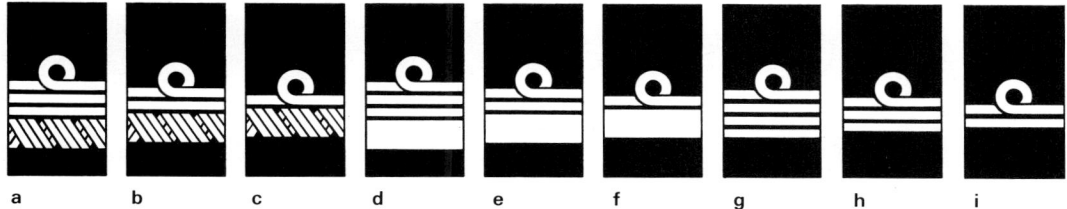

a: *Admiral*, Admiral   b: *Vice-Admiral*, Vice Admiral   c: *Kontradmiral*, Rear Admiral   d: *Komandor*, Captain   e: *Komandor Porucznik*, Commander   f: *Komandor Podporucznik*, Lieutenant Commander   g: *Kapitan Marynarki*, Lieutenant   h: *Porucznik Marynarki*, Sub Lieutenant   i: *Podporuznik Marynarki*, Acting Sub Lieutenant

Gold on dark blue.

Portugal

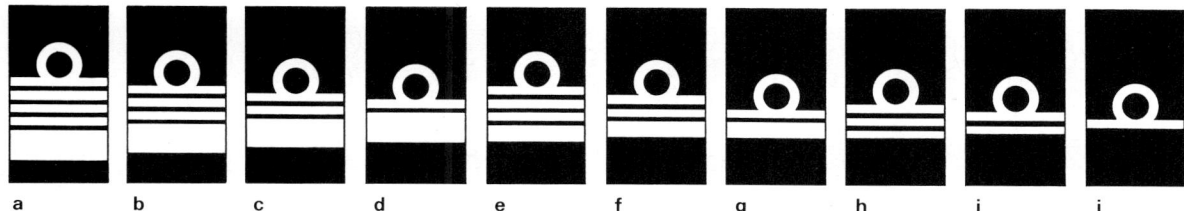

a: *Almirante da Armada*, Admiral of the Fleet   b: *Almirante*, Admiral   c: *Vice-Almirante*, Vice Admiral   d: *Contra-Almirante*, Rear Admiral
e: *Capitão-de-Mar-e-Guerra*, Captain   f: *Capitão-de-Fragata*, Commander   g: *Capitão-Tenente*, Lieutenant Commander   h: *Primeiro-Tenente*, Lieutenant   i: *Segundo-Tenente*, Sub Lieutenant   j: *Guarda-Marinha-ou-Subtenente*, Midshipman or Acting Sub Lieutenant

Gold on navy blue.

Romania

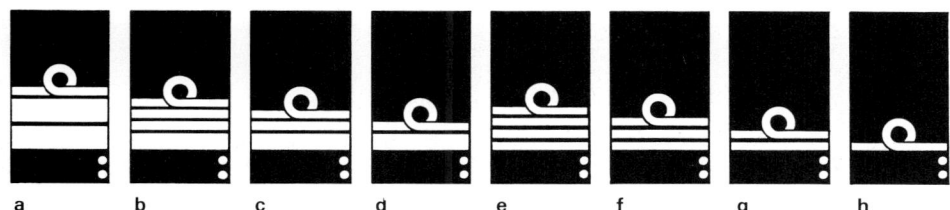

a: *Contra Amiral*, Rear Admiral   b: *Capitan de Rangel I*, Captain   c: *Capitan de Rangel II*, Commander   d: *Capitan de Rangel III*, Lieutenant Commander   e: *Capitan-Locotenent*, Senior Lieutenant   f: *Locotenent Major*, Lieutenant
g: *Locotenent*, Sub Lieutenant   h: *Sublocotenent*, Acting Sub Lieutenant

Gold on dark blue.

Russia

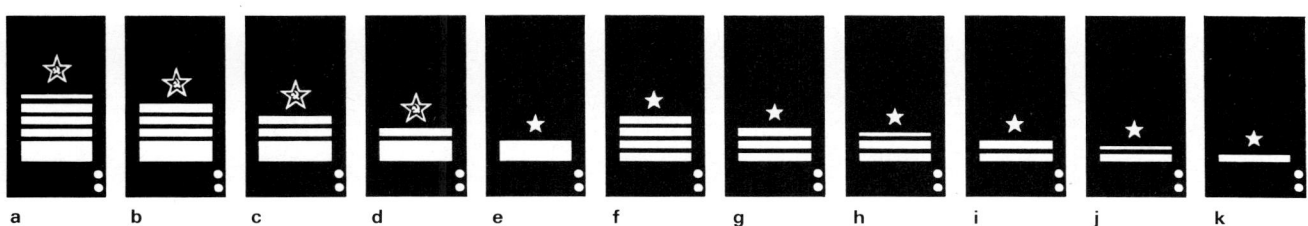

a: *Admiral Flota*, Admiral of the Fleet   b: *Admiral*, Admiral   c: *Vitse-Admiral*, Vice Admiral   d: *Kontr-Admiral*, Rear Admiral   e: *Kapitan Pervogo Ranga*, Captain
f: *Kapitan Vtorogo Ranga*, Commander   g: *Kapitan Tretyego Ranga*, Lieutenant Commander   h: *Kapitan-Leytenant*, Lieutenant   i: *Starshiy Leytenant*, Junior Lieutenant
j: *Leytenant*, Sub Lieutenant   k: *Mladshiy Leytenant*, Acting Sub Lieutenant

Gold on black.

RANKS AND INSIGNIA OF THE WORLD'S NAVIES

Saudi Arabia

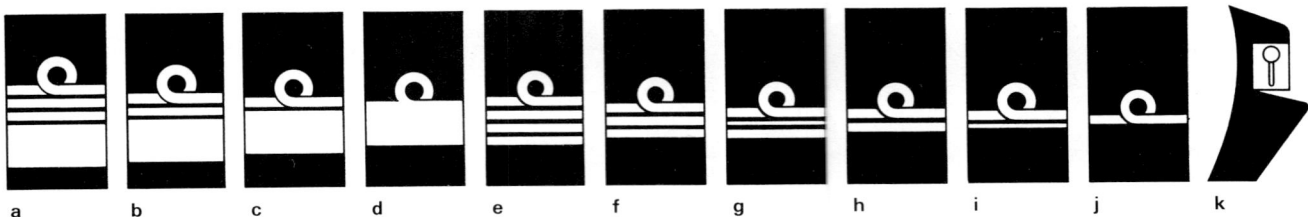

a: *Fariq Awwal*, Admiral   **b**: *Fariq*, Vice Admiral   **c**: *Liwa'*, Rear Admiral   **d**: *'Amid*, Commodore   **e**: *'Aqid*, Captain   **f**: *Muqaddam*, Commander   **g**: *Ra'id*, Lieutenant Commander   **h**: *Naqib*, Lieutenant   **i**: *Mulazim Awwal*, Sub Lieutenant   **j**: *Mulazim Thani*, Acting Sub Lieutenant   **k**: *Midshipman*, Midshipman
Gold on navy blue.

Senegal

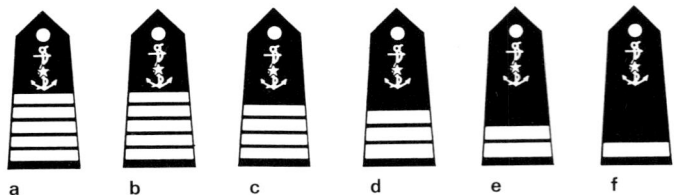

a: *Contre-Amiral*, Rear Admiral   **b**: *Capitaine de Vaisseau*, Captain   **c**: *Capitaine de Frégate*, Commander   **d**: *Capitaine de Corvette*, Lieutenant Commander   **e**: *Lieutenant de Vaisseau*, Lieutenant   **f**: *Enseigne de Vaisseau*, Sub Lieutenant
Gold on black. Captain, three gold and two silver stripes.

Singapore

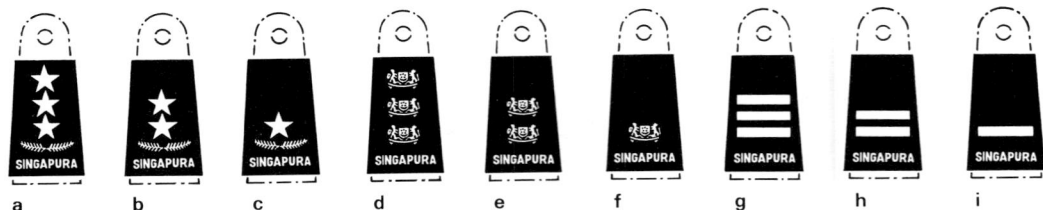

a: Vice Admiral   **b**: Rear Admiral   **c**: Commodore   **d**: Colonel   **e**: Lieutenant Colonel   **f**: Major   **g**: Captain   **h**: Lieutenant   **i**: Second Lieutenant
Gold on navy blue. Senior officers only have naval titles.

South Africa

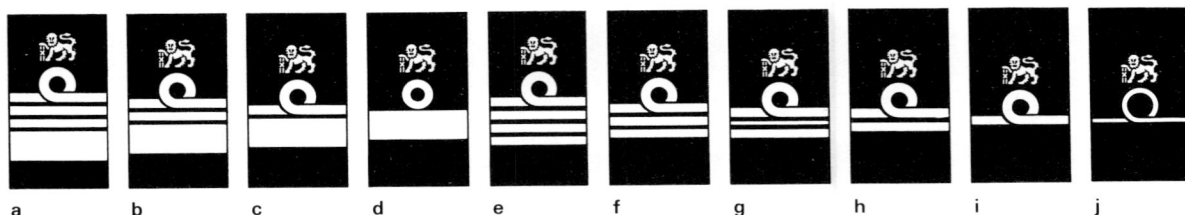

a: *Admiraal*, Admiral   **b**: *Vise-Admiraal*, Vice Admiral   **c**: *Skout-Admiraal*, Rear Admiral   **d**: *Kommodoor*, Commodore   **e**: *Kaptein*, Captain   **f**: *Kommandeur*, Commander   **g**: *Luitenant-Kommandeur*, Lieutenant Commander   **h**: *Luitenant*, Lieutenant   **i**: *Onder Luitenant*, Sub Lieutenant   **j**: *Vaandrig*, Ensign
Gold on navy blue.

Spain

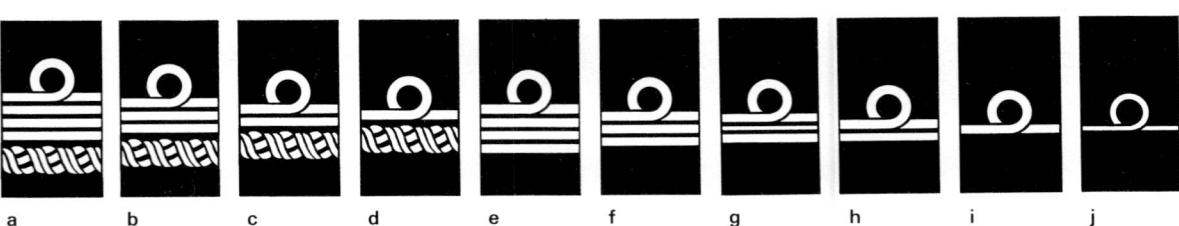

a: *Cap General de la Armada*, Admiral of the Fleet   **b**: *Almirante*, Admiral   **c**: *Vicealmirante*, Vice Admiral   **d**: *Contraalmirante*, Rear Admiral   **e**: *Capitán de Navío*, Captain   **f**: *Capitán de Fragata*, Commander   **g**: *Capitán de Corbeta*, Lieutenant Commander   **h**: *Teniente de Navío*, Lieutenant   **i**: *Alférez de Navío*, Sub Lieutenant   **j**: *Alférez de Fragata*, Acting Sub Lieutenant
Gold on navy blue.

RANKS AND INSIGNIA OF THE WORLD'S NAVIES

Sri Lanka

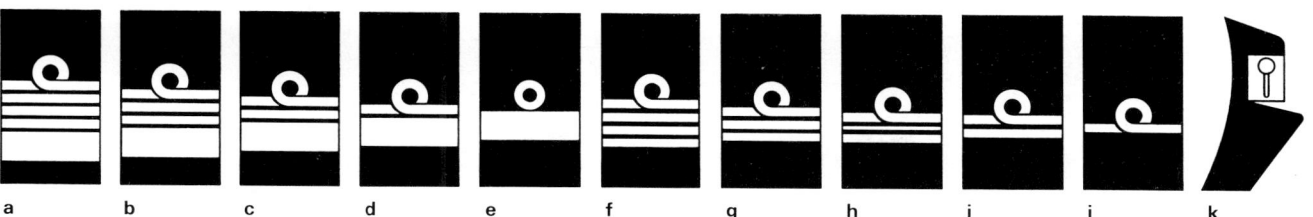

a: Admiral of the Fleet   b: Admiral   c: Vice Admiral   d: Rear Admiral   e: Commodore   f: Captain   g: Commander   h: Lieutenant Commander
i: Lieutenant   j: Sub Lieutenant   k: Midshipman

Gold on navy blue.

Sudan

a: *Fariq*, Vice Admiral   b: *Liwa'*, Rear Admiral   c: *'Awid*, Commodore   d: *'Aqid*, Captain   e: *Muqaddam*, Commander
f: *Ra'id*, Lieutenant Commander   g: *Naqib*, Lieutenant   h: *Mulazim Awwal*, Sub Lieutenant   i: *Mulazim Thani*, Acting Sub Lieutenant

Gold on black.

Suriname

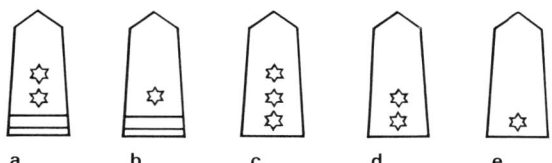

a: *Kapitein Ter Zee*, Commander   b: *Kapitein-Luitenant Ter Zee*, Lieutenant Commander   c: *Luitenant Ter Zee Der 1e Klasse*, Lieutenant   d: *Luitenant Ter Zee Der 2e Klasse Oudste Categorie*, Sub Lieutenant   e: *Luitenant Ter Zee Der 3e Klasse*, Acting Sub Lieutenant

Gold on white.

Sweden

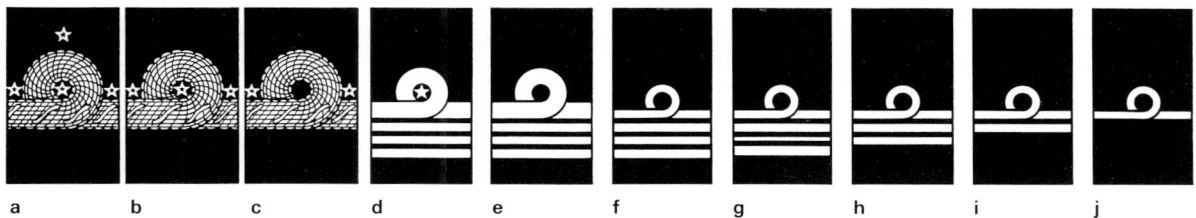

a: *Amiral*, Admiral   b: *Viceamiral*, Vice Admiral   c: *Konteramiral*, Rear Admiral   d: *Kommendör av 1. gr*, Commodore   e: *Kommendör*, Captain   f: *Kommendörkapten av 1. gr*, Commander   g: *Kommendörkapten av 2. gr*, Lieutenant Commander   h: *Kapten*, Lieutenant
i: *Löjtnant*, Sub Lieutenant   j: *Fänrik*, Acting Sub Lieutenant

Gold on dark blue.

Sweden (Coast Guard)

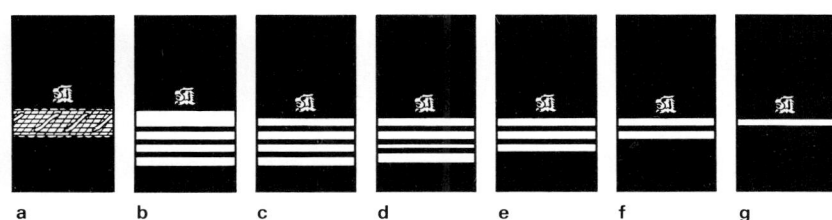

a: *Konteramiral*, Rear Admiral   b: *Kommendör*, Captain   c: *Kommendörkapten av 1. gr*, Commander
d: *Kommendörkapten av 2. gr*, Lieutenant Commander   e: *Kapten*, Lieutenant   f: *Löjtnant*, Sub Lieutenant   g: *Fänrik*, Acting Sub Lieutenant

Gold on dark blue.

RANKS AND INSIGNIA OF THE WORLD'S NAVIES

Syria

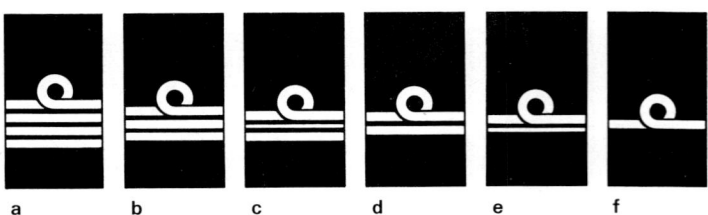

a: *'Aqid*, Captain   b: *Muqaddam*, Commander   c: *Ra'id*, Lieutenant Commander
d: *Naqib*, Lieutenant   e: *Mulazim Awwal*, Sub Lieutenant   f: *Mulazim*, Acting Sub Lieutenant

Gold on navy blue.

Taiwan

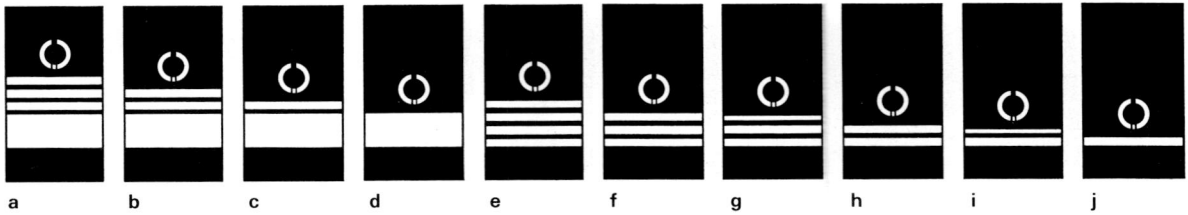

a: Admiral   b: Vice Admiral   c: Rear Admiral   d: Commodore   e: Captain   f: Commander   g: Lieutenant Commander   h: Lieutenant
i: Lieutenant JG (II)   j: Sub Lieutenant   k: Ensign   l: Acting Sub Lieutenant

Gold on navy blue.

Thailand

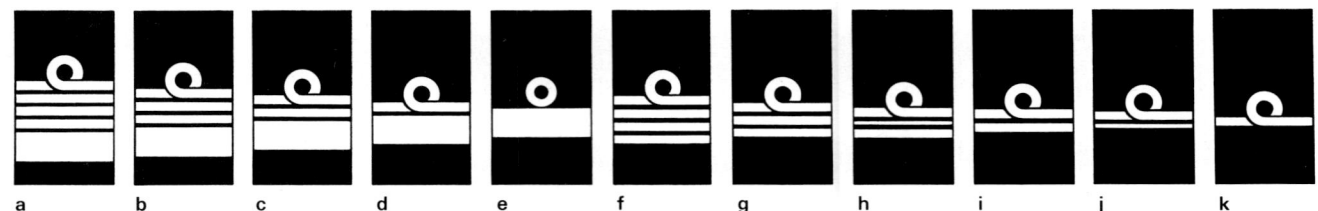

a: Admiral of the Fleet   b: Admiral   c: Vice Admiral   d: Rear Admiral   e: Commodore   f: Captain   g: Commander   h: Lieutenant Commander
i: Lieutenant   j: Sub Lieutenant   k: Acting Sub Lieutenant

Gold on navy blue.

Togo

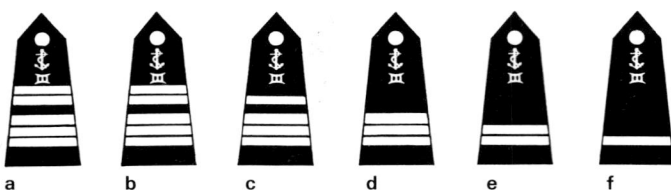

a: *Capitaine de Vaisseau*, Captain   b: *Capitaine de Frégate*, Commander
c: *Capitaine de Corvette*, Lieutenant Commander   d: *Lieutenant de Vaisseau*, Lieutenant   e: *Enseigne de Vaisseau 1re Classe*, Sub Lieutenant   f: *Enseigne de Vaisseau 2e classe*, Acting Sub Lieutenant

Gold on black. Commander, three gold two silver stripes.

Trinidad and Tobago

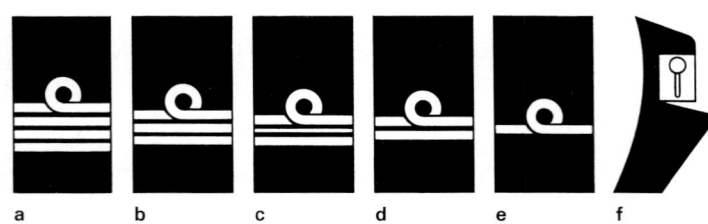

a: Captain   b: Commander   c: Lieutenant Commander   d: Lieutenant   e: Sub Lieutenant   f: Midshipman

Gold on navy blue.

RANKS AND INSIGNIA OF THE WORLD'S NAVIES

Turkey

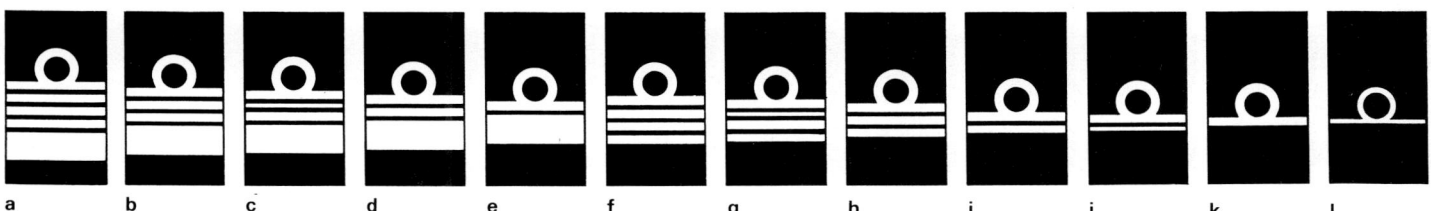

a: *Büyük Amiral*, Admiral of the Fleet   b: *Oramiral*, Admiral   c: *Koramiral*, Vice Admiral   d: *Tümamiral*, Rear Admiral   e: *Tugamiral*, Commodore   f: *Albay*, Captain   g: *Yarbay*, Commander   h: *Binbaşi*, Lieutenant Commander   i: *Yüzbaşi*, Lieutenant   j: *Üstegmen*, Sub Lieutenant   k: *Tegmen*, Acting Sub Lieutenant   l: *Astegmen*, Midshipman
Gold on black.

United Arab Emirates

a: *Fariq*, Vice Admiral   b: *Liwa*, Rear Admiral   c: *'Amid*, Commodore   d: *'Aqid*, Captain   e: *Muqaddam*, Commander   f: *Ra'id*, Lieutenant Commander   g: *Rais*, Lieutenant   h: *Awwal*, Sub Lieutenant   i: *Mulazim*, Acting Sub Lieutenant
Gold on navy blue.

United Kingdom (Navy)

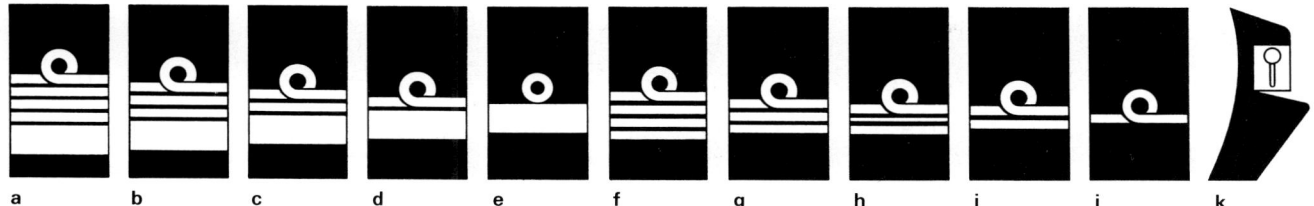

a: Admiral of the Fleet   b: Admiral   c: Vice Admiral   d: Rear Admiral   e: Commodore   f: Captain   g: Commander   h: Lieutenant Commander   i: Lieutenant   j: Sub Lieutenant   k: Midshipman
Gold on navy blue.

United Kingdom (RFA)

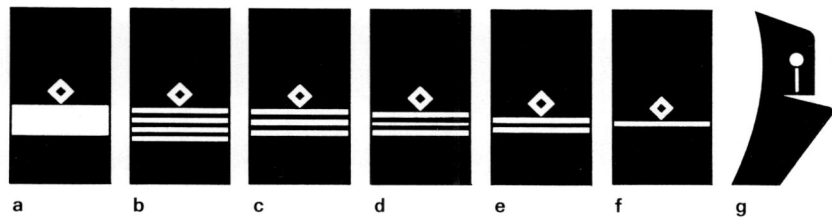

a: Commodore   b: Captain   c: Chief Officer   d: First Officer   e: 2nd Officer   f: 3rd Officer   g: Deck Cadet
Gold on navy blue.

United States (Navy)

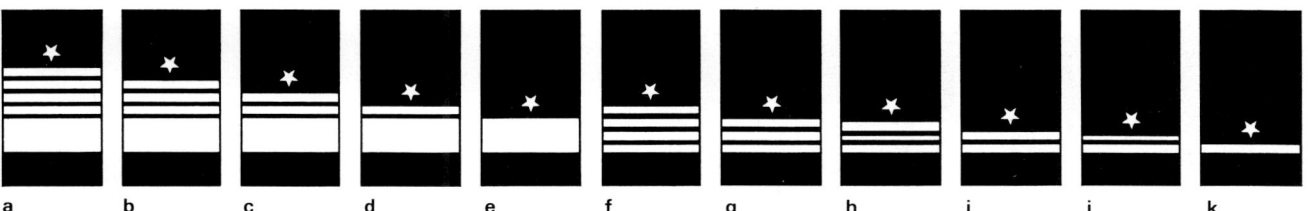

a: *Fleet Admiral*, Admiral of the Fleet   b: *Admiral*, Admiral   c: *Vice Admiral*, Vice Admiral   d: *Rear Admiral*, Rear Admiral   e: *Commodore Admiral*, Commodore   f: *Captain*, Captain   g: *Commander*, Commander   h: *Lieutenant Commander*, Lieutenant Commander   i: *Lieutenant*, Lieutenant   j: *Lieutenant Junior Grade*, Sub Lieutenant   k: *Ensign*, Acting Sub Lieutenant
Gold on navy blue.

RANKS AND INSIGNIA OF THE WORLD'S NAVIES

United States (Coast Guard)

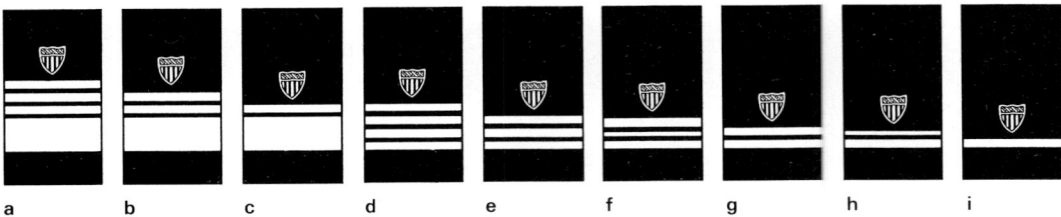

a: Admiral   **b:** Vice Admiral   **c:** Rear Admiral   **d:** Captain   **e:** Commander   **f:** Lieutenant Commander   **g:** Lieutenant   **h:** *Lieutenant Junior Grade*, Sub Lieutenant   **i:** *Ensign*, Acting Sub Lieutenant

Gold on navy blue.

Uruguay

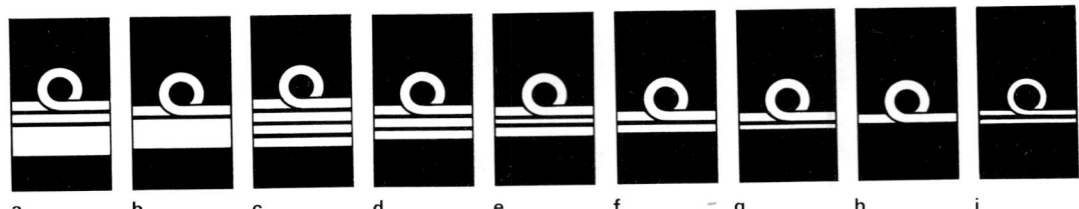

a: *Vicealmirante*, Vice Admiral   **b:** *Contraalmirante*, Rear Admiral   **c:** *Capitán de Navío*, Captain   **d:** *Capitán de Fragata*, Commander   **e:** *Capitán de Corbeta*, Lieutenant Commander   **f:** *Teniente de Navío*, Lieutenant   **g:** *Alférez de Navío*, Sub Lieutenant   **h:** *Alférez de Fragata*, Acting Sub Lieutenant   **i:** *Guardiamarina*, Midshipman

Gold on navy blue.

Venezuela

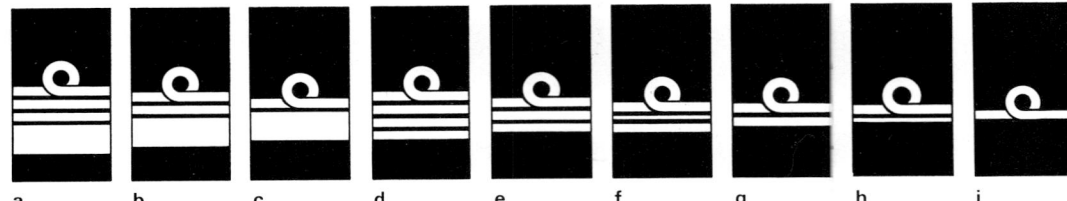

a: *Almirante*, Admiral   **b:** *Vicealmirante*, Vice Admiral   **c:** *Contraalmirante*, Rear Admiral   **d:** *Capitán de Navío*, Captain   **e:** *Capitán de Fragata*, Commander   **f:** *Capitán de Corbeta*, Lieutenant Commander   **g:** *Teniente de Navío*, Lieutenant   **h:** *Teniente de Fragata*, Sub Lieutenant   **i:** *Alférez de Navío*, Acting Sub Lieutenant

Gold on navy blue.

Vietnam

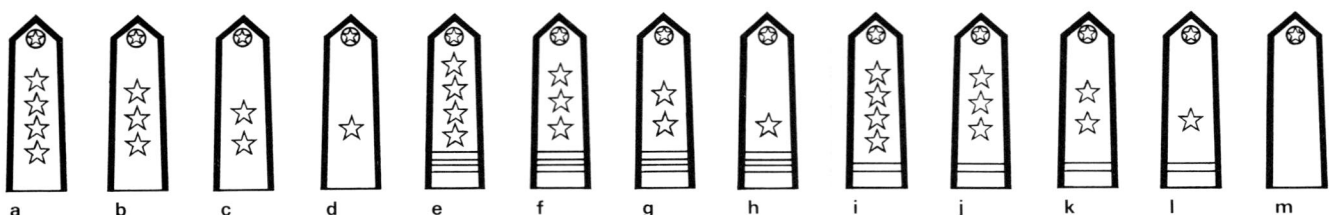

a: *Senior General*, Admiral of the Fleet   **b:** *Colonel General*, Admiral   **c:** *Lieutenant General*, Vice Admiral   **d:** *Major General*, Rear Admiral   **e:** *Senior Colonel*, Commodore   **f:** *Colonel*, Captain   **g:** *Lieutenant Colonel*, Commander   **h:** *Major*, Lieutenant Commander   **i:** *Senior Captain*, Senior Lieutenant   **j:** *Captain*, Lieutenant   **k:** *Senior Lieutenant*, Sub Lieutenant   **l:** *2d Lieutenant*, Acting Sub Lieutenant   **m:** *Student Officer*, Midshipman

Gold shoulder straps. Generals, edged red gold stars. Remainder, silver stars and lace.

Yemen

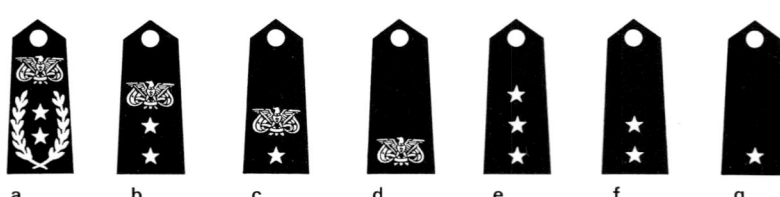

a: *'Amid*, Commodore   **b:** *'Aqid*, Captain   **c:** *Muqaddam*, Commander   **d:** *Ra'id*, Lieutenant Commander   **e:** *Naqib*, Lieutenant   **f:** *Mulazim Awwal*, Sub Lieutenant   **g:** *Mulazim Thani*, Acting Sub Lieutenant

Gold on black.

Yugoslavia

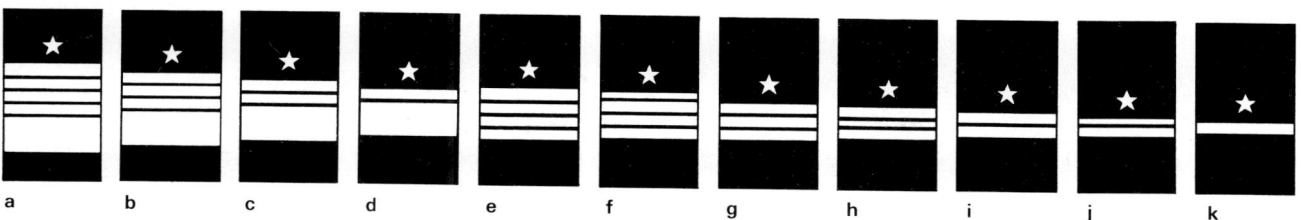

a: *Admiral Flote*, Admiral of the Fleet   b: *Admiral*, Admiral   c: *Viceadmiral*, Vice Admiral   d: *Kontraadmiral*, Rear Admiral   e: *Kapetan Bojnog Broda*, Captain
f: *Kapetan Fregate*, Commander   g: *Kapetan Korvete*, Lieutenant Commander   h: *Porucnik Bojnog Broda*, Lieutenant (Senior)   i: *Porucnik Fregate*, Lieutenant
j: *Porucnik Korvete*, Sub Lieutenant   k: *Potporucnik*, Acting Sub Lieutenant
Gold on dark blue.

Zaire

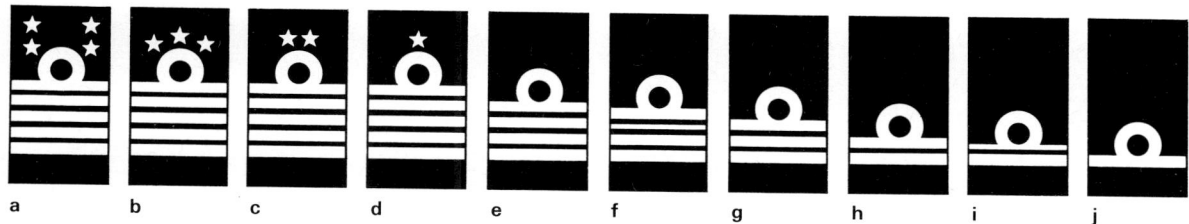

a: *Grand Amiral*, Admiral of the Fleet   b: *Amiral*, Admiral   c: *Vice-Amiral*, Vice Admiral   d: *Contre-Amiral*, Rear Admiral   e: *Capitaine de Vaisseau*, Captain   f: *Capitaine de Frégate*, Commander   g: *Capitaine de Corvette*, Lieutenant Commander   h: *Lieutenant de Vaisseau*, Lieutenant   i: *Enseigne de Vaisseau 1re Classe*, Sub Lieutenant   j: *Enseigne de Vaisseau 2e Classe*, Acting Sub Lieutenant
Gold on black.

AN ARCHITECT OF INTELLIGENT SYSTEMS

MICA

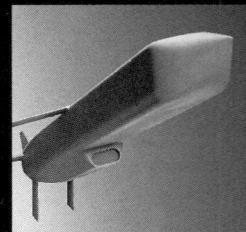
APACHE

BREVEL

MISTRAL

In a dangerous and unstable world, the intelligence and precision of weapon systems will be a major asset for the free nations that embrace the ideal of security.

MATRA DÉFENSE gathers men and women who are constantly integrating the evolution in their skills into the design and construction of efficient, reliable products which are adaptable to the security requirements of nations.

MATRA DÉFENSE is a major player in the "Europeanisation of Defence" across a wide range of systems and intelligent armament for the three services Army, Navy and Airforce.

MATRA DÉFENSE has experience of the future.

MATRA DÉFENSE

37, avenue Louis Bréguet
78140 Vélizy-Villacoublay - France
Tél. : (33-1) 34 88 30 00

Pennant list of major surface ships

Type abbreviations (for USA see page 755)

AD	Destroyer tender	BB	Battleship	FFLG	Guided missile light frigate or corvette
AEFS	Fleet replenishment ship	CA	Gun cruiser	HSS	Helicopter support ship
AFS	Combat stores ship	CG	Guided missile cruiser	LCC	Amphibious command ship
AG	Miscellaneous	CGH	Guided missile/helicopter cruiser	LHA	Amphibious assault ship (general purpose)
AG/FF	Frigate/FAC support ship	CGN	Guided missile cruiser (nuclear-powered)	LHD	Amphibious assault ship (multi-purpose)
AGI	Research and Survey ship	CL	Light cruiser	LKA	Amphibious cargo ship
AGOR	Research ship	CLT	Light cruiser, training	LPD	Amphibious transport dock
AGS	Surveying ship	CV	Multi-purpose aircraft carrier	LPH	Amphibious assault ship (helicopter)
AO	Oiler	CVA	Attack aircraft carrier		
AOE	Fast combat support ship	CVH	Helicopter carrier	LSD	Dock landing ship
AOF(L)	Large fleet tanker	CVL	Light aircraft carrier	LSI	Landing ship, infantry
AOF(S)	Small fleet tanker	CVN	Multi-purpose aircraft carrier (nuclear-powered)	LSL	Landing ship, logistic
AOR	Replenishment oiler			LST	Tank landing ship
AOS	Support tanker	CVS	ASW aircraft carrier	MH	Minehunter
AP	Transport	DD	Destroyer	ML	Minelayer
APA	Amphibious transport	DDG	Guided missile destroyer (including surface-to-air missile)	MSC	Coastal minesweeper
AR	Repair ship			MSO	Ocean minesweeper
ARS	Salvage ship	FF	Frigate	PV	Patrol vessel
AS	Submarine tender	FFG	Guided missile frigate (including surface-to-air missiles)	TCD	Landing ship dock
ATS	Training support ship				
AVT	Auxiliary aircraft landing training ship	FFL	Light frigate or corvette		

Pennant numbers of major surface ships in numerical order

Number	Ship's name	Type	Country	Number	Ship's name	Type	Country
A 00	Britannia	AG	UK	2	Sukhothai	FFLG	Thailand
01	Adelaide	FFG	Australia	2	Bang Rachan	MH/MSC	Thailand
01	Pohjanmaa	ML	Finland	2	Chula	AOR	Thailand
A 01	Panuco	LST	Mexico	2	General Artigas	FFG	Uruguay
A 01	Contramaestre Casado	AP	Spain	2/508	Al Hirasa	FF	Syria
B 01	Durango	AP	Mexico	A 2	Teniente Olivieri	PV	Argentina
C 01	Capitán de Navío Sebastian Jose Holzinger	PV	Mexico	A 2	Al Sultana	AFS	Oman
				AFS 2	Sylvania	AFS	USA
D 01	Admirable class	PV	Mexico	AOE 2	Camden	AOE	USA
FM 01	Presidente Eloy Alfaro	FFG	Ecuador	ATS 2	Beaufort	ATS	USA
G-01	Leandro Valle	PV	Mexico	D 2	Santisima Trinidad	DDG	Argentina
HL 01	Shoyo	AGS	Japan	L 2	Nasr Al Bahr	LSL	Oman
HQ 01	Pham Ngu Lao	FFG	Vietnam	LHA 2	Saipan	LHA	USA
LL 01	Tsushima	AG	Japan	LHD 2	Essex	LHD	USA
S 01	Gladan	ATS	Sweden	LST 2	Chang	LST	Thailand
1	Tachin	FF/ATS	Thailand	LSV 2	CW 3 Harold C Clinger	LSL	USA
1	Khamronsin	FFL	Thailand	M 2	Rio Negro	MSC	Argentina
1	Rattanakosin	FFLG	Thailand	MCM 2	Defender	MSO	USA
1	Thalang	MSC/AG	Thailand	PHM 2	Hercules	PV	USA
1	Uruguay	FFG	Uruguay	Q 2	Libertad	AG	Argentina
1/508	Petya III class	FF	Syria	V 2	Veinticinco de Mayo	CV	Argentina
A 1	Comandante General Irigoyen	PV	Argentina	03	Sydney	FFG	Australia
A 1	Al Mabrukah	PV/ATS	Oman	03	Turanmaa	FFL	Finland
AFS 1	Mars	AFS	USA	C 03	Brigadier Jose Maria de la Vega Gonzalez	PV	Mexico
AOE 1	Sacramento	AOE	USA				
ATS 1	Edenton	ATS	USA	D 03	Admirable class	PV	Mexico
D 1	Hercules	DDG	Argentina	E 03	Quetzalcoatl	DD	Mexico
L 1	Al Munassir	LSL	Oman	G-03	Mariano Escobedo	PV	Mexico
LHA 1	Tarawa	LHA	USA	HQ 03	Dai Ky	FFG	Vietnam
LHD 1	Wasp	LHD	USA	M 03	Visborg	ML/AG	Sweden
LSV 1	General Frank S Besson Jr	LSL	USA	P 03	Capitan Meza	PV	Paraguay
M 1	Neuquen	MSC	Argentina	3	Pin Klao	FF	Thailand
MCM 1	Avenger	MSO	USA	3	Longlom	FFL	Thailand
MSF 1	Phosamton	ATS	Thailand	3	Nongsarai	MH/MSC	Thailand
PHM 1	Pegasus	PV	USA	3	Maeklong	ATS	Thailand
S 1	Shabab Oman	AG	Oman	3	Montevideo	FFG	Uruguay
Z 1	Baltyk	AO	Poland	A 3	Francisco de Gurruchaga	PV	Argentina
02	Canberra	FFG	Australia	AFS 3	Niagara Falls	AFS	USA
02	Hameenmaa	ML	Finland	AGF 3	La Salle	AG	USA
A 02	Manzanillo	LST	Mexico	AOE 3	Seattle	AOE	USA
C 02	Capitán de Navío Blas Godinez Brito	PV	Mexico	AOR 3	Kansas City	AOR	USA
				ATS 3	Brunswick	ATS	USA
E 02	Cuitlahuac	DD	Mexico	B 3	Canal Beagle	AP	Argentina
FM 02	Moran Valverde	FFG	Ecuador	L 3	Fulk al Salamah	AP	Oman
G-02	Guillerrmo Prieto	PV	Mexico	LHA 3	Belleau Wood	LHA	USA
M 02	Älvsborg	ML/AS	Sweden	LHD 3	Kearsage	LHD	USA
P 02	Nanawa	PV	Paraguay	LST 3	Pangan	LST	Thailand
S 02	Falken	ATS	Sweden	LSV 3	General Brehon B Somervell	LSL	USA
2	Thayanchon	FFL	Thailand	M 3	Chubut	MSC	Argentina
2	Prasae	FF/ATS	Thailand	MCM 3	Sentry	MSO	USA

[97]

PENNANT LIST

Number	Ship's name	Type	Country
PHM 3	Taurus	PV	USA
Z 3	Krab	AO	Poland
04	Darwin	FFG	Australia
04	Karjala	FFL	Finland
C 04	General Felipe B Berriozabal	PV	Mexico
D 04	Admirable class	PV	Mexico
E 04	Netzahualcoyotl	DD	Mexico
HL 04	Tenyo	AGS	Japan
M 04	Carlskrona	ML/ATS	Sweden
N 04	Aktion	ML	Greece
P 04	Teneinte Farina	PV	Paraguay
4	Sattahip	PV	Thailand
AFS 4	White Plains	AFS	USA
AOE 4	Detroit	AOE	USA
AOR 4	Savannah	AOR	USA
B 4	Bahia San Blas	AP	Argentina
LHA 4	Nassau	LHA	USA
LHD 4	Boxer	LHD	USA
LPD 4	Austin	LPD	USA
LST 4	Lanta	LST	Thailand
LSV 4	Lt Gen William B Bunker	LSL	USA
M 4	Tierra del Fuego	MSC	Argentina
MCM 4	Champion	MSO	USA
PHM 4	Aquila	PV	USA
05	Melbourne	FFG	Australia
05	Uusimaa	ML	Finland
A 05	Vicente Guerrero	AG	Mexico
A 05	Tui	AGOR	New Zealand
D 05	Admirable class	PV	Mexico
G-05	Manuel Doblado	PV	Mexico
H 05	Altair	AGS	Mexico
L 05	President El Hadj Omar Bongo	LCC	Gabon
N 05	Amvrakia	ML	Greece
R 05	Invincible	CVSG	UK
5	Tapi	FF	Thailand
5	Ladya	MSC	Thailand
5	Klongyai	PV	Thailand
AOR 5	Wabash	AOR	USA
B 5	Cabo de Hornos	AP	Argentina
LHA 5	Peleliu	LHA	USA
LPD 5	Ogden	LPD	USA
LST 5	Prathong	LST	Thailand
LSV 5	Major General Charles P Gross	LSL	USA
M 5	Chaco	MH	Argentina
MCM 5	Guardian	MSO	USA
PC 5	Sukrip	PV	Thailand
PHM 5	Aries	PV	USA
Q 5	Almirante Irizar	AG	Argentina
Z 5	Moskit class	AO	Poland
06	Newcastle	FFG	Australia
06	Condell	FFG	Chile
A 06	Comodoro Manuel Azueta Perillos	FF	Mexico
A 06	Monowai	AGS	New Zealand
B 06	Usumacinta	FF	Mexico
G-06	Sebastian de la Tejada	PV	Mexico
H 06	Antares	AGS	Mexico
R 06	Illustrious	CVSG	UK
6	Khirirat	FF	Thailand
6	Bangkeo	MSC	Thailand
6	Takbai	PV	Thailand
AFS 6	San Diego	AFS	USA
AOE 6	Supply	AOE	USA
AOR 6	Kalamazoo	AOR	USA
LPD 6	Duluth	LPD	USA
LST 6	Sichang	LST	Thailand
M 6	Formosa	MH	Argentina
MCM 6	Devastator	MSO	USA
PC 6	Tongpliu	PV	Thailand
PHM 6	Gemini	PV	USA
07	Lynch	FFG	Chile
A 07	Cuauhtemoc	AG	Mexico
B 07	Coahuila	FF	Mexico
C 07	Guanajuata	PV	Mexico
G-07	Santos Degollado	PV	Mexico
HQ 07	Admirable class	FFL	Vietnam
P 07	Général d'Armée Ba Oumar	PV	Gabon
R 07	Ark Royal	CVSG	UK
7	Makut Rajakumarn	FF	Thailand
7	Kantang	PV	Thailand
AFS 7	San Jose	AFS	USA
AOE 7	Rainier	AOE	USA
AOR 7	Roanoke	AOR	USA
E 7	Inkadh	FF	Tunisia
FFG 7	Oliver Hazard Perry	FFG	USA
LPD 7	Cleveland	LPD	USA
LPH 7	Guadalcanal	LPH	USA
LST 7	Surin	LST	Thailand
MCM 7	Patriot	MSO	USA
PC 7	Liulom	PV	Thailand
PF 7	Andres Bonifacio	FF	Philippines
08	Ministro Zenteno	FFG	Chile
A 08	Plan de Iguala	AP	Mexico
B 08	Chihuahua	FF	Mexico
G-08	Ignacio de la Llave	PV	Mexico
P 08	Colonel Djoue Dabany	PV	Gabon
8	Donchedi	MSC	Thailand
8	Thepha	PV	Thailand
AR 8	Jason	AR	USA
FFG 8	McInerney	FFG	USA
LPD 8	Dubuque	LPD	USA
MCM 8	Scout	MSO	USA
Q 8	Puerto Deseado	AGS	Argentina
Z 8	Medusa	AO	Poland
09	General Baquedano	FFG	Chile
G-09	Juan N Alvares	PV	Mexico
HQ 09	Petya class	FF	Vietnam
9	Taimuang	PV	Thailand
A 9	Alferez Sobral	PV	Argentina
CGN 9	Long Beach	CGN	USA
FFG 9	Wadsworth	FFG	USA
LPD 9	Denver	LPD	USA
LPH 9	Guam	LPH	USA
MCM 9	Pioneer	MSO	USA
Z 9	Slimak	AO	Poland
A 10	Comodoro Somellera	PV	Argentina
D 10	Almirante Brown	DDG	Argentina
FFG 10	Duncan	FFG	USA
G-10	Manuel Gutierrez Zamora	PV	Mexico
L 10	Fearless	LPD	UK
LPD 10	Juneau	LPD	USA
LPH 10	Tripoli	LPH	USA
MCM 10	Warrior	MSO	USA
11	Smeli	FFG	Bulgaria
11	Prat	DDG	Chile
11	Kralj Petar Kresimir	FFLG	Croatia
11	Mahamiru	MH	Malaysia
A 11	Minas Gerais	CVS	Brazil
A 11	Endeavour	AEFS	New Zealand
A 11	Mar del Norte	AOF(L)	Spain
AGF 11	Coronado	AG	USA
AGS 11	Chanthara	AGS	Thailand
BE 11	Simon Bolivar	ATS	Venezuela
BO 11	Punta Brava	AGS	Venezuela
C 11	Cadete Virgilio Uribe Robles	PV	Mexico
CM 11	Esmeraldas	FFLG	Ecuador
D 11	La Argentina	DDG	Argentina
D 11	Admirable class	PV	Mexico
FFG 11	Clark	FFG	USA
G-11	Valentin G Farias	PV	Mexico
HQ 11	Petya class	FF	Vietnam
K 11	Felinto Perry	ARS	Brazil
K 11	Stockholm	FFLG	Sweden
L 11	Velasco	LST	Spain
L 11	Intrepid	LPD	UK
LPH 11	New Orleans	LPH	USA
M 11	Galeb	ATS	Yugoslavia
MCM 11	Gladiator	MSO	USA
MUL 11	Kalvsund	ML	Sweden
PF 11	Rajah Humabon	FF	Philippines
R 11	Vikrant	CV	India
R 11	Principe de Asturias	CV	Spain
12	Druzki	FF	Bulgaria
12	Cochrane	DDG	Chile
12	Kralj class	FFLG	Croatia
12	Jerai	MH	Malaysia
C 12	Teniente José Azueta Abad	PV	Mexico
CM 12	Manabi	FFLG	Ecuador
D 12	Heroina	DDG	Argentina
D 12	Admirable class	PV	Mexico
FFG 12	George Philip	FFG	USA
G-12	Ignacio Manuel Altamirano	PV	Mexico
K12	Malmö	FFLG	Sweden
L 12	Martin Alvarez	LST	Spain
LPD 12	Shreveport	LPD	USA
LPH 12	Inchon	LPH	USA
MCM 12	Ardent	MSO	USA
MUL 12	Arkösund	ML	Sweden
13	Reshitelni	FFLG	Bulgaria
13	Ledang	MH	Malaysia
13	Democratia	FFL	Romania
ASR 13	Kittiwake	ASR	USA
C 13	Capitan de Fragata Pedro Sáinz de Baranda Borreyro	PV	Mexico
CM 13	Los Rios	FFLG	Ecuador
D 13	Sarandi	DDG	Argentina

PENNANT LIST

Number	Ship's name	Type	Country
D 13	Admirable class	PV	Mexico
FFG 13	Samuel Eliot Morison	FFG	USA
G-13	Francisco Zarco	PV	Mexico
HQ 13	Petya class	FF	Vietnam
LPD 13	Nashville	LPD	USA
MCM 13	Dextrous	MSO	USA
MUL 13	Kalmarsund	ML	Sweden
14	Bodri	FFLG	Bulgaria
14	Latorre	DDG	Chile
14	Kinabalu	MH	Malaysia
14	Descatusaria	FFL	Romania
C 14	Comodoro Carlos Castillo Bretón Barrero	PV	Mexico
CM 14	El Oro	FFLG	Ecuador
D 14	Admirable class	PV	Mexico
FFG 14	John H Sides	FFG	USA
G-14	Ignacio L Vallarta	PV	Mexico
J 14	Nirupak	AGS	India
L 14	Ghorpad	LSM	India
LPD 14	Trenton	LPD	USA
MCM 14	Chief	MSO	USA
MUL 14	Alnösund	ML	Sweden
15	Blanco Encalada	DDG	Chile
15	Desrobirea	FFL	Romania
A 15	Nireehshak	ARS	India
C 15	Vicealmirante Othón Blanco Nunez de Caceres	PV	Mexico
CM 15	Los Galapagos	FFLG	Ecuador
D 15	Admirable class	PV	Mexico
F 15	Abu Bakr	FF	Bangladesh
FFG 15	Estocin	FFG	USA
G-15	Jesus G Ortega	PV	Mexico
HQ 15	Petya class	FF	Vietnam
J 15	Investigator	AGS	India
L 15	Kesari	LSM	India
LPD 15	Ponce	LPD	USA
M 15	Aratú	MSC	Brazil
MUL 15	Grundsund	ML	Sweden
V 15	Imperial Marinheiro	PV	Brazil
16	Dreptatea	FFL	Romania
C 16	Contraalmirante Angel Ortiz Monasterio	PV	Mexico
CG 16	Leahy	CG	USA
CM 16	Loja	FFLG	Ecuador
DE 16	Boyaca	PV	Colombia
F 16	Umar Farooq	FF	Bangladesh
FFG 16	Clifton Sprague	FFG	USA
G 16	Barroso Pereira	AP	Brazil
G-16	Melchor Ocampo	PV	Mexico
J 16	Jamuna	AGS	India
L 16	Shardul	LSM	India
M 16	Anhatomirim	MSC	Brazil
V 16	Iguatemi	PV	Brazil
CG 17	Harry E Yarnell	CG	USA
D 17	Admirable class	PV	Mexico
F 17	Ali Haider	FF	Bangladesh
HQ 17	Petya class	FF	Vietnam
J 17	Sutlej	AGS	India
L 17	Sharabh	LSM	India
M 17	Atalaia	MSC	Brazil
MUL 17	Skramsösund	AG	Sweden
18	Almirante Riveros	DDG	Chile
AD 18	Sierra	AD	USA
CG 18	Worden	CG	USA
D 18	Admirable class	PV	Mexico
F 18	Osman	FFG	Bangladesh
G-18	Juan Aldama	PV	Mexico
J 18	Sandhayak	AGS	India
L 18	Cheetah	LSM	India
M 18	Araçatuba	MSC	Brazil
MUL 18	Öresund	ML	Sweden
P 18	Armatolos	PV	Greece
V 18	Forte de Coimbra	PV	Brazil
19	Almirante Williams	DDG	Chile
AD 19	Yosemite	AD	USA
AS 19	Proteus	AS	USA
CG 19	Dale	CG	USA
D 19	Admirable class	PV	Mexico
FFG 19	John A Moore	FFG	USA
G-19	Hermenegildo Galeana	PV	Mexico
ID 19	Admirable class	PV	Mexico
J 19	Nirdeshak	AGS	India
L 19	Mahish	LSM	India
LCC 19	Blue Ridge	LCC	USA
M 19	Abrolhas	MSC	Brazil
MUL 19	Barösund	ML	Sweden
P 19	Navmachos	PV	Greece
PS 19	Miguel Malvar	FFL	Philippines
V 19	Caboclo	PV	Brazil
20	Capitan Miranda	ATS	Uruguay
A 20	Moawin	AR	Pakistan
ASL 20	Cormorant	AG	Canada
CG 20	Richmond K Turner	CG	USA
F 20	Godavari	FFG	India
FFG 20	Antrim	FFG	USA
G 20	Custódio de Mello	AP	Brazil
L 20	Magar	LST	India
LCC 20	Mount Whitney	LCC	USA
M 20	Albardão	MSC	Brazil
MH 20	Henri Christophe	PV	Haiti
MUL 20	Furusund	ML	Sweden
P 20	Murature	PV	Argentina
P 20	Deirdre	PV	Ireland
PS 20	Magat Salamat	FFL	Philippines
U 20	Gastão Moutinho	AR	Brazil
V 20	Angostura	PV	Brazil
21	Sour	PV	Lebanon
21	Musca class	MSC	Romania
A 21	Huasteco	AP/LSL	Mexico
AE 21	Suribachi	AEFS	USA
CG 21	Gridley	CG	USA
F 21	Gomati	FFG	India
F 21	Mariscal Sucre	FFG	Venezuela
FFG 21	Flatley	FFG	USA
G 21	Ary Parreiras	AP	Brazil
H 21	Sirius	AGS	Brazil
K 21	Göteborg	FFLG	Sweden
L 21	Guldar	LSM	India
L 21	Castilla	AP	Spain
M 21	Jucar	MSC	Spain
P 21	King	PV	Argentina
P 21	Emer	PV	Ireland
P 21	Anaga	PV	Spain
R 21	Tritão	AG	Brazil
V 21	Bahiana	PV	Brazil
22	Damour	PV	Lebanon
22	Musca class	MSC	Romania
A 22	Zapoteco	AP/LSL	Mexico
AE 22	Mauna Kea	AEFS	USA
ASR 22	Ortolan	ASR	USA
CG 22	England	CG	USA
F 22	Ganga	FFG	India
F 22	Almirante Brión	FFG	Venezuela
FFG 22	Fahrion	FFG	USA
G 22	Soares Dutra	AP	Brazil
H 22	Canopus	AGS	Brazil
K 22	Gälve	FFLG	Sweden
L 22	Kumbhir	LSM	India
L 22	Aragón	AP	Spain
M 22	Ebro	MSC	Spain
P 22	Aoife	PV	Ireland
P 22	Tagomago	PV	Spain
PS 22	Sultan Kudarat	FFL	Philippines
R 22	Tridente	AG	Brazil
R 22	Viraat	CV	India
V 22	Mearim	PV	Brazil
23	Musca class	MSC	Romania
AE 23	Nitro	AEFS	USA
CG 23	Halsey	CG	USA
F 23	General Urdaneta	FFG	Venezuela
FFG 23	Lewis B Puller	FFG	USA
G 23	Almirante Gastão Motta	AOS	Brazil
K 23	Kalmar	FFLG	Sweden
L 23	Gharial	LST	India
M 23	Duero	MSC	Spain
P 23	Aisling	PV	Ireland
P 23	Marola	PV	Spain
PS 23	Datu Marikudo	FFL	Philippines
R 23	Triunfo	AG	Brazil
V 23	Purus	PV	Brazil
24	Rahmat	FF	Malaysia
24	Musca class	MSC	Romania
AE 24	Pyro	AEFS	USA
CG 24	Reeves	CG	USA
F 24	General Soublette	FFG	Venezuela
FFG 24	Jack Williams	FFG	USA
G 24	Belmonte	AR	Brazil
K 24	Sundsvall	FFLG	Sweden
M 24	Tajo	MSC	Spain
P 24	Mouro	PV	Spain
V 24	Solimões	PV	Brazil
25	Kasturi	FFLG	Malaysia
A 25	Tarasco	AFS	Mexico
AE 25	Haleakala	AEFS	USA
ARS 25	Chang Won	ARS	Korea, Republic
AT 25	Ang Pangulo	AP	Philippines

PENNANT LIST

Number	Ship's name	Type	Country	Number	Ship's name	Type	Country
CGN 25	Bainbridge	CGN	USA	FFG 33	Jarrett	FFG	USA
D 25	Marcilio Dias	DD	Brazil	M 33	Brocklesby	MH/MSC	UK
F 25	General Salom	FFG	Venezuela	P 33	Abhay	FFLG	India
FFG 25	Copeland	FFG	USA	PH 33	Andrija Mohorovičić	AGS	Croatia
M 25	Genil	MSC	Spain	V 33	Frontin	FFG	Brazil
P 25	Grosa	PV	Spain	34	Ekstati Vinarov	MSC	Bulgaria
26	Lekir	FFLG	Malaysia	34	Audaz	MSC	Uruguay
26	Vanguardia	ARS	Uruguay	34	Pula	FFG	Yugoslavia
ARS 26	Gumi	ARS	Korea, Republic	AE 34	Mount Baker	AEFS	USA
CG 26	Belknap	CG	USA	AS 34	Canopus	AS	USA
D 26	Mariz E Barros	DD	Brazil	CG 34	Biddle	CG	USA
F 26	Almirante Garcia	FFG	Venezuela	F 34	Himgiri	FFG	India
FFG 26	Gallery	FFG	USA	F 34	Infanta Cristina	FFG	Spain
G 26	Duque de Caxais	LST	Brazil	FFG 34	Aubrey Fitch	FFG	USA
M 26	Odiel	MSC	Spain	M 34	Middleton	MH/MSC	UK
P 26	Medas	PV	Spain	P 34	Ajay	FFLG	India
AE 27	Butte	AEFS	USA	AE 35	Kiska	AEFS	USA
CG 27	Josephus Daniels	CG	USA	CGN 35	Truxtun	CGN	USA
D 27	Pará	FF	Brazil	D 35	Sergipe	DD	Brazil
FFG 27	Mahlon S Tisdale	FFG	USA	F 35	Udaygiri	FFG	India
M 27	Sil	MSC	Spain	F 35	Cazadora	FFG	Spain
P 27	Izaro	PV	Spain	M 35	Dulverton	MH/MSC	UK
U 27	Brasil	AG	Brazil	P 35	Akshay	FFLG	India
AE 28	Santa Barbara	AEFS	USA	AS 36	L Y Spear	AS	USA
CG 28	Wainwright	CG	USA	CGN 36	California	CGN	USA
D 28	Paraíba	FF	Brazil	D 36	Alagoas	DD	Brazil
FFG 28	Boone	FFG	USA	F 36	Dunagiri	FFG	India
M 28	Miño	MSC	Spain	F 36	Vencedora	FFG	Spain
P 28	Tabarca	PV	Spain	FFG 36	Underwood	FFG	USA
PS 28	Cebu	FFL	Philippines	LSD 36	Anchorage	LSD	USA
29	Uribe	AG	Chile	M 36	Bicester	MH/MSC	UK
AE 29	Mount Hood	AEFS	USA	P 36	Agray	FFLG	India
CG 29	Jouett	CG	USA	37	Papudo	PV	Chile
D 29	Paraná	FF	Brazil	AD 37	Samuel Gompers	AD	USA
FFG 29	Stephen W Groves	FFG	USA	AS 37	Dixon	AS	USA
M 29	Brecon	MH/MSC	UK	CGN 37	South Carolina	CGN	USA
P 29	Deva	PV	Spain	D 37	Rio Grande do Norte	DD	Brazil
PS 29	Negros Occidental	FFL	Philippines	FFG 37	Crommelin	FFG	USA
CG 30	Horne	CG	USA	LSD 37	Portland	LSD	USA
D 30	Pernambuco	FF	Brazil	M 37	Chiddingfold	MH/MSC	UK
FFG 30	Reid	FFG	USA	38	Perth	DDG	Australia
G 30	Ceará	LSD	Brazil	AD 38	Puget Sound	AD	USA
M 30	Ledbury	MH/MSC	UK	ARS 38	Bolster	ARS	USA
P 30	Kondori class	PV	Malta	CGN 38	Virginia	CGN	USA
P 30	Bergantin	PV	Spain	D 38	Espirito Santo	DD	Brazil
V 30	Inhaúma	FFG	Brazil	FFG 38	Curts	FFG	USA
31	Drummond	FFG	Argentina	LSD 38	Pensacola	LSD	USA
31	Iskar	MSC	Bulgaria	M 38	Atherstone	MH/MSC	UK
31	Poti class	FFL	Romania	39	Hobart	DDG	Australia
31	Temerario	MSC	Uruguay	ARS 39	Conserver	ARS	USA
31	Split class	FFG	Yugoslavia	AS 39	Emory S Land	AS	USA
A 31	Malaspina	AGOR	Spain	CGN 39	Texas	CGN	USA
AS 31	Hunley	AS	USA	FFG 39	Doyle	FFG	USA
CG 31	Sterett	CG	USA	LSD 39	Mount Vernon	LSD	USA
F 31	Descubierta	FFG	Spain	M 39	Hurworth	MH/MSC	UK
FFG 31	Stark	FFG	USA	ARS 40	Hoist	ARS	USA
G 31	Rio de Janeiro	LSD	Brazil	AS 40	Frank Cable	AS	USA
M 31	Cattistock	MH/MSC	UK	CGN 40	Mississippi	CGN	USA
P 31	Eithne	FFL	Ireland	F 40	Niteroi	FFG	Brazil
P 31	Kondori class	PV	Malta	FFG 40	Halyburton	FFG	USA
PS 31	Pangasinan	FFL	Philippines	H 40	Antares	AGS	Brazil
Q 31	Piloto Alsina	AG	Argentina	K 40	Veer	FFLG	India
V 31	Jaceguay	FFG	Brazil	LSD 40	Fort Fisher	LSD	USA
32	Guerrico	FFG	Argentina	M 40	Berkeley	MH/MSC	UK
32	Zibar	MSC	Bulgaria	P 40	Graúna	PV	Brazil
32	Poti class	FFL	Romania	41	Brisbane	DDG	Australia
32	Valiente	MSC	Uruguay	41	Espora	FFG	Argentina
32	Zagreb	FFG	Yugoslavia	41	Poti class	FFL	Bulgaria
A 32	Tofiño	AGOR	Spain	41	Yan Taing Aung	FFL	Burma
AE 32	Flint	AEFS	USA	A 41	Dacca	AOR	Pakistan
AS 32	Holland	AS	USA	AD 41	Yellowstone	AD	USA
CG 32	William H Standley	CG	USA	ARS 41	Opportune	ARS	USA
F 32	Diana	FFG	Spain	AS 41	McKee	AS	USA
FFG 32	John L Hall	FFG	USA	CGN 41	Arkansas	CGN	USA
M 32	Cottesmore	MH/MSC	UK	F 41	Defensora	FFG	Brazil
PS 32	Iloilo	FFL	Philippines	F 41	Taragiri	FFG	India
V 32	Julio de Noronha	FFG	Brazil	FFG 41	McClusky	FFG	USA
33	Granville	FFG	Argentina	H 41	Almirante Câmara	AGS	Brazil
33	Dobrotich	MSC	Bulgaria	K 41	Nirbhik	FFLG	India
33	Poti class	FFL	Romania	LSD 41	Whidbey Island	LSD	USA
33	Fortuna	MSC	Uruguay	M 41	Guadalete	MSO	Spain
33	Kotor	FFG	Yugoslavia	M 41	Quorn	MH/MSC	UK
A 33	Hespérides	AGOR	Spain	P 41	Goiana	PV	Brazil
AE 33	Shasta	AEFS	USA	P 41	Orla	PV	Ireland
AS 33	Simon Lake	AS	USA	42	Rosales	FFG	Argentina
CG 33	Fox	CG	USA	42	Strogij	FFL	Bulgaria
F 33	Nilgiri	FFG	India	42	Yan Gyi Aung	FFL	Burma
F 33	Infanta Elena	FFG	Spain	AD 42	Acadia	AD	USA

PENNANT LIST

Number	Ship's name	Type	Country	Number	Ship's name	Type	Country
ARS 42	Reclaimer	ARS	USA	CG 52	Bunker Hill	CG	USA
DDG 42	Mahan	DDG	USA	CM 52	Caldas	FFG	Colombia
F 42	Constituição	FFG	Brazil	D 52	Rana	DDG	India
F 42	Vindhyagiri	FFG	India	DDG 52	Barry	DDG	USA
FFG 42	Klakring	FFG	USA	FFG 52	Carr	FFG	USA
H 42	Barao de Teffé	AGS	Brazil	FM 52	Manuel Villavicencio	FFG	Peru
K 42	Nipat	FFLG	India	K 52	Vinash	FFLG	India
LSD 42	Germantown	LSD	USA	MHC 52	Heron	MH	USA
M 42	Guadalmedina	MSO	Spain	N 52	Vidar	ML	Norway
P 42	Grajaú	PV	Brazil	P 52	Suvarna	PV	India
P 42	Ciara	PV	Ireland	P 52	Ulla	PV	Spain
Q 42	Cabo San Antonio	LST	Argentina	53	Torrens	FF	Australia
43	Spiro	FFG	Argentina	53	Araucano	AOF(L)	Chile
43	Poti class	FFL	Bulgaria	A 53	Oker	AGI	Germany
43	Esmeralda	AG	Chile	ARS 53	Grapple	ARS	USA
AD 43	Cape Cod	AD	USA	CG 53	Mobile Bay	CG	USA
ARS 43	Recovery	ARS	USA	CM 53	Antioquia	FFG	Colombia
F 43	Liberal	FFG	Brazil	D 53	Ranjit	DDG	India
F 43	Trishul	FFG	India	DDG 53	John Paul Jones	DDG	USA
FFG 43	Thach	FFG	USA	FFG 53	Hawes	FFG	USA
H 43	Almirante Alvaro Alberto	AGS	Brazil	FM 53	Montero	FFG	Peru
K 43	Nishank	FFLG	India	MHC 53	Pelican	MH	USA
LSD 43	Fort McHenry	LSD	USA	N 53	Vale	ML	Norway
M 43	Guadalquivir	MSO	Spain	P 53	Savitri	PV	India
N 43	Lindormen	ML	Denmark	A 54	Amba	AS	India
P 43	Guaiba	PV	Brazil	CG 54	Antietam	CG	USA
44	Parker	FFG	Argentina	CM 54	Independiente	FFG	Colombia
44	Khrabri	FFL	Bulgaria	D 54	Ranvir	DDG	India
AD 44	Shenandoah	AD	USA	DDG 54	Curtis Wilbur	DDG	USA
F 44	Independencia	FFG	Brazil	FFG 54	Ford	FFG	USA
K 44	Nirghat	FFLG	India	FM 54	Mariategui	FFG	Peru
LSD 44	Gunston Hall	LSD	USA	MHC 54	Robin	MH	USA
M 44	Guadiana	MSO	Spain	P 54	Sarayu	PV	India
N 44	Lossen	ML	Denmark	P 54	Turia	PV	Spain
P 44	Kirpan	FFLG	India	55	Tonti class	AOS	RoK
T 44	Puerto Cabello	AFS	Venezuela	CG 55	Leyte Gulf	CG	USA
45	Robinson	FFG	Argentina	D 55	Ranvijay	DDG	India
45	Poti class	FFL	Bulgaria	DDG 55	Stout	DDG	USA
45	Piloto Pardo	AG	Chile	F 55	Waikato	FFG	New Zealand
F 45	União	FFG	Brazil	FFG 55	Elrod	FFG	USA
FFG 45	De Wert	FFG	USA	FV 55	Indaw	PV	Burma
K 45	Vibhuti	FFLG	India	MHC 55	Oriole	MH	USA
LSD 45	Comstock	LSD	USA	P 55	Sharada	PV	India
46	Gomez Roca	FFG	Argentina	56	Tonti class	AOS	RoK
46	Poti class	FFL	Bulgaria	CG 56	San Jacinto	CG	USA
FFG 46	Rentz	FFG	USA	DDG 56	John S McCain	DDG	USA
K 46	Vipul	FFLG	India	FFG 56	Simpson	FFG	USA
LSD 46	Tortuga	LSD	USA	FV 56	Inma	PV	Burma
P 46	Kuthar	FFLG	India	P 56	Sujata	PV	India
A 47	Nasr	AOR	Pakistan	A 57	Shakti	AOR	India
AP 47	Aquiles	AP	Chile	AO 57	Chun Jee	AOE	Korea, Republic
CG 47	Ticonderoga	CG	USA	CG 57	Lake Champlain	CG	USA
FFG 47	Nicholas	FFG	USA	DDG 57	Mitscher	DDG	USA
LSD 47	Rushmore	LSD	USA	F 57	Andromeda	FFG	UK
P 47	Khanjar	FFLG	India	FFG 57	Reuben James	FFG	USA
CG 48	Yorktown	CG	USA	FV 57	Inya	PV	Burma
FFG 48	Vandegrift	FFG	USA	LT 57	Sierra Madre	LST	Philippines
LSD 48	Ashland	LSD	USA	M 57	Arkö	MSC	Sweden
49	Derwent	FF	Australia	P 57	Sukanya class	PV	India
CG 49	Vincennes	CG	USA	CG 58	Philippine Sea	CG	USA
FFG 49	Robert G Bradley	FFG	USA	DDG 58	Laboon	DDG	USA
LSD 49	Harpers Ferry	LSD	USA	FFG 58	Samuel B Roberts	FFG	USA
P 49	Khukri	FFLG	India	AVT 59	Forrestal	AVT	USA
50	Swan	FF	Australia	CG 59	Princeton	CG	USA
50	Al Manama	FFLG	Bahrain	FFG 59	Kauffman	FFG	USA
A 50	Alster	AGI	Germany	60	Vidal Gormaz	AGOR	Chile
A 50	Deepak	AOR	India	A 60	Gorch Fock	AG	Germany
ARS 50	Safeguard	ARS	USA	CG 60	Normandy	CG	USA
CG 50	Valley Forge	CG	USA	CV 60	Saratoga	CV	USA
FFG 50	Taylor	FFG	USA	FFG 60	Rodney M Davis	FFG	USA
L 50	Tobruk	LSH	Australia	61	Briz	MSC	Bulgaria
P 50	Sukanya	PV	India	61	Babr	DDG	Iran
51	Al Muharraq	FFLG	Bahrain	A 61	Contramaestre Castelló	AG	Spain
51	Damavand	DDG	Iran	CG 61	Monterey	CG	USA
ARS 51	Grasp	ARS	USA	FFG 61	Ingraham	FFG	USA
CG 51	Thomas S Gates	CG	USA	M 61	Pondicherry	MSO	India
CM 51	Almirante Padilla	FFG	Colombia	P 61	Chilreu	PV	Spain
D 51	Rajput	DDG	India	T 61	Capana	LST	Venezuela
DDG 51	Arleigh Burke	DDG	USA	TR 61	Hualcopo	LST	Ecuador
FFG 51	Gary	FFG	USA	62	Shkval	MSC	Bulgaria
FM 51	Meliton Carvajal	FFG	Peru	62	Palang	DDG	Iran
MHC 51	Osprey	MH	USA	CG 62	Chancellorsville	CG	USA
P 51	Subhadra	PV	India	CV 62	Independence	CV	USA
P 51	Nalón	PV	Spain	M 62	Porbandar	MSO	India
T 51	Amazonas	LST	Venezuela	P 62	Niki	FFL	Greece
52	Almirante Jorge Montt	AOF(L)	Chile	T 62	Esequibo	LST	Venezuela
A 52	Oste	AGI	Germany	63	Ppiboy	MSC	Bulgaria
ARS 52	Salvor	ARS	USA	63	Sargento Aldea	PV	Chile

[101]

PENNANT LIST

Number	Ship's name	Type	Country	Number	Ship's name	Type	Country
A 63	Main	AG	Germany	M 76	Ven	MH	Sweden
CG 63	Cowpens	CG	USA	DD 77	Villar	DD	Peru
CV 63	Kitty Hawk	CV	USA	M 77	Ulvön	MH	Sweden
M 63	Bedi	MSO	India	DD 78	Galvez	DD	Peru
P 63	Doxa	FFL	Greece	P 78	Kadmath	FF	India
T 63	Goajira	LST	Venezuela	DD 79	Diez Canseco	DD	Peru
64	Shtorm	MSC	Bulgaria	F 79	Lamine Sadji Kaba	PV	Guinea
64	Yelcho	AGS	Chile	N 80	Falster	ML	Denmark
CG 64	Gettysburg	CG	USA	81	Zhenghe	AT	China
CV 64	Constellation	CV	USA	81	Bayandor	FFL	Iran
M 64	Bhavnagar	MSO	India	A 81	Aka	ARS	Iraq
P 64	Eleftheria	FFL	Greece	A 81	Brambleleaf	AOS	UK
T 64	Los Llanos	LST	Venezuela	CH 81	Almirante Grau	CG	Peru
CG 65	Chosin	CG	USA	F 81	Santa Maria	FFG	Spain
CVN 65	Enterprise	CVN	USA	N 81	Fyen	ML	Denmark
M 65	Alleppey	MSO	India	82	Naghdi	FFL	Iran
P 65	Carteria	FFL	Greece	F 82	Otobo	FFL	Nigeria
CG 66	Hue City	CG	USA	F 82	Victoria	FFG	Spain
CV 66	America	CV	USA	N 82	Møen	ML	Denmark
M 66	Ratnagiri	MSO	India	F 83	Erinomi	FFLG	Nigeria
P 66	Thetis class	FFL	Greece	F 83	Numancia	FFG	Spain
CG 67	Shiloh	CG	USA	N 83	Sjaelland	ML	Denmark
CV 67	John F Kennedy	CV	USA	C 84	Babur	DDG	Pakistan
M 67	Karwar	MSO	India	CH 84	Aguirre	CG	Peru
M 67	Nämdo	MSC	Sweden	F 84	Enyimiri	FFLG	Nigeria
ATF 68	Leucoton	AG	Chile	F 84	Reina Sofía	FFG	Spain
CG 68	Anzio	CG	USA	F 85	Cumberland	FFG	UK
CVN 68	Nimitz	CVN	USA	A 86	Tir	ATS	India
M 68	Cannanore	MSO	India	D 86	Birmingham	DDG	UK
M 68	Blidö	MSC	Sweden	F 86	Campbeltown	FFG	UK
P 68	Arnala	FF	India	LT 86	Zamboanga del Sur	LST	Philippines
A 69	Donau	AG	Germany	D 87	Newcastle	DDG	UK
ATF 69	Colo Colo	AG	Chile	F 87	Obuma	FF	Nigeria
CG 69	Vicksburg	DDG	USA	F 87	Chatham	FFG	UK
CVN 69	Dwight D Eisenhower	CVN	USA	LT 87	South Cotobato	LST	Philippines
F 69	Wellington	FFG	New Zealand	D 88	Glasgow	DDG	UK
M 69	Cuddalore	MSO	India	F 88	Broadsword	FFG	UK
P 69	Androth	FF	India	P 88	Victory	FFLG	Singapore
70	Angamos	AS	Chile	D 89	Exeter	DDG	UK
CG 70	Lake Erie	CG	USA	F 89	Aradu	FFG	Nigeria
CVN 70	Carl Vinson	CVN	USA	F 89	Battleaxe	FFG	UK
M 70	Kakinada	MSO	India	P 89	Valour	FFLG	Singapore
PS 70	Quezon	FFL	Philippines	AC 90	Mactan	AFS	Philippines
71	Alvand	FFG	Iran	D 90	Southampton	DDG	UK
A 71	Juan Sebastian de Elcano	ATS	Spain	F 90	Brilliant	FFG	UK
CG 71	Cape St George	CG	USA	P 90	Vigilance	FFLG	Singapore
CVN 71	Theodore Roosevelt	CVN	USA	BI 91	Orion	AGOR	Ecuador
F 71	Baleares	FFG	Spain	D 91	Nottingham	DDG	UK
F 71	Scylla	FFL	UK	F 91	Brazen	FFG	UK
K 71	Vijay Durg	FFLG	India	P 91	Valiant	FFLG	Singapore
M 71	Kozhikoda	MSO	India	R 91	Charles de Gaulle	CVN	France
M 71	Landsort	MH	Sweden	D 92	Liverpool	DDG	UK
P 71	Serviola	PV	Spain	F 92	Boxer	FFG	UK
72	Alborz	FFG	Iran	P 92	Vigour	FFLG	Singapore
A 72	Arosa	ATS	Spain	F 93	Beaver	FFG	UK
CG 72	Vella Gulf	CG	USA	P 93	Vengeance	FFLG	Singapore
CVN 72	Abraham Lincoln	CVN	USA	F 94	Brave	FFG	UK
F 72	Andalucia	FFG	Spain	D 95	Manchester	DDG	UK
K 72	Sindhu Durg	FFLG	India	F 95	London	FFG	UK
M 72	Konkan	MSO	India	D 96	Gloucester	DDG	UK
M 72	Arholma	MH	Sweden	F 96	Sheffield	FFG	UK
P 72	Centinela	PV	Spain	D 97	Edinburgh	DDG	UK
RM 72	Pedro de Heredia	PV	Colombia	R 97	Jeanne d'Arc	CVH	France
73	Sabalan	FFG	Iran	D 98	York	DDG	UK
A 73	Moresby	AGS	Australia	F 98	Coventry	FFG	UK
A 73	Hispania	ATS	Spain	R 98	Clemenceau	CV	France
CG 73	Port Royal	CG	USA	F 99	Cornwall	FFG	UK
CVN 73	George Washington	CVN	USA	R 99	Foch	CV	France
DM 73	Palacios	DDG	Peru	101	Mulniya	FFLG	Bulgaria
F 73	Cataluña	FFG	Spain	M 101	Sandown	MH	UK
K 73	Hos Durg	FFLG	India	N 101	Mordoğan	ML	Turkey
M 73	Koster	MH	Sweden	102	Kan	AGOR	China
P 73	Anjadip	FF	India	A 102	Agnadeen	AOR	Iraq
P 73	Vigia	PV	Spain	M 102	Inverness	MH	UK
RM 73	Sebastion de Belal Calzar	PV	Colombia	M 103	Cromer	MH	UK
A 74	Aris	AG	Greece	F 104	Southland	FFG	New Zealand
A 74	La Graciosa	ATS	Spain	L 104	Inouse	LST	Greece
DM 74	Ferré	DDG	Peru	M 104	Walney	MH	UK
F 74	Asturias	FFG	Spain	N 104	Mersin	ML	Turkey
M 74	Kullen	MH	Sweden	P 104	Bakassi	PVG	Cameroon
P 74	Atalaya	PV	Spain	105	Jinan	DDG	China
PS 74	Rizal	FFL	Philippines	M 105	Bridport	MH	UK
RM 74	Rodrigo de Bastidas	PV	Colombia	N 105	Mürefte	ML	Turkey
F 75	Extremadura	FFG	Spain	106	Xian	DDG	China
M 75	Vinga	MH	Sweden	107	Yinchuan	DDG	China
P 75	Amini	FF	India	108	Xining	DDG	China
76	Hang Tuah	FF	Malaysia	D 108	Cardiff	DDG	UK
DD 76	Quiñones	DD	Peru	109	Kaifeng	DDG	China

PENNANT LIST

Number	Ship's name	Type	Country	Number	Ship's name	Type	Country
A 109	Bayleaf	AOS	UK	DD 154	Amagiri	DDG	Japan
110	Dalian	DDG	China	L 154	Ikaria	LST	Greece
A 110	Orangeleaf	AOS	UK	155	Providencia	AGS	Colombia
MSA 110	Anticosti	MSC	Canada	DD 155	Hamagiri	DDG	Japan
N 110	Nusret	ML	Turkey	156	Malpelo	AGS	Colombia
111	Al Tiyar	MSO	Libya	ATP 156	Parinas	AOR	Peru
A 111	Alerta	AGI	Spain	DD 156	Setogiri	DDG	Japan
A 111	Oakleaf	AOS	UK	DD 157	Sawagiri	DDG	Japan
P 111	Sultanhisar	PV	Turkey	L 157	Rodos	LST	Greece
112	Luhu	DDG	China	ATP 158	Zorritos	AOS	Peru
MSA 112	Moresby	MSC	Canada	DD 158	Umigiri	DDG	Japan
P 112	Demirhisar	PV	Turkey	ATP 159	Lobitos	AOS	Peru
113	Al Isar	MSO	Libya	F 159	Tabuk	FFG	Pakistan
P 113	Yarhisar	PV	Turkey	PBL 159	Fundy	PV	Canada
LKA 114	Durham	LKA	USA	160	Musytari	PV	Malaysia
P 114	Akhisar	PV	Turkey	D 160	Alamgir	DDG	Pakistan
115	Ras al Hamman	MSO	Libya	M 160	Mahmood	MSC	Pakistan
DD 115	Asagumo	DD	Japan	PBL 160	Chignecto	PV	Canada
LKA 115	Mobile	LKA	USA	161	Changsha	DDG	China
N 115	Mehmetcik	ML	Turkey	161	Marikh	PV	Malaysia
P 115	Sivrihisar	PV	Turkey	F 161	Badr	FFG	Pakistan
DD 116	Minegumo	DD	Japan	M 161	Gradac	MH/MSC	Yugoslavia
L 116	Kos	LST	Greece	PBL 161	Thunder	PV	Canada
P 116	Koçhisar	PV	Turkey	162	Nanning	DDG	China
117	Ras al Fulaijah	MSO	Libya	PBL 162	Cowichan	PV	Canada
DD 117	Natsugumo	DD	Japan	163	Nanchang	DDG	China
LKA 117	El Paso	LKA	USA	DD 163	Amatsukaze	DDG	Japan
DD 118	Murakumo	DD	Japan	F 163	Khaibar	FFG	Pakistan
119	Ras al Qula	MSO	Libya	PBL 163	Miramichi	PV	Canada
DD 119	Aokumo	DD	Japan	164	Guilin	DDG	China
DD 120	Akigumo	DD	Japan	DD 164	Takatsuki	DDG	Japan
NL 120	Bayraktar	LST	Turkey	M 164	Mujahid	MSC	Pakistan
121	Ras al Madwar	MSO	Libya	PBL 164	Chaleur	PV	Canada
AG 121	Riverton	AGOR	Canada	165	Zhanjiang	DDG	China
DD 121	Yugumo	DD	Japan	DD 165	Kikuzuki	DDG	Japan
J 121	Changxingdao	AS	China	166	Zhuhai	DDG	China
NL 121	Sancaktar	LST	Turkey	D 166	Taimur	DDG	Pakistan
A 122	Olwen	AOF (L)	UK	DD 166	Mochizuki	DDG	Japan
DD 122	Hatsuyuki	DDG	Japan	M 166	Munsif	MH	Pakistan
NL 122	Çakabey	LST	Turkey	D 167	Tughril	DDG	Pakistan
123	Ras al Massad	MSO	Libya	DD 167	Nagatsuki	DDG	Japan
A 123	Olna	AOF (L)	UK	D 168	Tippu Sultan	DDG	Pakistan
DD 123	Shirayuki	DDG	Japan	DD 168	Tachikaze	DDG	Japan
NL 123	Sarucabey	LST	Turkey	DD 169	Asakaze	DDG	Japan
A 124	Olmeda	AOF (L)	UK	F 169	Hunain	FFG	Pakistan
DD 124	Mineyuki	DDG	Japan	DD 170	Sawakaze	DDG	Japan
NL 124	Karamürselbey	LST	Turkey	A 171	Endurance	PV	UK
125	Ras al Hani	MSO	Libya	AGOR 171	Endeavour	AGOR	Canada
DD 125	Sawayuki	DDG	Japan	DD 171	Hatakaze	DDG	Japan
NL 125	Osman Gazi	LST	Turkey	F 171	Active	FFG	UK
DD 126	Hamayuki	DDG	Japan	L 171	Kriti	LST	Greece
DD 127	Isoyuki	DDG	Japan	AGOR 172	Quest	AGOR	Canada
DD 128	Haruyuki	DDG	Japan	DD 172	Shimakaze	DDG	Japan
DD 129	Yamayuki	DDG	Japan	DD 173	Kongo	DDG	Japan
A 130	Roebuck	AGS	UK	L 173	Chios	LST	Greece
DD 130	Matsuyuki	DDG	Japan	F 174	Alacrity	FFG	UK
131	Nanjing	DDG	China	L 174	Samos	LST	Greece
ATC 131	Ilo	AP	Peru	L 176	Lesbos	LST	Greece
DD 131	Setoyuki	DDG	Japan	AO 177	Cimarron	AO	USA
132	Hefei	DDG	China	AO 178	Monongahela	AO	USA
132	Ibn Ouf	LST	Libya	AO 179	Merrimack	AO	USA
A 132	Diligence	AR	UK	AO 180	Willamette	AO	USA
DD 132	Asayuki	DDG	Japan	D 181	Hamburg	DDG	Germany
133	Chongqing	DDG	China	D 182	Schleswig-Holstein	DDG	Germany
A 133	Hecla	AGS	UK	D 183	Bayern	DDG	Germany
DD 133	Shimayuki	DDG	Japan	A 185	Salmoor	ARS	UK
134	Zunyi	DDG	China	D 185	Lütjens	DDG	Germany
134	Ibn Harissa	LST	Libya	F 185	Avenger	FFG	UK
A 135	Argus	AVT	UK	A 186	Salmaster	ARS	UK
A 138	Herald	AGS	UK	AO 186	Platte	AO	USA
DD 141	Haruna	DDG	Japan	D 186	Mölders	DDG	Germany
DT 141	Paita	LST	Peru	A 187	Salmaid	ARS	UK
DD 142	Hiei	DDG	Japan	D 187	Rommel	DDG	Germany
DT 142	Pisco	LST	Peru	189	Pescarusul	FFLG	Romania
DD 143	Shirane	DDG	Japan	190	Lastunul	FFLG	Romania
DT 143	Callao	LST	Peru	191	Zborul	FFLG	Romania
DD 144	Kurama	DDG	Japan	192	Cheng Hai	LSD	Taiwan
DT 144	Eten	LST	Peru	O 195	Westralia	AOR	Australia
L 144	Siros	LST	Greece	201	Chung Hai	LST	Taiwan
ATP 150	Bayovar	AO	Peru	A 201	Orion	AGI	Sweden
DD 151	Asagiri	DDG	Japan	L 201	Endurance	LST	Singapore
152	Mutiara	AGS	Malaysia	UAM 201	Creoula	ATS	Portugal
ATP 152	Talara	AOR	Peru	202	Dimiter A Dimitrov	AOS	Bulgaria
DD 152	Yamagiri	DDG	Japan	L 202	Excellence	LST	Singapore
M 152	Podgora	MH/MSC	Yugoslavia	M 202	Atalanti	MSC	Greece
DD 153	Yuugiri	DDG	Japan	203	Chung Ting	LST	Taiwan
L 153	Nafkratoussa	LSD	Greece	GT 203	Jervis Bay	AG	Australia
M 153	Blitvenica	MH/MSC	Yugoslavia	L 203	Intrepid	LST	Singapore

PENNANT LIST

Number	Ship's name	Type	Country
204	Chung Hsing	LST	Taiwan
L 204	Resolution	LST	Singapore
P 204	Indépendencia	PV	Dominican Republic
205	Chung Chien	LST	Taiwan
L 205	Persistence	LST	Singapore
M 205	Antiope	MSC	Greece
P 205	Libertad	PV	Dominican Republic
206	Kapitan Dmitry Dobrev	AG	Bulgaria
206	Chung Chi	LST	Taiwan
M 206	Faedra	MSC	Greece
P 206	Restauracion	PV	Dominican Republic
207	Skeena	FF	Canada
F 207	Bremen	FFG	Germany
P 207	Cambiaso	FFL	Dominican Republic
208	Chung Shun	LST	Taiwan
F 208	Niedersachsen	FFG	Germany
P 208	Separacion	FFL	Dominican Republic
209	Chung Lien	LST	Taiwan
F 209	Rheinland-Pfalz	FFG	Germany
P 209	Calderas	FFL	Dominican Republic
210	Chung Yung	LST	Taiwan
F 210	Emden	FFG	Germany
F 210	Mussa Ben Nussair	FFG	Iraq
M 210	Thalia	MSC	Greece
F 211	Köln	FFG	Germany
F 211	Dat Assawari	FFG	Libya
M 211	Alkyon	MSC	Greece
P 211	Meghna	PV	Bangladesh
D 212	Kanaris	DDG	Greece
F 212	Karlsruhe	FFG	Germany
F 212	Tariq Ibn Ziad	FFG	Iraq
F 212	Al Hani	FFG	Libya
P 212	Jamuna	PV	Bangladesh
D 213	Kountouriotis	DDG	Greece
F 213	Augsburg	FFG	Germany
F 213	Al Qirdabiyah	FFG	Libya
M 213	Klio	MSC	Greece
A 214	Belos	ARS	Sweden
D 214	Sachtouris	DDG	Greece
F 214	Lübeck	FFG	Germany
M 214	Avra	MSC	Greece
D 215	Tompazis	DDG	Greece
DE 215	Chikugo	FF	Japan
F 215	Brandenburg	FFG	Germany
216	Chung Kuang	LST	Taiwan
D 216	Apostolis	DDG	Greece
DE 216	Ayase	FF	Japan
217	Chung Suo	LST	Taiwan
D 217	Kriezis	DDG	Greece
DE 217	Mikuma	FF	Japan
D 218	Kimon	DDG	Greece
DE 218	Tokachi	FF	Japan
219	Kao Hsiung	AG	Taiwan
D 219	Nearchos	DDG	Greece
DE 219	Iwase	FF	Japan
D 220	Formion	DDG	Greece
DE 220	Chitose	FF	Japan
221	Chung Chuan	LST	Taiwan
D 221	Themistocles	DDG	Greece
DE 221	Niyodo	FF	Japan
222	Chung Sheng	LST	Taiwan
DE 222	Teshio	FF	Japan
223	Chung Fu	LST	Taiwan
DE 223	Yoshino	FF	Japan
DE 224	Kumano	FF	Japan
225	Chung Chiang	LST	Taiwan
DE 225	Noshiro	FF	Japan
226	Chung Chih	LST	Taiwan
DE 226	Ishikari	FFG	Japan
227	Chung Ming	LST	Taiwan
DE 227	Yubari	FFG	Japan
228	Chung Shu	LST	Taiwan
DE 228	Yubetsu	FFG	Japan
229	Chung Wan	LST	Taiwan
DE 229	Abukuma	FFG	Japan
F 229	Lancaster	FFG	UK
P 229	Tolmi	PV	Greece
230	Chung Pang	LST	Taiwan
DE 230	Jintsu	FFG	Japan
F 230	Norfolk	FFG	UK
P 230	Ormi	PV	Greece
231	Chung Yeh	LST	Taiwan
DE 231	Ohyodo	FFG	Japan
F 231	Argyll	FFG	UK
DE 232	Sendai	FFG	Japan
233	Fraser	FF	Canada
DE 233	Chikuma	FFG	Japan
F 233	Marlborough	FFG	UK
DE 234	Tone	FFG	Japan
F 234	Iron Duke	FFG	UK
F 235	Monmouth	FFG	UK
236	Gatineau	FFG	Canada
F 236	Montrose	FFG	UK
F 237	Westminster	FFG	UK
F 238	Northumberland	FFG	UK
P 239	Peacock	PV	UK
240	Kaszub	FFG	Poland
F 240	Yavuz	FFG	Turkey
M 240	Pleias	MSC	Greece
P 240	Plover	PV	UK
DBM 241	Silba	LCT/ML	Yugoslavia
F 241	Turgutreis	FFG	Turkey
M 241	Kichli	MSC	Greece
P 241	Starling	PV	UK
F 242	Fatih	FFG	Turkey
M 242	Kissa	MSC	Greece
A 243	Tafelberg	AOR	South Africa
F 243	Yildirim	FFG	Turkey
M 246	Aigli	MSC	Greece
M 247	Dafni	MSC	Greece
M 248	Aedon	MSC	Greece
251	Wodnik	ATS	Poland
252	Gryf	ATS	Poland
M 254	Niovi	MSC	Greece
257	Restigouche	FFG	Canada
258	Kootenay	FFG	Canada
P 258	Leeds Castle	PV	UK
259	Terra Nova	FFG	Canada
P 259	Redpole	PV	UK
260	Tetal class	FF	Romania
P 260	Kingfisher	PV	UK
261	Kopernik	AGI	Poland
261	Tetal class	FF	Romania
A 261	Uto	AG	Sweden
P 261	Cygnet	PV	UK
262	Saskatchewan	FF	Canada
262	Navigator	AGI	Poland
262	Tetal class	FF	Romania
F 262	Zulfiquar	FFG	Pakistan
263	Yukon	FF	Canada
263	Hydrograf	AGI	Poland
263	Tetal class	FF	Romania
F 263	Shamser	FFG	Pakistan
264	Tetal class	FF	Romania
F 264	Saif	FF	Pakistan
265	Annapolis	FF	Canada
265	Heweliusz	AGOR	Poland
F 265	Aslat	FF	Pakistan
P 265	Dumbarton Castle	PV	UK
266	Nipigon	FF	Canada
266	Arctowski	AGOR	Poland
F 266	Harbah	FF	Pakistan
F 267	Siqqat	FF	Pakistan
271	Warszawa	DDG	Poland
271	Cosar class	ML	Romania
A 271	Gold Rover	AOF (S)	UK
A 273	Black Rover	AOF (S)	UK
274	Cosar class	ML	Romania
P 277	Anglesey	PV	UK
P 278	Alderney	PV	UK
280	Iroquois	DDG	Canada
281	Huron	DDG	Canada
281	Piast	ARS	Poland
281	Constanta	AFS	Romania
282	Athabaskan	DDG	Canada
282	Lech	ARS	Poland
283	Algonquin	DDG	Canada
283	Midia	AFS	Romania
A 285	Auricula	AG	UK
P 295	Jersey	PV	UK
P 297	Guernsey	PV	UK
P 298	Shetland	PV	UK
P 299	Orkney	PV	UK
F 300	Oslo	FFG	Norway
P 300	Lindisfarne	PV	UK
301	Shahrokh	MSC	Iran
A 301	Drakensberg	AOR	South Africa
F 301	Bergen	FFG	Norway
MSO 301	Yaeyama	MSO/MH	Japan
P 301	Bizerte	PV	Tunisia
302	Atiya	AOS	Bulgaria
302	Simorgh	MSC	Iran
F 302	Trondheim	FFG	Norway
J 302	Chongmingdao	AS	China
MSO 302	Tsushima	MSO/MH	Japan
P 302	Horria	PV	Tunisia

PENNANT LIST

Number	Ship's name	Type	Country	Number	Ship's name	Type	Country
303	Karkas	MSC	Iran	M 371	Ohue	MH/MSC	Nigeria
F 303	Stavanger	FFG	Norway	M 372	Marabai	MH/MSC	Nigeria
MSO 303	Hachijyo	MSO/MH	Japan	A 373	Hermis	AGS	Greece
F 304	Narvik	FFG	Norway	A 377	Arethousa	AOS	Greece
OR 304	Success	AOR	Australia	A 378	Kinterbury	AG	UK
P 304	Monastir	PV	Tunisia	A 382	Arrochar	AG	UK
308	El Hahiq	PV	Morocco	383	Koni class	FFG	Cuba
309	El Tawfiq	PV	Morocco	A 385	Fort Grange	AEFS	UK
310	L V Rabhi	PV	Morocco	A 386	Fort Austin	AEFS	UK
311	Errachio	PV	Morocco	Y 386	Agdlek	PV	Denmark
312	El Akid	PV	Morocco	A 387	Fort Victoria	AOR	UK
313	El Maher	PV	Morocco	Y 387	Agpa	PV	Denmark
M 313	Tana	MH	Norway	A 388	Fort George	AOR	UK
314	El Majid	PV	Morocco	Y 388	Tulugaq	PV	Denmark
M 314	Alta	MSC	Norway	401	Admiral Branimir Ormanov	AGS	Bulgaria
315	El Bachir	PV	Morocco	L 401	Ertuğrul	LST	Turkey
316	El Hamiss	PV	Mexico	P 401	Cassiopea	PV	Italy
317	El Karib	PV	Mexico	ASR 402	Fushimi	ARS	Japan
A 317	Bulldog	AGS	UK	L 402	Serdar	LST	Turkey
318	Haiyun	AFS	China	P 402	Libra	PV	Italy
A 319	Beagle	AGS	UK	403		Haijui	China
321	Pauk II class	FFLG	Cuba	P 403	Spica	PV	Italy
324	Ta Hu	ARS	Taiwan	P 404	Vega	PV	Italy
A 324	Protea	AGS	South Africa	405	Ad Dakhla	AFS	Morocco
330	Halifax	FFG	Canada	AS 405	Chiyoda	AS	Japan
F 330	Vasco da Gama	FFG	Portugal	406	El Aigh	AFS	Morocco
331	Vancouver	FFG	Canada	407	Arrafiq	AP	Morocco
331	Martha Kristina Tiyahahu	FFG	Indonesia	411	Kangan	AOS	Iran
F 331	Alvares Cabral	FFG	Portugal	412	Taheri	AOS	Iran
M 331	Tista	MSC	Norway	412	Assad Al Bihar	FFLG	Libya
332	Ville de Québec	FFG	Canada	MSC 412	Addriyah	MH/MSC	Saudi Arabia
332	W Zakarias Yohannes	FFG	Indonesia	413	Assad El Tougour	FFLG	Libya
F 332	Corte Real	FFG	Portugal	414	Assad Al Khali	FFLG	Libya
M 332	Kvina	MSC	Norway	A 414	Ariadni	AOS	Greece
333	Toronto	FFG	Canada	MSC 414	Al Quysumah	MH/MSC	Saudi Arabia
333	Hasanuddin	FFG	Indonesia	415	Assad Al Hudud	FFLG	Libya
334	Regina	FFG	Canada	A 415	Evros	AG	Greece
M 334	Utla	MSC	Norway	416	Tariq Ibn Ziyad	FFLG	Libya
335	Calgary	FFG	Canada	MSC 416	Al Wadeeah	MH/MSC	Saudi Arabia
336	Montreal	FFG	Canada	417	Ean Al Gazala	FFLG	Libya
337	Fredericton	FFG	Canada	418	Ean Zara	FFLG	Libya
P 339	Bora	PV	Turkey	MSC 418	Safwa	MH/MSC	Saudi Arabia
F 340	Beskytteren	FF	Denmark	420	Al Jawf	MSC	Saudi Arabia
M 340	Oksøy	MH	Norway	421	Bandar Abbas	AFS	Iran
341	Samadikun	FF	Indonesia	421	Orkan	FFLG	Poland
342	Martadinata	FF	Indonesia	AOE 421	Sagami	AOE	Japan
343	Monginsidi	FF	Indonesia	F 421	Canterbury	FFG	New Zealand
344	Ngurah Rai	FF	Indonesia	422	Booshehr	AFS	Iran
D 345	Yücetepe	DDG	Turkey	422	Piorun	FFLG	Poland
D 346	Alcitepe	DD	Turkey	422	Shaqra	MSC	Saudi Arabia
D 347	Anittepe	DD	Turkey	AOE 422	Towada	AOE	Japan
D 348	Savaştepe	DDG	Turkey	423	Huragan	FFLG	Poland
D 349	Kiliç Ali Paşa	DDG	Turkey	423	Yung Chou	MSC	Taiwan
350	Koni class	FFG	Cuba	AOE 423	Tokiwa	AOE	Japan
D 350	Piyale Paşa	DDG	Turkey	424	Al Kharj	MSC	Saudi Arabia
V 350	Xiangyang Hong 09	AGS	China	AOE 424	Hamana	AOE	Japan
351	Djebel Chinoise	FFL	Algeria	426	Al Zahraa	AP	Iraq
351	Ahmed Yani	FFG	Indonesia	428	Khawla	AP	Iraq
D 351	M Fevzi Çakmak	DDG	Turkey	429	Balqees	AP	Iraq
352	Djebel Chinoise class	FFL	Algeria	431	Kharg	AFS	Iran
352	Slamet Riyadi	FFG	Indonesia	434	Gornik	FFLG	Poland
D 352	Gayret	DDG	Turkey	435	Hutnik	FFLG	Poland
353	Djebel Chinoise class	FFL	Algeria	436	Metalowiec	FFLG	Poland
353	Yos Sudarso	FFG	Indonesia	437	Folnik	FFLG	Poland
D 353	Adatepe	DDG	Turkey	441	Chah Bahar	AR	Iran
354	Oswald Siahann	FFG	Indonesia	441	Yung Cheng	MSC	Taiwan
D 354	Kocatepe	DDG	Turkey	441	Sonya class	MSC	Yemen
F 354	Niels Juel	FFG	Denmark	MSO 441	Exultant	MSO	USA
355	Abdul Halim Perdana Kusuma	FFG	Indonesia	449	Yung An	MSC	Taiwan
F 355	Olfert Fischer	FFG	Denmark	F 450	Elli	FFG	Greece
356	Koni class	FFG	Cuba	F 451	Mella	FF	Dominican Republic
356	Karel Satsuitubun	FFG	Indonesia	F 451	Limnos	FFG	Greece
D 356	Zafer	DD	Turkey	F 452	Hydra	FFG	Greece
F 356	Peter Tordenskiold	FFG	Denmark	F 453	Spetsai	FFG	Greece
F 357	Thetis	FF	Denmark	BM 454	Prestol	FFL	Dominican Republic
D 358	Berk	FF	Turkey	455	Chao Phraya	FFG	Thailand
F 358	Triton	FF	Denmark	BM 455	Tortuguero	FFL	Dominican Republic
AKL 359	Yung Kang	AGI	Taiwan	MSO 455	Implicit	MSO	USA
D 359	Peyk	FF	Turkey	456	Bangpakong	FFG	Thailand
F 359	Vaedderen	FF	Denmark	F 456	Epirus	FFG	Greece
D 360	Gelibolu	FF	Turkey	457	Yung Ju	MSC	Taiwan
F 360	Hvidbjørnen	FF	Denmark	457	Kraburi	FFG	Thailand
361	Fatahillah	FFG	Indonesia	F 457	Thrace	FFG	Greece
D 361	Gemlik	FF	Turkey	458	Saiburi	FFG	Thailand
362	Malahayati	FFG	Indonesia	F 458	Makedonia	FFG	Greece
363	Nala	FFG	Indonesia	F 460	Aegeon	FFG	Greece
364	Hajar Dewantara	FFG	Indonesia	462	Yung Sui	MSC	Taiwan
A 367	Newton	AG	UK	MST 462	Hayase	AG	Japan

PENNANT LIST

Number	Ship's name	Type	Country	Number	Ship's name	Type	Country
A 464	Axios	AFS	Greece	512	Wuxi	FFG	China
469	Yung Lo	MSC	Taiwan	512	Teluk Semangka	LST	Indonesia
F 471	Antonio Enes	FF	Portugal	512	Larak	LSL	Iran
472	Kalaat Beni Hammad	LSL	Algeria	A 512	Mosel	AG	Germany
473	Kalaat Beni Rached	LSL	Algeria	AOG 512	Wan Shou	AOS	Taiwan
475	Pyhäranta	ML	Finland	M 512	Surmene	MSC	Turkey
F 475	João Coutinho	FF	Portugal	513	Huayin	FFG	China
476	Yung Shan	MSC	Taiwan	513	Sinai	MSO	Egypt
F 476	Jacinto Candido	FF	Portugal	513	Teluk Penju	LST	Indonesia
F 477	General Pereira d'Eça	FF	Portugal	513	Tonb	LSL	Iran
A 478	Naftilos	AGS	Greece	A 513	Shahjalal	PV	Bangladesh
479	Yung Nien	MSC	Taiwan	A 513	Rhein	AG	Germany
A 480	Resource	AEFS	UK	M 513	Seddulbahir	MSC	Turkey
F 480	Comandante João Belo	FF	Portugal	514	Zhenjiang	FFG	China
F 481	Comandante Hermenegildo Capelo	FF	Portugal	514	Lavan	LSL	Iran
				514	Teluk Mandar	LST	Indonesia
482	Yung Fu	MSC	Taiwan	A 514	Werra	AG	Germany
ARC 482	Muroto	AG	Japan	M 514	Silifke	MSC	Turkey
F 482	Comandante Roberto Ivens	FF	Portugal	515	Xiamen	FFG	China
F 483	Comandante Sacadura Cabral	FF	Portugal	515	Teluk Sampit	LST	Indonesia
F 484	Augusto de Castilho	FF	Portugal	515	Lung Chuan	AOS	Taiwan
485	Yung Jen	MSC	Taiwan	A 515	Khan Jahan Ali	AOS	Bangladesh
F 485	Honorio Barreto	FF	Portugal	A 515	Main	AG	Germany
F 486	Baptista de Andrade	FF	Portugal	M 515	Saros	MSC	Turkey
F 487	João Roby	FF	Portugal	516	Jiujiang	FFG	China
488	Yung Hsin	MSC	Taiwan	516	Assiout	MSO	Egypt
F 488	Afonso Cerqueira	FF	Portugal	516	Teluk Banten	LST	Indonesia
MSO 488	Conquest	MSO	USA	A 516	Donau	AG	Germany
F 489	Oliveira E Carmo	FF	Portugal	LT 516	Kalinga Apayao	LST	Philippines
MSO 489	Gallant	MSO	USA	M 516	Sigacik	MSC	Turkey
MSO 492	Pledge	MSO	USA	517	Nanping	FFG	China
P 495	Bambu	PV	Italy	517	Teluk Ende	LST	Indonesia
P 496	Mango	PV	Italy	M 517	Sapanca	MSC	Turkey
497	Yung Chi	MSC	Taiwan	518	Jian	FFG	China
P 497	Mogano	PV	Italy	518	Yun Tai	AP	Taiwan
498	Lana	AGS	Nigeria	M 518	Sariyer	MSC	Turkey
P 500	Palma	PV	Italy	519	Changzhi	FFG	China
501	Nawarat	FFL	Burma	520	Kaifeng	FFG	China
501	Xiaguan	FF	China	A 520	Sagres	ATS	Portugal
501	Gharbiya	MSO	Egypt	AP 520	Tai Wu	AP	Taiwan
501	Teluk Langsa	LST	Indonesia	M 520	Karamürsel	MSC	Turkey
501	Eilat class	FFLG	Israel	521	Yu Tai	AR	Taiwan
501	Lieutenant Colonel Errhamani	FFG	Morocco	M 521	Kerempe	MSC	Turkey
LT 501	Laguna	LST	Philippines	522	Tai Hu	AP	Taiwan
502	Nagakyay	FFL	Burma	M 522	T 43 class	MSO	Algeria
502	Nanchong	FF	China	M 522	Kilimli	MSC	Turkey
502	Teluk Bajur	LST	Indonesia	523	Yuen Feng	AP	Taiwan
502	Eilat class	FFLG	Israel	M 523	Kozlu	MSC	Turkey
AOTL 502	Dundurn	AOF(S)	Canada	524	Yuen Feng class	AP	Taiwan
HQ 502	Qui Nonh	LST	Vietnam	M 524	Kuşadasi	MSC	Turkey
503	Kaiyuan	FF	China	525	Wu Kang	AP	Taiwan
503	Teluk Amboina	LST	Indonesia	M 525	Kemer	MSC	Turkey
HQ 503	Vung Tau	LST	Vietnam	526	Wu Kang class	AP	Taiwan
504	Dongchuan	FF	China	527	Wu Kang class	AP	Taiwan
504	Teluk Kau	LST	Indonesia	A 527	Almeida Carvalho	AGS	Portugal
504	Hittin	MSO	Syria	528	Wu Kang class	AP	Taiwan
LT 504	Lanao del Norte	LST	Philippines	529	Haikou	FF	China
505	Kunming	FFG	China	529	Wu Kang class	AP	Taiwan
505	Chang Pei	AOS	Taiwan	530	Aswan	MSO	Egypt
HQ 505	Da Nang	LST	Vietnam	530	Wu Yi	AFS	Taiwan
506	Chengdu	FFG	China	A 530	Horten	AG	Norway
J 506	Yongxingdao	AS	China	P 530	Trabzon	MSC/PV	Turkey
507	Pingxiang	FFG	China	531	Yingtan	FFG	China
507	Daqahliya	MSO	Egypt	P 531	Terme	MSC/PV	Turkey
507	Ibn Marjid	FF	Iraq	532	Zhongdong	FFG	China
507	Hsin Lung	AOS	Taiwan	532	Sonya class	MSO	Syria
LT 507	Benguet	LST	Philippines	P 532	Tirebolu	MSC/PV	Turkey
M 507	Seymen	MSC	Turkey	533	Ningbo	FFG	China
508	Xichang	FFG	China	533	Giza	MSO	Egypt
508	Teluk Tomini	LST	Indonesia	N 533	Norge	AG	Norway
AOR 508	Provider	AOR	Canada	534	Jinhua	FFG	China
M 508	Selçuk	MSC	Turkey	535	Huangshi	FFG	China
509	Chang De	FFG	China	536	Wu Hu	FFG	China
509	Teluk Ratai	LST	Indonesia	536	Qena	MSO	Egypt
AOR 509	Protecteur	AOR	Canada	537	Zhoushan	FFG	China
M 509	Seyhan	MSC	Turkey	539	Anqing	FFG	China
510	Shaoxing	FFG	China	539	Sohag	MSO	Egypt
510	Teluk Saleh	LST	Indonesia	540	Huainan	FFG	China
AOR 510	Preserver	AOR	Canada	A 540	Dannebrog	AG	Denmark
LT 510	Northern Samar	LST	Philippines	541	Jiangwei class	FFG	China
M 510	Samsun	MSC	Turkey	543	Dandong	FFG	China
511	Nantong	FFG	China	544	Siping	FFG	China
511	Teluk Bone	LST	Indonesia	545	Tianshan	FFG	China
511	Hengam	LSL	Iran	C 550	Vittorio Veneto	CGH	Italy
A 511	Elbe	AG	Germany	D 550	Ardito	DDG	Italy
M 511	Sinop	MSC	Turkey	F 550	Salvatore Todaro	FFL	Italy
MSO 511	Affray	MSO	USA	LC 550	Bacolod City	LSL	Philippines
512	Haijui	AS	China	P 550	Flyvefisken	PV/MH/ML	Denmark

[106]

PENNANT LIST

Number	Ship's name	Type	Country	Number	Ship's name	Type	Country
551	Maoming	FFG	China	A 590	Yunus	AGS	Turkey
551	Mornar	FFL	Yugoslavia	600	Haijiu	AFS	China
C 551	Giuseppe Garibaldi	CVL	Italy	A 601	Monge	AGOR	France
D 551	Audace	DDG	Italy	A 601	Tekirdag	MSC/AG	Turkey
F 551	Minerva	FFLG	Italy	P 601	Jayesagara	PV	Sri Lanka
LC 551	Cagayan de Oro City	LSL	Philippines	D 602	Suffren	DDG	France
MSC 551	Kum San	MSC	Korea, Republic	P 602	Sagarawardene	PV	Sri Lanka
P 551	Hajen	PV	Denmark	D 603	Duquesne	DDG	France
552	Yibin	FFG	China	A 607	Meuse	AOR	France
552	Borač	FFL	Yugoslavia	A 608	Var	AOR	France
F 552	Urania	FFLG	Italy	D 609	Aconit	DDG	France
MSC 552	Ko Hung	MSC	Korea, Republic	A 610	Ile d'Oléron	AG	France
P 552	Havkatten	PV	Denmark	D 610	Tourville	DDG	France
553	Shaoguan	FFG	China	M 610	Ouistreham	MSO	France
F 553	Danaide	FFLG	Italy	D 611	Duguay-Trouin	DDG	France
MSC 553	Kum Kok	MSC	Korea, Republic	612	Badr	FFLG	Saudi Arabia
P 553	Laxen	PV	Denmark	D 612	De Grasse	DDG	France
554	Anshun	FFG	China	M 612	Alençon	MSO	France
F 554	Sfinge	FFLG	Italy	614	Al Yarmook	FFLG	Saudi Arabia
P 554	Makrelen	PV	Denmark	D 614	Cassard	DDG	France
555	Zhaotong	FFG	China	A 615	Loire	AG	France
F 555	Driade	FFLG	Italy	D 615	Jean Bart	DDG	France
MSC 555	Nam Yang	MSC	Korea, Republic	X 615	Dongyun	AOR	China
P 555	Støren	PV	Denmark	616	Hitteen	FFLG	Saudi Arabia
556	Xiangtan	FFG	China	616	Kormoran	MSO	Poland
F 556	Chimera	FFLG	Italy	A 617	Garonne	AG	France
MSC 556	Ha Dong	MSC	Korea, Republic	AP 617	Yakal	AR	Philippines
P 556	Svaerdfisken	PV	Denmark	618	Albatros	MSO	Poland
557	Jishou	FFG	China	618	Tabuk	FFLG	Saudi Arabia
F 557	Fenice	FFLG	Italy	A 618	Rance	AG	France
MSC 557	Sam Kok	MSC	Korea, Republic	619	Pelikan	MSO	Poland
P 557	Glenten	PV	Denmark	620	Tukan	MSO	Poland
F 558	Sibilla	FFLG	Italy	A 620	Jules Verne	AR	France
MSC 558	Yong Dong	MSC	Korea, Republic	621	Flamingo	MSO	Poland
P 558	Gribben	PV	Denmark	A 621	Rhin	AG	France
MSC 559	Ok Cheon	MSC	Korea, Republic	622	Rybitwa	MSO	Poland
P 559	Lommen	PV	Denmark	A 622	Rhône	AG	France
560	Jianghu class	FFG	China	623	Mewa	MSO	Poland
560	Sonya class	MSC/MH	Cuba	624	Czajka	MSO	Poland
D 560	Luigi Durand de La Penne	DDG	Italy	625	Leniwka class	MSC	Poland
P 560	Raunen	PV	Denmark	626	Leniwka class	MSC	Poland
561	Sonya class	MSC/MH	Cuba	A 629	Durance	AOR	France
561	Multatuli	AS	Indonesia	630	Goplo	MSC	Poland
D 561	Francesco Mimbelli	DDG	Italy	A 630	Marne	AOR	France
P 561	Skaden	PV	Denmark	631	Gardno	MSC	Poland
P 562	Viben	PV	Denmark	A 631	Somme	AOR	France
AGS 563	Chiu Lien	AGS	Taiwan	632	Bukowo	MSC	Poland
F 564	Lupo	FFG	Italy	633	Dabie	MSC	Poland
F 565	Sagittario	FFG	Italy	634	Jamno	MSC	Poland
F 566	Perseo	FFG	Italy	634	Natya class	MSO	Yemen
F 567	Orsa	FFG	Italy	635	Mielno	MSC	Poland
A 568	Rimfaxe	AOS	Denmark	636	Wicko	MSC	Poland
A 569	Skinfaxe	AOS	Denmark	637	Resko	MSC	Poland
570	Sonya class	MSC/MH	Cuba	638	Sarbsko	MSC	Poland
A 570	Taşkizak	AOS	Turkey	639	Necko	MSC	Poland
F 570	Maestrale	FFG	Italy	640	Naklo	MSC	Poland
A 571	Yüzbaşi Tolunay	AOS	Turkey	D 640	Georges Leygues	DDG	France
F 571	Grecale	FFG	Italy	641	Druzno	MSC	Poland
A 572	Albay Hakki Burak	AOS	Turkey	641	Natya class	MSO	Yemen
F 572	Libeccio	FFG	Italy	D 641	Dupleix	DDG	France
A 573	Binbaşi Saadettin Gürçan	AOS	Turkey	M 641	Éridan	MH	France
F 573	Scirocco	FFG	Italy	642	Hancza	MSC	Poland
F 574	Aliseo	FFG	Italy	642	Natya class	PV	Syria
M 574	Grønsund	MSC	Denmark	D 642	Montcalm	DDG	France
A 575	Inebolu	AOS	Turkey	M 642	Cassiopée	MH	France
F 575	Euro	FFG	Italy	D 643	Jean de Vienne	DDG	France
X 575	Taicang	AOR	China	M 643	Andromède	MH	France
A 576	Derya	AD	Turkey	A 644	Berry	AGOR	France
F 576	Espero	FFG	Italy	D 644	Primauguet	DDG	France
A 577	Sokullu Mehmet Paşa	ATS	Turkey	M 644	Pégase	MH	France
F 577	Zeffiro	FFG	Italy	D 645	La Motte-Picquet	DDG	France
578	Sonya class	MSC/MH	Cuba	M 645	Orion	MH	France
M 578	Vilsund	MSC	Denmark	A 646	Triton	AS	France
A 579	Cezayirli Gazi Hasan Pasa	ATS	Turkey	D 646	Latouche-Treville	DDG	France
A 580	Akar	AOR	Turkey	M 646	Croix du Sud	MH	France
F 580	Alpino	FF	Italy	M 647	Aigle	MH	France
A 581	Onaran	AR	Turkey	M 648	Lyre	MH	France
F 581	Carabiniere	FFG	Italy	M 649	Persée	MH	France
A 582	Başaran	AR	Turkey	MSC 649	Hatsushima	MH/MSC	Japan
F 582	Artigliere	FFG	Italy	MSC 650	Ninoshima	MH/MSC	Japan
F 583	Aviere	FFG	Italy	651	Singa	PV	Indonesia
A 584	Kurtaran	ARS	Turkey	MSC 651	Miyajima	MH/MSC	Japan
F 584	Bersagliere	FFG	Italy	MSC 652	Enoshima	MH/MSC	Japan
A 585	Akin	ARS	Turkey	653	Ajak	PV	Indonesia
F 585	Granatiere	FFG	Italy	MSC 653	Ukishima	MH/MSC	Japan
A 586	Ülkü	AS	Turkey	MSC 654	Ooshima	MH/MSC	Japan
A 588	Umur Bey	AS	Turkey	MSC 655	Niijima	MH/MSC	Japan
A 589	Işin	ARS	Turkey	MSC 656	Yakushima	MH/MSC	Japan

PENNANT LIST

Number	Ship's name	Type	Country
MSC 657	Narushima	MH/MSC	Japan
MSC 658	Chichijima	MH/MSC	Japan
MSC 659	Torishima	MH/MSC	Japan
MSC 660	Hahajima	MH/MSC	Japan
MSC 661	Takashima	MH/MSC	Japan
MSC 662	Nuwajima	MH/MSC	Japan
MSC 663	Etajima	MH/MSC	Japan
MSC 664	Kamishima	MH/MSC	Japan
MSC 665	Himeshima	MH/MSC	Japan
MSC 666	Ogishima	MH/MSC	Japan
MSC 667	Moroshima	MH/MSC	Japan
MSC 668	Yurishima	MH/MSC	Japan
MSC 669	Hikoshima	MH/MSC	Japan
MSC 670	Awashima	MH/MSC	Japan
LST 671	Un Bong	LST	Korea, Republic
MSC 671	Sakushima	MH/MSC	Japan
MSC 672	Uwajima	MH/MSC	Japan
LST 673	Bi Bong	LST	Korea, Republic
MSC 673	Ieshima	MH/MSC	Japan
MSC 674	Tsukishima	MH/MSC	Japan
MSC 675	Hatsushima class	MH/MSO	Japan
LST 675	Kae Bong	LST	Korea, Republic
LST 676	Wee Bong	LST	Korea, Republic
LST 677	Su Yong	LST	Korea, Republic
LST 678	Buk Han	LST	Korea, Republic
LST 679	Hwa San	LST	Korea, Republic
P 679	Grèbe	PV	France
P 680	Sterne	PV	France
P 681	Albatros	PV	France
P 682	L'Audacieuse	PV	France
P 683	La Boudeuse	PV	France
P 684	La Capricieuse	PV	France
P 685	La Fougueuse	PV	France
P 686	La Glorieuse	PV	France
P 687	La Gracieuse	PV	France
P 688	La Moqueuse	PV	France
P 689	La Railleuse	PV	France
P 690	La Rieuse	PV	France
P 691	La Tapageuse	PV	France
701	Pulau Rani	PV/MSO	Indonesia
702	Pulau Ratewo	PV/MSO	Indonesia
702	Madina	FFG	Saudi Arabia
704	Hofouf	FFG	Saudi Arabia
706	Abha	FFG	Saudi Arabia
708	Taif	FFG	Saudi Arabia
F 710	La Fayette	FFLG	France
711	Pulau Rengat	MH/MSC	Indonesia
711	Zeltin	AR	Libya
712	Pulau Rupat	MH/MSC	Indonesia
M 712	Cybèle	MH	France
M 713	Calliope	MH	France
M 714	Clio	MH	France
P 714	Abheetha	AG	Sri Lanka
M 715	Circé	MH	France
P 715	Edithara	AG	Sri Lanka
M 716	Cérès	MH	France
P 716	Wickrama	AG	Sri Lanka
A 721	Khadem	AG	Bangladesh
722	Al Munjed	ARS	Libya
725	Sariwon class	PV	Korea, Democratic People's Republic
726	Sariwon class	PV	Korea, Democratic People's Republic
F 726	Commandant Bory	FFLG	France
727	Sariwon class	PV	Korea, Democratic People's Republic
F 729	Balny	FFLG	France
F 730	Floreal	FFLG	France
F 731	Prairial	FFLG	France
F 732	Nivose	FFLG	France
F 733	Ventose	FFLG	France
F 734	Vendémiaire	FFLG	France
F 735	Germinal	FFLG	France
F 749	Enseigne de Vaisseau Henry	FFLG	France
751	Dong Hae	FFL	Korea, Republic
752	Su Won	FFL	Korea, Republic
753	Kang Reung	FFL	Korea, Republic
755	An Yang	FFL	Korea, Republic
756	Po Hang	FFLG	Korea, Republic
A 756	L'Espérance	AGS	France
757	Kun San	FFLG	Korea, Republic
A 757	D'Entrecasteaux	AGS	France
758	Kyong Ju	FFLG	Korea, Republic
759	Mok Po	FFLG	Korea, Republic
761	Kim Chon	FFLG	Korea, Republic
762	Chung Ju	FFLG	Korea, Republic
763	Jin Ju	FFLG	Korea, Republic
765	Yo Su	FFLG	Korea, Republic
766	An Dong	FFLG	Korea, Republic
767	Sun Chon	FFLG	Korea, Republic
768	Yee Ree	FFLG	Korea, Republic
769	Won Ju	FFLG	Korea, Republic
771	Je Chon	FFLG	Korea, Republic
772	Chon An	FFLG	Korea, Republic
773	Song Nam	FFLG	Korea, Republic
775	Bu Chon	FFLG	Korea, Republic
775	Kadisia	MSC	Syria
776	Dae Chon	FFLG	Korea, Republic
776	Yarmuk	MSC	Syria
777	Porkkala	ML	Finland
777	Jin Hae	FFLG	Korea, Republic
778	Sok Cho	FFLG	Korea, Republic
779	Yong Ju	FFLG	Korea, Republic
781	Nam Won	FFLG	Korea, Republic
F 781	D'Estienne d'Orves	FFLG	France
782	Kwan Myong	FFLG	Korea, Republic
F 782	Amyot d'Inville	FFLG	France
F 783	Drogou	FFLG	France
F 784	Détroyat	FFLG	France
F 785	Jean Moulin	FFLG	France
F 786	Quartier Maître Anquetil	FFLG	France
F 787	Commandant De Pimodan	FFLG	France
F 788	Second Maître Le Bihan	FFLG	France
F 789	Lieutenant de Vaisseau Le Hénaff	FFLG	France
F 790	Lieutenant de Vaisseau Lavallée	FFLG	France
A 791	Lapérouse	AGS	France
F 791	Commandant l'Herminier	FFLG	France
A 792	Borda	AGS	France
F 792	Premier Maitre L'Her	FFLG	France
A 793	Laplace	AGS	France
F 793	Commandant Blaison	FFLG	France
F 794	Enseigne de Vaisseau Jacoubet	FFLG	France
A 795	Arago	AGS	France
F 795	Commandant Ducuing	FFLG	France
F 796	Commandant Birot	FFLG	France
F 797	Commandant Bouan	FFLG	France
801	Rais Hamidou	FFLG	Algeria
801	Yukan class	AFS	China
801	Pandbong	PV	Indonesia
F 801	Tromp	FFG	Netherlands
802	Salah Rais	FFLG	Algeria
802	Sura	PV	Indonesia
803	Rais Ali	FFLG	Algeria
F 806	De Ruyter	FFG	Netherlands
F 807	Kortenaer	FFG	Netherlands
M 809	Naaldwijk	MSC	Netherlands
M 810	Abcoude	MSC	Netherlands
811	Kakap	PV	Indonesia
811	Grunwald	LST	Poland
F 811	Piet Heyn	FFG	Netherlands
812	Kerapu	PV	Indonesia
F 812	Jacob van Heemskerck	FFG	Netherlands
M 812	Drachten	MSC	Netherlands
813	Tongkol	PV	Indonesia
F 813	Witte de With	FFG	Netherlands
M 813	Ommen	MSC	Netherlands
814	Bervang	PV	Indonesia
815	Tien Shan	FF	Taiwan
F 816	Abraham Crijnssen	FFG	Netherlands
821	Lublin	LST/ML	Poland
822	Gniezno	LST/ML	Poland
823	Krakow	LST/ML	Poland
F 823	Philips van Almonde	FFG	Netherlands
M 823	Naarden	MSC	Netherlands
824	Poznan	LST/ML	Poland
F 824	Bloys van Treslong	FFG	Netherlands
825	Torun	LST/ML	Poland
F 825	Jan van Brakel	FFG	Netherlands
F 826	Pieter Florisz	FFG	Netherlands
827	Tai Yuan	FF	Taiwan
F 827	Karel Doorman	FFG	Netherlands
F 829	Willem van der Zaan	FFG	Netherlands
F 830	Tjerk Hiddes	FFG	Netherlands
M 830	Sittard	MSC	Netherlands
F 831	Van Amstel	FFG	Netherlands
832	Yu Shan	FF	Taiwan
A 832	Zuiderkruis	AOE	Netherlands
F 832	Abraham van der Hulst	FFG	Netherlands
833	Hua Shan	FF	Taiwan
F 833	Van Nes	FFG	Netherlands
F 834	Van Galen	FFG	Netherlands
835	Fu Shan	FF	Taiwan
A 835	Poolster	AOE	Netherlands
836	Lu Shan	FF	Taiwan
837	Shou Shan	FF	Taiwan

PENNANT LIST

Number	Ship's name	Type	Country	Number	Ship's name	Type	Country
841	Dadie class	AGI	China	930	Lao Yang	DDG	Taiwan
843	Chung Shan	FF	Taiwan	931	Tariq	FF	Egypt
M 850	Alkmaar	MH	Netherlands	931	Burujulasad	AGS	Indonesia
HQ 851	Yurka class	MSO	Vietnam	932	Dewa Kembar	AGS	Indonesia
M 851	Delfzyl	MH	Netherlands	932	Chin Yang	FFG	Taiwan
HQ 852	Yurka class	MSO	Vietnam	933	Jalanidhi	AGOR	Indonesia
M 852	Dordrecht	MH	Netherlands	933	Fong Yang	FFG	Taiwan
M 853	Haarlem	MH	Netherlands	934	Feng Yang	FFG	Taiwan
M 854	Harlingen	MH	Netherlands	F 941	Abu Qir	FFG	Egypt
M 855	Scheveningen	MH	Netherlands	F 946	El Suez	FFG	Egypt
M 856	Maasluis	MH	Netherlands	951	Dayun class	AFS	China
V 856	Xing Fengshan	AGI	China	951	Najim al Zaffer	FFG	Egypt
M 857	Makkum	MH	Netherlands	951	Talaud	AP	Indonesia
M 858	Middelburg	MH	Netherlands	FF 951	Ulsan	FFG	Korea, Republic
M 859	Hellevoetsluis	MH	Netherlands	MMC 951	Souya	ML	Japan
M 860	Schiedam	MH	Netherlands	952	Nan Yun	AFS	China
M 861	Urk	MH	Netherlands	952	Nusa Telu	AP	Indonesia
M 862	Zierikzee	MH	Netherlands	FF 952	Seoul	FFG	Korea, Republic
M 863	Vlaardingen	MH	Netherlands	953	Natuna	AP	Indonesia
M 864	Willemstad	MH	Netherlands	FF 953	Chung Nam	FFG	Korea, Republic
867	Ping Jin	FFL	Taiwan	FF 955	Masan	FFG	Korea, Republic
876	Pansio	ML	Finland	956	El Nasser	FFG	Egypt
U 891	Dagushan	AR	China	956	Teluk Mentawai	AP	Indonesia
A 900	Mercuur	AS	Netherlands	FF 956	Kyong Buk	FFG	Korea, Republic
901	Mourad Rais	FFG	Algeria	957	Karimundsa	AP	Indonesia
902	Rais Kellich	FFG	Algeria	FF 957	Chon Nam	FFG	Korea, Republic
902	Boraida	AOR	Saudi Arabia	FF 958	Che Ju	FFG	Korea, Republic
M 902	J E Van Haverbeke	MSO	Belgium	960	Karimata	AP	Indonesia
903	Rais Korfou	FFG	Algeria	A 960	Godetia	AG	Belgium
903	Arun	AOF(S)	Indonesia	A 961	Zinnia	AG	Belgium
903	Hua Yang	DDG	Taiwan	A 962	Belgica	AGOR	Belgium
M 903	A F Dufour	MSO	Belgium	DD 963	Spruance	DDG	USA
904	Yunbou	AOR	Saudi Arabia	DD 964	Paul F Foster	DDG	USA
M 904	De Brouwer	MSO	Belgium	DD 965	Kinkaid	DDG	USA
906	Huei Yang	DDG	Taiwan	DD 966	Hewitt	DDG	USA
A 906	Tydeman	AGS	Netherlands	DD 967	Elliott	DDG	USA
M 906	Breydel	MSO	Belgium	DD 968	Arthur W Radford	DDG	USA
907	Fu Yang	DDG	Taiwan	DD 969	Peterson	DDG	USA
908	Kwei Yang	DDG	Taiwan	DD 970	Caron	DDG	USA
M 908	G Truffaut	MSO	Belgium	971	Tangung Pandan	AP	Indonesia
909	Chiang Yang	DDG	Taiwan	971	Tarantul class	FFLG	Yemen
M 909	F Bovesse	MSO	Belgium	DD 971	David R Ray	DDG	USA
F 910	Wielingen	FFG	Belgium	972	Tanjung Oisina	AP	Indonesia
911	Sorong	AOR	Indonesia	DD 972	Oldendorf	DDG	USA
911	Dang Yang	DDG	Taiwan	DD 973	John Young	DDG	USA
F 911	Westdiep	FFG	Belgium	DD 974	Comte de Grasse	DDG	USA
912	Chien Yang	DDG	Taiwan	DD 975	O'Brien	DDG	USA
F 912	Wandelaar	FFG	Belgium	976	Taruntul class	FFLG	Yemen
F 913	Westhinder	FFG	Belgium	DD 976	Merrill	DDG	USA
914	Lo Yang	DDG	Taiwan	DD 977	Briscoe	DDG	USA
915	Han Yang	DDG	Taiwan	DD 978	Stump	DDG	USA
DD 915	Chung Buk	DDG	Korea, Republic	DD 979	Conolly	DDG	USA
M 915	Aster	MH	Belgium	DD 980	Moosbrugger	DDG	USA
DD 916	Jeon Buk	DDG	Korea, Republic	DD 981	John Hancock	DDG	USA
M 916	Bellis	MH	Belgium	DD 982	Nicholson	DDG	USA
917	Nan Yang	DDG	Taiwan	DD 983	John Rodgers	DDG	USA
DD 917	Dae Gu	DDG	Korea, Republic	DD 984	Leftwich	DDG	USA
M 917	Crocus	MH	Belgium	DD 985	Cushing	DDG	USA
918	An Yang	DDG	Taiwan	DD 986	Harry W Hill	DDG	USA
DD 918	Inchon	DDG	Korea, Republic	DD 987	O'Bannon	DDG	USA
M 918	Dianthus	MH	Belgium	DD 988	Thorn	DDG	USA
919	Kun Yang	DDG/ML	Taiwan	DD 989	Deyo	DDG	USA
DD 919	Taejon	DDG	Korea, Republic	DD 990	Ingersoll	DDG	USA
M 919	Fuchsia	MH	Belgium	DD 991	Fife	DDG	USA
920	Dazhi	AS	China	DD 992	Fletcher	DDG	USA
920	Lai Yang	DDG	Taiwan	DDG 993	Kidd	DDG	USA
M 920	Iris	MH	Belgium	DDG 994	Callaghan	DDG	USA
921	El Fateh	DD	Egypt	DDG 995	Scott	DDG	USA
921	Jaya Wijaya	AR	Indonesia	DDG 996	Chandler	DDG	USA
921	Liao Yang	DDG	Taiwan	DD 997	Hayler	DDG	USA
DD 921	Kwang Ju	DDG	Korea, Republic	M 1060	Weiden	MH	Germany
M 921	Lobelia	MH	Belgium	M 1061	Rottweil	MH	Germany
DD 922	Kang Won	DDG	Korea, Republic	M 1063	Bad Bevensen	MH	Germany
M 922	Myosotis	MH	Belgium	M 1066	Frankenthal	MH	Germany
923	Chen Yang	DDG	Taiwan	M 1067	Bad Rappenau	MH	Germany
DD 923	Kyong Ki	DDG	Korea, Republic	FF 1070	Downes	FF	USA
M 923	Narcis	MH	Belgium	M 1070	Göttingen	MH	Germany
924	Kai Yang	DDG	Taiwan	M 1071	Koblenz	MH	Germany
M 924	Primula	MH	Belgium	M 1072	Lindau	MH	Germany
925	Te Yang	DDG	Taiwan	M 1073	Schleswig	MSC	Germany
DD 925	Jeon Ju	DDG	Korea, Republic	M 1074	Tübingen	MH	Germany
926	Shao Yang	DDG	Taiwan	M 1075	Wetzlar	MH	Germany
927	Yukan class	LST	China	M 1076	Paderborn	MSC	Germany
927	Yun Yang	DDG	Taiwan	M 1077	Weilheim	MH	Germany
928	Yukan class	LST	China	FF 1078	Joseph Hewes	FFG	USA
928	Shen Yang	DDG	Taiwan	M 1078	Cuxhaven	MH	Germany
929	Yukan class	LST	China	FF 1079	Bowen	FFG	USA
929	Chao Yang	DDG	Taiwan	M 1079	Düren	MSC	Germany

PENNANT LIST

Number	Ship's name	Type	Country
M 1080	Marburg	MH	Germany
M 1081	Konstanz	MSC	Germany
M 1082	Wolfsburg	MSC	Germany
M 1083	Ulm	MSC	Germany
FF 1084	McCandless	FFG	USA
FF 1085	Donald B Beary	FFG	USA
M 1085	Minden	MH	Germany
M 1087	Volklingen	MH	Germany
FF 1089	Jesse L Brown	FFG	USA
FF 1090	Ainsworth	FFG	USA
M 1090	Pegnitz	MSC	Germany
M 1091	Kulmbach	MSC	Germany
M 1092	Hameln	MSC	Germany
M 1093	Auerbach	MSC	Germany
M 1094	Ensdorf	MSC	Germany
FF 1095	Truett	FFG	USA
M 1095	Überherrn	MSC	Germany
M 1096	Passau	MSC	Germany
FF 1097	Moinester	FFG	USA
M 1097	Laboe	MSC	Germany
M 1098	Siegburg	MSC	Germany
M 1099	Herten	MSC	Germany
1101	Cheng Kung	FFG	Taiwan
1103	Cheng Ho	FFG	Taiwan
M 1114	Brinton	MH	UK
M 1116	Wilton	ATS	UK
M 1166	Nurton	MH	UK
M 1181	Sheraton	MH	UK
LST 1182	Fresno	LST	USA
LST 1183	Peoria	LST	USA
LST 1184	Frederick	LST	USA
LST 1185	Schenectady	LST	USA
LST 1186	Cayuga	LST	USA
LST 1187	Tuscaloosa	LST	USA
LST 1188	Saginaw	LST	USA
LST 1189	San Bernardino	LST	USA
LST 1190	Boulder	LST	USA
LST 1191	Racine	LST	USA
LST 1192	Spartanburg County	LST	USA
LST 1193	Fairfax County	LST	USA
LST 1194	La Moure County	LST	USA
LST 1196	Harlan County	LST	USA
LST 1197	Barnstable County	LST	USA
LST 1198	Bristol County	LST	USA
M 1210	Kimberley	MSC	South Africa
M 1214	Walvisbaai	MSC	South Africa
M 1215	East London	MSC	South Africa
LST 1312	Ambe	LST	Nigeria
LST 1313	Ofiom	LST	Nigeria
A 1407	Wittensee	AOS	Germany
A 1411	Lüneburg	AG	Germany
A 1413	Freiburg	AG	Germany
A 1414	Glücksburg	AG	Germany
A 1415	Saarburg	AG	Germany
A 1416	Nienburg	AG	Germany
A 1418	Meersburg	AG	Germany
A 1424	Walchensee	AOR	Germany
A 1425	Ammersee	AOR	Germany
A 1426	Tegernsee	AOR	Germany
A 1427	Westensee	AOR	Germany
A 1435	Westerwald	AG	Germany
A 1436	Odenwald	AG	Germany
A 1438	Steigerwald	AG	Germany
A 1442	Spessart	AOR	Germany
A 1443	Rhön	AOR	Germany
A 1450	Planet	AGOR	Germany
A1456	Alliance	AGOR	NATO
M 1498	Windhoek	MSC	South Africa
1501	Sri Banggi	LST	Malaysia
1501	Jacmin	ARS	RoK
1502	Rajah Jarom	LST	Malaysia
1503	Sri Indera Sakti	AFS/ATS	Malaysia
1504	Mahawangsa	AFS/ATS	Malaysia
F 1616	Petya II class	FF	Ethiopia
F 1617	Petya II class	FF	Ethiopia
M 2003	Waveney	MSC	UK
M 2004	Carron	MSC	UK
M 2005	Dovey	MSC	UK
M 2006	Helford	MSC	UK
M 2007	Humber	MSC	UK
M 2008	Blackwater	MSC	UK
M 2009	Itchen	MSC	UK
M 2010	Helmsdale	MSC	UK
M 2011	Orwell	MSC	UK
M 2012	Ribble	MSC	UK
M 2013	Spey	MSC	UK
M 2014	Arun	MSC	UK
3001	Tae Pung Yang	ARS	RoK
L 3004	Sir Bedivere	LSL	UK
L 3005	Sir Galahad	LSL	UK
L 3027	Sir Geraint	LSL	UK
L 3036	Sir Percivale	LSL	UK
TV 3501	Katori	ATS	Japan
L 3505	Sir Tristram	LSL	UK
TV 3506	Yamagumo	ATS	Japan
TV 3507	Makigumo	ATS	Japan
L 4001	Ardennes	LSL	UK
L 4003	Arakan	LSL	UK
LST 4101	Atsumi	LST	Japan
LST 4102	Motobu	LST	Japan
LST 4103	Nemuro	LST	Japan
LST 4151	Miura	LST	Japan
LST 4152	Ojika	LST	Japan
LST 4153	Satsuma	LST	Japan
ATS 4201	Azuma	ATS	Japan
ATS 4202	Kurobe	ATS	Japan
AGB 5002	Shirase	AG	Japan
AGS 5101	Akashi	AGS	Japan
AGS 5102	Futami	AGS	Japan
AGS 5103	Suma	AGS	Japan
AGS 5104	Wakasa	AGS	Japan
AOS 5201	Hibiki	AGS	Japan
AOS 5202	Harima	AGS	Japan
A 5206	São Gabriel	AOR	Portugal
A 5208	São Miguel	AFS	Portugal
A 5210	Berrio	AOF(S)	Portugal
A 5301	Pietro Cavezzale	AG	Italy
A 5303	Ammiraglio Magnaghi	AGS	Italy
A 5309	Anteo	ARS	Italy
A 5310	Proteo	ARS	Italy
A 5311	Palinuro	ATS	Italy
A 5312	Amerigo Vespucci	ATS	Italy
A 5327	Stromboli	AOR	Italy
A 5329	Vesuvio	AOR	Italy
A 5354	Piave	AG	Italy
A 5375	Simeto	AG	Italy
M 5504	Castagno	MH	Italy
M 5505	Cedro	MH	Italy
M 5509	Gelso	MH	Italy
M 5516	Platano	MH	Italy
M 5519	Mandorlo	MH/ATS	Italy
M 5550	Lerici	MH/MSC	Italy
M 5551	Sapri	MH/MSC	Italy
M 5552	Milazzo	MH/MSC	Italy
M 5553	Vieste	MH/MSC	Italy
M 5554	Gaeta	MH/MSC	Italy
M 5555	Termoli	MH/MSC	Italy
M 5556	Alghero	MH/MSC	Italy
M 5557	Numana	MH/MSC	Italy
M 5558	Crotone	MH/MSC	Italy
M 5559	Viareggio	MH/MSC	Italy
P 6501	Muray Jip	FFLG	UAE
P 6502	Das	FFLG	UAE
ASU 7010	Akizuki	AD	Japan
ASU 7012	Teruzuki	AS	Japan
ASU 7016	Kitikami	ATS	Japan
L 9011	Foudre	TCD	France
L 9021	Ouragan	TCD	France
L 9022	Orage	TCD	France
L 9030	Champlain	LST	France
L 9031	Francis Garnier	LST	France
L 9032	Dumont D'Urville	LST	France
L 9033	Jacques Cartier	LST	France
L 9034	La Grandière	LST	France
L 9077	Bougainville	TCD	France
L 9892	San Giorgio	LPD	Italy
L 9893	San Marco	LPD/AG	Italy
L 9894	San Giusto	LPD	Italy

Ship Reference Section

(See also Glossary)

1. Details of major warships are grouped under six separate non-printable headings. These are:-

   (a) **Number and Class Name**. Totals of vessels per class are listed as 'active + building (proposed)'.
   (b) **Building Programme**. This includes builders' names and key dates. In general the 'laid down' column reflects keel laying but modern shipbuilding techniques are making it increasingly difficult to be specific about the start date of actual construction. In this edition any date after March 1993 is projected or estimated and therefore liable to change.
   (c) **Hull**. This section tends to have only specification and performance parameters and contains little free text. Hull related details such as **Military lift** and **Cargo capacity** may be included when appropriate. **Displacement** and **Measurement** tonnages, **Dimensions**, **Horsepower** etc are defined in the Glossary. Throughout the life of a ship its displacement tends to creep upwards as additional equipment is added and redundant fixtures and fittings are left in place. For the same reasons, ships of the same class, active in different navies, frequently have different displacements and other dissimilar characteristics. Unless otherwise stated the lengths given are overall. Sustained maximum horsepower is given where the information is available and may not be the same for similar engines operating in different hulls under different conditions.
   (d) **Weapon Systems**. This section contains operational details and some free text on weapons and sensors which are laid out in a consistent order using the same sub-headings throughout the book. The titles are:- **Missiles** (sub-divided into SLBM, SSM, SAM, A/S); **Guns** (numbers of barrels are given and the rate of fire is 'per barrel' unless stated otherwise); **Torpedoes**; **A/S mortars**; **Depth charges**; **Mines**; **Countermeasures**; **Combat data systems**; **Fire control**; **Radars**; **Sonars**. The Fire control heading is used for weapons' direction equipment. In most cases the performance specifications are those of the manufacturer and may therefore be considered to be at the top end of the spectrum of effective performance. So-called 'operational effectiveness' is difficult to define, depends upon many variables and in the context of range may be considerably less than the theoretical maximum. Numbers inserted in the text refer to similar numbers included on line drawings.
   (e) **Aircraft**. Only the types and numbers are included here. Where appropriate each country has a separate section listing overall numbers and operational parameters of frontline shipborne and land-based maritime aircraft, normally included after the Frigate section. The main exception to this is that in the countries which only have Light Forces the aircraft details will be towards the end of the warship section.
   (f) **General Comments**. A maximum of six sub-headings are used to sweep up the variety of additional information which is available but has no logical place in the other sections. These headings are: **Programmes**; **Modernisation**; **Structure**; **Operational**; **Sales** and **Opinion**. The last of these allows space for informed comment.

2. Minor or less important ship entries follow the same format except that there is often much less detail in the first four headings and all additional remarks are put together under the single heading of **Comment**. The distinction between major and minor depends upon editorial judgement and is primarily a function of firepower. The age of the ship or class and its relative importance within the Navy concerned is also taken into account.

3. The space devoted to frontline maritime aircraft reflects the importance of air power as an addition to the naval weapon systems armoury, but the format used is necessarily brief and covers only numbers, roles and operational characteristics. Greater detail can be found in *Jane's All the World's Aircraft* and the appropriate volume of the *Jane's Weapon Systems* series.

4. Other than for coastal navies, tables are included at the front of each country section with such things as strength of the fleet, senior appointments, personnel numbers, bases etc. There is also a list of pennant numbers and a deletions column covering the previous three years. If you can't find your favourite ship, always look in the Deletions list first.

5. No addenda is included because modern typesetting technology allows changes to the main text to be made up to a few weeks before publication.

6. Shipbuilding companies and weapons manufacturers frequently change their names by merger or takeover. As far as possible the published name shows the title when the ship was completed or weapon system installed. It is therefore historically accurate.

7. Like many descriptive terms in international naval nomenclature, differences between Coast Guards, Armed Police craft, Customs and other paramilitary maritime forces are often indistinct and particular to an individual nation. Such vessels are usually included if they have a paramilitary function.

8. Where major defence industries build a speculative or demonstrator vessel, it is usually mentioned in a **Note**. Full details are only given if the ship is commissioned into the Navy.

9. When selecting photographs for inclusion, priority is given to those that have been taken most recently. A glossy picture five years old may look nice but often does not show the ship as it is now.

10. The Ship Reference section is geared to the professional user who needs to be able to make an assessment of the fighting characteristics of a Navy or class of ship without having to cross refer to other Navies and sections of the book. Much effort has also been made to prevent entries spilling across from one page to another.

ALBANIA

Personnel

(a) 1993: 3300 including 400 coastal defence
(b) Ratings on three year military service

Bases

Durazzo (Durresi), Valona (Vlorë), Sazan Island (Gulf of Vlorë), Sarande, Shingjin, Himara.

General

The Navy is slowly emerging from years of isolation following the loss of Soviet and Chinese support in the 1980s. Operational effectiveness is very low due to a lack of spares and the age of most of the ships.

Pennant Numbers

Pennant numbers are changed at intervals.

Mercantile Marine

Lloyd's Register of Shipping:
 24 vessels of 59 060 tons gross

DELETIONS

1990 3 Huchuan class, 3 PO 2 class
1991 1 T 43

SUBMARINES

2 Ex-SOVIET WHISKEY CLASS

522   523

Displacement, tons: 1080 surfaced; 1350 dived
Dimensions, feet (metres): 249.3 × 21.3 × 16.1 *(76 × 6.5 × 4.9)*
Main machinery: Diesel-electric; 2 Type 37-D diesels; 4000 hp(m) *(2.94 MW)*; 2 motors; 2700 hp(m) *(1.98 MW)*; 2 shafts
Speed, knots: 18 surfaced; 14 dived; 7 snorting
Range, miles: 8500 at 10 kts surfaced
Complement: 54

Torpedoes: 6—21 in *(533 mm)* tubes (4 bow, 2 stern). 12 obsolescent Soviet Type 53; dual purpose; pattern active/passive homing up to 20 km *(10.8 nm)* at up to 45 kts; warhead 400 kg.
Mines: 24 instead of torpedoes.
Radars: Surface search: Snoop Plate; I band.
Sonars: Tamir; passive; high frequency.

Programmes: Two transferred from USSR in 1960 and two others acquired from the USSR in mid-1961.
Structure: Diving depth, 150 m *(500 ft)*.
Operational: A third submarine of the class is used as a harbour training boat and charging station. The fourth has been deleted. Based at Sazan and probably unfit to dive.

WHISKEY   1989

LIGHT FORCES

Note: 12 P4 patrol craft still have limited operational status.

2 Ex-SOVIET KRONSHTADT CLASS (LARGE PATROL CRAFT)

414   415

Displacement, tons: 303 standard; 335 full load
Dimensions, feet (metres): 170.9 × 21.3 × 6.9 *(52.1 × 6.5 × 2.1)*
Main machinery: 3 Kolomna Type 9-D-8 diesels; 3000 hp(m) *(2.2 MW)* sustained; 3 shafts
Speed, knots: 18. **Range, miles:** 1400 at 12 kts
Complement: 51 (4 officers)

Guns: 1—3.5 in *(85 mm)*/52; 85° elevation; 18 rounds/minute to 15.5 km *(8.5 nm)*; weight of shell 9.5 kg.
 1—37 mm/63; 85° elevation; 160 rounds/minute to 4 km *(2.2 nm)*; weight of shell 0.7 kg.
 6—12.7 mm (3 vertical twin) MGs.
A/S mortars: 2 RBU 1200 five-tubed rocket launchers; range 2 km; warhead 34 kg.
Depth charges: 2 projectors; 2 racks.
Mines: 2 rails; approx 8 mines.
Radars: Surface search: Ball Gun; E/F band; range 37 km *(20 nm)*.
 Navigation: Neptun; I band.
IFF: High Pole.

Programmes: Four were transferred from the USSR in 1958. Albania sent two for A/S updating in 1960 and two others in 1961. Two subsequently deleted, but the two survivors were operational in 1992.

KRONSHTADT   1989

29 Ex-CHINESE HUCHUAN CLASS
(FAST ATTACK HYDROFOIL—TORPEDO)

121-129   227-232   311-315   410-418

Displacement, tons: 39 standard; 45 full load
Dimensions, feet (metres): 71.5 × 20.7 × 11.8 (hullborne) *(21.8 × 6.3 × 3.6)*
Main machinery: 3 Type M 50F diesels; 2200 hp(m) *(1.6 MW)* sustained; 2 shafts
Speed, knots: 50 foilborne. **Range, miles:** 500 at 30 kts
Complement: 11

Guns: 4—14.5 mm (2 twin) MGs.
Torpedoes: 2—21 in *(533 mm)* tubes. Obsolescent Soviet Type 53.
Radars: Surface search/fire control: Skin Head; I band; range 37 km *(20 nm)*.

Programmes: Built in Shanghai and transferred as follows; six in 1968, 15 in 1969, two in 1970, seven in 1971, two in June 1974. Three deleted.
Structure: Have foils forward while the stern planes on the surface.
Operational: Not all are seaworthy. One escaped to Italy in May 1991 and was seized by the Italian authorities.

HUCHUAN   1983

6 Ex-CHINESE SHANGHAI II CLASS (FAST ATTACK CRAFT—GUN)

150-152   614-616

Displacement, tons: 113 standard; 131 full load
Dimensions, feet (metres): 127.3 × 17.7 × 5.6 *(38.8 × 5.4 × 1.7)*
Main machinery: 2 Type L-12V-180 diesels; 2400 hp(m) *(1.76 MW)* (forward)
 2 Type 12-D-6 diesels; 1820 hp(m) *(1.34 MW)* (aft); 4 shafts
Speed, knots: 30. **Range, miles:** 700 at 16.5 kts
Complement: 34

Guns: 4 China 37 mm/63 (2 twin); 85° elevation; 180 rounds/minute to 8.5 km *(4.6 nm)*; weight of shell 1.42 kg.
 4 USSR 25 mm/60 (2 twin); 85° elevation; 270 rounds/minute to 3 km *(1.6 nm)*; weight of shell 0.34 kg.
Depth charges: 2 projectors; 8 depth charges.
Mines: Rails can be fitted; probably only 10 mines.
Radars: Surface search/fire control: Skin Head; I band; range 37 km *(20 nm)*.
Sonars: Hull-mounted set probably fitted.

Comment: Four transferred in mid-1974 and two in 1975. Doubtful operational status.

SHANGHAI II (old number)   1990

3 Ex-SOVIET PO 2 CLASS (COASTAL PATROL CRAFT)

Displacement, tons: 56 full load
Dimensions, feet (metres): 70.5 × 11.5 × 3.3 *(21.5 × 3.5 × 1)*
Main machinery: 1 Type 3-D-12 diesel; 300 hp(m) *(220 kW)* sustained; 1 shaft
Speed, knots: 12
Complement: 8
Guns: 2—12.7 mm MGs.

Comment: At least three have survived from a total of 11 transferred 1957-60. Previous minesweeping gear has been removed and the craft are used for utility roles.

PO 2   10/1990

4 ARCOR 25 CLASS (HARBOUR PATROL CRAFT)

Displacement, tons: 2.1 full load
Dimensions, feet (metres): 25.3 × 9.8 × 2.6 *(7.7 × 3 × 0.8)*
Speed, knots: 35
Complement: 2
Guns: 1—7.62 mm MG.

Comment: Delivered in November 1990. Four more may be acquired in due course.

ARCOR 25 *1990, Arcor*

LAKE AND HARBOUR PATROL CRAFT

Comment: A number of patrol boats are stationed on the lakes bordering Greece and the former Yugoslavia.

NAVAL PATROL CRAFT *5/1992*

MINE WARFARE FORCES

1 Ex-SOVIET T 43 CLASS (MINESWEEPERS—OCEAN)

Displacement, tons: 500 standard; 580 full load
Dimensions, feet (metres): 190.2 × 27.6 × 6.9 *(58 × 8.4 × 2.1)*
Main machinery: 2 Kolomna Type 9-D-8 diesels; 2000 hp(m) *(1.47 MW)* sustained; 2 shafts
Speed, knots: 15. **Range, miles:** 3000 at 10 kts; 2000 at 14 kts
Complement: 65

Guns: 2—37 mm/63 (twin); 85° elevation; 160 rounds/minute to 9 km *(5 nm)*; weight of shell 0.7 kg.
8—12.7 mm MGs.
Depth charges: 2 projectors.
Mines: 16.
Radars: Air/surface search: Ball End; E/F band.
Navigation: Neptun; I band.
Sonars: Hull-mounted set probably fitted.

Programmes: Two transferred in 1960. One deleted and the last survivor is probably non-operational.

T 43 (old number) *1988*

4 Ex-SOVIET T 301 CLASS (MINESWEEPERS—INSHORE)

Displacement, tons: 146 standard; 160 full load
Dimensions, feet (metres): 124.7 × 16.7 × 5.2 *(38 × 5.1 × 1.6)*
Main machinery: 3—6-cyl diesels; 1440 hp(m) *(1.06 MW)*; 3 shafts
Speed, knots: 12. **Range, miles:** 2200 at 9 kts
Complement: 25
Guns: 2—37 mm/63; 160 rounds/minute to 8.5 km *(5 nm)*; weight of shell 0.7 kg.
4—12.7 mm (2 twin) MGs.
Mines: Mine rails fitted.

Comment: Transferred from the USSR—two in 1957, two in 1959 and two in 1960. Two marginally operational since 1979; two in reserve; two deleted.

T 301 (old number) *1988*

TANKERS

2 Ex-SOVIET KHOBI CLASS (SUPPORT TANKERS)

PATOS **SEMANI**

Displacement, tons: 700 light; 1500 full load
Measurement, tons: 1600 dwt
Dimensions, feet (metres): 206.6 × 33 × 14.8 *(63 × 10.1 × 4.5)*
Main machinery: 2 diesels; 1600 hp(m) *(1.18 MW)*; 2 shafts
Speed, knots: 13. **Range, miles:** 2500 at 12 kts
Complement: 35
Cargo capacity: 500 tons; oil fuel
Radars: Navigation: Neptun; I band.

Comment: Launched in 1956. Transferred from the USSR in September 1958 and February 1959. *Semani* is civilian manned.

1 Ex-SOVIET TOPLIVO I CLASS (YARD TANKER)

TOMB

Displacement, tons: 425 full load
Dimensions, feet (metres): 115 × 22 × 9.6 *(34.5 × 6.5 × 3)*
Main machinery: 1 diesel; 1 shaft
Speed, knots: 10. **Range, miles:** 400 at 7 kts
Complement: 16

Cargo capacity: 200 tons oil fuel
Comment: Transferred from the USSR in March 1960. Similar to Khobi class in appearance though smaller.

TOPLIVO *4/1992, van Ginderen Collection*

TUGS

Note: There are also two small harbour tugs; one is named *Bregdeti*.

2 Ex-SOVIET TUGUR CLASS

MUJOULQINAKU +1

Displacement, tons: 300 full load
Dimensions, feet (metres): 100.7 × 25.3 × 7.5 *(30.7 × 7.7 × 2.3)*
Main machinery: 2 boilers; 2 triple expansion steam reciprocating engines; 500 ihp(m) *(376 kW)*; 1 shaft
Speed, knots: 10

Comment: Built in Finland for the USSR in the 1950s.

TUGUR *7/1991, Erik Laursen*

ALBANIA — Auxiliaries

AUXILIARIES

Note: There are reported to be a dozen or so harbour and port tenders including a Duna class floating power barge, a water carrier and a barrack ship. The Atrek class submarine tender transferred from the USSR in 1961 as a depot ship was converted into a merchant ship.

2 Ex-SOVIET SHALANDA I CLASS

SERANDE   SAZAN

Comment: Civilian freighters transferred in early 1960s. One used as AKL and one as YF.

SHALANDA   3/1991, Erik Laursen

1 Ex-SOVIET POLUCHAT I CLASS

SKENDERBEU

Displacement, tons: 70 standard; 100 full load
Dimensions, feet (metres): 97.1 × 19 × 4.8 (29.6 × 5.8 × 1.5)
Main machinery: 2 Type M 50 diesels; 2200 hp(m) (1.6 MW) sustained; 2 shafts
Speed, knots: 20. Range, miles: 1500 at 10 kts
Complement: 15
Guns: 2—14.5 mm MGs.

Comment: Used for torpedo recovery. Transferred in 1958.

POLUCHAT   1989

1 Ex-SOVIET SEKSTAN CLASS (DEGAUSSING SHIP)

SHENJIN

Displacement, tons: 280 standard; 400 full load
Dimensions, feet (metres): 133.8 × 30.5 × 14.1 (40.8 × 9.3 × 4.3)
Main machinery: 1 diesel; 400 hp(m) (294 kW); 1 shaft
Speed, knots: 11. Range, miles: 1000 at 11 kts
Complement: 24
Cargo capacity: 115 tons

Comment: Built in Finland in 1956. Transferred from the USSR in 1960.

1 Ex-SOVIET NYRYAT 1 CLASS (DIVING TENDER)

SQIPETARI

Displacement, tons: 120 full load
Dimensions, feet (metres): 93 × 18 × 5.5 (28.4 × 5.5 × 1.7)
Main machinery: Diesel; 450 hp(m) (330 kW); 1 shaft
Speed, knots: 12.5. Range, miles: 1600 at 10 kts
Complement: 15

Comment: Built about 1955.

NYRYAT 1   4/1992, van Ginderen Collection

ALGERIA

Headquarters' Appointments

Commander of the Navy:
General Chabane Ghodbane
Inspector General of the Navy:
Colonel Abdelmadjid Taright

Personnel

(a) 1993: 6800 (Navy); 630 (Coast Guard)
(b) Voluntary service

Bases

Algiers, Annaba, Mers-el-Kebir

Mercantile Marine

Lloyd's Register of Shipping:
149 vessels of 921 496 tons gross

Strength of the Fleet

Type	Active	Building
Submarines	2	(2)
Frigates	3	—
Corvettes	4	2
Fast Attack Craft (Missile)	11	—
Fast Attack Craft (Gun)	12	3
Minesweepers—Ocean	1	(2)
LSLs	2	—
LCT	1	—
Miscellaneous	6	—
Coast Guard	39	—

SUBMARINES

2 + (2) SOVIET KILO CLASS (TYPE 877)

Displacement, tons: 2325 surfaced; 3076 dived
Dimensions, feet (metres): 243.8 × 32.8 × 21.7 (74.3 × 10 × 6.6)
Main machinery: Diesel-electric; 2 diesels; 3650 hp(m) (2.68 MW); 2 generators; 1 motor; 5900 hp(m) (4.34 MW); 1 shaft
Speed, knots: 20 dived; 10 surfaced; 9 snorting
Range, miles: 6000 at 7 kts surfaced; 400 at 3 kts dived
Complement: 45

Torpedoes: 6—21 in (533 mm) tubes. 18 Soviet Type 53; dual purpose; pattern active/passive homing up to 20 km (10.8 nm) at up to 45 kts; warhead 400 kg.
Mines: 36 in lieu of torpedoes.
Countermeasures: ESM: Brick Group; radar warning.
Radars: Surface search: Snoop Tray; I band.
Sonars: Sharks Teeth; hull-mounted; passive/active search and attack; medium frequency.
Mouse Roar; active attack; high frequency.

Programmes: New construction hulls; first one delivered in October 1987, second in January 1988 as replacements for the Romeo class. Two more expected in due course when funds are available.
Structure: Diving depth, 300 m (985 ft).

KILO   1987

FRIGATES

Note: Three new frigate orders projected for 1994. First to be built in lead shipyard, remainder in Algeria.

3 SOVIET KONI CLASS (TYPE II)

Name	No	Builders	Commissioned
MOURAD RAIS	901	Zelenodolsk Shipyard	Dec 1980
RAIS KELLICH	902	Zelenodolsk Shipyard	Apr 1982
RAIS KORFOU	903	Zelenodolsk Shipyard	Jan 1985

Displacement, tons: 1440 standard; 1900 full load
Dimensions, feet (metres): 316.3 × 41.3 × 11.5 *(96.4 × 12.6 × 3.5)*
Main machinery: CODAG; 1 SGW, Nikolayev, M8B gas turbine (centre shaft); 18 000 hp(m) *(13.25 MW)* sustained; 2 Russki B-68 diesels; 15 820 hp(m) *(11.63 MW)* sustained; 3 shafts
Speed, knots: 27 gas; 22 diesel. **Range, miles:** 1800 at 14 kts
Complement: 130

Missiles: SAM: SA-N-4 Gecko twin launcher ❶; semi-active radar homing to 15 km *(8 nm)* at 2.5 Mach; height envelope 9-3048 m *(29.5-10 000 ft)*; warhead 50 kg; 20 missiles. Some anti-surface capability.
Guns: 4—3 in *(76 mm)*/60 (2 twin) ❷; 80° elevation; 90 rounds/minute to 15 km *(8 nm)*; weight of shell 6.8 kg.
4—30 mm/65 (2 twin) ❸; 85° elevation; 500 rounds/minute to 5 km *(2.7 nm)*; weight of shell 0.54 kg.
A/S mortars: 2—12-barrelled RBU 6000 ❹; range 6000 m; warhead 31 kg.
Depth charges: 2 racks.
Mines: Rails; capacity 22.
Countermeasures: Decoys: 2—16-barrelled chaff launchers.
ESM: Watch Dog. Cross Loop D/F.
Radars: Air/surface search: Strut Curve ❺; F band; range 110 km *(60 nm)* for 2 m² target.
Navigation: Don 2; I band.
Fire Control: Hawk screech ❻; I band; range 27 km *(15 nm)* (for guns).
Drum tilt ❼; H/I band (for search and acquisition).
Pop Group ❽; F/H/I band (for missile control).
IFF: High Pole B. Two Square Head.
Sonars: Hull-mounted; active search and attack; medium frequency.

Programmes: New construction ships with hull numbers 5, 7 and 10 in sequence. Others of the class built for Cuba, Yugoslavia, East Germany and Libya. Interest was shown in ex-GDR ships in 1991 but sale was rejected by the German Government.
Modernisation: New generators being fitted in 1992/93.
Structure: The deck house aft in Type II Konis is thought to house air-conditioning machinery. No torpedo tubes.

MOURAD RAIS *(Scale 1 : 900), Ian Sturton*

MOURAD RAIS — *1992*

CORVETTES

3 SOVIET NANUCHKA II CLASS (MISSILE CORVETTES)

RAIS HAMIDOU 801   SALAH RAIS 802   RAIS ALI 803

Displacement, tons: 850 full load
Dimensions, feet (metres): 194.5 × 38.7 × 8.5 *(59.3 × 11.8 × 2.6)*
Main machinery: 3 Type M 507 diesels; 21 600 hp(m) *(15.9 MW)* sustained; 3 shafts
Speed, knots: 36. **Range, miles:** 2500 at 12 kts; 900 at 31 kts
Complement: 70 (12 officers)

Missiles: SSM: 4 SS-N-2B; active radar or IR homing to 46 km *(25 nm)* at 0.9 Mach; warhead 513 kg. Preset altitude up to 300 m.
SAM: SA-N-4 Gecko twin launcher; semi-active radar homing to 15 km *(8 nm)* at 2.5 Mach; height envelope 9-3048 m *(29.5-10 000 ft)*; warhead 50 kg; 20 missiles. Some anti-surface capability.
Guns: 2—57 mm/80 (twin); 85° elevation; 120 rounds/minute to 6 km *(3.3 nm)*; weight of shell 2.8 kg.
Countermeasures: Decoys: 2—16-barrelled chaff launchers.
ESM: Bell Tap. Cross Loop; D/F.
Radars: Surface search: Square Tie (Radome); I band; range 73 km *(40 nm)* or limits of radar horizon.
Navigation: Don 2; I band.
Fire control: Pop Group; F/H/I band (SAN-4). Muff Cob; G/H band.
IFF: Square Head. High Pole.

Programmes: Delivered 4 July 1980, 9 February 1981, 8 May 1982 from Baltic. New construction.
Modernisation: Plans to re-engine with new diesels.

1 + 2 DJEBEL CHINOISE CLASS (CORVETTE)

DJEBEL CHINOISE 351   352   353

Displacement, tons: 496 standard; 540 full load
Dimensions, feet (metres): 191.6 × 27.9 × 8.5 *(58.4 × 8.5 × 2.6)*
Main machinery: 3 MTU 20V 538 TB92 diesels; 12 800 hp(m) *(9.4 MW)*; 3 shafts
Speed, knots: 31
Complement: 52 (6 officers)

Guns: 1 OTO Melara 3 in *(76 mm)*/62 (not fitted).
2 Breda 40 mm/70 (twin); 85° elevation; 300 rounds/minute to 12.5 km *(6.8 nm)*; weight of shell 0.96 kg.
4 USSR 23 mm (2 twin).
Fire control: Optronic director for 76 mm.
Radars: Surface search: Racal Decca 1226; I band.

Programmes: Ordered July 1983. Project 802 is a class of corvette building at ECRN, Mers-el-Kebir with Bulgarian assistance. First one launched 3 February 1985 and completed trials in 1988. Second launched in early 1990 but progress has been very slow due to shipyard debt problems.
Structure: Hull size suggests association with Bazan Cormoran class for Morocco.

RAIS ALI *1982, Ralf Bendfeldt*

DJEBEL CHINOISE (without 76 mm gun or optronic director) *11/1988, French Navy*

6 ALGERIA / Light forces — Amphibious forces

LIGHT FORCES

9 Ex-SOVIET OSA II and 2 OSA I CLASSES (TYPE 205)
(FAST ATTACK CRAFT—MISSILE)

OSA II—644-652
OSA I—642-643

Displacement, tons: 171 standard; 210 full load (Osa I); 245 full load (Osa II)
Dimensions, feet (metres): 126.6 × 24.9 × 8.8 *(38.6 × 7.6 × 2.7)*
Main machinery: 3 Type M 504 diesels; 10 800 hp(m) *(7.94 MW)* sustained; 3 shafts (Osa II)
3 Type M 503A diesels; 8025 hp(m) *(5.9 MW)* sustained; 3 shafts (Osa I)
Speed, knots: 35 (Osa I); 37 (Osa II). **Range, miles:** 400 at 34 kts (Osa I); 500 at 35 kts (Osa II)
Complement: 30

Missiles: SSM: 4 SS-N-2A Styx (Osa I) or 2B (Osa II); active radar or IR homing to 46 km *(25 nm)* at 0.9 Mach; warhead 513 kg.
Guns: 4—30 mm/65 (2 twin); 85° elevation; 500 rounds/minute to 5 km *(2.7 nm)*; weight of shell 0.54 kg.
Radars: Surface search: Square Tie; I band.
Fire Control: Drum Tilt; H/I band.
IFF: Two Square Head. High Pole B.

Programmes: One Osa I was delivered by the USSR on 7 October 1967. Two others transferred later in same year. Osa II transferred 1976-77 (four), fifth in September 1978, sixth in December 1978, next pair in 1979 and one from the Black Sea on 7 December 1981. Osa II No 643 was rebuilt after an explosion in 1981.
Modernisation: Plans to re-engine were reported as starting in late 1992.

OSA 652   1989

12 + 3 KEBIR CLASS (FAST ATTACK CRAFT—GUN)

| EL YADEKH | 341 | EL KECHEF | 343 | EL RASSED | 345 | 347-349 |
| EL MOURAKEB | 342 | EL MOUTARID | 344 | EL DJARI | 346 | 360-365 |

Displacement, tons: 166 standard; 200 full load
Dimensions, feet (metres): 123 × 22.6 × 5.6 *(37.5 × 6.9 × 1.7)*
Main machinery: 2 MTU 12V 538 TB92 diesels; 5110 hp(m) *(3.8 MW)*; 2 shafts (see *Structure*)
Speed, knots: 27. **Range, miles:** 3300 at 12 kts; 2600 at 15 kts
Complement: 27 (3 officers)

Guns: 1 OTO Melara 3 in *(76 mm)*/62 compact (in first five); 85° elevation; 85 rounds/minute to 16 km *(9 nm)* anti-surface; 12 km *(6.5 nm)* anti-aircraft; weight of shell 6 kg.
4 USSR 25 mm/60 (2 twin) (remainder); 85° elevation; 270 rounds/minute to 3 km *(1.6 nm)*; weight of shell 0.34 kg.
2 USSR 23 mm (twin).
Fire control: Lawrence Scott optronic director.
Radars: Surface search: Racal Decca 1226; I band.

Programmes: Design and first pair ordered from Brooke Marine in June 1981. First left for Algeria without armament in September 1982, second arrived Algiers 12 June 1983. The remainder assembled or built at ECRN, Mers-el-Kebir with assistance from Vosper Thornycroft. 346 commissioned 10 November 1985. *347-349* ordered June 1986, and delivered in 1988-89; *360-362* ordered in August 1989 and in service by the end of 1991. *363-365* were still under construction in early 1993. More of the class may be built in due course.
Structure: Same hull as Barbados *Trident*. There are some variations in armament and *363-365* are reported as having lower powered engines.
Operational: Six of the class may have been transferred temporarily to the Coast Guard.

EL MOURAKEB and EL YADEKH   5/1990

MINE WARFARE FORCES

Note: Orders for two new vessels projected for the mid-1990s.

1 Ex-SOVIET T 43 CLASS (MINESWEEPERS—OCEAN)

M 522

Displacement, tons: 500 standard; 580 full load
Dimensions, feet (metres): 190.2 × 27.6 × 6.9 *(58 × 8.4 × 2.1)*
Main machinery: 2 Kolomna Type 9-D-8 diesels; 2000 hp(m) *(1.47 MW)* sustained; 2 shafts
Speed, knots: 15. **Range, miles:** 3000 at 10 kts
Complement: 65

Guns: 2—45 mm/85; 90° elevation; 75 rounds/minute to 9 km *(5 nm)*; weight of shell 2.2 kg.
A/S mortars: 2 projectors.
Mines: Can carry 16.
Radars: Navigation: Neptun; I band.

Programmes: Two transferred in 1968. One cannibalised for spares.

T 43 (old number)   1988

AMPHIBIOUS FORCES

2 LANDING SHIPS (LOGISTIC)

Name	No	Builders	Commissioned
KALAAT BENI HAMMAD	472	Brooke Marine, Lowestoft	Apr 1984
KALAAT BENI RACHED	473	Vosper Thornycroft Ltd	Oct 1984

Displacement, tons: 2450 full load
Dimensions, feet (metres): 305 × 50.9 × 8.1 *(93 × 15.5 × 2.5)*
Main machinery: 2 MTU 16V 1163 TB82 diesels; 8880 hp(m) *(6.5 MW)* sustained; 2 shafts
Speed, knots: 15. **Range, miles:** 3000 at 12 kts
Complement: 81
Military lift: 240 troops; 7 MBTs and 380 tons other cargo; 2 ton crane with athwartships travel

Guns: 2 Breda 40 mm/70 (twin); 85° elevation; 300 rounds/minute to 12.5 km *(6.8 nm)*; weight of shell 0.96 kg.
Countermeasures: Decoys: Wallop Barricade double layer chaff launchers.
Fire control: CSEE Naja optronic.
Radars: Navigation: Racal Decca TM 1226; I band.
Helicopters: Platform only.

Programmes: First ordered in June 1981, and launched 18 May 1983; second ordered 18 October 1982 and launched 15 May 1984. Similar hulls to Omani *Nasr El Bahr*.
Structure: These ships have a through tank deck closed by bow and stern ramps. The forward ramp is of two sections measuring length 18 m (when extended) × 5 m breadth, and the single section stern ramp measures 4.3 × 5 m with the addition of 1.1 m finger flaps. Both hatches can support a 60 ton tank, and are winch operated. In addition, side access doors are provided on each side forward. The tank deck side bulkheads extend 2.25 m above the upper deck between the forecastle and the forward end of the superstructure, and provide two hatch openings to the tank deck below.

KALAAT BENI RACHED   1985, Vosper Thornycroft

1 Ex-SOVIET POLNOCHNY B CLASS (TYPE 771) (LCT)

471

Displacement, tons: 760 standard; 834 full load
Dimensions, feet (metres): 246.1 × 31.5 × 7.5 *(75 × 9.6 × 2.3)*
Main machinery: 2 Kolomna Type 40-D diesels; 4400 hp(m) *(3.2 MW)* sustained; 2 shafts
Speed, knots: 19. **Range, miles:** 1000 at 18 kts
Complement: 40
Military lift: 180 troops; 350 tons including up to 6 tanks

Guns: 2—30 mm/65 (twin); 85° elevation; 500 rounds/minute to 5 km *(2.7 nm)*; weight of shell 0.54 kg.
2—140 mm 18-tubed rocket launchers; shore bombardment; range 9 km *(5 nm)*.
Radars: Navigation: Don 2; I band.
Fire Control: Drum Tilt; H/I band.
IFF: Square Head. High Pole A.

Programmes: Class built in Poland 1968-70. Transferred in August 1976.

POLNOCHNY 471   1990, van Ginderen Collection

LAND-BASED MARITIME AIRCRAFT

Numbers/Type: 2 Beechcraft Super King Air 200T.
Operational speed: 282 kts *(523 km/h)*.
Service ceiling: 35 000 ft *(10 670 m)*.
Range: 2030 nm *(3756 km)*.
Role/Weapon systems: Operated by air force for close-range EEZ operations. Sensors: Weather radar only. Weapons: Unarmed.

Numbers/Type: 8 Fokker F27-400/600.
Operational speed: 250 kts *(463 km/h)*.
Service ceiling: 25 000 ft *(7620 m)*.
Range: 2700 nm *(5000 km)*.
Role/Weapon systems: Visual reconnaissance duties in support of EEZ, particularly offshore platforms. Sensors: Weather radar and visual means only. Weapons: Limited armament.

MISCELLANEOUS

1 Ex-SOVIET POLUCHAT I CLASS (TRV)

A 641

Displacement, tons: 70 standard; 100 full load
Dimensions, feet (metres): 97.1 × 19 × 4.8 *(29.6 × 5.8 × 1.5)*
Main machinery: 2 Type M 50F diesels; 2200 hp(m) *(1.6 MW)* sustained; 2 shafts
Speed, knots: 20. **Range, miles:** 1500 at 10 kts
Complement: 15

1 Ex-SOVIET NYRYAT 1 CLASS (DIVING TENDER)

YAVDEZAN VP 650

Displacement, tons: 120 full load
Dimensions, feet (metres): 93 × 18 × 5.5 *(28.4 × 5.5 × 1.7)*
Main machinery: Diesel; 450 hp(m) *(330 kW)*; 1 shaft
Speed, knots: 12.5. **Range, miles:** 1600 at 10 kts
Complement: 15

Comment: Delivered in 1965.

1 SURVEY SHIP

EL IDRISSI A 673

Displacement, tons: 540 full load
Speed, knots:. **Complement:** 28 (6 officers)

Comment: Built by Matsukara, Japan and delivered 17 April 1980.

EL IDRISSI *9/1990*

2 SURVEY CRAFT

RAS TARSA   ALIDADE

Comment: Both of about 18 tons acquired in the early 1980s.

1 HARBOUR TUG

KADER A 210

Displacement, tons: 265 full load
Dimensions, feet (metres): 85.3 × 21.7 × 9.2 *(26 × 6.6 × 2.8)*
Main machinery: 2 diesels; 1900 hp(m) *(1.4 MW)*; 2 shafts
Speed, knots: 11

Comment: Acquired in 1989.

KADER *7/1989, van Ginderen Collection*

COAST GUARD

Note: Six Kebir class have been transferred temporarily from the Navy.

1 CHINESE SUPPORT SHIP

GC 261

Displacement, tons: 600 full load
Dimensions, feet (metres): 193.6 × 27.6 × 6.9 *(59 × 8.4 × 2.1)*
Main machinery: 2 diesels; 2200 hp(m) *(1.6 MW)*; 2 shafts
Speed, knots: 14
Complement: 60

Comment: Delivered by transporter ship in April 1990. The design appears to be a derivative of the T43 minesweeper but with a stern gantry.

GC 261 *7/1991*

7 CHINESE CHUI-E CLASS

GC 251-GC 257

Displacement, tons: 380 full load
Dimensions, feet (metres): 192.8 × 23.6 × 6 *(58.8 × 7.2 × 2.2)*
Main machinery: 2 PCR/Kolomna diesels; 2200 hp(m) *(1.6 MW)*; 2 shafts
Speed, knots: 24. **Range, miles:** 1400 at 15 kts
Complement: 42
Guns: 2 China 37 mm/63 (twin).

Comment: Two delivered by transporter ship in April 1990 and described as training vessels. Two more acquired in January 1991, and the last three in late 1992. Hainan class hull with modified propulsion and superstructure.

GC 253 *1992*

10 BAGLIETTO TYPE 20 GC

| GC 100 | GC 113 | GC 221 | GC 235 | GC 237 |
| GC 112 | GC 114 | GC 222 | GC 236 | GC 329 |

Displacement, tons: 44 full load
Dimensions, feet (metres): 66.9 × 17.1 × 5.5 *(20.4 × 5.2 × 1.7)*
Main machinery: 2 CRM 18DS diesels; 2660 hp(m) *(2 MW)*; 2 shafts
Speed, knots: 36. **Range, miles:** 445 at 20 kts
Complement: 11 (3 officers)
Guns: 1 Oerlikon 20 mm.

Comment: The first pair delivered by Baglietto, Varazze in August 1976 and the remainder in pairs at two monthly intervals. Fitted with three radar sets and optical fire control. Some may have been scrapped.

BAGLIETTO 20 GC CRAFT *1978, Baglietto*

8   ALGERIA / Customs service — ANGOLA / Amphibious forces

6 MANGUSTA CLASS

OMBRINE GC 323	REQUIN GC 331	MARSOUIN GC 333
DORADE GC 324	ESPADON GC 332	MURÈNE GC 334

Displacement, tons: 91 full load
Dimensions, feet (metres): 98.4 × 19 × 7.2 *(30 × 5.8 × 2.2)*
Main machinery: 3 MTU diesels; 4000 hp(m) *(2.94 MW)*; 3 shafts
Speed, knots: 32.5. **Range, miles:** 800 at 24 kts
Complement: 14 (3 officers)
Guns: Can carry 1 Breda Bofors 40 mm/70 and 1 Oerlikon 20 mm.
Radars: Navigation: SMA 3 RM; I band; range 73 km *(40 nm)*.

Comment: First delivered early 1977 by Baglietto, Varazze, Italy. Some may have been scrapped.

3 CHINESE SAR CRAFT

GC 231-GC 233

Comment: 25 m SAR craft delivered by transporter ship which arrived in Algiers in April 1990. A fourth of class may be acquired. Unarmed.

GC 231-GC 233   1991

12 FISHERY PROTECTION CRAFT

| JEBEL ANTAR | JEBEL HANDA | +10 |

Displacement, tons: 18
Speed, knots: 15

Comment: Completed 1982/83 at Mers-el-Kebir.

CUSTOMS SERVICE

3 P 1200 CLASS

| BOUZAGZA | DJURDJURA | HODNA |

Displacement, tons: 39 full load
Dimensions, feet (metres): 68.2 × 18.4 × 5.2 *(20.8 × 5.6 × 1.6)*
Main machinery: 2 MAN D2540 diesels; 1300 hp(m) *(955 kW)*; 2 shafts
Speed, knots: 33. **Range, miles:** 300 at 22 kts
Complement: 4
Guns: 2—7.62 mm MGs.

Comment: Ordered from Watercraft Ltd, Shoreham, England in late 1984. Completed 21 November 1985. GRP construction.

2 P 802 CLASS

| AURES | HOGGAR |

Comment: Ordered from Watercraft Ltd, Shoreham, England in late 1984. 8 m craft with two Volvo AQAD 40 inboard/outboard diesels for speed of 30+ kts. Completed 21 November 1985.

ANGOLA

Personnel
(a) 1993: 1200
(b) Voluntary service

Bases
Luanda, Lobito, Namibe. (There are other good harbours available on the 1000 mile coastline.) Naval HQ at Luanda on Ila de Luanda is fortified, as is Namibe.

Mercantile Marine
Lloyd's Register of Shipping:
   113 vessels of 93 942 tons gross

LIGHT FORCES

Note: In the late 1970s and early 1980s six Osa II, four Shershen, one Zhuk and two Poluchat patrol vessels was acquired from the former Soviet Union to join the four Portuguese Argos class commissioned in the mid-1960s. None of these vessels was seaworthy at the end of 1992 although most of them are still, in theory, in the Naval order of battle.

0 + 4 BAZAN TYPE T 26.5 (COASTAL PATROL CRAFT)

| MANDUME P 101 | POLAR P 102 | ATLANTICO P 103 | GOLFINHO P 104 |

Displacement, tons: 105 full load
Dimensions, feet (metres): 95.6 × 19.5 × 4.9 *(29.1 × 5.9 × 1.5)*
Main machinery: 2 Paxman Vega 16 CM diesels; 3914 hp *(2.92 MW)* sustained; 2 shafts
Speed, knots: 25. **Range, miles:** 800 at 15 kts
Complement: 11 (1 officer)

Guns: 1 Oerlikon 20 mm. 1—12.7 mm MG.
Radars: Surface search: I band.

Comment: Ordered 27 March 1991. First two laid down November 1991 at Bazan Shipyard, San Fernando; launched 11 September 1992, to commission in April 1993 if delivery is not delayed by UN embargoes. Subsequent in-service dates at three month intervals.

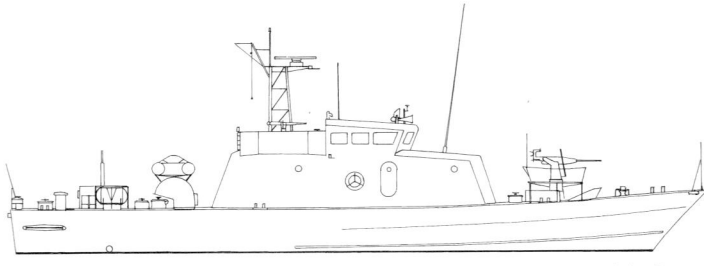

MANDUME   *(not to scale), Ian Sturton*

MINE WARFARE FORCES

2 Ex-SOVIET YEVGENYA CLASS

Displacement, tons: 77 standard; 90 full load
Dimensions, feet (metres): 80.4 × 18 × 4.6 *(24.5 × 5.5 × 1.4)*
Main machinery: 2 Type 3-D-12 diesels; 600 hp(m) *(440 kW)* sustained; 2 shafts
Speed, knots: 11. **Range, miles:** 300 at 10 kts
Complement: 10
Guns: 2 USSR 25 mm/80 (twin).
Radars: Navigation: Don 2; I band.
Sonars: VDS (lifted over stern on crane); minehunting; high frequency.

Comment: Both transferred in September 1987.

YEVGENYA class   *1988, P D Jones*

AMPHIBIOUS FORCES

Notes: (a) In addition to those below there are four derelict ex-Soviet T-4 class originally transferred in 1976. Also four out of nine ex-Portuguese LDM 400 class and three LDP 200 are in service but in very poor condition.
(b) 14 ex-GDR Frosch class acquired in 1991 for 'civilian' use.

3 Ex-SOVIET POLNOCHNY B CLASS (TYPE 771) (LCT)

Displacement, tons: 760 standard; 834 full load
Dimensions, feet (metres): 246.1 × 31.5 × 7.5 *(75 × 9.6 × 2.3)*
Main machinery: 2 Kolomna Type 40-D diesels; 4400 hp(m) *(3.2 MW)* sustained; 2 shafts
Speed, knots: 19. **Range, miles:** 1000 at 18 kts
Complement: 40
Military lift: 180 troops; 350 tons including up to 6 tanks

Guns: 4—30 mm/65 (2 twin); 85° elevation; 500 rounds/minute to 5 km *(2.7 nm)*; weight of shell 0.54 kg.
   2—140 mm 18-tubed rocket launchers; shore bombardment; range 9 km *(5 nm)*.
Radars: Navigation: Don 2 or Spin Trough; I band.
Fire control: Drum Tilt; H/I band.
IFF: Square Head.

Programmes: First transferred November 1977, the second 10 February 1979 and the third 11 December 1979.

POLNOCHNY class (Group B)

1 Ex-PORTUGUESE ALFANGE CLASS (LCT)

Name	No	Builders	Commissioned
Ex-**ALFANGE**	LDG 101	Estaleiros Navais do Mondego	1965

Displacement, tons: 500
Dimensions, feet (metres): 187 × 39 × 6.2 *(57 × 12 × 1.9)*
Main machinery: 2 diesels; 1000 hp(m) *(735 kW)*; 2 shafts
Speed, knots: 11
Complement: 20 (plus 35 troops)

Ex-ALFANGE *Portuguese Navy*

LAND-BASED MARITIME AIRCRAFT

Note: Two Aviocar C-218-300N may be delivered in 1993.

Numbers/Type: 2 Embraer EMB-111 Bandeirante.
Operational speed: 194 kts *(360 km/h)*.
Service ceiling: 25 500 ft *(7770 m)*.
Range: 1590 nm *(2945 km)*.
Role/Weapon systems: Armed MR and coastal patrol delivered in 1988. Sensors: APS-128 radar, limited EW. Weapons: ASV; 70 mm or 127 mm pods or rockets.

Numbers/Type: 4 Aerospatiale SA 365F Dauphin.
Operational speed: 140 kts *(260 km/h)*.
Service ceiling: 15 000 ft *(4575 m)*.
Range: 410 nm *(758 km)*.
Role/Weapon systems: ASV reconnaissance. Sensors: Possible radar fit.

DAUPHIN SA365F *1988 Aerospatiale*

Numbers/Type: 1 Fokker F27-600.
Operational speed: 250 kts *(46.3 km/h)*.
Service ceiling: 25 000 ft *(7620 m)*.
Range: 2700 nm *(5000 km)*.
Role/Weapon systems: Visual/radar reconnaissance. Sensors: Litton 360° radar. Weapons: None.

MARITIME POLICE

Note: A total of 11 Bazan-built harbour patrol craft acquired in 1992/93. One of 16 m, ten of 11 m and two of 7.9 m.

ANGUILLA

Commissioner of Police

Elliot Mc N Richardson CPM, JP

Mercantile Marine

Lloyd's Register of Shipping:
18 vessels of 5304 tons gross

DELETIONS

1991 *Mapleleaf,* 1 Interceptor class
1992 *Anguilletta*

1 HALMATIC M160 CLASS (INSHORE PATROL CRAFT)

DOLPHIN

Displacement, tons: 18 light
Dimensions, feet (metres): 52.5 × 15.4 × 4.6 *(16 × 4.7 × 1.4)*
Main machinery: 2 Detroit Diesels 6V-92TA; 520 hp *(390 kW)* sustained; 2 shafts
Speed, knots: 27. **Range, miles:** 500 at 17 kts
Complement: 8

Comment: Built by Halmatic and delivered 22 December 1989. Identical craft to Montserrat and Turks and Caicos Islands. GRP hulls. Rigid inflatable boat launched by gravity davit.

1 INSHORE PATROL CRAFT

LAPWING

Comment: 28 ft launch acquired in 1974 from Fairey Marine. Re-engined in 1992 with two Evinrude outboards; 450 hp *(330 kW)*.

DOLPHIN *1989, Halmatic*

ANTIGUA and BARBUDA

Headquarters' Appointment

Commanding Officer, Coastguard:
  Lieutenant Commander M J Wright

Base

St John's (capital).

Mercantile Marine

Lloyd's Register of Shipping:
  292 vessels of 611 795 tons gross

PATROL FORCES

1 SWIFT 65 ft CLASS

Name	No	Builders	Commissioned
LIBERTA	P 01	Swiftships, Morgan City	30 Apr 1984

Displacement, tons: 31.7 full load
Dimensions, feet (metres): 65.5 × 18.4 × 5 *(20 × 5.6 × 1.5)*
Main machinery: 2 Detroit Diesel 12V-71TA diesels; 840 hp *(616 kW)* sustained; 2 shafts
Speed, knots: 22. **Range, miles:** 250 at 18 kts
Complement: 9
Guns: 1—12.7 mm MG. 2—7.62 mm MGs.
Radars: Surface search: Furuno; I band.

Comment: Ordered in November 1983. Aluminium construction.

LIBERTA *1991, Antigua Coastguard*

ARGENTINA

Headquarters' Appointments

Chief of Naval General Staff:
  Admiral Jorge Osvaldo Ferrer
Deputy Commander-in-Chief Navy:
  Vice Admiral Fausto Juan Lopez
Naval Operations Commander:
  Vice Admiral Emilio Molina Pico

Senior Appointments

Commander Fleet:
  Rear Admiral Horacio F Reyser
Naval Area South:
  Rear Admiral Daniel Antonio Fusari
Naval Area Puerto Belgrano:
  Rear Admiral Eduardo Alfredo Rosenthal
Naval Area Fluvial:
  Captain Alfonso E Nicolas

Diplomatic Representation

Naval Attaché in Spain:
  Captain Raul Pueyrredon
Naval Attaché in Japan:
  Captain Luis A Garcia Bourimborde
Naval Attaché in Italy:
  Captain Fernando Sola
Naval Attaché in Germany and Holland:
  Captain Rodolfo Hasenbal
Naval Attaché in France:
  Captain Roberto O Roscoe
Naval Attaché in Brazil:
  Captain Arturo Massat
Naval Attaché in Chile:
  Captain Luis Posse
Naval Attaché in London:
  Captain Alberto C Secchi

Personnel

(a) 1993: 27 500 (4000 officers, 17 500 petty officers and ratings and 6000 conscripts)
Marine Corps: 6000 officers and men
(b) Volunteers plus 12 months' national service (being phased out)

Organisation

Naval Area Centre (HQ Puerto Belgrano) covers area from River Plate to Valdes Peninsula.
Naval Area South (HQ Ushuaia) covers coastal area from Valdes Peninsula to Drake Passage.
Naval Area Fluvial (HQ Buenos Aires) covers coast of River Plate.
Naval Area Antarctica (HQ Buenos Aires) covers Antarctica.

Bases

Buenos Aires (Dársena Norte): Some naval training establishments.
Rio Santiago (La Plata): Schools, naval shipbuilding yard (AFNE), 1 slipway, 1 floating crane.
Mar del Plata: Submarine base with slipway.
Puerto Belgrano: Main naval base, schools, 2 dry docks, 1 floating dock.
Ushuaia, Deseado, Dársena Sur: Small naval bases.

Naval Building Yards (being privatised)

(a) Astilleros y Fábricas Navales del Estado (AFNE), Rio Santiago.
(b) Tandanor, Dársena Norte (Planta 1) and Dársena Este (Planta 2); sold in 1991.
Planta 1 has two dry docks and two floating cocks. Planta 2 has two floating docks (A and B) and a synchrolift of 185 × 32 m.
(c) Astillero Domecq Garcia, Buenos Aires. Submarine building yard.

Coast Guard (Prefectura Naval Argentina)

In January 1992 the Coast Guard was limited to operations inside 12 mile territorial seas but this legislation was then cancelled in favour of the previous 200 mile operating zone.

Prefix to Ships' Names

ARA (Armada Republica Argentina)

Naval Aviation

Personnel: 2500
1st Naval Air Wing (Punta del Indio Naval Air Base): Naval Aviation School with Beech T-34Cs, Beech King Airs and Turbo Mentor T-34s.
2nd Naval Air Wing (Comandante Espora Naval Air Base): Anti Submarine Squadron with Grumman S-2E Trackers; 2nd Naval Helicopter Squadron with Agusta/Sikorsky S-H-3D and S-61D.
3rd Naval Air Wing (Comandante Espora Naval Air Base): 2nd Naval Fighter/Attack Squadron with Super Étendards; 1st Naval Helicopter Squadron with Alouette III.
4th Naval Air Wing (Punta Indio Naval Air Base): 1st Naval Attack Squadron with Macchi MB 326B and Embraer EMB 326 Xavantes; Naval Aerophotographic Squadron with Beech Queen Airs and Beech King Air 200s.
5th Naval Air Wing (Almirante Zar Naval Air Base): 1st Naval Logistic Support Squadron with Lockheed Electra; 2nd Naval Logistic Support Squadron with Fokker F28s
6th Naval Air Wing (Almirante Zar Naval Air Base): Naval Reconnaissance Squadron with Beech Queen Airs, Lockheed Electra L-188E and Pilatus PC-6.
Approximately half the aircraft, including most of the Super Étendards, are reported out of service due to shortage of spare parts but this situation was improving in early 1993.

Marine Corps

Organisation and Deployment

1st Marine Infantry Force (HQ Río Gallegos)
1st Marine Infantry Brigade (Baterías)
Amphibious Support Group (Puerto Belgrano)

1st Marine Infantry Battalion (HQ Baterías)
2nd Marine Infantry Battalion (Baterías)
3rd Marine Infantry Battalion (La Plata)
4th Marine Infantry Battalion (Río Gallegos)
5th Marine Infantry Battalion (Río Grande)

Marine Field Artillery Battalion (Puerto Belgrano)
Logistics Support Battalion (Baterías)
Amphibious Vehicles Battalion (Baterías)
Communications Battalion (Puerto Belgrano)
Marine A/A Battalion (Puerto Belgrano)
Scout Company (Baterías)
Marine A/T Company (Baterías)
Amphibious Engineers Company (Puerto Belgrano)
Amphibious Commandos Company (Baterías)
Navy Chief of Staff Security Battalion (Buenos Aires)
Puerto Belgrano Security Battalion (Puerto Belgrano)
There are Marine Security Companies in Buenos Aires, Rio Santiago, Punta Indio, Azul, Mar del Plata, Comandante Espora Naval Air Base, Zárate, Ezeiza, Trelew, Ushuaia and Rio Grande.

Strength of the Fleet

Type	Active (Reserve)	Building (Planned)
Patrol Submarines	4	3
Aircraft Carriers	(1)	—
Destroyers	6	—
Frigates	7	2
Patrol Ships	8	—
Fast Attack Craft (Gun)	2	—
Coastal Patrol Craft	4	—
Minehunters/sweepers	6	—
Landing Ship (Tank)	1	—
Minor Landing Craft	20	—
Survey/Oceanographic Ships	3	—
Survey Launches	2	—
Transports	4	(1)
Training Ships	2	—
Tugs	13	—
Floating Docks	5	—
Sail Training Ships	4	—

Mercantile Marine

Lloyd's Register of Shipping:
  423 vessels of 876 477 tons gross

DELETION

1992 *Tequara* (for sale)

PENNANT LIST

Submarines

S 31	Salta
S 32	San Luis
S 41	Santa Cruz
S 42	San Juan
S 43	Santa Fé (bldg)
S 44	Santiago del Estero (bldg)

Aircraft Carrier

V 2	Veinticinco de Mayo

Destroyers

D 1	Hercules
D 2	Santisima Trinidad
D 10	Almirante Brown
D 11	La Argentina
D 12	Heroina
D 13	Sarandi

Frigates

31	Drummond
32	Guerrico
33	Granville
41	Espora
42	Rosales
43	Spiro
44	Parker
45	Robinson (bldg)
46	Gomez Roca (bldg)

Patrol Ships

A 1	Com G Irigoyen
A 2	Teniente Olivieri
A 3	Francisco de Gurruchaga
A 9	Alferez Sobral
A 10	Comodoro Somellera
P 20	Murature
P 21	King

Light Forces

P 61	Baradero
P 62	Barranqueras
P 63	Clorinda
P 64	Concepcion del Uruguay
P 85	Intrepida
P 86	Indomita

Amphibious Force

Q 42	Cabo San Antonio

Mine Warfare Forces

M 1	Neuquen
M 2	Rio Negro
M 3	Chubut
M 4	Tierra del Fuego
M 5	Chaco
M 6	Formosa

Miscellaneous

A 8	Sanaviron
B 3	Canal Beagle
B 4	Bahia San Blas
B 5	Cabo de Hornos
Q 2	Libertad
Q 5	Almirante Irizar
Q 8	Puerto Deseado
Q 11	Comodoro Rivadavia
15	Cormoran
16	Petrel
Q 25	Fortuna I
Q 26	Fortuna II
Q 31	Piloto Alsina
Q 73	Itati II
R 1	Huarpe
R 2	Querandi
R 3	Tehuelche
R 4	Mataco
R 5	Mocovi
R 6	Calchaqui
R 7	Ona
R 8	Toba
R 10	Chulupi
R 16	Capayan
R 18	Chiquillan
R 19	Morcoyan

SUBMARINES

2 + 3 TR 1700 TYPE

Name	No	Builders	Laid down	Launched	Commissioned
SANTA CRUZ	S 41	Thyssen Nordseewerke	6 Dec 1980	28 Sep 1982	18 Oct 1984
SAN JUAN	S 42	Thyssen Nordseewerke	18 Mar 1982	20 June 1983	19 Nov 1985
SANTA FÉ	S 43	Astilleros Domecq Garcia	4 Oct 1983	—	—
SANTIAGO DEL ESTERO	S 44	Astilleros Domecq Garcia	5 Aug 1985	—	—
—	S 45	Astilleros Domecq Garcia	June 1992	—	—

Displacement, tons: 2116 surfaced; 2264 dived
Dimensions, feet (metres): 216.5 × 23.9 × 21.3 *(66 × 7.3 × 6.5)*
Main machinery: Diesel-electric; 4 MTU 16V 652 MB81 diesels; 6720 hp(m) *(4.94 MW)* sustained; 4 alternators; 4.4 MW; 1 Siemens Type 1HR4525 + 1HR 4525 four circuit DC motor; 6.6 MW; 1 shaft
Speed, knots: 15 surfaced; 15 snorting; 25 dived
Range, miles: 12 000 at 8 kts surfaced; 20 at 25 kts; 460 at 6 kts dived
Complement: 26 plus 6 spare berths

Torpedoes: 6—21 in *(533 mm)* bow tubes. 22 AEG SST 4; wire-guided; active/passive homing to 12/28 km *(6.5/15 nm)* at 35/23 kts; warhead 260 kg; automatic reload in 50 seconds. Swim-out discharge. US Mk 37 are also carried.
Mines: Capable of carrying ground mines.
Countermeasures: ESM: Sea Sentry III; Radar warning.
Fire control: Signaal Sinbads; can handle 5 targets and 3 torpedoes simultaneously.
Radars: Navigation: Thomson-CSF Calypso IV; I band.
Sonars: Atlas Elektronik CSU 3/4; active/passive search and attack; medium frequency.
Thomson Sintra DUUX 5; passive ranging.

Programmes: Contract signed 30 November 1977 with Thyssen Nordseewerke for two submarines to be built at Emden with parts and overseeing for four more boats to be built in Argentina by Astilleros Domecq Garcia, Buenos Aires. At the beginning of 1993 it appears that S 43 is 70 per cent complete, S 44 50 per cent and S 45 has started construction. Other reports indicate either that completion depends on sales of Meko 140s, or that the unfinished hulls may be shipped back to Germany.
Structure: Diving depth, 270 m *(890 ft)*.
Operational: Maximum endurance is 70 days.

SANTA CRUZ   *5/1987, van Ginderen Collection*

2 SALTA CLASS (209 CLASS—1200 TYPE)

Name	No	Builders	Laid down	Launched	Commissioned
SALTA	S 31	Howaldtswerke, Kiel	30 Apr 1970	9 Nov 1972	7 Mar 1974
SAN LUIS	S 32	Howaldtswerke, Kiel	1 Oct 1970	3 Apr 1973	24 May 1974

Displacement, tons: 1248 surfaced; 1440 dived
Dimensions, feet (metres): 183.4 × 20.5 × 17.9 *(55.9 × 6.3 × 5.5)*
Main machinery: Diesel-electric; 4 MTU 12V 493 AZ80 diesels; 2400 hp(m) *(1.76 MW)* sustained; 4 alternators; 1.7 MW; 1 motor; 4600 hp(m) *(3.36 MW)*; 1 shaft
Speed, knots: 10 surfaced; 22 dived; 11 snorting
Range, miles: 6000 at 8 kts surfaced; 230 at 8 kts; 400 at 4 kts dived
Complement: 32

Torpedoes: 8—21 in *(533 mm)* bow tubes. 14 AEG SST 4; wire-guided; active/passive homing to 12/28 km *(6.5/15 nm)* at 35/23 kts; warhead 260 kg or US Mk 37; wire-guided; active/passive homing to 8 km *(4.4 nm)* at 24 kts; warhead 150 kg. Swim-out discharge.
Mines: Capable of carrying ground mines.
Countermeasures: ESM: DR 2000; radar warning.
Fire control: Signaal M8 digital; computer-based; up to 3 targets engaged simultaneously.
Radars: Navigation: Thomson-CSF Calypso II.
Sonars: Atlas Elektronik CSU 3 (AN 526/AN 5039/41); active/passive search and attack; medium frequency.
Thomson Sintra DUUX 2C and DUUG 1D; passive ranging.

Programmes: Ordered in 1968. Built in sections by Howaldtswerke Deutsche Werft AG, Kiel from the IK 68 design of Ingenieurkontor, Lübeck. Sections were shipped to Argentina for assembly at Tandanor, Buenos Aires.

Modernisation: *Salta* is undergoing a mid-life modernisation at the Domecq Garcia Shipyard. New engines, weapons and electrical systems are being fitted and the last 15 m of the hull have been separated from the main hull to allow work in the main engineering section. Work was suspended in May 1990 for lack of funds. By October 1991 *San Luis* was also being refitted and work had restarted on *Salta*. Both were still in shipyard hands in early 1993.
Structure: Diving depth, 250 m *(820 ft)*.

ALTA   *1988*

SALTA   *1982, Argentine Navy*

ARGENTINA / Aircraft carriers — Destroyers

AIRCRAFT CARRIER

1 Ex-BRITISH COLOSSUS CLASS

Name	No	Builders	Laid down	Launched	Commissioned
VEINTICINCO DE MAYO	V 2	Cammell Laird & Co Ltd, Birkenhead	3 Dec 1942	30 Dec 1943	17 Jan 1945

(ex-HrMs *Karel Doorman*, ex-HMS *Venerable*)

Displacement, tons: 15 892 standard; 19 896 full load
Dimensions, feet (metres): 630 pp; 693.2 oa × 80 × 25 *(192; 211.3 × 24.4 × 7.6)*
Flight deck, feet (metres): 697.7 × 133.4 *(212.6 × 40.6)*
Main machinery: 2 shafts (see *Modernisation*)
Speed, knots: 24
Complement: 1000 plus up to 500 air crew

Guns: 9 Bofors 40 mm/70; 85° elevation; 300 rounds/minute to 12 km *(6.5 nm)* anti-surface; 4 km *(2.2 nm)* anti-aircraft; weight of shell 0.96 kg.
Combat data systems: Signaal SEWACO; Link 10.
Radars: Air search: Signaal LW 08; D band.
Surface/Air search: Signaal DA 08; F band.
Height finder: VI/SGR-109.
Surface search: Signaal LW 02; E/F band.
Navigation: Signaal ZW 01; I/J band.
Racal Decca 1226; I band.
CCA: Selenia MM/SPN 720; I band.
Tacan: URN 20.

Fixed wing aircraft: 12 Super Étendards and 6 S-2E Trackers (see *Shipborne Aircraft* section).
Helicopters: 4 SH-3D Sea King ASW and 1 A 103 Alouette III.

Programmes: Purchased from the UK on 1 April 1948 and commissioned in the Royal Netherlands Navy on 28 May 1948. Damaged by boiler fire on 29 April 1968. Sold to Argentina on 15 October 1968 and refitted at Rotterdam by N V Dok en Werf Mij Wilton-Fijenoord, being fitted with new turbines from HMS *Leviathan*. Commissioned in the Argentine Navy on 12 March 1969. Completed refit on 22 August 1969 and sailed for Argentina on 3 September 1969.
Modernisation: In 1980-81 her flight deck area was increased allowing for two extra aircraft in the deck-park and at the same time all necessary modifications, including lengthening and strengthening of catapult, were made to allow for operation of Super Étendards. In 1983 Plessey CAAIS was replaced by a SEWACO system compatible with the Meko 360 class. Major refit was planned to start in 1988 for modifications to main engines, flight deck, electrical systems, NBCD and the bridge. At that stage alternative main engine plans included COSAG (new boilers plus GT boost) or CODOG (4 Sulzer diesels plus GT boost). In June 1990 Fincantieri won an initial contract to give technical assistance to AFNE, Santiago, to replace the Parsons turbines with GE/Fiat Aviazione LM 2500 gas turbines, vp propellers, and a DMD power generation system. Also included was the repair of flight deck and lifts, modernisation of the C 41 system and a new steam plant for the catapults. By the end of 1992, old systems had been stripped out and work was ready to start if the funds can be found.

VEINTICINCO DE MAYO *1987, Argentine Navy*

Structure: Hangar dimensions, feet (metres): 455 × 52 × 17.5 *(138.7 × 15.8 × 5.3)*. Modified bridge superstructure, tripod radar mast and tall raked funnel are distinctive changes from the original Colossus class.
Operational: The ship has not been fully operational since 1985 and in early 1993 was moored at the Puerto Belgrano Naval Base.

DESTROYERS

4 MEKO 360 TYPE

Name	No	Builders	Laid down	Launched	Commissioned
ALMIRANTE BROWN	D 10	Blohm and Voss, Hamburg	8 Sep 1980	28 Mar 1981	26 Jan 1983
LA ARGENTINA	D 11	Blohm and Voss, Hamburg	30 Mar 1981	25 Sep 1981	4 May 1983
HEROINA	D 12	Blohm and Voss, Hamburg	24 Aug 1981	17 Feb 1982	31 Oct 1983
SARANDI	D 13	Blohm and Voss, Hamburg	9 Mar 1982	31 Aug 1982	16 Apr 1984

Displacement, tons: 2900 standard; 3360 full load
Dimensions, feet (metres): 413.1 × 46 × 19 (screws) *(125.9 × 14 × 5.8)*
Main machinery: COGOG; 2 RR Olympus TM3B gas turbines; 50 000 hp *(37.4 MW)* sustained; 2 RR Tyne RM1C gas turbines; 9900 hp *(7.4 MW)* sustained; 2 shafts; cp props
Speed, knots: 30.5; 20.5 cruising. **Range, miles:** 4500 at 18 kts
Complement: 200 (26 officers)

Missiles: SSM: 8 Aerospatiale MM 40 Exocet (2 quad) launchers ❶; inertial cruise; active radar homing to 70 km *(40 nm)*; warhead 165 kg; sea-skimmer.
SAM: Selenia/Elsag Albatros octuple launcher ❷; 24 Aspide; semi-active homing to 13 km *(7 nm)* at 2.5 Mach; height envelope 15-5000 m *(49.2-16 405 ft)*; warhead 30 kg.
Guns: 1 OTO Melara 5 in *(127 mm)*/54 automatic ❸; 85° elevation; 45 rounds/minute to 16 km *(8.7 nm)* anti-surface; 7 km *(3.6 nm)* anti-aircraft; weight of shell 32 kg; ready ammunition 69 rounds using 3 loading drums; also fires chaff and illuminants.
8 Breda/Bofors 40 mm/70 (4 twin) ❹; 85° elevation; 300 rounds/minute to 12.6 km *(6.8 nm)* anti-surface; 4 km *(2.2 nm)* anti-aircraft; weight of shell 0.96 kg; ready ammunition 736 (or 444) using AP Tracer, impact or proximity fuzing.
Torpedoes: 6—324 mm ILAS 3 (2 triple) tubes ❺. Whitehead A 244; anti-submarine; active/passive homing to 7 km *(3.8 nm)* at 33 kts; warhead 34 kg (shaped charge); 18 reloads.
Countermeasures: Decoys: CSEE Dagaie double mounting; Graseby G1738 towed torpedo decoy system.
2 Breda 105 mm SCLAR chaff rocket launchers; 20 tubes per launcher; can be trained and elevated; chaff to 5 km *(2.7 nm)*; illuminants to 12 km *(6.6 nm)*.
ESM/ECM: Sphinx/Scimitar.
Combat data systems: Signaal SEWACO; Link 10/11. SATCOMs can be fitted.
Fire control: 2 Signaal LIROD radar/optronic systems ❻ each controlling 2 twin 40 mm mounts; Signaal WM 25 FCS ❼.
Radars: Air/surface search: Signaal DA 08A ❽; F band; range 204 km *(110 nm)* for 2 m² target.
Surface search: Signaal ZW 06 ❾; I band.
Navigation: Decca 1226; I band.
Fire control: Signaal STIR ❿; I/J/K band; range 140 km *(76 nm)* for 1 m² target.
Sonars: Atlas Elektronik 80; hull-mounted; active search and attack; medium frequency.
DSQS 21BZ.

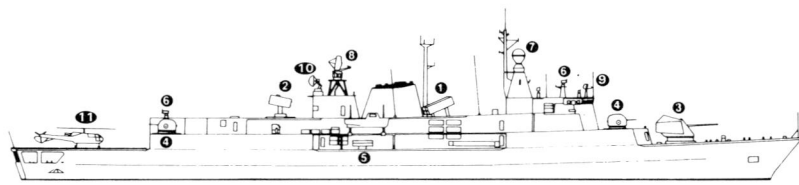

ALMIRANTE BROWN *(Scale 1 : 1200), Ian Sturton*

ALMIRANTE BROWN *11/1990*

Helicopters: 2 SA 319B Alouette III ⓫.

Programmes: Six were originally ordered in 1978, but later restricted to four when Meko 140 frigates were ordered in 1979.
Structure: Pennant numbers are displayed without the D prefix.
Operational: High operational availability was reflected in decision to send one of the class to take part in allied Gulf operations in late 1990.
Opinion: Currently deficient in ASW capability with obsolete helicopter equipment after order for Lynx cancelled in 1982. AB 212ASW was selected but acquisition not funded. Suitable helicopters are being sought in the United States which may provide Kaman SH-2 in due course.

Destroyers — Frigates / ARGENTINA 13

2 BRITISH TYPE 42

Name	No	Builders	Laid down	Launched	Commissioned
HERCULES	D 1 (ex-28)	Vickers, Barrow	16 June 1971	24 Oct 1972	12 July 1976
SANTISIMA TRINIDAD	D 2	AFNE, Rio Santiago	11 Oct 1971	9 Nov 1974	July 1981

Displacement, tons: 3150 standard; 4100 full load
Dimensions, feet (metres): 412 × 47 × 19 (screws) *(125.6 × 14.3 × 5.8)*
Main machinery: COGOG; 2 RR Olympus TM3B gas turbines; 50 000 hp *(37.3 MW)* sustained
2 RR Tyne RM1A gas turbines; 8500 hp *(6.3 MW)* sustained; 2 shafts; cp props
Speed, knots: 29; 18 (Tynes). **Range, miles:** 4000 at 18 kts
Complement: 300

Missiles: SSM: 4 Aerospatiale MM 38 Exocet ❶; inertial cruise; active homing to 42 km *(23 nm)* at 0.9 Mach; warhead 165 kg; sea-skimmer.
SAM: British Aerospace Sea Dart Mk 30 twin launcher ❷; semi-active radar homing to 40 km *(21.5 nm)* at 2 Mach; height envelope 100-18 300 m *(328-60 042 ft)*; 22 missiles; limited anti-ship capability.
Guns: 1 Vickers 4.5 in *(115 mm)*/55 Mk 8 automatic ❸; 25 rounds/minute to 22 km *(12 nm)*; weight of shell 21 kg; also fires chaff and illuminants.
2 Oerlikon 20 mm Mk 7 ❹.
Torpedoes: 6—324 mm ILAS 3 (2 triple) tubes ❺. Whitehead A 244/S; anti-submarine; active/passive homing to 7 km *(3.8 nm)* at 33 kts; warhead 34 kg (shaped charge).
Countermeasures: Decoys; Graseby Gl 738 towed torpedo decoy. Knebworth Corvus 8-tubed trainable launchers for chaff ❻.
ESM: Racal RDL 257; FH5 DF; radar intercept and DF.
ECM: Racal RCM 2 *(Hercules* only); jammer.
Combat data systems: Plessey-Ferranti ADAWS-4; Link 10.
Radars: Air search: Marconi Type 965P with double AKE2 array and 1010/1011 IFF ❼; A band.
Surface search: Marconi Type 992Q ❽; E/F band.
Navigation, HDWS and helicopter control: Kelvin Hughes Type 1006; I band.
Fire control: Two Marconi Type 909 ❾; I/J band (for Sea Dart missile control).
Sonars: Graseby Type 184M; hull-mounted; active search and attack; medium frequency 6-9 kHz.
Kelvin Hughes Type 162M classification set; sideways looking; active; high frequency.

Helicopters: 1 SA 319B Alouette III ❿.

Programmes: Contract signed 18 May 1970 between the Argentine Government and Vickers Ltd. This provided for the construction of these two ships, one to be built at Barrow-in-Furness and the second at Rio Santiago with British assistance and overseeing. *Santisima Trinidad* was sabotaged on 22

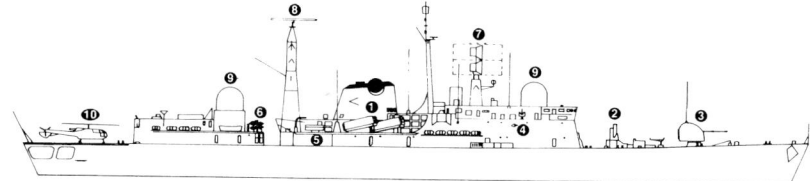

HERCULES *(Scale 1 : 1200), Ian Sturton*

HERCULES *1982, Argentine Navy*

August 1975 whilst fitting-out and subsequently placed in floating-dock at AFNE. Began trials early 1981.
Modernisation: Combat Data Systems have been improved with local modifications.

Operational: Although laid up for some time between 1983 and 1986, both ships were at sea for short periods in 1987 and back with the Fleet from 1988. *Santisima Trinidad* is used as a Flagship.

FRIGATES

3 FRENCH TYPE A 69

Name	No	Builders	Laid down	Launched	Completed
DRUMMOND (ex-*Good Hope*, ex-*Lieutenant de Vaisseau le Hénaff* F 789)	31	Lorient Naval Dockyard	12 Mar 1976	5 Mar 1977	Mar 1978
GUERRICO (ex-*Transvaal*, ex-*Commandant l'Herminier* F 791)	32	Lorient Naval Dockyard	1 Oct 1976	13 Sep 1977	Oct 1978
GRANVILLE	33	Lorient Naval Dockyard	1 Dec 1978	28 June 1980	22 June 1981

Displacement, tons: 950 standard; 1170 full load
Dimensions, feet (metres): 262.5 × 33.8 × 9.8; 18 (sonar) *(80 × 10.3 × 3; 5.5)*
Main machinery: 2 SEMT-Pielstick 12 PC2.2 V 400 diesels; 12 000 hp(m) *(8.82 MW)* sustained; 2 shafts; cp props
Speed, knots: 23. **Range, miles:** 4500 at 15 kts; 3000 at 18 kts
Complement: 93 (10 officers)

Missiles: SSM: 4 Aerospatiale MM 38 Exocet (2 twin) launchers ❶; inertial cruise; active radar homing to 42 km *(23 nm)*; warhead 165 kg; sea-skimmer.
Guns: 1 Creusot Loire 3.9 in *(100 mm)*/55 Mod 1953 ❷; 80° elevation; 60 rounds/minute to 17 km *(9 nm)* anti-surface; 8 km *(4.4 nm)* anti-aircraft; weight of shell 13.5 kg.
2 Breda 40 mm/70 (twin) ❸; 300 rounds/minute to 12.5 km *(6.8 nm)*; weight of shell 0.96 kg; ready ammunition 736 (or 444) using AP tracer, impact or proximity fuzing.
2 Oerlikon 20 mm ❹; 1000 rounds/minute.
Torpedoes: 6—324 mm Mk 32 (2 triple) tubes ❺. Whitehead A 244; anti-submarine; active/passive homing to 7 km *(3.8 nm)* at 33 kts; warhead 34 kg.
Countermeasures: Decoys: CSEE Dagaie double mounting; 10 or 6 replaceable containers; trainable; chaff to 12 km *(6.5 nm)*; illuminants to 4 km *(2.2 nm)*; decoys in H-J bands.
ESM: DR 2000/DALIA 500; radar warning.
ECM: Thomson-CSF Alligator; jammer.
Fire control: Thomson-CSF Vega system. CSEE Naja optronics director *(Granville)*. CSEE Panda Mk 2 optical director ❻ *(Drummond* and *Guerrico)*.
Radars: Air/surface search: Thomson-CSF DRBV 51A ❼ with UPX12 IFF; G band.
Navigation: Decca 1226; I band.
Fire control: Thomson-CSF DRBC 32E ❽; I/J band (for 100 mm gun).
Sonars: Thomson Sintra Diodon; hull-mounted; active search and attack; selectable 11, 12 or 13 kHz.

Programmes: The first pair was originally built for the French Navy and sold to the South African Navy in 1976 while under construction. As a result of a UN embargo on arms sales to South Africa this sale was cancelled. Purchased by Argentina in Autumn 1978. Both arrived in Argentina 2 November 1978 (third ship being ordered some time later) and all have proved very popular ships in the Argentine Navy.

DRUMMOND

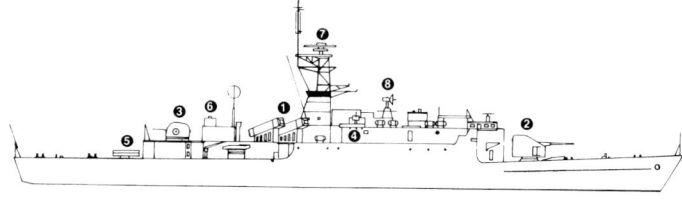

(Scale 1 : 900), Ian Sturton

DRUMMOND *2/1988*

Modernisation: *Drummond* has had her armament updated to the same standard as the other two, replacing the Bofors 40/60.

Operational: Endurance, 15 days. Very economical in fuel consumption.

4 + 2 MEKO 140 TYPE

Name	No	Builders	Laid down	Launched	Commissioned
ESPORA	41	AFNE, Rio Santiago	3 Oct 1980	23 Jan 1982	5 July 1985
ROSALES	42	AFNE, Rio Santiago	1 July 1981	4 Mar 1983	14 Nov 1986
SPIRO	43	AFNE, Rio Santiago	4 Jan 1982	24 June 1983	24 Nov 1987
PARKER	44	AFNE, Rio Santiago	2 Aug 1982	31 Mar 1984	17 Apr 1990
ROBINSON	45	AFNE, Rio Santiago	6 June 1983	15 Feb 1985	—
GOMEZ ROCA	46	AFNE, Rio Santiago	1 Dec 1983	14 Nov 1986	—

Displacement, tons: 1470 standard; 1790 full load
Dimensions, feet (metres): 299.1 × 36.4 × 11.2 *(91.2 × 11.1 × 3.4)*
Main machinery: 2 SEMT-Pielstick 16 PC2-5V 400 diesels; 20 400 hp(m) *(15 MW)* sustained; 2 shafts
Speed, knots: 27. **Range, miles:** 4000 at 18 kts
Complement: 93 (11 officers)

Missiles: SSM: 4 Aerospatiale MM 38 Exocet ❶ or 8 MM 40; inertial cruise; active radar homing to 42 km *(23 nm)* (MM 38); 70 km *(40 nm)* (MM 40); warhead 165 kg; sea-skimmer. Intention is to convert to 8 MM 40 and *Espora* was first to be fitted.
Guns: 1 OTO Melara 3 in *(76 mm)*/62 compact ❷; 85° elevation; 85 rounds/minute to 16 km *(8.7 nm)* anti-surface; 12 km *(6.5 nm)* anti-aircraft; weight of shell 6 kg; also fires chaff and illuminants.
4 Breda 40 mm/70 (2 twin) ❸; 85° elevation; 300 rounds/minute to 12.5 km *(6.8 nm)*; weight of shell 0.96 kg; ready ammunition 736 (or 444) using AP tracer, impact or proximity fuzing.
2—12.7 mm MGs.
Torpedoes: 6—324 mm ILAS 3 (2 triple) tubes ❹. Whitehead A 244/S; anti-submarine; active/passive homing to 7 km *(3.8 nm)* at 33 kts; warhead 34 kg (shaped charge).
Countermeasures: Decoys: CSEE Dagaie double mounting; 10 or 6 replaceable containers; trainable; chaff to 12 km *(6.5 nm)*; illuminants to 4 km *(2.2 nm)*; decoys in H-J bands.
ESM: Racal RQN-3B; radar warning.
ECM: Racal TQN-2X; jammer.
Combat data systems: Signaal SEWACO.
Fire control: Signaal WM 22/41 integrated system; 1 LIROD 8 optronic director ❺ (plus 2 sights—one on each bridge wing).
Radars: Air/surface search: Signaal DA 05 ❻; E/F band; range 137 km *(75 nm)* for 2 m² target.
Navigation: Decca TM 1226; I band.
Fire Control: Signaal WM 28 ❼; I/J band; range 46 km *(25 nm)*.
IFF: Mk 10.
Sonars: Atlas Elektronik ASQ 4; hull-mounted; active search and attack; medium frequency.

Helicopters: 1 SA 319B Alouette III.

Programmes: A contract was signed with Blohm & Voss on 1 August 1979 for this group of ships which are scaled down Meko 360s. All six have been fabricated in AFNE, Rio Santiago. *Parker* flooded while fitting out which delayed commissioning. Completion of the last pair depends upon funds from foreign sales and no work was being done at the end of 1992.
Structure: *Parker* and later ships fitted with a telescopic hangar which will be retrofitted in first three. Fitted with stabilisers. At least two of the class have flight deck extensions for SH-2F or AS-555 helicopters in due course.
Operational: Mostly used for offshore patrol and fishery protection duties but *Spiro* and *Rosales* sent to the Gulf in 1990/91.

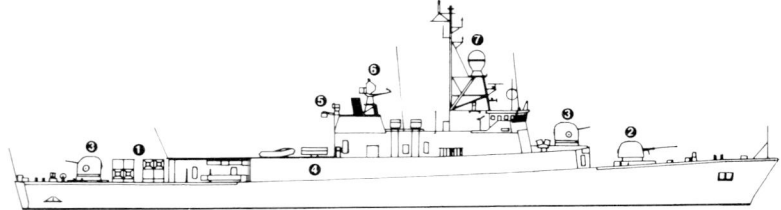

ESPORA   *(Scale 1 : 900), Ian Sturton*

SPIRO   *12/1990*

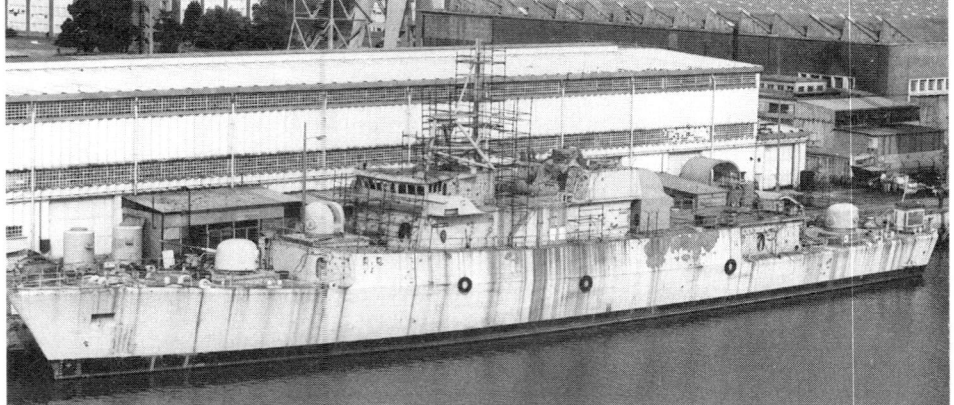

ROBINSON   *4/1992, Hartmut Ehlers*

SHIPBORNE AIRCRAFT

Notes: (i) New ASW helicopters are the highest procurement priority, with 6-8 Kaman SH-2F Seasprite or Aerospatiale AS-555 the most likely.
(ii) Fixed wing aircraft fly once a year from USN aircraft carriers.

Numbers/Type: 4/4 Agusta-Sikorsky ASH-3H/AS-61D Sea King.
Operational speed: 120 kts *(222 km/h)*.
Service ceiling: 12 205 ft *(3720 m)*.
Range: 630 nm *(1165 km)*.
Role/Weapon systems: ASW Helicopter; carrier or land-based for ASW with limited surface search capability. Sensors: Search radar, Bendix sonar. Weapons: ASW; up to 4 × A 244 torpedoes or 4 × depth bombs.

Numbers/Type: 6 Aerospatiale SA 319B Alouette III.
Operational speed: 113 kts *(210 km/h)*.
Service ceiling: 10 500 ft *(3200 m)*.
Range: 290 nm *(540 km)*.
Role/Weapon systems: ASW Helicopter; used for liaison in peacetime; wartime role includes commando assault and ASW/ASVW. Reported that there is a requirement for 12 Kaman SH-2G in due course as replacements. Sensors: Nose-mounted search radar. Weapons: ASW; 2 × Mk 44 torpedoes. ASV; 2 × AS12 missiles.

SEA KING   *1990, Argentine Navy*

ALOUETTE III   *1992*

Numbers/Type: 11 Dassault-Breguet Super Etendard.
Operational speed: Mach 1.
Service ceiling: 44 950 ft *(13 700 m)*.
Range: 920 nm *(1700 km)*.
Role/Weapon systems: Strike Fighter with anti-shipping ability proved in South Atlantic; carrier-borne strike, air defence and ASV roles, can also be land-based. Eight in service, three in reserve in 1992. Hi-lo-hi combat radius 460 nm *(850 km)*. Sensors: Agave multi-mode radar, ECM. Weapons: Strike; 2.1 tons of 'iron' bombs. ASVW; 1 × Exocet or 1 × Martin Pescador missiles. Self-defence; 2 × Magic AAMs. Standard; 2 × 30 mm cannon.

SUPER ETENDARD   *1985, Argentine Navy*

Numbers/Type: 5/3 Grumman S-2E/G Tracker.
Operational speed: 130 kts *(241 km/h)*.
Service ceiling: 25 000 ft *(7620 m)*.
Range: 1350 nm *(2500 km)*.
Role/Weapon systems: Carrier-borne medium-range ASW aircraft; also used for shore-based MR and EEZ patrol. One shipped to Israel in 1989 for Garrett turboprop installation. Possible prototype for fleet conversion. Three turboprop aircraft to be acquired from the US in 1993. Sensors: Search radar up to 32 sonobuoys, echo-ranging depth charges. Weapons: ASW; torpedoes, bombs and depth charges.

TRACKER   *1985, Argentine Navy*

LAND-BASED MARITIME AIRCRAFT

Notes: (i) MB 339A aircraft were for sale in 1992.
(ii) In addition there are three Fokker F28 for Logistic Support; One Pilatus PC-6 for reconnaissance and 10 Turbo Mentor T-34 training aircraft.
(iii) Up to 20 Skyhawk A4M may be acquired by the Air Force from the USA in 1993, with a further 16 in 1994/95.

Numbers/Type: 15 Aermacchi MB 326GB.
Operational speed: 468 kts *(867 km/h)*.
Service ceiling: 47 000 ft *(14 325 m)*.
Range: 1320 nm *(2446 km)*.
Role/Weapon systems: Light Attack; supplements anti-shipping/strike; also has training role. Weapons: ASV; 1.8 tons of 'iron' bombs. Strike; 6 × rockets. Recce; underwing camera pod.

Numbers/Type: 3/1 Lockheed L-188/188E Electra.
Operational speed: 389 kts *(721 km/h)*.
Service ceiling: 28 400 ft *(8655 m)*.
Range: 3000 nm *(5570 km)*.
Role/Weapon systems: At least one converted from transport aircraft for overwater Elint/EW role. Three more used for maritime reconnaissance. Sensors: Various EW systems including Elisra ESM. Weapons: Unarmed.

Numbers/Type: 7 Beechcraft Queen Air 80.
Operational speed: 260 kts *(482 km/h)*.
Service ceiling: 25 000 ft *(7620 m)*.
Range: 2000 nm *(3705 km)*.
Role/Weapon systems: Naval reconnaissance for protection of port installations; also has training role. Sensors: Bendix search radar. Weapons: Unarmed.

PATROL SHIPS

2 KING CLASS

Name	No	Builders	Commissioned
MURATURE	P 20	Base Nav Rio Santiago	12 Apr 1945
KING	P 21	Base Nav Rio Santiago	28 July 1946

Displacement, tons: 913 standard; 1000 normal; 1032 full load
Dimensions, feet (metres): 252.7 × 29.5 × 13.1 *(77 × 9 × 4)*
Main machinery: 2 Werkspoor diesels; 2500 hp(m) *(1.8 MW)*; 2 shafts
Speed, knots: 18. **Range, miles:** 9000 at 12 kts
Complement: 130
Guns: 3 Vickers 4 in *(105 mm)*/45; 80° elevation; 16 rounds/minute to 19 km *(10 nm)*; weight of shell 16 kg.
4 Bofors 40 mm/60 (1 twin, 2 single); 80° elevation; 120 rounds/minute/barrel to 10 km *(5.5 nm)*; weight of shell 0.89 kg.
5—12.7 mm MGs.
Depth charges: 4 projectors.
Radars: Surface search: Racal Decca 1226; I band.

Comment: Named after Captain John King, an Irish follower of Admiral Brown, who distinguished himself in the war with Brazil, 1826-28; and Captain Jose Murature, who performed conspicuous service against the Paraguayans at the Battle of Cuevas in 1865. *King* laid down June 1938, launched 3 November 1943. *Murature* laid down March 1940, launched July 1943. Used for cadet training.

MURATURE and KING   *4/1992, Hartmut Ehlers*

MURATURE (alongside *King*)   *4/1992, Hartmut Ehlers*

3 Ex-US CHEROKEE CLASS

Name	No	Builders	Commissioned
COMANDANTE GENERAL IRIGOYEN (ex-USS *Cahuilla*)	A 1	Charleston S B and D D Co	10 Mar 1945
FRANCISCO DE GURRUCHAGA (ex-USS *Luiseno* ATF 156)	A 3	Charleston S B and D D Co	16 June 1945
— (ex-USS *Takelma* ATF 113)	—	United Engineering Co, Alameda	3 Aug 1944

Displacement, tons: 1235 standard; 1731 full load
Dimensions, feet (metres): 205 × 38.5 × 17 *(62.5 × 11.7 × 5.2)*
Main machinery: Diesel-electric; 4 GM 12-278 diesels; 4400 hp *(3.28 MW)*; 4 generators; 1 motor; 3000 hp *(2.24 MW)*; 1 shaft
Speed, knots: 16. **Range, miles:** 6500 at 15 kts; 15 000 at 8 kts
Complement: 85
Guns: 6 Bofors 40 mm/60 (2 twin; 2 single); 80° elevation; 120 rounds/minute to 10 km *(5.5 nm)* anti-surface; 3 km *(1.6 nm)* anti-aircraft; weight of shell 0.89 kg.
2 Oerlikon 20 mm (mounted only in *Comandante General Irigoyen*); 800 rounds/minute to 2 km.
Radars: Surface search: Racal Decca 626; I band.
Navigation: Racal Decca 1230; I band.

Comment: Fitted with powerful pumps and other salvage equipment. *Comandante General Irigoyen* transferred by sale to Argentina at San Diego, California, on 9 July 1961. Classified as a tug until 1966 when she was re-rated as patrol vessel. *Francisco De Gurruchaga* transferred on 1 July 1975 by sale. Ex-*Takelma* to be transferred in 1993.

GURRUCHAGA   *1989, Argentine Navy*

16 ARGENTINA / Patrol ships — Amphibious forces

1 OLIVIERI CLASS

Name	No	Builders	Commissioned
TENIENTE OLIVIERI (ex-*Marsea 10*)	A 2	Quality SB, Louisiana	Dec 1987

Displacement, tons: 1640 full load
Dimensions, feet (metres): 184.8 × 40 × 14 *(56.3 × 12.2 × 4.3)*
Main machinery: 2 GM/EMD 16-645 E6; 3230 hp *(2.4 MW)* sustained; 2 shafts
Speed, knots: 16
Complement: 15 (4 officers)
Guns: 2—12.7 mm MGs.

Comment: Built by Quality Shipyards, New Orleans, as a large tug but rated as an Aviso. Acquired from US Maritime Administration in December 1987.

2 Ex-US SOTOYOMO CLASS

Name	No	Builders	Commissioned
ALFEREZ SOBRAL (ex-USS *Salish* ATA 187)	A 9	Levingstone S B Co, Orange	9 Sep 1944
COMODORO SOMELLERA (ex-USS *Catawba* ATA 210)	A 10	Levingstone S B Co, Orange	7 Dec 1944

Displacement, tons: 800 full load
Dimensions, feet (metres): 143 × 33.9 × 13 *(43.6 × 10.3 × 4)*
Main machinery: Diesel-electric; 2 GM 12-278A diesels; 2200 hp *(1.64 MW)*; 2 generators; 1 motor; 1500 hp *(1.12 MW)*; 1 shaft
Speed, knots: 12.5. **Range, miles:** 16 500 at 8 kts
Complement: 49

Comment: Former US ocean tugs transferred on 10 February 1972. *Sanaviron* (A 8) operates as a tug. *Alferez Sobral* was paid off in 1987 but is now back in service.

COMODORO SOMELLERA   1986, Argentine Navy

LIGHT FORCES

2 TYPE TNC 45 (FAST ATTACK CRAFT—GUN)

Name	No	Builders	Commissioned
INTREPIDA	P 85	Lürssen, Bremen	20 July 1974
INDOMITA	P 86	Lürssen, Bremen	12 Dec 1974

Displacement, tons: 268 full load
Dimensions, feet (metres): 147.3 × 24.3 × 7.9 *(44.9 × 7.4 × 2.4)*
Main machinery: 4 MTU MD 16V 538 TB90 diesels; 12 000 hp(m) *(8.82 MW)*; 4 shafts
Speed, knots: 38. **Range, miles:** 1450 at 20 kts
Complement: 39 (2 officers)
Guns: 1 OTO Melara 3 in *(76 mm)*/62 compact; 85 rounds/minute to 16 km *(9 nm)* anti-surface; 12 km *(6.5 nm)* anti-aircraft; weight of shell 6 kg.
2 Bofors 40 mm/70; 330 rounds/minute to 12 km *(6.5 nm)* anti-surface; 4 km *(2.2 nm)* anti-aircraft; weight of shell 0.89 kg.
2 Oerlikon 81 mm rocket launchers for illuminants.
Torpedoes: 2—21 in *(533 mm)* launchers. AEG SST-4; wire-guided; active/passive homing to 28 km *(15 nm)* at 23 kts.
Countermeasures: ESM: Racal RDL 1; radar warning.
Fire control: Signaal WM22 optronic for guns. Signaal M11 for torpedo guidance and control.
Radars: Surface search: Decca 626; I band.

Comment: These two vessels were ordered in 1970. *Intrepida* launched on 2 December 1973, *Indomita* on 8 April 1974.

INDOMITA   1986, van Ginderen Collection

4 DABUR CLASS (COASTAL PATROL CRAFT)

Name	No	Builders	Commissioned
BARADERO	P 61	Israel Aircraft Industries	1978
BARRANQUERAS	P 62	Israel Aircraft Industries	1978
CLORINDA	P 63	Israel Aircraft Industries	1978
CONCEPCIÓN DEL URUGUAY	P 64	Israel Aircraft Industries	1978

Displacement, tons: 33.7 standard; 39 full load
Dimensions, feet (metres): 64.9 × 18 × 5.8 *(19.8 × 5.5 × 1.8)*
Main machinery: 2 GM 12V-71TA diesels; 840 hp *(627 kW)* sustained; 2 shafts
Speed, knots: 19. **Range, miles:** 450 at 13 kts
Complement: 9
Guns: 2 Oerlikon 20 mm. 4—12.7 mm (2 twin) MGs.
Depth charges: 2 portable rails.
Radars: Navigation: Decca 101; I band.

Comment: Of all aluminium construction. Employed in 1991 and 1992 as part of the UN Central American peace-keeping force but now returned to normal duties.

DABUR class   1978, RAMTA

AMPHIBIOUS FORCES

1 LANDING SHIP (TANK)

Name	No	Builders	Commissioned
CABO SAN ANTONIO	Q 42	AFNE, Rio Santiago	1971

Displacement, tons: 4164 light; 8000 full load
Dimensions, feet (metres): 472.3 × 68.9 × 9.8 *(144 × 21 × 3)*
Main machinery: 6 diesels; 13 700 hp *(10.2 MW)*; 2 shafts
Speed, knots: 16
Complement: 124
Military lift: 700 troops; 23 medium tanks; 8 LCVPs each capable of carrying 36 troops or 3.5 tons
Guns: 12 Bofors 40/60 mm (3 quad); 120 rounds/minute to 10 km *(5.5 nm)* anti-surface; 3 km *(1.6 nm)* anti-aircraft; weight of shell 0.89 kg.
4 Oerlikon 20 mm (2 twin).
Fire control: 3 US Mk 5 Mod 2 optical GFCS.
Radars: Navigation: Plessey AWS-1; E/F band; has some air search capability.
Helicopters: Capable of operating up to CH-47 Chinook transport helicopter cross-deck.

Comment: Modified US De Soto County class—principal difference being the fitting of 60 tons Stülcken heavy-lift gear and different armament.

CABO SAN ANTONIO   1978, Argentine Navy

4 Ex-US LCM 6 CLASS

EDM 1, 2, 3, 4

Displacement, tons: 56 full load
Dimensions, feet (metres): 56 × 14 × 3.9 *(17.1 × 4.3 × 1.2)*
Main machinery: 2 Gray 64 HN9 diesels; 330 hp *(246 kW)* sustained; 2 shafts
Speed, knots: 11. **Range, miles:** 130 at 10 kts
Military lift: 30 tons
Guns: 2—12.7 mm MGs.

Comment: Acquired in June 1971.

8 Ex-US LCVPs

EDVP 30-37

Displacement, tons: 13 full load
Dimensions, feet (metres): 35.8 × 10.5 × 3.6 *(10.9 × 3.2 × 1.1)*
Main machinery: 1 Gray 64 HN9 diesel; 165 hp *(123 kW)* sustained; 1 shaft
Speed, knots: 9. **Range, miles:** 110 at 9 kts
Military lift: 3.5 tons or 36 troops

Comment: Acquired in May 1970.

8 ARGENTINIAN LCVPs

Displacement, tons: 7.5
Dimensions, feet (metres): 35.8 × 10.5 × 1.6 *(10.9 × 3.2 × 0.5)*
Main machinery: Fiat diesel; 200 hp(m) *(147 kW)*; 1 shaft
Speed, knots: 9

Comment: Built by AFNE and El Tigre since 1971.

MINE WARFARE FORCES

6 Ex-BRITISH TON CLASS
(4 MINESWEEPERS—COASTAL and 2 MINEHUNTERS)

Name	No	Builders	Launched
NEUQUEN (ex-HMS *Hickleton*)	M 1	Thornycroft	26 Jan 1955
RIO NEGRO (ex-HMS *Tarlton*)	M 2	Doig	10 Nov 1954
CHUBUT (ex-HMS *Santon*)	M 3	Fleetlands	18 Aug 1955
TIERRA DEL FUEGO (ex-HMS *Bevington*)	M 4	Whites	17 Mar 1953
CHACO (ex-HMS *Rennington*)	M 5	Richards	27 Nov 1958
FORMOSA (ex-HMS *Ilmington*)	M 6	Camper & Nicholson	8 Mar 1954

Displacement, tons: 360 standard; 440 full load
Dimensions, feet (metres): 153 × 28.9 × 8.2 *(46.6 × 8.8 × 2.5)*
Main machinery: 2 Paxman Deltic/Mirrlees JVSS-12 diesels; 3000 hp *(2.24 MW)*; 2 shafts
Speed, knots: 15. **Range, miles:** 2500 at 12 kts
Complement: Minesweepers 27; Minehunters 36

Guns: 1 or 2 Bofors 40 mm/60 (in some); 80° elevation; 120 rounds/minute to 10 km *(5.5 nm)* anti-surface; 3 km *(1.6 nm)* anti-aircraft; weight of shell 0.89 kg.
Radars: Navigation: Decca 45; I band. Type 955 IFF transponder.
Sonars: Plessey Type 193 (in minehunters); active minehunting; 100/300 kHz.

Programmes: Former British coastal minesweepers of the Ton class. Purchased in 1967.
Modernisation: In 1968 *Chaco* and *Formosa* were converted into minehunters in HM Dockyard, Portsmouth, and the other four were refitted and modernised as minesweepers by the Vosper Thornycroft Group with Vosper activated-fin stabiliser equipment. Of composite wooden and non-magnetic metal construction.
Operational: All were active in 1992 in spite of reports that they had been paid off.

NEUQUEN *1988, Argentine Navy*

SURVEY AND OCEANOGRAPHIC SHIPS

1 PUERTO DESEADO CLASS

Name	No	Builders	Commissioned
PUERTO DESEADO	Q 8	Astarsa, San Fernando	26 Feb 1979

Displacement, tons: 2133 standard; 2400 full load
Dimensions, feet (metres): 251.9 × 51.8 × 21.3 *(76.8 × 15.8 × 6.5)*
Main machinery: 2 Fiat-GMT diesels; 3600 hp(m) *(2.65 MW)*; 1 shaft
Speed, knots: 15. **Range, miles:** 12 000 at 12 kts
Complement: 61 (12 officers) plus 20 scientists
Radars: Navigation: I band.

Comment: Laid down on 17 March 1976 for Consejo Nacional de Investigaciones Tecnicas y Scientificas. Launched on 4 December 1976. For survey work fitted with: four Hewlett-Packard 2108-A, gravimeter, magnetometer, seismic systems, geological laboratory. Omega and NAVSAT equipped.

1 RESEARCH SHIP

Name	No	Builders	Commissioned
COMODORO RIVADAVIA	Q 11	Mestrina, Tigre	6 Dec 1974

Displacement, tons: 609 standard; 700 full load
Dimensions, feet (metres): 171.2 × 28.9 × 8.5 *(52.2 × 8.8 × 2.6)*
Main machinery: 2 Stork Werkspoor RHO-218K diesels; 1160 hp(m) *(853 kW)*; 2 shafts
Speed, knots: 12. **Range, miles:** 6000 at 12 kts
Complement: 33 (5 officers)
Helicopters: Provision for SA 319B Alouette III helicopter.

Comment: Laid down on 17 July 1971 and launched on 2 December 1972.

COMODORO RIVADAVIA *8/1988, van Ginderen Collection*

1 COASTAL SURVEY LAUNCH

Name	No	Builders	Commissioned
CORMORAN	15	AFNE, Rio Santiago	20 Feb 1964

Displacement, tons: 102 full load
Dimensions, feet (metres): 83 × 16.4 × 5.9 *(25.3 × 5 × 1.8)*
Main machinery: 2 diesels; 440 hp(m) *(323 kW)*; 2 shafts
Speed, knots: 11
Complement: 19 (3 officers)

Comment: Launched 10 August 1963.

CORMORAN *4/1992, Hartmut Ehlers*

1 COASTAL SURVEY LAUNCH

Name	No	Builders	Commissioned
PETREL	16	Cadenazzi, Tigre	1965

Displacement, tons: 50 full load
Dimensions, feet (metres): 64.8 × 14.8 × 5.6 *(19.7 × 4.5 × 1.7)*
Main machinery: 2 diesels; 340 hp(m) *(250 kW)*; 2 shafts
Speed, knots: 9
Complement: 9 (2 officers)

Comment: Built using hull of EM 128 transferred from Prefectura Naval.

PETREL *4/1992, Hartmut Ehlers*

TRANSPORTS

Note: There are plans for a large fleet replenishment ship to replace the *Punta Medanos* deleted in 1987. A lease from the USN seems the most likely way of meeting the requirement although the Navy would prefer a derivative of the Spanish *Mar del Norte*. Ex-US *Maumee* AOT 149 or *Yukon* AOT 152 are possible candidates.

3 COSTA SUR CLASS

Name	No	Builders	Commissioned
CANAL BEAGLE	B 3	Astillero Principe y Menghi SA	29 Apr 1978
BAHIA SAN BLAS	B 4	Astillero Principe y Menghi SA	27 Nov 1978
CABO DE HORNOS (ex-*Bahia Camarones*)	B 5	Astillero Principe y Menghi SA	28 June 1979

Measurement, tons: 5800 dwt; 4600 gross
Dimensions, feet (metres): 390.3 × 57.4 × 21 *(119 × 17.5 × 6.4)*
Main machinery: 2 AFNE-Sulzer diesels; 6400 hp(m) *(4.7 MW)*; 2 shafts
Speed, knots: 15

Comment: Ordered December 1975. Laid down 10 January 1977, 11 April 1977 and 29 April 1978. Launched 19 October 1977, 29 April 1978 and 4 November 1978. Used to supply off-shore research installations in Naval Area South. One operated in the Gulf in 1991.

BAHIA SAN BLAS *4/1992, Hartmut Ehlers*

18 ARGENTINA / Transports — Army watercraft

1 ICEBREAKER

Name	No	Builders	Commissioned
ALMIRANTE IRIZAR	Q 5	Wärtsilä, Helsinki	15 Dec 1978

Displacement, tons: 14 900 full load
Dimensions, feet (metres): 392 × 82 × 31.2 *(119.3 × 25 × 9.5)*
Main machinery: Diesel-electric; 4 Wärtsilä-SEMT-Pielstick 8 PC2.5 L diesels; 18 720 hp(m) *(13.77 MW)* sustained; 4 generators; 2 motors; 16 200 hp(m) *(11.9 MW)*; 2 shafts
Speed, knots: 16.5
Complement: 133 ship's company plus 100 passengers
Guns: 2 Bofors 40 mm/70; 300 rounds/minute to 12 km *(6.5 nm)* anti-surface; 4 km *(2.2 nm)* anti-aircraft; weight of shell 0.96 kg.
Radars: Air/surface search: Plessey AWS 2; E/F band.
Navigation: Two Decca; I band.
Helicopters: 2 ASH-3H Sea King.

Comment: Fitted for landing craft with two 16 ton cranes, fin stabilisers, Wärtsilä bubbling system and a 60 ton towing winch. Red hull with white upperworks and red funnel. Designed for Antarctic support operations and able to remain in polar regions throughout the Winter with 210 people aboard. Used as a transport to South Georgia in December 1981 and as a hospital ship during the Falklands campaign April to June 1982. Currently used as the Patagonian supply ship.

ALMIRANTE IRIZAR *7/1992, Miguel A Soto*

TRAINING SHIPS

Note: There are also three small yachts: *Itati II* (Q 73), *Fortuna I* (Q 25) and *Fortuna II* (Q 26).

Name	No	Builders	Commissioned
LIBERTAD	Q 2	AFNE, Rio Santiago	28 May 1963

Displacement, tons: 3025 standard; 3765 full load
Dimensions, feet (metres): 262 wl; 301 oa × 45.3 × 21.8 *(79.9; 91.7 × 13.8 × 6.6)*
Main machinery: 2 Sulzer diesels; 2400 hp(m) *(1.76 MW)*; 2 shafts
Speed, knots: 13.5 under power. **Range, miles:** 12 000
Complement: 220 crew plus 150 cadets
Guns: 1—3 in *(76 mm)* and 4—40 mm (fitted for but not with). 4—47 mm saluting guns.
Radars: Navigation: Decca; I band.

Comment: Launched 30 May 1956. She set record for crossing the North Atlantic under sail in 1966, a record which still stands. Sail area, 27 265 sq m.

LIBERTAD *4/1992, Marina Fraccaroli*

Name	No	Builders	Commissioned
PILOTO ALSINA (ex-MV *Ciudad de Formosa*)	Q 31	U N Levante, Spain	1963

Displacement, tons: 2800 full load
Measurement, tons: 720 dwt; 3986 gross
Dimensions, feet (metres): 346 × 57.1 × 26.9 *(105.5 × 17.4 × 8.2)*
Main machinery: 3 Maquinista/B&W diesels; 4500 hp(m) *(3.3 MW)*; 1 shaft
Speed, knots: 14

Comment: Commissioned in Navy 17 March 1981. Former ferry.

PILOTO ALSINA *4/1992, Hartmut Ehlers*

TUGS

Name	No	Builders	Commissioned
SANAVIRON (ex-US ATA 228)	A 8	Levingstone S B Co, Orange	5 Aug 1947

Comment: Details as for Sotoyomo class under *Patrol Ships*.

SANAVIRON *8/1989, van Ginderen Collection*

Name	No	Builders	Commissioned
QUERANDI	R 2	Ast Vicente Forte, Buenos Aires	22 Aug 1978
TEHUELCHE	R 3	Ast Vicente Forte, Buenos Aires	2 Nov 1978

Displacement, tons: 270 full load
Dimensions, feet (metres): 110.2 × 27.6 × 9.8 *(33.6 × 8.4 × 3)*
Main machinery: 2 MAN diesels; 1320 hp(m) *(970 kW)*; 2 shafts
Speed, knots: 12. **Range, miles:** 1100 at 12 kts
Complement: 30
Radars: Navigation: Decca; I band.

Comment: Ordered 1973. Launched 20 December 1977.

Name	No	Name	No
HUARPE	R 1	ONA	R 7
MATACO	R 4	TOBA	R 8

Displacement, tons: 208 full load
Dimensions, feet (metres): 99.4 × 27.6 × 10.5 *(30.3 × 8.4 × 3.2)*
Main machinery: 2 MAN diesels; 830 hp(m) *(610 kW)*; 1 shaft
Speed, knots: 12
Complement: 10 (2 officers)

Comment: Transferred from the River Flotilla to the Navy in 1988.

Name	No	Name	No
MOCOVI	R 5 (ex-US YTL 441)	CAPAYAN	R 16 (ex-US YTL 443)
CALCHAQUI	R 6 (ex-US YTL 445)	CHIQUILLAN	R 18 (ex-US YTL 444)
CHULUPI	R 10 (ex-US YTL 426)	MORCOYAN	R 19 (ex-US YTL 448)

Displacement, tons: 70
Dimensions, feet (metres): 63 × 16.4 × 7.2 *(19.2 × 5 × 2.2)*
Main machinery: 1 Hoover-Owens-Rentscheer diesel; 310 hp(m) *(228 kW)*; 1 shaft
Speed, knots: 10
Complement: 5

Comment: YTL Type built in USA and transferred on lease in March 1965 (R 16, 18, 19), remainder in March 1969. All purchased on 16 June 1977.

FLOATING DOCKS

Number	Dimensions, feet (metres)	Capacity, tons
Y 1 (ex-ARD 23)	492 × 88.6 × 56 *(150 × 27 × 17.1)*	3500
2	300.1 × 60 × 41 *(91.5 × 18.3 × 12.5)*	1500
—	215.8 × 46 × 45.5 *(65.8 × 14 × 13.7)*	750
A	565.8 × 85.3 *(172.5 × 26)*	12 000
B	360.8 × 110 × 18	2800
—	623.4 × 78.7 *(190 × 24)*	12 000

Comment: First one is at Mar del Plata naval base, the second at Dársena Norte, Buenos Aires, the third at Puerto Belgrano and last two at Dársena Este. No 2 was built in 1913, A in 1957-58 and B in 1956. Another 12 000 ton dock was built in 1987 at Rio Santiago Shipyard. There are also at least four floating cranes.

ARMY WATERCRAFT

Comment: Several LCPs (BDPs) are operated by Batallón de Ingenieros Anfibios 601 at Santa Fé. Built by Ast Vicente Forte. Ferries for crossing Rio Paraná include two built in 1969. In addition there are over 1000 Ferramar 'Asalto' and 'Comando' inflatable craft.

FERRAMAR ASALTO *1990, Ferramar*

PREFECTURA NAVAL ARGENTINA (COAST GUARD)

Headquarters' Appointments

Commander:
   Prefecto General Jorge H Maggi
Vice Commander:
   Prefecto General Jorge A Gentiluomo

Senior Appointments

Director of Prefectura's Zones:
   Prefecto General Raimundo Pelinsky
Director of Administration:
   Prefecto General Carlos J Leyes
Director of Pilot Services:
   Prefecto General Pedro L Bustamante
Director of Navigation Police and Safety:
   Prefecto General Juan C Babich
Director of Materiel:
   Prefecto General Andres R Lorenzo
nDirector of Personnel:
   Prefecto General Fortunato C Benasulin
Director of Judicial Police:
   Prefecto Mayor Juan M Redón

Personnel

1993: 12 960 (1470 officers) including 830 civilians

Tasks

Under the General Organisation Act the PNA is charged with:
(a) Enforcement of Federal Laws on the high seas and waters subject to the Argentine Republic.
(b) Enforcement of environmental protection laws in Federal waters.
(c) Search and Rescue.
(d) Security of waterfront facilities and vessels in port.
(e) Operations of certain Navaids.
(f) Operation of some Pilot Services.
(g) Management and operation of Aviation Department, Coast-guard Vessels, Salvage, Fire and Anti-Pollution Service, Yachtmaster School, National Diving School and several Fire Brigades.

Organisation

Formed in 10 districts; High Parana River, Upper Parana and Paraguay Rivers, Lower Parana River, Upper Uruguay River, Lower Uruguay River, Delta, River Plate, Northern Argentine Sea, Southern Argentine Sea, Lakes and Comahue.

History

The Spanish authorities in South America established similar organisations to those in Spain. In 1756 the Captainship of the Port came into being in Buenos Aires—in 1810 the Ship Registry office was added to this title. On 29 October 1896 the title of Capitania General de Puertos was established by Act of Congress, the beginning of the PNA. Today, as a security and safety force, it has responsibilities throughout the rivers of Argentina, the ports and harbours as well as within territorial waters out to the 200 mile EEZ. An attempt was made in January 1992 to restrict operations to a 12 mile limit but the legislation was cancelled.

Identity markings

Two unequal blue stripes with, superimposed, crossed white anchors followed by the title Prefectura Naval.

Strength of Prefectura

Patrol Ships	6
Large Patrol Craft	4
Coastal Patrol Craft	53
Training Ships	3
Pilot Stations	2
Pilot Craft	23

PENNANT LIST

Prefectura Naval Argentina

No	Name
GC 13	Delfin
GC 21	Lynch
GC 22	Toll
GC 24	Mantilla
GC 25	Azopardo
GC 26	Thompson
GC 27	Prefecto Fique
GC 28	Prefecto Derbes
GC 43	Mandubi
GC 47	Tonina
GC 48-61	Patrol Craft
GC 64	Mar del Plata
GC 65	Martin Garcia
GC 66	Rio Lujan
GC 67	Rio Uruguay
GC 68	Rio Paraguay
GC 69	Rio Parana
GC 70	Rio de la Plata
GC 71	La Plata
GC 72	Buenos Aires
GC 73	Cabo Corrientes
GC 74	Rio Quequen
GC 75	Bahia Blanca
GC 76	Ingeniero White
GC 77	Golfo San Matias
GC 78	Madryn
GC 79	Rio Deseado
GC 80	Ushuaia
GC 81	Canal de Beagle
GC 88-95	Patrol Craft
GC 101	Dorado
GC 102-114	Patrol Craft
GC 119	Lago Alumine

PATROL FORCES

Note: In addition to the ships and craft listed below the PNA operates 450 craft, including floating cranes, runabouts and inflatables of all types including LS 11201-3, LS 11001-4, LS 9500-9, LS 6301-17, LS 6801-12, LS 5801-5865, SB9.

5 HALCON CLASS (B 119)

Name	No	Builders	Commissioned
MANTILLA	GC 24	Bazán, El Ferrol	20 Dec 1982
AZOPARDO	GC 25	Bazán, El Ferrol	28 Apr 1983
THOMPSON	GC 26	Bazán, El Ferrol	20 June 1983
PREFECTO FIQUE	GC 27	Bazán, El Ferrol	29 July 1983
PREFECTO DERBES	GC 28	Bazán, El Ferrol	20 Nov 1983

Displacement, tons: 910 standard; 1084 full load
Dimensions, feet (metres): 219.9 × 34.4 × 13.8 *(67 × 10.5 × 4.2)*
Main machinery: 2 Bazán-MTU 16V 956 TB91 diesels; 7500 hp(m) *(5.52 MW)* sustained; 2 shafts
Speed, knots: 20. **Range, miles:** 5000 at 18 kts
Complement: 33 (10 officers)
Guns: 1 Breda 40 mm/70; 300 rounds/minute to 12.5 km *(7 nm)*; weight of shell 0.96 kg.
   2—12.7 mm MGs.
Radars: Navigation: Decca 1226; I band.
Helicopters: Hangar and Platform for 1 light.

Comment: Ordered in 1979 from Bazán, El Ferrol, Spain. All have helicopter hangar and Magnavox MX 1102 SATNAV. Hospital with four beds. Carry one rigid rescue craft *(6.1 m)* with Perkins outboard and a capacity of 12 and two inflatable craft *(4.1 m)* with Evinrude outboard. Esquilo helicopters were to have replaced the Alouettes loaned from the Navy but as this acquisition was cancelled in 1992, helicopters are currently no longer carried.

MANTILLA   *4/1992, Hartmut Ehlers*

1 PATROL SHIP

Name	No	Builders	Completed
DELFIN	GC 13	Ijsselwerf, Netherlands	14 May 1957

Displacement, tons: 700 standard; 1000 full load
Dimensions, feet (metres): 193.5 × 29.8 × 13.8 *(59 × 9.1 × 4.2)*
Main machinery: 2 MAN diesels; 2300 hp(m) *(1.69 MW)*; 2 shafts
Speed, knots: 15. **Range, miles:** 6720 at 10 kts
Complement: 27
Guns: 1 Oerlikon 20 mm. 2—12.7 mm Browning MGs.
Radars: Navigation: Decca; I band.

Comment: Whaler acquired for PNA in 1969. Commissioned 23 January 1970.

PREFECTO FIQUE   *6/1992, Miguel A Soto*

DELFIN   *4/1992, Hartmut Ehlers*

ARGENTINA / Patrol forces

2 LYNCH CLASS (LARGE PATROL CRAFT)

Name	No	Builders	Commissioned
LYNCH	GC 21	AFNE, Rio Santiago	20 May 1964
TOLL	GC 22	AFNE, Rio Santiago	7 July 1966

Displacement, tons: 100 standard; 117 full load
Dimensions, feet (metres): 98.4 × 21 × 5.6 *(30 × 6.4 × 1.7)*
Main machinery: 2 MTU Maybach diesels; 2700 hp(m) *(1.98 MW)*; 2 shafts
Speed, knots: 22. **Range, miles:** 2000
Complement: 11
Guns: 1 Oerlikon 20 mm.

TOLL   1990, Prefectura Naval Argentina

1 LARGE PATROL CRAFT

Name	No	Builders	Commissioned
MANDUBI	GC 43	Base Naval Rio Santiago	1940

Displacement, tons: 270 full load
Dimensions, feet (metres): 108.9 × 20.7 × 6.2 *(33.2 × 6.3 × 1.9)*
Main machinery: 2 MAN G6V-23.5/33 diesels; 500 hp(m) *(367 kW)*; 1 shaft
Speed, knots: 14. **Range, miles:** 800 at 14 kts; 3400 at 10 kts
Complement: 12
Guns: 2—12.7 mm Browning MGs.

Comment: Since 1986 has acted as training craft for PNA Cadets School carrying 20 cadets.

MANDUBI   1990, Prefectura Naval Argentina

1 RIVER PATROL SHIP

Name	No	Builders	Commissioned
TONINA	GC 47	SANYM SA San Fernando, Argentina	30 June 1978

Displacement, tons: 103 standard; 153 full load
Dimensions, feet (metres): 83.8 × 21.3 × 10.1 *(25.5 × 6.5 × 3.3)*
Main machinery: 2 GM 16V-71TA diesels; 1000 hp *(746 kW)* sustained; 2 shafts
Speed, knots: 10. **Range, miles:** 2800 at 10 kts
Complement: 11 (3 officers)
Guns: 1 Oerlikon 20 mm.
Radars: Navigation: Decca 1226; I band.

Comment: Served as training ship for PNA Cadets School until 1986. Now acts as salvage ship with salvage pumps and recompression chamber. Capable of operating divers and underwater swimmers.

TONINA   1989, Prefectura Naval Argentina

18 BLOHM & VOSS Z-28 TYPE (COASTAL PATROL CRAFT)

MAR DEL PLATA GC 64	RIO DE LA PLATA GC 70	INGENIERO WHITE GC 76
MARTIN GARCIA GC 65	LA PLATA GC 71	GOLFO SAN MATIAS GC 77
RIO LUJAN GC 66	BUENOS AIRES GC 72	MADRYN GC 78
RIO URUGUAY GC 67	CABO CORRIENTES GC 73	RIO DESEADO GC 79
RIO PARAGUAY GC 68	RIO QUEQUEN GC 74	USHUAIA GC 80
RIO PARANA GC 69	BAHIA BLANCA GC 75	CANAL DE BEAGLE GC 81

Displacement, tons: 81 full load
Dimensions, feet (metres): 91.8 × 17.4 × 5.2 *(28 × 5.3 × 1.6)*
Main machinery: 2 MTU 8V 331 TC92 diesels; 1770 hp(m) *(1.3 MW)* sustained; 2 shafts
Speed, knots: 22. **Range, miles:** 1200 at 12 kts; 780 at 18 kts
Complement: 14 (3 officers)
Guns: 1 Oerlikon 20 mm. 2—12.7 mm Browning MGs.
Radars: Navigation: Decca 1226; I band.

Comment: Ordered 24 November 1978. First delivered mid-1979 and then at monthly intervals. Steel hulls. GC 82 and 83 were captured by the British Forces in 1982.

RIO LUJAN   4/1992, Hartmut Ehlers

1 COASTAL PATROL CRAFT

Name	No	Builders	Commissioned
DORADO	GC 101	Base Naval, Rio Santiago	17 Dec 1939

Displacement, tons: 43 full load
Dimensions, feet (metres): 69.5 × 14.1 × 4.9 *(21.2 × 4.3 × 1.5)*
Main machinery: 2 GM 6071-6A diesels; 360 hp *(268 kW)*; 1 shaft
Speed, knots: 12. **Range, miles:** 1550
Complement: 7 (1 officer)

DORADO   4/1992, Tomas Lozada

34 SMALL PATROL CRAFT

GC 48-61   GC 88-95   GC 102-108   GC 110-114

Displacement, tons: 15 full load
Dimensions, feet (metres): 41 × 11.8 × 3.6 *(12.5 × 3.6 × 1.1)*
Main machinery: 2 GM diesels; 514 hp *(383 kW)*; 2 shafts
Speed, knots: 20. **Range, miles:** 400 at 18 kts
Complement: 3
Guns: 12.7 mm Browning MG.

Comment: First delivered September 1978. First 14 built by Cadenazzi, Tigre 1977-79, remainder by Ast Belen de Escobar 1984-86. GC 102-114 are slightly smaller.

GC 61   7/1992, Julio Caufero

3 TRAINING SHIPS

ESPERANZA   ADHARA II   TALITA II

Displacement, tons: 33.5 standard
Dimensions, feet (metres): 62.3 × 14.1 × 8.9 *(19 × 4.3 × 2.7)*
Main machinery: 1 VM diesel; 90 hp(m) *(66 kW)*; 1 shaft
Speed, knots: 6; 15 sailing
Complement: 6 plus 6 cadets

Comment: Details given are for *Esperanza* built by Ast Central de la PNA. Launched and commissioned 20 December 1968 as a sail training ship. In addition there are two 30 ton training craft *Adhara II* and *Talita II* of similar dimensions.

TALITA II *11/1988, Prefectura Naval Argentina*

6 HARBOUR TUGS

CANAL EMILIO MITRE SB 8   **+SB** 3, 4, 5, 9 and 10

Comment: *Canal Emilio Mitre* is of 53 tons full load and has a speed of 10 kts and was built by Damen Shipyard, Netherlands in 1982.

CANAL EMILIO MITRE *1986, van Ginderen Collection*

PILOT VESSELS

1 PILOT STATION

Name	No	Builders	Commissioned
LAGO LACAR	DF 14	Brodogradiliste, Split	1962

Displacement, tons: 10 900 full load
Dimensions, feet (metres): 515.1 × 65.6 × 25 *(157 × 20 × 7.6)*
Main machinery: 1 Fiat 759S diesel; 1 shaft
Speed, knots: 14
Complement: 28 (3 officers)

Comment: Commissioned as a Coast Guard ship 24 December 1986. Has a helicopter deck and a hospital with 40 beds.

LAGO LACAR *6/1992, Miguel A Soto*

1 PILOT STATION

Name	No	Builders	Commissioned
RIO LIMAY	DF —	Astillero Astarsa	30 May 1972

Displacement, tons: 10 070 full load
Dimensions, feet (metres): 482.3 × 65.6 × 28 *(147 × 20 × 8.5)*
Speed, knots: 13
Complement: 28 (3 officers)

Comment: Commissioned as a Coast Guard ship 24 December 1991. Has a helicopter deck and a 20 bed hospital.

RIO LIMAY *1990, Prefectura Naval Argentina*

23 PILOT CRAFT

ALUMINE GC 119 (ex-SP 14)	SAN MARTIN SP 21	ROCA SP 28
TRAFUL SP 15	BUENOS AIRES SP 22	PUELO SP 29
COLHUE SP 16	FAGNANO SP 23	FUTALAUFQUEN SP 30
MASCARDI SP 17	LACAR SP 24	FALKNER SP 31
MARIO L PENDO SP 18	CARDIEL SP 25	FONTANA SP 32
NAHUEL HUAPI SP 19	MUSTERS SP 26	COLHUE HUAPI SP 33
VIEDMA SP 20	QUILLEN SP 27	HUECHULAFQUEN SP 34
		YEHUIN SP 35

(All names preceded by **LAGO**)

Comment: There are five different types of named pilot craft. SP 14-15 of 33.7 tons built in 1981; SP 16-18 of 47 tons built since 1981; SP 19-23 of 51 tons built since 1981; SP 24-27 of 20 tons built in 1981; SP 28-30 of 16.5 m built in 1983; SP 31-35 of 7 tons built in 1986-1991. Most built by Damen SY, Netherlands. The last three built by Astillero Mestrina, Tigre. No armament.

LAGO MUSTERS *8/1992, Juan Sanchez*

LAND-BASED MARITIME AIRCRAFT

Note: 10 Helibras Esquilo or Bell shipborne helicopters will not now be acquired until at least 1994. Until then no helicopters are embarked.

Numbers/Type: 2 Aerospatiale SA 330 Super Puma.
Operational speed: 151 kts *(279 km/h)*.
Service ceiling: 15 090 ft *(4600 m)*.
Range: 335 nm *(620 km)*.
Role/Weapon systems: Support and SAR helicopter for Patrol work. Sensors: Omera search radar. Weapons: Can carry pintle-mounted machine guns but are usually unarmed.

Numbers/Type: 5 CASA C-212 Aviocar.
Operational speed: 190 kts *(353 km/h)*.
Service ceiling: 24 000 ft *(7315 m)*.
Range: 1650 nm *(3055 km)*.
Role/Weapon systems: Two acquired in 1989, three more in 1990. Medium-range reconnaissance and coastal surveillance duties in EEZ. Sensor: Bendix RDS 32 surface search radar. Omega Global GNS-500. Weapons: ASW; can carry torpedoes, depth bombs or mines. ASV; 2 × rockets or machine gun pods not normally fitted.

AUSTRALIA

Headquarters' Appointments

Chief of Defence Force:
　Vice Admiral A L Beaumont, AC
Chief of Naval Staff:
　Vice Admiral I D G MacDougall, AO
Deputy Chief of Naval Staff:
　Rear Admiral R G Taylor, AO
Assistant Chief of Naval Staff (Personnel):
　Rear Admiral D B Chalmers, AO
Assistant Chief of Naval Staff (Materiel):
　Rear Admiral N D H Hammond

Senior Appointments

Maritime Commander, Australia:
　Rear Admiral R A K Walls, AO
Flag Officer Naval Support Command:
　Rear Admiral A L Hunt, AO
Commodore Flotillas:
　Commodore R A Christie, AM
Commodore Naval Training Command:
　Commodore P D Briggs, AM

Diplomatic Representation

Naval Attaché in Jakarta:
　Captain K J Jordan
Defence Adviser in Kuala Lumpur:
　Captain K F Pitt
Assistant Defence Attaché in Kuala Lumpur:
　Commander M Adams
Head of Australian Defence Staff in London:
　Commodore G P Kable
Naval Adviser in London:
　Captain P J Parkins
Defence Adviser in New Delhi:
　Captain R G Dagworthy
Defence Attaché in Manila:
　Captain M C Webster
Naval Attaché in Washington and Ottawa:
　Commodore T A A Roach, AM
Defence Attaché in Bonn/Berlin:
　Captain J G J Newman
Defence Attaché in Tokyo:
　Captain J W Hewett
Naval Adviser in Honiara:
　Commander K R Eglen

Personnel

1993: 15 000 officers and sailors
　　　4500 Reserves (active and inactive)

RAN Reserve

The Naval Reserve is integrated into the Permanent Force. Personnel are either Active Reservists with regular commitments or Inactive Reservists with periodic or contingent duty. The missions undertaken by the Reserve include Naval Control of Shipping, Aviation, MCM, Intelligence, Diving and patrol boat/landing craft operations. In addition, members of the Ready Reserve (a component of the Active Reserve) are shadow posted to selected major fleet units.

Navy Estimates

　　　A$
1990-91: 2 198 700 000
1991-92: 2 593 000 000
1992-93: 2 501 162 000

Shore Establishments

Sydney: Maritime Headquarters Australia, Fleet Base East (Garden Island), *Platypus* (Submarines), *Waterhen* (Mine warfare), *Watson* (Warfare Training), *Penguin* (Diving, NBCD, Hospital, Staff College), *Kuttabul* (Administration).
Jervis Bay Area: *Albatross* (Air Station), *Creswell* (Naval College and Fleet Support), Jervis Bay Range Facility.
Cockburn Sound (WA): Fleet Base West, *Stirling* (Administration and Maintenance Support), Submarine School.
Darwin: Minor warship base, *Coonawarra* (Communications Station).
Cairns: Headquarters Patrol Boat Force, *Cairns* (Minor warship base).
Canberra: Navy Office, *Harman* (Communications Station).
Westernport: *Cerberus* (Major training facility, minor warship base).
Brisbane: *Moreton* (Reserve training/minor warship base).
Adelaide: *Encounter* (Reserve training/minor warship base).
Hobart: *Huon* (Reserve training/minor warship base).
North West Cape: Harold E Holt Communications Station.

Fleet Deployment 1993

Fleet Base East (and other Sydney bases): 3 SS, 3 DDG, 4 FFG, 1 AOR, 1 GT, 1 LSH, 1 ASR, 2 MHI, 4 MSA, 1 PTF, 2 LCH.
Fleet Base West: 1 SS, 2 FFG, 3 DE, 1 AO, 1 AGS, 2 PTF.
Darwin Naval Base: 6 PTF, 1 LCH.
Cairns: 5 PTF, 2 LCH, 5 AGS.
Westernport, Hobart, Adelaide: 1 PTF/PC each.
Brisbane: 1 LCH.

Fleet Air Arm (see *Shipborne Aircraft* section).

Squadron	Aircraft
HC-723	Squirrel AS 350B, utility, FFG embarked flights, SAR
	HS 748, Fixed wing, EW operations and training
	Bell 206B, survey support
HS-817	Sea King Mk 50, ASW
HS-816	Seahawk S-70B-2, ASW, ASST

Prefix to Ships' Names

HMAS.　Her Majesty's Australian Ship

Strength of the Fleet

Type	Active (Reserve)	Building (Projected)
Patrol Submarines (SS)	5	6
Destroyers (DDG)	3	—
Frigates (FFG)	5	8
Destroyer Escorts (DE)	3	—
Minehunters (Coastal)	—	(6)
Minehunters (Inshore)	2	—
Minesweepers (Auxiliary)	4	(1)
Offshore Patrol Vessels (OPV)	—	(12)
Large Patrol Craft (PTF)	15 (2 RANR)	—
Amphibious Heavy Lift Ship (LSH)	1	—
Heavy Landing Craft (LCH)	6 (3 RANR)	—
Light Landing Craft (LCVP)	1	3
Marine Science Ships (AGS)	6	(3)
Replenishment Ships (AO)	2	—
Training Ships	3	(1)
Trials and Safety Ship (ASR)	1	—
Tugs (AT)	5	—
Torpedo Recovery Vessels (TRV)	3	—

Surface Ship Development Plan

The surface combatant force is being developed under a two Tier concept. Tier One are destroyers and frigates, while Tier Two are offshore patrol vessels. A force of 16 Tier One and 12 Tier Two ships is envisaged.

Mercantile Marine

Lloyd's Register of Shipping:
　695 vessels of 2 676 087 tons gross

DELETIONS

Submarines

1992　*Oxley*

Frigates

1991　*Parramatta* (old), *Stuart* (old)

Minesweepers

1990　*Curlew*
1991　*Wave Rider* (returned to civilian use)
1992　*Salvatore V*

Miscellaneous

1990　*Cook*
1991　TB 1536 (sold)
1992　*Adroit, Bass*

PENNANT LIST

Submarines

59	Otway
60	Onslow
61	Orion
62	Otama
70	Ovens
71	Collins (bldg)
72	Farncomb (bldg)
73	Waller (bldg)
74	Dechaineux (bldg)
75	Sheean (bldg)
76	Rankin (bldg)

Destroyers

38	Perth (old)
39	Hobart
41	Brisbane

Frigates

01	Adelaide
02	Canberra
03	Sydney
04	Darwin
05	Melbourne
06	Newcastle (bldg)
49	Derwent
50	Swan
53	Torrens
150	Anzac (bldg)
151	Arrernte (bldg)
152	Warumungu (bldg)
153	Stuart (bldg)
154	Parramatta (planned)
155	Ballarat (planned)
156	Toowoomba (planned)
157	Perth (new) (planned)

Mine Warfare Vessels

M 80	Rushcutter
M 81	Shoalwater
Y 298	Bandicoot
Y 299	Wallaroo
1102	Brolga
1185	Koraaga

Training Ships

GT 203	Jervis Bay
P 225	Argus (RANR)
AG 244	Banks

Large Patrol Craft

87	Ardent (RANR)
91	Aware (RANR)
203	Fremantle (RANR)
204	Warrnambool (RANR)
205	Townsville
206	Wollongong
207	Launceston
208	Whyalla
209	Ipswich
210	Cessnock
211	Bendigo
212	Gawler
213	Geraldton
214	Dubbo
215	Geelong
216	Gladstone
217	Bunbury

Amphibious Heavy Lift Ship

| L 50 | Tobruk |

Landing Craft

L 126	Balikpapan (RANR)
L 127	Brunei
L 128	Labuan (RANR)
L 129	Tarakan
L 130	Wewak
L 133	Betano

Survey Ships

A 73	Moresby
A 312	Flinders
A 01	Paluma
A 02	Mermaid
A 03	Shepparton
A 04	Benalla

Replenishment Ships

| O 195 | Westralia |
| OR 304 | Success |

Trials and Safety Ship

| ASR 241 | Protector |

Torpedo Recovery Vessels

TRV 801	Tuna
TRV 802	Trevally
TRV 803	Tailor

SUBMARINES

0 + 6 COLLINS CLASS

Name	No	Builders	Laid down	Launched	Commissioned
COLLINS	71	Australia Submarine Corp, Adelaide	14 Feb 1990	Aug 1993	Jan 1995
FARNCOMB	72	Australia Submarine Corp, Adelaide	1 Mar 1991	Sep 1994	Feb 1996
WALLER	73	Australia Submarine Corp, Adelaide	19 Mar 1992	Aug 1995	Jan 1997
DECHAINEUX	74	Australia Submarine Corp, Adelaide	Mar 1993	Aug 1996	Dec 1997
SHEEAN	75	Australia Submarine Corp, Adelaide	Mar 1994	Aug 1997	Nov 1998
RANKIN	76	Australia Submarine Corp, Adelaide	Mar 1995	Aug 1998	Oct 1999

Displacement, tons: 3051 surfaced; 3353 dived
Dimensions, feet (metres): 254 × 25.6 × 23 *(77.5 × 7.8 × 7)*
Main machinery: Diesel-electric; 3 Hedemora/Garden Island Type V18B/14Sub diesels; 6020 hp *(4.42 MW)* sustained snorting; 1 Jeumont Schneider motor; 7344 hp(m) *(5.4 MW)*; 1 shaft
Speed, knots: 10 surfaced; 10 snorting; 20 dived
Range, miles: 9000 at 10 kts
Complement: 42 plus 5 trainees

Missiles: SSM: McDonnell Douglas Sub Harpoon.
Torpedoes: 6—21 in *(533 mm)* fwd tubes. Air turbine pump discharge. Total of 23 weapons including Mk 48 and Sub Harpoon.
Mines: In lieu of torpedoes. The Swedish external attachment is an option.
Countermeasures: Decoys: 2 SSDE.
ESM: Argo AR 740; radar warning.
Fire control: Librascope weapons control system.
Radars: Navigation: GEC Marconi; I band.
Sonars: Thomson Sintra Scylla bow and flank arrays.
Kariwara or Thomson Sintra retractable passive towed array.

Programmes: Contract signed on 3 June 1987 for construction of six Swedish-designed Kockums Type 471. Fabrication work started in June 1989; bow and stern sections of the first submarine are being built in Sweden. The option on two additional boats, recommended by the Navy, was not taken up.
Structure: Air independent propulsion (AIP) developments will be monitored but acquisition is a low priority. Scylla is an updated Eledone sonar suite. Diving depth, greater than 175 m *(574 ft)*.
Operational: All will be based at Fleet Base West with one or two deploying regularly to the east coast. A 'two crew' cycle was considered and rejected. *Collins* is scheduled to start sea trials early in 1994.

COLLINS (artist's impression) — *1992, Jeff Isaacs*

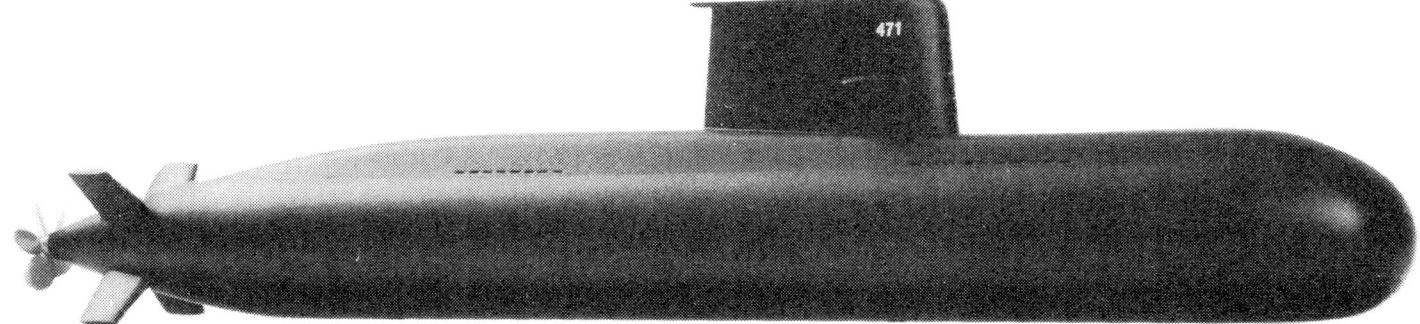

COLLINS (model) — *1989, Kockums*

5 BRITISH OBERON CLASS

Name	No	Builders	Laid down	Launched	Commissioned
OTWAY	59	Scotts' Shipbuilding & Eng Co Ltd, Greenock	29 June 1965	29 Nov 1966	23 Apr 1968
ONSLOW	60	Scotts' Shipbuilding & Eng Co Ltd, Greenock	4 Dec 1967	3 Dec 1968	22 Dec 1969
ORION	61	Scotts' Shipbuilding & Eng Co Ltd, Greenock	6 Oct 1972	16 Sep 1974	15 June 1977
OTAMA	62	Scotts' Shipbuilding & Eng Co Ltd, Greenock	25 May 1973	3 Dec 1975	27 Apr 1978
OVENS	70	Scotts' Shipbuilding & Eng Co Ltd, Greenock	17 June 1966	4 Dec 1967	18 Apr 1969

Displacement, tons: 1610 standard; 2030 surfaced; 2410 dived
Dimensions, feet (metres): 295.2 × 26.5 × 18 *(90 × 8.1 × 5.5)*
Main machinery: Diesel-electric; 2 ASR 16 VVS-ASR1 diesels; 3680 hp *(2.74 MW)*; 2 AEI motors; 6000 hp *(4.48 MW)*; 2 shafts
Speed, knots: 12 surfaced; 17 dived; 11 snorting
Range, miles: 9000 at 12 kts surfaced
Complement: 64 (8 officers)

Missiles: SSM: McDonnell Douglas Sub Harpoon; active radar homing to 130 km *(70 nm)* at 0.9 Mach; warhead 227 kg.
Torpedoes: 6—21 in *(533 mm)* bow tubes (HP air discharge). Gould Mk 48 Mod 4; dual purpose; wire-guided; active/passive homing to 38 km *(21 nm)* at 55 kts; 50 km *(27 nm)* at 40 kts; warhead 267 kg. Combined total of 20 SSM and torpedoes carried.
Countermeasures: Decoys: 2 SSDE.
ESM: MEL Manta; radar warning.
Fire control: Singer Librascope SFCS Mk 1 data handling and fire control system.
Radars: Surface search: Kelvin Hughes Type 1006; I band.
Sonars: Atlas Elektronik Type CSU3-41; bow array; active/passive; medium frequency; has intercept and UWT capability.
BAC Type 2007; flank array; passive; long range; low frequency.
Sperry BQQ 4 micropuffs; passive; range-finding.

Programmes: In 1963 an order was placed for four submarines. Two more were ordered in October 1971. Scheduled deletion dates are *Otway* 1993, *Ovens* 1994, *Orion* 1996, *Onslow* 1997. If *Otama* is refitted as planned she will scrap in 1998.

ORION — *10/1992, Hachiro Nakai*

Modernisation: Between October 1977 and October 1985 all submarines of the class were given a mid-life modernisation at Vickers, Cockatoo. Trials are continuing on one submarine for the Kariwara towed array but this is not yet an operational system and may not be until 1994. Sub Harpoon fitted in 1985-86. The two short stern tubes have been removed.
Operational: 1st Submarine Squadron is based at *Platypus*, Neutral Bay, Sydney. *Orion* is based at *Stirling* in Western Australia.

DESTROYERS

3 MODIFIED US DDG-2 CLASS (DDGs)

Name	No	Builders	Laid down	Launched	Commissioned
PERTH	38	Defoe Shipbuilding Co, Bay City, Michigan	21 Sep 1962	26 Sep 1963	17 July 1965
HOBART	39	Defoe Shipbuilding Co, Bay City, Michigan	26 Oct 1962	9 Jan 1964	18 Dec 1965
BRISBANE	41	Defoe Shipbuilding Co, Bay City, Michigan	15 Feb 1965	5 May 1966	16 Dec 1967

Displacement, tons: 3370 standard; 4618 full load
Dimensions, feet (metres): 440.8 × 47.1 × 20.1 *(134.3 × 14.3 × 6.1)*
Main machinery: 4 Foster-Wheeler boilers; 1200 psi *(84.37 kg/cm sq)*, 950°F *(510°C)*; 2 GE turbines; 70 000 hp *(52 MW)*; 2 shafts
Speed, knots: 30+. **Range, miles:** 6000 at 15 kts; 2000 at 30 kts
Complement: 325 (25 officers)

Missiles: SSM: McDonnell Douglas Harpoon (fitted for but not with).
SAM: 40 GDC Pomona Standard SM-1MR; Mk 13 Mod 6 launcher ❶; command guidance; semi-active radar homing to 46 km *(25 nm)* at 2 Mach; height 45.7-18 288 m *(150-60 000 ft)*. Dual capability launcher for SSM.
Guns: 2 FMC 5 in *(127 mm)*/54 Mk 42 Mod 10 automatic ❷; 85° elevation; 40 rounds/minute to 24 km *(13 nm)* anti-surface; 14 km *(8 nm)* anti-aircraft; weight of shell 32 kg.
2 GE/GDC 20 mm Mk 15 Vulcan Phalanx ❸; 6 barrels per mounting; 3000 rounds/minute combined to 1.5 km. Mountings rotated between ships.
Up to 6—12.7 mm MGs.
Torpedoes: 6—324 mm Mk 32 Mod 5 (2 triple) tubes ❹. Honeywell Mk 46 Mod 5; anti-submarine; active/passive homing to 11 km *(5.9 nm)* at 40 kts; warhead 44 kg. Some obsolete Mk 44 torpedoes still in service.
Countermeasures: Decoys: 2 Loral Hycor SRBOC 6-barrelled fixed Mk 36; chaff and IR flares to 1-4 km *(0.6-2.2 nm)*. Nulka quad expendable decoy launcher fitted in *Brisbane* for trials. SLQ 25; towed torpedo decoy.
ESM/ECM: WLR-1H; intercept.
Combat data systems: NCDS with NTDS consoles and Univac UYK-7 computers; Link 11. OE-2 SATCOM ❺.
Fire control: GFCS Mk 68. Missile control Mk 74 Mod 13. Electro-optic sights may be fitted.
Radars: Air search: Hughes SPS 52C ❻; E/F band; range 439 km *(240 nm)*.
Lockheed SPS 40C ❼; E/F band; range 320 km *(175 nm)*.
Surface search: Norden SPS 67V ❽; G band.
Fire control: Two Raytheon SPG 51C ❾; G/I band (for Standard missile system).
Western Electric SPG 53F ❿; I/J band (for guns).
IFF: AIMS Mk 12.
Tacan: URN 20.
Sonars: Sangamo SQS 23KL; hull-mounted; active; medium frequency; with limited bottom bounce capability.

Modernisation: *Perth* was first modernised in 1974 in the USA with the installation of Standard missiles, replacement gun mountings, new combat data system and modern radars. *Hobart* and *Brisbane* were brought to the same standard in 1978 and 1979 at the Garden Island Dockyard in Sydney. A second modernisation programme: *Brisbane* completed 1987; *Perth* in 1989; *Hobart* in 1991. Major equipment upgraded: search and fire control radars, naval combat data system, gun systems, the Mk 13 missile launcher (to take Harpoon). Missile modernisation included decoy and improved ECM equipment; three-dimensional radar SPS 52B upgraded to SPS 52C. In 1990/91 all ships were fitted for Phalanx CIWS, although the mountings are rotated in a fleet pool system. To accommodate Phalanx the ship's boats have been replaced by RIBs. Ikara launchers and magazines have been removed. Nulka stand off decoys installed in *Brisbane* for trials in 1992/93.

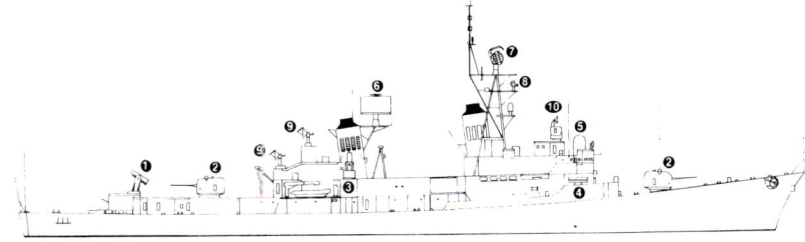

HOBART *(Scale 1 : 1200), Ian Sturton*

BRISBANE (with Phalanx) *11/1991, John Mortimer*

Structure: Generally similar to the US Charles F Adams class, but they differ by the addition of a broad deckhouse between the funnels which was the magazine for the now deleted Ikara system. In *Hobart* this space has been modified to include Flag accommodation.

Operational: Operational deployments include communications enhancements and portable RAM panels. All ships are capable of fighter control.

PERTH *10/1992, S Poynton, RAN*

FRIGATES

5 + 1 US FFG 7 CLASS

Name	No	Builders	Laid down	Launched	Commissioned
ADELAIDE	01	Todd Pacific Shipyard Corporation, Seattle, USA	29 July 1977	21 June 1978	15 Nov 1980
CANBERRA	02	Todd Pacific Shipyard Corporation, Seattle, USA	1 Mar 1978	1 Dec 1978	21 Mar 1981
SYDNEY	03	Todd Pacific Shipyard Corporation, Seattle, USA	16 Jan 1980	26 Sep 1980	29 Jan 1983
DARWIN	04	Todd Pacific Shipyard Corporation, Seattle, USA	3 July 1981	26 Mar 1982	21 July 1984
MELBOURNE	05	Australian Marine Eng (Consolidated), Williamstown	12 July 1985	5 May 1989	15 Feb 1992
NEWCASTLE	06	Australian Marine Eng (Consolidated), Williamstown	21 July 1989	21 Feb 1992	Nov 1993

Displacement, tons: 3962 (4000 *Melbourne*, 4100 *Newcastle*) full load

Dimensions, feet (metres): 453 × 45 × 24.5 (sonar); 14.8 (keel) *(138.1 × 13.7 × 7.5; 4.5)*

Main machinery: 2 GE LM 2500 gas turbines; 41 000 hp *(30.6 MW)* sustained; 1 shaft; cp prop; 2 auxiliary electric retractable propulsors fwd; 650 hp *(490 kW)*

Speed, knots: 29 (4 on propulsors). **Range, miles:** 4500 at 20 kts

Complement: 184 (15 officers) plus aircrew

Missiles: SSM: 8 McDonnell Douglas Harpoon; active radar homing to 130 km *(70 nm)* at 0.9 Mach; warhead 227 kg.
SAM: GDC Pomona Standard SM-1MR; Mk 13 Mod 4 launcher for both SAM and SSM systems ❶; command guidance; semi-active radar homing to 46 km *(25 nm)* at 2 Mach; height 45.7-18 288 m *(150-60 000 ft)*; 40 missiles (combined SSM and SAM).

Guns: 1 OTO Melara 3 in *(76 mm)*/62 US Mk 75 compact ❷; 85° elevation; 85 rounds/minute to 16 km *(9 nm)* anti-surface; 12 km *(6.5 nm)* anti-aircraft; weight of shell 6 kg. Guns for 05 and 06 manufactured in Australia.
1 General Electric/GDC 20 mm Mk 15 Vulcan Phalanx ❸; anti-missile system with 6 barrels; 3000 rounds/minute combined to 1.5 km. Retrofitted in 01 and 02 in 1985; 03-06 fitted on completion.
Up to 6—12.7 mm MGs.

Torpedoes: 6—324 mm Mk 32 (2 triple) tubes ❹. Honeywell Mk 46 Mod 5; anti-submarine; active/passive homing to 11 km *(5.9 nm)* at 40 kts; warhead 44 kg. Some Mk 44 torpedoes are still in service.

Countermeasures: Decoys: 2 Loral Hycor SRBOC Mk 36 chaff and IR decoy launchers; fixed 6-barrelled system; range 1-4 km. 4 Nulka quad expendable decoy launchers may be fitted in due course.
SLQ 25; towed torpedo decoy.

ESM/ECM: Raytheon SLQ-32C; intercept; J band.

Combat data systems: NCDS using NTDS consoles and Sperry Univac UYK 7 computers. OE-2 SATCOM; Link 11.

Fire control: Sperry Mk 92 Mod 2 gun and missile control (HSA derivative). Electro-optic sights.

Radars: Air search: Raytheon SPS 49 ❺; C/D band; range 457 km *(250 nm)*.
Surface search/navigation: ISC Cardion SPS 55 ❻; I/J band.
Fire control: Lockheed SPG 60 ❼; I/J band; range 110 km *(60 nm)*; Doppler search and tracking.
Sperry Mk 92 (Signaal WM 28) ❽; I/J band; range 46 km *(25 nm)*.

IFF: AIMS Mk XII.
Tacan: URN-25.

Sonars: Raytheon SQS 56; hull-mounted; active; medium frequency. Commercial derivative of DE 1160 series. 05 and 06 will have EMI/Honeywell Mulloka system instead of SQS 56. Kariwara towed passive array in due course.

Helicopters: 2 Sikorsky S-70B-2 Seahawks ❾ or 1 Seahawk and 1 Squirrel (see *Shipborne Aircraft* section).

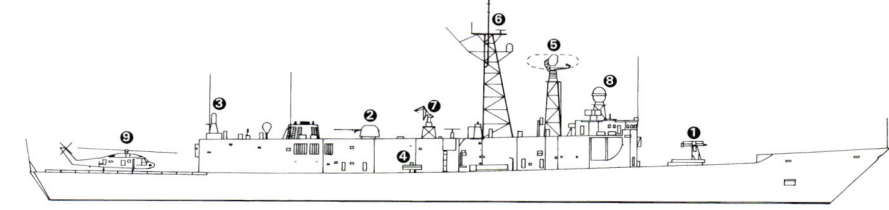

ADELAIDE *(Scale 1 : 1200), Ian Sturton*

ADELAIDE *10/1992, Vic Jeffery, RAN*

Programmes: US numbers: *Adelaide* FFG 17; *Canberra* FFG 18; *Sydney* FFG 35; *Darwin* FFG 44.

Modernisation: *Adelaide* in November 1989, *Sydney* February 1989 and *Canberra* December 1991 completed a 12 month Helicopter Modification Programme to allow operation of Seahawk helicopters. The modification, fitted to *Darwin* during construction, involved angling the transom (increasing the ship's overall length by 8 ft) and fitting the RAST helo recovery system. *Melbourne* and *Newcastle* fitted during construction which also includes longitudinal strengthening and buoyancy upgrades. A mid-life modernisation is being considered—to include SM2 missiles, towed array sonars and improved AAW fire control.

Operational: *Adelaide* based at Fleet Base West from October 1992, to be joined by *Sydney* in 1993. The remainder are based at Fleet Base East. For operational tasks ships are fitted with enhanced communications, electro-optical sights, rigid inflatable boats and portable RAM panels. All ships are fighter control capable.

CANBERRA *10/1992, S Connolly, RAN*

26 AUSTRALIA / Frigates

3 RIVER CLASS

Name	No	Builders	Laid down	Launched	Commissioned
DERWENT	49	HMA Naval Dockyard, Melbourne	16 June 1958	17 Apr 1961	30 Apr 1964
SWAN	50	HMA Naval Dockyard, Melbourne	18 Aug 1965	16 Dec 1967	20 Jan 1970
TORRENS	53	Cockatoo Island Dockyard, Sydney	18 Aug 1965	28 Sep 1968	19 Jan 1971

Displacement, tons: 2100 standard; 2700 full load
Dimensions, feet (metres): 360 wl; 370 oa × 41 × 17.3 (screws) *(109.8; 112.8 × 12.5 × 5.3)*
Main machinery: 2 B&W boilers; 550 psi *(38.7 kg/cm sq)*; 850°F *(450°C)*; 2 steam turbines; 30 000 hp *(22.4 MW)*; 2 shafts
Speed, knots: 30. **Range, miles:** 3400 at 12 kts
Complement: 234 (20 officers); 224 (21 officers) (in 49)

Guns: 2 Vickers 4.5 in *(114 mm)*/45 Mk 6 (twin) ❶; 80° elevation; 20 rounds/minute to 19 km *(10 nm)* anti-surface; 6 km *(3 nm)* anti-aircraft; weight of shell 25 kg.
  4—12.7 mm MGs.
Torpedoes: 6—324 mm (2 triple) Mk 32 tubes ❷. Honeywell Mk 46; anti-submarine; active/passive homing to 11 km *(5.9 nm)* at 40 kts; warhead 44 kg. Some US Mk 44 torpedoes still in service.
Countermeasures: Decoys: SLQ 25 (50 and 53) and Type 182 (49) towed torpedo decoy.
  ESM: ELT 901.
Radars: Air search: Signaal LW 02 ❸; D band; range 183 km *(100 nm)*.
  Surface search: ISC Cardion SPS 55 (in 49) ❹; I/J band.
    Atlas Elektronik 8600 ARPA (in 50 and 53); I band.
  Fire control: Signaal M 22 ❺; I/J band; range 46 km *(25 nm)*.
  IFF: AIMS Mk XII.
Sonars: EMI/Honeywell Mulloka; hull-mounted; active search and attack; medium frequency.
  Kelvin Hughes Type 162 M; sideways looking classification; 50 kHz.

Modernisation: *Derwent* half-life modernisation completed December 1985. This programme included improved accommodation consequent on reduction in complement, installation of M22 system, the fitting of Australian Mulloka sonar, the conversion of the boilers to burn diesel fuel, installation of Mk 32 torpedo tubes in lieu of Mk 10 mortar and new navigation radar. *Swan* and *Torrens* had a half-life refit which completed in September 1985. This refit included installation of Mulloka sonar, Mk 32 torpedo tubes in lieu of Mk 10 mortar and a torpedo decoy. Seacat and Ikara deleted from operational service in 1991.
Structure: The design of *Derwent* is basically similar to that of British Type 12 (now deleted), the other pair to that of the Leander frigates. Note difference in silhouette between *Swan/Torrens* and *Derwent*, the former pair having a straight-run upper deck.
Operational: Classified as Destroyer Escorts. Based at Fleet Base West as part of the deployment of the fleet as a 'Two Ocean Navy'. An RBS 70 Mk 2 missile detachment can be embarked if required.

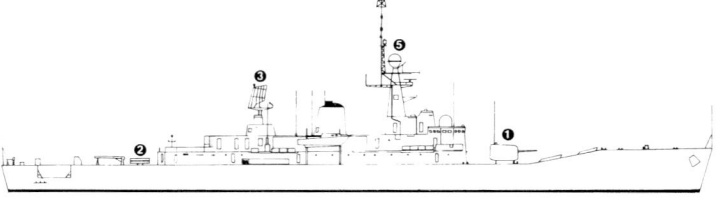
TORRENS (Scale 1 : 1200), Ian Sturton

TORRENS 10/1992, S Connolly, RAN

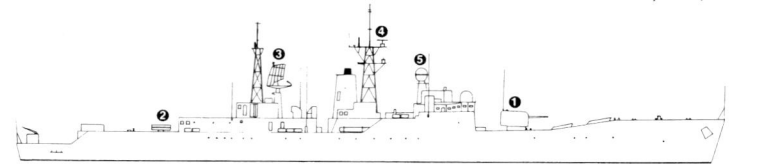
DERWENT (Scale 1 : 1200), Ian Sturton

SWAN 8/1991, P. Steel, RAN

DERWENT 3/1992, John Mortimer

Frigates — Shipborne aircraft / AUSTRALIA

0 + 8 ANZAC CLASS

Name	No	Builders	Laid down	Launched	Commissioned
ANZAC	150	Amecon, Williamstown	27 Mar 1992	Nov 1994	Oct 1995
ARRERNTE	151	Amecon, Williamstown	Nov 1993	June 1995	Nov 1997
WARUMUNGU	152	Amecon, Williamstown	1995	June 1997	Nov 1999
STUART	153	Amecon, Williamstown	1996	June 1998	Nov 2000
PARRAMATTA	154	Amecon, Williamstown	1997	1999	2001
BALLARAT	155	Amecon, Williamstown	1998	2000	2002
TOOWOOMBA	156	Amecon, Williamstown	1999	2001	2003
PERTH	157	Amecon, Williamstown	2000	2002	2004

Displacement, tons: 3600 full load
Dimensions, feet (metres): 387.1 oa; 357.6 wl × 48.6 × 14.3 *(118; 109 × 14.8 × 4.35)*
Main machinery: CODOG: 1 GE LM 2500 gas turbine; 30 172 hp *(22.5 MW)* sustained; 2 MTU 12V 1163 TB83 diesels; 8840 hp(m) *(6.5 MW)* sustained; 2 shafts; cp props
Speed, knots: 27. **Range, miles:** 6000 at 18 kts
Complement: 163

Missiles: SAM: Raytheon Sea Sparrow RIM-7P; Martin Marietta Mk 41 Mod 5 octuple vertical launcher ❶; 8 missiles total.
Guns: 1 FMC 5 in (127 mm)/54 Mk 45 Mod 2 ❷. 2—12.7 mm MGs.
Torpedoes: 6—324 mm (2 triple) Mk 32 tubes; to be fitted after ship acceptance into the Navy.
Countermeasures: Decoys: G & D Aircraft GD 36 Mod 1 chaff launchers ❸ for SRBOC. 4 Nulka quad launchers may be fitted. SLQ-25 Nixie towed torpedo decoy (probably).
ESM: THORN EMI modified Sceptre A; radar intercept. Telefunken Telegon 10.
Combat data systems: NobelTech 9LV 453 Mk 3. Link 11.
Fire control: NobelTech 9LV 453 optronic director. Raytheon CW Mk 73 (for SAM).
Radars: Air search: Raytheon SPS 49(V)8 ANZ ❹; C/D band.
Air/surface search: NobelTech 9LV 453 TIR (Ericsson Tx/Rx) ❺; G band.
Navigation: Atlas Elektronik 8600 ARPA; I band.
Fire control: NobelTech 9LV 453 ❻; J band.
IFF: Cossor AIMS Mk XII.
Sonars: Thomson Sintra Spherion B; hull-mounted; active search and attack; medium frequency. Provision for Kariwara towed array; passive search; very low frequency.

Helicopters: 1 S-70B Seahawk ❼.

Programmes: Contract signed with Australian Marine Engineering Consolidated on 19 November 1989 to build eight Blohm & Voss designed MEKO 200 ANZ frigates for Australia and two for New Zealand, which has an option for two more. Modules are being constructed at Newcastle and shipped to Melbourne for assembly. The second and fourth ships are for New Zealand. The second four Australian ships will be Batch 2 fitted with Evolved Sea Sparrow. It is possible that a stretched version of this class may be ordered in due course as replacements for the DDGs.

Structure: 'Space and weight' reserved for a CIWS, Harpoon SSM, an additional octuple VLS, second channel of fire for VLS, towed array sonar, offboard active ECM, extended ESM frequency coverage, Helo data link and SATCOM. Stealth features are incorporated in the design. All steel construction. Fin stabilisers. Torpedo tubes will be taken from older classes and fitted after ship acceptance from the builders. Indal RAST helicopter recovery system.

ANZAC *(Scale 1 : 900), Ian Sturton*

ANZAC (artist's impression) *1990, RAN*

SHIPBORNE AIRCRAFT

Note: Six maritime utility helicopters are to be ordered in the mid-1990s.

Numbers/Type: 6 Aerospatiale AS 350B Squirrel.
Operational speed: 125 kts *(232 km/h)*.
Service ceiling: 10 000 ft *(3050 m)*.
Range: 390 nm *(720 km)*.
Role/Weapon systems: Support helicopter for operational training of naval personnel on new FFG-7 frigates prior to delivery of S-70B, then for utility tasks and training duties. Sensors: None. Weapons: ASV; two Mag 58 MGs.

SEAHAWK *1992, S Connolly, RAN*

Numbers/Type: 6 Westland Sea King HAS 50/50A.
Operational speed: 125 kts *(230 km/h)*.
Service ceiling: 10 500 ft *(3200 m)*.
Range: 630 nm *(1165 km)*.
Role/Weapon systems: Utility helicopter; embarked periodically for operations from Afloat Support Ships. Sensors: MEL 5955 radar. Weapons: Disarmed in 1992.

SQUIRREL *8/1990, RAN*

Numbers/Type: 16 Sikorsky S-70B-2 Seahawk.
Operational speed: 135 kts *(250 km/h)*.
Service ceiling: 12 000 ft *(3810 m)*.
Range: 600 nm *(1110 km)*.
Role/Weapon systems: Seahawk derivative aircraft designed by Sikorsky to meet RAN specifications for ASW and ASST operations. Eight assembled by ASTA in Victoria. Helicopters embarked in FFG-7 and may be utilised in ANZAC frigates. Sensors: MEL Surface surveillance radar, CDC Sonobuoy Processor and Barra Side Processor, and CAE Magnetic Anomaly Detector Set controlled by a versatile Tactical Display/Management System, FLIR and ESM, possibly dipping sonar in due course. Weapons: ASW; two Mk 46 Mod 5 torpedoes. ASV; two Mag 58 MGs, possibly Sea Skua ASM in due course.

SEA KING *1992, RAN*

28 AUSTRALIA / Land-based maritime aircraft — Mine warfare forces

LAND-BASED MARITIME AIRCRAFT

Numbers/Type: 2 British Aerospace HS 748.
Operational speed: 140 kts *(259 km/h)*.
Service ceiling: 25 000 ft *(7620 m)*.
Range: 2675 nm *(4950 km)*.
Role/Weapon systems: ELINT aircraft operated by Squadron RAN HC 723 specially equipped by Sanders Associates, USA. Sensors: Complete EW suite classified.

Numbers/Type: 22 General Dynamics F-111C.
Operational speed: 793 kts *(1469 km/h)*.
Service ceiling: 60 000 ft *(18 290 m)*.
Range: 2540 nm *(4700 km)*.
Role/Weapon systems: Royal Australian Air Force operates the F-111 for anti-shipping strike and its small force of RF-111 for coastline surveillance duties using EW/ESM and photographic equipment underwing. Plans to acquire 18 more F-111 from US. Sensors: GE AN/APG-144, podded EW. Weapons: ASV; 4 × Harpoon missiles. Strike; 4 × Snakeye bombs. Self-defence; 2 × AIM-9P.

Numbers/Type: 19 Lockheed P-3C/Update II Orion.
Operational speed: 410 kts *(760 km/h)*.
Service ceiling: 28 300 ft *(8625 m)*.
Range: 4000 nm *(7410 km)*.
Role/Weapon systems: Operated by air force for long-range ocean surveillance and ASW. Being upgraded from 1992 with improvements to radar, acoustic processors, navigation and communications. Sensors: APS-115 radar, AQS-901 processor, AQS-81 MAD, ECM, Elta/IAI, ESM, 80 × BARRA sonobuoys. Weapons: ASW; 8 × Mk 44 or Mk 46 torpedoes, Mk 25 mines, 8 × Mk 54 depth bombs. ASV; up to six Harpoon.

Numbers/Type: 72 McDonnell Douglas F-18 Hornet.
Operational speed: 1032 kts *(1910 km/h)*.
Service ceiling: 50 000 ft *(15 240 m)*.
Range: 1000 nm *(1829 km)*.
Role/Weapon systems: Air defence and strike aircraft operated by RAAF but with fleet defence and anti-shipping secondary roles. Sensors: APG-65 attack radar, AAS-38 FLIR/ALR-67 radar warning receiver. Weapons: ASV; 4 × Harpoon missiles. Strike; 1 × 20 mm cannon, up to 7.7 tons of 'iron' bombs. Fleet defence; 4 × AIM-7 Sparrow and 4 × AIM-9L Sidewinder.

LIGHT FORCES

Note: The plan is to build 12 Tier Two Offshore Patrol Vessels starting in 1997. The class will have better seakeeping, endurance, weapons and sensors than the Fremantle class. Provisional design includes 55 m length, range 5500 nm, speed 26 kts in sea state 4, medium range gun, hard and soft kill defences and search radar.

15 FREMANTLE CLASS (LARGE PATROL CRAFT)

Name	No	Builders	Commissioned
FREMANTLE	203	Brooke Marine, Lowestoft	17 Mar 1980
WARRNAMBOOL	204	NQEA Australia, Cairns	14 Mar 1981
TOWNSVILLE	205	NQEA Australia, Cairns	18 July 1981
WOLLONGONG	206	NQEA Australia, Cairns	28 Nov 1981
LAUNCESTON	207	NQEA Australia, Cairns	1 Mar 1982
WHYALLA	208	NQEA Australia, Cairns	3 July 1982
IPSWICH	209	NQEA Australia, Cairns	13 Nov 1982
CESSNOCK	210	NQEA Australia, Cairns	5 Mar 1983
BENDIGO	211	NQEA Australia, Cairns	28 May 1983
GAWLER	212	NQEA Australia, Cairns	27 Aug 1983
GERALDTON	213	NQEA Australia, Cairns	10 Dec 1983
DUBBO	214	NQEA Australia, Cairns	10 Mar 1984
GEELONG	215	NQEA Australia, Cairns	2 June 1984
GLADSTONE	216	NQEA Australia, Cairns	8 Sep 1984
BUNBURY	217	NQEA Australia, Cairns	15 Dec 1984

Displacement, tons: 211 full load
Dimensions, feet (metres): 137.1 × 23.3 × 5.9 *(41.8 × 7.1 × 1.8)*
Main machinery: 2 MTU 16V 538 TB91 diesels; 6140 hp(m) *(4.5 MW)* sustained 1 centre line Dorman cruising diesel; 3 shafts
Speed, knots: 30; 8 on cruising diesel. **Range, miles:** 1450 at 30 kts; 4800 cruising
Complement: 22 (3 officers)

Guns: 1 Bofors AN 4—40 mm/60; 120 rounds/minute to 10 km *(5.5 nm)*. The 40 mm mountings were designed by Australian Government Ordnance Factory and although the guns are of older manufacture, this mounting gives greater accuracy particularly in heavy weather. 1—81 mm mortar. 2—12.7 mm MGs.
Countermeasures: ESM: AWA Defence Industries Type 133 PRISM; radar warning.
Radars: Navigation: Kelvin Hughes Type 1006; I band.

Programmes: The decision to buy these PCF 420 class patrol craft was announced in September 1977. The design is by Brooke Marine Ltd, Lowestoft which built the lead ship.
Modernisation: A life extension programme, including sensor upgrade, is being given to keep these craft in service until OPV replacements are built. ESM being fitted from 1993.
Operational: Bases: Cairns—P 205, 208, 209, 211, 216. Darwin—P 206, 207, 210, 212, 214, 215. Sydney—P 203 (reserve training). Melbourne—P 204 (reserve training). Fremantle—P 213, 217.

BENDIGO   *6/1992, John Mortimer*

2 ATTACK CLASS (LARGE PATROL CRAFT)

Name	No	Builders	Commissioned
ARDENT	87	Evans Deakin Ltd	26 Oct 1968
AWARE	91	Evans Deakin Ltd	21 June 1968

Displacement, tons: 146 full load
Dimensions, feet (metres): 107.5 × 20 × 7.3 *(32.8 × 6.1 × 2.2)*
Main machinery: 2 Paxman 16YJCM diesels; 4000 hp *(2.98 MW)* sustained; 2 shafts
Speed, knots: 24. **Range, miles:** 1220 at 13 kts
Complement: 19 (3 officers)

Guns: 1 Bofors 40 mm/60 Mk 7; 85° elevation; 300 rounds/minute to 12 km *(6.5 nm)*; weight of shell 0.96 kg.
2—7.62 mm MGs.
Radars: Navigation: Racal Decca RM 916; I band.

Programmes: Steel construction. First ordered in November 1965.
Operational: Bases are: Adelaide PD—91 (Reserve Training). Hobart PD—87 (Reserve Training). In addition *Bayonet* is an unarmed training platform at *Cerberus* but is still seagoing and in good condition.
Sales: *Bandolier* transferred to Indonesia 1973; *Archer* 1974. *Aitape, Ladava, Lae, Madang,* and *Samarei* transferred to Papua New Guinea Defence Force 1975. *Barricade* to Indonesia 1982; *Acute, Bombard* 1983; *Barbette, Assail, Attack* 1985; *Buccaneer* disposed of in 1984 and sunk as a target in October 1988. *Advance* to National Maritime Museum.

ATTACK class (old number)   *6/1991, Vic Jeffery, RAN*

MINE WARFARE FORCES

Notes: (1) Six (or four) MCMV of a proven design are to be acquired as a matter of priority. Orders expected in 1993 from a short list of Vosper Sandown, Intermarine Gaeta and Kockums Landsort. All these companies are acting in consort with different Australian shipbuilding industries. It is planned to have the first vessel in service in 1995.
(2) Of the four vessels involved in the early COOP programme, *Wave Rider* and *Salvatore V* were returned to their owners, and a replacement *Gunundaal* acquired in May 1992. This ship had hull problems and will in turn be replaced in mid-1993. The full programme involves having equipment available for large numbers of earmarked fishing vessels.

2 BAY CLASS (MINEHUNTERS—INSHORE)

Name	No	Builders	Commissioned
RUSHCUTTER	M 80	Carrington Slipways	1 Nov 1986
SHOALWATER	M 81	Carrington Slipways	10 Oct 1987

Displacement, tons: 170 approx
Dimensions, feet (metres): 101.7 × 29.5 × 6.6 *(30.9 × 9 × 2)*
Main machinery: 2 Poyaud/Grossel diesel generator sets; 2 Schottel hydraulic transmission and steering systems (one to each hull)
Speed, knots: 10. **Range, miles:** 1200 at 10 kts
Complement: 14 (3 officers)

Guns: 4—12.7 mm MGs.
Countermeasures: MCM system is containerised allowing for rapid replacement or removal. As well as the hull sonar the MWS 80-5 has Satam command system, NBD navigation and track control, and the DDSX-11 active classification sonar. Four subsystems are located in the container—sonar, tactical data, precision navigation and mine disposal weapon control. The latter operates a remote-controlled ECA 38 system using two PAP 104 vehicles.
Radars: Navigation: Kelvin Hughes Type 1006; I band.
Sonars: Atlas Elektronik DSQS 11M; hull-mounted; minehunting; high frequency.

Programmes: Ordered January 1983. First launched 3 May 1986; second 20 June 1987.
Structure: The catamaran hull form was chosen as it provides stability, a large deck area, greater manoeuvrability than a mono-hull and reduction in signatures by placing heavy machinery high in the ship. Each hull is 3 m beam with 3 m space between. Foam sandwich construction was adopted and a policy of repair by replacement. *Shoalwater* fitted with two funnels in 1992 to assess impact on noise reduction.
Operational: Due to performance deficiencies of the MWS 80 minehunting weapon system, comparative trials were conducted in 1992 between the Atlas MWS 80-5 and the Thomson Sintra Ibis V Mk 2 systems. The Atlas system has been selected. The two ships are based in Sydney and used for training and operations in confined waters.

SHOALWATER (with twin funnels)   *10/1992, John Mortimer*

2 MINESWEEPERS AUXILIARY (TUGS) (MSA(T))

BANDICOOT (ex-*Grenville VII*) Y 298   **WALLAROO** (ex-*Grenville V*) Y 299

Displacement, tons: 242 full load
Dimensions, feet (metres): 95.8 × 28 × 11.3 *(29.6 × 8.5 × 3.4)*
Main machinery: 2 Stork Werkspoor diesels; 2400 hp(m) *(1.76 MW)*; 2 shafts
Speed, knots: 11. **Range, miles:** 6300 at 10 kts
Complement: 10
Radars: Navigation: Furuno 7040D; I band.

Comment: Built in Singapore 1982 and operated by Maritime (PTE) Ltd. Purchased by the RAN and refurbished prior to delivery 11 August 1990. Initially being used for minesweeping trials towing large influence and mechanical sweeps. No side scan sonar. Also used as berthing tugs. Bollard pull, 30 tons. Both painted grey in early 1993.

BANDICOOT   *11/1992, John Mortimer*

1 MINESWEEPER AUXILIARY (SMALL) (MSA(S))

BROLGA (ex-*Lumen*) 1102

Displacement, tons: 268 full load
Dimensions, feet (metres): 93.2 × 26.6 × 11.5 *(28.4 × 8.1 × 3.5)*
Main machinery: 1 Mirrlees Blackstone diesel; 540 hp *(403 kW)*; 1 shaft; cp prop
Speed, knots: 10.5
Complement: 8 (1 officer)

Comment: Acquired from the Department of Transport on 10 February 1988 for the COOP programme. The COOP tow a magnetic body and acoustic noise makers for influence minesweeping, a mechanical sweep to counter moored mines and a Klein side scan sonar for route surveillance. Painted grey in late 1992.

BROLGA   *11/1992, John Mortimer*

1 MINESWEEPER AUXILIARY (SMALL) (MSA(S))

KORAAGA (ex-*Grozdana 'A'*) 1185

Displacement, tons: 119 full load
Dimensions, feet (metres): 71.9 × 21 × 9.8 *(21.9 × 6.4 × 3)*
Main machinery: 1 Caterpillar D346 diesel; 480 hp *(358 kW)* sustained; 1 shaft
Speed, knots: 11
Complement: 8 (1 officer)

Comment: Acquired 16 February 1989 for the COOP programme. Painted grey in late 1992.

KORAAGA   *11/1992, John Mortimer*

3 MINESWEEPING DRONES

MSO 01-03

Comment: Remote-controlled drones with twin Yamaha outboard engines. GRP hulls made by Hydrofield

MSO 03   *11/1992, John Mortimer*

AMPHIBIOUS FORCES

1 AMPHIBIOUS HEAVY LIFT SHIP (LSH)

Name	No	Builders	Laid down	Launched	Commissioned
TOBRUK	L 50	Carrington Slipways Pty Ltd	7 Feb 1978	1 Mar 1980	23 Apr 1981

Displacement, tons: 3300 standard; 5700 full load
Dimensions, feet (metres): 417 × 60 × 16 *(127 × 18.3 × 4.9)*
Main machinery: 2 Mirrlees Blackstone KDMR8 diesels; 9600 hp *(7.2 MW)*; 2 shafts
Speed, knots: 18. **Range, miles:** 8000 at 15 kts
Complement: 144 (13 officers)
Military lift: 350-500 troops; 1300 tons cargo; 70 tons capacity derrick; 2—4.25 ton cranes; 2 LCVP; 2 LCM

Guns: 2 Bofors 40 mm/60; dual purpose; 80° elevation; 120 rounds/minute to 10 km *(5.5 nm)* anti-surface.
2—12.7 mm MGs.
Radars: Surface search: Kelvin Hughes Type 1006; I band.
Navigation: Racal Decca RM 916; I band.

Helicopters: Platform only for up to 4 Sea King.

Structure: The design is an update of the British Sir Bedivere class and provides facilities for the operation of helicopters, landing craft, amphibians or side-carried pontoons for ship-to-shore movement. A special feature is the ship's heavy lift derrick system for handling heavy loads. The LSH is able to embark a squadron of Leopard tanks plus a number of wheeled vehicles and artillery in addition to its troop lift. Bow and stern ramps are fitted. Carries two 20 kt waterjet LCVPs at davits. Fitted for side-carrying two NLE pontoons. Two LCM 8 carried on deck. Helicopters can be operated from the well deck or the after platform.
Operational: A comprehensive communication fit and minor hospital facilities are provided. Can operate all in-service helicopters. Based at Sydney.

TOBRUK   *3/1992, John Mortimer*

30 AUSTRALIA / Amphibious forces — General purpose vessels

6 LANDING CRAFT (HEAVY) (LCH)

Name	No	Builders	Commissioned
BALIKPAPAN	L 126	Walkers Ltd, Queensland	8 Dec 1971
BRUNEI	L 127	Walkers Ltd, Queensland	5 Jan 1973
LABUAN	L 128	Walkers Ltd, Queensland	9 Mar 1973
TARAKAN	L 129	Walkers Ltd, Queensland	15 June 1973
WEWAK	L 130	Walkers Ltd, Queensland	10 Aug 1973
BETANO	L 133	Walkers Ltd, Queensland	8 Feb 1974

Displacement, tons: 310 light; 503 full load
Dimensions, feet (metres): 146 × 33 × 6.5 *(44.5 × 10.1 × 2)*
Main machinery: 2 GM 6-71 diesels; 348 hp *(260 kW)* sustained; 2 shafts
Speed, knots: 10. **Range, miles:** 3000 at 10 kts
Complement: 13 (2 officers)
Military lift: 3 medium tanks or equivalent
Guns: 2—7.62 mm MGs.
Radars: Navigation: Racal Decca RM 916; I band.

Comment: Originally this class was ordered for the Army with which *Balikpapan* remained until June 1974, being commissioned for naval service on 27 September 1974. The remainder were built for the Navy. *Brunei* and *Betano* act as diving tenders. *Labuan* at Brisbane and *Balikpapan* at Darwin for reserve training. *Wewak* in operational reserve at Cairns but could be made operational quickly. *Tarakan* operates from Cairns in a survey ship role and for general duties. All are available for amphibious duties and the plan is to base more of them in the north. *Buna* and *Salamaua* transferred to Papua New Guinea Defence Force in November 1974.

TARAKAN 3/1992, John Mortimer

1 + 3 LANDING CRAFT (LIGHT) (LCVP)

Displacement, tons: 6.5 full load
Dimensions, feet (metres): 43.3 × 11.5 × 2.3 *(13.2 × 3.5 × 0.7)*
Main machinery: 2 Volvo Penta Sterndrives; 400 hp(m) *(294 kW)*
Speed, knots: 22; 15 (fully laden)
Complement: 3
Military lift: 4.5 tons cargo or 36 troops

Comment: Prototype built by Geraldton, Western Australia. Trials conducted in late 1992. Total of four to be acquired: two for *Tobruk*, one for *Success* and one spare to be attached to *Penguin*.

LCVP 10/1992, RAN

OCEANOGRAPHIC AND SURVEY SHIPS (MARINE SCIENCE FORCE)

Notes: (i) In addition to the ships listed below there are four civilian survey vessels; *Icebird, Franklin, Rig Seismic* and *Lady Franklin*. Also an arctic supply ship *Aurora Australis* started operating in the Antarctic in 1990; this vessel carries 70 scientists and has a helicopter hangar.
(ii) Three ships, one for oceanography and two for hydrography to be built in due course. Contracts for Project Definition studies to be let in mid-1993. Common hull and machinery is anticipated.

Name	No	Builders	Commissioned
MORESBY	A 73	Dockyard, Newcastle	6 Mar 1964

Displacement, tons: 1714 standard; 2351 full load
Dimensions, feet (metres): 314 × 42 × 15 *(95.7 × 12.8 × 4.6)*
Main machinery: Diesel-electric; 3 diesel generators; 2 motors; 3990 hp *(2.9 MW)*; 2 shafts
Speed, knots: 19
Complement: 138 (12 officers)
Guns: 2 Bofors 40 mm (removed).
Radars: Navigation: Racal Decca TM 916C; I band.
Sonars: Simrad SU2; high definition; retractable dome.
Helicopters: 1 Bell 206B.

Comment: The RAN's first specifically designed survey ship. Launched 7 September 1963. During refit in 1973 *Moresby*'s funnel was heightened, her 40 mm guns removed and an exhaust outlet fitted on her forecastle. Three new survey launches with jet drive embarked in 1982. Has Qubit Hydlaps data logging and processing system. Based at *Stirling* (Cockburn Sound WA).

MORESBY 1/1992, S Connolly, RAN

Name	No	Builders	Commissioned
FLINDERS	A 312	HMA Dockyard, Williamstown	27 Apr 1973

Displacement, tons: 750
Dimensions, feet (metres): 161 × 33 × 12 *(49.1 × 10 × 3.7)*
Main machinery: 2 Paxman 8YJCM diesels; 2000 hp *(1.98 MW)* sustained; 2 shafts; cp props
Speed, knots: 13.5. **Range, miles:** 5000 at 9 kts
Complement: 43 (5 officers)
Radars: Navigation: Racal Decca TM 916C; I band.
Sonars: Simrad SU2; high definition; retractable dome.

Comment: Launched 29 July 1972. Similar in design to *Atyimba* built for the Philippines. New survey launch with jet drive embarked in 1982. Has Qubit Hydlaps data logging and processing system. The ship is based at Cairns, with primary responsibility in the Barrier Reef area.

FLINDERS 10/1986, John Mortimer

4 PALUMA CLASS (SURVEY SHIPS)

Name	No	Builders	Commissioned
PALUMA	A 01	Eglo, Adelaide	27 Feb 1989
MERMAID	A 02	Eglo, Adelaide	4 Dec 1989
SHEPPARTON	A 03	Eglo, Adelaide	24 Jan 1990
BENALLA	A 04	Eglo, Adelaide	20 Mar 1990

Displacement, tons: 320 full load
Dimensions, feet (metres): 118.9 × 45.3 × 6.2 *(36.6 × 13.8 × 1.9)*
Main machinery: 2 Detroit 12V-92TA diesels; 1020 hp *(760 kW)* sustained; 2 shafts
Speed, knots: 12. **Range, miles:** 3500 at 11 kts
Complement: 12 (2 officers)
Radars: Navigation: JRC JMA-3710-6; I band.
Sonars: Skipper S113; hull-mounted; active; high frequency. ELAC LAZ 72; hull-mounted side scan; active; high frequency.

Comment: Catamaran design based on Prince class Ro-Ro passenger ferries. Steel hulls and aluminium superstructure. Contract signed in November 1987. Although she commissioned in February 1989, *Paluma* was not accepted into service until September 1989 because of noise problems. As a result other members of the class were about six months late completing. Qubit Hydlaps data logging and processing system fitted. All are based at Cairns and are fitted out for operations in shallow waters of Northern Australia. Normally operate in pairs.

MERMAID 5/1990, John Mortimer

GENERAL PURPOSE VESSELS

1 TRAINING SHIP

Name	No	Builders	Commissioned
BANKS	AG 244	Walkers, Maryborough, Queensland	16 Feb 1960

Displacement, tons: 207 standard; 255 and 260 full load respectively
Dimensions, feet (metres): 90 pp; 101 oa × 22 × 8 *(27.5; 30.8 × 6.7 × 2.4)*
Main machinery: 2 diesels; 260 hp *(190 kW)*; 2 shafts
Speed, knots: 10
Complement: 12 (2 officers)
Radars: Navigation: Racal Decca 916; I band.

Comment: Explorer class; all steel construction. Fitted for fishery surveillance but is now used for navigation training based at *Waterhen*.

BANKS 10/1990, van Ginderen Collection

SERVICE FORCES

Note: A Training and Helicopter Support ship of about 20 000 tons is required to replace *Jervis Bay* and complement the amphibious capability of *Tobruk*. Capabilities should include carrying a battalion of troops, up to 12 utility helicopters and 4 LCM, plus an 80 bed hospital. A project office was formed on 21 December 1992 to examine the concept. The ship is planned to enter service in 1999.

1 LEAF CLASS (UNDERWAY REPLENISHMENT TANKER)

Name	No	Builder	Laid down	Launched	Commissioned
WESTRALIA (ex-*Hudson Cavalier*, ex-*Appleleaf*)	O 195 (ex-A 79)	Cammell Laird, Birkenhead	1974	24 July 1975	Nov 1979

Displacement, tons: 40 870 full load
Measurement, tons: 20 761 gross; 10 851 net; 33 595 dwt
Dimensions, feet (metres): 560 × 85 × 38.9 *(170.7 × 25.9 × 11.9)*
Main machinery: 2 SEMT-Pielstick 14 PC2.2 V400 diesels; 14 000 hp(m) *(10.3 MW)* sustained; 1 shaft
Speed, knots: 16 (11 on one engine). **Range, miles:** 7260 at 15 kts
Complement: 61 (8 officers) plus 9 spare berths
Cargo capacity: 22 000 tons dieso; 3800 tons aviation fuel
Radars: Navigation: 2 Kelvin Hughes ARPA; I and E/F bands.

Comment: Part of an order by the Hudson Fuel and Shipping Co which was subsequently cancelled. Leased by the RN from 1979 until transferred on 9 October 1989 on a five year lease to the RAN, arriving in Fremantle 20 December 1989. Option to purchase in 1994. Has three 3 ton cranes and two 5 ton derricks. Hospital facilities. Two beam and one stern replenishment stations. Based at *Stirling*. RBS 70 SAM systems (with Army detachment) and 4—12.7 mm MGs may be embarked for operations. Also modified to provide a large Vertrep platform aft.

WESTRALIA *3/1992, John Mortimer*

1 DURANCE CLASS (UNDERWAY REPLENISHMENT TANKER)

Name	No	Builders	Laid down	Launched	Commissioned
SUCCESS	OR 304	Cockatoo Dockyard	9 Aug 1980	3 Mar 1984	19 Feb 1986

Displacement, tons: 17 933 full load
Dimensions, feet (metres): 515.7 × 69.5 × 38.4 *(157.2 × 21.2 × 10.8)*
Main machinery: 2 SEMT-Pielstick 16 PC2.5 V400 diesels; 20 800 hp(m) *(15.3 MW)* sustained; 2 shafts; cp props
Speed, knots: 20. **Range, miles:** 9000 at 15 kts
Complement: 205 (26 officers)
Cargo capacity: 10 088 tons: 8220 dieso; 1300 Avcat; 259 distilled water; 183 victuals; 250 munitions including SM1 missiles and Mk 46 torpedoes; 45 naval stores and spares

Guns: 3 Bofors 40 mm (2 fwd, 1 aft). 4—12.7 mm MGs.
Radars: Navigation. Two Kelvin Hughes Type 1006; I band.
Helicopters: 1 AS 350B Squirrel or Sea King.

Comment: Based on French Durance class design. Replenishment at sea from four beam positions (two having heavy transfer capability) and vertrep. Hangar modified to take Sea Kings.

SUCCESS *3/1991, van Ginderen Collection*

1 HELICOPTER AND LOGISTIC SUPPORT SHIP

Name	No	Builders	Laid down	Launched	Commissioned
JERVIS BAY (ex-*Australian Trader*)	GT 203	State Dockyard, Newcastle, NSW	18 Aug 1967	17 Feb 1969	17 June 1969

Displacement, tons: 8915 full load
Dimensions, feet (metres): 445.1 × 70.6 × 20.1 *(135.7 × 21.5 × 6.1)*
Main machinery: 2 Crossley Pielstick 16 PC2.2 V400 diesels; 16 000 hp(m) *(11.8 MW)* sustained; 2 shafts; bow thruster
Speed, knots: 19.5
Complement: 177 (14 officers) plus 76 trainees

Guns: 2—12.7 mm MGs.
Radars: Surface search: Kelvin Hughes Type 1006; I band. Navigation: Atlas Elektronik 8600; I band.
Helicopters: Platform only for 1 Sea King.

Comment: Classified as a Helicopter, Logistic Support and Training Ship, the former roll-on roll-off vessel commissioned in the RAN on 25 August 1977. For the training role a navigation bridge was added in 1978. In 1987 the deckhouse was removed and the after deck strengthened for a Sea King sized helicopter. More ambitious plans to carry up to six aircraft were shelved. Based at Sydney.

JERVIS BAY *3/1992, John Mortimer*

TUGS

Note: In addition the two MSA(L) ships are used as tugs. Details under Mine Warfare Forces.

TAMMAR DT 2601

Displacement, tons: 265
Dimensions, feet (metres): 84.3 × 26.9 × 6.6 *(25.7 × 8.2 × 2)*
Main machinery: 2 diesels; 2800 hp *(2.09 MW)*; 2 shafts
Speed, knots: 11. **Range, miles:** 1450 at 11 kts
Complement: 6

Comment: Built by Australian Shipbuilding Industries, South Coogee, WA. Launched 10 March 1984 for service at *Stirling*, Cockburn Sound, completed 15 March 1984. Bollard pull 35 tons. Also used for torpedo recovery.

TAMMAR   8/1992, Vic Jeffery, RAN

QUOKKA DT 1801

Displacement, tons: 110
Dimensions, feet (metres): 59.4 × 19.4 × 7.9 *(18.1 × 5.9 × 2.4)*
Main machinery: 2 Detroit 6V-53 diesels; 300 hp *(224 kW)* sustained; 2 shafts
Speed, knots: 9
Complement: 4

Comment: Built by Shoreline Engineering Pty Ltd, Portland, Victoria. Launched October 1983 for service at *Stirling*, Cockburn Sound. Bollard pull 8 tons.

QUOKKA   3/1991, Vic Jeffery, RAN

BRONZEWING HTS 501   **MOLLYMAWK** HTS 504
CURRAWONG HTS 502

Displacement, tons: 47.5
Dimensions, feet (metres): 50 × 15 × 6.2 *(15.2 × 4.6 × 1.9)*
Main machinery: 2 GM diesels; 340 hp *(250 kW)*; 2 shafts
Speed, knots: 8
Complement: 3

Comment: First pair with bipod mast funnel built by Stannard Bros, Sydney in 1969 and second pair (including 503) with conventional funnel by Perrin Engineering, Brisbane in 1972. Bollard pull 5 tons. 503 transferred to Papua New Guinea in 1974. *Mollymawk* has been modified with twin funnels following a berthing accident with *Tobruk*.

BRONZEWING   11/1991, John Mortimer

TORPEDO RECOVERY VESSELS

Note: *Tammar* (see *Tugs*) is also modified to recover torpedoes.

3 FISH CLASS

TUNA TFV 801   **TREVALLY** TRV 802   **TAILOR** TRV 803

Displacement, tons: 91.6
Dimensions, feet (metres): 88.5 × 20.9 × 4.5 *(27 × 6.4 × 1.4)*
Main machinery: 3 GM diesels; 890 hp *(664 kW)*; 3 shafts
Speed, knots: 13
Complement: 9

Comment: All built at Williamstown completed between January 1970 and April 1971. Can transport eight torpedoes.

TAILOR   1/1991, Vic Jeffery, RAN

AUXILIARIES

1 TRIALS AND SAFETY VESSEL

Name	No	Builders	Commissioned
PROTECTOR (ex-*Blue Nabilla*)	ASR 241	Stirling Marine Services, WA	1984

Displacement, tons: 670 full load
Dimensions, feet (metres): 140.1 × 31.2 × 9.8 *(42.7 × 9.5 × 3)*
Main machinery: 2 Detroit 12V-92TA diesels; 1020 hp *(760 kW)* sustained; 2 Heimdal cp props
Speed, knots: 11.5. **Range, miles:** 10 000 at 11 kts
Complement: 13
Radars: Navigation: JRC 310; I band. Decca RM 970BT; I band.
Sonars: Klein; side scan; high frequency.
Helicopters: Platform for one light.

Comment: A former National Safety Council of Australia vessel commissioned in November 1990 to be used to support contractor's sea trials of the Collins class submarines, and for mine warfare trials and diving operations. LIPS dynamic positioning, two ROVs and a recompression chamber. Helicopter deck and a submersible were removed in 1992 and the ship is now painted grey. Probably to be based at *Stirling* from 1994.

PROTECTOR   6/1992, Nikolaus Sifferlinger

1 RESERVE TRAINING CRAFT

ARGUS P 225

Displacement, tons: 8.8 full load
Dimensions, feet (metres): 34.1 × 11.2 × 3.3 *(10.4 × 3.4 × 1)*
Main machinery: 2 Volvo TAMD60C diesels; 304 hp(m) *(223 kW)* sustained; 2 shafts
Speed, knots: 25. **Range, miles:** 400
Complement: 3
Radars: Navigation: FCR 1411; I band.

Comment: Former Federal Police craft built by Stebercraft in 1984 and commissioned into the Navy 8 June 1990. GRP construction. Based at Thursday Island and used for Reserve Port Division training.

4 SELF-PROPELLED LIGHTERS

WARRIGAL WFL 8001 **WOMBAT** WFL 8003
WALLABY WFL 8002 **WYULDA** WFL 8004

Displacement, tons: 265 light; 1206 full load
Dimensions, feet (metres): 124.6 × 33.5 × 12.5 *(38 × 10.2 × 3.8)*
Main machinery: 2 Harbourmaster outdrives (1 fwd, 1 aft)

Comment: First three were laid down at Williamstown in 1978. The fourth, for HMAS *Stirling*, was ordered in 1981 from Williamstown Dockyard. Total cost A$7 million. Used for water/fuel transport. Steel hulls with twin, swivelling, outboard propellers. Based at Jervis Bay and Cockburn Sound (WFL 8001, 8004), other pair at Garden Island, Sydney.

WYULDA *9/1991, van Ginderen Collection*

4 LIGHTERS—CATAMARAN

WATTLE CSL 01 **BORONIA** CSL 02 **TELOPEA** CSL 03 **AWL 304**

Comment: 175 ton self-propelled lighters used for general cargo duties.

WATTLE *9/1988, Hachiro Nakai*

SAIL TRAINING VESSELS

Note: In addition to *Young Endeavour* there are five Fleet class. Of 36.1 ft *(11 m)*. GRP yachts named *Charlotte of Cerberus*, *Friendship of Leeuwin*, *Scarborough of Cerberus*, *Lady Penrhyn of Nirimba* and *Alexander of Creswell*. The names are a combination of Australia's first colonising fleet and the training base to which each yacht is allocated.

YOUNG ENDEAVOUR

Displacement, tons: 200
Dimensions, feet (metres): 144 × 26 × 13 *(44 × 7.8 × 4)*
Main machinery: 2 Perkins diesels; 334 hp *(294 kW)*; 1 shaft
Speed, knots: 14 sail; 7 diesel. **Range, miles:** 1500 at 7 kts
Complement: 32 (8 RAN crew, 24 youth crew)

Comment: Built to Lloyds 100 Al LMC yacht classification. Sail area, 5500 sq ft *(510 m)*. Presented to Australia by UK Government 25 January 1987 as a Bicentennial gift. Operated by RAN as a tender to HMAS *Waterhen* for benefit of Australian youth.

YOUNG ENDEAVOUR *4/1992, Giorgio Ghiglione*

WORK BOATS

OTTER NWBD 1281 **DOLPHIN** NWBD 1286
WALRUS NWBD 1282 **DUGONG** NWBD 1287
BEAVER NWBD 1283 **TURTLE** NWBD 1292
GRAMPUS NWBD 1285 **AWB 400-445**

Comment: Of 12 tons and 39.3 ft *(12 m)* long. Built by North Queensland Engineers and Agents, Cairns of aluminium with varying superstructures. There are also four hydrofoil Cheetah remote-controlled surface targets capable of 35 kts.

WALRUS *11/1991, John Mortimer*

ARMY WATERCRAFT

Notes: (i) Operated by Royal Australian Army Corps of Transport. Personnel: 300-400 as required. (ii) In addition to the craft listed below there are some 150 assault boats 16.4 ft *(5 m)* in length and capable of 30 kts. Can carry 12 troops or 1200 kg of equipment.

16 US LCM(8) CLASS

AB 1050-1053, 1055, 1056, 1058-1067

Displacement, tons: 116 full load
Dimensions, feet (metres): 73.5 × 21 × 5.2 *(22.4 × 6.4 × 1.6)*
Main machinery: 2 GM 12V-71 diesels; 680 hp *(508 kW)* sustained; 2 shafts
Speed, knots: 10. **Range, miles:** 480 at 10 kts
Complement: 3-5

Comment: Built by North Queensland Engineers, Cairns and Dillinghams, Fremantle to US design. Based at Sydney, Darwin, Fremantle and Brisbane (some in dry storage). More are to be based at Darwin in 1992. Can carry 55 tons of cargo. Three of these craft carry names: 1050 *Coconut Queen*; 1052 *Reluctant Lady* and 1053 *Sea Widow*. AB 1057 transferred to Tonga 1982.

AB 1063 *3/1992, John Mortimer*

2 TUGS

JOE MANN AT 2700 **THE LUKE** AT 2701

Displacement, tons: 60
Dimensions, feet (metres): 60.5 × 17.3 × 5.5 *(18.4 × 5.3 × 1.7)*
Main machinery: 2 GM 6-71 diesels; 348 hp *(260 kW)* sustained; 2 shafts
Speed, knots: 10.5. **Range, miles:** 5060 at 10 kts

Comment: Built in 1962. Fitted for firefighting, the first at Sydney, the second at Brisbane.

JOE MANN *1983, Graeme Andrews*

34 AUSTRALIA / Army watercraft — Non-naval patrol craft / AUSTRIA / River patrol craft

7 WORK BOATS

| OOLAH AM 417 | KEWOL 418 | SEA HORSE ONE 419 | BOONGAREE AM 420 |
| MENA II 421 | AKUNA 422 | GABINGA 423 | |

Comment: Similar to naval NWBD 1280 type. Based at Sydney, Melbourne, Brisbane, Townsville. Have poor handling qualities.

BOONGAREE 7/1989, John Mortimer

2 SHARK CAT CLASS

AIR EAGLE 08-002   **AIR CONDOR** 08-003

Comment: Sisters to the Army Shark Cats. Based at Townsville for range safety, and rescue. Two others deleted.

AIR EAGLE 11/1992, John Mortimer

6 SHARK CAT CLASS

AM 215-220

Comment: Multi-hulled craft with twin Johnson engines from 175-200 hp. Length 27.2 ft *(8.3 m)*. Speed, 35 kts. Operated by Army Safety Organisation.

AM 215 11/1983, van Ginderen Collection

P SERIES

CASTOR 201   **POLLUX** 202

Comment: Self-propelled lighters; speed, 7 kts; load capacity 90 tons; based at Sydney.

WARANA 016-100

Comment: Of 76 ft *(23 m)*, 49 tons standard, 18 kts, range 400 nm. Deployed in support of RAAF Townsville.

RAAF

1 STEBER 36 CLASS

AIR HAWK 011-001

Comment: Replaced one of the Shark Cats in October 1989. Twin diesels 750 hp *(560 kW)* giving 27 kts. Length 36 ft *(11 m)*. Has a crew of eight. Based at Crook Point.

AIR HAWK 1989, Dennis Hersey

NON-NAVAL PATROL CRAFT

Notes: 1. Various State and Federal agencies, including some fishery departments, have built off-shore patrol craft up to 25 m and 26 kts.
2. Cocos Island patrol carried out by *Sir Zelman Cowan* of 47.9 × 14 ft *(14.6 × 4.3 m)* with two Cummins diesels; 20 kts, range 400 nm at 17 kts, complement 13 (3 officers). Operated by West Australian Department of Harbours and Lights.
3. The Naval Police operate 4 Shark Cat class (0801-0804) which are similar to Army and Air Force versions. These craft are based at Sydney and Rockingham.

AUSTRIA

Commanding Officer

Major Ing Friedrich Hegna

Diplomatic Representation

Defence Attaché in London:
 Major General A Radauer

Personnel

(a) 1993: 32 (cadre personnel and national service), plus a small shipyard unit
(b) 6 months' national service plus 2 months a year for 12 years

Base

Marinekaserne Tegetthof, Wien-Kuchelau (under command of Austrian School of Military Engineering)

Mercantile Marine

Lloyd's Register of Shipping:
 26 vessels of 123 612 tons gross

RIVER PATROL CRAFT

Name	No	Builders	Commissioned
NIEDERÖSTERREICH	A 604	Korneuberg Werft AG	16 Apr 1970

Displacement, tons: 75 full load
Dimensions, feet (metres): 96.8 × 17.8 × 3.6 *(29.4 × 5.4 × 1.1)*
Main machinery: 2 MWM V16 diesels; 1600 hp(m) *(1.18 MW)*; 2 shafts
Speed, knots: 22
Complement: 9 (1 officer)
Guns: 1 Oerlikon 20 mm SPz Mk 66; 50° elevation; 800 rounds/minute to 2 km.
 1—12.7 mm MG. 1—7.62 mm MG. 1—84 mm PAR 66 'Carl Gustav' AT mortar.

Comment: Fully welded. Only one built of a projected class of 12. Re-engined in 1985.

NIEDERÖSTERREICH 7/1991, Austrian Government

Name	No	Builders	Commissioned
OBERST BRECHT	A 601	Korneuburg Werft AG	14 Jan 1958

Displacement, tons: 10 full load
Dimensions, feet (metres): 40.3 × 8.2 × 2.5 *(12.3 × 2.5 × 0.75)*
Main machinery: 2 MAN 6-cyl diesels; 290 hp(m) *(213 kW)*; 2 shafts
Speed, knots: 10
Complement: 5
Guns: 1—12.7 mm MG. 1—84 mm PAR 66 Carl Gustav AT mortar.

10 M-BOOT 80 PATROL CRAFT

Displacement, tons: 4.7 full load
Dimensions, feet (metres): 24.6 × 8.2 × 2 *(7.5 × 2.5 × 0.6)*
Main machinery: 1 Klöckner-Humboldt-Deutz V diesel; 1 shaft
Speed, knots: 14

Comment: Built by Schottel-Werft, Spay, West Germany. Unarmed, they are general-purpose work boats.

OBERST BRECHT   *7/1992, Austrian Government*

M-BOOT 80   *5/1991, van Ginderen Collection*

AZERBAIJAN

General

Coast Guard formed in September 1992 with ships transferred from the Russian Caspian Flotilla and Border Guard.

Base

Baku

Russian Caspian Flotilla

More ships may transfer to Azerbaijan in 1993. Caspian Flotilla candidates include Osa I and II missile attack craft, Yurka, Sonya, Vanya, T 43 and Yevgenya minesweepers, Polnochny LSTs, and a number of support ships.

PATROL FORCES

2 PETYA II CLASS (LIGHT FRIGATES)

Displacement, tons: 950 standard; 1180 full load
Dimensions, feet (metres): 268.3 (270.6, Mod Petya II) × 29.9 × 9.5 *(81.8 (82.5) × 9.1 × 2.9)*
Main machinery: CODAG; 2 gas turbines; 30 000 hp(m) *(22 MW)*; 1 Type 61V-3 diesel; 6000 hp(m) *(4.4 MW)* (centre shaft); 3 shafts
Speed, knots: 32. **Range, miles:** 4870 at 10 kts; 450 at 29 kts
Complement: 98

Guns: 4—3 in *(76 mm)*/60 (2 twin); (1 twin in some Mod Petya I); 80° elevation; 90 rounds/minute to 15 km *(8 nm)*; weight of shell 6.8 kg.
Torpedoes: 10—16 in *(406 mm)* (2 quin) tubes. Type 40; anti-submarine; active/passive homing to 15 km *(8.1 nm)* at 40 kts; warhead 100 kg.
A/S mortars: 2 RBU 6000 12-tubed trainable; range 6000 m; warhead 31 kg.
Mines: Capacity for 22.
Countermeasures: ESM: 2 Watch Dog; radar warning.
Radars: Air/surface search: Strut Curve; F band; range 110 km *(60 nm)* for 2 m² target.
Navigation: Don 2; I band.
Fire control: Hawk Screech; I band; range 27 km *(15 nm)*.
IFF: High Pole B.
Sonars: Hull-mounted; active search and attack; high/medium frequency.
VDS; active search; high frequency.

Comment: Transferred from Russian control in September 1992. Probably built in the mid-1960s.

6 STENKA CLASS (FAST ATTACK CRAFT—PATROL)

Displacement, tons: 170 standard; 210 full load
Dimensions, feet (metres): 127.9 × 25.6 × 5.9 *(39 × 7.8 × 1.8)*
Main machinery: 3 Type M 503A diesels; 10 125 hp(m) *(7.44 MW)* sustained; 3 shafts
Speed, knots: 36. **Range, miles:** 800 at 24 kts; 500 at 35 kts
Complement: 30

Guns: 4—30 mm/65 (2 twin).
Torpedoes: 2—16 in *(406 mm)* tubes. Type 40.
Depth charges: 2 racks.
Radars: Surface search: Pot Drum or Peel Cone; H/I or E band.
Fire control: Drum Tilt; H/I band.
IFF: High Pole. 2 Square Head.
Sonars: VDS; high frequency; Hormone type dipping sonar.

Comment: Transferred from Russian control in September 1992. Based on the hull design of the Osa class. Construction started in 1967 and continued until 1988 for the Border Guard. Type name is *pogranichny storozhevoy korabl* meaning border patrol ship.

PETYA II   *1992*   STENKA   *1992*

BAHAMAS

Headquarters' Appointments

Commander Royal Bahamas Defence Force:
 Commodore L L Smith
Base Commander:
 Commander A J Allens

Base

HMBS *Coral Harbour*, New Providence Island

Personnel

1993: 870

Prefix to Ships' Names

HMBS

Mercantile Marine

Lloyd's Register of Shipping:
 1061 vessels of 20 054 161 tons gross

DELETIONS

1990 *Fort Charlotte* (old)
1992 *P 106* (sunk)

PATROL CRAFT

3 PROTECTOR CLASS

YELLOW ELDER P 03   **PORT NELSON** P 04
SAMANA P 05

Displacement, tons: 110 standard; 180 full load
Dimensions, feet (metres): 108.3 × 22 × 6.9 *(33 × 6.7 × 2.1)*
Main machinery: 3 Detroit 16V-149TI diesels; 3483 hp *(2.6 MW)* sustained; 3 shafts
Speed, knots: 30. **Range, miles:** 300 at 24 kts; 600 at 14 kts on 1 engine
Complement: 20 plus 5 spare berths
Guns: 1 Rheinmetall 20 mm. 3—7.62 mm MGs.

Comment: Ordered December 1984 from Fairey Marine Ltd, Cowes, delivered in November 1986. All commissioned 20 November 1986.

AUSTIN SMITH   12/1989, Giorgio Arra

1 VOSPER TYPE

Name	No	Builders	Commissioned
MARLIN	P 01	Vosper Thornycroft	23 May 1978

Displacement, tons: 96 standard; 109 full load
Dimensions, feet (metres): 103 × 19.8 × 5.5 *(31.4 × 6 × 1.7)*
Main machinery: 2 Paxman 12YJCM diesels; 3000 hp *(2.24 MW)* sustained; 2 shafts
Speed, knots: 25. **Range, miles:** 2000 at 13 kts
Complement: 19 (3 officers)
Guns: 1 Rheinmetall 20 mm. 2 MGs. 2 flare launchers.
Radars: Surface Search: Racal Decca; I band.

Comment: *Marlin* laid down 22 November 1976, launched 20 June 1977. Sister ship *Flamingo* sunk by Cuban aircraft on 10 May 1980.

MARLIN   1/1992, A Sheldon Duplaix

YELLOW ELDER   6/1992, RBDF

6 Ex-USCG CAPE CLASS

Name	No	Name	No
FENRICK STURRUP (ex-*Shoalwater*)	P 06	EDWARD WILLIAMS (ex-*York*)	P 09
DAVID TUCKER (ex-*Upright*)	P 07	SAN SALVADOR II (ex-*Fox*)	P 10
AUSTIN SMITH (ex-*Current*)	P 08	FORT FINCASTLE (ex-*Morgan*)	P 11

Displacement, tons: 98 standard; 148 full load
Dimensions, feet (metres): 95 × 20.2 × 6.6 *(28.9 × 6.2 × 2)*
Main machinery: 2 Detroit 16V-149TI diesels; 2322 hp *(1.73 MW)* sustained; 2 shafts
Speed, knots: 20. **Range, miles:** 2500 at 10 kts
Complement: 18 (2 officers)
Guns: 2—12.7 mm MGs.
Radars: Navigation: Raytheon SPS 64; I band.

Comment: Built at the Coast Guard Yard, Maryland between 1953 and 1959 and modernised 1977-81. Modernisation included new engines, electronics and improved habitability. P 06, 07, 09 and 10 commissioned into the Bahamian Navy in February 1989 and the remaining two in November 1989. Designed for port security and search and rescue, they are a formidable addition to the surveillance capabilities of the RBDF.

5 KEITH NELSON TYPE

Name	No	Builders	Commissioned
ELEUTHERA	P 22	Vosper Thornycroft	5 Mar 1971
ANDROS	P 23	Vosper Thornycroft	5 Mar 1971
ABACO	P 25	Vosper Thornycroft	10 Dec 1977
EXUMA	P 26	Vosper Thornycroft	10 Dec 1977
INAGUA	P 27	Vosper Thornycroft	10 Dec 1977

Displacement, tons: 30 standard; 37 full load
Dimensions, feet (metres): 60 × 15.8 × 4.6 *(18.3 × 4.8 × 1.4)*
Main machinery: 2 Detroit 12V-71 diesels (P 22-23); 680 hp *(508 kW)*
 2 Caterpillar 3408BTA diesels (P 25-27); 1070 hp *(800 kW)* sustained; 2 shafts
Speed, knots: 20. **Range, miles:** 650 at 16 kts
Complement: 11
Guns: 3—7.62 mm MGs.
Radars: Surface Search: Racal Decca; I band.

Comment: The first two were the original units of the Bahamas Police Marine Division. With air-conditioned living spaces, these craft are designed for patrol among the many islands of the Bahamas Group. Light machine guns mounted in sockets either side of the bridge. Main engines replaced in the first pair in 1990.

ABACO   1984, RBDF

Support craft — BAHAMAS / Patrol craft — BAHRAIN   37

9 LAUNCHES

P 30-P 33   P 101-P 105

Displacement, tons: 8 standard *(P 30-33)*
Dimensions, feet (metres): 28.9 × 10 × 2.3 *(8.8 × 3 × 0.7) (P 30-33)*
Main machinery: 2 Volvo TAMD40A diesels; 220 hp(m) *(162 kW)* sustained; 2 shafts
Speed, knots: 24+. **Range, miles:** 350 at 21 kts
Complement: 4
Guns: 2—7.62 mm MGs.

Comment: P 30-33 are GRP launches built by Phoenix Marine, Florida and commissioned in 1981-82. P 101-105 are between 28 and 40 ft in length; P 102 and 104 have Mercruises inboard engines, the remainder Mercury, Johnson or Yamaha twin outboards. P 106 sunk in a hurricane in 1992.

P 31   4/1992, RBDF

4 Ex-FISHING VESSELS

P 34 —(ex-*Lady Hero*)
P 35 —(ex-*Carey*)
P 36 —Hatteras 45 ft motor yacht
P 37 —(ex-*Maria Mercedes II*)

Comment: P 34, P 35 and P 37 have a single GM diesel; 12 kts. P 36 has twin diesels; 15 kts.

SUPPORT CRAFT

FORT CHARLOTTE A 02 (ex-YFU 97, ex-LCU 1611)

Displacement, tons: 339 full load
Dimensions, feet (metres): 134.9 × 29 × 6.1 *(41.1 × 8.8 × 1.9)*
Main machinery: 2 Detroit 12V-71 diesels; 680 hp *(508 kW)* sustained; 2 shafts
Speed, knots: 11. **Range, miles:** 1200 at 10 kts
Complement: 15 (2 officers)
Guns: 2—7.62 mm MGs.
Radars: Navigation: Raytheon AN/SPS-66; I band.

Comment: Constructed by the Christy Corporation, Sturgeon Bay, in 1958; later converted and assigned to AUTEC in 1978 as harbour utility craft. Commissioned in the RBDF on 19 June 1991. Large cargo capacity and main deck area. Used primarily as a supply ship and mobile support platform.

FORT CHARLOTTE   6/1991, RBDF

FORT MONTAGUE A 01

Displacement, tons: 90 full load
Dimensions, feet (metres): 94 × 23 × 6 *(28.6 × 7 × 1.8)*
Main machinery: 2 Detroit 12V-71 diesels; 680 hp *(508 kW)* sustained; 2 shafts
Speed, knots: 13. **Range, miles:** 3000 at 10 kts
Complement: 16
Guns: 2—7.62 mm MGs.
Radars: Navigation: Racal Decca; I band.

Comment: Acquired 6 August 1980. Used as a supply ship.

FORT MONTAGUE   1984, RBDF

BAHRAIN

Headquarters' Appointments

Chief of Naval Staff:
  Brigadier Shaikh Abdullah Bin Salman Bin Khalid Al Khalifa
Commander of Navy:
  Major Yusuf Ahmad Malullah
Director of Coast Guard:
  Colonel Abdul-Aziz Attiyatullah Al Khalifa

Personnel

(a) 1993: 650 (Navy), 250 (Coast Guard—seagoing)
(b) Voluntary service

Base

Mina Sulman.

Coast Guard

This unit is under the direction of the Ministry of the Interior.

Mercantile Marine

Lloyd's Register of Shipping:
  87 vessels of 155 472 tons gross

DELETIONS

1990 *Dera'a 2* (old)
1992 *Al-Bayneh, Junnan, Quaimas*

PATROL FORCES

2 LÜRSSEN FPB 38 TYPE (FAST ATTACK CRAFT—GUN)

Name	No	Builders	Commissioned
AL RIFFA	10	Lürssen	Aug 1981
HAWAR	11	Lürssen	Nov 1981

Displacement, tons: 188 half load; 205 full load
Dimensions, feet (metres): 126.3 × 22.9 × 7.2 *(38.5 × 7 × 2.2)*
Main machinery: 2 MTU 16V 538 TB92 diesels; 6810 hp(m) *(5 MW)* sustained; 2 shafts
Speed, knots: 32. **Range, miles:** 1100 at 16 kts
Complement: 27 (3 officers)
Guns: 2 Breda 40 mm/70 (twin); dual purpose; 85° elevation; 300 rounds/minute to 12 km *(6.5 nm)* anti-surface; 4 km *(2.2 nm)*; weight of shell 0.96 kg.
1—57 mm Starshell rocket launcher.
Mines: Mine rails fitted.
Fire control: CSEE Lynx optical director with Philips 9LV 100 optronic system.
Radars: Surface search: Philips 9GR 600; I band.
Navigation: Racal Decca 1226; I band.

Comment: Ordered in 1979. *Al Riffa* launched April 1981. *Hawar* launched July 1981.

HAWAR   8/1990

38 BAHRAIN / Patrol forces — Coast Guard

2 SWIFT FPB 20 TYPE (FAST ATTACK CRAFT—GUN)

AL JARIM 30   AL JASRAH 31

Displacement, tons: 33 full load
Dimensions, feet (metres): 63 × 18.4 × 6.5 *(19.2 × 5.6 × 2)*
Main machinery: 2 Detroit 12V-71TA diesels; 840 hp(m) *(627 kW)* sustained; 2 shafts
Speed, knots: 30. Range, miles: 1200 at 18 kts
Guns: 1 Oerlikon 20 mm.
Radars: Navigation: Decca 110; I band.

Comment: Built by Swiftships, Morgan City, USA. Both commissioned in February 1982. Aluminium hulls.

MISSILE CORVETTES

2 LÜRSSEN FPB 62 TYPE (FAST ATTACK CRAFT)

Name	No	Builders	Commissioned
AL MANAMA	50	Lürssen	14 Dec 1987
AL MUHARRAQ	51	Lürssen	3 Feb 1988

Displacement, tons: 632 full load
Dimensions, feet (metres): 206.7 × 30.5 × 9.5 *(63 × 9.3 × 2.9)*
Main machinery: 4 MTU 20V 538 TB92 diesels; 12 820 hp(m) *(9.42 MW)* sustained; 4 shafts
Speed, knots: 32. Range, miles: 4000 at 16 kts
Complement: 43 (7 officers)

Missiles: SSM: 4 Aerospatiale MM 38 Exocet launchers (2 twin); inertial cruise; active radar homing to 42 km *(23 nm)* at 0.9 Mach; warhead 165 kg; sea-skimmer.
Guns: 1 OTO Melara 3 in *(76 mm)*/62 compact; 85° elevation; 85 rounds/minute to 16 km *(8.7 nm)* anti-surface; 12 km *(6.5 nm)* anti-aircraft; weight of shell 6 kg.
2 Breda 40 mm/70 (twin); 85° elevation; 300 rounds/minute to 12.5 km *(6.8 nm)*; weight of shell 0.96 kg.
2 Oerlikon GAM-BO1 20 mm/93.
Countermeasures: Decoys: CSEE Dagaie; chaff and IR flares.
ESM/ECM: Racal Decca Cutlass/Cygnus; intercept and jammer.
Fire control: CSEE Panda Mk 2 optical director. Philips TV/IR optronic director.
Radars: Air/surface search: Philips Sea Giraffe 50 HC; G band.
Navigation: Racal Decca 1226; I band.
Fire control: Philips 9LV 331; J band.

Helicopters: 1 SA 365F Dauphin 2.

Programmes: Ordered February 1984.
Structure: Similar to Abu Dhabi and Singapore designs. Steel hull, aluminium superstructure. Fitted with a helicopter platform which incorporates a lift to lower the aircraft into the hangar.
Operational: SA 365F armed with Aerospatiale AS 15TT anti-ship missiles, eight of which are carried on board ship.

AL MUHARRAQ   4/1992

4 LÜRSSEN FPB 45 TYPE (FAST ATTACK CRAFT)

Name	No	Builders	Commissioned
AHMAD EL FATEH	20	Lürssen	5 Feb 1984
AL JABIRI	21	Lürssen	3 May 1984
ABDUL RAHMAN AL FADEL	22	Lürssen	10 Sep 1986
AL TAWEELAH	23	Lürssen	25 Mar 1989

Displacement, tons: 228 half load; 259 full load
Dimensions, feet (metres): 147.3 × 22.9 × 8.2 *(44.9 × 7 × 2.5)*
Main machinery: 4 MTU 16V 538 TB92 diesels; 13 640 hp(m) *(10 MW)* sustained; 4 shafts
Speed, knots: 40. Range, miles: 1600 at 16 kts
Complement: 36 (6 officers)

Missiles: SSM: 4 Aerospatiale MM 40 Exocet (2 twin); inertial cruise; active radar homing to 70 km *(40 nm)* at 0.9 Mach; warhead 165 kg; sea-skimmer.
Guns: 1 OTO Melara 3 in *(76 mm)*/62; dual purpose; 85° elevation; 85 rounds/minute to 16 km *(8.7 nm)* anti-surface; 12 km *(6.5 nm)* anti-aircraft; weight of shell 6 kg.
2 Breda 40 mm/70 (twin); 85° elevation; 300 rounds/minute to 12.5 km *(6.8 nm)*; weight of shell 0.96 kg.
3—7.62 mm MGs.
Countermeasures: Decoys: CSEE Dagaie launcher; trainable mounting; 10 containers firing chaff decoys and IR flares.
ESM: RDL 2 ABC; radar warning.
ECM: Racal Cygnus (not in 20 and 21); jammer.
Fire control: 1 Panda optical director for 40 mm guns.
Radars: Surface search/fire control: Philips LV223; J band.
Navigation: Racal Decca 1226; I band.

Programmes: First pair ordered in 1979, second pair in 1985.

ABDUL RAHMAN AL FADEL   9/1991

SUPPORT SHIP

AJEERA 41

Displacement, tons: 420 full load
Dimensions, feet (metres): 129.9 × 36.1 × 5.9 *(39.6 × 11 × 1.8)*
Main machinery: 2 Detroit 16V-71 diesels; 811 hp *(605 kW)* sustained; 2 shafts
Speed, knots: 13. Range, miles: 1500 at 10 kts
Complement: 21
Guns: 2—12.7 mm MGs.

Comment: Built by Swiftships, Morgan City, USA. Commissioned in October 1982. Used as a general purpose cargo ship and can carry up to 200 tons of fuel and water. Built to an LCU design with a bow ramp and 15 ton crane.

AJEERA   9/1990

SHIPBORNE AIRCRAFT

Numbers/Type: 2 Aerospatiale SA 365F Dauphin.
Operational speed: 140 kts *(260 km/h)*.
Service ceiling: 15 000 ft *(4575 m)*.
Range: 410 nm *(758 km)*.
Role/Weapon systems: Reconnaissance and anti-shipping role. Sensors: Thomson-CSF Agrion radar. Weapons: ASV; AS 15TT air-to-surface missiles.

COAST GUARD

Notes: 1. In addition to the craft listed below about ten small open fibreglass boats are used for patrol duties.
2. Eight 13 ft Diver Support craft ordered in April 1992, from RTK Marine.

1 WASP 30 METRE CLASS

AL MUHARRAQ

Displacement, tons: 90 standard; 103 full load
Dimensions, feet (metres): 98.5 × 21 × 5.5 *(30 × 6.4 × 1.6)*
Main machinery: 2 Detroit 16V-149TI diesels; 2322 hp *(1.73 MW)* sustained; 2 shafts
Speed, knots: 25. Range, miles: 500 at 22 kts
Complement: 9
Guns: 1—30 mm. 2—7.62 mm MGs.

Comment: Ordered from Souters, Cowes, Isle of Wight in 1984. Laid down November 1984, launched August 1985, shipped 21 October 1985. GRP hull.

4 HALMATIC 20 METRE CLASS

DERA'A 2, 6, 7 and 8

Displacement, tons: 31.5 full load
Dimensions, feet (metres): 65.9 × 17.3 × 5.1 *(20.1 × 5.3 × 1.5)*
Main machinery: 2 Detroit 12V-71TA diesels; 840 hp *(626 kW)* sustained; 2 shafts
Speed, knots: 25. Range, miles: 500 at 20 kts
Complement: 7
Guns: 2—7.62 mm MG.

Comment: Three delivered in late 1991, the last in early 1992. GRP hulls.

DERA'A 6   1991, Bahrain Coast Guard

2 WASP 20 METRE

DERA'A 4 and **5**

Displacement, tons: 36.3 full load
Dimensions, feet (metres): 65.6 × 16.4 × 4.9 (20 × 5 × 1.5)
Main machinery: 2 Detroit 12V-71TA diesels; 840 hp (626 kW) sustained; 2 shafts
Speed, knots: 24.5. Range, miles: 500 at 20 kts
Complement: 8
Guns: 2—7.62 mm MGs.

Comment: Built by Souters, Cowes, Isle of Wight. Delivered 1983. GRP hulls.

DERA'A 4 and 5   *1983, Beken of Cowes Ltd*

2 TRACKER CLASS

DERA'A 1 and **3**

Displacement, tons: 31 full load
Dimensions, feet (metres): 64 × 16 × 5 (19.5 × 4.9 × 1.5)
Main machinery: 2 General Motors diesels; 1120 hp (823 kW); 2 shafts
Speed, knots: 29
Guns: 1 Oerlikon 20 mm.

Comment: All built by Fairey Marine Ltd. The first purchased in 1974, the other two in 1980. One deleted in 1990.

1 CHEVERTON TYPE

Name	No	Builders	Commissioned
MASHTAN	6	Cheverton Ltd, Isle of Wight	1976

Displacement, tons: 17.3 full load
Dimensions, feet (metres): 50 × 14.7 × 4.5 (15.2 × 4.5 × 1.4)
Main machinery: 2 GM 8V-71 diesels; 460 hp (344 kW) sustained; 2 shafts
Speed, knots: 22. Range, miles: 660 at 12 kts

Comment: GRP hull.

6 HALMATIC 14 METRE CLASS

SAIF 5, 6, 7, 8, 9 and **10**

Displacement, tons: 17 full load
Dimensions, feet (metres): 47.2 × 12.8 × 3.9 (14.4 × 3.9 × 1.2)
Main machinery: 2 Detroit 6V-92TA diesels; 520 hp (388 kW) sustained; 2 shafts
Speed, knots: 27. Range, miles: 500 at 22 kts
Complement: 4

Comment: Delivered in 1990/91. GRP hulls. More could be ordered for delivery in 1992.

SAIF 9   *1991, Bahrain Coast Guard*

4 FAIREY SWORD CLASS

SAIF 1, 2, 3 and **4**

Displacement, tons: 15
Dimensions, feet (metres): 44.9 × 13.4 × 4.3 (13.7 × 4.1 × 1.3)
Main machinery: 2 GM 8V-71 diesels; 590 hp (440 kW) sustained; 2 shafts
Speed, knots: 28
Complement: 6

Comment: Purchased in 1980. Built by Fairey Marine Ltd.

SAIF 1   *1982, Bahrain Coast Guard*

3 WASP 11 METRE CLASS

SAHAM 1, 2 and **3**

Displacement, tons: 7.25 full load
Dimensions, feet (metres): 36.1 × 10.5 × 2 (11 × 3.2 × 0.6)
Main machinery: 2 Perkins diesels; 612 hp (462 kW); 2 waterjets
Speed, knots: 24
Guns: 1—7.62 mm MG.

Comment: Built by Souters, Cowes, Isle of Wight. Delivered 1983.

SAHAM 1   *1983, Beken of Cowes Ltd*

3 CHEVERTON TYPE

Name	No	Builders	Commissioned
NOON	15	Cheverton Ltd, Isle of Wight	1977
ASKAR	16	Cheverton Ltd, Isle of Wight	1977
SUWAD	17	Cheverton Ltd, Isle of Wight	1977

Displacement, tons: 3.5 full load
Dimensions, feet (metres): 27 × 9 × 2.8 (8.2 × 2.7 × 0.8)
Main machinery: 2 diesels; 150 hp (111 kW); 2 shafts
Speed, knots: 15

Comment: Purchased 1976.

1 SUPPORT CRAFT

Name	No	Builders	Commissioned
SAFRA 3	—	Halmatic, Havant	1992

Displacement, tons: 165 full load
Dimensions, feet (metres): 85 × 25.9 × 5.2 (25.9 × 7.9 × 1.6)
Main machinery: 2 Detroit 16V-92TA diesels; 1380 hp (1.03 MW); 2 shafts
Speed, knots: 13. Range, miles: 700 at 12 kts
Complement: 6

Comment: Delivered in early 1992. General purpose workboat equipped for towing and fire fighting. Can carry 15 tons.

SAFRA 3   *1992, Halmatic*

1 LANDING CRAFT

Name	No	Builders	Commissioned
SAFRA 2	40	Fairey Marine Ltd	1981

Displacement, tons: 150 full load
Measurement, tons: 90 dwt
Dimensions, feet (metres): 73.9 × 24.9 × 4 (22.5 × 7.5 × 1.2)
Main machinery: 2 Detroit 12V-71 diesels; 680 hp (508 kW) sustained; 2 shafts
Speed, knots: 8
Complement: 8

1 60 ft LOADMASTER

Name	No	Builders	Commissioned
SAFRA 1	7	Cheverton Ltd, Isle of Wight	Dec 1977

Displacement, tons: 90 full load
Dimensions, feet (metres): 60 × 20 × 3.5 (18.3 × 6.1 × 1.1)
Main machinery: 2 diesels; 348 hp (260 kW); 2 shafts
Speed, knots: 9
Complement: 13
Military lift: 45 tons of equipment

1 TIGER CLASS HOVERCRAFT

Displacement, tons: 4.5 full load
Dimensions, feet (metres): 26.2 × 12.5 × 7.5 (7.97 × 3.8 × 2.26)
Main machinery: 1 AMC 5900 cc petrol engine; 180 hp (134 kW)
Speed, knots: 35

Comment: Built by AVL Cowes.

1 HARBOUR TUG

JIDA

Displacement, tons: 12
Main machinery: 1 GM 6-71 diesel; 174 hp (130 kW) sustained; 1 shaft

Comment: Purchased in 1981.

BANGLADESH

Headquarters' Appointments

Chief of Naval Staff:
  Rear Admiral Mohammad Mohaiminul Islam
Assistant Chief of Naval Staff (Personnel):
  Commodore F Ahmed
Assistant Chief of Naval Staff (Logistics):
  Commodore A M A Alam
Assistant Chief of Naval Staff (Material):
  Commodore M G Rabbani
Assistant Chief of Naval Staff (Operations):
  Commodore S I Mujtaba

Senior Appointments

Commodore Commanding Chittagong:
  Commodore A Z Nizam
Commodore Commanding BN Flotilla:
  Commodore M N Islam

Bases

Chittagong (BNS *Issa Khan*, BN Dockyard Complex). Naval Academy (BNS *Patenga*). Dhaka (BNS *Haji Mohsin*). Khulna (BNS *Titumir* and *Mongla*). Kaptai (BNS *Shaheed Moazzam*)

Personnel

(a) 1993: 8000 (650 officers)
(b) Voluntary service

Prefix to Ships' Names

BNS

Mercantile Marine

Lloyd's Register of Shipping:
  301 vessels of 410 402 tons gross

Strength of the Fleet

Type	Active
Frigates	4
Fast Attack Craft (Missile)	8
Fast Attack Craft (Torpedo)	8
Fast Attack Craft (Patrol)	2
Fast Attack Craft (Gun)	8
Large Patrol Craft	7
Coastal Patrol Craft	1
Riverine Patrol Craft	5
Training Ship	1
Repair Ship	1
Tanker	1
Coastal Survey Craft	2
Landing Craft	7

DELETIONS

1991 1 Huangfen class, 1 Hegu class

PENNANT LIST

Frigates

F 15	Abu Bakr
F 16	Umar Farooq
F 17	Ali Haider
F 18	Osman

Light Forces

P 111	Pabna
P 112	Noakhali
P 113	Patuakhali
P 114	Rangamati
P 115	Bogra
P 211	Meghna
P 212	Jamuna
P 311	Bishkhali

P 312	Padma
P 313	Surma
P 314	Karnaphuli (reserve)
P 315	Tista
P 411	Shaheed Daulat
P 412	Shaheed Farid
P 413	Shaheed Mohibullah
P 414	Shaheed Akhtaruddin
P 611	Tawheed
P 612	Tawfiq
P 613	Tawjeed
P 614	Tanveer
P 811	Durjoy
P 812	Nirbhoy
P 8111	Durbar
P 8112	Duranta
P 8113	Durvedya
P 8114	Durdam

P 8125	Durdharsha
P 8126	Durdanta
P 8127	Durnibar
P 8128	Dordanda
A 513	Shahjalal

Auxiliaries

A 511	Shaheed Ruhul Amin
A 512	Shahayak
A 515	Khan Jahan Ali
A 581	Darshak
A 582	Tallashi
A 721	Khadem
L 900	Shahamanat

FRIGATES

1 CHINESE JIANGHU I CLASS (TYPE 053 H1)

Name	No	Builders	Laid down	Launched	Commissioned
OSMAN	F 18	Hutong SY, Shanghai	—	—	4 Nov 1989

Displacement, tons: 1425 standard; 1702 full load
Dimensions, feet (metres): 338.6 × 35.4 × 10.2 *(103.2 × 10.7 × 3.1)*
Main machinery: 2 Type 12 PA6 280 BTC (Type 12 E 390V) diesels; 14 400 hp(m) *(10.6 MW)* sustained; 2 shafts
Speed, knots: 26. **Range, miles:** 2700 at 18 kts
Complement: 300 (27 officers)

Missiles: SSM: 4 Hai Ying 2 (2 twin) launchers ❶; active radar or IR homing to 80 km *(43.2 nm)* at 0.9 Mach; warhead 513 kg.
Guns: 4 China 3.9 in *(100 mm)*/56 (2 twin) ❷; 85° elevation; 18 rounds/minute to 22 km *(12 nm)*; weight of shell 15.9 kg.
8 China 37 mm/76 (4 twin) ❸; 85° elevation; 180 rounds/minute to 8.5 km *(4.6 nm)* anti-aircraft; weight of shell 1.42 kg.
A/S mortars: 2 RBU 1200 5-tubed fixed launchers ❹; range 1200 m; warhead 34 kg.
Depth charges: 2 BMB-2 projectors; 2 racks.
Mines: Can carry up to 60.
Countermeasures: Decoys: 2 Loral Hycor SRBOC Mk 36 6-barrelled chaff launchers.
ESM: Watchdog; radar warning.
Radars: Air/surface search: MX 902 Eye Shield (922-1) ❺; possible E band.
Surface search/fire control: Square Tie (254) ❻; I band.

Navigation: Fin Curve (352); I band.
Fire control: Wok Won (752A) ❼.
IFF: High Pole A.
Sonars: Echo Type 5; hull-mounted; active search and attack; medium frequency.

Programmes: First transferred 26 September 1989, arrived Bangladesh 8 October 1989. Second expected in 1991 but was either postponed or cancelled.

Structure: This is a Jianghu Type I (version 4) hull with twin 100 mm guns (vice the 57 mm in the ships sold to Egypt), Wok Won fire control system, and a rounded funnel.
Operational: Damaged in collision with a merchant ship in August 1991. One 37 mm mounting uprooted and SSM and RBU mountings misaligned. Being repaired in 1992/93.

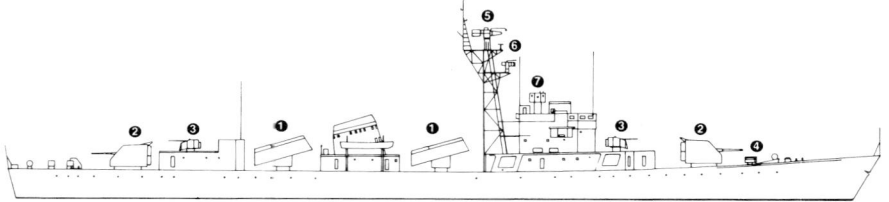

OSMAN *(Scale 1 : 900), Ian Sturton*

OSMAN *6/1990, G Jacobs*

Frigates / BANGLADESH 41

1 Ex-BRITISH SALISBURY CLASS (TYPE 61)

Name	No	Builders	Laid down	Launched	Commissioned
UMAR FAROOQ (ex-HMS *Llandaff*)	F 16	Hawthorn Leslie Ltd	27 Aug 1953	30 Nov 1955	11 Apr 1958

Displacement, tons: 2170 standard; 2408 full load
Dimensions, feet (metres): 339.8 × 40 × 15.5 (screws) *(103.6 × 12.2 × 4.7)*
Main machinery: 8 VVS ASR 1 diesels; 12 380 hp *(9.2 MW)* sustained; 2 shafts
Speed, knots: 24. **Range, miles:** 2300 at full power; 7500 at 16 kts
Complement: 237 (14 officers)

Guns: 2 Vickers 4.5 in *(115 mm)*/45 (twin) Mk 6 ❶; dual purpose; 80° elevation; 20 rounds/minute to 19 km *(10 nm)* anti-surface; 6 km *(3.3 nm)* anti-aircraft; weight of shell 25 kg.
2 Bofors 40 mm/60 Mk 9 ❷; 80° elevation; 120 rounds/minute to 3 km *(1.6 nm)* anti-aircraft; 10 km *(5.5 nm)* maximum.
A/S mortars: 1 triple-barrelled Squid Mk 4 ❸; fires pattern of 3 depth charges to 300 m ahead of ship.
Fire control: 1 Mk 6M gun director.
Radars: Air search: Marconi Type 965 with double AKE 2 array ❹; A band.
Air/surface search: Plessey Type 993 ❺; E/F band.
Height finder: Type 278M ❻; E band.
Surface search: Kelvin Hughes Type 1007 ❼; I/J band.
Navigation: Decca Type 978; I band.
Fire control: Type 275 ❽; F band.
Sonars: Type 174; hull-mounted; active search; medium frequency.
Graseby Type 170B; hull-mounted; active attack; 15 kHz.

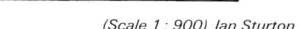

UMAR FAROOQ *(Scale 1 : 900), Ian Sturton*

Programmes: Transferred to Bangladesh at Royal Albert Dock, London 10 December 1976.
Operational: Suffered major machinery accident in 1985 but is now fully operational. The radar Type 982 aerial is still retained on the after mast but the set is non-operational.

UMAR FAROOQ *5/1990, John Mortimer*

2 Ex-BRITISH LEOPARD CLASS (TYPE 41)

Name	No	Builders	Laid down	Launched	Commissioned
ABU BAKR (ex-HMS *Lynx*)	F 15	John Brown & Co Ltd, Clydebank	13 Aug 1953	12 Jan 1955	14 Mar 1957
ALI HAIDER (ex-HMS *Jaguar*)	F 17	Wm Denny & Bros Ltd, Dumbarton	2 Nov 1953	30 July 1957	12 Dec 1959

Displacement, tons: 2300 standard; 2520 full load
Dimensions, feet (metres): 339.8 × 40 × 15.5 (screws) *(103.6 × 12.2 × 4.7)*
Main machinery: 8 VVS ASR 1 diesels; 12 380 hp *(9.2 MW)* sustained; 2 shafts
Speed, knots: 24. **Range, miles:** 2300 at full power; 7500 at 16 kts
Complement: 235 (15 officers)

Guns: 4 Vickers 4.5 in *(115 mm)*/45 (2 twin) Mk 6 ❶; dual purpose; 80° elevation; 20 rounds/minute to 19 km *(10 nm)* anti-surface; 6 km *(3.3 nm)* anti-aircraft; weight of shell 25 kg.
1 Bofors 40 mm/60 Mk 9 ❷; 80° elevation; 120 rounds/minute to 3 km *(1.6 nm)* anti-aircraft; 10 km *(5.5 nm)* maximum.
Countermeasures: ESM: Radar warning.
Fire control: Mk 6M gun director.
Radars: Air search: Marconi Type 965 with single AKE 1 array ❸; A band.
Air/surface search: Plessey Type 993 ❹; E/F band.
Navigation: Decca Type 978; Kelvin Hughes 1007; I band.
Fire control: Type 275 ❺; F band.

ABU BAKR *(Scale 1 : 900), Ian Sturton*

Programmes: *Ali Haider* transferred 16 July 1978 and *Abu Bakr* on 12 March 1982. *Ali Haider* refitted at Vosper Thornycroft August-October 1978. *Abu Bakr* extensively refitted in 1982. Could be replaced by British Type 21 if the funds can be found.

Structure: All welded. Fitted with stabilisers. Sonars removed while still in service with RN. Fuel tanks have a water compensation system to improve stability.
Operational: Designed as air-defence ships.

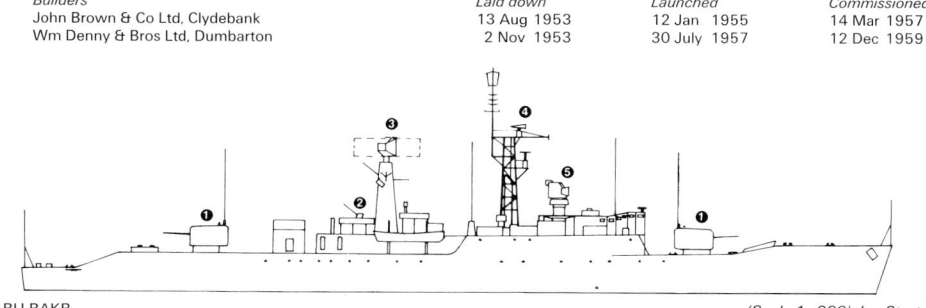

ALI HAIDER *5/1990, John Mortimer*

LIGHT FORCES

4 TYPE 021 (CHINESE HUANGFEN CLASS)
(FAST ATTACK CRAFT—MISSILE)

DURDHARSHA P 8125	DURNIBAR P 8127
DURDANTA P 8126	DORDANDA P 8128

Displacement, tons: 171 standard; 205 full load
Dimensions, feet (metres): 110.2 × 24.9 × 8.9 *(33.6 × 7.6 × 2.7)*
Main machinery: 3 Type 42-160 diesels; 12 000 hp(m) *(8.8 MW)*; 3 shafts
Speed, knots: 35. **Range, miles:** 800 at 30 kts
Complement: 65 (5 officers)
Missiles: SSM: 4 Hai Ying 2; active radar or IR homing to 95 km *(51 nm)* at 0.9 Mach; warhead 513 kg.
Guns: 4 USSR 30 mm/69 (2 twin); 85° elevation; 1000 rounds/minute to 3 km *(1.6 nm)* anti-aircraft.
Radars: Surface search: Square Tie; I band.
IFF: High Pole A.

Comment: Commissioned in Bangladesh Navy on 10 November 1988. Chinese equivalent of the Soviet Osa class which started building in 1985. All damaged in April 1991 typhoon and one sunk. A replacement was delivered in June 1992.

DURDHARSHA   6/1990, G Jacobs

4 TYPE 024 (CHINESE HEGU CLASS)
(FAST ATTACK CRAFT—MISSILE)

DURBAR P 8111	DURVEDYA P 8113
DURANTA P 8112	DURDAM P 8114

Displacement, tons: 68 standard; 79.2 full load
Dimensions, feet (metres): 88.6 × 20.7 × 4.3 *(27 × 6.3 × 1.3)*
Main machinery: 4 Type L-12V-180 diesels; 4800 hp(m) *(3.53 MW)*; 4 shafts
Speed, knots: 37.5. **Range, miles:** 400 at 30 kts
Complement: 17 (4 officers)
Missiles: SSM: 2 SY-1; active radar or IR homing to 45 km *(24.3 nm)* at 0.9 Mach; warhead 513 kg.
Guns: 2—25 mm/80 (twin); dual purpose; 85° elevation; 270 rounds/minute to 3 km *(1.6 nm)*; weight of shell 0.34 kg.
Radars: Surface search: Square Tie; I band.

Comment: First pair commissioned in Bangladesh Navy on 6 April 1983, second pair on 10 November 1983. Two badly damaged in April 1991 typhoon. One was scrapped and replaced in June 1992.

DURANTA   6/1990, G Jacobs

8 TYPE 026 (CHINESE HUCHUAN CLASS)
(FAST ATTACK CRAFT—TORPEDO)

TB 8235-TB 8238 + 4

Displacement, tons: 46 full load
Dimensions, feet (metres): 73.8 × 16.4 × 6.9 (foil) *(22.5 × 5 × 2.1)*
Main machinery: 3 Type L-12V-180 diesels; 3600 hp(m) *(2.64 MW)*; 3 shafts
Speed, knots: 50. **Range, miles:** 500 cruising
Complement: 23 (3 officers)
Guns: 4 China 14.5 mm (2 twin); 85° elevation; 600 rounds/minute to 7 km *(3.8 km)*.
Torpedoes: 2—21 in *(533 mm)*; anti-ship; active/passive homing; warhead 380 kg.
Radars: Surface search: Skin Head; I band.

Comment: This is the newer version of the Huchuan class with some minor differences. Two damaged in April 1991 typhoon, 4 more from Pakistan in 1993.

TB 8235   4/1988, Bangladesh Navy

TB 8237   6/1990, G Jacobs

2 CHINESE HAINAN CLASS (FAST ATTACK CRAFT—PATROL)

DURJOY P 811   NIRBHOY P 812

Displacement, tons: 375 standard; 392 full load
Dimensions, feet (metres): 192.8 × 23.6 × 6 *(58.8 × 7.2 × 2.2)*
Main machinery: 4 PCR/Kolomna Type 9-D-8 diesels; 4000 hp(m) *(2.94 MW)* sustained; 4 shafts
Speed, knots: 30.5. **Range, miles:** 1300 at 15 kts
Complement: 70
Guns: 4 China 57 mm/70 (2 twin); 85° elevation; 120 rounds/minute to 12 km *(6.5 nm)* anti-aircraft; weight of shell 6.31 kg.
4—25 mm (2 twin); 85° elevation; 270 rounds/minute to 3 km *(1.6 nm)* anti-aircraft.
A/S mortars: 4 RBU 1200 fixed 5-barrelled launchers; range 1200 m; warhead 34 kg.
Depth charges: 2 racks; 2 throwers.
Mines: Fitted with rails.
Radars: Surface search: Pot Head (Skin Head in some); I band.
IFF: High Pole.
Sonars: Tamir II; hull-mounted; short range attack; high frequency.

Comment: First transferred and commissioned in BN 10 September 1982 and the second 1 December 1985. Form part of Escort Squadron 81 at Chittagong. Some previous confusion over numbers of this class. Both damaged in April 1991 typhoon and may not have been repaired.

DURJOY   1984, Bangladesh Navy

2 Ex-YUGOSLAV KRALJEVICA CLASS (LARGE PATROL CRAFT)

Name	No	Builders	Commissioned
KARNAPHULI (ex-*PBR 502*)	P 314	Yugoslavia	1956
TISTA (ex-*PBR 505*)	P 315	Yugoslavia	1956

Displacement, tons: 195 standard; 245 full load
Dimensions, feet (metres): 141.4 × 20.7 × 5.7 *(43.1 × 6.3 × 1.8)*
Main machinery: 2 MAN V8V 30/38 diesels; 3300 hp(m) *(2.42 MW)*; 2 shafts
Speed, knots: 19. **Range, miles:** 1500 at 12 kts
Complement: 44 (4 officers)
Guns: 2 Bofors 40 mm/70. 4 Oerlikon 20 mm. 2—128 mm rocket launchers (5 barrels per mounting).
Depth charges: 2 racks; 2 Mk 6 projectors.
Radars: Surface search: Decca 45; I band.
Sonars: QCU 2; hull-mounted; active; high frequency.

Comment: Transferred and commissioned 6 June 1975. *Karnaphuli* placed in Class III reserve in 1988.

KARNAPHULI   1984, Bangladesh Navy

Light forces / BANGLADESH 43

2 Ex-INDIAN AKSHAY CLASS (LARGE PATROL CRAFT)

Name	No	Builders	Commissioned
PADMA (ex-INS *Akshay*)	P 312	Hooghly D & E Co, Calcutta	1962
SURMA (ex-INS *Ajay*)	P 313	Hooghly D & E Co, Calcutta	1962

Displacement, tons: 120 standard; 150 full load
Dimensions, feet (metres): 117.2 × 20 × 5.5 *(35.7 × 6.1 × 1.7)*
Main machinery: 2 Paxman YHAXM diesels; 1100 hp *(820 kW)*; 2 shafts
Speed, knots: 18
Complement: 35 (3 officers)
Guns: 8 Oerlikon 20 mm (2 quad).
Radars: Surface search: Racal Decca; I band.

Comment: Generally similar to the Royal Navy's former Ford class. Transferred and commissioned 12 April 1973 and 26 July 1974 respectively. *Surma* refitted in 1983.

PADMA 1984, Bangladesh Navy

2 MEGHNA CLASS (LARGE PATROL CRAFT)

MEGHNA P 211   **JAMUNA** P 212

Displacement, tons: 410 full load
Dimensions, feet (metres): 152.5 × 24.6 × 6.6 *(46.5 × 7.5 × 2)*
Main machinery: 2 Paxman Valenta 12CM diesels; 5000 hp *(3.73 MW)* sustained; 2 shafts
Speed, knots: 20. **Range, miles:** 2000 at 16 kts
Complement: 47 (3 officers)
Guns: 1 Bofors 57 mm/70 Mk 1; 75° elevation; 200 rounds/minute to 17 km *(9.3 nm)*; weight of shell 2.4 kg.
 1 Bofors 40 mm/70; 90° elevation; 300 rounds/minute to 12 km *(6.5 nm)*; weight of shell 0.96 kg.
 2—7.62 mm MGs; launchers for illuminants on the 57 mm gun.
Fire control: Selenia NA 18 B optronic system.
Radars: Surface search: Decca 1229; I band.

Comment: Built by Vosper Private Ltd, Singapore for EEZ work under the Ministry of Agriculture. *Meghna* launched 19 January 1984, *Jamuna* 19 March 1984. Both completed late 1984. Reported that MTU diesels may have been fitted giving a top speed of 24 kts. Both damaged in April 1991 typhoon.

MEGHNA 6/1990, G Jacobs

1 RIVER CLASS (LARGE PATROL CRAFT)

Name	No	Builders	Commissioned
BISHKHALI (ex-PNS *Jessore*)	P 311	Brooke Marine Ltd	20 May 1965

Displacement, tons: 115 standard; 143 full load
Dimensions, feet (metres): 107 × 20 × 6.9 *(32.6 × 6.1 × 2.1)*
Main machinery: 2 MTU 12V 538 TB90 diesels; 4500 hp(m) *(3.3 MW)* sustained; 2 shafts
Speed, knots: 24
Complement: 30
Guns: 2 Breda 40 mm/70; 85° elevation; 300 rounds/minute to 12.5 km *(6.8 nm)*; weight of shell 0.96 kg.
Radars: Surface search: Racal Decca; I band.

Comment: PNS *Jessore*, which was sunk during the 1971 war, was salvaged and extensively repaired at Khulna Shipyard and recommissioned as *Bishkhali* on 23 November 1978.

BISHKHALI 1984, Bangladesh Navy

8 Ex-CHINESE SHANGHAI II CLASS (FAST ATTACK CRAFT—GUN)

SHAHEED DAULAT	P 411	TAWHEED	P 611
SHAHEED FARID	P 412	TAWFIQ	P 612
SHAHEED MOHIBULLAH	P 413	TAWJEED	P 613
SHAHEED AKHTARUDDIN	P 414	TANVEER	P 614

Displacement, tons: 113 standard; 131 full load
Dimensions, feet (metres): 127.3 × 17.7 × 5.6 *(38.8 × 5.4 × 1.7)*
Main machinery: 4 Type M 50 diesels; 4400 hp(m) *(3.2 MW)* sustained; 4 shafts
Speed, knots: 30. **Range, miles:** 800 at 16.5 kts
Complement: 36
Guns: 4—37 mm/63 (2 twin); 85° elevation; 180 rounds/minute to 8.5 km *(4.6 nm)*; weight of shell 1.4 kg.
 4—25 mm/80 (2 twin); 85° elevation; 270 rounds/minute to 3 km *(1.6 nm)* anti-aircraft.
Depth charges: 2 throwers; 8 charges.
Mines: 10 can be carried.
Radars: Surface search: Skin Head/Pot Head; I band.
Sonars: Hull-mounted; active; short range; high frequency. Some reported to have VDS.

Comment: First four transferred March 1980, remainder in 1982. Different engine arrangement from Chinese craft. Four based at Chittagong form Patrol Squadron 41.

SHAHEED FARID 1984, Bangladesh Navy

TAWJEED 6/1990, G Jacobs

5 PABNA CLASS (RIVERINE PATROL CRAFT)

Name	No	Builders	Commissioned
PABNA	P 111	DEW Narayangonj, Dhaka	12 June 1972
NOAKHALI	P 112	DEW Narayangonj, Dhaka	8 July 1972
PATUAKHALI	P 113	DEW Narayangonj, Dhaka	7 Nov 1974
RANGAMATI	P 114	DEW Narayangonj, Dhaka	11 Feb 1977
BOGRA	P 115	DEW Narayangonj, Dhaka	15 July 1977

Displacement, tons: 69.5
Dimensions, feet (metres): 75 × 20 × 3.5 *(22.9 × 6.1 × 1.1)*
Main machinery: 2 Cummins diesels; 2 shafts
Speed, knots: 10.8. **Range, miles:** 700 at 8 kts
Complement: 33 (3 officers)
Guns: 1 Bofors 40 mm/60; 80° elevation; 120 rounds/minute to 10 km *(5.5 nm)*; weight of shell 0.89 kg.

Comment: The first indigenous naval craft built in Bangladesh. Form River Patrol Squadron 11 at Mongla.

RANGAMATI 1984, Bangladesh Navy

44 BANGLADESH / Light forces — Auxiliaries

1 COASTAL PATROL CRAFT

SHAHJALAL A 513

Displacement, tons: 600 full load
Dimensions, feet (metres): 131.8 × 29.7 × 12.6 *(40.2 × 9.1 × 3.8)*
Main machinery: 1 V-16 cyl Type diesel; 1 shaft
Speed, knots: 12. **Range, miles:** 7000 at 12 kts
Complement: 55 (3 officers)
Guns: 2 Oerlikon 20 mm.

Comment: Ex-Thai fishing vessel SMS *Gold 4*. Probably built in Tokyo. Commissioned into BN on 15 January 1987 and used as a patrol craft in spite of its A pennant number.

SHAHJALAL   8/1987, Bangladesh Navy

AUXILIARIES

Note: Two LSLs built by Narayanganj Dockyard and launched in 1992 may be taken over by the Navy. Names are *Barkat* and *Bahasha Shaeed*.

1 TRAINING SHIP

SHAHEED RUHUL AMIN (ex-MV *Anticosti*) A 511

Displacement, tons: 710 full load
Dimensions, feet (metres): 155.8 × 36.5 × 10 *(47.5 × 11.1 × 3.1)*
Main machinery: 1 Caterpillar diesel; 1 shaft
Speed, knots: 11.5. **Range, miles:** 4000 at 10 kts
Complement: 80 (8 officers)
Guns: 1 Bofors 40 mm/60.

Comment: Built by Atlantic Shipbuilding Co, Montreal. Laid down 1956, completed March 1957. Sold to India as MV *Anticosti*. After use in relief work was handed over to BN in 1972, modified at Khulna and commissioned 10 December 1974 as a training ship.

SHAHEED RUHUL AMIN   6/1990, G Jacobs

1 TANKER

KHAN JAHAN ALI A 515

Displacement, tons: 2900 full load
Measurement, tons: 1343 gross
Dimensions, feet (metres): 250.8 × 37.5 × 18.4 *(76.4 × 11.4 × 5.6)*
Main machinery: 1 diesel; 1350 hp(m) *(992 kW)*; 1 shaft
Speed, knots: 12
Complement: 26 (3 officers)
Cargo capacity: 1500 tons

Comment: Completed in Japan in 1983.

KHAN JAHAN ALI   6/1987, Gilbert Gyssels

1 REPAIR SHIP

SHAHAYAK A 512

Displacement, tons: 477 full load
Dimensions, feet (metres): 146.6 × 26.2 × 6.6 *(44.7 × 8 × 2)*
Main machinery: 1 Type 12 VTS 6 diesel; 1 shaft
Speed, knots: 11.5. **Range, miles:** 3800 at 11.5 kts
Complement: 45 (1 officer)
Guns: 1 Oerlikon 20 mm.

Comment: Re-engined and modernised at Khulna Shipyard and commissioned in 1978 to act as repair vessel.

SHAHAYAK   1984, Bangladesh Navy

1 OCEAN TUG

KHADEM A 721

Displacement, tons: 1472 full load
Dimensions, feet (metres): 197.5 × 38 × 16.1 *(60.2 × 11.6 × 4.9)*
Main machinery: 2 diesels; 2 shafts
Speed, knots: 14. **Range, miles:** 7200 at 14 kts
Complement: 56 (7 officers)
Guns: 2—12.7 mm MGs.

Comment: Commissioned 6 May 1984.

KHADEM   6/1990, G Jacobs

2 Ex-CHINESE YUCH'IN CLASS (TYPE 069)

DARSHAK   A 581   **TALLASHI**   A 582

Displacement, tons: 83 full load
Dimensions, feet (metres): 79.1 × 17.1 × 4.3 *(24.1 × 5.2 × 1.3)*
Main machinery: 2 Type 12V 150 diesels; 600 hp(m) *(440 kW)*; 2 shafts
Speed, knots: 11.5. **Range, miles:** 700 at 11.5 kts
Complement: 26 (1 officer)

Comment: Transferred from China in 1983 and used as coastal survey craft.

TALLASHI   1984, Bangladesh Navy

1 LANDING CRAFT LOGISTIC (LSL)

SHAHAMANAT L 900

Displacement, tons: 366 full load
Dimensions, feet (metres): 154.2 × 34.1 × 8 *(47 × 10.4 × 2.4)*
Main machinery: 2 Caterpillar D 343 diesels; 730 hp *(544 kW)* sustained; 2 shafts
Speed, knots: 9.5
Complement: 31 (3 officers)

Comment: One of two Danyard-built LSLs delivered in 1988 for civilian use and transferred to the Navy in 1990. The second may also be taken over by the Navy in due course.

SHAHAMANAT   6/1990, Bangladesh Navy

4 Ex-CHINESE YUCH'IN CLASS (TYPE 068)

LCT 101-LCT 104   A 584-587

Displacement, tons: 85 full load
Dimensions, feet (metres): 81.2 × 17.1 × 4.3 *(24.8 × 5.2 × 1.3)*
Main machinery: 2 Type 12V 150 diesels; 600 hp(m) *(440 kW)*; 2 shafts
Speed, knots: 11.5. **Range, miles:** 450 at 11.5 kts
Complement: 23
Military lift: Up to 150 troops
Guns: 4 China 14.5 mm (2 twin) MGs.

Comment: First two transferred 4 May 1986; second pair 1 July 1986. Probably built in the late 1960s. Two badly damaged in April 1991 typhoon.

A 586   6/1990, G Jacobs

3 LCVP

LCVP 011, 012, 013

Displacement, tons: 83 full load
Dimensions, feet (metres): 69.9 × 17.1 × 4.9 *(21.3 × 5.2 × 1.5)*
Main machinery: 2 Cummins diesels; 365 hp *(272 kW)*; 2 shafts
Speed, knots: 12.
Complement: 10 (1 officer)

Comment: First two built at Khulna Shipyard and *013* at DEW Narayangong; all completed in 1984.

LCVP 012   1984, Bangladesh Navy

1 Ex-FISHING VESSEL

MFV 66

Displacement, tons: 96 full load
Dimensions, feet (metres): 91.9 × 19.7 × 5.9 *(28 × 6 × 1.8)*
Main machinery: 1 diesel; 1 shaft
Speed, knots: 8. **Range, miles:** 750 at 8 kts
Complement: 24 (1 officer)
Guns: 1 Oerlikon 20 mm.

Comment: Ex-Thai steel hulled fishing vessel. Confiscated and taken into naval service.

MFV 66   1989, Bangladesh Navy

SANKET

Displacement, tons: 80 full load
Dimensions, feet (metres): 96.5 × 20 × 5.9 *(29.4 × 6.1 × 1.8)*
Main machinery: 2 Deutz Sea diesels; 1215 hp(m) *(893 kW)*; 2 shafts
Speed, knots: 18. **Range, miles:** 1000 at 16 kts
Complement: 24 (1 officer)
Guns: 1 Oerlikon 20 mm.

Comment: Acquired in 1989. Used for general harbour duties.

1 FLOATING DOCK and 1 FLOATING CRANE

Comment: Floating Dock (*Sundarban*) acquired from Brodogradiliste Joso Lozovina-Mosor, Trogir, Yugoslavia in 1980; capacity 3500 tons. Floating crane (*Balaban*) is self-propelled at 9 kts and has a lift of 70 tons; built at Khulna Shipyard and commissioned 18 May 1988, she has a complement of 29 (2 officers).

SUNDARBAN   1984, Bangladesh Navy

BALABAN   1990, Bangladesh Navy

BARBADOS

Headquarters' Appointment

Chief of Staff, Barbados Defence Force:
 Brigadier Rudyard E C Lewis

Commanding Officer Coast Guard Squadron

 Lieutenant Commander D A Dowridge

Personnel

(a) 1993: 110 (12 officers)
(b) Voluntary service

Coast Guard

This was formed early in 1973. In 1979 it became the naval arm of the Barbados Defence Force.

Base

Bridgetown (HMBS *Willoughby Fort*)

Headquarters

St Ann's Fort, Garrison, St Michael

Prefix to Ships' Names

HMBS

Mercantile Marine

Lloyd's Register of Shipping:
 37 vessels of 53 445 tons gross

PATROL FORCES

1 KEBIR CLASS (LARGE PATROL CRAFT)

Name	No	Builders	Commissioned
TRIDENT	P 01	Brooke Marine Ltd	Nov 1981

Displacement, tons: 155.5 standard; 190 full load
Dimensions, feet (metres): 123 × 22.6 × 5.6 *(37.5 × 6.9 × 1.7)*
Main machinery: 2 Paxman Valenta 12CM diesels; 5000 hp *(3.73 MW)* sustained; 2 shafts
Speed, knots: 29. **Range, miles:** 3000 at 12 kts
Complement: 28
Guns: 2—12.7 mm MGs.
Radars: Surface search: Racal Decca TM 1226C; I band.

Comment: Launched 14 April 1981. Similar to Algerian vessels. Refitted by Bender Shipyard in 1990.

TRIDENT 11/1990, Bob Hanlon

3 GUARDIAN II CLASS (COASTAL PATROL CRAFT)

Name	No	Builders	Commissioned
T T LEWIS	P 04	Halmatic/Aquarius UK	Dec 1973
COMMANDER MARSHALL	P 05	Halmatic/Aquarius UK	Dec 1973
J T C RAMSEY	P 06	Halmatic/Aquarius UK	Nov 1974

Displacement, tons: 11
Dimensions, feet (metres): 41 × 12.1 × 3.3 *(12.5 × 3.7 × 1)*
Main machinery: 2 Caterpillar D 334TA diesels; 480 hp *(358 kW)*; 2 shafts
Speed, knots: 24
Complement: 4
Guns: 1—7.62 mm MG (fitted for but not with).

Comment: GRP hulls. Designed for coastal patrol/SAR duties by T T Boat Designs Ltd. Fitted out by Aquarius Boat Co Ltd, Christchurch.

EXCELLENCE 11/1990, Bob Hanlon

3 INSHORE PATROL CRAFT

Comment: One Arctic 22 ft craft for SAR duties; speed 30 kts; commissioned November 1985. Two Boston Whalers 22 ft craft for law enforcement role; speed 40 kts; commissioned early 1989.

COMMANDER MARSHALL 1988, BDF

1 ENTERPRISE CLASS (OFFSHORE PATROL CRAFT)

Name	No	Builders	Commissioned
EXCELLENCE	P 03	Desco Marine	Dec 1981

Displacement, tons: 87 full load
Dimensions, feet (metres): 73.7 × 22 × 9 *(22.5 × 6.7 × 2.7)*
Main machinery: 1 Caterpillar diesel; 1 shaft
Speed, knots: 9.5
Complement: 9
Guns: 1—12.7 mm MG.
Radars: Surface search: Racal Decca TM 1229C; I band.

Comment: Shrimp boat converted for patrol duties by Swan Hunter (Trinidad) in 1980-81.

ARCTIC 22 1988, BDF

BELGIUM

Headquarters' Appointments

Chief of Naval Staff:
  Vice Admiral J de Wilde
Deputy Chief of Naval Staff:
  Captain J L Barbieux

Diplomatic Representation

Naval, Military and Air Attaché in London:
  Captain P A C Lavaert
Naval, Military and Air Attaché in Washington:
  Commodore J Ceux (Navy)

Personnel

(a) 1993: 4500 (1500 national service). Numbers reducing to 2500
(b) 10 months' national service (to end in 1994)

Note: 70 per cent of junior ratings are regulars.

Strength of the Fleet

Type	Active	Building
Frigates	4	—
Minehunters (Ocean)	6	—
Minehunters (Coastal)	10	(6)
River Patrol Craft	1	(1)
Command and Support Ships	2	—
Training Ship	1	—
Research Ships	1	—
Auxiliary and Service Craft	9	—

Bases

Zeebrugge: Frigates, MCMV, Reserve Units.
Ostend: Clearance Diving.
Koksijde: Naval aviation.
Antwerp: *Liberation*.

Mercantile Marine

Lloyd's Register of Shipping:
  232 vessels of 255 648 tons gross

DELETIONS

Mine Warfare Vessels

1990 *Seraing, Huy*
1991 *Andenne* (marine cadets), *Turnhout, Tongeren* (marine cadets), *Herstal, Vise* (marine cadets), *Nieuwport, Koksijde*
1992 *Merksem, Ougrée, Dinant, Heist, Rochefort*

PENNANT LIST

Frigates

F 910	Wielingen
F 911	Westdiep
F 912	Wandelaar
F 913	Westhinder

Mine Warfare Forces

M 902	Van Haverbeke
M 903	Dufour
M 904	De Brouwer
M 906	Breydel
M 908	Truffaut
M 909	Bovesse
M 915	Aster
M 916	Bellis
M 917	Crocus
M 918	Dianthus
M 919	Fuchsia
M 920	Iris
M 921	Lobelia
M 922	Myosotis
M 923	Narcis
M 924	Primula

River Patrol Craft

P 902	Liberation

Support Ships

A 960	Godetia
A 961	Zinnia

Research Ships

A 962	Belgica

Training Ships

A 958	Zenobe Gramme

Auxiliary and Service Craft

A 950	Valcke
A 951	Hommel
A 953	Bij
A 954	Zeemeeuw
A 956	Krekel
A 963	Spa
A 981	Avila
A 997	Spin
A 998	Ekster

FRIGATES

4 WIELINGEN CLASS (E-71)

Name	No	Builders	Laid down	Launched	Commissioned
WIELINGEN	F 910	Boelwerf, Temse	5 Mar 1974	30 Mar 1976	20 Jan 1978
WESTDIEP	F 911	Cockerill, Hoboken	2 Sep 1974	8 Dec 1975	20 Jan 1978
WANDELAAR	F 912	Boelwerf, Temse	28 Mar 1975	21 June 1977	27 Oct 1978
WESTHINDER	F 913	Cockerill, Hoboken	8 Dec 1975	28 Jan 1977	27 Oct 1978

Displacement, tons: 1940 light; 2430 full load
Dimensions, feet (metres): 349 × 40.3 × 18.4 *(106.4 × 12.3 × 5.6)*
Main machinery: CODOG; 1 RR Olympus TM3B gas turbine; 25 440 hp *(19 MW)* sustained; 2 Cockerill 240 CO V 12 diesels; 6000 hp(m) *(4.4 MW)*; 2 shafts; cp props
Speed, knots: 26; 15 on 1 diesel; 20 on 2 diesels
Range, miles: 4500 at 18 kts; 6000 at 15 kts
Complement: 159 (13 officers)

Missiles: SSM: 4 Aerospatiale MM 38 Exocet (2 twin) launchers ❶; inertial cruise; active radar homing to 42 km *(23 nm)* at 0.9 Mach; warhead 165 kg; sea-skimmer.
SAM: Raytheon Sea Sparrow Mk 29 octuple launcher ❷; semi-active radar homing to 14.6 km *(8 nm)* at 2.5 Mach; warhead 39 kg.
Guns: 1 Creusot Loire 3.9 in *(100 mm)/*55 Mod 68 ❸; 80° elevation; 60-80 rounds/minute to 17 km *(9 nm)* anti-surface; 8 km *(4.4 nm)* anti-aircraft; weight of shell 13.5 kg.
Torpedoes: 2—21 in *(533 mm)* launchers. ECAN L5 Mod 4; anti-submarine; active/passive homing to 9.5 km *(5 nm)* at 35 kts; warhead 150 kg; depth to 550 m *(1800 ft)*.
A/S Mortars: 1 Creusot Loire 375 mm 6-barrelled trainable launcher ❹; Bofors rockets to 1600 m; warhead 107 kg.
Countermeasures: Decoys: 2 Tracor MBA SRBOC 6-barrelled Mk 36 launchers; chaff decoys and IR flares to 4 km *(2.2 nm)*.
Nixie SLQ 25; towed anti-torpedo decoy.
ESM: CSF DR 2000; radar warning.

Combat data systems: Signaal SEWACO IV action data automation; Link 11. SATCOM.
Fire control: 2 CSEE DMAb optical directors ❺.
Radars: Air/surface search: Signaal DA 05 ❻; E/F band; range 137 km *(75 nm)* for 2 m² target.
Surface search/fire control: Signaal WM 25 ❼; I/J band; range 46 km *(25 nm)*.
Navigation: Raytheon TM 1645/9X; I/J band.
IFF: Mk XII.
Sonars: Westinghouse SQS 505A; hull-mounted; active search and attack; medium frequency.

WIELINGEN   *(Scale 1 : 900), Ian Sturton*

Programmes: This compact, well-armed class of frigate is the first class fully designed by the Belgian Navy and built in Belgian yards. The programme was approved on 23 June 1971 and design studies completed July 1973. An order was placed in October 1973 and F 910 and F 911 were first delivered in December 1976 and returned to the yard for engine overhaul which was completed a year later.
Modernisation: Plans to fit Goalkeeper and new ESM have been shelved but Sea Sparrow has been updated from 7M to 7P and L5 Mod 4 torpedoes acquired.
Structure: Fully air-conditioned. Fin stabilisers fitted.
Operational: Based at Zeebrugge. Two to be paid off by 1994 as part of defence cuts.

WANDELAAR   *9/1992, van Ginderen Collection*

MINE WARFARE FORCES

0 + (6) NEW MINESWEEPERS (COASTAL)

Displacement, tons: 620 full load
Dimensions, feet (metres): 171.9 oa; 157.5 wl × 34.1 × 10.2 *(52.4; 48 × 10.4 × 3.1)*
Speed, knots: 15; 10 (sweeping). **Range, miles:** 3000 at 12 kts
Complement: 25 plus 5 spare

Guns: 1 DCN 20 mm/20.
Radars: Navigation: I band.

Programmes: Memorandum of Understanding signed 6 April 1989 for a joint Belgium/Netherlands minesweeper project. Design contract awarded November 1990 to van der Giessen-de Noord Marinebouw in a joint venture with Beliard Polyship NV, completed in August 1992. Orders of up to six vessels for Belgium, eight for the Netherlands and four for Portugal were expected in 1993 until the project was suspended as part of defence cuts.
Operational: The ship is to be equipped with a newly developed magnetic sweeping gear, 'Sterne M', by Thomson Sintra. This development, ordered by the joint navies, is based upon the concept of 'target simulation' and consists of six bodies, towed in array, each carrying two coils. By automatically computed coil settings a simulated ship's signature is generated without any assumption concerning the mine itself. In addition, proven acoustic and mechanic sweeping capabilities are installed. The requirement is to be able to sweep bottom mines which have sunk so far into soft sand that they are not detected by hunters.

NEW MINESWEEPER (artist's impression)   *1992, van der Giessen-de Noord*

10 FLOWER CLASS (TRIPARTITE) (MINEHUNTERS—COASTAL)

Name	No	Builders	Laid down	Launched	Commissioned
ASTER	M 915	Beliard S. Y., Ostend and Rupelmonde	26 Apr 1983	6 June 1985	17 Dec 1985
BELLIS	M 916	Beliard S. Y., Ostend and Rupelmonde	9 Feb 1984	14 Feb 1986	14 Aug 1986
CROCUS	M 917	Beliard S. Y., Ostend and Rupelmonde	9 Oct 1984	6 Aug 1986	5 Feb 1987
DIANTHUS	M 918	Beliard S. Y., Ostend and Rupelmonde	4 Apr 1985	26 Feb 1987	17 Aug 1987
FUCHSIA	M 919	Beliard S. Y., Ostend and Rupelmonde	31 Oct 1985	23 Sep 1987	18 Feb 1988
IRIS	M 920	Beliard S. Y., Ostend and Rupelmonde	23 May 1986	21 Apr 1987	6 Oct 1988
LOBELIA	M 921	Beliard S. Y., Ostend and Rupelmonde	4 Dec 1986	6 Jan 1988	9 May 1989
MYOSOTIS	M 922	Beliard S. Y., Ostend and Rupelmonde	6 July 1987	4 Aug 1988	14 Dec 1989
NARCIS	M 923	Beliard S. Y., Ostend and Rupelmonde	25 Feb 1988	30 Mar 1990	27 Sep 1990
PRIMULA	M 924	Beliard S. Y., Ostend and Rupelmonde	10 Nov 1988	17 Dec 1990	29 May 1991

Displacement, tons: 562 standard; 595 full load
Dimensions, feet (metres): 168.9 × 29.2 × 8.2 *(51.5 × 8.9 × 2.5)*
Main machinery: 1 Brons/Werkspoor A-RUB 215X-12 diesel; 1860 hp(m) *(1.37 MW)* sustained; 1 shaft; Lips cp prop; 2 motors; 240 hp(m) *(176 kW)*; 2 active rudders; 2 bow thrusters
Speed, knots: 15. **Range, miles:** 3000 at 12 kts
Complement: 46 (5 officers)

Guns: 1 DCN 20 mm/20; 60° elevation; 720 rounds/minute to 10 km *(5.5 nm)*. 1—12.7 mm MG.
Countermeasures: MCM: 2 PAP 104 remote-controlled mine locators; 39 charges.
Mechanical sweep gear (medium depth).
Radars: Navigation: Racal Decca 1229; I band.
Sonars: Thomson Sintra DUBM 21A; hull-mounted; active minehunting; 100 KHz ± 10 KHz.

Programmes: Developed in co-operation with France and the Netherlands. A 'ship factory' for the hulls was built at Ostend and the hulls were towed to Rupelmonde for fitting out. Each country built its own hulls but for all 35 ships France provided MCM gear and electronics, Belgium electrical installation and the Netherlands the engine room equipment.
Structure: GRP hull fitted with active tank stabilisation, full NBC protection and air-conditioning. Has automatic pilot and buoy tracking.
Operational: A 5 ton container can be carried, stored for varying tasks—HQ support, research, patrol, extended diving, drone control. The ship's company varies from 23-46 depending on the assigned task. Six divers are carried when minehunting. All of the class are based at Zeebrugge.

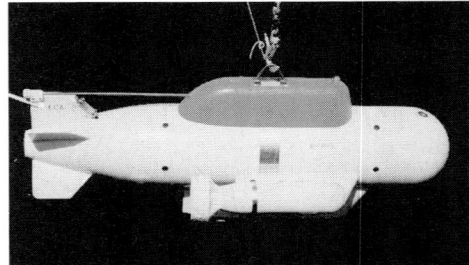

PAP 104   *3/1991, van Ginderen Collection*

NARCIS   *4/1992, Harald Carstens*

Mine warfare forces — Command and support ships / BELGIUM 49

6 Ex-US AGGRESSIVE CLASS (MINEHUNTERS/SWEEPERS — OCEAN)

Name	No	Builders	Laid down	Launched	Commissioned
J E VAN HAVERBEKE (ex-MSO 522)	M 902	Peterson Builders Inc, Sturgeon Bay, Wisc.	2 Mar 1959	29 Oct 1959	7 Nov 1960
A F DUFOUR (ex-*Lagen* M 950, ex-MSO 498, ex-AM 498)	M 903	Bellingham Shipyard Inc, Wash.	11 Feb 1954	13 Aug 1954	27 Sep 1955
DE BROUWER (ex-*Namsen* M 951, ex-MSO 499, ex-AM 499)	M 904	Bellingham Shipyard Inc, Wash.	25 Apr 1954	15 Oct 1954	1 Nov 1955
BREYDEL (ex-MSO 504, ex-AM 504)	M 906	Tacoma Boatbuilding Co, Tacoma, Wash.	25 Nov 1954	25 Mar 1955	24 Jan 1956
G TRUFFAUT (ex-MSO 515, ex-AM 515)	M 908	Tampa Marine Co Inc, Tampa, Fla.	1 Feb 1955	1 Nov 1955	21 Sep 1956
F BOVESSE (ex-MSO 516, ex-AM 516)	M 909	Tampa Marine Co Inc, Tampa, Fla.	1 Apr 1954	8 Feb 1956	21 Dec 1956

Displacement, tons: 720 standard; 780 full load
Dimensions, feet (metres): 172.5 × 35.1 × 14.1 *(52.6 × 10.7 × 4.3)*
Main machinery: 4 GM 8-268A diesels; 1760 hp *(1.3 MW)*; 2 shafts; cp props
Speed, knots: 14. **Range, miles:** 2400 at 12 kts; 3000 at 10 kts
Complement: 40 (3 officers)

Guns: 2 Oerlikon 20 mm (twin). 2—12.7 mm MGs (M 906 and M 908).
Radars: Navigation: Racal Decca 1229; I band.
Sonars: GE SQQ 14; VDS; minehunting; high frequency.

Programmes: Transfer dates; M 902 9 December 1960, M 903 14 April 1966, M 904 14 April 1966, M 906 15 February 1956, M 908 12 October 1956, M 909 25 January 1957. M 903 and M 904 originally served in Royal Norwegian Navy (1955-66).
Structure: Wooden hulls and non-magnetic structure. Capable of sweeping mines of all types. Diesels of non-magnetic stainless steel alloy. LIPS cp propellers.
Operational: Based at Zeebrugge. Most to pay off in 1993.

BREYDEL   7/1992, G Toremans

LIGHT FORCES

Note: A new fast patrol craft is planned probably to be funded by the Ministry of Agriculture but naval manned. Could be built in 1993 and in service in 1995.

1 RIVER PATROL CRAFT

Name	No	Builders	Commissioned
LIBERATION	P 902	Hitzler, Regensburg	4 Aug 1954

Displacement, tons: 275 full load
Dimensions, feet (metres): 85.5 × 13.1 × 3.2 *(26.1 × 4 × 1)*
Main machinery: 2 diesels; 440 hp(m) *(323 kW)*; 2 shafts
Speed, knots: 19
Complement: 7
Guns: 2—12.7 mm MGs.
Radars: Navigation: Racal Decca; I band.

Comment: Laid down 12 March 1954 and launched 29 July 1954. Paid off 12 June 1987 but put back in active service 15 September 1989 after repairs. Last of a class of ten.

LIBERATION   6/1991, van Ginderen Collection

SHIPBORNE AIRCRAFT

Numbers/Type: 3 Aerospatiale SA 316B Alouette III.
Operational speed: 113 kts *(210 km/h)*.
Service ceiling: 10 500 ft *(3200 m)*.
Range: 290 nm *(540 km)*.
Role/Weapon systems: CG helicopter; used for close-range search and rescue and support for commando forces. Sensors: Carries French-design search radar. Weapons: Unarmed. One SA 319B is used for transport on shore.

ALOUETTE III   3/1991, van Ginderen Collection

LAND-BASED MARITIME AIRCRAFT

Numbers/Type: 5 Westland Sea King Mk 48.
Operational speed: 140 kts *(260 km/h)*.
Service ceiling: 10 500 ft *(3200 m)*.
Range: 630 nm *(1165 km)*.
Role/Weapon systems: SAR helicopter; operated by air force; used for surface search and combat rescue tasks. Sensors: MEL ARI 5955 search radar. Weapons: Unarmed.

SEA KING Mk 48   1989, Paul Beaver

COMMAND AND SUPPORT SHIPS

Note: Also serve as Royal Yachts when required.

Name	No	Builders	Commissioned
ZINNIA	A 961	Cockerill, Hoboken	22 Sep 1967

Displacement, tons: 1705 light; 2620 full load
Dimensions, feet (metres): 324.7 × 45.9 × 11.8 *(99 × 14 × 3.6)*
Main machinery: 2 Cockerill Ougree 240 CO 12 TR diesels; 5000 hp(m) *(3.68 MW)*; 1 shaft; cp prop
Speed, knots: 18. **Range, miles:** 14 000 at 12.5 kts
Complement: 125 (13 officers)
Guns: 3 Bofors 40 mm/60.
Radars: Surface search: Racal Decca 1229; I band.
Helicopters: 1 Alouette III.

Comment: Laid down 8 November 1966, launched on 6 May 1967. Design includes a telescopic hangar. Rated as Command and Logistic Support Ship with an oil fuel capacity of 500 tons. Fitted with chaff launchers for prolonged operations. Based at Zeebrugge.

ZINNIA   1/1992, van Ginderen Collection

50 BELGIUM / Command and support ships — Training ships

Name	No	Builders	Commissioned
GODETIA	A 960	Boelwerf, Temse	3 June 1966

Displacement, tons: 2000 standard; 2260 full load
Dimensions, feet (metres): 301 × 46 × 11.5 *(91.8 × 14 × 3.5)*
Main machinery: 4 ACEC-MAN diesels; 5400 hp(m) *(3.97 MW)*; 2 shafts; cp props
Speed, knots: 19. **Range, miles:** 8700 at 12.5 kts
Complement: 100 (10 officers) plus 35 spare billets
Guns: 1 Bofors 40 mm/60. 2 midships sponsons for 12.7 mm MGs.
Radars: Surface search: Racal Decca 1229; I band.

Comment: Laid down 15 February 1965 and launched 7 December 1965. Rated as Command and Logistic Support Ship. Refit (1979-80) and mid-life conversion (1981-82) included helicopter hangar and replacement cranes. Minesweeping cables fitted either side of helo deck. Refitted in early 1992.

BELGICA — 5/1992, van Ginderen Collection

TRAINING SHIPS

1 SAIL TRAINING VESSEL

Name	No	Builders	Commissioned
ZENOBE GRAMME	A 958	Boel and Zonen, Temse	27 Dec 1961

Displacement, tons: 149
Dimensions, feet (metres): 92 × 22.5 × 7 *(28 × 6.8 × 2.1)*
Main machinery: 1 MWM diesel; 200 hp(m) *(147 kW)*; 1 shaft
Speed, knots: 10
Complement: 14

Comment: Auxiliary sail ketch. Laid down 7 October 1960 and launched 23 October 1961. Designed for scientific research but now only used as a training ship.

GODETIA — 7/1992, van Ginderen Collection

ZENOBE GRAMME — 4/1992, Giorgio Ghiglione

AUXILIARIES

1 AMMUNITION TRANSPORT

Name	No	Builders	Commissioned
SPA	A 963 (ex-M 9 953 271-78)	Boel and Zonen, Temse	10 Mar 1955

Displacement, tons: 390 full load
Dimensions, feet (metres): 144.3 × 27.9 × 8.9 *(44 × 8.5 × 2.7)*
Main machinery: 2 GM 8-268A diesels; 880 hp *(656 kW)*; 2 shafts
Speed, knots: 13.5. **Range, miles:** 3000 at 10 kts
Complement: 36 (4 officers)
Guns: 1 Bofors 40 mm/60.
Radars: Navigation: Racal Decca 1229; I band.

Comment: Ex-MSC launched 21 June 1954 and converted in 1978 to Ammunition Transport for guided missiles. Based at Zeebrugge.

SPA — 7/1992, Maritime Photographic

3 MARINE CADET SHIPS

TONGEREN (ex-*M 475*)   **VISE** (ex-*M 482*)   **ANDENNE** (ex-*M 485*)

Displacement, tons: 190 full load
Dimensions, feet (metres): 111.5 × 19.7 × 6.9 *(34 × 6 × 2.1)*
Main machinery: 2 Fiat-Mercedes Benz diesels; 1260 hp(m) *(926 kW)*; 2 shafts
Speed, knots: 15. **Range, miles:** 2300 at 10 kts
Complement: 14 (2 officers)
Radars: Navigation: Racal Decca 1229; I band.

Comment: Herstal class ex-Inshore minesweepers built in 1957-59, paid off in 1991 and now used by marine cadets.

RESEARCH SHIP

Name	No	Builders	Commissioned
BELGICA	A 962	Boelwerf, Temse	5 July 1984

Displacement, tons: 1085
Dimensions, feet (metres): 167 × 32.8 × 14.4 *(50.9 × 10 × 4.4)*
Main machinery: 1 ABC 6DZC diesel; 1600 hp(m) *(1.18 MW)* sustained; 1 Kort nozzle prop
Speed, knots: 13.5. **Range, miles:** 5000 at 12 kts
Complement: 26 (11 civilian)
Radars: Navigation: Racal Decca 1229; I band.

Comment: Ordered 1 December 1982. Laid down 17 October 1983, launched 6 January 1984. Used for hydrography, oceanography, meteorology and fishery control. Based at Zeebrugge. Painted white.

MARINE CADET SHIP — 9/1992, G Toremans

TUGS and MISCELLANEOUS

Note: There are four Government patrol craft of 16.6 m completed by SKB Antwerp in 1992/93. Names are *Nele 35, Tiji 36, Zannefin 37, Jan Bart 38.*

2 COASTAL TUGS

VALCKE (ex-*Steenbank*, ex-*Astroloog*) A 950
EKSTER (ex-*Schouwenbank*, ex-*Astronoom*) A 998

Displacement, tons: 183
Dimensions, feet (metres): 99.7 × 24.9 × 11.8 *(30.4 × 7.6 × 3.6)*
Main machinery: Diesel-electric; 2 Deutz diesel generators; 1240 hp(m) *(911 kW)*; 1 shaft
Speed, knots: 12
Complement: 12

Comment: Originally Netherlands civilian tugs built by H H Bodewes, Millingen in 1960. Bought by Belgian Navy in April 1980. Based at Zeebrugge.

VALCKE *7/1992, G Toremans*

BIJ A 953 **KREKEL** A 956

Comment: Harbour tugs with firefighting facilities. Of 71 tons and twin shafts; 400 hp(m) *(294 kW)* with Voith-Schneider propellers; 10 kts. A 953 built at Akerboom, Lisse 1959 and based at Ostend, A 956 by Scheepswerf van Rupelmonde at Rupelmonde 1961 and based at Antwerp.

BIJ *7/1992, G Toremans*

HOMMEL A 951

Comment: Harbour tug of 22 tons, 300 hp(m) *(220 kW)* diesels with Voith-Schneider propellers. Built by Clausen, Remagen-Oberwinter in 1953. Based at Ostend.

SPIN A 997 **AVILA** A 981

Comment: *Spin* is a harbour launch of 32 tons built in Netherlands 1958. Based at Ostend.

AVILA *7/1991, Gilbert Gyssels*

ZEEMEEUW A 954

Displacement, tons: 220
Dimensions, feet (metres): 91.8 × 23.6 × 11.8 *(28 × 7.2 × 3.6)*
Speed, knots: 10

Comment: Ex-civilian tug (same name) built in 1971 at Hemiksem, acquired 8 December 1981. Based at Zeebrugge.

ZEEMEEUW *10/1992, van Ginderen Collection*

BELIZE

Headquarters' Appointment

Officer Commanding Defence Force Maritime Wing:
Maritime Wing Major H H Cain

Personnel

(a) 1993: 50 (8 officers)
(b) The Maritime Wing of the Belize Defence Force comprises volunteers from the Army.

Bases

Belize City, Punta Gorda

Mercantile Marine

Lloyd's Register of Shipping:
32 vessels of 30 100 tons gross

2 WASP 20 METRE (COASTAL PATROL CRAFT)

DANGRIGA PB 01 **TOLEDO** PB 02

Displacement, tons: 36.3 full load
Dimensions, feet (metres): 65.6 × 16.4 × 4.9 *(20 × 5 × 1.5)*
Main machinery: 2 Detroit 16V-71 diesels; 812 hp *(606 kW)* sustained; 2 shafts
Speed, knots: 18
Complement: 10 (2 officers)
Guns: 1—12.7 mm MG. 2—7.62 mm MGs.

Comment: Built by Souters, Cowes, Isle of Wight. Completed August 1983 and commissioned 19 September 1984. GRP hulls. It is reported that these vessels have too great a draught for the shallow waters frequented by smugglers.

DANGRIGA *8/1983, W Sartori*

8 INSHORE PATROL CRAFT

Comment: The BDFMW has two Mexican Skiffs and two Avon type boats. The Police Maritime Wing has three armed Seacraft (P1-P3) with two outboard motors capable of 35 kts; one 12.7 mm MG. Also one Mexican Skiff.

LAND-BASED MARITIME AIRCRAFT

Numbers/Type: 2 Pilatus Britten-Norman Defender.
Operational speed: 150 kts *(280 km/h)*.
Service ceiling: 18 900 ft *(5760 m)*.
Range: 1500 nm *(2775 km)*.
Role/Weapon systems: Coastal patrol, EEZ protection and anti-drug operations. Sensors: Nose-mounted search radar, underwing searchlight. Weapons: Underwing rocket and gun pods possible

POLICE CRAFT *7/1989, BDFMW*

DEFENDER *1990*

BENIN

General

In 1978 a decision was taken to found a naval force. As the coastline of Benin is no more than 75 miles long the Patrol Craft can cover the whole coast in a little over two hours. Four Zhuk patrol craft still exist but are unlikely to go to sea again. There are also a Dornier Do 128 and a DHC-6 Twin Otter reconnaissance aircraft.

Base

Cotonou

Personnel

1993: 150

Mercantile Marine

Lloyd's Register of Shipping:
12 vessels of 1666 tons gross

1 PR 360T COASTAL PATROL CRAFT

PATRIOTE

Displacement, tons: 70 full load
Dimensions, feet (metres): 124.7 × 22.3 × 4.3 *(38 × 6.8 × 1.3)*
Main machinery: 3 Baudouin 12P15.2SR diesels; 3000 hp(m) *(2.2 MW)* sustained; 3 waterjets
Speed, knots: 35. **Range, miles:** 1500 at 16 kts
Complement: 23
Guns: 1 Oerlikon 20 mm. 2—12.7 mm MGs.

Comment: Laid down by Société Bretonne de Construction Navale (Loctudy) in October 1986. Launched January 1988 and completed 15 May 1988. Has a wood/epoxy resin composite hull. Endurance 10 days. The craft was damaged shortly after delivery and has never been fully operational.

1 COASTAL TUG

KONDO

Displacement, tons: 350
Main machinery: Deutz diesel; 2000 hp(m) *(1.47 MW)*; 1 shaft
Speed, knots: 12.5

Comment: Ordered from Oelkers, West Germany, in February 1984. Completed late 1985.

BERMUDA

General

A small group operated by the Bermuda Police under the charge of Inspector P J Every. There are also two tugs, *Powerful* and *Faithful*, operated by the Department of Port Services.

Base

Hamilton

Mercantile Marine

Lloyd's Register of Shipping:
94 vessels of 3 139 164 tons gross

PATROL FORCES

BLUE HERON

Comment: Delivered 22 May 1978 by Harris Boat, Newburyport, Massachusetts, USA. Of 7 tons, 36 ft *(10.9 m)* with two GM 8 2 Y diesels; 420 hp *(313 kW)*. Complement three.

HERON I   HERON II   HERON III

Comment: *Heron II* delivered in December 1988 and *Heron I* in August 1991. A new *Heron III* delivered in June 1992 to replace the craft of the same name. All are Boston Whaler type craft of 1.5 tons, 22 ft *(6.7 m)* and have twin Yamaha 115 hp(m) *(84.5 kW)* outboard engines.

BLUE HERON *1982, Bermuda Police*

RESCUE I   RESCUE II

Comment: First one delivered September 1986 and second May 1988 by Osborne Rescue Boats Ltd. An 'Arctic' rigid hull inflatable. Of 1.45 tons, 24 ft *(7.3 m)* with twin Yamaha 115 hp(m) *(84.5 kW)* outboard engines. Complement three.

HERON III *7/1992, Bermuda Police*

BOLIVIA

Headquarters' Appointments

Commander Armada Boliviana:
Vice Admiral Anibal Gutierrez Chavez
Chief of Staff:
Rear Admiral Rolando Herrera

General

A small navy, Armada Boliviana, used for patrolling Lake Titicaca and the Beni, Madre de Dios, Mamoré and Paraguay river systems was founded in 1963, receiving its present name in 1982. These rivers cover over 10 000 miles. Most of the advanced training of officers and senior ratings is carried out in friendly countries. The junior ratings are almost entirely converted soldiers. The vessels listed were those operational at the end of 1991, all the others have been deleted.

Personnel

(a) 1993: 5000 officers and men
(b) 12 months' selective military service

Organisation

The country is divided into five naval districts, each with one flotilla.
1st Naval District (HQ Riberalta). Patrol craft and two BTL logistic vessels on the Beni/Mamoré river system.
2nd Naval District (HQ Trinidad). Patrol craft and two BTL logistic vessels on the northern portion of Lake Titicaca.
3rd Naval District (HQ Puerto Guayaramerin). Four patrol craft and two BTL logistic vessels on the Madre de Dios river.
4th Naval District (HQ Tiquina). Patrol craft and the hospital ship on the southern portion of Lake Titicaca.
5th Naval District (HQ Puerto Quijarro). Three patrol craft and one BTL logistic vessel on the upper Paraguay river.

Marine Corps

Infanteria de Marina of 600 men based at Tiquina (Almirante Grau battalion)
Equipment: light infantry weapons and Unimos trucks

Prefix to Ships' Names

ARB

Mercantile Marine

Lloyd's Register of Shipping:
1 vessel of 9610 tons gross

PATROL FORCES

9 RIVER/LAKE PATROL CRAFT

Name	No	Tonnage
COMANDO	LP-01	10
TACTICA	LP-02	10
INTI	LP-04	10
MALLCU	LP-05	10
AUXILIAR	LP-08	10
SANTA CRUZ DE LA SIERRA	PR-51	50
TAMENGO	LP-502	10
SUAREZ ARANA	LP-510	10
MARISCAL SANTA CRUZ	LP-512	10

Comment: In addition to the above, four Boston Whalers were acquired from the US in late 1989 and 11 more in early 1991. A 55 ft craft *General Banzer* was launched in September 1990.

17 LOGISTIC SUPPORT and PATROL CRAFT

Name	No	Tonnage
GENERAL PANDO	BTL-01	40
NICOLAS SUAREZ	BTL-02	40
MARISCAL CRUZ	BTL-03	40
MAX PAREDES	BTL-04	40
V A H UGARTECHE	BTL-06	45
MANURIPI	BTL-07	40
ALMIRANTE GRAU	M-101	20
COMANDANTE ARANDIA	M-103	20
LIBERTADOR	M-223	20
TRINIDAD	M-224	20
LITORAL	M-18	20
J CHAVEZ SUAREZ	M-225	20
ING PALACIOS	M-315	20
ITENEZ	M-322	20
BRUNO RACUA	M-329	20
TF R RIOS V	M-331	20
ING GUMUCIO	M-341	70

Comment: The craft with BTL numbers have a liquid cargo capacity of 250 000 litres.

4 AUXILIARIES

Name	No	Tonnage
JULIAN APAZA	AH 01	150
GENERAL BELGRANO	LT 01	30
PIONERA	LH 01	30
CENTAURO	LH 03	30

Comment: AH 01 is a hospital ship given by the USA in 1972. LT 01 is a transport vessel and LH 01 and LH 03 are survey ships.

LAND-BASED MARITIME AIRCRAFT

Numbers/Type: 8 Helibras (Aerospatiale) SA 315B Gavião (Lama).
Operational speed: 124 kts *(230 km/h)*.
Service ceiling: 7710 ft *(2350 m)*.
Range: 390 nm *(720 km)*.
Role/Weapon systems: Support helicopter for SAR/commando forces. Sensors: Visual reconnaissance. Weapons: Unarmed.

Numbers/Type: 1 Cessna 402-C.
Operational speed: 210 kts *(389 km/h)*.
Service ceiling: 27 000 ft *(9000 m)*.
Range: 1080 nm *(2000 km)*.
Role/Weapon systems: Fixed-wing MR for short-range operations. Sensors: Visual reconnaissance. Weapons: Unarmed.

BRAZIL

Headquarters' Appointments

Chief of Naval Staff:
Admiral Sergio Alves Lima
Chief of Naval Operations:
Admiral Carlos Eduardo Cezar de Andrade
Chief of Naval Personnel:
Admiral José Julio Pedrosa
Commandant General Brazilian Marines:
Admiral Luiz Carlos da Silva Cantidio
Vice Chief of Naval Staff:
Vice Admiral Paulo Augusto Garcia Dumont

Senior Officer

Flag Officer Commanding Fleet:
Vice Admiral Carlos Augusto Bastos de Oliveira

Personnel

(a) 1993: 50 000 (5700 officers)
Figures include 14 600 marines and also auxiliary corps
(b) 1 year's national service

Organisation

Naval Districts as follows:
I Naval District (HQ Rio de Janeiro)
II Naval District (HQ São Salvador)
III Naval District (HQ Natal)
IV Naval District (HQ Belém)
V Naval District (HQ Rio Grande)
VI Naval District (HQ Ladário)
VII Naval District (HQ Manaus)
Comando Naval de Brasilia (HQ Brasilia)

Bases

Arsenal de Marinha do Rio de Janeiro – Rio de Janeiro (Naval shipyard with three dry docks and one floating dock with graving docks of up to 70 000 tons capacity)
Base Naval do Rio de Janeiro – Rio de Janeiro (Main Naval Base with two dry docks)
Base Almirante Castro e Silva – Rio de Janeiro (Naval Base for submarines)
Base Naval de Aratu – Bahia (Naval Base and repair yard with one dry dock and synchrolift)
Base Naval de Val-de-Cães – Pará (Naval River and repair yard with one dry dock)
Base Naval Almirante Ary Parreiras – Rio Grande do Norte (Small Naval Base and repair yard with one floating dock)
Base Fluvial de Ladário – Mato Grosso do Sul (Small Naval River Base and repair yard with one dry dock)
Base Aérea Naval de São Pedro d'Aldeia – Rio de Janeiro (Naval Air Station)
Estação Naval do Rio Negro – Amazonas (Small Naval River Station and repair yard with one floating dock)

Naval Aviation

A Fleet Air Arm was formed on 26 January 1965.
Squadrons: HA-1 Lynx; HS-1 Sea King; HI-1 Jet Ranger; HU-1 Ecureuil; HU-2 Super Puma.

Marines (Corpo de Fuzileiros Navais)

14 600 officers and men.

Headquarters at Fort São José, Rio de Janeiro
Divisão Anfibia: 1 Command Battalion, 3 Infantry Battalions (Riachuelo, Humaita and Paissandu), 1 Artillery group, 1 Service Battalion.
Tropa de Reforço: 1 Special Forces Battalion (Tonelero), 1 Commander Battalion, 1 Engineer Battalion, 1 Amphib Vehicles Battalion, 1 Maintenance and Supply Battalion.
Grupos Regionais: One security group in each naval district (Rio de Janeiro, Salvador, Natal, Belém, Rio Grande, Ladário, Manaus, Brasilia).

Strength of the Fleet (mid-1993)

Type	Active	Building (Planned)
Submarines (Patrol)	4	2 (2)
Aircraft Carrier (light)	1	—
Destroyers	6	—
Frigates	13	1
Coastal Patrol Ships	9	—
Landing Ships	3	—
River Monitor	1	—
River Patrol Ships	5	—
Large Patrol Craft	10	2 (2)
Coastal Patrol Craft	4	—
Minesweepers (Coastal)	6	—
Survey Ships	9	(1)
Survey Launches	12	—
Buoy Tenders	9	—
S/M Rescue Ship	1	—
Repair and Support Ships	2	—
Large Tanker	1	—
Small Tanker	1	—
Training Ships	7	—
Transports	16	—
Tugs—Ocean	5	—

Mercantile Marine

Lloyd's Register of Shipping:
635 vessels of 5 573 175 tons gross

54 BRAZIL / Introduction — Submarines

DELETIONS

Submarines

1990 *Goias*
1992 *Amazonas*
1993 *Bahia*

Destroyers

1990 *Maranhão, Mato Grosso*

Miscellaneous

1991 *Marajó, Almirante Saldanha, Rio Doce*

PENNANT LIST

Submarines

S 20	Humaitá
S 21	Tonelero
S 22	Riachuelo
S 30	Tupi
S 31	Tamoio (bldg)
S 32	Timbira (bldg)

Aircraft Carrier

A 11	Minas Gerais

Destroyers

D 25	Marcílio Dias
D 26	Mariz E Barros
D 27	Pará
D 28	Paraiba
D 29	Paraná
D 30	Pernambuco
D 35	Sergipe
D 36	Alagoas
D 37	Rio Grande do Norte
D 38	Espírito Santo

Frigates

F 40	Niteroi
F 41	Defensora
F 42	Constituição
F 43	Liberal
F 44	Independência
F 45	União
V 30	Inhaúma
V 31	Jaceguay
V 32	Julio de Noronha
V 33	Frontin (bldg)

Amphibious Forces

G 26	Duque de Caxais
G 30	Ceará
G 31	Rio de Janeiro
(ex-L 10)	Guarapari
(ex-L 11)	Tambaú
(ex-L 12)	Camboriú

Patrol Forces

V 15	Imperial Marinheiro
V 16	Iguatemi
V 18	Forte De Coimbra
V 19	Caboclo
V 20	Angostura
V 21	Bahiana
V 22	Mearim
V 23	Purus
V 24	Solimões
P 10	Piratini
P 11	Pirajá
P 12	Pampeiro
P 13	Parati
P 14	Penedo
P 15	Poti
P 20	Pedro Teixeira
P 21	Raposo Tavares
P 30	Roraima
P 31	Rondônia
P 32	Amapá
P 40	Graúna
P 41	Goiana
P 42	Grajaú
P 43	Guaiba (bldg)
P 44	Guajará (bldg)
P 45	Guaporé (bldg)
P 46	Gurupá (planned)
P 47	Gurupi (planned)

Mine Warfare Forces

M 15	Aratú
M 16	Anhatomirim
M 17	Atalaia
M 18	Araçatuba
M 19	Abrolhos
M 20	Albardão

Oceanographic Vessels and Tenders

(ex-H 11)	Paraibano
(ex-H 12)	Rio Branco
H 13	Mestre João dos Santos
(ex-H 14)	Nogueira da Gama
(ex-H 15)	Itacurussá
(ex-H 16)	Camocim
(ex-H 17)	Caravelas
H 18	Comandante Varella
H 19	Tenente Castelo
H 20	Comandante Manhães
H 21	Sirius
H 22	Canopus
H 24	Castelhanos
H 25	Tenente Boanerges
H 26	Faroleiro Mário Seixas
H 27	Faroleiro Areas
H 30	Faroleiro Nascimento
H 31	Argus
H 32	Orion
H 33	Taurus
H 34	Almirante Graça Aranha
H 40	Antares
H 41	Almirante Câmara
H 42	Barão de Teffé
H 43	Almirante Alvaro Alberto

Miscellaneous

G 15	Paraguassú
G 16	Barroso Pereira
G 17	Potengi
G 20	Custódio de Mello
G 21	Ary Parreiras
G 22	Soares Dutra
G 23	Almirante Gastao Motta
G 24	Belmonte
K 11	Felinto Perry
(ex-R 15)	Comandante Marroig
(ex-R 16)	Comandante Didier
(ex-R 17)	Tenente Magalhães
(ex-R 18)	Cabo Schramm
R 21	Tritão
R 22	Tridente
R 23	Triunfo
R 24	Almirante Guilhem
R 25	Almirante Guillobel
U 10	Aspirante Nascimento
U 11	Guarda Marinha Jensen
U 12	Guarda Marinha Brito
(ex-U 15)	Suboficial Oliveira
U 16	Trindade
U 17	Parnaiba
U 18	Oswaldo Cruz
U 19	Carlos Chagas
U 20	Gastão Moutinho
U 27	Brasil
U 29	Piraim
(ex-U 30)	Almirante Hess

SUBMARINES

Notes: (a) Plans for the construction of nuclear powered submarines are advancing with a prototype nuclear reactor being built at São Paulo. A uranium enrichment plant was inaugurated at Ipero in April 1988. The prototype SSN (S-NAC-2) to be about 2800 tons and have a power plant developing 50 MW for a speed of 25 kts. In spite of delays in the diesel submarine programme, the SSN has a very high priority.
(b) Two improved Tupi class to be called S-NAC-1 may be built. These may be of 2425 tons to a design advanced by the Naval Engineering Directorate in January 1990. First one to be called *Tapajos* S 33, second one *Tocantins* S 34. An industry group COPSEP is looking for technology transfers with the aim of placing contracts in 1993 to start building in 1996.

1 + 2 TUPI CLASS (209 TYPE 1400)

Name	No	Builders	Laid down	Launched	Commissioned
TUPI	S 30	Howaldtswerke-Deutsche Werft (Kiel)	8 Mar 1985	28 Apr 1987	6 May 1989
TAMOIO	S 31	Arsenal de Marinha, Rio de Janeiro	15 July 1986	1993	1994
TIMBIRA	S 32	Arsenal de Marinha, Rio de Janeiro	15 Sep 1987	1995	1996

Displacement, tons: 1260 surfaced; 1440 dived
Dimensions, feet (metres): 200.1 × 20.3 × 18 *(61 × 6.2 × 5.5)*
Main machinery: Diesel-electric; 4 MTU 12V 493 AZ80 GA31L diesels; 2400 hp(m) *(1.76 MW)*; 4 alternators; 1.7 MW; 1 Siemens motor; 4600 hp(m) *(3.36 MW)* sustained; 1 shaft
Speed, knots: 11 surfaced/snorting; 21.5 dived
Range, miles: 8200 at 8 kts surfaced; 400 at 4 kts dived
Complement: 30

Torpedoes: 8—21 in *(533 mm)* bow tubes. 16 Marconi Mk 24 Tigerfish Mod 1; wire-guided; active homing to 13 km *(7 nm)* at 35 kts; passive homing to 29 km *(15.7 nm)* at 24 kts; warhead 134 kg. Swim-out discharge.
Countermeasures: ESM: Thomson-CSF DR-4000; electronic warfare suite.
Fire control: Ferranti KAFS-A10 action data automation. Sperry Mk 29 inertial navigation. 2 Kollmorgen Mod 76 periscopes.
Radars: Navigation: Thomson-CSF Calypso III; I band.
Sonars: Atlas Elektronik CSU-83/1; hull-mounted; passive/active search and attack; medium frequency.

Programmes: Contract signed with Howaldtswerke in February 1984. Financial negotiations were completed with the West German Government in October 1984. Original plans included building four followed by two improved Tupis for a total of six by the end of the 1990s. However only three are now to be built followed by S-NAC-1.
Structure: Diving depth, 250 m *(820 ft)*.
Operational: IPqM designed A/S torpedoes may also be carried.

TUPI   *5/1992, Miguel Soto*

3 HUMAITÁ (OBERON) CLASS

Name	No	Builders	Laid down	Launched	Commissioned
HUMAITÁ	S 20	Vickers, Barrow	3 Nov 1970	5 Oct 1971	18 June 1973
TONELERO	S 21	Vickers, Barrow	18 Nov 1971	22 Nov 1972	10 Dec 1977
RIACHUELO	S 22	Vickers, Barrow	26 May 1973	6 Sep 1975	12 Mar 1977

Displacement, tons: 1610 standard; 2030 surfaced; 2410 dived
Dimensions, feet (metres): 295.2 × 26.5 × 18 *(90 × 8.1 × 5.5)*
Main machinery: Diesel-electric; 2 ASR 16 VVS-ASR1 diesels; 3680 hp *(2.74 MW)*; 2 AEI motors; 6000 hp *(4.48 MW)*; 2 shafts
Speed, knots: 12 surfaced; 17 dived; 10 snorting
Range, miles: 9000 surfaced at 12 kts
Complement: 70 (6 officers)

Torpedoes: 8—21 in *(533 mm)* (6 bow, 2 stern) tubes. 22 Marconi Mk 24 Tigerfish Mod 1; wire-guided; active homing to 13 km *(7 nm)* at 35 kts; passive homing to 29 km *(15.7 nm)* at 24 kts; warhead 134 kg.
4 Honeywell Mk 37 Mod 2 (stern tubes); wire-guided; active/passive homing to 8 km *(4.4 nm)* at 24 kts; warhead 150 kg. Some Mk 8 Mod 4 anti-ship torpedoes (4.5 km at 45 kts) are still in service.
Countermeasures: ESM: Radar warning.
Fire control: Ferranti DCH tactical data system.
Radars: Navigation: Kelvin Hughes Type 1006; I band.

Sonars: Thorn-EMI Type 187; hull-mounted; search and attack; medium frequency.
BAC Type 2007; flank array; passive search; low frequency.

Programmes: Two ordered from Vickers in 1969, the third in 1972. Completion of *Tonelero* was much delayed by a serious fire on board originating in the cabling. It was this fire which resulted in re-cabling of all Oberon class under construction.
Modernisation: The previously planned modernisation programme was finally cancelled in 1990.
Operational: Two short torpedo tubes aft are still in service.

AIRCRAFT CARRIER

1 Ex-BRITISH COLOSSUS CLASS

Name	No	Builders	Laid down	Launched	Commissioned
MINAS GERAIS (ex-HMS *Vengeance*)	A 11	Swan Hunter & Wigham Richardson, Ltd, Wallsend on Tyne	16 Nov 1942	23 Feb 1944	15 Jan 1945

Displacement, tons: 15 890 standard; 17 500 normal; 19 890 full load (13 190 standard; 18 010 full load before reconstruction)
Dimensions, feet (metres): 695 × 80 × 24.5 *(211.8 × 24.4 × 7.5)*
Flight deck, feet (metres): 690 × 119.6 *(210.3 × 36.4)*
Main machinery: 4 Admiralty boilers; 400 psi *(28.1 kg/cm sq)*, 700°F *(371°C)*; 2 Parsons turbines; 40 000 hp *(30 MW)*; 2 shafts
Speed, knots: 24. **Range, miles:** 12 000 at 14 kts; 6200 at 23 kts
Complement: 1300 (300 aircrew)

Guns: 10 Bofors 40 mm/60 (2 quad Mk 2, 1 twin Mk 1); 330 rounds/minute to 3 km *(1.6 nm)* anti-aircraft; weight of shell 0.89 kg.
2—47 mm saluting guns.
Countermeasures: Decoys: Plessey Shield chaff launcher.
ESM: SLR-2; radar warning.
Combat data systems: Ferranti Link system compatible with CAAIS fitted ships. SATCOM.
Fire control: 2 Mk 63 GFCS. 1 Mk 51 Mod 2 GFCS.
Radars: Air search: Lockheed SPS 40B; E/F band; range 320 km *(175 nm)*.
Air/surface search: Plessey AWS 4; E/F band.
Navigation: Scanter Mil; I band.
Fire control: Two SPG 34; I/J band.
CCA: Scanter Mil-Par; I band.

Fixed wing aircraft: 6 Grumman S-2G Trackers.
Helicopters: 4-6 Agusta SH-3A Sea Kings; 2 Aerospatiale UH-13 Ecureuil II; 3 Aerospatiale UH-14 Super Puma.

Programmes: Served in the Royal Navy from 1945 onwards. Fitted out 1948-49 for experimental cruise to the Arctic. Lent to the RAN early in August 1953, returned to the Royal Navy in 1955. Purchased by the Brazilian Government on 14 December 1956 and commissioned in the Brazilian Navy on 6 December 1960.
Modernisation: During reconstruction in 1957-60 at Rotterdam the steam capacity was increased when the boilers were retubed. New lifts were installed; also included were one MacTaggart-Scott single track steam catapult for launching, and arrester wires for recovering 30 000 lb aircraft at 60 kts. The conversion and overhaul also included the installation of the 8½ degrees angled deck, mirror-sight deck landing system, armament fire control, a new island and radar equipment. Completed refit in 1981 but further modernisation was postponed until 1991 when Plessey and Scanter Mil radars were fitted. Combat data systems, internal communications, generators and boilers are all being replaced/renewed and the ship is expected to be operational again in 1994.
Structure: Hangar dimensions: length, 135.6 m *(445 ft)*; width, 15.8 m *(52 ft)*; clear depth, 5.3 m *(17.5 ft)*. Aircraft lifts: 13.7 × 10.4 m *(45 × 34 ft)*. The ship's overall length quoted does not include the catapult spur.
Opinion: Plans delayed but still under consideration for a new 35 000-40 000 ton ship. It is reported that she will, if built, have a speed of 28 kts with two steam catapults, carry 30-40 aircraft and have modern anti-aircraft defences. The more likely alternative is a smaller 25 000 ton ship for use as a helicopter carrier.

MINAS GERAIS 1992

MINAS GERAIS 1992

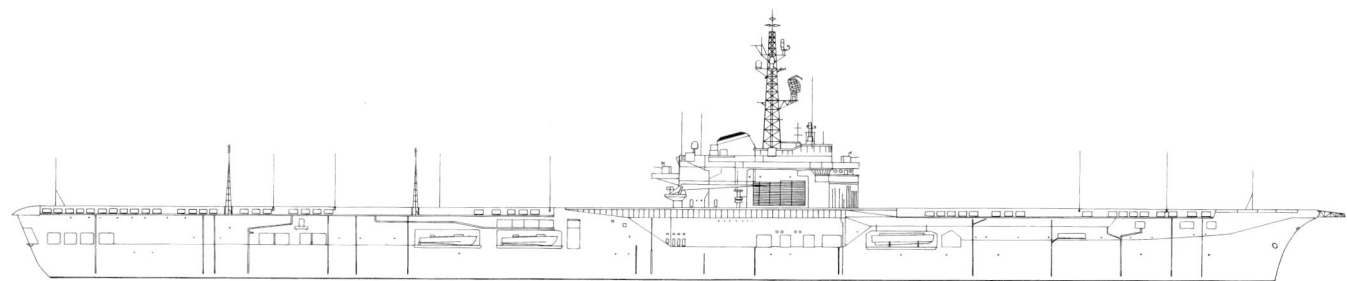

MINAS GERAIS (Scale 1 : 1200), Ian Sturton

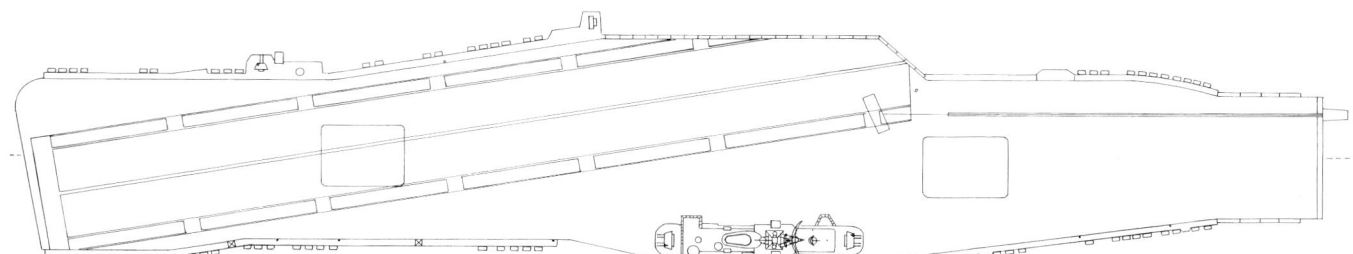

MINAS GERAIS (Scale 1 : 1200), Ian Sturton

56 BRAZIL / Destroyers

DESTROYERS

Note: There were provisional plans to acquire up to four ex-USN Charles F Adams class, but these had been indefinitely postponed by the end of 1992.

2 Ex-US GEARING (FRAM I) CLASS

Name	No	Builders	Laid down	Launched	Commissioned
MARCILIO DIAS (ex-USS *Henry W Tucker* DD 875)	D 25	Consolidated Steel	29 May 1944	8 Nov 1944	12 Mar 1945
MARIZ E BARROS (ex-USS *Brinkley Bass* DD 887)	D 26	Consolidated Steel	20 Dec 1944	26 May 1945	1 Oct 1945

Displacement, tons: 2425 standard; 3500 full load
Dimensions, feet (metres): 390.5 × 41.2 × 19 *(119 × 12.6 × 5.8)*
Main machinery: 4 Babcock & Wilcox boilers; 600 psi *(43.3 kg/cm sq)*; 850°F *(454°C)*; 2 GE turbines; 60 000 hp *(45 MW)*; 2 shafts
Speed, knots: 32. **Range, miles:** 5800 at 15 kts
Complement: 274 (14 officers)

Missiles: A/S: Honeywell ASROC Mk 116 octuple launcher ❶. Not operational.
Guns: 4—5 in *(127 mm)*/38 (2 twin) Mk 38 ❷; 15 rounds/minute to 17 km *(9.2 nm)* anti-surface; 11 km *(5.9 nm)* anti-aircraft; weight of shell 25 kg.
Torpedoes: 6—324 mm Mk 32 (2 triple) tubes ❸. Honeywell Mk 46 Mod 5; anti-submarine; active/passive homing to 11 km *(5.9 nm)* at 40 kts; warhead 44 kg.
Countermeasures: ESM: WLR 3; radar warning.
ECM: VLQ 6; jammer.
Fire control: Mk 37 GFCS.
Radars: Air search: Lockheed SPS 40 ❹; E/F band; range 320 km *(175 nm)*.
Surface search: Raytheon/Sylvania SPS 10 ❺; G band.
Fire control: Western Electric Mk 25 ❻; I/J band.
Sonars: Sangamo SQS 23; hull-mounted; active search and attack; medium frequency; with bottom bounce.

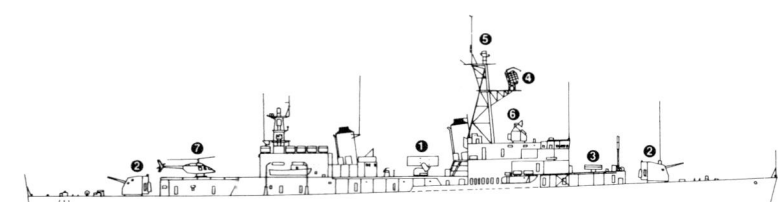

MARCILIO DIAS (Scale 1 : 1200), Ian Sturton

Helicopters: 1 Bell JetRanger III ❼.

Programmes: Transferred 8 December 1973.
Operational: Plans for new engines and re-arming have been dropped. JetRanger helicopter has replaced the deleted Wasp. ASROC is not operational.

MARCILIO DIAS 7/1990

4 Ex-US ALLEN M SUMNER (FRAM II) CLASS

Name	No	Builders	Laid down	Launched	Commissioned
SERGIPE (ex-USS *James C Owens* DD 776)	D 35	Bethlehem Steel Co (San Pedro)	9 Apr 1944	1 Oct 1944	17 Feb 1945
ALAGOAS (ex-USS *Buck* DD 761)	D 36	Bethlehem Steel Co (San Francisco)	1 Feb 1944	11 Mar 1945	28 June 1946
RIO GRANDE DO NORTE (ex-USS *Strong* DD 758)	D 37	Bethlehem Steel Co (San Francisco)	25 July 1943	23 Apr 1944	8 Mar 1945
ESPIRITO SANTO (ex-USS *Lowry* DD 770)	D 38	Bethlehem Steel Co (San Pedro)	1 Aug 1943	6 Feb 1944	23 July 1944

Displacement, tons: 2200 standard; 3320 full load
Dimensions, feet (metres): 376.5 × 40.9 × 19 *(114.8 × 12.5 × 5.8)*
Main machinery: 4 Babcock & Wilcox boilers; 600 psi *(43.3 kg/cm sq)*; 850°F *(454°C)*; 2 GE turbines; 60 000 hp *(45 MW)*; 2 shafts
Speed, knots: 34. **Range, miles:** 4600 at 15 kts; 1260 at 30 kts
Complement: 274 (15 officers)

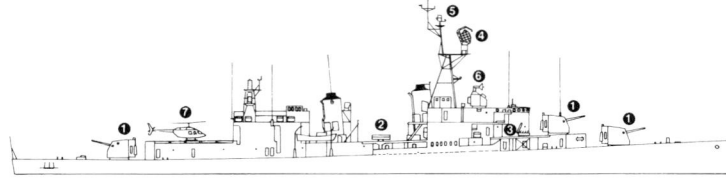

ALAGOAS (Scale 1 : 1200), Ian Sturton

Guns: 6—5 in *(127 mm)*/38 (3 twin) Mk 38 ❶; 15 rounds/minute to 17 km *(9.2 nm)* anti-surface; 11 km *(5.9 nm)* anti-aircraft; weight of shell 25 kg.
Torpedoes: 6—324 mm Mk 32 (2 triple) tubes ❷. Honeywell Mk 46 Mod 5; anti-submarine; active/passive homing to 11 km *(5.9 nm)* at 40 kts; warhead 44 kg.
A/S mortars: 2 Hedgehogs ❸; 24 manually loaded rockets; range 350 m.
Countermeasures: ESM: WLR 3; radar warning.
ECM: ULQ-6 *(Espirito Santo)*; jammer.
Fire control: Mk 37 GFCS.
Radars: Air search: Westinghouse SPS 29 *(Espirito Santo)*; B/C band; range 457 km *(250 nm)*.
Lockheed SPS 40 (others) ❹; E/F band; range 320 km *(175 nm)*.
Surface search: Raytheon/Sylvania SPS 10 ❺; G band.
Fire control: Western Electric Mk 25 ❻; I/J band
Sonars: SQS 40; hull-mounted; active search and attack; medium frequency.

Helicopters: 1 Bell JetRanger ❼.

Programmes: Transferred to Brazil by sale as follows: *Sergipe* and *Alagoas* 16 July 1973, *Espirito Santo* 29 October 1973 and *Rio Grande do Norte* 31 October 1973.
Operational: *Sergipe* VDS removed.

ESPIRITO SANTO 5/1990, Brazilian Navy

FRIGATES

6 NITEROI CLASS

Name	No	Builders	Laid down	Launched	Commissioned
NITEROI	F 40	Vosper Thornycroft Ltd	8 June 1972	8 Feb 1974	20 Nov 1976
DEFENSORA	F 41	Vosper Thornycroft Ltd	14 Dec 1972	27 Mar 1975	5 Mar 1977
CONSTITUIÇÃO	F 42*	Vosper Thornycroft Ltd	13 Mar 1974	15 Apr 1976	31 Mar 1978
LIBERAL	F 43*	Vosper Thornycroft Ltd	2 May 1975	7 Feb 1977	18 Nov 1978
INDEPENDÊNCIA	F 44	Arsenal de Marinha, Rio de Janeiro	11 June 1972	2 Sep 1974	3 Sep 1979
UNIÃO	F 45	Arsenal de Marinha, Rio de Janeiro	11 June 1972	14 Mar 1975	12 Sep 1980

*GP design.

Displacement, tons: 3200 standard; 3707 full load
Dimensions, feet (metres): 424 × 44.2 × 18.2 (sonar) *(129.2 × 13.5 × 5.5)*
Main machinery: CODOG; 2 RR Olympus TM3B gas turbines; 50 880 hp *(37.9 MW)* sustained; 4 MTU 16V 956 TB91 diesels; 15 000 hp(m) *(11 MW)* sustained; 2 shafts; cp props
Speed, knots: 30 gas; 22 diesels. **Range, miles:** 5300 at 17 kts on 2 diesels; 4200 at 19 kts on 4 diesels; 1300 at 28 kts on gas
Complement: 209 (22 officers)

Missiles: SSM: 4 Aerospatiale MM 40 Exocet (2 twin) launchers ❶; inertial cruise; active radar homing to 70 km *(40 nm)* at 0.9 Mach; warhead 165 kg; sea-skimmer.
SAM: 2 Short Bros Seacat triple launchers ❷; optical/radar guidance to 5 km *(2.7 nm)*; warhead 10 kg; 60 missiles. To be replaced.
A/S: 1 Ikara launcher (Branik standard) (A/S version) ❸; command radio/radar guidance to 24 km *(13 nm)* at 0.8 Mach; 10 missiles; payload Mk 46 torpedoes.
Guns: 2 Vickers 4.5 in *(115 mm)*/55 Mk 8 (GP version) ❹; 55° elevation; 25 rounds/minute to 22 km *(12 nm)* anti-surface; 6 km *(3.2 nm)* anti-aircraft; weight of shell 21 kg. A/S version only has 1 mounting.
2 Bofors 40 mm/70 ❺; 90° elevation; 300 rounds/minute to 12 km *(6.5 nm)* anti-surface; 4 km *(2.2 nm)* anti-aircraft; weight of shell 0.96 kg.
Torpedoes: 6—324 mm Plessey STWS-1 (2 triple) tubes ❻. Honeywell Mk 46 Mod 5; anti-submarine; active/passive homing to 11 km *(5.9 nm)* at 40 kts; warhead 44 kg.
A/S mortars: 1 Bofors 375 mm trainable rocket launcher (twin-tube) ❼; automatic loading; range 1600 m.
Depth charges: 1 rail; 5 charges (GP version).
Countermeasures: Decoys: 2 Plessey Shield chaff launchers.
ESM: SDR-2 and SDR-7; radar warning. FH5 HF/DF.
Combat data systems: Ferranti CAAIS 400 with FM 1600B computers.
Fire control: Ikara tracker (A/S version).
Radars: Air/surface search: Plessey AWS 2 with Mk 10 IFF ❽; E/F band; range 110 km *(60 nm)*.
Surface search: Signaal ZW 06 ❾; I band; range 26 km *(14 nm)*.
Fire control: Two Selenia Orion RTN 10X ❿; I/J band; range 40 km *(22 nm)*.
Sonars: EDO 610E; hull-mounted; active search and attack; medium frequency.
EDO 700E VDS (F 40 and 41); active search and attack; medium frequency.

Helicopters: 1 Westland Lynx SAH-11 ⓫.

Programmes: A contract announced on 29 September 1970 was signed between the Brazilian Government and Vosper Thornycroft for the design and building of six Vosper Thornycroft Mark 10 frigates.
Modernisation: The modernisation plan in late 1992 included replacing Seacat/RTN 10X by Matra Sadral, Plessey AWS 2 radar by AWS 5, ZW 06 radar by Kelvin Hughes Type 1007, updating the Bofors gun and fitting the same SAAB Optronic FCS, Plessey Shield countermeasures and Racal Cutlass ESM equipment as the Inhaúma class. ESM systems are being developed by the Instituto de Pesquisas da Marinas. In early 1993 contracts were being negotiated for the first two (probably the GP versions).

CONSTITUIÇÃO (GP)   *(Scale 1 : 1200), Ian Sturton*

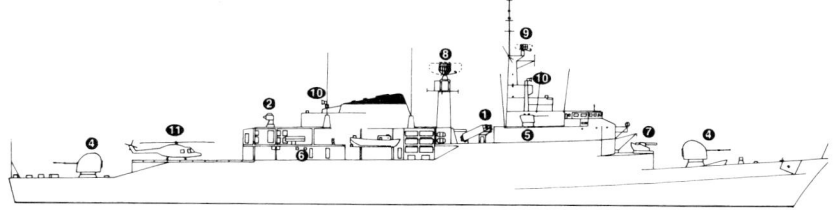

LIBERAL (GP design)   *4/1992, van Ginderen Collection*

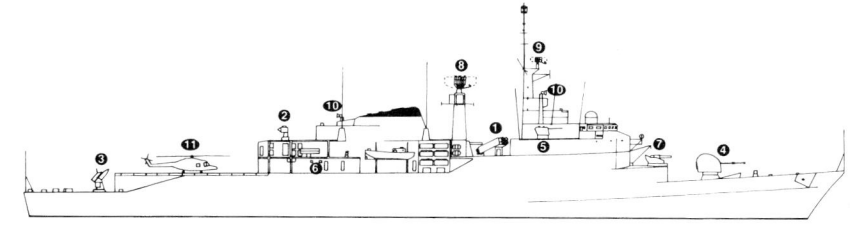

NITEROI (A/S)   *(Scale 1 : 1200), Ian Sturton*

Structure: F 40, 41, 44 and 45 are of the A/S configuration. F 42 and 43 are General Purpose design. Materials, equipment and lead-yard services supplied by Vosper Thornycroft at Navyard, Rio de Janeiro. Fitted with retractable stabilisers. Seventh ship with differing armament was ordered from Navyard, Rio de Janeiro in June 1981 and is used as a training ship.

Operational: At the time they were built these ships were economical in personnel, amounting to a 50 per cent reduction of manpower in relation to previous warships of this size and complexity. Endurance, 45 days' stores, 60 days' provisions. Oil fuel, 530 tons. The helicopter has Sea Skua ASM.

INDEPENDÊNCIA (A/S design)   *4/1992, van Ginderen Collection*

58 BRAZIL / Frigates

4 Ex-US GARCIA CLASS

Name	No	Builders	Laid down	Launched	Commissioned	Recommissioned
PARÁ (ex-*Albert David*)	D 27 (ex-FF 1050)	Lockheed S B & Construction Co	29 Apr 1964	19 Dec 1964	19 Oct 1968	18 Sep 1989
PARAÍBA (ex-*Davidson*)	D 28 (ex-FF 1045)	Avondale Shipyards	20 Sep 1963	2 Oct 1964	7 Dec 1965	25 July 1989
PARANÁ (ex-*Sample*)	D 29 (ex-FF 1048)	Lockheed S B & Construction Co	19 July 1963	28 Apr 1964	23 Mar 1968	24 Aug 1989
PERNAMBUCO (ex-*Bradley*)	D 30 (ex-FF 1041)	Bethlehem Steel, San Francisco	17 Jan 1963	26 Mar 1964	15 May 1965	25 Sep 1989

Displacement, tons: 2620 standard; 3403 full load
Dimensions, feet (metres): 414.5 × 44.2 × 24 sonar; 14.5 keel *(126.3 × 13.5 × 7.3; 4.4)*
Main machinery: 2 Foster-Wheeler boilers; 1200 psi *(83.4 kg/cm sq)*; 950°F *(510°C)*; 1 Westinghouse or GE turbine; 35 000 hp *(26 MW)*; 1 shaft
Speed, knots: 27.5. **Range, miles:** 4000 at 20 kts
Complement: 270 (18 officers)

Missiles: A/S: Honeywell ASROC Mk 112 octuple launcher ❶; inertial guidance to 1.6-10 km *(1-5.4 nm)*; payload Mk 46 torpedo. *Pará* and *Paraná* have automatic ASROC reload system.
Guns: 2 USN 5 in *(127 mm)*/38 Mk 30 ❷; 85° elevation; 15 rounds/minute to 17 km *(9.3 nm)*; weight of shell 25 kg.
Torpedoes: 6—324 mm Mk 32 (2 triple) tubes ❸. 14 Honeywell Mk 46 Mod 5; anti-submarine; active/passive homing to 11 km *(5.9 nm)* at 40 kts; warhead 44 kg.
Countermeasures: Decoys: 2 Loral Hycor Mk 33 RBOC 6 tubed chaff launchers. T-Mk 6 Fanfare; torpedo decoy system. Prairie/Masker; hull/blade rate noise suppression.
ESM: WLR-1; WLR-6; radar warning.
ECM: ULQ-6; jammer.
Fire control: Mk 56 GFCS. Mk 114 ASW FCS. SATCOM.
Radars: Air search: Lockheed SPS 40 ❹; E/F band; range 320 km *(175 nm)*.
Surface search: Raytheon SPS 10 ❺; G band.
Navigation: Marconi LN 66; I band.
Fire control: General Electric Mk 35 ❻; I/J band.
Tacan: SRN 15.
Sonars: EDO/General Electric SQS 26 AXR (D 29 and 30) or SQS 26B; bow-mounted; active search and attack; medium frequency.

Helicopters: Westland Lynx SAH-11 ❼.

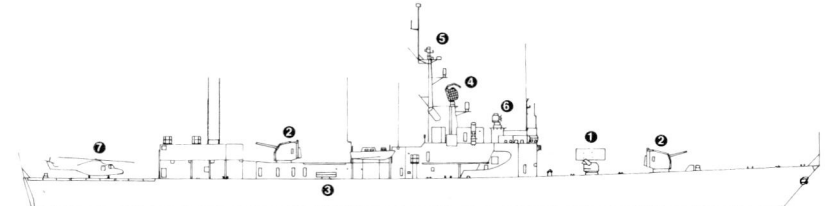

PARAÍBA *(Scale 1 : 1200), Ian Sturton*

PERNAMBUCO *5/1992, Hartmut Ehlers*

Programmes: First three transferred by five year lease 15 April 1989 and last one 1 October 1989. All arrived in Brazil on 13 December 1989.

Structure: All four have the enlarged hangar capable of taking a Sea King size helicopter but in USN service *Pará* and *Paraná* had the flight deck area converted to take SQR 15 towed array which was removed on transfer.

3 + 1 INHAÚMA CLASS

Name	No	Builders	Laid down	Launched	Commissioned
INHAÚMA	V 30	Arsenal de Marinha do Rio de Janeiro	23 Sep 1983	13 Dec 1986	12 Dec 1989
JACEGUAY	V 31	Arsenal de Marinha do Rio de Janeiro	15 Oct 1984	8 June 1987	2 Apr 1991
JULIO DE NORONHA	V 32	Verolme, Angra dos Reis	8 Dec 1986	15 Dec 1989	27 Oct 1992
FRONTIN	V 33	Verolme, Angra dos Reis	14 May 1987	6 Feb 1992	Oct 1993

Displacement, tons: 1600 standard; 1970 full load
Dimensions, feet (metres): 314.2 × 37.4 × 12.1; 17.4 (sonar) *(95.8 × 11.4 × 3.7; 5.3)*
Main machinery: CODOG; 1 GE LM2500 gas turbine; 27 500 hp *(20.52 MW)* sustained; 2 MTU 16V 396 TB94 diesels; 5800 hp(m) *(4.26 MW)* sustained; 2 shafts; cp props
Speed, knots: 27. **Range, miles:** 4000 at 15 kts
Complement: 162 (19 officers)

Missiles: SSM: 4 Aerospatiale MM 40 Exocet ❶; inertial cruise; active radar homing to 70 km *(40 nm)* at 0.9 Mach; warhead 165 kg; sea-skimmer.
Guns: 1 Vickers 4.5 in *(115 mm)* Mk 8 ❷; 55° elevation; 25 rounds/minute to 22 km *(12 nm)* anti-surface; 6 km *(3.3 nm)* anti-aircraft; weight of shell 21 kg.
2 Bofors 40 mm/70 ❸; 90° elevation; 300 rounds/minute to 12 km *(6.5 nm)* anti-surface; 4 km *(2.2 nm)* anti-aircraft; weight of shell 0.96 kg.
Torpedoes: 6—324 mm Mk 32 (2 triple) tubes ❹. Honeywell Mk 46 Mod 5; anti-submarine; active/passive homing to 11 km *(5.9 nm)* at 40 kts; warhead 44 kg.
Countermeasures: Decoys: 2 Plessey Shield chaff launchers ❺; fires chaff and IR flares in distraction, decoy or centroid patterns.
ESM/ECM: IPqM SDR-2 (V 30) or Racal Cygnus B1 (remainder) radar intercept ❻ and IPqM SDR-7 jammer ❼.
Combat data systems: Ferranti CAAIS 450.

Fire control: Saab EOS-400 missile and gun FCS with optronic ❽ director and two optical ❾ directors.
Radars: Surface search: Plessey ASW 4 ❿; E/F band; range 101 km *(55 nm)*.
Navigation: Kelvin Hughes Type 1007; I/J band.
Fire control: Selenia Orion RTN 10X ⓫; I/J band; range 40 km *(22 nm)*.
Sonars: Atlas Elektronik ASO 4 Mod 2; hull-mounted; active; medium frequency.

Helicopters: 1 Westland Lynx ⓬.

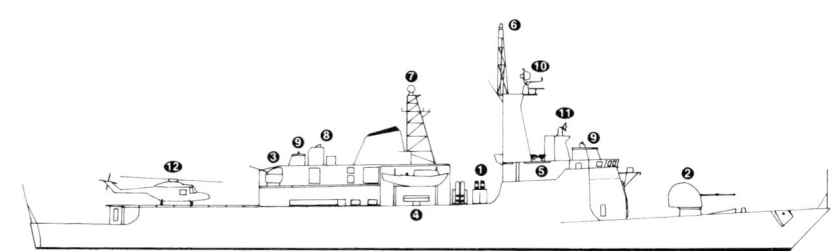

INHAÚMA *(Scale 1 : 900), Ian Sturton*

Programmes: Designed by Brazilian Naval Design Office with advice from West German private Marine Technik design company. Signature of final contract on 1 October 1981. First pair ordered on 15 February 1982 and second pair 9 January 1986. In mid-1986 the government approved in principle construction of a total of 16 ships but this has been reduced to four and a cheaper stretched design has been authorised to follow on possibly to start building in 1993.

Structure: Plans to fit more Brazilian-made weapon systems have apparently been cancelled.

INHAÚMA *1992*

SHIPBORNE AIRCRAFT (FRONT LINE)

Note: 5 Super Lynx authorised in 1992.

Numbers/Type: 10 Aerospatiale UH-12 (AS 350B Ecureuil).
Operational speed: 120 kts *(222 km/h)*.
Service ceiling: 10 000 ft *(3050 m)*.
Range: 240 nm *(445 km)*.
Role/Weapon systems: Support helicopters for Fleet liaison and Marine Corps transportation. Sensors: None. Weapons: 1 axial MG or 1 lateral MG or 2 rocket pods.

UH-12   *1990, Brazilian Navy*

Numbers/Type: 4/3 Agusta/Sikorsky SH 3A/SH 3D Sea King.
Operational speed: 100 kts *(182 km/h)*.
Service ceiling: 12 200 ft *(3720 m)*.
Range: 400 nm *(740 km)*.
Role/Weapon systems: ASW helicopter; carrier-borne and shore-based for medium-range ASW, ASVW and SAR. Sensors: 1 APS-705(V)II Search radar. Weapons: ASW; up to 4 × Mk 44/46 torpedoes, or 4 × depth bombs. ASVW; 4 × AM 39 Exocet missiles.

SEA KING (with Exocet)   *8/1992, Mário R V Carneiro*

Numbers/Type: 5 Aerospatiale UH-14 (AS 332F1 Super Puma).
Operational speed: 100 kts *(182 km/h)*.
Service ceiling: 20 000 ft *(6100 m)*.
Range: 345 nm *(635 km)*.
Role/Weapon systems: SAR, troop transport and ASVW. Sensors: Search radar. Weapons: None. Total of 15 planned.

UH-14   *1989, Brazilian Navy*

Numbers/Type: 12 Grumman S-2A/E/H P16 Tracker (Air Force).
Operational speed: 229 kts *(426 km/h)*.
Service ceiling: 25 000 ft *(7620 m)*.
Range: 799 nm *(1480 km)*.
Role/Weapon systems: Air Force operated; carrier-borne surveillance and medium-range ASW aircraft re-engined with PT6A-67-CF turbos; supplemented by Sea King; land-based for coastal and EEZ surveillance. Sensors: Thomson-CSF Varan Search radar, MAD. Weapons: ASW; various internally stored bombs, mines or depth bombs, rockets on wings.

Numbers/Type: 9 Aerospatiale UH-13 (AS 355F2 Ecureuil 2).
Operational speed: 121 kts *(224 km/h)*.
Service ceiling: 11 150 ft *(3400 m)*.
Range: 240 nm *(445 km)*.
Role/Weapon systems: SAR, liaison and utility in support of Marine Corps. Sensors: Search radar. Weapons: 2 axial MGs or 1 lateral MG or 2 rocket pods.

UH-13   *1990, Brazilian Navy*

Numbers/Type: 16 UH-6B (Bell JetRanger III).
Operational speed: 115 kts *(213 km/h)*.
Service ceiling: 20 000 ft *(6100 m)*.
Range: 368 nm *(682 km)*.
Role/Weapon systems: Utility and training helicopters. Sensors: None. Weapons: 2 MGs or 2 rocket pods.

JETRANGER   *8/1992, Mário R V Carneiro*

Numbers/Type: 6 Westland Lynx SAH-11 (HAS 21).
Operational speed: 125 kts *(232 km/h)*.
Service ceiling: 12 000 ft *(3650 m)*.
Range: 160 nm *(296 km)*.
Role/Weapon systems: ASW helicopter; embarked in Niteroi, Inhaúma and Pará classes for ASW patrol and support; additional ASVW role from 1988. May be upgraded in due course to Super Lynx standard with Mk 3 radar and Racal Kestrel EW suite. Sensors: Sea Spray Mk 1 radar. Weapons: ASW; 2 × Mk 44 or Mk 46 torpedoes, or depth bombs. ASV; 4 × Sea Skua missiles.

LYNX (with Sea Skua)   *8/1992, Mário R V Carneiro*

LAND-BASED MARITIME AIRCRAFT (FRONT LINE)

Numbers/Type: 10 Bandeirante P-95 (EMB-111(A)).
Operational speed: 194 kts *(360 km/h)*.
Service ceiling: 25 500 ft *(7770 m)*.
Range: 1590 nm *(2945 km)*.
Role/Weapon systems: Air Force operated for coastal surveillance role by three squadrons in 7 Group. Sensors: AN/APS-128 search radar, ECM, searchlight pod on starboard wing. Weapons: ASW; various internally stored bombs, mines or depth bombs, rockets on wings.

Numbers/Type: 10 Bandeirante P-95B (EMB-111(B)).
Operational speed: 194 kts *(360 km/h)*.
Service ceiling: 25 500 ft *(7770 m)*.
Range: 1590 nm *(2945 km)*.
Role/Weapon systems: Air Force operated for coastal surveillance role by three squadrons in 7 Group. Sensors: MEL sea search radar, ECM, searchlight pod on starboard wing, EFIS-74 (electronic flight instrumentation) and Collins APS-65 (autopilot); ESM Thomson-CSF DR2000A/Dalia 1000A Mk II, Marconi Canada CMA-771 Mk III (Omega navigation system). Weapons: Strike; 6 or 8 × 127 mm rockets, or up to 28 × 70 mm rockets.

Numbers/Type: 16 Xavante AT-26 (EMB-326GB).
Operational speed: 468 kts *(867 km/h)*.
Service ceiling: 47 000 ft *(14 325 m)*.
Range: 1320 nm *(2446 km)*.
Role/Weapon systems: Air Force operated for light attack; supplements anti-shipping/strike; also has reconnaissance role by 3/10 Group. Sensors: None. Weapons: ASV; 1.8 tons of bombs. Strike; 28 × 70 mm rockets. Recce; underwing camera pod.

Numbers/Type: 8 Tucano AT-27 (EMB-312).
Operational speed: 270 kts *(500 km/h)*.
Service ceiling: 30 000 ft *(9150 m)*.
Range: 995 nm *(1844 km)*.
Role/Weapon systems: Air Force operated for liaison and attack by 2 ELO. Sensors: None. Weapons: 6 or 8 × 127 mm rockets or bombs and 1 MG pod in each wing.

AMPHIBIOUS FORCES

2 Ex-US THOMASTON CLASS (LSD)

Name	No	Builders	Laid Down	Launched	Commissioned	Recommissioned
CEARÁ (ex-*Hermitage*)	G 30 (ex-LSD 34)	Ingalls, Pascagoula	11 April 1955	12 June 1956	14 Dec 1956	28 Nov 1989
RIO DE JANEIRO (ex-*Alamo*)	G 31 (ex-LSD 33)	Ingalls, Pascagoula	11 Oct 1954	20 Jan 1956	24 Aug 1956	21 Nov 1990

Displacement, tons: 6880 light; 12 150 full load
Dimensions, feet (metres): 510 × 84 × 19 *(155.5 × 25.6 × 5.8)*
Main machinery: 2 Babcock & Wilcox boilers; 580 psi *(40.8 kg/cm sq)*; 2 GE turbines; 24 000 hp *(17.9 MW)*; 2 shafts
Speed, knots: 22.5. **Range, miles:** 10 000 at 18 kts
Complement: 345 (20 officers)
Military lift: 340 troops; 21 LCM 6s or 3 LCUs and 6 LCMs or 50 LVTs; 30 LVTs on upper deck
Guns: 6 USN 3 in *(76 mm)*/50 (3 twin) Mk 33; 85° elevation; 50 rounds/minute to 12.8 km *(7 nm)*; weight of shell 6 kg.
Countermeasures: Decoys: 2 Loral Hycor SRBOC Mk 36 6-tubed chaff launchers.
Radars: Air search: Westinghouse SPS 6C; D band (in G 30). Surface search: Raytheon SPS 10; G band. Navigation: CRP 3100; I band.
Helicopters: Platform (over docking well).

Programmes: The original plan to build a 4500 ton LST was overtaken by the acquisition of these two LSDs.
Structure: Have two 50 ton capacity cranes and a docking well of 391 × 48 ft *(119.2 × 14.6 m)*. Phalanx guns removed before transfer. *Rio de Janeiro* has been fitted with a more modern air search radar.

RIO DE JANEIRO   5/1992, Hartmut Ehlers

1 Ex-US DE SOTO COUNTY CLASS (LST)

Name	No	Builders	Commissioned
DUQUE DE CAXAIS (ex-USS *Grant County* LST 1174)	G 26	Avondale, New Orleans	8 Nov 1957

Displacement, tons: 4164 light; 7804 full load
Dimensions, feet (metres): 445 × 62 × 17.5 *(135.6 × 18.9 × 5.3)*
Main machinery: 4 Fairbanks-Morse 38D8-1/8-12 diesels; 8500 hp *(6.34 MW)* sustained; 2 shafts; cp props
Speed, knots: 16.5. **Range, miles:** 13 000 at 10 kts
Complement: 175 (11 officers)
Military lift: 575 troops
Guns: 6 FMC 3 in *(76 mm)*/50 (3 twin) Mk 33; 85° elevation; 50 rounds/minute to 12.8 km *(6.9 nm)*; weight of shell 6 kg.
Fire control: 1 Mk 51 Mod 5 GFCS.
Radars: Surface search: Raytheon SPS 21; G/H band. Navigation: Racal Decca; I band.

Comment: Launched 12 October 1956 and transferred 15 January 1973, purchased 11 February 1980. Now has Stülcken 60 tons heavy-lift gear fitted. Four LCVPs carried on davits; helicopter platform.

DUQUE DE CAXAIS   1987, Brazilian Navy

3 US LCU 1610 TYPE (EDCG)

Name	No	Builders	Commissioned
GUARAPARI	(ex-L 10)	Arsenal de Marinha, Rio de Janeiro	27 Mar 1978
TAMBAÚ	(ex-L 11)	Arsenal de Marinha, Rio de Janeiro	27 Mar 1978
CAMBORIÚ	(ex-L 12)	Arsenal de Marinha, Rio de Janeiro	6 Jan 1981

Displacement, tons: 390 full load
Dimensions, feet (metres): 134.5 × 27.6 × 6.6 *(41 × 8.4 × 2.0)*
Main machinery: 2 GM 12V-71 diesels; 874 hp *(650 kW)* sustained; 2 shafts; cp props
Speed, knots: 11. **Range, miles:** 1200 at 8 kts
Military lift: 172 tons
Guns: 3—12.7 mm MGs.
Radars: Navigation: Racal Decca; I band.

Comment: Status changed in 1991 when all of the class were reclassified EDCG (landing craft) and lost their pennant numbers having been decommissioned from the Navy. They remain in service as support vessels to establishments.

CAMBORIÚ   1985, Ronaldo S Olive

6 EDVM CLASSES (LCM)

Displacement, tons: 55 full load
Dimensions, feet (metres): 55.8 × 14.4 × 3.9 *(17 × 4.4 × 1.2)*
Main machinery: 2 Saab Scania diesels; 470 hp(m) *(345 kW)*; 2 shafts
Speed, knots: 9
Military lift: 80 troops plus 31 tons equipment

Comment: Three are EDVM 300 type and three are EDVM 17 of similar characteristics.

EDVM 301   1985, Ronaldo S Olive

5 EDVM 25 CLASS (LCM)

Displacement, tons: 130 full load
Dimensions, feet (metres): 72.2 × 21.7 × 4.9 *(22 × 6.6 × 1.5)*
Speed, knots: 9
Military lift: 80 troops plus 70 tons equipment

Comment: Built in 1992/93.

39 EDVP CLASSES 400 and 500 (LCP)

Displacement, tons: 13 full load
Dimensions, feet (metres): 35.8 × 9.8 × 3 *(10.9 × 3 × 0.9)*
Main machinery: Saab Scania diesel; 235 hp(m) *(173 kW)*; 1 shaft
Speed, knots: 10
Military lift: 3.7 tons or 36 men

Comment: GRP hulls built in Brazil. Some in Mato Grosso Flotilla at Ladario, and some in Amazonas Flotilla at Manaus.

EDVP 512   1985, Ronaldo S Olive

PATROL FORCES

Note: The *Porto Esperança* (P 8) River Patrol Craft project was postponed in 1990 but may be resurrected in 1993/94.

9 IMPERIAL MARINHEIRO CLASS (COASTAL PATROL SHIPS)

Name	No	Builders	Commissioned
IMPERIAL MARINHEIRO	V 15	Smit, Kinderdijk, Netherlands	8 June 1955
IGUATEMI	V 16	Smit, Kinderdijk, Netherlands	17 Sep 1955
FORTE DE COIMBRA	V 18	Smit, Kinderdijk, Netherlands	26 July 1955
CABOCLO	V 19	Smit, Kinderdijk, Netherlands	5 Apr 1955
ANGOSTURA	V 20	Smit, Kinderdijk, Netherlands	21 May 1955
BAHIANA	V 21	Smit, Kinderdijk, Netherlands	27 June 1955
MEARIM	V 22	Smit, Kinderdijk, Netherlands	3 Aug 1955
PURUS	V 23	Smit, Kinderdijk, Netherlands	17 Apr 1955
SOLIMÕES	V 24	Smit, Kinderdijk, Netherlands	3 Aug 1955

Displacement, tons: 911 standard; 960 full load
Dimensions, feet (metres): 184 × 30.5 × 11.7 *(56 × 9.3 × 3.6)*
Main machinery: 2 Sulzer diesels; 2160 hp(m) *(1.59 MW)*; 2 shafts
Speed, knots: 16
Complement: 60
Guns: 1—3 in *(76 mm)*/50 Mk 33; 85° elevation; 50 rounds/minute to 12.8 km *(6.9 nm)*; weight of shell 6 kg.
2 or 4 Oerlikon 20 mm; 55° elevation.
Radars: Surface search: Racal Decca; I band.

Comment: Fleet tugs classed as corvettes. Equipped for firefighting. *Imperial Marinheiro* has acted as a submarine support ship but gave up the role in 1990.

IMPERIAL MARINHEIRO *1989, Brazilian Navy*

2 PEDRO TEIXEIRA CLASS (RIVER PATROL SHIPS)

Name	No	Builders	Commissioned
PEDRO TEIXEIRA	P 20	Arsenal de Marinha, Rio de Janeiro	17 Dec 1973
RAPOSO TAVARES	P 21	Arsenal de Marinha, Rio de Janeiro	17 Dec 1973

Displacement, tons: 690 standard
Dimensions, feet (metres): 208.7 × 31.8 × 5.6 *(63.6 × 9.7 × 1.7)*
Main machinery: 2 MAN V6 V16/18 TL diesels; 1920 hp(m) *(1.41 MW)*; 2 shafts
Speed, knots: 16. **Range, miles**: 6800 at 13 kts
Complement: 60 (6 officers)
Guns: 1 Bofors 40 mm/60; 90° elevation; 300 rounds/minute to 12 km *(6.5 nm)* anti-surface; 4 km *(2.2 nm)* anti-aircraft; weight of shell 0.89 kg.
6—12.7 mm MGs. 2—81 mm Mk 2 mortars.
Radars: Surface search: 2 Racal Decca; I band.
Helicopters: 1 Bell JetRanger.

Comment: *Pedro Teixeira* launched 14 October 1970, *Raposo Tavares* 11 June 1972. Belong to Amazon Flotilla. Can carry two armed LCVPs and 85 marines in deck accommodation.

RAPOSO TAVARES *1988*

1 THORNYCROFT TYPE (RIVER MONITOR)

Name	No	Builders	Commissioned
PARNAIBA	U 17 (ex-P 2)	Arsenal de Marinha, Rio de Janeiro	6 Nov 1938

Displacement, tons: 620 standard; 720 full load
Dimensions, feet (metres): 180.5 × 33.3 × 5.1 *(55 × 10.1 × 1.6)*
Main machinery: 2 Thornycroft triple expansion; 1300 ihp *(970 kW)*; 2 shafts
Speed, knots: 12. **Range, miles**: 1350 at 10 kts
Complement: 90
Guns: 1—3 in *(76 mm)*/50 Mk 33; 85° elevation; 50 rounds/minute to 12.8 km *(6.9 nm)*; weight of shell 6 kg.
2 Bofors 40 mm/60 (twin). 6 Oerlikon 20 mm.
Radars: Surface search: Racal Decca; I band.

Comment: Laid down 11 June 1936. Launched 2 September 1937. In Mato Grosso Flotilla. Re-armed with new guns in 1960. 3 in *(76 mm)* side armour and partial deck protection. Oil fuel, 70 tons. Was to have been replaced by *Porto Esperança* in 1991 but will now run on until 1994.

PARNAIBA *1992, Brazilian Navy*

3 RORAIMA CLASS (RIVER PATROL SHIPS)

Name	No	Builders	Commissioned
RORAIMA	P 30	Maclaren, Niteroi	21 Feb 1975
RONDÔNIA	P 31	Maclaren, Niteroi	3 Dec 1975
AMAPÁ	P 32	Maclaren, Niteroi	12 Jan 1976

Displacement, tons: 340 standard; 365 full load
Dimensions, feet (metres): 151.9 × 27.9 × 4.6 *(46.3 × 8.5 × 1.4)*
Main machinery: 2 MAN V6 V16/18TL diesels; 1920 hp(m) *(1.41 MW)*; 2 shafts
Speed, knots: 14. **Range, miles**: 6000 at 12 kts
Complement: 40 (9 officers)
Guns: 1 Bofors 40 mm/60; 90° elevation; 300 rounds/minute to 12 km *(6.5 nm)* anti-surface; 4 km *(2.2 nm)* anti-aircraft; weight of shell 0.89 kg.
2 Oerlikon 20 mm. 2—81 mm mortars. 6—12.7 mm MGs.
Radars: Surface search: 2 Racal Decca; I band.

Comment: *Roraima* launched 2 November 1972, *Rondônia* 10 January, *Amapá* 9 March 1973. Carry two armed LCVPs. Belong to Amazon Flotilla.

RONDÔNIA *1989, Brazilian Navy*

4 + 2 (2) GRAÚNA CLASS (LARGE PATROL CRAFT)

Name	No	Builders	Commissioned
GRAÚNA	P 40	Estaleiro Mauá, Niteroi	1993
GOIANA	P 41	Estaleiro Mauá, Niteroi	1993
GRAJAÚ	P 42	Estaleiro Mauá, Niteroi	1994
GUAIBA	P 43	Estaleiro Mauá, Niteroi	1994
GUAJARÁ	P 44	Arsenal de Marinha, Rio de Janeiro	1995
GUAPORÉ	P 45	Arsenal de Marinha, Rio de Janeiro	1995
GURUPÁ	P 46	Estaleiro Mauá, Niteroi	1996
GURUPI	P 47	Estaleiro Mauá, Niteroi	1996

Displacement, tons: 410 full load
Dimensions, feet (metres): 152.6 × 24.6 × 7.5 *(46.5 × 7.5 × 2.3)*
Main machinery: 2 MTU 16V 396 TB94 diesels; 5800 hp(m) *(4.26 MW)* sustained; 2 shafts
Speed, knots: 22. **Range, miles**: 2000 at 12 kts
Complement: 25 (4 officers)
Guns: 1 Bofors 40 mm/70. 2 Oerlikon 20 mm.
Radars: Surface search: Racal Decca 1290A; I band.

Comment: Two ordered in late 1987 to a Vosper QAF design similar to Bangladesh Meghna class. Technology transfer in February 1988 and construction started in July 1988 for the first pair which were launched on 9 December 1988. Second pair started construction in September 1990, and third pair in June 1992. The last two have still to be authorised. Used for patrol duties and diver support.

VOSPER TYPE (larger gun) *1988, Vosper QAF*

62　BRAZIL / Patrol forces — Oceanographic and survey ships

6 PIRATINI CLASS (LARGE PATROL CRAFT)

Name	No	Builders	Commissioned
PIRATINI (ex-PGM 109)	P 10	Arsenal de Marinha, Rio de Janeiro	Nov 1970
PIRAJÁ (ex-PGM 110)	P 11	Arsenal de Marinha, Rio de Janeiro	Mar 1971
PAMPEIRO (ex-PGM 118)	P 12	Arsenal de Marinha, Rio de Janeiro	May 1971
PARATI (ex-PGM 119)	P 13	Arsenal de Marinha, Rio de Janeiro	July 1971
PENEDO (ex-PGM 120)	P 14	Arsenal de Marinha, Rio de Janeiro	Sep 1971
POTI (ex-PGM 121)	P 15	Arsenal de Marinha, Rio de Janeiro	Oct 1971

Displacement, tons: 105 standard
Dimensions, feet (metres): 95 × 19 × 6.5 *(29 × 5.8 × 2)*
Main machinery: 4 Cummins VT-12M diesels; 1100 hp *(820 kW)*; 2 shafts
Speed, knots: 17. **Range, miles:** 1700 at 12 kts
Complement: 15 (2 officers)
Guns: 1 Oerlikon 20 mm. 2—12.7 mm MGs.
Radars: Surface search: Racal Decca; I band.

Comment: Built under offshore agreement with the USA. 81 mm mortar removed in 1988. Carries an inflatable launch.

ATALAIA　　　　　　　　　　　　　　　　　　　　　　　　　1988, Brazilian Navy

PENEDO　　　　　　　　　　　　　　　　　　　　　　　　　1991, Brazilian Navy

4 TRACKER II CLASS (COASTAL PATROL CRAFT)

P 8002　　P 8003　　P 3004　　P 3005

Displacement, tons: 37 full load
Dimensions, feet (metres): 68.6 × 17 × 4.8 *(20.9 × 5.2 × 1.5)*
Main machinery: 2 MTU 8V 396 TB83 diesels; 2100 hp(m) *(1.54 MW)* sustained; 2 shafts
Speed, knots: 27. **Range, miles:** 600 at 15 kts
Complement: 12 (4 officers)
Guns: 2—12.7 mm MGs.
Radars: Racal Decca RM 1070A.

Comment: First four ordered in February 1987 to a Fairey design and built at Estaleiro Shipyard, Porto Alegre. National input is 60 per cent. First of class completed building 22 February 1990. All entered service in May 1991; plans for more were postponed indefinitely in 1991 when the shipbuilder went bankrupt. Designed for EEZ patrol.

P 8002　　　　　　　　　　　　　　　　　　　　　　　　　1991, Brazilian Navy

MINE WARFARE FORCES

6 ARATÚ CLASS (MINESWEEPERS—COASTAL)

Name	No	Builders	Commissioned
ARATÚ	M 15	Abeking & Rasmussen	5 May 1971
ANHATOMIRIM	M 16	Abeking & Rasmussen	30 Nov 1971
ATALAIA	M 17	Abeking & Rasmussen	13 Dec 1972
ARAÇATUBA	M 18	Abeking & Rasmussen	13 Dec 1972
ABROLHOS	M 19	Abeking & Rasmussen	25 Feb 1976
ALBARDÃO	M 20	Abeking & Rasmussen	25 Feb 1976

Displacement, tons: 230 standard; 280 full load
Dimensions, feet (metres): 154.9 × 23.6 × 6.9 *(47.2 × 7.2 × 2.1)*
Main machinery: 4 MTU Maybach diesels; 4500 hp(m) *(3.3 MW)*; 2 shafts; 2 Escher-Weiss cp props
Speed, knots: 24. **Range, miles:** 710 at 20 kts
Complement: 39 (4 officers)
Guns: 1 Bofors 40 mm/70.
Radars: Surface search: Signaal ZW 06; I band.

Comment: Wooden hulled. First four ordered in April 1969 and last pair in November 1973. Same design as West German Schütze class. Can carry out wire, magnetic and acoustic sweeping. Modernisation expected in the mid-1990s.

OCEANOGRAPHIC AND SURVEY SHIPS

0 + (1) ANTARCTIC SURVEY SHIP

Displacement, tons: 6000
Dimensions, feet (metres): 328 oa; 305 wl × 65.6 × 23 *(100; 93 × 20 × 7)*
Main machinery: 2 diesels; 10 000 hp(m) *(7.35 MW)*; 2 motors; 1300 kW; 2 pumpjets
Speed, knots: 17 (diesels); 3 (motors). **Range, miles:** 20 000 at 13 kts
Complement: 95 (22 officers) plus 40 scientists
Helicopters: 2 light.

Comment: Replacement for *Barão de Teffé* to be built by Caneco, Rio de Janeiro to a Cleaver and Walkinshaw (Vancouver) design. Six laboratories (seismic, meteorology, oceanography, geology, geophysical and marine biology) are planned. Cost (1987 prices) US $36 million for the ship and probably as much again for the equipment. Originally ordered in September 1987 but the project was still suspended at the beginning of 1993 for lack of funds.

Name	No	Builders	Commissioned
BARÃO DE TEFFÉ (ex-*Thala Dan*)	H 42	Aalborg Vaerft	1957

Measurement, tons: 2183 gross
Dimensions, feet (metres): 246.6 × 45.2 × 20.8 *(75.2 × 14.2 × 6.3)*
Main machinery: 1 Burmeister & Wain diesel; 1970 hp(m) *(1.45 MW)*; 1 shaft; cp prop
Speed, knots: 12
Complement: 46 (11 officers)
Helicopters: 2 Aerospatiale UH-13 Ecureuil 2.

Comment: A Danish polar supply ship commissioned into the Navy on 28 September 1982. Planned to run on until 1999. Strengthened for ice. SATCOM fitted. This ship has a red hull, mast and funnel and a pale brown superstructure.

BARÃO DE TEFFÉ　　　　　　　　　　　　　　　　　　　　　　　　　1992

Name	No	Builders	Commissioned
ANTARES (ex-M/V *Lady Harrison*)	H 40	Mjellem and Karlsen A/S, Bergen	1984

Displacement, tons: 1076 full load
Dimensions, feet (metres): 180.3 × 33.8 × 14.1 *(55 × 10.3 × 4.3)*
Main machinery: 1 Burmeister & Wain Alpha diesel; 1860 hp(m) *(1.37 MW)*; 1 shaft; bow thruster
Speed, knots: 13.5. **Range, miles:** 10 000 at 12 kts
Complement: 49 (9 officers)
Radars: Navigation: 2 Racal Decca; I band.

Comment: Research vessel acquired from Racal Energy Resources. Used for seismographic survey. Recommissioned 6 June 1988. Painted white with orange masts and funnels.

ANTARES　　　　　　　　　　　　　　　　　　　　　　　　　1989, Brazilian Navy

Oceanographic and survey ships / BRAZIL   63

1 Ex-US ROBERT D CONRAD CLASS

Name	No	Builders	Commissioned
ALMIRANTE CÂMARA (ex-USNS *Sands* T-AGOR 6)	H 41	Marietta Co, Point Pleasant, West Va.	8 Feb 1965

Displacement, tons: 1200 standard; 1380 full load
Dimensions, feet (metres): 208.9 × 40 × 15.3 *(63.7 × 12.2 × 4.7)*
Main machinery: Diesel-electric; 2 Caterpillar diesel generators; 1 motor; 1000 hp *(746 kW)*; 1 shaft; bow thruster
Speed, knots: 13.5. **Range, miles:** 12 000 at 12 kts
Complement: 36 (7 officers) plus 15 scientists
Radars: Navigation: RCA CRM-NIA-75; I/J band.

Comment: Built specifically for oceanographic research. Equipped for gravimetric, magnetic and geological research. 10 ton crane and 620 hp gas turbine for providing 'quiet power'. Transferred 1 July 1974. Has a white hull and orange masts and funnel.

ALMIRANTE CÂMARA   *1989, Brazilian Navy*

2 SIRIUS CLASS

Name	No	Builders	Commissioned
SIRIUS	H 21	Ishikawajima Co Ltd, Tokyo	1 Jan 1958
CANOPUS	H 22	Ishikawajima Co Ltd, Tokyo	15 Mar 1958

Displacement, tons: 1463 standard; 1800 full load
Dimensions, feet (metres): 255.7 × 39.3 × 12.2 *(78 × 12.1 × 3.7)*
Main machinery: 2 Sulzer 7T6-36 diesels; 2700 hp(m) *(1.98 MW)*; 2 shafts; cp props
Speed, knots: 15.7. **Range, miles:** 12 000 at 11 kts
Complement: 116 (16 officers) plus 14 scientists
Radars: Navigation: Racal Decca (H 21); Signaal ZW 06 (H 22); I band.
Helicopters: 1 Bell JetRanger.

Comment: Laid down 1955-56. Painted white with orange funnels and masts. Special surveying apparatus, echo sounders, Raydist equipment, sounding machines installed, and landing craft (LCVP), jeep, and survey launches carried. All living and working spaces are air-conditioned.

CANOPUS   *1987, Brazilian Navy*

3 ARGUS CLASS

Name	No	Builders	Commissioned
ARGUS	H 31	Arsenal de Marinha, Rio de Janeiro	29 Jan 1959
ORION	H 32	Arsenal de Marinha, Rio de Janeiro	11 June 1959
TAURUS	H 33	Arsenal de Marinha, Rio de Janeiro	23 Apr 1959

Displacement, tons: 250 standard; 343 full load
Dimensions, feet (metres): 146.7 × 21.3 × 9.2 *(44.7 × 6.5 × 2.8)*
Main machinery: 2 Caterpillar D 379 diesels; 1098 hp *(818 kW)* sustained; 2 shafts
Speed, knots: 15. **Range, miles:** 3000 at 15 kts
Complement: 42 (6 officers)
Guns: 2 Oerlikon 20 mm (removed).
Radars: Navigation: 2 Racal Decca; I band.
Helicopters: 1 Bell JetRanger (when carried).

Comment: All laid down in 1955 and launched between December 1957–February 1958. *Orion* re-engined in 1974. Replacement ships are needed. White hull and superstructure, orange funnel.

ORION   *1985, Brazilian Navy*

Name	No	Builders	Commissioned
ALMIRANTE ALVARO ALBERTO (ex-M V *Grant Mariner*)	H 43	Burton S B Co, Texas	1973

Displacement, tons: 1517 light; 2688 full load
Dimensions, feet (metres): 217.1 × 44 × 15.4 *(66.2 × 13.4 × 4.7)*
Main machinery: 3 Fairbanks-Morse diesels; 7200 hp *(5.37 MW)*; 3 shafts; bow thruster
Speed, knots: 13.5
Complement: 48 (10 officers)
Radars: Navigation: 2 Racal Decca; I band.

Comment: Supply vessel acquired in October 1987 from Grant Norfac (USA). Recommissioned 6 June 1988 as a seismic survey ship. Has a platform for one light helicopter. Hull and superstructure white, mast and funnels orange.

ALVARO ALBERTO   *1989, Brazilian Navy*

1 LIGHTHOUSE TENDER

Name	No	Builders	Commissioned
ALMIRANTE GRAÇA ARANHA	H 34	Ebin, Niteroi	9 Sep 1976

Displacement, tons: 2390 full load
Dimensions, feet (metres): 245.3 × 42.6 × 13.8 *(74.8 × 13 × 4.2)*
Main machinery: 1 diesel; 2440 hp(m) *(1.8 MW)*; 1 shaft; bow thruster
Speed, knots: 14
Complement: 95 (13 officers)
Radars: Navigation: 2 Racal Decca; I band.
Helicopters: 1 Bell JetRanger.

Comment: Laid down in 1971 and launched 23 May 1974. Fitted with telescopic hangar, 10 ton crane, two landing craft, GP launch and two Land Rovers. Omega navigation system. White hull and superstructure, orange mast and funnel.

ALMIRANTE GRAÇA ARANHA   *5/1990, Mário R V Carneiro*

5 BUOY TENDERS

MESTRE JOÃO DOS SANTOS H 13   FAROLEIRO AREAS H 27
CASTELHANOS H 24   FAROLEIRO NASCIMENTO H 30
FAROLEIRO MÁRIO SEIXAS H 26
  (ex-*Mestre Jerânimo*)

Displacement, tons: 195 (H 13); 110 (H 24, 27 and 30); 242 (H 26)
Complement: 17 (1 or 2 officers)

Comment: Four taken over 1973–H 26 on 21 January 1984. H 13 launched in 1950 and H 26 in 1962; remainder 1954-57. All are white with orange masts and funnels.

4 BUOY TENDERS

Name	No	Builders	Commissioned
COMANDANTE VARELLA	H 18	Arsenal de Marinha, Rio de Janeiro	20 May 1982
TENENTE CASTELO	H 19	Estanave, Manaus	15 Aug 1984
COMANDANTE MANHÃES	H 20	Estanave, Manaus	15 Dec 1983
TENENTE BOANERGES	H 25	Estanave, Manaus	29 Mar 1985

Displacement, tons: 440 full load
Dimensions, feet (metres): 123 × 28.2 × 8.5 *(37.5 × 8.6 × 2.6)*
Main machinery: 2—8-cyl diesels; 1300 hp(m) *(955 kW)*; 2 shafts
Speed, knots: 12. **Range, miles:** 2880 at 10 kts
Complement: 28 (2 officers)
Radars: Navigation: Racal Decca; I band.

Comment: Dual purpose minelayers. *Tenente Castelo* is based at Santana, *Tenente Boanerges* at Sao Luiz. White hull and superstructure, orange mast and funnel.

COMANDANTE VARELLA   *1987, Brazilian Navy*

SURVEY LAUNCHES

Note: In addition there are 5 trawler type vessels, first in service in October 1982. Names are *Cabo Branco, Cabo Calcanhar, Cabo Frio, Cabo Orange, Tubarão*.

SUBOFICIAL OLIVEIRA (ex-U 15)

Displacement, tons: 170 full load
Dimensions, feet (metres): 116.4 × 22 × 15.7 *(35.5 × 6.7 × 4.8)*
Main machinery: 2 diesels; 740 hp(m) *(544 kW)*; 2 shafts
Speed, knots: 8. **Range, miles:** 1400 at 8 kts
Complement: 10 (2 officers)

Comment: Commissioned at Fortaleza for Naval Research Institute on 6 May 1981. Decommissioned in 1991 but retained in service as an AvPqOc (ocean survey craft).

SUBOFICIAL OLIVEIRA   *1990, Brazilian Navy*

PARAIBANO (ex-H 11)   **ITACURUSSÁ** (ex-H 15)
RIO BRANCO (ex-H 12)   **CAMOCIM** (ex-H 16)
NOGUEIRA DA GAMA (ex-*Jaceguai*) (ex-H 14)   **CARAVELAS** (ex-H 17)

Displacement, tons: 32 standard; 50 full load
Dimensions, feet (metres): 52.5 × 15.1 × 4.3 *(16 × 4.6 × 1.3)*
Main machinery: 2 GM diesels; 330 hp *(246 kW)*; 2 shafts
Speed, knots: 11. **Range, miles:** 600 at 11 kts
Complement: 10 (1 officer)

Comment: First pair commissioned 7 November 1969, second pair 8 March 1971 and last two 22 September 1972. Built by Bormann, Rio de Janeiro. Majority work in Amazon Flotilla. Wooden hulls. All decommissioned in 1991 but retained in service as support to naval establishments and reclassified AvHi (inshore survey craft).

PARAIBANO   *1985, Brazilian Navy*

SUBMARINE RESCUE SHIP

Name	No	Builders	Commissioned
FELINTO PERRY (ex-*Holger Dane*, ex-*Wildrake*)	K 11	Stord Verft, Norway	1979

Displacement, tons: 1380 full load
Dimensions, feet (metres): 256.6 × 57.4 × 15.1 *(78.2 × 17.5 × 4.6)*
Main machinery: Diesel-electric; 2 BMK KVG B12 and 2 KVGB 16 diesels; 11 400 hp(m) *(8.4 MW)*; 2 motors; 7000 hp(m) *(5.15 MW)*; 2 shafts; cp props; 2 bow thrusters; 2 stern thrusters
Speed, knots: 14.5
Complement: 65 (9 officers)
Helicopters: Platform only.

Comment: Former oilfield support ship acquired 28 December 1988. Has an octagonal heliport (62.5 ft diameter) above the bridge. Has replaced *Gastão Moutinho* as the submarine rescue ship. Dynamic positioning system.

FELINTO PERRY   *11/1988, W Sartori*

Name	No	Builders	Commissioned
BELMONTE (ex-USS *Helios* ARE 12, ex-LST 1127)	G 24	Maryland D D Co, Baltimore	26 Feb 1945

Displacement, tons: 1625 light; 2030 standard; 4100 full load
Dimensions, feet (metres): 328 × 50 × 11 *(100 × 15.2 × 3.4)*
Main machinery: 2 GM 12-567A diesels; 1800 hp *(1.34 MW)*; 2 shafts
Speed, knots: 11.6. **Range, miles:** 6000 at 9 kts
Guns: 8 Bofors 40 mm/60 (2 quad); 90° elevation; 300 rounds/minute to 12 km *(6.5 nm)* anti-surface; 4 km *(2.2 nm)* anti-aircraft; weight of shell 0.89 kg.

Comment: Former US battle damage repair ship (ex-LST). Laid down 23 November 1944. Launched 14 February 1945. Transferred by lease to Brazil by USA 16 April 1963 under MAP and purchased 28 December 1977. Oil fuel, 1000 tons.

BELMONTE   *1985, Brazilian Navy*

REPAIR SHIPS

Name	No	Builders	Launched
GASTÃO MOUTINHO (ex-USS *Skylark* ASR 20)	U 20 (ex-K 10)	Charleston S B & D D Co	19 Mar 1946

Displacement, tons: 1653 standard; 2320 full load
Dimensions, feet (metres): 251.5 × 44 × 16 *(76.7 × 13.4 × 4.9)*
Main machinery: Diesel-electric; 4 GM 12-278A diesel generators; 4400 hp *(3.58 MW)*; 1 motor; 3000 hp *(2.2 MW)*; 1 shaft
Speed, knots: 15. **Range, miles:** 15 000 at 8 kts
Complement: 85
Guns: 2 Oerlikon 20 mm.
Radars: Surface search: Westinghouse SPS 5; G/H band.

Comment: Fitted with special pumps, compressors and submarine rescue chamber in 1947. Transferred 30 June 1973 and used as the submarine rescue ship until replaced by *Felinto Perry*. Now employed as a tender for the MCMV force at Aratu naval base.

GASTÃO MOUTINHO (old number)   1988, Brazilian Navy

TRANSPORTS

4 BARROSO PEREIRA CLASS

Name	No	Builders	Commissioned
BARROSO PEREIRA	G 16	Ishikawajima Co Ltd, Tokyo	22 Mar 1955
CUSTÓDIO DE MELLO	G 20 (ex-U 26)	Ishikawajima Co Ltd, Tokyo	8 Feb 1955
ARY PARREIRAS	G 21	Ishikawajima Co Ltd, Tokyo	6 Mar 1957
SOARES DUTRA	G 22	Ishikawajima Co Ltd, Tokyo	27 May 1957

Displacement, tons: 4800 standard; 7300 full load
Measurement, tons: 4200 dwt; 4879 gross (Panama)
Dimensions, feet (metres): 362 pp; 391.8 oa × 52.5 × 20.5 *(110.4; 119.5 × 16 × 6.3)*
Main machinery: 2 Ishikawajima boilers and turbines; 4800 hp(m) *(3.53 MW)*; 2 shafts
Speed, knots: 15
Complement: 127
Military lift: 1972 troops (overload); 497 troops (normal)
Cargo capacity: 425 m³ refrigerated cargo space; 4000 tons
Guns: 2—3 in *(76 mm)* Mk 33; 85° elevation; 50 rounds/minute to 12.8 km *(6.9 nm)* anti-aircraft; weight of shell 6 kg.
2 or 4 Oerlikon 20 mm; 55° elevation; 800 rounds/minute to 2 km.
Radars: Navigation: SPS 4 (*Custódio de Mello* only). Two unknown types (others).

Comment: Transports and cargo vessels. Helicopter landing platform aft except in *Custódio de Mello* and *Barroso Pereira*. Medical, hospital and dental facilities. Working and living quarters are mechanically ventilated with partial air-conditioning. Refrigerated cargo space 15 500 cu ft. *Custódio de Mello* was classified as a training ship in July 1961, replaced by *Brasil* in 1987 and has now reverted to being a transport. All operate commercially from time to time.

BARROSO PEREIRA   8/1987, van Ginderen Collection

1 RIVER TRANSPORT

PIRAIM U 29

Displacement, tons: 91.5 full load
Dimensions, feet (metres): 82.0 × 18.0 × 3.2 *(25.0 × 5.5 × 0.97)*
Main machinery: 2 MWM diesels; 400 hp(m) *(294 kW)*; 2 shafts
Speed, knots: 7. **Range, miles:** 700 at 7 kts
Complement: 17 (2 officers)

Comment: Built by Estaleiro SNBP, Mato Grosso. Commissioned 10 March 1982.

Name	No	Builders	Commissioned
PARAGUASSU (ex-*Guarapunava*)	G 15	Amsterdam Drydock	1951

Displacement, tons: 285 full load
Dimensions, feet (metres): 131.2 × 23 × 6.6 *(40 × 7 × 2)*
Main machinery: 3 diesels; 2505 hp(m) *(1.84 MW)*; 1 shaft
Speed, knots: 13. **Range, miles:** 2500 at 10 kts
Complement: 43 (4 officers)
Military lift: 178 troops

Comment: Passenger ship converted into a troop carrier in 1957 and acquired in 1971.

PARAGUASSU   1989, Brazilian Navy

HOSPITAL SHIPS

Name	No	Builders	Commissioned
OSWALDO CRUZ	U 18	Arsenal de Marinha, Rio de Janeiro	29 May 1984
CARLOS CHAGAS	U 19	Arsenal de Marinha, Rio de Janeiro	7 Dec 1984

Displacement, tons: 500 full load
Dimensions, feet (metres): 154.2 × 26.9 × 5.9 *(47.2 × 8.5 × 1.8)*
Main machinery: 2 diesels; 714 hp(m) *(525 kW)*; 2 shafts
Speed, knots: 9. **Range, miles:** 4000 at 9 kts
Complement: 46 (4 officers) plus 21 medical (6 doctors/dentists)
Radars: Navigation: Racal Decca; I band.
Helicopters: 1 Helibras HB-350B.

Comment: *Oswaldo Cruz* launched 11 July 1983, and *Carlos Chagas* 16 April 1984. Have two sick bays, dental surgery, a laboratory, two clinics and X-ray centre. The design is a development of the Roraima class with which they operate in the Amazon Flotilla.

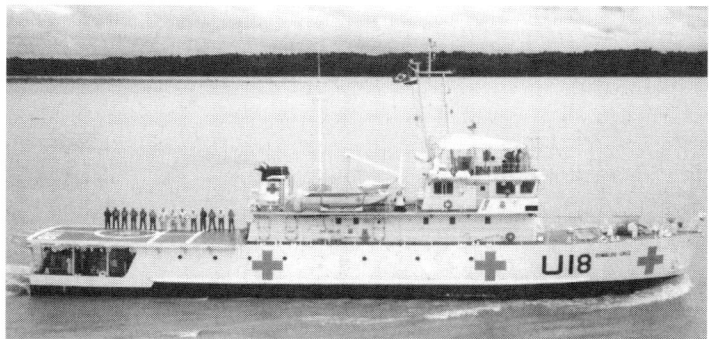

OSWALDO CRUZ   1992, Brazilian Navy

TANKERS/SUPPLY SHIPS

Name	No	Builders	Commissioned
POTENGI	G 17	Papendrecht, Netherlands	28 June 1938

Displacement, tons: 600 full load
Dimensions, feet (metres): 178.8 × 24.5 × 6 *(54.5 × 7.5 × 1.8)*
Main machinery: 2 diesels; 550 hp(m) *(404 kW)*; 2 shafts
Speed, knots: 10. **Range, miles:** 600 at 8 kts
Complement: 19
Cargo capacity: 450 tons

Comment: Launched 16 March 1938. Employed in the Mato Grosso Flotilla on river service.

POTENGI   1992, Brazilian Navy

66 BRAZIL / Tankers/supply ships — Training ships

Name	No	Builders	Commissioned
ALMIRANTE GASTÃO MOTTA	G 23	Ishibras, Rio de Janeiro	26 Nov 1991

Measurement, tons: 10 300 dwt
Dimensions, feet (metres): 442.9 × 62.3 × 24.6 *(135 × 19 × 7.5)*
Main machinery: Diesel electric; 2 Wärtsilä 12V32 diesel generators; 11 700 hp(m) *(8.57 MW)* sustained; 1 motor; 1 shaft
Speed, knots: 20. **Range, miles:** 10 000 at 15 kts
Complement: 121 (13 officers)
Cargo capacity: 5000 tons liquid; 200 tons dry

Comment: Ordered March 1987 to replace *Marajó*. Laid down 11 December 1989 and launched 1 June 1990. Fitted for abeam and stern refuelling. Probably armed with light guns.

ALMIRANTE GASTÃO MOTTA   *4/1992, Brazilian Navy*

Name	No	Builders	Commissioned
TRINDADE (ex-*Nobistor*)	U 16	J G Hitzler, Lavenburg	1969

Displacement, tons: 590 light; 1308 full load
Dimensions, feet (metres): 176.1 × 20 × 6.9 *(53.7 × 6.1 × 2.1)*
Main machinery: 2 MWM diesels; 2740 hp(m) *(2 MW)* sustained; 2 shafts
Speed, knots: 12.7 kts
Complement: 22 (2 officers)

Comment: Ex-Panamanian tug seized for smuggling in 1989 and commissioned in the Navy 31 January 1990. Used for target towing.

TRINDADE   *1990, Mário R V Carneiro*

TRAINING SHIPS

1 MODIFIED NITEROI CLASS

Name	No	Builders	Commissioned
BRASIL	U 27	Arsenal de Marinha, Rio de Janeiro	21 Aug 1986

Displacement, tons: 2380 light; 3400 full load
Dimensions, feet (metres): 430.7 × 44.3 × 13.8 *(131.3 × 13.5 × 4.2)*
Main machinery: 2 Pielstick/Ishikawajima (Brazil) 6 PC 2.5 L400 diesels; 7020 hp(m) *(5.17 MW)* sustained; 2 shafts
Speed, knots: 18. **Range, miles:** 7000 at 15 kts
Complement: 221 (27 officers) plus 200 midshipmen
Guns: 2 Bofors 40 mm. 4 saluting guns.
Countermeasures: ESM: Racal RDL; radar intercept.
Fire control: Saab Scania TVT 300 optronic director.
Radars: Surface search: Racal Decca RMS 1230C; E/F band.
Navigation: Racal Decca TM 1226C; I band.
Helicopters: Platform for 2 Sea King.

Comment: A modification of the Vosper Thornycroft Mk 10 Frigate design ordered in June 1981. Laid down 18 September 1981, launched 23 September 1983. Designed to carry midshipmen and other trainees from the Naval and Merchant Marine Academies. Minimum electronics as required for training.

BRASIL   *8/1992, Giorgio Ghiglione*

Name	No	Builders	Commissioned
ASPIRANTE NASCIMENTO	U 10	Ebrasa	13 Dec 1980
GUARDA MARINHA JENSEN	U 11	Ebrasa	22 July 1981
GUARDA MARINHA BRITO	U 12	Ebrasa	22 July 1981

Displacement, tons: 108.5 standard; 130 full load
Dimensions, feet (metres): 91.8 × 21.3 × 5.9 *(28 × 6.5 × 1.8)*
Main machinery: 2 MWM D232V12 diesels; 650 hp(m) *(478 kW)*; 2 shafts
Speed, knots: 10. **Range, miles:** 700 at 10 kts
Complement: 12
Guns: 1—12.7 mm MG.
Radars: Navigation: Racal Decca; I band.

Comment: Can carry 24 trainees overnight. All of the class are attached to the Naval Academy.

GUARDA MARINHA JENSEN   *1985, Ronaldo S Olive*

ROSCA FINA (ex-U 31)   **VOGA PICADA** (ex-U 32)   **LEVA ARRIBA** (ex-U 33)

Displacement, tons: 50
Dimensions, feet (metres): 61 × 15.4 × 3.9 *(18.6 × 4.7 × 1.2)*
Main machinery: 1 diesel; 650 hp(m) *(477 kW)*; 1 shaft
Speed, knots: 11. **Range, miles:** 200
Complement: 5 plus trainees
Radars: Navigation: Racal Decca; I band.

Comment: Built by Carbrasmar, Rio de Janeiro. All commissioned 21 February 1984 and attached to the Naval College. Pennant numbers removed in 1989. In addition the former American fishing vessel *Night Hawk* is in use for training at Centro de Instrucao Almirante Braz de Aguiar.

VOGA PICADA   *1984, Brazilian Navy*

8 SAIL TRAINING VESSELS

SAFGACO BL 177   **BREKELE** (ex-*Carro Chefe*) BL 898
SITIO FORTE BL 1130   **VENDAVAL**
ALBATROZ (ex-*Cisne Branco*)   **CISNE BRANCO** (ex-*Ondine*) BL 810
ITAPOA (ex-*Cri-Cri*)   **JACANA II**

Comment: Some are used for civilian training as well.

TUGS

Note: In addition to the vessels listed below there are three harbour tugs: *Wandenkolk* (R 20), *Antonio Joao* (R 26) and *Etchebarne* (R 28).

2 ALMIRANTE GUILHEM CLASS (FLEET OCEAN TUGS)

Name	No	Builders	Commissioned
ALMIRANTE GUILHEM (ex-*Superpesa 4*)	R 24	Sumitomo Heavy Industry, Japan	1976
ALMIRANTE GUILLOBEL (ex-*Superpesa 5*)	R 25	Sumitomo Heavy Industry, Japan	1976

Displacement, tons: 1200 dwt
Dimensions, feet (metres): 207 × 44 × 14.8 *(63.2 × 13.4 × 4.5)*
Main machinery: 2 GM EMD 20-645F7B diesels; 7120 hp *(5.31 MW)* sustained; 2 shafts; cp props; bow thruster
Speed, knots: 14
Complement: 40
Guns: 2 Oerlikon 20 mm (not always carried).

Comment: Originally built as civilian tugs. Bollard pull, 84 tons. Commissioned into the Navy 22 January 1981.

ALMIRANTE GUILLOBEL *1985, Mário R V Carneiro*

3 TRITÃO CLASS (FLEET OCEAN TUGS)

Name	No	Builders	Commissioned
TRITÃO (ex-*Sarandi*)	R 21	Estanave, Manaus	19 Feb 1987
TRIDENTE (ex-*Sambaiba*)	R 22	Estanave, Manaus	8 Oct 1987
TRIUNFO (ex-*Sorocaba*)	R 23	Estanave, Manaus	5 July 1986

Displacement, tons: 1680 full load
Dimensions, feet (metres): 181.8 × 38.1 × 11.2 *(55.4 × 11.6 × 3.4)*
Main machinery: 2 diesels; 2480 hp(m) *(1.82 MW)*; 2 shafts
Speed, knots: 12
Complement: 49
Guns: 2 Oerlikon 20 mm.
Radars: Navigation: Racal Decca; I band.

Comment: Offshore supply vessels acquired from National Oil Company of Brazil and converted for naval use. Assumed names of previous three ships of Sotoyomo class. Fitted to act both as tugs and patrol vessels. Bollard pull, 23.5 tons. Firefighting capability. Endurance, 45 days.

TRIUNFO *1987, Brazilian Navy*

2 COASTAL TUGS

AHMEYER D. N. O. G.

Comment: Built at Servimar, Rio de Janeiro. Both commissioned in 1972. Of 100 tons and 105 ft *(32 m)* long. Based at Aratu naval base.

4 COASTAL TUGS

| INTREPIDO BNRJ 16 | VALENTE BNRJ 18 |
| ARROJADO BNRJ 17 | IMPAVIDO BNRJ 19 |

Displacement, tons: 200 full load
Dimensions, feet (metres): 73.8 × 23 × 9.2 *(22.5 × 7 × 2.8)*
Main machinery: 2 Caterpillar 3508A DI-TA diesels; 1572 hp(m) *(1.16 MW)* sustained; 2 shafts
Speed, knots: 11.7
Complement: 6

Comment: Damen Shipyards Stan Tug 2207 type. First two delivered in May 1992, second pair in September 1992. Bollard pull 22.5 tons. The second pair have external firefighting equipment.

INTREPIDO and ARROJADO *6/1992, van Ginderen Collection*

4 COASTAL TUGS

| COMANDANTE MARROIG (ex-R 15) | TENENTE MAGALHÃES (ex-R 17) |
| COMANDANTE DIDIER (ex-R 16) | CABO SCHRAMM (ex-R 18) |

Displacement, tons: 115 standard
Dimensions, feet (metres): 65 × 23 × 6.5 *(19.8 × 7 × 2)*
Main machinery: 2 GM diesels; 900 hp(m) *(661 kW)*; 2 shafts
Complement: 6

Comment: Built by Turn-Ship Limited, USA. First pair commissioned 30 April 1981, second pair 14 September 1982. *Comandante Marroig* sank in 1990 in an incident with *Ceará* but was salvaged and active again in 1991. Decommissioned in 1991 but retained in service as support ships to naval establishments and designated Rb.

CABO SCHRAMM *6/1989, Mário R V Carneiro*

SERVICE CRAFT

Note: In addition to the vessels listed below there are (1) three 485 ton water tankers *Dr Gondim* (R 38), *Itapura* (R 42) and *Paulo Afonso* (R 43); (2) two general purpose auxiliaries *Guairia* (R 40) and *Iguacu* (R 41); (3) six river patrol launches *Arenque* (R 55), *Atum* (R 56), *Acara* (R 57), *Agulha* (R 58), *Aruana* (R 59) and *Argentina* (R 60). There are also large numbers of small service craft.

9 RIO DOCE and RIO PARDO CLASSES

RIO DAS CONTAS (ex-U 21)	RIO PARDO (ex-U 40)
RIO FORMOSO (ex-U 22)	RIO NEGRO (ex-U 41)
RIO REAL (ex-U 23)	RIO CHUI (ex-U 42)
RIO TURVO (ex-U 24)	RIO OIAPOQUE (ex-U 43)
RIO VERDE (ex-U 25)	

Displacement, tons: 150 full load
Dimensions, feet (metres): 120 × 21.3 × 6.2 *(36.6 × 6.5 × 1.9)*
Main machinery: 2 Sulzer 6-TD24; 900 hp(m) *(661 kW)*; 2 shafts
Speed, knots: 14. **Range, miles:** 700 at 14 kts
Complement: 10

Comment: Can carry 600 passengers. The first five were built by Holland Nautic, commissioned in 1954 and the second group by Inconav de Niteroi in 1975/76. Pennant numbers removed in 1989. *Rio Doce* (ex-U 20) sold for civilian use in 1986.

SARGENTO BORGES (ex-R 47)

Displacement, tons: 108.5
Dimensions, feet (metres): 91.8 × 21.3 × 4.9 *(28 × 6.5 × 1.5)*
Main machinery: 2 diesels; 650 hp(m) *(478 kW)*; 2 shafts
Speed, knots: 10. **Range, miles:** 400 at 10 kts
Complement: 10

Comment: Built by Ebrasa, Itajai. Launched 29 August 1974. Can carry 106 passengers. Pennant number removed in 1989.

68 BRAZIL / Torpedo transports/TRV — BRUNEI / Light forces

TORPEDO TRANSPORTS/TRV

ALMIRANTE HESS (ex-U 30)

Displacement, tons: 91 full load
Dimensions, feet (metres): 77.4 × 19.7 × 6.6 *(23.6 × 6 × 2)*
Speed, knots: 13

Comment: Built by Inace S/A, Fortaleza and commissioned 2 December 1983. Attached to Trem da Esquadra. Can transport up to four torpedoes. Decommissioned in 1991 but retained in service as an AvPpCo (coast support craft).

FLOATING DOCKS

CIDADE DE NATAL (ex-AFDL 39) G 27
AFONSO PENA (ex-*Ceara*, ex-ARD 14) G 25
ALMIRANTE SCHIECK
ALMIRANTE JERONIMO GONÇALVES (ex-*Goiaz* AFDL 4) G 26

Comment: The first three are floating docks loaned to Brazil by US Navy in the mid-1960s and purchased 11 February 1980. Ship lifts of 2800 tons, 1800 tons and 1000 tons respectively. *Almirante Schieck* was built by Arsenal de Marinha, Rio de Janeiro and commissioned 12 October 1989. There are also two Floating Cranes, *Campos Salles* and *Atlas* of 100 tons and 30 tons capacity respectively.

BRUNEI

Headquarters' Appointment

Lieutenant Colonel Abdel Latif

Personnel

(a) 1993: 700 (60 officers)
This total includes Special Combat Squadron and River Division
(b) Voluntary service

Base

Flotilla Base—Muara

Prefix to Ships' Names

KDB (Kapal Di-Raja Brunei)

General

Tentera Laut Diraja Brunei (Royal Brunei Navy).

Mercantile Marine

Lloyd's Register of Shipping:
51 vessels of 362 109 tons gross

DELETIONS

1991 *Abadi, Penang*

CORVETTES

Note: Order placed in October 1989 for three Vosper Vigilance class was not confirmed. Tenders re-opened but further delays have been caused by priority being given to the purchase of Hawk aircraft. A further Invitation to Tender for three vessels of 1000 tons is expected in 1993. A Landing Craft may also be ordered.

LIGHT FORCES

3 WASPADA CLASS (FAST ATTACK CRAFT—MISSILE)

Name	No	Builders	Commissioned
WASPADA	P 02	Vosper (Singapore)	1978
PEJUANG	P 03	Vosper (Singapore)	1979
SETERIA	P 04	Vosper (Singapore)	1979

Displacement, tons: 206 full load
Dimensions, feet (metres): 121 × 23.5 × 6 *(36.9 × 7.2 × 1.8)*
Main machinery: 2 MTU 20V 538 TB91 diesels; 7680 hp(m) *(5.63 MW)* sustained; 2 shafts
Speed, knots: 32. Range, miles: 1200 at 14 kts
Complement: 24 (4 officers)

Missiles: SSM: 2 Aerospatiale MM 38 Exocet; inertial cruise; active radar homing to 42 km *(23 nm)* at 0.9 Mach; warhead 165 kg.
Guns: 2 Oerlikon 30 mm GCM-B01 (twin); 85° elevation; 650 rounds/minute to 10 km *(5.5 nm)*; weight of shell 1 kg.
2—7.62 mm MGs. 2 MOD(N) 2 in launchers for illuminants.
Countermeasures: ESM: Decca RDL; radar warning.
Fire control: Sea Archer system with Sperry Co-ordinate Calculator and 1412A digital computer.
Radars: Surface search: Racal Decca TM 1629AC; I band.

Programmes: *Waspada* launched in August 1977, the remaining two in March and June 1978 respectively.
Modernisation: Started in 1988 and included improved gun fire control and ESM equipment. OMM 40 Exocet may be fitted in due course.
Structure: Welded steel hull with aluminium alloy superstructure. *Waspada* has an enclosed upper bridge for training purposes.

WASPADA 5/1990, John Mortimer

24 FAST ASSAULT BOATS

Comment: Rigid Raider type with one 140 hp *(103 kW)* outboard mostly 16.4-19.7 ft *(5-6 m)* long. One 7.62 mm MG. Operated in rivers and estuaries by River Division for Infantry Battalions.

3 PERWIRA CLASS (COASTAL PATROL CRAFT)

Name	No	Builders	Commissioned
PERWIRA	P 14	Vosper (Singapore)	9 Sep 1974
PEMBURU	P 15	Vosper (Singapore)	17 June 1975
PENYERANG	P 16	Vosper (Singapore)	24 June 1975

Displacement, tons: 38 full load
Dimensions, feet (metres): 71 × 20 × 5 *(21.7 × 6.1 × 1.2)*
Main machinery: 2 MTU MB 12V 331 TC81 diesels; 2450 hp(m) *(1.8 MW)* sustained; 2 shafts
Speed, knots: 32. Range, miles: 600 at 22 kts; 1000 at 16 kts
Complement: 14 (2 officers)
Guns: 2 Hispano Suiza 20 mm; 720 rounds/minute to 10 km *(5.5 nm)*.
2—7.62 mm MGs.
Radars: Surface search: Racal Decca RM 1290; I band.

Comment: *Perwira* launched May 1974, other two in January and March 1975 respectively. Of all wooden construction on laminated frames. Fitted with enclosed bridges—modified July 1976.

PENYERANG 6/1990, James Goldrick

2 CHEVERTON LOADMASTERS

Name	No	Builders	Commissioned
DAMUAN	L 31	Cheverton Ltd, Isle of Wight	May 1976
PUNI	L 32	Cheverton Ltd, Isle of Wight	Feb 1977

Displacement, tons: 60; 64 *(Puni)*
Dimensions, feet (metres): 65 × 20 × 3.6 *(19.8 × 6.1 × 1.1)* (length 74.8 *(22.8)* Puni)
Main machinery: 2 Detroit 6-71 diesels; 442 hp *(305 kW)* sustained; 2 shafts
Speed, knots: 9. Range, miles: 1000 at 9 kts
Complement: 8
Military lift: 32 tons
Radars: Navigation: Racal Decca RM 1216; I band.

DAMUAN 1988, Royal Brunei Armed Forces

Patrol forces — Marine police / BRUNEI 69

3 ROTORK TYPE (INSHORE PATROL CRAFT)

S 24, 25, 26

Displacement, tons: 8.8 full load
Dimensions, feet (metres): 41.5 × 10.5 × 4.8 *(12.7 × 3.2 × 1.5)*
Main machinery: 2 Ford Mermaid diesels; 430 hp *(320 kW)*; 2 Castoldi 06 waterjets
Speed, knots: 27 light; 12 heavy. **Range, miles:** 100 at 12 kts
Complement: 3
Guns: 3—7.62 mm MGs.
Radars: Navigation: Decca 60; I band.

Comment: Rotork Marine FPB 512 type. S 24 was delivered in November 1980 for patrol and transport duties. S 25 and 26 delivered May 1981.

S 26   *1982, Royal Brunei Armed Forces*

2 UTILITY CRAFT

BURONG NURI

Displacement, tons: 23 full load
Dimensions, feet (metres): 58.4 × 14.1 × 4.9 *(17.8 × 4.3 × 1.5)*
Main machinery: 2 diesels; 400 hp *(298 kW)*; 2 shafts
Speed, knots: 12
Complement: 5

Comment: Built by Cheverton in 1982. Serves as tug, tender or anti-pollution vessel.

BURONG NURI   *6/1990, James Goldrick*

1 SAR TENDER

NORAIN

Displacement, tons: 25
Dimensions, feet (metres): 62 × 16 × 4.5 *(18.9 × 4.8 × 1.4)*
Main machinery: 2 diesels; 1250 hp *(932 kW)*; 2 shafts
Speed, knots: 26
Complement: 5

Comment: Built by Cheverton in 1982. Serves as SAR vessel or tender and as VIP transport.

NORAIN   *6/1990, James Goldrick*

LAND-BASED MARITIME AIRCRAFT

Numbers/Type: 3 ASA/IPTN CN-235.
Operational speed: 240 kts *(445 km/h)*.
Service ceiling: 26 600 ft *(8110 m)*.
Range: 669 nm *(1240 km)*.
Role/Weapon systems: Long-range maritime patrol for surface surveillance and ASW. Sensors: Search radar: Litton AN/APS 504(V)5; MAD; acoustic processors; sonobuoys. Weapons: Mk 46 torpedoes.

CN235   *1989*

MARINE POLICE

Note: In addition to the vessels listed below there are two 36 ft launches with Sabre engines, some 30 GRP patrol boats of 19 ft with outboard engines, and 17 miscellaneous small craft.

4 COASTAL PATROL CRAFT

PDB 12-15

Displacement, tons: 20 full load
Dimensions, feet (metres): 47.7 × 13.9 × 3.9 *(14.5 × 4.2 × 1.2)*
Main machinery: 2 MAN D 2840 LE diesels; 1040 hp(m) *(764 kW)* sustained; 2 shafts
Speed, knots: 30. **Range, miles:** 310 at 22 kts
Complement: 7
Guns: 1—7.62 mm MG

Comment: Built by Singapore Shipbuilding and Engineering Ltd. First three handed over in October 1987, last one in 1988. Aluminium hulls.

PDB 13   *10/1987, Royal Brunei Police Force*

3 + 4 COASTAL PATROL CRAFT

BENDEHARU P 21   KEMAINDERA P 23
MAHARAJALELA P 22   + P 24-27

Displacement, tons: 68 full load
Dimensions, feet (metres): 91.8 × 17.7 × 5.9 *(28.5 × 5.4 × 1.7)*
Main machinery: 2 MTU diesels; 2260 hp(m) *(1.6 MW)*; 2 shafts
Complement: 19
Guns: 1—12.7 mm MG.

Comment: Reported ordered for the Police from PT Pal Surabaya, Indonesia in 1989. Three delivered in 1991, remainder not confirmed by early 1993. Similar to Indonesian craft.

POLICE CRAFT (Indonesian colours)   *1991*

BULGARIA

Headquarters' Appointments

Commander-in-Chief:
  Vice Admiral Ventseslav Velkov
Deputy Commander-in-Chief:
  Rear Admiral Christo Kontrov
Chief of Staff:
  Rear Admiral Iliya Popov

General

The Navy is being restructured. The first stage (1992/93) sees the reduction of 22 per cent of the officers and 14 per cent of ratings, and the conscript ratio changed from 44 to 35 per cent. The second stage (1993-2000) will involve a reduction to 52 ships paying off obsolete vessels and replacing others. By 2000 the Fleet is planned to be: 3 submarines, 10 patrol vessels, 8 FAC (M), 20 minehunters/sweepers, 12 minelayers and 12 helicopters.

Personnel

(a) 1993: 5880 (1760 afloat, 2840 ashore, 1000 training, 280 aviation)
(b) 18 months' national service, to reduce to 12 months

Bases

Varna; Naval HQ, Naval Base, Air Station
Burgas; Naval Base
Sozopol; Naval Base
Higher Naval School *(Nikola Yonkov Vaptsarov)* at Varna. Missile, gun, radar and signal stations on Black Sea coast under Navy command.

Strength of the Fleet

Type	Active
Patrol Submarines	3
Frigates	2
Corvettes	9
Fast Attack Craft (Missile)	6
Coastal Patrol Craft (Border Guard)	10
Minesweepers (Coastal)	8
Minesweepers (Inshore)	13
Landing Craft	25
Surveying Ships	3
Support Tankers	2
Training Ship	1

Mercantile Marine

Lloyd's Register of Shipping:
  222 vessels of 1 346 085 tons gross

DELETIONS

Submarine

1990 *Slava* (old)

Frigates

1990 *Smeli* (old), *Habri, Strogi, Bodri* (old)

Minesweepers

1991 1 T 43, 3 PO 2
1992 2 Vanya class, 8 PO 2

Light Forces

1990 2 SOI, 2 Shershen class
1992 4 Shershen class

Amphibious Forces

1991 4 MFP D-3 Type

Miscellaneous

1990 *Vessletz*
1991 *Nikola Vaptzarov* (civilian), *Perun* (civilian)
1992 *Kiril Khalachev, Vladimir Zaimov*

SUBMARINES (PATROL)

3 Ex-SOVIET ROMEO CLASS

POSEDA 81   NADEZHDA 83   SLAVA 84

Displacement, tons: 1475 surfaced; 1830 dived
Dimensions, feet (metres): 251.3 × 22 × 16.1 *(76.6 × 6.7 × 4.9)*
Main machinery: Diesel-electric; 2 Type 37-D diesels; 4000 hp(m) *(2.94 MW)*; 2 motors; 2700 hp(m) *(1.98 MW)*; 2 creep motors; 2 shafts
Speed, knots: 16 surfaced; 13 dived. **Range, miles:** 9000 at 9 kts surfaced
Complement: 54

Torpedoes: 8—21 in *(533 mm)* tubes (6 bow, 2 stern). 14 Soviet Type 53; dual purpose; pattern active/passive homing up to 20 km *(10.8 nm)* at up to 45 kts; warhead 400 kg.
Mines: Can carry up to 28 in lieu of torpedoes.
Radars: Surface search: Snoop Plate; I band.
Sonars: Hull-mounted; active/passive search and attack; high frequency.

Programmes: Built between 1958 and 1961. First pair transferred in 1972-73, one of which was scrapped in 1990. Third transferred during 1985 and a fourth in 1986.
Operational: In 1992 the remaining three were operational but probably restricted to diving to periscope depth.

ROMEO   *1992, S S Breyer*

FRIGATES

1 Ex-SOVIET RIGA CLASS

DRUZKI 12

Displacement, tons: 1260 standard; 1510 full load
Dimensions, feet (metres): 300.1 × 33.1 × 10.5 *(91.5 × 10.1 × 3.2)*
Main machinery: 2 boilers; 2 turbines; 20 000 hp(m) *(14.7 MW)*; 2 shafts
Speed, knots: 30. **Range, miles:** 2000 at 13 kts
Complement: 175

Guns: 3 USSR 3.9 in *(100 mm)*/56; 40° elevation; 15 rounds/minute to 16 km *(8.7 nm);* weight of shell 13.5 kg.
  4—37 mm/63 (2 twin); 80° elevation; 160 rounds/minute to 9 km *(5 nm);* weight of shell 0.7 kg.
  2—25 mm (twin).
Torpedoes: 3—21 in *(533 mm)* tubes. Soviet Type 53; active/passive homing up to 20 km *(10.8 nm)* at up to 45 kts; warhead 400 kg.
A/S mortars: 4 RBU 1200 5-tubed fixed launchers; range 1200 m; warhead 34 kg.
Depth charges: 4 projectors.
Mines: 28.
Countermeasures: ESM: Watch Dog; radar intercept.
Radars: Surface search: Slim Net; E/F band.
  Navigation: Neptun; I band.
  Fire control: Wasp Head/Sun Visor B; G/H/I band.
IFF: High Pole. Square Head.
Sonars: Hull-mounted; active search and attack; high frequency.

Programmes: Transferred in November 1985. The last of three of the class, the other two being scrapped in 1990 at a Turkish Shipyard.
Operational: Probably to be scrapped in 1993.

DRUZKI   *1992 Bulgarian Navy*

Frigates — Corvettes / BULGARIA 71

1 Ex-SOVIET KONI CLASS

SMELI (ex-*Delfin*) 11

Displacement, tons: 1440 standard; 1900 full load
Dimensions, feet (metres): 316.3 × 41.3 × 11.5 *(96.4 × 12.6 × 3.5)*
Main machinery: CODAG; 1 SGW, Nikayev M8B gas turbine (centre shaft); 18 000 hp(m) *(13.25 MW)* sustained; 2 Russki B-68 diesels; 15 820 hp(m) *(11.63 MW)* sustained; 3 shafts
Speed, knots: 27 gas; 22 diesel. **Range, miles:** 1800 at 14 kts
Complement: 110

Missiles: SAM: SA-N-4 Gecko twin launcher ❶; semi-active radar homing to 15 km *(8 nm)* at 2.5 Mach; warhead 50 kg; altitude 9.1-3048 m *(30-10 000 ft)*; 20 missiles.
Guns: 4—3 in *(76 mm)*/60 (2 twin) ❷; 80° elevation; 60 rounds/minute to 15 km *(8 nm)*; weight of shell 7 kg.
4—30 mm/65 (2 twin) ❸; 85° elevation; 500 rounds/minute to 5 km *(2.7 nm)*; weight of shell 0.54 kg.
A/S mortars: 2 RBU 6000 12-tubed trainable ❹; range 6000 m; warhead 31 kg.
Depth charges: 2 racks.
Mines: Capacity for 22.
Countermeasures: Decoys: 2—16-tubed chaff launchers. ESM: 2 Watch Dog.
Radars: Air search: Strut Curve ❺; F band; range 110 km *(60 nm)* for 2 m² target.
Surface search: Don 2; I band.
Fire control: Hawk Screech ❻; I band (for 76 mm). Drum Tilt ❼; H/I band (for 30 mm). Pop Group ❽; F/H/I band (for SA-N-4).
IFF: High Pole B.
Sonars: Hull-mounted; active search and attack; medium frequency.

Programmes: First reported in the Black Sea in 1976. Type I retained by the USSR for training foreign crews but transferred in February 1990 when the Koni programme terminated. Others of the class acquired by the former East German Navy, Yugoslavia, Algeria, Cuba and Libya.

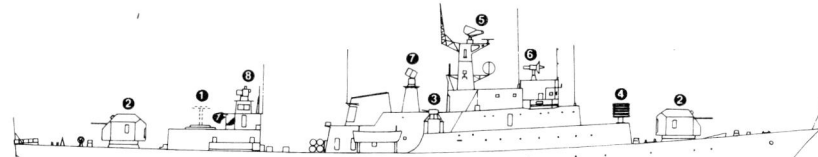

SMELI

(Scale 1 : 900), Ian Sturton

SMELI 7/1992

LAND-BASED MARITIME AIRCRAFT (FRONT LINE)

Numbers/Type: 10 Mil Mi-14PL Haze A.
Operational speed: 120 kts *(222 km/h)*.
Service ceiling: 15 000 ft *(4570 m)*.
Range: 240 nm *(445 km)*.
Role/Weapon systems: Primary role as inshore/coastal ASW and Fleet support helicopter; coastal patrol and surface search. Sensors: Search radar, MAD, sonobuoys, dipping sonar. Weapons: ASW; up to 2 × torpedoes, or mines, or depth bombs.

HAZE 1992, Bulgarian Navy

CORVETTES

1 Ex-SOVIET TARANTUL II CLASS

MULNIYA 101

Displacement, tons: 385 standard; 455 full load
Dimensions, feet (metres): 184.1 × 37.7 × 8.2 *(56.1 × 11.5 × 2.5)*
Main machinery: COGOG; 2 Nikolayev Type DR 77 gas turbines; 16 016 hp(m) *(11.77 MW)* sustained; 2 Nikolayev Type DR 76 gas turbines with reversible gearboxes; 4993 hp(m) *(3.76 MW)* sustained; 2 shafts
Speed, knots: 36 on 4 turbines. **Range, miles:** 400 at 36 kts; 2000 at 20 kts
Complement: 34 (5 officers)

Missiles: SSM: 4 SS-N-2C Styx (2 twin) launchers; active radar or IR homing to 83 km *(45 nm)* at 0.9 Mach; warhead 513 kg; sea-skimmer at end of run.
SAM: SA-N-5 Grail quad launcher; manual aiming; IR homing to 6 km *(3.2 nm)* at 1.5 Mach; altitude to 2500 m *(8000 ft)*; warhead 1.5 kg.
Guns: 1—3 in *(76 mm)*/60; 85° elevation; 120 rounds/minute to 7 km *(3.8 nm)*; weight of shell 7 kg.
2—30 mm/65; 6 barrels per mounting; 3000 rounds/minute to 2 km.
Countermeasures: Decoys: 2—16-barrelled chaff launchers. ESM: 2 receivers.
Fire control: Hood Wink optronic director.
Radars: Air/surface search: Plank Shave (also for missile control); E band.
Navigation: Spin Trough; I band.
Fire control: Bass Tilt; H/I band.
IFF: Square Head. High Pole.

Programmes: Built at Volodarski, Rybinsk. Transferred in December 1989.

2 Ex-SOVIET PAUK I CLASS

RESHITELNI 13 **BODRI 14**

Displacement, tons: 440 full load
Dimensions, feet (metres): 195.2 × 33.5 × 11.2 *(59.5 × 10.2 × 3.4)*
Main machinery: 2 Type M 507 diesels; 14 400 hp(m) *(10.6 MW)* sustained; 2 shafts
Speed, knots: 32. **Range, miles:** 2300 at 18 kts
Complement: 32

Missiles: SAM: SA-N-5 Grail quad launcher; manual aiming; IR homing to 6 km *(3.2 nm)* at 1.5 Mach; altitude to 2500 m *(8000 ft)*; warhead 1.5 kg; 8 missiles.
Guns: 1—3 in *(76 mm)*/60; 85° elevation; 120 rounds/minute to 7 km *(3.8 nm)*; weight of shell 7 kg.
1—30 mm/65; 6 barrels; 3000 rounds/minute combined to 2 km.
Torpedoes: 4—16 in *(406 mm)* tubes. Type 40; anti-submarine; active/passive homing up to 15 km *(8 nm)* at up to 40 kts; warhead 100-150 kg.
A/S mortars: 2 RBU 1200 5-tubed fixed; range 1200 m; warhead 34 kg.
Depth charges: 2 racks (12).
Countermeasures: Decoys: 2—16-barrelled chaff launchers. ESM: Passive receivers.
Radars: Air/surface search: Peel Cone; E band.
Surface search: Spin Trough; I band.
Fire control: Bass Tilt; H/I band.
Sonars: Rat Tail VDS (mounted on transom); active attack; high frequency.

Programmes: *Reshitelni* transferred in September 1989, *Bodri* in December 1990.

MULNIYA 7/1992

BODRI 1992, S S Breyer

72 BULGARIA / Corvettes — Mine warfare forces

6 Ex-SOVIET POTI CLASS

| STROGIJ 45 | LETYASHTI 41 | NAPORISTI 43 |
| KHRABRI 44 | BDIJELNI 45 | BEZSTRASHNI 46 |

Displacement, tons: 400 full load
Dimensions, feet (metres): 196.8 × 26.2 × 6.6 *(60 × 8 × 2)*
Main machinery: CODAG; 2 gas turbines; 30 000 hp(m) *(22.4 MW)*; 2 Type M 503A diesels; 5350 hp(m) *(3.91 MW)* sustained; 2 shafts
Speed, knots: 38. **Range, miles:** 4500 at 10 kts; 500 at 37 kts
Complement: 80

Guns: 2 USSR 57 mm/80 (twin); 85° elevation; 120 rounds/minute to 6 km *(3 nm)*; weight of shell 2.8 kg.
Torpedoes: 4—16 in *(406 mm)* tubes. Soviet Type 40; anti-submarine; active/passive homing up to 15 km *(8 nm)* at up to 40 kts; warhead 100-150 kg.
A/S mortars: 2 RBU 6000 12-tubed trainable launchers; automatic loading; range 6000 m; warhead 31 kg.
Countermeasures: ESM: Watch Dog; radar warning.
Radars: Air search: Strut Curve; F band; range 110 km *(60 nm)* for 2 m² target.
Surface search: Don; I band.
Fire control: Muff Cob; G/H band.
IFF: Square Head. High Pole.
Sonars: Hull-mounted; active search and attack; high frequency.

Programmes: Series built between 1961 and 1968. Three transferred December 1975, the fourth at the end of 1986 and the last two in 1990.

KHRABRI 7/1992

LIGHT FORCES

4 Ex-SOVIET OSA II and 2 OSA I CLASSES (TYPE 205)
(FAST ATTACK CRAFT—MISSILE)

| URAGON 102 | GRUM 104 | TYPFOON 112 (OSA I) |
| BURYA 103 (OSA I) | SVETKAVISTA 111 | SMERCH 113 |

Displacement, tons: 245 full load
Dimensions, feet (metres): 126.6 × 24.9 × 8.8 *(38.6 × 7.6 × 2.7)*
Main machinery: 3 Type M 504 diesels; 10 800 hp(m) *(7.94 MW)* sustained; 3 shafts
Speed, knots: 37. **Range, miles:** 500 at 35 kts
Complement: 30
Missiles: SSM: 4 SS-N-2 Styx B; active radar/IR homing to 46 km *(25 nm)* at 0.9 Mach; warhead 513 kg.
Guns: 4 USSR 30 mm/65 (2 twin); 85° elevation; 500 rounds/minute to 5 km *(2.7 nm)*; weight of shell 0.54 kg.
Radars: Surface search/fire control: Square Tie; I band; range 73 km *(40 nm)*.
Fire control: Drum Tilt; H/I band.
IFF: High Pole. Square Head.

Comment: Details given are for the Osa IIs built between 1965 and 1970, and transferred between 1977 and 1982. Both Osa Is transferred in 1971 and have survived longer than expected.

OSA II 104 1992, Bulgarian Navy

10 Ex-SOVIET ZHUK CLASS (COASTAL PATROL CRAFT)

| 511-513 | 515 | 521-523 | 531-533 |

Displacement, tons: 50 full load
Dimensions, feet (metres): 75.4 × 17 × 6.2 *(23 × 5.2 × 1.9)*
Main machinery: 2 Type M 50 diesels; 2200 hp(m) *(1.6 MW)* sustained; 2 shafts
Speed, knots: 30. **Range, miles:** 1100 at 15 kts
Complement: 17
Guns: 4 USSR 14.5 mm (2 twin) MGs.
Radars: Surface search: Spin Trough; I band.

Comment: Transferred 1980-81. Belong to the Border Police under the Minister of the Interior.

ZHUKs 522 and 523 7/1992

MINE WARFARE FORCES

Note: 10 Vydra class (see *Amphibious Forces*) converted to minelayers in 1992.

4 Ex-SOVIET SONYA CLASS (MINESWEEPERS—COASTAL)

| BRIZ 61 | SHKVAL 62 | PPIBOY 63 | SHTORM 64 |

Displacement, tons: 450 full load
Dimensions, feet (metres): 157.4 × 28.9 × 6.6 *(48 × 8.8 × 2)*
Main machinery: 2 Kolomna Type 9-D-8 diesels; 2000 hp(m) *(1.47 MW)* sustained; 2 shafts
Speed, knots: 15. **Range, miles:** 1500 at 14 kts
Complement: 43
Guns: 2 USSR 30 mm/65 (twin); 85° elevation; 500 rounds/minute to 5 km *(2.7 nm)*; weight of shell 0.54 kg.
2 USSR 25 mm/60 (twin); 85° elevation; 270 rounds/minute to 3 km *(1.6 nm)* anti-aircraft; weight of shell 0.34 kg.
Mines: 5.
Radars: Surface search/navigation: Don 2; I band.
IFF: Two Square Head. High Pole B.

Comment: Wooden hulled ships transferred in 1981-84. Based at Varna.

BRIZ 1984

4 Ex-SOVIET VANYA CLASS (MINESWEEPERS—COASTAL)

| ISKAR 31 | ZIBAR 32 | DOBROTICH 33 | EKSTATI VINAROV 34 |

Displacement, tons: 260 full load
Dimensions, feet (metres): 131.2 × 23.9 × 5.9 *(40 × 7.3 × 1.8)*
Main machinery: 2 Kolomna Type 9-D-8 diesels; 2000 hp(m) *(1.47 MW)* sustained; 2 shafts
Speed, knots: 16. **Range, miles:** 2400 at 10 kts
Complement: 30
Guns: 2 USSR 30 mm/65 (twin); 85° elevation; 500 rounds/minute to 5 km *(2.7 nm)*; weight of shell 0.54 kg.
Mines: Can carry 8.
Radars: Surface search: Don 2; I band.

Comment: Built 1961 to 1973. Transferred from the USSR—two in 1970, two in 1971 and two in 1985. Can act as minehunters. Two deleted in 1992.

VANYA class (old number) 1991, S S Breyer

4 Ex-SOVIET YEVGENYA CLASS (MINESWEEPERS—INSHORE)

65   66   67   68

Displacement, tons: 77 standard; 90 full load
Dimensions, feet (metres): 80.4 × 18 × 4.6 *(24.5 × 5.5 × 1.4)*
Main machinery: 2 Type 3-D-12 diesels; 600 hp(m) *(440 kW)* sustained; 2 shafts
Speed, knots: 11. Range, miles: 300 at 10 kts
Complement: 10
Guns: 2—14.5 mm MGs.
Radars: Navigation: Spin Trough; I band.
IFF: High Pole.

Comment: GRP hulls built at Kolpino. Transferred 1977.

YEVGENYA 65-68   7/1992

5 OLYA (TYPE 1259) CLASS (MINESWEEPERS—INSHORE)

51   52   53   54   55

Displacement, tons: 66 full load
Dimensions, feet (metres): 74.8 × 14.8 × 4.6 *(22.8 × 4.5 × 1.4)*
Main machinery: 2 Type 3-D-12 diesels; 600 hp(m) *(440 kW)* sustained; 2 shafts
Speed, knots: 12. Range (miles): 500 at 10 kts
Complement: 15
Guns: 2—12.7 mm MGs (twin).
Radars: Navigation: Pechora; I band.

Comment: Built between 1988 and 1992 in Bulgaria to the Russian Olya design.

OLYA   *1992, Bulgarian Navy*

4 PO 2 (501) CLASS (MINESWEEPERS—INSHORE)

57   58   218   219

Displacement, tons: 56 full load
Dimensions, feet (metres): 70.5 × 11.5 × 3.3 *(21.5 × 3.5 × 1)*
Main machinery: 1 Type 3-D-12 diesel; 300 hp(m) *(220 kW)* sustained; 2 shafts
Speed, knots: 12
Complement: 8

Comment: Built in Bulgaria—first units completed in early 1950s and last in early 1960s. Originally a class of 24 and these four are the last to survive into 1993. Belonged to Danube flotilla. Occasionally carry a 12.7 mm MG.

AMPHIBIOUS FORCES

2 Ex-SOVIET POLNOCHNY A CLASS (TYPE 770)

SIRIUS (ex-*Ivan Zagubanski*) 701   ANTARES 702

Displacement, tons: 750 standard; 800 full load
Dimensions, feet (metres): 239.5 × 27.9 × 5.8 *(73 × 8.5 × 1.8)*
Main machinery: 2 Kolomna Type 40-D diesels; 4400 hp(m) *(3.2 MW)* sustained; 2 shafts
Speed, knots: 19. Range, miles: 1000 at 18 kts
Complement: 40
Military lift: 350 tons including 6 tanks; 180 troops
Guns: 2 USSR 30 mm (twin). 2—140 mm 18-barrelled rocket launchers.
Radars: Navigation: Spin Trough; I band.

Comment: Built 1963 to 1968. Transferred 1986/87. Not fitted either with the SA-N-5 Grail SAM system or with Drum Tilt fire control radars. To be converted to minelayers.

SIRIUS   *9/1989, S S Breyer*

23 SOVIET VYDRA (104K) CLASS

601-613   703-712

Displacement, tons: 425 standard; 550 full load
Dimensions, feet (metres): 179.7 × 25.3 × 6.6 *(54.8 × 7.7 × 2)*
Main machinery: 2 Type 3-D-12 diesels; 600 hp(m) *(440 kW)* sustained; 2 shafts
Speed, knots: 12. Range, miles: 2500 at 10 kts
Complement: 20
Military lift: 200 tons or 100 troops or 3 MBTs
Radars: Navigation: Spin Trough; I band.
IFF: High Pole.

Comment: Built 1963 to 1969. Ten transferred from the USSR in 1970, the remainder built in Bulgaria between 1974 and 1978. In 1992 ten *(703-712)* converted to be used as minelayers.

VYDRA 705   *11/1989, S S Breyer*

SURVEY SHIPS

1 MOMA CLASS (AGS)

ADMIRAL BRANIMIR ORMANOV 401

Displacement, tons: 1580 full load
Dimensions, feet (metres): 240.5 × 36.8 × 12.8 *(73.3 × 11.2 × 3.9)*
Main machinery: 2 Zgoda-Sulzer 6TD48 diesels; 3300 hp(m) *(2.43 MW)* sustained; 2 shafts
Speed, knots: 17. Range, miles: 9000 at 12 kts
Complement: 37 (5 officers)
Radars: Navigation: Two Don-2; I band.

Comment: Built in Poland in 1977.

MOMA AGS (Russian number)   *1990 G. Jacobs*

2 COASTAL SURVEY VESSELS

231   331

Displacement, tons: 114 full load
Dimensions, feet (metres): 86.9 × 19 × 9.5 *(26.5 × 5.8 × 2.9)*
Main machinery: 2 Type 3-D-12 diesels; 600 hp(m) *(440 kW)* sustained; 2 shafts
Speed, knots: 12. Range, miles: 600 at 10 kts
Complement: 9

Comment: Built in Bulgaria in 1986 and 1988 respectively.

231   *1991, S S Breyer*

74 BULGARIA / Auxiliaries

AUXILIARIES

1 SALVAGE TUG

JUPITER 221

Displacement, tons: 792 full load
Dimensions, feet (metres): 146.6 × 35.1 × 12.7 (44.7 × 10.7 × 3.9)
Main machinery: 2—12 KVD 21 diesels; 1760 hp(m) (1.3 MW); 2 shafts
Speed, knots: 12.5. Range, miles: 3000 at 12 kts
Complement: 39 (6 officers)
Guns: 4—25 mm/70 (2 twin) automatic.

Comment: Bollard pull, 16 tons. Former DDR Type 700.

2 SUPPORT TANKERS

DIMITER A DIMITROV (ex-Mesar, ex-Anlene) 202   ATIYA 302

Displacement, tons: 3500 full load
Dimensions, feet (metres): 319.8 × 43.3 × 16.4 (97.5 × 13.2 × 5)
Main machinery: 2 diesels; 12 000 hp(m) (8.82 MW); 2 shafts
Speed, knots: 20
Guns: 4 USSR 30 mm/65 (2 twin).

Comment: Both built in Bulgaria in 1979 and 1987 respectively. Abeam fuelling to port and astern fuelling. Mount 1.5 ton crane amidships. Also carry dry stores.

DIMITER A DIMITROV   7/1992

ATIYA   7/1992

5 AUXILIARIES

204   205   222   224   321

Comment: 204 is a water barge; 205 a torpedo recovery vessel; 222 a tug; 224 and 321 firefighting vessels.

1 Ex-SOVIET T 43 CLASS (TRAINING SHIP)

N I VAPTSAROV 421

Displacement, tons: 500 standard; 580 full load
Dimensions, feet (metres): 190.2 × 27.6 × 6.9 (58 × 8.4 × 2.1)
Main machinery: 2 Kolomna Type 9-D-8 diesels; 2000 hp(m) (1.47 MW) sustained; 2 shafts
Speed, knots: 14. Range, miles: 3000 at 10 kts
Complement: 65
Guns: 2 USSR 37 mm/63 (twin); 80° elevation; 160 rounds/minute to 9 km (5 nm); weight of shell 0.7 kg.
  4—12.7 mm (2 twin) MGs.
Mines: Can carry 16.
Radars: Surface search: Ball End; E/F band.
Navigation: Neptun; I band.

Comment: Built 1948 to 1957. The survivor of three transferred from the USSR in 1953, this is now the only short-hulled, low bridge, tripod mast T 43 in commission. Converted to a training ship in 1986.

N I VAPTSAROV   1992, Bulgarian Navy

2 DIVING TENDERS

223   323

Dimensions, feet (metres): 91.5 × 17.1 × 7.2 (27.9 × 5.2 × 2.2)
Main machinery: Diesel electric; 2 MCK 83-4 diesel generators; 1 motor; 300 hp(m) (220 kW); 1 shaft
Speed, knots: 10. Range, miles: 400 at 10 kts
Complement: 13

Comment: Built in Bulgaria in mid-1980s.

DIVING TENDER   (not to scale), S S Breyer

1 BEREZA CLASS (TYPE 130)

KAPITAN DIMITER DOBREV 206

Displacement, tons: 2051 full load
Dimensions, feet (metres): 228 × 45.3 × 13.1 (69.5 × 13.8 × 4)
Main machinery: 2 Zgoda-Sulzer 8 AL 25/30 diesels; 2925 hp(m) (2.16 MW) sustained; 2 shafts; cp props
Speed, knots: 13. Range, miles: 1000 at 13 kts
Complement: 48
Radars: Navigation: Kivach; I band.

Comment: New construction built in Poland and transferred July 1988. Used as a degaussing ship. Fitted with an NBC citadel and upper deck wash-down system. The ship has three laboratories.

KAPITAN DIMITER DOBREV   1992, Bulgarian Navy

BORDER GUARD

Comment: Total of 60 small craft including 12 ex-Soviet PO2 class.

BURMA

General

The title used by the current government is Myanmar. The unique characteristic of this Navy is that no ship ever seems to be scrapped. Although some of the hulls are very old, operating in predominantly fresh water has kept corrosion to within containable limits.

Bases

Bassein, Mergui, Moulmein, Rangoon, Seikyi, Sittwe (Akyab), Sinmalaik, Hanggyi Island.

Strength of the Fleet

Type	Active	Building
Corvettes	3 (1)	—
Offshore Patrol Vessels	3	—
Fast Attack Craft (Gun)	—	2
Coastal Patrol Craft	22	—
River Patrol Craft and Gunboats	64	—
Amphibious Vessels	15	—
Survey Vessels	3	—

Headquarters' Appointment

Vice-Chief of Staff, Defence Services (Navy):
Vice Admiral Than Nyunt

Personnel

(a) 1993: 12 400
(b) Voluntary service

Mercantile Marine

Lloyd's Register of Shipping:
144 vessels of 977 251 tons gross

CORVETTES

Note: All Corvettes come under the Major War Vessels Command.

1 Ex-US PCE 827 CLASS

Name	No	Builders	Commissioned
YAN TAING AUNG (ex-USS *Farmington* PCE 894)	41	Willamette Iron & Steel Co, Portland, Oregon	10 Aug 1943

Displacement, tons: 640 standard; 903 full load
Dimensions, feet (metres): 184 × 33 × 9.5 *(56 × 10.1 × 2.9)*
Main machinery: 2 GM 12-567A diesels; 1800 hp *(1.34 MW)*; 2 shafts
Speed, knots: 15
Complement: 72

Guns: 1 US 3 in *(76 mm)*/50 Mk 26; 85° elevation; 20 rounds/minute to 12 km *(6.6 nm)*; weight of shell 6 kg.
2 Bofors 40 mm/60. 8 Oerlikon 20 mm (4 twin).
A/S mortars: 1 Hedgehog Mk 10; 24 rockets; manual loading; range 350 m; warhead 26 kg.
Depth charges: 2 racks. 2 Mk 6 projectors; range 160 m; warhead 150 kg.
Radars: Surface search: Raytheon SPS 5; G/H band; range 37 km *(20 nm)*.
Sonars: RCA QCU-2; hull-mounted; active attack; high frequency.

Programmes: Laid down on 7 December 1942 and launched on 15 May 1943. Transferred on 18 June 1965.
Operational: In poor condition but still operational.

1 Ex-US ADMIRABLE CLASS

Name	No	Builders	Commissioned
YAN GYI AUNG (ex-USS *Creddock* MSF 356)	42	Willamette Iron & Steel Co, Portland, Oregon	1944

Displacement, tons: 650 standard; 945 full load
Dimensions, feet (metres): 184.5 × 33 × 9.8 *(56.2 × 10.1 × 3)*
Main machinery: 2 Busch-Sulzer BS-539 diesels; 1500 hp(m) *(1.1 MW)*; 2 shafts
Speed, knots: 14.8. **Range, miles:** 4300 at 10 kts
Complement: 73

Guns: 1 US 3 in *(76 mm)*/50 Mk 26; 85° elevation; 20 rounds/minute to 12 km *(6.6 nm)*; weight of shell 6 kg.
4 Bofors 40 mm/60 (2 twin). 4 Oerlikon 20 mm (2 twin).
A/S mortars: 1 Hedgehog Mk 10; 24 rockets; manual loading; range 350 m; warhead 26 kg.
Depth charges: 2 racks. 2 Mk 6 projectors; range 160 m; warhead 150 kg.
Radars: Surface search: Raytheon SPS 5; G/H band; range 37 km *(20 nm)*.
Sonars: RCA QCU-2; hull-mounted; active attack; high frequency.

Programmes: Laid down on 10 November 1943 and launched on 22 July 1944. Transferred at San Diego on 31 March 1967.
Operational: Minesweeping gear removed. Fully operational.

YAN GYI AUNG   12/1991

YAN TAING AUNG   1987

OFFSHORE PATROL VESSELS

2 NAWARAT CLASS

Name	No	Builders	Commissioned
NAWARAT	501	Government Dockyard, Dawbon, Rangoon	26 Apr 1960
NAGAKYAY	502	Government Dockyard, Dawbon, Rangoon	3 Dec 1960

Displacement, tons: 400 standard; 450 full load
Dimensions, feet (metres): 163 × 26.8 × 5.8 *(49.7 × 8.2 × 1.8)*
Main machinery: 2 Paxman Ricardo diesels; 1160 hp(m) *(865 kW)*; 2 shafts
Speed, knots: 12
Complement: 43
Guns: 2—25 pdr (88 mm) QF. 2 Bofors 40 mm.

Comment: In spite of their size, these vessels are used mostly for river patrols and are in good condition.

3 OSPREY CLASS

Name	No	Builders	Commissioned
INDAW	FV 55	Frederikshavn Dockyard	30 May 1980
INMA	FV 56	Frederikshavn Dockyard	25 Mar 1982
INYA	FV 57	Frederikshavn Dockyard	25 Mar 1982

Displacement, tons: 385 standard; 505 full load
Dimensions, feet (metres): 164 × 34.5 × 9 *(50 × 10.5 × 2.8)*
Main machinery: 2 Burmeister and Wain Alpha diesels; 4640 hp(m) *(3.4 MW)*; 2 shafts
Speed, knots: 20. **Range, miles:** 4500 at 16 kts
Complement: 20 (5 officers) (accommodation for 35)
Guns: 1 Bofors 40 mm/60. 2 Oerlikon 20 mm.

Comment: Operated by Burmese Navy for the People's Pearl and Fishery Department. Helicopter deck with hangar in *Indaw*. Carry David Still craft capable of 25 kts.

NAWARAT

INYA   1990

76　BURMA / Light forces

LIGHT FORCES

0 + 2 FAST ATTACK CRAFT (GUN)

Displacement, tons: 213 full load
Dimensions, feet (metres): 147.3 × 23 × 8.2 *(45 × 7 × 2.5)*
Main machinery: 2 Mercedes Benz diesels; 2 shafts
Speed, knots: 30+
Complement: 34 (7 officers)
Guns: 2 Bofors 40 mm/60.
Radars: Surface search: I band.

Comment: Under construction in 1991 for completion in 1993.

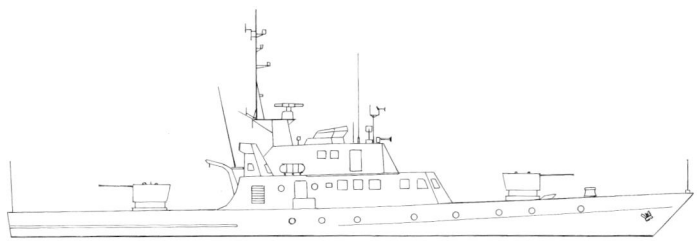

FAC(G)   *(not to scale), Ian Sturton*

6 CHINESE HAINAN CLASS (TYPE 037) (COASTAL PATROL CRAFT)

Name	No	Name	No
YAN SIT AUNG	43	YAN KHWIN AUNG	46
YAN MYAT AUNG	44	YAN MIN AUNG	47
YAN NYEIN AUNG	45	YAN YE AUNG	48

Displacement, tons: 375 standard; 392 full load
Dimensions, feet (metres): 192.8 × 23.6 × 6 *(58.8 × 7.2 × 2.2)*
Main machinery: 4 PCR/Kolomna Type 9-D-8 diesels; 4000 hp(m) *(2.94 MW)* sustained; 4 shafts
Speed, knots: 30.5. Range, miles: 1300 at 15 kts
Complement: 69
Guns: 4 China 57 mm/70 (2 twin); dual purpose; 120 rounds/minute to 12 km *(6.5 nm)*; weight of shell 6.31 kg.
    4 USSR 25 mm/60 (2 twin); 85° elevation; 270 rounds/minute to 3 km *(1.6 nm)* anti-aircraft; weight of shell 0.34 kg.
A/S mortars: 4 RBU 1200 5-tubed fixed launchers; range 1200 m; warhead 34 kg.
Depth charges: 2 BMB-2 projectors; 2 racks.
Mines: Rails fitted.
Radars: Surface search: Pot Head; I band.
Navigation: Raytheon Pathfinder; I band.
IFF: High Pole.
Sonars: Hull-mounted; active search and attack; high frequency.

Comment: Later variant of this class with tripod masts. Delivered in January 1991.

YAN SIT AUNG   *1991*

3 YUGOSLAV PB 90 CLASS (COASTAL PATROL CRAFT)

424   425   426

Displacement, tons: 80 standard
Dimensions, feet (metres): 89.9 × 21.5 × 7.2 *(27.4 × 6.6 × 2.2)*
Main machinery: 3 diesels; 4290 hp(m) *(3.15 MW)*; 3 shafts
Speed, knots: 32. Range, miles: 400 at 25 kts
Complement: 17
Guns: 8—20 mm M75 (two quad). 2—128 mm launchers for illuminants.
Radars: Navigation: I band.

Comment: Built by Brodotechnika, Yugoslavia for an African country and completed in 1986-87. Laid up when the sale did not go through and shipped to Burma arriving in October 1990.

PB 90 (old number)   *1990, Yugoslav FDSP*

4 PGM TYPE (COASTAL PATROL CRAFT)

PGM 412-PGM 415

Displacement, tons: 128 full load
Dimensions, feet (metres): 110 × 22 × 6.5 *(33.5 × 6.7 × 2)*
Main machinery: 2 Deutz SBA16MB816 LLKR diesels; 2720 hp(m) *(2 MW)*; 2 shafts
Speed, knots: 16. Range, miles: 1400 at 14 kts
Complement: 17
Guns: 2 Bofors 40 mm/60.

Comment: First two completed 1983. Two more built in Burma Naval Dockyard.

PGM 412   *9/1991*

6 Ex-US PGM TYPE (COASTAL PATROL CRAFT)

PGM 401-PGM 406

Displacement, tons: 141 full load
Dimensions, feet (metres): 101 × 21.1 × 7.5 *(30.8 × 6.4 × 2.3)*
Main machinery: 8 GM 6-71 diesels; 1920 hp *(1.43 MW)* sustained; 2 shafts
Speed, knots: 17. Range, miles: 1000 at 15 kts
Complement: 17
Guns: 2 Bofors 40 mm/60. 2 Oerlikon 20 mm (twin). 2—12.7 mm MGs.
Radars: Navigation: Raytheon 1500 (PGM 405-406).
    EDO 320 (PGM 401-404); I/J band.

Comment: Built by the Marinette Marine Corporation, USA in 1959-61. Ex-US PGM 43-46, 51 and 52 respectively.

PGM 406   *3/1992*

3 SWIFT TYPE PGM (COASTAL PATROL CRAFT)

421   422   423

Displacement, tons: 111 full load
Dimensions, feet (metres): 103.3 × 23.8 × 6.9 *(31.5 × 7.2 × 3.1)*
Main machinery: 2 MTU 12V 331 TC81 diesels; 2450 hp(m) *(1.8 MW)* sustained; 2 shafts
Speed, knots: 27. Range, miles: 1800 at 18 kts
Complement: 25
Guns: 2 Bofors 40 mm. 2 Oerlikon 20 mm. 2—12.7 mm MGs.

Comment: Swiftships construction completed in 1979. Acquired 1980 through Vosper, Singapore.

PGM 421   *6/1991*

Light forces / BURMA

2 IMPROVED Y 301 CLASS (RIVER GUNBOATS)

Y 311   Y 312

Displacement, tons: 250 full load
Dimensions, feet (metres): 121.4 × 24 × 3.9 *(37 × 7.3 × 1.2)*
Main machinery: 2 MTU MB diesels; 1000 hp(m) *(735 kW)*; 2 shafts
Speed, knots: 12
Complement: 37
Guns: 2 Bofors 40 mm. 4 Oerlikon 20 mm.

Comment: Built at Simmilak in 1969 and based on similar Yugoslav craft.

Y 311   6/1992

10 Y 301 CLASS (RIVER GUNBOATS)

Y 301-Y 310

Displacement, tons: 120 full load
Dimensions, feet (metres): 104.8 × 24 × 3 *(32 × 7.3 × 0.9)*
Main machinery: 2 MTU MB diesels; 1000 hp(m) *(735 kW)*; 2 shafts
Speed, knots: 13
Complement: 29
Guns: 2 Bofors 40 mm/60 or 1 Bofors 40 mm/60 and 1—2 pdr.

Comment: All of these boats were completed in 1958 at the Uljanik Shipyard, Pula, Yugoslavia.

Y 304   1991

4 RIVER GUNBOATS (Ex-TRANSPORTS)

SAGU   SEINDA   SHWETHIDA   SINMIN

Displacement, tons: 98 full load
Dimensions, feet (metres): 94.5 × 22 × 4.5 *(28.8 × 6.7 × 1.4)*
Main machinery: 1 Crossley ERL 6 cyl diesel; 160 hp *(119 kW)*; 1 shaft
Speed, knots: 12
Complement: 32
Guns: 1—40 mm/60 *(Sagu)*. 1—20 mm (3 in *Sagu*).

Comment: Built in mid-1950s. *Sinmin*, *Seinda* and *Shwethida* have a roofed-in upper deck with a 20 mm gun forward of the funnel. *Sagu* has an open upper deck aft of the funnel but with a 40 mm gun forward and mountings for 20 mm aft on the upper deck and midships either side on the lower deck. Four other ships of the same type are probably unarmed and are listed under *Miscellaneous*.

SINMIN   1989

SAGU   1990

2 Ex-US CGC TYPE (RIVER GUNBOATS)

MGB 102   MGB 110

Displacement, tons: 49 standard; 66 full load
Dimensions, feet (metres): 83 × 16 × 5.5 *(25.3 × 4.9 × 1.7)*
Main machinery: 4 GM diesels; 800 hp *(596 kW)*; 2 shafts
Speed, knots: 11
Complement: 16
Guns: 1 Bofors 40 mm. 1 Oerlikon 20 mm.

Comment: Ex-USCG type cutters with new hulls built in Burma. Completed in 1960.

MGB 110

9 RIVER PATROL CRAFT

RPC 11   12   13   14   15   + 4

Displacement, tons: 37 full load
Dimensions, feet (metres): 50 × 14 × 3.5 *(15.2 × 4.3 × 1.1)*
Main machinery: 2 Thornycroft RZ 6 diesels; 250 hp *(186 kW)*; 2 shafts
Speed, knots: 10. **Range, miles:** 400 at 8 kts
Complement: 8
Guns: 1 Oerlikon 20 mm or 2—12.7 mm MGs (twin). 1—12.7 mm MG.

Comment: Built by the Naval Engineering Depot. First five in mid-1980s; second batch of a modified design in 1990/91.

6 RIVER PATROL CRAFT

PBR 211-216

Displacement, tons: 9 full load
Dimensions, feet (metres): 32 × 11 × 2.6 *(9.8 × 3.4 × 0.8)*
Main machinery: 2 GM 6V-53 diesels; 348 hp *(260 kW)* sustained; 2 waterjets
Speed, knots: 25. **Range, miles:** 180 at 20 kts
Complement: 4 or 5
Guns: 2—12.7 mm (twin, fwd) MGs. 1—7.9 mm LMG (aft).

Comment: Acquired in 1978. Built by Uniflite, Washington.

PBR 211   1987

25 YUGOSLAV-BUILT RIVER PATROL CRAFT

001-025

Comment: Small craft, 52 ft *(15.8 m)* long, acquired from Yugoslavia in 1965.

6 CARPENTARIA CLASS (RIVER PATROL CRAFT)

112-117

Displacement, tons: 26 full load
Dimensions, feet (metres): 51.5 × 15.7 × 4.3 *(15.7 × 4.8 × 1.3)*
Main machinery: 2 diesels; 1360 hp *(1.01 MW)*; 2 shafts
Speed, knots: 29. **Range, miles:** 950 at 18 kts
Complement: 10
Guns: 1 Oerlikon 20 mm or 1—12.7 mm MG.

Comment: Built by De Havilland Marine, Sydney. First two delivered 1979, remainder in 1980. Similar to craft built for Indonesia and South Africa.

CARPENTARIA 113   1991

78 BURMA / Shipborne aircraft — Survey vessels

SHIPBORNE AIRCRAFT

Numbers/Type: 10 Aerospatiale SA 316B Alouette III.
Operational speed: 113 kts *(210 km/h)*.
Service ceiling: 10 500 ft *(3200 m)*.
Range: 290 nm *(540 km)*.
Role/Weapon systems: Embarked in offshore patrol craft for support duties. Sensors: None. Weapons: 7.62 mm machine gun mountings.

LAND-BASED MARITIME AIRCRAFT

Numbers/Type: 10 Kawasaki-Bell 47G-3.
Operational speed: 74 kts *(137 km/h)*.
Service ceiling: 13 200 ft *(4023 m)*.
Range: 261 nm *(483 km)*.
Role/Weapon systems: Light liaison and utility tasks. Sensors: None. Weapons: Unarmed, but single 7.62 mm mounting has been supplied.

Numbers/Type: 3 Fokker F27M.
Operational speed: 250 kts *(463 km/h)*.
Service ceiling: 25 000 ft *(7620 m)*.
Range: 2700 nm *(5000 km)*.
Role/Weapon systems: Long-range patrol of coastlines. Sensors: Bendix weather radar, wingtip searchlight. Weapons: Unarmed.

AMPHIBIOUS FORCES

Note: As well as the vessels listed below there are at least three Army Landing Craft (001-003) of about 75 tons.

LANDING CRAFT 001(2)   7/1992

4 LCUs

AIYAR MAI 604   **AIYAR MINTHAMEE** 606
AIYAR MAUNG 605   **AIYAR MINTHAR** 607

Displacement, tons: 250 full load
Dimensions, feet (metres): 125.6 × 29.8 × 4.6 *(38.3 × 9.1 × 1.4)*
Main machinery: 2 diesels; 600 hp(m) *(441 kW)*; 2 shafts
Speed, knots: 10
Complement: 10
Military lift: 100 tons

Comment: All built at Yokohama in 1969.

AIYAR MAUNG   1991

1 LCU

AIYAR LULIN 603

Displacement, tons: 360 full load
Dimensions, feet (metres): 119 × 34 × 6 *(36.3 × 10.4 × 1.8)*
Main machinery: 2 diesels; 600 hp *(448 kW)*; 2 shafts
Speed, knots: 10
Complement: 14
Military lift: 168 tons
Guns: 1—12.7 mm MG.

Comment: Built in Rangoon in 1966.

AIYAR LULIN   1990

10 Ex-US LCM 3 TYPE

LCM 701-710

Displacement, tons: 52 full load
Dimensions, feet (metres): 50 × 14 × 4 *(15.2 × 4.3 × 1.2)*
Main machinery: 2 Gray Marine 64 HN9 diesels; 330 hp *(246 kW)*; 2 shafts
Speed, knots: 9

Comment: US-built LCM type landing craft. Used as local transports for stores and personnel. Cargo capacity, 30 tons. Guns have been removed.

LCM 710   1991

SURVEY VESSELS

Note: Thu Tay Thi means 'survey vessel'.

Name	No	Builders	Commissioned
—	801	Brodogradiliste Tito, Belgrade, Yugoslavia	1965

Displacement, tons: 1059 standard
Dimensions, feet (metres): 204 × 36 × 11.8 *(62.2 × 11 × 3.6)*
Main machinery: 2 MTU 12V 493 TY7 diesels; 2120 hp(m) *(1.62 MW)* sustained; 2 shafts
Speed, knots: 15
Complement: 99 (7 officers)
Guns: 1 Bofors 40 mm. 2 Oerlikon 20 mm (twin) can be fitted.

Comment: Fitted with helicopter platform and two surveying motor boats.

801

Name	No	Builders	Commissioned
— (ex-*Changi*)	802	Miho Shipyard, Shimizu	20 June 1969

Measurement, tons: 387 gross; 118 dwt
Dimensions, feet (metres): 154.2 × 28.6 × 11.9 *(47 × 8.7 × 3.6)*
Main machinery: 1 Niigata diesel; 1 shaft
Speed, knots: 13
Complement: 35
Guns: 2 Oerlikon 20 mm.

Comment: A fishery research ship of Singapore origin, arrested on 8 April 1974 and taken into service as a survey vessel in about 1981. Stern trawler type.

802   3/1992

807

Comment: Inshore launch of about 50 tons armed with one 12.7 mm MG. Used for river surveys.

807   1990

MISCELLANEOUS

Note: As well as the ships listed below there is a small coastal oil tanker, a harbour tug and several harbour launches and personnel carriers.

1 TRANSPORT VESSEL

Comment: Acquired in 1991. Of unknown origin. Looks like a mini liner.

TRANSPORT VESSEL 12/1991

1 TANKER

INTERBUNKER

Displacement, tons: 4000 full load
Dimensions, feet (metres): 180.5 × 78.5 × 9.8 *(55 × 23.9 × 3)*
Main machinery: 2 diesels; 2 shafts
Speed, knots: 15
Complement: 15

Comment: Singapore registered tanker arrested in October 1991 and taken into the Navy.

INTERBUNKER 12/1991

1 DIVING SUPPORT VESSEL

YAN LON AUNG 200

Displacement, tons: 536 full load
Dimensions, feet (metres): 179 × 30 × 8 *(54.6 × 9.1 × 2.4)*
Speed, knots: 12
Complement: 88
Guns: 1 Bofors 40 mm/60. 2—12.7 mm MGs.

Comment: Light forces support diving ship acquired from Japan in 1967.

YAN LON AUNG

4 TRANSPORT VESSELS

SABAN   SETHYA   SHWEPAZUN   SETYAHAT

Displacement, tons: 98 full load
Dimensions, feet (metres): 94.5 × 22 × 4.5 *(28.8 × 6.7 × 1.4)*
Main machinery: 1 Crossley ERL 6 cyl diesel; 160 hp *(119 kW)*; 1 shaft
Speed, knots: 12
Complement: 30

Comment: These are sister ships to the armed gunboats shown under *Light Forces*. It is possible that a 20 mm gun may be mounted on some occasions.

SHWEPAZUN 1991

1 BUOY TENDER

HSAD DAN

Displacement, tons: 706 full load
Dimensions, feet (metres): 130.6 × 37.1 × 8.9 *(39.8 × 11.3 × 2.7)*
Main machinery: 2 Deutz BA8M816 diesels; 1341 hp(m) *(986 kW)*; 2 shafts
Speed, knots: 10
Complement: 23

Comment: Built by Italthai in 1986. Operated by the Rangoon Port Authority.

HSAD DAN 5/1992

1 TRANSPORT VESSEL

PYI DAW AYE

Measurement, tons: 700 dwt
Dimensions, feet (metres): 160 × 27 × 11 *(48.8 × 8.2 × 3.4)*
Main machinery: 2 diesels; 600 hp *(447 kW)*; 2 shafts
Speed, knots: 11
Complement: 12

Comment: Completed in about 1975. Dimensions are approximate. Naval manned.

PYI DAW AYE 1991

1 PRESIDENTIAL YACHT

YADANABON

Comment: Built in Burma and used for VIP cruises on the Irrawaddy river and in coastal waters. Armed with 2—7.62 mm MGs and manned by the Navy.

PRESIDENT'S YACHT 1990

8 MFVs

511   520-523   901   905   906

Comment: Armed vessels of approximately 200 tons *(901)*, 80 tons *(905, 906)* and 50 tons (remainder) with a 12.7 mm MG mounted above the bridge in some.

MFV 901 12/1991

CAMBODIA

General
The Marine Royale Khmer was established on 1 March 1954 and became Marine Nationale Khmer (MNK) on 9 October 1970. Originally Cambodia, became known as the Khmer Republic, then The People's Republic of Kampuchea and is now back to being Cambodia again. In 1992 all naval units were under UN command and painted white.

Personnel
1993: 950

Bases
Ream (coastal), Phnom Penn (river), Kompongson (civil)

Operational
The Riverine branch has 10 battalions, only two of which man the patrol craft.

Mercantile Marine
Lloyd's Register of Shipping:
3 vessels of 3558 tons gross

PATROL FORCES

2 Ex-SOVIET TURYA CLASS
(FAST ATTACK CRAFT—HYDROFOIL)

Displacement, tons: 190 standard; 250 full load
Dimensions, feet (metres): 129.9 × 24.9 (41 foils) × 5.9 (13.1 foils) *(39.6 × 7.6 (12.5) × 1.8 (4))*
Main machinery: 3 Type M 504 diesels; 10 800 hp(m) *(7.94 MW)* sustained; 3 shafts
Speed, knots: 40 foils. **Range, miles:** 600 at 35 kts foils; 1450 at 14 kts hull
Complement: 30
Guns: 2—57 mm (twin). 2—25 mm (twin).
Radars: Search: Pot Drum.
Fire control: Muff Cob; G/H band.
IFF: High Pole B. Square Head.

Comment: Transferred March 1984 and February 1985 without torpedo tubes and dipping sonars. Used mostly as Floating Barracks.

TURYA 1987

4 Ex-SOVIET MODIFIED STENKA CLASS
(FAST ATTACK CRAFT—PATROL)

1131   1132   1133   1134

Displacement, tons: 170 standard; 210 full load
Dimensions, feet (metres): 127.9 × 25.6 × 5.9 *(39 × 7.8 × 1.8)*
Main machinery: 3 Type M 503A diesels; 8025 hp(m) *(5.9 MW)* sustained; 3 shafts
Speed, knots: 36. **Range, miles:** 800 at 24 kts; 500 at 35 kts
Complement: 30
Guns: 4—30 mm/65 (2 twin).
Radars: Search: Pot Drum.
Fire control: Muff Cob; G/H band.
IFF: High Pole. Two Square Head.

Comment: Transferred in November 1987. All are the export model without torpedo tubes and sonar.

2 SOVIET ZHUK CLASS (RIVER PATROL CRAFT)

Displacement, tons: 50 full load
Dimensions, feet (metres): 75.4 × 17 × 6.2 *(23 × 5.2 × 1.9)*
Main machinery: 2 Type M 50 diesels; 2200 hp(m) *(1.6 MW)* sustained; 2 shafts
Speed, knots: 30. **Range, miles:** 1100 at 15 kts
Complement: 17
Guns: 2—14.5 mm (twin, fwd) MGs. 1—12.7 mm (aft) MG.
Radars: Surface search: Spin Trough; I band.

Comment: Transferred via Vietnam between 1985 and 1987.

ZHUK 1992

2 Ex-SOVIET T 4 CLASS (LCVPs)

Displacement, tons: 70 full load
Dimensions, feet (metres): 62.3 × 14 × 3.3 *(19 × 4.3 × 1)*
Main machinery: 2 diesels; 316 hp(m) *(232 kW)*; 2 shafts
Speed, knots: 10
Complement: 4

Comment: Transferred January 1985. Both operational in 1993.

STENKA 1134 1992, Ships of the World

T 4 1992, Ships of the World

4 Ex-SOVIET SHMEL CLASS (RIVER PATROL CRAFT)

Displacement, tons: 85 full load
Dimensions, feet (metres): 91.8 × 14.1 × 3 6 (28 × 4.3 × 1.1)
Main machinery: 2 Type M 50 diesels; 2200 hp(m) (1.6 MW) sustained; 2 shafts
Speed, knots: 22. **Range, miles:** 600 at 12 kts
Complement: 12
Guns: 1—3 in (76 mm). 2—25 mm (twin). 5—7.62 mm MGs. 1 BP6 rocket launcher.
Mines: 9.
Radars: Spin Trough; I band

Comment: Two transferred March 1984, two in January 1985. All operational in 1992.

2 SWIFT PBR Mk II

Displacement, tons: 8 full load
Dimensions, feet (metres): 32 × 11 × 2.6 (9 8 × 3.4 × 0.8)
Main machinery: 2 diesels; 2 waterjets
Speed, knots: 25
Complement: 5
Guns: 3—12.7 mm MGs.

Comment: Transferred in 1974. Sole survivors of many and deleted in error some years ago.

SHMEL *1992, Ships of the World*

5 KANO and 20 ZODIAC CLASSES (RIVER PATROL CRAFT)

Comment: Small patrol boats. Of a total of about 20 Kano class, five were operational in 1992. There are also some 20 Zodiac rubber boats imported by the United Nations.

CAMEROON

Headquarters' Appointment

Chief of Naval Staff:
Commander Guillaume Ngouah Ngally

Diplomatic Representation

Naval Attaché in London:
Lieutenant Commander E Babou

Personnel

1993: 1300

Bases

Douala, Limbe, Kribi

Mercantile Marine

Lloyd's Register of Shipping:
47 vessels of 34 765 tons gross

DELETIONS

1990 *Quartier Maître Alfred Motto*
1992 *Indépendance, Reunification, Souellaba, Machtigal, Manoka*

PATROL FORCES

1 P 48S TYPE (MISSILE PATROL CRAFT)

Name	No	Builders	Commissioned
BAKASSI	P 104	SFCN, Villeneuve-La-Garenne	9 Jan 1984

Displacement, tons: 308 full load
Dimensions, feet (metres): 172.5 × 23.6 × 7.9 (52.6 × 7.2 × 2.4)
Main machinery: 2 SACM 195 V16 CZSHR diesels; 8000 hp(m) (5.88 MW) sustained; 2 shafts
Speed, knots: 25. **Range, miles:** 2000 at 16 kts
Complement: 39 (6 officers)

Missiles: SSM: 8 Aerospatiale MM 40 Exocet (2 quad) launchers; inertial cruise; active radar homing to 70 km (40 nm) at 0.9 Mach; warhead 165 kg; sea-skimmer.
Guns: 2 Bofors 40 mm/70; 85° elevation; 300 rounds/minute to 12.8 km (7 nm); weight of shell 0.96 kg.
Fire control: Two Naja optronic systems. Raca Decca Cane 100 command system.
Radars: Navigation/surface search: Two Racal Decca 1226; I band.

Programmes: Ordered January 1981. Laid down 16 December 1981. Launched 22 October 1982.
Modernisation: Radars have been updated.

BAKASSI *1984, SFCN*

1 PR 48 TYPE (LARGE PATROL CRAFT)

Name	No	Builders	Commissioned
L'AUDACIEUX	P 103	SFCN, Villeneuve-La-Garenne	11 May 1976

Displacement, tons: 250 full load
Dimensions, feet (metres): 157.5 × 23.3 × 7.5 (48 × 7.1 × 2.3)
Main machinery: 2 SACM 195 V12 CZSHR diesels; 6000 hp(m) (4.41 MW) sustained; 2 shafts; cp props
Speed, knots: 23. **Range, miles:** 2000 at 16 kts
Complement: 25 (4 officers)
Missiles: SSM: Fitted for 8 Aerospatiale SS 12M; wire-guided to 5.5 km (3 nm) subsonic; warhead 30 kg.
Guns: 2 Bofors 40 mm/70; 85° elevation; 300 rounds/minute to 12.8 km (7 nm); weight of shell 0.96 kg.

Comment: L'Audacieux ordered in September 1974. Laid down on 10 February 1975, launched on 31 October 1975. Similar to Bizerte class in Tunisia.

2 SIMONNEAU 36 TYPE (RIVER PATROL CRAFT)

Displacement, tons: 8 full load
Dimensions, feet (metres): 36.4 × 11.5 × 3.3 (11.1 × 3.5 × 1)
Main machinery: 2 Volvo-TAMD 61 diesels; 504 hp(m) (368 kW); 2 shafts
Speed, knots: 27. **Range, miles:** 230 at 18 kts
Complement: 6
Guns: 1—7.62 mm MG.

Comment: Delivered in early 1991 for use by Customs.

SIMONNEAU 36 *1991, Simonneau Marine*

4 SIMONNEAU 30 TYPE (RIVER PATROL CRAFT)

Displacement, tons: 4 full load
Dimensions, feet (metres): 30.5 × 9.8 × 2.6 (9.3 × 3 × 0.8)
Main machinery: 2 Volvo-TAMD 41 diesels; 330 hp(m) (243 kW); 2 shafts
Speed, knots: 27. **Range, miles:** 240 at 12 kts
Complement: 4
Guns: 1—7.62 mm MG.

Comment: Delivered in early 1991 for use by Customs.

SIMONNEAU 30 *1991, Simonneau Marine*

82 CAMEROON / Patrol forces — CANADA / Introduction

30 RIVER PATROL CRAFT

PR 01-30

Displacement, tons: 12 full load
Dimensions, feet (metres): 38 × 12.5 × 3.2 *(11.6 × 3.8 × 1)*
Main machinery: 2 Stewart and Stevenson 6V-92TA diesels; 520 hp *(388 kW)* sustained; 2 shafts
Speed, knots: 32. **Range, miles:** 210 at 20 kts
Complement: 4
Guns: 2—12.7 mm MGs. 2—7.62 mm MGs.

Comment: Built by Swiftships and supplied under the US Military Assistance Programme. First 10 delivered in March 1987, second 10 in September 1987 and the remainder by the end of 1987. Ten of the craft are used by the gendarmerie.

PR 01   4/1992

LAND-BASED MARITIME AIRCRAFT

Numbers/Type: 3 Dornier Do 128-6MPA.
Operational speed: 165 kts *(305 km/h)*.
Service ceiling: 32 600 ft *(9335 m)*.
Range: 790 nm *(1460 km)*.
Role/Weapon systems: Sole MR assets with short-range EEZ protection and coastal surveillance. Sensors: MEL Marec radar. Weapons: Unarmed.

MISCELLANEOUS

2 LCMs

BETIKA   **BIBUNDI**

Comment: *Betika* built by Carena, Abidjan, Ivory Coast and refitted in 1987. *Bibundi* built by Tanguy Marine, France in 1982/83. Both are 56 ft *(17.1 m)* in length and have a speed of 10 kts.

3 RAIDER CRAFT

Comment: Supplied by Napco Int in 1987. 19.7 or 23 ft *(6 or 7 m)* in length Boston Whaler Type with twin 140 hp *(104 kW)* outboards giving a speed of 40 kts and a range in excess of 200 miles. Fitted for two 12.7 mm machine guns.

1 TUG

GRAND BATANGA

Comment: Completed by La Manche Dieppe 30 October 1985. Of 96.4 × 29.5 × 12.1 ft *(29.4 × 9 × 3.7 m)*. Fitted with 2 Sacha AGO diesels; 2000 hp(m) *(1.47 MW)*. Speed 12.8 kts.

8 AUXILIARIES

Comment: *Tornade* and *Ouragan*—built in 1966. *St Sylvestre*—built in 1967. *Mungo* operated by Transport Ministry. *Dr Jamot* operated by Health Ministry. *Sanaga* and *Bimbia* harbour launches. *Nyong* at 218 grt buoy tender was built by Cassens, Emden and delivered in December 1990.

CANADA

Headquarters' Appointments

Chief of Defence Staff:
  Admiral J R Anderson, CMM, CD
Vice Chief of Defence Staff:
  Vice Admiral L E Murray, OMM, CD
Director General Maritime Development
  Commodore J A King, CD

Flag Officers

Commander, Maritime Command:
  Vice Admiral P W Cairns, CMM, CD
Commander, Maritime Forces, Atlantic:
  Rear Admiral L G Mason, CD
Commander, Maritime Forces, Pacific:
  Rear Admiral R C Waller, OMM, CD

Diplomatic Representation

Military Representative, Brussels
  Vice Admiral R E George, CMM, CD
Commander, Canadian Defence Liaison Staff, Washington:
  Rear Admiral K J Summers, MSC, OMM, CD
Naval Adviser, London:
  Captain (N) E E Davie, CD
Naval Attaché, Moscow:
  Commander J J Olivier, CD
Naval Attaché, Washington:
  Commodore J D S Reilley, CD
Naval Attaché, Oslo
  Captain D E Pollard, CD
Naval Attaché, The Hague
  Captain J Nethercott, CD
Naval Attaché, Tokyo
  Captain G V Davidson
Naval Attaché, Paris
  Commander J C A Nabeau

Establishment

The Royal Canadian Navy (RCN) was officially established on 4 May 1910. On Royal Assent was given to the Naval Service Act. On 1 February 1968 the Canadian Forces Reorganisation Act unified the three branches of the Canadian Forces and the title 'Royal Canadian Navy' was dropped.

Personnel

(a) 11 800 (Navy)
(b) 7500 (Civilian)
(c) 4600 (Reserves)

Prefix to Ships' Names

HMCS

Bases

Halifax and Esquimalt

Maritime Air Group (MAG)

Commander MAG (Chief of Staff (Air) Marcom)—based in Halifax

Squadron/ Unit	Base	Aircraft	Function
MP 404	Greenwood, NS	Aurora/ Arcturus	LRMP/ Training
MP 405	Greenwood, NS	Aurora	LRMP
HT 406	Shearwater, NS	Sea King	Training
MP 407	Comox, BC	Aurora	LRMP
MP 415	Greenwood, NS	Aurora	LRMP
HS 423	Shearwater, NS	Sea King	ASW
HS 443	Victoria, BC	Sea King	ASW
HOTEF	Shearwater, NS	Sea King	Test
MPEU	Greenwood, NS	Aurora	Test
420 ARS	Shearwater, NS	CP144/CT133	Fleet Support/ Coastal Patrol

Notes

(a) Detachments from HS 423 and HS 443 meet ships' requirements in Atlantic and Pacific Fleets respectively.
(b) No 420 ARS is an Air Reserve Group (ARG) formation under the operational control of Maritime Air Group.
(c) The Department of National Defence is currently in contract with European Helicopter Industries (Canada) for the replacement of the Sea King fleet with EH 101s.
(d) 413 Sqn based in Greenwood, NS, and 442 Sqn based in Comox, BC, are two maritime search and rescue squadrons under the command of Air Transport Group (ATG).
(e) 434 and 414 Squadrons are Fighter Group resources, based in Shearwater, NS, and Comox, BC, respectively, providing resources to Maritime operations with CP-144 Challengers and CT-133 Silver Stars.

Strength of the Fleet

Type	Active	Building (Projected)
Submarines (Patrol)	3	(6)
Destroyers	4	—
Frigates	14	8
Corvettes	—	(6)
MCM Vessels	2	12
Operational Support Ships	3	—
Diving Support Ship	1	—
Patrol Vessels	7	—
Gate Vessels	5	—
Yacht	1	—
Research Vessels	3	—
Transport Oiler, small	1	—
Tenders	8	(6)
Tugs	13	—
Torpedo and Ship Ranging Vessels	4	—
Naval Reserve Unit Tenders	8	—

Fleet Deployment

Atlantic:
1st Destroyer Squadron (Operational East Coast ships)
5th Destroyer Squadron (Ships under refit, trials and work up)
3 Oberon class submarines
Preserver
Diving Support Vessel *Cormorant*

Pacific:
2nd Destroyer Squadron (Operational West Coast ships)
4th Destroyer Squadron (Training ships)
Provider, Protecteur

Mercantile Marine

Lloyd's Register of Shipping:
  1185 vessels of 2 642 795 tons gross

DELETIONS

Frigates

1990 *Saguenay*
1992 *Margaree, Ottawa, Qu'Appelle*
1993 *Mackenzie*

Research Vessels

1990 *Bluethroat*

Tenders

1991 *Songhee, Nimpkish, Ehkoli, YPT 4, Cavalier, Burrard, Queensville, Plainsville, Youville, Loganville*
1992 *Nicholson, Caribou, Beamsville, Rally, Rapid*

PENNANT LIST

Submarines		FFH 338	Winnipeg (building)	Gate Vessels		Tugs	
		FFH 339	Charlottetown (building)				
SS 72	Ojibwa	FFH 340	St John's (building)	YNG 180	Porte St Jean	ATA 531	Saint Anthony
SS 73	Onondaga	FFH 341	Ottawa (building)	YNG 183	Porte St Louis	ATA 533	Saint Charles
SS 74	Okanagan			YNG 184	Porte de la Reine	YTB 640	Glendyne
		Operational Support Ships		YNG 185	Porte Quebec	YTB 641	Glendale
Destroyers				YNG 186	Porte Dauphine	YTB 642	Glenevis
		AOR 508	Provider			YTB 643	Glenbrook
DDH 280	Iroquois	AOR 509	Protecteur			YTB 644	Glenside
DDH 281	Huron	AOR 510	Preserver	Sail Training Ship		YTL 533	Wildwood
DDH 282	Athabaskan					YTL 590	Lawrenceville
DDH 283	Algonquin			YAC 3	Oriole	YTL 591	Parksville
		Diving Support Ship				YTL 592	Listerville
Frigates						YTL 593	Merrickville
		ASL 20	Cormorant	Research Vessels		YTL 594	Marysville
DDH 207	Skeena						
DDH 233	Fraser			AGOR 171	Endeavour	TSRVs	
DD 236	Gatineau	Patrol Vessels		AGOR 172	Quest		
DD 257	Restigouche			AG 121	Riverton	YPT 610	Sechelt
DD 258	Kootenay	PB 140	Fort Steele			YPT 611	Sikanni
DD 259	Terra Nova	PBL 159	Fundy			YPT 612	Sooke
DD 262	Saskatchewan	PBL 160	Chignecto			YPT 613	Stikine
DD 263	Yukon	PBL 161	Thunder	Transport Oiler			
DDH 265	Annapolis	PBL 162	Cowichan			Naval Reserve Unit Tenders	
DDH 266	Nipigon	PBL 163	Miramichi	AOTL 502	Dundurn		
FFH 330	Halifax	PBL 164	Chaleur			PB 191	Adversus
FFH 331	Vancouver					PB 193	Captor
FFH 332	Ville de Québec			Tenders		PB 194	Acadian
FFH 333	Toronto					PB 195	Sydney
FFH 334	Regina (building)	Minesweepers		YDT	6, 8, 9, 10, 11, 12	PB 197	Crossbow
FFH 335	Calgary (building)			YTR 561	Firebird	PB 198	Service
FFH 336	Montreal (building)	MSA 110	Anticosti	YTR 562	Firebrand	PB 199	Standoff
FFH 337	Fredericton (building)	MSA 112	Moresby			YFL 104	Pogo

SUBMARINES

Note: (a) The April 1992 Defence Policy Announcement stated that in a project continuing past the fifteen year planning period, the navy will replace its current submarine fleet with up to six modern conventional submarines in order to provide an under-water capability in both the Atlantic and the Pacific. A request for proposals is expected in 1994 unless it is overtaken by an off-the-shelf purchase of British or Dutch submarines.

(b) Ex-British *Olympus* was purchased in August 1989 and is used for alongside training in Halifax. *Osiris* acquired in 1992 and cannibalised for spares.

3 OBERON CLASS (PATROL SUBMARINES)

Name	No	Builders	Laid down	Launched	Commissioned
OJIBWA (ex-*Onyx*)	72	HM Dockyard, Chatham	27 Sep 1962	29 Feb 1964	23 Sep 1965
ONONDAGA	73	HM Dockyard, Chatham	18 June 1964	25 Sep 1965	22 June 1967
OKANAGAN	74	HM Dockyard, Chatham	25 Mar 1965	17 Sep 1966	22 June 1968

Displacement, tons: 2030 surfaced; 2410 dived
Dimensions, feet (metres): 295.2 × 26.5 × 18 *(90 × 8.1 × 5.5)*
Main machinery: Diesel-electric; 2 ASR 16 VVS-ASR1 diesels; 3680 hp *(2.74 MW)*; 2 AEI motors; 6000 hp *(4.48 MW)*; 2 shafts
Speed, knots: 12 surfaced; 17 dived; 10 snorting
Range, miles: 9000 surfaced at 12 kts
Complement: 65 (7 officers)

Torpedoes: 6—21 in *(533 mm)* bow tubes. 2C Gould Mk 48 Mod 4; dual purpose; active/passive homing to 50 km *(27 nm)*/ 38 km *(21 nm)* at 40/55 kts; warhead 267 kg.
Countermeasures: ESM: Radar warning.
Fire control: Singer Librascope TFCS with Sperry UYK 20 computer.
Radars: Navigation: Kelvin Hughes Type 1006; I band.
Sonars: Plessey Triton Type 2051; hull-mounted; passive/active search and attack; medium frequency.
BAC Type 2007; flank array; passive search; long range; low frequency.
BQG 501 Sperry Micropuffs; passive ranging.
Hermes Electronics/MUSL towed arrays to be fitted from 1993.

Programmes: In 1962 the Ministry of National Defence announced that Canada was to buy three Oberon class submarines in the UK. The first of these patrol submarines was obtained by the Canadian Government from the Royal Navy construction programme. She was laid down as *Onyx* but launched as *Ojibwa*. The other two were Canadian orders. There were some design changes to meet specific new needs including installation of RCN communications equipment and increase of air-conditioning capacity to meet the wide extremes of climate encountered in Canadian operating areas. All are to have their service lives extended until the end of the century.

Modernisation: All underwent SOUP (Submarine Operational Update Project) with more modern sonar and fire control equipment fitted. *Ojibwa* 1980-82, *Onondaga* 1982-84 and *Okanagan* 1984-86. Starting in 1987 weapon launching and fire control systems were upgraded to take the US Mk 48 torpedo which replaced the Mk 37. Plessey Triton Type 2051 sonar purchased in 1989 and is being fitted to replace Type 187C. It is intended to fit all three submarines with towed array sonars starting with *Okanagan* in 1993. TFCS is also being updated at the same time.
Structure: Diving depth, 200 m *(656 ft)*. Stern tubes have been blanked off.

OJIBWA *9/1992, Giorgio Arra*

ONONDAGA *1992, Canadian Maritime Command*

84 CANADA / Destroyers

DESTROYERS

4 IROQUOIS

Name	No	Builders	Laid down	Launched	Commissioned
IROQUOIS	280	Marine Industries Ltd, Sorel	15 Jan 1969	28 Nov 1970	29 July 1972
HURON	281	Marine Industries Ltd, Sorel	15 Jan 1969	3 Apr 1971	16 Dec 1972
ATHABASKAN	282	Davie S B Co, Lauzon	1 June 1969	27 Nov 1970	30 Nov 1972
ALGONQUIN	283	Davie S B Co, Lauzon	1 Sep 1969	23 Apr 1971	30 Sep 1973

Displacement, tons: 5 100 full load
Dimensions, feet (metres): 398 wl; 426 oa × 50 × 15.5 keel/21.5 screws *(121.4; 129.8 × 15.2 × 4.7/6.6)*
Main machinery: COGOG; 2 Pratt & Whitney FT4A2 gas turbines; 50 000 hp *(37 MW)*; 2 GM Allison 570-KF gas turbines; 12 700 hp *(9.5 MW)* sustained; 2 shafts; cp props
Speed, knots: 29+. **Range, miles:** 4500 at 20 kts

Complement: 255 (23 officers) plus aircrew 30 (11 officers)

Missiles: SAM: 1 Martin Marietta Mk 41 VLS ❶ for 29 GDC Standard SM-2MR; command/inertial guidance; semi active radar homing to 73 km *(40 nm)* at 2 Mach.
Guns: 1 OTO Melara 3 in *(76 mm)*/62 Super Rapid ❷; 85° elevation; 120 rounds/minute to 16 km *(8.7 nm)*; weight of shell 6 kg.
 1 GE/GDC 20 mm/76 6-barrelled Vulcan Phalanx Mk 15 ❸; 3000 rounds/minute combined to 1.5 km.
Torpedoes: 6—324 mm Mk 32 (2 triple) tubes ❹. Honeywell Mk 46 Mod 5 (from 1993); anti-submarine; active/passive homing to 11 km *(5.9 nm)* at 40 kts; warhead 44 kg.
Countermeasures: Decoys: 2 Plessey Shield 6-tubed trainable launchers ❺.
 SLQ 25 Nixie; torpedo decoy.
 ESM: MEL SLQ 504 Canews ❻; radar warning.
 ECM: ULQ-6; jammer.
Combat data systems: SHINPADS, automated data handling with UYQ-504 and UYK-505 processors. Links 11 and 14. WSC-IV and SSR-1 SATCOM.
Fire control: Signaal WM 25 including LIROD 8 ❼ optronic director. SAR-8 IRSTD will not now be fitted.
Radars: Air search: Signaal LW 08 ❽; D band.
 Surface search/navigation: Signaal DA 08 ❾; E/F band.
 Fire control: Two Signaal STIR 1.8 ❿; I/J band.
 Tacan: URN 25.
Sonars: Westinghouse SQS 505; combined VDS and hull-mounted; active search and attack; 7 kHz.
 Westinghouse SQS 501; hull-mounted; bottom target classification; high frequency.

Helicopters: 2 CH-124A Sea King ASW ⓫ to be replaced by 2 EH-101 in 1999.

Modernisation: A contract for the Tribal Class Update and Modernisation Project (TRUMP) was awarded to Litton Systems Canada Limited in June 1986. The new equipment reflects the changing role of the ship and replaces systems that did not meet the air defence requirement. *Algonquin* started modernisation in November 1987 at Mil Davie, Quebec, and completed October 1991, followed by *Iroquois*, started November 1988, and completed May 1992. *Athabaskan* entered the yard in September 1991 and is scheduled to complete in early 1995; *Huron* started in June 1992 and should complete in mid-1995.
Structure: These ships are also fitted with a landing deck equipped with double hauldown and Beartrap, pre-wetting system to counter NBC conditions, enclosed citadel, and bridge control of machinery. The flume type anti-roll tanks have been replaced during modernisation with a water displaced fuel system.
Operational: Helicopters can carry 12.7 mm MGs and ESM/FLIR instead of ASW gear.

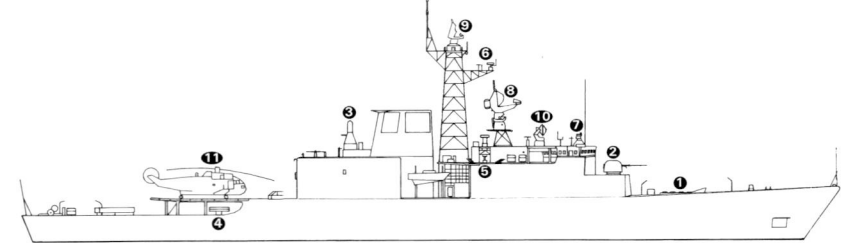

ALGONQUIN (Scale 1 : 1200), Ian Sturton

IROQUOIS 7/1992, Canadian Maritime Command

ALGONQUIN 7/1991, Canadian Maritime Command

FRIGATES

Note: Up to six corvettes are to be acquired in due course. These ships are referred to as CASSEVs (Canadian Sovereignty Surveillance and Enforcement Vessels).

4 + 8 HALIFAX CLASS (FFH)

Name	No	Builders	Laid down	Launched	Completed	Commissioned
HALIFAX	330	St John S B Ltd, New Brunswick	19 Mar 1987	30 Apr 1988	28 June 1991	29 June 1992
VANCOUVER	331	St John S B Ltd, New Brunswick	19 May 1988	8 July 1989	11 Sep 1992	Aug 1993
VILLE DE QUÉBEC	332	Marine Industries Ltd, Sorel	17 Jan 1989	16 May 1991	July 1993	1993
TORONTO	333	St John S B Ltd, New Brunswick	24 Apr 1989	18 Dec 1990	23 Dec 1993	1993
REGINA	334	Marine Industries Ltd, Sorel	6 Oct 1989	25 Oct 1991	Dec 1993	1993
CALGARY	335	Marine Industries Ltd, Sorel	15 June 1991	28 Aug 1992	Sep 1994	1994
MONTREAL	336	St John S B Ltd, New Brunswick	8 Feb 1991	28 Feb 1992	Sep 1993	1993
FREDERICTON	337	St John S B Ltd, New Brunswick	25 Apr 1992	June 1993	May 1994	1994
WINNIPEG	338	St John S B Ltd, New Brunswick	21 Mar 1993	Dec 1993	Jan 1995	1995
CHARLOTTETOWN	339	St John S B Ltd, New Brunswick	Dec 1993	July 1994	Sep 1995	1995
ST JOHN'S	340	St John S B Ltd, New Brunswick	July 1994	Mar 1995	Mar 1996	1996
OTTAWA	341	St John S B Ltd, New Brunswick	Mar 1995	Oct 1995	Sep 1996	1997

Displacement, tons: 5235 full load
Dimensions, feet (metres): 441.9 oa; 408.5 pp × 53.8 × 16.1; 23.3 (screws) *(134.7; 124.5 × 16.4 × 4.9; 7.1)*
Main machinery: CODOG; 2 GE LM 2500 gas turbines; 47 494 hp *(35.43 MW)* sustained
1 SEMT-Pielstick 20 PA6 V 280 diesel; 8800 hp(m) *(6.48 MW)* sustained; 2 shafts; cp props
Speed, knots: 28. **Range, miles:** 7100 at 15 kts (diesel); 4500 at 15 kts (gas)
Complement: 225 (23 officers)

Missiles: SSM: 8 McDonnell Douglas Harpoon Block 1C (2 quad) launchers ❶; active radar homing to 130 km *(70 nm)* at 0.9 Mach; warhead 227 kg.
SAM: 2 Raytheon Sea Sparrow Mk 48 octuple vertical launchers ❷; semi-active radar homing to 14.6 km *(8 nm)* at 2.5 Mach; warhead 39 kg; 28 missiles (16 normally carried).
Guns: 1 Bofors 57 mm/70 Mk 2 ❸; 77° elevation; 220 rounds/minute to 17 km *(9 nm)*; weight of shell 2.4 kg.
1 GE/GDC 20 mm Vulcan Phalanx Mk 15 Mod 1 ❹; anti-missile; 3000 rounds/minute (6 barrels combined) to 1.5 km.
8—12.7 mm MGs.
Torpedoes: 4—324 mm Mk 32 Mod 9 (2 twin) tubes ❺. 24 Honeywell Mk 46 Mod 5; anti-submarine; active/passive homing to 11 km *(5.9 nm)* at 40 kts; warhead 44 kg.
Countermeasures: Decoys: 4 Plessey Shield decoy launchers ❻; triple mountings; fires P8 chaff and P6 IR flares in distraction, decoy or centroid modes.
Nixie SLQ 25; towed acoustic decoy.
ESM: MEL/Lockheed Canews SLQ 504 ❼; radar intercept; (0.5-18 GHz). SRD 502.
ECM: MEL/Lockheed Ramses SLQ 503 ❽; jammer.
Combat data systems: UYC-501 SHINPADS action data automation with UYQ-504 and UYK-505 or 507 (336-341) processors. Links 11 and 14.
Fire control: SWG-1(V) for Harpoon. CDC UYS 503(V); sonobuoy processing system.
Radars: Air search: Raytheon SPS 49(V)5 ❾; C/D band; range 457 km *(250 nm)*.
Air/surface search: Ericsson Sea Giraffe HC 150 ❿; G/H band; range 40 km *(21.6 nm)* against missiles in clear conditions.
Fire control: Two Signaal VM 25 STIR ⓫; K/I band; range 140 km *(76 nm)* for 1 m² target.
Navigation: Sperry Mk 340; I band.
Tacan: URN 25. IFF Mk XII.
Sonars: Westinghouse SQS 505(V)6; hull-mounted; active search and attack; medium frequency.
CDC SQR 501 CANTASS towed array (uses part of Martin Marietta SQR 19 TACTASS).

Helicopters: 1 CH-124A ASW or 1 CH-124B Feltas Sea King ⓬.

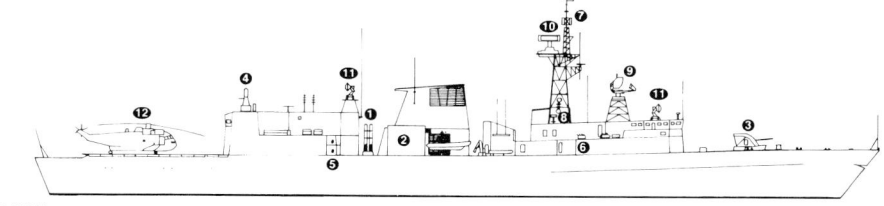
HALIFAX   *(Scale 1 : 1200), Ian Sturton*

Programmes: On 29 June 1983 St John Shipbuilding Ltd won the long running competition for the first six of a new class of patrol frigates to be assisted by Paramax Electronics Inc of Montreal, a subsidiary of Unisys Co (formerly Sperry). Three were subcontracted to Marine Industries Ltd in Lauzon and Sorel. On 18 December 1987 six additional ships of the same design were ordered from St John S. B. Ltd with delivery by 1997. Sometimes referred to as the Halifax class. There have been problems keeping to the planned construction programme. Legal action taken by SJSL to cancel the MIL contract in 1991.

Structure: Plans to lengthen some of the class to increase SAM capacity and improve accommodation have been shelved which means there is limited reserve for mid-life modernisation. Much effort has gone into stealth technology. Gas turbine engines are raft mounted. It is claimed there is more equipment per cubic volume of space than in any other comparable NATO frigate.
Operational: Problems on first of class trials have included higher than designed radiated noise levels which are reported as speed associated. These are in process of being rectified.

VANCOUVER   *9/1992, Canadian Maritime Command*

TORONTO   *10/1992, St John Shipbuilding*

86 CANADA / Frigates

2 ANNAPOLIS CLASS

Name	No	Builders	Laid down	Launched	Commissioned
ANNAPOLIS	265	Halifax Shipyards Ltd, Halifax	July 1960	27 Apr 1963	19 Dec 1964
NIPIGON	266	Marine Industries Ltd, Sorel	Apr 1960	10 Dec 1961	30 May 1964

Displacement, tons: 2400 standard; 2930 full load
Dimensions, feet (metres): 371 × 42 × 14.4 *(113.1 × 12.8 × 4.4)*
Main machinery: 2 Babcock & Wilcox boilers; 600 psi *(43.3 kg/cm sq)*; 850°F *(454°C)*; 2 English Electric turbines; 30 000 hp *(22.4 MW)*; 2 shafts
Speed, knots: 28 (30 on trials). **Range, miles:** 4570 at 14 kts
Complement: 210 (11 officers)

Guns: 2 FMC 3 in *(76 mm)*/50 Mk 33 (twin) ❶; 85° elevation; 50 rounds/minute to 12.8 km *(7 nm)*; weight of shell 6 kg.
Torpedoes: 6—324 mm Mk 32 (2 triple) tubes ❷. Honeywell Mk 46 Mod 5; anti-submarine; active/passive homing to 11 km *(5.9 nm)* at 40 kts; warhead 44 kg.
Countermeasures: Decoys: 4 Loral Hycor SRBOC; chaff and IR flares to 4 km *(2.2 nm)*.
ESM: MEL Canews; radar warning; 0.5-18 GHz.
Combat data systems: Litton ADLIPS automated tactical data handling; Links 11 and 14.
Fire control: GFCS Mk 60.
Radars: Air/surface search: Marconi SPS 503 (CMR 1820) ❸; E/F band; range 128 km *(70 nm)*.
Surface search: Raytheon/Sylvania SPS 10 ❹; G band.
Fire control: Bell SPG 48 ❺; I/J band.
Tacan: URN 25.
Sonars: Westinghouse SQS 505 *(Annapolis)*, SQS 510 *(Nipigon)*; hull-mounted; active search and attack.
SQS 501; hull-mounted; bottom target classification; high frequency.
CDC SQR 501 CANTASS; trials towed array; passive; very low frequency. Uses part of SQR-19.

Helicopters: 1 CH-124A Sea King ASW ❻.

Programmes: Officially classified as DDH. These two ships represented the logical development of the original St Laurent class, through the Restigouche and Mackenzie designs.
Modernisation: A full Delex (Destroyer Life Extension Programme) took place in 1982-85 including new air radar, GFC, communications, sonar and EW equipment. Extension until 1994-96. Both ships fitted with a trials CANTASS vice VDS in 1987/88.
Operational: *Annapolis* is based in the Pacific Fleet.

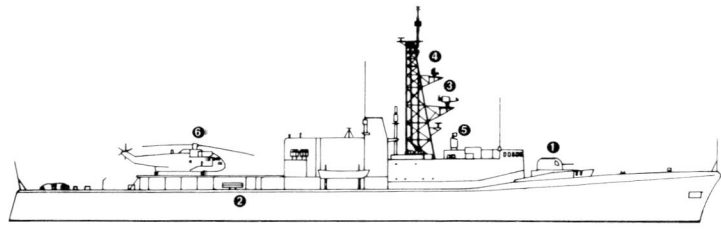
ANNAPOLIS *(Scale 1 : 1200), Ian Sturton*

NIPIGON *11/1991, Harald Carstens*

2 MACKENZIE CLASS

Name	No	Builders	Laid down	Launched	Commissioned
SASKATCHEWAN	262	Victoria Machinery (and Yarrows Ltd)	16 July 1959	1 Feb 1961	16 Feb 1963
YUKON	263	Burrard Dry Dock & Shipbuilding	25 Oct 1959	27 July 1961	25 May 1963

Displacement, tons: 2380 standard; 2880 full load
Dimensions, feet (metres): 366 × 42 × 13.5 *(111.6 × 12.8 × 4.1)*
Main machinery: 2 Babcock & Wilcox boilers; 600 psi *(43.3 kg/cm sq)*; 850°F *(454°C)*; 2 English Electric turbines; 30 000 hp *(22.4 MW)*; 2 shafts
Speed, knots: 28. **Range, miles:** 4750 at 14 kts
Complement: 210 (11 officers)

Guns: 2 Vickers 3 in *(76 mm)*/70 Mk 6 mounting (twin) ❶; 90° elevation; 90 rounds/minute to 17 km *(9 nm)*; weight of shell 7 kg.
2 FMC 3 in *(76 mm)*/50 Mk 33 mounting (twin) ❷; 85° elevation; 50 rounds/minute to 12.8 km *(7 nm)*; weight of shell 6 kg.
Torpedoes: 6—324 mm Mk 32 (2 triple) tubes ❸. Honeywell Mk 46; anti-submarine; active/passive homing to 11 km *(5.9 nm)* at 40 kts; warhead 44 kg.
Countermeasures: ESM: WLR 1; radar warning.
Combat data systems: Litton ADLIPS; automated tactical data handling; Links 11 and 14.
Fire control: GFCS Mk 69. GFCS Mk 63.

Radars: Air search: RCA SPS 12 ❹; D band; range 119 km *(65 nm)*.
Surface search: Raytheon SPS 10 ❺; G band.
Fire control: SPG 48 ❻; I/J band.
SPG 34; I/J band.
Sonars: Westinghouse SQS 505; combined VDS and hull-mounted; active search and attack; medium frequency.
SQS 501; hull-mounted; bottom target classification; high frequency.

Programmes: Officially classified as DD.
Modernisation: Both modernised at Esquimalt by Burrard/Yarrow Inc under Delex (Destroyer Life Extension Programme) 1982-85 including improved sonar and communications, and modifications to SPS 12 radar.
Operational: These last two of the class are part of the Training Squadron in the Pacific Fleet.

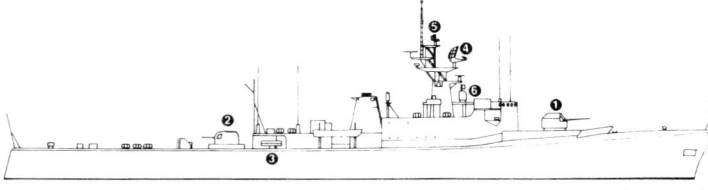
SASKATCHEWAN *(Scale 1 : 1200), Ian Sturton*

SASKATCHEWAN *10/1991, John Mortimer*

Frigates / CANADA

4 IMPROVED RESTIGOUCHE CLASS

Name	No	Builders	Laid down	Launched	Commissioned
GATINEAU	236	Davie Shipbuilding & Repairing	30 Apr 1953	3 June 1957	17 Feb 1959
RESTIGOUCHE	257	Canadian Vickers, Montreal	15 July 1953	22 Nov 1954	7 June 1958
KOOTENAY	258	Burrard Dry Dock & Shipbuilding	21 Aug 1952	15 June 1954	7 Mar 1959
TERRA NOVA	259	Victoria Machinery Depot Co	14 Nov 1952	21 June 1955	6 June 1959

Displacement, tons: 2390 standard; 2900 full load
Dimensions, feet (metres): 371 × 42 × 14.1 *(113.1 × 12.8 × 4.3)*
Main machinery: 2 Babcock & Wilcox boilers; 600 psi *(43.3 kg/cm sq)*; 850°F *(454°C)*; 2 English Electric turbines; 30 000 hp *(22.4 MW)*; 2 shafts
Speed, knots: 28. **Range, miles:** 4750 at 14 kts
Complement: 214 (13 officers)

Missiles: SSM: 8 McDonnell Douglas Harpoon 2 quad launchers ❶ (Gulf 1991/92); active radar homing to 130 km *(70 nm)* at 0.9 Mach; warhead 227 kg.
A/S: Honeywell ASROC Mk 112 octuple launcher ❷; 8 reloads; inertial guidance to 1.6-10 km *(1-5.4 nm)*; payload Mk 46 torpedo. Replaced by 8 Harpoon during Gulf 1991/92.
Guns: 2 Vickers 3 in *(76 mm)*/70 (twin) Mk 6 ❸; dual purpose; 90° elevation; 90 rounds/minute to 17 km *(9 nm)*; weight of shell 7 kg.
1 GE/GDC 20 mm/76 6-barrelled Vulcan Phalanx Mk 15 (modified) ❹ (Gulf 1991/92); 3000 rounds/minute combined to 1.5 km.
2 Bofors 40 mm/60 ❺ (Gulf 1991/92).
Torpedoes: 6—324 mm Mk 32 (2 triple) tubes ❻. Honeywell Mk 46 Mod 5; anti-submarine; active/passive homing to 11 km *(5.9 nm)* at 40 kts; warhead 44 kg.
Countermeasures: Decoys: 4 Loral Hycor SRBOC Mk 36 ❼; 4 launchers with 4 fixed barrels firing chaff decoys and IR flares to 4 km *(2.2 nm)*. Plessey Shield chaff launchers (Gulf 1991/92).
ESM: Canews ❽; radar warning.
ECM: ULQ-6; jammer.
Combat data systems: Litton ADLIPS; automated data handling; Links 11 and 14. SATCOM ❾.
Fire control: GFCS Mk 69.
Radars: Air search: Marconi SPS 503 (CMR 1820); E/F band; or Ericsson Sea Giraffe HC 150 ❿; G/H band.
Surface search: Raytheon SPS 10 ⓫; G band.
Navigation: Sperry 127E; I band.
Fire control: Bell SPG 48 ⓬; I/J band.
Tacan: URN 25.
Sonars: Westinghouse SQS 505; combined VDS and hull-mounted; active search and attack; medium frequency.
C-Tech mine avoidance active; high frequency.
SQS 501; hull-mounted; bottom target classification; high frequency.

Programmes: Officially classified as DD.
Modernisation: These four ships were first refitted with ASROC aft and lattice foremast. Work included removing the after 3 in/50 twin gun mounting and one Limbo A/S Mk 10 triple mortar, to make way for ASROC and variable depth sonar. Refits also included improvements to communications fit and completed 1968-73. Three other ships of the class were paid off without being refitted. All four modernised again under Delex programme 1983-86 with new air radar, GFCS, communications and EW equipment. The Bofors rocket launcher replaced by Super RBOC and Tacan fitted on a pole mast replacing the top section of the lattice mast. Triple Mark 32 torpedo tubes fitted. Air search radars are also being replaced again from 1992.
Operational: For operational deployments to the Gulf in 1991 and 1992 two ships had the ASROC launcher replaced by 8 Harpoon SSM, the Limbo Mk 10 by Phalanx, and the ships boats by two single Bofors 40 mm/60. All reverted to standard fit by the end of 1992 except that the Limbo launchers have been removed and SATCOM fitted. *Restigouche* and *Kootenay* based in the Pacific Fleet. *Columbia* (paid off in 1974) is used as a harbour training ship at Esquimalt. Additional 12.7 mm MGs can be carried plus Blowpipe and Javelin shoulder-launched SAM.

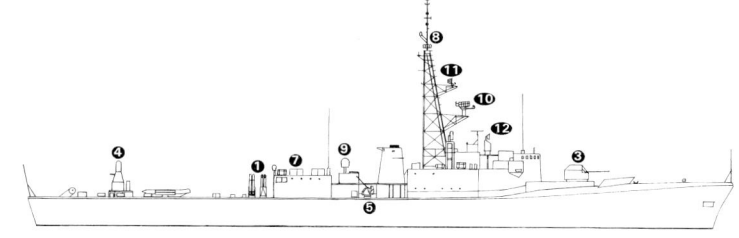
GULF 1991/92 *(Scale 1 : 1200), Ian Sturton*

RESTIGOUCHE (Gulf 1991/92 – see *Operational*) *5/1991, David Warren*

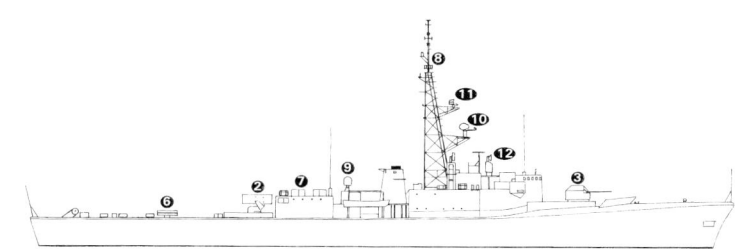
GATINEAU *(Scale 1 : 1200), Ian Sturton*

GATINEAU *7/1992, Maritime Photographic*

88 CANADA / Frigates

2 ST LAURENT CLASS

Name	No	Builders	Laid down	Launched	Commissioned
SKEENA	207	Burrard Dry Dock & Shipbuilding	1 June 1951	19 Aug 1952	30 Mar 1957
FRASER	233	Yarrows Ltd, Esquimalt, BC	11 Dec 1951	19 Feb 1953	28 June 1957

Displacement, tons: 2260 standard; 3051 full load (after conversion)
Dimensions, feet (metres): 366 × 42 × 14 (hull) *(111.6 × 12.8 × 5.4)*
Main machinery: 2 Babcock & Wilcox boilers; 600 psi *(43.3 kg/cm sq)*; 850°F *(454°C)*; 2 English Electric turbines; 30 000 hp *(22.4 MW)*; 2 shafts
Speed, knots: 27. **Range, miles:** 4570 at 12 kts
Complement: 213 (16 officers) plus 20 aircrew (7 officers)

Guns: 2 FMC 3 in *(76 mm)*/50 Mk 33 (twin) ❶; dual purpose; 85° elevation; 50 rounds/minute to 12.8 km *(7 nm)*; weight of shell 6 kg.
Torpedoes: 6—324 mm Mk 32 (2 triple) tubes ❷. Honeywell Mk 46; anti-submarine; active/passive homing to 11 km *(5.9 nm)* at 40 kts; warhead 44 kg.
Countermeasures: ESM: WLR 1 ❸; radar warning.
Fire control: GFCS Mk 63.
Radars: Air search: RCA SPS 12 ❹; D band; range 119 km *(65 nm)*.
Surface search: Raytheon SPS 10 ❺; G band.
Fire control: Bell SPG 48; I/J band.
Navigation: Sperry Mk II; I band.
Tacan: URN 20 ❻.
Sonars: SQS 503; hull-mounted; active search and attack; medium frequency.
SQS 504; VDS; active search; medium frequency *(Skeena)*.
SQR 19 ETASS (wet end with experimental processor) *(Fraser)*; passive towed array; low frequency.
SQS 502; hull-mounted; active attack; high frequency.
SQS 501; hull-mounted; bottom target classification; high frequency.
Helicopters: 1 CH-124B Sea King Heltas *(Fraser)* ❼; 1 CH-124A Sea King ASW *(Skeena)* ❽.

Programmes: Officially classified as DDH. The first major warships to be designed in Canada.
Modernisation: Both modernised under Delex programme 1979-84 although no new sensors were included. Experimental towed array sonar system (ETASS) fitted to *Fraser* in 1988. In providing helicopter platforms and hangars, an after 3 in/50 Mk 33 was removed and the twin Mk 10 Limbo A/S Mortar was reduced to a single mount. The mortars have since been removed from all Canadian ships. *Fraser's* mortar mount was removed during installation of ETASS. *Fraser* has a lattice radar-mast between the funnels for the TACAN aerial while *Skeena* has this aerial on a pole mast.
Structure: Twin funnels to permit fwd extension of the helicopter hangar. Fitted with fin stabilisers. Gunhouses are of glass fibre.
Operational: *Assiniboine* paid off in 1989 and is used as a harbour training ship at Halifax. These last two survivors of the class are planned to pay off by 1995.

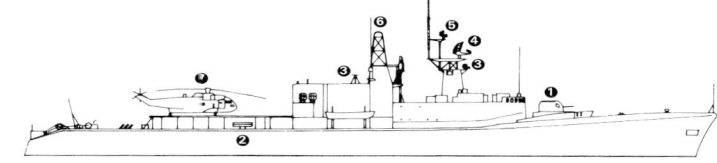

FRASER (Scale 1 : 1200), Ian Sturton

FRASER 10/1988, Maritime Photographic

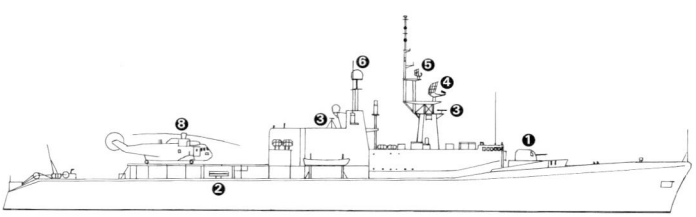

SKEENA (Scale 1 : 1200), Ian Sturton

SKEENA 7/1992, Maritime Photographic

OPERATIONAL SUPPORT SHIPS

Name	No	Builders	Laid down	Launched	Commissioned
PROTECTEUR	AOR 509	St John Dry Dock Co Ltd, NB	17 Oct 1967	18 July 1968	30 Aug 1969
PRESERVER	AOR 510	St John Dry Dock Co Ltd, NB	17 Oct 1967	29 May 1969	30 July 1970

Displacement, tons: 8380 light; 24 700 full load
Dimensions, feet (metres): 564 × 76 × 30 *(171.9 × 23.2 × 9.1)*
Main machinery: 2 boilers; 1 GE Canada turbine; 21 000 hp *(15.7 MW)*; 1 shaft; bow thruster
Speed, knots: 21. **Range, miles:** 4100 at 20 kts; 7500 at 11.5 kts
Complement: 290 (28 officers)
Cargo capacity: 13 700 tons fuel; 400 tons aviation fuel; 1048 tons dry cargo; 1250 tons ammunition; 2 cranes (15 ton lift)
Guns: 2 FMC 3 in *(76 mm)*/50 Mk 33 (twin). Mounted in the bow and under local control it was removed from both ships in 1983 but replaced in *Protecteur* in 1990 for Gulf deployment only.
2 GE/GDC 20 mm/76 6-barrelled Vulcan Phalanx Mk 15.
Countermeasures: Decoys: 4 Plessey Shield chaff launchers.
ESM: Racal Kestrel SLQ 504; radar warning.
Combat data systems: ADLIPS with Link 11; SATCOM WSC-3(V).
Radars: Surface search: SPS 502 with Mk XII IFF.
Navigation: Sperry Mk II. Racal Decca TM 969; I band.
Tacan: URN 20.
Sonars: Westinghouse SQS 505; hull-mounted; active search.
C-Tech mine avoidance for Gulf.
Helicopters: 3 CH-124A ASW or CH-124B Heltas Sea King.

Comment: An improved design based on the prototype *Provider*. Four replenishment positions. Both have been used as Flagships and troop carriers. They can carry anti-submarine helicopters, military vehicles and bulk equipment for sealift purposes; also four LCVPs. For the Gulf deployment in 1991, the 76 mm gun was remounted, two Vulcan Phalanx and two Bofors 40/60 guns were fitted, 4 Plessey Shield chaff launchers and ESM equipment were provided for *Protecteur*. Additionally, all helicopters carried 12.7 mm MGs and ESM/FLIR equipment instead of ASW gear. Bofors and 76 mm gun later removed from *Protecteur*. Remaining equipment retained and also installed in *Preserver* during her 1992 refit. Weapon system positions in *Protecteur* to be changed during her 1993 refit. *Protecteur* transferred to the Pacific Fleet November 1992.

PRESERVER *1992, Canadian Maritime Command*

Name	No	Builders	Laid down	Launched	Commissioned
PROVIDER	AOR 508	Davie Shipbuilding Ltd, Lauzon	1 May 1961	5 July 1962	28 Sep 1963

Displacement, tons: 7300 light; 22 000 full load
Dimensions, feet (metres): 555 × 76 × 32 *(169.2 × 23.2 × 9.8)*
Main machinery: 2 boilers; 1 GE Canada steam turbine; 21 000 hp *(15.7 MW)*; 1 shaft
Speed, knots: 21. **Range, miles:** 3600 at 20 kts
Complement: 166 (15 officers)
Cargo capacity: 12 000 tons fuel; 900 tons aviation fuel; 250 tons dry cargo
Countermeasures: ESM: Racal Kestrel SLQ 504; radar warning.
Combat data systems: ADLIPS with Link 11; SATCOM WSC-3(V).
Radars: Navigation: Racal Decca TM 969; I band.
Helicopters: 3 CH-124A Sea King ASW.

Comment: The flight deck can receive the largest and heaviest helicopters. A total of 20 electrohydraulic winches is fitted on deck for ship-to-ship movements of cargo and supplies, as well as shore-to-ship requirements when alongside. Based in the Pacific Fleet. Can be fitted with Bofors and Vulcan Phalanx guns, chaff and ESM if sent on operational deployments.

PROVIDER *10/1991, John Mortimer*

1 DUN CLASS TANKER

DUNDURN AOTL 502 (ex-AOC 502)

Displacement, tons: 950 light; 1500 full load
Dimensions, feet (metres): 178.8 × 32.2 × 13 *(54.5 × 9.8 × 3.9)*
Main machinery: 1 Fairbanks-Morse 38D8-1/8-4 diesel; 708 hp *(528 kW)* sustained; 1 shaft
Speed, knots: 10
Complement: 24
Cargo capacity: 790 tons fuel; 25 tons dry cargo

Comment: Small tanker, classed as fleet auxiliary. Based on West Coast.

DUNDURN *10/1992, Canadian Maritime Command*

FLEET DIVING SUPPORT SHIP

Name	No	Builder	Commissioned
CORMORANT (ex-*Aspa Quarto*)	ASL 20	Marelli, Italy	10 Nov 1978 (CAF)

Displacement, tons: 2350 full load
Dimensions, feet (metres): 245 × 39 × 16.5 *(74.7 × 11.9 × 5)*
Main machinery: Diesel-electric; 3 Marelli-Deutz ACR 12456 EV diesels; 1800 hp(m) *(1.32 MW)*; 1 shaft; cp prop
Speed, knots: 14. **Range, miles:** 13 000 at 12 kts
Complement: 74
Radars: Navigation: Two Decca 1229; I band.

Comment: Ex-Italian stern trawler bought in 1975 which underwent maintenance and design modification until 1977. She was then taken in hand for conversion by Davie Shipbuilding Ltd, Lauzon, returning to Halifax a year later to commission. She carries two submersibles, *SDL-1* and *PISCES IV*, in a heated hangar, side-scan sonar and a ROV. She is capable of conducting mixed gas diving operations to 330 ft *(100 m)*. *SDL-1* and *PISCES IV* are both untethered craft capable of operations to 2000 ft *(610 m)*. *SDL-1* has a lock-out compartment to support diving operations on air to 150 ft *(45 m)*. Several high frequency sonic devices are fitted. In 1980, this was the first ship in the Canadian Navy to carry women crew members.

CORMORANT *1990, van Ginderen Collection*

SHIPBORNE AIRCRAFT

Note: In 1992 the decision was taken to order 35 Anglo/Italian EH-101 naval helicopters, to start replacing the Sea Kings in 1999.

Numbers/Type: 27/6 Sikorsky CH-124A ASW/CH-124B Heltas Sea King.
Operational speed: 110 kts *(203 km/h)*.
Service ceiling: 17 000 ft *(5150 m)*.
Range: 410 nm *(760 km)*.
Role/Weapon systems: ASW, surface surveillance and support; Tribal class carry two helicopters, AORs three. CH-124B Heltas Sea Kings dedicated to *Fraser*, Annapolis class and City class ships. Sensors: CH-124A ASW – APS-503 radar, sonobuoys, ASQ-13 dipping sonar. Some modified for FLIR and GPS. During Gulf operations, FLIR modified aircraft were also fitted with APR-39, ALE-37 chaff dispenser and ALQ-144 IR countermeasures. CH-124B Heltas – APS-503 radar, UYS-503 sonobuoy processor, GPS and ASQ-504 MAD. Weapons: Up to four Mk 46 torpedoes for both aircraft types.

SEA KING CH-124A *1992, Canadian Maritime Command*

LAND-BASED MARITIME AIRCRAFT (FRONT LINE)

Numbers/Type: 18/3 Lockheed CP-140 Aurora/P-3C Arcturus.
Operational speed: 410 kts *(760 km/h)*.
Service ceiling: 28 300 ft *(8625 m)*.
Range: 4000 nm *(7410 km)*.
Role/Weapon systems: Aurora operated for long-range maritime surveillance on Atlantic and Pacific Oceans; roles include ASW/ASV and SAR; three Arcturus delivered in 1992 for unarmed High Arctic patrol. Sensors: APS-116 radar, IFF, ESM, ECM. Aurora also has DIFAR processor, ASQ-81 MAD, OL 5004 processor. Weapons: 8 Mk 46 Mod 5 torpedoes.

MINE WARFARE FORCES

2 MINESWEEPERS AUXILIARY (MSA)

Name	No	Builders	Commissioned
ANTICOSTI (ex-*Jean Tide*)	MSA 110	Allied SB, Vancouver	Sep 1973
MORESBY (ex-*Joyce Tide*)	MSA 112	Allied SB, Vancouver	Apr 1973

Displacement, tons: 2205 full load
Dimensions, feet (metres): 191 × 43 × 17 *(58.2 × 13.1 × 5.2)*
Main machinery: 4 Nohab Polar SF 16RS diesels; 4600 hp(m) *(3.38 MW)*; 2 shafts; Gil Jet bow thruster; 575 hp *(429 kW)*
Speed, knots: 13.5. **Range, miles:** 12 000 at 13 kts
Complement: 18 (5 officers)
Guns: 2—7.62 mm MGs.
Countermeasures: MCM: BAJ Mk 9 mechanical sweep with WSMF (monitoring equipment).
Radars: Navigation: 2 Racal Decca; I band.
Sonars: Side scan towed VDS; high frequency.

Comment: Former offshore towing/supply vessels Ice class 3, suitable for navigation in light ice. Purchased in March 1988 and commissioned 7 May 1989. Mechanical sweeps, sonar, Hyperfix and PINS 9000 navigation system completed fitting in mid-1991. Mixed crews of Regulars and Reservists. They will operate until the MCDV vessels start to enter service in 1995.

MORESBY *8/1991, Canadian Maritime Command*

0 + 12 MARITIME COASTAL DEFENCE VESSELS (MCDV)

Displacement, tons: 962 full load
Dimensions, feet (metres): 180.4 × 37.1 × 11.2 *(55 × 11.3 × 3.4)*
Main machinery: Diesel-electric; 3000 hp(m) *(2.2 MW)*; 2 shafts; 2 azimuth thrusters
Speed, knots: 15. **Range, miles:** 5000 at 12 kts
Complement: 37
Guns: 1 Bofors 40 mm/60 Mk 5C. 2—12.7 mm MGs.
Countermeasures: MCM: Double Oropesa team sweep; wire sweep WS Mk 9; acoustic and magnetic sweeps; 1 ROV.
Radars: Surface search: E/F band.
Navigation: I band.
Sonars: Towfish sidescan; high frequency; for route survey.

Comment: Tenders requested 31 August 1988. Contract awarded to Fenco Engineers on 2 October 1991. The design is by German Marine, Dartmouth and the ships are to be built by Halifax-Dartmouth Industries starting in 1993 with a first of class delivery in 1995. Thomson-CSF are to provide combat system support. The vessels are to combine MCM capabilities with general patrol duties and will be stationed on both coasts and in the St Lawrence. Reserve manpower is to be increased from 6500 to 8500 to allow continuous operation on both coasts.

MCDV (artist impression) *1991, Canadian Maritime Command*

SAIL TRAINING SHIP

Name	No	Builders	Launched
ORIOLE	YAC 3	Owens	4 June 1921

Displacement, tons: 78.2 full load
Dimensions, feet (metres): 102 × 19 × 9 *(31.1 × 5.8 × 2.7)*
Main machinery: 1 Cummins diesel; 165 hp *(123 kW)*; 1 shaft
Speed, knots: 8
Complement: 24 (2 officers)

Comment: Commissioned in the Navy in 1948 and based at Esquimalt. Sail area (with spinnaker) 11 000 sq ft. Height of mainmast 94 ft *(28.7 m)*, mizzen 55.2 ft *(16.8 m)*. Usually cruises with 14 trainee officers at a time.

PATROL VESSELS

Note: There are plans for a new 46 m coastal patrol vessel.

1 FORT CLASS PATROL VESSEL (PB)

Name	No	Builders	Commissioned
FORT STEELE	PB 140	Canadian S B and Eng Co	Nov 1955

Displacement, tons: 85
Dimensions, feet (metres): 118 × 21 × 7 *(36 × 6.4 × 2.1)*
Main machinery: 2 Paxman 12 YJCM diesels; 3000 hp *(2.24 MW)*; 2 shafts; KaMeWa cp props
Speed, knots: 18. **Range, miles:** 1200 at 16 kts
Complement: 16

Comment: Steel hull aluminium superstructure. Twin rudders. Acquired by DND in 1973 from RCMP—acts as Reserve Training ship based at Halifax.

FORT STEELE *11/1989, van Ginderen Collection*

6 BAY CLASS Ex-MSC (PBL)

Name	No	Builders	Commissioned
FUNDY	PBL 159	Davie Shipbuilding Co, Lauzon	27 Nov 1956
CHIGNECTO	PBL 160	Davie Shipbuilding Co, Lauzon	1 Aug 1957
THUNDER	PBL 161	Port Arthur S B Co	3 Oct 1957
COWICHAN	PBL 162	Yarrows Ltd, Esquimalt	19 Dec 1957
MIRAMICHI	PBL 163	Victoria Machinery Depot Co	28 Oct 1957
CHALEUR	PBL 164	Marine Industries Ltd, Sorel	12 Sep 1957

Displacement, tons: 370 standard; 470 full load
Dimensions, feet (metres): 164 × 30.2 × 9.2 *(50 × 9.2 × 2.8)*
Main machinery: 2 GM 12-278A diesels; 2200 hp *(1.64 MW)*; 2 shafts
Speed, knots: 15. **Range, miles:** 4500 at 11 kts
Complement: 35 (4 officers)
Guns: 1 Bofors 40 mm/60 (fitted for but not with).
Radars: Surface Search: Racal Decca; I band.

Comment: Wooden hulls with aluminium frames and decks. There were originally 20 vessels of this class of which six were transferred to France, four to Turkey and four sold commercially. Named after Canadian straits and bays. Designation changed from AMC to MCB in 1954. They were redesignated as Patrol Escorts (small) (PF) in 1972, being used as training ships and PB from 1979. *Fundy* and *Thunder* in reserve in 1992.

THUNDER   7/1987, van Ginderen Collection

5 PORTE CLASS (GATE VESSELS)

Name	No	Builders	Commissioned
PORTE ST JEAN	YNG 180	Geo T Davie, Lauzon	4 June 1952
PORTE ST LOUIS	YNG 183	Geo T Davie, Lauzon	28 Aug 1952
PORTE DE LA REINE	YNG 184	Victoria Machinery	19 Sep 1952
PORTE QUEBEC	YNG 185	Burrard Dry Dock	7 Oct 1952
PORTE DAUPHINE	YNG 186	Ferguson Ind.	12 Dec 1952

Displacement, tons: 429 full load
Dimensions, feet (metres): 125.5 × 26.3 × 13 *(38.3 × 8 × 4)*
Main machinery: Diesel-electric; 1 Fairbanks-Morse 38D8-1/8-6 diesel generator; 724 kW sustained; 1 shaft
Speed, knots: 11. **Range, miles:** 4000 at 10 kts
Complement: 23 (3 officers)
Radars: Navigation: Racal Decca; I band.

Comment: Of trawler design. Multi-purpose vessels used for operating gates in A/S booms, fleet auxiliaries, anti-submarine netlayers for entrances to defended harbours. Can be fitted for minesweeping. First four used during Summer for training Reserves. *Porte Dauphine* was re-acquired from DOT in 1974 and employed on West Coast with *Porte de la Reine* and *Porte Quebec*.

PORTE DE LA REINE   1989, van Ginderen Collection

RESEARCH VESSELS

Name	No	Builders	Commissioned
QUEST	AGOR 172	Burrard Dry Dock Co, Vancouver	21 Aug 1969

Displacement, tons: 2130
Dimensions, feet (metres): 235 × 42 × 15.5 *(71.6 × 12.8 × 4.6)*
Main machinery: Diesel-electric; 4 Fairbanks-Morse 38D8-1/8-9 diesel generators; 4.37 MW sustained; 2 shafts; cp props
Speed, knots: 16. **Range, miles:** 10 000 at 12 kts
Complement: 55
Helicopters: Platform only.

Comment: Built for the Naval Research Establishment of the Defence Research Board for acoustic, hydrographic and general oceanographic work. Capable of operating in heavy ice in the company of an icebreaker. Launched on 9 July 1968. Based at Halifax and does line array acoustic research in the straits of the northern archipelago.

QUEST   1986, Canadian Maritime Command

Name	No	Builders	Commissioned
ENDEAVOUR	AGOR 171	Yarrows Ltd, Esquimalt, BC	9 Mar 1965

Displacement, tons: 1560
Dimensions, feet (metres): 236 × 38.5 × 13 *(71.9 × 11.7 × 4)*
Main machinery: Diesel-electric; 4 Fairbanks-Morse 38D8-1/8-9 diesel generators; 4.36 MW; 2 shafts; cp props
Speed, knots: 16. **Range, miles:** 10 000 at 12 kts
Complement: 50 (10 officers, 13 scientists, 2 aircrew)
Helicopters: 1 light.

Comment: A naval research ship designed primarily for anti-submarine research. Flight deck 48 × 31 ft *(14.6 × 9.4 m)*. Stiffened for operating in ice-covered areas. Able to turn in 2.5 times her own length. Two 9 ton Austin-Weston telescopic cranes are fitted. There are two oceanographical winches each holding 5000 fathoms of wire, two bathythermograph winches and a deep-sea anchoring and coring winch. She has acoustic insulation in her machinery spaces.

ENDEAVOUR   1990, Canadian Maritime Command

Name	No	Builders	Commissioned
RIVERTON (ex-*Smit-Lloyd* 112)	AG 121	De Waal, Netherlands	1975

Displacement, tons: 2563 full load
Dimensions, feet (metres): 209 × 43.5 × 16.5 *(63.9 × 13.3 × 5.1)*
Main machinery: 2 6TM-410 Stork-Werkspoor diesels; 10 100 hp(m) *(7.44 MW)* sustained; 2 shafts; Kort nozzle bow thrusters
Speed, knots: 15.5. **Range, miles:** 13 000 at 12 kts
Complement: 10 (5 officers) plus 16 scientists

Comment: An offshore supply and support vessel acquired 3 March 1989 for conversion to a general purpose auxiliary research and support ship. Replaced *Bluethroat* in mid-1990 and used for the CPF first of class trials.

RIVERTON   1991, Canadian Maritime Command

SUPPORT VESSELS AND TENDERS

5 NAVAL RESERVE TENDERS

Name	No	Name	No
ADVERSUS	PB 191	SYDNEY	PB 195
CAPTOR	PB 193	STANDOFF	PB 199
ACADIAN	PB 194		

Displacement, tons: 48 full load (191-195); 85 (199)
Main machinery: 2 Paxman YJCM diesels; 2800 hp *(2.1 MW)*; 2 shafts
Speed, knots: 16. **Range, miles:** 900 at 13 kts
Complement: 18

Comment: 191 to 195, completed by Smith and Rhulorel, Lunenburg, NS in 1968 transferred from RCMP in 1975. 199 transferred in 1980. Some deleted in 1992.

CAPTOR   1991, van Ginderen Collection

92 CANADA / Support vessels and tenders — Tugs

4 TORPEDO AND SHIP RANGING VESSELS (TSRV)

Name	No	Builders	Commissioned
SECHELT	YPT 610	West Coast Manly	10 Nov 1990
SIKANNI	YPT 611	West Coast Manly	10 Nov 1990
SOOKE	YPT 612	West Coast Manly	10 Nov 1990
STIKINE	YPT 613	West Coast Manly	10 Nov 1990

Displacement, tons: 290 full load
Dimensions, feet (metres): 108.5 × 27.8 × 7.8 *(33.1 × 8.5 × 2.4)*
Main machinery: 2 Caterpillar 3412T diesels; 1080 hp *(806 kW)* sustained; 2 shafts
Speed, knots: 12.5
Complement: 4

Comment: Based at the Nanoose Bay Maritime Experimental and Test Range. Replaced the 1940s vintage TRVs.

SECHELT *1991, Canadian Maritime Command*

5 SERVICE CRAFT

CROSSBOW PB 197   FIREBIRD YTR 561
SERVICE PB 198   FIREBRAND YTR 562
POGO YFL 104

Comment: The two YTRs are 130 ton firefighting craft. The other three craft are used as Naval Reserve Unit tenders.

6 DIVING TENDERS

YDT 6, 8, 9, 10, 11, 12

Displacement, tons: 70; 110 (YDT 11-12)
Main machinery: 2 GM diesels; 165 hp *(123 kW)* (228 hp *(170 kW)* in YDT 11-12); 2 shafts
Speed, knots: 11
Complement: 23 (3 officers)

Comment: Can operate four divers at a time to 75 m. Recompression chamber.

TUGS

2 SAINT CLASS

Name	No	Builders	Commissioned
SAINT ANTHONY	ATA 531	St John Dry Dock Co	22 Feb 1957
SAINT CHARLES	ATA 533	St John Dry Dock Co	7 June 1957

Displacement, tons: 840
Dimensions, feet (metres): 151.5 × 33 × 17 *(46.2 × 10 × 5.2)*
Main machinery: Diesel; 1920 hp *(1.43 MW)*; 1 shaft
Speed, knots: 14
Complement: 21

Comment: Ocean tugs. Authorised under the 1951 Programme. Originally class of three. There are plans to replace them in the mid-1990s with two 1500 ton support vessels.

SAINT ANTHONY *1983, Giorgio Arra*

5 GLEN CLASS (HARBOUR/COASTAL)

Name	No	Builders	Commissioned
GLENDYNE	YTB 640	Yarrows, Esquimalt	8 Aug 1975
GLENDALE	YTB 641	Yarrows, Esquimalt	16 Sep 1975
GLENEVIS	YTB 642	Georgetown S Y, PEI	9 Aug 1976
GLENBROOK	YTB 643	Georgetown S Y, PEI	16 Dec 1976
GLENSIDE	YTB 644	Georgetown S Y, PEI	20 May 1977

Displacement, tons: 255
Dimensions, feet (metres): 92.5 × 28 × 14.5 *(28.2 × 8.5 × 4.4)*
Main machinery: 2 diesels; 1300 hp *(970 kW)*; 2 Voith-Schneider props
Speed, knots: 11.5
Complement: 6

Comment: Two of the class reported in error as sold to McKiel Workboats in late 1980s.

GLENEVIS *10/1986, Giorgio Arra*

GLENDYNE *6/1992, van Ginderen collection*

5 VILLE CLASS

Name	No	Builders	Commissioned
LAWRENCEVILLE	YTL 590	Vito Steel & Barge Co	17 Jan 1974
PARKSVILLE	YTL 591	Vito Steel & Barge Co	17 Jan 1974
LISTERVILLE	YTL 592	Georgetown S Y, PEI	31 July 1974
MERRICKVILLE	YTL 593	Georgetown S Y, PEI	11 Sep 1974
MARYSVILLE	YTL 594	Georgetown S Y, PEI	11 Sep 1974

Displacement, tons: 70 full load
Dimensions, feet (metres): 64 × 15.5 × 9 *(19.5 × 4.7 × 2.7)*
Main machinery: 1 Diesel; 365 hp *(272 kW)*; 1 shaft
Speed, knots: 9.8

Comment: Small harbour tugs employed at Esquimalt and Halifax.

1 WOOD CLASS

Name	No	Builders	Commissioned
WILDWOOD	YTL 553	Falconer Marine	1944

Displacement, tons: 65 full load
Dimensions, feet (metres): 60 × 16 × 5 *(18.3 × 4.9 × 1.5)*
Main machinery: 1 diesel; 250 hp; 1 shaft
Speed, knots: 10
Complement: 3

Comment: Used as target towing vessel. Deleted in error in 1990.

COAST GUARD

Administration

Commissioner Canadian Coast Guard/Associate Deputy Minister Transport:
R A Quail

Ships

The Canadian Coast Guard comprises 112 ships and craft of all types, operating in the Atlantic and Pacific coastal waters and from the head of the Great Lakes to the northernmost reaches of Canada's Arctic. The Fleet is composed of icebreakers of various sizes, buoy tenders and lighthouse resupply vessels, specialised vessels for tasks such as search and rescue, oil pollution clean-up, submarine communication cable laying and repair, channel sounding and shallow-draught operations in areas such as the Mackenzie River system and Lake Winnipeg. In addition, the Fleet is supplemented by a wide variety of small craft such as shore-based workboats, landing craft and inflatable boats, used on all navigable waterways within Canadian waters.

Establishment

In January 1962 all ships owned and operated by the Federal Department of Transport, with the exception of pilotage and canal craft, were amalgamated into the Canadian Coast Guard Fleet. The Canadian Coast Guard is a civilian organisation and its members are public servants. Its Headquarters are in Ottawa while field operations are administered from five regional offices located in Vancouver, British Columbia; Toronto, Ontario; Quebec, Quebec; Dartmouth, Nova Scotia; and St John's, Newfoundland. The principal bases for the ships and aircraft are: St John's, Newfoundland; Dartmouth, NS; Saint John, NB; Charlottetown, PEI; Quebec and Sorel, Quebec; Prescott, Amherstburg and Parry Sound, Ontario; Victoria and Prince Rupert, BC; and Hay River, Northwest Territories.

Flag and Identity Markings

The Canadian Coast Guard has its own distinctive jack, a red maple leaf on a white ground at the hoist and two gold dolphins on a blue ground at the fly.
Canadian Coast Guard vessels have red hulls with white superstructures. The funnel is white with a red maple leaf on each side. A white diagonal stripe extends aft on the hull below the bridge on both sides. The words 'Coast Guard — Garde Côtière' appear aft of the stripe preceded by a stylised Canadian flag. The markings include the word 'Canada' on each side of the vessel near the stern. Search and Rescue vessels' superstructures are international yellow in colour.

Missions

The Canadian Coast Guard carries out the following missions:
(a) Icebreaking and Escort. Icebreaking and escort of commercial ships is carried out in waters off the Atlantic seaboard, in the Gulf of St Lawrence, St Lawrence River and the Great Lakes in Winter and in Arctic waters in Summer.
(b) Aids to Navigation. Installation, supply and maintenance of fixed and floating aids to navigation in Canadian waters.
(c) Organise and provide icebreaker escort to commercial shipping in support of the annual Northern Sealift which supplies bases and settlements in the Canadian Arctic, Hudson Bay and Foxe Basin.
(d) Provide and operate a wide range of marine search and rescue vessels.
(e) Provide and operate hydrographic survey and sounding vessels for the St Lawrence River Ship Channel.
(f) Provide and operate a vessel for the laying, maintenance and repair of submarine communication cables.
(g) Operate a fleet of one fixed wing aircraft and 35 helicopters primarily used for aids to navigation, ice reconnaissance when based in icebreakers, and pollution control work.

Strength of the Fleet

Type	Active
Heavy Icebreakers	6 + 1 (leased)
Heavy Icebreaker/Cable Ship	1
Light Icebreaker/Navaids Tenders	11
Ice Strengthened Navaids Tenders	11
Small Navaids Tenders	6
Small River Navaids Tenders	5
Offshore SAR Cutters	3
Intermediate SAR Cutters	2
Small SAR Cutters	6
SAR Lifeboats	18
Small Ice Strengthened SAR Cutters	2
Small SAR Utility Craft	10
Training Vessel	1
Survey and Sounding Vessel	1
Total	83 + 1

(plus approximately 28 Inshore Rescue Craft)

Note: This list does not include lifeboats, surfboats, self-propelled barges and other small craft which are carried on board the larger vessels. Also excluded are shore-based workboats, floating oil spill boats, oil slick-lickers or any of the small boats which are available for use at the various Canadian Coast Guard Bases and lighthouse stations.

DELETIONS

1990 William, Montmorency
1991 Thomas Carleton, George E Darby, Ready, Racer, John A MacDonald, Kenoki, Jackman
1992 Spindrift

HEAVY GULF ICEBREAKER

1 GULF CLASS (Type 1300)

Name	No	Builders	Commissioned
LOUIS S ST LAURENT	—	Canadian Vickers Ltd, Montreal	Oct 1969

Displacement, tons: 13 800 full load
Measurement, tons: 10 908 gross; 5370 net
Dimensions, feet (metres): 392.7 × 80.1 × 32.2 *(119.7 × 24.4 × 9.8)*
Main machinery: Diesel-electric; 5 Krupp MaK 4SA 16-cyl diesels; 39 400 hp(m) *(28.96 MW)*; 3 motors; 27 000 hp(m) *(19.85 MW)*; 3 shafts
Speed, knots: 18. **Range, miles:** 23 000 at 17 kts
Complement: 59
Helicopters: 2 light type, such as BO 105CBS.

Comment: Launched on 3 December 1966. Larger than any of the former Coast Guard icebreakers. Helicopter hangar fitted below the flight deck, with an elevator to raise the two helicopters to the deck when required. Two 49.2 ft *(15 m)* landing craft embarked. Mid-life modernisation July 1988 to early 1993 included replacing main engines with a diesel-electric system, adding a more efficient *Henry Larsen* type ice breaking bow (adds 8 m to length) with an air bubbler system and improving helicopter facilities with a new fixed hangar. In addition the complement was reduced to 59. Based in the Maritimes at Dartmouth, NS.

JOHN CABOT 6/1992, D Maginley

LOUIS S ST LAURENT 10/1992, D Maginley

HEAVY ICEBREAKER/CABLE SHIP

Name	No	Builders	Commissioned
JOHN CABOT	—	Canadian Vickers Ltd, Montreal	July 1965

Displacement, tons: 6375 full load
Measurement, tons: 5234 gross; 2069 net
Dimensions, feet (metres): 291 × 60 × 22 *(88.7 × 18.3 × 6.7)*
Main machinery: Diesel-electric; 4 Fairbanks-Morse 38D8-1/8-12 diesel generators; 5.8 MW sustained; 2 motors; 2 shafts
Speed, knots: 15. **Range, miles:** 10 000 at 12 kts
Complement: 76
Helicopters: 1 light type, such as Bell 206L.

Comment: Launched on 15 April 1964. Combination cable repair ship and icebreaker. Designed to repair and lay cable over the bow only. For use in East Coast and Arctic waters. Bow waterjet reaction manoeuvring system, heeling tanks and Flume stabilisation system. Three circular storage holds handle a total of 400 miles of submarine cable. Type 1200 based in Newfoundland.

MEDIUM GULF/RIVER ICEBREAKERS

3 R CLASS (Type 1200)

Name	No	Builders	Commissioned
PIERRE RADISSON	—	Burrard D D Co Ltd, Vancouver, BC	June 1978
SIR JOHN FRANKLIN	—	Burrard D D Co Ltd, Vancouver, BC	Mar 1979
DES GROSEILLIERS	—	Port Weller D D Co Ltd, Ontario	Aug 1983

Displacement, tons: 6400 standard; 8180 (7594, *Des Groseilliers*) full load
Measurement, tons: 5910 gross; 1678 net
Dimensions, feet (metres): 322 × 64 × 23.6 *(98.1 × 19.5 × 7.2)*
Main machinery: Diesel-electric; 6 Montreal Loco 251V-16F diesels; 17 580 hp *(13.1 MW)*; 6 GEC generators; 11.1 MW sustained; 2 motors; 13 600 hp *(10.14 MW)*; 2 shafts
Speed, knots: 16. **Range, miles:** 15 000 at 13.5 kts
Complement: 48
Helicopters: 1 Bell 212.

Comment: First two ordered on 1 May 1975. *Pierre Radisson* launched on 3 June 1977, *Franklin* on 10 March 1978 and *Des Groseilliers* on 20 February 1982. *Franklin* is based at Newfoundland, the other two in the Laurentides at Quebec.

PIERRE RADISSON 2/1989, van Ginderen Collection

1 MODIFIED R CLASS (Type 1200)

Name	No	Builders	Commissioned
HENRY LARSEN	—	Versatile Pacific S Y, Vancouver, BC	29 June 1988

Displacement, tons: 5798 light; 8290 full load
Measurement, tons: 6172 gross; 1741 net
Dimensions, feet (metres): 327.3 × 64.6 × 24 *(99.8 × 19.7 × 7.3)*
Main machinery: Diesel-electric; 3 Wärtsilä Vasa 16V32 diesel generators; 17.13 MW/60 Hz sustained; 3 motors; 16 320 hp(m) *(12 MW)*; 3 shafts
Speed, knots: 16. **Range, miles:** 15 000 at 13.5 kts
Complement: 52 (15 officers) plus 20 spare berths
Helicopters: 1 Bell 212.

Comment: Contract date 25 May 1984, laid down 23 August 1985, launched 3 January 1987; she is officially designated as 'Medium Gulf/River Icebreaker'. Although similar in many ways to the R class she has a different hull form particularly at the bow and a very different propulsion system. Fitted with Wärtsilä air bubbling system which is also in the *Sir Humphrey Gilbert*. Based at Dartmouth for operations in the Maritimes.

HENRY LARSEN　　　　　　　　　　　　　　　　　3/1989, D Maginley

Name	No	Builders	Commissioned
NORMAN McLEOD ROGERS	—	Canadian Vickers Ltd, Montreal	Oct 1969

Displacement, tons: 6320 full load
Measurement, tons: 4179 gross; 1847 net
Dimensions, feet (metres): 294.9 × 62.5 × 20 *(89.9 × 19.1 × 6.1)*
Main machinery: CODLAG; 4 Fairbanks-Morse 38D8-1/8-12 diesels; 8496 hp *(6.34 MW)* sustained; 4 GE generators; 4.8 MW; 2 Ruston RK3CZ diesels; 7520 hp *(5.6 MW)* sustained; 2 GE generators; 2.76 MW; 2 GE motors; 12 000 hp *(8.95 MW)*; 2 shafts
Speed, knots: 15. **Range, miles:** 12 000 at 12 kts
Complement: 33
Helicopters: 1 light type, such as BO 105CBS.

Comment: Type 1200 based on the West Coast at Victoria.

NORMAN McLEOD ROGERS　　　　　　　　　　　3/1988, van Ginderen Collection

HEAVY ICEBREAKER/SUPPLY TUG

Name	No	Builders	Commissioned
TERRY FOX	—	Burrard Yarrow, Vancouver	1983

Measurement, tons: 4233 gross; 1955 net
Dimensions, feet (metres): 288.7 × 58.7 × 27.2 *(88 × 17.9 × 8.3)*
Main machinery: 4 Werkspoor 8-cyl 4SA diesels; 23 200 hp(m) *(17 MW)*; 2 shafts; cp props
Speed, knots: 15
Complement: 24

Comment: Leased for two years from Gulf Canada Resources during the completion of *Louis S St Laurent* conversion. Commissioned in Coast Guard colours 1 November 1991. Based in the Maritimes at Dartmouth.

TERRY FOX　　　　　　　　　　　　　　　　　　7/1992, D Maginley

LIGHT ICEBREAKERS/MAJOR NAVAIDS TENDERS (Type 1100)

Name	No	Builders	Commissioned
MARTHA L BLACK	—	Versatile Pacific, Vancouver, BC	30 Apr 1986
GEORGE R PEARKES	—	Versatile Pacific, Vancouver, BC	17 Apr 1986
EDWARD CORNWALLIS	—	Marine Industries Ltd, Tracy, Quebec	14 Aug 1986
SIR WILLIAM ALEXANDER	—	Marine Industries Ltd, Tracy, Quebec	13 Feb 1987
SIR WILFRID LAURIER	—	Canadian Shipbuilding Ltd, Collingwood, Ontario	15 Nov 1986
ANN HARVEY	—	Halifax Industries Ltd, Halifax, NS	29 June 1987

Displacement, tons: 4662
Measurement, tons: 3818 *(Martha L Black)*; 3809 *(George R Pearkes)*; 3812 *(Sir Wilfrid Laurier)*; 3727 *(Edward Cornwallis* and *Sir William Alexander)*; 3823 *(Ann Harvey)* gross
Dimensions, feet (metres): 272.2 × 53.1 × 18.9 *(83 × 16.2 × 5.8)*
Main machinery: Diesel-electric; 3 Bombardier/Alco 12V-251 diesels; 8019 hp *(6 MW)* sustained; 3 Canadian GE generators; 6 MW; 2 Canadian GE motors; 7040 hp *(5.25 MW)*; 2 shafts; thrusters
Speed, knots: 15.5. **Range, miles:** 6500 at 15 kts
Complement: 28
Helicopters: 1 light type, such as Bell 206L.

Comment: *Black*, *Laurier* and *Pearkes* based in the Laurentides at Quebec, *Cornwallis* and *Alexander* in the Maritimes at Dartmouth and *Ann Harvey* in Newfoundland.

SIR WILLIAM ALEXANDER　　　　　　　　　　　1990, Canadian Coast Guard

ANN HARVEY　　　　　　　　　　　　　　　　　1989, R Cotie

Name	No	Builders	Commissioned
GRIFFON	—	Davie Shipbuilding Ltd, Lauzon	Dec 1970

Displacement, tons: 3096
Measurement, tons: 2212 gross; 752 net
Dimensions, feet (metres): 233.9 × 49 × 15.5 *(71.3 × 14.9 × 4.7)*
Main machinery: Diesel-electric; 4 Fairbanks-Morse 38D8-1/8-12 diesel generators; 5.8 MW sustained; 2 motors; 5340 hp *(3.98 MW)*; 2 shafts
Speed, knots: 14. **Range, miles:** 5500 at 10 kts
Complement: 28
Helicopters: Platform for 1 light type, such as Bell 206L.

Comment: Based in the Central Region at Prescott, Ontario.

GRIFFON　　　　　　　　　　　　　　　　　　　1989, M Wills

Light icebreakers/navaids tenders — Ice strengthened navaids tenders / CANADA (COAST GUARD)

Name	No	Builders	Commissioned
J E BERNIER	—	Davie Shipbuilding Ltd, Lauzon	Aug 1967

Displacement, tons: 3096
Measurement, tons: 2457 gross; 705 net
Dimensions, feet (metres): 231 × 49 × 16 *(70.5 × 14.9 × 4.9)*
Main machinery: Diesel-electric; 4 Fairbanks-Morse 4SA 8-cyl diesels; 5600 hp *(4.12 MW)*; 4 generators; 3.46 MW; 2 motors; 4250 hp *(3.13 MW)*; 2 shafts
Speed, knots: 13.5. **Range, miles:** 8000 at 11 kts
Complement: 28
Helicopters: 1 Bell 206L/L-1.

Comment: Based in Newfoundland.

J E BERNIER   *12/1984, van Ginderen Collection*

Name	No	Builders	Commissioned
SIR HUMPHREY GILBERT	—	Davie Shipbuilding Ltd, Lauzon	June 1959

Displacement, tons: 3000 full load
Measurement, tons: 2152 gross; 728 net
Dimensions, feet (metres): 228 × 48 × 16.3 *(69.5 × 14.6 × 5)*
Main machinery: Diesel-electric; 4 Fairbanks-Morse 2SA 8-cyl diesels; 5120 hp *(3.77 MW)*; 4 generators; 3.46 MW; 2 motors; 4240 hp *(3.13 MW)*; 2 shafts
Speed, knots: 13. **Range, miles:** 10 000 at 11 kts
Complement: 41
Helicopters: 1 Bell 206L/L-1.

Comment: First Canadian Coast Guard vessel to be fitted with an air-bubbling system. In 1984-85 completed a major refit which included a diesel-electric a/c-a/c propulsion system, the fitting of a new bow and a new derrick. Based at Newfoundland.

SIR HUMPHREY GILBERT   *1989, B Briggs*

LIGHT ICEBREAKERS/MEDIUM NAVAIDS TENDERS
(Type 1050)

Name	No	Builders	Commissioned
SAMUEL RISLEY	—	Vito Construction Ltd, Delta, BC	4 July 1985
EARL GREY	—	Pictou Shipyards Ltd, Pictou, NS	30 May 1986

Displacement, tons: 2935 full load
Measurement, tons: 1988 gross *(Grey)*; 1967 gross *(Risley)*; 642 net *(Grey)*; 649.5 net *(Risley)*
Dimensions, feet (metres): 228.7 × 44.9 × 17.4 *(69.7 × 13.7 × 5.3)*
Main machinery: Diesel-electric; 4 Wärtsilä 4SA 12-cyl diesels; 8644 hp(m) *(6.4 MW) (Samuel Risley)*; 4 Deutz 4SA 9-cyl diesels; 8836 hp(m) *(6.5 MW) (Earl Grey)*; 2 shafts; cp props
Speed, knots: 13
Complement: 24

Comment: *Risley* based in the Central Region at Thunder Bay, Ontario, *Grey* in the Maritimes at Charlottetown, PEI.

SAMUEL RISLEY   *5/1990, van Ginderen Collection*

ICE STRENGTHENED MEDIUM NAVAIDS TENDERS
(Type 1000)

Name	No	Builders	Commissioned
TUPPER	—	Marine Industries Ltd, Sorel	Dec 1959
SIMON FRASER	—	Burrard Dry Dock Co Ltd, Vancouver	Feb 1960

Displacement, tons: 1375 full load
Measurement, tons: 1358 gross; 419 net
Dimensions, feet (metres): 204.5 × 42 × 15.1 *(62.4 × 12.8 × 4.6)*
Main machinery: Diesel-electric; 2 Fairbanks-Morse 2SA 8-cyl diesels *(Tupper)*; 2 Alco 4SA 12-cyl diesels *(Simon Fraser)*; 3330 hp *(2.45 MW)*; 2 generators; 2.3 MW; 2 motors; 1900 hp *(2.16 MW)*; 2 shafts
Speed, knots: 13. **Range, miles:** 5000 at 10 kts
Complement: 37; 25 *(Simon Fraser)*
Helicopters: Platform for 1 Bell 206L/L-1.

Comment: Both based in the Maritimes; *Simon Fraser* at Dartmouth and *Tupper* at Charlottetown, PEI.

TUPPER   *1989, R Cotie*

Name	No	Builders	Commissioned
NARWHAL	—	Canadian Vickers Ltd, Montreal	July 1963

Displacement, tons: 2220 full load
Measurement, tons: 2064 gross; 935 net
Dimensions, feet (metres): 259.8 × 42 × 12.5 *(79.2 × 12.8 × 3.8)*
Main machinery: 2 Cooper-Bessemer diesels; 3000 hp *(2.9 MW)*; 2 shafts
Speed, knots: 12. **Range, miles:** 9500 at 10 kts
Complement: 38
Helicopters: 1 light type, such as BO 105CBS.

Comment: Re-engined in 1985. Helicopter deck and hangar added. Based on the West Coast at Victoria.

NARWHAL   *6/1992, van Ginderen Collection*

Name	No	Builders	Commissioned
TRACY	—	Port Weller Drydocks, Ontario	1968

Displacement, tons: 1300
Measurement, tons: 963 gross; 290 net
Dimensions, feet (metres): 181.1 × 38 × 12.1 *(55.2 × 11.6 × 3.7)*
Main machinery: Diesel-electric; 2 Fairbanks-Morse 38D8-1/8-8 diesel generators; 1.94 MW sustained; 2 motors; 2000 hp *(1.49 MW)*; 2 shafts
Speed, knots: 13. **Range, miles:** 5000 at 11 kts
Complement: 30

Comment: Based in Laurentides at Sorel.

TRACY   *1992, Canadian Coast Guard*

CANADA (COAST GUARD) / Ice strengthened navaids tenders — Ice strengthened small navaids tenders

Name	No	Builders	Commissioned
BARTLETT	—	Marine Industries, Sorel	1969
PROVO WALLIS	—	Marine Industries, Sorel	1969

Displacement, tons: 1620
Measurement, tons: 1317 gross; 491 net
Dimensions, feet (metres): 189.3; 209 *(Provo Wallis)* × 42.5 × 15.4 *(57.7; 63.7 × 13 × 4.7)*
Main machinery: 2 National Gas 6-cyl diesels; 2100 hp *(1.55 MW)*; 2 shafts; cp props
Speed, knots: 12.5. **Range, miles:** 3300 at 11 kts
Complement: 29

Comment: Both Type 1000. *Bartlett* based in Western Region at Victoria, *Wallis* in the Maritimes at St Johns, New Brunswick. *Bartlett* was modernised in 1988 and *Wallis* completed one year modernisation at Marystown, Newfoundland at the end of 1990. Work included lengthening the hull by 6 m, installing new equipment and improving accommodation.

BARTLETT   *1988, Larry Ferris*

PROVO WALLIS   *4/1991, Canadian Coast Guard*

Name	No	Builders	Commissioned
SIMCOE	—	Canadian Vickers Ltd, Montreal	1962

Displacement, tons: 1300 full load
Measurement, tons: 961 gross; 361 net
Dimensions, feet (metres): 179.1 × 38 × 12.5 *(54.6 × 11.6 × 3.8)*
Main machinery: Diesel-electric; 2 Paxman 4SA 12-cyl diesels; 3000 hp *(2.24 MW)*; 2 motors; 2000 hp *(1.49 MW)*; 2 shafts
Speed, knots: 13. **Range, miles:** 5000 at 10 kts
Complement: 29

Comment: Based in Central Region at Prescott, Ontario.

SIMCOE   *10/1989, van Ginderen Collection*

ICE STRENGTHENED SMALL NAVAIDS TENDERS
(Type 900)

Name	No	Builders	Commissioned
SIR JAMES DOUGLAS	—	Burrard Dry Dock Co Ltd	Nov 1956

Measurement, tons: 564 gross; 173 net
Dimensions, feet (metres): 149.6 × 30.8 × 10.5 *(45.6 × 9.4 × 3.2)*
Main machinery: 2 diesels; 850 hp *(634 kW)*; 2 shafts
Speed, knots: 12
Complement: 31

Comment: Based in the Western Region at Victoria.

SIR JAMES DOUGLAS   *6/1992, van Ginderen Collection*

Name	No	Builders	Commissioned
MONTMAGNY	—	Russel Bros, Owen Sound, Ontario	May 1963

Displacement, tons: 565 full load
Measurement, tons: 497 gross; 195 net
Dimensions, feet (metres): 148 × 28.9 × 8.5 *(45.1 × 8.8 × 2.6)*
Main machinery: Diesel; 1000 hp *(746 kW)*; 2 shafts
Speed, knots: 12
Complement: 23

Comment: Based in Laurentides at Sorel. To be paid off in April 1994.

MONTMAGNY   *12/1990, Gilbert Gyssels*

Name	No	Builders	Commissioned
ROBERT FOULIS	—	St John Drydock, NB	1969

Displacement, tons: 260
Measurement, tons: 258 gross; 29 net
Dimensions, feet (metres): 104 × 25 × 7.9 *(31.7 × 7.6 × 2.4)*
Main machinery: 2 diesels; 960 hp *(716 kW)*; 2 shafts
Speed, knots: 12
Complement: 12

Comment: Used as CG College training ship and based at Charlottetown, PEI.

ROBERT FOULIS (at CG College)   *6/1992, D Maginley*

Name	No	Builders	Commissioned
NAMAO	—	Riverton Boat Works, Manitoba	1975

Displacement, tons: 380
Measurement, tons: 318 gross; 107 net
Dimensions, feet (metres): 110 × 28 × 7 *(33.5 × 8.5 × 2.1)*
Main machinery: 2 diesels; 1350 hp *(1 MW)*; 2 shafts
Speed, knots: 12
Complement: 11

Comment: Based in the Central Region on Lake Winnipeg at Selkirk.

SHIPBORNE AIRCRAFT

Numbers/Type: 6 Bell 206B JetRanger.
Operational speed: 115 kts *(213 km/h)*.
Service ceiling: 13 500 ft *(4115 m)*.
Range: 368 nm *(682 km)*.
Role/Weapon systems: Liaison and limited SAR helicopter. Sensors: None. Weapons: None.

Numbers/Type: 5/2 Bell 206L/206L-1 LongRanger.
Operational speed: 108 kts *(200 km/h)*.
Service ceiling: 19 000 ft *(5795 m)*.
Range: 304 nm *(563 km)*.
Role/Weapon systems: Liaison and limited SAR. Sensors: None. Weapons: None.

Numbers/Type: 5 Bell 212.
Operational speed: 100 kts *(185 km/h)*.
Service ceiling: 13 200 ft *(4023 m)*.
Range: 224 nm *(415 km)*.
Role/Weapon systems: Liaison and medium support helicopter. Sensors: None. Weapons: None.

Numbers/Type: 16 MBB BO 105CBS.
Operational speed: 110 kts *(204 km/h)*.
Service ceiling: 20 000 ft *(6090 m)*.
Range: 278 nm *(515 km)*.
Role/Weapon systems: Liaison, SAR and shipborne reconnaissance duties; replaces older single-engined types. Sensors: None. Weapons: None.

BO 105   *1991*

Numbers/Type: 1 Sikorsky S-61N.
Operational speed: 121 kts *(224 km/h)*.
Service ceiling: 12 500 ft *(3810 m)*.
Range: 440 nm *(815 km)*.
Role/Weapon systems: Based on West Coast for long-range SAR and navigational aids. Sensors: Bendix search radar. Weapons: None.

SMALL NAVAIDS TENDERS (Type 800)

Name	No	Builders	Commissioned
PARTRIDGE ISLAND	—	Breton Industries, Port Hawkesbury, N S	31 Oct 1985
ILE DES BARQUES	—	Breton Industries, Port Hawkesbury, N S	26 Nov 1985
ILE SAINT-OURS	—	Breton Industries, Port Hawkesbury, N S	15 May 1986
CARIBOU ISLE	—	Breton Industries, Port Hawkesbury, N S	16 June 1986

Measurement, tons: 92 gross; 36 net
Dimensions, feet (metres): 75.5 × 19.7 × 4.4 *(23 × 6 × 1.4)*
Main machinery: 2 diesels; 475 hp *(354 kW)*; 2 shafts
Speed, knots: 11
Complement: 5

Comment: *Partridge Island* based in the Maritimes at St Johns, New Brunswick, *Caribou Isle* in the Central Region at Sault Ste Marie, Ontario, and the other two in the Laurentides at Sorel.

ILE SAINT-OURS   *4/1992, van Ginderen Collection*

Name	No	Builders	Commissioned
COVE ISLE	—	Canadian D and D, Kingston, Ontario	1980
GULL ISLE	—	Canadian D and D, Kingston, Ontario	1980

Measurement, tons: 80 gross; 33 net
Dimensions, feet (metres): 65.6 × 19.7 × 4.6 *(20 × 6 × 1.4)*
Main machinery: 2 diesels; 373 hp *(278 kW)*; 2 shafts
Speed, knots: 10
Complement: 5

Comment: Based in Central Region at Parry Sound, Ontario.

SPECIAL RIVER NAVAIDS TENDERS (Type 700)

Name	No	Builders	Commissioned
NAHIDIK	—	Allied Shipbuilders Ltd, N Vancouver	1974

Measurement, tons: 856 gross; 392 net
Dimensions, feet (metres): 175.2 × 49.9 × 6.6 *(53.4 × 15.2 × 2)*
Main machinery: 2 diesels; 4290 hp *(3.2 MW)*; 2 shafts
Speed, knots: 14
Complement: 15

Comment: Based at Hay River, North West Territories.

NAHIDIK   *1991, Canadian Coast Guard*

Name	No	Builders	Commissioned
DUMIT	—	Allied Shipbuilders Ltd, N Vancouver	1979

Measurement, tons: 569 gross; 176 net
Dimensions, feet (metres): 160.1 × 40 × 5.2 *(48.8 × 12.2 × 1.6)*
Main machinery: 2 diesels; 839 hp *(626 kW)*; 2 shafts
Speed, knots: 12
Complement: 10

Comment: Similar to *Eckaloo*. Based at Hay River, North West Territories.

Name	No	Builders	Commissioned
TEMBAH	—	Allied Shipbuilders Ltd, N Vancouver	1963

Measurement, tons: 189 gross; 58 net
Dimensions, feet (metres): 123 × 25.9 × 3 *(37.5 × 7.9 × 0.9)*
Main machinery: 2 diesels; 500 hp *(373 kW)*; 2 shafts
Speed, knots: 13
Complement: 9

Comment: Based at Hay River, North West Territories.

TEMBAH   *1978, Canadian Coast Guard*

Name	No	Builders	Commissioned
MISKINAW	—	Allied Shipbuilders Ltd, N Vancouver	1958

Measurement, tons: 104 gross; 47 net
Dimensions, feet (metres): 64 × 19.7 × 3.9 *(19.5 × 6 × 1.2)*
Main machinery: 2 diesels; 358 hp *(267 kW)*; 2 shafts
Speed, knots: 10
Complement: 8

Comment: Based at Fort McMurray, Alta.

98   CANADA (COAST GUARD) / Special river navaids tenders (Type 700) — Small search and rescue cutters (Type 400)

Name	No	Builders	Commissioned
ECKALOO	—	Vancouver S Y Ltd	July 1988

Displacement, tons: 534
Measurement, tons: 661 gross; 213 net
Dimensions, feet (metres): 160.8 × 44 × 4 *(49 × 13.4 × 1.2)*
Main machinery: 2 Caterpillar 3512TA; 2420 hp *(1.8 MW)* sustained; 2 shafts
Speed, knots: 13
Complement: 9
Helicopters: Platform for 1 Bell 206L/L-1.

Comment: Replaced vessel of the same name. Similar design to *Dumit*. Based at Hay River, North West Territories.

Name	No	Builders	Commissioned
MARY HICHENS	—	Marystown Shipyard Ltd, Newfoundland	1983

Displacement, tons: 3262
Measurement, tons: 1684 gross; 696 net
Dimensions, feet (metres): 210 × 45 × 19.7 *(64 × 13.8 × 6)*
Main machinery: 2 Burmeister & Wain Alpha 18 V 28/32-VO diesels; 10 800 hp(m) *(7.94 MW)* sustained; 2 shafts; 2 Kort nozzle cp props; bow thrusters
Speed, knots: 15
Complement: 18

Comment: Based in the Maritimes Region at Dartmouth.

ECKALOO   *7/1988, Murray McLellan*

MARY HICHENS   *7/1992, D Maginley*

LARGE SEARCH AND RESCUE CUTTERS (Type 600)

Name	No	Builders	Commissioned
ALERT	—	Davie Shipbuilding Ltd, Lauzon	1969

Displacement, tons: 2025
Measurement, tons: 1752 gross; 495 net
Dimensions, feet (metres): 234.3 × 39.7 × 16.1 *(71.4 × 12.1 × 4.9)*
Main machinery: 4 Fairbanks-Morse 2SA 12-cyl diesels; 10 560 hp *(7.77 MW)*; 2 shafts
Speed, knots: 18.5
Complement: 25
Helicopters: 1 light type, such as BO 105CBS.

Comment: Based in the Maritimes at Dartmouth.

INTERMEDIATE SAR CUTTERS (Type 500)

Name	No	Builders	Commissioned
GORDON REID	—	Versatile Pacific, Vancouver	Oct 1990
JOHN JACOBSON	—	Versatile Pacific, Vancouver	Nov 1990

Measurement, tons: 836 gross
Dimensions, feet (metres): 163.9 × 36.1 × 13.1 *(49.9 × 11 × 4)*
Main machinery: 4 Deutz SBV-6M-628 diesels; 2475 hp(m) *(1.82 MW)* sustained; 2 shafts; bow thruster; 400 hp *(294 kW)*
Speed, knots: 16. **Range, miles:** 2500 at 15 kts
Complement: 14 plus 8 spare

Comment: Type 500 Intermediate cutters. Designed for long-range patrols along the British Columbian coast out to 200 mile limit. They have a stern ramp for launching Zodiac Hurricane 733 rigid inflatables in up to Sea State 6. The Zodiac has a speed of 50 kts and is radar equipped. Both based in the Western Region at Victoria.

ALERT   *1983, Canadian Coast Guard*

Name	No	Builders	Commissioned
SIR WILFRED GRENFELL	—	Marystown S Y, Newfoundland	1987

Displacement, tons: 3753
Measurement, tons: 2403 gross; 664.5 net
Dimensions, feet (metres): 224.7 × 49.2 × 16.4 *(68.5 × 15 × 5)*
Main machinery: 4 Deutz 4SA (2—16-cyl, 2—9-cyl) diesels; 12 862 hp(m) *(9.46 MW)*; 2 shafts; cp props
Speed, knots: 16
Complement: 20

Comment: Built on speculation in 1984/85. Modified to include an 85 tonne towing winch and additional SAR accommodation and equipment; replaced *Grenfell* in December 1987. Based at St John's, Newfoundland.

GORDON REID   *1992, Canadian Coast Guard*

SMALL SEARCH AND RESCUE CUTTERS (Type 400)

Name	No	Builders	Commissioned
SPRAY	—	J J Taylor & Sons Ltd, Toronto	1964
SPUME	—	Crew Ltd, Prescott, Ontario	1963

Measurement, tons: 56 gross; 17 net
Dimensions, feet (metres): 69.9 × 16.7 × 4.6 *(21.3 × 5.1 × 1.4)*
Main machinery: 2 diesels; 1064 hp *(794 kW)*; 2 shafts
Speed, knots: 12.5
Complement: 4

Comment: Employed on Great Lakes Patrol in the Central Region. *Spume* at Meaford and *Spray* at Port Dover, Ontario.

SIR WILFRED GRENFELL   *1989, Canadian Coast Guard*

SPINDRIFT (deleted 1992)   *1986, Canadian Coast Guard*

Small search and rescue cutters (Type 400) — Small sar utility craft (Type 100) / CANADA (COAST GUARD)

Name	No	Builders	Commissioned
POINT HENRY	—	Breton Industrial and Machinery	1980
ISLE ROUGE	—	Breton Industrial and Machinery	1980
POINT RACE	—	Pt Hawkesbury, NS	1982
CAPE HURD	—	Pt Hawkesbury, NS	1982

Displacement, tons: 49
Measurement, tons: 57 gross; 14 net
Dimensions, feet (metres): 70.8 × 18 × 5.6 *(21.6 × 5.5 × 1.7)*
Main machinery: 2 MTU 8V 396 TC82 diesels; 1740 hp(m) *(1.28 MW)* sustained; 2 shafts
Speed, knots: 20
Complement: 5

Comment: Aluminium alloy hulls. *Point Henry* based in Western Region, *Cape Hurd* in Central Region, and the other two in the Laurentides.

CAPE HURD *1992, D N Glen*

SAR SELF-RIGHTING LIFEBOATS (Type 300)

Name	Builders	Commissioned
WESTPORT	Paspediac, Quebec	1969
BAMFIELD	McKay Cormack Ltd, Victoria, BC	1970
TOFINO	McKay Cormack Ltd, Victoria, BC	1970
PORT HARDY (ex-*Bull Harbour*)	McKay Cormack Ltd, Victoria, BC	1970
BURIN	Georgetown Shipyard, Georgetown, PEI	1973
TOBERMORY	Georgetown Shipyard, Georgetown, PEI	1974
WESTFORT (ex-*Thunder Bay*)	Georgetown Shipyard, Georgetown, PEI	1974
BURGEO	Georgetown Shipyard, Georgetown, PEI	1974
SHIPPEGAN	Eastern Equipment, Montreal, Quebec	1975
CLARK'S HARBOUR	Eastern Equipment, Montreal, Quebec	1975
SAMBRO	Eastern Equipment, Montreal, Quebec	1975
LOUISBOURG	Eastern Equipment, Montreal, Quebec	1975
PORT MOUTON	Georgetown Shipyard, Georgetown, PEI	1982
CAP AUX MEULES	Georgetown Shipyard, Georgetown, PEI	1982
SOURIS	Hike Metal Products Ltd, Wheatley, Ontario	1985
CAP GOÉLANDS	Hike Metal Products Ltd, Wheatley, Ontario	1985
CGR 100	—	1986

Measurement, tons: 10 gross
Dimensions, feet (metres): 44.1 × 12.7 × 3.4 *(13.5 × 3.9 × 1)*
Main machinery: 2 diesels; 485 hp *(362 kW)*; 2 shafts
Speed, knots: 12.5
Complement: 3 or 4

Comment: Including *Bickerton*, eight based in the Maritimes, three Western, three Central, two Newfoundland and two in Laurentides. CGR 100 is a self-righting Medina lifeboat (Type 300B) and has a speed of 26 kts.

TOFINO *7/1988, Florian Jentsch*

Name	No	Builders	Commissioned
BICKERTON	—	Halmatic, Havant	Aug 1989

Measurement, tons: 34 gross
Dimensions, feet (metres): 52 × 17.5 × 4.6 *(15.9 × 5.3 × 1.5)*
Main machinery: 2 Caterpillar 3408BTA diesels; 1170 hp *(872 kW)* sustained; 2 shafts
Speed, knots: 18

Comment: Arun Type 300. Final total has not been decided. To replace up to 10 Westport class.

BICKERTON *7/1989, J Carter*

SMALL ICE STRENGTHENED SAR CUTTERS (Type 200)

Name	No	Builders	Commissioned
HARP	—	Georgetown SY, Georgetown, PEI	12 Dec 1986
HOOD	—	Georgetown SY, Georgetown, PEI	12 Dec 1986

Displacement, tons: 225
Measurement, tons: 179 gross; 69 net
Dimensions, feet (metres): 80.4 × 27.6 × 7.9 *(24.5 × 8.5 × 2.4)*
Main machinery: 2 diesels; 850 hp *(634 kW)*; 2 shafts
Speed, knots: 10. **Range, miles:** 500 at 10 kts
Complement: 7 plus 10 spare berths

Comment: Ordered 26 April 1985 and launched in September and November 1986. Based in Newfoundland.

HARP *1992, Canadian Coast Guard*

SMALL SAR UTILITY CRAFT (Type 100)

Note: There are also 28 Inshore Rescue boats with CG numbers.

Name	Builders	Commissioned
MALLARD	Matsumoto Shipyard, Vancouver, B C	1985
SKUA	Matsumoto Shipyard, Vancouver, B C	1986
OSPREY	Matsumoto Shipyard, Vancouver, B C	1986
STERNE	Matsumoto Shipyard, Vancouver, B C	1987

Measurement, tons: 15 gross
Dimensions, feet (metres): 40.8 × 13.2 × 4.2 *(12.4 × 4.1 × 1.3)*
Main machinery: 2 diesels; 637 hp *(475 kW)*; 2 shafts
Speed, knots: 26
Complement: 3

Comment: *Sterne* based at Quebec, remainder in Western Region.

Name	Measurement, tons	Speed, knots	Built
BITTERN	20 gross	26	1982
SORA	20 gross	12	1968
SWIFT	5 gross	36	1981
CG 119	20 gross	18	1973
AVOCET (ex-*Sterne*)	20 gross	15	1973

Comment: All based in Central Region except *Swift* which is in reserve at Vancouver.

CG 119 *1990, van Ginderen Collection*

CCG COLLEGE CADET SEA TRAINING VESSELS

Note: In addition to *Mikula* there are three 10.5 m craft, *Mink*, *Martin* and *Muskrat*.

Name	No	Builders	Commissioned
MIKULA (ex-*Lurcher*)	—	Kingston S Y, Ontario	1959

Displacement, tons: 617
Measurement, tons: 526 gross; 135 net
Dimensions, feet (metres): 128 × 30.5 × 11 *(39 × 9.3 × 3.4)*
Main machinery: 1 diesel; 372 hp *(277 kW)*; 1 shaft
Speed, knots: 10
Complement: 6 plus 21 cadets

Comment: Former Lightship. May be retained for alongside training.

MIKULA   1986, R Allan

SURVEY AND SOUNDING VESSELS

Note: 2 catamaran vessels are planned for 1994.

Name	No	Builders	Commissioned
NICOLET	—	Collingwood S Y, Ontario	1966

Displacement, tons: 935 full load
Measurement, tons: 887 gross; 147 net
Dimensions, feet (metres): 169.6 × 36.4 × 10.2 *(51.7 × 11.1 × 3.1)*
Main machinery: 2 diesels; 1237 hp *(923 kW)*; 2 shafts; cp props
Speed, knots: 13
Complement: 27

Comment: Based in Laurentides. To be paid off in 1994.

NICOLET   1990, van Ginderen Collection

HOVERCRAFT

3 SRN 6 TYPE

CG 039   CG 045   CG 086

Displacement, tons: 10.9 full load
Dimensions, feet (metres): 48.5 × 23 × 3.9 (skirt) *(14.8 × 7 × 1.2)*
Main machinery: 1 RR Gnome 1050 gas turbine; 1050 hp *(783 kW)* sustained
Speed, knots: 60. **Range, miles:** 170 at 54 kts
Complement: 3

Comment: Built in 1968 and 1977. Based at Sea Island and Parksville, both in the Western Region. Can carry up to 6 tons of equipment.

SRN 6 Type   1986, Canadian Coast Guard

1 + 1 AP. I-88/200/400 TYPES

Name	No	Builders	Commissioned
WABAN-AKI	—	Westland Aerospace	15 July 1987

Displacement, tons: 47.6 light
Dimensions, feet (metres): 80.4 × 36.7 × 19.6 *(24.5 × 11.2 × 6.6)* (height on cushion)
Main machinery: 4 diesels
Speed, knots: 50; 35 cruising
Complement: 3
Cargo capacity: 12 tons

Comment: *Waban-Aki* is based at Quebec and capable of year round operation as a Navaid Tender for flood control operations in the St Lawrence. Fitted with a hydraulic crane. The name means People of the Dawn. Second of class (Type 400) with a crane for buoy tending operations is planned to be in service in September 1994.

WABAN-AKI   1989, Canadian Coast Guard

DEPARTMENT OF FISHERIES AND OCEANS

Senior Appointment

Director, Ship Branch:
   Commodore J M Cutts

General

The department has two separate fleets. The hydrographic, oceanographic and fishery research vessels are painted white with buff masts and buff funnels with black tops. They are based on the East Coast at the Bedford Institute of Oceanography, Dartmouth NS and at St Johns, Newfoundland; on the West Coast at the Pacific Institute of Ocean Sciences, Sidney, BC; and in the Great Lakes at the Canada Centre for Inland Waters at Burlington, Ontario.

The fishery patrol vessels are painted grey with the departmental crest on the funnel. They are based in their respective patrol areas. These vessels are armed with machine guns and carry armed boarding parties.

Apart from the major vessels whose details are given below there are some 700 medium and small patrol craft.

DELETION

1992   *Louisbourg*

FISHERY PATROL VESSELS

Name	Builders	Commissioned
LEONARD J COWLEY	Manly Shipyard, RivTow Ind, Vancouver BC	1985

Measurement, tons: 2244 grt
Dimensions, feet (metres): 236.2 × 45.9 × 16.1 *(72 × 14 × 4.9)*
Main machinery: 2 Nohab diesels; 2325 hp(m) *(1.71 MW)*; 1 shaft
Speed, knots: 14. **Range, miles:** 12 000 at 14 kts
Complement: 19
Guns: 2—12.7 mm MGs.

Helicopters: Capability for one light.

Comment: Based in Newfoundland.

LEONARD J COWLEY   6/1992, Harald Carstens

Fishery patrol vessels — Hydrographic and oceanographic vessels / CANADA   101

Name	Builders	Commissioned
CYGNUS	Marystown Shipyard, Nfld	1981
CAPE ROGER	Ferguson Industries, Pictou NS	1977

Measurement, tons: 1255 grt
Dimensions, feet (metres): 205 × 40 × 13 *(62.5 × 12.2 × 4.1)*
Main machinery: 2 Nohab diesels, 2400 hp(m) *(1.76 MW)*; 1 shaft
Speed, knots: 16. **Range, miles:** 2450 at 10 kts
Complement: 19
Guns: 2—12.7 mm MGs.
Helicopters: Capability for one light.

Comment: *Cygnus* based in Nova Scotia, *Cape Roger* in Newfoundland. Two crews per ship work a 14 day patrol cycle.

Name	Builders	Commissioned
CHEBUCTO	Ferguson Industries, Pictou NS	1966

Measurement, tons: 751 grt
Dimensions, feet (metres): 179 × 31 × 15 *(54.6 × 9.4 × 3.6)*
Main machinery: 2 Fairbanks-Morse diesels; 2560 hp *(1.91 MW)*; 2 shafts
Speed, knots: 14. **Range, miles:** 7320 at 10 kts
Complement: 21
Guns: 2—12.7 mm MGs.

Comment: Based in Nova Scotia. Mid-life refit in 1987. Operates a two crew system changing every 14 days.

CYGNUS   *1989, DFO*

CHEBUCTO   *1989, DFO*

Name	Builders	Commissioned
JAMES SINCLAIR	Manly Shipyard, RivTow Ind, Vancouver BC	1981

Measurement, tons: 323 grt
Dimensions, feet (metres): 124 × 27.5 × 12 *(37.8 × 8.4 × 3.7)*
Main machinery: 2 MTU diesels; 4600 hp(m) *(3.38 MW)*; 2 shafts
Speed, knots: 16.5
Complement: 14
Guns: 2—12.7 mm MGs.

Comment: Based in British Columbia.

HYDROGRAPHIC AND OCEANOGRAPHIC VESSELS

Note: *Baffin* and *Dawson* deleted in 1991.

Name	Commissioned	Based	Complement
HUDSON	1963	East Coast	65 (25 scientists)
MATTHEW	1990	East Coast	—
F C G SMITH	1986	East Coast	11 (4 scientists)
MAXWELL	1962	East Coast	19 (7 scientists)
JOHN P TULLY	1985	West Coast	36 (15 scientists)
PARIZEAU	1967	East Coast	45 (13 scientists)
VECTOR	1967	West Coast	25 (8 scientists)
LOUIS M LAUZIER (ex-*Cape Harrison*)	1977	St Lawrence	14 (6 scientists)
LIMNOS	1968	St Lawrence	30 (14 scientists)
BAYFIELD (ex-*Hildur*)	1966	St Lawrence	16 (6 scientists)
R B YOUNG	1990	West Coast	11 (5 scientists)

JAMES SINCLAIR   *6/1992, Harald Carstens*

Name	Builders	Commissioned
TANU	Yarrows Ltd, Victoria BC	1968

Measurement, tons: 746 grt
Dimensions, feet (metres): 179.5 × 32.8 × 10.8 *(54.7 × 10 × 3.3)*
Main machinery: 1 diesel; 2624 hp *(1.96 MW)*; 1 shaft
Speed, knots: 12.
Complement: 18
Guns: 2—12.7 mm MGs.

Comment: Based in British Columbia.

HUDSON   *1989, DFO*

TANU   *1990, van Ginderen Collection*

MATTHEW   *1991, Bedford Institute of Oceanography*

FISHERY RESEARCH VESSELS

Name	Commissioned	Based	Complement
ALFRED NEEDLER	1982	Nova Scotia	37 (15 scientists)
WILFRED TEMPLEMAN	1982	Nova Scotia	37 (15 scientists)
E E PRINCE	1966	Nova Scotia	20 (6 scientists)
W E RICKER (ex-*Callistratus*)	1978	West Coast	36 (12 scientists)

E E PRINCE 1990, DFO

ALFRED NEEDLER 1989, DFO

CAPE VERDE

Personnel

1993: 225

Bases

Praia, main naval base.
Porto Grande (Isle de Sao Vicente), naval repair yard built with Soviet assistance.

Mercantile Marine

Lloyd's Register of Shipping:
42 vessels of 21 723 tons gross

PATROL FORCES

3 Ex-SOVIET ZHUK CLASS (COASTAL PATROL CRAFT)

Displacement, tons: 50
Dimensions, feet (metres): 75.4 × 17 × 6.2 *(23 × 5.2 × 1.9)*
Main machinery: 2 Type M 50 diesels; 2200 hp(m) *(1.6 MW)* sustained; 2 shafts
Speed, knots: 30. **Range, miles:** 1100 at 15 kts
Complement: 17
Guns: 4—14.5 mm (2 twin) MGs.
Radars: Surface search: Spin Trough; I band.

Comment: Transferred 1980. Only one was operational in 1992.

ZHUK 1988, S S Breyer

1 Ex-SOVIET BIYA CLASS (SURVEY SHIP)

5th JULY A 450

Displacement, tons: 750 full load
Dimensions, feet (metres): 180.4 × 32.1 × 8.5 *(55 × 9.8 × 2.6)*
Main machinery: 2 diesels; 1200 hp(m) *(882 kW)*; 2 shafts; cp props
Speed, knots: 13. **Range, miles:** 4700 at 11 kts
Complement: 25

Comment: Transferred in 1979. Class built in Poland 1972-76. Probably non-operational.

0 + 5 (3) PETERSON TYPE (COASTAL PATROL CRAFT)

Displacement, tons: 22 full load
Dimensions, feet (metres): 51.3 × 14.8 × 4.3 *(15.6 × 4.5 × 1.3)*
Main machinery: 2 Detroit 6V 92TA diesels; 900 hp *(672 kW)*; 2 shafts
Speed, knots: 24. **Range, miles:** 500 at 20 kts
Complement: 6
Guns: 2—12.7 mm MGs (twin). 2—7.62 mm MGs.
Radars: Surface search: I band.

Comment: Ordered from Peterson Builders Inc (PBI) under FMS programme on 25 September 1992. First of five to be delivered in late 1993; option on three more. Aluminium hulls. The 12.7 mm mounting is aft with the smaller guns on the bridge roof.

2 Ex-SOVIET SHERSHEN CLASS (FAST ATTACK CRAFT)

451   452

Displacement, tons: 145 standard; 170 full load
Dimensions, feet (metres): 113.8 × 22 × 4.9 *(34.7 × 6.7 × 1.5)*
Main machinery: 3 Type M 503A diesels; 8025 hp(m) *(5.9 MW)* sustained; 3 shafts
Speed, knots: 45. **Range, miles:** 460 at 42 kts; 850 at 30 kts
Complement: 23
Guns: 4 USSR 30 mm/65 (2 twin); 85° elevation; 500 rounds/minute to 5 km *(2.7 nm)*; weight of shell 0.54 kg.
Depth charges: 12.
Radars: Surface search: Pot Head; I band; range 37 km *(20 nm)*.
Fire control: Drum Tilt; H/I band.

Comment: Supplied without the usual four torpedo tubes. Delivered March and July 1979. Class built in period 1962-74.

SHERSHEN 451 and 452 1991, van Ginderen Collection

1 LANDING CRAFT LOGISTIC

ILHEN RASO

Comment: A 28.5 m craft built by Sürken, West Germany and delivered in October 1988. Probably a civilian manned Ro-Ro.

CHILE

Headquarters' Appointments

Commander-in-Chief:
　Admiral Jorge Martinez
Chief of the Naval Staff:
　Vice Admiral Alfredo Gallesos
Flag Officer, Fleet:
　Vice Admiral Sergio O Jarpa
Flag Officer, Submarines:
　Rear Admiral Pedro Arrieta
Flag Officer, Naval Aviation:
　Rear Admiral Ariel Rosas
Flag Officer, Marines:
　Rear Admiral Miguel Alvarez
Flag Officer, Maritime Territory:
　Vice Admiral Juan Mackay
Flag Officer, 1st Naval Zone:
　Vice Admiral Jorge Llorente
Flag Officer, 2nd Naval Zone:
　Rear Admiral Eduardo Oelckers
Flag Officer, 3rd Naval Zone:
　Rear Admiral Hugo Bruna
Flag Officer, 4th Naval Zone:
　Rear Admiral Norman Fritis

Diplomatic Representation

Naval Attaché in London, The Hague and Stockholm:
　Rear Admiral Eduardo Berardi
Naval Attaché in Washington:
　Rear Admiral Arturo Oxley
Naval Attaché in Paris:
　Captain Carlos Valderrama
Naval Attaché in Buenos Aires:
　Captain Rodolfo Camacho
Naval Attaché in Brasilia:
　Captain Raul Silva
Naval Attaché in Quito:
　Captain Carlos Sanchez
Naval Attaché in Tel Aviv:
　Commander Daniel Arellano
Naval Attaché in Lima:
　Captain Juan Pattillo
Naval Attaché in Madrid:
　Captain Oscar Manzano
Naval Attaché in Bogota:
　Captain Ricardo Leon

Personnel

(a) 1993: 24 500 (excluding Marines) (2000 officers)
(b) 2 years' national service

Command Organisation

1st Naval Zone. HQ at Valparaiso. From 26°S to Topocalma Point (33°S).
2nd Naval Zone. HQ at Talcahuano. From Topocalma Point to 47°S.
3rd Naval Zone. HQ at Punta Arenas. From 47°S to South Pole including Beagle Naval District.
4th Naval Zone. HQ at Iquique. From Peruvian frontier to 26°S.

Naval Air Stations and Organisation

Having won the battle to own all military aircraft flying over the sea, a fixed wing squadron of about 20 CASA/ENAER Halcón is envisaged when finances permit.
Viña del Mar (Valparaiso); *Almirante Von Schroeders* (Punta Arenas); *Guardiamarina Zañartu* (Puerto Williams).
Four Squadrons: VP1 (MP) Bandeirante; HS1 (Helicopters) Alouette III, Super Puma, Dauphin; VC1 (GP) Bandeirante, Aviocar, JetRangers; VT1 (Training) Pilatus PC-7.

Infanteria de Marina

Personnel: 5200.
Organisation: 4 detachments each comprising Amphibious Warfare, Coast Defence and Local Security. Also embarked are detachments of commandos, engineering units and a logistic battalion.
1st Marine Infantry Detachment 'Patricio Lynch'. At Iquique.
2nd Marine Infantry Detachment 'Miller'. At Viña del Mar.
3rd Marine Infantry Detachment 'Sargento Aldea'. At Talcahuano.
4th Marine Infantry Detachment 'Cochrane'. At Punta Arenas.
51 Commando Group. At Valparaiso.
Some embarked units, commando and engineering units and a logistics battalion.
Equipment: Infantry personnel and support weapons; LVTP 5 amphibious assault vehicles; MOWAG Roland APCs; light field artillery.

Bases

Valparaiso. Main naval base, schools, repair yard. HQ 1st Naval Zone. Air station.
Talcahuano. Naval base, schools, major repair yard (two dry docks, three floating docks), two floating cranes. HQ 2nd Naval Zone. Submarine Base.
Punta Arenas. Naval base. Dockyard with slipway having building and repair facilities. HQ 3rd Naval Zone. Air station.
Iquique. Small naval base. HQ 4th Naval Zone.
Puerto Montt. Small naval base.
Puerto Williams (Beagle Channel). Small naval base. Air station.
Dawson Island (Magellan Straits). Small naval base.

Strength of the Fleet

Type	Active	Projected
Patrol Submarines	4	(4)
Cruiser	1	—
Destroyers	6	—
Frigates	4	—
Patrol Ships	2	(4)
Landing Ships (Tank)	3	—
Landing Craft	2	—
Fast Attack Craft (Missile)	4	—
Fast Attack Craft (Torpedo)	4	—
Large Patrol Craft	5	—
Coastal Patrol Craft	6	—
Survey Ships	2	—
Training Ships	3	—
Transports	3	—
Tankers	3	—
Tugs/Supply Ships	5	—
Submarine Support Ship	1	—
Coast Guard	37	2 (4)

Mercantile Marine

Lloyd's Register of Shipping:
　392 vessels of 604 419 tons gross

DELETIONS

Cruisers

1992　*O'Higgins*

Destroyers

1990　*Ministro Zenteno* (old), *Ministro Portales*

Patrol Forces

1990　*Lautaro* (old)

Miscellaneous

1990　*Grumete Perez*

PENNANT LIST

Note: Chilean naval vessels do not carry visible pennant numbers.

Submarines

20	Thomson
21	Simpson
22	O'Brien
23	Hyatt

Destroyers/Frigates

06	Condell
07	Lynch
08	Ministro Zenteno
09	General Baquedano
11	Prat
12	Cochrane
14	Latorre
15	Blanco Encalada
18	Almirante Riveros
19	Almirante Williams

Patrol Forces

45	Piloto Pardo
63	Sargento Aldea

Light Forces

30	Casma
31	Chipana
32	Iquique
33	Covadonga
37	Papudo
80	Guacolda
81	Fresia
82	Quidora
83	Tegualda
1814	Grumete Diaz
1815	Grumete Bolados
1816	Grumete Salinas
1817	Grumete Tellez
1818	Grumete Bravo
1819	Grumete Campos

Survey Ships

60	Vidal Gormaz
64	Yelcho

Training Ships

29	Uribe
43	Esmeralda

Submarine Support Ship

70	Angamos

Amphibious Forces

90	Elicura
91	Maipo
92	Rancagua
93	Chacabuco
94	Orompello

Transports

AP 47	Aquiles
AP 48	Aguila
YFB 110	Meteoro

Tankers

52	Almirante Jorge Montt
53	Araucano
YOG 101	Guardian Brito

Tugs/Supply Ships

ATF 65	Janequeo
ATF 66	Galvarino
ATF 67	Lautaro
ATF 68	Leucoton
ATF 69	Colo Colo

SUBMARINES

Note: Up to four new submarines are required. The equipment fit has been decided and an order for a new class of about 1400 tons may be placed in 1993. First to be built abroad, remainder by ASMAR.

2 TYPE 209 CLASS (TYPE 1300)

Name	No	Builders	Laid down	Launched	Commissioned
THOMSON	20	Howaldtswerke	1 Nov 1980	28 Oct 1982	31 Aug 1984
SIMPSON	21	Howaldtswerke	15 Feb 1982	29 July 1983	18 Sep 1984

Displacement, tons: 1260 surfaced; 1390 dived
Dimensions, feet (metres): 195.2 × 20.3 × 18 *(59.5 × 6.2 × 5.5)*
Main machinery: Diesel-electric; 4 MTU 12V 493 AZ80 GA31L diesels; 2400 hp(m) *(1.76 MW)* sustained; 4 Piller alternators; 1.7 MW; 1 Siemens motor; 4600 hp(m) *(3.38 MW)* sustained; 1 shaft
Speed, knots: 11 surfaced; 21.5 dived
Range, miles: 400 at 4 kts surfaced; 16 at 21.5 kts dived; 8200 at 8 kts snorkel
Complement: 32 (5 officers)

Torpedoes: 8—21 in *(533 mm)* bow tubes. 14 AEG SUT; wire-guided; active homing to 12 km *(6.5 nm)* at 35 kts; passive homing to 28 km *(15 nm)* at 23 kts; warhead 250 kg.
Radars: Surface search: Thomson-CSF Calypso II; I band.
Sonars: Atlas Elektronik CSU 3; hull-mounted; active/passive search and attack; medium frequency.

Programmes: Ordered from Howaldtswerke, Kiel in 1980. Two more projected in 1988 Five Year Plan but this has been overtaken by the requirement for a new class of four of similar displacement.

SIMPSON *1992, Chilean Navy*

Modernisation: *Thomson* refit completed at Talcahuano in late 1990, *Simpson* in 1991. Refit duration about 10 months each.

Structure: Fin and associated masts lengthened by 50 cm to cope with wave size off Chilean coast.

2 OBERON CLASS

Name	No	Builders	Laid down	Launched	Commissioned
O'BRIEN	22	Scott-Lithgow	17 Jan 1971	21 Dec 1972	15 Apr 1976
HYATT (ex-*Condell*)	23	Scott-Lithgow	10 Jan 1972	26 Sep 1973	27 Sep 1976

Displacement, tons: 1610 standard; 2030 surfaced; 2410 dived
Dimensions, feet (metres): 295.2 × 26.5 × 18.1 *(90 × 8.1 × 5.5)*
Main machinery: Diesel-electric; 2 ASR 16 VVS-ASR1 diesels; 3680 hp *(2.74 MW)*; 2 AEI motors; 6000 hp *(4.48 MW)*; 2 shafts
Speed, knots: 12 surfaced; 17 dived; 10 snorting
Complement: 65 (7 officers)

Torpedoes: 8—21 in *(533 mm)* tubes (6 bow, 2 stern). 22 AEG SUT; wire-guided; active homing to 12 km *(6.5 nm)* at 35 kts; passive homing to 28 km *(15 nm)* at 23 kts; warhead 250 kg.
Fire control: Sisdef TFCS.
Radars: Navigation: Kelvin Hughes Type 1006; I band.
Sonars: BAC Type 2007; flank array; passive; long range; low frequency.
EMI Type 187; bow-mounted; passive/active search and attack; medium frequency.

HYATT *1992, Chilean Navy*

Programmes: Ordered from Scott's Shipbuilding & Engineering Co Ltd, Greenock, late 1969. Both suffered delays in fitting out due to re-cabling and a minor explosion in *Hyatt* in January 1976.

Modernisation: Sisdef fire control system fitted in 1992. New sonars expected in 1993.
Operational: Stern tubes may no longer be used.

DESTROYERS

2 ALMIRANTE CLASS

Name	No	Builders	Laid down	Launched	Commissioned
ALMIRANTE RIVEROS	18	Vickers-Armstrong Ltd, Barrow	12 Apr 1957	12 Dec 1958	31 Dec 1960
ALMIRANTE WILLIAMS	19	Vickers-Armstrong Ltd, Barrow	20 June 1956	5 May 1958	26 Mar 1960

Displacement, tons: 2730 standard; 3300 full load
Dimensions, feet (metres): 402 × 43 × 13.3 *(122.5 × 13.1 × 4)*
Main machinery: 2 Babcock & Wilcox boilers; 600 psi *(43.3 kg/cm sq)*; 850°F *(454°C)*; 2 Parsons Pametrada turbines; 54 000 hp *(40 MW)*; 2 shafts
Speed, knots: 34.5. **Range, miles:** 6000 at 16 kts
Complement: 266 (17 officers)

Missiles: SSM: 4 Aerospatiale MM 38 Exocet ❶; inertial cruise; active radar homing to 42 km *(23 nm)* at 0.9 Mach; warhead 165 kg; sea-skimmer.
SAM: 2 Short Bros Seacat quad launchers ❷; optical/radar guidance to 5 km *(2.7 nm)*; warhead 10 kg; 16 reloads.
Guns: 3 or 4 Vickers 4 in *(102 mm)*/60 Mk(N)R ❸; 75° elevation; 40 rounds/minute to 18 km *(10 nm)* anti-surface; 12 km *(6.5 nm)* anti-aircraft; weight of shell 16 kg.
4 Bofors 40 mm/70 ❹; 90° elevation; 300 rounds/minute to 12 km *(6.5 nm)* anti-surface; 4 km *(2.2 nm)* anti-aircraft; weight of shell 2.4 kg.
Torpedoes: 6—324 mm Mk 32 (2 triple) tubes ❺. Honeywell Mk 44 Mod 1; active homing to 5.5 km *(3 nm)* at 30 kts; warhead 34 kg.
A/S mortars: 2 Admiralty Squid DC mortars (3-barrelled) ❻; range 800 m; warhead 52 kg.
Countermeasures: ESM: WLR-1; radar warning. Elta IR sensor.
Combat data systems: Ferranti action data with autonomous displays.
Fire control: 2 Signaal M-4 directors for Seacat SAMs
Radars: Air search: Plessey AWS 1 ❼; range 110 km *(60 nm)*.
Air/surface search: Marconi SNW 10 ❽; E/F band.
Navigation: Racal Decca 1629; I band.
Fire control: Two SGR 102 ❾; Signaal M4/3 ❿; I/J band.
Sonars: Graseby Type 184 B; hull-mounted; active search and attack; medium frequency (6/9 kHz).
Type 170; hull mounted; active attack; high frequency (15 kHz).

Programmes: Ordered in May 1955.
Modernisation: Both modernised by Swan Hunter in co-operation with Plessey: *Almirante Williams* in 1971-74 and *Almirante Riveros* in 1973-75. In the late 1980s both were given an a further extensive refit with the addition of modern electronic equipment including Netherlands M4 fire control radars. Israeli Barak I may replace Seacat but these ships have a lower priority than the County and Leander classes. Additional ESM equipment fitted in 1990.

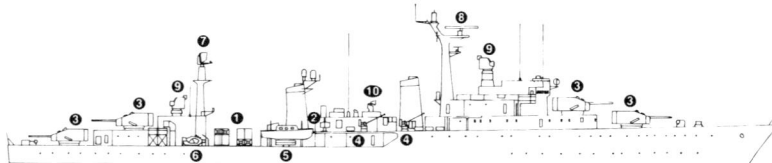

ALMIRANTE RIVEROS *(Scale 1 : 1200), Ian Sturton*

ALMIRANTE WILLIAMS *1992, Chilean Navy*

Operational: 4 in guns were removed one at a time for refurbishment in 1986-88 and ships operated minus one or two turrets each while the work was done.

Destroyers / CHILE

4 Ex-BRITISH COUNTY CLASS

Name	No	Builders	Laid down	Launched	Commissioned
PRAT (ex-HMS *Norfolk*)	11	Swan Hunter, Wallsend	15 Mar 1966	16 Nov 1967	7 Mar 1970
COCHRANE (ex-HMS *Antrim*)	12	Fairfield S. B. & Eng Co Ltd, Govan	20 Jan 1966	19 Oct 1967	14 July 1970
LATORRE (ex-HMS *Glamorgan*)	14	Vickers (Shipbuilding) Ltd, Newcastle-upon-Tyne	13 Sep 1962	9 July 1964	11 Oct 1966
BLANCO ENCALADA (ex-HMS *Fife*)	15	Fairfield S. B. & Eng Co Ltd, Govan	1 June 1962	9 July 1964	21 June 1966

Displacement, tons: 5440 standard; 6200 full load
Dimensions, feet (metres): 520.5 × 54 × 20.5 *(158.7 × 16.5 × 6.3)*
Main machinery: COSAG; 2 Babcock & Wilcox boilers; 700 psi *(49.2 kg/cm sq)*; 950°F *(510°C)*; 2 AEI steam turbines; 30 000 hp *(22.4 MW)*; 4 English Electric G6 gas turbines; 30 000 hp *(22.4 MW)*; 2 shafts
Speed, knots: 30. **Range, miles:** 3500 at 28 kts
Complement: 470 (36 officers)

Missiles: SSM: 4 Aerospatiale MM 38 Exocet ❶; inertial cruise; active radar homing to 42 km *(23 nm)* at 0.9 Mach; warhead 165 kg; sea-skimmer.
SAM: Short Bros Seaslug Mk 2 (11 and 14 only) ❷; range 45 km *(25 nm)* at 2 Mach; warhead HE; beam riding. Limited anti-surface role.
2 Shorts Seacat quad launchers (not in 14) ❸; optical/radar guidance to 5 km *(2.7 nm)*; warhead 10 kg. Israeli Barak I (15) command line of sight radar or optical guidance to 10 km *(5.5 nm)* at 2 Mach; warhead 22 kg. To be fitted in all.
Guns: 2 Vickers 4.5 in *(115 mm)* Mk 6 semi-automatic (twin) ❹; 80° elevation; 20 rounds/minute to 19 km *(10.3 nm)* anti-surface; 6 km *(3.2 nm)* anti-aircraft; weight of shell 25 kg.
2 or 4 Oerlikon 20 mm Mk 9 ❺; 55° elevation; 800 rounds/minute to 2 km.
2 Bofors 40 mm/60 (14 only) ❺ᴀ.
12.7 mm (single or twin) MGs.
Torpedoes: 6—324 mm Mk 32 (2 triple) tubes ❻; Honeywell Mk 44 Mod 1; active homing to 5.5 km *(3 nm)* at 30 kts; warhead 34 kg.
Countermeasures: Decoys: 2 Corvus 8-barrelled trainable chaff launchers ❼; distraction or centroid patterns to 1 km.
2 Wallop Barricade double layer chaff launchers ❽; 6 sets triple-barrelled with four modes of fire.
ESM: UA 8/9; radar warning.
Combat data systems: ADAWS-1 being replaced by Sisdef Imagen starting in 1993. SATCOM.
Fire control: Gunnery MRS 3 system. Seacat 2 GWS 22 systems (not in 14).
Radars: Air search: Marconi Type 965 M ❾ or 966 (14 and 15); A band.
Admiralty Type 277 M ❿; E band. For height finding.
Surface search: Marconi Type 992 Q or R ⓫; E/F band; range 55 km *(30 nm)*.
Navigation: Decca Type 978/1006; I band.
Fire control: Plessey Type 903 ⓬; I band (for Guns).
Marconi Type 901 (in 11 and 14) ⓭; G/H band (for Seaslug).
Two Plessey Type 904 (not in 14) ⓮; I band (for Seacat).
Sonars: Kelvin Hughes Type 162 M; hull-mounted; sideways looking classification; high-frequency.
Graseby Type 184 M or Type 184 S (15); hull-mounted; active search and attack; medium range; 7-9 kHz.

Helicopters: 1 Aerospatiale SA 319B Alouette III or Bell 206B (11 and 14) ⓯. 2 NAS 332F Super Puma (12 and 15) ⓰.

Programmes: Transferred 6 April 1982 *(Prat)*, 22 June 1984 *(Cochrane)*, 3 October 1986 *(Latorre)* and 12 August 1987 *(Blanco Encalada)*. Extensive refits carried out after transfer. *Glamorgan* renamed *Latorre* after the Swedish-built cruiser which paid off in 1986. Although all are named after senior officers, the titles Almirante and Capitan are not used.
Modernisation: *Blanco Encalada* converted at Talcahuano into helicopter carrier for two Super Pumas completed May 1988; *Cochrane* similar conversion completed in 1992. The remaining two will serve as Flagships. All of the class to get the Israeli Barak I (*Blanco Encalada* in 1992/93) and new communications, optronic directors and ECM equipment. VDS sonars and torpedo decoys are also a possibility. New combat data system to be fitted starting in 1993. *Latorre* was transferred with 40 mm guns in lieu of Seacats (damaged in the Falklands War). There are no plans to remove Seaslug from the remaining two ships.
Structure: *Blanco Encalada* and *Cochrane* are now markedly different in appearance from their two half-sisters with a greatly enlarged flight deck continued right aft to accommodate two large helicopters simultaneously, making them effectively flush-decked. The hangar has also been completely rebuilt.

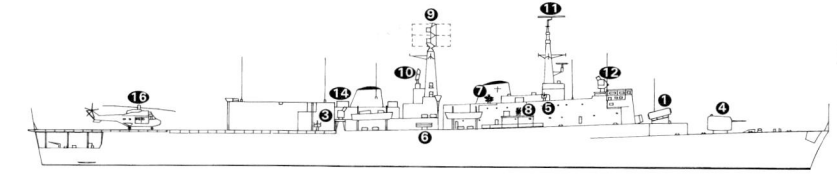

COCHRANE (Scale 1 : 1500), Ian Sturton

BLANCO ENCALADA 1991, Chilean Navy

LATORRE (Scale 1 : 1500), Ian Sturton

PRAT 1991, Chilean Navy

FRIGATES

4 BRITISH LEANDER CLASS

Name	No	Builders	Laid down	Launched	Commissioned
CONDELL	06	Yarrow & Co, Scotstoun	5 June 1971	12 June 1972	21 Dec 1973
LYNCH	07	Yarrow & Co, Scotstoun	6 Dec 1971	6 Dec 1972	25 May 1974
MINISTRO ZENTENO (ex-*Achilles*)	08 (ex-F 12)	Yarrow & Co, Scotstoun	1 Dec 1967	21 Nov 1968	9 July 1970
GENERAL BAQUEDANO (ex-*Ariadne*)	09 (ex-F 72)	Yarrow & Co, Scotstoun	1 Nov 1969	10 Sep 1971	10 Feb 1973

Displacement, tons: 2500 standard; 2962 full load
Dimensions, feet (metres): 372 oa; 360 wl × 43 × 18 (screws) *(113.4; 109.7 × 13.1 × 5.5)*
Main machinery: 2 Babcock & Wilcox boilers; 550 psi *(38.7 kg/cm sq)*; 850°F *(450°C)*; 2 White/English Electric turbines; 30 000 hp *(22.4 MW)*; 2 shafts
Speed, knots: 29. **Range, miles:** 4500 at 12 kts
Complement: 263 (20 officers)

Missiles: SSM: 4 Aerospatiale MM 40 Exocet (06, 07) ❶; inertial cruise; active radar homing to 70 km *(40 nm)* at 0.9 Mach; warhead 165 kg; sea-skimmer.
SAM: Short Bros Seacat GWS 22 quad launcher ❷; optical/radar guidance to 5 km *(2.7 nm)*; warhead 10 kg; 16 reloads. Being replaced by Israeli Barak I vertical launch canisters.
Guns: 2 Vickers 4.5 in *(115 mm)*/45 Mk 6 (twin) semi-automatic ❸; 80° elevation; 20 rounds/minute to 19 km *(10 nm)* anti-surface; 6 km *(3.2 nm)* anti-aircraft; weight of shell 45 kg.
2 Oerlikon 20 mm Mk 9 ❹; 55° elevation; 800 rounds/minute to 2 km.
Torpedoes: 6—324 mm Mk 32 (2 triple) tubes ❺ (not in 09). Honeywell Mk 44 Mod 1; active homing to 5.5 km *(3 nm)* at 30 kts; warhead 34 kg. To be replaced by Murene in due course.
Countermeasures: Decoys: 2 Corvus 8-barrelled trainable chaff rocket launchers ❻; distraction or centroid patterns to 1 km. Wallop Barricade double layer chaff launchers.
ESM: UA 8/9; radar intercept. FH12 HF/DF. Elta IR sensor.
Combat data systems: Sisdef Imagen in two of the class in due course.
Fire control: MRS 3 system for gunnery. GWS 22 system for Seacat.
Radars: Air search: Marconi Type 965/966 ❼; A band.
Surface search: Marconi Type 992 Q ❽ (06 and 07); Plessey Type 994 ❾ (08 and 09); E/F band.
Navigation: Kelvin Hughes Type 1006; I band.
Fire control: Plessey Type 903 ❿; I band (for guns).
Plessey Type 904 ⓫; I band (for Seacat). Both radars may be replaced by IAI/Elta in due course.
Sonars: Graseby Type 184 M; hull-mounted; active search and attack; medium frequency (6/9 kHz).
Graseby Type 170 B; hull-mounted; active attack; high frequency (15 kHz).
Kelvin Hughes Type 162 M; hull-mounted; sideways looking classification; high frequency.

Helicopters: 1 Aerospatiale SA 319B Alouette III ⓬ or Bell 206B. Platform for Super Puma (06 and 07).

Programmes: First two ordered from Yarrow & Co Ltd, Scotstoun in the late 1960s. Third ship purchased in September 1990 and fourth in June 1992.
Modernisation: In 1989 *Lynch* was considerably modified at Talcahuano Dockyard with two twin MM 40 Exocet launchers being mounted on each side of the hangar (instead of the MM 38 aft) and by moving the torpedo tubes down one deck. The enlarged flight deck can now take a Super Puma aircraft. Other modifications include Barak VLS canisters to replace Seacat in due course, improvements to the fire control radars and Israeli EW systems. Two ships are to be fitted with Sisdef Imagen combat data system. It is reported that *Condell* started a similar modernisation to *Lynch* in mid-1992. *General Baquedano* may have torpedo tubes replaced in 1993.
Structure: *Condell* and *Lynch* have slightly taller foremasts than ex-British Leander class.

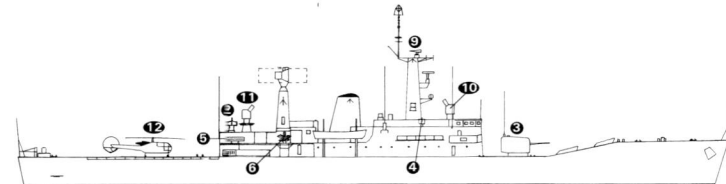
MINISTRO ZENTENO *(Scale 1 : 1200), Ian Sturton*

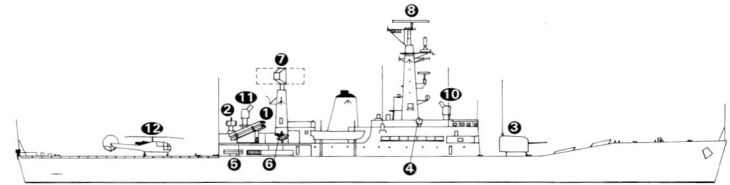
LYNCH *(Scale 1 : 1200), Ian Sturton*

LYNCH *1992, Chilean Navy*

MINISTRO ZENTENO *1992, Chilean Navy*

GENERAL BAQUEDANO *6/1992, Maritime Photographic*

SHIPBORNE AIRCRAFT

Numbers/Type: 7 Aerospatiale SA 319B Alouette III.
Operational speed: 113 kts *(210 km/h)*.
Service ceiling: 10 500 ft *(3200 m)*.
Range: 290 nm *(540 km)*.
Role/Weapon systems: Operated as standard shipborne helicopter; some shore-based in similar ASW role and for SAR utility duties. There is a report that these aircraft may be sold to South Africa. Sensors: Omera search radar, hand-mounted FLIR. Weapons: ASW; 1 × Mk 44 torpedo.

ALOUETTE III *2/1990, Maritime Photographic*

Numbers/Type: 7 Bell 206B JetRanger.
Operational speed: 115 kts *(213 km/h)*.
Service ceiling: 13 500 ft *(4115 m)*.
Range: 368 nm *(682 km)*.
Role/Weapon systems: Some tasks and training carried out by torpedo-armed liaison helicopter; emergency war role for ASW. Weapons: ASW; 1 × Mk 44 torpedo.

JETRANGER *1992, Chilean Navy*

Numbers/Type: 4 Nurtanio (Aerospatiale) NAS 332SC Super Puma.
Operational speed: 151 kts *(279 km/h)*.
Service ceiling: 15 090 ft *(4600 m)*.
Range: 335 nm *(620 km)*.
Role/Weapon systems: ASV/ASW helicopters for DLG conversions; surface search and SAR secondary roles. Sensors: Thomson-CSF radar and Alcatel dipping sonar. Weapons: ASW; 2 × Mk 46 torpedoes (to be replaced by Murene) or depth bombs. ASV; 1 or 2 × AM 39 Exocet anti-ship missile.

SUPER PUMA *1992, Chilean Navy*

Numbers/Type: 5 MBB BO 105C.
Operational speed: 113 kts *(210 km/h)*.
Service ceiling: 9845 ft *(3000 m)*.
Range: 407 nm *(754 km)*.
Role/Weapon systems: Coastal patrol helicopter for patrol, training and liaison duties; SAR as secondary role. Sensors: Bendix search radar. Weapons: Unarmed.

BO 105C *1992, Chilean Navy*

Numbers/Type: 4 Aerospatiale SA 365F Dauphin.
Operational speed: 140 kts *(260 km/h)*.
Service ceiling: 15 000 ft *(4575 m)*.
Range: 410 nm *(758 km)*.
Role/Weapon systems: ASW helicopters for escorts to replace SA 319B Alouette IIIs ordered in October 1988. Possibly cancelled in favour of more BO 105s. Sensors: Thomson-CSF Agrion 15 radar. Weapons: 2 × Mk 44 torpedoes (to be replaced by Murene).

LAND-BASED MARITIME AIRCRAFT (FRONT LINE)

Note: In addition there are EMB 110, Falcon 200 and Casa Aviocar 212 support aircraft.

Numbers/Type: 6 Embraer EMB-111 Bandeirante.
Operational speed: 194 kts *(360 km/h)*.
Service ceiling: 25 500 ft *(7770 m)*.
Range: 1590 nm *(2945 km)*.
Role/Weapon systems: Designated EMB-111N for peacetime EEZ and wartime MR. Sensors: Eaton-AIL AN/APS-128 search radar, ECM/ESM, searchlight. Weapons: Strike; 6 × 127 mm or 28 × 70 mm rockets.

EMB-111 *1992, Chilean Navy*

Numbers/Type: 8 Pilatus PC-7 Turbo-Trainer.
Operational speed: 270 kts *(500 km/h)*.
Service ceiling: 32 000 ft *(9755 m)*.
Range: 1420 nm *(2630 km)*.
Role/Weapon systems: Training includes simulated attacks to exercise ships' AA defences; emergency war role for strike operations. Sensors: None. Weapons: 4 × 127 mm or similar rockets and machine gun pods.

Numbers/Type: 2 Dassault-Breguet Gardian.
Operational speed: 470 kts *(870 km/h)*.
Service ceiling: 45 000 ft *(13 715 m)*.
Range: 2425 nm *(4490 km)*.
Role/Weapon systems: Maritime reconnaissance role with limited strike capability. Sensors: Thomson-CSF Varan radar. Omega navigation. ESM/ECM pods. Weapons: ASV; can carry 4 × AM 39 Exocet or podded guns or rocket launchers.

PATROL FORCES

Note: Project Zonomac is the planned building of four offshore patrol vessels with a helo deck and light gun. Orders should have been placed in 1992 but have been delayed by lack of funds. Former ocean-going tugs are being purchased for both patrol and survey duties.

1 Ex-US CHEROKEE CLASS

Name	No	Builders	Commissioned
SARGENTO ALDEA (ex-USS *Arikara* ATF 98)	63	Charleston S. B. & D. D. Co	5 Jan 1944

Displacement, tons: 1235 standard; 1640 full load
Dimensions, feet (metres): 205 × 38.5 × 17 *(62.5 × 11.7 × 5.2)*
Main machinery: Diesel-electric; 4 Busch-Sulzer BS-539 diesels; 4 generators; 1 motor; 3000 hp *(2.24 MW)*; 1 shaft
Speed, knots: 16. **Range, miles:** 7000 at 15 kts; 15 000 at 8 kts
Complement: 85
Guns: 1 USN 3 in *(76 mm)*/50 Mk 26; 85° elevation; 20 rounds/minute to 12 km *(6.5 nm)* anti-surface; 9 km *(5 nm)* anti-aircraft; weight of shell 6 kg.
2 Oerlikon 20 mm; 55° elevation; 800 rounds/minute to 2 km.
Radars: Surface search: Westinghouse SPS 5; G/H band; range 37 km *(20 nm)*.

Comment: Launched on 22 June 1943. Transferred by lease on 1 July 1971, and by sale on 30 September 1992.

SARGENTO ALDEA *1991, Chilean Navy*

108 CHILE / Patrol forces — Light forces

1 ANTARCTIC PATROL SHIP

Name	No	Builders	Commissioned
PILOTO PARDO	45	Haarlemsche Scheepsbouw, Netherlands	Aug 1958

Displacement, tons: 1250 light; 2750 full load
Dimensions, feet (metres): 269 × 39 × 15 *(82 × 11.9 × 4.6)*
Main machinery: Diesel-electric; 2000 hp(m) *(1.47 MW)*; 1 shaft
Speed, knots: 14. **Range, miles:** 6000 at 10 kts
Complement: 56 (8 officers)
Military lift: 24 troops
Guns: 1–3 in *(76 mm)* (not always embarked).
Helicopters: 1 Aerospatiale SA 319B Alouette III.

Comment: Antarctic patrol ship, transport and research vessel with reinforced hull to navigate in ice. Launched on 11 June 1958. Also listed as a survey ship by the International Hydrographic Bureau. Possible replacement being sought together with an Icebreaker Tug.

PILOTO PARDO   1991, Chilean Navy

LIGHT FORCES

2 ISRAELI SAAR 3 CLASS (FAST ATTACK CRAFT—MISSILE)

Name	No	Builders	Commissioned
IQUIQUE (ex-*Hamit*)	32	CMN Cherbourg	1969
COVADONGA (ex-*Hefz*)	33	CMN Cherbourg	1969

Displacement, tons: 220 standard; 250 full load
Dimensions, feet (metres): 147.6 × 23 × 8.2 *(45 × 7 × 2.5)*
Main machinery: 4 MTU MD 16V 537 TB80 diesels; 10 000 hp(m) *(7.35 MW)* sustained; 4 shafts
Speed, knots: 40+. **Range, miles:** 2500 at 15 kts; 1600 at 20 kts; 1000 at 30 kts
Complement: 35-40 (5 officers)

Missiles: SSM: 6 IAI Gabriel II; active radar or optical TV guidance; semi-active radar homing to 36 km *(20 nm)* at 0.7 Mach; warhead 75 kg.
Guns: 1 OTO Melara 3 in *(76 mm)*/62 DP; 85° elevation; 65 rounds/minute to 8 km *(4.4 nm)*; weight of shell 6 kg.
2—12.7 mm MGs.
Countermeasures: Decoys: 6—24 tube, 4 single tube chaff launchers.
ESM: Elta Electronics MN-53; intercept.
ECM: Jammer.
Radars: Air/surface search: Thomson-CSF TH-D 1040 Neptune; G band; range 33 km *(18 nm)* for 2 m² target.
Fire control: Selenia Orion RTN 10X; I/J band; range 40 km *(22 nm)*.

Programmes: Both acquired from Israel in December 1988 and commissioned into the Chilean Navy 3 May 1989. There are no immediate plans to transfer any more of the class.

IQUIQUE   1992, Chilean Navy

2 ISRAELI SAAR 4 CLASS (FAST ATTACK CRAFT—MISSILE)

Name	No	Builders	Commissioned
CASMA (ex-*Romah*)	30	Haifa Shipyard	Mar 1974
CHIPANA (ex-*Keshet*)	31	Haifa Shipyard	Oct 1973

Displacement, tons: 415 standard; 450 full load
Dimensions, feet (metres): 190.6 × 25 × 8 *(58 × 7.8 × 2.4)*
Main machinery: 4 MTU 16V 538 TB82 diesels; 11 880 hp(m) *(8.74 MW)* sustained; 4 shafts
Speed, knots: 32. **Range, miles:** 1650 at 30 kts; 4000 at 17.5 kts
Complement: 45

Missiles: SSM: 4 IAI Gabriel I; radar or optical guidance; semi-active radar homing to 20 km *(10.8 nm)* at 0.7 Mach; warhead 75 kg HE.
Guns: 2 OTO Melara 3 in *(76 mm)*/62 compact; 85° elevation; 85 rounds/minute to 16 km *(8.7 nm)* anti-surface; 12 km *(6.5 nm)* anti-aircraft; weight of shell 6 kg.
2 Oerlikon 20 mm; 55° elevation; 800 rounds/minute to 2 km.
Countermeasures: Decoys: 4 Rafael LRCR chaff decoy launchers.
Radars: Surface search: Thomson-CSF THD 1040 Neptune; E/F band; range 110 km *(60 nm)*.
Fire control: Elta Electronics M 2221; I/J band; range 40 km *(22 nm)*.

Programmes: One transferred late 1979 and second in February 1981 for refit and deployment to Beagle Channel.

CASMA   1988, Chilean Navy

4 LÜRSSEN TYPE (FAST ATTACK CRAFT—TORPEDO)

Name	No	Builders	Commissioned
GUACOLDA	80	Bazán, San Fernando	30 July 1965
FRESIA	81	Bazán, San Fernando	9 Dec 1965
QUIDORA	82	Bazán, San Fernando	28 Mar 1966
TEGUALDA	83	Bazán, San Fernando	1 July 1966

Displacement, tons: 134 full load
Dimensions, feet (metres): 118.1 × 18.4 × 7.2 *(36 × 5.6 × 2.2)*
Main machinery: 2 MTU MB 16V 652 SB60 diesels; 3200 hp(m) *(2.35 MW)* sustained; 2 shafts
Speed, knots: 32. **Range, miles:** 1500 at 15 kts
Complement: 20
Guns: 2 Bofors 40 mm/70.
Torpedoes: 4—21 in *(533 mm)* tubes for heavyweight anti-ship torpedoes.
Radars: Navigation: Decca 505; I band.

Comment: Built to West German Lürssen design from 1963 to 1966. First launched 1964.

FRESIA   1989, Chilean Navy

1 + 3 MICALVI CLASS (LARGE PATROL CRAFT)

Name	No	Builders	Commissioned
CONTRAMAESTRE MICALVI	PSG 71	Asmar Talcahuano	3 Mar 1993
CONTRAMAESTRE ORTIZ	PSG 72	Asmar Talcahuano	Nov 1993
ASPIRANTE ISAZA	PSG 73	Asmar Talcahuano	Jan 1994
ASPIRANTE MOREL	PSG 74	Asmar Talcahuano	June 1994

Displacement, tons: 518 full load
Dimensions, feet (metres): 139.4 × 27.9 × 9.5 *(42.5 × 8.5 × 2.9)*
Main machinery: 2 diesels; 2560 hp(m) *(1.88 MW)*; 2 shafts
Speed, knots: 15. **Range, miles:** 4200 at 12 kts
Complement: 23 (5 officers)
Guns: 1 Bofors 40 mm/60. 2 Oerlikon 20 mm.
Radars: Surface search: I band.

Comment: Built by ASMAR Talcahuano under design project Taitao. First in service December 1992, remainder 1993. Multi-purpose patrol vessels with a secondary mission of transport and servicing navigational aids. Provision for bow thruster, sonar and mine rails. Can carry 35 tons cargo in holds and 18 tons in containers. Crane lift of 2.5 tons.

CONTRAMAESTRE MICALVI   1992, ASMAR, Chile

Light forces — Survey ships / CHILE   109

1 US PC-1638 CLASS (LARGE PATROL CRAFT)

Name	No	Builders	Commissioned
PAPUDO (ex-US *PC 1646*)	37	Asmar, Talcahuano	27 Nov 1971

Displacement, tons: 412 full load
Dimensions, feet (metres): 173.7 × 23 × 10.2 *(53 × 7 × 3.1)*
Main machinery: 2 GM 16—567 diesels; 2300 hp *(2.1 MW)*; 2 shafts
Speed, knots: 19. **Range, miles:** 5000 at 10 kts
Complement: 69 (4 officers)
Guns: 1 Bofors 40 mm/60; 90° elevation; 300 rounds/minute to 12 km *(6.5 nm)* anti-surface; 4 km *(2.2 nm)* anti-aircraft; weight of shell 0.89 kg.
 4 Oerlikon 20 mm; 50° elevation; 800 rounds/minute to 2 km.
Depth charges: 2 K-type throwers; 4 racks

Comment: Of similar design to the Turkish Hisar class built to the US PC plan. Hedgehog mortar has been removed.

PAPUDO   *1990, Chilean Navy*

6 ISRAELI DABUR CLASS (COASTAL PATROL CRAFT)

GRUMETE DIAZ	1814	**GRUMETE TELLEZ**	1817
GRUMETE BOLADOS	1815	**GRUMETE BRAVO**	1818
GRUMETE SALINAS	1816	**GRUMETE CAMPOS**	1819

Displacement, tons: 39 full load
Dimensions, feet (metres): 64.9 × 18 × 5.9 *(19.8 × 5.5 × 1.8)*
Main machinery: 2 Detroit 12V-71TA diesels; 840 hp *(627 kW)* sustained; 2 shafts
Speed, knots: 19. **Range, miles:** 450 at 13 kts
Complement: 8 (2 officers)
Guns: 1 Oerlikon 20 mm. 1—12.7 mm MG.
Radars: Surface search: Racal Decca Super 101 Mk 3; I band.

Comment: Transferred from Israel and commissioned 3 January 1991. A fast inflatable boat is carried on the stern. Deployed in the Fourth Naval Zone.

GRUMETE TELLEZ   *1991, Chilean Navy*

AMPHIBIOUS FORCES

2 ELICURA CLASS (LSMs)

Name	No	Builders	Commissioned
ELICURA	90	Talcahuano	10 Dec 1968
OROMPELLO	94	Dade Dry Dock Co, Miami	15 Sep 1964

Displacement, tons: 290 light; 750 full load
Dimensions, feet (metres): 145 × 34 × 12.8 *(44.2 × 10.4 × 3.9)*
Main machinery: 2 Cummins VT-17-700M diesels; 900 hp *(660 kW)*; 2 shafts
Speed, knots: 10.5. **Range, miles:** 2900 at 9 kts
Complement: 20
Military lift: 350 tons
Guns: 3 Oerlikon 20 mm (can be carried).
Radars: Navigation: Raytheon 1500B; I/J band.

Comment: Two of similar class operated by Chilean Shipping Co. Oil fuel, 77 tons.

ELICURA   *1991, Chilean Navy*

3 BATRAL CLASS (LSTs)

Name	No	Builders	Launched	Commissioned
MAIPO	91	Asmar, Talcahuano	26 Sep 1981	1 Jan 1982
RANCAGUA	92	Asmar, Talcahuano	6 Mar 1982	8 Aug 1983
CHACABUCO	93	Asmar, Talcahuano	16 July 1985	15 Apr 1986

Displacement, tons: 873 standard; 1409 full load
Dimensions, feet (metres): 260.4 × 42.7 × 8.2 *(79.4 × 13 × 2.5)*
Main machinery: 2 SACM Type 195 V12 CSHR diesels; 3600 hp(m) *(2.65 MW)* sustained; 2 shafts; cp props
Speed, knots: 16. **Range, miles:** 3500 at 13 kts
Complement: 49
Military lift: 180 troops; 350 tons
Guns: 1 Bofors 40 mm/60. 1 Oerlikon 20 mm. 2—81 mm mortars.
Radars: Navigation: Decca; I/J band.
Helicopters: Platform for 1 Super Puma.

Comment: First pair laid down in 1980 to standard French design with French equipment.

RANCAGUA   *1992, Chilean Navy*

SURVEY SHIPS

Notes: 1. *Piloto Pardo* also listed—see *Patrol Forces*.
2. A projected Hydrographic vessel of 2000 tons, ice strengthened, is planned. To be built by ASMAR in due course.

1 Ex-US ROBERT D CONRAD CLASS

Name	No	Builders	Commissioned
VIDAL GORMAZ (ex-*Thomas Washington*)	60 (ex-AGOR 10)	Marinette Marine, Wisconsin	27 Sep 1965

Displacement, tons: 1370 full load
Dimensions, feet (metres): 208.9 × 40 × 15.3 *(63.7 × 12.2 × 4.7)*
Main machinery: Diesel-electric; 2 Cummins diesel generators; 1 motor; 1000 hp *(746 kW)*; 1 shaft
Speed, knots: 13.5. **Range, miles:** 12 000 at 12 kts
Complement: 41 (9 officers, 15 scientists)
Radars: Navigation: TM 1660/12S; I band.

Comment: Transferred on 28 September 1992. This is the first class of ships designed and built by the US Navy for oceanographic research. Fitted with instrumentation and laboratories to measure gravity and magnetism, water temperature, sound transmission in water, and the profile of the ocean floor. Special features include 10 ton capacity boom and winches for handling over-the-side equipment; 620 hp gas turbine (housed in funnel structure) for providing 'quiet' power when conducting experiments; can propel the ship at 6.5 kts.
 Ships of this class are in service with Brazil *(Sands)*, Mexico *(James M Gilliss* and *S P Lee)* and New Zealand *(Charles H Davies)*.

VIDAL GORMAZ   *1992, Chilean Navy*

110 CHILE / Survey ships — Transports

1 Ex-US CHEROKEE CLASS

Name	No	Builders	Commissioned
YELCHO (ex-USS *Tekesta* ATF 93)	64	Commercial Iron Works, Portland, Oregon	16 Aug 1943

Displacement, tons: 1235 standard; 1640 full load
Dimensions, feet (metres): 205 × 38.5 × 17 *(62.5 × 11.7 × 5.2)*
Main machinery: Diesel-electric; 4 GM 12-278A diesels; 4400 hp *(3.28 MW)*; 4 generators; 1 motor; 3000 hp *(2.24 MW)*; 1 shaft
Speed, knots: 16. **Range, miles:** 7000 at 15 kts; 15 000 at 8 kts
Complement: 72 (7 officers)
Guns: 1—3 in *(76 mm)* Mk 26; 85° elevation; 20 rounds/minute to 12 km *(6 nm)* anti-surface; 9 km *(5 nm)* anti-aircraft; weight of shell 6 kg.
2 Oerlikon 20 mm; 55° elevation; 800 rounds/minute to 2 km.

Comment: Was fitted with powerful pumps and other salvage equipment although these were removed on conversion for surveying. Laid down on 7 September 1942, launched on 20 March 1943 and loaned to Chile by the USA on 15 May 1960. Transferred by sale on 30 September 1992. Employed as Antarctic research ship and surveying vessel. Similar to *Sargento Aldea* listed under *Patrol Forces*.

YELCHO 1987, Pedro del Fierro Carmona

TRAINING SHIPS

Note: There is also a small training yacht *Blanca Estela* which can carry a crew of 14 cadets.

Name	No	Builders	Commissioned
URIBE (ex-USS *Daniel Griffin*, APD 38)	29	Bethlehem, Hingham	9 June 1943

Displacement, tons: 2130 full load
Dimensions, feet (metres): 306 × 37 × 12.6 *(93.3 × 11.3 × 3.8)*
Main machinery: Turbo-electric; 2 Foster-Wheeler boilers; 435 psi *(30.6 kg/cm sq)*; 750°F *(399°C)*; 2 GE turbo-generators; 12 000 hp *(9 MW)*; 2 motors; 2 shafts
Speed, knots: 22. **Range, miles:** 5000 at 15 kts
Complement: 209
Guns: 1—5 in *(127 mm)*/38 Mk 30. 6 Bofors 40 mm/60 (2 twin).
Radars: Surface search: SPS 4; E/F band.

Comment: Ex-US Charles Lawrence class converted transport transferred 1 December 1966. Paid off in 1984 but was back in commission again in 1988 as a training and general purpose vessel based at Talcahuano.

URIBE 1991, Chilean Navy

Name	No	Builders	Commissioned
ESMERALDA (ex-*Don Juan de Austria*)	43	Bazán, Cadiz	15 June 1954

Displacement, tons: 3420 standard; 3754 full load
Dimensions, feet (metres): 269.2 pp; 360 oa × 44.6 × 23 *(82; 109.8 × 13.1 × 7)*
Main machinery: 1 Fiat diesel; 1400 hp(m) *(1.03 MW)*; 1 shaft
Speed, knots: 11. **Range, miles:** 8000 at 8 kts
Complement: 271 plus 80 cadets
Guns: 2—37 mm saluting guns.

Comment: Four-masted schooner originally intended for the Spanish Navy. Near sister ship of *Juan Sebastian de Elcano* in the Spanish Navy. Refitted Saldanha Bay, South Africa, 1977. Sail area, 26 910 sq ft.

ESMERALDA 4/1992, van Ginderen Collection

TRANSPORTS

Name	No	Builders	Commissioned
AQUILES	AP 47	Asmar, Talcahuano	15 July 1988

Displacement, tons: 2767 light; 4550 full load
Dimensions, feet (metres): 337.8 × 55.8 × 18 *(103 × 17 × 5.5 (max))*
Main machinery: 2 Krupp MaK 8 M 453B diesels; 7080 hp(m) *(5.10 MW)* sustained; 1 shaft
Speed, knots: 18
Complement: 80
Military lift: 250 troops
Helicopters: Platform for up to Super Puma size.

Comment: Ordered 4 October 1985, launched 4 December 1987. Can be converted rapidly to act as hospital ship. Has replaced the old *Aquiles* (ex-*Tjaldur*).

AQUILES 1992, Chilean Navy

Name	No	Builders	Commissioned
AGUILA (ex-*Australgas*)	AP 48	Suendborg, Denmark	1957

Displacement, tons: 735 full load
Dimensions, feet (metres): 168.3 × 28.5 × 11.8 *(51.3 × 8.7 × 3.6)*
Main machinery: 1 Burmeister & Wain Alpha diesel; 480 hp(m) *(353 kW)*; 1 shaft
Speed, knots: 9. **Range, miles:** 6000 at 9 kts
Complement: 13
Guns: 3 Oerlikon 20 mm.

Comment: Acquired in 1984 and commissioned into the Navy in 1985. Former commercial liquid gas carrier, now used as a transport.

AGUILA 1990, Chilean Navy

Name	No	Builders	Commissioned
METEORO	YFB 110	Asmar, Talcahuano	1967

Displacement, tons: 205 full load
Dimensions, feet (metres): 80 × 22 × 8.5 *(24.4 × 6.7 × 2.6)*
Main machinery: 1 diesel; 1 shaft
Speed, knots: 8
Military lift: 220 troops

Comment: Transferred to Seaman's School as harbour transport.

METEORO *1990, Chilean Navy*

TANKERS

Name	No	Builders	Commissioned
ALMIRANTE JORGE MONTT (ex-RFA *Tidepool*)	52	Hawthorn Leslie, Hebburn	28 June 1963

Displacement, tons: 8531 light; 27 400 full load
Measurement, tons: 18 900 dwt; 14 130 gross
Dimensions, feet (metres): 583 × 71 × 32 *(177.6 × 21.6 × 9.8)*
Main machinery: 2 Babcock & Wilcox boilers; 850 psi *(60 kg/cm sq)*; 950°F *(510°C)*; Pametrada turbines; 15 000 hp *(11.2 MW)*; 1 shaft
Speed, knots: 18.3
Complement: 110
Cargo capacity: 18 000 tons liquids
Guns: 4 Oerlikon 20 mm Mk 9; 4 Browning 12.7 mm (2 twin) MGs.
Radars: Navigation: Kelvin Hughes 14/12; I band.
Helicopter Control: Kelvin Hughes 14/16; I band.
Helicopters: Platform for up to 3 Super Puma.

Comment: Eventually transferred August 1982, after being delayed by the British in April 1982 for use in the Falklands' campaign. In poor condition and may soon be scrapped.

ALMIRANTE JORGE MONTT *1992, Chilean Navy*

Name	No	Builders	Commissioned
ARAUCANO	53	Burmeister & Wain, Copenhagen	10 Jan 1967

Displacement, tons: 17 300
Dimensions, feet (metres): 497.6 × 74.9 × 28.8 *(151.7 × 22.8 × 8.8)*
Main machinery: 1 Burmeister & Wain Type 62 VT 2BF140 diesel; 10 800 hp(m) *(7.94 MW)*; 1 shaft
Speed, knots: 17. **Range, miles:** 12 000 at 15.5 kts
Cargo capacity: 21 126 m³ liquid; 1444 m³ dry
Guns: 8 Bofors 40 mm/70 (4 twin); 80° elevation; 120 rounds/minute to 10 km *(5 nm)* anti-surface; 3 km *(1.6 nm)* anti-aircraft; weight of shell 0.89 kg.

Comment: Launched on 21 June 1966.

ARAUCANO *1992, Chilean Navy*

Name	No	Builders	Commissioned
GUARDIAN BRITO (ex-M. S. *Sylvia*)	YOG 101	Marco Chilena Sa-Iquique	1966

Displacement, tons: 482 full load
Dimensions, feet (metres): 129.9 × 23.9 × 10.8 *(39.6 × 7.3 × 3.3)*
Main machinery: 1 MWM diesel; 400 hp(m) *(294 kW)*; 1 shaft
Speed, knots: 10. **Range, miles:** 3000 at 8 kts
Complement: 8 (1 officer)

Comment: Small former commercial tanker. Enlarged for naval service at Asmar, Talcahuano after acquisition 13 January 1983.

GUARDIAN BRITO *1990, Chilean Navy*

SUBMARINE SUPPORT VESSEL

Note: *Huascar*, completed 1865, previously Peruvian monitor, now harbour Flagship at Talcahuano and open to the public as a museum.

Name	No	Builders	Commissioned
ANGAMOS (ex-M/V *Puerto Montt*, ex-M/V *Kobenhavn*)	70	Orenstein & Koppel, West Germany	1966

Measurement, tons: 4616 gross
Dimensions, feet (metres): 308.2 × 53.2 × 13.6 *(93.9 × 16.2 × 4.1)*
Main machinery: 2 Lind-Pielstick diesels; 6500 hp(m) *(4.78 MW)*; 2 shafts
Speed, knots: 17

Comment: Acquired from Chilean state shipping company early 1977 for conversion to submarine support vessel. Entered service early 1979. Former Chilean and Danish ferry.

ANGAMOS *1992, Chilean Navy*

TUGS/SUPPLY VESSELS

Note: Small harbour tugs *Caupolican*, *Reyes*, *Galvez* and *Cortés*, and the small personnel transport *Sobenes* are also in commission.

SOBENES *1991, Chilean Navy*

112 CHILE / Tugs/supply vessels — Coast guard

3 VERITAS CLASS (TUG/SUPPLY VESSELS)

Name	No	Builders	Commissioned
JANEQUEO (ex-*Maersk Transporter*)	ATF 65	Salthammex Batbyggeri, Vestness	1974
GALVARINO (ex-*Maersk Traveller*)	ATF 66	Aukra Bruk, Aukra	1974
LAUTARO (ex-*Maersk Tender*)	ATF 67	Aukra Bruk, Aukra	1973

Displacement, tons: 941 light; 2380 full load
Dimensions, feet (metres): 191.3 × 41.4 × 12.8 *(58.3 × 12.6 × 3.9)*
Main machinery: 2 Krupp MaK 8 M 453AK diesels; 6400 hp(m) *(4.7 MW)*; 2 shafts; cp props; bow thruster
Speed, knots: 14
Complement: 11 plus 12 spare berths
Cargo capacity: 1400 tons
Radars: Navigation: Terma Pilot 7T-48; Furuno FR 240; I band.

Comment: First two delivered from Maersk and commissioned into Navy 26 January 1988. Third one delivered in 1991. Bollard pull, 70 metric tons; towing winch, 100 tons. Fully air-conditioned. Designed for towing large semi-submersible platform in extreme weather conditions. Ice strengthened.

JANEQUEO 1990, Chilean Navy

2 SMIT LLOYD CLASS

Name	No	Builders	Commissioned
LEUCOTON (ex-*Smit Lloyd* 44)	ATF 68	de Waal, Zaltbommel	1972
COLO COLO (ex-*Smit Lloyd* —)	ATF 69	de Waal, Zaltbommel	1972

Displacement, tons: 1750 full load
Dimensions, feet (metres): 174.2 × 39.4 × 14.4 *(53.1 × 12 × 4.4)*
Main machinery: 2 Burmeister & Wain Alpha diesels; 4000 hp(m) *(2.94 MW)*; 2 shafts
Speed, knots: 13

Comment: Acquired in February 1991 and 1992 respectively. Modified at Punta Arenas and now used mainly as supply ships.

LEUCOTON 1992, Chilean Navy

FLOATING DOCKS

Name	No	Lift	Commissioned
INGENIERO MERY (ex-*ARD 25*)	131	3000 tons	1944 (1973)
MUTILLA (ex-*ARD 32*)	132	3000 tons	1944 (1960)
MARINERO GUTIERREZ	—	1200 tons	1991

COAST GUARD

2 BUOY TENDERS

Name	No	Builders	Commissioned
MARINERO FUENTEALBA	75	Asmar, Talcahuano	22 July 1966
CABO ODGER	76	Asmar, Talcahuano	21 Apr 1967

Displacement, tons: 215
Dimensions, feet (metres): 80 × 21 × 9 *(24.4 × 6.4 × 2.7)*
Main machinery: 1 Cummins diesel; 340 hp *(254 kW)*; 1 shaft
Speed, knots: 9. **Range, miles:** 2600 at 9 kts
Complement: 19
Guns: 1 Oerlikon 20 mm. 3 Browning 12.7 mm MGs.

MARINERO FUENTEALBA 1991, Chilean Navy

2 + 2 (4) PROTECTOR CLASS

ALACALUFE LEP 1603	HALLEF LEP 1604

Displacement, tons: 107 full load
Dimensions, feet (metres): 107.3 × 22 × 6.6 *(32.7 × 6.7 × 2)*
Main machinery: 2 MTU diesels; 5200 hp(m) *(3.82 MW)*; 2 shafts
Speed, knots: 20. **Range, miles:** 1000 at 15 kts
Complement: 16

Comment: Built under licence from FBM at Asmar, Talcahuano, in conjunction with FBM Marine. First commissioned 24 June 1989; options on six more and it is reported that two gun armed variants were building in 1992. Manned by the Navy for patrol and Pilot Service duties in the Magellan Straits.

HALLEF 1991, Chilean Navy

10 COASTAL PATROL CRAFT

PILLAN GC 1801	LLAIMA GC 1806
TRONADOR GC 1802	ANTUCO GC 1807
RANO KAU GC 1803	OSORNO GC 1808
VILLARRICA GC 1804	CHOSHUENCO GC 1809
CORCOVADO GC 1805	COPAHUE GC 1810

Displacement, tons: 43 full load
Dimensions, feet (metres): 61 × 17.3 × 5.6 *(18.6 × 5.3 × 1.7)*
Main machinery: 2 MTU 8V 331 TC82 diesels; 1740 hp(m) *(1.28 MW)* sustained; 2 shafts
Speed, knots: 30. **Range, miles:** 700 at 15 kts
Guns: 2 Oerlikon 20 mm; 85° elevation; 800 rounds/minute.
Depth charges: 2 racks.

Comment: Built by Maclaren, Niteroi, Brazil. Ordered 1977. GRP hulls. *Pillan* commissioned August 1979 (approx); *Tronador*, August 1980 (approx); *Rano Kau* and *Villarrica*, November 1980; *Corcovado*, 6 March 1981; *Llaima*, 10 April 1981; *Choshuenco* and *Copahue*, 16 April 1982.

CORCOVADO 1991, Chilean Navy

Coast guard / CHILE

1 PATROL VESSEL

CASTOR WPC 113

Displacement, tons: 149 full load
Dimensions, feet (metres): 70.8 × 20.7 × 10.5 *(21.6 × 6.3 × 3.2)*
Main machinery: 1 Cummins diesel; 365 hp *(272 kW)*; 1 shaft
Speed, knots: 8
Complement: 14
Guns: 2 Oerlikon 20 mm. 2 Browning 12.7 mm MGs.

Comment: Built in 1968 and commissioned into the Coast Guard in 1975.

2 COASTAL PATROL CRAFT

ONA LEP 1601   **YAGAN** LEP 1602

Displacement, tons: 79 full load
Dimensions, feet (metres): 80.7 × 17.4 × 9.5 *(24.6 × 5.3 × 2.9)*
Main machinery: 2 MTU 6V 331 TC82 diesels; 1300 hp(m) *(960 kW)* sustained; 2 shafts
Speed, knots: 22
Complement: 5
Guns: 2—12.7 mm MGs.

Comment: Built by Asenav and commissioned in 1980.

15 INSHORE PATROL CRAFT

MAULE LPM 1901	**LOA** LPM 1906	**RIO RINIHUE** LPM 1911
LAUCA LPM 1902	**MAULIN** LPM 1907	**CHADMO** LPM 1912
ACONCAGUA LPM 1903	**COPIAPO** LPM 1908	**CASPANA** LPM 1914
RAPEL LPM 1904	**CAU-CAU** LPM 1909	**PETROHUE** LPM 1916
ISLUGA LPM 1905	**PUDETO** LPM 1910	**RIO BUENO** LPM 1917

Displacement, tons: 14 full load
Dimensions, feet (metres): 43.3 × 11.5 × 3.5 *(13.2 × 3.5 × 1.1)*
Main machinery: 2 MTU 6V 331 TC82 diesels; 1300 hp(m) *(960 kW)* sustained; 2 shafts
Speed, knots: 18
Guns: 1 Browning 12.7 mm MG.

Comment: LPM 1901-1910 ordered in August 1981. Completed by Asenav 1982-83. Remainder built in the late 1980s.

2 COASTAL PATROL CRAFT

KIMITAHI LPC 1701   **GUALE** LPC 1811

Comment: Details not known.

1 INSHORE PATROL CRAFT

BELLATRIX

Dimensions, feet (metres): 31.8 × 10.2 × 3 *(9.7 × 3.1 × 0.9)*
Main machinery: 2 Volvo diesels; 500 hp(m) *(367 kW)*; 1 shaft
Speed, knots: 24

Comment: Built in 1953.

1 HOSPITAL SHIP

Name	No	Builders	Commissioned
CIRUJANO VIDELA	GC 111	Asmar, Talcahuano	1964

Displacement, tons: 140 full load
Dimensions, feet (metres): 101.7 × 21.3 × 6.6 *(31 × 6.5 × 2)*
Main machinery: 2 Cummins VT-12-700M diesels; 1400 hp *(1.05 MW)*; 2 shafts
Speed, knots: 14

Comment: Hospital and dental facilities are fitted. A modified version of US PGM 59 design with larger superstructure and less power. Owned by Ministry of Health and operated by Coast Guard.

CIRUJANO VIDELA   *1991, Chilean Navy*

1 SAR CRAFT

Displacement, tons: 10 full load
Dimensions, feet (metres): 41.7 × 12.8 × 1.6 *(12.7 × 3.9 × 0.5)*
Main machinery: 2 Volvo Penta TAMD41A diesels; 400 hp(m) *(294 kW)* maximum; 2 waterjets
Speed, knots: 25
Complement: 4 + 32 survivors
Guns: 1—7.62 mm MG.

Comment: Built at Asmar, Talcahuano and completed 8 August 1991. GRP hull.

COPIAPO   *1992, Chilean Navy*

ALACALUFE   *6/1989 FBM Marine*

CHINA, People's Republic

Note: Chinese names are transliterated in Pin Yin.

Headquarters' Appointments

Commander-in-Chief of the Navy:
  Vice Admiral Zhang Lianzhong
Political Commissar of the Navy:
  Vice Admiral Wei Jinshan
Deputy Commanders-in-Chief of the Navy:
  Vice Admiral Shi Yunsheng
  Vice Admiral Chen Mingshan
  Vice Admiral He Peng Fei

Fleet Commanders

North Sea Fleet:
  Vice Admiral Qu Zhenmou
East Sea Fleet:
  Vice Admiral Wang Jiying
South Sea Fleet:
  Vice Admiral Gao Zhenjia

Personnel

(a)
1993: 260 000 officers and men, including 25 000 naval air force, 6000 marines (28 000 in time of war) and 28 000 for coastal defence
(b)
4 years' national service for sailors afloat; 3 years for those in shore service. Some stay on for up to 15 years.

General

The Soviet involvement with China after 1949 included plans to develop a Sino-Soviet naval presence in the Pacific. These fell apart in the early 1960s as the rift between the two countries deepened but, when Lin Biao was in charge of defence, there was a resurgence of naval programmes. With Lin's death in 1971 these again suffered an eclipse which was intensified in the later years of the Cultural Revolution. The results of this national disaster were the swingeing cuts made in scientific and industrial improvements which delayed any notable advance in naval architecture or weapons systems development. It was only by the mid-1980s that there were signs that this dead period had been put aside and the naval export market was probing beyond the transfer of current designs to Bangladesh, Egypt and Pakistan. New designs of submarines, frigates and patrol craft were advertised and assistance was actively sought from Western Defence industries. Unfortunately the events of 1989 caused a check in co-operation with the West but an active market was maintained in Thailand and Bangladesh. The last two years to 1993 have seen the introduction into service of new classes of Destroyers and Frigates as well as further modifications to the older types. In addition there are new types of patrol, amphibious and support vessels. Some interest is also being taken in aircraft carrier designs with unconfirmed rumours of both new construction in China and foreign purchase from Russia/Ukraine.

Operational Numbers

Because large numbers of vessels are kept in operational reserve, the Chinese version of the order of battle tends to show many fewer ships than are counted by western observers.

Bases

North Sea Fleet. Major bases: Qingdao (HQ), Lushun, Xiaopingdao. Minor bases: Weihai Wei, Qingshan, Luda, Huludao, Lien Yun, Ling Shan, Ta Ku Shan, Changshandao, Liuzhuang, Dayuanjiadun
East Sea Fleet. Major bases: Ningbo (HQ), Zhoushan, Shanghai, Fujan. Minor bases: Zhenjiangguan, Wusong, Xinxiang, Wenzhou, Sanduao, Xiamen, Xingxiang, Quandou, Wen Zhou SE, Wuhan
South Sea Fleet. Major bases: Zhanjiang (HQ), Yulin, Guangzhou (Canton). Minor bases: Haikou, Huangfu, Shantou, Humen, Kuanchuang, Tsun, Kuan Chung, Mawai, Beihai, Ping Tan, San Chou Shih, Tang-Chiah Huan, Longmen, Bailong, Dongcun, Baimajing, Xiachuandao
(The fleet is split with the main emphasis on the North Sea Fleet).

Strength of the Fleet (1 January 1993)

Type	Active (Reserve)	Building (Planned)
SSBN	1	(1)
SSB	(1)	—
Fleet Submarines (SSN)	5	(1)
Cruise Missile Submarine (SSG)	1	—
Patrol Submarines	29 (50)	1 (2)
Destroyers (DDG)	16	2 (2)
Frigates	39 (1)	2 (2)
Fast Attack Craft (Missile)	155 (60)	3
Fast Attack Craft (Gun)	110 (200)	8
Fast Attack Craft (Torpedo)	90 (50)	—
Fast Attack Craft (Patrol)	101	4
River Patrol Craft	13 (40)	—
Minesweepers (Ocean)	27 (60)	—
Minesweepers (Coastal)	35 (50)	2
Mine Warfare Drones	4 (56)	—
Minelayer	1	—
Hovercraft	1	—
Troop Transports	9	—
LSTs	14 (2)	?
LSMs	33	—
LCMs—LCUs	110 (200)	—
Submarine Support Ships	5	—
Salvage and Repair Ships	7	—
Survey and Research Ships	60	—
Supply Ships	26+	3
Tankers	33+	—
Boom Defence Vessels	5+	—
Icebreakers	4	—
Degaussing Ships	10	—
Miscellaneous	450+	—

Training

The main training centres are:

Dalian: First Surface Vessel Academy, Political School
Canton: Second Surface Vessel Academy
Qingdao: Submarine Academy, Aviation School
Wuhan: Engineering College
Nanjing: Naval Staff College, Medical School, Electronic Engineering College
Yan Tai: Aviation Engineering College

Naval Air Force

With 25 000 officers and men and over 700 aircraft, this is a considerable naval air force primarily land-based and with a defensive role. There is also some ASW capability. Interest has been shown in the possibility of an aircraft carrier either in the form of a new construction ship of some 48 000 tons or as a Ro-Ro conversion of an existing vessel.

Mercantile Marine

Lloyd's Register of Shipping:
  2390 vessels of 13 946 326 tons gross

DELETIONS

Submarines

1990-92   10 Whiskey class, 10 Romeo class

Destroyers

1992   *Anshan, Fushun, Changchun, Qingdao*

Patrol Forces

1989-92
12 Kronshtadt class, 50 Shantou class, 60 P 4 class, Yingkou class (militia), Beihai class, 20 Yulin class

Minesweepers

1990-92   5 Fushun class

Amphibious Vessels

1990-92   20 Yuchai class, 14 Hua class, 7 ex-US LSIL

Support Vessels

1990-92   3 Ding Hai class, *Haiyun* (merchant)

PENNANT LIST

Destroyers		Frigates					
				518	Jian	553	Shaoguan
				519	Changzhi	554	Anshun
105	Jinan	501	Xiaguan	520	Kaifeng	555	Zhaotong
106	Xian	502	Nanchong	529	Haikou	556	Xiangtan
107	Yinchuan	503	Kaiyuan	531	Yingtan	557	Jishou
108	Xining	504	Dongchuan	532	Zhongdong	560	—
109	Kaifeng	505	Kunming	533	Ningpo		
110	Dalian	506	Chengdu	534	Jinhua	**Principal Support Ships**	
112	Luhu	507	Pingxiang	535	Huangshi		
131	Nanjing	508	Xichang	536	Wu Hu	81	Zhenghe
132	Hefei	509	Chang De	537	Zhoushan	920	Dazhi
133	Chongqing	510	Shaoxing	539	Anqing	J 121	Changxingdao
134	Zunyi	511	Nantong	540	Huainan	J 302	Chongmingdao
161	Changsha	512	Wuxi	541	—	J 506	Yongxingdao
162	Nanning	513	Huayin	543	Dandong	U 891	Dagushan
163	Nanchang	514	Zhenjiang	544	Siping	X 575	Taicang
164	Guilin	515	Xiamen	545	Tianshan	X 615	Dongyun
165	Zhanjiang	516	Jiujiang	551	Maoming	AK 952	Nan Yun
166	Zhuhai	517	Nanping	552	Yibin		

SUBMARINES

Strategic Missile Submarines

1 SOVIET GOLF CLASS (SSB)

200

Displacement, tons: 2350 surfaced; 2950 dived
Dimensions, feet (metres): 321.5 × 28.2 × 21.7 *(98 × 8.6 × 6.6)*
Main machinery: Diesel-electric; 3 Type 37-D diesels; 6000 hp(m) *(4.41 MW)*; 3 motors; 5500 hp(m) *(4 MW)*; 3 shafts
Speed, knots: 17 surfaced; 13 dived
Range, miles: 6000 surfaced at 15 kts
Complement: 86 (12 officers)

Missiles: SLBM: 2 CSS-N-3; two stage solid fuel; inertial guidance to 2700 km *(1460 nm)*; warhead nuclear 2 MT.
Torpedoes: 10—21 in *(533 mm)* tubes (6 bow, 4 stern). 12 Soviet Type 53; dual purpose; pattern active/passive homing up to 20 km *(10.8 nm)* at up to 45 kts; warhead 400 kg.
Radars: Navigation: Snoop Plate; I band.

GOLF   *1988*

Programmes: Ballistic missile submarine similar but not identical to the Soviet Golf class. Built at Dalian and launched in 1964.
Structure: Two Missile tubes only because the Chinese missile is reported as having a larger diameter than the Soviet SS-N-5.

Operational: This was the trials submarine for the CSS-N-3 ballistic missile which was successfully launched to 1800 km in October 1982. As the missile is now operational it is probable that the submarine is in reserve but still available if needed.

1 XIA CLASS (TYPE 092) (SSBN)

Name	No	Builders	Laid down	Launched	Commissioned
XIA	406	Huludao Shipyard	1978	30 Apr 1981	1987

Displacement, tons: 8000 dived
Dimensions, feet (metres): 393.6 × 33 × 26 2 *(120 × 10 × 8)*
Main machinery: Nuclear; turbo-electric; 1 PWR; 90 MW; 1 shaft
Speed, knots: 22 dived
Complement: 104

Missiles: SLBM: 12 CSS-N-3; two stage solid fuel; inertial guidance to 2700 km *(1460 nm)*; warhead single nuclear 2 MT. An improved version called CSS-NX-4 is being developed.
Torpedoes: 6—21 in *(533 mm)* bow tubes.

Programmes: A second of class was reported launched in 1982 and an unconfirmed report suggests that one of the two was lost in an accident in 1985. A new design Type 094 is being developed with a longer range missile.
Modernisation: CSS-N-3 may be replaced by CSS-NX-4 possibly with MIRV but not until sometime in the mid-1990s.
Structure: Diving depth about 300 m *(985 ft)*.
Operational: First test launch of the two stage CSS-NX-3 missile took place on 30 April 1982 from a submerged pontoon near Huludao (Yellow Sea). Range 1800 km. Second launched on 12 October 1982, from a Golf class trials submarine. The first firing from Xia was in 1985 and was unsuccessful (delaying final acceptance into service of the submarine) and it was not until September 1988 that a satisfactory launch took place.
Opinion: To maintain one submarine on continuous patrol takes a minimum of three and, to be absolutely safe, an optimum number of five hulls. Because of this known requirement there has been a tendency in the West to exaggerate the Chinese SSBN programme both in terms of numbers and timescales.

XIA   1987, Xinhua

XIA   1987, Xinhua

XIA   1988, Chinese Gazette

116 CHINA / Submarines

Attack Submarines

Notes: 1. A new SSN design is being worked on.
2. A new patrol submarine building programme is reported to be based on the French Agosta class.
3. A few residual Whiskey V submarines are in reserve and unlikely to go to sea again.

5 HAN CLASS (SSN)

401 402 403 404 405

Displacement, tons: 5000 dived
Dimensions, feet (metres): 330; 356 (403 onwards) × 36 × 27.9 approx *(100; 108 × 11 × 8.5)*
Main machinery: Nuclear; turbo-electric; 1 PWR; 90 MW; 1 shaft
Speed, knots: 25 dived
Complement: 75

Missiles: SSM (403 onwards); Ying Ji (Eagle Strike) (C-801); inertial cruise; active radar homing to 40 km *(22 nm)* at 0.9 Mach; warhead 165 kg; sea-skimmer.
Torpedoes: 6—21 in *(533 mm)* bow tubes.
Sonars: May include French DUUX-5, some having been delivered in 1985.

Programmes: These are the first Chinese nuclear submarines. With an Albacore hull the first of this class was laid down about 1968 in Huludao shipyard. Her construction may have been delayed as problems were encountered with the power plant, but she appears to have been launched in 1972 and ran trials in 1974. Second Han class was launched in 1977, third in 1983, the fourth in 1987 and the fifth on 8 April 1990. A successor design is being worked on with Western assistance but no date has been given for construction work to start.
Structure: From 403 onwards the hull has been extended by some 8 m and Ying Ji SSM tubes fitted aft of the fin.
Operational: In North Sea Fleet. The first pair were thought to be non-operational for a time in the late 1980s but have probably been extensively refitted and are now back in service.
Opinion: Nuclear submarines remain a high priority but high internal radiation levels and other problems seem to have led to a cessation in the building of this class.

HAN 402   1990

Patrol Submarines

1 MODIFIED ROMEO CLASS (SSG)

351

Displacement, tons: 1650 surfaced; 2100 dived
Dimensions, feet (metres): 251.3 × 22 × 17.1 *(76.6 × 6.7 × 5.2)*
Main machinery: Diesel-electric; 2 Type 37-D diesels; 4000 hp(m) *(2.94 MW)*; 2 motors; 2700 hp(m) *(1.98 MW)*; 2 creep motors; 2 shafts
Speed, knots: 13 dived; 15 surfaced; 10 snorting
Complement: 54 (10 officers)

Missiles: SSM: 6 YJ-1 (Eagle Strike) (C-801); three launchers either side of fin; inertial cruise; active radar homing to 40 km *(22 nm)* at 0.9 Mach; warhead 165 kg; sea-skimmer.
Torpedoes: 8—21 in *(533 mm)* (6 bow, 2 stern) tubes. 16 Soviet Type 53; dual purpose; pattern active/passive homing up to 20 km *(10.8 nm)* at up to 45 kts; warhead 400 kg.
Mines: 20 in lieu of torpedoes.
Radars: Surface search: Snoop Plate and Snoop Tray; I band.
Sonars: Hercules or Tamir 5; hull-mounted; active/passive search and attack; high frequency.

Programmes: This design, designated ES5G, is a modified Romeo (Wuhan) rebuilt as a trials SSM platform. Others may be converted in due course.

MOD ROMEO 351 (firing YJ-1)   1987, Xinhua

Structure: The six missile tubes are built into the casing abreast the fin and elevate to fire much as in the Soviet Juliett class. To provide target acquisition an additional radar mast (Snoop Tray) is mounted between the two periscopes.
Operational: Has to surface to fire missiles.

9 MING CLASS (TYPE 035)

232 233 342 352 353 354 356 357 358

Displacement, tons: 1584 surfaced; 2113 dived
Dimensions, feet (metres): 249.3 × 24.9 × 16.7 *(76 × 7.6 × 5.1)*
Main machinery: Diesel-electric; 2 diesels; 5200 hp(m) *(3.82 MW)*; 2 shafts
Speed, knots: 15 surfaced; 18 dived; 10 snorting
Range, miles: 8000 at 8 kts snorting; 330 at 4 kts dived
Complement: 57 (12 officers)

Torpedoes: 8—21 in *(533 mm)* (6 fwd, 2 aft) tubes. Soviet Type 53; dual purpose; pattern active/passive homing up to 20 km *(10.8 nm)* at up to 45 kts; warhead 400 kg. Total of 16.
Mines: 32 in lieu of torpedoes.
Radars: Surface search: Snoop Plate or Snoop Tray; I band.
Sonars: Hercules/Feniks; hull-mounted; active/passive search and attack; high frequency.

MING 353   1991

Programmes: First three completed between 1971 and 1979 one of which was scrapped after a fire. These were Type ES5C/D. Building resumed in 1987 at the rate of about one per year to a modified design ES5E but probably terminated again in 1992. This is to be superseded by Type 039 of which the first of class may have been laid down in 1992 at Wuzhang Shipyard. It is reported that the new design is based on the French Agosta class.
Structure: Diving depth, 300 m *(985 ft)*.
Operational: Active in the East Sea Fleet. Fitted with Magnavox SATNAV.

20 (+ 50 RESERVE) SOVIET and CHINESE ROMEO CLASS (TYPE 033)

Displacement, tons: 1475 surfaced; 1830 dived
Dimensions, feet (metres): 251.3 × 22 × 17.1 *(76.6 × 6.7 × 5.2)*
Main machinery: Diesel-electric; 2 Type 37-D diesels; 4000 hp(m) *(2.94 MW)*; 2 motors; 2700 hp(m) *(1.98 MW)*; 2 creep motors; 2 shafts
Speed, knots: 15.2 surfaced; 13 dived; 10 snorting
Range, miles: 9000 at 9 kts surfaced
Complement: 54 (10 officers)

Torpedoes: 8—21 in *(533 mm)* (6 bow, 2 stern) tubes. 14 Soviet Type 53; dual purpose; pattern; active/passive homing up to 20 km *(10.8 nm)* at up to 45 kts; warhead 400 kg.
Mines: 28 in lieu of torpedoes.
Radars: Surface search: Snoop Plate or Snoop Tray; I band.
Sonars: Hercules or Tamir 5; hull-mounted; active/passive search and attack; high frequency. Thomson Sintra DUUX 5 in some of the class.

Programmes: The Chinese continued to construct their own submarines to the Soviet Romeo design up until the end of 1984. The first boats of this class were built at Jiangnan SY, Shanghai in mid-1962 with Wuzhang being used later. The basic Romeo class design is at least 30 years old and has evolved from the Type 031 (ES3B). Construction stopped around 1987 with the resumption of the Ming Class programme.
Modernisation: Battery refits are being done and the more modern boats have French passive ranging sonar; Italian torpedoes have also been reported but not confirmed.
Structure: Diving depth, 300 m *(984 ft)*. There are probably some dimensional variations between newer and older ships of the class.
Operational: Operational numbers are difficult to assess as no submarine spends more than a few days at sea each year because there are insufficient trained men. Of the original 84, at least 50 are in various states of operational reserve and some have been scrapped. ASW capability is virtually non-existent.
Sales: Seven to North Korea in 1973-75. Two to Egypt February/March 1982, two in 1984. All new construction.

ROMEO 250   *12/1989, G Jacobs*

DESTROYERS

0 + 1 + 1 (2) LUHU (TYPE 052) CLASS (DDG)

Name	No	Builders	Laid down	Launched	Commissioned
LUHU	112	Jiangnan Shipyard	1988	June 1991	1993

Displacement, tons: 4200 standard
Measurement, tons: 492 × 52.5 × 16.4 *(150 × 16 × 5)*
Main machinery: CODOG: 2 GE LM 2500 gas turbines, 55 000 hp *(41 MW)* sustained; 2 MTU 12V 1163 TB83 diesels; 8840 hp(m) *(6.5 MW)* sustained; 2 shafts; cp props
Speed, knots: 30
Complement: 300

Missiles: SSM: 8 YJ-1 (Eagle Strike) (C-801) ❶; active radar homing to 40 km *(22 nm)* (possibly extended range version) at 0.9 Mach; warhead 165 kg; sea-skimmer.
SAM: 1 Thomson-CSF Crotale octuple launcher ❷; line of sight guidance to 13 km *(7 nm)* at 2.4 Mach; warhead 14 kg.
Guns: 2—3.9 in *(100 mm)*/56 (twin) ❸; 85° elevation; 18 rounds/minute to 22 km *(12 nm)*; weight of shell 15 kg.
8—37 mm/63 (4 twin) ❹; 85° elevation; 180 rounds/minute to 8.5 km *(4.6 nm)* anti-aircraft; weight of shell 1.42 kg.
Torpedoes: 6—324 mm Whitehead B515 (2 triple) tubes ❺. Whitehead A 244S; anti-submarine.
A/S mortars: 2 FQF 2500 ❻ 12-tubed fixed launchers.
Countermeasures: Decoys: 2 SRBOC Mk 33; 6-barrelled chaff launchers. 2 China 26-barrelled chaff launchers.
ESM/ECM: Intercept and jammer.
Combat data systems: Thomson-CSF TAVITAC; action data automation.
Radars: Air search: Rice Screen ❼; 3D; G band.
Hai Ying ❽; G band.
Air/surface search: Thomson-CSF Sea Tiger ❾; E/F band.
Navigation: I band.
Fire control: Type 347G ❿; I band (for SSM and 100 mm).
Two Rice Lamp ⓫; I band.
Sonars: Hull-mounted; active search and attack; medium frequency.
VDS; active attack; medium frequency.
Helicopters: 2 Harbin Z9A (Dauphin) ⓬.

LUHU   *5/1992, Henry Dodds*

Programmes: First of a new class expected for some years but delayed by priority being given to export orders for Thailand. Now in series production probably replacing the Luda class.
Structure: The most notable features are the new SAM launcher, improved radar and fire control systems and a modern 100 mm gun. The SSM is possibly an extended range version of the C-801 but not yet the C-802, which is still to achieve production status.
Operational: Started trials in late 1992.
Opinion: By Chinese standards this is an impressive looking ship and the assiduous wooing of Western manufacturers has achieved a major step forward in operational capabilities.

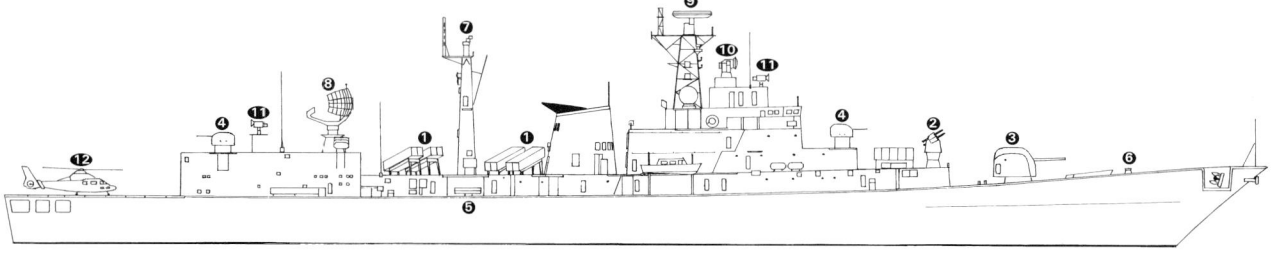

LUHU   *(Scale 1 : 900), Ian Sturton*

16 LUDA (TYPE 051) CLASS (DDG)

Name	No	Name	No	Name	No
JINAN	105 (Type II)	NANJING	131	CHANGSHA	161
XIAN	106	HEFEI	132	NANNING	162
YINCHUAN	107	CHONGQING	133	NANCHANG	163
XINING	108	ZUNYI	134	GUILIN	164
KAIFENG	109			ZHANJIANG	165
DALIAN	110			ZHUHAI	166 (Type III)

Displacement, tons: 3250 standard; 3670 full load
Dimensions, feet (metres): 433.1 × 42 × 15.1 *(132 × 12.8 × 4.6)*
Main machinery: 2 boilers; 2 turbines; 72 000 hp(m) *(53 MW)*; 2 shafts
Speed, knots: 32. **Range, miles:** 2970 at 18 kts
Complement: 280 (45 officers)

Missiles: SSM: 6 HY-2 (C-201) (2 triple) launchers ❶; (Types I and II); active radar or IR homing to 95 km *(51 nm)* at 0.9 Mach; warhead 513 kg.
8 YJ-1 (Eagle Strike) (C-801) (4 twin) launchers (Type III) ❷; active radar homing to 40 km *(22 nm)* at 0.9 Mach; warhead 165 kg; sea-skimmer.
SAM: Thomson-CSF Crotale octuple launcher *(Kaifeng)*; fitted aft; line of sight guidance to 13 km *(7 nm)* at 2.4 Mach; warhead 14 kg.
A/S: The after set of launchers in *Zhuhai* may also be used for CY-1 anti-submarine missiles; range 8-15 nm *(4.4-8.3 nm)*; payload anti-submarine torpedoes.
Guns: 4 (Type I) or 2 (Type II) USSR 5.1 in *(130 mm)*/58 (2 twin) (Type I) ❸; 85° elevation; 17 rounds/minute to 29 km *(16 nm)*; weight of shell 33.4 kg.
8 China 57 mm/70 (4 twin) ❹; 85° elevation; 120 rounds/minute to 12 km *(6.5 nm)*; weight of shell 6.31 kg. These guns are fitted in some of the class, the others have 37 mm.
8 China 37 mm/63 (4 twin) (some Type I and Type III) ❺; 85° elevation; 180 rounds/minute to 8.5 km *(4.6 nm)*; weight of shell 1.42 kg.
8 USSR 25 mm/60 (4 twin) ❻; 85° elevation; 270 rounds/minute to 3 km *(1.6 nm)* anti-aircraft; weight of shell 0.34 kg.
Torpedoes: 6—324 mm Whitehead B515 (2 triple tubes) ❼ (fitted in some Type I and Type III); Whitehead A 244S; anti-submarine.
A/S mortars: 2 FQF 2500 12-tubed fixed launchers ❽; 120 rockets; range 1200 m; warhead 34 kg. Similar in design to the Soviet RBU 1200.
Depth charges: 2 or 4 projectors; 2 or 4 racks.
Mines: 38.
Countermeasures: Decoys: chaff launchers (fitted to some).
ESM: Jug Pair (RW-23-1); 2-18 GHz; radar warning.
Combat data systems: Thomson-CSF TAVITAC with Vega FCS (in some).
Radars: Air search: Knife Rest or Cross Slot; A band or Bean Sticks or Pea Sticks ❾; E/F band.
Rice Screen ❿ (on mainmast in some); 3D; G band. Similar to Hughes SPS-39A.
Surface search: Eye Shield ⓫; E band or Thomson-CSF Sea Tiger; E/F band.
Square Tie (not in all); I band.
Navigation: Fin Curve; I band.
Fire control: Wasp Head (also known as Wok Won) or Type 343 Sun Visor B (series 2) ⓬; G/H band.
2 Rice Lamp (series 2) ⓭; I band.
2 Type 347G ⓮; I band.
IFF: High Pole.
Sonars: Pegas 2M and Tamir 2; hull-mounted; active search and attack; high frequency.
VDS (Type III); active attack.
Helicopters: 2 Harbin Z-9A (Dauphin) (Type II).

Programmes: The first Chinese-designed destroyers of such a capability to be built. First of class completed in 1971. 105-110 built at Luda; 131-134 at Shanghai and 161-166 at Guangzhou. Similar to the deleted Soviet Kotlin class. The programme was much retarded after 1971 by drastic cuts in the defence budget. In early 1977 building of series two of this class was put in hand and includes those after 109, with the latest 164 in April 1987, and 165 and 166 in 1992. The order of completion was 105, 160 (scrapped), 106, 161, 107, 162, 131, 108, 132, 109, 163, 110, 133, 134, 164, 165 and 166. The building programme may have terminated in favour of Luhu class or more Type IIIs may be built or converted.
Modernisation: First of class 105 completed a major refit in 1987 as a Type II trials ship, with the after armament replaced by a twin helicopter hangar and deck. *Zhuhai* is the first Type III

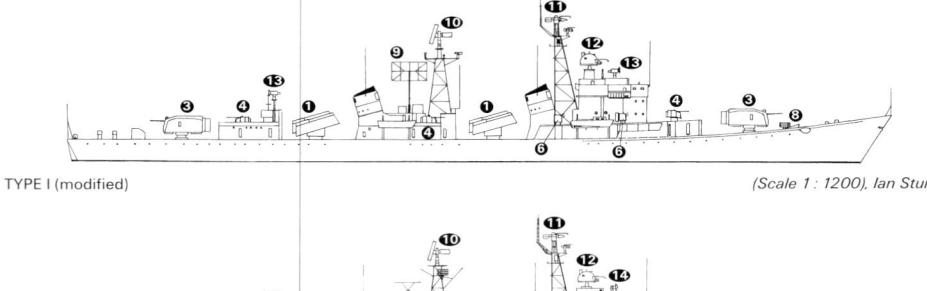

TYPE I (modified) *(Scale 1 : 1200), Ian Sturton*

TYPE III *(Scale 1 : 1200), Ian Sturton*

KAIFENG (with Crotale) *1992*

ZHUHAI (Type III) *5/1992, Henry Dodds*

and shows many changes from the Type Is, including modified after SSM launchers which may fire the CY-1 anti-submarine missile.
Structure: Electronics vary in later ships. Some ships have 57 mm guns, others 37 mm. *Jinan* may have Alcatel 'Safecopter' landing aid. *Zhuhai* is Type III with Ying Ji launchers. Thomsea combat data system including Vega FCS has been installed in at least two of the class and Crotale SAM is fitted in *Kaifeng* in X gun position.

Operational: Capable of foreign deployment, although command and control is limited. Underway refuelling is practised. Deployment; 105 series in North and East Sea Fleets; 131 series in East Sea Fleet; 161 series in South Sea Fleet. 160 was damaged by an explosion in 1978, and was scrapped.
Opinion: There have long been reports of a ballistic trajectory ASW weapon CY-1 and the different types of SSM launchers in *Zhuhai* indicate that the weapon may now be operational.

NANJING *5/1992*

JINAN (Type II) 1992

FRIGATES

5 JIANGNAN (TYPE 065) CLASS (FF)

XIAGUAN	501	KAIYUAN	503		
NANCHONG	502	DONGCHUAN	504	HAIKOU	529

Displacement, tons: 1350 standard; 1600 full load
Dimensions, feet (metres): 300.1 × 33.1 × 10.5 *(91.5 × 10.1 × 3.2)*
Main machinery: 2 SEMT-Pielstick 12 PA6 280 BTC diesels; 14 400 hp(m) *(10.6 MW)* sustained; 2 shafts
Speed, knots: 28. **Range, miles:** 3000 at 10 kts; 900 at 26 kts
Complement: 180 (15 officers)

Guns: 3 China 3.9 in *(100 mm)*/56 (1 fwd, 2 aft) ❶; 85° elevation; 18 rounds/minute to 22 km *(12 nm)*; weight of shell 15.9 kg.
8 China 37 mm/63 (4 twin) ❷; 85° elevation; 180 rounds/minute to 8.5 km *(4.6 nm)*; weight of shell 1.42 kg.
4 China 14.5 mm/93 (2 twin); 85° elevation; 600 rounds/minute to 7 km *(3.8 nm)*.
A/S mortars: 2 RBU 1200 5-tubed fixed launchers ❸; range 1200 m; warhead 34 kg.
Depth charges: 4 BMB-2 projectors; 2 racks.
Mines: Can carry up to 60.
Radars: Surface search: Ball End ❹; E/F band; range 37 km *(20 nm)*.
Navigation: Neptun or Fin Curve; I band.
Fire control: Twin Eyes ❺.
Sonars: Pegas-2M and Tamir 2; hull-mounted; active search and attack; medium/high frequency.

Programmes: The Chinese Navy embarked on a new building programme in 1965 of which this class was the first. All five built at Guangzhou and commissioned in 1967-68. Development of Soviet Riga class. All had major refits since 1974.
Operational: Four with South Sea Fleet and one with East Sea Fleet. One may have been used as an early trials ship for the HY 2 SSM.

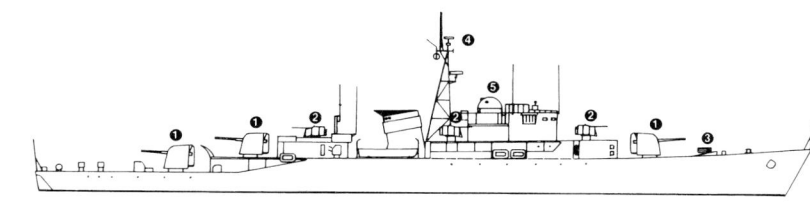

JIANGNAN *(Scale 1 : 900), Ian Sturton*

KAIYUAN 1986

3 (+ 1 RESERVE) CHENGDU (TYPE 01) CLASS (FFG)

Name	No	Builders	Laid down	Launched	Commissioned
KUNMING	505	Hutong, Shanghai	1955	26 Sep 1956	1958
CHENGDU	506	Guangzhou	1955	1957	1959
PINGXIANG	507	Hutong, Shanghai	1955	28 Apr 1956	1958
XICHANG	508	Guangzhou	1955	1957	1959

Displacement, tons: 1240 standard; 1460 full load
Dimensions, feet (metres): 300.1 × 33.1 × 10.5 *(91.5 × 10.1 × 3.2)*
Main machinery: 2 boilers; 2 turbines; 20 000 hp(m) *(14.7 MW)*; 2 shafts
Speed, knots: 28. **Range, miles:** 2000 at 10 kts
Complement: 170 (16 officers)

Missiles: SSM: 2 HY-2 (twin) launcher ❶; active radar or IR homing to 80 km *(43.2 nm)* at 0.9 Mach; warhead 513 kg.
Guns: 2 or 3 China 3.9 in *(100 mm)*/56 ❷; 85° elevation; 18 rounds/minute to 22 km *(12 nm)*; weight of shell 15.9 kg.
4 China 37 mm/63 (2 twin) ❸; 85° elevation; 180 rounds/minute to 8.5 km *(4.6 nm)* anti-aircraft; weight of shell 1.42 kg.
4 China 14.5 mm/93 (2 twin) ❹; 85° elevation; 600 rounds/minute to 7 km *(3.8 nm)*.
Depth charges: 4 BMB-2 projectors; 2 racks.
Mines: Can be carried.
Radars: Air/surface search: Slim Net ❺; E/F band.
Navigation: Neptun; I band.
Fire control: Sun Visor B ❻; G/H/I band (for guns).
Square Tie ❼; I or G/H band (for missiles).
IFF: High Pole A.
Sonars: Hull-mounted; active search and attack; medium/high frequency.

Programmes: Similar to the Soviet Riga class and assembled from Soviet components. Designated 'Old Missile Frigates'.
Modernisation: Two started conversion in 1971 for the replacement of the torpedo tubes by a twin SS-N-2 launcher. All converted at Hudong SY. In 1978-79 additional 37 mm and 14.5 mm guns added.
Structure: All had light tripod mast and high superstructure, but later converted with heavier mast and larger bridge. Two were redesigned with modified superstructure and not all have the after 100 mm gun.
Operational: All stationed in South Sea Fleet. One is being cannibalised for spares for the other three.

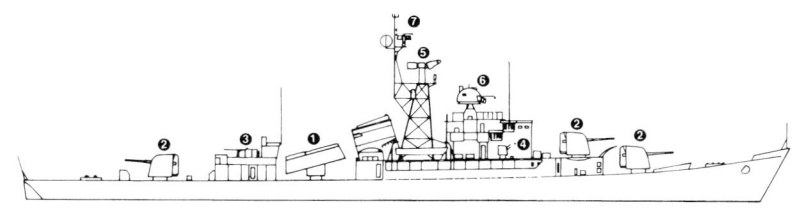

CHENGDU *(Scale 1 : 900), Ian Sturton*

XICHANG 1988

120 CHINA / Frigates

24 + 1 JIANGHU I and II (TYPE 053) CLASS (FFG)

Name	No	Name	No	Name	No
CHANG DE	509	NANPING	517	TIANSHAN	545
SHAOXING	510	JIAN	518	MAOMING	551
NANTONG	511	CHANGZHI	519	YIBIN	552
WUXI	512	KAIFENG	520	SHAOGUAN	553
HUAYIN	513	NINGPO	533	ANSHUN	554
ZHENJIANG	514	JINHUA	534	ZHAOTONG	555
XIAMEN	515	DANDONG	543	XIANGTAN	556
JIUJIANG	516	SIPING	544 (Type II)	JISHOU	557
				—	560

Displacement, tons: 1425 standard; 1702, 1820 (Type II) full load
Dimensions, feet (metres): 338.5 × 35.4 × 10.2 *(103.2 × 10.8 × 3.1)*
Main machinery: 2 SEMT-Pielstick 12 PA6 280 BTC diesels; 14 400 hp(m) *(10.6 MW)* sustained; 2 shafts
Speed, knots: 26. **Range, miles:** 4000 at 15 kts; 2700 at 18 kts
Complement: 200 (30 officers)

Missiles: SSM: 4 HY-2 (C-201) (2 twin) launchers (2 in Type II) ❶; active radar or IR homing to 80 km *(43.2 nm)* at 0.9 Mach; warhead 513 kg.
Guns: 4 China 3.9 in *(100 mm)*/56 ❷ (2 twin, none in Type II); 85° elevation; 18 rounds/minute to 22 km *(12 nm)*; weight of shell 15.9 kg.
1 Creusot Loire 3.9 in *(100 mm)*/55 ❸ (Type II); 85° elevation; 60-80 rounds/minute to 17 km *(9.3 nm)*; weight of shell 13.5 kg.
12 China 37 mm/63 (6 twin) ❹ (8 (4 twin), in some); 85° elevation; 180 rounds/minute to 8.5 km *(4.6 nm)* anti-aircraft; weight of shell 1.42 kg.
Torpedoes: 6—324 mm ILAS (2 triple) tubes ❺ (Type II). Whitehead A 244S; anti-submarine.
A/S mortars: 2 RBU 1200 5-tubed fixed launchers (4 in some) ❻; range 1200 m; warhead 34 kg.
Depth charges: 2 BMB-2 projectors; 2 racks.
Mines: Can carry up to 60.
Countermeasures: Decoys: 2 SRBOC Mk 33 6-barrelled chaff launchers or 2 China 26-barrelled launchers.
ESM: Jug Pair or Watchdog; radar warning.
Fire control: Naja optronic director (Type II) for 100 mm gun.
Radars: Air/surface search: MX 902 Eye Shield ❼; possible E band.
Surface search/fire control: Square Tie ❽; I band.
Navigation: Don 2 or Fin Curve; I band.
Fire control: Wok Won or Rice Lamp ❾; I/J band.
Sun Visor (some Type I) ❿; I band.
IFF: High Pole A. Yard Rake or Square Head.
Sonars: Echo Type 5; hull-mounted; active search and attack; medium frequency.

Helicopters: Harbin Z-9A (Dauphin) (in Type II) ⓫.

Programmes: A modification of Jiangdong class with SSM in place of SAM. Pennant numbers changed in 1979. All built in Shanghai starting in the mid-1970s at the Hudong and Jiangnan shipyards and still continuing at least into 1993 for the completion of the Thailand order. Ships were completed in the following order: 515, 516, 517, 511, 512, 513, 514, 518, 509, 510, 519, 520, 551, 552, 533, 534, two for Egypt, 543, 553, 554, 555, 545, 556, 557, 544, one for Bangladesh, two for Thailand. The latest of the class still building is 560 which is another Type I.
Modernisation: Fire control and electronics equipment is being modernised. Sun Visor and Rice Lamp have been seen on newly refitted Type Is. Possible VDS or sonar towed array may be fitted in one of the class.
Structure: All of the class have the same hull dimensions. Previously reported Type numbers have been superseded by the following designations:
Type I has four versions. Version 1 has an oval funnel and square bridge wings; version 2 a square funnel with bevelled bridge face; version 3 an octagonal funnel and version 4 reverts back to the oval funnel.
Type II (No 544) has a hangar and flight deck and only two Hai Ying (twin) SSM and is referred to as 053 HT(H). Has CSEE Naja optronic director and Alcatel 'Safecopter' landing aid. A candidate for the second conversion is 511 seen in September 1990 with its after superstructure stripped to deck level.
Types III and IV. See separate entry.
Sales: Two have been transferred to Egypt, one in September 1984, the other in March 1985, and one to Bangladesh in November 1989. Two built for Thailand (Type II) and delivered in 1992.

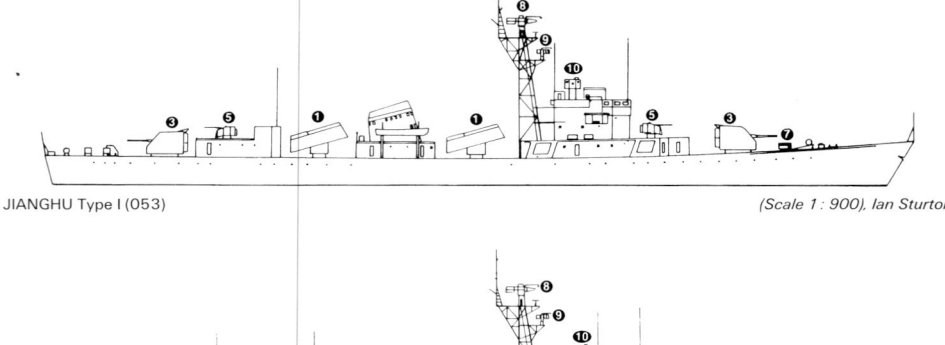

JIANGHU Type I (053) *(Scale 1 : 900), Ian Sturton*

JIANGHU Type II (053 HT(H)) *(Scale 1 : 900), Ian Sturton*

XIANGTAN 1988

SIPING 1990

DANDONG 1991

3 + 1 JIANGHU III and IV (TYPE 053 HT) CLASS (FFG)

HUANGSHI 535 (Type III)   **WU HU** 536 (Type III)   **ZHOUSHAN** 537 (Type IV)

Displacement, tons: 1924 full load
Dimensions, feet (metres): 338.5 × 35.4 × 10.2 *(103.2 × 10.8 × 3.1)*
Main machinery: 2 SEMT-Pielstick 12 PA6 280 STC diesels; 14 400 hp(m) *(10.6 MW)* sustained; 2 shafts
Speed, knots: 26. **Range, miles:** 4000 at 15 kts; 2700 at 18 kts
Complement: 200 (30 officers)

Missiles: SSM: 8 YJ-1 (Eagle Strike) (C-801) ❶; active radar homing to 40 km *(22 nm)* at 0.9 Mach; warhead 165 kg. Type IV has an improved version of this missile with an extended range to 85 km *(45.9 nm)*.
Guns: 4 China 3.9 in *(100 mm)*/56 (2 twin) ❷; 85° elevation; 18 rounds/minute to 22 km *(12 nm)*; weight of shell 15.9 kg.
  8 China 37 mm/63 (4 twin) ❸; 85° elevation; 180 rounds/minute to 8.5 km *(4.6 nm)* anti-aircraft; weight of shell 1.42 kg.
A/S mortars: 2 RBU 1200 5-tubed fixed launchers ❹; range 1200 m; warhead 34 kg.
Depth charges: 2 BMB-2 projectors; 2 racks.
Mines: Can carry up to 60.
Countermeasures: Decoys: 2 China 26-barrelled chaff launchers.
  ESM: Elettronica Newton; radar warning.
  ECM: Elettronica 929; jammer.
Radars: Air/surface search: MX 902 Eye Shield ❺; possible E band.
  Surface search/fire control: Square Tie ❻; I band.
  Navigation: Fin Curve; I band.
  Fire Control: Rice Lamp ❼; I/J band.
  IFF: High Pole A. Square Head.
Sonars: Echo Type 5; hull-mounted; active search and attack; medium frequency.

Programmes: These ships are Jianghu hulls 27, 28 and 30 and are referred to as New Missile Frigates. *Zhoushan* completed in early 1993 and a fourth of the class was launched in July 1992.
Structure: The main deck is higher in the midships section and the lower part of the mast is solid. Type IV has an improved SSM missile which is probably a longer range version of C-801 rather than the turbojet C-802 which is not yet thought to be in operational service.
Sales: Two Type III to Thailand in 1991.

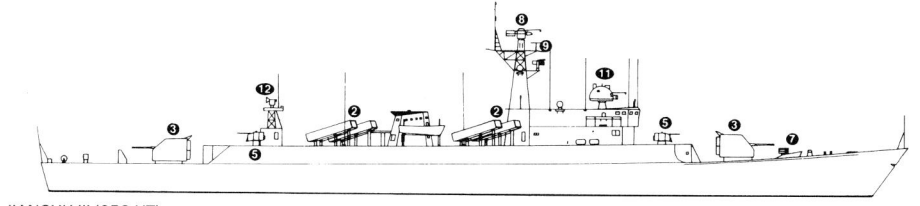

JIANGHU III (053 HT)   *(Scale 1 : 1200), Ian Sturton*

WU HU   *10/1992, Ships of the World*

ZHOUSHAN   *10/1992, Ships of the World*

WU HU   *5/1992*

122 CHINA / Frigates — Shipborne aircraft

2 + 2 (2) JIANGWEI CLASS (FFG)

Name	No
ANQING	539
HUAINAN	540
—	541

Builders	Laid down	Launched	Completed
Hudong Shipyard	1988	July 1991	Dec 1991
Hudong Shipyard	1989	Dec 1991	Dec 1992
Hudong Shipyard	1990	1993	Aug 1993

Displacement, tons: 2250 standard
Dimensions, feet (metres): 377.3 × 45.9 × 13.1 *(115 × 14 × 4)*
Main machinery: 2 SEMT-Pielstick 12 PA6 280 BTC diesels; 14 400 hp(m) *(10.6 MW)* sustained; 2 shafts
Speed, knots: 25
Complement: 200

Missiles: SSM: 6 YJ-1 (Eagle Strike) (C-801) (2 triple) launchers ❶; active radar homing to 40 km *(22 nm)* at 0.9 Mach; warhead 165 kg; sea-skimmer. May have an extended range.
SAM: 1 HQ-61 sextuple launcher ❷; PL-9; command guidance; semi-active radar homing to 10 km *(5.5 nm)* at 3 Mach.
Guns: 2 China 3.9 in *(100 mm)*/56 (twin) ❸; 85° elevation; 18 rounds/minute to 22 km *(12 nm)*; weight of shell 15.9 kg.
8 China 37 mm/63 (4 twin) ❹; 85° elevation; 180 rounds/minute to 8.5 km *(4.6 nm)* anti-aircraft; weight of shell 1.42 kg.
A/S mortars: 2 RBU 1200 ❺; 5-tubed fixed launchers; range 1200 m; warhead 34 kg.
Countermeasures: 2 SRBOC Mk 33 6-barrelled chaff launchers ❻.
2 China 26-barrelled chaff launchers ❼.
Fire control: Fog Lamp IR system.
Radars: Air search: Rice Screen ❽; G band.
Surface search: Square Tie ❾; I band.
Fire control: Sun Visor ❿; I band.
2 Rice Lamp ⓫; I band.
Navigation: Fin Curve; I band.
Sonars: Echo Type 5; hull-mounted; active search and attack; medium frequency.

Helicopters: 1 Harbin Z9A (Dauphin) ⓬.

Programmes: New programme started in 1988. First one conducted sea trials in late 1991. In series production with up to six expected to be in service by 1995.
Structure: The sextuple launcher is a much needed multiple launch SAM system using the PL-9 missile. Early reports indicated a possible ASW capability but this was not correct. There is a possibility that CY-1 A/S missiles may also be launched from the YJ-1 launchers as in Luda III.

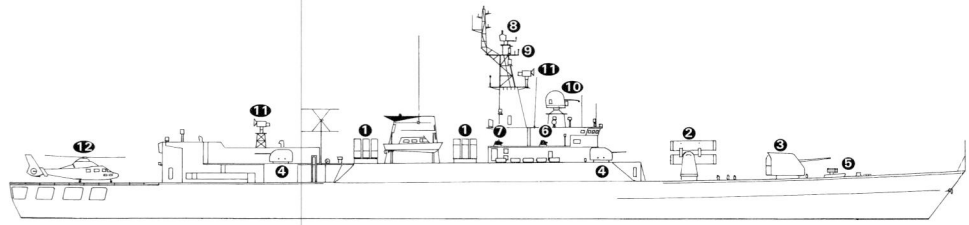
ANQING   *(Scale 1 : 900), Ian Sturton*

ANQING   *8/1992, Ships of the World*

ANQING   *8/1992, Ships of the World*

2 JIANGDONG (TYPE 053K) CLASS (FFG)

YINGTAN 531   **ZHONGDONG** 532

Displacement, tons: 1674 standard; 1924 full load
Dimensions, feet (metres): 338.5 × 35.1 × 10.2 *(103.2 × 10.7 × 3.1)*
Main machinery: 2 SEMT-Pielstick 12 PA6 280 BTC diesels; 14 400 hp(m) *(10.6 MW)* sustained; 2 shafts
Speed, knots: 26. **Range, miles:** 4000 at 15 kts; 1800 at 25 kts
Complement: 198 (30 officers)

Missiles: SAM: 2 HQ-61 twin arm launchers ❶; PL-9; command guidance; semi-active radar homing to 10 km *(5.5 nm)* at 3 Mach.
Guns: 4 China 3.9 in *(100 mm)*/56 (2 twin) ❷; 85° elevation; 18 rounds/minute to 22 km *(12 nm)*; weight of shell 15.9 kg.
8 China 37 mm/63 (4 twin) ❸; 85° elevation; 180 rounds/minute to 8.5 km *(4.6 nm)* anti-aircraft; weight of shell 1.42 kg.
A/S mortars: 2 RBU 1200 5-tubed fixed launchers ❹; range 1200 m; warhead 34 kg.
Depth charges: 2 BMB-2 projectors; 2 racks.
Countermeasures: ESM: 2 Jug Pair.
Fire control: Fog Lamp ❺; IR system fitted in 531 in 1985.
Radars: Air search: Rice Screen ❻; 3D; G band.
Surface search: Square Tie ❼; I band.
Navigation: Fin Curve; I band.
Fire control: Sun Visor B ❽; G/H/I band (for 57 mm guns).
2 Rice Lamp ❾; I band.
IFF: Ski Pole. Yard Rake.
Sonars: Probably Pegas-2M and Tamir 2; hull-mounted; active search and attack; medium/high frequency.

Programmes: *Yingtan* was laid down at Hudong, Shanghai in 1970 and commissioned in 1977. *Zhongdong* built two years later at Jiuxin, Shanghai but has not been reported since it was photographed in 1982 without SAM systems. Jiangdong class is called an 'Anti-Air Missile Frigate'.

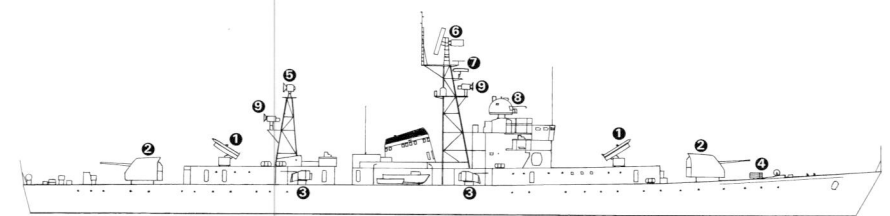
JIANGDONG   *(Scale 1 : 900), Ian Sturton*

YINGTAN   *1989, Chinese Gazette*

Modernisation: These ships may have started modernisation with some western weapon systems in 1992.
Structure: First SAM armed Chinese ship(s). Rice Screen is also the first modern air search radar to be fitted.
Operational: The SAM system in these ships has a long history of problems.

SHIPBORNE AIRCRAFT

Note: Reported that 2 Kamov Ka-27 ASW helicopters are to be delivered in 1993 for evaluation.

Numbers/Type: 10/2 Aerospatiale SA 321G/Zhi-8 Super Frelon.
Operational speed: 134 kts (248 km/h).
Service ceiling: 10 000 ft (3100 m).
Range: 440 nm (815 km).
Role/Weapon systems: ASW helicopter; SA 321G delivered from France but now being supplemented by locally built Zhi-8, of which the first operational aircraft was delivered in late 1991. Plans to fit Thomson Sintra HS-12 in three SA 321Gs completed for SSBN escort role. Sensors: Early dipping sonar and processor, some have French-built search radar. Weapons: ASW; probably Whitehead A244 torpedo carried.

Numbers/Type: 50 Harbin Z-9A Haitun (Dauphin 2).
Operational speed: 140 kts (260 km/h).
Service ceiling: 15 000 ft (4575 m).
Range: 410 nm (758 km).
Role/Weapon systems: New doctrine being developed for these licence-built helicopters, which are embarked in latest Chinese escorts. China has an option to continue building after these first 50 have been produced. Not all are naval. Sensors: Thomson-CSF Agrion; HS-12 dipping sonar; Crouzet MAD. Weapons: ASV; up to 4 × locally built radar-guided anti-ship missiles and Whitehead A244 torpedoes or locally built Mk 46 Mod 2.

LAND-BASED MARITIME AIRCRAFT (FRONT LINE)

Numbers/Type: 25 Sukhoi Su-27 Flanker.
Operational speed: 1345 kts (2500 km/h).
Service ceiling: 59 000 ft (18 000 m).
Range: 2160 nm (4000 km).
Role/Weapon systems: Air defence fighter first acquired in 1991 for trials. 24 more purchased in 1992. Sensors: Doppler radar. Weapons: 1 × 30 mm cannon; 10 × AAMs.

Numbers/Type: 10 Beriev Be-6 (Madge).
Operational speed: 224 kts (415 km/h).
Service ceiling: 20 000 ft (6100 m).
Range: 2645 nm (4900 km).
Role/Weapon systems: Flying-boat of obsolescent design now thought to be operated by one squadron only. Weapons: ASW/ASV; up to 4 tons of bombs and other weapons. Standard; 5 × 23 mm cannon.

Numbers/Type: 4 Harbin SH-5.
Operational speed: 243 kts (450 km/h).
Service ceiling: 23 000 ft (7000 m).
Range: 2563 nm (4750 km).
Role/Weapon systems: Multi-purpose amphibian introduced into service in 1986. ASW and avionics upgrade planned. Sensors: Doppler radar; MAD; sonobuoys. Weapons: ASV; 4 C 101, two gun turret, bombs. ASW; Whitehead A 244 torpedoes, mines, depth bombs.

Numbers/Type: 3 Hanzhong Y-8MPA.
Operational speed: 351 kts (650 km/h).
Service ceiling: 34 120 ft (10 400 m).
Range: 3020 nm (5600 km).
Role/Weapon systems: Maritime patrol version of Y-8 (AN-12) transport; first flown 1985; now being evaluated to replace Be-6 for ASW and AEW roles. Sensors: Litton APSO-504(V)3 search radar in undernose radome. 2 Litton LTN 72R INS and Omega/Loran. Weapons: No weapons carried.

Numbers/Type: 80 Harbin H-5 (Il-28 Beagle).
Operational speed: 487 kts (902 km/h).
Service ceiling: 40 350 ft (12 300 m).
Range: 1175 nm (2180 km).
Role/Weapon systems: Overwater strike aircraft with ASW/ASVW roles; some recently moved into second line roles such as target towing and ECM training. Weapons: ASW; 2 × torpedoes or 4 × depth bombs. ASVW; 1 × torpedo + mines. Standard; 4 × 23 mm cannon.

Numbers/Type: 40 Harbin Z-5 (Mi-4 Hound).
Operational speed: 113 kts (210 km/h).
Service ceiling: 18 000 ft (5500 m).
Range: 217 nm (400 km).
Role/Weapon systems: ASW and SAR helicopter; normally shore-based but some have been embarked for short periods, mainly for SAR. Sensors: Search radar only. Weapons: ASW; 1 × ASW torpedo.

Numbers/Type: 70 Shenyang J-8-II Finback.
Operational speed: 701 kts (1300 km/h).
Service ceiling: 65 620 ft (20 000 m).
Range: 1187 nm (2200 km).
Role/Weapon systems: Dual role, all weather fighter introduced into service in 1990. Weapons: 23 mm twin barrel cannon; AAM; 90 mm ASM.

Numbers/Type: 75 Nanchang Q-5 (Fantan).
Operational speed: 643 kts (1190 km/h).
Service ceiling: 52 500 ft (16 000 m).
Range: 650 nm (1188 km).
Role/Weapon systems: Strike aircraft developed from Shenyang J-6; operated by Chinese People's Naval Aviation Arm (CPNAA) in the beachhead and coastal shipping attack role. Q-5I version adapted to carry 2 torpedoes or C-801 ASM. Weapons: 2 × 23 mm cannon, 2 × cluster bombs, 1 or 2 × air-to-air missiles. Capable of carrying 1 ton warload.

Numbers/Type: 110 Shenyang J-5 (MiG-17F Fresco).
Operational speed: 618 kts (1145 km/h).
Service ceiling: 54 450 ft (16 600 m).
Range: 755 nm (1400 km).
Role/Weapon systems: Coastal strike and inshore Fleet support fighter; some aircraft modified for limited all-weather defence role. Weapons: Strike; 1 × 37 mm and 2 × 23 mm cannon, 32 rockets, or 500 kg of bombs underwing.

Numbers/Type: 280 Shenyang J-6 (MiG-19 Farmer).
Operational speed: 831 kts (1540 km/h).
Service ceiling: 58 725 ft (17 900 m).
Range: 1187 nm (2200 km).
Role/Weapon systems: Strike fighter operated by CPNAA (supported by Air Force of PLA) for Fleet air defence and anti-shipping strike; is replacing the obsolete Shenyang J-5 Fresco although a few of these aircraft may still be in service. Weapons: Fleet air defence role; 4 × AA-1 ('Alkali') beam-riding missiles. Attack; some 1000 kg of underwing bombs or depth charges, PL-2 missile has anti-ship capability.

Numbers/Type: 30 Xian H-6 (Tu-16 Badger).
Operational speed: 535 kts (992 km/h).
Service ceiling: 40 350 ft (12 300 m).
Range: 2605 nm (4800 km).
Role/Weapon systems: Bomber and maritime reconnaissance aircraft. Sensors: Search/attack radar. Weapons: ASV; 2 × underwing anti-shipping missiles of local manufacture, including C-601. Self-protection; ECM, up to 5 × 23 mm cannon.

Numbers/Type: 180 Xian J-7 (MiG-21 Fishbed).
Operational speed: 1175 kts (2175 km/h).
Service ceiling: 61 680 ft (18 800 m).
Range: 804 nm (1490 km).
Role/Weapon systems: Land-based Fleet air defence fighter with limited strike role against enemy shipping or beachhead. Sensors: Search attack radar, some ECM. Weapons: Strike; 500 kg bombs or 36 × rockets. Standard; 2 × 30 mm cannon. AD; 2 × 'Atoll' AAMs.

LIGHT FORCES

Note: A few obsolete Kronshtadt, Shantou and P 4 class patrol craft may still be in reserve but none were operational in late 1992.

1 HOUJIAN (OR HUANG) (TYPE 520) CLASS
(FAST ATTACK CRAFT—MISSILE)

Name	No	Builders	Commissioned
—	770	Huangpo Shipyard	July 1991

Displacement, tons: 520 standard
Dimensions, feet (metres): 214.6 × 27.6 × 7.9 (65.4 × 8.4 × 2.4)
Main machinery: 3 SEMT-Pielstick 12 PA6 280 MPC diesels; 15 840 hp(m) (11.7 MW) sustained; 3 shafts
Speed, knots: 32. **Range, miles:** 1800 at 18 kts
Complement: 75

Missiles: SSM: 6 YJ-1 (Eagle Strike) (C-801) (2 triple); inertial cruise; active radar homing to 40 km (22 nm) at 0.9 Mach; warhead 165 kg.
Guns: 2—37 mm/63 (twin) Type 76A; 85° elevation; 180 rounds/minute to 8.5 km (4.6 nm) anti-aircraft; weight of shell 1.42 kg.
4—30 mm/65 (2 twin) Type 69; 500 rounds/minute to 5 km (2.7 nm); weight of shell 0.54 kg.
Countermeasures: ESM/ECM: Intercept and jammer.
Fire control: China Type 88C WCS.
Radars: Surface search: Square Tie; I band.
Fire control: Rice Lamp; I band.

Programmes: Laid down in 1989 and built in a very short time probably with the export market in mind. Sometimes called the Huang class. No reports of more of the class by early 1993.

HOUJIAN 770   1991

124 CHINA / Light forces

5 + 3 HOUXIN CLASS (FAST ATTACK CRAFT—MISSILE)

751-755

Displacement, tons: 480 full load
Dimensions, feet (metres): 213.3 × 23.6 × 7.5 *(65 × 72 × 2.3)*
Main machinery: 4 diesels; 13 200 hp(m) *(9.7 MW)* 4 shafts
Speed, knots: 32. **Range, miles:** 750 at 18 kts
Complement: 60

Missiles: SSM: 4 YJ-1 (Eagle Strike) (C-801) (2 twin); active radar homing to 40 km *(22 nm)* at 0.9 Mach; warhead 165 kg; sea-skimmer.
Guns: 4—37 mm/63 (2 twin); 180 rounds/minute to 8.5 km *(4.6 nm)* anti-aircraft; weight of shell 1.42 kg.
4—14.5 mm (2 twin); 600 rounds/minute to 7 km *(3.8 nm)*.
Countermeasures: ESM/ECM: Intercept and jammer.
Radars: Surface search: Square Tie; I band.
Fire control: Rice Lamp; I band.

Programmes: First seen in 1991 and building at the rate of up to three per year at Qiuxin Shipyard to replace the Hegu/Hoku class.
Structure: This is a missile armed version of the prototype Haijui class.

HOUXIN 1991, CSSC

HOUXIN 751 1992

79 (+ 35 RESERVE) CHINESE HUANGFEN (TYPE 021) (OSA I TYPE) and 1 HOLA CLASS (FAST ATTACK CRAFT—MISSILE)

215, 218, 3103, 3113, 3114, 3115, 3128-3131, 5100, 7100 *et al*

Displacement, tons: 171 standard; 205 full load
Dimensions, feet (metres): 110.2 × 24.9 × 8.9 *(33.6 × 7.6 × 2.7)*
Main machinery: 3 Type M 503A diesels; 8025 hp(m) *(7.94 MW)* sustained; 3 shafts
Speed, knots: 35. **Range, miles:** 800 at 30 kts
Complement: 28

Missiles: SSM: 6 or 8 YJ-1 (Eagle Strike) (C-801); inertial cruise; active radar homing to 40 km *(22 nm)* at 0.9 Mach; warhead 165 kg; sea-skimmer. Some still have the older Hai Ying missiles.
4 HY-2 (2 twin) launchers (still fitted in some).
Guns: 4 USSR 25 mm/60 (2 twin); 85° elevation; 270 rounds/minute to 3 km *(1.6 nm)* anti-aircraft.
Being replaced in some by 4 Soviet 30 mm/65 (2 twin); 85° elevation; 500 rounds/minute to 5 km *(2.7 nm)*; weight of shell 0.54 kg.
Radars: Surface search: Square Tie; I band; range 73 km *(40 nm)* or limits of radar horizon.
Fire control: Round Ball (in 30 mm boats); H/I band.
IFF: 2 Square Head; High Pole A.

Programmes: Most of the original Osas transferred in the 1960s have been scrapped and replaced by a rolling programme of Huangfens, which was first reported in 1985.
Modernisation: The Ying Ji missile is slowly replacing the Hai Yings. With its launcher being half the weight of the Hai Ying 2 this means the doubling of the original missile armament of this class.
Structure: The only boat of the Hola class has a radome aft, four launchers, no guns, slightly larger dimensions (137.8 ft *(42 m)* long) and a folding mast. This radome is also fitted in others which carry 30 mm guns. Pennant numbers: Hola, 5100 and the remainder 200, 1100 and 3100/7100 series.
Operational: China credits this class with a speed of 39 kts. At least 35 are in reserve, leaving an operational strength of 79 at the start of 1993.
Sales: Four to North Korea in 1980. Four to Pakistan in 1984. Four to Bangladesh in 1988 and one more in 1992 to replace one which sank.

HUANGFEN 3115 1990

70 (+ 25 RESERVE) CHINESE HEGU or HOKU (TYPE 024) and 1 HEMA CLASS (FAST ATTACK CRAFT—MISSILE)

Displacement, tons: 68 standard; 79.2 full load
Dimensions, feet (metres): 88.6 × 20.7 × 4.3 *(27 × 6.3 × 1.3) (28.6 m*—Hema class)
Main machinery: 4 Type L-12V-180 diesels; 4800 hp(m) *(3.53 MW)*; 4 shafts
Speed, knots: 37.5. **Range, miles:** 400 at 30 kts
Complement: 17 (2 officers)

Missiles: SSM: 2 SY-1; inertial cruise; active radar homing to 45 km *(24.3 nm)* at 0.9 Mach; warhead 513 kg.
Guns: 2 USSR 25 mm/60 (twin) (4 (2 twin) in Hema class); 85° elevation; 270 rounds/minute to 3 km *(1.6 nm)* anti-aircraft; weight of shell 0.34 kg.
Radars: Surface search: Square Tie; I band; range 73 km *(40 nm)* or limits of radar horizon.
IFF: High pole A.

Programmes: The Komars delivered from the USSR in the 1960s have been deleted. They were followed by a building programme of ten a year (probably now stopped) of the Hegu class, a Chinese variant of the Komar with a steel hull instead of wooden. Pennant numbers: 1100 and 3100 series as some of the Huangfen class.
Modernisation: Plans to replace the missiles with C-801 have been shelved although a few may be fitted.
Structure: The chief external difference is the siting of the launchers clear of the bridge and further inboard, eliminating sponsons and use of pole instead of lattice mast. A hydrofoil variant, the Hema class, has a semi-submerged foil fwd. The extra 6 ft length allows for the mounting of a second twin 25 mm abaft the missile launchers.
Operational: 25 were in reserve in early 1993 leaving an operational strength of 70.
Sales: Four to Pakistan, 1981; four to Bangladesh, February 1983; six to Egypt, 1984; ten ordered for Iran in 1992.

HEGU 4/1988, A Sheldon Duplaix

4 HAIJUI CLASS (FAST ATTACK CRAFT—PATROL)

688   693   694   697

Displacement, tons: 430 standard
Dimensions, feet (metres): 203.4 × 23.6 × 7.2 *(62 × 7.2 × 2.2)*
Main machinery: 4 diesels; 8800 hp(m) *(6.47 MW)*; 4 shafts
Speed, knots: 28. **Range, miles:** 750 at 18 kts
Complement: 72

Guns: 4 China 57 mm/70 (2 twin); dual purpose; 85° elevation; 120 rounds/minute to 12 km *(6.5 nm)*; weight of shell 6.31 kg.
4 USSR 30 mm/65 (2 twin); 85° elevation; 500 rounds/minute to 5 km *(2.7 nm)* anti-aircraft; weight of shell 0.54 kg.
A/S mortars: 4 RBU 1200 5-tubed fixed launchers; range 1200 m; warhead 34 kg.
Depth charges: 2 rails.
Radars: Surface search: Pot Head; I band.
Fire control: I band.

Comment: A lengthened version of the Hainan class probably used as a prototype for the Houxin class now in series production. 688 seen in 1989 with a Thomson Sintra SS 12 VDS Sonar and again in 1990 with twin missile tubes replacing the forward 57 mm gun. At least one of the class has no funnel.

HAIJUI 1986

HAIJUI 4/1990, John Mapletoft

Light forces / CHINA   125

93 + 3 HAINAN CLASS (TYPE 037)
(FAST ATTACK CRAFT—PATROL)

Nos 267-285, 290, 302, 305, 609, 610, 628, 636-687, 689-692, 695, 696, 698, 699, 723-731

Displacement, tons: 375 standard; 392 full load
Dimensions, feet (metres): 192.8 × 23.6 × 6 *(58.8 × 7.2 × 2.2)*
Main machinery: 4 PCR/Kolomna Type 9-D-8 diesels; 4000 hp(m) *(2.94 MW)* sustained; 4 shafts
Speed, knots: 30.5. **Range, miles:** 1300 at 15 kts
Complement: 78

Missiles: Can be fitted with four YJ-1 launchers in lieu of the after 57 mm gun.
Guns: 4 China 57 mm/70 (2 twin); dual purpose; 120 rounds/minute to 12 km *(6.5 nm)*; weight of shell 6.31 kg.
  4 USSR 25 mm/60 (2 twin); 85° elevation; 270 rounds/minute to 3 km *(1.6 nm)* anti-aircraft; weight of shell 0.34 kg.
A/S mortars: 4 RBU 1200 5-tubed fixed launchers; range 1200 m; warhead 34 kg.
Depth charges: 2 BMB-2 projectors; 2 racks.
Mines: Rails fitted.
Radars: Surface search: Pot Head or Skin Head; I band.
IFF: High Pole.
Sonars: Hull-mounted; active search and attack; high frequency.
  Thomson Sintra SS 12 (on at least two of the class); VDS.

Programmes: A larger Chinese-built version of Soviet SO 1. Low freeboard. Programme started 1963-64 and continues into 1993 with new hulls replacing the first ships of the class.
Structure: Later ships have a tripod foremast in place of a pole and a short stub mainmast. Two trials SS 12 sonars fitted in 1987.
Sales: Two to Bangladesh, one in 1982 and one in 1985; eight to Egypt in 1983/84; six to North Korea 1975-78; four to Pakistan, two in 1976 and two in 1980; six to Burma in 1991.

HAINAN 686   4/1988

HAINAN 649   5/1992, Henry Dodds

4 + 1 HULUDAO CLASS (TYPE 206)
(FAST ATTACK CRAFT—PATROL)

65   77   101   109

Displacement, tons: 180 full load
Dimensions, feet (metres): 147.6 × 21 × 5.6 *(45 × 6.4 × 1.7)*
Main machinery: 3 MWM TBD604BV12 diesels; 5204 hp(m) *(3.82 MW)* sustained; 3 shafts
Speed, knots: 29. **Range, miles:** 1000 at 15 kts
Complement: 24 (6 officers)
Guns: 4 China 14.5 mm Type 82 (2 twin); 85° elevation; 600 rounds/minute to 7 km *(3.8 nm)*; weight of shell 1.42 kg.

Comment: New class of EEZ patrol craft first seen at Wuxi Shipyard in 1988. Fourth and fifth of class reported ordered in May 1991. The craft looks like a scaled down version of the Pakistan Barkat class and has probably been built for export. First three are expected to go to Tunisia in 1993.

HULUDAO 109   8/1992, Dr Chien Chung

110 (+ 200 RESERVE) SHANGHAI CLASS (TYPE 062)
(FAST ATTACK CRAFT—GUN)

E 277, 321   N 1121, 1127, 3215, 3313, 4301, 4324, 9342 *et al*

Displacement, tons: 113 standard; 134 full load
Dimensions, feet (metres): 127.3 × 17.7 × 5.6 *(38.8 × 5.4 × 1.7)*
Main machinery: 2 Type L-12V-180 diesels; 2400 hp(m) *(1.76 MW)* (forward); 2 Type 12-D-6 diesels; 1820 hp(m) *(1.34 MW)* (aft); 4 shafts
Speed, knots: 30. **Range, miles:** 700 at 16.5 kts on one engine
Complement: 38

Guns: 4 China 37 mm/63 (2 twin); 85° elevation; 180 rounds/minute to 8.5 km *(4.6 nm)*; weight of shell 1.42 kg.
  4 USSR 25 mm/60 (2 twin); 85° elevation; 270 rounds/minute to 3 km *(1.6 nm)* anti-aircraft; weight of shell 0.34 kg.
  Some are fitted with a twin 57 mm/70, some have a twin 75 mm Type 56 recoilless rifle mounted fwd and some have a twin 14.5 mm MG.
Depth charges: 2 projectors; 8 weapons.
Mines: Mine rails can be fitted for 10 mines.
Radars: Surface search: Skin Head or Pot Head; I band.
IFF: High Pole.
Sonars: It is reported that a hull-mounted set is fitted, with VDS in some.

Programmes: Construction began in 1961 and continued at Shanghai and other yards at rate of about ten a year for 30 years but is now beginning to tail off.
Structure: The five versions of this class vary slightly in the outline of their bridges. A few of the class have been reported as fitted with RBU 1200 anti-submarine mortars. Displacement and dimensions are for the Shanghai II class.
Sales: Eight to North Vietnam in May 1966, plus Romanian craft of indigenous construction. Seven to Tanzania in 1970-71, six to Guinea, twelve to North Korea, twelve to Pakistan, five to Sri Lanka in 1972, six to Albania, eight to Bangladesh in 1980-82, three to Congo, four to Egypt in 1984, three to Sri Lanka in 1991 and two to Tanzania in 1992. Many of these have since been deleted.

SHANGHAI II (with 57 mm gun)   1989

SHANGHAI II (with twin 14.5 mm MG)   1989

10 (+ 30 RESERVE) P 6 CLASS (TYPE 083)
(FAST ATTACK CRAFT—TORPEDO)

Displacement, tons: 64 standard; 73 full load
Dimensions, feet (metres): 85.3 × 20 × 4.9 *(26 × 6.1 × 1.5)*
Main machinery: 4 Type M 50 diesels; 4400 hp(m) *(3.2 MW)* sustained; 4 shafts
Speed, knots: 41. **Range, miles:** 450 at 30 kts; 600 at 15 kts
Complement: 15
Guns: 4 USSR 25 mm/60 (2 twin); 85° elevation; 270 rounds/minute to 3 km *(1.6 nm)*.
Torpedoes: 2—21 in *(533 mm)* tubes (or mines or 12 DCs); anti-surface.
Depth charges: Up to 12.
Mines: Can be carried.
Radars: Surface search: Skin Head; I band.
IFF: High Pole.

Comment: This class has wooden hulls. Some were constructed in Chinese yards largely at Shanghai. Most built prior to 1966. Pennant numbers; in 5200 series. Six sold to North Vietnam in 1967. Some already deleted, another 30 are in reserve in early 1993.

P 6 class   1980

126 CHINA / Light forces — Mine warfare forces

80 (+ 20 RESERVE) HUCHUAN CLASS (TYPE 025/026)
(FAST ATTACK CRAFT—TORPEDO)

205, 207-209, 248, 2201, 2203, 3206, 3214, 6218, 7230 *et al*

Displacement, tons: 39 standard; 45.8 full load
Dimensions, feet (metres): 71.5 × 20.7 oa × 11.8 (hullborne) *(21.8 × 6.3 × 3.6 (max))*
Main machinery: 3 Type M 50 diesels; 2200 hp(m) *(1.6 MW)* sustained; 2 shafts
Speed, knots: 50 foilborne. **Range, miles:** 500 cruising
Complement: 16

Guns: 4 China 14.5 mm (2 twin); 85° elevation; 600 rounds/minute to 7 km *(3.8 nm)*.
Torpedoes: 2—21 in *(533 mm)* tubes. Probably fires older Soviet Type 53.
Radars: Surface search: Skin Head (some variations); I band.

Programmes: Hydrofoils designed and built by China, in the Hutong yard, Shanghai. Construction started in 1966. Previously Hu Chwan class. Construction discontinued in 1988-89 and numbers are now declining. Another 18 are in reserve in early 1993.
Structure: Of all-metal construction with a bridge well fwd and a low superstructure extending aft. Fwd pair of foils can be withdrawn into recesses in the hull. There are two variants. Older boats have a twin mounting amidships and one aft with the front of the bridge well fwd of the lips of the tubes. Newer versions have the front of the bridge in line with the lips of the tubes and the first mounting on the fo'c'sle and have differences in their electronics. Not all are hydrofoil fitted.
Sales: 32 to Albania, four to Pakistan, four to Tanzania, three to Romania plus additional craft of indigenous construction. Four to Bangladesh in 1989. Some have been deleted.

HUCHUAN 3214 (older version)   *3/1988, DTM*

HUCHUAN 2201 (newer version)   *1988*

5 (+ 40 RESERVE) HUANGPU CLASS (RIVER PATROL CRAFT)

Displacement, tons: 42 standard; 50 full load
Dimensions, feet (metres): 88.6 × 13 × 5 *(27 × 4 × 1.5)*
Main machinery: 2 diesels; 1000 hp(m) *(735 kW)*; 2 shafts
Speed, knots: 14. **Range, miles:** 400 at 9 kts
Complement: 25
Guns: 2 or 4 USSR 25 mm/60 (1 or 2 twin); 85° elevation; 270 rounds/minute to 3 km *(1.6 nm)*. Recently rearmed.
Radars: Surface search: Skin Head; I band; range 37 km *(20 nm)*.

Comment: Armament varies—above is the most common fit. Built in Guangzhou and Shanghai 1950-55 probably for riverine duties. Underpowered with low freeboard although some have been modified for greater crew safety. Previously Whampoa class. 30 in East Sea Fleet, six in North Sea Fleet and nine in South Sea Fleet. Most of these are in reserve.

HUANGPU class   *1989*

8 + 4 HUXIN CLASS (RIVER PATROL CRAFT)

62   233   *et al*

Displacement, tons: 165 full load
Dimensions, feet (metres): 91.9 × 13.8 × 5.2 *(28 × 4.2 × 1.6)*
Main machinery: 2 diesels; 1000 hp(m) *(735 kW)*; 2 shafts
Speed, knots: 13. **Range, miles:** 400 at 10 kts
Complement: 26
Guns: 4 China 14.5 mm/93 (2 twin); 85° elevation; 600 rounds/minute to 7 km *(3.8 nm)*.
Radars: Surface search: Skin Head; I band.

Comment: This is a class of modified Huangpu design with a greater freeboard and a slightly larger displacement. First seen in 1989 and now in series production.

HUXIN 62   *1989, P D Jones*

MINE WARFARE FORCES

Notes: 1. There are also some 60 auxiliary minesweepers of various types including trawlers and motor-driven junks.
2. There are reported to be plans to build a Lerici type minehunter.

27 (+ 6 RESERVE) SOVIET T 43 CLASS (TYPE 010)
(MINESWEEPERS—OCEAN)

124, 364-6, 377-9, 386-9, 396-9, 801-3, 807-9, 821-3, 829-832, 853-4, 863, 994-6 *et al*

Displacement, tons: 520 standard; 590 full load (Chinese built)
Dimensions, feet (metres): 196.8 × 27.6 × 6.9 *(60 × 8.8 × 2.3)*
Main machinery: 2 PCR/Kolomna Type 9-D-8 diesels; 2200 hp(m) *(1.62 MW)*; 2 shafts
Speed, knots: 14. **Range, miles:** 3000 at 10 kts
Complement: 70 (10 officers)

Guns: 2 or 4 China 37 mm/63 (1 or 2 twin) (3 of the class have a 65 mm/52 forward instead of one twin 37 mm/63); dual purpose; 85° elevation; 180 rounds/minute to 8.5 km *(4.6 nm)*; weight of shell 1.42 kg.
4 USSR 25 mm/60 (2 twin); 85° elevation; 270 rounds/minute to 3 km *(1.6 nm)*.
4 China 14.5 mm/93 (2 twin); 85° elevation; 600 rounds/minute to 7 km *(3.8 nm)*.
Some ships also carry 1—85 mm/52 Mk 90K; 18 rounds/minute to 15 km *(8 nm)*; weight of shell 9.6 kg.
Depth charges: 2 BMB-2 projectors; 20 depth charges.
Mines: Can carry 12-16.
Countermeasures: MCMV; MPT-1 paravanes; MPT-3 mechanical sweep; acoustic and magnetic gear.
Radars: Surface search: Ball End; E/F band; range 37 km *(20 nm)*.
Navigation: Fin Curve or Neptun; I band.
IFF: High Pole or Yard Rake.
Sonars: Tamir II; hull-mounted; active search and attack; high frequency.

Programmes: Four were acquired from USSR in 1954-55, one being returned 1960; 26 more were built in Chinese shipyards, the first two in 1956. The construction of T 43 class fleet minesweepers started again in mid-1980s at Wuzhang and at Guangzhou.
Structure: Displacement figures are for Chinese-built ships. Three (Soviet ships) converted for surveying, three transferred as civilian research ships.
Operational: Seven in North Sea Fleet (364-6, 801-3, 807), nine in East Sea Fleet (821, 829, 830, 832, 853-4, 994-6) and eight in South Sea Fleet (386-9, 396-9). Remainder not known. Some are used as patrol ships with sweep gear removed. Three units reported as having a 65 mm/52 gun forward. Another six of the class were in reserve at the beginning of 1993.

T 43 831   *5/1992, Henry Dodds*

T 43 class   *12/1989, G Jacob*

Mine warfare forces — Amphibious warfare forces / CHINA   127

1 BELEIJAN CLASS (MINELAYER)

814

Comment: First of a new class probably built at Shanghai and completed successful sea trials in 1988. Displacement about 1000 tons, 93 × 14 m.

5 + 2 WOSAO CLASS (MINESWEEPER—COASTAL)

4422   + 4

Displacement, tons: 310 full load
Dimensions, feet (metres): 147 × 20.3 × 7.5 *(44.8 × 6.2 × 2.3)*
Main machinery: 2 diesels; 2000 hp(m) *(1.47 MW)*; 2 shafts
Speed, knots: 15.5. **Range, miles:** 500 at 15 kts
Complement: 25
Guns: 4 China 25 mm/60 (2 twin); 85° elevation; 270 rounds/minute to 3 km *(1.6 nm)*.
Countermeasures: Acoustic, magnetic and mechanical sweeps.

Comment: Building programme started in 1986. First of class commissioned in 1988 and now building at about one per year. Steel hull with low magnetic properties.

WOSAO   1990, CSSC

5 FUSHUN CLASS (MINESWEEPERS—COASTAL)

Displacement, tons: 275
Dimensions, feet (metres): 131.2 × 18 × 9.8 *(40 × 5.5 × 3)*
Main machinery: 2 Type M 50 diesels; 2200 hp(m) *(1.6 MW)* sustained; 2 Type 12-D-6 diesels; 1820 hp(m) *(1.34 MW)*; 4 shafts
Speed, knots: 18. **Range, miles:** 750 at 16 kts
Guns: 2 USSR 25 mm/60 (twin); forward.
   4 China 14.5 mm/9 (2 twin); midships.

Comment: A modification of the Shanghai II class fast attack craft fitted with minesweeping winch and two davits. Several have been deleted and these last five are expected to be scrapped in 1993/94.

FUSHUN class   1986

25 (+ 50 RESERVE) LIENYUN CLASS (MINESWEEPERS—COASTAL)

Displacement, tons: 400
Dimensions, feet (metres): 131.2 × 26.2 × 11.5 *(40 × 8 × 3.5)*
Main machinery: 1 diesel; 400 hp(m) *(294 kW)*; 1 shaft
Speed, knots: 8
Guns: 2—12.7 mm MGs.

Comment: Built to a converted trawler design with steel hulls. Have a minesweeping winch and davits aft. Approximately 50 more hulls were in reserve in early 1993.

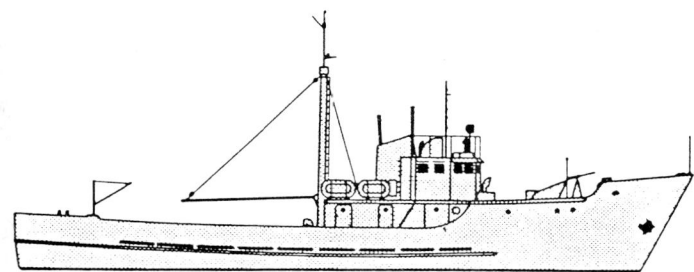

LIENYUN class   1990

4 (+ 56 RESERVE) TYPE 312 DRONE MINESWEEPERS

Displacement, tons: 47 standard
Dimensions, feet (metres): 68.6 × 12.8 × 6.9 *(20.9 × 3.9 × 2.1)*
Main machinery: Diesel-electric; 1 Type 12V 150C diesel; 300 hp(m) *(220 kW)*; 1 motor; cp prop
Speed, knots: 12. **Range, miles:** 144 at 12 kts
Complement: 3

Comment: A large number of these craft, similar to the German Troikas, have been built since the early 1970s. Fitted to carry out magnetic and acoustic sweeping under remote control up to 5 km *(2.7 nm)* from shore control station. Most were in reserve in early 1993.

DRONE Type 312   1988, CSSC

AMPHIBIOUS WARFARE FORCES

Notes: (i) In addition to the ships listed below there are up to 500 minor LCM/LCVP types used to transport stores and personnel. There is also a 67 ton DAGU class research hovercraft designed by Shanghai SB R&D Institute.
(ii) A Ro-Ro conversion to an aviation support ship is being actively studied as one option to improve amphibious capability out of range of shore based aircraft. If taken up the Navy may introduce STOVL aircraft to the Fleet. The alternative of a 48 000 ton fixed wing carrier is also under consideration. The Ministry of Communications ship *Huayuankou* has been mentioned as a possible candidate for conversion.
(iii) All of the ex-US LSM Hua type, the Yuchai class LCMs and the ex-US LSILs have been scrapped.

9 QIONSHA (7 AP + 2 AH) CLASS

Y 831   Y 832   Y 833   + 6

Displacement, tons: 2150 full load
Dimensions, feet (metres): 282.1 × 44.3 × 13.1 *(86 × 13.5 × 4)*
Main machinery: 3 SKL 8 NVD 48 A-2U diesels; 3960 hp(m) *(2.91 MW)* sustained; 3 shafts
Speed, knots: 16
Complement: 59
Military lift: 400 troops; 350 tons cargo
Guns: 8 China 14.5/93 mm (4 twin); 85° elevation; 600 rounds/minute to 7 km *(3.8 nm)*.

Comment: Personnel attack transports begun about 1980 at Guangzhou. All South Sea Fleet. Have four sets of davits, light cargo booms serving fwd and aft. No helicopter pad. Twin funnels. Carry a number of LCAs. Two converted to Hospital Ships (AH) and painted white.

QIONSHA Y 832   1985, G Jacobs

QIONSHA AH (Hospital ship alongside YUKAN class)   12/1988, G Jacobs

11 (+ 2 RESERVE) Ex-US 1-511 (SHAN) CLASS (LST)

351, 355, 902-3, 905-7, 921-6

Displacement, tons: 1653 standard; 4080 full load
Dimensions, feet (metres): 328 × 50 × 14 *(100 × 15.3 × 4.3)*
Main machinery: 2 GM 12-567A diesels; 1800 hp(m) *(1.32 MW)*; 2 shafts
Speed, knots: 11
Military lift: 165 troops; 2100 tons cargo; 2 LCVP
Guns: 2—76 mm/50; dual purpose; 85° elevation; 18 rounds/minute to 12.8 km *(7 nm)*; weight of shell 5.92 kg.
   9 China 37 mm/63 (3 twin, 3 single); 180 rounds/minute to 8.5 km *(4.6 nm)*; weight of shell 1.42 kg.
Mines: All capable of minelaying.

Comment: Two transferred to North Vietnam as tankers. Some other ex-US LSTs are in the merchant service or used as tenders. Some armed with rocket launchers. All built between 1942 and 1945. Five (902-3, 905-7) in North Sea Fleet at Luda, six (921-6) in East Sea Fleet at Shanghai and two (351, 355) in South Sea Fleet at Guangzhou. Two were in reserve in early 1993.

SHAN 926   1/1990

128 CHINA / Amphibious warfare forces

3 YUKAN CLASS (TYPE 072) (LST)

927   928   929

Displacement, tons: 3110 standard
Dimensions, feet (metres): 393.6 × 50 × 9.5 *(120 × 15.3 × 2.9)*
Main machinery: 2 SEMT-Pielstick 12PA 6V 280 diesels; 9600 hp(m) *(7.1 MW)* sustained; 2 shafts
Speed, knots: 18. **Range, miles:** 3000 at 14 kts
Complement: 109
Military lift: 200 troops; 10 tanks; 2 LCVP
Guns: 8 China 57 mm/50 (4 twin) (some carry 4—57 mm (2 twin) and 4—37 mm (2 twin)); 85°
 elevation; 120 rounds/minute to 12 km *(6.5 nm)*; weight of shell 6.31 kg.
 4—25 mm/60 (2 twin) (some also have 4—25 mm (2 twin) mountings amidships above the tank
 deck); 85° elevation; 270 rounds/minute to 3 km *(1.6 nm)*.
Radars: Navigation: 2 Neptun; I band.

Comment: First completed in 1980. Bow and stern ramps fitted. Carry two LCVPs. Some reports
 indicate up to 14 of this class may be completed with 10 earmarked for the South Fleet and four
 for the East Fleet. At least two of the class are active off the Spratley Islands. Bow ramp maximum
 load 50 tons, stern ramp 20 tons.

YUKAN 927   *9/1990, John Mapletoft*

YUKAN 929   *9/1990, John Mapletoft*

28 YULIANG CLASS (TYPE 079) and 1 YULING CLASS (LSM)

Displacement, tons: 800 standard; 1600 full load
Dimensions, feet (metres): 236.2 × 45.3 × 10.8 *(72 × 13.8 × 3.3)*
Main machinery: 2 diesels; 2 shafts
Military lift: 3 tanks
Guns: 4 China 37 mm/63 (2 twin) (Type I only); 85° elevation; 180 rounds/minute to 8.5 km
 (4.6 nm); weight of shell 1.42 kg.
 4—25 mm/60 (2 twin); 85° elevation; 270 rounds/minute to 3 km *(1.6 nm)*.
 2 BM 21 MRL rocket launchers; range about 9 km *(5 nm)*.

Comment: Yuling started in China in 1971. Stationed at Qingdao. Yuliang class is a variation of
 what may have been a prototype. Data is similar but there are variations in the superstructure.
 Series production started in 1980 in three or four smaller shipyards (Shantou etc). Numbers have
 been overestimated in the past and production has stopped in favour of newer classes.

YULIANG 1122   *5/1992, Henry Dodds*

3 CHINESE TYPE (LSM)

972   + 2

Displacement, tons: 600 full load
Dimensions, feet (metres): 185.7 × 34.1 × 7.5 *(56.6 × 10.4 × 2.3)*
Main machinery: 2 diesels; 2 shafts
Speed, knots: 15. **Range, miles:** 1000 at 12 kts
Complement: 25
Military lift: 150 tons
Guns: 4—25 mm/60 (2 twin).

Comment: Logistic supply LSM first seen in 1991 on sea trials. Probably in series production and
 could be for export. At least three of the class completed by the end of 1992.

LSM 972   *8/1992, Dr Chien Chung*

4 YUDAO CLASS (LSM)

Displacement, tons: 1460 full load
Dimensions, feet (metres): 285.4 × 41.3 × 10.2 *(87 × 12.6 × 3.1)*
Guns: 8—25 mm/60 (2 quad); 85° elevation; 270 rounds/minute to 3 km *(1.6 nm)*.

Comment: Probably first entered service in early 1980s. In South Fleet.

YUDAO   *12/1988, G Jacobs*

110 (+ 200 RESERVE) YUNNAN CLASS (TYPE 067) (LCU)

Displacement, tons: 128 full load
Dimensions, feet (metres): 93.8 × 17.7 × 4.6 *(28.6 × 5.4 × 1.4)*
Main machinery: 2 diesels; 600 hp(m) *(441 kW)*; 2 shafts
Speed, knots: 12. **Range, miles:** 500 at 10 kts
Complement: 12
Military lift: 46 tons
Guns: 2—12.7 mm MGs.

Comment: Built in China 1968-72 although a continuing programme was reported in 1982. Pennant numbers in 3000 series (3313, 3321, 3344 seen). 5000 series (5526 seen) and 7000 series (7566 and 7568 seen). Numbers split evenly between the three fleets. One to Sri Lanka in 1991. Numbers have been overestimated in the past but another 200 are probably in reserve.

YUNNAN   *1992*

40-50 YUCH'IN CLASS (LCU/LCP)

Displacement, tons: 58 standard; 85 full load
Dimensions, feet (metres): 81.2 × 17.1 × 4.3 *(24.8 × 5.2 × 1.3)*
Main machinery: 2 Type 12V 150C diesels; 600 hp(m) *(441 kW)*; 2 shafts
Speed, knots: 11.5. **Range, miles:** 450 at 11.5 kts
Military lift: Up to 150 troops
Guns: 4—14.5 mm (2 twin) MGs.

Comment: Built in Shanghai 1962-72. Smaller version of Yunnan class with a shorter tank deck and longer poop deck. Primarily intended for personnel transport.

YUCH'IN class

1 JINGSAH CLASS (HOVERCRAFT)

Displacement, tons: 70
Dimensions, feet (metres): 72.2 × 26.2 *(22 × 8)*
Main machinery: 2 propulsion motors; 2 lift motors
Speed, knots: 55
Military lift: 15 tons

Comment: Built at Dagu in 1979. A single prototype so far. All of the Payi class have been scrapped.

JINGSAH 5/1988, DTM

TRAINING SHIP

1 DAXIN CLASS

ZHENGHE 81

Displacement, tons: 4500 standard
Dimensions, feet (metres): 390.4 × 51.8 × 15.7 *(119 × 15.8 × 4.8)*
Main machinery: 2 diesels; 7800 hp(m) *(5.73 MW)*; 2 shafts
Speed, knots: 15
Complement: 170 plus 30 instructors plus 200 Midshipmen
Guns: 4 China 57 mm/70 (2 twin). 4—37 mm/63 (2 twin). 4—12.7 mm MGs.
A/S mortars: 2 FQF 2500 fixed 12 tubed launchers.
Radars: Navigation: 2 Racal Decca; I band.
Helicopters: Platform only.

Comment: Built at Qiuxin SY, Shanghai. Launched 12 July 1986, commissioned 27 April 1987. Resembles a small cruise liner. Subordinate to the Naval Academy and replaced *Huian*.

ZHENGHE 1992, Ships of the World

SUBMARINE SUPPORT SHIPS

1 DAZHI CLASS

DAZHI 920

Displacement, tons: 5600 full load
Dimensions, feet (metres): 350 × 50 × 20 *(106.7 × 15.3 × 6.1)*
Main machinery: 2 diesels; 3500 hp(m) *(2.57 MW)*; 2 shafts
Speed, knots: 14. **Range, miles:** 6000 at 14 kts
Complement: 290
Cargo capacity: 500 tons dieso
Guns: 4 China 37 mm/63 (2 twin). 4—25 mm/60 (2 twin).
Radars: Navigation: Fin Curve; I band.

Comment: Built at Hudung, Shanghai 1963-65. Has four electro-hydraulic cranes. Carries large stock of torpedoes and stores.

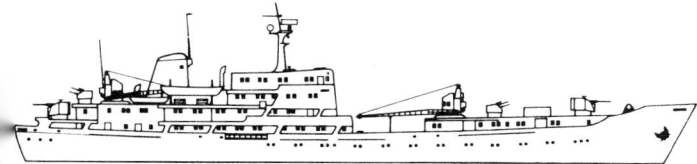

DAZHI (not to scale)

---

3 DAJIANG CLASS

| CHANGXINGDAO J 121 | YONGXINGDAO J 506 |
| CHONGMINGDAO J 302 | |

Displacement, tons: 10 975 full load
Dimensions, feet (metres): 511.7 × 67.2 × 22.3 *(156 × 20.5 × 6.8)*
Main machinery: 2 MAN K9Z60/105E diesels; 9000 hp(m) *(6.6 MW)*; 2 shafts
Speed, knots: 20
Guns: Light MGs. Can carry 6—37 mm (3 twin).
Radars: Surface search: Eye Shield; E band.
Navigation: Two Fin Curve; I band.
Helicopters: 2 Aerospatiale SA 321 G Super Frelon.

Comment: Submarine support and salvage ships built at Shanghai. First launched in mid-1973, operational in 1976. *Yongxingdao* has a smoke deflector on funnel and appears to have been fitted with a new foremast. Provision for DSRV on fwd well deck aft of launching crane. A fourth and fifth of the class are listed under *Research Ships*. New foremast on *Yongxingdao* suggests possible conversion to research ship role with long range communications similar to Russian *Fedor Vidyaev*.

CHANGXINGDAO 1991

YONGXINGDAO (with new foremast) 7/1989

---

1 DA DONG CLASS AND 1 DADAO CLASS

J 304 + 1

Displacement, tons: 2500 approx
Dimensions, feet (metres): 269 × 36.1 × 8.9 *(82 × 11 × 2.7)*

Comment: J304 reported to have been built at Hudung in late 1970s. Has a large and conspicuous crane aft. A second ship of approximately same dimensions and designed for the same duties was launched at Huludao shipyard and commissioned 12 January 1986 possibly with a civilian crew. Principal role is wreck location and salvage.

DADAO class 1989, Gilbert Gyssels

130 CHINA / Submarine support ships / Research and survey ships

2 DALANG and 1 DONGXIU CLASS

J 503   J 504   U 911

Displacement, tons: 3700 standard; 4300 full load (est)
Dimensions, feet (metres): 367 × 47.9 × 14.1 *(111.9 × 14.6 × 4.3)*
Main machinery: 2 diesels; 4000 hp(m) *(2.94 MW)*; 2 shafts
Speed, knots: 16. Range, miles: 8000 at 14 kts
Guns: 8 China 37 mm/63 (4 twin). 4 or 8 China 14.5 mm (2 or 4 twin) MGs.
Radars: Navigation: Fin Curve; I band.

Comment: First two built at Guangzhou Shipyard. First one commissioned November 1975, second in 1986. The Dongxiu class ship (U 911) is slightly larger and was built at Wuhu shipyard, commissioning in late 1986. Bulbous bow with notable rake to funnel amidships.

DALANG 504   12/1990, DTM

1 HUDUNG CLASS (ASR)

HAIJUI 512 (ex-J 301)   **HAIJUI** 403

Displacement, tons: 4500 standard (est); 4900+ full load (est)
Dimensions, feet (metres): 308.5 × 55.8 × 15.1 *(94 × 17 × 4.6)*
Main machinery: 2 diesels; 3600 hp(m) *(2.64 MW)*; 2 shafts
Speed, knots: 16. Range, miles: 5000 at 12 kts
Complement: 225 (est)
Guns: 6 China 37 mm/63 (3 twin).
Radars: Navigation: Fin Curve; I band.

Comment: Both built at Hudung Shipyard, Shanghai. Laid down 1965, launched 1967. Design revised before completion. 512 has two bow and two stern anchors. Two 5 ton booms and stern gantry for submarine rescue bell. 403 may be slightly smaller.

HAIJUI 512   1987

SALVAGE SHIPS

2 DSRV

Dimensions, feet (metres): 48.9 × 13.1 × 8.5 *(15 × 4 × 2.6)*
Speed, knots: 4
Complement: 4

Comment: First tested in 1986 and can be carried on large salvage ships. Capable of 'wet' rescue at 200 m and of diving to 600 m. Capacity for six survivors. Underwater TV, high frequency active sonar and a manipulator arm are all fitted.

DSRV   1991, CSSC

1 KANSHA CLASS

Displacement, tons: 1325
Dimensions, feet (metres): 229.3 × 34.4 × 11.8 *(69.9 × 10.5 × 3.6)*
Main machinery: 2 Type 8300 ZC diesels; 2200 hp(m) *(1.62 MW)*; 2 shafts
Speed, knots: 13.5. Range, miles: 2400 at 13 kts

Comment: Built at Chunghua SY, Shanghai in 1980-81. Trials July 1981. Designed by Chinese Marine Design and Research Institute. Carries one French SM-358-S DSRV (deep submergence recovery vehicle), 7 m long with a crew of five and an operating depth of 985 ft *(300 m)*. Ship has one 5 ton crane fwd and a 2 ton crane aft. Based in East China Sea.

4 YEN TING CLASS (ARS)

HAI LAO 456, 520, 523, 666

Displacement, tons: 260-275 standard
Dimensions, feet (metres): 103.3 × 23 × 8.2 *(31.5 × 7 × 2.5)*
Main machinery: 1 Type 3-D-12 diesel; 300 hp(m) *(220 kW)* sustained; 1 shaft
Speed, knots: 10
Complement: 18
Guns: 2 China 14.5 mm/93 (twin).

Comment: Trawler-type hull, similar to enlarged FT series. Built in 1972-74.

YEN TING 666   12/1989, G Jacobs

REPAIR SHIPS

1 Ex-US ACHELOUS CLASS

DAGUSHAN (ex-*Hsiang An*, ex-USS *Achilles* ARL 41, ex-LST 455) U 891

Displacement, tons: 1625 light; 4325 full load
Dimensions, feet (metres): 328 × 50 × 14 *(100 × 15.2 × 4.3)*
Main machinery: 2 GM 12-567A diesels; 1800 hp *(1.34 MW)*; 2 shafts
Speed, knots: 12
Complement: 270
Guns: 12 China 37 mm/63 (6 twin). 4 China 14.5 mm/93 (2 twin).
Radars: Navigation: Fin Curve; I band.

Comment: Launched on 17 October 1942. Transferred to Nationalist China as *Hsiang An* in September 1947. Burned and grounded in 1949, salvaged and refitted. Has 60 ton A-frame and 25 ton crane. Mostly alongside in Shanghai.

DAGUSHAN   7/1985, Fischer/Donko

1 DA LIANG CLASS (AR)

HAI WU 809

Comment: Built in 1968-69 possibly as a repair ship for small craft.

RESEARCH AND SURVEY SHIPS

Notes: (a) In addition to naval ships listed the following ships work for the Hydrographic Bureau of the Ministry of Communications and therefore act as AGIs: *Sui Hang Biao No 1*, *Hu Hang Biao No 3* and *Jin Hang Biao No 1* (all of 1400 tons) and *Sui Hang CE Nos 1* and *2*, *Hu Hang CE Nos 11-15*, and *Jin Hang CE Nos 1* and *2* (all of 300 tons).
(b) *Qionsha* H 263 is a survey ship which is armed with 2—37 mm twins and 2—25 mm twins. This is probably an adaptation of the class of same name listed in *Amphibious Warfare Forces* section as an AP.

1 RESEARCH SHIP

JI DI HAO

Displacement, tons: 1050 full load
Dimensions, feet (metres): 164 × 34 × 16.4 *(50 × 10.4 × 5)*
Main machinery: 1 Burmeister and Wain Alpha 12V 23/30-V diesel; 2200 hp(m) *(1.62 MW)* sustained; 1 shaft
Speed, knots: 14. Range, miles: 12 000 at 11 kts
Complement: 26 plus 15 scientists

Comment: Ordered from Mjellem and Karlsen, Bergen, Norway in 1983. Laid down 15 Novembe 1983. Similar to civilian research ships built for Mexico.

Research and survey ships / CHINA

2 DAJIANG CLASS (RESEARCH SHIPS)

R 327   YUAN WANG 3

Displacement, tons: 10 975 full load
Dimensions, feet (metres): 511.7 × 67.2 × 37.7 *(156 × 20.5 × 11.5)*
Main machinery: 2 MAN K9Z60/105E diesels; 9000 hp(m) *(6.6 MW)*; 2 shafts
Speed, knots: 20
Helicopters: 2 Aerospatiale SA 321G Super Frelon (*R 237* only).

Comment: Built at Hutong, Shanghai. Completed 1981-82. Sisters of submarine support and salvage ships and operate for Academy of Sciences.

R 327   1980, RNZAF

YUAN WANG 3   1984

1 SHIH YEN CLASS (AGOR)

SHIH YEN (ex-*Kim Guam*)

Displacement, tons: 2500 full load
Dimensions, feet (metres): 213.3 × 38.1 × 16.4 *(65 × 11.6 × 5)*
Main machinery: 2 UK Polar diesels; 1200 hp *(895 kW)*; 2 shafts
Speed, knots: 11 (est)
Radars: Navigation: Fin Curve or Japan OKI NXE-12c; I band.

Comment: Former coastal steamer purchased by China from Quan Quan Shipping Ltd (Singapore) about 1973. Cargo holds forward and amidships. Believed rebuilt in late 1970s for oceanographic duties. Operated by one of China's research academies or China Institute of Oceanography. Painted white.

2 SPACE EVENT SHIPS

YUAN WANG 1 and 2

Displacement, tons: 17 100 standard; 21 000 full load
Dimensions, feet (metres): 623.2 × 74.1 × 24.6 *(190 × 22.6 × 7.5)*
Main machinery: 1 diesel; 1 shaft
Speed, knots: 20

Comment: Built by Shanghai Jiangnan Yard. Probably commissioned in 1979. Have helicopter platform but no hangar. New communications. SATNAV and meteorological equipment fitted in Jiangnan SY in 1986-87. Both being refitted in 1991.

YUAN WANG 2   9/1988

2 SHIJIAN CLASS (AGOR)

SHIJIAN   KEXUEYIHAO

Displacement, tons: 3700 full load
Dimensions, feet (metres): 311.6 × 46 × 16.4 *(95 × 14 × 5)*
Main machinery: 2 Type 6 ESDZ 48/82 diesels; 4000 hp(m) *(2.94 MW)*; 2 shafts
Speed, knots: 15. **Range, miles:** 10 000 at 12 kts
Complement: 125 approx
Guns: 8 China 14.5 mm/93 (4 twin).
Radars: Navigation: Fin curve; I band.

Comment: *Shijian* built at Shanghai in 1965-68 as enlarged unit of Dong Fang Hong class AGOR. Electronics updated in 1991. Operates in East China Sea area under civil authority of the State Bureau of Oceanography and with scientists of the Chinese Academy of Sciences. Twelve labs on board. Painted white. *Kexueyihao* was first seen in late 1989 and is a slightly modified version.

SHIJIAN   5/1992, Henry Dodds

1 DADIE CLASS (AGI)

841

Displacement, tons: 2300 standard
Dimensions, feet (metres): 308.4 × 37.1 × 13.1 *(94 × 11.3 × 4)*
Main machinery: 2 diesels; 2 shafts
Speed, knots: 17
Complement: 170 (18 officers)
Guns: 4 China 37 mm/63 (2 twin).

Comment: Built at Wuhan shipyard, Wuchang and commissioned in 1986. North Sea Fleet and seen regularly in Sea of Japan and East China Sea.

841   1991, Ships of the World

2 HAI YING CLASS (AGOR)

KE XUE YIHAO 1   KE XUE YIHAO 2

Displacement, tons: 4500 standard
Dimensions, feet (metres): 412 × 51 × 24 *(125.6 × 15.5 × 7.3)*
Main machinery: 2 Type ESDZ diesels; 2 shafts
Speed, knots: 22
Complement: 148 (20 officers)
Radars: Navigation: 2 Fin Curve.

Comment: Successor design to Xiangyang Hong 9 series of civilian research ship. Believed to have been built in 1987-89. Fitted with deep sea cable reel on stern. Observed in East China Sea in March and September 1990 and Sea of Japan in 1991.

KE XUE YIHAO   12/1990, G Jacobs

132 CHINA / Research and survey ships

1 KAN CLASS (AGOR)

KAN 102

Displacement, tons: 2300 standard
Dimensions, feet (metres): 225 × 22.5 × 9 *(68.6 × 6.9 × 2.7)*
Main machinery: 2 diesels; 2 shafts
Speed, knots: 18
Radars: Navigation: Fin Curve; I band.

Comment: Believed built in 1985-87, possibly at Shanghai. Large open stern area. Aft main deck area covered and may have cable reel system. Operated in East China Sea and Sea of Japan during 1991.

KAN 102   9/1990, G Jacobs

1 XING FENGSHAN CLASS (AGI)

XING FENGSHAN V 856

Displacement, tons: 5500

Comment: Launched in June 1987. Similar to Dalang class.

XING FENGSHAN   1987, Ships of the World

XIANGYANG HONG 01

Displacement, tons: 1100 standard; 1150 full load
Dimensions, feet (metres): 219.8 × 32.8 × 13.1 *(67 × 10 × 4)*
Main machinery: 2 diesels; 2 shafts
Guns: 2 China 37 mm/63 (twin). 8 China 14.5 mm/93 (2 quad).
Radars: Navigation: Fin Curve; I band.

Comment: The generic name Xiangyang Hong means 'The East is Red'. Initial vessel built either at Jiangnan or Tsingdao about 1970. Commissioned in 1971 and employed as research vessel but painted grey as if naval subordinated. Weapons not normally included on vessels subordinated to the Chinese Academy of Sciences.

XIANGYANG HONG 04, 06

Displacement, tons: 2000
Speed, knots: 15

Comment: Research ships built 1971-73.

XIANGYANG HONG 04   1980, USN

XIANGYANG HONG 02, 03, 08

Displacement, tons: 800 standard; 1000 full load
Dimensions, feet (metres): 236.2 × 26.2 × 8.2 *(72 × 8 × 2.5)*
Main machinery: 2 diesels; 2 shafts
Speed, knots: 14
Radars: Navigation: Fin Curve; I band.

Comment: Built in 1971-73 at Guangzhou. Operated by Chinese Academy of Sciences for coastal survey. Painted white.

XIANGYANG HONG 05

Displacement, tons: 14 500 full load
Dimensions, feet (metres): 500 × 64 × 28.9 *(152.5 × 19.5 × 8.8)*
Main machinery: 2 diesels; 2 shafts
Speed, knots: 16. **Range, miles:** 12-15 000
Radars: Navigation: Square Tie; I band.

Comment: Built as Polish B41 Type *(Francesco Nullo)* in 1967. Purchased by China and rebuilt 1970-72 in Guangzhou. Stationed at Guangzhou. Acts as environmental research ship. Four sister ships in Chinese mercantile fleet. Operated by Academy of Science. The goal post with a parabolic aerial has been removed from its position aft.

XIANGYANG HONG 05   1980, RNZAF

XIANGYANG HONG 09 (ex-*21*) V 350

Displacement, tons: 4435 standard
Dimensions, feet (metres): 400.3 × 49.9 × 23.6 *(122 × 15.2 × 7.2)*
Main machinery: 2 Type ESDZ 43/82B diesels; 8600 hp(m) *(6.32 MW)*; 2 shafts
Speed, knots: 22. **Range, miles:** 11 000 at 15 kts
Complement: 145 (20 officers)
Radars: Navigation: Type 756; I band.

Comment: Originally built as Xiang Yang Hong 21 (AGOR) at Hudong Shipyard, Shanghai, in 1978. Conversion to AGI completed about 1986 and has since been observed monitoring US-ROK 'Team Spirit' military exercises in Sea of Japan and Yellow Sea. Prominent 5 ton cargo boom aft and two forward kingposts with extensive electronics mounted. Painted dark grey. Operated in East China Sea in 1989.

XIANGYANG HONG 09   6/1988, G Jacobs

XIANGYANG HONG 10

Displacement, tons: 10 975
Dimensions, feet (metres): 512.3 × 67.6 × 22.3 *(156.2 × 20.6 × 6.8)*
Main machinery: 2 diesels; 2 shafts
Speed, knots: 20
Helicopters: 1 Aerospatiale SA 321G Super Frelon.

Comment: Built at Jiangnan Shipyard, Shanghai in 1979. Operates in conjunction with the Academy of Science.

XIANGYANG HONG 10   3/199*

XIANGYANG HONG 11-16

Measurement, tons: 2894 grt (14 and 16)
Dimensions, feet (metres): 364.2 × 49.9 × 23.3 *(111 × 15.2 × 7.1)*
Main machinery: 2 diesels; 2 shafts

Comment: A series of research ships of varying dimensions but similar appearance. 14 and 16 built in 1981.

XIANGYANG HONG 12   7/1987

1 YEN HSI CLASS (AGM)

HSUN 701

Displacement, tons: 930 standard; 1200 full load
Dimensions, feet (metres): 196.86 × 35.3 × 11.48 *(60 × 11 × 3.5)*
Main machinery: 2 diesels; 1800 hp(m) *(1.32 MW)*; 2 shafts
Speed, knots: 16 max; 11 cruise. **Range, miles:** 4500 at 11 kts
Complement: 110
Guns: 2 China 37 mm/63 (twin). 4 China 14.5 mm (2 twin) MGs.
Radars: Navigation: Fin Curve; I band.

Comment: Built in Shanghai in 1968-70. Has pronounced flare fwd and bow bulwark. Appearance is that of Hsiang Yang Hung 02-series of AGORs, though lighter in displacement and may have originally been planned as an AGOR/AGS unit.

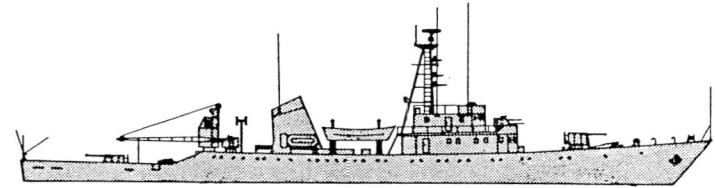

3 GEOPHYSICAL RESEARCH SHIPS

NAN HAI 502   **BIN HAI** 511   —

Measurement, tons: 697 dwt; 1257 gross
Dimensions, feet (metres): 215.5 × 36.9 × 13.5 *(65.7 × 11.2 × 4.1)*
Main machinery: 2 Yanmar CG-ST diesels; 2000 hp(m) *(1.47 MW)*; 1 shaft; cp prop
Speed, knots: 15
Complement: 50 (31 plus 19 scientists)

Comment: Built by Mitsubishi Heavy Industries in 1979. Designed for bathymetric and seismic research using satellite and terrestrial fixing. 511 modified in 1983 to include a helicopter deck. Arrays up to 3600 m can be towed.

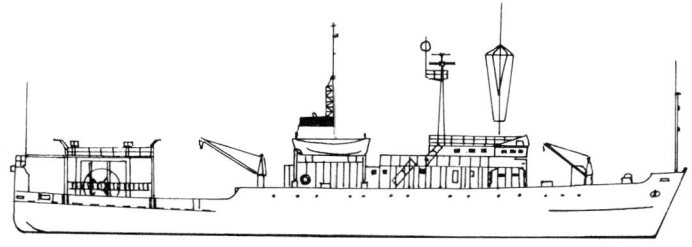

NAN HAI

1 YENLUN CLASS (AGS) + 2 Ex-US ARMY (AGS)

HAITSE 583   **HAITSE** 502   **HAITSE** 601

Displacement, tons: 1250 standard; 2000 full load (583)
Dimensions, feet (metres): 229.7 × 65.6 × 9.8 *(70 × 20 × 3)* (583)
Main machinery: 2 PRC/Kolomna Type 9-D-8 diesels; 2000 hp(m) *(1.47 MW)* sustained; 2 shafts
Speed, knots: 17
Guns: 4—25 mm/60 (2 twin).
Radars: Navigation: Fin Curve; I band.

Comment: 583 has prominent twin funnels amidships. First twin-hulled vessel built by PRC, with open well deck aft for supporting diving equipment and deep ocean survey work. Two small cranes aft. 502 and 601 are smaller ex-US Army craft of about 800 tons.

3 SHUGUANG CLASS (ex T-43) (AGOR/AGH)

SHUGUANG 1, 2 and 3

Displacement, tons: 500 standard; 570 full load
Dimensions, feet (metres): 190.3 × 28.9 × 11.5 *(58 × 8.8 × 3.5)*
Main machinery: 2 PRC/Kolomna Type 9-D-8 diesels; 2000 hp(m) *(1.47 MW)* sustained; 2 shafts
Speed, knots: 15. **Range, miles:** 5300 at 8 kts
Complement: 55-60

Comment: Converted from ex-Soviet T43 Minesweepers in late 1960s. All painted white. One used for hydro-acoustic work in the East Sea Fleet has the number S994.

SHUGUANG 3   1980

5 SHUGUANG 04 CLASS (AGOR)

SHUGUANG 04, 05, 06, 07, 08

Displacement, tons: 1700 standard; 2400 full load
Dimensions, feet (metres): 214.9 × 32.8 × — *(65.5 × 10 × —)*
Main machinery: 2 diesels; 2 shafts
Speed, knots: 16
Guns: 2 China 37 mm/63 (twin). 4 China 25 mm/80 (2 twin).
Radars: Navigation: Fin Curve; I band.

Comment: Built at Guangzhou from 1970 to about 1975, based on modified design of *Hsiang Yan Hung 1* AGOR. Units differ slightly in superstructure appearance. At least three units subordinated to the Chinese Academy of Sciences and are without armament. Operated in East China and South China Seas.

SHUGUANG 04 class   9/1990, John Mapletoft

5 YENLAI CLASS (AGS)

K 200   226   426   427   943

Displacement, tons: 1100 full load
Dimensions, feet (metres): 229.6 × 32.1 × 9.7 *(70 × 9.8 × 3)*
Main machinery: 2 PRC/Kolomna Type 9-D-8 diesels; 2000 hp(m) *(1.47 MW)* sustained; 2 shafts
Speed, knots: 16. **Range, miles:** 4000 at 14 kts
Complement: 100
Guns: 4 China 37 mm/63 (2 twin). 4—25 mm/60 (2 twin).
Radars: Navigation: Fin Curve; I band.

Comment: Built at Zhonghua Shipyard, Shanghai in early 1970s. Carry four survey motor boats.

YENLAI 427   1987, G Jacobs

134 CHINA / Research and survey ships — Boom defence vessels

2 HAI YANG CLASS (AGOR)

HAI YANG 01   HAI YANG 02

Displacement, tons: 3300 standard; 4500 full load
Dimensions, feet (metres): 341.2 × 42.7 × 14.8 *(104 × 13 × 4.5)*
Main machinery: 2 diesels; 8000 hp(m) *(5.9 MW)*; 2 shafts
Speed, knots: 21. Range, miles: 10 000 at 18 kts
Complement: 150 including scientists
Guns: 4 China 37 mm/63 (2 twin).
Radars: Navigation: Fin Curve; I band.

Comment: Built at Shanghai during 1969-71. *Hai Yang 01* commissioned in 1972; *Hai Yang 02* in 1973 or 1974. Funnel amidships. Subordinated to Chinese Academy of Sciences. Painted white.

HAI YANG class   7/1989, G Jacobs

1 DONG FANG HONG CLASS (AGOR)

Displacement, tons: 3000 full load
Dimensions, feet (metres): 282.2 × 37.7 × 14.8 *(86 × 11.5 × 4.5)*
Main machinery: 2 diesels; 2 shafts
Speed, knots: 14
Radars: Navigation: Fin Curve; I band.

Comment: Built at Hutong, Shanghai 1964-66.

DONG FANG HONG   1988

1 HAI CLASS (AGOR)

HAI 521

Displacement, tons: 550 full load
Dimensions, feet (metres): 164 × 32.8 × 11.5 *(50 × 10 × 3.5)*
Main machinery: 2 Niigata Type 6M26KHHS diesels; 1600 hp(m) *(1.18 MW)*; 2 shafts; bow thruster
Speed, knots: 14. Range, miles: 5000 at 11 kts
Complement: 15 (7 officers) plus 25 scientists
Radars: Navigation: Japanese AR-M31; I band.

Comment: Built by Niigata Engineering Co., Niigata (Japan) in 1974-75. Launched 10 March 1975. Commissioned July 1975. First operated by the China National Machinery Export-Import Corp. on oceanographic duties. Operates on East and South China research projects but based in North China. For small vessel, has unique cruiser stern with raked bow, and small funnel well aft. Capability to operate single DSRV and the Chinese Navy has a number of Japanese-built KSWB-300 submersibles. Painted white.

1 GANZHU CLASS (AGS)

K 420

Displacement, tons: 850 standard; 1000 full load
Dimensions, feet (metres): 213.2 × 29.5 × 9.7 *(65 × 9 × 3)*
Main machinery: 4 diesels; 4400 hp(m) *(3.23 MW)*; 2 shafts
Speed, knots: 20
Complement: 125 (est)
Guns: 4—37 mm/63 (2 twin). 4—25 mm/60 (2 twin).

Comment: Built in Zhu Zhiang 1973-75. Frigate-type bridge. Prominent raked funnel.

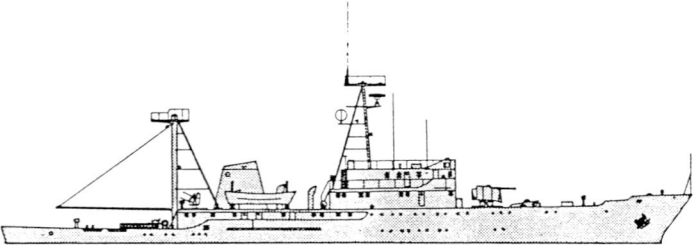

GANZHU   1990

1 YANXI CLASS (AGS)

V 201

Displacement, tons: 1150 standard
Dimensions, feet (metres): 213.9 × 34.4 × 10.8 *(65.2 × 10.5 × 3.3)*
Main machinery: 2 diesels; 4000 hp(m) *(2.9 MW)*; 2 shafts
Speed, knots: 16
Guns: 4 China 37 mm/63 Type 61/74 (2 twin); 4 China 25 mm/80 Type 61 (2 twin).

Comment: Built 1968-69; commissioned 1970. Outfitted initially to provide electronic monitoring support for China's SLBM missile tests.

2 YANNAN CLASS (AGS)

K 982   983

Displacement, tons: 1750 standard
Dimensions, feet (metres): 237.2 × 38.7 × 13.1 *(72.3 × 11.8 × 4)*
Main machinery: 1 diesel; 500 hp(m) *(367 kW)*; 1 shaft
Speed, knots: 12
Complement: 95

Comment: Built 1978-79; commissioned 1980.

YANNAN 982   1992

2 DING HAI CLASS and 1 KAIBOBAN CLASS (AGS)

HAI SHENG 701, 702 and 623

Displacement, tons: 330 full load (701, 702)
Dimensions, feet (metres): 128 × 24.6 × 11.5 *(39 × 7.5 × 3.5)* (701, 702)
Main machinery: 2 PRC/Kolomna Type 3-D-12 diesels; 600 hp(m) *(440 kW)* sustained; 2 shafts
Speed, knots: 13
Guns: 4—14.5 mm/93 (2 twin).

Comment: Coastal trawler design. Naval subordinated. 701 and 702 are South Sea Fleet units. 623 is a larger craft of 67.5 m assigned to the North Sea Fleet.

CABLE SHIPS

Note: Several classes of cable layers are in service. These carry 'B' pennant numbers while similar ships with 'H' numbers act as buoy tenders and those with 'N' numbers are based at Nanjing. Examples are B 873, H 263 and N 2304, all of the same class.

1 WULAI CLASS (ARC)

230

Displacement, tons: 500 full load
Dimensions, feet (metres): 177.1 × 28.9 × 7.5 *(54 × 8.8 × 2.3)*
Complement: 50 approx
Guns: 4—25 mm/60 (2 twin).
Radars: Navigation: Skin Head; I band.

Comment: Built at Guangzhou in 1968-69 as coastal cable repair ship. Has noticeable davits aft. Fitted with bow sheaves. Also acts as salvage ship in South Sea Fleet.

BOOM DEFENCE VESSELS

Note: There are several classes of vessel including Yen Tai, Yen Bai, Yen Kuan, Hang Feng and some trawler conversions. Most are armed with at least 14.5 mm MGs.

5 Ex-US AILANTHUS CLASS

Displacement, tons: 560 standard; 805 full load
Dimensions, feet (metres): 194.5 × 34.5 × 14.8 *(59.3 × 10.5 × 4.5)*
Main machinery: Diesel-electric; 1200 hp(m) *(895 kW)*
Speed, knots: 14
Complement: 55
Guns: 1—14.5 mm MG.

Comment: Probably now used as service vessels.

SUPPLY SHIPS

Note: In addition to the following there may be another 12 coastal merchant ships operating under naval control as well as several 450 ton cargo ships wearing 'N' numbers.

2 DAYUN CLASS (AK)

— 951   NAN YUN 952

Displacement, tons: 11 000 full load
Dimensions, feet (metres): 511.7 × 67.2 × 22.5 (156 × 20.5 × 6.9)
Main machinery: 2 diesels; 9000 hp(m) (6.6 MW); 2 shafts
Speed, knots: 20
Guns: 4—37 mm/63 (2 twin).
Helicopters: 2 Super Frelon SA 321.

Comment: First of class completed in late 1991, second in 1992. Same hull as Dajiang class support ships and with a similar crane on the foredeck.

NAN YUN   7/1992, Ships of the World

1 YUKAN CLASS (AK)

801

Displacement, tons: 3330 full load
Dimensions, feet (metres): 393.6 × 50 × 9.8 (120 × 15.3 × 3)
Main machinery: 2 diesels; 2 shafts
Speed, knots: 17
Complement: 100
Guns: 2 China 57 mm/50 (twin).

Comment: Either a new construction or a converted Yukan class hull. First seen in 1992.

AK 801   5/1992, Henry Dodds

1 DAMEN CLASS (AK)

Y 529

Displacement, tons: 1050 standard; 1400 full load
Dimensions, feet (metres): 205.1 × 30.8 × 11.8 (62.5 × 9.4 × 3.6)
Complement: 30
Cargo capacity: 450 tons

Comment: Built at CSSC Shipyard, Xiamen in 1983.

4 DANLIN CLASS (AK)

HAI LENG L 191, L 201   HAI YUN L 790, L 794

Displacement, tons: 900 standard; 1290 full load
Dimensions, feet (metres): 198.5 × 29.5 × 13.1 (60.5 × 9 × 4)
Main machinery: 1 Soviet/PRC Type 6DRN 30/50 diesel; 750 hp(m) (551 kW); 1 shaft
Speed, knots: 15
Complement: 35
Cargo capacity: 750-800 tons
Guns: 4—25 mm/80 (2 twin).
Radars: Navigation: Fin Curve or Skin Head; I band.

Comment: Built in China in early 1960-62. Have a refrigerated stores capability. Two serve in each of South and East Sea Fleets. Two or more in civilian service.

DANLIN 794   5/1992, Henry Dodds

2 GALATI CLASS (AK)

HAIYUN 318   HAIJIU 600

Displacement, tons: 5300
Dimensions, feet (metres): 328 × 45.6 × 21.6 (100 × 13.9 × 6.6)
Main machinery: 1 Sulzer 5TAD56 diesel; 2500 hp(m) (1.84 MW); 1 shaft
Speed, knots: 12.5. Range, miles: 5000 at 12 kts
Complement: 50
Cargo capacity: 3750 tons; 20 ton; 3-5 ton cranes

Comment: Built at Santiereal Shipyard, Galati, Romania in 1960s. Nine ships purchased of which these two were converted to AKs in early 1970s. Both reported operating in South Sea Fleet.

4 HONGQI CLASS (AK)

Y 443   Y 528   Y 755   Y 771

Displacement, tons: 1950 full load
Dimensions, feet (metres): 203.4 × 39.4 × 14.4 (62 × 12 × 4.4)
Main machinery: 1 diesel; 1 shaft
Speed, knots: 14. Range, miles: 2500 at 11 kts
Guns: 4 China 25/80 (2 twin).

Comment: Used to support offshore military garrisons. A further ship, L 202, appears to be similar but carries no armament.

HONGQI 755   5/1992, Henry Dodds

3 LEIZHOU CLASS (WTL)

HAI SHUI 412, 555, 558

Comment: Details under same class in Tankers section. Two in South Sea and one in East Sea Fleets.

9 FUZHOU CLASS (WTL)

HAI SHUI 416, HAI SHUI 419, HAI SHUI 556, HAI SHUI 557, HAI SHUI 608 et al

Displacement, tons: 1100 standard
Dimensions, feet (metres): 196.8 × 29.5 × 11.5 (60 × 9 × 3.5)
Main machinery: 1 diesel; 600 hp(m) (441 kW); 1 shaft
Speed, knots: 12
Complement: 35
Guns: 4—25 mm (2 twin). 4—12.7 mm (2 twin) (not in all).

Comment: Built in Shanghai 1964-70. Large water carriers. Four in North Sea Fleet, two in East Sea Fleet, two in South Sea Fleet. Fourteen of same class in Tanker section.

FUZHOU 608   7/1989

DEGAUSSING SHIPS

Note: In addition to the vessels listed below four ex-US LSIL conversions, Hai Dzu 741, 742, 804 and 821 act as degaussing ships.

2 YEN FANG CLASS (ADG)

HAI DZU 950   HAI DZU 951

Displacement, tons: 110 standard; 125 full load
Dimensions, feet (metres): 101.7 × 20 × 5.9 (31 × 6.1 × 1.8)
Main machinery: 2 Soviet/PRC Type 3-D-6 diesels; 600 hp(m) (440 kW) sustained; 2 shafts
Speed, knots: 9
Complement: 14-16

Comment: Trawler hull conversion. Cable reels on stern. Converted mid-1960s.

136 CHINA / Degaussing ships — Tankers

2 YEN PAI CLASS (ADG)

HAI DZU 746   **DONG QIN 863**

Displacement, tons: 746 standard
Dimensions, feet (metres): 213.3 × 29.5 × 8.5 *(65 × 9 × 2.6)*
Main machinery: Diesel-electric; 2 12VE 230ZC diesels; 2200 hp(m) *(1.62 MW)*; 2 ZDH-99/57 motors; 2 shafts
Speed, knots: 16. **Range, miles:** 800 at 15 kts
Complement: 55 (est)
Guns: 4—37 mm/63 (2 twin). 4—25 mm/80 (2 twin).

Comment: Enlarged version of T 43 MSF with larger bridge and funnel amidships. Reels on quarterdeck for degaussing function. Not all the guns are embarked.

HAI DZU   1991, CSSC

2 YENKA CLASS (ADG)

HAI DZU 745   **+1**

Displacement, tons: 395 full load
Dimensions, feet (metres): 154.2 × 24.6 × 7.2 *(47 × 7.5 × 2.2)*
Main machinery: 2 PRC/Kolomna 9-D-8 diesels; 2000 hp(m) *(1.47 MW)* sustained; 2 shafts
Speed, knots: 18. **Range, miles:** 3000 at 11 kts
Complement: 50
Guns: 2—37 mm/63 (twin). 2 or 4—14.5 mm/93 (1 or 2 twin) MGs.

Comment: Built at Chunghua Shipyard, Shanghai about 1966-68. Modified trawler hull. Prominent angled funnel and transom stern.

TANKERS

Note: In addition to the ships listed below there are some elderly coastal tankers of the Kuangzhou (X 624, X 627), Fuzhi and Mettawge classes.

2 FUQING CLASS (AOR)

TAICANG X 575   **DONGYUN** (ex-*Fenfcang*) X 615

Displacement, tons: 7500 standard; 21 750 full load
Dimensions, feet (metres): 552 × 71.5 × 30.8 *(168.2 × 21.8 × 9.4)*
Main machinery: 1 Sulzer 8RL B66 diesel; 15 000 hp(m) *(11 MW)* sustained; 1 shaft
Speed, knots: 18. **Range, miles:** 18 000 at 14 kts
Complement: 130 (24 officers)
Cargo capacity: 10 550 tons fuel; 1000 tons dieso; 200 tons feed water; 200 tons drinking water; 4 small cranes
Guns: 8—37 mm (4 twin) (fitted for but not with).
Radars: Navigation: Two Fin Curve; I band.

Comment: Operational in late 1979. This is the first class of ships built for underway replenishment in the Chinese Navy. Helicopter platform but no hangar. No armament. All built at Talien. Two liquid replenishment positions each side with one solid replenishment position each side by the funnel. X 615 has a rounded funnel vice the square shape of the X 575. A third of the class *Hongcang* (X 950) was converted to merchant use in 1989 and renamed *Hai Lang*, registered at Dalian. A fourth (X 350) was sold to Pakistan in 1987.

DONGYUN   1992

2 SHENGLI CLASS (AOT)

X 620   **X 621**

Displacement, tons: 3300 standard; 4950 full load
Dimensions, feet (metres): 331.4 × 45.3 × 18 *(101 × 13.8 × 5.5)*
Main machinery: 1 6 ESDZ 43/82B diesel; 2600 hp(m) *(1.91 MW)*; 1 shaft
Speed, knots: 14. **Range, miles:** 2400 at 11 kts
Cargo capacity: 3400 tons dieso
Guns: 2—57 mm (twin). 2—25 mm (twin).

Comment: Built at Hudong SY, Shanghai in late 1970s. Others of the class in commercial service.

SHENGLI 621   5/1992, Henry Dodds

3 JINYOU CLASS (AOT)

X 622   **X 625**   **X 675**

Displacement, tons: 2500 standard; 4800 full load
Dimensions, feet (metres): 324.8 × 45.3 × 18.7 *(99 × 31.8 × 5.7)*
Main machinery: 1 SEMT-Pielstick 8 PC2.2 L diesel; 4000 hp(m) *(2.94 MW)* sustained; 1 shaft
Speed, knots: 15. **Range, miles:** 4000 at 9 kts

Comment: Built at Kanashashi SY, Japan.

JINYOU 625   9/1990, John Mapletoft

7 FULIN CLASS

X 583   **X 606**   **X 607**   **X 609**   **X 628**   **X 629**   **X 633**

Displacement, tons: 2300 standard
Dimensions, feet (metres): 216.5 × 42.6 × 13.1 *(66 × 13 × 4)*
Main machinery: 1 diesel; 600 hp(m) *(441 kW)*; 1 shaft
Speed, knots: 10. **Range, miles:** 1500 at 8 kts
Complement: 30
Guns: 4—25 mm/80 (2 twin).
Radars: Navigation: Fin Curve; I band.

Comment: A total of 20 of these ships built at Hutong, Shanghai, beginning 1972. Thirteen in civilian service. Naval ships painted dark grey. Some having single underway replenishment rig. One in South Sea Fleet.

FULIN 607   5/1992, Henry Dodds

14 FUZHOU CLASS (AOT)

X 573   **X 580**   **X 606**   **X 629**   *et al*

Cargo capacity: 600 tons fuel

Comment: Details under same class in Supply Ships. Built in Hudung SY, Shanghai 1964-70. Five in South Sea Fleet.

FUZHOU 606   5/1992, Henry Dodds

Tankers — Tugs / CHINA   137

5 LEIZHOU CLASS (AOTL)

Displacement, tons: 900 standard
Dimensions, feet (metres): 173.9 × 32.2 × 10.5 *(53 × 9.8 × 3.2)*
Main machinery: 1 diesel; 500 hp(m) *(367 kW)*; 1 shaft
Speed, knots: 12. **Range, miles:** 1200 at 10 kts
Complement: 25-30
Cargo capacity: 450 tons
Guns: 4—37 mm (2 twin).
Radars: Navigation: Skin Head; I band.

Comment: Built in late 1960s probably at Qingdao or Wutong.

LEIZHOU 1104   *5/1992, Henry Dodds*

ICEBREAKERS

2 HAIBING CLASS (AGB)

101 (ex-C723)   102 (ex-C721)

Displacement, tons: 2900 standard; 3400 full load
Dimensions, feet (metres): 275 × 50 × 16.4 *(83.8 × 15.3 × 5)*
Main machinery: Diesel-electric; 2 diesel generators; 5250 hp(m) *(3.86 MW)*; 1 motor; 1 shaft
Speed, knots: 16
Complement: 90-95
Guns: 8—37 mm/63 (4 twin). 4 or 8—25 mm/80 (2 or 4 twin).
Radars: Navigation: Fin Curve; I band.

Comment: Built in 1969-73 at Chiu Hsin SY, Shanghai. Employed as icebreaking tugs in Bo Hai Gulf for port clearance. Sometimes deployed as AGIs.

102   *1982, G Jacobs*

1 MOD YANHA CLASS (AGB)

723

Displacement, tons: 4000 full load
Dimensions, feet (metres): 310 × 56 × 19.5 *(94.5 × 17.1 × 5.9)*
Main machinery: Diesel-electric; 2 diesels; 2 shafts
Speed, knots: 17.5
Complement: 95
Guns: 8—37 mm/63 Type 61/74 (4 twin).
Radars: Navigation: Fin Curve; I band.

Comment: Enlarged version of Yanha class icebreaker, with greater displacement, longer and wider hull, added deck level and curved upper funnel. In October 1990, painted white while operating in Sea of Japan.

723   *1991, Ships of the World*

1 YANHA CLASS (AGB)

519

Displacement, tons: 3400 full load
Dimensions, feet (metres): 290 × 53 × 17 *(88.4 × 16.2 × 5.2)*
Main machinery: Diesel-electric; 2 diesels; 1 shaft
Speed, knots: 17.5
Complement: 90
Guns: 8—37 mm/63 Type 61/74 (4 twin); 4—25 mm/80 Type 61.
Radars: Navigation: Fin Curve; I band.

Comment: Commissioned in 1989. Similar to Haibing class with minor differences. Painted in PLAN grey colour. Operated in East China Sea in late 1990.

519   *10/1991, G Jacobs*

SERVICE CRAFT

Note: There are probably over 500 armed motor junks, launches and miscellaneous service craft.

TUGS

Note: The vessels below represent a small cross-section of the craft available.

5 YUNG GANG CLASS (ATA)

Displacement, tons: 320
Dimensions, feet (metres): 87 × 31.4 × 10.8 *(26.5 × 9.6 × 3.3)*
Main machinery: 2 Daihatsu 6DLM-24 diesels; 3000 hp(m) *(2.2 MW)* sustained; 2 shafts
Speed, knots: 15

Comment: *Yung Gang 16* launched 29 July 1981 at Ishikawajima, built in Japan. It is not known whether these are for naval or civilian use.

1 YAN JIU CLASS (ATA)

YAN JIU 14

Comment: Probably one of a series with dual military civilian use.

YAN JIU 14   *9/1991, G Jacobs*

16 GROMOVOY CLASS (ATA)

HAITO 210, 221, 230, 231, 235, 319, T 147, T 716, T 802, T 814   +6

Displacement, tons: 795 standard; 890 full load
Dimensions, feet (metres): 149.9 × 31.2 × 15.1 *(45.7 × 9.5 × 4.6)*
Main machinery: 2 diesels; 1300 hp(m) *(956 kW)*; 2 shafts
Speed, knots: 11. **Range, miles:** 7000 at 7 kts
Complement: 25-30 (varies)
Guns: 4—14.5 mm (2 twin) or 12.7 mm (2 twin) MGs.
Radars: Navigation: Fin Curve or Oki X-NE-12 (Japanese); I band.

Comment: Built at Luda Shipyard and Shanghai International, 1958-62. Nine in North Sea Fleet and seven in East Sea Fleet. Oil fuel, 175 tons.

GROMOVOY 802   *5/1992, Henry Dodds*

138 CHINA / Tugs — COLOMBIA / Introduction

4 HUJIU CLASS (ATA)

T 155   T 711   T 842   T 867

Displacement, tons: 750 full load
Dimensions, feet (metres): 160.8 × 31.2 × 12.1 *(49 × 9.5 × 3.7)*
Main machinery: 2 LVP 24 diesels; 1800 hp(m) *(1.32 MW)*; 2 shafts
Speed, knots: 13.5. Range, miles: 2200 at 13 kts

Comment: Built in 1980s.

HUJIU 155   1991

4 TUZHONG CLASS (ATR)

T 154   T 710   T 830   T 890

Displacement, tons: 3600 full load
Dimensions, feet (metres): 278.5 × 46 × 18 *(84.9 × 14 × 5.5)*
Main machinery: 2 10 ESDZ 43/82B diesels; 8600 hp(m) *(6.32 MW)*; 2 shafts
Speed, knots: 18.5
Radars: Navigation: Fin Curve; I band.

Comment: Built in late 1970s. Can be fitted with twin 37 mm AA armament and at least one of the class has been fitted with a Square Tie radar. 35 ton towing winch.

TUZHONG   1991

1 JIN JIAN XUN 05 CLASS (ARS)

Displacement, tons: 559 standard
Dimensions, feet (metres): 196.9 × 24.3 × 8.5 *(60 × 7.4 × 2.6)*
Main machinery: 2 Niigata 6M26BGT diesels; 1700 hp(m) *(1.25 MW)* sustained; 2 shafts
Speed, knots: 18.4

Comment: Built by Osaka Shipyard, Niigata, Japan in early 1986. Commissioned November 1986. Identified as a rescue ship and towing vessel.

4 ROSLAVL CLASS (ARS)

J 120, HAITO 302, 403   + 1

Displacement, tons: 670 full load
Dimensions, feet (metres): 149.9 × 31 × 15.1 *(45.7 × 9.5 × 4.6)*
Main machinery: Diesel-electric; 2 diesel generators; 1200 hp(m) *(882 kW)*; 1 shaft
Speed, knots: 12. Range, miles: 6000 at 11 kts
Complement: 28
Guns: 4—14.5 mm (2 twin) MGs.

Comment: First ship *(302)* transferred by the USSR late 1950s. Remainder built in China in mid-1960s. One carries diving bell and submarine rescue gear on stern. Fuel, 90 tons.

HARBOUR TUGS

HARBOUR TUG   1990

MARITIME MILITIA (M. B. D. F.)

Note: In the early 1950s certain ships of the deep-sea and coastal fishing fleets were formed into the Maritime Militia. These ships, under the control of the local branch of the party, act in support or as cover for naval forces. Their normal task is reconnaissance and surveillance but, on occasions, they have been armed with machine guns. About 100 ex-Soviet T 4 LCMs are used by the M. B. D. F. Some Fuzhou class coastal tankers are operated by M. B. D. F. to support East Sea Fleet island garrisons.

MBDF 136   12/1991, 92 Wing RAAF

COLOMBIA

Headquarters' Appointments

Fleet Commander:
  Admiral Gustavo Adolfo Angel Mejia
Deputy Fleet Commander and Chief of Operations:
  Vice Admiral Alvaro Campos Castaneda
Commander, Atlantic Force:
  Vice Admiral Holdan Delgado Villamil
Commander, Pacific Force:
  Vice Admiral Roberto Serrano Avila

Personnel

(a) 1993: 14 000 (including 6800 marines)
(b) 2 years' national service (few conscripts in the Navy)

Organisation

Atlantic Force Command: HQ at Cartagena.
Pacific Force Command: HQ at Bahia Malaga.
Naval Force South: HQ at Puerto Leguizamo.
River Forces Command: HQ at Bogota.

Bases

Cartagena, ARC *Bolivar*: Main naval base (floating dock, 1 slipway), schools.
ARC *Bahia Malaga*: Major Pacific base.
ARC *Barranquilla*: Naval Training base.
Puerto Leguizamo: Putumayo River base.
Leticia: Meta River base.
Puerto Orocué, Puerto Carreño: River bases.

Naval and Maritime Air

A Fleet Air Arm has been established with one fixed wing squadron and one helicopter squadron.
The Colombian Air Force with 50 helicopters and a number of attack/reconnaissance aircraft provides support including Type A 37B.

Cuerpo de Infanteria de Marina

Organisation: Atlàntico Brigade: 1st Battalion (San Andrés).
3rd Battalion (Cartagena).
5th Battalion (Coveñas also has Amphibious Warfare School).
Pacífico Brigade: 2nd Battalion (Tumaco).
4th (Jungle) Battalion, subordinate to Western River Forces Command (Puerto Leguizamo).
6th Battalion (Buenaventura).

Prefix to Ships' Names

ARC (Armada Republica de Colombia)

Dimar

Maritime authority in charge of hydrography and navigational aids.

Customs

The Coast Guard was established in 1979 but has now given way to the Customs Service. Some of the former CG vessels transferred to the Navy, others have been retained by Customs.

Strength of the Fleet

Type	Active
Patrol Submarines	2
Midget Submarines	2
Frigates	4
Patrol Ships	4
Fast Attack Craft (Gun)	2 + (2)
Coastal/River Patrol Craft	22 + 15
Gunboats	3
Survey/Research Vessels	4
Transports	14
Training Ship	1
Tugs	15

Mercantile Marine

Lloyd's Register of Shipping:
  101 vessels of 265 727 tons gross

DELETIONS

Auxiliaries

1990 *Jurado, Mario Serpa*
1992 *Turbo, Bahia Cupica*

Customs

1990 *Rodriguez, Nito Restrepo*

PENNANT LIST

Submarines
- SS 20 Intrepido
- SS 21 Indomable
- SS 28 Pijao
- SS 29 Tayrona

Frigates
- CM 51 Almirante Padilla
- CM 52 Caldas
- CM 53 Antioquia
- CM 54 Independiente

Patrol Ships
- DE 16 Boyaca
- RM 72 Pedro de Heredia
- RM 73 Sebastion de Belal Calzar
- RM 74 Rodrigo de Bastidas

Light Forces
- 111 Albuquerque
- 112 Quita Sueno
- CF 135 Riohacha
- CF 136 Leticia
- CF 137 Arauca
- GC 100 Espartana
- GC 101 Capitan R D Binney
- GC 102 Rafael del Castillo y Rada
- GC 103 Jose Maria Palas
- GC 104 Medardo Monzon
- GC 105 Jaime Gomez
- GC 106 Nepomuceno Peña
- LR I Rio Magdalena
- LR II Rio Cauca
- LR III Rio Sinu
- LR IV Rio Atrato
- LR V Rio San Jorge
- LR 122 Juan Lucio
- LR 123 Alfonso Vargas
- LR 124 Fritz Hagale
- LR 126 Humberto Cortes
- LR 127 Calibio
- LR 128 Carlos Galindo

Survey Vessels
- 155 Providencia
- 156 Malpelo
- BO 153 Quindio
- BO 161 Gorgona

Auxiliaries
- BD 33 Socorro
- BD 35 Hernando Gutierrez
- RR 73 Teniente Sorzano
- RM 76 Josué Alvarez
- RR 81 Capitan Castro
- RR 84 Capitan Alvaro Ruiz
- RR 86 Capitan Rigoberto Giraldo
- RR 87 Capitan Vladimir Valek
- RR 88 Teniente Luis Bernal Baquero
- RR 89 Teniente Miguel Silva
- RR 90 Néstor Orpina
- RM 93 Segeri
- RR 96 Inirida
- TM 44 Tolú
- TM 45 Serranilla
- TM 60 San Andres
- LR 92 Igaraparana
- LR 95 Manacasias
- NF 141 Filogonio Hichamón
- DF 141 Mayor Jaime Arias
- TM 246 Morrosquillo
- TN 247 Uraba
- TM 248 Bahia Honda
- TM 249 Bahia Portete
- TM 251 Bahia Solano
- TM 252 Bahia Cupica
- TM 253 Bahia Utria
- TM 254 Bahia Malaga

SUBMARINES

2 209 CLASS (TYPE 1200) PATROL SUBMARINES

Name	No	Builders	Laid down	Launched	Commissioned
PIJAO	SS 28	Howaldtswerke, Kiel	1 Apr 1972	10 Apr 1974	18 Apr 1975
TAYRONA	SS 29	Howaldtswerke, Kiel	1 May 1972	16 July 1974	16 July 1975

Displacement, tons: 1180 surfaced; 1285 dived
Dimensions, feet (metres): 183.4 × 20.5 × 17.9 *(55.9 × 6.3 × 5.4)*
Main machinery: Diesel-electric; 4 MTU 12V 493 AZ80 diesels; 2400 hp(m) *(1.76 MW)* sustained; 4 AEG alternators; 1.7 MW; 1 Siemens motor; 4600 hp(m) *(3.38 MW)* sustained; 1 shaft
Speed, knots: 22 dived; 11 surfaced
Range, miles: 8000 at 8 kts surfaced; 4000 at 4 kts dived
Complement: 34 (7 officers)

Torpedoes: 8—21 in *(533 mm)* bow tubes. 14 AEG SUT; dual purpose; wire-guided; active/passive homing to 12 km *(6.5 nm)* at 35 kts; 28 km *(15 nm)* at 23 kts; warhead 250 kg. Swim-out discharge.
Fire control: Signaal M8/24 action data automation.
Radars: Surface search: Thomson-CSF Calypso II; I band.
Sonars: Atlas Elektronik CSU 3-2; hull-mounted; active/passive search and attack; medium frequency.
Atlas Elektronik PRS 3-4; passive ranging; integral with CSU 3.

Programmes: Ordered in 1971. Two more are required but money is not available. Both refitted by HDW at Kiel; *Pijao* completed refit in July 1990 and *Tayrona* in September 1991. Main batteries were replaced.
Structure: Diving depth, 820 ft *(250 m)*.

TAYRONA   *8/1991, Foto Flite*

2 MIDGET SUBMARINES

INTREPIDO SS 20   **INDOMABLE SS 21**

Displacement, tons: 40 surfaced; 70 dived
Dimensions, feet (metres): 75.5 × 13.1 *(23 × 4)*
Speed, knots: 11 surfaced; 6 dived
Range, miles: 1200 surfaced; 60 dived
Complement: 4

Comment: Similar to those in service with Pakistan Navy. They can carry eight swimmers with 2 tons of explosive as well as two swimmer delivery vehicles (SDVs). Built by Cosmos, Livorno and commissioned in 1972.

INDOMABLE   *10/1990, Hartmut Ehlers*

140 COLOMBIA / Frigates — Patrol ships

FRIGATES

4 ALMIRANTE PADILLA CLASS (TYPE FS 1500)

Name	No	Builders	Laid down	Launched	Commissioned
ALMIRANTE PADILLA	CM 51	Howaldtswerke, Kiel	17 Mar 1981	6 Jan 1982	31 Oct 1983
CALDAS	CM 52	Howaldtswerke, Kiel	14 June 1981	23 Apr 1982	14 Feb 1984
ANTIOQUIA	CM 53	Howaldtswerke, Kiel	22 June 1981	28 Aug 1982	30 Apr 1984
INDEPENDIENTE	CM 54	Howaldtswerke, Kiel	22 June 1981	21 Jan 1983	24 July 1984

Displacement, tons: 1500 standard; 2100 full load
Dimensions, feet (metres): 325.1 × 37.1 × 12.1 *(99.1 × 11.3 × 3.7)*
Main machinery: 4 MTU 20V 1163 TB92 diesels; 23 400 hp(m) *(17.2 MW)* sustained; 2 shafts; cp props
Speed, knots: 27; 18 on 2 diesels. **Range, miles:** 7000 at 14 kts; 5000 at 18 kts
Complement: 94

Missiles: SSM: 8 Aerospatiale MM 40 Exocet ❶; inertial cruise; active radar homing to 70 km *(40 nm)* at 0.9 Mach; warhead 165 kg; sea-skimmer.
SAM: ❷ To be fitted forward of the bridge when funds become available.
Guns: 1 OTO Melara 3 in *(76 mm)*/62 compact ❸; 85° elevation; 85 rounds/minute to 16 km *(8.7 nm)*; weight of shell 6 kg.
2 Breda 40 mm/70 (twin) ❹; 85° elevation; 300 rounds/minute to 12.5 km *(6.8 nm)* anti-surface; weight of shell 0.96 kg.
4 Oerlikon 30 mm/75 Mk 74 (2 twin); 85° elevation; 650 rounds/minute to 10 km *(5.5 nm)*; 950 ready use rounds.
Torpedoes: 6—324 mm Mk 32 (2 triple) tubes ❺; anti-submarine.
Countermeasures: Decoys: 1 CSEE Dagaie double mounting; IR flares and chaff decoys (H-J band).
ESM: AC672; radar warning.
ECM: Scimitar; jammer.
Combat data systems: Thomson-CSF TAVITAC action data automation. Possibly Link Y fitted.
Fire control: 2 Canopus optronic directors. Thomson-CSF Vega II GFCS.
Radars: Combined search: Thomson-CSF Sea Tiger ❻; E/F band; range 110 km *(60 nm)* for 2 m² target.
Fire control: Castor II B ❼; I/J band; range 15 km *(8 nm)* for 1 m² target.
IFF: Mk 10.
Sonars: Atlas Elektronik ASO 4-2; hull-mounted; active attack; medium frequency.

Helicopters: 1 MBB BO 105 CB, ASW ❽.

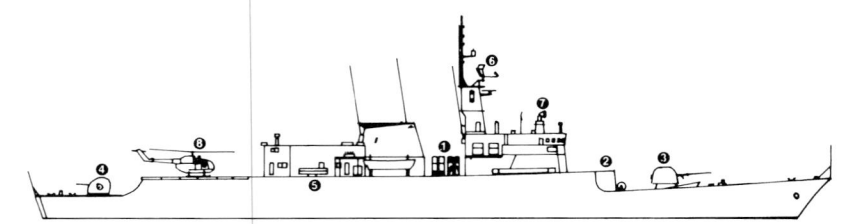

ALMIRANTE PADILLA *(Scale 1 : 900), Ian Sturton*

INDEPENDIENTE *11/1990, Hartmut Ehlers*

Programmes: Order for four Type FS 1500 placed late 1980. *Almirante Padilla* started trials July 1982. Near sisters to Malaysian frigates.

Modernisation: No confirmation yet of SAM fit. Albatros/Aspide, Crotale and Barak have all been mentioned. A modernisation programme remains the top priority in 1993.

ANTIOQUIA *11/1990, Hartmut Ehlers*

PATROL SHIPS

1 Ex-US COURTNEY CLASS

Name	No	Builders	Commissioned
BOYACA (ex-USS *Hartley*)	DE 16	New York SB	26 Jan 1957

Displacement, tons: 1450 standard; 1914 full load
Dimensions, feet (metres): 314.5 × 36.8 × 13.6 *(95.9 × 11.2 × 4.1)*
Main machinery: 2 Foster-Wheeler boilers; 300 psi *(42 kg/cm sq)*; 950°F *(510°C)*; 1 De Laval turbine; 20 000 hp *(15 MW)*; 1 shaft
Speed, knots: 24. **Range, miles:** 4500 at 15 kts
Complement: 161 (11 officers)

Guns: 2 USN 3 in *(76 mm)*/50 Mk 33 (twin); 85° elevation; 50 rounds/minute to 12.8 km *(7 nm)*; weight of shell 6 kg.
Torpedoes: 6—324 mm Mk 32 (2 triple tubes); anti-submarine.
Depth charges: 1 rack.
Fire control: Mk 63 GFCS.
Radars: Surface search: Raytheon SPS 10; G band.
Fire control: Western Electric SPG 34; I/J band.
Sonars: Sangamo SQS 23; hull-mouunted active search and attack; medium frequency.

Helicopters: Platform only.

Programmes: Transferred 8 July 1972; paid off into reserve in 1983. Brought out of retirement in 1988 for use mostly as a Headquarters ship.

BOYACA *11/1990, Hartmut Ehlers*

Patrol ships — Light forces / COLOMBIA 141

3 Ex-US CHEROKEE CLASS

Name	No	Builders	Commissioned
PEDRO DE HEREDIA (ex-*Choctaw*)	RM 72	Charleston SB & DD Co	21 Apr 1943
SEBASTION DE BELAL CALZAR (ex-*Carib*)	RM 73	Charleston SB & DD Co	24 July 1943
RODRIGO DE BASTIDAS (ex-*Hidatsa*)	RM 74	Charleston SB & DD Co	25 Apr 1944

Displacement, tons: 1235 standard; 1640 full load
Dimensions, feet (metres): 205 × 38.5 × 17 *(62.5 × 11.7 × 5.2)*
Main machinery: Diesel-electric; 4 GM 12-278 diesels; 4400 hp *(3.28 MW)*; 4 generators; 1 motor; 3000 hp *(2.24 MW)*; 1 shaft
Speed, knots: 15
Complement: 75
Guns: 1 USN 3 in *(76 mm)*/50 Mk 22.

Comment: Transferred by sale on 15 March 1979 and paid off in 1987. Reactivated in 1990. Originally built as tugs but used as patrol ships.

PEDRO DE HEREDIA   11/1990, Hartmut Ehlers

SHIPBORNE AIRCRAFT

Note: 4 more BO 105 are planned. 4 A37B Dragonfly aircraft acquired from the Air Force in 1991.

Numbers/Type: 2 MBB BO 105CB.
Operational speed: 113 kts *(210 km/h)*.
Service ceiling: 9854 ft *(3000 m)*.
Range: 407 nm *(754 km)*.
Role/Weapon systems: Shipborne surface search and limited ASW helicopter. Sensors: Search/weather radar. Weapons: ASW; provision to carry depth bombs. ASV; light attack role with machine gun pods.

BO 105   1990, Colombian Navy

LIGHT FORCES

3 ARAUCA CLASS RIVER GUNBOATS

Name	No	Builders	Commissioned
RIOHACHA	CF 135 (ex-35)	Union Industrial de Barranquilla	1956
LETICIA	CF 136 (ex-36)	Union Industrial de Barranquilla	1956
ARAUCA	CF 137 (ex-37)	Union Industrial de Barranquilla	1956

Displacement, tons: 184 full load
Dimensions, feet (metres): 163.5 × 23.5 × 2.8 *(49.9 × 7.2 × 0.9)*
Main machinery: 2 Caterpillar diesels; 916 hp *(683 kW)*; 2 shafts
Speed, knots: 14. **Range, miles:** 1890 at 14 kts
Complement: 43; 39 plus 6 orderlies (*Leticia*)
Guns: 2 USN 3 in *(76 mm)*/50. 4 Oerlikon 20 mm.

Comment: Launched in 1955. *Leticia* has been equipped as a hospital ship with six beds and reported as disarmed.

ARAUCA   1991, Colombian Navy

2 Ex-US ASHEVILLE CLASS (FAST ATTACK CRAFT—GUN)

Name	No	Builders	Commissioned
ALBUQUERQUE (ex-USS *Welch*)	111	Peterson Builders	8 Sep 1969
QUITA SUENO (ex-USS *Tacoma*)	112	Tacoma Boat Building	14 July 1969

Displacement, tons: 225 standard; 245 full load
Dimensions, feet (metres): 164.5 × 23.8 × 9.5 *(50.1 × 7.3 × 2.9)*
Main machinery: CODOG; 2 Cummins VT12-875M diesels; 1450 hp *(1.08 MW)*; 1 GE LM-1500 gas turbine; 13 300 hp *(9.92 MW)*; 2 shafts; cp props
Speed, knots: 40. **Range, miles:** 1700 at 16 kts on diesels; 325 at 37 kts
Complement: 24
Guns: 1 US 3 in *(76 mm)*/50 Mk 34; 85° elevation; 50 rounds/minute to 12.8 km *(7 nm)*; weight of shell 6 kg.
 1 Bofors 40 mm/56; 45° elevation; 160 rounds/minute to 11 km *(5.9 nm)* anti-aircraft; weight of shell 0.96 kg.
 2—12.7 mm (twin) MGs.
Fire control: Mk 63 GCFS.
Radars: Surface search: Marconi LN 66/LP; I band.
Fire control: Western Electric SPG 50; I/J band.

Comment: Decommissioned in US Navy 30 September 1981. Transferred by lease 16 May 1983. Two more of this class may be transferred in 1993.

QUITA SUENO   11/1992, Paul Campbell

2 SWIFT 110 ft CLASS (LARGE PATROL CRAFT)

Name	No	Builders	Commissioned
JOSE MARIA PALAS	GC 103	Swiftships Inc, Berwick	Sep 1989
MEDARDO MONZON	GC 104	Swiftships Inc, Berwick	July 1990

Displacement, tons: 95 full load
Dimensions, feet (metres): 109.9 × 24.6 × 6.6 *(33.5 × 7.5 × 2)*
Main machinery: 2 MTU diesels; 2 shafts
Speed, knots: 25. **Range, miles:** 2250 at 15 kts
Complement: 19 (3 officers)
Guns: 1 Bofors 40 mm/60. 1—12.7 mm MG. 2—7.62 mm MGs.

JOSE MARIA PALAS   1990, Colombian Navy

1 SWIFT 105 ft CLASS (LARGE PATROL CRAFT)

Name	No	Builders	Commissioned
RAFAEL DEL CASTILLO Y RADA (ex-AN 102)	GC 102	Swiftships Inc, Berwick	Feb 1983

Displacement, tons: 103 full load
Dimensions, feet (metres): 105 × 22 × 7 *(31.5 × 6.7 × 2.1)*
Main machinery: 4 MTU 12V331 TC92 diesels; 5320 hp(m) *(3.97 MW)* sustained; 4 shafts
Speed, knots: 25. **Range, miles:** 1200 at 18 kts
Complement: 19 (3 officers)
Guns: 1 Bofors 40 mm/60. 2—12.7 mm MGs.

Comment: Second of two delivered in the early 1980s. The other craft was badly damaged in 1986 but is now back in service with the Customs. *Castillo y Rada* transferred to the Navy in 1989.

RAFAEL DEL CASTILLO Y RADA   1988

142 COLOMBIA / Light forces

1 LARGE PATROL CRAFT

Name	No	Builders	Commissioned
ESPARTANA	GC 100	Ast Naval, Cartagena	1950

Displacement, tons: 50
Dimensions, feet (metres): 96 × 13.5 × 4 *(29.3 × 4.1 × 1.2)*
Main machinery: 2 diesels; 300 hp *(224 kW)*; 2 shafts
Speed, knots: 13.5
Guns: 1 Oerlikon 20 mm.

Comment: May be decommissioned in 1993.

1 COASTAL PATROL CRAFT

Name	No	Builders	Commissioned
CAPITAN R D BINNEY	GC 101	Ast Naval, Cartagena	1947

Displacement, tons: 23 full load
Dimensions, feet (metres): 67 × 10.7 × 3.5 *(20.4 × 3.3 × 1.1)*
Main machinery: 2 Diesels; 115 hp(m) *(85 kW)*; 2 shafts
Speed, knots: 13

Comment: Buoy and lighthouse inspection boat. Named after first head of Colombian Naval Academy, Lieutenant Commander Ralph Douglas Binney, RN. May finally be paid off in 1993.

CAPITAN R D BINNEY   *1991, Colombian Navy*

2 Ex-US Mk III PBs (COASTAL PATROL CRAFT)

JAIME GOMEZ GC 105   **NEPOMUCENO PEÑA** GC 106

Displacement, tons: 34 full load
Dimensions, feet (metres): 64.9 × 18 × 5.1 *(19.8 × 5.5 × 1.6)*
Main machinery: 3 Detroit 8V-71 diesels; 690 hp *(515 kW)* sustained; 3 shafts
Speed, knots: 28. **Range, miles:** 450 at 26 kts
Complement: 7 (1 officer)
Guns: 2—12.7 mm MGs. 2—7.62 mm MGs. 1 Mk 19 Grenade launcher.

Comment: Swiftships 65 ft type delivered in 1990. Original 40 mm and 20 mm guns replaced by lighter armament.

JAIME GOMEZ   *1990, Colombian Navy*

6 RIVER PATROL CRAFT

Name	No	Builders	Commissioned
JUAN LUCIO	LR 122	Ast Naval, Cartagena	1953
ALFONSO VARGAS	LR 123	Ast Naval, Cartagena	1952
FRITZ HAGALE	LR 124	Ast Naval, Cartagena	1952
HUMBERTO CORTES	LR 126	Ast Naval, Cartagena	1953
CALIBIO	LR 127	Ast Naval, Cartagena	1953
CARLOS GALINDO	LR 128	Ast Naval, Cartagena	1954

Displacement, tons: 33 full load
Dimensions, feet (metres): 76 × 12 × 2.8 *(23.2 × 3.7 × 0.8)*
Main machinery: 2 GM diesels; 280 hp *(209 kW)*; 2 shafts
Speed, knots: 13
Complement: 10
Guns: 2 Oerlikon 20 mm or 1 Oerlikon and 4 mortars.

Comment: Some may be unserviceable.

JUAN LUCIO   *1991, Colombian Navy*

2 SWIFT 45 ft CLASS (RIVER PATROL CRAFT)

8 DE OCTUBRE   **27 DE OCTUBRE**

Displacement, tons: 18 full load
Dimensions, feet (metres): 45 × 15 × 1.8 *(13.7 × 4.6 × 0.5)*
Main machinery: 2 Detroit diesels; 2 waterjets
Speed, knots: 32. **Range, miles:** 600 at 22 kts
Complement: 4 plus 8 troops
Guns: 2—12.7 mm MGs. 2—7.62 mm MGs.

Comment: Delivered by the US Navy in September 1992 to assist in anti-narcotics patrols.

5 + 15 RIO CLASS (RIVER PATROL CRAFT)

RIO MAGDALENA LR I   **RIO ATRATO** LR IV
RIO CAUCA LR II   **RIO SAN JORGE** LR V
RIO SINU LR III

Displacement, tons: 9 full load
Dimensions, feet (metres): 31 × 11.1 × 2 *(9.8 × 3.5 × 0.6)*
Main machinery: 2 Detroit 6V-53 diesels; 296 hp *(221 kW)* sustained; 2 waterjets
Speed, knots: 24. **Range, miles:** 150 at 22 kts
Complement: 4
Guns: 2—12.7 mm (twin) MGs. 1—7.62 mm MG. 1—60 mm mortar.
Radars: Surface search: Raytheon 1900; I band.

Comment: Acquired in 1989-90. Ex-US PBR Mk II built by Uniflite. GRP hulls. May be numbered 176-180. Reported that 15 more are to be acquired for riverine operations by the Marines.

RIO SAN JORGE   *11/1990, Hartmut Ehlers*

2 ROTORK CRAFT

MANUELA SAENZ   **JAMIE ROOK**

Displacement, tons: 9 full load
Dimensions, feet (metres): 41.7 × 10.5 × 2.3 *(12.7 × 3.2 × 0.7)*
Main machinery: 2 Caterpillar diesels; 240 hp *(179 kW)*; 2 shafts
Speed, knots: 25
Complement: 4
Military lift: 4 tons
Guns: 1—12.7 mm MG. 2—7.62 mm MGs.

Comment: Acquired in 1989-90. Capable of transporting eight fully equipped marines.

JAMIE ROOK   *1990, Colombian Navy*

0 + 45 PIRANA CRAFT

Comment: These are 6.8 m river assault boats reported as being acquired from the US for use by Marines. Armed with 1—12.7 mm and 2—7.62 mm MGs. The plan is to have 15 patrol units each operating with one Rio class and three Piranas. Capable of 25-30 kts depending on load.

1 ADMIRAL'S YACHT

CONTRALMIRANTE BELL SALTER

Comment: Could be used as a patrol craft in an emergency.

CONTRALMIRANTE BELL SALTER   *10/1990, Hartmut Ehlers*

SURVEY VESSELS

Name	No	Builders	Commissioned
PROVIDENCIA	155	Martin Jansen SY. Leer	24 July 1981
MALPELO	156	Martin Jansen SY. Leer	24 July 1981

Displacement, tons: 1040 full load
Measurement, tons: 830 gross
Dimensions, feet (metres): 164.3 × 32.8 × 13.1 *(50.3 × 10 × 4)*
Main machinery: 1 MAN-Augsburg diesel; 1570 hp(m) *(1.15 MW)*; 1 shaft; bow thruster
Speed, knots: 13. **Range, miles:** 15 000 at 12 kts
Complement: 21 (5 officers) plus 6 scientists

Comment: Both launched in January 1981. *Malpelo* employed on fishery research and *Providencia* on geophysical research. Both are operated by DIMAR, the naval authority in charge of hydrographic, pilotage, navigational and ports services. Painted white.

MALPELO   *1992, Colombian Navy*

Name	No	Builders	Commissioned
GORGONA	BO 161 (ex-FB 161)	Lidingoverken, Sweden	1955

Displacement, tons: 574 full load
Dimensions, feet (metres): 135 × 29.5 × 9.3 *(41.2 × 9 × 2.8)*
Main machinery: 2 diesels; 910 hp(m) *(669 kW)*; 2 shafts
Speed, knots: 13
Complement: 45

Comment: Paid off in 1982 but after a complete overhaul at Cartagena naval base was back in service in late 1992.

Name	No	Builders	Commissioned
QUINDIO (ex-US YFR 443)	BO 153	Niagara S. B. Corporation	11 Nov 1943

Displacement, tons: 380 light; 600 full load
Dimensions, feet (metres): 131 × 29.8 × 9 *(40 × 9.1 × 2.7)*
Main machinery: 2 Union diesels; 300 hp *(224 kW)*; 2 shafts
Speed, knots: 10
Complement: 17 (2 officers)

Comment: Transferred by lease in July 1964 and by sale on 31 March 1979.

QUINDIO   *11/1990, Hartmut Ehlers*

TRANSPORTS

Name	No	Builders	Commissioned
SAN ANDRES (ex-*Philip P*)	TM 60 (ex-BO 154)	H Rancke, Hamburg	1956

Measurement, tons: 680 dwt
Dimensions, feet (metres): 170.3 × 27.6 × 11.5 *(51.9 × 8.4 × 3.5)*
Main machinery: 1 diesel; 300 hp(m) *(220 kW)*; 1 shaft
Speed, knots: 9

Comment: Former Honduran coaster confiscated for smuggling and commissioned in the Navy in 1986. Used as a transport ship.

SAN ANDRES   *10/1990, Hartmut Ehlers*

Name	No	Builders	Commissioned
HERNANDO GUTIERREZ	BD 35 (ex-TF 52)	Ast Naval, Cartagena	1955
SOCORRO (ex-*Alberto Gomez*)	BD 33	Ast Naval, Cartagena	1956

Displacement, tons: 70
Dimensions, feet (metres): 82 × 18 × 2.8 *(25 × 5.5 × 0.9)*
Main machinery: 2 GM diesels; 260 hp *(194 kW)*; 2 shafts
Speed, knots: 9. **Range, miles:** 650 at 9 kts
Complement: 12 plus berths for 48 troops and medical staff
Guns: 2—12.7 mm MGs.

Comment: River transports. Named after Army officers. *Socorro* was converted in July 1967 into a floating surgery. *Hernando Gutierrez* was converted into a dispensary ship in 1970.

HERNANDO GUTIERREZ   *10/1990, Hartmut Ehlers*

TOLÚ TM 44   FILOGONIO HICHAMÓN NF 141
SERRANILLA TM 45

Comment: Captured drug running vessels of various characteristics and now 'poachers turned gamekeepers'. *Tolú* is used as a diving tender.

TOLÚ   *10/1990, Hartmut Ehlers*

8 LCU 1466A CLASS

MORROSQUILLO	TM 246	BAHIA SOLANO	TM 251
URABA	TM 247	BAHIA CUPICA	TM 252
BAHIA HONDA	TM 248	BAHIA UTRIA	TM 253
BAHIA PORTETE	TM 249	BAHIA MALAGA	TM 254

Displacement, tons: 347 full load
Dimensions, feet (metres): 119 × 34 × 6 *(36.3 × 10.4 × 1.8)*
Main machinery: 3 Detroit 6-71 diesels; 522 hp *(389 kW)* sustained; 3 shafts
Speed, knots: 7. **Range, miles:** 700 at 7 kts
Complement: 14
Cargo capacity: 167 tons
Guns: 2—12.7 mm MGs.

Comment: Former US Army craft built in 1954 and transferred in 1991 and 1992 with new engines. Used as inshore transports. Speed quoted is fully laden.

FLOATING DOCKS

Note: It is reported that the 6700 ton *Rodriguez Zamora* (ex-ARD 28), the small floating dock *Manuel Lara*, the floating workshop *Mantilla* (ex-YR 66) purchased April 1979 and the repair craft *Victor Cubillos* (ex-USS YFND 6) purchased on 31 March 1978, are in use by Compania Colombiana de Astilleros Limitada (CONASTIL), Cartagena which is the former naval dockyard still owned by the Navy.

MAYOR JAIME ARIAS DF 141 (ex-170)

Displacement, tons: 700

Comment: Capacity of 165 tons, length 140 ft *(42.7 m)*. Used as a non self-propelled depot ship for the midget submarines.

MAYOR JAIME ARIAS (old number)   *10/1990, Hartmut Ehlers*

144 COLOMBIA / Tugs — Sail training ships

TUGS

CAPITAN CASTRO RR 81
CAPITAN ALVARO RUIZ RR 84
CAPITAN RIGOBERTO GIRALDO RR 86
CAPITAN VLADIMIR VALEK RR 87
TENIENTE LUIS BERNAL BAQUERO RR 88

Displacement, tons: 50
Dimensions, feet (metres): 63 × 14 × 2.5 *(19.2 × 4.3 × 0.8)*
Main machinery: 2 GM diesels; 260 hp *(194 kW)*; 2 shafts
Speed, knots: 9

TENIENTE SORZANO (ex-USS YTL 231) RR 73

Displacement, tons: 54
Dimensions, feet (metres): 65.7 × 17.5 × 9 *(20 × 5.3 × 2.7)*
Main machinery: 6-cyl diesel; 240 hp(m) *(176 kW)*; 1 shaft
Speed, knots: 9

Comment: Formerly on loan—purchased on 31 March 1978. Dockyard tug at CONASTIL, Cartagena.

TENIENTE MIGUEL SILVA RR 89   **NÉSTOR ORPINA** RR 90

Dimensions, feet (metres): 73.3 × 17.5 × 3 *(22.4 × 5.3 × 0.9)*
Main machinery: 2 diesels; 260 hp *(194 kW)*; 2 shafts
Speed, knots: 9

Comment: River tugs built by Union Industrial (UNIMAL), Barranquilla.

IGARAPARANA LR 92   **MANACASIAS** LR 95

Displacement, tons: 104 full load
Dimensions, feet (metres): 102.4 × 23.6 × 2.8 *(31.2 × 7.2 × 0.9)*
Main machinery: 2 Detroit 4-71 diesels; 330 hp *(238 kW)* sustained; 2 shafts
Speed, knots: 7. **Range, miles:** 1600 at 7 kts
Complement: 7 (1 officer)

Comment: River tugs built by Servicio Naviero Armada R. de Colombia at Puerto Leguizamo. Completed June 1985 (LR 92) and June 1986 (LR 95). Used to transport materials to places difficult to reach by road.

MANACASIAS   *1988, Juan Mazuero*

SEGERI RM 93   **INIRIDA** RR 96   **JOSUÉ ALVAREZ** RM 76
MITU RR —   **CALIMA** RM —

Comment: Probably captured drug running vessels. Characteristics unknown.

CUSTOMS (ADUANAS)

Note: Pennant numbers are in the 200 series. When the Coast Guard was abolished, its assets were divided between the Navy and Customs services.

Name	No	Builders	Commissioned
OLAYA HERRERA	AN 201	Swiftships, Berwick	16 Oct 1981

Displacement, tons: 103 full load
Dimensions, feet (metres): 105 × 22 × 7 *(31.5 × 6.7 × 2.1)*
Main machinery: 4 MTU 12V 331 TC92 diesels; 5320 hp *(3.97 MW)*; 4 shafts
Speed, knots: 25. **Range, miles:** 1200 at 18 kts
Complement: 19
Guns: 1 Bofors 40 mm/60. 2—12.7 mm MGs.

Comment: Badly damaged in 1986 but repaired and brought back into service in 1991. Sister craft *Castillo y Rada* transferred to the Navy.

Name	No	Builders	Commissioned
CARLOS ALBAN	AN 208	Rauma Repola, Finland	1971

Displacement, tons: 130 full load
Dimensions, feet (metres): 108 × 18 × 5.9 *(33 × 5.5 × 1.8)*
Main machinery: 2 MTU diesels; 2500 hp(m) *(1.84 MW)*; 2 shafts; cp props
Speed, knots: 17
Complement: 20
Guns: 2 Oerlikon 20 mm.

Comment: Similar to Finnish Ruissalo class. Acquired in 1980. Second of class deleted in 1990.

CARLOS ALBAN

SAIL TRAINING SHIP

Name	No	Builders	Commissioned
GLORIA	—	A T Celaya, Bilbao	May 1969

Displacement, tons: 1150 full load
Dimensions, feet (metres): 249.3 oa; 211.9 wl; × 34.8 × 21.7 *(76; 64.6 × 10.6 × 6.6)*
Main machinery: 1 auxiliary diesel; 530 hp(m) *(389 kW)*; 1 shaft
Speed, knots: 10.5
Complement: 51 (10 officers) plus 88 trainees

Comment: Sail training ship. Barque rigged. Hull is entirely welded. Sail area, 1675 sq yards *(1400 sq m)*. Endurance, 60 days.

GLORIA   *11/1990, Hartmut Ehlers*

COMORO ISLANDS

General

Three of the four main islands of this group joined in a unilateral Declaration of Independence in July 1975. This has been legitimised by France.

Base

Moroni.

Mercantile Marine

Lloyd's Register of Shipping:
6 vessels of 2296 tons gross

PATROL FORCES

2 JAPANESE YAMAYURI CLASS

Name	No	Builders	Commissioned
KARTHALA	—	Ishihara Dockyard Co Ltd	Oct 1981
NTRINGUI	—	Ishihara Dockyard Co Ltd	Oct 1981

Displacement, tons: 26.5 standard; 41 full load
Dimensions, feet (metres): 59 × 14.1 × 3.6 *(18 × 4.3 × 1.1)*
Main machinery: 2 Nissan RD10TA06 diesels; 900 hp(m) *(661 kW)* maximum; 2 shafts
Speed, knots: 20
Complement: 6
Guns: 2—12.7 mm (twin) MGs.

Comment: These two patrol vessels of the 18M type (steel-hulled) supplied under Japanese Government co-operation plan. Used for fishery protection services.

KARTHALA *10/1981, Ishihara D Y*

CONGO

Senior Officer

Head of the Navy:
Captain Jean-Felix Ongouya

General

The People's Republic of Congo became independent on 15 August 1960 and formed a naval service.

Personnel

(a) 1993: 300 officers and men
(b) Voluntary service

Base

Pointe-Noire.

Mercantile Marine
Lloyd's Register of Shipping:
22 vessels of 8598 tons gross

DELETIONS

1989-90   4 Yulin class
1990-91   3 Shanghai II class

PATROL FORCES

3 Ex-SOVIET ZHUK CLASS

301   302   303

Displacement, tons: 50 full load
Dimensions, feet (metres): 75.4 × 17 × 6.2 *(23 × 5.2 × 1.9)*
Main machinery: 2 M 50 diesels; 2200 hp(m) *(1.6 MW)* sustained; 2 shafts
Speed, knots: 30. **Range, miles:** 1100 at 15 kts
Complement: 17
Guns: 4—14.5 mm (2 twin) MGs.

Comment: Transferred in 1982. Three more were expected in 1984 but did not materialise.

ZHUK *1987*

4 ARCO RIVER PATROL CRAFT

Comment: Two of 42.6 ft *(13 m)* and two of 37.4 ft *(11.4 m)* with Volvo Penta diesels. Delivered 1982. Used for river patrols together with a number of small boats with outboard motors.

3 SPANISH PIRAÑA CLASS (FAST ATTACK CRAFT—PATROL)

Name	No	Builders	Completed
MARIEN N'GOUABI (ex-*L'Intrepide*)	P 601	Bazán, Cadiz	Nov 1982
LES TROIS GLORIEUSES (ex-*Le Vaillant*)	P 602	Bazán, Cadiz	Jan 1983
LES MALOANGO (ex-*Le Terrible*)	P 603	Bazán, Cadiz	Mar 1983

Displacement, tons: 140 full load
Dimensions, feet (metres): 107.3 × 20.2 × 5.1 *(32.7 × 6.2 × 1.6)*
Main machinery: 2 MTU 12V 538 TB92 diesels; 5110 hp(m) *(3.76 MW)* sustained; 2 shafts
Speed, knots: 28. **Range, miles:** 700 at 17 kts
Complement: 19 (3 officers)
Guns: 1 Breda 40 mm/70; 85° elevation; 300 rounds/minute to 12.5 km *(6.8 nm)*; weight of shell 0.96 kg.
  1 Oerlikon 20 mm. 2—12.7 mm MGs.
Fire control: CSEE Panda optronic director.
Radars: Navigation: Decca; I band.

Comment: Ordered in 1980. Steel hulls. Derivative of Barcelo class. All were officially commissioned on arrival at Pointe-Noire 3 April 1983. All probably unserviceable.

MARIEN N'GOUABI *1983, Bazán*

1 TUG

HINDA

Displacement, tons: 200 full load
Dimensions, feet (metres): 96.8 × — × 12.5 *(29.5 × — × 3.8)*
Main machinery: 1 MGO diesel; 900 hp(m) *(661 kW)*; 1 shaft
Speed, knots: 11
Complement: 16

Comment: Ordered from La Manche, St Malo. Laid down 16 February 1981, launched 31 March 1981, completed 3 October 1981.

COOK ISLANDS

General

A group of islands which are self governing in free association with New Zealand. Defence is the responsibility of New Zealand in consultation with the islands' government.

1 PACIFIC FORUM TYPE (LARGE PATROL CRAFT)

Name	Builders	Commissioned
TE KUKUPA	Australian Shipbuilding Industries	1 Sep 1989

Displacement, tons: 162 full load
Dimensions, feet (metres): 103.3 × 26.6 × 6.9 *(31.5 × 8.1 × 2.1)*
Main machinery: 2 Caterpillar 3516TA diesels; 2820 hp *(2.1 MW)* sustained; 2 shafts
Speed, knots: 20. **Range, miles:** 2500 at 12 kts
Complement: 17 (3 officers)
Radars: Surface search: Furuno 1011; I band.

Comment: Laid down 16 May 1988 and launched 27 January 1989. Cost, training and support provided by Australia under Defence Co-operation. Acceptance date was 9 March 1989 but the handover was deferred another six months because of the change in local government. Has Furuno D/F equipment, SATNAV and a seaboat with a 40 hp outboard engine.

TE KUKUPA   10/1991, John Mortimer

COSTA RICA

Personnel

(a) 1993: 160 officers and men
(b) Voluntary service

Bases

Golfito, Puntarenas, Puerto Limon

Mercantile Marine

Lloyd's Register of Shipping:
24 vessels of 12 446 tons gross

PATROL FORCES

1 Ex-USCG CAPE CLASS (LARGE PATROL CRAFT)

Name	No	Builders	Commissioned
ASTRONAUTA FRANKLIN CHANG (ex-*Cape Henlopen*)	95-1	Coast Guard Yard, Curtis Bay	5 Dec 1958

Displacement, tons: 98 standard; 148 full load
Dimensions, feet (metres): 94.8 × 20.3 × 6.6 *(28.9 × 6.2 × 2)*
Main machinery: 2 Detroit 16V-149TI diesels; 2070 hp *(1.54 MW)* sustained; 2 shafts
Speed, knots: 20. **Range, miles:** 2500 at 10 kts
Complement: 14 (1 officer)
Guns: 2—12.7 mm MGs.
Radars: Surface search: Raytheon SPS 64(V)1; I band.

Comment: Transferred from US Coast Guard 28 September 1989 after a refit by Bender SB and Repair Co. Painted white.

ISLA DEL COCO   2/1989

1 Ex-USCG POINT CLASS (COASTAL PATROL CRAFT)

— (ex-*Point Hope*)

Displacement, tons: 67 full load
Dimensions, feet (metres): 83 × 17.2 × 5.8 *(25.3 × 5.2 × 1.8)*
Main machinery: 2 Cummins diesels; 1600 hp *(1.19 MW)*; 2 shafts
Speed, knots: 23. **Range, miles:** 1500 at 8 kts
Complement: 10
Guns: 2—12.7 mm MGs.
Radars: Navigation: Raytheon SPS 64; I band.

Comment: Transferred 3 May 1991.

ASTRONAUTA FRANKLIN CHANG   1989, Bender SB & R Co

1 SWIFT 105 ft CLASS (FAST PATROL CRAFT)

ISLA DEL COCO 1055

Displacement, tons: 118 full load
Dimensions, feet (metres): 105 × 23.3 × 7.2 *(32 × 7.1 × 2.2)*
Main machinery: 3 MTU 12V-1163 TC92 diesels; 10 530 hp(m) *(7.74 MW)*; 3 shafts
Speed, knots: 33. **Range, miles:** 1200 at 18 kts; 2000 at 12 kts
Complement: 21 (3 officers)
Guns: 1—12.7 mm MG. 4—7.62 mm (2 twin) MGs. 1—60 mm mortar.
Radars: Navigation: Decca RM 916; I band.

Comment: Built by Swiftships, Morgan City in 1978. Refitted in 1985-86 under FMS funding. The twin MGs are fitted abaft the bridge and the mortar is on the stern.

POINT class (US colours)   10/1991, Giorgio Arra

4 SWIFT 65 ft CLASS (COASTAL PATROL CRAFT)

| CABO VELAS | 656 | CABO BLANCO | 658 |
| ISLA UVITA | 657 | PUNTA BURICA | 659 |

Displacement, tons: 35 full load
Dimensions, feet (metres): 65.5 × 18.4 × 6.6 *(20 × 5.6 × 2)*
Main machinery: 2 MTU 8V 331 TC92 diesels; 1770 hp(m) *(1.3 MW)*; 2 shafts
Speed, knots: 23. Range, miles: 500 at 18 kts
Complement: 7 (2 officers)
Guns: 1—12.7 mm MG. 4—7.62 mm (2 twin) MGs. 1—60 mm mortar.
Radars: Navigation: Decca RM 916; I band.

Comment: Built by Swiftships, Morgan City in 1979. Refitted 1985-86 under FMS funding.

2 SWIFT 36 ft CLASS (INSHORE PATROL CRAFT)

TELAMANCA 361   CARIARI 362

Displacement, tons: 11 full load
Dimensions, feet (metres): 36 × 10 × 2.6 *(11 × 3.1 × 0.8)*
Main machinery: 2 Detroit diesels; 500 hp *(373 kW)*; 2 shafts
Speed, knots: 24. Range, miles: 250 at 18 kts
Complement: 4 (1 officer)
Guns: 1—12.7 mm MG. 1—60 mm mortar.

Comment: Built by Swiftships, Morgan City in 1986.

ISLA UVITA   12/1987

CARIARI   1991

1 SWIFT 42 ft CLASS (INSHORE PATROL CRAFT)

DONNA MARGARITA (ex-*Puntarena*) 421

Displacement, tons: 11 full load
Dimensions, feet (metres): 42 × 14.1 × 3 *(12.8 × 4.3 × 0.9)*
Main machinery: 2 Detroit 8V-92TA diesels; 700 hp *(522 kW)*; 2 shafts
Speed, knots: 33. Range, miles: 300 at 30 kts; 450 at 18 kts.
Complement: 4 (1 officer)

Comment: Built by Swiftships, Morgan City in 1986. The original name has been changed and she is now used as a hospital ship with armament removed.

8 BOSTON WHALERS

181-188

Comment: The survivors of 13 delivered in 1983. Craft of 18 ft with 70 hp *(52 kW)* outboard engines.

DONNA MARGARITA   1989

BOSTON WHALER   1988

CROATIA

Flag Officers

Commander-in-Chief:
  Vice Admiral Sveto Letica
Deputy Commander and Chief of Staff:
  Vice Admiral Carlo Grbac

General

The Navy was established on 11 September 1991. Ships captured from the Yugoslav federation form the bulk of the Fleet. The main task is the control and protection of territorial waters; border guard duties are left to police multi-purpose craft.

Personnel

1993: 1000 (95 officers)

Bases and Organisation

Headquarters: Lora-Split.
Main bases: Sibenik, Split, Pula, Ploce.
There are three coastal command sectors: North Adriatic, North Dalmatia and South Dalmatia. Radar surveillance stations and coastal batteries are established on key islands and peninsulas. All the bases and naval installations of the former federal Navy have been taken over with the exception of those in the Bay of Cattaro.

Naval Infantry

Headquarters in Split. Companies deployed to Pula, Losinj, Zadar, Sibenik, Brac, Peljesac, Korcula, Dubrovnik and Jelsa (Hvar).

Mercantile Marine

Lloyd's Register of Shipping:
  203 vessels of 133 670 tons gross

148 CROATIA / Submarines — Light forces

SUBMARINES

Note: It is reported, but not confirmed, that one Una class midget submarine and at least two Mala class swimmer delivery vehicles were captured and are in use. Details are in the Yugoslav section.

CORVETTES

1 + 1 (2) KRALJ CLASS (TYPE 400)

Name	No	Builders	Commissioned
KRALJ PETAR KRESIMIR IV	11	Kraljevica Shipyard	1993
—	12	Kraljevica Shipyard	1994

Displacement, tons: 385 full load
Dimensions, feet (metres): 175.9 × 27.9 × 7.5 *(53.6 × 8.5 × 2.3)*
Main machinery: 3 diesels; 14 550 hp(m) *(10.7 MW)*; 3 shafts
Speed, knots: 32. **Range, miles:** 1500 at 20 kts
Complement: 33 (5 officers)

Missiles: SSM: 4 or 8 Saab RBS 15; active radar homing to 70 km *(37.8 nm)* at 0.8 Mach; warhead 150 kg.
Guns: 1 Bofors 57 mm/70; 75° elevation; 200 rounds/minute to 17 km *(9.3 nm)*; weight of shell 2.4 kg. Launchers for illuminants on side of mounting.
1—30 mm/65 AK 630; 6 barrels; 85° elevation; 3000 rounds/minute combined to 2 km.
2 Oerlikon 20 mm or 2—12.7 mm MGs.
Mines: 4 AIM-70 magnetic or 6 SAG-1 acoustic.
Countermeasures: Decoys: Wallop Barricade chaff launcher.
Fire control: BEAB 9LV 249 Mk 2 director.
Radars: Surface search: Racal BT 502; E/F band.
Fire control: BEAB 9LV 249 Mk 2; I/J band.

Programmes: The building of this class (formerly called Kobra) was officially announced as 'suspended' in 1989 but was restarted in 1991. First of class launched 21 March 1992. Projected numbers are uncertain after the first two. Designated as a missile Gunboat.
Structure: Derived from the Koncar class with a stretched hull and a new superstructure. Mine rails may be removed in favour of increasing SSM capability to eight missiles once the missiles have been acquired. There may also be a small mine detection high frequency active sonar.

KRALJ PETAR KRESIMIR IV   *3/1992, S S Breyer collection*

KRALJ PETAR KRESIMIR IV   *3/1992, S S Breyer collection*

LIGHT FORCES

Note: In addition to the listed vessels, there are large numbers of high speed small craft and rubber boats, many civilian manned but naval controlled. Some have machine guns and rocket launchers.

1 KONČAR CLASS (TYPE 240) (FAST ATTACK CRAFT—MISSILE)

Name	No	Builders	Commissioned
SIBENIC (ex-*Vlado Cetkovič*)	21 (ex-402)	Tito SY, Kraljevica	Mar 1978

Displacement, tons: 242 full load
Dimensions, feet (metres): 147.6 × 27.6 × 8.2 *(45 × 8.4 × 2.5)*
Main machinery: CODAG; 2 RR Proteus gas turbines; 7200 hp *(5.37 MW)* sustained; 2 MTU 20V 538 TB92 diesels; 8530 hp(m) *(6.27 MW)* sustained; 4 shafts
Speed, knots: 39. **Range, miles:** 500 at 35 kts; 880 at 23 kts (diesels)
Complement: 30 (5 officers)

Missiles: SSM: 2 SS-N-2B Styx; active radar or IR homing to 46 km *(25 nm)* at 0.9 Mach; warhead 513 kg. May be replaced by RBS-15.
Guns: 1 Bofors 57 mm/70; 75° elevation; 200 rounds/minute to 17 km *(9.3 nm)*; weight of shell 2.4 kg. 128 mm rocket launcher for illuminants.
1—30 mm/65 AK 630; 6 barrels; 85° elevation; 3000 rounds/minute to 2 km.
Countermeasures: Decoys: Wallop Barricade double layer chaff launcher.
Fire control: PEAB 9LV 200 GFCS.
Radars: Surface search: Decca 1226; I band.
Fire control: Philips TAB; I/J band.

Programmes: Type name, Raketna Topovnjaca. A second of this class may have been captured, but this is not confirmed. Four or five others of the class serve with the Yugoslav Navy.
Structure: Aluminium superstructure. Designed by the Naval Shipping Institute in Zagreb based on Swedish Spica class with bridge amidships like Malaysian boats. The after 57 mm gun has been replaced by a 30 mm AK 630.

SIBENIC   *8/1992, S S Breyer collection*

2 Ex-SOVIET OSA I CLASS (TYPE 205)
(FAST ATTACK CRAFT—MISSILE)

MITAR ACEV 41 (ex-301)   **VELIMIR ŠKORPIK** 42 (ex-310)

Displacement, tons: 171 standard; 210 full load
Dimensions, feet (metres): 126.6 × 24.9 × 8.8 *(38.6 × 7.6 × 2.7)*
Main machinery: 3 Type M 503A diesels; 8025 hp(m) *(5.9 MW)* sustained; 3 shafts
Speed, knots: 35. **Range, miles:** 400 at 34 kts
Complement: 30 (4 officers)

Missiles: SSM: 4 SS-N-2A Styx; active radar or IR homing to 46 km *(25 nm)* at 0.9 Mach; warhead 513 kg.
Guns: 4 USSR 30 mm/65 (2 twin); 85° elevation; 500 rounds/minute to 5 km *(2.7 nm)*; weight of shell 0.54 kg.
Radars: Surface search: Square Tie; I band.
Fire control: Drum Tilt; H/I band.
IFF: High Pole. 2 Square Head.

Programmes: Type name, Raketni Čamac. These two were captured from the Yugoslav Navy which still has eight others.
Operational: *Mitar Acev* was badly damaged and nearly scrapped, but eventually repaired at Sibenik navy yard.

OSA 1 (Yugoslav number)   *1982*

1 SOVIET SHERSHEN CLASS (TYPE 201)
(FAST ATTACK CRAFT—TORPEDO)

VUKOVAR (ex-*Partizan II*) 51 (ex-221)

Displacement, tons: 145 standard; 170 full load
Dimensions, feet (metres): 113.8 × 22.3 × 4.9 *(34.7 × 6.7 × 1.5)*
Main machinery: 3 M 503A diesels; 8025 hp(m) *(5.9 MW)* sustained; 3 shafts
Speed, knots: 45. **Range, miles:** 850 at 30 kts
Complement: 23
Guns: 4 USSR 30 mm/65 (2 twin); 85° elevation; 500 rounds/minute to 5 km *(2.7 nm)*; weight of shell 0.54 kg.
Torpedoes: 4—21 in *(533 mm)* tubes. Soviet Type 53.
Mines: 6.
Radars: Surface search: Pot Head; I band.
Fire control: Drum Tilt; H/I band.
IFF: High Pole. Square Head

Comment: Built under licence by Tito Shipyard, Kraljevica. Type name, Torpedni Čamac. A second of class, *Streljko*, was also captured but was damaged beyond repair in late 1991.

SHERSHEN   *10/1989, Gilbert Gyssels*

Light forces — Amphibious forces / CROATIA   149

3 MIRNA CLASS (TYPE 140) (FAST ATTACK CRAFT—PATROL)

SOLTA (ex-*Mukos*) 62 (ex-176)   **HRVATSKA KOSTAJNICA** (ex-*Cer*) 63 (ex-180)   +1

Displacement, tons: 120 full load
Dimensions, feet (metres): 104.9 × 22 × 7.5 *(32 × 6.7 × 2.3)*
Main machinery: 2 SEMT-Pielstick 12 PA4 200 VGDS diesels; 5292 hp(m) *(3.89 MW)* sustained; 2 shafts
Speed, knots: 30. **Range, miles:** 400 at 20 kts
Complement: 19 (3 officers)
Missiles: SAM: 1 SA-N-5 Grail quad mounting; manual aiming; IR homing to 6 km *(3.2 nm)* at 1.5 Mach; altitude to 2500 m *(8000 ft)*; warhead 1.5 kg.
Guns: 1 Bofors 40 mm/70. 1 Oerlikon 20 mm. 2—128 mm illuminant launchers.
Depth charges: 8 rails.
Sonars: Simrad SQS 3D/SF; active high frequency.

Comment: Builders, Kraljevica Yard. Commissioned 1981-85. A most unusual feature of this design is the fitting of an electric outboard motor giving a speed of up to 6 kts. Both named craft were captured after sustaining heavy damage, one by a missile fired from Brac island and the other by a torpedo. Both fully repaired. A third of this class is also in service with the Croatian Navy.

HRVATSKA KOSTAJNICA   8/1992

2 GALEB CLASS (RIVER PATROL CRAFT)

CISTA VELIKA   + 1

Displacement, tons: 19.5 full load
Dimensions, feet (metres): 55.4 × 12.8 × 2.3 *(16.9 × 3.9 × 0.7)*
Main machinery: 2 diesels; 330 hp(m) *(242 kW)*; 2 shafts
Speed, knots: 16. **Range, miles:** 160 at 12 kts
Complement: 6
Guns: 1 Oerlikon 20 mm; 2—7.62 mm MGs.
Radars: Surface search: Racal Decca 110; I band.

Comment: Commissioned in August 1992 for use in shallow water. Steel hulls with GRP superstructure.

RIVER PATROL CRAFT

Comment: A number of naval tenders have been converted to serve as river patrol vessels, some of them heavily armed. The one shown below has a Bofors 40 mm/70 gun forward and a quadruple 12.7 mm MG aft.

PB 92   1992, J P Husson

MINE WARFARE FORCES

Note: The former federal Navy retained the whole inventory of mines. There is therefore an urgent requirement for more MCMV capabilities.

1 BRITISH HAM CLASS (MINESWEEPER—INSHORE)

OLIB M 143

Displacement, tons: 120 standard; 159 full load
Dimensions, feet (metres): 106.5 × 21.3 × 5.5 *(32.5 × 6.5 × 1.7)*
Main machinery: 2 Paxman YHAXM diesels; 1100 hp *(821 kW)*; 2 shafts
Speed, knots: 14. **Range, miles:** 2000 at 9 kts
Complement: 22
Guns: 2 Oerlikon 20 mm (twin).

Comment: Built in Yugoslavia 1964-66 under the US Military Aid Programme. Wooden hull. Three others in service with the Yugoslav Navy.

1 SIRIUS CLASS (MINEHUNTER)

Name	No	Builders	Commissioned
VUKOV KLANAC (ex-*Hrabri*)	M 151 (ex-D 25)	A Normand, France	Sep 1957

Displacement, tons: 365 standard; 424 full load
Dimensions, feet (metres): 152 × 28 × 8.2 *(46.4 × 8.6 × 2.5)*
Main machinery: 2 SEMT-Pielstick PA1 175 diesels; 1620 hp(m) *(1.19 MW)*; 2 shafts
Speed, knots: 15. **Range, miles:** 3000 at 10 kts
Complement: 40
Guns: 2 Oerlikon 20 mm.
Countermeasures: MCMV: PAP 104; remote controlled submersibles.
Radars: Navigation: Thomson-CSF DRBN 30; I band.
Sonars: Plessey Type 193M; hull-mounted; active minehunting; high frequency.

Comment: Built as a US 'off-shore' order and converted to a minehunter in 1981. Upper deck extensively damaged in November 1991, but has been repaired.

VUKOV KLANAC   10/1990, Eric Grove

AMPHIBIOUS FORCES

1 SILBA CLASS (LCT/MINELAYER)

Name	No	Builders	Launched
CETINA (ex-*Rab*)	81	Brodosplit Shipyard, Split	18 July 1992

Displacement, tons: 880 full load
Measurement, tons: 163.1 oa; 144 wl × 33.5 × 8.5 *(49.7; 43.9 × 10.2 × 2.6)*
Main machinery: 2 Alpha 10V23L-VO diesels; 3100 hp(m) *(2.28 MW)* sustained; 2 shafts; cp props
Speed, knots: 12. **Range, miles:** 1200 at 12 kts
Complement: 33 (3 officers)
Military lift: 460 tons or 6 medium tanks or 7 APCs or 4—130 mm guns plus towing vehicles or 300 troops with equipment
Missiles: SAM: 1 SA-N-5 Grail quad mounting.
Guns: 4—30 mm/65 (2 twin) AK 230.
  4—20 mm M75 (quad). 2—128 mm illuminant launchers.
Mines: 94 Type SAG-1.
Radars: Surface search: I band.

Comment: Ro-Ro design with bow and stern ramps. Can be used for minelaying, transporting weapons or equipment and personnel. This is the second of class, the first being commissioned in 1990 into the Yugoslav Navy.

CETINA   7/1992, S S Breyer collection

4 MFPD-3 (DTM) TYPE + 1 DSM 501 TYPE (LCTs/MINELAYERS)

JASTREB

Displacement, tons: 410 full load
Dimensions, feet (metres): 155.1 × 21 × 7.5 *(47.3 × 6.4 × 2.3)*
Main machinery: 3 Gray Marine 64 HN9 diesels; 495 hp *(369 kW)*; 3 shafts
Speed, knots: 9
Complement: 15
Military lift: 200 troops or 3 heavy tanks
Guns: 2—12.7 mm MGs.
Mines: Can carry 100.

Comment: Unlike other tank landing craft in that the centre part of the bow drops to form a ramp down which the tanks go ashore, the vertical section of the bow being articulated to form outer end of ramp. Built in Yugoslavia. Can also act as minelayers. DTM (Desantni Tenkonosac/Minopolagac means landing ship tank/minelayer). Up to 12 more of the class operate with the Yugoslav Navy.

150 CROATIA / Amphibious forces — Service forces

3 TYPE 22 (LCUs)

Displacement, tons: 48 full load
Dimensions, feet (metres): 73.2 × 15.7 × 3.3 *(22.3 × 4.8 × 1)*
Main engines: 2 MTU diesels; 1740 hp(m) *(1.28 MW)*; 2 waterjets
Speed, knots: 35. **Range, miles:** 320 at 22 kts
Complement: 8
Military lift: 40 troops or 15 tons cargo
Guns: 2—20 mm M71. 1—30 mm Grenade launcher.
Radars: Navigation: Decca 101; I band.

Comment: Built of polyester and glass fibre. Last one completed in 1987. A total of 12 was built with numbers DJC 620-632.

LCU TYPE 22   1989

4 TYPE 21 (LCUs)

Displacement, tons: 32 full load
Dimensions, feet (metres): 69.9 × 15.7 × 5.2 *(21.3 × 4.8 × 1.6)*
Main machinery: 1 diesel; 1450 hp(m) *(1.07 MW)*; 1 shaft
Speed, knots: 23. **Range, miles:** 320 at 22 kts
Complement: 6
Military lift: 6 tons
Guns: 1—20 mm M71. 2—30 mm Grenade launchers.

Comment: Built between 1976 and 1979. Two more were damaged and may be repaired. A total of 18 of the class were produced with numbers DJC 601-620.

SURVEY SHIP

1 MOMA CLASS (AGS)

Name	No	Builders	Commissioned
ANDRIJA MOHOROVIČIĆ	PH 33	Gdansk Shipyard, Poland	1972

Displacement, tons: 1200 standard; 1475 full load
Dimensions, feet (metres): 240.5 × 33.5 × 12.8 *(73.3 × 10.2 × 3.9)*
Main machinery: 2 Zgoda-Sulzer 6TD48 diesels; 3300 hp(m) *(2.4 MW)* sustained; 2 shafts; cp props
Speed, knots: 15. **Range, miles:** 9000 at 12 kts
Complement: 37 (4 officers)
Radars: Navigation: Don 2; I band.

Comment: Built in 1971 at the shipyard in Gdansk, Poland, and added to the Yugoslav Navy List in 1972. Soviet Moma class type.

ANDRIJA MOHOROVIČIĆ   1982

SERVICE FORCES

1 PO TYPE (AET)

PO 51

Displacement, tons: 700
Main machinery: 2 Burmeister and Wain diesels; 600 hp(m) *(440 kW)*; 2 shafts
Speed, knots: 16
Complement: 43
Cargo capacity: 150 troops plus all types of ammunition

Comment: Built at Split in 1950s. Ammunition transport vessel.

1 SPASILAC CLASS (ASR)

SPASILAC (ex-PS 12)

Displacement, tons: 1590 full load
Dimensions, feet (metres): 182 × 39.4 × 14.1 *(55.5 × 12 × 4.3)*
Main engines: 2 diesels; 4340 hp(m) *(3.19 MW)*; 2 shafts; Kort nozzle props; bow thruster
Speed, knots: 13. **Range, miles:** 4000 at 12 kts
Complement: 53 plus 19 spare berths

Comment: Built at Tito SY, Belgrade. In service 10 September 1976. Fitted for firefighting and fully equipped for salvage work. Decompression chamber, and can support a manned rescue submersible. Can be fitted with two quadruple M 75 and two single M 71 20 mm guns. Sister ship in Libyan Navy.

SPASILAC   1988

1 WATER CARRIER (AWT)

ALGA (ex-PV 17)

Displacement, tons: 600 full load
Dimensions, feet (metres): 144.4 × 25.6 × 10.5 *(44 × 7.8 × 3.2)*
Main machinery: 1 diesel; 350 hp(m) *(257 kW)*; 1 shaft
Speed, knots: 8
Cargo capacity: 380 tons
Guns: 1 Bofors 40 mm/60. 1—20 mm M71.

Comment: Used to supply off-shore islands.

ALGA   10/1990, Eric Grove

1 HARBOUR TANKER

(ex-PN 25)

Displacement, tons: 430 full load
Dimensions, feet (metres): 151 × 23.6 × 10.2 *(46 × 7.2 × 3.1)*
Main machinery: 1 diesel; 300 hp(m) *(220 kW)*; 1 shaft
Speed, knots: 7

Comment: Built at Split in mid-1950s.

2 COASTAL TUGS

Displacement, tons: 550 full load
Dimensions, feet (metres): 105 × 26.2 × 16.4 *(32 × 8 × 5)*
Speed, knots: 11

Comment: Built at Split in 1950s. Type name, PR (Pomorski Remorker).

CUBA

Headquarters' Appointment

Chief of the Navy:
Vice Admiral Pedro Perez Betancourt

Personnel

(a) 1993: 12 000 (7500 conscripts) including 1000 marines
(b) 2 years' national service

Naval Establishments

Naval Academy:
At Punta Santa Ana, for officers and cadets.
Naval School:
At Playa Del Salado, for petty officers and men.
Naval Bases:
Cabanas, Nicaro, Cienfuegos, Havana, Mariel, Punta Ballenatos, Varadero, Canasi.

Command Organisation

Territorial:
Western Naval District (HQ Cabanas).
Central Naval District (HQ Cienfuegos).
Eastern Naval District (HQ Holguin).
Operational:
Missile Boat Flotilla, Torpedo Boat Flotilla, ASW Flotilla, Mine Warfare Division. These are deployed in whole or part amongst the Territorial Flotillas. Submarine Flotilla is based at Cienfuegos. Guard Flotilla consists of 1000 marines.

Mercantile Marine

Lloyd's Register of Shipping:
393 vessels of 714 900 tons gross

Strength of the Fleet

Type	Active
Submarines	3
Frigates	3
Corvette	1
Fast Attack Craft (Missile)	18
Fast Attack Craft (Patrol)	12
Minesweepers	16
LSMs	2
Survey Vessels	7
Border Guard	34

DELETIONS

1990 2 SO 1 class, 2 T 4 class, *XX Aniversario*
1991 *Gaviota Primero*
1992 2 Eichstaden class, *Caribe*, 1 Poluchat 1 class

SUBMARINES

3 Ex-SOVIET FOXTROT CLASS (TYPE 641)

725   727   729

Displacement, tons: 1950 surfaced; 2475 dived
Dimensions, feet (metres): 299.5 × 24.6 × 19.7 *(91.3 × 7.5 × 6)*
Main machinery: Diesel-electric; 3 Type 37-D diesels; 6000 hp(m) *(4.4 MW)*; 3 motors; (1 × 2700, 2 × 1350); 5400 hp(m) *(3.97 MW)*; 3 shafts; 1 auxiliary motor; 140 hp(m) *(103 kW)*
Speed, knots: 16 surfaced; 15 dived; 9 snorting
Range, miles: 20 000 at 8 kts surfaced; 380 at 2 kts dived
Complement: 75

Torpedoes: 10—21 in *(533 mm)* (6 bow, 4 stern) tubes. 22 Soviet Type 53; dual purpose; pattern active/passive homing up to 20 km *(10.8 nm)* at up to 45 kts; warhead 400 kg.
Mines: 44 in lieu of torpedoes.
Radars: Surface search: Snoop Tray; I band.
Sonars: Herkules/Feniks hull-mounted; active/passive search and attack; high frequency.

Programmes: First arrived Cuba 7 February 1979, second in January 1980 and third on 7 February 1984.
Structure: Diving depth, 250 m *(820 ft)* reducing with age.
Operational: An ex-Soviet Whiskey class is used as a non-operational charging station and training submarine. *725* started a five year refit in Havana in March 1986 which completed in 1992. *727* started a similar refit in July 1989.

FOXTROT 729   *1991*

FRIGATES

3 SOVIET KONI CLASS

350   356   383 (ex-*353*)

Displacement, tons: 1440 standard; 1900 full load
Dimensions, feet (metres): 316.3 × 41.3 × 11.5 *(96.4 × 12.6 × 3.5)*
Main machinery: CODAG; 1 SGW, Nikolayev, M8B gas turbine (centre shaft); 18 000 hp(m) *(13.25 MW)* sustained; 2 Russki B-68 diesels; 15 820 hp(m) *(11.63 MW)* sustained; 3 shafts
Speed, knots: 27 gas; 22 diesel. **Range, miles:** 1800 at 14 kts
Complement: 110

Missiles: SAM: SA-N-4 Gecko twin launcher ❶; semi-active radar homing to 15 km *(8 nm)* at 2.5 Mach; height envelope 9-3048 m *(29.5-10 000 ft)*; warhead 50 kg; magazine silo holds missiles. Some anti-surface capability.
Guns: 4 USSR 3 in *(76 mm)*/60 (2 twin) ❷; 80° elevation; 90 rounds/minute to 15 km *(8 nm)*; weight of shell 6.8 kg.
4 USSR 30 mm/65 (2 twin) (353 and 356) ❸; 85° elevation; 500 rounds/minute to 5 km *(2.7 nm)* anti-aircraft; weight of shell 0.54 kg.
2—6-barrelled Gatlings (350 only); 3000 rounds/minute combined to 2 km anti-missile.
A/S mortars: 2 RBU 6000 12-tubed trainable launchers ❹; range 6000 m; warhead 31 kg.
Depth charges: 2 rails.
Mines: Can lay 22 mines.
Countermeasures: Decoys: 2—16-barrelled chaff launchers.
ESM: Watch Dog; radar warning.
Radars: Air search: Strut Curve ❺; F band; range 110 km *(60 nm)* for 2 m² target.
Navigation: Don 2; I band.
Fire control: Hawk Screech ❻; I band; range 27 km *(15 nm)*.
Drum Tilt ❼; H/I band.
Pop Group ❽; F/H/I band (for SAM).
IFF: Two Square Head. High Pole A.
Sonars: Hull-mounted; active search and attack; medium frequency.

Programmes: First transferred 24 September 1981; second 8 February 1984; third 10 April 1988. These ships have no names. Based at Cienfuegos. *353* was redesignated *383* in October 1988.
Structure: Similar to the Algerian Konis.

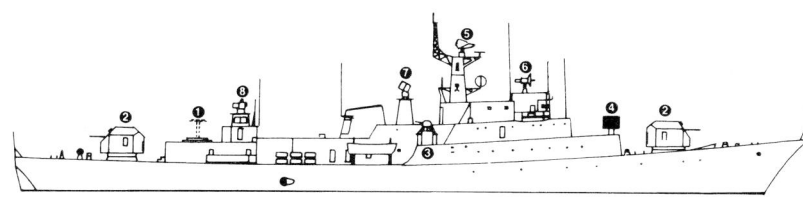

KONI   *(Scale 1 : 900), Ian Sturton*

KONI 353 (old number)   *3/1988, van Boeijen*

CUBA / Corvette — Mine warfare forces

CORVETTE

1 SOVIET PAUK II CLASS

321

Displacement, tons: 520 full load
Dimensions, feet (metres): 195.2 × 33.5 × 11.2 *(59.5 × 10.2 × 3.4)*
Main machinery: 2 Type M 507 diesels; 14 400 hp(m) *(10.6 MW)* sustained; 2 shafts
Speed, knots: 32. **Range, miles:** 2200 at 18 kts
Complement: 32

Missiles: SAM — SA-N-5 quad launcher; manual aiming, IR homing to 10 km *(5.4 nm)* at 1.5 Mach; warhead 1.1 kg.
Guns: 1 USSR 76 mm/60; 85° elevation; 120 rounds/minute to 7 km *(3.8 nm)*; weight of shell 16 kg.
1—30 mm/65; 6 barrels; 3000 rounds/minute combined to 2 km.
Torpedoes: 4—21 in *(533 mm)* (2 twin) tubes. Soviet type 53; active/passive homing up to 20 km *(11 nm)* at up to 45 kts; warhead 400 kg.
A/S mortars: 2 RBU 1200 5-tubed fixed; range 1200 m; warhead 34 kg.
Countermeasures: 2—16-tubed chaff launchers.
Radars: Air/surface search: Positive E; E/F band.
Navigation: Pechora; I band.
Fire control: Bass Tilt; H/I band.
Sonars: Rat Tail; VDS (on transom); attack; high frequency.

Programmes: Built at Yaroslav Shipyard and transferred in May 1990. Similar to the ships building for India.
Structure: Has a longer superstructure than the Pauk I and new electronics with a radome similar to the Parchim II class.

PAUK II (Russian number)   *1991, van Ginderen Collection*

LIGHT FORCES

5 Ex-SOVIET OSA I and 13 OSA II CLASS (TYPE 205)
(FAST ATTACK CRAFT—MISSILE)

251-255 (Osa I)
212, 225, 256-262, 267, 268, 271, 274 (Osa II)

Displacement, tons: 171 standard; 210 full load (Osa I); 245 full load (Osa II)
Dimensions, feet (metres): 126.6 × 24.9 × 8.8 *(38.6 × 7.6 × 2.7)*
Main machinery: 3 Type M 503A diesels; 8025 hp(m) *(5.9 MW)* sustained; 3 shafts (Osa I); 3 Type M 504 diesels; 10 800 hp(m) *(7.94 MW)* sustained; 3 shafts (Osa II)
Speed, knots: 35 (Osa I); 37 (Osa II)
Range, miles: 400 at 34 kts (Osa I); 500 at 35 kts (Osa II)
Complement: 30
Missiles: SSM — 4 SS-N-2 Styx; active radar or IR homing to 46 km *(25 nm)* at 0.9 Mach; warhead 513 kg.
Guns: 4—30 mm/65 (2 twin); 80° elevation; 500 rounds/minute to 5 km *(2.7 nm)*; weight of shell 0.54 kg.
Radars: Surface search: Square Tie; I band.
Fire control: Drum Tilt; H/I band.
IFF: Square Head. High Pole A (Osa I). High Pole B (Osa II).

Comment: Two boats of Osa I class were transferred to Cuba from the USSR in January 1972 and three in 1973. These were followed by one Osa I and one Osa II in mid-1976, one Osa II in January 1977 and one Osa II in March 1978. Further two Osa II delivered in December 1978, one in April 1979, one in October 1979, two from Black Sea November 1981, four in February 1982. One Osa I deleted in 1981.

OSA I 252   *1988*

9 Ex-SOVIET TURYA CLASS
(FAST ATTACK CRAFT—HYDROFOIL)

| 101 | 102 | 108 | 112 | 130 |
| 165 | 178 | 180 | 193 | |

Displacement, tons: 190 standard; 250 full load
Dimensions, feet (metres): 129.9 × 24.9 (41 over foils) × 5.9 (13.1 over foils) *(39.6 × 7.6 (12.5) × 1.8 (4))*
Main machinery: 3 Type M 504 diesels; 10 800 hp(m) *(7.94 MW)* sustained; 3 shafts
Speed, knots: 40 foilborne. **Range, miles:** 600 at 35 kts foilborne; 1450 at 14 kts
Complement: 30
Missiles: SAM — SA-N-5 Grail; IR homing to 6 km *(3.2 nm)* at 1.5 Mach; warhead 1.5 kg.
Guns: 2—57 mm/80 (twin, aft); 85° elevation; 120 rounds/minute to 6 km *(3.3 nm)*; weight of shell 2.8 kg.
2—25 mm/80 (twin, fwd); 85° elevation; 270 rounds/minute to 3 km *(1.6 nm)*; weight of shell 0.34 kg.
Torpedoes: 4—21 in *(533 mm)* tubes (some). 4 Soviet Type 53; dual purpose; pattern active/passive homing up to 20 km *(10.8 nm)* at up to 45 kts; warhead 400 kg.
Radars: Surface search: Pot Drum; H/I band.
Fire control: Muff Cob; G/H band.
IFF: High Pole. Square Head.
Sonars: May have helicopter type VDS.

Comment: Transferred February 1979 (first pair); February 1980 (second pair); from the Pacific 17 February 1981 (third pair); 9 January 1983 (fourth pair); 13 November 1983 (single craft). Three of the class in reserve in late 1992.

TURYA 102   *1988*

LAND-BASED MARITIME AIRCRAFT

Numbers/Type: 4 Mil Mi-14 ('Haze A').
Operational speed: 120 kts *(222 km/h)*.
Service ceiling: 15 000 ft *(4572 m)*.
Range: 240 nm *(445 km)*.
Role/Weapon systems: Fleet defence helicopter; shore-based for coastal duties; possibly operated by Soviet crews in support of Soviet naval forces. Sensors: Search radar, dipping sonar, MAD. Weapons: ASW; 2 × torpedoes, depth bombs or mines.

Numbers/Type: 4 Kamov Ka-28 ('Helix A').
Operational speed: 135 kts *(250 km/h)*.
Service ceiling: 19 685 ft *(6000 m)*.
Range: 432 nm *(800 km)*.
Role/Weapon systems: Probably intended as replacements for the Haze. Delivered in 1988. Sensors: Search radar, dipping sonar, sonobuoys, MAD, ECM. Weapons: 3 torpedoes, depth bombs, mines.

Numbers/Type: 6 Mikoyan MiG-29 Fulcrum.
Operational speed: 1320 kts *(1520 mph)*.
Service ceiling: 56 000 ft *(17 000 m)*.
Range: 1130 nm *(2100 km)*.
Role/Weapon systems: Air force manned air defence or Ground Attack fighters acquired with two training aircraft in 1989. Sensors: Pulse Doppler radar, IR scanner, laser rangefinder. Weapons: 1 × 30 mm cannon; 6 × AA-10 or AA-11.

MINE WARFARE FORCES

12 Ex-SOVIET YEVGENYA CLASS (MINEHUNTERS—INSHORE)

501, 502, 504, 507, 509, 510-514, 531, 538

Displacement, tons: 77 standard; 90 full load
Dimensions, feet (metres): 80.7 × 18 × 4.9 *(24.6 × 5.5 × 1.5)*
Main machinery: 2 Type 3-D-12 diesels; 600 hp(m) *(440 kW)* sustained; 2 shafts
Speed, knots: 11. **Range, miles:** 300 at 10 kts
Complement: 10
Guns: 2—14.5 mm (twin) MGs.
Countermeasures: Minehunting gear is lowered on a crane at the stern.
Radars: Navigation: Don 2; I band.

Comment: First pair transferred in November 1977, one in September 1978, two in November 1979, two in December 1980, two from the Baltic on 10 December 1981, one in October 1982 and four on 1 September 1984. There are two squadrons, one central and one west. At least two are non-operational.

YEVGENYA (Russian number)   *1990*

4 Ex-SOVIET SONYA CLASS (MINESWEEPERS/HUNTERS)

560   561   570   578

Displacement, tons: 400 full load
Dimensions, feet (metres): 157.4 × 28.9 × 6 6 *(48 × 8.8 × 2)*
Main machinery: 2 Kolomna Type 9-D-8 diesels; 2000 hp(m) *(1.47 MW)* sustained; 2 shafts
Speed, knots: 15. **Range, miles:** 3000 at 10 kts
Complement: 43
Guns: 2—30 mm/65 (twin); 85° elevation; 500 rounds/minute to 5 km *(2.7 nm)*; weight of shell 0.54 kg.
  2—25 mm/80 (twin); 85° elevation; 270 rounds/minute to 3 km *(1.6 nm)*.
Mines: Can carry 8.
Radars: Navigation: Don 2; I band.
IFF: Two Square Head. High Pole B.

Comment: Transferred August, December 1980, January and December 1985. First two are probably non-operational.

SONYA (Russian number)   5/1990

4 Ex-SOVIET NYRYAT-1 CLASS

H 93-96

Displacement, tons: 120 full load
Dimensions, feet (metres): 93 × 18 × 5.5 *(28.4 × 5.5 × 1.7)*
Main machinery: 1 diesel; 450 hp(m) *(330 kW)*; 1 shaft
Speed, knots: 12.5
Complement: 15

Comment: Mostly used for surveying. Two (*H 91-92*) deleted so far and the remainder may be scrapped soon.

NYRYAT-1   1990

AMPHIBIOUS FORCES

2 POLNOCHNY B CLASS (TYPE 771) (LSM)

690   601

Displacement, tons: 760 standard; 834 full load
Dimensions, feet (metres): 246.1 × 31.5 × 7.5 *(75 × 9.6 × 2.3)*
Main machinery: 2 Kolomna Type 40-D diesels; 4400 hp(m) *(3.2 MW)* sustained; 2 shafts
Speed, knots: 19. **Range, miles:** 1000 at 18 kts
Complement: 40
Military lift: 350 tons including 6 tanks and 200 troops
Guns: 4—30 mm/65 (2 twin); 85° elevation; 500 rounds/minute to 5 km *(2.7 nm)*; weight of shell 0.54 kg.
  2—140 mm rocket launchers; 18 tubes; range 9 km *(5 nm)*.
Radars: Navigation: Don 2 or Spin Trough; I band.
Fire control: Drum Tilt; H/I band.

Comment: Transferred September/December 1982. *601* is probably providing spares for *690*.

SURVEY VESSELS

1 Ex-SOVIET BIYA CLASS (AGS)

GUAMA H 103

Displacement, tons: 750 full load
Dimensions, feet (metres): 180.4 × 32.1 × 8.5 *(55 × 9.8 × 2.6)*
Main machinery: 2 diesels; 1200 hp(m) *(882 kW)*; 2 shafts; cp props
Speed, knots: 13. **Range, miles:** 4700+ at 11 kts
Complement: 25
Radars: Navigation: Don 2; I band.

Comment: Has laboratory facilities, one survey launch and a five ton crane. Built in Poland and acquired from USSR in 1970. Subordinate to Institute of Hydrography.

BIYA class   1976

SIBONEY H 101

Displacement, tons: 530
Dimensions, feet (metres): 138.5 × 27.2 × 8.5 *(42.2 × 8.3 × 2.6)*
Main machinery: 2 diesels; 910 hp(m) *(669 kW)*; 2 shafts
Speed, knots: 11

Comment: An ex-fishing trawler/buoy tender also used for cadet training. Acquired from Spain in 1968.

TAINO H 102

Displacement, tons: 1100
Dimensions, feet (metres): 173.9 × 34.1 × 11.5 *(53 × 10.4 × 3.5)*
Main machinery: 2 diesels; 1550 hp(m) *(1.14 MW)*; 2 shafts
Speed, knots: 12

Comment: Mostly used as a buoy tender. Acquired from Spain in 1979.

MISCELLANEOUS

Notes: 1. Tanker *Las Guasimas* of 8300 tons is capable of alongside refuelling. Civilian manned.
2. Chemical tanker *Capitan Olo Pantoja* converted to carry oil fuel.

1 ARMINZA CLASS (AGI)

ISLA DE LA JUVENTUD

Measurement, tons: 1556 gross
Dimensions, feet (metres): 230 × 41.3 × 17.7 *(70 × 12.6 × 5.4)*
Main machinery: 1 diesel; 2200 hp(m) *(1.62 MW)*; 1 shaft
Speed, knots: 13

Comment: Ex-trawler used as an intelligence collection ship since 1982.

ISLA DE LA JUVENTUD   7/1984, US Navy

1 Ex-SOVIET POLUCHAT 1 CLASS

RT 84

Displacement, tons: 100 full load
Dimensions, feet (metres): 97.1 × 19 × 4.8 *(29.6 × 5.8 × 1.5)*
Main machinery: 2 Type M 50 diesels; 2200 hp(m) *(1.6 MW)* sustained; 2 shafts
Speed, knots: 20. **Range, miles:** 1500 at 10 kts
Complement: 15
Guns: 4—14.7 mm (2 twin) MGs.

Comment: Used as a torpedo recovery vessel. Others of the class have been cannibalised for spares.

2 TRAINING SHIPS

VIETNAM HEROICO   TAINO (ex-*Jose Marti*)

Comment: Different types of ships. *Taino* is also the name of a survey vessel.

1 Ex-SOVIET PELYM CLASS (DEGAUSSING SHIP)

ADG 40

Displacement, tons: 1300 full load
Dimensions, feet (metres): 214.8 × 38 × 11.2 *(65.5 × 11.6 × 3.4)*
Main machinery: 2 diesels; 2400 hp(m) *(1.76 MW)*; 2 shafts
Speed, knots: 14
Complement: 70

Comment: Built in USSR in mid-1970s. Transferred in 1982.

154 CUBA / Miscellaneous — CYPRUS, REPUBLIC / Patrol forces

1 Ex-SOVIET YELVA CLASS (DIVING TENDER)

B-015

Displacement, tons: 300 full load
Dimensions, feet (metres): 134.2 × 26.2 × 6.6 *(40.9 × 8 × 2)*
Main machinery: 2 Type 3-D-12 diesels; 600 hp(m) *(440 kW)* sustained; 2 shafts
Speed, knots: 12.5
Complement: 30
Radars: Navigation: Spin Trough; I band.

Comment: Built in early 1970s, transferred 1973. Two 1.5 ton cranes.

YELVA class   1973

4 OREL CLASS (SALVAGE TUGS)

R 21   R 23   R 27   R 29

Displacement, tons: 1750 full load
Dimensions, feet (metres): 201.2 × 39.2 × 14.8 *(61.4 × 12 × 4.5)*
Main machinery: 1 diesel; 1700 hp(m) *(1.25 MW)*; 1 shaft
Speed, knots: 15. Range, miles: 14 000 at 13.5 kts
Complement: 40

Comment: Built in Finland in the late 1950s. Probably acquired from Russian Ministry of Fisheries.

BORDER GUARD

Note: Operates under the Ministry of the Interior. Pennant numbers painted in red.

3 Ex-SOVIET STENKA CLASS (FAST ATTACK CRAFT—PATROL)

Displacement, tons: 170 standard; 210 full load
Dimensions, feet (metres): 127.9 × 25.6 × 5.9 *(39 × 7.8 × 1.8)*
Main machinery: 3 Type M 503A diesels; 8025 hp(m) *(5.9 MW)* sustained; 3 shafts
Speed, knots: 36. Range, miles: 800 at 24 kts; 500 at 35 kts
Complement: 30
Guns: 4—30 mm/65 (2 twin); dual purpose; 85° elevation; 500 rounds/minute to 5 km *(2.7 nm)*; weight of shell 0.54 kg.
Radars: Surface search: Pot Drum; H/I band.
Fire control: Muff Cob; G/H band.
IFF: High Pole. Square Head.

Comment: Similar to class operated by KGB with torpedo tubes and sonar removed. Transferred in February 1985 (two) and August 1985 (one).

STENKA   1990

31 Ex-SOVIET ZHUK CLASS (FAST ATTACK CRAFT—PATROL)

Displacement, tons: 50 full load
Dimensions, feet (metres): 75.4 × 17 × 6.2 *(23 × 5.2 × 1.9)*
Main machinery: 2 Type M 50 diesels; 2200 hp(m) *(1.6 MW)* sustained; 2 shafts
Speed, knots: 30. Range, miles: 1100 at 15 kts
Complement: 17
Guns: 4—14.5 mm (2 twin) MGs.
Radars: Surface search: Spin Trough; I band.

Comment: A total of 40 acquired since 1971. Last batch of two arrived December 1989. Some transferred to Nicaragua. The total has been reduced to allow for wastage.

ZHUK   1990

CYPRUS, Republic

Senior Officer

Chief of Navy:
Captain J Vragalis, HN

Personnel

1993: 320

General

In November 1983 Turkey set up an independent republic in the northern part of the island. Subsequently the UN declared this to be illegal. At least one unit of the Turkish Navy, *Caner Gönyeli* (P 145), is permanently based at Girne (Kyrenia) as are units of the Turkish Coast Guard flying the North Cyprus flag. For details of these vessels see Turkey section.

Base

Limassol

Mercantile Marine

Lloyd's Register of Shipping:
1416 vessels of 20 385 718 tons gross

PATROL FORCES

Name	No	Builders	Commissioned
SALAMIS	P 01	Chantiers de l'Esterel	24 May 1983

Displacement, tons: 98 full load
Dimensions, feet (metres): 105.3 × 21.3 × 5.9 *(32.1 × 6.5 × 1.8)*
Main machinery: 2 SACM 195 CZSHRY 12 diesels; 4680 hp(m) *(3.44 MW)* sustained; 2 shafts
Speed, knots: 30. Range, miles: 1200 at 15 kts
Complement: 22
Guns: 1 Breda 40 mm/70; 85° elevation; 300 rounds/minute to 12.5 km *(6.8 nm)* anti-surface; weight of shell 0.96 kg.
1 Rheinmetall Wegmann 20 mm. 2—12.7 mm MGs.
Radars: Surface search: I band.

Comment: Laid down in December 1981, completed in 1983 for Naval Command of National Guard.

SALAMIS   1992, Cyprus Navy

Name	No	Builders	Commissioned
EVAGORAS	PV 20	Brodotehnika SY, Belgrade	21 Nov 1991
POSIDON	PV 21	Brodotehnika SY, Belgrade	21 Nov 1991

Displacement, tons: 57 full load
Dimensions, feet (metres): 80.7 × 18.7 × 3.9 *(24.6 × 5.7 × 1.2)*
Main machinery: 2 diesels; 4270 hp(m) *(3.14 MW)*; 2 KaMeWa waterjets
Speed, knots: 42. **Range, miles:** 600 at 20 kts
Complement: 9
Guns: 1 Rheinmetall 20 mm; ISBRS rocket launcher. 2—7.62 mm MGs.
Radars: Surface search: I band.

Comment: Designated as FAC-23 Jets. Aluminium construction. Maritime Police.

5 Ex-GDR SAB 12 TYPE

ex-*G 50/GS 10*   ex-*G 52/GS 25*   ex-*G 54/GS 27*   ex-*G 55/GS 12*   ex-*G 57/GS 28*

Comment: Harbour patrol craft of the former GDR MAB 12 class transferred in December 1992. Controlled by Maritime Police.

SAB 12 (German colours)   *10/1991, Hartmut Ehlers*

EVAGORAS   *11/1991*

Name	No	Builders	Commissioned
KINON	PL 2	C N de l'Esterel	1982

Main machinery: 2 MTU diesels; 2 shafts

Comment: Of 58.1 ft *(17.7 m)*. Controlled by Maritime Police. Second of class deleted in 1991.

LAND-BASED MARITIME AIRCRAFT

Numbers/Type: 1 Pilatus Britten-Norman Maritime Defender.
Operational speed: 150 kts *(280 km/h)*.
Service ceiling: 18 900 ft *(5760 m)*.
Range: 1500 nm *(2775 km)*.
Role/Weapon systems: Operated around southern coastline of Cyprus to prevent smuggling and terrorist activity. Sensors: Search radar, searchlight mounted on wings. Weapons: ASV; various machine gun pods and rockets.

DENMARK

Headquarters' Appointment

Flag Officer Denmark:
Rear Admiral K E J Borck
Inspector Naval Home Guard
Captain S V Andersen

Diplomatic Representation

Defence Attaché, Bonn:
Colonel S S Jensen (Army)
Defence Attaché, London:
Captain S Lund
Defence Attaché, Stockholm:
Commander (S G) N Friis
Defence Attaché, Warsaw:
Colonel C Barløse (Army)
Defence Attaché, Washington and Ottawa:
Brigadier K D Andersen (Air Force)
Defence Attaché, Paris:
Colonel M Christensen (Air Force)
Defence Attaché, Moscow:
Colonel S V Fandrup (Army)

Personnel

a) 1993: 1006 officers, 2963 regular ratings, 800 national service ratings.
Reserves: 5500.
Naval Home Guard: 4030.
b) 9 months' national service

Bases

Korsør (Corvettes, FACs, Stanflex), Frederikshavn (Submarines, MCMV, Fishery Protection Ships), Grønnedal (Greenland)

Naval Air Arm

Naval helicopters owned and operated by Navy in naval squadron based at Värlöse near Copenhagen. All servicing and maintenance by air force. LRMP are flown by the Air Force.

Coast Defence

There are forts at Stevns and Langeland (on southern approaches to Sound and Great Belt) armed with 150 mm and 40 mm guns. Six radar stations and a number of coast watching stations in the area. There are also two mobile batteries planned to be operational in 1994. Linked by a Terma command and control system they will each consist of three trailers, one for command and two for carrying Harpoon missiles taken from deleted frigates.

Command and Control

It was originally the intention to have all government vessels under The Directorate of Waters (Farvandsdirektoratet). However the Ministry of Trade and Shipping now runs the icebreakers and some training ships (the icebreakers are maintained by the Navy and are based at Frederikshavn in the Summer) while the Ministry of the Environment (Miljøministeriet) controls two environmental protection divisions based at Copenhagen (being phased out) and Korsør (both manned and maintained by the Navy). Survey ships are run by the Farvandsdirektoratet Nautisk Afdeling (Administration of Navigation and Hydrography) under the Ministry of Defence and the Ministry of Fisheries has four rescue vessels and an Osprey class.

Appearance

Ships are painted in 6 different colours as follows:
Grey: Frigates, corvettes and patrol frigates.
Olive-green: FACs and tankers.
Black: Submarines.
Orange: Survey Vessels.
White: The Royal Yacht and the Sail Training Yawls.
Black/yellow: Service Vessels, tugs and ferryboats.

Prefix to Ships' Names

HDMS

Mercantile Marine

Lloyd's Register of Shipping:
1276 vessels of 5 780 551 tons gross

Strength of the Fleet

Type	Active	Building (Projected)
Submarines (Coastal)	5	—
Frigates	8	—
Fast Attack Craft (Missile)	10	—
Large Patrol Craft	22	3 (3)
Coastal Patrol Craft	3	—
Naval Home Guard	36	9 (6)
Minelayers	6	—
Minesweepers (Coastal)	2	—
Minesweepers (Drones)	2	(10)
Support Ship	1	—
Tankers (Small)	2	—
Icebreakers	4	—
Royal Yacht	1	—
Tugs	2	—
TRVs	3	—
Survey and Training Craft	11	—
Environment Craft	6	—

DELETIONS

Submarines

1990 *Spaekhuggeren, Springeren* (old)

Frigates

1990 *Peder Skram, Herluf Trolle*
1991 *Fylla*
1992 *Ingolf, Vaedderen* (old), *Hvidbjørnen* (old)

Light Forces

1990 *Søløven, Søridderen, Søbjørnen, Søhesten, Søhunden, Søulve*
1992 *Dryaden, Najaden, Nymfen, Maagen, Mallemukken*

Naval Home Guard

1992 *Aldebaran* (old), *Andromeda* (old)
1993 *Aries* (old), *Carina* (old)

Minesweepers

1991 *Guldborgsund*

Miscellaneous

1990 SKB 3
1992 *Havørnen* (civilian)

PENNANT LIST

Submarines

S 320	Narhvalen
S 321	Nordkaperen
S 322	Tumleren
S 323	Saelen
S 324	Springeren

Frigates

F 340	Beskytteren
F 354	Niels Juel
F 355	Olfert Fischer
F 356	Peter Tordenskiold
F 357	Thetis
F 358	Triton
F 359	Vaedderen
F 360	Hvidbjørnen

Light Forces

P 540	Bille
P 541	Bredal
P 542	Hammer
P 543	Huitfeld
P 544	Krieger
P 545	Norby
P 546	Rodsteen
P 547	Sehested
P 548	Suenson
P 549	Willemoes
P 550	Flyvefisken
P 551	Hajen
P 552	Havkatten
P 553	Laxen
P 554	Makrelen
P 555	Støren
P 556	Svaerdfisken
P 557	Glenten
P 558	Gribben
P 559	Lommen
P 560	Raunen (building)
P 561	Skaden (building)
P 562	Viben (building)
Y 300	Barsø
Y 301	Drejø
Y 302	Romsø
Y 303	Samsø
Y 304	Thurø
Y 305	Vejrø
Y 306	Farø
Y 307	Laesø
Y 308	Rømø
Y 343	Lunden
Y 386	Agdlek
Y 387	Agpa
Y 388	Tulugaq

Mine Warfare Forces

N 43	Lindormen
N 44	Lossen
N 80	Falster
N 81	Fyen
N 82	Møen
N 83	Sjaelland
M 574	Grønsund
M 578	Vilsund

Auxiliaries

A 540	Dannebrog
A 559	Sleipner
A 568	Rimfaxe
A 569	Skinfaxe
TO 8	Hugin
TO 9	Munin
TO 10	Mimer
—	MSA 4
Y 101	Svanen
Y 102	Thyra

SUBMARINES

3 TUMLEREN (ex-KOBBEN) CLASS (TYPE 207)

Name	No	Builders	Laid down	Launched	Commissioned	Recommissioned
TUMLEREN (ex-*Utvaer*)	S 322	Rheinstahl-Nordseewerke, Emden	24 Mar 1965	30 July 1965	1 Dec 1965	20 Oct 1989
SAELEN (ex-*Uthaug*)	S 323	Rheinstahl-Nordseewerke, Emden	31 May 1965	3 Oct 1965	16 Feb 1966	5 Oct 1990
SPRINGEREN (ex-*Kya*)	S 324	Rheinstahl-Nordseewerke, Emden	26 May 1963	20 Feb 1964	15 Jan 1964	10 Oct 1991

Displacement, tons: 459 surfaced; 524 dived
Dimensions, feet (metres): 155.5 × 15 × 14 *(47.4 × 4.6 × 4.3)*
Main machinery: Diesel-electric; 2 MTU 12V 493 AZ80 diesels; 1200 hp(m) *(880 kW)*; 1 motor; 1700 hp(m) *(1.25 MW)*; 1 shaft
Speed, knots: 12 surfaced; 18 dived
Range, miles: 5000 at 8 kts snorting
Complement: 18 (5 officers)

Torpedoes: 8—21 in *(533 mm)* bow tubes. FFV Type 61; anti-surface; wire-guided; passive homing to 25 km *(13.7 nm)* at 45 kts; warhead 240 kg.
Countermeasures: ESM: Racal/Sea Lion; radar warning.
Fire control: Terma TFCS.
Radars: Surface search: Terma; I band.
Sonars: Atlas Elektronik PSU 83; passive search and attack; medium frequency.

Programmes: First two acquired from Norway in 1986 for modernisation; the third in late 1989. Have replaced Delfinen class.

Modernisation: Work done at Urivale Shipyard, Bergen between 1987 and 1991 included lengthening by 5.2 ft *(1.6 m)* (which has increased displacement) and new communications, ESM, navigation and fire control equipment. New sonar fitted in 1992/93.
Structure: Diving depth, 200 m *(650 ft)*.
Operational: *Saelen* sank in the Kattegat while unmanned and under tow in late 1990. Salvaged and repaired using spares taken from the ex-Norwegian *Kaura*, which was purchased for cannibalisation. Planned to be back in service in December 1993.

SAELEN *1992, Royal Danish Navy*

2 NARHVALEN CLASS

Name	No	Builders	Laid down	Launched	Commissioned
NARHVALEN	S 320	Royal Dockyard, Copenhagen	16 Feb 1965	10 Sep 1968	27 Feb 1970
NORDKAPEREN	S 321	Royal Dockyard, Copenhagen	4 Mar 1966	18 Dec 1969	22 Dec 1970

Displacement, tons: 420 surfaced; 450 dived
Dimensions, feet (metres): 145.3 × 15 × 13.8 *(44.3 × 4.6 × 4.2)*
Main machinery: Diesel-electric; 2 MTU 12V 493 TY7; 2250 hp(m) *(1.62 MW)*; 1 motor; 1200 hp(m) *(882 kW)*; 1 shaft
Speed, knots: 12 surfaced; 17 dived
Complement: 21 (4 officers)

Torpedoes: 8—21 in *(533 mm)* bow tubes. Combination of FFV Type 61; wire-guided; passive homing to 25 km *(13.7 nm)* anti-surface at 45 kts; warhead 240 kg and FFV Type 41; anti-submarine; passive homing to 20 km *(10.8 nm)* at 25 kts; warhead 45 kg; no reloads.
Fire control: Signaal M8.
Radars: Surface search: Thomson-CSF Calypso; I band.
Sonars: Atlas Elektronik CSU 3-2; hull-mounted; active/passive search and attack; medium frequency.
PRS 3-4; passive ranging; part of CSU 3.

Programmes: These coastal submarines are similar to the West German Improved Type 205 and were built under licence at the Royal Dockyard, Copenhagen with modifications for Danish needs.
Modernisation: A programme update has been approved for an equipment update similar to the Tumleren class to enable both submarines to serve until the end of the decade. Work starts on *Narhvalen* in late 1993 and *Nordkaperen* in mid-1995 and includes new periscopes, an optronic mast, ESM, radar and sonar.

NARHVALEN *10/1990, Maritime Photographic*

FRIGATES

3 NIELS JUEL CLASS

Name	No
NIELS JUEL	F 354
OLFERT FISCHER	F 355
PETER TORDENSKIOLD	F 356

Builders	Laid down	Launched	Commissioned
Aalborg Vaerft	20 Oct 1976	17 Feb 1978	26 Aug 1980
Aalborg Vaerft	6 Dec 1978	10 May 1979	16 Oct 1981
Aalborg Vaerft	3 Dec 1979	30 Apr 1980	2 Apr 1982

Displacement, tons: 1320 full load
Dimensions, feet (metres): 275.5 × 33.8 × 10.2 *(84 × 10.3 × 3.1)*
Main machinery: CODOG; 1 GE LM 2500 gas turbine; 24 600 hp *(18.35 MW)* sustained; 1 MTU 20 V 956 TB82 diesel; 5210 hp(m) *(3.83 MW)* sustained; 2 shafts
Speed, knots: 28 (gas); 20 (diesel). **Range, miles:** 2500 at 18 kts
Complement: 98 (18 officers)

Missiles: SSM: 8 McDonnell Douglas Harpoon (2 quad) launchers ❶; active radar homing to 130 km *(70 nm)* at 0.9 Mach; warhead 227 kg.
SAM: Raytheon NATO Sea Sparrow Mk 29 octuple launcher ❷; semi-active radar homing to 14.6 km *(8 nm)* at 2.5 Mach; warhead 39 kg; 8 missiles.
Guns: 1 OTO Melara 3 in *(76 mm)*/62 compact ❸; 85° elevation; 85 rounds/minute to 16 km *(8.7 nm)* anti-surface; 12 km *(6.6 nm)* anti-aircraft; weight of shell 6 kg.
4 Oerlikon 20 mm (one each side of the funnel and two abaft the mast) ❹.
Depth charges: 1 rack.
Countermeasures: Decoys: 2 THORN EMI Sea Gnat 6-barrelled chaff launchers ❺.
ESM: Racal Cutlass; radar warning.
Combat data systems: Ericsson EPLO action data automation; Link 11. SATCOMs ❻.
Fire control: Philips 9LV 200 Mk 2 GFCS with TV tracker. Raytheon Mk 91 Mod 1 MFCS with two directors. Harpoon to 1A(V) standard.
Radars: Air search: Plessey AWS 5 ❼; 3D; E/F band; range 155 km *(85 nm)* for 4 m² target.
Surface search: Philips 9GR 600 ❽; I band.
Fire control: Two Mk 95 ❾; I/J band (for SAM).
Philips 9LV 200 ❿; J band (for guns and SSM).
Navigation: Burmeister & Wain Elektronik Scanter Mil 009; E/I band.
Sonars: Plessey PMS 26; hull-mounted; active search and attack; 10 kHz.

Programmes: YARD Glasgow designed the class to Danish order.
Modernisation: A mid-life update is planned including 2 RAM launchers and new combat data and communications systems. Air search radar is to be replaced by TST TRS-3D in 1993/94. The seaboat was replaced by a rigid inflatable type in 1989.

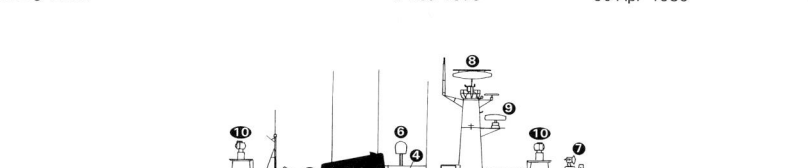

OLFERT FISCHER   *(Scale 1 : 900), Ian Sturton*

OLFERT FISCHER   *5/1992, Guy Toremans*

OLFERT FISCHER   *5/1992, Gilbert Gyssels*

1 MODIFIED HVIDBJØRNEN CLASS

Name	No
BESKYTTEREN	F 340

Builders	Laid down	Launched	Commissioned
Aalborg Vaerft	11 Dec 1974	29 May 1975	27 Feb 1976

Displacement, tons: 1970 full load
Dimensions, feet (metres): 245 × 40 × 17.4 *(74.7 × 12.2 × 5.3)*
Main machinery: 3 MAN/Burmeister & Wain Alpha diesels; 7440 hp(m) *(5.47 MW)*; 1 shaft; cp prop
Speed, knots: 18. **Range, miles:** 4500 at 16 kts on 2 engines; 6000 at 13 kts on 1 engine
Complement: 67 (8 officers)

Guns: 1 USN 3 in *(76 mm)*/50; dual purpose.
Countermeasures: Decoys: THORN EMI Sea Gnat 6-barrelled chaff launchers.
ESM: Racal Cutlass; radar warning.
Combat data systems: Terma TDS; SATCOM.
Radars: Air/surface search: Plessey AWS 6; G band.
Navigation: Burmeister & Wain Elektronik Scanter Mil 009; E/I band.
Sonars: Plessey PMS 26; hull-mounted; active search and attack; 10 kHz.

Helicopters: 1 Westland Lynx Mk 80/91.

Modernisation: May be modernised in due course.
Structure: Strengthened for ice operations.
Operational: Used for similar fishery protection duties.

BESKYTTEREN   *2/1991, Royal Danish Navy*

DENMARK / Frigates — Land-based maritime aircraft

4 THETIS CLASS

Name	No	Builders	Laid down	Launched	Commissioned
THETIS	F 357	Svenborg Vaerft	10 Oct 1988	14 July 1989	1 July 1991
TRITON	F 358	Svenborg Vaerft	27 June 1989	16 Mar 1990	2 Dec 1991
VAEDDEREN	F 359	Svenborg Vaerft	19 Mar 1990	21 Dec 1990	9 June 1992
HVIDBJØRNEN	F 360	Svenborg Vaerft	2 Jan 1991	11 Oct 1991	30 Nov 1992

Displacement, tons: 2600 standard; 3500 full load
Dimensions, feet (metres): 369.1 oa; 327.4 wl × 47.2 × 19.7 *(112.5; 99.8 × 14.4 × 6.0)*
Main machinery: 3 MAN/Burmeister & Wain Alpha 12V 28/32A diesels; 10 800 hp(m) *(7.94 MW)* sustained; 1 shaft; cp prop; bow and azimuth thrusters; 880 hp(m) *(647 kW)*, 1100 hp(m) *(800 kW)*
Speed, knots: 20; 8 on thrusters. **Range, miles:** 8500 at 15.5 kts
Complement: 61 (11 officers) plus 12 spare berths

Guns: 1 OTO Melara 3 in *(76 mm)*/62; Super Rapid ❶; dual purpose; 85° elevation; 120 rounds/minute to 16 km *(8.7 nm)*; weight of shell 6 kg.
1 or 2 Oerlikon 20 mm.
Depth charges: 2 Rails (door in stern).
Countermeasures: ESM: Racal Cutlass; radar warning.
Combat data systems: Terma TDS; SATCOM ❷.
Fire control: Bofors 9LV 200 Mk 3 optronic director.
Radars: Air/surface search: Plessey AWS 6 ❸; G band; range 88 km *(48 nm)*.
Surface search: Terma Scanter Mil ❹; I band.
Navigation: Furuno FR1505DA; I band.
Fire control: Bofors Electronic 9LV 200; I/J band.
Sonars: Thomson Sintra TSM 2640 Salmon; hull-mounted and VDS; active search and attack; medium frequency.

Helicopters: 1 Westland Lynx Mk 80/91 ❺.

Programmes: Preliminary study by YARD in 1986 led to Dwinger Marine Consultants being awarded a contract for a detailed design completed in mid-1987. All four ordered in October 1987.
Structure: The hull is some 30 m longer than the Hvidbjørnen class to improve sea-keeping qualities and allow considerable extra space for additional armament. The design allows the use of containerised equipment to be shipped depending on role and there is some commonality with the Flex 300 ships. Some sensors have been transferred from the Hvidbjørnen class as the latter paid off. The hull is ice strengthened to enable penetration of 1 m thick ice and efforts have been made to incorporate stealth technology, for instance by putting anchor equipment, bollards and winches below the upper deck. There is a double skin up to 2 m below the waterline. The flight deck (28 × 14 m) is strengthened to take Sea King or Merlin helicopters. A rigid inflatable boarding craft plumbed by a hydraulic crane is fitted alongside the fixed hangar. The bridge and ops room are combined. Thetis has a modified stern for seismological equipment.

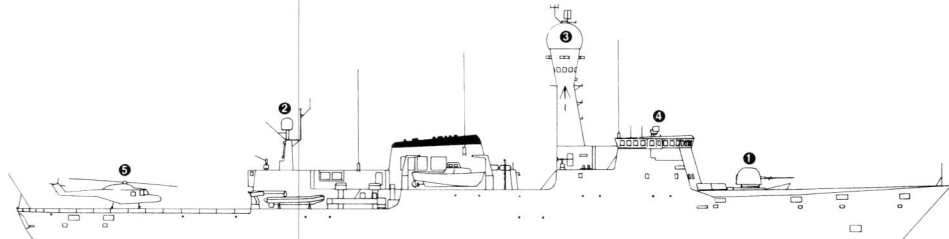

THETIS *(Scale 1 : 900), Ian Sturton*

TRITON *6/1992, Gunnar Olsen*

Operational: Primary role is fishery protection. *Thetis* is employed for 3-4 months a year doing seismological surveys in the Greenland EEZ. A 4000 m towed array is used to receive signals generated by pneumatic noise guns towed 800 m astern.

Opinion: It seems likely that the built-in flexibility of the design may allow the development of a fully armed frigate in due course. The following systems have been considered: Harpoon, VLS Sea Sparrow, triple torpedo tubes, RAM PDMS, SRBOC or Sea Gnat decoys, Nixie, fire control radars and passive sonar towed array.

THETIS (modified stern) *6/1992, Royal Danish Navy*

SHIPBORNE AIRCRAFT

Numbers/Type: 8/2 Westland Lynx Mk 80/91.
Operational speed: 125 kts *(232 km/h)*.
Service ceiling: 12 500 ft *(3810 m)*.
Range: 320 nm *(593 km)*.
Role/Weapon systems: Shipborne helicopter for EEZ and surface search tasks. Sensors: Bendix weather radar to be replaced by Ferranti Seaspray; Kestrel ESM. Weapons: Unarmed.

LAND-BASED MARITIME AIRCRAFT

Numbers/Type: 3 Gulfstream Aerospace SMA-3 Gulfstream III.
Operational speed: 500 kts *(926 km/h)*.
Service ceiling: 45 000 ft *(13 720 m)*.
Range: 3940 nm *(7300 km)*.
Role/Weapon systems: MR and liaison aircraft; flown on EEZ patrol around Greenland coast and in Danish sea areas in Baltic; EW work undertaken. Sensors: APS-127 surveillance radar. Weapons: Unarmed.

Numbers/Type: 7 Sikorsky S-61A-1 Sea King.
Operational speed: 118 kts *(219 km/h)*.
Service ceiling: 14 700 ft *(4480 m)*.
Range: 542 nm *(1005 km)*.
Role/Weapon systems: Land-based SAR helicopter for peacetime search and rescue; wartime combat rescue and surface search. Sensors: Bendix weather radar; GEC Avionics FLIR to be fitted. Weapons: Unarmed.

LYNX *1989, Royal Danish Nav*

LIGHT FORCES

10 + 3 (1) FLYVEFISKEN CLASS
(LARGE PATROL CRAFT AND MINEHUNTERS/LAYERS)

Name	No	Builders	Commissioned
FLYVEFISKEN	P 550	Danyard A/S, Aalborg	19 Dec 1989
HAJEN	P 551	Danyard A/S, Aalborg	19 July 1990
HAVKATTEN	P 552	Danyard A/S, Aalborg	1 Nov 1990
LAXEN	P 553	Danyard A/S, Aalborg	22 Mar 1991
MAKRELEN	P 554	Danyard A/S, Aalborg	1 Oct 1991
STØREN	P 555	Danyard A/S, Aalborg	Apr 1992
SVAERDFISKEN	P 556	Danyard A/S, Aalborg	Oct 1991
GLENTEN	P 557	Danyard A/S, Aalborg	June 1992
GRIBBEN	P 558	Danyard A/S, Aalborg	Dec 1992
LOMMEN	P 559	Danyard A/S, Aalborg	June 1993
RAUNEN	P 560	Danyard A/S, Aalborg	Dec 1993
SKADEN	P 561	Danyard A/S, Aalborg	June 1994
VIBEN	P 562	Danyard A/S, Aalborg	Dec 1994

Displacement, tons: 320 standard; 450 full load
Dimensions, feet (metres): 177.2 × 29.5 × 8.2 *(54 × 9 × 2.5)*
Main machinery: CODAG; 1 GE LM 500 gas turbine (centre shaft); 5450 hp *(4.1 MW)* sustained; 1 GM 12V-71 diesel; 340 hp *(254 kW)* sustained (centre shaft) (also powers the hydraulic drive); 2 MTU 16V 396 TB94 diesels (outer shafts); 5800 hp(m) *(4.26 MW)* sustained; 3 shafts; cp props on outer shafts; bow thruster
Speed, knots: 30; 20 on diesels; 6 on electric propulsion. **Range, miles:** 2400 at 18 kts
Complement: 15-18 plus 10 spare berths

Missiles: SSM: 8 McDonnell Douglas Harpoon; active radar homing to 130 km *(70 nm)* at 0.9 Mach; warhead 227 kg.
Guns: 1 OTO Melara 3 in *(76 mm)*/62 Super Rapid; dual purpose; 85° elevation; 120 rounds/minute to 16 km *(8.7 nm)*; weight of shell 6 kg.
2—12.7 mm MGs.
Torpedoes: 2—21 in *(533 mm)* tubes; FFV Type 613; wire-guided passive homing.
Mines: Can be carried.
Countermeasures: MCMV: Ibis 43 minehunting system with Thomson Sintra 2061 tactical system and 2054 sidescan sonar in a towed body.
Decoys: 1 Sea Gnat 6-barrelled launcher for chaff.
ESM: Racal Mermaid or Sabre; radar warning.
Combat data systems: Terma system primarily for control of MCMV robot drones.
Fire control: Bofors Electronic 9LV Mk 3 optronic director. Harpoon to 1A(V) standard.
Radars: Air/surface search: Plessey AWS 6; G band (P 550-P 556).
Telefunken SystemTechnik TRS-3D; G/H band (P 557-P 562).
Navigation: Terma Pilot; E/I band.
Fire control: Philips 9LV 200; J band.
Sonars: Thomson Sintra TSM 2640 hull-mounted and VDS; active search and attack; medium frequency.

Programmes: Standard Flex 300 which has replaced Daphne class (seaward defence craft) and Søløven class (fast attack craft torpedo), and will replace Sund (MCM) class. First batch of seven with option on a further nine contracted with Danyard on 27 July 1985. Second batch of six ordered 14 June 1990. Building rate is two per year completing in 1997 with a total of 14 which is two less than originally planned.
Structure: GRP hulls. Positions prepared to plug in armament and operations rooms containers, extra guns, up to four SSMs, one SAM system, two 533 mm torpedo tubes, ASW and MCM equipment. As MCMVs these ships operate a tethered underwater vehicle for classification and control two surface 'robot' boats each with a Thomson Sintra TSM 2054 sidescan sonar. The controlling radio antenna is fitted on top of the bridge. Details of the robots can be found in the *Mine Warfare Forces* section under SAV class.
Operational: The first seven are equipped for surveillance except that *Flyvefisken* is being fitted out as the prototype MCMV ship. Then four ships have the combat fit of SSM and torpedo tubes, four to be equipped as minehunters and one as a minelayer. In times of tension the surveillance vessels are to be reconfigured for mine warfare or combat. The overall design allows ships to change roles as required. Requirement is to be able to change within 48 hours.

HAVKATTEN (surveillance)   *6/1992, Gunnar Olsen*

FLYVEFISKEN (MCM in 1993)   *6/1992, Gunnar Olsen*

SVAERDFISKEN (surveillance)   *5/1992, Per Kornefeldt*

MRF 1 ROBOT (see *Mine Warfare Forces* section)   *4/1991, Royal Danish Navy*

HAJEN (combat)   *1990, Royal Danish Navy*

160 DENMARK / Light forces

10 WILLEMOES CLASS (FAST ATTACK CRAFT—MISSILE)

Name	No	Builders	Commissioned
BILLE	P 540	Frederikshavn V and F	1 Oct 1976
BREDAL	P 541	Frederikshavn V and F	21 Jan 1977
HAMMER	P 542	Frederikshavn V and F	1 Apr 1977
HUITFELD	P 543	Frederikshavn V and F	15 June 1977
KRIEGER	P 544	Frederikshavn V and F	22 Sep 1977
NORBY	P 545	Frederikshavn V and F	22 Nov 1977
RODSTEEN	P 546	Frederikshavn V and F	16 Feb 1978
SEHESTED	P 547	Frederikshavn V and F	19 May 1978
SUENSON	P 548	Frederikshavn V and F	10 Aug 1978
WILLEMOES	P 549	Frederikshavn V and F	21 June 1976

Displacement, tons: 260 full load
Dimensions, feet (metres): 151 × 24 × 8.2 *(46 × 7.4 × 2.5)*
Main machinery: CODOG; 3 RR 52M/544 gas turbines; 12 750 hp *(9.51 MW)*; 2 GM 8V-71 diesels for cruising on wing shafts; 460 hp *(343 kW)* sustained; 3 shafts; cp props
Speed, knots: 38 (12 on diesels)
Complement: 25 (5 officers)

Missiles: SSM: 4 or 8 McDonnell Douglas Harpoon; active radar homing to 130 km *(70 nm)* at 0.9 Mach; warhead 227 kg.
   Numbers carried depend on task and numbers of torpedoes.
Guns: 1 OTO Melara 3 in *(76 mm)*/62 compact; 85° elevation; 85 rounds/minute to 16 km *(8.7 nm)*; weight of shell 6 kg.
   2 triple 103 mm illumination rocket launchers.
Torpedoes: 2 or 4—21 in *(533 mm)* tubes. FFV Type 61; wire-guided; passive homing to 25 km *(13.7 nm)* at 45 kts; warhead 240 kg.
Countermeasures: Decoys: Sea Gnat chaff dispensers.
   ESM: Racal Cutlass; radar warning.
Combat data systems: EPLO action data automation. Being replaced by Terma.
Radars: Air/surface search: 9GA 208; E/F band.
   Navigation: Terma Elektronik 20T 48 Super; E/I band.
   Fire control: Philips 9LV 200; J band.

Programmes: Designed by Lürssen to Danish order. Very similar to Swedish Spica II class (also Lürssen). Original order to Frederikshavn for four boats, increased to eight and finally ten. *Willemoes* (prototype) laid down in July 1974.
Modernisation: *Norby* has conducted trials with a Simbad light SAM system fitted on the platform aft of the mast. It is reported that this may now be fitted in all of the class in due course probably starting in 1993. Sea Gnat decoy launchers were fitted in 1991/92, otherwise there are no further modernisation plans.
Operational: Patrols do not normally exceed 36 hours. The mix of weapons varies.

3 AGDLEK CLASS (LARGE PATROL CRAFT)

Name	No	Builders	Commissioned
AGDLEK	Y 386	Svendborg Vaerft	12 Mar 1974
AGPA	Y 387	Svendborg Vaerft	14 May 1974
TULUGAQ	Y 388	Svendborg Vaerft	26 June 1979

Displacement, tons: 300; 330 (Y 388) full load
Dimensions, feet (metres): 103 × 25.3 × 11.2 *(31.4 × 7.7 × 3.4)*
Main machinery: 1 Burmeister & Wain Alpha A08-26 VO diesel; 800 hp(m) *(588 kW)*; 1 shaft
Speed, knots: 12
Complement: 14
Guns: 2 Oerlikon 20 mm.
Radars: Surface search: Terma 20T 48 Super; E/I band.
   Navigation: Skanter 009; I band.

Comment: Designed for service off Greenland. Ice strengthened. SATCOM fitted.

TULUGAQ   1990, Royal Danish Navy

9 Ø CLASS (LARGE PATROL CRAFT)

Name	No	Builders	Commissioned
BARSØ	Y 300	Svendborg Vaerft	13 June 1969
DREJØ	Y 301	Svendborg Vaerft	1 July 1969
ROMSØ	Y 302	Svendborg Vaerft	21 July 1969
SAMSØ	Y 303	Svendborg Vaerft	15 Aug 1969
THURØ	Y 304	Svendborg Vaerft	12 Sep 1969
VEJRØ	Y 305	Svendborg Vaerft	17 Oct 1969
FARØ	Y 306	Svendborg Vaerft	17 May 1973
LAESØ	Y 307	Svendborg Vaerft	23 July 1973
ROMØ	Y 308	Svendborg Vaerft	3 Sep 1973

Displacement, tons: 155 full load
Dimensions, feet (metres): 84 × 19.7 × 9.2 *(25.6 × 6 × 2.8)*
Main machinery: 1 diesel; 385 hp(m) *(283 kW)*; 1 shaft
Speed, knots: 11
Complement: 20
Guns: 2 Oerlikon 20 mm (not always fitted). 1—12.7 mm MG.
Radars: Navigation: Skanter 009; I band.

Comment: Rated as patrol cutters. *Laesø* acts as diver support ship with a recompression chamber. The last three have a wheelhouse which extends over the full beam.

FARØ   1988, Royal Danish Navy

SEHESTED   5/1992, Antonio Moreno

HUITFELD   1992, Royal Danish Navy

LAESØ (diver support)   1992, Royal Danish Navy

2 LARGE BOTVED TYPE (COASTAL PATROL CRAFT)

Y 375   Y 376

Displacement, tons: 12 (Y 376); 13.5 (Y 375) full load
Dimensions, feet (metres): 43.6 × 14.8 × 3.7 *(13.3 × 4.5 × 1.1)*
Main machinery: 2 diesels; 680 hp(m) *(500 kW)*; 2 shafts
Speed, knots: 26
Guns: 1—7.62 mm MG
Radars: Navigation: NWS 3; I band.

Comment: Built in 1974 by Botved Boats. Y 375 is 45.9 ft *(14 m)* in length overall having a stern ladder extension for divers.

Y 376   *1988, Royal Danish Navy*

1 Y TYPE (COASTAL PATROL CRAFT)

LUNDEN Y 343

Displacement, tons: 71.5 full load
Dimensions, feet (metres): 64.6 × 17.7 × 9.2 *(19.7 × 5.4 × 2.8)*
Speed, knots: 8
Guns: 1—7.62 mm MG.

Comment: Cutter of a similar type to trawlers MHV 51 and 76, built in 1941.

LUNDEN   *1988, Royal Danish Navy*

NAVAL HOME GUARD

6 MHV 90 CLASS (COASTAL PATROL CRAFT)

BOPA MHV 90   HOLGER DANSKE MHV 92   RINGEN MHV 94
BRIGADEN MHV 91   HVIDSTEN MHV 93   SPEDITØREN MHV 95

Displacement, tons: 85 full load
Dimensions, feet (metres): 64.9 × 18.7 × 8.2 *(19.8 × 5.7 × 2.5)*
Main machinery: 1 Burmeister & Wain diesel; 400 hp(m) *(294 kW)*; 1 shaft
Speed, knots: 11
Guns: 2—7.62 mm MGs.
Radars: Navigation: RM 1290S; I band.

Comment: Built between 1973 and 1975.

HVIDSTEN   *7/1992, Gunnar Olsen*

Light forces— Naval home guard / DENMARK   161

11 KUTTER CLASS (COASTAL PATROL CRAFT)

ANTARES MHV 51   CRUX MHV 64   JUPITER MHV 74
APOLLO MHV 56   DUBHE MHV 66   LUNA MHV 75
BETELGEUSE MHV 61   GEMINI MHV 67   LYRA MHV 76 (ex-Y 339)
CASSIOPEIA MHV 63   HERCULES MHV 73

Displacement, tons: 35 *(Gemini)* full load
Dimensions, feet (metres): 60.4 × 17.1 × 7.5 *(18.4 × 5.2 × 2.3)*
Speed, knots: 9
Guns: 2—7.62 mm MGs.

Comment: Built between 1922 and 1941. Details above apply only to *Gemini* but the rest are similar. Apart from *Hercules* all are veterans of the Second World War. Being paid off as the 800 class come into service.

LUNA   *7/1992, Gunnar Olsen*

3 + 9 (6) MHV 800 CLASS (COASTAL PATROL CRAFT)

Name	No	Builders	Commissioned
ALDEBARAN	MHV 801	Soby Shipyard	9 July 1992
CARINA	MHV 802	Soby Shipyard	30 Sep 1992
ARIES	MHV 803	Soby Shipyard	Mar 1993
ANDROMEDA	MHV 804	Soby Shipyard	Sep 1993
GEMINI	MHV 805	Soby Shipyard	Feb 1994
DUBHE	MHV 806	Soby Shipyard	June 1994

Displacement, tons: 83 full load
Dimensions, feet (metres): 77.8 × 18.4 × 6.6 *(23.7 × 5.6 × 2)*
Main machinery: 2 Saab Scania DSI-14 diesels; 900 hp(m) *(661 kW)*; 2 shafts
Speed, knots: 13. **Range, miles:** 990 at 11 kts
Complement: 8 + 4 spare
Guns: 2—7.62 mm MGs. 2—20 mm (can be fitted).
Radars: Navigation: Furuno 1505; I band.

Comment: A new class of Home Guard patrol craft. First six ordered in April 1991, second six in July 1992. Final total of 25 planned. Steel hulls with a moderate ice capability.

ALDEBARAN   *7/1992, Gunnar Olsen*

ALDEBARAN   *7/1992, Royal Danish Navy*

162 DENMARK / Light forces — Mine warfare forces

7 MHV 80 CLASS (COASTAL PATROL CRAFT)

Name	No	Builders	Commissioned
FAENØ (ex-MHV 69, ex-MS 6)	MHV 80	Denmark	July 1941
ASKØ (ex-Y 386, ex-M 560, ex-MS 2)	MHV 81	Denmark	1 Aug 1941
ENØ (ex-Y 388, ex-M 562, ex-MS 5)	MHV 82	Denmark	18 Aug 1941
MANØ (ex-Y 391, ex-M 566, ex-MS 9)	MHV 83	Denmark	30 Oct 1941
BAAGØ (ex-Y 387, ex-M 561, ex-MS 3)	MHV 84	Denmark	9 Aug 1941
HJORTØ (ex-Y 389, ex-M 564, ex-MS 7)	MHV 85	Denmark	24 Sep 1941
LYØ (ex-Y 390, ex-M 565, ex-MS 8)	MHV 86	Denmark	22 Oct 1941

Displacement, tons: 80 full load
Dimensions, feet (metres): 80.1 × 15.1 × 5.2 *(24.4 × 4.6 × 1.6)*
Main machinery: 1 diesel; 350 hp(m) *(257 kW)*; 1 shaft
Speed, knots: 11
Guns: 2—7.62 mm MGs.
Radars: Navigation: RM 1290S; I band.

Comment: Of wooden construction. All launched in 1941. Former inshore minesweepers.

ENØ *6/1992, van Ginderen Collection*

3 MHV 70 CLASS (COASTAL PATROL CRAFT)

SATURN MHV 70   **SCORPIUS** MHV 71   **SIRIUS** MHV 72

Displacement, tons: 76 full load
Dimensions, feet (metres): 64 × 16.7 × 8.2 *(19.5 × 5.1 × 2.5)*
Main machinery: 1 diesel; 200 hp(m) *(147 kW)*; 1 shaft
Speed, knots: 10
Guns: 2—7.62 mm MGs.
Radars: Navigation: RM 1290S; I band.

Comment: Patrol boats and training craft for the Naval Home Guard. Built in the Royal Dockyard, Copenhagen and commissioned in 1958. Formerly designated DMH, but allocated MHV numbers in 1969.

SCORPIUS *7/1992, Gunnar Olsen*

6 MHV 20 CLASS (COASTAL PATROL CRAFT)

BAUNEN MHV 20	**KUREREN** MHV 22	**PATRIOTEN** MHV 24
BUDSTIKKEN MHV 21	**PARTISAN** MHV 23	**SABOTØREN** MHV 25

Displacement, tons: 60 full load
Dimensions, feet (metres): 54.1 × 13.8 × 4.9 *(16.5 × 4.2 × 1.5)*
Main machinery: 2 MTU diesels; 500 hp(m) *(367 kW)*; 2 shafts
Speed, knots: 15
Complement: 9
Guns: 2—7.62 mm MGs.
Radars: Navigation: Terma 9T48/9; I band.

Comment: Built of GRP by Ejvinds Plastikbodevaerft, Svendborg between 1978 and 1982. Used for patrols in The Sound.

SABOTØREN *8/1991, Gunnar Olsen*

MINE WARFARE FORCES

Note: See also Flyvefisken class under *Light Forces*.

4 FALSTER CLASS (MINELAYERS)

Name	No	Builders	Commissioned
FALSTER	N 80	Nakskov Skibsvaerft	7 Nov 1963
FYEN	N 81	Frederikshavn Vaerft	18 Sep 1963
MØEN	N 82	Frederikshavn Vaerft	29 Apr 1964
SJAELLAND	N 83	Nakskov Skibsvaerft	7 July 1964

Displacement, tons: 1880 full load
Dimensions, feet (metres): 252.6 × 42 × 11.8 *(77 × 12.8 × 3.6)*
Main machinery: 2 GM/EMD 16-567D3 diesels; 4800 hp *(3.58 MW)* sustained; 2 shafts
Speed, knots: 17
Complement: 133 (10 officers)

Guns: 4 US 3 in *(76 mm)*/50 Mk 33 (2 twin); 85° elevation; 25 rounds/minute to 12.8 km *(7 nm)*; weight of shell 6 kg.
  4 Oerlikon 20 mm. To be replaced by 2 twin Stinger SAM mountings.
Mines: 4 rails; 400.
Countermeasures: Decoys: 2—57 mm multiple chaff launchers.
Combat data systems: Terma TDS.
Fire control: Contraves.
Radars: Air/surface search: CWS 2; E/F band.
  Fire control: CGS 1; I band.
  Surface search: NWS 2; I band.
  Navigation: Terma Pilot; E/I band.

Programmes: Ordered in 1960-61 and launched 1962-63. All are named after Danish islands. Similar to Turkish *Nusret*. *Sjaelland* converted in 1976 to act as depot ship for submarines and FAC but retains minelaying capability.
Modernisation: Refitted to allow them to serve until late 1990s; included Terma command and control system. Mine stocks updated in collaboration with Germany. Twin Stinger SAM mountings to be fitted in 1993/94.
Structure: The steel hull is flush-decked with a raking stem, a full stern and a prominent knuckle fwd. The hull has been specially strengthened for ice navigation. In 1987 *Sjaelland* after mast was raised; *Falster* and *Fyen* similarly modified in 1989-91, *Møen* completed in 1993.
Operational: *Sjaelland* is used as a Command ship. *Møen* and sometimes *Fyen* employed on midshipmen's training.

FALSTER (new guns) *1992, Royal Danish Navy*

SJAELLAND *10/1991, Erik Laursen*

2 LINDORMEN CLASS (COASTAL MINELAYERS)

Name	No	Builders	Commissioned
LINDORMEN	N 43	Svendborg Vaerft	16 Feb 1978
LOSSEN	N 44	Svendborg Vaerft	14 June 1978

Displacement, tons: 570 full load
Dimensions, feet (metres): 146 × 29.5 × 8 *(44.5 × 9 × 2.6)*
Main machinery: 2 Frichs diesels; 1600 hp(m) *(1.2 MW)*; 2 shafts
Speed, knots: 14
Complement: 30
Guns: 3 Oerlikon 20 mm.
Mines: 50-60 (depending on type).
Radars: NWS 3; I band.

Comment: Controlled Minelayers. *Lindormen* laid down on 2 February 1977, launched on 7 June 1977 and *Lossen* laid down on 9 July 1977, launched on 11 October 1977.

MRF 1   *4/1991, Royal Danish Navy*

SERVICE FORCES

Note: There is a road-borne support unit (MOBA) for the Fast Attack Craft with two sections. The first, of eight vehicles with radar, W/T and control offices is MOBA (Ops) and the second, of 25 vehicles for stores, fuel, provisions, torpedoes and workshops is MOBA (Log).

Name	No	Builders	Commissioned
SLEIPNER	A 559	Åbenrå Vaerft og A/S	18 July 1986

Displacement, tons: 150 full load
Dimensions, feet (metres): 119.6 × 24.9 × 8.8 *(36.5 × 7.6 × 2.7)*
Main machinery: 1 Callesen diesel; 1 shaft
Speed, knots: 11
Complement: 6
Cargo capacity: 150 tons

LOSSEN   *1992, Royal Danish Navy*

2 Ex-US BLUEBIRD CLASS (SUND CLASS)
(Ex-AMS) (MINESWEEPERS—COASTAL)

Name	No	Builders	Commissioned
GRØNSUND (ex-*MSC 256*)	M 574	USA	21 Sep 1956
VILSUND (ex-*MSC 264*)	M 578	USA	15 Nov 1956

Displacement, tons: 350 standard; 376 full load
Dimensions, feet (metres): 147.6 × 27.9 × 8.5 *(45 × 8.5 × 2.6)*
Main machinery: 2 GM 8-268A diesels; 880 hp *(656 kW)*; 2 shafts
Speed, knots: 13. **Range, miles:** 3000 at 10 kts
Complement: 35
Guns: 1 Bofors 40 mm/60.
Radars: Navigation: Terma Pilot; E/I band.

Comment: MSC (ex-AMS) 60 class NATO coastal minesweepers. *Grønsund* has been fitted with a charthouse between bridge and funnel, and has been employed on surveying duties. *Vilsund* has a deckhouse abaft the bridge after modernisation in 1985. Being replaced by Flyvefisken class.

SLEIPNER   *5/1990, Gilbert Gyssels*

2 Ex-US YO 65 CLASS (TANKERS)

Name	No	Builders	Commissioned
RIMFAXE (ex-US YO 226)	A 568	Jefferson Bridge & Machine Co, USA	2 Nov 1945
SKINFAXE (ex-US YO 229)	A 569	Jefferson Bridge & Machine Co, USA	7 Dec 1945

Displacement, tons: 1400 full load
Dimensions, feet (metres): 174 × 32.9 × 13.3 *(53.1 × 10 × 4.1)*
Main machinery: 1 GM diesel; 560 hp *(418 kW)*; 1 shaft
Speed, knots: 10
Complement: 19
Cargo capacity: 900 tons fuel
Guns: 1 Oerlikon 20 mm.

Comment: Transferred from the USA on 2 August 1962. Act as tenders for the Willemoes class.

GRØNSUND   *5/1992, Wright & Logan*

2 + (10) SAV CLASS (MINESWEEPER—DRONES)

MRF 1   MRF 2

Displacement, tons: 32 full load
Dimensions, feet (metres): 59.7 × 15.6 × 3.9 *(18.2 × 4.8 × 1.2)*
Main machinery: 1 Schottel pump jet propulsor
Speed, knots: 12
Combat data systems: Terma link to Flyvefisken class (in MCMV configuration).
Radars: Navigation: Furuno; I band.
Sonars: Thomson Sintra TSM 2054 sidescan; high frequency active.

Comment: Being built by Danyard with GRP hulls. First one completed in March 1991, second in December 1991. Trials continue into 1993. If satisfactory it is planned to order 10 more of the class. The vessels are robot drones (or Surface Auxiliary Vessels (SAV)) operated in pairs by the Flyvefisken class in MCMV configuration. Hull is based on the Hugin class TRVs with low noise propulsion. The towfish with sidescan sonar is lowered and raised from the stern-mounted gantry. Further trials in 1993 include the Sutec Double Sea Eagle ROV.

RIMFAXE   *1990, Royal Danish Navy*

1 ROYAL YACHT

Name	No	Builders	Commissioned
DANNEBROG	A 540	R Dockyard, Copenhagen	20 May 1932

Displacement, tons: 1130 full load
Dimensions, feet (metres): 246 × 34 × 12.1 *(75 × 10.4 × 3.7)*
Main machinery: 2 Burmeister & Wain Alpha T23L-KVO diesels; 1800 hp(m) *(1.32 MW)*; 2 shafts; cp props
Speed, knots: 14
Complement: 55
Guns: 2—37 mm saluting guns.

Comment: Laid down 2 January 1931, launched on 10 October 1931. Major refit 1980 included new engines and electrical gear. SATCOM fitted in 1992.

DANNEBROG 6/1992, Gunnar Olsen

1 MINE TRANSPORT

Name	No	Builders	Commissioned
MSA 4	(ex-MK 5, ex-Y 383)	Holbaek Bädevaerft	1949

Displacement, tons: 34 full load
Dimensions, feet (metres): 62.3 × 13.8 × 4.9 *(19 × 4.2 × 1.5)*
Main machinery: 1 diesel; 1 shaft
Speed, knots: 8

MSA 4 1992, Royal Danish Navy

3 HUGIN CLASS (TORPEDO RECOVERY VESSELS)

HUGIN TO 8   MUNIN TO 9   MIMER TO 10

Displacement, tons: 23 full load
Dimensions, feet (metres): 53.1 × 13.8 × 3.9 *(16.2 × 4.2 × 1.2)*
Main machinery: 1 MWM diesel; 450 hp(m) *(330 kW)*; 1 shaft
Speed, knots: 15

Comment: Built by Ejvinds, Svenborg. The same hull, slightly lengthened, is the basis of the robot boats for MCM systems.

MUNIN 1988, Royal Danish Navy

2 HARBOUR TUGS

BALDER   HERMOD

Dimensions, feet (metres): 39 × 13.1 × 3.9 *(11.9 × 4 × 1.2)*
Main machinery: 1 GM diesel; 300 hp *(224 kW)*; 1 shaft
Speed, knots: 8.5

Comment: Berthing tugs based at Korsør. Built in 1983 at Assens.

HERMOD 8/1991, Gunnar Olsen

ICEBREAKERS

Note: Icebreakers, once controlled by the Ministry of Trade and Shipping are being transferred to the Navy but will continue to have a combined naval and civilian crew. Maintenance is done at Frederikshavn in Summer. During Summer period one icebreaker may be employed on surveying duties in Danish waters for the Administration of Navigation and Hydrography.

Name	No	Builders	Commissioned
THORBJØRN	—	Svendborg Vaerft	1981

Displacement, tons: 2344 full load
Dimensions, feet (metres): 221.4 × 50.2 × 15.4 *(67.5 × 15.3 × 4.7)*
Main machinery: Diesel-electric; 4 Burmeister & Wain Alpha diesels; 6800 hp(m) *(5 MW)*; 2 motors; 2 shafts
Speed, knots: 16.5
Complement: 29 (8 officers)

Comment: No bow thruster. Side rolling tanks. Fitted for surveying duties in non-ice periods.

THORBJØRN 7/1990, A Sheldon Duplaix

Name	No	Builders	Commissioned
DANBJØRN	—	Lindø Vaerft, Odense	1965
ISBJØRN	—	Lindø Vaerft, Odense	1966

Displacement, tons: 3685
Dimensions, feet (metres): 252 × 56 × 20 *(76.8 × 17.1 × 6.1)*
Main machinery: Diesel-electric; 2 diesel generators; 10 500 hp(m) *(7.72 MW)*; 2 shafts
Speed, knots: 14
Complement: 34

ISBJØRN 6/1990, van Ginderen Collection

Name	No	Builders	Commissioned
ELBJØRN	—	Frederikshavn Vaerft	1966

Displacement, tons: 893 standard; 1400 full load
Dimensions, feet (metres): 156.5 × 40.3 × 14.5 *(47 × 12.1 × 4.4)*
Main machinery: Diesel-electric; 2 diesel generators; 3600 hp(m) *(2.64 MW)*; 2 shafts
Speed, knots: 12

ELBJØRN 7/1990, A Sheldon Duplaix

FISHERY PROTECTION

4 RESCUE VESSELS

NORDJYLLAND NORDSØEN VESTKYSTEN JENS VAEVER

Displacement, tons: 475; 657 (*Vestkysten*); 141 (*Jens Vaever*)
Dimensions, feet (metres): 134.5 × 32.8 × 13 *(41 × 10 × 4)*
163.7 × 32.8 × 10.8 *(49.9 × 10 × 3.3)* (*Vestkysten*)
95.1 × 19.7 × 9.8 *(29 × 6 × 3)* (*Jens Vaever*)

Comment: Three for the North Sea, one for the Baltic. *Jens Vaever* commissioned 1960; *Nordjylland* 1967 and *Nordsøen* 1968. *Vestkysten* commissioned in 1987 and replaced the old ship of the same name.

NORDSØEN 1/1992, Harald Carstens

TRAINING AND SURVEY VESSELS

Notes: 1. *Thorbjorn* also used as a survey ship.
2. There are two small Sail Training Ships, *Svanen* Y 101 and *Thyra* Y 102.

SKB 1 SKB 2 SKB 4

Displacement, tons: 27
Speed, knots: 9

Comment: Built 1958-68. Length 42.7 ft *(13 m)*. Training vessels.

SKB 1 7/1991, Antonio Moreno

SKA 11 12 13 14 15 16

Displacement, tons: 52
Dimensions, feet (metres): 65.6 × 17.1 × 6.9 *(20 × 5.2 × 2.1)*
Main machinery: 1 GM diesel; 540 hp *(403 kW)*; 1 shaft
Speed, knots: 12
Complement: 6 (1 officer)

Comment: GRP hulls. Built 1981-84. Have red hulls. Survey motor launches.

SKA 11 1989, Royal Danish Navy

ENVIRONMENT CRAFT

2 POLLUTION CONTROL CRAFT

MILJØ 101 and 102

Displacement, tons: 16 full load
Dimensions, feet (metres): 53.8 × 14.4 × 7.1 *(16.2 × 4.2 × 2.2)*
Main machinery: 1 MWM TBD232V12 diesel; 454 hp(m) *(334 kW)* sustained; 1 shaft
Speed, knots: 15. **Range, miles:** 350 at 8 kts
Complement: 3

Comment: Built by Ejvinds Plastikbodevaerft, Svendborg. Carry derricks and booms for framing oil slicks and dispersant fluids. Naval manned. Delivered 1 November and 1 December 1977.

MILJØ 102 1987, Royal Danish Navy

2 SEA TRUCKS

METTE MILJØ MARIE MILJØ

Displacement, tons: 157 full load
Dimensions, feet (metres): 97.7 × 26.2 × 5.2 *(29.8 × 8 × 1.6)*
Main machinery: 2 Grenaa diesels; 660 hp(m) *(485 kW)*; 2 shafts
Speed, knots: 10
Complement: 8

Comment: Built by Carl B Hoffmann A/S, Esbjerg and Søren Larsen & Sønners Skibsvaerft A/S, Nykøbing Mors. Delivered 22 February 1980. Have orange and yellow superstructure.

METTE MILJØ 5/1991, Gunnar Olsen

2 OIL POLLUTION CRAFT

GUNNAR THORSON   GUNNAR SEIDENFADEN

Displacement, tons: 750 full load
Dimensions, feet (metres): 183.7 × 40.3 × 12.8 *(56 × 12.3 × 3.9)*
Main machinery: 2 Burmeister and Wain Alpha diesels; 2320 hp(m) *(1.7 MW)*; 2 shafts
Speed, knots: 12.5
Complement: 17

Comment: Built by Ørnskov Stålskibsvaerft, Frederikshavn. Delivered May and July 1981 respectively. *G Thorson* at Copenhagen, *G Seidenfaden* at Korsør. Carry firefighting equipment. Large hydraulic crane fitted in 1988 for the secondary task of buoy tending. Orange painted hulls.

GUNNAR SEIDENFADEN   *1988, Royal Danish Navy*

DJIBOUTI

Headquarters' Appointment

Commander of the Navy:
  Colonel Ahmad Hossein

Personnel

1993: 92

Base

Djibouti

French Navy

The permanent French naval contingent usually includes a command ship, four frigates, EDIC 9091, three small landing craft and two repair ships.

Mercantile Marine

Lloyd's Register of Shipping:
  10 vessels of 3642 tons gross

LIGHT FORCES

2 PLASCOA CLASS (COASTAL PATROL CRAFT)

MOUSSA ALI   P 10   MONT ARREH   P 11

Displacement, tons: 35 full load
Dimensions, feet (metres): 75.5 × 18 × 4.9 *(23 × 5.5 × 1.5)*
Main machinery: 2 SACM Poyaud diesels; 1700 hp(m) *(1.25 MW)*; 2 shafts
Speed, knots: 25. **Range, miles:** 750 at 12 kts
Complement: 15
Guns: 1 Giat 20 mm. 1 Browning 12.7 mm MG.
Radars: Navigation: Decca; I band.

Comment: Completed by Plascoa, Cannes on 8 June 1985 (P 10) and 16 February 1986 (P 11) as gift from France. GRP hulls.

3 SEA RIDERS and 2 ZODIACS

Comment: Rigid inflatable craft acquired from UK 25 October 1988.

1 TECIMAR CLASS (COASTAL PATROL CRAFT)

ZENA

Displacement, tons: 30 full load
Dimensions, feet (metres): 43.6 × 13.8 × 3.6 *(13.3 × 4.2 × 1.1)*
Main machinery: 2 GM 6V 71 diesels; 480 hp(m) *(350 kW)*; 2 shafts
Speed, knots: 25
Guns: 1—12.7 mm MG. 1—7.62 mm MG.

Comment: Built in 1974 and transferred by France after Declaration of Independence in 1977.

5 SAWARI CLASS (INSHORE PATROL CRAFT)

Displacement, tons: 7 full load
Dimensions, feet (metres): 36.1 × 8.2 × 2 *(11 × 2.5 × 0.6)*
Speed, knots: 22

Comment: Acquired from Iraq in 1989. Can be armed with MGs and rocket launchers. Outboard engines.

DOMINICA

Headquarters' Appointments

Commissioner of Police:
  D Blanchard
RN Liaison Officer:
  Lieutenant Commander B W Halliday
Head of Coast Guard:
  Sergeant Frederick

General

An independent island in the British Commonwealth situated north of Martinique.

Personnel

1993: 32

Bases

Roseau, Portsmouth, Ange-de-Mai

Mercantile Marine

Lloyd's Register of Shipping:
  7 vessels of 2107 tons gross

1 SWIFT 65 ft CLASS

MELVILLE   D 4

Displacement, tons: 33
Dimensions, feet (metres): 64.9 × 18.4 × 6.6 *(19.8 × 5.6 × 2)*
Main machinery: 2 Detroit 12V-71TA diesels; 840 hp *(616 kW)* sustained; 2 shafts
Speed, knots: 23. **Range, miles:** 500 at 18 kts
Complement: 10
Radars: Navigation: Furuno; I/J band.

Comment: Ordered from Swiftships, Morgan City in November 1983. Commissioned 1 May 1984. Similar craft supplied to Antigua and St Lucia.

2 PATROL CRAFT

VIGILANCE   OBSERVER

Displacement, tons: 2.4 full load
Dimensions, feet (metres): 27 × 8.4 × 1 *(8.2 × 2.6 × 0.3)*
Main machinery: 1 Johnson outboard motor; 225 hp *(168 kW)* sustained
Speed, knots: 28
Complement: 3

Comment: Boston Whalers acquired in 1988.

MELVILLE   *1989, Dominica CG*

VIGILANCE   *1989, Dominica CG*

DOMINICAN REPUBLIC

Headquarters' Appointments

Chief of Naval Staff:
Vice Admiral Ivan Vargas Cespedes
Vice Chief of Naval Staff:
Rear Admiral Victor F Garcia Alecont

Personnel

(a) 1993: 3900 officers and men (including naval infantry)
(b) Selective military service

Bases

27 de Febrero, Santo Domingo: HQ of CNS, Naval School. Supply base.
Las Calderas: Las Calderas, Bani: Naval dockyard, 700 ton synchrolift. Training centre. Supply base.
Haina: Dockyard facility. Supply base.
Puerto Plata. Small naval base.

General

Not all the ships listed are operational. Some of the older vessels are seaworthy but of questionable fighting capability.

Mercantile Marine

Lloyd's Register of Shipping:
28 vessels of 11 574 tons gross

DELETION

1990 Atlantida

FRIGATE

1 Ex-CANADIAN RIVER CLASS

Name	No	Builders	Laid down	Launched	Commissioned
MELLA (ex-*Presidente Trujillo*, ex-HMCS *Carlplace*)	F 451	Davie S B & Repairing Co, Lauzon, Canada	30 Nov 1943	6 July 1944	13 Dec 1944

Displacement, tons: 1445 standard; 2125 full load
Dimensions, feet (metres): 304 × 37.5 × 12.5 *(92.7 × 11.4 × 4.1)*
Main machinery: 2 boilers; 2 triple expansion reciprocating engines; 5500 ihp *(4.1 MW)*; 2 shafts
Speed, knots: 20. **Range, miles:** 7200 at 12 kts
Complement: 195 (15 officers, 50 midshipmen)
Guns: 1 Vickers 4 in *(102 mm)*/45 Mk 23; 80° elevation; 16 rounds/minute to 19 km *(10.4 nm)*; weight of shell 16 kg. Fitted for 2—40 mm (twin) and 4—20 mm but these are not all always carried.
2—47 mm saluting guns.
Radars: Navigation: Raytheon SPS 64; I band.

Programmes: Transferred to the Dominican Navy in 1946. Pennant number as a frigate was F 101, but now carries pennant number 451 as flagship of Dominican naval forces. Renamed *Mella* in 1962.
Structure: Modified for use as Presidential yacht with extra accommodation and deckhouses built up aft in place of some armament.
Operational: Used by staff in naval operations and as a cadet training ship.

MELLA *1/1993, A Sheldon Duplaix*

CORVETTES

3 Ex-US COHOES CLASS

Name	No	Builders	Commissioned
CAMBIASO (ex-USS *Etlah* AN 79)	P 207	Marietta Manufacturing Co	16 Apr 1945
SEPARACION (ex-USS *Passaconaway* AN 86)	P 208	Marine S B Co	27 Apr 1945
CALDERAS (ex-USS *Passaic* AN 87)	P 209	Leatham D Smith S B Co	6 Mar 1945

Displacement, tons: 650 standard; 855 full load
Dimensions, feet (metres): 162.3 × 33.8 × 11.7 *(49.5 × 10.3 × 3.6)*
Main machinery: Diesel-electric; 2 Busch-Sulzer BS-539 diesels; 1500 hp(m) *(1.1 MW)*; 2 generators; 1 motor; 1 shaft
Speed, knots: 12
Complement: 64 (5 officers)
Guns: 2—3 in *(76 mm)*. 3 Oerlikon 20 mm.

Comment: Ex-netlayers in reserve in USA by 1963. Transferred by sale on 29 September 1976. Now used for patrol duties. P 207 and 208 modified in 1980 with the removal of the bow horns. P209 has only one 76 mm gun and is used as a survey ship.

PRESTOL *1/1993, A Sheldon Duplaix*

SEPARACION *6/1989, Hartmut Ehlers*

2 Ex-US ADMIRABLE CLASS

Name	No	Builders	Commissioned
PRESTOL (ex-*Separacion*, ex-USS *Skirmish* MSF 303)	BM 454	Associated SB	16 Aug 1943
TORTUGUERO (ex-USS *Signet* MSF 302)	BM 455	Associated SB	16 Aug 1943

Displacement, tons: 650 standard; 900 full load
Dimensions, feet (metres): 184.5 × 33 × 14.4 *(56.3 × 10.1 × 4.4)*
Main machinery: 2 Cooper-Bessemer GSB8 diesels; 1710 hp *(1.28 MW)*; 2 shafts
Speed, knots: 15. **Range, miles:** 4300 at 10 kts
Complement: 90 (8 officers)
Guns: 1—3 in *(76 mm)*/50. 2 Bofors 40 mm/60. 6 Oerlikon 20 mm.
Radars: Surface search: SPS 69; I band.

Comment: Former US fleet minesweepers. Purchased on 13 January 1965. BM 454 renamed early 1976. Sweep-gear removed. Classified as Cañoneros.

LIGHT FORCES

3 (RESERVE) Ex-USCG ARGO CLASS (LARGE PATROL CRAFT)

Name	No	Builders	Commissioned
INDÉPENDENCIA (ex-USCGC *Icarus*)	P 204 (ex-P 105)	Bath Iron Works	1932
LIBERTAD (ex-*Rafael Atoa*, ex-USCGC *Thetis*)	P 205 (ex-P 106)	Bath Iron Works	1931
RESTAURACION (ex-USCGC *Galatea*)	P 206 (ex-P 104)	John H Mathis & Co, Camden, NJ	1933

Displacement, tons: 337 standard
Dimensions, feet (metres): 165 × 25.2 × 9.5 *(50.3 × 7.7 × 2.9)*
Main machinery: 2 diesels; 1280 hp *(955 kW)*; 2 shafts
Speed, knots: 15. **Range, miles:** 1300 at 15 kts
Complement: 49 (5 officers)
Guns: 1—3 in *(76 mm)*. 1 Bofors 40 mm/60. 2 Oerlikon 20 mm.

Comment: Ex-US Coast Guard Cutters. Rebuilt in 1975. In reserve and may not go to sea again.

INDÉPENDENCIA *1982, Dominican Navy*

168　DOMINICAN REPUBLIC / Light forces — Auxiliaries

1 LARGE PATROL CRAFT

Name	No	Builders	Commissioned
CAPITAN ALSINA (ex-RL 101)	GC 105	—	1944

Displacement, tons: 100 standard
Dimensions, feet (metres): 104.8 × 19.2 × 5.8 *(32 × 5.9 × 1.8)*
Main machinery: 2 GM diesels; 1000 hp *(746 kW)*; 2 shafts
Speed, knots: 17
Complement: 20
Guns: 2 Oerlikon 20 mm.

Comment: Former US SAR craft of wooden construction. Launched in 1944. Renamed in 1957. Rebuilt 1977 and used as an alongside training vessel.

CAPITAN ALSINA

2 SWIFTSHIPS 110 ft CLASS (LARGE PATROL CRAFT)

Name	No	Builders	Commissioned
CANOPUS	GC 107	Swiftships, Morgan City	June 1984
ORION	GC 109	Swiftships, Morgan City	Aug 1984

Displacement, tons: 93.5 full load
Dimensions, feet (metres): 109.9 × 23.9 × 5.9 *(33.5 × 7.3 × 1.8)*
Main machinery: 3 Detroit 12V-92TA diesels; 1020 hp *(760 kW)* sustained; 3 shafts
Speed, knots: 23. **Range, miles:** 1500 at 12 kts
Complement: 19 (3 officers)
Guns: 1 Bofors 40 mm/60. 2—12.7 mm MGs.

Comment: Built of aluminium.

ORION　　　　　　　　　　　　　　　　　　　　　1/1993, A Sheldon Duplaix

4 BELLATRIX CLASS (COASTAL PATROL CRAFT)

Name	No	Builders	Commissioned
PROCION	GC 103	Sewart Seacraft Inc, Berwick, La.	1967
ALDEBARÁN	GC 104	Sewart Seacraft Inc, Berwick, La.	1972
BELLATRIX	GC 106	Sewart Seacraft Inc, Berwick, La.	1967
CAPELLA	GC 108	Sewart Seacraft Inc, Berwick, La.	1968

Displacement, tons: 60
Dimensions, feet (metres): 85 × 18 × 5 *(25.9 × 5.5 × 1.5)*
Main machinery: 2 GM 16V-71 diesels; 811 hp *(605 kW)* sustained; 2 shafts
Speed, knots: 18.7. **Range, miles:** 800 at 15 kts
Complement: 12
Guns: 3—12.7 mm MGs.

Comment: Transferred to the Dominican Navy by the USA. *Procion* and *Capella* are probably non-operational in 1993.

ALDEBARÁN　　　　　　　　　　　　　　　　　　6/1989, Hartmut Ehlers

1 US PGM 71 CLASS (LARGE PATROL CRAFT)

Name	No	Builders	Commissioned
BETELGEUSE (ex-US PGM 77)	GC 102	Peterson, USA	1966

Displacement, tons: 130 standard; 145 full load
Dimensions, feet (metres): 101.5 × 21 × 5 *(30.9 × 6.4 × 1.5)*
Main machinery: 2 Caterpillar D 348 diesels; 1450 hp *(1.08 MW)* sustained; 2 shafts
Speed, knots: 21. **Range, miles:** 1500 at 10 kts
Complement: 20
Guns: 1 Oerlikon 20 mm. 2—12.7 mm MGs.

Comment: Built in the USA and transferred to the Dominican Republic under the Military Aid Programme on 14 January 1966.

1 COASTAL PATROL CRAFT

LUPERON GC 110

Comment: This is not a Swiftships 110 ft class as previously listed. Length about 60 ft *(18 m)*.

LAND-BASED MARITIME AIRCRAFT (FRONT LINE)

Numbers/Type: 2 Aerospatiale SA 316B Alouette III.
Operational speed: 113 kts *(210 km/h)*.
Service ceiling: 10 500 ft *(3200 m)*.
Range: 290 nm *(540 km)*.
Role/Weapon systems: Operated by air force liaison and SAR tasks. Sensors: None. Weapons: Possibly 7.62 mm machine gun.

Numbers/Type: 7 Cessna T-41D.
Operational speed: 102 kts *(188 km/h)*.
Service ceiling: 13 100 ft *(3995 m)*.
Range: 535 nm *(990 km)*.
Role/Weapon systems: Inshore/coastal reconnaissance reporting role; also used for training. Sensors: Hand-held cameras only. Weapons: Unarmed.

AUXILIARIES

1 LCU

Name	No	Builders	Commissioned
SAMANA (ex-LA 2)	LDM 302	Ast Navales Dominicanos	1958

Displacement, tons: 150 standard; 310 full load
Dimensions, feet (metres): 119.5 × 36 × 3 *(36.4 × 11 × 0.9)*
Main machinery: 3 GM 6X4NY diesels; 441 hp *(329 kW)*; 3 shafts
Speed, knots: 8
Complement: 17
Guns: 1—12.7 mm MG.

Comment: Similar characteristics to US LCT 5 type although slightly larger. Oil fuel, 80 tons.

SAMANA　　　　　　　　　　　　　　　　　　　1972, Dominican Navy

1 SURVEY CRAFT

Name	No	Builders	Commissioned
NEPTUNO (ex-Toro)	BA 10	John H Mathis, New Jersey	Feb 1954

Displacement, tons: 72 full load
Dimensions, feet (metres): 64 × 18.1 × 8 *(19.5 × 5.7 × 2.4)*
Main machinery: 1 GM 6-71 diesel; 174 hp *(130 kW)* sustained; 1 shaft
Speed, knots: 10
Complement: 7 (1 officer)

Comment: Deleted in error in 1989. Also used as a buoy tender.

NEPTUNO　　　　　　　　　　　　　　　　　　11/1990, Hartmut Ehlers

Auxiliaries — Floating dock / DOMINICAN REPUBLIC 169

1 Ex-US OIL BARGE

Name	No	Builders	Commissioned
CAPITAN BEOTEGUI (ex-US *YO 215*)	BT 5	Ira S Bushey, Brooklyn	17 Dec 1945

Displacement, tons: 422 light; 1400 full load
Dimensions, feet (metres): 174 × 32.9 × 13.3 *(53.1 × 10 × 4.1)*
Main machinery: 1 Union diesel; 525 hp *(392 kW)*; 1 shaft
Speed, knots: 8
Complement: 23
Cargo capacity: 6570 barrels
Guns: 2 Oerlikon 20 mm.

Comment: Former US self-propelled fuel oil barge. Lent by the USA in April 1964. Lease renewed 31 December 1980. Sister ship sank 21 February 1989.

CAPITAN BEOTEGUI *1/1993, A. Sheldon Duplaix*

TRAINING SHIPS AND TENDERS

Note: In addition to those listed below there are various tenders mostly acquired 1986-88: *Cojinoa* BA 01, *Bonito* BA 02, *Beata* BA 14, *Albacora* BA 18, *Salinas* BA 19, *Carey* BA 20.

Name	No	Builders	Commissioned
CARITE	BA 3	Ast Navales Dominicanos	1975
ATÚN	BA 6	Ast Navales Dominicanos	1975
PICÚA	BA 9	Ast Navales Dominicanos	1975
JUREL	BA 15	Ast Navales Dominicanos	1975

Displacement, tons: 24
Dimensions, feet (metres): 45 × 13 × 6.6 *(13.7 × 4 × 1.9)*
Main machinery: 1 GM diesel; 101 hp *(75 kW)*; 1 shaft
Speed, knots: 9
Complement: 4
Guns: 1—7.62 mm MG.

Comment: Auxiliary sailing craft with a sail area of 750 sq ft and a cargo capacity of 7 tons. Used for training. There may be more of this class.

NUBE DEL MAR BA 7

Displacement, tons: 40
Dimensions, feet (metres): 42 × 12 × 1 *(12.8 × 3.6 × 0.3)*
Main machinery: 1 Volvo MD21A; 75 hp *(55 kW)* maximum; 1 shaft
Speed, knots: 10

Comment: Auxiliary yacht used for sail training at the Naval School. Completed 1979.

TUGS

1 Ex-US CHEROKEE CLASS

Name	No	Builders	Commissioned
MACORIX (ex-USS *Kiowa* ATF 72)	RM 21	Charleston S B and D D Co	7 June 1943

Displacement, tons: 1235 standard; 1675 full load
Dimensions, feet (metres): 205 × 38.5 × 15.5 *(62.5 × 11.7 × 4.7)*
Main machinery: Diesel-electric; 4 GM 12-278 diesels; 4400 hp *(3.28 MW)*; 4 generators; 1 motor; 3000 hp *(2.24 MW)*; 1 shaft
Speed, knots: 16.5
Complement: 85
Guns: 1 US 3 in *(76 mm)*/50. 1 Oerlikon 20 mm.
Radars: Navigation: Raytheon SPS 5D; G/H band.

Comment: Carries additional salvage equipment. Transferred on 6 October 1972. Lease renewed 31 December 1980.

MACORIX *1975, Dominican Navy*

2 Ex-US SOTOYOMO CLASS

Name	No	Builders	Commissioned
CAONABO (ex-USS *Sagamore* ATA 208)	RM 18	Gulfport Boiler and Welding Works	19 Mar 1945
ENRIQUILLO (ex-USS *Stallion* ATA 193)	RM 22	Levington S B Co, Orange, Texas	26 Feb 1945

Displacement, tons: 534 standard; 860 full load
Dimensions, feet (metres): 143 × 33.9 × 13 *(43.6 × 10.3 × 4)*
Main machinery: Diesel-electric; 2 GM 12-278A diesels; 2200 hp *(1.64 MW)*; 2 generators; 1 motor; 1500 hp *(1.12 MW)*; 1 shaft
Speed, knots: 13
Complement: 45
Guns: 1 US 3 in *(76 mm)* (RM 18). 2 Oerlikon 20 mm (RM 22).
Radars: Surface search: Raytheon SPS 5D; G/H band.

Comment: RM 18 transferred on lease 1 February 1972 and RM 22 transferred by sale 30 October 1980.

ENRIQUILLO *6/1989, Hartmut Ehlers*

2 HERCULES CLASS

Name	No	Builders	Commissioned
HERCULES (ex-*R 2*)	RP 12	Ast Navales Dominicanos	1960
GUACANAGARIX (ex-*R 5*)	RP 13	Ast Navales Dominicanos	1960

Displacement, tons: 200 approx
Dimensions, feet (metres): 70 × 15.6 × 9 *(21.4 × 4.8 × 2.7)*
Main machinery: 1 Caterpillar diesel; 500 hp *(373 kW)*; 1 shaft
Complement: 8

1 LCU TUG

Name	No	Builders	Commissioned
OCOA	LDP 303	Ast Navales Dominicanos	1976

Displacement, tons: 50 full load
Dimensions, feet (metres): 56.2 × 14 × 3.9 *(17.1 × 4.3 × 1.2)*
Main machinery: 2 GM 6-71 diesels; 348 hp *(260 kW)* sustained; 2 shafts
Speed, knots: 9. **Range, miles:** 130 at 9 kts
Complement: 5
Cargo capacity: 30 tons

Comment: Converted for use as a tug, retaining bow ramp.

OCOA *1979, Dominican Navy*

2 HARBOUR TUGS

BOHECHIO (ex-US *YTL 600*) RP 16   CAYACCA RP 19

Comment: Small tugs for harbour and coastal use. Not of uniform type and dimensions. RP 16 transferred January 1971. Lease extended 31 December 1980.

FLOATING DOCK

1 FLOATING DOCK

ENDEAVOR   DF 1 (ex-AFDL 1)

Comment: Lift, 1000 tons. Commissioned in 1943. Transferred on loan 8 March 1986.

ECUADOR

Headquarters' Appointments

Commander-in-Chief of the Navy:
　Rear Admiral Yezid Jaramillo Santos
Chief of Naval Operations:
　Rear Admiral Jorge Donoso Moran
Chief of Naval Staff:
　Rear Admiral Oswaldo Viteri Jerez
Chief of Naval Personnel:
　Rear Admiral Belisario Pinto Tapia
Chief of Naval Materiel:
　Captain Enrique Monteverde

Diplomatic Representation

Naval Attaché in Rome and Bonn:
　Captain Edgar Guerra
Naval Attaché in London and Paris:
　Captain Jaime Samaniego
Naval Attaché in Washington:
　Captain Jorge Endara

Personnel

(a) 1993: Total 8000 including 1900 marines
(b) 1 years' selective national service

Bases

Guayaquil (main naval base), Jaramijo, Salinas.
San Lorenzo and Galapagos Islands (small bases).

Establishments

The Naval Academy in Salinas; Naval War College and Merchant Navy Academy in Guayaquil.

Naval Aviation

Naval Aviation wing is based at Guayaquil Air Base. Annual budget comprises 5-7.5 per cent of naval budget.
Personnel: 35 pilots, 75 aircrew, and 200 enlisted maintenance/other rating. Pilot training is conducted at foreign flight training facilities.

Naval Infantry

A force of naval infantry is based at Guayaquil, on the Galapagos Islands and at Oriente (Esmeraldas Manta).

Coast Guard

Small force formed in 1980.

Prefix to Ships' Names

BAE

Strength of the Fleet

Type	Active
Patrol Submarines	2
Frigates	2
Corvettes	6
Fast Attack Craft (Missile)	6
LST	1
Depot Ship	1
Survey Vessels	2
Tugs	9
Floating Docks	2
Sail Training Ship	1
Coast Guard Craft	27

Mercantile Marine

Lloyd's Register of Shipping:
　154 vessels of 369 902 tons gross

DELETIONS

Frigates

1991　*Presidente Eloy Alfaro* (old)

Coast Guard

1992　*9 de Octubre* (old)

PENNANT LIST

Submarines

S 101	Shyri
S 102	Huancavilca

Frigates

FM 01	Presidente Eloy Alfaro (new)
FM 02	Moran Valverde (new)

Corvettes

CM 11	Esmeraldas
CM 12	Manabi
CM 13	Los Rios
CM 14	El Oro
CM 15	Los Galapagos
CM 16	Loja

Light Forces

LM 21	Quito
LM 23	Guayaquil
LM 24	Cuenca
LM 25	Manta
LM 26	Tulcan
LM 27	Nuevo Rocafuerte

Amphibious Forces

TR 61	Hualcopo

Survey/Research Vessels

BI 91	Orion
LH 94	Rigel

Tugs

RA 70	Chimborazo
RA 71	Cayambe
RB 72	Sangay
RB 73	Cotopaxi
RB 74	Antizana
RB 75	Sirius
RB 76	Altar
RB 77	Tungurahua
RB 78	Quilotoa

Miscellaneous

TR 62	Calicuchima
TR 63	Atahualpa
TR 64	Quisquis
TR 65	Taurus
BE 51	Guayas
BT 84	Putumayo
DF 81	Amazonas
DF 82	Napo
UT 111	Isla de la Plata
UT 112	Isla Puná

Coast Guard

LGC 31	25 de Julio
LGC 32	24 de Mayo
LGC 33	10 de Agosto
LGC 34	3 de Noviembre
LGC 35	5 de Agosto
LGC 36	21 de Febrero
LGC 37	9 de Octubre
LGC 38	27 de Octubre
LGC 41	Rio Puyango
LGC 42	Rio Mataje
LGC 43	Rio Zarumilla
LGC 44	Rio Chone
LGC 45	Rio Daule
LGC 46	Rio Babahoyo

SUBMARINES

2 TYPE 209 CLASS (TYPE 1300)

Name	No	Builders	Laid down	Launched	Commissioned
SHYRI	S 101 (ex-S 11)	Howaldtswerke, Kiel	5 Aug 1974	6 Oct 1976	5 Nov 1977
HUANCAVILCA	S 102 (ex-S 12)	Howaldtswerke, Kiel	2 Jan 1975	15 Mar 1977	16 Mar 1978

Displacement, tons: 1285 surfaced; 1390 dived
Dimensions, feet (metres): 195.1 × 20.5 × 17.9 *(59.5 × 6.3 × 5.4)*
Main machinery: Diesel-electric; 4 MTU 12V 493 AZ80 GA31L diesels; 2400 hp(m) *(1.76 MW)* sustained; 4 Siemens alternators; 1.7 MW; 1 Siemens motor; 4600 hp(m) *(3.38 MW)* sustained; 1 shaft
Speed, knots: 11 surfaced/snorting; 21.5 dived
Complement: 33 (5 officers)

Torpedoes: 8—21 in *(533 mm)* bow tubes. 14 AEG SUT; dual purpose; wire-guided; active/passive homing to 28 km *(15 nm)* at 23 kts; 12 km *(6.5 nm)* at 35 kts; warhead 250 kg.
Fire control: Signaal M8 Mod 24.
Radars: Surface search: Thomson-CSF Calypso; I band.
Sonars: Atlas Elektronik CSU 3; hull-mounted; active/passive search and attack; medium frequency.
Thomson Sintra DUUX 2; passive ranging.

Programmes: Ordered in March 1974. *Shyri* underwent major refit in West Germany in 1983; *Huancavilca* in 1984. Second refits authorised in 1992 and may be done by ASMAR starting in 1993.
Operational: Based at Guayaquil.

TYPE 209　　　1988

FRIGATES

2 Ex-BRITISH LEANDER CLASS

Name	No	Builders	Laid down	Launched	Commissioned
PRESIDENTE ELOY ALFARO (ex-*Penelope*)	FM 01 (ex-F 127)	Vickers Armstrong, Newcastle	14 Mar 1961	17 Aug 1962	31 Oct 1963
MORAN VALVERDE (ex-*Danae*)	FM 02 (ex-F 47)	HM Dockyard, Devonport	16 Dec 1964	31 Oct 1965	7 Sep 1967

Displacement, tons: 2450 standard; 3200 full load
Dimensions, feet (metres): 360 wl; 372 oa × 41 × 14.8 (keel); 19 (screws) *(109.7; 113.4 × 12.5 × 4.5; 5.8)*
Main machinery: 2 Babcock & Wilcox boilers; 38.7 kg/cm sq; 850°F *(450°C)*; 2 English Electric/White turbines; 30 000 hp *(22.4 MW)*; 2 shafts
Speed, knots: 28. **Range, miles:** 4000 at 15 kts
Complement: 248 (20 officers)

Missiles: SSM: 4 Aerospatiale MM 38 Exocet ❶; inertial cruise; active radar homing to 42 km *(23 nm)* at 0.9 Mach; warhead 165 kg.
SAM: 3 Shorts Seacat GWS 22 quad launchers ❷; radar guidance to 5 km *(2.7 nm)*; warhead HE; sea-skimmer; anti-ship capability.
Guns: 2 Bofors 40 mm/60 Mk 9 ❸; 80° elevation; 120 rounds/minute to 10 km *(5.4 nm)* anti-surface; 3 km *(1.6 nm)* anti-aircraft; weight of shell 0.89 kg.
2 Oerlikon/BMARC 20 mm GAM-BO1 can be fitted midships or aft.
Countermeasures: Decoys: Graseby Type 182; towed torpedo decoy.
2 Vickers Corvus 8-barrelled trainable launchers ❹; chaff to 1 km.
ESM: UA-8/9; radar warning.
ECM: Type 667/668; jammer.
Combat data systems: CAAIS action data automation. Links 10 and 14 (receive).
Fire control: GWS 50.
Radars: Air search: Marconi Type 966 ❺; A band.
Surface search: Plessey Type 994 ❻; E/F band.
Navigation: Kelvin Hughes Type 1006; I band.
Fire control: Two Plessey Type 903/904 (for Seacat) ❼.
Sonars: Kelvin Hughes Type 162M; hull-mounted; bottom classification; 50 kHz.
Graseby Type 184P; hull-mounted; active search and attack; 7-9 kHz.

Helicopters: 1 Bell 206 B ❽.

Programmes: Both ships acquired 25 April 1991 and sailed for Ecuador after working up in July and August respectively.
Structure: These are Batch 2 Exocet conversions completed in 1980 and 1982. Torpedo tubes were subsequently removed in 1988/89. The ships were transferred without Exocet or Seacat ammunition.

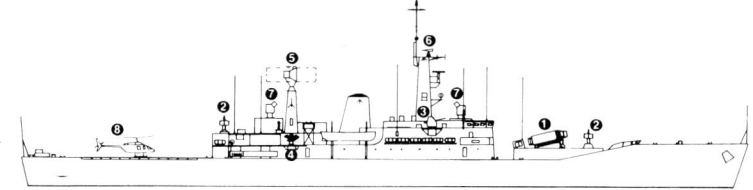

MORAN VALVERDE *(Scale 1 : 1200), Ian Sturton*

MORAN VALVERDE *6/1991, D & B Teague*

CORVETTES

6 ESMERALDAS CLASS (CORVETTES)

Name	No	Builders	Laid down	Launched	Commissioned
ESMERALDAS	CM 11	Fincantieri Muggiano	27 Sep 1979	1 Oct 1980	7 Aug 1982
MANABI	CM 12	Fincantieri Ancona	19 Feb 1980	9 Feb 1981	21 June 1983
LOS RIOS	CM 13	Fincantieri Muggiano	5 Dec 1979	27 Feb 1981	9 Oct 1983
EL ORO	CM 14	Fincantieri Ancona	20 Mar 1980	9 Feb 1981	11 Dec 1983
LOS GALAPAGOS	CM 15	Fincantieri Muggiano	4 Dec 1980	4 July 1981	26 May 1984
LOJA	CM 16	Fincantieri Ancona	25 Mar 1981	27 Feb 1982	26 May 1984

Displacement, tons: 685 full load
Dimensions, feet (metres): 204.4 × 30.5 × 8 *(62.3 × 9.3 × 2.5)*
Main machinery: 4 MTU 20V 956 TB92 diesels; 22 140 hp(m) *(16.27 MW)* sustained; 4 shafts
Speed, knots: 37. **Range, miles:** 4400 at 14 kts
Complement: 51

Missiles: SSM: 6 Aerospatiale MM 40 Exocet (2 triple) launchers ❶; inertial cruise; active radar homing to 70 km *(40 nm)* at 0.9 Mach; warhead 165 kg; sea-skimmer.
SAM: Selenia Elsag Albatros quad launcher ❷; Aspide; semi-active radar homing to 13 km *(7 nm)* at 2.5 Mach; height envelope 15-5000 m *(49.2-16 405 ft)*; warhead 30 kg.
Guns: 1 OTO Melara 3 in *(76 mm)*/62 compact ❸; 85° elevation; 85 rounds/minute to 16 km *(8.7 nm)*; weight of shell 6 kg.
2 Breda 40 mm/70 (twin) ❹; 85° elevation; 300 rounds/minute to 12.5 km *(6.8 nm)* anti-surface; weight of shell 0.96 kg.
Torpedoes: 6—324 mm ILAS-3 (2 triple) tubes ❺; Whitehead Motofides A244; anti-submarine; self adaptive patterns to 6 km *(3.3 nm)* at 30 kts; warhead 34 kg.
Countermeasures: Decoys: 1 Breda 105 mm SCLAR launcher; chaff to 5 km *(2.7 nm)*; illuminants to 12 km *(6.6 nm)*.
ESM/ECM: Elettronika Gamma ED; radar intercept and jammer.
Combat data systems: Selenia IPN 10 action data automation.
Fire control: 2 Selenia NA21 with C03 directors.
Radars: Air/surface search: Selenia RAN 10S ❻; E/F band; range 155 km *(85 nm)*.
Navigation: SMA 3 RM 20; I band; range 73 km *(40 nm)*.
Fire control: 2 Selenia Orion 10X ❼; I/J band; range 40 km *(22 nm)*.
Sonars: Thomson Sintra Diodon; hull-mounted; active search and attack; 11, 12 or 13 kHz.

Helicopters: 1 Bell 206B can be embarked (platform only).

Programmes: Ordered in 1979. *El Oro* out of commission for two years from mid-1985 after a bad fire.
Modernisation: Contracts for updating command and weapons control systems are to be placed in 1993. The priority is for a Link system compatible with the frigates.
Structure: Similar to Libyan and Iraqi corvettes, with a helicopter deck and larger engines.

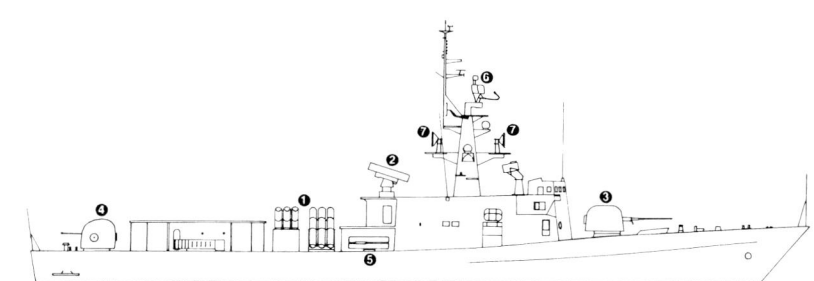

ESMERALDAS *(Scale 1 : 600), Ian Sturton*

ESMERALDAS *1985*

172 ECUADOR / Shipborne aircraft — Survey/research vessels

SHIPBORNE AIRCRAFT

Numbers/Type: 3 Bell 206B JetRanger.
Operational speed: 115 kts *(213 km/h)*.
Service ceiling: 13 500 ft *(4115 m)*.
Range: 368 nm *(682 km)*.
Role/Weapon systems: Support helicopter for afloat reconnaissance and SAR. Sensors: None. Weapons: None.

JETRANGER   1989, Textron

LAND-BASED MARITIME AIRCRAFT (FRONT LINE)

Numbers/Type: 3 Beech T-34C-1 Turbo-Mentor.
Operational speed: 250 kts *(404 km/h)*.
Service ceiling: 30 000 ft *(9145 m)*.
Range: 650 nm *(1205 km)*.
Role/Weapon systems: Operated for training and surveillance tasks. Sensors: None. Weapons: Underwing pylons for rockets, cannon and bombs.

Numbers/Type: 1 Beech Super King 200T.
Operational speed: 282 kts *(523 km/h)*.
Service ceiling: 35 000 ft *(10 670 m)*.
Range: 2030 nm *(3756 km)*.
Role/Weapon systems: Maritime reconnaissance and drug interdiction. Sensors: Weather radar only. Weapons: Unarmed.

LIGHT FORCES

3 LÜRSSEN 45 CLASS (FAST ATTACK CRAFT—MISSILE)

Name	No	Builders	Commissioned
QUITO	LM 21	Lürssen, Vegesack	13 July 1976
GUAYAQUIL	LM 23	Lürssen, Vegesack	22 Dec 1977
CUENCA	LM 24	Lürssen, Vegesack	17 July 1977

Displacement, tons: 255
Dimensions, feet (metres): 147.6 × 23 × 8.1 *(45 × 7 × 2.5)*
Main machinery: 4 MTU 16V 538 TB91 diesels; 12 240 hp(m) *(9.11 MW)* sustained; 4 shafts
Speed, knots: 40. **Range, miles:** 700 at 40 kts; 1800 at 16 kts
Complement: 35

Missiles: SSM: 4 Aerospatiale MM 38 Exocet; inertial cruise; active radar homing to 42 km *(23 nm)* at 0.9 Mach; warhead 165 kg; sea-skimmer.
Guns: 1 OTO Melara 3 in *(76 mm)*/62 compact; 85° elevation; 85 rounds/minute to 16 km *(8.7 nm)*; weight of shell 6 kg.
2 Oerlikon 35 mm/90 (twin); 85° elevation; 550 rounds/minute to 6 km *(3.3 nm)*; weight of shell 1.55 kg.
Fire control: Thomson-CSF Vega system.
Radars: Air/surface search: Thomson-CSF Triton; G band; range 33 km *(18 nm)* for 2 m² target.
Fire control: Thomson-CSF Pollux; I/J band; range 31 km *(17 nm)* for 2 m² target.
Navigation: Racal Decca; I band.

Programmes: Launched—*Quito* on 20 November 1975; *Guayaquil* on 5 April 1976; *Cuenca* in December 1976.

QUITO   9/1981, USN

3 MANTA CLASS (FAST ATTACK CRAFT—MISSILE)

Name	No	Builders	Commissioned
MANTA	LM 25	Lürssen, Vegesack	11 June 1971
TULCAN	LM 26	Lürssen, Vegesack	2 Apr 1971
NUEVO ROCAFUERTE	LM 27	Lürssen, Vegesack	23 June 1971

Displacement, tons: 119 standard; 134 full load
Dimensions, feet (metres): 119.4 × 19.1 × 6 *(36.4 × 5.8 × 1.8)*
Main machinery: 3 Mercedes-Benz diesels; 9000 hp(m) *(6.61 MW)*; 3 shafts
Speed, knots: 42. **Range, miles:** 700 at 30 kts; 1500 at 15 kts
Complement: 19

Missiles: SSM: 4 IAI Gabriel II; radar or optical guidance; semi-active radar homing to 36 km *(19.4 nm)* at 0.7 Mach; warhead 75 kg.
Guns: 2 Emerson Electric 30 mm (twin); 80° elevation; 1200 rounds/minute combined to 6 km *(3.3 nm)*; weight of shell 0.35 kg.
Fire control: Thomson-CSF Vega system.
Radars: Fire control: Thomson-CSF Pollux; I/J band; range 31 km *(17 nm)* for 2 m² target.
Navigation: I band.

Modernisation: Rearmed in 1980 with new electronic fit and missiles. Torpedo tubes have been removed.
Structure: Similar design to the Chilean Guacolda class with an extra diesel, 3 kts faster.
Operational: Missiles are not carried when used on EEZ surveillance.

AMPHIBIOUS SHIPS

1 Ex-US 512-1152 SERIES (LST)

Name	No	Builders	Commissioned
HUALCOPO	TR 61	Chicago Bridge and	9 June 1945
(ex-USS *Summit County* LST 1146)	(ex-T 61)	Iron Co	

Displacement, tons: 1653 standard; 4080 full load
Dimensions, feet (metres): 328 × 50 × 14 *(100 × 16.1 × 4.3)*
Main machinery: 2 GM 12-567A diesels; 1800 hp *(1.34 MW)*; 2 shafts
Speed, knots: 11.6. **Range, miles:** 7200 at 10 kts
Complement: 119
Military lift: 147 troops
Guns: 8 Bofors 40 mm. 2 Oerlikon 20 mm.

Comment: Purchased on 14 February 1977. Commissioned in November 1977 after extensive refit. May still have the ice strengthened bow fitted in the early 1950s. Plans for replacement not yet realised.

HUALCOPO (old number)   10/1984, R E Parkinson

6 ROTORK CRAFT

LF 91-96

Displacement, tons: 9 full load
Dimensions, feet (metres): 41.5 × 10.5 × 3 *(12.6 × 3.2 × 0.9)*
Main machinery: 2 Volvo AQD40A diesels; 182 hp(m) *(134 kW)* sustained; 2 shafts
Speed, knots: 26
Complement: 4
Military lift: 4 tons

Comment: Purchased 1979 from UK.

SURVEY/RESEARCH VESSELS

Name	No	Builders	Commissioned
RIGEL	LH 94 (ex-LH 92)	Halter Marine	1975

Displacement, tons: 50
Dimensions, feet (metres): 64.5 × 17.1 × 3.6 *(19.7 × 5.2 × 1.1)*
Main machinery: 2 diesels; 2 shafts
Speed, knots: 10
Complement: 10 (2 officers)

Comment: Used for inshore oceanographic work.

Name	No	Builders	Commissioned
ORION (ex-*Dometer*)	BI 91 (ex-HI 91, ex-HI 92)	Ishikawajima, Tokyo	10 Nov 1982

Measurement, tons: 1105 gross
Dimensions, feet (metres): 210.6 pp × 35.1 × 11.8 *(64.2 × 10.7 × 3.6)*
Main machinery: Diesel-electric; 3 Detroit 16V-92TA diesels; 2070 hp *(1.54 MW)* sustained; 2 motors; 1900 hp *(1.42 MW)*; 1 shaft
Speed, knots: 12.6. **Range, miles:** 6000 at 12 kts
Complement: 45 (6 officers) plus 14 civilians
Radars: Navigation: Two Decca; I band.

Comment: Research vessel for oceanographic, hydrographic and meteorological work.

ORION (old number) *3/1990, T J Gander*

AUXILIARIES

Note: An ex-German Darss class was to have been acquired in 1991 but the sale was cancelled.

1 Ex-US YW CLASS WATER CARRIER

Name	No	Builders	Commissioned
ATAHUALPA (ex-US *YW 131*)	TR 63 (ex-T 63, ex-T 62, ex-T 33, ex-T 41, ex-A 01)	Leatham D Smith S B Co	1945

Displacement, tons: 415 light; 1235 full load
Dimensions, feet (metres): 174 × 32 × 15 *(53.1 × 9.8 × 4.6)*
Main machinery: 2 GM 8-278A diesels; 1500 hp *(1.12 MW)*; 2 shafts
Speed, knots: 11.5

Comment: Acquired by the Ecuadorian Navy on 2 May 1963. Purchased on 1 December 1977. Paid off in 1988 but back in service in 1990.

1 TANKER

Name	No	Builders	Commissioned
TAURUS	TR 65 (ex-T 66)	Astinave, Guayaquil	1985

Measurement, tons: 1175 dwt; 1110 gross
Dimensions, feet (metres): 174.2 × 36 × 14.4 *(53.1 × 11 × 4.4)*
Main machinery: 1 GM diesel; 1050 hp *(783 kW)*; 1 shaft
Speed, knots: 11

Comment: Acquired for the Navy in 1987.

1 TRAINING SHIP

Name	No	Builders	Commissioned
GUAYAS	BE 51 (ex-BE 01)	Ast Celaya, Spain	23 July 1977

Measurement, tons: 234 dwt; 934 gross
Dimensions, feet (metres): 264 × 33.5 × 13.4 *(80 × 10.2 × 4.2)*
Main machinery: 1 GM 12V-149T diesel; 875 hp *(652 kW)* sustained; 1 shaft
Speed, knots: 11.3

Comment: Three masted sail training ship. Launched 23 September 1976. Has accommodation for 180.

GUAYAS *4/1992, Hartmut Ehlers*

1 ARMAMENT STORES CARRIER (AKF)

Name	No	Builders	Commissioned
CALICUCHIMA (ex-*Throsk*)	TR 62 (ex-A 379)	Cleland S B Co, Wallsend	20 Sep 1977

Displacement, tons: 2207 full load
Dimensions, feet (metres): 231.2 × 39 × 15 *(70.5 × 11.9 × 4.6)*
Main machinery: 2 Mirrlees-Blackstone diesels; 3000 hp *(2.2 MW)*; 1 shaft
Speed, knots: 14.5. **Range, miles:** 4000 at 11 kts
Complement: 24 (8 officers)

Comment: Acquired from the UK in November 1991. Recommissioned 24 March 1992.

CALICUCHIMA (old number) *8/1982, Mike Lennon*

1 WATER CLASS

Name	No	Builders	Commissioned
QUISQUIS (ex-*Waterside*)	TR 64 (ex-Y 20)	Drypool Engineering & Drydock Co, Hull	1968

Measurement, tons: 285 gross
Dimensions, feet (metres): 131.5 × 24.8 × 8 *(40.1 × 7.5 × 2.4)*
Main machinery: 1 Lister-Blackstone ERS-8-MCR diesel; 660 hp *(492 kW)*; 1 shaft
Speed, knots: 11
Complement: 8

Comment: Acquired from the UK in November 1991.

QUISQUIS (old number) *1989*

2 Ex-US YP TYPE

ISLA DE LA PLATA UT 111   ISLA PUNA UT 112

Displacement, tons: 11
Dimensions, feet (metres): 42 × 11.5 × 3.9 *(12.8 × 3.5 × 1.2)*

Comment: Transferred 1962. Ex US Coast Guard utility boats.

1 Ex-US YR TYPE

Name	No	Builders	Commissioned
PUTUMAYO (ex-US *YR 34*)	BT 84 (ex-BT 123, ex-BT 62)	New York Navy Yard	—

Displacement, tons: 770 full load

Comment: Repair barge leased July 1962. Purchased on 1 December 1977. Used in conjunction with the Floating Docks.

2 Ex-US ARD 12 CLASS FLOATING DOCK

Name	No	Builders	Commissioned
AMAZONAS (ex-US *ARD 17*)	DF 81 (ex-DF 121)	USA	1944
NAPO (ex-US *ARD 24*)	DF 82	USA	1944

Dimensions, feet (metres): 492 × 81 × 17.7 *(150 × 24.7 × 5.4)*

Comment: *Amazonas* leased in 1961 and bought outright in 1982; *Napo* bought in 1988. Suitable for docking ships up to 3200 tons.

174 ECUADOR / Auxiliaries — Coast guard

2 Ex-US CHEROKEE CLASS

Name	No	Builders	Commissioned
CAYAMBE (ex-USS *Cusabo* ATF 155)	RA 71 (ex-R 711, ex-R 101, ex-R 51)	Charleston S B & D D Co	28 Apr 1945
CHIMBORAZO (ex-USS *Chowanoc* ATF 100)	RA 70 (ex-R 710, ex-R 71, ex-R 105)	Charleston S B & D D Co	21 Feb 1945

Displacement, tons: 1235 standard; 1640 full load
Dimensions, feet (metres): 205 × 38.5 × 17 *(62.5 × 11.7 × 5.2)*
Main machinery: Diesel-electric; 4 GM 12-278 diesels; 4400 hp *(3.28 MW)*; 4 generators; 1 motor; 3000 hp *(2.24 MW)*; 1 shaft *(Cayambe)*
Diesel-electric; 4 Busch-Sulzer BS-539 diesels; 4 generators; 1 motor; 3000 hp *(2.24 MW)*; 1 shaft *(Chimborazo)*
Speed, knots: 16.5. **Range, miles:** 7000 at 15 kts
Complement: 85
Guns: 1—3 in *(76 mm)*. 2 Bofors 40 mm. 2 Oerlikon 20 mm (not all fitted).

Comment: *Cayambe* launched on 26 February 1945. Fitted with powerful pumps and other salvage equipment. Transferred to Ecuador by lease on 2 November 1960 and renamed *Los Rios*. Again renamed *Cayambe* in 1966 and purchased on 30 August 1978. *Chimborazo* transferred 1 October 1977.

CAYAMBE (old number)   *1970, Ecuadorean Navy*

Name	No	Builders	Commissioned
SANGAY (ex-*Loja*)	RB 72 (ex-R 720, ex-R 102, ex-R 53)	—	1952

Displacement, tons: 295 light; 390 full load
Dimensions, feet (metres): 107 × 26 × 14 *(32.6 × 7.9 × 4.3)*
Main machinery: 1 Fairbanks-Morse diesel; 1 shaft
Speed, knots: 12

Comment: Acquired in 1964. Renamed in 1966.

Name	No	Builders	Commissioned
COTOPAXI (ex-USS *R T Ellis*)	RB 73 (ex-R 721, ex-R 103, ex-R 52)	Equitable Building Corporation	1945

Displacement, tons: 150
Dimensions, feet (metres): 82 × 21 × 8 *(25 × 6.4 × 2.4)*
Main machinery: 1 Diesel; 650 hp *(478 kW)*; 1 shaft
Speed, knots: 9

Comment: Purchased from the USA in 1947.

ANTIZANA	RB 74 (ex-R 723)	TUNGURAHUA	RB 77 (ex-R 722)
SIRIUS	RB 75 (ex-R 724)	QUILOTOA	RB 78 (ex-R 726)
ALTAR	RB 76 (ex-R 725)		

Displacement, tons: 490
Dimensions, feet (metres): 100.4 × — × 8.2 *(30.6 × — × 2.5)*
Speed, knots: 8

COAST GUARD

2 US PGM-71 CLASS (LARGE PATROL CRAFT)

Name	No	Builders	Commissioned
25 DE JULIO (ex-*Quito*)	LG 31 (ex-LGC 31, ex-LC 71)	Peterson, USA	30 Nov 1965
24 DE MAYO (ex-*Guayaquil*)	LG 32 (ex-LGC 32, ex-LC 72)	Peterson, USA	30 Nov 1965

Displacement, tons: 130 standard; 146 full load
Dimensions, feet (metres): 101.5 × 21 × 5 *(30.9 × 6.4 × 1.5)*
Main machinery: 4 diesels; 880 hp *(656 kW)*; 2 shafts
Speed, knots: 21. **Range, miles:** 1000 at 12 kts
Complement: 15
Guns: 1 Bofors 40 mm/60. 4 Oerlikon 20 mm (2 twin). 2—12.7 mm MGs.

Comment: Transferred to the Navy under MAP on 30 November 1965 and then to the Coast Guard in 1980. Paid off into reserve in 1983 and deleted from the order of battle. Refitted with new engines in 1988-89.

2 COASTAL PATROL CRAFT

Name	No	Builders	Commissioned
10 DE AGOSTO	LG 33	Schurenstedt, Bardenfleth	Aug 1954
3 DE NOVIEMBRE	LG 34	Schurenstedt, Bardenfleth	Aug 1954

Displacement, tons: 45 standard; 64 full load
Dimensions, feet (metres): 76.8 × 13.5 × 6.2 *(23.4 × 4.6 × 1.9)*
Main machinery: 2 Bohn & Kähler diesels; 1200 hp(m) *(882 kW)*; 2 shafts
Speed, knots: 22. **Range, miles:** 550 at 16 kts
Complement: 9
Guns: 1 or 2—7.62 mm MGs.

Comment: Ordered in 1954. One deleted in 1992.

2 ESPADA CLASS (LARGE PATROL CRAFT)

Name	No	Builders	Commissioned
5 DE AGOSTO	LG 35	Moss Point Marine, Escatawpa	May 1991
21 DE FEBRERO	LG 36	Moss Point Marine, Escatawpa	Nov 1991

Displacement, tons: 190 full load
Dimensions, feet (metres): 112 × 22.5 × 7 *(34.1 × 6.9 × 2.1)*
Main machinery: 2 Detroit 16V-149TI diesels; 2322 hp *(1.73 MW)* sustained; 1 Detroit 16V-92TA; 690 hp *(514 kW)* sustained; 3 shafts
Speed, knots: 27
Complement: 19 (5 officers)
Guns: 1 Bofors 40 mm/60. 2—12.7 mm MGs.
Radars: Surface search: Racal Decca; I band.

Comment: Steel hulls and aluminium superstructure. Accommodation is air-conditioned. Carry a 10 man RIB and launching crane on the stern.

5 DE AGOSTO (gun not fitted)   *1991, Trinity Marine*

2 SWIFTSHIPS TYPE (RIVERINE PATROL CRAFT)

Name	No	Builders	Commissioned
9 DE OCTUBRE	LG 37	Swiftships	1 Oct 1992
27 DE OCTUBRE	LG 38	Swiftships	1 Oct 1992

Displacement, tons: 17 full load
Dimensions, feet (metres): 45.5 × 11.8 × 1.8 *(13.9 × 3.6 × 0.6)*
Main machinery: 2 Detroit 6V 92 TA diesels; 900 hp *(671 kW)*; 2 Hamilton waterjets
Speed, knots: 22. **Range, miles:** 600 at 22 kts
Complement: 4
Guns: 2 M2HB 12.7 mm MGs; 2 M60D 7.62 mm MGs.
Radars: Navigation: I band.

Comment: Transferred under MAP to the Navy and thence to the Coast Guard. Hard chine modified V hull form. Can carry up to 8 troops.

9 DE OCTUBRE   *9/1992, Swiftships*

6 RIO PUYANGO CLASS (RIVERINE PATROL CRAFT)

Name	No	Builders	Commissioned
RIO PUYANGO	LG 41 (ex-LGC 40)	Halter Marine, New Orleans	15 June 1986
RIO MATAGE	LG 42 (ex-LGC 41)	Halter Marine, New Orleans	15 June 1986
RIO ZARUMILLA	LG 43 (ex-LGC 42)	Astinave, Guayaquil	11 Mar 1988
RIO CHONE	LG 44 (ex-LGC 43)	Astinave, Guayaquil	11 Mar 1988
RIO DAULE	LG 45 (ex-LGC 44)	Astinave, Guayaquil	17 June 1988
RIO BABAHOYO	LG 46 (ex-LGC 45)	Astinave, Guayaquil	17 June 1988

Displacement, tons: 17
Dimensions, feet (metres): 44 × 13.5 × 3.5 *(13.4 × 4.1 × 1.1)*
Main machinery: 2 Detroit 8V-71 diesels; 460 hp *(343 kW)* sustained; 2 shafts
Speed, knots: 26. **Range, miles:** 500 at 18 kts
Complement: 5 (1 officer)
Guns: 1—12.7 mm MG. 2—7.62 mm MGs.
Radars: Surface search: Furuno 2400; I band.

Comment: Two delivered by Halter Marine in June 1986. Four more ordered in February 1987; assembled under licence at Astinave shipyard, Guayaquil. Used mainly for drug interdiction.

14 US 40 ft BAYCRAFT (RIVER PATROL CRAFT)

Comment: Modified civilian sporting craft purchased in 1980.

RIO PUYANGO (old number)   1/1988, Halter Marine

EGYPT

Headquarters' Appointment

Commander of Naval Forces:
Vice Admiral Ahmed Ali Fadel

General

The cancellation of US debts on older contracts has released money to upgrade the Fleet. In 1992 operational availability improved to the point where more than two-thirds of all units were active.

Personnel

(a) 1993: 16 000 officers and men, including the Coast Guard (Reserves of about 15 000)
(b) 1-3 years' national service (depending on educational qualifications)

Bases

Alexandria, Port Said, Mersa Matru, Abu Qir, Suez, Safaqa and Hurghada on the Red Sea.
Naval Academy: Abu Qir.

Coastal Defences

The Samlet, Otomat and modified CSS-N-1 Styx missiles employed for Coastal Defence by the Border Guard are naval-manned. There are two Coastal Artillery Brigades.

Maritime Air

Although the navy has no air arm the Air Force has a number of E2Cs, ASW Sea Kings and Gazelles with an ASM capability (see *Land-based Maritime Aircraft* section). The Sea Kings are controlled by the Anti-Submarine Brigade and have naval sensor operators.

Prefix to Ships' Name

ENS

Strength of the Fleet

Type	Active	Building (Projected)
Submarines (Patrol)	8	(2)
Destroyer	1	—
Frigates	5	—
Fast Attack Craft (Missile)	22 (+ 2 Komar)	—
Fast Attack Craft (Torpedo)	2	—
Fast Attack Craft (Gun)	8	—
Fast Attack Craft (Patrol)	8 (+ 5 P6)	—
LSMs	3	—
LCUs	9	—
Minesweepers (Ocean)	8	—
Minehunters (Inshore)	—	3
Route Survey Vessels	2	2
Support Ships	20	—
Coast Guard	79	1

Mercantile Marine

Lloyd's Register of Shipping:
444 vessels of 1 200 054 tons gross

DELETIONS

Amphibious Forces

1991   2 SMB 1 class, 3 Winchester Hovercraft

Mine Warfare Forces

1991   *El Fayoum, El Manufieh*

Miscellaneous

1990   *Rashid*
1991   1 Nyryat class

Coast Guard

1990   *Nimr, Nur, Al Bahr*

SUBMARINES

Note: After several attempts to buy second-hand had come to nothing, a request for quotation on two new construction submarines was made in September 1991. The German-built 209 or Dolphin class seem to be the most likely candidates when funds become available, which may not be for some years.

4 Ex-SOVIET and 4 Ex-CHINESE ROMEO CLASS

831, 840, 843, 846—ex-Soviet
849, 852, 855, 858—ex-Chinese

Displacement, tons: 1475 surfaced; 1830 dived
Dimensions, feet (metres): 251.3 × 22 × 16.1 *(76.6 × 6.7 × 4.9)*
Main machinery: Diesel-electric; 2 Type 37-D diesels; 4000 hp(m) *(2.94 MW)*; 2 motors; 2700 hp(m) *(1.98 MW)*; 2 creep motors; 2 shafts
Speed, knots: 16 surfaced; 13 dived
Range, miles: 9000 at 9 kts surfaced
Complement: 54

Torpedoes: 8—21 in *(533 mm)* tubes (6 bow, 2 stern). 14 Soviet Type 53; dual purpose; pattern active/passive homing up to 20 km *(10.8 nm)* at up to 45 kts; warhead 400 kg.
Mines: 28 in lieu of torpedoes.
Countermeasures: ESM: Argo or Racal; radar warning
Fire control: Singer Librascope Mk 2 (in 4).
Radars: Surface search: Snoop Plate; I band.
Sonars: Hull-mounted; active/passive; high frequency.

Programmes: One Romeo class was transferred to Egypt by the USSR in 1966. Two more replaced Whiskey class in May 1966 and another pair was delivered later that year. The sixth boat joined in 1969. Two transferred from China 22 March 1982. Second pair arrived 3 January 1984, commissioned 21 May 1984.
Modernisation: The ex-Soviet submarines have been refitted with limited up-date to bridge the gap until completion of a full modernisation programme of the four ex-Chinese vessels. In early 1988 a five year contract was signed with Tacoma, Washington to retrofit the ex-Chinese submarines with Harpoon, and convert them to fire Mk 37 wire-guided torpedoes; weapon systems improvements to include Loral active sonar, Atlas Elektronik passive sonar and fire control system. The US Congress did not give approval to start work until July 1989 and a further series of delays in the Tacoma shipyard meant that work did not start until April 1992.
Operational: Two Soviet submarines deleted in 1989 and of the remaining four Soviet type, only two are operating regularly.

ROMEO class (ex-Chinese) (old number)   1984

ROMEO class (old number)   1987

DESTROYER

1 Ex-BRITISH Z CLASS

Name	No	Builders	Laid down	Launched	Commissioned
EL FATEH (ex-*Zenith*, ex-*Wessex*)	921	Wm Denny & Bros, Dumbarton	19 May 1942	5 June 1944	22 Dec 1944

Displacement, tons: 1730 standard; 2575 full load
Dimensions, feet (metres): 362.8 × 35.7 × 16 *(110.6 × 10.9 × 4.9)*
Main machinery: 2 Admiralty boilers; 2 Parsons turbines; 40 000 hp *(30 MW)*; 2 shafts
Speed, knots: 31. **Range, miles:** 2800 at 20 kts
Complement: 186

Guns: 4 Vickers 4.5 in *(115 mm)*/45 hand loaded Mk 5 mounting; 50° elevation; 14 rounds/minute to 17 km *(9.3 nm)*; weight of shell 25 kg.
  6 China 37 mm/63 (3 twin); 180 rounds/minute to 8.5 km *(4.6 nm)*; weight of shell 1.42 kg.
Torpedoes: 4—21 in *(533 mm)* (quad) tubes. Probably Soviet anti-surface Type 53.
Depth charges: 4 projectors.
Fire control: Fly 4 director.
Radars: Air search: Marconi SNW 10; D band.
Surface search: Racal Decca 916; I band.
Fire control: Marconi Type 275; F band.

Programmes: Purchased from the UK in 1955. Before being taken over by Egypt, *El Fateh* was refitted by John I. Thornycroft & Co Ltd, Woolston, Southampton in July 1956, subsequently modernised by J S White & Co Ltd, Cowes, completed in July 1964.
Modernisation: Bofors replaced by Chinese 37 mm guns. Sonars removed.
Operational: Is still being used for sea training.

EL FATEH   *5/1985, van Ginderen Collection*

FRIGATES

2 CHINESE JIANGHU I CLASS

Name	No	Builders	Commissioned
NAJIM AL ZAFFER	951	Hutong, Shanghai	27 Oct 1984
EL NASSER	956	Hutong, Shanghai	16 Apr 1985

Displacement, tons: 1425 standard; 1702 full load
Dimensions, feet (metres): 338.5 × 35.4 × 10.2 *(103.2 × 10.8 × 3.1)*
Main machinery: 2 SEMT-Pielstick 12 PA6 280 BTC diesels; 14 400 hp(m) *(10.6 MW)* sustained; 2 shafts
Speed, knots: 26. **Range, miles:** 4000 at 15 kts
Complement: 195

Missiles: SSM: 4 Hai Ying 2 (Flying Dragon) (2 twin) ❶; active radar or passive IR homing to 80 km *(43.2 nm)* at 0.9 Mach; warhead 513 kg.
Guns: 4 China 57 mm/70 (2 twin) ❷; 85° elevation; 120 rounds/minute to 12 km *(6.5 nm)*; weight of shell 6.31 kg.
  12 China 37 mm/63 (6 twin) ❸; 85° elevation; 180 rounds/minute to 8.5 km *(4.6 nm)*; weight of shell 1.42 kg.
A/S mortars: 2 RBU 1200 5-tubed fixed launchers ❹; range 1200 m; warhead 34 kg.
Depth charges: 2 projectors; 2 racks.
Mines: Up to 60.
Countermeasures: ESM: Elettronica SpA Beta; radar intercept.
Radars: Air search: Type 765 ❺.
Surface search: Eye Shield ❻; E band.
Surface search/gun direction: Square Tie; I band; range 73 km *(40 nm)*.
Navigation: Decca; I band.
Sonars: Hull-mounted; active search and attack; high frequency.

NAJIM AL ZAFFER   *(Scale 1 : 900), Ian Sturton*

Programmes: Ordered in 1982. This is a Jianghu I class modified with 57 mm guns vice the standard 100 mm.
Modernisation: Combat data system to be fitted together with optronic fire control directors. There are also plans to remove the after superstructure and guns and build a flight deck for a LAMPS helicopter.
Structure: The funnel is the rounded type of the Jianghu class.

EL NASSER   *5/1992, Hartmut Ehlers*

2 DESCUBIERTA CLASS

Name	No
ABU QIR (ex-*Serviola*)	F 941
EL SUEZ (ex-*Centinela*)	F 946

Builders	Laid down	Launched	Commissioned
Bazán	28 Feb 1979	20 Dec 1979	27 Oct 1984
Bazán	31 Oct 1978	6 Oct 1979	21 May 1984

Displacement, tons: 1233 standard; 1479 full load
Dimensions, feet (metres): 291.3 × 34 × 12.5 *(88.8 × 10.4 × 3.8)*
Main machinery: 4 MTU-Bazán 16V 956 TB91 diesels; 15 000 hp(m) *(11 MW)* sustained; 2 shafts; cp props
Speed, knots: 25.5; 28 trials. **Range, miles:** 4000 at 18 kts
Complement: 116

Missiles: SSM: 8 McDonnell Douglas Harpoon (2 quad) launchers ❶; active radar homing to 130 km *(70 nm)* at 0.9 Mach; warhead 227 kg.
SAM: Selenia Elsag Albatros octuple launcher ❷; 24 Aspide; semi-active radar homing to 13 km *(7 nm)* at 2.5 Mach; height envelope 15-5000 m *(49.2-16 405 ft)*; warhead 30 kg.
Guns: 1 OTO Melara 3 in *(76 mm)*/62 compact ❸; 85° elevation; 85 rounds/minute to 16 km *(8.7 nm)*; weight of shell 6 kg.
2 Bofors 40 mm/70 ❹; 85° elevation; 300 rounds/minute to 12.5 km *(6.8 nm)*; weight of shell 0.96 kg.
Torpedoes: 6—324 mm Mk 32 (2 triple) tubes ❺. MUSL Stingray; anti-submarine; active/passive homing to 11 km *(5.9 nm)* at 45 kts; warhead 35 kg (shaped charge); depth to 750 m *(2460 ft)*.
A/S mortars: 1 Bofors 375 mm twin-barrelled trainable launcher ❻; automatic loading; range 1600 m or 3600 m depending on type of rocket.
Countermeasures: ESM: Elettronica SpA Beta; radar intercept. Prairie Masker; acoustic signature suppression.
Combat data systems: Signaal SEWACO action data automation. Link Y.
Radars: Air/surface search: Signaal DA 05 ❼; E/F band; range 137 km *(75 nm)* for 2 m² target.
Navigation: Signaal ZW 06; I band.
Fire control: Signaal WM 25 ❽; I/J band; range 46 km *(25 nm)*.
Sonars: Raytheon 1160B; hull-mounted; active search and attack; medium frequency.
Raytheon 1167 ❾; VDS; active search; 12-7.5 kHz.

Programmes: Ordered September 1982 from Bazán, Spain. The two Spanish ships *Centinela* and *Serviola* were sold to Egypt prior to completion and transferred after completion at Ferrol and modification at Cartagena. *El Suez* completed 28 February 1984 and *Abu Qir* on 31 July 1984.
Operational: Stabilisers fitted. Modern noise insulation of main and auxiliary machinery.

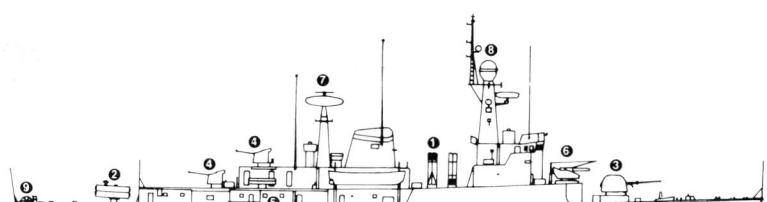
EL SUEZ *(Scale 1 : 900), Ian Sturton*

EL SUEZ 10/1991

ABU QIR 10/1991

1 Ex-BRITISH BLACK SWAN CLASS

Name	No	Builders	Laid down	Launched	Commissioned
TARIQ (ex-*Malek Farouk*, ex-*Whimbrel*)	931	Yarrows, Glasgow	31 Oct 1941	25 Aug 1942	13 Jan 1943

Displacement, tons: 1925 full load
Dimensions, feet (metres): 299 × 38.5 × 11.5 *(91.2 × 11.7 × 3.5)*
Main machinery: 2 Admiralty boilers; 2 Parsons geared turbines; 3600 hp *(2.69 MW)*; 2 shafts
Speed, knots: 18. **Range, miles:** 4500 at 12 kts
Complement: 180

Guns: 6 Vickers 4 in *(102 mm)*/45 (3 twin) Mk 19.
4 Bofors 4 mm/60 (2 twin).
Depth charges: 4 projectors; 2 racks.
Radars: Surface search: 2 Decca; I band.

Programmes: Transferred in November 1949.
Structure: Still has the original class appearance with some minor modifications to the armament.
Operational: Relegated for a time in the mid-1980s to an accommodation ship and offered as part of a deal involving the acquisition of two Oberon class submarines in 1989. When this project was cancelled, the ship resumed service as a training platform and was seen at sea in 1991 and 1992.

TARIQ 10/1988, F Sadek

EGYPT — Land-based maritime aircraft — Light forces

LAND-BASED MARITIME AIRCRAFT (FRONT LINE)

Note: All Badger and Beagle aircraft non-operational by late 1991.

Numbers/Type: 9 Aerospatiale SA 342L Gazelle.
Operational speed: 142 kts *(264 km/h)*.
Service ceiling: 14 105 ft *(4300 m)*.
Range: 407 nm *(755 km)*.
Role/Weapon systems: Land-based helicopter for coastal anti-shipping strike, particularly against FAC and insurgents. Sensors: SFIM sight. Weapons: ASV; 2 × AS-12 wire-guided missiles.

Numbers/Type: 5 Grumman E-2C Hawkeye.
Operational speed: 269 kts *(499 km/h)*.
Service ceiling: 30 800 ft *(9390 m)*.
Range: 1350 nm *(2500 km)*.
Role/Weapon systems: Airborne early warning and control tasks; capable of handling up to 30 tracks over water or land. Sensors: APS-125 search/warning radar, various ESM/ECM systems. Weapons: Unarmed.

Numbers/Type: 10 Westland Sea King Mk 47.
Operational speed: 112 kts *(208 km/h)*.
Service ceiling: 14 700 ft *(4480 m)*.
Range: 664 nm *(1230 km)*.
Role/Weapon systems: Shore-based helicopter for ASW and surface search; secondary role as SAR helicopter; may be embarked in due course. Airframe and engine refurbishment in 1990 for first five. Sensors: MEL search radar. Weapons: ASW; 4 × Mk 46 or Stingray torpedoes or depth bombs. ASV; Otomat.

Numbers/Type: 2 Beechcraft 1900C.
Operational speed: 267 kts *(495 km/h)*.
Service ceiling: 25 000 ft *(7620 m)*.
Range: 1569 nm *(2907 km)*.
Role/Weapon systems: Two (of six) Air Force aircraft acquired in 1988 and used for maritime surveillance. Sensors: Litton search radar; Motorola multi-mode SLAMMR radar; Singer S-3075 ESM; Data Link Y. Weapons: Unarmed.

LIGHT FORCES

Note: 1. Five modified ex-Soviet P 6 class (Fast Attack Craft—Patrol) with BM 21 rocket launchers were active in 1991 and 1992 (pennant numbers 201, 202, 205, 206 and 253).
2. Two Komar class were also brought out of reserve in 1991.

6 RAMADAN CLASS (FAST ATTACK CRAFT—MISSILE)

Name	No	Builders	Laid down	Launched	Commissioned
RAMADAN	670	Vosper Thornycroft	22 Sep 1978	6 Sep 1979	20 July 1981
KHYBER	672	Vosper Thornycroft	23 Feb 1979	31 Jan 1980	15 Sep 1981
EL KADESSAYA	674	Vosper Thornycroft	24 Apr 1979	19 Feb 1980	6 Apr 1982
EL YARMOUK	676	Vosper Thornycroft	15 May 1979	12 June 1980	18 May 1982
BADR	678	Vosper Thornycroft	29 Sep 1979	17 June 1981	17 June 1982
HETTEIN	680	Vosper Thornycroft	29 Feb 1980	25 Nov 1980	28 Oct 1982

Displacement, tons: 307 full load
Dimensions, feet (metres): 170.6 × 25 × 7.5 *(52 × 7.6 × 2.3)*
Main machinery: 4 MTU 20V 538 TB91 diesels; 15 360 hp(m) *(11.29 MW)* sustained; 4 shafts
Speed, knots: 40. **Range, miles:** 1600 at 18 kts
Complement: 30 (4 officers)

Missiles: SSM: 4 OTO Melara/Matra Otomat Mk 1; active radar homing to 80 km *(43.2 nm)* at 0.9 Mach; warhead 210 kg.
Guns: 1 OTO Melara 3 in *(76 mm)* compact; 85° elevation; 85 rounds/minute to 16 km *(8.7 nm)*; weight of shell 6 kg.
2 Breda 40 mm/70 (twin); 85° elevation; 300 rounds/minute to 12.5 km *(6.8 nm)* anti-surface; weight of shell 0.96 kg.
Countermeasures: Decoys: 4 Protean fixed launchers each with 4 magazines containing 36 chaff decoy and IR flare grenades.
ESM: Racal Cutlass; radar intercept.
ECM: Racal Cygnus; jammer.
Combat data systems: Ferranti CAAIS action data automation.
Fire control: Marconi Sapphire System with 2 radar/TV and 2 optical directors.
Radars: Air/surface search: Marconi S 820; E/F band; range 73 km *(40 nm)*.
Navigation: Marconi S 810; I band; range 48 km *(25 nm)*.
Fire control: Two Marconi ST 802; I band.

Programmes: The contract was carried out at the Porchester yard of Vosper Thornycroft Ltd with some hulls built at Portsmouth Old Yard, being towed to Porchester for fitting out.
Modernisation: The intention is to double the SSM capability with eight lightweight Otomat or Harpoon.
Operational: Portable SAM SA-N-5 sometimes carried.

BADR 6/1992, G Toremans

RAMADAN

Light forces / EGYPT 179

4 Ex-SOVIET OSA I CLASS (TYPE 205) (FAST ATTACK CRAFT—MISSILE)

633   637   641   643

Displacement, tons: 171 standard; 210 full load
Dimensions, feet (metres): 126.6 × 24.9 × 8.9 *(38.6 × 7.6 × 2.7)*
Main machinery: 3 MTU diesels; 12 000 hp(m) *(8.82 MW)*; 3 shafts
Speed, knots: 35. **Range, miles:** 400 at 34 kts
Complement: 30

Missiles: SSM: 4 SS-N-2A Styx; active radar or IR homing to 46 km *(25 nm)* at 0.9 Mach; altitude pre-set up to 300 m *(984.3 ft)*; warhead 513 kg.
SAM: SA-N-5 Grail; manual aiming; IR homing to 6 km *(3.2 nm)* at 1.5 Mach; altitude to 2500 m *(8000 ft)*; warhead 1.5 kg.
Guns: 4 USSR 30 mm/65 (2 twin); 85° elevation; 500 rounds/minute to 5 km *(2.7 nm)* anti-aircraft; weight of shell 0.54 kg.
2—12.7 mm MGs.
Countermeasures: ESM: Radar warning.
Radars: Air/surface search: Kelvin Hughes; I band.
Navigation: Racal Decca 916; I band.
Fire control: Drum Tilt; H/I band.
IFF: High Pole. Square Head.

Programmes: Thirteen reported to have been delivered to Egypt by the Soviet Navy in 1966-68 but some were sunk in war with Israel, October 1973. Four of the remaining seven were derelict in 1989 but one more was back in service in 1991.
Modernisation: Refitted with MTU diesels and two machine guns.

OSA 633 1986

6 EGYPTIAN OCTOBER CLASS (FAST ATTACK CRAFT—MISSILE)

781   783   785   787   789   791

Displacement, tons: 82 full load
Dimensions, feet (metres): 84 × 20 × 5 *(25.5 × 6.1 × 1.3)*
Main machinery: 4 CRM 12 D/SS diesels; 5000 hp(m) *(3.67 MW)* sustained; 4 shafts
Speed, knots: 40. **Range, miles:** 400 at 30 kts
Complement: 20

Missiles: SSM: 2 OTO Melara/Matra Otomat Mk 1; active radar homing to 80 km *(43.2 nm)* at 0.9 Mach; warhead 210 kg.
Guns: 4 BMARC/Oerlikon 30 mm/75 (2 twin); 85° elevation; 650 rounds/minute to 10 km *(5.5 nm)* anti-surface; 3 km *(1.6 nm)* anti-aircraft; weight of shell 1 kg and 0.36 kg mixed.
Countermeasures: Decoys: 2 Protean fixed launchers each with 4 magazines containing 36 chaff decoy and IR flare grenades.
ESM: Matilda; radar warning.
Fire control: Marconi Sapphire radar/TV system.
Radars: Air/surface search: Marconi S 810; range 48 km *(25 nm)*.
Fire control: Marconi/ST 802; I band.

Programmes: Built in Alexandria 1975-76. Hull of same design as Soviet Komar class. Refitted by Vosper Thornycroft, completed 1979-81. 791 was washed overboard on return trip, recovered and returned to Portsmouth for refit. Left UK after repairs on 12 August 1982.

OCTOBER 7/1980, van Ginderen Collection

6 CHINESE HEGU CLASS (FAST ATTACK CRAFT—MISSILE)

609   611   613   615   617   619

Displacement, tons: 68 standard; 79.2 full load
Dimensions, feet (metres): 88.6 × 20.7 × 4.3 *(27 × 6.3 × 1.3)*
Main machinery: 4 Type L-12V-180 diesels; 4800 hp(m) *(3.53 MW)*; 4 shafts
Speed, knots: 37.5. **Range, miles:** 400 at 30 kts
Complement: 17 (2 officers)

Missiles: SSM: 2 SY-1; active radar or passive IR homing to 40 km *(22 nm)* at 0.9 Mach; warhead 513 kg.
Guns: 2—23 mm (twin); locally constructed to fit 25 mm mounting.
Radars: Air/surface search: Square Tie; I band; range 73 km *(40 nm)* (mounted in radome).
IFF: High Pole A.

Programmes: All commissioned in Egypt on 27 October 1984. Reported that one may be non-operational.

HEGU 615 4/1988, A Sheldon Duplaix

6 Ex-SOVIET SHERSHEN CLASS
(FAST ATTACK CRAFT—2 TORPEDO, 4 GUN)

751   753   755   757   759   761

Displacement, tons: 145 standard; 170 full load
Dimensions, feet (metres): 113.8 × 22 × 4.9 *(34.7 × 6.7 × 1.5)*
Main machinery: 3 Type M 503A diesels; 8025 hp(m) *(5.9 MW)* sustained; 3 shafts
Speed, knots: 45. **Range, miles:** 850 at 30 kts
Complement: 23

Missiles: SAM: SA-N-5 Grail *(755-761)*; manual aiming; IR homing to 6 km *(3.2 nm)* at 1.5 Mach; warhead 1.5 kg.
Guns: 4 USSR 30 mm/65 (2 twin); 85° elevation; 500 rounds/minute to 5 km *(2.7 nm)*; weight of shell 0.54 kg.
2 USSR 122 mm rocket launchers *(755-761* in lieu of torpedo tubes); 20 barrels per launcher; range 9 km *(5 nm)*.
Torpedoes: 4—21 in *(533 mm)* tubes *(751* and *753)*. Soviet Type 53; dual purpose; pattern active/passive homing up to 20 km *(10.8 nm)* at up to 45 kts; warhead 400 kg.
Depth charges: 12.
Radars: Surface search: Pot Drum; H/I band.
Fire control: Drum Tilt, H/I band.
IFF: High Pole.

Programmes: Five delivered from USSR in 1967 and two more in 1968. One deleted. 753 completed an extensive refit at Ismailia in 1987; 751 in 1988.
Structure: The last four have had their torpedo tubes removed to make way for multiple BM21 rocket-launchers and one SA-N-5 Grail.

SHERSHEN 757 1990 US Navy

4 Ex-CHINESE SHANGHAI II CLASS
(FAST ATTACK CRAFT—GUN)

793   795   797   799

Displacement, tons: 113 standard; 131 full load
Dimensions, feet (metres): 127.3 × 17.7 × 5.6 *(38.8 × 5.4 × 1.7)*
Main machinery: 2 Type L12-180 diesels; 2400 hp(m) *(1.76 MW)* (forward); 2 Type L12-180Z diesels; 1820 hp(m) *(1.34 MW)* (aft); 4 shafts
Speed, knots: 30. **Range, miles:** 700 at 16.5 kts
Complement: 34

Guns: 4 China 37 mm/63 (2 twin); 85° elevation; 180 rounds/minute to 8.5 km *(4.6 nm)*; weight of shell 1.42 kg.
4—23 mm (2 twin); locally constructed to fit the 25 mm mountings.
Mines: Rails can be fitted for 10 mines.
Radars: Surface search: Pot Head; I band; range 37 km *(20 nm)*.
IFF: High Pole.

Programmes: Transferred in 1984.
Structure: Painted black.

SHANGHAI II 793 3/1987

180 EGYPT / Light forces — Mine warfare forces

8 Ex-CHINESE HAINAN CLASS (FAST ATTACK CRAFT—PATROL)

AL NOUR 430	AL HADY 433	AL HAKIM 436	AL WAKIL 439
AL QATAR 442	AL SADDAM 445	AL SALAM 448	AL RAFIA 451

Displacement, tons: 375 standard; 392 full load
Dimensions, feet (metres): 192.8 × 23.6 × 6 *(58.8 × 7.2 × 2.2)*
Main machinery: 4 PRC/Kolomna Type 9-D-8 diesels; 4000 hp *(2.94 MW)* sustained; 4 shafts
Speed, knots: 30.5. **Range, miles:** 1300 at 15 kts
Complement: 69

Guns: 4 China 57 mm/70 (2 twin); 85° elevation; 120 rounds/minute to 12 km *(6.5 nm)*; weight of shell 6.31 kg.
  4—23 mm (2 twin); locally constructed to fit the 25 mm mountings.
A/S mortars: 4 RBU 1200 fixed 5-tubed launchers; range 1200 m; warhead 34 kg.
Depth charges: 2 projectors; 2 racks.
Mines: Rails fitted.
Radars: Surface search: Pot Head; I band; range 37 km *(20 nm)*.
  Navigation: Decca; I band.
IFF: High Pole.
Sonars: Hull-mounted; active search and attack; high frequency.

Programmes: First pair transferred to Egypt in October 1983, next three in February 1984 (commissioned 21 May 1984) and last three late 1984.
Modernisation: Two to be fitted with 6—324 mm (2 triple) tubes for MUSL Stingray torpedoes and with Singer Librascope fire control in due course. If successful the remainder of the class may follow.

HAINAN (old number) 9/1991

AMPHIBIOUS FORCES

Note: There are plans to build landing craft locally, probably to a Chinese design. There is also the possibility of leasing an LST/LSM from the US.

3 Ex-SOVIET POLNOCHNY A CLASS (TYPE 770) (LSMs)

301   303   305

Displacement, tons: 800 full load
Dimensions, feet (metres): 239.5 × 27.9 × 5.8 *(73 × 8.5 × 1.8)*
Main machinery: 2 Kolomna Type 40-D diesels; 4400 hp(m) *(3.2 MW)* sustained; 2 shafts
Speed, knots: 19. **Range, miles:** 1000 at 18 kts
Complement: 40
Military lift: 6 tanks; 350 tons
Guns: 2 USSR 30 mm/65 (twin); 85° elevation; 500 rounds/minute to 5 km *(2.7 nm)*; weight of shell 0.54 kg.
  2—140 mm rocket launchers; 18 barrels to 9 km *(4.9 nm)*.
Radars: Surface search: Don 2; I band.
  Fire control: Drum Tilt; H/I band.

Comment: Transferred 1973-74. All used for Gulf logistic support in 1990-91.

POLNOCHNY A 1987

10 SEAFOX TYPE (SWIMMER DELIVERY CRAFT)

21-30

Displacement, tons: 11.3 full load
Dimensions, feet (metres): 36.1 × 9.8 × 2.6 *(11 × 3 × 0.8)*
Main machinery: 2 GM 6V-92TA diesels; 520 hp *(388 kW)* sustained; 2 shafts
Speed, knots: 30
Complement: 3
Guns: 2—12.7 mm MGs. 2—7.62 mm MGs.

Comment: Ordered from Uniflite, Washington in 1982. GRP construction painted black. There is a strong underwater team in the Egyptian Navy which is also known to use commercial two-man underwater chariots.

---

9 Ex-SOVIET VYDRA CLASS (LCUs)

330	332	334	336	338
340	342	344	346	

Displacement, tons: 425 standard; 600 full load
Dimensions, feet (metres): 179.7 × 25.3 × 6.6 *(54.8 × 7.7 × 2)*
Main machinery: 2 Type 3-D-12 diesels; 600 hp(m) *(440 kW)* sustained; 2 shafts
Speed, knots: 11. **Range, miles:** 2500 at 10 kts
Complement: 20
Military lift: 200 troops; 250 tons.

Comment: Built in late 1960s, transferred 1968-69. For a period after the Israeli war of October 1973 several were fitted with rocket launchers and two 37 or 40 mm guns, all of which have now been removed. At least two are in reserve.

VYDRA 332 10/1992, F Sadek

MINE WARFARE FORCES

4 Ex-SOVIET T 43 CLASS (MINESWEEPERS—OCEAN)

ASSIOUT 516	SINAI 513	GHARBIYA 501	DAQAHLIYA 507

Displacement, tons: 580 full load
Dimensions, feet (metres): 190.2 × 27.6 × 6.9 *(58 × 8.4 × 2.1)*
Main machinery: 2 Kolomna Type 9-D-8 diesels; 2000 hp(m) *(1.47 MW)* sustained; 2 shafts
Speed, knots: 15. **Range, miles:** 3000 at 10 kts
Complement: 65
Guns: 4—37 mm/63 (2 twin); 85° elevation; 160 rounds/minute to 9 km *(5 nm)*; weight of shell 0.7 kg.
  8—12.7 mm MGs.
Mines: Can carry 20.

Comment: Delivered in the early 1970s. Others of the class have been sunk or used as targets or cannibalised for spares. The plan to fit them with VDS sonars and ROVs has been shelved in favour of new minehunters.

SINAI 7/1992, F Sadek

4 Ex-SOVIET YURKA CLASS (MINESWEEPERS—OCEAN)

GIZA 533	ASWAN 530	QENA 536	SOHAG 539

Displacement, tons: 460 full load
Dimensions, feet (metres): 171.9 × 30.8 × 8.5 *(52.4 × 9.4 × 2.6)*
Main machinery: 2 Type M 503 diesels; 5350 hp(m) *(3.91 MW)* sustained; 2 shafts
Speed, knots: 17. **Range, miles:** 1500 at 12 kts
Complement: 60
Guns: 4 USSR 30 mm/65 (2 twin); 85° elevation; 500 rounds/minute to 5 km *(2.7 nm)*; weight of shell 0.54 kg.
Mines: Can lay 10.
Radars: Navigation: Don; I band.

Comment: Steel-hulled minesweepers transferred from the USSR in 1969. Built 1963-69. Egyptian Yurka class do not carry Drum Tilt radar and have a number of ship's-side scuttles. The plan to equip them with VDS sonar and ROVs may have been shelved in favour of new minehunters.

ASWAN 10/1986

0 + 3 SWIFTSHIPS TYPE (COASTAL MINEHUNTERS)

Displacement, tons: 175 full load
Dimensions, feet (metres): 110 × 27 × 8 *(33.5 × 8.2 × 2.4)*
Main machinery: 2 MTU 12V 183 TE61 DB51L diesels; 1034 hp(m) *(760 kW)* sustained; 2 shafts
Speed, knots: 12.4. **Range, miles:** 2000 at 10 kts
Complement: 25 (5 officers)
Guns: 2—12.7 mm MGs.
Radars: Navigation: I band.
Sonars: Thoray/Thomson Sintra TSM 2022; hull-mounted; active minehunting; high frequency.

Comment: MCM vessels with GRP hulls ordered from Swiftships in 1991 with FMS funding. First one to be delivered in 1994. Probably to be fitted with a Unisys command data handling system and may also have a towfish sonar. GPS and line of sight navigation system.

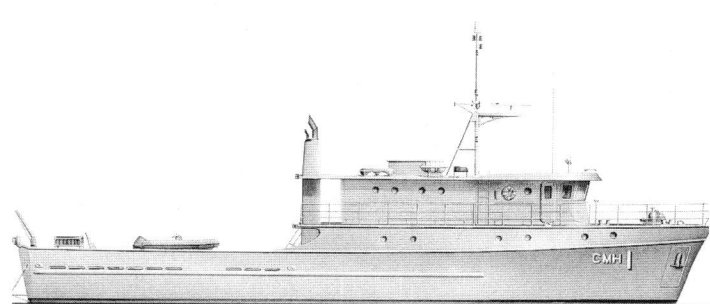

SWIFTSHIPS MCMV (artist's impression)   *1991, Swiftships*

2 ROUTE SURVEY VESSELS

SAFAGA 610   ABU EL GHOSON 613

Displacement, tons: 20
Complement: 18 (4 officers)

Comment: Launched in 1968. Route survey vessels belonging to the Minesweeper flotilla.

0 + 2 SWIFTSHIPS TYPE (ROUTE SURVEY VESSELS)

Displacement, tons: 165 full load
Dimensions, feet (metres): 90 × 24.8 × 8 *(27.4 × 7.6 × 2.4)*
Main machinery: 2 MTU 12V 183 TAW diesels; 900 hp(m) *(662 kW)*; 2 shafts; bow thruster; 60 hp(m) *(44 kW)*
Speed, knots: 12. **Range, miles:** 1500 at 10 kts
Complement: 16 (2 officers)
Guns: 1—12.7 mm MG.
Radars: Navigation: I band.

Comment: Route survey vessels ordered from Swiftships in 1991. Both to be delivered in mid-1993.

SUPPORT SHIPS

6 SOVIET TOPLIVO 2 CLASS (YARD TANKERS)

AKDU 214   MARYUT ATBARAH 215   AYEDA 3 216   + 3

Displacement, tons: 1200 full load
Dimensions, feet (metres): 178.1 × 30.8 × 11.2 *(54.3 × 9.4 × 3.4)*
Main machinery: 1 diesel; 600 hp(m) *(441 kW)*; 1 shaft
Speed, knots: 10. **Range, miles:** 400 at 7 kts
Complement: 16
Cargo capacity: 500 tons diesel (some used for water)

Comment: Built in Egypt in 1972-77.

1 Ex-SOVIET NYRYAT I CLASS

Displacement, tons: 120 full load
Dimensions, feet (metres): 93 × 18 × 5.5 *(28.4 × 5.5 × 1.7)*
Main machinery: 1 diesel; 450 hp(m) *(330 kW)*; 1 shaft
Speed, knots: 12
Complement: 15

Comment: Diving support ship transferred in 1964.

2 Ex-SOVIET POLUCHAT I CLASS

Displacement, tons: 100 full load
Dimensions, feet (metres): 97.1 × 19 × 4.8 *(29.6 × 5.8 × 1.5)*
Main machinery: 2 Type M 50 diesels; 2200 hp(m) *(1.6 MW)* sustained; 2 shafts
Speed, knots: 20
Complement: 15

Comment: Torpedo recovery craft.

POLUCHAT I   *11/1992*

6 Ex-SOVIET OKHTENSKY CLASS (TUGS)

AL MEKS 103	ANTAR 107	AL ISKANDARANI 111
AL AGAMI 105	AL DIKHILA 109	— 113

Displacement, tons: 930 full load
Dimensions, feet (metres): 156.1 × 34 × 13.4 *(47.6 × 10.4 × 4.1)*
Main machinery: Diesel-electric; 2 BM diesel generators; 1 motor; 1500 hp(m) *(1.1 MW)*; 1 shaft
Speed, knots: 13. **Range, miles:** 6000 at 13 kts
Complement: 38

Comment: Two transferred to the Egyptian Navy in 1966, others assembled in Egypt.

AL AGAMI   *5/1991, F Sadek*

AMIRA RAMA

Comment: An ex-trawler used as a lighthouse tender and acquired by the Navy in 1987.

5 TRAINING SHIPS

Comment: *Al Kousser* is a 1000 ton vessel belonging to the Naval Academy. *Intishat* is a 500 ton training ship. Pennant number 160 is a USSR Sekstan class used as a cadet training ship. Two YSB training craft acquired from the USA in 1989. A 3300 ton training ship *Aida IV* presented by Japan in 1988 for delivery in March 1992 belongs to the Arab Maritime Transport Academy.

1 PRESIDENTIAL YACHT

EL HORRIYA

Comment: Taken out of retirement in 1992 and prepared for the Columbus celebrations in Italy. In the end she did not go but is reported to be serviceable.

COAST GUARD

13 + 1 TIMSAH CLASS (LARGE PATROL CRAFT)

01-13

Displacement, tons: 106 full load
Dimensions, feet (metres): 101.8 × 17 × 4.8 *(30.5 × 5.2 × 1.5)*
Main machinery: 2 MTU 8V 331 TC92 diesels; 1770 hp *(1.3 MW)* sustained; 2 shafts (first 6); 2 MTU 12V 331 TC92 diesels; 2660 hp(m) *(1.96 MW)* sustained; 2 shafts (second 6)
Speed, knots: 25
Complement: 13
Guns: 2 Oerlikon 30 mm (twin) or 2 Oerlikon 20 mm.

Comment: First three completed December 1981, second three December 1982 at Timsah SY, Ismailia. Further six ordered in January 1985 and completed in 1988-89 with a different type of engine and with waterline exhaust vice a funnel. Thirteenth of class in service in 1992 and more are being built.

TIMSAH 2 (with funnel)   *7/1992, F Sadek*

182 EGYPT / Coast guard

10 SWIFTSHIPS 93 ft CLASS

| 322 | 332 | 336 | 346 | + 6 |

Displacement, tons: 102 full load
Dimensions, feet (metres): 93.2 × 18.7 × 4.9 *(28.4 × 5.7 × 1.5)*
Main machinery: 2 MTU 12V 331 TC92 diesels; 2660 hp(m) *(1.96 MW)* sustained; 2 shafts
Speed, knots: 27. **Range, miles:** 900 at 12 kts
Complement: 14 (2 officers)
Guns: 2 Oerlikon 20 mm.

Comment: Ordered November 1983. First three built in USA, remainder assembled in Egypt. First four commissioned 16 April 1985.

SWIFTSHIPS 336   1/1985

6 CRESTITALIA 70 ft CLASS (COASTAL PATROL CRAFT)

Displacement, tons: 36 full load
Dimensions, feet (metres): 68.9 × 17.4 × 3 *(21 × 5.3 × 0.9)*
Main machinery: 2 MTU 12V 331 TC92 diesels; 2660 hp(m) *(1.96 MW)* sustained; 2 shafts
Speed, knots: 35. **Range, miles:** 500 at 32 kts
Guns: 2 Oerlikon 30 mm A32 (twin). 1 Oerlikon 20 mm.

Comment: Ordered 1980—GRP hulls. Naval manned, employed on Coast Guard duties.

CRESTITALIA 70 ft   1980, Crestitalia

3 NISR CLASS (LARGE PATROL CRAFT)

| NISR 713 | THAR | + 1 |

Displacement, tons: 110 full load
Dimensions, feet (metres): 102 × 18 × 4.9 *(31 × 5.2 × 1.5)*
Main machinery: 2 Maybach diesels; 3000 hp(m) *(2.2 MW)*; 2 shafts
Speed, knots: 24
Guns: 1 Oerlikon 20 mm.

Comment: Built by Castro, Port Said. First three launched in May 1963, two of which have been scrapped. Two more completed 1983.

6 SMALL PATROL CRAFT

Displacement, tons: 10
Main machinery: 1 diesel; 1 shaft

Comment: Ordered from Canal Naval Construction, Port Fuad on 12 December 1983. Two more delivered for port service in Alexandria in October 1989.

7 BERTRAM TYPE (COASTAL PATROL CRAFT)

702-708

Displacement, tons: 3 full load
Dimensions, feet (metres): 28 × 10.2 × 1.3 *(8.5 × 3.1 × 0.4)*
Main machinery: 2 Mercury diesels; 340 hp *(254 kW)*; 2 shafts
Speed, knots: 36
Guns: 2—7.62 mm MGs.

Comment: GRP hulls. Built in Miami, Florida in 1973. Armament changed on transfer. One of the original 20 craft is part of a permanent military Panorama Exhibition in Cairo.

BERTRAM Type   10/1974

30 DC 35 TYPE

Displacement, tons: 4
Dimensions, feet (metres): 35.1 × 11.5 × 2.6 *(10.7 × 3.5 × 0.8)*
Main machinery: 2 diesels; 390 hp *(287 kW)*; 2 shafts
Speed, knots: 25
Complement: 4

Comment: Built by Dawncraft, Wroxham, UK, 1982.

4 DAMEN TYPE TUGS

| KHOUFAN | KHAFRA | RAMSES | KARIR |

Comment: Delivered by Damen, Netherlands in 1982.

ABU QIR and KHYBER   10/1991

EL SALVADOR

Senior Officer

Commander of the Navy:
Captain Fernando Menjivar Campos

Personnel

(a) 1993: 2200 (including 700 Marines and 650 Commandos)
(b) Voluntary service

Bases

Acajutla, La Libertad, El Triunfo y La Union

Mercantile Marine

Lloyd's Register of Shipping:
15 vessels of 1836 tons gross

DELETIONS

1988-90 GC 1, GC 5 (sunk)

3 CAMCRAFT TYPE

GC 6, GC 7, GC 8

Displacement, tons: 100 full load
Dimensions, feet (metres): 100 × 21 × 4.9 (30.5 × 6.4 × 1.5)
Main machinery: 3 Detroit 12V-71TA diesels; 1260 hp (939 kW) sustained; 3 shafts
Speed, knots: 25. **Range, miles:** 780 at 24 kts
Complement: 10
Guns: 1 Oerlikon 20 mm or 1—12.7 mm MG. 2—7.62 mm MGs.
Radars: Surface search: Racal Decca; I band.

Comment: Delivered October, November, December 1975. Refitted in 1986. Sometimes carry a combined 12.7 mm MG/81 mm mortar mounting in the stern.

CG 8

1 SWIFTSHIPS 77 ft CLASS

GC 11

Displacement, tons: 48 full load
Dimensions, feet (metres): 77.1 × 20 × 4.9 (23.5 × 6.1 × 1.5)
Main machinery: 3 Detroit 12V-71TA diesels; 1260 hp (939 kW) sustained; 3 shafts
Speed, knots: 26
Guns: 2—12.7 mm MGs. Aft MG combined with 81 mm mortar.
Radars: Surface search: Furuno; I band.

Comment: Aluminium hull. Delivered by Swiftships, Morgan City in June 1985.

GC 11   1989

6 PIRANHA CLASS

LOF 1-6

Displacement, tons: 8.2 full load
Dimensions, feet (metres): 36 × 10.1 × 1.6 (11 × 3.1 × 0.5)
Main machinery: 2 Caterpillar 3208TA diesels; 680 hp (507 kW) sustained; 2 shafts
Speed, knots: 26
Complement: 5
Guns: 2—12.7 mm (twin) MGs. 2—7.62 mm (twin) MGs.
Radars: Surface search: Furuno 3600; I band.

Comment: Riverine craft with Kevlar hulls. Completed in March 1987 by Lantana Boatyard, Florida. Same type supplied to Honduras.

PIRANHAs   1988, Julio Montes

1 SWIFTSHIPS 65 ft CLASS

GC 10

Displacement, tons: 36 full load
Dimensions, feet (metres): 65.6 × 18.3 × 5 (20 × 6 × 1.5)
Main machinery: 2 Detroit 12V-71TA diesels; 840 hp (626 kW) sustained; 2 shafts
Speed, knots: 23. **Range, miles:** 600 at 18 kts
Complement: 6
Guns: 1 Oerlikon 20 mm. 1 or 2—12.7 mm MGs.
Radars: Surface search: Furuno; I band.

Comment: Aluminium hull. Delivered by Swiftships, Morgan City in June 1984. Was laid up for a time in 1989/90 but became operational again in 1991.

GC 10   1986, Julio Montes

10 PROTECTOR CLASS

LP 03 1-10

Displacement, tons: 9 full load
Dimensions, feet (metres): 40.4 × 13.4 × 1.4 (12.3 × 4 × 0.4)
Main machinery: 2 Caterpillar 3208TA diesels; 680 hp (507 kW) sustained; 2 shafts
Speed, knots: 28. **Range, miles:** 350 at 20 kts
Complement: 4
Guns: 2—12.7 mm MGs. 2—7.62 mm MGs.
Radars: Navigation: Furuno 3600; I band.

Comment: Ordered in December 1987 from SeaArk Marine (ex-MonArk). Five delivered in December 1988 and the remainder in February and March 1989.

PROTECTOR   1989, SeaArk Marine

10 MERCOUGAR RIVERINE CRAFT

LP 04 1-5   LOF 7-11

Comment: Five 40 ft monohulls (LP 04) and five 35 ft catamarans (LOF) completed by Mercougar, Miami in 1988-89. Both types are powered by two Ford Merlin diesels, 600 hp (448 kW), giving speeds up to 40 kts. The 40 ft craft have a range of 556 km (300 nm) which extends to 741 km (400 nm) in the 35 ft version. One 40 ft craft is equipped as a hospital vessel.

3 LCMs

Comment: One LCM 6 (LD 1) and two LCM 8s (LD 2-3) transferred by the USA in April 1986 and January 1987 respectively.

EQUATORIAL GUINEA

Personnel

1993: 120 officers and men

Bases

Malabo (Fernando Po), Bata (Rio Muni)

Mercantile Marine

Lloyd's Register of Shipping:
3 vessels of 6527 tons gross

2 EX-CHINESE SHANTOU CLASS

Displacement, tons: 60 standard; 80 full load
Dimensions, feet (metres): 83.5 × 19 × 6.5 *(25.5 × 5.8 × 2)*
Main machinery: 2 Type 3-D-12 diesels; 600 hp(m) *(460 kW)* sustained; 2 Type M 50 diesels; 2200 hp(m) *(1.6 MW)* sustained; 4 shafts
Speed, knots: 28. **Range, miles:** 500 at 28 kts
Complement: 17
Guns: 4—37 mm/63 (2 twin). 2—12.7 mm MGs.
Radars: Surface search: Skin Head; I band; range 37 km *(20 nm)*.

Comment: Transferred in 1983. Doubtful operational status but seen alongside in 1991 and 1992.

1 LANTANA TYPE

ISLA DE BIOKO

Displacement, tons: 33 full load
Dimensions, feet (metres): 68.8 × 18 × 4 *(21 × 5.5 × 1.5)*
Main machinery: 2 Detroit 8V-92TA diesels; 700 hp *(522 kW)* sustained; 2 shafts
Speed, knots: 24. **Range, miles:** 800 at 15 kts
Guns: 2—12.7 mm MGs. 2—7.62 mm MGs.
Radars: Surface search: Furuno; I band.

Comment: Completed in July 1988 by Lantana Boatyard, Florida, and paid for by USA.

1 VAN MILL TYPE

RIOWELE (ex-*P 220*)

Displacement, tons: 45 full load
Dimensions, feet (metres): 66.3 × 17.4 × 5.9 *(20.2 × 5.3 × 1.8)*
Main machinery: 2 MTU diesels; 2200 hp(m) *(1.62 MW)*; 2 shafts
Speed, knots: 35. **Range, miles:** 950 at 25 kts
Complement: 12 (2 officers)
Guns: 1 Rheinmetall 20 mm. 2—7.62 mm MGs.

Comment: Built by Van Mill, Netherlands in 1986 and transferred from Nigeria. This was one of the second group of three fitted with MTU diesels vice the GM type of the first batch.

ISLA DE BIOKO

1987, Lantana Boatyard

ESTONIA

General

Negotiations started in 1992 to form an independent Coast Guard. Finland and Sweden have offered patrol craft at no cost.

Base

Tallinn

Mercantile Marine

Lloyd's Register of Shipping:
234 vessels of 640 792 tons gross

PATROL FORCES

2 RUSSIAN ZHUK CLASS (COASTAL PATROL CRAFT)

Displacement, tons: 50 full load
Dimensions, feet (metres): 75.4 × 17 × 6.2 *(23 × 5.2 × 1.9)*
Main machinery: 2 Type M 50 diesels; 2200 hp(m) *(1.6 MW)* sustained; 2 shafts
Speed, knots: 30. **Range, miles:** 1100 at 15 kts
Complement: 17
Guns: 2—14.5 mm (twin) MGs.
Radars: Surface search: Spin Trough; I band.

Comment: Transferred in late 1992. In poor condition but seaworthy.

ZHUK

1990

KOSKELO

1991, Finnish Frontier Guard

1 Ex-FINNISH COMMAND SHIP

ex-*Kemio*

Displacement, tons: 340 full load
Dimensions, feet (metres): 118.1 × 29.5 × 9.8 *(36 × 9 × 3)*
Main machinery: 1 diesel; 670 hp(m) *(492 kW)*; 1 shaft
Speed, knots: 11
Complement: 10
Guns: 2—23 mm/60 (twin).

Comment: Built in 1958 as a buoy tender and converted to a command ship in 1983. Transferred in December 1992 having paid off from the Finnish Navy. Armament changed in 1988.

3 Ex-FINNISH KOSKELO CLASS (COASTAL PATROL CRAFT)

Displacement, tons: 95 full load
Dimensions, feet (metres): 95.1 × 16.4 × 4.9 *(29 × 5 × 1.5)*
Main machinery: 2 Mercedes Benz/MTU diesels; 2700 hp(m) *(1.98 MW)*; 2 shafts
Speed, knots: 23
Complement: 11
Guns: 1 Oerlikon 20 mm.

Comment: Transferred from the Finnish Coast Guard in November 1992. Steel hulled craft built between 1955 and 1960 and modernised in 1973.

Ex-KEMIO (old number and old gun)

1987, Finnish Navy

1 Ex-SWEDISH COAST GUARD TYPE (INSHORE PATROL CRAFT)

ex-*KBV 257*

Displacement, tons: 17 full load
Dimensions, feet (metres): 63 × 13.1 × 4.3 *(19.2 × 4 × 1.3)*
Main machinery: 2 Volvo Penta TAMD 120A diesels; 700 hp(m) *(515 kW)*; 2 shafts
Speed, knots: 22
Complement: 5

Comment: Transferred in April 1992. Former Coast Guard vessel built in 1970. Similar craft to Latvia and Lithuania.

COAST GUARD TYPE (Swedish colours)   *1990, Hartmut Ehlers*

SERVICE FORCES

1 MAYAK CLASS (TRANSPORT)

TORI

Displacement, tons: 920 full load
Dimensions, feet (metres): 178.1 × 30.5 × 11.8 *(54.3 × 9.3 × 3.6)*
Main machinery: 1 diesel; 1000 hp(m) *(735 kW)*; 1 shaft
Speed, knots: 12. **Range, miles:** 11 000 at 11 kts
Cargo capacity: 240 tons
Radars: Navigation: Spin Trough; I band.

Comment: Converted trawler transferred from Russia in 1992.

TORI   *1992*

1 AKEDEMIK SHULEYKIN CLASS

ARNOLD VEIMER

Displacement, tons: 2000 full load
Dimensions, feet (metres): 236.2 × 42.6 × 15.4 *(72 × 13 × 4.7)*
Main machinery: 2 Gorkiy G-74 diesels; 3060 hp(m) *(2.25 MW)*; 2 shafts
Speed, knots: 14
Complement: 70

Comment: Built by Laivateollisuus, Finland in 1983. Ice strengthened. Works for Estonia Academy and is painted dark blue.

ARNOLD VEIMER   *3/1989, van Ginderen Collection*

ETHIOPIA AND ERITREA

Headquarters' Appointment

Commander of the Ethiopian Navy:
Rear Admiral Yehuwalashet Girma

Personnel

(a) 1993: 3000
(b) Volunteers (Navy)

Bases

Massawa, Aseb, Dahlak, Djibouti

General

The picture was very confused in early 1993. It seems likely that Eritrea is to form a separate Navy based at Massawa and Dahlak, while the remains of the Ethiopian fleet either uses Aseb or retreats to Djibouti. Of the 10 ships which sought sanctuary in Yemen in May 1991, most have been scuttled, but those that went to Saudi Arabian ports have now returned. One or two of the patrol craft listed under *Deletions* may, in time, be recovered.

Mercantile Marine

Lloyd's Register of Shipping:
27 vessels of 69 481 tons gross

DELETIONS

Note: One or two of the patrol craft may be salvaged and repaired in due course.

Frigates

1991-92   *Ethiopia* (Hulk in Yemen port)

Light Forces

1990-92   3 Osa II class, 2 Turya class, 1 Mol class, 1 Swiftships 105 ft class, 2 Zhuk class, 4 Boghammar, 4 Sewart class

Amphibious Forces

1990-92   2 Chamo class (civilian), 4 T 4 class, 1 Edic class

---

FRIGATES

2 Ex-SOVIET PETYA II CLASS

F 1616   F 1617

Displacement, tons: 950 standard; 1180 full load
Dimensions, feet (metres): 268.3 × 29.9 × 9.5
(81.8 × 9.1 × 2.9)
Main machinery: CODAG; 1 Type 61V-3 diesel on centre shaft; 5400 hp(m) *(3.97 MW)* sustained; 2 gas turbines on outer shafts; 30 000 hp(m) *(22 MW)*; 3 shafts; cp prop on centre shaft
Speed, knots: 32. **Range, miles:** 4870 at 10 kts; 450 at 29 kts
Complement: 98 (8 officers)

Guns: 4 USSR 3 in *(76 mm)*/60 (2 twin) ❶; 80° elevation; 90 rounds/minute to 15 km *(8 nm)*; weight of shell 6.8 kg.
1 Multi Barrelled Rocket Launcher (MBRL) is mounted on the stern ❷.
1—12.7 mm MG.
Torpedoes: 5—16 in *(406 mm)* (1 quin) tubes ❸. Soviet Type 40; anti-submarine; active/passive homing up to 15 km *(8 nm)* at up to 40 kts; warhead 100-150 kg.
A/S mortars: 2 RBU 6000 12-tubed trainable mountings ❹; range 6000 m; warhead 31 kg.
Depth charges: 2 racks.
Mines: 22.
Countermeasures: ESM: Watch Dog; radar warning.
Radars: Air search: Strut Curve ❺; F band; range 110 km *(60 nm)* for 2 m² target.
Navigation: Don 2; I band.
Fire control: Hawk Screech ❻; I band; range 27 km *(15 nm)*.
IFF: High Pole B.
Sonars: Hull-mounted; active search and attack; medium frequency.

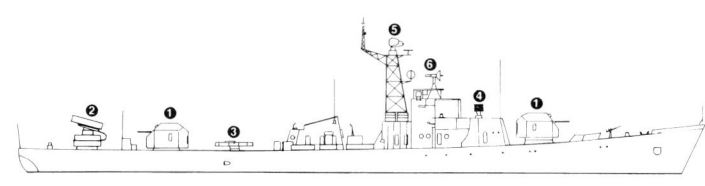

F 1616   *(Scale 1 : 900), Ian Sturton*

F 1616   *1990, Ethiopian Navy*

Programmes: First transferred 21 July 1983; second 19 March 1984. Both were towed to Massawa by Soviet warships. F 1616 was named *Zerai Deres* but this had been expunged by 1990.

Structure: This is the standard armament except that one MBRL replaces the after quintuple torpedo tubes.
Operational: In early 1993 F 1616 was at Dahlak and may be the first unit in the Eritrean Navy; F 1617 was at Djibouti.

186 ETHIOPIA / Light forces — Amphibious forces

LIGHT FORCES

1 Ex-SOVIET OSA II CLASS (FAST ATTACK CRAFT—MISSILE)

FMB 163

Displacement, tons: 245 full load
Dimensions, feet (metres): 126.6 × 24.9 × 8.8 *(38.6 × 7.6 × 2.7)*
Main machinery: 3 Type M 504 diesels; 10 800 hp(m) *(7.94 MW)* sustained; 3 shafts
Speed, knots: 37. **Range, miles:** 800 at 30 kts
Complement: 30

Missiles: SSM: 4 SS-N-2A Styx; active radar or IR homing to 46 km *(25 nm)* at 0.9 Mach; warhead 513 kg.
Guns: 4—30 mm/65 (2 twin); 85° elevation; 500 rounds/minute to 5 km *(2.7 nm)* anti-aircraft; weight of shell 0.54 kg.
Radars: Surface search: Square Tie; I band.
Fire control: Drum Tilt; H/I band.
IFF: Square Head. High Pole B.

Programmes: Acquired on 13 January 1981. The rest of the class have been sunk or scuttled.

FMB 163 *1991*

1 Ex-SOVIET MOL CLASS (FAST ATTACK CRAFT—TORPEDO)

FTB 111

Displacement, tons: 160 standard; 200 full load
Dimensions, feet (metres): 127.9 × 26.6 × 5.9 *(39 × 8.1 × 1.8)*
Main machinery: 3 Type M 504 diesels; 10 800 hp(m) *(7.94 MW)* sustained; 3 shafts
Speed, knots: 36. **Range, miles:** 1250 at 14 kts
Complement: 25 (3 officers)

Guns: 4—30 mm/65 (2 twin); 85° elevation; 500 rounds/minute to 5 km *(2.7 nm)*; weight of shell 0.54 kg.
Torpedoes: 4—21 in *(533 mm)* tubes. Soviet Type 53; dual purpose; pattern active/passive homing up to 20 km *(10.8 nm)* at up to 45 kts; warhead 400 kg.
Depth charges: 12.
Radars: Surface search: H/I band.
Fire control: Drum Tilt; H/I band.
IFF: Square Head. High Pole B.

Comment: Transferred January 1978. Seen in Djibouti in late 1992.

FTB 111 *1989*

2 SWIFTSHIPS 105 ft CLASS (LARGE PATROL CRAFT)

P 203   P 204

Displacement, tons: 118 full load
Dimensions, feet (metres): 105 × 23.6 × 6.5 *(32 × 7.2 × 2)*
Main machinery: 2 MTU MD 16V 538 TB90 diesels; 6000 hp(m) *(4.41 MW)* sustained; 2 shafts
Speed, knots: 30. **Range, miles:** 1200 at 18 kts
Complement: 21
Guns: 4 Emerlec 30 mm (2 twin); 80° elevation; 600 rounds/minute to 6 km *(3.3 nm)*; weight of shell 0.35 kg.
2—23 mm (twin) (201). 2—12.7 mm (twin) (203, 204).
Radars: Surface search: Decca RM 916; I band.

Comment: Six ordered in 1976 of which four were delivered in April 1977 before the cessation of US arms sales to Ethiopia. Built by Swiftships, Louisiana. One deserted to Somalia and served in that Navy for a time. These two are probably the only survivors and may be based at Djibouti.

P 203 *1989*

1 Ex-US PGM 53 CLASS (LARGE PATROL CRAFT)

P 15

Displacement, tons: 146 full load
Dimensions, feet (metres): 95 × 19 × 5.2 *(29 × 5.8 × 1.6)*
Main machinery: 4 diesels; 2200 hp *(1.64 MW)*; 2 shafts
Speed, knots: 21. **Range, miles:** 1500 at 18 kts
Complement: 20
Guns: 1 Bofors 40 mm/60. 1—12.7 mm MG.

Comment: Built by Peterson for the US Navy and commissioned in 1962. Transferred and then paid off in 1986. Seen again at sea in 1992.

PGM 53 *1980*

2 Ex-SOVIET ZHUK CLASS (COASTAL PATROL CRAFT)

P 206 *(ex-PC 17)*   **P 207**

Displacement, tons: 50 full load
Dimensions, feet (metres): 75.4 × 17 × 6.2 *(23 × 5.2 × 1.9)*
Main machinery: 2 Type M 50 diesels; 2200 hp(m) *(1.6 MW)* sustained; 2 shafts
Speed, knots: 30. **Range, miles:** 1100 at 15 kts
Complement: 17
Guns: 2—14.5 mm (twin) MGs.
Radars: Surface search: Spin Trough; I band.

Comment: First two delivered 9 October 1982 in Fizik Korchatov. Second pair arrived in Assad on 9 June 1990. Two destroyed in 1991; the other two may also be deleted.

P 206 (old number) *1985*

AMPHIBIOUS FORCES

2 Ex-SOVIET POLNOCHNY B CLASS (TYPE 771)

LTC 1037   LTC 1038

Displacement, tons: 760 standard; 834 full load
Dimensions, feet (metres): 246.1 × 31.5 × 7.5 *(75 × 9.6 × 2.3)*
Main machinery: 2 Kolomna Type 40-D diesels; 4400 hp(m) *(3.2 MW)* sustained; 2 shafts
Speed, knots: 19. **Range, miles:** 1000 at 18 kts
Complement: 40
Military lift: 350 tons including 6 tanks; 180 troops
Guns: 4—30 mm (2 twin). 2—140 mm rocket launchers; range 9 km *(4.9 nm)*.
Radars: Surface search: Don 2; I band.
Fire control: Drum Tilt; H/I band.

Comment: First transferred under tow from USSR 9 November 1981, second 8 January 1983. Both still operational in 1992.

POLNOCHNY 1038 *1990, Ethiopian Navy*

1 FRENCH EDIC CLASS

LTC 1036

Displacement, tons: 250 standard; 670 full load
Dimensions, feet (metres): 193.5 × 39.2 × 4.2 *(59 × 12 × 1.3)*
Main machinery: 2 SACM MGO 175 V12 diesels; 1200 hp(m) *(882 kW)* sustained; 2 shafts
Speed, knots: 12. **Range, miles:** 1800 at 8 kts
Complement: 16 (1 officer)
Military lift: 5 heavy vehicles or 11 personnel carriers
Guns: 2 DCN 20 mm (twin).

Comment: Two of the class completed by SFCN. Villeneuve la Garenne, France in May 1977. Cargo deck space 28.5 × 5 m *(93.5 × 16.4 ft)*. One deleted in 1990. This one was non-operational in 1992 but may be repairable.

SUPPORT SHIP

1 COASTAL TANKER

A 502

Displacement, tons: 1029 full load
Dimensions, feet (metres): 176.2 × 31.8 × 10.5 *(53.7 × 9.7 × 3.2)*
Main machinery: 1 6DR 30/50-5 diesel; 600 hp(m) *(441 kW)*; 1 shaft
Speed, knots: 10.5
Complement: 23
Guns: 2—12.7 mm MGs.
Radars: Navigation: Don; I band.

Comment: Acquired in 1989-90. May be deleted.

LTC 1036   *1990, Ethiopian Navy*

A 502   *1990, Ethiopian Navy*

FAEROES

COAST GUARD

1 PATROL CRAFT

TJALDRID

Displacement, tons: 650 full load
Dimensions, feet (metres): 146 × 33.1 × 10.5 *(44.5 × 10.1 × 3.2)*
Main machinery: 2 MWM diesels; 2400 hp(m) *(1.76 MW)*; 2 shafts
Speed, knots: 14.5
Complement: 18
Guns: 1—57 mm of late 19th century vintage can be carried.

Comment: Originally a commercial tug built in 1976 by Svolvaer, Verksted and acquired by the local government in 1987. Although Denmark retains control of defence, the Coast Guard and Fisheries come under the Landsstyri which is the islands' local government. The ship is based at Tórshavn on the island of Streymoy.

TJALDRID   *6/1987, Gunnar Olsen*

FALKLAND ISLANDS

General

A dependent territory of the United Kingdom. The capital and principle town is at Stanley. In 1987 Britain declared a fishing zone off the Falklands within which only licensed ships may work. On 26 December 1990 a further outer zone was declared, extending the original zones. No fishing is allowed in this outer area. Both zones are patrolled by two vessels throughout the year. Both ships have red hulls and white superstructures.

Aircraft

There are also two Pilatus Britten-Norman Defender unarmed maritime surveillance aircraft.

Mercantile Marine

Lloyd's Register of Shipping:
7 vessels of 13 982 tons gross

DELETIONS

1989-90	*Falkland Right* (ex-*Lancella*), *Beaulieu* (sold to Chile), *Blakeney* (sunk)	
1991	*Falkland Sound* (civilian), *Mount Kent* (civilian)	

FALKLAND PROTECTOR (ex-*Falkland Right*, ex-*G A Reay*, ex-*Arctic Privateer*)

Measurement, tons: 1878 grt
Dimensions, feet (metres): 227 × 39.4 × 16.4 *(69.2 × 12 × 5)*
Main machinery: 1 diesel; 2500 hp(m) *(1.84 MW)*; 1 shaft
Speed, knots: 14.5
Complement: 23 plus 6 spare

Comment: Ex-trawler built at Gdynia, Poland and first leased in February 1987. The ship returned to Gdynia to refit in 1989-90, being replaced by the ex-*Lancella* which was also called *Falkland Right*. Refit completed in March 1990 and returned to station in September 1990, now named *Falkland Protector*.

FALKLAND DESIRE (ex-*Southella*)

Measurement, tons: 1496 grt
Dimensions, feet (metres): 229 × 41.6 × 15.1 *(69.6 × 12.7 × 4.6)*
Main machinery: 1 Mirrlees KMR8 diesel; 2880 hp *(2.15 MW)*; 1 shaft; cp prop; Jetsam bow thruster; 250 hp *(186 kW)*
Speed, knots: 15
Complement: 40 + 21 spare

Comment: Research Vessel Ice Class III built in 1969, refitted in 1981 and again in 1987.

FALKLAND PROTECTOR   *1991, Government House*

FALKLAND DESIRE   *1991, Government House*

FIJI

Headquarters' Appointments

Commander, Military Forces:
  Brigadier E G Ganilau MC, MSD
Commander, Navy:
  Commander T Lesikivatukoula

Personnel

1993: 294

Base

FNS *Viti*, at Togalevu (Training).
Operation base at Walu Bay, Suva.

General

On 12 June 1975 the then Royal Fiji Military Forces were authorised to raise a Naval Division to carry out Fishery Protection, Surveillance, Hydrographic Surveying and Coast Guard duties. On 14 May 1987 a military coup overthrew the government and Fiji became a Republic on 10 October 1987. The Fiji Navy comes under the authority of the Minister of Home Affairs, and has been accountable to the CinC Military Forces since June 1989.

Prefix to Ships' Names

FNS

Mercantile Marine

Lloyd's Register of Shipping:
  64 vessels of 58 761 tons gross

DELETIONS

1990 *Kula*
1991 *Kikau*

PATROL FORCES

1 Ex-US REDWING CLASS (TRAINING SHIP)

Name	No	Builders	Commissioned
KIRO (ex-USS *Warbler*, MSC 206)	206	Bellingham SY, USA	23 July 1955

Displacement, tons: 370 full load
Dimensions, feet (metres): 144 × 28 × 8.5 *(43.9 × 8.5 × 2.5)*
Main machinery: 2 GM 8-268A diesels; 880 hp *(656 kW)*; 2 shafts
Speed, knots: 12. **Range, miles:** 3300 at 8 kts
Complement: 28
Guns: 1 Oerlikon 20 mm. 2—12.7 mm MGs.
Radars: Navigation: SPS 5C; I band.
Sonars: UQS-1B; hull-mounted; high frequency active.

Comment: Transferred in June 1976. Formerly a minesweeper but retained in 1991 as a training ship. *Kula* (deleted in 1990) was the only one of the class to have a helicopter platform.

4 Ex-ISRAEL DABUR CLASS (COASTAL PATROL CRAFT)

VAI 301   SAKU 303
OGO 302   SAQA 304

Displacement, tons: 39 full load
Dimensions, feet (metres): 64.9 × 18 × 5.8 *(19.8 × 5.5 × 1.8)*
Main machinery: 4 GM 12V-71TA diesels; 1680 hp *(1.25 MW)* sustained; 4 shafts
Speed, knots: 19. **Range, miles:** 450 at 13 kts
Complement: 9
Guns: 1 Oerlikon 20 mm. 1—12.7 mm MG.
Radars: Surface search: Racal Decca Super 101 Mk 3; I band.

Comment: Built in mid-1970s by Israeli Aircraft Industries and commissioned in the Fiji Navy 22 November 1991. Torpedo tubes are not fitted.

KIRO   *1989, Ships of the World*

DABUR   *1989, Rupert Pengelly*

0 + 3 PACIFIC FORUM TYPE (LARGE PATROL CRAFT)

Displacement, tons: 162 full load
Dimensions, feet (metres): 103.3 × 26.6 × 6.9 *(31.5 × 8.1 × 2.1)*
Main machinery: 2 Caterpillar 3516TA diesels; 2820 hp *(2.09 MW)* sustained; 2 shafts
Speed, knots: 20. **Range, miles:** 2500 at 12 kts
Complement: 17
Guns: 1—12.7 mm MG.

Comment: Ordered from Australian Shipbuilding Industries in December 1992. An improved design is expected.

2 COASTAL PATROL CRAFT

LEVUKA 101   **LAUTOKA** 102

Displacement, tons: 97 full load
Dimensions, feet (metres): 110 × 24 × 5 *(33.8 × 7.4 × 1.5)*
Main machinery: 4 GM 12V-71TA diesels; 1680 hp *(1.25 MW)* sustained; 4 shafts
Speed, knots: 12
Guns: 1—12.7 mm MG.

Comment: Built in 1979-80 by Beaux's Bay Craft Inc, Louisiana as oil rig support craft. Purchased in September 1987 and commissioned on 22 and 28 October 1987 respectively. All aluminium construction.

1 HYDROGRAPHIC SURVEY SHIP

TOVUTO (ex-*Babale*, ex-*Eugene McDermott II*)

Displacement, tons: 920 full load
Dimensions, feet (metres): 171 × 38 × 11 *(52.6 × 11.7 × 3.4)*
Main machinery: 2 Caterpillar D 399; 2250 hp *(1.67 MW)* sustained; 2 shafts
Speed, knots: 12. **Range, miles:** 9400 at 10 kts
Complement: 41 (5 officers)

Comment: Originally a commercial exploration vessel launched by Carrington Slipways in 1971. Delivered April 1987. Transferred 9 December 1989 to the Marine Department of the Ministry of Transport, then later to the Ministry of Works and Communications. Civilian manned.

TOVUTO   *1987, Fiji Navy*

1 TRAINING VESSEL

VANIDORO

Comment: Presidential yacht taken over in March 1991 and now used as a training ship. Has crew of 20.

LAUTOKA   *10/1987, Fiji Navy*

FINLAND

Headquarters' Appointments

Commander-in-Chief Defence Forces:
  Admiral Jan Klenberg
Commander-in-Chief Finnish Navy:
  Rear Admiral Sakari Visa
Chief Engineer Defence Forces:
  Rear Admiral (E) Auvo Vappula
Chief of Staff FNHQ:
  Captain Seppo Lintula

Diplomatic Representation

Defence Attaché in London:
  Captain Juhani Kaskeala
Defence Attaché in Moscow:
  Colonel Kalevi Rissanen
Defence Attaché in Paris:
  Lieutenant Colonel Harri Vilkuna
Defence Attaché in Washington:
  Colonel Kari Savolainen
Defence Attaché in Bonn:
  Commander Matti Mäkinen

Treaty Limitations

The Treaty of Paris (1947) limited the Navy to 10 000 tons of ships and 4500 personnel with submarines and torpedo boats prohibited. In September 1990 the government 'disengaged' from parts of the Treaty so allowing a reappraisal of defence requirements, including submarines.

Personnel

(a) 1993: 1800 (200 officers, 500 POs and 1100 conscripts)
(b) 11 months' national service
(c) 600 Frontier Guards

Fleet Organisation

Organisation changed on 1 January 1993.
Gulf of Finland Naval Command; main base Uppinniemi, Helsinki.
Archipelago Sea Naval Command; main base Turku.
Not all ships are fully manned all the time but all are rotated on a regular basis.

Coastal Artillery

The following vessels are used by the Coastal Artillery: *Vahakari, Vaarlahti, Väno, Kampela 1* and *2, Pyhäranta*, 2 Lohi class, 6 Hauki class, *Askeri, Parainen, Träskö, Torsö*. There are also numerous smaller vessels.

Strength of the Fleet

Type	Active	Building (Planned)
Corvettes	2	—
Fast Attack Craft (Missile)	12	—
Fast Attack Craft (Gun)	5	—
Large Patrol Craft	5	—
Coastal Patrol Craft	1	—
Minelayers	6	—
Minesweepers, Inshore	13	—
Tugs	2	—
Command Craft	8	1 (1)
Transports (Landing Craft)	47	—
Cable Ship	1	—
Icebreakers	9	1
Support and Transport Ships	12	2

Frontier Guard

All Frontier Guard vessels come under the Ministry of the Interior.

Type	Active	Building
Large Patrol Craft	8	(2)
Coastal Patrol Craft	57 app	7

Hydrographic Department

This office and the survey ships come under the Ministry of Trade and Industry.

Icebreakers

All these ships work for the Board of Navigation.

Mercantile Marine

Lloyd's Register of Shipping:
  263 vessels of 1 186 691 tons gross

DELETIONS

Minelayers

1992 *Keihässalmi*

Light Forces

1992 *Kuikka, Tavi, Kurki, Telkkä* (three to Estonia, November 1992), *Nuoli 5*

Support Ships

1990 *Kave 1-4, 6, Pyhäranta* (old)
1991 *Pansio* (old), *Porkkala* (old)
1992 *Kemiö* (to Estonia), *Kala 2, Kala 5, Vihuri*

PENNANT LIST

Corvettes

03	Turunmaa
04	Karjala

Light Forces

11	Tuima
12	Tuisku
14	Tuuli
15	Tyrsky
30	Hurja
38	Nuoli 8
40	Nuoli 10
41	Nuoli 11
42	Nuoli 12
43	Nuoli 13
51	Rihtniemi
52	Rymättylä
53	Ruissalo
54	Raisio
55	Röytta
60	Helsinki
61	Turku
62	Oulu
63	Kotka
70	Rauma
71	Raahe
72	Porvoo
73	Naantali

Mine Warfare Forces

01	Pohjanmaa
02	Hämeenmaa
05	Uusimaa
21-26	Kuha 21-26
475	Pyhäranta
521-	
527	Kiiski 1-7
777	Porkkala
876	Pansio (new)

Support Ships and Miscellaneous

91	Viiri
92	Putsaari
97	Valas
98	Mursu
99	Kustaanmiekka
121	Vahakari
133	Havouri
222	Vaarlahti
232	Hauki
235	Hirsala
237	Hila
238	Harun
241	Askeri
251	Lohi
272	Kampela 2
323	Väno
334	Hankoniemi
420	Parainen
431	Hakuni
436	Houtskar
452	Lohm
471	Kampela 1
511	Vinha
521	Raju
531	Syöksy
557	Kampela 3
731	Haukipää
773	Kala 3
776	Kala 6
799	Hylje
826	Isku
831	Kallanpää
871	Kala 1
874	Kala 4
899	Halli
992	Träskö
993	Torsö

CORVETTES

2 TURUNMAA CLASS

Name	No	Builders	Laid down	Launched	Commissioned
TURUNMAA	03	Wärtsilä, Helsinki	Mar 1967	11 July 1967	29 Aug 1968
KARJALA	04	Wärtsilä, Helsinki	Mar 1967	16 Aug 1967	21 Oct 1968

Displacement, tons: 660 standard; 770 full load
Dimensions, feet (metres): 243.1 × 25.6 × 7.9 *(74.1 × 7.8 × 2.4)*
Main machinery: CODOG; 1 RR Olympus TM1A gas turbine; 15 000 hp *(11.2 MW)* sustained; 3 MTU MB diesels; 3000 hp(m) *(2.2 MW)*; 3 shafts; cp props
Speed, knots: 35; 17 diesel. **Range, miles:** 2500 at 14 kts
Complement: 70

Guns: 1 Bofors 4.7 in *(120 mm)*/46 ❶; 80° elevation; 80 rounds/minute to 18.5 km *(10 nm)*; weight of shell 21 kg. 6—103 mm rails for illuminants are fitted on the side of the mounting.
2 Bofors 40 mm/70 ❷; 90° elevation; 300 rounds/minute to 12 km *(6.6 nm)*; weight of shell 0.96 kg.
4 USSR 23 mm/87 (2 twin) ❸.
A/S mortars: 2 RBU 1200 5-tubed fixed launchers ❹ (mounted inside main deck superstructure abaft the pennant number); range 1200 m; warhead 34 kg.
Depth charges: 2 racks.
Countermeasures: Decoys: Wallop Barricade double chaff launcher.
ESM: Argo ❺; radar intercept.
Fire control: SAAB EOS-400 optronic director ❻.
Radars: Surface search: Terma 20T 48 Super ❼; E/F band.
Fire control: Signaal WM 22 ❽; I/J band; range 46 km *(25 nm)*.
Navigation: Raytheon ARPA; I band.
Sonars: Hull-mounted; active search and attack; high frequency. Optimised for operations in archipelago waters.

Programmes: Ordered on 18 February 1965.
Modernisation: Both completed refit at the Wärtsilä Shipyard, Turku in 1986. New equipment included radar, EW and sonar.
Structure: Flush decked. Fitted with Vosper Thornycroft fin stabiliser equipment. The exhaust system is trunked on either side of the quarter-deck, the two plumes coalescing some 50 ft abaft the stern.

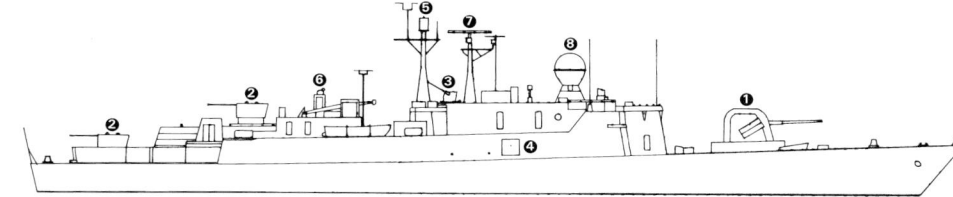

TURUNMAA (Scale 1 : 600), Ian Sturton

TURUNMAA 1992, Finnish Navy

LIGHT FORCES

4 HELSINKI CLASS (FAST ATTACK CRAFT—MISSILE)

Name	No	Builders	Commissioned
HELSINKI	60	Wärtsilä, Helsinki	1 Sep 1981
TURKU	61	Wärtsilä, Helsinki	3 June 1985
OULU	62	Wärtsilä, Helsinki	1 Oct 1985
KOTKA	63	Wärtsilä, Helsinki	16 June 1986

Displacement, tons: 280 standard; 300 full load
Dimensions, feet (metres): 147.6 × 29.2 × 9.9 *(45 × 8.9 × 3)*
Main machinery: 3 MTU 16V 538 TB92 diesels; 10 230 hp(m) *(7.52 MW)* sustained; 3 shafts
Speed, knots: 30
Complement: 30

Missiles: SSM: 8 Saab RBS 15; inertial guidance; active radar homing to 70 km *(37.8 nm)* at 0.8 Mach; warhead 150 kg; sea-skimmer.
Guns: 1 Bofors 57 mm/70; 75° elevation; 200 rounds/minute to 17 km *(9.3 nm)*; weight of shell 2.4 kg. 6—103 mm rails for rocket illuminants.
4 USSR 23 mm/87 (2 twin); can be replaced by Sadral SAM launcher.
Depth charges: 2 rails.
Countermeasures: Decoys: Philax chaff and IR flare launcher.
ESM: Argo; radar intercept.
Fire control: Saab EOS 400 optronic.
Radars: Surface search: 9GA 208; I band.
Fire control: Philips 9LV 225; J band.
Sonars: Simrad Marine SS 304; high resolution active scanning.

Programmes: *Helsinki* was launched 5 November 1980. Next three ordered to a revised design on 13 January 1983.
Modernisation: *Helsinki's* bridge and armament have been modified and are now the same as the other three of the class. A *Kotka* type barbet can take either twin 23 mm guns or a Sadral SAM launcher.
Structure: The light armament can be altered to suit the planned role. Hull and superstructure of light alloy.

4 RAUMA CLASS (FAST ATTACK CRAFT—MISSILE)

Name	No	Builders	Commissioned
RAUMA	70	Hollming, Rauma	18 Oct 1990
RAAHE	71	Hollming, Rauma	20 Aug 1991
PORVOO	72	Finnyards, Rauma	27 Apr 1992
NAANTALI	73	Finnyards, Rauma	23 June 1992

Displacement, tons: 215 standard; 248 full load
Dimensions, feet (metres): 157.5 × 26.2 × 4.5 *(48 × 8 × 1.5)*
Main machinery: 2 MTU 16V 538 TB93 diesels; 7510 hp(m) *(5.52 MW)* sustained; 2 Riva Calzoni waterjets
Speed, knots: 30
Complement: 19 (5 officers)

Missiles: SSM: 6 Saab RBS 15SF (could embark 8); active radar homing to 150 km *(80 nm)* at 0.8 Mach; warhead 200 kg.
SAM: Matra Sadral sextuple launcher; Mistral; IR homing to 4 km *(2.2 nm)*; warhead 3 kg.
Guns: Bofors 40 mm/70; 90° elevation; 300 rounds/minute to 12 km *(6.6 nm)*; weight of shell 96 kg.
6—103 mm rails for rocket illuminants.
2 USSR 23 mm/87 (twin); can be fitted instead of Sadral.
A/S mortars: 4 Saab Elma LLS-920 9-tubed launchers; range 300 m; warhead 4.2 kg shaped charge.
Depth charges: 1 rail.
Countermeasures: Decoys: Philax chaff and IR flares.
ESM: MEL Matilda; radar intercept.
Fire control: Bofors Electronic 9LV200 Mk 3 optronic director with TV camera; infra-red and laser telemetry.
Radars: Surface search: 9GA 208; I band.
Fire control: Bofors Electronic 9LV 225; J band.
Navigation: Raytheon ARPA; I band.
Sonars: Simrad Subsea toadfish sonar; search and attack; high frequency.

Programmes: Four ordered 27 August 1987. Another eight of these craft are planned for the future, but further orders are uncertain.
Structure: Developed from Helsinki class. Hull and superstructure of light alloy. SAM and 23 mm guns are interchangeable within the same barbet.
Operational: Primary function is the anti-ship role but there is some ASW capability and mention is also made of a secondary role in mine warfare, as it is in all Finnish war vessels.

KOTKA *10/1990, Antonio Moreno*

HELSINKI *1992, Finnish Navy*

KOTKA (left) and HELSINKI *6/1991, Harald Carstens*

RAUMA (with SAM) *6/1992, Marko Enqvist*

RAAHE (with 23 mm gun) *1992, Finnish Nav*

RAUMA (with SAM) *1992, Finnish Nav*

FINLAND / Light forces

4 TUIMA CLASS (FAST ATTACK CRAFT—MISSILE)

TUIMA 11	TUISKU 12	TUULI 14	TYRSKY 15

Displacement, tons: 210 standard; 245 full load
Dimensions, feet (metres): 110.2 × 24.9 × 8.8 *(33.6 × 7.6 × 2.7)*
Main machinery: 3 Type M 504 diesels; 10 800 hp(m) *(7.94 MW)* sustained; 3 shafts
Speed, knots: 37. **Range, miles:** 500 at 35 kts
Complement: 30

Missiles: SSM: 4 SS-N-2B Styx; active radar or IR homing to 46 km *(25 nm)* at 0.9 Mach; warhead 513 kg.
Guns: 4 USSR 30 mm/65 (2 twin); 85° elevation; 500 rounds/minute to 5 km *(2.7 nm)*; weight of shell 0.54 kg.
Radars: Surface search: Square Tie; I band.
Fire control: Drum Tilt; H/I band.
Navigation: Racal Decca; I band.

Programmes: Ex-Soviet Osa II class purchased from the USSR 1974-75.
Modernisation: New construction but with Finnish electronics and Western navigational radar. *Tuima* converted in 1993 to a minelayer with the missile system removed. The others may also be converted in due course.

TUISKU *1991, Finnish Navy*

5 NUOLI CLASS (FAST ATTACK CRAFT—GUN)

Name	No	Builders	Commissioned
NUOLI 8, 10—13	38, 40—43	Laivateollisuus, Turku	1961-66

Displacement, tons: 40 standard
Dimensions, feet (metres): 72.2 × 21.7 × 5 *(22 × 6.6 × 1.5)*
Main machinery: 3 Type M 50 diesels; 3300 hp(m) *(2.4 MW)* sustained; 3 shafts
Speed, knots: 40
Complement: 15
Guns: 1 Bofors 40 mm/70 or 2 USSR 23 mm/87 (twin, aft). 1 Oerlikon 20 mm or 12.7 mm (fwd) MG.
Depth charges: 4
Radars: Surface search: Decca; I band.

Comment: Delivery dates: 22 August 1962, 5 May 1964, 5 May 1964, 30 November 1964, 12 October 1966. This class is split into two: *Nuoli 1* (8) and *Nuoli 2* (10-13). The main difference is a lower superstructure in *Nuoli 2*. These five were modernised under the 1979 estimates.

NUOLI 13 (with 40 mm gun) *1991, Finnish Navy*

2 RIHTNIEMI CLASS (LARGE PATROL CRAFT)

Name	No	Builders	Commissioned
RIHTNIEMI	51	Rauma-Repola, Rauma	21 Feb 1957
RYMÄTTYLÄ	52	Rauma-Repola, Rauma	20 May 1957

Displacement, tons: 90 standard; 110 full load
Dimensions, feet (metres): 101.7 × 18.7 × 5.9 *(31 × 5.6 × 1.8)*
Main machinery: 2 MTU MB diesels; 2500 hp(m) *(1.84 MW)*; 2 shafts; cp props
Speed, knots: 18
Complement: 20
Guns: 4 USSR 23 mm/87 (2 twin).
A/S mortars: 2 RBU 1200 fixed 5-tubed launchers; range 1200 m; warhead 34 kg.
Mines: Can lay mines.
Radars: Navigation: Decca; I band.
Sonars: Hull-mounted; active search and attack; high frequency.

Comment: Ordered in June 1955, launched in 1956. Both modernised for A/S work—further modernisation completed 1981.

RIHTNIEMI *1990, van Ginderen Collection*

3 RUISSALO CLASS (LARGE PATROL CRAFT)

Name	No	Builders	Commissioned
RUISSALO	53	Laivateollisuus, Turku	11 Aug 1959
RAISIO	54	Laivateollisuus, Turku	12 Sep 1959
RÖYTTÄ	55	Laivateollisuus, Turku	14 Oct 1959

Displacement, tons: 110 standard; 130 full load
Dimensions, feet (metres): 108.9 × 18.5 × 5.9 *(33 × 5.6 × 1.8)*
Main machinery: 2 MTU MB diesels; 2500 hp(m) *(1.84 MW)*; 2 shafts
Speed, knots: 17
Complement: 20
Guns: 2 or 4 USSR 23 mm/87 (1 or 2 twin).
A/S mortars: 2 RBU 1200 fixed 5-tubed launchers; range 1200 m; warhead 34 kg.
Mines: Can lay mines.
Radars: Navigation: Decca; I band.
Sonars: Hull-mounted; active search and attack; high frequency.
Sonac/PTA towed array; passive search; low frequency.

Comment: Ordered in January 1958. Launched on 16 June, 2 July and 2 June 1959. *Ruissalo* was modernised in 1976, other pair in 1980. In 1991 *Ruissalo* was fitted with a lightweight towed sonar array replacing the after gun mounting. Others of the class may also be fitted.

RAISIO *1988, Finnish Navy*

RUISSALO (with towed array) *1992, Finnish Navy*

1 TRIALS SHIP

Name	No	Builders	Commissioned
ISKU	826 (ex-16)	Reposaaron Konepaja	1970

Displacement, tons: 180 standard
Dimensions, feet (metres): 108.5 × 28.5 × 5.9 *(33 × 8.7 × 1.8)*
Main machinery: 4 Type M 50 diesels; 4400 hp(m) *(3.3 MW)* sustained; 4 shafts
Speed, knots: 18
Complement: 25
Radars: Navigation: Raytheon ARPA; I band

Comment: Formerly a missile experimental craft, now used for various equipment trials. Modernised in 1989-90 by Uusikaupunki Shipyard and lengthened by 7 metres. Can quickly be converted to a minelayer.

ISKU *1990, Finnish Navy*

1 EXPERIMENTAL COASTAL PATROL CRAFT

HURJA 30

Displacement, tons: 30
Dimensions, feet (metres): 72.2 × 16.4 × 6.6 *(22 × 5 × 2)*
Main machinery: 3 diesels; 3800 hp(m) *(2.2 MW)*; 3 waterjets
Speed, knots: 30
Complement: 10

Comment: Built by Fiskars, Turun, Turku. Completed 1981. GRP hull. Probably did not come up to expectations and is now used as trials craft.

HURJA *1991, Finnish Navy*

FINLAND / Mine warfare forces

MINE WARFARE FORCES

Note: *Tuima* (see *Light Forces*) converted to a fast minelayer in 1993. Others of the class may follow.

2 HÄMEENMAA CLASS (MINELAYERS)

Name	No	Builders	Laid down	Launched	Commissioned
HÄMEENMAA	02	Finnyards, Rauma	2 Apr 1991	11 Nov 1991	15 Apr 1992
UUSIMAA	05	Finnyards, Rauma	12 Nov 1991	June 1992	2 Dec 1992

Displacement, tons: 1000 standard
Dimensions, feet (metres): 249.3 × 38.1 × 9.8 *(76 × 11.6 × 3)*
Main machinery: 2 Wärtsilä 16V22 diesels; 6300 hp(m) *(4.64 MW)* sustained; 2 KaMeWa cp props; bow thruster
Speed, knots: 19
Complement: 70

Missiles: SAM: Matra Sadral sextuple launcher; Mistral; IR homing to 4 km *(2.2 nm)*; warhead 3 kg.
Guns: 2 Bofors 40 mm/70. 4 or 6—23 mm/87 (2 or 3 twin) (the third mounting is interchangeable with Sadral launcher).
A/S mortars: 2 RBU 1200 fixed 5-tubed launchers; range 1200 m; warhead 34 kg.
Mines: 4 rails for 100-150.
Countermeasures: Decoys: 2 ML/Wallop Superbarricade multi-chaff launchers.
ESM: Radar warning.
Fire control: Radamec System 2400 optronic director; 2 Galileo optical directors.
Radars: Surface search and Navigation: Three Selesmar ARPA; I band.
Sonars: Hull-mounted high frequency mine detection set.

Programmes: First one ordered 29 December 1989 after the original order in July from Wärtsilä had been cancelled. Second ordered 13 February 1991. Dual role as a transport and support ship.
Structure: Steel hull and alloy superstructure. Ice-strengthened and capable of breaking up to 40 nm ice. Ramps in bow and stern. The Sadral launcher is mounted at the stern. The after 40 mm gun is on the after end of the superstructure. SAM system can be replaced by a third twin 23 mm mounting within the same barbet.

HÄMEENMAA *1992, Finnish Navy*

1 MINELAYER

Name	No	Builders	Laid down	Launched	Commissioned
POHJANMAA	01	Wärtsilä, Helsinki	4 May 1978	28 Aug 1978	8 June 1979

Displacement, tons: 1000 standard; 1100 full load
Dimensions, feet (metres): 255.8 × 37.7 × 9.8 *(78.2 × 11.6 × 3)*
Main machinery: 2 Wärtsilä Vasa 16V22 diesels; 6300 hp(m) *(4.64 MW)* sustained; 2 shafts; cp props; bow thruster
Speed, knots: 19. **Range, miles:** 3500 at 15 kts
Complement: 90

Guns: 1 Bofors 4.7 in *(120 mm)*/46; 80° elevation; 80 rounds/minute to 18.5 km *(10 nm)*; weight of shell 21 kg. 6—103 mm launchers for illuminants fitted to the mounting.
2 Bofors 40 mm/70; 90° elevation; 300 rounds/minute to 12 km *(6.6 nm)*; weight of shell 0.96 kg.
4 USSR 23 mm/87 (2 twin). 2—12.7 mm MGs.
A/S mortars: 2 RBU 1200 fixed 5-tubed launchers; range 1200 m; warhead 34 kg.
Depth charges: 2 rails.
Mines: 120 including UK Stonefish.
Countermeasures: Decoys: Philax chaff and IR flare launcher.
ESM: Argo; radar intercept.
Radars: Air search: Signaal DA 05; E/F band; range 137 km *(75 nm)* for 2 m² target.
Fire control: Phillips 9LV 200; J band.
Navigation: I band.
Sonars: Hull-mounted; active search and attack; high frequency. Bottom classification; search; high frequency.

POHJANMAA *6/1992, Finnish Navy*

Programmes: Design completed 1976. Ordered late 1977.
Modernisation: In 1992 the forward 23 mm guns were replaced by 12.7 mm MGs.
Operational: Also serves as training ship. Carries 70 trainees accommodated in Portakabins on the mine deck. Helicopter area on quarter-deck but no hangar.

3 PANSIO CLASS (MINELAYERS—LCU TYPE)

Name	No	Builders	Commissioned
PANSIO	876	Olkiluoto Shipyard	25 Sep 1991
PYHÄRANTA	475	Olkiluoto Shipyard	26 May 1992
PORKKALA	777	Olkiluoto Shipyard	29 Oct 1992

Displacement, tons: 450 standard
Dimensions, feet (metres): 144.3 oa; 128.6 wl × 32.8 × 6.6 *(44; 39.2 × 10 × 2)*
Main machinery: 2 MTU 12V 183 diesels; 1500 hp(m) *(1.1 MW)*; 2 shafts; bow thruster
Speed, knots: 10
Complement: 12
Guns: 2 USSR 23 mm/87 (twin). 1—12.7 mm MG.
Mines: 50.
Radars: Navigation: Raytheon ARPA; I band.

Comment: Ordered in May 1990. Used for inshore minelaying and transport with a capacity of 100 tons. Ice strengthened with ramps in bow and stern. Has a 15 ton crane fitted aft.

6 KUHA CLASS (MINESWEEPERS—INSHORE)

Name	No	Builders	Commissioned
KUHA 21—26	21—26	Laivateollisuus, Turku	1974-75

Displacement, tons: 90 full load
Dimensions, feet (metres): 87.2 × 22.7 × 6.6 *(26.6 × 6.9 × 2)*
Main machinery: 2 Cummins MT-380M diesels; 600 hp(m) *(448 kW)*; 1 shaft; cp prop; active rudder
Speed, knots: 12
Complement: 15
Guns: 2 USSR 23 mm/60 (twin). 1—12.7 mm MG.
Radars: Navigation: Decca; I band.

Comment: All ordered 1972. *Kuha 21* completed 28 June 1974, *Kuha 26* in late 1975. Fitted for magnetic, acoustic and pressure-mine clearance. Hulls are of GRP.

PANSIO *1991, Finnish Navy*

KUHA 24 *1992, Finnish Navy*

7 KIISKI CLASS (MINESWEEPERS—INSHORE)

Name	No	Builders	Commissioned
KIISKI 1-7	521-527	Fiskars, Turku	1983-84

Displacement, tons: 20
Dimensions, feet (metres): 49.9 × 13.4 × 3.3 *(15.2 × 4.1 × 1.2)*
Main machinery: 2 Valmet 611 CSMP diesels; 340 hp(m) *(250 kW)*; 2 waterjets
Speed, knots: 11
Complement: 4

Comment: Ordered January 1983. All completed by 24 May 1984. GRP hull. Built to be used with Kuha class for unmanned teleguided sweeping, but this was not successful and they are now used for manned sweeping operations with crew of four.

KIISKI 4 *1992, Finnish Navy*

2 MINELAYING BARGES

721   821

Displacement, tons: 130 full load
Dimensions, feet (metres): 49.2 × 23 × 4.9 *(15 × 7 × 1.5)*

Comment: Built by Lehtinen, Rauma in 1987. Dumb barges used to transport and lay mines in port approaches.

ICEBREAKERS

Note: Controlled by Board of Navigation which also operates 14 transport ships and 9 oil recovery vessels. There is also the German-owned, Finnish manned, icebreaker *Hansa*, of the Karhu class, completed on 25 November 1966, which operates off Germany in Winter and off Finland at other times.

HANSA *8/1988, Gilbert Gyssels*

2 KARHU 2 CLASS

OTSO   KONTIO

Measurement, tons: 9200 dwt
Dimensions, feet (metres): 324.7 × 79.4 × 26.2 *(99 × 24.2 × 8)*
Main machinery: Diesel-electric; 4 Wärtsilä Vasa 16V32 diesel generators; 22.84 MW 60 Hz sustained; 2 motors; 17 700 hp(m) *(13 MW)*; 2 shafts
Speed, knots: 18.5
Complement: 28
Helicopters: 1 light.

Comment: First ordered from Wärtsilä 29 March 1984, completed 30 January 1986. Second ordered 29 November 1985, delivered 29 January 1987.

KONTIO *1/1987, Wärtsilä*

2 URHO CLASS

URHO   SISU

Displacement, tons: 7800 *Urho* (7900, *Sisu*) standard; 9500 full load
Dimensions, feet (metres): 343.1 × 78.1 × 27.2 *(104.6 × 23.8 × 8.3)*
Main machinery: Diesel-electric; 5 Wärtsilä-SEMT-Pielstick diesels; 25 000 hp(m) *(18.37 MW)*; 4 motors; 22 000 hp(m) *(16.2 MW)*; 4 shafts (2 fwd, 2 aft)
Speed, knots: 18
Complement: 47
Helicopters: 1 light.

Comment: Built by Wärtsilä and commissioned on 5 March 1975 and 28 January 1976 respectively. Fitted with two screws aft, taking 60 per cent of available power and two fwd, taking the remainder. Sisters to Swedish Atle class.

URHO and SISU *6/1988, A Sheldon Duplaix*

3 TARMO CLASS

TARMO   VARMA   APU

Displacement, tons: 4890 full load
Dimensions, feet (metres): 281 × 71 × 23.9 *(85.7 × 21.7 × 7.3)*
Main machinery: Diesel-electric; 4 Wärtsilä-Sulzer diesels; electric drive; 12 000 hp(m) *(8.82 MW)*; 4 shafts (2 screws fwd, 2 aft)
Speed, knots: 17
Complement: 45-55
Helicopters: 1 light.

Comment: Built by Wärtsilä and commissioned in 1963, 1968 and 1970 respectively.

TARMO *1989, Finnish Navy*

1 + 1 FENNICA CLASS

FENNICA

Measurement, tons: 4800 dwt
Dimensions, feet (metres): 380.5 × 85.3 × 27.6 *(116 × 26 × 8.4)*
Main machinery: Diesel-electric; 2 Wärtsilä Vasa 16V32D/ABB Strömberg diesel generators; 12 MW; 2 Wärtsilä Vasa 12V32D/ABB Strömberg diesel generators; 9 MW; 2 ABB Strömberg motors; 2 Aquamaster US ARC 1 nozzles; 20 400 hp(m) *(15 MW)*; 3 Brunvoll bow thrusters; 6120 hp(m) *(4.5 MW)*
Speed, knots: 16
Complement: 86
Helicopters: 1 light.

Comment: Ordered in October 1991 from Finnyards, Rauma. *Fennica* launched 10 September 1992 and completed in March 1993. Second of class to complete in January 1994. Bollard pull 200 tons. Capable of 8 kts at 0.8 m level ice and continuous slow speed at 1.8 m arctic level ice. 120 ton A frame and two deck cranes of 15 and 5 tons each. Combination of azimuth propulsion units and bow thrusters gives full dynamic positioning capability.

FENNICA (artist's impression) *1992, Finnyards*

194 FINLAND / Icebreakers — Support ships

1 VOIMA CLASS

VOIMA

Displacement, tons: 4415 full load
Dimensions, feet (metres): 274 × 63.7 × 23 (83.6 × 19.4 × 7)
Main machinery: Diesel-electric; 6 Wärtsilä Vasa 16V22 diesel generators; 16.8 MW sustained; 4 motors; 13 600 hp(m) (10 MW); 4 shafts (2 fwd, 2 aft)
Speed, knots: 16.5
Complement: 45

Comment: Launched in 1953. Modernised in 1978-79 with new main machinery and a remodelled superstructure and living quarters by Wärtsilä. This has given her a life expectancy until 1994. *Voima* when built was sister to the Soviet Kapitan Belousov class and the Swedish *Oden* (since deleted).

VOIMA
1991, van Ginderen Collection

SUPPORT SHIPS

1 COMMAND SHIP

KUSTAANMIEKKA (ex-*Valvoja III*) 99

Displacement, tons: 340 full load
Dimensions, feet (metres): 118.1 × 29.5 × 9.8 (36 × 9 × 3)
Main machinery: 1 diesel; 670 hp(m) (492 kW); 1 shaft
Speed, knots: 11
Complement: 10
Guns: 2—12.7 mm MGs (not always carried).

Comment: Completed in 1963. Former buoy tender transferred from Board of Navigation and converted by Hollming, Rauma in 1989. Bofors 40 mm gun replaced in 1988.

5 VALAS CLASS (GP TRANSPORTS)

| VALAS 97 | MURSU 98 | VAHAKARI 121 | VAARLAHTI 222 | VANO 323 |

Displacement, tons: 300 full load
Dimensions, feet (metres): 100.4 × 26.5 × 10.4 (30.6 × 8.1 × 3.2)
Main machinery: 1 Wärtsilä Vasa 8V22 diesel; 1576 hp(m) (1.16 MW) sustained; 1 shaft
Speed, knots: 12
Complement: 11
Military lift: 35 tons
Guns: 2—23 mm/60 (twin). 1—12.7 mm MG.
Mines: 28 can be carried.

Comment: Completed 1979-80. *Mursu* acts as a diving tender; *Vahakari*, *Vaarlahti* and *Vano* are used by the Coastal Artillery. Funnel is offset to starboard. Can be used as minelayers or transport/cargo carriers and are capable of breaking thin ice.

VAARLAHTI
10/1990, van Ginderen Collection

3 KAMPELA CLASS (LCU TRANSPORTS)

Name	No	Builders	Commissioned
KAMPELA 1	471	Enso Gutzeit	29 July 1976
KAMPELA 2	272	Enso Gutzeit	21 Oct 1976
KAMPELA 3	557 (ex-77)	Finnmekano	23 Oct 1979

Displacement, tons: 90 light; 260 full load
Dimensions, feet (metres): 106.6 × 26.2 × 4.9 (32.5 × 8 × 1.5)
Main machinery: 2 Scania diesels; 460 hp(m) (338 kW); 2 shafts
Speed, knots: 9
Complement: 10
Guns: 2 or 4 USSR 23 mm/60 (1 or 2 twin).
Mines: About 20 can be carried.

Comment: Can be used as amphibious craft, transports, minelayers or for shore support. Armament can be changed to suit role. *Kampela 1* and *2* are used by the Coastal Artillery.

KAMPELA 2
1988, Finnish Navy

4 KALA CLASS (LCU TRANSPORTS)

| KALA 1 871 | KALA 3 773 | KALA 4 874 | KALA 6 776 |

Displacement, tons: 60 light; 200 full load
Dimensions, feet (metres): 88.6 × 26.2 × 6 (27 × 8 × 1.8)
Main machinery: 2 Valmet diesels; 360 hp(m) (265 kW); 2 shafts
Speed, knots: 9
Complement: 10
Guns: 1 Oerlikon 20 mm (not in all).
Mines: 34.

Comment: Completed between 20 June 1956 (*Kala 1*) and 4 December 1959 (*Kala 6*). Can be used as transports, amphibious craft, minelayers or for shore support. Armament can be changed to suit role. Pennant numbers changed in 1990. Two deleted in 1992.

KALA 6
1991, Finnish Navy

6 HAUKI CLASS (TRANSPORTS)

| HAVOURI 133 | HIRSALA 235 | HAKUNI 431 |
| HAUKI 232 | HANKONIEMI 334 | HOUTSKÄR 436 |

Displacement, tons: 45 full load
Dimensions, feet (metres): 47.6 × 15.1 × 7.2 (14.5 × 4.6 × 2.2)
Main machinery: 2 Valmet 611 CSM diesels; 586 hp(m) (431 kW); 1 shaft
Speed, knots: 12
Complement: 4
Cargo capacity: 6 tons or 40 passengers

Comment: Completed 1979. Ice-strengthened; two serve isolated island defences. Four converted in 1988 as tenders to the Marine War College, but from 1990 back in service as light transports. All used by the Coastal Artillery.

HIRSALA
1991, Finnish Navy

Support ships / FINLAND 195

2 + 2 HILA CLASS (TRANSPORTS)

| HILA 237 | HARUN 238 |

Displacement, tons: 50 full load
Dimensions, feet (metres): 49.2 × 13.1 × 5.9 *(15 × 4 × 1.8)*
Main machinery: 2 diesels; 416 hp(m) *(306 kW)*; 2 shafts
Speed, knots: 12
Complement: 4

Comment: Ordered from Kotkan Telakka in August 1990. Second pair to complete late 1993. Ice-strengthened. All for use by Coastal Artillery.

HILA 10/1991, Finnish Navy

2 LOHI CLASS (LCU TRANSPORTS)

| LOHI 251 | LOHM 452 |

Displacement, tons: 38 full load
Dimensions, feet (metres): 65.6 × 19.7 × 3 *(20 × 6 × 0.9)*
Main machinery: 2 WMB diesels; 1200 hp(m) *(882 kW)*; 2 waterjets
Speed, knots: 20. **Range, miles:** 240 at 20 kts
Complement: 4
Guns: 2 USSR 23 mm/60 (twin). 1—14.5 mm MG.

Comment: Commissioned September 1984. Used as troop carriers and for light cargo by the Coastal Artillery. Guns not always carried.

LOHI 1992, Finnish Navy

2 TRANSPORT and COMMAND LAUNCHES

| ASKERI 241 | VIIRI 91 |

Displacement, tons: 20
Dimensions, feet (metres): 52.6 × 14.5 × 4.5 *(16 × 4.4 × 1.4)*
Speed, knots: 20

Comment: Closely resemble Spanish PVC II class. *Askeri* is used by the Coastal Artillery.

VIIRI 1991, Finnish Navy

5 + 1 (1) VIHURI CLASS (COMMAND LAUNCHES)

| VINHA 511 | SYÖKSY 531 | TORSÖ 993 |
| RAJU 521 | TRÄSKÖ 992 | + 1 |

Displacement, tons: 13 full load
Dimensions, feet (metres): 42.7 × 13.1 × 3 *(13 × 4 × 0.9)*
Main machinery: 2 diesels; 772 hp(m) *(567 kW)*; 2 waterjets
Speed, knots: 30

Comment: First of class *Vihuri* delivered in 1988 and the next five in 1991. *Träskö, Torsö* and one to be delivered in 1993 act as fast transports for Coastal Artillery. *Vinha, Raju* and *Syöksy* are command launches for Navy squadrons. *Vihuri* was destroyed by fire in late 1991 and a replacement may be built in due course.

VIHURI class (old number) 1988, Finnish Navy

38 MERIUISKO CLASS (LCAs)

U 201-U 238

Displacement, tons: 9.8 full load
Dimensions, feet (metres): 36 × 11.5 × 2.9 *(11 × 3.5 × 0.9)*
Main machinery: 2 Volvo TAMD70E diesels; 418 hp(m) *(307 kW)* sustained; 2 waterjets
Speed, knots: 36; 30 full load
Military lift: 48 troops

Comment: First batch of eleven completed by Alumina Varvet from 1983 to 1986. Last four ordered in 1989. Constructed of light alloy. Two of the class equipped with cable handling system for boom defence work. Batch one has smaller cabins.

U 207 (small cabin) 1991, Finnish Navy

U 214 (large cabin) 1991, Finnish Navy

196 FINLAND / Support ships — Surveying and research vessels

1 SUPPORT SHIP

PARAINEN (ex-*Pellinki*, ex-*Meteor*) 420 (ex-210)

Displacement, tons: 404
Dimensions, feet (metres):126.3 × 29.5 × 14.8 *(38.5 × 9 × 4.5)*
Main machinery: 1 diesel; 1800 hp(m) *(1.32 MW)*; 1 shaft
Speed, knots: 13
Complement: 17
Guns: 1 Madsen 20 mm.

Comment: Built as a tug in 1960. Acquired late 1980 from Oy Neptun Ab and modernised in 1987 by Teijon Telakka. Used by the Coastal Artillery.

2 HARBOUR TUGS

HAUKIPÄÄ 731   **KALLANPÄÄ** 831

Displacement, tons: 38
Dimensions, feet (metres): 45.9 × 16.4 × 7.5 *(14 × 5 × 2.3)*
Main machinery: 2 diesels; 360 hp(m) *(265 kW)*; 2 shafts
Speed, knots: 9
Complement: 2

Comment: Delivered by Teijon Telakka Oy in December 1985. Similar to Hauki class.

PARAINEN   *9/1988, Antonio Moreno*

KALLANPÄÄ   *1988, Finnish Navy*

MISCELLANEOUS

Note: In addition to the vessels listed below there is a fuel/water barge PA3 of 540 tons, self-propelled at 2 kts (normally towed). Built in 1979.

1 CABLE SHIP

PUTSAARI 92

Displacement, tons: 45
Dimensions, feet (metres): 149.5 × 28.6 × 8.2 *(45.6 × 8.7 × 2.5)*
Main machinery: 1 Wärtsilä diesel; 510 hp(m) *(375 kW)*; 1 shaft; active rudder; bow thruster
Speed, knots: 10
Complement: 20

Comment: Built by Rauma-Repola, Rauma and commissioned in 1966. Modernised by Wärtsilä in 1987. Fitted with two 10 ton cable winches. Strengthened for ice operations.

SURVEYING AND RESEARCH VESSELS

Note: Controlled by Ministry of Trade and Industry

Name	Displacement	Launched	Complement
PRISMA	1080 tons	1978	50 (12)
KALLA	920 tons	1963	50 (12)
SAARISTO	537 tons	1965	32 (7)
LINSSI	444 tons	1979	29 (6)
AIRISTO	350 tons	1972	13 (6)
TAUVO	187 tons	1963	13 (4)
SESTA	119 tons	1979	11 (2)

Plus 36 surveying launches.

ARANDA

Displacement, tons: 1800 full load
Dimensions, feet (metres): 193.6 × 44.6 × 15.7 *(59 × 13.6 × 4.8)*
Main machinery: 1 Wärtsilä diesel; 2720 hp(m) *(2 MW)*; 1 shaft; bow and stern thrusters
Speed, knots: 12
Complement: 12 plus 12-25 research staff
Helicopters: Platform only.

Comment: Ordered from Laivateollisuus, Turku, to a Wärtsilä design in February 1988 and delivered in Spring 1989. Has 270 square metres of laboratory space. Replacement for old *Aranda* whose conversion in 1985 was not satisfactory.

PUTSAARI   *1992, Finnish Navy*

POLLUTION CONTROL VESSELS

HYLJE 799   **HALLI** 899

Displacement, tons: 1500
Dimensions, feet (metres): 164 × 41 × 9.8 *(50 × 12.5 × 3)*
Main machinery: 2 Saab diesels; 680 hp(m) *(500 kW)*; 2 shafts; active rudders; bow thruster
Speed, knots: 7

Comment: Painted grey. Strengthened for ice. Owned by Board of Navigation, civilian manned but operated by Navy from Turku. *Hylje* commissioned 3 June 1981, *Halli* in January 1987. Capacity is about 1400 cu m of contaminated seawater. The ships have slightly different superstructure lines aft.

ARANDA   *1991, van Ginderen Collection*

HYLJE   *1992, Finnish Navy*

ARANDA

FRONTIER GUARD

Note: Controlled by Ministry of the Interior.

2 TURSAS CLASS (LARGE PATROL CRAFT)

TURSAS   **UISKO**

Displacement, tons: 700
Dimensions, feet (metres): 149 × 34.1 × 13.1 *(45.4 × 10.4 × 4)*
Main machinery: 2 Wärtsilä Vasa 8R22 diesels; 3152 hp(m) *(2.32 MW)* sustained; 2 shafts
Speed, knots: 16
Guns: 2 USSR 23 mm/60 (twin).
Sonars: Simrad SS105; active scanning; 14 kHz.

Comment: First ordered from Rauma-Repola on 21 December 1984. Launched 31 January 1986. Delivered June 1986. Second ordered 20 March 1986. Delivered 27 January 1987. Operate as offshore patrol craft and can act as salvage tugs. Ice-strengthened.

TURSAS   *1991, Finnish Frontier Guard*

1 IMPROVED VALPAS CLASS (LARGE PATROL CRAFT)

TURVA

Displacement, tons: 550
Dimensions, feet (metres): 159.1 × 28 × 12.8 *(48.5 × 8.6 × 3.9)*
Main machinery: 2 Wärtsilä diesels; 2000 hp(m) *(1.47 MW)*; 1 shaft
Speed, knots: 15
Guns: 1 Oerlikon 20 mm.
Sonars: Simrad SS105; active scanning; 14 kHz.

Comment: Built by Laivateollisuus, Turku and commissioned 15 December 1977.

TURVA   *1991, Finnish Navy*

1 VALPAS CLASS (LARGE PATROL CRAFT)

VALPAS

Displacement, tons: 545
Dimensions, feet (metres): 159.1 × 27.9 × 12.5 *(48.5 × 8.5 × 3.8)*
Main machinery: 1 Werkspoor diesel; 2000 hp(m) *(1.47 MW)*; 1 shaft
Speed, knots: 15
Complement: 22
Guns: 1 Oerlikon 20 mm.
Sonars: Simrad SS105; active scanning; 14 kHz.

Comment: An improvement on the *Silmä* design. Built by Laivateollisuus, Turku, and commissioned 21 July 1971. Ice-strengthened.

VALPAS   *1/1990, van Ginderen Collection*

1 SILMÄ CLASS (LARGE PATROL CRAFT)

SILMÄ

Displacement, tons: 530
Dimensions, feet (metres): 158.5 × 27.2 × 14.1 *(48.3 × 8.3 × 4.3)*
Main machinery: 1 Werkspoor diesel; 1800 hp(m) *(1.32 MW)*; 1 shaft
Speed, knots: 15
Complement: 22
Guns: 1 Oerlikon 20 mm.
Sonars: Simrad SS105; active scanning; 14 kHz.

Comment: Built by Laivateollisuus, Turku and commissioned 19 August 1963.

SILMÄ   *4/1990, van Ginderen Collection*

2 + (2) KIISLA CLASS

KIISLA   **KURKI**

Displacement, tons: 270 full load
Dimensions, feet (metres): 158.5 × 28.9 × 7.2 *(48.3 × 8.8 × 2.2)*
Main machinery: 2 MTU 16V 538 TB93 diesels; 7510 hp(m) *(6.9 MW)* sustained; 2 KaMeWa waterjets
Speed, knots: 25
Complement: 22
Guns: 2 USSR 23 mm/60 (twin) or 1 Madsen 20 mm.
Sonars: Simrad SS304 hull-mounted and VDS; active search; high frequency.

Comment: First ordered from Hollming on 23 November 1984 and commissioned 25 May 1987 after lengthy trials. Three more of an improved type ordered 22 November 1988, the first of which was laid down 3 August 1989 and commissioned in late 1990. Work on the last pair has been postponed. To replace Koskelo class. The design allows for rapid conversion to attack craft, ASW craft, minelayer, minesweeper or minehunter. A central telescopic crane over the engine room casing is used to launch a 5.7 m rigid inflatable sea boat. A fire monitor is mounted in the bows. The KaMeWa steerable waterjets extend the overall hull length by 2 m.

KIISLA   *1992, Finnish Navy*

1 LARGE PATROL CRAFT

VIIMA

Displacement, tons: 135
Dimensions, feet (metres): 118.1 × 21.7 × 7.5 *(36 × 6.6 × 2.3)*
Main machinery: 3 MTU MB diesels; 4050 hp(m) *(2.98 MW)*; 3 shafts; cp props
Speed, knots: 25
Complement: 13
Guns: 1 Oerlikon 20 mm.

Comment: Built by Laivateollisuus, Turku and commissioned in 1964.

VIIMA   *1991, Gilbert Gyssels*

198 FINLAND / Frontier guard — Land-based maritime aircraft

4 LOKKI CLASS (COASTAL PATROL CRAFT)

LOKKI   TIIRA   KAJAVA   KIHU

Displacement, tons: 59 *(Lokki)*; 64 (remainder)
Dimensions, feet (metres): 87.9 × 18 × 6.2 *(26.8 × 5.5 × 1.9)*
  87.9 × 17.1 × 8.5 *(26.8 × 5.2 × 2.1)* (*Lokki*)
Main machinery: 2 MTU 8V 396 TB82 diesels; 1740 hp(m) *(1.28 MW)* sustained *(Lokki)*
  2 MTU 8V 396 TB84 diesels; 2100 hp(m) *(1.54 MW)* sustained (remainder); 2 shafts
Speed, knots: 25
Complement: 8

Comment: Under a contract signed on 12 May 1980 Valmet/Laivateollisuus Oy (Turku) built the prototype craft *Lokki* which completed in Autumn 1981. *Tiira* completed 1 November 1985, *Kajava* 28 August 1986 and *Kihu* in December 1986. Built in light metal alloy. *Lokki* has a V-shaped hull.

LOKKI   1991, Finnish Navy

7 COASTAL PATROL CRAFT

RV 37-41   RV 142   RV 243

Displacement, tons: 20 full load
Dimensions, feet (metres): 46.9 × 11.8 × 5.2 *(14.3 × 3.6 × 1.6)*
Main machinery: 1 MTU MB diesel; 300 hp(m) *(220 kW)*; 1 shaft
Speed, knots: 12

Comment: Built by Hollming Oy, Rauma. Two completed January 1978, the third 1 September 1978, two more in early 1984 and the last two in 1985. For patrol, towing and salvage.

RV 38   1978, Finnish Frontier Guard

14 COASTAL PATROL CRAFT

PV 11, 12, 104, 108, 120, 205, 209, 210, 306, 307, + 4

Displacement, tons: 10
Speed, knots: 28
Complement: 2

Comment: Built by Fiskars, Turku. First nine launched by June 1983, first *(209)* completed September 1984. Five more ordered in 1989 from Waterman-Teiso, to replace older craft.

PV 120   1992, Finnish Navy

3 + 7 COASTAL PATROL CRAFT

RV 90 series

Displacement, tons: 25 full load
Dimensions, feet (metres): 49.2 × 13.1 × 5.9 *(15 × 4 × 1.8)*
Main machinery: 1 Caterpillar 3408 diesel; 476 hp(m) *(350 kW)*; 1 shaft
Speed knots: 12

Comment: Building at Uusikaupunki Yard. First in service in 1992; all to be completed by 1996. Ice-strengthened for use at Coast Guard stations.

COASTAL PATROL CRAFT

Class	Total	Tonnage	Speed	Commissioned
RV 1 (ex-RV 41)	1	17	10	1965
RV 8	1	10	10	1958
RV 9	9	12	10	1959-60
RV 10	11	18	10	1961-63
RV 30	7	19	10	1973-74
TENDERS	2	6	13	1986

TENDER   6/1988, A Sheldon Duplaix

LAND-BASED MARITIME AIRCRAFT

Note: Both Mi-8s transferred to the Air Force in 1990.

Numbers/Type: 2 Agusta AB 412 Griffon.
Operational speed: 122 kts *(226 km/h)*.
Service ceiling: 14 200 ft *(4330 m)*.
Range: 227 nm *(420 km)*.
Role/Weapon systems: Operated by Coast Guard/Frontier force for patrol and SAR. Sensors: Possible radar. Weapons: Unarmed at present but possible mountings for machine guns.

Numbers/Type: 2 Aerospatiale AS 332B Super Puma.
Operational speed: 151 kts *(279 km/h)*.
Service ceiling: 15 090 ft *(4600 m)*.
Range: 335 nm *(620 km)*.
Role/Weapon systems: Coastal patrol, surveillance and SAR helicopters. Sensors: Surveillance radar, tactical navigation systems and SAR equipment. Weapons: Unarmed.

SUPER PUMA   1991

Numbers/Type: 3 Agusta AB 206B JetRanger.
Operational speed: 116 kts *(215 km/h)*.
Service ceiling: 13 500 ft *(4120 m)*.
Range: 311 nm *(576 km)*.
Role/Weapon systems: Coastal patrol and inshore surveillance helicopters. Sensors: Visual means only. Weapons: Unarmed.

Numbers/Type: 2 Piper PA-31 Navajo.
Operational speed: 220 kts *(410 km/h)*.
Service ceiling: 27 200 ft *(8290 m)*.
Range: 755 nm *(1400 km)*.
Role/Weapon systems: Medium range maritime patrol aircraft. Sensors: Weather/search radar. Weapons: Unarmed.

FRANCE

Headquarters' Appointments

Chief of the Naval Staff:
  Amiral Coatanea
Inspector General of the Navy:
  Amiral Calmon
Director of Personnel:
  Vice-Amiral d'escadre Bonnot
Major General of the Navy:
  Vice-Amiral d'escadre Turcat

Senior Appointments

C-in-C Atlantic Theatre (CECLANT):
  Vice-Amiral d'escadre R Merveilleux du Vignaux
C-in-C Mediterranean Theatre (CECMED):
  Vice-Amiral d'escadre Tripier
Flag Officer ASW Action Group (GASM):
  Contre-Amiral Rouyer
Flag Officer Naval Action Force (FAN):
  Vice-Amiral Lefebvre
Flag Officer, Cherbourg:
  Vice-Amiral Cannone
Flag Officer French Forces Polynesia:
  Vice-Amiral Quérat
Flag Officer Indian Ocean:
  Contre-Amiral Foillard
Flag Officer (Submarines):
  Vice-Amiral Guilhem-Ducléon
Flag Officer (Naval Air):
  Vice-Amiral d'escadre Deramond
Flag Officer (Embarked Aviation):
  Contre-Amiral Wild
Flag Officer Mine Warfare Force (FGM):
  Contre-Amiral Delbrel
Commandant Marines:
  Capitaine de Vaisseau Lorin

Diplomatic Representation

Naval Attaché in London:
  Vice-Amiral Garibal
Naval Attaché in Washington:
  Capitaine de Vaisseau Viriot
Military Attaché in Saudi Arabia:
  Contre-Amiral La Tourette
Military Attaché to SACLANT:
  Capitaine de Vaisseau Deschamps
Military Attaché to CINC South:
  Contre-Amiral Desgrées du Lou

Personnel

(a) 1993: 64 471 (4645 officers)
(b) 10 months' national service (18 760) (15 months for seagoers)

Bases

Cherbourg: Channel Command base
Brest: Main Atlantic base. SSBN base
Lorient: Atlantic submarine base (until 1995)
Toulon: Mediterranean Command base
Papeete (Tahiti): Refitting base with 3800 ton capacity floating docks, 23 ton floating crane and earth stations for Syracuse communications
Fort-de-France (Martinique): Small base; Syracuse communications
Nouméa (New Caledonia): Small base
Degrad des Cannes (French Guiana): Small base
Saint Denis (La Réunion): Small base; Syracuse communications

Shipyards (Naval)

Cherbourg: Submarines and Fast Attack Craft (private shipyard)
Brest: Major warships and refitting
Lorient: Destroyers and Frigates, MCMVs, Patrol Craft
Toulon: Major warships and refits.

Dates

Armement pour essais: After launching when the ship is sufficiently advanced to allow a crew to live on board, and the commanding officer has joined. From this date the ship hoists the French flag and is ready to undertake her first harbour trials.
Armement définitif: On this date the ship has received her full complement and is able to undergo sea trials.
Clôture d'armement: Trials are completed and the ship is now able to undertake her first endurance cruise.
Croisière de longue durée or traversée de longue durée: The endurance cruise follows the clôture d'armement and lasts until the ship is accepted with all systems fully operational.
Admission au service actif: Commissioning date.

Reserve

A ship in 'Reserve Normale' has no complement but is available at short notice. 'Reserve Speciale' means that a refit will be required before the ship can go to sea again. 'Condamnation' is the state before being broken up or sold; at this stage a Q number is allocated.

Prefix

FS is used in NATO communications but is not official.

Mercantile Marine

Lloyd's Register of Shipping:
  890 vessels of 4 205 310 tons gross

Strength of the Fleet

Type	Active (Reserve)	Building (Projected)
Submarines (Ballistic Missile)	5	2 (2)
Submarines (Fleet)	5	1
Submarines (Patrol)	8	—
Aircraft Carriers	2	1 (1)
Helicopter Carrier	1	—
Destroyers	15	(4)
Frigates	24	8
Public Service Force	3	3
Fast Attack Craft (Patrol)	10	—
LSDs	4	(1)
LCTs	12 (1)	—
LCMs	26	—
Minesweepers	2	3
Minehunters	14	1
Diving Support Ships	4	—
Surveying Ships	6	—
Tankers (URs)	5	—
Maintenance Ship	1	(1)
Depot Ships	5	—
Trials Ships	7	1 (1)
Boom Defence Vessels	7	—
Supply Tenders	8	—
Transports	15	—
Tenders	16	—
Training Ships	16	—

Fleet Air Arm Bases

Base/Squadron No	Aircraft	Task

Embarked Squadrons (68 fixed wing aircraft; 40 helicopters)

Base/Squadron No	Aircraft	Task
Lann Bihoué/4F	Alizé (modernised)	Surveillance
Nîmes Garons/6F	Alizé (modernised)	Surveillance
Landivisiau/11F	Super Étendard	Assault
Landivisiau/12F	F-8E(FN) Crusader	Fighters
Landivisiau/17F	Super Étendard	Assault
Landivisiau/16F	Étendard IVP	Reconnaissance
St Mandrier/31F	Lynx	ASW
Lanvéoc-Poulmic/32F	Super Frelon	Support
St Mandrier/33F	Super Frelon	Support
Lanvéoc-Poulmic/34F	Lynx	ASW
J d'Arc, Lanvéoc-Poulmic/35F	Lynx/Alouette II/III (later Dauphin (Panther))	Training/Support

Support Squadrons

Base/Squadron No	Aircraft	Task
Lann Bihoué/2S	Xingu/Nord 262 A/E	Support Atlantic Region
Hyères/3S	Falcon 10 MER/ Nord 262 A/E/ Navajo	Support Mediterranean Region
Hyères/10S	Navajo Alouette II/III Super Frelon	Trials CEPA
Dugny-Le-Bourget/11S	Nord 262A/Xingu	Support
Lanvéoc-Poulmic/22S	Alouette III	Support Atlantic Region, SAR
St Mandrier/23S	Alouette II/III Dauphin	Support Mediterranean Region, SAR
Landivisiau/57S	Falcon 10 MER/Paris	Support

Maritime Patrol Squadrons

Base/Squadron No	Aircraft	Task
Nîmes-Garons/21F	Atlantic Mk 1 (NATO)	MP
Nîmes-Garons/22F	Atlantic Mk 1	MP
Lann Bihoué/23F	Atlantique Mk 2	MP
Lann Bihoué/24F	Atlantique Mk 2	MP

Training Squadrons

Base/Squadron No	Aircraft	Task
Lann Bihoué/52S	Xingu	Flying School
Nimes Garons/56S	Nord 262E/Navajo	Flying School
Hyères/59S	Super Étendard/ Zéphyr	Fighter School
Lanvéoc-Poulmic/50S	MS 880 Rallye	Naval School Recreational
Dax/SME Dax	Alouette II	Helicopter School
Rochefort/51S	CAP 10/MS 880 Rallye	Initial Flying School

Overseas Detachments

Base/Squadron No	Aircraft	Task
Tontouta/9S	Gardian	MP
Faaa (Papeete)/12S	Gardian Alouette III	MP Support

In addition, Atlantic Mk 1 aircraft are permanently deployed to Dakar, Fort-de-France and Djibouti.

Approximate Fleet Dispositions mid-1993

	FAN	GASM	FOST	FGM	Mediterranean	Atlantic	Channel	Indian Ocean	Pacific	Antilles
Carriers	2	—	—	—	—	1 (hel)	—	—	—	—
SSBN	—	—	5	—	—	—	—	—	—	—
SSN	—	—	6	—	—	—	—	—	—	—
SS	—	—	6	—	—	—	—	—	—	—
DDG/DD	9	6	—	—	—	—	—	—	—	—
FF	—	10	—	—	6	1	—	4/3	3/4	1
MCMV (incl tenders)	—	—	—	20	—	—	—	—	—	—
Light Forces	—	—	—	—	2	16	2	3	5	4
LPD	3	—	—	—	—	—	—	—	—	—
AOR	3	1	—	—	—	—	—	1	—	—

FAN = Force d'Action Navale (based at Toulon). All foreign operational deployments
GASM = Groupe d'Action Sous-Marine (based at Brest)
FOST = Force Océanique Stratégique (HQ at Houilles, near Paris). SSBNs based at l'Ile Longue near Brest. All SSNs and two SSs based at Toulon. Four SSs based at Lorient (Brest by 1995)
FGM = Force de Guerre des Mines (HQ and main base at Brest). One diving tender based at Cherbourg. Three MHCs and one diving tender at Toulon. Remainder plus one tender and one trials ship at Brest

Notes: (1) CEP Nuclear Test Range Pacific: *Bougainville*; EDICs, L 9051; L 9072; L 9074;
Supply Tenders, *Taape, Chamois, Rari, Revi; Tugs, Maroa, Maito, Manini.*
(2) Craft counted in the Light Forces total are:
(a) All patrol craft manned by the Navy
(b) Training ships which have a secondary EEZ patrol role: eight Leopard class vessels and two Glycine class trawlers
(c) Major patrol craft manned by the Gendarmerie Maritime: four Patras and two 24 m patrol craft (P 775-776)
(d) Excluded are *Tourmaline* (firing range surveillance craft, manned by civilians) and smaller patrol craft from the Gendarmerie Maritime

200 FRANCE / Introduction

DELETIONS

Submarines

1990 *Vénus*
1991 *Le Redoutable, Galatée*
1992 *Dauphin*

Cruisers

1991 *Colbert*

Destroyers

1990 *La Galissonnière*
1991 *Du Chayla*
1992 *Duperré*

Frigates

1990 *Commandant Bourdais, Amiral Charner* (both to Uruguay)
1991 *Doudart de Lagrée*
1992 *Protet*

Light Forces

1991 *Mercure*
1992 *Iris* (civilian)

Mine Warfare Forces

1992 *Phénix, Sagittaire* (old) (sold to Pakistan)
1993 *Baccarat*

Amphibious Forces

1990 L 9092, L 9096, LCM 1055-56
1991 L 9094, CTM 5

Survey and Research Ships

1990 *Boussole, Corail*
1991 *L'Estafette*
1992 *Henri Poincaré, Agnes 200, Commandant Rivière*

Service Forces

1990 *Palangrin, Dahlia, Abeille Supporter*
1991 *Engageante, Vigilante*
1993 *Papenoo, Punaruu, Tapatai* (civilian)

Tugs

1990 *Okoume, Aigrette, Héron*
1991 *Hercule, Balsa, Geyser*
1992 *Robuste*
1993 *Acajou, Charme, Latanier, Pin, Alouette, Vanneau, Sarcell Oued*

Gendarmerie

1992 *La Combattante*

PENNANT LIST

Submarines

S 601	Rubis
S 602	Saphir
S 603	Casabianca
S 604	Emeraude
S 605	Amethyste
S 606	Perle (bldg)
S 610	Le Foudroyant
S 612	Le Terrible
S 613	L'Indomptable
S 614	Le Tonnant
S 615	L'Inflexible
S 616	Le Triomphant (bldg)
S 617	Le Téméraire (bldg)
S 620	Agosta
S 621	Bévéziers
S 622	La Praya
S 623	Ouessant
S 643	Doris
S 648	Junon
S 650	Psyché
S 651	Sirène

Aircraft and Helicopter Carriers

R 91	Charles de Gaulle (bldg)
R 97	Jeanne d'Arc
R 98	Clemenceau
R 99	Foch

Destroyers

D 602	Suffren
D 603	Duquesne
D 609	Aconit
D 610	Tourville
D 611	Duguay-Trouin
D 612	De Grasse
D 614	Cassard
D 615	Jean Bart
D 640	Georges Leygues
D 641	Dupleix
D 642	Montcalm
D 643	Jean de Vienne
D 644	Primauguet
D 645	La Motte-Picquet
D 646	Latouche-Tréville

Frigates

F 710	La Fayette (bldg)
F 711	Surcouf (bldg)
F 712	Amiral Courbet (bldg)
F 726	Commandant Bory
F 729	Balny
F 730	Floréal
F 731	Prairial
F 732	Nivôse
F 733	Ventôse
F 734	Vendémiaire (bldg)
F 735	Germinal (bldg)
F 749	Enseigne de Vaisseau Henry
F 781	D'Estienne d'Orves
F 782	Amyot d'Inville
F 783	Drogou
F 784	Détroyat
F 785	Jean Moulin
F 786	Quartier Maître Anquetil
F 787	Commandant de Pimodan
F 788	Second Maître Le Bihan
F 789	Lieutenant de Vaisseau le Hénaff
F 790	Lieutenant de Vaisseau Lavallée
F 791	Commandant l'Herminier
F 792	Premier Maître l'Her
F 793	Commandant Blaison
F 794	Enseigne de Vaisseau Jacoubet
F 795	Commandant Ducuing
F 796	Commandant Birot
F 797	Commandant Bouan

Mine Warfare Forces

M 610	Ouistreham
M 611	Vulcain
M 612	Alençon
M 614	Styx
M 622	Pluton
M 641	Éridan
M 642	Cassiopée
M 643	Andromède
M 644	Pégase
M 645	Orion
M 646	Croix du Sud
M 647	Aigle
M 648	Lyre
M 649	Persée
M 650	Sagittaire
M 660	Narvik (bldg) (trials)
M 712	Cybèle
M 713	Calliope
M 714	Clio
M 715	Circé
M 716	Cérès

Light Forces

P 670	Trident GM
P 671	Glaive GM
P 672	Épée GM
P 673	Pertuisane GM
P 679	Grèbe
P 680	Sterne
P 681	Albatros
P 682	L'Audacieuse
P 683	La Boudeuse
P 684	La Capricieuse
P 685	La Fougueuse
P 686	La Glorieuse
P 687	La Gracieuse
P 688	La Moqueuse
P 689	La Railleuse
P 690	La Rieuse
P 691	La Tapageuse

Amphibious Forces

L 9011	Foudre
L 9021	Ouragan
L 9022	Orage
L 9030	Champlain
L 9031	Francis Garnier
L 9032	Dumont D'Urville
L 9033	Jacques Cartier
L 9034	La Grandière
L 9051	EDIC
L 9052	EDIC
L 9061	CDIC
L 9062	CDIC
L 9070	EDIC
L 9072	EDIC
L 9074	EDIC
L 9077	Bougainville
L 9090	Gapeau
L 9096	EDIC (Harbour support)

Auxiliaries Survey and Support Ships

A 601	Monge
A 607	Meuse
A 608	Var
A 610	Ile d'Oléron
A 613	Achéron
A 615	Loire
A 617	Garonne
A 618	Rance
A 620	Jules Verne
A 621	Rhin
A 622	Rhône
A 629	Durance
A 630	Marne
A 631	Somme
A 633	Taape
A 634	Rari
A 635	Revi
A 636	Maroa
A 637	Maito
A 638	Manini
A 644	Berry
A 646	Triton
A 649	L'Étoile
A 650	La Belle Poule
A 652	Mutin
A 653	La Grande Hermine
A 664	Malabar
A 669	Tenace
A 671	Le Fort
A 672	Utile
A 673	Lutteur
A 674	Centaure
A 675	Fréhel
A 676	Saire
A 677	Armen
A 678	La Houssaye
A 679	Kereon
A 680	Lardier
A 686	Actif
A 687	Laborieux
A 688	Valeureux
A 692	Travailleur
A 693	Acharné
A 694	Efficace
A 695	Bélier
A 696	Buffle
A 697	Bison
A 702	Girelle
A 712	Athos
A 713	Aramis
A 714	Tourmaline
A 722	Poséidon
A 731	Tianée
A 743	Denti
A 748	Léopard
A 749	Panthère
A 750	Jaguar
A 751	Lynx
A 752	Guépard
A 753	Chacal
A 754	Tigre
A 755	Lion
A 756	L'Espérance
A 757	D'Entrecasteaux
A 767	Chamois
A 768	Élan
A 770	Glycine
A 771	Eglantine
A 774	Chevreuil
A 775	Gazelle
A 776	Isard
A 785	Thétis
A 790	Coralline
A 791	Lapérouse
A 792	Borda
A 793	Laplace
A 795	Arago

Auxiliaries

GFA 1-3	Floating Cranes
Y 604	Ariel
Y 611	Bengali
Y 613	Faune
Y 617	Mouette
Y 618	Cascade
Y 620	Chataigner
Y 621	Mésange
Y 624	Chêne
Y 625	Cigogne
Y 628	Colibri
Y 629	Cormier
Y 630	Bonite
Y 632	Cygne
Y 634	Rouget
Y 636	Martinet
Y 637	Fauvette
Y 644	Frêne
Y 645	Gave
Y 648	Goéland
Y 654	Hêtre
Y 655	Hévéa
Y 661	Korrigan
Y 662	Dryade
Y 666	Manguier
Y 667	Tupa
Y 668	Mélèze
Y 669	Merisier
Y 670	Merle
Y 671	Morgane
Y 673	Moineau
Y 675	Martin Pêcheur
Y 686	Palétuvier
Y 687	Passereau
Y 688	Peuplier
Y 691	Pinson
Y 692	Telenn Mor
Y 694	Pivert
Y 695	Platane
Y 696	Alphée
Y 698	Calmar
Y 700	Nereide
Y 701	Ondine
Y 702	Naiade
Y 706	Chimère
Y 708	Saule
Y 709	Sycomore
Y 710	Sylphe
Y 711	Farfadet
Y 717	Ébène
Y 718	Érable
Y 719	Olivier
Y 720	Santal
Y 723	Engoulevent
Y 725	Marabout
Y 726	Toucan
Y 727	Macreuse
Y 728	Grand Duc
Y 729	Eider
Y 730	Ara
Y 732	DGV—S de D No 3
Y 735	Merlin
Y 736	Mélusine
Y 738	Maronnier
Y 739	Noyer
Y 740	Papayer
Y 741	Elfe
Y 745	Aiguière
Y 746	Embrun
Y 747	Loriot
Y 748	Gélinotte
Y 749	La Prudente
Y 750	La Persévérante
Y 751	La Fidèle
Y 790-799	Tenders

GM = Gendarmerie Maritime

SUBMARINES

Strategic Missile Submarines (Sous-Marins Nucléaires Lanceurs d'Engins (SNLE))

Note: Continuous patrols reduced from three to two submarines in 1992.

0 + 2 + 1 (1) LE TRIOMPHANT CLASS (SNLE-NG)

Name	No	Builders	Laid down	Launched	Operational
LE TRIOMPHANT	S 616	Cherbourg Naval Dockyard	9 June 1989	1993	July 1995
LE TÉMÉRAIRE	S 617	Cherbourg Naval Dockyard	1992	1996	July 1998
—	S 618	Cherbourg Naval Dockyard	1994	1998	June 2000

Displacement, tons: 12 640 surfaced; 14 120 dived
Dimensions, feet (metres): 453 × 41; 55.8 (aft planes) × 41 *(138 × 12.5; 17 × 12.5)*
Main machinery: Nuclear; turbo-electric; 1 PWR Type K15 (enlarged CAS 48); 150 MW; 2 turbo-alternators; 1 motor; 41 500 hp(m) *(30.5 MW)*; diesel-electric auxiliary propulsion; 2 SEMT-Pielstick 8 PA4 V 200 SM diesels; 900 kW; 1 emergency motor; 1 shaft; pump jet propulsor
Speed, knots: 25 dived
Complement: 111 (15 officers) (2 crews)

Missiles: SLBM: 16 Aerospatiale M45/TN 71; three stage solid fuel rockets; inertial guidance to 5300 km *(2860 nm)*; thermonuclear warhead with 6 MRV each of 150 kT. (To be replaced by M5/TN 75 which has a planned range of 11 000 km *(6000 nm)* and 10-12 MRVs).
SSM: Aerospatiale SM 39 Exocet; launched from 21 in *(533 mm)* torpedo tubes; inertial cruise; active radar homing to 50 km *(27 nm)* at 0.9 Mach; warhead 165 kg.
Torpedoes: 4—21 in *(533 mm)* tubes. ECAN L5 Mod 3; dual purpose; active/passive homing to 9.5 km *(5.1 nm)* at 35 kts; warhead 150 kg; depth to 550 m *(1800 ft)*; total of 18 torpedoes and SSM carried in a mixed load.
Countermeasures: ESM: Warning.
Fire control: SAD (Système d'Armes de Dissuasion) tactical data system (for SLBMs); SAT (Système d'Armes Tactique) and DLA 4A weapon control system (for SSM and torpedoes).
Radars: Search: Dassault; I band.
Sonars: Thomson Sintra DMUX 80 'multi-function' passive bow and flank arrays.
DUUX 5; passive ranging and intercept; low frequency.
DSUV 61; towed array.

Programmes: First of class ordered 10 March 1986 with building decision taken 18 June 1987. Second of class ordered in 1990; third delayed into 1993 and fourth into 1995. Class of six originally planned but this is now reduced to a total of four. Trials of Le Triomphant planned to start in mid-1993. Will replace the Redoutable class. SNLE-NG (Sous-Marins Nucléaires Lanceurs Engins Nouvelle Génération).

Modernisation: The M5 missile development was first funded in the 1988 budget and the programme has been brought forward to start in 1993, which is earlier than planned. Hull No 3 will be the first to commission with M5, the others being back fitted in due course. Four sets of missiles were to have been ordered but this number may now be reduced.

Structure: Later versions may be longer, up to 170 m. Diving depth greater than 300 m *(984 ft)*. Height from keel to top of fin is 21.3 m *(69.9 ft)*.

LE TRIOMPHANT (artist's impression)   1990, DCN

5 L'INFLEXIBLE CLASS (SNLE)

Name	No	Builders	Laid down	Launched	Operational
LE FOUDROYANT	S 610	Cherbourg Naval Dockyard	12 Dec 1969	4 Dec 1971	6 June 1974
LE TERRIBLE	S 612	Cherbourg Naval Dockyard	24 June 1967	12 Dec 1969	1 Jan 1973
L'INDOMPTABLE	S 613	Cherbourg Naval Dockyard	4 Dec 1971	17 Sep 1974	23 Dec 1976
LE TONNANT	S 614	Cherbourg Naval Dockyard	19 Oct 1974	17 Sep 1977	3 May 1980
L'INFLEXIBLE	S 615	Cherbourg Naval Dockyard	21 Mar 1980	23 June 1982	1 Apr 1985

Displacement, tons: 8080 surfaced; 8920 dived
Dimensions, feet (metres): 422.1 × 34.8 × 32.8 *(128.7 × 10.6 × 10)*
Main machinery: Nuclear; turbo-electric; 1 PWR; 2 turbo-alternators; 1 Jeumont Schneider motor; 16 000 hp(m) *(11.76 MW)*; twin SEMT-Pielstick/Jeumont Schneider 8 PA4 V 185 SM diesel-electric auxiliary propulsion; 1.5 MW; 1 emergency motor; 1 shaft
Speed, knots: 25 dived; 20 surfaced
Range, miles: 5000 at 4 kts on auxiliary propulsion only
Complement: 114 (14 officers) (2 crews)

Missiles: SLBM: 16 Aerospatiale M4; three stage solid fuel rockets; inertial guidance to 5300 km *(2860 nm)*; thermonuclear warhead with 6 MRV each of 150 kT.
SSM: Aerospatiale SM 39 Exocet; launched from 21 in *(533 mm)* torpedo tubes; inertial cruise; active radar homing to 50 km *(27 nm)* at 0.9 Mach; warhead 165 kg (to be carried in all in due course).
Torpedoes: 4—21 in *(533 mm)* tubes. ECAN L5 Mod 3; dual purpose; active/passive homing to 9.5 km *(5.1 nm)* at 35 kts; warhead 150 kg; depth to 550 m *(1800 ft)*; and ECAN F17 Mod 2; wire-guided; active/passive homing to 20 km *(10.8 nm)* at 40 kts; warhead 250 kg; depth 600 m *(1970 ft)*; total of 18 torpedoes and SSM carried in a mixed load.
Countermeasures: ESM: Intercept.
Fire control: SAD (Système d'Armes de Dissuasion) tactical data system (for SLBMs); SAT (Système d'Armes Tactique) and DLA 1A weapon control system (for SSM and torpedoes).
Radars: Navigation: Thomson-CSF DRUA 33; I band.
Sonars: Thomson Sintra DSUX 21 'multi-function' passive bow and flank arrays.
DUUX 5; passive ranging and intercept; low frequency.
DSUV 61; towed array.

Programmes: With the paying off of Le Redoutable in December 1991, the remaining submarines of the class are now known as L'Inflexible class SNLE M4.
Modernisation: All are fitted with M4 missiles. Le Tonnant recommissioned 15 October 1987; L'Indomptable 15 June 1989; Le Terrible 7 June 1990; Le Foudroyant 9 February 1993. As well as replacing the missile system, work included an improved reactor core, noise reduction efforts, updating sonar and other equipment to the same standard as L'Inflexible on build.
Structure: Diving depth, 250 m *(820 ft)* approx. Improved streamlining of M4 conversion submarines changes the silhouette so that they resemble L'Inflexible.
Operational: First operational launch of M4 by Le Tonnant on 15 September 1987 in the Atlantic.

LE TERRIBLE   1992, DCN

Attack Submarines (Sous-Marins Nucléaires d'Attaque (SNA))

5 + 1 RUBIS CLASS (SNA 72)

Name	No	Builders	Laid down	Launched	Operational
RUBIS	S 601	Cherbourg Naval Dockyard	11 Dec 1976	7 July 1979	23 Feb 1983
SAPHIR	S 602	Cherbourg Naval Dockyard	1 Sep 1979	1 Sep 1981	6 July 1984
CASABIANCA	S 603	Cherbourg Naval Dockyard	19 Sep 1979	22 Dec 1984	21 Apr 1987
EMERAUDE	S 604	Cherbourg Naval Dockyard	1 Mar 1983	12 Apr 1986	16 Sep 1988
AMETHYSTE	S 605	Cherbourg Naval Dockyard	11 Oct 1984	14 May 1988	3 Mar 1992
PERLE	S 606	Cherbourg Naval Dockyard	27 Mar 1987	22 Sep 1990	Dec 1993

Displacement, tons: 2385 (2410, S 605 onwards) surfaced; 2670 dived
Dimensions, feet (metres): 236.5 (241.5, S 605 onwards) × 24.9 × 21 *(72.1 (73.6) × 7.6 × 6.4)*
Main machinery: Nuclear; turbo-electric; 1 PWR CAS 48; 48 MW; 2 turbo-alternators; 1 motor; 9500 hp(m) *(7 MW)*; SEMT-Pielstick/Jeumont Schneider 8 PA4 V 185 SM diesel-electric auxiliary propulsion; 450 kW; 1 emergency motor; 1 shaft
Speed, knots: 25
Complement: 2 alternating crews each of 70 (8 officers)

Missiles: SSM: Aerospatiale SM 39 Exocet; launched from 21 in *(533 mm)* torpedo tubes; inertial cruise; active radar homing to 50 km *(27 nm)* at 0.9 Mach; warhead 165 kg.
Torpedoes: 4—21 in *(533 mm)* tubes. ECAN L5 Mod 3; dual purpose; active/passive homing to 9.5 km *(5.1 nm)* at 35 kts; warhead 150 kg; depth to 550 m *(1800 ft)*; and ECAN F17 Mod 2; wire-guided; active/passive homing to 20 km *(10.8 nm)* at 40 kts; warhead 250 kg; depth 600 m *(1970 ft)*. Total of 18 torpedoes and missiles carried in a mixed load.
Mines: Up to 32 FG 29 in lieu of torpedoes.
Countermeasures: ESM: ARUR, ARUD; intercept and warning.
Fire control: SAT (Système d'Armes Tactique) and DLA 2B or 3 weapon control system.
Radars: Search: Thomson-CSF DRUA 33; I band.
Sonars: Thomson Sintra DMUX 20 multi-function; passive search; low frequency.
DUUA 2B; active; medium frequency; 8 kHz.
DUUX 5; passive ranging and intercept.
DSUV 62C; towed passive array; very low frequency.

Programmes: The programme has been slowed down by defence economies with the seventh of class *Turquoise* (may be completed for export with diesel propulsion) and eighth of class *Diamant* being cancelled. SNA No 7 (displacement: 4000 tons) will be of a new and improved class with VLS SSM and may be funded under the 1995-97 Loi de Programmation.
Modernisation: Between 1989 and 1995 the first four boats of this class are being converted under operation Améthyste (AMÉlioration Tactique HYdrodynamique Silence Transmission Ecoute) to bring them to the same standard of ASW (includes new sonars) efficiency as the later boats rather than that required for the original anti-surface ship role. *Saphir* recommissioned 1 July 1991. *Casabianca* completed August 1992; *Rubis* is scheduled to complete in December 1993 and *Emeraude* in December 1995.
Structure: Diving depth, greater than 300 m *(984 ft)*. As this is the smallest class of SSNs ever designed except for the 400 ton NR-1 of the US Navy there has clearly been a marked reduction in the size of the reactor compared with the Le Redoutable class. S 605 and onwards have had their length increased to 241.5 ft (73.6 m) and are being built to a modified design. This includes a new bow form, Syracuse 2 SATCOM System, a new design sonar DMUX 20 in place of DSUV 22, a new DSUV 62C towed array sonar, a major silencing programme, a streamlining of the superstructure as well as new tactical and attack systems and improved electronics.
Operational: All operational SSNs are based at Toulon. Endurance rated at 45 days (food).

AMETHYSTE *1991, DCN*

EMERAUDE *4/1992, W Sartor*

Patrol Submarines (Sous-Marins d'Attaque)

4 AGOSTA CLASS

Name	No	Builders	Laid down	Launched	Commissioned
AGOSTA	S 620	Cherbourg Naval Dockyard	1 Nov 1972	19 Oct 1974	28 July 1977
BÉVÉZIERS	S 621	Cherbourg Naval Dockyard	17 May 1973	14 June 1975	27 Sep 1977
LA PRAYA	S 622	Cherbourg Naval Dockyard	1974	15 May 1976	9 Mar 1978
OUESSANT	S 623	Cherbourg Naval Dockyard	1974	23 Oct 1976	27 July 1978

Displacement, tons: 1230 standard; 1510 surfaced; 1760 dived
Dimensions, feet (metres): 221.7 × 22.3 × 17.7 *(67.6 × 6.8 × 5.4)*
Main machinery: Diesel-electric; 2 SEMT-Pielstick 16 PA4 V 185 VG diesels; 3600 hp(m) *(2.65 MW)*; 2 alternators; 1.7 MW; 1 motor; 4600 hp(m) *(3.4 MW)*; 1 cruising motor; 31 hp(m) *(23 kW)*; 1 shaft
Speed, knots: 12 surfaced; 20 dived
Range, miles: 8500 at 9 kts snorting; 350 at 3.5 kts dived
Complement: 58 (7 officers)

Missiles: SSM: Aerospatiale SM 39 Exocet; launched from 21 in *(533 mm)* tubes; inertial cruise; active radar homing to 50 km *(27 nm)* at 0.9 Mach; warhead 165 kg.
Torpedoes: 4—21 in *(533 mm)* bow tubes. ECAN L5 Mod 3; dual purpose; active/passive homing to 9.5 km *(5.1 nm)* at 35 kts; warhead 150 kg; depth to 550 m *(1800 ft)* and ECAN F17 Mod 2; wire-guided; active/passive homing to 20 km *(10.8 nm)* at 40 kts; warhead 250 kg; depth 600 m *(1970 ft)*. Total of 20 torpedoes and missiles carried in a mixed load.
Mines: Up to 36 in lieu of torpedoes.
CounterMainmeasures: ESM: ARUR, ARUD; intercept and warning.
Fire control: DLA 2A weapon control system.
Radars: Search: Thomson-CSF DRUA 33; I band.
Sonars: Thomson Sintra DSUV 22; passive search; medium frequency.
DUUA 2D; active search and attack; 8 kHz.
DUUA 1D; active search. DUUX 2; passive ranging.
DSUV 62A; passive towed array; very low frequency.

Programmes: Building of this class was announced in 1970 under the third five-year new construction plan 1971-75. Considerable efforts have been made to improve noise reduction, including a clean casing and the damping of internal noise. Service lives: *Ouessant* 2003, remainder 2002 but these dates may be extended.
Modernisation: Included fitting of SM 39 Exocet and better torpedo discharge and reloading. Completed in 1987.
Structure: First diesel submarines in the French Navy to be fitted with 21 in *(533 mm)* tubes. Diving depth, 320 m *(1050 ft)*. Has twice the battery capacity of the Daphne class.
Operational: All based at Lorient. Endurance, 45 days. Torpedoes can be fired at all speeds and down to full diving depth.

AGOSTA 10/1992

Rapid reloading gear fitted.
Sales: Four built at Cartagena for Spanish Navy and two for Pakistan by Dubigeon (with a possible three more to follow in due course).

LA PRAYA 5/1991, D & B Teague

4 DAPHNÉ CLASS

Name	No	Builders	Laid down	Launched	Commissioned
DORIS	S 643	Cherbourg Naval Dockyard	Sep 1958	14 May 1960	26 Aug 1964
JUNON	S 648	Cherbourg Naval Dockyard	July 1961	11 May 1964	25 Feb 1966
PSYCHÉ	S 650	Brest Naval Dockyard	May 1965	28 June 1967	1 July 1969
SIRÈNE	S 651	Brest Naval Dockyard	May 1965	28 June 1967	1 Mar 1970

Displacement, tons: 860 surfaced; 1038 dived
Dimensions, feet (metres): 189.6 × 22.3 × 15.1 *(57.8 × 6.8 × 4.6)*
Main machinery: Diesel-electric; 2 SEMT-Pielstick 12 PA1 diesels (S 643 and 648); 2 SEMT-Pielstick 12 PA4 V 185 diesels (S 650 and 651); 2450 hp(m) *(1.8 MW)*; 2 Jeumont Schneider alternators; 900 kW; 2 motors; 2600 hp(m) *(1.9 MW)*; 2 shafts
Speed, knots: 13.5 surfaced; 16 dived
Range, miles: 2700 at 12.5 kts; 10 000 at 7 kts surfaced; 4500 at 5 kts; 3000 at 7 kts snorting
Complement: 53 (7 officers)

Torpedoes: 12—21.7 in *(550 mm)* (8 bow, 4 stern) tubes. 12 ECAN E15; dual purpose; passive homing to 12 km *(6.6 nm)* at 25 kts; warhead 300 kg. Larger version of shorter range E14. Submarine target must be cavitating; no reloads.
Fire control: DLT D3 torpedo control.
Radars: Search: Thomson-CSF Calypso; I/J band.
Sonars: Thomson Sintra DSUV 2; passive search; medium frequency.
DUUA 2; active search and attack.
DUUX 2; passive ranging.

Programmes: Service lives have been extended as SSN completion rate is slower than planned. *Flore* paid off in 1989 and is used as a training submarine.
Modernisation: Carried out between 1971 and 1981.
Structure: Diving depth, 300 m *(984 ft)*; crushing at 575 m *(1886 ft)*.
Operational: *Doris* and *Junon* based at Toulon, *Psyché* and *Sirène* at Lorient. *Doris* to pay off in 1994.
Sales: South Africa (1967) (3), Pakistan (1966) (3), (1 from Portugal later), Portugal (1964) (4), Spain (built in Spain) (1965) (4).

JUNON 1/1988, Gilbert Gyssels

AIRCRAFT CARRIERS (Porte-Avions)

0 + 1 + (1) CHARLES DE GAULLE CLASS (Porte-Avions Nucléaires PAN) (CVN)

Name	No	Builders	Laid down	Launched	Commissioned
CHARLES DE GAULLE	R 91	Brest Naval Dockyard	24 Apr 1989	Apr 1994	Dec 1998

Displacement, tons: 35 500 standard; 39 680 full load
Dimensions, feet (metres): 857.7 oa; 780.8 wl × 211.3 oa; 103.3 wl × 27.8 *(261.5; 238 × 64.4; 31.5 × 8.5)*
Flight deck, feet (metres): 857.7 × 211.3 *(261.5 × 64.4)*
Main machinery: Nuclear; 2 PWR Type K15; 300 MW; 2 turbines; 83 000 hp(m) *(61 MW)*; 2 shafts
Speed, knots: 27
Complement: 1150 ship's company plus 550 aircrew plus 50 Flag Staff; (accommodation for 1950) (plus temporary 800 marines)

Missiles: SAM: 4 Thomson-CSF SAAM VLS octuple launchers ❶; Aerospatiale ASTER 15; anti-missile system with inertial guidance and midcourse update; active radar homing to 15 km *(8.1 nm)*; warhead 3 kg.
2 Matra Sadral PDMS sextuple launchers ❷; Mistral; IR homing to 4 km *(2.2 nm)*; warhead 3 kg; anti-sea-skimmer; able to engage targets down to 10 ft above sea level.
Guns: 8 Giat 20F2 20 mm; 60° elevation; 720 rounds/minute to 8 km *(4.3 nm)*; weight of shell: 0.25 kg.
Countermeasures: Decoys: 4 CSEE Sagaie 10-barrelled trainable launchers ❸; medium range; chaff to 8 km *(4.3 nm)*; IR flares to 3 km *(1.6 nm)*.
ESM: ARBR 17; radar warning. DIBV 1A Vampir ❹; IR detector.
ECM: 2 ARBB 33 ❺; jammers.
Combat data systems: SENIT; Links 11, 14 and 16. Syracuse 2 SATCOM ❻. AIDCOMER command support system.
Radars: Air search: Thomson-CSF DRBJ 11D/E ❼; 3D; E/F band; range 366 km *(200 nm)*.
Thomson-CSF DRBV 26D ❽; D band; range 183 km *(100 nm)* for 2 m² target.
Air/surface search: Thomson-CSF DRBV 15C ❾; E/F band; range 50 km *(27 nm)*.
Navigation: Two Racal 1229; I band.
Fire control: Arabel ❿; I/J band (for SAAM).
Tacan: NRBP 20A ⓫.
Sonars: To include SLAT torpedo attack warning.

Fixed wing aircraft: 35-40 including Rafale M (SU 0), Super Étendards (to be replaced by Rafale SU 2), AEW aircraft (possibly E-2C Hawkeye).

Programmes: On 23 September 1980 the Defence Council decided to build two nuclear-propelled carriers to replace *Clemenceau* in 1996 and *Foch* some years later. First of class ordered 4 February 1986, first metal cut 24 November 1987. Hull floated for technical trials on 20 December 1992. Second ship, if built, will probably be called *Clemenceau* and was to have been ordered in 1992 but this has been postponed to 1997 for an in-service date of 2004. Funds for preliminary work at Brest provided in 1984 estimates and for the construction and trials of the nuclear-power plant at Cadarache in the 1982-83 estimates. A 19.8 m *(65 ft)* long one-twelfth scale model has been built. Constructed of light alloy, and with a crew of three, it is used for hydrodynamic trials. Building programme delayed two years due to defence budget cuts but sea trials are planned to start in July 1997.
Structure: Two lifts 62.3 × 41 ft *(19 × 12.5 m)* of 36 tons capacity. Hangar for 20-25 aircraft; dimensions 454.4 × 96.5 × 20 ft *(138.5 × 29.4 × 6.1 m)*. Angled deck 8.5°. Catapults: 2 USN Type C13; length 75 m *(246 ft)* for Super Étendards and up to 22 tonne aircraft. Enhanced weight capability of flight deck to allow operation of AEW aircraft. Island placed well fwd so that both lifts can be abaft it and thus protected from the weather. CSEE Dallas (Deck Approach and Landing Laser System) fitted, later to be replaced by MLS system.
Operational: Five years continuous steaming at 25 kts available before refuelling (same reactors as *Le Triomphant*).

CHARLES DE GAULLE (model) — 1990, DCN

CHARLES DE GAULLE — 8/1992, J Y Robert

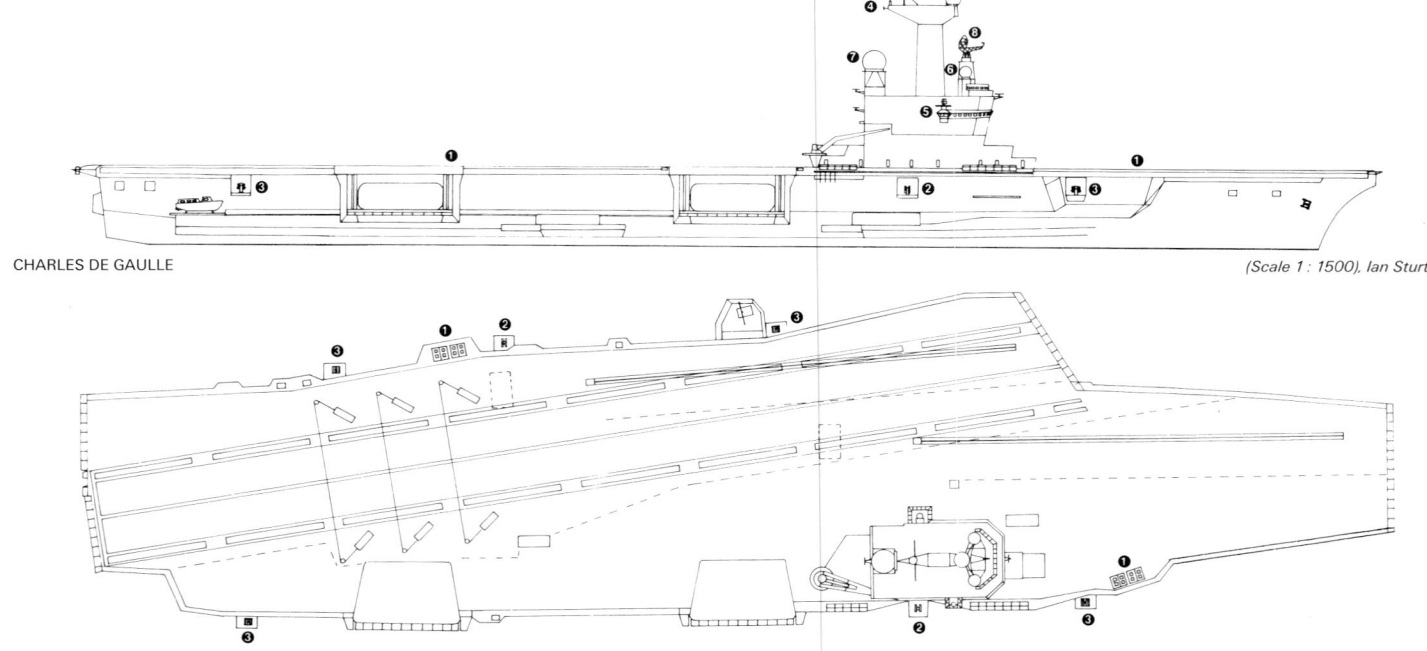

CHARLES DE GAULLE (Scale 1 : 1500), Ian Sturton

2 CLEMENCEAU CLASS (CV)

Name	No	Builders	Laid down	Launched	Commissioned
CLEMENCEAU	R 98	Brest Naval Dockyard	Nov 1955	21 Dec 1957	22 Nov 1961
FOCH	R 99	Chantiers de l'Atlantique, St. Nazaire	Feb 1957	28 July 1960	15 July 1963

Displacement, tons: 27 307 standard; 32 780 full load
Dimensions, feet (metres): 869.4 × 104.1 hull (168 oa) × 28.2 *(265 × 31.7 (51.2) × 8.6)*
Flight deck, feet (metres): 543 × 96.8 *(165.5 × 29.5)*
Main machinery: 6 boilers; 640 psi *(45 kg/cm sq)*; 840°F *(450°C)*; 2 Parsons turbines; 126 000 hp(m) *(93 MW)*; 2 shafts
Speed, knots: 32. **Range, miles:** 7500 at 18 kts; 4800 at 24 kts; 3500 at full power
Complement: 1017 (47 officers) plus 672 aircrew

Missiles: SAM: 2 Thomson-CSF Crotale EDIR octuple launchers ❶; 18 missiles per magazine; radar and IR line of sight guidance to 13 km *(7 nm)* at 2.4 Mach; warhead 14 kg. Replaced 4 of the 100 mm guns.
Guns: 4 DCN 3.9 in *(100 mm)*/55 Mod 1953 automatic ❷; 80° elevation; 60 rounds/minute to 17 km *(9 nm)* anti-surface; 8 km *(4.4 nm)* anti-aircraft; weight of shell 13.5 kg. Several M2 12.7 mm MGs.
Countermeasures: Decoys: 2 CSEE Sagaie 10-barrelled trainable launchers ❸; medium range decoy rockets; chaff to 8 km *(4.3 nm)*; IR flares to 3 km *(1.6 nm)*.
ESM: ARBR 17; radar warning.
ECM: ARBB 33; jammer.
Combat data systems: SENIT 2 tactical data automation system; Links 11 and 14 (later 16); Syracuse 1 SATCOM. AIDCOMER command support system.
Fire control: Two C T Analogiques; two Sagem DMAa optical sights.
Radars: Air search: Thomson-CSF DRBV 23B ❹; D band; range 201 km *(110 nm)*.
Air/surface search: Two DRBI 10 ❺; E/F band; range 256 km *(140 nm)*.
DRBV 15 ❻; E/F band.
Navigation: Racal Decca 1226; I band.
Fire control: Two Thomson-CSF DRBC 32B ❼ (for guns); I band; two Crotale ❶ (for SAM); I band.
Tacan: SRN-6.
Landing approach control: NRBA 51 ❽; I band.
Sonars: Westinghouse SQS 505; hull-mounted; active search; medium frequency; 7 kHz.

Fixed wing aircraft: 18 Super Étendard; 4 Étendard IVP; 8 Crusaders; 7 Alizé.
Helicopters: 2 SA 365F Dauphin 2.

Programmes: First aircraft carriers designed as such and built from the keel to be completed in France. Authorised in 1953 and 1955 respectively. Under current plans *Clemenceau* is due to pay off (when *Charles de Gaulle* commissions) in 1998 and *Foch* in 2004.
Modernisation: *Clemenceau* refitted in 1978 to accommodate Super Étendard aircraft and tactical nuclear weapons. *Foch* had a similar refit to *Clemenceau*'s in 1980-81. *Clemenceau* started a refit 1 September 1985, ended October 1986. This included the replacement of four of the 100 mm guns by two Crotale EDIR, retubing of boilers and other major engine overhauls, fitting of stronger aircraft lifts and catapults, modernisation of communications (including Syracuse 1 SATCOM) and electronics, fitting of Sagaie, new long range air warning radar and passive radar detection system, and modernised combat data system. *Foch* similarly modified in her 1987-88 refit, which also included a trial CSEE Dallas (Deck Approach and Landing Laser System), and a capability to accommodate ASMP nuclear missiles for Super Étendard. *Foch* was fitted in 1992/93 with a removable mini ski-jump (10 × 4.2 × 0.2 m) on the forward catapult as well as a nose gear launch device. The landing mirror has been moved forward, and the combat system of the ship has been slightly modified. *Clemenceau* has received similar modifications (but to a lesser extent).
In 1995/96, more work will be done on *Foch* to enable the carrier to operate Rafale M aircraft permanently. A foldable mini ski-jump (wider) will be fitted to both catapults. The jet deflectors will be enlarged (this implies reducing the area of the forward lift).
Structure: Flight deck, island superstructure and bridges, hull (over machinery spaces and magazines) are all armour plated. There are 3 bridges: Flag, Command and Aviation.
2 Mitchell-Brown steam catapults; Mk BS 5; able to launch 20 ton aircraft at 110 kts. The flight deck is angled at 8 degrees. Two lifts 52.5 × 36 ft *(16 × 10.97 m)* one of which is on the starboard deck edge. Dimensions of the hangar are 590.6 × 78.7 × 23 ft *(180 × 24 × 7 m)*. *Clemenceau* mainmast shortened in 1990.
Operational: Oil fuel capacity is 3720 tons. Flight deck letters: F = *Foch*, U = *Clemenceau*. The aircraft complement for the helicopter carrier role includes between 30 and 40 with a mixture of Super Frelon, Lynx, Super Puma, Puma and Gazelle (the last three types being army owned). Crusaders refitted to be able to fly until 1995. Deck trials of Rafale M aircraft scheduled for May 1993 in *Foch*.

CLEMENCEAU 6/1991, van Ginderen Collection

FOCH 4/1992, French Navy

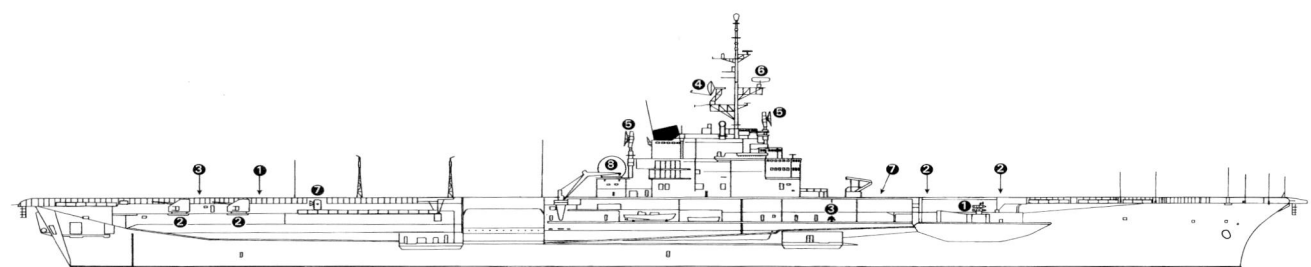

CLEMENCEAU (Scale 1 : 1500), Ian Sturton

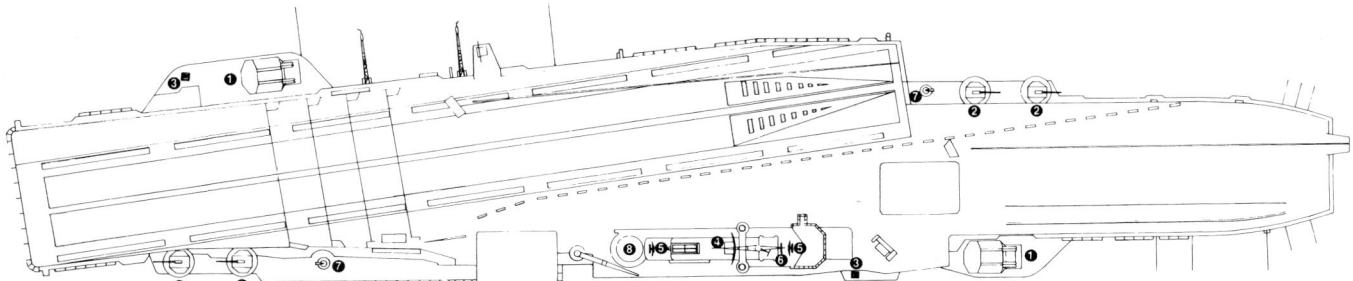

CLEMENCEAU (Scale 1 : 1500), Ian Sturton

206 FRANCE / Helicopter carrier — Destroyers

HELICOPTER CARRIER (Porte-Hélicoptères) (CVH)

Name	No	Builders	Laid down	Launched	Commissioned
JEANNE D'ARC (ex-*La Résolue*)	R 97	Brest Naval Dockyard	7 July 1960	30 Sep 1961	16 July 1964

Displacement, tons: 10 000 standard; 13 270 full load
Dimensions, feet (metres): 597.1 × 78.7 hull × 24 *(182 × 24 × 7.3)*
Flight deck, feet (metres): 203.4 × 68.9 *(62 × 21)*
Main machinery: 4 boilers; 640 psi *(45 kg/cm sq)*; 840°F *(450°C)*; 2 Rateau-Bretagne turbines; 40 000 hp(m) *(29.4 MW)*; 2 shafts
Speed, knots: 26.5. **Range, miles:** 6000 at 15 kts
Complement: 626 (30 officers) plus 140 cadets

Missiles: SSM: 6 Aerospatiale MM 38 Exocet ❶; inertial cruise; active radar homing to 42 km *(23 nm)* at 0.9 Mach; warhead 165 kg; sea-skimmer.
Guns: 4 DCN 3.9 in *(100 mm)*/55 Mod 1964 CADAM automatic ❷; 80° elevation; 80 rounds/minute to 17 km *(9 nm)* anti-surface; 8 km *(4.4 nm)* anti-aircraft; weight of shell 13.5 kg.
Countermeasures: Decoys: 2 CSEE/VSEL Syllex 8-barrelled trainable launchers for chaff (may not be fitted).
ESM: ARBR 16; radar warning.
Fire control: Three C T Analogiques; two Sagem DMAa optical sights. SATCOM ❸.
Radars: Air search: Thomson-CSF DRBV 22D ❹; D band; range 366 km *(200 nm)*.
Air/surface search: DRBV 51 ❺; G band (from 1992).
Navigation: DRBN 32 (Decca 1226); I band.
Fire control: Three Thomson-CSF DRBC 32A ❻; I band.
Tacan: SRN-6.
Sonars: Thomson Sintra DUBV 24; hull-mounted; active search; medium frequency; 5 kHz.

Helicopters: 4 Alouette III (to be replaced by Dauphin). War inventory includes 8 Super Puma and Lynx.

Programmes: Due to pay off after 2005.
Modernisation: Long refits in the Summers of 1989 and 1990 have allowed equipment to be updated to enable the ship to continue well into the next century. SENIT 2 combat data system was to have been fitted but this was cancelled as a cost saving measure. DRBV 51 radar fitted in 1992.
Structure: Flight deck lift has a capacity of 12 tons. Some of the hangar space is used to accommodate officers under training. The ship is almost entirely air-conditioned. Carries two LCVPs.
Operational: Used for training officer cadets in peacetime. In wartime, after rapid modification, she would be used as a commando ship, helicopter carrier or troop transport with commando equipment and a battalion of 700 men. Flagship of the Training Squadron for an Autumn/Spring cruise with Summer refit.

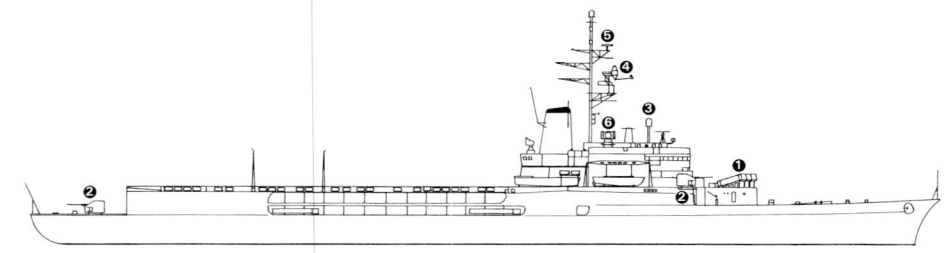
JEANNE D'ARC (Scale 1 : 1500), Ian Sturton

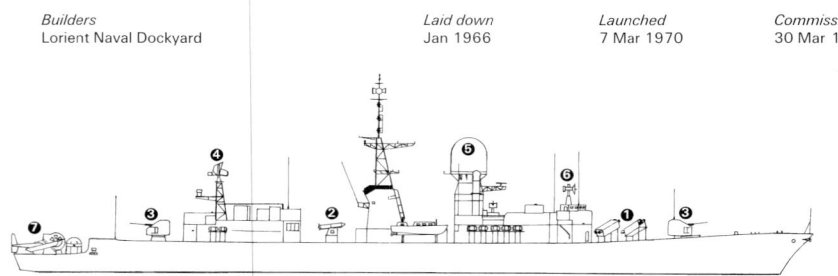
JEANNE D'ARC (old radar) 2/1992, Hachiro Nakai

DESTROYERS (Frégates)

1 TYPE F 65 (ASW)

Name	No	Builders	Laid down	Launched	Commissioned
ACONIT	D 609 (ex-*F 703*)	Lorient Naval Dockyard	Jan 1966	7 Mar 1970	30 Mar 1973

Displacement, tons: 3500 standard; 3900 full load
Dimensions, feet (metres): 416.7 × 44 × 18.9 *(127 × 13.4 × 5.8)*
Main machinery: 2 boilers; 640 psi *(45 kg/cm sq)*; 842°F *(450°C)*; 1 Rateau turbine; 28 650 hp(m) *(21 MW)*; 1 shaft
Speed, knots: 27. **Range, miles:** 5000 at 18 kts
Complement: 228 (15 officers)

Missiles: SSM: 8 Aerospatiale MM 40 Exocet ❶; inertial cruise; active radar homing to 70 km *(40 nm)* at 0.9 Mach; warhead 165 kg; sea-skimmer.
SAM: 2 Matra Simbad twin launchers for Mistral (can be fitted on 20 mm gun pedestals).
A/S: Latecoere Malafon ❷; range 13 km *(7 nm)* at 450 kts; payload L4 acoustic homing torpedo; warhead 100 kg; 13 missiles.
Guns: 2 DCN 3.9 in *(100 mm)*/55 Mod 68 CADAM automatic ❸; 80° elevation; 80 rounds/minute to 17 km *(9 nm)* anti-surface; 8 km *(4.4 nm)* anti-aircraft; weight of shell 13.5 kg.
2 Oerlikon 20 mm; 2—12.7 mm MGs.
Torpedoes: 2 launchers. 10 ECAN L5; anti-submarine; active/passive homing to 9.5 km *(5.1 nm)* at 35 kts; warhead 150 kg; depth to 550 m *(1800 ft)*.
Countermeasures: Decoys: 2 CSEE/VSEL Syllex 8-barrelled trainable launchers; chaff to 1 km in distraction and centroid patterns. Nixie; towed torpedo decoy.
ESM: ARBR 16; radar warning.
ECM: ARBB 32; jammer.
Combat data systems: SENIT 3 action data automation; Links 11 and 14. SATCOM.
Fire control: SENIT 3 radar/TV tracker (possibly SAT Murène in due course). Two Sagem DMAa optical directors.
Radars: Air search: DRBV 22A ❹; D band.
Air/surface search: Thomson-CSF DRBV 15A ❺; E/F band.
Navigation: DRBN 32 (Decca 1226); I band.
Fire control: DRBC 32D ❻; I band (for guns).
Sonars: Thomson Sintra DUBV 23; bow-mounted; active search and attack; 5 kHz.
DUBV 43C ❼; VDS; medium frequency 5 kHz; tows at up to 24 kts at 200 m.
DSBV 62C; passive linear towed array; very low frequency.

Programmes: Forerunner of the F 67 Type. A one-off class ordered under 1965 programme. Due to pay off in 2004.
Modernisation: A second quadruple Exocet launcher has been fitted. Mid-life refit from June 1991 to April 1992 included DSBV 62 passive sonar towed array, a lightweight DRBC 32D fire control radar and SATCOM.
Operational: Assigned to GASM.

ACONIT (Scale 1 : 1200), Ian Sturton

ACONIT 6/1992, French Navy

7 GEORGES LEYGUES CLASS (TYPE F 70 (ASW))

Name	No	Builders	Laid down	Launched	Commissioned
GEORGES LEYGUES	D 640	Brest Naval Dockyard	16 Sep 1974	17 Dec 1976	10 Dec 1979
DUPLEIX	D 641	Brest Naval Dockyard	17 Oct 1975	2 Dec 1978	13 June 1981
MONTCALM	D 642	Brest Naval Dockyard	5 Dec 1975	31 May 1980	28 May 1982
JEAN DE VIENNE	D 643	Brest Naval Dockyard	26 Oct 1979	17 Nov 1981	25 May 1984
PRIMAUGUET	D 644	Brest Naval Dockyard	19 Nov 1981	17 Mar 1984	7 Nov 1986
LA MOTTE-PICQUET	D 645	Brest Naval Dockyard/Lorient	12 Feb 1982	6 Feb 1985	18 Feb 1988
LATOUCHE-TRÉVILLE	D 646	Brest Naval Dockyard/Lorient	15 Feb 1984	19 Mar 1988	16 July 1990

Displacement, tons: 3830 standard; 4300 (D 640-643); 4490 (D 644-646) full load
Dimensions, feet (metres): 455.9 × 45.9 × 18.7 *(139 × 14 × 5.7)*
Main machinery: CODOG; 2 RR Olympus TM3B gas turbines; 46 200 hp *(34.5 MW)* sustained; 2 SEMT-Pielstick 16PA6 V280 diesels; 12 800 hp(m) *(9.41 MW)* sustained; 2 shafts; cp props
Speed, knots: 30; 21 on diesels. **Range, miles:** 8500 at 18 kts on diesels; 2500 at 28 kts
Complement: 218 (16 officers) plus 16 spare billets

Missiles: SSM: 4 Aerospatiale MM 38 Exocet (MM 40 in D 642-646) ❶; inertial cruise; active radar homing to 42 km *(23 nm)* at 0.9 Mach (MM 38); active radar homing to 70 km *(40 nm)* at 0.9 Mach (MM 40); warhead 165 kg; sea-skimmer. 4 additional Exocet missiles can be carried as a warload (D 644-646).
SAM: Thomson-CSF Crotale Naval EDIR octuple launcher ❷; command line of sight guidance; radar/IR homing to 13 km *(7 nm)* at 2.4 Mach; warhead 14 kg; 26 missiles.
Guns: 1—3.9 in *(100 mm)*/55 Mod 68 CADAM automatic ❸; dual purpose; 80° elevation; 78 rounds/minute to 17 km *(9 nm)* anti-surface; 8 km *(4.4 nm)* anti-aircraft; weight of shell 13.5 kg.
2 Oerlikon 20 mm ❹; 720 rounds/minute to 10 km *(5.5 nm)*.
4 M2HB 12.7 mm MGs.
Torpedoes: 2 fixed launchers. 10 ECAN L5; anti-submarine; active/passive homing to 9.5 km *(5.1 nm)* at 35 kts; warhead 150 kg; depth to 550 m *(1800 ft)*. 12 Honeywell Mk 46 for helicopters.
Countermeasures: Decoys: 2 CSEE Dagaie 10-barrelled double trainable launcher (replacing Syllex) ❺; chaff and IR flares; H-J band.
ESM: ARBR 17 ❻; radar warning. DIBV 1A Vampir; IR detector (D 644-646).
ECM: ARBB 32 B; jammer.
Combat data systems: SENIT 4 action data automation; Links 11 and 14. SLASM integrated ASW (to be fitted in due course). Syracuse 1 SATCOM ❼.
Fire control: Thomson-CSF Vega (D 640-643) and DCN CTMS (D 644-646) optronic/radar systems. SAT Murène IR tracker to be added to CTMS and possibly Vega systems. CSEE Panda optical director. DLT L4 (D 640-643) and DLT L5 (D 644-646) torpedo control system.
Radars: Air search: DRBV 26 (not in D 644-646) ❽; D band; range 182 km *(100 nm)* for 2 m² target.
Air/surface search: Thomson-CSF DRBV 51C (DRBV 15A in D 644-646) ❾; G band; range 120 km *(65 nm)* for 2 m² target.
Navigation: Two Decca 1226; I band (one for close-range helicopter control).
Fire control: Thomson-CSF Vega with DRBC 32E (D 640-643) ❿; I band; DRBC 33A (D 644-646) ⓫; I band.
Crotale ❷; I band (for SAM).
Sonars: Thomson Sintra DUBV 23D (DUBV 24C in D 644-646); bow-mounted; active search and attack; 5 kHz.
DUBV 43B (43C in D 643-646) ⓬; VDS; search; medium frequency; paired with DUBV 23D/24; tows at 24 kts down to 200 m *(650 ft)*, *(700 m (3000 ft)* for 43C). Length of tow 600 m *(2000 ft)*; being upgraded to 43C.
DSBV 61B (in D 644 onward); passive linear towed array; very low frequency; 365 m *(1200 ft)*. DSBV 62C may be fitted in first four during mid-life refits in 1990s.

Helicopters: 2 Lynx Mk 4 ⓭.

Programmes: First three were in the 1971-76 new construction programme, fourth in 1978 estimates, fifth in 1980 estimates, sixth in 1981 estimates, seventh in 1983 estimates. D 645 and 646 were towed from Brest to Lorient for completion. Service lives: *Georges Leygues*, 2004; *Dupleix* and *Montcalm*, 2006; *Jean de Vienne*, 2008; *Primauguet*, 2011; *La Motte-Picquet*, 2012; *Latouche-Tréville*, 2014. Re-rated F 70 'frégates antisous-marines (FASM)' (ex-C 70) on 6 June 1988.
Modernisation: The class is to receive the new OTO Melara/Matra ASW missile Milas. The projected SLASM update from 1997 includes a new bow sonar and a VLF towed active sonar with separate passive array. The first four may be back-fitted with towed arrays in mid-life refits in 1990s.
Structure: Bridge raised one deck in the last three of the class.
Operational: The ships' helicopters are dual roled, either carrying sonar or sonobuoy dispenser and ASW weapons or AS 12 anti-ship missiles. *Primauguet* and *Latouche-Tréville* allocated to GASM, remainder to FAN. SIMBAD may be fitted.

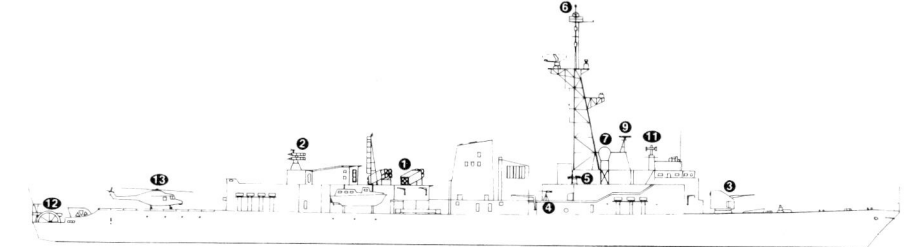

PRIMAUGUET *(Scale 1 : 1200), Ian Sturton*

MONTCALM (low bridge) *7/1992, B Sullivan*

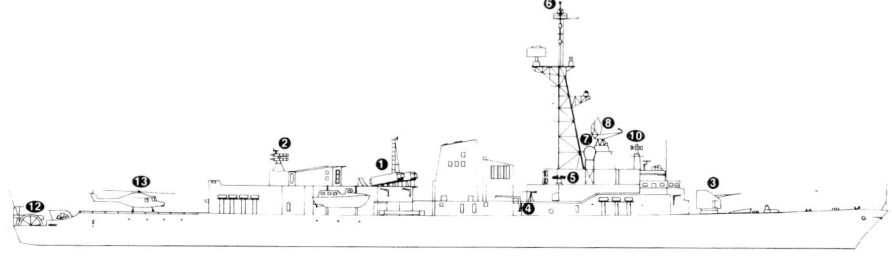

GEORGES LEYGUES *(Scale 1 : 1200), Ian Sturton*

LATOUCHE-TRÉVILLE (high bridge) *6/1992, Guy Toremans*

LATOUCHE-TRÉVILLE (VDS and towed array) *6/1992, Guy Toremans*

208 FRANCE / Destroyers

2 CASSARD CLASS (TYPE F 70 (A/A))

Name	No	Builders	Laid down	Launched	Commissioned
CASSARD	D 614	Lorient Naval Dockyard	3 Sep 1982	6 Feb 1985	28 July 1988
JEAN BART	D 615	Lorient Naval Dockyard	12 Mar 1986	19 Mar 1988	21 Sep 1991

Displacement, tons: 4230 standard; 4700 full load
Dimensions, feet (metres): 455.9 × 45.9 × 21.3 (sonar) *(139 × 14 × 6.5)*
Main machinery: 4 SEMT-Pielstick 18 PA6 V 280 BTC diesels; 43 200 hp(m) *(31.75 MW)* sustained; 2 shafts
Speed, knots: 29.5. **Range, miles:** 8200 at 17 kts; 4800 at 24 kts
Complement: 244 (22 officers) accommodation for 251

Missiles: SSM: 8 Aerospatiale MM 40 Exocet ❶; inertial cruise; active radar homing to 70 km *(40 nm)* at 0.9 Mach; warhead 165 kg; sea-skimmer.
SAM: 40 GDC Pomona Standard SM-1MR; Mk 13 Mod 5 launcher ❷; semi-active radar homing to 46 km *(25 nm)* at 2 Mach; height envelope 45-18 288 m *(150-60 000 ft)*. Launchers taken from T 47 (DDG) ships.
2 Matra Sadral PDMS sextuple launchers ❸; Mistral; IR homing to 4 km *(2.2 nm)*; warhead 3 kg; anti-sea-skimmer; able to engage targets down to 10 ft above sea level.
Guns: 1 DCN 3.9 in *(100 mm)*/55 Mod 68 CADAM automatic ❹; 80° elevation; 80 rounds/minute to 17 km *(9 nm)* anti-surface; 8 km *(4.4 nm)* anti-aircraft; weight of shell 13.5 kg.
2 Oerlikon 20 mm ❺; 720 rounds/minute to 10 km *(5.5 nm)*.
4—12.7 mm MGs.
Torpedoes: 2 fixed launchers model KD 59E ❻. 10 ECAN L5 Mod 4; anti-submarine; active/passive homing to 9.5 km *(5.1 nm)* at 35 kts; warhead 150 kg; depth to 550 m *(1800 ft)*. Honeywell Mk 46 torpedoes for the helicopter.
Countermeasures: Decoys: 2 CSEE Dagaie ❼ and 2 Sagaie 10-barrelled trainable launchers ❽; fires a combination of chaff and IR flares. Nixie; towed torpedo decoy.
ESM: ARBR 17B ❾; radar warning. DIBV 1A Vampir ❿; IR detector (integrated with search radar for active/passive tracking in all weathers). Saigon radio intercept at masthead.
ECM: ARBB 33; jammer; H, I and J bands.
Combat data systems: SENIT 6 action data automation; Links 11 and 14 (later 16). Syracuse 1 SATCOM ⓫.
Fire control: DCN CTMS optronic/radar system with DIBC 1A Piranha II IR/TV tracker; CSEE Najir optronic secondary director.
Radars: Air search: Thomson-CSF DRBJ 11B ⓬; 3D; range 366 km *(200 nm)*.
Air/surface search: DRBV 26C ⓭; D band; range 182 km *(100 nm)*.
Navigation: Two Racal DRBN 34A; I band (one for close-range helicopter control ⓮).
Fire control: Thomson-CSF DRBC 33A ⓯; I band (for guns).
Two Raytheon SPG 51C ⓰; G/I band (for missiles).
Sonars: Thomson Sintra DUBA 25A (D 614) or DUBV 24C (D 615); hull-mounted; active search and attack; medium frequency. May be fitted later with DSBV 62C passive towed array; very low frequency.

Helicopters: 1 Lynx Mk 4 ⓱.

Programmes: On the same hull as the F 70 (A/S) a very different armament and propulsion system has been introduced. Funds for the first ship allotted in 1978 estimates, for the second in 1979 estimates (ordered 27 September 1979), and for the third and fourth in 1983 estimates. Third and fourth ships ordered 27 February 1984, but then cancelled. The building programme was considerably slowed down by finance problems and doubts about the increasingly obsolescent Standard SM 1 missile system, and the SM 2 is reported as being too expensive. Service lives: First, 2013; second, 2015. Re-rated F 70 (ex-C 70) on 6 June 1988, officially 'frégates anti-aériennes (FAA)'.
Structure: Samahe 210 helicopter handling system. It is reported that both ships are to be fitted with Aster SAM during their first refits. *Cassard* fitted with DRBJ 11B radar (replacing DRBV 15) in 1992. Displacement is creeping up to over 4700 tons.
Operational: Helicopter used for third party targeting for the SSM. Both ships are assigned to FAN.

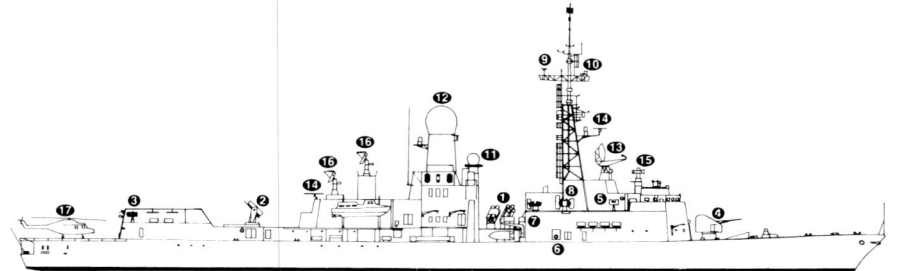
JEAN BART *(Scale 1 : 1200), Ian Sturton*

JEAN BART *7/1992, Giorgio Ghiglione*

JEAN BART *5/1991 Fotoflite*

0 + (4) FRANCO-BRITISH NEW GENERATION TYPE

Displacement, tons: 6200 app
Dimensions, feet (metres): 472.1 × 61.7 × 15.7 *(143.9 × 18.8 × 4.8)*
Main machinery: CODLAG; 2 gas turbines; 4 diesels; 2 motors; 2 shafts
Speed, knots: 30. **Range, miles:** 6000 at 18 kts
Complement: 200 plus 35 spare

Missiles: SSM: 8 (2 quad) ❶ or VLS.
SAM: Aster VLS ❷ PAMS (principal AAW missile system).
Guns: 1—100/114 mm ❸; anti-surface.
2—30 mm ❹. 2 ILMS (inner layer missile system) ❺.
Torpedoes: 4 (2 twin) fixed launchers ❻.
Countermeasures: Decoys: Chaff and IR flare launchers. Torpedo defence system.
Combat data systems: Link 16 included.
Radars: Air/surface search ❼.
Surveillance/fire control ❽; multi-function.
Sonars: Hull-mounted; active search and attack; medium frequency.

Helicopters: 1 Marine Nationale NH 90 ❾.

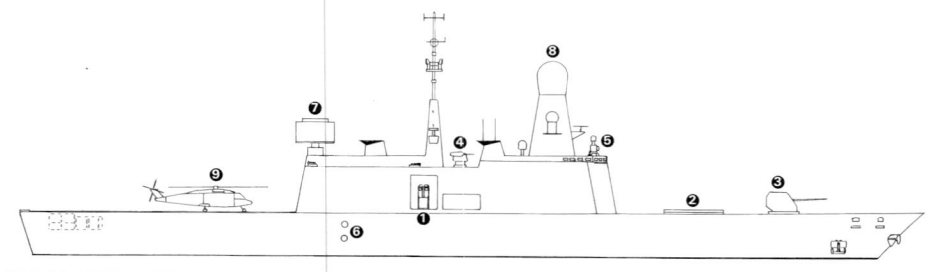
FRANCO-BRITISH NG TYPE *(Scale 1 : 1200), Ian Sturton*

Programmes: Bilateral project for a new AAW ship with the possibility of Italian participation. Warship design contract expected in late 1994 for first order in 1996 and an in service date of 2002.
Structure: Details given are speculative and the drawing should be compared with the same entry in the UK section.

Destroyers / FRANCE 209

2 SUFFREN CLASS

Name	No	Builders	Laid down	Launched	Commissioned
SUFFREN	D 602	Lorient Naval Dockyard	21 Dec 1962	15 May 1965	20 July 1967
DUQUESNE	D 603	Brest Naval Dockyard	1 Feb 1965	12 Feb 1966	1 Apr 1970

Displacement, tons: 5090 standard; 6910 full load
Dimensions, feet (metres): 517.1 × 50.9 × 20 *(157.6 × 15.5 × 6.1)*
Main machinery: 4 boilers; 640 psi *(45 kg/cm sq)*; 842°F *(450°C)*; 2 Rateau turbines; 72 500 hp(m) *(53 MW)*; 2 shafts
Speed, knots: 34. **Range, miles:** 5100 at 18 kts; 2400 at 29 kts
Complement: 355 (23 officers)

Missiles: SSM: 4 Aerospatiale MM 38 Exocet ❶; inertial cruise; active radar homing to 42 km *(23 nm)* at 0.9 Mach; warhead 165 kg; sea-skimmer.
 SAM: ECAN Ruelle Masurca twin launcher ❷; Mk 2 Mod 3 semi-active radar homers; range 55 km *(30 nm)*; warhead 98 kg; 48 missiles.
A/S: Latecoere Malafon ❸; range 13 km *(7 nm)* at 450 kts; payload L4 acoustic homing torpedo; warhead 100 kg; 13 missiles.
Guns: 2 DCN 3.9 in *(100 mm)*/55 Mod 1964 CADAM automatic ❹; 80° elevation; 80 rounds/minute to 17 km *(9 nm)* anti-surface; 8 km *(4.4 nm)* anti-aircraft; weight of shell 13.5 kg.
 4 or 6 Oerlikon 20 mm; 720 rounds/minute to 10 km *(5.5 nm)*.
Torpedoes: 4 launchers (2 each side) ❺. 10 ECAN L5; anti-submarine; active/passive homing to 9.5 km *(5.1 nm)* at 35 kts; warhead 150 kg; depth to 550 m *(1800 ft)*.
Countermeasures: Decoys: 2 CSEE Sagaie 10-barrelled trainable launchers; chaff to 8 km *(4.4 nm)* and IR flares to 3 km *(1.6 nm)*. 2 Dagaie launchers ❻.
 ESM: ARBR 17; intercept.
 ECM: ARBB 33; jammer.
Combat data systems: SENIT 2 action data automation; Links 11 and 14. Syracuse 1 SATCOM ⓬.
Fire control: DCN CTMS radar/optronic control system with SAT DIBC 1A Piranha IR and TV tracker. 2 Sagem DMA optical directors.
Radars: Air search (radome): DRBI 23 ❼; D band.
 Air/surface search: DRBV 15A ❽; E/F band.
 Navigation: Racal Decca 1226; I band.
 Fire control: Two Thomson-CSF DRBR 51 ❾; G/I band (for Masurca).
 Thomson-CSF DRBC 33A ❿; I band (for guns).
 Tacan: URN 20.
Sonars: Thomson Sintra DUBV 23; hull-mounted; active search and attack; 5 kHz.
 DUBV 43 ⓫; VDS; medium frequency 5 kHz; tows at up to 24 kts at 200 m *(656 ft)*.

Programmes: Ordered under the 1960 programme. Service lives: Both extended to over 2000.

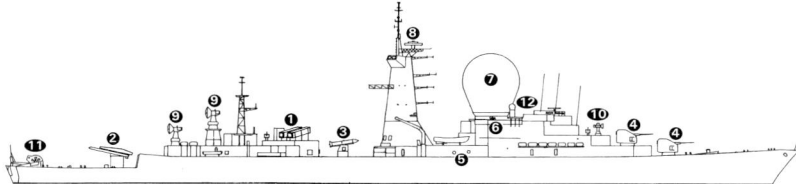
SUFFREN *(Scale 1 : 1500), Ian Sturton*

DUQUESNE *9/1992, C D Yaylali*

Modernisation: MM 38 Exocet fitted in 1977 *(Duquesne)* and 1979 *(Suffren)*; Masurca modernised in 1984-85 *(Duquesne)* and 1988-89 *(Suffren)*, with new computers. DRBV 15A radars replaced DRBV 50. *Suffren* had a major refit from May 1988 to September 1989 and *Duquesne* from June 1990 to March 1991: modernisation of the DRBI-23 radar; new computers for the SENIT combat data system; new CTMS fire control system for 100 mm guns fitted (with DRBC-33A radar, TV camera and DIBC-1A Piranha IR tracker). New ESM/ECM suite: ARBR 17 radar interceptor, ARBB 33 jammer and Sagaie decoy launchers. Two 20 mm guns fitted either side of DRBC 33A.
Structure: Equipped with gyro-controlled stabilisers operating three pairs of non-retractable fins. NBC citadel fitted during modernisation. Air-conditioning of accommodation and operational areas. Excellent sea boats and weapon platforms.
Operational: Both ships operate in the Mediterranean under FAN. Officially frégates lance-missiles (FLM).

3 TOURVILLE CLASS (TYPE F 67)

Name	No	Builders	Laid down	Launched	Commissioned
TOURVILLE	D 610	Lorient Naval Dockyard	16 Mar 1970	13 May 1972	21 June 1974
DUGUAY-TROUIN	D 611	Lorient Naval Dockyard	25 Feb 1971	1 June 1973	17 Sep 1975
DE GRASSE	D 612	Lorient Naval Dockyard	14 June 1972	30 Nov 1974	1 Oct 1977

Displacement, tons: 4580 standard; 5950 full load
Dimensions, feet (metres): 501.6 × 52.4 × 18.7 *(152.8 × 16 × 5.7)*
Main machinery: 4 boilers; 640 psi *(45 kg/cm sq)*; 840°F *(450°C)*; 2 Rateau turbines; 58 000 hp(m) *(43 MW)*; 2 shafts
Speed, knots: 32. **Range, miles:** 5000 at 18 kts
Complement: 301 (21 officers)

Missiles: SSM: 6 Aerospatiale MM 38 Exocet ❶; inertial cruise; active radar homing to 42 km *(23 nm)* at 0.9 Mach; warhead 165 kg; sea-skimmer.
 SAM: Thomson-CSF Crotale Naval EDIR octuple launcher ❷; command line of sight guidance; radar/IR homing to 13 km *(7 nm)* at 2.4 Mach; warhead 14 kg.
A/S: Latecoere Malafon (to be replaced by Milas from 1997) ❸; range 13 km *(7 nm)* at 450 kts; payload L4 acoustic homing torpedo; warhead 100 kg; 13 missiles.
Guns: 2 DCN 3.9 in *(100 mm)*/55 Mod 68 CADAM automatic ❹; dual purpose; 80° elevation; 80 rounds/minute to 17 km *(9 nm)* anti-surface; 8 km *(4.4 nm)* anti-aircraft; weight of shell 13.5 kg.
 2 Oerlikon 20 mm ❺; 720 rounds/minute to 10 km *(5.5 nm)*.
Torpedoes: 2 launchers ❻. 10 ECAN L5; anti-submarine; active/passive homing to 9.5 km *(5.1 nm)* at 35 kts; warhead 150 kg; depth to 550 m *(1800 ft)*. Honeywell Mk 46 torpedoes for helicopters.
Countermeasures: Decoys: 2 CSEE/VSEL Syllex 8-barrelled trainable launcher (to be replaced by 2 Dagaie systems) ❼; chaff to 1 km in centroid and distraction patterns.
 ESM: ARBR 16; radar warning.
 ECM: ARBB 32; jammer.
Combat data systems: SENIT 3 action data automation; Links 11 and 14. Syracuse 1 SATCOM ⓭. AIDCOMER command support system *(Duguay-Trouin)*.
Fire control: SENIT 3 radar/TV tracker (possibly SAT Murène in due course). Two Sagem DMAa optical directors.
Radars: Air search: DRBV 26 ❽; D band; range 182 km *(100 nm)* for 2 m² target.
 Air/surface search: Thomson-CSF DRBV 51B ❾; G band; range 29 km *(16 nm)*.
 Navigation: Two Racal Decca Type 1226; I band (one for helicopter control).
 Fire control: Thomson-CSF DRBC 32D ❿; I band.
 Crotale ❷; J band (for SAM).
Sonars: Thomson Sintra DUBV 23; bow-mounted; active search and attack; 5 kHz.
 DUBV 43C ⓫; VDS; medium frequency 5 kHz; tows at up to 24 kts at 200 m.
 DSBV 62C; passive linear towed array; very low frequency.

Helicopters: 2 Lynx Mk 4 ⓬.

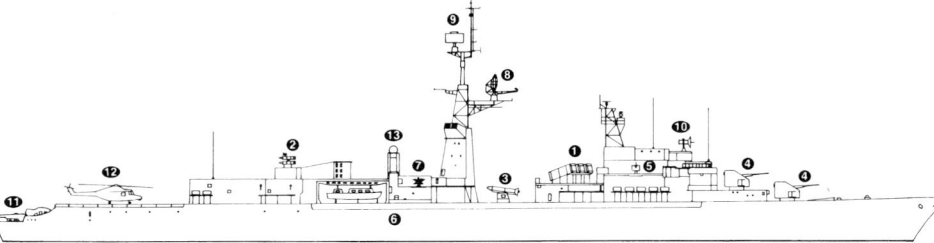
TOURVILLE *(Scale 1 : 1200), Ian Sturton*

TOURVILLE *1992, DCN*

Programmes: Developed from the Aconit design. Originally rated as corvettes but reclassified as 'frégates anti-sous-marins (FASM)' on 8 July 1971 and given D pennant numbers like destroyers. *De Grasse* completed major refit September 1981, *Duguay-Trouin* in 1984-85.
 Service lives: *Tourville*, 2000; *Duguay-Trouin* , 2001; *De Grasse*, 2003. These will probably be extended.
Modernisation: Planned to complete *Tourville* August 1994, *De Grasse* October 1995, *Duguay-Trouin* 1996; to include new bow sonar plus VLF towed active sonar with separate towed passive array (SLASM), Murene torpedoes launched from (a) helicopter (b) ships' tubes and (c) using OTO Melara/Matra Milas vice Malafon as stand off delivery vehicle. Passive towed arrays fitted to all three ships in 1990.
Operational: All assigned to GASM. Helicopters are dual roled either with sonar or sonobuoy dispenser and ASW weapons, or AS 12 anti-ship missiles.

210 FRANCE / Frigates

FRIGATES (Frégates, Avisos-escorteurs, Avisos)

4 + 2 FLORÉAL CLASS (PATROL FRIGATES)

Name	No	Builders	Laid down	Launched	Commissioned
FLORÉAL	F 730	Chantiers de L'Atlantique, St Nazaire	2 Apr 1990	6 Oct 1990	27 May 1992
PRAIRIAL	F 731	Chantiers de L'Atlantique, St Nazaire	11 Sep 1990	23 Mar 1991	20 May 1992
NIVÔSE	F 732	Chantiers de L'Atlantique, St Nazaire	16 Jan 1991	10 Aug 1991	15 Oct 1992
VENTÔSE	F 733	Chantiers de L'Atlantique, St Nazaire	28 June 1991	14 Mar 1992	4 May 1993
VENDÉMIAIRE	F 734	Chantiers de L'Atlantique, St Nazaire	17 Jan 1992	22 Aug 1992	Oct 1993
GERMINAL	F 735	Chantiers de L'Atlantique, St Nazaire	17 Aug 1992	Mar 1993	June 1994

Displacement, tons: 2600 standard; 2950 full load
Dimensions, feet (metres): 306.8 × 45.9 × 14.1 *(93.5 × 14 × 4.3)*
Main machinery: CODAD; 4 SEMT-Pielstick 6 PA6 L 280 diesels; 8820 hp(m) *(6.5 MW)* sustained; 2 shafts; cp props; bow thruster; 340 hp(m) *(250 kW)*
Speed, knots: 20. **Range, miles:** 9000 at 15 kts
Complement: 86 (11 officers) (including air crew) plus 38 spare

Missiles: SSM: 2 Aerospatiale MM 38 Exocet ❶; inertial cruise; active radar homing to 42 km *(23 nm)* at 0.9 Mach; warhead 165 kg; sea-skimmer.
SAM: 2 Matra Simbad twin launchers to replace 20 mm guns in due course.
Guns: 1 DCN 3.9 in *(100 mm)*/55 Mod 68 CADAM ❷; 80° elevation; 80 rounds/minute to 17 km *(9 nm)*; weight of shell 13.5 kg.
2 Giat 20 F2 20 mm ❸; 720 rounds/minute to 10 km *(5.5 nm)*.
Countermeasures: Decoys: 2 CSEE Dagaie II; 10-barrelled trainable launchers ❹; chaff and IR flares.
ESM: Thomson-CSF ARBR 17 ❺; radar intercept.
Fire control: CSEE Najir optronic director ❻. Syracuse 2 SATCOM ❼.
Radars: Air/surface search: Thomson-CSF Mars DRBV 21A ❽; D band.
Navigation: Two Racal Decca DRBN 34A (1226); I band (one for helicopter control ❾).

Helicopters: 1 Dauphin II/Panther or 1 Alouette III or 1 AS 332F Super Puma ❿.

Programmes: Officially described as 'Frégates de Surveillance' or 'Ocean capable patrol vessel' and designed to operate in the offshore zone in low intensity operations. First two ordered on 20 January 1989; built at Chantiers de L'Atlantique, St Nazaire, with weapon systems fitted by DCAN Lorient. Second pair ordered 9 January 1990; third pair in January 1991. Named after the months of the Revolutionary calendar.
Structure: Built to merchant passenger marine standards with stabilisers and air-conditioning. New funnel design improves airflow over the flight deck. Has one freight bunker aft for about 100 tons cargo. Second-hand Exocet MM 38 has been fitted instead of planned MM 40.
Operational: Endurance, 50 days. Range proved to be better than expected during sea trials. Able to operate a helicopter up to seastate 5. Stations planned as follows: *Floreal* in South Indian Ocean, *Ventose* in Antilles, *Germinal* tender to *Jeanne d'Arc*, remainder in the Pacific.

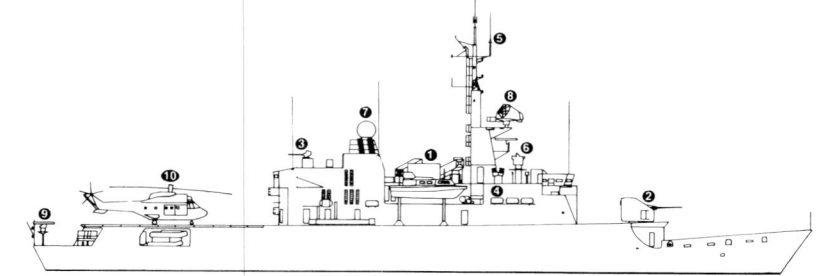
FLORÉAL (Scale 1 : 900), Ian Sturton

PRAIRIAL 3/1992, Giorgio Arra

FLORÉAL 11/1992, S Poynton, RAN

Frigates / FRANCE

3 COMMANDANT RIVIÈRE CLASS (Avisos Escorteurs)

Name	No	Builders	Laid down	Launched	Commissioned
COMMANDANT BORY	F 726	Lorient Naval Dockyard	14 Mar 1958	11 Oct 1958	5 Mar 1964
BALNY	F 729	Lorient Naval Dockyard	24 Mar 1960	17 Mar 1962	1 Feb 1970
ENSEIGNE DE VAISSEAU HENRY	F 749	Lorient Naval Dockyard	15 Sep 1962	14 Dec 1963	1 Jan 1965

Displacement, tons: 1750 standard; 2250 full load
1650 standard; 2150 full load *(Balny)*
Dimensions, feet (metres): 336.9 × 38.4 × 14.1 *(102.7 × 11.7 × 4.3)*
Main machinery: 4 SEMT-Pielstick 12PC series diesels; 16 000 hp(m) *(11.8 MW)*; 2 shafts *(Enseigne de Vaisseau Henry)*
CODAG; 2 AGO V16 diesels; 6528 hp(m) *(4.8 MW)*; 1 Turbomeca M38 gas turbine; 10 600 hp(m) *(7.8 MW)*; 1 shaft; cp prop *(Balny)*
2 SEMT-Pielstick 12 PC2 V 400 diesels; 12 000 hp(m) *(8.2 MW)*; 2 shafts; cp props *(Commandant Bory)*
Speed, knots: 25. **Range, miles:** 7500 at 15 kts; 8000 at 12 kts *(Balny)*
Complement: 159 (9 officers)

Missiles: SSM: 4 Aerospatiale MM 38 Exocet (not fitted in *Balny*) ❶; active radar homing to 42 km *(23 nm)* at 0.9 Mach; warhead 165 kg; sea-skimmer.
Guns: 2 DCN 3.9 in *(100 mm)*/55 Mod 1953 automatic ❷; dual purpose; 80° elevation; 60 rounds/minute to 17 km *(9 nm)* anti-surface; 8 km *(4.4 nm)* anti-aircraft; weight of shell 13.5 kg.
2 Bofors 40/60 ❸. 2—12.7 mm MGs.
Torpedoes: 6—21.7 in *(550 mm)* (2 triple) tubes ❹. ECAN L3; anti-submarine; active homing to 5.5 km *(3 nm)* at 25 kts; warhead 200 kg; depth to 300 m *(985 ft)*.
A/S mortars: 1 Mortier 305 mm 4-barrelled launcher ❺; automatic loading; range 2700 m; warhead 227 kg. Removed from *Enseigne de Vaisseau Henry*.
Countermeasures: Decoys: 2 CSEE Dagaie 10-barrelled trainable launchers ❻; chaff and IR flares; H-J band.
ESM: ARBR 16; radar warning.
Fire control: C T Analogique; Sagem DMAa optical secondary director.
Radars: Air/surface search: Thomson-CSF DRBV 22A ❼; D band.
Surface search: Racal Decca 1226 ❽; I band.
Fire control: Thomson-CSF DRBC 32C ❾; I band.
Sonars: EDO SQS 17; hull-mounted; active search; medium frequency.
Thomson Sintra DUBA 3; active attack; high frequency.

Programmes: Survivors of a large class. *Balny* was made the CODAG trials ship in 1964 but later again became fully operational.
Service lives: 1995. To be replaced by La Fayette class.
Operational: Can carry a senior officer and staff. If necessary a force of 80 soldiers can be embarked as well as two 30 ft *(9 m)* LCPs with a capacity of 25 men at 11 kts. Pacific, one ship; Indian Ocean, one ship. *Enseigne de Vaisseau Henry* acts as tender to *Jeanne d'Arc*.
Sales: *Victor Schoelcher* sold to Uruguay 30 September 1988, *Commandant Bourdais* and *Amiral Charner*, 14 March 1990.

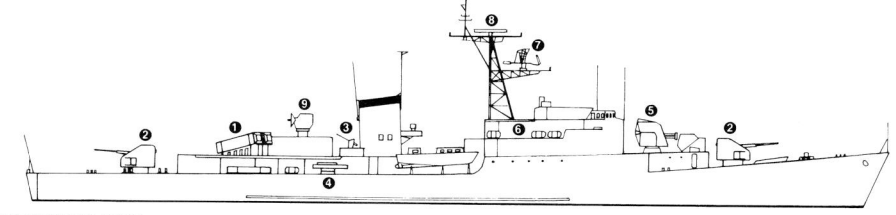

COMMANDANT BORY *(Scale 1 : 900), Ian Sturton*

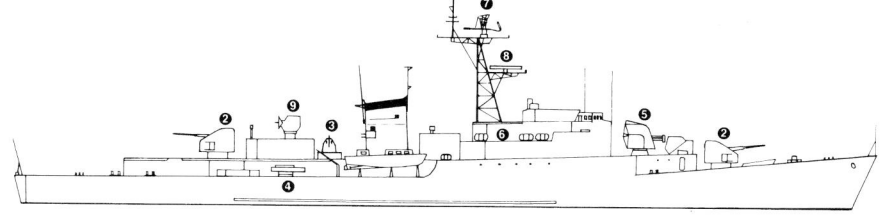

BALNY *(Scale 1 : 900), Ian Sturton*

ENSEIGNE DE VAISSEAU HENRY *2/1992, Hachiro Nakai*

BALNY *6/1991, John Mortimer*

212 FRANCE / Frigates

17 D'ESTIENNE D'ORVES (TYPE A 69) CLASS

Name	No	Builders	Laid down	Launched	Commissioned
D'ESTIENNE D'ORVES	F 781	Lorient Naval Dockyard	1 Sep 1972	1 June 1973	10 Sep 1976
AMYOT D'INVILLE	F 782	Lorient Naval Dockyard	Sep 1973	30 Nov 1974	13 Oct 1976
DROGOU	F 783	Lorient Naval Dockyard	1 Oct 1973	30 Nov 1974	30 Sep 1976
DÉTROYAT	F 784	Lorient Naval Dockyard	15 Dec 1974	31 Jan 1976	4 May 1977
JEAN MOULIN	F 785	Lorient Naval Dockyard	15 Jan 1975	31 Jan 1976	11 May 1977
QUARTIER MAÎTRE ANQUETIL	F 786	Lorient Naval Dockyard	1 Aug 1975	7 Aug 1976	4 Feb 1978
COMMANDANT DE PIMODAN	F 787	Lorient Naval Dockyard	1 Sep 1975	7 Aug 1976	20 May 1978
SECOND MAÎTRE LE BIHAN	F 788	Lorient Naval Dockyard	1 Nov 1976	13 Aug 1977	7 July 1979
LIEUTENANT DE VAISSEAU LE HÉNAFF	F 789	Lorient Naval Dockyard	21 Mar 1977	16 Sep 1978	13 Feb 1980
LIEUTENANT DE VAISSEAU LAVALLÉE	F 790	Lorient Naval Dockyard	1 Nov 1977	29 May 1979	16 Aug 1980
COMMANDANT L'HERMINIER	F 791	Lorient Naval Dockyard	29 May 1979	7 Mar 1981	22 Feb 1986
PREMIER MAÎTRE L'HER	F 792	Lorient Naval Dockyard	24 July 1979	28 June 1980	5 Dec 1981
COMMANDANT BLAISON	F 793	Lorient Naval Dockyard	15 Nov 1979	7 Mar 1981	28 Apr 1982
ENSEIGNE DE VAISSEAU JACOUBET	F 794	Lorient Naval Dockyard	June 1980	28 Sep 1981	23 Oct 1982
COMMANDANT DUCUING	F 795	Lorient Naval Dockyard	1 Oct 1980	28 Sep 1981	17 Mar 1983
COMMANDANT BIROT	F 796	Lorient Naval Dockyard	23 Mar 1981	22 May 1982	14 Mar 1984
COMMANDANT BOUAN	F 797	Lorient Naval Dockyard	12 Oct 1981	23 Apr 1983	1 Nov 1984

Displacement, tons: 1175 standard; 1250 (1330, later ships) full load
Dimensions, feet (metres): 262.5 × 33.8 × 18 (sonar) *(80 × 10.3 × 5.5)*
Main machinery: 2 SEMT-Pielstick 12 PC2 V 400 diesels; 12 000 hp(m) *(8.82 MW)*; 2 shafts; cp props
2 SEMT-Pielstick 12 PA6 V 280 BTC diesels; 14 400 hp(m) *(10.6 MW)* sustained; 2 shafts; cp props *(Commandant L'Herminier)*
Speed, knots: 23. **Range, miles:** 4500 at 15 kts
Complement: 90 (7 officers)

Missiles: SSM: 4 Aerospatiale MM 40 (or 2 MM 38) Exocet ❶; inertial cruise; active radar homing to 70 km *(40 nm)* (or 42 km *(23 nm)*) at 0.9 Mach; warhead 165 kg; sea-skimmer. Most will get dual fit capability ITL in due course (see *Modernisation*) but a few only have MM 38 capability (ITS) and some none at all.
Guns: 1 DCN 3.9 in *(100 mm)*/55 Mod 68 CADAM automatic ❷; 80° elevation; 80 rounds/minute to 17 km *(9 nm)* anti-surface; 8 km *(4.4 nm)* anti-aircraft; weight of shell 13.5 kg.
2 Oerlikon 20 mm ❸; 720 rounds/minute to 10 km *(5.5 nm)*.
Torpedoes: 4 fixed tubes ❹. ECAN L5; dual purpose; active/passive homing to 9.5 km *(5.1 nm)* at 35 kts; warhead 150 kg; depth to 550 m *(1800 ft)*.
A/S mortars: 1 Creusot Loire 375 mm Mk 54 6-tubed trainable launcher ❺; range 1600 m; warhead 107 kg.
Countermeasures: Decoys: 2 CSEE Dagaie 10-barrelled trainable launchers (fitted from F 792 onwards; remainder being fitted at refit) ❻; chaff and IR flares; H-J band.
Nixie torpedo decoy.
ESM: ARBR 16; radar warning.
Fire control: Thomson-CSF Vega system; CSEE Panda optical secondary director.
Radars: Air/surface search: Thomson-CSF DRBV 51A ❼; G band.
Navigation: Racal Decca 1226; I band.
Fire control: Thomson-CSF DRBC 32E ❽; I band.
Sonars: Thomson Sintra DUBA 25; hull-mounted; search and attack; medium frequency.

Programmes: Classified as 'Avisos'. Service lives: Extended to 2000 and beyond.
Modernisation: In 1985 *Commandant L'Herminier*, F 791, fitted with 12PA6 BTC Diesels Rapides as trial for Type F 70. Most have dual MM 38/MM 40 ITL (Installation de Tir Légère) capability. Weapon fit depends on deployment and operational requirement. Those without ITL are being retrofitted with ITS (Installation de Tir Standard) as Commandant Rivière class pay off.
Operational: Endurance, 30 days and primarily intended for coastal A/S operations. Also available for overseas patrols. Ten assigned to GASM; remainder to Commander Mediterranean Flotilla or abroad.
Sales: The original *Lieutenant de Vaisseau Le Hénaff* and *Commandant l'Herminier* sold to South Africa in 1976 while under construction. As a result of the UN embargo on arms sales to South Africa, they were sold to Argentina in September 1978 followed by a third, specially built.

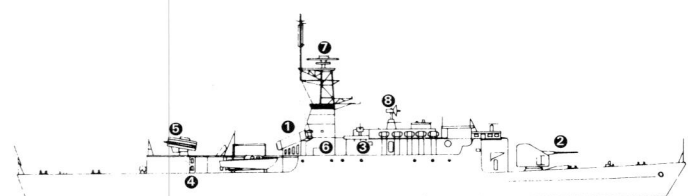

D'ESTIENNE D'ORVES (Scale 1 : 900), Ian Sturton

SECOND MAÎTRE LE BIHAN 6/1992, Stefan Terzibaschitsch

DROGOU 5/1992, Giorgio Ghiglione

ENSEIGNE DE VAISSEAU JACOUBET 11/1991, Giorgio Arr.

Frigates — Shipborne aircraft / FRANCE

0 + 6 LA FAYETTE CLASS (LIGHT FRIGATES)

Name	No	Builders	Laid down	Launched	Commissioned
LA FAYETTE	F 710	Lorient Naval Dockyard	15 Dec 1990	13 June 1992	Dec 1994
SURCOUF	F 711	Lorient Naval Dockyard	6 July 1992	1994	May 1996
AMIRAL COURBET	F 712	Lorient Naval Dockyard	May 1993	1996	Jan 1998

Displacement, tons: 3500 full load
Dimensions, feet (metres): 410.1 oa; 377.3 pp × 50.5 × 13.1 *(125; 115 × 15.4 × 4)*
Main machinery: CODAD; 4 SEMT-Pielstick 12 PA6 V 280 STC diesels; 21 107 hp(m) *(15.52 MW)* sustained or 23 228 hp(m) *(17.08 MW)* with 2 turbochargers; 2 shafts
Speed, knots: 25. **Range, miles:** 7000 at 15 kts; 9000 at 12 kts
Complement: 139 (15 officers) plus 25 spare

Missiles: SSM: 8 Aerospatiale MM 40 Exocet ❶; inertial cruise; active radar homing to 70 km *(40 nm)* at 0.9 Mach; warhead 165 kg; sea-skimmer.
SAM: Thomson-CSF Crotale Naval CN 2 (variant of NG) octuple launcher ❷; command line of sight guidance; radar/IR homing to 13 km *(7 nm)* at 3.5 Mach; warhead 14 kg. To be replaced by SAAM VLS ❸ with 16 Aster 15 missiles in second three.
Guns: 1 DCN 3.9 in *(100 mm)*/55 Mod 68 CADAM ❹; 80° elevation; 80 rounds/minute to 17 km *(9 nm)*; weight of shell 13.5 kg.
2 Giat 20F2 20 mm ❺; 720 rounds/minute to 10 km *(5.5 nm)*. 2—12.7 mm MGs.
Countermeasures: Decoys: 2 CSEE Dagaie ❻ 10-barrelled trainable launchers; chaff and IR flares. SLAT anti-wake homing torpedoes system (when available).
ESM: Thomson-CSF ARBR 17 (DR 3000-S) ❼; radar intercept. DIBV 10 Vampir ❽; IR detector.
ECM: Dassault ARBB 33; jammer.
Combat data systems: Thomson-CSF TAVITAC 2000. Syracuse 2 SATCOM ❾.
Fire control: Thomson-CSF CTM radar/IR system.
Radars: Air/surface search: Thomson-CSF Sea Tiger (DRBV 15C) ❿; E/F band.
Navigation: Racal Decca 1226 ⓫; I band. A second set fitted for helicopter control.
Fire control: Thomson-CSF Castor II ⓬; J band; range 15 km *(8 nm)* for 1 m² target.
Crotale ❷; J band (for SAM).
Arabel for SAAM (for second three).
Helicopters: 1 Dauphin 2/Panther ⓭ or 1 NFH 90.

Programmes: Originally described as 'Frégates Légères' but this was changed in 1992 to 'Frégates type La Fayette'. First three ordered 25 July 1988; three more 24 September 1992. Planned total of up to 10 but may stop at 6. The programme was delayed by up to one year by the 1989 defence budget. First steel cut for each hull about 14 months before the keel is laid.
Structure: Space left for a SAAM launcher forward of the bridge which will replace Crotale in the second three of the class on build and the first three at refit. This might mean putting the Arabel fire control radar on top of a more solid looking foremast once Crotale is removed. Superstructure inclines at 10° to the vertical to reduce radar echoing area. External equipment such as capstans, bollards etc either 'hidden' or installed as low as possible. Radar absorbent paint is used extensively. Sensitive areas are armour-plated. SLAT anti-torpedo system may be fitted when available. Magazine for AM 39 Exocet and AS 15 for the NFH-90 helicopter.
Operational: *La Fayette* planned to start trials in 1993, *Surcouf* in 1994 and *Courbet* in 1996. These frigates are designed for out of area operations on overseas stations and the first three are to be assigned to the Indian Ocean.
Sales: Three of an improved design to Saudi Arabia if the order is confirmed and the first six of a possible 16 are building for Taiwan.
Opinion: Plans to fit sonar have been dropped but in the future an ASW version of the ship could be built with hull and towed array sonars, lightweight torpedo launchers, and an ASW configured helicopter.

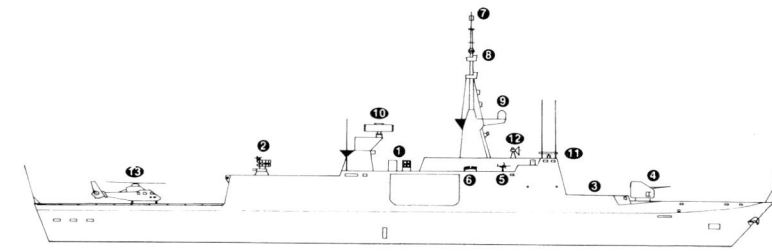

LA FAYETTE *(Scale 1 : 1200), Ian Sturton*

LA FAYETTE *6/1992, DCN*

SHIPBORNE AIRCRAFT

Numbers/Type: 2 Dassault Aviation ACM Rafale M.
Operational speed: Mach 2.
Service ceiling: 50 000 ft *(15 240 m)*.
Range: 1800 nm *(3335 km)*.
Role/Weapon systems: Fighter (SU 0) and strike/recce (SU 2) variants. Deck trials in 1993. 86 aircraft required; first production aircraft funded in 1992 for delivery in 1997. Sensors: Thomson-CSF/Dassault RBE2 radar, Spectra EW suite. Weapons: Strike; Exocet AM 39, Aerospatiale AS 30L stand off ASM (SU 2), Apache weapon dispenser, 30 mm cannon (SU 0), ASMP nuclear bomb. Air defence; 8 Matra MICA AAMs (SU 0), 8 tons of weapons total limited to 6 tons for carrier operations.

RAFALE M *1991, Dassault Aviation*

Numbers/Type: 59 Dassault-Bréguet Super Étendard.
Operational speed: Approx Mach 1.
Service ceiling: 45 000 ft *(13 700 m)*.
Range: 920 nm *(1682 km)*.
Role/Weapon systems: Carrier-borne strike fighter with limited air defence role with nuclear strike. 50 are being modernised, of which 20 are to carry ASMP missiles. Sensors: Thomson-CSF Agave radar, ECM/ESM. Weapons: Strike; 1 × Aerospatiale ASMP stand-off weapon; range 300 km; nuclear warhead, 2.1 tons of underwing stores including AM 39 Exocet. Defence; 2 × Magic AAM and drop tanks. Self protection; 2 × 30 mm DEFA cannon. 56 are being modernised (14 by the end of 1993): radar (Dassault Electronique Anémone), computer (SAGEM UAT 90), displays, ESM/ECM and AS 30L (laser) missile.

SUPER ÉTENDARD *5/1992, F Gámez*

Numbers/Type: 11 Dassault Étendard IV-P.
Operational speed: Mach 1.02.
Service ceiling: 49 000 ft *(15 000 m)*.
Range: 1520 nm *(2817 km)*.
Role/Weapon systems: Primary role is photo-reconnaissance and overwater surveillance; carrier-borne and land-based depending on needs and updated in 1991/92. Sensors: Up to 5 × Omera cameras, ESM pods. Weapons: 2 × Magic 1 or 2 AAMs.

ÉTENDARD IV-P *1988, French Navy*

Numbers/Type: 19 LTV F-8E(FN) Crusader.
Operational speed: 868 kts *(1610 km/h)*.
Service ceiling: 50 000 ft *(15 240 m)*.
Range: 740 nm *(1370 km)*.
Role/Weapon systems: Carrier-borne air defence fighter modified for French needs. 17 being refurbished to last until replaced by Rafale (5 delivered by early 1993). Sensors: Search/attack radar, ESM/ECM. Weapons: AD; 2 × Magic 1 or 2 AAM or 2 × R530 AAM. Self protection; 4 × 20 mm cannon.

CRUSADER *1984*

214 FRANCE / Shipborne aircraft — Amphibious forces

Numbers/Type: 26 Bréguet Br 1050 Alizé (modernised).
Operational speed: 254 kts *(470 km/h)*.
Service ceiling: 26 250 ft *(8000 m)*.
Range: 1350 nm *(2500 km)*.
Role/Weapon systems: ASW and strike aircraft embarked in CVLs for surface search, ASV and ASW roles; updated 1985-86 and again in 1992-93. Sensors: Thomson-CSF Iguane surveillance radar, sonobuoys, ECM/ESM. Weapons: ASW; 1 × torpedo or 3 × 160 kg depth bombs or 1 × nuclear depth bomb. ASV; 2 × AS12 missiles and 6 × rockets.

ALIZÉ   *1987, Breguet*

Numbers/Type: 17 Aerospatiale SA 321G Super Frelon.
Operational speed: 148 kts *(275 km/h)*.
Service ceiling: 10 170 ft *(3100 m)*.
Range: 442 nm *(820 km)*.
Role/Weapon systems: Formerly ASW helicopter; now used for assault and support tasks embarked on carriers and LSDs; possible update for ASV not proceeded with but radar updated; provision for 27 passengers. Sensors: Omera ORB search radar. Weapons: Provision for 20 mm gun.

SUPER FRELON   *10/1992, Peter Felstead*

Numbers/Type: 34 Westland Lynx Mk 4 (FN).
Operational speed: 125 kts *(232 km/h)*.
Service ceiling: 12 500 ft *(3810 m)*.
Range: 320 nm *(593 km)*.
Role/Weapon systems: Sole French ASW helicopter, all now of the Mk 4 variant; embarked in destroyers and deployed on training tasks. Sensors: Omera 31 search radar, Alcatel (HS-12 in Mk 2, DUAV 4 in Mk 4) dipping sonar, sonobuoys. Weapons: ASV; 4 × AS12 missiles/SFIM M335 sight. ASW; 2 × Mk 46 Mod 1 (or MU 90 in due course) torpedoes, or depth charges.

LYNX   *10/1992, Peter Felstead*

Numbers/Type: 6/15 Aerospatiale SA 365F/AS 565MA Dauphin 2 (Panther).
Operational speed: 140 kts *(260 km/h)*.
Service ceiling: 15 000 ft *(4575 m)*.
Range: 410 nm *(758 km)*.
Role/Weapon systems: SA 365F replace Alouette III for carrier-borne SAR and three (operated for the Navy) in English Channel. 15 AS 565 ordered in several batches for light and patrol frigates, first two delivered in 1993. Sensors: Agrion search radar. Weapons: Unarmed (SA 365F); ASV Aerospatiale AS 15TT ASM (AS 565).

DAUPHIN 2   *5/1992, Camil Busquets i Vilanova*

Numbers/Type: 32 Aerospatiale SA 319B Alouette III.
Operational speed: 113 kts *(210 km/h)*.
Service ceiling: 10 500 ft *(3200 m)*.
Range: 290 nm *(540 km)*.
Role/Weapon systems: General purpose helicopter; replaced by Lynx for ASW; now used for trials, surveillance and training tasks. Sensors: Some radar. Weapons: Unarmed.

ALOUETTE III   *1988, French Navy*

LAND-BASED MARITIME AIRCRAFT (FRONT LINE)

Numbers/Type: 28 Bréguet Atlantic (NATO) Mk 1.
Operational speed: 355 kts *(658 km/h)*.
Service ceiling: 32 800 ft *(10 000 m)*.
Range: 4855 nm *(8995 km)*.
Role/Weapon systems: Maritime reconnaissance carried out in Atlantic and Mediterranean; regularly deployed overseas. Primarily ASW but useful ASV role; being replaced by Atlantique 2. Sensors: Thomson-CSF radar, ECM/ESM, MAD, sonobuoys. Weapons: ASW; 9 × torpedoes (including Mk 46) or depth bombs and mines. ASV; 3/4 Martel ARM.

Numbers/Type: 22 Dassault Aviation Atlantique Mk 2.
Operational speed: 355 kts *(658 km/h)*.
Service ceiling: 32 800 ft *(10 000 m)*.
Range: 8 hours patrol at 1000 nm from base; 4 hours patrol at 1500 nm from base.
Role/Weapon systems: Maritime reconnaissance. ASW, ASV, COMINT/ELINT roles. 28 ordered by late 1992 with 22 delivered by late 1993. Sensors: Thomson-CSF Iguane radar, ARAR 13 ESM, ECM, FLIR, MAD, sonobuoys (with DSAX-1 Thomson-CSF Sadang processing equipment). Link 11 (in due course). COMINT/ELINT equipment optional. Integrated sensor/weapon system built around a CIMSA 15/125X computer. Weapons: 2 × AM 39 Exocet ASMs in ventral bay, or up to eight lightweight torpedoes (Mk 46 and later MU 90), or depth charges, mines or bombs.

Numbers/Type: 4 Boeing E-3F Sentry AWAC.
Operational speed: 460 kts *(853 km/h)*.
Service ceiling: 30 000 ft *(9145 m)*.
Range: 870 nm *(1610 km)*.
Role/Weapon systems: Air defence early warning aircraft with secondary role to provide coastal AEW for the Fleet; six hours endurance at the range given above. Sensors: Westinghouse APY-2 surveillance radar, Bendix weather radar, Mk XII IFF, Yellow Gate, ESM, ECM. Weapons: Unarmed. Operated by the Air Force.

Numbers/Type: 6 Dassault-Bréguet Falcon 10MER.
Operational speed: 492 kts *(912 km/h)*.
Service ceiling: 35 500 ft *(10 670 m)*.
Range: 1920 nm *(3560 km)*.
Role/Weapon systems: Primary aircrew/ECM training role in peacetime but also has overwater surveillance role in wartime; France sole user. Sensors: Search radar. Weapons: Unarmed.

Numbers/Type: 5 Dassault-Bréguet Gardian.
Operational speed: 470 kts *(870 km/h)*.
Service ceiling: 45 000 ft *(13 715 m)*.
Range: 2425 nm *(4490 km)*.
Role/Weapon systems: Maritime reconnaissance role in French Pacific area. Sensors: Thomson-CSF Varan radar, Omega navigation, ECM/ESM pods. Weapons: Unarmed.

AMPHIBIOUS FORCES

2 CDIC CLASS (LCT)

| L 9061 | L 9062 |

Displacement, tons: 380 light; 710 full load
Dimensions, feet (metres): 194.9 × 39 × 5.9 *(59.4 × 11.9 × 1.8)*
Main machinery: 2 SACM Uni Diesel UD 30 V12 M1 diesels; 1200 hp(m) *(882 kW)* sustained; 2 shafts
Speed, knots: 10.5. **Range, miles:** 1000 at 10 kts
Complement: 12 (1 officer)
Military lift: 336 tons
Guns: 2 Giat 20F2 20 mm. 2—12.7 mm MGs.

Comment: First laid down September 1987 at SFCN, Villeneuve la Garenne. Commissioned 19 October 1988 and 2 March 1989 respectively. CDIC (Chaland de Débarquement d'Infanterie et de Chars) designed to replace the EDICs and specially built to work with Foudre class. The wheelhouse can be lowered to facilitate docking manoeuvres in the LPDs. Assigned to FAN.

L 9061   *10/199.*

1 + (1) FOUDRE CLASS (LANDING SHIPS (DOCK)) (TYPE TCD 90)

Name	No	Builders	Laid down	Launched	Commissioned
FOUDRE	L 9011	Brest Naval Dockyard	26 Mar 1986	19 Nov 1988	7 Dec 1990

Displacement, tons: 8190 light; 11 900 full load
Dimensions, feet (metres): 551 × 77.1 × 17 (30.2 flooded) *(168 × 23.5 × 5.2 (9.2))*
Main machinery: 2 SEMT-Pielstick 16 PC2.5 V 400 diesels; 15 600 hp(m) *(11.48 MW)* sustained; 2 shafts; cp props; bow thruster; 1000 hp(m) *(735 kW)*
Speed, knots: 21. **Range, miles:** 11 000 at 15 kts
Complement: 210 (13 officers)
Military lift: 470 troops plus 1810 tons load; 2 CDIC or 10 CTM or 1 P 400 patrol craft

Missiles: SAM: 2 Matra Sadral sextuple launchers ❶ (to be replaced by 2 twin Simbad launchers); Mistral; IR homing to 4 km *(2.2 nm)*; warhead 3 kg.
Guns: 1 Bofors 40 mm/60 ❷. 2 Giat 20F2 20 mm guns ❸. 2—12.7 mm MGs.
Combat data systems: Syracuse SATCOM ❹.
Radars: Air/surface search: Thomson-CSF Rodeo (Army type) ❺.
Surface search: Racal Decca 2459 ❻; I band.
Navigation: 2 Racal Decca RM 1229; I band (1 for helo control ❼).

Helicopters: 4 AS 332F Super Puma ❽ or 2 Super Frelon.

Programmes: First ordered 5 November 1984. Second and third (L 9012 and 9013) orders postponed until 1994. Transports de Chalands de Débarquement (TCD).

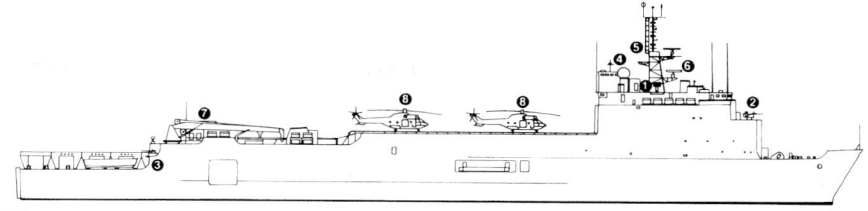

FOUDRE *(Scale 1 : 1500), Ian Sturton*

Structure: Designed to take a mechanised regiment of the Rapid Action Force and act as a logistic support ship. Extensive command and hospital facilities include two operating theatres and 47 beds. Sadral SAM to be replaced by two lightweight Simbad SAMs either side of bridge. Hangar capacity: two Super Frelons or four Super Pumas. Two landing spots. Well dock 122 × 14.2 × 7.7 m. Lift of 52 tons capacity. Flight deck 1450 m² with Samahe haul down system. Flume stabilisation to be fitted in 1993.
Operational: Two landing spots on flight deck plus one on deck well rolling cover. Can operate up to seven Super Puma helicopters. Could carry up to 1600 troops in emergency. Endurance, 30 days (with 700 persons aboard). A 400 ton ship can be docked. Assigned to FAN.

FOUDRE *7/1992, B Sullivan*

FOUDRE *7/1992, B Sullivan*

2 OURAGAN CLASS (LANDING SHIPS (DOCK) (TCDs))

Name	No	Builders	Laid down	Launched	Commissioned
OURAGAN	L 9021	Brest Naval Dockyard	June 1962	9 Nov 1963	1 June 1965
ORAGE	L 9022	Brest Naval Dockyard	June 1966	22 Apr 1967	1 Apr 1968

Displacement, tons: 5800 light; 8500 full load; 15 000 when fully docked down
Dimensions, feet (metres): 488.9 × 75.4 × 17.7 (28.5 flooded) *(149 × 23 × 5.4 (8.7))*
Main machinery: 2 SEMT-Pielstick diesels; 8600 hp(m) *(6.32 MW)*; 2 shafts; cp props
Speed, knots: 17. **Range, miles:** 9000 at 15 kts
Complement: 213 (10 officers)
Military lift: 343 troops (plus 129 short haul only); 2 LCTs (EDIC) with 11 light tanks each or 8 loaded CTMs; logistic load 1500 tons; 2 cranes (35 tons each)

Guns: 2—4.7 in *(120 mm)* mortars; 42 rounds/minute to 20 km *(10.8 nm)*; weight of shell 24 kg.
4 Bofors 40 mm; 300 rounds/minute to 12 km *(6.5 nm)*.
Radars: Navigation: Racal Decca 1226; I band.
Sonars: EDO SQS-17 *(Ouragan)*; search; medium frequency.

Helicopters: 4 SA 321G Super Frelon or Super Pumas or 10 SA 319B Alouette III.

Programmes: Service lives will be extended until L 9012 and L 9013 are commissioned.
Structure: Normal helicopter platform for operating three Super Frelon or 10 Alouette III plus a portable platform for a further one Super Frelon or three Alouette III. Bridge is on the starboard side. Three LCVPs can also be carried. Extensive workshops.
Operational: Typical loads—18 Super Frelon or 80 Alouette III helicopters or 120 AMX 13 tanks or 84 DUKWs or 340 Jeeps or 12—50 ton barges. A 400 ton ship can be docked. Command facilities for directing amphibious and helicopter operations. Both ships assigned to FAN and transferred to Toulon.

OURAGAN *5/1991, A Campanera i Rovira*

216   FRANCE / Amphibious forces

1 BOUGAINVILLE CLASS (BTS)

Name	No	Builders	Laid down	Launched	Commissioned
BOUGAINVILLE	L 9077	Chantier Dubigeon, Nantes	28 Jan 1986	3 Oct 1986	June 1988

Displacement, tons: 4876 standard; 5100 full load
Dimensions, feet (metres): 372.3; 344.4 wl × 55.8 × 14.1 *(113.5; 105 × 17 × 4.3)*
Flight deck, feet (metres): 85.3 × 55.8 *(26 × 17)*
Main machinery: 2 SACM AGO 195 V12 RVR diesels; 4410 hp(m) *(3.24 MW)* sustained; 2 shafts; cp props; bow thruster; 400 hp(m) *(294 kW)*
Speed, knots: 15. **Range, miles:** 6000 at 12 kts
Complement: 53 (5 officers) plus 10 staff
Military lift: 500 troops for 8 days; 1180 tons cargo; 2 LCU in support or 10 LCP plus 2 LCM for amphibious role

Guns: 2—12.7 mm MGs.
Radars: Navigation: Two Decca 1226; I band.

Helicopters: Platform for 2 AS 332B Super Puma.

Programmes: Ordered November 1984 for the Direction du Centre d'Experimentations Nucléaires (DIRCEN). As Chantier Dubigeon closed down after her launch she was completed by Chantier de l'Atlantique of the Alsthom group. Bâtiment de Transport et de Soutien (BTS).
Structure: Well size is 78 × 10.2 m *(256 × 33.5 ft)*. It can receive tugs and one BSR or two CTMs, a supply tender of the Chamois class, containers, mixed bulk cargo. Has extensive repair workshops and repair facilities for helicopters. Can act as mobile crew accommodation and has medical facilities. Storerooms for spare parts, victuals and ammunition. Hull to civilian standards. Carries a 37 ton crane.
Operational: Completed sea trials 25 February 1988. Based in the Pacific Squadron for use at the nuclear test base. Can dock a 400 ton ship.

BOUGAINVILLE   *1988, Alsthom*

5 BATRAL TYPE (LIGHT TRANSPORTS and LANDING SHIPS)

Name	No	Builders	Commissioned
CHAMPLAIN	L 9030	Brest Naval Dockyard	5 Oct 1974
FRANCIS GARNIER	L 9031	Brest Naval Dockyard	27 Oct 1974
DUMONT D'URVILLE	L 9032	CMN, Cherbourg	5 Feb 1983
JACQUES CARTIER	L 9033	CMN, Cherbourg	29 Sep 1983
LA GRANDIÈRE	L 9034	CMN, Cherbourg	20 Jan 1987

Displacement, tons: 750 standard; 1330 (1400, second pair) full load
Dimensions, feet (metres): 262.4 × 42.6 × 7.9 *(80 × 13 × 2.4)*
Main machinery: 2 SACM AGO 195 V12 diesels; 3600 hp(m) *(2.65 MW)* sustained; 2 shafts; cp props
Speed, knots: 16. **Range, miles:** 4500 at 13 kts
Complement: 50 (5 officers)
Military lift: 138 troops (180 in second pair); 12 vehicles; 350 tons load; 10 ton crane

Guns: 2 Bofors 40 mm/60 (L 9030, L 9031). 2 Giat 20F2 20 mm (L 9032, L 9033). 1—81 mm mortar. 2—12.7 mm MGs.
Radars: Navigation: DRBN 32; I band.
Sonars: Two; hull-mounted.

Helicopters: 1 SA 319B Alouette III.

Programmes: Classified as Batral 3F. Bâtiments d'Assaut et de TRansport Légers (BATRAL). First two launched 17 November 1973. *Dumont D'Urville* floated out 27 November 1981. *Jacques Cartier* launched 28 April 1982 and *La Grandière* 15 December 1985.
Structure: 40 ton bow ramp; stowage for vehicles above and below decks. One LCVP and one LCPS carried. Helicopter landing platform. Last three of class have bridge one deck higher.
Operational: Deployment: *La Grandière*, Indian Ocean; *F Garnier*, Antilles/French Guiana; *D D'Urville*, Papeete; *J Cartier*, New Caledonia; *Champlain*, Toulon (FAN).
Sales: Ships of this class built for Chile, Gabon, Ivory Coast and Morocco. *La Grandière* was also built for Gabon under Clause 29 arrangements but funds were not available.

CHAMPLAIN   *11/1992, van Ginderen Collection*

CHAMPLAIN   *11/1992 van Ginderen collection*

2 EDIC 700 CLASS (LCT)

L 9051   L 9052

Displacement, tons: 736 full load
Dimensions, feet (metres): 193.6 × 38.1 × 5.8 *(59 × 11.6 × 1.7)*
Main machinery: 2 SACM Uni Diesel UD 30 V12 M1 diesels; 1200 hp(m) *(882 kW)* sustained; 2 shafts
Speed, knots: 12. **Range, miles:** 1800 at 12 kts
Complement: 17
Military lift: 350 tons
Guns: 2 Giat 20F2 20 mm. 2—12.7 mm MGs.

Comment: Ordered 10 March 1986 from SFCN, Villeneuve la Garenne. Commissioned on 13 June 1987 and 19 December 1987 respectively. Rated as Engins de Débarquement d'Infanterie et Chars (EDIC III). Based at the Pacific Test Centre (*L 9051*) and Djibouti (*L 9052*).

L 9052   *4/1991, Guy Toremans*

4 EDIC CLASS (LCT)

L 9070 (29 Mar 1967)   L 9074 (7 Feb 1970)
L 9072 (1968)   L 9096 (see *Comment*)

Displacement, tons: 635 (L 9070)
Dimensions, feet (metres): 193.5 × 39.2 × 4.5 *(59 × 12 × 1.3)*
Main machinery: 2 SACM MGO 175 V12 diesels; 1000 hp(m) *(753 kW)* sustained; 2 shafts
Speed, knots: 8. **Range, miles:** 1800 at 8 kts
Complement: 17
Military lift: 5 LVTs or 11 lorries
Guns: 2 Oerlikon 20 mm.

Comment: *L 9095* to Senegal 1 July 1974 as *La Falence*. *L 9082* transferred to Madagascar in 1985 and renamed *Aina Vao Vao*. Of the remainder *L 9072* is deployed to the Pacific Test Range *L 9070* is at Lorient and *L 9074* at Toulon. Being replaced by the CDICs. *L 9096* was paid off in 1990 but is now employed as special harbour craft at Brest.

L 9074   *8/1990, J Y Rober*

24 CTMs (LCMs)

CTM 2, 3, 5, 9, 10, 12, 14-31

Displacement, tons: 56 standard; 150 full load
Dimensions, feet (metres): 78 × 21 × 4.2 *(23.8 × 6.4 × 1.3)*
Main machinery: 2 Poyaud 520 V8 diesels; 225 hp(m) *(165 kW)*; 2 shafts
Speed, knots: 9.5. **Range, miles:** 350 at 8 kts
Complement: 6
Military lift: 90 tons (maximum); 48 tons (normal)

Comment: First series of 16 built 1966-70 and so far seven have been deleted. Second series built at CMN, Cherbourg 1982-92. All have a bow ramp but the second series has a different shaped pilot house. Chalands de Transport de Matériel (CTM). Many are deployed overseas.

CTM 12   *8/1990, J Y Robert*

2 LCM 6s

1057   1058

Comment: Of 52 tons full load and 8 kts. Built in Réunion for service at Mayotte Naval Base. Completed March 1983. Some others operated by French Army overseas.

LIGHT FORCES

Note: The Thomson-CSF demonstrator *Iris* P 696 was returned by the Navy in 1992.

10 P 400 CLASS (FAST ATTACK CRAFT—PATROL)

Name	No	Builders	Commissioned
L'AUDACIEUSE	P 682	CMN, Cherbourg	18 Sep 1986
LA BOUDEUSE	P 683	CMN, Cherbourg	15 Jan 1987
LA CAPRICIEUSE	P 684	CMN, Cherbourg	13 Mar 1987
LA FOUGUEUSE	P 685	CMN, Cherbourg	13 Mar 1987
LA GLORIEUSE	P 686	CMN, Cherbourg	18 Apr 1987
LA GRACIEUSE	P 687	CMN, Cherbourg	17 July 1987
LA MOQUEUSE	P 688	CMN, Cherbourg	18 Apr 1987
LA RAILLEUSE	P 689	CMN, Cherbourg	16 May 1987
LA RIEUSE	P 690	CMN, Cherbourg	13 June 1987
LA TAPAGEUSE	P 691	CMN, Cherbourg	11 Feb 1988

Displacement, tons: 406 standard; 454 full load
Dimensions, feet (metres): 178.6 × 26.2 × 8.5 *(54.5 × 8 × 2.5)*
Main machinery: 2 SEMT-Pielstick 16 PA4 200 VGDS diesels; 8000 hp(m) *(5.88 MW)* sustained; 2 shafts; cp props
Speed, knots: 24.5. **Range, miles:** 4200 at 15 kts
Complement: 26 (3 officers) plus 20 passengers

Guns: 1 Bofors 40 mm/60; 1 Giat 20F2 20 mm; 2—12.7 mm MGs.
Radars: Surface search: Racal Decca 1226; I band.

Programmes: First six ordered in May 1982, with further four in March 1984. The original engines of this class were unsatisfactory. Replacements were ordered and construction was slowed. Those completed were laid up at Lorient until new engines became available. This class relieved the Patra fast patrol craft which have all transferred to the Gendarmerie.
Structure: Steel hull and superstructure protected by an upper deck bulwark. Design modified from original missile craft configuration. Now capable of transporting personnel with appropriate store-rooms. Of more robust construction than previously planned—to be used as overseas transports. Can be converted for missile armament (MM 38) with dockyard assistance and Sadral PDMS has been considered. L'Audacieuse has done trials with a VDS-12 sonar. Twin funnels replaced the unsatisfactory submerged diesel exhausts in 1990/91.
Operational: Deployments: Antilles/French Guiana; P 684, 685. Noumea; P 686, 688. Mayotte (Indian Ocean); P 683. Djibouti; 690. Tahiti; P 687, 689, 691. Cherbourg; P 682. Endurance, 15 days with 45 people aboard.

L'AUDACIEUSE   *8/1992, Guy Toremans*

FORCE DE SURFACE A MISSIONS CIVILES—FSMC

Note: This designation is applied to a programme of ships and craft designed for offshore and coastal patrol, fishery protection, maritime traffic surveillance, anti-pollution duties and search and rescue, all being manned by the Navy.

Name	No	Builders	Commissioned
ALBATROS (ex-*Névé*)	P 681	Ch de la Seine Maritime	1967

Displacement, tons: 2800 full load
Dimensions, feet (metres): 278.1 × 44.3 × 18.4 *(84.8 × 13.5 × 5.6)*
Main machinery: Diesel-electric; 2 Uni Diesel UD 33 V12 M6 diesels; 4410 hp(m) *(3.24 MW)* sustained; 2 motors; 3046 hp(m) *(2.24 MW)*; 1 shaft
Speed, knots: 15
Complement: 46 (5 officers) plus 16 passengers
Guns: 1 Bofors 40 mm/60. 2—12.7 mm MGs.
Helicopters: Platform for Alouette III.

Comment: Former trawler bought in April 1983 from Compagnie Nav. Caennaise for conversion into a patrol ship. Commissioned 19 May 1984. Conducts patrols from Réunion to Kerguelen, Crozet, St Paul and Amsterdam Islands with occasional deployments to South Pacific. Can carry 200 tons cargo, has extensive sick berth arrangements and VIP accommodation. Major refit in Lorient from June 1990 to March 1991 which included new diesel-electric propulsion. Service life: 2015.

ALBATROS   *1986, French Navy*

Name	No	Builders	Commissioned
STERNE	P 680	La Perrière, Lorient	25 Oct 1980

Displacement, tons: 380 full load
Dimensions, feet (metres): 160.7 × 24.6 × 9.2 *(49 × 7.5 × 2.8)*
Main machinery: 2 SACM 195 V12 CZSHR diesels; 4340 hp(m) *(3.19 MW)* sustained; electro-hydraulic auxiliary propulsion on starboard shaft; 150 hp(m) *(110 kW)*; 2 shafts
Speed, knots: 20; 6 on auxiliary propulsion. **Range, miles:** 4900 at 12 kts; 1500 at 20 kts
Complement: 18 (3 officers); 2 crews
Guns: 2—12.7 mm MGs.
Radars: Navigation: Racal Decca; I band.

Comment: *Sterne* was the first ship for the FSMC. Has active tank stabilisation. Paid for by shipping owners but manned and operated by Navy.

STERNE   *5/1992, French Navy*

1 + 3 GRÈBE CLASS

Name	No	Builders	Commissioned
GRÈBE	P 679	SFCN, Villeneuve La Garenne	6 Apr 1991

Displacement, tons: 410 full load
Dimensions, feet (metres): 170.6 × 32.2 × 9 *(52 × 9.8 × 2.8)*
Main machinery: 2 Uni Diesel UD 33 V12 M6 diesels; 4410 hp(m) *(3.24 MW)*; diesel-electric auxiliary propulsion; 2 shafts; cp props
Speed, knots: 23; 7.5 on auxiliary propulsion. **Range, miles:** 4500 at 12 kts
Complement: 19 (4 officers); accommodation for 24; 2 crews
Guns: 2—12.7 mm MGs.
Radars: Navigation: Racal Decca; I band.

Comment: Type Espadon 50 ordered 17 July 1988 and launched 16 November 1989; three more ordered from CMN Cherbourg in July 1992. 'Deep V' hull; stern ramp for craft handling. Large deck area (8 × 8 m) for Vertrep operations. Pollution control equipment and remotely operated waterjet gun for firefighting. Based at Lorient.

GRÈBE   *10/1992*

MINE WARFARE FORCES

Note: Narvik class project cancelled in 1992. For details see *Trials/Research Ships* section.

9 + 1 ÉRIDAN (TRIPARTITE) CLASS (MINEHUNTERS)

Name	No	Laid down	Launched	Commissioned
ÉRIDAN	M 641	20 Dec 1977	2 Feb 1979	16 Apr 1984
CASSIOPÉE	M 642	26 Mar 1979	28 Sep 1981	5 May 1984
ANDROMÈDE	M 643	6 Mar 1980	22 May 1982	18 Oct 1984
PÉGASE	M 644	22 Oct 1980	23 Apr 1983	30 May 1985
ORION	M 645	17 Aug 1981	6 Feb 1985	14 Jan 1986
CROIX DU SUD	M 646	22 Apr 1982	6 Feb 1985	14 Nov 1986
AIGLE	M 647	2 Dec 1982	8 Mar 1986	1 July 1987
LYRE	M 648	14 Oct 1983	15 Nov 1986	16 Dec 1987
PERSÉE	M 649	30 Oct 1984	19 Apr 1988	4 Nov 1988
SAGITTAIRE	M 650	1993	1995	1995

Displacement, tons: 562 standard; 595 full load
Dimensions, feet (metres): 168.9 × 29.2 × 8.2 *(51.5 × 8.9 × 2.5)*
Main machinery: 1 Brons Werkspoor A-RUB 215X-12 diesel; 1860 hp(m) *(1.37 MW)* sustained; 1 shaft; Lips cp prop
  Auxiliary propulsion; 2 motors; 240 hp(m) *(179 kW)*; 2 active rudders; 2 bow thrusters
Speed, knots: 15; 7 on auxiliary propulsion. **Range, miles:** 3000 at 12 kts
Complement: 46 (5 officers)

Guns: 1 Giat 20F2 20 mm; 1—12.7 mm MG.
Countermeasures: MCM: 2 PAP 104 systems; mechanical sweep gear. AP-4 acoustic sweep.
Radars: Navigation: Racal Decca 1229; I band.
Sonars: Thomson Sintra DUBM 21B; hull-mounted; active; high frequency; 100 kHz (±10 kHz).

Programmes: All built in Lorient. Belgium, France and the Netherlands each agreed to build 15 (10 in Belgium with option on five more). Subsequently the French programme was cut to 10. Each country provided people to man a joint bureau de programme in Paris and built its own GRP hulls to a central design. Belgium provided all the electrical installations, France all the minehunting gear and some electronics and the Netherlands the propulsion systems. Replacement for the last of class (sold to Pakistan) was ordered in January 1992.
Structure: GRP hull. Equipment includes: autopilot and hovering; automatic radar navigation; navigation aids by Loran and Syledis; Evec data system; Decca Hifix.
Operational: Minehunting, minesweeping, patrol, training, directing ship for unmanned minesweeping, HQ ship for diving operations and pollution control. Pre-packed 5 ton modules of equipment to be embarked for separate tasks. M 641-646 based at Brest, remainder at Toulon. Chasseurs de Mines Tripartites (CMT).
Sales: The original tenth ship of the class, completed in 1989, was transferred to Pakistan 24 September 1992 as part of an order for three; the second is being built in Lorient, the third in Karachi.

ÉRIDAN *6/1992, H M Steele*

5 CIRCÉ CLASS (MINEHUNTERS)

Name	No	Builders	Commissioned
CYBÈLE	M 712	CMN, Cherbourg	28 Sep 1972
CALLIOPE	M 713	CMN, Cherbourg	28 Sep 1972
CLIO	M 714	CMN, Cherbourg	18 May 1972
CIRCÉ	M 715	CMN, Cherbourg	18 May 1972
CÉRÈS	M 716	CMN, Cherbourg	8 Mar 1973

Displacement, tons: 460 standard; 495 normal; 510 full load
Dimensions, feet (metres): 167 × 29.2 × 11.2 *(50.9 × 8.9 × 3.4)*
Main machinery: 1 MTU diesel; 1800 hp(m) *(1.32 MW)*; 2 active rudders; 1 shaft
Speed, knots: 15. **Range, miles:** 3000 at 12 kts
Complement: 48 (5 officers)

Guns: 1 Oerlikon 20 mm.
Countermeasures: MCM: The 9 ft *(2.74 m)* long PAP is propelled by two electric motors at 6 kts and is wire-guided to a maximum range of 500 m. Fitted with a television camera, this machine detects the mine and lays its 100 kg charge nearby. This is then detonated by an ultrasonic signal. These ships carry no normal minesweeping equipment.
Radars: Navigation: Racal Decca 1229; I band.
Sonars: Thomson Sintra DUBM 20B; hull-mounted; active search; high frequency.

Programmes: Ordered in 1968. Due for deletion 1991-93 but will be retained until BAMOs come into service.
Modernisation: Programmes completed 1989 included computer-aided sonar classification.
Operational: All based at Brest.

CALLIOPE *7/1992, van Ginderen Collection*

2 Ex-US AGGRESSIVE CLASS (MINESWEEPERS)

OUISTREHAM (ex-MSO 513) M 610   ALENÇON (ex-MSO 453) M 612

Displacement, tons: 700 standard; 780 full load
Dimensions, feet (metres): 172 × 36 × 13.6 *(52.4 × 11 × 4.1)*
Main machinery: 4 GM 8-268A diesels; 1760 hp *(1.31 MW)*; 2 shafts; cp props
Speed, knots: 13.5. **Range, miles:** 3000 at 10 kts
Complement: 58 (5 officers)

Guns: 1 Bofors 40 mm/60; 2—12.7 mm MGs.
Countermeasures: MCM: Mechanical minesweeping capabilities; AP 4 acoustic sweep.
Radars: Navigation: Racal Decca 1229; I band.
Sonars: DUBM 41B; towed; side scanning; active search; high frequency.

Programmes: The USA transferred MSOs to France in three batches during 1953. Four paid off in 1987 and three more in 1989 and one in 1992. To be replaced by BINRS class.
Modernisation: Modernised with improved DUBM 41 and AP 4 acoustic sweep.
Structure: *Alençon* has a shorter funnel.

OUISTREHAM *2/1991, van Ginderen Collection*

0 + 3 BINRS CLASS (MINEHUNTERS)

Displacement, tons: 295 full load
Dimensions, feet (metres): 92.8 × 25.3 × 12.5 *(28.3 × 7.7 × 3.8)*
Main machinery: 1 Baudouin diesel; 800 hp(m) *(590 kW)*; 1 shaft
Speed, knots: 10. **Range, miles:** 3600 at 10 kts
Complement: 10
Radars: Navigation: I band.
Sonars: Thomson Sintra DUBM 41B; towed side scan; active search; high frequency.

Comment: Being built by Socarenam, Boulogne to complete in 1994 and replace the Aggressive class for Navigation training and route survey at Brest. BINRS—Bâtiments d'Instruction à la Navigation Remorquers de Sonars. Trawler type similar to Glycine class (see *Training Ships* section).

MCM DIVING TENDERS

4 MCM DIVING SUPPORT SHIPS

Name	No	Builders	Commissioned
VULCAIN	M 611	La Perrière, Lorient	11 Oct 1986
PLUTON	M 622	La Perrière, Lorient	10 Dec 1986
ACHÉRON	A 613	CMN, Cherbourg	21 Apr 1987
STYX	M 614	CMN, Cherbourg	22 July 1987

Displacement, tons: 375 standard; 505 full load
Dimensions, feet (metres): 136.5 × 24.6 × 12.5 *(41.6 × 7.5 × 3.8)*
Main machinery: 2 SACM MGO 175 V16 ASHR diesels; 2200 hp(m) *(1.62 MW)*; 2 shafts; bow thruster; 70 hp(m) *(51 kW)*
Speed, knots: 13.7. **Range, miles:** 2800 at 13 kts; 7400 at 9 kts
Complement: 14 (1 officer) plus 12 divers
Guns: 1—12.7 mm MG.
Radars: Navigation: Decca 1226; I band.

Comment: First pair ordered in December 1984. Second pair ordered July 1985. Designed to act as support ships for clearance divers. (Bâtiments Bases pour Plongeurs Démineurs — BBPD). *Vulcain* launched 17 January 1986, based at Cherbourg. *Pluton* launched 13 May 1986, based at Toulon. *Achéron* launched 9 November 1986, based at Toulon as a diving school tender and *Styx* launched 3 March 1987, based at Brest. Modified Chamois (BSR) class design. 5 ton hydraulic crane.

VULCAIN *7/1992, van Ginderen Collection*

OCEANOGRAPHIC AND SURVEY SHIPS

Notes: (a) These ships are painted white.
(b) A total of about 100 officers and technicians with oceanographic and hydrographic training is employed in addition to the ships' companies listed here. They occupy the extra billets marked as 'scientists'.

4 BH2 CLASS (Bâtiments Hydrographiques de 2e classe)

Name	No	Builders	Commissioned
LAPÉROUSE	A 791	Lorient Naval Dockyard	20 Apr 1988
BORDA	A 792	Lorient Naval Dockyard	18 June 1988
LAPLACE	A 793	Lorient Naval Dockyard	5 Oct 1989
ARAGO	A 795	Lorient Naval Dockyard	9 July 1991

Displacement, tons: 970 standard; 1100 full load
Dimensions, feet (metres): 193.5 × 35.8 × 11.9 *(59 × 10.9 × 3.6)*
Main machinery: 2 SACM MGO 175 V12 RVR diesels; 2500 hp(m) *(1.84 MW)*; 2 cp props; bow thruster
Speed, knots: 15. **Range, miles:** 6000 at 12 kts
Complement: 27 (2 officers) plus 11 scientists plus 7 spare berths
Radars: Navigation: Decca 1226; I band.
Sonars: Thomson-Sintra DUBM 42 or DUBM 21C (A 791); active search; high frequency.

Comment: Have replaced L'Espérance and L'Astrolabe classes. Ordered under 1982 and 1986 estimates, first pair on 24 July 1984, third 22 January 1986 and fourth 12 April 1988. Two variants: BH2A (A 791)—Carry Thomson Sintra DUBM 21C sonar for detection of underwater obstacles. Based at Brest; BH2C (remainder)—Carry two VH8 survey launches for hydrographic work. A 793 sailed for the Pacific 9 October 1989, joined by A 795 on 1 October 1991. A 792 based at Brest. *Borda* has the TSM 5260 Lennermor multi-path echo sounder.

LAPÉROUSE *3/1992, H M Steele*

Name	No	Builders	Commissioned
D'ENTRECASTEAUX	A 757	Brest Naval Dockyard	10 Oct 1970

Displacement, tons: 2400 full load
Dimensions, feet (metres): 292 × 42.7 × 14.4 *(89 × 13 × 4.4)*
Main machinery: Diesel-electric; 2 diesel generators; 2720 hp(m) *(2 MW)*; 2 motors; 2 shafts; cp props
Auxiliary propulsion; 2 Schottel trainable and retractable props
Speed, knots: 15. **Range, miles:** 10 000 at 12 kts
Complement: 88 (6 officers) plus 38 scientific staff
Radars: Navigation: Two Racal Decca 1226; I band.
Helicopters: 1 SA 319B Alouette III.

Comment: This ship was specially designed for oceanographic surveys capable of working to 6000 m *(19 686 ft)*. Bâtiment Océanographique (BO). Carries one LCP and three survey launches. Telescopic hangar. Serves in the Mediterranean.

D'ENTRECASTEAUX *7/1991, J Y Robert*

Name	No	Builders	Commissioned
L'ESPÉRANCE (ex-*Jacques Coeur*)	A 756	Gdynia	25 June 1969

Displacement, tons: 956 standard; 1360 full load
Dimensions, feet (metres): 208.3 × 32.1 × 19.4 *(63.5 × 9.8 × 5.9)*
Main machinery: 2 MAN diesels; 1850 hp(m) *(1.36 MW)*; 2 shafts
Speed, knots: 15. **Range, miles:** 7500 at 13 kts
Complement: 32 (3 officers) plus 14 scientists

Comment: Former trawler first commissioned in 1962 at Gdynia and purchased by the Navy in 1968. Adapted as survey ship. Based in Atlantic. Has a TSM 5260 Lennermor multi-path echo sounder.

L'ESPÉRANCE *1/1989, van Ginderen Collection*

SERVICE FORCES

Notes: 1. The support tankers *Vendres*, *Penhors* and *Mascarin* (included in 1988-89 edition) are fitted for replenishment at sea and are available for loan to the Navy.
2. A mobile support ship may be ordered in 1993/94.

5 RHIN CLASS (DEPOT and SUPPORT SHIPS)

Name	No	Builders	Commissioned
LOIRE	A 615	Lorient Naval Dockyard	10 Oct 1967
GARONNE	A 617	Lorient Naval Dockyard	1 Sep 1965
RANCE	A 618	Lorient Naval Dockyard	5 Feb 1966
RHIN	A 621	Lorient Naval Dockyard	1 Mar 1964
RHÔNE	A 622	Lorient Naval Dockyard	1 Dec 1964

Displacement, tons: 2075 (2320, *Garonne* and *Loire*) standard; 2445 full load
Dimensions, feet (metres): 331.5 × 43 × 12.1 *(101.1 × 13.1 × 3.7)*
Main machinery: 2 SEMT-Pielstick 16 PA2 V 400 diesels (*Rhin* and *Rhône*); 3300 hp(m) *(2.43 MW)*; 1 shaft
2 SEMT-Pielstick 12 PA4 V 400 diesels (*Rance*, *Loire* and *Garonne*); 4000 hp(m) *(2.94 MW)*; 1 shaft
Speed, knots: 16.5; 13 *(Rance)*. **Range, miles:** 13 000 at 13 kts
Complement: 165 (11 officers) (*Rhin* and *Rhône*); 120 (7 officers) and about 118 passengers *(Rance)*; 167 (19 officers) *(Garonne)*; 156 (12 officers) *(Loire)*
Guns: 3 Bofors 40 mm/60 (*Loire*, *Rhin* and *Rhône*). 1 Bofors 40 mm/60. 2 Oerlikon 20 mm (*Garonne*). None in *Rance*. 3—12.7 mm MGs.
Radars: Air search: DRBV 23C (in *Rance* in addition).
Air/surface search: Thomson-CSF DRBV 50; D band.
Helicopters: 1-3 SA 310B Alouette III (except *Garonne*). Platform only *(Rhône)*.

Comment: Designed for supporting various classes of ships. Have a 5 ton crane, carry two LCPs and have a helicopter platform (except *Garonne*). *Rhin* has a hangar and carries two helicopters; *Rance* has two platforms and carries three in her hangar. *Loire* has a hangar for one. *Garonne* is designed as a Repair Workshop, *Loire* for minesweeper support, *Rhin* for electronic maintenance and *Rhône* for submarines. *Rance* has been converted as a command and medical support ship for La Force d'Assistance Rapide with several modifications, and is also used as flagship of the Fleet Training Centre (Mediterranean). *Rhône* operates in the Atlantic, *Garonne* in the Indian Ocean/Pacific, *Loire* at Brest and *Rhin* in the Indian Ocean. Another ship (Bâtiment de Soutien Logistique—BSL) was to have been ordered in 1992 but this has been postponed. *Rhin* to pay off in 1993, *Rhône* in 1994 and *Garonne* in 1995.

GARONNE *2/1992, van Ginderen Collection*

RHÔNE *7/1990, Giorgio Arra*

RANCE *6/1991, van Ginderen Collection*

5 DURANCE CLASS (UNDERWAY REPLENISHMENT TANKERS)

Name	No	Builders	Laid down	Launched	Commissioned
MEUSE	A 607	Brest Naval Dockyard	2 June 1977	2 Dec 1978	21 Nov 1980
VAR	A 608	Brest Naval Dockyard	8 May 1979	1 June 1981	29 Jan 1983
DURANCE	A 629	Brest Naval Dockyard	12 Dec 1973	6 Sep 1975	1 Dec 1976
MARNE	A 630	Brest Naval Dockyard	4 Aug 1982	2 Feb 1985	16 Jan 1987
SOMME	A 631	Normed, la Seyne	3 May 1985	3 Oct 1987	7 Mar 1990

Displacement, tons: 17 900 full load
Dimensions, feet (metres): 515.9 × 69.5 × 38.5 *(157.3 × 21.2 × 10.8)*
Main machinery: 2 SEMT-Pielstick 16 PC2.5 V 400 diesels; 20 800 hp(m) *(15.3 MW)* sustained; 2 shafts; cp props
Speed, knots: 19. **Range, miles:** 9000 at 15 kts
Complement: 164 (18 officers)
Cargo capacity: 7500 tons FFO; 1500 diesel; 500 TR5 Avcat; 140 distilled water; 170 victuals; 150 munitions; 50 naval stores *(Durance)*. 5000 tons FFO; 3200 diesel; 1800 TR5 Avcat; 130 distilled water; 170 victuals; 150 munitions; 50 naval stores *(Meuse)*. 5090 tons FFO; 3310 diesel; 1090 TR5 Avcat; 260 distilled water; 180 munitions; 15 stores *(Var and Marne)*.

Guns: 2 Bofors 40 mm/60 *(Durance)*. 1 Bofors 40 mm/60. 2 Oerlikon 20 mm (remainder). 4—12.7 mm MGs.
Radars: Navigation: 2 Racal Decca 1226; I band.

Helicopters: 1 Lynx Mk 2/4.

Programmes: First two classed as Pétroliers Ravitailleurs d'Escadres (PRE). Last three classed as Bâtiments de Commandement et de Ravitaillement (BCR; Command and Replenishment Ships).
Structure: Four beam transfer positions and two astern, two of the beam positions having heavy transfer capability. *Var, Marne* and *Somme* differ from the others in several respects. The bridge extends further aft, boats are located either side of the funnel and a crane is located between the gantries. Also fitted with Syracuse SATCOM.
Operational: *Var, Marne* and *Somme* are designed to carry a Maritime Zone staff or Commander of a Logistic Formation and a commando unit of up to 45 men. Capable of accommodating 250 men. *Durance* assigned to GASM, others to FAN with one of the three BCR ships deployed to the Indian Ocean as a Flagship.
Sales: One to Australia built locally; two of similar but smaller design to Saudi Arabia.

SOMME *12/1992, B Sullivan*

MEUSE *5/1992, Guy Toremans*

JULES VERNE *9/1989, Photo Sami*

2 RR 4000 TYPE (SUPPLY TENDERS)

Name	No	Builders	Commissioned
RARI	A 634	Breheret	21 Feb 1985
REVI	A 635	Breheret	9 Mar 1985

Displacement, tons: 900 light; 1450 full load
Dimensions, feet (metres): 167.3 × 41.3 × 13.1 *(51 × 12.6 × 4)*
Main machinery: 2 SACM AGO 195 V12 diesels; 4410 hp(m) *(3.24 MW)*; 2 shafts; cp props; bow thruster
Speed, knots: 14.5. **Range, miles:** 6000 at 12 kts
Complement: 22 plus 18 passengers

Comment: Two 'remorqueurs ravitailleurs' for le Centre d'Expérimentation du Pacifique. Can carry 400 tons of cargo on deck.

1 MAINTENANCE and REPAIR SHIP

Name	No	Builders	Commissioned
JULES VERNE (ex-*Achéron*)	A 620	Brest Naval Dockyard	1 June 1976

Displacement, tons: 6485 standard; 10 250 full load
Dimensions, feet (metres): 482.2 × 70.5 × 21.3 *(147 × 21.5 × 6.5)*
Main machinery: 2 SEMT-Pielstick 18 PC2.2 V 400 diesels; 18 000 hp(m) *(13.2 MW)* sustained; 2 shafts
Speed, knots: 18. **Range, miles:** 9500 at 18 kts
Complement: 294 (15 officers)
Guns: 2 Bofors 40 mm/60. Several 12.7 mm MGs.
Helicopters: 2 SA 319B Alouette III.

Comment: Ordered in 1961 budget, originally as an Armament Supply Ship. Role and design changed whilst building—now rated as Engineering and Electrical Maintenance Ship. Launched 30 May 1970. Serves in Indian Ocean, providing general support for all ships. Carries stocks of torpedoes and ammunition. Refit in France November 1988-June 1989.

RARI *8/1985, J Y Rober*

6 CHAMOIS CLASS (SUPPLY TENDERS)

Name	No	Builders	Commissioned
TAAPE	A 633	La Perrière, Lorient	2 Nov 1983
CHAMOIS	A 767	La Perrière, Lorient	24 Sep 1976
ÉLAN	A 768	La Perrière, Lorient	7 Apr 1978
CHEVREUIL	A 774	La Perrière, Lorient	7 Oct 1977
GAZELLE	A 775	La Perrière, Lorient	13 Jan 1978
ISARD	A 776	La Perrière, Lorient	15 Dec 1978

Displacement, tons: 495 (500, *Taape*) full load
Dimensions, feet (metres): 136.1 × 24.6 × 10.5 *(41.5 × 7.5 × 3.2)*
Main machinery: 2 SACM AGO 175 V16 diesels; 2700 hp(m) *(1.98 MW)*; 2 shafts; cp props; bow thruster
Speed, knots: 14.2. **Range, miles:** 6000 at 12 kts
Complement: 13 plus 7 spare berths
Radars: Navigation: Racal Decca 1226; I band.

Comment: Similar to the standard Fish oil rig support ships. Can act as tugs, oil pollution vessels, salvage craft (two 30 ton and two 5 ton winches), coastal and harbour controlled minelaying, torpedo recovery, diving tenders and a variety of other tasks. Bollard pull 25 tons. Can carry 100 tons of stores on deck or 125 tons of fuel and 40 tons of water or 65 tons of fuel and 120 tons of water. *Taape* ordered in March 1982 from La Perrière—of improved design but basically similar with bridge one deck higher. *Taape* and *Chamois* based at Centre d'Expérimentation du Pacifique. Remainder based in France. *Isard* serves as a special diving support ship with an extra deckhouse. Seventh of class *Tapatai* returned to owners in 1992.

ISARD 6/1991, van Ginderen Collection

GAZELLE 5/1991, J Y Robert

TAAPE (high bridge) 1990, van Ginderen Collection

1 TRANSPORT LANDING SHIP

Name	No	Builders	Commissioned
GAPEAU	L 9090	Chantier Serra, la Seyne	2 Oct 1987

Displacement, tons: 509 standard; 1058 full load
Dimensions, feet (metres): 216.5 × 40 × 11.2 *(66 × 12.2 × 3.4)*
Main machinery: 2 diesels; 2 shafts
Speed, knots: 10
Complement: 6 + 30 scientists
Cargo capacity: 460 tons

Comment: Supply ship with bow doors. Operates for Centre d'Essais de la Mediterranée, Levant Island (missile range).

GAPEAU 5/1991, Giorgio Ghiglione

TRIALS/RESEARCH SHIPS

Notes: (a) In addition to the ships listed below there is a civilian manned 25 m trawler *L'Aventurière II* (launched July 1986) operated by GESMA, Brest for underwater research which comes under DCN.
(b) A new *Berry* is to be ordered as soon as possible as a purpose-built Electronics intelligence gathering ship.
(c) *Agnes 200* A 786 returned to owners 13 March 1992 and may now be used for commercial service.

Name	No	Builders	Commissioned
MONGE	A 601	Chantiers de l'Atlantique, St Nazaire	4 Nov 1992

Displacement, tons: 21 040 full load
Dimensions, feet (metres): 740.2 × 81.4 × 25.3 *(225.6 × 24.8 × 7.7)*
Main machinery: 2 SEMT-Pielstick 8 PC2.5 L 400 diesels; 10 400 hp(m) *(7.65 MW)* sustained; 1 shaft; bow thruster
Speed, knots: 16. **Range, miles:** 15 000 at 15 kts
Complement: 110 plus 100 military and 98 civilian technicians
Guns: 2 Giat F2 20 mm.
Combat data systems: Tavitac 2000 for trials.
Radars: Air search: Thomson-CSF DRBV 15C; E/F band.
Missile tracking: L band (new model); Gascogne; two Armor; Savoie; two Antares.
Navigation: Two Racal Decca (one for helo control); I band.
Helicopters: 2 Super Frelon.

Comment: Ordered 25 November 1988. Rated as a BEM (Bâtiment d'Essais et de Mesures). Laid down 26 March 1990, and launched 6 October 1990. She has 14 telemetry antennas; optronic tracking unit; LIDAR; Syracuse SATCOM. Flume tank stabilisation restricts the ship to a maximum of 9° roll at slow speed in Sea State 6. Flagship of the Trials Squadron.

MONGE 6/1992, French Navy

Name	No	Builders	Commissioned
ILE D'OLÉRON (ex-*München*, ex-*Mür*)	A 610	Weser, Bremen	1939

Displacement, tons: 5500 standard; 6500 full load
Dimensions, feet (metres): 378 × 50 × 21.3 *(115.2 × 15.2 × 6.5)*
Main machinery: 2 MAN 6-cyl diesels; 3500 hp(m) *(2.57 MW)*; 1 shaft
Speed, knots: 14.5. **Range, miles:** 7200 at 12 kts
Complement: 195 (12 officers)
Radars: Various, according to experiments (DRBV 22C, DRBV 50).
Navigation: Racal Decca 1226; I band.
Helicopters: Platform only for Alouette III.

Comment: Taken as a war prize. Commissioned in French Navy 29 August 1945. Formerly rated as a transport. Converted to experimental guided missile ship in 1957-58 by Chantiers de Provence and l'Arsenal de Toulon. Commissioned early in 1959. Fitted with one launcher for target planes. Has been fitted with various equipment and weapon systems for trials: Masurca, Crotale, Otomat, MM 40 Exocet, Sadral, 100 mm gun with CTMS fire control system, Crotale Modulaire, Sagaie, Simbad. Fitted for sea trials of Milas in 1992 (ASW torpedo delivery missile with a range of 50 km). Also trials continue on prototype Sylver launchers for VLS Aster 15 PDMS and Aster 30 Area SAM. Based at Toulon.

ILE D'OLÉRON 5/1991, Camil Busquets i Vilanova

222 FRANCE / Trials/research ships — Boom and mooring vessels

Name	No	Builders	Commissioned
BERRY (ex-M/S *Médoc*)	A 644	Roland Werft, Bremen	26 Nov 1964

Displacement, tons: 1148 standard; 2700 full load
Dimensions, feet (metres): 284.5 × 38 × 15 *(86.7 × 11.6 × 4.6)*
Main machinery: 2 MWM diesels; 2400 hp(m) *(1.76 MW)*; 1 shaft
Speed, knots: 13. **Range, miles:** 7000 at 15 kts
Guns: 2—12.7 mm MGs.
Radars: Navigation: Racal Decca 1226; I band.

Comment: Launched on 10 May 1958. In 1976-77 converted at Toulon from victualling stores ship to Mediterranean electronic trials ship. Recommissioned February 1977. Deleted in error in 1991. It is planned to replace her as soon as possible, her performance as an AGI having been inadequate in the Gulf in 1991.

BERRY *7/1992, J Y Robert*

Name	No	Builders	Commissioned
THÉTIS (ex-*Nereide*)	A 785	Lorient Naval Dockyard	9 Nov 1988

Displacement, tons: 720 standard; 1000 full load
Dimensions, feet (metres): 185.4 × 35.8 × 11.8 *(56.5 × 10.9 × 3.6)*
Main machinery: 2 Uni Diesel UD 30 V16 M4 diesels; 2710 hp(m) *(1.99 MW)* sustained; 1 shaft; cp prop
Speed, knots: 15. **Range, miles:** 6000
Complement: 36 (2 officers) plus 7 passengers
Guns: 2—12.7 mm MGs.
Radars: Navigation: Racal Decca 1226; I band.
Sonars: VDS; Thomson Sintra DUBM 42 and DUBM 60A; active search; high frequency.

Comment: Same hull as Lapérouse class. Classified as Bâtiment Experimental Guerre de Mines (BEGM). Operated by the Centre d'Études, d'Instruction et d'Entraînement de la Guerre des Mines (CETIEGM) in Brest. Launched 19 March 1988. Renamed to avoid confusion with Y 700. Equipped to conduct trials on all underwater weapons and sensors for mine warfare. Can lay mines. Can support six divers. Fitted with the Thomson Sintra mine warfare combat system designed for the cancelled Narvik class.

THÉTIS *11/1992, van Ginderen Collection*

Name	No	Builders	Commissioned
TRITON	A 646	Lorient	20 Jan 1972

Displacement, tons: 1410 standard; 1510 full load
Dimensions, feet (metres): 242.7 × 38.9 × 12 *(74 × 11.8 × 3.7)*
Main machinery: 2 MGO V12 diesels; 1800 hp(m) *(1.32 MW)*; 1 Voith-Schneider screw (aft); 2 motors; 800 kW; 1 Voith-Schneider screw (fwd)
Speed, knots: 13. **Range, miles:** 4000 at 13 kts
Complement: 54 (5 officers) plus 5 officers and 12 men for diving
Radars: Navigation: Racal Decca 1226; I band.

Comment: Launched on 7 March 1970. Support ship for the two-man submarine *Griffon*. Painted white. Operated by Groupe d'Intervention sous la Mer (GISMER) for trials of submarines and deep-sea diving equipment. Underwater TV, recompression chamber, four-man diving bell of 13.5 tons and laboratories are fitted. Available as submarine rescue ship. Also carries a number of diving saucers. Special sonar equipment is fitted and there is a helicopter platform. The midget submarine *Griffon* is carried amidships on the starboard side of *Triton*. She is 25 ft *(7.8 m)* long, displaces 16 tons and is driven by an electric motor. Her diving depth is 600 m *(2000 ft)* and her endurance 24 miles at 4 kts. Can be used for deep recovery operations. Fitted with manipulating arm.

TRITON *9/1991, H M Steele*

Name	No	Builders	Commissioned
DENTI	A 743	DCAN Toulon	15 July 1976

Displacement, tons: 170 full load
Dimensions, feet (metres): 113.8 × 21.6 × 7.5 *(34.7 × 6.6 × 2.3)*
Main machinery: 2 Baudouin DP8 diesels; 960 hp(m) *(706 kW)*; 2 shafts; cp props
Speed, knots: 12. **Range, miles:** 800 at 12 kts
Complement: 6 (2 officers)

Comment: Launched 7 October 1975. Employed on ammunition trials off Toulon.

DENTI *6/1991, van Ginderen Collection*

Name	No	Builders	Commissioned
NARVIK	M 660	Lorient Naval Dockyard	22 Mar 1991

Displacement, tons: 905 full load
Dimensions, feet (metres): 170.6 oa; 152.9 wl × 48.6 × 11.8 *(52; 46.6 × 14.8 × 3.6)*
Main machinery: 2 diesels; 2700 hp(m) *(1.98 MW)*; 2 shafts; cp props; auxiliary propulsion: diesel-electric; 500 kW; bow thruster; 204 hp(m) *(150 kW)*
Speed, knots: 15. **Range, miles:** 5000 at 10 kts
Complement: 46
Guns: 1 Giat 20 mm F2. 2—12.7 mm MGs.
Countermeasures: MCM: One or two remote controlled minehunting PAP Mk 5 with DUBM 60 sonar and television. Mechanical, magnetic and acoustic (DCN AP4) sweeps.
Sonars: Thomson Sintra DUBM 42; towed; active; high frequency; can be towed at 10 kts down to 300 m *(984 ft)*.

Comment: Designed by DCN. BAMO (Bâtiment Anti-Mines Océanique). Programme of six cancelled in 1992 leaving an unfinished *Narvik* at Lorient. May be used as a trials ship. GRP hull with a catamaran design. This type of hull offers a larger working area than a monohull of equivalent displacement. Other claimed advantages include seakeeping, stability and manoeuvrability.

NARVIK *8/1992, J Y Robert*

BOOM AND MOORING VESSELS

Name	No	Builders	Commissioned
LA PRUDENTE	Y 749	AC Manche	27 July 1969
LA PERSÉVÉRANTE	Y 750	AC La Rochelle	3 Mar 1969
LA FIDÈLE	Y 751	AC Manche	10 June 1969

Displacement, tons: 626 full load
Dimensions, feet (metres): 142.8 × 32.8 × 9.2 *(43.5 × 10 × 2.8)*
Main machinery: Diesel-electric; 2 Baudouin diesels; 620 hp(m) *(441 kW)*; 1 shaft
Speed, knots: 10. **Range, miles:** 4000 at 10 kts
Complement: 30 (1 officer)

Comment: Net layers and tenders. Launched on 13 May 1968 (*La Prudente*), 14 May 1968 (*La Persévérante*) and 26 August 1968 (*La Fidèle*). Have a 25 ton lift. Based at Brest, Toulon and Cherbourg respectively.

LA FIDÈLE *9/1992, Guy Toreman*

Boom and mooring vessels — Transports / FRANCE

Name	No	Builders	Commissioned
TIANÉE	A 731	Arsenal de Brest	8 July 1975

Displacement, tons: 842 standard; 905 full load
Dimensions, feet (metres): 178.1 × 34.8 × 11.2 *(54.3 × 10.6 × 3.4)*
Main machinery: Diesel-electric; 2 diesel generators; 1300 hp(m) *(960 kW)*; 1 motor; 1200 hp(m) *(880 kW)*; 1 shaft
Speed, knots: 12. **Range, miles:** 5200 at 12 kts
Complement: 37 (1 officer)

Comment: Launched 17 November 1973. Fitted with lateral screws in bow tunnel. Refitted early 1985, based at Toulon.

TIANÉE *10/1991, Aldo Fraccaroli*

TUPA Y 667   **TELENN MOR** Y 692

Comment: 292 tons with 210 hp(m) *(154 kW)* diesel. *Tupa* commissioned 16 March 1974, *Telenn Mor* on 16 January 1986. Mooring vessels. *Tupa* based at Papeete.

TELENN MOR *8/1988, J Y Robert*

CALMAR Y 698

Comment: A 270 ton harbour tug converted for raising moorings. One diesel engine. Commissioned 12 August 1970. Based at Lorient.

CALMAR *8/1990, J Y Robert*

TRANSPORTS

REBERON

Comment: Commissioned at Brest 26 November 1979.

REBERON *8/1988, J Y Robert*

ARIEL Y 604   **DRYADE** Y 662   **ONDINE** Y 701
FAUNE Y 613   **ALPHÉE** Y 696   **NAIADE** Y 702
KORRIGAN Y 661   **NEREIDE** Y 700   **ELFE** Y 741

Displacement, tons: 195 standard; 225 full load
Dimensions, feet (metres): 132.8 × 24.5 × 10.8 *(40.5 × 7.5 × 3.3)*
Main machinery: 2 SACM MGO or Poyaud diesels; 1640 hp(m) *(1.21 MW)* or 1730 hp(m) *(1.27 MW)*; 2 shafts
Speed, knots: 15.3. **Range, miles:** 940 at 14 kts
Complement: 9

Comment: All built by Société Française de Construction Naval (ex-Franco-Belge) except for *Nereide*, *Ondine* and *Naiade* by DCAN Brest. *Ariel* in service 1964, *Elfe* in 1980; the remainder at approximately two year intervals. Can carry 400 passengers (250 seated). *Naiade* based with CEM Toulon.

ALPHÉE *8/1992, J Y Robert*

SYLPHE Y 710

Displacement, tons: 171 standard; 189 full load
Dimensions, feet (metres): 126.5 × 22.7 × 8.2 *(38.5 × 6.9 × 2.5)*
Main machinery: 1 SACM MGO diesel; 833 hp(m) *(612 kW)*; 1 shaft
Speed, knots: 12
Complement: 9

Comment: Small transport for passengers, built by Chantiers Franco-Belges in 1959-60. Based at Brest since 1981.

SYLPHE *8/1992, J Y Robert*

MORGANE Y 671   **MERLIN** Y 735   **MÉLUSINE** Y 736

Displacement, tons: 170 full load
Dimensions, feet (metres): 103.3 × 23.2 × 7.9 *(31.5 × 7.1 × 2.4)*
Main machinery: 2 SACM MGO diesels; 940 hp(m) *(691 kW)*; 2 shafts
Speed, knots: 11

Comment: Small transports for 400 passengers built by Chantiers Navals Franco-Belges at Châlons-sur-Saône *(Mélusine* and *Merlin)* and Toulon Dockyard *(Morgane)*. First one commissioned in June 1968. Based at Toulon.

MORGANE *6/1987, A Toremans*

224 FRANCE / Tenders

TENDERS

Note: In addition to the craft listed below an EDIC class L 9096 is in service at Brest (see *Amphibious Forces* section for details).

POSÉIDON A 722

Displacement, tons: 220 full load
Dimensions, feet (metres): 132.9 × 23.6 × 7.3 *(40.5 × 7.2 × 2.2)*
Main machinery: 1 diesel; 600 hp(m) *(441 kW)*; 1 shaft
Speed, knots: 13
Complement: 42

Comment: Base ship for assault swimmers. Completed 6 August 1975.

POSÉIDON 6/1991, van Ginderen Collection

TOURMALINE A 714

Displacement, tons: 45
Dimensions, feet (metres): 88 × 16.8 × 4.8 *(26.8 × 5.1 × 1.5)*
Main machinery: 2 diesels; 1120 hp(m) *(823 kW)*; 2 shafts
Speed, knots: 27

Comment: Commissioned 14 February 1974. Built by Chantiers Navals de L'Esterel. Attached to Mediterranean Test Range. Civilian manned. Based at Port Pothau near Toulon.

TOURMALINE 6/1985, Giorgio Arra

ATHOS A 712   ARAMIS A 713

Displacement, tons: 100 full load
Dimensions, feet (metres): 105.3 × 21.3 × 6.2 *(32.1 × 6.5 × 1.9)*
Main machinery: 2 SACM diesels; 4400 hp(m) *(3.23 MW)*; 2 shafts
Speed, knots: 32. Range, miles: 1500 at 15 kts
Complement: 12 plus 6 passengers
Guns: 1 Oerlikon 20 mm. 2—12.7 mm MGs.
Radars: Navigation: Racal Decca 1226; I band.

Comment: Built by Chantiers Navals de l'Esterel for Missile Trials Centre of Les Landes (CEL). Based at Bayonne, forming Groupe des Vedettes de l'Adour. Commissioned 1980.

ATHOS 9/1983, van Ginderen Collection

Y 732

Comment: Built in Lorient. Commissioned 3 March 1979. Based at Brest. Designated 'Station de Démagnétisation No 3'.

Y 732 8/1992, J Y Robert

CORALLINE A 790   Y 790-798

Displacement, tons: 44 full load
Dimensions, feet (metres): 68.9 × 14.8 × 3.6 *(21 × 4.5 × 1.1)*
Main machinery: 2 diesels; 264 hp(m) *(194 kW)*; 2 shafts
Speed, knots: 13
Complement: 4 plus 14 divers

Comment: Diving tenders building at Lorient. First one delivered in February 1990. *Coralline* is used for radioactive monitoring in Cherbourg. Y 790-791 are Divers training craft (VIP) at Toulon. Y 792-793 are clearance diver support craft (VIPD) based at Brest. Others are to be based at Cherbourg and Toulon.

Y 790 6/1991, van Ginderen Collection

Y 753-755   Y 776-777   Y 783-785
Y 762-765   Y 779-781   Y 786-789

Displacement, tons: 18-21 full load
Dimensions, feet (metres): 47.9 × 15.1 × 3.3 *(14.6 × 4.6 × 1)*
Main machinery: 2 Baudouin diesels; 900 or 500 hp(m) *(661 kW or 368 kW)*; 2 shafts
Speed, knots: 20 or 13. Range, miles: 400 at 11 kts
Complement: 4

Comment: All built by DCN Lorient between 1988 and 1992. Y 762-765 are patrol craft and can carry one 12.7 mm MG; Y 779-781 are pilot craft; Y 753-755 and Y 786-789 are transport craft based in the Pacific; Y 783-785 are for fire-fighting and Y 776-777 are radiological monitoring craft and have smaller engines.

Y 765 8/1992, J Y Robert

TRAINING SHIPS

8 LÉOPARD CLASS

Name	No	Builders	Commissioned
LÉOPARD	A 748	ACM, St Malo	4 Dec 1982
PANTHÈRE	A 749	ACM, St Malo	4 Dec 1982
JAGUAR	A 750	ACM, St Malo	18 Dec 1982
LYNX	A 751	La Perrière, Lorient	18 Dec 1982
GUÉPARD	A 752	ACM, St Malo	1 July 1983
CHACAL	A 753	ACM, St Malo	10 Sep 1983
TIGRE	A 754	La Perrière, Lorient	1 July 1983
LION	A 755	La Perrière, Lorient	10 Sep 1983

Displacement, tons: 463 full load
Dimensions, feet (metres): 141 × 27.1 × 10.5 *(43 × 8.3 × 3.2)*
Main machinery: 2 SACM MGO 175 V16 ASHR diesels; 2200 hp(m) *(1.62 MW)*; 2 shafts
Speed, knots: 15. **Range, miles:** 4100 at 12 kts
Complement: 14 plus 21 trainees
Guns: 2 Oerlikon 20 mm.
Radars: Navigation: Racal Decca 1226; I band.

Comment: First four ordered May 1980. Further four ordered April 1981. Form 20ème Divec (Training division) for shiphandling training and occasional EEZ patrols.

CHACAL *11/1992, van Ginderen Collection*

2 GLYCINE CLASS

Name	No	Builders	Commissioned
GLYCINE	A 770	Socarenam, Boulogne	11 Apr 1992
EGLANTINE	A 771	Socarenam, Boulogne	Sep 1992

Displacement, tons: 295 full load
Dimensions, feet (metres): 92.8 × 25.3 × 12.5 *(28.3 × 7.7 × 3.8)*
Main machinery: 1 Baudouin diesel; 800 hp(m) *(588 kW)*; 1 shaft
Speed, knots: 10. **Range, miles:** 3600 at 10 kts
Complement: 10 + 16 trainees
Radars: Navigation: 2 Furuno; I band.

Comment: Trawler type. Three more building as route survey craft (included under *Mine Warfare Forces* section).

GLYCINE *11/1992, van Ginderen Collection*

CHIMÈRE Y 706   **FARFADET** Y 711

Displacement, tons: 100
Main machinery: 1 diesel; 200 hp(m) *(147 kW)*; 1 shaft
Speed, knots: 11

Comment: Built at Bayonne in 1971. Tenders to the Naval School. Re-engined in 1991/92.

LA GRANDE HERMINE (ex-*La Route Est Belle*, ex-*Ménestrel*) A 653

Comment: Ex-sailing fishing boat built in 1932 by Chantiers Fidèle, Marseilles. Purchased in 1964 as the Navigation School (EOR) training ship. Length 46 ft *(14.02 m)*.

L'ÉTOILE A 649   **LA BELLE POULE** A 650

Displacement, tons: 227
Dimensions, feet (metres): 105.9 × 22.9 × 10.5 *(32.3 × 7 × 3.2)*
Main machinery: Sulzer diesel; 125 hp(m) *(92 kW)*; 1 shaft
Speed, knots: 6

Comment: Auxiliary sail vessels. Built by Chantiers de Normandie (Fécamp) in 1932. Accommodation for three officers, 30 cadets, 5 petty officers, 12 men. Attached to Naval School.

L'ÉTOILE *6/1991, Guy Toremans*

MUTIN A 652

Comment: A 57 ton coastal tender built in 1927 by Chaffeteau, Les Sables d'Olonne. Auxiliary diesel and sails. Attached to the Navigation School. Launched 18 May 1927. Length 33 m and has a sail area of 240 sq m.

TUGS

OCEAN TUGS (Remorqueurs de Haute Mer RHM)

MALABAR A 664   **TENACE** A 669   **CENTAURE** A 674

Displacement, tons: 1080 light; 1454 full load
Dimensions, feet (metres): 167.3 × 37.8 × 18.6 *(51 × 11.5 × 5.7)*
Main machinery: 2 Krupp MAK 9 M US2 AK diesels; 4600 hp(m) *(3.38 MW)*; 1 shaft; Kort nozzles
Speed, knots: 15. **Range, miles:** 9500 at 15 kts
Complement: 42

Comment: *Malabar* and *Tenace* built by J. Oelkers, Hamburg, *Centaure* built at La Pallice. *Tenace* commissioned 15 November 1973, *Centaure* on 15 November 1974 and *Malabar* on 7 October 1975. All based at Brest with one operating as Fishery Protection ship off US coast. Carry fire-fighting equipment. Bollard pull, 60 tons.

CENTAURE *8/1990, Photo Sami*

COASTAL TUGS (Remorqueurs Côtiers RC)

BÉLIER A 695   **BUFFLE** A 696   **BISON** A 697

Displacement, tons: 500 standard; 800 full load
Dimensions, feet (metres): 104.9 × 28.9 × 10.5 *(32 × 8.8 × 3.2)*
Main machinery: 2 SACM AGO 195 V8 CSHR diesels; 2600 hp(m) *(1.91 MW)*; 2 Voith-Schneider props
Speed, knots: 11
Complement: 12

Comment: Built at Cherbourg. *Bélier* commissioned 10 July 1980, *Buffle* on 19 July 1980, *Bison* on 16 April 1981. All based at Toulon. Bollard pull, 25 tons.

BÉLIER *6/1991, van Ginderen Collection*

226 FRANCE / Tugs

MAROA A 636   **MAITO** A 637   **MANINI** A 638

Displacement, tons: 245 full load
Dimensions, feet (metres): 90.5 × 27.2 × 11.5 *(27.6 × 8.9 × 3.5)*
Main machinery: 2 SACM diesels; 1280 hp(m) *(941 kW)*; 2 Voith-Schneider props
Speed, knots: 11. Range, miles: 1200 at 10 kts
Complement: 10

Comment: Built by SFCN and Villeneuve La Garonne (A 638) for CEP Nuclear Test Range. *Maito* commissioned 25 July 1984, *Maroa* 28 July 1984, *Manini* 12 September 1985. Bollard pull, 12 tons.

LE FORT A 671 (12 July 1971)	VALEUREUX A 688 (17 Oct 1960)
UTILE A 672 (8 Apr 1971)	TRAVAILLEUR A 692 (11 July 1963)
LUTTEUR A 673 (19 July 1963)	ACHARNÉ A 693 (5 July 1974)
ACTIF A 686 (11 July 1963)	EFFICACE A 694 (17 Oct 1974)
LABORIEUX A 687 (14 Aug 1963)	

Displacement, tons: 230 full load
Dimensions, feet (metres): 92 × 26 × 13 *(28.1 × 7.9 × 4)*
Main machinery: 1 SACM MGO diesel; 1050 hp(m) *(773 kW)* or 1450 hp(m) *(1.07 MW)* (later ships); 1 shaft
Speed, knots: 11. Range, miles: 2400 at 10 kts
Complement: 15

Comment: Commissioning dates in brackets. Bollard pull, 13 tons. A 688 due to scrap in 1993.

ACHARNÉ   6/1990, Gilbert Gyssels

FRÉHEL A 675	ARMEN A 677	KEREON (ex-*Sicie*) A 679
SAIRE A 676	LA HOUSSAYE A 678	LARDIER A 680

Displacement, tons: 259 full load
Dimensions, feet (metres): 82 × 27.6 × 11.2 *(25 × 8.4 × 3.4)*
Main machinery: 2 diesels; 1280 hp(m) *(941 kW)* (1320 hp(m) *(970 kW)* in later vessels); 2 Voith-Schneider props
Speed, knots: 10. Range, miles: 800 at 10 kts
Complement: 8 (coastal); 5 (harbour)

Comment: Building at Lorient Naval et Industries shipyard (formerly Chantiers et Ateliers de la Perrière, now part of Leroux et Lotz). *Fréhel* in service 23 May 1989, based at Cherbourg, *Saire* 16 October 1989 at Cherbourg, *Armen* commissioned 6 December 1991, based at Brest, *La Houssaye* and *Kereon* commissioned in 1992 and based at Lorient and Brest respectively, *Lardier* commissioned in 1993 and based at Toulon. It is planned to build craft on this pattern until 2005. Bollard pull 12 tons.

ARMEN   8/1992, J Y Robert

HARBOUR TUGS (Remorqueurs de port)

21—105 TON TYPE

Chataigner Y 620, *Chêne* Y 624, *Cormier* Y 629, *Frêne* Y 644, *Hêtre* Y 654, *Hevea* Y 655, *Manguier* Y 666, *Méléze* Y 668, *Merisier* Y 669, *Paletuvier* Y 686, *Peuplier* Y 688, *Platane* Y 695, *Saule* Y 708, *Sycomore* Y 709, *Ébène* Y 717, *Érable* Y 718, *Olivier* Y 719, *Santal* Y 720, *Maronnier* Y 738, *Noyer* Y 739, *Papayer* Y 740.

Comment: Of 105 tons, 10 ton bollard pull with 700 hp(m) *(514 kW)* diesel and maximum speed of 11 kts. Being deleted.

ÉBÈNE   8/1992, J Y Robert

2—93 TON TYPE

Bonite Y 630   *Rouget* Y 634

Comment: Of 93 tons, 7 ton bollard pull with 380 hp(m) *(279 kW)* and maximum speed of 10 kts. Based at Brest.

ROUGET and BONITE   8/1990, J Y Robert

24—65 TON TYPE

Bengali Y 611, *Mouette* Y 617, *Mésange* Y 621, *Cigogne* Y 625, *Colibri* Y 628, *Cygne* Y 632, *Martinet* Y 636, *Fauvette* Y 637, *Goéland* Y 648, *Merle* Y 670, *Moineau* Y 673, *Martin Pêcheur* Y 675, *Passereau* Y 687, *Pinson* Y 691, *Pivert* Y 694, *Engoulevent* Y 723, *Marabout* Y 725, *Toucan* Y 726, *Macreuse* Y 727, *Grand Duc* Y 728, *Eider* Y 729, *Ara* Y 730, *Loriot* Y 747, *Gélinotte* Y 748.

Comment: Of 65 tons, 3.5 ton bollard pull with 250 hp(m) *(184 kW)* diesel and maximum speed of 9 kts. *Ibis* Y 658 loaned to Senegal.

65 TON TYPE   8/1990, J Y Robert

23 WATER TRACTORS

P 1-23

Displacement, tons: 24
Dimensions, feet (metres): 37.7 × 14.1 × 4.6 *(11.5 × 4.3 × 1.4)*
Main machinery: 2 SACM Poyaud 520 V8M diesels; 440 hp(m) *(323 kW)*; 2 shafts
Speed, knots: 9.2

Comment: Pusher-tugs built by Ch et A de La Perrière. First of the second series (P13) delivered 23 December 1980, P20 in service 2 May 1989. P 21 in service December 1990, P 22 January 1991, P 23 15 February 1991. Bollard push, 4 tons.

P 16   5/1991, J Y Robert

4 FIREFIGHTING TUGS

CASCADE Y 618   AIGUIÈRE Y 745
GAVE Y 645   EMBRUN Y 746

Displacement, tons: 85 full load
Dimensions, feet (metres): 78.1 × 17.4 × 5.6 *(23.8 × 5.3 × 1.7)*
Main machinery: 2 SACM Poyaud diesels; 410 hp(m) *(301 kW)*; 2 shafts
Speed, knots: 11.3

Comment: Have red hulls and white superstructure. Beginning to be paid off.

GAVE   *8/1992, J Y Robert*

MISCELLANEOUS

Note: In addition there are 11 harbour oil barges (CIC), 5 water barges (CIE), 6 oily bilge barges (CIEM) and 3 anti-pollution barges (CIEP/BAPM). Most have a capability of 400 cu m and CIC and CIE craft are self-propelled.

CIE 23   *8/1992, J Y Robert*

1 FLOATING DOCK

Comment: Of 3800 tons capacity, built at Brest in 1975. Based at Papeete for use by Centre Expérimentation du Pacifique. 150 × 33 m.

6 FLOATING CRANES

FA 1-6

Comment: With lifts of 7.5-15 tons. One in Cherbourg, three in Brest, two in Toulon. Self-propelled. Grue Flottante Automotrice (GFA).

30 HARBOUR SUPPORT CRAFT

CHA 8   14   17   19   23-38

Comment: Of 20 tons based at Cherbourg, Brest, Lorient, Toulon, Rochefort. Used as harbour craft. CHA 27-34 in service 1988, 35-38 in service 1989.

CHA 32   *8/1992, J Y Robert*

FLOTTE AUXILIAIRE OCCASIONNELLE (FAO)

Note: The ships listed below were on the 'taken up from trade' list at the beginning of 1993.

ABEILLE FLANDRE (ex-*Neptun Suecia*)   **ABEILLE LANGUEDOC** (ex-*Neptun Gothia*)
ABEILLE BRETAGNE

Displacement, tons: 1577
Dimensions, feet (metres): 208 × 48.2 × 2.9 *(63.4 × 14.7 × 0.9)*
Main machinery: 4 Atlas diesels; 23 000 hp(m) *(16.9 MW)*; 2 shafts
Speed, knots: 17

Comment: Details given are for *Abeille Flandre* and *Abeille Languedoc*. *Abeille Bretagne* is of 670 tons and 43.7 m. Built by Ulstein Hatlo in Norway in 1978. *Abeille Flandre* based at Brest, *Abeille Languedoc* at Cherbourg, and *Abeille Bretagne* at Tahiti. Used as salvage tugs.

ABEILLE FLANDRE   *7/1990, M Voss*

ALBACORE (ex-*Beryl Fish*)   **MÉROU** (ex-*King Fish*)
GIRELLE (ex-*Moon Fish*) A 702

Comment: All of about 55 m in length and capable of 12 kts. *Mérou* and *Girelle* built in the Netherlands in 1981-82 and based in Toulon. *Albacore* on loan from Feronica International and also based in the Mediterranean. Used as supply ships.

ALBACORE   *10/1990, J Y Robert/M Pouget*

MÉROU   *6/1991, van Ginderen Collection*

AILETTE (ex-*Cyrus*)   **ALCYON** (ex-*Bahram*)

Displacement, tons: 1500 full load
Dimensions, feet (metres): 173.9 × 43.6 × 14.8 *(53 × 13.3 × 4.5)*
Main machinery: 2 diesels; 5200 hp(m) *(3.8 MW)*; 2 shafts
Speed, knots: 12
Complement: 7

Comment: Built in 1981/82. Replaced deleted boom defence vessels. Bollard pull, 62 tons. Fitted with a 30 ton stern gantry. Have green hulls and white superstructures.

228 FRANCE / Flotte auxiliaire occasionnelle (FAO) — Government maritime forces

LANGEVIN (ex-*Percy Navigator*, ex-*Martin Fish*)

Displacement, tons: 1650 full load
Dimensions, feet (metres): 222.1 × 44 × 16.1 *(67.7 × 13.4 × 4.9)*
Main machinery: Diesel-electric; 3 GM 16V-149TI diesels; 2 motors; 3483 hp(m) *(2.6 MW)*; 2 shafts
Speed, knots: 12

Comment: Built in 1980 by Halter Marine. Leased in May 1990 by DCN for use as an SNLE trials support ship.

GOVERNMENT MARITIME FORCES

GENDARMERIE MARITIME AND GENDARMERIE DÉPARTEMENTALE

Notes: 1. These ships are operated and maintained by the Navy but are manned by Gendarmes. Total of 1200 people (276 conscripts) tasked to protect naval bases and establishments ashore.
2. The Gendarmerie Départementale operates minor craft in territorial waters and overseas.

4 PATRA CLASS (FAST PATROL CRAFT)

Name	No	Builders	Commissioned
TRIDENT	P 670	Auroux, Arcachon	17 Dec 1976
GLAIVE	P 671	Auroux, Arcachon	2 Apr 1977
ÉPÉE	P 672	CMN, Cherbourg	9 Oct 1976
PERTUISANE	P 673	CMN, Cherbourg	20 Jan 1977

Displacement, tons: 115 standard; 147.5 full load
Dimensions, feet (metres): 132.5 × 19.4 × 5.2 *(40.4 × 5.9 × 1.6)*
Main machinery: 2 SACM AGO 195 V12 diesels; 4410 hp(m) *(3.24 MW)*; 2 shafts; cp props
Speed, knots: 26. **Range, miles:** 1750 at 10 kts; 750 at 20 kts
Complement: 18 (1 officer)
Guns: 1 Bofors 40 mm/60. 1 or 2—12.7 mm MGs.
Radars: Surface search: Racal Decca 1226; I band.

Comment: P 672 transferred to Gendarmerie in February 1986, P 670 in June 1987, P 671 in September 1987 and P 673 in November 1987. The class proved to be too small for their intended naval role. SS-12 SSM removed. P 670 and 672 based at Lorient, P 671 at Cherbourg and P 673 at Toulon.

ÉPÉE   6/1989, Gilbert Gyssels

P 772   **P 774**

Displacement, tons: 14 full load
Dimensions, feet (metres): 43.6 × 13.5 × 3.6 *(13.3 × 4.1 × 1.1)*
Main machinery: 2 diesels; 440 hp(m) *(323 kW)*; 2 shafts
Speed, knots: 25
Guns: 1—12.7 mm MG. 2—7.62 mm MGs.

Comment: Tecimar Volte 43 class. Commissioned in 1975 and based at Toulon and Brest respectively. P 770 deleted in November 1991.

P 772 (with P 791)   8/1990, J Y Robert

P 775   **P 776**

Displacement, tons: 52 full load
Dimensions, feet (metres): 81.7 × 20 × 5.6 *(24.9 × 6.1 × 1.7)*
Main machinery: 3 diesels; 2500 hp(m) *(1.8 MW)*; 2 shafts; 1 waterjet
Speed, knots: 28; 10 (waterjet only). **Range, miles:** 700 at 22 kts
Complement: 8
Guns: 1—12.7 mm MG. 2—7.62 mm MGs.

Comment: Built by DCN Lorient and completed late 1992/early 1993 for transfer to Guyana. GRP hulls. More to be built to replace older craft.

P 779-781

Displacement, tons: 30 full load
Dimensions, feet (metres): 81.7 × 17.4 × 5.2 *(24.9 × 5.3 × 1.6)*
Main machinery: 2 Detroit 8V-71 diesels; 460 hp *(343 kW)* sustained; 2 shafts
Speed, knots: 24
Complement: 4
Guns: 1—12.7 mm MG.

Comment: Built in 1977. Unofficial names: *Gyane* P 780 and *Karukera* P 781 in Antilles/French Guiana; P 779 at Papeete.

P 760 (ex-Y 760)   **P 761**   **P 778**   **P 789-791**   **P 794**

Displacement, tons: 18 full load
Dimensions, feet (metres): 47.9 × 15.1 × 3.3 *(14.6 × 4.6 × 1)*
Main machinery: 2 Baudouin 12 F11 SM diesels; 800 hp(m) *(588 kW)*; 2 shafts
Speed, knots: 20. **Range, miles:** 360 at 18 kts
Guns: 2—12.7 mm MGs.

Comment: Type V14 SC. Built 1985-1993. Similar to naval tenders with Y pennant numbers.

P 791   8/1992, J Y Robert

DOUANES FRANÇAISES

Note: The French customs service has a number of tasks not normally associated with such an organisation. In addition to the usual duties of dealing with ships entering either its coastal area or ports it also has certain responsibilities for rescue at sea, control of navigation, fishery protection and pollution protection. For these purposes 650 officers and men operate a number of craft of various dimensions: Class I of 30 m, 24 kts and a range of 1200 miles; Class II of 27 m, 24 kts and with a range of 900 miles; Class III of 17-20 m, 24 kts and a range of 400 miles; Class IV of 12-17 m, 24 kts and a range of 400 miles. In addition it operates a number of helicopters and fixed wing aircraft. All vessels have DF numbers painted on the bow.

DF 28   6/1991, van Ginderen Collection

AFFAIRES MARITIMES

Note: A force of some 30 patrol ships and craft of varying sizes. The vessels are unarmed and manned by civilians on behalf of the Préfectures Maritimes. Their duties mainly involve navigation and pilotage supervision as well as search and rescue. All have PM numbers painted on the bow and Préfectures Maritime written on the superstructure in the vicinity of the bridge.

PM 30   7/1992, A Sheldon Dupl

GABON

Headquarters' Appointment

Commanding Officer of the Navy:
Captain Major Jean-Léonard Mbini

Bases

Port Gentil, Mayumba

Personnel

(a) 1993: 505 (54 officers)

Coast Guard

Has a number of small inshore patrol launches. Three named *N'Djolé*, *N'Gombé* and *Omboué* are of doubtful operational status but eleven smaller 'vedettes' are in regular service.

Mercantile Marine

Lloyd's Register of Shipping:
29 vessels of 25 171 tons gross

DELETIONS

1990 *N'Guene*, *President A B Bongo* (ex-*Colonel D Dabany*)

PATROL FORCES

2 FRENCH P 400 CLASS (FAST ATTACK CRAFT—PATROL)

Name	No	Builders	Commissioned
GÉNÉRAL d'ARMÉE BA OUMAR	P 07	CMN, Cherbourg	27 June 1988
COLONEL DJOUE DABANY	P 08	CMN, Cherbourg	14 Sep 1990

Displacement, tons: 446 full load
Dimensions, feet (metres): 179 × 26.2 × 8.5 *(54.6 × 8 × 2.5)*
Main machinery: 2 SACM UD 33 V16 M7 diesels; 8000 hp(m) *(5.88 MW)* sustained; 2 shafts; cp props
Speed, knots: 24. **Range, miles:** 4200 at 15 kts
Complement: 32 (4 officers)
Military lift: 20 troops

Guns: 1 Bofors 57 mm/70 SAK 57 Mk 2 (P 07); 75° elevation; 220 rounds/minute to 17 km *(9 nm)*; weight of shell 2.4 kg. Not in P 08 which has a second Oerlikon 20 mm.
2 Giat F2 20 mm (twin) (P 08).
Fire control: CSEE Naja optronic director (P 07).
Radars: Navigation: Racal Decca 1226C; I band.

Programmes: Contract signed May 1985 with CMN Cherbourg. First laid down 2 July 1986, launched 18 December 1987 and arrived in Gabon 6 August 1988 for a local christening ceremony. Second ordered in February 1989 and launched 29 March 1990.
Structure: There is space on the quarterdeck for two MM 40 Exocet surface-to-surface missiles. These craft are similar to the French vessels but with different engines. *Ba Oumar* had twin funnels fitted in 1992, similar to French P 400 class conversions.

GÉNÉRAL d'ARMÉE BA OUMAR   *1988, CMN Cherbourg*

1 FAST ATTACK CRAFT (MISSILE)

Name	No	Builders	Commissioned
GENERAL NAZAIRE BOULINGUI (ex-*President Omar Bongo*)	P 10	Chantiers Navals de l'Estérel	7 Aug 1978

Displacement, tons: 150 full load
Dimensions, feet (metres): 138 × 25.3 × 6.5 *(42 × 7.7 × 1.9)*
Main machinery: 3 SACM 195 V12 CSHR diesels; 5400 hp(m) *(3.97 MW)*; 3 shafts
Speed, knots: 32. **Range, miles:** 1500 at 15 kts
Complement: 20 (3 officers)

Missiles: SSM: 4 Aerospatiale SS 12M; wire-guided to 5.5 km *(3 nm)* subsonic; warhead 30 kg.
Guns: 1 Bofors 40 mm/60; 90° elevation; 300 rounds/minute to 12 km *(6.5 nm)* anti-surface; 4 km *(2.2 nm)* anti-aircraft; weight of shell 0.89 kg.
1 DCN 20 mm; 50° elevation; 800 rounds/minute to 2 km; weight of shell 0.24 kg.
Radars: Navigation: Racal Decca RM1226; I band.

Programmes: Launched 21 November 1977. Engines changed in 1985.
Structure: Triple skinned mahogany hull.

GENERAL NAZAIRE BOULINGUI   *1978, Chantiers Navals de l'Estérel*

AMPHIBIOUS FORCES

1 BATRAL TYPE

Name	No	Builders	Commissioned
PRESIDENT EL HADJ OMAR BONGO	L 05	CMN, Cherbourg	3 Nov 1984

Displacement, tons: 1336 full load
Dimensions, feet (metres): 262.4 × 42.6 × 7.9 *(80 × 13 × 2.4)*
Main machinery: 2 SACM Type 195 V12 CSHR diesels; 3600 hp(m) *(2.65 MW)*; 2 shafts; cp props
Speed, knots: 16. **Range, miles:** 4500 at 13 kts
Complement: 39
Military lift: 188 troops; 12 vehicles; 350 tons cargo
Guns: 1 Bofors 40 mm; 90° elevation; 300 rounds/minute to 12 km *(6.5 nm)* anti-surface; 4 km *(2.2 nm)* anti-aircraft; weight of shell 0.89 kg.
2 Oerlikon 20 mm; 50° elevation; 800 rounds/minute to 2 km; weight of shell 0.24 kg.
2—81 mm mortars. 2 Browning 12.7 mm MGs. 1—7.62 mm MG.
Radars: Navigation: Racal Decca 1226; I band.
Helicopters: Capable of operating up to SA 330 Puma size.

Comment: Sister to French *La Grandière*. Carries one LCVP and one LCP.

BATRAL Type (French number)   *6/1989, Hartmut Ehlers*

1 LCM

Name	No	Builders	Commissioned
MANGA	—	DCAN, Dakar	11 May 1976

Displacement, tons: 150 full load
Dimensions, feet (metres): 78.8 × 21 × 4.2 *(24 × 6.4 × 1.3)*
Main machinery: 2 Poyaud V8-250 diesels; 480 hp(m) *(353 kW)*; 2 shafts
Speed, knots: 8. **Range, miles:** 600 at 5 kts
Complement: 10
Guns: 2 Browning 12.7 mm MGs.
Radars: Navigation: Racal Decca 110; I band.

Comment: Fitted with bow doors.

2 SEA TRUCKS

Comment: Built by Tanguy Marine, Le Havre in 1985. One of 12.2 m with two 165 hp(m) *(121 kW)* engines and one of 10.2 m with one engine.

LAND-BASED MARITIME AIRCRAFT

Note: In addition there are also two EMB 110s.

Numbers/Type: 1 Embraer EMB-111 Bandeirante.
Operational speed: 194 kts *(360 km/h)*.
Service ceiling: 25 500 ft *(7770 m)*.
Range: 1590 nm *(2945 km)*.
Role/Weapon systems: Coastal surveillance and EEZ protection tasks are primary roles. Sensors: APS-128 search radar, limited ECM, searchlight. Weapons: ASV; 8 × 127 mm rockets or 28 × 70 mm rockets.

GENDARMERIE

Note: The Police have a number of 6.8 m LCVPs and Simmoneau 11 m patrol craft delivered in 1989.

SIMMONEAU SM 360   *1989, Simmoneau Marine*

GAMBIA

Headquarters' Appointment

Commander, Marine Unit:
Captain Saho

General

On 1 February 1982 the two countries of Senegal and Gambia united to form the confederation of Senegambia, which included merging the armed forces. Confederation was cancelled on 30 September 1989 and the forces again became national and independent of each other. The patrol craft come under the Marine Unit of the National Army. A Nigerian liaison officer replaced the British in 1992.

Personnel

(a) 1993: 60 officers and men
(b) Voluntary service

Base

Banjul

Mercantile Marine

Lloyd's Register of Shipping:
11 vessels of 2720 tons gross

---

2 Ex-CHINESE SHANGHAI II CLASS (FAST ATTACK CRAFT—GUN)

GUNJUR 101   **BRUFUT** 102

Displacement, tons: 113 standard; 131 full load
Dimensions, feet (metres): 127.3 × 17.4 × 5.2 *(38.8 × 5.3 × 1.6)*
Main machinery: 2 L12-180 diesels (fwd); 2400 hp(m) *(1.76 MW)*; 2 L12-180Z diesels (aft); 1820 hp(m) *(1.34 MW)*; 4 shafts
Speed, knots: 26. **Range, miles:** 700 at 16 kts (on 2 diesels)
Complement: 34
Guns: 6—25 mm/80 (3 twin).
Radars: Surface search: Furuno 1505; I band.

Comment: Built in May 1979 and refitted in China in mid-1988. Delivered as a gift from the PLA(N) on 2 February 1989 and commissioned in May 1989. The 37 mm gun normally mounted aft in this class has been replaced by a boat davit. Both craft need refits in 1993.

JATO   *1/1990, E Grove*

1 FAIREY MARINE LANCE CLASS (COASTAL PATROL CRAFT)

Name	No	Builders	Commissioned
SEA DOG	P 11	Fairey Marine, UK	28 Oct 1976

Displacement, tons: 17 full load
Dimensions, feet (metres): 48.7 × 15.3 × 4.3 *(14.8 × 4.7 × 1.3)*
Main machinery: 2 GM 8V-71TA diesels; 650 hp *(485 kW)* sustained; 2 shafts
Speed, knots: 24. **Range, miles:** 500 at 16 kts
Complement: 9
Guns: 2—7.62 mm MGs (not carried).
Radars: Surface search: Racal Decca 110; I band.

Comment: Delivered 28 October 1976. Unarmed and used for training.

GUNJUR   *1/1990, E Grove*

1 FAIREY MARINE TRACKER 2 CLASS (COASTAL PATROL CRAFT)

Name	No	Builders	Commissioned
JATO	P 12	Fairey Marine, UK	1978

Displacement, tons: 31.5 full load
Dimensions, feet (metres): 65.7 × 17 × 4.8 *(20 × 5.2 × 1.5)*
Main machinery: 2 GM 12V-71TA diesels; 840 hp *(617 kW)* sustained; 2 shafts
Speed, knots: 29. **Range, miles:** 650 at 20 kts
Complement: 11
Guns: 1 Oerlikon 20 mm. 2—7.62 mm MGs.
Radars: Surface search: Racal Decca; I band.

Comment: Hull and superstructure of GRP. Air-conditioned accommodation. The other two of the class returned to Senegal in 1989.

SEA DOG   *1/1990, E Grove*

GEORGIA

General

By early 1993, the Georgian element of the Black Sea Fleet was insufficiently distinct to establish a separate order of battle. Nonetheless Georgia intends to control its own Coast Guard in due course.

Base

Poti

Patrol Ships Based at Poti

1 Grisha I, 1 Grisha V, 1 Turya, 10 Stenka, 2 Muravey. There is also a support ship.

GRISHA V   *1992*

TURYA   *199*

GERMANY

Headquarters' Appointments

Chief of Naval Staff:
　Vice Admiral Hein-Peter Weyher
Chief of Staff:
　Rear Admiral Dirk Horten

Commander-in-Chief

Commander-in-Chief, Fleet:
　Vice Admiral Dieter Franz Braun
Deputy Commander-in-Chief, Fleet:
　Rear Admiral Hans Rudolf Boehmer

Diplomatic Representation

Defence and Naval Attaché in London:
　Rear Admiral Karlheinz Reichert
Naval Assistant in London:
　Commander U P Stickdorn

Personnel

(a) 1993: 32 200 (5430 officers) (includes Naval Air Arm)
(b) 12 months' national service (7680)

Squadron Allocations

Lütjens class, 1st DS; Hamburg class, 2nd DS; 4 Bremen class, 2nd FS; 4 Bremen class, 4th FS.

Naval Air Arm

MFG (Marine Flieger Geschwader)
MFG 1 (Fighter Bomber Wing at Schleswig-Jagel)
　PA 200 Tornado (to be reallocated to the Air Force)
MFG 2 (Fighter Bomber and Reconnaissance Wing at Eggebek)
　PA 200 Tornado
MFG 3 'Graf Zeppelin' (LRMP Wing at Nordholz). To take over the assets of MFG 5
　Breguet Atlantic of which 5 converted for Sigint, Sea Lynx (landbase for embarkation and maintenance)
MFG 5 (SAR and Liaison Wing at Kiel). To be evacuated and returned to civil use in due course
　Sea King Mk 41, Do 28D-2 Skyservant of which 2 converted for pollution control plus 1 Dornier Do 228
MF Hubschraubergruppe (SAR and Liaison Wing at Parow/Stralsund)
　Mi-8 Hip, Mi-14 Haze

Volksmarine

The former GDR Navy ceased to exist after reunification on 3 October 1990. Most of the warships organised into a Coastal Guard Squadron subordinate to the District Command at Rostock were paid off in 1991 and have either been sold or are waiting to be scrapped. A few auxiliaries have been retained.

Bases

C-in-C Fleet: Glücksburg. Flag Officer Naval Command: Rostock.
Baltic: Kiel, Olpenitz (all mine warfare forces in due course), Flensburg*, Eckernförde*, Neustadt*, Warnemunde (all patrol craft in due course)
North Sea: Wilhelmshaven, Borkum*, Emden*.
Naval Arsenal: Wilhelmshaven (all frigates in due course), Kiel (all destroyers and submarines in due course).
Training (other than in Bases above): Bremerhaven, Brake*, Glückstaat, List/Sylt, Plön, Grossenbrode*, Stralsund.

The administration of the bases is vested in the Naval Support Command at Wilhelmshaven. Those marked with an asterisk are to close by 2005 although Flensburg, Eckernförde, Neustadt, Peenmünde and Emden may retain some minor support facilities.

Prefix to Ships' Names

Prefix FGS is used in communications.

Strength of the Fleet (1 June 1993)

Type	Active	Building (Projected)
Submarines—Patrol	20	(12)
Destroyers	6	—
Frigates	8	4 (4)
Fast Attack Craft—Missile	38	—
LCUs	5	—
LCMs	16	—
Minehunters	12	8
Minesweepers—Coastal	16	—
Minesweepers—Inshore	10	—
Minesweepers—Drones	18	—
Diver Support Vessels	1	—
Tenders	3	5
Support Ships	6	—
Replenishment Tankers	6	—
Support Tankers	2	—
Accommodation Ships	5	—
Ammunition Transports	2	—
Mine Transports	1	—
Water Boats	2	—
Tugs—Salvage	5	—
Tugs—Icebreaking	2	—
Tugs—Coastal/Harbour	16	6
Surveillance Ships	3	—
Training Ships	4	—
Sail Training Ships	2	—
TRVs	4	—
Trials Ships	16	—
Miscellaneous	25	(2)
Non-naval Vessels		
Coast Guard Patrol Craft	27	—
Police Patrol Craft	17+	—
Fishery Protection Ships	8	—
Research and Survey Ships	14	—
Army craft	43	—

Future Projects

Building:
4 + (8) submarines to replace the Type 205 and unmodernised Type 206 in late 1990s (early 2000s). Type 212
4 frigates to replace the Type 103 destroyers from 2004 onwards. Type 124
4 combat store ships in early 2000s. Type 702
1 floating dock to replace Schwimmdock B
Note: Projects Type 748, 751 and 752 have all been deferred

Naval Aviation:
12 LRAACA to replace the BR 1150 Atlantic not before 1997
Helicopters to replace Sea King and Sea Lynx after 2000

Weapons:
New SSMs 'Anti-Navire Supersonique' (ANS) for Type 143B, 143A and 123 in late 1990s
262 ASMs 'Kormoran 2' for PA 200 Tornado in early 1990s
58 RAM launchers with 1923 SAMs in 1992-96
4432 SAMs 'Fliegerfaust 2' in 1989-98
New torpedoes for modernised submarines
New influence mines 'SGM 80' in 1990-96

Modernisation

10 FAC Type 143 in mid-1990s including new SSMs
　RAM-ASDM launchers for Types 103(2), 122(2), 123(2), 143(1) 1992-96
Light SAMs 'Fliegerfaust 2' (similar to USSR SA-N-5, with Stinger-SAM) for support ships and minor combatants

Hydrographic Service

This service, under the direction of the Ministry of Transport, is civilian manned with HQ at Hamburg. Survey ships are listed at the end of the section.

Mercantile Marine

Lloyd's Register of Shipping:
　1375 vessels of 5 552 094 tons gross

DELETIONS

Submarines

1991　U 1 (TNSW trials)
1992　U 2
1993　U 9, U 10

Destroyers

1990　Hessen

Frigates

1990　Berlin (ex-GDR)
1991　Rostock (ex-GDR), Halle (ex-GDR)

Corvettes

1990　4 Tarantul I class (ex-GDR)
1991　16 Parchim I class (ex-GDR) (to Indonesia in 1992)
　　　Thetis, Najade (both to Greece)
1992　Hermes, Triton, Theseus (all to Greece)

Light Forces

1990　6 Shershen class (ex-GDR), 14 Libelle class (ex-GDR), 12 Osa I class (ex-GDR)
1992　Iltis, Storch

Mine Warfare Vessels

1990　Rigel, Skorpion, Sirius, Regulus, 23 Kondor II class (ex-GDR) (one to Uruguay) (12 to Indonesia in 1992)
1991　Castor, Flensburg, Tangerhütte, Bitterfeld, Eisleben, Bernau, Eilenburg (last five ex-GDR, last three to Uruguay)
1992　Spica, Schütze, Waage, Freya, Hertha, Nymphe, Nixe, Pollux, Mars, Fulda, Ariadne, Vineta, Amazone, Gazelle, Hansa, Sömmerda (to Indonesia)

Landing Craft

1990　12 Frosch I class (ex-GDR), 2 Frosch II class (ex-GDR) (all to Indonesia in 1992)
1991　LCM 1-11, Barbe, Delphin, Dorsch, Felchen, Forelle, Makrele (all to Greece)
1992　Rochen, Brasse, Muräne, Butt, Karpfen, Stör, Tümmler, Wels, Inger

Auxiliaries

1990　Deutschland, Mosel, 4 Support Ships (ex-GDR) (Jasmund to Spain in 1992)
1991　Saar, Lahn, Werra, Sachsenwald, Odin, Wotan, Wittow, Mönchgut, Darss, Kühlung, Werdau (last five ex-GDR), Coburg (to Greece)
1992　Eifel, Harz, Rhein (old), Elbe (old), Havelland (ex-GDR), Kölpinsee (ex-GDR), Förde, Jade
1993　Offenburg

Miscellaneous

1990　TF 106 and TF 108, TF 4, Mellum, Trischen, Knechtsand (old), Scharhörn (old), Hans Bürckner, Lütje Hörn (old) (all to Greece)
　　　30+ Tugs and Miscellaneous (ex-GDR)
1991　EF 3, FW 4 (to Turkey), FW 6 (to Greece), Kollicker Ort (ex-GDR), KW 3, Otto Von Guericke, Zingst (last two to Uruguay)
1992　H 13, TF 2, Ummanz, Havel, Oder, Saale (last four ex-GDR)

Coast Guard

1990　Uelzen, 9 Kondor I class (ex-GDR) (one to Guinea Bissau)
1992　6 Kondor I class (ex-GDR) (four to Tunisia, two to Malta), 9 Bremse class (ex-GDR) (five to Tunisia, two to Malta, two to Jordan)

PENNANT LIST

Submarines

S 170	U 21
S 171	U 22
S 172	U 23
S 173	U 24
S 174	U 25
S 175	U 26
S 176	U 27
S 177	U 28
S 178	U 29
S 179	U 30
S 190	U 11
S 191	U 12
S 192	U 13
S 193	U 14
S 194	U 15
S 195	U 16
S 196	U 17
S 197	U 18
S 198	U 19
S 199	U 20

Destroyers

D 181	Hamburg
D 182	Schleswig-Holstein (old)
D 183	Bayern (old)
D 185	Lütjens
D 186	Mölders
D 187	Rommel

Frigates

F 207	Bremen
F 208	Niedersachsen
F 209	Rheinland-Pfalz
F 210	Emden
F 211	Köln
F 212	Karlsruhe
F 213	Augsburg
F 214	Lübeck
F 215	Brandenburg (bldg)
F 216	Schleswig-Holstein (new) (bldg)
F 217	Bayern (new) (bldg)
F 218	Mecklenburg-Vorpommern (bldg)

Light Forces

P 6111	S 61 Albatros
P 6112	S 62 Falke
P 6113	S 63 Geier
P 6114	S 64 Bussard
P 6115	S 65 Sperber
P 6116	S 66 Greif
P 6117	S 67 Kondor
P 6118	S 68 Seeadler
P 6119	S 69 Habicht
P 6120	S 70 Kormoran
P 6121	S 71 Gepard
P 6122	S 72 Puma
P 6123	S 73 Hermelin
P 6124	S 74 Nerz
P 6125	S 75 Zobel
P 6126	S 76 Frettchen
P 6127	S 77 Dachs
P 6128	S 78 Ozelot
P 6129	S 79 Wiesel
P 6130	S 80 Hyäne
P 6141	S 41 Tiger
P 6143	S 43 Luchs
P 6144	S 44 Marder
P 6145	S 45 Leopard
P 6146	S 46 Fuchs
P 6147	S 47 Jaguar
P 6148	S 48 Löwe
P 6149	S 49 Wolf
P 6150	S 50 Panther
P 6151	S 51 Häher
P 6153	S 53 Pelikan
P 6154	S 54 Elster
P 6155	S 55 Alk
P 6156	S 56 Dommel
P 6157	S 57 Weihe
P 6158	S 58 Pinguin
P 6159	S 59 Reiher
P 6160	S 60 Kranich

232 GERMANY / Introduction — Submarines

Mine Warfare Forces

No	Name
M 1050	TB 1
M 1053	Stier
M 1060	Weiden
M 1061	Rottweil (bldg)
M 1062	Sulzbach-Rosenberg (bldg) (new)
M 1063	Bad Bevensen (bldg)
M 1064	Grömitz (bldg)
M 1065	Dillingen (bldg)
M 1066	Frankenthal
M 1067	Bad Rappenau (bldg)
M 1068	Datteln (bldg)
M 1069	Homburg (bldg)
M 1070	Göttingen
M 1071	Koblenz
M 1072	Lindau
M 1073	Schleswig
M 1074	Tübingen
M 1075	Wetzlar
M 1076	Paderborn
M 1077	Weilheim
M 1078	Cuxhaven
M 1079	Düren
M 1080	Marburg
M 1081	Konstanz
M 1082	Wolfsburg
M 1083	Ulm
M 1085	Minden
M 1087	Völklingen
M 1090	Pegnitz
M 1091	Kulmbach
M 1092	Hameln
M 1093	Auerbach
M 1094	Ensdorf
M 1095	Überherrn
M 1096	Passau
M 1097	Laboe
M 1098	Siegburg
M 1099	Herten
M 2658	Frauenlob
M 2659	Nautilus
M 2660	Gefion
M 2661	Medusa
M 2662	Undine
M 2663	Minerva
M 2664	Diana
M 2665	Loreley
M 2666	Atlantis
M 2667	Acheron

Amphibious Forces

No	Name
L 760	Flunder
L 762	Lachs
L 763	Plötze
L 765	Schlei
L 769	Zander
LCM 12	Sprotte
LCM 13	Sardine
LCM 14	Sardelle
LCM 15	Hering
LCM 16	Orfe
LCM 18	Saibling
LCM 19	Stint
LCM 20	Aesche
L 780	LCM 21 Hummer
L 781	LCM 22 Krill
L 782	LCM 23 Krabbe
L 783	LCM 24 Auster
L 784	LCM 25 Muschel
L 785	LCM 26 Koralle
L 786	LCM 27 Garnele
L 787	LCM 28 Languste

Support Ships and Auxiliaries

No	Name
A 50	Alster
A 52	Oste
A 53	Oker
A 60	Gorch Fock
A 63	Main (old)
A 69	Donau (old)
A 511	Elbe
A 512	Mosel (bldg)
A 513	Rhein (bldg)
A 514	Werra (bldg)
A 515	Main (new) (bldg)
A 516	Donau (new) (bldg)
A 1400	Holnis
A 1401	Eisvogel
A 1402	Eisbär
A 1403	FW 1
A 1405	FW 5
A 1407	Wittensee
A 1408	SP 1
A 1409	Wilhelm Pullwer
A 1410	Walther von Ledebur
A 1411	Lüneburg
A 1413	Freiburg
A 1414	Glücksburg
A 1415	Saarburg
A 1416	Nienburg
A 1418	Meersburg
A 1424	Walchensee
A 1425	Ammersee
A 1426	Tegernsee
A 1427	Westensee
A 1435	Westerwald
A 1436	Odenwald
A 1438	Steigerwald
A 1439	Baltrum
A 1440	Juist
A 1441	Langeoog
A 1442	Spessart
A 1443	Rhön
A 1450	Planet
A 1451	Wangerooge
A 1452	Spiekeroog
A 1455	Norderney
A 1457	Helgoland
A 1458	Fehmarn
Y 811	Knurrhahn
Y 812	Lütje Hörn
Y 814	Knechtsand
Y 815	Scharhorn
Y 816	Vogelsand
Y 817	Nordstrand
Y 819	Langeness
Y 820	Sylt
Y 821	Föhr
Y 822	Amrum
Y 823	Neuwerk
Y 827	KW 15
Y 830	KW 16
Y 832	KW 18
Y 834	Nordwind
Y 842	Schwimmdock A
Y 844	Barbara
Y 845	KW 17
Y 846	KW 20
Y 851	TF 1
Y 853	TF 3
Y 855	TF 5
Y 856	TF 6
Y 857	H 11
Y 860	Schwedeneck
Y 861	Kronsort
Y 862	Helmsand
Y 863	Stollergrund
Y 864	Mittelgrund
Y 865	Kalkgrund
Y 866	Breitgrund
Y 867	Bant
Y 871	Heinz Roggenkamp
Y 875	Hiev
Y 876	Griep
Y 879	Schwimmdock B
Y 890	Vogtland
Y 891	Altmark
Y 893	Uckermark
Y 894	Borde
Y 895	Wische
Y 1643	Bottsand
Y 1644	Eversand
Y 1651	Koos
Y 1656	Wustrow
Y 1657	Fleesensee
Y 1658	Dranske
Y 1670	MT 1
Y 1671	AK 1
Y 1672	AK 3
Y 1673	AK 5
Y 1674	AM 6
Y 1675	AM 8
Y 1676	MA 2
Y 1677	MA 3
Y 1679	AM 7
Y 1680	Neuende
Y 1681	Heppens
Y 1682	Ellerbek
Y 1683	AK 6
Y 1684	Peter Bachmann
Y 1686	AK 2
Y 1687	Borby
Y 1689	Bums
Y 1690	LP 3

SUBMARINES

2 TYPE 205

Name	No	Builders	Laid down	Launched	Commissioned
U 11	S 190	Howaldtswerke, Kiel	1 Apr 1966	9 Feb 1968	21 June 1968
U 12	S 191	Howaldtswerke, Kiel	1 Sep 1966	10 Sep 1968	14 Jan 1969

Displacement, tons: 419 surfaced; 450 dived
Dimensions, feet (metres): 144 × 15.1 × 14.1 *(43.9 × 4.6 × 4.3)*
Main machinery: Diesel-electric; 2 MTU 12V 493 AZ80 GA 31L diesels; 1200 hp(m) *(882 kW)* sustained; 2 alternators; 810 kW; 1 Siemens motor; 1800 hp(m) *(1.32 MW)* sustained; 1 shaft
Speed, knots: 10 surfaced; 17 dived
Complement: 22 (4 officers)

Torpedoes: 8—21 in *(533 mm)* tubes. AEG Seeal; wire-guided; active homing to 13 km *(7 nm)* at 35 kts; passive homing to 28 km *(15 nm)* at 23 kts; warhead 260 kg; no reloads.
Mines: 16 in place of torpedoes.
Countermeasures: ESM: Radar warning.
Fire control: Signaal Mk 8.
Radars: Surface search: Thompson-CSF Calypso II; I band.
Sonars: Atlas Elektronik SRS M1H; passive/active search and attack; high frequency.

Programmes: Built in floating docks. First submarines designed and built by West Germany after the Second World War.
Structure: Diving depth, 159 m *(490 ft)*. Hulls of steel alloys with non-magnetic properties. U 11 (Type 205A) converted as a padded target in 1988; U 12 (Type 205B) acts as a sonar trials platform.
Operational: The boats are trimmed by the stern to load through the bow caps.
Sales: U 1 decommissioned 29 November 1991 and is on loan to TNSW for trials of a 250 kW closed cycle diesel developed by Carlton Deep Sea Systems (Cosworth) and TNSW.

U 12   6/1992, Stefan Terzibaschitsch

U 11   2/1992, Horst Dehns

Submarines / GERMANY 233

0 + (4) TYPE 212

Displacement, tons: 1320 surfaced; 1800 dived
Dimensions, feet (metres): 174.5 × 22.3 × 19 *(53.2 × 6.8 × 5.8)*
Main machinery: Diesel-electric; 1 MTU 16V 396 diesel; 1440 hp(m) *(1.06 MW)*; 1 Siemens Permasyn motor; 2400 hp(m) *(1.76 MW)*; 1 shaft; HDW fuel cell (AIP); Sodium Sulphide high energy batteries
Speed, knots: 20 dived; 12 surfaced
Complement: 23 + 5 training

Torpedoes: 6 or 8—21 in *(533 mm)* bow tubes; water ram discharge; DMT (formerly AEG) Seeal 3 or Seehecht.
Mines: Abeking & Rasmussen external belt.
Countermeasures: ESM: TST FL 1800U; radar warning.
Fire control: NFT (formerly Kongsberg) MFI-90U weapons control system.
Radars: Navigation: Kelvin Hughes 1007; I band.
Sonars: Atlas Elektronik DBQS-21DG; passive ranging and intercept.
Atlas Elektronik DBQS-90FTC; flank and clip-on passive towed array.
Ferranti FMS 52; high frequency; active.

Programmes: Design phase completed in 1990 by IKL in conjunction with HDW and TNSW. The HDW/TNSW consortium expects to contract the building of the first batch of four in 1995. First of class to enter service in 1999 if the project survives defence cutbacks in 1993.
Structure: Primarily equipped for Baltic and North Sea operations with a hybrid fuel cell/battery propulsion based on the HDW prototype successfully evaluated in *U1* in 1988-89. This prototype had 16 fuel cells each generating 25 kW of power. It is hoped to achieve a five-fold increase in power by replacing the liquid electrolyte with solid polymer technology. The submarine is designed with a partial double hull which has a larger diameter forward. This is joined to the after end by a short conical section which houses the fuel cell plant. Two LOX tanks and 38 Hydrogen cylinders are carried around the circumference of the smaller hull section.

TYPE 212 (artist's impression) *1990, HDW*

6 TYPE 206 and 12 TYPE 206A

Name	No	Builders	Laid down	Launched	Commissioned
U 13	S 192	Howaldtswerke, Kiel	15 Nov 1969	28 Sep 1971	19 Apr 1973
U 14	S 193	Rheinstahl Nordseewerke, Emden	1 Mar 1970	1 Feb 1972	19 Apr 1973
U 15*	S 194	Howaldtswerke, Kiel	1 June 1970	15 June 1972	17 July 1974
U 16*	S 195	Rheinstahl Nordseewerke, Emden	1 Nov 1970	29 Aug 1972	9 Nov 1973
U 17*	S 196	Howaldtswerke, Kiel	1 Oct 1970	10 Oct 1972	28 Nov 1973
U 18*	S 197	Rheinstahl Nordseewerke, Emden	1 Apr 1971	31 Oct 1972	19 Dec 1973
U 19	S 198	Howaldtswerke, Kiel	5 Jan 1971	15 Dec 1972	9 Nov 1973
U 20	S 199	Rheinstahl Nordseewerke, Emden	3 Sep 1971	16 Jan 1973	24 May 1974
U 21	S 170	Howaldtswerke, Kiel	15 Apr 1971	9 Mar 1973	16 Aug 1974
U 22*	S 171	Rheinstahl Nordseewerke, Emden	18 Nov 1971	27 Mar 1973	26 July 1974
U 23*	S 172	Rheinstahl Nordseewerke, Emden	5 Mar 1973	25 May 1974	2 May 1975
U 24*	S 173	Rheinstahl Nordseewerke, Emden	20 Mar 1972	26 June 1973	16 Oct 1974
U 25*	S 174	Howaldtswerke, Kiel	1 July 1971	23 May 1973	14 June 1974
U 26*	S 175	Rheinstahl Nordseewerke, Emden	14 July 1972	20 Nov 1973	13 Mar 1975
U 27	S 176	Howaldtswerke, Kiel	1 Oct 1971	21 Aug 1973	16 Oct 1974
U 28*	S 177	Rheinstahl Nordseewerke, Emden	4 Oct 1972	22 Jan 1974	18 Dec 1974
U 29*	S 178	Howaldtswerke, Kiel	10 Jan 1972	5 Nov 1973	27 Nov 1974
U 30*	S 179	Rheinstahl Nordseewerke, Emden	5 Dec 1972	26 Mar 1974	13 Mar 1975

* Type 206A (see *Modernisation*)

Displacement, tons: 450 surfaced; 498 dived
Dimensions, feet (metres): 159.4 × 15.1 × 14.8 *(48.6 × 4.6 × 4.5)*
Main machinery: Diesel-electric; 2 MTU 12V 493 AZ80 GA 31L diesels; 1200 hp(m) *(882 kW)* sustained; 2 alternators; 810 kW; 1 Siemens motor; 1800 hp(m) *(1.32 MW)* sustained; 1 shaft
Speed, knots: 10 surfaced; 17 dived
Range, miles: 4500 at 5 kts surfaced
Complement: 22 (4 officers)

Torpedoes: 8—21 in *(533 mm)* bow tubes. AEG Seeschlenge (Type 206); wire-guided; active homing to 6 km *(3.3 nm)* at 35 kts; passive homing to 14 km *(7.6 nm)* at 23 kts; warhead 100 kg.
DMT (ex-AEG) Seeal 3 (Type 206A); wire-guided; active homing to 13 km *(7 nm)* at 35 kts; passive homing to 28 km *(15 nm)* at 23 kts; warhead 260 kg.
Mines: GRP container secured outside hull each side. Each container holds 12 mines, carried in addition to the normal torpedo or mine armament (16 in place of torpedoes).
Countermeasures: ESM: Radar warning.

Fire control: Signaal Mk 8 (Type 206). CSU 83 (Type 206A).
Radars: Surface search: Thomson-CSF Calypso II; I band; range 31 km *(17 nm)* for 10 m² target.
Sonars: Thomson Sintra DUUX 2; passive ranging.
Atlas Elektronik 410 A4 (Type 206); Atlas Elektronik DBQS-21D (Type 206A); passive/active search and attack; medium frequency.

Programmes: Authorised on 7 June 1969 from Howaldtswerke Deutsche Werft (8) and Rheinstahl Nordseewerke, Emden (10).
Modernisation: Mid-life conversion of 12 of the class (Type 206A) was a very extensive one, including the installation of new sensors (sonar DBQS-21D with training simulator STU-5), periscopes, weapon control system (LEWA), weapons (torpedo Seeal), GPS navigation, and a comprehensive refitting of the propulsion system, as well as habitability improvements. Conversion work was shared between Thyssen Nordseewerke *(U 23, 30, 22, 27, 15, 26)* at Emden and HDW *(U 29, 16, 25, 28, 17, 18)* at Kiel. The work started in mid-1987 and completed in February 1992.

Structure: Type 206 hulls are built of high-tensile non-magnetic steel. In this the West German submarines are unique. Modernised Type 206A submarines have a slight difference in superstructure shape.
Operational: First squadron *(Meersburg)*: four Type 205; six unmodernised Type 206; based at Kiel.
Third squadron: 12 Type 206A; based at Eckernförde.

6/1992, Maritime Photographic

U 30 *5/1992, Horst Dehnst*

DESTROYERS

3 Ex-US MODIFIED CHARLES F ADAMS CLASS (TYPE 103B) (DDGs)

Name	No	Builders	Laid down	Launched	Commissioned
LÜTJENS (ex-US DDG 28)	D 185	Bath Iron Works Corporation	1 Mar 1966	11 Aug 1967	22 Mar 1969
MÖLDERS (ex-US DDG 29)	D 186	Bath Iron Works Corporation	12 Apr 1966	13 Apr 1968	20 Sep 1969
ROMMEL (ex-US DDG 30)	D 187	Bath Iron Works Corporation	22 Aug 1967	1 Feb 1969	2 May 1970

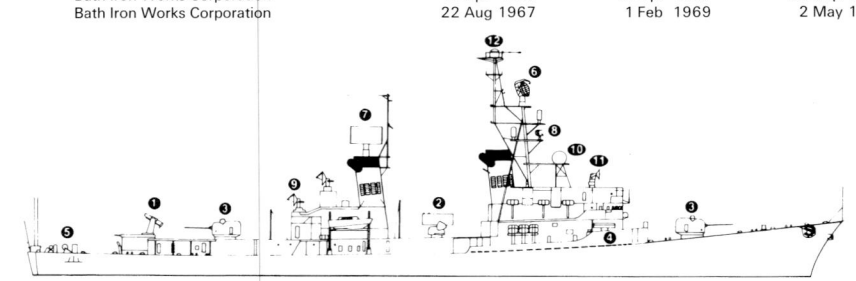

MÖLDERS   (Scale 1 : 1200), Ian Sturton

Displacement, tons: 3370 standard; 4500 full load
Dimensions, feet (metres): 437 × 47 × 20
  (133.2 × 14.3 × 6.1)
Main machinery: 4 Combustion Engineering boilers; 1200 psi
  (84.4 kg/cm sq); 950°F *(510°C)*; 2 turbines; 70 000 hp *(52.2 MW)*; 2 shafts
Speed, knots: 32. **Range, miles:** 4500 at 20 kts
Complement: 337 (19 officers)

Missiles: SSM: McDonnell Douglas Harpoon; active radar homing to 130 km *(70 nm)* at 0.9 Mach; warhead 227 kg. Combined Mk 13 single-arm launcher with SAM system ❶.
  SAM: GDC Pomona Standard SM-1MR; Mk 13 Mod 0 launcher; command guidance; semi-active radar homing to 46 km *(25 nm)* at 2 Mach; 40 missiles—combined SSM and SAM.
  2 RAM 21 cell Mk 49 launchers being fitted; passive IR/anti-radiation homing to 9.6 km *(5.2 nm)* at 2 Mach; warhead 9.1 kg.
A/S: Honeywell ASROC Mk 112 octuple launcher ❷; inertial guidance to 1.6-10 km *(1-5.4 nm)*; payload Mk 46 torpedo.
Guns: 2 FMC 5 in *(127 mm)*/54 Mk 42 Mod 10 automatic ❸; 65° elevation; 20 rounds/minute to 23 km *(12.4 nm)* anti-surface; 15 km *(8 nm)* anti-aircraft; weight of shell 32 kg.
Torpedoes: 6—324 mm US Mk 32 (2 triple) tubes ❹. Honeywell Mk 46; anti-submarine; active/passive homing to 11 km *(5.9 nm)* at 40 kts; warhead 44 kg.
Depth charges: 1 projector ❺.
Countermeasures: Decoys: Loral Hycor Mk 36 SRBOC 6-barrelled chaff launcher; range 1-4 km *(0.6-2.2 nm)*.
  ESM/ECM: AEG FL-1800S; radar intercept and jammer. To be replaced by Stage II in 1995.
Combat data systems: SATIR 1 action data automation; Link 11. SATCOM to be fitted.
Fire control: Mk 86 GFCS. Mk 74 MFCS.
Radars: Air search: Lockheed SPS 40 ❻; E/F band; range 320 km *(175 nm)*.
  Hughes SPS 52 ❼; 3D; E/F band; range 439 km *(240 nm)*.
  Surface search: Raytheon/Sylvania SPS 10 ❽; G band.
  Fire control: Two Raytheon SPG 51 ❾; G/I band (for missiles).
  Lockheed SPQ 9 ❿; I/J band; range 37 km *(20 nm)*.
  Lockheed SPG 60 ⓫; I/J band; range 110 km *(60 nm)*.
Tacan: URN 20 ⓬.
Sonars: Atlas Elektronik DSQS 21B; hull-mounted; active search and attack; medium frequency.
Programmes: Modified to suit West German requirements and practice. 1965 contract.
Modernisation: The Type 103B modernisation and other modifications included:
  (a) Installation of one single-arm Mk 13 launcher for Standard SAM and Harpoon SSM.
  (b) Improved fire control with digital in place of analogue computers.
  (c) Higher superstructure abaft bridge with SPG 60 and SPQ 9 on a mast platform.

Carried out by Naval Arsenal, Kiel and Howaldtswerke, Kiel: *Mölders* completed 29 March 1984, *Rommel* 26 July 1985, *Lütjens* 16 December 1986. RAM launchers are being fitted in front of the bridge and aft of the Mk 13 launcher. First in *Mölders* in late 1992. EW update in 1995/96.

Structure: Some differences from Charles F Adams in W/T aerials and general outline, particularly the funnels.
Operational: These ships are planned to have a life of at least 30 years.

MÖLDERS   3/1992, F Gámez

3 HAMBURG CLASS (TYPE 101A)

Name	No	Builders	Laid down	Launched	Commissioned
HAMBURG	D 181	H C Stülcken Sohn, Hamburg	29 Jan 1959	26 Mar 1960	23 Mar 1964
SCHLESWIG-HOLSTEIN	D 182	H C Stülcken Sohn, Hamburg	20 Aug 1959	20 Aug 1960	12 Oct 1964
BAYERN	D 183	H C Stülcken Sohn, Hamburg	14 Sep 1960	14 Aug 1962	6 July 1965

Displacement, tons: 3340 standard; 4680 full load
Dimensions, feet (metres): 438.5 × 44 × 20.3
  (133.7 × 13.4 × 6.2)
Main machinery: 4 Wahodag boilers; 910 psi *(64 kg/cm sq)*; 860°F *(460°C)*; 2 Wahodag turbines; 68 000 hp *(51 MW)*; 2 shafts
Speed, knots: 34. **Range, miles:** 6000 at 13 kts; 920 at 34 kts
Complement: 268 (19 officers)

Missiles: SSM: 4 Aerospatiale MM 38 Exocet (2 twin) launchers ❶; inertial cruise; active radar homing to 42 km *(23 nm)* at 0.9 Mach; warhead 165 kg; sea-skimmer.
Guns: 3 DCN 3.9 in *(100 mm)*/55 Mod 1954 ❷; 80° elevation; 60-80 rounds/minute to 17 km *(9 nm)* anti-surface; 8 km *(4.4 nm)* anti-aircraft; weight of shell 13.5 kg.
  8 Breda 40 mm/70 (4 twin) ❸; 85° elevation; 300 rounds/minute to 12.5 km *(6.8 nm)*; weight of shell 0.96 kg.
Torpedoes: 4—21 in *(533 mm)* single tubes ❹.
A/S mortars: 2 Bofors 375 mm 4-barrelled trainable mortars ❺; automatic loading; range 1600 m.
Depth charges: 2 projectors ❻; DC rails.
Mines: Can lay mines.
Countermeasures: Decoys: 2 Breda 105 mm SCLAR; 20 barrels per launcher; chaff to 5 km *(2.7 nm)*; illuminants to 12 km *(6.6 nm)*.
ESM: WLR-6; radar warning.
Fire control: Signaal M 45 series.
Radars: Air search: Signaal LW 04 ❼; D band; range 219 km *(120 nm)* for 2 m² target.
  Air/surface search: Signaal DA 08 ❽; F band; range 204 km *(110 nm)* for 2 m² target.
  Surface search: Signaal ZW 01 ❾; I/J band.
  Navigation: Kelvin Hughes 14/9; I band.
  Fire control: Three Signaal M 45 ❿; I/J band; short range.
Sonars: Atlas Elektronik ELAC 1BV; hull-mounted; active search and attack; medium frequency.

Modernisation: Replacement of 100 mm gun by four MM 38 Exocet, 40 mm Breda/Bofors guns and LW 02 radar by LW 04. Two extra A/S torpedo tubes were also added. *Hamburg* completed modernisation mid-1976; *Schleswig-Holstein* February 1977 and *Bayern* November 1977. During refit bridges were re-modelled. There are no plans to fit RAM and further limited

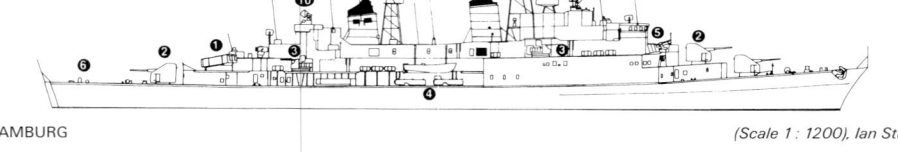

HAMBURG   (Scale 1 : 1200), Ian Sturton

HAMBURG   6/1992, Giorgio Arra

modernisation has been shelved. Due to be replaced by the Type 123 class. *Bayern* planned to pay off in December 1993

FRIGATES

Note: Four Type 124 air defence ships will be needed from 2004 onwards to replace the Lütjens class. A collaborative design with the Netherlands and Spain is evolving with a common AAW system based on the Evolved Seasparrow missile.

8 BREMEN CLASS (TYPE 122)

Name	No	Builders	Laid down	Launched	Commissioned
BREMEN	F 207	Bremer Vulkan	9 July 1979	27 Sep 1979	7 May 1982
NIEDERSACHSEN	F 208	AG Weser/Bremer Vulkan	9 Nov 1979	9 June 1980	15 Oct 1982
RHEINLAND-PFALZ	F 209	Blohm & Voss/Bremer Vulkan	29 Sep 1979	3 Sep 1980	9 May 1983
EMDEN	F 210	Thyssen Nordseewerke, Emden/Bremer Vulkan	23 June 1980	17 Dec 1980	7 Oct 1983
KÖLN	F 211	Blohm & Voss/Bremer Vulkan	16 June 1980	29 May 1981	19 Oct 1984
KARLSRUHE	F 212	Howaldtswerke, Kiel/Bremer Vulkan	10 Mar 1981	8 Jan 1982	19 Apr 1984
AUGSBURG	F 213	Bremer Vulkan	4 Apr 1987	17 Sep 1987	3 Oct 1989
LÜBECK	F 214	Thyssen Nordseewerke, Emden/Bremer Vulkan	1 June 1987	15 Oct 1987	19 Mar 1990

Displacement, tons: 3600 full load
Dimensions, feet (metres): 426.4 × 47.6 × 21.3 *(130 × 14.5 × 6.5)*
Main machinery: CODOG; 2 GE LM 2500 gas turbines; 51 000 hp *(38 MW)* sustained; 2 MTU 20V 956 TB92 diesels; 11 070 hp(m) *(8.14 MW)* sustained; 2 shafts; cp props
Speed, knots: 30; 20 on diesels. **Range, miles:** 4000 at 18 kts
Complement: 207 (aircrew 18)

Missiles: SSM: 8 McDonnell Douglas Harpoon (2 quad) launchers ❶; active radar homing to 130 km *(70 nm)* at 0.9 Mach; warhead 227 kg.
SAM: 16 Raytheon NATO Sea Sparrow; Mk 29 octuple launcher ❷; semi-active radar homing to 14.6 km *(8 nm)* at 2.5 Mach; warhead 39 kg.
2 GDC RAM 21 cell point-defence systems (to be fitted on hangar roof 1993-96) ❸; passive IR/anti-radiation homing to 9.6 km *(5.2 nm)* at 2 Mach; warhead 9.1 kg. Goalkeeper fitted as a contingency in three of the class in 1991.
Guns: 1 OTO Melara 3 in *(76 mm)*/62 Mk 75 ❹; 85° elevation; 85 rounds/minute to 16 km *(8.6 nm)* anti-surface; 12 km *(6.5 nm)* anti-aircraft; weight of shell 6 kg.
Torpedoes: 4—324 mm Mk 32 (2 twin) tubes ❺. 8 Honeywell Mk 46 Mod 1; anti-submarine; active/passive homing to 11 km *(5.9 nm)* at 40 kts; warhead 44 kg.
Countermeasures: Decoys: 4 Loral Hycor SRBOC ❻ 6-barrelled fixed Mk 36; chaff and IR flares to 4 km *(2.2 nm)*.
SLQ 25 Nixie; towed torpedo decoy. Prairie bubble noise reduction.
ESM/ECM: AEG FL 1800 ❼; radar warning and jammers. To be replaced by TST 1800S by 1994.
Combat data systems: SATIR action data automation; Link 11; SCOT 1A SATCOM ❽ (in some).
Fire control: Signaal WM 25/STIR.
Radars: Air/surface search: Signaal DA 08 ❾; F band; range 204 km *(110 nm)* for 2 m² target.
Navigation: SMA 3 RM 20; I band; range 73 km *(40 nm)*.
Fire control: Signaal WM 25 ❿; I/J band; range 46 km *(25 nm)*.
Signaal STIR ⓫; I/J/K band; range 140 km *(76 nm)* for 1 m² target.
Sonars: Atlas Elektronik DSQS 21 BZ (BO); hull-mounted; active search and attack; medium frequency.

Helicopters: 2 Westland Sea Lynx Mk 88 ⓬.

Programmes: Approval given in early 1976 for first six of this class, a modification of the Netherlands Kortenaer class. Replaced the deleted Fletcher and Köln classes. Equipment ordered February 1986 after order placed 6 December 1985 for last pair. Hulls and some engines are provided in the five building yards. Ships are then towed to the prime contractor Bremer Vulkan where weapon systems and electronics are fitted and trials conducted. The three names for F210-212 were changed from the names of Länder to take the well known town names of the Köln class as they were paid off.
Modernisation: RAM to be fitted from 1993; first in F 208. Updated EW fit from 1994.
Operational: Form 2nd and 4th Frigate Squadrons. Three containerised SCOT 1A terminals acquired in 1988 and when fitted are mounted on the hangar roof. Dutch Goalkeeper CIWS was installed on the port side of the hangar roof in F 207, 208 and 212 as a short-term contingency in 1991.

BREMEN *(Scale 1 : 1200), Ian Sturton*

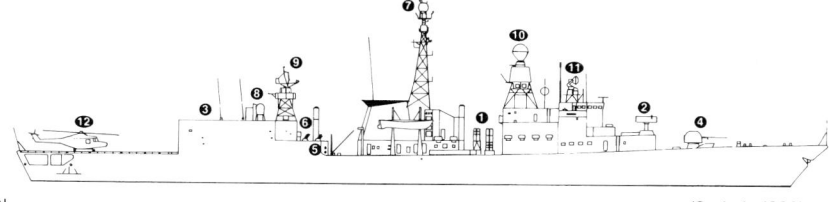

NIEDERSACHSEN *8/1992, H M Steele*

RHEINLAND-PFALZ *7/1992, Maritime Photographic*

236 GERMANY / Frigates — Land-based maritime aircraft (front line)

0 + 4 BRANDENBURG CLASS (TYPE 123)

Name	No	Builders	Laid down	Launched	Commissioned
BRANDENBURG	F 215	Blohm & Voss, Hamburg	20 Jan 1992	28 Aug 1992	Dec 1994
SCHLESWIG-HOLSTEIN	F 216	Howaldtswerke, Kiel	July 1993	June 1994	Dec 1995
BAYERN	F 217	Thyssen Nordseewerke, Emden	1 Mar 1993	July 1994	May 1996
MECKLENBURG-VORPOMMERN	F 218	Blohm & Voss/Bremer Vulkan	May 1994	Nov 1994	Nov 1996

Displacement, tons: 4490 full load
Dimensions, feet (metres): 455.7 oa; 417.7 wl × 54.8 × 14.4 *(138.9; 126.1 × 16.7 × 4.4)*
Main machinery: CODOG; 2 GE LM 2500 gas turbines; 51 000 hp *(38 MW)* sustained; 2 MTU 20V 956 TB92 diesels; 11 070 hp(m) *(8.14 MW)* sustained; 2 shafts; cp props
Speed, knots: 29; 18 on diesels. **Range, miles:** 4000 at 18 kts
Complement: 197 plus 22 aircrew

Missiles: SSM: 4 Aerospatiale MM 38 Exocet ❶ (from Type 101A); later ANS (if not cancelled).
SAM: Martin Marietta VLS Mk 41 ❷ for 16 NATO Sea Sparrow.
2 RAM 21 cell Mk 49 launchers ❸.
Guns: 1 OTO Melara 76 mm/62 ❹.
Torpedoes: 4—324 mm Mk 32 (2 twin) tubes ❺; anti-submarine. Honeywell Mk 46; anti-submarine.
Countermeasures: Decoys: 2 Breda SCLAR ❻.
ESM/ECM: TST FL 1800S Stage II; intercept and jammers.
Combat data systems: SATIR action data automation with Unisys UYK 43 computer; Link 11.
Fire control: Signaal MWCS.
Radars: Air search: Signaal LW 08 ❼; D band.
Air/Surface search ❽: Signaal SMART; 3D; F band.
Fire control: Two Signaal STIR 180 trackers ❾.
Navigation: Two Raypath; I band.
Sonars: Atlas Elektronik DSQS 23BZ; hull-mounted; medium frequency.
Towed array (provision only).

Helicopters: 2 Sea Lynx Mk 88 ❿.

Programmes: Formerly Deutschland class. Four ordered 28 June 1989. Developed by Blohm & Voss whose design was selected in October 1988. To replace Hamburg class. First metal cut 5 February 1991.
Structure: The design is a mixture of MEKO and improved serviceability Type 122 having the same propulsion as the Type 122. Contemporary stealth features. All steel. Fin stabilisers.

BRANDENBURG (Scale 1 : 1200), Ian Sturton

BRANDENBURG 8/1992, Michael Nitz

BRANDENBURG (artist's impression) 1988, Jochen Sachse

SHIPBORNE AIRCRAFT

Numbers/Type: 19 Westland Sea Lynx Mk 88.
Operational speed: 125 kts *(232 km/h)*.
Service ceiling: 12 500 ft *(3010 m)*.
Range: 320 nm *(593 km)*.
Role/Weapon systems: Shipborne ASW/ASV role in support of coastal defence roles and North/Baltic Seas anti-submarine warfare. Sensors: Ferranti Sea Spray Mk 1 radar, ECM and Bendix AQS-18 dipping sonar. Weapons: ASW; up to 2 × Mk 46 torpedoes or depth charges. ASV; possible update.

LAND-BASED MARITIME AIRCRAFT (FRONT LINE)

Note: 13 Mi-8 Hip retained for SAR and liaison duties until due next major inspection (latest 1994). Mi-14 Haze taken out of service in 1992.

SEA LYNX 1991, German Navy

HIP 6/1992, Hartmut Ehler

Numbers/Type: 22 Westland Sea King Mk 41 KWS.
Operational speed: 140 kts *(260 km/h)*.
Service ceiling: 10 500 ft *(3200 m)*.
Range: 630 nm *(1165 km)*.
Role/Weapon systems: Role change from primary combat rescue helicopter to ASV started in 1988 with new camouflage appearance and an update programme by MBB with BAe/Ferranti support which completed in 1992. Sensors: Ferranti Sea Spray Mk 3 radar, Link 11, ECM. Weapons: ASW; limited ability with torpedoes and depth charges. ASV; 4 × Sea Skua missiles.

SEA KING *11/1989, Ralf Bendfeldt*

Numbers/Type: 16 Breguet Atlantic 1.
Operational speed: 355 kts *(658 km/h)*.
Service ceiling: 32 800 ft *(10 000 m)*.
Range: 4850 nm *(8990 km)*.
Role/Weapon systems: Long-range/endurance MR tasks carried out in North and Baltic Seas, also Atlantic Ocean; five aircraft also allocated to Elint/SIGINT tasks in Baltic Sea area; to be replaced in the late 1990s. Sensors: Thomson-CSF radar, Loral ESM/ECM, MAD, sonobuoys. Weapons: ASW; 9 × torpedoes (including Mk 46) or mines or depth bombs. ASV; 2 × AS30 missiles.

Numbers/Type: 18/2 Dornier Do 28D-2/Do 228-212.
Operational speed: 156 kts *(290 km/h)*.
Service ceiling: 20 700 ft *(6300 m)*.
Range: 667 nm *(1235 km)*.
Role/Weapon systems: Short-range surveillance tasks flown; SAR and EEZ protection. Two converted for pollution control. Sensors: Weather radar; converted aircraft also have SLAR, IR/UR scanner, microwave radiometer, LLL TV camera and data downlink. Weapons: Unarmed.

Numbers/Type: 106 Panavia Tornado IDS.
Operational speed: Mach 2.2.
Service ceiling: 80 000 ft *(24 385 m)*.
Range: 1500 nm *(2780 km)*.
Role/Weapon systems: Swing-wing strike and recce; shore-based for fleet air defence and ASV strike primary roles; two wings have been equipped for North and Baltic Sea defence; update with Kormoran 2 and Texas Instruments HARM; 40 are to be transferred to the Air Force on 1 January 1994. Sensors: Texas Instruments nav/attack system. Weapons: ASV; 4 × Kormoran missiles. Fleet AD; 2 × 27 mm cannon, 4 × AIM-9L Sidewinder.

LIGHT FORCES

Note: Vessels in this section have an 'S' number as part of their name as well as a 'P' pennant number. The 'S' number is shown in the Pennant List at the front of this country.

10 GEPARD CLASS (TYPE 143 A) (FAST ATTACK CRAFT—MISSILE)

Name	No	Builders	Commissioned
GEPARD	P 6121	AEG/Lürssen	13 Dec 1982
PUMA	P 6122	AEG/Lürssen	24 Feb 1983
HERMELIN	P 6123	AEG/Kröger	5 May 1983
NERZ	P 6124	AEG/Lürssen	14 July 1983
ZOBEL	P 6125	AEG/Kröger	25 Sep 1983
FRETTCHEN	P 6126	AEG/Lürssen	15 Dec 1983
DACHS	P 6127	AEG/Kröger	22 Mar 1984
OZELOT	P 6128	AEG/Lürssen	3 May 1984
WIESEL	P 6129	AEG/Lürssen	12 July 1984
HYÄNE	P 6130	AEG/Lürssen	13 Nov 1984

Displacement, tons: 391 full load
Dimensions, feet (metres): 190 × 25.6 × 8.5 *(57.6 × 7.8 × 2.6)*
Main machinery: 4 MTU MA 16V 956 SB80 diesels; 13 200 hp(m) *(9.7 MW)* sustained; 4 shafts
Speed, knots: 40. **Range, miles:** 2600 at 16 kts; 600 at 33 kts
Complement: 34 (4 officers)
Missiles: SSM: 4 Aerospatiale MM 38 Exocet; inertial cruise; active radar homing to 42 km *(23 nm)* at 0.9 Mach; warhead 165 kg; sea-skimmer. Possibly to be replaced by ANS in due course.
SAM: GDC RAM 21 cell point defence system (being fitted behind Exocet 1992-95); passive IR/anti-radiation homing to 9.6 km *(5.2 nm)* at 2 Mach; warhead 9.1 kg.
Guns: 1 OTO Melara 3 in *(76 mm)*/62 compact; 85° elevation; 85 rounds/minute to 16 km *(8.6 nm)* anti-surface; 12 km *(6.5 nm)* anti-aircraft; weight of shell 6 kg.
Mines: Can lay mines.
Countermeasures: Decoys: Buck-Wegmann Hot Dog/Silver Dog; IR/chaff dispenser.
ESM/ECM: AEG FL 1800s; radar intercept and jammer. Stage II to be fitted in 1994.
Combat data systems: AEG AGIS action data automation; Link 11.
Radars: Surface search/fire control: Signaal WM 27; I/J band; range 46 km *(25 nm)*.
Navigation: SMA 3 RM 20; I band; range 73 km *(40 nm)*.

Programmes: Ordered mid-1978 from AEG-Telefunken with sub-contracting to Lürssen (P 6121, 6122, 6124-6128) and Kröger (P 6123, 6129, 6130). First of class laid down 11 July 1979.
Modernisation: Includes plans for new SSM in mid-1990s and an updated EW fit in 1994. First RAM fit in *Puma* in 1992.
Structure: Wooden hulls on aluminium frames.
Operational: Form 7th Squadron based at Kiel.

GEPARD *5/1992, Giorgio Ghiglione*

PUMA (with RAM launcher) *1/1993 German Navy*

DACHS *5/1992, van Ginderen Collection*

238 GERMANY / Light forces

10 ALBATROS CLASS (TYPE 143/143B)
(FAST ATTACK-CRAFT—MISSILE)

Name	No	Builders	Commissioned
ALBATROS	P 6111	Lürssen, Vegesack	1 Nov 1976
FALKE	P 6112	Lürssen, Vegesack	13 Apr 1976
GEIER	P 6113	Lürssen, Vegesack	2 June 1976
BUSSARD	P 6114	Lürssen, Vegesack	14 Aug 1976
SPERBER	P 6115	Kröger, Rendsburg	27 Sep 1976
GREIF	P 6116	Lürssen, Vegesack	25 Nov 1976
KONDOR	P 6117	Kröger, Rendsburg	17 Dec 1976
SEEADLER	P 6118	Lürssen, Vegesack	28 Mar 1977
HABICHT	P 6119	Kröger, Rendsburg	23 Dec 1977
KORMORAN	P 6120	Lürssen, Vegesack	29 July 1977

Displacement, tons: 398 full load
Dimensions, feet (metres): 189 × 25.6 × 8.5 *(57.6 × 7.8 × 2.6)*
Main machinery: 4 MTU 16V 956 TB91 diesels; 17 700 hp(m) *(13 MW)* sustained; 4 shafts
Speed, knots: 40. **Range, miles:** 1300 at 30 kts
Complement: 40 (4 officers)

Missiles: SSM: 4 Aerospatiale MM 38 Exocet (2 twin) launchers; inertial cruise; active radar homing to 42 km *(23 nm)* at 0.9 Mach; warhead 165 kg; sea-skimmer.
Guns: 2 OTO Melara 3 in *(76 mm)*/62 compact; 85° elevation; 85 rounds/minute to 16 km *(8.6 nm)* anti-surface; 12 km *(6.5 nm)* anti-aircraft; weight of shell 6 kg.
Torpedoes: 2—21 in *(533 mm)* aft tubes. AEG Seeal; wire-guided; active homing to 13 km *(7 nm)* at 35 kts; passive homing to 28 km *(15 nm)* at 23 kts; warhead 260 kg.
Countermeasures: Decoys: Buck-Wegmann Hot Dog/Silver Dog; IR/chaff dispenser.
ESM/ECM: Thomson-CSF DR 2000 (radar warning) or Racal Octopus (Cutlass intercept, Scorpion jammer).
Combat data systems: Fully automatic data processing command and fire control system; Link 11.
Fire control: ORG7/3 optronics GFCS.
Radars: Surface search/fire control: Signaal WM 27; I/J band; range 46 km *(25 nm)*.
Navigation: SMA 3 RM 20; I band; range 73 km *(40 nm)*.

Programmes: AEG-Telefunken main contractor with construction by sub-contractors. Ordered in 1972.
Modernisation: *Habicht* started trials with RAM-ASDM mounting in 1983. Plans for major modernisation have been reduced to fitting a new EW system, Racal Octopus, which started in 1992. Then to be classified Type 143B.
Structure: Wooden hulled craft.
Operational: Form 2nd Squadron at Olpenitz. Tender *Donau*.

HABICHT (with GD RAM-ASDM SAM aft)   5/1983, Michael D J Lennon

KORMORAN   5/1992, Per Kornefeldt

SPERBER   6/1992, Horst Dehnst

18 TIGER CLASS (TYPE 148) (FAST ATTACK CRAFT—MISSILE)

Name	No	Builders	Commissioned
TIGER	P 6141	CMN, Cherbourg	30 Oct 1972
LUCHS	P 6143	CMN, Cherbourg	9 Apr 1973
MARDER	P 6144	CMN, Cherbourg	14 June 1973
LEOPARD	P 6145	CMN, Cherbourg	21 Aug 1973
FUCHS	P 6146	CMN, Cherbourg	17 Oct 1973
JAGUAR	P 6147	CMN, Cherbourg	13 Nov 1973
LÖWE	P 6148	CMN, Cherbourg	9 Jan 1974
WOLF	P 6149	CMN, Cherbourg	26 Feb 1974
PANTHER	P 6150	CMN, Cherbourg	27 Mar 1974
HÄHER	P 6151	CMN, Cherbourg	12 June 1974
PELIKAN	P 6153	CMN, Cherbourg	24 Sep 1974
ELSTER	P 6154	CMN, Cherbourg	14 Nov 1974
ALK	P 6155	CMN, Cherbourg	7 Jan 1975
DOMMEL	P 6156	CMN, Cherbourg	12 Feb 1975
WEIHE	P 6157	CMN, Cherbourg	3 Apr 1975
PINGUIN	P 6158	CMN, Cherbourg	22 May 1975
REIHER	P 6159	CMN, Cherbourg	24 June 1975
KRANICH	P 6160	CMN, Cherbourg	6 Aug 1975

Displacement, tons: 234 standard; 265 full load
Dimensions, feet (metres): 154.2 × 23 × 8.9 *(47 × 7 × 2.7)*
Main machinery: 4 MTU MD 16V 538 TB90 diesels; 12 000 hp(m) *(8.82 MW)* sustained; 4 shafts
Speed, knots: 36. **Range, miles:** 570 at 30 kts; 1600 at 15 kts
Complement: 30 (4 officers)

Missiles: SSM: 4 Aerospatiale MM 38 Exocet (2 twin) launchers; inertial cruise; active radar homing to 42 km *(23 nm)* at 0.9 Mach; warhead 165 kg; sea-skimmer.
Guns: 1 OTO Melara 3 in *(76 mm)*/62 compact; 85° elevation; 85 rounds/minute to 16 km *(8.6 nm)* anti-surface; 12 km *(6.5 nm)* anti-aircraft; weight of shell 6 kg.
1 Bofors 40 mm/70; 80° elevation; 330 rounds/minute to 12 km *(6.5 nm)* anti-surface; 4 km *(2.2 nm)* anti-aircraft; weight of shell 0.96 kg; fitted with GRP dome (1984) (see *Modernisation*).
Mines: Laying capability.
Countermeasures: Decoys: Wolke chaff launcher.
ESM/ECM: Racal Octopus (Cutlass B1 radar intercept and Scorpion jammer).
Combat data systems: PALIS and Link 11.
Fire control: CSEE Panda optical director. Thomson-CSF Vega PCET system, controlling missiles and guns.
Radars: Air/surface search: Thomson-CSF Triton; G band; range 33 km *(18 nm)* for 2 m² target.
Navigation: SMA 3 RM 20; I band; range 73 km *(40 nm)*.
Fire control: Thomson-CSF Castor; I/J band.

Programmes: Ordered in December 1970 from DTCN as main contractors. Some hulls contracted to Lürssen (P 6146, 6148, 6150, 6154, 6156, 6158, 6160) but all fitted out in France.
Modernisation: New Triton search and Castor fire control radars fitted to the whole class; also Racal EW systems as part of a mid-life update. *Dommel* had the 40 mm/70 gun replaced by a Mauser Vierling Taifun CIWS for trials in September 1991. The gun has four 27 mm barrels and a combined rate of fire of 6800 rounds/minute.
Structure: Steel-hulled craft. Similar to Combattante II craft.
Operational: 3rd Sqn: P 6141-6150 based at Flensburg.
5th Sqn: P 6151-6160 based at Olpenitz. Two deleted in 1992, more will pay off in 1993.

MARDER   8/1992, Hartmut Ehlers

PANTHER   6/1992, Horst Dehnst

AMPHIBIOUS FORCES

Note: As with Light Forces, most LCMs have an LCM number as part of their name. These numbers are in the Pennant List. The exceptions are LCMs 12-20 which have no L pennant number.

16 TYPE 521 (LCMs)

SPROTTE LCM 12	STINT LCM 19	MUSCHEL L 784
SARDINE LCM 13	AESCHE LCM 20	KORALLE L 785
SARDELLE LCM 14	HUMMER L 780	GARNELE L 786
HERING LCM 15	KRILL L 781	(ex-A 1406)
ORFE LCM 16	KRABBE L 782	LANGUSTE L 787
SAIBLING LCM 18	AUSTER L 783	(ex-A 1410)

Displacement, tons: 168 full load
Dimensions, feet (metres): 77.4 × 20.9 × 4.9 *(23.6 × 6.4 × 1.5)*
Main machinery: 2 MWM 8-cyl diesels; 685 hp(m) *(503 kW)*; 2 shafts
Speed, knots: 10.5
Complement: 7
Military lift: 60 tons or 50 troops

Comment: Built by Rheinwerft, Walsam (first two of class by Blohm & Voss). Completed in 1964-67 and later placed in reserve. LCM 21-28 recommissioned 4 September 1980 as L 780-787 but all except the last two were decommissioned again on 31 December 1992 and placed in reserve. LCM 12-20 are rated as 'floating equipment' without permanent crews. The design is similar to US LCM 8—LCM 12-20 have a derrick and can be used for carrying 18 torpedoes. LCM 1-11 sold to Greece in April 1991.
Bases: Kiel; LCM 12, LCM 16, L 780-L 785. Flensburg; LCM 13. Wilhelmshaven; LCM 14. Borkum; LCM 15. Olpenitz; LCM 18. Neustadt; LCM 19. Eckernförde; LCM 20. Coastal Services School, Grossenbrode; L 786-L 787.

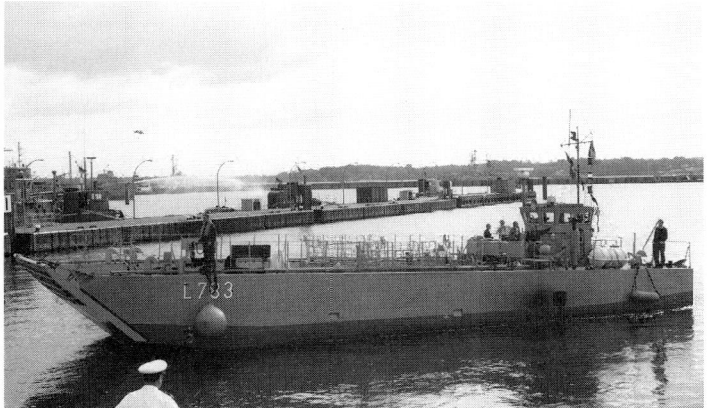

AUSTER 8/1992, Hartmut Ehlers

5 TYPE 520 (LCUs)

FLUNDER L 760	LACHS L 762	PLOTZE L 763	SCHLEI L 765	ZANDER L 769

Displacement, tons: 430 full load
Dimensions, feet (metres): 131.2 × 28.9 × 7.2 *(40 × 8.8 × 2.2)*
Main machinery: 2 MWM 12-cyl diesels; 1020 hp(m) *(750 kW)*; 2 shafts
Speed, knots: 11
Complement: 17
Military lift: 150 tons
Guns: 2 Oerlikon 20 mm; 55° elevation; 800 rounds/minute to 2 km; weight of shell 0.24 kg.

Comment: Similar to the US LCU (Landing Craft Utility) type. Provided with bow and stern ramp. Built by Howaldtswerke, Hamburg, 1965-66. Two sold to Greece in November 1989 and six more in 1992. Based at Olpenitz from 1 April 1993.

SCHLEI 6/1992, Antonio Moreno

MINE WARFARE FORCES

Note: Squadrons

Minesweeper Squadron 1 (Olpenitz)	10 Frankenthal class
Minesweeper Squadron 4 (Wilhelmshaven)	10 Lindau class
Minesweeper Squadron 5 (Olpenitz)	10 Hameln class
Minesweeper Squadron 6 (Wilhelmshaven)	6 Lindau class
	18 Seehund class
Minesweeper Squadron 7 (Neustadt)	10 Frauenlob class
Clearance Diver Company (Eckernförde)	Stier (diver support ship)

16 LINDAU CLASS
(TYPE 331, MINEHUNTERS (10); TYPE 351, TROIKA (6))
(MINESWEEPERS—COASTAL and MINEHUNTERS)

Name	No	Builders	Commissioned
GÖTTINGEN	M 1070	Burmester, Bremen	31 May 1958
KOBLENZ	M 1071	Burmester, Bremen	8 July 1958
LINDAU	M 1072	Burmester, Bremen	24 Apr 1958
SCHLESWIG*	M 1073	Burmester, Bremen	30 Oct 1958
TÜBINGEN	M 1074	Burmester, Bremen	25 Sep 1958
WETZLAR	M 1075	Burmester, Bremen	20 Aug 1958
PADERBORN*	M 1076	Burmester, Bremen	16 Dec 1958
WEILHEIM	M 1077	Burmester, Bremen	28 Jan 1959
CUXHAVEN	M 1078	Burmester, Bremen	11 Mar 1959
DÜREN*	M 1079	Burmester, Bremen	22 Apr 1959
MARBURG	M 1080	Burmester, Bremen	11 June 1959
KONSTANZ*	M 1081	Burmester, Bremen	23 July 1959
WOLFSBURG*	M 1082	Burmester, Bremen	8 Oct 1959
ULM*	M 1083	Burmester, Bremen	7 Nov 1959
MINDEN	M 1085	Burmester, Bremen	22 Jan 1960
VOLKLINGEN	M 1087	Burmester, Bremen	21 May 1960

* Troika control ships

Displacement, tons: 463 full load (Hunters); 465 full load (Troika)
Dimensions, feet (metres): 154.5 × 27.2 × 9.8 (9.2 Troika) *(47.1 × 8.3 × 3) (2.8)*
Main machinery: 2 MTU MD diesels; 4000 hp(m) *(2.94 MW)*; 2 shafts (Hunters)
2 MTU MD 16V 538 TB90 diesels; 5000 hp(m) *(3.68 MW)*; 2 shafts
Speed, knots: 16.5. **Range, miles:** 850 at 16.5 kts
Complement: 43 (5 officers) (Hunters); 44 (4 officers) (Troika)

Guns: 1 Bofors 40 mm/70; 90° elevation; 330 rounds/minute to 12 km *(6.5 nm)* anti-surface; 4 km *(2.2 nm)* anti-aircraft; weight of shell 0.96 kg.
Radars: Navigation: Kelvin Hughes 14/9; I band or Atlas Elektronik TRS N. Being replaced by Raytheon.
Sonars: Atlas Elektronik DSQS 11; minehunting; high frequency or Plessey 193 m; minehunting; high frequency (100/300 kHz).

Programmes: *Lindau*, first West German-built vessel for the Navy since the Second World War, launched on 16 February 1957. *Volklingen* was to have been scrapped in 1992 but was reprieved.
Modernisation: Minehunter conversions (Type 331) were completed in 1978/79. This conversion involved the fitting of Plessey 193M sonar and ECA/PAP 105 disposal vehicles. Prime contractor was VFW-Fokker.
Troika conversions: (Type 351) The six ships *(Düren, Konstanz, Paderborn, Ulm, Schleswig* and *Wolfsburg)* not being converted to minehunters but converted as guide ships for Troika between 1981 and 1983. Each guide three of these unmanned minesweeping vehicles as well as maintaining their moored minesweeping capabilities. *Göttingen, Koblenz, Lindau, Schleswig, Tübingen* and *Wetzlar* were modified with lower bridges in 1958-59. All were lengthened by 6.8 ft *(2.07 m)* in 1960-64. New gun mountings fitted in some in 1992.
Structure: The hull is of wooden construction, laminated with plastic glue. The engines are of non-magnetic materials.

TÜBINGEN (Hunter) (new gun mounting) 8/1992, Hartmut Ehlers

WOLFSBURG (Troika) 3/1992, Harald Carstens

240 GERMANY / Mine warfare forces

18 TROIKA (MINESWEEPERS—DRONES)

SEEHUND 1-18

Displacement, tons: 99
Dimensions, feet (metres): 88.5 × 15 × 4.5 *(26.9 × 4.6 × 1.4)*
Main machinery: 1 Deutz MWM D602 diesel; 446 hp(m) *(328 kW)*; 1 shaft
Speed, knots: 10. **Range, miles:** 520 at 9 kts
Complement: 3 (passage crew)

Comment: Built by MaK, Kiel and Blohm & Voss, Hamburg between August 1980 and May 1982. Commissioned in groups of three with the converted parent vessels. Remote-control using magnetic and acoustic sweeping gear.

SEEHUND 14   *3/1992, Harald Carstens*

10 FRAUENLOB CLASS (TYPE 394)
(MINESWEEPERS—INSHORE)

Name	No	Builders	Commissioned
FRAUENLOB	M 2658	Krögerwerft, Rendsburg	27 Sep 1966
NAUTILUS	M 2659	Krögerwerft, Rendsburg	26 Oct 1966
GEFION	M 2660	Krögerwerft, Rendsberg	17 Feb 1967
MEDUSA	M 2661	Krögerwerft, Rendsburg	17 Feb 1967
UNDINE	M 2662	Krögerwerft, Rendsburg	20 Mar 1967
MINERVA	M 2663	Krögerwerft, Rendsburg	16 June 1967
DIANA	M 2664	Krögerwerft, Rendsburg	21 Sep 1967
LORELEY	M 2665	Krögerwerft, Rendsburg	29 Mar 1968
ATLANTIS	M 2666	Krögerwerft, Rendsburg	29 Mar 1968
ACHERON	M 2667	Krögerwerft, Rendsburg	10 Feb 1969

Displacement, tons: 246 full load
Dimensions, feet (metres): 124.6 × 26.9 × 6.6 *(38 × 8.2 × 2)*
Main machinery: 2 MTU MB 12V 493 TY70 diesels; 2200 hp(m) *(1.62 MW)* sustained; 2 shafts
Speed, knots: 12+. **Range, miles:** 700 at 14 kts
Complement: 25 (2 officers)

Guns: 1 Bofors 40 mm/70; 90° elevation; 330 rounds/minute to 12 km *(6.5 nm)* anti-surface; 4 km *(2.2 nm)* anti-aircraft; weight of shell 0.96 kg.
Mines: Laying capability.
Radars: Navigation: I band.

Programmes: Launched in 1965-67. Originally designed coast guard boats with W numbers. Rated as inshore minesweepers in 1968 with the M numbers. All subsequently allocated Y numbers and later re-allocated M numbers.

DIANA   *8/1992, Hartmut Ehlers*

1 SCHÜTZE CLASS (TYPE 732) (DIVER—SUPPORT SHIP)

Name	No	Builders	Commissioned
STIER	M 1053 (ex-Y 849)	Abeking & Rasmussen	1961

Displacement, tons: 305 full load
Dimensions, feet (metres): 155.5 × 22.9 × 7.2 *(47.4 × 7 × 2.2)*
Main machinery: 2 Maybach diesels; 4500 hp(m) *(3.31 MW)*; 2 shafts
Speed, knots: 24. **Range, miles:** 2000 at 13 kts
Complement: 36 (4 officers)
Guns: Bofors 40 mm/70.
Radars: Navigation: Atlas Elektronik TRS N; I band.

Comment: Deckhouse and recompression chamber added. Original pennant number M 1061. Operates clearance divers.

STIER   *4/1989, Hartmut Ehlers*

2 + 8 FRANKENTHAL CLASS (TYPE 332)
(MINEHUNTERS—COASTAL)

Name	No	Builders	Commissioned
FRANKENTHAL	M 1066	Lürssenwerft	16 Dec 1992
WEIDEN	M 1060	Abeking & Rasmussen	16 Mar 1993
ROTTWEIL	M 1061	Krögerwerft	July 1993
BAD BEVENSEN	M 1063	Lürssenwerft	Dec 1993
BAD RAPPENAU	M 1067	Abeking & Rasmussen	Apr 1994
GRÖMITZ	M 1064	Krögerwerft	Aug 1994
DATTELN	M 1068	Lürssenwerft	Dec 1994
DILLINGEN	M 1065	Abeking & Rasmussen	Apr 1995
HOMBURG	M 1069	Krögerwerft	Aug 1995
SULZBACH-ROSENBERG	M 1062	Lürssenwerft	Nov 1995

Displacement, tons: 650 full load
Dimensions, feet (metres): 178.8 × 30.2 × 8.5 *(54.5 × 9.2 × 2.6)*
Main machinery: 2 MTU 16V 396 TB84 diesels; 5550 hp(m) *(4.08 MW)* sustained; 2 shafts; cp props. 1 motor (minehunting)
Speed, knots: 18
Complement: 40 (5 officers)

Missiles: SAM: 2 Stinger quad launchers.
Guns: 1 Bofors 40 mm/70; 90° elevation; 330 rounds/minute to 12 km *(6.5 nm)* anti-surface; 4 km *(2.2 nm)* anti-aircraft; weight of shell 0.96 kg.
Radars: Navigation: Raytheon; I band.
Sonars: Atlas Elektronik DSQS-11M; hull-mounted; high frequency.

Programmes: Ordered in September 1988 with MBB as main contractor. M 1066 laid down at Lürssen 6 December 1989 and launched 6 February 1992. M 1060 launched 14 May 1992, M 1061 12 March 1992, M 1063 21 January 1993.
Structure: Same hull, similar superstructure and high standardisation as Type 343. Built of amagnetic steel. Two Pinguin-B3 drones with sonar and TV cameras but not Troika control and minelaying capabilities. Fitted with Atlas Elektronik MWS 80-4 minehunting control system.

ROTTWEIL   *12/1992, Harald Carstens*

10 HAMELN CLASS (TYPE 343) (MINESWEEPERS—COASTAL)

Name	No	Builders	Launched	Commissioned
HAMELN	M 1092	Lürssenwerft	15 Mar 1988	29 June 1989
ÜBERHERRN	M 1095	Abeking & Rasmussen	30 Aug 1988	19 Sep 1989
LABOE	M 1097	Krögerwerft	13 Sep 1988	7 Dec 1989
PEGNITZ	M 1090	Lürssenwerft	14 Mar 1989	8 Mar 1990
KULMBACH	M 1091	Abeking & Rasmussen	20 June 1989	23 May 1990
SIEGBURG	M 1098	Krögerwerft	18 Apr 1989	26 July 1990
ENSDORF	M 1094	Lürssenwerft	14 Dec 1989	14 Oct 1990
PASSAU	M 1096	Abeking & Rasmussen	13 Mar 1990	18 Dec 1990
HERTEN	M 1099	Krögerwerft	21 Dec 1989	26 Mar 1991
AUERBACH	M 1093	Lürssenwerft	23 Aug 1990	7 May 1991

Displacement, tons: 635 full load
Dimensions, feet (metres): 178.5 × 30.2 × 8.2 *(54.4 × 9.2 × 2.5)*
Main machinery: 2 MTU 16V 538 TB91 diesels; 6140 hp(m) *(4.5 MW)* sustained; 2 shafts; cp props
Speed, knots: 18
Complement: 37 (4 officers)

Missiles: SAM: 2 Stinger quad launchers.
Guns: 2 Bofors 40 mm/70; 90° elevation; 330 rounds/minute to 12 km *(6.5 nm)* anti-surface; 4 km *(2.2 nm)* anti-aircraft; weight of shell 0.96 kg.
Mines: 60.
Countermeasures: Decoys: 2 Silver Dog chaff rocket launchers.
ESM: Thomson-CSF DR 2000; radar warning.
Radars: Surface Search/fire control: Signaal WM 20/2; I/J band; range 46 km *(25 nm)*.
Navigation: Raytheon SPS 64; I band.
Sonars: Atlas Elektronik DSQS-11M; hull-mounted; high frequency.

Programmes: On 3 January 1985 an MBB-headed consortium was awarded the order. The German designation of 'Schnelles Minenkampfboot' was changed in 1989 to 'Minensuchboot'.
Structure: Ships built of amagnetic steel adapted from submarine construction. Signaal M 20 System removed from the deleted Zobel class fast attack craft. PALIS active link. Sonar fitted from 1991.
Operational: Primary task is minesweeping. Plans to fit Troika control from 1995 may be shelved.

PASSAU   *9/1991, Harald Carstens*

1 TRIALS SHIP (TYPE 740) (Ex-MINESWEEPER)

Name	No	Builders	Commissioned
HOLNIS	A 1400 (ex-A 836)	Abeking & Rasmussen	31 Mar 1966

Displacement, tons: 150 standard; 180 full load
Dimensions, feet (metres): 116.8 × 24.3 × 6.9 *(35.6 × 7.4 × 2.1)*
Main machinery: 2 MTU MB 12V 493 TY70 diesels; 2200 hp(m) *(1.62 MW)* sustained; 2 shafts
Speed, knots: 14.5
Complement: 21

Comment: Now serving for trials and evaluation. *Holnis* was launched on 22 May 1965 as the prototype of a new design projected as a class of 20 such vessels but she is the only unit of this type, the other 19 boats having been cancelled. Hull number changed from M 2651 to Y 836 in 1970, to A 836 in 1985 and to A 1400 in 1987.

HOLNIS 10/1992, van Ginderen Collection

1 SACHSENWALD CLASS (TYPE 762) (MINE TRANSPORT)

Name	No	Builders	Commissioned
STEIGERWALD	A 1438	Blohm & Voss, Hamburg	20 Aug 1969

Displacement, tons: 3380 full load
Dimensions, feet (metres): 363.8 × 45.6 × 12.5 *(110.9 × 13.9 × 3.8)*
Main machinery: 2 Maybach MD 874 diesels; 5600 hp(m) *(4.1 MW)*; 2 shafts
Speed, knots: 17.8. **Range, miles:** 3500 at 14 kts
Complement: 65
Guns: 4 Bofors 40 mm/70 (2 twin); 80° elevation; 300 rounds/minute to 12 km *(6.5 nm)* anti-surface; 4 km *(2.2 nm)* anti-aircraft; weight of shell 0.96 kg.
Mines: Laying capacity.

Comment: Built as a mine transport. Mine ports in the stern and can be used as a minelayer. Planned to pay off in November 1993.

STEIGERWALD 11/1991, Horst Dehnst

SERVICE FORCES

Note: Four KSV 90 combat support ships (Type 702) are projected for completion not before 2003. Of 18 000 tons for underway replenishment of fuel, ammunition and solids. Will carry helicopters for VERTREP.

1 + 5 ELBE CLASS (TYPE 404) (TENDERS)

Name	No	Builders	Commissioned
ELBE	A 511	Bremer Vulkan	27 Jan 1993
MOSEL	A 512	Bremer Vulkan	July 1993
RHEIN	A 513	Flensburger Schiffbau	Oct 1993
WERRA	A 514	Flensburger Schiffbau	Dec 1993
MAIN	A 515	Lürssen/Krögerwerft	July 1994
DONAU	A 516	Lürssen/Krögerwerft	Nov 1994

Displacement, tons: 3586 full load
Dimensions, feet (metres): 329.7 oa; 285.4 wl × 49.2 × 13.5 *(100.5; 87 × 15 × 4.1)*
Main machinery: 1 Deutz MWM 8V 12M 628 diesel; 3335 hp(m) *(2.45 MW)*; 1 shaft; bow thruster
Speed, knots: 15. **Range, miles:** 2000 at 15 kts
Complement: 40 (4 officers) plus 12 squadron staff plus 50 maintainers
Cargo capacity: 450 tons dieso; 150 tons water; 11 tons luboil; 130 tons ammunition
Missiles: SAM: 2 Stinger (Fliegerfaust 2) quad launchers.
Guns: 4 Mauser 27 mm (quad) may be fitted.
Helicopters: Platform for 1 medium.

Comment: Funds released in November 1990 for the construction of six ships to replace the Rhein class. *Elbe* launched 24 June 1992. Containers for maintenance and repairs, spare parts and supplies for fast attack craft and minesweepers. Waste disposal capacity: 270 cu m liquids, 60 cu m solids. The use of the Darss class (all sold in 1991) was investigated as an alternative but rejected on the grounds of higher long-term costs because of the age of the ships.

ELBE 1/1993, Mod Bonn

2 RHEIN CLASS (TYPE 401) (TENDERS)

Name	No	Builders	Commissioned
MAIN	A 63	Lindenau, Kiel	29 June 1963
DONAU	A 69	Schlichting, Travemünde	23 May 1964

Displacement, tons: 2940 full load
Dimensions, feet (metres): 322.1 × 38.8 × 14.4/19.7 *(98.2 × 11.8 × 4.4/6)*
Main machinery: 6 Maybach diesels; 14 400 hp(m) *(10.58 MW)*; 2 shafts
Speed, knots: 20.5. **Range, miles:** 1625 at 15 kts
Complement: 153; 163 *(Elbe)*

Guns: 2 DCN 3.9 in *(100 mm)*; 80° elevation; 60-80 rounds/minute to 17 km *(9.2 nm)* anti-surface; 8 km *(4.4 nm)* anti-aircraft; weight of shell 13.5 kg.
  2 or 4 Bofors 40 mm/70 (2 singles or 2 twin); 90° elevation; 300 rounds/minute to 12 km *(6.5 nm)* anti-surface; 4 km *(2.2 nm)* anti-aircraft; weight of shell 0.96 kg.
Fire control: 2 Signaal M 45 GFCS for gunnery.
Radars: Surface search: Signaal ZW 01; I/J band.
  Signaal DA 02; E/F band; range 73 km *(40 nm)*.
Navigation: Kelvin Hughes 14/9; I band.
Fire control: Two Signaal M 45; I/J band; short range for gunnery.
Sonars: Atlas Elektronik; hull-mounted; active search; medium frequency.

Programmes: Originally a class of 13. The survivors are rated as tenders for fast attack craft.
Operational: *Donau*, 2nd FPB Squadron; *Main*, 5th FPB Squadron. *Main* planned to pay off in November 1993, *Donau* December 1994.
Sales: *Weser* to Greece 1975. *Ruhr* to Turkey 1976, *Isar* to Turkey October 1982.

MAIN 6/1992, Hartmut Ehlers

2 REPLENISHMENT TANKERS (TYPE 704)

Name	No	Builders	Commissioned
SPESSART (ex-*Okapi*)	A 1442	Kröger, Rendsburg	1974
RHÖN (ex-*Okene*)	A 1443	Kröger, Rendsburg	1974

Displacement, tons: 14 169 full load
Measurement, tons: 6103 grt; 10 800 dwt
Dimensions, feet (metres): 427.1 × 63.3 × 26.9 *(130.2 × 19.3 × 8.2)*
Main machinery: 1 MAK 12-cyl diesel; 8000 hp(m) *(5.88 MW)*; 1 shaft
Speed, knots: 16. **Range, miles:** 7400 at 16 kts
Complement: 42
Cargo capacity: 11 000 cu m fuel; 400 cu m water

Comment: Completed for Terkol Group as tankers. Acquired in 1976 for conversion *(Spessart* at Bremerhaven, *Rhön* at Kröger). The former commissioned for naval service on 5 September 1977 and the latter on 23 September 1977. Unarmed and civilian manned.

RHÖN 6/1992, Giorgio Arra

242 · GERMANY / Service forces

4 WALCHENSEE CLASS (TYPE 703) (REPLENISHMENT TANKERS)

Name	No	Builders	Commissioned
WALCHENSEE	A 1424	Lindenau, Kiel	29 June 1966
AMMERSEE	A 1425	Lindenau, Kiel	2 Mar 1967
TEGERNSEE	A 1426	Lindenau, Kiel	23 Mar 1967
WESTENSEE	A 1427	Lindenau, Kiel	6 Oct 1967

Displacement, tons: 2191
Dimensions, feet (metres): 235.8 × 36.7 × 13.5 *(71.9 × 11.2 × 4.1)*
Main machinery: 2 MWM 12-cyl diesels; 1370 hp(m) *(1 MW)*; 2 shafts
Speed, knots: 12.6. **Range, miles:** 3250 at 12 kts
Complement: 21

Comment: Civilian manned.

WALCHENSEE 5/1992, Per Kornefeldt

1 TYPE 763 (SUPPORT TANKER)

Name	No	Builders	Commissioned
WITTENSEE (ex-*Sioux*)	A 1407	Lindenau, Kiel	26 Mar 1959

Displacement, tons: 1854 full load
Dimensions, feet (metres): 221.4 × 32 × 14.1 *(67.5 × 9.8 × 4.3)*
Main machinery: 1 MAK diesel; 1050 hp(m) *(772 kW)*; 1 shaft
Speed, knots: 12
Complement: 21

Comment: Civilian manned. *Bodensee* sold to Turkey in 1977. Planned to pay off in late 1996.

WITTENSEE 6/1990, Stefan Terzibaschitsch

1 GUSTAV KÖNIGS CLASS (TYPE 670) (HARBOUR TANKERS)

FLEESENSEE Y 1657 (ex-C 40)

Displacement, tons: 1010 full load
Dimensions, feet (metres): 219.8 × 26.9 × 7.2 *(67 × 8.2 × 2.2)*
Main machinery: 1 R8DV 148 diesel; 420 hp(m) *(308 kW)*; 1 shaft
Speed, knots: 8

Comment: Ex-GDR built by VEB/Rosslau-Elbe. Based at Warnemünde. Able to pass under river bridges. Sister ship *Kölpinsee* was sold for civilian use in September 1992.

FLEESENSEE 6/1991, Hartmut Ehlers

6 LÜNEBURG CLASS (TYPE 701) (SUPPORT SHIPS)

Name	No	Builders	Commissioned
LÜNEBURG	A 1411	Flensburger Schiffbau/Bremer Vulkan	31 Jan 1966
FREIBURG*	A 1413	Blohm & Voss	27 May 1968
GLÜCKSBURG*	A 1414	Bremer Vulkan/Flensburger Schiffbau	9 July 1968
SAARBURG*	A 1415	Blohm & Voss	30 July 1968
NIENBURG	A 1416	Bremer Vulkan/Flensburger Schiffbau	1 Aug 1968
MEERSBURG*	A 1418	Bremer Vulkan/Flensburger Schiffbau	25 June 1968

*conversions

Displacement, tons: 3483; 3709 (conversions); 3900 *Freiburg*
Dimensions, feet (metres): 341.2 × 43.3 × 13.8 *(104 × 13.2 × 4.2)*
 (374.9 ft *(114.3 m)* for conversions; 388.1 ft *(118.3 m)* for *Freiburg*)
Main machinery: 2 MTU MD 16V 538 TB90 diesels; 6000 hp(m) *(4.1 MW)* sustained; 2 shafts; cp props; bow thruster
Speed, knots: 17. **Range, miles:** 3200 at 14 kts
Complement: 71
Cargo capacity: 1100 tons
Guns: 4 Bofors 40 mm/70 (2 twin) (cocooned or removed in most).

Comment: Four of this class were lengthened in 1975-76 by 33.7 ft *(10.3 m)* and modernised to serve the missile installations of the new classes of fast attack craft and converted destroyers, including MM 38 Exocet maintenance. *Freiburg* was lengthened in 1984 by 46.9 ft *(14.3 m)*, has a helicopter deck, portside larger crane and will act as support ship for Bremen class carrying nine spare Harpoons. Most serve as support ships for fast attack craft or MCM squadrons. *Meersburg* replaced *Lahn* as depot ship for 1st Submarine Squadron and *Nienburg* replaced *Werra* in 1991. *Coburg* transferred to Greece 25 September 1991. *Offenburg* decommissioned in April 1993 and *Lüneburg* and *Saarburg* are scheduled to scrap in mid-1994.

GLÜCKSBURG (with SATCOM) 6/1992, Giorgio Arra

NIENBURG (with guns) 4/1992, Horst Dehnst

FREIBURG (with helo deck) 6/1989, Gilbert Gyssels

5 OHRE CLASS (ACCOMMODATION SHIPS)

VOGTLAND Y 890 (ex-H 71) BÖRDE Y 894 (ex-H 72)
ALTMARK Y 891 (ex-H 11) WISCHE (ex-*Harz*) Y 895 (ex-H 31)
UCKERMARK Y 893 (ex-H 91)

Displacement, tons: 1320 full load
Dimensions, feet (metres): 231 × 39.4 × 5 *(70.4 × 12 × 1.6)*
Main machinery: 2 SKL VEB 6V D18/15 AL-1 diesels; 944 hp(m) *(694 kW)* sustained; 2 shafts; bow thruster

Comment: Ex-GDR-built by Peenewerft, Wolgast. One hydraulic 8 ton crane fitted. First commissioned 1985. Classified as 'Schwimmende Stuetzpunkte'. Propulsion and armament is being removed and they are used as non self-propelled accommodation ships for crews of vessels in refit. Civilian manned. Two based at Warnemünde and the other three at Wilhelmshaven.

ALTMARK 1/1992, Hartmut Ehlers

2 WESTERWALD CLASS (TYPE 760) (AMMUNITION TRANSPORTS)

Name	No	Builders	Commissioned
WESTERWALD	A 1435	Orenstein and Koppel, Lübeck	11 Feb 1967
ODENWALD	A 1436	Orenstein and Koppel, Lübeck	23 Mar 1967

Displacement, tons: 3460 standard; 4042 full load
Dimensions, feet (metres): 344.4 × 46 × 12.2 (105 × 14 × 3.7)
Main machinery: 2 MTU MD 16V 538 TB90 diesels; 6000 hp(m) (4.1 MW) sustained; 2 shafts; cp props; bow thruster
Speed, knots: 17. **Range, miles:** 3500 at 17 kts
Complement: 60 (Westerwald); 31 (Odenwald) (civilian manned)
Cargo capacity: 1080 tons ammunition
Guns: 4 Bofors 40 mm/70 (2 twin) (cocooned in Odenwald).

Comment: Both based at Wilhelmshaven.

ODENWALD 5/1992, Antonio Moreno

2 TYPE 705 (WATER BOATS)

FW 1 A 1403 (ex-Y 864) **FW 5** A 1405 (ex-Y 868)

Displacement, tons: 626 full load
Dimensions, feet (metres): 144.4 × 25.6 × 8.2 (44.1 × 7.8 × 2.5)
Main machinery: 1 MWM diesel; 230 hp(m) (169 kW); 1 shaft
Speed, knots: 9.5
Complement: 6
Cargo capacity: 340 tons

Comment: Originally class of six built in pairs by Schiffbarges, Unterweser, Bremerhaven; H. Rancke, Hamburg and Jadewerft, Wilhelmshaven, in 1963-64. FW 2 (3 December 1975) and FW 4 (12 April 1991) to Turkey; FW 3 (22 April 1976) and FW 6 (5 March 1991) to Greece.

FW 5 6/1992, Stefan Terzibaschitsch

1 KNURRHAHN CLASS (TYPE 730) (ACCOMMODATION SHIP)

Name	No	Builders	Commissioned
KNURRHAHN	Y 811	Sietas, Hamburg	Nov 1989

Displacement, tons: 1424 full load
Dimensions, feet (metres): 157.5 × 45.9 × 5.9 (48 × 14 × 1.8)

Comment: Based at Bremerhaven. Accommodation for 230 people.

KNURRHAHN 10/1992, van Ginderen Collection

3 BATTERY CHARGING CRAFT (TYPE 718)

Name	No	Builders	Commissioned
LP 1	—	Jadewerft, Wilhelmshaven	18 Feb 1964
LP 2	—	Oelkers, Hamburg	17 Apr 1964
LP 3	Y 1690	Jadewerft, Wilhelmshaven	12 Sep 1974

Displacement, tons: 234 (267 LP 3) full load
Dimensions, feet (metres): 90.6 × 23 × 5.2 (27.6 × 7.0 × 1.6)
Main machinery: 1 MTU MB diesel; 250 hp(m) (184 kW); 1 shaft
Speed, knots: 9
Complement: 6

Comment: Have diesel charging generators for submarine batteries. LP 3 is 1.6 ft (0.5 m) more in beam than the first two.

LP 1 6/1992, Gunnar Olsen

5 TOWING LAUNCHES (TYPE 946)

AK 1 Y 1671	MA 2 Y 1676	BORBY Y 1687
AK 3 Y 1672	MA 3 Y 1677	

Dimensions, feet (metres): 39.4 × 12.8 × 6.2 (12.0 × 3.9 × 1.9)
Main machinery: 1 MAN D2540MTE diesel; 366 hp(m) (269 kW); 1 shaft

Comment: Built by Hans Boost, Trier. All completed in 1985.

AK 1 6/1991, Antonio Moreno

2 UTILITY LAUNCHES (TYPE 945)

MA 1 Y 1678 **SCHIRNAU** Y 1685

Dimensions, feet (metres): 53.1 × 14.8 × 6.6 (16.2 × 4.5 × 2)
Main machinery: 1 MAN D2866TE diesel; 300 hp(m) (221 kW); 1 shaft

Comment: Built by Hans Boost, Trier and delivered in September 1992.

12 OIL BARGES (TYPE 737)

Comment: Numbered Ölschute 1-12 and completed in 1986-87. 65.6 ft (20 m) dumb barges with 150 tons capacity.

GERMANY / Auxiliary and trials ships

AUXILIARY AND TRIALS SHIPS

Notes: 1. Type 749 project to build new torpedo and sonar trials vessels has been deferred until 2005.
2. In addition to those listed below there are two SES trials craft:
(a) *Corsair* which is owned by Blohm & Voss and has a 57 mm Bofors.
(b) *Moses* completed by Lürssen in October 1990 with two Tohatsu outboard engines giving a speed of 25 kts. This is a scaled down version of the Type 751 below.

CORSAIR *1991, van Ginderen Collection*

0 + (1) SES TRIALS CRAFT (TYPE 751)

Displacement, tons: 720 full load
Dimensions, feet (metres): 219.8 × 52.8 × 9.4 (hullborne) *(67.0 × 16.1 × 2.8)*
Main machinery: 4 Allison 571-KF gas turbines, 30 776 hp(m) *(23 MW)* sustained; 2 KaMeWa waterjets
Speed, knots: 50+

Comment: MTG Marinetechnik Hamburg has been contracted to design a craft characterised by a top speed of 50 knots for construction in the 1990s.
Prior to construction of the full scale SES a manned and self-propelled model in scale 1:6.3 has been built at Lürssen and completed on 21 Aug 1990.

3 OSTE CLASS (TYPE 423) (AGI)

Name	No	Builders	Commissioned
ALSTER	A 50	Schiffsbaugesellschaft, Flensburg	5 Oct 1989
OSTE	A 52	Schiffsbaugesellschaft, Flensburg	30 June 1988
OKER	A 53	Schiffsbaugesellschaft, Flensburg	10 Nov 1988

Displacement, tons: 3200 full load
Dimensions, feet (metres): 273.9 × 47.9 × 13.8 *(83.5 × 14.6 × 4.2)*
Main machinery: 2 Deutz-MWM BV 16M 628 diesels; 8980 hp(m) *(6.6 MW)* sustained; 1 shaft; 1 motor (for slow speed)
Speed, knots: 19
Complement: 40 plus 40 specialists (2 crews)

Comment: Three new vessels ordered in March 1985 and December 1986 and have replaced the Radar Trials Ships of the same name (old *Oker* and *Alster* transferred to Greece and Turkey respectively). *Oste* launched 15 May 1987, *Oker* 24 September 1987, *Alster* 4 November 1988. Carry Atlas Elektronik passive sonar and optical ELAM and electronic surveillance equipment. Particular attention has been given to accommodation standards.

OKER *6/1992, Horst Dehnst*

1 TRIALS SHIP (TYPE 742)

Name	No	Builders	Commissioned
WALTHER VON LEDEBUR	A 1410 (ex-Y 841)	Burmester, Bremen	21 Dec 1967

Displacement, tons: 775 standard; 825 full load
Dimensions, feet (metres): 206.6 × 34.8 × 8.9 *(63 × 10.6 × 2.7)*
Main machinery: 2 Maybach MTU 16-cyl diesels; 5200 hp(m) *(3.82 MW)*; 2 shafts
Speed, knots: 19
Complement: 11 plus 10 trials party

Comment: Wooden hulled vessel. Launched on 30 June 1966 as a prototype minesweeper but completed as a trials ship. To be replaced in 1995 by fourth Type 748.

WALTHER VON LEDEBUR *6/1992, Hartmut Ehlers*

3 SCHWEDENECK CLASS (TYPE 748) (MULTI-PURPOSE)

Name	No	Builders	Commissioned
SCHWEDENECK	Y 860	Krögerwerft, Rendsburg	20 Oct 1987
KRONSORT	Y 861	Elsflether Werft	2 Dec 1987
HELMSAND	Y 862	Krögerwerft, Rendsburg	4 Mar 1988

Displacement, tons: 1018 full load
Dimensions, feet (metres): 185.3 × 35.4 × 17 *(56.5 × 10.8 × 5.2)*
Main machinery: Diesel-electric; 3 MTU 6V 396 TB53 diesel generators; 1485 kW 60 Hz sustained; 1 motor; 1 shaft
Speed, knots: 13. **Range, miles:** 2400 at 13 kts
Complement: 13 plus 10 trials parties
Radars: Navigation: Two Raytheon; I band.

Comment: Order for first three placed in mid-1985. One more planned after 1995 to replace *Walther von Ledebur* but may not now be funded.

HELMSAND *6/1992, Stefan Terzibaschitsch*

5 STOLLERGRUND CLASS (TYPE 745) (MULTI-PURPOSE)

Name	No	Builders	Commissioned
STOLLERGRUND	Y 863	Krögerwerft	31 May 1989
MITTELGRUND	Y 864	Elsflether Werft	23 Aug 1989
KALKGRUND	Y 865	Krögerwerft	23 Nov 1989
BREITGRUND	Y 866	Elsflether Werft	19 Dec 1989
BANT	Y 867	Krögerwerft	28 May 1990

Displacement, tons: 450 full load
Dimensions, feet (metres): 126.6 × 30.2 × 10.5 *(38.6 × 9.2 × 3.2)*
Main machinery: 1 Deutz-MWM BV6M628 diesel; 1690 hp(m) *(1.24 MW)* sustained; 1 shaft
Speed, knots: 12. **Range, miles:** 1000 at 12 kts.
Complement: 7 plus 6 trials personnel

Comment: Five ordered from Lürssen in November 1987; two subcontracted to Elsflether. Equipment includes two I band radars and an intercept sonar. The first four are based at the Armed Forces Technical Centre; *Bant* at Wilhelmshaven. Two more planned for the mid-1990s may be cancelled.

BANT *6/1991, van Ginderen Collection*

1 RESEARCH SHIP (TYPE 750)

Name	No	Builders	Commissioned
PLANET	A 1450	Norderwerft, Hamburg	15 Apr 1967

Displacement, tons: 1943 full load
Dimensions, feet (metres): 263.8 × 41.3 × 13.1 *(80.4 × 12.6 × 4)*
Main machinery: Diesel-electric; 4 MWM diesel generators; 1 motor; 1390 hp(m) *(1.02 MW)*; 1 shaft; bow thruster
Speed, knots: 13. **Range, miles:** 9400 at 13 kts
Complement: 39 plus 22 scientists
Radars: Navigation: Two Raytheon; I band.
Sonars: Hull-mounted; high frequency search.
Helicopters: 1 Bell 206B or MBB BO105CB can be embarked.

Comment: Weapons research ship launched 23 September 1965. Planned to be replaced by SWATH type ship (Type 751).

PLANET 9/1992, Horst Dehnst

1 TRIALS SHIP (TYPE 740)

Name	No	Builders	Commissioned
HEINZ ROGGENKAMP	Y 871	Weser, Bremerhaven	30 Dec 1952

Displacement, tons: 996 full load
Dimensions, feet (metres): 187.7 × 29.5 × 10.2 *(57.2 × 9 × 3.1)*
Main machinery: 1 KHD diesel; 1145 hp(m) *(841 kW)*; 1 shaft
Speed, knots: 12
Complement: 19

Comment: Built as a trawler and converted in 1964 as a torpedo trials ship with both 533 mm and 324 mm tubes. Was to have been paid off in late 1992 but once again has been reprieved.

HEINZ ROGGENKAMP 6/1991, Stefan Terzibaschitsch

2 TRIALS SHIPS (TYPE 741)

Name	No	Builders	Commissioned
SP 1	A 1408 (ex-A 837)	Schürenstadt, Bardenfleth	29 June 1967
WILHELM PULLWER	A 1409 (ex-Y 838)	Schürenstadt, Bardenfleth	22 Dec 1967

Displacement, tons: 160 full load
Dimensions, feet (metres): 103.3 × 24.6 × 7.2 *(31.5 × 7.5 × 2.2)*
Main machinery: 2 MTU MB diesels; 700 hp(m) *(514 kW)*; 2 Voith-Schneider props
Speed, knots: 12.5
Complement: 17

Comment: Wooden hulled trials ships for barrage systems. *SP 1* works for the Naval Service Test Command.

SP 1 6/1992, Stefan Terzibaschitsch

1 DIVING TENDER (TYPE 732)

Name	No	Builders	Commissioned
TB 1	M 1050	Burmeister, Bremen	21 June 1972

Displacement, tons: 70 full load
Dimensions, feet (metres): 91.2 × 19 × 6.2 *(27.8 × 5.8 × 1.9)*
Main machinery: 1 MWM diesel; 950 hp(m) *(698 kW)*; 1 shaft
Speed, knots: 17
Complement: 6 plus divers

Comment: Similar to Type 430 TRVs.

TB 1 6/1991, van Ginderen Collection

1 TRIALS PLATFORM

BARBARA Y 844

Comment: Artillery testing ship of 3500 tons and 170.9 ft *(52.1 m)*. Commissioned in June 1964. No propulsion. Named after the patron saint of artillery.

BARBARA 1990, van Ginderen Collection

5 FLOATING DOCKS (TYPES 712-715) and 2 CRANES (TYPE 711)

SCHWIMMDOCKS A	Y 842	HIEV	Y 875
SCHWIMMDOCKS B	Y 879	GRIEP	Y 876
C, 2 and 3			

Comment: Dock lift capacity: 3 (8000 tons); B (4500 tons); A and 2 (1000 tons). C is used for submarine pressure tests; Cranes (100 tons).

Y 879 6/1991, Stefan Terzibaschitsch

SAIL TRAINING SHIPS

Note: In addition to the two listed below there are 54 other sail training vessels (Types 910-915).

Name	No	Builders	Commissioned
GORCH FOCK	A 60	Blohm & Voss, Hamburg	17 Dec 1958

Displacement, tons: 1760 standard; 1870 full load
Dimensions, feet (metres): 293 × 39.2 × 16.1 *(89.3 × 12 × 4.9)*
Main machinery: Auxiliary 1 Deutz MWM BV6M628 diesel; 1690 hp(m) *(1.24 MW)* sustained; 1 shaft; KaMeWa cp prop
Speed, knots: 11 power; 15 sail. **Range, miles:** 1990 at 10 kts
Complement: 206 (10 officers, 140 cadets)

Comment: Sail training ship of the improved Horst Wessel type. Barque rig. Launched on 23 August 1958. Sail area, 21 141 sq ft. Major modernisation in 1985 at Howaldtswerke. Second major refit in 1991 at Motorenwerke, Bremerhaven included a new propulsion engine and three diesel generators.

GORCH FOCK   *4/1992, van Ginderen Collection*

Name	No	Builders	Commissioned
NORDWIND	Y 834	—	1944

Displacement, tons: 110
Dimensions, feet (metres): 78.8 × 21 × 8.2 *(24 × 6.4 × 2.5)*
Main machinery: 1 Demag diesel; 150 hp(m) *(110 kW)*; 1 shaft
Speed, knots: 8. **Range, miles:** 1200 at 7 kts
Complement: 10

Comment: Ketch rigged. Sail area, 2037.5 sq ft. Ex-Second World War patrol craft. Taken over from Border Guard in 1956.

NORDWIND   *6/1992, Stefan Terzibaschitsch*

MISCELLANEOUS

Notes: 1. The trials submarine *Jonas* (ex-Swedish *Valen*) is a hulk without propulsion machinery at Eckernförde.
2. There is also a 30 kt reconnaissance craft VB 2 built by Lürssen and completed in September 1987. Used by the 2nd FPB Squadron at Olpenitz.

VB 2   *6/1992, Hartmut Ehlers*

1 TRIAL BOAT (TYPE 740)

Name	No	Builders	Commissioned
BUMS	Y 1689	Howaldtswerke, Kiel	—

Dimensions, feet (metres): 86.6 × 22.3 × 4.9 *(26.4 × 6.8 × 1.5)*

Comment: Single diesel engine. Has a 3 ton crane.

BUMS   *1983, Ralf Bendfeldt*

8 GENERAL SERVICE LAUNCHES (TYPES 740, 743, 744, 744A)

MT 1 (ex-*MT-Boot*) Y 1670   AM 7 Y 1679
AK 5 Y 1673   AK 6 Y 1683
AM 6 Y 1674   PETER BACHMANN Y 1684
AM 8 Y 1675   AK 2 Y 1686

Dimensions, feet (metres): 52.5 × 13.1 × 3.9 *(16 × 4 × 1.2)* approx
Main machinery: 1 or 2 diesels

Comment: For personnel transport and trials work. Types 744 and 744A (AK 2) are radio calibration craft; Type 740 (AK 5) is a radar trials craft.

AK 6   *6/1991, Antonio Moreno*

AK 2   *8/1992, Hartmut Ehlers*

27 PERSONNEL TENDERS (TYPES 934 and GDR 407)

V 2-V 21   B 03   B 11   B 30   B 33   B 83   B 86   B 88

Comment: V 2-V 21 built in 1987/88 by Hatecke. The B series are ex-GDR craft built by Yachtwerft, Berlin.

V 14   *5/1992, Erik Laurser*

6 + 5 RANGE SAFETY CRAFT (5 TYPE 369, 1 TYPE 909 + 5 TYPE 905)

KW 15 Y 827	KW 17 Y 845	KW 20 Y 846
KW 16 Y 830	KW 18 Y 832	H 11 Y 857

Displacement, tons: 70 full load
Dimensions, feet (metres): 93.5 × 15.4 × 4.9 *(28.9 × 4.7 × 1.5)*
Main machinery: 2 MTU MB diesels; 2000 hp(m) *(1.47 MW)*; 2 shafts
Speed, knots: 25
Complement: 17

Comment: First six built in 1951-53 for Weser river patrol. Can be fitted with two Oerlikon 20 mm. For Todedorf AAW range. One paid off in early 1992, four more are planned to go in late 1993, and *KW 17* and *KW 20* in 1994 when they will be replaced by Type 905 contracted to Lürssen in 1991 for delivery by December 1993.

KW 15   *6/1991, Stefan Terzibaschitsch*

2 TWIN HULL OIL RECOVERY SHIPS (TYPE 738)

Name	No	Builders	Commissioned
BOTTSAND	Y 1643	Lühring, Brake	24 Jan 1985
EVERSAND	Y 1644	Lühring, Brake	11 June 1988

Measurement, tons: 500 gross; 650 dwt
Dimensions, feet (metres): 151.9 × 39.4 (137.8, bow opened) × 10.2 *(46.3 × 12 (42) × 3.1)*
Main machinery: 1 Deutz BA12M816 diesel; 1000 hp(m) *(759 kW)* sustained; 2 shafts
Speed, knots: 10
Complement: 6

Comment: Built with two hulls which are connected with a hinge in the stern. During pollution clearance the bow will be opened. Ordered by Ministry of Transport but taken over by West German Navy. Normally used as tank cleaning vessels. Civilian manned. *Bottsand* based at Olpenik, *Eversand* at Wilhelmshaven. A third of class *Thor* belongs to the Ministry of Transport.

BOTTSAND   *8/1992, Hartmut Ehlers*

4 TORPEDO RECOVERY VESSELS (TYPE 430A)

TF 1 Y 851   TF 3 Y 853   TF 5 Y 855   TF 6 Y 856

Comment: All built in 1966 of approximately 56 tons. Provided with stern ramp for torpedo recovery. One sold to the Turkish Navy, two to Greece in 1989 and two more in 1991. Being replaced by Type 745 multi-purpose vessels.

TF 6   *6/1992, Stefan Terzibaschitsch*

TUGS

2 HELGOLAND CLASS (TYPE 720) (SALVAGE TUGS)

Name	No	Builders	Commissioned
HELGOLAND	A 1457	Unterweser, Bremerhaven	8 Mar 1966
FEHMARN	A 1458	Unterweser, Bremerhaven	1 Feb 1967

Displacement, tons: 1310 standard; 1643 full load
Dimensions, feet (metres): 223.1 × 41.7 × 14.4 *(68 × 12.7 × 4.4)*
Main machinery: Diesel-electric; 4 MWM 12-cyl diesel generators; 2 motors; 3300 hp(m) *(2.43 MW)*; 2 shafts
Speed, knots: 17. **Range, miles:** 6400 at 16 kts
Complement: 34
Guns: 2 Bofors 40 mm/70 (twin) (cocooned or removed)
Mines: Laying capacity.
Radars: Navigation: Raytheon; I band.
Sonars: High definition, hull-mounted for wreck search.

Comment: Launched on 25 November 1965 and 9 April 1965. Carry firefighting equipment and have an ice strengthened hull. *Fehmarn* (Type 720B) modernised and employed as safety ship for the submarine training group.

HELGOLAND   *6/1992, Maritime Photographic*

6 WANGEROOGE CLASS (3 TYPE 722 and 3 TYPE 754)

Name	No	Builders	Commissioned
WANGEROOGE	A 1451	Schichau, Bremerhaven	9 Apr 1968
SPIEKEROOG	A 1452	Schichau, Bremerhaven	14 Aug 1968
NORDERNEY	A 1455	Schichau, Bremerhaven	15 Oct 1970
BALTRUM	A 1439	Schichau, Bremerhaven	8 Oct 1968
JUIST	A 1440	Schichau, Bremerhaven	1 Oct 1971
LANGEOOG	A 1441	Schichau, Bremerhaven	14 Aug 1968

Displacement, tons: 854 standard; 1024 full load
Dimensions, feet (metres): 170.6 × 39.4 × 12.8 *(52 × 12.1 × 3.9)*
Main machinery: Diesel-electric; 4 MWM 16-cyl diesel generators; 2 motors; 2400 hp(m) *(1.76 MW)*; 2 shafts
Speed, knots: 14. **Range, miles:** 5000 at 10 kts
Complement: 24 plus 33 trainees (A 1439-1441)
Guns: 1 Bofors 40 mm/70 (cocooned in some, not fitted in all).

Comment: First three are salvage tugs with firefighting equipment and ice-strengthened hulls. *Wangerooge* sometimes used for pilot training and *Spiekeroog* and *Norderney* as submarine safety ships. The second three were converted 1974-78 to training ships with *Baltrum* and *Juist* being used as diving training vessels with recompression chambers and civilian crews.

SPIEKEROOG   *6/1992, Stefan Terzibaschitsch*

4 HARBOUR TUGS (TYPE 724)

Name	No	Builders	Commissioned
SYLT	Y 820	Schichau, Bremerhaven	1962
FÖHR	Y 821	Schichau, Bremerhaven	1962
AMRUM	Y 822	Schichau, Bremerhaven	1963
NEUWERK	Y 823	Schichau, Bremerhaven	1963

Displacement, tons: 244 standard; 266 full load
Dimensions, feet (metres): 100.7 × 24.6 × 13.1 *(30.6 × 7.5 × 4)*
Main machinery: 1 Deutz MAK 8-cyl diesel; 1000 hp(m) *(735 kW)*; 1 shaft
Speed, knots: 12
Complement: 10

Comment: Launched in 1961. Civilian manned. Carry firefighting equipment.

NEUWERK   *5/1992, Antonio Moreno*

248 GERMANY / Tugs — River engineers (Army)

3 HARBOUR TUGS (TYPE 724)

Name	No	Builders	Commissioned
NEUENDE	Y 1680	Schichau, Bremerhaven	27 Oct 1971
HEPPENS	Y 1681	Schichau, Bremerhaven	17 Dec 1971
ELLERBEK	Y 1682	Schichau, Bremerhaven	26 Nov 1971

Displacement, tons: 232
Dimensions, feet (metres): 87.2 × 24.3 × 8.5 *(26.6 × 7.4 × 2.6)*
Main machinery: 1 MWM 8-cyl diesel; 800 hp(m) *(588 kW)*; 1 shaft
Speed, knots: 12
Complement: 6

ELLERBEK 8/1992, Hartmut Ehlers

6 + 6 HARBOUR TUGS (TYPE 725)

Name	No	Builders	Commissioned
VOGELSAND	Y 816	Orenstein und Koppel, Lübeck	14 Apr 1987
NORDSTRAND	Y 817	Orenstein und Koppel, Lübeck	20 Jan 1987
LANGENESS	Y 819	Orenstein und Koppel, Lübeck	5 Mar 1987
LÜTJE HORN	Y 812	Husumer Schiffswerft	31 May 1990
KNECHTSAND	Y 814	Husumer Schiffswerft	16 Nov 1990
SCHARHÖRN	Y 815	Husumer Schiffswerft	1 Oct 1990

Displacement, tons: 445
Dimensions, feet (metres): 99.3 × 29.8 × 8.5 *(30.3 × 9.1 × 2.6)*
Main machinery: 2 Deutz MWM BV6M628 diesels; 3360 hp(m) *(2.47 MW)* sustained; 2 Voith-Schneider props
Speed, knots: 12
Complement: 10

Comment: Bollard pull, 23 tons. Six more to complete 1994-97, to replace Type 724.

LÜTJE HORN 6/1992, Hartmut Ehlers

3 HARBOUR TUGS (TYPE 414)

KOOS (ex-*Delphin*) Y 1651 (ex-A 08) **DRANKSE** (ex-*Kormoran*) Y 1658 (ex-A 68)
WUSTROW (ex-*Zander*) Y 1656 (ex-A 45)

Displacement, tons: 320 full load
Dimensions, feet (metres): 96.1 × 27.2 × 12.1 *(29.3 × 8.3 × 3.7)*
Main machinery: 2 diesels; 1200 hp(m) *(882 kW)*; 2 shafts
Speed, knots: 11. **Range, miles:** 1800 at 11 kts
Complement: 3

Comment: Ex-GDR vessels being retained in service until 1998.

KOOS 3/1991, Hartmut Ehlers

4 WARNOW CLASS HARBOUR TUGS

A 15 A 16 A 42 A 43

Comment: Ex-GDR Type 1344 berthing tugs built by Yachtwerft Berlin. Retained in service at Peenemünde and Warnemünde.

A 16 9/1992, Hartmut Ehlers

ICEBREAKERS

Name	No	Builders	Commissioned
EISVOGEL	A 1401	J G Hitzler, Lauenburg	11 Mar 1961
EISBÄR	A 1402	J G Hitzler, Lauenburg	1 Nov 1961

Displacement, tons: 560 standard
Dimensions, feet (metres): 125.3 × 31.2 × 15.1 *(38.2 × 9.5 × 4.6)*
Main machinery: 2 Maybach 12-cyl diesels; 2400 hp(m) *(1.76 MW)*; 2 shafts
Speed, knots: 13
Complement: 16

Comment: Launched on 28 April and 9 June 1960 respectively. Icebreaking tugs of limited capability. Civilian manned. Fitted for but not with one Bofors 40 mm/70.

EISVOGEL 4/1992, Harald Carstens

RIVER ENGINEERS (ARMY)

Note: Four companies are located along the River Rhine at Krefeld, Koblenz, Neuwied and Wiesbaden. Each company is provided with Landing Craft (Mannheim 59 or Bodan class), River Patrol Craft and one River Tug and each has its own numbered series: 80101-31, 80111-31, 85011-31, 85111-31.

14 MANNHEIM 59 CLASS (RIVER LANDING CRAFT) (LCMs)

Displacement, tons: 89 standard
Dimensions, feet (metres): 89.9 × 23.6 × 3.9 *(27.4 × 7.2 × 1.2)*
Main machinery: 2 MWM RHS518A diesels; 440 hp(m) *(323 kW)*; 2 shafts
Speed, knots: 9
Complement: 9
Guns: 4—7.62 mm MGs.

Comment: Ordered in April 1959 and built by Schiffs und Motorenwerke AG, Mannheim. Normal load 70 tons but can carry 90 tons. One transferred to Tonga in 1989. Eight paid off for sale in August 1991.

LCM 85131 9/1991, van Ginderen Collection

13 BODAN CLASS (RIVER LANDING CRAFT) (LCMs)

Dimensions, feet (metres): 98.4 × 19 *(30 × 5.8)* (loading area)
Main machinery: 4 diesels; 596 hp(m) *(438 kW)*; 4 Schottel props
Guns: 1 Oerlikon 20 mm.

Comment: Built of 12 pontoons, provided with bow and stern ramp. Can carry 90 tons.

BODAN 85031   6/1992, Horst Dehnst

12 RIVER PATROL CRAFT

Dimensions, feet (metres): 82 × 12.5 × 3.3 *(25 × 3.8 × 1)*
Main machinery: 2 MWM RHS518A diesels; 440 hp(m) *(323 kW)*; 2 shafts
Speed, knots: 20.5
Complement: 7
Guns: 4—12.7 mm Browning MGs.

Comment: Resemble the Belgian river patrol craft *Liberation*.

S 80102   1991, van Ginderen Collection

4 RIVER TUGS

T 80001   T 80101   T 85001   T 85101

Dimensions, feet (metres): 91.8 × 19.4 × 3.9 *(28 × 5.9 × 1.2)*
Main machinery: 2 KHD SBF 12M716 diesels; 760 hp(m) *(559 kW)*; 2 shafts
Speed, knots: 11
Complement: 7
Guns: 2—7.62 mm MGs.

T 80101   8/1984, Gunnar Olsen

COAST GUARD VESSELS

(Bundesgrenzschutz—See)

Notes: (a) This police force consists of about 600 men. Headquarters is at Neustadt and bases at Warnemünde, Sassnitz, Karnin, Stralsund and Frankfurt/Oder.
(b) A maritime section of the anti-terrorist force GSG 9 is attached to the Bundesgrenzschutz.
(c) Craft have blue hulls and white superstructures.

3 KONDOR I CLASS (COASTAL PATROL CRAFT)

BOLTENHAGEN BG 31 (ex-GS 09, ex-G 443)   AHRENSHOOP BG 33 (ex-GS 08, ex-G 415)
KÜHLUNGSBORN BG 32 (ex-GS 07, ex-G 445)

Displacement, tons: 327 standard; 377 full load
Dimensions, feet (metres): 170.3 × 23.3 × 7.2 *(51.9 × 7.1 × 2.2)*
Main machinery: 2 Russki Kolomna 40DM diesels; 4408 hp(m) *(3.24 MW)* sustained; 2 shafts
Speed, knots: 20
Complement: 24
Guns: 2—25 mm (twin) automatic (can be carried).
Radars: Navigation; Racal Decca 360; I band.

Comment: Built by Peenewerft, Wolgast in 1969-71. Ex-GDR Grenzbrigade Küste (GBK) former minesweepers originally taken over from the Navy. All mining and sonar gear removed. Form 3rd Flotilla based at Warnemünde. Four of the class sold to Tunisia in May 1992 and two to Malta in July 1992.

AHRENSHOOP   7/1992, German Coast Guard

1 BREDSTEDT CLASS (LARGE PATROL CRAFT)

Name	No	Builders	Commissioned
BREDSTEDT	BG 21	Elsflether Werft	24 May 1989

Displacement, tons: 673 full load
Dimensions, feet (metres): 214.6 × 30.2 × 10.5 *(65.4 × 9.2 × 3.2)*
Main machinery: 1 MTU 20V 1163 TB93 diesel; 8325 hp(m) *(6.12 MW)* sustained; 1 shaft; bow thruster; 1 auxiliary diesel generator; 1 motor
Speed, knots: 25 (12 on motor). **Range, miles:** 2000 at 25 kts; 7000 at 10 kts
Complement: 18 plus 4 spare
Guns: 1 Bofors 40 mm/70; 90° elevation; 300 rounds/minute to 12 km *(6.5 nm)*; weight of shell 0.96 kg.
Radars: Surface search; Racal AC 2690 BT; I band.
Helicopters: Platform for 1 light.

Comment: Ordered 27 November 1987, laid down 3 March 1988 and launched 18 December 1988. An Avon Searider rigid inflatable craft can be lowered by a stern ramp. A second RIB on the port side is launched by crane. Based in the German Bight.

BREDSTEDT   6/1991, Harald Carstens

3 SASSNITZ CLASS (TYPE 153) (LARGE PATROL CRAFT)

Name	No	Builders	Commissioned
NEUSTRELITZ (ex-*Sassnitz*)	BG 22 (ex-P 6165, ex-591)	Peenewerft, Wolgast	31 July 1990
SELLIN	BG 23 (ex-592)	Peenewerft, Wolgast	2 Oct 1990
BINZ	BG 24 (ex-593)	Peenewerft, Wolgast	23 Dec 1990

Displacement, tons: 369 full load
Dimensions, feet (metres): 160.4 oa; 147.6 wl × 28.5 × 7.2 *(48.9; 45 × 8.7 × 2.2)*
Main machinery: 2 MTU 12V 595 TE90 diesels; 8800 hp(m) *(6.48 MW)* sustained; 2 shafts
Speed, knots: 25. **Range, miles:** 2400 at 20 kts
Complement: 33 (7 officers)
Guns: 1 Bofors 40 mm/70; 90° elevation; 300 rounds/minute to 12 km *(6.5 nm)*; weight of shell 0.96 kg.
Radars: Surface search; Racal AC 2690 BT; I band.
Navigation: I band.

Comment: Ex-GDR designated Balcom 10 and seen for the first time in the Baltic in August 1988. The original intention was to build up to 50 for the USSR, Poland and the GDR. In 1991 the first three were transferred to the Border Guard, based at Neustadt. Fitted with German engines and electronics in 1992/93. The original design had the SS-N-25 SSM and three engines. Three hulls transferred to Poland for completion at Gdynia.

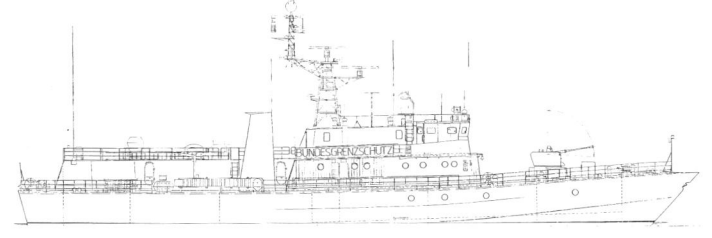

NEUSTRELITZ   (not to scale)

7 NEUSTADT CLASS (LARGE PATROL CRAFT)

Name	No	Name	No
NEUSTADT	BG 11	ALSFELD	BG 16
BAD BRAMSTEDT	BG 12	BAYREUTH	BG 17
DUDERSTADT	BG 14	ROSENHEIM	BG 18
ESCHWEGE	BG 15		

Displacement, tons: 218 full load
Dimensions, feet (metres): 127.1 × 23 × 5 *(38.5 × 7 × 2.2)*
Main machinery: 2 MTU MD diesels; 6000 hp(m) *(4.41 MW)*; 1 MWM diesel; 685 hp(m) *(500 kW)*; 3 shafts
Speed, knots: 30. **Range, miles:** 450 at 27 kts
Complement: 24
Guns: 1 Bofors 40 mm/70; 90° elevation; 300 rounds/minute to 12 km *(6.5 nm)*; weight of shell 0.96 kg.
Radars: Surface search; Selenia ARP 1645; I band.
Navigation: I band.

Comment: All built between 1969 and late 1970 by Lürssen, Vegesack. Form two flotillas: BG 11-14 the first and BG 15-18 the second. BG 13 was sold to Mauritania in February 1990. The after gun mounting has been removed from all.

DUDERSTADT   6/1991, Hartmut Ehlers

2 RIVER PATROL CRAFT

BG 6   BG 7

Comment: Former river engineers craft acquired in the 1970s. Length 15 m and capable of about 6 kts.

BG 7   10/1991, Hartmut Ehlers

4 BREMSE CLASS (TYPE GB 23) (INSHORE PATROL CRAFT)

Name	No	Name	No
PRIGNITZ	BG 61 (ex-G 20, ex-GS 31)	ALTMARK	BG 63 (ex-G 21, ex-GS 21)
UCKERMARK	BG 62 (ex-G 34, ex-GS 23)	BÖRDE	BG 64 (ex-G 35, ex-GS 50)

Displacement, tons: 42 full load
Dimensions, feet (metres): 74.1 × 15.4 × 3.6 *(22.6 × 4.7 × 1.1)*
Main machinery: 2 DM 6VD 18/5 AL-1 diesels; 1020 hp(m) *(750 kW)*; 2 shafts
Speed, knots: 14
Complement: 6
Guns: 2—14.5 mm (twin) MGs can be carried.
Radars: Navigation: TSR 333; I band.

Comment: Built in 1971-72 for the ex-GDR GBK. BG 61 and 62 based at Warnemünde, BG 63 and 64 at Sassnitz. Five of the class sold to Tunisia, two to Malta and two to Jordan, all in 1992.

PRIGNITZ (old number)   4/1991, Hartmut Ehlers

4 TYPE SAB 12 (HARBOUR PATROL CRAFT)

Name	No	Name	No
VOGTLAND	BG 51 (ex-G 56, ex-GS 17)	SPREEWALD	BG 53 (ex-G 51, ex-GS 16)
RHON	BG 52 (ex-G 53, ex-GS 26)	ODERBRUCH	BG 54

Comment: Ex-GDR MAB 12 craft based at Karnin, Stralsund and Frankfurt/Oder. Five sold to Cyprus in 1992.

VOGTLAND   7/1992, German Coast Guard

1 ICEBREAKING TUG (TYPE 724)

Name	No	Builders	Commissioned
RETTIN	BG 5	Mützelfeldwerft	3 Dec 1976

Measurement, tons: 120 grt
Dimensions, feet (metres): 73.8 × 21.7 × 9.5 *(22.5 × 6.6 × 2.9)*
Main machinery: 2 MWM diesels; 590 hp(m) *(434 kW)*; 2 Voith-Schneider props
Speed, knots: 9
Complement: 4

Comment: Launched 29 October 1976. Bollard pull, 7.5 tons. Carries firefighting equipment.

RETTIN   7/1992, German Coast Guard

FISHERY PROTECTION AND RESEARCH SHIPS

(Operated by Ministry of Agriculture and Fisheries)

WARNEMÜNDE of 399 tons and 18 kts. Ex-Kondor I class completed 1969
FRITHJOF of 2150 tons and 16 kts. Completed September 1968
MEERKATZE of 2250 tons and 15 kts. Completed December 1977
SEEFALKE of 1820 tons gross and 20 kts. Completed August 1981
SOLEA of 340 tons and 12 kts. Completed May 1974
UTHÖRN of 200 tons and 10 kts. Completed June 1982
WALTHER HERWIG of 2500 tons and 15 kts. Completed October 1972
HEINCKE of 1322 tons gross and 13 kts. Completed in June 1990

Comment: First four are Fishery Protection ships serving the fleet in the North Atlantic. *Seefalcke* has a helicopter platform. The remainder are research ships carrying scientists. A new ship ordered in 1991 from Peenewerft should complete in 1993.

MEERKATZE   11/1992, van Ginderen Collection

SURVEY AND RESEARCH SHIPS

Note: The following ships operate for the Bundesamt für Seeschiff-fahrt und Hydrographie (BSH), either under the Ministry of Transport or the Ministry of Research and Technology (*Polarstern, Meteor, Poseidon, Sonne* and *Alkor*).

ATAIR (survey), **ALKOR** (research), **WEGA** (survey) 1050 tons, diesel-electric, 11.5 kts. Complement 16 plus 6 scientists. Built by Krögerwerft, completed 3 August 1987, 2 May 1990 and 26 October 1990 respectively
METEOR (research) 97.5 × 16.5 × 4.8 m, diesel-electric, 14 kts, range 10 000 nm. Complement 33 plus 29 research staff. Completed by Schlichting, Travemünde 15 March 1986
KOMET (survey and research) 1535 grt, speed 15 kts. Complement 42 plus 4 scientists. Completed 26 August 1969 by Jadewerft
GAUSS (survey and research) 1813 grt, completed 6 May 1980 by Schlichting, speed 13.5 kts, complement 19 + 12 scientists. Modernised 1985
CARL FR GAUSS (survey) 490 tons; speed 19 kts. Kondor II hull built at Peenewerft in 1976
DENEB (ex-*Wega*) (survey) 157 grt; speed 10 kts. Complement 12. Completed 4 May 1962 by Schlichting
POLARSTERN (polar research) 10 878 grt; completed 1982
POSEIDON (research) 1049 grt; completed 1976
SONNE (research) 1200 grt; completed 1990

CARLF FR. GAUSS   *6/1990, Hartmut Ehlers*

METEOR   *1991, Harald Carstens*

POLARSTERN   *1/1991, Robert Pabst*

CUSTOMS SERVICE

Notes: (a) Operated by Ministry of Finance with a total of over 100 craft. Green hulls with grey superstructure and sometimes carry machine guns.
(b) Seaward patrol craft include *Hamburg, Bremerhaven, Schleswig-Holstein, Emden, Kniepsand, Alte Liebe, Priwall, Glückstadt, Helgoland, Oldenburg, Laboe, Ner Darchau* and *Hohwacht*.

HOHWACHT   *8/1991, Maritime Photographic*

POLICE

Notes: (a) Under the control of regional governments. Blue hulls with white superstructure.
(b) There are 10 seaward patrol craft: *Wasserschutzpolizei 5, WSP 1* and *4, Bremen 2* and *3, Helgoland, Sylt, Fehmarn, Birknack* and *Falshöft*.
(c) Harbour craft include *Dithmarchen, Probstei, Schwansen, Vossbrook, Angela, Brunswick, Habicht*.

WSP 4   *11/1991, Antonio Moreno*

WATER AND NAVIGATION BOARD

Notes: (a) Comes under the Ministry of Transport. Most ships have black hulls with black/red/yellow stripes.
(b) Three icebreakers: *Polarstern, Hanse* and *Max Waldeck*.
(c) Eight buoy tenders: *Walter Körte, Kurt Burkowitz, Otto Treplin, Gustav Meyer, Bruno Illing, Konrad Meisel, Barsemeister Brehme, J G Repsold*.
(d) Five oil recovery ships: *Scharhörn, Oland, Nordsee, Mellum, Kiel*.

OTTO TREPLIN   *6/1992, Antonio Moreno*

GHANA

Headquarters' Appointment	Personnel	Bases	Mercantile Marine
Commander, Navy: Commodore Tom Kwesi Annan	(a) 1993: 850 (b) Voluntary service	Sekondi (Western Naval Command) Tema, near Accra (Eastern Naval Command)	Lloyd's Register of Shipping: 155 vessels of 133 333 tons gross

GHANA / Patrol forces

PATROL FORCES

2 LÜRSSEN PB 57 CLASS (FAST ATTACK CRAFT—GUN)

Name	No.	Builders	Commissioned
ACHIMOTA	P 28	Lürssen, Vegesack	27 Mar 1981
YOGAGA	P 29	Lürssen, Vegesack	27 Mar 1981

Displacement, tons: 389 full load
Dimensions, feet (metres): 190.6 × 25 × 9.2 *(58.1 × 7.6 × 2.8)*
Main machinery: 3 MTU 16V 538 TB91 diesels; 9210 hp(m) *(6.78 MW)* sustained; 3 shafts
Speed, knots: 30
Complement: 45 plus 2 VIPs
Guns: 1 OTO Melara 3 in *(76 mm)* compact; 85° elevation; 85 rounds/minute to 16 km *(8.6 nm)* anti-surface; 12 km *(6.5 nm)* anti-air; weight of shell 6 kg; 250 rounds.
1 Breda 40 mm/70; 85° elevation; 300 rounds/minute to 12.5 km *(6.8 nm)* anti-surface; weight of shell 0.96 kg; 750 rounds.
Fire control: LIOD optronic director.
Radars: Surface search/fire control: Thomson-CSF Canopus B; I/J band.
Navigation: Decca TM 1226C; I band.

Comment: Ordered in 1977. *Yogaga* completed a major overhaul at Swan Hunter's Wallsend, Tyneside yard 8 May 1989. *Achimota* started a similar refit at CMN Cherbourg in May 1991 and was joined by *Yogaga* for repairs in late 1991. Both completed by August 1992. Employed on Fishery Protection duties.

YOGAGA   5/1989, Swan Hunter

2 LÜRSSEN FPB 45 CLASS (FAST ATTACK CRAFT—GUN)

Name	No.	Builders	Commissioned
DZATA	P 26	Lürssen, Vegesack	4 Dec 1979
SEBO	P 27	Lürssen, Vegesack	2 May 1980

Displacement, tons: 269 full load
Dimensions, feet (metres): 147.3 × 23 × 8.9 *(44.9 × 7 × 2.7)*
Main machinery: 2 MTU 16V 538 TB91 diesels; 6140 hp(m) *(4.5 MW)* sustained; 2 shafts
Speed, knots: 27. **Range, miles:** 1800 at 16 kts; 700 at 25 kts
Complement: 55 (5 officers)
Guns: 2 Breda 40 mm/70; 80° elevation; 300 rounds/minute to 12.5 km *(6.8 nm)*; weight of shell 0.96 kg.
Fire control: LIOD optronic director.
Radars: Surface search/fire control: Thomson-CSF Canopus B; I/J band.
Navigation: Decca Type 978; I band.

Comment: Ordered in 1976. *Dzata* completed a major overhaul at Swan Hunter's Wallsend, Tyneside yard on 8 May 1989. *Sebo* started a similar refit at CMN Cherbourg in May 1991 which completed in August 1992. Employed in Fishery Protection role.

DZATA   5/1989, Swan Hunter

LAND-BASED MARITIME AIRCRAFT

Note: In addition four Skyvan and four Defender aircraft are available for maritime reconnaissance.

Numbers/Type: 2 Fokker F27 400M.
Operational speed: 250 kts *(463 km/h)*.
Service ceiling: 25 000 ft *(7 620 m)*.
Range: 2700 nm *(5000 km)*.
Role/Weapon systems: Operated for coastal surveillance, SAR and shipping control tasks. Sensors: Weather radar. Weapons: Unarmed.

GREECE

Headquarters' Appointments

Chief of the Hellenic Navy:
  Vice Admiral H Drikos
Deputy Chief of the Hellenic Navy:
  Rear Admiral I Panagiotopoulos
Deputy Chief, National Defence Staff:
  Vice Admiral N Fostieris
Commander, Navy Training Command:
  Rear Admiral P Kavlieros
Commander, Navy Logistics Command:
  Rear Admiral N Themelidis

Fleet Command

Commander of the Fleet:
  Vice Admiral G Demestihas
Chief of Staff, Fleet HQ:
  Rear Admiral E Zarokostas

Diplomatic Representation

Naval Attaché in Ankara:
  Commander K Mayatis
Naval Attaché in Bonn:
  Captain G Voulgarakis
Naval Attaché in Cairo:
  Captain G Antonopoulos
Naval Attaché in London:
  Captain I Theofanidis
Naval Attaché in Paris:
  Captain D Hatzidakis
Naval Attaché in Washington:
  Captain A Kopitsas

Personnel

(a) 1993: 19 500 (2900 officers)
(b) Between 19 and 23 months' national service depending on location

Bases

Salamis and Suda Bay

Naval Commands

Commander of the Fleet has under his flag all combatant ships. Navy Logistic Command is responsible for the bases at Salamis and Suda Bay, the Supply Centre and all auxiliary ships. Navy Training Command is in charge of the Naval Officers' Academy, Petty Officers' School, three training centres and a training ship.

Naval Districts

Aegean, Ionian and Northern Greece

Strength of the Fleet

Type	Active (Reserve)	Building (Planned)
Patrol Submarines	10	—
Destroyers	8(2)	—
Frigates	6	6
Corvettes	5	—
Fast Attack Craft—Missile	14	—
Fast Attack Craft—Torpedo	10	—
Fast Attack Craft—Patrol	4	2
Large Patrol Craft	2	—
Coastal Patrol Craft	5	—
Major Landing Ships	11	5
LCUs	7	—
LCTs	2	—
Minor Landing Craft	77	—
Minelayers—Coastal	2	—
Minesweepers—Coastal	14	—
Survey and Research Vessels	6	—
Support Ship	1	—
Training Ship	1	—
Support Tankers	2	—
Harbour Tankers	4	—
Lighthouse Tenders	2	—
Tugs	17	—
Netlayer	1	—
Water Boats	8	—
Auxiliary Transports	2	—
Ammunition Ship	1	—

Prefix to Ships' Names

HS (Hellenic Ship)

Naval Aviation

Alouette III helicopters (No 1 Squadron).
AB 212ASW helicopters (No 2 and 3 Squadrons).
HU-16B Albatros are operated under naval command by mixed Air Force and Navy crews.

Mercantile Marine

Lloyd's Register of Shipping:
  1872 vessels of 24 542 087 tons gross

DELETIONS

Note: Many of the deleted ships are in unmaintained reserve in anchorages.

Destroyers

1991 *Aspis, Velos, Lonchi, Sfendoni*
1992 *Miaoulis, Themistocles* (old)
1993 *Sachtouris, Apostolis*

Frigates

1991 *Aetos*
1992 *Panthir, Ierax, Leon*

Light Forces

1990 *N I Goulandris 1*
1991 *E Panagopoulos 1*
1992 *Adamidis*

Amphibious Forces

1990 *I Tournas, Kea, Skopelos*
1991 *Lesbos* (old), *Kassos, Karpathos*
1992 *Kimolos, Sifnos, Skiathos*

Miscellaneous

1990 *Minotaurus, Perseus*
1991 *Argo* (sold), *Aegeon, Arhikelefstis Stassis*
1992 *Kastoria*

Introduction — Submarines / GREECE

PENNANT LIST

Submarines

- S 110 Glavkos
- S 111 Nereus
- S 112 Triton
- S 113 Proteus
- S 114 Papanikolis
- S 115 Katsonis
- S 116 Posydon
- S 117 Amphitrite
- S 118 Okeanos
- S 119 Pontos

Destroyers

- D 212 Kanaris
- D 213 Kountouriotis
- D 215 Tompazis
- D 217 Kriezis
- D 218 Kimon
- D 219 Nearchos
- D 220 Formion
- D 221 Themistocles

Frigates

- F 450 Elli
- F 451 Limnos
- F 452 Hydra
- F 453 Spetsai (bldg)
- F 454 Psara (bldg)
- F 455 Salamis (bldg)
- F 456 Epirus
- F 457 Thrace
- F 458 Makedonia
- F 460 Aegeon

Corvettes

- P 62 Niki
- P 63 Doxa
- P 64 Eleftheria
- P 65 Carteria
- P 66 Andreia

Light Forces

- P 14 Anthipoploiarhos Anninos
- P 15 Ipoploiarhos Arliotis
- P 16 Ipoploiarhos Konidis
- P 17 Ipoploiarhos Batsis
- P 18 Armatolos
- P 19 Navmachos
- P 20 Antiploiarhos Laskos
- P 21 Plotarhis Blessas
- P 22 Ipoploiarhos Mikonios
- P 23 Ipoploiarhos Troupakis
- P 24 Simeoforos Kavaloudis
- P 25 Anthipoploiarhos Kostakos
- P 26 Ipoploiarhos Deyiannis
- P 27 Simeoforos Xenos
- P 28 Simeoforos Simitzopoulos
- P 29 Simeoforos Starakis
- P 50 Hesperos
- P 52 Kentauros
- P 53 Kyklon
- P 54 Lelaps
- P 55 Skorpios
- P 56 Tyfon
- P 70 E Panagopoulos 2
- P 96 E Panagopoulos 3
- P 196 Andromeda
- P 198 Kyknos
- P 199 Pigasos
- P 228 Toxotis
- P 229 Tolmi
- P 230 Ormi
- P 267 Dilos
- P 268 Knossos
- P 269 Lindos
- P 286 Diopos Antoniou
- P 287 Kelefstis Stamou

Amphibious Forces

- L 104 Inouse
- L 116 Kos
- L 144 Siros
- L 149 Kithnos
- L 153 Nafkratoussa
- L 154 Ikaria (old)
- L 157 Rodos (old)
- L 161 I Grigoropoulos
- L 163 I Daniolos
- L 164 I Roussen
- L 165 I Krystalidis
- L 167 Ios
- L 168 Sikinos
- L 169 Irakleia
- L 170 Folegrandos
- L 171 Kriti
- L 173 Chios (bldg)
- L 174 Samos (bldg)
- L 175 Ikaria (bldg)
- L 176 Lesbos (bldg)
- L 177 Rodos (bldg)
- L 178 Naxos
- L 179 Paros
- L 185 Kithera
- L 189 Milos

Minelayers

- N 04 Aktion
- N 05 Amvrakia

Minesweepers

- M 202 Atalanti
- M 205 Antiopi
- M 206 Faedra
- M 210 Thalia
- M 211 Alkyon
- M 213 Klio
- M 214 Avra
- M 240 Pleias
- M 241 Kichli
- M 242 Kissa
- M 246 Aigli
- M 247 Dafni
- M 248 Aedon
- M 254 Niovi

Service Forces

- A 74 Aris
- A 307 Thetis
- A 373 Hermis
- A 375 Zeus
- A 376 Orion
- A 377 Arethousa
- A 407 Antaios
- A 408 Atlas
- A 409 Acchileus
- A 410 Atromitos
- A 411 Adamastos
- A 412 Aias
- A 413 Pilefs
- A 414 Ariadni
- A 415 Evros
- A 416 Ouranos
- A 417 Hyperion
- A 419 Pandora
- A 420 Pandrosos
- A 422 Kadmos
- A 423 Heraklis
- A 424 Iason
- A 425 Odisseus
- A 426 Kiklops
- A 427 Danaos
- A 428 Nestor
- A 430 Pelops
- A 431 Titan
- A 432 Gigas
- A 433 Kerkini
- A 434 Prespa
- A 435 Kekrops
- A 436 Minos
- A 437 Pelias
- A 438 Aegeus
- A 460 Evrotas
- A 461 Arachthos
- A 462 Strymon
- A 463 Nestos
- A 464 Axios
- A 465 Yliki
- A 466 Trichonis
- A 467 Doirani
- A 468 Kalliroe
- A 469 Stimfalia
- A 474 Pytheas
- A 475 Doris
- A 476 Strabon
- A 478 Naftilos
- A 479 I Karavoyiannos Theophilopoulos
- A 481 St Likoudis

SUBMARINES

1 Ex-US GUPPY III CLASS

Name	No	Builders	Laid down	Launched	Commissioned
KATSONIS (ex-USS *Remora* SS 487)	S 115	Portsmouth Navy Yard	5 Mar 1945	12 July 1945	3 Jan 1946

Displacement, tons: 1975 standard; 2450 dived
Dimensions, feet (metres): 326.5 × 27 × 17 *(99.4 × 8.2 × 5.2)*
Main machinery: Diesel-electric; 4 Fairbanks-Morse 38D8 1/8-10 diesels; 6000 hp *(4.48 MW)*; 2 motors; 5600 hp *(4.18 MW)*; 2 shafts
Speed, knots: 20 surfaced; 15 dived
Range, miles: 12 000 at 10 kts surfaced
Complement: 85

Torpedoes: 10—21 in *(533 mm)* tubes (6 bow, 4 stern). 24 probably Honeywell Mk 37 Mod 1; wire-guided; active/passive homing to 8 km *(4.4 nm)* at 24 kts; warhead 150 kg.
Countermeasures: ESM: WLR-1; radar warning.
Radars: Surface search: I band.
Sonars: EDO BQR 2B; hull-mounted; passive; medium frequency. Sperry/Raytheon BQG 4; fire control; hull-mounted; passive; medium frequency.

Programmes: Transferred 29 October 1973 by sale.
Operational: Training boat.

KATSONIS

1989, Hellenic Navy

1 Ex-US GUPPY IIA CLASS

Name	No	Builders	Laid down	Launched	Commissioned
PAPANIKOLIS (ex-USS *Hardhead* SS 365)	S 114	Manitowoc SB Co	7 July 1943	12 Dec 1943	Apr 1944

Displacement, tons: 1840 standard; 2445 dived
Dimensions, feet (metres): 306 × 27 × 17 *(93.2 × 8.2 × 5.2)*
Main machinery: Diesel-electric; 3 GM 16-278A diesels; 4500 hp *(3.36 MW)*; 2 motors; 5400 hp *(4.3 MW)*; 2 shafts
Speed, knots: 17 surfaced; 15 dived
Range, miles: 12 000 at 10 kts surfaced
Complement: 84

Torpedoes: 10—21 in *(533 mm)* tubes (6 bow, 4 stern). 24 probably Honeywell Mk 37 Mod 1; wire-guided; active/passive homing to 8 km *(4.3 nm)* at 24 kts; warhead 150 kg.
Countermeasures: ESM: WLR-1; radar warning.
Radars: Surface search: I band.
Sonars: EDO BQR 2B; hull-mounted; passive search; medium frequency.

Programmes: Transferred 26 July 1972 by sale.
Operational: Training boat.

PAPANIKOLIS

1990, Hellenic Navy

254 GREECE / Submarines — Destroyers

8 GLAVKOS CLASS (209 TYPES 1100 and 1200)

Name	No	Builders	Laid down	Launched	Commissioned
GLAVKOS	S 110	Howaldtswerke, Kiel	1 Sep 1968	15 Sep 1970	6 Sep 1971
NEREUS	S 111	Howaldtswerke, Kiel	15 Jan 1969	7 June 1971	10 Feb 1972
TRITON	S 112	Howaldtswerke, Kiel	1 June 1969	14 Oct 1971	8 Aug 1972
PROTEUS	S 113	Howaldtswerke, Kiel	1 Oct 1969	1 Feb 1972	8 Aug 1972
POSYDON	S 116	Howaldtswerke, Kiel	15 Jan 1976	21 Mar 1978	22 Mar 1979
AMPHITRITE	S 117	Howaldtswerke, Kiel	26 Apr 1976	14 June 1978	14 Sep 1979
OKEANOS	S 118	Howaldtswerke, Kiel	1 Oct 1976	16 Nov 1978	15 Nov 1979
PONTOS	S 119	Howaldtswerke, Kiel	25 Jan 1977	21 Mar 1979	29 Apr 1980

Displacement, tons: 1100 surfaced; 1210 (1285, S 112 and 116-119) dived
Dimensions, feet (metres): 178.4; 183.4 (112, 116-119) × 20.3 × 17.9 *(54.4; 55.9 × 6.2 × 5.5)*
Main machinery: Diesel-electric; 4 MTU 12V 493 AZ80 diesels; 2400 hp(m) *(1.76 MW)* sustained; 4 Siemens alternators; 1.7 MW; 1 Siemens motor; 4600 hp(m) *(3.38 MW)* sustained; 1 shaft
Speed, knots: 11 surfaced; 21.5 dived
Complement: 31 (6 officers)

Missiles: McDonnell Douglas Sub Harpoon (after modernisation); active radar homing to 130 km *(70 nm)* at 0.9 Mach; warhead 258 kg. Can be discharged from 4 tubes only.
Torpedoes: 8—21 in *(533 mm)* bow tubes. 14 probably AEG SST 4; wire-guided; active homing to 13 km *(7 nm)* at 35 kts; passive homing to 28 km *(15 nm)* at 23 kts; warhead 260 kg. Swim-out discharge. Probably to be replaced by AEG SEEAL 3.
Countermeasures: ESM: Racal Sealion (after modernisation). Thomson-CSF DR 2000U (unmodernised); radar warning.
Fire control: Signaal (S 116-S 119). Unisys (after modernisation). Kanaris (unmodernised).
Radars: Surface search: Thomson-CSF Calypso II; I band.
Sonars: Atlas Elektronik CSU 3-2 (unmodernised); hull-mounted; active/passive search and attack; medium frequency.
Atlas Elektronik PRS-3-4; passive ranging.
Atlas Elektronik CSU 83-90 (DBQS-21) (after modernisation)

Atlas Elektronik CSU-3-4 (S 112, 116-119); hull-mounted; active/passive search and attack; medium frequency.
Thomson Sintra DUUX 2; passive ranging.

Programmes: Designed by Ingenieurkontor, Lübeck for construction by Howaldtswerke, Kiel and sale by Ferrostaal, Essen all acting as a consortium.
Modernisation: Contract signed 5 May 1989 with HDW and Ferrostaal to implement a Neptune update programme to bring first four up to the same standard as the others and along the same lines as the German S 206A class. Also to include Sub

AMPHITRITE   *1987, van Ginderen Collection*

Harpoon. *Triton* completed refit at Kiel in early 1993, remainder are being done at Salamis between 1993 and 1996 in a Synchrolift purchased by the Navy. A quarter of the cost is covered by German Military Aid.
Structure: A single-hull design with two ballast tanks and fwd and after trim tanks. Fitted with snort and remote machinery control. The single screw is slow revving. Very high capacity batteries with GRP lead-acid cells and battery cooling—by Wilh Hagen and VARTA. Diving depth, 250 m *(820 ft)*. Fitted with two periscopes.
Operational: Endurance, 50 days.

DESTROYERS

4 Ex-US CHARLES F ADAMS CLASS

Name	No	Builders	Laid down	Launched	Commissioned	Recommissioned
KIMON (ex-*Semmes*)	D 218 (ex-DDG 18)	Avondale Marine Ways	18 Aug 1960	20 May 1961	10 Dec 1962	12 Sep 1992
NEARCHOS (ex-*Waddell*)	D 219 (ex-DDG 24)	Todd Shipyards	6 Feb 1962	26 Feb 1963	28 Aug 1964	1 Oct 1992
FORMION (ex-*Miltiadis*, ex-*Strauss*)	D 220 (ex-DDG 16)	New York Shipbuilding	27 Dec 1960	9 Dec 1961	20 Apr 1963	1 Oct 1992
THEMISTOCLES (ex-*Konon*, ex-*Berkeley*)	D 221 (ex-DDG 15)	New York Shipbuilding	1 June 1960	29 July 1961	15 Dec 1962	1 Oct 1992

Displacement, tons: 3370 standard; 4825 full load
Dimensions, feet (metres): 437 × 47 × 15.6; 21 (sonar) *(133.2 × 14.3 × 4.8; 6.4)*
Main machinery: 4 boilers (Foster-Wheeler in D 219, 221, Combustion Engineering in D 218, 220); 2 turbines (General Electric in D 218, 220, Westinghouse in D 219, 221); 70 000 hp *(52.2 MW)*; 2 shafts
Speed, knots: 30. **Range, miles:** 6000 at 15 kts; 1600 at 30 kts
Complement: 340 (22 officers)

Missiles: SSM: 6 McDonnell Douglas Harpoon; active radar homing to 130 km *(70 nm)* at 0.9 Mach; warhead 227 kg.
SAM: 34 GDC Standard SM-1MR; command guidance; semi-active radar homing to 46 km *(25 nm)* at 2 Mach; height 150-60 000 ft *(45.7-18 288 m)*.
1 single Mk 13 launcher ❶; can load, direct, and fire about 6 missiles per minute. There are 40 missiles carried. 6 Harpoons are stored in the magazines as part of the load.
A/S: Honeywell ASROC Mk 16 octuple launcher ❷; inertial guidance to 1.6-10 km *(1-5.4 nm)*; payload Mk 46 Mod 5.
Guns: 2 FMC 5 in *(127 mm)*/54 Mk 42 ❸; 85° elevation; 20-40 rounds/minute to 24 km *(13 nm)*; weight of shell 32 kg.
4—12.7 mm MGs.
Torpedoes: 6—324 mm Mk 32 (2 triple) tubes ❹. Honeywell Mk 46; anti-submarine; active/passive homing to 11 km *(5.9 nm)* at 40 kts; warhead 44 kg.
Countermeasures: Decoys: 4 Loral Hycor SRBOC 6-barrelled fixed Mk 36; IR flares and chaff to 4 km *(2.2 nm)*.
T—Mk-6 Fanfare; torpedo decoy.
ESM/ECM: SLQ 32V(2); radar warning.
Combat data systems: Link 14 receive only. SATCOM. NTDS being replaced by Signaal STACOS.
Fire control: Mk 68 GFCS. Mk 4 WDS. Mk 70 MFCS. Mk 114 FCS ASW. SYS-1 IADT.
Radars: Air search: Hughes SPS 52B/C ❺; 3D; E/F band; range 439 km *(240 nm)*.
Lockheed SPS 40B/D ❻; E/F band; range 320 km *(175 nm)*.
Surface search: Raytheon SPS 10D/F ❼; G band.
Navigation: Marconi LN 66; I band.
Fire control: Two Raytheon SPG 51D ❽; G/I band.
Lockheed SPG 53A ❾; K band.
Tacan: URN 25/SRN 6. IFF Mk XII.
Sonars: Sangamo SQS 23D; hull-mounted (bow-mounted SQQ 23 Pair in D 219); active/passive search and attack; medium frequency. To be replaced by DE 1191.

Programmes: Leased as part of the Defence Co-operation Agreement signed with the USA on 8 July 1990. *Kimon* recommissioned at Salamis, the remainder in San Diego prior to sailing for Greece in late 1992.
Modernisation: DE 1191 sonars being fitted at the expense of the Gearing class. A Signaal STACOS command system is to replace NTDS.
Structure: *Nearchos* has a stern anchor because of the sonar Pair arrangement.

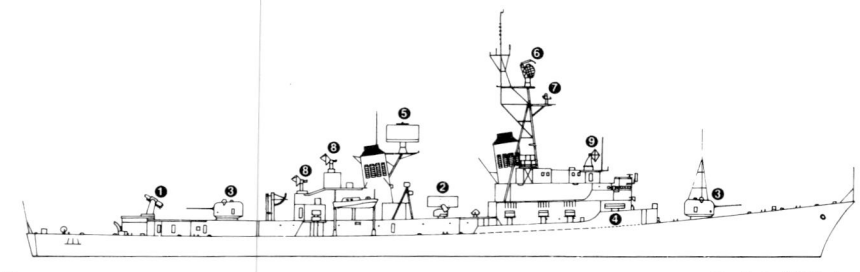

KIMON   *(Scale 1 : 1200), Ian Sturton*

NEARCHOS   *11/1991, Paul Campbe*

Destroyers / GREECE

6 Ex-US GEARING (FRAM I) CLASS

Name	No	Builders	Laid down	Launched	Commissioned
KANARIS (ex-USS *Stickell* DD 888)	D 212	Consolidated Steel Corporation	5 Jan 1945	16 June 1945	26 Sep 1945
KOUNTOURIOTIS (ex-USS *Rupertus* DD 851)	D 213	Bethlehem (Quincy)	2 May 1945	21 Sep 1945	8 Mar 1946
SACHTOURIS (ex-USS *Arnold J Isbell* DD 869)	D 214	Bethlehem (Staten Island)	14 Mar 1945	6 Aug 1945	5 Jan 1946
TOMPAZIS (ex-USS *Gurke* DD 783)	D 215	Todd Pacific Shipyards	Oct 1944	15 Feb 1945	12 May 1945
APOSTOLIS (ex-USS *Charles P Cecil* DD 835)	D 216	Bath Iron Works	2 Dec 1944	22 Apr 1945	29 June 1945
KRIEZIS (ex-USS *Corry* DD 817)	D 217	Consolidated Steel Corporation	5 Apr 1945	28 July 1945	26 Feb 1946

Displacement, tons: 2425 standard; 3500 full load
Dimensions, feet (metres): 390.5 × 41.2 × 19 *(119 × 12.6 × 5.8)*
Main machinery: 4 Babcock & Wilcox boilers; 600 psi *(43.3 kg/cm sq)*; 850°F *(454°C)*; 2 Westinghouse turbines; 60 000 hp *(45 MW)*; 2 shafts
Speed, knots: 32.5. **Range, miles:** 4800 at 15 kts
Complement: 269 (16 officers)

Missiles: SSM: 4 McDonnell Douglas Harpoon (not in D 216-217) ❶; active radar homing to 130 km *(70 nm)* at 0.9 Mach; warhead 227 kg.
SAM: Portable Redeye; shoulder-launched; short range.
A/S: Honeywell ASROC Mk 112 octuple launcher ❷; inertial guidance to 10 km *(5.4 nm)*. Mk 46 torpedo; active/passive homing to 11 km *(5.9 nm)* at 40 kts; warhead 45 kg.
Guns: 4 USN 5 in *(127 mm)*/38 (2 twin) Mk 38 ❸; 85° elevation; 15 rounds/minute to 17 km *(9 nm)* anti-surface; 11 km *(5.9 nm)* anti-aircraft; weight of shell 25 kg.
1 OTO Melara 3 in *(76 mm)*/62 compact aft ❹; 85° elevation; 85 rounds/minute to 16 km *(8.6 nm)* anti-surface; 12 km *(6.5 nm)* anti-aircraft; weight of shell 6 kg.
1 Bofors 40 mm/70 (D 216-217); 90° elevation; 300 rounds/minute to 12 km *(6.5 nm)*; weight of shell 2.4 kg.
2—12.7 mm MGs.
Torpedoes: 6—324 mm Mk 32 (2 triple) tubes ❺. Honeywell Mk 46; anti-submarine; active/passive homing to 11 km *(5.9 nm)* at 40 kts; warhead 44 kg.
Depth charges: 2 racks.
Countermeasures: Decoys: 2 Loral Hycor SRBOC fixed triple 6-barrelled chaff launchers; range 1-4 km *(0.6-2.2 nm)*.
ESM: WLR-1; radar warning.
ECM: ULQ-6; jammer.
Fire control: Mk 37 GFCS. Elsag NA 21/30.
Radars: Air search: Westinghouse SPS 37 (D 212, D 215, D 216) ❻; B/C band; range 556 km *(300 nm)*.
Lockheed SPS 40 (remainder); E/F band; range 320 km *(175 nm)*.
Surface search: Raytheon/Sylvania SPS 10 ❼; G band.
Navigation: Decca; I band.
Fire control: Western Electric Mk 25 ❽; I/J band.
Selenia RTN 10X ❾; I/J band; range 40 km *(22 nm)*.
Sonars: Sangamo SQS 23; hull-mounted; active search and attack; medium frequency.

Programmes: From USA: D 214, 4 Dec 1973 (sold 11 July 1978); D 212, 1 July 1972; D 213, 10 July 1973 (sold 11 July 1978); D 215, by sale 17 Mar 1977, commissioned 20 Mar 1977; D 216 and ex-USS *Myles C Fox* 2 August 1980. D 217 and ex-USS *Dyess* DD 880 transferred 27 February 1981 by sale.
Modernisation: Major modernisation programme in 1987-88 for all. Included Harpoon, OTO Melara 76 mm/62 gun placed aft and a new FCS (NA-30 or NA-21). D 216 and D 217 completed in 1987 without Harpoon but with a forward Bofors 40 mm/70 mounted between the torpedo tubes. Harpoon is not always carried. SQS 23 was to have been replaced by DE 1191 but the new sonars are now being fitted in newer ships.
Operational: All to be paid off by the end of 1994. D 214 and 216 in reserve and to be scrapped in 1993.

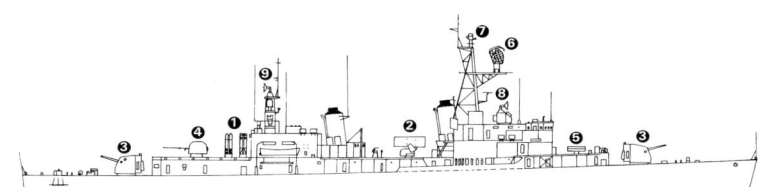

KOUNTOURIOTIS *(Scale 1 : 1200), Ian Sturton*

KOUNTOURIOTIS *9/1991, van Ginderen Collection*

SACHTOURIS *5/1992, G Toremans*

KANARIS *10/1990, Hellenic Navy*

256 GREECE / Frigates

FRIGATES

1 + 3 HYDRA CLASS (MEKO 200HN)

Name	No	Builders	Laid down	Launched	Commissioned
HYDRA	F 452	Blohm & Voss, Hamburg	17 Dec 1990	25 June 1991	12 Nov 1992
SPETSAI	F 453	Blohm & Voss/Hellenic Shipyards, Skaramanga	11 Aug 1992	June 1993	May 1995
PSARA	F 454	Hellenic Shipyards, Skaramanga	Dec 1993	Sep 1994	Feb 1997
SALAMIS	F 455	Hellenic Shipyards, Skaramanga	Feb 1995	Nov 1995	Mar 1998

Displacement, tons: 2710 light; 3200 full load
Dimensions, feet (metres): 383.9; 357.6 (wl) × 48.6 × 13.5 *(117; 109 × 14.8 × 4.1)*
Main machinery: CODOG; 2 GE LM 2500 gas turbines; 60 000 hp *(44.76 MW)* sustained; 2 MTU 20V 956 TB82 diesels; 10 420 hp(m) *(7.66 MW)* sustained; 2 shafts; cp props
Speed, knots: 31 gas; 20 diesel. **Range, miles:** 4100 at 16 kts
Complement: 173 (22 officers) plus 16 flag staff

Missiles: SSM: 8 McDonnell Douglas Harpoon Block 1C; 2 quad launchers ❶; active radar homing to 130 km *(70 nm)* at 0.9 Mach; warhead 227 kg.
SAM: Raytheon NATO Sea Sparrow Mk 48 Mod 2A vertical launcher ❷; 16 missiles; semi-active radar homing to 14.6 km *(8 nm)* at 2.5 Mach; warhead 39 kg.
Guns: 1 FMC Mk 45 Mod 2A 5 in *(127 mm)*/54 ❸; dual purpose.
2 GD/GE Vulcan Phalanx 20 mm Mk 15 Mod 12 ❹; 6 barrels per mounting; 3000 rounds/minute combined to 1.5 km.
Torpedoes: 6—324 mm Mk 32 Mod 5 (2 triple) tubes ❺. Honeywell Mk 46; anti-submarine; active/passive homing to 11 km *(5.9 nm)* at 40 kts; warhead 44 kg.
Countermeasures: Decoys: 4 Mk 36 Mod 2 SRBOC chaff launchers ❻.
SLQ-25 Nixie; torpedo decoy.
ESM: Argo AR 700; Telegon 10; intercept.
ECM: Argo APECS II; jammer.
Combat data systems: Signaal STACOS Mod 2; Links 11 and 14.
Fire control: Two Signaal Mk 73 Mod 1 (for SAM). Vesta Helo transponder with data link for OTHT. SAR-8 IR search. SWG 1 A(V) Harpoon LCS.
Radars: Air search: Signaal MW 08 ❼; 3D; F/G band.
Air Surface search: Signaal/Magnavox; DA 08 ❽, F band.
Navigation: Racal Decca 2690 BT; I band.
Fire Control: 2 Signaal STIR ❾; I/J/K band.
IFF: Mk XII Mod 4.
Sonars: Raytheon SQS-56/DE 1160; hull-mounted and VDS.

Helicopters: 1 Sikorsky S-70B6 Seahawk ❿ (from 1995).

Programmes: Decision to buy four Meko 200 Mod 3HN announced on 18 April 1988. West German Government 'offset' of tanks and aircraft went with the sale, and the electronics and some of the weapon systems are being secured through US FMS credits. The first ship ordered 10 February 1989 built by Blohm & Voss, Hamburg and the remainder ordered 10 May 1989 at Hellenic Shipyards, Skaramanga, with German technical assistance. Programme has been delayed by financial problems at Hellenic Shipyards in 1992 and some of the prefabrication of *Spetsai* has been done in Hamburg.
Structure: The design follows the Portuguese Vasco da Gama class. All steel fin stabilisers.

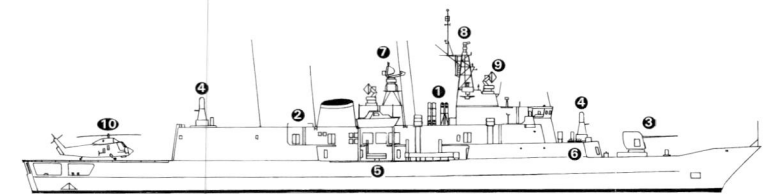
HYDRA *(Scale 1 : 1200), Ian Sturton*

HYDRA *6/1992, Hartmut Ehlers*

HYDRA *11/1992, Harald Carstens*

2 + 3 NETHERLANDS KORTENAER CLASS

Name	No	Builders	Laid down	Launched	Commissioned
ELLI (ex-*Pieter Florisz* F 812)	F 450	Koninklijke Maatschappij de Schelde, Flushing	1 July 1977	15 Dec 1979	10 Oct 1981
LIMNOS (ex-*Witte de With* F 813)	F 451	Koninklijke Maatschappij de Schelde, Flushing	13 June 1978	27 Oct 1979	18 Sep 1982
AEGEON (ex-*Banckert* F 810)	F 460	Koninklijke Maatschappij de Schelde, Flushing	25 Feb 1976	13 July 1978	29 Oct 1980
— (ex-*Callenburgh* F 808)	—	Koninklijke Maatschappij de Schelde, Flushing	30 June 1975	12 Mar 1977	26 July 1979
— (ex-*Van Kinsbergen* F 809)	—	Koninklijke Maatschappij de Schelde, Flushing	2 Sep 1975	16 Apr 1977	24 Apr 1980

Displacement, tons: 3050 standard; 3630 full load
Dimensions, feet (metres): 428 × 47.9 × 20.3 (screws) *(130.5 × 14.6 × 6.2)*
Main machinery: COGOG; 2 RR Olympus TM3B gas turbines; 50 880 hp *(39.7 MW)* sustained; 2 RR Tyne RM1C gas turbines; 9900 hp *(7.4 MW)* sustained; 2 shafts; cp props
Speed, knots: 30. **Range, miles:** 4700 at 16 kts
Complement: 176 (17 officers)

Missiles: SSM: 8 McDonnell Douglas Harpoon (2 quad) launchers ❶; active radar homing to 130 km *(70 nm)* at 0.9 Mach; warhead 227 kg; 16 missiles.
SAM: Raytheon NATO Sea Sparrow ❷; 24 missiles; semi-active radar homing to 14.6 km *(8 nm)* at 2.5 Mach; warhead 39 kg.
Portable Redeye; shoulder-launched; short range.
Guns: 2 OTO Melara 3 in *(76 mm)*/62 compact ❸; 85° elevation; 85 rounds/minute to 16 km *(8.6 nm)* anti-surface; 12 km *(6.5 nm)* anti-aircraft; weight of shell 6 kg.
2 GE/GD Vulcan Phalanx 20 mm Mk 15 6-barrelled ❹; 90° elevation; 3000 rounds/minute combined to 1.5 km.
Torpedoes: 4—324 mm Mk 32 (2 twin) tubes ❺. 16 Honeywell Mk 46 Mod 1/2; anti-submarine; active/passive homing to 11 km *(5.9 nm)* at 40 kts; warhead 44 kg.
Countermeasures: Decoys: 2 Loral Hycor Mk 36 SRBOC chaff launchers.
ESM: Elettronika Sphinx; radar warning.
ECM: Jammer.
Combat data systems: Signaal SEWACO II action data automation; Links 10 and 11.
Radars: Air search: Signaal LW 08 ❻; D band; range 264 km *(145 nm)* for 2 m² target.
Surface search: Signaal ZW 06 ❼; I band; range 26 km *(14 nm)*.
Fire control: Signaal WM 25 ❽; I/J band; range 46 km *(25 nm)*.
Signaal STIR ❾; I/J/K band; range 140 km *(76 nm)* for 1 m² target.
Sonars: Canadian Westinghouse SQS 505; hull-mounted; active search and attack; 7 kHz.

Helicopters: 2 AB 212ASW ❿.

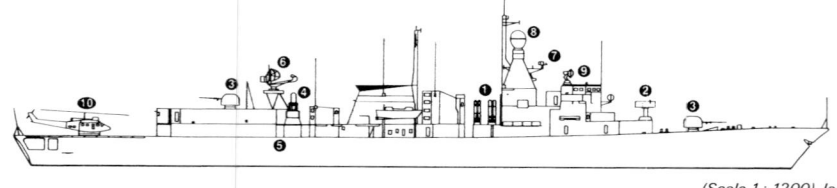
ELLI *(Scale 1 : 1200), Ian Sturton*

LIMNOS *10/1992, D Dervissis*

Programmes: A contract was signed with the Netherlands on 15 September 1980 for the purchase of one of the Kortenaer class building for the Netherlands' Navy, and an option on a second of class, which was taken up 7 June 1981. A second contract, signed on 9 November 1992, transferred three more of the class. Planned delivery dates are May 1993, April 1994 and February 1995.
Modernisation: The original plan was to fit one Phalanx CIWS in place of the after 76 mm gun but for Gulf deployments in 1990-91 the gun was retained and two Phalanx fitted on the deck above the torpedo tubes. Corvus chaff launchers replaced by SRBOC (fitted either side of the bridge). The three ex-Netherlands ships will be modified to the same standard with a second 76 mm gun, 2 Phalanx (vice Goalkeeper) and a larger hangar.
Structure: Hangar is 2 m longer than in Netherlands' ships to accommodate AB 212ASW helicopters.

Frigates — Land-based maritime aircraft / GREECE   257

3 Ex-US KNOX CLASS

Name	No	Builders	Laid down	Launched	Commissioned	Recommissioned
EPIRUS (ex-*Connole*)	F 456 (ex-FF 1056)	Avondale Shipyards	23 Mar 1967	20 July 1968	30 Aug 1969	30 Aug 1992
THRACE (ex-*Trippe*)	F 457 (ex-FF 1075)	Avondale Shipyards	29 July 1968	1 Nov 1969	19 Sep 1970	30 July 1992
MAKEDONIA (ex-*Vreeland*)	F 458 (ex-FF 1068)	Avondale Shipyards	20 Mar 1968	14 June 1969	13 June 1970	25 July 1992

Displacement, tons: 3011 standard; 3877 full load
Dimensions, feet (metres): 439.6 × 46.8 × 15; 24.8 (sonar) *(134 × 14.3 × 4.6; 7.8)*
Main machinery: 2 Combustion Engineering/Babcock & Wilcox boilers; 1200 psi *(84.4 kg/cm sq)*; 950°F *(510°C)*; 1 turbine; 35 000 hp *(26 MW)*; 1 shaft
Speed, knots: 27. **Range, miles:** 4000 at 22 kts on 1 boiler
Complement: 288 (17 officers)

Missiles: SSM: 8 McDonnell Douglas Harpoon; active radar homing to 130 km *(70 nm)* at 0.9 Mach; warhead 227 kg.
  A/S: Honeywell ASROC Mk 16 octuple launcher with reload system (has 2 cells modified to fire Harpoon) ❶; inertial guidance to 1.6-10 km *(1-5.4 nm)*; payload Mk 46.
Guns: 1 FMC 5 in *(127 mm)*/54 Mk 42 Mod 9 ❷; 85° elevation; 20-40 rounds/minute to 24 km *(13 nm)* anti-surface; 14 km *(7.7 nm)* anti-aircraft; weight of shell 32 kg.
  1 General Electric/General Dynamics 20 mm/76 6-barrelled Mk 15 Vulcan Phalanx ❸; 3000 rounds/minute combined to 1.5 km.
Torpedoes: 4—324 mm Mk 32 (2 twin) fixed tubes ❹. 22 Honeywell Mk 46; anti-submarine; active/passive homing to 11 km *(5.9 nm)* at 40 kts; warhead 44 kg.
Countermeasures: Decoys: 2 Loral Hycor SRBOC 6-barrelled fixed Mk 36 ❺; IR flares and chaff to 4 km *(2.2 nm)*. T Mk-6 Fanfare/SLQ-25 Nixie; torpedo decoy. Prairie Masker hull and blade rate noise suppression.
  ESM/ECM: SLQ 32(V)2 ❻; radar warning. Sidekick modification adds jammer and deception system.
Combat data systems: Link 14 receive only. FFISTS (Frigate Integrated Shipboard Tactical Systems) (see *Modernisation*).
Fire control: SWG-1A Harpoon LCS. Mk 68 GFCS. Mk 114 ASW FCS. Mk 1 target designation system. MMS target acquisition sight (for mines, small craft and low flying aircraft).
Radars: Air search: Lockheed SPS 40B ❼; E/F band; range 320 km *(175 nm)*.
  Surface search: Raytheon SPS 10 or Norden SPS 67 ❽; G band.
  Navigation: Marconi LN 66; I band.
  Fire control: Western Electric SPG 53 ❾; I/J band.
  Tacan: SRN 15. IFF: UPX-12.
Sonars: EDO/General Electric SQS 26 CX; bow-mounted; active search and attack; medium frequency.
  EDO SQS 35; independent VDS.

Helicopters: 1 AB 212ASW ❿.

Programmes: Officially announced on 11 February 1992 that three Knox class would be leased and then transferred to the Hellenic Navy. The names in English translation are Epirus, Thrace and Macedonia, three of the Greek border provinces. *Makedonia* arrived at Salamis 25 August 1992, *Thrace* 15 September 1992 and *Epirus* in early 1993.
Modernisation: From 1972 to 1976 they were modified to accommodate the Light Airborne Multi-Purpose System (LAMPS) and the SH-2F Seasprite anti-submarine helicopter; hangar and flight deck are enlarged. In 1979 a programme was initiated to fit 3.5 ft bow bulwarks and spray strakes adding 9.1

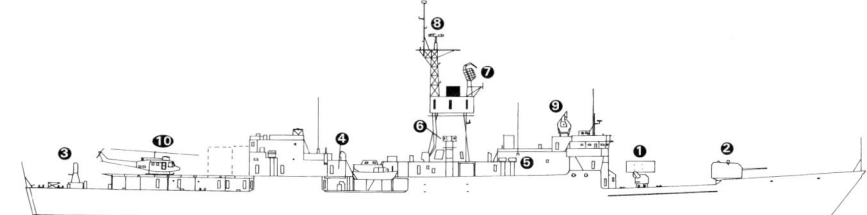

MAKEDONIA   *(Scale 1 : 1200), Ian Sturton*

THRACE   *9/1992, Diego Quevedo*

tons to the displacement. Sea Sparrow SAM replaced by Phalanx 1982-88. FFISTS is a combat system using desktop computers to integrate ASW data from Link and from ships' sonars. There are plans to improve air defence capabilities.
Structure: Improved ASROC-torpedo reloading capability (note slanting face of bridge structure immediately behind ASROC).

Four Mk 32 torpedo tubes are fixed in the midships structure, two to a side, angled out at 45 degrees. The arrangement provides improved loading capability over exposed triple Mk 32 torpedo tubes. A 4000 lb lightweight anchor is fitted on the port side and an 8000 lb anchor fits into the after section of the sonar dome. 4 SAM launchers for Stinger.

SHIPBORNE AIRCRAFT

Numbers/Type: 5 Sikorsky S-70B6 Seahawk.
Operational speed: 135 kts *(250 km/h)*.
Service ceiling: 10 000 ft *(3050 m)*.
Range: 600 nm *(1110 km)*.
Role/Weapon systems: Ordered 25 July 1991 with an option for three more. First one to be delivered in 1994. To be used on the Hydra class. Sensors: Telephonica APS 143(V)3 search radar, Bendix AQS 18(V)3 dipping sonar, Litton ALR 606(V)2 ESM, ASN 150(V) tactical data system with CD22 or Link 11. Weapons: ASV; possible Penguin Mk 2 Mod 7. ASW; 2 × Mk 46 torpedoes.

SEAHAWK   *1990 Sikorsky*

Numbers/Type: 3 Aerospatiale SA 319B Alouette III.
Operational speed: 113 kts *(210 km/h)*.
Service ceiling: 10 500 ft *(3200 m)*.
Range: 290 nm *(540 km)*.
Role/Weapon systems: Shipborne ASW/SAR role on older escorts and for training; limited to daylight operations only. Sensors: None. Weapons: ASW; 1 or 2 × Mk 44/46 torpedoes.

Numbers/Type: 9 Agusta AB 212ASW.
Operational speed: 106 kts *(196 km/h)*.
Service ceiling: 14 200 ft *(4330 m)*.
Range: 230 nm *(425 km)*.
Role/Weapon systems: Shipborne ASW/Elint and surface search role from new escorts. Sensors: Selenia APS-705 radar, AQS-18 dipping sonar. Weapons: ASW; 2 × Mk 46 or 2 × A244/S homing torpedoes.

AB 212ASW   *1987, Hellenic Navy*

LAND-BASED MARITIME AIRCRAFT

Numbers/Type: 8 Grumman HU-16B Albatross.
Operational speed: 130 kts *(241 km/h)*.
Service ceiling: 25 000 ft *(7620 m)*.
Range: 2480 nm *(4590 km)*.
Role/Weapon systems: Aegean Sea reconnaissance amphibian; update programme abandoned in favour of procurement of six P-3A Orion replacement aircraft by 1992. Sensors: Search radar. Weapons: ASW; 6 × torpedoes or depth bombs or mines.

Numbers/Type: 4/6 Lockheed P-3B/C Orion.
Operational speed: 410 kts *(760 km/h)*.
Service ceiling: 28 300 ft *(8625 m)*.
Range: 4000 nm *(7410 km)*.
Role/Weapon systems: Four maritime reconnaissance aircraft transferred from the USN in 1992/93 as part of the Defence Co-operation Agreement signed in July 1990; six P-3C may be acquired in 1995. Sensors: APS 115 radar; sonobuoys; ESM. Weapons: ASW; Mk 44/46 torpedoes, depth bombs and mines.

CORVETTES

5 Ex-GERMAN THETIS CLASS (GUNBOATS)

Name	No	Commissioned		Recommissioned	
NIKI (ex-*Thetis*)	P 62 (ex-P 6052)	1 July	1961	6 Sep	1991
DOXA (ex-*Najade*)	P 63 (ex-P 6054)	12 May	1962	6 Sep	1991
ELEFTHERIA (ex-*Triton*)	P 64 (ex-P 6055)	10 Nov	1962	7 Sep	1992
CARTERIA (ex-*Hermes*)	P 65 (ex-P 6053)	16 Dec	1961	7 Sep	1992
ANDREIA (ex-*Theseus*)	P 66 (ex-P 6056)	15 Aug	1963	Dec	1992

Displacement, tons: 575 standard; 732 full load
Dimensions, feet (metres): 229.7 × 26.9 × 8.6 *(70 × 8.2 × 2.7)*
Main machinery: 2 MAN V84V diesels; 6800 hp(m) *(5 MW)*; 2 shafts
Speed, knots: 19.5. **Range, miles:** 2760 at 15 kts
Complement: 64 (4 officers)

Guns: 2 Breda 40 mm/70 (twin); 85° elevation; 300 rounds/minute to 12.5 km *(6.7 nm)*; weight of shell 0.96 kg.
Torpedoes: 4—324 mm single tubes. 4 Honeywell Mk 46; active/passive homing to 11 km *(5.9 nm)* at 40 kts; warhead 44 kg.
A/S mortars: 1 Bofors 375 mm 4-barrelled trainable launcher; automatic loading; range 1600 m; 20 rockets.
Depth charges: 2 rails.
Fire control: Signaal Mk 9 TFCS.
Radars: Surface search: Thomson-CSF TRS 3001; E/F band.
Navigation: Kelvin Hughes 14/9; I band.
Sonars: Atlas Elektronik ELAC 1 BV; hull-mounted; active search and attack; high frequency.

Programmes: All built by Rolandwerft, Bremen. The fifth may be used for spares.
Structure: *Doxa* has a deckhouse before bridge for sick bay. Torpedo tubes have liners effectively reducing their diameter to 324 mm.

ELEFTHERIA (old number) *3/1991, Horst Dehnst*

LIGHT FORCES

2 OSPREY 55 CLASS (FAST ATTACK CRAFT—PATROL)

Name	No	Builders	Commissioned
ARMATOLOS	P 18	Hellenic Shipyards, Skaramanga	27 Mar 1990
NAVMACHOS	P 19	Hellenic Shipyards, Skaramanga	15 July 1990

Displacement, tons: 555 full load
Dimensions, feet (metres): 179.8; 166.7 (wl) × 34.4 × 8.5 *(54.8; 50.8 × 10.5 × 2.6)*
Main machinery: 2 MTU 16V 1163 TB63 diesels; 10 000 hp(m) *(7.3 MW)* sustained; 2 shafts; cp props
Speed, knots: 25. **Range, miles:** 500 at 25 kts, 2800 at 12 kts
Complement: 36 plus 25 troops
Missiles: SSM: 2 McDonnell Douglas Harpoon (to be fitted in 1993).
Guns: 1 OTO Melara 3 in *(76 mm)*/62 compact; 85° elevation; 85 rounds/minute to 16 km *(8.6 nm)* anti-surface; 12 km *(6.6 nm)* anti-aircraft; weight of shell 6 kg (to be fitted in 1993).
2 Bofors 40 mm/70 (twin) (to be replaced by OTO Melara 76 mm).
2 Rheinmetall 20 mm.
Mines: Rails.
Countermeasures: Decoys: 2 chaff launchers.
Fire control: Selenia Elsag NA 21.
Radars: Surface search: Thomson-CSF Triton; G band.
Fire control: Selenia RTNX; I/J band.

Comment: Built in co-operation with Danyard A/S. Ordered in March 1988. First one laid down 8 May 1989 and launched 19 December 1989. Second laid down 9 November 1989 and launched 16 May 1990. Armament is of modular design and therefore can be changed. Harpoon and 76 mm guns are to be fitted in 1993 after being taken from decommissioned Gearing class destroyers. Options on more of the class were shelved in favour of the Hellenic 56 design.

NAVMACHOS (with 40 mm gun) *5/1991, Erik Laursen*

0 + 2 HELLENIC 56 CLASS (FAST ATTACK CRAFT—PATROL)

Name	No	Builders	Commissioned
PIRPOLITIS	P 57	Hellenic Shipyard, Skaramanga	1993
POLEMISTIS	P 61	Hellenic Shipyard, Skaramanga	1994

Displacement, tons: 550 full load
Dimensions, feet (metres): 185.4 × 32.8 × 8.9 *(56.5 × 10 × 2.7)*
Main machinery: 2 Wärtsilä Nohab 16V25 diesels; 9200 hp(m) *(6.76 MW)* sustained; 2 shafts
Speed, knots: 24. **Range, miles:** 2200 at 15 kts; 500 at 24 kts
Complement: 36 plus 23 spare
Guns: 1 Bofors 40 mm/70. 2 Rheinmetall 20 mm.
Mines: 2 rails.
Fire control: Selenia Elsag NA 21.
Radars: Surface search: Thomson-CSF Triton; I band.

Comment: Ordered 20 February 1990. This is a design by Hellenic which uses the modular concept so that weapons and sensors can be changed as required. Appearance is similar to Osprey 55 class. *Pirpolitis* launched 16 September 1992 and the second of class was laid down on the same day. Completion delayed by the shipyard's financial problems. Alternative guns and 2 Harpoon SSM can be fitted. 25 fully equipped troops can be carried.

10 LA COMBATTANTE III CLASS (FAST ATTACK CRAFT—MISSILE)

Name	No	Builders	Commissioned
ANTIFLOIARHOS LASKOS	P 20	CMN Cherbourg	20 Apr 1977
PLOTARHIS BLESSAS	P 21	CMN Cherbourg	7 July 1977
IPOPLOIARHOS MIKONIOS	P 22	CMN Cherbourg	10 Feb 1978
IPOPLOIARHOS TROUPAKIS	P 23	CMN Cherbourg	8 Nov 1977
SIMEOFOROS KAVALOUDIS	P 24	Hellenic Shipyards, Skaramanga	14 July 1980
ANTIPOPLOIARHOS KOSTAKOS	P 25	Hellenic Shipyards, Skaramanga	9 Sep 1980
IPOPLOIARHOS DEYIANNIS	P 26	Hellenic Shipyards, Skaramanga	Dec 1980
SIMEOFOROS XENOS	P 27	Hellenic Shipyards, Skaramanga	31 Mar 1981
SIMEOFOROS SIMITZOPOULOS	P 28	Hellenic Shipyards, Skaramanga	June 1981
SIMEOFOROS STARAKIS	P 29	Hellenic Shipyards, Skaramanga	12 Oct 1981

Displacement, tons: 359 standard; 425 full load (P 20-23)
329 standard; 429 full load (P 24-29)
Dimensions, feet (metres): 184 × 26.2 × 7 *(56.2 × 8 × 2.1)*
Main machinery: 4 MTU 20V 538 TB92 diesels; 17 060 hp(m) *(12.54 MW)* sustained; 4 shafts (P 20-23)
4 MTU 20V 538 TB91 diesels; 15 360 hp(m) *(11.29 MW)* sustained; 4 shafts (P 24-29)
Speed, knots: 36 (P 20-23); 32.5 (P 24-29). **Range, miles:** 700 at 32 kts; 2700 at 15 kts
Complement: 42 (5 officers)

Missiles: SSM: 4 Aerospatiale MM 38 Exocet (P 20-P 23); inertial cruise; active radar homing to 42 km *(23 nm)* at 0.9 Mach; warhead 165 kg.
6 Kongsberg Penguin Mk 2 (P 24-P 29); inertial/IR homing to 27 km *(15 nm)* at 0.8 Mach; warhead 120 kg.
Guns: 2 OTO Melara 3 in *(76 mm)*/62 compact; 85° elevation; 85 rounds/minute to 16 km *(8.6 nm)* anti-surface; 12 km *(6.5 nm)* anti-aircraft; weight of shell 6 kg.
4 Emerson Electric 30 mm (2 twin); multi-purpose; 80° elevation; 1200 rounds/minute combined to 6 km *(3.2 nm)*; weight of shell 0.35 kg.
Torpedoes: 2—21 in *(533 mm)* aft tubes. AEG SST-4; anti-surface; wire-guided; active homing to 12 km *(6.5 nm)* at 35 kts; passive homing to 28 km *(15 nm)* at 23 kts; warhead 250 kg.
Countermeasures: Decoys: Wegmann chaff launchers.
Fire control: 2 CSEE Panda optical directors for 30 mm guns. Thomson-CSF Vega I or II system.
Radars: Surface search: Thomson-CSF Triton; G band; range 33 km *(18 nm)* for 2 m² target.
Navigation: Decca 1226C; I band.
Fire control: Thomson-CSF Castor II; I/J band; range 31 km *(17 nm)* for 2 m² target.
Thomson-CSF Pollux; I/J band; range 31 km *(17 nm)* for 2 m² target.

Programmes: First four ordered in September 1974. Second group of six ordered 1978.
Structure: First four fitted with SSM Exocet; remainder have Penguin.

PLOTARHIS BLESSAS (with Exocet) *1988, Hellenic Navy*

IPOFLOIARHOS DEYIANNIS (with Penguin) *1988, Hellenic Navy*

4 LA COMBATTANTE II CLASS (FAST ATTACK CRAFT—MISSILE)

Name	No	Builders	Commissioned
ANTHIPOPLOIARHOS ANNINOS (ex-*Navsithoi*)	P 14	CMN Cherbourg	June 1972
IPOPLOIARHOS ARLIOTIS (ex-*Evniki*)	P 15	CMN Cherbourg	Apr 1972
IPOPLOIARHOS KONIDIS (ex-*Kymothoi*)	P 16	CMN Cherbourg	July 1972
IPOPLOIARHOS BATSIS (ex-*Calypso*)	P 17	CMN Cherbourg	Dec 1971

Displacement, tons: 234 standard; 255 full load
Dimensions, feet (metres): 154.2 × 23.3 × 8.2 *(47 × 7.1 × 2.5)*
Main machinery: 4 MTU MD 16V 538 TB90 diesels; 12 000 hp(m) *(8.82 MW)* sustained; 4 shafts
Speed, knots: 36.5. **Range, miles:** 850 at 25 kts
Complement: 40 (4 officers)

Missiles: SSM: 4 Aerospatiale MM 38 Exocet; inertial cruise; active radar homing to 42 km *(23 nm)* at 0.9 Mach; warhead 165 kg; sea-skimmer.
Guns: 4 Oerlikon 35 mm/90 (2 twin); 85° elevation; 550 rounds/minute to 6 km *(3.2 nm)* anti-surface; 5 km *(2.7 nm)* anti-aircraft; weight of shell 1.55 kg.
Torpedoes: 2—21 in *(533 mm)* tubes. AEG SST-4; wire-guided; active homing to 12 km *(6.5 nm)* at 35 kts; passive homing to 28 km *(15 nm)* at 23 kts; warhead 250 kg.
Fire control: Thomson-CSF Vega system.
Radars: Surface search: Thomson-CSF Triton; G band; range 33 km *(18 nm)* for 2 m² target.
Navigation: Decca 1226C; I band.
Fire Control: Thomson-CSF Pollux; I/J band; range 31 km *(17 nm)* for 2 m² target.
IFF: Plessey Mk 10.

Programmes: Ordered in 1969. P 15 launched 8 September 1971; P 14 on 20 December 1971; P 17 on 27 April 1971; P 16 on 26 January 1972.
Modernisation: Plans to modernise include updating the fire control system.

IPOPLOIARHOS BATSIS *1989, Hellenic Navy*

6 Ex-FDR JAGUAR CLASS (FAST ATTACK CRAFT—TORPEDO)

Name	No	Builders	Commissioned
HESPEROS (ex-*Seeadler* P 6068)	P 50	Lürssen, Vegesack	29 Aug 1958
KENTAUROS (ex-*Habicht* P 6075)	P 52	Krogerwerft, Rendsburg	15 Nov 1958
KYKLON (ex-*Greif* P 6071)	P 53	Lürssen, Vegesack	3 Mar 1959
LELAPS (ex-*Kondor* P 6070)	P 54	Lürssen, Vegesack	24 Feb 1959
SKORPIOS (ex-*Kormoran* P 6077)	P 55	Krogerwerft, Rendsburg	9 Nov 1959
TYFON (ex-*Geier* P 6073)	P 56	Lürssen, Vegesack	3 June 1959

Displacement, tons: 160 standard; 190 full load
Dimensions, feet (metres): 139.4 × 23.6 × 7.9 *(42.5 × 7.2 × 2.4)*
Main machinery: 4 MTU MD 16V 538 TB90 diesels; 12 000 hp(m) *(8.82 MW)* sustained; 4 shafts
Speed, knots: 42. **Range, miles:** 500 at 40 kts; 1000 at 32 kts
Complement: 39
Guns: 2 Bofors 40 mm/70; 90° elevation; 300 rounds/minute to 12 km *(6.5 nm)* anti-surface; 4 km *(2.2 nm)* anti-aircraft; weight of shell 2.4 kg.
Torpedoes: 4—21 in *(533 mm)* tubes. Probably AEG SST-4; anti-surface; wire-guided; passive homing to 28 km *(15.3 nm)* at 23 kts; active homing to 12 km *(6.6 nm)* at 35 kts; warhead 260 kg.
Mines: 2 in lieu of each torpedo.

Comment: Transferred 1976-77. P 53 and P 56 commissioned in Hellenic Navy 12 December 1976. P 50 and P 54 on 24 March 1977, P 52 and P 55 on 22 May 1977. Three others (ex-*Albatros*, ex-*Bussard*, and ex-*Sperber*) transferred at same time for spares.

ESPEROS *1989, Hellenic Navy*

4 Ex-NASTY CLASS (FAST ATTACK CRAFT—TORPEDO)

Name	No	Builders	Commissioned
ANDROMEDA	P 196	Mandal, Norway	Nov 1966
KYKNOS	P 198	Mandal, Norway	Feb 1967
PIGASOS	P 199	Mandal, Norway	Apr 1967
TOXOTIS	P 228	Mandal, Norway	May 1967

Displacement, tons: 72 full load
Dimensions, feet (metres): 80.4 × 24.6 × 6.9 *(24.5 × 7.5 × 2.1)*
Main machinery: 2 MTU 12V 331 TC92 diesels; 2660 hp(m) *(1.96 MW)* sustained; 2 shafts
Speed, knots: 40. **Range, miles:** 676 at 17 kts
Complement: 20
Guns: 1 Bofors 40 mm/70. 1 Rheinmetall 20 mm.
Torpedoes: 4—21 in *(533 mm)* tubes.
Radars: Navigation: I band.

Comment: Six of the class acquired from Norway in 1967 and paid off into reserve in the early 1980s. Four re-engined and brought back into service in 1988.

KYKNOS *1988, Hellenic Navy*

2 Ex-US ASHEVILLE CLASS (LARGE PATROL CRAFT)

Name	No	Builders	Commissioned
TOLMI (ex-*Green Bay*)	P 229	Peterson, Wisconsin	5 Dec 1969
ORMI (ex-*Beacon*)	P 230	Peterson, Wisconsin	21 Nov 1969

Displacement, tons: 225 standard; 245 full load
Dimensions, feet (metres): 164.5 × 23.8 × 9.5 *(50.1 × 7.3 × 2.9)*
Main machinery: 2 Cummins VT12-875 diesels; 1450 hp *(1.07 MW)*; 2 shafts
Speed, knots: 16. **Range, miles:** 1700 at 16 kts
Complement: 24 (3 officers)
Missiles: SSM: 4 Aerospatiale SS 12M; wire-guided to 5.5 km *(3 nm)* subsonic; warhead 30 kg.
Guns: 1 USN 3 in *(76 mm)*/50 Mk 34; 85° elevation; 50 rounds/minute to 12.8 km *(7 nm)*; weight of shell 6 kg.
1 Bofors 40 mm/56 Mk 10. 4—12.7 mm (2 twin) MGs.
Fire control: Mk 63 GFCS.
Radars: Surface search: Sperry SPS 53; I/J band.
Fire control: Western Electric SPG 50; I/J band.

Comment: Transferred from the USN in mid-1990 after a refit and recommissioned 18 June 1991. Both were in reserve from April 1977 having originally been built for the Cuban crisis. Similar craft in Turkish, Colombian and South Korean navies. Gas turbine propulsion engine removed prior to transfer.

TOLMI *1990, Hellenic Navy*

2 FAST ATTACK CRAFT (PATROL)

Name	No	Builders	Commissioned
DIOPOS ANTONIOU	P 286	Ch N de l'Esterel	4 Dec 1975
KELEFSTIS STAMOU	P 287	Ch N de l'Esterel	28 July 1975

Displacement, tons: 115 full load
Dimensions, feet (metres): 105 × 19 × 5.3 *(32 × 5.8 × 1.6)*
Main machinery: 2 MTU 12V 331 TC81 diesels; 2610 hp(m) *(1.92 MW)* sustained; 2 shafts
Speed, knots: 30. **Range, miles:** 1500 at 15 kts
Complement: 17
Missiles: SSM: 4 Aerospatiale SS 12M; wire-guided to 5.5 km *(3 nm)* subsonic; warhead 30 kg.
Guns: 1 Rheinmetall 20 mm. 1—12.7 mm MG.

Comment: Originally ordered for Cyprus, later transferred to Greece. Wooden hulls.

DIOPOS ANTONIOU *1990, Hellenic Navy*

260 GREECE / Light forces — Amphibious forces

3 DILOS CLASS (COASTAL PATROL CRAFT)

DILOS P 267   **KNOSSOS** P 268   **LINDOS** P 269

Displacement, tons: 74.5 standard; 86 full load
Dimensions, feet (metres): 95.1 × 16.2 × 5.6 *(29 × 5 × 1.7)*
Main machinery: 2 MTU 12V 331 TC92 diesels; 2660 hp(m) *(1.96 MW)* sustained; 2 shafts
Speed, knots: 27. **Range, miles:** 1600 at 24 kts
Complement: 15
Guns: 2 Rheinmetall 20 mm.
Radars: Surface search: Racal Decca 1226C; I band.

Comment: Ordered from Hellenic Shipyards, Skaramanga in May 1976 to a design by Abeking & Rasmussen. The Navy uses these craft for air-sea rescue duties. Based at the National SAR centre. Four more of this class serve in Coast Guard and three in Customs service.

KNOSSOS   *7/1989, D Dervissis*

2 COASTAL PATROL CRAFT

Name	No	Builders	Commissioned
E PANAGOPOULOS 2	P 70	Hellenic Shipyards, Skaramanga	1980
E PANAGOPOULOS 3	P 96	Hellenic Shipyards, Skaramanga	1981

Displacement, tons: 35 full load
Dimensions, feet (metres): 75.5 × 16.4 × 3.3 *(23 × 5 × 1)*
Main machinery: 2 MTU 12V 331 TC92 diesels; 2660 hp(m) *(1.96 MW)* sustained; 2 shafts
Speed, knots: 38
Complement: 6
Guns: 2—6-barrelled 106 mm rocket launchers. 1—12.7 mm MG.
Radars: Navigation: Decca; I band.

Comment: Officially classified as 'pursuit vessels'. Have aluminium hulls. The first of class paid off in 1991.

E PANAGOPOULOS 3   *5/1990, Erik Laursen*

AMPHIBIOUS FORCES

Note: There are a number of paid off LSTs and LSMs in unmaintained reserve at Salamis.

0 + 5 JASON CLASS (LST)

Name	No	Builders	Commissioned
CHIOS	L 173	Eleusis Shipyard	1993
SAMOS	L 174	Eleusis Shipyard	1993
LESBOS	L 176	Eleusis Shipyard	1994
IKARIA	L 175	Eleusis Shipyard	1994
RODOS	L 177	Eleusis Shipyard	1995

Displacement, tons: 4400 full load
Dimensions, feet (metres): 380.5 × 50.2 × 11.3 *(116 × 15.3 × 3.4)*
Main machinery: 2 Wärtsilä Nohab 16V25 diesels; 9200 hp(m) *(6.76 MW)* sustained; 2 shafts
Speed, knots: 16
Military lift: 300 troops plus vehicles; 4 LCVPs
Guns: 1 OTO Melara 76 mm/62 Mod 9 compact; 85° elevation; 100 rounds/minute to 16 km *(8.6 nm)* anti-surface; 12 km *(6.5 nm)* anti-aircraft; weight of shell 6 kg.
  4 Breda 40 mm/70 (2 twin) compact Fast 40; 85° elevation; 900 rounds/minute to 12 km *(6.5 nm)*; weight of shell 2.4 kg.
  4 Rheinmetall 20 mm (2 twin).
Fire control: 1 CSEE Panda optical director. Thomson-CSF Canopus GFCS.
Radars: Thomson-CSF Triton; G band.
  Fire control: Thomson-CSF Pollux; I/J band.
  Navigation: Kelvin Hughes Type 1007; I band.
Helicopters: Platform for one.

Comment: Contract for construction of five LSTs by Eleusis Shipyard signed 15 May 1986. Bow and stern ramps, drive through design. First laid down 18 April 1987, second in September 1987, third in May 1988, fourth April 1989 and fifth November 1989. First launched 16 December 1988, second 6 April 1989, third 5 July 1990. Completion of all five severely delayed by shipyard financial problems.

CHIOS (model)   *1989, Eleusis Shipyard*

2 Ex-US TERREBONNE PARISH CLASS (LSTs)

Name	No	Builders	Commissioned
INOUSE (ex-USS *Terrell County* LST 1157)	L 104	Bath Iron Works Corporation	19 Mar 1953
KOS (ex-USS *Whitfield County* LST 1169)	L 116	Christy Corporation	14 Sep 1954

Displacement, tons: 2590 light; 5800 full load
Dimensions, feet (metres): 384 × 55 × 17 *(117.1 × 16.8 × 5.2)*
Main machinery: 4 GM 16-278A diesels; 6000 hp *(4.48 MW)*; 2 shafts; cp props
Speed, knots: 15
Complement: 115
Military lift: 400 troops; 4 LCVPs
Guns: 6 USN 3 in *(76 mm)*/50 Mk 21 (3 twin); 85° elevation; 20 rounds/minute to 12 km *(6.5 nm)* anti-surface; 9 km *(4.9 nm)* anti-aircraft; weight of shell 6 kg.
  3 Rheinmetall 20 mm S 20.
Fire control: 2 Mk 63 GFCS.
Radars: Surface search: Raytheon/Sylvania SPS 10; G band.
  Fire control: Two Western Electric Mk 34; I/J band.

Comment: Part of class of 16 of which these two were transferred 17 March 1977 by sale.

KOS   *1988, Hellenic Navy*

4 Ex-US 511—1152 and 1—510 CLASSES (LSTs)

Name	No	Builders	Commissioned
IKARIA (ex-USS *Potter County* LST 1086)	L 154	AM Bridge Co	14 Mar 1945
KRITI (ex-USS *Page County* LST 1076)	L 171	Bethlehem Steel Co, Hingham	1 May 1945
SIROS (ex-USS LST 325)	L 144	Philadelphia Navy Yard	1 Feb 1943
RODOS (ex-USS *Bowman County* LST 391)	L 157	Newport News	3 Dec 1942

Displacement, tons: 1653 standard; 2366 beaching; 4080 full load
Dimensions, feet (metres): 328 × 50 × 14 *(100 × 15.3 × 4.3)*
Main machinery: 2 GM 12-567A diesels; 1800 hp *(1.34 MW)*; 2 shafts
Speed, knots: 11.6. **Range, miles:** 9500 at 9 kts
Complement: 93 (8 officers)
Military lift: 2100 tons; 4 LCVPs
Guns: 8 Bofors 40 mm/60 (2 twin, 4 single) (10 in L 157).
  4 Oerlikon 20 mm/2 Rheinmetall 20 mm S 20.
Radars: Navigation: I band.

Comment: Former US tank landing ships. L 154 and 171 are 511—1152 class and L 144 and 157 are 1—510 class. L 157 and 154 were transferred to the Hellenic Navy in May 1960 and August 1960 respectively. L 144 was transferred on 29 May 1964, L 171 in March 1971. To be replaced by the Jason class.

LST 1-510 class (old number)   *5/1990, Gilbert Gyssels*

4 Ex-US LSM 1 CLASS

Name	No	Builders	Commissioned
IPOPLOIARHOS GRIGOROPOULOS (ex-USS *LSM 45*)	L 161	Brown SB Co, Houston	3 July 1944
IPOPLOIARHOS DANIOLOS (ex-USS *LSM 227*)	L 163	Dravo Corp, Wilmington	5 Oct 1944
IPOPLOIARHOS ROUSSEN (ex-USS *LSM 399*)	L 164	Charleston Navy Yard	13 Aug 1945
IPOPLOIARHOS KRYSTALIDIS (ex-USS *LSM 541*)	L 165	Brown SB Co, Houston	7 Dec 1945

Displacement, tons: 743 beaching; 1095 full load
Dimensions, feet (metres): 203.5 × 34.2 × 8.3 *(62.1 × 10.4 × 2.5)*
Main machinery: 2 Fairbanks-Morse 38D8-1/8-10 diesels; 3540 hp *(2.64 MW)* sustained; 2 shafts (L 161, 163 and 165); 4 GM 16-278A diesels; 3000 hp *(2.24 MW)*; 2 shafts (L 164)
Speed, knots: 13. **Range, miles:** 4900 at 12 kts
Complement: 60
Guns: 2 Bofors 40 mm/60 (twin). 8 Oerlikon 20 mm.

Comment: LSM 541 was handed over to Greece at Salamis on 30 October 1958 and LSM 45, LSM 227 and 399 at Portsmouth, Virginia on 3 November 1958. All were renamed after naval heroes killed during the Second World War.

I GRIGOROPOULOS   *5/1990, Erik Laursen*

Amphibious forces — Mine warfare forces / GREECE 261

1 Ex-US CABILDO CLASS (LSD)

Name	No	Builders	Commissioned
NAFKRATOUSSA (ex-USS *Fort Mandan* LSD 21)	L 153	Boston Navy Yard	31 Oct 1945

Displacement, tons: 4790 light; 9357 full load
Dimensions, feet (metres): 457.8 × 72.2 × 18 *(139.6 × 22 × 5.5)*
Main machinery: 2 boilers; 435 psi *(30.6 kg/cm sq)*; 750°F *(393°C)*; 2 turbines; 7000 hp *(5.22 MW)*; 2 shafts
Speed, knots: 15.4. **Range, miles:** 8000 at 12 kts
Complement: 250
Military lift: 18 LCMs; 2—35 ton cranes
Guns: 12 Bofors 40 mm/60 (2 quad and 2 twin); 90° elevation; 300 rounds/minute to 12 km *(6.5 nm)* anti-surface; 4 km *(2.2 nm)* anti-aircraft; weight of shell 0.89 kg.
Radars: Air search: Bendix SPS 6; D band; range 146 km *(80 nm)*.
Surface search: Westinghouse SPS 5; G/H band; range 37 km *(20 nm)*.
Helicopters: Platform for 1 light.

Comment: Laid down on 2 January 1945. Launched on 22 May 1945. Taken over on lease from USA in 1971, acquired by sale 5 February 1980. Headquarters ship for Captain Landing Forces.

NAFKRATOUSSA *7/1988, D Dervissis*

6 Ex-GERMAN LCUs (TYPE 520)

NAXOS (ex-*Renke*) L 178 **IOS** (ex-*Barbe*) L 167 **IRAKLEIA** (ex-*Forelle*) L 169
PAROS (ex-*Salm*) L 179 **SIKINOS** (ex-*Dorsch*) L 168 **FOLEGRANDOS** (ex-*Delphin*) L 169

Displacement, tons: 430 full load
Dimensions, feet (metres): 131.2 × 28.9 × 7.2 *(40 × 8.8 × 2.2)*
Main machinery: 2 MWM 12-cyl diesels; 1020 hp(m) *(750 kW)*; 2 shafts
Speed, knots: 11
Complement: 17
Military lift: 150 tons
Guns: 2 Oerlikon 20 mm.

Comment: First two transferred 16 November 1989, remainder in 1992. Built by HDW, Hamburg in 1966. Bow and stern ramps similar to US Type. Two others used for spares.

LCU TYPE 520 (German number) *8/1992, Hartmut Ehlers*

1 Ex-US LCU 501 CLASS (Ex-LCT 6)

Name	No	Builders	Commissioned
KITHNOS (ex-*LCU 763*)	L 149	Missouri Valley Bridge	24 Dec 1944

Displacement, tons: 143 standard; 309 full load
Dimensions, feet (metres): 119 × 32.7 × 5 *(36.3 × 10 × 1.5)*
Main machinery: 3 GM 6-71 diesels; 522 hp *(389 kW)* sustained; 3 shafts
Speed, knots: 8
Complement: 13
Guns: 2 Oerlikon 20 mm.

Comment: Former US Utility Landing Craft of the LCU (ex-LCT 6) type acquired 1959.

KITHNOS *9/1987, van Ginderen Collection*

2 Ex-BRITISH LCTs

Name	No	Builders	Commissioned
KITHERA (ex-*LCT 1198*)	L 185	UK	1945
MILOS (ex-*LCT 1300*)	L 189	UK	1945

Displacement, tons: 400 full load
Dimensions, feet (metres): 187.2 × 38.7 × 4.3 *(57 × 11.8 × 1.3)*
Main machinery: 2 Paxman diesels; 1000 hp *(746 kW)*; 2 shafts
Speed, knots: 7. **Range, miles:** 3000 at 7 kts
Complement: 12
Military lift: 350 tons
Guns: 2 Oerlikon 20 mm.

Comment: The survivors of a class of 12 acquired in 1946.

11 Ex-GERMAN LCMs (TYPE 521)

Displacement, tons: 168 full load
Dimensions, feet (metres): 77.4 × 20.9 × 4.9 *(23.6 × 6.4 × 1.5)*
Main machinery: 1 MWM 8-cyl diesel; 685 hp(m) *(503 kW)*; 2 shafts
Speed, knots: 10.5
Complement: 7
Military lift: 60 tons or 50 troops

Comment: Built in 1964-67 but spent much of their time in reserve. Transferred in April 1991 and numbered ABM 20-30.

LCM Type 521 (German number) *7/1991, Hartmut Ehlers*

11 Ex-US LCMs

Displacement, tons: 56 full load
Dimensions, feet (metres): 56 × 14.4 × 3.9 *(17 × 4.4 × 1.2)*
Main machinery: 2 Gray Marine 64 HN9 diesels; 330 hp *(264 kW)*; 2 shafts
Speed, knots: 10. **Range, miles:** 130 at 10 kts
Military lift: 30 tons

Comment: Transferred from the USA in 1956-58.

34 Ex-US LCVPs + 14 LCPs + 7 LCAs

Displacement, tons: 13 full load
Speed, knots: 6-9
Military lift: 36 troops or 3 tons equipment

Comment: LCVPs transferred from the USA between 1956-71, LCPs built in Greece in 1977 and LCAs in 1981.

MINE WARFARE FORCES

2 COASTAL MINELAYERS

Name	No	Builders	Commissioned
AKTION (ex-*LSM 301*, ex-*MMC 6*)	N 04	Charleston Naval Shipyard	1 Jan 1945
AMVRAKIA (ex-*LSM 303*, ex-*MMC 7*)	N 05	Charleston Naval Shipyard	6 Jan 1945

Displacement, tons: 720 standard; 1100 full load
Dimensions, feet (metres): 203.5 × 34.5 × 8.3 *(62.1 × 10.5 × 2.5)*
Main machinery: 2 GM 16-278A diesels; 3000 hp *(2.24 MW)*; 2 shafts
Speed, knots: 12.5. **Range, miles:** 3000 at 12 kts
Complement: 65
Guns: 8 Bofors 40 mm/60 (4 twin). 6 Oerlikon 20 mm.
Mines: Capacity 100-130; 2 rails.
Fire control: 4 Mk 51 optical directors for 40 mm guns.
Radars: Navigation: I band.

Comment: Former US LSM 1 class. N 04 was launched on 1 January 1945 and N 05 on 14 November 1944. Converted in the USA into minelayers for the Hellenic Navy. Underwent extensive rebuilding from the deck up. Twin rudders. Transferred on 1 December 1953.

AKTION *9/1987, van Ginderen Collection*

262 GREECE / Mine warfare forces — Survey and research vessels

9 US MSC 294 CLASS (MINESWEEPERS—COASTAL)

Name	No	Builders	Commissioned
ALKYON (ex-MSC 319)	M 211	Peterson Builders	3 Dec 1968
KLIO (ex-Argo, ex-MSC 317)	M 213	Peterson Builders	7 Aug 1968
AVRA (ex-MSC 318)	M 214	Peterson Builders	3 Oct 1968
PLEIAS (ex-MSC 314)	M 240	Peterson Builders	22 June 1967
KICHLI (ex-MSC 308)	M 241	Peterson Builders	14 July 1964
KISSA (ex-MSC 309)	M 242	Peterson Builders	1 Sep 1964
AIGLI (ex-MSC 299)	M 246	Tacoma, California	4 Jan 1965
DAFNI (ex-MSC 307)	M 247	Peterson Builders	23 Sep 1964
AEDON (ex-MSC 310)	M 248	Peterson Builders	13 Oct 1964

Displacement, tons: 320 standard; 370 full load
Dimensions, feet (metres): 144 × 28 × 8.2 *(43.3 × 8.5 × 2.5)*
Main machinery: 2 Waukesha L-1616 diesels (being replaced); 1200 hp *(882 kW)*; 2 shafts
Speed, knots: 13. **Range, miles:** 2500 at 10 kts
Complement: 39 (4 officers)
Guns: 2 Oerlikon 20 mm (twin).
Radars: Navigation: I band.
Sonars: UQS 1D; active; high frequency.

Comment: Built in the USA for Greece, wooden hulls. *Doris* acts as survey ship. Modernisation programme started in 1990 with replacement main engines and navigation radar. New sonar under consideration.

KISSA 9/1992, B Sullivan

5 Ex-US ADJUTANT CLASS (MINESWEEPERS—COASTAL)

Name	No
ATALANTI (ex-Belgian *St Truiden* M 919, ex-USS *MSC 169*)	M 202
ANTIOPI (ex-Belgian *Herve* M 921, ex-USS *MSC 153*)	M 205
FAEDRA (ex-Belgian *Malmedy* M 922, ex-USS *MSC 154*)	M 206
THALIA (ex-Belgian *Blankenberge* M 923, ex-USS *MSC 170*)	M 210
NIOVI (ex-Belgian *Laroche* M 924, ex-USS *MSC 171*)	M 254

Displacement, tons: 330 standard; 402 full load
Dimensions, feet (metres): 145 × 27.9 × 8 *(44.2 × 8.5 × 2.4)*
Main machinery: 2 GM 8-268A diesels; 880 hp *(656 kW)*; 2 shafts
Speed, knots: 14. **Range, miles:** 2500 at 10 kts
Complement: 38 (4 officers)
Guns: 1 Oerlikon 20 mm.

Comment: Originally supplied to Belgium under MDAP. All built in 1954 in the USA—M 202, M 210 and M 254 by Consolidated SB Corp, Morris Heights and the other pair by Hodgson Bros, Goudy and Stevens, East Booth Bay. Subsequently returned to the USA and simultaneously transferred to Greece as follows: 29 July 1969 (*Herve* and *St Truiden*) and 26 September 1969 (*Laroche*, *Malmedy* and *Blankenberge*).

ATALANTI 1989, Hellenic Navy

4 MINESWEEPING LAUNCHES

Displacement, tons: 21 full load
Dimensions, feet (metres): 49.9 × 13.1 × 4.3 *(15.2 × 4 × 1.3)*
Main machinery: 1 diesel; 60 hp(m) *(44 kW)*; 1 shaft
Speed, knots: 8
Complement: 6

Comment: Transferred from USA in 1971 on loan and bought in 1981.

SURVEY AND RESEARCH VESSELS

Name	No	Builders	Commissioned
NAFTILOS	A 478	Annastadiades Tsortanides (Perama)	3 Apr 1976

Displacement, tons: 1400
Dimensions, feet (metres): 207 × 38 × 13.8 *(63.1 × 11.6 × 4.2)*
Main machinery: 2 Burmeister & Wain SS28LM diesels; 2640 hp(m) *(1.94 MW)*; 2 shafts
Speed, knots: 15
Complement: 74 (8 officers)

Comment: Launched 19 November 1975. Of similar design to the two lighthouse tenders.

NAFTILOS 1989, Hellenic Navy

Name	No	Builders	Commissioned
HERMIS (ex-*Oker*, ex-*Hoheweg*)	A 373	Unterweser, Bremen	19 Oct 1960

Displacement, tons: 1497 full load
Dimensions, feet (metres): 237.7 × 34.4 × 16.1 *(72.5 × 10.5 × 4.9)*
Main machinery: Diesel-electric: 1 KHD diesel; 1800 hp(m) *(1.32 MW)*;
  1 KHD auxiliary diesel; 400 hp(m) *(294 kW)*; 1 shaft
Speed, knots: 15
Complement: 30

Comment: First converted in 1972 to serve as an AGI in the West German Navy. Transferred 12 February 1988 and now based at Suda Bay. Serves as an AGI.

HERMIS 9/1989, Hellenic Navy

Name	No	Builders	Commissioned
PYTHEAS	A 474	Annastadiades Tsortanides (Perama)	Dec 1983

Displacement, tons: 670 standard; 840 full load
Dimensions, feet (metres): 164.7 × 31.5 × 21.6 *(50.2 × 9.6 × 6.6)*
Main machinery: 2 Detroit 12V-92TA diesels; 1020 hp *(760 kV)* sustained; 2 shafts
Speed, knots: 14
Complement: 58 (8 officers)

Comment: *Pytheas* ordered in May 1982. Launched 19 September 1983. A similar ship, *Aigeo*, was constructed to Navy specification in 1985 but belongs to the National Maritime Research Centre.

PYTHEAS 10/1987, D Dervissis

Survey and research vessels — Service forces / GREECE

Name	No	Builders	Commissioned
STRABON	A 476	Emanuil-Maliris, Perama	27 Feb 1989

Displacement, tons: 252 full load
Dimensions, feet (metres): 107.3 × 20 × 8.2 *(32.7 × 6.1 × 2.5)*
Main machinery: 1 MAN D2842LE; 571 hp(m) *(420 kW)* sustained; 1 shaft
Speed, knots: 12.5
Complement: 20 (2 officers)

Comment: Ordered in 1987, launched September 1988.

STRABON (*Pytheas* behind)   1991, Hellenic Navy

Name	No	Builders	Commissioned
DORIS (ex-*MSC 298*)	A 475 (ex-M 245)	Tacoma, California	9 Nov 1964

Comment: Of same details as MSC 294 class in *Mine Warfare* section except that her displacement is now 383 tons full load and complement 35 (3 officers).

OLYMPIAS

Dimensions, feet (metres): 121.4 × 17.1 × 4.9 *(37 × 5.2 × 1.5)*
Main machinery: 170 oars (85 each side in three rows)
Speed, knots: 9-12
Complement: 180

Comment: Construction started in 1985 and completed in 1987. Made of Oregon pine. Built for historic research and as a reminder of the naval hegemony of ancient Greeks. Part of the Hellenic Navy. Started refit in 1992.

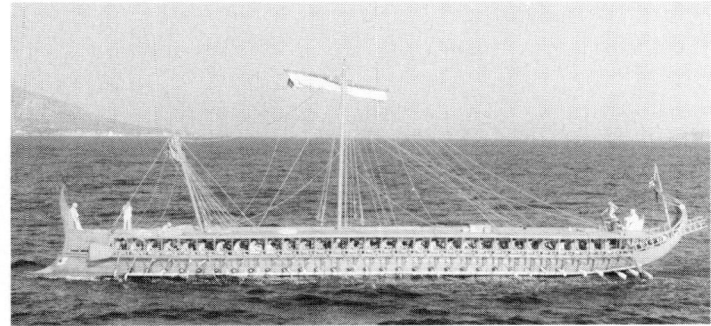

OLYMPIAS   1988, Hellenic Navy

SERVICE FORCES

Note: Tenders requested by September 1992 for a hospital ship.

Ex-GERMAN LÜNEBURG CLASS (SUPPORT SHIP)

Name	No	Builders	Commissioned	Recommissioned
AXIOS (ex-*Coburg*)	A 464 (ex-A 1412)	Bremer Vulcan	9 July 1968	30 Sep 1991

Displacement, tons: 3709 full load
Dimensions, feet (metres): 374.9 × 43.3 × 13.8 *(114.3 × 13.2 × 4.2)*
Main machinery: 2 MTU MD 16V 538 TB90 diesels; 6000 hp(m) *(4.41 MW)* sustained; 2 shafts; cp props; bow thruster
Speed, knots: 17. **Range, miles:** 3200 at 14 kts
Complement: 71
Cargo capacity: 1100 tons
Guns: 4 Bofors 40 mm/70 (2 twin); 90° elevation; 300 rounds/minute to 12 km *(6.5 nm)*; weight of shell 0.96 kg.

Comment: Lengthened by 33.7 ft *(10.3 m)* and modified in 1975. Serves as a depot ship for fast attack craft and is capable of servicing all weapons including missiles.

AXIOS (old number)   6/1991, Wright & Logan

1 TRAINING SHIP

Name	No	Builders	Commissioned
ARIS	A 74	Salamis	Jan 1980

Displacement, tons: 2400 standard; 2630 full load
Dimensions, feet (metres): 328 × 48.2 × 14.8 *(100 × 14.7 × 4.5)*
Main machinery: 2 MAK diesels; 10 000 hp(m) *(7.35 MW)*; 2 shafts
Speed, knots: 18
Complement: 500 (21 officers, up to 370 cadets)
Guns: 2 US 3 in *(76 mm)* Mk 26; 85° elevation; 50 rounds/minute to 12 km *(6.5 nm)*; weight of shell 6 kg.
    2 Bofors 40 mm/70 (twin); 90° elevation; 300 rounds/minute to 12 km *(6.5 nm)* anti-surface; 4 km *(2.2 nm)* anti-aircraft; weight of shell 0.96 kg.
    4 Rheinmetall 20 mm.
Radars: Surface search: Two Racal Decca 1226C; I band.
Helicopters: 1 Aerospatiale SA 319B Alouette III.

Comment: Laid down October 1976 at Salamis. Launched 4 October 1978. Hangar reactivated in 1986. The 76 mm guns are mounted on sponsons forward of the funnel. Can be used as transport or hospital ship. SATCOM fitted.

ARIS   7/1991, W Sartori

2 Ex-US PATAPSCO CLASS (SUPPORT TANKERS)

Name	No	Builders	Commissioned
ARETHOUSA (ex-USS *Natchaug* AOG 54)	A 377	Cargill Inc, Savage, Minn	11 June 1945
ARIADNI (ex-USS *Tombigbee* AOG 11)	A 414	Cargill Inc, Savage, Minn	12 July 1944

Displacement, tons: 1850 light; 4335 full load
Measurement, tons: 2575 dwt
Dimensions, feet (metres): 292 wl; 310.8 oa × 48.5 × 15.7 *(89.1; 94.8 × 14.8 × 4.8)*
Main machinery: 2 GM 16-278A diesels; 3000 hp *(2.24 MW)*; 2 shafts
Speed, knots: 14
Complement: 43 (6 officers)
Cargo capacity: 2040 tons
Guns: 1 USN 3 in *(76 mm)*/50; 85° elevation; 20 rounds/minute to 12 km *(6.6 nm)*; weight of shell 6 kg.
    2 Oerlikon 20 mm/85; 55° elevation; 800 rounds/minute to 2 km.
Fire control: 1 Mk 26 system for guns.
Radars: Surface search: Westinghouse SPS 5; G/H band; range 37 km *(20 nm)*.
    Navigation: Decca; I band.

Comment: Former US petrol carriers. A 377 laid down on 15 August 1944. Launched on 16 December 1944. Transferred from the USA to Greece under the Mutual Defense Assistance Program in July 1959 and A 414 transferred 7 July 1972 (sold 11 July 1978), both at Pearl Harbour.

ARETHOUSA   1988, Hellenic Navy

4 HARBOUR TANKERS

Name	No	Builders	Commissioned
OURANOS	A 416	Kinosoura Shipyard	27 Jan 1977
HYPERION	A 417	Kinosoura Shipyard	27 Apr 1977
ORION	A 376	Hellenic Shipyards	5 May 1989
ZEUS	A 375	Hellenic Shipyards	21 Feb 1989

Displacement, tons: 1900 full load
Dimensions, feet (metres): 219.8; 198.2 (wl) × 32.8 × 13.8 *(67; 60.4 × 10 × 4.2)*
Main machinery: 1 MAN-Burmeister & Wain 12V 20/27 diesel; 1632 hp(m) *(1.2 MW)* sustained; 1 shaft
Speed, knots: 12
Complement: 28
Cargo capacity: 1323 cu m
Guns: 2 Rheinmetall 20 mm.

Comment: First two are oil tankers. The others were ordered from Hellenic Shipyards, Skaramanga in December 1986 and are used as petrol tankers. There are some minor superstructure differences between the first two and the last two which have a forward crane.

ZEUS (old number)   *1989, Hellenic Shipyards*

1 AMMUNITION SHIP

Name	No	Builders	Commissioned
EVROS (ex-FDR *Schwarzwald* A 1400, ex-*Amalthee*)	A 415	Ch Dubigeon Nantes	1957

Displacement, tons: 2400
Measurement, tons: 1667 gross
Dimensions, feet (metres): 263.1 × 39 × 15.1 *(80.2 × 11.9 × 4.6)*
Main machinery: 1 Sulzer 6SD60 diesel; 3000 hp(m) *(2.2 MW)*; 1 shaft
Speed, knots: 15
Guns: 4 Bofors 40 mm/60.

Comment: Bought by FDR from Société Navale Caënnaise in February 1960. Transferred to Greece 6 June 1976.

EVROS   *1987, Hellenic Navy*

1 NETLAYER

Name	No	Builders	Commissioned
THETIS (ex-USS *AN 103*)	A 307	Kröger, Rendsburg	Apr 1960

Displacement, tons: 680 standard; 805 full load
Dimensions, feet (metres): 169.5 × 33.5 × 11.8 *(51.7 × 10.2 × 3.6)*
Main machinery: Diesel-electric; 1 MAN GTV-40/60 diesel generator; 1 motor; 1470 hp(m) *(1.08 MW)*; 1 shaft
Speed, knots: 12. **Range, miles:** 6500 at 10 kts
Complement: 48 (5 officers)
Guns: 1 Bofors 40 mm/60. 3 Rheinmetall 20 mm.

Comment: US offshore order. Launched in 1959. Some guns not always embarked.

THETIS   *1988, Hellenic Navy*

2 AUXILIARY TRANSPORTS

Name	No	Builders	Commissioned
PANDORA	A 419	Perama Shipyard	26 Oct 1973
PANDROSOS	A 420	Perama Shipyard	1 Dec 1973

Displacement, tons: 390 full load
Dimensions, feet (metres): 153.5 × 27.2 × 6.2 *(46.8 × 8.3 × 1.9)*
Main machinery: 2 diesels; 2 shafts
Speed, knots: 12
Military lift: 500 troops

Comment: Launched 1972 and 1973.

PANDROSOS   *6/1986, van Ginderen Collection*

4 Ex-GERMAN TORPEDO RECOVERY VESSELS (TYPE 430A)

EVROTAS (ex-*TF 106*) A 460 (ex-Y 872)   STRYMON (ex-*TF 104*) A 462 (ex-Y 870)
ARACHTHOS (ex-*TF 108*) A 461 (ex-Y 874)   NESTOS (ex-*TF 4*) A 463 (ex-Y 854)

Comment: First two acquired on 16 November 1989, second pair on 5 March 1991. Of about 56 tons with stern ramps for torpedo recovery. Built in 1966.

EVROTAS (old number)   *5/1989, Ralf Bendfeldt*

2 LIGHTHOUSE TENDERS

Name	No	Builders	Commissioned
I KARAVOYIANNOS THEOPHILOPOULOS	A 479	Perama Shipyard	17 Mar 1976
ST LIKOUDIS	A 481	Perama Shipyard	2 Jan 1976

Displacement, tons: 1450 full load
Dimensions, feet (metres): 207.3 × 38 × 13.1 *(63.2 × 11.6 × 4)*
Main machinery: 1 Deutz MWM TBD5008UD diesel; 2400 hp(m) *(1.76 MW)*; 1 shaft
Speed, knots: 15
Complement: 40
Radars: Navigation: Racal Decca; I band.
Helicopters: Platform for 1 light.

I KARAVOYIANNOS THEOPHILOPOULOS   *5/1991, Erik Laursen*

3 COASTAL TUGS

HERAKLIS A 423   IASON A 424   ODISSEUS A 425

Displacement, tons: 345 full load
Dimensions, feet (metres): 98.5 × 26 × 11.3 *(30 × 7.9 × 3.4)*
Main machinery: 1 Deutz MWM diesel; 1200 hp(m) *(882 kW)*; 1 shaft
Speed, knots: 12

Comment: Laid down 1977 at Perama Shipyard. Commissioned 6 April, 6 March and 28 June 1978 respectively.

18 HARBOUR TUGS

Name	No	Commissioned
ANTAIOS (ex-USS *Busy* YTM 2012)	A 407	1947
ATLAS (ex-HMS *Mediator*)	A 408	1944
ACCHILEUS (ex-USS *Confident*)	A 409	1947
ATROMITOS	A 410	1968
ADAMASTOS	A 411	1968
AIAS (ex-USS *Ankachak* YTM 767)	A 412	1972
PILEFS (ex-German)	A 413	1991
KADMOS (ex-US)	A 422	1989
KIKLOPS	A 426	1947
DANAOS (ex-US)	A 427	1989
NESTOR (ex-US)	A 428	1989
PELOPS	A 430	1989
TITAN	A 431	1962
GIGAS	A 432	1961
KEKROPS	A 435	1989
MINOS (ex-German)	A 436	1991
PELIAS (ex-German)	A 437	1991
AEGEUS (ex-German)	A 438	1991

1 FLOATING DOCK and 5 FLOATING CRANES

Comment: The floating dock is 45 m *(147.6 ft)* in length and has a 6000 ton lift. Built at Eleusis with Swedish assistance and launched 5 May 1988; delivered 1989. The cranes were all built in Greece.

7 WATER BOATS

KERKINI (ex-German *FW 3*) A 433
PRESPA A 434
YLIKI A 465
TRICHONIS (ex-German *FW 6*) A 466
DOIRANI A 467
KALLIROE A 468
STIMFALIA A 469

Comment: All built between 1964 and 1972. Capacity, 600 tons except A 433 and A 466 which can carry 300 tons and A 469 which can carry 1000 tons. Three in reserve.

ACCHILEUS   1982

DOIRANI   6/1986, van Ginderen Collection

COAST GUARD (Limenikon Soma)

Senior Officers

Commander-in-Chief:
Vice Admiral N Hasiotis
Deputy Commander-in-Chief:
Rear Admiral M Plakiotis

Bases

HQ: Piraeus
Main bases: Piraeus, Eleusis, Thessalonika, Volos, Patra, Corfu, Rhodes, Mytilene, Heraklion (Crete), Chios, Kavala, Chalcis
Minor bases: Every port and island of Greece

Ships and Craft

In general very similar in appearance to naval ships, being painted grey. Since 1990 pennant numbers have been painted white and on both sides of the hull they carry a blue and white band with two crossed anchors. In addition to the Coast Guard vessels about 20 very similar craft are operated by the Customs Service's Anti-Smuggling Flotilla.

Personnel

1993: 4300 (850 officers). Includes about 230 women.

General

This force consists of some 158 patrol craft and anti-pollution vessels made up of four Dilos class offshore patrol craft, 33 coastal craft of 45 ft *(13.7 m)*, 108 up to 27.5 ft *(8.4 m)* plus 18 inflatables for the 48 man Underwater Missions Squad and 12 anti-pollution vessels. There is also a special SAR ship. Administration in peacetime is by the Ministry of Merchant Marine. In wartime it would be transferred to naval command.
Officers are trained at the Naval Academy and ratings at two special schools.
The Dilos class of four craft (details of same class in main section under *Light Forces*), pennant numbers 80-83, are the largest currently in use. The pennant numbers are all preceded as in the accompanying photographs by Greek 'Lambda Sigma' for Limenikon Soma. New plans include eight more 45 ft craft and three anti-pollution vessels.
Three more Abeking & Rasmussen craft are operated by the Customs Service.

Duties

The policing of all Greek harbours, coasts and territorial waters, navigational safety, SAR operations, anti-pollution surveillance and operations, supervision of port authorities, merchant navy training, inspection of Greek merchant ships world-wide.

Coast Guard Air Service

In October 1981 the Coast Guard acquired two Cessna Cutlass 172 RG aircraft and in July 1988 two Socata TB 20s. Maintenance and training by the Air Force. Based at Dekelia air base. New plans include larger aircraft.

LS 80   1990, Greek Coast Guard

LS 24   5/1991, Erik Laursen

GRENADA

Headquarters' Appointments

Commissioner of Police:
Lieutenant Colonel Nestor Ogilvie
Coast Guard Commander:
Superintendent Charles

Personnel

1993: 42

Bases

Prickly Bay (main), St George, Grenville, Hillsborough

General

Grenada was granted self-government, in association with the UK (which was responsible for its defence) on 3 March 1967. Independence was achieved in February 1974. Coast Guard craft are operated under the direction of the Commissioner of Police.

Mercantile Marine

Lloyd's Register of Shipping:
3 vessels of 623 tons gross

DELETIONS

1990 1 Brooke Marine class (PB 02), 1 Spear class

266 GRENADA / Patrol forces — GUATEMALA / Patrol forces

1 GUARDIAN CLASS (COASTAL PATROL CRAFT)

Name	No	Builders	Commissioned
TYRREL BAY	PB 01	Lantana, Florida	21 Nov 1984

Displacement, tons: 90 full load
Dimensions, feet (metres): 105 × 20.6 × 7 *(32 × 6.3 × 2.1)*
Main machinery: 3 Detroit 12V-71TA diesels; 1260 hp *(939 kW)* sustained; 3 shafts
Speed, knots: 24. **Range, miles:** 1500 at 18 kts
Complement: 15 (2 officers)
Guns: 3—12.7 mm MGs. 2—7.62 mm MGs.
Radars: Surface search: Furuno 1411 Mk II; I band.

Comment: Similar to Jamaican and Honduras vessels.

2 BOSTON WHALERS

Displacement, tons: 1.3 full load
Dimensions, feet (metres): 22.3 × 7.4 × 1.2 *(6.7 × 2.3 × 0.4)*
Main machinery: 2 outboards; 240 hp *(179 kW)*
Speed, knots: 40+
Complement: 4
Guns: 1—12.7 mm MG.

Comment: Acquired in 1988-89.

TYRREL BAY   11/1990, Bob Hanlon

BOSTON WHALER   11/1990, Bob Hanlon

GUATEMALA

Senior Appointments

Commander Atlantic Naval Base:
  Captain Edgar Abdiel Villanueva Vargas
Commander Pacific Naval Base:
  Captain Miguel Posadas Perez

Personnel

(a) 1993: 1230 (125 officers) including 700 Marines (2 battalions) (mostly volunteers)
(b) 2¼ years' national service

Note: With army logistic support the total employed on naval work is about 1500 (including 900 conscripts).

Bases

Santo Tomás de Castillas (Atlantic); Sipacate and Puerto Quetzal (Pacific)

Mercantile Marine

Lloyd's Register of Shipping:
  8 vessels of 1797 tons gross

PATROL FORCES

Notes: (a) There is also a naval manned Ferry *15 de Enero* (T 691).
(b) Still trying to acquire new patrol craft possibly with assistance from the USA. Three 32 m patrol boats reportedly ordered from CMN Cherbourg in February 1990 were cancelled.

1 BROADSWORD CLASS (COASTAL PATROL CRAFT)

Name	No	Builder	Commissioned
KUKULKÁN	P 1051	Halter Marine	4 Aug 1976

Displacement, tons: 90.5 standard; 110 full load
Dimensions, feet (metres): 105 × 20.4 × 6.3 *(32 × 6.2 × 1.9)*
Main machinery: 2 GM 16V-149TI diesels; 3483 hp *(2.6 MW)* sustained; 2 shafts
Speed, knots: 32. **Range, miles:** 1150 at 20 kts
Complement: 20 (5 officers)
Guns: 1—75 mm recoilless. 2 Oerlikon 20 mm. 2—7.62 mm MGs.
Radars: Surface search: Racal Decca; I band.

Comment: As the flagship she used to rotate between Pacific and Atlantic bases every two years but has remained in the Pacific since 1989. Rearmed with 20 mm guns in 1989.

KUKULKÁN   5/1985

2 SEWART CLASS (COASTAL PATROL CRAFT)

Name	No	Builders	Commissioned
UTATLAN	P 851	Sewart, Louisiana	May 1967
SUBTENIENTE OSORIO SARAVIA	P 852	Sewart, Louisiana	Nov 1972

Displacement, tons: 43 standard; 54 full load
Dimensions, feet (metres): 85 × 18.7 × 7.2 *(25.9 × 5.7 × 2.2)*
Main machinery: 2 GM 16V-71TI diesels; 2000 hp *(1.49 MW)* sustained; 2 shafts
Speed, knots: 23. **Range, miles:** 400 at 12 kts
Complement: 17 (4 officers)
Guns: 2—75 mm recoilless. 2 Oerlikon 20 mm. 2—7.62 mm MGs.
Radars: Surface search: Racal Decca; I band.

Comment: Aluminium superstructure. P 851 rearmed with 20 mm guns in 1989 and is based in the Atlantic; P 852 in the Pacific.

UTATLAN   8/1987

6 US CUTLASS CLASS (5 COASTAL PATROL CRAFT AND 1 SURVEY CRAFT)

Name	No	Builders	Commissioned
TECUN UMAN	P 651	Halter Marine	26 Nov 1971
KAIBIL BALAM	P 652	Halter Marine	8 Feb 1972
AZUMANCHE	P 653	Halter Marine	8 Feb 1972
TZACOL	P 654	Halter Marine	10 Mar 1976
BITOL	P 655	Halter Marine	4 Aug 1976
GUCUMAZ	BH 656	Halter Marine	15 May 1981

Displacement, tons: 45 full load
Dimensions, feet (metres): 64.5 × 17 × 3 *(19.7 × 5.2 × 0.9)*
Main machinery: 2 GM 12V-71 diesels; 680 hp *(507 kW)* sustained; 2 shafts
Speed, knots: 25. **Range, miles:** 400 at 15 kts
Complement: 10 (2 officers)
Guns: 2 Oerlikon 20 mm or 2—12.7 mm MGs. 3—7.62 mm (triple) MGs.
Radars: Surface search: Racal Decca; I band.

Comment: *Gucumaz* used for Survey duties. All rearmed with 20 mm guns in 1991. P 651, 654 and 655 are in the Atlantic, remainder in the Pacific.

BITOL   1987

2 MACHETE CLASS (TROOP CARRIERS)

Name	No	Builders	Commissioned
PICUDA	D 361	Halter Marine	4 Aug 1976
BARRACUDA	D 362	Halter Marine	4 Aug 1976

Displacement, tons: 8.3 full load
Dimensions, feet (metres): 36 × 12.5 × 2 *(11 × 3.8 × 0.6)*
Main machinery: 2 GM 6V-53; 296 hp *(221 kW)* sustained; 2 waterjets
Speed, knots: 36
Complement: 2
Military lift: 20 troops

Comment: Armoured, open deck, aluminium craft. Both based in the Pacific.

RIVER PATROL CRAFT

KOCHAB	PAMPANU	SPICA	PAMPANO
ALIOTH	PROCYON	SCHEDAR	ESCUINTLA
SIRIES	VEGA	STELLA MARIS	MAZATENANGO
MERO	POLUX	SARDINA	RETALHULEU
			LAGO DE ATITLAN

Comment: Small wooden or aluminium hulled craft of various types. When older craft are replaced, the names are transferred to the new hulls. Overall numbers are uncertain.

BARRACUDA   1986

GUINEA

Senior Appointment

Commander of the Navy:
Commander Amara Bangoura

General

Some of the craft listed below are probably non-operational.

Personnel

(a) 1993: 400 officers and men
(b) 2 years' conscript service

Bases

Conakry, Kakanda

Mercantile Marine

Lloyd's Register of Shipping:
23 vessels of 5426 tons gross

DELETIONS

1989-90   6 Shanghai II class, 3 Shershen class

PATROL FORCES

1 Ex-SOVIET T 58 CLASS (PATROL SHIP)

LAMINE SADJI KABA F 79

Displacement, tons: 790 standard; 860 full load
Dimensions, feet (metres): 229.9 × 29.5 × 7.9 *(70.1 × 9 × 2.4)*
Main machinery: 2 diesels; 4000 hp(m) *(2.94 MW)*; 2 shafts
Speed, knots: 17. **Range, miles:** 2500 at 13 kts
Complement: 82
Guns: 4—57 mm/70 (2 twin); 85° elevation; 120 rounds/minute to 8 km *(4.4 nm)*; weight of shell 2.8 kg.
   4—25 mm/60 (2 twin); 85° elevation; 270 rounds/minute to 3 km *(1.6 nm)*; weight of shell 0.34 kg.
Mines: Laying capability.
Radars: Surface search: Don 2; I band.
   Fire control: Muff Cob; G/H band.

Comment: Transferred May 1979. MCM equipment removed. Refitted in Luanda 1984. Not in good condition and last reported at sea in 1989.

58 (old number)   1990

SOVIET BOGOMOL CLASS (FAST ATTACK CRAFT—GUN)

Displacement, tons: 245 full load
Dimensions, feet (metres): 127.9 × 25.6 × 5.9 *(39 × 7.8 × 1.8)*
Main machinery: 3 Type M 504 diesels; 10 100 hp(m) *(7.94 MW)* sustained; 3 shafts
Speed, knots: 37. **Range, miles:** 500 at 35 kts
Complement: 30
Guns: 1 USSR 3 in *(76 mm)*/66; 85° elevation; 120 rounds/minute to 15 km *(8 nm)*; weight of shell 7 kg.
   2 USSR 30 mm/65 (twin); 85° elevation; 500 rounds/minute to 5 km *(2.7 nm)*; weight of shell 0.54 kg.
Radars: Surface search: Pot Head; H/I band.
   Fire control: Bass Tilt; H/I band.

Comment: Built by Isora (Kolpino) in the Pacific and completed in April 1989. A Soviet export model with an Osa hull and machinery.

BOGOMOL (in transporter)   1989, G Jacobs

1 SWIFTSHIPS 77 ft CLASS

Name	No	Builders	Commissioned
INTREPIDE	P 328	Swiftships, Morgan City	Feb 1987

Displacement, tons: 47.5 full load
Dimensions, feet (metres): 77.1 × 20 × 4.9 *(23.5 × 6.1 × 1.5)*
Main machinery: 3 Detroit 12V-71TA diesels; 1260 hp *(993 kW)* sustained; 3 shafts
Speed, knots: 26. **Range, miles:** 600 at 18 kts
Complement: 10
Guns: 2 Browning 12.7 mm MGs. 2—7.62 mm MGs.

Comment: Ordered in July 1985 and completed 18 December 1986. Aluminium hull.

INTREPIDE   1987, Swiftships

268 GUINEA / Patrol forces — GUINEA-BISSAU / Patrol forces

1 COASTAL PATROL CRAFT

Name	No	Builder	Commissioned
ALMAMY BOCAR BIRO BARRY	P 400	Chantiers Navals d l'Esterel	Aug 1979

Displacement, tons: 56 full load
Dimensions, feet (metres): 91.8 × 17.1 × 5.2 *(28 × 5.2 × 1.6)*
Main machinery: 2 MTU 12V 331 TC82 diesels; 2605 hp(m) *(1.91 MW)* sustained; 2 shafts
Speed, knots: 35. **Range, miles:** 750 at 15 kts
Complement: 13
Guns: 1—12.7 mm MG.

Comment: Two more of the class were expected in 1987 but the order was cancelled.

1 SWIFTSHIPS 65 ft CLASS

Name	No	Builders	Commissioned
VIGILANTE	P 300	Swiftships, Morgan City	6 Jan 1986

Displacement, tons: 36.5
Dimensions, feet (metres): 64.9 × 18.4 × 5.2 *(19.8 × 5.6 × 1.6)*
Main machinery: 2 Detroit 12V-71TA diesels; 840 hp *(627 kW)* sustained; 2 shafts
Speed, knots: 24. **Range, miles:** 500 at 18 kts
Complement: 10
Guns: 2 Browning 12.7 mm MGs. 2—7.62 mm MGs.

Comment: Ordered in October 1984. Aluminium hull.

2 Ex-SOVIET ZHUK CLASS (COASTAL PATROL CRAFT)

Displacement, tons: 50
Dimensions, feet (metres): 75.4 × 17 × 6.2 *(23 × 5.2 × 1.9)*
Main machinery: 2 Type M 50 diesels; 2200 hp(m) *(1.6 MW)* sustained; 2 shafts
Speed, knots: 30. **Range, miles:** 1100 at 15 kts
Complement: 17
Guns: 2—14.5 mm (twin) MGs. 1—12.7 mm MG.

Comment: Transferred July 1987 after refurbishment.

2 STINGER CLASS

P 30   P 35

Displacement, tons: 2.9 full load
Dimensions, feet (metres): 26.3 × 11.1 × 1.5 *(8 × 3.4 × 0.5)*
Main machinery: 2 MC outboards; 310 hp *(231 kW)*
Speed, knots: 35
Complement: 4
Guns: 2—12.7 mm MGs.
Radars: Navigation: Raytheon 1200; I band.

Comment: Coastal/river patrol craft delivered in 1986 by SeaArk Marine (ex-MonArk).

VIGILANTE   *1985, Swiftships*

STINGER   *1987, MonArk Boats*

GUINEA-BISSAU

Personnel

(a) 1993: 350 officers and men
(b) Voluntary service

Base

Bissau

General

A Cessna 337 patrol aircraft is used for offshore surveillance. Several small craft including some ex-Soviet and Chinese LCU types may still be in service.

Mercantile Marine

Lloyd's Register of Shipping:
  19 vessels of 4380 tons gross

DELETIONS

1990 2 Poluchat class, *Cabo Roxo, Ilha de Poilao*
1991 4 Bazán type

PATROL FORCES

1 Ex-GERMAN KONDOR I CLASS (COASTAL PATROL CRAFT)

(ex-*Greifswald*) (ex-G 413)

Displacement, tons: 377 full load
Dimensions, feet (metres): 170.3 × 23.3 × 7.2 *(51.9 × 7.1 × 2.2)*
Main machinery: 2 Russki Kolomna Type 40DM diesels; 4408 hp(m) *(3.24 MW)* sustained; 2 shafts
Speed, knots: 20
Complement: 24
Radars: Navigation: TSR 333; I band.

Comment: Built by Peenewerft in 1970; transferred in early 1991 having been 'demilitarised'. Probably now carries a 20 mm gun or 12.7 mm MG.

3 SOVIET BOGOMOL CLASS (FAST ATTACK CRAFT—GUN)

Displacement, tons: 245 full load
Dimensions, feet (metres): 127.9 × 25.6 × 5.9 *(39 × 7.8 × 1.8)*
Main machinery: 3 Type M 504 diesels; 10 100 hp(m) *(7.94 MW)* sustained; 3 shafts
Speed, knots: 37. **Range, miles:** 500 at 35 kts
Complement: 30
Guns: 1 USSR 3 in *(76 mm)*/60; 85° elevation; 120 rounds/minute to 15 km *(8 nm)*; weight of shell 7 kg.
  2 USSR 30 mm/65 (twin); 85° elevation; 500 rounds/minute to 5 km *(2.7 nm)*; weight of shell 0.54 kg.
Radars: Surface search: Pot Head; H/I band.
Fire control: Bass Tilt; H/I band.

Comment: Built in the Pacific by Isora (Kolpino), Soviet export model with an Osa hull and machinery. First one delivered in early 1988, second in June 1990 from Vladivostock. Possibly one more in 1991.

KONDOR I (old number)   *1990, Erik Laursen*

BOGOMOL (in transporter)   *1989, G Jacob*

2 Ex-CHINESE SHANTOU CLASS

Displacement, tons: 80 full load
Dimensions, feet (metres): 83.3 × 19 × 6.5 *(25.5 × 5.8 × 2)*
Main machinery: 2 Type 3-D-12 diesels; 600 hp(m) *(440 kW)* sustained; 2 Type M 50 diesels; 2200 hp(m) *(1.6 MW)* sustained; 4 shafts
Speed, knots: 28. **Range, miles:** 500 at 28 kts
Complement: 36
Guns: 4—37 mm/63 (2 twin); 85° elevation; 160 rounds/minute to 8.5 km *(4.6 nm)*; weight of shell 1.46 kg.
2—12.7 mm MGs.
Depth charges: 8.
Radars: Surface search: Skin Head; I band; range 37 km *(20 nm)*.

Comment: Two delivered in 1983, two more in March 1986. First two used to provide spares for the others.

3 BAZÁN TYPE (COASTAL PATROL CRAFT)

Displacement, tons: 21.2 full load
Dimensions, feet (metres): 52.2 × 14.4 × 4.3 *(15.9 × 4.4 × 1.3)*
Main machinery: 2 Baudouin DNP-8 M1R diesels; 768 hp(m) *(564 kW)*; 2 shafts
Speed, knots: 25.7. **Range, miles:** 430 at 18 kts
Complement: 5
Guns: 1—12.7 mm MG.

Comment: Three ordered from Bazán, Ferrol in 1978. Four more ordered in September 1981. At least four deleted.

2 ALFEITE TYPE (COASTAL PATROL CRAFT)

Displacement, tons: 55 full load
Dimensions, feet (metres): 64.6 × 19 × 10.6 *(19.7 × 5.8 × 3.2)*
Main machinery: 3 MTU 12V 183 TE92 diesels; 3000 hp(m) *(2.2 MW)* maximum; 3 Hamilton MH 521 waterjets
Speed, knots: 28
Complement: 9 (1 officer)
Radars: Navigation, Furuno FR 2010

Comment: Ordered from Arsenal do Alfeite in 1991 for delivery in 1993.

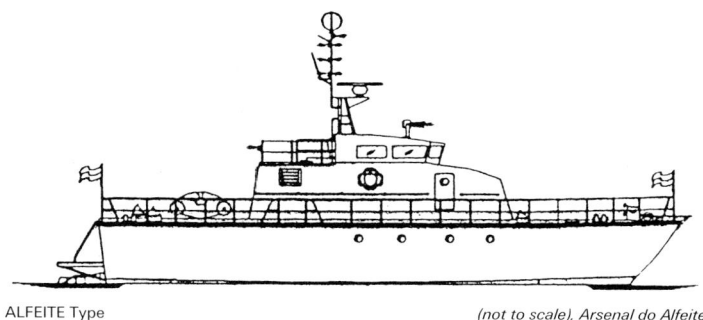

ALFEITE Type *(not to scale), Arsenal do Alfeite*

GUYANA

Headquarters' Appointment

Commanding Officer Coast Guard:
Captain Harry B Hinds

Personnel

(a) 1993: 190 members of Guyana Defence Force
(b) Voluntary

Bases

Georgetown, New Amsterdam

Prefix to Ships' Names

GDFS

Mercantile Marine

Lloyd's Register of Shipping:
82 vessels of 16 937 tons gross

DELETIONS

1990 *Hymara, Pirai*
1991 *Kimbia*
1992 *Peccari, Ekereku*

PATROL FORCES

2 Ex-US 45 FT CLASS (INSHORE PATROL CRAFT)

HOURI DFS 1018   **SEAFOOD** DFS 1021

Dimensions, feet (metres): 45 × 16 × 7 *(13.7 × 4.9 × 2.1)*
Main machinery: 1 diesel; 1 shaft
Speed, knots: 14
Complement: 4

Comment: Supplied by the USA. The survivors of six, salvaged in 1992.

2 Ex-FISHING VESSELS (INSHORE PATROL CRAFT)

WAITIPU DFS 1008   **MAIPURI** DFS 1017

Dimensions, feet (metres): 69 × 18 × 7 *(21 × 5.5 × 2.1)*
Main machinery: 1 Caterpillar 343 diesel; 1 shaft
Speed, knots: 9
Complement: 4

Comment: Converted fishing boats. Put back in service in 1992.

HAITI

Headquarters' Appointments

Commander of the Coast Guard:
Commander Charles A André
Deputy Commander:
Lieutenant Commander Yves Celestin

Personnel

(a) 1993: 165 (Total Armed Forces 7000)
(b) Voluntary service

Bases

Main: Port Au Prince
Secondary: Les Cayes, Port de Paix

Mercantile Marine

Lloyd's Register of Shipping:
4 vessels of 916 tons gross

State Yacht

Also reported, though not confirmed, that *Sans Souci* has been retained as a state yacht.

DELETIONS

1990   *MH 22, MH 23*
1991-92   *MH 11-16*

PATROL FORCES

1 Ex-US SOTOYOMO CLASS

Name	No	Builders	Commissioned
HENRI CHRISTOPHE (ex-USS *Samoset* ATA 190)	MH 20	Levingston S B Co, Orange, Texas	1 Jan 1945

Displacement, tons: 534 standard; 860 full load
Dimensions, feet (metres): 143 × 33.9 × 13 *(43.6 × 10.3 × 4)*
Main machinery: Diesel-electric; 2 GM 12-278A diesels; 2200 hp *(1.64 MW)*; 2 generators; 1 motor; 1500 hp *(1.12 MW)*; 1 shaft
Speed, knots: 13. **Range, miles:** 16 500 at 9 kts
Complement: 49
Guns: 1 Bofors 40 mm/60. 2—12.7 mm (twin) MGs.

Comment: Transferred by sale 16 October 1978.

HENRI CHRISTOPHE *1988, van Ginderen Collection*

270 HAITI / Patrol forces — HONDURAS / Patrol forces

3 US 3812-VCF CLASS (COASTAL PATROL CRAFT)

CHARLEMAGNE PERRAULT MH 17   **SONTHONAX** MH 18
BOIS ROND TONNERRE MH 19

Displacement, tons: 15 full load
Dimensions, feet (metres): 40.8 × 13.3 × 1.4 *(12.4 × 4.1 × 0.4)*
Main machinery: 2 Detroit 6-71 diesels; 348 hp *(260 kW)* sustained; 2 shafts
Speed, knots: 25. **Range, miles:** 350 at 20 kts
Complement: 4
Guns: 1 Browning 12.7 mm MG. 2 FN Herstal 7.62 mm (twin) MGs.

Comment: Built by MonArk, Monticello, Arkansas in 1981. By the end of 1992 only three were operational, six others had either been scrapped or cannibalised for spares.

SONTHONAX   *1988, van Ginderen Collection*

HONDURAS

Headquarters' Appointments

Chief of the Armed Forces:
  Brigadier Luis Discua Elvir
Commander of Honduran Navy:
  Colonel Reynaldo Andino Flores

Personnel

(a) 1993: 900 (95 officers)
(b) 24 months' conscript service

Bases

Puerto Cortés, Amapala, Puerto Castilla, La Ceiba, Puerto Trujillo

General

Two ex-Polish Polnochny class LCTs were seen flying the Honduran flag at Kiel in April 1990. These ships had been bought commercially for scrapping in a Spanish shipyard, and not to be transferred to the Honduran Navy.

Mercantile Marine

Lloyd's Register of Shipping:
  966 vessels of 945 067 tons gross

PATROL FORCES

3 SWIFT 105 ft CLASS (FAST ATTACK CRAFT—GUN)

GUAYMURAS FNH 101   **HONDURAS** FNH 102   **HIBUERAS** FNH 103

Displacement, tons: 103 full load
Dimensions, feet (metres): 105 × 20.6 × 7 *(32 × 6.3 × 2.1)*
Main machinery: 2 MTU 16V 538 TB90 diesels; 6000 hp(m) *(4.4 MW)* sustained; 2 shafts
Speed, knots: 30. **Range, miles:** 1200 at 18 kts
Complement: 17 (3 officers)
Guns: 1 General Electric Sea Vulcan 20 mm Gatling (FNH 101-102). 2—12.7 mm MGs.
  6 Hispano-Suiza 20 mm (2 triple) (FNH 103).

Comment: First delivered by Swiftships, Morgan City in April 1977 and last two in March 1980. Gatling guns acquired in 1987 with HSV-20NCS fire control system.

HONDURAS   *4/1991*

2 GUARDIAN CLASS (COASTAL PATROL CRAFT)

COPAN FNH 106   **TEGUCIGALPA** FNH 107

Displacement, tons: 94 full load
Dimensions, feet (metres): 106 × 20.6 × 7 *(32.3 × 6.3 × 2.1)*
Main machinery: 3 Detroit 16V-92TA diesels; 2070 hp *(1.54 MW)* sustained; 3 shafts
Speed, knots: 30. **Range, miles:** 1500 at 18 kts
Complement: 17 (3 officers)
Guns: 1 General Electric Sea Vulcan 20 mm Gatling.
  3 Hispano Suiza 20 mm (1 triple). 2—12.7 mm MGs.
Radars: Navigation: Furuno; I band.

Comment: Delivered by Lantana Boatyard, Florida in January 1983 and August 1986. A third of the class, completed in May 1984, became the Jamaican *Paul Bogle*.

COPAN   *7/1986, Giorgio Arra*

1 COASTAL PATROL CRAFT

CHAMELECON FN 8501

Displacement, tons: 50 full load
Dimensions, feet (metres): 85.3 × 19 × 3.3 *(26 × 5.8 × 1)*
Main machinery: 2 GM 12V-71TA diesels; 840 hp *(627 kW)* sustained; 2 shafts
Speed, knots: 23. **Range, miles:** 780 at 18 kts
Complement: 10 (2 officers)
Guns: 1 Oerlikon 20 mm. 2—12.7 mm MGs.

Comment: Built by Swiftships, Morgan City in 1967. Ex-*Rio Kuringuras* defected from Nicaragua in 1979.

CHAMELECON and GOASCORAN   *1988*

5 SWIFT 65 ft CLASS (COASTAL PATROL CRAFT)

NACAOME (ex-*Aguan*, ex-*Gral*) FNH 651   **ULUA** FNH 654
GOASCORAN (ex-*General J T Cabanas*) FNH 652   **CHOLUTECA** FNH 655
PETULA FNH 653

Displacement, tons: 33 full load
Dimensions, feet (metres): 69.9 × 17.1 × 5.2 *(21.3 × 5.2 × 1.6)*
Main machinery: 2 GM 12V-71TA diesels; 840 hp *(627 kW)* sustained; 2 shafts (FNH 6501-2)
  2 MTU 8V 396 TB93 diesels; 2180 hp(m) *(1.6 MW)* sustained; 2 shafts (FNH 6503-5)
Speed, knots: 25 (FNH 6501-2); 36 (FNH 6503-5). **Range, miles:** 2000 at 22 kts (FNH 6501-2)
Complement: 9 (2 officers)
Guns: 1 Oerlikon 20 mm. 2 Browning 12.7 mm (twin) MGs.

Comment: First pair built by Swiftships, Morgan City originally for Haiti. Contract cancelled and Honduras bought the two which had been completed in 1973-74. Delivered in 1977. Last three ordered in 1979 and delivered 1980.

CHOLUTECA   *4/199*

10 PIRANHA CLASS (RIVER PATROL CRAFT)

Displacement, tons: 8.2
Dimensions, feet (metres): 36 × 10 × 1.6 *(11 × 3.1 × 0.5)*
Main machinery: 2 Caterpillar diesels; 630 hp *(470 kW)*; 2 shafts
Speed, knots: 26
Complement: 5
Guns: 2—12.7 mm MGs. 2—7.62 mm MGs.

Comment: Eight built by Lantana Boatyard, Florida, and delivered on 3 February 1986. Three more in 1991. Also supplied to El Salvador. One reported sunk in September 1988 in a clash with Nicaraguan craft.

PIRANHA *1988, Honduras Navy*

12 OUTRAGE CLASS (RIVER PATROL CRAFT)

Displacement, tons: 2.2
Dimensions, feet (metres): 24.9 × 7.9 × 1.3 *(7.6 × 2.4 × 0.4)*
Main machinery: 2 Evinrude outboards; 300 hp *(224 kW)*
Speed, knots: 30. **Range:** 200 at 30 kts
Complement: 4
Guns: 1—12.7 mm MG. 2—7.62 mm MGs.

Comment: Built by Boston Whaler in 1982.

OUTRAGE *4/1991*

SERVICE FORCES

1 Ex-US HOLLYHOCK CLASS (BUOY TENDER)

YOJOA (ex-USS *Walnut*) FNH 252

Displacement, tons: 989 full load
Dimensions, feet (metres): 175.2 × 34.1 × 12.1 *(53.4 × 10.4 × 3.7)*
Main machinery: 2 diesels; 1350 hp *(1 MW)*; 2 shafts
Speed, knots: 12
Complement: 40 (4 officers)

Comment: Transferred in July 1982. Built by Moore Drydock Co in 1939.

YOJOA *8/1989*

1 LANDING CRAFT (LCU)

PUNTA CAXINAS FNH 1491

Displacement, tons: 625 full load
Dimensions, feet (metres): 149 × 33 × 6.5 *(45.4 × 10 × 2)*
Main machinery: 3 Caterpillar 3412 diesels; 1821 hp *(1.4 MW)*; 3 shafts
Speed, knots: 14. **Range:** 3500 at 12 kts
Complement: 18 (3 officers)
Military lift: 100 tons equipment or 50 000 gallons dieso plus 4 standard containers

Comment: Ordered in 1986 from Lantana, Florida, and commissioned 12 January 1988.

PUNTA CAXINAS *1988, Honduras Navy*

10 TRANSPORT CRAFT

Comment: In addition to the above, three old ex-US LCM 8 (*Warunta* FNH 7401, *Tansin* FNH 7402, *Caratasca* FNH 7403) transferred in 1987, and six ex-Fishing Boats (*Juliana* FNH 7501, *San Rafael* FNH 7502, *Carmen* FNH 7503, *Mairy* FNH 7504, *Yosuro* FNH 7505, *Gregori* FNH 7506) are used as transport vessels. There is also a 75 m former commercial vessel *Tatubla II* built in 1959 in Germany and taken over in the late 1980s.

LCM 8 *8/1989*

HONG KONG

General

All the listed craft are operated by the Marine Region of the Royal Hong Kong Police Force (RHKP). This is a Coast Guard Force responsible for the territorial waters of Hong Kong including the colony's 244 islands. The four main tasks are the prevention of illegal immigration from China, the detention of Vietnamese boat people, the prevention of smuggling by water between Hong Kong and mainland China and SAR operations.

Organisation

Marine Police Regional HQ, Tsim Sha Tsui, Kowloon
Bases at Ma Liu Shui, Tui Min Hoi, Tai Lam Chung, Aberdeen, Sai War Ho

Senior Officers

Regional Commander:
  B J Deegan, QPM, CPM
Deputy Regional Commander:
  Lim Sak-Yeung

Personnel

(a) 1993: 2600
(b) Voluntary service

Mercantile Marine

Lloyd's Register of Shipping:
  387 vessels of 6 925 724 tons gross

DELETIONS

1992 Sea Cat, Sea Puma, Sea Leopard, Sea Eagle, Sea Hawk, Sea Lynx, Sea Falcon, PL 37-45
1993 Sea Lion, Sea Tiger

PATROL FORCES

2 COMMAND VESSELS

SEA PANTHER PL 3   **SEA HORSE** PL 4

Displacement, tons: 420
Dimensions, feet (metres): 131.2 × 28.2 × 10.5 *(40 × 8.6 × 3.2)*
Main machinery: 2 Caterpillar 3512TA diesels; 2420 hp *(1.81 MW)* sustained; 2 shafts
Speed, knots: 14. Range, miles: 1500 at 14 kts
Complement: 33
Guns: 2—12.7 mm MGs.
Radars: Surface search: Two Racal Decca; I band.

Comment: Built by Hong Kong SY, PL 3 completed 27 July 1987, PL 4 on 29 September 1987. Both commissioned 1 February 1988. Steel hulls. Both have a Racal Cane command system.

SEA PANTHER   *1987, RHKP*

6 ASI 315 CLASS (COMMAND/PATROL CRAFT)

| PROTECTOR PL 51 | DEFENDER PL 53 | RESCUER PL 55 |
| GUARDIAN PL 52 | PRESERVER PL 54 | DETECTOR PL 56 |

Displacement, tons: 170 full load
Dimensions, feet (metres): 107 × 26.9 × 5.2 *(32.6 × 8.2 × 1.6)*
Main machinery: 2 Caterpillar 3516TA diesels; 4400 hp *(3.28 MW)* sustained; 2 shafts; 1 Caterpillar 3412TA; 1860 hp *(1.24 MW)* sustained; Hamilton jet (centre line); 764 hp *(570 kW)*
Speed, knots: 24. Range, miles: 600 at 18 kts
Complement: 18
Guns: 1 Browning 12.7 mm MG.
Fire control: GEC V3901 optronic director.
Radars: Surface search: 2 Racal Decca; I band.

Comment: Ordered from Australian Shipbuilding Industries in August 1991. First one in service 23 November 1992, the remainder at monthly intervals from January 1993. As well as patrol work, the craft provide command platforms for Divisional commanders.

DEFENDER   *12/1992, Australian Shipbuilding Industries*

15 DAMEN Mk III (PATROL CRAFT)

KING LAI PL 70	KING DAI PL 74	KING CHI PL 78	KING YAN PL 82
KING YEE PL 71	KING CHUNG PL 75	KING TAI PL 79	KING YUNG PL 83
KING LIM PL 72	KING SHUN PL 76	KING KWAN PL 80	KING KAN PL 84
KING HAU PL 73	KING TAK PL 77	KING MEI PL 81	

Displacement, tons: 95
Dimensions, feet (metres): 87 × 19 × 6 *(26.5 × 5.8 × 1.8)*
Main machinery: 2 MTU 12V 396 TC82 diesels; 2610 hp(m) *(1.92 MW)* sustained; 2 shafts
1 Mercedes-Benz OM 424A 12V diesel; 341 hp(m) *(251 kW)* sustained; 1 KaMeWa waterjet
Speed, knots: 26 on 3 diesels; 8 on waterjet and cruising diesel. Range, miles: 600 at 14 kts
Complement: 17
Guns: 1 Browning 12.7 mm MG.
Radars: Surface search: Racal Decca.

Comment: Steel-hulled craft constructed by Chung Wah SB & Eng Co Ltd 1984/85.

KING CHUNG   *1988, RHKP*

9 DAMEN CLASS (PATROL CRAFT)

PL 60-68

Displacement, tons: 86
Dimensions, feet (metres): 85.9 × 19.4 × 5.9 *(26.2 × 5.9 × 1.8)*
Main machinery: 2 MTU 12V 396 TC82 diesels; 2610 hp(m) *(1.92 MW)* sustained; 2 shafts
1 MAN D2566 diesel; 195 hp(m) *(143 kW)*; Schottel prop (centre line)
Speed, knots: 23 MTU; 6 MAN. Range, miles: 600 at 14 kts
Complement: 14
Guns: 1 Browning 12.7 mm MG.
Radars: Surface search: Racal Decca; I band.

Comment: Designed by Damen SY, Netherlands. Steel-hulled craft built by Chung Wah SB & Eng Co Ltd. Delivered February 1980 to January 1981.

PL 65   *11/1985, Giorgio Arra*

7 HARBOUR PATROL CRAFT

PETREL PL 11	TERN PL 14	PUFFIN PL 16
AUK PL 12	SKUA PL 15	GANNET PL 17
GULL PL 13		

Displacement, tons: 36
Dimensions, feet (metres): 52.5 × 15.1 × 4.9 *(16 × 4.6 × 1.5)*
Main machinery: 2 Cummins NTA-855-M diesels; 700 hp *(522 kW)* sustained; 2 waterjets
Speed, knots: 12
Complement: 7

Comment: Built by Chung Wah SB & Eng Co Ltd in 1986-87. Replaced old patrol craft some of which had the same names.

3 SHALLOW WATER PATROL CRAFT (JET)

JETSTREAM PL 6   **SWIFTSTREAM** PL 7   **TIDESTREAM** PL 8

Displacement, tons: 24
Dimensions, feet (metres): 53.8 × 14.8 × 2.8 *(16.4 × 4.5 × 0.8)*
Main machinery: 2 Daimler-Benz OM 422A 8V diesels; 490 hp(m) *(434 kW)* sustained; 2 Hamilton 421 waterjets
Speed, knots: 18. Range, miles: 300 at 15 kts
Complement: 8

Comment: Fibreglass hull built by Choy Lee Shipyards Limited. Completed April 1986 *(Jetstream)*, May 1986 *(Swiftstream)*, and June 1986 *(Tidestream)*.

JETSTREAM   *1986, RHKP*

3 DAMEN LOGISTIC CRAFT

MERCURY PL 57   **VULCAN** PL 58   **CERES** PL 59

Displacement, tons: 86
Dimensions, feet (metres): 85.9 × 19.4 × 5.9 *(26.2 × 5.9 × 1.8)*
Main machinery: 2 MTU 12V 396 TC82 diesels; 2610 hp(m) *(1.92 MW)* sustained; 2 shafts
   1 Daimler-Benz OM 422 8V diesel; 245 hp(m) *(217 kW)* sustained; 1 Hamilton 421 waterjet
Speed, knots: 23+ MTU; 7 waterjet and cruising diesels. **Range, miles:** 600 at 14 kts
Complement: 5 (10 for patrol work)
Military lift: 2 platoons of troops
Guns: 1 Browning 12.7 mm MG.
Radars: Navigation: Decca 150; I band.

Comment: Modified PL 60 design by Damen SY, Netherlands. Built by Chung Wah SB & Eng Co Ltd. Completed 26 January 1982 *(Mercury)*, 22 March 1982 *(Vulcan)*, 29 March 1982 *(Ceres)*. To be converted to patrol craft in 1993, with improved communications and accommodation, the addition of an RIB and launching davit and an MG mounting.

CERES *1987, Giorgio Arra*

11 SEASPRAY INSHORE PATROL CRAFT

PL 22-32

Dimensions, feet (metres): 32.5 × 13.8 × 4.3 *(9.9 × 4.2 × 1.3)*
Main machinery: 2 Caterpillar 3208TA diesels; 680 hp *(508 kW)*; 2 shafts
Speed, knots: 35
Complement: 4

Comment: Built by Seaspray Boats, Fremantle. First three delivered in mid-1992, remainder by early 1993.

PL 22 *1992, RHKP*

2 SHARK CAT INTERCEPTORS

PL 20-21

Displacement, tons: 4.5
Dimensions, feet (metres): 27 × 9.2 × 1.6 *(8.3 × 2.8 × 0.5)*
Main machinery: 2 outboards; 540 hp *(403 kW)*
Speed, knots: 40+
Complement: 4

Comment: Catamaran construction. Commissioned in October 1988.

PL 20 *10/1988, RHKP*

4 SEASPRAY LOGISTIC CRAFT

PL 46-49

Dimensions, feet (metres): 37.4 × 13.8 × 4.3 *(11.4 × 4.2 × 1.3)*
Main machinery: 2 Caterpillar 3208TA diesels; 550 hp *(410 kW)* sustained; 2 shafts
Speed, knots: 30
Complement: 4 + 16 fully equipped men

Comment: Built by Seaspray Boats, Fremantle. First one in service in June 1992, remainder by the end of the year. Catamaran hulls capable of carrying 6 people in VIP conditions or 16 for operational purposes.

7 WIN CLASS POLICE MOTOR BOATS

PL 35, 36, PL 85-89

Comment: Built by Choy Lee SY in 1970. Of 4.8 tons and 20 kts with a range of 160 miles at full speed.

WIN class *1987, RHKP*

11 HIGH SPEED INTERCEPTORS

PV 10-12   PV 30-37

Comment: *PV 10-12* are 9.5 m and *PV 30-37* are 7.5 m Typhoon RHIBs. Operated by the Small Boat Unit. Others of this type (fluctuating numbers) are operated as tenders to larger patrol craft.

CUSTOMS SERVICE

Note: Among other craft three Damen 26 metre Sector command launches were completed in 1986 by Chung Wah SB & Eng Co Ltd, Kowloon. In all essentials these craft are sisters of the 15 operated by the Royal Hong Kong Police with the exception of the latter's slow speed waterjet. Names: *Sea Glory* (Customs 6), *Sea Guardian* (Customs 5), *Sea Leader* (Customs 2).

LAND-BASED MARITIME AIRCRAFT

Note: Eight S-76A helicopters on order for SAR/transport duties.

Numbers/Type: 1 Cessna 404 Titan.
Operational speed: 258 kts *(478 km/h)*.
Service ceiling: 30 200 ft *(9200 m)*.
Range: 1485 nm *(2748 km)*.
Role/Weapon systems: Coastal surveillance for smugglers and 'boat people'. Sensors: Weather radar and cameras. Weapons: Unarmed.

Numbers/Type: 1 Pilatus Britten-Norman Islander.
Operational speed: 150 kts *(280 km/h)*.
Service ceiling: 18 900 ft *(5760 m)*.
Range: 1500 nm *(2775 km)*.
Role/Weapon systems: Supports RHKP in inter-island surveillance and against smugglers. Sensors: Weather radar and cameras. Weapons: Unarmed.

ISLANDER *1989*

HUNGARY

Headquarters' Appointment

Chief of General Staff:
Lieutenant General Janos Deak

Diplomatic Representation

Defence Attaché in London:
Colonel Peter Szücs

Personnel

(a) 1993: 400 officers and men
(b) 12 months' national service

General

The Navy was dissolved by 1968 but a maritime wing of the Army is active on the Danube in the form of an independent maritime brigade. Based in Budapest to patrol 420 km of the Danube. The future of this force is uncertain but live ordnance is still a hazard in the river.

Mercantile Marine

Lloyd's Register of Shipping:
15 vessels of 93 204 tons gross

DELETION

1991 1 Transport Barge 511-001

---

6 Ex-YUGOSLAV NESTIN CLASS
(RIVER MINESWEEPERS)

ÚJPEST AM 11	SZASZHALOMBATTA AM 21	DUNAÚJVÁROS AM 31
BAJA AM 12	ÓBUDA AM 22	DUNAFOLDVAR AM 32

Displacement, tons: 72 full load
Dimensions, feet (metres): 88.6 × 20.7 × 5.2 *(27 × 6.3 × 1.6)*
Main machinery: 2 Torpedo 12-cyl diesels; 520 hp(m) *(382 kW)*; 2 shafts
Speed, knots: 15. **Range, miles:** 860 at 11 kts
Complement: 17 (1 officer)
Guns: 5 Hispano 20 mm (1 triple fwd, 2 single aft).
Mines: 24 ground mines.
Radars: Navigation: Decca; I band.

Comment: Built by Brodotehnika, Belgrade in 1979-80. Full magnetic/acoustic and wire sweeping capabilities. Kram minesweeping system employs a towed sweep at 200 m. Two more, *AM 14* and *AM 24* are in reserve.

45 AN-2 CLASS MINE WARFARE/PATROL CRAFT

542-001 to 542-053

Displacement, tons: 11.5
Dimensions, feet (metres): 44 × 12.5 × 2 *(13.4 × 3.8 × 0.6)*
Main machinery: 2 diesels; 220 hp(m) *(162 kW)*; 2 shafts
Speed, knots: 9
Complement: 6
Guns: 2—12.7 mm (twin) MGs.
Mines: Can lay ground mines.

Comment: Aluminium hulls built between 1955 and 1965. Act as MCMV/patrol craft using mechanical sweeps and countermining. About 40 are active each Summer, being laid up in the Winter. Can be taken by road transport to the Tisza river. One of the craft, *542-004*, acts as a diving tender.

SZASZHALOMBATTA *2/1992, Eric Grove*

542-051 *9/1990, Per Kornefeldt*

SERVICE FORCES

One transport barge (CSS-001 ex-511-002) can double as landing craft (one tank) or bridging elements. New engines fitted in 1990.
One fireboat 531-001.
Two Volvo motor boats 583-001/002.
Two dumb diving pontoons and one tug.
Additional craft are taken up from civilian trade when required.

CSS-001 (old number) *1989, S Breyer*

ICELAND

Senior Officer

Director of Coast Guard:
Gunnar K Bergsteinsson

Duties

The Coast Guard Service deals with fishery protection, salvage, rescue, hydrographic research, surveying and lighthouse duties. All ships have at least double the number of berths required for the complement.

Personnel

1993: 127 officers and men

Colours

In 1990 all vessels were marked with red, white and blue diagonal stripes on the ships' side and the Coast Guard name (Landhelgisgaeslan).

Base

Reykjavik

Research Ships

A number of government Research Ships bearing RE pennant numbers operate off Iceland.

Mercantile Marine

Lloyd's Register of Shipping:
394 vessels of 172 812 tons gross

COAST GUARD

Name	No	Builders	Commissioned
AEGIR	—	Aalborg Vaerft, Denmark	1968
TYR	—	Dannebrog Vaerft, Denmark	15 Mar 1975

Displacement, tons: 1200 (1300 *Tyr*) standard; 1500 full load
Dimensions, feet (metres): 229.6 × 33 × 14.8 *(70 × 10 × 4.6)*
Main machinery: 2 MAN/Burmeister & Wain diesels; 8000 hp(m) *(5.88 MW)*; 2 shafts
Speed, knots: 19 *(Aegir)*; 20 *(Tyr)*
Complement: 22
Guns: 1 Bofors 40 mm/60.
Radars: Navigation: Sperry and Furuno; I band.
Sonars: Hull-mounted; active search; high frequency (*Tyr*).
Helicopters: Platform for 1 light.

Comment: Similar ships but *Tyr* has a slightly improved design and *Aegir* has no sonar. The hangar is between the funnels. The 57 mm gun has been replaced.

TYR — *1990, Iceland Coast Guard*

Name	No	Builders	Commissioned
BALDUR	—	Vélsmiöja Seyöisfjaröar	8 May 1991

Displacement, tons: 54 full load
Dimensions, feet (metres): 65.6 × 17.1 × 4.3 *(20 × 5.2 × 1.3)*
Main machinery: 2 Caterpillar 3406TA diesels; 640 hp *(480 kW)*; 2 shafts
Speed, knots: 12
Complement: 5
Radars: Navigation: Furuno; I band.

Comment: Built in an Icelandic Shipyard. Used for survey work.

Name	No	Builders	Commissioned
ODINN	—	Aalborg Vaerft, Denmark	Jan 1960

Displacement, tons: 1200 full load
Dimensions, feet (metres): 210 × 33 × 13 *(64 × 10 × 4)*
Main machinery: 2 MAN/Burmeister & Wain diesels; 5050 hp(m) *(3.71 MW)*; 2 shafts
Speed, knots: 18
Complement: 22
Guns: 1 Bofors 40 mm/60.
Radars: Navigation: Sperry and Furuno; I band.
Helicopters: Platform for 1 light.

Comment: Refitted in Denmark by Aarhus Flydedock AS late 1975. Has twin funnels and helicopter hangar. A large crane was fitted in 1989 on the starboard side at the forward end of the flight deck. The 57 mm gun has been replaced.

BALDUR — *5/1991, Iceland Coast Guard*

ODINN — *1992, Iceland Coast Guard*

LAND-BASED MARITIME AIRCRAFT

Note: In addition there is the single engined Ecureil A8 350B helicopter.

Numbers/Type: 1 Aerospatiale SA 365N Dauphin 2.
Operational speed: 140 kts *(260 km/h)*.
Service ceiling: 15 000 ft *(4575 m)*.
Range: 410 nm *(758 km)*.
Role/Weapon systems: Coast Guard SAR and surveillance helicopter with no armed role. Sensors: Flir weather radar. Weapons: Unarmed.

Numbers/Type: 1 Fokker F27 Friendship.
Operational speed: 250 kts *(463 km/h)*.
Service ceiling: 25 000 ft *(7620 m)*.
Range: 2700 nm *(5000 km)*.
Role/Weapon systems: Longer-range surveillance, especially fisheries patrol and SAR operations. Sensors: Bendix 1500B search radar. Weapons: Unarmed.

INDIA

Headquarters' Appointments

Chief of Naval Staff:
  Admiral L Ramdas, PVSM, AVSM, VrC, VSM, ADC
Vice Chief of Naval Staff:
  Vice Admiral V S Shekhawat, PVSM, AVSM, VrC
Deputy Chief of Naval Staff:
  Vice Admiral Vishnu Bhagwat, AVSM
Chief of Personnel:
  Vice Admiral R B Suri, AVSM, VSM
Chief of Material:
  Vice Admiral I C Rao, AVSM
Chief of Logistics Support:
  Vice Admiral A C Bhatia
Assistant Chief of Naval Staff (Policy and Plans):
  Rear Admiral S Kumar, UYSM
Assistant Chief of Naval Staff (Operations):
  Rear Admiral K R Menon
Assistant Chief of Naval Staff (Materials):
  Rear Admiral P Datey, VSM

Senior Appointments

Flag Officer C-in-C Western Naval Command:
  Vice Admiral K A S Z Raju, PVSM, AVSM, NM
Flag Officer C-in-C Eastern Naval Command:
  Vice Admiral B Guha, AVSM
Flag Officer C-in-C Southern Naval Command:
  Vice Admiral S K Chand, AVSM
Flag Officer Commanding Western Fleet:
  Rear Admiral Madhvendra Singh, AVSM
Flag Officer Commanding Eastern Fleet:
  Rear Admiral P J Jacob, AVSM, VSM
Fortress Commander, Andaman and Nicobar Islands:
  Vice Admiral P S Das, UYSM, VSM
Flag Officer, Naval Aviation and Goa Area (at Goa):
  Rear Admiral P Debrass, AVSM
Flag Officer, Submarines (Vishakapatnam):
  Rear Admiral S C Anand

Naval Air Arm

Squadron	Aircraft	Role
300 (Goa)	Sea Harrier FRS Mk 51	Fighter/Strike
	Sea Harrier T Mk 60	Trainer
312 (Madras)	Tu-142M 'Bear F'	LRMP/ASW
315 (Goa)	Il-38 May	LRMP/ASW
318 (Goa)	PBN Defender	Utility
321 (Goa)	HAL Chetak	Utility/SAR (Flight)
330 (Cochin)	Sea King Mk 42/42A	ASW
331 (Cochin)	HAL Chetak	Utility/SAR
333 (ships) (Goa)	Kamov Ka-25 'Hormone'	ASW
	Kamov Ka-28 'Helix'	ASW
336 (Cochin)	Sea King Mk 42/42A	ASW
339 (Bombay)	Sea King 42B	ASW/ASVW
550 (Vishwanath)	Tu-142M 'Bear F'	LRMP/ASW (Flight)
551 (Goa)	HAL HJT-16 Kiran	Training (OCU)
561 (Cochin)	HAL Chetak	Training
562 (Cochin)	Hughes 300, Chetak	Training
	HAL Jaguar	Strike

Air Stations

Name	Location	Role
INS *Garuda*	Wellington Island, Cochin	Helicopters
INS *Hansa*	Goa	HQ Flag Officer Naval Air Stations, LRMP, Strike/Fighter
INS *Sea Bird*	Karwar	Fleet Support (mid-1990s)
INS *Utkrosh*	Port Blair, Andaman Isles	Maritime Patrol
	Uchipuli, Tamil Nadu	Maritime Patrol
	Ramanathuram	Maritime Patrol
	Vishakapatnam	Fleet support and maritime patrol building
	Tiruchirapalli	LRMP, Helo Training
INS *Rajali*	Arakonam	
	Bangalore	LRMP building Naval Air Technical School

Personnel

(a) 1993: 55 000 officers and ratings (including 5000 Naval Air Arm)
(b) Voluntary service
(c) A Marine Commando Force was formed in 1986.

Prefix to Ships' Names

INS

Bases and Establishments

New Delhi, HQ (INS *India*)
Bombay, C-in-C **Western Command**, barracks and main Dockyard; with one 'Carrier' dock. New submarine pens being built. Supply school (INS *Hamla*). The region includes Mazagon and Goa shipyards.
Vishakapatnam, C-in-C **Eastern Command**, submarine base (INS *Virbahu*), submarine school (INS *Satyavahana*) and major dockyard built with Soviet support and being extended. Naval Air Station (INS *Dega*). New entry training (INS *Chilka*). At Vijayaraghavapuram is the submarine VLF W/T station completed in September 1986. Facilities at Madras and Calcutta. The region includes Hindustan and Garden Reach shipyards.
Cochin, C-in-C **Southern Command**, Naval Air Station, and professional schools (INS *Venduruthy*) (all naval Training now comes under Southern Command). Ship repair yard. Trials establishment (INS *Dronacharya*).
Goa is HQ Flag Officer Naval Air Stations.
Karwar (near Goa) has been selected as the site for a new naval base; first phase due for completion after 1994. Alongside berthing for Aircraft Carriers and a naval air station are planned. At Lakshadweep in the Laccadive Islands there is a patrol craft base. There are also limited support facilities including a floating dock at Andaman and Nicobar bases.
Naval Academy at Goa to move to Ezhimala, new base called INS *Jawarhalal Nehru*. A college of naval warfare has been established at Karanja.
Shipbuilding: Bombay (submarines, destroyers, frigates, corvettes); Calcutta (frigates, corvettes, LSTs, auxiliaries); Goa (patrol craft, LCU, MCMV facility planned).

Weapons and Sensors

Indian developments include:
SSM: Prithvi test fired in 1987; range 240 km; warhead 1000 kg.
SAM: Agni, Akash and Trishul; all being developed, at least one for the Navy. Trishul has a reported range of 10 km and is to be in service in 1994.
Medium range chaff decoy rocket. Sonar towed arrays. Remote piloted vehicle (RPV).

Strength of the Fleet

Type	Active (Reserve)	Building (Projected)
Patrol Submarines	14 (3)	1
Attack Carriers (Medium)	2	(2)
Destroyers	5	3 (1)
Frigates	15	3
Corvettes	18 (1)	8 (11)
Patrol Ships	7	3
Fast Attack Craft—Missile	4 (4)	—
Fast Attack Craft—Patrol/Torpedo	12	1
Landing Ships	10	(1)
LCUs	7	—
Minesweepers—Ocean	12	—
Minesweepers—Inshore	10	—
Minehunters	—	(6)
Survey Ships	10	—
Training Ships	1	(1)
Submarine Tender	1	—
Diving Support/Rescue Ships	1	2
Replenishment Tankers	2	1
Support Tankers	4	—
Water Carriers	3	—
Tugs	15	—
Coast Guard	40	13

Mercantile Marine

Lloyd's Register of Shipping:
  888 vessels of 6 457 275 tons gross

DELETIONS

Submarines

1991 *Chakra, Kanderi*
1992 *Kalvari*

Frigates

1990 *Andaman* (sunk)
1991 *Kamorta, Betwa*
1992 *Beas*

Light Forces

1990 *Vinash, Vidyut, Vijeta, Nashat, Nirghat*

Service Forces

1990 *Desh Deep*

PENNANT LIST

Submarines

S 20	Kursura
S 21	Karanj
S 40	Vela
S 41	Vagir
S 42	Vagli
S 43	Vagsheer
S 44	Shishumar
S 45	Shankush
S 46	Shalki
S 47	Shankul
S 55	Sindhughosh
S 56	Sindhudvaj
S 57	Sindhuraj
S 58	Sindhuvir
S 59	Sindhuratna
S 60	Sindhukesari
S 61	Sindhukiri
S 62	Sindhuvijay

Aircraft Carriers

R 11	Vikrant
R 22	Viraat

Destroyers

—	Delhi (bldg)
—	Mysore (bldg)
D 51	Rajput
D 52	Rana
D 53	Ranjit
D 54	Ranvir
D 55	Ranvijay

Frigates

F 20	Godavari
F 21	Gomati
F 22	Ganga
F 33	Nilgiri
F 34	Himgiri
F 35	Udaygiri
F 36	Dunagiri
F 41	Taragiri
F 42	Vindhyagiri
F 43	Trishul
P 68	Arnala
P 69	Androth
P 73	Anjadip
P 75	Amini
P 78	Kadmath

Corvettes

P 33	Abhay
P 34	Ajay
P 35	Akshay
P 36	Agray
P 44	Kirpan
P 46	Kuthar
P 47	Khanjar
P 49	Khukri
—	Kora
—	Kirch
K 40	Veer
K 41	Nirbhik
K 42	Nipat
K 43	Nishank
K 44	Nirghat
K 45	Vibhuti
K 46	Vipul
K 52	Vinash
K 71	Vijay Durg
K 72	Sindhu Durg
K 73	Hos Durg

Patrol Ships

P 50	Sukanya
P 51	Subhadra
P 52	Saryu
P 53	Savitri
P 54	Saryu
P 55	Sharada
P 56	Sujata

Light Forces

K 90	Prachand
K 91	Pralaya
K 92	Pratap
K 93	Prabal
K 94	Chapal
K 95	Chamak
K 96	Chatak
K 97	Charag

Mine Warfare Forces

M 61	Pondicherry
M 62	Porbandar
M 63	Bedi
M 64	Bhavnagar
M 65	Alleppey
M 66	Ratnagiri
M 67	Karwar
M 68	Cannanore
M 69	Cuddalore
M 70	Kakinada
M 71	Kozhikoda
M 72	Konkan
M 83	Mahé
M 84	Malvan
M 85	Mangalore
M 86	Malpe
M 87	Mulki
M 88	Magdala
M 89	Bulsar
M 90	Bhatkal
M 2705	Bimlipitan
M 2707	Bassein

Amphibious Forces

L 14	Ghorpad
L 15	Kesari
L 16	Shardul
L 17	Sharabh
L 18	Cheetah
L 19	Mahish
L 20	Magar
L 21	Guldar
L 22	Kumbhir
L 23	Gharial
L 34	Vasco da Gama
L 38	Midhur
L 39	Mangala

Service Forces

A —	Aditya
A 15	Nireekshak
A 50	Deepak
A 51	Gaj
A 54	Amba
A 57	Shakti
A 86	Tir
J 14	Nirupak
J 15	Investigator
J 16	Jamuna
J 17	Sutlej
J 18	Sandhayak
J 19	Nirdeshak
J 33	Makar
J 34	Mithun
J 35	Meen
J 36	Mesh

SUBMARINES

Notes: 1. The ex-Soviet Charlie class nuclear-powered submarine *Chakra* was leased for three years from January 1988. The lease was not extended and she returned to Vladivostock in January 1991. Although interest is still being taken in buying a modern SSN, the likely plan now is to build a nuclear propelled submarine in India. For this purpose there is an R&D project called the Advanced Technology Vessel which is reasonably well funded and has facilities in Delhi, Hyderabad, Vishakapatnam and Kalpakkam. A Navy-Defence Research and Development Organisation (DRDO) runs the project and since the mid-1980s has had a Vice Admiral in charge. The submarine will be a development of a Russian design with an Indian PWR. The nuclear reactor facility should be tested in 1993. This project has priority over the new aircraft carrier.

2. It is probable that India has acquired at least three midget submarines including two of the Italian Cosmos SX-756 type, which displace 80 tons dived and were bought commercially in 1988. The third may be slightly larger at 110 tons. There may be additional units together with a number of two-man chariot underwater vehicles.

3 + 1 SHISHUMAR (209) CLASS (TYPE 1500)

Name	No	Builders	Laid down	Launched	Commissioned
SHISHUMAR	S 44	Howaldtswerke, Kiel	1 May 1982	13 Dec 1984	22 Sep 1986
SHANKUSH	S 45	Howaldtswerke, Kiel	1 Sep 1982	11 May 1984	20 Nov 1986
SHALKI	S 46	Mazagon Dock Ltd, Bombay	5 June 1984	30 Sep 1989	7 Feb 1992
SHANKUL	S 47	Mazagon Dock Ltd, Bombay	3 Sep 1989	21 Mar 1992	1994

Displacement, tons: 1450 standard; 1660 surfaced; 1850 dived
Dimensions, feet (metres): 211.2 × 21.3 × 19.7 *(64.4 × 6.5 × 6)*
Main machinery: Diesel-electric; 4 MTU 12V 493 AZ80 GA31L diesels; 2400 hp(m) *(1.76 MW)* sustained; 4 alternators; 1.8 MW; 1 Siemens motor; 4600 hp(m) *(3.38 MW)* sustained; 1 shaft
Speed, knots: 11 surfaced; 22 dived
Range, miles: 8000 snorting at 8 kts; 13 000 surfaced at 10 kts
Complement: 40 (8 officers)

Torpedoes: 8—21 in *(533 mm)* tubes. 14 AEG SUT; wire-guided; active/passive homing to 28 km *(15.3 nm)* at 23 kts; 12 km *(6.6 nm)* at 35 kts; warhead 250 kg.
Mines: External 'strap-on' type.
Countermeasures: ESM: Phoenix II; radar warning.
Fire control: Singer Librascope Mk 1.
Radars: Surface search: Thomson-CSF Calypso; I band.
Sonars: Atlas Elektronik CSU 83; active/passive search and attack; medium frequency.
Thomson Sintra DUUX-5 (S 46 and 47); passive ranging and intercept.

Programmes: After several years of discussion Howaldtswerke concluded an agreement with the Indian Navy on 11 December 1981. This was in four basic parts: the building in West Germany of two Type 1500 submarines; the supply of 'packages' for the building of two more boats at Mazagon, Bombay; training of various groups of specialists for the design and construction of the Mazagon pair; logistic services during the trials and early part of the commissions as well as consultation services in Bombay.
The first two sailed for India February 1987. The second two delayed by assembly problems caused by faulty welding.
In 1984 it was announced that a further two submarines would be built at Mazagon for a total of six but this was overtaken by events in 1987-88 and the agreement with HDW terminated at four although this was being reconsidered in 1992. The medium term plan is for an indigenous design of 2000 tons to be built at Bombay after the 209 class programme is completed and Western designs have been evaluated.
Structure: The Type 1500 has a central bulkhead and an IKL-designed integrated escape sphere which can carry the full crew of up to 40 men, has an oxygen supply for eight hours, and can withstand pressures at least as great as those that can be withstood by the submarine's pressure hull. Diving depth 260 m *(853 ft)*. DUUX-5 sonar will be back-fitted to the first pair in the mid-1990s.

SHALKI   6/1992, G Toremans

8 SOVIET KILO CLASS (TYPE 877E)

Name	No	Builders	Commissioned
SINDHUGHOSH	S 55	Sudomekh, Leningrad	30 Apr 1986
SINDHUDHVAJ	S 56	Sudomekh, Leningrad	12 June 1987
SINDHURAJ	S 57	Sudomekh, Leningrad	20 Oct 1987
SINDHUVIR	S 58	Sudomekh, Leningrad	26 Aug 1988
SINDHURATNA	S 59	Sudomekh, Leningrad	16 Feb 1989
SINDHUKESARI	S 60	Sudomekh, Leningrad	10 Mar 1989
SINDHUKIRI	S 61	Sudomekh, Leningrad	4 Mar 1990
SINDHUVIJAY	S 62	Sudomekh, Leningrad	8 Mar 1991

Displacement, tons: 2325 surfaced; 3076 dived
Dimensions, feet (metres): 243.8 × 32.8 × 21.7 *(74.3 × 10 × 6.6)*
Main machinery: Diesel-electric; 2 diesels; 3650 hp(m) *(2.68 MW)*; 2 generators; 1 motor; 5900 hp(m) *(4.34 MW)*; 1 shaft
Speed, knots: 10 surfaced; 20 dived
Range, miles: 6000 at 7 kts surfaced; 400 at 3 kts dived
Complement: 60

Missiles: SAM: SA-N-8/14 (S 58 onwards, but not confirmed).
Torpedoes: 6—21 in *(533 mm)* tubes. 18 Indian (based on Type 53); pattern; active/passive homing up to 20 km *(10.8 nm)* at up to 45 kts; warhead 400 kg.
Mines: 36 in lieu of torpedoes.
Countermeasures: ESM: Stop Light; radar warning. Quad Loop D/F.
Radars: Navigation: Snoop Tray; I band.
Sonars: Shark Teeth; hull-mounted; active/passive search and attack; medium frequency.
Whale series; passive search; low frequency.

Programmes: The Kilo class was launched in the Soviet Navy in 1979 and although India was the first country to acquire one they have since been transferred to Algeria, Poland and Romania. Because of the slowness of the S 209 programme and its early termination, the original order in 1983 for six Kilo class expanded to ten but was then cut back again to eight. Plans to manufacture the class under licence in India have been shelved for the time being but design drawings are held should this project be resurrected.

SINDHUVIJAY   2/1992

Structure: Diving depth, 350 m *(1150 ft)*. Reported that from *Sindhuvir* onwards these submarines have an SA-N-8/14 SAM capability.
Operational: Based at Vishakapatnam and Bombay.

6 SOVIET FOXTROT CLASS (TYPE 641)

KURSURA S 20   **KARANJ** S 21   **VELA** S 40   **VAGIR** S 41   **VAGLI** S 42   **VAGSHEER** S 43

Displacement, tons: 1952 surfaced; 2475 dived
Dimensions, feet (metres): 299.5 × 24.6 × 19.7 *(91.3 × 7.5 × 6)*
Main machinery: Diesel-electric; 3 Type 37-D diesels; 6000 hp(m) *(4.4 MW)*; 3 motors (1 × 2700 and 2 × 1350); 5400 hp(m) *(3.97 MW)*; 3 shafts; 1 auxiliary motor; 140 hp(m) *(103 kW)*
Speed, knots: 16 surfaced; 15 dived
Range, miles: 20 000 at 8 kts surfaced; 380 at 2 kts dived
Complement: 75 (8 officers)

Torpedoes: 10—21 in *(533 mm)* (6 fwd, 4 aft) tubes. 22 Soviet Type 53; pattern active/passive homing up to 20 km *(10.8 nm)* at up to 45 kts; warhead 400 kg.
Mines: 44 in lieu of torpedoes.
Countermeasures: ESM: Stop Light; radar warning.
Radars: Surface search: Snoop Tray; I band.
Sonars: Bow-mounted; passive search and attack; medium frequency.
Bow-mounted; active search and attack; high frequency.

Programmes: *Karanj* arrived in India in October 1970, *Kursura* in December 1970, *Vela* November 1973, *Vagir* December 1973, *Vagli* September 1974, *Vagsheer* December 1975. All new construction. At least two have been refitted in the USSR.
Structure: Diving depth 250 m *(820 ft)*, reducing with age.
Operational: First one paid off in 1990 and has been cannibalised for spares, second in 1992 and at least one other is unlikely to go to sea again. Up to three are operational at any one time and used mostly for training.

VAGLI   11/1987, G Jacobs

AIRCRAFT CARRIERS

Note: The plan announced in 1989 was to build two new aircraft carriers, the first to replace *Vikrant* in 1997. A design study contract was signed with DCN (France) for a ship of about 28 000 tons and with a speed in excess of 30 kts. Size restricted by available construction dock capacity. Options included Ski Jump and CTOL. The Indian Naval Design Organisation was to translate the design study into the production model with construction to start at Cochin in 1993. However in mid-1991 the Committee on Defence Expenditure told the Navy to abandon plans for large carriers, and design effort has shifted to Italian *Garibaldi* type. The whole project takes second priority to the nuclear submarine effort.

1 Ex-BRITISH HERMES CLASS

Name	No	Builders	Laid down	Launched	Commissioned
VIRAAT (ex-HMS *Hermes*)	R 22	Vickers Shipbuilding Ltd, Barrow-in-Furness	21 June 1944	16 Feb 1953	18 Nov 1959

Displacement, tons: 23 900 standard; 28 700 full load
Dimensions, feet (metres): 685 wl; 744.3 oa × 90; 160 oa × 28.5 *(208.8; 226.9 × 27.4; 48.8 × 8.7)*
Main machinery: 4 Admiralty boilers; 400 psi *(28 kg/cm sq)*; 700°F *(370°C)*; 2 Parsons geared turbines; 76 000 hp *(57 MW)*; 2 shafts
Speed, knots: 28
Complement: 1350 (143 officers)

Missiles: SAM: 2 Shorts Seacat quad launchers; radar guidance to 5 km *(3.3 nm)*.
Guns: Some 30 mm/65 6-barrelled ADGs may be fitted.
Countermeasures: Decoys: 2 Knebworth Corvus chaff launchers.
ESM: Radar intercept and jamming.
Combat data systems: CAAIS action data automation; Link 10.
Fire control: GWS 22 for SAM.

Radars: Air search: Marconi Type 996; E/F band with IFF 1010.
Air/surface search: Plessey Type 994; E/F band.
Navigation: Two Racal Decca 1006; I band.
Fire control: Two Plessey Type 904; I/J band.
Tacan: FT 13-S/M.
Sonars: Graseby Type 184M; hull-mounted; active search and attack; 6-9 kHz.

Fixed wing aircraft: 12 Sea Harriers FRS Mk 51 (capacity for 30).
Helicopters: 7 Sea King Mk 42B/C ASW/ASV/Vertrep and Ka-25 Hormone.

Programmes: Purchased in May 1986 for £50 million thence to an extensive refit in Devonport Dockyard costing £15 million. Life extension of at least 10 years. Commissioned in Indian Navy 20 May 1987.

Modernisation: Devonport refit included new fire control equipment, navigation radars, and deck landing aids. Boilers were converted to take distillate fuel and the ship was given improved NBC protection. Seacat launchers removed but subsequently replaced. It is reported that a Soviet CIWS is to be fitted during further modernisation.
Structure: Fitted with 12° ski jump. Reinforced flight deck (0.75 in); 1-2 inches of armour over magazines and machinery spaces. Four LCVP on after davits. Magazine capacity includes 80 lightweight torpedoes.
Operational: The Sea Harrier complement will normally be no more than 12 or 18 aircraft leaving room for a greater mix of Sea King and Hormone helicopters (see *Shipborne Aircraft* section).

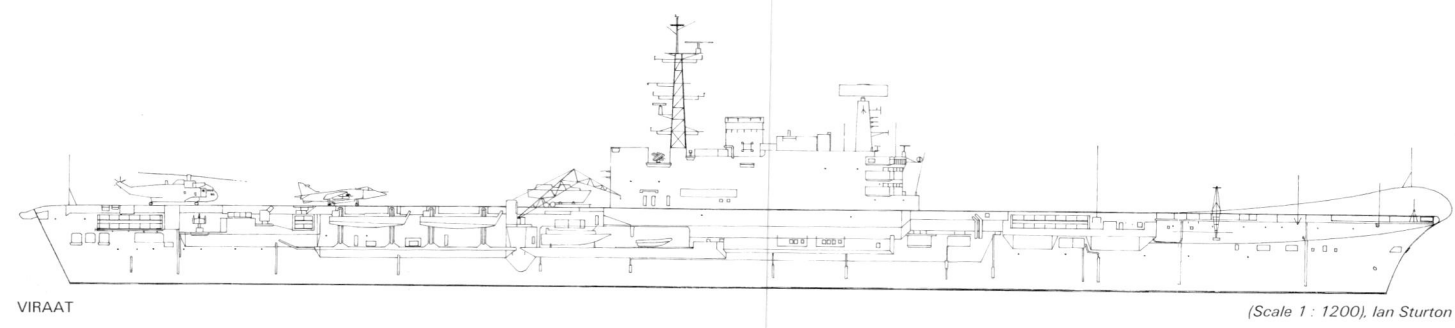

VIRAAT *(Scale 1 : 1200), Ian Sturton*

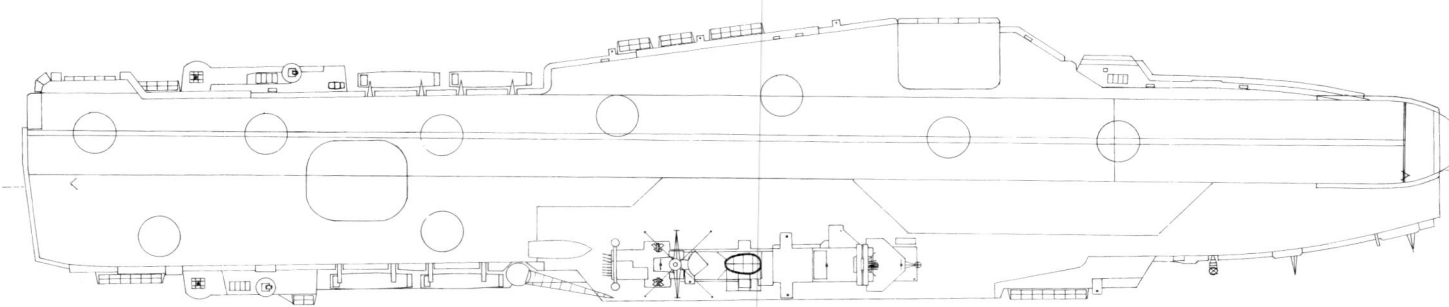

VIRAAT *(Scale 1 : 1200), Ian Sturton*

VIRAAT *1989, Indian Navy*

Aircraft carriers / INDIA

1 Ex-BRITISH MAJESTIC CLASS

Name	No	Builders	Laid down	Launched	Commissioned
VIKRANT (ex-HMS *Hercules*)	R 11	Vickers-Armstrong Ltd, Tyne	14 Oct 1943	22 Sep 1945	4 Mar 1961

Displacement, tons: 16 000 standard; 19 500 full load
Dimensions, feet (metres): 700 × 80; 128 oa × 24 *(213.4 × 24.4; 39 oa × 7.3)*
Flight deck, feet (metres): 690 × 112 *(210 × 34)*
Main machinery: 4 Admiralty boilers, 400 psi *(28 kg/cm sq)*; 700°F *(370°C)*; 2 Parsons turbines; 40 000 hp *(30 MW)*; 2 shafts
Speed, knots: 24.5
Range, miles: 12 000 at 14 kts; 6200 at 23 kts
Complement: 1075 peace; 1345 war

Guns: 7 Bofors 40 mm/70; 90° elevation; 300 rounds/minute to 12 km *(6.6 nm)* anti-aircraft; weight of shell 2.4 kg. Some may have been replaced by 30 mm/65 6-barrelled ADGs.
Combat data systems: Selenia IPN-10 action data automation.
Radars: Air search: Signaal LW 08; D band; range 264 km *(145 nm)* for 2 m^2 target.
Air/surface search: Signaal DA 05; E/F band; range 137 km *(75 nm)* for 2 m^2 target.
Navigation: Signaal ZW 06; I band.
Sonars: Graseby 750; hull-mounted; active search and attack; medium frequency.

Fixed wing aircraft: 6 Sea Harriers FRS Mk 51.
Helicopters: 9 Sea Kings Mk 42 ASW/ASV. 1 Chetak SAR.

Programmes: Acquired from the UK in January 1957 after having been suspended in May 1946 when structurally almost complete and 75% fitted out. Taken in hand by Harland & Wolff Ltd, Belfast, in April 1957 for completion in 1961. Commissioned on 4 March 1961 and renamed *Vikrant*.
Modernisation: Major two-year refit began in January 1979. Re-entered service 3 January 1982. Second major refit in 1983. Third refit in 1987-89 (recommissioned 12 February 1989) to increase life expectancy to 1997 at least; ski jump fitted and possible improvements made to CIWS.
Structure: Flight deck: Two electrically operated lifts. 9.75° ski-ramp to take '150 ton lift' installed during 1987-89 modernisation; steam catapults removed. The original ski jump structure was not strong enough for a fully loaded Sea Harrier and further modifications were made in 1990/91.
Operational: Total capacity for 22 aircraft.

VIKRANT (modified ski jump)   1992

VIKRANT   1992

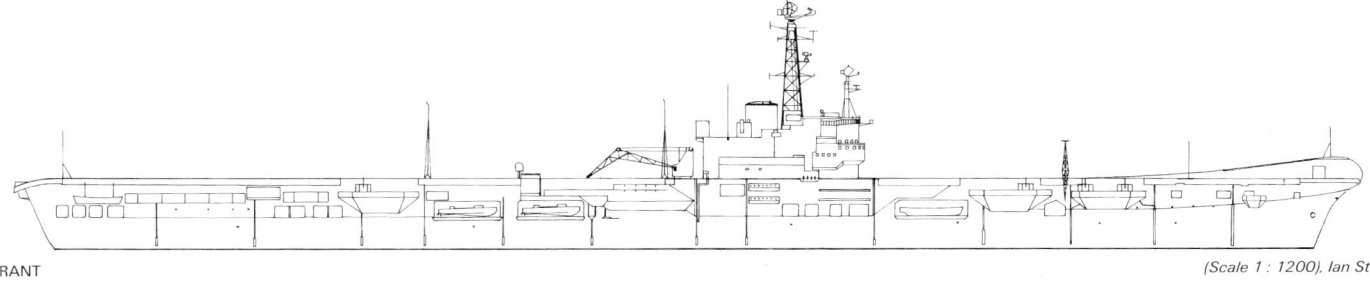

VIKRANT   *(Scale 1 : 1200), Ian Sturton*

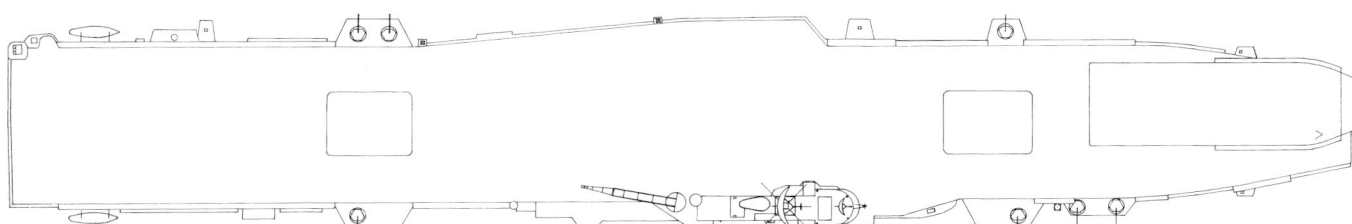

VIKRANT   *(Scale 1 : 1200), Ian Sturton*

VIKRANT   1992

DESTROYERS

5 SOVIET KASHIN II CLASS (TYPE 61MP)

Name	No	Builders	Commissioned
RAJPUT	D 51	Kommuna, Nikolayev	30 Sep 1980
RANA	D 52	Kommuna, Nikolayev	28 June 1982
RANJIT	D 53	Kommuna, Nikolayev	24 Nov 1983
RANVIR	D 54	Kommuna, Nikolayev	28 Aug 1986
RANVIJAY	D 55	Kommuna, Nikolayev	15 Jan 1988

Displacement, tons: 3950 standard; 4950 full load
Dimensions, feet (metres): 480.5 × 51.8 × 15.7 *(146.5 × 15.8 × 4.8)*
Main machinery: 4 gas turbines; 72 000 hp(m) *(53 MW)*; 2 shafts
Speed, knots: 35. **Range, miles:** 4500 at 18 kts; 2600 at 30 kts
Complement: 320 (35 officers)

Missiles: SSM: 4 SS-N-2D Styx ❶; IR homing to 83 km *(45 nm)* at 0.9 Mach; warhead 513 kg; sea-skimmer at end of run.
SAM: 2 SA-N-1 Goa twin launchers ❷; command guidance to 31.5 km *(17 nm)* at 2 Mach; height 91-22 860 m *(300-75 000 ft)*; warhead 60 kg; 44 missiles. Some SSM capability.
Guns: 2—3 in *(76 mm)*/60 (twin, fwd) ❸; 80° elevation; 90 rounds/minute to 15 km *(8 nm)*; weight of shell 6.8 kg.
8—30 mm/65 (4 twin) *(Rajput, Rana* and *Ranjit)* ❹; 85° elevation; 500 rounds/minute to 5 km *(2.7 nm)*; weight of shell 0.54 kg.
4—30 mm/65 (6-barrels per mounting) *(Ranvir* and *Ranvijay)*; 85° elevation; 3000 rounds/minute combined to 2 km.
Torpedoes: 5—21 in *(533 mm)* (quin) tubes ❺. Probably Soviet Type 53; pattern active/passive homing up to 20 km *(10.8 nm)* at up to 45 kts; warhead 400 kg.
A/S mortars: 2 RBU 6000 12-tubed trainable ❻; range 6000 m; warhead 31 kg.
Countermeasures: 4—16-barrelled chaff launchers for radar decoy and distraction.
ESM: Two Watch Dog. Two Top Hat A and B; radar warning.
Radars: Air search: Big Net A ❼; C band; range 183 km *(100 nm)* for 2 m² target.
Air/surface search: Head Net C ❽; 3D; E band; range 128 km *(70 nm)*.
Navigation: Two Don Kay; I band.
Fire control: Two Peel Group ❾; H/I band; range 73 km *(40 nm)* for 2 m² target.
Owl Screech ❿; G band.
Two Drum Tilt ⓫ or Two Bass Tilt *(Ranvir* and *Ranvijay)*; H/I band.
IFF: Two High Pole B.
Sonars: Hull-mounted and VDS; active search and attack; medium frequency.

Helicopters: 1 Ka-25 Hormone B or 1 Ka-28 Helix *(Ranvir* and *Ranvijay)* (to be retrofitted in earlier ships) ⓬.

Programmes: First batch of three ordered in the mid-1970s. *Ranvir* was the first of the second batch ordered on 20 December 1982.
Structure: All built as new construction for India at Nikolayev with considerable modifications to the Soviet design. Helicopter hangar, which is reached by a lift from the flight deck, replaces after 76 mm twin mount and the SS-N-2D launchers are sited forward of the bridge. *Ranvir* and *Ranvijay* differ from previous ships in class by being fitted with ADGM-630 30 mm guns, two Bass Tilt fire control radars and possibly infra-red attachment to SS-N-2D missile launchers. It is possible that an Italian combat data system is installed. Inmarsat fitted.

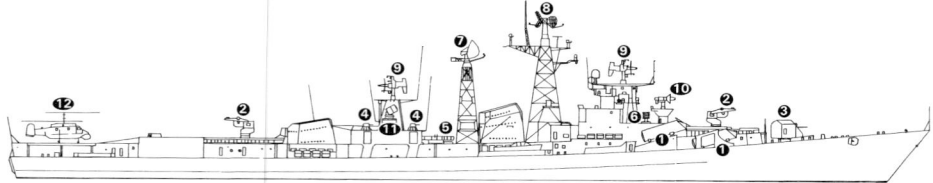

RANA (Scale 1 : 1200), Ian Sturton

RANJIT 1991

RANVIJAY 6/1992

0 + 3 (1) DELHI CLASS (DDG)

Name	No	Builders	Laid down	Launched	Commissioned
DELHI	—	Mazagon Dock Ltd, Bombay	14 Nov 1987	1 Feb 1991	1995
MYSORE	—	Mazagon Dock Ltd, Bombay	2 Feb 1991	1994	1998
—	—	Mazagon Dock Ltd, Bombay	1992	1996	2000

Displacement, tons: 6200 full load
Dimensions, feet (metres): 524.9 × 55.8 × 21.3 *(160 × 17 × 6.5)*
Main machinery: CODAG; 2 AM-50 Soviet gas turbines (GE/HAL LM 2500 in later ships); 54 000 hp(m) *(49 MW)*; 2 Bergen/Garden Reach KVM-18 diesels; 9920 hp(m) *(7.73 MW)* sustained; 2 shafts
Speed, knots: 28

Missiles: SSM: 4 SS-N-22.
SAM: SA-N-7 twin launcher (aft of the 76 mm gun) and/or 2 Trishul.
Guns: 1 USSR 3 in *(76 mm)*/60 (on the forecastle).
4 USSR 30 mm/65; 6 barrels per mounting (2 each side).
Torpedoes: 6 Whitehead 324 mm (2 triple tubes)
Depth charges: 2 rails.
Countermeasures: ESM/ECM DRDO/Selenia EW equipment
Radars: Air search: Bharat/Signaal RALW (LW 08); D band.
Surface search: Indra; E band.
Fire control: Bass Tilt; H/I/J band.
Sonars: Thomson Sintra TSM 2633 Spherion; hull-mounted; active search; medium frequency.
Indian developed VDS or linear towed array.

Helicopters: 2 Westland Sea Kings Mk 42B or 2 Hindustan Aeronautics ALH.

Programmes: Being built with Russian assistance. *Delhi* ordered in March 1986. *Mysore* ordered in 1990 and laid down as soon as *Delhi* was launched. Third of class laid down in late 1992. *Mysore* is launched. Programme is called Project 15.
Structure: The design is described as a 'stretched *Rajput*' with some *Godavari* features. Soviet gas turbines have been fitted in *Delhi* (and may be in *Mysore*), later ships will have LM 2500 built in India by HAL under licence. A combination of Russian and Indian weapon systems is being fitted but delays in supplying Russian equipment may mean bringing forward plans to fit later vessels with Western technology.

DELHI 2/1991

FRIGATES

3 + 3 GODAVARI CLASS

Name	No	Builders	Laid down	Launched	Commissioned
GODAVARI	F 20	Mazagon Dock Ltd, Bombay	2 June 1978	15 May 1980	10 Dec 1983
GOMATI	F 21	Mazagon Dock Ltd, Bombay	1981	19 Mar 1984	16 Apr 1988
GANGA	F 22	Mazagon Dock Ltd, Bombay	1980	21 Oct 1981	30 Dec 1985
—	—	Garden Reach SY, Calcutta	1989	1993	1995

Displacement, tons: 3600 standard; 4000 full load
Dimensions, feet (metres): 414.9 × 47.6 × 14.8 (29.5 sonar) *(126.5 × 14.5 × 4.5 (9))*
Main machinery: 2 Babcock & Wilcox boilers; 550 psi *(38.7 kg/cm sq)*; 850°F *(450°C)*; 2 turbines; 30 000 hp *(22.4 MW)*; 2 shafts
Speed, knots: 27. **Range, miles:** 4500 at 12 kts
Complement: 313 (40 officers including 13 aircrew)

Missiles: SSM: 4 SS-N-2D Styx ❶; IR homing to 83 km *(45 nm)* at 0.9 Mach; warhead 513 kg; sea-skimmer at end of run. Indian designation P 20 or P 21.
SAM: SA-N-4 Gecko twin launcher ❷; semi-active radar homing to 15 km *(8 nm)* at 2.5 Mach; height 9.1-3048 m *(130-10 000 ft)*; warhead 50 kg; limited surface-to-surface capability; 20 missiles. System called 'Osa-M'.
Trishul being fitted in second batch.
Guns: 2—57 mm/70 (twin) ❸; 90° elevation; 120 rounds/minute to 8 km *(4.4 nm)*; weight of shell 2.8 kg.
8—30 mm/65 (4 twin) ❹; 85° elevation; 500 rounds/minute to 5 km *(2.7 nm)*; weight of shell 0.54 kg.
Torpedoes: 6—324 mm ILAS 3 (2 triple) tubes ❺. Whitehead A244S; anti-submarine; active/passive homing to 7 km *(3.8 nm)* at 33 kts; warhead 34 kg (shaped charge). *Godavari* has tube modifications for the Indian NST 58 version of A244S.
Countermeasures: Decoys: 2 chaff launchers (Super Barricade in due course). Graseby G738 towed torpedo decoy.
ESM/ECM: Selenia INS-3; intercept and jammer.
Combat data systems: Selenia IPN-10 action data automation. Inmarsat communications (JRC) ❻.
Fire control: MR 301 MFCS. MR 103 GFCS.
Radars: Air search: Signaal LW 08 ❼; D band; range 264 km *(145 nm)* for 2 m² target.
Air/surface search: Head Net C ❽; 3D; E band; range 128 km *(70 nm)*.
Navigation/helo control: 2 Signaal ZW 06 ❾; or Don Kay; I band.
Fire control: Two Drum Tilt ❿; H/I band (for 30 mm).
Pop Group ⓫; F/H/I band (for SA-N-4).
Muff Cob ⓬; G/H band (for 57 mm).
Sonars: Graseby 750 *(Godavari)*; Bharat APSOH *(Ganga* and *Gomati)*; hull-mounted; active panoramic search and attack; medium frequency.
Fathoms Oceanic VDS (not in *Godavari*).
Type 162M; bottom classification; high frequency.

Helicopters: 2 Sea King or 1 Sea King and 1 Chetak ⓭.

Programmes: The second batch of three ordered from Garden Reach SY, Calcutta. This is Project 16A, indicating an improved Godavari design but probably with the same hull. Work is proceeding very slowly and hull number 5 is unlikely to be laid down until 1993.
Structure: The first three were a further modification of the original Leander design with an indigenous content of 72% and a larger hull. Poor welding is noticeable in *Godavari*. *Gomati* is the first Indian ship to have digital electronics in her combat data system. The second three have structural modifications based on lessons learned from the first of class. Trishul SAM to be fitted and Bhopal Engineering steam turbines.
Operational: French helicopter handling equipment is fitted. Usually only one helo is carried with more than one crew. The first three have a unique mixture of Soviet, Western and Indian weapon systems which has inevitably led to some equipment compatibility problems. The first ship of the second batch is scheduled for sea trials in 1994.

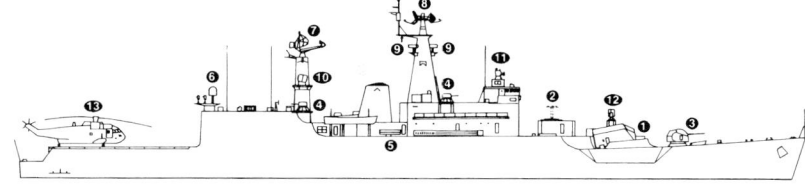

GODAVARI (Scale 1 : 1200), Ian Sturton

GANGA 5/1990, John Mortimer

GOMATI 8/1992, 92 Wing RAAF

GOMATI 4/1992

282 INDIA / Frigates

Name	No
NILGIRI	F 33
HIMGIRI	F 34
UDAYGIRI	F 35
DUNAGIRI	F 36
TARAGIRI	F 41
VINDHYAGIRI	F 42

Displacement, tons: 2682 standard; 2962 full load
Dimensions, feet (metres): 372 × 43 × 18 *(113.4 × 13.1 × 5.5)*
Main machinery: 2 Babcock & Wilcox boilers; 550 psi *(38.7 kg/cm sq)*; 850°F *(450°C)*; 2 turbines; 30 000 hp *(22.4 MW)*; 2 shafts
Speed, knots: 27; 28 *(Taragiri and Vindhyagiri).* **Range, miles:** 4500 at 12 kts
Complement: 267 (17 officers)

Missiles: SSM: 4 SSN-2B Styx *(Taragiri and Vindhyagiri)*; not always embarked.
 SAM: 1 or 2 Short Bros Seacat quad launchers ❶; optical radar guidance to 5 km *(2.7 nm)*; warhead 10 kg; 32 missiles. *Nilgiri* and *Himgiri* have 1 Seacat with GWS22 control. Remainder have 2 Seacat with 2 Dutch M44 directors.
Guns: 2 Vickers 4.5 in *(114 mm)*/45 (twin) Mk 6 ❷; 80° elevation; 20 rounds/minute to 19 km *(10.4 nm)* anti-surface; 6 km *(3.3 nm)* anti-aircraft; weight of shell 25 kg.
 2 Oerlikon 20 mm/70 ❸; 800 rounds/minute to 2 km.
Torpedoes: 6—324 mm ILAS 3 (2 triple) tubes *(Taragiri and Vindhyagiri)* ❹. Whitehead A244S or Indian NST 58 version; anti-submarine; active/passive homing to 7 km *(3.8 nm)* at 33 kts; warhead 34 kg (shaped charge).
A/S mortars: 1 Bofors 375 mm twin-tubed launcher *(Taragiri and Vindhyagiri)* ❺; range 1600 m.
 1 Limbo Mk 10 triple-tubed launcher (remainder) ❻; range 1000 m; warhead 92 kg.
Countermeasures: Decoys: Graseby G 738; towed torpedo decoy; effective against both active and passive torpedoes.
ESM: Racal UA 8/9; radar intercept. FH5 Telegon D/F (in some).
ECM: Type 667; jammer.
Fire control: 2 M44 MFCS. 1 GWS 22 *(Nilgiri)*. MRS 3 GFCS *(Nilgiri)*.
Radars: Air search: Signaal LW 08 ❼; D band; range 265 km *(145 nm)* for 2 m² target.
 Marconi Type 965M *(Nilgiri)* ❽; A band.
 Surface search: Signaal ZW 06 ❾; I band; range 26 km *(14 nm)*.
 RN Type 993 *(Nilgiri)* ❿; E/F band.
 Navigation: Decca 978; I band.
 Fire control: Two Signaal M44 (not in *Nilgiri* and *Himgiri*) ⓫; I/J band (for Seacat).
 Plessey Type 904 *(Nilgiri* and *Himgiri)* ⓬; I band (for Seacat).
 Signaal M 45 ⓭; I/J band.
 Plessey Type 903 ⓮ *(Nilgiri* and *Himgiri)*; I band.
IFF: Type 944; 954M.
Sonars: Graseby 750 (APSOH fitted in *Himgiri* as trials ship); hull-mounted; active search and attack; medium frequency. Type 170; active attack; high frequency.
 EMI Type 199 or Westinghouse VDS (first four only); active; medium frequency. Thomson Sintra VDS in *Taragiri* and *Vindhyagiri*. Type 162M; bottom classification; high frequency.

Helicopters: 1 Chetak (in first 4) ⓯.
 1 Sea King Mk 42 (in *Taragiri* and *Vindhyagiri*) ⓰.

Programmes: The first major warships built in Indian yards with a 60% indigenous component.
Modernisation: At future refits earlier ships are to have their armament brought into line with later ships. *Taragiri* and *Vindhyagiri* are fitted for two SSN-2 Styx launchers; these may have come from Osa class. Westinghouse has supplied the Indian Navy with ASW sonar systems, two hull-mounted arrays and three variable depth sonar (VDS) arrays for Leander class frigates. The VDS arrays are installed inside towed bodies built by Fathom Oceanology Ltd of Canada. The transducer elements in both cases are identical.

6 BRITISH LEANDER CLASS

Builders	Laid down	Launched	Commissioned
Mazagon Dock Ltd, Bombay	Oct 1966	23 Oct 1968	3 June 1972
Mazagon Dock Ltd, Bombay	1967	6 May 1970	23 Nov 1974
Mazagon Dock Ltd, Bombay	Jan 1973	9 Mar 1974	5 May 1977
Mazagon Dock Ltd, Bombay	14 Sep 1970	24 Oct 1972	18 Feb 1976
Mazagon Dock Ltd, Bombay	1974	25 Oct 1976	16 May 1980
Mazagon Dock Ltd, Bombay	1975	12 Nov 1977	8 July 1981

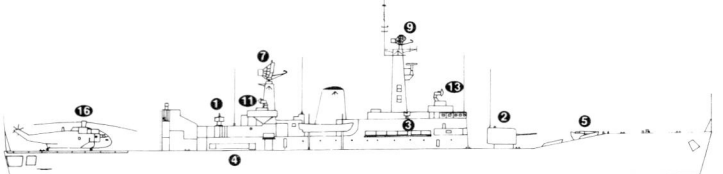
TARAGIRI *(Scale 1 : 1200), Ian Sturton*

TARAGIRI *10/1992, van Ginderen Collection*

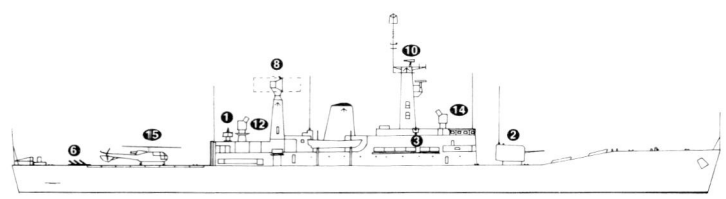
NILGIRI *(Scale 1 : 1200), Ian Sturton*

DUNAGIRI *1985*

Structure: Of similar design to the Broad-beam Leanders but with several differences. In the first four the hangar was provided with telescopic extension to take the Alouette III helicopter while in the last pair, a much-changed design, the Mk 10 Mortar has been removed as well as VDS and the aircraft space increased to make way for a Sea King helicopter with a telescopic hangar and Canadian Beartrap haul-down gear. In these two an open deck has been left below the flight deck for handling mooring gear and there is a cut-down to the stern.
Operational: It is reported that *Vindhyagiri* and *Taragiri* have more powerful engines than the remainder. Form 14th Frigate Squadron. Oil fuel, 382 tons plus 10 tons avgas.

5 SOVIET PETYA II CLASS

ARNALA P 68	ANDROTH P 69	ANJADIP P 73	AMINI P 75	KADMATH P 78

Displacement, tons: 950 standard; 1100 full load
Dimensions, feet (metres): 270 × 29.9 × 10.5 *(82.3 × 9.1 × 3.2)*
Main machinery: CODOG; 2 gas turbines; 30 000 hp(m) *(22 MW)*; 1 Type 6I-V3 diesel (centre shaft); 5400 hp(m) *(3.97 MW)* sustained; 3 shafts
Speed, knots: 32. **Range, miles:** 4000 at 20 kts
Complement: 98

Guns: 4 USSR 3 in *(76 mm)*/60 (2 twin) ❶; 80° elevation; 90 rounds/minute to 15 km *(8 nm)*; weight of shell 6.8 kg.
Torpedoes: 3—21 in *(533 mm)* (triple) tubes ❷. Probably Soviet Type 53; pattern active/passive homing up to 20 km *(10.8 nm)* at up to 45 kts; warhead 400 kg.
A/S mortars: 4 RBU 2500 16-tubed trainable launchers ❸; range 2500 m; warhead 21 kg.
Depth charges: 2 racks.
Mines: 2 rails.
Radars: Surface search: Slim Net ❹; E/F band.
 Navigation: Don 2; I band.
 Fire control: Hawk Screech ❺; I band; range 27 km *(15 nm)*.
IFF: High Pole B.
Sonars: Hercules; hull-mounted; active search and attack; medium/high frequency.

Programmes: An export version of Petya II class with simplified communications.
 Transfers: *Kadmath* (originally built for Egypt) February 1969; *Arnala* and *Androth* August 1972; *Anjadip* (built at Khabarovsk) February 1973; *Amini* (built at Khabarovsk) March 1974.
Operational: Form 31st and 32nd Frigate Squadrons. *Andaman* (P 74) sank in heavy weather in the Bay of Bengal 22 August 1990. Fourteen of the crew were lost. Four deleted so far, last one in October 1991. The remainder to pay off in 1993/94.

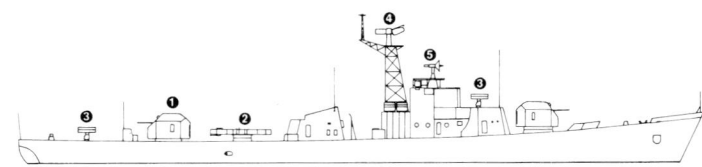
PETYA II class *(Scale 1 : 900), Ian Sturton*

PETYA II class (old number) *7/1987, G Jacobs*

Frigates — Corvettes / INDIA 283

1 BRITISH WHITBY CLASS (TYPE 12)

Name	No	Builders	Laid down	Launched	Commissioned
TRISHUL	F 43	Harland & Wolff Ltd, Belfast	1957	18 June 1959	Jan 1960

Displacement, tons: 2144 standard; 2557 full load
Dimensions, feet (metres): 369.8 × 41 × 17.8 (screws) *(112.7 × 12.5 × 5.4)*
Main machinery: 2 Babcock & Wilcox boilers; 550 psi *(38.7 kg/cm sq)*; 850°F *(450°C)*; 2 turbines; 30 000 hp *(22.4 MW)*; 2 shafts
Speed, knots: 30. **Range, miles:** 4500 at 12 kts
Complement: 231 (11 officers)

Missiles: SSM: 3 SS-N-2A Styx ❶; active radar or IR homing to 46 km *(25 nm)* at 0.9 Mach; warhead 513 kg.
Guns: 4 USSR 30 mm/65 (2 twin) ❷; 85° elevation; 500 rounds/minute to 5 km *(2.7 nm)*; weight of shell 0.54 kg.
A/S mortars: 1 Limbo Mk 10 launcher ❸; range 1000 m.
Countermeasures: Decoys: 2 UK Mk 5 chaff launchers. Graseby G738; towed torpedo decoy.
ESM: Telegon IV D/F.
Radars: Air/surface search: Signaal DA 05 ❹; E/F band; range 137 km *(75 nm)* for 2 m² target.
Surface search: Square Tie ❺; I band; range 73 km *(40 nm)* or limits of radar horizon.
Navigation: Signaal ZW 06 ❻; I band.
Fire control: Two Drum Tilt ❼; H/I band (for 30 mm).
Sonars: Graseby Type 177; hull-mounted; active search; 7-9 kHz.
Graseby Type 170B; hull-mounted; active search; 15 kHz.
Type 162M; bottom classification; high frequency.

Helicopters: 1 Chetak ❽.

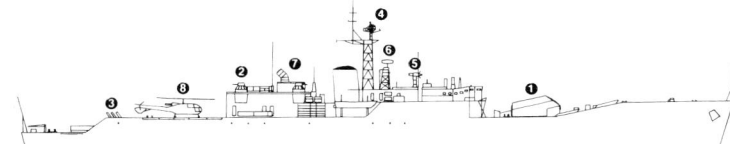

TRISHUL *(Scale 1 : 1200), Ian Sturton*

TRISHUL *1989*

Modernisation: SS-N-2 missile launchers from an Osa class were fitted in place of the 4.5 in gun in 1977-78. *Trishul* reconstructed at Mazagon Dock Ltd, Bombay, 1982-83. Rebuilt after section included construction of helicopter deck and hangar and Bofors guns were replaced by Soviet 30 mm.

Structure: Generally similar to the British frigates of the deleted Whitby class, but modified to suit Indian conditions.
Operational: Used mostly as an alongside training ship and may soon be scrapped.

CORVETTES

4 + 4 (4) KHUKRI CLASS (PROJECTS 25 and 25A)

Name	No	Builders	Laid down	Launched	Commissioned
KHUKRI	P 49	Mazagon Dock Ltd, Bombay	27 Sep 1985	3 Dec 1986	23 Aug 1989
KUTHAR	P 46	Mazagon Dock Ltd, Bombay	13 Sep 1986	15 Apr 1989	7 June 1990
KIRPAN	P 44	Garden Reach SY, Calcutta	15 Nov 1985	16 Aug 1988	12 Jan 1991
KHANJAR	P 47	Garden Reach SY, Calcutta	15 Nov 1985	16 Aug 1988	22 Oct 1991
KORA	—	Garden Reach SY, Calcutta	10 Jan 1990	10 Oct 1992	1994
KIRCH	—	Garden Reach SY, Calcutta	31 Jan 1992	1994	1996
—	—	Garden Reach SY, Calcutta	1993	1995	1997
—	—	Garden Reach SY, Calcutta	1995	1997	1999

Displacement, tons: 1350 full load
Dimensions, feet (metres): 298.6 × 34.4 × 8.2 *(91 × 10.5 × 2.5)*
Main machinery: 2 SEMT-Pielstick/Kirloskar 18 PA6 V 280 diesels; 14 400 hp(m) *(10.58 MW)* sustained; 2 shafts; cp props
Speed, knots: 25. **Range, miles:** 4000 at 16 kts
Complement: 79 (10 officers)

Missiles: SSM: 2 or 4 SS-N-2D Styx (1 or 2 twin) launchers ❶; IR homing to 83 km *(45 nm)* at 0.9 Mach; warhead 513 kg; seaskimmer at end of run.
SAM: SA-N-5 Grail ❷; manual aiming; IR homing to 6 km *(3.2 nm)* at 1.5 Mach; altitude to 2500 m *(8000 ft)*; warhead 1.5 kg.
Guns: 1 USSR AK 176 3 in *(76 mm)*/60 ❸; 85° elevation; 120 rounds/minute to 15 km *(8 nm)*; weight of shell 7 kg.
2—30 mm/65 (twin) AK 630 ❹; 85° elevation; 500 rounds/minute to 5 km *(2.7 nm)*; weight of shell 0.54 kg.
Countermeasures: Decoys: 2—16-barrelled chaff launchers ❺. NPOL (Cochin); towed torpedo decoy.
ESM: Bharat Ajanta P; radar warning.
Combat data systems: Selenia system *(Khukri)*; Bharat Vympal system (remainder).
Radars: Air search: Positive E/Cross Sword ❻; E/F band; range 130 km *(70 nm)*.

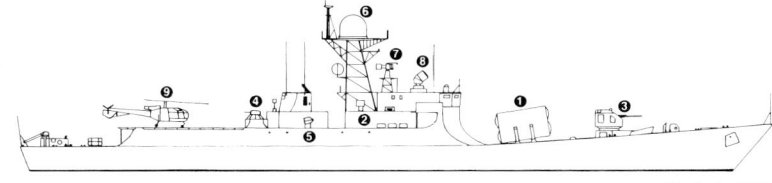

KHUKRI *(Scale 1 : 900), Ian Sturton*

Air/surface search: Plank Shave ❼; I band.
Fire control: Bass Tilt ❽; H/I band.
Navigation: Bharat 1245; I band.

Helicopters: Platform only ❾ for Chetak (to be replaced by Hindustan Aeronautics ALH in due course).

Programmes: First two ordered December 1983; two more ordered in 1985 and the next batch of four from Garden Reach/Mazagon in April 1990. Total of 12 planned. The diesels are assembled in India under licence by Kirloskar. Indigenous content of the whole ship is about 65 per cent. This class is replacing the Petyas. The follow-on class is an upgraded version and the first should start sea trials in 1993/94.
Structure: SA-N-4 may be fitted in the second batch of four. The reported plan was to make the first four ASW ships, and the remainder anti-aircraft or general purpose. However *Khukri* has neither torpedo tubes nor a sonar (apart from an Atlas Elektronik echo sounder), so if the plan is correct these ships will rely on an ALH helicopter which will have dunking sonar and ASW torpedoes and depth charges. All have fin stabilisers and full air-conditioning.
Operational: Based in Bombay. The advanced light helicopter (ALH) to have Sea Eagle SSM, torpedoes and dipping sonar.

KIRPAN *11/1992, RAN*

284 INDIA / Corvettes

4 ABHAY (PAUK) CLASS

Name	No	Builders	Commissioned
ABHAY	P 33	Volodarski, Rybinsk	Mar 1989
AJAY	P 34	Volodarski, Rybinsk	24 Jan 1990
AKSHAY	P 35	Volodarski, Rybinsk	Dec 1990
AGRAY	P 36	Volodarski, Rybinsk	Feb 1991

Displacement, tons: 520 full load
Dimensions, feet (metres): 195.2 × 33.5 × 10.8 *(59.5 × 10.2 × 3.3)*
Main machinery: 2 Type M 507T diesels; 11 520 hp(m) *(8.47 MW)* sustained; 2 shafts
Speed, knots: 32. **Range, miles:** 2200 at 18 kts
Complement: 32

Missiles: SAM: SA-N-5 Grail quad launcher; manual aiming, IR homing to 6 km *(3.2 nm)* at 1.5 Mach; warhead 1.5 kg.
Guns: 1 USSR 3 in *(76 mm)*/60; 85° elevation; 120 rounds/minute to 15 km *(8 nm)*; weight of shell 7 kg.
 1—30 mm/65; 6 barrels; 3000 rounds/minute combined to 2 km.
Torpedoes: 4—21 in *(533 mm)* (2 twin) tubes. Soviet type 53; active/passive homing up to 20 km *(11 nm)* at up to 45 kts; warhead 400 kg.
A/S mortars: 2 RBU 1200 5-tubed fixed; range 1200 m; warhead 34 kg.
Countermeasures: 2—16-tubed chaff launchers.
Radars: Air/Surface search: Positive E; E/F band.
 Navigation: Pechora; I band.
 Fire Control: Bass Tilt; H/I band.
Sonars: Rat Tail VDS (on transom); attack; high frequency.

Programmes: Modified Pauk II class built in the USSR for export. Original order in late 1983 but completion of the first delayed by lack of funds and the order for the others was not reinstated until 1987. A fifth of class has probably been cancelled. Names associated with former coastal patrol craft. One of the same class has been acquired by Cuba.
Structure: Has a longer superstructure than the Pauk I and new electronics with a radome similar to the Parchim II class.

AGRAY 1/1991, Photo Sami

8 + 4 (7) VEER (TARANTUL I) CLASS (TYPE 1241)

Name	No	Builders	Laid down	Launched	Commissioned
VEER	K 40	Volodarski, Rybinsk	—	—	May 1987
NIRBHIK	K 41	Volodarski, Rybinsk	—	—	Jan 1988
NIPAT	K 42	Volodarski, Rybinsk	—	—	Jan 1989
NISHANK	K 43	Volodarski, Rybinsk	—	—	Sep 1989
NIRGHAT	K 44	Volodarski, Rybinsk	—	—	Feb 1990
VIBHUTI	K 45	Mazagon Dock Ltd, Bombay	Mar 1988	26 Apr 1990	3 June 1991
VIPUL	K 46	Mazagon Dock Ltd, Bombay	July 1988	3 Jan 1991	16 Mar 1992
VINASH	K 52	Mazagon Dock Ltd, Goa	June 1990	24 Jan 1992	1993
—	K 47-50	Mazagon Dock Ltd, Bombay	—	—	—
—	K 53-59	Mazagon Dock Ltd, Goa	—	—	—

Displacement, tons: 385 standard; 450 full load
Dimensions, feet (metres): 184.1 × 37.7 × 8.2 *(56.1 × 11.5 × 2.5)*
Main machinery: COGOG; 2 Type NK-12MV gas turbines; 18 936 hp(m) *(13.92 MW)* sustained; 2 gas turbines with reversible gear box; 8000 hp(m) *(5.9 MW)*; 2 shafts (K 40-44)
 CODOG; 1 GE LM 2500 gas turbine; 23 300 hp *(17.38 MW)* sustained; 2 MTU 12V 538 TB92 diesels; 5110 hp(m) *(3.76 MW)* sustained; 2 shafts (K 45 onwards)
Speed, knots: 36. **Range, miles:** 2000 at 20 kts; 400 at 36 kts
Complement: 41 (5 officers)

Missiles: SSM: 4 SS-N-2D Styx; IR homing to 83 km *(45 nm)* at 0.9 Mach; warhead 513 kg; sea-skimmer at end of run.
 SAM: SA-N-5 Grail quad launcher; manual aiming, IR homing to 6 km *(3.2 nm)* at 1.5 Mach; warhead 1.5 kg.
Guns: 1 USSR 3 in *(76 mm)*/60; 85° elevation; 120 rounds/minute to 15 km *(8 nm)*; weight of shell 7 kg.
 2—30 mm/65; 85° elevation; 500 rounds/minute to 5 km *(2.7 nm)*; weight of shell 0.54 kg.
Fire control: Hood Wink optronic director.
Radars: Air/surface search: Plank Shave; E band.
 Navigation: Pechora; I Band.
 Fire Control: Bass tilt; H/I band.
IFF: Salt Pot, Square Head A.

NIRGHAT 1991

Programmes: First five are Soviet Tarantul I class built for export. Remainder of this type are building in India. Because of supply problems from Russia, numbers to be built are uncertain but are likely to be revised downwards and the programme may even be suspended.

Structure: Variations in the Indian-built ships include CODOG propulsion (with one gas turbine and two diesels) and improved countermeasures equipment. It is possible that the early Indian-built ships also have Russian gas turbines.

VIBHUTI 1992

3 Ex-SOVIET NANUCHKA II CLASS

Name	No	Commissioned
VIJAY DURG	K 71	Apr 1976
SINDHU DURG	K 72	Sep 1977
HOS DURG	K 73	Apr 1978

Displacement, tons: 850 full load
Dimensions, feet (metres): 194.5 × 38.7 × 8.5 *(59.3 × 11.8 × 2.6)*
Main machinery: 3 Type M 507 diesels; 21 600 hp(m) *(15.9 MW)* sustained; 3 shafts
Speed, knots: 34. **Range, miles:** 2500 at 12 kts; 900 at 31 kts
Complement: 60

Missiles: SSM: 4 SS-N-2C Styx; active radar or IR homing to 46 km *(25 nm)* at 0.9 Mach; warhead 513 kg.
SAM: SA-N-4 Gecko twin launcher; semi-active radar homing to 15 km *(8 nm)* at 2.5 Mach; height envelope 9-3048 m *(29.5-10 000 ft)*; warhead 50 kg; 20 missiles.
Guns: 2 USSR 57 mm/80 (twin); 90° elevation; 120 rounds/minute to 8 km *(4.4 nm)*; weight of shell 2.8 kg.
Countermeasures: 2—16-barrelled chaff launchers.
ESM: Radar warning.
Radars: Air/surface search: Square Tie; I band; range 73 km *(40 nm)* (mounted in radome).
Fire control: Pop Group; F/H/I band (for SAN-4).
Muff Cob; G/H band.
Navigation: Don 2; I band.
IFF: High Pole. Two Square Head.

Structure: The radome is mounted lower than in Soviet ships of this class due to the absence of Fish Bowl because of the use of SS-N-2 missiles in place of SS-N-9.
Operational: At least one is non-operational, supplying spares for the others.

VIJAY DURG *1990*

PATROL SHIPS

7 + 3 SUKANYA CLASS (OFFSHORE PATROL SHIPS)

Name	No	Builders	Launched	Commissioned
SUKANYA	P 50	Korea Tacoma, Masan	1989	31 Aug 1989
SUBHADRA	P 51	Korea Tacoma, Masan	1989	25 Jan 1990
SUVARNA	P 52	Korea Tacoma, Masan	22 Aug 1990	4 Apr 1991
SAVITRI	P 53	Hindustan SY, Vishakapatnam	23 May 1989	27 Nov 1990
SARYU	P 54	Hindustan SY, Vishakapatnam	16 Oct 1989	8 Oct 1991
SHARADA	P 55	Hindustan SY, Vishakapatnam	22 Aug 1990	27 Oct 1991
SUJATA	P 56	Hindustan SY, Vishakapatnam	25 Oct 1991	1993
—	P 57	Mazagon Dock Ltd, Goa	26 Aug 1992	1993
—	P 58-59	Mazagon Dock Ltd, Goa	—	—

Displacement, tons: 1890 full load
Dimensions, feet (metres): 334.6 oa; 315 wl × 37.7 × 11.2 *(102; 96 × 11.5 × 3.4)*
Main machinery: 2 SEMT-Pielstick 16 PA6 V 280 diesels; 12 800 hp(m) *(9.41 MW)* sustained; 2 shafts
Speed, knots: 21. **Range, miles:** 7000 at 15 kts
Complement: 145 (12 officers)

Guns: 1 Oerlikon 20 mm.
Radars: Surface search: Selenia; I band.
Navigation: Racal Decca; I band.
Helicopters: 1 Chetak.

Comment: First three ordered in March 1987 from Korea Tacoma to an Ulsan class design. Second four ordered in August 1987. The Korean-built ships commissioned at Masan and then sailed for India where the armament was fitted. Three more reported ordered from Goa in April 1990. Lightly armed and able to 'stage' helicopters, they are fitted out for offshore patrol work only but have the capacity to be much more heavily armed. Fin stabilisers fitted. Firefighting pump on hangar roof aft. These are naval ships (not Coast Guard) used for harbour defence, protection of offshore installations and patrol of the EEZ. Potential for role change is considerable. Inmarsat can be fitted on the hangar roof.

SUBHADRA *4/1992*

SHIPBORNE AIRCRAFT

Note: Naval versions of the Advanced Light Aircraft are being developed.

Numbers/Type: 23/3 British Aerospace Sea Harrier FRS Mk 51/Mk 60 (trainers).
Operational speed: 640 kts *(1186 km/h)*.
Service ceiling: 51 200 ft *(15 600 m)*.
Range: 800 nm *(1480 km)*.
Role/Weapon systems: Fleet air defence, strike and reconnaissance STOVL fighter with future ASV role with Sea Eagle missiles; mid-life update planned after 1995; seven on order. Sensors: Ferranti Blue Fox air interception radar, limited ECM/RWR. Weapons: Air defence; 2 × Magic AAMs, 2 × 30 mm Aden cannon. Strike; 2 × Sea Eagle missiles or 3.6 tons of 'iron' bombs.

Numbers/Type: 20/5 Westland Sea King Mks 42B/42C.
Operational speed: 112 kts *(208 km/h)*.
Service ceiling: 11 500 ft *(3500 m)*.
Range: 664 nm *(1230 km)*.
Role/Weapon systems: Advanced shipborne helicopter for embarked and shore-based role; Mk 42B has primary ASV capability; Mk 42C for commando assault/vertrep; Mk 42D for AEW were not acquired and an Indian AEW radar is being developed. Intention is to buy up to nine more. Sensors: MEL Super Searcher radar, Thomson Sintra H/S-12 dipping sonar, AQS 902B acoustic processor; Marconi Hermes ESM (Mk 42B); Bendix weather radar (Mk 42C). Weapons: ASW; 2 Whitehead A244S torpedoes; Mk 11 depth bombs, mines (Mk 42B only). ASV; 2 × Sea Eagle (Mk 42B only). Unarmed (Mk 42C).

SEA HARRIER *1991, Indian Navy*

SEA KING 42B *4/1992*

286 INDIA / Shipborne aircraft — Light forces

Numbers/Type: 7 Westland Sea King Mks 42/42A.
Operational speed: 112 kts *(208 km/h)*.
Service ceiling: 11 500 ft *(3500 m)*.
Range: 664 nm *(1230 km)*.
Role/Weapon systems: Primary ASW helicopter for large escorts and CVL; some are shore-based for training and surface search. Sensors: MEL search radar, Alcatel dipping sonar. Weapons: ASW; 4 × Whitehead A244S torpedoes, BAe Mk 11 depth bombs or mines.

Numbers/Type: 18 Kamov Ka-27 (Helix A).
Operational speed: 110 kts *(204 km/h)*.
Service ceiling: 12 000 ft *(3660 m)*.
Range: 270 nm *(500 km)*.
Role/Weapon systems: ASW helicopter embarked in new generation/updated Soviet-designed escorts. Total of 18 ordered; will replace Ka-25. Sensors: Search radar, dipping sonar, sonobuoys. Weapons: ASW; 2 × Whitehead A244S torpedoes or 4 × depth bombs.

Numbers/Type: 5 Kamov Ka-25 ('Hormone').
Operational speed: 104 kts *(193 km/h)*.
Service ceiling: 11 500 ft *(3500 m)*.
Range: 217 nm *(400 km)*.
Role/Weapon systems: ASW helicopter embarked in Soviet-built Kashin class destroyers for ASW tasks. Sensors: Search radar, dipping sonar, sonobuoys. Weapons: ASW; 2 × torpedoes or 4 × depth bombs.

HORMONE *4/1992*

Numbers/Type: 9 Aerospatiale (HAL) SA 319B Chetak (Alouette III).
Operational speed: 113 kts *(210 km/h)*.
Service ceiling: 10 500 ft *(3200 m)*.
Range: 290 nm *(540 km)*.
Role/Weapon systems: Several helicopter roles still performed including embarked ASW and carrier-based SAR, utility and support to commando forces. Sensors: Some helicopters have search radar. Weapons: ASW; 2 × Whitehead A244S torpedoes.

CHETAK *1991, Indian Navy*

Numbers/Type: HAL Advanced Light Helicopter (ALH).
Operational speed: 156 kts *(290 km/h)*.
Service ceiling: 9850 ft *(3000 m)*.
Range: 216 nm *(400 km)*.
Role/Weapon systems: Full production expected from 1994 to replace Chetak.

LAND-BASED MARITIME AIRCRAFT (FRONT LINE)

Numbers/Type: 36 Dornier 228.
Operational speed: 200 kts *(370 km/h)*.
Service ceiling: 28 000 ft *(8535 m)*.
Range: 940 nm *(1740 km)*.
Role/Weapon systems: Coastal surveillance and EEZ protection duties for Navy and Coast Guard. Sensors: MEL Marec 2 search radar, cameras and searchlight. Weapons: Unarmed, but will carry anti-ship missiles eventually, type unknown.

Numbers/Type: 6 Ilyushin Il-38 (May).
Operational speed: 347 kts *(645 km/h)*.
Service ceiling: 32 800 ft *(10 000 m)*.
Range: 3887 nm *(7200 km)*.
Role/Weapon systems: Shore-based long-range ASW reconnaissance into Indian Ocean. Sensors: Search radar, MAD, sonobuoys, ESM. Weapons: ASW; various torpedoes, mines and depth bombs.

Numbers/Type: 18 Pilatus Britten-Norman Maritime Defender.
Operational speed: 150 kts *(280 km/h)*.
Service ceiling: 18 900 ft *(5760 m)*.
Range: 1500 nm *(2775 km)*.
Role/Weapon systems: Coastal and short-range reconnaissance tasks undertaken in support of Navy (5) and Coast Guard. Sensors: Search radar, camera. Weapons: Unarmed.

Numbers/Type: 10 Tupolev Tu-142M (Bear F).
Operational speed: 500 kts *(925 km/h)*.
Service ceiling: 45 000 ft *(13 720 m)*.
Range: 6775 nm *(12 550 km)*.
Role/Weapon systems: First entered service in April 1988 for long-range surface surveillance and ASW. Air Force manned. Sensors: Search and attack radars, MAD, cameras. Active and passive sonobuoys. Weapons: ASW; 12 × torpedoes, depth bombs. ASV; 2 × 23 mm cannon (no AS-4 ASM).

Numbers/Type: 2 Fokker F-27 Friendship.
Operational speed: 250 kts *(463 km/h)*.
Service ceiling: 29 500 ft *(8990 m)*.
Range: 2700 nm *(5000 km)*.
Role/Weapon systems: Operated by Coast Guard for long-range patrol. Sensors: Search radar only. Weapons: Unarmed.

Numbers/Type: 12 SEPECAT/HAL Jaguar International.
Operational speed: 917 kts *(1699 km/h)* (max).
Service ceiling: 36 000 ft *(11 000 m)*.
Range: 760 nm *(1408 km)*.
Role/Weapon systems: A maritime strike squadron. Sensors: Thomson-CSF Agave radar. Weapons: ASV; 2 BAe Sea Eagle anti-ship missiles underwing; 2 DEFA 30 mm cannon or up to 8—1000 lb bombs. Can carry two air-to-air missiles overwing.

LIGHT FORCES

8 OSA II CLASS (FAST ATTACK CRAFT—MISSILE)

PRACHAND K 90	CHAPAL K 94
PRALAYA K 91	CHAMAK K 95
PRATAP K 92	CHATAK K 96
PRABAL K 93	CHARAG K 97

Displacement, tons: 245 full load
Dimensions, feet (metres): 126.6 × 24.9 × 8.6 *(38.6 × 7.6 × 2.7)*
Main machinery: 3 Type M 504 diesels; 10 800 hp(m) *(7.94 MW)* sustained; 3 shafts
Speed, knots: 37. **Range, miles:** 800 at 25 kts
Complement: 30

Missiles: SSM: 4 SS-N-2A or B Styx; active radar or IR homing to 46 km *(25 nm)* at 0.9 Mach; warhead 513 kg.
Guns: 4 USSR 30 mm/65 (2 twin); 85° elevation; 500 rounds/minute to 5 km *(2.7 nm)*; weight of shell 0.54 kg.
Radars: Surface search: Square Tie; I band.
Fire control: Drum Tilt; H/I band.
IFF: High Pole. Square Head.

Programmes: Eight Osa II class delivered January 1976-September 1977. Being replaced by Tarantul class and beginning to be paid off. Most are in reserve.

CHAPAL *2/1989, G Jacob*

7 SDB Mk 3 CLASS (FAST ATTACK CRAFT—PATROL)

Displacement, tons: 210 full load
Dimensions, feet (metres): 124 × 24.6 × 6.2 *(37.8 × 7.5 × 1.9)*
Main machinery: 2 MTU 16V 538 TB92 diesels; 6820 hp(m) *(5 MW)* sustained; 2 shafts
Speed, knots: 30
Complement: 32
Guns: 2 Bofors 40 mm/60; 80° elevation; 120 rounds/minute to 10 km *(5.5 nm)*; weight of shell 0.89 kg.

Comment: First pair and Nos 4 and 5 ordered from Garden Reach SY, Calcutta, remainder from Mazagon Dock Ltd, Goa. First three completed in 1984, remainder in 1985-86.

SDB Mk 3 *1989, G Jaco*

5 SDB Mk 2 CLASS (FAST ATTACK CRAFT—PATROL)

Displacement, tons: 203 full load
Dimensions, feet (metres): 123 × 24.6 × 5.9 *(37.5 × 7.5 × 1.8)*
Main machinery: 2 Paxman Deltic 18-42K diesels; 6240 hp *(4.66 MW)*; 2 shafts. Auxiliary propulsion; 1 Kirloskar-Cummins diesel; 165 hp *(123 kW)*
Speed, knots: 29; 4 on auxiliary diesel
Range, miles: 1400 at 14 kts
Complement: 28 (4 officers)
Guns: 1 Bofors 40 mm/60; 80° elevation; 120 rounds/minute to 10 km *(5.5 nm)*; weight of shell 0.89 kg.
1—7.62 mm MG.
Depth charges: 18 Mk 7; 10 Mk 12.
Sonars: Hull-mounted; active attack; high frequency.

Comment: First three commissioned in 1977-78; last two in 1984. All built by Garden Reach SY, Calcutta. Reported that problems delayed launchings of the first group. This might be due to use of GRP hulls. All with Eastern Naval Command. Same class built for Coast Guard.

0 + 1 FAST ATTACK CRAFT (TORPEDO)

Displacement, tons: 90 full load
Dimensions, feet (metres): 84.6 × 22.6 × 3.9 *(25.8 × 6.9 × 1.2)*
Main machinery: 2 diesels; 5000 hp *(3.73 MW)*; 2 shafts
Speed, knots: 30. **Range, miles:** 400 at 20 kts
Complement: 7 (3 officers)
Guns: 2—12.7 mm MGs.
Torpedoes: 2—21 in *(533 mm)* tubes; anti-surface.
Radars: Surface search: I band.

Comment: A Mazagon design reported building for the Indian Navy. Numbers not known.

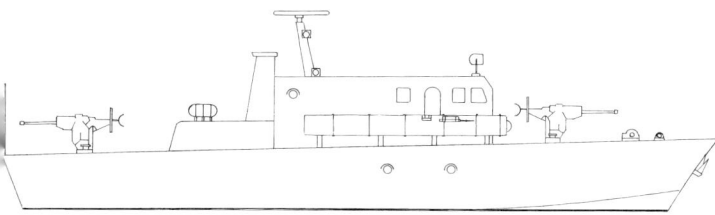

FAST ATTACK CRAFT *(not to scale), Ian Sturton*

AMPHIBIOUS FORCES

Note: An agreement has been reached for the production of US LCAs in India. Project definition started 1 April 1990 and full production is expected by 1995.

1 + 1 (1) MAGAR CLASS (LST)

Name	No	Builders	Commissioned
MAGAR	L 20	Garden Reach SY, Calcutta	15 July 1987
GHARIAL	L 23	Hindustan/Garden Reach	Dec 1993

Displacement, tons: 5655 full load
Dimensions, feet (metres): 409.4 oa; 393.7 wl × 57.4 × 13.1 *(124.8; 120 × 17.5 × 4)*
Main machinery: 2 SEMT-Pielstick 8 PC2 V 400 Mk 3 diesels; 8560 hp(m) *(6.29 MW)* sustained; 2 shafts
Speed, knots: 15. **Range, miles:** 3000 at 14 kts
Complement: 136 (16 officers)
Guns: 4 Bofors 40 mm/60. 2 multi-barrel rocket launchers in the bow.
Helicopters: 1 Sea King 42C; platform for 2.

Comment: A new *Magar*, maintaining the name of the deleted ex-British LST 3 and based on the *Sir Lancelot* design, was launched on 7 November 1984. *Gharial* ordered in 1985, launched 1 April 1991 at Hindustan Shipyard but is fitting out at Garden Reach. A third of class is scheduled to be laid down in 1993. Carries four LCVPs on davits. Bow door. Can beach on gradients 1 in 40 or more. Original plan was for eight of the class.

MAGAR *10/1990, 92 Wing RAAF*

8 SOVIET POLNOCHNY C (TYPE 773) and D CLASS (LSMs)

GHORPAD L 14	SHARABH L 17	GULDAR L 21
KESARI L 15	CHEETAH L 18	KUMBHIR L 22
SHARDUL L 16	MAHISH L 19	

Displacement, tons: 1120 standard; 1305 (D class); 1150 full load
Dimensions, feet (metres): 266.7; 275.3 (D class) × 31.8 × 7.9 *(81.3; 83.9 × 9.7 × 2.4)*
Main machinery: 2 Kolomna Type 40-D diesels; 4400 hp(m) *(3.2 MW)* sustained; 2 shafts
Speed, knots: 15. **Range, miles:** 2000 at 12 kts
Complement: 45
Military lift: 350 tons; 160 troops
Guns: 4—30 mm (2 twin). 2—140 mm 18-tubed rocket launchers.
Radars: Navigation: Don 2 or Krivach (SRN 745); I band.
Fire control: Drum Tilt; H/I band (in D class).
Helicopters: Platform only (in D class).

Comment: All new construction direct from Poland. *Ghorpad* and *Kesari* transferred in March 1975, *Shardul* and *Sharabh* in February 1976, *Cheetah* in February 1985, *Mahish* in July 1985, *Guldar* in March 1986 and *Kumbhir* in November 1986. The last four are Polnochny Ds with the flight deck forward of the bridge and different radars. At least two are in reserve.

CHEETAH *12/1992 92 Wing RAAF*

7 Mk 3 LANDING CRAFT (LCU)

VASCO DA GAMA L 34	MANGALA L 39
MIDHUR L 38	L 35-37, L 40

Displacement, tons: 500 full load
Dimensions, feet (metres): 188.6 oa; 174.5 pp × 26.9 × 5.2 *(57.5; 53.2 × 8.2 × 1.6)*
Main machinery: 3 Kirloskar-MAN V8V 17.5/22 AMAL diesels; 1686 hp(m) *(1.24 MW)*; 3 shafts
Speed, knots: 11. **Range, miles:** 1000 at 8 kts
Complement: 287 including troops
Military lift: 250 tons; 2 PT 76 or 2 APC
Guns: 2 Bofors 40 mm/60 (aft).
Mines: Can be embarked.

Comment: First two built by Hooghly D and E Co and remainder at Goa SY (subsidiary of Mazagon Dock Ltd). First craft *(Vasco da Gama)* launched 29 November 1978 and the last one commissioned 25 March 1987.

MANGALA *1987, Mazagon Dock Ltd*

MINE WARFARE FORCES

Note: A need for at least 10 minehunters has been accepted with the lead vessels to be built overseas and the remainder at Goa. An alternative is to build all 10 to a Soviet design. Hulls to be of GRP. In 1990 it was reported that six (M 89-M 94) were to be ordered from Goa Shipyard which is installing GRP facilities. Progress is slow.

6 SOVIET YEVGENYA CLASS (MINESWEEPERS—INSHORE)

MAHÉ M 83	MANGALORE M 85	MULKI M 87
MALVAN M 84	MALPE M 86	MAGDALA M 88

Displacement, tons: 77 standard; 90 full load
Dimensions, feet (metres): 80.7 × 18 × 4.9 *(24.6 × 5.5 × 1.5)*
Main machinery: 2 Type 3-D-12 diesels; 600 hp(m) *(440 kW)* sustained; 2 shafts
Speed, knots: 11. **Range, miles:** 300 at 10 kts
Complement: 10
Guns: 2 USSR 25 mm/80 (twin).
Radars: Navigation: Don 2; I band.
Sonars: A small transducer streamed over the stern on a crane.

Comment: First three delivered as deck cargo 16 May 1983 and second three on 3 February 1984. A mid-1960s design with GRP hulls built at Kolpino. All based at Cochin.

MAHÉ *2/1992*

288　INDIA / Mine warfare forces — Service forces

12 SOVIET NATYA I CLASS (MINESWEEPERS—OCEAN)

PONDICHERRY M 61	ALLEPPEY M 65	CUDDALORE M 69
PORBANDAR M 62	RATNAGIRI M 66	KAKINADA M 70
BEDI M 63	KARWAR M 67	KOZHIKODA M 71
BHAVNAGAR M 64	CANNANORE M 68	KONKAN M 72

Displacement, tons: 770 full load
Dimensions, feet (metres): 200.1 × 31.8 × 8.9 *(61 × 9.7 × 2.7)*
Main machinery: 2 Type 504 diesels; 7200 hp(m) *(5.29 MW)* sustained; 2 shafts
Speed, knots: 19. **Range, miles:** 4000 at 10 kts
Complement: 58

Guns: 4—30 mm/65 (2 twin); 85° elevation; 500 rounds/minute to 5 km *(2.7 nm)*; weight of shell 0.54 kg.
　4—25 mm/70 (2 twin); 85° elevation; 270 rounds/minute to 3 km *(1.6 nm)*.
A/S mortars: 2 RBU 1200 5-tubed fixed; range 1200 m; warhead 34 kg.
Mines: Can carry 10.
Radars: Navigation: Don 2; I band.
Fire control: Drum Tilt; H/I band.
IFF: Two Square Head. High Pole B.
Sonars: Hull-mounted; active mine detection; high frequency.

Programmes: Built for export at Isora Yard, Leningrad. First pair transferred April 1978, second pair July 1979, third pair August 1980, one in October 1986, one in June 1987, one in December 1987, one in May 1988, one in November 1988 and the last in early 1989. Last six have been delivered out of pennant number order.
Structure: Steel hulls but do not have stern ramp as in Soviet class.
Operational: Some are fitted with two quad SA-N-5 systems. All are capable of magnetic, acoustic and mechanical sweeping. *Pondicherry* was painted white and used as the Presidential yacht for the Indian Fleet Review by President R Venkataramen on 15 February 1989; she reverted to her normal role and colour on completion. One serves as an AGI.

CANNANORE　　　　　　　　　　　　　　　　　　　　　　1989, van Ginderen Collection

4 HAM CLASS (MINESWEEPERS—INSHORE)

Name	No	Builders	Commissioned
BULSAR	M 89	Mazagon Dock Ltd, Bombay	1970
BHATKAL	M 90	Mazagon Dock Ltd, Bombay	1968
BIMLIPITAN (ex-HMS *Hildersham*)	M 2705	Vosper, Portsmouth	1954
BASSEIN (ex-HMS *Littleham*)	M 2707	Brooke Marine, Lowestoft	1954

Displacement, tons: 120 standard; 159 full load
Dimensions, feet (metres): 107.5 × 22 × 5.8 *(32.8 × 6.7 × 1.8)*
Main machinery: 2 Paxman YHAZM diesels; 1100 hp *(821 kW)*; 2 shafts
Speed, knots: 14; 9 sweeping
Complement: 15 (2 officers)
Guns: 1 Oerlikon 20 mm.
Radars: Decca 978; I band.

Comment: Of wooden construction; two were built for the Royal Navy but transferred from the UK to the Indian Navy in 1955. *Bassein* was launched on 4 May 1954, *Bimlipitan* on 5 February 1954, *Bhatkal* in April 1967, and *Bulsar* on 17 May 1969.

SURVEY AND OCEANOGRAPHIC SHIPS

Note: The National Institute of Oceanography operates several research and survey ships including *Sagar Kanya, Samudra Manthan, Sagar Sampada, Samudra Sarvekshak, Samudra Nidhi* and *Samudra Sandhari*. A new acoustic research ship *Mars* was launched in May 1991 at Garden Reach SY, Calcutta.

4 MAKAR CLASS (SURVEY CRAFT)

MAKAR J 33	MEEN J 35
MITHUN J 34	MESH J 36

Displacement, tons: 210 full load
Dimensions, feet (metres): 123 × 24.6 × 6.2 *(37.5 × 7.5 × 1.9)*
Main machinery: 2 diesels; 1124 hp(m) *(826 kW)*; 2 shafts
Speed, knots: 12. **Range, miles:** 1500 at 12 kts
Complement: 36 (4 officers)
Guns: 1 Bofors 40 mm/60.

Comment: Launched at Goa in 1981-82. Similar hulls to SDB Mk 2 class but with much smaller engines.

MAKAR　　　　　　　　　　　　　　　　　　　　　　　　　　　4/1992

6 SANDHAYAK CLASS (SURVEY SHIPS)

Name	No	Builders	Commissioned
SANDHAYAK	J 18	Garden Reach, Calcutta	1 Mar 1981
NIRDESHAK	J 19	Garden Reach, Calcutta	4 Oct 1982
NIRUPAK	J 14	Garden Reach, Calcutta	14 Aug 1985
INVESTIGATOR	J 15	Garden Reach, Calcutta	11 Jan 1990
JAMUNA	J 16	Garden Reach, Calcutta	31 Aug 1991
SUTLEJ	J 17	Garden Reach, Calcutta	Feb 1993

Displacement, tons: 1929 full load
Dimensions, feet (metres): 281.3 × 42 × 11 *(85.8 × 12.8 × 3.3)*
Main machinery: 2 GRSE MAN G8V 30/45 ATL diesels; 3860 hp(m) *(2.84 MW)*; 2 shafts; active rudder
Speed, knots: 16. **Range, miles:** 6000 at 14 kts; 14 000 at 10 kts
Complement: 189 (14 officers) plus 30 scientists
Guns: 1 Bofors 40 mm/60.
Countermeasures: ESM: Telegon IV HF D/F.
Radars: Navigation: Racal Decca 1629; I band.
Helicopters: 1 Alouette III.

Comment: *Investigator* launched 8 August 1987 and *Jamuna* in September 1989. *Sutlej* laid down in 1990. Total of seven planned but programme may terminate at six. Telescopic hangar. Fitted with three echo sounders, extensively equipped laboratories, and carries four GRP survey launches on davits amidships. Painted white with yellow funnels. An active rudder with a DC motor gives speeds of up to 5 kts.

NIRUPAK　　　　　　　　　　　　　　　　　　　　　　　1987, Gilbert Gyssel

SERVICE FORCES

1 DIVING SUPPORT SHIP

Name	No	Builders	Commissioned
NIREEKSHAK	A 15	Mazagon Dock Ltd, Bombay	8 June 1989

Displacement, tons: 3600 full load
Dimensions, feet (metres): 231.3 × 57.4 × 16.4 *(70.5 × 17.5 × 5)*
Main machinery: 2 Bergen KRM-8 diesels; 4410 hp(m) *(3.24 MW)* sustained; 2 shafts; cp prop 2 bow thrusters; 2 stern thrusters; 990 hp(m) *(727 kW)*
Speed, knots: 12
Complement: 63 (15 officers)

Comment: Laid down in August 1982 and launched January 1984. Acquired on three year lease with an option for purchase. The vessel was built for offshore support operations but has been modified for naval requirements. Two DSRV, capable of taking 12 men to 300 m, are carried together with two six-man recompression chambers and one three-man bell. Kongsberg ADP-503 Mk II. Dynamic positioning system. The ship will be used for submarine SAR until the purpose-built ships are completed.

NIREEKSHAK

Service forces / INDIA 289

1 TIR CLASS (TRAINING SHIP)

Name	No	Builders	Commissioned
TIR	A 86	Mazagon Dock Ltd, Bombay	21 Feb 1986

Displacement, tons: 2400 full load
Dimensions, feet (metres): 347.4 × 43.3 × 15.7 *(105.9 × 13.2 × 4.8)*
Main machinery: 2 Crossley-Pielstick 8 PC2 V Mk 2 diesels; 8000 hp(m) *(5.88 MW)* sustained; 2 shafts
Speed, knots: 18. **Range, miles:** 6000 at 12 kts
Complement: 239 (35 officers) plus 120 cadets
Guns: 2 Bofors 40 mm/60 (twin) with launchers for illuminants. 4 saluting guns.
Countermeasures: ESM: Telegon IV D/F.
Radars: Navigation: Two Indian design.
Helicopters: Platform for Alouette III.

Comment: First launched 15 April 1983. Second reported ordered May 1986 but may have been cancelled. Built to commercial standards, Decca collision avoidance plot and SATNAV. Can carry up to 120 cadets and 20 instructors.

TIR   5/1991, 92 Wing RAAF

1 Ex-SOVIET UGRA CLASS (SUBMARINE TENDER)

AMBA A 54

Displacement, tons: 6750 standard; 9650 full load
Dimensions, feet (metres): 462.6 × 57.7 × 23 *(141 × 17.6 × 7)*
Main machinery: Diesel-electric; 4 Kolomna Type 2-D-42 diesel generators; 2 motors; 8000 hp(m) *(5.88 MW)*; 2 shafts
Speed, knots: 17. **Range, miles:** 21 000 at 10 kts
Complement: 400
Guns: 4 USSR 3 in *(76 mm)*/60 (2 twin); 80° elevation; 90 rounds/minute to 15 km *(8 nm)*; weight of shell 6.8 kg.
Radars: Air/surface search: Slim Net; E/F band.
Fire control: Two Hawk Screech; I band.
Navigation: Don 2; I band.
IFF: Two Square Head. High Pole A.

Comment: Acquired from the USSR in 1968. Provision for helicopter. Can accommodate 750. Two cranes, one of 6 tons and one of 10 tons. Differs from others of the class by having 76 mm guns.

AMBA   4/1992

0 + 2 SUPPORT AND RESCUE SHIPS

Displacement, tons: 7000 full load
Dimensions, feet (metres): 334 × 298.6 × 28.5 *(101.8 × 91 × 8.7)*
Main machinery: Diesel-electric; 5 diesel generators; 11.6 MW; 2 motors; 1 shaft; cp prop; 2 bow thrusters; 4020 hp(m) *(2.95 MW)*; 2 stern thrusters; 4830 hp(m) *(3.5 MW)*
Speed, knots: 13. **Range, miles:** 19 500 at 12 kts
Complement: 84 (28 officers) plus 26 spare berths

Comment: Reported authorised in mid-1990 to a Rauma Repola design for delivery of the first in the mid-1990s. Kongsberg ADP 503 Mk II dynamic positioning system. One 120 ton crane. Two DSRVs for 12 men to 300 m. Helicopter platform forward. Two hospitals. One might be used by the Coast Guard as an SAR and pollution control ship.

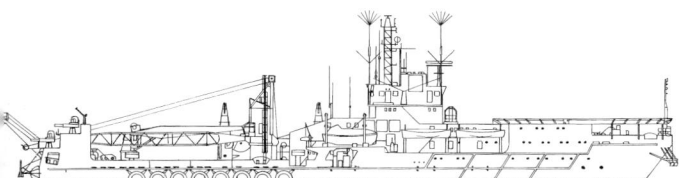

SUPPORT SHIP   (not to scale), Ian Sturton

2 DEEPAK CLASS (REPLENISHMENT TANKERS)

Name	No	Builders	Commissioned
DEEPAK	A 50	Bremer-Vulkan	20 Nov 1967
SHAKTI	A 57	Bremer-Vulkan	31 Dec 1975

Displacement, tons: 6785 light; 15 828 full load
Measurement, tons: 12 013 gross
Dimensions, feet (metres): 552.4 × 75.5 × 30 *(168.4 × 23 × 9.2)*
Main machinery: 2 Babcock & Wilcox boilers; 1 BV/BBC steam turbine; 16 500 hp(m) *(12.13 MW)*; 1 shaft
Speed, knots: 18.5. **Range, miles:** 5500 at 16 kts
Complement: 169
Cargo capacity: 1280 tons diesel; 12 624 tons FFO; 1495 tons avcat; 812 tons FW
Guns: 4 Bofors 40 mm/60. 2 Oerlikon 20 mm.
Countermeasures: ESM: Telegon IV HF D/F.
Radars: Navigation: Decca Type 1006; I band.
Helicopters: 1 Chetak.

Comment: *Deepak* on charter to Indian Navy from Mogul Lines which paid for the construction when the Navy could not afford the expense. Automatic tensioning fitted to replenishment gear. Heavy and light jackstays. Stern fuelling as well as alongside. DG fitted.

DEEPAK   3/1992

0 + 1 MODIFIED DEEPAK CLASS (REPLENISHMENT AND REPAIR SHIP)

Name	No	Builders	Commissioned
ADITYA (ex-*Rajaba Gan Palan*)	—	Garden Reach SY, Calcutta	1994

Displacement, tons: 22 000 full load
Dimensions, feet (metres): 564.3 × 75.5 × 29.9 *(172 × 23 × 9.1)*
Main machinery: 2 diesels; 24 000 hp(m) *(17.6 MW)*; 1 shaft
Speed, knots: 20. **Range, miles:** 10 000 at 16 kts
Complement: 191 plus 6 spare berths
Cargo capacity: 14 200 cu m diesel and avcat; 2250 cu m water; 2170 cu m ammunition and stores
Guns: 3 Bofors 40 mm/60.
Helicopters: 1 Chetak.

Comment: Ordered in July 1987 to a Bremer-Vulkan design. Lengthened version of Deepak class but with a multi-purpose workshop. The bridge and accommodation superstructure are towards the stern, with the helicopter platform right aft. Fully air-conditioned. A second one may follow in due course.

3 POSHAK CLASS (SUPPORT TANKERS)

POSHAK   PURAN   PUSHPA

Displacement, tons: 650 full load
Dimensions, feet (metres): 197.2 × 32.2 × 9.8 *(60.1 × 9.8 × 3)*
Main machinery: 2 diesels; 1540 hp(m) *(1.13 MW)* sustained; 2 shafts
Speed, knots: 12
Complement: 22
Cargo capacity: 200 tons

Comment: Built at Mazagon Dock Ltd, Bombay. *Poshak* completed April 1982, and *Puran* in November 1988.

PUSHPA   1990, Mazagon Dock

2 PRADHAYAK CLASS (SUPPORT TANKERS)

PRADHAYAK   PURAK

Displacement, tons: 960 full load
Dimensions, feet (metres): 163 × 26.2 × 9.8 *(49.7 × 8 × 3)*
Main machinery: 1 diesel; 560 hp(m) *(412 kW)*; 1 shaft
Speed, knots: 9
Cargo capacity: 376 tons

Comment: Built at Rajabagan Yard, Calcutta. *Pradhayak* completed February 1978, *Purak* June 1977.

290 INDIA / Service forces

3 WATER CARRIERS

AMBUDA   COCHIN   +1

Displacement, tons: 200
Dimensions, feet (metres): 108.3 × — × 8 *(32 × — × 2.4)*
Speed, knots: 9

Comment: First laid down Rajabagan Yard 18 January 1977. Second and third built at Mazagon Dock Ltd, Bombay.

AMBUDA   *4/1992*

1 HOSPITAL SHIP

LAKSHADWEEP

Dimensions, feet (metres): 171 × 29.5 × 10.5 *(52 × 9 × 3.2)*
Main machinery: 2 diesels; 900 hp(m) *(661 kW)*; 2 shafts
Speed, knots: 12
Complement: 35 (including 16 medical)

Comment: Ordered from Hindok, Calcutta in 1980. Launched 28 August 1981. Has accommodation for 90 patients.

1 SAIL TRAINING SHIP

VARUNA

Displacement, tons: 105

Comment: Completed in April 1981 by Alcock-Ashdown, Bhavnagar. Can carry 26 cadets.

VARUNA   *1/1988, van Ginderen Collection*

2 TUGS (OCEAN)

GAJ A 51   MATANGA

Displacement, tons: 1465 *(Gaj)*; 1600 *(Matanga)* full load
Dimensions, feet (metres): 216.5 × 37.7 × 13.1 *(66 × 11.5 × 4) (Gaj)*
Main machinery: 2 GRSE/MAN G7V diesels; 3920 hp(m) *(2.88 MW)*; 2 shafts
Speed, knots: 15. Range, miles: 8000 at 12 kts.
Guns: 1 Bofors 40 mm/60.

Comment: Built by Garden Reach SY. *Gaj* completed September 1973, *Matanga* launched 29 October 1977. Bollard pull of 40 tons and capable of towing a 20 000 ton ship at 8 kts. *Matanga* is 3 m longer and 1 m broader.

GAJ   *4/1992*

1 TUG (COASTAL)

RAJAJI

Displacement, tons: 428
Dimensions, feet (metres): 100 × 31.3 × 12.5 *(30.5 × 9.5 × 3.8)*
Main machinery: 2 GRSE-MAN diesels; 2120 hp(m) *(1.56 MW)*; 2 shafts; Kort nozzles
Speed, knots: 12.5

Comment: Built by Garden Reach SY. Completed July 1982.

12 HARBOUR TUGS

AGARAL   ARJUN   BALSHIL   BALRAM   BAJRANG   ANAND   + 6

Measurement, tons: 216 grt
Dimensions, feet (metres): 96.1 × 27.9 × 8.5 *(29.3 × 8.5 × 2.6)*
Main machinery: 2 SEMT-Pielstick 8 PA4 V 200 diesels; 3200 hp(m) *(2.35 MW)*; 2 shafts
Speed, knots: 11
Complement: 12

Comment: First three built by Mazagon Dock Ltd, Bombay in 1973-74. Five more delivered in 1988-89, and four more in 1991 from Mazagon Dock Ltd, Goa. Details given are for *Balram* and *Bajrang*; the others are smaller and of varying types.

HARBOUR TUG   *4/1992*

3 TORPEDO RECOVERY VESSELS

A 71   A 72   ASTRAVAHINI

Displacement, tons: 110
Dimensions, feet (metres): 93.5 × 20 × 4.6 *(28.5 × 6.1 × 1.4)*
Main machinery: 2 Kirloskar V12 diesels; 720 hp(m) *(529 kW)*; 2 shafts
Speed, knots: 11
Complement: 13

Comment: Details above apply only to *A 71* and *A 72*. First completed early 1980, second 1981 at Goa Shipyard. *Astravahini* completed in 1984 at Vishakapatnam.

TRV A 72   *2/1989, G Jacob*

3 DIVING TENDERS

Displacement, tons: 36
Dimensions, feet (metres): 48.9 × 14.4 × 3.9 *(14.9 × 4.4 × 1.2)*
Main machinery: 2 diesels; 130 hp(m) *(96 kW)*; 2 shafts
Speed, knots: 12

Comment: Built at Cleback Yard. First completed 1979; second and third in 1984.

COAST GUARD

Administration

Director General:
Vice Admiral K K Kohli, AVSM
Deputy Director General:
Inspector General A K Sharma, NM, PTM

Future plans

Future plans include the following total strength by 2000: 24 OPVs, six for each region and six for offshore oil platform protection; 36 IPVs for regional work; six Deep Sea Patrol Vessels for deep water surveillance; four specialised pollution control vessels; six medium range surveillance aircraft; 36 light surveillance aircraft; six twin-engined helicopters for SAR and 30 light helicopters for shipborne operations.

General

An Interim Coast Guard Force started operations as a part of the Indian Navy on 1 February 1977. It was constituted as an independent paramilitary service on 19 August 1978 with the passing of the Coast Guard Act, 1978 by the Indian Parliament. It functions under the Ministry of Defence but with the budget met by the Department of Revenue.

Its responsibilities include:
(a) Ensuring the safety and protection of artificial islands, offshore terminals and other installations in the Maritime Zones.
(b) Measures for the safety of life and property at sea including assistance to mariners in distress.
(c) Measures to preserve and protect the marine environment and control marine pollution.
(d) Assisting the Customs and other authorities in anti-smuggling operations.
(e) Enforcing the provisions of enactments in force in the Maritime Zones.

Bases

The Headquarters of the Coast Guard is located in Delhi with Regional Headquarters in Bombay, Madras and Port Blair. District Headquarters established at Bombay, Haldia, New Mangalore, Paradip, Porbandar, Cochin, Vishakhapatnam, Campbell Bay and Diglipur. Stations at Vadinar, Mandapam, Okha and Tuticorin.
Air Squadrons at Daman CGAS 750 (5 Dorniers 228), Madras CGAS 744 and CGAS 800 (6 Dorniers 228 and 2 Chetaks), Calcutta CGAS 700 (2 F 27), Goa CGAS 800 (3 Chetaks) and Bombay CGAS 841 (2 Chetaks).

Personnel

1993: 5290 (660 officers)

PATROL FORCES

0 + 3 SAMAR CLASS (OFFSHORE PATROL VESSELS)

Name	No	Builders	Commissioned
SAMAR	42	Goa Shipyard	1994
SANGRAM	43	Goa Shipyard	1995
SARANG	44	Goa Shipyard	1996

Displacement, tons: 1950 full load
Dimensions, feet (metres): 334.6 oa; 315 wl × 37.7 × 11.5 *(102; 96 × 11.5 × 3.5)*
Main machinery: 2 SEMT-Pielstick 16 PA6 V 280 diesels; 12 800 hp(m) *(9.41 MW)* sustained; 2 shafts
Speed, knots: 21. **Range, miles:** 7000 at 15 kts
Complement: 45 (2 officers)
Guns: 2—30 mm (twin). 2—7.62 mm MGs.
Radars: Surface search: F/I band.

Comment: Ordered in 1991. These are the largest Coast Guard vessels built so far. Almost identical to the Navy's Sukanya class but more heavily armed.

9 VIKRAM CLASS (OFFSHORE PATROL VESSELS TYPE P 957)

Name	No	Builders	Commissioned
VIKRAM	33	Mazagon Dock, Bombay	20 Dec 1983
VIJAYA	34	Mazagon Dock, Bombay	12 Apr 1985
VEERA	35	Mazagon Dock, Bombay	3 May 1986
VARUNA	36	Mazagon Dock, Bombay	27 Feb 1988
VAJRA	37	Mazagon Dock, Bombay	22 Dec 1988
VIVEK	38	Mazagon Dock, Bombay	19 Aug 1989
VIGRAHA	39	Mazagon Dock, Bombay	12 Apr 1990
VARAD	40	Goa Shipyard	19 July 1990
VARAHA	41	Goa Shipyard	11 Mar 1992

Displacement, tons: 1224 full load
Dimensions, feet (metres): 243.1 × 37.4 × 10.5 *(74.1 × 11.4 × 3.2)*
Main machinery: 2 SEMT-Pielstick 16 PA6 V 280 diesels; 12 800 hp(m) *(9.41 MW)* sustained; 2 shafts; cp props
Speed, knots: 22. **Range, miles:** 4000 at 16 kts
Complement: 96 (11 officers)
Guns: 1 or 2 Bofors 40 mm/60. 2—7.62 mm MGs.
Fire control: Lynx optical sights.
Radars: Navigation: Two Decca 1226; I band.
Helicopters: 1 HAL (Aerospatiale) Chetak or 1 Sea King.

Comment: Owes something to a NEVESBU (Netherlands) design, being a stretched version of its 750 ton offshore patrol vessels. Ordered in 1979. Fin stabilisers. Diving equipment. 4.5 ton deck crane. External firefighting pumps. Has one GRP boat and two inflatable craft. This class is considered too small for its required task and hence the need for the larger Samar class.

VAJRA   *12/1988, Indian Coast Guard*

TARA BAI   *5/1987, Singapore SB & E Ltd*

RAZIA SULTANA   *12/1992, Garden Reach*

7 JIJA BAI CLASS (INSHORE PATROL CRAFT TYPE 956)

JIJA BAI 64	RANI JINDAN 67	RAMADEVI 69
CHAND BIBI 65	HABBAKHATUN 68	AVVAYAR 70
KITTUR CHINNAMA 66		

Displacement, tons: 181 full load
Dimensions, feet (metres): 144.3 × 24.3 × 7.5 *(44 × 7.4 × 2.3)*
Main machinery: 2 MTU 12V 538 TB82 diesels; 5940 hp(m) *(4.37 MW)* sustained; 2 shafts
Speed, knots: 25. **Range, miles:** 2375 at 14 kts
Complement: 34 (7 officers)
Guns: 1 Bofors 40 mm/60. 2—7.62 mm MGs.
Radars: Surface search: Racal Decca 1226; I band.

Comment: The first three were completed by Sumidagawa and subsequent four craft built at Garden Reach, Calcutta. First of class commissioned 20 June 1983 and the last on 19 October 1985.

AVVAYAR   *1985, Indian Coast Guard*

11 JIJA BAI MOD I CLASS (INSHORE PATROL CRAFT)

TARA BAI 71	NAIKI DEVI 75	ANNIE BESANT 223
AHALYA BAI 72	GANGA DEVI 76	KAMLA DEVI 224
LAKSHMI BAI 73	PRIYADARSHINI 221	AMRIT KAUR 225
AKKA DEVI 74	RAZIA SULTANA 222	

Displacement, tons: 306 full load
Dimensions, feet (metres): 147.3 × 24.6 × 8.5 *(44.9 × 7.5 × 2.6)*
Main machinery: 2 MTU 12V 538 TB82 diesels; 5940 hp(m) *(4.37 MW)* sustained; 2 shafts
Speed, knots: 23. **Range, miles:** 2400 at 12 kts
Complement: 33 (5 officers)
Guns: 1 Bofors 40 mm/60. 2—7.62 mm MGs.
Radars: Surface search: Racal Decca 1226 or BEL 1245/6X (221-225); I band.

Comment: Two ordered in June 1986 from Singapore Shipbuilding and Engineering Ltd and built at Singapore to a Lürssen 45 design; completed May and July 1987. Four more laid down in 1987 at Garden Reach, Calcutta, first completed in April 1989, *Akka Devi* in September 1989, and the last two December 1989 and April 1990 respectively. A further batch of five followed with *Priyadarshini* commissioning 25 May 1992, *Razia Sultana* in December 1992, *Annie Besant* 7 December 1991, *Kamla Devi* 20 May 1992 and *Amrit Kaur* in December 1992. This is a 'follow-on' class to the Type 956 and is known as the Jija Bai Mod I class.

0 + 10 INSHORE PATROL CRAFT

Displacement, tons: 49 full load
Dimensions, feet (metres): 68.2 × 19 × 5.9 *(20.8 × 5.8 × 1.8)*
Main machinery: 2 Deutz MWM TBD234V12 diesels; 1360 hp(m) *(1.00 MW)*; 1 Deutz MWM TBD234V8 diesel; 550 hp(m) *(404 kW)*; 3 Hamilton 402 waterjets
Speed, knots: 25. **Range, miles:** 600 at 15 kts
Complement: 10 (4 officers)
Guns: 1 Oerlikon 20 mm. 1—7.62 mm MG.
Radars: Navigation: I band.

Comment: Ordered from Anderson Marine, Goa in September 1990 to a P-2000 design by Amgram, similar to British Archer class. GRP hull. First one to be delivered in 1993. Official description is 'Interceptor Boats'.

5 SDB Mk 2 RAJ CLASS (INSHORE PATROL CRAFT)

RAJHANS 56	RAJKIRAN 59	RAJKAMAL 61
RAJTARANG 57	RAJSHREE 60	

Displacement, tons: 203 full load
Dimensions, feet (metres): 123 × 24.6 × 5.9 (37.5 × 7.5 × 1.8)
Main machinery: 2 Paxman Deltic 18-42K diesels; 6240 hp (4.66 MW); 2 shafts. Auxiliary propulsion; 1 Kirloska-Cummins diesel; 165 hp (123 kW)
Speed, knots: 29; 4 auxiliary. Range, miles: 1400 at 14 kts
Complement: 28
Guns: 2 Bofors 40 mm/60.

Comment: Built by Garden Reach SY, Calcutta. Commissioned—*Rajhans*, 23 December 1980; *Rajtarang*, 25 November 1981; *Rajkiran* March 1984; *Rajshree* September 1984 and *Rajkamal* September 1986. All other previously reported vessels of this class belong to the Navy.

8 INSHORE PATROL CRAFT

C 01-08

Displacement, tons: 32 full load
Dimensions, feet (metres): 65.6 × 15.4 × 5 (20 × 4.7 × 1.5)
Main machinery: 2 Detroit 12V-71TA diesels; 840 hp (627 kW) sustained; 2 shafts
Speed, knots: 20. Range, miles: 400 at 20 kts
Complement: 8
Guns: 1—7.62 mm MG.
Radars: Navigation: I band.

Comment: Built by Swallow Craft Co, Pusan, South Korea. Six commissioned 24 September 1980, and two on 22 May 1982 having been taken over from India Oil Corporation.

RAJKAMAL   1989, Indian Coast Guard

C 03 (old number)   1982, Swallow Craft

INDONESIA

Headquarters' Appointments

Chief of the Naval Staff:
  Admiral Mohammad Arifin
Deputy Chief of the Naval Staff (Operations):
  Rear Admiral Soemartono
Deputy Chief of the Naval Staff (Logistics):
  Rear Admiral Nyoman Suharta
Deputy Chief of the Naval Staff (Personnel):
  Rear Admiral Tonny Soekaton
Inspector General of the Navy:
  Major General Mar Hartarto Radem

Fleet Command

Commander-in-Chief Western Fleet (Barat):
  Rear Admiral Yusuf Effendi
Commander-in-Chief Eastern Fleet (Timur):
  Rear Admiral Tanto Kuswanto
Commandant of Navy Marine Corps:
  Major General Mar Gafur Chalik
Commander Military Sealift Command:
  Rear Admiral Mochamad Sochid

Personnel

(a) 1993: 41 000 including 12 000 Marine Commando Corps and 1000 Naval Air Arm
(b) Selective national service

Prefix to Ships' Names

KRI (Kapal di Republik Indonesia)

Bases

Tanjung Priok (Jakarta), Ujung (Surabaya), Sabang, Medan (Sumatra), Makasar (Celebes), Balikpapan (East Borneo), Biak (New Guinea), Tanjung Pinang, Manado (Celebes), Teluk Ratai (South Sumatra). Naval Air Arm at Ujung, Biak and Pekan Baru. Ujung (Surabaya) is concerned with building, particularly naval patrol craft, and is the main naval dockyard as well as housing Eastern Command. New base to be built at Teluk Ratai in Lampung.

Strength of the Fleet

Type	Active (Reserve)	Building/Transfers (Projected)
Patrol Submarines	2	(2)
Frigates	17	—
Corvettes	—	16
Fast Attack Craft—Missile	4	—
Large Patrol Craft	19	(4)
Coastal Patrol Craft	18	—
Hydrofoils	5	4
LSTs/LSM	14	12
LCM/LCU	44+	—
MCMV	4	9
Survey Ships	6	—
Submarine Tender	1	—
Repair Ship	1	—
Replenishment Tankers	2	—
Coastal Tankers	2	—
Transports	2	2
Cable Ship	1	—
Tugs	4	—
Sail Training Ship	1	—

Command Structure

Eastern Command (Surabaya)
Western Command (Teluk Ratai)
Training Command
Military Sea Communications Command (Maritime Security Agency)
Military Sealift Command (Logistic Support)

Mercantile Marine

Lloyd's Register of Shipping:
  2014 vessels of 2 338 604 tons gross

DELETIONS

Submarines

1990 *Pasopati*

Amphibious Forces

1992 *Amurang*

Auxiliaries

1990 *Ratulangi*

PENNANT LIST

Submarines

| 401 | Cakra |
| 402 | Nanggala |

Frigates

331	Martha Kristina Tiyahahu
332	W Zakarias Yohannes
333	Hasanuddin
341	Samadikun
342	Martadinata
343	Monginsidi
344	Ngurah Rai
351	Ahmed Yani
352	Slamet Riyadi
353	Yos Sudarso
354	Oswald Siahann
355	Abdul Halim Perdana Kusuma
356	Karel Satsiutubun
361	Fatahillah
362	Malahayati
363	Nala
364	Ki Hajar Dewantara

Light Forces

621	Mandau
622	Rencong
623	Badik
624	Keris
651	Singa
653	Ajak
801	Pandbong
802	Sura
811	Kakap
812	Kerapu
813	Tongkol
814	Bervang
819	Lajang
822	Dorang
823	Todak
829	Tohok
830	Sembilang
847	Sibarau
848	Siliman
851	Samadar
852	Sasila
853	Sabola
854	Sawangi
855	Sadarin
856	Salmaneti
857	Sigalu
858	Silea
859	Siribua
862	Siada
863	Sikuda
864	Sigurot

Amphibious Forces

501	Teluk Langsa
502	Teluk Bajur
503	Teluk Amboina
504	Teluk Kau
508	Teluk Tomini
509	Teluk Ratai
510	Teluk Saleh
511	Teluk Bone
512	Teluk Semangka
513	Teluk Penju
514	Teluk Mandar
515	Teluk Sampit
516	Teluk Banten
517	Teluk Ende
580	Dore
582	Kupang
583	Dili
584	Nusantara

Mine Warfare Forces

701	Pulau Rani
702	Pulau Retewo
711	Pulau Rengat
712	Pulau Rupat

Support Ship

| 561 | Multatuli |

Service Forces

901	Balikpapan
903	Arun
909	Pakan Baru
911	Sorong
921	Jaya Wijaya
922	Rakata
934	Lampo Batang
935	Tambora
936	Bromo
951	Talaud
952	Nusa Telu
953	Natuna
956	Teluk Mentawai
957	Karimundsa
960	Karimata
971	Tangung Pandan
972	Tangung Oisina

Survey Ships

931	Burujulasad
932	Dewa Kembar
933	Jalanidhi

Submarines — Frigates / INDONESIA

SUBMARINES

2 + (2) TYPE 209 CLASS (1300 TYPE)

Name	No	Builders	Laid down	Launched	Commissioned
CAKRA	401	Howaldtswerke, Kiel	25 Nov 1977	10 Sep 1980	19 Mar 1981
NANGGALA	402	Howaldtswerke, Kiel	14 Mar 1978	10 Sep 1980	6 July 1981

Displacement, tons: 1285 surfaced; 1390 dived
Dimensions, feet (metres): 195.2 × 20.3 × 17.9 *(59.5 × 6.2 × 5.4)*
Main machinery: Diesel-electric; 4 MTU 12V 493 AZ80 GA31L diesels; 2400 hp(m) *(1.76 MW)* sustained; 4 Siemens alternators; 1.7 MW; 1 Siemens motor; 4600 hp(m) *(3.38 MW)* sustained; 1 shaft
Speed, knots: 11 surfaced; 21.5 dived
Range, miles: 8200 at 8 kts
Complement: 34 (6 officers)

Torpedoes: 8—21 in *(533 mm)* bow tubes. 14 AEG SUT; dual purpose; wire-guided; active/passive homing to 12 km *(6.5 nm)* at 35 kts; 28 km *(15 nm)* at 23 kts; warhead 250 kg.
Fire control: Signaal Sinbad system.
Radars: Surface search: Thomson-CSF Calypso; I band.
Sonars: Atlas Elektronik CSU 3-2; active/passive search and attack; medium frequency.
PRS-3/4; (integral with CSU) passive ranging.

Programmes: First pair ordered on 2 April 1977. Designed by Ingenieurkontor, Lübeck for construction by Howaldtswerke, Kiel and sale by Ferrostaal, Essen—all acting as a consortium. Orders for two 1400 Type planned but the contract may depend on German credits.
Modernisation: Major refits at HDW spanning three years from 1986 to 1989. These refits were expensive, and lengthy, and may have discouraged further orders.
Structure: Have high capacity batteries with GRP lead-acid cells and battery cooling supplied by Wilhelm Hagen AG. Diving depth, 240 m *(790 ft)*.
Operational: Endurance, 50 days.

NANGGALA 9/1991, 92 Wing RAAF

FRIGATES

Note: Ambitious plans for new frigates have probably been indefinitely postponed in favour of German corvettes.

3 FATAHILLAH CLASS

Name	No	Builders	Laid down	Launched	Commissioned
FATAHILLAH	361	Wilton Fijenoord, Schiedam	31 Jan 1977	22 Dec 1977	16 July 1979
MALAHAYATI	362	Wilton Fijenoord, Schiedam	28 July 1977	19 June 1978	21 Mar 1980
NALA	363	Wilton Fijenoord, Schiedam	27 Jan 1978	11 Jan 1979	4 Aug 1980

Displacement, tons: 1200 standard; 1450 full load
Dimensions, feet (metres): 276 × 36.4 × 10.7 *(84 × 11.1 × 3.3)*
Main machinery: CODOG; 1 RR Olympus TM3B gas turbine; 25 440 hp *(19 MW)* sustained; 2 MTU 20V 956 TB92 diesels; 11 070 hp(m) *(8.14 MW)* sustained; 2 shafts; LIPS cp props
Speed, knots: 30. **Range, miles:** 4250 at 16 kts
Complement: 89 (11 officers)

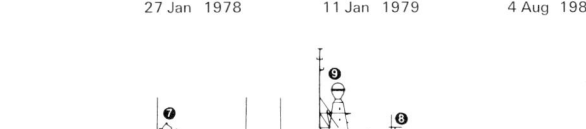

NALA FATAHILLAH *(Scale 1 : 1200), Ian Sturton*

Missiles: SSM: 4 Aerospatiale MM 38 Exocet ❶; inertial cruise; active radar homing to 42 km *(23 nm)* at 0.9 Mach; warhead 165 kg; sea-skimmer.
Guns: 1 Bofors 4.7 in *(120 mm)*/46 ❷; 80° elevation; 80 rounds/minute to 18.5 km *(10 nm)*; weight of shell 21 kg.
1 or 2 Bofors 40 mm/70 (2 in *Nala*) ❸; 90° elevation; 300 rounds/minute to 12 km *(6.6 nm)*; weight of shell 0.96 kg.
2 Rheinmetall 20 mm; 55° elevation; 1000 rounds/minute to 2 km anti-aircraft; weight of shell 0.24 kg.
Torpedoes: 6—324 mm Mk 32 or ILAS 3 (2 triple) tubes (none in *Nala*) ❹. 12 Mk 46 (or A244S); anti-submarine; active/passive homing to 11 km *(5.9 nm)* at 40 kts; warhead 44 kg.
A/S mortars: 1 Bofors 375 mm twin-barrelled trainable ❺; 54 Erika; range 1600 m and Nelli; range 3600 m.
Countermeasures: Decoys: 2 Knebworth Corvus 8-tubed trainable chaff launchers ❻; radar distraction or centroid modes to 1 km. 1 T-Mk 6; torpedo decoy.
ESM: MEL Susie 1; radar intercept.
Combat data systems: Signaal SEWACO-RI action data automation.
Fire control: GFCS has Signaal LIROD laser/TV directors.
Radars: Air/surface search: Signaal DA 05 ❼; E/F band; range 137 km *(75 nm)* for 2 m² target.
Surface search: Racal Decca AC 1229 ❽; I band.
Fire control: Signaal WM 28 ❾; I/J band; range 46 km *(25 nm)*.
Sonars: Signaal PHS 32; hull-mounted; active search and attack; medium frequency.

Helicopters: 1 Westland Wasp (*Nala* only) ❿.

Programmes: Ordered August 1975. Officially rated as Corvettes.
Structure: NEVESBU design. *Nala* is fitted with a folding hangar/landing deck.

FATAHILLAH 9/1991, 92 Wing RAAF

6 Ex-NETHERLANDS VAN SPEIJK CLASS

Name	No	Builders	Laid down	Launched	Commissioned
AHMAD YANI (ex-*Tjerk Hiddes*)	351	Nederlandse Dok en Scheepsbouw Mij, Amsterdam	1 June 1964	17 Dec 1965	16 Aug 1967
SLAMET RIYADI (ex-*Van Speijk*)	352	Nederlandse Dok en Scheepsbouw Mij, Amsterdam	1 Oct 1963	5 Mar 1965	14 Feb 1967
YOS SUDARSO (ex-*Van Galen*)	353	Koninklijke Maatschappij de Schelde, Flushing	25 July 1963	19 June 1965	1 Mar 1967
OSWALD SIAHAAN (ex-*Van Nes*)	354	Koninklijke Maatschappij de Schelde, Flushing	25 July 1963	26 Mar 1966	9 Aug 1967
ABDUL HALIM PERDANA KUSUMA (ex-*Evertsen*)	355	Koninklijke Maatschappij de Schelde, Flushing	6 July 1965	18 June 1966	21 Dec 1967
KAREL SATSUITUBUN (ex-*Isaac Sweers*)	356	Nederlandse Dok en Scheepsbouw Mij, Amsterdam	5 May 1965	10 Mar 1967	15 May 1968

Displacement, tons: 2225 standard; 2835 full load
Dimensions, feet (metres): 372 × 41 × 13.8 *(113.4 × 12.5 × 4.2)*
Main machinery: 2 Babcock & Wilcox boilers; 550 psi *(38.7 kg/cm sq)*; 850°F *(450°C)*; 2 Werkspoor/English Electric turbines; 30 000 hp *(22.4 MW)*; 2 shafts
Speed, knots: 28.5. **Range, miles:** 4500 at 12 kts
Complement: 180

Missiles: SSM: 8 McDonnell Douglas Harpoon ❶; active radar homing to 130 km *(70 nm)* at 0.9 Mach; warhead 227 kg.
SAM: 2 Short Bros Seacat quad launchers ❷; optical/radar guidance to 5 km *(2.7 nm)*; warhead 10 kg.
Guns: 1 OTO Melara 3 in *(76 mm)*/62 compact ❸; 85° elevation; 85 rounds/minute to 16 km *(8.7 nm)* anti-surface; 12 km *(6.6 nm)* anti-aircraft; weight of shell 6 kg.
Torpedoes: 6—324 mm Mk 32 (2 triple) tubes ❹. Honeywell Mk 46; anti-submarine; active/passive homing to 11 km *(5.9 nm)* at 40 kts; warhead 44 kg.
Countermeasures: Decoys: 2 Knebworth Corvus 8-tubed trainable; radar distraction or centroid chaff to 1 km.
ESM: UA 8/9; UA 13 (355 and 356); radar warning. FH5 D/F.
Combat data systems: SEWACO V action data automation and Daisy data processing.
Fire control: Signaal LIROD optronic director.
Radars: Air search: Signaal LW 03 ❺; D band; range 219 km *(120 nm)* for 2 m² target.
Air/surface search: Signaal DA 05 ❻; E/F band; range 137 km *(75 nm)* for 2 m² target.
Navigation: Racal Decca 1229; I band.
Fire control: Signaal M 45 ❼; I/J band (for 76 mm gun).
2 Signaal M 44 ❽; I/J band (for Seacat).
Sonars: Signaal CWE 610; hull-mounted; active search and attack; medium frequency. VDS; medium frequency.

Helicopters: 1 Westland Wasp ❾.

Programmes: On 11 February 1986 agreement signed for transfer of two of this class with an option on two more *(Van Galen, Van Nes)*. Transfer dates:—*Tjerk Hiddes*, 31 October 1986; *Van Speijk*, 1 November 1986; *Van Galen*, 2 November 1987; *Van Nes*, 31 October 1988. Contract of sale for the last two of the class signed 13 May 1989. *Evertsen* transferred 1 November 1989 and *Isaac Sweers* 1 November 1990. Ships provided with all spare parts but not towed arrays or helicopters.
Modernisation: This class underwent mid-life modernisation at Rykswerf Den Helder from 1976. This included replacement of 4.5 in turret by 76 mm, A/S mortar by torpedo tubes, new electronics and electrics, updating combat data system, improved communications, extensive automation with reduction in complement, enlarged hangar for Lynx and improved habitability. Update on transfer included LIROD optronic director. Harpoon for first two only initially because there was no FMS funding for the others. However the USN then provided sufficient SWG 1A panels for all of the class to be retrofitted again with Harpoon missiles.

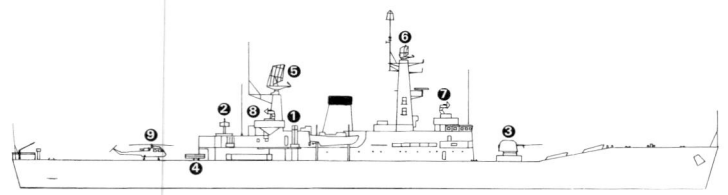

AHMAD YANI

(Scale 1 : 1200), Ian Sturton

OSWALD SIAHAAN

3/1992

AHMAD YANI

8/1991, L P Duane, RAN

3 Ex-BRITISH TRIBAL CLASS

Name	No	Builders	Laid down	Launched	Commissioned
MARTHA KRISTINA TIYAHAHU (ex-HMS *Zulu*)	331	Alex Stephen & Sons Ltd, Govan	13 Dec 1960	3 July 1962	17 Apr 1964
WILHELMUS ZAKARIAS YOHANNES (ex-HMS *Gurkha*)	332	J I Thornycroft Ltd, Woolston	3 Nov 1958	11 July 1960	13 Feb 1963
HASANUDDIN (ex-HMS *Tartar*)	333	HM Dockyard, Devonport	22 Oct 1959	19 Sep 1960	26 Feb 1962

Displacement, tons: 2300 standard; 2700 full load
Dimensions, feet (metres): 350 wl; 360 oa × 42.5 × 18 (screws), 12.5 (keel) *(106.7; 109.7 × 13 × 5.5, 3.8)*
Main machinery: COSAG; 1 Babcock & Wilcox boiler; 550 psi *(38.7 kg/cm sq)*; 850°F *(450°C)*; 1 Parsons Metrovick turbine; 12 500 hp *(9.3 MW)*; 2 Yarrow/AEI G-6 gas turbines; 7500 hp *(5.6 MW)*; 1 shaft; cp prop
Speed, knots: 25; 17 gas turbines. **Range, miles:** 5400 at 12 kts
Complement: 250 (19 officers)

Missiles: SAM: 2 Short Bros Seacat quad launchers ❶; optical/radar guidance to 5 km *(2.7 nm)*; warhead 10 kg.
Guns: 2 Vickers 4.5 in *(114 mm)* ❷; 50° elevation; 14 rounds/minute to 17 km *(9.3 nm)*; weight of shell 25 kg.
2 Oerlikon 20 mm ❸; 55° elevation; 800 rounds/minute to 2 km anti-aircraft.
2—12.7 mm MGs.
A/S mortars: 1 Limbo 3-tubed Mk 10 ❹; range 1000 m; warhead 92 kg.
Countermeasures: Decoys: 2 Knebworth Corvus 8-tubed chaff launchers; distraction or centroid modes to 1 km.
ESM: Radar warning.
Fire control: MRS 3 (for guns). 2 GWS 21 ❽ optical directors (for SAM).
Radars: Air search: Marconi Type 965 ❺; A band.
Surface search: Type 993 ❻; E/F band.
Navigation: Decca 978; I band.
Fire control: Plessey Type 903 ❼; I band (for guns).
Sonars: Graseby Type 177; hull-mounted; active search; 7-9 kHz.
Graseby Type 170 B; hull-mounted; active attack; 15 kHz.
Kelvin Hughes Type 162; classification; 50 kHz.

Helicopters: 1 Westland Wasp ❾.

Programmes: Refitted by Vosper Thornycroft Ltd. 331 commissioned in Indonesian Navy on 2 May 1985, 332 on 16 October 1985 and 333 on 3 April 1986.
Structure: Helicopter descends by flight deck lift and is covered by portable panels. MGs fitted just aft of the GWS 21 directors.

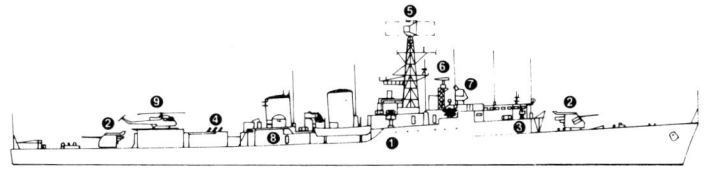
HASANUDDIN (Scale 1 : 1200), Ian Sturton

WILHELMUS ZAKARIAS YOHANNES 7/1991, 92 Wing RAAF

4 Ex-US CLAUD JONES CLASS

Name	No	Builders	Laid down	Launched	Commissioned
SAMADIKUN (ex-USS *John R Perry* DE 1034)	341	Avondale Marine Ways	1 Oct 1957	29 July 1958	5 May 1959
MARTADINATA (ex-USS *Charles Berry* DE 1035)	342	American S B Co, Toledo, Ohio	29 Oct 1958	17 Mar 1959	25 Nov 1959
MONGINSIDI (ex-USS *Claud Jones* DE 1033)	343	Avondale Marine Ways	1 June 1957	27 May 1958	10 Feb 1959
NGURAH RAI (ex-USS *McMorris* DE 1036)	344	American S B Co, Toledo, Ohio	5 Nov 1958	26 May 1959	4 Mar 1960

Displacement, tons: 1720 standard; 1968 full load
Dimensions, feet (metres): 310 × 38.7 × 18 *(95 × 11.8 × 5.5)*
Main machinery: 2 Fairbanks-Morse 38TD 8-1/8-12 diesels (not in 343); 7000 hp *(5.2 MW)* sustained; 1 shaft
Speed, knots: 22. **Range, miles:** 3000 at 18 kts
Complement: 171 (12 officers)

Guns: 1 US 3 in *(76 mm)*/50 Mk 34 ❶; 85° elevation; 50 rounds/minute to 12.8 km *(7 nm)*; weight of shell 6 kg.
2 USSR 37 mm/63 (twin) ❷; 80° elevation; 160 rounds/minute to 9 km *(5 nm)*; weight of shell 0.7 kg.
2 USSR 25 mm/80 (twin) ❸; 85° elevation; 270 rounds/minute to 3 km *(1.6 nm)*; weight of shell 0.34 kg.
Torpedoes: 6—324 mm Mk 32 (2 triple) tubes ❹. Probably fires Honeywell Mk 46; anti-submarine; active/passive homing to 11 km *(5.9 nm)* at 40 kts; warhead 44 kg.
A/S mortars: 2 Hedgehog 24-tubed launchers ❺; range 350 m; warhead 26 kg.
Countermeasures: ESM: WLR-1C (except *Samadikun*); radar warning.
Fire control: Mk 70 for guns. Mk 105 for A/S weapons.
Radars: Air search: Westinghouse SPS 6E ❻; D band; range 146 km *(80 nm)* (for fighter).
Surface search: Raytheon SPS 5D ❼; G/H band; range 37 km *(20 nm)*.
Raytheon SPS 4 *(Ngurah Rai)*; G/H band.
Navigation: Racal Decca 1226; I band.
Fire control: Lockheed SPG 52 ❽; K band.
Sonars: EDO *(Samadikun)*; SQS 45V *(Martadinata)*; SQS 39V *(Monginsidi)*; SQS 42V *(Ngurah Rai)*; hull-mounted; active search and attack; medium/high frequency.

Programmes: *Samadikun* transferred 20 February 1973; *Martadinata*, 31 January 1974; *Monginsidi* and *Ngurah Rai*, 16 December 1974. All refitted at Subic Bay 1979-82.
Operational: Replaced by Van Speijk class and all are reported to be in reserve.

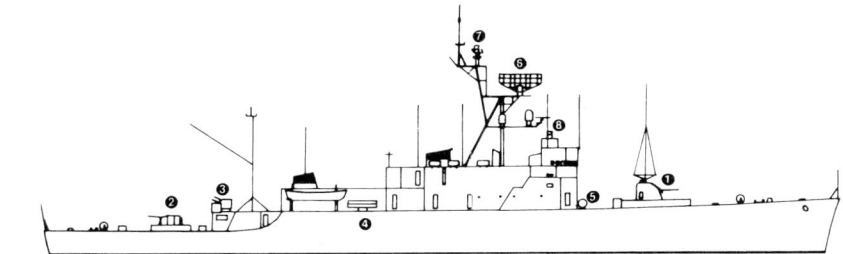
MARTADINATA (Scale 1 : 900), Ian Sturton

MARTADINATA 6/1989, 92 Wing RAAF

296 INDONESIA / Frigates — Corvettes

1 KI HAJAR DEWANTARA CLASS

Name	No	Builders	Laid down	Launched	Commissioned
KI HAJAR DEWANTARA	364	Split SY, Yugoslavia	11 May 1979	11 Oct 1980	31 Oct 1981

Displacement, tons: 2050 full load
Dimensions, feet (metres): 317.3 × 36.7 × 15.7 *(96.7 × 11.2 × 4.8)*
Main machinery: CODOG; 1 RR Olympus TM3B gas turbine; 24 525 hp *(18.3 MW)* sustained; 2 MTU 16V 956 TB92 diesels; 11 070 hp(m) *(8.14 MW)* sustained; 2 shafts; cp props
Speed, knots: 26 gas; 20 diesels. **Range, miles:** 4000 at 18 kts; 1150 at 25 kts
Complement: 76 (11 officers) plus 14 instructors and 100 cadets

Missiles: SSM: 4 Aerospatiale MM 38 Exocet; inertial cruise; active radar homing to 42 km *(23 nm)* at 0.9 Mach; warhead 165 kg; sea-skimmer.
Guns: 1 Bofors 57 mm/70; 75° elevation; 200 rounds/minute to 17 km *(9.3 nm)*; weight of shell 2.4 kg.
4 Rheinmetall 20 mm (2 twin); anti-aircraft.
Torpedoes: 2—21 in *(533 mm)* tubes. AEG SUT; dual purpose; wire-guided; active/passive homing to 28 km *(15 nm)* at 23 kts; 12 km *(6.5 nm)* at 35 kts; warhead 250 kg.
Depth charges: 1 projector/mortar.
Countermeasures: Decoys: 2—128 mm twin-tubed flare launchers.
ESM: Susie; radar intercept.
Fire control: Signaal SEWACO-RI action data automation.
Radars: Surface search: Racal Decca 1229; I band.
Fire control: Signaal WM 28; I/J band; range 46 km *(25 nm)*.
Sonars: Signaal PHS 32; hull-mounted; active search and attack; medium frequency.

Helicopters: Platform for 1 NBO 105 helicopter.

Programmes: First ordered 14 March 1978 from Split SY, Yugoslavia where the hull was built and engines fitted. Armament and electronics fitted in the Netherlands and Indonesia. Near sister to Iraqi *Ibn Khaldoum*.
Structure: Two LCVPs on davits either side of the funnel. For the training role there is a classroom and additional wheelhouse, navigation and radio rooms.
Operational: Used for training and troop transport. War roles include escort, ASW and troop transport. This ship is rarely seen outside the Indonesian archipelago.

KI HAJAR DEWANTARA 12/1992

CORVETTES

0 + 16 Ex-GERMAN PARCHIM I CLASS

(ex-*Wismar*) (ex-241, ex-P 6170)
(ex-*Parchim*) (ex-242)
(ex-*Perleberg*) (ex-243)
(ex-*Bützow*) (ex-244)
(ex-*Lübz*) (ex-221, ex-P 6169)
(ex-*Bad Doberan*) (ex-222)
(ex-*Güstrow*) (ex-223)
(ex-*Waren*) (ex-224)
(ex-*Prenzlau*) (ex-231)
(ex-*Ludwigslust*) (ex-232)
(ex-*Ribnitz-Damgarten*) (ex-233)
(ex-*Teterow*) (ex-234, ex-P 6168)
(ex-*Gadebusch*) (ex-211, ex-P 6167)
(ex-*Grevesmühlen*) (ex-212)
(ex-*Bergen*) (ex-213)
(ex-*Angermünde*) (ex-214)

Displacement, tons: 769 standard
Dimensions, feet (metres): 246.7 × 32.2 × 11.5 *(75.2 × 9.8 × 3.5)*
Main machinery: 3 Type M 504A diesels; 10 812 hp(m) *(7.95 MW)* sustained; 3 shafts
Speed, knots: 28
Complement: 60

Guns: 2 USSR 57 mm/80 (twin) ❶ automatic; 85° elevation; 120 rounds/minute to 6 km *(3.2 nm)*; weight of shell 2.8 kg.
2—30 mm (twin) ❷; 85° elevation; 500 rounds/minute to 5 km *(2.7 nm)* anti-aircraft; weight of shell 0.54 kg.
Torpedoes: 4—400 mm tubes ❸.
A/S mortars: 2 RBU 6000 12-barrelled trainable launchers ❹; automatic loading; range 6000 m; warhead 31 kg.
Depth charges: 2 racks.
Mines: Mine rails fitted.
Countermeasures: Decoys: 2—16-tubed chaff rocket launchers.
ESM: 2 Watch Dog; radar warning.
Radars: Air/surface search: Strut Curve ❺; F band; range 110 km *(60 nm)* for 2 m² target.
Navigation: TSR 333; I band.
Fire control: Muff Cob ❻; G/H band.
IFF: High Pole B.
Sonars: Hull-mounted; active search and attack; high frequency. VDS system on starboard side (in some hulls).

Programmes: Ex-GDR built by Peenewerft, Wolgast between 1981 and 1985. Provisional acceptance in August 1992 subject to price negotiations which had not been concluded in early 1993.
Structure: Basically very similar to Soviet Grisha class but with a higher freeboard and different armament. Details listed are as found at the end of 1992. It is expected that the range of the vessels is to be increased and air-conditioning added to accommodation spaces.

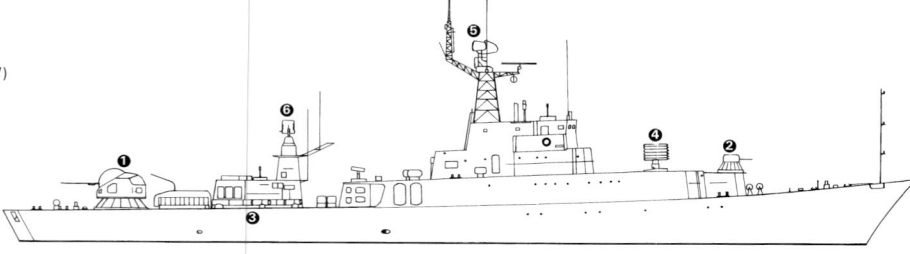

PARCHIM I *(Scale 1 : 600), Ian Sturton*

PARCHIM Is *9/1992, Hartmut Ehlers*

SHIPBORNE AIRCRAFT

Numbers/Type: 2 Aerospatiale SA 316B Alouette III.
Operational speed: 113 kts *(210 km/h)*.
Service ceiling: 10 500 ft *(3200 m)*.
Range: 290 nm *(540 km)*.
Role/Weapon systems: Embarked for support duties. Sensors: None. Weapons: Unarmed.

Numbers/Type: 4 Bell 47J.
Operational speed: 74 kts *(137 km/h)*.
Service ceiling: 13 200 ft *(4025 m)*.
Range: 261 nm *(483 km)*.
Role/Weapon systems: Embarked for survey ship liaison duties. Sensors: None. Weapons: Unarmed.

Numbers/Type: 28 Nurtanio (Aerospatiale) NAS-332 Super Puma.
Operational speed: 151 kts *(279 km/h)*.
Service ceiling: 15 090 ft *(4600 m)*.
Range: 335 nm *(620 km)*.
Role/Weapon systems: ASW and assault operations with secondary role in utility and SAR; ASVW development possible with Exocet or similar. Sensors: Thomson-CSF Omera radar and Alcatel dipping sonar in some. Weapons: ASW; 2 × Mk 46 torpedoes or depth bombs. ASV; planned for future.

Numbers/Type: 6 Nurtanio (MBB) NBO 105C.
Operational speed: 113 kts *(210 km/h)*.
Service ceiling: 9845 ft *(3000 m)*.
Range: 407 nm *(754 km)*.
Role/Weapon systems: Embarked for liaison and support duties. Numbers are increasing slowly. Sensors: None. Weapons: Unarmed.

NBO 105C *11/1990*

Numbers/Type: 9 Westland Wasp (HAS Mk 1).
Operational speed: 96 kts *(177 km/h)*.
Service ceiling: 12 200 ft *(3720 m)*.
Range: 263 nm *(488 km)*.
Role/Weapon systems: Shipborne ASW helicopter weapons carrier and reconnaissance; SAR and utility as secondary roles. Preferred replacement is Westland Navy Lynx. Sensors: None. Weapons: ASW; 2 × Mk 44 or 1 × Mk 46 torpedoes, depth bombs or mines.

LAND-BASED MARITIME AIRCRAFT (FRONT LINE)

Numbers/Type: 3 Boeing 737-200 Surveiller.
Operational speed: 462 kts *(856 km/h)*.
Service ceiling: 50 000 ft *(15 240 m)*.
Range: 2530 nm *(4688 km)*.
Role/Weapon systems: Land-based for long-range maritime surveillance roles. Sensors upgraded in 1991 to include IFF. Sensors: 2 × Motorola APS-135(v) SLAM MR radars, various specialist radars. Weapons: Unarmed.

Numbers/Type: 10/6 GAF Searchmaster B/L.
Operational speed: 168 kts *(311 km/h)*.
Service ceiling: 21 000 ft *(6400 m)*.
Range: 730 nm *(1352 km)*.
Role/Weapon systems: Short-range maritime patrol, EEZ protection and anti-smuggler duties. Nomad type built in Australia. Sensors: Nose-mounted search radar. Weapons: Unarmed.

Numbers/Type: 4 Grumman HU-16B Albatross.
Operational speed: 205 kts *(379 km/h)*.
Service ceiling: 21 000 ft *(6400 m)*.
Range: 2850 nm *(3280 km)*.
Role/Weapon systems: Peacetime role as SAR amphibian; in wartime could operate for ASW, surface search and combat rescue tasks. Sensors: Search radar. Weapons: Generally unarmed but can carry depth bombs or 'iron' bombs.

Numbers/Type: 3 Lockheed C-130H-MP Hercules.
Operational speed: 325 kts *(602 km/h)*.
Service ceiling: 33 000 ft *(10 060 m)*.
Range: 4250 nm *(7876 km)*.
Role/Weapon systems: Long-range maritime reconnaissance role. Sensors: Search/weather radar. Weapons: Unarmed.

Numbers/Type: 16 Northrop F-5E Tiger II.
Operational speed: 940 kts *(1740 km/h)*.
Service ceiling: 51 800 ft *(15 790 m)*.
Range: 300 nm *(556 km)*.
Role/Weapon systems: Fleet air defence and strike fighter, formed 'naval co-operation unit'. Sensors: AI radar. Weapons: AD; 2 × AIM-9 Sidewinder, 2 × 20 mm cannon. Strike; 3175 tons of underwater stores.

Numbers/Type: 5 CASA/Nurtanio CN-235 MPA
Operational speed: 240 kts *(445 km/h)*.
Service ceiling: 26 600 ft *(8110 m)*.
Range: 669 nm *(1240 km)*.
Role/Weapon systems: Medium-range maritime reconnaissance role; 12 transport variants also in service. Sensors: Search/weather radar. Weapons: ASV; may have ASMs.

LIGHT FORCES

Note: It is reported that two ex-Soviet Kronshtadt class patrol craft (*Tohok* 829 and *Sembilang* 830) were resurrected in 1988.

4 DAGGER CLASS (FAST ATTACK CRAFT—MISSILE)

Name	No	Builders	Commissioned
MANDAU	621	Korea Tacoma, Masan	20 July 1979
RENCONG	622	Korea Tacoma, Masan	20 July 1979
BADIK	623	Korea Tacoma, Masan	Feb 1980
KERIS	624	Korea Tacoma, Masan	Feb 1980

Displacement, tons: 270 full load
Dimensions, feet (metres): 164.7 × 23.9 × 7.5 *(50.2 × 7.3 × 2.3)*
Main machinery: CODOG; 1 GE LM 2500 gas turbine; 23 000 hp *(17.16 MW)* sustained; 2 MTU 12V 331 TC81 diesels; 2240 hp(m) *(1.65 MW)* sustained; 2 shafts; cp props
Speed, knots: 41 gas; 17 diesel. **Range, miles:** 2000 at 17 kts
Complement: 43 (7 officers)

Missiles: SSM: 4 Aerospatiale MM 38 Exocet; inertial cruise; active radar homing to 42 km *(23 nm)* at 0.9 Mach; warhead 165 kg; sea-skimmer.
Guns: 1 Bofors 57 mm/70 Mk 1; 75° elevation; 200 rounds/minute to 17 km *(9.3 nm)*; weight of shell 0.96 kg. Launchers for illuminants on each side.
 1 Bofors 40 mm/70; 90° elevation; 300 rounds/minute to 12 km *(6.6 nm)*; weight of shell 2.4 kg.
 2 Rheinmetall 20 mm.
Countermeasures: ESM (in 623 and 624).
Fire Control: Selenia NA-18 optronic director.
Radars: Surface search: Racal Decca 1226; I band.
 Fire control: Signaal WM 28; I/J band; range 46 km *(25 nm)*.

Programmes: PSMM Mk 5 type craft ordered in 1975.
Structure: Shorter in length and smaller displacement than South Korean units. *Mandau* has a different shaped mast with a tripod base.

KERIS *1992*

4 + (4) LÜRSSEN PB 57 CLASS (NAV III and IV)
(LARGE PATROL CRAFT)

Name	No	Builders	Commissioned
KAKAP	811	Lürssen/PT Pal Surabaya	Oct 1988
KERAPU	812	Lürssen/PT Pal Surabaya	5 Apr 1989
TONGKOL	813	PT Pal Surabaya	1991
BERVANG	814	PT Pal Surabaya	1992

Displacement, tons: 423 full load
Dimensions, feet (metres): 190.6 × 25 × 9.2 *(58.1 × 7.6 × 2.8)*
Main machinery: 2 MTU 16V 956 TB92 diesels; 8850 hp(m) *(6.5 MW)* sustained; 2 shafts
Speed, knots: 27. **Range, miles:** 6100 at 15 kts; 2200 at 27 kts
Complement: 40 plus 17 spare berths
Guns: 1 Bofors 40 mm/60. 90° elevation; 240 rounds/minute to 12.6 km *(6.8 nm)*; weight of shell 0.96 kg. 2—12.7 mm MGs.
Radars: Surface search: Racal Decca 2459; I band.
 Navigation: KH 1007; I band.
Helicopters: Platform for 1 NBO 105 or Wasp.

Comment: Ordered in 1982. First pair shipped from West Germany and completed at P T Pal Surabaya. Second pair assembled at Surabaya. The first pair are NAV III SAR versions and by comparison with NAV I are very lightly armed and have a 13 × 7.1 m helicopter deck in place of the after guns and torpedo tubes. The ship can be used for Patrol purposes as well as SAR, and can transport two rifle platoons. There is also a fast seaboat with launching crane at the stern and two water guns for firefighting. The NAV IV version has some minor variations. These are naval craft not Maritime Security Agency as previously indicated. Four more may be ordered in 1993.

KAKAP *5/1990, John Mortimer*

298 INDONESIA / Light forces

4 LÜRSSEN PB 57 CLASS (NAV I and II) (LARGE PATROL CRAFT)

Name	No	Builders	Commissioned
SINGA	651	Lürssen/PT Pal Surabaya	Apr 1988
AJAK	653	Lürssen/PT Pal Surabaya	5 Apr 1989
PANDBONG	801	PT Pal Surabaya	1990
SURA	802	PT Pal Surabaya	1991

Displacement, tons: 447 full load (NAV I); 428 full load (NAV II)
Dimensions, feet (metres): 190.6 × 25 × 9.2 *(58.1 × 7.6 × 2.8)*
Main machinery: 2 MTU 16V 956 TB92 diesels; 8850 hp(m) *(6.5 MW)* sustained; 2 shafts
Speed, knots: 27. **Range, miles:** 6100 at 15 kts; 2200 at 27 kts
Complement: 42 (6 officers)
Guns: 1 Bofors SAK 57 mm/70 Mk 2; 75° elevation; 220 rounds/minute to 14 km *(7.6 nm)*; weight of shell 2.4 kg.
  1 Bofors SAK 40 mm/70; 90° elevation; 300 rounds/minute to 12 km *(6.6 nm)*; weight of shell 0.96 kg.
  2 Rheinmetall 20 mm (NAV II).
Torpedoes: 2—21 in *(533 mm)* Toro tubes (NAV I). AEG SUT; anti-submarine; wire-guided; active/passive homing to 12 km *(6.6 nm)* at 35 kts; 28 km *(15 nm)* at 23 kts; warhead 250 kg.
Countermeasures: Decoys: CSEE Dagaie single trainable launcher; automatic dispenser for IR flares and chaff; H/J band.
  ESM: DR 2000 S3 with Dalia analyser; radar intercept. Telegon VIII D/F.
Fire control: Signaal LIOD 73 Ri optronic director. Signaal WM 22 72 Ri WCS.
Radars: Surface search: Racal Decca 2459; I band.
  Fire control: Signaal WM 22; I/J band; range 46 km *(25 nm)*.
Sonars: Signaal PMS 32 (NAV I); active search and attack; medium frequency.

Comment: Class ordered from Lürssen in 1982. First launched and shipped incomplete to P T Pal Surabaya for fitting out in January 1984. Second shipped July 1984. The first two are NAV I ASW versions with torpedo tubes and sonars. The second pair are NAV II AAW versions with an augmented gun armament but without torpedo tubes and sonars.

SINGA *10/1992, van Ginderen Collection*

AJAK *5/1990, 92 Wing RAAF*

3 Ex-YUGOSLAV KRALJEVICA CLASS (LARGE PATROL CRAFT)

LAJANG (ex-*PBR 515*) 819   TODAK (ex-*PBR 518*) 823
DORANG (ex-*PBR 514*) 822

Displacement, tons: 195 standard; 245 full load
Dimensions, feet (metres): 141.4 × 20.7 × 5.5 *(43.1 × 6.3 × 1.7)*
Main machinery: 2 MAN/Burmeister & Wain V8V 30/38 diesels; 3300 hp(m) *(2.43 MW)*; 2 shafts
Speed, knots: 19. **Range, miles:** 1500 at 12 kts
Complement: 52 (4 officers)
Guns: 1 US 3 in *(76 mm)*/50; 85° elevation; 20 rounds/minute to 12 km *(6.6 nm)*; weight of shell 6 kg.
  1 Bofors 40 mm/60. 4—12.7 mm (2 twin) MGs.
A/S mortars: 2—24-tubed Hedgehogs; range 350 m; warhead 26 kg.
Depth charges: 2 racks.
Radars: Surface search: Decca 974; I band.
Sonars: US QCU 2; hull-mounted; active attack; high frequency.

Comment: Purchased and transferred March-April 1959. All built at Tito SY. All in reserve and soon to be scrapped.

TODAK *7/1983, P D Jones*

8 Ex-AUSTRALIAN ATTACK CLASS (LARGE PATROL CRAFT)

Name	No	Builders	Commissioned
SIBARAU (ex-HMAS *Bandolier*)	847	Walkers, Australia	14 Dec 1968
SILIMAN (ex-HMAS *Archer*)	848	Walkers, Australia	15 May 1968
SIGALU (ex-HMAS *Barricade*)	857	Walkers, Australia	26 Oct 1968
SILEA (ex-HMAS *Acute*)	858	Evans Deakin	24 Apr 1968
SIRIBUA (ex-HMAS *Bombard*)	859	Walkers, Australia	5 Nov 1968
SIADA (ex-HMAS *Barbette*)	862	Walkers, Australia	16 Aug 1968
SIKUDA (ex-HMAS *Attack*)	863	Evans Deakin	17 Nov 1967
SIGUROT (ex-HMAS *Assail*)	864	Evans Deakin	12 July 1968

Displacement, tons: 146 full load
Dimensions, feet (metres): 107.5 × 20 × 7.3 *(32.8 × 6.1 × 2.2)*
Main machinery: 2 Paxman 16YJCM diesels; 4000 hp *(2.98 MW)* sustained; 2 shafts
Speed, knots: 21. **Range, miles:** 1220 at 13 kts
Complement: 19 (3 officers)
Guns: 1 Bofors 40 mm/60. 1—12.5 mm MG.
Radars: Surface search: Decca 916; I band; range 88 km *(48 nm)*.

Comment: Transferred from RAN after refit—*Bandolier* 16 November 1973, *Archer* in 1974, *Barricade* March 1982, *Acute* 6 May 1983, *Bombard* September 1983, *Attack* 22 February 1985 (recommissioned 24 May 1985), *Barbette* February 1985, *Assail* February 1986. All carry rocket/flare launchers. Two similar craft with pennant numbers 860 and 861 have been reported.

SIGUROT *10/1992, van Ginderen Collection*

18 KAL KANGEAN CLASS (COASTAL PATROL CRAFT)

Displacement, tons: 44.7 full load
Dimensions, feet (metres): 80.4 × 14.1 × 3.3 *(24.5 × 4.3 × 1)*
Main machinery: 2 diesels; 2 shafts
Speed, knots: 18
Guns: 2 USSR 25 mm/80 (twin). 2 USSR 14.5 mm (twin) MGs.

Comment: Ordered from PT Kabrick Kapal in about 1984 and completed between 1987 and 1990.

KAL KANGEAN 1112 *10/1988, Trevor Brown*

5 + 4 BOEING JETFOILS

BIMA SAMUDERA 1   + 4

Displacement, tons: 117 full load
Dimensions, feet (metres): 102 × 30 × 17.5/7.8 *(31 × 9.1 × 5.3/2.4)*
Main machinery: 2 Allison 501-K20A gas turbines; 7560 hp *(5.64 MW)*; 2 shafts; 2 Detroit 8V-92TA diesels; 700 hp *(522 kW)* sustained; 2 waterjets
Speed, knots: 48. **Range, miles:** 900 at 40 kts; 1500 at 15 kts
Complement: 12
Military lift: 100 troops
Guns: Combinations of 1 Bofors 40 mm/60. 1 Rheinmetall 20 mm. 2—12.7 mm MGs.
Radars: Navigation: Decca; I band.

Comment: First ordered for evaluation in sundry naval and civilian roles including gunboat and troop transporter. Launched 22 October 1981, arrived Indonesia January 1982 for start of trials in March. In 1983 further four ordered from Boeing for delivery in 1984, 1985 and 1986. Plans to increase the total to 47 seem to have been abandoned, but in 1992 four more were building at Surabaya.

BOEING JETFOIL *1987*

AMPHIBIOUS FORCES

Notes: 1. Four LSTs authorised in 1992. Possibly to be built in South Korea.
2. This section includes some vessels of the Military Sealift Command—Kolinlamil.

7 Ex-US LST 1-511 and 512-1152 CLASSES

Name	No	Builders	Commissioned
TELUK LANGSA (ex-USS *LST 1128*)	501	Chicago Bridge and Iron Works	9 Mar 1945
TELUK BAJUR (ex-USS *LST 616*)	502	Chicago Bridge and Iron Works	29 May 1944
TELUK KAU (ex-USS *LST 652*)	504	Chicago Bridge and Iron Works	1 Jan 1945
TELUK TOMINI (ex-MV *Inagua Crest*, ex-MV *Brunei*, ex-USS *Bledsoe County, LST 356*)	508	Charleston NY	22 Dec 1942
TELUK RATAI (ex-Liberian *Inagua Shipper*, ex-USS *Presque Isle*, APB 44, ex-*LST 678*, ex-*Teluk Sindoro*)	509	American Bridge Co, Pennsylvania	30 June 1944
TELUK SALEH (ex-USS *Clark County, LST 601*)	510	Chicago Bridge and Iron Works	25 Mar 1944
TELUK BONE (ex-USS *Iredell County, LST 839*)	511	American Bridge Co, Pennsylvania	6 Dec 1944

Displacement, tons: 1653 standard; 4080 full load
Dimensions, feet (metres): 328 × 50 × 14 *(100 × 15.2 × 4.3)*
Main machinery: 2 GM 12-567A diesels; 1800 hp *(1.34 MW)*; 2 shafts
Speed, knots: 11.6. **Range, miles:** 11 000 at 10 kts
Complement: 119 (accommodation for 266)
Military lift: 2100 tons

Guns: 7—40 mm. 2—20 mm *(Teluk Langsa)*. 6—37 mm (remainder).
 Older units and previously unarmed ships now fitted with ex-Soviet 37 mm guns.
Radars: Surface search: SPS 21 *(Teluk Tomini, Teluk Sindoro)*.
 SPS 53 *(Teluk Saleh, Teluk Bone)*. SO-1 *(Teluk Kau)*. SO-6 *(Teluk Langsa)*.

Programmes: *Teluk Bajur, Teluk Saleh* and *Teluk Bone* transferred in June 1961 (and purchased 22 February 1979). *Teluk Kau* and *Teluk Langsa* in July 1970.
Operational: *Teluk Bajur* and *Teluk Tomini* in Military Sealift Command and are classified as LCCs. May be scrapped when Frosch I class are delivered.

TELUK KAU *3/1991, 92 Wing RAAF*

1 JAPANESE TYPE LST

Name	No	Builders	Commissioned
TELUK AMBOINA	503	Sasebo, Japan	17 Mar 1961

Displacement, tons: 2378 standard; 4200 full load
Dimensions, feet (metres): 327 × 50 × 15 *(99.7 × 15.3 × 4.6)*
Main machinery: 2 MAN V6V 22/30 diesels; 3425 hp(m) *(2.52 MW)*; 2 shafts
Speed, knots: 13.1. **Range, miles:** 4000 at 13.1 kts
Complement: 88
Military lift: 212 troops; 2100 tons

Guns: 6—37 mm; anti-aircraft.

Programmes: Launched on 17 March 1961 and transferred in June 1961.
Structure: A faster copy of US LST 511 class with 30 ton crane forward of bridge.
Operational: Military Sealift Command.

TELUK AMBOINA *10/1992, van Ginderen Collection*

6 TACOMA TYPE LST

Name	No	Builders	Commissioned
TELUK SEMANGKA	512	Korea-Tacoma, Masan	20 Jan 1981
TELUK PENJU	513	Korea-Tacoma, Masan	20 Jan 1981
TELUK MANDAR	514	Korea-Tacoma, Masan	July 1981
TELUK SAMPIT	515	Korea-Tacoma, Masan	June 1981
TELUK BANTEN	516	Korea-Tacoma, Masan	May 1982
TELUK ENDE	517	Korea-Tacoma, Masan	2 Sep 1982

Displacement, tons: 3750 full load
Dimensions, feet (metres): 328 × 47.2 × 13.8 *(100 × 14.4 × 4.2)*
Main machinery: 2 diesels; 6860 hp(m) *(5.04 MW)*; 2 shafts
Speed, knots: 15. **Range, miles:** 7500 at 13 kts
Complement: 90 (13 officers)
Military lift: 1800 tons (including 17 MBTs); 2 LCVPs; 200 troops

Guns: 3—40 mm/60. 2 Rheinmetall 20 mm.
Radars: Navigation: Racal Decca; I band.

Helicopters: 1 Westland Wasp; 3 NAS-332 Super Pumas can be carried in last pair.

Programmes: First four ordered in June 1979, last pair June 1981.
Structure: No hangar in *Teluk Semangka* and *Teluk Mandar*. Two hangars in *Teluk Ende*. First four ordered June 1979, last pair June 1981. The last pair differ in silhouette having drowned exhausts in place of funnels and having their LCVPs carried forward of the bridge.
Operational: Battalion of marines can be embarked if no tanks are carried. One of the class is fitted out as a hospital ship and the last pair act as Command ships.

TELUK SEMANGKA *1/1991, 92 Wing RAAF*

TELUK ENDE *12/1992*

1 LCU TYPE

DORE 580

Displacement, tons: 182 standard; 275 full load
Dimensions, feet (metres): 125.7 × 32.8 × 5.9 *(38.3 × 10 × 1.8)*
Main machinery: 2 diesels; 600 hp(m) *(441 kW)*; 2 shafts
Speed, knots: 8
Complement: 17
Military lift: 4 light tanks or 9 trucks
Guns: 1—12.7 mm MG.

Comment: Military Sealift Command. Built by Korneuberg SY, Austria in 1968. A second of class sank in September 1992. Two of same class are civilian operated in West Irian.

3 LCUs

KUPANG 582   **DILI** 583   **NUSANTARA** 584

Displacement, tons: 400 full load
Dimensions, feet (metres): 140.7 × 29.9 × 4.6 *(42.9 × 9.1 × 1.4)*
Main machinery: 2 diesels; 2 shafts
Speed, knots: 12. **Range, miles:** 700 at 11 kts
Complement: 17
Military lift: 200 tons

Comment: Built at Naval Training Centre, Surabaya in 1978-80. Military Sealift Command.

0 + 12 Ex-GERMAN FROSCH I CLASS (LSM)

Name	No	Builders	Commissioned
(ex-*Hoyerswerda*)	(ex-611)	Peenewerft, Wolgast	12 Nov 1976
(ex-*Hagenow*)	(ex-632)	Peenewerft, Wolgast	1 Dec 1976
(ex-*Frankfurt/Oder*)	(ex-613)	Peenewerft, Wolgast	2 Feb 1977
(ex-*Eberswalde-Finow*)	(ex-634)	Peenewerft, Wolgast	28 May 1977
(ex-*Lübben*)	(ex-631)	Peenewerft, Wolgast	15 Mar 1978
(ex-*Schwerin*)	(ex-612)	Peenewerft, Wolgast	19 Oct 1977
(ex-*Neubrandenburg*)	(ex-633)	Peenewerft, Wolgast	28 Dec 1977
(ex-*Cottbus*)	(ex-614)	Peenewerft, Wolgast	26 May 1978
(ex-*Anklam*)	(ex-635)	Peenewerft, Wolgast	14 July 1978
(ex-*Schwedt*)	(ex-636)	Peenewerft, Wolgast	7 Sep 1979
(ex-*Eisenhüttenstadt*)	(ex-615)	Peenewerft, Wolgast	4 Jan 1979
(ex-*Grimmen*)	(ex-616)	Peenewerft, Wolgast	4 Jan 1979

Displacement, tons: 1950 full load
Dimensions, feet (metres): 321.5 × 36.4 × 9.2 *(98 × 11.1 × 2.8)*
Main machinery: 2 diesels; 5000 hp(m) *(3.68 MW)*; 2 shafts
Speed, knots: 18
Military lift: 600 tons
Guns: 4—57 mm/70 (2 twin). 4—30 mm/65 (2 twin). 2—122 mm rocket launchers.
Mines: Can lay mines through stern doors.
Radars: Air/surface search: Strut Curve; F band.
Navigation: TSR 333; I band.
Fire control: Muff Cob; G/H band.

Comment: Provisional acceptance in August 1992 subject to satisfactory financial negotiations, not completed by early 1993. Some of the guns may be removed or replaced as in theory the sale is for demilitarised vessels.

FROSCH Is   *9/1992, Hartmut Ehlers*

40+ LCMs

Displacement, tons: 62
Main machinery: 2 Gray Marine 64 HN9 diesels; 330 hp *(264 kW)*; 2 shafts
Speed, knots: 8

Comment: A programme which has continued since 1960 although some of the details may have changed. Some may have come from Taiwan.

MINE WARFARE FORCES

2 TRIPARTITE TYPE (MINE WARFARE VESSELS)

Name	No	Builders	Commissioned
PULAU RENGAT	711	van der Giessen-de Noord	26 Mar 1988
PULAU RUPAT	712	van der Giessen-de Noord	26 Mar 1988

Displacement, tons: 502 standard; 568 full load
Dimensions, feet (metres): 168.9 × 29.2 × 8.2 *(51.5 × 8.9 × 2.5)*
Main machinery: 2 MTU 12V 396 TC82 diesels; 2610 hp(m) *(1.92 MW)* sustained; 2 shafts; auxiliary propulsion; 3 Turbomeca gas turbine generators; 2 motors; 2400 hp(m) *(1.76 MW)*; 2 retractable Schottel propulsors; 2 bow thrusters; 150 hp(m) *(110 kW)*
Speed, knots: 15; 7 auxiliary propulsion. **Range, miles:** 3000 at 12 kts
Complement: 46 plus 4 spare berths

Guns: 2 Rheinmetall 20 mm. An additional short range missile system may be added for patrol duties or a third 20 mm gun.
Countermeasures: MCM: OD3 Oropesa mechanical sweep gear; Fiskars F-82 magnetic and SA Marine AS 203 acoustic sweeps; Ibis V minehunting system; 2 PAP 104 Mk 4 minehunting vehicles.
Combat data systems: Signaal SEWACO-RI action data automation.
Radars: Navigation: Racal Decca AC 1229C; I band.
Sonars: Thomson Sintra TSM 2022; active minehunting; high frequency.

Programmes: First ordered on 29 March 1985, laid down 22 July 1985 and launched 23 July 1987. Second ordered 30 August 1985, laid down 15 December 1985 and launched 27 August 1987. More were to have been built in Indonesia up to a total of 12 but this programme has been suspended by lack of funds.
Structure: There are differences in design between these ships and the European Tripartites, apart from their propulsion. Deck-houses and general layout are different as they will be required to act as minehunters, minesweepers and patrol ships. Hull construction is GRP shock proven Tripartite design.
Operational: Endurance, 15 days. Automatic operations, navigation and recording systems, Thomson-CSF Naviplot TSM 2060 tactical display. A 5 ton container can be shipped, stored for varying tasks—research; patrol; extended diving; drone control.

PULAU RENGAT   *6/1988, Gilbert Gyssels*

0 + 9 Ex-GERMAN KONDOR II CLASS
(MINESWEEPERS—COASTAL)

(ex-*Kamenz*) (ex-351)   (ex-*Bitterfeld*) (ex-332, ex-M 2672)   (ex-*Jüterbog*) (ex-342)
(ex-*Röbel*) (ex-324)   (ex-*Zerbst*) (ex-335)   (ex-*Sömmerda*) (ex-311, ex-M 2670)
(ex-*Pritzwalk*) (ex-325)   (ex-*Oranienburg*) (ex-341)   (ex-*Hettstedt*) (ex-353)

Displacement, tons: 414 standard
Dimensions, feet (metres): 186 × 24.6 × 7.9 *(56.7 × 7.5 × 2.4)*
Main machinery: 2 Russki Kolomna Type 40DM diesels; 4408 hp(m) *(3.24 MW)* sustained; 2 shafts; cp props
Speed, knots: 21
Complement: 40
Guns: 6—25 mm (3 twin).
Mines: 2 rails.
Radars: Navigation: TSR 333; I band.
Sonars: Bendix AQS 17(V) VDS; minehunting; 200 kHz

Comment: Planned to be transferred in 1993 if negotiations are concluded. All built by Peenewerft, Wolgast in the early 1970s. Guns may be replaced. New sonars fitted.

KONDOR IIs   *9/1992, Hartmut Ehlers*

2 Ex-SOVIET T 43 CLASS (MINESWEEPERS—OCEAN)

PULAU RANI 701   PULAU RATEWO 702

Displacement, tons: 580 full load
Dimensions, feet (metres): 190.2 × 27.6 × 6.9 *(58 × 8.4 × 2.1)*
Main machinery: 2 Kolomna 9-D-8 diesels; 2000 hp(m) *(1.6 MW)* sustained; 2 shafts
Speed, knots: 15. **Range, miles:** 3000 at 10 kts
Complement: 77
Guns: 4—37 mm/63 (2 twin). 8—12.7 mm (4 twin) MGs.
Depth charges: 2 projectors.
Radars: Navigation: Decca 110; I band.
Sonars: Hull-mounted; active search and attack; high frequency.

Comment: Transferred in 1964. Mostly used as patrol craft.

PULAU RANI   *1983, W Sartori*

SURVEY SHIPS

1 Ex-BRITISH HECLA CLASS

Name	No	Builders	Commissioned
DEWA KEMBAR	932	Yarrow and Co., Blythswood	5 May 1966
(ex-HMS *Hydra*)			

Displacement, tons: 1915 light; 2733 full load
Dimensions, feet (metres): 260.1 × 49.1 × 15.4 *(79.3 × 15 × 4.7)*
Main machinery: Diesel-electric; 3 Paxman 12YJCZ diesels; 3780 hp *(2.82 MW)*; 3 generators 1 motor; 2000 hp(m) *(1.49 MW)*; 1 shaft; bow thruster
Speed, knots: 14. **Range, miles:** 12 000 at 11 kts
Complement: 123 (14 officers)
Radars: Navigation: Kelvin Hughes Type 1006; I band.
Helicopters: 1 Westland Wasp.

Comment: Transferred 18 April 1986 for refit. Commissioned in Indonesian Navy 10 September 1986. SATCOM fitted. Two survey launches on davits.

DEWA KEMBAR   *9/1986, W Sarto*

3 HYDROGRAPHIC/RESEARCH SHIPS

Name	No	Builders	Commissioned
BARUNAJAYA I	—	CMN, Cherbourg	15 Sep 1989
BARUNAJAYA II	—	CMN, Cherbourg	Dec 1989
BARUNAJAYA III	—	CMN, Cherbourg	Apr 1990

Displacement, tons: 1180 full load
Dimensions, feet (metres): 198.2 × 38 × 13.8 *(60.4 × 11.6 × 4.2)*
Main machinery: 2 Niigata/SEMT-Pielstick 5 PA5 L 255 diesels; 2990 hp(m) *(2.2 MW)* sustained; 2 shafts; cp props
Speed, knots: 14. **Range, miles:** 7500 at 12 kts
Complement: 24 plus 26 scientists

Comment: Ordered from La Manche, Dieppe in February 1985 by the office of Technology, Ministry of Industry and Research. Badly delayed by the closing down of the original shipbuilders (ACM, Dieppe) and construction taken over by CMN at St Malo. *Barunajaya 1* is employed entirely on hydrography, the second on oceanography and the third combines both tasks.

BARUNAJAYA II   *1989, CMN, Cherbourg*

Name	No	Builders	Commissioned
BURUJULASAD	931	Schlichting, Lübeck-Travemünde	1967

Displacement, tons: 2165 full load
Dimensions, feet (metres): 269.5 × 37.4 × 11.5 *(82.2 × 11.4 × 3.5)*
Main machinery: 4 MAN V6V 22/30 diesels; 6850 hp(m) *(5.03 MW)*; 2 shafts
Speed, knots: 19.1. **Range, miles:** 14 500 at 15 kts
Complement: 108 (15 officers) plus 28 scientists
Guns: 1—37 mm. 4—12.7 mm (2 twin) MGs.
Radars: Surface search: Decca TM 262; I band.
Helicopters: 1 Bell 47J.

Comment: *Burujulasad* was launched in August 1965; her equipment includes laboratories for oceanic and meteorological research and a cartographic room. Carries one LCVP and three surveying motor boats.

BURUJULASAD   *5/1991, 92 Wing RAAF*

Name	No	Builders	Commissioned
JALANIDHI	933	Sasebo Heavy Industries	12 Jan 1963

Displacement, tons: 985 full load
Dimensions, feet (metres): 176.8 × 31.2 × 14.1 *(53.9 × 9.5 × 4.3)*
Main machinery: 1 MAN G6V 30/42 diesel; 1000 hp(m) *(735 kW)*; 1 shaft
Speed, knots: 11.5. **Range, miles:** 7200 at 10 kts
Complement: 87 (13 officers) plus 26 scientists
Radars: Navigation: Nikkon Denko; I band.

Comment: Launched in 1962. Oceanographic research ship with hydromet facilities. Three ton boom aft. Operated by Hydrographic Office.

JALANIDHI   *1990, Indonesian Navy*

COMMAND AND SUPPORT SHIPS

1 SUBMARINE TENDER

Name	No	Builders	Commissioned
MULTATULI	561	Ishikawajima-Harima Heavy Industries Co Ltd	Aug 1961

Displacement, tons: 3220 standard; 6741 full load
Dimensions, feet (metres): 365.3 × 52.5 × 23 *(111.4 × 16 × 7)*
Main machinery: 1 Burmeister & Wain diesel; 5500 hp(m) *(4.04 MW)*; 1 shaft
Speed, knots: 18.5. **Range, miles:** 6000 at 16 kts
Complement: 130

Guns: 6 USSR 37 mm/63 (2 twin, 2 single); 85° elevation; 160 rounds/minute to 9 km *(5 nm)*; weight of shell 0.7 kg.
8—12.7 mm MGs.
Radars: Surface search: Ball End; E/F band; range 37 km *(20 nm)*.
Navigation: I band.

Helicopters: Platform for Alouette size.

Programmes: Built as a submarine tender. Launched on 15 May 1961. Delivered to Indonesia August 1961.
Modernisation: Original after 76 mm mounting replaced by helicopter deck.
Structure: Living and working spaces air-conditioned.
Operational: Capacity for replenishment at sea (fuel oil, fresh water, provisions, ammunition, naval stores and personnel). Medical and hospital facilities. Now used as fleet flagship (Eastern Force) and is fitted with ICS-3 communications.

MULTATULI   *9/1988, 92 Wing RAAF*

SERVICE FORCES

1 Ex-US ACHELOUS CLASS (REPAIR SHIP)

Name	No	Builders	Commissioned
JAYA WIJAYA (ex-USS *Askari*, ex-ARL 30, ex-LST 1131)	921	Chicago Bridge and Iron Co.	15 Mar 1945

Displacement, tons: 1625 light; 4325 full load
Dimensions, feet (metres): 328 × 50 × 14 *(100 × 15.3 × 4.3)*
Main machinery: 2 GM 12-567A diesels; 1800 hp *(1.34 MW)*; 2 shafts
Speed, knots: 12. **Range, miles:** 17 000 at 7 kts
Complement: 180 (11 officers)
Cargo capacity: 300 tons; 60 ton crane

Guns: 8 Bofors 40 mm/56 (2 quad); 45° elevation; 160 rounds/minute to 11 km *(5.9 nm)*; weight of shell 0.9 kg.
Radars: Air/surface search: Sperry SPS 53; I/J band.
Navigation: Raytheon 1900; I/J band.
IFF: UPX 12B.

Programmes: In reserve from 1956-66. She was recommissioned and reached Vietnam in 1967 to support River Assault Flotilla One. She was used by the US Navy and Vietnamese Navy working up the Mekong in support of the Cambodian operations in May 1970. Transferred on lease to Indonesia at Guam on 31 August 1971 and purchased 22 February 1979.
Structure: Bow doors welded shut. Carries two LCVPs.

JAYA WIJAYA   *9/1988, 92 Wing RAAF*

302 INDONESIA / Service forces

1 REPLENISHMENT TANKER

Name	No	Builders	Commissioned
SORONG	911	Trogir SY, Yugoslavia	Apr 1965

Measurement, tons: 5100 dwt; 4090 gross
Dimensions, feet (metres): 367.4 × 50.5 × 21.6 *(112 × 15.4 × 6.6)*
Main machinery: 1 diesel; 1 shaft
Speed, knots: 15
Cargo capacity: 4200 tons fuel; 300 tons water
Guns: 4—12.7 mm (2 twin) MGs.
Radars: Navigation: Don; I band.

Comment: Has limited under way replenishment facilities.

SORONG 12/1992

1 Ex-BRITISH ROVER CLASS (AOL)

Name	No	Builders	Commissioned
ARUN (ex-*Green Rover*)	903	Swan Hunter, Tyneside	15 Aug 1969

Displacement, tons: 4700 light; 11 522 full load
Dimensions, feet (metres): 461 × 63 × 24 *(140.6 × 19.2 × 7.3)*
Main machinery: 2 SEMT-Pielstick 16 PA4 diesels; 15 360 hp(m) *(11.46 MW)*; 1 shaft; cp prop; bow thruster
Speed, knots: 19. **Range, miles:** 15 000 at 15 kts
Complement: 49
Cargo capacity: 6600 tons fuel
Guns: 2 Oerlikon 20 mm
Radars: Navigation: Kelvin Hughes Type 1006; I band
Helicopters: Platform for Westland Sea King type

Comment: Small fleet tanker designed to replenish ships at sea with fuel, fresh water, limited dry cargo and refrigerated stores under all conditions while under way. No hangar but helicopter landing platform is served by a stores lift, to enable stores to be transferred at sea by 'vertical lift'. Capable of HIFR. Sailed for Indonesia in September 1992 after a refit at Swan Hunter.

ARUN 9/1992, Swan Hunter

2 Ex-SOVIET KHOBI CLASS (COASTAL TANKERS)

BALIKPAPAN 901   **PAKAN BARU** (ex-*Aragua*) 909

Displacement, tons: 1525 full load
Dimensions, feet (metres): 206.6 × 33 × 14.8 *(63 × 10.1 × 4.5)*
Main machinery: 2 diesels; 1600 hp(m) *(1.18 MW)*; 2 shafts
Speed, knots: 13. **Range, miles:** 2500 at 12 kts
Complement: 37 (4 officers)
Cargo capacity: 550 tons dieso
Guns: 4—12.7 mm (2 twin) MGs.
Radars: Navigation: Neptun; I band.

Comment: Transferred 1959.

BALIKPAPAN 6/1990, 92 Wing RAAF

0 + 2 Ex-GERMAN FROSCH II CLASS (SUPPORT SHIPS)

Name	No	Builders	Commissioned
(ex-*Nordperd*)	(ex-E 171)	Peenewerft, Wolgast	3 Oct 1979
(ex-*Sudperd*)	(ex-E 172)	Peenewerft, Wolgast	26 Feb 1980

Displacement, tons: 1700 full load
Dimensions, feet (metres): 297.6 × 36.4 × 9.2 *(90.7 × 11.1 × 2.8)*
Main machinery: 2 diesels; 4408 hp(m) *(3.24 MW)* sustained; 2 shafts
Speed, knots: 18
Cargo capacity: 650 tons
Radars: Air/surface search: Strut Curve; F band.

Comment: Disarmed and scheduled for transfer in 1993. 5 ton crane amidships. In GDR service these ships had two twin 57 mm and two twin 25 mm guns plus Muff Cob fire control radar.

Ex-NORDPERD 9/1990, Hartmut Ehlers

6 TISZA CLASS (AKL)

TALAUD 951	NATUNA 953	KARIMUNDSA 957
NUSA TELU 952	TELUK MENTAWAI 956	KARIMATA 960

Displacement, tons: 2400 full load
Dimensions, feet (metres): 258.4 × 35.4 × 15.1 *(78.8 × 10.8 × 4.6)*
Main machinery: 1 MAN diesel; 1000 hp(m) *(735 kW)*; 1 shaft
Speed, knots: 12. **Range, miles:** 3000 at 11 kts
Complement: 26
Cargo capacity: 875 tons dry; 11 tons liquid
Guns: 4—12.7 mm (2 twin) MGs.
Radars: Navigation: Spin Trough; I band.

Comment: Built in Hungary. All transferred in 1963-64. Military Sealift Command since 1978.

2 TRANSPORTS

TANJUNG PANDAN 971   **TANJUNG OISINA** 972

Measurement, tons: 8000 grt

Comment: Passenger liners built in the 1940s and purchased in 1978. Ex-Mecca pilgrim transports now used for troop transfers between islands. Unarmed. Military Sealift Command.

TANJUNG OISINA 1992, van Ginderen Collection

1 CABLE SHIP

Name	No	Builders	Commissioned
BIDUK	—	J & K Smit, Kinderijk	30 July 1952

Displacement, tons: 1250 standard
Dimensions, feet (metres): 213.2 × 39.5 × 11.5 *(65 × 12 × 3.5)*
Main machinery: 2 boilers; 1 triple expansion engine; 1600 ihp(m) *(1.12 MW)*; 1 shaft
Speed, knots: 12
Complement: 66

Comment: Launched on 30 October 1951. Cable layer, lighthouse tender, and multi-purpose auxiliary.

Service forces — Customs patrol craft / INDONESIA   303

1 SAIL TRAINING SHIP

Name	No	Builders	Commissioned
DEWARUTJI	—	H C Stülcken & Sohn, Hamburg	9 July 1953

Displacement, tons: 810 standard; 1500 full load
Dimensions, feet (metres): 136.2 pp; 191.2 oa × 31.2 × 13.9 *(41.5; 58.3 × 9.5 × 4.2)*
Main machinery: 1 MAN diesel; 600 hp(m) *(441 kW)*; 1 shaft
Speed, knots: 10.5
Complement: 110 (includes 78 midshipmen)

Comment: Barquentine of steel construction. Sail area, 1305 sq yards *(1091 sq m)*. Launched on 24 January 1953.

DEWARUTJI   5/1990, Guy Toremans

2 BUOY TENDERS

MAJANG   **MIZAN**

Displacement, tons: 2150 full load
Dimensions, feet (metres): 255.9 × 44.9 × 13.1 *(7.8 × 13.7 × 4)*
Complement: 70

Comment: Have three 20 ton derricks and a survey launch.

FLOATING DOCKS

Comment: There are three large floating docks in Surabaya which are used for naval purposes.

TUGS

Note: Two BIMA VIII class of 423 tons completed in 1991 are not naval.

1 Ex-US CHEROKEE CLASS

RAKATA (ex-USS *Menominee* ATF 73) 922

Displacement, tons: 1235 standard; 1640 full load
Dimensions, feet (metres): 205 × 38.5 × 17 *(62.5 × 11.7 × 5.2)*
Main machinery: Diesel-electric; 4 GM 12-278 diesels; 4400 hp *(3.28 MW)*; 4 generators; 1 motor; 3000 hp *(2.24 MW)*; 1 shaft
Speed, knots: 15. **Range, miles:** 6500 at 15 kts
Complement: 67
Guns: 1 US 3 in *(76 mm)*/50. 2 Bofors 40 mm/60 aft. 4—25 mm (2 twin) (bridge wings).
Radars: Surface search: Raytheon SPS 5B; G/H band; range 37 km *(20 nm)*.

Comment: Launched on 14 February 1942 by United Eng. Alameda. Commissioned 25 September 1942. Transferred at San Diego in March 1961.

Name	No	Builders	Commissioned
LAMPO BATANG	934	Ishikawajima-Harima	Sep 1961

Displacement, tons: 154 light; 280 full load
Dimensions, feet (metres): 92.3 × 23.2 × 11.3 *(28.2 × 7.1 × 3.4)*
Main machinery: 2 MAN diesels; 600 hp(m) *(441 kW)*; 2 shafts
Speed, knots: 11. **Range, miles:** 1000 at 11 kts
Complement: 13

Comment: Ocean tug. Launched in April 1961.

Name	No	Builders	Commissioned
TAMBORA (Army)	935	Ishikawajima-Harima	June 1961
BROMO	936	Ishikawajima-Harima	Aug 1961

Displacement, tons: 150 light; 250 full load
Dimensions, feet (metres): 79 × 21.7 × 9.7 *(24.1 × 6.6 × 3)*
Main machinery: 2 MAN diesels; 600 hp(m) *(441 kW)*; 2 shafts
Speed, knots: 10.5. **Range, miles:** 690 at 10.5 kts
Complement: 15

Comment: Harbour tugs.

MARITIME SECURITY AGENCY

Note: Established in 1978 to control the 200 mile EEZ and to maintain navigational aids. Comes under the Military Sea Communications Command.

5 SAR CRAFT

KUJANG 201	CELURIT 203	BELATI 205
PARANG 202	CUNDRIK 204	

Displacement, tons: 162 full load
Dimensions, feet (metres): 125.6 × 19.6 × 6.8 *(38.3 × 6 × 2.1)*
Main machinery: 2 AGO SACM 195 V12 CZSHR diesels; 4410 hp(m) *(3.24 MW)*; 2 shafts
Speed, knots: 28. **Range, miles:** 1500 at 18 kts
Complement: 18
Guns: 1—12.7 mm MG.

Comment: Built by SFCN, Villeneuve la Garenne. Completed April 1981 (*Kujang* and *Parang*), August 1981 (*Celurit*), October 1981 (*Cundrik*), December 1981 (*Belati*).

KUJANG   8/1988, 92 Wing RAAF

4 SAR CRAFT

GOLOK 206	PANAN 207	PEDANG 208	KAPAK 209

Displacement, tons: 190 full load
Dimensions, feet (metres): 123 pp × 23.6 × 6.6 *(37.5 × 7.2 × 2)*
Main machinery: 2 MTU 16V 652 TB91 diesels; 4610 hp(m) *(3.39 MW)* sustained; 2 shafts
Speed, knots: 25. **Range, miles:** 1500 at 18 kts
Complement: 18
Guns: 1 Rheinmetall 20 mm.

Comment: All launched 5 November 1981. First pair completed 12 March 1982. Last pair completed 12 May 1982. Built by Deutsche Industrie Werke, Berlin. Fitted out by Schlichting, Travemünde.

6 PAT CLASS

PAT 01	PAT 02	PAT 03	PAT 04	PAT 05	PAT 06

Displacement, tons: 12 full load
Dimensions, feet (metres): 40 × 14.1 × 3.3 *(12.2 × 4.3 × 1)*
Main machinery: 1 diesel; 260 hp(m) *(191 kW)*; 1 shaft
Speed, knots: 14
Guns: 1—7.62 mm MG.

Comment: Built at Tanjung Priok Shipyard 1978-79.

CUSTOMS PATROL CRAFT

17 COASTAL PATROL CRAFT

BC 1001-1010   **BC 3001-3007**

Displacement, tons: 55 (1001 class); 62 (3001 class)
Dimensions, feet (metres): 92.5 × 17 × 5.3 *(28.2 × 5.2 × 1.6)*
Main machinery: 2 MTU 12V 331 TC81 diesels; 2610 hp(m) *(1.92 MW)* sustained; 2 shafts
Speed, knots: 34. **Range, miles:** 750 at 15 kts
Complement: 18
Guns: 1—20 mm (BC 3001 class). 1—12.7 mm MG (BC 1001 class).

Comment: Built by Chantiers Navals de l'Esterel. BC 1001-3 commissioned April, June and November 1975, BC 3001-2 and BC 1004-6 in 1979, BC 3003-3005 and 1007-9 in 1980, BC 3006-7 in January 1981 and BC 1010 in April 1981.

BC 3006   10/1986, van Ginderen Collection

INDONESIA / Customs patrol craft — Police craft

7 COASTAL PATROL CRAFT

BC 2001-2007

Displacement, tons: 70.3 full load
Dimensions, feet (metres): 93.5 × 17.7 × 5.5 *(28.5 × 5.4 × 1.7)*
Main machinery: 2 MTU 12V 331 TC92 diesels; 2660 hp(m) *(1.96 MW)* sustained; 2 shafts
Speed, knots: 29.7
Guns: 1—12.7 mm MG.

Comment: Built CMN Cherbourg to Lürssen design. Ordered in January 1979. Last two commissioned 7 November 1980 (2006) and 10 February 1981 (2007).

BC 2007   1/1990, 92 Wing RAAF

48 LÜRSSEN 28 METRE TYPE

BC 4001-3, 5001-3, 6001-24, 7001-6, 8001-6, 9001-6

Displacement, tons: 68 full load
Dimensions, feet (metres): 91.8 × 17.7 × 5.9 *(28 × 5.4 × 1.8)*
Main machinery: 2 Deutz diesels; 2720 hp(m) *(2 MW)*; or 2 MTU diesels; 2260 hp(m) *(1.66 MW)*; 2 shafts
Speed, knots: 30. **Range, miles:** 1100 at 15 kts; 860 at 28 kts
Complement: 19 (6 officers)
Guns: 1—12.7 mm MG.

Comment: Replacements for the deleted BT series. Lürssen design, some built by Fulton Marine and Scheepswerven van Langebrugge of Belgium, some by Lürssen Vegesack and some by PT Pal Surabaya (which also assembled most of them). Programme started in 1980 and continues into the 1990s. Some of these craft are operated by the Navy, the Police and the Maritime Security Agency.

BC 8003   8/1991, 92 Wing RAAF

BC 5003   8/1991, 92 Wing RAAF

ARMY CRAFT

Note: The Army (ADRI) craft have mostly been transferred to the Military Sealift Command (Logistic Support). More LSLs are reported to be planned.

28 LANDING CRAFT LOGISTICS

ADRI XXXI-ADRI LVIII

Displacement, tons: 580 full load
Dimensions, feet (metres): 137.8 × 35.1 × 5.9 *(42 × 10.7 × 1.8)*
Main machinery: 2 Detroit 6-71 diesels; 348 hp(m) *(260 kW)* sustained; 2 shafts
Speed, knots: 10. **Range, miles:** 1500 at 10 kts
Complement: 15
Military lift: 122 tons equipment

Comment: Built in Tanjung Priok Shipyard 1979-82.

POLICE CRAFT

Note: The police operates a number of craft of varying sizes including 14 Bango class of 194 tons and 32 Hamilton waterjet craft of 7.9 m, 234 hp giving a speed of 28 kts. The Carpentaria class have been transferred from the Navy, and the Lürssen type (619-623) are identical to Customs craft.

POLICE 620   9/1991, van Ginderen Collection

10 COASTAL PATROL CRAFT

DKN 504-DKN 513

Displacement, tons: 440 full load
Dimensions, feet (metres): 157.8 × 24.6 × 9.5 *(48.1 × 7.5 × 2.9)*
Main machinery: 2 MAN V8V 22/30 diesels; 4560 hp(m) *(3.35 MW)*; 2 shafts
Speed, knots: 15. **Range, miles:** 2700 at 14 kts
Complement: 35
Guns: 1 Rheinmetall 20 mm. 2—12.7 mm MGs.

Comment: Built in Japan in the early 1960s. Can carry 70 tons equipment.

9 COASTAL PATROL CRAFT

DKN 908-DKN 916

Displacement, tons: 159 full load
Dimensions, feet (metres): 137.8 × 21.3 × 5.9 *(42 × 6.5 × 1.8)*
Main machinery: 2 MTU MD 655 diesels; 3000 hp(m) *(2.2 MW)*; 2 shafts
Speed, knots: 24.5. **Range, miles:** 1500 at 18 kts
Complement: 22
Guns: 4 Rheinmetall 20 mm.

Comment: Built by Baglietto and Riva Trigosa 1961-64.

DKN 915   7/1983

6 CARPENTARIA CLASS (COASTAL PATROL CRAFT)

Name	No	Builders	Commissioned
SAMADAR	851	Hawker-De Havilland Australia	Aug 1976
SASILA	852	Hawker-De Havilland Australia	Sep 1976
SABOLA	853	Hawker-De Havilland Australia	Oct 1976
SAWANGI	854	Hawker-De Havilland Australia	Nov 1976
SADARIN	855	Hawker-De Havilland Australia	Jan 1977
SALMANETI	856	Hawker-De Havilland Australia	Jan 1977

Displacement, tons: 27
Dimensions, feet (metres): 51.5 × 15.7 × 4.3 *(15.7 × 4.8 × 1.3)*
Main machinery: 2 MTU 8V 331 TC92 diesels; 1770 hp(m) *(1.3 MW)* sustained; 2 shafts
Speed, knots: 29. **Range, miles:** 950 at 18 kts
Complement: 10
Guns: 2—12.7 mm MGs.
Radars: Surface search: Decca; I band.

Comment: First delivered June 1976. Endurance, 4-5 days. Transferred from the Navy in the mid-1980s and probably have new numbers.

CARPENTARIA

IRAN

Headquarters' Appointments

Commander of the Iranian Navy:
  Rear Admiral Ali Shamkhani
Deputy Commander:
  Commodore Abbas Mohtaj
Commander of the Pasdaran Naval Forces:
  Hussein Alai

Personnel

(a) 1993: 16 000 officers and men (Navy)
(b) 2 years' national service

Bases

Persian Gulf: Bandar Abbas (MHQ), Boushehr (also a Dockyard), Kharg Island, Khorramshar (Light Forces)
Indian Ocean: Chah Bahar
Caspian Sea: Bandar—Pahlavi (Training)

Strength of the Fleet

Type	Active	Building
Submarines	1	1 (2)
Midget Submarines	3	—
Destroyers	3	—
Frigates	3	—
Corvettes	2	—
Fast Attack Craft—Missile	11	10
Fast Attack Craft—Gun	3	—
Large Patrol Craft	7	—
Coastal Patrol Craft	87	—
Inshore Patrol Craft	77	—
Landing Ships (Logistic)	4	—
Landing Ships (Tank)	8	—
LCU	14	—
Hovercraft	14	—
Minesweepers—Coastal	3	—
Minesweeper—Inshore	2	—
Replenishment Ship	1	—
Supply Ships	2	—
Repair Ship	1	—
Support Ships	7	—

Type	Active	Building
Water Tankers	4	—
Service Craft	57	—
Tugs	14	—
Ex-Yacht	1	—
Floating Dock	2	—
Customs Craft	2	—

Prefix to Ships' Names

IS

Mercantile Marine

Lloyd's Register of Shipping:
  403 vessels of 4 558 219 tons

PENNANT LIST

Destroyers

51	Damavand
61	Babr
62	Palang

Frigates

71	Alvand
72	Alborz
73	Sabalan

Corvettes

81	Bayandor
82	Naghdi

Light Forces

201	Kaivan
202	Azadi
204	Mahvan
211	Parvin
212	Bahram
213	Nahid
P 221	Kaman
P 222	Zoubin
P 223	Khadang
P 226	Falakhon
P 227	Shamshir
P 228	Gorz
P 229	Gardouneh
P 230	Khanjar
P 231	Neyzeh
P 232	Tabarzin

Mine Warfare Forces

301	Shahrokh
302	Simorgh
303	Karkas
311	Harischi
312	Riazi

Amphibious Forces

21	LCT
22	LCT
23	LCT
24	LST
25	LST
26	LST

Service Forces

411	Kangan
412	Taheri
421	Bandar Abbas
422	Boushehr
431	Kharg
441	Chah Bahar
511	Hengam
512	Larak
513	Tonb
514	Lavan

SUBMARINES

1 + 1 (2) RUSSIAN KILO CLASS (TYPE 877E)

Name	No	Builders	Laid down	Launched	Commissioned
TAREQ	901	Admiralty Yard, St Petersburg	1988	1991	21 Nov 1992

Displacement, tons: 2356 surfaced; 3076 dived
Dimensions, feet (metres): 243.8 × 32.8 × 21.7 *(74.3 × 10 × 6.6)*
Main machinery: Diesel-electric; 2 diesels; 3650 hp(m) *(2.68 MW)*; 2 generators; 1 motor; 5900 hp(m) *(4.34 MW)*; 1 shaft
Speed, knots: 20 dived; 9 snorting; 10 surfaced
Range, miles: 6000 at 7 kts surfaced; 400 at 3 kts dived
Complement: 45

Torpedoes: 6—2 in *(533 mm)* tubes; 18 Type 53; dual purpose; pattern active/passive homing up to 20 km *(10.8 nm)* at up to 45 kts; warhead 400 kg.
Mines: In lieu of torpedoes.
Countermeasures: ESM: Squid Head or Brick Pulp; radar warning. Quad Loop D/F.
Radars: Surface search; Snoop Tray; I band.
Sonars: Sharks Teeth; hull-mounted; passive/active search and attack; medium frequency.
Mouse Roar; active attack; high frequency.

Programmes: The CinC Navy revealed in 1990 that sailors were being trained at Riga with the aim of establishing a submarine force. The first submarine to be transferred sailed from the Baltic in October 1992 flying the Russian flag and with a predominantly Russian crew. A second is expected to transfer in 1993, and a third and fourth in due course.
Structure: Diving depth, 300 m *(985 ft)*.
Operational: Based at Chah Bahar which is outside the Persian Gulf on the northern shore of the Gulf of Oman.
Opinion: Operational effectiveness will initially depend on the number of experienced Russian submariners retained either on loan service or employed as mercenaries. The northern Gulf of Oman and the few deep water parts of the Persian Gulf are notoriously bad areas for anti-submarine warfare. These submarines will be vulnerable to attack when alongside in harbour but could pose a severe threat to merchant shipping either from torpedoes or mines.

TAREQ *10/1992*

3 MIDGET SUBMARINES

Displacement, tons: 27 surfaced; 30 dived
Dimensions, feet (metres): 51.3 × 5.7 × 5.7 *(15.6 × 1.7 × 1.7)*
Main machinery: Diesel; 1 shaft
Speed, knots: 6.5 surfaced; 6 dived
Range, miles: 1200 at 6 kts
Complement: 5

Mines: Two side cargoes each of 2 tons or 14 limpets.

Programmes: Initial submarine constructed in Iran and assembled at Bandar Abbas, combining Japanese and German Second World War design drawings with locally available fabrication and imported equipment. Initially completed in May 1987 but shipped to Tehran in late 1988 for modifications, as diving tests were unsuccessful. Second midget submarine of North Korean (DPRK) design delivered in June 1988 and a third in 1991. Although the programme has not so far been successful, developments continue with the possibility of a Pakistan model.

Structure: The listed characteristics are based on a Second World War design which observers report the first submarine closely resembles, but this one has a more powerful engine and larger diesel exhaust. Diving depth, approx 300 ft *(90 m)*. There is a 'wet and dry' compartment for divers.
Operational: Based at Boushehr. Side cargoes can be released from inside the hull but limpet mines require a diver to exit, attach the mines to the target and then re-enter.

DESTROYERS

1 Ex-BRITISH BATTLE CLASS

Name	No	Builders	Laid down	Launched	Commissioned
DAMAVAND (ex-HMS *Sluys* D 60, ex-*Artemiz*)	51	Cammell Laird & Co Ltd, Birkenhead	24 Nov 1943	28 Feb 1945	30 Sep 1946

Displacement, tons: 2288 standard; 3404 full load
Dimensions, feet (metres): 379 × 40.3 × 17.1 (screws) *(115.5 × 12.3 × 5.2)*
Main machinery: 2 Admiralty boilers; 2 Parsons turbines; 50 000 hp *(37 MW)*; 2 shafts
Speed, knots: 31. **Range, miles:** 3200 at 20 kts; 4400 at 12 kts
Complement: 270

Missiles: SAM: 4 GDC Pomona Standard SM-1MR box launchers ❶; command guidance; semi-active radar homing to 46 km *(25 nm)* at 2 Mach; height envelope 45.7-18 288 m *(150-60 000 ft)*; 4 missiles.
Guns: 4 Vickers 4.5 in *(114 mm)*/45 (2 twin, fwd) ❷; 80° elevation; 15 rounds/minute to 18 km *(10 nm)* anti-surface; 8 km *(4.4 nm)* anti-aircraft; weight of shell 25 kg.
2 Bofors 40 mm/60 ❸; 80° elevation; 120 rounds/minute to 10 km *(5.5 nm)*; weight of shell 0.89 kg.
4 USSR 23 mm/80 (2 twin) ❹; (one replaced Seacat launcher and one mounted forward of bridge).
A/S mortars: 1 Mk 4 3-tubed Squid ❺; range 350 m.
Countermeasures: ESM: Decca RDL 1. Racal FH 5-HF/DF.
Fire control: US Mk 25 for 4.5 in guns and MR SAM. MCS 2 for Squid.
Radars: Air/surface search: Plessey AWS 1 ❻; E/F band; range 110 km *(60 nm)*.
Surface search: Decca 629 ❼; I band.
Fire control: Contraves Sea Hunter Mk 4 ❽; I/J band.
IFF: UK Mk 10.
Sonars: Plessey PMS 26; hull-mounted; lightweight; active search and attack; 10 kHz.

Programmes: Transferred to Iran at Southampton on 26 January 1967, and handed over to the Imperial Iranian Navy after a three-year modernisation refit by the Vosper Thornycroft Group. Refitted again in South Africa 1976.
Operational: Standard SAM has some surface-to-surface capability. Seacat has been removed except for the optical director and two twin 23 mm guns are mounted. Regularly seen at sea in 1989, but not much since then.

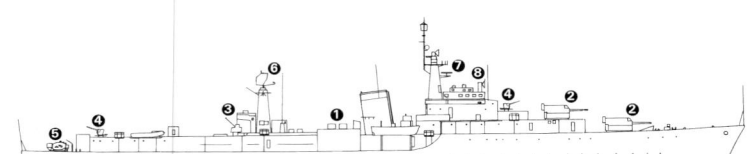

DAMAVAND *(Scale 1 : 1200), Ian Sturton*

DAMAVAND 3/1987

2 Ex-US ALLEN M SUMNER (FRAM II) CLASS

Name	No	Builders	Laid down	Launched	Commissioned
BABR (ex-USS *Zellers* DD 777)	61	Todd Pacific Shipyards	24 Dec 1943	19 July 1944	25 Oct 1944
PALANG (ex-USS *Stormes* DD 780)	62	Todd Pacific Shipyards	15 Apr 1944	4 Nov 1944	27 Jan 1945

Displacement, tons: 2388 standard; 3254 full load
Dimensions, feet (metres): 376.5 × 41 × 21.4 *(114.8 × 12.5 × 6.5)*
Main machinery: 2 Babcock & Wilcox and 2 Foster-Wheeler boilers; 600 psi *(43.3 kg/cm sq)*; 850°F *(454°C)*; 2 turbines; 60 000 hp *(45 MW)*; 2 shafts
Speed, knots: 34. **Range, miles:** 3740 at 12.5 kts
Complement: 290 (14 officers)

Missiles: SAM: 4 GDC Pomona Standard SM-1MR box launchers ❶; command guidance; semi-active radar homing to 46 km *(25 nm)* at 2 Mach; height envelope 45.7-18 288 m *(150-60 000 ft)*; 8 missiles.
Guns: 4 US 5 in *(127 mm)*/38 (2 twin) Mk 38 ❷; 85° elevation; 15 rounds/minute to 17 km *(9.3 nm)* anti-surface; 11 km *(5.9 nm)* anti-aircraft; weight of shell 25 kg.
2 USSR 23 mm/80 (twin) ❸; (replaced VDS right aft).
Torpedoes: 6—324 mm Mk 32 (2 triple) tubes ❹. Possibly Honeywell Mk 44 or 46.
Countermeasures: ESM: WLR-1; radar warning.
ECM: ULQ/6; jammers.
Fire control: Mk 37 GFCS. Mk 105 TFCS.
Radars: Air search: Westinghouse SPS 29C ❺; B/C band; range 457 km *(250 nm)*.
Surface search: Raytheon SPS 10B ❻; G band.
Navigation: LN 66; I band.
Fire control: Western Electric Mk 25 ❼; I/J band.
IFF: UPX-1/UPX-12.
Sonars: SQS 43 *(Babr)*, SQS 44 *(Palang)*; hull-mounted; active search and attack; medium/high frequency.

Helicopters: 1 Agusta AB 204AS ❽.

Programmes: Two FRAM II conversion destroyers of the Allen M Sumner class transferred to Iran from the US Navy 19 March 1971 and 16 February 1972 respectively, both by sale.
Modernisation: Both ships received a full refit as well as conversion at Philadelphia NSY before sailing for Iran. This included a much-improved air-conditioning layout, the removal of B gunmount with its magazine, altered accommodation, the fitting of a Canadian telescopic hangar, the siting of the four Standard missile launchers athwartships beside the torpedo stowage between the funnels, the rigging of VDS and fitting of Hedgehogs in B position. VDS and Hedgehogs subsequently removed and a 23 mm gun fitted right aft.
Operational: Both ships reported doing regular patrols. The pennant numbers have the second digit painted out.

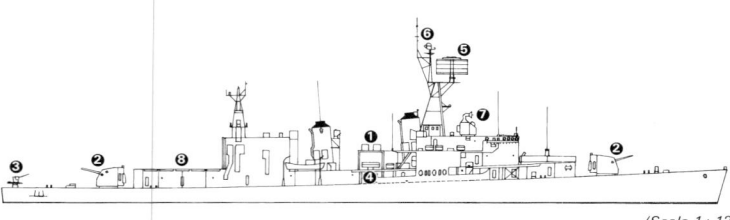

BABR *(Scale 1 : 1200), Ian Sturton*

PALANG 7/198

FRIGATES

3 VOSPER MARK 5 CLASS

Name	No
ALVAND (ex-Saam)	71
ALBORZ (ex-Zaal)	72
SABALAN (ex-Rostam)	73

Builders	Laid down	Launched	Commissioned
Vosper Thornycroft, Woolston	22 May 1967	25 July 1968	20 May 1971
Vickers, Barrow	3 Mar 1968	4 Mar 1969	1 Mar 1971
Vickers, Newcastle & Barrow	10 Dec 1967	4 Mar 1969	June 1972

Displacement, tons: 1100 standard; 1350 full load
Dimensions, feet (metres): 310 × 36.4 × 14.1 (screws) (94.5 × 11.1 × 4.3)
Main machinery: CODOG; 2 RR Olympus TM2A gas turbines; 40 000 hp (29.8 MW) sustained; 2 Paxman 16YJCM diesels; 3800 hp (2.83 MW) sustained; 2 shafts
Speed, knots: 39 gas; 18 diesel. **Range, miles:** 3650 at 18 kts; 550 at 36 kts
Complement: 125 (accommodation for 146)

Missiles: SSM: 1 Sistel Sea Killer II quin launcher ❶; beam rider radio command or optical guidance to 25 km (13.5 nm) at 0.8 Mach; warhead 70 kg. May have been modified by removal of top row of cassettes to incorporate a BM-21 MRL.
Guns: 1 Vickers 4.5 in (114 mm)/55 Mk 8 ❷; 55° elevation; 25 rounds/minute to 22 km (12 nm) anti-surface; 6 km (3.3 nm) anti-aircraft; weight of shell 21 kg.
2 Oerlikon 35 mm/90 (twin) ❸; 85° elevation; 550 rounds/minute to 6 km (3.3 nm); weight of shell 1.55 kg.
3 Oerlikon GAM-B01 20 mm ❹ (replaced 23 mm and both seaboats).
2—12.7 mm MGs.
A/S mortars: 1—3-tubed Limbo Mk 10 ❺; automatic loading; range 1000 m; warhead 92 kg.
Countermeasures: Decoys: 2 UK Mk 5 rocket flare launchers.
ESM: Decca RDL 2AC; radar warning. Racal FH 5-HF/DF.
Radars: Air/surface search: Plessey AWS 1 ❻; E/F band; range 110 km (60 nm).
Surface search: Racal Decca 1226 ❼; I band.
Navigation: Decca 629; I band.
Fire control: Two Contraves Sea Hunter ❽; I/J band.
IFF: UK Mk 10.
Sonars: Graseby 174; hull-mounted; active search; medium/high frequency.
Graseby 170; hull-mounted; active attack; 15 kHz.

Programmes: It was announced on 25 August 1966 that Vosper Ltd, Portsmouth, had received an order for four Mark 5 frigates for the Iranian Navy, two of which were to be built by Vickers. Sabalan was towed to Barrow for completion.
Modernisation: Alvand and Alborz taken in hand by HM Dockyard Devonport July/August 1975 for major refit including replacement of Mk 5 4.5 in gun by Mk 8. Completed 1977. Modifications in 1988 included replacing Seacat with a 23 mm gun and boat davits with minor armaments. By 1990 the 23 mm and both boats had been replaced by GAM-B01 20 mm guns.
Structure: Air-conditioned throughout. Fitted with Vosper stabilisers.
Operational: Sahand sunk by USN on 18 April 1988. Sabalan had her back broken by a laser-guided bomb in the same skirmish but was out of dock by the end of 1990 and was operational again in late 1991.

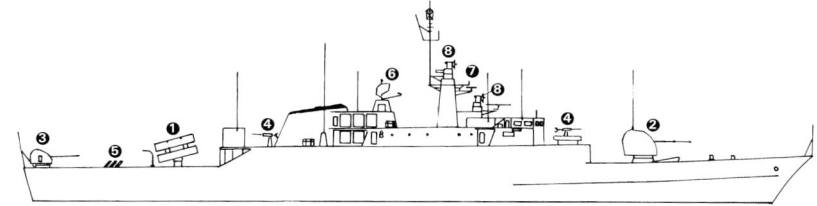

ALVAND *(Scale 1 : 900), Ian Sturton*

ALBORZ *1/1991*

CORVETTES

2 Ex-US PF 103 CLASS

Name	No
BAYANDOR (ex-US PF 103)	81
NAGHDI (ex-US PF 104)	82

Builders	Laid down	Launched	Commissioned
Levingstone Shipbuilding Co, Orange, Texas	20 Aug 1962	7 July 1963	18 May 1964
Levingstone Shipbuilding Co, Orange, Texas	12 Sep 1962	10 Oct 1963	22 July 1964

Displacement, tons: 900 standard; 1135 full load
Dimensions, feet (metres): 275.6 × 33.1 × 10.2 (84 × 10.1 × 3.1)
Main machinery: 2 Fairbanks-Morse 38TD8-1/8-9 diesels; 5250 hp (3.92 MW) sustained; 2 shafts
Speed, knots: 20. **Range, miles:** 2400 at 18 kts; 4800 at 12 kts
Complement: 140

Guns: 2 US 3 in (76 mm)/50 Mk 34 ❶; 85° elevation; 50 rounds/minute to 12.8 km (7 nm); weight of shell 6 kg.
2 Bofors 40 mm/60 (twin) ❷; 80° elevation; 120 rounds/minute to 10 km (5.5 nm); weight of shell 0.89 kg.
2 Oerlikon GAM-B01 20 mm ❸. 2—12.7 mm MGs.
Fire control: Mk 63 for 76 mm gun. Mk 51 for 40 mm gun.
Radars: Air/surface search: Westinghouse SPS 6C ❹; D band; range 146 km (80 nm) (for fighter).
Surface search: Racal Decca ❺; I band.
Navigation: Raytheon 1650 ❻; I/J band.
Fire control: Western Electric Mk 36 ❼; I/J band.
IFF: UPX-12B.

Sonars: EDO SQS 17A; hull-mounted; active attack; high frequency.

Programmes: Transferred from the USA to Iran under the Mutual Assistance programme in 1964.
Modernisation: Naghdi change of engines and reconstruction of accommodation completed in mid-1988. 23 mm gun and depth charge racks replaced by 20 mm guns in 1990.
Operational: Milanian and Khanamuie sunk in 1982 during war with Iraq.

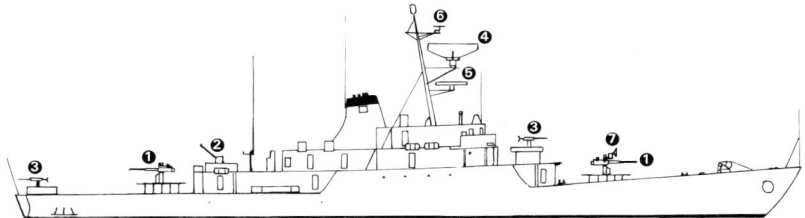

BAYANDOR *(Scale 1 : 900), Ian Sturton*

BAYANDOR *9/1990*

SHIPBORNE AIRCRAFT

Numbers/Type: 8 Agusta AB 204ASW.
Operational speed: 104 kts *(193 km/h)*.
Service ceiling: 11 500 ft *(3505 m)*.
Range: 332 nm *(615 km)*.
Role/Weapon systems: Only small ship helicopter in service, mainly engaged in ASV operations in defence of oil installations. Sensors: APS 705 search radar, dipping sonar (if carried). Weapons: ASW; 2 × torpedoes. ASV; 2 × AS 12 missiles.

LAND-BASED MARITIME AIRCRAFT (FRONT LINE)

Numbers/Type: 6 Agusta-Sikorsky ASH-3D Sea King.
Operational speed: 120 kts *(222 km/h)*.
Service ceiling: 12 200 ft *(3720 m)*.
Range: 630 nm *(1165 km)*.
Role/Weapon systems: Shore-based ASW helicopter to defend major port and oil installations. Sensors: Selenia search radar, dipping sonar. Weapons: ASW; 4 × A244/S torpedoes or depth bombs.

Numbers/Type: 2 Lockheed P-3F Orion.
Operational speed: 410 kts *(760 km/h)*.
Service ceiling: 28 300 ft *(8625 m)*.
Range: 4000 nm *(7410 km)*.
Role/Weapon systems: One of the remaining aircraft used for early warning and control duties for strikes. Sensors: Search radar, sonobuoys. Weapons: ASW; various weapons can be carried.

Numbers/Type: 4 Sikorsky RH-53D.
Operational speed: 125 kts *(232 km/h)*.
Service ceiling: 11 100 ft *(3385 m)*.
Range: 405 nm *(750 km)*.
Role/Weapon systems: Mine clearance and surface search helicopter. Sensors: Weather radar. Weapons: Unarmed.

Numbers/Type: 5 Lockheed C-130H-MP Hercules.
Operational speed: 325 kts *(602 km/h)*.
Service ceiling: 33 000 ft *(10 060 m)*.
Range: 4250 nm *(7876 km)*.
Role/Weapon systems: Long-range maritime reconnaissance role. Sensors: Search/weather radar. Weapons: Unarmed.

LIGHT FORCES

10 COMBATTANTE II (KAMAN) CLASS
(FAST ATTACK CRAFT—MISSILE)

Name	No	Builders	Commissioned
KAMAN	P 221	CMN, Cherbourg	12 Aug 1977
ZOUBIN	P 222	CMN, Cherbourg	12 Sep 1977
KHADANG	P 223	CMN, Cherbourg	15 Mar 1978
FALAKHON	P 226	CMN, Cherbourg	31 Mar 1978
SHAMSHIR	P 227	CMN, Cherbourg	31 Mar 1978
GORZ	P 228	CMN, Cherbourg	22 Aug 1978
GARDOUNEH	P 229	CMN, Cherbourg	11 Sep 1978
KHANJAR	P 230	CMN, Cherbourg	1 Aug 1981
NEYZEH	P 231	CMN, Cherbourg	1 Aug 1981
TABARZIN	P 232	CMN, Cherbourg	1 Aug 1981

Displacement, tons: 249 standard; 275 full load.
Dimensions, feet (metres): 154.2 × 23.3 × 6.2 *(47 × 7.1 × 1.9)*.
Main machinery: 4 MTU 16V 538 TB91 diesels; 12 280 hp(m) *(9.03 MW)* sustained; 4 shafts
Speed, knots: 37.5. **Range, miles:** 2000 at 15 kts; 700 at 33.7 kts
Complement: 31

Missiles: SSM: 4 McDonnell Douglas Harpoon or Chinese YJ-1.
Guns: 1 OTO Melara 3 in *(76 mm)*/62 compact; 85° elevation; 85 rounds/minute to 16 km *(8.7 nm)* anti-surface; 12 km *(6.6 nm)* anti-aircraft; weight of shell 6 kg; 320 rounds.
1 Breda Bofors 40 mm/70; 90° elevation; 300 rounds/minute to 12 km *(6.6 nm)*; weight of shell 0.96 kg; 900 rounds.
Countermeasures: ESM: TMV 433 Dalia; radar intercept
ECM: Alligator; jammer.
Radars: Surface search/fire control: Signaal WM 28; I/J band.
Navigation: Racal Decca 1226; I band.
IFF: UPZ 27N/APX 72.

Programmes: Ordered in February 1974. The transfer of the last three craft was delayed by the French Government after the Iranian revolution. On 12 July 1981 France decided to hand them over. This took place on 1 August—on 2 August they sailed and soon after *Tabarzin* was seized by a pro-Royalist group off Cadiz. After the latter surrendered to the French in Toulon further problems were prevented by sending all three to Iran in a merchant ship.
Structure: The last three were not fitted with Harpoon tubes on delivery. Portable SA-7 launchers may be embarked in some. Harpoon may have been replaced by Chinese SSM.
Operational: *Peykan* was sunk in 1980 by Iraq; *Joshan* in April 1988 by the USN.

GORZ 8/1992

0 + 10 Ex-CHINESE HEGU CLASS (FAST ATTACK CRAFT—MISSILE)

Displacement, tons: 68 standard; 79.2 full load
Dimensions, feet (metres): 88.6 × 20.7 × 4.3 *(27 × 6.3 × 1.3)*
Main machinery: 4 Type L-12V-180 diesels; 4800 hp(m) *(3.53 MW)*; 4 shafts
Speed, knots: 37.5. **Range, miles:** 400 at 30 kts
Complement: 17 (2 officers)

Missiles: SSM: 4 YJ-1 (Eagle Strike); possibly the extended range version will be fitted.
Guns: 2 USSR 25 mm/60 (twin); 85° elevation; 270 rounds/minute to 3 km *(1.6 nm)* anti-aircraft; weight of shell 0.34 kg.
Radars: Surface search: Square Tie; I band.
IFF: High Pole A.

Programmes: Chinese variant of the Komar class with a steel hull which has been building since the late 1970s. Sometimes called the Hoku class. Negotiations for sale started in late 1991; the date of transfer may depend on whether these vessels are new or second hand. Not much progress in 1992 because of arguments over the type of missile to be fitted. Similar craft transferred to Bangladesh, Pakistan and Egypt.

1 Ex-IRAQI OSA II CLASS (FAST ATTACK CRAFT—MISSILE)

Displacement, tons: 245 full load
Dimensions, feet (metres): 126.6 × 24.9 × 8.8 *(38.6 × 7.6 × 2.7)*
Main machinery: 3 Type M 504 diesels; 10 800 hp(m) *(7.94 MW)* sustained; 3 shafts
Speed, knots: 37. **Range, miles:** 500 at 35 kts
Complement: 30

Missiles: 4 SS-N-2B Styx; active radar or IR homing to 46 km *(25 nm)* at 0.9 Mach; warhead 513 kg.
Guns: 4—30 mm/65 (2 twin); 85° elevation; 500 rounds/minute to 5 km *(2.7 nm)*; weight of shell 0.54 kg.
Radars: Surface search/fire control: Square Tie; I band.
Fire control: Drum Tilt; H/I band.

Comment: Delivered to Iraq in the mid-1970s. Sailed to Iran in January 1991 to escape the Gulf War and taken over by the Navy. Operational in November 1991.

OSA II 1991

3 Ex-NORTH KOREA CHAHO CLASS (FAST ATTACK CRAFT—GUN)

Displacement, tons: 70 standard; 82 full load
Dimensions, feet (metres): 85.3 × 19 × 6.6 *(26 × 5.8 × 2)*
Main machinery: 4 Type M 50 diesels; 4400 hp(m) *(3.2 MW)* sustained; 4 shafts
Speed, knots: 40
Complement: 17
Guns: 2 USSR 23 mm/80 (twin) (aft). 2—14.5 mm (twin) MG (forward). 1 BM-21 40-barrelled rocket launcher (MRL).
Radars: Surface search: Racal Decca; I band.

Comment: Built in North Korea. Transferred to Iran in April 1987 and re-engined (type unknown) so top speed may be reduced. Called the Zafar class by the Iranians. Hull based on Soviet P 6 class.

CHAHO 4/1988

3 US COAST GUARD CAPE CLASS (LARGE PATROL CRAFT)

Name	No	Builders	Commissioned
KAIVAN	201	USA	14 Jan 1956
AZADI (ex-*Tiran*)	202	US Coast Guard, Curtis Bay, Maryland	1957
MAHVAN	204	USA	1959

Displacement, tons: 98 standard; 148 full load
Dimensions, feet (metres): 95 × 20.2 × 6.6 *(28.9 × 6.2 × 2)*
Main machinery: 4 Cummins NYHMS-1200 diesels; 2120 hp *(1.58 MW)*; 2 shafts
Speed, knots: 21. **Range, miles:** 460 at 20 kts; 2324 at 8 kts
Complement: 15
Guns: 1 Bofors 40 mm/60. 2 USSR 23 mm/80 (twin). 2—12.7 mm MGs.
Depth charges: 2 racks; 8—136 kg charges.
Sonars: Hull-mounted; active attack; high frequency (probably not operational).

Comment: *Mehran* (203) destroyed during war with Iraq. *Kaivan* and *Mahvan* damaged but have been made operational again. The Mk 22 Mousetrap was replaced by the USSR ZU 23 mm/80 twin mounting which may in turn have been replaced by an Oerlikon 20 mm.

1 Ex-IRAQI BOGOMOL CLASS (LARGE PATROL CRAFT)

Displacement, tons: 245 full load
Dimensions, feet (metres): 127.9 × 25.6 × 5.9 *(39 × 7.8 × 1.8)*
Main machinery: 3 Type M 504 diesels; 10 800 hp(m) *(7.94 MW)* sustained; 3 shafts
Speed, knots: 37. **Range, miles:** 500 at 35 kts
Complement: 30
Guns: 1 USSR 3 in *(76 mm)*/66; 85° elevation; 120 rounds/minute to 15 km *(8 nm)*; weight of shell 7 kg.
2 USSR 30 mm/65 (twin); 85° elevation; 500 rounds/minute to 5 km *(2.7 nm)*; weight of shell 0.54 kg.
Radars: Surface search: Pot Head; H/I band.
Fire control: Bass Tilt; H/I band.

Comment: Delivered in March 1990 to Iraq. Escaped to Iran in January 1991 and in service with the Iranian Navy in early 1993.

3 IMPROVED PGM-71 CLASS (LARGE PATROL CRAFT)

Name	No	Builders	Commissioned
PARVIN (ex-US *PGM 103*)	211	Peterson Builders Inc	1967
BAHRAM (ex-US *PGM 112*)	212	Peterson Builders Inc	1969
NAHID (ex-US *PGM 122*)	213	Peterson Builders Inc	1970

Displacement, tons: 98 standard; 148 full load
Dimensions, feet (metres): 101 × 21.3 × 8.3 *(30.8 × 6.5 × 2.5)*
Main machinery: 2 GM 6-71 diesels; 2040 hp *(1.52 MW)* sustained; 2 shafts
Speed, knots: 22. **Range, miles:** 1140 at 17 kts
Complement: 20
Guns: 1 Bofors 40 mm/60. 2 Oerlikon 20 mm. 2—12.7 mm MGs.
Depth charges: 4 racks (8 US Mk 6).
Radars: Surface search: Decca 303; I band.
Sonars: SQS 17B; hull-mounted active attack; high frequency.

Comment: The heavier 40 mm gun is mounted aft and the 20 mm forward to compensate for the large SQS 17B sonar dome under the bows.

14 US Mk III CLASS (COASTAL PATROL CRAFT)

Displacement, tons: 41.6 full load
Dimensions, feet (metres): 65 × 18.1 × 6 *(19.8 × 5.5 × 1.8)*
Main machinery: 3 GM 8V-71TI diesels; 690 hp *(515 kW)* sustained; 3 shafts
Speed, knots: 30. **Range, miles:** 500 at 28 kts
Complement: 5
Guns: 3—12.7 mm (1 twin, 1 single) MGs.
Radars: Surface search: RCA LN-66; I band

Comment: Twenty ordered from Marinette Marine Corp, Wisconsin, USA; the first delivered in December 1975 and the last in December 1976. A further 50 were ordered in 1976 to be shipped out and completed in Iran. It is not known how many were finally assembled. Six lost in the Gulf War, others have been scrapped. A vessel named *Qa'am 6* was launched at Bandar Anzali on 6 February 1992. This was probably a Mk III which suggests the assembly of more of the class continues.

US Mk III 1991

70 PBI TYPE (COASTAL PATROL CRAFT)

Displacement, tons: 20.1 full load
Dimensions, feet (metres): 50 × 15 × 4 *(15.2 × 4.6 × 1.2)*
Main machinery: 2 GM 8V-71TI diesels; 460 hp *(343 kW)* sustained; 2 shafts
Speed, knots: 28. **Range, miles:** 750 at 26 kts
Complement: 5 (1 officer)
Missiles: SSM: Tigercat; range 6 km *(3.2 nm)*.
Guns: 2—12.7 mm MGs.
Radars: Surface search: I band.

Comment: Ordered by Iranian Arvandan Maritime Company. First 19 completed by Petersons and remainder shipped as kits for completion in Iran. The SSM is crude and unguided.

PBI Type 1991

6 US Mk II CLASS (COASTAL PATROL CRAFT)

Displacement, tons: 22.9 full load
Dimensions, feet (metres): 49.9 × 15.1 × 4.3 *(15.2 × 4.6 × 1.3)*
Main machinery: 2 GM 8V-71TI diesels; 460 hp *(343 kW)* sustained; 2 shafts
Speed, knots: 28. **Range, miles:** 750 at 26 kts
Complement: 6
Guns: 4—12.7 mm (2 twin) MGs.
Radars: Surface search: SPS 6; I band.

Comment: Twenty-six ordered from Peterson, USA in 1976-77. Six were for the Navy and the remainder for the Imperial Gendarmerie. All were built in association with Arvandan Maritime Corporation, Abadan. The six naval units operate in the Caspian sea. Of the remaining 20, six were delivered complete and the others were only 65 per cent assembled on arrival in Iran. Some were lost when the Iraqi army captured Kormansaar. Others have been lost at sea.

12 ENFORCER TYPE (INSHORE PATROL CRAFT)

Displacement, tons: 4.7 full load
Dimensions, feet (metres): 30.5 × 11.2 × 3 *(9.3 × 3.4 × 0.9)*
Main machinery: 2 GM 6V-53 diesels; 296 hp *(221 kW)* sustained; 2 shafts
Speed, knots: 28. **Range, miles:** 146 at 16 kts
Complement: 4
Guns: 1—12.7 mm MG.
Radars: Surface search: Apelco AD7-7; I band.

Comment: Built by Bertram Yacht, Miami in 1972. Thirty-six units delivered; so far twenty-four deleted.

3 SEWART TYPE (INSHORE PATROL CRAFT)

MAHNAVI-HAMRAZ   MAHNAVI-VAHEDI   MAHNAVI-TAHERI

Displacement, tons: 9.1 full load
Dimensions, feet (metres): 40 × 12.1 × 3.3 *(12.2 × 3.7 × 1)*
Main machinery: 2 GM 6-71 diesels; 348 hp *(260 kW)* sustained; 2 shafts
Speed, knots: 31
Complement: 6
Guns: 1—12.7 mm MG.

Comment: Small launches for port duties of Sewart (USA) standard 40 ft type. Six transferred in 1970 and six in 1986. *Mardjan, Morvarid* and *Sadaf* given to Sudan in December 1975, remainder deleted.

30 BOGHAMMAR CRAFT

Displacement, tons: 6.4 full load
Dimensions, feet (metres): 41.2 × 8.6 × 2.3 *(13 × 2.7 × 0.7)*
Main machinery: 2 Volvo Penta TAMD71A diesels; 714 hp(m) *(525 kW)*; or 2 Seatek 6-4V-9 diesels; 1160 hp *(853 kW)*; 2 shafts
Speed, knots: 46. **Range, miles:** 500 at 40 kts
Complement: 5/6
Guns: 1—12.7 mm MG. 1 RPG-7 rocket launcher or 106 mm recoilless rifle. 1—12-barrelled 107 mm rocket launcher (MRL)
Radars: Surface search: Decca 170; I band

Comment: Ordered in 1983 and completed in 1984-85 for Customs Service. Total of 51 delivered. Used extensively by the Pasdaran (Islamic Revolutionary Guard) for operations against merchant vessels in the Persian Gulf. Maximum payload 450 kg. Speed is dependent on load carried. They can be transported by Amphibious Lift Ships and can operate from bases at Farsi, Sirri and Abu Musa Islands with a main base at Bandar Abbas. Being re-engined with Seatek diesels from 1991.
There are also a further 10—11 Metre craft with similar characteristics. Known as TORAGH boats.

BOGHAMMAR 1988

32 BOSTON WHALER CRAFT (TYPE 1)

Displacement, tons: 1.3 full load
Dimensions, feet (metres): 22.3 × 7.4 × 1.2 *(6.7 × 2.3 × 0.4)*
Main machinery: 2 outboards; 240 hp *(179 kW)*
Speed, knots: 40+
Complement: 4
Guns: Various, but can include 1—12-barrelled 107 mm MRL or 1—12.7 mm MG.

Comment: Designed for coastal law enforcement by Boston Whaler Inc, USA. GRP hulls. Numerous indigenously constructed hulls.

BOSTON WHALER 1988

310 IRAN / Light forces — Amphibious forces

RIVER ROADSTEAD PATROL AND HOVERCRAFT

Comment: Numerous craft used by the Revolutionary Guard include:
Type 2: Dimensions, feet (metres): 22.0 × 7.2 *(6.7 × 2.2)*; single outboard engine; 1—12.7 mm MG.
Type 3: Dimensions, feet (metres): 16.4 × 5.2 *(5.0 × 1.6)*; single outboard engine; small arms.
Type 4: Dimensions, feet (metres): 13.1-26.2 × 7.9 *(4-8 × 1.6)*; two outboard engines; small arms.
Type 5: Dimensions, feet (metres): 24.6 × 9.2 *(7.5 × 2.8)*; Damen assault craft.
Type 6: Dimensions, feet (metres): 30.9 × 11.8 *(9.4 × 3.6)*; single outboard engine; 1—12.7 mm MG.
Dhows: Dimensions, feet (metres): 77.1 × 20 *(23.5 × 6.1)*; single diesel engine; mine rails.
Yunus: Dimensions, feet (metres): 27.6 × 9.8 *(8.4 × 3)*; speed 32 kts.

MINE WARFARE FORCES

3 Ex-US MSC 292 and 268 CLASS (MINESWEEPERS—COASTAL)

Name	No	Builders	Commissioned
SHAHROKH (ex-*MSC 276*)	301	Bellingham Shipyards	1960
SIMORGH (ex-*MSC 291*)	302	Tacoma Boat	1962
KARKAS (ex-*MSC 292*)	303	Peterson Builders	1959

Displacement, tons: 376 (*Shahrokh*); 384 (others) full load
Dimensions, feet (metres): 145.8 × 28 × 8.3 *(44.5 × 8.5 × 2.5)*
Main machinery: 2 GM 8-268A diesels (*Shahrokh*); 880 hp *(656 kW)*; 2 shafts
4 GM 6-71 diesels (others); 696 hp *(519 kW)* sustained; 2 shafts
Speed, knots: 13. **Range, miles:** 2400 at 10 kts
Complement: 40 (6 officers)
Guns: 2 Oerlikon 20 mm (twin).
Radars: Surface search: Decca; I band.

Comment: Originally class of four. Of wooden construction with mechanical, acoustic and magnetic sweeps. Transferred from the USA to Iran under MAP in 1959-62. *Shahrokh* in the Caspian Sea as a training ship. *Karkas* still active but rarely seen at sea. *Simorgh* paid off some years ago but reactivated in 1992.

2 US CAPE CLASS (MINESWEEPER—INSHORE)

Name	No	Builders	Commissioned
HARISCHI (ex-*MSI 14*)	311	Tacoma Boat	3 Sep 1964
RIAZI (ex-*MSI 13*)	312	Tacoma Boat	15 Oct 1964

Displacement, tons: 239 full load
Dimensions, feet (metres): 111 × 23 × 7.9 *(33.9 × 7 × 2.4)*
Main machinery: 4 Type 2490 8V diesels; 1300 hp *(970 kW)*; 2 shafts
Speed, knots: 13. **Range, miles:** 1200 at 12 kts; 3500 at 8 kts
Complement: 21 (5 officers)
Guns: 1—12.7 mm MG.
Radars: Surface search: Decca 303N; I band

Comment: Delivered to Iran under MAP and transferred at Seattle, Washington, on 15 October 1964. *Riazi* is still operational with mechanical, acoustic and magnetic sweep gear. *Harischi* was put back in service in 1992.

RIAZI (old number) *1975, Imperial Iranian Navy*

AMPHIBIOUS FORCES

Note: One Polnochny class LST escaped from Iraq in January 1991 and took shelter in Iran. Although it has been retained, no attempt had been made to make it operational by the end of 1992.

2 IRAN AJR CLASS (LSTs)

IRAN ASIR (ex-*Arya Akian*)   **IRAN GHAYDR** (ex-*Arya Sahand*)

Displacement, tons: 2274 full load
Measurement, tons: 1691 gross
Dimensions, feet (metres): 176 × 35.4 × 9.9 *(53.7 × 10.8 × 3)*
Main machinery: 2 diesels; 2200 hp(m) *(1.62 MW)*; 2 shafts
Speed, knots: 12.5
Complement: 30
Military lift: 650 tons
Guns: 2—12.7 mm MGs.

Comment: Five built by Teraoka, Japan in 1978-79. Ro-Ro landing craft acquired by the Iranian Navy in 1980 primarily for minelaying. The *Iran Ajr* was captured and scuttled by the US Navy in September 1987 and two others of the class were sunk by Iraq in 1980. Probably only one is operational.

3 IRAN HORMUZ 24 CLASS (LSTs)

24-26

Displacement, tons: 2014 full load
Dimensions, feet (metres): 239.8 × 46.6 × 8.2 *(73.1 × 14.2 × 2.5)*
Main machinery: 2 Daihatsu 6DLM-22 diesels; 2400 hp(m) *(1.76 MW)*; 2 shafts
Speed, knots: 12
Complement: 30 plus 110 berths
Military lift: 9 tanks, 140 troops

Comment: Built by Inchon, South Korea in 1985-86 and as with the Iran Hormuz 21 class officially classed as Merchant Ships. Large bow doors. Have been used to support Pasdaran activities.

4 HENGAM CLASS (LSL)

Name	No	Builders	Commissioned
HENGAM	511	Yarrow (Shipbuilders) Ltd, Clyde	12 Aug 1974
LARAK	512	Yarrow (Shipbuilders) Ltd, Clyde	12 Nov 1974
TONB	513	Yarrow (Shipbuilders) Ltd, Clyde	21 Feb 1985
LAVAN	514	Yarrow (Shipbuilders) Ltd, Clyde	16 Jan 1985

Displacement, tons: 2540 full load
Dimensions, feet (metres): 305 × 49 × 7.3 *(93 × 15 × 2.4)*
Main machinery: 4 Paxman 12YJCM diesels (*Hengam, Larak*); 3000 hp *(2.24 MW)* sustained; 2 shafts
4 MTU 16V 652 TB81 diesels (*Tonb, Lavan*); 4600 hp(m) *(3.38 MW)* sustained; 2 shafts
Speed, knots: 14.5. **Range, miles:** 4000+ at 12 kts
Complement: 80
Military lift: Up to 9 tanks depending on size; 600 tons cargo; 227 troops; 10 ton crane

Guns: 4 Bofors 40 mm/60 (*Hengam* and *Larak*). 8 USSR 23 mm/80 (4 twin) (*Tonb* and *Lavan*). 2—12.7 mm MGs.
1 BM-21 multiple rocket launcher.
Countermeasures: Decoys: 2 UK Mk 5 rocket flare launchers.
Radars: Navigation: Racal Decca 1229; I band.
IFF: SSR 1520 (*Hengam* and *Larak*).
Tacan: URN 25.

Helicopters: Can embark 1 medium.

Programmes: Named after islands in the Gulf. First two ordered 25 July 1972. Four more ordered 20 July 1977. The material for the last two ships of the second order had been ordered by Yarrows when the order was cancelled in early 1979. *Tonb* carried out trials in October 1984 followed by *Lavan* later in the year and both were released by the UK in 1985 as 'Hospital Ships'.
Structure: Smaller than British *Sir Lancelot* design with no through tank deck.
Operational: Two LCVPs and a number of small landing craft can be carried. Can act as Depot Ships for MCMV and small craft and have been used to ferry Pasdaran small craft around the Gulf.

LAVAN *2/1991, 92 Wing RAAF*

3 IRAN HORMUZ 21 CLASS (LCT)

21-23

Displacement, tons: 1400 full load
Measurement, tons: 750 dwt
Dimensions, feet (metres): 213.3 × 39.4 × 8.5 *(65 × 12 × 2.6)*
Main machinery: 2 MAN V12V-12.5/14 diesels; 730 hp(m) *(537 kW)*; 2 shafts
Speed, knots: 9
Complement: 28
Military lift: 600 tons

Comment: Officially ordered for 'civilian use' and built by Ravenstein, Netherlands in 1984-85. Similar but slightly smaller than the Iran Ajr class. No 21 is operational but the others are in a poor state of repair.

8 WINCHESTER (SR. N6) CLASS (HOVERCRAFT)

01-08

Displacement, tons: 10.9 full load
Dimensions, feet (metres): 48.5 × 23 × 3.9 (skirt) *(14.8 × 7 × 1.2)*
Main machinery: 1 RR Gnome Model 1050 gas turbine; 1050 hp *(783 kW)* sustained
Speed, knots: 60. **Range, miles:** 170 at 54 kts
Complement: 3
Guns: 1 or 2—12.7 mm MGs.
Radars: Surface search: Decca 202; I band.

Comment: Ordered 1970-72 and commissioned 1973-75. First three were Mk 3, remainder Mk 4. Some refitted in UK in 1984. Can carry 20 troops and 5 tons of cargo. Can also be fitted with four 500 kg mines on the side decks. Probably only half are operational.

WINCHESTER 03

Amphibious forces — Service forces / IRAN   311

6 WELLINGTON (BH.7) CLASS (HOVERCRAFT)

101-106

Displacement, tons: 53.8 full load
Dimensions, feet (metres): 78.3 × 45.6 × 5.6 (skirt) *(23.9 × 13.9 × 1.7)*
Main machinery: 1 RR Proteus 15 M/541 gas turbine; 4250 hp *(3.17 MW)* sustained
Speed, knots: 70; 30 in sea state 5 or more. **Range, miles:** 620 at 66 kts
Guns: 2 Browning 12.7 mm MGs.
Radars: Surface search: Decca 1226; I band.

Comment: First pair are British Hovercraft Corporation 7 Mk 4 commissioned in 1970-71 and the next four are Mk 5 craft commissioned in 1974-75. Mk 5 craft fitted for, but not with Standard missiles. Some refitted in UK in 1984. Can embark troops and vehicles or normal support cargoes. All were in reasonable condition in late 1992.

WELLINGTON 103   9/1985, Michael D J Lennon

14 ROTORK CRAFT (LCU)

Displacement, tons: 9 full load
Dimensions, feet (metres): 41.7 × 10.5 × 3 *(12.7 × 3.2 × 0.9)*
Main machinery: 2 Volvo Penta diesels; 240 hp(m) *(176 kW)*; 2 shafts
Speed, knots: 28
Military lift: 30 troops
Guns: Up to 4—7.62 mm MGs.

Comment: Some are used by the Coast Guard. Some of these craft have been deleted and numbers are uncertain.

SERVICE FORCES

1 REPLENISHMENT SHIP

Name	No	Builders	Commissioned
KHARG	431	Swan Hunter Ltd, Wallsend	5 Oct 1984

Displacement, tons: 11 064 light; 33 014 full load
Measurement, tons: 9367 dwt; 18 582 gross
Dimensions, feet (metres): 679 × 86.9 × 30 *(207.2 × 26.5 × 9.2)*
Main machinery: 2 Babcock & Wilcox boilers; 2 Westinghouse turbines; 26 870 hp *(19.75 MW)*; 1 shaft
Speed, knots: 21.5
Complement: 248
Guns: 1 OTO Melara 76 mm/62 compact. 4 USSR 23 mm/80 (2 twin).
Radars: Navigation: Two Decca 1229; I band.
IFF: 955M.
Helicopters: Three can be embarked (twin hangar).

Comment: Ordered October 1974. Laid down 27 January 1976. Launched 3 February 1977. Ship handed over to Iranian crew on 25 April 1980 but remained in UK. In 1983 Iranian Government requested this ship's transfer. The British Government delayed approval until January 1984. On 10 July 1984 began refit at Tyne Ship Repairers. Trials began 4 September 1984 and ship was then delivered without guns which were subsequently fitted. A design incorporating some of the features of the British Ol class but carrying ammunition and dry stores in addition to fuel. Inmarsat fitted.

KHARG   3/1987, Michael D J Lennon

2 FLEET SUPPLY SHIPS

Name	No	Builders	Commissioned
BANDAR ABBAS	421	C Lühring Yard, Brake, West Germany	Apr 1974
BOUSHEHR	422	C Lühring Yard, Brake, West Germany	Nov 1974

Displacement, tons: 4673 full load
Measurement, tons: 3250 dwt; 3186 gross
Dimensions, feet (metres): 354.2 × 54.4 × 14.8 *(108 × 16.6 × 4.5)*
Main machinery: 2 MAN 6L 52/55 diesels; 12 060 hp(m) *(8.86 MW)* sustained; 2 shafts
Speed, knots: 20. **Range, miles:** 3500 at 16 kts
Complement: 59
Guns: 2 USSR 23 mm/80 (twin). 2 Oerlikon 20 mm. 8—14.5 mm (2 quad) MGs.
Radars: Navigation: Two Decca 1226; I band.
Helicopters: 1 light reconnaissance.

Comment: *Bandar Abbas* launched 11 August 1973, *Boushehr* launched 23 March 1974. Combined tankers and store-ships carrying victualling, armament and general stores. Telescopic hangar for Bell UH-1N size helicopter. Both carry 2 SA-7 portable SAM and 20 mm guns have been fitted alongside the hangar.

BOUSHEHR   2/1990

1 Ex-US AMPHION CLASS (REPAIR SHIP)

Name	No	Builders	Commissioned
CHAH BAHAR (ex-USS *Amphion*, ex-AR 13)	441	Tampa Shipbuilding Co	30 Jan 1946

Displacement, tons: 8941 standard; 14 803 full load
Dimensions, feet (metres): 492 × 69.6 × 27.5 *(150.1 × 21.2 × 8.4)*
Main machinery: 2 Foster-Wheeler boilers; 435 psi *(30.6 kg/cm sq)*; 2 Westinghouse turbines; 8560 hp *(6.4 MW)*; 1 shaft
Speed, knots: 18. **Range, miles:** 13 950 at 11.5 kts
Complement: 880

Comment: Launched on 15 May 1945. Transferred on loan to the Iran Navy on 2 October 1971. Purchased 1 March 1977. Non-operational and based at Bandar Abbas as permanent repair facility. Two US 3 in (76 mm)/50 guns have been removed but navigational radar (SPS 4) is retained.

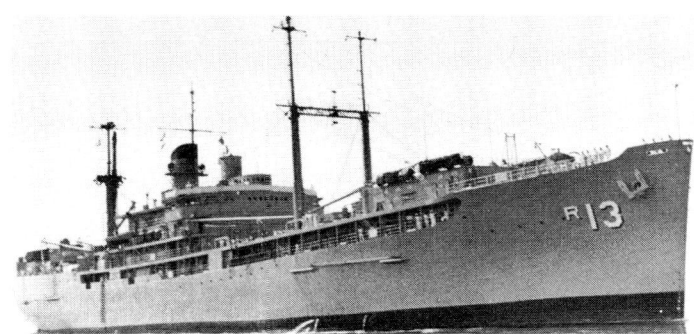

CHAH BAHAR (old number)   1972, Imperial Iranian Navy

4 KANGAN CLASS (WATER TANKERS)

KANGAN 411	SHAHID MARJANI —
TAHERI 412	AMIR —

Displacement, tons: 12 000 full load
Measurement, tons: 9430 dwt
Dimensions, feet (metres): 485.6 × 70.5 × 16.4 *(148 × 21.5 × 5)*
Main machinery: 1 MAN 7L52/55A diesel; 7385 hp(m) *(5.43 MW)* sustained; 1 shaft
Speed, knots: 15
Complement: 14
Cargo capacity: 9000 cu m of water
Guns: 2 USSR 23 mm/80 (twin). 2—12.7 mm MGs.
Radars: Navigation: Decca 1229; I band.

Comment: The first two were built in Mazagon Dock, Bombay in 1978 and 1979. The second pair to a slightly modified design were acquired in 1991/92. Some of the largest water tankers afloat and are used to supply remote coastal towns and islands. Accommodation is air-conditioned.

TAHERI   5/1989

7 DELVAR CLASS (SUPPORT SHIPS)

CHARAK (AK)	CHIROO (AK)	DELVAR (AE)	DILIM (AW)
SOURU (AK)	SIRJAN (AE)	DAYER (AW)	

Measurement, tons: 890 gross; 765 dwt
Dimensions, feet (metres): 210 × 34.4 × 10.9 *(64 × 10.5 × 3.3)*
Main machinery: 2 MAN G6V 23.5/33ATL diesels; 1560 hp(m) *(1.15 MW)*; 2 shafts
Speed, knots: 11
Guns: 2 USSR 23 mm/80 (twin).
Radars: Navigation: Decca 1226; I band.

Comment: All built by Karachi SY in 1980-82. *Delvar* and *Sirjan* are ammunition ships, *Dayer* and *Dilim* water carriers and the other three are general cargo ships. The water carriers have only one crane (against two on the other types), and have rounded sterns (as opposed to transoms).

IRAN / Service forces — IRAQ / Frigates

14 HARBOUR TUGS

No 1 (ex-West German *Karl*)	MENAB	SEFID-RUD
No 2 (ex-West German *Ise*)	HARI-RUD	ATRAK
HAAMOON	ARAS	+5 (YTM class)
HIRMAND		

Comment: All between 70 and 90 ft in length. All but the first two (which were built in the early 1960s and acquired in June 1974) built in 1984-85.

2 FLOATING DOCKS

400 (ex-US *ARD 29*, ex-*FD 4*)　　　DOLPHIN

Dimensions, feet (metres): 487 × 80.2 × 32.5 *(149.9 × 24.7 × 10)* (400)
786.9 × 172.1 × 58.4 *(240 × 52.5 × 17.8)* (*Dolphin*)

Comment: *400* is an ex-US ARD 12 class built by Pacific Bridge, California and transferred in 1977; lift 3556 tons. *Dolphin* built by MAN-GHH Nordenham, West Germany and completed in November 1985; lift 28 000 tons.

1 Ex-YACHT

KISH

Displacement, tons: 178 full load
Dimensions, feet (metres): 122 × 24.9 × 7.3 *(37.2 × 7.6 × 2.2)*
Main machinery: 2 MTU diesels; 2920 hp(m) *(2.15 MW)*; 2 shafts
Speed, knots: 20
Complement: 20
Radars: Navigation: I band

Comment: Completed in 1970 by Yacht und Bootswerft, West Germany. Refitted in Bandar Abbas and used for training.

8 + 1 HENDIJAN CLASS (TENDERS) (AG)

HENDIJAN	KONARAK	SIRIK	GENO
KALAT	GENAVEH	SAVATAR	MOGAM

Measurement, tons: 445 grt
Dimensions, feet (metres): 154.3 × 28.1 × 11.5 *(47 × 8.6 × 3.5)*
Main machinery: 2 diesels; 2 shafts
Cargo capacity: 40 tons

Comment: Built by Damen, Netherlands 1988-90. Two more delivered in 1991. One more reported launched at Bandar Abbas in November 1992. There are five other names: *Rostani*, *Mayband*, *Maqam*, *Koramshahr* and *Bamregan* which are used in conjunction with this class which suggests a local building programme.

KONARAK　　　　　　　　　　　　　　　　　　　　　　*6/1989, Gilbert Gyssels*

45+ BARGES AND SERVICE CRAFT

Comment: Many built in Karachi 1976-79 the largest being a 260 ft *(79.2 m)* self-propelled lighter. One delivered from Iran Marine is of 1000 grt and was launched on 2 March 1987.

IRAQ

Administration

Commander-in-Chief:
　Rear Admiral Abd Muhammad Abdullah
Chief of Staff:
　Commander Samad Sat Al Mufti

Bases

Basra, Umm Qasr, Az Zubayr
The UN decision on the status of Umm Qasr could deprive the Navy of its base, but leaves the commercial port still in Iraq. In 1992 little progress was made in clearing the Shatt-al-Arab passage to Basra.

Mercantile Marine

Lloyd's Register of Shipping:
　131 vessels of 919 740 tons

DELETIONS

Note: Captured Kuwaiti vessels destroyed in 1991 are shown in *Kuwait* section.

Frigates

1992　*Hittin*, *Thi Qar*, *Al Qadisiya*, *Al Yarmouk* (retained by Italy)

Corvettes

1992　*Abdulla Ben Abi Sarh*, *Khalid Ibn Al Walid*, *Saad Ibn Abi Waccade*, *Salah Ad Deen Al Ayoori* (retained by Italy and at least two sold to Morocco in 1992)

Patrol Forces

1991　1 Osa I (to Iran), 5 Osa II (one to Iran), 6 P 6, 3 SO 1, 1 Poluchat I, 3 Zhuk, 8 PO 2, 1 Bogomol (to Iran), 3 PB 90, 1 Winchester Hovercraft, 6 Rotork Type 412
1992　3 PB 90

Mine Warfare Forces

1991　1 Yevgenya, 1 T 43

Amphibious Forces

1991　3 Polnochny (one to Iran)

FRIGATES

Notes: 1. Four Modified Lupo class frigates completed between 1985 and 1988 were not transferred and are being taken on by the Italian Navy.
2. Two Jianghu class frigates were to have been acquired from China in 1991 and this contract may be honoured in due course.

2 ASSAD CLASS

Name	No	Builders	Laid down	Launched	Completed
MUSSA BEN NUSSAIR	F 210	Fincantieri, Muggiano	15 Jan 1982	22 Oct 1982	17 Sep 1986
TARIQ IBN ZIAD	F 212	Fincantieri, Muggiano	20 May 1982	8 July 1983	29 Oct 1986

Displacement, tons: 685 full load
Dimensions, feet (metres): 204.4 × 30.5 × 8 *(62.3 × 9.3 × 2.5)*
Main machinery: 4 MTU 20V 956 TB92 diesels; 20 120 hp(m) *(14.8 MW)* sustained; 4 shafts
Speed, knots: 37. **Range, miles:** 4000 at 18 kts
Complement: 51 (without aircrew)

Missiles: SSM: 2 OTO Melara/Matra Otomat Teseo Mk 2 (fitted for).
SAM: 1 Selenia/Elsag Albatros launcher (4 cell—2 reloads); Aspide; semi-active radar homing to 13 km *(7 nm)* at 2.5 Mach; height envelope 15-5000 m *(49.2-16 405 ft)*; warhead 30 kg.
Guns: 1 OTO Melara 3 in *(76 mm)*/62 compact; 85° elevation; 85 rounds/minute to 16 km *(8.7 nm)* anti-surface; 12 km *(6.6 nm)* anti-aircraft; weight of shell 6 kg.
2 Breda 40 mm/70 (twin) (not in helicopter ships); 85° elevation; 300 rounds/minute to 12.5 km *(6.8 nm)*; weight of shell 0.96 kg.
Countermeasures: Decoys: 2 Breda 105 mm six-tubed fixed multi-purpose launchers; chaff to 5 km *(2.7 nm)*; illuminants to 12 km *(6.6 nm)*.
ESM: Selenia INS-3; intercept.
ECM: Selenia TQN-2; jammer.
Combat data systems: Selenia IPN-10; action data automation.
Fire control: 2 Selenia 21 (for SAM); Dardo (for guns).
Radars: Air/surface search: Selenia RAN 12L/X; D/I band; range 82 km *(45 nm)*.
Navigation: SMA SPN 703 (3 RM 20); I band; range 73 km *(40 nm)*.
Fire control: 2 Selenia RTN 10X; I/J band; range 40 km *(22 nm)*.
Sonars: KAe ASO 84-41; hull-mounted; active search and attack.

Helicopters: 1 Agusta AB 212 type.

Programmes: Ordered in February 1981. Formally handed over in 1986 but without operational weapon systems. Started trials with Iraqi crews in mid-1990 but the invasion of Kuwait brought to a halt any prospects of final delivery until UN embargoes are lifted. Four other similar ships (but without helicopter facilities) were not paid for and are now being sold, at least two to Morocco.
Structure: Flight deck and telescopic hangar, similar to Ecuadorean Esmeraldas class.
Operational: Moored at La Spezia.

TARIQ IBN ZIAD　　　　　　　　　　　　　　　　　　*4/1990, van Ginderen Collection*

Frigates — Light forces / IRAQ   313

1 YUGOSLAV TYPE

Name	No	Builders	Laid down	Launched	Commissioned
IBN MARJID (ex-*Ibn Khaldoum*)	507	Uljanic, Yugoslavia	1977	1978	20 Mar 1980

Displacement, tons: 1850 full load
Dimensions, feet (metres): 317.3 × 36.7 × 14.8 *(96.7 × 11.2 × 4.5)*
Main machinery: CODOG; 1 RR Olympus TM3B gas turbine; 21 500 hp *(16 MW)* sustained; 2 MTU 16V 956 TB91 diesels; 7500 hp(m) *(5.5 MW)* sustained; 2 shafts
Speed, knots: 26 gas; 20 diesels. **Range, miles:** 4000 at 20 kts
Complement: 93 plus 100 trainees

Missiles: Can carry 4 Aerospatiale SSM Exocet ❶ (but not fitted).
Guns: 1 Bofors 57 mm/70 ❷. 1 Bofors 40 mm/70 ❸. 8 Oerlikon 20 mm (4 twin) ❹.
Torpedoes: Fitted for 2—21 in *(533 mm)* tubes.
Depth charges: 1 rail.
Countermeasures: ESM/ECM: Radar intercept and jammer.
Radars: Surface search/navigation: Two Racal Decca 1229 ❺; I band.
Fire control: Philips Elektronik 9LV200 Mk 2 ❻; J band.
Sonars: Hull-mounted; active search and attack; medium frequency.

IBN MARJID   *(Scale 1 : 900), Ian Sturton*

Structure: Near sister to Indonesian *Hajar Dewantara* but with no helicopter deck. Training ship with frigate capability.
Operational: Mainly used as a training ship and transport during war with Iran. Subsequently used mostly as an accommodation and supply ship and is unlikely to become operational again as a frigate. The superstructure was badly damaged during the Gulf War in 1991.

LIGHT FORCES

Note: In addition to the vessels listed, there are two damaged SO 1 class patrol craft and three Rotork craft which may be salvaged. One ex-Kuwaiti TNC-45 is also moored but looks to be beyond repair.

1 SOVIET OSA I CLASS (TYPE 205) (FAST ATTACK CRAFT—MISSILE)

Displacement, tons: 210 full load
Dimensions, feet (metres): 126.6 × 24.9 × 8.8 *(38.6 × 7.6 × 2.7)*
Main machinery: 3 Type M 503A diesels; 8025 hp(m) *(5.9 MW)* sustained; 3 shafts
Speed, knots: 35. **Range, miles:** 400 at 34 kts
Complement: 30
Missiles: SSM: SS-N-2A Styx; active radar or IR homing to 46 km *(25 nm)* at 0.9 Mach; warhead 513 kg.
Guns: 4—30 mm/65 (2 twin); 85° elevation; 500 rounds/minute to 5 km *(2.7 nm)*; weight of shell 0.54 kg.
Radars: Surface search/fire control: Square Tie; I band.
Fire control: Drum Tilt; H/I band.

Comment: A surprising survivor from the Gulf War but operational in late 1992. A second of class defected to Iran together with an Osa II but only the latter had joined the Iranian Navy by early 1993.

OSA I   1989

1 SOVIET BOGOMOL CLASS (LARGE PATROL CRAFT)

Displacement, tons: 245 full load
Dimensions, feet (metres): 127.9 × 25.6 × 5.9 *(39 × 7.8 × 1.8)*
Main machinery: 3 Type M 504 diesels; 10 800 hp(m) *(7.94 MW)* sustained; 3 shafts
Speed, knots: 37. **Range, miles:** 500 at 35 kts
Complement: 30
Guns: 1 USSR 3 in *(76 mm)*/66; 85° elevation; 120 rounds/minute to 15 km *(8 nm)*; weight of shell 7 kg.
2 USSR 30 mm/65 (twin); 85° elevation; 500 rounds/minute to 5 km *(2.7 nm)*; weight of shell 0.54 kg.
Radars: Surface search: Pot Head; H/I band.
Fire control: Bass Tilt; H/I band.

Comment: Delivered in March 1990. Similar to craft delivered to Guinea and Guinea-Bissau. Another of this class defected to Iran in 1992. Doubtful operational status in 1993.

3 THORNYCROFT TYPE (COASTAL PATROL CRAFT)

Displacement, tons: 40 full load
Dimensions, feet (metres): 78 × 15.5 × 4.5 *(23.8 × 4.7 × 1.4)*
Main machinery: 2 diesels; 1116 hp *(833 kW)*; 2 shafts
Speed, knots: 20. **Range, miles:** 700 at 15 kts
Complement: 12
Guns: 1—12.7 mm MG.
Radars: Surface search: Decca 202; I band.

Comment: Acquired by Kuwait in early 1970s and captured in 1991.

THORNYCROFT Type   1982

1 Ex-SOVIET POLUCHAT I CLASS (LARGE PATROL CRAFT)

Displacement, tons: 70 standard; 100 full load
Dimensions, feet (metres): 97.1 × 19 × 4.8 *(29.6 × 5.8 × 1.5)*
Main machinery: 2 Type M 50 diesels; 2200 hp(m) *(1.6 MW)* sustained; 2 shafts
Speed, knots: 20. **Range, miles:** 1500 at 10 kts
Complement: 20
Guns: 2—14.5 mm (twin) MGs.
Radars: Surface search: Spin Trough; I band.

Comment: Transferred by the USSR in late 1960s. Also used for torpedo recovery.

2 Ex-SOVIET ZHUK CLASS (COASTAL PATROL CRAFT)

Displacement, tons: 50 full load
Dimensions, feet (metres): 75.4 × 17 × 6.2 *(23 × 5.2 × 1.9)*
Main machinery: 2 Type M 50 diesels; 2200 hp(m) *(1.6 MW)* sustained; 2 shafts
Speed, knots: 30. **Range, miles:** 1100 at 15 kts
Complement: 17
Guns: 4—14.5 mm (2 twin) MGs. 1—12.7 mm MG.
Radars: Surface search: Spin Trough; I band.
IFF: High Pole B.

Comment: Transferred in 1975. Survivors of a class of five. Both still in need of repair in late 1992.

ZHUK   1981

3 PB 90 CLASS (COASTAL PATROL CRAFT)

Displacement, tons: 90
Dimensions, feet (metres): 100 × 19.5 × 10 *(30.5 × 5.9 × 3.1)*
Main machinery: 3 diesels; 4290 hp(m) *(3.15 MW)*; 3 shafts
Speed, knots: 27. **Range, miles:** 800 at 20 kts
Complement: 17
Guns: 1 Bofors 40 mm/70. 4 Oerlikon 20 mm (quad). 2 twin 128 mm MRL.
Countermeasures: Decoys: 2 twin-barrelled chaff launchers.
Radars: Surface search: Decca 1226; I band.

Comment: Built by Tito, Yugoslavia. Four of the class delivered via Kuwait in July 1984 and the remainder in 1985. Six sunk in war with Iran, and three more in Desert Storm. Three more scrapped in 1992 leaving three survivors.

PB 90 Type   1986

314 IRAQ / Light forces — Services forces

4 SRN 6 MK 6 WINCHESTER CLASS (HOVERCRAFT)

Displacement, tons: 10.9 full load
Dimensions, feet (metres): 48.4 × 23 × 3.9 (skirt) *(14.8 × 7 × 1.2)*
Main machinery: 1 RR Gnome Model GT; 1050 hp *(783 kW)* sustained
Speed, knots: 60. **Range, miles:** 170 at 54 kts
Complement: 3
Guns: 1—12.7 mm MG.

Comment: Six built by British Hovercraft, Cowes in 1981. Can carry five tons of cargo plus 20 troops. Two destroyed in Desert Storm.

70 + SAWARI CLASS (INSHORE PATROL BOATS)

Comment: This is a range of Iraqi-built boats, the largest types being Sawari 4 of 7 tons (11 × 2.5 × 0.6 m) and 22 kts and Sawari 6 of 12.5 m and 25 kts. Most have outboard engines and are capable of 25 kts in calm conditions. Used as patrol boats and landing craft armed with MGs and rocket launchers. Five exported to Djibouti in 1989.

MINE WARFARE FORCES

Note: One ex-Soviet T 43 minesweeper is possibly still available, but in poor condition.

2 Ex-SOVIET YEVGENYA CLASS (MINEHUNTERS—INSHORE)

Displacement, tons: 90 full load
Dimensions, feet (metres): 80.7 × 18 × 4.9 *(24.6 × 5.5 × 1.5)*
Main machinery: 2 Type 3-D-12 diesels; 600 hp(m) *(440 kW)* sustained; 2 shafts
Speed, knots: 11. **Range, miles:** 300 at 10 kts
Complement: 10
Guns: 2—25 mm/80 (twin).
Radars: Navigation: Spin Trough; I band.
IFF: High Pole.
Sonars: Helo type VDS (on stern); minehunting; high frequency.

Comment: GRP hulls. Delivered in January 1975 under cover-name of 'oceanographic craft'. One sunk in Desert Storm; these two damaged but have been repaired.

3 YUGOSLAV NESTIN CLASS (MINESWEEPERS—INSHORE)

Displacement, tons: 72 full load
Dimensions, feet (metres): 88.6 × 21.3 × 3.9 *(27 × 6.5 × 1.2)*
Main machinery: 2 Torpedo 12-cyl diesels; 520 hp(m) *(382 kW)*; 2 shafts
Speed, knots: 12. **Range, miles:** 860 at 11 kts
Complement: 17
Guns: 3 Hispano 20 mm (triple). 2 Hispano 20 mm.
Mines: Can lay 24.
Radars: Navigation: I band.

Comment: Built Brodotehnika, Belgrade. Transferred 1979-80. Have magnetic, acoustic and explosive sweep gear. All survived Desert Storm although one was damaged.

NESTIN   1988

SERVICE FORCES

Note: One Polnochny LST was sunk in Desert Storm and one defected to Iran. The third was badly damaged but may be repaired in due course.

3 CHEVERTON LOADMASTERS

Displacement, tons: 350 full load
Dimensions, feet (metres): 108.2 × 33.5 × 5.8 *(33 × 10.2 × 1.8)*
Main machinery: 2 Caterpillar 3412 DTA diesels; 1214 hp *(906 kW)*; 2 shafts
Speed, knots: 10.5. **Range, miles:** 1000 at 10 kts
Complement: 7
Military lift: 60 tons liquid; 90 tons deck cargo

Comment: Built for Kuwait in 1985 and captured in 1991. Probably only two are fully operational. A fourth was sunk in Desert Storm.

LOADMASTER   1985

1 STROMBOLI CLASS (REPLENISHMENT TANKER)

Name	No	Builders	Commissioned
AGNADEEN	A 102	Castellamare di Stabia, Naples	29 Oct 1984

Displacement, tons: 3556 light; 8706 full load
Dimensions, feet (metres): 423.1 × 59 × 21.3 *(129 × 18 × 6.5)*
Main machinery: 2 GMT A 420.8 H diesels; 9400 hp(m) *(6.91 MW)* sustained; 1 shaft
Speed, knots: 18.5. **Range, miles:** 5080 at 18.5 kts
Complement: 115

Guns: 1 OTO Melara 3 in *(76 mm)*/62; 85° elevation; 60 rounds/minute to 16 km *(8.7 nm)* anti-surface; 5 km *(2.7 nm)* anti-aircraft; weight of shell 6 kg.
Radars: Navigation: SMA 3 RM; I band; range 73 km *(40 nm)*.
Fire control: Selenia RTN 10X; I/J band; range 40 km *(22 nm)*.

Programmes: Ordered 1 February 1981. Laid down 29 January 1982 under sub-contract from Fincantieri, Muggiano. Launched 22 October 1982. Completed 20 December 1983.
Structure: Underway replenishment facilities on both sides of the ship.
Operational: Laid up in Alexandria since 1986 but still capable of going to sea.

AGNADEEN   7/1988

3 TRANSPORT SHIPS

Name	No	Builders	Commissioned
AL ZAHRAA	426	Helsingør SY	21 Apr 1983
KHAWLA	428	Helsingør SY	July 1983
BALQEES	429	Helsingør SY	Oct 1983

Displacement, tons: 5800 full load
Measurement, tons: 3681 gross
Dimensions, feet (metres): 347.8 × 61.7 × 17.4 *(106 × 18.8 × 5.3)*
Main machinery: 2 MTU 12V 1163 TB82 diesels; 6600 hp(m) *(4.85 MW)* sustained; 2 shafts
Speed, knots: 15.5
Complement: 35
Military lift: 250 troops; 16 tanks

Comment: Fitted with helicopter deck. A Ro-Ro design based on civilian requirements and therefore cannot beach. Fitted with a stern ramp capable of handling 55 ton tanks to shore and launching amphibious 41 ton tanks. 55 ton lift between decks. A 1200 ton trim arrangement allows the embarkation of small landing craft. At least one of the class sails under Iraqi Line colours. Based in Aden since Desert Storm but still sea-going.

AL ZAHRAA   1992, van Ginderen Collection

1 SPASILAC CLASS (SALVAGE SHIP)

Name	No	Builders	Commissioned
AKA	A 81 (ex-A 51)	Tito SY, Belgrade	1978

Displacement, tons: 1600 full load
Dimensions, feet (metres): 182 × 37.6 × 12.2 *(55.5 × 11.5 × 3.8)*
Main machinery: 2 diesels; 4340 hp(m) *(3.19 MW)*; 2 shafts; cp props
Speed, knots: 15. **Range, miles:** 1700 at 12 kts
Complement: 50
Guns: 4—14.5 mm MGs.
Radars: Navigation: Racal Decca; I band.

Comment: Similar to Libyan and Yugoslav naval ships. Can carry 750 tons of equipment and liquids. Has facilities for divers. Damaged in Desert Storm but may be repaired.

1 Ex-SOVIET POZHARNY (FIRE BOAT)

A 82

Displacement, tons: 180 full load
Dimensions, feet (metres): 114.5 × 20 × 6 *(34.9 × 6.1 × 1.8)*
Main machinery: 2 Type M 50 diesels; 2200 hp(m) *(1.6 MW)* sustained; 2 shafts
Speed, knots: 10

Comment: Built in the mid-1950s. Survived Desert Storm but in poor repair.

A 82   *1989, Peter Jones*

AKA   *1989, Peter Jones*

1 DIVING TENDER

Displacement, tons: 119 full load
Dimensions, feet (metres): 93.5 × 21 × 5.9 *(28.5 × 6.4 × 1.8)*
Main machinery: 1 MTU 8V 396 TC82 diesel; 870 hp(m) *(640 kW)*; 1 shaft
Speed, knots: 15
Complement: 6

Comment: Built in the Netherlands and completed in October 1980.

1 PRESIDENTIAL YACHT

QADISSIYAT SADDAM

Displacement, tons: 1660 full load
Dimensions, feet (metres): 269 × 42.8 × 10.8 *(82 × 13 × 3.3)*
Main machinery: 2 MTU 12V 1163 TB82 diesels; 6600 hp(m) *(4.85 MW)*; 2 shafts
Speed, knots: 19

Comment: Built by Helsingør SY, Denmark. Completed September 1981. Helicopter deck. Accommodation for 56 passengers.

IRELAND

Senior Appointment

Flag Officer Commanding Naval Service:
Commodore J Kavanagh

Bases

Haulbowline Island (Cork), Headquarters' naval base and dockyard, sea-going replacement section, ship support and maintenance and communications section. Haulbowline Naval Base and Ballincollig Barracks, Cork, are the centres for all recruit and continuation training. A new training establishment is to be set up at Ringaskiddy in Cork Harbour.

Naval Requirement

If the EEZ is to be policed effectively, the OPV requirement is for 12 vessels (two at 2000 tons, six at 1000 tons and four at 500 tons).

Personnel

Establishment: 1266 (158 officers, 568 petty officers, 540 ratings)
(a) 1993: Currently under strength at 1040 (135 officers)
(b) Voluntary service

Operational

All seven ships are in full commission in 1993.

Prefix to Ships' Names

L. É (Long Éirennach = Irish Ship)

Mercantile Marine

Lloyd's Register of Shipping:
189 vessels of 197 579 tons gross

CORVETTE

1 + (1) EITHNE CLASS

Name	No	Builders	Laid down	Launched	Commissioned
EITHNE	P 31	Verolme, Cork	15 Dec 1982	19 Dec 1983	7 Dec 1984

Displacement, tons: 1760 standard; 1910 full load
Dimensions, feet (metres): 265 × 39.4 × 14.1 *(80.8 × 12 × 4.3)*
Main machinery: 2 Ruston 12RKC diesels; 6800 hp *(5.07 MW)* sustained; 2 shafts
Speed, knots: 20+; 19 normal. **Range, miles:** 7000 at 15 kts
Complement: 85 (9 officers)

Guns: 1 Bofors 57 mm/70 Mk 1 ❶; 75° elevation; 200 rounds/minute to 17 km *(9.3 nm)*; weight of shell 2.4 kg.
2 Rheinmetall 20 mm/20 ❷.
2 Wallop 57 mm launchers for illuminants.
Fire control: Signaal LIOD director ❸.
Radars: Air/surface search: Signaal DA 05 Mk 4 ❹; E/F band; range 137 km *(75 nm)* for 2 m² target.
Navigation: Two Racal Decca ❺; I band.
IFF: MEL RRB transponder.
Sonars: Plessey PMS 26; hull-mounted; lightweight; active search and attack; 10 kHz.

Helicopters: 1 SA 365F Dauphin 2 ❻.

Programmes: Ordered 23 April 1982 from Verolme, Cork, this was the last ship to be built at this yard. A bid for funding a second of class is to be made to the EC in 1993.
Structure: Fitted with retractable stabilisers. Closed circuit TV for flight deck operations. Satellite navigation and communications.
Operational: Manpower problems have made it difficult to operate the helicopter but progress is being made with naval aircrew training.

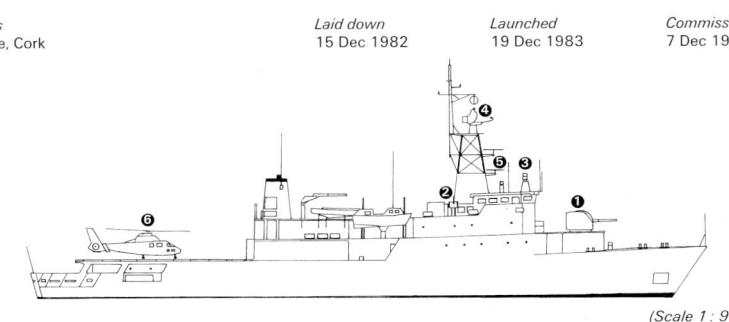

EITHNE   *(Scale 1 : 900), Ian Sturton*

EITHNE   *1991, T Smith, Irish Navy*

PATROL FORCES

4 P 21 and DEIRDRE CLASSES

Name	No	Builders	Commissioned
DEIRDRE	P 20	Verolme, Cork	19 June 1972
EMER	P 21	Verolme, Cork	16 Jan 1978
AOIFE	P 22	Verolme, Cork	29 Nov 1979
AISLING	P 23	Verolme, Cork	21 May 1980

Displacement, tons: 972 *(Deirdre)*; 1019.5 (remainder)
Dimensions, feet (metres): 184.3 pp × 34.1 × 14.4 *(56.2 × 10.4 × 4.4) (Deirdre)*
 213.7 × 34.4 × 14 *(65.2 × 10.5 × 4.4)* (remainder)
Main machinery: 2 British Polar SF112 VS-F diesels; 4200 hp *(3.13 MW)*; 1 shaft *(Deirdre)*
 2 SEMT-Pielstick 6 PA6 L 280 diesels; 4800 hp *(3.53 MW)*; 1 shaft (remainder)
Speed, knots: 17. Range, miles: 4000 at 17 kts; 6750 at 12 kts
Complement: 46 (5 officers)

Guns: 1 Bofors 40 mm/60; may be uprated from 120 to 180 rounds/minute.
 2 GAMB-01 20 mm (except *Deirdre*); 60° elevation; 900 rounds/minute to 2 km.
 2—12.7 mm MGs *(Deirdre)*.
Radars: Surface search: Selesmar/Selescan 1024; I band.
Navigation: Racal Decca RM 1229; I band.
Sonars: Simrad Marine; hull-mounted; active search; 34 kHz.

Programmes: *Deirdre* was the first vessel ever built for the Naval Service in Ireland.
Structure: All of Nevesbu design. Stabilisers fitted. *Aoife* and *Aisling* are of similar construction to *Emer* with the addition of a bow thruster and KaMeWa four-bladed skewed propeller. Satellite navigation and communications.
Operational: Decca Mk 53 Navigator and SATNAV. The practice of keeping one in reserve and rotating every six months was stopped at the end of 1990 and all have been operational since then.

DEIRDRE 6/1991, Stefan Terzibaschitsch

AISLING 6/1989, Bram Risseeuw

MISCELLANEOUS

Note: In addition there are a number of mostly civilian manned auxiliaries including: *Seabhac* a small tug acquired in 1983; *Fainleog*, *David F* (built in 1962) and *Fiachdubh* passenger craft, the last two taken over after lease in 1988 and the first in 1983; *Tailte* a Dufour 35 ft sail training yacht bought in 1979 and two elderly training yachts *Nancy Bet* and *Creidne*. *Gray Seal* (ex-*Seaforth Clansman*) is a lighthouse tender operated by the Commissioners of Irish Lights.

2 P 41 PEACOCK CLASS

Name	No	Builders	Commissioned
ORLA (ex-HMS *Swift*)	P 41	Hall Russell, Aberdeen	3 May 1985
CIARA (ex-HMS *Swallow*)	P 42	Hall Russell, Aberdeen	17 Oct 1984

Displacement, tons: 712 full load
Dimensions, feet (metres): 204.1 × 32.8 × 8.9 *(62.6 × 10 × 2.7)*
Main machinery: 2 Crossley SEMT-Pielstick 18 PA6 V 280 diesels; 14 400 hp(m) *(10.58 MW)* sustained; 2 shafts; auxiliary drive; Schottel prop; 181 hp(m) *(133 kW)*
Speed, knots: 25. Range, miles: 2500 at 17 kts
Complement: 39 (6 officers)

Guns: 1—3 in (76 mm)/62 OTO Melara compact; 85° elevation; 85 rounds/minute to 16 km *(8.6 nm)*; weight of shell 6 kg.
 2—12.7 mm MGs. 4—7.62 mm MGs.
Fire control: BAe Sea Archer (for 76 mm).
Radars: Surface search: Kelvin Hughes Type 1006; I band.

Programmes: *Orla* launched 11 September 1984 and *Ciara* 31 March 1984. Both served in Hong Kong from mid-1985 until early 1988. Acquired by the Irish Navy and commissioned 21 November 1988.
Structure: Can carry Sea Rider craft. Have loiter drive. Displacement increased by the addition of more electronic equipment including Satellite navigation and communications.
Operational: Sprint speed is nearly 30 kts. Complement augmented by boarding party personnel.

CIARA 1991, T Smith, Irish Navy

SHIPBORNE AIRCRAFT

Numbers/Type: 5 Aerospatiale SA 365F Dauphin 2.
Operational speed: 140 kts *(260 km/h)*.
Service ceiling: 15 000 ft *(4575 m)*.
Range: 410 nm *(758 km)*.
Role/Weapon systems: Embarked helicopter for MR/SAR tasks in *Eithne*; some shore land-based training by Army Air Corps and SAR. Sensors: Bendix RDR 1500 radar. Weapons: Unarmed.

DAUPHIN 2 1989

LAND-BASED MARITIME AIRCRAFT

Note: 2 civilian operated Sikorsky S-61 helicopters provide long-range SAR services.

Numbers/Type: 1 Casa CN-235.
Operational speed: 210 kts *(384 km/h)*.
Service ceiling: 24 000 ft *(7315 m)*.
Range: 2000 nm *(3218 km)*.
Role/Weapon systems: EEZ surveillance. Delivered in June 1992 with two more to follow in 1993/94 to replace the Beechcraft sold in 1992. Sensors: Search radar Bendix APS 504(V)5 FLIR. Weapons: Unarmed.

ISRAEL

Headquarters' Appointment

Commander-in-Chief:
 Rear Admiral Ami Ayalon

Personnel

(a) 1993: 6600 (900 officers) of whom 2500 are conscripts. Includes a Naval Commando
(b) 3 years' national service for Jews and Druses

Note: An additional 4000 Reserves available on mobilisation.

Bases

Haifa, Ashdod, Eilat
(The repair base at Eilat has a synchrolift)

Prefix to Ships' Names

INS (Israeli Naval Ship)

Deployment

About 7 Dabur class and some smaller vessels are based at Eilat. Remainder of fleet in the Mediterranean.

Strength of the Fleet

Type	Active	Building (Planned)
Patrol Submarines	3	2 (1)
Corvettes	0	3
Fast Attack Craft—Missile	19 (1)	—
Fast Attack Craft—Gun	14	4
Coastal Patrol Craft	14	—
LCTs	3	(2)
LCPs	1	—
Support Ship	1	—

Mercantile Marine

Lloyd's Register of Shipping:
 58 vessels of 652 287 tons gross

DELETIONS

Light Forces

1990 *Saar, Gaash, Herev*, 9 Yatush class
1991 1 Dvora, 10 Super Dvora (6 to Chile, 4 to Fiji)
1992 *Shimrit, Livnit, Snapirit*

Amphibious Forces

1990 2 LCPs
1991 *Etzion Geuber, Shiqmona, Kessaraya*

Support Ship

1991 *Ma'oz*

SUBMARINES

0 + 2 (1) DOLPHIN CLASS

Displacement, tons: 1550 surfaced; 1720 dived
Dimensions, feet (metres): 187 × 22.3 × 20.3
(57 × 6.8 × 6.2)
Main machinery: 3 MTU 16V 396 SE* diesels; 2910 hp(m) *(2.14 MW)* sustained; 1 Siemens motor; 2850 hp(m) *(2.09 MW)* sustained; 1 shaft
Speed, knots: 20 dived; 11 snorting
Complement: 35

Torpedoes: 10—21 in *(533 mm)* bow tubes.
Countermeasures: ESM: Radar warning.
Fire control: Atlas Elektronik or Litton TCS.
Radars: Surface search.
Sonars: Atlas Elektronik; hull-mounted; passive/active search and attack.

Programmes: In mid-1988 Ingalls Shipbuilding Division of Litton Corporation was chosen as the prime contractor for two IKL-designed Dolphin class submarines to be built in West Germany with FMS funds by HDW in conjunction with Thyssen Nordseewerke. Funds approved in July 1989 with an effective contract date of January 1990 but the project was cancelled in November 1990 due to pressures on defence funds. After the Gulf War in April 1991 the contract was resurrected, this time with German funding for two submarines with an option on a third. First steel cut on 15 February 1992 at Kiel by HDW; the hull is to move to Emden for completion by TNSW starting in January 1994. The second hull is following the first by six months. Projected completion in 1997.
Structure: Diving depth at least 200 m *(650 ft)*. Similar to German Type 212 in design but with a 'wet and dry' compartment for underwater swimmers, and a greater torpedo capacity.
Operational: Endurance, 30 days. To be used for interdiction, surveillance and special boat operations.

3 IKL/VICKERS TYPE 540

Name	No	Builders	Laid down	Launched	Commissioned
GAL	—	Vickers Ltd, Barrow	1973	2 Dec 1975	Jan 1977
TANIN	—	Vickers Ltd, Barrow	1974	25 Oct 1976	June 1977
RAHAV	—	Vickers Ltd, Barrow	1974	1977	Dec 1977

Displacement, tons: 420 surfaced; 600 dived
Dimensions, feet (metres): 146.7 × 15.4 × 12
(45 × 4.7 × 3.7)
Main machinery: Diesel-electric; 2 MTU 12V 483 AZ80 GA31L diesels; 1200 hp(m) *(882 kW)* sustained; 2 alternators; 810 kW; 1 motor; 1800 hp(m) *(1.32 MW)* sustained; 1 shaft
Speed, knots: 11 surfaced; 17 dived
Complement: 22
Missiles: SSM: McDonnell Douglas Sub Harpoon launched from torpedo tubes; active radar homing to 130 km *(70 nm)* at 0.9 Mach; warhead 227 kg.
Torpedoes: 8—21 in *(533 mm)* bow tubes. Honeywell NT 37E; active/passive homing to 20 km *(10.8 nm)* at 35 kts; warhead 150 kg. Total of 10 missiles and torpedoes can be embarked.
Countermeasures: ESM: Elisra NS 9034; radar warning.
Fire control: Tios System.
Radars: Surface search: Plessey; I band.
Sonars: Plessey; hull-mounted; passive search and attack; medium/high frequency.

Programmes: A contract was signed by Vickers in April 1972.
Modernisation: Sub Harpoon and associated fire control equipment installed in 1983 and the NT 37E torpedoes replaced the obsolete Mk 37 in 1987-88. A local contract has been let to update sensors and fire control equipment. Atlas Elektronik is the most likely supplier of equipment.

RAHAV   1988

CORVETTES

0 + 3 EILAT (SAAR 5) CLASS

Name	No	Builders	Laid down	Launched	Commissioned
EILAT	501	Ingalls, Pascagoula	24 Feb 1992	9 Feb 1993	Oct 1993
—	502	Ingalls, Pascagoula	25 Sep 1992	1993	Apr 1994
—	503	Ingalls, Pascagoula	Feb 1993	1994	Oct 1994

Displacement, tons: 1075 standard; 1227 full load
Dimensions, feet (metres): 280.8 oa; 251.3 wl × 39 × 10.5
(85.6; 76.6 × 11.9 × 3.2)
Main machinery: CODOG; 1 GE LM 2500 gas turbine; 30 000 hp *(22.38 MW)* sustained; 2 MTU 12V 1163 TB82 diesels; 6600 hp(m) *(4.86 MW)* sustained; 2 shafts; KaMeWa cp props
Speed, knots: 33 gas; 20 diesels. **Range, miles:** 3500 at 17 kts
Complement: 64 (16 officers) plus 10 (4 officers) aircrew

Missiles: SSM: 8 McDonnell Douglas Harpoon (2 quad) launchers ❶; active radar homing to 130 km *(70 nm)* at 0.9 Mach; warhead 227 kg.
8 IAI Gabriel II ❷; radar or optical guidance; semi-active homing to 36 km *(19.4 nm)* at 0.7 Mach; warhead 75 kg.
SAM: 2 Israeli Industries Barak I (vertical launch) ❸; 2 × 32 cells; command line of sight radar or optical guidance to 10 km *(5.5 nm)* at 2 Mach; warhead 22 kg.
Guns: OTO Melara 3 in *(76 mm)*/62 compact ❹; 85° elevation; 85 rounds/minute to 16 km *(8.7 nm)*; weight of shell 6 kg. Interchangeable with a Bofors 57 mm gun or Vulcan Phalanx CIWS.
2 Sea Vulcan 25 mm CIWS ❺; range 1 km.
Torpedoes: 6—324 mm Mk 32 (2 triple) tubes ❻. Honeywell Mk 46; anti-submarine.
Countermeasures: Decoys: 4 chaff launchers ❼; Nixie SLQ 25 towed torpedo decoy
ESM/ECM: Elisra NS 9003/5; intercept and jammer.
Combat data systems: Possibly ELBIT NTCCS using Elta EL/S 9000 computers. Data link.
Fire control: 3 Elop optronic directors ❽.
Radars: Air search ❾.
Air/surface search ❿.
Navigation.
Fire control: 2 Elta EL/M 2221 GM STGR; I/K band ⓫.
Sonars: Hull-mounted; search and attack; medium frequency.
VDS or towed array; active and passive search; medium/low frequency.

Helicopters: 1 Dauphin SA 366G ⓬ or SH-2F or Hellstar RPV.

Programmes: A design (QU-09-35) prepared by Israeli Shipyards, Haifa in conjunction with Ingalls Shipbuilding Division of Litton Corporation which was authorised to act as main contractor using FMS funding. Ships building at Pascagoula with some final fitting out in Israel. Contract awarded 8 February 1989. An option for a fourth is unlikely to be taken up.

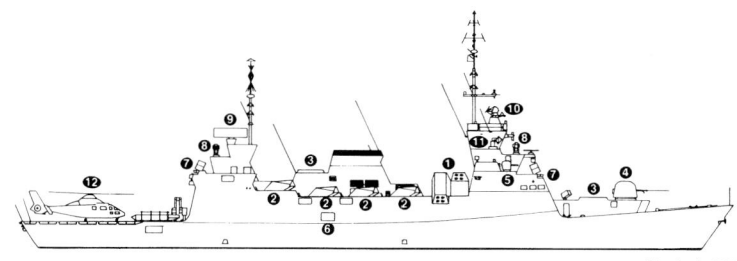

LAHAV   *(Scale 1 : 900), Ian Sturton*

EILAT   2/1993, Ingalls

Structure: Steel hull. Stealth features including resilient mounts for main machinery, and Prairie Masker Bubbler system. A secondary operations room is fitted aft.
Operational: Endurance, 20 days. The main role will be to counter threats in main shipping routes.
Opinion: The Israeli Navy wanted eight in two batches of four so unless more are subsequently ordered, updated versions of the Saar 4 class will be needed to replace some of the other FAC hulls.

318 ISRAEL / Light forces

LIGHT FORCES

Note: The *Shaldag* was launched by Israeli Shipyards on 25 December 1989. This is a 55 ton, 50 kt fast patrol boat demonstrator, which had not been taken into service by the Navy by early 1993.

5 ALIYA/ROMAT/HETZ (SAAR 4.5) CLASS
(FAST ATTACK CRAFT—MISSILE)

Name	Builders	Launched	Commissioned
ALIYA	Israel Shipyards, Haifa	11 July 1980	Aug 1980
GEOULA	Israel Shipyards, Haifa	Oct 1980	31 Dec 1980
ROMAT	Israel Shipyards, Haifa	30 Oct 1981	Oct 1981
KESHET	Israel Shipyards, Haifa	Oct 1982	Nov 1982
HETZ (ex-*Nirit*)	Israel Shipyards, Haifa	Oct 1990	Feb 1991

Displacement, tons: 488 full load
Dimensions, feet (metres): 202.4 × 24.9 × 8.2 *(61.7 × 7.6 × 2.5)*
Main machinery: 4 MTU/Bazán 16V 956 TB91 diesels; 15 000 hp(m) *(11.03 MW)* sustained; 4 shafts
  4 MTU 16V 538 TB93 diesels; 16 600 hp(m) *(12.2 MW)*; 4 shafts *(Hetz)*
Speed, knots: 31. **Range, miles:** 3000 at 17 kts; 1500 at 30 kts
Complement: 53 *(Aliya, Hetz* and *Geoula);* 45 *(Romat* and *Keshet)*

Missiles: SSM: McDonnell Douglas Harpoon; active radar homing to 130 km *(70 nm)* at 0.9 Mach; warhead 227 kg.
  IAI Gabriel II; radar or optical guidance; semi-active radar plus anti-radiation homing to 36 km *(19.4 nm)* at 0.7 Mach; warhead 75 kg.
  4 Harpoon (2 twin) plus 4 Gabriel *(Aliya* and *Geoula).*
  8 Harpoon (2 quad) plus 6 or 8 Gabriel *(Romat, Keshet* and *Hetz).*
SAM: Israeli Industries Barak I (vertical launch) *(Hetz);* 32 cells in four 8 pack launchers; command line-of-sight radar or optical guidance to 10 km *(5.5 nm)* at 2 Mach; warhead 22 kg.
Guns: 1 OTO Melara 3 in *(76 mm)*/62 *(Romat, Keshet* and *Hetz);* 85° elevation; 85 rounds/minute to 16 km *(8.7 nm);* weight of shell 6 kg.
  2 Oerlikon 20 mm; 55° elevation; 800 rounds/minute to 2 km.
  1 General Electric/General Dynamics Vulcan Phalanx 6-barrelled 20 mm Mk 15; 3000 rounds/minute combined to 1.5 km anti-missile.
  2 or 4—12.7 mm (twin or quad) MGs.
Countermeasures: Decoys: 1—45 tube, 4—24 tube, 4 single tube chaff launchers.
ESM/ECM: Elisra NS 9003/5; intercept and jammer.
Combat data systems: IAI Reshet data link.
Radars: Air/surface search: Thomson-CSF TH-D 1040 Neptune; G band; range 33 km *(18 nm)* for 2 m² target.
  Fire control: Selenia Orion RTN-10X; I/J band; range 40 km *(22 nm).*
  Elta EL/M-2221 GM STGR *(Hetz);* I/K band

Helicopters: 1 SA 366G Dauphin reconnaissance for OTH targeting *(Aliya* and *Geoula).* Can be replaced by Hellstar RPV.

Programmes: *Hetz* started construction in 1984 as the fifth of the class but was not completed, as an economy measure. Taken in hand again in 1989 and fitted out as the trials ship for some of the systems to be fitted in the Saar 5 class.
Modernisation: It is reported that *Romat* and *Keshet* and perhaps the other pair are to be fitted with Barak VLS and new fire control radar in due course. The Gabriel III missile did not go into production.
Structure: In the second pair the hangar was replaced by a 76 mm gun aft and four additional Gabriel launchers. The CIWS is mounted in the eyes of the ship in all cases replacing the 40 mm gun. *Hetz* has four 8 pack Barak launchers which are fully containerised and require no deck penetration or onboard maintenance. They are fitted aft in place of two of the Gabriel launchers. She has a quite central mast to house the various new sensors being tested for the Saar 5 class, including the fire control system for Barak, which is to be fitted on the platform aft of the bridge on the port side. The system should be operational by the end of 1993. *Hetz* also has more powerful engines.

KESHET   1990

HETZ   1991, Israel Shipyards

ALIYA   1991

8 RESHEF (SAAR 4) CLASS (FAST ATTACK CRAFT—MISSILE)

Name	Builders	Launched	Commissioned
RESHEF	Israel Shipyards, Haifa	19 Feb 1973	Apr 1973
KIDON	Israel Shipyards, Haifa	4 July 1974	Sep 1974
TARSHISH	Israel Shipyards, Haifa	17 Jan 1975	Mar 1975
YAFFO	Israel Shipyards, Haifa	3 Feb 1975	Apr 1975
NITZHON	Israel Shipyards, Haifa	10 July 1978	Sep 1978
ATSMOUT	Israel Shipyards, Haifa	3 Dec 1978	Feb 1979
MOLEDET	Israel Shipyards, Haifa	22 Mar 1979	May 1979
KOMEMIUT	Israel Shipyards, Haifa	19 July 1978	Aug 1980

Displacement, tons: 415 standard; 450 full load
Dimensions, feet (metres): 190.6 × 25 × 8 *(58 × 7.8 × 2.4)*
Main machinery: 4 MTU/Bazán 16V 956 TB91 diesels; 15 000 hp(m) *(11.03 MW)* sustained; 4 shafts
Speed, knots: 32. **Range, miles:** 1650 at 30 kts; 4000 at 17.5 kts
Complement: 45

Missiles: SSM: 2-4 McDonnell Douglas Harpoon (twin or quad) launchers; active radar homing to 130 km *(70 nm)* at 0.9 Mach; warhead 227 kg.
  4-6 Gabriel II or III; radar or TV optical guidance; semi-active radar plus anti-radiation homing to 36 km *(20 nm)* at 0.7 Mach; warhead 75 kg.
  Harpoons fitted with Israeli homing systems. The Gabriel II system carries a TV camera which can transmit a homing picture to the firing ship beyond the radar horizon. The missile fit currently varies in training boats—2 Harpoon, 5 Gabriel II.
Guns: 1 or 2 OTO Melara 3 in *(76 mm)*/62 compact; 85° elevation; 85 rounds/minute to 16 km *(8.7 nm);* weight of shell 6 kg. Adapted for shore bombardment.
  2 Oerlikon 20 mm; 55° elevation; 800 rounds/minute to 2 km.
  1 General Electrics/General Dynamics Vulcan Phalanx 6-barrelled 20 mm Mk 15 (fitted fwd of the bridge); 3000 rounds/minute combined to 1.5 km anti-missile.
  2—12.7 mm MGs.
Countermeasures: Decoys: 1—45 tube, 4 or 6—24 tube, 4 single tube chaff launchers.
ESM: Elta MN-53; intercept.
ECM: Jammer.
Combat data systems: IAI Reshet data link.
Radars: Air/surface search: Thomson-CSF TH-D 1040 Neptune; G band; range 33 km *(18 nm)* for 2 m² target.
  Fire control: Selenia Orion RTN 10X; I/J band; range 40 km *(22 nm).*
Sonars: EDO 780; VDS; occasionally fitted in some of the class.

Helicopters: *Tarshish* had her after 76 mm gun removed to make way for a helicopter platform, temporary trial in 1979, but there is an option for replacing the after gun with a Hellstar RPV.

Modernisation: It is planned to replace Vulcan Phalanx by the Barak SAM system. VDS sonars can be fitted. Gabriel III SSM did not go into production.
Operational: This very interesting class has a long range at cruising speed, two pairs having made the passage from Israel to the Red Sea via the Strait of Gibraltar and Cape of Good Hope, relying only on refuelling at sea. This is a tribute not only to their endurance but also to their seakeeping qualities. All now deployed in Mediterranean.
Sales: Eight of this class built for South Africa in Haifa and Durban. One transferred to Chile late 1979 and one in February 1981.

RESHEF   19

6 MIVTACH (SAAR 2) and 1 SAAR (SAAR 3) CLASSES
(FAST ATTACK CRAFT—MISSILE)

Name	No	Builders	Commissioned
Saar 2			
MIVTACH	311	CMN, Cherbourg	1968
MIZNAG	312	CMN, Cherbourg	1968
MIFGAV	313	CMN, Cherbourg	1968
EILATH	321	CMN, Cherbourg	1968
HAIFA	322	CMN, Cherbourg	1968
AKKO	323	CMN, Cherbourg	1968
Saar 3			
SOUFA	332	CMN, Cherbourg	1969

Displacement, tons: 220 standard; 250 full load
Dimensions, feet (metres): 147.6 × 23 × 8.2 *(45 × 7 × 2.5)*
Main machinery: 4 MTU MD 16V 538 TB90 diesels; 12 000 hp(m) *(8.82 MW)* sustained; 4 shafts
Speed, knots: 40+. **Range, miles:** 2500 at 15 kts; 1600 at 20 kts; 1000 at 30 kts
Complement: 35-40 (5 officers)

Missiles: SSM: 2 or 4 McDonnell Douglas Harpoon; active radar homing to 130 km *(70 nm)* at 0.9 Mach; warhead 227 kg. Harpoon is replacing Gabriel to reduce top weight.
6 or 3 IAI Gabriel II; active radar or optical guidance; semi-active radar homing to 36 km *(19.4 nm)* at 0.7 Mach; warhead 75 kg.
Guns: 1 OTO Melara 3 in *(76 mm)*/62 DP; 85° elevation; 65 rounds/minute to 8 km *(4.4 nm)*; weight of shell 6 kg.
1-3 Breda 40 mm/70; 85° elevation; 300 rounds/minute to 4 km *(2.2 nm)* anti-aircraft; weight of shell 0.96 kg (see *Operational*).
2 or 4—12.7 mm MGs.
Torpedoes: 2 or 4—324 mm Mk 32 tubes (Saar 2 class only and not fitted in all). Honeywell Mk 46; anti-submarine; active/passive homing to 11 km *(5.9 nm)* at 40 kts; warhead 44 kg.
Countermeasures: Decoys: 6—24 tube, 4 single tube chaff launchers.
ESM: Elta MN-53; intercept.
ECM: Jammer.
Combat data systems: IAI Reshet data link.
Radars: Air/surface search: Thomson-CSF TH-D 1040 Neptune; G band; range 33 km *(18 nm)* for 2 m² target. Being replaced.
Fire control: Selenia Orion RTN 10X; I/J band; range 40 km *(22 nm)*.
Sonars: EDO 780 (Saar 2 class only and not fitted in all); VDS; active search and attack; 13.7 and 5 kHz.

Programmes: Built from designs by Lürssen Werft of Bremen. Political problems caused their building in France instead of West Germany. Two batches: the first six being ordered in 1965, the second six in 1966. Five of these ships were delivered to Israel after the 1969 French arms embargo and two *(Akko* and *Saar)* made the journey on completion of local trials. The last five arrived off Haifa in January 1970 after a much-publicised passage which began on Christmas Eve off the west coast of France and proved the remarkable endurance of this class.
Structure: Steel hulls and light alloy superstructure. The class suffers from top weight problems, being alleviated to some extent by substituting Harpoon for Gabriel and fitting a lightweight radar aerial.
Operational: Saar 2 can mount an armament varying from one 40 mm gun and Harpoon or Gabriel missiles to three 40 mm guns and four A/S torpedo tubes plus VDS. Saar 3 can mount Harpoon and Gabriel missiles as well as the 76 mm gun forward but does not have sonar. The plan was for Saar 2 to concentrate on ASW and to pay off Saar 3 as Saar 5 are commissioned, but by early 1991 all but one of the Saar 3 were already paid off and by early 1992 even that one was permanently moored.
Sales: *Hanit* and *Hetz* (Saar 3 class) transferred to Chile in 1988; more may follow if funds become available.

SAAR 2 (with torpedo tubes)   1989

14 + 4 SUPER DVORA CLASS (FAST ATTACK CRAFT—GUN)

810-821

Displacement, tons: 54 full load
Dimensions, feet (metres): 71 × 18 × 5.9 screws *(21.6 × 5.5 × 1.8)*
Main machinery: 2 MTU 12V 396 TB93 diesels; 3260 hp(m) *(2.4 MW)* sustained; 2 shafts (Mk I)
2 Detroit 16V-92TA diesels; 1380 hp *(1.03 MW)* sustained; 2 shafts (Mk II)
3 Detroit 16V-92TA diesels; 2070 hp *(1.54 MW)* sustained; 3 shafts (Mk III)
Speed, knots: 36 or 46 (Mk III). **Range, miles:** 1200 at 17 kts
Complement: 9 (1 officer)

Guns: 2 Oerlikon 20 mm/80. 2—12.7 or 7.62 mm MGs. 1—84 mm rocket launcher.
Depth charges: 2 racks.
Fire control: Elop optronic director.
Radars: Surface search: Raytheon; I band.

Programmes: A further improvement on the Dabur design ordered in March 1987 from Israeli Aircraft Industries (RAMTA). First started trials in November 1988, and first two commissioned in June 1989. Remainder following at about two to four per year.
Structure: All gun armament and improved speed and endurance compared with the prototype Dvora. SSM, depth charges, torpedoes or a 130 mm MRL can be fitted if required. The first 10 are probably Mk I and II with the much faster Mk III version coming in at about hull number 11.
Sales: The Mk III version is being deployed to the US to bid for the USN Mk V SEALS contract planned for FY 1993.

SAAR 2 (with VDS)   1990

SUPER DVORA   1989, Israeli Aircraft Industries

SAAR 2 (both with VDS, one with new radar aerial)   10/1992, Erik Laursen

SUPER DVORA   10/1992, Erik Laursen

320 ISRAEL / Light forces — Support ship

14 DABUR CLASS (COASTAL PATROL CRAFT)

Displacement, tons: 39 full load
Dimensions, feet (metres): 64.9 × 18 × 5.8 *(19.8 × 5.5 × 1.8)*
Main machinery: 2 GM 12V-71TA diesels; 840 hp *(627 kW)* sustained; 2 shafts
  About 6 have more powerful GE engines.
Speed, knots: 19; 30 (GE engines). **Range, miles:** 450 at 13 kts
Complement: 6/9 depending on armament

Guns: 2 Oerlikon 20 mm; 55° elevation; 800 rounds/minute to 2 km.
  2—12.7 mm MGs. Carl Gustav 84 mm portable rocket launchers.
Torpedoes: 2—324 mm tubes. Honeywell Mk 46; anti-submarine; active/passive homing to 11 km *(5.9 nm)* at 40 kts; warhead 44 kg.
Depth charges: 2 racks in some.
Fire control: Elop optronic director.
Radars: Surface search: Decca Super 101 Mk 3; I band.
Sonars: Active search and attack; high frequency.

Programmes: Twelve built by Sewart Seacraft USA and remainder by Israel Aircraft Industries (RAMTA) between 1973 and 1977. Final total of 34.
Structure: Aluminium hull. Several variations in the armament. Seven of the class are fitted with more powerful General Electric engines to increase speed to 30 kts.
Operational: Deployed in the Mediterranean and Red Sea, these craft have been designed for over-land transport. Good rough weather performance. Portable rocket launchers are carried for anti-terrorist purposes. Not considered fast enough to cope with modern terrorist speedboats and are being sold as more Super Dvoras are commissioned.
Sales: Four to Argentina in 1978; four to Nicaragua in 1978; two to Sri Lanka in 1984; four to Fiji and six to Chile in 1991. Five also given to Lebanon Christian Militia in 1976 but these were returned.

DABUR 882 *5/1989, Rupert Pengelley*

SHIPBORNE AIRCRAFT

Numbers/Type: 2 Aerospatiale SA 366G Dauphin.
Operational speed: 140 kts *(260 km/h)*.
Service ceiling: 15 000 ft *(4575 m)*.
Range: 410 nm *(758 km)*.
Role/Weapon systems: SAR/MR helicopter embarked for trials; primarily SAR/MR but growing submarine threat could mean upgrading; 20 more on order in 1987. Sensors: Israeli-designed radar/FLIR systems. Weapons: Unarmed at present but plans for ASV/ASW.

DAUPHIN *1986, Ofer Karni*

Numbers/Type: IAI/Mata Hellstar.
Operational speed: 55 kts *(102 km/h)*.
Service ceiling: 15 000 ft *(4575 m)*.
Range: 245 nm *(454 km)*.
Role/Weapons systems: Unmanned reconnaissance and surveillance helicopter, started trials in July 1990. Sensors: Israeli-designed radar/FLIR systems with data link; Elop optronic trackers. Weapons: ASV/ASW in due course.

HELLSTAR *1991, IAI*

Numbers/Type: 6 Agusta AB 206B JetRanger.
Operational speed: 115 kts *(213 km/h)*.
Service ceiling: 13 500 ft *(4115 m)*.
Range: 368 nm *(682 km)*.
Role/Weapon systems: Liaison and limited SAR helicopter. Sensors: None. Weapons: Unarmed.

LAND-BASED MARITIME AIRCRAFT

Note: Army helicopters can be used including Cobras.

Numbers/Type: 25 Bell 212.
Operational speed: 100 kts *(185 km/h)*.
Service ceiling: 13 200 ft *(4025 m)*.
Range: 224 nm *(415 km)*.
Role/Weapon systems: SAR and coastal helicopter surveillance tasks undertaken. Sensors: IAI EW systems. Weapons: Unarmed except for self-defence machine guns.

Numbers/Type: 4 Grumman E-2C Hawkeye.
Operational speed: 269 kts *(499 km/h)*.
Service ceiling: 30 800 ft *(9390 m)*.
Range: 1350 nm *(2500 km)*.
Role/Weapon systems: Airborne early warning and control aircraft; operated for air defence and strike direction by the Air Force. Sensors: APS-125 radar, various EW systems. Weapons: Unarmed.

Numbers/Type: 3 IAI 1124 Sea Scan.
Operational speed: 471 kts *(873 km/h)*.
Service ceiling: 45 000 ft *(13 725 m)*.
Range: 2500 nm *(4633 km)*.
Role/Weapon systems: Coastal surveillance tasks with long endurance; used for intelligence gathering. Sensors: Include radar, IFF, MAD and various EW systems of IAI manufacture.

AMPHIBIOUS FORCES

Note: Two new construction landing ships are planned by the Navy to transport large numbers of troops. No funds available. A Ro-Ro ship may be in use for research and development.

3 ASHDOD CLASS (LCTs)

Name	No	Builders	Commissioned
ASHDOD	61	Israel Shipyards, Haifa	1966
ASHKELON	63	Israel Shipyards, Haifa	1967
ACHZIV	65	Israel Shipyards, Haifa	1967

Displacement, tons: 400 standard; 730 full load
Dimensions, feet (metres): 205.5 × 32.8 × 5.8 *(62.7 × 10 × 1.8)*
Main machinery: 3 MWM diesels; 1900 hp(m) *(1.4 MW)*; 3 shafts
Speed, knots: 10.5
Complement: 20
Guns: 2 Oerlikon 20 mm.

Comment: At least one has a helicopter deck aft. *Ashdod* was an early trials ship for Barak VLS.

ASHDOD *198*

1 Ex-US LCP TYPE

Displacement, tons: 24 full load
Dimensions, feet (metres): 52.5 × 14.4 × 5.6 *(16 × 4.4 × 1.7)*
Main machinery: 2 Saturn gas turbines; 2000 hp *(1.49 MW)*; 2 shafts
Speed, knots: 35
Complement: 8
Military lift: 22 troops; 1 ton equipment

Comment: The survivor of four transferred in 1968. Used for swimmer operations.

SUPPORT SHIP

1 BAT SHEVA CLASS (TRANSPORT)

Name	No	Builders	Commissioned
BAT SHEVA	—	Netherlands	1967

Displacement, tons: 1150 full load
Dimensions, feet (metres): 311.7 × 36.7 × 26.9 *(95.1 × 11.2 × 8.2)*
Main machinery: 2 diesels; 2 shafts
Speed, knots: 10
Complement: 26
Guns: 4 Oerlikon 20 mm. 4—12.7 mm MGs.

Comment: Purchased from South Africa in 1968.

ITALY

Headquarters' Appointments

Chief of Naval Staff:
 Admiral Guido Venturoni
Vice Chief of Naval Staff:
 Admiral Gianfranco Ginesi
Chief of Naval Personnel:
 Vice Admiral Enrico Siviero
Chief of Procurement and Technical Support:
 Engineer Admiral Alberto Pacini

Principal Commands

Commander, Allied Naval Forces, Southern Europe (Naples) and
 Commander-in-Chief Basso Tirreno:
  Admiral Carlo Alberto Vandini
Commander-in-Chief of Fleet (and Comedcent):
  Admiral Angelo Mariani
Commander-in-Chief Alto Tirreno (La Spezia):
  Admiral Mario Strigini
Commander-in-Chief Adriatico (Ancona):
  Vice Admiral Achille Zanoni
Commander-in-Chief dello Jonio e Canale d'Otranto (Taranto):
  Admiral Alfeo Battelli
Commander Sicilian Naval Area (Messina):
  Vice Admiral Umberto Battigelli
Commander Sardinian Naval Area (La Maddalena):
  Vice Admiral Franco di Girolamo
Commander Submarine Force:
  Captain Armando Molaschi
1st Naval Division:
  Rear Admiral Leandro Papa
2nd Naval Division:
  Rear Admiral Paolo Mancinelli
3rd Naval Division:
  Rear Admiral Vincenzo Pellegrino
Naval Commandos and Special Naval Group (La Spezia):
  Rear Admiral Vezio Vascotto
Mine Countermeasures Force:
  Captain Franco Eccher
Naval Training Command:
  Rear Admiral Gianfranco Coviello

Diplomatic Representation

Naval Attaché in Bonn:
  Captain Attilio Panella-Fabrello
Naval Attaché in London:
  Captain Mario Maguolo
Naval Attaché in Moscow:
  Captain Franco Paoli
Naval Attaché in Paris:
  Captain Gianluca Assettati
Naval Attaché in Washington:
  Captain Luciano Callini

Bases

Main—La Spezia (Alto Tirreno), Taranto (Jonio e Canale d'Otranto)
Regional—Ancona (Adriatico), Naples (Basso Tirreno)
Secondary—Brindisi, Augusta, Messina, La Maddalena, Cagliari, Venice

Organisation

Name	Base	Units
First Division	La Spezia	Major warships
Second Division	Taranto	Major warships
Third Division	Brindisi	Amphibious ships; Hydrofoils
Submarine Command	Taranto	Submarines
Mine Countermeasures Command	La Spezia	MCMVs

In addition there is a 'Special Force and Underwater Swimmers (COMSUBIN)' including Commandos plus support and minor craft, located near La Spezia. The former Auxiliary Force has been disbanded.

Strength of the Fleet

Type	Active	Building (Planned)
Submarines	8	2 (2)
Light Aircraft Carrier	1	(1)
Cruisers	1	—
Destroyers	4	—
Frigates	14	4
Corvettes	9	(4)
Offshore Patrol Vessels	10	—
Hydrofoils—Missile	6	—
LPDs	2	1
Minehunters/sweepers—Ocean	7	5
Minesweepers/hunters—Coastal	5	—
Survey/Research Vessels	3	2
Replenishment Tankers	2	(1)
Harbour Tankers	7	—
Experimental Ships	4	—
Fleet Support Ship	1	—
Coastal Transports	8	—
Commando Support Craft	2	—
Transports (MTM/MTP/MEN)	41	—
Sail Training Ships	6	—
Training Ships	6	—
Lighthouse Tenders	5	—
Salvage Ships	2	—
Repair Craft	5	—
Large Water Carriers	11	2
Tugs	51	—
Floating Docks	14	—

Personnel

(a) 1993: 49 000 (5500 officers) plus 1900 Naval Air Arm and 3500 marines
(b) 1 year's national service (about 20 000 of the Navy are conscripts)

Naval Air Arm—Planned strength and deployment

2 LRMP Squadrons—Bréguet Atlantique (No 41, Catania; No 30, Cagliari/Elmas); operated by Navy with Air Force support and maintenance
2 SH-3D/H helicopter squadrons (1st and 3rd based at Luni and Catania respectively)
3 AB-212 helicopter squadrons (2nd, 4th and 5th based at Luni, Taranto and Catania respectively)
1 AV-8B Harrier II squadron at Grottaglie, Taranto (2 TAV-8B plus 16 AV-8B)

Marines

San Marco Battalion became a Group in late 1990 absorbing the Security and Base Defence Units and the related School formerly held at the Special Forces Command (COMSUBIN). In 1993 the Group becomes a Regiment.
The Italian Army also operates an autonomous 'Amphibious Command' composed of an Amphibious Assault Battalion and an Amphibious and Marine Crafts Battalion, both operating in the Venice Lagoons area. There are rumours that it may amalgamate with the marines to create an Amphibious Brigade.

Mercantile Marine

Lloyd's Register of Shipping:
 1636 vessels of 7 730 054 tons gross

DELETIONS

Submarines

1991 *Attilio Bagnolini*
1992 *Lazzaro Mocenigo*

Cruisers

1990 *Caio Duilio*
1992 *Andrea Doria*

Destroyers

1991 *Intrepido*
1992 *Impavido*

Frigates

1990 *Virginio Fasan*

Corvettes

1992 *Aquila, Alcione* (harbour training), *Airone* (harbour training), *Licio Visintini*
1993 *Pietro de Cristofaro, Umberto Grosso*

Light Forces

1991 *Sparviero*

Minesweepers

1990 *Salmone, Sgombro, Gelsomino, Giaggiolo*
1991 *Frassino, Timo, Vischio*
1992 *Loto, Alloro*

Amphibious Forces

1990 *Grado*

Miscellaneous

1990 *Vigoroso* (tug), *Ustica* (tug), *Panaria* (tug), *Albenga* (tug), *San Benedetto* (tug)
1991 *Arzachena* (tug), *Ustica* (tug), *Quarto, Alicudi, MOC 1207*
1992 *MTC 1001, MTC 1006, Mincio*

PENNANT LIST

Submarines

506	Enrico Toti
513	Enrico Dandolo
518	Nazario Sauro
519	Fecia di Cossato
520	Leonardo da Vinci
521	Guglielmo Marconi
522	Salvatore Pelosi
523	Giuliano Prini
524	Primo Longobardo (bldg)
525	Gazzana Priaroggia (bldg)

Light Aircraft Carrier

551	Giuseppe Garibaldi

Cruisers

550	Vittorio Veneto

Destroyers

550	Ardito
551	Audace
560	Luigi Durand de la Penne
561	Francesco Mimbelli

Frigates

564	Lupo
565	Sagittario
566	Perseo
567	Orsa
570	Maestrale
571	Grecale
572	Libeccio
573	Scirocco
574	Aliseo
575	Euro
576	Espero
577	Zeffiro
580	Alpino
581	Carabiniere
F 582	Artigliere
F 583	Aviere
F 584	Bersagliere
F 585	Granatiere

Corvettes

F 550	Salvatore Todaro
F 551	Minerva
F 552	Urania
F 553	Danaide
F 554	Sfinge
F 555	Driade
F 556	Chimera
F 557	Fenice
F 558	Sibilla

Offshore Patrol Vessels

P 401	Cassiopea
P 402	Libra
P 403	Spica
P 404	Vega
P 495	Bambù
P 496	Mango
P 497	Mogano
P 500	Palma
P —	Storione
P —	Squalo

Light Forces

P 421	Nibbio
P 422	Falcone
P 423	Astore
P 424	Grifone
P 425	Gheppio
P 426	Condor
P 492	Barbara

Minesweepers/Hunters

M 5504	Castagno*
M 5505	Cedro*
M 5509	Gelso*
M 5516	Platano*
M 5519	Mandorlo*
M 5550	Lerici*
M 5551	Sapri*
M 5552	Milazzo*
M 5553	Vieste*
M 5554	Gaeta
M 5555	Termoli
M 5556	Alghero
M 5557	Numana
M 5558	Crotone (bldg)
M 5559	Viareggio (bldg)
M 5560	Chioggia (bldg)
M 5561	Rimini (bldg)

* Hunters

Amphibious Forces

L 9892	San Giorgio
L 9893	San Marco
L 9894	San Giusto (bldg)

Service Forces

A 5301	Pietro Cavezzale
A 5302	Caroly
A 5303	Ammiraglio Magnaghi
A 5304	Alicudi
A 5305	Murena
A 5306	Mirto
A 5307	Pioppo
A 5308	Alloro
A 5309	Anteo
A 5310	Proteo
A 5311	Palinuro
A 5312	Amerigo Vespucci
A 5313	Stella Polare
A 5315	Raffaele Rossetti
A 5316	Corsaro II
A 5317	Atlante
A 5318	Prometeo
A 5319	Ciclope
A 5320	Vincenzo Martellotta
A 5324	Titano
A 5325	Polifemo
A 5327	Stromboli
A 5328	Gigante
A 5329	Vesuvio
A 5330	Saturno
A 5331-5	MOC 1201-5
A 5347	Gorgona
A 5348	Tremiti
A 5349	Caprera
A 5351	Pantelleria
A 5352	Lipari
A 5353	Capri
A 5354	Piave
A 5356	Basento
A 5357	Bradano
A 5358	Brenta
A 5359	Bormida
A 5364	Ponza
A 5365	Tenace
A 5366	Levanzo
A 5367	Tavolara
A 5368	Palmaria
A 5370-3	MCC 1101-4
A 5375	Simeto
A 5378	Aragosta
A 5379	Astice
A 5380	Mitilo
A 5381	Polipo
A 5382	Porpora
A 5383	Procida
Y 413	Porto Fossone
Y 416	Porto Torres
Y 417	Porto Corsini
Y 421	Porto Empedocle
Y 422	Porto Pisano
Y 423	Porto Conte
Y 425	Portoferraio
Y 426	Portovenere
Y 428	Porto Salvo
Y 436	Porto d'Ischia
Y 443	Riva Trigoso
Y 498	Mario Marino
Y 499	Alcide Pedretti

SUBMARINES

0 +(2) TYPE S 90 CLASS

Displacement, tons: 2500 surfaced; 2780 dived
Dimensions, feet (metres): 228.7 × 26.9 × 20.1 (69.7 × 8.2 × 6.3)
Main machinery: Diesel-electric; 3 Fincantieri GMT 210.16 SM diesels; 6400 hp(m) *(4.7 MW)* sustained; 1 motor; 6000 hp(m) *(4.41 MW)*; 1 shaft
Speed, knots: 20 dived; 11 surfaced
Range, miles: 6000 at 6 kts dived
Complement: 50 (8 officers)

Torpedoes: 6—21 in *(533 mm)* (2 triple) bow tubes. Total of 24 missiles, guided and unguided torpedoes.

Programmes: The programme is uncertain because overall submarine numbers have been cut from 10 to eight. The characteristics shown above are still subject to the completion of Project Definition. The original plan was to order in 1993 for completion in 1998, but this has been delayed.

Structure: Diving depth is expected to be about 400 m *(1300 ft)*. This is to be a high performance conventional submarine and although gaseous storage toroidal designs have been tested in midget submarines built by Maritalia and the concept could be applied to larger (2800 or 1400 ton) submarines, this technology will not be incorporated in the S 90.
Opinion: Future European collaboration is possible as an alternative to this project, perhaps using the German Type 212 as the basic design.

2 + 2 IMPROVED SAURO CLASS

Name	No	Builders	Laid down	Launched	Commissioned
SALVATORE PELOSI	S 522	Fincantieri, Monfalcone	24 May 1984	29 Dec 1986	14 July 1988
GIULIANO PRINI	S 523	Fincantieri, Monfalcone	30 May 1985	12 Dec 1987	11 Nov 1989
PRIMO LONGOBARDO	S 524	Fincantieri, Monfalcone	19 Dec 1991	20 June 1992	July 1993
GAZZANA PRIAROGGIA	S 525	Fincantieri, Monfalcone	12 Nov 1992	Feb 1993	Feb 1994

Displacement, tons: 1476 (1653, S 524-5) surfaced; 1662 (1862, S 524-5) dived
Dimensions, feet (metres): 211.2 (217.8 S 524-5) × 22.3 × 18.4 *(64.4 (66.4) × 6.8 × 5.6)*
Main machinery: Diesel-electric; 3 Fincantieri GMT 210.16 SM diesels; 6400 hp(m) *(4.7 MW)* sustained; 3 alternators; 2.16 MW; 1 motor; 4270 hp(m) *(3.14 MW)*; 1 shaft
Speed, knots: 11 surfaced; 19 dived; 12 snorting
Range, miles: 11 000 at 11 kts surfaced; 250 at 4 kts dived
Complement: 45 (7 officers)

Missiles: Capability to launch Harpoon being considered.
Torpedoes: 6—21 in *(533 mm)* bow tubes. 12 Whitehead A184; dual purpose; wire-guided; active/passive homing to 25 km *(13.7 nm)* at 24 kts; 17 km *(9.2 nm)* at 38 kts; warhead 250 kg. Swim-out discharge.
Countermeasures: ESM: Elettronica BLD-727; radar warning; 2 aerials—1 on a mast, second in search periscope.
Fire control: SMA BSN 716(V)2; SACTIS including Link 11 (receive only).
Radars: Search/navigation: SMA BPS 704; I band; also periscope radar for attack ranging.
Sonars: Selenia Elsag IPD 70/S; linear passive array; 200 Hz-7.5 kHz; active and UWT transducers in bow (15 kHz).
Selenia Elsag MD 100S; passive ranging.

Programmes: The first two were ordered in March 1983 and the second pair in July 1988.
Structure: Pressure hull of HY 80 steel with a central bulkhead for escape purposes. Diving depth, 300 m *(985 ft)* (test) and 600 m *(1970 ft)* (crushing). The second pair have a slightly longer hull.
Periscopes: Kollmorgen; S 76 Mod 322 with laser rangefinder and ESM—attack; S 76 Mod 323 with radar rangefinder and ESM—search. Wave contour snort head has a very low radar profile.
Operational: Litton Italia PL 41 inertial navigation; Ferranti auto pilot Omega and Transit. Endurance, 45 days possibly increased in second pair.

GIULIANO PRINI　　　　　　　　　　　　　　　　　　*1991, van Ginderen Collection*

4 SAURO CLASS (1081 TYPE)

Name	No	Builders	Laid down	Launched	Commissioned
NAZARIO SAURO	S 518	Italcantieri, Monfalcone	27 June 1974	9 Oct 1976	12 Feb 1980
FECIA DI COSSATO	S 519	Italcantieri, Monfalcone	15 Nov 1975	16 Nov 1977	5 Nov 1979
LEONARDO DA VINCI	S 520	Italcantieri, Monfalcone	8 June 1978	20 Oct 1979	23 Oct 1981
GUGLIELMO MARCONI	S 521	Italcantieri, Monfalcone	23 Oct 1979	20 Sep 1980	11 Sep 1982

Displacement, tons: 1456 surfaced; 1631 dived
Dimensions, feet (metres): 210 × 22.5 × 18.9 *(63.9 × 6.8 × 5.7)*
Main machinery: Diesel-electric; 3 Fincantieri GMT 210.16 NM diesels; 3350 hp(m) *(2.46 MW)* sustained; 3 alternators; 2.16 MW; 1 motor; 3210 hp(m) *(2.36 MW)*; 1 shaft
Speed, knots: 11 surfaced; 19 dived; 12 snorting
Range, miles: 11 000 surfaced at 11 kts; 250 dived at 4 kts
Complement: 45 (7 officers) plus 4 trainees

Torpedoes: 6—21 in *(533 mm)* bow tubes. 12 Whitehead A184; dual purpose; wire-guided; active/passive homing to 25 km *(13.7 nm)* at 24 kts; 17 km *(9.2 nm)* at 38 kts; warhead 250 kg. Swim-out discharge.
Countermeasures: ESM: Elettronica BLD 726; radar warning.
Fire control: SMA BSN 716(V)1; SACTIS data processing and computer-based TMA. CCRG FCS.
Radars: Search/navigation: SMA BPS 704; I band.
Sonars: Selenia Elsag IPD 70/S; linear passive array; 200 Hz-7.5 kHz; active and UWT transducers in bow (15 kHz).
Selenia Elsag MD 100; passive ranging.

LEONARDO DA VINCI　　　　　　　　　　　　　　　*9/1991, van Ginderen Collection*

Programmes: Two of this class were originally ordered in 1967 but were cancelled in the following year. Reinstated in the building programme in 1972. Second pair provided for in Legge Navale and ordered 12 February 1976.
The discrepancy in commissioning dates of *N Sauro* and *F di Cossato* was due to problems over the main batteries. *F di Cossato* was provided with a new CGA battery which was satisfactory. *N Sauro* was then similarly fitted.
Modernisation: All being modernised. *Fecia di Cossato* in 1990, *Nazario Sauro* in 1991, *Guglielmo Marconi* in 1992 and *Leonardo da Vinci* in 1993. New batteries have greater capacity; some auxiliary machinery replaced and habitability improved.
Structure: Diving depth, 300 m *(985 ft)* (max) and 250 m *(820 ft)* (normal).
Operational: Endurance, 35 days. Reliability improved by the mid-life modernisation programme. *Leonardo da Vinci* damaged in a dived collision with *Ardito* in 1992.

2 TOTI CLASS (1075 TYPE)

Name	No	Builders	Laid down	Launched	Commissioned
ENRICO TOTI	S 506	Italcantieri, Monfalcone	15 Apr 1965	12 Mar 1967	22 Jan 1968
ENRICO DANDOLO	S 513	Italcantieri, Monfalcone	10 Mar 1967	16 Dec 1967	25 Sep 1968

Displacement, tons: 460 standard; 524 surfaced; 582 dived
Dimensions, feet (metres): 151.5 × 15.4 × 13.1 *(46.2 × 4.7 × 4)*
Main machinery: Diesel-electric; 2 Fiat/MTU 12V 493 TY7 diesels; 2200 hp(m) *(1.62 MW)* sustained; 2 alternators; 1.08 MW; 1 motor; 2200 hp(m) *(1.62 MW)*; 1 shaft
Speed, knots: 14 surfaced; 15 dived. **Range, miles:** 3000 at 5 kts surfaced
Complement: 26 (4 officers)

Torpedoes: 4—21 in *(533 mm)* bow tubes. 6 Whitehead A184; dual purpose; wire-guided; active/passive homing to 25 km *(13.7 nm)* at 24 kts; 17 km *(9.2 nm)* at 38 kts; warhead 250 kg.
Countermeasures: ESM: BPR-2; radar warning.
Fire control: Selenia IPD 64 TFCS.
Radars: Search/navigation: SMA 3RM 20A/SMG; I band.
Sonars: Selenia Elsag IPD 64; passive/active search and attack; medium frequency.
Selenia Elsag MD 64; passive ranging.

Programmes: Italy's first indigenously built submarines after the Second World War. First of class paid off to reserve in July 1990. Second of class *Enrico Toti* paid off in 1991 but was reactivated and taken back into service 1 April 1992, when the fourth of the class was deleted. The two survivors will pay off in 1995 when the second pair of Improved Sauro class are fully operational.
Structure: Diving depth, 180 m *(600 ft)*.

TOTI class (old number)　　　　　　　　　　　　　*7/1992, van Ginderen Collection*

LIGHT AIRCRAFT CARRIER

Note: A second carrier is a high priority naval project. The design might be about 16 000 tons with twin funnels and include two VLS Aster 15 SAAM silos and three CIWS mountings. An amphibious role might also be included with extra berths for marines, 2 LCVPs on davits, Rigid Raiders and a stern well dock.

Name	No	Builders	Laid down	Launched	Commissioned
GIUSEPPE GARIBALDI	C 551	Italcantieri, Monfalcone	26 Mar 1981	4 June 1983	9 Aug 1987

Displacement, tons: 10 100 standard; 13 370 full load
Dimensions, feet (metres): 591 × 110.2 × 22 *(180 × 33.4 × 6.7)*
Flight deck, feet (metres): 570.2 × 99.7 *(173.8 × 30.4)*
Main machinery: COGAG; 4 Fiat/GE LM 2500 gas turbines; 81 000 hp *(60 MW)* sustained; 2 shafts
Speed, knots: 30. **Range, miles:** 7000 at 20 kts
Complement: 550 ship plus 230 air group (accommodation for 825 including Flag and staff)

Missiles: SSM: 4 OTO Melara Teseo Mk 2 (TG 2) ❶; active radar homing to 180 km *(98.4 nm)* at 0.9 Mach; warhead 210 kg; sea-skimmer for last 4 km *(2.2 nm)*.
SAM: 2 Selenia Elsag Albatros octuple launchers ❷; 48 Aspide; semi-active radar homing to 13 km *(7 nm)* at 2.5 Mach; height envelope 15-5000 m *(49.2-16 405 ft)*; warhead 30 kg.
Guns: 6 Breda 40 mm/70 (3 twin) MB ❸; 85° elevation; 300 rounds/minute to 12.5 km *(6.8 nm)* anti-surface; 4 km *(2.2 nm)* anti-aircraft; weight of shell 0.96 kg.
Torpedoes: 6—324 mm B-515 (2 triple) tubes ❹. Honeywell Mk 46; anti-submarine; active/passive homing to 11 km *(5.9 nm)* at 40 kts; warhead 44 kg. Being replaced by new A 290.
Countermeasures: Decoys: AN/SLQ 25 Nixie; noisemaker. 2 Breda SCLAR 105 mm 20-barrelled launchers; trains and elevates; chaff to 5 km *(2.7 nm)*, illuminants to 12 km *(6.6 nm)*.
ESM/ECM: Elettronica Nettuno SLQ 732; integrated intercept and jamming system.
Combat data systems: IPN 20 (SADOC 2) action data automation including Links 11 and 14. SATCOM ❺.
Fire control: 3 NA 30 electro-optical backup for SAM. 3 Dardo NA21 for guns.
Radars: Long range air search: Hughes SPS 52C ❻; 3D; E/F band; range 440 km *(240 nm)*.
Air search: Selenia SPS 768 (RAN 3L) ❼; D band; range 220 km *(120 nm)*.
SMA SPN 728; I band; range 73 km *(40 nm)*; TV indicator.
Air/surface search: Selenia SPS 774 (RAN 10S) ❽; E/F band; range 155 km *(85 nm)*.
Surface search/target indication: SMA SPS 702 UPX; 718 beacon; I band.
Navigation: SMA SPN 749(V)2; I band.
Fire control: Three Selenia SPG 75 (RTN 30X) ❾; I/J band; range 15 km *(8 nm)* (for Albatros).
Three Selenia SPG 74 (RTN 20X) ❿; I/J band; range 13 km *(7 nm)* (for Dardo).
CCA: Selenia SPN 728(V)1; I band.
IFF: Mk XII. Tacan: SRN-15A.
Sonars: Raytheon DE 1160 LF; bow-mounted; active search; medium frequency.

Fixed wing aircraft: 16 AV-8B Harrier II (1993).
Helicopters: 18 SH-3D Sea King helicopters (12 in hangar, 6 on deck). The total capacity is either 16 Harriers or 18 helicopters. In practice a combination will be embarked.

Programmes: Contract awarded 21 November 1977. The design was changed considerably. Design work completed February 1980 and engineering work began in March 1980. Started sea trials 3 December 1984. Refitted late 1986-January 1987. A sister ship, *Giuseppe Mazzini*, was to replace *Vittorio Veneto* in the mid-1990s. This project was suspended in 1990 but may be revived in a different design (see Note at head of page).
Structure: Six decks with 13 vertical watertight bulkheads. Fitted with 6.5° ski-jump and VSTOL operating equipment. Two 15 ton lifts 18 × 10 m *(59 × 32.8 ft)*. Hangar size 110 × 15 × 6 m *(361 × 49.2 × 19.7 ft)*. Has a slightly narrower flight deck than UK Invincible class. Two MEN class fast personnel launches (capacity 250) can be embarked for amphibious operations or disaster relief.
Operational: Fleet Flagship. The long-standing dispute between the Navy and the Air Force concerning the former's operation of fixed-wing aircraft (dating back to pre-World War II legislation) was finally resolved by legislation passed on 29 January 1989. Embarked aircraft are operated by the Navy with the Air Force providing evaluation and maintenance and any additional pilots required. Two trainer TAV-8B aircraft acquired in early 1991. First operational aircraft embarked in 1993.

GIUSEPPE GARIBALDI *8/1991, Giorgio Arra*

GIUSEPPE GARIBALDI *8/1991, Giorgio Arra*

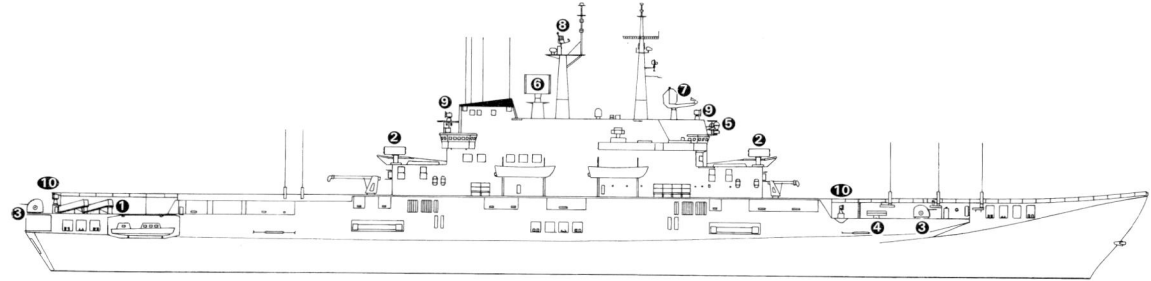

GIUSEPPE GARIBALDI *(Scale 1 : 1200), Ian Sturton*

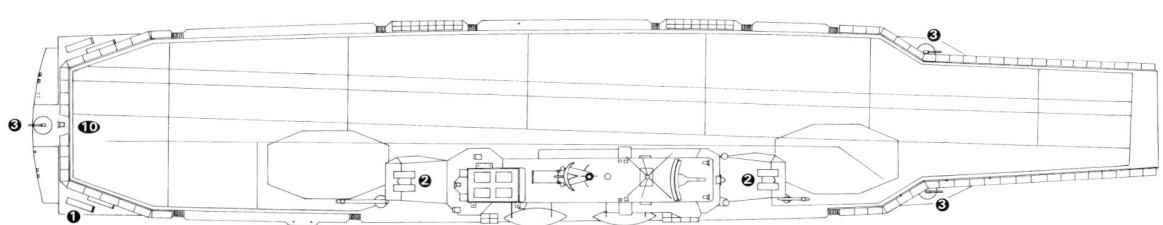

GIUSEPPE GARIBALDI *(Scale 1 : 1200), Ian Sturton*

CRUSIERS

Name	No	Builders	Laid down	Launched	Commissioned
VITTORIO VENETO	C 550	Italcantieri, Castellammare	10 June 1965	5 Feb 1967	12 July 1969

Displacement, tons: 7500 standard; 9500 full load
Dimensions, feet (metres): 589 × 63.6 × 19.7 *(179.6 × 19.4 × 6)*
Flight deck, feet (metres): 131 × 61 *(40 × 18.6)*
Main machinery: 4 Foster-Wheeler boilers (Ansaldo); 700 psi *(50 kg/cm sq)*; 850°F *(450°C)*; 2 Tosi turbines; 73 000 hp(m) *(54 MW)*; 2 shafts
Speed, knots: 32. **Range, miles:** 5000 at 17 kts
Complement: 550 (53 officers)

Missiles: SSM: 4 OTO Melara Teseo Mk 2 (TG 2) ❶; inertial cruise; active radar homing to 180 km *(98.4 nm)* at 0.9 Mach; warhead 210 kg; sea-skimmer.
SAM: GDC Pomona Standard SM-1ER; Aster twin Mk 10 Mod 9 launcher ❷; capacity for 60 missiles (including ASROC) on 3 drums; command guidance; semi-active radar homing to 64 km *(35 nm)* at 2.5 Mach.
A/S: Honeywell ASROC; inertial guidance to 1.6-10 km *(1-5.4 nm)*; payload Mk 46 torpedo.
Guns: 8 OTO Melara 3 in *(76 mm)*/62 MMK ❸; 85° elevation; 55-65 rounds/minute to 8 km *(4.4 nm)*; weight of shell 6 kg.
6 Breda 40 mm/70 (3 twin) ❹; 85° elevation; 300 rounds/minute to 12.5 km *(6.8 nm)* anti-surface; 4 km *(2.2 nm)* anti-aircraft; weight of shell 0.96 kg.
Torpedoes: 6—324 mm US Mk 32 (2 triple) tubes ❺. Honeywell Mk 46; anti-submarine; active/passive homing to 11 km *(5.9 nm)* at 40 kts; warhead 44 kg.
Countermeasures: Decoys: 2 Breda SCLAR 105 mm 20-barrelled trainable ❻; chaff to 5 km *(2.7 nm)*; illuminants to 12 km *(6.6 nm)*. SLQ 25 Nixie; towed torpedo decoy.
ESM: SLR 4; intercept.
ECM: 3 SLQ-B; 2 SLQ-C; jammers.
Combat data systems: SADOC 1 action data automation; Link 11. SATCOM.
Fire control: 4 Argo 10 systems for 76 mm guns. 2 Dardo systems for 40 mm guns.
Radars: Long range air search: Hughes SPS 52C ❼; 3D; E/F band; range 440 km *(240 nm)*.
Air search: Selenia SPS 768 (RAN 3L) ❽; D band; range 220 km *(120 nm)*.
Surface search/target indication: SMA SPS 702 ❾; I band.
Navigation: SMA SPS 748; I band; range 73 km *(40 nm)*.
Fire control: Four Selenia SPG 70 (RTN 10X) ❿; I/J band; range 40 km *(22 nm)* (for Argo).
Two Selenia SPG 74 (RTN 20X) ⓫; I/J band; range 13 km *(7 nm)* (for Dardo).
Two Sperry/RCA SPG 55C ⓬; G/H band; range 51 km *(28 nm)* (for Standard).
IFF: Mk XII. Tacan: SRN-15A.
Sonars: Sangamo SQS 23G; bow-mounted; active search and attack; medium frequency.

Helicopters: 6 AB 212ASW ⓭.

VITTORIO VENETO
1991, Camil Busquets i Vilanova

Programmes: Projected under the 1959-60 New Construction Programme, but her design was recast several times. Started trials 30 April 1969. Defined as a Guided Missile Helicopter Cruiser.
Modernisation: In hand from 1981 to early 1984 for modernisation which included the four Teseo launchers and the three twin Breda compact 40 mm.
Structure: Developed from the Andrea Doria class but with much larger helicopter squadron and improved facilities for anti-submarine operations. Fitted with two sets of stabilisers.

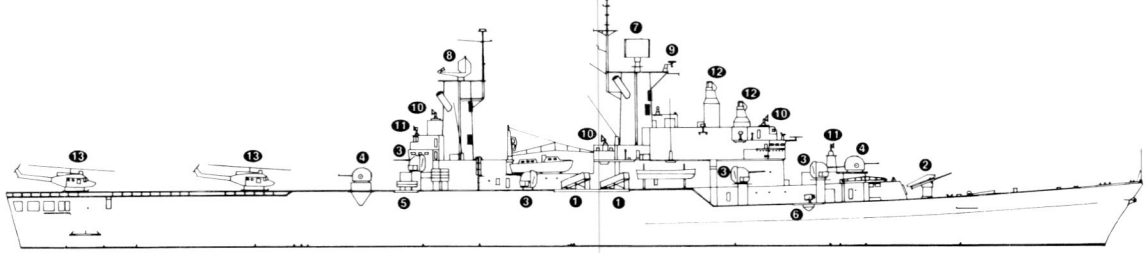

VITTORIO VENETO
(Scale 1 : 1200), Ian Sturton

VITTORIO VENETO
10/1992, C D Yayla

VITTORIO VENETO
10/1992, C D Yay

DESTROYERS

Note: It seems likely that Italy will join the Anglo-French Air Defence ship project in 1993. Requirement is for six ships at the end of the decade.

2 AUDACE CLASS (DDG)

Name	No	Builders	Laid down	Launched	Commissioned
ARDITO	D 550	Italcantieri, Castellammare	19 July 1968	27 Nov 1971	5 Dec 1972
AUDACE	D 551	Fincantieri, Riva Trigoso/Muggiano	27 Apr 1968	2 Oct 1971	16 Nov 1972

Displacement, tons: 3600 standard; 4400 full load
Dimensions, feet (metres): 448 × 46.6 × 15.1 *(136.6 × 14.2 × 4.6)*
Main machinery: 4 Foster-Wheeler boilers; 600 psi *(43 kg/cm sq)*; 850°F *(450°C)*; 2 turbines; 73 000 hp(m) *(54 MW)*; 2 shafts
Speed, knots: 34. **Range, miles:** 3000 at 20 kts
Complement: 380 (30 officers)

Missiles: SSM: 8 OTO Melara/Matra Teseo Mk 2 (TG 2) (4 twin) ❶; mid-course guidance; active radar homing to 180 km *(98.4 nm)* at 0.9 Mach; warhead 210 kg; sea-skimmer.
SAM: 40 GDC Pomona Standard SM-1MR; Mk 13 Mod 4 launcher ❷; command guidance; semi-active radar homing to 46 km *(25 nm)* at 2 Mach; height envelope 45.7-18 288 m *(150-60 000 ft)*.
Selenia Albatros octuple launcher for Aspide ❸; semi-active radar homing to 13 km *(7 nm)* at 2.5 Mach.
Guns: 1 OTO Melara 5 in *(127 mm)*/54 ❹; 85° elevation; 45 rounds/minute to 16 km *(8.7 nm)* anti-surface; 7 km *(3.8 nm)* anti-aircraft; weight of shell 32 kg.
3 OTO Melara 3 in *(76 mm)*/62 Compact *(Ardito)* and 1 *(Ardito)* or 4 *(Audace)* Super Rapid ❺; 85° elevation; 85 rounds/minute (Compact) or 120 rounds/minute (Super Rapid) to 16 km *(8.7 nm)* anti-surface; 12 km *(6.6 nm)* anti-aircraft; weight of shell 6 kg.
Torpedoes: 6—324 mm US Mk 32 (2 triple) tubes ❻. Honeywell Mk 46; anti-submarine; active/passive homing to 11 km *(5.9 nm)* at 40 kts; warhead 44 kg. Transom tubes have been removed.
Countermeasures: Decoys: 2 Breda 105 mm SCLAR 20-barrelled trainable; chaff to 5 km *(2.7 nm)*; illuminants to 12 km *(6.6 nm)*. SLQ 25 Nixie; towed torpedo decoy.
ESM/ECM: Elettronica SLQ 732 Nettuno; integrated intercept and jammer.
Combat data systems: Selenia Elsag IPN-20 action data automation; Links 11 and 14. SATCOM ❼.
Fire control: 3 Dardo E FCS (3 channels for Aspide). Selenia NA 30 optronic director.
Radars: Long range air search: Hughes SPS 52C ❽; 3D; E/F band; range 440 km *(240 nm)*.
Air search: Selenia SPS 768 (RAN 3L) ❾; D band; range 220 km *(120 nm)*.
Air/surface search: Selenia SPS 774 (RAN 10S) ❿; E/F band; range 155 km *(85 nm)*.
Surface search: SMA SPQ 2D ⓫; I band.
Navigation: SMA SPN 748; I band.
Fire control: Three Selenia SPG 76 (RTN 30X) ⓬; I/J band; range 40 km *(22 nm)* (for Dardo E).
Two Raytheon SPG 51 ⓭; G/I band (for Standard).
IFF: Mk XII.
Tacan: SRN-15A.
Sonars: CWE 610; hull-mounted; active search and attack; medium frequency.

Helicopters: 2 AB 212ASW ⓮.

Programmes: It was announced in April 1966 that two new guided missile destroyers would be built. They are basically similar to, but an improvement in design on, that of the Impavido class (now deleted).

Modernisation: B gun has been replaced by Albatros PDMS. Stern torpedo tubes removed. *Audace* fitted with four and *Ardito* one Super Rapid guns vice the 76 mm Compacts. *Ardito* should get three more by 1994. *Ardito* completed modernisation in March 1988 and *Audace* in early 1991. Improved EW equipment also fitted.

Structure: Both fitted with stabilisers.
Operational: First deck landing trials of EH 101 helicopter were carried out on 14 May 1992.

AUDACE *(Scale 1 : 1200), Ian Sturton*

AUDACE *1/1992, Giorgio Ghiglione*

AUDACE *7/1991, Giorgio Ghiglione*

326 ITALY / Destroyers — Frigates

2 ANIMOSO CLASS (DDG)

Name	No	Builders	Laid down	Launched	Commissioned
LUIGI DURAND DE LA PENNE (ex-*Animoso*)	D 560	Fincantieri, Riva Trigoso/Muggiano	20 Jan 1988	29 Oct 1989	Dec 1992
FRANCESCO MIMBELLI (ex-*Ardimentoso*)	D 561	Fincantieri, Riva Trigoso/Muggiano	15 Nov 1989	13 Apr 1991	June 1993

Displacement, tons: 4330 standard; 5400 full load
Dimensions, feet (metres): 487.4 × 52.8 × 16.5 *(147.7 × 16.1 × 5)*
Flight deck, feet (metres): 78.7 × 42.7 *(24 × 13)*
Main machinery: CODOG; 2 Fiat/GE LM2500 gas turbines; 54 000 hp *(40.3 MW)* sustained; 2 GMT BL 230.20 DVM diesels; 12 600 hp(m) *(9.3 MW)* sustained; 2 shafts; cp props
Speed, knots: 31.5. **Range, miles:** 7000 at 18 kts
Complement: 400 approx (35 officers)

Missiles: SSM: 4 or 8 OTO Melara/Matra Teseo Mk 2 (TG 2) (2 or 4 twin) ❶; mid-course guidance; active radar homing to 180 km *(98.4 nm)* at 0.9 Mach; warhead 210 kg; sea-skimmer. 4 SSM may be replaced by 4 Milas A/S launchers.
SAM: 40 GDC Pomona Standard SM-1MR; Mk 13 Mod 4 launcher ❷; command guidance; semi-active radar homing to 46 km *(25 nm)* at 2 Mach.
Selenia Albatros Mk 2 octuple launcher for Aspide ❸; semi-active radar homing to 13 km *(7 nm)* at 2.5 Mach; 16 missiles. Automatic reloading.
Guns: 1 OTO Melara 5 in *(127 mm)*/54 ❹; 85° elevation; 45 rounds/minute to 16 km *(8.7 nm)*; weight of shell 32 kg.
3 OTO Melara 3 in *(76 mm)*/62 Super Rapid ❺; 85° elevation; 120 rounds/minute to 16 km *(8.7 nm)*; weight of shell 6 kg.
Torpedoes: 6—324 mm B-515 (2 triple) tubes ❻. Whitehead A 290; anti-submarine.
Countermeasures: Decoys: 2 CSEE Sagaie chaff launchers. 1 Elmer anti-torpedo system.
ESM/ECM: Elettronica SLQ 732 Nettuno; integrated intercept and jamming system. SLC 705.
Combat data systems: Selenia Elsag IPN 20; Links 11 and 14. SATCOM.
Fire control: 4 Dardo E systems (3 channels for Aspide). Milas TFCS.
Radars: Long range air search: Hughes SPS 52C; 3D ❼; E/F band; range 440 km *(240 nm)*.
Air search: Selenia SPS 768 (RAN 3L) ❽; D band; range 220 km *(120 nm)*.
Air/surface search: Selenia SPS 774 (RAN 10S) ❾; E/F band; range 155 km *(85 nm)*.
Surface search: SMA SPS 702 ❿; I band.
Fire control: Four Selenia SPG 76 (RTN 30X) ⓫; I/J band (for Dardo).
Two Raytheon SPG 51D ⓬; G/I band (for SAM).
Navigation: SMA SPN 748 (3 RM 20); I band; range 73 km *(40 nm)*.
IFF: Mk XII. Tacan: SRN-15A.
Sonars: Raytheon/Elsag DE 1167LF and DE 1164; integrated hull and VDS; active search and attack; medium frequency (3.75 kHz (hull); 7.5 kHz (VDS)).

Helicopters: 2 AB 212ASW ⓭; SH-3D Sea King and EH 101 capable.

Programmes: Order placed 9 March 1986 with Riva Trigoso. All ships built at Riva Trigoso are completed at Muggiano after launching. Names changed on 10 June 1992 to honour former naval heroes. Acceptance dates have been delayed by reduction gear radiated noise problems which have been resolved.
Structure: Kevlar armour fitted. Prairie Masker noise suppression system. The 127 mm guns are ex-Audace class B turrets. Fully stabilised. Hangar is 18.5 m in length.
Operational: GPS and Meteosat receivers fitted. The three Super Rapid 76 mm guns are used as a combined medium range anti-surface armament and CIWS against missiles.

FRANCESCO MIMBELLI *(Scale 1 : 1200), Ian Sturton*

LUIGI DURAND DE LA PENNE 9/1991, Milpress

FRIGATES

2 ALPINO CLASS

Name	No	Builders	Laid down	Launched	Commissioned
ALPINO (ex-*Circe*)	F 580	Fincantieri, Riva Trigoso	27 Feb 1963	10 June 1967	14 Jan 1968
CARABINIERE (ex-*Climene*)	F 581	Fincantieri, Riva Trigoso	9 Jan 1965	30 Sep 1967	28 Apr 1968

Displacement, tons: 2400 standard; 2700 full load
Dimensions, feet (metres): 371.7 × 43.6 × 12.7 *(113.3 × 13.3 × 3.9)*
Main machinery: CODAG; 2 Metrovick gas turbines; 15 000 hp(m) *(11.2 MW)*; 4 Tosi OTV-320 diesels; 16 800 hp(m) *(12.35 MW)*; 2 shafts
Speed, knots: 20 diesel; 28 diesel and gas. **Range, miles:** 3500 at 18 kts
Complement: 163 (13 officers)

Missiles: SAM: VLS for Aster 15 trials *(Carabiniere)*.
Guns: 6 OTO Melara 3 in *(76 mm)*/62 ❶ *(Alpino)*; 85° elevation; 60 rounds/minute to 16 km *(8.7 nm)*; weight of shell 6 kg.
Torpedoes: 6—324 mm US Mk 32 (2 triple) tubes ❷. Honeywell Mk 46; anti-submarine; active/passive homing to 11 km *(5.9 nm)* at 40 kts; warhead 44 kg.
A/S mortars: 1 Whitehead K 113 single-barrelled automatic *(Alpino)* ❸; range 900 m; warhead 160 kg. MILAS launchers *(Carabiniere)*.
Countermeasures: Decoys: 2 Breda 105 mm SCLAR 20-tubed trainable ❹; chaff to 5 km *(2.7 nm)*; illuminants to 12 km *(6.6 nm)*.
ESM/ECM: Selenia SLQ 747; integrated intercept and jammer.
Fire control: 2 Argo 'O' for 3 in guns.
Radars: Air search: RCA SPS 12 ❺; D band; range 120 km *(65 nm)*.
Surface search: SMA SPS 702(V)3 ❻; I band.
Navigation: SMA SPN 748; I band.
Fire control: Two Selenia SPG 70 (RTN 10X) ❼; I/J band; range 40 km *(22 nm)* (for Argo).
SPY 790 *(Carabiniere)*; for SAAM.
Sonars: Raytheon DE 1164; integrated hull and VDS; active search and attack; medium frequency.

Helicopters: 1 AB 212ASW ❽ (not in *Carabiniere*).

Modernisation: Both have been updated with new sonar, CCIC and EW. *Carabiniere* has been modified to replace *Quarto* as a trials ship. B gun turret and the Whitehead mortar have been replaced by MILAS launchers, and the two after 76 mm guns by the VLS for the Aster 15 SAAM system. An oil rig type mast on the flight deck carries the SAAM system radar SPY 790.
Structure: Stabilisers fitted.

ALPINO *(Scale 1 : 1200), Ian Sturton*

CARABINIERE (modified for SAM trials) 5/1991, Giorgio Ghiglione

Frigates / ITALY 327

8 MAESTRALE CLASS

Name	No	Builders	Laid down	Launched	Commissioned
MAESTRALE	F 570	Fincantieri, Riva Trigoso	8 Mar 1978	2 Feb 1981	6 Mar 1982
GRECALE	F 571	Fincantieri, Muggiano	21 Mar 1979	12 Sep 1981	5 Feb 1983
LIBECCIO	F 572	Fincantieri, Riva Trigoso	1 Aug 1979	7 Sep 1981	5 Feb 1983
SCIROCCO	F 573	Fincantieri, Riva Trigoso	26 Feb 1980	17 Apr 1982	20 Sep 1983
ALISEO	F 574	Fincantieri, Riva Trigoso	10 Aug 1980	29 Oct 1982	7 Sep 1983
EURO	F 575	Fincantieri, Riva Trigoso	15 Apr 1981	25 Apr 1983	24 Jan 1984
ESPERO	F 576	Fincantieri, Riva Trigoso	29 July 1982	19 Nov 1983	4 May 1984
ZEFFIRO	F 577	Fincantieri, Riva Trigoso	15 Mar 1983	19 May 1984	4 May 1985

Displacement, tons: 2500 standard; 3200 full load
Dimensions, feet (metres): 405 × 42.5 × 15.1 *(122.7 × 12.9 × 4.6)*
Flight deck, feet (metres): 89 × 39 *(27 × 12)*
Main machinery: CODOG; 2 Fiat/GE LM 2500 gas turbines; 50 000 hp *(37.3 MW)* sustained; 2 GMT BL 230.20 DVM diesels; 12 600 hp(m) *(9.3 MW)* sustained; 2 shafts; cp props
Speed, knots: 32 gas; 21 diesels. **Range, miles:** 6000 at 16 kts
Complement: 232 (24 officers)

Missiles: SSM: 4 OTO Melara Teseo Mk 2 (TG 2) ❶; mid-course guidance; active radar homing to 180 km *(98.4 nm)*; warhead 210 kg; sea-skimmer.
  SAM: Selenia Albatros octuple launcher; 16 Aspide ❷; semi-active homing to 13 km *(7 nm)* at 2.5 Mach; height envelope 15-5000 m *(49.2-16 405 ft)*; warhead 30 kg.
Guns: 1 OTO Melara 5 in *(127 mm)*/54 automatic ❸; 85° elevation; 45 rounds/minute to 16 km *(8.7 nm)* anti-surface; 7 km *(3.8 nm)* anti-aircraft; weight of shell 32 kg; fires chaff and illuminants.
  4 Breda 40 mm/70 (2 twin) compact ❹; 85° elevation; 300 rounds/minute to 12.5 km *(6.8 nm)* anti-surface; 4 km *(2.2 nm)* anti-aircraft; weight of shell 0.96 kg.
  2 Oerlikon 20 mm fitted for Gulf deployments in 1990-91. 2 Breda Oerlikon 25 mm (twin) tested in *Espero* in 1992.
Torpedoes: 6—324 mm US Mk 32 (2 triple) tubes ❺. Honeywell Mk 46; anti-submarine; active/passive homing to 11 km *(5.9 nm)* at 40 kts; warhead 44 kg.
  2—21 in *(533 mm)* B516 tubes in transom ❻. Whitehead A184; dual purpose; wire-guided; active/passive homing to 17 km *(9.2 nm)* at 38 kts; 25 km *(13.7 nm)* at 24 kts; warhead 250 kg.
Countermeasures: Decoys: 2 Breda 105 mm SCLAR 20-tubed trainable chaff rocket launchers ❼; chaff to 5 km *(2.7 nm)*; illuminants to 12 km *(6.6 nm)*. 2 Dagaie chaff launchers being fitted in all.
  SLQ 25; towed torpedo decoy. Prairie Masker; noise suppression system.
ESM: SLR-4; intercept.
ECM: 2 SLQ-D; jammers.
Combat data systems: IPN 20 (SADOC 2) action data automation; Link 11. SATCOM ❽.
Fire control: NA 30 for Albatros and 5 in guns. 2 Dardo for 40 mm guns.
Radars: Air/surface search: Selenia SPS 774 (RAN 10S) ❾; E/F band; range 155 km *(85 nm)*.
  Surface search: SMA SPS 702 ❿; I band.
  Navigation: SMA SPN 703; I band.
  Fire control: Selenia SPG 75 (RTN 30X) ⓫; I/J band (for Albatros and 12.7 mm gun).
  Two Selenia SPG 74 (RTN 20X) ⓬; I/J band; range 15 km *(8 nm)* (for Dardo).
  IFF: Mk XII.
Sonars: Raytheon DE 1164; hull-mounted; VDS; active/passive attack; medium frequency. VDS can be towed at up to 28 kts. Maximum depth 300 m.

Helicopters: 2 AB 212ASW ⓭.

Programmes: First six ordered December 1976 and last pair in October 1980. All Riva Trigoso ships completed at Muggiano after launch.
Structure: There has been a notable increase of 34 ft in length and 5 ft in beam over the Lupo class to provide for the fixed hangar and VDS, the result providing more comfortable accommodation but a small loss of top speed. Fittted with stabilisers.
Operational: A towed passive LF array may be attached to the VDS body. F 576 fitted with an Oerlikon Breda 25 mm gun for evaluation in 1991 and 1992.

MAESTRALE *(Scale 1 : 1200), Ian Sturton*

ALISEO *5/1992, F Gámez*

ESPERO *11/1992, Harald Carstens*

LIBECCIO *4/1992, Giorgio Ghiglione*

4 LUPO CLASS

Name	No	Builders	Laid down	Launched	Commissioned
LUPO	F 564	Fincantieri, Riva Trigoso	11 Oct 1974	29 July 1976	12 Sep 1977
SAGITTARIO	F 565	Fincantieri, Riva Trigoso	4 Feb 1976	22 June 1977	18 Nov 1978
PERSEO	F 566	Fincantieri, Riva Trigoso	28 Feb 1977	12 July 1978	1 Mar 1980
ORSA	F 567	Fincantieri, Muggiano	1 Aug 1977	1 Mar 1979	1 Mar 1980

Displacement, tons: 2208 standard; 2525 full load
Dimensions, feet (metres): 371.3 × 37.1 × 12.1 *(113.2 × 11.3 × 3.7)*
Main machinery: CODOG; 2 Fiat/GE LM 2500 gas turbines; 50 000 hp *(37.3 MW)* sustained; 2 GMT BL 230.20 M diesels; 10 000 hp(m) *(7.3 MW)* sustained; 2 shafts; cp props
Speed, knots: 35 turbines; 21 diesels. **Range, miles:** 4350 at 16 kts on diesels
Complement: 185 (16 officers)

Missiles: SSM: 8 OTO Melara Teseo Mk 2 (TG 2) ❶; mid-course guidance; active radar homing to 180 km *(98.4 nm)* at 0.9 Mach; warhead 210 kg; sea-skimmer.
SAM: Raytheon NATO Sea Sparrow Mk 29 octuple launcher ❷; semi-active radar homing to 14.6 km *(8 nm)* at 2.5 Mach; warhead 39 kg. 8 reloads. Updated for RIM-7H so cannot now fire Aspide.
Guns: 1 OTO Melara 5 in *(127 mm)*/54 ❸; 85° elevation; 45 rounds/minute to 16 km *(8.7 nm)* anti-surface; 7 km *(3.8 nm)* anti-aircraft; weight of shell 32 kg.
4 Breda 40 mm/70 (2 twin) compact ❹; 85° elevation; 300 rounds/minute to 12.5 km *(6.8 nm)* anti-surface; 4 km *(2.2 nm)* anti-aircraft; weight of shell 0.96 kg.
2 Oerlikon 20 mm can be fitted.
Torpedoes: 6—324 mm US Mk 32 tubes ❺. Honeywell Mk 46; anti-submarine; active/passive homing to 11 km *(5.9 nm)* at 40 kts; warhead 44 kg.
Countermeasures: Decoys: 2 Breda 105 mm SCLAR 20-tubed trainable ❻; chaff to 5 km *(2.7 nm)*; illuminants to 12 km *(6.6 nm)*.
SLQ 25 Nixie; towed torpedo decoy.
ESM: SLR-4; intercept.
ECM: 2 SLQ-D; jammers.
Combat data systems: IPN 20 (SADOC 2) action data automation; Link 11. SATCOM.
Fire control: Argo NA10 Mod 2 for missiles and 5 in gun. 2 Dardo for 40 mm guns.
Radars: Air search: Selenia SPS 774 (RAN 10S) ❼; E/F band; range 155 km *(85 nm)*.
Surface search/target indication: SMA SPS 702 ❼ₐ; I band (after modernisation).
Surface search: SMA SPQ2 F ❽; I band.
Navigation: SMA SPN 748; I band.
Fire control: Selenia SPG 70 (RTN 10X) ❾; I/J band; range 40 km *(22 nm)* (for Argo).
Two Selenia SPG 74 (RTN 20X) ❿; I/J band; range 15 km *(8 nm)* (for Dardo).
US Mk 95 Mod 1 (for SAM) ⓫; I band.
IFF: Mk XII.
Sonars: Raytheon DE 1160B; hull-mounted; active search and attack; medium frequency.

Helicopters: 1 AB 212ASW ⓬.

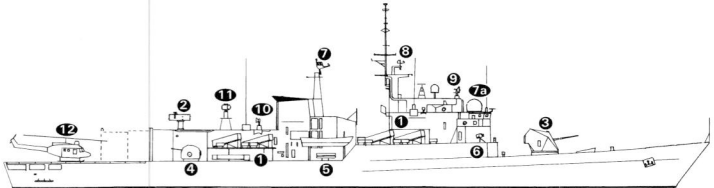

LUPO

(Scale 1 : 1200), Ian Sturton

ORSA (with SPS 702 radome)

11/1992, G. Toremans

Modernisation: Mid-life update started in 1991 and includes low altitude CORA SPS 702 search radar (radome on bridge roof), new gyros and improved communications. All should complete by late 1993.
Structure: 14 watertight compartments; fixed-fin stabilisers; telescopic hangar.
Sales: Similar ships built for Peru (4), Venezuela (6) and Iraq (4). Iraqi ships not delivered and transferred to the Italian Navy on 20 January 1992 (see Artigliere class).
Operational: Ships deploying to the Gulf in 1991 had SATCOM fitted above the bridge.

0 + 4 ARTIGLIERE (LUPO) CLASS

Name	No	Builders	Laid down	Launched	Commissioned
ARTIGLIERE (ex-*Hittin*)	F 582 (ex-F 14)	Fincantieri, Ancona	31 Mar 1982	27 July 1983	1993
AVIERE (ex-*Thi Qar*)	F 583 (ex-F 15)	Fincantieri, Ancona	3 Sep 1982	19 Dec 1984	1993
BERSAGLIERE (ex-*Al Qadisiya*)	F 584 (ex-F 16)	Fincantieri, Ancona	1 Dec 1983	1 June 1985	1994
GRANATIERE (ex-*Al Yarmouk*)	F 585 (ex-F 17)	Fincantieri, Riva Trigoso	12 Mar 1984	18 Apr 1985	1994

Displacement, tons: 2208 standard; 2525 full load
Dimensions, feet (metres): 371.3 × 37.1 × 12.1 *(113.2 × 11.3 × 3.7)*
Main machinery: CODOG; 2 Fiat/GE LM 2500 gas turbines; 50 000 hp *(37.3 MW)* sustained; 2 GMT BL 230.20 M diesels; 10 000 hp(m) *(7.3 MW)* sustained; 2 shafts; cp props
Speed, knots: 35 turbines; 21 diesels. **Range, miles:** 4350 at 16 kts on diesels
Complement: 185 (16 officers)

Missiles: SSM: 8 OTO Melara Teseo Mk 2 (TG 2) ❶; mid-course guidance; active radar homing to 180 km *(98.4 nm)* at 0.9 Mach; warhead 210 kg; sea-skimmer.
SAM: Selenia Elsag Aspide octuple launcher ❷; semi-active radar homing to 14.6 km *(8 nm)* at 2.5 Mach; warhead 39 kg. 8 reloads.
Guns: 1 OTO Melara 5 in *(127 mm)*/54 ❸; 85° elevation; 45 rounds/minute to 16 km *(8.7 nm)* anti-surface; 7 km *(3.8 nm)* anti-aircraft; weight of shell 32 kg.
4 Breda 40 mm/70 (2 twin) compact ❹; 85° elevation; 300 rounds/minute to 12.5 km *(6.8 nm)* anti-surface; 4 km *(2.2 nm)* anti-aircraft; weight of shell 0.96 kg.
2 Oerlikon 20 mm can be fitted.
Countermeasures: Decoys: 2 Breda 105 mm SCLAR 20-tubed trainable ❺; chaff to 5 km *(2.7 nm)*; illuminants to 12 km *(6.6 nm)*.
SLQ 25 Nixie; towed torpedo decoy.
ESM/ECM: Selenia SLQ 747 (INS-3M); intercept and jammer.
Combat data systems: IPN 10 mini SADOC action data automation; Link 11. SATCOM.
Fire control: 2 Elsag Mk 10 Argo with NA 21 directors for missiles and 5 in gun. 2 Dardo for 40 mm guns.
Radars: Air search: Selenia SPS 774 (RAN 10S) ❻; E/F band; range 155 km *(85 nm)*.
Surface search: Selenia SPQ 712 (RAN 12 L/X) ❼; I band.
Navigation: SMA SPN 748; I band.
Fire control: 2 Selenia SPG 70 (RTN 10X) ❽; I/J band; range 40 km *(22 nm)* (for Argo).
Two Selenia SPG 74 (RTN 20X) ❾; I/J band; range 15 km *(8 nm)* (for Dardo).
IFF: Mk XII.

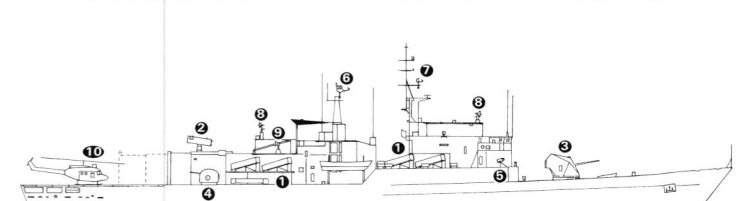

ARTIGLIERE

(Scale 1 : 1200), Ian Sturton

GRANATIERE (old number)

5/1991, van Ginderen Collection

Helicopters: 1 AB 212 ❿.

Programmes: On 20 January 1992 it was decided to transfer the four ships built for Iraq to the Italian Navy. The original sale to Iraq was first delayed by payment problems and then cancelled in 1990 when UN embargoes were placed on military sales to Iraq. The ships should enter service as offshore patrol vessels in 1993/94 although the refit programme was subject to continuous delays in 1992 as a result of the Defence Committee trying to cancel it, and the outcome remains uncertain in early 1993.
Modernisation: The details given are for the ships on completion of modernisation for Italian service. All ASW equipment removed, new combat and communications systems to Italian standards and a major upgrading of damage control and accommodation facilities.

CORVETTES

Note: Albatros class *Alcione* F 544 and *Airone* F 545 are used only for harbour training.

8 + (4) MINERVA CLASS

Name	No	Builders	Laid down	Launched	Commissioned
MINERVA	F 551	Fincantieri, Riva Trigoso	11 Mar 1985	3 Apr 1986	10 June 1987
URANIA	F 552	Fincantieri, Riva Trigoso	4 Apr 1985	21 June 1986	1 June 1987
DANAIDE	F 553	Fincantieri, Muggiano	26 June 1985	18 Oct 1986	9 Sep 1987
SFINGE	F 554	Fincantieri, Muggiano	2 Sep 1986	16 May 1987	13 Feb 1988
DRIADE	F 555	Fincantieri, Riva Trigoso	18 Mar 1988	11 Mar 1989	19 Apr 1990
CHIMERA	F 556	Fincantieri, Riva Trigoso	21 Dec 1988	7 Apr 1990	15 Jan 1991
FENICE	F 557	Fincantieri, Riva Trigoso	6 Sep 1988	9 Sep 1989	11 Sep 1990
SIBILLA	F 558	Fincantieri, Muggiano	16 Oct 1989	15 Sep 1990	16 May 1991

Displacement, tons: 1029 light; 1285 full load
Dimensions, feet (metres): 284.1 × 34.5 × 10.5 *(86.6 × 10.5 × 3.2)*
Main machinery: 2 Fincantieri GMT BM 230.20 DVM diesels; 12 600 hp(m) *(9.26 MW)* sustained; 2 shafts; cp props
Speed, knots: 24. **Range, miles:** 3500 at 18 kts
Complement: 123 (10 officers)

Missiles: SSM: Fitted for but not with 4 or 6 Teseo Otomat between the masts.
SAM: Selenia Elsag Albatros octuple launcher ❶; 8 Aspide; semi-active radar homing to 13 km *(7 nm)* at 2.5 Mach; height envelope 15-5000 m *(49.2-16 405 ft)*; warhead 30 kg. Capacity for larger magazine.
Guns: 1 OTO Melara 3 in *(76 mm)*/62 Compact ❷; 85° elevation; 85 rounds/minute to 16 km *(8.7 nm)* anti-surface; 12 km *(6.6 nm)* anti-aircraft; weight of shell 6 kg.
Torpedoes: 6—324 mm Whitehead B 515 (2 triple) tubes ❸. Honeywell Mk 46; active/passive homing to 11 km *(5.9 nm)* at 40 kts; warhead 44 kg. Being replaced by Whitehead A 290.
Countermeasures: Decoys: 2 Wallop Barricade double layer launchers for chaff and IR flares. SLQ 25 Nixie; towed torpedo decoy.
ESM/ECM: Selenia SLQ 747 intercept and jammer.
Combat data systems: Selenia IPN 10 Mini SADOC action data automation; Link 11. SATCOM.
Fire control: 1 Elsag Dardo E system. Selenia/Elsag NA 18L Pegaso optronic director ❹. Elmer TLC system.
Radars: Air/surface search: Selenia SPS 774 (RAN 10S) ❺; E/F band; range 155 km *(85 nm)*.
Navigation: SMA SPN 728(V)2 ❻; I band.
Fire control: Selenia SPG 76 (RTN 30X) ❼; I/J band (for Albatros and gun).
Sonars: Raytheon/Elsag DE 1167; hull-mounted; active search and attack; 7.5-12 kHz.

Programmes: First four ordered in November 1982, second four in January 1987. A third four are planned, allowing all other corvette classes to be scrapped.
Structure: The funnels remodelled to reduce turbulence and IR signature. Two fin stabilisers.
Operational: Omega transit fitted. Intended for a number of roles including EEZ patrol, fishery protection and Commanding Officers training. First four based at Augusta, Sicily.

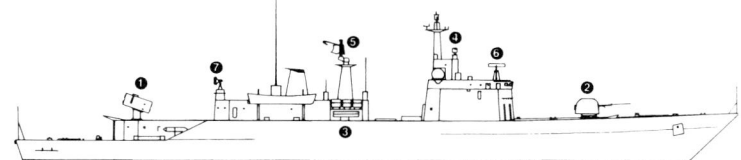
MINERVA *(Scale 1 : 900), Ian Sturton*

FENICE *6/1992, Harald Carstens*

1 DE CRISTOFARO CLASS

Name	No	Builders	Laid down	Launched	Commissioned
SALVATORE TODARO	F 550	Cantieri Ansaldo, Leghorn	21 Oct 1962	24 Oct 1964	25 Apr 1966

Displacement, tons: 850 standard; 1020 full load
Dimensions, feet (metres): 263.2 × 33.7 × 9 *(80.2 × 10.3 × 2.7)*
Main machinery: 2 Fiat 3012 RSS diesels; 8400 hp(m) *(6.17 MW)*; 2 shafts
Speed, knots: 23. **Range, miles:** 4000 at 16 kts
Complement: 131 (8 officers)

Guns: 2 OTO Melara 3 in *(76 mm)*/62 ; 85° elevation; 60 rounds/minute to 16 km *(8.7 nm)*; weight of shell 6 kg.
Torpedoes: 6—324 mm US Mk 32 (2 triple) tubes. Honeywell Mk 46; anti-submarine; active/passive homing to 11 km *(5.9 nm)*; warhead 44 kg.
A/S mortars: 1 Whitehead K 113 single-barrelled automatic ; range 900 m; warhead 160 kg.
Countermeasures: ESM: Elettronica SPR; intercept.
Fire control: OG3 director for guns. DLB 1 for A/S weapons.
Radars: Air/surface search: SMA SPQ 2B; I band.
Navigation: BX 732; I band.
Fire control: Selenia Orion 7; I/J band (for OG3); range 73 km *(40 nm)*.
Sonars: EDO SQS 36; hull-mounted and VDS; active search and attack; medium frequency.

Structure: The design is an improved version of the Albatros class.
Operational: The last of the class to survive and expected to pay off in 1994.

DE CRISTOFARO class (old number) *7/1991, van Ginderen Collection*

SHIPBORNE AIRCRAFT

Numbers/Type: 1 Westland/Agusta EH 101 Merlin.
Operational speed: 160 kts *(296 km/h)*.
Service ceiling: 15 000 ft *(4572 m)*.
Range: 550 nm *(1019 km)*.
Role/Weapon systems: Primary anti-submarine role with secondary anti-surface and troop carrying capabilities. Up to 30 planned in due course. Sensors: Radar, dipping sonar, sonobuoy acoustic processor, ESM, ECM. Weapons: ASW; 4 Whitehead torpedoes. ASV; 4 Sea Killer or replacement, capability for guidance of ship-launched SSM.

MERLIN *1991, Italian Navy*

ITALY / Shipborne aircraft — Offshore patrol vessels (OPV)

Numbers/Type: 16/2 AV-8B/TAV-8B Harrier II Plus.
Operational speed: 562 kts *(1041 km/h)*.
Service ceiling: 50 000 ft *(15 240 m)*.
Range: 800 nm *(1480 km)*.
Role/Weapon systems: Two trainers delivered in July 1991 plus 16 front line aircraft to be delivered from 1993. 13 more to be ordered in 1993. Sensors: Radar derived from APG-65, FLIR and ECM. Weapons: Strike and AD missiles, bombs and cannon.

SEA HARRIER *1991, Italian Navy*

Numbers/Type: 57/5 Agusta-Bell 212ASW/EW.
Operational speed: 106 kts *(196 km/h)*.
Service ceiling: 17 000 ft *(5180 m)*.
Range: 360 nm *(667 km)*.
Role/Weapon systems: ASW/ECM helicopter; mainly deployed to escorts, but also shore-based for ASW support duties. Five more being acquired for ex-Iraqi frigates. Sensors: Selenia APS 705 (APS 707 in 5 ex-Iraqi aircraft) search/attack radar, AQS-13B dipping sonar or GUFO (not in Iraqi aircraft) ESM/ECM. Weapons: ASW; 2 × Mk 46 torpedoes (not in Iraqi aircraft).

AB 212 *6/1992, Barbara Fraccaroli*

AB 212 *1992, Camil Busquets i Vilanova*

Numbers/Type: 36 Agusta-Sikorsky SH-3D/H Sea King.
Operational speed: 120 kts *(222 km/h)*.
Service ceiling: 12 200 ft *(3720 m)*.
Range: 630 nm *(1165 km)*.
Role/Weapon systems: ASW helicopter; embarked in larger ASW ships, including CVL; also shore-based for medium ASV-ASW in Mediterranean Sea; several sub-variants operated. Sensors: Selenia APS 705 search radar, AQS-13B dipping sonar, sonobuoys. Weapons: ASW; 4 × Mk 46 torpedoes. ASV; 2 × Marte 2/Sea Killer missiles.

SEA KING *1989, Aldo Fraccaroli*

LAND-BASED MARITIME AIRCRAFT

Numbers/Type: 18 Bréguet Atlantique 1.
Operational speed: 355 kts *(658 km/h)*.
Service ceiling: 22 800 ft *(10 000 m)*.
Range: 4855 nm *(8995 km)*.
Role/Weapon systems: Shore-based for long-range MR and shipping surveillance; wartime role includes ASW support to helicopters. Sensors: Thomson-CSF radar, ECM/ESM, MAD, sonobuoys. Weapons: ASW; 9 × torpedoes (including Mk 46 torpedoes) or depth bombs or mines.

Numbers/Type: 18 Panavia Tornado IDS.
Operational speed: Mach 2.2.
Service ceiling: 80 000 ft *(24 385 m)*.
Range: 1500 nm *(2780 km)*.
Role/Weapon systems: Swing wing strike and recce; part of a force of a total of 100 aircraft of which 18 are used for maritime operations based near Bari. Sensors: Texas instruments nav/attack systems. Weapons: ASV; 4 Kormoran missiles; 2 × 27 mm cannon. AD; 4 AIM-9L Sidewinder.

OFFSHORE PATROL VESSELS (OPV)

4 CASSIOPEA CLASS

Name	No	Builders	Laid down	Launched	Commissioned
CASSIOPEA	P 401	Fincantieri, Muggiano	16 Dec 1987	20 July 1988	6 July 1989
LIBRA	P 402	Fincantieri, Muggiano	17 Dec 1987	27 July 1988	28 Nov 1989
SPICA	P 403	Fincantieri, Muggiano	5 Sep 1988	27 May 1989	3 May 1990
VEGA	P 404	Fincantieri, Muggiano	20 June 1989	24 Feb 1990	25 Oct 1990

Displacement, tons: 1002 standard; 1475 full load
Dimensions, feet (metres): 261.8 × 38.7 × 11.5 *(79.8 × 11.8 × 3.5)*
Flight deck, feet (metres): 72.2 × 26.2 *(22 × 8)*
Main machinery: 2 Fincantieri/GMT BL 230.16 M diesels; 7940 hp(m) *(5.84 MW)* sustained; 2 shafts
Speed, knots: 20. **Range, miles:** 3300 at 17 kts
Complement: 78 (8 officers)

Guns: 1 OTO Melara 3 in *(76 mm)*/62; 85° elevation; 60 rounds/minute to 16 km *(8.7 nm)*; weight of shell 6 kg.
2—12.7 mm MGs.
Fire control: Argo NA 10.
Radars: Surface search: SMA SPS 702(V)2; I band.
Navigation: SMA SPN 748(V)2; I band.
Fire control: Selenia SPG 70 (RTN 10X); I/J band.

Helicopters: 1 AB 212ASW.

Programmes: Ordered in December 1986 for operations in EEZ. Officially 'pattugliatori marittimi'. Funded by the Ministry of the Merchant Navy but all operated by the Navy. The projected fifth of the class was cancelled in 1991.
Structure: Fitted for firefighting, rescue and supply tasks. Telescopic hangar. The guns and fire control radars are old stock taken from Bergamini class. There is a 500 cu m tank for storing oil polluted water.

VEGA *12/1990, Giorgio Ghiglione*

4 AGAVE CLASS

BAMBU P 495 (ex-M 5521)   **MANGO** P 496 (ex-M 5523)
MOGANO P 497 (ex-M 5524)   **PALMA** P 500 (ex-M 5525)

Displacement, tons: 375 standard; 405 full load
Dimensions, feet (metres): 144 × 25.6 × 8.5 *(43 × 7.8 × 2.6)*
Main machinery: 2 GM 8-268A diesels; 880 hp *(656 kW)*; 2 shafts
Speed, knots: 13.5. **Range, miles:** 2500 at 10 kts
Complement: 38 (5 officers)
Guns: 2 Oerlikon 20 mm (twin).
Radars: Navigation: SPN 750; I band.

Comment: Non-magnetic minesweepers of composite wooden and alloy construction similar to those transferred from the USA but built in Italian yards; all completed November 1956-April 1957. Originally class of 19. *Mirto* now used for surveying and *Alloro* as training ship for Petty Officers' School, La Maddalena. These four were converted for patrol duties with UN force in Red Sea, carry P numbers and are painted white. When the Italian commitment to the UN force comes to an end, the ships will be scrapped.

MANGO   *7/1992, F Sadek*

2 Ex-US AGGRESSIVE CLASS

Name	No	Builders	Commissioned
STORIONE (ex-*MSO 506*)	(ex-M 5431)	Martinolich S B Co	23 Feb 1956
SQUALO (ex-*MSO 518*)	(ex-M 5433)	Tampa Marine Co	20 June 1957

Displacement, tons: 665 standard; 720 full load
Dimensions, feet (metres): 172 × 36 × 13.6 *(52.4 × 11 × 4.1)*
Main machinery: 4 GM 8-268A diesels; 1760 hp *(1.31 MW)*; 2 shafts; cp props
Speed, knots: 14. **Range, miles:** 2400 at 10 kts
Complement: 62 (4 officers)
Guns: 1 US/Bofors 40 mm/56.
Radars: Navigation: SMA SPN 703; I band; range 73 km *(40 nm)*.
Sonars: GE UQS-1; active mine detection; high frequency.

Comment: Converted to offshore patrol vessels in 1992/93. New pennant numbers allocated. All minesweeping gear removed.

STORIONE (old number)   *1990, van Ginderen Collection*

MINE WARFARE FORCES

4 LERICI AND 3 + 5 GAETA CLASS (MINEHUNTERS/SWEEPERS)

Name	No	Builders	Commissioned
LERICI	M 5550	Intermarine, Sarzana	22 Mar 1985
SAPRI	M 5551	Intermarine, Sarzana	4 June 1985
MILAZZO	M 5552	Intermarine, Sarzana	6 Aug 1985
VIESTE	M 5553	Intermarine, Sarzana	2 Dec 1985
GAETA	M 5554	Intermarine, Sarzana	3 July 1992
TERMOLI	M 5555	Intermarine, Sarzana	7 Oct 1992
ALGHERO	M 5556	Intermarine, Sarzana	24 Feb 1993
NUMANA	M 5557	Intermarine, Sarzana	July 1993
CROTONE	M 5558	Intermarine, Sarzana	Dec 1993
VIAREGGIO	M 5559	Intermarine, Sarzana	May 1994
CHIOGGIA	M 5560	Intermarine, Sarzana	1995
RIMINI	M 5561	Intermarine, Sarzana	1995

Displacement, tons: 485 standard; 502 (672, *Gaeta* onwards) full load
Dimensions, feet (metres): 164 (167.3 *Gaeta*) × 31.5 × 8.6 *(50 (51) × 9.6 × 2.6)*
Main machinery: 1 Fincantieri GMT BL 230.8 M diesel (passage); 1985 hp(m) *(1.46 MW)* sustained; 1 shaft; cp prop; 3 Isotta Fraschini ID 36 SS 6V diesels (hunting); 1481 hp(m) *(1.1 MW)* sustained; 3 hydraulic thrust props (1 fwd, 2 aft)
Speed, knots: 15; 7 hunting. **Range, miles:** 2500 at 12 kts
Complement: 47 (4 officers) including 7 divers

Guns: 1 Oerlikon 20 mm/70 or 2 Oerlikon 20 mm/70 (twin) (*Gaeta* onwards). 2 additional 20 mm guns added for deployments.
Countermeasures: Minehunting: 1 Min 77 Mk 2 ROV; 1 Pluto mine destruction system; diving equipment and recompression chamber.
Minesweeping: Oropesa Mk 4 wire sweep.
Combat data systems: Motorola MRS III/GPS Eagle precision navigation system with Datamat SMA SSN-714V(2) automatic plotting and radar indicator IP-7113.
Radars: Navigation: SMA SPN 728V(3); I band; range 73 km *(40 nm)*.
Sonars: FIAR SQQ 14(IT) VDS (lowered from keel fwd of bridge); classification and route survey; high frequency.

Programmes: First four ordered 7 January 1978 under Legge Navale. Next six ordered from Intermarine 30 April 1988 and two more in 1991. From No 5 onwards ships are 1 m longer and are of an improved design with a better minehunting sonar which has been retrofitted in the first four in 1991. Construction of Gaetas started in 1988, with *Gaeta* launched 28 July 1990, *Termoli* 15 December 1990, *Alghero* 11 May 1991, *Numana* 26 October 1992, *Crotone* 11 Apr 1992 and *Viareggio* 4 October 1992. The last pair delayed by budget cuts in 1992, then cancelled but are now to be ordered in 1993.
Structure: Of heavy GRP throughout hull, decks and bulkheads, with frames eliminated. All machinery is mounted on vibration dampers and main engines made of amagnetic material. Fitted with Galeazzi 2 man compression chambers and a telescopic crane for launching Callegari frogmen boats.
Operational: Endurance, 12 days. For long passages passive roll-stabilising tanks can be used for extra fuel increasing range to 4000 miles at 12 kts.
Sales: Four to Malaysia, two to Nigeria and 12 of a modified design being built by the USA.

GAETA   *7/1992, Giorgio Ghiglione*

SAPRI   *9/1992, B Sullivan*

332 ITALY / Mine warfare forces — Amphibious forces

5 Ex-US ADJUTANT CLASS (MINEHUNTERS—COASTAL)

CASTAGNO M 5504	GELSO M 5509	MANDORLO M 5519
CEDRO M 5505	PLATANO M 5516	

Displacement, tons: 378 (360, *Mandorlo*) standard; 390 full load
Dimensions, feet (metres): 144 × 27.9 × 8 *(43.9 × 8.5 × 2.4)*
Main machinery: 2 GM 8-268A diesels; 880 hp *(656 kW)*; 2 shafts
Speed, knots: 13.5. **Range, miles:** 3000 at 10 kts
Complement: 41 (3 officers)
Guns: 2 Oerlikon 20 mm (twin) (in some).
Countermeasures: Pluto remote control system (minehunting).
Radars: Navigation: SMA 3 RM 20R (SPN 703); I band; range 73 km *(40 nm)*.
Sonars: GE SQQ 14; VDS; mine detection; high frequency.

Comment: Wooden hulled and constructed throughout of anti-magnetic materials. All commissioned August 1953-December 1954 and transferred by the USA in 1953-54. Originally class of 18. *Pioppo* used for surveying (see Survey Vessels). Minehunting conversion: *Mandorlo* completed 1975, *Platano* in 1979, *Cedro* in 1982, *Castagno* in 1983 and *Gelso* in 1984. *Mandorlo* used for alongside training and the rest are scheduled to pay off at one a year from 1993-96.

MANDORLO   *7/1992, Giorgio Ghiglione*

AMPHIBIOUS FORCES

2 + 1 SAN GIORGIO CLASS (LPDs)

Name	No	Builders	Laid down	Launched	Commissioned
SAN GIORGIO	L 9892	Fincantieri, Riva Trigoso	27 June 1985	25 Feb 1987	9 Oct 1987
SAN MARCO	L 9893	Fincantieri, Riva Trigoso	28 June 1986	21 Oct 1987	18 Mar 1988
SAN GIUSTO	L 9894	Fincantieri, Riva Trigoso	30 Nov 1992	Oct 1993	Feb 1994

Displacement, tons: 6687 standard; 7665 (8000 *San Giusto*) full load
Dimensions, feet (metres): 437.2 × 67.3 × 17.4 *(133.3 × 20.5 × 5.3)*
Flight deck, feet (metres): 328.1 × 67.3 *(100 × 20.5)*
Main machinery: 2 Fincantieri GMT A 420.12 diesels; 16 800 hp(m) *(12.35 MW)* sustained; 2 shafts; cp props
Speed, knots: 21. **Range, miles:** 7500 at 16 kts; 4500 at 20 kts
Complement: 170
Military lift: Battalion of 400 plus 30-36 APCs or 30 medium tanks. 3 LCMs in stern docking well. 3 LCVPs on upper deck

Guns: 1 OTO Melara 3 in *(76 mm)*/62 ❶; 85° elevation; 60 rounds/minute to 16 km *(8.7 nm)*; weight of shell 6 kg.
2 Oerlikon 20 mm ❷. 2—12.7 mm MGs.
Countermeasures: ESM: SLR 730.
Combat data systems: Selenia IPN 20 (*San Giusto* only).
Fire control: Elsag NA 10.
Radars: Surface search: SMA SPS 702 ❸; I band.
Navigation: SMA SPN 748; I band.
Fire control: Selenia SPG 70 (RTN 10X) ❹; I/J band; range 40 km *(22 nm)*.

Helicopters: 3 SH-3D Sea King or 5 AB 212.

Programmes: *San Giorgio* ordered 26 November 1983, *San Marco* on 5 March 1984 and *San Giusto* 1 March 1991. Launching dates of the first two are slightly later than the 'official' launching ceremony because of poor weather.
Structure: Aircraft carrier type flight deck with island to starboard. Three landing spots. Bow ramp for amphibious landings. Stern docking well 20.5 × 7 m. Fitted with a 30 ton lift and two 40 ton travelling cranes for LCMs. *San Giusto* is 300 tons heavier, of similar design except for more accommodation, a slightly longer island and different LCVP davit arrangement. Also no bow doors and therefore no beaching capability.
Operational: *San Giorgio* replaced *Caio Duilio* for midshipmen training and amphibious squadron but will be relieved by *San Giusto* in 1994. *San Marco*, being run in conjunction with and paid for by the Ministry of Civil Protection, is specially fitted for disaster relief but will be transferred to the Navy in a crisis. Both are based at Brindisi and assigned to the Third Naval Division. *San Giusto* is expected to be fully operational in October 1994 and will be attached to the Naval Academy at Livorno in peacetime.
Opinion: An imaginative but cheap and versatile design which has applications in Amphibious, ASW support or disaster relief operations. Being studied by a number of other navies.

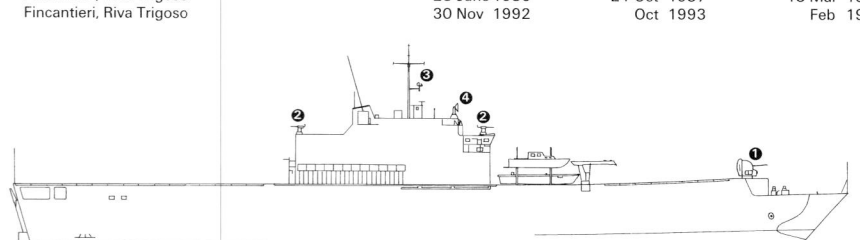

SAN GIORGIO   *(Scale 1 : 1200), Ian Sturton*

SAN GIORGIO   *7/1992, Giorgio Arra*

SAN GIORGIO   *1991, Milpress*

LIGHT FORCES

Notes: 1. *Saettia* (P 920) is a private Fincantieri venture and will not be bought by the Italian Navy.
2. The Navy plans to build up to eight 23 m Fast Patrol Craft in due course.

6 SPARVIERO CLASS (HYDROFOIL—MISSILE)

Name	No	Builders	Commissioned
NIBBIO	P 421	Fincantieri, Muggiano	6 Mar 1982
FALCONE	P 422	Fincantieri, Muggiano	6 Mar 1982
ASTORE	P 423	Fincantieri, Muggiano	5 Feb 1983
GRIFONE	P 424	Fincantieri, Muggiano	5 Feb 1983
GHEPPIO	P 425	Fincantieri, Muggiano	20 Jan 1983
CONDOR	P 426	Fincantieri, Muggiano	18 Jan 1984

Displacement, tons: 60.6 full load
Dimensions, feet (metres): 80.7 × 23.1 × 14.4 *(24.6 × 7 × 4.4)* (length and beam foils extended, draught hullborne); 75.4 × 22.9 × 5.2 *(23 × 7 × 1.6)* (hull size)
Main machinery: Foilborne: 1 RR Proteus 15 M/560 gas turbine; 4250 hp *(3.17 MW)* sustained; 1 waterjet
Hullborne: 1 Isotta Fraschini ID 38 N 6V diesel; 290 hp(m) *(213 kW)* sustained; 1 retractable prop
Speed, knots: 48; 8 hullborne on diesel. **Range, miles:** 400 at 45 kts; 1200 at 8 kts
Complement: 10 (2 officers)

Missiles: SSM: 2 OTO Melara/Matra Otomat Teseo Mk 2 (TG 1); active radar homing to 80 km *(43.2 nm)* at 0.9 Mach; warhead 210 kg; sea-skimmer.
Guns: 1 OTO Melara 3 in *(76 mm)*/62 compact; 85° elevation; 85 rounds/minute to 16 km *(8.7 nm)* anti-surface; 12 km *(6.6 nm)* anti-aircraft; weight of shell 6 kg.
Fire control: Elsag NA 10 Mod 3.
Radars: Surface search: SMA SPQ 701 (3 RM 7-250 in P 420); I band; range 73 km *(40 nm)*; IFF.
Fire control: Selenia SPG 70 (RTN 10X); I/J band; range 40 km *(22 nm)*.

Modernisation: Plans to change to a more powerful GT engine have been postponed but a new diesel has been fitted.
Structure: Aluminium hull and superstructure. Payload equal to 25 per cent of displacement.
Operational: Day running capability—no sleeping accommodation. Prototype paid off in October 1991.
Sales: Six of the class being built under licence in Japan.

GHEPPIO   *1990, Camil Busquets i Vilanova*

SURVEY VESSELS

Note: Two 300 ton 38 m GRP hulls to be built by Intermarine, Sarzana. These ships are planned to replace *Mirto* and *Pioppo* in due course if the contract goes ahead, which is doubtful.

Name	No	Builders	Commissioned
AMMIRAGLIO MAGNAGHI	A 5303	Fincantieri, Riva Trigoso	2 May 1975

Displacement, tons: 1700 full load
Dimensions, feet (metres): 271.3 × 44.9 × 11.5 *(82.7 × 13.7 × 3.5)*
Main machinery: 2 GMT B 306 SS diesels; 3000 hp(m) *(2.2 MW)*; 1 shaft; cp prop; auxiliary motor; 240 hp(m) *(176 kW)*; bow thruster
Speed, knots: 16. **Range, miles:** 6000 at 12 kts (1 diesel); 4200 at 16 kts (2 diesels)
Complement: 148 (14 officers, 15 scientists)
Guns: 1 Breda 40 mm/70 (not fitted).
Radars: Navigation: SMA 3 RM 20; I band; range 73 km *(40 nm)*.
Helicopters: Platform only.

Comment: Ordered under 1972 programme. Laid down 13 June 1973. Launched 11 October 1974. Full air-conditioning, bridge engine controls, flume-type stabilisers. Equipped for oceanographical studies including laboratories and underwater TV. Two Qubit Trac V integrated navigation and logging systems and a Chart V data processing system installed in 1992 to augment the existing Trac 100-based HODAPS. Carries six surveying motor boats.

AMMIRAGLIO MAGNAGHI   *5/1991, Giorgio Ghiglione*

Name	No	Builders	Commissioned
MIRTO	A 5306	Breda, Porta Marghera	4 Aug 1956
PIOPPO	A 5307	Bellingham SY, Seattle	31 July 1954

Comment: *Mirto* of the Agave class and *Pioppo* of the Adjutant class (see *OPV* and *Mine Warfare* sections for details) have been converted for surveying duties with complement of four officers and 36 men. To be replaced by two new construction ships in due course.

MIRTO   *9/1989, Marina Fraccaroli*

SERVICE FORCES

0 + (1) ETNA CLASS (REPLENISHMENT TANKER)

Displacement, tons: 12 660 full load
Dimensions, feet (metres): 464.2 × 68.9 × 24.3 *(141.5 × 21 × 7.4)*
Main machinery: 2 GMT A 420.16 H diesels; 23 000 hp(m) *(16.9 MW)* sustained; 2 shafts
Speed, knots: 21. **Range, miles:** 6300 at 22 kts
Complement: 230
Cargo capacity: 5000 tons gas oil; 500 tons JP5; 2000 m³ ammunition and stores
Guns: 1 OTO Melara 76 mm/62. 2 Breda 40 mm/70 (twin). 1—25 mm Gatling.
Helicopters: 2 EH-101 size.

Comment: Details revised in 1992 for a possible order in 1993. Hangar for 2 helicopters.

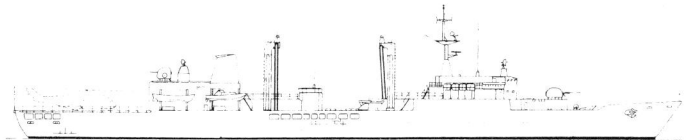

ETNA   *Lieut Comdr Erminio Bagnasco*

2 STROMBOLI CLASS (REPLENISHMENT TANKERS)

Naame	No	Builders	Commissioned
STROMBOLI	A 5327	Fincantieri, Riva Trigoso	20 Nov 1975
VESUVIO	A 5329	Fincantieri, Muggiano	18 Nov 1978

Displacement, tons: 3556 light; 8706 full load
Dimensions, feet (metres): 423.1 × 59 × 21.3 *(129 × 18 × 6.5)*
Main machinery: 2 GMT C428 SS diesels; 9600 hp(m) *(7.06 MW)*; 1 shaft; Lips cp prop
Speed, knots: 18.5. **Range, miles:** 5080 at 18 kts
Complement: 115 (9 officers)
Cargo capacity: 3000 tons FFO; 1000 tons dieso; 400 tons JP5; 300 tons other stores
Guns: 1 OTO Melara 3 in *(76 mm)*/62.
2 Breda 40 mm/70 (not fitted).
4 Oerlikon 20 mm (2 twin) fitted for Gulf deployments 1987-91.
Fire control: Argo NA 10 system.
Radars: Surface search: SMA SPQ 2; I band.
Navigation: SMA SPN 748; I band.
Fire control: Selenia SPG 70 (RTN 10X); I/J band; range 40 km *(22 nm)*.
Helicopters: Flight deck but no hangar.

Comment: *Stromboli* launched 20 February 1975, *Vesuvio* 4 June 1977. *Vesuvio* was the first large ship to be built at Muggiano (near La Spezia) since the war and the first with funds under Legge Navale 1975. Beam and stern refuelling stations for fuel and stores. Also Vertrep. The two ships have different midships crane arrangements. Similar ship built for Iraq and laid up in Alexandria since 1986.

VESUVIO   *9/1991, van Ginderen Collection*

334 ITALY / Service forces

4 EXPERIMENTAL SHIPS

Name	No	Builders	Commissioned
RAFFAELE ROSSETTI	A 5315	Picchiotti, Viareggio	20 Dec 1986

Displacement, tons: 320 full load
Dimensions, feet (metres): 146.3 × 25.9 × 6.9 *(44.6 × 7.9 × 2.1)*
Main machinery: 2 Fincantieri Isotta Fraschini ID 36 N 12V diesels; 1320 hp(m) *(970 kW)* sustained; 2 shafts; bow thruster
Speed, knots: 17.5. **Range, miles:** 700 at 15 kts
Complement: 17 (1 officer, 8 technicians)

Comment: Launched on 12 July 1986. Five different design torpedo tubes fitted for above and underwater testing and trials. Other equipment for research into communications, surface and air search as well as underwater weapons. There is a stern doorway which is partially submerged and the ship has a set of 96 batteries to allow 'silent' propulsion. Operated by the Permanent Commission for Experiments of War Materials at La Spezia.

RAFFAELE ROSSETTI 7/1987, Marina Fraccaroli

Name	No	Builders	Commissioned
VINCENZO MARTELLOTTA	A 5320	Picchiotti, Viareggio	22 Dec 1990

Displacement, tons: 340 full load
Dimensions, feet (metres): 146.3 × 25.9 × 7.5 *(44.6 × 7.9 × 2.3)*
Main machinery: 2 Fincantieri Isotta Fraschini ID 36 SS 16V diesels; 3520 hp(m) *(2.59 MW)* sustained; 2 shafts; bow thruster
Speed, knots: 17. **Range, miles:** 700 at 15 kts
Complement: 17 (1 officer)

Comment: Launched on 28 May 1988. Has one 21 in *(533 mm)* and three 12.75 in *(324 mm)* torpedo tubes and acoustic equipment to operate a 3D tracking range for torpedoes or underwater vehicles. Like *Rossetti* she is operated by the Commission at La Spezia.

V MARTELLOTTA 6/1990, Aldo Fraccaroli

BARBARA P 492

Displacement, tons: 195 full load
Dimensions, feet (metres): 98.4 × 20.7 × 4.9 *(30 × 6.3 × 1.5)*
Main machinery: 2 diesels; 600 hp(m) *(441 kW)*; 2 shafts
Speed, knots: 12

Comment: Built by Castracani, Ancona. A fishing vessel purchased and converted for research work in 1975. Converted in 1986 to Coastal Patrol Boat. Operates under the Technical and Scientific Council of Defence for missile testing at Perdasdefogu, Sardinia.

BARBARA 1989, Aldo Fraccaroli

MURENA (ex-*Scampo*) A 5305

Displacement, tons: 188 full load
Dimensions, feet (metres): 106 × 21 × 6 *(32.5 × 6.4 × 1.8)*
Main machinery: 2 Fiat/MTU MB 12V 493 TY7 diesels; 2200 hp(m) *(1.62 MW)* sustained; 2 shafts
Speed, knots: 14. **Range, miles:** 2000 at 9 kts
Complement: 16 (4 officers)

Comment: Built in 1957. Converted Aragosta class MSI used as a torpedo launching and support vessel.

MURENA 11/1990, Giorgio Ghiglione

1 Ex-US BARNEGAT CLASS (SUPPORT SHIP)

Name	No	Builders	Commissioned
PIETRO CAVEZZALE (ex-USS *Oyster Bay*, ex-AGP 6, AVP 28)	A 5301	Lake Washington Shipyard	17 Nov 1943

Displacement, tons: 1766 standard; 2800 full load
Dimensions, feet (metres): 310.8 × 41 × 13.5 *(94.7 × 12.5 × 4.1)*
Main machinery: 2 Fairbanks-Morse 38D8-1/8-10 diesels; 3540 hp *(2.64 MW)* sustained; 2 shafts
Speed, knots: 16. **Range, miles:** 10 000 at 11 kts
Complement: 114 (7 officers)
Guns: 1 US 3 in *(76 mm)*/50. 2 US/Bofors 40 mm/56.
Radars: Air search: Westinghouse SPS 6C; D band; range 146 km *(80 nm)* against fighter aircraft.
Surface search: SMA SPN 748; I band.

Comment: Former US seaplane tender (subsequently motor torpedo boat tender). Launched on 7 September 1942. Transferred to the Italian Navy on 23 October 1957. Was to have been paid off in 1991 but this has been delayed until late 1993.

PIETRO CAVEZZALE 9/1991, van Ginderen Collection

6 MTC 1011 CLASS (RAMPED TRANSPORTS)

Name	No	Builders	Commissioned
GORGONA (1011)	A 5347	C N Mario Marini	23 Dec 1986
TREMITI (1012)	A 5348	C N Mario Marini	2 Mar 1987
CAPRERA (1013)	A 5349	C N Mario Marini	10 Apr 1987
PANTELLERIA (1014)	A 5351	C N Mario Marini	26 May 1987
LIPARI (1015)	A 5352	C N Mario Marini	10 July 1987
CAPRI (1016)	A 5353	C N Mario Marini	16 Sep 1987

Displacement, tons: 631 full load
Dimensions, feet (metres): 186 × 32.8 × 8.2 *(56.7 × 10 × 2.5)*
Main machinery: 2 CRM 12D/SS diesels; 1760 hp(m) *(1.29 MW)*; 2 shafts
Speed, knots: 14.5. **Range, miles:** 1500 at 14 kts
Complement: 32 (4 officers)
Guns: 1 Oerlikon 20 mm (fitted for). 2—7.62 mm MGs.
Radars: Navigation: SMA SPN 748; I band.

Comment: As well as transporting stores, oil or water they can act as support ships for Light Forces, salvage ships or minelayers. 1015 and 1016 are attached to the Italian Naval Academy at Livorno, 1011 based at La Spezia, 1012 at Ancona, 1013 at La Maddalena and 1014 at Taranto.

PANTELLERIA 9/1992, B Sullivan

2 PEDRETTI CLASS (COMMANDO SUPPORT CRAFT)

Name	No	Builders	Commissioned
ALCIDE PEDRETTI	Y 499 (ex-MEN 213)	Crestitalia-Ameglia	23 Oct 1984
MARIO MARINO	Y 498 (ex-MEN 214)	Crestitalia-Ameglia	21 Dec 1984

Displacement, tons: 75.4 *(Alcide Pedretti)*, 69.5 *(Mario Marino)* full load
Dimensions, feet (metres): 86.6 × 22.6 × 3.3 *(26.4 × 6.9 × 1)*
Main machinery: 2 Isotta Fraschini ID 36 SS 12V diesels; 2640 hp(m) *(1.94 MW)* sustained; 2 shafts
Speed, knots: 25. **Range, miles:** 450 *(Alcide Pedretti)*, 250 *(Mario Marino)* at 23 kts
Complement: 6

Comment: Both laid down 8 September 1983. For use by assault swimmers of COMSUBIN. Both have decompression chambers. *Alcide Pedretti* has a floodable dock aft and is used for combat swimmers and special operations, while *Mario Marino* is fitted for underwater work and rescue missions. Based at Varignano, La Spezia. A similar but more heavily equipped vessel serves with the UAE coastguard.

ALCIDE PEDRETTI 9/1987, Aldo Fraccaroli

2 MEN 215 CLASS (LCVP)

MEN 215 MEN 216

Displacement, tons: 82 full load
Dimensions, feet (metres): 89.6 × 23 × 3.6 *(27.3 × 7 × 1.1)*
Main machinery: 2 Isotta Fraschini ID 36 SS 12V diesels; 2640 hp(m) *(1.94 MW)* sustained; 2 shafts
Speed, knots: 28. **Range, miles:** 250 at 14 kts
Complement: 4

Comment: Fast personnel launches completed in June 1986 by Crestitalia. Usually attached to *G Garibaldi* and can transport 250 men. Can also be used for amphibious operations or disaster relief.

MEN 215   *1987, Crestitalia*

1 SAR CRAFT

Name	No	Builders	Commissioned
PAOLUCCI	—	Picchiotti, Viareggio	12 Sep 1970

Displacement, tons: 70 full load
Dimensions, feet (metres): 90.9 × 24.3 × 3.3 *(27.7 × 7.4 × 1)*
Speed, knots: 21
Complement: 8 (1 officer)

Comment: Used as an air/sea rescue and ambulance craft.

PAOLUCCI   *1991, Italian Navy*

1 MEN 212 CLASS (TRV)

MEN 212

Displacement, tons: 32 full load
Dimensions, feet (metres): 58.4 × 16.7 × 3.3 *(17.8 × 5.1 × 1)*
Main machinery: 2 HP diesels; 1380 hp(m) *(1.01 MW)*; 2 shafts
Speed, knots: 22. **Range, miles:** 250 at 20 kts
Complement: 4

Comment: Torpedo Recovery Vessel completed in October 1983 by Crestitalia. GRP construction with a stern ramp.

MEN 212 (and assorted harbour launches)   *9/1991, Nikolaus Sifferlinger*

15 Ex-US LCMs

MTM 542-556 (9908-9922)

Displacement, tons: 56 full load
Dimensions, feet (metres): 56.1 × 14.4 × 3.9 *(17.1 × 4.4 × 1.2)*
Main machinery: 2 Gray Marine 64 NH9 diesels; 330 hp *(264 kW)*; 2 shafts
Speed, knots: 11. **Range, miles:** 130 at 10 kts
Cargo capacity: 30 tons
Guns: 2—12.7 mm MGs.

Comment: Transferred in 1953.

MTM 545   *11/1988, Aldo Fraccaroli*

11 MTM 217 CLASS (LCMs)

MTM 217-227 (9923-9933)

Displacement, tons: 64.6 full load
Dimensions, feet (metres): 60.7 × 16.7 × 3 *(18.5 × 5.1 × 0.9)*
Speed, knots: 9. **Range, miles:** 300 at 9 kts
Complement: 3
Cargo capacity: 30 tons

Comment: Built at Muggiano, La Spezia by Fincantieri. Three completed 9 October 1987 for *San Giorgio*, three completed 8 March 1988 for *San Marco*. Two commissioned in 1989. Three more ordered in March 1991 from a different shipyard.

MTM 220   *9/1991, van Ginderen Collection*

6 US LCVP TYPE

MTP 9726	MTP 9748	MTP 9750
MTP 9731	MTP 9749	MTP 9751

Displacement, tons: 11 full load
Dimensions, feet (metres): 36.5 × 10.8 × 3 *(11.1 × 3.3 × 0.9)*
Main machinery: 1 Gray Marine 64 HN9 diesel; 165 hp *(123 kW)*; 1 shaft
Speed, knots: 10. **Range, miles:** 110 at 9 kts
Guns: 2—12.7 mm MGs.

Comment: Italian construction but built to a basic US design. Pennant numbers in the 523-539 series.

12 MTP 96 CLASS (LCVP)

MTP 96-107 (9755-9766)

Displacement, tons: 14.3 full load
Dimensions, feet (metres): 44.9 × 12.5 × 2.3 *(13.7 × 3.8 × 0.7)*
Main machinery: 2 diesels; 700 hp(m) *(515 kW)*; 2 shafts
Speed, knots: 22. **Range, miles:** 100 at 12 kts
Complement: 3

Comment: Built by Crestitalia 1987 (three) and 1988 (five). Can carry 45 men or 4.5 tons of cargo. Speed reduced to 9 kts fully laden. Four more delivered in 1991. These craft have Kevlar armour.

HARBOUR TANKERS

GRS TYPE

Displacement, tons: 500 approx

Comment: Have GRS numbers. The old 170 series is being replaced by the 1010 series.

GRS Type   *3/1991, Giorgio Ghiglione*

336   ITALY / Training ships — Salvage ships

TRAINING SHIPS

Note: In addition to the ships listed *San Giorgio* is used in the training role until *San Giusto* takes over.

Name	No	Builders	Commissioned
AMERIGO VESPUCCI	A 5312	Castellammare	15 May 1931

Displacement, tons: 3543 standard; 4146 full load
Dimensions, feet (metres): 229.5 pp; 270 oa hull; 330 oa bowsprit × 51 × 22 *(70; 82.4; 100 × 15.5 × 7)*
Main machinery: Diesel-electric; 2 Fiat B 306 ESS diesel generators; 2 Marelli motors; 2000 hp(m) *(1.47 MW)*; 1 shaft
Speed, knots: 10. **Range, miles:** 5450 at 6.5 kts
Complement: 243 (13 officers)
Radars: Navigation: Two SMA SPN 748; I band.

Comment: Launched on 22 March 1930. Hull, masts and yards are of steel. Sail area, 22 604 sq ft. Extensively refitted at La Spezia Naval Dockyard in 1973 and again in 1984. Used for Naval Academy Summer cruise.

AMERIGO VESPUCCI   7/1992, van Ginderen Collection

Name	No	Builders	Commissioned
PALINURO (ex-*Commandant Louis Richard*)	A 5311	Ch Dubigeon, Nantes	1934

Displacement, tons: 1042 standard; 1450 full load
Measurement, tons: 858 gross
Dimensions, feet (metres): 193.5 × 32.8 × 15.7 *(59 × 10 × 4.8)*
Main machinery: 1 diesel; 450 hp(m) *(331 kW)*; 1 shaft
Speed, knots: 7.5. **Range, miles:** 5390 at 7.5 kts
Complement: 47

Comment: Barquentine launched in 1934. Purchased in 1951. Rebuilt in 1954-55 and commissioned in Italian Navy on 1 July 1955. Sail area, 1152 sq ft. She was one of the last two French Grand Bank cod-fishing barquentines. Owned by the Armement Glâtre she was based at St Malo until bought by Italy. Used for seamanship basic training.

PALINURO   5/1990, van Ginderen Collection

ARAGOSTA A 5378   MITILO A 5380   PORPORA A 5382
ASTICE A 5379   POLIPO A 5381

Displacement, tons: 188 full load
Dimensions, feet (metres): 106 × 21 × 6 *(32.5 × 6.4 × 1.8)*
Main machinery: 2 Fiat-MTU 12V 493 TY7 diesels; 2200 hp(m) *(1.62 MW)* sustained; 2 shafts
Speed, knots: 14. **Range, miles:** 2000 at 9 kts
Complement: 15 (2 officers)
Radars: Navigation: BX 732; I band.

Comment: Builders: CRDA, Monfalcone: *Aragosta, Astice*. Picchiotti, Viareggio: *Mitilo*. Costaguta, Voltri: *Polipo, Porpora*.
Similar to the late British Ham class. All constructed to the order of NATO in 1955-57. Designed armament of one 20 mm gun not mounted. Originally class of 20. Remaining five converted for training 1986. *Polipo* and *Porpora* used by the Naval Academy. *Aragosta* has large deckhouse aft as support ship for frogmen. Others of the class include *Murena* the experimental ship and GLS 501-502 ferries.

ASTICE   9/1991, van Ginderen Collection

ALLORO A 5308 (ex-*M 5532*)

Displacement, tons: 405 full load
Dimensions, feet (metres): 144 × 25.6 × 8.5 *(43 × 7.8 × 2.6)*
Main machinery: 2 Fiat diesels; 1200 hp(m) *(882 kW)*; 2 shafts
Speed, knots: 13.5. **Range, miles:** 2500 at 10 kts
Complement: 38 (5 officers)
Guns: 2 Oerlikon 20 mm.
Radars: Navigation: SPN 750; I band.

Comment: Agave class minesweeper built in 1957. Used by the Petty Officers training school at La Maddalena.

Name	No	Builders	Commissioned
CAROLY	A 5302	Baglietto, Varazze	1948
STELLA POLARE	A 5313	Sangermani, Chiavari	7 Oct 1965
CORSARO II	A 5316	Costaguta, Voltri	5 Jan 1961
CRISTOFORO COLOMBO II		Sai Ambrosini	Oct 1991

Comment: The first three are sail training ships of between 40 and 60 tons with a crew including trainees of about 16. *C Colombo II* built for the 1992 regatta to commemorate the 500th anniversary of the discovery of America. She displaces 82 tons and has a crew of 20. Sail area of 9900 sq ft.

SALVAGE SHIPS

Name	No	Builders	Commissioned
PROTEO (ex-*Perseo*)	A 5310	Cantieri Navali Riuniti, Ancona	24 Aug 1951

Displacement, tons: 1865 standard; 2147 full load
Dimensions, feet (metres): 248 × 38 × 21 *(75.6 × 11.6 × 6.4)*
Main machinery: 2 Fiat diesels; 4800 hp(m) *(3.53 MW)*; 1 shaft
Speed, knots: 16. **Range, miles:** 7500 at 13 kts
Complement: 122 (8 officers)
Guns: 3 Oerlikon 20 mm.
Radars: Navigation: SMA SPN 748; I band.

Comment: Laid down at Cantieri Navali Riuniti, Ancona, in 1943. Suspended in 1944. Seized by Germans and transferred to Trieste. Construction re-started at Cantieri Navali Riuniti, Ancona, in 1949. Formerly mounted one 3.9 in gun and two 20 mm. May be paid off in late 1993.

PROTEO   11/1988 Giorgio Ghiglione

Name	No	Builders	Commissioned
ANTEO	A 5309	C N Breda-Mestre	31 July 1980

Displacement, tons: 3200 full load
Dimensions, feet (metres): 322.8 × 51.8 × 16.7 *(98.4 × 15.8 × 5.1)*
Main machinery: 2 GMT A 230.12 diesels; 5000 hp(m) *(3.68 MW)*; 2 motors; 6000 hp(m) *(4.41 MW)*; 1 shaft; 2 bow thrusters; 1000 hp(m) *(735 kW)*
Speed, knots: 20. **Range, miles:** 4000 at 14 kts
Complement: 121 (including salvage staff)
Guns: 2 Oerlikon 20 mm fitted during deployments.
Radars: Surface search: SMA SPN 751; I band.
Navigation: SMA SPN 748; I band.
Helicopters: 1 AB 212.

Comment: Ordered mid-1977, launched 11 November 1978. Comprehensively fitted with flight deck and hangar, extensive salvage gear, including rescue bell, and recompression chambers. Carries four lifeboats of various types. Three firefighting systems. Full towing equipment. Carries midget submarine, *Usel*, of 13.2 tons dived with dimensions 26.2 × 6.2 × 8.9 ft *(8 × 1.9 × 2.7 m)*. Carries two men and can dive to 600 m. Endurance, 120 hours at 5 kts. Also has a McCann rescue chamber.

ANTEO   7/1990, J Y Robert

LIGHTHOUSE TENDERS

5 PONZA CLASS

Name	No	Builders	Commissioned
PONZA	A 5364	Morini Yard, Ancona	9 Dec 1988
LEVANZO	A 5366	Morini Yard, Ancona	24 Jan 1989
TAVOLARA	A 5367	Morini Yard, Ancona	12 Apr 1989
PALMARIA	A 5368	Morini Yard, Ancona	12 May 1989
PROCIDA	A 5383	Morini Yard, Ancona	14 Nov 1990

Displacement, tons: 608 full load
Dimensions, feet (metres): 186 × 35.4 × 8.2 *(56.7 × 10.8 × 2.5)*
Main machinery: 2 Fincantieri Isotta Fraschini ID 36 SS 8V diesels; 1760 hp(m) *(1.29 MW)* sustained; 2 shafts
Speed, knots: 14.5. **Range, miles:** 1500 at 14 kts
Complement: 34
Guns: 2—7.62 mm MGs.

Comment: MTF 1304-1308. Similar to MTC 1011 class.

PALMARIA   9/1991, van Ginderen Collection

REPAIR CRAFT

5 Ex-BRITISH LCT 3 TYPE

MOC 1201 A 5331   MOC 1203 A 5333   MOC 1205 A 5335
MOC 1202 A 5332   MOC 1204 A 5334

Displacement, tons: 350 standard; 640 full load
Dimensions, feet (metres): 192 × 31 × 7 *(58.6 × 9.5 × 2.1)*
Main machinery: 2 diesels; 1000 hp *(746 kW)*; 2 shafts
Speed, knots: 8
Complement: 24 (3 officers)
Guns: 2 Bofors 40 mm/70. 2 Oerlikon 20 mm.
  2 ships have 2—40 mm and 1 ship has 3—20 mm.

Comment: Built in 1943. Originally converted as repair craft. Other duties have been taken over—*MOC 1201* is used for torpedo trials and *MOC 1203* is the minesweepers' support ship.

MOC 1203   1990, Milpress

MOC 1201   8/1991, Aldo Fraccaroli

FERRIES

TARANTOLA

Comment: Based at Taranto. To be replaced by *Cheradi* in 1993.

TARANTOLA   9/1991, van Ginderen Collection

WATER CARRIERS

Name	No	Builders	Commissioned
PIAVE	A 5354	Orlando, Leghorn	23 May 1973

Displacement, tons: 4973 full load
Dimensions, feet (metres): 320.8 × 44 × 19.4 *(97.8 × 13.4 × 5.9)*
Main machinery: 2 diesels; 2560 hp(m) *(1.88 MW)*; 2 shafts
Speed, knots: 13. **Range, miles:** 1500 at 12 kts
Complement: 55 (7 officers)
Cargo capacity: 3500 tons
Guns: 4 Breda 40 mm/70 (2 twin) (not mounted).
Radars: Navigation: SMA SPN 748; I band.

PIAVE   1989, Aldo Fraccaroli

Name	No	Builders	Commissioned
BASENTO	A 5356	Inma di La Spezia	19 July 1971
BRADANO	A 5357	Inma di La Spezia	29 Dec 1971
BRENTA	A 5358	Inma di La Spezia	18 Apr 1972

Displacement, tons: 1914 full load
Dimensions, feet (metres): 225.4 × 33.1 × 12.8 *(68.7 × 10.1 × 3.9)*
Main machinery: 2 Fiat LA 230 diesels; 1730 hp(m) *(1.27 MW)*; 2 shafts
Speed, knots: 13. **Range, miles:** 1650 at 12 kts
Complement: 24 (3 officers)
Cargo capacity: 1200 tons
Guns: 2 Oerlikon 20 mm (not fitted in all ships).

BRADANO   9/1989, Marina Fraccaroli

BORMIDA (ex-*GGS 1011*) A 5359

Displacement, tons: 736
Dimensions, feet (metres): 131.9 × 23.6 × 10.5 *(40.2 × 7.2 × 3.2)*
Complement: 11 (1 officer)
Cargo capacity: 260 tons

Comment: Converted at La Spezia in 1974.

BORMIDA   9/1991, van Ginderen Collection

338 ITALY / Water carriers — Tugs

GGS 185, 186, 500, 501, 502, 503, 507, 1009

Displacement, tons: 200

Comment: 185 and 502 at Taranto, 500 and 501 at Naples, 503 and 1009 at La Maddalena, 507 at Brindisi, 186 at La Spezia. GGS indicates water carriers.

GGS 186   9/1991, van Ginderen Collection

MCC 1101	A 5370	MCC 1103	A 5372
MCC 1102	A 5371	MCC 1104	A 5373

Displacement, tons: 898 full load
Dimensions, feet (metres): 155.2 × 32.8 × 10.8 *(47.3 × 10 × 3.3)*
Main machinery: 2 Fincantieri Isotta Fraschini ID 36 SS 6V diesels; 1320 hp(m) *(970 kW)* sustained; 2 shafts
Speed, knots: 13. Range, miles: 1500 at 12 kts
Complement: 12
Cargo capacity: 550 tons

Comment: Built by Ferrari, La Spezia and completed one in 1986, two in May 1987, one in May 1988.

MCC 1101   9/1991, van Ginderen Collection

Name	No	Builders	Commissioned
SIMETO	A 5375	Cinet, Molfetta	9 July 1988
—	—	Poli Shipyard, Pellestrina	Mar 1994
—	—	Poli Shipyard, Pellestrina	June 1994

Displacement, tons: 1858 full load
Dimensions, feet (metres): 224 × 32.8 × 12.8 *(68.3 × 10 × 3.9)*
Main machinery: 2 GMT B 230.6 M diesels; 2980 hp(m) *(2.1 MW)* sustained; 2 shafts
Speed, knots: 13. Range, miles: 1500 at 12 kts
Complement: 27 (2 officers)
Cargo capacity: 1130 tons

Comment: Two units of a slightly improved version building. Increased displacement of 1968 tons and cargo capacity of 1200 tons.

TUGS

CICLOPE	A 5319	POLIFEMO	A 5325	SATURNO	A 5330
TITANO	A 5324	GIGANTE	A 5328	TENACE	A 5365

Displacement, tons: 658 full load
Dimensions, feet (metres): 127.6 × 32.5 × 12.1 *(38.9 × 9.9 × 3.7)*
Main machinery: 2 GMT B 230.8 M diesels; 3970 hp(m) *(2.02 MW)* sustained; 2 shafts
Speed, knots: 14.5. Range, miles: 3000 at 14 kts
Complement: 12

Comment: Built by C N Ferrari, La Spezia. Completed *Ciclope*, 5 September 1985; *Titano*, 7 December 1985; *Polifemo*, 21 April 1986; *Gigante*, 18 July 1986; *Saturno* 5 April 1988 and *Tenace* 9 July 1988. All fitted with firefighting equipment and two portable submersible pumps. Bollard pull 45 tons.

TENACE   9/1991, van Ginderen Collection

Name	No	Builders	Commissioned
ATLANTE	A 5317	Visentini-Donada	14 Aug 1975
PROMETEO	A 5318	Visentini-Donada	14 Aug 1975

Displacement, tons: 750 full load
Dimensions, feet (metres): 127.9 × 32.1 × 13.4 *(39 × 9.6 × 4.1)*
Main machinery: 1 Tosi QT 320/8 SS diesel; 2670 hp(m) *(1.96 MW)*; 1 shaft; cp prop
Speed, knots: 13.5. Range, miles: 4000 at 12 kts
Complement: 25

PROMETEO   1990, van Ginderen Collection

9 COASTAL TUGS

PORTO EMPEDOCLE Y 421	PORTO FERRAIO Y 425	PORTO FOSSONE Y 413
PORTO PISANO Y 422	PORTO VENERE Y 426	PORTO TORRES Y 416
PORTO CONTE Y 423	PORTO SALVO Y 428	PORTO CORSINI Y 417

Displacement, tons: 412 full load
Measurement, tons: 122 dwt
Dimensions, feet (metres): 106.3 × 27.9 × 10.8 *(32.4 × 8.5 × 3.3)*
Main machinery: 2 GMT B 230.8 M diesels; 3970 hp(m) *(2.92 MW)* sustained; 2 shafts
Speed, knots: 12.7. Range, miles: 4000 at 12 kts
Complement: 13
Radars: Navigation: GEM BX 132; I band.
Sonars: Honeywell/Elac Type LAZ-50.

Comment: Six ordered from CN De Poli (Pallestrina) and further three from Ferbex (Naples) in 1986.
Delivery dates *Porto Salvo* (13 Sep 1985), *Porto Pisano* (22 Oct 1985), *Porto Ferraio* (20 July 1985), *Porto Conte* (21 Nov 1985), *Porto Empedocle* (19 Mar 1986), *Porto Venere* (16 May 1989), *Porto Fossone* (24 Sep 1990), *Porto Torres* (16 Jan 1991) and *Porto Corsini* (4 Mar 1991). Fitted for firefighting and anti-pollution. Carry a 1 ton telescopic crane. Based at Taranto, La Spezia, Augusta and La Maddalena.

PORTO TORRES   7/1992, Giorgio Ghiglione

PORTO D'ISCHIA Y 436	RIVA TRIGOSO Y 443

Displacement, tons: 296 full load
Dimensions, feet (metres): 89.5 × 23.3 × 10.8 *(27.3 × 7.1 × 3.3)*
Main machinery: Diesel; 850 hp(m) *(625 kW)*; 1 shaft; cp prop
Speed, knots: 12.1

Comment: Both launched in September 1969 by CNR, Riva Trigoso. *Porto d'Ischia* commissioned 1970 and based at La Spezia; *Riva Trigoso*, 1969 and based at Taranto.

RIVA TRIGOSO   9/1991, van Ginderen Collection

32 HARBOUR TUGS

RP 101 Y 403 (1972)	RP 113 Y 463 (1978)	RP 125 Y 478 (1983)
RP 102 Y 404 (1972)	RP 114 Y 464 (1980)	RP 126 Y 479 (1983)
RP 103 Y 406 (1974)	RP 115 Y 465 (1980)	RP 127 Y 480 (1984)
RP 104 Y 407 (1974)	RP 116 Y 466 (1980)	RP 128 Y 481 (1984)
RP 105 Y 408 (1974)	RP 118 Y 468 (1980)	RP 129 Y 482 (1984)
RP 106 Y 410 (1974)	RP 119 Y 470 (1980)	RP 130 Y 483 (1985)
RP 108 Y 452 (1975)	RP 120 Y 471 (1980)	RP 131 Y 484 (1985)
RP 109 Y 456 (1975)	RP 121 — (1984)	RP 132 Y 485 (1985)
RP 110 Y 458 (1975)	RP 122 Y 473 (1981)	RP 133 Y 486 (1985)
RP 111 Y 460 (1975)	RP 123 Y 467 (1981)	RP 134 Y 487 (1985)
RP 112 Y 462 (1975)	RP 124 Y 477 (1981)	

Comment: RP 126 by Cantieri Navali Vittoria of Adria and RP 121 by Baia, Naples. RP 127-131 and 134 built by Ferrari Yard, La Spezia. RP 132 and 133 built by CINET Yard, Molfetta. RP 113-126 are of slightly larger dimensions and differ somewhat in appearance. RP 127-134 are larger and slower.

RP 121   10/1991, Aldo Fraccaroli

FLOATING DOCKS

Number	Date	Capacity-tons
GO 1	1942	1000
GO 5	1893	100
GO 8	1904	3800
GO 10	1900	2000
GO 11	1920	2700
GO 17	1917	500
GO 18A	1920	800
GO 18B	1920	600
GO 20	1935	1600
GO 22	1935	1000
GO 23	1935	1000
GO 51	1971	2000
GO 52	1988	6000
GO 53	1991	6000

Comment: Stationed at La Spezia (GS 52) and Augusta (GS 53).

ITALIAN ARMY, AMPHIBIOUS COMMAND

Note: The following units are operated by the 'Sile Amphibious Battalion' in the Venice Lagoons area. EIG means Italian Army Craft and is part of the hull number. Four LCM (EIG 29, 30, 31, 32), 60 tons; two LCVP (EIG 26, 27), 13 tons; four recce craft (EIG 3, 48, 49, 206), 5 tons; two command craft (EIG 208, 210), 21.5 tons; one rescue tug (EIG 209), 45 tons; one inshore tanker (EIG 44), 95 tons; one ambulance and rescue craft (EIG 28) and 15 minor craft (ferries, barges, rigid inflatable raiders).

GOVERNMENT MARITIME FORCES

GUARDIA COSTIERA—CAPITANERIE DI PORTO (COAST GUARD)

Note: This is a force of 130 craft which is affiliated with the Marina Militare under whose command it would be placed in an emergency. The Coast Guard denomination was given after the Sea Protection Law in 1988. All vessels now have a red diagonal stripe painted on the hull. There are some 4700 naval personnel including 770 officers of which 2550 are doing national service.
SAR craft; 8 CP 400 class of 100 tons. *Michelle Fiorillo* CP 307 (84 tons); *Bruno Gregoretti* CP 312 (65 tons); *Dante Novaro* CP 313; CP 314-315 (43 tons); CP 301-306, 308-311 (29 tons); CP 303-304 (18 tons).
Fast patrol craft; CP 239-245 (25 tons), CP 254-256 (22.5 tons), CP 246-253 (21.5 tons), CP 226-30 (18-20 tons), CP 231-238 (14 tons), CP 257-258 (24 tons).
Coastal patrol craft; CP 2069-2081 (13 tons), CP 2049-2051, 2053-2058, 2060-2068 (12.5 tons), CP 2043-2047 (12.4 tons), CP 2033-2035 (12 tons), CP 2010-2017 (10 tons), CP 2001-2005 (9 tons), CP 207 (8 tons), CP 502-505 (6.6 tons), CP 1001-1006 (5.2 tons), CP 501, 601-605 (3 tons). In addition there are five patrol craft of the CP 100 designation, 50 of the CP 5000 class with a speed of 25-30 kts, six inflatable rescue craft and 12 Crestitalia small patrol craft CP 6001-6012. Several of the larger craft are armed.
Aircraft include 12 Piaggio P 166 DL3 maritime patrol. Four Griffon AB 412 helicopters in service in 1992.

CP 406   5/1991, Giorgio Ghiglione

CP 251   9/1992, Aldo Fraccaroli

SERVIZIO NAVALE CARABINIERI

Note: The Carabinieri established its maritime force in 1969. This currently numbers 163 craft which operate in coastal waters within the three-mile limit and in inshore waters. The following are typical of the craft concerned;
8—700 class of 22 tons; 25—600 class of 12 tons; 30 N 500 class of 6 tons; 3 S 500 class of 7 tons; 23—500 class of 2.6 tons; 54—400 class of 1.4 tons.
All but the 500 and 400 classes are equipped with radar and all but the N 500 class (18 kts) are capable of 20-25 kts. 18 Rio 630 class ordered in mid-1989.

500 class   11/1991, van Ginderen Collection

SERVIZIO NAVALE GUARDIA DI FINANZA

Notes: 1. This force is operated by the Ministry of Finance but in time of war would come under the command of the Marina Militare. It is divided into 16 areas, 20 operational sectors and 28 squadrons. Their task is to patrol ports, lakes and rivers. The total manpower is 5300 operating 445 craft. Nearly all the larger craft are armed with a 20 mm gun or a machine gun. The first P-166 patrol aircraft was delivered by Piaggio in early 1991. A total of 10 has been ordered.

2. Patrol craft, 2 of 210 tons; Offshore patrol craft, *Genna* G 96 (120 tons); 4 of 57 tons G 72, 75, 77, 79; 2 of 54 tons G 70-71; 56 of 40 tons G 10-G 37, G 39-G 44, G 46-G 66; Coastal patrol craft, 2 of 20.4 tons building by Intermarine, 18 of 16.4 tons GL 314-331; 2 of 13.3 tons GL 432-433; 2 of 7.1 tons GL 103, 106; Local patrol craft; 34 of 15 tons V 5800-5833; 2 of 10.5 tons V 5901-5902; 81 of 7.8 tons V 5500-5581; 15 of 6.9 tons V 4000-4014; 3 of 5.1 tons V 5300-5302; 3 of 4.9 tons V 2911-2913; 1 of 2.9 tons V 3000; 1 of 1.8 tons V 2901; Training craft, *Giorgio Cini* of 800 tons; *Gian Maria Paolini* G 95 of 348 tons.
In addition 210 small craft operate on Italian lakes and rivers.

GIAN MARIA PAOLINI   9/1991, van Ginderen Collection

ITALY / Government maritime forces — IVORY COAST / Patrol forces

2 + 2 ANTONIO ZARA CLASS

ANTONIO ZARA P 01   **VIZZARI** P 02

Displacement, tons: 320 full load
Dimensions, feet (metres): 167 × 24.6 × 6.2 *(51 × 7.5 × 1.9)*
Main machinery: 2 GMT BL 230.12 M diesels; 5956 hp(m) *(4.38 MW)* sustained; 2 shafts
Speed, knots: 28. **Range, miles:** 2700 at 15 kts
Complement: 30 (1 officer)
Guns: 2 Breda 30 mm (twin). 2—7.62 mm MGs.
Fire control: Selenia Pegaso optronic director.

Comment: Built by Fincantieri at Muggiano, La Spezia. Similar to the Ratcharit class built for Thailand in 1976-79. Ordered in August 1987. *Antonio Zara* delivered 23 February 1990, *Vizzari* 27 April 1990. Two more to start building in 1993/94 with a modified armament of a single 30 mm gun with a Medusa optronic director. This is a second attempt by the Customs Service to create a force of high capability craft able to control the EEZ. Many years ago two 300 ton patrol boats were built and rejected as not meeting the operational requirement.

12 + 6 CORRUBIA and 8 + 10 BIGLIANI CLASSES

BIGLIANI G 80   **CORRUBIA** G 90
CAVAGLIA G 81   **GIUDICE** G 91

Displacement, tons: 80 full load
Dimensions, feet (metres): 86.6 × 23 × 3.6 *(26.4 × 7 × 1.1)*
Main machinery: 2 MTU 16V 396 TB94 diesels; 5800 hp(m) *(4.26 MW)* sustained; 2 shafts
Speed, knots: 40-45. **Range, miles:** 700 at 25 kts
Complement: 11
Guns: 1 Breda 30 mm. 2—7.62 mm MGs.
Fire control: Elsag Medusa optronic director.

Comment: Details given are for the Bigliani class built by Crestitalia and delivered October 1987 at La Spezia. G 90 and G 91 built by Cantieri Navale, Gaeta and delivered in 1990. Six more Corrubia class and ten more Bigliani class are being built. The Corrubia class displace 81 tons and are capable of only 40 kts having slightly less powerful engines.

ANTONIO ZARA   *1/1990, Giorgio Ghiglione*

BIGLIANI   *7/1987, Crestitalia*

IVORY COAST

Headquarters' Appointment

Chief of Naval Staff
  Capitaine de Vaisseau C V Timité Lassana

Bases

Use made of ports at Abidjan, Sassandra, Tabou and San-Pédro

Personnel

1993: 700 (70 officers)

General

This force is primarily concerned, in conjunction with aircraft, with offshore, riverine and coastal protection. Particular emphasis is placed on environmental protection, anti-pollution operations and dealing with fires. There are also some Halter and Arcor craft which are non-naval.

Mercantile Marine

Lloyd's Register of Shipping:
  51 vessels of 82 002 tons gross

DELETIONS

1991 *Comoe*
1992 6 Arcor class

PATROL FORCES

2 PATRA CLASS (FAST ATTACK CRAFT—MISSILE)

Name	No	Builders	Commissioned
L'ARDENT	—	Auroux, Arcachon	6 Oct 1978
L'INTRÉPIDE	—	Auroux, Arcachon	6 Oct 1978

Displacement, tons: 147.5 full load
Dimensions, feet (metres): 132.5 × 19.4 × 5.2 *(40.4 × 5.9 × 1.6)*
Main machinery: 2 SACM AGO 195 V12 CZSHR diesels; 4340 hp(m) *(3.19 MW)* sustained; 2 shafts
Speed, knots: 26. **Range, miles:** 1750 at 10 kts; 750 at 20 kts
Complement: 19 (2 officers)
Missiles: SSM: 4 Aerospatiale SS 12M; wire-guided to 5.5 km *(3 nm)* subsonic; warhead 30 kg.
Guns: 1 Breda 40 mm/70. 1 Oerlikon 20 mm. 2—7.62 mm MGs.
Radars: Surface search: Racal Decca 1226; I band.

Comment: Of similar design to French Patra class. Laid down 7 July 1977 *(Intrépide)* and 7 May 1977 *(Ardent)*. Both launched 21 July 1978. Patrol endurance of five days.

2 FRANCO-BELGE TYPE (LARGE PATROL CRAFT)

Name	No	Builders	Commissioned
LE VIGILANT	—	SFCN, Villeneuve	1968
LE VALEUREUX	—	SFCN, Villeneuve	25 Oct 1976

Displacement, tons: 235 standard; 250 full load
Dimensions, feet (metres): 155.8 × 23.6 × 7.5 *(47.5 × 7 × 2.3)*
Main machinery: 2 AGO diesels; 4220 hp(m) *(3 MW)*; 2 shafts *(Valeureux)*
  2 MGO diesels; 2400 hp(m) *(1.76 MW)*; 2 shafts *(Vigilant)*
Speed, knots: 22 *(Valeureux)*; 18.5 *(Vigilant)*. **Range, miles:** 2000 at 15 kts
Complement: 34 (4 officers)
Guns: 2 Breda 40 mm/70. 2—12.7 mm MGs.
Radars: Surface search: Racal Decca; I band.

Comment: *Le Vigilant* laid down in February 1967; launched on 23 May 1967. *Le Valeureux*, laid down 20 October 1975; launched 8 March 1976. Have been reported as Exocet fitted but this is not confirmed. *Le Valeureux* received new engines in 1987.

PATRA   *1989, Gilbert Gyssels*

LE VIGILANT   *8/198*

1 BATRAL TYPE (LIGHT TRANSPORT)

Name	No	Builders	Commissioned
L'ÉLÉPHANT	—	A Français de l'Ouest, Grand Queville	2 Feb 1977

Displacement, tons: 750 standard; 1330 full load
Dimensions, feet (metres): 262.4 × 42.6 × 7.9 *(80 × 13 × 2.4)*
Main machinery: 2 SACM Type 195 V12 diesels; 3600 hp(m) *(2.65 MW)*; 2 shafts; cp props
Speed, knots: 16. **Range, miles:** 4500 at 13 kts
Complement: 47 (5 officers)
Military lift: 180 troops; 12 vehicles; 350 tons cargo
Guns: 2 Breda 40 mm/70. 2—81 mm mortars.
Helicopters: Platform only.

Comment: Ordered 20 August 1974. Laid down 1975.

L'ÉLÉPHANT   1983

3 ROTORK TYPE 412

Displacement, tons: 9 full load
Dimensions, feet (metres): 41.7 × 10.5 × 3 *(12.7 × 3.2 × 0.9)*
Main machinery: 2 Volvo Penta AQD 40A diesels; 240 hp(m) *(176 kW)*; 2 shafts
Speed, knots: 28
Military lift: 30 troops

Comment: One fast assault boat supplied in 1980. Two others supplied for civilian use at the same time have now been taken over. More are still in civilian use.

2 LCVPs

Displacement, tons: 9 full load
Dimensions, feet (metres): 34.4 × 10.5 × 3.3 *(10.5 × 3.2 × 1.0)*
Main machinery: 1 Baudouin diesel; 1 shaft
Speed, knots: 9
Guns: 1—12.7 mm MG.

Comment: Built by DCAN, Cherbourg in 1976.

3 ARCOR TYPE

Displacement, tons: 5 full load
Dimensions, feet (metres): 31 × 11.5 × 2.6 *(9.5 × 3.5 × 0.8)*
Main machinery: 2 Baudouin diesels; 320 hp(m) *(235 kW)*; 2 shafts
Speed, knots: 20
Military lift: 30 troops

Comment: Delivered between 1982 and 1985. Six deleted so far.

JAMAICA

Headquarters' Appointment

Commanding Officer Jamaica Defence Force Coast Guard:
Commander H M Lewin

Defence Force Coast Guard

Jamaica, which became independent within the Commonwealth on 6 August 1962, formed the Sea Squadron on 25 August 1963 as the Maritime Arm of the Defence Force. The squadron was renamed the Defence Force Coast Guard on 1 January 1966.

Personnel

1993: (a) 178 (26 officers) Regulars
(b) 57 (18 officers) Reserve Forces

Training

(a) Officers: JDF Training depot, BRNC Dartmouth and other RN Establishments, RCN and Canadian Coast Guard, USN and US Coast Guard.
(b) Ratings: JDF Training depot, RN, RCN and Canadian Coast Guard, US Coast Guard and MTU Engineering Germany.

Bases

HMJS *Cagway*, Port Royal. Discovery Bay CG station

Mercantile Marine

Lloyd's Register of Shipping:
12 vessels of 11 096 tons gross

PATROL FORCES

1 FORT CLASS

Name	No	Builders	Commissioned
FORT CHARLES	P 7	Sewart Seacraft Inc, Berwick, La, USA	Sep 1974

Displacement, tons: 130 full load
Dimensions, feet (metres): 115 × 24 × 7 *(34.5 × 7.3 × 2.1)*
Main machinery: 2 MTU 16V 538 TB90 diesels; 6000 hp(m) *(4.41 MW)* sustained; 2 shafts
Speed, knots: 32. **Range, miles:** 1500 at 18 kts
Complement: 20 (4 officers)
Guns: 1 Oerlikon 20 mm. 2—12.7 mm MGs.

Comment: Of all-aluminium construction, launched July 1974. Underwent refit at Jacksonville, Fla, in 1980-81 which included extensive modifications to the bow resulting in increased length. Accommodation for 18 soldiers and may be used as 18-bed mobile hospital in an emergency.

FORT CHARLES   10/1990, JDFCG

3 BAY CLASS

Name	No	Builders	Commissioned
DISCOVERY BAY	P 4	Sewart Seacraft Inc, Berwick, La, USA	3 Nov 1966
HOLLAND BAY	P 5	Sewart Seacraft Inc, Berwick, La, USA	4 Apr 1967
MANATEE BAY	P 6	Sewart Seacraft Inc, Berwick, La, USA	9 Aug 1967

Displacement, tons: 72 full load
Dimensions, feet (metres): 85 × 18 × 6 *(25.9 × 5.7 × 1.8)*
Main machinery: 3 MTU 8V 396 TC82 diesels; 2610 hp(m) *(1.92 MW)* sustained; 3 shafts
Speed, knots: 25. **Range, miles:** 800 at 15 kts
Complement: 14 (3 officers)
Guns: 3—12.7 mm MGs.

Comment: All-aluminium construction. *Discovery Bay*, the prototype, was launched in August 1966. *Holland Bay* and *Manatee Bay* were supplied under the US Military Assistance programme. All three boats were extensively refitted and modified in 1972-73 by the builders with General Motors 12V 71 turbo-injected engines to give greater range, speed and operational flexibility. They were again re-engined and refitted at Swiftships, Louisiana, 1975-77. Between 1981 and 1984 a third engine change to MTU 396 diesels was done by Atlantic Dry Docks at Jacksonville.

MANATEE BAY   10/1990, JDFCG

1 HERO CLASS

Name	No	Builders	Commissioned
PAUL BOGLE	P 8	Lantana Boatyard Inc, Fla, USA	17 Sep 1985

Displacement, tons: 93 full load
Dimensions, feet (metres): 105 × 20.6 × 7 *(32 × 6.3 × 2.1)*
Main machinery: 3 MTU 8V 396 TB93 diesels; 3270 hp(m) *(2.4 MW)* sustained; 3 shafts
Speed, knots: 30+
Complement: 20 (4 officers)
Guns: 1 Oerlikon 20 mm. 2—12.7 mm MGs.
Radars: Surface search: Furuno; I band.

Comment: Of all-aluminium construction, launched in 1984. *Paul Bogle* was originally intended for Honduras as the third of the Guardian class. Similar to patrol craft in Honduras and Grenada navies.

PAUL BOGLE   10/1990, JDFCG

3 DAUNTLESS CLASS (INSHORE PATROL CRAFT)

CG 121   CG 122   CG 123

Displacement, tons: 11 full load
Dimensions, feet (metres): 40 × 14 × 4.3 *(12.2 × 4.3 × 1.3)*
Main machinery: 2 Caterpillar 3208TA diesels; 2 shafts
Speed, knots: 28. **Range, miles:** 420 at 22 kts
Complement: 5
Guns: 1—7.62 mm MG.
Radars: Surface search: Raytheon; I band.

Comment: Delivered in September and November 1992 and January 1993. Built by SeaArk Marine, Monticello. Aluminium construction.

CG 102   5/1992, JDFCG

2 BOSTON WHALER TYPE (INSHORE PATROL CRAFT)

CG 091   CG 092

Displacement, tons: 2.2 full load
Dimensions, feet (metres): 27 × 10 × 1.5 *(8.2 × 3 × 0.5)*
Main machinery: 2 Johnson OMC outboards; 400 hp *(298 kW)*
Speed, knots: 35
Complement: 3
Guns: 1—7.62 mm MG.
Radars: Surface search: Raytheon; I band.

Comment: Delivered in July 1992. Built by Boston Whaler, Rockland.

CG 121   10/1992, JDFCG

3 OFFSHORE PERFORMANCE TYPE (INSHORE PATROL CRAFT)

CG 101   CG 102   CG 103

Displacement, tons: 3 full load
Dimensions, feet (metres): 33 × 8 × 1.8 *(10.1 × 2.4 × 0.6)*
Main machinery: 2 Johnson OMC outboards; 450 hp *(336 kW)*
Speed, knots: 48
Complement: 3
Guns: 1—7.62 mm MG.
Radars: Surface search: Raytheon; I band.

Comment: Delivered in April 1992. Built by Offshore Performance Marine, Miami. Used in the anti-narcotics role.

CG 092   8/1992, JDFCG

JAPAN (MSDF)

MARITIME SELF-DEFENCE FORCE

Naval Board

Chief of Staff, Maritime Self-Defence Force:
   Admiral Fumio Okabe
Commander-in-Chief, Self-Defence Fleet:
   Vice Admiral Tatsuji Ito
Director, Administration, Maritime Staff Office:
   Rear Admiral Yujiro Koga

Senior Appointments

Commander Fleet Escort Force:
   Vice Admiral Toshio Muranaka
Commander Submarine Force:
   Vice Admiral Makotu Satou

Diplomatic Representation

Defence (Naval) Attaché in London:
   Captain Kazuo Tohyama

Personnel

1993: 46 630 (including Naval Air) plus 3969 civilians

District Flotillas

In addition to the Escort Fleet there are two Submarine Flotillas (Kure and Yokosuka), two MCM Flotillas (Kure and Yokosuka) and five District Flotillas (Yokosuka, Maizuru, Oominato, Sasebo and Kure). The District Flotillas are made up of up to six destroyers/frigates, an LST and a number of MCMV and patrol craft.

Bases

Naval—Yokosuka, Kure, Sasebo, Maizuru, Oominato
Naval Air—Atsugi, Hachinohe, Iwakuni, Kanoya, Komatsujima, Naha, Ozuki, Oominato, Omura, Shimofusa, Tateyama, Tokushima

Strength of the Fleet

Type	Active (Auxiliary)	Building (Projected)
Submarines—Patrol	15 (2)	2 (1)
Destroyers	42 (4)	5
Frigates	20 (1)	—
Fast Attack Hydrofoil—Missile	2	1
Fast Attack Craft—Torpedo	1	—
Patrol Craft—Coastal	5	—
LSTs	6	(1)
LSUs	2	—
Landing Craft (LCU/LSM/LCVP)	29	1
M/S Support Ships	3	(1)
Minehunters—Ocean	2	1 (3)
Minesweepers—Coastal	29	4
MSBs	4	—
Training Ships	1*	1
Training Support Ships	2	—
S/M Rescue Vessels	2	—
Fleet Support Ships	4	—
Tenders	10	—
Harbour Tankers	34	—
Icebreaker	1	—
Survey Ships	4	—
Cable Layer	1	—
Experimental Ships	1	1
Surtass Ships	2	—

* not including conversions

New Construction Programme

1990 1—7200 ton DDG, 1—2400 ton SS, 1—1000 ton MSO, 1—490 ton MSC, 2—50 ton PG, 1—2800 ton AOS, 1—420 ton LCU.
1991 1—7200 ton DDG, 1—4400 ton DD, 1—2400 ton SS, 1—490 ton MSC.
1992 1—4400 ton DD, 1—2500 ton SS, 3—490 ton MSC, 1—5C ton PG, 1—4000 ton TV, 1—4200 ton ASE.
1993 1—7200 ton DDG, 1—2700 ton SS, 1—8900 ton LST.

Fleet Air Arm

16 Air ASW Sqns: P-3C, P-2J, HSS-2, SH-60J
Six Air Training Sqns: P-3C, YS-11, TC-90, B-65, KM-2, Mentor, OH-6, HSS-2, U-36A, SH-60J
One Transport Sqn: YS-11
One MCM Sqn: MH-53E
Air Training Command (Shimofusa)
Air Wings at Kanoya (Wing 1), Hachinohe (Wing 2), Atsugi (Wing 4), Naha (Wing 5), Tateyama (Wing 21), Omura (Wing 22), Iwakuni (Wing 31)
The 1991-95 procurement plan includes eight P-3C, three EP-3, 36 SH-60J, eight UH-60J and one MH-53E

Mercantile Marine

Lloyd's Register of Shipping:
10 091 vessels of 25 403 270 tons gross

Introduction / JAPAN (MSDF)

Organisation of the Major Surface Units of Japan (MSDF)

Four escort flotillas each consisting of DDH (Flagship); two Air Defence ships and three or so ASW/general purpose Divisions of up to three ships each.

Escort Fleet (Yokosuka)
Murakumo (DD 118) Flagship

Escort Flotilla 1 (Yokosuka)
Shirane (DDH 143)
48th Destroyer Division
Umigiri (DD 158)
Hamagiri (DD 155)
Setogiri (DD 156)
46th Destroyer Division
Yuugiri (DD 153)
Amagiri (DD 154)
61st Destroyer Division
Asakaze (DDG 169)
Hatakaze (DDG 171)

Escort Flotilla 2 (Sasebo)
Kurama (DDH 144)
47th Destroyer Division
Asagiri (DD 151)
Yamagiri (DD 152)
Sawagiri (DD 157)
44th Destroyer Division
Yamayuki (DD 129)
Matsuyuki (DD 130)
62nd Destroyer Division
Sawakaze (DDG 170)
Kongo (DDG 173)

Escort Flotilla 3 (Maizuru)
Haruna (DDH 141)
42nd Destroyer Division
Mineyuki (DD 124)
Hamayuki (DD 126)
45th Destroyer Division
Setoyuki (DD 131)
Asayuki (DD 132)
Shimayuki (DD 133)
63rd Destroyer Division
Amatsukaze (DDG 163)
Shimakaze (DD 172)

Escort Flotilla 4 (Yokosuka)
Hiei (DDH 142)
1st Destroyer Division
Takatsuki (DD 164)
Kikuzuki (DD 165)
Tachikaze (DDG 168)
41st Destroyer Division
Hatsuyuki (DD 122)
Shirayuki (DD 123)
Sawayuki (DD 125)
43rd Destroyer Division
Isoyuki (DD 127)
Haruyuki (DD 128)

DELETIONS and CONVERSIONS

Submarines

1990 *Narushio* (converted May)
1991 *Kuroshio* (converted Mar)
1992 *Isoshio* (Mar), *Takashio* (converted July)
1993 *Narushio* (Mar)

Destroyers

1990 *Oonami* (Mar), *Makinami* (Mar)
1991 *Yamagumo, Makigumo* (both converted June)

Frigates

1990 *Ooi* (converted Jan), *Kitakami* (converted Jan)
1991 *Mogami* (June)
1992 *Isuzu* (Mar)
1993 *Ooi* (Feb)

Light Forces

1990 *Ash 6* (Mar), *PT 811* (Nov)
1991 *PT 12-13* (Oct)
1992 *PB 19-22* (Oct)
1993 *PT 14* (Mar)

Amphibious Forces

1992 YF 2097-98, YF 2066-67, YF 2091, YF 2110

Mine Warfare Forces

1990 2 MSC (640, 641) (converted Nov)
1992 2 MSC (642, 643) (converted Mar), 2 MSB (707, 708) (Mar)
1993 2 MSC (644, 645) (converted Mar)

Support Ships

1990 ASU 7001 *(Tsugaru)*, YAS 79 *(Minase)*, YAS 81 *(Katsura)*
1991 YO 5, YW 1-2, YW 7-9, YO 7-8, YT 35, YT 34
1992 YAS 82 *(Takami)*, YAS 83 *(Iou)*, YW 10
1993 *Utone*, YAS 85 *(Awaji)*, YAS 86 *(Toushi)*

PENNANT LIST

Submarines—Patrol

SS 572	Yaeshio
SS 573	Yuushio
SS 574	Mochishio
SS 575	Setoshio
SS 576	Okishio
SS 577	Nadashio
SS 578	Hamashio
SS 579	Akishio
SS 580	Takeshio
SS 581	Yukishio
SS 582	Sachishio
SS 583	Harushio
SS 584	Natsushio
SS 585	Hayashio
SS 586	Arashio
SS 587	Wakashio (bldg)
SS 588	— (bldg)

Submarines—Auxiliary

ATSS 8003	Kuroshio
ATSS 8004	Takashio

Destroyers

DD 115	Asagumo
DD 116	Minegumo
DD 117	Natsugumo
DD 118	Murakumo
DD 119	Aokumo
DD 120	Akigumo
DD 121	Yugumo
DD 122	Hatsuyuki
DD 123	Shirayuki
DD 124	Mineyuki
DD 125	Sawayuki
DD 126	Hamayuki
DD 127	Isoyuki
DD 128	Haruyuki
DD 129	Yamayuki
DD 130	Matsuyuki
DD 131	Setoyuki
DD 132	Asayuki
DD 133	Shimayuki
DD 141	Haruna
DD 142	Hiei
DD 143	Shirane
DD 144	Kurama
DD 151	Asagiri
DD 152	Yamagiri
DD 153	Yuugiri
DD 154	Amagiri
DD 155	Hamagiri
DD 156	Setogiri
DD 157	Sawagiri
DD 158	Umigiri
DD 163	Amatsukaze
DD 164	Takatsuki
DD 165	Kikuzuki
DD 166	Mochizuki
DD 167	Nagatsuki
DD 168	Tachikaze
DD 169	Asakaze
DD 170	Sawakaze
DD 171	Hatakaze
DD 172	Shimakaze
DD 173	Kongo
DD 174	— (bldg)

Frigates

DE 215	Chikugo
DE 216	Ayase
DE 217	Mikuma
DE 218	Tokachi
DE 219	Iwase
DE 220	Chitose
DE 221	Niyodo
DE 222	Teshio
DE 223	Yoshino
DE 224	Kumano
DE 225	Noshiro
DE 226	Ishikari
DE 227	Yubari
DE 228	Yubetsu
DE 229	Abukuma
DE 230	Jintsu
DE 231	Ohyodo
DE 232	Sendai
DE 233	Chikuma
DE 234	Tone

Light Forces

815	PT 15
923-927	PB 23-27
821-822	PG 01-02
823	PG 03 (bldg)

Minehunters/Sweepers—Ocean

MSO 301	Yaeyama
MSO 302	Tsushima
MSO 303	Hachijyo (bldg)

Minesweepers—Coastal

MSC 646	Okitsu
MSC 647	Hashira
MSC 648	Iwai
MSC 649	Hatsushima
MSC 650	Ninoshima
MSC 651	Miyajima
MSC 652	Enoshima
MSC 653	Ukishima
MSC 654	Ooshima
MSC 655	Niijima
MSC 656	Yakushima
MSC 657	Narushima
MSC 658	Chichijima
MSC 659	Torishima
MSC 660	Hahajima
MSC 661	Takashima
MSC 662	Nuwajima
MSC 663	Etajima
MSC 664	Kamishima
MSC 665	Himeshima
MSC 666	Ogishima
MSC 667	Moroshima
MSC 668	Yurishima
MSC 669	Hikoshima
MSC 670	Awashima
MSC 671	Sakushima
MSC 672	Uwajima
MSC 673	Ieshima
MSC 674	Tsukishima
MSC 675	— (bldg)

Minesweeping Boats

709	Kyuu-Go
710	Jyuu-Go
711	Jyuu-Ichi-Go
712	Jyuu-Ni-Go

MCM Support Ships

MMC 951	Souya
MST 462	Hayase
MST 476	Fukue

Amphibious Forces

LST 4101	Atsumi
LST 4102	Motobu
LST 4103	Nemuro
LST 4151	Miura
LST 4152	Ojika
LST 4153	Satsuma
LSU 4171	Yura
LSU 4172	Noto
LCU 2001	Yusotei-Ichi-Go
LCU 2002	Yusotei-Ni-Go

Submarine Depot/Rescue Ships

AS 405	Chiyoda
ASR 402	Fushimi

Fleet Support Ships

AOE 421	Sagami
AOE 422	Towada
AOE 423	Tokiwa
AOE 424	Hamana

Training Ships

TV 3501	Katori
TV 3506	Yamagumo
TV 3507	Makigumo

Training Support Ships

ATS 4201	Azuma
ATS 4202	Kurobe

Cable Layer

ARC 482	Muroto

Icebreaker

AGB 5002	Shirase

Surveying Ships

AGS 5101	Akashi
AGS 5102	Futami
AGS 5103	Suma
AGS 5104	Wakasa

Surtass Ships

AOS 5201	Hibiki
AOS 5202	Harima

Tenders

ASE 6101	Kurihama
ASU 81-85	
ASY 92	Hiyodori
ASU 7010	Akizuki
ASU 7012	Teruzuki
ASU 7016	Kitakami
YAS 84	Miyake
YAS 87	Teuri
YAS 88	Murotsu
YAS 89	Tashiro
YAS 90	Miyato
YAS 91	Takane
YAS 92	Muzuki
YAS 93	Yokoze
YAS 94	Sakate
YAS 95	Oumi

SUBMARINES

Notes: 1. Operational numbers are to be maintained at 14-16 hulls.
2. The first Improved Harushio class (S 589) should be laid down at Mitsubishi, Kobe in 1993. Displacement is 100 tons more than Harushio and the complement has reduced to 71 (10 officers). In service date 1997. Possibly to be fitted with air-independent propulsion. More of the class to follow at intervals of about 12 months.

4 + 2 HARUSHIO CLASS

Name	No	Builders	Laid down	Launched	Commissioned
HARUSHIO	SS 583	Mitsubishi, Kobe	21 Apr 1987	26 July 1989	30 Nov 1990
NATSUSHIO	SS 584	Kawasaki, Kobe	8 Apr 1988	20 Mar 1990	20 Mar 1991
HAYASHIO	SS 585	Mitsubishi, Kobe	9 Dec 1988	17 Jan 1991	25 Mar 1992
ARASHIO	SS 586	Kawasaki, Kobe	8 Jan 1990	17 Mar 1992	17 Mar 1993
WAKASHIO	SS 587	Mitsubishi, Kobe	12 Dec 1990	22 Jan 1993	Mar 1994
—	SS 588	Kawasaki, Kobe	12 Dec 1991	Feb 1994	Mar 1995

Displacement, tons: 2450 standard; 2750 dived
Dimensions, feet (metres): 262.5 × 35.4 × 25.6 *(80 × 10.8 × 7.8)*
Main machinery: Diesel-electric; 2 Kawasaki 12V25/25S diesels; 5520 hp(m) *(4.1 MW)*; 2 Kawasaki alternators; 3.7 MW; 1 Fuji motor; 7200 hp(m) *(5.3 MW)*; 1 shaft
Speed, knots: 12 surfaced; 20+ dived
Complement: 75 (10 officers)

Missiles: SSM: McDonnell Douglas Sub-Harpoon; active radar homing to 130 km *(70 nm)* at 0.9 Mach; warhead 227 kg (fired from torpedo tubes).
Torpedoes: 6—21 in *(533 mm)* tubes. Japanese Type 89; high speed active homing.
Countermeasures: ESM: ZLR 3-6; radar warning.
Radars: Surface search: JRC ZPS 6; I band.
Sonars: Hughes/Oki ZQQ 5B; hull-mounted; active/passive search and attack; medium/low frequency.
ZQR 1 towed array similar to BQR 15; passive search; very low frequency.

Programmes: First approved in 1986 estimates and one per year since then.
Structure: The slight growth in all dimensions suggests a natural evolution from the Yuushio class. Anechoic coating.

ARASHIO
10/1992, Hachiro Nakai

10 YUUSHIO CLASS

Name	No	Builders	Laid down	Launched	Commissioned
YUUSHIO	SS 573	Mitsubishi, Kobe	3 Dec 1976	29 Mar 1979	26 Feb 1980
MOCHISHIO	SS 574	Kawasaki, Kobe	9 May 1978	12 Mar 1980	5 Mar 1981
SETOSHIO	SS 575	Mitsubishi, Kobe	17 Apr 1979	10 Feb 1981	17 Mar 1982
OKISHIO	SS 576	Kawasaki, Kobe	17 Apr 1980	5 Mar 1982	1 Mar 1983
NADASHIO	SS 577	Mitsubishi, Kobe	16 Apr 1981	27 Jan 1983	6 Mar 1984
HAMASHIO	SS 578	Kawasaki, Kobe	8 Apr 1982	1 Feb 1984	5 Mar 1985
AKISHIO	SS 579	Mitsubishi, Kobe	15 Apr 1983	22 Jan 1985	5 Mar 1986
TAKESHIO	SS 580	Kawasaki, Kobe	3 Apr 1984	9 Feb 1986	3 Mar 1987
YUKISHIO	SS 581	Mitsubishi, Kobe	11 Apr 1985	23 Jan 1987	11 Mar 1988
SACHISHIO	SS 582	Kawasaki, Kobe	11 Apr 1986	17 Feb 1988	24 Mar 1989

Displacement, tons: 2200; 2250 (SS 574 and 577-582); 2300 (SS 576) standard; 2450 dived
Dimensions, feet (metres): 249.3 × 32.5 × 24.3 *(76 × 9.9 × 7.4)*
Main machinery: Diesel-electric; 2 Kawasaki-MAN V8V24/30ATL diesels; 6800 hp(m) *(5 MW)*; 1 motor; 7200 hp(m) *(5.3 MW)*; 1 shaft
Speed, knots: 12 surfaced; 20+ dived
Complement: 75 (10 officers)

Missiles: SSM: McDonnell Douglas Sub-Harpoon (SS 574, SS 577-582, others may be back fitted); active radar homing to 130 km *(70 nm)* at 0.9 Mach; warhead 227 kg; fired from torpedo tubes.
Torpedoes: 6—21 in *(533 mm)* tubes amidships. Probably a combination of Japanese Type 89 and US Mk 37C.
Countermeasures: ESM: ZLR 3-6; radar warning.
Radars: Surface search: JRC ZPS 6; I band.
Sonars: Hughes/Oki ZQQ 4 (or 5 in some) (modified BQS 4); bow-mounted; passive/active search and attack; medium/low frequency.
ZQR 1 towed array similar to BQR 15 (in most of the class); passive search; very low frequency.

Programmes: SS 573 approved in FY 1975, SS 574 in FY 1977, SS 575 in FY 1978, SS 576 in FY 1979, SS 577 in FY 1980, SS 578 in FY 1981, SS 579 in FY 1982, SS 580 in FY 1983, SS 581 in FY 1984 and SS 582 in FY 1985.

Modernisation: Towed sonar array fitted in *Okishio* in 1987 and now back-fitted to others in the class. ZQQ 5 is also being retrofitted.
Structure: An enlarged version of the Uzushio class with improved diving depth to 275 m *(900 ft)*. Double hull construction. Probably carries 18 torpedoes and missiles. The towed array is stowed in a conduit on the starboard side of the casing.
Operational: In July 1988 *Nadashio* on the surface collided with a fishing boat which caused much loss of life.

OKISHIO
10/1992, Hachiro Nakai

Submarines — Destroyers / JAPAN (MSDF)

3 UZUSHIO CLASS

Name	No	Builders	Laid down	Launched	Commissioned
KUROSHIO	ATSS 8003 (ex-SS 570)	Kawasaki, Kobe	5 July 1972	22 Feb 1974	27 Nov 1974
TAKASHIO	ATSS 8004 (ex-SS 571)	Mitsubishi, Kobe	6 July 1973	30 June 1975	30 Jan 1976
YAESHIO	SS 572	Kawasaki, Kobe	14 Apr 1975	19 May 1977	7 Mar 1978

Displacement, tons: 1850 standard; 1900 surfaced; 2430 dived
Dimensions, feet (metres): 236.2 × 32.5 × 24.6 *(72 × 9.9 × 7.5)*
Main machinery: Diesel-electric; 2 Kawasaki-MAN V8V24/30ATL diesels; 6800 hp(m) *(5 MW)*; 1 motor; 7200 hp(m) *(5.3 MW)*; 1 shaft
Speed, knots: 12 surfaced; 20 dived
Complement: 80 (10 officers); 70 plus 20 trainees (ATSS)

Torpedoes: 6—21 in *(533 mm)* tubes amidships. Japanese Type 89 high speed active homing.
Countermeasures: ESM: ZLR 3-6; radar warning.
Radars: Surface search: JRC ZPS 4; I band.
Sonars: Hughes/Oki ZQQ 2 (SS 572 has ZQQ 3 in lieu); bow-mounted; passive/active search and attack; medium/low frequency.

Programmes: Being paid off at one a year as new constructions commission.
Structure: Diving depth, 200 m *(656 ft)*. Double-hull construction and 'tear-drop' form, built of high tensile steel to increase diving depth.
Operational: *Kuroshio* became an auxiliary training submarine in May 1991 and *Takashio* 6 July 1992. One of the class may have been fitted with a Sterling engine for trials starting in late 1991.

YAESHIO *3/1992, Hachiro Nakai*

DESTROYERS

2 HATAKAZE CLASS

Name	No	Builders	Laid down	Launched	Commissioned
HATAKAZE	DD 171	Mitsubishi, Nagasaki	20 May 1983	9 Nov 1984	27 Mar 1986
SHIMAKAZE	DD 172	Mitsubishi, Nagasaki	13 Jan 1985	30 Jan 1987	23 Mar 1988

Displacement, tons: 4600 (4650, DD 172) standard; 5500 full load
Dimensions, feet (metres): 492 × 53.8 × 15.7 *(150 × 16.4 × 4.8)*
Main machinery: COGAG; 2 RR Olympus TM3B gas turbines; 49 400 hp *(36.8 MW)* sustained; 2 RR Spey SM1A gas turbines; 26 650 hp *(19.9 MW)* sustained; 2 shafts; cp props
Speed, knots: 30
Complement: 260

Missiles: SSM: 8 McDonnell Douglas Harpoon ❶; active radar homing to 130 km *(70 nm)* at 0.9 Mach; warhead 227 kg.
SAM: 40 GDC Pomona Standard SM-1MR; Mk 13 Mod 4 launcher ❷; command guidance; semi-active radar homing to 46 km *(25 nm)* at 2 Mach; height envelope 45-18 288 m *(150-60 000 ft)*.
A/S: Honeywell ASROC Mk 112 octuple launcher ❸; inertial guidance to 1.6-10 km *(1-5.4 nm)* at 0.9 Mach; payload Mk 46 Mod 5 Neartip. Reload capability.
Guns: 2 FMC 5 in *(127 mm)*/54 Mk 42 automatic ❹; 85° elevation; 20-40 rounds/minute to 24 km *(13 nm)* anti-surface; 14 km *(7.6 nm)* anti-aircraft; weight of shell 32 kg.
2 General Electric/General Dynamics 20 mm Phalanx Mk 15 CIWS ❺; 6 barrels per mounting; 3000 rounds/minute combined to 1.5 km.
Torpedoes: 6—324 mm Type 68 (2 triple) tubes ❻. Honeywell Mk 46 Mod 5 Neartip; anti-submarine; active/passive homing to 11 km *(5.9 nm)* at 40 kts; warhead 44 kg.

Countermeasures: Decoys: 2 Loral Hycor SRBOC 6-barrelled Mk 36 chaff launchers; range 4 km *(2.2 nm)*.
ESM: Melco NOLQ 1; intercept.
ECM: Fujitsu OLT 3; jammer.
Combat data systems: OYQ-4 Mod 1 action data automation; Links 11 and 14. SATCOM ❼.
Fire control: Type 2-21C for 127 mm guns. General Electric Mk 74 Mod 13 for Standard.
Radars: Air search: Hughes SPS 52C ❽; 3D; E/F band; range 439 km *(240 nm)*.
Melco OPS 11C ❾.
Surface search: JRC OPS 28 B ❿; G/H band.
Fire control: Two Raytheon SPG 51C ⓫; G/I band.
Melco 2-21 ⓬; I/J band. Type 2-12 ⓭; I band.
Tacan: Nec ORN-6.
Sonars: Nec OQS 4; hull-mounted; active search and attack; medium frequency.

Helicopters: Platform for 1 Mitsubishi HSS-2B Sea King or SH-60J Sea Hawk ⓮.

Programmes: DD 171 provided for in 1981 programme. DD 172 provided for in 1983 programme, ordered 29 March 1984.

HATAKAZE *(Scale 1 : 1200), Ian Sturton*

ATAKAZE *4/1992, Hachiro Nakai*

1 + 3 KONGO CLASS

Name	No	Builders	Laid down	Launched	Commissioned
KONGO	DD 173	Mitsubishi, Nagasaki	8 May 1990	26 Sep 1991	25 Mar 1993
—	DD 174	Mitsubishi, Nagasaki	7 Apr 1992	Sep 1993	Mar 1995
—	DD 175	Mitsubishi, Nagasaki	Apr 1993	Sep 1994	Mar 1996
—	DD 176	Ishikawajima Harima, Tokyo	Apr 1995	Sep 1996	Mar 1998

Displacement, tons: 7250 standard; 9485 full load
Dimensions, feet (metres): 528.2 × 68.9 × 20.3 *(161 × 21 × 6.2)*
Main machinery: COGAG; 4 GE LM 2500 gas turbines; 102 160 hp *(76.21 MW)* sustained; 2 shafts; cp props
Speed, knots: 30. **Range, miles:** 4500 at 20 kts
Complement: 300

Missiles: SSM: 8 McDonnell Douglas Harpoon (2 quad) ❶ launchers; active radar homing to 130 km *(70 nm)* at 0.9 Mach; warhead 227 kg.
SAM: GDC Pomona Standard SM-2MR. FMC Mk 41 (29 cells) forward ❷. Martin Marietta Mk 41 VLS (61 cells) aft ❸; command/inertial guidance; semi-active radar homing to 73 km *(40 nm)* at 2 Mach. Total of 90 Standard and ASROC weapons.
A/S: Vertical launch ASROC; inertial guidance to 1.6-10 km *(1-5.4 nm)*; payload Mk 46 Mod 5 Neartip.
Guns: 1 OTO Melara 5 in *(127 mm)*/54 Compatto ❹; 85° elevation; 45 rounds/minute to 16 km *(8.7 nm)*; weight of shell 32 kg. 2 GE/GD 20 mm/76 Mk 15 Vulcan Phalanx ❺. 6 barrels per mounting; 3000 rounds/minute combined to 1.5 km.
Torpedoes: 6—324 mm (2 triple) tubes ❻. Honeywell Mk 46 Mod 5 Neartip; anti-submarine; active/passive homing to 11 km *(5.9 nm)* at 40 kts; warhead 44 kg.
Countermeasures: Decoys: 4 Mk 36 SRBOC ❼ 6-barrelled Mk 36 chaff launchers; towed torpedo decoy.
ESM: Melko NOLQ 2; intercept.
ECM: Fujitsu OLT-3; jammer.
Combat data systems: Aegis NTDS with Links 11 and 14; Link 16 in due course. SATCOM OE-82C ❽
Fire control: 3 Mk 99 Mod 1 MFCS. Type 2-21 GFCS. Mk 116 Mod 7 for ASW.
Radars: Air search: RCA SPY 1D ❾; 3D; E/F band.
Surface search: JRC OPS 28C or D ❿; G/H band.
Navigation: JRC OPS 19C; I band.
Fire control: 3 SPG 62 ⓫; 1 Mk 2/21 ⓬; I/J band.
Tacan: UPX 29 IFF.
Sonars: Nec OQS 102 (SQS 53B/C) hull-mounted; active search and attack.
Oki OQR 2 (SQR 19A (V)) TACTASS; towed array; passive; very low frequency.

Helicopters: Platform ⓭ and fuelling facilities for SH-60J Seahawk.

Programmes: Proposed in the FY 1987 programme; first one accepted in FY 1988 estimates, second in FY 1990, third in FY 1991, fourth in FY 1993. Designated as destroyers but these ships are of cruiser size.
Structure: This is an enlarged and improved version of the USN *Arleigh Burke* with a lightweight version of the Aegis system. There are two missile magazines. OQS 102 plus OQR 2 towed array is the equivalent of SQQ 89.
Opinion: The combination of cost and US Congressional reluctance to release Aegis technology slowed the programme down but the plan is to complete all four by the end of 1998.

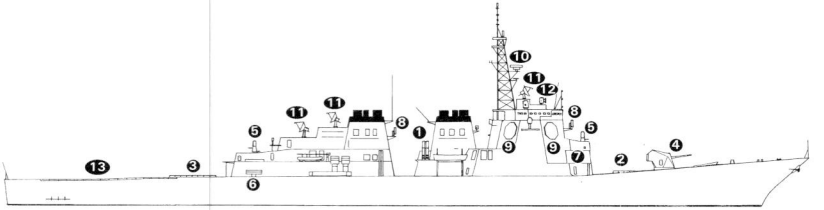

KONGO *(Scale 1 : 1500), Ian Sturton*

KONGO *6/1992, Hachiro Nakai*

KONGO *6/1992, Hachiro Nakai*

Destroyers /JAPAN (MSDF) 347

2 SHIRANE CLASS

Name	No	Builders	Laid down	Launched	Commissioned
SHIRANE	DD 143	Ishikawajima Harima, Tokyo	25 Feb 1977	18 Sep 1978	17 Mar 1980
KURAMA	DD 144	Ishikawajima Harima, Tokyo	17 Feb 1978	20 Sep 1979	27 Mar 1981

Displacement, tons: 5200 standard
Dimensions, feet (metres): 521.5 × 57.5 × 17.5 *(159 × 17.5 × 5.3)*
Main machinery: 2 boilers; 850 psi *(60 kg/cm sq)*; 900°F *(480°C)*; 2 turbines; 70 000 hp(m) *(51.5 MW)*; 2 shafts
Speed, knots: 32
Complement: 350; 360 *(Kurama)*

Missiles: SAM: Raytheon Sea Sparrow Mk 29 octuple launcher ❶; semi-active radar homing to 14.6 km *(8 nm)* at 2.5 Mach; warhead 39 kg; 24 missiles.
A/S: Honeywell ASROC Mk 112 octuple launcher ❷; inertial guidance to 10 km *(5.4 nm)* at 0.9 Mach; payload Mk 46 Mod 5 Neartip.
Guns: 2 FMC 5 in *(127 mm)*/54 Mk 42 automatic ❸; 85° elevation; 20-40 rounds/minute to 24 km *(13 nm)* anti-surface; 14 km *(7.6 nm)* anti-aircraft; weight of shell 32 kg.
2 General Electric/General Dynamics 20 mm Phalanx Mk 15 CIWS ❹; 6 barrels per mounting; 3000 rounds/minute combined to 1.5 km.
Torpedoes: 6—324 mm Type 68 (2 triple) tubes ❺. Honeywell Mk 46 Mod 5 Neartip; anti-submarine; active/passive homing to 11 km *(5.9 nm)* at 40 kts; warhead 44 kg.
Countermeasures: ESM: Melco NOLQ 1; intercept.
ECM: Fujitsu OLR-9B; jammer.
Prairie Masker; blade rate suppression system.
Combat data systems: OYQ-6; Links 11 and 14. SATCOM.
Fire control: Singer Mk 114 for ASROC system. Type 72-1A GFCS.
Radars: Air search: Nec OPS 12 ❻; 3D; D band; range 119 km *(65 nm)*.
Surface search: JRC OPS 28 ❼; G/H band.
Navigation: Koden OPN-11; I band.
Fire control: Signaal WM 25 ❽; I/J band; range 46 km *(25 nm)*.
Two Type 72-1A FCS ❾; I/J band.
Tacan: ORN-6.
Sonars: EDO/Nec SQS 35(J); VDS; active/passive search; medium frequency.
Nec OQS 101; hull-mounted; low frequency.
EDO/Nec SQR 18A; towed array; passive; very low frequency.

Helicopters: 3 Mitsubishi HSS-2B Sea King ❿ or SH-60J Sea Hawk (DD 143).

Programmes: One each in 1975 and 1976 programmes.
Modernisation: DD 143 refit in 1989-90. Both fitted with CIWS and towed array sonars by mid-1990.
Structure: Fitted with Vosper Thornycroft fin stabilisers. The after funnel is set to starboard and the forward one to port. The crane is on the starboard after corner of the hangar.

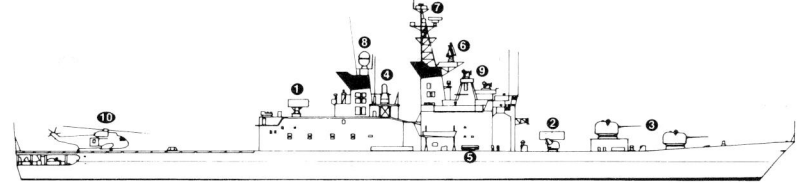
KURAMA *(Scale 1 : 1500), Ian Sturton*

SHIRANE *8/1992, Hachiro Nakai*

2 HARUNA CLASS

Name	No	Builders	Laid down	Launched	Commissioned
HARUNA	DD 141	Mitsubishi, Nagasaki	19 Mar 1970	1 Feb 1972	22 Feb 1973
HIEI	DD 142	Ishikawajima Harima, Tokyo	8 Mar 1972	13 Aug 1973	27 Nov 1974

Displacement, tons: 4950 (4700, DD 142) standard
Dimensions, feet (metres): 502 × 57.4 × 17.1 *(153 × 17.5 × 5.2)*
Main machinery: 2 boilers; 850 psi *(60 kg/cm sq)*; 900°F *(480°C)*; 2 GE/Ishikawajima turbines; 70 000 hp *(51.5 MW)*; 2 shafts
Speed, knots: 31
Complement: 370 (360, DD 142) (36 officers)

Missiles: SAM: Raytheon Sea Sparrow Mk 29 octuple launcher ❶; semi-active radar homing to 14.6 km *(8 nm)* at 2.5 Mach; warhead 39 kg; 24 missiles.
A/S: Honeywell ASROC Mk 112 octuple launcher ❷; inertial guidance to 1.6-10 km *(1-5.4 nm)* at 0.9 Mach; payload Mk 46 Mod 5 Neartip.
Guns: 2 FMC 5 in *(127 mm)*/54 Mk 42 automatic ❸; 85° elevation; 20-40 rounds/minute to 24 km *(13 nm)* anti-surface; 14 km *(7.6 nm)* anti-aircraft; weight of shell 32 kg.
2 General Electric/General Dynamics 20 mm Phalanx Mk 15 CIWS ❹; 6 barrels per mounting; 3000 rounds/minute combined to 1.5 km.
Torpedoes: 6—324 mm Type 68 (2 triple) tubes ❺. Honeywell Mk 46 Mod 5 Neartip; anti-submarine; active/passive homing to 11 km *(5.9 nm)* at 40 kts; warhead 44 kg.
Countermeasures: Decoys: 4 Loral Hycor SRBOC Mk 36 multi-barrelled chaff launchers.
ESM: Melco NOLQ 1; intercept.
ECM: Fujitsu OLR 9; jammer.
Combat data systems: OYQ-6 action data automation; Links 11 and 14. SATCOM.
Fire control: 2 Type 2-12 FCS (one for guns, one for SAM).
Radars: Air search: Melco OPS 11C ❻; D band.
Surface search: JRC OPS 28 ❼; G/H band.
Fire control: One Type 1A ❽; I/J band (guns).
One Type 2-12 ❾; I/J band (SAM).
IFF: US Mk 10.
Tacan: Nec ORN-6.
Sonars: Sangamo/Mitsubishi OQS 3; hull-mounted; active search and attack; low frequency with bottom bounce.

Helicopters: 3 Mitsubishi HSS-2B Sea King ❿.

Programmes: Ordered under the third five-year defence programme (from 1967-71).
Modernisation: DD 141 taken in hand from 31 March 1986 to 31 October 1987 for FRAM at Mitsubishi, Nagasaki; DD 142 received FRAM from 31 August 1987 to 30 March 1989 at IHI, Tokyo; included Sea Sparrow, two CIWS and chaff launchers.
Structure: The funnel is offset slightly to port. Fitted with fin stabilisers. A heavy crane has been fitted on the top of the hangar, starboard side.
Operational: Fitted with Canadian Beartrap hauldown gear.

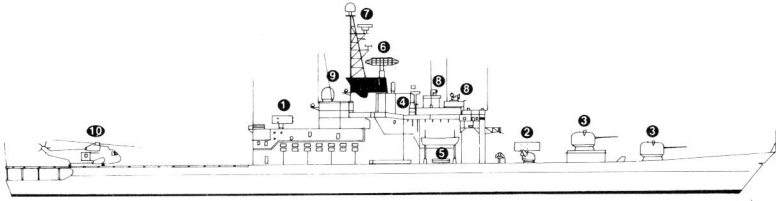
HARUNA *(Scale 1 : 1500), Ian Sturton*

HIEI *7/1992, Hachiro Nakai*

8 ASAGIRI CLASS

Name	No	Builders	Laid down	Launched	Commissioned
ASAGIRI	DD 151	Ishikawajima Harima, Tokyo	13 Feb 1985	19 Sep 1986	17 Mar 1988
YAMAGIRI	DD 152	Mitsui, Tamano	5 Feb 1986	8 Oct 1987	25 Jan 1989
YUUGIRI	DD 153	Sumitomo, Uraga	25 Feb 1986	21 Sep 1987	28 Feb 1989
AMAGIRI	DD 154	Ishikawajima Harima, Tokyo	3 Mar 1986	9 Sep 1987	17 Mar 1989
HAMAGIRI	DD 155	Hitachi, Maizuru	20 Jan 1987	4 June 1988	31 Jan 1990
SETOGIRI	DD 156	Sumitomo, Uraga	9 Mar 1987	12 Sep 1988	14 Feb 1990
SAWAGIRI	DD 157	Mitsubishi, Nagasaki	14 Jan 1987	25 Nov 1988	6 Mar 1990
UMIGIRI	DD 158	Ishikawajima Harima, Tokyo	31 Oct 1988	9 Nov 1989	12 Mar 1991

Displacement, tons: 3500 standard; 4200 full load
Dimensions, feet (metres): 449.4 × 48 × 14.6 *(137 × 14.6 × 4.5)*
Main machinery: COGAG; 4 RR Spey SM1A gas turbines; 53 300 hp *(39.8 MW)* sustained; 2 shafts; cp props
Speed, knots: 30+
Complement: 220

Missiles: SSM: 8 McDonnell Douglas Harpoon (2 quad) launchers ❶; active radar homing to 130 km *(70 nm)* at 0.9 Mach; warhead 227 kg.
SAM: Raytheon Sea Sparrow Mk 29 octuple launcher ❷; semi-active radar homing to 14.6 km *(8 nm)* at 2.5 Mach; warhead 39 kg; 20 missiles.
A/S: Honeywell ASROC Mk 112 octuple launcher ❸; inertial guidance to 1.6-10 km *(1-5.4 nm)* at 0.9 Mach; payload Mk 46 Mod 5 Neartip. Reload capability.
Guns: 1 OTO Melara 3 in *(76 mm)*/62 compact ❹; 85° elevation; 85 rounds/minute to 16 km *(8.6 nm)* anti-surface; 12 km *(6.5 nm)* anti-aircraft; weight of shell 6 kg.
2 General Electric/General Dynamics 20 mm Phalanx Mk 15 CIWS ❺; 6 barrels per mounting; 3000 rounds/minute combined to 1.5 km.
Torpedoes: 6—324 mm Type 68 (2 triple) HOS 301 tubes ❻. Honeywell Mk 46 Mod 5 Neartip; anti-submarine; active/passive homing to 11 km *(5.9 nm)* at 40 kts; warhead 44 kg.
Countermeasures: Decoys: 2 Loral Hycor SRBOC 6-barrelled Mk 36 chaff launchers ❼; range 4 km *(2.2 nm)*.
1 SLQ 51 Nixie; towed anti-torpedo decoy.
ESM: Nec NOLR 6C ❽; intercept.
ECM: Fujitsu OLT-3; jammer.
Combat data systems: OYQ-6 action data automation; Link 11. SATCOM. Helicopter datalink ❾ for SH-60J.
Radars: Air search: Melco OPS 14C (DD 151-154) ❿.
Melco OPS 24 (DD 155-158) ⓫; 3D; D band.
Surface search: JRC OPS 28C ⓬; G/H band.
Fire control: Type 2-22 (for guns) ⓭. Type 2-12E (for SAM) ⓮ (DD 151-154); Type 2-12G (for SAM) ⓯ (DD 155-158).
Tacan: ORN-6.
Sonars: Mitsubishi OQS 4A (II); hull-mounted; active search and attack; low frequency.
OQR-1; towed array; passive search; very low frequency.

Helicopters: 1 Mitsubishi HSS-2B Sea King ⓰ or SH-60J Sea Hawk ⓱ (DD 153-156, 158).

Programmes: DD 151 in 1983 estimates, DD 152-154 in 1984, DD 155-157 in 1985 and DD 158 in 1986.
Modernisation: The last four have been fitted on build with improved air search radar, updated fire control radars and a helicopter datalink. *Umigiri* also commissioned with a sonar towed array which has been fitted to the rest of the class, as are the other improvements in due course. Sea Hawk helos are replacing the Sea Kings.
Structure: Because of the enhanced IR signature and damage to electronic systems on the mainmast caused by after funnel gases there have been modifications to help contain the problem. The mainmast is now slightly higher than originally designed and in *Asagiri* the mast was moved to port. In the others of the class the mast has retained its central position but the after funnel has been offset to starboard. The hangar structure is asymmetrical extending to the after funnel on the starboard side but only to the mainmast to port. SATCOM is fitted at the after end of the hangar roof.
Operational: Beartrap helicopter hauldown system.

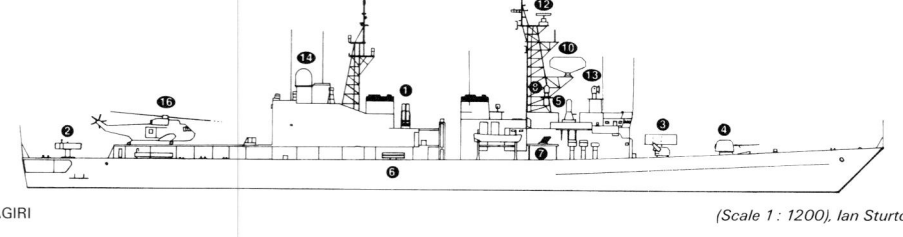

ASAGIRI *(Scale 1 : 1200), Ian Sturton*

UMIGIRI *(Scale 1 : 1200), Ian Sturton*

YUUGIRI (with OPS 14C radar) *8/1992, Hachiro Nakai*

UMIGIRI (with OPS 24 radar) *4/1992, Hachiro Nakai*

12 HATSUYUKI CLASS

Name	No
HATSUYUKI	DD 122
SHIRAYUKI	DD 123
MINEYUKI	DD 124
SAWAYUKI	DD 125
HAMAYUKI	DD 126
ISOYUKI	DD 127
HARUYUKI	DD 128
YAMAYUKI	DD 129
MATSUYUKI	DD 130
SETOYUKI	DD 131
ASAYUKI	DD 132
SHIMAYUKI	DD 133

Builders	Laid down	Launched	Commissioned
Sumitomo, Uraga	14 Mar 1979	7 Nov 1980	23 Mar 1982
Hitachi, Maizuru	3 Dec 1979	4 Aug 1981	8 Feb 1983
Mitsubishi, Nagasaki	7 May 1981	19 Oct 1982	26 Jan 1984
Ishikawajima Harima, Tokyo	22 Apr 1981	21 June 1982	15 Feb 1984
Mitsui, Tamano	4 Feb 1981	27 May 1982	18 Nov 1983
Ishikawajima Harima, Tokyo	20 Apr 1982	19 Sep 1983	23 Jan 1985
Sumitomo, Uraga	11 Mar 1982	6 Sep 1983	14 Mar 1985
Hitachi, Maizuru	25 Feb 1983	10 July 1984	3 Dec 1985
Ishikawajima Harima, Tokyo	7 Apr 1983	25 Oct 1984	19 Mar 1986
Mitsui, Tamano	26 Jan 1984	3 July 1985	11 Dec 1986
Sumitomo, Uraga	22 Dec 1983	16 Oct 1985	20 Feb 1987
Mitsubishi, Nagasaki	8 May 1984	29 Jan 1986	17 Feb 1987

Displacement, tons: 2950 (3050 from DD 129 onwards) standard; 3700 (3800) full load
Dimensions, feet (metres): 426.4 × 44.6 × 13.8 (14.4 from 129 onwards) *(130 × 13.6 × 4.2) (4.4)*
Main machinery: COGOG; 2 Kawasaki-RR Olympus TM3B gas turbines; 49 400 hp *(36.8 MW)* sustained; 2 RR Type RM1C gas turbines; 9900 hp *(7.4 MW)* sustained; 2 shafts; cp props
Speed, knots: 30
Complement: 195 (200, DD 124 onwards)

Missiles: SSM: 8 McDonnell Douglas Harpoon (2 quad) launchers ❶; active radar homing to 130 km *(70 nm)* at 0.9 Mach; warhead 227 kg.
SAM: Raytheon Sea Sparrow Type 3 (A-1) launcher ❷; semi-active radar homing to 14.6 km *(8 nm)* at 2.5 Mach; warhead 39 kg; 12 missiles.
A/S: Honeywell ASROC Mk 112 octuple launcher ❸; inertial guidance to 1.6-10 km *(1-5.4 nm)* at 0.9 Mach; payload Mk 46 Mod 5 Neartip.
Guns: 1 OTO Melara 3 in *(76 mm)*/62 compact ❹; 85° elevation; 85 rounds/minute to 16 km *(8.6 nm)* anti-surface; 12 km *(6.5 nm)* anti-aircraft; weight of shell 6 kg.
2 General Electric/General Dynamics 20 mm Phalanx Mk 15 CIWS ❺; 6 barrels per mounting; 3000 rounds/minute combined to 1.5 km.
Torpedoes: 6—324 mm Type 68 (2 triple) tubes ❻. Honeywell Mk 46 Mod 5 Neartip; anti-submarine; active/passive homing to 11 km *(5.9 nm)* at 40 kts; warhead 44 kg.
Countermeasures: Decoys: 2 Loral Hycor SRBOC 6-barrelled Mk 36 chaff launchers; range 4 km *(2.2 nm)*.
ESM: Nec NOLR 6C: intercept.
ECM: Fujitsu OLT 3; jammer.
Combat data systems: OYQ-5 action data automation; Link 14 (receive only).
Radars: Air search: Melco OPS 14B ❼.
Surface search: JRC OPS 18 ❽; G/H band.
Fire control: Type 2-12 A ❾; I/J band (for SAM).
Two Type 2-21/21A ❿; I/J band (for guns).
Tacan: URN 25.
Sonars: Nec OQS 4A (II) (SQS 23 type); hull-mounted; active search and attack; low frequency.
OQR 1 TACTASS (being fitted in all); passive; low frequency.

Helicopters: 1 Mitsubishi HSS-2B Sea King ⓫.

Modernisation: *Shirayuki* retrofitted with Phalanx in early 1992, *Hatsuyuki* in 1993. *Matsuyuki* first to get sonar towed array in 1990; the others are being fitted.
Structure: Fitted with fin stabilisers. Steel in place of aluminium alloy for bridge etc after DD 129 which increased displacement.
Operational: Canadian Beartrap helicopter landing aid. Improved ECM equipment in the last three of the class.

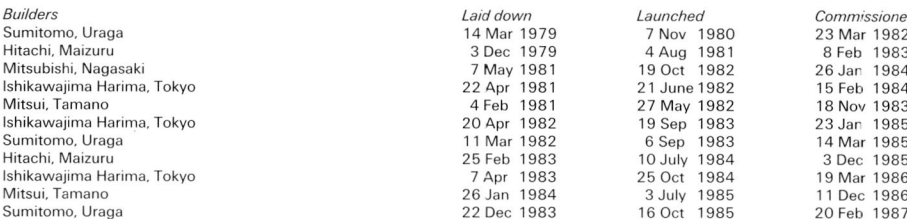

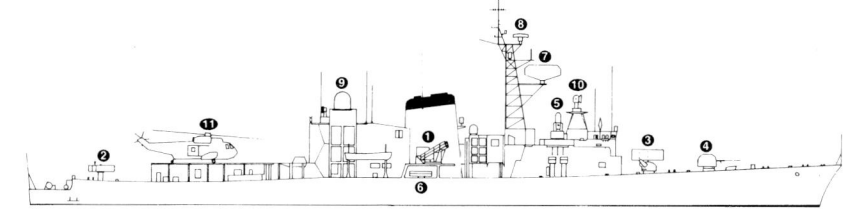

MINEYUKI (Scale 1 : 1200), Ian Sturton

SHIMAYUKI 7/1992, John Mortimer

YAMAYUKI 9/1991, Horst Dehnst

YAMAYUKI 11/1991, 92 Wing RAAF

350 JAPAN (MSDF) / Destroyers

3 TACHIKAZE CLASS

Name	No	Builders	Laid down	Launched	Commissioned
TACHIKAZE	DD 168	Mitsubishi, Nagasaki	19 June 1973	17 Dec 1974	26 Mar 1976
ASAKAZE	DD 169	Mitsubishi, Nagasaki	27 May 1976	15 Oct 1977	27 Mar 1979
SAWAKAZE	DD 170	Mitsubishi, Nagasaki	14 Sep 1979	4 June 1981	30 Mar 1983

Displacement, tons: 3850 (3950, DD 170) standard
Dimensions, feet (metres): 469 × 47 × 15.4 *(143 × 14.3 × 4.7)*
Main machinery: 2 boilers; 600 psi *(60 kg/cm sq)*; 850°F *(454°C)*; 2 Mitsubishi turbines; 70 000 hp(m); *(51.5 MW)*; 2 shafts
Speed, knots: 32
Complement: 250; 255 (D 170)

Missiles: SSM: 8 McDonnell Douglas Harpoon; active radar homing to 130 km *(70 nm)* at 0.9 Mach; warhead 227 kg HE.
SAM: GDC Pomona Standard SM-1MR; Mk 13 Mod 3 or 4 launcher ❶; command guidance; semi-active radar homing to 46 km *(25 nm)* at 2 Mach; height envelope 45-18 288 m *(150-60 000 ft)*; 40 missiles (SSM and SAM combined).
A/S: Honeywell ASROC Mk 112 octuple launcher ❷; inertial guidance to 1.6-10 km *(1-5.4 nm)* at 0.9 Mach; payload Mk 46 Mod 5 Neartip. Reloads in DD 170 only.
Guns: 2 FMC 5 in *(127 mm)*/54 Mk 42 automatic ❸; 85° elevation; 20-40 rounds/minute to 24 km *(13 nm)* anti-surface; 14 km *(7.6 nm)* anti-aircraft; weight of shell 32 kg.
2 General Electric/General Dynamics 20 mm Phalanx CIWS Mk 15 ❹; 6 barrels per mounting; 3000 rounds/minute combined to 1.5 km.
Torpedoes: 6—324 mm Type 68 (2 triple) tubes ❺. Honeywell Mk 46 Mod 5 Neartip; anti-submarine; active/passive homing to 11 km *(5.9 nm)* at 40 kts; warhead 44 kg.
Countermeasures: Decoys: 4 Loral Hycor SRBOC Mk 36 multi-barrelled chaff launchers.
ESM: Nec NOLR 6 (DD 168); Nec NOLQ 1 (others); intercept.
ECM: Fujitsu OLT 3; jammer.
Combat data systems: OYQ-5 action data automation; Link 14. SATCOM.
Fire control: 2 Mk 74 Mod 13 missile control directors. US Mk 114 ASW control. GFCS-2 for gun (DD 170). GFCS-1A for gun (others).
Radars: Air search: Melco OPS 11 ❻.
Hughes SPS 52C ❼; 3D; E/F band; range 439 km *(240 nm)*.
Surface search: JRC OPS 16 ❽; D band.
JRC OPS 28 (DD 170); G/H band.
Fire control: Two Raytheon SPG 51 ❾; G/I band.
Type 2 FCS ❿; I/J band.
IFF: US Mk 10.

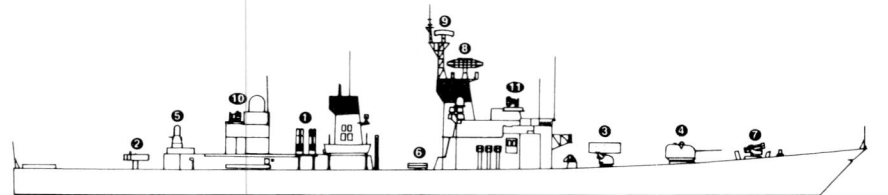

TACHIKAZE *(Scale 1 : 1200), Ian Sturton*

ASAKAZE *8/1992, Hachiro Nakai*

Sonars: Nec ORS-3 (DD 168); Nec OQS-3A (DD 169-170); hull-mounted; active search and attack; low frequency.

Modernisation: Harpoon and CIWS added to DD 168 in 1983, DD 169 and 170 in 1987.

4 TAKATSUKI CLASS

Name	No	Builders	Laid down	Launched	Commissioned
TAKATSUKI	DD 164	Ishikawajima Harima, Tokyo	8 Oct 1964	7 Jan 1966	15 Mar 1967
KIKUZUKI	DD 165	Mitsubishi, Nagasaki	15 Mar 1966	25 Mar 1967	27 Mar 1968
MOCHIZUKI	DD 166	Ishikawajima Harima, Tokyo	22 Nov 1966	15 Mar 1968	25 Mar 1969
NAGATSUKI	DD 167	Mitsubishi, Nagasaki	2 Mar 1968	19 Mar 1969	12 Feb 1970

Displacement, tons: 3250 standard; 3100 (DD 166, 167)
Dimensions, feet (metres): 446.1 × 44 × 14.8 *(136 × 13.4 × 4.5)*
Main machinery: 2 boilers; 600 psi *(60 kg/cm sq)*; 850°F *(454°C)*; 2 Mitsubishi turbines; 70 000 hp(m); *(51.5 MW)*; 2 shafts
Speed, knots: 31. **Range, miles:** 7000 at 20 kts
Complement: 260; 270 (DD 166, 167)

Missiles: SSM: 8 McDonnell Douglas Harpoon (2 quad) launchers ❶; active radar homing to 130 km *(70 nm)* at 0.9 Mach; warhead 227 kg.
SAM: Raytheon Sea Sparrow Mk 29 octuple launcher (DD 164, 165) ❷; semi-active radar homing to 14.6 km *(8 nm)* at 2.5 Mach; warhead 39 kg; 16 missiles.
A/S: Honeywell ASROC Mk 112 octuple launcher ❸; inertial guidance to 10 km *(5.4 nm)* at 0.9 Mach; payload Mk 46 Mod 5 Neartip.
Guns: 1 or 2 (DD 166, 167) FMC 5 in *(127 mm)*/54 Mk 42 automatic ❹; 85° elevation; 20-40 rounds/minute to 24 km *(13 nm)* anti-surface; 14 km *(7.6 nm)* anti-aircraft; weight of shell 32 kg.
1 General Electric/General Dynamics 20 mm Phalanx CIWS Mk 15 (DD 164, 165) ❺; 6 barrels per mounting; 3000 rounds/minute combined to 1.5 km.
Torpedoes: 6—324 mm Type 68 (2 triple) tubes ❻. Honeywell Mk 46 Mod 5 Neartip; anti-submarine; active/passive homing to 11 km *(5.9 nm)* at 40 kts; warhead 44 kg.
A/S mortars: 1—375 mm Bofors Type 71 4-barrelled trainable rocket launcher ❼; automatic loading; range 1.6 km.
Countermeasures: Decoys: 2 Loral Hycor SRBOC 6-barrelled Mk 36 chaff launchers; range 4 km *(2.2 nm)*.
ESM: Nec NOLR 6C (NOLR 9 in DD 165); intercept.
ECM: Fujitsu OLT 3; jammer.
Combat data systems: OYQ-5 action data automation; Link 14. SATCOM.
Fire control: US Mk 56 or GFCS-1 for 127 mm guns. Type 2-12B for Sea Sparrow system (DD 164, 165).
Radars: Air search: Melco OPS 11B ❽.
Surface search: JRC OPS 17 ❾; G/H band.
Fire control: Type 2-12B ❿; I/J band (DD 164, 165).
General Electric Mk 35 ⓫; I/J band.
Sonars: Nec SQS 35J; hull-mounted; active search and attack; low frequency.
EDO SQR 18 TACTASS (DD 164, 165); passive; low frequency.

Modernisation: From 1 April 1984 to 31 October 1985 DD 164 taken in hand for modifications to include removal of after 5 in gun and Dash hangar, fitting of Harpoon and Sea Sparrow, removal of VDS and its replacement by TASS, installation of FCS-2, and fittings for one 20 mm Phalanx mounting on after superstructure. Similar alterations carried out in DD 165 from May 1985 to December 1986. Phalanx not fitted in DD 164 until 1989. NOLR 9 installed in DD 165 for trials in 1991/92.
Operational: Two unmodified ships of the class were expected to pay off in 1992 but have been retained in service.

TAKATSUKI *(Scale 1 : 1200), Ian Sturton*

TAKATSUKI (modified) *4/1992, Hachiro Nakai*

NAGATSUKI (unmodified) *4/1992, Hachiro Nakai*

Destroyers / JAPAN (MSDF) 351

4 YAMAGUMO CLASS

Name	No	Builders	Laid down	Launched	Commissioned
ASAGUMO	DD 115	Hitachi, Maizuru	24 June 1965	25 Nov 1966	29 Aug 1967
AOKUMO	DD 119	Sumitomo, Uraga	2 Oct 1970	30 Mar 1972	25 Nov 1972
AKIGUMO	DD 120	Sumitomo, Uraga	7 July 1972	23 Oct 1973	24 July 1974
YUGUMO	DD 121	Sumitomo, Uraga	4 Feb 1976	31 May 1977	24 Mar 1978

Displacement, tons: 2150 standard
Dimensions, feet (metres): 377.2 × 38.7 × 13.1 *(114.9 × 11.8 × 4)*
Main machinery: 6 Mitsubishi 12UEV30/40N diesels; 21 600 hp(m) *(15.9 MW)*; 2 shafts
Speed, knots: 27. **Range, miles:** 7000 at 20 kts
Complement: 210 (19 officers)

Missiles: A/S: Honeywell ASROC Mk 112 octuple launcher ❶; inertial guidance to 1.6-10 km *(1-5.4 nm)* at 0.9 Mach; payload Mk 46 Mod 5 Neartip.
Guns: 4 USN 3 in *(76 mm)*/50 Mk 33 (2 twin) ❷; 85° elevation; 50 rounds/minute to 12.8 km *(6.9 nm)*; weight of shell 6 kg.
Torpedoes: 6—324 mm Type 68 (2 triple) tubes ❸. Honeywell Mk 46 Mod 5 Neartip; anti-submarine; active/passive homing to 11 km *(5.9 nm)* at 40 kts; warhead 44 kg.
A/S mortars: 1 Bofors 375 mm Type 71 4-barrelled trainable rocket launcher ❹; automatic loading; range 1.6 km.
Countermeasures: ESM: Nec NOLR 5 (DD 119-121); Nec NOLR 1B (DD 115); radar intercept.
Fire control: US Mk 56 or 63 for 76 mm guns (DD 115, 119). Japanese GFCS-1 for 76 mm guns (DD 120, 121).
Radars: Air search: Melco OPS 11 ❺.
Surface search: JRC OPS 17 ❻; G/H band.
Fire control: Two General Electric Mk 35 ❼; I/J band.
IFF: US Mk 10.
Sonars: Sangamo SQS 23 (DD 115); hull mounted; active search and attack; low frequency.
Nec OQS 3A (DD 119, 120, 121); hull mounted; active search and attack.
EDO SQS 35(J) (DD 120, 121); VDS; active/passive search; medium frequency.

YUGUMO *(Scale 1 : 1200), Ian Sturton*

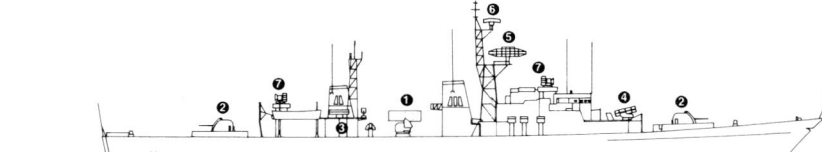

ASAGUMO (tripod mast) *3/1992, A Sheldon Duplaix*

Structure: DD 115 has a tripod mainmast and the remainder lattice mainmasts.

Operational: The first two of the class were converted to Training Ships on 20 June 1991.

AOKUMO *10/1992, Hachiro Nakai*

3 MINEGUMO CLASS

Name	No	Builders	Laid down	Launched	Commissioned
MINEGUMO	DD 116	Mitsui, Tamano	14 Mar 1967	16 Dec 1967	31 Aug 1968
NATSUGUMO	DD 117	Sumitomo, Uraga	30 June 1967	25 July 1968	15 May 1969
MURAKUMO	DD 118	Hitachi, Maizuru	19 Oct 1968	15 Nov 1969	21 Aug 1970

Displacement, tons: 2100 (2150, DD 118) standard
Dimensions, feet (metres): 373.9 (377.2, DD 118) × 38.7 × 13.1 *(114 (115) × 11.8 × 4)*
Main machinery: 6 Mitsubishi 12UEV30/40N diesels; 21 600 hp(m) *(15.9 MW)*; 2 shafts
Speed, knots: 27. **Range, miles:** 7000 at 20 kts
Complement: 210 (220, DD 118) (19 officers)

Missiles: A/S: Honeywell ASROC Mk 112 octuple launcher ❶; inertial guidance to 1.6-10 km *(1-5.4 nm)* at 0.9 Mach; payload Mk 46 Mod 5 Neartip.
Guns: 4 USN 3 in *(76 mm)*/50 Mk 33 (2 twin) (only 2 in DD 118) ❷; 85° elevation; 50 rounds/minute to 12.8 km *(6.9 nm)*; weight of shell 6 kg.
1 FMC/OTO Melara 3 in *(76 mm)*/62 Mk 75 compact (DD 118 only) ❸; 85° elevation; 50 rounds/minute to 16 km *(8.6 nm)* anti-surface; 12 km *(6.5 nm)* anti-aircraft; weight of shell 6 kg.
Torpedoes: 6—324 mm Type 68 (2 triple) tubes ❹. Honeywell Mk 46 Mod 5 Neartip; anti-submarine; active/passive homing to 11 km *(5.9 nm)* at 40 kts; warhead 44 kg.
A/S mortars: 1 Bofors 375 mm Type 71 4-barrelled trainable rocket launcher ❺; automatic loading; range 1.6 km.
Countermeasures: ESM: Nec NOLR 5; intercept.
Fire control: Japanese Type 2 for guns.
Radars: Air search: Melco OPS 11 ❻.
Surface search: JRC OPS 17 ❼; G/H band.
Fire control: Type 2-12B ❽; I/J band.
Western Electric SPG 34 (DD 118 only).
Type 1A FCS ❾.
IFF: US Mk 10.
Sonars: Nec OQS 3; hull-mounted; active/passive; low frequency.
EDO SQS 36(J) (DD 118); VDS; active/passive search; medium frequency.

Programmes: As completed the three Minegumo class had the same basic characteristics as the early Yamagumo.
Modernisation: ASROC replaced the Dash ASW helicopter. In 1978 DD 118 was rearmed with an OTO Melara 76 mm replacing one USN Mk 33 mounting. SATCOM fitted for deployments.

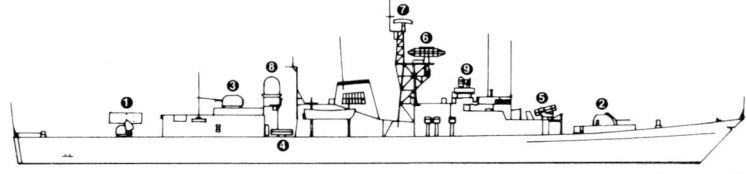

MURAKUMO *(Scale 1 : 1200), Ian Sturton*

MURAKUMO (with OTO Melara gun) *4/1992, Hachiro Nakai*

MINEGUMO (with SATCOM) *3/1992, Hachiro Nakai*

0 + 2 MODIFIED ASAGIRI CLASS

Name	No	Builders	Laid down	Launched	Commissioned
—	—	Ishikawajima Harima, Yokohama	Aug 1993	Aug 1994	Mar 1996
—	—	Mitsui, Tamano	July 1994	Aug 1995	Mar 1997

Displacement, tons: 4400 full load
Main machinery: COGAG; 2 RR Spey SM1C gas turbines; 26 650 hp *(19.9 MW)* sustained; 2 GE LM 2500 gas turbines; 46 000 hp *(34.3 MW)* sustained; 2 shafts
Speed, knots: 30
Complement: 160

Missiles: SSM: 8 SSM-1B ❶.
SAM: Raytheon Mk 48 VLS ❷ Sea Sparrow.
A/S: VL ASROC ❸.
Guns: 1 OTO Melara 76 mm/62 ❹; 2 Vulcan Phalanx 20 mm ❺.
Torpedoes: 6—324 mm Type 68 (2 triple) tubes ❻ Type 89.
Countermeasures: Decoys: 4 chaff launchers ❼.
ESM/ECM: intercept and jammer.
Radars: Air search: OPS 24 ❽.
Surface search: OPS 28C ❾.
Fire control: Two Type 2-21 ❿.

Helicopters: 1 SH-60J Seahawk ⓫.

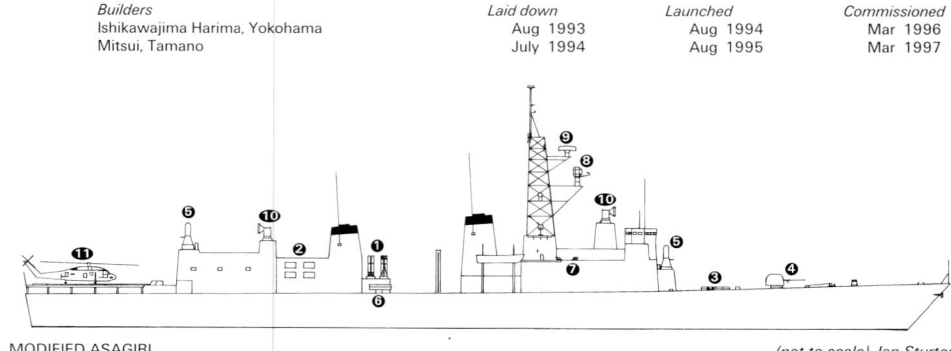

MODIFIED ASAGIRI *(not to scale), Ian Sturton*

Programmes: First one approved in FY 1991 as an addition to the third Aegis type destroyer. Second approved in FY 1992. Total numbers are uncertain but the programme may stop at these two.

Structure: Enlarged Asagiri class with VLS and a much reduced complement. Some of the weapons systems have still to be decided.

1 AMATSUKAZE CLASS

Name	No	Builders	Laid down	Launched	Commissioned
AMATSUKAZE	DD 163	Mitsubishi, Nagasaki	29 Nov 1962	5 Oct 1963	15 Feb 1965

Displacement, tons: 3050 standard; 4000 full load
Dimensions, feet (metres): 429.8 × 44 × 13.8 *(131 × 13.4 × 4.2)*
Main machinery: 2 boilers 540 psi *(38 kg/cm sq)*; 820°F *(438°C)*; 2 Ishikawajima turbines; 60 000 hp(m) *(44 MW)*; 2 shafts
Speed, knots: 33. **Range, miles:** 7000 at 18 kts
Complement: 290

Missiles: SAM: 40 GDC Pomona Standard SM-1MR; Mk 13 Mod 0 launcher ❶; command guidance; semi-active radar homing to 46 km *(25 nm)* at 2 Mach; height envelope 45-18 288 m *(150-60 000 ft)*.
A/S: Honeywell ASROC Mk 112 octuple launcher ❷; inertial guidance to 1.6-10 km *(1-5.4 nm)* at 0.9 Mach; payload Mk 46 Mod 5 Neartip.
Guns: 4 USN 3 in *(76 mm)*/50 Mk 33 (2 twin) ❸; 85° elevation; 50 rounds/minute to 12.8 km *(6.9 nm)*; weight of shell 6 kg. To be replaced by OTO Melara 76 mm. Vulcan Phalanx CIWS to be fitted.
Torpedoes: 6—324 mm Type 68 (2 triple) tubes ❹. Honeywell Mk 46 Mod 5 Neartip; anti-submarine; active/passive homing to 11 km *(5.9 nm)* at 40 kts; warhead 44 kg.
A/S mortars: 2 USN Hedgehog Mk 15 trainable rocket launchers; manually loaded; range 350 m; warhead 26 kg.
Countermeasures: ESM: Nec NOLR 6; intercept.

ECM: Fujitsu OLT 3; jammer.
Fire control: Japanese Type 2-21 system for 76 mm guns.
Radars: Air search: Hughes SPS 39 ❺; 3D; E/F band.
Westinghouse SPS 29A ❻; B/C band; range 457 km *(250 nm)*.
Surface search: JRC OPS 17 ❼; G/H band.
Fire control: Two Raytheon SPG 51C ❽; G/I band (for Standard). SPG 34 Mod 16 ❾; I/J band.
Sonars: Sangamo SQS 23G; hull-mounted; active search and attack; low frequency.

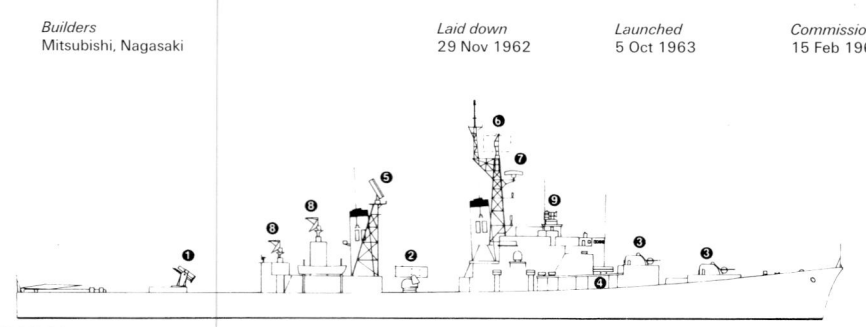

AMATSUKAZE *(Scale 1 : 1200), Ian Sturton*

Programmes: Ordered under the 1960 programme.
Modernisation: Refitted in 1967 when A/S tubes and new sonar were fitted. In 1968 equipped with ASROC launcher between funnels. SATCOM fitted in 1991. Further planned modernisation (life extension programme) to include OTO Melara 76 mm guns and Phalanx CIWS have been cancelled and it is reported that the ship will pay off in 1993.

AMATSUKAZE *4/1992, Hachiro Naka*

FRIGATES

6 ABUKUMA CLASS

Name	No	Builders	Laid down	Launched	Commissioned
ABUKUMA	DE 229	Mitsui, Tamano	17 Mar 1988	21 Dec 1988	12 Dec 1989
JINTSU	DE 230	Hitachi, Maizuru	14 Apr 1988	31 Jan 1989	28 Feb 1990
OHYODO	DE 231	Mitsui, Tamano	8 Mar 1989	19 Dec 1989	23 Jan 1991
SENDAI	DE 232	Sumitomo, Uraga	14 Apr 1989	26 Jan 1990	15 Mar 1991
CHIKUMA	DE 233	Hitachi, Maizuru	14 Feb 1991	22 Jan 1992	24 Feb 1993
TONE	DE 234	Sumitomo, Uraga	8 Feb 1991	6 Dec 1991	8 Feb 1993

Displacement, tons: 2050 standard; 2550 full load
Dimensions, feet (metres): 357.6 × 44 × 12.5 *(109 × 13.4 × 3.8)*
Main machinery: CODOG; 2 RR Spey SM1A gas turbines; 26 650 hp *(19.9 MW)* sustained; 2 Mitsubishi S12U-MTK diesels; 6000 hp(m) *(4.4 MW)*; 2 shafts
Speed, knots: 27
Complement: 115

Missiles: SSM: 8 McDonnell Douglas Harpoon (2 quad) launchers ❶; active radar homing to 130 km *(70 nm)* at 0.9 Mach; warhead 227 kg.
A/S: Honeywell ASROC Mk 112 octuple launcher ❷; inertial guidance to 1.6-10 km *(1-5.4 nm)* at 0.9 Mach; payload Mk 46 Mod 5 Neartip.
Guns: 1 OTO Melara 3 in *(76 mm)*/62 compact ❸; 85° elevation; 85 rounds/minute to 16 km *(8.6 nm)* anti-surface; 12 km *(6.5 nm)* anti-aircraft; weight of shell 6 kg.
1 General Electric/General Dynamics 20 mm Phalanx CIWS Mk 15 ❹; 6 barrels per mounting; 3000 rounds/minute combined to 1.5 km.
Torpedoes: 6—324 mm Type 68 (2 triple) tubes ❺. Honeywell Mk 46 Mod 5 Neartip; anti-submarine; active/passive homing to 11 km *(5.9 nm)* at 40 kts; warhead 44 kg.
Countermeasures: Decoys: 2 Loral Hycor SRBOC 6-barrelled Mk 36 chaff launchers.
ESM: Nec NOLQ-6C; intercept.
ECM: Fujitsu OLT-3; jammer.
Combat data systems: OYQ action data automation.
Fire control: Type 2-21; GFCS.
Radars: Air search: Melco OPS 14C ❻.
Surface search: JRC OPS 28 ❼; G/H band.
Fire control: Mk 2-21 ❽.
Sonars: Hitachi OQS-8 (DE 1167); hull-mounted; active search and attack; medium frequency.
SQR 19A towed passive array in due course.

Programmes: First pair of this class approved in 1986 estimates, ordered March 1987; second pair in 1987 estimates, ordered February 1988; last two in 1989 estimates, ordered 24 January 1989. The name of the first of class was last used for a light cruiser which was sunk in the battle of Leyte Gulf in October 1944.
Structure: Stealth features include non-vertical and rounded surfaces. German RAM PDMS may be fitted later and space has been left for a towed sonar array.

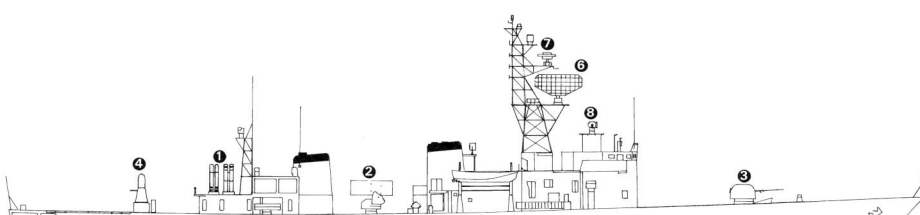
ABUKUMA *(Scale 1 : 900), Ian Sturton*

SENDAI *3/1992, Hachiro Nakai*

2 YUBARI CLASS

Name	No	Builders	Laid down	Launched	Commissioned
YUBARI	DE 227	Sumitomo, Uraga	9 Feb 1981	22 Feb 1982	18 Mar 1983
YUBETSU	DE 228	Hitachi, Maizuru	14 Jan 1982	25 Jan 1983	14 Feb 1984

Displacement, tons: 1470 standard; 1690 full load
Dimensions, feet (metres): 298.5 × 35.4 × 11.8 *(91 × 10.8 × 3.6)*
Main machinery: CODOG; 1 Kawasaki/RR Olympus TM3B gas turbine; 24 700 hp *(18.4 MW)* sustained; 1 Mitsubishi/MAN 6DRV diesel; 4700 hp(m) *(3.45 MW)*; 2 shafts; cp props
Speed, knots: 25
Complement: 95

Missiles: SSM: 8 McDonnell Douglas Harpoon (2 quad) launchers ❶; active radar homing to 130 km *(70 nm)* at 0.9 Mach; warhead 227 kg.
Guns: 1 OTO Melara 3 in *(76 mm)*/62 compact ❷; 85° elevation; 85 rounds/minute to 16 km *(8.6 nm)* anti-surface; 12 km *(6.5 nm)* anti-aircraft; weight of shell 6 kg.
1 General Electric/General Dynamics 20 mm Phalanx CIWS Mk 15 (not yet fitted) ❸; 6 barrels per mounting; 3000 rounds/minute combined to 1.5 km.
Torpedoes: 6—324 mm Type 68 (2 triple) tubes ❹. Honeywell Mk 46 Mod 5 Neartip; anti-submarine; active/passive homing to 11 km *(5.9 nm)* at 40 kts; warhead 44 kg.
A/S mortars: 1—375 mm Bofors Type 71 4-6-barrelled trainable rocket launcher ❺; automatic loading; range 1.6 km.
Countermeasures: Decoys: 2 Loral Hycor SRBOC 6-barrelled Mk 36 chaff launchers ❻; range 4 km *(2.2 nm)*.
ESM: Nec NOLQ 6C ❼; intercept.
ECM: Fujitsu OLT 3; jammer.
Combat data systems: OYQ action data automation.
Fire control: Type 2-21 system for 76 mm guns.
Radars: Surface search: JRC OPS 28C ❽; G/H band.
Navigation: Fujitsu OPS 19B; I band.
Fire control: Type 2-21 ❾; I/J band.
Sonars: Nec SQS 36J; hull-mounted; active/passive; medium frequency.

Programmes: The *Yubari* design is based on experience with *Ishikari* (DE 226).
Structure: The increased space for the same weapons systems as *Ishikari* has meant improved accommodation and an increase in fuel oil carried.

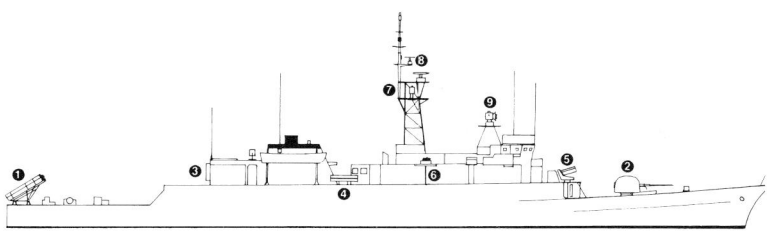
YUBARI *(Scale 1 : 900), Ian Sturton*

YUBARI (Phalanx not fitted) *3/1992, Hachiro Nakai*

354   JAPAN (MSDF) / Frigates

1 ISHIKARI CLASS

Name	No	Builders	Laid down	Launched	Commissioned
ISHIKARI	DE 226	Mitsui, Tamano	17 May 1979	18 Mar 1980	28 Mar 1981

Displacement, tons: 1290 standard; 1450 full load
Dimensions, feet (metres): 278.8 × 34.7 × 11.5 *(85 × 10.6 × 3.5)*
Main machinery: CODOG; 1 Kawasaki/RR Olympus TM3B gas turbine; 24 700 hp *(18.4 MW)*; 1 Mitsubishi/MAN 6DRV diesel; 4700 hp(m) *(3.45 MW)*; 2 shafts; cp props
Speed, knots: 25
Complement: 90

Missiles: SSM: 8 McDonnell Douglas Harpoon (2 quad) launchers ❶; active radar homing to 130 km *(70 nm)* at 0.9 Mach; warhead 227 kg.
Guns: 1 OTO Melara 3 in *(76 mm)*/62 compact ❷; 85° elevation; 85 rounds/minute to 16 km *(8.6 nm)* anti-surface; 12 km *(6.5 nm)* anti-aircraft; weight of shell 6 kg.
Torpedoes: 6—324 mm Type 68 (2 triple) tubes ❸. Honeywell Mk 46 Mod 5 Neartip; anti-submarine; active/passive homing to 11 km *(5.9 nm)* at 40 kts; warhead 44 kg.
A/S mortars: 1—375 mm Bofors Type 71 4-barrelled trainable rocket launcher ❹; automatic loading; range 1.6 km.
Countermeasures: Decoys: 1 Loral Hycor SRBOC 6-barrelled Mk 36 chaff launcher ❺; range 4 km *(2.2 nm)*.
ESM: Nec NOLQ 6C ❻; intercept.
ECM: Fujitsu OLT 2; jammer.
Fire control: Type 2-21 system for 76 mm gun.
Radars: Surface search: JRC OPS 28 ❼; G/H band.
Navigation: Fujitsu OPS 19B; I band.
Fire control: Type 2-21 FCS ❽; I/J band.
Sonars: Nec SQS 36D(J); hull-mounted; active/passive; low frequency.

Programmes: The Japanese had not constructed a frigate since the Chikugo class, which was designed in the mid-1960s. The development of so many new systems since that time probably dictated the need for a prototype.
Modernisation: To be fitted with Vulcan Phalanx when available.

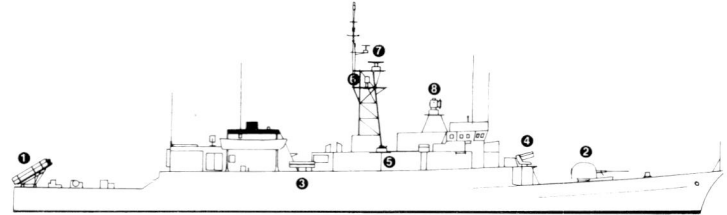

ISHIKARI   *(Scale 1 : 900), Ian Sturton*

ISHIKARI   *11/1987, Hachiro Nakai*

11 CHIKUGO CLASS

Name	No	Builders	Laid down	Launched	Commissioned
CHIKUGO	DE 215	Mitsui, Tamano	9 Dec 1968	13 Jan 1970	31 July 1970
AYASE	DE 216	Ishikawajima Harima	5 Dec 1969	16 Sep 1970	20 May 1971
MIKUMA	DE 217	Mitsui, Tamano	17 Mar 1970	16 Feb 1971	26 Aug 1971
TOKACHI	DE 218	Mitsui, Tamano	11 Dec 1970	25 Nov 1971	17 May 1972
IWASE	DE 219	Mitsui, Tamano	6 Aug 1971	29 June 1972	12 Dec 1972
CHITOSE	DE 220	Hitachi, Maizuru	7 Oct 1971	25 Jan 1973	31 Aug 1973
NIYODO	DE 221	Mitsui, Tamano	20 Sep 1972	28 Aug 1973	8 Feb 1974
TESHIO	DE 222	Hitachi, Maizuru	11 July 1973	29 May 1974	10 Jan 1975
YOSHINO	DE 223	Mitsui, Tamano	28 Sep 1973	22 Aug 1974	6 Feb 1975
KUMANO	DE 224	Hitachi, Maizuru	29 May 1974	24 Feb 1975	19 Nov 1975
NOSHIRO	DE 225	Mitsui, Tamano	27 Jan 1976	23 Dec 1976	30 June 1977

Displacement, tons: 1470 (DE 215, 217-219 and 221); 1480 (DE 216, 220); 1500 (DE 222 onwards) standard
Dimensions, feet (metres): 305 × 35.5 × 11.5 *(93 × 10.8 × 3.5)*
Main machinery: 4 Mitsubishi-Burmeister & Wain UEV 30/40 diesels; 16 000 hp(m) *(11.8 MW)* (Mitsui ships)
4 Matsui 228 V 3BU-38V diesels; 16 000 hp(m) *(11.8 MW)* (Hitachi ships); 2 shafts
Speed, knots: 25. **Range, miles:** 10 900 at 12 kts
Complement: 160 (12 officers)

Missiles: A/S: Honeywell ASROC Mk 112 octuple launcher ❶; inertial guidance to 1.6-10 km *(1-5.4 nm)* at 0.9 Mach; payload Mk 46 Mod 5 Neartip.
Guns: 2 USN 3 in *(76 mm)*/50 Mk 33 (twin) ❷; 85° elevation; 50 rounds/minute to 12.8 km *(6.9 nm)*; weight of shell 6 kg.
2 Bofors 40 mm/60 Mk 1 (twin) ❸; 80° elevation; 120 rounds/minute to 10 km *(5.4 nm)* anti-surface; 3 km *(1.6 nm)* anti-aircraft; weight of shell 0.89 kg.
Torpedoes: 6—324 mm Type 68 (2 triple) tubes ❹. Honeywell Mk 46 Mod 5 Neartip; anti-submarine; active/passive homing to 11 km *(5.9 nm)* at 40 kts; warhead 44 kg.

Countermeasures: ESM: Nec NORL 5 ❺; intercept.
Fire control: GFCS-1 for 76 mm gun. Mk 51 GFCS for 40 mm gun.
Radars: Air search: Melco OPS 14 ❻.
Surface search: JRC OPS 16 ❼; D band.
Fire control: Type 1B ❽; I/J band.
IFF: US Mk 10.

Sonars: Hitachi OQS 3A; hull-mounted; active search and attack; medium frequency.
EDO SPS 35(J) (in last five ships only); VDS; active/passive search; medium frequency.
Structure: These are the smallest warships to mount ASROC.

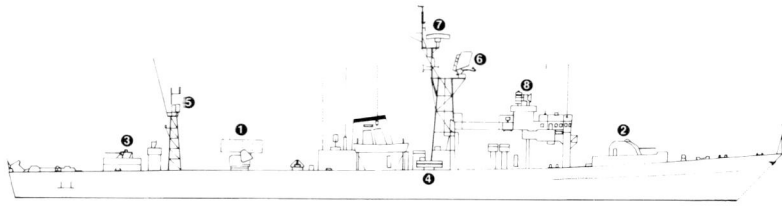

TESHIO   *(Scale 1 : 900), Ian Sturton*

IWASE   *4/1992, Hachiro Nakai*

SHIPBORNE AIRCRAFT

Numbers/Type: 72 Mitsubishi SH-3A (HSS-2B) Sea King.
Operational speed: 120 kts *(222 km/h).*
Service ceiling: 12 200 ft *(3720 m).*
Range: 630 nm *(1165 km).*
Role/Weapon systems: Shipborne ASW helicopter and surface search. Production completed in 1990. Sensors: Search radar, ESM ALR 66(V)1, Bendix AQS-13 dipping sonar. Weapons: ASW; 4 × Mk 46 torpedoes or depth bombs.

SEA KING *3/1992, A Sheldon Duplaix*

Numbers/Type: 25 Sikorsky/Mitsubishi SH-60J Seahawk.
Operational speed: 135 kts *(250 km/h).*
Service ceiling: 12 500 ft *(3810 m).*
Range: 600 nm *(1110 km).*
Role/Weapon systems: ASW and ASV helicopter; started replacing SH-3A/HSS-2 in July 1991; being built in Japan; prototypes fitted by Mitsubishi with Japanese avionics and mission equipment. Total of 48 authorised by the end of 1992. Plans include up to 100 plus 18 UH-60J for SAR. Sensors: Search radar; sonobuoys plus datalink; Bendix AQS 18/Nippon HQS 103 dipping sonar, ECM, HLR 108 ESM. Weapons: ASW; 2 × Mk 46 torpedoes or depth bombs. ASV; possible missile armament.

SEAHAWK *9/1992, Hachiro Nakai*

LAND-BASED MARITIME AIRCRAFT (FRONT LINE)

Numbers/Type: 6 Kawasaki P-2J.
Operational speed: 217 kts *(402 km/h).*
Service ceiling: 30 000 ft *(9150 m).*
Range: 2400 nm *(4450 km).*
Role/Weapon systems: Long-range MR/ASW being phased out. Remainder to be deleted in 1994. Sensors: APS-80 search radar, ESM, ALQ 101, MAD, smoke detector, Tacan and sonobuoy processor, EW, some aircraft equipped for Elint. Weapons: ASW; Mk 46 torpedoes, depth bombs or mines.

Numbers/Type: 87/4 Kawasaki P-3C/EP3B Update II Orion.
Operational speed: 410 kts *(760 km/h).*
Service ceiling: 28 300 ft *(8625 m).*
Range: 4000 nm *(7410 km).*
Role/Weapon systems: Long-range MR/ASW and surface surveillance and attack to supplement and replace P-2Js. Four EW version EP-3. The aim is a total of 104 by 1995. Sensors: APS-115 radar, ASQ-81 MAD, AQA 7 processor, AQS-114 computer, IFF, ECM, ALQ 78, ESM, ALR 66, sonobuoys. Weapons: ASW; 8 × Mk 46 torpedoes, depth bombs or mines, 10 underwing stations for Harpoon and ASM-1.

Numbers/Type: 8 Shin Meiwa US-1A.
Operational speed: 295 kts *(546 km/h).*
Service ceiling: 29 500 ft *(9000 m).*
Range: 2060 nm *(3817 km).*
Role/Weapon systems: Long-range patrol and SAR amphibian aircraft. Sensors: Search radar, MAD, sonobuoys, ECM. Weapons: ASW; Mk 46 torpedoes, depth bombs, mines, life rafts and flares.

US-1A *10/1992, Hachiro Nakai*

Numbers/Type: 10 Sikorsky/Mitsubishi S-80M-1 Sea Dragon (MH53E).
Operational speed: 170 kts *(315 km/h).*
Service ceiling: 18 500 ft *(5640 m).*
Range: 1120 nm *(2000 km).*
Role/Weapon systems: Improved, three-engined AMCM helicopter with mechanical, magnetic and acoustic sweep equipment; self-deployed if necessary. 11 authorised by the end of 1991 with one more to come. Sensors: None. Weapons: 2 × 12.7 mm guns for self-defence.

SEA DRAGON *10/1992, Hachiro Nakai*

LIGHT FORCES

1 FAST ATTACK CRAFT—TORPEDO

Name	No	Builders	Commissioned
PT 15	PT 815	Mitsubishi, Shimonoseki	10 July 1975

Displacement, tons: 100 standard; 125 full load
Dimensions, feet (metres): 114.8 × 30.2 × 3.9 *(35 × 9.2 × 1.2)*
Main machinery: CODAG; 2 IHI IM-300 gas turbines; 11 000 hp(m) *(8.08 MW)*; 2 Mitsubishi 24WZ-31MC diesels; 3 shafts
Speed, knots: 40. **Range, miles:** 1000 at 18 kts; 300 at 40 kts
Complement: 26-28
Guns: 2 Bofors 40 mm/70 Mk 3; 90° elevation; 300 rounds/minute to 12 km *(6.5 nm)* anti-surface; 4 km *(2.2 nm)* anti-aircraft; weight of shell 0.96 kg.
Torpedoes: 4—21 in *(533 mm)* tubes; anti-surface.
Radars: Surface search: Fujitsu OPS 19; G/H band.

Comment: Deployed to Yoichi, Hokkaido. *PT 14* deleted in March 1993.

PT 14 (now deleted) *10/1991, Hachiro Nakai*

5 COASTAL PATROL CRAFT

Name	No	Builders	Commissioned
PB 23	PB 923	Ishikawajima, Yokohama	31 Mar 1972
PB 24	PB 924	Ishikawajima, Yokohama	31 Mar 1972
PB 25	PB 925	Ishikawajima, Yokohama	29 Mar 1973
PB 26	PB 926	Ishikawajima, Yokohama	29 Mar 1973
PB 27	PB 927	Ishikawajima, Yokohama	29 Mar 1973

Displacement, tons: 18 standard
Dimensions, feet (metres): 55.8 × 14.1 × 2.3 *(17 × 4.3 × 0.7)*
Main machinery: 2 Isuzu V170T diesels; 760 hp(m) *(560 kW)*; 2 shafts
Speed, knots: 20. **Range, miles:** 400 at 20 kts
Complement: 6
Guns: 1 USN 20 mm/80 Mk 10; 55° elevation; 800 rounds/minute to 2 km; weight of shell 0.24 kg.
Radars: Navigation: Koden OPS 29.

Comment: GRP hulls. Some of the class have a 12.7 mm MG instead of the 20 mm gun. Four paid off in October 1992.

PB 24 *8/1989, Hachiro Nakai*

JAPAN (MSDF) / Light forces — Amphibious forces

2 + 1 ITALIAN SPARVIERO TYPE (PG)
(FAST ATTACK HYDROFOIL—MISSILE)

Name	No	Builders	Commissioned
PG 01	821	Sumitomo, Uraga	22 Mar 1993
PG 02	822	Sumitomo, Uraga	22 Mar 1993
PG 03	823	Sumitomo, Uraga	Mar 1995

Displacement, tons: 50 standard
Dimensions, feet (metres): 71.5 × 22.9 × 5.6 *(21.8 × 7 × 1.7)* (hull)
80.7 × 23.1 × 14.4 *(24.6 × 7 × 4.4)* (foilborne)
Main machinery: 1 GE/IHI LM 500 gas turbine; 5522 hp *(4.12 MW)* sustained; 1 pumpjet (foilborne); 1 diesel; 1 retractable prop (hullborne)
Speed, knots: 46; 8 (diesel). **Range, miles:** 400 at 45 kts; 1200 at 8 kts
Complement: 10 (2 officers)
Missiles: SSM: 4 Mitsubishi SSM-1B (derivative of land-based system); range 150 km *(81 nm)*.
Guns: 1 GE 20 mm/76 Sea Vulcan; 3 barrels per mounting; 55° elevation; 1500 rounds/minute combined to 4 km *(2.2 nm)*.
Countermeasures: Decoys: 2 Loral Hycor Mk 36 SRBOC chaff launchers.
ESM/ECM: intercept and jammer.
Combat data systems: Link 11.
Radars: Surface search; I band.

Comment: First two approved in FY 1990 and both laid down 25 March 1991 and launched 17 July 1992. One more approved in FY 1992. Being built with Italian assistance from Fincantieri. Final total expected to be six. Planned to improve the Navy's interceptor capabilities, this is an ambitious choice of vessel bearing in mind the falling popularity of the hydrofoil in the few navies (US, Italy and USSR) that have built them up to now.

PG 02   *2/1993, Ships of the World*

AMPHIBIOUS FORCES

3 MIURA CLASS (LSTs)

Name	No	Builders	Commissioned
MIURA	LST 4151	Ishikawajima Harima, Tokyo	29 Jan 1975
OJIKA	LST 4152	Ishikawajima Harima, Tokyo	22 Mar 1976
SATSUMA	LST 4153	Ishikawajima Harima, Tokyo	17 Feb 1977

Displacement, tons: 2000 standard
Dimensions, feet (metres): 321.4 × 45.9 × 9.8 *(98 × 14 × 3)*
Main machinery: 2 Kawasaki-MAN V8V22/30ATL diesels; 4000 hp(m) *(2.94 MW)*; 2 shafts
Speed, knots: 14
Complement: 115
Military lift: 200 troops; 2 LCMs; 2 LCVPs; 10 Type 74 main battle tanks
Guns: 2 USN 3 in *(76 mm)*/50 Mk 33 (twin); 85° elevation; 50 rounds/minute to 12.8 km *(6.9 nm)*; weight of shell 6 kg.
2 Bofors 40 mm/70 (twin) (LST 4151-4152); 90° elevation; 300 rounds/minute to 12 km *(6.5 nm)* anti-surface; 4 km *(2.2 nm)* anti-aircraft; weight of shell 0.96 kg.
Fire control: Type 72-1B for 76 mm guns *(Miura)*; US Mk 63 for 76 mm guns (remainder). US Mk 51 for 40 mm guns.
Radars: Air search: Melco OPS 14.
Surface search: JRC OPS 16 *(Miura)*; JRS OPS 18 (remainder); D/G/H band.

Comment: Used primarily for logistic support. SATCOM fitted.

SATSUMA   *10/1992, Hachiro Nakai*

0 + 1 LST

Displacement, tons: 8900 standard
Dimensions, feet (metres): 557.7 × 75.5 × 24.6 *(170 × 23 × 7.5)*
Main machinery: 2 diesels; 2 shafts
Speed, knots: 22
Complement: 130
Military lift: 1000 troops; 2 LCAC; 10 Type 90 tanks or equivalent in weight
Guns: 2 GE/GD 20 mm Vulcan Phalanx Mk 15.
Helicopters: C-47 type.

Comment: A 5500 ton LSD was requested and not approved in the 1989 or 1990 estimates. The published design resembled the Italian San Giorgio with a large flight deck and a stern dock. No further action was taken for two years but the FY 1993 request included a larger ship showing the design of a USN LPH, although smaller in size. This vessel, with some modifications, was authorised in the 1993 estimates. Such a ship would be capable of operating VSTOL aircraft, should such a development become politically acceptable, at some time in the future.

3 ATSUMI CLASS (LSTs)

Name	No	Builders	Commissioned
ATSUMI	LST 4101	Sasebo Heavy Industries	27 Nov 1972
MOTOBU	LST 4102	Sasebo Heavy Industries	21 Dec 1973
NEMURO	LST 4103	Sasebo Heavy Industries	27 Oct 1977

Displacement, tons: 1480 (LST 4101), 1550 (LST 4102-4103) standard
Dimensions, feet (metres): 291.9 × 42.6 × 8.9 *(89 × 13 × 2.7)*
Main machinery: 2 Kawasaki-MAN V8V22/30ATL diesels; 4000 hp(m) *(2.94 MW)*; 2 shafts
Speed, knots: 13 (LST 4102-4103); 14 (LST 4101). **Range, miles:** 9000 at 12 kts
Complement: 100 (LST 4101); 95 (LST 4102-4103)
Military lift: 130 troops; 400 tons cargo including 5 Type 74 tanks; 2 LCVPs
Guns: 4 Bofors 40 mm/70 Mk 1 (2 twin); 90° elevation; 300 rounds/minute to 12 km *(6.5 nm)*; weight of shell 0.96 kg.
Fire control: 2 US Mk 51 for 40 mm guns.
Radars: Navigation: Fujitsu OPS 9; I band.

Comment: *Nemuro* has an electric crane at the after end of the cargo deck. SATCOM fitted.

MOTOBU   *10/1992, Hachiro Nakai*

2 YURA CLASS (LSU)

Name	No	Builders	Commissioned
YURA	4171	Sasebo Heavy Industries	27 Mar 1981
NOTO	4172	Sasebo Heavy Industries	27 Mar 1981

Displacement, tons: 590 standard
Dimensions, feet (metres): 190.2 × 31.2 × 5.6 *(58 × 9.5 × 1.7)*
Main machinery: 2 Fuji 6L27.5XF diesels; 3250 hp(m) *(2.39 MW)*; 2 shafts; cp props
Speed, knots: 12
Complement: 30
Military lift: 70 troops
Guns: 1 GE 20 mm/76 Sea Vulcan 20; 3 barrels per mounting; 55° elevation; 1500 rounds/minute combined to 4 km *(2.2 nm)*.

Comment: Both laid down 23 April 1980. LST 4171 launched 15 October 1980 and LST 4172 on 12 November 1980.

NOTO   *8/1989, Hachiro Nak*

Amphibious forces — Mine warfare forces / JAPAN (MSDF) 357

2 YUSOTEI CLASS (LCU)

Name	No	Builders	Commissioned
YUSOTEI-ICHI-GO	2001	Sasebo Heavy Industries	17 Mar 1988
YUSOTEI-NI-GO	2002	Sasebo Heavy Industries	11 Mar 1992

Displacement, tons: 420 standard
Dimensions, feet (metres): 170.6 × 28.5 × 5.2 *(52 × 8.7 × 1.6)*
Main machinery: 2 Mitsubishi S16MTK diesels; 3040 hp(m) *(2.23 MW)*; 2 shafts
Speed, knots: 12
Complement: 28
Guns: 1 GE 20 mm/76 Sea Vulcan; 3 barrels per mounting; 1500 rounds/minute combined to 4 km *(2.2 nm)*.

Comment: First approved in 1986 estimates, laid down 11 May 1987, launched 9 October 1987. Second approved in FY 1990 estimates, laid down 15 May 1991, launched 7 October 1991; plans for a third have been scrapped.

YUSOTEI-NI-GO *3/1992, Hachiro Nakai*

10 + 1 LCM TYPE

YF 2075   2121   2124-25   2127-29   2132-33

Displacement, tons: 25 standard
Dimensions, feet (metres): 56.2 × 14 × 3.9 *(17.1 × 4.3 × 1.2)*
Main machinery: 2 Isuzu E120-MF6R diesels; 480 hp(m) *(353 kW)*; 2 shafts
Speed, knots: 10. **Range, miles:** 130 at 9 kts
Complement: 3
Military lift: 34 tons or 80 troops

Comment: Built in Japan. These are in addition to the six LCMs carried in the Miura class which do not have pennant numbers. YF 2127-29 commissioned in March 1992.

YF 2125 *10/1991, Hachiro Nakai*

17 LCVP TYPE

YF 2068-74   2078-81   2083-87   2116

Displacement, tons: 12 full load
Dimensions, feet (metres): 35.8 × 10.5 × 3.3 *(10.9 × 3.2 × 1)*
Main machinery: 1 Yanmar 6CH-DTE diesel; 190 hp(m) *(140 kW)*; 1 shaft
Speed, knots: 9
Complement: 3
Military lift: 40 troops

Comment: Built in Japan with wooden hulls. In addition to these there are 12 more carried in the LSTs which have no pennant numbers.

YF 2070 *2/1991, Hachiro Nakai*

MINE WARFARE FORCES

Note: Two 3000 ton new Minesweeper Support Ships are in the 1991-95 ship construction plan.

1 SOUYA CLASS (MINELAYER/SUPPORT SHIP)

Name	No	Builders	Commissioned
SOUYA	MMC 951	Hitachi, Maizuru	30 Sep 1971

Displacement, tons: 2150 standard; 3300 full load
Dimensions, feet (metres): 324.8 × 49.5 × 13.9 *(99 × 15 × 4.2)*
Main machinery: 4 Kawasaki-MAN V6V 22/30 ATL diesels; 6400 hp(m) *(4.7 MW)*; 2 shafts
Speed, knots: 18. **Range, miles:** 7500 at 14 kts
Complement: 185

Guns: 2 USN 3 in *(76 mm)*/50 Mk 33 (twin); 85° elevation; 50 rounds/minute to 12.8 km *(6.9 nm)*; weight of shell 6 kg.
  2 GE 20 mm/76 Sea Vulcan; 3 barrels per mounting; 1500 rounds/minute combined to 4 km *(2.2 nm)*.
Torpedoes: 6—324 mm Type 68 (2 triple) tubes. Honeywell Mk 46 Mod 5 Neartip; anti-submarine; active/passive homing to 11 km *(5.9 nm)* at 40 kts; warhead 44 kg.
Mines: 6 internal plus 2 external rails; 460 buoyant.
Fire control: GFCS-1 for 76 mm guns.
Radars: Air search: Melco OPS 14.
  Surface search: JRC OPS 16; D band.
IFF: US Mk 10.
Sonars: SQS 11A; hull-mounted; active search and attack; medium frequency.
  ZQS 1B; bow-mounted; active search and attack; high frequency.

Helicopters: Platform for one Sea Dragon.

Operational: Dual purpose ship used as minelayer with a minesweeper support capability. Flagship for Second MCM Flotilla based at Yukosuka.

SOUYA *2/1990, Hachiro Nakai*

1 HAYASE CLASS (MINESWEEPER SUPPORT SHIP)

Name	No	Builders	Commissioned
HAYASE	MST 462	Ishikawajima Harima, Tokyo	6 Nov 1971

Displacement, tons: 2000 standard
Dimensions, feet (metres): 324.8 × 47.6 × 13.8 *(99 × 14.5 × 4.2)*
Main machinery: 2 Kawasaki-MAN V6V22/30ATL diesels; 6400 hp(m) *(4.7 MW)*; 2 shafts
Speed, knots: 18
Complement: 180

Guns: 2 USN 3 in *(76 mm)*/50 Mk 33 (twin); 85° elevation; 50 rounds/minute to 12.8 km *(6.9 nm)*; weight of shell 6 kg.
  2 GE 20 mm/76 Sea Vulcan; 3 barrels per mounting; 1500 rounds/minute combined to 4 km *(2 nm)*.
Torpedoes: 6—324 mm Type 68 (2 triple) tubes. Honeywell Mk 46 Mod 5 Neartip; anti-submarine; active/passive homing to 11 km *(5.9 nm)* at 40 kts; warhead 44 kg.
Mines: 5 internal rails; 116 buoyant mines.
Fire control: US Mk 63 for 76 mm guns.
Radars: Air search: Melco OPS 14.
  Surface search: JRC OPS 16; D band.
  Fire control: Western Electric Mk 34; I/J band.
Sonars: SQS 11A; hull-mounted; active search and attack; medium frequency.

Helicopters: Platform for 1 Sea Dragon.

Operational: Flagship of historic Gulf deployment in 1991. Also flagship for First MCM Flotilla based at Kure.

HAYASE *2/1993 Hachiro Nakai*

358 JAPAN (MSDF) / Mine warfare forces

2 + 1 (3) YAEYAMA CLASS (MINEHUNTER/SWEEPER—OCEAN)

Name	No	Builders	Commissioned
YAEYAMA	MSO 301	Hitachi, Kanagawa	16 Mar 1993
TSUSHIMA	MSO 302	Nippon Steel Tube Co, Tsurumi	23 Mar 1993
HACHIJYO	MSO 303	Nippon Steel Tube Co, Tsurumi	Mar 1994

Displacement, tons: 1275 full load
Dimensions, feet (metres): 219.8 × 38.7 × 10.2 *(67 × 11.8 × 3.1)*
Main machinery: 2 Mitsubishi 6NMU-TAI diesels; 2400 hp(m) *(1.76 MW)*; 2 shafts; 1 hydrojet bow thruster; 350 hp(m) *(257 kW)*
Speed, knots: 14
Complement: 60
Guns: 1 GE 20 mm/76 Sea Vulcan; 3 barrels per mounting; 1500 rounds/minute combined to 4 km *(2.2 nm)*.
Radars: Surface search: Fujitsu OPS 9; I band.
Sonars: Raytheon SQQ 32 VDS; high frequency; active.

Comment: First two approved in 1989 estimates, third in 1990. First laid down 30 August 1990 and launched 29 August 1991; second laid down 20 July 1990 and launched 20 September 1991; third laid down 17 May 1991 and launched 15 December 1992. Wooden hulls. Probable class of six. Fitted with S 7 deep sea minehunting system and S 8 deep sea moored minesweeping equipment. Appears to be a derivative of the USN Avenger class. Second batch of three may have a Japanese sonar fitted.

YAEYAMA *3/1993, Hachiro Nakai*

TSUSHIMA *3/1993, NKK*

3 TAKAMI CLASS (MINEHUNTERS/SWEEPERS—COASTAL)

Name	No	Builders	Commissioned
OKITSU	MSC 646	Hitachi, Kanagawa	20 Sep 1977
HASHIRA	MSC 647	Nippon Steel Tube Co	28 Mar 1978
IWAI	MSC 648	Hitachi, Kanagawa	28 Mar 1978

Displacement, tons: 380 standard; 530 full load
Dimensions, feet (metres): 170.6 × 28.9 × 7.9 *(52 × 8.8 × 2.4)*
Main machinery: 2 Mitsubishi YV12ZC-15/20 diesels; 1440 hp(m) *(1.06 MW)*; 2 shafts
Speed, knots: 14
Complement: 45
Guns: 1 GE 20 mm/76 Sea Vulcan 20; 3 barrels per mounting; 55° elevation; 1500 rounds/minute combined to 4 km *(2.2 nm)*.
Radars: Surface search: Fujitsu OPS 9; I band.
Sonars: Nec/Hitachi ZQS 2 (Type 193M); hull-mounted; minehunting; high frequency.

Comment: Numbers gradually being reduced (converted to auxiliaries) as Hatsushima class complete. Wooden hulls. Fitted with wire and acoustic minesweeping gear. Also carry four clearance divers.

IWAI *2/1992, Hachiro Nakai*

26 + 4 HATSUSHIMA CLASS (MINEHUNTERS/SWEEPERS—COASTAL)

Name	No	Builders	Commissioned
HATSUSHIMA	MSC 649	Nippon Steel Tube Co (Tsurumi)	30 Mar 1979
NINOSHIMA	MSC 650	Hitachi, Kanagawa	19 Dec 1979
MIYAJIMA	MSC 651	Nippon Steel Tube Co (Tsurumi)	29 Jan 1980
ENOSHIMA	MSC 652	Nippon Steel Tube Co (Tsurumi)	25 Dec 1980
UKISHIMA	MSC 653	Hitachi, Kanagawa	27 Nov 1980
OOSHIMA	MSC 654	Hitachi, Kanagawa	26 Nov 1981
NIIJIMA	MSC 655	Nippon Steel Tube Co (Tsurumi)	26 Nov 1981
YAKUSHIMA	MSC 656	Nippon Steel Tube Co (Tsurumi)	17 Dec 1982
NARUSHIMA	MSC 657	Hitachi, Kanagawa	17 Dec 1982
CHICHIJIMA	MSC 658	Hitachi, Kanagawa	16 Dec 1983
TORISHIMA	MSC 659	Nippon Steel Tube Co (Tsurumi)	16 Dec 1983
HAHAJIMA	MSC 660	Nippon Steel Tube Co (Tsurumi)	18 Dec 1984
TAKASHIMA	MSC 661	Hitachi, Kanagawa	18 Dec 1984
NUWAJIMA	MSC 662	Hitachi, Kanagawa	12 Dec 1985
ETAJIMA	MSC 663	Nippon Steel Tube Co (Tsurumi)	12 Dec 1985
KAMISHIMA	MSC 664	Nippon Steel Tube Co (Tsurumi)	16 Dec 1986
HIMESHIMA	MSC 665	Hitachi, Kanagawa	16 Dec 1986
OGISHIMA	MSC 666	Hitachi, Kanagawa	17 Dec 1987
MOFOSHIMA	MSC 667	Nippon Steel Tube Co (Tsurumi)	17 Dec 1987
YURISHIMA	MSC 668	Nippon Steel Tube Co (Tsurumi)	15 Dec 1988
HIKOSHIMA	MSC 669	Hitachi, Kanagawa	15 Dec 1988
AWASHIMA	MSC 670	Hitachi, Kanagawa	13 Dec 1989
SAKUSHIMA	MSC 671	Nippon Steel Tube Co (Tsurumi)	13 Dec 1989
UWAJIMA	MSC 672	Nippon Steel Tube Co (Tsurumi)	19 Dec 1990
IESHIMA	MSC 673	Hitachi, Kanagawa	19 Dec 1990
TSUKISHIMA	MSC 674	Hitachi, Kanagawa	18 Mar 1993
—	MSC 675	Hitachi, Kanagawa	Dec 1993
—	MSC 676	Hitachi, Kanagawa	Dec 1994
—	MSC 677	Hitachi, Kanagawa	Dec 1994
—	MSC 678	Nippon Steel Tube Co (Tsurumi)	Mar 1995

Displacement, tons: 440 (490, MSC 670 onwards) standard; 510 full load
Dimensions, feet (metres): 180.4 (189.3, MSC 670 onwards) × 30.8 × 7.9 *(55 (57.7) × 9.4 × 2.4)*
Main machinery: 2 Mitsubishi YV122C-15/20 diesels (MSC 649-665); 1440 hp(m) *(1.06 MW)*; 2 Mitsubishi 6NMU-TAI diesels (MSC 666 onwards); 1400 hp(m) *(1.03 MW)*; 2 shafts
Speed, knots: 14
Complement: 45
Guns: 1 GE 20 mm/76 Sea Vulcan 20; 55° elevation; 3 barrels per mounting; 1500 rounds/minute combined to 4 km *(2.2 nm)*.
Radars: Surface search: Fujitsu OPS 9; I band.
Sonars: Nec/Hitachi ZQS 2B or ZQS 3 (MSC 672 onwards); hull-mounted; minehunting; high frequency.

Programmes: First ordered in 1976. Last three authorised in FY 1992. Because of the new sonar and mine detonating equipment vessels from MSC 672 onwards are sometimes known as the Uwajima class.
Structure: From MSC 670 onwards the hull is lengthened by 2.7 m in order to improve the sleeping accommodation from three tier to two tier bunks. Hulls are made of wood.
Operational: Fitted with new S 4 (S 7 from MSC 672 onwards) mine detonating equipment, a remote-controlled counter-mine charge. MSC 668, 669, 670 and 671 formed the Minesweeper Squadron to deploy to the Gulf in 1991.

IESHIMA *10/1992, Hachiro Nakai*

OGISHIMA *2/1992, Hachiro Nakai*

Mine warfare forces — Service forces and auxiliaries / JAPAN (MSDF)   359

1 MCM SUPPORT SHIP

Name	No	Builders	Commissioned
FUKUE	MST 476 (ex-MSC 645)	Nippon Steel Tube Co	18 Nov 1976

Displacement, tons: 380 standard; 530 full load
Dimensions, feet (metres): 170.6 × 28.9 × 7.9 *(52 × 8.8 × 2.4)*
Main machinery: 2 Mitsubishi YV12ZC-15/20 diesels; 1440 hp(m) *(1.06 MW)*; 2 shafts
Speed, knots: 14
Complement: 38
Guns: 1 GE 20 mm/76 Sea Vulcan 20; 55° elevation; 3 barrels per mounting; 1500 rounds/minute combined to 4 km *(2.2 nm)*.
Radars: Surface search: Fujitsu OPS 9.
Sonars: Nec/Hitachi ZQS 2; hull-mounted; minehunting.

Comment: Takami class; minesweeping gear removed and fitted as MCM command ship, recommissioned February 1993 and replaced *Utone*. Used as tender for Nana-Go class MSBs.

FUKUE   *2/1993, Hachiro Nakai*

4 NANA-GO CLASS (MSBs)

Name	No	Builders	Commissioned
KYUU-GO	709	Nippon Steel Tube Co	28 Mar 1974
JYUU-GO	710	Nippon Steel Tube Co	29 Mar 1974
JYUU-ICHI-GO	711	Hitachi, Kanagawa	10 May 1975
JYUU-NI-GO	712	Nippon Steel Tube Co	22 Apr 1975

Displacement, tons: 58 standard
Dimensions, feet (metres): 73.8 × 17.7 × 3.3 *(22.5 × 5.4 × 1)*
Main machinery: 2 Mitsubishi 4ZV20M diesels; 480 hp(m) *(353 kW)*; 2 shafts
Speed, knots: 11
Complement: 10
Radars: Navigation: Koden OPS 29D.

Comment: Wooden hulls. *Fukue* is the depot ship. Two deleted in March 1992.

KYUU-GO   *5/1992, Hachiro Nakai*

SERVICE FORCES AND AUXILIARIES

0 + 1 TRAINING SHIP

Name	No	Builders	Commissioned
—	—	Hitachi, Maizuru	Jan 1995

Displacement, tons: 4060 standard
Dimensions, feet (metres): 465.9 × 59.1 × 15.1 *(142 × 18 × 4.6)*
Main machinery: CODOG; 2 RR Spey SM1C gas turbines; 26 650 hp *(19.9 MW)* sustained; 2 Mitsubishi S16U diesels; 8000 hp(m) *(5.88 MW)*; 2 shafts
Speed, knots: 25
Complement: 389 (includes 140 midshipmen)
Guns: 1 OTO Melara 76 mm/62. 2—40 mm saluting guns.
Torpedoes: 6—324 mm (2 triple) tubes.
Radars: Air search: E/F band.
Surface search: I band.
Sonars: Hull-mounted; active search and attack; medium frequency.
Helicopters: Platform for 1 medium.

Comment: Approved in FY 1991 as a dedicated training ship to replace *Katori* but the project postponed to FY 1992 as a budget saving measure. Laid down April 1993 and due to be launched in February 1994.

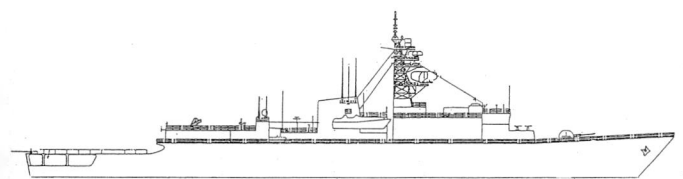

TRAINING SHIP   *(not to scale)*

2 AKIZUKI CLASS

Name	No	Builders	Commissioned
AKIZUKI	ASU 7010 (ex-DD 161)	Mitsubishi, Nagasaki	13 Feb 1960
TERUZUKI	ASU 7012 (ex-TV 3504) (ex-DD 162)	Shin Mitsubishi, Kobe	29 Feb 1960

Displacement, tons: 2350 standard; 2890 full load
Dimensions, feet (metres): 387.2 × 39.4 × 13.1 *(118 × 12 × 4)*
Main machinery: 4 boilers; 2 Mitsubishi turbines; 45 000 hp(m) *(33 MW)*; 2 shafts
Speed, knots: 32
Complement: 310; 190 (TV 3504)
Guns: 2 or 3 USN 5 in *(127 mm)*/54 Mk 39; 80° elevation; 15 rounds/minute to 22 km *(12 nm)* anti-surface; 13 km *(7 nm)* anti-aircraft; weight of shell 32 kg. Originally mounted in US Midway class.
4 USN 3 in *(76 mm)*/50 Mk 33 (2 twin); 85° elevation; 50 rounds/minute to 12.8 km *(6.9 nm)*; weight of shell 6 kg.
Torpedoes: 6—324 mm Type 68 (2 triple) tubes. Honeywell Mk 46 Mod 5 Neartip; anti-submarine; active/passive homing to 11 km *(5.9 nm)* at 40 kts; warhead 44 kg.
A/S mortars: 1 Bofors 375 mm Type 71 4-barrelled trainable rocket launcher; automatic loading; range 1.6 km.
Fire control: US Mk 63 for 127 mm guns. US Mk 57 for 76 mm guns.
Radars: Air search: Melco OPS 1; G band.
Surface search: JRC OPS 15; D band; range 146 km *(80 nm)*.
Fire control: Western Electric Mk 34; I/J band (for Mk 63 system).
IFF: US Mk 10.
Sonars: Sangamo SQS 23; hull-mounted; active search and attack; medium frequency.
Towed array for trials *(Akizuki)*.

Comment: Built under the 1957 Military Aid Programme as destroyers. *Akizuki* converted to ASU in 1985 and *Teruzuki* 27 Mar 1986. *Teruzuki* transferred to training duties 1 July 1987 and back again to ASU 20 June 1991 as a submarine depot or target ship. Both have had 21 in torpedo tubes and VDS removed and *Akizuki* had Y gun turret replaced by a trials towed sonar array in 1989.

AKIZUKI   *7/1992, Hachiro Nakai*

TERUZUKI   *7/1991, Hachiro Nakai*

2 YAMAGUMO CLASS

Name	No	Builders	Commissioned
YAMAGUMO	TV 3506 (ex-DD 113)	Mitsui, Tamano	29 Jan 1966
MAKIGUMO	TV 3507 (ex-DD 114)	Sumitomo, Uraga	19 Mar 1966

Displacement, tons: 2050 standard
Dimensions, feet (metres): 373.9 × 38.7 × 13.1 *(114 × 11.8 × 4)*
Main machinery: 6 Mitsubishi 12UEV30/40 diesels; 21 600 hp(m) *(15.9 MW)*; 2 shafts
Speed, knots: 27. **Range, miles:** 7000 at 20 kts
Complement: 210 (19 officers)
Missiles: A/S: Honeywell ASROC Mk 112 octuple launcher; inertial guidance to 1.6-10 km *(1-5.4 nm)* at 0.9 Mach; payload Mk 46 Mod 5 Neartip.
Guns: 4 USN 3 in *(76 mm)*/50 Mk 33 (2 twin); 85° elevation; 50 rounds/minute to 12.8 km *(6.9 nm)*; weight of shell 6 kg.
Torpedoes: 6—324 mm Type 68 (2 triple) tubes. Honeywell Mk 46 Mod 5 Neartip; anti-submarine; active/passive homing to 11 km *(5.9 nm)* at 40 kts; warhead 44 kg.
A/S mortars: 1 Bofors 375 mm Type 71 4-barrelled trainable rocket launcher; automatic loading; range 1.6 km.
Countermeasures: ESM: Nec NOLR 1B; radar intercept.
Fire control: US Mk 56 and Mk 57 for 76 mm guns.
Radars: Air search: Melco OPS 11.
Surface search: JRC OPS 17; G/H band.
Fire control: Two GE Mk 35; I/J band.
IFF: US Mk 10.
Sonars: Sangamo SQS 23; hull-mounted; active search and attack; low frequency.
EDO SQS 35(J); VDS; active/passive search; medium frequency.

Comment: Converted as training ships on 20 June 1991. Lecture room added under ASROC, chart room on the signal deck and accommodation for 16 women.

MAKIGUMO   *10/1991, Hachiro Nakai*

360 JAPAN (MSDF) / Service forces and auxiliaries

1 ISUZU CLASS

Name	No	Builders	Commissioned
KITAKAMI	ASU 7016 (ex-DE 213)	Ishikawajima Harima, Tokyo	27 Feb 1964

Displacement, tons: 1490 standard; 1788 full load
Dimensions, feet (metres): 308.3 × 34.2 × 11.5 *(94 × 10.4 × 3.5)*
Main machinery: 4 Mitsubishi 12UEV30/40 diesels; 14 400 hp(m) *(10.6 MW)*; 2 shafts
Speed, knots: 25
Complement: 160
Guns: 4 USN 3 in *(76 mm)*/50 Mk 33 (2 twin); 85° elevation; 50 rounds/minute to 12.8 km *(6.9 nm)*; weight of shell 6 kg.
A/S mortars: 1—375 mm Bofors Type 71 4-barrelled trainable rocket launchers; automatic loading; range 1.6 km.
Countermeasures: ESM: BLR-1; intercept.
Fire control: 2 US Mk 63 for 76 mm guns. US Mk 105 for ASW.
Radars: Air search: Melco OPS 1; G band.
Surface search: JRC OPS 16; D band.
Navigation: ORD 1; I band.
Fire control: Two Western Electric Mk 34; I/J band.
IFF: US Mk 10.
Sonars: SQS 29; hull-mounted; active search and attack; medium frequency.

Comment: Converted 31 January 1990 to training role with lecture hall replacing torpedo tubes and VDS removed. *Ooi* paid off in February 1993.

ISUZU class (old number)   5/1992, *Hachiro Nakai*

1 TRAINING SHIP

Name	No	Builders	Commissioned
KATORI	TV 3501	Ishikawajima Harima, Tokyo	10 Sep 1969

Displacement, tons: 3350 standard
Dimensions, feet (metres): 419.8 × 49.2 × 14.1 *(128 × 15 × 4.3)*
Flight deck, feet (metres): 98.4 × 42.6 *(30 × 13)*
Main machinery: 2 Ishikawajima boilers; 610 psi *(43 kg/cm sq)*; 850°F *(454°C)*; 2 Ishikawajima geared turbines; 20 000 hp(m) *(14.7 MW)*; 2 shafts; 454°C
Speed, knots: 25. **Range, miles:** 7000 at 18 kts
Complement: 463 (165 trainees)
Guns: 4 USN 3 in *(76 mm)*/50 Mk 33 (2 twin); 85° elevation; 50 rounds/minute to 12.8 km *(6.9 nm)*; weight of shell 6 kg.
Torpedoes: 6—324 mm Type 68 (2 triple) tubes. Honeywell Mk 46 Mod 5 Neartip; anti-submarine; active/passive homing to 11 km *(5.9 nm)* at 40 kts; warhead 44 kg.
A/S mortars: 1—375 mm Bofors Type 71 4-barrelled trainable rocket launcher; automatic loading; range 1.6 km.
Countermeasures: ESM: Nec NOLR 1B; radar warning.
Radars: Air search: RCA SPS 12; D band; range 119 km *(65 nm)*.
Air/surface search: JRC OPS 17; D band.
Navigation: JRC OPS 20; I band.
Sonars: Sangamo/General Electric SQS 4; hull-mounted; active; short-range; high frequency.

Comment: Provided with a large auditorium amidships and an open deck space aft which is used as a parade ground. Used for training officers. To be replaced in 1995.

KATORI   3/1992, *Hachiro Nakai*

1 AZUMA CLASS (TRAINING SUPPORT SHIP)

Name	No	Builders	Commissioned
AZUMA	ATS 4201	Hitachi, Maizuru	26 Nov 1969

Displacement, tons: 1950 standard
Dimensions, feet (metres): 321.5 × 42.7 × 12.5 *(98 × 13 × 3.8)*
Main machinery: 2 Kawasaki-MAN V8V22/30ATL diesels; 4000 hp(m) *(2.94 MW)*; 2 shafts
Speed, knots: 18
Complement: 185
Guns: 1 USN 3 in *(76 mm)*/50; 85° elevation; 50 rounds/minute to 12.8 km *(6.9 nm)*; weight of shell 6 kg.
Torpedoes: 2—483 mm Mk 4 tubes. USN Mk 32; active/passive homing to 8 km *(4.4 nm)* at 12 kts; warhead 49 kg.
Fire control: US Mk 51 Mod 2 for 76 mm gun system.
Radars: Air/Surface search: JRC OPS 16; D band; range 146 km *(80 nm)*.
Lockheed SPS 40; E/F band; range 320 km *(175 nm)*.
Fire control: Target control and tracking system (TCATS) (for drones).
Sonars: SQS 11A; hull-mounted; active search and attack.

Comment: Drone hangar amidships and catapult on flight deck. Can operate towed target. In 1982 target control and tracking system (TCATS) fitted to work with high-speed drones. Carries 10 Northrop KD2R-5 and 4 BQM-34-AJ Chaca II drones. Training support ship for AA gunnery.

AZUMA   7/1986, *Hachiro Nakai*

1 KUROBE CLASS (TRAINING SUPPORT SHIP)

Name	No	Builders	Commissioned
KUROBE	ATS 4202	Nippon Steel Tube Co, Tsurumi	23 Mar 1989

Displacement, tons: 2270 standard; 3200 full load
Dimensions, feet (metres): 331.4 × 54.1 × 13.1 *(101 × 16.5 × 4)*
Main machinery: 4 Fuji 8L27.5XF diesels; 8700 hp(m) *(6.4 MW)*; 2 shafts; cp props
Speed, knots: 20
Complement: 156
Guns: 1 FMC/OTO Melara 3 in *(76 mm)*/62 Mk 75; 85° elevation; 85 rounds/minute to 16 km *(8.6 nm)* anti-surface; 12 km *(6.5 nm)* anti-aircraft; weight of shell 6 kg.
Radars: Air search: Melco OPS 14.
Surface search: JRC OPS 18.

Comment: Approved under 1986 estimates, laid down 31 July 1987, launched 23 May 1988. Carries four BQM-34AJ high speed drones and four Northrop Chukar II drones with two stern launchers. Used for training crews in anti-aircraft operations and evaluating the effectiveness and capability of ships' anti-aircraft missile systems.

KUROBE   4/1992, *Hachiro Nakai*

1 CHIYODA CLASS
(SUBMARINE DEPOT AND RESCUE SHIP)

Name	No	Builders	Commissioned
CHIYODA	AS 405	Mitsui, Tamano	27 Mar 1985

Displacement, tons: 3650 standard; 4450 full load
Dimensions, feet (metres): 370.6 × 57.7 × 15.1 *(113 × 17.6 × 4.6)*
Main machinery: 2 Mitsui 8L42M diesels; 10 540 hp(m) *(8.8 MW)*; 2 shafts; cp props; bow and stern thrusters
Speed, knots: 17
Complement: 120
Helicopters: Platform for up to Sea King size.

Comment: Laid down 19 January 1983, launched 7 December 1983. Carries a Deep Submergence Rescue Vehicle (DSRV), built by Kawasaki Heavy Industries, Kobe, of 40 tons, 40.7 × 10.5 × 14.1 ft *(12.4 × 3.2 × 4.3 m)* with a 30 hp(m) *(22 kW)* electric motor and speed of 4 kts, it has space for 12 people. Flagship Second Submarine Flotilla based at Yokosuka.

CHIYODA   9/1992, *Hachiro Nakai*

Service forces and auxiliaries / JAPAN (MSDF) 361

1 SUBMARINE RESCUE SHIP

Name	No	Builders	Commissioned
FUSHIMI	ASR 402	Sumitomo, Uraga	10 Feb 1970

Displacement, tons: 1430 standard
Dimensions, feet (metres): 249.5 × 41 × 12.5 *(76 × 12.5 × 3.8)*
Main machinery: 2 Kawasaki-MAN V6V22/30ATL diesels; 3200 hp(m) *(2.35 MW)*; 1 shaft
Speed, knots: 16
Complement: 100
Radars: Surface search: Fujitsu OPS 9; I band.
IFF: US Mk 10.
Sonars: SQS 11A; hull-mounted.

Comment: Laid down on 5 November 1968, launched 10 September 1969. Equipped with rescue chamber and two recompression chambers. Flagship First Submarine Flotilla based at Kure.

FUSHIMI *7/1991, Hachiro Nakai*

3 TOWADA CLASS (FLEET SUPPORT SHIP)

Name	No	Builders	Commissioned
TOWADA	AOE 422	Hitachi, Maizuru	24 Mar 1987
TOKIWA	AOE 423	Ishikawajima Harima, Tokyo	12 Mar 1990
HAMANA	AOE 424	Hitachi, Maizuru	29 Mar 1990

Displacement, tons: 8150 standard; 15 850 full load
Dimensions, feet (metres): 547.8 × 72.2 × 26.9 *(167 × 22 × 8.2)*
Main machinery: 2 Mitsui 16V42MA diesels; 23 950 hp(m) *(17.6 MW)*; 2 shafts
Speed, knots: 22
Complement: 140
Cargo capacity: 5700 tons
Guns: 1—20 mm/76 Mk 15 Vulcan Phalanx *(Hamana)*.
Radars: Surface search: JRC OPS 18; I band.
Helicopters: Platform for 1 Sea King size.

Comment: First approved under 1984 estimates, laid down 17 April 1985, launched 25 March 1986. Second and third of class in 1987 estimates. AOE 423 laid down 12 May 1988, launched 23 March 1989. AOE 424 laid down 8 July 1988, launched 18 May 1989. Two replenishment at sea positions on each side (one fuel only, one fuel or stores). All to be fitted with Vulcan Phalanx guns in due course.

TOWADA *4/1992, Hachiro Nakai*

1 FLEET SUPPORT SHIP

Name	No	Builders	Commissioned
SAGAMI	AOE 421	Hitachi, Maizuru	30 Mar 1979

Displacement, tons: 5000 standard; 11 600 full load
Dimensions, feet (metres): 478.9 × 62.3 × 24 *(146 × 19 × 7.3)*
Main machinery: 2 Type 12DRV diesels; 18 000 hp(m) *(13.23 MW)*; 2 shafts
Speed, knots: 22. **Range, miles:** 9500 at 18 kts
Complement: 130
Cargo capacity: 5000 tons
Radars: Surface search: JRC OPS 18; D band.
Helicopters: Platform for 1 Sea King size.

Comment: Merchant type hull. Ordered December 1976. Laid down 28 September 1977, launched 4 September 1978. Two fuel stations each side. No armament but can be fitted.

SAGAMI *4/1992, Hachiro Nakai*

34 HARBOUR TANKERS

Comment: There are: 12 of 490 tons (YO 9, 14, 21-27, 29-31); three of 310 tons (YW 17-19); four of 290 tons (YO 10-13); nine of 270 tons (YO 19, 28, 32 and YG 201-206); five of 160 tons (YW 12-16); one of 100 tons (YO 18). YO (oil), YW (water) and YG (gasoline). Most are propelled by two diesels at about 9 kts. The latest to commission was YO 32 on 20 October 1992.

YW 13 *10/1991, Hachiro Nakai*

6 TAKAMI CLASS (EOD TENDERS)

MIYAKE (ex-*MSC 632*) YAS 84	**MIYATO** (ex-*MSC 639*) YAS 90
TEURI (ex-*MSC 636*) YAS 87	**YOKOSE** (ex-*MSC 642*) YAS 93
TASHIRO (ex-*MSC 638*) YAS 89	**SAKATE** (ex-*MSC 643*) YAS 94

Displacement, tons: 380 standard; 510 full load
Dimensions, feet (metres): 170.6 × 28.9 × 7.9 *(52 × 8.8 × 2.4)*
Main machinery: 2 Mitsubishi YV12ZC-15/20 diesels; 1440 hp(m) *(1.06 MW)*; 2 shafts
Speed, knots: 14
Complement: 43
Guns: 1 Oerlikon 20 mm.

Comment: Transferred after conversion to Explosive Ordnance Disposal (EOD) Unit (Mine Hunting Diver) duties which includes removal of minesweeping gear to provide for divers' room and equipment.

MIYATO *9/1991, Hachiro Nakai*

SAKATE *1/1993, Hachiro Nakai*

1 CABLE LAYER

Name	No	Builders	Commissioned
MUROTO	ARC 482	Mitsubishi, Shimonoseki	27 Mar 1980

Displacement, tons: 4544 standard
Dimensions, feet (metres): 436.2 × 57.1 × 18.7 *(133 × 17.4 × 5.7)*
Main machinery: 4 Kawasaki-MAN V8V22/30ATL diesels; 8000 hp(m) *(5.88 MW)*; 2 shafts
Speed, knots: 18
Complement: 135

Comment: Ocean survey capability. Laid down 28 November 1978, launched 25 July 1979.

MUROTO *10/1991, Hachiro Nakai*

362 JAPAN (MSDF) / Service forces and auxiliaries — Survey and experimental ships

5 81-GO CLASS

Name	Laid down	Launched	Commissioned
ASU 81	21 Oct 1967	18 Jan 1968	30 Mar 1968
ASU 82	25 Sep 1968	20 Dec 1968	31 Mar 1969
ASU 83	2 Apr 1971	24 May 1971	30 Sep 1971
ASU 84	4 Feb 1972	15 June 1972	13 Sep 1972
ASU 85	20 Feb 1973	16 July 1973	19 Sep 1973

Displacement, tons: 500 (ASU 85), 490 (ASU 82-84), 480 (ASU 81) standard
Dimensions, feet (metres): 170.6 × 32.8 × 8.3 *(52 × 10 × 2.5)*
Main machinery: 2 Akasaka diesels; 1600 hp(m) *(1.18 MW)*; 2 shafts
Speed, knots: 14
Complement: 25; 35 (ASU 81-83)
Radars: Navigation: Fujitsu OPS 19 (ASU 84/85). Oki OPS 10 (others).

Comment: Training support and rescue. The after deck crane is able to lift a helicopter. *ASU 82* and *ASU 83* can launch propeller-driven drones by catapult.

ASU 84   2/1991, Hachiro Nakai

1 MIZUTORI CLASS

Name	No	Builders	Commissioned
HIYODORI	ASY 92 (ex-PC 320)	Sasebo Heavy Industries	28 Feb 1966

Displacement, tons: 390 standard
Dimensions, feet (metres): 197 × 23.3 × 8.3 *(60 × 7.1 × 2.5)*
Main machinery: 2 Kawasaki-MAN V8V22/30ATL diesels; 4000 hp(m) *(2.94 MW)*; 2 shafts
Speed, knots: 20
Complement: 35 (90 passengers)

Comment: Built under FY 1964 programme as large patrol craft. Reconstructed as Auxiliary Special Service Yacht (ASY) at Yokohama Yacht Co Ltd, completed 27 April 1987.

HIYODORI   3/1992, A Sheldon Duplaix

4 TAKAMI CLASS (TENDERS)

Name	No	Builders	Commissioned
MUROTSU	YAS 88 (ex-MSC 637)	Hitachi, Kanagawa	30 Mar 1972
TAKANE	YAS 91 (ex-MSC 640)	Nippon Steel Tube Co	28 Aug 1974
MUZUKI	YAS 92 (ex-MSC 641)	Hitachi, Kanagawa	28 Aug 1974
OUMI	YAS 95 (ex-MSC 644)	Hitachi, Kanagawa	18 Nov 1976

Comment: Details as for Takami class under Mine Warfare Forces. YAS 83 converted 27 March 1986, YAS 86 24 March 1987, YAS 88 23 March 1988, YAS 91 and 92 in December 1990 and YAS 95 in 1992. Various roles. YAS 95 used as noise range support ship.

MUROTSU   4/1992, Hachiro Nakai

SURVEY AND EXPERIMENTAL SHIPS

Note: The SES trials ship *Merguro* does not belong to the MSDF.

2 HIBIKI CLASS (AOS)

Name	No	Builders	Commissioned
HIBIKI	AOS 5201	Mitsui, Tamano	30 Jan 1991
HARIMA	AOS 5202	Mitsui, Tamano	10 Mar 1992

Displacement, tons: 2850 standard
Dimensions, feet (metres): 219.8 × 98.1 × 24.6 *(67 × 29.9 × 7.5)*
Main machinery: Diesel-electric; 4 Mitsubishi 6SU diesels; 6700 hp(m) *(4.93 MW)*; 4 generators; 2 motors; 3000 hp(m) *(2.2 MW)*; 2 shafts
Speed, knots: 11 (3 towing). **Range, miles:** 3800 at 10 kts
Complement: 40
Radars: Navigation: JRC OPS 16; I band.
Sonars: UQQ 2 SURTASS; passive surveillance.
Helicopters: Platform only.

Comment: First authorised 24 January 1989, laid down 28 November 1989 and launched 27 July 1990. Second approved in FY 1990, laid down 26 December 1990 and launched 11 September 1991. Total of five planned originally but subsequently reduced to two. Auxiliary Ocean Surveillance (AOS) ships to a SWATH design similar to USN TAGOS-19 class; the first of class embarks US civilians. A data collection station is based at Yokosuka Bay using WSC-6 satellite data relay to the AOS.

HIBIKI   1/1991, Hachiro Nakai

1 SUMA CLASS (AGS)

Name	No	Builders	Commissioned
SUMA	AGS 5103	Hitachi, Maizuru	30 Mar 1982

Displacement, tons: 1180 standard
Dimensions, feet (metres): 236.2 × 42 × 11.1 *(72 × 12.8 × 3.4)*
Main machinery: 2 Fuji 6L27.5XF diesels; 3250 hp(m) *(2.39 MW)*; 2 shafts; cp props
Speed, knots: 15
Complement: 64

Comment: Laid down 24 September 1980, launched 1 September 1981. Carries an 11 m launch for surveying work.

SUMA   10/1992, Hachiro Nakai

2 FUTAMI CLASS (AGS)

Name	No	Builders	Commissioned
FUTAMI	AGS 5102	Mitsubishi, Shimonoseki	27 Feb 1979
WAKASA	AGS 5104	Hitachi Zosen, Maizuru	25 Feb 1986

Displacement, tons: 2050 standard; 3175 full load
Dimensions, feet (metres): 318.2 × 49.2 × 13.8 *(97 × 15 × 4.2)*
Main machinery: 2 Kawasaki-MAN V8V22/30ATL diesels; 4000 hp(m) *(2.94 MW)* (AGS 5102); 2 Fuji 6L27.5XF diesels; 3250 hp(m) *(2.39 MW)* (AGS 5104); 2 shafts; cp props; bow thruster
Speed, knots: 16
Complement: 105
Radars: Navigation: JRC OPS 18; I band.

Comment: AGS 5102 laid down 20 January 1978. Launched 9 August 1978. AGS 5104 laid down 21 August 1984, launched 21 May 1985. Built to merchant marine design. Carry an RCV-22 remote controlled rescue/underwater survey submarine. *Wakasa* has a slightly taller funnel.

FUTAMI   7/1992, Hachiro Nakai

Survey and experimental ships — Tugs / JAPAN (MSDF) 363

1 AKASHI CLASS (AGS)

Name	No	Builders	Commissioned
AKASHI	AGS 5101	Nippon Steel Tube Co	25 Oct 1969

Displacement, tons: 1420 standard
Dimensions, feet (metres): 242.7 × 42.2 × 14.2 *(74 × 13 × 4.3)*
Main machinery: 2 Kawasaki-MAN V6V22/30ATL diesels; 3200 hp(m) *(2.35 MW)*; 2 shafts; bow thruster
Speed, knots: 16. **Range, miles:** 16 500 at 14 kts
Complement: 65 plus 10 scientists
Countermeasures: ESM: Nec NOLR-5; radar intercept.
Radars: Navigation: Fujitsu OPS 9; I band.

Comment: Has a large number of electronic intercept aerials.

AKASHI 1990, JMSDF

1 KURIHAMA CLASS (ASE)

Name	No	Builders	Commissioned
KURIHAMA	ASE 6101	Sasebo Heavy Industries	8 Apr 1980

Displacement, tons: 959 standard
Dimensions, feet (metres): 223 × 37.9 × 9.8 (screws) *(68 × 11.6 × 3)*
Main machinery: 2 Fuji 6S30B diesels; 4800 hp(m) *(3.5 MW)*; 2 shafts; 2 cp props; bow thruster
Speed, knots: 15
Complement: 40 plus 12 scientists

Comment: Experimental ship built for the Technical Research and Development Institute and used for testing underwater weapons and sensors.

KURIHAMA 12/1984, Hachiro Nakai

0 + 1 ASE

Name	No	Builders	Commissioned
—	—	Sumitomo, Uraga	Mar 1995

Displacement, tons: 4200 standard
Main machinery: 2 gas turbines; 2 shafts
Speed, knots: 27
Complement: 170 plus 100 scientists

Comment: Included in the FY 1992 programme. To be laid down in 1993. For experimental and weapon systems testing.

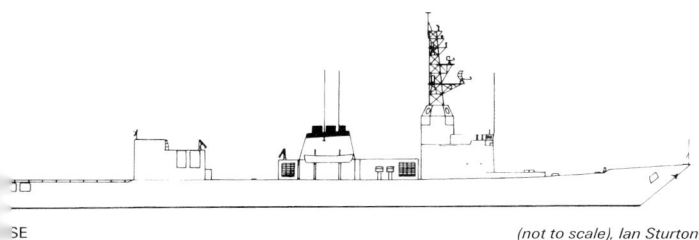

ASE (not to scale), Ian Sturton

ICEBREAKER

Name	No	Builders	Commissioned
SHIRASE	AGB 5002	Nippon Steel Tube Co, Tsurumi	12 Nov 1982

Displacement, tons: 11 600 standard; 17 600 full load
Dimensions, feet (metres): 439.5 × 91.8 × 30.2 *(134 × 28 × 9.2)*
Main machinery: Diesel-electric; 6 Mitsui 12V42M diesels; 53 900 hp(m) *(39.6 MW)*; 6 generators; 3 motors; 30 000 hp(m) *(22 MW)*; 3 shafts
Speed, knots: 19. **Range, miles:** 25 000 at 15 kts
Complement: 174 (37 officers) plus 60 scientists
Cargo capacity: 1000 tons
Helicopters: 2 Mitsubishi S-61A; 1 Kawasaki OH-6J.

Comment: Laid down 5 March 1981 and launched 11 December 1981. Fully equipped for marine and atmospheric research. Stabilised.

SHIRASE 5/1992, Ships of the World

TUGS

13 OCEAN TUGS

YT 58 YT 63-74

Displacement, tons: 260 standard
Dimensions, feet (metres): 93 × 28 × 8.2 *(28.4 × 8.6 × 2.5)*
Main machinery: 2 Niigata 6L25B diesels; 1800 hp(m) *(1.32 MW)*; 2 shafts
Speed, knots: 11
Complement: 10

Comment: YT 58 entered service on 31 October 1978, YT 63 on 27 September 1982, YT 64 on 30 September 1983, YT 65 on 20 September 1984, YT 66 on 20 September 1985, YT 67 on 4 September 1986, YT 68 on 9 September 1987, YT 69 on 16 September 1987, YT 70 on 2 September 1988, YT 71 on 28 July 1989, YT 72 on 27 July 1990, YT 73 on 31 July 1991 and YT 74 on 30 September 1991. All built by Yokohama Yacht.

YT 73 3/1992, Hachiro Nakai

4 COASTAL TUGS

YT 53, 55-57

Displacement, tons: 190 standard
Dimensions, feet (metres): 84.8 × 23 × 7.5 *(25.7 × 7 × 2.3)*
Main machinery: 2 Kubota M6D20BUCS diesels; 1500 hp(m) *(1.1 MW)*; 2 shafts
Speed, knots: 11
Complement: 10

Comment: YT 53 entered service on 8 March 1975, YT 55 on 22 August 1975, YT 56 on 13 July 1976, YT 57 on 22 August 1977.

YT 56 3/1992, Hachiro Nakai

364 JAPAN (MSDF) / Tugs — JAPAN (MSA) / Large patrol vessels

7 COASTAL TUGS

YT 37, YT 40-41, YT 44-46, YT 48

Displacement, tons: 100 standard
Dimensions, feet (metres): 78.1 × 17.7 × 7.9 *(23.8 × 5.4 × 2.4)*
Main machinery: 1 diesel; 400 hp(m) *(294 kW)*; 1 shaft
Speed, knots: 10

YT 75   *10/1992, Ships of the World*

HARBOUR CRAFT

Comment: Large numbers of harbour craft fly the naval ensign.

YT 45   *8/1990, Hachiro Nakai*

13 + 2 HARBOUR TUGS

YT 38-39, YT 42-43, YT 47, YT 49, YT 51, YT 54, YT 59-62, YT 75

Comment: Of varying sizes from 26-50 tons. Two more YT 75 type building by Yokohama Yacht to complete in 1993. YT 75 commissioned 30 September 1992.

YAL 01   *4/1992, Hachiro Nakai*

MARITIME SAFETY AGENCY
(KAIJO HOANCHO)

Commandant of the MSA

Tsuguo Iyama

Establishment

Established in May 1948 as an external organisation of the Ministry of Transport to carry out patrol and rescue duties as well as hydrographic and navigation aids services. Since then a very considerable organisation with HQ in Tokyo has been built up. The Academy for the Agency is in Kure and the School in Maizuru. The main operational branches are the Guard and Rescue, the Hydrographic and the Aids to Navigation Departments. Regional Maritime Safety offices control the 11 districts with their location as follows (air bases in brackets): RMS 1—Otaru (Chitose, Hakodate, Kushiro); 2—Shiogama (Sendai); 3—Yokohama (Haneda); 4—Nagoya (Ise); 5—Kobe (Yao); 6—Hiroshima (Hiroshima); 7—Kitakyushu (Fukuoka); 8—Maizuru (Miho); 9—Niigata (Niigata); 10—Kagoshima (Kagoshima); 11—Naha (Naha, Ishigaki). This organisation includes, as well as the RMS HQ, 66 MS offices, 57 MS stations, 26 MS detachments, 14 MS air stations, 9 district communication centres, 3 traffic advisory service centres, 4 hydrographic observatories and 119 aids to navigation offices.

Personnel

1993: 12 500 (2630 officers)

Strength of the Fleet

Type	Active	Building
GUARD AND RESCUE SERVICE		
Patrol Vessels:		
Large with helicopter (PLH)	11	—
Large (PL)	37	1
Medium (PM)	47	—
Small (PS)	19	1
Firefighting Vessels (FL)	5	—
Patrol Craft:		
Patrol Craft (PC)	61	—
Patrol Craft (CL)	170	—
Firefighting Craft (FM)	10	—
Special Service Craft:		
Monitoring Craft (MS)	4	—
Guard Boats (GS)	2	—
Surveillance Craft (SS)	34	—
Oil Recovery Craft (OR)	5	—
Oil Skimming Craft (OS)	3	—
Oil Boom Craft (OX)	19	—
Miscellaneous (NO)	3	—

Type	Active	Building
HYDROGRAPHIC SERVICE		
Surveying Vessels:		
Large (HL)	4	1
Medium (HM)	1	—
Small (HS)	17	1
AIDS TO NAVIGATION SERVICE		
Aids to Navigation Research Vessel (LL)	1	—
Buoy Tenders:		
Large (LL)	3	—
Medium (LM)	1	—
Aids to Navigation Tenders:		
Medium (LM)	10	—
Small (LS)	62	—

DELETIONS

1990 *Takanawa* PS 36, *Takahikari* LS 202, *Sekihikari* LS 156 *Meiyo* HL 03 (old)
1991 *Ojika* PL 12 (old), *Rokko* PS 35, *Hamashio* HS 01, *Sekiur* LM 105, *Houn* LM 111
1992 *Amami* PM 62, *Takatsuki* PS 39, *Reiun* LM 102, *Kinugasa* MS 01 (old), CL 50-51, CL 53-55, CL 66, CL 78, LS 102
1993 *Kojima* PL 21 (old), *Genun* LM 113, CL 65-77

LARGE PATROL VESSELS

1 SHIKISHIMA CLASS

Name	No	Builders	Commissioned
SHIKISHIMA	PLH 31	Ishikawajima Harima, Tokyo	8 Apr 1992

Displacement, tons: 6500 standard
Dimensions, feet (metres): 492.1 × 55.8 × 19.7 *(150 × 17 × 6)*
Main machinery: 2 SEMT-Pielstick 16 PC2.5 V 400; 20 800 hp(m) *(15.29 MW)*; 2 shafts
Speed, knots: 25. **Range, miles:** 20 000 at 18 kts
Guns: 4 Oerlikon 35 mm/90 (2 twin). 2 JM-61 MB 20 mm Gatling.
Radars: Air/surface search: Melco Ops 14; D/E band.
Surface search: JMA 1576; I band.
Navigation: JMA 1596; I band.
Helicopter control: I band.
Helicopters: 2 medium type.

Comment: Authorised in the FY 1989 programme in place of the third Mizuho class. Laid down 24 August 1990 and launched 27 June 1991. Used to escort the plutonium transport ship. Armament and command and control systems seem barely adequate for escort duties. SATCOM fitted.

SHIKISHIMA   *4/1992, Ships of the World*

SHIKISHIMA 8/1992, Hachiro Nakai

2 MIZUHO CLASS

Name	No	Builders	Commissioned
MIZUHO	PLH 21	Mitsubishi, Nagasaki	19 Mar 1986
YASHIMA	PLH 22	Nippon Kokan, Tsurumi	1 Dec 1988

Displacement, tons: 4900 standard; 5204 full load
Dimensions, feet (metres): 426.5 × 50.9 × 17.7 *(130 × 15.5 × 5.4)*
Main machinery: 2 SEMT-Pielstick 14 PC2.5 V 400 diesels; 18 200 hp(m) *(13.38 MW)* sustained; 2 shafts; cp props; bow thruster
Speed, knots: 23. **Range, miles:** 8500 at 22 kts
Complement: 100 plus 30 aircrew
Guns: 1 Oerlikon 35 mm/90; 85° elevation; 550 rounds/minute to 6 km *(3.2 nm)* anti-surface; 5 km *(2.7 nm)* anti-aircraft; weight of shell 1.55 kg.
1 JM-61 MB 20 mm Gatling.
Radars: Navigation: Two sets.
Helicopter control: One set.
Helicopters: 2 Sikorsky S-62 Seaguard or Fuji-Bell 212.

Comment: PLH 21 ordered under the FY 1983 programme laid down 27 August 1984 and launched 5 June 1985. PLH 22 in 1986 estimates, laid down 3 October 1987 and launched 20 January 1988. Two sets of fixed electric fin stabilisers that have a lift of 26 tons × 2 and reduce rolling by 90 per cent at 18 kts. Employed in search and rescue beyond 200 miles from the base line.

MIZUHO 5/1992, Hachiro Nakai

8 SOYA CLASS

Name	No	Builders	Commissioned
SOYA	PLH 01	Nippon Kokan, Tsurumi	22 Nov 1978
TSUGARU	PLH 02	IHI, Tokyo	17 Apr 1979
OOSUMI	PLH 03	Mitsui Tamano	18 Oct 1979
URAGA	PLH 04	Hitachi, Maizuru	5 Mar 1980
ZAO	PLH 05	Mitsubishi, Nagasaki	19 Mar 1982
CHIKUZEN	PLH 06	Kawasaki, Kobe	28 Sep 1983
SETTSU	PLH 07	Sumitomo, Oppama	27 Sep 1984
ECHIGO	PLH 08	Mitsui Tamano	28 Feb 1990

Displacement, tons: 3200 normal; 3744 full load
Dimensions, feet (metres): 323.4 × 51.2 × 17.1 *(98.6 × 15.6 × 5.2)* (PLH 01) 345.8 × 47.9 × 15.7 *(105.4 × 14.6 × 4.8)*
Main machinery: 2 SEMT-Pielstick 12 PC2.5 V 400 diesels; 15 604 hp(m) *(11.47 MW)* sustained; 2 shafts; cp props; bow thruster
Speed, knots: 21 (PLH 01); 22 (others). **Range, miles:** 5700 at 18 kts
Complement: 71 (PLH 01-04); 69 (others)
Guns: 1 Bofors 40 mm or Oerlikon 35 mm. 1 Oerlikon 20 mm (PLH 01, 02, 05-07).
Radars: Surface search: JMA 1576; I band.
Navigation: JMA 1596; I band.
Helicopter control: CCA Type.
Helicopters: 1 Fuji-Bell 212.

Comment: PLH 01 has an icebreaking capability while the other ships are only ice strengthened. Fitted with both fin stabilisers and anti-rolling tanks of 70 tons capacity. The fixed electric hydraulic fins have a lift of 26 tons × 2 at 18 kts which reduces rolling by 90 per cent at that speed. At slow speed the reduction is 50 per cent, using the tanks.

ECHIGO 5/1992, Hachiro Nakai

2 IZU CLASS

Name	No	Builders	Commissioned
IZU	PL 31	Hitachi, Mukaishima	31 July 1967
MIURA	PL 32	Hitachi, Maizuru	15 Mar 1969

Displacement, tons: 2081 normal
Dimensions, feet (metres): 313.3 × 38 × 12.8 *(95.5 × 11.6 × 3.9)*
Main machinery: 2 SEMT-Pielstick 12 PC2.5 V 400 diesels; 15 604 hp(m) *(11.47 MW)* sustained; 2 shafts; cp props; bow thruster
Speed, knots: 20. **Range, miles:** 6000 at 18.8 kts
Complement: 72
Guns: 1 Bofors 40 mm/70.
Radars: Surface search: JMA 1576; I band.
Navigation: JMA 1596; I band.

Comment: PL 31 was laid down in August 1966, launched in January 1967. PL 32 was laid down in May 1968, launched in October 1968. Equipped with various types of marine instruments. Ice-strengthened hull. Armament may be removed depending on employment. Based at Yokohama and employed in long-range rescue and patrol duties.

IZU 5/1992, Hachiro Nakai

1 KOJIMA CLASS

Name	No	Builders	Commissioned
KOJIMA	PL 21	Hitachi, Maizuru	11 Mar 1993

Displacement, tons: 2650 normal; 2950 full load
Dimensions, feet (metres): 377.3 × 45.9 × 16.4 *(115 × 14 × 5)*
Main machinery: 2 diesels; 8000 hp(m) *(5.9 MW)*; 2 shafts
Speed, knots: 18. **Range, miles:** 7000 at 15 kts
Complement: 118
Guns: 1 Oerlikon 35 mm/90. 1—20 mm JM-61B Gatling. 1—12.7 mm MG.

Comment: Authorised in the FY 1990 programme and ordered in March 1991. Laid down 7 November 1991, launched 10 September 1992. Training ship which has replaced the old ship of the same name and pennant number.

KOJIMA 1/1993, Hachiro Nakai

28 SHIRETOKO CLASS

Name	No	Builders	Commissioned
SHIRETOKO	PL 101	Mitsui Tamano	8 Nov 1978
ESAN	PL 102	Sumitomo	16 Nov 1978
WAKASA	PL 103	Kawasaki, Kobe	29 Nov 1978
YAHIKO	PL 104	Mitsubishi, Shimonoseki	16 Nov 1978
MOTOBU	PL 105	Sasebo	29 Nov 1978
RISHIRI	PL 106	Shikoku	12 Sep 1979
MATSUSHIMA	PL 107	Tohoku	14 Sep 1979
IWAKI	PL 108	Naikai	10 Aug 1979
SHIKINE	PL 109	Usuki	20 Sep 1979
SURUGA	PL 110	Kurushima	28 Sep 1979
REBUN	PL 111	Narasaki	21 Nov 1979
CHOKAI	PL 112	Nihonkai	30 Nov 1979
ASHIZURI	PL 113	Sanoyasu	31 Oct 1979
OKI	PL 114	Tsuneishi	16 Nov 1979
NOTO	PL 115	Miho	30 Nov 1979
YONAKUNI	PL 116	Hayashikane	31 Oct 1979
KUDAKA (ex-*Daisetsu*)	PL 117	Hakodate	31 Jan 1980
SHIMOKITA	PL 118	Ishikawajima, Kakoki	12 Mar 1980
SUZUKA	PL 119	Kanazashi	7 Mar 1980
KUNISAKI	PL 120	Kouyo	29 Feb 1980
GENKAI	PL 121	Oshima	31 Jan 1980
GOTO	PL 122	Onomichi	29 Feb 1980
KOSHIKI	PL 123	Kasado	25 Jan 1980
HATERUMA	PL 124	Osaka	12 Mar 1980
KATORI	PL 125	Tohoku	21 Oct 1980
KUNIGAMI	PL 126	Kanda	17 Oct 1980
ETOMO	PL 127	Naikai	17 Mar 1982
MASHU	PL 128	Shiikoku	12 Mar 1982

Displacement, tons: 974 normal; 1360 full load
Dimensions, feet (metres): 255.8 × 31.5 × 10.5 *(78 × 9.6 × 3.2)*
Main machinery: 2 Fuji 8S40B; 8120 hp(m) *(5.97 MW)*; or 2 Niigata 8MA40 diesels; 2 shafts; cp props
Speed, knots: 20. **Range, miles:** 4400 at 17 kts
Complement: 41
Guns: 1 Bofors 40 mm or 1 Oerlikon 35 mm. 1 Oerlikon 20 mm (PL 101-105, 127 and 128).
Radars: Navigation: One set.

Comment: Average time from launch to commissioning was about four to five months. Designed for EEZ patrol duties. PL 117 changed her name on 1 April 1988.

KATORI 5/1992, Hachiro Nakai

4 ERIMO and DAIO CLASSES

Name	No	Builders	Commissioned
ERIMO	PL 13	Hitachi, Mukaishima	30 Nov 1965
SATSUMA	PL 14	Hitachi, Mukaishima	30 July 1966
DAIO	PL 15	Hitachi, Maizuru	28 Sep 1973
MUROTO	PL 16	Naikai	30 Nov 1974

Displacement, tons: 1010 (1206, PL 15-16) normal
Dimensions, feet (metres): 251.3 × 30.2 × 9.9 *(76.6 × 9.2 × 3)* (PL 13-14)
  251.3 × 31.5 × 10.7 *(76.6 × 9.6 × 3.3)* (PL 15-16)
Main machinery: 2 Burmeister & Wain diesels (PL 13-14); 2 Fuji 8S40B (PL 15-16); 8120 hp(m) *(5.97 MW)*; 2 shafts; cp props
Speed, knots: 20. **Range, miles:** 5000 at 18 kts (PL 13-14); 4400 at 18 kts (PL 15-16)
Complement: 72 (PL 13-14); 50 (PL 15-16)
Guns: 1 Oerlikon 20 mm. 1 Bofors 40 mm (PL 15-16). 1 Oerlikon 20 mm (PL 13-14).
Radars: Navigation: JMA 1576. JMA 1596.

Comment: PL 13's structure is strengthened against ice. Based at Kamaishi (PL 13); Kagoshima (PL 14); Kushiro (PL 15); Aburatsu (PL 16).

SATSUMA 1990, Ships of the World

1 NOJIMA CLASS

Name	No	Builders	Commissioned
NOJIMA	PL 01	Ishikawajima Harima, Tokyo	21 Sep 1989

Displacement, tons: 1500 normal
Dimensions, feet (metres): 285.4 × 34.4 × 11.5 *(87 × 10.5 × 3.5)*
Main machinery: 2 Fuji 8S40B diesels; 8120 hp(m) *(5.97 MW)*; 2 shafts
Speed, knots: 19
Guns: 1—20 mm JM-61B Gatling.
Radars: Navigation.
Helicopters: Platform for 1 Bell 212.

Comment: Laid down 16 August 1988 and launched 30 May 1989. Equipped as surveillance and rescue command ship. SATCOM fitted.

NOJIMA 5/1992, Hachiro Nakai

1 + 1 OJIKA CLASS

Name	No	Builders	Commissioned
OJIKA	PL 02	Mitsui, Tamano	31 Oct 1991
—	PL 03	Hakodate Dock	Oct 1994

Displacement, tons: 1883 normal
Dimensions, feet (metres): 299.9 × 36.1 × 16.4 *(91.4 × 11 × 5)*
Main machinery: 2 Fuji 8S40B diesels; 7000 hp(m) *(5.15 MW)*; 2 shafts
Speed, knots: 18
Guns: 1—20 mm JM-61B Gatling.
Helicopters: Platform for 1 Bell 212.

Comment: First of class launched 23 April 1991. Second ordered in 1992. Equipped as SAR command ships. SATCOM fitted.

OJIKA 5/1992, Hachiro Nakai

SHIPBORNE AIRCRAFT

Numbers/Type: 36 Bell 212.
Operational speed: 100 kts *(185 km/h)*.
Service ceiling: 10 000 ft *(3048 m)*.
Range: 412 nm *(763 km)*.
Role/Weapon systems: Liaison, medium range support and SAR. Sensors: Search radar. Weapons: Unarmed.

BELL 212 5/1992, Hachiro Nakai

LAND-BASED MARITIME AIRCRAFT (FRONT LINE)

Numbers/Type: 16 Beech Super King Air 200T.
Operational speed: 245 kts *(453 km/h)*.
Service ceiling: 35 000 ft *(10 670 m)*.
Range: 1460 nm *(2703 km)*.
Role/Weapon systems: Visual reconnaissance in support of EEZ. Sensors: Weather/search radar. Weapons: Unarmed.

Numbers/Type: 4 Bell 206B JetRanger.
Operational speed: 115 kts *(213 km/h)*.
Service ceiling: 10 000 ft *(3048 m)*.
Range: 312 nm *(577 km)*.
Role/Weapon systems: Liaison and training. Sensors: None. Weapons: Unarmed.

Numbers/Type: 5 NAMC YS-11A.
Operational speed: 230 kts *(425 km/h)*.
Service ceiling: 21 600 ft *(6580 m)*.
Range: 1960 nm *(3629 km)*.
Role/Weapon systems: Maritime surveillance and associated tasks. Sensors: Weather/search radar. Weapons: Unarmed.

Numbers/Type: 2 Shorts Skyvan 3.
Operational speed: 175 kts *(324 km/h).*
Service ceiling: 10 000 ft *(3048 m).*
Range: 847 nm *(1568 km).*
Role/Weapon systems: Coastal patrol and support aircraft. Sensors: Weather radar. Weapons: Unarmed.

Numbers/Type: 2 Falcon 900.
Operational speed: 428 kts *(792 km/h).*
Service ceiling: 51 000 ft *(15 544 m).*
Range: 4170 nm *(7722 km).*
Role/Weapon systems: Maritime surveillance. Sensors: Weather/search radar. Weapons: Unarmed.

MEDIUM PATROL VESSELS

14 TESHIO CLASS

Name	No	Builders	Commissioned
TESHIO	PM 01	Shikoku	30 Sep 1980
OIRASE	PM 02	Naikai	29 Aug 1980
ECHIZEN	PM 03	Usuki	30 Sep 1980
TOKACHI	PM 04	Narazaki	24 Mar 1981
HITACHI	PM 05	Tohoku	19 Mar 1981
OKITSU	PM 06	Usuki	17 Mar 1981
ISAZU	PM 07	Naikai	18 Feb 1982
CHITOSE	PM 08	Shikoku	15 Mar 1983
KUWANO	PM 09	Naikai	10 Mar 1983
SORACHI	PM 10	Tohoku	30 Aug 1984
YUBARI	PM 11	Usuki	28 Nov 1985
MOTOURA	PM 12	Shikoku	21 Nov 1986
KANO	PM 13	Naikai	13 Nov 1986
SENDAI	PM 14	Shikoku	1 June 1988

Displacement, tons: 630 normal; 670 full load
Dimensions, feet (metres): 222.4 × 25.9 × 6.6 *(67.8 × 7.9 × 2.7)*
Main machinery: 2 Fuji 6S32F diesels; 3650 hp(m) *(2.69 MW);* 2 shafts
Speed, knots: 18. **Range, miles:** 3200 at 16 kts
Complement: 33
Guns: 1 JN-61B 20 mm Gatling.
Radars: Navigation: Two JMA 159B; I band.

Comment: First three built under FY 1979 programme and second three under FY 1980, seventh under FY 1981, PM 08-09 under FY 1982, PM 10 under FY 1983, PM 11 under FY 1984, PM 12-13 under FY 1985, PM 14 under FY 1987.

ISAZU *5/1992, Hachiro Nakai*

20 BIHORO CLASS (350-M4 TYPE)

Name	No	Builders	Commissioned
BIHORO	PM 73	Tohoku	28 Feb 1974
KUMA	PM 74	Usuki	28 Feb 1974
FUJI	PM 75	Usuki	7 Feb 1975
KABASHIMA	PM 76	Usuki	25 Mar 1975
SADO	PM 77	Tohoku	7 Feb 1975
ISHIKARI	PM 78	Tohoku	13 Mar 1976
ABUKUMA	PM 79	Tohoku	30 Jan 1976
ISUZU	PM 80	Naikai	10 Mar 1976
KIKUCHI	PM 81	Usuki	6 Feb 1976
KUZURYU	PM 82	Usuki	18 Mar 1976
HOROBETSU	PM 83	Tohoku	27 Jan 1977
SHIRAKAMI	PM 84	Tohoku	24 Mar 1977
SAGAMI	PM 85	Naikai	30 Nov 1976
TONE	PM 86	Usuki	30 Nov 1976
YOSHINO	PM 87	Usuki	28 Jan 1977
KUROBE	PM 88	Shikoku	15 Feb 1977
CHIKUGO	PM 90	Naikai	27 Jan 1978
YAMAKUNI	PM 91	Usuki	26 Jan 1978
KATSURA	PM 92	Shikoku	15 Feb 1978
SHINANO	PM 93	Tohoku	23 Feb 1978

Displacement, tons: 615 normal; 636 full load
Dimensions, feet (metres): 208 × 25.6 × 8.3 *(63.4 × 7.8 × 2.5)*
Main machinery: 2 Niigata 6M31EX diesels; 3000 hp(m) *(2.21 MW);* 2 shafts; cp props
Speed, knots: 18. **Range, miles:** 3200 at 16 kts
Complement: 34
Guns: 1 USN 20 mm/80 Mk 10.
Radars: Navigation: JMA 1596 and JMA 1576; I band.

Comment: Average time from launch to commissioning, four months. Fitted with Loran.

ISUZU *1990, Ships of the World*

2 TAKATORI CLASS

Name	No	Builders	Commissioned
TAKATORI	PM 89	Naikai	24 Mar 1978
KUMANO	PM 94	Namura	23 Feb 1979

Displacement, tons: 634 normal
Dimensions, feet (metres): 152.5 × 30.2 × 9.3 *(46.5 × 9.2 × 2.9)*
Main machinery: 2 Niigata 6M31EX diesels; 3000 hp(m) *(2.21 MW);* 2 shafts; cp props
Speed, knots: 15. **Range, miles:** 700 at 14 kts
Complement: 34

Comment: SAR vessels equipped for salvage and firefighting.

KUMANO *7/1990, Hachiro Nakai*

7 KUNASHIRI CLASS (350-M3 TYPE)

Name	No	Builders	Commissioned
KUNASHIRI	PM 65	Hitachi, Maizuru	28 Mar 1969
MINABE	PM 66	Hitachi, Maizuru	28 Mar 1970
SAROBETSU	PM 67	Hitachi, Maizuru	30 Mar 1971
KAMISHIMA	PM 68	Usuki	31 Jan 1972
MIYAKE	PM 70	Tohoku	25 Jan 1973
AWAJI	PM 71	Usuki	25 Jan 1973
YAEYAMA	PM 72	Usuki	20 Dec 1972

Displacement, tons: 498 normal
Dimensions, feet (metres): 190.4 × 24.3 × 7.9 *(58 × 7.4 × 2.4)*
Main machinery: 2 Niigata 6MF32H or 6M31EX (PM 70-72) diesels; 2600 hp(m) *(1.91 MW)* or 3000 hp(m) *(2.21 MW)* (PM 70-72); 2 shafts
Speed, knots: 17 or 18. **Range, miles:** 3000 at 16 kts
Complement: 40
Guns: 1 USN 20 mm Mk 10.
Radars: Navigation: JMA 1576 or 1596 (PM 70-72).

Comment: The last three have slightly more powerful diesels and a top speed of 18 kts.

MINABE *7/1992, Hachiro Nakai*

2 MATSUURA CLASS (350-M2 TYPE)

Name	No	Builders	Commissioned
NATORI	PM 63	Hitachi, Mukaishima	20 Jan 1966
KARATSU	PM 64	Hitachi, Mukaishima	29 Mar 1967

Displacement, tons: 455 normal
Dimensions, feet (metres): 181.4 × 23 × 7.5 *(55.3 × 7 × 2.3)*
Main machinery: 2 Ikegai 6MSB3HS diesels (PM 63); 1800 hp(m) *(1.32 MW)*; 2 Ikegai 6MA31X diesels (PM 64); 2600 hp(m) *(1.91 MW)*; 2 shafts
Speed, knots: 17. **Range, miles:** 3500 at 13 kts
Complement: 40
Guns: 1 USN 20 mm Mk 10.
Radars: Navigation: One set.

NATORI　　　　　　　　　　　　　　　　　　　　　*1990, Ships of the World*

1 ANAMI CLASS

Name	No	Builders	Commissioned
ANAMI	PM 95	Hitachi, Kanagawa	28 Sep 1992

Displacement, tons: 230 normal
Dimensions, feet (metres): 183.7 × 24.6 × 6.6 *(56 × 7.5 × 2)*
Main machinery: 2 Fuji 8S40B diesels; 8120 hp(m) *(5.97 MW)*; 2 shafts; cp props
Speed, knots: 25
Guns: 1—20 mm JM-61B Gatling.
Radars: Navigation: I band.

Comment: Authorised in the FY 1991 programme. Laid down 22 October 1991.

ANAMI　　　　　　　　　　　　　　　　　　　　　*9/1992, Ships of the World*

1 YAHAGI CLASS (350 TYPE)

Name	No	Builders	Commissioned
MISASA (ex-*Okinawa*)	PM 69	Usuki	23 Oct 1970

Displacement, tons: 376 normal
Dimensions, feet (metres): 164.9 × 24 × 7.4 *(50.3 × 7.3 × 2.3)*
Main machinery: 2 diesels; 1400 hp(m) *(1.03 MW)*; 2 shafts
Speed, knots: 15.5. **Range, miles:** 2900 at 14 kts
Complement: 44
Guns: 1 USN 20 mm Mk 10.
Radars: Navigation: One set.

Comment: Transferred to MSA in 1972. Changed her name 1 April 1988.

MISASA　　　　　　　　　　　　　　　　　　　　　　*1988, JMSA*

SMALL PATROL VESSELS

4 MIHASHI CLASS (180 TYPE)

Name	No	Builders	Commissioned
MIHASHI	PS 01	Mitsubishi, Shimonoseki	9 Sep 1988
SAROMA	PS 02	Hitachi, Kanagawa	24 Nov 1989
INASA	PS 03	Mitsubishi, Shimonoseki	31 Jan 1990
KIRISHIMA	PS 04	Hitachi, Kanagawa	22 Mar 1991

Displacement, tons: 195 normal
Dimensions, feet (metres): 141.1 × 24.6 × 5.6 *(43 × 7.5 × 1.7)*
Main machinery: 2 Mitsubishi S12U diesels; 6700 hp(m) *(4.92 MW)*; 2 shafts
1 Mitsubishi S8U diesel; 2230 hp(m) *(1.64 MW)*; KaMeWa waterjet
Speed, knots: 35. **Range, miles:** 650 at 34 kts
Complement: 34
Guns: 1—12.7 mm MG.

Comment: First one launched 28 June 1988, second 28 June 1989 and third 20 October 1989. Fourth laid down 10 May 1990. Capable of 15 kts on the waterjet alone.

INASA　　　　　　　　　　　　　　　　　　　　　*5/1992, Hachiro Nakai*

7 AKAGI CLASS

Name	No	Builders	Commissioned
AKAGI	PS 101	Sumidagawa	26 Mar 1980
TSUKUBA	PS 102	Sumidagawa	24 Feb 1982
KONGOU	PS 103	Ishihara	16 Mar 1987
KATSURAGI	PS 104	Ishihara	24 Mar 1988
HIROMINE	PS 105	Yokohama Yacht Co	24 Mar 1988
SHIZUKI	PS 106	Sumidagawa	24 Mar 1988
TAKACHIHO	PS 107	Sumidagawa	24 Mar 1988

Displacement, tons: 115 full load
Dimensions, feet (metres): 114.8 × 20.7 × 4.3 *(35 × 6.3 × 1.3)*
Main machinery: 2 Pielstick 16 PA4 V 185 diesels; 5344 hp(m) *(3.93 MW)* sustained; 2 shafts
Speed, knots: 28. **Range, miles:** 500 at 20 kts
Complement: 22
Guns: 1 Browning 12.7 mm MG.
Radars: Navigation: One set.

Comment: Carry a 25-man inflatable rescue craft. The last four were ordered on 31 August 1987 and commissioned less than seven months later.

KONGOU　　　　　　　　　　　　　　　　　　　　　*5/1992, Hachiro Nakai*

2 TAKATSUKI CLASS

Name	No	Builders	Commissioned
TAKATSUKI	PS 108	Mitsubishi, Shimonoseki	23 Mar 1992
NOBARU	PS 109	Hitachi, Kanagawa	Mar 1993

Displacement, tons: 115 normal
Dimensions, feet (metres): 114.8 × 22 × 4.3 *(35 × 6.7 × 1.3)*
Main machinery: 2 diesels; 5200 hp(m) *(3.82 MW)*; 2 KaMeWa waterjets
Speed, knots: 35
Guns: 1—12.7 mm MG.

Comment: Authorised in the FY 1991 programme.

TAKATSUKI　　　　　　　　　　　　　　　　　　　　*9/1992, Hachiro Nakai*

6 HIDAKA CLASS

Name	No	Builders	Commissioned
KUNIMI	PS 38	Hayashikane	15 Feb 1965
KAMUI	PS 41	Hayashikane	15 Feb 1966
ASHITAKA	PS 43	Usuki	10 Feb 1967
KURAMA	PS 44	Usuki	28 Feb 1967
IBUKI	PS 45	Usuki	5 Mar 1968
TOUMI	PS 46	Usuki	20 Feb 1968

Displacement, tons: 169 normal
Dimensions, feet (metres): 104 × 20.8 × 5.5 *(31.7 × 6.3 × 1.7)*
Main machinery: 1 Ikegai 6MSB31A diesel; 700 hp(m) *(515 kW)*; 1 shaft
Speed, knots: 12.5. Range, miles: 1000 at 12 kts
Complement: 17
Radars: Navigation: One set.

Comment: Occasionally carry a 12.7 mm MG. Being replaced by Mihashi and Takatsuki classes.

KURAMA   1/1992, Hachiro Nakai

1 BIZAN CLASS

Name	No	Builders	Commissioned
SHIRAMINE	PS 48	Mitsubishi, Shimonoseki	15 Dec 1969

Displacement, tons: 42 full load
Dimensions, feet (metres): 85.3 × 18.3 × 2.8 *(26 × 5.6 × 0.9)*
Main machinery: 2 MTU diesels; 2200 hp(m) *(1.62 MW)*; 2 shafts
Speed, knots: 25. Range, miles: 250 at 25 kts
Complement: 14
Radars: Navigation: MD 808.

Comment: Aluminium alloy construction. Soon to be paid off.

SHIRAMINE   10/1991, Hachiro Nakai

COASTAL PATROL CRAFT

1 MATSUNAMI CLASS

Name	No	Builders	Commissioned
MATSUNAMI	PC 53	Hitachi, Kanagawa	30 Mar 1971

Displacement, tons: 59 normal
Dimensions, feet (metres): 82 × 19.7 × 7.9 *(25 × 6 × 2.4)*
Main machinery: 2 MTU MB 12V 493 TY7 diesels; 2200 hp(m) *(1.62 MW)* sustained; 2 shafts
Speed, knots: 20. Range, miles: 270 at 18 kts
Complement: 30

Comment: Used for Oceanographic survey and specially fitted out for the Emperor.

MATSUNAMI   5/1992, Hachiro Nakai

23 MURAKUMO CLASS

Name	No	Builders	Commissioned
MURAKUMO	PC 201	Mitsubishi, Shimonoseki	24 Mar 1978
KITAGUMO	PC 202	Hitachi, Kanagawa	17 Mar 1978
YUKIGUMO	PC 203	Hitachi, Kanagawa	27 Sep 1978
ASAGUMO	PC 204	Mitsubishi, Shimonoseki	21 Sep 1978
HAYAGUMO	PC 205	Mitsubishi, Shimonoseki	30 Jan 1979
AKIGUMO	PC 206	Hitachi, Kanagawa	28 Feb 1979
YAEGUMO	PC 207	Hitachi, Kanagawa	16 Mar 1979
NATSUGUMO	PC 208	Hitachi, Kanagawa	22 Mar 1979
YAMAGIRI	PC 209	Hitachi, Kanagawa	29 June 1979
KAWAGIRI	PC 210	Hitachi, Kanagawa	27 July 1979
TERUZUKI	PC 211	Mitsubishi, Shimonoseki	26 June 1979
NATSUZUKI	PC 212	Mitsubishi, Shimonoseki	26 July 1979
MIYAZUKI	PC 213	Hitachi, Kanagawa	13 Mar 1980
NIJIGUMO	PC 214	Mitsubishi, Shimonoseki	29 Jan 1981
TATSUGUMO	PC 215	Mitsubishi, Shimonoseki	19 Mar 1981
HAMAYUKI	PC 216	Hitachi, Kanagawa	27 Feb 1981
ISONAMI	PC 217	Mitsubishi, Shimonoseki	19 Mar 1981
NAGOZUKI	PC 218	Hitachi, Kanagawa	29 Jan 1981
YAEZUKI	PC 219	Hitachi, Kanagawa	19 Mar 1981
YAMAYUKI	PC 220	Hitachi, Kanagawa	16 Feb 1982
KOMAYUKI	PC 221	Hitachi, Kanagawa	10 Feb 1982
UMIGIRI	PC 222	Hitachi, Kanagawa	17 Feb 1983
ASAGIRI	PC 223	Mitsubishi, Shimonoseki	23 Feb 1983

Displacement, tons: 85 normal
Dimensions, feet (metres): 98.4 × 20.7 × 7.2 *(30 × 6.3 × 2.2)*
Main machinery: 2 Ikegai MTU MB 16V 652 SB70 diesels; 4400 hp(m) *(3.23 MW)* sustained; 2 shafts
Speed, knots: 30. Range, miles: 350 at 28 kts
Complement: 13
Guns: 1 Browning 12.7 mm MG.

NATSUZUKI   5/1992, Hachiro Nakai

12 AKIZUKI CLASS

Name	No	Builders	Commissioned
AKIZUKI	PC 64	Mitsubishi, Shimonoseki	28 Feb 1974
SHINONOME	PC 65	Mitsubishi, Shimonoseki	25 Mar 1974
URAYUKI	PC 72	Mitsubishi, Shimonoseki	31 May 1975
ISEYUKI	PC 73	Mitsubishi, Shimonoseki	31 July 1975
HATAGUMO	PC 75	Mitsubishi, Shimonoseki	21 Feb 1976
MAKIGUMO	PC 76	Mitsubishi, Shimonoseki	19 Mar 1976
HAMAZUKI	PC 77	Mitsubishi, Shimonoseki	29 Nov 1976
ISOZUKI	PC 78	Mitsubishi, Shimonoseki	18 Mar 1977
SHIMANAMI	PC 79	Mitsubishi, Shimonoseki	23 Dec 1977
YUZUKI	PC 80	Mitsubishi, Shimonoseki	22 Mar 1979
HANAYUKI	PC 81	Mitsubishi, Shimonoseki	27 Mar 1981
AWAGIRI	PC 82	Mitsubishi, Shimonoseki	24 Mar 1983

Displacement, tons: 77 normal
Dimensions, feet (metres): 85.3 × 20.7 × 6.9 *(26 × 6.3 × 2.1)*
Main machinery: 3 Mitsubishi 12DM20MTK diesels; 3000 hp(m) *(2.21 MW)*; 3 shafts
Speed, knots: 22. Range, miles: 220 at 21.5 kts
Complement: 10
Radars: Navigation: FRA 10 Mk 2.

Comment: Aluminium hulls.

HANAYUKI   8/1990, Hachiro Nakai

370 JAPAN (MSA) / Coastal patrol craft

3 SHIMAGIRI CLASS

Name	No	Builders	Commissioned
SHIMAGIRI	PC 83	Hitachi, Kanagawa	7 Feb 1985
SETOGIRI	PC 84	Hitachi, Kanagawa	22 Mar 1985
HAYAGIRI	PC 85	Mitsubishi, Shimonoseki	22 Feb 1985

Displacement, tons: 51 normal
Dimensions, feet (metres): 75.5 × 17.4 × 6.2 *(23 × 5.3 × 1.9)*
Main machinery: 2 Ikegai 12V 175 RTC diesels; 3000 hp(m) *(2.21 MW)*; 2 shafts
Speed, knots: 30
Complement: 10
Guns: 1—12.7 mm MG (not in all).

Comment: Aluminium hulls.

SETOGIRI *7/1992, Hachiro Nakai*

17 SHIKINAMI CLASS

Name	No	Builders	Commissioned
SHIKINAMI	PC 54	Mitsubishi, Shimonoseki	25 Feb 1971
TOMONAMI	PC 55	Mitsubishi, Shimonoseki	20 Mar 1971
WAKANAMI	PC 56	Mitsubishi, Shimonoseki	30 Oct 1971
ISENAMI	PC 57	Hitachi, Kanagawa	29 Feb 1972
TAKANAMI	PC 58	Mitsubishi, Shimonoseki	30 Nov 1971
MUTSUKI	PC 59	Hitachi, Kanagawa	18 Dec 1972
MOCHIZUKI	PC 60	Hitachi, Kanagawa	18 Dec 1972
HARUZUKI	PC 61	Mitsubishi, Shimonoseki	30 Nov 1972
KIYOZUKI	PC 62	Mitsubishi, Shimonoseki	18 Dec 1972
URAZUKI	PC 63	Hitachi, Kanagawa	30 Jan 1973
URANAMI	PC 66	Hitachi, Kanagawa	22 Dec 1973
TAMANAMI	PC 67	Mitsubishi, Shimonoseki	25 Dec 1973
MINEGUMO	PC 68	Mitsubishi, Shimonoseki	30 Nov 1973
KIYONAMI	PC 69	Mitsubishi, Shimonoseki	30 Oct 1973
OKINAMI	PC 70	Hitachi, Kanagawa	8 Feb 1974
WAKAGUMO	PC 71	Hitachi, Kanagawa	25 Mar 1974
ASOYUKI	PC 74	Hitachi, Kanagawa	16 June 1975

Displacement, tons: 46 normal
Dimensions, feet (metres): 69 × 17.4 × 3.3 *(21 × 5.3 × 1)*
Main machinery: 2 MTU MB 12V 493 TY7 diesels; 2200 hp(m) *(1.62 MW)* sustained; 2 shafts
Speed, knots: 26. **Range, miles:** 230 at 23.8 kts
Complement: 10
Radars: Navigation: MD 806.

Comment: Built completely of light alloy.

URANAMI *7/1990, Hachiro Nakai*

2 HAMAGIRI CLASS

Name	No	Builders	Commissioned
HAMAGIRI	PC 48	Sumidagawa	19 Mar 1970
HAMANAMI	PC 52	Sumidagawa	22 Mar 1971

Displacement, tons: 51 normal
Dimensions, feet (metres): 69 × 16.6 × 3.3 *(21 × 5.1 × 1)*
Main machinery: 2 MTU MB 12V 493 TY7 diesels (PC 52); 2200 hp(m) *(1.62 MW)* sustained
  2 Mitsubishi DH12TK diesels (PC 48); 1140 hp(m) *(838 kW)*; 2 shafts
Speed, knots: 14.6 (PC 48); 21.8 (PC 52). **Range, miles:** 300 at 9 kts (PC 52); 270 at 13 kts (PC 48)
Complement: 10
Guns: 1 Browning 12.7 mm MG.
Radars: Navigation: MD 808.

Comment: Steel hulls. Both to be paid off in 1993.

1 HAYANAMI CLASS

Name	No	Builders	Commissioned
HAYANAMI	PC 11	Sumidagawa	Mar 1990

Displacement, tons: 110 normal
Dimensions, feet (metres): 114.8 × 20.7 × 7.5 *(35 × 6.3 × 2.3)*
Main machinery: 2 diesels; 4000 hp(m) *(2.94 MW)*; 2 shafts
Speed, knots: 25

Comment: Launched 7 January 1993. More may be built.

2 NATSUGIRI CLASS

Name	No	Builders	Commissioned
NATSUGIRI	PC 86	Sumidagawa	29 Jan 1990
SUGANAMI	PC 87	Sumidagawa	29 Jan 1990

Displacement, tons: 68 normal
Dimensions, feet (metres): 88.6 × 18.4 × 3.9 *(27 × 5.6 × 1.2)*
Main machinery: 2 diesels; 3000 hp(m) *(2.21 MW)*; 2 shafts
Speed, knots: 27

Comment: Built under FY 1988 programme. Steel hulls.

SUGANAMI *5/1990, Hachiro Nakai*

170 COASTAL PATROL AND RESCUE CRAFT

CL 01-04, 11-27, 70-71, 79-156, 201-264

Displacement, tons: 23 *(01-04, 11-17)*, 19 *(65-156)*, 27 *(201-264)* normal
Main machinery: 2 diesels; 900 hp(m) *(01-02)*, 1400 hp(m) *(03-04)*, 1820 hp(m) *(11-17)*, 500 hp(m) *(65-156)*, 900 hp *(201-264)*; 2 shafts
Speed, knots: 18-30
Complement: 6

Comment: This total includes five similar classes all of about 20 m in length. Some have firefighting capability. Built by Shigi, Ishihara, Sumidagawa and Yokohama Yacht Co. *CL 01-04* completed 1989-91. *CL 11-17* completed in 1992 and ten more of the class built in 1993. For coastal patrol and rescue duties. Built of high tensile steel.

CL 12 *3/1992, Hachiro Nakai*

CL 79 *3/1991, Hachiro Naka*

FIREFIGHTING VESSELS AND CRAFT

5 HIRYU CLASS

Name	No	Builders	Commissioned
HIRYU	FL 01	Nippon Kokan, Tsurumi	4 Mar 1969
SHORYU	FL 02	Nippon Kokan, Tsurumi	4 Mar 1970
NANRYU	FL 03	Nippon Kokan, Tsurumi	4 Mar 1971
KAIRYU	FL 04	Nippon Kokan, Tsurumi	18 Mar 1977
SUIRYU	FL 05	Yokohama Yacht Co	24 Mar 1978

Displacement, tons: 215 normal
Dimensions, feet (metres): 90.2 × 34.1 × 7.2 *(27.5 × 10.4 × 2.2)*
Main machinery: 2 Ikegai MTU MB 12V 493 TY7 diesels; 2200 hp(m) *(1.62 MW)* sustained; 2 shafts
Speed, knots: 13.2. **Range, miles:** 300 at 13 kts
Complement: 14

Comment: Catamaran type fire boats designed and built for firefighting services to large tankers.

HIRYU 5/1992, Hachiro Nakai

10 NUNOBIKI CLASS

Name	No	Builders	Commissioned
NUNOBIKI	FM 01	Yokohama Yacht Co	25 Feb 1974
YODO	FM 02	Sumidagawa	30 Mar 1975
OTOWA	FM 03	Yokohama Yacht Co	25 Dec 1974
SHIRAITO	FM 04	Yokohama Yacht Co	25 Feb 1975
KOTOBIKI	FM 05	Yokohama Yacht Co	31 Jan 1976
NACHI	FM 06	Sumidagawa	14 Feb 1976
KEGON	FM 07	Yokohama Yacht Co	29 Jan 1977
MINOO	FM 08	Sumidagawa	27 Jan 1978
RYUSEI	FM 09	Yokohama Yacht Co	24 Mar 1980
KIYOTAKI	FM 10	Sumidagawa	25 Mar 1981

Displacement, tons: 89 normal
Dimensions, feet (metres): 75.4 × 19.7 × 5.2 *(23 × 6 × 1.6)*
Main machinery: 1 MTU MB 12V 493 TY7 diesel; 1100 hp(m) *(810 kW)* sustained; 1 shaft
2 Nissan diesels; 500 hp(m) *(515 kW)*; 3 shafts
Speed, knots: 14. **Range, miles:** 180 at 13.5 kts
Complement: 12
Radars: Navigation: FRA 10.

Comment: Equipped for chemical firefighting.

OTOWA 5/1992, Hachiro Nakai

HYDROGRAPHIC SERVICE

Name	No	Builders	Commissioned
TAKUYO	HL 02	Nippon Kokan, Tsurumi	31 Aug 1983

Displacement, tons: 3000 normal
Dimensions, feet (metres): 314.9 × 46.6 × 15.1 *(96 × 14.2 × 4.6)*
Main machinery: 2 Fuji 6S40B diesels; 6090 hp(m) *(4.47 MW)*; 2 shafts; cp props
Speed, knots: 17. **Range, miles:** 12 000 at 16 kts
Complement: 60 (24 officers)
Radars: Navigation: Two sets.

Comment: Laid down on 14 April 1982, launched on 24 March 1983. Based at Tokyo.

TAKUYO 5/1992, Hachiro Nakai

Name	No	Builders	Commissioned
SHOYO	HL 01	Hitachi, Maizuru	26 Feb 1972

Displacement, tons: 2200 normal
Dimensions, feet (metres): 268 × 41.3 × 13.8 *(81.7 × 12.6 × 4.2)*
Main machinery: 2 Fuji 12VM32 H2F diesels; 4800 hp(m) *(3.53 MW)*; 1 shaft
Speed, knots: 17. **Range, miles:** 11 000 at 14 kts
Complement: 58 (23 officers)
Radars: Navigation: Two sets.

Comment: Launched 18 September 1971. Fully equipped for all types of hydrographic and oceanographic work. Carries MX702 SATNAV and Loran. Based at Tokyo.

SHOYO 1/1992, Hachiro Nakai

Name	No	Builders	Commissioned
TENYO	HL 04	Sumitomo, Oppama	27 Nov 1986

Displacement, tons: 770 normal
Dimensions, feet (metres): 183.7 × 32.2 × 9.5 *(56 × 9.8 × 2.9)*
Main machinery: 2 Akasaka diesels; 1300 hp(m) *(955 kW)*; 2 shafts
Speed, knots: 13. **Range, miles:** 5400 at 12 kts
Complement: 43 (18 officers)

Comment: Laid down 11 April 1986, launched 5 August 1986. Based at Tokyo.

TENYO 1986, Maritime Safety Agency

372 JAPAN (MSA) / Hydrographic service — Aids to navigation service

Name	No	Builders	Commissioned
MEIYO	HL 03	Kawasaki, Kobe	24 Oct 1990
—	HL 05	Mitsubishi, Shimonoseki	1993

Displacement, tons: 550 normal
Dimensions, feet (metres): 196.9 × 34.4 × 10.2 *(60 × 10.5 × 3.1)*
Main machinery: 2 Daihatsu 6 DLM-24 diesels; 3000 hp(m) *(2.2 MW)*; 2 shafts; bow thruster
Speed, knots: 15. **Range, miles:** 5280 at 11 kts
Complement: 25 + 13 scientists

Comment: *Meiyo* laid down 24 July 1989 and launched 29 June 1990; second of class authorised in FY 1992 programme. Have anti-roll tanks and resiliently mounted main machinery. A large survey launch is carried on the port side.

MEIYO *10/1990, Hachiro Nakai*

Name	No	Builders	Commissioned
KAIYO	HM 06	Nagoya	14 Mar 1964

Displacement, tons: 380 normal
Dimensions, feet (metres): 106 × 26.5 × 7.8 *(44.5 × 8.1 × 2.4)*
Main machinery: 1 Sumiyoshi Tekko S6 NBS diesel; 450 hp(m) *(331 kW)*; 1 shaft; cp prop
Speed, knots: 10
Complement: 35 (13 officers)

Comment: Flume tanks fitted.

KAIYO *1990, Ships of the World*

SURVEYING CRAFT

10 ISESHIO CLASS

ISESHIO HS 02	ISOSHIO HS 06	OYASHIO HS 10
SETOSHIO HS 03	TAKASHIO HS 07	KUROSHIO HS 11
UZUSHIO HS 04	WAKASHIO HS 08	
HAYASHIO HS 05	YUKISHIO HS 09	

Displacement, tons: 6
Dimensions, feet (metres): 32.8 *(10)* long
Main machinery: 1 Nissan UD326 diesel; 90 hp(m) *(66 kW)*; 1 shaft
Speed, knots: 8.8
Complement: 7

Comment: Completed 1969-72. GRP hulls. One carried in *Shoyo* (HL 01). All to pay off in 1993.

WAKASHIO *4/1991, Hachiro Nakai*

5 AKASHI CLASS

AKASHI HS 31	KURIHAMA HS 34
KERAMA HS 32	KURUSHIMA HS 35
HAYATOMO HS 33	

Displacement, tons: 21
Dimensions, feet (metres): 49.2 *(15)* long
Main machinery: 1 Nissan UD626 diesel; 180 hp(m) *(132 kW)*; 1 shaft
Speed, knots: 9. **Range, miles:** 400 at 9 kts
Complement: 7

Comment: Completed 1973-77. Steel hulls.

KURIHAMA *5/1991, Hachiro Nakai*

2 HAMASHIO CLASS

HAMASHIO HS 21   ISOSHI HS 22

Displacement, tons: 42 normal
Dimensions, feet (metres): 68.9 × 14.8 × 3.9 *(21 × 4.5 × 1.2)*
Main machinery: 3 diesels; 1015 hp(m) *(746 kW)*; 3 shafts
Speed, knots: 15
Complement: 10

Comment: *Hamashio* built by Yokohama Yacht Co and completed 25 March 1991. Second of class completed in March 1993.

HAMASHIO *6/1991, Ships of the World*

AIDS TO NAVIGATION SERVICE

Name	No	Builders	Commissioned
TSUSHIMA	LL 01	Mitsui, Tamano	9 Sep 1977

Displacement, tons: 1950 normal
Dimensions, feet (metres): 246 × 41 × 13.8 *(75 × 12.5 × 4.2)*
Main machinery: 1 Fuji-Sulzer 8S40C diesel; 4200 hp(m) *(3.09 MW)*; 1 shaft; cp prop; bow thruster
Speed, knots: 15.5. **Range, miles:** 10 000 at 15 kts
Complement: 54

Comment: Lighthouse Supply Ship. Fitted with tank stabilisers. Equipped with modern electronic instruments for carrying out research on electronic aids to navigation.

TSUSHIMA *5/1992, Hachiro Nakai*

Aids to navigation service — Miscellaneous / JAPAN (MSA)   373

3 HOKUTO CLASS

Name	No	Builders	Commissioned
HOKUTO	LL 11	Sasebo	29 June 1979
KAIO	LL 12	Sasebo	11 Mar 1980
GINGA	LL 13	Kawasaki, Kobe	18 Mar 1980

Displacement, tons: 700 normal
Dimensions, feet (metres): 180.4 × 34.8 × 8.7 *(55 × 10.6 × 2.7)*
Main machinery: 2 Asakasa MH23R diesels; 1030 hp(m) *(757 kW)*; 2 shafts
Speed, knots: 12. **Range, miles:** 3900 at 12 kts
Complement: 31

KAIO   8/1990, Hachiro Nakai

Name	No	Builders	Commissioned
MYOJO	LM 11	Nippon Kokan, Tsurumi	25 Mar 1974

Displacement, tons: 303 normal
Dimensions, feet (metres): 88.6 × 39.4 × 8.8 *(27 × 12 × 2.7)*
Main machinery: 2 Niigata 6M9 16HS diesels; 600 hp(m) *(441 kW)*; 2 shafts; cp props
Speed, knots: 10.5. **Range, miles:** 1360 at 10.5 kts
Complement: 18

Comment: Catamaran type buoy tender, this ship is employed in maintenance and position adjustment service to floating aids to navigation.

MYOJO   10/1991, Hachiro Nakai

AIDS TO NAVIGATION TENDERS

1 ZUIUN CLASS

Name	No	Builders	Commissioned
ZUIUN	LM 101	Usuki	27 July 1983

Displacement, tons: 370 normal
Dimensions, feet (metres): 146.3 × 24.6 × 7.2 *(44.6 × 7.5 × 2.2)*
Main machinery: 2 Mitsubishi-Asakasa MH23R diesels; 1030 hp(m) *(757 kW)*; 2 shafts
Speed, knots: 13.5. **Range, miles:** 1000 at 13 kts
Complement: 20

Comment: Classed as a medium tender.

ZUIUN   1988, JMSA

1 AYABANE CLASS

Name	No	Builders	Commissioned
AYABANE	LM 112	Shimoda	25 Dec 1972

Displacement, tons: 187 normal
Dimensions, feet (metres): 107.3 × 21.3 × 6.6 *(32.7 × 6.5 × 2)*
Main machinery: 1 diesel; 500 hp(m) *(368 kW)*; 1 shaft
Speed, knots: 12
Complement: 18

8 HAKUUN CLASS

Name	No	Builders	Commissioned
HAKUUN	LM 106	Sumidagawa	28 Feb 1978
TOUN	LM 107	Sumidagawa	14 Mar 1979
TOKUUN	LM 114	Yokohama Yacht Co	23 Mar 1981
SHOUN	LM 201	Sumidagawa	26 Mar 1986
SEIUN	LM 202	Sumidagawa	22 Feb 1989
SEKIUN	LM 203	Ishihara	12 Mar 1991
HOUUN	LM 204	Ishihara	22 Feb 1991
REIUN	LM 205	Ishihara	28 Feb 1992

Displacement, tons: 58 full load
Dimensions, feet (metres): 75.5 × 19.7 × 3.3 *(23 × 6 × 1)*
Main machinery: 2 GM 12V-71TA diesels; 840 hp *(627 kW)* sustained; 2 shafts
Speed, knots: 14. **Range, miles:** 250 at 14 kts
Complement: 9

SEKIUN   6/1991, Ships of the World

62 SMALL TENDERS

LS 103, 105, 114, 116-118, 123, 137, 141-146, 148-149, 154-155, 157-158, 160-161, 164-170, 180-182, 185-195, 204-221

Displacement, tons: 25 full load
Dimensions, feet (metres): 54.4 × 14.1 × 2.6 *(17.5 × 4.3 × 0.9)*
Main machinery: 2 diesels; 560 hp(m) *(412 kW)*; 2 shafts
Speed, knots: 15. **Range, miles:** 230 at 14.5 kts
Complement: 8

Comment: Details given are for *LS 204-221*. Last one completed 31 January 1990. Others with varying characteristics.

LS 211   9/1992, Hachiro Nakai

MISCELLANEOUS

32 SURVEILLANCE CRAFT

SS 04-35

Comment: Craft of 6 m completed between 1972-79. *SS 15* is equipped with waterjet. *SS 35* of 7 m completed 1984.

3 OIL SKIMMERS

OS 01-03

Comment: Completed 1974-75 by Lockheed.

374 JAPAN (MSA) / Miscellaneous — JORDAN / Patrol forces

1 KINUGASA CLASS

Name	No	Builders	Commissioned
KINUGASA	MS 01	Ishihara, Takasago	31 Jan 1992

Displacement, tons: 39 normal
Dimensions, feet (metres): 59.1 × 29.5 × 4.3 *(18 × 9 × 1.3)*
Main machinery: 2 diesels; 1000 hp(m) *(735 kW)*; 2 shafts
Speed, knots: 15
Complement: 8

Comment: Used for monitoring pollution. Replaced craft of the same name. Catamaran hull.

KINUGASA 2/1992, Hachiro Nakai

2 + 1 MONITORING CRAFT

SAIKAI MS 02   KATSUREN MS 03

Comment: *Saikai* of 10 m, *Katsuren* of 16 m. One more building in 1993.

SAIKAI 3/1990, Hachiro Nakai

2 GUARD BOATS

HAYATE GS 01   INAZUMA GS 02

Displacement, tons: 7.9 full load
Dimensions, feet (metres): 39 × 10.5 × 4.9 *(11.9 × 3.2 × 1.5)*
Main machinery: 2 Mitsubishi S6M2 diesels; 580 hp(m) *(426 kW)*; 2 shafts
Speed, knots: 30. **Range, miles:** 150 at 28 kts

Comment: Built by Yokohama Yacht Co and commissioned 21 December 1987.

HAYATE 7/1991, Hachiro Nakai

5 OIL RECOVERY CRAFT

SHIRASAGI OR 01   MIZUNANGI OR 03   ISOSHIGI OR 05
SHIRATORI OR 02   CHIDORI OR 04

Displacement, tons: 153 normal
Dimensions, feet (metres): 72.3 × 21 × 2.6 *(22 × 6.4 × 0.9)*
Main machinery: 2 Nissan UD626 diesels; 360 hp(m) *(265 kW)*; 2 shafts
Speed, knots: 6. **Range, miles:** 160 at 6 kts
Complement: 7

Comment: Completed by Sumidagawa (OR 01), Shigi (OR 02 and 04) and Ishihara (OR 03 and 05) between 31 January 1977 and 23 March 1979.

SHIRASAGI 5/1990, Hachiro Nakai

JORDAN

Headquarters' Appointments

Chief of Staff:
  Major General Abu Taleb
Chief of the Navy:
  Colonel Hussein Ali Mahmoud Al Khasaweh

Organisation

The Royal Jordanian Naval Force comes under the Director of Operations at General Headquarters. There has been a considerable expansion in the years 1990-93.

Base

Aqaba

Personnel

(a) 1993: 600 officers and men
(b) Voluntary service

Mercantile Marine

Lloyd's Register of Shipping:
  5 vessels of 61 266 tons gross

DELETION

1992 *Ali Abdullah*

PATROL FORCES

4 BERTRAM TYPE (COASTAL PATROL CRAFT)

FAYSAL   HAN   HASAYU   MUHAMMED

Displacement, tons: 8 full load
Dimensions, feet (metres): 38 × 13.1 × 1.6 *(11.6 × 4 × 0.5)*
Main machinery: 2 diesels; 600 hp *(441 kW)*; 2 shafts
Speed, knots: 25
Complement: 8
Guns: 1—12.7 mm MG. 1—7.62 mm MG.

Comment: Acquired from Bertram, Miami in 1974.

3 ROTORK CRAFT

AL HASHM   AL FAISAL   AL HAMZA

Displacement, tons: 9 full load
Dimensions, feet (metres): 41.7 × 10.5 × 3 *(12.7 × 3.2 × 0.9)*
Main machinery: 2 diesels; 240 hp *(179 kW)*; 2 shafts
Speed, knots: 28
Military lift: 30 troops
Guns: 1—7.62 mm MG.

Comment: Delivered in late 1990 for patrolling the Dead Sea.

Patrol forces / JORDAN — Patrol forces / KENYA   375

3 HAWK CLASS (FAST ATTACK CRAFT—GUN)

AL HUSSEIN 101   **AL HUSSAN** 102   **ABDULLAH** 103

Displacement, tons: 124 full load
Dimensions, feet (metres): 100 × 22.5 × 4.9 *(30.5 × 6.9 × 1.5)*
Main machinery: 2 MTU 16V 396 TB94 diesels; 5800 hp(m) *(4.26 MW)* sustained; 2 shafts
Speed, knots: 32. **Range, miles:** 750 at 15 kts; 1500 at 11 kts
Complement: 16 (3 officers)
Guns: 2 Oerlikon GCM-A03 30 mm (twin). 1 Oerlikon GAM-B01 20 mm. 2—12.5 mm MGs.
Countermeasures: Decoys: 2 Wallop Stockade chaff launchers.
Combat data systems: Racal Cane 100.
Fire control: Radamec Series 2000 optronic for 30 mm gun.
Radars: Surface search: Kelvin Hughes 1007; I band.

Comment: Ordered from Vosper Thornycroft in December 1987. GRP structure. First one on trials in May 1989 and completed December 1989. Second completed in March 1990 and the third in early 1991. All transported to Aqaba in September 1991.

2 Ex-GERMAN BREMSE CLASS (INSHORE PATROL CRAFT)

— (ex-G 30/GS 30)   — (ex-G 31/GS 42)

Displacement, tons: 42 full load
Dimensions, feet (metres): 74.1 × 15.4 × 3.6 *(22.6 × 4.7 × 1.1)*
Main machinery: 2 DM 6VD 18/5 AL-1 diesels; 1020 hp(m) *(750 kW)*; 2 shafts
Speed, knots: 14
Complement: 8
Guns: 1—12.7 mm MG.
Radars: Surface search: TSR 333; I band.

Comment: Built in 1971-72 for the former GDR border guard. Transferred in 1992. Similar craft sold to Tunisia and Malta.

AL HUSSAN   7/1990, W Sartori

BREMSE GS 42 (old number)   4/1991, Hartmut Ehlers

KENYA

Administration

Commander, Navy:
  Major General J R E Kibwana

Personnel

(a) 1993: 1400 officers and men
(b) Voluntary service

Base

Mombasa

Customs/Police

There are some 18 Customs and Police patrol craft of between 12 and 14 metres. Mostly built by Cheverton, Performance Workboats and Fassmer in the 1980s.

Mercantile Marine

Lloyd's Register of Shipping:
  29 vessels of 12 312 tons gross

DELETIONS

1992   *Simba, Chui, Ndovu, Kiongozi* (civilian)

PATROL FORCES

1 BROOKE MARINE TYPE (FAST ATTACK CRAFT—MISSILE)

Name	No	Builders	Commissioned
MAMBA	P 3100	Brooke Marine, Lowestoft	7 Feb 1974

Displacement, tons: 125 standard; 160 full load
Dimensions, feet (metres): 123 × 22.5 × 5.2 *(37.5 × 6.9 × 1.6)*
Main machinery: 2 Paxman 16YJCM diesels; 4000 hp *(2.98 MW)* sustained; 2 shafts
Speed, knots: 25. **Range, miles:** 3300 at 13 kts
Complement: 25 (3 officers)

Missiles: SSM: 4 IAI Gabriel II; active radar or optical guidance; semi-active homing to 36 km *(19.4 nm)* at 0.7 Mach; warhead 75 kg.
Guns: 2 Oerlikon/BMARC 30 mm GCM-A02 (twin); 85° elevation; 650 rounds/minute to 10 km *(5.4 nm)* anti-surface; 3 km *(1.6 nm)* anti-aircraft; weight of shell 0.36 kg.
Radars: Navigation: Decca AC 1226; I band.
Fire control: Selenia RTN 10X; I/J band; range 40 km *(22 nm)*.

Programmes: Laid down 17 February 1972.
Modernisation: In 1982 missiles, new gunnery equipment and an optronic director fitted.
Operational: Arrived Vosper Thornycroft, Portchester on 4 May 1989 for a long refit. Returned to Kenya with *Madaraka* as deck cargo in a transport ship leaving Portsmouth on 7 November 1990.

2 NYAYO CLASS (FAST ATTACK CRAFT—MISSILE)

Name	No	Builders	Commissioned
NYAYO	P 3126	Vosper Thornycroft	23 July 1987
UMOJA	P 3127	Vosper Thornycroft	16 Sep 1987

Displacement, tons: 310 light; 400 full load
Dimensions, feet (metres): 186 × 26.9 × 7.9 *(56.7 × 8.2 × 2.4)*
Main machinery: 4 Paxman Valenta 18CM diesels; 15 000 hp *(11.19 MW)* sustained; 4 shafts; 2 motors (slow speed patrol); 100 hp *(74.6 kW)*
Speed, knots: 40. **Range, miles:** 2000 at 18 kts
Complement: 40

Missiles: SSM: 4 OTO Melara/Matra Otomat Mk 2 (2 twin); active radar homing to 160 km *(86.4 nm)* at 0.9 Mach; warhead 210 kg; sea-skimmer for last 4 km *(2.2 nm)*.
Guns: 1 OTO Melara 3 in *(76 mm)*/62; 85° elevation; 85 rounds/minute to 16 km *(8.7 nm)* anti-surface; 12 km *(6.5 nm)* anti-aircraft; weight of shell 6 kg.
   2 Oerlikon/BMARC 30 mm GCM-A02 (twin); 85° elevation; 650 rounds/minute to 10 km *(5.4 nm)* anti-surface; 3 km *(1.6 nm)* anti-aircraft; weight of shell 0.36 kg.
   2 Oerlikon/BMARC 20 mm A41A; 50° elevation; 800 rounds/minute to 2 km; weight of shell 0.24 kg.
Countermeasures: Decoys: 2 Wallop Barricade 18-barrelled launchers; Stockade and Palisade rockets.
ESM: Racal Cutlass; radar warning.
ECM: Racal Cygnus; jammer.
Fire control: CAAIS 450 including Signaal 423; action data automation.
Radars: Surface search: Plessey AWS 4; E/F band; range 101 km *(55 nm)*.
   Navigation: Decca AC 1226; I band.
   Fire control: Marconi/Ericsson ST802; I band.

Programmes: Ordered in September 1984. Sailed in company from the UK, arriving at Mombasa 30 August 1988. Similar to Omani Province class.
Operational: First live Otomat firing in February 1989. Form Squadron 86.

MAMBA (alongside *Madaraka*)   11/1990, Colin Rossiter

UMOJA   3/1988, van Ginderen Collection

376 KENYA / Patrol forces — KOREA (DPR) / Submarines

3 BROOKE MARINE TYPE (FAST ATTACK CRAFT—MISSILE)

Name	No	Builders	Commissioned
MADARAKA	P 3121	Brooke Marine, Lowestoft	16 June 1975
JAMHURI	P 3122	Brooke Marine, Lowestoft	16 June 1975
HARAMBEE	P 3123	Brooke Marine, Lowestoft	22 Aug 1975

Displacement, tons: 120 standard; 145 full load
Dimensions, feet (metres): 107 × 20 × 5.6 *(32.6 × 6.1 × 1.7)*
Main machinery: 2 Paxman Valenta 16CM diesels; 6650 hp *(4.96 MW)* sustained; 2 shafts
Speed, knots: 25.5. **Range, miles:** 2500 at 12 kts
Complement: 21 (3 officers)

Missiles: SSM: 4 IAI Gabriel II; active radar or optical guidance; semi-active homing to 36 km *(19.4 nm)* at 0.7 Mach; warhead 75 kg.
Guns: 2 Oerlikon/BMARC 30 mm GCM (twin); 85° elevation; 650 rounds/minute to 10 km *(5.4 nm)* anti-surface; 3 km *(1.6 nm)* anti-aircraft; weight of shell 0.36 kg.
Radars: Navigation: Decca AC 1226; I band.
Fire control: Selenia RTN 10X; I/J band; range 40 km *(22 nm)*.

Programmes: Ordered 10 May 1973. *Madaraka* launched 28 January 1975, *Jamhuri* 14 March 1975, *Harambee* 2 May 1975.
Modernisation: *Madaraka* (1981), *Harambee* (1982), *Jamhuri* (1983) all received SSM, new guns and an optronic director.
Operational: *Madaraka* started a long refit at Vosper Thornycroft, Portchester, on 4 May 1989 and completed in August 1990. *Harambee* refitted in Mombasa 1991-92. Form Squadron 76.

MADARAKA 8/1990, Maritime Photographic

HARAMBEE 6/1991

1 TUG

NGAMIA

Measurement, tons: 298 grt
Dimensions, feet (metres): 115.8 × 30.5 × 12.8 *(35.3 × 9.3 × 3.9)*
Main machinery: 2 diesels; 1200 hp *(895 kW)*; 1 shaft
Speed, knots: 14

Comment: Tug built in 1969. Acquired from merchant marine in 1982.

KOREA, Democratic People's Republic (North)

Headquarters' Appointment

Commander of the Navy:
Vice Admiral Kim Il-Choi

Bases

East coast: Wonsan (main), Mayang-do, Cha-ho (submarines).
Minor bases: Najin, Sanjin-dong, Kimchaek, Yohori, Songjon, Pando, Munchon-up, Namae-ri, Kosong-up.
West coast: Nampo (main), Pipa-got (submarines).
Minor bases: Yogampo-ri, Tasa-ri, Sohae-ri, Chodo, Sunwi-do, Pupo-ri, Sagon-ri.
A number of these bases has underground berthing facilities.

Personnel

(a) 1993: 43 000 officers and men plus 40 000 reserves
(b) 5 years' national service

Strength of the Fleet

Type	Active
Submarines—Patrol	25
Submarines—Midgets	48+
Frigates	3
Fast Attack Craft—Missile	39
Fast Attack Craft—Gun/Torpedo	304
Patrol Craft	55+
Amphibious Craft	131
Hovercraft (LCP)	70+
Minesweepers	29
Depot Ships for Midget Submarines	8
Survey Vessels	4

Mercantile Marine

Lloyd's Register of Shipping:
100 vessels of 598 955 tons gross

Maritime Coastal Security Force

In addition to the Navy there is a Coastal and Port Security Police Force which would be subordinate to the Navy in war. It is reported that the strength of this force is one Sariwon class PGF, 10-15 Chong-Ju patrol craft and 130 patrol boats of the Sin Hung, Kimjin and Yongdo classes.

DELETIONS

Note: Changes to the order of battle represent the most up-to-date information available.

SUBMARINES

Note: There are also four obsolete ex-Soviet Whiskey class based at Pipa-got and used for training. Probably restricted to periscope depth when dived.

24 + 2 Ex-CHINESE and NORTH KOREAN ROMEO CLASS (PATROL TYPE)

Displacement, tons: 1475 surfaced; 1830 dived
Dimensions, feet (metres): 251.3 × 22 × 17.1 *(76.6 × 6.7 × 5.2)*
Main machinery: Diesel-electric; 2 Type 37-D diesels; 4000 hp(m) *(2.94 MW)*; 2 motors; 2700 hp(m) *(1.98 MW)*; 2 creep motors; 2 shafts
Speed, knots: 15 surfaced; 13 dived. **Range, miles:** 9000 at 9 kts surfaced
Complement: 54 (10 officers)

Torpedoes: 8—21 in *(533 mm)* tubes (6 bow, 2 stern). 14 probably Soviet Type 53; dual purpose; pattern active/passive homing up to 20 km *(10.8 nm)* at up to 45 kts; warhead 400 kg.
Mines: 28 in lieu of torpedoes.
Radars: Surface search: Snoop Plate; I band.
Sonars: Tamir 5L; hull-mounted; active.
Feniks; hull-mounted; passive.

Programmes: Two transferred from China 1973, two in 1974 and three in 1975. First three of class built in North Korea in 1975. Local building at Mayang-do and Sinpo Shipyards provided two more in 1976. Programme now seems to be running at about one every two years. One reported sunk in February 1985.
Operational: Most are stationed on east coast and occasionally operate in Sea of Japan. Four ex-Chinese units are based on the west coast. By modern standards these are basic attack submarines with virtually no anti-submarine performance or potential.

ROMEO 1989

MIDGET SUBMARINES

Note: In addition to those listed below a new series has been building since 1988. These are of similar size but have two diesels and a dived speed of up to 8 kts. So far 12 have been completed.

55 NORTH KOREAN DESIGN

Displacement, tons: 76 surfaced; 90 dived
Dimensions, feet (metres): 65.6 × 6.6 × 5.2 *(20 × 2 × 1.6)*
Main machinery: 1 MTU MB diesel, 160 hp(m) *(118 kW)*; 1 shaft
Speed, knots: 10 surfaced; 4 dived
Range, miles: 550 at 10 kts surfaced; 50 at 4 kts dived
Complement: 2 plus 6-7 divers

Comment: Built at Yukdaeso-ri shipyard since early 1960s. Forty-eight confirmed in 1992. Some lost on operations against South Korea. One reported captured by South Korean Navy in 1965 or 1966. Some stationed on Songjong peninsula. Later type imported from Yugoslavia, which began in mid-1970s. Some have two short torpedo tubes. Operate from eight merchant mother ships (see *Service Forces*).

FRIGATES

1 SOHO CLASS

Displacement, tons: 1600 standard; 1845 full load
Dimensions, feet (metres): 246 × 49.2 × 12.5 *(75 × 15 × 3.8)*
Main machinery: 2 diesels; 15 000 hp(m) *(11.03 MW)*; 2 shafts
Speed, knots: 27
Complement: 190

Missiles: SSM: 4 SS-N-2A Styx; active radar or IR homing to 46 km *(25 nm)* at 0.9 Mach; warhead 513 kg.
Guns: 1—3.9 in *(100 mm)*/56; 40° elevation; 15 rounds/minute to 16 km *(8.6 nm)*; weight of shell 13.5 kg.
4—37 mm/63 (2 twin); 80° elevation; 160 rounds/minute to 9 km *(4.9 nm)*; weight of shell 0.7 kg.
4—25 mm/60 (quad); 85° elevation; 270 rounds/minute to 3 km *(1.6 nm)*; weight of shell 0.34 kg.
A/S mortars: 2 RBU 1200 5-tubed fixed launchers; range 1200 m; warhead 34 kg.

Helicopters: Platform for one medium.

Programmes: Built at Najin Shipyard; laid down 1980; commissioned 1983.
Structure: This is reported as a unique twin hull design with a large helicopter flight deck aft.
Operational: Little time is spent at sea so the design is probably unsuccessful.

LIGHT FORCES

Note: A few obsolete P 4 patrol craft are still active.

19 SOVIET and NORTH KOREAN SO 1 CLASSES
(LARGE PATROL CRAFT)

Displacement, tons: 170 light; 215 normal
Dimensions, feet (metres): 137.8 × 19.7 × 5.9 *(42 × 6 × 1.8)*
Main machinery: 3 Kolomna Type 40-D diesels; 6600 hp(m) *(4.85 MW)* sustained; 3 shafts
Speed, knots: 28. **Range, miles:** 1100 at 13 kts
Complement: 31
Guns: 1—85 mm/52; 85° elevation; 18 rounds/minute to 15 km *(8 nm)*; weight of shell 9.5 kg.
2—37 mm/63 (twin); 80° elevation; 160 rounds/minute to 9 km *(4.9 nm)*; weight of shell 0.7 kg.
4—25 mm/60 (2 twin); 85° elevation; 270 rounds/minute to 3 km *(1.6 nm)*; weight of shell 0.34 kg.
4—14.5 mm/93 MGs.
A/S mortars: 2 RBU 1200 5-tubed launchers; range 1200 m; warhead 34 kg.
Radars: Surface search: Pot Head; I band; range 37 km *(20 nm)*.
Navigation: Don 2; I band.
IFF: Ski Pole or Dead Duck.
Sonars: Tamir 2; hull-mounted; active.

Comment: Eight transferred by the USSR in early 1960s, with RBU 1200 ASW rocket launchers and depth charges instead of the 85 mm and 37 mm guns. Remainder built in North Korea to modified design. Thirteen are fitted out for ASW with sonar and depth charges; the other six are used as gunboats.

SO 1 (Russian type)   1988

2 NAJIN CLASS

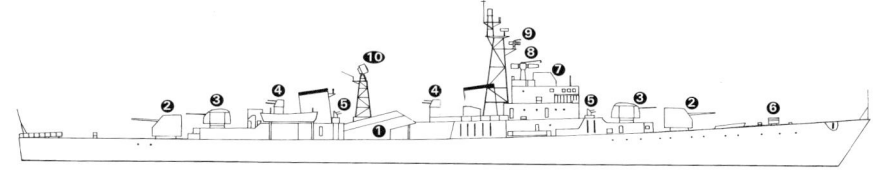

NAJIN   *(Scale 1 : 900), Ian Sturton*

Displacement, tons: 1500 full load
Dimensions, feet (metres): 334.6 × 32.8 × 8.9 *(102 × 10 × 2.7)*
Main machinery: 2 diesels; 15 000 hp(m) *(11.03 MW)*; 2 shafts
Speed, knots: 24. **Range, miles:** 4000 at 13 kts
Complement: 180

Missiles: SSM: 2 SS-N-2A Styx ❶; active radar or IR homing to 46 km *(25 nm)* at 0.9 Mach; warhead 513 kg HE. Replaced torpedo tubes on both ships.
Guns: 2—3.9 in *(100 mm)*/56 ❷; 40° elevation; 15 rounds/minute to 16 km *(8.6 nm)*; weight of shell 13.5 kg.
4—57 mm/80 (2 twin) ❸; 85° elevation; 120 rounds/minute to 6 km *(3.2 nm)*; weight of shell 2.8 kg.
8—25 mm/70 (2 quad) ❹; 85° elevation; 270 rounds/minute to 3 km *(1.6 nm)*; weight of shell 0.34 kg.
8—14.5 mm (4 twin) MGs ❺; anti-aircraft.
A/S mortars: 2 RBU 1200 5-tubed fixed launchers ❻; range 1200 m; warhead 34 kg.
Depth charges: 2 projectors; 2 racks.
Mines: 30 (estimated).
Fire control: Optical director ❼.
Radars: Air search: Slim Net ❽; E/F band.
Surface search: Pot Head ❾; I band; range 37 km *(20 nm)*.
Navigation: Pot Drum; H/I band.
Fire control: Drum Tilt ❿; H/I band.
IFF: Ski Pole.
Sonars: One hull-mounted type. One VDS type.

Programmes: Built in North Korea. First completed 1973, second completed 1975.
Structure: There is some resemblance to the ex-Soviet Kola class, now deleted. Pennant numbers are changed at intervals.

NAJIN 631   1990

NAJIN 531   1988

378 KOREA (DPR) / Light forces

8 Ex-SOVIET OSA I (TYPE 205) and 4 Ex-CHINESE HUANGFEN CLASSES (FAST ATTACK CRAFT—MISSILE)

Displacement, tons: 171 standard; 210 full load
Dimensions, feet (metres): 126.6 × 24.9 × 8.9 *(38.6 × 7.6 × 2.7)*
Main machinery: 3 Type M 503A diesels; 8025 hp(m) *(5.9 MW)* sustained; 3 shafts
Speed, knots: 35. **Range, miles:** 800 at 30 kts
Complement: 30

Missiles: SSM: 4 SS-N-2A Styx; active radar or IR homing to 46 km *(25 nm)* at 0.9 Mach; warhead 513 kg.
Guns: 4—30 mm/65 (2 twin); 85° elevation; 500 rounds/minute to 5 km *(2.7 nm)*; weight of shell 0.54 kg.
Radars: Surface search: Square Tie; I band.
Fire control: Drum Tilt; H/I band.
IFF: High Pole B. Square Head.

Programmes: Twelve Osa I class transferred in 1968 and four more in 1972-83. Eight deleted so far. Four Huangfen class acquired in 1980.

OSA I

10 Ex-SOVIET KOMAR and 9 SOHUNG CLASSES (FAST ATTACK CRAFT—MISSILE)

Displacement, tons: 75 standard; 85 full load
Dimensions, feet (metres): 87.9 × 20.3 × 4.9 *(26.8 × 6.2 × 1.5)* (Sohung)
Main machinery: 4 Type M 50 diesels; 4400 hp(m) *(3.3 MW)* sustained; 4 shafts
Speed, knots: 40. **Range, miles:** 400 at 30 kts
Complement: 19

Missiles: SSM: 2 SS-N-2A Styx; active radar or IR homing to 46 km *(25 nm)* at 0.9 Mach; warhead 513 kg.
Guns: 2—25 mm/80 (twin); 85° elevation; 270 rounds/minute to 3 km *(1.6 nm)*; weight of shell 0.34 kg.
Radars: Surface search: Square Tie; I band.
IFF: Ski Pole. Dead Duck.

Programmes: Ten Komar class transferred by USSR, all still in service but with wood hulls replaced by steel. The Sohung class is a North Korean copy of the Komar class, first built in 1980-81.

KOMAR

6 Ex-CHINESE HAINAN CLASS (LARGE PATROL CRAFT)

Displacement, tons: 375 standard; 392 full load
Dimensions, feet (metres): 192.8 × 23.6 × 6.6 *(58.8 × 7.2 × 2)*
Main machinery: 4 Kolomna/PCR Type 9-D-8 diesels; 4000 hp(m) *(2.94 MW)*; 4 shafts
Speed, knots: 30.5. **Range, miles:** 1300 at 15 kts
Complement: 69
Guns: 4—57 mm/70 (2 twin); 85° elevation; 120 rounds/minute to 8 km *(4.4 nm)*; weight of shell 2.8 kg.
4—25 mm/80 (2 twin); 85° elevation; 270 rounds/minute to 3 km *(1.6 nm)*; weight of shell 0.34 kg.
A/S mortars: 4 RBU 1200 5-tubed launchers; range 1200 m; warhead 34 kg.
Depth charges: 2 projectors; 2 racks.
Mines: Laying capability.
Radars: Surface search: Pot Head; I band.
Sonars: Hull-mounted; active search and attack; high frequency.

Comment: Transferred in 1975 (2), 1976 (2), 1978 (2).

HAINAN (Chinese number) 1988

14 SOJU CLASS (FAST ATTACK CRAFT—MISSILE)

Displacement, tons: 220 full load
Dimensions, feet (metres): 141 × 24.6 × 5.6 *(43 × 7.5 × 1.7)*
Main machinery: 3 Type M 503A diesels; 8025 hp(m) *(5.9 MW)* sustained; 3 shafts
Speed, knots: 34
Missiles: SSM: 4 SS-N-2 Styx; active radar or IR homing to 46 km *(25 nm)* at 0.9 Mach; warhead 513 kg.
Guns: 4—30 mm AKM-30 (2 twin).
Radars: Surface search: Square Tie; I band.
Fire Control: Drum Tilt; H/I band.

Comment: North Korean-built and enlarged version of Osa class. First completed in 1981; building at about one per year.

3 SARIWON (TRAL) CLASS (LARGE PATROL CRAFT)

725 726 727

Displacement, tons: 600 standard; 650 full load
Dimensions, feet (metres): 203.7 × 23.9 × 7.8 *(62.1 × 7.3 × 2.4)*
Main machinery: 2 diesels; 3000 hp(m) *(2.21 MW)*; 2 shafts
Speed, knots: 21. **Range, miles:** 2700 at 18 kts
Complement: 65-70
Guns: 2—3.9 in *(100 mm)*/56; 40° elevation; 15 rounds/minute to 16 km *(8.6 nm)*; weight of shell 13.5 kg.
12/16—14.5 mm (3/4 quad) MGs (possibly ZPU-4 type).
Depth charges: 2 rails.
Mines: 30.
Radars: Surface search: Skin Head; I band.
Navigation: Don 2; I band.
IFF: Ski Pole.
Sonars: Hull-mounted type.

Comment: Built in North Korea in the mid-1960s. Design similar to that of obsolete Soviet Tral class. Another of the class is the Flagship of the Maritime Coastal Security Forces.

SARIWON 1991

8 TAECHONG I and 4 TAECHONG II (MAYANG) CLASSES (LARGE PATROL CRAFT)

Displacement, tons: 385 standard; 410 full load (I); 425 full load (II)
Dimensions, feet (metres): 196.3 (I); 199.5 (II) × 23.6 × 6.6 *(59.8; 60.8 × 7.2 × 2)*
Main machinery: 4 Kolomna Type 40-D diesels; 8800 hp(m) *(6.4 MW)* sustained; 4 shafts
Speed, knots: 30. **Range, miles:** 2000 at 12 kts
Complement: 80
Guns: 1—3.9 in *(100 mm)*/56 (Taechong II); 40° elevation; 15 rounds/minute to 16 km *(8.6 nm)*; weight of shell 13.5 kg.
2—57 mm/70 (twin); 90° elevation; 120 rounds/minute to 8 km *(4.4 nm)*; weight of shell 2.8 kg.
1—37 mm/63 (Taechong I); 85° elevation; 160 rounds/minute to 4 km *(2.2 nm)*; weight of shell 0.7 kg.
4—30 mm/65 (2 twin). 4—14.5 mm/93 (2 twin) MGs.
A/S mortars: 2 RBU 1200 5-tubed fixed launchers; range 1200 m; warhead 34 kg.
Depth charges: 2 racks.
Radars: Surface search: Pot Head; I band; range 37 km *(20 nm)*.
Fire control: Drum Tilt; H/I band.
IFF: High Pole A. Square Head.
Sonars: Stag Ear; hull-mounted; active attack; high frequency.

Comment: North Korean class of mid-1970s design, slightly larger than Hainan class. The first eight are Taechong I class. The last four are slightly longer and are heavily armed for units of this size. Taechong II still building at about one per year and may now be called Mayang class.

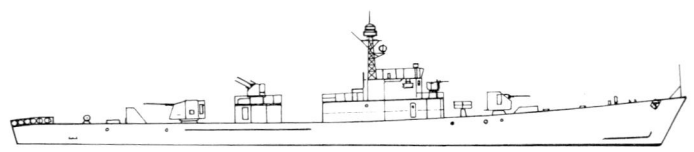

TAECHONG (not to scale)

TAECHONG II (with *Najin*) 1988

Light forces / KOREA (DPR) 379

1 SOMAN CLASS (LARGE PATROL CRAFT)

Displacement, tons: 190 full load
Dimensions, feet (metres): 91.6 × 19 × 6.2 *(27.9 × 5.8 × 1.9)*
Main machinery: 1 Kolomna Type 3-D-12 diesel; 300 hp(m) *(220 kW)*; 1 shaft
Speed, knots: 10. **Range, miles:** 1200 at 9 kts
Complement: 50 (7 officers)
Guns: 4—25 mm/60 (2 twin); 85° elevation; 270 rounds/minute to 3 km *(1.6 nm)*; weight of shell 0.34 kg.
  4—14.5 mm/93 (2 twin) MGs.
Mines: 2 rails for 16.
Radars: Surface search: Skin Head; I band.
IFF: High Pole A; Square Head.

Comment: The only one of its kind possibly used as a command gunboat or may have a secondary role as a minelayer.

13 SHANGHAI II CLASS (FAST ATTACK CRAFT—GUN)

Displacement, tons: 113 standard; 131 full load
Dimensions, feet (metres): 126.3 × 17.7 × 5.6 *(38.5 × 5.4 × 1.7)*
Main machinery: 2 Type L12-180 diesels; 2400 hp(m) *(1.76 MW)* (forward)
  2 Type 12-D-6 diesels; 1820 hp(m) *(1.34 MW)* (aft); 4 shafts
Speed, knots: 30. **Range, miles:** 700 at 16.5 kts
Complement: 34
Guns: 4—37 mm/63 (2 twin); 80° elevation; 160 rounds/minute to 9 km *(4.9 nm)*; weight of shell 0.7 kg.
  4—25 mm/60 (2 twin); 85° elevation; 270 rounds/minute to 3 km *(1.6 nm)*; weight of shell 0.34 kg.
  2—3 in *(76 mm)* recoilless rifles.
Depth charges: 8.
Mines: Rails can be fitted for 10 mines.
Radars: Surface search: Pot Head; I band or Skin Head; I band.

Comment: Acquired from China since 1967. One deleted in 1988 and one more in 1990.

SHANGHAI II

3 CHODO CLASS (FAST ATTACK CRAFT—GUN)

Displacement, tons: 130 full load
Dimensions, feet (metres): 140 × 19 × 8.5 *(42.7 × 5.8 × 2.6)*
Main machinery: 4 diesels; 6000 hp(m) *(4.41 MW)*; 2 shafts
Speed, knots: 25. **Range, miles:** 2000 at 10 kts
Complement: 40
Guns: 1—3 in *(76 mm)*/66 automatic; 85° elevation; 120 rounds/minute to 15 km *(8 nm)*; weight of shell 7 kg.
  2—37 mm/63; 85° elevation; 160 rounds/minute to 4 km *(2.2 nm)*; weight of shell 0.7 kg.
  4—25 mm/60 (2 twin); 85° elevation; 270 rounds/minute to 3 km *(1.6 nm)*; weight of shell 0.34 kg.
Radars: Surface search: Skin Head; I band.
IFF: Ski Pole.

Comment: Built in North Korea in mid-1960s.

CHODO

62 CHAHO CLASS (FAST ATTACK CRAFT—GUN)

Displacement, tons: 82 full load
Dimensions, feet (metres): 85.3 × 19 × 6.6 *(26 × 5.8 × 2)*
Main machinery: 4 Type M 50 diesels; 4400 hp(m) *(3.2 MW)* sustained; 4 shafts
Speed, knots: 40
Complement: 12
Guns: 1 BM 21 multiple rocket launcher. 2 USSR 23 mm/87 (twin). 2—14.5 mm (twin) MGs.
Radars: Surface search: Pot Head; I band.

Comment: Building in North Korea since 1974. Based on P 6 hull. Three transferred to Iran in April 1987. Four deleted in 1990/91.

CHAHO   4/1988

52 CHONG-JIN and 4 CHONG-JU CLASSES (FAST ATTACK CRAFT—GUN or TORPEDO)

Displacement, tons: 80 full load
Dimensions, feet (metres): 90.9 × 20 × 5.9 *(27.7 × 6.1 × 1.8)*
  139.4 × 22.3 × 6.2 *(42.5 × 6.8 × 1.9)* (Chong-Ju class)
Main machinery: 4 Type M 50 diesels; 4400 hp(m) *(3.2 MW)* sustained; 4 shafts
Speed, knots: 40
Complement: 12
Guns: 1—85 mm/52; 85° elevation; 18 rounds/minute to 15 km *(8 nm)*; weight of shell 9.5 kg.
  4 or 8—14.5 mm (2 or 4 twin) MGs (Chong-Jin). 1 BM 21 MRL and quad 14.5 mm (Chong-Ju).
Radars: Surface search: Pot Head; I band.
IFF: High Pole B; Square Head.

Comment: Particulars similar to Chaho class of which this is an improved version. Building began about 1975. About one third reported to be a hydrofoil development. A further class, Chong-Ju (an enlarged Chong-Jin) started building in 1985; one of these has been converted to fire torpedoes.

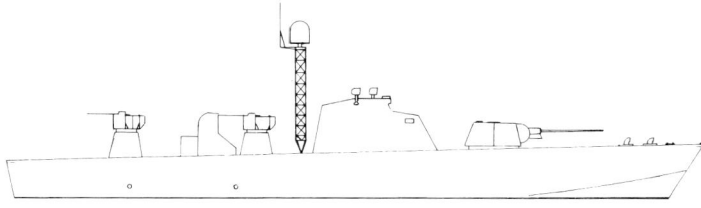
CHONG-JIN   *(not to scale), Ian Sturton*

24 SOVIET AND CHINESE P 6 CLASS (FAST ATTACK CRAFT—TORPEDO) and 21 SINPO or SINNAM CLASS (FAST ATTACK CRAFT—GUN)

Displacement, tons: 64 standard; 73 full load
Dimensions, feet (metres): 85.3 × 20 × 4.9 *(26 × 6.1 × 1.5)*
Main machinery: 4 Type M 50 diesels; 4400 hp(m) *(3.2 MW)* sustained; 4 shafts
Speed, knots: 45. **Range, miles:** 450 at 30 kts; 600 at 15 kts
Complement: 15
Guns: 4—25 mm/80 (2 twin) (original). 2—37 mm (others). 6—14.5 mm MGs (Sinpo class).
Torpedoes: 2—21 in *(533 mm)* tubes (in some). Sinpo class has no tubes.
Depth charges: 8 in some.
Radars: Surface search: Skin Head; I band (some have Furuno).
IFF: Dead Duck. High Pole.

Comment: There is a growing number of the Sinpo class with local building programme in hand of a modified form. Originally 27 P 6 class were transferred by the USSR and 15 from China. The Sinpos are replacing the P 6s.

P 6

SINPO

88 KU SONG, SIN HUNG and 37 MOD SIN HUNG CLASSES (FAST ATTACK CRAFT—TORPEDO)

Displacement, tons: 40 full load
Dimensions, feet (metres): 72.2 × 11 × 5.5 *(22 × 3.4 × 1.7)*
Main machinery: 2 Type M 50 diesels; 2200 hp(m) *(1.6 MW)* sustained; 2 shafts
Speed, knots: 40
Guns: 4—14.5 mm (2 twin) MGs.
Torpedoes: 2—18 in *(457 mm)* or 2—21 in *(533 mm)* tubes (not fitted in all).
Radars: Surface search: Skin Head; I band.
IFF: Dead Duck.

Comment: Ku Song and Sin Hung built in North Korea mid-1950s to 1970. Frequently operated on South Korean border. A modified version of Sin Hung with hydrofoils built from 1981 to 1985.

SIN HUNG (no torpedo tubes)   1991

380 KOREA (DPR) / Light forces — Service forces

MODIFIED FISHING VESSELS (COASTAL PATROL CRAFT)

Comment: An unknown number of fishing vessels have been converted for naval use. Two seen in 1991 include 801 which has a twin 25 mm gun forward and a twin 14.5 mm MG aft of the funnel, and 177 which was acting as a survey ship in the Sea of Japan.

801   7/1991, G Jacobs

177   7/1991, G Jacobs

10 TB 11PA AND 6 TB 40A CLASSES (INSHORE PATROL CRAFT)

Displacement, tons: 8
Dimensions, feet (metres): 36.7 × 8.6 × 3.3 (11.2 × 2.7 × 1)
Main machinery: 2 diesels; 520 hp(m) (382 kW); 2 shafts
Speed, knots: 35. **Range, miles:** 200 at 15 kts
Complement: 4
Guns: 1—7.62 mm MG.
Radars: Surface search/navigation: Radar-24.

Comment: New construction high speed patrol boats. Reinforced fibreglass hull. Design closely resembles a number of UK/Western European commercial craft. Twenty ordered by Zaire for delivery in late 1990 but this was probably delayed by lack of funds. Larger hull design, known as 'TB 40A' also building. Both classes being operated by the MSCF.

HIGH SPEED INFILTRATION CRAFT (HSIC)

Displacement, tons: 5
Dimensions, feet (metres): 30.5 × 8.2 × 3.1 (9.3 × 2.5 × 1)
Main machinery: 1 diesel; 260 hp(m) (191 kW); 1 shaft
Speed, knots: 35
Complement: 2
Guns: 1—7.62 mm MG.
Radars: Navigation: Furuno 701; I band.

Comment: Large numbers built for Agent infiltration and covert operations. These craft have a very low radar cross section and 'squat' at high speeds.

HSIC   1991, J Bermudez

AMPHIBIOUS FORCES

16 HUNGNAM AND 8 HANTAE CLASSES (LSM)

Comment: Both classes started building in 1980-82 and are capable of taking four to five medium tanks. Hungnam is slightly larger.

7 HANCHON CLASS (LCM)

Displacement, tons: 145 full load
Dimensions, feet (metres): 117.1 × 25.9 × 3.9 (35.7 × 7.9 × 1.2)
Main machinery: 2 Type 3-D-12 diesels; 600 hp(m) (443 kW) sustained; 2 shafts
Speed, knots: 10. **Range, miles:** 600 at 6 kts
Complement: 15 (1 officer)
Military lift: 2 tanks or 200 troops
Guns: 2—14.5 mm/93 (twin) MG.
Radars: Surface search: Skin Head; I band.

Comment: Built in North Korea.

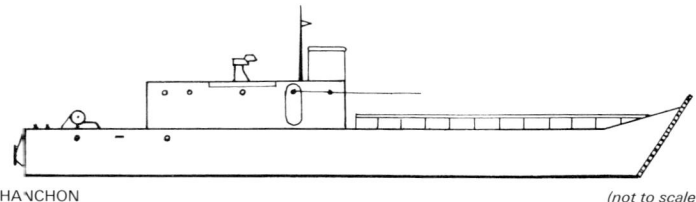

HANCHON   (not to scale)

100 NAMPO CLASS (LCP)

Displacement, tons: 80 full load
Dimensions, feet (metres): 84.2 × 20 × 6 (27.7 × 6.1 × 1.8)
Main machinery: 4 Type M 50 diesels; 4400 hp(m) (3.2 MW) sustained; 4 shafts
Speed, knots: 40. **Range, miles:** 375 at 40 kts
Complement: 19
Military lift: 20-30 troops
Guns: 4—14.5 mm (2 twin) MGs.
Radars: Surface search: Pot Head; I band.

Comment: A class of assault landing craft. Almost identical to the Chong-Jin class but with a smaller forward gun mounting and with retractable ramp in bows. Building began about 1975. Four or five have probably been deleted due to damage. Numbers uncertain. About 20 used for patrol duties with bow doors welded shut. Four sold to Madagascar in 1979.

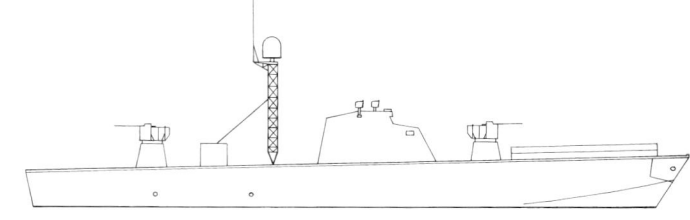

NAMPO   (not to scale), Ian Sturton

70 + SONGJONG CLASS (LCP—HOVERCRAFT)

Comment: Three types: one Type I, 31 Type II and 20 + 6 Type III. Type III is building at 6-10 per year. Length about 25 m (I) and 18 m (II). A series of high speed air-cushion landing craft first reported in 1987. Use of air-cushion technology is an adoption of commercial technology imported from the UK. Estimated to carry 35 to 55 (or more) light infantry troops. Songjong II may be called the Hwanghae class.

MINESWEEPERS

19 YUKTO I and 4 YUKTO II CLASSES (COASTAL MINESWEEPERS)

Displacement, tons: 60 full load
Dimensions, feet (metres): 78.7 × 13.1 × 5.6 (24 × 4 × 1.7)
Main machinery: 2 diesels; 2 shafts
Speed, knots: 18
Complement: 22 (4 officers)
Guns: 1—37 mm/63 or 2—25 mm/80 (twin). 2—14.5 mm/93 (twin) MGs.
Mines: 2 rails for 4.
Radars: Surface search: Skin Head; I band.

Comment: North Korean design built in the 1980s and replaced the obsolete ex-Soviet KN-14 class. A total of four Yukto IIs was built; they are 3 m shorter (at 21 m length) overall and have no after gun. Wooden construction.

6 PIPA-GOT CLASS (INSHORE MINESWEEPERS)

Comment: A new class of MSI. No details.

SURVEY VESSELS

Note: The Hydrographic Department has four survey ships but also uses a number of converted fishing vessels.

Name	Displacement	Launched	Complement
DONGHAE 101	260 tons	1970	22 (8 officers)
DONGHAE 102	1100 tons	1979	35 (20 officers)
SOHAI 201	260 tons	1972	22 (14 officers)
SOHAI 202	300 tons	1981	26 (16 officers)

SERVICE FORCES

Notes: (1) One Kowan class ASR built recently for submarine rescue, possibly catamaran construction. Trawlers operate as AGIs on the South Korean border where several have been sunk over the years. In addition many ocean-going commercial vessels are used for carrying weapons and ammunition worldwide in support of international terrorism.
(2) There are also eight ocean cargo ships adapted as mother ships for midget submarines. Their names are *Soo Gun-Ho*, *Dong Geon Ae Gook-Ho*, *Dong Hae-Ho*, *Choong Seong-Ho Number One*, *Choong Seong-Ho Number Two*, *Choong Seong-Ho Number Three*, *Hae Gum Gang-Ho* and the *Song Rim-Ho*.

KOREA, Republic (South)

Headquarters' Appointments

Chief of Naval Operations:
Admiral Kim Chul-Woo
Commandant Marine Corps:
Lieutenant General Cho Ki-Yup
Commandant Naval Academy:
Vice Admiral Choi Il-Kun

Operational Commands

Commander First Fleet:
Rear Admiral Jong Dae Kim
Commander Second Fleet:
Rear Admiral An Pyong-Tae
Commander Third Fleet:
Rear Admiral Kim Man Chong

Diplomatic Representation

Defence Attaché in London:
Captain S J Kim

Personnel

(a) 1993: 35 500 Navy, 25 000 Marine Corps
(b) 2¼ years' (Navy) national service with a proportion of ratings and all marines being volunteers

Bases

Major: Chinhae (Fleet HQ), Pukpyong (1st Fleet)
Minor: Cheju, Mokpo, Mukho, Pohang, Inchon (2nd Fleet), Pusan (3rd Fleet)
Aviation: Pohang, Chinhae

Organisation

In 1986 the Navy was reorganised into three Fleets, each commanded by a Rear Admiral, whereas the Marines retain two Divisions and one brigade plus smaller and support units. From October 1973 the RoK Marine Force was placed directly under the RoK Navy command with a Vice Chief of Naval Operations for Marine Affairs replacing the Commandant of Marine Corps. The Marine Corps was re-established as an independent service on 1 November 1987.

1st Fleet: No 11, 12, 13 DD/FF Sqn; No 101, 102 Coastal Defence Sqn; 181, 191, 111, 121 Coastal Defence Units; 121st Minesweeper Sqn.
2nd Fleet: No 21, 22, 23 DD/FF Sqn; No 201, 202 Coastal Defence Sqn; 211, 212 Coastal Defence Units; 522nd Minesweeper Sqn.
3rd Fleet: 301, 302, 303 DD/FF Sqn; 304, 406th Coastal Defence Units.

Pennant Numbers

Pennant numbers are changed at unspecified intervals. The numbers 0 and 4 are not used as they are unlucky.

Strength of the Fleet

Type	Active	Building (Proposed)
Submarines (Patrol)	1	8 (9)
Submarines (Midget)	4	—
Destroyers	9	(4)
Frigates	10	1 (9)
Corvettes	26	—
Fast Attack Craft—Missile	11	—
Fast Attack Craft—Patrol	66	—
Minehunters	3	5 (10)
Minesweepers	8	—
Minelayers	0	(1)
LSTs	7	2
LSMs	8	—
LCU/LCM	16	—
Logistic Support Ship	1	(1)
Salvage Ships	4 (one CG)	1
Tankers	4	—
Survey Ships and Craft	7	—

Mercantile Marine

Lloyd's Register of Shipping:
2138 vessels of 7 518 485 tons gross

DELETIONS

Service Forces

1992 Chun Ji, Hwa Chon

SUBMARINES

1 + 8 CHANG BOGO (TYPE 209) CLASS (1200)

Name	No	Builders	Laid down	Launched	Commissioned
CHANG BOGO	—	HDW, Kiel	1989	June 1992	Jan 1993
YI CHON	—	Daewoo, Okpo	1990	14 Oct 1992	1994
—	—	Daewoo, Okpo	1991	1993	1994

Displacement, tons: 1100 surfaced; 1285 dived
Dimensions, feet (metres): 183.7 × 20.3 × 18 *(56 × 6.2 × 5.5)*
Main machinery: Diesel-electric; 4 MTU 12V 396 SE diesels; 3800 hp(m) *(2.8 MW)* sustained; 4 alternators; 1 motor; 4600 hp(m) *(3.38 MW)* sustained; 1 shaft
Speed, knots: 11 surfaced/snorting; 22 dived
Range, miles: 7500 at 8 kts surfaced
Complement: 33 (6 officers)

Torpedoes: 8—21 in *(533 mm)* bow tubes. 14 probably AEG SS4; wire-guided; active/passive homing to 28 km *(15.3 nm)* at 23 kts; 12 km *(6.6 nm)* at 35 kts; warhead 260 kg. Swim-out discharge.
Mines: 28 in lieu of torpedoes.
Countermeasures: ESM: Radar warning.
Fire control: Atlas Elektronik ISUS TFCS.
Radars: Navigation: I band.
Sonars: Atlas Elektronik CSU 83; hull-mounted; passive/active; medium frequency.

Programmes: First three ordered in late 1987, one built at Kiel by HDW, and two being assembled at Okpo by Daewoo from material packages transported from Germany. Key Korean personnel have been trained in Germany. Second three ordered in October 1989 and a further batch of three reported ordered in January 1993, all to be built at Okpo. The final total could be as many as 18 split between the three fleets and the aim is eventually to be independent of European shipbuilding assistance.
Structure: Type 1200 similar to those built for the Turkish Navy with a heavy dependence on Atlas Elektronik sensors and AEG torpedoes. Air independent propulsion using a Cosworth Argo diesel is an option in some of the later hulls, which may be of a larger size.

CHANG BOGO *11/1992, HDW*

YI CHON *10/1992, Daewoo*

1 KSS-1 TOLGORAE and 3 COSMOS CLASSES

Displacement, tons: 150 surfaced; 175 dived (Tolgorae); 70 surfaced (Cosmos)
Torpedoes: 2—406 mm tubes (Tolgorae).
Sonars: Atlas Elektronik; hull-mounted; passive search; high frequency.

Comment: Tolgorae in service in 1983. A report that more had been ordered was incorrect. There are also three Cosmos type used by Marines for a total of four of both classes. Limited endurance, for use only in coastal waters. There is an unconfirmed report that six KSS-1s may have been sold to Saudi Arabia.

TOLGORAE *11/1985, G Jacobs*

KOREA (REPUBLIC) / Destroyers

DESTROYERS

Note: A new class of heavy destroyers is projected. Design work to start in 1993 for an air defence ship of 7-8000 tons. Planned in-service date is 2003.

7 Ex-US GEARING (FRAM I and II) CLASS

Name	No	Builders	Laid down	Launched	Commissioned
CHUNG BUK (ex-USS *Chevalier* DD 805)	DD 915	Bath Iron Works Corporation, Bath, Maine	12 June 1944	29 Oct 1944	9 Jan 1945
JEON BUK (ex-USS *Everett F Larson* DD 830)	DD 916	Bath Iron Works Corporation, Bath, Maine	4 Sep 1944	28 Jan 1945	6 Apr 1945
TAEJON (ex-USS *New* DD 818)	DD 919	Consolidated Steel Corporation	14 Apr 1945	18 Aug 1945	5 Apr 1946
KWANG JU (ex-USS *Richard E Kraus* DD 849)	DD 921	Bath Iron Works Corporation, Bath, Maine	31 July 1945	2 Mar 1946	23 May 1946
KANG WON (ex-USS *William R Rush* DD 714)	DD 922	Federal S B and D D Co, Newark	19 Oct 1944	8 July 1945	21 Sep 1945
KYONG KI (ex-USS *Newman K Perry* DD 883)	DD 923	Consolidated Steel Corporation	10 Oct 1944	17 Mar 1945	26 July 1945
JEON JU (ex-USS *Rogers* DD 876)	DD 925	Consolidated Steel Corporation	3 June 1944	20 Nov 1944	26 Mar 1945

Displacement, tons: 2425 standard; 3470 full load approx
Dimensions, feet (metres): 390.5 × 41.2 × 19 *(119 × 12.6 × 5.8)*
Main machinery: 4 Babcock & Wilcox boilers; 600 psi *(43.3 kg/cm sq)*; 850°F *(454°C)*; 2 GE turbines; 60 000 hp *(45 MW)*; 2 shafts
Speed, knots: 32.5. **Range, miles:** 3275 at 11 kts; 975 at 32 kts
Complement: 280

Missiles: SSM: 8 McDonnell Douglas Harpoon (2 quad) launchers ❶(all except DD 923 and 925); active radar homing to 130 km *(70 nm)* at 0.9 Mach; warhead 227 kg.
A/S: Honeywell ASROC Mk 112 octuple launcher (DD 923 and 925); inertial guidance to 1.6-10 km *(1-6 nm)*; payload Mk 46 torpedo.
Guns: 4 or 6—5 in *(127 mm)*/38 (2 twin) Mk 38 (3 twin in DD 915-916) ❷; 85° elevation; 15 rounds/minute to 17 km *(9 nm)* anti-surface; 11 km *(5.9 nm)* anti-aircraft; weight of shell 25 kg.
2 USN/Bofors 40 mm/56 (twin) (except DD 915 and 916); 45° elevation; 160 rounds/minute to 11 km *(5.9 nm)* anti-surface; 6 km *(3.3 nm)* anti-aircraft; weight of shell 0.9 kg.
2 General Electric/General Dynamics 20 mm Vulcan Gatling (except DD 923); 3000 rounds/minute combined to 1.5 km.
Torpedoes: 6—324 mm Mk 32 (2 triple) tubes ❸. Honeywell Mk 46; anti-submarine; active/passive homing to 11 km *(5.9 nm)* at 40 kts; warhead 44 kg.
A/S mortars: 2 USN Hedgehog Mk 11 fixed rocket launchers (DD 915-916) ❹; manually loaded; range 350 m; warhead 26 kg; 24 missiles.
Depth charges: 1 Mk IX rack.
Countermeasures: ESM: WLR-1; radar warning. WJ 1140 (DD 916).
ECM: ULQ-6; jammer.
Fire control: 1 Mk 37 GFCS. 1 Mk 51 Mod 2 (except DD 915 and 916) (for 40 mm).
Radars: Air search: Lockheed SPS 40 ❺ (DD 921 has SPS 37); E/F band; range 320 km *(175 nm)*.
Surface search: Raytheon/Sylvania SPS 10 ❻; G band.
Fire control: Western Electric Mk 25 ❼; I/J band.
IFF: UPX 1-12 (DD 919 and 921).
Sonars: SQS 29 (DD 915-916); hull-mounted; active search and attack; high frequency.
Sangamo SQS 23 (remainder); active search and attack; medium frequency.

Helicopters: 1 Aerospatiale SA 316B Alouette III or 1 Westland Super Lynx ❽ (all except DD 923 and 925).

Programmes: First pair on loan on 5 July 1972 and 30 October 1972 respectively and by purchase 31 January 1977. Second pair 23 February 1977 by sale. DD 922 by sale 1 July 1978. Last pair by sale February/March 1981.
Modernisation: DD 915 and DD 916 were converted to radar picket destroyers (DDR) in 1949. All subsequently modernised under the US Navy's Fleet Rehabilitation and Modernisation (FRAM) programme—first pair to FRAM II standards, others to FRAM I. Fitted with small helicopter hangar and flight deck. Anti-ship torpedo tubes have been removed. In DD 915 and DD 919 the helicopter deck has been strengthened and in 925 two Vulcan Gatling guns have been positioned at the after end. Harpoon fitted in 1979 and some ships may still only carry two twin launchers. Most are now Tacan and SATCOM fitted.

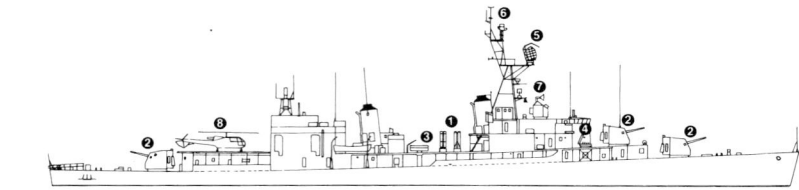
CHUNG BUK
(Scale 1 : 1200), Ian Sturton

KANG WON (with Harpoon and Gatling midships plus 40 mm guns forward) 9/1988

CHUNG BUK (with 3 twin 127 mm guns) 9/1988

JEON JU (ASROC and Gatling aft)

Destroyers — Frigates / KOREA (REPUBLIC) 383

2 Ex-US ALLEN M SUMNER (FRAM II) CLASS

Name	No	Builders	Laid down	Launched	Commissioned
DAE GU (ex-USS *Wallace L Lind* DD 703)	DD 917	Bath Iron Works Corporation, Bath, Maine	Apr 1944	14 June 1944	8 Sep 1944
INCHON (ex-USS *De Haven* DD 727)	DD 918	Federal S B & D D Co, Kearney, New Jersey	Oct 1943	9 Jan 1944	31 Mar 1944

Displacement, tons: 2200 standard; 3320 full load
Dimensions, feet (metres): 376.5 × 40.9 × 19 *(114.8 × 12.4 × 5.8)*
Main machinery: 4 Babcock & Wilcox boilers; 600 psi *(43.3 kg/cm sq)*; 850°F *(454°C)*; 2 GE turbines; 60 000 hp *(45 MW)*; 2 shafts
Speed, knots: 34. **Range, miles:** 4500 at 16 kts
Complement: 235

Guns: 6 USN 5 in *(127 mm)*/38 (3 twin) Mk 38; 85° elevation; 15 rounds/minute to 17 km *(9 nm)* anti-surface; 11 km *(5.9 nm)* anti-aircraft; weight of shell 25 kg.
 2 USN/Bofors 40 mm/56 (twin); 45° elevation; 160 rounds/minute to 11 km *(5.9 nm)* anti-surface; 6 km *(3.3 nm)* anti-aircraft; weight of shell 0.9 kg.
 1 General Electric/General Dynamics 20 mm Vulcan Gatling (DD 918); 3000 rounds/minute combined to 1.5 km.
Torpedoes: 6—324 mm Mk 32 (2 triple) tubes. Honeywell Mk 46; anti-submarine; active/passive homing to 11 km *(5.9 nm)* at 40 kts; warhead 44 kg.
A/S mortars: 2 USN Hedgehog Mk 11 fixed rocket launchers; manually loaded; range 350 m; warhead 20 kg; 24 missiles.
Countermeasures: Decoys: 2 Loral-Hycor RBOC 6-barrelled Mk 33 launchers; range 4 km *(2.2 nm)*.
Fire control: USN Mk 37 for 127 mm gunnery. 2 Mk 51 for 40 mm gunnery.
Radars: Air search: Lockheed SPS 40 (DD 917); E/F band; range 320 km *(175 nm)*.
 Westinghouse SPS 37 (DD 918); B/C band; range 556 km *(300 nm)*.
 Surface search: Raytheon/Sylvania SPS 10; G band.
Fire control: Western Electric Mk 25; I/J band.
IFF: UPX 1-12.
Sonars: Sangamo SQS 23; hull-mounted; active search and attack; medium frequency.
 Litton SQA 10; VDS; active/passive search; medium frequency.

Helicopters: 1 Aerospatiale SA 316B Alouette III or 1 Westland Super Lynx.

Programmes: Transferred by sale December 1973.
Modernisation: Both ships were modernised under the US Navy's Fleet Rehabilitation and Modernisation (FRAM II) programme.
Structure: DD 917 fitted with strengthened helicopter deck and hangar.

JEON BUK (similar to *Dae Gu*) 1984

FRIGATES

0 + 1 + (9) KDX-2000 CLASS

Displacement, tons: 3900 full load
Dimensions, feet (metres): 444.2 × 46.6 × 13.8 *(135.4 × 14.2 × 4.2)*
Main machinery: CODOG; 2 GE LM 2500 gas turbines; 58 200 hp *(43.42 MW)* sustained; 2 MTU or SEMT-Pielstick diesels; 8000 hp(m) *(5.88 MW)*; 2 shafts
Speed, knots: 30. **Range, miles:** 4000 at 18 kts
Complement: 170 (15 officers)

Missiles: SSM: 8 McDonnell Douglas Harpoon (2 quad) launchers ❶.
 SAM: Raytheon Sea Sparrow Mk 48; VLS launcher ❷ for 16 cells RIM-7M. Mk 41 for Standard in later ships.
Guns: 1 OTO Melara 5 in *(127 mm)*/54 ❸.
 2 Signaal 30 mm Goalkeeper ❹; 7 barrels per mounting.
Torpedoes: 6—324 mm (2 triple) Mk 32 tubes ❺; Mk 46; anti-submarine.
Countermeasures: Decoys: 4 chaff launchers ❻. SLQ-25 Nixie towed torpedo decoy.
ESM/ECM: Argo AR 700/APECS II or TST FI 1800S; intercept and jammer.
Combat data systems: BAe Dowty-Sema SSCS Mk 7 or Atlas/Contraves COSYS 200. Link 11.
Radars: Air search: Raytheon SPS 49(V)5 ❼; C/D band.
 Surface search: Cardion SPS 55M ❽; I/J/K band.
 Fire control: 2 Signaal or Contraves ❾.
IFF: UPX-27.
Sonars: Ferranti/Thomson Sintra Spherion B; hull-mounted active search; medium frequency.

Helicopters: 1 Westland Super Lynx ❿.

Programmes: A much delayed programme. The first keel was to have been laid down at Daewoo in late 1992 for completion in 1996, but definition studies have been extended to late 1993 and the whole project may be overtaken by the 8000 ton destroyer. If the project goes ahead subsequent units will be shared with Hyundai, but may not be ordered until after first of class trials.
Structure: Later ships of the class may be fitted with vertical launch Standard missiles and towed sonar arrays. Configuration shown in the line drawing still has some minor amendments to come.

KDX-2000 (Scale 1 : 1200), Ian Sturton

384 KOREA (REPUBLIC) / Frigates

9 ULSAN CLASS

Name	No	Builders	Laid down	Launched	Commissioned
ULSAN	FF 951	Hyundai, Ulsan	1979	8 Apr 1980	1 Jan 1981
SEOUL	FF 952	Hyundai, Ulsan	1982	1984	30 June 1985
CHUNG NAM	FF 953	Korean SEC, Pusan	1984	1985	1 June 1986
MASAN	FF 955	Korea Tacoma	1983	26 Oct 1984	20 July 1985
KYONG BUK	FF 956	Daewoo, Okpo	1984	15 Jan 1986	30 May 1986
CHON NAM	FF 957	Hyundai, Ulsan	1986	19 Apr 1988	17 June 1989
CHE JU	FF 958	Daewoo, Okpo	1986	3 May 1988	1 Jan 1990
CHUNG JU	—	Daewoo, Okpo	1990	20 Mar 1992	1993
BUSAN	—	Hyundai, Ulsan	1990	18 Feb 1992	1993

Displacement, tons: 1496 light; 2180 full load (2300 for FF 957-959)
Dimensions, feet (metres): 334.6 × 37.7 × 11.5 *(102 × 11.5 × 3.5)*
Main machinery: CODOG; 2 GE LM 2500 gas turbines; 53 640 hp *(40 MW)* sustained; 2 MTU 16V 538 TB82 diesels; 5940 hp(m) *(4.37 MW)* sustained; 2 shafts; cp props
Speed, knots: 34; 18 on diesels. **Range, miles:** 4000 at 15 kts
Complement: 150 (16 officers)

Missiles: SSM: 8 McDonnell Douglas Harpoon (4 twin) launchers ❶; active radar homing to 130 km *(70 nm)* at 0.9 Mach; warhead 227 kg.
Guns: 2—3 in *(76 mm)*/62 OTO Melara compact ❷; 85° elevation; 85 rounds/minute to 16 km *(8.6 nm)* anti-surface; 12 km *(6.5 nm)* anti-aircraft; weight of shell 6 kg.
8 Emerson Electric 30 mm (4 twin) (FF 951-955) ❸; 6 Breda 40 mm/70 (3 twin) (FF 956-959) ❹.
Torpedoes: 6—324 mm Mk 32 (2 triple) tubes ❺. Honeywell Mk 46 Mod 1; anti-submarine; active/passive homing to 11 km *(5.9 nm)* at 40 kts; warhead 44 kg.
Depth charges: 12.
Countermeasures: Decoys: 4 Loral Hycor SRBOC 6-barrelled Mk 36 launchers ❻; range 4 km *(2.2 nm)*.
Nixie; towed torpedo decoy.
ESM/ECM: Intercept and jammer.
Combat data systems: Samsung/Ferranti WSA 423 action data automation (FF 957-959). Litton systems may be retrofitted to others.
Fire control: 1 Signaal Lirod optronic director (FF 951-956) ❼; 1 Radamec System 2400 optronic director (FF 957-959) ❽.
Radars: Air/surface search: Signaal DA 05 ❾; E/F band.
Surface search: Signaal ZW 06 (FF 951-956) ❿; Marconi S 1810 (FF 957-959) ⓫; I band.
Fire control: Signaal WM 28 (FF 951-956) ⓬; Marconi ST 1802 (FF 957-959) ⓭; I/J band.
Navigation: Raytheon SPS 10C (FF 957-959) ⓮; I band.
Tacan: SRN 15.
Sonars: Signaal PHS 32; hull-mounted; active search and attack; medium frequency.

Structure: Steel hull with aluminium alloy superstructure. There are three versions. The first five ships are the same but *Kyong Buk* has the 4 Emerson Electric twin 30 mm guns replaced by 3 Breda twin 40 mm, and the last four of the class have a built-up gun platform aft and a different combination of surface search, target indication and navigation radars. Weapon systems integration caused earlier concern and a Ferranti combat data system has been installed in the last three; it is reported that a Litton Systems CDS will be retrofitted in the earlier ships of the class.
Operational: *Che Ju* and *Chung Nam* conducted the first ever deployment of South Korean warships to Europe during a four month tour from September 1991 to January 1992. Trainees were embarked.

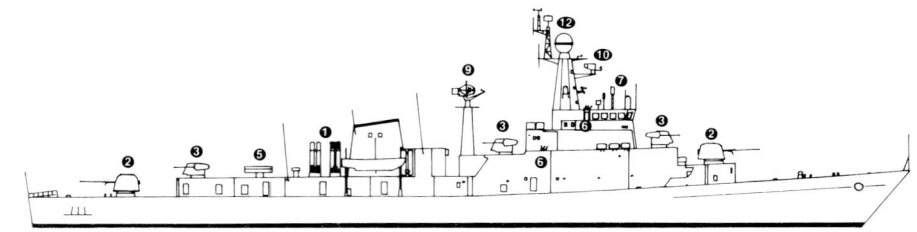
ULSAN (Scale 1 : 900), Ian Sturton

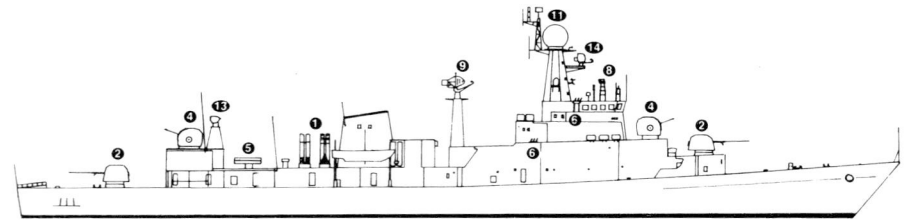
CHE JU (Scale 1 : 900), Ian Sturton

CHE JU (with Marconi FC radar and 40 mm guns) 10/1991, Foto Flite

KYONG BUK (with Signaal FC radar and 40 mm guns) 10/1985

CHUNG NAM (with Signaal FC radar and 30 mm guns) 11/1991, Maritime Photograph

CORVETTES

22 PO HANG CLASS

Name	No	Builders	Commissioned
PO HANG	756	Korea SEC, Pusan	Dec 1984
KUN SAN	757	Korea Tacoma	Dec 1984
KYONG JU	758	Hyundai	1986
MOK PO	759	Daewoo, Okpo	1986
KIM CHON	761	Korea SEC, Pusan	1987
CHUNG JU	762	Korea Tacoma	1987
JIN JU	763	Hyundai, Ulsan	1988
YO SU	765	Daewoo, Okpo	1988
AN DONG	766	Korea SEC, Pusan	Feb 1989
SUN CHON	767	Korea Tacoma	June 1989
YEE REE	768	Hyundai, Ulsan	June 1989
WON JU	769	Daewoo, Okpo	1989
JE CHON	771	Korea Tacoma	1989
CHON AN	772	Korea SEC, Pusan	Nov 1989
SONG NAM	773	Daewoo, Okpo	1990
BU CHON	775	Hyundai, Ulsan	1990
DAE CHON	776	Korea Tacoma	1990
JIN HAE	777	Korea SEC, Pusan	1990
SOK CHO	778	Korea Tacoma	1991
YONG JU	779	Hyundai, Ulsan	1991
NAM WON	781	Daewoo, Okpo	1991
KWAN MYONG	782	Korea SEC, Pusan	1991

Displacement, tons: 1220 full load
Dimensions, feet (metres): 289.7 × 32.8 × 9.5 *(88.3 × 10 × 2.9)*
Main machinery: CODOG; 1 GE LM 2500 gas turbine; 26 820 hp *(20 MW)* sustained; 2 SEMT-Pielstick 12 PA6 V 280 diesels; 9600 hp(m) *(7.08 MW)* sustained; 2 shafts
Speed, knots: 32. **Range, miles:** 4000 at 15 kts
Complement: 95 (10 officers)

Missiles: SSM: 2 Aerospatiale MM 38 Exocet (756-765) ❶; inertial cruise; active radar homing to 42 km *(23 nm)* at 0.9 Mach; warhead 165 kg; sea-skimmer. Not in all.
Guns: 1 or 2 OTO Melara 3 in *(76 mm)*/62 compact ❷; 85° elevation; 85 rounds/minute to 16 km *(8.6 nm)* anti-surface; 12 km *(6.5 nm)* anti-aircraft; weight of shell 6 kg.
 4 Emerson Electric 30 mm (2 twin) (756-765) ❸; 2 Breda 40 mm/70 (766 onwards) ❹.
Torpedoes: 6—324 mm Mk 32 (2 triple) tubes (766 onwards) ❺. Honeywell Mk 46; anti-submarine; active/passive homing to 11 km *(5.9 nm)* at 40 kts; warhead 44 kg.
Depth charges: 12 (766 onwards).
Countermeasures: Decoys: 4 MEL Protean fixed launchers; 36 grenades.
 2 Loral Hycor SRBOC 6-barrelled Mk 36 launchers (in some); range 4 km *(2.2 nm)*.
ESM/ECM: THORN EMI or NobelTech; intercept/jammer.
Combat data systems: Signaal Sewaco ZK (756-765); Ferranti WSA 423 (766 onwards).
Fire control: Signaal Lirod or Radamec 2400 optronic director ❻.
Radars: Surface search: Marconi 1810 ❼ and/or Raytheon SPS 64 ❽; I band.
Fire control: Signaal WM 28 ❾; I/J band; or Marconi 1802 ❿; I/J band.
Sonars: Signaal PHS 32 (766 onwards); hull-mounted; active search and attack; medium frequency.

Programmes: First laid down early 1983 by Korea SEC. The pennant number/name attribution shown above is uncertain but names and shipbuilders are correct. At least two more of the class were scheduled for completion in 1992 but the status of further orders is uncertain.
Structure: It is probable that there are three groups specialising in surface-to-surface warfare, anti-submarine, and possibly to come, air defence. The first group therefore has no ASW equipment and starting with *An Dong* (766) the second group has no SSM. The second group also has an improved combat data system with Ferranti/Radamec/Marconi fire control systems and radars as in the Ulsan class later versions.

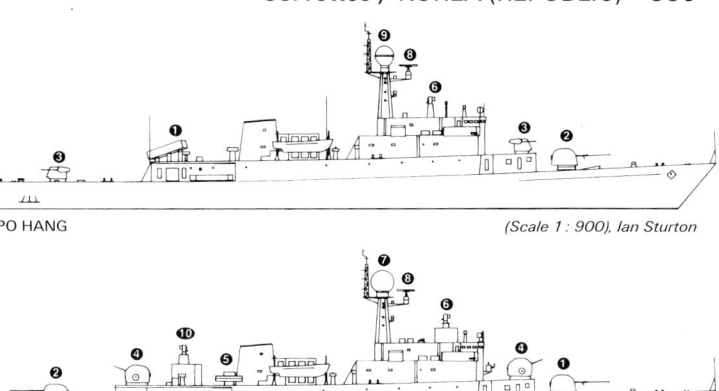

PO HANG *(Scale 1 : 900), Ian Sturton*

AN DONG *(Scale 1 : 900), Ian Sturton*

WON JU *1989, Daewoo*

4 DONG HAE CLASS

Name	No	Builders	Commissioned
DONG HAE	751	Korea SEC, Pusan	1982
SU WON	752	Korea Tacoma	1983
KANG REUNG	753	Hyundai, Ulsan	1983
AN YANG	755	Daewoo, Okpo	1983

Displacement, tons: 950 full load
Dimensions, feet (metres): 256.2 × 31.5 × 8.5 *(78.1 × 9.6 × 2.6)*
Main machinery: CODOG; 1 GE LM 2500 gas turbine; 26 820 hp *(20 MW)* sustained; 2 MTU 12V 956 TB82 diesels; 6260 hp(m) *(4.6 MW)* sustained; 2 shafts; cp props
Speed, knots: 31. **Range, miles:** 4000 at 15 kts
Complement: 95 (10 officers)

Guns: 1 OTO Melara 3 in *(76 mm)*/62 compact ❶; 85° elevation; 85 rounds/minute to 16 km *(8.6 nm)*; weight of shell 6 kg.
 4 Emerson Electric 30 mm (2 twin) ❷. 2 Oerlikon 20 mm (twin) ❸.
Torpedoes: 6—324 mm Mk 32 (2 triple) tubes ❹. Honeywell Mk 46.
Depth charges: 12.
Countermeasures: Decoys: 4 MEL Protean chaff launchers.
ESM/ECM: THORN EMI or NobelTech; intercept and jammer.
Combat data systems: Signaal Sewaco ZK.
Fire control: Signaal Lirod optronic director ❺.
Radars: Surface search: Raytheon SPS 64 ❻; I band.
Fire control: Signaal WM 28 ❼; I/J band; range 46 km *(25 nm)*.
Sonars: Signaal PHS 32; hull-mounted; active search and attack; medium frequency.

Programmes: This was the first version of the corvette series, with four being ordered in 1980, one each from the four major warship building yards.
Structure: The design was almost certainly too small for the variety of different weapons which were intended to be fitted for different types of warfare and was therefore discontinued in favour of the Po Hang class.

KUN SAN *1987, Korea Tacoma*

NAM WON *1992, Ships of the World*

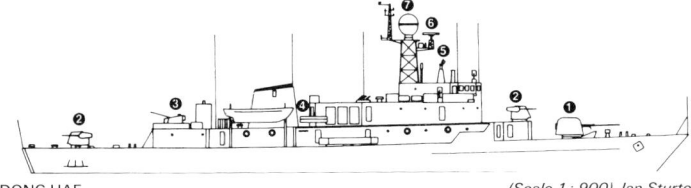

DONG HAE *(Scale 1 : 900), Ian Sturton*

SU WON *1987, Korea Tacoma*

SHIPBORNE AIRCRAFT

Numbers/Type: 12 Westland Super Navy Lynx Mk 99.
Operational speed: 125 kts *(231 km/h).*
Service ceiling: 12 000 ft *(3660 m).*
Range: 320 nm *(593 km).*
Role/Weapon systems: Shipborne ASV helicopter delivered in 1991 to replace Alouette III; a further order of six ASW versions is expected in 1992 with 12 more in due course. Sensors: Ferranti Sea Spray Mk 3 radar and Racal ESM. Weapons: 4 BAe Sea Skua missiles. Mk 46 torpedo (in ASW version).

SUPER LYNX   11/1989, Westland

Numbers/Type: 11 Aerospatiale SA 316B/SA 319B Alouette III.
Operational speed: 113 kts *(210 km/h).*
Service ceiling: 10 500 ft *(3200 m).*
Range: 290 nm *(540 km).*
Role/Weapon systems: Marine support helicopter; operated by RoK Marine Corps. Sensors: None. Weapons: Unarmed.

ALOUETTE III   1990

LAND-BASED MARITIME AIRCRAFT (FRONT LINE)

Note: 10 UH-60 to replace UH-1H starting in 1993.

Numbers/Type: 14 Grumman S-2A/F Tracker.
Operational speed: 130 kts *(241 km/h).*
Service ceiling: 25 000 ft *(7620 m).*
Range: 1350 nm *(2500 km).*
Role/Weapon systems: Maritime surveillance and limited ASW operations; coastal surveillance and EEZ patrol. Sensors: Search radar, ECM. Weapons: ASW; torpedoes, depth bombs and mines. ASV; underwing 127 mm rockets.

Numbers/Type: 8 Lockheed P-3C Orion.
Operational speed: 411 kts *(761 km/h).*
Service ceiling: 28 300 ft *(8625 m).*
Range: 4000 nm *(7410 km).*
Role/Weapon systems: Maritime patrol aircraft ordered in December 1990 for delivery in 1995. This is the Update III version. Sensors: To include AAS-36 IR. Weapons: To include Harpoon ASM if approved.

LIGHT FORCES

8 TACOMA PSMM 5 TYPE (FAST ATTACK CRAFT—MISSILE)

Name	No	Builders	Commissioned
PAE KU 52	PGM 582 (ex-PGM 352)	Tacoma Boatbuilding Co, Tacoma, Wash.	14 Mar 1975
PAE KU 53	PGM 583 (ex-PGM 353)	Tacoma Boatbuilding Co, Tacoma, Wash.	14 Mar 1975
PAE KU 55	PGM 585 (ex-PGM 355)	Tacoma Boatbuilding Co, Tacoma, Wash.	1 Feb 1976
PAE KU 56	PGM 586 (ex-PGM 356)	Korea Tacoma Marine	1 Feb 1976
PAE KU 57	PGM 587 (ex-PGM 357)	Korea Tacoma Marine	1977
PAE KU 58	PGM 588 (ex-PGM 358)	Korea Tacoma Marine	1977
PAE KU 59	PGM 589 (ex-PGM 359)	Korea Tacoma Marine	1977
PAE KU 61	PGM 591 (ex-PGM 361)	Korea Tacoma Marine	1978

Displacement, tons: 268 full load
Dimensions, feet (metres): 176.2 × 23.9 × 9.5 *(53.7 × 7.3 × 2.9)*
Main machinery: 6 Avco Lycoming TF-35 gas turbines; 16 800 hp *(12.53 MW);* 2 shafts; cp props
Speed, knots: 40+. **Range, miles:** 2400 at 18 kts
Complement: 32 (5 officers)

Missiles: SSM: 2 GDC Standard ARM launchers (PGM 352-355); anti-radiation homing to 35 km *(18.9 nm)* at 2 Mach; warhead 98 kg; 2 reloads.
4 McDonnell Douglas Harpoon (PGM 356-361); active radar homing to 130 km *(70 nm)* at 0.9 Mach; warhead 227 kg.
Guns: 1 OTO Melara 3 in *(76 mm)*/62 compact (PGM 356-361); 85° elevation; 85 rounds/minute to 16 km *(8.6 nm)* anti-surface; 12 km *(6.5 nm)* anti-aircraft; weight of shell 6 kg.
1 USN 3 in *(76 mm)*/50 Mk 34 (PGM 352-355); 85° elevation; 50 rounds/minute to 12.8 km *(6.9 nm);* weight of shell 6 kg.
2 Emerson Electric 30 mm (twin); 80° elevation; 1200 rounds/minute combined to 6 km *(3.2 nm);* weight of shell 0.35 kg.
2 Browning 12.7 mm MGs.
Countermeasures: Decoys: Loral RBOC 4-barrelled Mk 33 launchers; range 4 km *(2.2 nm).*
Fire control: Mk 63 GFCS (PGM 352-355). Honeywell H 930 Mod 0 (PGM 356-361).
Radars: Air search: SPS 58; E/F band.
Surface search: Marconi Canada HC 75; I band; range 88 km *(48 nm).*
Fire control: Western Electric SPG 50 or Westinghouse W-120; I/J band.

Programmes: Tacoma design designation was PSMM for multi-mission patrol ship.
Structure: Aluminium hulls, based on the US Navy's Asheville (PG 84) design, but appearance of Korean-built ships' superstructure differs.
Operational: The six TF 35 gas turbines turn two propeller shafts; the Asheville class ships have combination gas turbine-diesel power plants. In the South Korean units one, two, or three turbines can be selected to provide each shaft with a variety of power settings.

PAE KU 53 (with Standard) (old number)   3/1987, G Jacobs

PAE KU 58 (with Harpoon) (old number)   3/1987, G Jacobs

1 Ex-US ASHEVILLE CLASS (FAST ATTACK CRAFT—MISSILE)

Name	No	Builders	Commissioned
PAE KU 51 (ex-USS *Benicia* PG 96)	PGM 581 (ex-PGM 351, ex-PGM 11, ex-PGM 101)	Tacoma Boatbuilding Co, Tacoma, Wash.	25 Apr 1970

Displacement, tons: 225 standard; 245 full load
Dimensions, feet (metres): 164.5 × 23.9 × 9.5 *(50.1 × 7.3 × 2.9)*
Main machinery: CODOG; 1 GE LM-1500 gas turbine; 13 300 hp *(9.92 MW);* 2 Cummins VT12-875M diesels; 1450 hp *(1.08 MW);* 2 shafts
Speed, knots: 40; 16 diesels. **Range, miles:** 1700 at 16 kts
Complement: 42 (5 officers)
Missiles: SSM: 2 GDC Standard ARM launchers; anti-radiation homing to 35 km *(18.9 nm)* at 2 Mach; warhead 98 kg; 2 reloads.
Guns: 1 USN 3 in *(76 mm)*/50 Mk 34; 85° elevation; 50 rounds/minute to 12.8 km *(6.9 nm);* weight of shell 6 kg.
1 Bofors 40 mm/60 Mk 3; 80° elevation; 120 rounds/minute to 10 km *(5.4 nm)* anti-surface; 3 km *(1.6 nm)* anti-aircraft; weight of shell 0.89 kg.
4 Browning 12.7 mm MGs.
Fire control: USN Mk 63 Mod 29 for 76 mm gunnery.
Radars: Surface search: Raytheon 1645; I/J band.
Fire control: Western Electric SPG 50; I/J band.
IFF: APX 72.

Comment: Former US Asheville class patrol gunboat. Launched 20 December 1969; transferred on lease 15 October 1971 and arrived in South Korea in January 1972. Probably paid off in 1991.

PAE KU 51 (old number)   9/1988

2 SOUTH KOREAN-BUILT WILDCAT CLASS
(FAST ATTACK CRAFT—MISSILE)

PKM 271-272

Displacement, tons: 140 full load
Dimensions, feet (metres): 108.9 × 22.6 × 7.9 *(33.9 × 6.9 × 2.4)*
Main machinery: 2 MTU MB 20V 672 TY90 (PKM 271); 5800 hp(m) *(4.26 MW)* sustained; 2 shafts
3 MTU MD 16V 538 TB90 diesels (PKM 272); 9000 hp(m) *(6.61 MW)* sustained; 3 shafts
Speed, knots: 40. **Range, miles:** 800 at 17 kts
Complement: 29 (5 officers)
Missiles: SSM: 2 Aerospatiale MM 38 Exocet; inertial cruise; active radar homing to 42 km *(23 nm)* at 0.9 Mach; warhead 165 kg; sea-skimmer.
Guns: 2 Bofors 40 mm/60; 80° elevation; 120 rounds/minute to 10 km *(5.4 nm)* anti-surface; 3 km *(1.6 nm)* anti-aircraft; weight of shell 0.89 kg.
2 Browning 12.7 mm MGs.
Radars: Surface search: Raytheon 1645; I band.
IFF: UPX 17.

Comment: Built by Korea Tacoma, Masan 1971-72. Steel hull and aluminium superstructure.

WILDCAT 12/1985, G Jacobs

8 SEA DOLPHIN CLASS (FAST ATTACK CRAFT—PATROL)

PKM 200 series

Displacement, tons: 170 full load
Dimensions, feet (metres): 121.4 × 22.6 × 5.6 *(37 × 6.9 × 1.7)*
Main machinery: 2 MTU MD 16V 538 TB90 diesels; 6000 hp(m) *(4.41 MW)* sustained; 2 shafts
Speed, knots: 37. **Range, miles:** 600 at 20 kts
Complement: 31
Guns: 2 Emerson Electric 30 mm (twin). 2 GE/GD 20 mm Vulcan Gatlings. 2 Browning 12.7 mm (twin) MGs.
Fire control: Optical director.
Radars: Surface search: I band.

Comment: Built by Korea SEC, Korea Tacoma and Daewoo. First laid down 1978. The class has some gun armament variations and some minor superstructure changes in later ships of the class.

SEA DOLPHIN 292 1991, Daewoo

7 SEA HAWK and SEA FOX CLASSES
(FAST ATTACK CRAFT—PATROL)

151-189 series

Displacement, tons: 80 full load
Dimensions, feet (metres): 84.3 × 17.7 × 4.9 *(25.7 × 5.4 × 1.5)*
Main machinery: 2 MTU MD 16V 538 TB90 diesels; 6000 hp(m) *(4.41 MW)* sustained; 2 shafts
Speed, knots: 41. **Range, miles:** 600 at 17 kts; 500 at 20 kts
Complement: 15 (6 officers)
Guns: 4 Oerlikon 20 mm (2 twin). 4 Browning 12.7 mm (2 twin) MGs.

Comment: Built by Korea Tacoma Marine Industries Ltd, Korea SEC and Hyundai between 1975-1978. The term Schoolboy class was also applied to this class. Ordered in three batches: 1973, 1976, 1978. Armament varies amongst boats. Some have a US Bofors 40 mm Mk 3 forward while later boats have a Korean 40 mm mount forward. Some have two MM 38 Exocet. At least even paid off in 1991/92.

SEA HAWK 1986, Hyundai

1 SWATH TYPE (COASTAL PATROL CRAFT)

Displacement, tons: 310 full load
Dimensions, feet (metres): 113.2 × 49.2 × 11.5 *(34.5 × 15 × 3.5)*
Main machinery: 1 MTU 16V 396 TE74L diesel; 2680 hp(m) *(2 MW)*; 1 shaft
Speed, knots: 20. **Range, miles:** 600 at 16 kts
Complement: 25

Comment: Experimental design built by Hyundai. Laid down June 1992, launched November 1992 and completed April 1993.

MINE WARFARE FORCES

Note: Project definition for a minelayer of 100 m length is to complete in late 1993. First of class to be in service by 1996.

3 + 5 SWALLOW CLASS (MINEHUNTERS)

KAN KEONG 561 562 563

Displacement, tons: 470 standard; 520 full load
Dimensions, feet (metres): 164 × 27.2 × 8.6 *(50 × 8.3 × 2.6)*
Main machinery: 2 MTU diesels; 2040 hp(m) *(1.5 MW)*; 2 shafts; bow thruster
Speed, knots: 15. **Range, miles:** 2000 at 10 kts
Complement: 48
Guns: 1 Oerlikon 20 mm.
Countermeasures: MCM: 2 Gaymarine Pluto remote-control submersibles.
Radars: Navigation: Racal Decca; I band.
Sonars: Plessey/MUSL 193M Mod I; minehunting; high frequency.

Comment: Built to a design similar to the Italian Lerici class by Kangnam Shipyard. GRP hull. Decca/Racal plotting system. First delivered at the end of 1986 for trials. Two more with some modifications ordered in 1987, three more in 1989 and two more in 1991. Could lead to a class of 18. The first six should be in service by 1996.

KAN KEONG 1990, Kangnam Corp

3 Ex-US MSC 268 and 5 289 CLASSES
(MINESWEEPERS—COASTAL)

Name	No	Builders	Commissioned
KUM SAN (ex-US *MSC 284*)*	MSC 551	Harbour Boat Building, Terminal Island, Calif	June 1959
KO HUNG (ex-US *MSC 285*)*	MSC 552	Harbour Boat Building, Terminal Island, Calif	Aug 1959
KUM KOK (ex-US *MSC 286*)*	MSC 553	Harbour Boat Building, Terminal Island, Calif	Oct 1959
NAM YANG (ex-US *MSC 295*)	MSC 555	Peterson Builders, Wisconsin	Aug 1963
HA DONG (ex-US *MSC 296*)	MSC 556	Peterson Builders, Wisconsin	Nov 1963
SAM KOK (ex-US *MSC 316*)	MSC 557	Peterson Builders, Wisconsin	July 1968
YONG DONG (ex-US *MSC 320*)	MSC 558	Peterson Builders, Wisconsin	Oct 1975
OK CHEON (ex-US *MSC 321*)	MSC 559	Peterson Builders, Wisconsin	Oct 1975

* MSC 268 class

Displacement, tons: 320 light; 370 full load
  (268 class) 315 light; 380 full load (289 class)
Dimensions, feet (metres): 141.1 × 26.2 × 8.5 *(43 × 8 × 2.6)* (268 class)
  145.4 × 27.2 × 12 (screws) *(44.3 × 8.3 × 2.7)* (289 class)
Main machinery: 2 GM 8-268A diesels; 880 hp *(656 kW)* (268 class); 2 shafts
  4 GM 6-71 diesels; 696 hp *(519 kW)* sustained (289 class); 2 shafts
Speed, knots: 14. **Range, miles:** 2500 at 14 kts
Complement: 40
Guns: 2 Oerlikon 20 mm (twin) (268 class); 2 Oerlikon 20 mm (289 class).
  3 Browning 12.7 mm MGs.
Radars: Navigation: Decca 45; I band.
Sonars: General Electric UQS 1 or Thomson Sintra; hull-mounted; minehunting; high frequency.

Comment: Built by the USA specifically for transfer under the Military Aid Programme with wooden hulls and non-magnetic metal fittings. MSC 551 transferred to South Korea in June 1959, MSC 552 in September 1959, MSC 553 in November 1959, MSC 555 in September 1963, MSC 556 in November 1963, MSC 557 in July 1968, MSC 558 and 559 on 2 October 1975. The last four may have been retrofitted with Thomson Sintra mine detection sonars. Planned to pay off as Swallow class commission.

KO HUNG 1982, G Jacobs

AMPHIBIOUS FORCES

0 + 2 LANDING SHIP TANKS (LST)

Displacement, tons: 4200 full load
Dimensions, feet (metres): 350.7 × 50.2 × 9.8 *(106.9 × 15.3 × 3)*
Main machinery: 2 SEMT-Pielstick 16 PA6 V 280; 12 800 hp(m) *(9.41 MW)* sustained; 2 shafts
Speed, knots: 16. Range, miles: 10 000 at 12 kts
Complement: 120 (14 officers)
Military lift: 700 tons vehicles; 200 tons landing craft
Guns: 4 Breda 40 mm/70 (2 twin). 2 Oerlikon 20 mm.
Fire control: Optronic director.
Radars: Navigation: I band.
Helicopters: Platform for 1 medium.

Comment: Ordered in June 1990 from Korea Tacoma, Masan. Characteristics listed are for the Hyundai HDL-4000. First of class sea trials are scheduled for late 1993.

7 Ex-US 1-510 and 511-1152 CLASSES (LSTs)

Name	No	Commissioned
UN BONG (ex-USS *LST 1010*)	LST 671	25 Apr 1944
BI BONG (ex-USS *LST 218*)	LST 673	12 Aug 1943
KAE BONG (ex-USS *Berkshire County* LST 288)	LST 675	20 Dec 1943
WEE BONG (ex-USS *Johnson County* LST 849)	LST 676	16 Jan 1945
SU YONG (ex-USS *Kane County* LST 853)	LST 677	11 Dec 1945
BUK HAN (ex-USS *Lynn County* LST 900)	LST 678	28 Dec 1944
HWA SAN (ex-USS *Pender County* LST 1080)	LST 679	29 May 1945

Displacement, tons: 1653 standard; 2366 beaching; 4080 full load
Dimensions, feet (metres): 328 × 50 × 14 (screws) *(100 × 15.2 × 4.3)*
Main machinery: 2 GM 12-567A diesels; 1800 hp *(1.34 MW)*; 2 shafts
Speed, knots: 11.6
Complement: 80
Military lift: 2100 tons including 20 tanks and 2 LCVPs
Guns: 8 Bofors 40 mm (2 twin, 1 quad). 2 Oerlikon 20 mm.

Comment: Former US Navy tank landing ships. Transferred to South Korea between 1955 and 1959. All purchased 15 November 1974.

BUK HAN *1982, G Jacobs*

8 Ex-US LSM 1 CLASS

Name	No
UL RUNG (ex-USS *LSM 17*)	LSM 652
—	LSM 653
KO MUN (ex-USS *LSM 30*)	LSM 655
PI AN (ex-USS *LSM 96*)	LSM 656
WOL MI (ex-USS *LSM 57*)	LSM 657
KI RIN (ex-USS *LSM 19*)	LSM 658
NUNG RA (ex-USS *LSM 84*)	LSM 659
SIN MI (ex-USS *LSM 316*)	LSM 661

Displacement, tons: 743 beaching; 1095 full load
Dimensions, feet (metres): 203.5 × 34.6 × 8.2 *(62 × 10.5 × 2.5)*
Main machinery: 2 Fairbanks-Morse 38D8-1/8-10 diesels; 3540 hp *(2.64 MW)* sustained; 2 shafts
Speed, knots: 13
Complement: 75
Guns: 2 Bofors 40 mm (twin). 4 Oerlikon 20 mm.

Comment: Former US Navy medium landing ships, built 1944-45. Transferred in 1956. All purchased 15 November 1974. Arrangement of 20 mm guns differs; some ships have two single mounts adjacent to forward 40 mm mount on forecastle; other 20 mm guns along sides of cargo well.

PI AN *3/1987, G Jacobs*

6 FURSEAL CLASS (LCU)

MULKAE 72, 73, 75, 76, 77, 78

Displacement, tons: 415 full load
Dimensions, feet (metres): 134.8 × 28.8 × 5.9 *(41.1 × 8.8 × 1.8)*
Main machinery: 2 GM 6-71 diesels; 348 hp *(260 kW)* sustained; 2 Kort nozzles
Speed, knots: 13. Range, miles: 560 at 11 kts
Complement: 14 (2 officers)
Military lift: 200 tons including battle tanks
Guns: 2 Oerlikon 20 mm.

Comment: In service 1979-81. Built by Korea Tacoma Marine Industries Ltd based on a US design.

FURSEAL 76 *1987, Korea Tacoma*

10 Ex-US LCM 8 CLASS

Displacement, tons: 115 full load
Dimensions, feet (metres): 74.5 × 21 × 4.6 *(22.7 × 6.4 × 1.4)*
Main machinery: 4 GM 6-71 diesels; 696 hp *(519 kW)* sustained; 2 shafts
Speed, knots: 11

Comment: Previously US Army craft. Transferred 1978.

LCVP TYPES

Comment: A considerable number of US type built of GRP in South Korea. In addition there are plans to build up to 30 small hovercraft for special forces.

SERVICE FORCES

Notes: 1. The South Korean Navy also operates nine small harbour tugs (designated YTLs). These include one ex-US Navy craft (YTL 550) and five ex-US Army craft. There are also approximately 35 small service craft in addition to the YO-type tankers listed and the harbour tugs. These craft include oper lighters, floating cranes, diving tenders, dredgers, ferries, non self-propelled fuel barges, pontoon barges, and sludge removal barges; most are former US Navy craft.
2. The ex-US *Cavallaro* high speed transport (APD 822) was in service in 1992.

1 + (1) CHUN JEE CLASS (HDA 8000) (AOE)

Name	No	Builders	Commissioned
CHUN JEE	AO 57	Hyundai, Ulsan	Dec 1990

Displacement, tons: 7500 full load
Dimensions, feet (metres): 426.5 × 58.4 × 21.3 *(130 × 17.8 × 6.5)*
Main machinery: 2 SEMT-Pielstick 12 PC2.5 V 400; 15 650 hp(m) *(11.5 MW)* sustained; 2 shafts
Speed, knots: 20. Range, miles: 4500 at 15 kts
Cargo capacity: 4200 tons liquids; 450 tons solids
Guns: 4 Emerlec 30 mm (2 twin). 2 GE/GD 20 mm Vulcan Gatlings.
Radars: Navigation: I band.
Helicopters: 1 medium.

Comment: Laid down September 1989 and launched in May 1990. Second of class planned in due course. Underway replenishment stations on both sides. Helicopter for Vertrep. Called a logistic support ship. There are three 6 ton lifts.

CHUN JEE *1991, Hyundai*

Service forces — Hydrographic service / KOREA (REPUBLIC)   389

0 + 1 SUBMARINE SALVAGE SHIP

Displacement, tons: 4300 full load
Dimensions, feet (metres): 337.3 × 53.8 × 15.1 *(102.8 × 16.4 × 4.6)*
Main machinery: Diesel-electric; 4 MAN Burmeister & Wain 16V 28/32 diesels; 11 800 hp(m) *(8.67 MW)*; 2 motors; 5440 hp(m) *(4 MW)*; 2 shafts; cp props; 3 bow and 2 stern thrusters
Speed, knots: 18. **Range, miles:** 9500 at 15 kts
Complement: 130
Guns: 1 GE/GD 20 mm Vulcan Gatling. 6—12.7 mm MGs.
Radars: Navigation: I band.
Sonars: Hull-mounted; active search; high frequency.
Helicopters: Platform for 1 light.

Comment: Ordered in 1992 from Daewoo, Okpo. To be laid down in 1993 for completion in 1995. A multi-purpose salvage and rescue ship which carries a 300 m ROV as well as two LCVPs on davits plus a diving bell for nine men and a decompression chamber. Two large hydraulic cranes fore and aft and one towing winch. There are also two salvage ships which belong to the Coast Guard.

DW 4000R (model)   *1992, Daewoo*

2 Ex-US TONTI CLASS (GASOLINE TANKERS)

55 (ex-*Tarland*, ex-USNS *Rincon* T-AOG 77)
56 (ex-*Racoon Bend*, ex-USNS *Petaluma* T-AOG 79)

Displacement, tons: 2100 light; 6047 full load
Dimensions, feet (metres): 325.2 × 48.2 × 19.1 *(99.1 × 14.7 × 5.8)*
Main machinery: 2 Nordberg diesels; 1400 hp *(1.04 MW)*; 1 shaft
Speed, knots: 10. **Range, miles:** 6000 at 10 kts
Complement: 41
Cargo capacity: 31 284 barrels light fuel

Comment: Launched as merchant tankers 9 August 1945 and 5 January 1945 respectively. Transferred 21 February 1982 on lease. Probably armed.

2 Ex-US 174-ft YO TYPE (HARBOUR TANKERS)

KU YONG (ex-USS *YO 118*) YO 1   — (ex-USS *YO 179*) YO 6

Displacement, tons: 1400 full load
Dimensions, feet (metres): 174 × 32 × 13.1 *(53 × 9.8 × 4)*
Main machinery: 1 Union diesel; 560 hp *(418 kW)*; 1 shaft
Speed, knots: 7 kts
Complement: 36
Cargo capacity: 900 tons
Guns: Several 20 mm.

Comment: Former US Navy self-propelled fuel barges. Transferred to South Korea on 3 December 1946 and 13 September 1971, respectively.

2 Ex-US DIVER CLASS (SALVAGE SHIPS)

Name	No	Builders	Launched
GUMI (ex-USS *Deliver* ARS 23)	ARS 26	Basalt Rock Co, Napa, Calif.	18 July 1944
CHANG WON (ex-USS *Grasp* ARS 24)	ARS 25	Basalt Rock Co, Napa, Calif.	22 Aug 1944

Displacement, tons: 1530 standard; 1970 full load
Dimensions, feet (metres): 213.5 × 41 × 13 *(65.1 × 12.5 × 4)*
Main machinery: Diesel-electric; 4 Cooper Bessemer GSB8 diesels; 3420 hp *(2.55 MW)*; 4 generators; 2 motors; 3060 hp *(2.28 MW)*; 2 shafts
Speed, knots: 14.8. **Range, miles:** 9000 at 14 kts
Complement: 83
Guns: 2 Oerlikon 20 mm.
Radars: Surface search: Sperry SPS 53; I/J band.
IFF: UPX 12.

Comment: ARS 26 purchased 15 August 1979 and ARS 25 on 31 March 1978. Operated by Service Squadron 51. Equipped for salvage, diver support and towage.

CHANG WON   *1982, G Jacobs*

2 Ex-US SOTOYOMO CLASS (TUGS)

Name	No	Builders	Launched
YONG MUN (ex-USS *Keosanqua* ATA 198)	31 (ex-*ATA 2*)	Levingston S B Co, Orange, Texas	17 Jan 1945
DO BONG (ex-USS *Pinola* ATA 206)	32 (ex-*ATA (S) 3*)	Gulfport Boiler & Welding Works, Port Arthur, Texas	14 Dec 1944

Displacement, tons: 534 standard; 860 full load
Dimensions, feet (metres): 143 × 33.9 × 13 *(43.6 × 10.3 × 4)*
Main machinery: Diesel-electric; 2 GM 12-278A diesels; 2200 hp *(1.64 MW)*; 2 generators; 1 motor; 1500 hp *(1.12 MW)*; 1 shaft
Speed, knots: 13
Complement: 45
Guns: 1 USN 3 in *(76 mm)*/50. 4 Oerlikon 20 mm.

Comment: Former US Navy auxiliary ocean tugs. Both transferred to South Korea in February 1962. 32 modified for salvage work.

DO BONG   *1985, G Jacobs*

HYDROGRAPHIC SERVICE

Note: The listed craft are operated by the South Korean Hydrographic Service which is responsible to the Ministry of Transport.

7 SURVEY CRAFT

Name	Displacement, tons	Launched	Complement
PUSAN 801	494	1980	15 (8 officers)
PUSAN 802	240	1982	9 (5 officers)
PUSAN 803	125	1979	8 (5 officers)
PUSAN 805	156	1983	5 (5 officers)
CH'UNGNAM 821	65	1981	5 (3 officers)
KANGWON 831	65	1981	5 (3 officers)
PUSAN 806	22	1987	2 (2 officers)

PUSAN 801   *1990, Ships of the World*

390 KOREA (REPUBLIC) / Coast guard

COAST GUARD

Note: The South Korean Coast Guard operates a number of small ships and several hundred craft including tugs and rescue craft.

3 MAZINGER CLASS

PC 1001–PC 1003

Displacement, tons: 1200 full load
Dimensions, feet (metres): 264.1 × 32.2 × 11.5 *(80.5 × 9.8 × 3.2)*
Main machinery: 2 Niigata diesels; 10 560 hp(m) *(7.76 MW)*; 2 shafts
Speed, knots: 22. Range, miles: 7000 at 18 kts
Complement: 69 (11 officers)
Guns: 1 Bofors 40 mm/70. 4 Oerlikon 20 mm (2 twin).

Comment: Ordered 7 November 1980 from Korea Tacoma. *PC 1001* delivered 29 November 1981. All welded mild steel construction. Used for offshore surveillance and general coast guard duties. *PC 1001* is reported to be the Coast Guard Command ship. Only three of this class were completed.

MAZINGER *1987, Korea Tacoma*

1 HAN KANG CLASS

HAN KANG PC 1005

Displacement, tons: 1180 full load
Dimensions, feet (metres): 289.7 × 32.8 × 9.5 *(88.3 × 10 × 2.9)*
Main machinery: CODOG; 1 GE LM 2500 gas turbine; 26 820 hp *(20 MW)* sustained; 2 MTU 12V 956 TB82 diesels; 6260 hp(m) *(4.6 MW)* sustained; 3 shafts
Speed, knots: 32. Range, miles: 4000 at 15 kts
Complement: 72 (11 officers)
Guns: 1 OTO Melara 76/62 compact. 1 Bofors 40 mm/70. 2 GE/GD 20 mm Vulcan Gatlings.
Fire control: Signaal LIOD optronic director.
Radars: Surface search: Raytheon SPS 64(V); I band.
Fire control: Signaal WM 28; I/J band.

Comment: Built between May 1984 and December 1985 by Daewoo. Same hull as Po Hang class but much more lightly armed. Only one of the class was completed.

HAN KANG *1989, Ships of the World*

1 + 1 HYUNDAI TYPE

402

Displacement, tons: 430 full load
Dimensions, feet (metres): 176.2 × 24.3 × 7.9 *(53.7 × 7.4 × 2.4)*
Main machinery: 2 MTU 16V 396 TB83 diesels; 1990 hp(m) *(1.49 MW)*; 2 shafts; cp props
Speed, knots: 19. Range, miles: 2100 at 17 kts
Complement: 14
Guns: 1 GD/GE 20 mm Vulcan Gatling. 4—12.7 mm MGs.

Comment: Built by Hyundai. First of class delivered in December 1991, second to complete in 1993. Multi-purpose patrol craft.

402 *1992, Hyundai*

6 SEA DRAGON/WHALE CLASS

FC 501, 502, 503, 505, 506, 507

Displacement, tons: 640 full load
Dimensions, feet (metres): 200.1 × 26.2 × 8.9 *(61 × 8 × 2.7)*
Main machinery: 2 MTU diesels; 9000 hp(m) *(6.61 MW)*; 2 shafts
Speed, knots: 24. Range, miles: 6000 at 15 kts
Complement: 40 (7 officers)
Guns: 1 Bofors 40 mm. 2 Oerlikon 20 mm. 2 Browning 12.7 mm MGs.
Radars: Navigation: Two sets.

Comment: Ordered in 1980 from Korea SEC and Korea Tacoma. Fitted with SATNAV. Welded steel hull. Armament varies between ships, one 76 mm gun can be mounted on the forecastle.

SEA DRAGON 507 *1987, Korea Tacoma*

22 SEA WOLF/SHARK CLASS

Displacement, tons: 310 full load
Dimensions, feet (metres): 158.1 × 23.3 × 8.2 *(48.2 × 7.1 × 2.5)*
Main machinery: 2 diesels; 7320 hp(m) *(5.38 MW)*; 2 shafts
Speed, knots: 25. Range, miles: 2400 at 15 kts
Complement: 35 (3 officers)
Guns: 4 Oerlikon 20 mm (2 twin or 1 twin, 2 single). Some have a twin Bofors 40 mm/70 vice the twin Oerlikon. 2 Browning 12.7 mm MGs.

Comment: First four ordered in 1979-80 from Korea SEC (Sea Shark), Hyundai and Korea Tacoma (Sea Wolf). Programme terminated in 1988. Pennant numbers in 200 series up to 277.

SEA WOLF 251 *1987, Korea Tacoma*

2 BUKHANSAN CLASS

BUKHANSAN 278   CHULMASAN 279

Displacement, tons: 380 full load
Dimensions, feet (metres): 174.2 × 24 × 7.2 *(53.1 × 7.3 × 2.2)*
Main machinery: 2 MTU diesels; 8300 hp(m) *(6.1 MW)* sustained; 2 shafts
Speed, knots: 28. Range, miles: 2500 at 15 kts
Complement: 35 (3 officers)
Guns: 2 Breda 40 mm/70 (twin). 1 GE/GD 20 mm Vulcan Gatling. 2—12.7 mm MGs.
Fire control: Radamec optronic director.
Radars: Surface search: I band.

Comment: Follow on to Sea Wolf class developed by Hyundai in 1987. Ordered in 1988 from Hyundai and Daewoo respectively. Both in service in 1989.

CHULMASAN *1989, Daewoo*

18 SEAGULL CLASS

Displacement, tons: 80 full load
Dimensions, feet (metres): 78.7 × 18 × 6.6 *(24 × 5.5 × 2)*
Main machinery: 2 diesels; 3700 hp(m) *(2.72 MW)*; 2 shafts
Speed, knots: 30. Range, miles: 950 at 20 kts
Complement: 18
Guns: 4 Oerlikon 20 mm.

Comment: First ordered in 1971 and 1972 from Korea SEC. Some sold to Kuwait.

INSHORE PATROL CRAFT

Displacement, tons: 47
Dimensions, feet (metres): 69.9 × 17.7 × 4.6 *(21.3 × 5.4 × 1.4)*
Main machinery: 2 diesels; 1800 hp(m) *(1.32 MW)*; 2 shafts
Speed, knots: 22. **Range, miles:** 400 at 12 kts
Complement: 11
Guns: 3—12.7 mm MGs.

Comment: Details are for the latest design of patrol craft. There are large numbers of this type of vessel used for inshore patrol work.

IPC *1991, Kangnam Corp*

SUPPORT SHIPS

1 SALVAGE SHIP

Name	No	Builders	Commissioned
TAE PUNG YANG	3001	Hyundai, Ulsan	Dec 1992

Displacement, tons: 3200 standard; 4300 full load
Dimensions, feet (metres): 343.5 × 49.2 × 17 *(104.7 × 15 × 5.2)*
Main machinery: 4 Ssangyoung MAN Burmeister & Wain 16V 28/32 diesels; 4800 hp(m) *(3.53 MW)*; 2 shafts; cp props; bow and stern thrusters
Speed, knots: 21. **Range, miles:** 8500 at 15 kts
Complement: 121
Guns: 1 GD/GE 20 mm Vulcan Gatling.
Helicopters: 1 light.

Comment: Laid down February 1991, launched October 1991. Has a helicopter deck and hangar, an ROV capable of diving to 300 m and a firefighting capability. Dynamic positioning system. Operates for the Coast Guard.

TAE PUNG YANG *12/1992, Hyundai*

1 SALVAGE SHIP

Name	No	Builders	Commissioned
JACMIN	1501	Daewoo, Okpo	28 Dec 1992

Displacement, tons: 2072 full load
Dimensions, feet (metres): 254.6 × 44.3 × 13.8 *(77.6 × 13.5 × 4.2)*
Main machinery: 2 MTU diesels; 8000 hp(m) *(5.88 MW)*; 2 shafts
Speed, knots: 18. **Range, miles:** 4500 at 12 kts
Complement: 92
Guns: 1 GD/GE 20 mm Vulcan Gatling.

Comment: Ordered in 1990. Fitted with diving equipment and has a four point mooring system.

JACMIN *1992, Daewoo*

KUWAIT

Headquarters' Appointment

Commander of the Navy:
  Commodore Ahmed Yousuf Al Mulla

Iraq Invasion

In August 1990 Iraq invaded Kuwait. All Naval and Coast Guard ships and aircraft were captured with the exception of two fast attack craft. Subsequently the Iraqi Navy used the captured craft in Operation Desert Storm and most were either sunk or damaged by Allied Forces. A few are still in service with Iraq.

New Construction Plan

A proposed ten year reconstruction plan includes two corvettes and two 34 m landing craft to be built in 1994. Subsequent orders may include three minehunters, two diving support ships and a training vessel. Eight large patrol craft are expected to be ordered in 1993, probably from France and at least four possibly to the Combattante IV design, if the intention projected in August 1992 is confirmed.

Bases

Navy: Ras Al Qalayah
Coast Guard: Shuwaikh, Umm Al-Hainan

Mercantile Marine

Lloyd's Register of Shipping:
  209 vessels of 1 910 180 tons gross

DELETIONS (Captured by Iraq in August 1990)

Fast Attack Craft (Missile):	5 Lürssen TNC 45 and 1 Lürssen FPB 57
Patrol Craft:	5 Seagull, 15 Thornycroft, 1 Halter Marine, 7 Magnum Sedan
Landing Craft:	4 Loadmasters, 6 Vosper Singapore Type
Miscellaneous:	10 tugs and launches
Aircraft:	12 Super Puma
Customs:	3 Azimut launches

PATROL FORCES

2 + 2 OPV 310 CLASS (LARGE PATROL CRAFT)

Name	No	Builders	Commissioned
INTTISAR	P 301	Australian Shipbuilding Industries	20 Jan 1993
AMAN	P 302	Australian Shipbuilding Industries	20 Jan 1993
—	P 303	Australian Shipbuilding Industries	June 1993
—	P 304	Australian Shipbuilding Industries	June 1993

Displacement, tons: 150 full load
Dimensions, feet (metres): 103.3 oa; 88.9 wl × 21.3 × 6.6 *(31.5; 27.1 × 6.5 × 2)*
Main machinery: 2 MTU 16V 396 TB94 diesels; 5800 hp(m) *(4.26 MW)* sustained; 2 shafts; 1 MTU 8V 183 TE62 diesel; 750 hp(m) *(550 kW)* maximum; 1 Hamilton 422 waterjet
Speed, knots: 28. **Range, miles:** 300 at 28 kts
Complement: 11 (3 officers)
Guns: 1 Oerlikon 20 mm. 1—12.7 mm MG
Radars: Surface search.

Comment: First two ordered from Australian Shipbuilding Industries in 1991. Second pair ordered in July 1992. Steel hulls, aluminium superstructure. The third engine drives a small waterjet to provide a loiter capability.

AMAN *1992, Australian Shipbuilding Industries*

1 TNC 45 TYPE (FAST ATTACK CRAFT—MISSILE)

AL SANBOUK P 4505

Displacement, tons: 255 full load
Dimensions, feet (metres): 147.3 × 23 × 7.5 *(44.9 × 7 × 2.3)*
Main machinery: 4 MTU 16V 538 TB92 diesels; 13 640 hp(m) *(10 MW)* sustained; 4 shafts
Speed, knots: 41. **Range, miles:** 1800 at 16 kts
Complement: 35 (5 officers)

Missiles: SSM: 4 Aerospatiale MM 40 Exocet; inertial cruise; active radar homing to 70 km *(40 nm)* at 0.9 Mach; warhead 165 kg; sea-skimmer.
Guns: 1 OTO Melara 3 in *(76 mm)*/62 compact; 85° elevation; 85 rounds/minute to 16 km *(8.6 nm)* anti-surface; 12 km *(6.5 nm)* anti-aircraft; weight of shell 6 kg.
2 Breda 40 mm/70 (twin); 85° elevation; 300 rounds/minute to 12.5 km *(6.6 nm)*; weight of shell 0.96 kg.
Countermeasures: Decoys: CSEE Dagaie trainable mounting; automatic dispenser; IR flares and chaff; H/J band.
ESM: Racal Cutlass; radar intercept.
Fire control: PEAB 9LV 228 system. CSEE Lynx optical sight.
Radars: Surface search: Decca TM 1226C; I band.
Fire control: Philips 9LV 200; J band.

Programmes: Six ordered from Lürssen in 1980 and delivered in 1983/84.
Operational: *Al Sanbouk* escaped to Bahrain when the Iraqis invaded in August 1990, but the rest of this class were taken over by the Iraqi Navy, and either sunk or severely damaged by Allied forces in February 1991.

TNC 45 Type   *1984, G Koop*

12 SIMMONEAU STANDARD 12 CLASS
(INSHORE PATROL CRAFT)

Displacement, tons: 10 full load
Dimensions, feet (metres): 45.9 × 12.5 × 2.3 *(14 × 3.8 × 0.7)*
Main machinery: 2 Caterpillar 3208 diesels; 850 hp(m) *(625 kW)*; 2 shafts
Speed, knots: 40
Complement: 4
Guns: 1—12.7 mm MG. 1—7.62 mm MG.
Radars: Surface search: I band.

Comment: Ordered in September 1992 from Simmoneau Marine for delivery in 1993. Aluminium construction. This version has two inboard engines.

SIMMONEAU 12   *1992, Simmoneau Marine*

1 FPB 57 TYPE (FAST ATTACK CRAFT—MISSILE)

ISTIQLAL P 5702

Displacement, tons: 410 full load
Dimensions, feet (metres): 190.6 × 24.9 × 8.9 *(58.1 × 7.6 × 2.7)*
Main machinery: 4 MTU 16V 956 TB91 diesels; 15 000 hp(m) *(11 MW)* sustained; 4 shafts
Speed, knots: 36. **Range, miles:** 1300 at 30 kts
Complement: 40 (5 officers)

Missiles: SSM: 4 Aerospatiale MM 40 Exocet; inertial cruise; active radar homing to 70 km *(40 nm)* at 0.9 Mach; warhead 165 kg; sea-skimmer.
Guns: 1 OTO Melara 3 in *(76 mm)*/62 compact; 85° elevation; 85 rounds/minute to 16 km *(8.6 nm)* anti-surface; 12 km *(6.5 nm)* anti-aircraft; weight of shell 6 kg.
2 Breda 40 mm/70 (twin); 85° elevation; 300 rounds/minute to 12.5 km *(6.6 nm)*; weight of shell 0.96 kg.
Mines: Fitted for minelaying.
Countermeasures: Decoys: CSEE Dagaie trainable mounting; automatic dispenser; IR flares and chaff; H/J band.
ESM: Racal Cutlass; radar intercept.
Fire control: PEAB 9LV 228 system. CSEE Lynx optical sight.
Radars: Surface search: Marconi S 810 (after radome); I band; range 43 km *(25 nm)*.
Navigation: Decca TM 1226C; I band.
Fire control: Philips 9LV 200; J band.

Programmes: Two ordered from Lürssen in 1980. In service November 1982 and March 1983.
Operational: *Istiqlal* escaped to Bahrain when the Iraqis invaded in August 1990. The second of this class was captured and sunk in February 1991.

ISTIQLAL   *1986*

17 COUGAR TYPE (INSHORE PATROL CRAFT)

Comment: Three Cat 900 (32 ft), three Cat 1000 (33 ft) and three Predator 1100 (35 ft) all powered by 2 Yamaha outboards (400 hp(m) *(294 kW)*). Four Type 1200 (38 ft) and four Type 1300 (41 ft) all powered by 2 Sabre diesels (760 hp(m) *(559 kW)*). All based on the high performance planing hull developed for racing, and acquired in 1991/92. Most have a 7.62 mm MG and an I band radar.

COUGAR 1200   *1991, Cougar Marine*

33 AL-SHAALI TYPE (INSHORE PATROL CRAFT)

Comment: Ten 33 ft and twenty-three 28 ft patrol craft built by Al-Shaali Marine, Dubai, and delivered in June 1992.

LAOS

General

It is reported that the Marine section of the Army has eight patrol craft, four LCMs and four service craft which are used for patrolling the Mekong river. In addition some 40 patrol boats were acquired from the USSR in 1985. Most vessels are probably ex-Soviet types but there may still be a few relics left behind by the US Navy.

Personnel

(a) 1993: 600 officers and men
(b) 18 months' national service

Bases

Luang Prabang, Chinaimo, Savanmma Khet, Pakse

Mercantile Marine

Lloyd's Register of Shipping:
1 ship of 483 tons gross

LATVIA

Headquarters' Appointments

Commander Defence Forces:
Colonel Dainis Turlais
Commander of the Navy:
Captain Gaidis Zeibots

Bases

Liepāja, Riga

Personnel

1 Jan 1993: 284 (37 officers)
(to increase to 1100 by 1994)

Mercantile Marine

Lloyd's Register of Shipping:
261 ships of 1 235 573 tons gross

PATROL FORCES

Note: There is no intention of taking ex-Russian vessels.

1 SELGA CLASS

SAMS KA 104

Displacement, tons: 147.4 standard; 174.4 full load
Dimensions, feet (metres): 78.9 × 19.6 × 7.2 *(24.08 × 6 × 2.2)*
Main machinery: 1 GNVD2B-K-2 diesel; 300 hp(m) *(221 kW)*; 1 shaft
Speed, knots: 9.5
Complement: 12
Guns: 1—12.7 mm MG.
Radars: Surface search: MIUS; I band.

Comment: Ex-fishing vessel conversion in 1992.

2 RIBNADZOR-4 CLASS

SPULGA KA 102   **COMETA** KA 103

Displacement, tons: 143 standard; 173.3 full load
Dimensions, feet (metres): 112.8 × 19 × 8 *(34.4 × 5.8 × 2.45)*
Main machinery: 1 40 DMM3 diesel; 2200 hp(m) *(1.62 MW)*; 1 shaft
Speed, knots: 15
Complement: 17 (4 officers)
Guns: 1—12.7 mm MG.
Radars: Surface search: MIUS; I band.

Comment: Ex-fishing vessels built in the late 1970s and converted in 1992.

1 Ex-SWEDISH COAST GUARD TYPE

ex-*KBV 244*

Displacement, tons: 17 full load
Dimensions, feet (metres): 63 × 13.1 × 4.3 *(19.2 × 4 × 1.3)*
Main machinery: 2 Volvo Penta TAMD 120A diesels; 700 hp(m) *(515 kW)*; 2 shafts
Speed, knots: 22
Complement: 5

Comment: Transferred in April 1993. Former Coast Guard vessel built in 1970. Similar craft to Estonia and Lithuania.

COAST GUARD TYPE (Swedish colours)   *1992, Swedish Navy*

AUXILIARIES

1 DIVING SUPPORT VESSEL

GEFESTS A 101

Displacement, tons: 92 standard; 116.1 full load
Dimensions, feet (metres): 93.7 × 17.05 × 5.5 *(28.58 × 5.2 × 1.7)*
Main machinery: 1 6CSP 28/3C diesel; 450 hp(m) *(331 kW)*; 1 shaft
Speed, knots: 11
Complement: 6
Radars: Navigation: SNN-7; I band.

Comment: Ex-fishing vessel converted to a diver support ship in 1992.

SPULGA   *1992, Latvian Navy*

COMETA   *1992, Latvian Navy*

GEFESTS   *1992, Latvian Navy*

LEBANON

Naval Commander

Rear Admiral Alberto Ghorayeb

Personnel

1993: 400 officers and men

Bases

Beirut, Jounieh

Operational

The Syrian Navy does not patrol off the coast of Lebanon.

Mercantile Marine

Lloyd's Register of Shipping:
163 vessels of 286 149 tons gross

DELETIONS

1990 *Byblos, Sidon, Beyrouth*
1991 *Trablous* (L'Esterel craft), 1 Aztec class

394 LEBANON / Patrol forces — LIBERIA / Introduction

PATROL FORCES

2 FRENCH EDIC CLASS (LANDING CRAFT)

Name	No	Builders	Commissioned
SOUR	21	SFCN, Villeneuve la Garonne	28 Mar 1985
DAMOUR	22	SFCN, Villeneuve la Garonne	28 Mar 1985

Displacement, tons: 670 full load
Dimensions, feet (metres): 193.5 × 39.2 × 4.2 *(59 × 12 × 1.3)*
Main machinery: 2 SACM MGO 175 V12 M1 diesels; 1200 hp(m) *(882 kW)*; 2 shafts
Speed, knots: 10. **Range, miles:** 1800 at 9 kts
Complement: 20 (2 officers)
Military lift: 33 troops; 11 trucks or 5 APCs
Guns: 2 Oerlikon 20 mm (twin). 1—81 mm mortar.

Comment: Both were damaged in early 1990 but repaired in 1991 and are fully operational.

SOUR *11/1985*

3 Ex-BRITISH ATTACKER CLASS (COASTAL PATROL CRAFT)

Displacement, tons: 38 full load
Dimensions, feet (metres): 65.6 × 17 × 4.9 *(20 × 5.2 × 1.5)*
Main machinery: 2 Detroit 12V-71TA diesels; 840 hp *(616 kW)* sustained; 2 shafts
Speed, knots: 21. **Range, miles:** 650 at 14 kts
Complement: 14 (2 officers)
Guns: 1 Oerlikon 20 mm (can be fitted).
Radars: Surface search: Racal Decca 1216; I band.

Comment: Built at Cowes and Southampton, and commissioned in March 1983. Transferred 17 July 1992 after serving as patrol craft for the British base in Cyprus. Former names, *Attacker*, *Hunter* and *Striker*.

ATTACKER *7/1992*

2 TRACKER Mk 2 (COASTAL PATROL CRAFT)

Displacement, tons: 31 full load
Dimensions, feet (metres): 63.3 × 16.4 × 4.9 *(19.3 × 5 × 1.5)*
Main machinery: 2 Detroit 12V-71TA diesels; 840 hp *(616 kW)* sustained; 2 shafts
Speed, knots: 25. **Range, miles:** 650 at 20 kts
Complement: 11
Guns: 2—23 mm (twin).
Radars: Surface search: Racal Decca; I band.

Comment: Built in 1980 by Fairey Allday, UK. Both held by the Navy in 1991.

TRACKER 2 *1991, Lebanese Navy*

5 AZTEC CLASS (COASTAL PATROL CRAFT)

CP 1000-1005

Displacement, tons: 5.2 full load
Dimensions, feet (metres): 29.5 × 8.5 × 1.6 *(9 × 2.6 × 0.5)*
Main machinery: 2 diesels; 320 hp(m) *(235 kW)*; 2 shafts
Speed, knots: 24

Comment: Six supplied by Crestitalia in 1979. GRP hulls. One deleted and five held by Lebanese Customs. All were damaged in 1990, but in 1991 were being repaired by the Navy.

AZTEC 1003

LIBERIA

General

The Liberian National Coast Guard became the Liberian Navy in 1987. During the civil war the remaining naval vessels were taken over by rebels. One Cessna 337 aircraft was reported as under naval control in 1992.

Bases

Elijah Johnson, Monrovia;
Buchanan, Bassa;
Greenville, Sinoe;
Harper, Cape Palmas.

Mercantile Marine

Lloyd's Register of Shipping:
1672 vessels of 55 166 948 tons gross

DELETIONS

1990 *Samuel K Doe, Thomas Quiwonkpa*

1 KOREA TACOMA CRAFT (FAST ATTACK CRAFT—GUN)

FARANDUGU

Displacement, tons: 170 full load
Dimensions, feet (metres): 108.6 × 22.6 × 8.2 *(33.1 × 6.9 × 2.5)*
Main machinery: 2 MTU MD 16V 538 TB90 diesels; 6000 hp(m) *(4.41 MW)* sustained; 2 shafts
Speed, knots: 38. **Range, miles:** 700 at 20 kts
Complement: 31
Guns: 2 Oerlikon 20 mm. 2—12.7 mm MGs.

Comment: Ordered from Korea Tacoma and delivered in October 1989. Armament is uncertain but the hull is a variation of the South Korean Navy's Sea Dolphin class but less heavily armed. Taken over by the rebels and painted in camouflage colours.

SEA DOLPHIN class *1989, Korea Tacoma*

1 COASTAL PATROL CRAFT

Name	No	Builders	Commissioned
C G C ALBERT PORTE	CG 8802	Karlskrona Varvet	27 Aug 1980

Displacement, tons: 50
Dimensions, feet (metres): 87.6 × 17.1 × 3.6 *(26.7 × 5.2 × 1.1)*
Main machinery: 2 MTU 8V 331 TC82 diesels; 1740 hp(m) *(1.28 MW)* sustained; 2 shafts
Speed, knots: 25. **Range, miles:** 1000 at 18 kts
Complement: 8
Guns: 1 Browning 12.7 mm MG. 2 FN 7.62 mm MGs.
Radars: Navigation: Decca 1226C; I band.

Comment: Aluminium alloy hull. Karlskrona TV 103 design. The survivor of a class of three taken over by the rebels and painted in camouflage colours. The other two of the class were destroyed in 1990.

TV 103 Type *8/1986, van Ginderen Collection*

LIBYA

Headquarters' Appointments

Commander-in-Chief Libyan Armed Forces:
Colonel Abu Bahr Yunis Jabir
Senior Officer, Libyan Navy:
Captain Abdullah Al Latif El Shaksuki

Personnel

(a) 1993: Total 8000 officers and ratings, including Coast Guard
(b) Voluntary service

Bases

Operating Ports at Tripoli, Darnah (Derna) and Benghazi.
Naval bases at Al Khums and Tobruq.
Submarine base at Ras Hilal.
Naval air station at Al Girdabiyah.
Naval infantry battalion at Sidi Bilal.

Strength of the Fleet

Type	Active
Submarines	5 (+6 small)
Frigates	3
Corvettes (Missile)	7
Minesweepers—Ocean	8
Fast Attack Craft—Missile	24
Large Patrol Craft	8
Landing Ships	5
LCTs	3
Support Ships	7
Tugs	7
Diving Tender	1
Salvage Ship	1
Floating Docks	2

Camouflage

Photographs of Libyan naval vessels taken since 1991 indicate that some ships have been painted in striped shades of green and black.

General

Specialist teams in unconventional warfare are a threat and almost any Libyan vessel can lay mines, but overall operational effectiveness is not high, not least because of poor maintenance and stores support. Sanctions imposed by the UN in April 1992 have not helped.

Mercantile Marine

Lloyd's Register of Shipping:
150 vessels of 727 228 tons gross

DELETION

Submarines

1992 *Al Fateh*

SUBMARINES

5 Ex-SOVIET FOXTROT CLASS (TYPE 641)

| AL BADR | 311 | AL MITRAQA | 314 | AL HUNAIN | 316 |
| AL AHAD | 313 | AL KHYBER | 315 | | |

Displacement, tons: 1950 surfaced; 2475 dived
Dimensions, feet (metres): 299.5 × 24.6 × 19.7 *(91.3 × 7.5 × 6)*
Main machinery: Diesel-electric; 3 Type 37-D diesels (1 × 2700 and 2 × 1350); 6000 hp(m) *(4.4 MW)*; 3 motors; 5400 hp(m) *(3.97 MW)*; 3 shafts; 1 auxiliary motor; 140 hp(m) *(103 kW)*
Speed, knots: 16 surfaced; 15 dived
Range, miles: 20 000 at 8 kts surfaced; 380 at 2 kts dived
Complement: 75 (8 officers)

Torpedoes: 10—21 in *(533 mm)* (6 bow, 4 stern) tubes. 22 Soviet Type 53; pattern active/passive homing up to 20 km *(10.8 nm)* at up to 45 kts; warhead 400 kg.
Mines: 44 in place of torpedoes.
Countermeasures: ESM: Stop Light; radar warning.
Radars: Surface search: Snoop Tray; I band.
Sonars: Herkules; hull-mounted; active; medium frequency.
Feniks; hull-mounted; passive.

Programmes: Came from a re-activated building line in Leningrad. *Al Badr* arrived in Tripoli December 1976; the second in February 1978, the third in March 1978, the fourth in February 1982, the fifth in April 1982 and the sixth in February 1983.
Structure: HF masts not fitted. Diving depth 250 m *(820 ft)* reducing with age.
Operational: Libyan crews trained in the USSR and much of the maintenance was done by Russian personnel. No routine patrols have been seen since 1984. *Al Fateh* in refit in Lithuania in 1992 when UN sanctions were applied to Libya and work stopped. She has now been abandoned and has been deleted.

AL KHYBER *6/1992, van Ginderen Collection*

6 YUGOSLAV R-2 MALA CLASS

Displacement, tons: 1.4 full load
Dimensions, feet (metres): 16.1 × 4.1 *(4.9 × 1.4)*
Main machinery: 1 motor; 6.2 hp(m) *(4.6 kW)*; 1 shaft
Speed, knots: 4.4
Range, miles: 18 at 4.4 kts; 23 at 3.7 kts
Complement: 2

Mines: Can carry 249 kg of limpet mines and other weapons.

Programmes: Two transferred in 1977, 1981 and 1982 each. A further pair may be on order, possibly of the Una class.
Structure: This is a free-flood craft with the main motor, battery, navigation-pod and electronic equipment housed in separate watertight cylinders. Instrumentation includes aircraft type gyro-compass, magnetic compass, depth gauge (with 0-100 m scale), echo sounder, sonar and two searchlights. Constructed of light aluminium and plexiglass, it is fitted with fore- and after-hydroplanes, the tail being a conventional cruciform with a single rudder abaft the screw. Large perspex windows give a good all-round view.
Operational: Details given are for lead-acid batteries and could be much improved by use of silver-zinc batteries. Operating depth, 60 m max. Passage to the target area can be as pick-a-back on a submarine or as deck cargo on any surface vessel with a 25-ton crane—lacking in all Libyan surface warships. However they could be floated out from *Zeltin's* dock. This class of submarine does not look very suitable for towing. Operational status doubtful.

R-2 MALA class (on Swedish submarine) *12/1988, Gilbert Gyssels*

FRIGATES

2 SOVIET KONI CLASS

AL HANI F 212	AL QIRDABIYAH F 213

Displacement, tons: 1440 standard; 1900 full load
Dimensions, feet (metres): 316.3 × 41.3 × 11.5 *(96.4 × 12.6 × 3.5)*
Main machinery: CODAG; 1 SGW, Nikolayev, M8B gas turbine (centre shaft); 18 000 hp(m) *(13.25 MW)* sustained; 2 Russki B-68 diesels; 15 820 hp(m) *(11.63 MW)* sustained; 3 shafts
Speed, knots: 27 on gas; 22 on diesel. **Range, miles:** 1800 at 14 kts
Complement: 120

Missiles: SSM: 4 Soviet SS-N-2C Styx (2 twin) launchers ❶; active radar/IR homing to 83 km *(45 nm)* at 0.9 Mach; warhead 513 kg; sea-skimmer at end of run.
SAM: SA-N-4 Gecko twin launcher ❷; semi-active radar homing to 15 km *(8 nm)* at 2.5 Mach; altitude 9.1-3048 m *(29.5-10 000 ft)*; warhead 50 kg; 20 missiles.
Guns: 4 USSR 3 in *(76 mm)*/60 (2 twin) ❸; 80° elevation; 60 rounds/minute to 15 km *(8 nm)* anti-surface; 14 km *(7.6 nm)* anti-aircraft; weight of shell 16 kg.
4 USSR 30 mm/65 (2 twin) automatic ❹; 85° elevation; 500 rounds/minute to 5 km *(2.7 nm)*; weight of shell 0.54 kg.
Torpedoes: 4—406 mm (2 twin) tubes amidships ❺. Soviet Type 40; anti-submarine; active/passive homing up to 15 km *(8 nm)* at up to 40 kts; warhead 150 kg.
A/S mortars: 1 RBU 6000 12-tubed trainable launcher ❻; automatic loading; range 6000 m; warhead 31 kg.
Depth charges: 2 racks.
Mines: Capacity for 20.
Countermeasures: Decoys: 2—16-barrelled chaff launchers. Towed torpedo decoys.
ESM: 2 Watch Dog; radar warning.
Radars: Air search: Strut Curve ❼; F band; range 110 km *(60 nm)* for 2 m² target.
Surface search: Plank Shave ❽; I band.
Navigation: Don 2; I band.
Fire control: Drum Tilt ❾; H/I band (for 30 mm).
Hawk Screech ❿; I band; range 27 km *(15 nm)* (for 76 mm).
Pop Group ⓫; F/H/I band (for SAM).
IFF: High Pole B. Square Head.
Sonars: Hull-mounted; active search and attack; medium frequency.

Programmes: Type III Konis built at Zelenodolsk and transferred from the Black Sea. 212 commissioned 28 June 1986 and 213 on 24 October 1987.
Structure: SSMs mounted either side of small deckhouse on forecastle behind gun. A deckhouse amidships contains air-conditioning machinery. Changes to the standard Koni include SSM, four torpedo tubes, only one RBU 6000 and Plank Shave surface search and target indication radar. Camouflage paint applied in 1991.

AL HANI *(Scale 1 : 900), Ian Sturton*

AL HANI *7/1991, van Ginderen Collection*

1 VOSPER THORNYCROFT MARK 7

Name	No	Builders	Laid down	Launched	Commissioned
DAT ASSAWARI	F 211	Vosper Thornycroft	27 Sep 1968	Sep 1969	1 Feb 1973

Displacement, tons: 1360 standard; 1780 full load
Dimensions, feet (metres): 333 × 38.3 × 11.2 *(101.5 × 11.7 × 3.4)*
Main machinery: CODOG; 2 RR Olympus TM2A gas turbines; 40 000 hp *(29.8 MW)* sustained; 2 Paxman 16YJCM diesels; 3800 hp *(2.83 MW)* sustained; 2 shafts; KaMeWa cp props
Speed, knots: 37.5 gas turbines; 17 diesels. **Range, miles:** 5700 at 17 kts
Complement: 130

Missiles: SSM: 4 OTO Melara/Matra Otomat ❶; active radar homing to 180 km *(100 nm)* at 0.9 Mach; warhead 210 kg.
SAM: 1 Selenia/Elsag Albatros quad launcher ❷; 64 Aspide; semi-active homing to 13 km *(7 nm)* at 2.5 Mach; height envelope 15-5000 m *(49.2-16 405 ft)*; warhead 30 kg.
Guns: 1 Vickers 4.5 in *(114 mm)*/55 Mk 8 ❸; 55° elevation; 25 rounds/minute to 22 km *(11.9 nm)* anti-surface; 6 km *(3.3 nm)* anti-aircraft; warhead 21 kg.
2 Oerlikon GDM-A 35 mm/90 (twin) ❹; 85° elevation; 550 rounds/minute to 6 km *(3.3 nm)* anti-surface; 5 km *(2.7 nm)* anti-aircraft; weight of shell 1.55 kg.
2 Oerlikon A41A 20 mm ❺; 50° elevation; 800 rounds/minute to 2 km; weight of shell 0.24 kg.
Torpedoes: 6—324 mm ILAS 3 (2 triple) tubes ❻. Whitehead Motofides A244; anti-submarine; active/passive homing to 7 km *(3.8 nm)* at 33 kts; warhead 34 kg (shaped charge).
Countermeasures: ESM: Selenia INS-1; radar intercept.
Decca RDS-1. Marconi FH-12 HFD/F.
Combat data systems: Selenia IPN/10 action data automation.
Fire control: 2 Selenia Elsag NA 10 Mod 2 for guns and missiles.
Radars: Air/surface search: Selenia RAN 12 ❼; D/I band; range 82 km *(45 nm)*.
Surface search: Selenia RAN 10S ❽; E/F band; range 155 km *(85 nm)*.
Fire control: Two Selenia RTN 10X ❾; I/J band; range 40 km *(22 nm)*.
Sonars: Thomson Sintra TSM 2310 Diodon; hull-mounted; active search and attack; 11-13 kHz.

Programmes: Mk 7 Frigate ordered from Vosper Thornycroft on 6 February 1968. Generally similar in design to the two Iranian Mk 5s built by this firm, but larger and with different armament. After trials she carried out work-up at Portland, UK, reaching Tripoli Autumn 1973.
Modernisation: In 1979 modernisation of SAM, ASW armament and sensors was started by CNR, Genoa but was interrupted by onboard explosion on 29 October 1980. Completed including trials October 1983. Returned to Italy for major engine repairs in 1984 which completed in 1985.
Operational: In 1990 the ship was in a partly disarmed state and back in Genoa once again. In 1992 she was in Tripoli and still non-operational.

DAT ASSAWARI *(Scale 1 : 900), Ian Sturton*

DAT ASSAWARI *5/1984, Aldo Fraccaroli*

SHIPBORNE AIRCRAFT

Numbers/Type: 8 Aerospatiale SA 316B Alouette III.
Operational speed: 113 kts *(210 km/h)*.
Service ceiling: 10 500 ft *(3200 m)*.
Range: 290 nm *(540 km)*.
Role/Weapon systems: Support helicopter; can be operated from amphibious warfare ships. Sensors: None. Weapons: Unarmed.

ALOUETTE III

LAND-BASED MARITIME AIRCRAFT

Numbers/Type: 4 Aerospatiale SA 321M Super Frelon.
Operational speed: 134 kts *(248 km/h)*.
Service ceiling: 10 000 ft *(3050 m)*.
Range: 440 nm *(815 km)*.
Role/Weapon systems: Obsolescent helicopter; used for naval support tasks but non-operational due to lack of spares. Sensors: None. Weapons: Modified to carry Exocet AM 39.

Numbers/Type: 25 Mil Mi-14 Haze A.
Operational speed: 120 kts *(222 km/h)*.
Service ceiling: 15 000 ft *(4570 m)*.
Range: 240 nm *(445 km)*.
Role/Weapon systems: ASW and surface search helicopter. Sensors: Search radar, ECM, dipping sonar, MAD. Weapons: ASW; internal torpedoes, depth bombs or mines.

CORVETTES

Note: Tobruk is still used as an alongside training hulk.

3 SOVIET NANUCHKA II CLASS (MISSILE CORVETTES)

TARIQ IBN ZIYAD (ex-*Ean Mara*) 416   **EAN AL GAZALA** 417   **EAN ZARA** 418

Displacement, tons: 850 full load
Dimensions, feet (metres): 194.5 × 38.7 × 8.5 *(59.3 × 11.8 × 2.6)*
Main machinery: 3 Type M 507 diesels; 21 600 hp(m) *(15.9 MW)* sustained; 3 shafts
Speed, knots: 34. **Range, miles:** 2500 at 12 kts; 900 at 31 kts
Complement: 60

Missiles: SSM: 4 Soviet SS-N-2C Styx launchers; auto-pilot; active radar/IR homing to 83 km *(45 nm)* at 0.9 Mach; warhead 513 kg HE; sea-skimmer at end of run.
 SAM: SA-N-4 Gecko twin launcher; semi-active radar homing to 15 km *(8 nm)* at 2.5 Mach; altitude 9.1-3048 m *(29.5-10 000 ft)*; warhead 50 kg HE; 20 missiles.
Guns: 2 USSR 57 mm/80 (twin) automatic; 85° elevation; 120 rounds/minute to 6 km *(3.2 nm)*; weight of shell 2.8 kg.
Countermeasures: Decoys: 2 chaff 16-barrelled launchers.
 ESM: Bell Top; radar warning.
Radars: Surface search: Square Tie; I band (Bandstand radome).
 Navigation: Don 2; I band.
 Fire control: Muff Cob; G/H band.
 Pop Group; F/H/I band (for SAM).

Programmes: First reached Libya in October 1981; second in February 1983; third in February 1984; fourth in September 1985.
Structure: Camouflage paint applied in 1991.
Operational: *Ean Zaquit* (419) sunk on 24 March 1986. *Ean Mara* (416) severely damaged on 25 March 1986 by forces of the US Sixth Fleet; repaired in Leningrad and returned to Libya in early 1991 as the *Tariq Ibn Ziyad*.

TARIQ IBN ZIYAD   *7/1991, van Ginderen Collection*

4 ASSAD CLASS (MISSILE CORVETTES)

Name	No	Builders	Launched	Commissioned
ASSAD AL BIHAR	412	Fincantieri, Muggiano	29 Apr 1977	14 Sep 1979
ASSAD EL TOUGOUR	413	Fincantieri, Muggiano	20 Apr 1978	12 Feb 1980
ASSAD AL KHALI	414	Fincantieri, Muggiano	15 Dec 1978	28 Mar 1981
ASSAD AL HUDUD	415	Fincantieri, Muggiano	21 June 1979	28 Mar 1981

Displacement, tons: 670 full load
Dimensions, feet (metres): 202.4 × 30.5 × 7.2 *(61.7 × 9.3 × 2.2)*
Main machinery: 4 MTU-Bazán 16V 956 TB91 diesels; 15 000 hp(m) *(11 MW)* sustained; 4 shafts
Speed, knots: 34. **Range, miles:** 4400 at 14 kts
Complement: 58

Missiles: SSM: 4 OTO Melara/Matra Otomat Teseo Mk 2 (TG1); active radar homing to 80 km *(43.2 nm)* at 0.9 Mach; warhead 210 kg.
Guns: 1 OTO Melara 3 in *(76 mm)*/62 compact; 85° elevation; 85 rounds/minute to 16 km *(8.6 nm)* anti-surface; 12 km *(6.5 nm)* anti-aircraft; weight of shell 6 kg.
 2 Oerlikon GDM-A 35 mm/90 (twin); 85° elevation; 550 rounds/minute to 6 km *(3.3 nm)* anti-surface; 5 km *(2.7 nm)* anti-aircraft.
Torpedoes: 6—324 mm ILAS (2 triple) tubes. Whitehead Motofides A244; anti-submarine; self-adaptive patterns to 7 km *(3.8 nm)* at 33 kts; warhead 34 kg (shaped charge).
Mines: Can lay 16 mines.
Countermeasures: ESM: Selenia INS-1; radar intercept.
Combat data systems: Selenia IPN/10 action data automation.
Fire control: Selenia Elsag NA 10 Mod 2.
Radars: Air/surface search: Selenia RAN 11X; D/I band; range 82 km *(45 nm)*.
 Navigation: Decca TM 1226C; I band.
 Fire control: Selenia RTN 10X; I/J band; range 40 km *(22 nm)*.
Sonars: Thomson Sintra TSM Diodon; hull-mounted; active search and attack; 11-13 kHz.

Programmes: Ordered in 1974. Previously Wadi class—renamed 1982-83. Similar hull to Ecuador corvettes.
Structure: Fin stabilisers and degaussing equipment fitted.
Operational: At the beginning of 1990 only one was operational with the others cannibalised for spares. By 1993 all were non-operational.

ASSAD AL HUDUD   *1986, W Magrawa*

LIGHT FORCES

Notes: (i) More than 50 remote-control explosive craft acquired from Cyprus. Based on Q-Boats with Q-26 GRP hulls and speed of about 30 kts. Also reported that fifteen 31 ft craft delivered by Storebro, and 60 more built locally are similarly adapted.
(ii) The 1985 order for four Improved Končar class FAC(M) from Yugoslavia was cancelled because of contract problems.
(iii) 14 SAR 33 FAC(G) were reported delivered to the Customs Service by Turkey in 1986-87. In fact the order was cancelled.
(iv) There is also a 37 m patrol craft *Al Kifah* 206.

9 COMBATTANTE II G CLASS (FAST ATTACK CRAFT—MISSILE)

SHARABA (ex-*Beir Grassa*) 518
SHEHAB (ex-*Beir Gtifa*) 522
WAHAG (ex-*Beir Gzir*) 524
SHOUAIAI (ex-*Beir Algandula*) 528
SHOULA (ex-*Beir Ktitat*) 532
SHAFAK (ex-*Beir Alkrarim*) 534
BARK (ex-*Beir Alkardmen*) 536
RAD (ex-*Beir Alkur*) 538
LAHEEB (ex-*Beir Alkuefat*) 542

Displacement, tons: 311 full load
Dimensions, feet (metres): 160.7 × 23.3 × 6.6 *(49 × 7.1 × 2)*
Main machinery: 4 MTU 20V 538 TB91 diesels; 15 360 hp(m) *(11.29 MW)* sustained; 4 shafts
Speed, knots: 39. **Range, miles:** 1600 at 15 kts
Complement: 27

Missiles: SSM: 4 OTO Melara/Matra Otomat Mk 2 (TG1); active radar homing to 80 km *(43.2 nm)* at 0.9 Mach; warhead 210 kg.
Guns: 1 OTO Melara 3 in *(76 mm)*/62 compact; 85° elevation; 85 rounds/minute to 16 km *(8.6 nm)* anti-surface; 12 km *(6.8 nm)* anti-aircraft; weight of shell 6 kg.
 2 Breda 40 mm/70 (twin); 85° elevation; 300 or 450 rounds/minute to 12.5 km *(6.8 nm)* anti-surface; 4 km *(2.2 nm)* anti-aircraft; weight of shell 0.96 kg.
Fire control: CSEE Panda director. Thomson-CSF Vega II system.
Radars: Surface search: Thomson-CSF Triton; G band; range 33 km *(18 nm)* for 2 m² target.
 Fire control: Thomson-CSF Castor IIB; I band; range 15 km *(8 nm)* (associated with Vega fire control system).

Programmes: Ordered from CMN Cherbourg in May 1977. 518 completed February 1982; 522 3 April 1982; 524 29 May 1982; 528 5 September 1982; 532 29 October 1982; 534 17 December 1982; 536 11 March 1983; 538 10 May 1983; 542 29 July 1983.
Structure: Steel hull with alloy superstructure.
Operational: In 1983 an unexpected change of names took place. *Waheed* (526) sunk on 24 March 1986 and one other severely damaged on 25 March 1986 by forces of the US Sixth Fleet.

RAD   *10/1982, van Ginderen Collection*

398 LIBYA / Light forces — Mine warfare forces

12 Ex-SOVIET OSA II CLASS (FAST ATTACK CRAFT—MISSILE)

AL KATUM 511	AL NABHA 519	AL MOSHA 527
AL ZUARA 513	AL SAFHRA 521	AL SAKAB 529
AL RUHA 515	AL FIKAH 523	AL BITAR 531
AL BAIDA 517	AL MATHUR 525	AL SADAD 533

Displacement, tons: 245 full load
Dimensions, feet (metres): 126.6 × 24.9 × 8.8 *(38.6 × 7.6 × 2.7)*
Main machinery: 3 Type M 504 diesels; 10 800 hp(m) *(7.94 MW)* sustained; 3 shafts
Speed, knots: 37. **Range, miles:** 800 at 30 kts; 500 at 35 kts
Complement: 30

Missiles: SSM: 4 Soviet SS-N-2C Styx; active radar or IR homing to 83 km *(45 nm)* at 0.9 Mach; warhead 513 kg HE; sea-skimmer at end of run.
Guns: 4 USSR 30 mm/65 (2 twin) automatic; 85° elevation; 500 rounds/minute to 5 km *(2.7 nm)*; weight of shell 0.54 kg.
Radars: Surface search: Square Tie; I band; range 73 km *(45 nm)*.
Fire control: Drum tilt; H/I band.
IFF: Two Square Head. High Pole.

Programmes: The first craft arrived in October 1976, four more in August-October 1977, a sixth in July 1978, three in September-October 1979, one in April 1980, one in May 1980 (521) and one in July 1980 (529).
Structure: Some painted with camouflage stripes in 1991.

AL BAIDA — *1986, van Ginderen Collection*

3 SUSA CLASS (FAST ATTACK CRAFT—MISSILE)

Name	No	Builders	Commissioned
SUSA	512	Vosper Ltd, Portsmouth	23 Jan 1969
SIRTE	514	Vosper Ltd, Portsmouth	23 Jan 1969
SEBHA (ex-*Sokna*)	516	Vosper Ltd, Portsmouth	23 Jan 1969

Displacement, tons: 95 standard; 114 full load
Dimensions, feet (metres): 100 × 25.5 × 7 *(30.5 × 7.8 × 2.1)*
Main machinery: CODOG; 3 RR Proteus gas turbines; 12 750 hp *(9.51 MW)* sustained; 2 GM 6-71 diesels; 348 hp *(260 kW)* sustained; 3 shafts
Speed, knots: 54
Complement: 20

Missiles: SSM: 8 Aerospatiale SS 12M; wire-guided to 5.5 km *(3 nm)* subsonic; warhead 30 kg.
Guns: 2 Bofors 40 mm/60.
Fire control: Aerospatiale/Nord optical director.
Radars: Surface search: Decca 626; I band.

Programmes: The order for these three fast patrol boats was announced on 12 October 1966. They are generally similar to the RN Brave class (now deleted) and the Søloven class designed and built by Vosper for the Royal Danish Navy.
Modernisation: All three overhauled in Italy in 1977 with new electronics. Further Italian refit 1983-84.

SEBHA — *Wright and Logan*

3 THORNYCROFT TYPE (LARGE PATROL CRAFT)

Name	No	Builders	Commissioned
BENINA	CG 3	Vosper Thornycroft	29 Aug 1968
FARWA (ex-*Homs*)	CG 2	Vosper Thornycroft	early 1969
MISURATA	CG 4	Vosper Thornycroft	29 Aug 1968

Displacement, tons: 100
Dimensions, feet (metres): 100 × 21 × 5.5 *(30.5 × 6.4 × 1.7)*
Main machinery: 3 RR DV8TM diesels; 1740 hp *(1.3 MW)*; 3 shafts
Speed, knots: 18. **Range, miles:** 1800 at 14 kts
Complement: 18
Guns: 1 Oerlikon 20 mm.

Comment: Welded steel construction. Two transferred to Malta in 1978. Used for Coast Guard duties.

THORNYCROFT Type — *Vosper Thornycroft*

4 GARIAN CLASS (LARGE PATROL CRAFT)

Name	No	Builders	Commissioned
SABRATA	611	Brooke Marine, Lowestoft	early 1970
ZLEITAN (ex-*Garian*)	612	Brooke Marine, Lowestoft	30 Aug 1969
KAWLAN	613	Brooke Marine, Lowestoft	30 Aug 1969
MERAWA	614	Brooke Marine, Lowestoft	early 1970

Displacement, tons: 120 standard; 159 full load
Dimensions, feet (metres): 106 × 21.2 × 5.5 *(32.3 × 6.5 × 1.7)*
Main machinery: 2 Paxman 12YJCM diesels; 3000 hp *(2.24 MW)* sustained; 2 shafts
Speed, knots: 24. **Range, miles:** 1500 at 12 kts
Complement: 15-22
Guns: 1 Bofors 40 mm/60. 1 Oerlikon 20 mm.

Comment: At least first pair refitted in Istanbul in 1984. Used for Coast Guard duties. 612 renamed after former MRC became a hulk. At least one has a 144 mm rocket launcher. All non-operational.

KAWLAN — *Brooke Marine*

1 Ex-SOVIET POLUCHAT CLASS (LARGE PATROL CRAFT)

723

Displacement, tons: 70 standard; 100 full load
Dimensions, feet (metres): 97.1 × 19 × 4.8 *(29.6 × 5.8 × 1.5)*
Main machinery: 2 Type M 50 diesels; 2200 hp(m) *(1.6 MW)* sustained; 2 shafts
Speed, knots: 20. **Range, miles:** 1500 at 10 kts
Complement: 15
Guns: 2 (twin) MGs.
Radars: Navigation: Spin Trough; I band.

Comment: Transferred May 1985. Used as Torpedo Recovery Vessel.

MINE WARFARE FORCES

8 Ex-SOVIET NATYA CLASS (OCEAN MINESWEEPERS)

AL TIYAR (ex-*Ras Hadad*) 111	RAS AL FULAIJAH 117	RAS AL MASSAD 123
AL ISAR (ex-*Ras El Gelais*) 113	RAS AL QULA 119	RAS AL HANI 125
RAS AL HAMMAN 115	RAS AL MADWAR 121	

Displacement, tons: 770 full load
Dimensions, feet (metres): 200.1 × 31.8 × 8.9 *(61 × 9.7 × 2.7)*
Main machinery: 2 Type M 504 diesels; 7200 hp(m) *(5.29 MW)* sustained; 2 shafts
Speed, knots: 19. **Range, miles:** 4000 at 10 kts
Complement: 60

Guns: 4 USSR 30 mm/65 (2 twin) automatic; 85° elevation; 500 rounds/minute to 5 km *(2.7 nm)*; weight of shell 0.54 kg.
4 USSR 25 mm/60 (2 twin); 85° elevation; 270 rounds/minute to 3 km *(1.6 nm)*; weight of shell 0.34 kg.
A/S mortars: 2 RBU 1200 5-tubed fixed launchers; elevating; range 1-2 km; warhead 34 kg.
Mines: 10.
Radars: Surface search: Don 2; I band.
Fire control: Drum Tilt; H/I band.
IFF: Two Square Head. One High Pole B.
Sonars: Hull-mounted; active search; high frequency.

Programmes: First pair transferred February 1981. Second pair arrived February 1983, one in August 1983, the sixth in January 1984 the seventh in January 1985 and the eighth in October 1986.
Structure: At least one of the class painted in green striped camouflage in 1991.
Operational: Capable of magnetic, acoustic and mechanical sweeping. Mostly used for coastal patrols.

RAS AL HANI — *2/1988*

AMPHIBIOUS FORCES

2 PS 700 CLASS (LSTs)

Name	No	Builders	Commissioned
IBN OUF	132	CNI de la Mediterranée	11 Mar 1977
IBN HARISSA	134	CNI de la Mediterranée	10 Mar 1978

Displacement, tons: 2800 full load
Dimensions, feet (metres): 326.4 × 51.2 × 7.9 *(99.5 × 15.6 × 2.4)*
Main machinery: 2 SEMT-Pielstick 16 PA4 V 185 diesels; 5344 hp(m) *(3.93 MW)* sustained; 2 shafts; cp props
Speed, knots: 15.4. **Range, miles:** 4000 at 14 kts
Complement: 35
Military lift: 240 troops; 11 tanks
Guns: 6 Breda 40 mm/70 (3 twin). 1—81 mm mortar.
Fire control: CSEE Panda director.
Radars: Air search: Thomson-CSF Triton; D band.
Surface search: Decca 1226; I band.
Helicopters: 1 Aerospatiale SA 316B Alouette III.

Comment: 132 laid down 1 April 1976 and launched 22 October 1976; 134 laid down 18 April 1977, launched 18 October 1977.

IBN HARISSA   1981

3 Ex-SOVIET POLNOCHNY D CLASS (TYPE 773U) (LSMs)

IBN AL HADRAMI 112   IBN UMAYAA 116   IBN AL FARAT 118

Displacement, tons: 1305 full load
Dimensions, feet (metres): 275.3 × 31.8 × 7.9 *(83.9 × 9.7 × 2.4)*
Main machinery: 2 Type 40-D diesels; 4400 hp(m) *(3.2 MW)* sustained; 2 shafts
Speed, knots: 15. **Range, miles:** 2900 at 12 kts
Complement: 45
Military lift: 160 troops; 5 MBT or 5 APC or 5 AA guns or 8 trucks
Guns: 4 USSR 30 mm (2 twin). 2—140 mm 18-tubed rocket launchers.
Mines: 100.
Radars: Surface search: Radwar SRN-745; I band.
Fire control: Drum Tilt; H/I band.
IFF: Salt Pot A. Square Head.
Helicopters: Platform for 1 medium.

Comment: The first to be transferred arrived in November 1977. On 14 September 1978 *Ibn Qis* (fourth of the class) was burned out during a landing exercise and was a total loss. 118 and 116 delivered June 1978. All are an export variant of the standard Soviet/Polish Polnochny class but with helicopter deck added. Built in Poland. Similar types built for India and Iraq (now deleted).

IBN UMAYAA   7/1990, van Ginderen Collection

IBN UMAYAA   6/1990

3 TURKISH TYPE (LCTs)

IBN AL IDRISI 130   IBN MARWAN 131   EL KOBAYAT 132

Displacement, tons: 280 standard; 600 full load
Dimensions, feet (metres): 183.7 × 37.8 × 3.6 *(56 × 11.6 × 1.1)*
Main machinery: 3 GM 6-71TI diesels; 930 hp *(694 kW)* maximum; 3 shafts
Speed, knots: 8.5 loaded; 10 max. **Range, miles:** 600 at 10 kts
Complement: 15
Military lift: 100 troops; 350 tons including 5 tanks
Guns: 2—30 mm (twin).

Comment: First two transferred 7 December 1979 (ex-Turkish *C130* and *C131*) from Turkish fleet. Third of class reported in 1991. Previously reported numbers were much exaggerated.

TURKISH LCT (Turkey number)   10/1991, Harald Carstens

SALVAGE SHIP

1 YUGOSLAV SPASILAC CLASS

AL MUNJED (ex-*Zlatica*) 722

Displacement, tons: 1590 full load
Dimensions, feet (metres): 182 × 39.4 × 14.1 *(55.5 × 12 × 4.3)*
Main machinery: 2 diesels; 4340 hp(m) *(3.19 MW)*; 2 shafts; cp props; bow thruster
Speed, knots: 13. **Range, miles:** 4000 at 12 kts
Complement: 50
Guns: 4—12.7 mm MGs. Can also be fitted with 8—20 mm (2 quad) and 2—20 mm.
Radars: Surface search: Racal Decca; I band.

Comment: Transferred in 1982. Fitted for firefighting, towing and submarine rescue—carries recompression chamber. Built at Tito SY, Belgrade.

SPASILAC (old number)   1988, Peter Jones

SUPPORT SHIPS

1 LSD TYPE

Name	No	Builders	Commissioned
ZELTIN	711	Vosper Thornycroft, Woolston	23 Jan 1969

Displacement, tons: 2200 standard; 2470 full load
Dimensions, feet (metres): 324 × 48 × 10.2 *(98.8 × 14.6 × 3.1)*; 19 *(5.8)* aft when flooded
Main machinery: 2 Paxman 16YJCM diesels; 4000 hp *(2.98 MW)*; 2 shafts
Speed, knots: 15. **Range, miles:** 3000 at 14 kts
Complement: As Senior Officer Ship: 101 (15 officers)

Guns: 2 Bofors 40 mm/70; 90° elevation; 300 rounds/minute to 12 km *(6.5 nm)* anti-surface; 4 km *(2.2 nm)* anti-aircraft; weight of shell 0.96 kg.
Fire control: Vega II-12 for 40 mm guns.
Radars: Surface search: Thomson-CSF Triton; G band; range 33 km *(18 nm)* for 2 m² target (associated with Vega fire control).

Programmes: Ordered in January 1967; launched 29 February 1968.
Structure: Fitted with accommodation for a flag officer or a senior officer and staff. Operational and administrative base of the squadron. Workshops with a total area of approximately 4500 sq ft are situated amidships with ready access to the dock, and there is a 3 ton travelling gantry fitted with outriggers to cover ships berthed alongside up to 200 ft long.
Operational: The ship provides full logistic support, including docking maintenance and repair facilities. Craft up to 120 ft can be docked. Used as tender for Light Forces and is probably no longer capable of going to sea.

ZELTIN   1980, van Ginderen Collection

LIBYA — Support ships

6 RO-RO TRANSPORTS

GARYOUNIS (ex-*Mashu*)   **EL TEMSAH**   **+ 4**

Measurement, tons: 2412 gross
Dimensions, feet (metres): 546.3 × 80.1 × 21.3 *(166.5 × 24.4 × 6.5)*
Main machinery: 2 SEMT-Pielstick diesels; 20 800 hp(m) *(15.29 MW)*; 2 shafts; bow thruster
Speed, knots: 20

Comment: Details are for *Garyounis*, a converted Ro-Ro passenger/car ferry used as a training vessel in 1989. In addition the 117 m *El Temsah* has been refitted and is back in service, and another four Ro-Ro vessels are in regular military service. All have minelaying potential.

TUGS

3 COASTAL TYPE

A 33   A 34   A 35

Measurement, tons: 150 grt
Dimensions, feet (metres): 87.3 × 26 × 8.2 *(26.6 × 7.9 × 2.5)*
Main machinery: 2 diesels; 2 shafts

Comment: Built by Jonker and Stans BV Shipyard, Netherlands. First launched 16 October 1979.

4 COASTAL TYPE

Name	No	Builders	Commissioned
RAS EL HELAL	A 31	Mondego, Portugal	22 Oct 1976
AL AHWEIRIF	A 32	Mondego, Portugal	17 Feb 1977
AL KERIAT	—	Mondego, Portugal	1 July 1977
AL TABKAH	—	Mondego, Portugal	29 July 1978

Measurement, tons: 200 grt
Dimensions, feet (metres): 114 × 29.5 × 13 *(34.8 × 9 × 4)*
Main machinery: 2 diesels; 2300 hp(m) *(1.69 MW)*; 2 shafts
Speed, knots: 14

DIVING TENDER

1 Ex-SOVIET YELVA CLASS

AL MANOUD VM 917

Displacement, tons: 300 full load
Dimensions, feet (metres): 134.2 × 26.2 × 6.6 *(40.9 × 8 × 2)*
Main machinery: 2 Type 3-D-12A diesels; 630 hp(m) *(463 kW)* sustained; 2 shafts
Speed, knots: 12.5
Complement: 30
Radars: Navigation: Spin trough; I band.
IFF: High Pole.

Comment: Built in early 1970s. Transferred December 1977. Carries two 1.5 ton cranes and has a portable decompression chamber.

YELVA class   *1973*

FLOATING DOCKS

Comment: One of 5000 tons capacity at Tripoli. One of 3200 tons capacity acquired in April 1985.

LITHUANIA

General

Coast Guard Force beginning to be formed in late 1992. The intention is for all Russian naval ships to withdraw by September 1993.

Colours

There is a distinctive green and yellow diagonal stripe on all Coast Guard vessels.

Mercantile Marine

Lloyd's Register of Shipping:
52 ships of 314 240 tons gross

FRIGATES

2 Ex-RUSSIAN GRISHA III (FFL)

Displacement, tons: 950 standard; 1200 full load
Dimensions, feet (metres): 236.2 × 32.8 × 12.1 *(72 × 10 × 3.7)*
Main machinery: CODAG; 1 gas turbine; 15 000 hp(m) *(11 MW)*; 2 diesels; 16 000 hp(m) *(11.8 MW)*; 3 shafts
Speed, knots: 30. **Range, miles:** 4500 at 10 kts; 1750 at 22 kts diesels; 950 at 27 kts
Complement: 48 (5 officers)

Missiles: SAM: SA-N-4 Gecko twin launcher; semi-active radar homing to 15 km *(8 nm)* at 2.5 Mach; warhead 50 kg; altitude 9.1-3048 m *(30-10 000 ft)*; 20 missiles.
Guns: 2—57 mm/80 (twin); 85° elevation; 120 rounds/minute to 6 km *(3.3 nm)*; weight of shell 2.8 kg.
1—30 mm/65; 6 barrels; 85° elevation; 3000 rounds/minute combined to 2 km.
Torpedoes: 4—21 in *(533 mm)* (2 twin) tubes. Type 53; dual purpose; pattern active/passive homing up to 20 km *(10.8 nm)* at up to 45 kts; warhead 400 kg.
A/S mortars: 2 RBU 6000 12-tubed trainable; range 6000 m; warhead 31 kg.
Depth charges: 2 racks (12).
Mines: Capacity for 18 in lieu of depth charges.
Countermeasures: ESM: 2 Watch Dog.
Radars: Air/surface search: Strut Curve; F band; range 110 km *(60 nm)* for 2 m² target.
Navigation: Don 2; I band.
Fire control: Pop Group; F/H/I band (for SA-N-4). Bass Tilt; H/I band (for 57/76 mm and 30 mm).
IFF: High Pole A or B. Square Head. Salt Pot.
Sonars: Hull-mounted; active search and attack; high/medium frequency.
VDS; active search; high frequency. Similar to Hormone helicopter dipping sonar.

Programmes: Built in the early 1980s. Transferred in November 1992.

PATROL FORCES

1 Ex-SWEDISH COAST GUARD TYPE

ex-*KBV 245*

Displacement, tons: 17 full load
Dimensions, feet (metres): 63 × 13.1 × 4.3 *(19.2 × 4 × 1.3)*
Main machinery: 2 Volvo Penta TAMD 120A diesels; 700 hp(m) *(515 kW)*; 2 shafts
Speed, knots: 22
Complement: 5

Comment: Transferred in April 1993. Former Coast Guard vessel built in 1970. Similar craft transferred to Estonia and Latvia.

COAST GUARD TYPE (Swedish colours)   *1992, Maritime Photographic*

GRISHA III (Russian number)   *4/1992, van Ginderen Collection*

2 TURYA CLASS (FAST ATTACK CRAFT—TORPEDO)

Displacement, tons: 190 standard; 250 full load
Dimensions, feet (metres): 129.9 × 24.9 (41 over foils) × 5.9 (13.1 over foils) *(39.6 × 7.6 (12.5) × 1.8 (4))*
Main machinery: 3 Type M 504 diesels; 10 800 hp(m) *(7.94 MW)* sustained; 3 shafts
Speed, knots: 40 foilborne. **Range, miles:** 600 at 35 kts foilborne; 1450 at 14 kts hullborne
Complement: 30

Guns: 2—57 mm/80 (twin, aft); 85° elevation; 120 rounds/minute to 6 km *(3.3 nm)*; weight of shell 2.8 kg.
2—25 mm/80 (twin, fwd); 85° elevation; 270 rounds/minute to 3 km *(1.6 nm)*; weight of shell 0.34 kg.
1—14.5 mm MG.
Torpedoes: 4—21 in *(533 mm)* tubes. Type 53; dual purpose; pattern active/passive homing up to 20 km *(10.8 nm)* at up to 45 kts; warhead 400 kg.
Depth charges: 1 rack.
Radars: Surface search: Pot Drum; H/I band.
Fire control: Muff Cob; G/H band.
IFF: High Pole B. Square Head.
Sonars: VDS; active search and attack; high frequency. Similar to Hormone dipping sonar. This sonar is not fitted in most export versions.

Programmes: Built in the mid-1970s. Transferred in early 1993. The class has been widely sold abroad.
Structure: Single hydrofoil forward on an Osa type hull.

SUPPORT SHIPS

1 VALERIAN URYVAYEV CLASS

VETRA (ex-*Rudolf Samoylovich*) 41

Displacement, tons: 1050 full load
Dimensions, feet (metres): 180.1 × 31.2 × 13.1 *(54.9 × 9.5 × 4)*
Main machinery: 1 Deutz diesel; 850 hp(m) *(625 kW)*; 1 shaft
Speed, knots: 12
Complement: 52

Comment: Built at Khabarovsk in early 1980s. Transferred from the Russian Navy in 1992 where she was used as a civilian oceanographic research vessel.

VALERIAN URYVAYEV   1989

TURYA (Russian number)   1992

MADAGASCAR

Personnel
(a) 1993: 500 officers and men (including Marine Company of 120 men)
(b) 18 months' national service

Bases
Diego-Suarez, Tamatave, Majunga, Tulear, Nossi-Be, Fort Dauphin, Manakara.

Mercantile Marine
Lloyd's Register of Shipping:
85 vessels of 67 385 tons gross

LIGHT FORCES

Note: Five police patrol craft (GC 1-5) were destroyed in 1990.

1 TYPE PR 48 (LARGE PATROL CRAFT)

Name	No	Builders	Commissioned
MALAIKA	—	Chantiers Navals Franco-Belges (SFCN)	Dec 1967

Displacement, tons: 235 light; 250 full load
Dimensions, feet (metres): 155.8 × 23.6 × 8.2 *(47.5 × 7.1 × 2.5)*
Main machinery: 2 SACM V12 CZSHR diesels; 3600 hp(m) *(2.65 MW)* sustained; 2 shafts
Speed, knots: 23. **Range, miles:** 2000 at 15 kts
Complement: 25 (3 officers)
Guns: 2 Bofors 40 mm/60; 90° elevation; 300 rounds/minute to 12 km *(6.5 nm)* anti-surface; 4 km *(2.2 nm)* anti-aircraft; weight of shell 0.89 kg.

Comment: Ordered by the French Navy for delivery to Madagascar. Laid down in November 1966, launched on 22 March 1967. Non-operational in early 1992.

AMPHIBIOUS FORCES

1 BATRAM CLASS

Name	No	Builders	Commissioned
TOKY	—	Arsenal de Diego Suarez	Oct 1974

Displacement, tons: 810
Dimensions, feet (metres): 217.8 × 41 × 6.2 *(66.4 × 12.5 × 1.9)*
Main machinery: 2 MGO diesels; 2400 hp(m) *(1.76 MW)*; 2 shafts
Speed, knots: 13. **Range, miles:** 3000 at 12 kts
Complement: 43
Military lift: 250 tons stores; 30 troops or 120 troops (short range)
Missiles: SSM: 8 Aerospatiale SS 12M; wire-guided to 5.5 km *(3 nm)* subsonic; warhead 30 kg.
Guns: 1 OTO Melara 3 in *(76 mm)*. 2 Oerlikon 20 mm. 1—81 mm mortar.

Comment: Paid for by the French Government as military assistance. Fitted with a bow ramp and similar to, though larger than, the French Edic but smaller than Batral. Non-operational in early 1992.

1 Ex-NORTH KOREAN NAMPO CLASS

Displacement, tons: 82 full load
Dimensions, feet (metres): 84.2 × 20 × 6 *(27.7 × 6.1 × 1.8)*
Main machinery: 4 Type M 50 diesels; 4400 hp(m) *(3.2 MW)* sustained; 4 shafts
Speed, knots: 40. **Range, miles:** 375 at 38 kts
Complement: 19
Guns: 4 USSR 14.5 mm (2 twin) MGs. 1—81 mm mortar.

Comment: Assault landing craft based on Soviet P 6 hull. Four transferred February 1979 and June 1979 but three were lost in a typhoon in April 1984. Non-operational in early 1992.

1 Ex-FRENCH EDIC

AINA VAO VAO (ex-*L9082*)

Displacement, tons: 250 standard; 670 full load
Dimensions, feet (metres): 193.5 × 39.2 × 4.5 *(59 × 12 × 1.3)*
Main machinery: 2 MGO diesels; 1000 hp(m) *(753 kW)*; 2 shafts
Speed, knots: 8. **Range, miles:** 1800 at 8 kts
Complement: 17
Military lift: 5 LVTs or 11 trucks
Guns: 2 Oerlikon 20 mm. 1—81 mm mortar.

Comment: Built in 1964. Transferred 28 September 1985 having been paid off by the French Navy in 1981. This was the only operational ship in the Navy in 1992.

EDIC   1990, J Y Robert

3 LCVP TYPE

FIHERENGA   MAROLA   SAMBATHRA

Comment: 14.3 m personnel launches acquired from West Germany in 1988.

TRAINING SHIP

Name	No	Builders	Commissioned
FANANTENANA (ex-*Richelieu*)	—	A G Weser, Bremen	1959

Displacement, tons: 1040 standard; 1200 full load
Dimensions, feet (metres): 206.4 × 30 × 14.8 *(62.9 × 9.2 × 4.5)*
Main machinery: 2 Deutz diesels; 2400 hp(m) *(1.76 MW)*; 1 shaft
Speed, knots: 12
Complement: 45
Guns: 2 Bofors 40 mm/60.

Comment: Trawler (691 tons gross) purchased and converted in 1966-67 for Coast Guard and as training ship/transport. Can accommodate up to 120 people as well as carrying 300 tons of cargo. Occasionally hired out to tourists.

MALAWI

Senior Appointment

Commander of the Navy:
Lieutenant Colonel M M B Gondwe

Base

Monkey Bay, Lake Malawi

Personnel

1993: 220

PATROL FORCES

Note: There are also one LCU and twelve RB 12 Zodiacs.

1 ANTARES CLASS

CHIKALA P 703

Displacement, tons: 36 full load
Dimensions, feet (metres): 68.9 × 16.1 × 4.9 *(21 × 4.9 × 1.5)*
Main machinery: 2 Poyaud 520 V12 M2 diesels; 1300 hp(m) *(956 kW)*; 2 shafts
Speed, knots: 22. Range, miles: 650 at 15 kts
Complement: 6
Guns: 1—12.7 mm MG.

Comment: Built in prefabricated sections by SFCN Villeneuve-la-Garenne and shipped to Malawi for assembly on 17 December 1984. Commissioned May 1985. Non-operational in early 1993.

CHIKALA *1984, van Ginderen Collection*

1 NAMACURRA TYPE

Displacement, tons: 5 full load
Dimensions, feet (metres): 29.5 × 9 × 2.8 *(9 × 2.7 × 0.8)*
Main machinery: 2 diesels; 2 shafts
Speed, knots: 32
Complement: 4
Guns: 1—12.7 mm MG. 2—7.62 mm MGs.

Comment: Delivered by South Africa on 29 October 1988. Operational in 1992.

2 SURVEY LAUNCHES

Displacement, tons: 70 full load
Dimensions, feet (metres): 68.9 *(21)* length
Main machinery: 2 Baudouin diesels; 2 shafts
Speed, knots: 10.5

Comment: Built by SFCN Villeneuve-la-Garenne and delivered at the end of 1988 for operations on Lake Malawi.

MALAYSIA

(including Sabah)

Headquarters' Appointments

Chief of the Navy:
Vice Admiral Dato Seri Mohd Shariff Bin Ishak
Deputy Chief of Navy:
Rear Admiral Ahmad Ramli Bin Nor
Fleet Commander:
Rear Admiral Dato Yaacob Bin Haji Daud
Commander Naval Area I (Peninsula):
Commodore Dato Abu Bakar Bin Abdul Jamal
Commander Naval Area II (Sabah and Sarawak):
Commodore Hj Ahmad Bin Haron

Diplomatic Representation

Defence Adviser in London:
Colonel Z Saidi

Personnel

(a) 1993: 12 500 officers and ratings
(b) Voluntary service
(c) RMNVR: Total, 1000 officers and sailors
Divisions at Penang, Selangor and Johore. Target of 7000 in 19 port divisions.

Future Plans

It is planned to build 15 small bases around the country with main emphasis on training reserves to man ships taken up in an emergency. Each base will provide a harbour for naval vessels and have up to 400 personnel.

Bases

KD *Malaya*, Lumut HQ Area 1 (West of 109°E); (Telok Muroh) Perak
Fleet Operation Command centre, main fleet base, dockyard and training centre on west coast
KD *Pelandok*, Lumut (Training Centre)
RMN Barrack Woodlands (Training and Support), Singapore
Kuantan—an advanced base completed in 1981 on east coast
Labuan—(KD *Sri Labuan*, KD *Sri Tawau*, KD *Sri Rejang*) HQ Area 2 (East of 109°E)
Sungei Antu in Sarawak
Sitiawan, Perak; site for planned new naval air station
Kota Kinabalu; site for planned patrol boat base in East Malaysia (1995-96).

Prefix to Ships' Names

The names of Malaysian warships are prefixed by KD (Kapal DiRaja meaning King's Ship).

Maritime Patrol Craft

There are large numbers of armed patrol craft belonging to the Police, Customs and Fisheries Departments. Details at the end of the section.

Strength of the Fleet

Type	Active	Building (Planned)
Frigates	2	2
Corvettes	2	—
Offshore Patrol Vessels	2	(4)
Logistic Support Vessels	2	—
Fast Attack Craft—Missile	8	—
Fast Attack Craft—Gun	6	—
Patrol Craft	21	—
Minehunters	4	—
Diving Tender	1	—
Survey Vessels	1	(1)
LSTs	2	—
Amphibious Craft	198	—
Tugs	17	—

Mercantile Marine

Lloyd's Register of Shipping:
552 vessels of 2 015 562 tons gross

DELETION

1990 *Perantau*

PENNANT LIST

Frigates		Light Forces					Mine Warfare Forces	
24	Rahmat	34	Kris	3144	Sri Sabah	11	Mahamiru
76	Hang Tuah	36	Sundang	3145	Sri Sarawak	12	Jerai
		37	Badek	3146	Sri Negri Sembilan	13	Ledang
		38	Renchong	3147	Sri Melaka	14	Kinabalu
		39	Tombak	3501	Perdana		
		40	Lembing	3502	Serang		
Corvettes		41	Serampang	3503	Ganas		
25	Kasturi	42	Panah	3504	Ganyang		
26	Lekir	43	Kerambit	3505	Jerong		
		44	Beledau	3506	Todak	Support Forces	
		45	Kelewang	3507	Paus		
		46	Rentaka	3508	Yu	152	Mutiara
		47	Sri Perlis	3509	Baung	1109	Duyong
Offshore Patrol Vessels		49	Sri Johor	3510	Pari	1501	Sri Banggi
		3139	Sri Selangor	3511	Handalan	1502	Rajah Jarom
160	Musytari	3142	Sri Kelantan	3512	Perkasa	1503	Sri Indera Sakti
161	Marikh	3143	Sri Trengganu	3513	Pendekar	1504	Mahawangsa
				3514	Gempita		

SUBMARINES

Note: Approved in principle in April 1988 to start a submarine squadron with up to two refurbished vessels as training boats while two new ones were to be built. On 28 November 1990 it was announced that the government had approved a naval request to buy two new construction and two second-hand Swedish hulls at a cost of over US$500 million spread over a period of several years. In 1991 the government announced that the programme had been postponed, although in 1992 a naval staff requirement was again raised. Training is being done in Pakistan, India and Australia.

FRIGATES

0 + 2 FRIGATE 2000

Name	No	Builders	Laid down	Launched	Commissioned
—	—	Yarrow (Shipbuilders), Glasgow	Dec 1992	1995	1996
—	—	Yarrow (Shipbuilders), Glasgow	1993	1996	1997

Displacement, tons: 1845 standard; 2270 full load
Dimensions, feet (metres): 346 oa; 319.9 wl × 42 × 11.8 *(105.5; 97.5 × 12.8 × 3.6)*
Main machinery: CODAD; 4 MTU 20V 1163 TB93 diesels; 33 300 hp(m) *(24.5 MW)* sustained; 2 shafts; cp props
Speed, knots: 28. **Range, miles:** 5000 at 18 kts
Complement: 146 (18 officers)

Missiles: SSM: 8 Aerospatiale MM 40 Exocet Block II ❶.
SAM: British Aerospace VLS Seawolf; 16 launchers ❷.
Guns: 1 Bofors 57 mm/70 SAK Mk 2 ❸.
2 MSI Defence Systems 30 mm DS 30B ❹.
Torpedoes: 6 Whitehead B 515 324 mm (2 triple) tubes ❺; anti-submarine; GEC Mk 46 Mod 5.
Countermeasures: Decoys: 2 Super Barricade 12-barrelled launchers for chaff ❻; Graseby Sea Siren torpedo decoy.
ESM/ECM: AEG Telefunken/Marconi Mentor/THORN EMI Scimitar; intercept and jammer.
Combat data systems: GEC/Marconi Nautis-F; Link Y.
Fire control: Radamec Series 2000 Optronic director ❼. Thomson-CSF ITL 70 (for Exocet); GEC/Marconi Type V 3901 thermal imager.
Radars: Air search: Signaal DA 08 ❽; E/F band.
Surface search: Ericsson Sea Giraffe 150HC ❾; G/H band.
Navigation: Racal; I band.
Fire control: 2 Marconi 1802 ❿; I/J band.
Sonars: Thomson Sintra Spherion; hull-mounted active search and attack; medium frequency.

Helicopters: 1 Westland Wasp HAS 1 ⓫ or Lynx.

Programmes: Contract announced 31 March 1992 for two ships originally classed as corvettes but uprated to light frigates.
Structure: GEC Naval Systems Frigate 2000 design with a modern combat data system and automated machinery control.

FRIGATE 2000 *(Scale 1 : 900), Ian Sturton*

FRIGATE 2000 (artist's impression) *1992, GEC Naval Systems*

1 YARROW TYPE

Name	No	Builders	Laid down	Launched	Commissioned
RAHMAT (ex-*Hang Jebat*)	24	Yarrow (Shipbuilders), Glasgow	Feb 1966	18 Dec 1967	31 Aug 1971

Displacement, tons: 1250 standard; 1600 full load
Dimensions, feet (metres): 308 × 34.1 × 14.8 *(93.9 × 10.4 × 4.5)*
Main machinery: CODOG; 1 Bristol Siddeley Olympus TM1B gas turbine; 20 626 hp *(15.4 MW)*; 1 Crossley Pielstick PC2.2 V diesel; 4000 hp *(2.94 MW)*; 2 shafts; cp props
Speed, knots: 26 gas; 16 diesel. **Range, miles:** 6000 at 16 kts; 1000 at 26 kts
Complement: 140

Guns: 1 Vickers 4.5 in *(114 mm)*/45 Mk 5 hand-loaded ❶; 50° elevation; 14 rounds/minute to 17 km *(9.2 nm)* anti-surface; 8 km *(4.4 nm)* anti-aircraft; weight of shell 25 kg. 103 mm rocket for illuminants on each side of mounting.
3 Bofors 40 mm/70 ❷; 90° elevation; 300 rounds/minute to 12 km *(6.5 nm)* anti-surface; 4 km *(2.2 nm)* anti-aircraft; weight of shell 0.96 kg.
A/S mortars: 1 Limbo Mk 10 3-tubed mortar ❸; automatic loading; range 900 m; warhead 92 kg.
Countermeasures: Decoys: 2 UK Mk I rail chaff launchers.
ESM: UA-3; radar intercept; FH4 HF D/F.
Combat data systems: Signaal Sewaco-MA. Link Y.
Radars: Air search: Signaal LW 02 ❹; D band; range 183 km *(100 nm)*.
Surface search: Decca 626 ❺; I band.
Navigation: Kelvin Hughes MS 32; I band.
Fire control: Signaal M 22 ❻; I/J band; short range.
Sonars: Graseby Type 170B and Type 174; hull-mounted; active search and attack; 15 kHz.

Programmes: Ordered on 11 February 1966. Arrived on station 23 December 1972.
Modernisation: Seacat system removed during refit in 1982-83 and replaced by an additional Bofors gun. A fourth Bofors was mounted (lashed) on the forward part of the flight deck in July 1990 but this appears to have been a temporary arrangement.
Operational: Can land helicopter on MacGregor hatch over Mk 10 well.

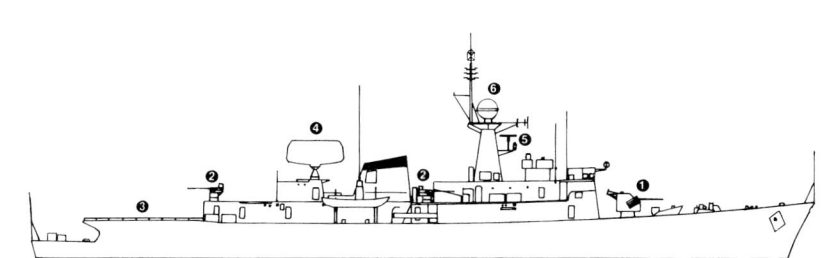

RAHMAT *(Scale 1 : 900), Ian Sturton*

RAHMAT *2/1991*

404 MALAYSIA / Frigates — Corvettes

1 Ex-BRITISH TYPE 41/61

Name	No	Builders	Laid down	Launched	Commissioned
HANG TUAH (ex-HMS *Mermaid*)	76	Yarrow (Shipbuilders), Glasgow	1965	29 Dec 1966	16 May 1973

Displacement, tons: 2300 standard; 2520 full load
Dimensions, feet (metres): 339.3 × 40 × 16 (screws) *(103.5 × 12.2 × 4.9)*
Main machinery: 8 VVS ASR 1 diesels; 12 380 hp *(9.2 MW)* sustained; 2 shafts; cp props
Speed, knots: 24. **Range, miles:** 4800 at 15 kts
Complement: 210

Guns: 2 Vickers 4 in *(102 mm)*/45 Mk 19 (twin) ❶; 80° elevation; 16 rounds/minute to 19 km *(10.3 nm)* anti-surface; 13 km *(7 nm)* anti-aircraft; weight of shell 16 kg.
 2 Bofors 40 mm/70 ❷; 90° elevation; 300 rounds/minute to 12 km *(6.5 nm)* anti-surface; 4 km *(2.2 nm)* anti-aircraft; weight of shell 0.96 kg.
A/S mortars: 1 RN Limbo 3-tubed Mk 10 mortar ❸; automatic loading; range 1000 m; warhead 92 kg.
Fire control: STD Mk 1 sight for 102 mm gun.
Radars: Air/surface search: Plessey AWS 1 ❹; E/F band; range 110 km *(60 nm)*.
 Navigation: Racal Decca 45 ❺; I band.
Sonars: Graseby Type 170B and Type 174; hull-mounted; active search and attack; 15 kHz.

Helicopters: Platform for 1 Westland Wasp HAS 1.

Programmes: Originally built for Ghana as a display ship for ex-President Nkrumah at a cost of £5 million but put up for sale after his departure. She was launched without ceremony on 29 December 1966 and completed in 1968. Commissioned in Royal Navy 16 May 1973, she was based at Singapore 1974-75 returning to the UK early 1976. Transferred to Royal Malaysian Navy May 1977 and refitted by Vosper Thornycroft before sailing for Malaysia in August 1977.
Structure: Similar in hull and machinery to former Leopard and Salisbury classes.
Operational: Refitted in 1991/92 to become a training ship in 1993.

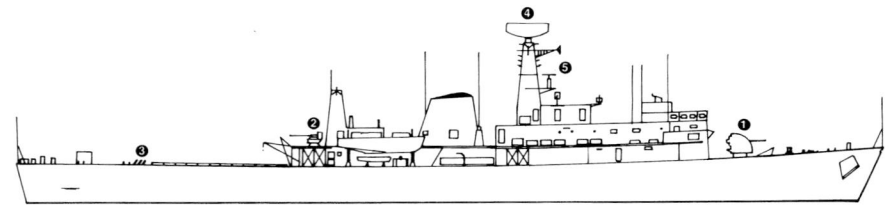

HANG TUAH *(Scale 1 : 900), Ian Sturton*

HANG TUAH *11/1988, Trevor Brown*

CORVETTES

2 TYPE FS 1500

Name	No	Builders	Laid down	Launched	Commissioned
KASTURI	25	Howaldtswerke, Kiel	3 Jan 1983	14 May 1983	15 Aug 1984
LEKIR	26	Howaldtswerke, Kiel	3 Jan 1983	14 May 1983	15 Aug 1984

Displacement, tons: 1500 standard; 1850 full load
Dimensions, feet (metres): 319.1 × 37.1 × 11.5 *(97.3 × 11.3 × 3.5)*
Main machinery: 4 MTU 20V 1163 TB92 diesels; 23 400 hp(m) *(17.2 MW)* sustained; 2 shafts
Speed, knots: 28; 18 on 2 diesels. **Range, miles:** 3000 at 18 kts; 5000 at 14 kts
Complement: 124 (13 officers)

Missiles: SSM: 4 Aerospatiale MM 38 Exocet ❶; inertial cruise; active radar homing to 42 km *(23 nm)* at 0.9 Mach; warhead 165 kg; sea-skimmer.
Guns: 1 Creusot-Loire 3.9 in *(100 mm)*/55 compact ❷; 80° elevation; 20/45/90 rounds/minute to 17 km *(9.2 nm)* anti-surface; 6 km *(3.2 nm)* anti-aircraft; weight of shell 13.5 kg.
 1 Bofors 57 mm/70 ❸; 75° elevation; 200 rounds/minute to 17 km *(9.2 nm)*; weight of shell 2.4 kg. Launchers for illuminants.
 4 Emerson Electric 30 mm (2 twin) ❹; 80° elevation; 1200 rounds/minute combined to 6 km *(3.2 nm)*; weight of shell 0.35 kg.
A/S mortars: 1 Bofors 375 mm twin trainable launcher ❺; automatic loading; range 3625 m.
Countermeasures: Decoys: 2 CSEE Dagaie trainable systems; replaceable containers for IR or chaff.
ESM: Rapids; radar intercept.
ECM: Scimitar; jammer.
Combat data systems: Signaal Sewaco-MA. Link Y.
Fire control: 2 Signaal LIOD optronic directors for gunnery.
Radars: Air/surface search: Signaal DA 08 ❻; F band; range 204 km *(110 nm)* for 2 m² target.
 Navigation: Decca TM 1226C; I band.
 Fire control: Signaal WM 22 ❼; I/J band; range 46 km *(25 nm)*.
 IFF: US Mk 10.
Sonars: Atlas Elektronik DSQS 21C; hull-mounted; active search and attack; medium frequency.

Helicopters: Platform for 1 Westland Wasp HAS 1 ❽.

Programmes: First two ordered in February 1981. Fabrication began early 1982. Rated as Corvettes even though they are bigger ships than *Rahmat*.
Modernisation: May be fitted with telescopic hangars in due course.
Structure: Near sisters to the Colombian ships with differing armament.

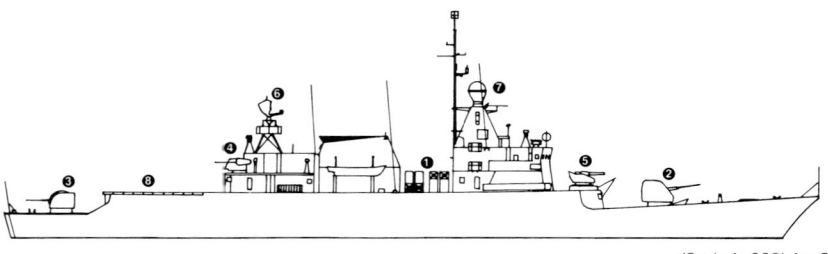

KASTURI *(Scale 1 : 900), Ian Sturton*

LEKIR *10/1991, John Mortime*

Offshore patrol vessels — Light forces / MALAYSIA 405

OFFSHORE PATROL VESSELS

Note: The new OPV project has taken second priority to the frigates. The plan is to place contracts in 1994 with the first of class to be built abroad and up to three more in Malaysian shipyards at Lumut and Johore. Required characteristics include about 1000 tons displacement, 20 kts speed, 6000 n miles at 12 kts endurance and a complement of 52 (7 officers). Weapons systems to include a helicopter (with telescopic hangar), medium and light guns, surveillance radar, optronic director and ESM.

2 OFFSHORE PATROL VESSELS

Name	No	Builders	Launched	Commissioned
MUSYTARI	160	Korea Shipbuilders, Pusan	20 July 1984	19 Dec 1985
MARIKH	161	Malaysia S B and E Co, Johore	21 Jan 1985	9 Apr 1987

Displacement, tons: 1300 full load
Dimensions, feet (metres): 246 × 35.4 × 12.1 *(75 × 10.8 × 3.7)*
Main machinery: 2 diesels; 12 720 hp(m) *(9.35 MW)*; 2 shafts
Speed, knots: 22. **Range, miles:** 5000 at 15 kts
Complement: 76

Guns: 1 Creusot Loire 3.9 in *(100 mm)*/55 compact; 80° elevation; 20/45/90 rounds/minute to 17 km *(9.2 nm)* anti-surface; 6 km *(3.2 nm)* anti-aircraft; weight of shell 13.5 kg.
  2 Emerson Electric 30 mm (twin); 80° elevation; 1200 rounds/minute combined to 6 km *(3.2 nm)*; weight of shell 0.35 kg.
Fire control: PEAB 9LV 230 optronic system.
Radars: Air/surface search: Signaal DA 05; E/F band; range 137 km *(75 nm)* for 2 m² target.
  Navigation: Racal Decca TM 1226; I band.
  Fire control: Philips 9LV; J band.

Programmes: Ordered in June 1983. Names translate to Jupiter and Mars.
Structure: Flight deck suitable for Sikorsky S-61A Nari army support helicopter.

MUSYTARI 5/1990, John Mortimer

SHIPBORNE AIRCRAFT

Numbers/Type: 16 Westland Wasp HAS 1.
Operational speed: 96 kts *(177 km/h)*.
Service ceiling: 12 200 ft *(3720 m)*.
Range: 268 nm *(488 km)*.
Role/Weapon systems: First naval air arm helicopter; six acquired in April 1988, six in 1989-90 and six more in 1991; more modern helicopters (up to a total of 40) planned (either Lynx or Dauphin) but may have to wait for next five year plan. Sensors: None. Weapons: ASW; 1 or 2 Mk 44 torpedoes, depth bombs.

LAND-BASED MARITIME AIRCRAFT

Note: 4 Beechcraft B 200T ordered 7 April 1992 for maritime surveillance role. Delivery expected in late 1993 for the Air Force.

Numbers/Type: 3 Lockheed C-130H-MP Hercules.
Operational speed: 325 kts *(602 km/h)*.
Service ceiling: 33 000 ft *(10 060 m)*.
Range: 4250 nm *(7880 km)*.
Role/Weapon systems: Long-range MR and SAR tasks; operated by the Air Force. Sensors: Search radar, cameras. Weapons: Unarmed.

LIGHT FORCES

4 SPICA-M CLASS (FAST ATTACK CRAFT—MISSILE)

Name	No	Builders	Commissioned
HANDALAN	3511	Karlskrona Varvet, Sweden	26 Oct 1979
PERKASA	3512	Karlskrona Varvet, Sweden	26 Oct 1979
PENDEKAR	3513	Karlskrona Varvet, Sweden	26 Oct 1979
GEMPITA	3514	Karlskrona Varvet, Sweden	26 Oct 1979

Displacement, tons: 240 full load
Dimensions, feet (metres): 142.6 × 23.3 × 7.4 (screws) *(43.6 × 7.1 × 2.4)*
Main machinery: 3 MTU 16V 538 TB91 diesels; 9180 hp(m) *(6.75 MW)* sustained; 3 shafts
Speed, knots: 34.5. **Range, miles:** 1850 at 14 kts
Complement: 40 (6 officers)

Missiles: SSM: 4 Aerospatiale MM 38 Exocet; inertial cruise; active radar homing to 42 km *(23 nm)* at 0.9 Mach; warhead 165 kg; sea-skimmer.
Guns: 1 Bofors 57 mm/70; 75° elevation; 200 rounds/minute to 17 km *(9.2 nm)*; weight of shell 2.4 kg. Illuminant launchers.
  1 Bofors 40 mm/70; 90° elevation; 300 rounds/minute to 12 km *(6.5 nm)* anti-surface; 4 km *(2.2 nm)* anti-aircraft; weight of shell 0.96 kg.
Countermeasures: ECM: MEL Susie.
Fire control: 1 PEAB 9LV200 Mk 2 weapon control system with TV tracking. LME anti-aircraft laser and TV rangefinder.
Radars: Surface search: Philips 9GR 600; I band (agile frequency).
  Navigation: Decca 616; I band.
  Fire control: Philips 9LV 212; J band.
Sonars: Simrad; hull-mounted; active search; high frequency.

Programmes: Ordered 15 October 1976. All named in one ceremony on 11 November 1978, arriving in Port Klang on 26 October 1979.
Structure: Bridge further forward than in Swedish class to accommodate Exocet. Provision has been made for fitting 324 mm torpedo tubes.
Operational: *Handalan* acts as squadron leader.

4 PERDANA CLASS (FAST ATTACK CRAFT—MISSILE)

Name	No	Builders	Commissioned
PERDANA	3501	Constructions Mécaniques de Normandie	21 Dec 1972
SERANG	3502	Constructions Mécaniques de Normandie	31 Jan 1973
GANAS	3503	Constructions Mécaniques de Normandie	28 Feb 1973
GANYANG	3504	Constructions Mécaniques de Normandie	20 Mar 1973

Displacement, tons: 234 standard; 265 full load
Dimensions, feet (metres): 154.2 × 23.1 × 12.8 *(47 × 7 × 3.9)*
Main machinery: 4 MTU MB 870 diesels; 14 000 hp(m) *(10.3 MW)*; 4 shafts
Speed, knots: 36.5. **Range, miles:** 800 at 25 kts; 1800 at 15 kts
Complement: 30 (4 officers)

Missiles: SSM: 2 Aerospatiale MM 38 Exocet; inertial cruise; active radar homing to 42 km *(23 nm)* at 0.9 Mach; warhead 165 kg; sea-skimmer.
Guns: 1 Bofors 57 mm/70; 75° elevation; 200 rounds/minute to 17 km *(9.2 nm)*; weight of shell 2.4 kg.
  1 Bofors 40 mm/70; 90° elevation; 300 rounds/minute to 12 km *(6.5 nm)* anti-surface; 4 km *(2.2 nm)* anti-aircraft; weight of shell 0.96 kg.
Countermeasures: Decoys: 4—57 mm chaff/flare launchers.
ESM: French type; radar warning.
Fire control: Thomson-CSF Vega optical for guns.
Radars: Air/surface search: Thomson-CSF TH-D 1040 Triton; G band; range 33 km *(18 nm)* for 2 m² target.
  Navigation: Racal Decca 616; I band.
  Fire control: Thomson-CSF Pollux; I/J band; range 31 km *(17 nm)* for 2 m² target.

Programmes: Left Cherbourg for Malaysia 2 May 1973.
Structure: All of basic La Combattante IID design.

PENDEKAR 5/1990, John Mortimer   GANAS 5/1991, 92 Wing RAAF

406 MALAYSIA / Light forces — Amphibious forces

6 JERONG CLASS (FAST ATTACK CRAFT—GUN)

Name	No	Builders	Commissioned
JERONG	3505	Hong Leong-Lürssen, Butterworth	27 Mar 1976
TODAK	3506	Hong Leong-Lürssen, Butterworth	16 June 1976
PAUS	3507	Hong Leong-Lürssen, Butterworth	16 Aug 1976
YU	3508	Hong Leong-Lürssen, Butterworth	15 Nov 1976
BAUNG	3509	Hong Leong-Lürssen, Butterworth	11 Jan 1977
PARI	3510	Hong Leong-Lürssen, Butterworth	23 Mar 1977

Displacement, tons: 244 full load
Dimensions, feet (metres): 147.3 × 23 × 8.3 *(44.9 × 7 × 2.5)*
Main machinery: 3 MTU MB 16V 538 TB90 diesels; 9000 hp(m) *(6.6 MW)* sustained; 3 shafts
Speed, knots: 32. **Range, miles:** 2000 at 14 kts
Complement: 36 (4 officers)
Guns: 1 Bofors 57 mm/70. 1 Bofors 40 mm/70.
Fire control: CSEE Naja optronic director.
Radars: Surface search: Racal Decca 626; I band.
Navigation: Kelvin Hughes MS 32.
Fire control: Signaal WM 28; I/J band; range 46 km *(25 nm)*.

Comment: Lürssen 45 type. Illuminant launchers on both gun mountings.

PARI *5/1990, John Mortimer*

21 KEDAH, SABAH and KRIS CLASSES (PATROL CRAFT)

Name	No	Builders	Commissioned
SRI SELANGOR	3139	Vosper Ltd, Portsmouth	25 Mar 1963
SRI KELANTAN	3142	Vosper Ltd, Portsmouth	12 Nov 1963
SRI TRENGGANU	3143	Vosper Ltd, Portsmouth	16 Dec 1963
SRI SABAH	3144	Vosper Ltd, Portsmouth	2 Sep 1964
SRI SARAWAK	3145	Vosper Ltd, Portsmouth	30 Sep 1964
SRI NEGRI SEMBILAN	3146	Vosper Ltd, Portsmouth	28 Sep 1964
SRI MELAKA	3147	Vosper Ltd, Portsmouth	2 Nov 1964
KRIS	34	Vosper Ltd, Portsmouth	1 Jan 1966
SUNDANG	36	Vosper Ltd, Portsmouth	29 Nov 1966
BADEK	37	Vosper Ltd, Portsmouth	15 Dec 1966
RENCHONG	38	Vosper Ltd, Portsmouth	17 Jan 1967
TOMBAK	39	Vosper Ltd, Portsmouth	2 Mar 1967
LEMBING	40*	Vosper Ltd, Portsmouth	12 Apr 1967
SERAMPANG	41	Vosper Ltd, Portsmouth	19 May 1967
PANAH	42	Vosper Ltd, Portsmouth	27 July 1967
KERAMBIT	43*	Vosper Ltd, Portsmouth	28 July 1967
BELEDAU	44*	Vosper Ltd, Portsmouth	12 Sep 1967
KELEWANG	45	Vosper Ltd, Portsmouth	4 Oct 1967
RENTAKA	46	Vosper Ltd, Portsmouth	22 Sep 1967
SRI PERLIS	47*	Vosper Ltd, Portsmouth	24 Jan 1968
SRI JOHOR	49*	Vosper Ltd, Portsmouth	14 Feb 1968

* Training

Displacement, tons: 96 standard; 109 full load
Dimensions, feet (metres): 103 × 19.8 × 5.5 *(31.4 × 6 × 1.7)*
Main machinery: 2 Bristol Siddeley or MTU MD 655/18 diesels; 3500 hp(m) *(2.57 MW)*; 2 shafts
Speed, knots: 27. **Range, miles:** 1400 (1660 Sabah class) at 14 kts
Complement: 22 (3 officers)
Guns: 2 Bofors 40 mm/60 (not in 3139, 3142-43).
Radars: Surface search: Racal Decca 616 or 707; I band.

Comment: The first six boats (of which three remain in service), constitute the Kedah class and were ordered in 1961 for delivery in 1963. The four Sabah class were ordered in 1963 for delivery in 1964. The boats of the Kris class were ordered in 1965 for delivery between 1966 and 1968. All are of prefabricated steel construction and are fitted with air-conditioning and Vosper roll damping equipment. The differences between the three classes are minor, the later ones having improved radar, communications, evaporators and engines of MTU, as opposed to Bristol Siddeley construction. *Sri Melaka* (P 3147) is on loan to Sabah. All 21 have been refitted to extend their operational lives. The three Kedah class have had their guns removed.

KELEWANG *5/1990, John Mortimer*

SRI MELAKA *5/1990, G Toremans*

MINE WARFARE FORCES

Note: Plans for more Lerici class have been shelved in favour of Inshore minehunters in due course.

4 LERICI CLASS (MINEHUNTERS)

Name	No	Builders	Commissioned
MAHAMIRU	11	Intermarine, Italy	11 Dec 1985
JERAI	12	Intermarine, Italy	11 Dec 1985
LEDANG	13	Intermarine, Italy	11 Dec 1985
KINABALU	14	Intermarine, Italy	11 Dec 1985

Displacement, tons: 470 standard; 610 full load
Dimensions, feet (metres): 167.3 × 31.5 × 9.2 *(51 × 9.6 × 2.8)*
Main machinery: 2 MTU 12V 396 TC82 diesels (passage); 2605 hp(m) *(1.91 MW)* sustained; 2 shafts; KaMeWa cp props; 3 Fincantieri Isotta Fraschini ID 36 SS 6V diesels; 1481 hp(m) *(1.09 MW)* sustained; 2 Riva Calzoni hydraulic thrust jets
Speed, knots: 16 diesels; 7 thrust jet. **Range, miles:** 2000 at 12 kts
Complement: 42 (5 officers)
Guns: 1 Bofors 40 mm/70; 85° elevation; 300 rounds/minute to 12.5 km *(6.8 nm)*; weight of shell 0.96 kg.
Countermeasures: Thomson-CSF IBIS II minehunting system; 2 improved PAP 104 vehicles. Oropesa 'O' MIS-4 mechanical sweep.
Radars: Navigation: Racal Decca 1226; Thomson-CSF Tripartite III; I band.
Sonars: Thomson Sintra TSM 2022 with Display 2060; minehunting; high frequency.

Comment: Ordered on 20 February 1981. First (14) launched 19 March 1983; second (13) 14 July 1983; third (12) 5 January 1984; fourth (11) 23 February 1984. All arrived in Malaysia on 26 March 1986. Heavy GRP construction without frames. Snach active tank stabilisers. Draeger Duocom decompression chamber. Slightly longer than Italian sisters. Endurance, 14 days. Based at Labuan and Lumut to cover both coasts.

JERAI *5/1990, John Mortimer*

AMPHIBIOUS FORCES

Note: Some interest shown in LCACs but no orders placed yet.

5 LCMs and 15 LCPs

LCM 1-5   LCP 1-15

Displacement, tons: 56 (LCM); 18.5 (LCVP) full load
Main machinery: 2 diesels; 330 hp *(246 kW)* (LCM); 400 hp *(298 kW)* (LCVP); 2 shafts
Speed, knots: 10 (LCM); 16 (LCVP)
Military lift: 30 tons (LCM)

Comment: Australian-built and transferred 1965-70. LCMs have light armour on sides and some have gun turrets.

LCM 3 (with gun turret) *5/1990, van Ginderen Collection*

2 Ex-US 511-1152 CLASS (LSTs)

SRI BANGGI (ex-USS *Henry County* LST 824) 1501
RAJAH JAROM (ex-USS *Sedgewick County* LST 1123) 1502

Displacement, tons: 1653 standard; 2366 beaching; 4080 full load
Dimensions, feet (metres): 328 × 50 × 12 *(100 × 15.3 × 3.7)*
Main machinery: 2 GM 12-567A diesels; 1800 hp(m) *(1.34 MW)*; 2 shafts
Speed, knots: 11.6
Complement: 128 (11 officers)
Military lift: 2100 tons; 500 tons beaching or 125 troops
Guns: 6 Bofors 40 mm (2 twin, 2 single).
Fire control: 2 Mk 51G for guns.
Radars: Surface search: Raytheon SPS 21C (1501); G/H band; range 22 km *(12 nm)*.
Sperry SPS 53 (1502); I/J band.

Comment: Built by Missouri Valley BY (1501) and Chicago Bridge Co in 1945. Transferred 1 August 1974, by sale 7 October 1976. Operate as harbour tenders to Light Forces and seldom go to sea.

SRI BANGGI *5/1991, 92 Wing RAAF*

9 RCPs and 4 LCUs

RCP 1-9   LCU 1-4

Displacement, tons: 30 full load
Main machinery: 2 diesels
Speed, knots: 17
Military lift: 35 troops
Guns: 1 Oerlikon 20 mm.

Comment: Malaysian built. RCPs in service 1974. LCUs in service 1984.

165 DAMEN ASSAULT CRAFT 540

Dimensions, feet (metres): 17.7 × 5.9 × 2 *(5.4 × 1.8 × 0.6)*
Main machinery: 1 outboard; 40 hp(m) *(29.4 kW)*
Speed, knots: 12
Military lift: 10 troops

Comment: First 65 built by Damen Gorinchem, Netherlands in 1986. Remainder built by Limbungan Timor SY. Army assault craft. Manportable and similar to Singapore craft.

SURVEY VESSELS

Note: A replacement survey ship for the deleted *Perantau* is a priority. Negotiations continue for a second-hand ship.

Name	No	Builders	Commissioned
MUTIARA	152	Hong Leong-Lürssen, Butterworth	12 Jan 1978

Displacement, tons: 1905
Dimensions, feet (metres): 232.9 × 42.6 × 13.1 *(71 × 13 × 4)*
Main machinery: 2 Deutz SBA12M528 diesels; 4000 hp(m) *(2.94 MW)*; 2 shafts
Speed, knots: 16. **Range, miles:** 4500 at 16 kts
Complement: 155 (14 officers)
Guns: 4 Oerlikon 20 mm (2 twin).
Radars: Navigation: Two-Racal Decca; I band.
Helicopters: Platform only.

Comment: Ordered in early 1975. Carries satellite navigation, auto-data system and computerised fixing system. Davits for six survey launches. Painted white. She acted as the Reviewing ship for the Penang Fleet Review in May 1990.

MUTIARA *5/1990, John Mortimer*

LOGISTIC SUPPORT SHIPS

Name	No	Builders	Commissioned
SRI INDERA SAKTI	1503	Bremer Vulkan	24 Oct 1980
MAHAWANGSA	1504	Korea Tacoma	16 May 1983

Displacement, tons: 4300 (1503); 4900 (1504) full load
Dimensions, feet (metres): 328; 337.9 (1504) × 49.2 × 15.7 *(100; 103 × 15 × 4.8)*
Main machinery: 2 KHD SBV6M540 diesels; 5865 hp(m) *(4.31 MW)*; 2 shafts; cp props; bow thruster
Speed, knots: 16.5. **Range, miles:** 4000 at 14 kts
Complement: 136 (14 officers) plus accommodation for 215
Military lift: 17 tanks; 600 troops
Cargo capacity: 1300 tons dieso; 200 tons fresh water (plus 48 tons/day distillers)

Guns: 2 Bofors 57 mm Mk 1 (1 only fwd in 1503). 2 Oerlikon 20 mm.
Fire control: 2 CSEE Naja optronic directors (1 only in 1503).
Radars: Navigation: I band.

Helicopters: 1 Sikorsky S-61A Nari (army support) can be carried.

Programmes: Ordered in October 1979 and 1981 respectively.
Modernisation: 100 mm gun included in original design but used for OPVs.
Structure: Fitted with stabilising system, vehicle deck, embarkation ramps port and starboard, recompression chamber and a stern anchor. Large operations room and a conference room are provided. Transfer stations on either beam and aft, light jackstay on both sides and a 15 ton crane for replenishment at sea. 1504 has additional capacity to transport ammunition and the funnel has been removed to enlarge the flight deck.
Operational: Used as training ships for cadets in addition to main roles of long-range support of Light Forces and MCM vessels, command and communications and troop or ammunition transport.

SRI INDERA SAKTI *9/1990, G Toremans*

MAHAWANGSA (no funnel) *10/1991, John Mortimer*

DIVING TENDER

Name	No	Builders	Commissioned
DUYONG	1109	Kall Teck (Pte) Ltd, Singapore	5 Jan 1971

Displacement, tons: 120 standard; 140 full load
Dimensions, feet (metres): 110 × 21 × 5.8 *(33.6 × 6.4 × 1.8)*
Main machinery: 2 Cummins diesels; 500 hp *(373 kW)*; 2 shafts
Speed, knots: 12. **Range, miles:** 1000
Complement: 23
Guns: 1 Oerlikon 20 mm (not fitted).

Comment: Launched on 18 August 1970 as TRV. Carries recompression chamber. Can act as support ship for 7-10 commandos.

DUYONG *5/1990, van Ginderen Collection*

MISCELLANEOUS

1 SAIL TRAINING SHIP

TUNAS SAMUDERA

Displacement, tons: 239 full load
Dimensions, feet (metres): 114.8 × 25.6 × 13.1 *(35 × 7.8 × 4)*
Main machinery: 2 Perkins diesels; 370 hp *(272 kW)*; 2 shafts
Speed, knots: 9
Complement: 10
Radars: Navigation: Racal Decca; I band.

Comment: Ordered from Brooke Yacht, Lowestoft. Laid down 1 December 1988, launched 4 August 1989 and completed 16 October 1989. Two-masted brig manned by the Navy but used for training all sea services.

TUNAS SAMUDERA 8/1991, 92 Wing RAAF

9 COASTAL SUPPLY SHIPS AND TANKERS

LANG HINDEK	LANG KANGOK	LANG SIPUT
LANG TIRAM	ENTERPRISE	KEPAH
MELEBAN	JERNIH	TERIJAH

Comment: Various auxiliaries mostly acquired in the early 1980s.

KEPAH 5/1990, John Mortimer

12 HARBOUR TUGS AND CRAFT

TUNDA SATU	KETAM	KUPANG	SOTONG
BELAWKAS	KEMPONG	MANGKASA	SIPUT
TEPURUK	TERITUP	PENYU	SELAR

TUNDA SATU 5/1990, van Ginderen Collection

SABAH SUPPLY SHIPS

Comment: There are a number of Sabah supply ships which are identified by M numbers.

KURAMAH (M 48) 9/1988, van Ginderen Collection

ROYAL MALAYSIAN POLICE

15 LANG HITAM CLASS

LANG HITAM PZ 1	BELIAN PZ 6	HARIMAU BELANG PZ 11
LANG MALAM PZ 2	KURITA PZ 7	HARIMAU AKAR PZ 12
LANG LEBAH PZ 3	SERANGAN BATU PZ 8	PERANGAN PZ 13
LANG KUIK PZ 4	HARIMAU BINTANG PZ 9	MERSUJI PZ 14
BALONG PZ 5	HARIMAU KUMBANG PZ 10	ALU-ALU PZ 15

Displacement, tons: 230 full load
Dimensions, feet (metres): 126.3 × 22.9 × 5.9 *(38.5 × 7 × 1.8)*
Main machinery: 2 MTU 20V 538 TB92 diesels; 8530 hp(m) *(6.27 MW)* sustained; 2 shafts
Speed, knots: 35. Range, miles: 1200 at 15 kts
Complement: 38 (4 officers)
Guns: 1 Bofors 40 mm/70 (in a distinctive plastic turret).
  1 Oerlikon 20 mm. 2 FN 7.62 mm MGs.
Radars: Navigation: Kelvin Hughes; I band.

Comment: Ordered from Hong Leong-Lürssen, Butterworth, Malaysia in 1979. First delivered August 1980, last in April 1983.

ALU-ALU 1991, RM Police

6 BROOKE MARINE 29 METRE CLASS

| SANGITAN PX 28 | DUNGUN PX 30 | TUMPAT PX 32 |
| SABAHAN PX 29 | TIOMAN PX 31 | SEGAMA PX 33 |

Displacement, tons: 114
Dimensions, feet (metres): 95.1 × 19.7 × 5.6 *(29 × 6 × 1.7)*
Main machinery: 2 Paxman Valenta 6CM diesels; 2250 hp *(1.68 MW)* sustained; 2 shafts
Speed, knots: 36. Range, miles: 1200 at 24 kts
Complement: 18 (4 officers)
Guns: 2 Oerlikon 20 mm.

Comment: Ordered 1979 from Penang Shipbuilding Co. First delivery June 1981, last pair completed June 1982. Brooke Marine provided lead yard services.

SANGITAN 1991, RM Police

9 IMPROVED PX CLASS

ALOR SETAR PX 19	JOHORE BAHRU PX 22	SRI GAYA PX 25
KOTA BAHRU PX 20	SRI MENANTI PX 23	SRI KUDAT PX 26
KUALA TRENGGANU PX 21	KUCHING PX 24	SRI TAWAU PX 27

Displacement, tons: 92 full load
Dimensions, feet (metres): 91 × 19 × 4.9 *(27.8 × 5.8 × 1.5)*
Main machinery: 2 MTU MB 12V 493 TY7 diesels; 2200 hp(m) *(1.62 MW)* sustained; 2 shafts
Speed, knots: 25. **Range, miles:** 900 at 15 kts
Complement: 17 (2 officers)
Guns: 2 Oerlikon 20 mm.
Radars: Kelvin Hughes Type 19; I band.

Comment: Built by Vosper Thornycroft (Private) Ltd, Singapore between 1972-73.

SRI MENANTI *1972, Yam Photos, Singapore*

18 PX CLASS

MAHKOTA PX 1	BENTARA PX 7	PEKAN PX 13
TEMENGGONG PX 2	PERWIRA PX 8	KELANG PX 14
HULUBALANG PX 3	PERTANDA PX 9	KUALA KANGSAR PX 15
MAHARAJASETIA PX 4	SHAHBANDAR PX 10	ARAU PX 16
MAHARAJALELA PX 5	SANGSETIA PX 11	GUMANTONG PX 17
PAHLAWAN PX 6	LAKSAMANA PX 12	LABUAN PX 18

Displacement, tons: 86.4 full load
Dimensions, feet (metres): 87.5 × 19 × 4.9 *(26.7 × 5.8 × 1.5)*
Main machinery: 2 MTU MB 12V 493 TY7 diesels; 2200 hp(m) *(1.62 MW)* sustained; 2 shafts
Speed, knots: 25. **Range, miles:** 550 at 20 kts; 900 at 15 kts
Complement: 15
Guns: 1 Oerlikon 20 mm. 1 FN 7.62 mm MG.
Radars: Kelvin Hughes Type 19; I band; range 117 km *(64 nm)*.

Comment: Built by Vosper Thornycroft (Private) Ltd, Singapore and completed between 1963 and 1970. PX 17 and PX 18 operated by Sabah Government, remainder by Royal Malaysian Police.

BENTARA *1991, RM Police*

122 INSHORE/RIVER PATROL CRAFT

Comment: Built in several batches and designs since 1964. Some are armed with 7.62 mm MGs. All have PA/PC/PGR/PSC numbers. The latest batch are 23 Simmoneau SM 465 type built between January 1992 and mid-1993.

PA 6 (with MG) *1992, RM Police*

PC 2 *1991, RM Police*

6 TRANSPORT VESSELS

PENJAGA PT 1   MARGHERITA PT 2
PLC 1-4

Comment: The PLCs are landing craft built in 1980 by Pasir Gudang. The two PT craft were built in 1985 by Brooke Dockyard, Sarawak.

PENJAGA *1991, RM Police*

ROYAL MALAYSIAN CUSTOMS AND EXCISE

Note: In addition there are 30 interceptor craft and 12 inflatable chase boats.

6 VOSPER 32 METRE PATROL CRAFT

| JUANG K 33 | JERAI K 35 | BAYU K 37 |
| PULAI K 34 | PERAK K 36 | HIJAU K 38 |

Displacement, tons: 143 full load
Dimensions, feet (metres): 106.2 × 23.6 × 5.9 *(32.4 × 7.2 × 1.8)*
Main machinery: 2 Paxman Valenta 16CM diesels; 6650 hp *(5 MW)* sustained; 2 shafts
1 Cummins diesel; 575 hp *(423 kW)* on 1 shaft
Speed, knots: 27; 8 on cruise diesel. **Range, miles:** 2000 at 8 kts
Complement: 26
Guns: 1 Oerlikon 20 mm. 2—7.62 mm MGs.

Comment: Ordered February 1981 from Malaysia Shipyard and Engineering Company with technical support from Vosper Thornycroft (Private) Ltd, Singapore. Two completed 1982, the remainder in 1983-84. Names are preceded by 'Bahtera'.

HIJAU *4/1990, 92 Wing RAAF*

4 PEMBANTERAS CLASS

Dimensions, feet (metres): 94.5 × 19.4 × 6.6 *(28.8 × 5.9 × 2)*
Main machinery: 2 Deutz SBA-16M 816C diesels; 3140 hp(m) *(2.31 MW)*; 2 shafts
Speed, knots: 20
Complement: 8

Comment: Built at Limbungan Timor shipyard, Terengganu.

23—13.7 METRE PATROL CRAFT

Comment: Some carry a 7.62 mm machine gun.

13.7 m Customs   *4/1990, 92 Wing RAAF*

1—18 METRE PATROL CRAFT

KUALA BENGKOKA KA 34

Comment: Built by Mengsina Ltd, Singapore and commissioned on 3 December 1976. Based in Sabah.

KUALA BENGKOKA   *9/1988, van Ginderen Collection*

27 PENUMPAS CLASS

Comment: 9 m fast interceptor craft capable of 65 kts. Built in 1991/92 at Penang and Johore.

ROYAL MALAYSIAN FISHERIES DEPARTMENT

Note: Patrol craft have a distinctive diagonal band on the hull and have been mistaken for a Coast Guard. All have P numbers. Latest to be built in 1992 were P 51-53 at Ironwood, Malaysia.

FISHERIES P 25   *12/1988, Hartmut Ehlers*

FISHEFIES P 202   *5/1991, G Toremans*

MALDIVES

Headquarters' Appointment	Personnel	Mercantile Marine
Chief of Coast Guard: Colonel Hussein I Fulhu	1993: 400	*Lloyd's Register of Shipping:* 44 vessels of 50 321 tons gross

PATROL FORCES

Note: All British craft transferred in 1976 have been scrapped as have three ex-Taiwanese trawlers. *Ufuli,* an LCM built in Singapore and delivered in 1991, is used as a civilian transport.

4 TRACKER II CLASS

11   12   13   14

Displacement, tons: 38 full load
Dimensions, feet (metres): 65.6 × 17.1 × 4.9 *(20 × 5.2 × 1.5)*
Main machinery: 2 Detroit 12V-71TA diesels; 840 hp *(627 kW)* sustained; 2 shafts
Speed, knots: 25. **Range, miles:** 450 at 20 kts
Guns: 2—7.62 mm MGs.

Comment: First one ordered June 1985 from Fairey Marinteknik and commissioned in April 1987. Three more acquired July 1987 ex-UK Customs craft. GRP hulls. Seven days normal endurance. Used for fishery protection and EEZ patrols.

TRACKER II   *1989, Maldives CG*

1 CHEVERTON PATROL CRAFT

7

Displacement, tons: 24 full load
Dimensions, feet (metres): 55.8 × 14.8 × 3.9 *(17 × 4.5 × 1.2)*
Main machinery: 2 Detroit 8V-71TI diesels; 850 hp *(634 kW)* sustained; 2 shafts
Speed, knots: 22. **Range, miles:** 590 at 18 kts
Complement: 9
Guns: 1 FN 7.62 mm MG.

Comment: GRP hull and aluminium superstructure. Originally built for Kiribati and subsequently sold to Maldives in 1984.

CHEVERTON *1989, Maldives CG*

MALTA

General

A coastal patrol force of small craft was formed in 1971. It is manned by the 2nd Regiment of the Armed Forces of Malta and primarily employed as a Coast Guard.

Commander, Maritime Squadron

Captain M Gatt, AFM

Personnel

1993: 190

Pennant Numbers

In 1992 all identification numbers were changed from C to P.

Mercantile Marine

Lloyd's Register of Shipping:
  889 vessels of 10 126 848 tons gross

DELETIONS

1990 *C 25*
1991 *C 20, C 22, C 26*
1992 *C 28*

PATROL FORCES

2 Ex-GERMAN KONDOR I CLASS

P 30 (ex-*Ückermünde* G 411/GS 01)   P 31 (ex-*Pasewalk* G 423/GS 05)

Displacement, tons: 377 full load
Dimensions, feet (metres): 170.3 × 23.3 × 7.2 *(51.9 × 7.1 × 2.2)*
Main machinery: 2 Russki/Kolomna Type 40DM diesels; 4408 hp(m) *(3.24 MW)* sustained; 2 shafts
Speed, knots: 20
Complement: 20
Guns: 3—12.7 mm MGs.
Radars: Surface search: TSR 333; I band.

Comment: Built by Peenewerft, Wolgast in 1969-71. Transferred with new armament and sonar removed in July 1992. Others of the class acquired by Tunisia and Guinea Bissau.

P 30 *8/1992, Armed Forces Malta*

P 30 and P 31 *7/1992, Hartmut Ehlers*

2 Ex-YUGOSLAV TYPE 131

PRESIDENT TITO (ex-*Cer* 138) P 38
GANNI BONNICI (ex-*Dom Mintoff*, ex-*Durmitor* 139) P 39

Displacement, tons: 85 standard; 120 full load
Dimensions, feet (metres): 91.9 × 14.8 × 8.3 *(28 × 4.5 × 2.5)*
Main machinery: 2 MTU diesels; 2000 hp(m) *(1.47 MW)*; 2 shafts
Speed, knots: 22
Guns: 6—30 mm/70 Hispano Suiza (2 triple).
Radars: Navigation: Kelvin Hughes; I band.

Comment: Built at Trogir Shipyard 1965-68. Transferred 31 March 1982.

PRESIDENT TITO *1/1992, van Ginderen Collection*

2 Ex-US NOAA PATROL CRAFT

P 25 (ex-*1255*)   P 26 (ex-*1257*)

Displacement, tons: 35 full load
Dimensions, feet (metres): 59 × 15 × 4 *(18 × 4.6 × 1.2)*
Main machinery: 2 GM 12V-71 diesels; 680 hp *(507 kW)* sustained; 2 shafts
Speed, knots: 20. **Range, miles:** 300 at 15 kts
Complement: 7
Guns: 2—7.62 mm MGs.

Comment: Acquired in 1991.

P 26 (old number) *1991, Armed Forces Malta*

412 MALTA / Patrol forces — MARSHALL ISLANDS / Introduction

2 Ex-GERMAN BREMSE CLASS

P 32 (ex-*G 33/GS 20*)   **P 33** (ex-*G 22/GS 22*)

Displacement, tons: 42 full load
Dimensions, feet (metres): 74.1 × 15.4 × 3.6 *(22.6 × 4.7 × 1.1)*
Main machinery: 2 DM 6VD 18/5 AL-1 diesels; 1020 hp(m) *(750 kW)*; 2 shafts
Speed, knots: 14
Complement: 6
Guns: 1—7.62 mm MG.
Radars: Surface search: TSR 333; I band.

Comment: Built in 1971-72 for the ex-GDR GBK. Transferred in mid-1992. Others of the class acquired by Tunisia and Jordan.

P 33   *8/1992, Armed Forces Malta*

2 Ex-US SWIFT CLASS

P 23 (ex-*US C 6823*)   **P 24** (ex-*US C 6824*)

Displacement, tons: 22.5
Dimensions, feet (metres): 50 × 13 × 4.9 *(15.6 × 4 × 1.5)*
Main machinery: 2 GM 12V-71 diesels; 680 hp *(507 kW)* sustained; 2 shafts
Speed, knots: 25
Complement: 6
Guns: 3—12.7 mm Browning M2 MGs (1 twin, 1 single). 1—81 mm mortar.
Radars: Surface search: I band.

Comment: Built by Sewart Seacraft Ltd in 1967. Bought in February 1971. Have an operational endurance of about 24 hours.

P 23 (old number)   *1/1992, van Ginderen Collection*

3 Ex-ITALIAN CUSTOMS CRAFT

P 34 (ex-*GL 316*)   **P 36** (ex-*GL 324*)   **P 37** (ex-*GL 326*)

Displacement, tons: 19 full load
Dimensions, feet (metres): 50.9 × 16.1 × 3.6 *(15.5 × 4.9 × 1.1)*
Main machinery: 2 Fiat SRM 828 diesels; 880 hp(m) *(649 kW)* sustained; 2 shafts
Speed, knots: 20
Complement: 7
Guns: 1—7.62 mm MG.
Radars: Surface search: I band.

Comment: Acquired from the Guardia Di Finanza on 9 June 1992.

P 34   *7/1992, Armed Forces Malta*

1 LCVP

Displacement, tons: 13.5 full load
Dimensions, feet (metres): 36 × 10.5 × 1.1 *(11 × 3.2 × 0.3)*
Main machinery: 1 Detroit 64 HN9 diesel; 225 hp *(168 kW)*; 1 shaft
Speed, knots: 10
Complement: 4

Comment: Built by Gulfstream Co, USA and acquired in January 1987.

LCVP   *1989, Armed Forces Malta*

2 PATROL CRAFT

P 27   **P 29**

Comment: Malta-built 9.5 m Barberis cabin cruisers acquired in 1989 and used for SAR.

MARSHALL ISLANDS

General

The Marshalls are a group of five main islands which became a self governing republic on 1 May 1979, but with the United States retaining responsibility for defence. Main port is Majuro.

Personnel

1993: 60 (Maritime Authority)

Mercantile Marine

Lloyd's Register of Shipping:
35 vessels of 2 098 671 tons gross

PATROL FORCES

Note: In addition there are two ex-US LCUs acquired in 1987 and used as ferries.

1 PACIFIC FORUM TYPE (LARGE PATROL CRAFT)

Name	No	Builders	Commissioned
—	—	Australian Shipbuilding Industries	29 June 1991

Displacement, tons: 162 full load
Dimensions, feet (metres): 103.3 × 26.6 × 6.9 *(31.5 × 8.1 × 2.1)*
Main machinery: 2 Caterpillar 3516TA diesels; 4400 hp *(3.3 MW)* sustained; 2 shafts
Speed, knots: 20. **Range, miles:** 2500 at 12 kts
Complement: 17 (3 officers)
Radars: Surface search: Furuno 1011; I band.

Comment: The 14th craft to be built in this series for a number of Pacific Island Coast Guards. Ordered in 1989. Capable of mounting a 20 mm gun or 12.7 mm MG.

PACIFIC FORUM Type *1988, Gilbert Gyssels*

1 Ex-OFFSHORE SUPPLY SHIP

IONMETO I (ex-*Southern Light*)

Displacement, tons: 110 full load
Dimensions, feet (metres): 100 × — × — *(30.5 × — × —)*
Main machinery: 2 diesels; 2 shafts
Speed, knots: 14
Complement: 12
Guns: Can carry 2—12.7 mm MGs.

Comment: Acquired in 1987 and refitted by Halter Marine for patrol duties in December 1987.

1 Ex-USCG CAPE CLASS

Name	No	Builders	Commissioned
IONMETO II (ex-*Cape Small*)	—	CG Yard, Curtis Bay	1953

Displacement, tons: 98 standard; 148 full load
Dimensions, feet (metres): 95 × 20.2 × 6.6 *(28.9 × 6.2 × 2)*
Main machinery: 4 Cummins VT-12 diesels; 2340 hp *(1.75 MW)*; 2 shafts
Speed, knots: 20. **Range, miles:** 2500 at 10 kts
Complement: 15
Guns: Can carry up to 2—12.7 mm MGs.
Radars: Navigation: Raytheon SPS 64(V)1; I band.

Comment: Acquired in April 1987.

CAPE class (old number) *1990*

2 TRINITY MARINE TYPE PATROL BOATS

HSPC 1-2

Dimensions, feet (metres): 40.5 × 12 × 2.5 *(12.3 × 3.6 × 0.8)*
Main machinery: 2 Merlin diesels; 800 hp *(597 kW)* sustained; 2 Arneson ASD 10 surface drives
Speed, knots: 47
Complement: 3 plus 8 troops
Guns: 1—7.62 mm MG (can be carried).
Radars: Surface search: FLIR.

Comment: Halter Marine Interceptor 41s delivered to the US Army in March 1992 for permanent basing in the Marshall Islands. Two Zodiac F 470 raiding craft embarked. Hulls of PVC/Kevlar.

HSPC 1 and 2 *3/1992, Trinity Marine*

MAURITANIA

Personnel

(a) 1993: 450 (32 officers)
(b) Voluntary service

Bases

Port Etienne, Nouadhibou
Port Friendship, Nouakchott

Future plans

Acquisition of two French Batral LCTs and small number of patrol craft under consideration if finances permit. Another possibility is the FGN Ariadne class with sweep gear removed.

Mercantile Marine

Lloyd's Register of Shipping:
126 vessels of 42 663 tons gross

DELETIONS

1990 Tichitt, Dar El Barka, Im Raq Ni

PATROL FORCES

1 PATRA CLASS

Name	No	Builders	Commissioned
EL NASR (ex-*Le Dix Juillet*, ex-*Rapière*)	P 411	Auroux, Arcachon	14 May 1982

Displacement, tons: 147.5 full load
Dimensions, feet (metres): 132.5 × 19.4 × 5.2 *(40.4 × 5.9 × 1.6)*
Main machinery: 2 SACM AGO 195 V12 CZSHR diesels; 4340 hp(m) *(3.2 MW)* sustained; 2 shafts
Speed, knots: 26.3. **Range, miles:** 1750 at 10 kts
Complement: 20 (2 officers)
Guns: 1 Bofors 40 mm/60. 1 Oerlikon 20 mm. 2—12.7 mm Browning MGs.
Radars: Surface search: Racal/Decca 1226; I band.

Comment: Originally built as a private venture by Auroux. Carried out trials with French crew as *Rapière*. Laid down February 1980, launched 3 June 1981, commissioned for trials 1 November 1981. Transferred to Mauritania in 1982. Doubtful operational status.

4 INDIAN PATROL CRAFT

Displacement, tons: 15 full load
Dimensions, feet (metres): 49.2 × 11.8 × 2.6 *(15 × 3.6 × 0.8)*
Main machinery: 2 Deutz MWM TBD232V12 Marine diesels; 750 hp(m) *(551 kW)*; 2 Hamilton waterjets
Speed, knots: 24
Complement: 8
Guns: 1—7.62 mm MG.
Radars: Navigation: Furuno FR 8030; I band.

Comment: Built by Garden Reach and delivered in 1990. Same type acquired by Mauritius.

3 LÜRSSEN FPB 36 CLASS

Name	No	Builders	Commissioned
EL VAIZ	P 361	Bazán-La Carraca	Oct 1979
EL BEIG	P 362	Bazán-La Carraca	May 1979
EL KINZ	P 363	Bazán-La Carraca	Aug 1982

Displacement, tons: 139 full load
Dimensions, feet (metres): 118.7 × 19 × 6.2 *(36.2 × 5.8 × 1.9)*
Main machinery: 2 MTU 16V 538 TB90 diesels; 7503 hp(m) *(5.51 MW)* sustained; 2 shafts
Speed, knots: 36. **Range, miles:** 1200 at 17 kts
Complement: 19 (3 officers)
Guns: 1 Bofors 40 mm/70. 1 Oerlikon 20 mm. 2—12.7 mm MGs.
Fire control: 1 CSEE Panda optical director (made in Spain).
Radars: Surface search: Raytheon RN 1220/6XB; I band.

Comment: First pair ordered 21 July 1976—third in 1979. Doubtful operational status.

EL BEIG *1980, Bazan*

414   MAURITANIA / Patrol forces — MAURITIUS / Patrol forces

1 Ex-GERMAN NEUSTADT CLASS

Name	No	Builders	Launched
Z'BAR (ex-Uelzen)	P 381 (ex-BG 13)	Schlichting, Travemünde	25 July 1969

Displacement, tons: 218 full load
Dimensions, feet (metres): 127.1 × 23 × 5 *(38.5 × 7 × 2.2)*
Main machinery: 2 MTU MD 16-cyl diesels; 6000 hp(m) *(4.41 MW)*
  1 MWM diesel; 685 hp(m) *(503 kW)*; 3 shafts
Speed, knots: 30. **Range, miles:** 450 at 27 kts
Complement: 23 (5 officers)
Guns: 2 Bofors 40 mm/70; 90° elevation; 300 rounds/minute to 12 km *(6.5 nm)* anti-surface;
  4 km *(2.2 nm)* anti-aircraft; weight of shell 0.96 kg.

Comment: Ex-West German Coast Guard vessel acquired in March 1990 and recommissioned 29 April 1990. Lürssen design larger but similar to the El Vaiz class.

1 JURA CLASS

N'MADI (ex-*Criscilla*, ex-*Jura*)

Displacement, tons: 1285 full load
Dimensions, feet (metres): 195.3 × 35 × 14.4 *(59.6 × 10.7 × 4.4)*
Main machinery: 2 British Polar SP 112VS-F diesels; 4200 hp *(3.13 MW)*; 1 shaft
Speed, knots: 15.5
Complement: 28

Comment: Built by Hall Russell, Aberdeen in 1975. Became a Scottish Fishery Protection vessel but was paid off in 1988 and acquired by J Marr Ltd. On lease from July 1989 for Fishery Patrol duties.

JURA class   *1982, van Ginderen Collection*

LAND-BASED MARITIME AIRCRAFT

Note: There are also 2 Cessna 337F and 2 Buffalo DHC-5D.

Numbers/Type: 2 Piper Cheyenne II.
Operational speed: 283 kts *(524 km/h)*.
Service ceiling: 31 600 ft *(9630 m)*.
Range: 1510 nm *(2796 km)*.
Role/Weapon systems: Coastal surveillance and EEZ protection acquired 1981. Sensors: Bendix 1400 weather radar; cameras. Weapons: Unarmed.

NEUSTADT class   *1989, Hartmut Ehlers*

MAURITIUS

Headquarters' Appointments

Commissioner of Police:
  Bhimsen Kowlessur MPM, QPM
Commandant Coast Guard:
  Commander K N Rao

Base

Port Louis (plus 12 manned CG stations)

Personnel

1993: 500

Mercantile Marine

Lloyd's Register of Shipping:
  35 vessels of 102 415 tons gross

PATROL FORCES

Note: In 1991 tenders were invited for a 1000 ton 60 m offshore patrol vessel. Contract expected in 1993. A second vessel may be ordered later.

1 Ex-INDIAN LARGE PATROL CRAFT

AMAR P 1

Displacement, tons: 120 standard; 151 full load
Dimensions, feet (metres): 117.2 × 20 × 5 *(35.7 × 6.1 × 1.5)*
Main machinery: 2 Paxman diesels; 1000 hp *(746 kW)*; 2 shafts
Speed, knots: 18. **Range, miles:** 500 at 12 kts
Complement: 20
Guns: 1 Bofors 40 mm/60.
Radars: Surface search: Racal Decca 978; I band.

Comment: The last of the old Abhay class built by Garden Reach Workshops Ltd, Calcutta 1969. Transferred April 1974. Retained original name.

AMAR   *1991, Mauritius CG*

32 PATROL BOATS

Comment: Two Rover 663 FPC donated by Australia and 30 Rigid Inflatable craft mostly RHIBS, AVONS and ZODIACS acquired in 1988-89.

9 INDIAN PATROL CRAFT

| MARLIN | CASTOR | SIRIUS | CAPELLA | RIGEL |
| BARRACUDA | POLARIS | POLLUX | CANOPUS | |

Displacement, tons: 15 full load
Dimensions, feet (metres): 49.2 × 11.8 × 2.6 *(15 × 3.6 × 0.8)*
Main machinery: 2 Deutz MWM TBD232V12 Marine diesels; 750 hp(m) *(551 kW)*; 2 Hamilton waterjets
Speed, knots: 24
Complement: 8
Guns: 1—7.62 mm MG.
Radars: Navigation: Furuno FR 8030; I band.

Comment: Ordered in 1987 from Mandovi Marine Private Ltd, courtesy of the Indian Government. First two delivered early in 1989; second batch of three with some modifications on 1 May 1990 and the last four at the end of 1990. SATNAV fitted.

MARLIN   *1990, Mauritius CG*

2 SOVIET ZHUK CLASS

RESCUER **RETRIEVER**

Displacement, tons: 50 full load
Dimensions, feet (metres): 75 × 17 × 6.2 *(23 × 5.2 × 1.9)*
Main machinery: 2 diesels; 2400 hp(m) *(1.76 MW)*; 2 shafts
Speed, knots: 30. **Range, miles:** 1100 at 15 kts
Complement: 17
Guns: 4—14.5 mm (2 twin) MGs.

Comment: Acquired from the Soviet Union in January 1990.

LAND-BASED MARITIME AIRCRAFT

Numbers/Type: 1 Dornier 228 (MPCG 01).
Operational speed: 200 kts *(370 km/h)*.
Service ceiling: 28 000 ft *(8535 m)*.
Range: 940 nm *(1740 km)*.
Role/Weapon systems: EEZ surveillance and SAR; acquired from Hindustan Aeronautics in 1990.
 Sensors: MEL search radar. Weapons: Unarmed.

RESCUER (alongside RETRIEVER and AMAR)   *1990, Mauritius CG*

MEXICO

Headquarters' Appointments

Secretary of the Navy:
 Admiral Luis Carlos Ruano Angulo
Under-Secretary of the Navy:
 Admiral David Zepeda Torres
Chief of Naval Operations:
 Admiral Jorge Mora Perez
Inspector General of the Navy:
 Vice Admiral Sergio Loperena Garcia
Chief of the Naval Staff:
 Rear Admiral Luis Cotero Bayardini

Flag Officers

Commander in Chief, Gulf and Caribbean:
 Vice Admiral David Leal Rodriguez
Commander in Chief, Pacific:
 Vice Admiral Augusto Esparza Rodriguez

Personnel

(a) 1993: 37 500 officers and men (including 1050 Naval Air Force and 8650 Marines)
(b) Voluntary service

Naval Air Force

Naval air bases at Mexico City, Las Bajadas, Tulum, Campeche, Chetumal, Puerto Cortes, Isla Mujeres, La Paz, Salina Cruz, Tapachula.

Marine Force

One Marine Paratroop Brigade of two battalions, one Presidential Guard Group (battalion), three battalions with HQs in Mexico City, Acapulco and Veracruz, and 35 independent companies.

Naval Bases and Commands

The Naval Command is split between the Pacific and Gulf areas each with a Commander-in-Chief with HQs at Veracruz (Gulf) and Acapulco (Pacific). Each area has three naval Regions which are further sub-divided into Zones (17) and Sectors (16).

Gulf Area
North Naval Region – HQ Veracruz.
 I Naval Zone – HQ Ciudad Madero (State of Tamaupilas).
  Naval Sectors – HQ Matamoros, HQ La Pesca.
 III Naval Zone – HQ Veracruz (State of Veracruz).
  Naval Sectors – HQ Tuxpan, HQ Coatzacoalcos.
East Naval Region – HQ Frontera.
 V Naval Zone – HQ Frontera (State of Tabasco).
 VII Naval Zone – HQ Lerma (State of Campeche).
  Naval Sectors – HQ Champotón, HQ Ciudad del Cármen.
Caribbean Sea Naval Region – HQ Chetumal.
 IX Naval Zone – HQ Yucalpeten (State of Yucatán).
  Naval Sector – HQ Progreso.
 XI Naval Zone – HQ Chetumal (State of Quintana Roo).
  Naval Sectors – HQ Isla Mujeres, HQ Isla Cozumel.
Pacific Area
Northwest Naval Region – HQ Mazatlán.
 II Naval Zone – HQ Ensenada (State of Baja California Norte).
 IV Naval Zone – HQ La Paz (State of Baja California Sur).
  Naval Sectors – HQ Puerto Cortes, HQ Santa Rosalía.
 VI Naval Zone – HQ Guaymas (State of Sonora).
  Naval Sector – HQ Puerto Peñasco.
 VIII Naval Zone – HQ Mazatlán (State of Sinaloa).
  Naval Sector – HQ Topolobampo.
West Naval Region – HQ Lazaro Cárdenas.
 X Naval Zone – HQ San Blas (State of Nayarit).
 XII Naval Zone – HQ Puerto Vallarta (State of Jalisco).
 XIV Naval Zone – HQ Manzanillo (State of Colima).
  Naval Sector – HQ Isla Socorro.
 XVI Naval Zone – HQ Lázaro Cardenas (State of Michoacán).
Southwest Naval Region – HQ Acapulco.
 XVIII Naval Zone – HQ Acapulco (State of Guerrero).
  Naval Sector – HQ Ixtapa-Zihuatanejo.
 XX Naval Zone – HQ Salina Cruz (State of Oaxaca).
  Naval Sector – HQ Puerto Angel.
 XXII Naval Zone – HQ Puerto Madero (State of Chiapas).

Strength of the Fleet

Type	Active
Destroyers	3
Frigates	4
Gunships	23
Large Patrol Craft	36
Coast Guard	17
Coastal and River Patrol Craft	26
Survey Ships	5
Support Ships	11
Tankers-Harbour	2
Tugs	6
Sail Training Ship	1
Floating Docks	4
Dredgers	5

General

One of the persistent problems facing the Mexican Navy is the incursion of foreign fishery poachers, frequently highly organised groups working from the USA. In addition there is a requirement for patrolling the Exclusive Economic Zone including the offshore oil fields. The drug smuggling menace is taking up more and more of the navy's time.

Mercantile Marine

Lloyd's Register of Shipping:
 635 vessels of 1 109 683 tons gross

DESTROYERS

1 Ex-US FLETCHER CLASS

Name	No	Builders	Laid down	Launched	Commissioned
CUITLAHUAC (ex-USS *John Rodgers* DD 574)	E 02 (ex-F 2)	Consolidated Steel Corporation	25 July 1941	7 May 1942	9 Feb 1943

Displacement, tons: 2100 standard; 3050 full load
Dimensions, feet (metres): 376.5 × 39.4 × 18 *(114.8 × 12 × 5.5)*
Main machinery: 4 Babcock & Wilcox boilers; 600 psi *(43.3 kg/cm sq)*; 850°F *(454°C)*; 2 GE turbines; 60 000 hp *(45 MW)*; 2 shafts
Speed, knots: 32. **Range, miles:** 5000 at 14 kts
Complement: 197

Guns: 5 USN 5 in *(127 mm)*/38 Mk 30 ❶; 85° elevation; 15 rounds/minute to 17 km *(9.3 nm)* anti-surface; 8 km *(4.4 nm)* anti-aircraft; weight of shell 25 kg.
 10 Bofors 40 mm/60 (5 twin) Mk 2 ❷; 80° elevation; 120 rounds/minute to 10 km *(5.5 nm)*; weight of shell 0.89 kg.
Torpedoes: 5—21 in *(533 mm)* (quin) tubes ❸; anti-surface.
Fire control: Mk 37 GFCS for 127 mm guns. 5 Mk 51 GFCS for 40 mm guns.
Radars: Surface search: Kelvin Hughes 17/9 ❹; I band.
 Navigation: Kelvin Hughes 14/9; I band.
 Fire control: Western Electric Mk 25 ❺; I/J band.

Programmes: Transferred to the Mexican Navy in August 1970.
Operational: In spite of its age this ship still has a formidable gun armament and is very active in drug enforcement patrols.

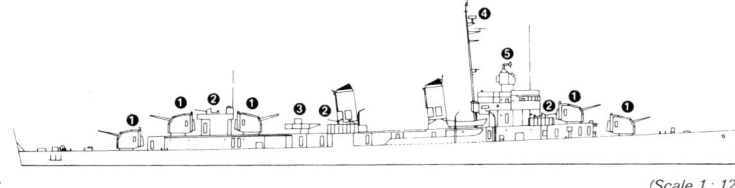

CUITLAHUAC   *(Scale 1 : 1200), Ian Sturton*

CUITLAHUAC (alongside E 03 and E 04)   *9/1990*

416 MEXICO / Destroyers — Frigates

2 Ex-US GEARING (FRAM I) CLASS

Name	No	Builders	Laid down	Launched	Commissioned
QUETZALCOATL (ex-USS *Vogelgesang* DD 862)	E 03	Bethlehem, Staten Island	3 Aug 1944	15 Jan 1945	28 Apr 1945
NETZAHUALCOYOTL (ex-USS *Steinaker* DD 863)	E 04	Bethlehem, Staten Island	1 Sep 1944	13 Feb 1945	26 May 1945

Displacement, tons: 2425 standard; 3690 full load
Dimensions, feet (metres): 390.2 × 41.9 × 15 *(118.7 × 12.5 × 4.6)*
Main machinery: 4 Babcock & Wilcox boilers; 600 psi *(43.3 kg/cm sq)*; 850°F *(454°C)*; 2 GE turbines; 60 000 hp *(45 MW)*; 2 shafts
Speed, knots: 32.5. **Range, miles:** 5800 at 15 kts
Complement: 300

Missiles: A/S: Honeywell ASROC Mk 112 octuple launcher ❶; inertial guidance to 1.6-10 km *(1-5.4 nm)*; payload Mk 46 torpedo.
Guns: 4 USN 5 in *(127 mm)*/38 (2 twin) Mk 38 ❷; 85° elevation; 15 rounds/minute to 17 km *(9.3 nm)* anti-surface; 11 km *(5.9 nm)* anti-aircraft; weight of shell 25 kg.
Torpedoes: 6—324 mm Mk 32 (2 triple) tubes ❸. Honeywell Mk 46; anti-submarine; active/passive homing to 11 km *(5.9 nm)* at 40 kts; warhead 44 kg.
Countermeasures: ESM: WLR-1; radar warning.
Fire control: Mk 37 GFCS.
Radars: Air search: Lockheed SPS 40; E/F band (E 03); range 320 km *(175 nm)*.
Westinghouse SPS 29 ❹; B/C band (E 04); range 457 km *(250 nm)*.
Surface search: Raytheon SPS 10 ❺; G band.
Navigation: Marconi LN 66; I band.
Fire control: Western Electric Mk 25 ❻; I/J band.
Sonars: Sangamo SQS 23; hull-mounted; active search and attack; medium frequency.

Helicopters: 1 MBB BO 105CB ❼.

Programmes: Transferred by sale 24 February 1982.
Structure: The devices on top of the funnel are to reduce IR signature.
Operational: E 03 rated as an 'escort vessel'.

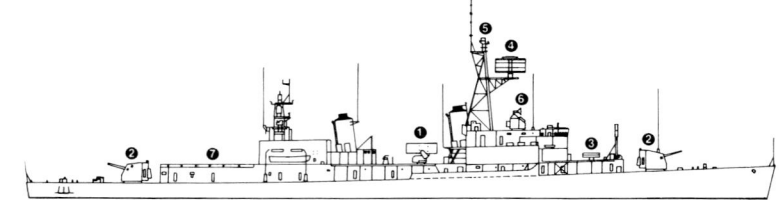
NETZAHUALCOYOTL *(Scale 1 : 1200), Ian Sturton*

NETZAHUALCOYOTL *1991, Mexican Navy*

FRIGATES

3 Ex-US CHARLES LAWRENCE and CROSLEY CLASSES

Name	No	Builders	Laid down	Launched	Commissioned
USUMACINTA (ex-USS *Don O Woods* APD 118, ex-*DE 721*)	B 06 (ex-H 6)	Consolidated Steel Corporation	1 Dec 1943	19 Feb 1944	28 May 1945
COAHUILA (ex-USS *Rednour* APD 102, ex-*DE 592*)	B 07	Bethlehem S B Co, Hingham, Mass	9 Jan 1944	1 Mar 1944	15 Mar 1945
CHIHUAHUA (ex-USS *Barber* APD 57, ex-*DE 161*)	B 08	Norfolk Navy Yard, Norfolk, Va	27 Apr 1943	20 May 1943	10 Oct 1943

Displacement, tons: 1400 standard; 2130 full load
Dimensions, feet (metres): 306 × 37 × 11.3 *(93.3 × 11.3 × 3.4)*
Main machinery: Turbo-electric; 2 Foster-Wheeler boilers; 435 psi *(30.6 kg/cm sq)*; 750°F *(399°C)*; 2 GE turbo generators; 12 000 hp *(9 MW)*; 2 motors; 2 shafts
Speed, knots: 20. **Range, miles:** 5000 at 15 kts
Complement: 204 plus 162 troops

Guns: 1 USN 5 in *(127 mm)*/38 Mk 30; 85° elevation; 15 rounds/minute to 17 km *(9.3 nm)*; weight of shell 25 kg.
6 Bofors 40 mm/60 (3 twin) Mk 1. 6 Oerlikon 20 mm/80.
Fire control: 3 Mk 51 GFCS for 40 mm guns.
Radars: Surface search: Kelvin Hughes 14/9; I band.

Programmes: B 06 purchased by Mexico in December 1963, B 07 in June 1969 and B 08 in December 1969.
Structure: B 07 is the only Charles Lawrence class; the others have a tripod after mast supporting the conspicuous 10 ton boom.

USUMACINTA *1992, Mexican Navy*

COAHUILA *1990*

Frigates — Patrol ships / MEXICO   417

1 Ex-US EDSALL CLASS

Name	No	Builders	Laid down	Launched	Commissioned
COMODORO MANUEL AZUETA PERILLOS (ex-USS *Hurst* DE 250)	A 06	Brown S B Co, Houston, Texas	27 Jan 1943	14 Apr 1943	30 Aug 1943

Displacement, tons: 1200 standard; 1850 full load
Dimensions, feet (metres): 302.7 × 36.6 × 13 *(92.3 × 11.3 × 4)*
Main machinery: 4 Fairbanks-Morse 38D8-1/8-10 diesels; 7080 hp *(5.3 MW)* sustained; 2 shafts
Speed, knots: 20. **Range, miles:** 13 000 at 12 kts
Complement: 216 (15 officers)

Guns: 3 USN 3 in *(76 mm)*/50 Mk 22; 85° elevation; 20 rounds/minute to 12 km *(6.6 nm)*; weight of shell 6 kg.
 8 Bofors 40 mm/60 (1 quad, 2 twin) Mk 2 and Mk 1; 80° elevation; 120 rounds/minute to 10 km *(5.5 nm)*; weight of shell 0.89 kg.
 2—37 mm saluting guns.
Fire control: Mk 52 (for 3 in); Mk 51 Mod 2 (for 40 mm).
Radars: Surface search: Kelvin Hughes Type 17; I band.
 Navigation: Kelvin Hughes Type 14; I band.
Fire control: RCA/GE Mk 26; I/J band.

Programmes: Transferred to Mexico 1 October 1973.
Operational: Employed as training ship with Gulf Area command. A/S weapons and sensors removed.

COMODORO MANUEL AZUETA PERILLOS   *1992, Mexican Navy*

PATROL SHIPS

Note: Called gunships by the Mexican Navy.

6 URIBE CLASS (GUNSHIPS)

Name	No	Builders	Laid down	Launched	Commissioned
CADETE VIRGILIO URIBE ROBLES	C 11 (ex-GH 01)	Bazán, San Fernando	1 July 1981	12 Nov 1981	2 June 1982
TENIENTE JOSÉ AZUETA ABAD	C 12 (ex-GH 02)	Bazán, San Fernando	7 Sep 1981	12 Dec 1981	30 Aug 1982
CAPITAN de FRAGATA PEDRO SÁINZ de BARANDA BORREYRO	C 13 (ex-GH 03)	Bazán, San Fernando	22 Oct 1981	29 Jan 1982	20 Oct 1982
COMODORO CARLOS CASTILLO BRETÓN BARRERO	C 14 (ex-GH 04)	Bazán, San Fernando	11 Nov 1981	26 Feb 1982	4 Nov 1982
VICEALMIRANTE OTHÓN P BLANCO NUNEZ DE CACERES	C 15 (ex-GH 05)	Bazán, San Fernando	18 Dec 1981	26 Mar 1982	16 Nov 1982
CONTRALMIRANTE ANGEL ORTIZ MONASTERIO	C 16 (ex-GH 06)	Bazán, San Fernando	30 Dec 1981	4 May 1982	17 Dec 1982

Displacement, tons: 910 full load
Dimensions, feet (metres): 219.9 × 34.4 × 10.2 *(67 × 10.5 × 3.1)*
Main machinery: 2 MTU-Bazán 16V 956 TB91 diesels; 7500 hp(m) *(5.52 MW)* sustained; 2 shafts
Speed, knots: 22. **Range, miles:** 5000 at 18 kts
Complement: 46 (7 officers)

Guns: 1 Bofors 40 mm/70.
Fire control: Naja optronic director.
Radars: Surface search: Decca AC 1226; I band.
Tacan: SRN 15.

Helicopters: 1 MBB BO 105CB.

Programmes: Ordered in 1980 to a Halcon class design. Contracts for a further eight of the class have been shelved. Pennant numbers changed in 1992.
Operational: Used for EEZ patrol.

VICEALMIRANTE OTHÓN P BLANCO   *1992, Mexican Navy*

4 HOLZINGER CLASS (GUNSHIPS)

Name	No	Builders	Commissioned
CAPITÁN DE NAVIO SEBASTIAN JOSE HOLZINGER (ex-*Uxmal*)	C 01 (ex-GA 01)	Tampico	Nov 1991
CAPITÁN DE NAVIO BLAS GODINEZ BRITO (ex-*Mitla*)	C 02 (ex-GA 02)	Veracruz	21 Apr 1992
BRIGADIER JOSE MARIA DE LA VEGA GONZALEZ (ex-*Peten*)	C 03 (ex-GA 03)	Tampico	Apr 1993
GENERAL FELIPE B BERRIOZABAL (ex-*Anahuac*)	C 04 (ex-GA 04)	Veracruz	May 1993

Displacement, tons: 1290 full load
Dimensions, feet (metres): 244.1 × 34.4 × 11.2 *(74.4 × 10.5 × 3.4)*
Main machinery: 2 MTU 20V 956 TB92 diesels; 11 700 hp(m) *(8.6 MW)* sustained; 2 shafts
Speed, knots: 22. **Range, miles:** 3820 at 18 kts
Complement: 75 (11 officers)

Guns: 1 Bofors 57 mm/70 Mk 2; 75° elevation; 220 rounds/minute to 17 km *(9.3 nm)*; weight of shell 2.4 kg. At least two of the class have a Bofors 40 mm/60.
Fire control: Elsag NA 18 optronic director.
Radars: Surface search: Raytheon SPS 64(V)6A; I band.
Helicopters: 1 MBB BO 105CB.

Programmes: Originally four were ordered from Tampico and Veracruz. First laid down November 1983, second in 1984 but the whole programme has been slowed down by financial problems.
Structure: An improved variant of the Bazán Halcon (Uribe) class. C 01 and C 02 commissioned with a Bofors 40 mm/60 in lieu of the 57 mm. This may be a temporary arrangement.

SEBASTIAN JOSE HOLZINGER   *1/1992, Mexican Navy*

418 MEXICO / Patrol ships — Land-based maritime aircraft

1 GUANAJUATO CLASS (GUNSHIP)

Name	No	Builders	Commissioned
GUANAJUATO	C 07	S E C N Ferrol	19 Mar 1936

Displacement, tons: 1950 full load
Dimensions, feet (metres): 264 × 37.8 × 13 *(80.5 × 11.5 × 4)*
Main machinery: 2 diesels; 5000 hp *(37.3 MW)*; 2 shafts
Speed, knots: 14
Complement: 140
Guns: 2 Vickers 4 in *(102 mm)*/45; 80° elevation; 16 rounds/minute to 19 km *(10.4 nm)*; weight of shell 16 kg.
    2 Bofors 40 mm/60. 2 Oerlikon 20 mm.
Radars: Surface search: I band.

Comment: Launched 29 May 1934. Originally used as a gunboat and troop transporter. Steam turbines replaced by diesels in the late 1960s.

GUANAJUATO　　　　　　　　　　　　　　　　　　　　　　　　　　　　1990, Mexican Navy

17 Ex-US AUK CLASS (COAST GUARD)

Name	No
LEANDRO VALLE (ex-USS *Pioneer* MSF 105)	G-01
GUILLERMO PRIETO (ex-USS *Symbol* MSF 123)	G-02
MARIANO ESCOBEDO (ex-USS *Champion* MSF 314)	G-03
MANUEL DOBLADO (ex-USS *Defense* MSF 317)	G-05
SEBASTIAN LERDO DE TEJADA (ex-USS *Devastator* MSF 318)	G-06
SANTOS DEGOLLADO (ex-USS *Gladiator* MSF 319)	G-07
IGNACIO DE LA LLAVE (ex-USS *Spear* MSF 322)	G-08
JUAN N ALVARES (ex-USS *Ardent* MSF 340)	G-09
MANUEL GUTIERREZ ZAMORA (ex-USS *Roselle* MSF 379)	G-10
VALENTIN GOMEZ FARIAS (ex-USS *Starling* MSF 64)	G-11
IGNACIO MANUEL ALTAMIRANO (ex-USS *Sway* MSF 120)	G-12
FRANCISCO ZARCO (ex-USS *Threat* MSF 124)	G-13
IGNACIO L VALLARTA (ex-USS *Velocity* MSF 128)	G-14
JESUS GONZALEZ ORTEGA (ex-USS *Chief* MSF 315)	G-15
MELCHOR OCAMPO (ex-USS *Scoter* MSF 381)	G-16
JUAN ALDAMA (ex-USS *Piloti* MSF 104)	G-18
HERMENEGILDO GALEANA (ex-USS *Sage* MSF 111)	G-19

Displacement, tons: 1090 standard; 1250 full load
Dimensions, feet (metres): 221.2 × 32.2 × 10.8 *(67.5 × 9.8 × 3.3)*
Main machinery: Diesel-electric; 2 GM 278A diesels; 2200 hp *(1.64 MW)*; 2 generators; 2 motors; 2 shafts
Speed, knots: 18. **Range, miles:** 4300 at 10 kts
Complement: 105 (9 officers)
Guns: 1 USN 3 in *(76 mm)*/50. 4 Bofors 40 mm/56 (2 twin). 2 Oerlikon 20 mm.
Radars: Surface search: Kelvin Hughes 14/9 (in most); I band.

Comment: Transferred six in February 1973, four in April 1973, nine in September 1973. Employed on Coast Guard duties. All built during Second World War. Variations are visible in the midships section where some have a bulwark running from the break of the fo'c'sle to the quarter-deck. Minesweeping gear removed. There is a variety of diesel engines, radars and even shipbuilders for this class. Starting to be paid off. One used as a survey vessel deleted in 1988.

JUAN N ALVARES　　　　　　　　　　　　　　　　　　　　　　　　　　　　　　3/1988

SEBASTIAN LERDO DE TEJADA　　　　　　　　　　　　　　　　　　　　　　　　6/1991

12 Ex-US ADMIRABLE CLASS

D 01 (ex-USS *Jubilant* AM 255)	D 13 (ex-USS *Knave* AM 256)
D 03 (ex-USS *Execute* AM 232)	D 14 (ex-USS *Rebel* AM 284)
D 04 (ex-USS *Specter* AM 306)	D 15 (ex-USS *Crag* AM 214)
D 05 (ex-USS *Scuffle* AM 298)	D 17 (ex-USS *Diploma* AM 221)
D 11 (ex-USS *Device* AM 220)	D 18 (ex-USS *Invade* AM 254)
D 12 (ex-USS *Ransom* AM 283)	D 19 (ex-USS *Intrigue* AM 253)

Displacement, tons: 650 standard; 900 full load
Dimensions, feet (metres): 184.5 × 33 × 14.4 *(56.3 × 10.1 × 4.4)*
Main machinery: 2 Cooper-Bessemer GSB-8 diesels; 1710 hp *(1.28 MW)*; 2 shafts
Speed, knots: 15. **Range, miles:** 4300 at 10 kts
Complement: 104 (8 officers)
Guns: 1 USN 3 in *(76 mm)*/50 Mk 22; 85° elevation; 20 rounds/minute to 12 km *(6.5 nm)* anti-surface; 9 km *(4.9 nm)* anti-aircraft; weight of shell 6 kg.
    2 Bofors 40 mm/70; 90° elevation; 300 rounds/minute to 12 km *(6.5 nm)* anti-surface; 4 km *(2.2 nm)* anti-aircraft; weight of shell 2.4 kg.
    6 or 8 Oerlikon 20 mm; 50° elevation; 800 rounds/minute to 2 km; weight of shell 0.24 kg.
Helicopters: Platform for 1 BO 105 *(D 11-13)*.

Comment: Former US steel hulled fleet minesweepers. All completed in 1943-44. D 20 now fitted for surveying (see *Survey Vessels*). Minesweeping gear removed. Four of the class deleted in 1986. Three others, D 11-13, converted in 1991/92 to provide a helicopter platform aft. In these conversions the funnel has been raised. Pennant numbers are now the same as the ship's name.

D 19　　　　　　　　　　　　　　　　　　　　　　　　　　　　　　1992, Mexican Navy

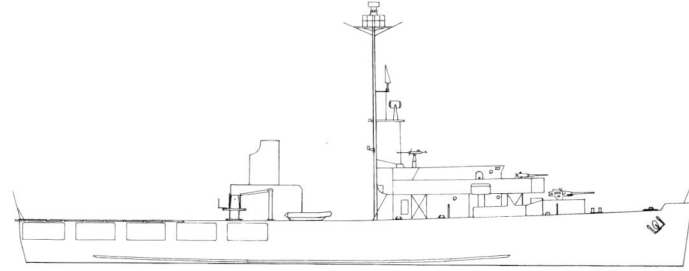

D 11 (helo deck)　　　　　　　　　　　　　　　　　　　　　(not to scale), Ian Sturton

SHIPBORNE AIRCRAFT

Numbers/Type: 12 MBB BO 105CB.
Operational speed: 113 kts *(210 km/h)*.
Service ceiling: 9845 ft *(3000 m)*.
Range: 407 nm *(754 km)*.
Role/Weapon systems: Coastal patrol helicopter for patrol, fisheries protection and EEZ protection duties; SAR as secondary role. Sensors: Bendix search radar. Weapons: MGs or rocket pods.

BO 105CB　　　　　　　　　　　　　　　　　　　　　　　　　　1988, Paul Jackson

Numbers/Type: 2 Aerospatiale AS 555 AF Fennec.
Operational speed: 121 kts *(225 km/h)*.
Service ceiling: 13 120 ft *(4000 m)*.
Range: 389 nm *(722 km)*.
Role/Weapon systems: Patrol helicopter for EEZ protection and SAR. Sensors: Bendix 1500 search radar. Weapons: Can carry up to 2 torpedoes, rocket pods or an MG.

LAND-BASED MARITIME AIRCRAFT (FRONT LINE)

Note: A number of confiscated drug-running aircraft are also in service, mostly Cessnas.

Numbers/Type: 9 CASA C-212 Aviocar.
Operational speed: 190 kts *(353 km/h)*.
Service ceiling: 24 000 ft *(7315 m)*.
Range: 1650 nm *(3055 km)*.
Role/Weapon systems: Acquired from 1987 and used for Maritime Surveillance. Have replaced the Albatross and Aravas. Sensors: Search radar; APS 504. Weapons: Unarmed.

LIGHT FORCES

3 Ex-US CAPE CLASS (LARGE PATROL CRAFT)

Name	No	Builders	Recommissioned
CABO CORRIENTES (ex-*Jalisco*, ex-*Cape Carter*)	P 42	C G Yard, Curtis Bay	1 Apr 1990
CABO CORZO (ex-*Nayarit*, ex-*Cape Hedge*)	P 43	C G Yard, Curtis Bay	21 Apr 1990
CABO CATOCHE (ex-*Cape Hattaras*)	P 44	C G Yard, Curtis Bay	18 Mar 1991

Displacement, tons: 98 standard; 148 full load
Dimensions, feet (metres): 95 × 20.2 × 6.6 *(28.9 × 6.2 × 2)*
Main machinery: 2 GM 16V-149TI diesels; 2322 hp *(1.73 MW)* sustained; 2 shafts
Speed, knots: 20. **Range, miles:** 2500 at 10 kts
Complement: 14 (1 officer)
Guns: 2—12.7 mm MGs.
Radars: Navigation: Raytheon SPS 64; I band

Comment: Built between 1953 and 1959; have been re-engined and extensively modernised. Transferred under the FMS programme, having paid off from the US Coast Guard.

CABO CORZO *1992, Mexican Navy*

31 AZTECA CLASS (LARGE PATROL CRAFT)

Name	No	Builders	Commissioned
ANDRES QUINTANA ROO	P 01	Ailsa Shipbuilding Co Ltd	1 Nov 1974
MATIAS DE CORDOVA	P 02	Scott & Sons, Bowling	22 Oct 1974
MIGUEL RAMOS ARIZPE	P 03	Ailsa Shipbuilding Co Ltd	23 Dec 1974
JOSE MARIA IZAZAGA	P 04	Ailsa Shipbuilding Co Ltd	19 Dec 1974
JUAN BAUTISTA MORALES	P 05	Scott & Sons, Bowling	19 Dec 1974
IGNACIO LOPEZ RAYON	P 06	Ailsa Shipbuilding Co Ltd	19 Dec 1974
MANUEL CRESCENCIO REJON	P 07	Ailsa Shipbuilding Co Ltd	4 July 1975
JUAN ANTONIO DE LA FUENTE	P 08	Ailsa Shipbuilding Co Ltd	4 July 1975
LEON GUZMAN	P 09	Scott & Sons, Bowling	7 Apr 1975
IGNACIO RAMIREZ	P 10	Ailsa Shipbuilding Co Ltd	17 July 1975
IGNACIO MARISCAL	P 11	Ailsa Shipbuilding Co Ltd	23 Sep 1975
HERIBERTO JARA CORONA	P 12	Ailsa Shipbuilding Co Ltd	7 Nov 1975
JOSE MARIA MATA	P 13	Lamont & Co Ltd	13 Oct 1975
FELIX ROMERO	P 14	Scott & Sons, Bowling	23 June 1975
FERNANDO M LIZARDI	P 15	Ailsa Shipbuilding Co Ltd	24 Dec 1975
FRANCISCO J MUJICA	P 16	Ailsa Shipbuilding Co Ltd	21 Nov 1975
PASTOR ROUAIX	P 17	Scott & Sons, Bowling	7 Nov 1975
JOSE MARIA DEL CASTILLO VELASCO	P 18	Lamont & Co Ltd	14 Jan 1975
LUIS MANUEL ROJAS	P 19	Lamont & Co Ltd	3 Apr 1976
JOSE NATIVIDAD MACIAS	P 20	Lamont & Co Ltd	2 Sep 1976
ESTEBAN BACA CALDERON	P 21	Lamont & Co Ltd	18 June 1976
GENERAL IGNACIO ZARAGOZA	P 22	Veracruz	1 June 1976
TAMAULIPAS	P 23	Veracruz	18 May 1977
YUCATAN	P 24	Veracruz	3 July 1977
TABASCO	P 25	Salina Cruz	1 Dec 1978
VERACRUZ	P 26	Veracruz	1 Dec 1978
CAMPECHE	P 27	Veracruz	1 Mar 1980
PUEBLA	P 28	Salina Cruz	1 June 1982
MARGARITA MAZA DE JUAREZ	P 29	Salina Cruz	29 Nov 1976
LEONA VICARIO	P 30	Veracruz	1 May 1977
JOSEFA ORTIZ DE DOMINGUEZ	P 31	Salina Cruz	1 June 1977

Displacement, tons: 148 full load
Dimensions, feet (metres): 111.8 × 28.1 × 6.8 *(34.1 × 8.6 × 2)*
Main machinery: 2 Paxman 12YJCM diesels; 3000 hp *(2.24 MW)* sustained; 2 shafts
Speed, knots: 24. **Range, miles:** 2500 at 12 kts
Complement: 24 (2 officers)
Guns: 1 Bofors 40 mm/70; 90° elevation; 300 rounds/minute to 12 km *(6.5 nm)* anti-surface; 4 km *(2.2 nm)* anti-aircraft; weight of shell 2.4 kg.
1 Oerlikon 20 mm; 55° elevation; 800 rounds/minute to 2 km; weight of shell 0.24 kg.

Comment: Ordered by Mexico on 27 March 1973 from Associated British Machine Tool Makers Ltd to a design by T T Boat Designs, Bembridge, Isle of Wight. The first 21 were modernised in 1987 in Mexico with spare parts and equipment supplied by ABMTM Marine Division who supervised the work which included engine refurbishment and the fitting of air-conditioning. The refit programme was designed to extend service lives by at least 10 years. Reports that more of the class were to be built were not correct.

JOSE MARIA IZAZAGA *1992, Mexican Navy*

2 Ex-US POINT CLASS (LARGE PATROL CRAFT)

Name	No	Builders	Recommissioned
PUNTA MORRO (ex-*Point Verde*)	P 45	C G Yard, Curtis Bay	12 June 1991
PUNTA MASTUN (ex-*Point Herron*)	P 46	C G Yard, Curtis Bay	21 June 199

Displacement, tons: 67 full load
Dimensions, feet (metres): 83 × 17.2 × 5.8 *(25.3 × 5.2 × 1.8)*
Main machinery: 2 Caterpillar diesels; 1600 hp *(1.19 MW)*; 2 shafts
Speed, knots: 23. **Range, miles:** 1500 at 8 kts
Complement: 10
Guns: 2—12.7 mm MGs (can be carried).
Radars: Surface search: Raytheon SPS 64; I band.

Comment: Ex-US Coast Guard craft built in the early 1960s. Steel hulls and aluminium superstructures.

PUNTA MASTUN *1992, Mexican Navy*

8 POLIMAR CLASS (COASTAL PATROL CRAFT)

Name	No	Builders	Commissioned
POLUNO	F 01	Astilleros de Tampico	1 Oct 1962
POLDOS	F 02	Icacas Shipyard, Guerrero	1968
POLTRES	F 03	Icacas Shipyard, Guerrero	1968
POLCUATRO	F 04	Astilleros de Tampico	1971
POLCINCO	F 05	Astilleros de Tampico	28 July 1953
ASPIRANTE JOSE V RAZCON	F 06	Astilleros de Tampico	18 Mar 1960
POLSIETE	F 07	—	1985
POLOCHO	F 08	—	1986

Displacement, tons: 37 standard; 57 full load
Dimensions, feet (metres): 67.2 × 14.8 × 4.3 *(20.1 × 4.5 × 1.3)*
Main machinery: 2 diesels; 456 hp *(335 kW)*; 2 shafts
Speed, knots: 11
Guns: 1 Oerlikon 20 mm (can be carried).
Radars: Surface search: I band.

Comment: Steel construction. Details given are for the first six. The last two were transferred from the USN on the dates shown and may have some structural differences.

POLCINCO *1992, Mexican Navy*

13 OLMECA II CLASS (RIVER PATROL CRAFT)

AM 11-AM 23

Displacement, tons: 18 full load
Dimensions, feet (metres): 54.8 × 14.4 × 7.9 *(16.7 × 4.4 × 2.4)*
Main machinery: 2 Detroit 8V-92TA diesels; 700 hp *(562 kW)* sustained; 2 shafts
Speed, knots: 20. **Range, miles:** 460 at 15 kts
Complement: 15 (2 officers)
Guns: 1—12.7 mm MG.
Radars: Navigation: Raytheon; I band.

Comment: Built at Acapulco from 1979-83 with GRP hulls.

AM 11 *1986, Mexican Navy*

420 MEXICO / Light forces — Survey vessels

5 FLUVIAL CLASS (RIVER PATROL CRAFT)

Name	No	Builders	Commissioned
AM 04	F 14	Vera Cruz	1957
AM 05	F 15	Tampico	1959
AM 06	F 16	Vera Cruz	1959
AM 07	F 17	Tampico	1961
AM 08	F 18	Vera Cruz	1981

Displacement, tons: 37
Dimensions, feet (metres): 56.1 × 16.4 × 8.2 *(17.1 × 5 × 2.5)*
Main machinery: 1 diesel; 1 shaft
Speed, knots: 6

Comment: Steel construction. One already deleted having been replaced by the last of the class which was built 20 years after the others.

AM 04   1989

SURVEY VESSELS

1 Ex-US ADMIRABLE CLASS

OCEANOGRAFICO (ex-DM 20, ex-USS *Harlequin* AM 365, ex-ID-20)   H 02

Comment: Details given in Admirable class under *Patrol Ships*. Now unarmed but has a complement of 62 (12 officers).

OCEANOGRAFICO   1990, Mexican Navy

1 HUMBOLT CLASS

Name	No	Builders	Recommissioned
ALEJANDRO DE HUMBOLT	H 03	J G Hitzler, Elbe	22 June 1987

Displacement, tons: 585 standard; 700 full load
Dimensions, feet (metres): 140.7 × 32 × 13.5 *(42.3 × 9.6 × 4.1)*
Main machinery: 2 diesels; 2 shafts
Speed, knots: 14
Complement: 20 (4 officers)

Comment: Built in 1970. Converted in 1982 to become a hydrographical and acoustic survey ship. Based at Sinaloa.

ALEJANDRO DE HUMBOLT   1989, Mexican Navy

1 ONJUKU CLASS

ONJUKU H 04

Displacement, tons: 494 full load
Dimensions, feet (metres): 121 × 26.2 × 11.5 *(36.9 × 8 × 3.5)*
Main machinery: 1 Yanmar 6UA-UT diesel; 700 hp(m) *(515 kW)*; 1 shaft
Speed, knots: 12. **Range, miles:** 5645 at 10.5 kts
Complement: 20 (4 officers)
Radars: Navigation: I band.
Sonars: Furuno; hull-mounted; high frequency.

Comment: Launched in 1977 and commissioned in 1980.

ONJUKU   1987, Mexican Navy

2 Ex-US ROBERT D CONRAD CLASS

Name	No	Builders	Commissioned
ALTAIR (ex-*James M Gilfss*)	H 05 (ex-AGOR 4)	Christy Corp, Wisconsin	5 Nov 1962
ANTARES (ex-*S P Lee*)	H 06 (ex-AG 192)	Defoe, Bay City	2 Dec 1962

Displacement, tons: 1370 full load
Dimensions, feet (metres): 208.9 × 40 × 15.4 *(63.7 × 12.2 × 4.7)*
Main machinery: Diesel-electric; 2 Caterpillar diesel generators; 1 motor; 1000 hp *(746 kW)*; 1 shaft; bow thruster
Speed, knots: 13.5. **Range, miles:** 12 000 at 12 kts
Complement: 34 (12 officers)
Radars: Navigation: Raytheon TM1600; I band.

Comment: *Altair* leased 14 June 1983. Refitted and modernised in Mexico. Recommissioned 27 November 1984. Primarily used for oceanography. *Antares* served as an AGI with the USN until February 1974 when she transferred on loan to the Geological Survey. Recommissioned into the Mexican Navy 7 December 1992.

ALTAIR   1989, Mexican Navy

ANTARES (old name)   1983, van Ginderen Collection

SERVICE FORCES

Note: US planned to lease at least one Thomaston class LSD, now in reserve in Mexico, in 1991. No sign of this offer being taken up. The ship would be employed in anti-smuggling and anti-drug war duties, which would require formation of a much larger Naval Aviation helicopter wing (UH-1Hs, and so on).

1 Ex-US FABIUS CLASS (LIGHT FORCES TENDER)

Name	No	Builders	Commissioned
VICENTE GUERRERO (ex-USS *Megara* ARVA-6)	A 05	American Bridge Co, Ambridge, Penn	27 June 1945

Displacement, tons: 3284 light; 4100 full load
Dimensions, feet (metres): 328 × 50 × 14 *(100 × 15.3 × 4.3)*
Main machinery: 2 GM 12-567A diesels; 1800 hp *(1.34 MW)*; 2 shafts
Speed, knots: 10.6. **Range, miles:** 6000 at 10 kts
Complement: 250
Guns: 12 Bofors 40 mm/60 (2 quad; 2 twin).
Fire control: 2 Mk 51 Mod 2 GFCS.

Comment: Ex-aircraft repair ship sold to Mexico 1 October 1973. Carries two LCVPs.

VICENTE GUERRERO　　　　　　　　　　　　　　　　1992, Mexican Navy

LCVP (embarked in A 05)　　　　　　　　　　　　　　　1988

2 Ex-US 511-1152 CLASS (LSTs)

Name	No	Builders	Commissioned
PANUCO (ex-*Park County*)	A 01	Bethlehem Steel	8 May 1945
MANZANILLO (ex-*Clearwater County*)	A 02	Chicago Bridge & Iron Co	31 Mar 1944

Displacement, tons: 4080 full load
Dimensions, feet (metres): 328 × 50 × 14 *(100 × 15.3 × 4.3)*
Main machinery: 2 GM 12-567A diesels; 1800 hp *(1.34 MW)*; 2 shafts
Speed, knots: 11. **Range, miles:** 6000 at 11 kts
Complement: 13
Guns: 8 Bofors 40 mm (2 twin, 4 single).

Comment: Transferred in 1971-72 and deployed as SAR and disaster relief ships. Were to have paid off when *Huasteco* and *Zapoteco* commissioned but have been retained in service.

PANUCO　　　　　　　　　　　　　　　　7/1991, Harald Carstens

2 LOGISTIC SUPPORT SHIPS

Name	No	Builders	Commissioned
HUASTECO	A 21	Tampico, Tampa	21 May 1986
ZAPOTECO	A 22	Salina Cruz	1 Sep 1986

Displacement, tons: 2650 full load
Dimensions, feet (metres): 227 × 42 × 18.6 *(69.2 × 12.8 × 5.7)*
Main machinery: 1 diesel; 3600 hp(m) *(2.65 MW)*; 1 shaft
Speed, knots: 16. **Range, miles:** 5500 at 14 kts
Complement: 57 plus 300 passengers
Guns: 1 Bofors 40/60.
Helicopters: 1 MBB BO 105C.

Comment: Can serve as troop transports, supply or hospital ships. Were to have replaced the ex-US LSTs but the latter have been retained in service.

HUASTECO　　　　　　　　　　　　　　　　6/1992, Mexican Navy

1 LOGISTIC SUPPORT SHIP

Name	No	Builders	Recommissioned
TARASCO (ex-*Sea Point*, ex-*Tricon*, ex-*Marika*, ex-*Arneb*)	A 25	Solvesborg, Sweden	1 Mar 1990

Displacement, tons: 1970 full load
Dimensions, feet (metres): 282.2 × 40.7 × 16.1 *(86 × 12.4 × 4.9)*
Main machinery: 1 Kloeckner Humboldt Deutz diesel; 2100 hp(m) *(1.54 MW)*; 1 shaft
Speed, knots: 14
Cargo capacity: 778 tons

Comment: Built in 1962 as a commercial ship and taken into the Navy in 1990.

TARASCO　　　　　　　　　　　　　　　　1990, Mexican Navy

1 DURANGO CLASS

Name	No	Builders	Commissioned
DURANGO	B 01 (ex-128)	Union Naval de Levante, Valencia	14 July 1936

Displacement, tons: 1600 standard; 2000 full load
Dimensions, feet (metres): 256.5 × 36.6 × 10.5 *(78.2 × 11.2 × 3.1)*
Main machinery: Diesel-electric; 2 Enterprise DMR-38 diesels; 5000 hp *(3.73 MW)*; 2 shafts
Speed, knots: 18. **Range, miles:** 3000 at 12 kts
Complement: 149 (24 officers)
Guns: 1—4 in *(102 mm)*. 2—57 mm. 4 Oerlikon 20 mm.

Comment: Laid down 28 October 1933 and launched 28 June 1935. Originally designed primarily as an armed transport with accommodation for 20 officers and 450 men, then reclassified as a frigate. Became non-operational in the 1970s but has since been refitted as a transport ship.

DURANGO　　　　　　　　　　　　　　　　1992, Mexican Navy

1 LOGISTIC SUPPORT SHIP

Name	No	Builders	Recommissioned
MAYA	A 23	Isla Gran Cayman, Ru	1 June 1988

Displacement, tons: 924 full load
Dimensions, feet (metres): 160.1 × 38.7 × 16.1 *(48.8 × 11.8 × 4.9)*
Main machinery: 1 MAN diesel; 1 shaft
Speed, knots: 12
Complement: 15 (8 officers)

Comment: First launched in 1962 and acquired for the Navy in 1988. Unarmed.

MAYA　　　　　　　　　　　　　　　　1989, Mexican Navy

422 MEXICO / Service forces

1 LOGISTIC SUPPORT SHIP

Name	No	Builders	Recommissioned
PROGRESO	A 24	Angulo, Del Carmen	27 Mar 1989

Displacement, tons: 152 full load
Dimensions, feet (metres): 73.8 × 21.7 × 4.9 *(22.5 × 6.6 × 1.5)*
Main machinery: 1 diesel; 1 shaft
Speed, knots: 10
Cargo capacity: 57 tons

Comment: First commissioned 27 February 1985. Converted in 1988 and taken into the Navy in 1989.

PROGRESO   *1992, Mexican Navy*

1 TRANSPORT VESSEL

Name	No	Builders	Recommissioned
PLAN DE IGUALA (ex-*La Paz*)	A 08	Kure Zosencho, Japan	16 Mar 1990

Displacement, tons: 4205 full load
Dimensions, feet (metres): 357.7 × 57.5 × 16.1 *(109 × 17.5 × 4.9)*
Main machinery: 2 Burmeister & Wain diesels; 5600 hp(m) *(4.1 MW)*; 2 shafts
Speed, knots: 17.5
Cargo capacity: 1227 tons

Comment: Former Ro-Ro ferry belonging to the Transport Ministry. Built in 1963.

PLAN DE IGUALA   *1990, Mexican Navy*

1 TRANSPORT VESSEL

Name	No	Builders	Commissioned
ZACATECAS	B 02	Ulua SY, Veracruz	1960

Displacement, tons: 785 standard
Dimensions, feet (metres): 158 × 27.2 × 10 *(48.2 × 8.3 × 2.7)*
Main machinery: 1 MAN diesel; 560 hp(m) *(412 kW)*; 1 shaft
Speed, knots: 8
Complement: 50 (13 officers)
Cargo capacity: 400 tons
Guns: 2 Bofors 40 mm/60.

Comment: Cargo ship type employed as a transport.

ZACATECAS   *1992, Mexican Navy*

2 Ex-US YOG/YO TYPE (HARBOUR TANKERS)

Name	No	Builders	Recommissioned
AGUASCALIENTES (ex-*YOG 6*)	A 03	Geo H Mathis Co Ltd, Camden, NJ	Nov 1964
TLAXCALA (ex-*YO 107*)	A 04	Geo Lawley & Son, Neponset, Mass	Nov 1964

Displacement, tons: 440 light; 1400 full load
Dimensions, feet (metres): 159.2 × 32.9 × 13.3 *(48.6 × 10 × 4.1)*
Main machinery: 1 Fairbanks-Morse diesel; 500 hp *(373 kW)*; 1 shaft
Speed, knots: 8
Complement: 26 (5 officers)
Cargo capacity: 6570 barrels
Guns: 1 Oerlikon 20 mm.

Comment: Former US self-propelled fuel oil barges built in 1943. Purchased in August 1964.

1 SAIL TRAINING SHIP

Name	No	Builders	Commissioned
CUAUHTEMOC	A 07	Astilleros Taleres Calaya, SA, Bilbao	29 July 1982

Displacement, tons: 1800 full load
Dimensions, feet (metres): 296.9 (bowsprit); 220.5 wl × 39.4 × 17.7 *(90.5; 67.2 × 12 × 5.4)*
Main machinery: 1 Detroit 12V-149T diesel; 875 hp *(652 kW)* sustained; 1 shaft
Speed, knots: 17 sail; 7 diesel
Complement: 268 (20 officers, 90 midshipmen)

Comment: Launched January 1982. Has 2368 sq m of sail.

CUAUHTEMOC   *7/1992, Giorgio Arra*

4 Ex-US ABNAKI CLASS (TUGS)

Name	No	Builders	Commissioned
OTOMI (ex-USS *Molala* ATF 106)	A 17	United Eng Co, Alameda, Calif	29 Sep 1943
YAQUI (ex-USS *Abnaki* ATF 96)	A 18	Charleston S B and D D Co	15 Nov 1943
SERI (ex-USS *Cocopa* ATF 101)	A 19	Charleston S B and D D Co	25 Mar 1944
CORA (ex-USS *Hitchiti* ATF 103)	A 20	Charleston S B and D D Co	27 May 1944

Displacement, tons: 1640 full load
Dimensions, feet (metres): 205 × 38.5 × 17 *(62.5 × 11.7 × 5.2)*
Main machinery: Diesel-electric; 4 Busch-Sulzer BS-539 diesels; 6000 hp *(4.48 MW)*; 4 generators; 1 motor; 3000 hp(m) *(2.24 MW)*; 1 shaft
Speed, knots: 15. **Range, miles:** 6500 at 15 kts
Complement: 75
Guns: 1 US 3 in *(76 mm)*/50.
Radars: Navigation: Marconi LN 66; I band.

Comment: *Otomi* transferred 1 August 1978, remainder 30 September 1978. All by sale.

SERI   *1990, Mexican Nav*

4 FLOATING DOCKS

— (ex-US ARD 2)   — (ex-US ARD 11)   AR 15 (ex-US ARD 15)
— (ex-US AFDL 28)

Comment: ARD 2 (150 × 24.7 m) transferred 1963 and ARD 11 (same size) 1974 by sale. Lift 3550 tons. Two 10 ton cranes and one 100 kW generator. ARD 15 has the same capacity and facilities—transferred 1971 by lease. AFDL 28 built in 1944, transferred 1973. Lift, 1000 tons.

Patrol forces / MEXICO — Introduction / MONTSERRAT   423

2 Ex-US MARITIME ADMINISTRATION V 4 CLASS (TUGS)

MAYO (ex-*Montauk*) A 12   MIXTECO (ex-*Point Vicente*) A 13

Displacement, tons: 1863 full load
Dimensions, feet (metres): 191.3 × 37 × 18 *(58.3 × 11.3 × 5.5)*
Main machinery: 2 Nat Supply 8-cyl diesels; 2250 hp *(1.68 MW)*; 1 Kort nozzle
Speed, knots: 14. **Range, miles:** 9000 at 14 kts
Complement: 90
Guns: 1—3 in *(76 mm)*/50. 2 Oerlikon 20 mm (*R 2*).
Radars: Navigation: Kelvin Hughes 14/9; I band.

Comment: Part of a large class built 1943-45 by US Maritime Administration for civilian use. Not a successful design; most were laid up on completion. In 1968 six were taken from reserve and transferred by sale in June 1969. All originally unarmed—guns fitted in Mexico. *Mayo* assigned to Gulf area, *Mixteco* to Pacific area. The other four have been scrapped.

5 DREDGERS

CHIAPAS A 30   CRISTOBAL COLON A 32   ISLA AZTECA A 34
MAZATLAN A 31   ISLA DEL CARMEN A 33

Comment: Various types.

MIXTECO   *1992, Mexican Navy*

MICRONESIA

Headquarters' Appointment

OIC Maritime Surveillance Centre
  Mr Lester Ruda

Bases

Kolonia (main base), Kosral, Moen, Takatik.

General

Pacific Islands of the Caroline archipelago comprising the states of Kosral, Pohnpei, Truk and Yap. The Federated States became a self-governing republic on 10 May 1979. The United States maintains responsibility for defence and has leased 3 Cape class Coast Guard patrol craft for anti-narcotics patrols.

Mercantile Marine

Lloyd's Register of Shipping:
  17 vessels of 8141 tons gross

PATROL FORCES

2 PACIFIC FORUM TYPE (LARGE PATROL CRAFT)

Name	No	Builders	Commissioned
PALIKIR	FSM 1	Australian Shipbuilding Industries	28 Apr 1990
MICRONESIA	FSM 2	Australian Shipbuilding Industries	3 Nov 1990

Displacement, tons: 162 full load
Dimensions, feet (metres): 103.3 × 26.6 × 6.9 *(31.5 × 8.1 × 2.1)*
Main machinery: 2 Caterpillar 3516TA diesels; 4400 hp *(3.28 MW)* sustained; 2 shafts
Speed, knots: 20. **Range, miles:** 2500 at 12 kts
Complement: 17 (3 officers)
Radars: Surface search: Furuno 1011; I band.

Comment: Ordered in June 1989 from Australian Shipbuilding Industries. Training and support provided by Australia at Port Kolonia.

3 Ex-US CAPE CLASS (LARGE PATROL CRAFT)

Name	No	Builders	Commissioned
— (ex-*Cape George*)	—	Coast Guard Yard, Curtis Bay	15 Mar 1958
— (ex-*Cape Cross*)	—	Coast Guard Yard, Curtis Bay	20 Aug 1958
— (ex-*Cape Corwin*)	—	Coast Guard Yard, Curtis Bay	14 Nov 1958

Displacement, tons: 148 full load
Dimensions, feet (metres): 95 × 20.2 × 6.6 *(28.9 × 6.2 × 2)*
Main machinery: 2 GM 16V-149TI diesels; 2070 hp *(1.54 MW)* sustained; 2 shafts
Speed, knots: 20. **Range, miles:** 2500 at 10 kts
Complement: 14
Guns: 2—12.7 mm MGs. 2—40 mm mortars.
Radars: Surface search: Raytheon SPS 64; I band.

Comment: Transferred on loan in early 1991.

MICRONESIA   *11/1990, Royal Australian Navy*

CAPE GEORGE (in USCG colours)   *1990*

MONTSERRAT

Senior Officer

Commissioner of Police:
  David H Crowther

Base

Plymouth

Mercantile Marine

Lloyd's Register of Shipping:
  1 vessel of 711 tons gross

1 HALMATIC M160 CLASS (COASTAL PATROL CRAFT)

SHAMROCK

Displacement, tons: 18 light
Dimensions, feet (metres): 52.5 × 15.4 × 4.6 *(16 × 4.7 × 1.4)*
Main machinery: 2 Detroit 6V-92TA diesels; 520 hp *(388 kW)* sustained; 2 shafts
Speed, knots: 27. **Range, miles:** 500 at 17 kts
Complement: 6
Guns: 1—7.62 mm MG.

Comment: Delivered on 7 January 1990; identical craft acquired by Anguilla and the Turks and Caicos Islands in December 1989.

SHAMROCK   *1989, Halmatic*

MOROCCO

Headquarters' Appointment

Inspector of the Navy:
Captain Mohamed Trikki

Diplomatic Representation

Defence Attaché in London:
Colonel Mustapha Jabrane

Personnel

(a) 1993: 7000 officers and ratings (including 1500 Marines)
(b) 18 months' national service

Bases

Casablanca, Safi, Agadir, Kenitra, Tangier, Dakhla, Al Hoceima

Mercantile Marine

Lloyd's Register of Shipping:
492 vessels of 468 101 tons gross

DELETION

1991 *Lieutenant Riffi*

FRIGATE

Note: Negotiations have been under way since 1985 for two more frigates. In 1989 credits were asked for to cover purchases of Spanish military equipment which included two lengthened Descubierta class of about 2150 tons with helicopter facilities; to be built by Bazán. Provisional order placed in early 1991 but still not confirmed by early 1993 and this project may have been overtaken by the acquisition of Assad class corvettes.

1 MODIFIED DESCUBIERTA CLASS

Name	No	Builders	Laid down	Launched	Commissioned
LIEUTENANT COLONEL ERRHAMANI	501	Bazán, Cartagena	20 Mar 1979	26 Feb 1982	28 Mar 1983

Displacement, tons: 1233 standard; 1479 full load
Dimensions, feet (metres): 291.3 × 34 × 12.5 *(88.8 × 10.4 × 3.8)*
Main machinery: 4 MTU-Bazán 16V 956 TB91 diesels; 15 000 hp(m) *(11 MW)* sustained; 2 shafts; cp props
Speed, knots: 25.5. **Range, miles:** 4000 at 18 kts (1 engine)
Complement: 100

Missiles: SSM: 4 Aerospatiale MM 38 Exocet ❶; inertial cruise; active radar homing to 42 km *(23 nm)* at 0.9 Mach; warhead 165 kg; sea-skimmer. Frequently not embarked.
SAM: Selenia/Elsag Albatros octuple launcher ❷; 24 Aspide; semi-active radar homing to 13 km *(8 nm)* at 2.5 Mach; height envelope 15-5000 m *(49.2-16 405 ft)*; warhead 30 kg.
Guns: 1 OTO Melara 3 in *(76 mm)*/62 compact ❸; 85° elevation; 85 rounds/minute to 16 km *(8.6 nm)* anti-surface; 12 km *(6.5 nm)* anti-aircraft; weight of shell 6 kg.
2 Breda Meccanica 40 mm/70 ❹; 85° elevation; 300 rounds/minute to 12.5 km *(6.7 nm)*; weight of shell 0.96 kg.
Torpedoes: 6—324 mm Mk 32 (2 triple) tubes ❺. Honeywell Mk 46 Mod 1; anti-submarine; active/passive homing to 11 km *(5.9 nm)* at 40 kts; warhead 44 kg.
A/S mortars: 1 Bofors SR 375 mm twin trainable launcher ❻; range 3.6 km *(1.9 nm)*; 24 rockets.
Countermeasures: Decoys: 2 CSEE Dagaie double trainable mounting; IR flares and chaff; H/J band.
ESM/ECM: Elettronica ELT 715; intercept and jammer.
Combat data systems: Signaal SEWACO-MR action data automation.
Radars: Air/surface search: Signaal DA 05 ❼; E/F band; range 137 km *(75 nm)* for 2 m² target.
Surface search: Signaal ZW 06 ❽; I band; range 26 km *(14 nm)*.
Fire control: Signaal WM 25/41 ❾; I/J band; range 46 km *(25 nm)*.
Sonars: Raytheon DE 1160 B; hull-mounted; active/passive; medium range; medium frequency.

Programmes: Ordered 7 June 1977.

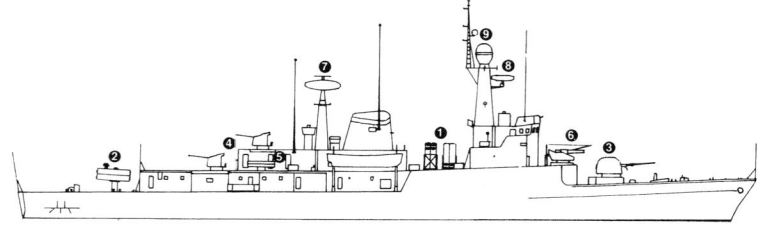

LIEUTENANT COLONEL ERRHAMANI   *(Scale 1 : 900), Ian Sturton*

LIEUTENANT COLONEL ERRHAMANI   1991

Operational: The ship is fitted to carry Exocet but the missiles are seldom embarked.

CORVETTES

2 + (2) ASSAD CLASS

Name	No	Builders	Laid down	Launched	Completed
(ex-*Abdulla Ben Abi Sarh*)	(ex-F 214)	Fincantieri, Breda, Mestre	22 Mar 1982	5 July 1983	1987
(ex-*Khalid Ibn Al Walid*)	(ex-F 216)	Fincantieri, Breda, Mestre	3 June 1982	5 July 1983	1987
(ex-*Saad Ibn Abi Waccade*)	(ex-F 218)	Fincantieri, Breda, Marghera	17 Sep 1982	30 Dec 1983	1988
(ex-*Salah Ad Deen Al Ayoori*)	(ex-F 220)	Fincantieri, Breda, Marghera	17 Sep 1982	30 Mar 1984	1988

Displacement, tons: 705 full load
Dimensions, feet (metres): 204.4 × 30.5 × 8 *(62.3 × 9.3 × 2.5)*
Main machinery: 4 MTU 20V 956 TB92 diesels; 20 120 hp(m) *(14.8 MW)* sustained; 4 shafts
Speed, knots: 37. **Range, miles:** 4000 at 18 kts
Complement: 47

Missiles: SSM: 6 OTO Melara/Matra Otomat Teseo Mk 2 (TG 2) (3 twin); active radar homing to 180 km *(98.4 nm)* at 0.9 Mach; warhead 210 kg; sea-skimmer.
SAM: 1 Selenia/Elsag Albatros launcher (4 cell—2 reloads); Aspide; semi-active radar homing to 13 km *(7 nm)* at 2.5 Mach; height envelope 15-5000 m *(49.2-16 405 ft)*; warhead 30 kg.
Guns: 1 OTO Melara 3 in *(76 mm)*/62 compact; 85° elevation; 85 rounds/minute to 16 km *(8.7 nm)* anti-surface; 12 km *(6.6 nm)* anti-aircraft; weight of shell 6 kg.
2 Breda 40 mm/70 (twin) (not in helicopter ships); 85° elevation; 300 rounds/minute to 12.5 km *(6.8 nm)*; weight of shell 0.96 kg.
Torpedoes: 6—324 mm ILAS 3 (2 triple) tubes. Whitehead A244S; anti-submarine; active/passive homing to 6 km *(3.3 nm)*; warhead 34 kg (shaped charge).
Countermeasures: Decoys: 2 Breda 105 mm six-tubed multi-purpose launchers; chaff to 5 km *(2.7 nm)*; illuminants to 12 km *(6.6 nm)*.
ESM: Selenia INS-3; intercept.
ECM: Selenia TQN-2; jammer.
Combat data systems: Selenia IPN 10; action data automation.
Fire control: 2 Selenia NA 21; Dardo.
Radars: Air/surface search: Selenia RAN 12L/X; D/I band; range 82 km *(45 nm)*.
Navigation: SMA SPN 703 (3 RM 20); I band.
Fire control: 2 Selenia RTN 10X; I/J band; range 40 km *(22 nm)*.
Sonars: Atlas Elektronik ASO 84-41; hull-mounted; active search and attack.

ABDULLA BEN ABI SARH   *3/1992, Melara Club*

Programmes: Ordered in February 1981 for the Iraqi Navy and fell foul of UN sanctions before they could either be paid for or delivered. Subsequently maintained by Fincantieri. Two near sister ships were paid for by Iraq and remain laid up in Italian ports. Two of the ships bought by Morocco in late 1992, and the intention is to acquire all four if money is available.

Structure: Same type as Libyan ships. NBC citadel and full air conditioning fitted.
Operational: All refitted for sale in 1992/93.

LIGHT FORCES

2 FRENCH PR 72 TYPE (FAST ATTACK CRAFT—GUN)

Name	No	Builders	Commissioned
OKBA	302	Soc Française de Construction Navale	16 Dec 1976
TRIKI	303	Soc Française de Construction Navale	12 July 1977

Displacement, tons: 375 standard; 445 full load
Dimensions, feet (metres): 188.8 × 25 × 7.1 *(57.5 × 7.6 × 2.1)*
Main machinery: 4 SACM AGO V16 ASHR diesels; 11 040 hp(m) *(8.11 MW)*; 4 shafts
Speed, knots: 28. **Range, miles:** 2500 at 16 kts
Complement: 53 (5 officers)
Guns: 1 OTO Melara 3 in *(76 mm)*/62 compact; 85° elevation; 85 rounds/minute to 16 km *(8.6 nm)* anti-surface; 12 km *(6.5 nm)* anti-aircraft; weight of shell 6 kg.
1 Bofors 40 mm/70; 85° elevation; 300 rounds/minute to 12.5 km *(6.7 nm)*; weight of shell 0.96 kg.
Fire control: 2 CSEE Panda optical directors.
Radars: Surface search: Decca; I band.

Comment: Ordered June 1973. *Okba* launched 10 October 1975, *Triki* 1 February 1976. Can be Exocet fitted (with Vega control system).

OKBA   1992

4 LAZAGA CLASS (FAST ATTACK CRAFT—MISSILE)

Name	No	Builders	Commissioned
EL KHATTABI	304	Bazán, San Fernando	26 July 1981
COMMANDANT AZOUGGARH	305	Bazán, San Fernando	2 Aug 1982
COMMANDANT BOUTOUBA	306	Bazán, San Fernando	20 Nov 1981
COMMANDANT EL HARTY	307	Bazán, San Fernando	25 Feb 1982

Displacement, tons: 425 full load
Dimensions, feet (metres): 190.6 × 24.9 × 8.9 *(58.1 × 7.6 × 2.7)*
Main machinery: 2 MTU-Bazán 16V 956 TB91 diesels; 7500 hp(m) *(5.51 MW)* sustained; 2 shafts
Speed, knots: 30. **Range, miles:** 3000 at 15 kts
Complement: 41
Missiles: SSM: 4 Aerospatiale MM 38 Exocet; inertial cruise; active radar homing to 42 km *(23 nm)* at 0.9 Mach; warhead 165 kg; sea-skimmer.
Guns: 1 OTO Melara 3 in *(76 mm)*/62 compact; 85° elevation; 85 rounds/minute to 16 km *(8.6 nm)* anti-surface; 12 km *(6.5 nm)* anti-aircraft; weight of shell 6 kg.
1 Breda Meccanica 40 mm/70; 85° elevation; 300 rounds/minute to 12.5 km *(6.7 nm)*; weight of shell 0.96 kg.
2 Oerlikon 20 mm/90 GAM-BO1; 55° elevation; 800 rounds/minute to 2 km.
Fire control: CSEE Panda optical director.
Radars: Surface search: Signaal ZW 06; I band; range 26 km *(14 nm)*.
Fire control: Signaal WM 25; I/J band; range 46 km *(25 nm)*.

Comment: Ordered from Bazán, San Fernando (Cadiz), Spain 14 June 1977.

COMMANDANT AZOUGGARH   5/1984

4 OSPREY MK II CLASS (LARGE PATROL CRAFT)

Name	No	Builders	Commissioned
EL HAHIQ	308	Danyard A/S, Frederickshaven	11 Nov 1987
EL TAWFIQ	309	Danyard A/S, Frederickshaven	31 Jan 1988
EL HAMISS	316	Danyard A/S, Frederickshaven	9 Aug 1990
EL KARIB	317	Danyard A/S, Frederickshaven	23 Sep 1990

Displacement, tons: 475 full load
Dimensions, feet (metres): 179.8 × 34 × 8.5 *(54.8 × 10.5 × 2.6)*
Main machinery: 2 MAN Burmeister & Wain Alpha 12V23/30-DVO diesels; 4440 hp(m) *(3.23 MW)* sustained; 2 waterjets
Speed, knots: 22. **Range, miles:** 4500 at 16 kts
Complement: 15 plus 20 spare berths
Guns: 1 Bofors 40 mm/60. 2 Oerlikon 20 mm (twin).
Radars: Surface search; Racal Decca; I band.

Comment: First two ordered in September 1986; two more on 30 January 1989 and a third pair in late 1990. First two were for the Customs Service and second pair for the Navy but this may have been reversed. There is a stern ramp with a hinged cover for launching the inspection boat.

EL TAWFIQ   9/1992, H M Steele

6 CORMORAN CLASS (LARGE PATROL CRAFT)

Name	No	Builders	Launched	Commissioned
L V RABHI	310	Bázan, San Fernando	23 Sep 1987	16 Sep 1988
ERRACHIQ	311	Bázan, San Fernando	23 Sep 1987	16 Dec 1988
EL AKID	312	Bázan, San Fernando	29 Mar 1988	4 Apr 1989
EL MAHER	313	Bázan, San Fernando	29 Mar 1988	20 June 1989
EL MAJID	314	Bázan, San Fernando	21 Oct 1988	26 Sep 1989
EL BACHIR	315	Bázan, San Fernando	21 Oct 1988	19 Dec 1989

Displacement, tons: 425 full load
Dimensions, feet (metres): 190.6 × 24.9 × 8.9 *(58.1 × 7.6 × 2.7)*
Main machinery: 2 MTU Bazán 16V 956 TB82 diesels; 8340 hp(m) *(6.13 MW)* sustained; 2 shafts
Speed, knots: 22. **Range, miles:** 6100 at 12 kts
Complement: 36 (4 officers)
Guns: 1 Bofors 40 mm/70. 2 Giat 20 mm.
Fire control: Lynx optronic director.
Radars: Surface search: Racal Decca; I band.

Comment: Three ordered from Bazán, Cadiz in October 1985 as a follow on to the Lazaga class of which these are a slower patrol version with a 10 day endurance. Option on three more taken up. Used for fishery protection.

EL MAHER   6/1989, Bazán

6 P 32 TYPE (COASTAL PATROL CRAFT)

Name	No	Builders	Commissioned
EL WACIL	203	CMN, Cherbourg	9 Oct 1975
EL JAIL	204	CMN, Cherbourg	3 Dec 1975
EL MIKDAM	205	CMN, Cherbourg	30 Jan 1976
EL KHAFIR	206	CMN, Cherbourg	16 Apr 1976
EL HARIS	207	CMN, Cherbourg	30 June 1976
EL ESSAHIR	208	CMN, Cherbourg	16 July 1976

Displacement, tons: 74 light; 89 full load
Dimensions, feet (metres): 105 × 17.7 × 4.6 *(32 × 5.4 × 1.4)*
Main machinery: 2 SACM MGO 12V BZSHR diesels; 2700 hp(m) *(1.98 MW)*; 2 shafts
Speed, knots: 28. **Range, miles:** 1500 at 15 kts
Complement: 17
Guns: 1 Oerlikon 20 mm.
Radars: Surface search: Decca; I band.

Comment: Ordered in February 1974. In July 1985 a further four of this class were ordered from the same builders but for the Customs Service. Wooden hull sheathed in plastic.

EL WACIL   1988

AMPHIBIOUS FORCES

3 BATRAL TYPE

Name	No	Builders	Commissioned
DAOUD BEN AICHA	402	Dubigeon, Normandie	28 May 1977
AHMED ES SAKALI	403	Dubigeon, Normandie	Sep 1977
ABOU ABDALLAH EL AYACHI	404	Dubigeon, Normandie	Mar 1978

Displacement, tons: 750 standard; 1409 full load
Dimensions, feet (metres): 262.4 × 42.6 × 7.9 *(80 × 13 × 2.4)*
Main machinery: 2 SACM Type 195 V12 CSHR diesels; 3600 hp(m) *(2.65 MW)* sustained; 2 shafts
Speed, knots: 16. **Range, miles:** 4500 at 13 kts
Complement: 47 (3 officers)
Military lift: 140 troops; 12 vehicles
Guns: 2 Bofors 40 mm/70. 2—81 mm mortars.
Radars: Surface search: Thomson-CSF DRBN 32; I band.
Helicopters: Platform only.

Comment: Two ordered on 12 March 1975. Third ordered 19 August 1975. Of same type as the French *Champlain*. Vehicle-stowage above and below decks.

AHMED ES SAKALI *8/1986, John G Callis*

1 EDIC CLASS

Name	No	Builders	Commissioned
LIEUTENANT MALGHAGH	401	Chantiers Navals Franco-Belges	1965

Displacement, tons: 250 standard; 670 full load
Dimensions, feet (metres): 193.5 × 39.2 × 4.3 *(59 × 12 × 1.3)*
Main machinery: 2 MGO diesels; 1000 hp(m) *(735 kW)*; 2 shafts
Speed, knots: 8. **Range, miles:** 1800 at 8 kts
Complement: 16 (1 officer)
Military lift: 11 vehicles
Guns: 2 Oerlikon 20 mm. 1—120 mm mortar.

Comment: Ordered early in 1963. Similar to the French landing craft of the Edic type built at the same yard.

LIEUTENANT MALGHAGH (EL KHAFIR alongside) *1989*

SERVICE FORCES

Note: There is also a yacht, *Essaouira*, 60 tons, from Italy in 1967, used as a training vessel for watchkeepers.

2 LOGISTIC SUPPORT SHIPS

AD DAKHLA (ex-*Merc Caribe*) 405   EL AIGH (ex-*Merc Nordia*) 406

Measurement, tons: 1500 grt
Dimensions, feet (metres): 252.6 × 40 × 15.4 *(77 × 12.2 × 4.7)*
Main machinery: 1 Burmeister & Wain diesel; 1250 hp(m) *(919 kW)*; 1 shaft
Speed, knots: 11
Guns: 2—14.5 mm MGs.

Comment: Logistic support vessels with four 5 ton cranes. Former cargo ships built by Fredrickshavn Vaerft in 1973 and acquired in 1981.

EL AIGH *1989*

1 TRANSPORT SHIP

ARRAFIQ (ex-*Thjelvar*, ex-*Gotland*) 407

Measurement, tons: 2990 grt, 784 dwt
Dimensions, feet (metres): 305.8 × 53.8 × 13.8 *(93.2 × 16.4 × 4.2)*
Main machinery: 4 Werkspoor 16V diesels; 8000 hp(m) *(5.88 MW)*; 4 shafts
Speed, knots: 18.5

Comment: Former Ro-Ro ferry converted as a troop transport.

ARRAFIQ *1990*

CUSTOMS/COAST GUARD

4 P 32 TYPE (COASTAL PATROL CRAFT)

Name	No	Builders	Commissioned
ERRAID	209	CMN, Cherbourg	18 Mar 1988
ERRACED	210	CMN, Cherbourg	15 Apr 1988
EL KACED	211	CMN, Cherbourg	17 May 1988
ESSAID	212	CMN, Cherbourg	4 July 1988

Displacement, tons: 89 full load
Dimensions, feet (metres): 105 × 17.7 × 4.6 *(32 × 5.4 × 1.4)*
Main machinery: 2 SACM MGO 12V BZSHR diesels; 2700 hp(m) *(1.98 MW)*; 2 shafts
Speed, knots: 28. **Range, miles:** 1500 at 15 kts
Complement: 17
Guns: 1 Oerlikon 20 mm.
Radars: Navigation: Decca; I band.

Comment: Almost identical to the El Wacil class listed under Light Forces. Ordered in July 1985.

P 32 TYPE *1988*

18 ARCOR 46 CLASS (COASTAL PATROL CRAFT)

D01-D18

Displacement, tons: 15 full load
Dimensions, feet (metres): 47.6 × 13.8 × 4.3 *(14.5 × 4.2 × 1.3)*
Main machinery: 2 Uni Diesel UD18 V8 M5; 1010 hp(m) *(742 kW)* sustained; 2 shafts
Speed, knots: 32
Complement: 6
Guns: 2 Browning 12.7 mm MGs.
Radars: Surface search: Racal Decca; I band.

Comment: Ordered from Arcor, La Teste in June 1985. GRP hulls. Delivered in groups of three from April to September 1987. Used for patrolling the Mediterranean coastline.

ARCOR 46 *1987, Arcor*

15 ARCOR 53 CLASS (COASTAL PATROL CRAFT)

Displacement, tons: 17 full load
Dimensions, feet (metres): 52.5 × 13 × 3.9 *(16 × 4 × 1.2)*
Main machinery: 2 diesels; 2 shafts
Speed, knots: 35
Complement: 6
Guns: 1—12.7 mm MG.
Radars: Surface search: Racal Decca; I band.

Comment: Ordered from Arcor, La Teste in 1990 for the Police Force. Delivered at one a month from October 1992.

3 SAR CRAFT

HAOUZ   ASSA   TARIK

Displacement, tons: 40 full load
Dimensions, feet (metres): 63.6 × 15.7 × 4.3 *(19.4 × 4.8 × 1.3)*
Main machinery: 2 diesels; 1400 hp(m) *(1.03 MW)*; 2 shafts
Speed, knots: 20
Complement: 6

Comment: Rescue craft built by Schweers, Bardenfleth, and delivered in 1991.

ARCOR 53   1992, Arcor

MOZAMBIQUE

Senior Appointment

Commander of the Navy:
  Captain Manuel Gimo Caetano

Personnel

(a) 1993: 900
(b) Voluntary

General

In addition to the vessels shown, some of those listed under *Deletions* may in time be repairable, but none has been operational for at least two years.

Bases

Maputo (Naval HQ); Nacala; Beira; Pemba (Porto Amelia); Metangula (Lake Malawi).

Mercantile Marine

Lloyd's Register of Shipping:
  107 vessels of 37 288 tons gross

DELETIONS

1991-92   2 SO 1 class, 2 Jupiter class, 1 Alfange class

PATROL FORCES

Note: A few 18 m patrol craft built in India may still be serviceable.

3 Ex-SOVIET ZHUK CLASS (COASTAL PATROL CRAFT)

Displacement, tons: 50 full load
Dimensions, feet (metres): 75.4 × 17 × 6.2 *(23 × 5.2 × 1.9)*
Main machinery: 2 Type M 50 diesels; 2200 hp(m) *(1.6 MW)* sustained; 2 shafts
Speed, knots: 30. **Range, miles:** 1100 at 15 kts
Complement: 17
Guns: 4 USSR 14.5 mm (2 twin) MGs.
Radars: Navigation: Spin Trough; I band.

Comment: Two transferred in February 1979, one in August 1979 and two in October 1980. Only one operational in 1992. At least two deleted.

2 Ex-SOVIET YEVGENYA CLASS (INSHORE MINESWEEPERS)

Displacement, tons: 77 standard; 90 full load
Dimensions, feet (metres): 80.7 × 18 × 4.9 *(24.6 × 5.5 × 1.5)*
Main machinery: 2 Type 3-D-12 diesels; 600 hp(m) *(440 kW)* sustained; 2 shafts
Speed, knots: 11. **Range, miles:** 300 at 10 kts
Complement: 10
Guns: 2 USSR 14.5 mm (twin) MGs.
Radars: Surface search: Don 2; I band.
Sonars: Small portable; active minehunting; high frequency.

Comment: Both transferred in 1985. One of them may be the minesweeper PM 525 reported to be called *Graciosa*. Neither were operational in 1992.

HUK   1985

YEVGENYA   1985

NAMIBIA

General

shery protection patrols are being carried out by shore-based elicopters and an assortment of civilian vessels leased by the government. Of these ships the largest is the *Globe*, a whaler built in 1952. Six Cessna aircraft have been offered by the United States but may be used for other duties. Other vessels mentioned are a former yacht *Oryx*, two RIBs, and a research ship *Benguela*.

The rationale for South Africa to continue holding Walvis Bay is weakening and in due course an opportunity may be found to return the port fully to Namibia. A Coast Guard service is being formed possibly with small second-hand USCG craft.

NATO

Note: The NATO frigate project NFR 90 died a predictable death as participating countries pulled out at the end of 1989. A number of more sensible bilateral projects are now being considered and some of these are taking advantage of the work done on NFR 90.

1 RESEARCH VESSEL

Name	No	Builders	Commissioned
ALLIANCE	A1456	Fincantieri, Muggiano	6 May 1988

Displacement, tons: 2466 standard; 3180 full load
Dimensions, feet (metres): 305.1 × 49.9 × 16.7 *(93 × 15.2 × 5.1)*
Main machinery: Diesel-electric; 2 Fincantieri GMT B 230.12 M diesels; 6079 hp(m) *(4.47 MW)* sustained; 2 AEG CC 3127 generators; 2 AEG motors; 5100 hp(m) *(3.75 MW)*; 2 shafts; bow thruster
Speed, knots: 16. **Range, miles:** 8000 at 12 kts
Complement: 27 (10 officers) plus 23 scientists

Comment: Built at La Spezia and launched 9 July 1986. NATO's first wholly owned ship is a Public Service vessel of the German Navy with a German, British and Italian crew. Designed for oceanography and acoustic research, replacing the *Maria Paolina*. Based at La Spezia and operated by SACLANT Undersea Research Centre. Facilities include extensive laboratories, position location systems, silent propulsion, and overside deployment equipment. Can tow a 20 ton load at 12 kts. A Kongsberg gas turbine on 02 deck provides silent propulsion power at 1945 hp *(1.43 MW)* up to speeds of 12 kts.

ALLIANCE 9/1992, H M Steele

NETHERLANDS

Headquarters' Appointments

Chief of the Naval Staff:
  Vice Admiral N W G Buis
Vice Chief of the Naval Staff:
  Rear Admiral C J van der Werf
Director, Material (Navy):
  Rear Admiral T J N van der Voort
Director, Personnel (Navy):
  Rear Admiral J L A van Aalst

Commands

Admiral Netherlands Fleet Command:
  Vice Admiral F J Haver Droeze
Commander Netherlands Task Group:
  Rear Admiral L Kroon
Commandant General Royal Netherlands Marine Corps:
  Major-General R Spiekerman van Weezelenburg
Flag Officer Netherlands Antilles:
  Brigadier F E van Kappen
Hydrographer:
  Commodore E Bakker

Diplomatic Representation

Naval Attaché in London, Dublin and NLR CINCHAN:
  Captain W F L van Leeuwen
Naval Attaché in Madrid:
  Captain D T Noffen
Naval Attaché in Paris and Lisbon:
  Captain W H Hoek
Naval Attaché in Washington and NLR SACLANT:
  Rear Admiral A van der Jande

Personnel

(a) 1993: 14 950 officers and ratings (including the Navy Air Service, 2800 Royal Netherlands Marine Corps and 850 female personnel)
(b) 12 months' national service

Bases

Naval HQ: The Hague
Main Base: Den Helder
Minor Bases: Flushing and Curacao
Fleet Air Arm: NAS Valkenburg (LRMP),
  NAS De Kooy (helicopters)
R Neth Marines: Rotterdam, Doorn and Texel
Training Base (Technical and Logistic): Amsterdam

Naval Air Arm (see *Shipborne Aircraft* section)

Personnel: 1500

Squadron	Aircraft	Task
7	Lynx (UH-14A)	Utility and Transport/SAR
320/321	P-3C Orion	LRMP
860	Lynx (SH-14)	Embarked

Royal Netherlands Marine Corps

4 Marine battalions; 1 combat support battalion and 1 logistic battalion. Based at Doorn and in the Netherlands Antilles and Aruba.

Prefix to Ships' Names

Hr Ms

Strength of the Fleet

Type	Active (Reserve)	Building (Projected)
Submarines (Patrol)	5	1
Frigates	15	4
Mine Hunters	10 (5)	—
Minesweepers—Coastal	6	? (8)
Submarine Support Ship	1	—
Landing Ship Dock (LPD)	—	(1)
Landing Craft	12	—
Surveying Vessels	3	—
Combat Support Ships	2	1
Training Ships	3	—
Tugs	12	—
Auxiliaries (Major)	9	—

Planned Deployments

All frigates and AOEs are deployed in two approximately equal task groups.
  5 Patrol Submarines (6 as from 1994)
  13 LRMP Aircraft in 2 squadrons
  1 MCM Group operating off Dutch ports
  1 MCM Group for Channel command
  2 R Neth Marine battalions (arctic trained)
  2 R Neth Marine battalions for operations overseas

Mercantile Marine

Lloyd's Register of Shipping:
  1230 vessels of 4 250 456 tons gross

DELETIONS

Submarines

1990	*Zeehond* (trials)
1991	*Tonijn* (museum)
1992	*Potvis* (trials)

Frigates

| 1990 | *Isaac Sweers* (Nov) (to Indonesia) |
| 1992 | *Banckert, Callenburgh, Van Kinsbergen* (all to Greece in 1993, 1994 and 1995 respectively) |

Minesweeper

| 1990 | *Woerden* |
| 1992 | *Hoogezand, Giethoorn, Venlo, Hoogeveen, Gemert* |

Miscellaneous

1990	*Gelderland, Itadda, Eems, L 9520*
1992	*Nautilus* (old), *Hydra* (old), *L 9512-9515, L 9518, Triton*
1993	*Wielingen*

PENNANT LIST

Submarines

S 802	Walrus
S 803	Zeeleeuw
S 806	Zwaardvis
S 807	Tijgerhaai
S 808	Dolfijn
S 810	Bruinvis (bldg)

Frigates

F 801	Tromp
F 806	De Ruyter
F 807	Kortenaer
F 811	Piet Heyn
F 812	Jacob van Heemskerck
F 813	Witte de With
F 816	Abraham Crijnssen
F 823	Philips van Almonde
F 824	Bloys van Treslong
F 825	Jan van Brakel
F 826	Pieter Florisz
F 827	Karel Doorman
F 828	Van Speijk (new) (bldg)
F 829	Willem van der Zaan
F 830	Tjerk Hiddes
F 831	Van Amstel
F 832	Abraham van der Hulst (bldg)
F 833	Van Nes (bldg)
F 834	Van Galen (bldg)

Mine Hunters

M 850	Alkmaar
M 851	Delfzyl
M 852	Dordrecht
M 853	Haarlem
M 854	Harlingen
M 855	Scheveningen
M 856	Maassluis
M 857	Makkum
M 858	Middelburg
M 859	Hellevoetsluis
M 860	Schiedam
M 861	Urk
M 862	Zierikzee
M 863	Vlaardingen
M 864	Willemstad

Coastal Minesweepers

M 809	Naaldwijk
M 810	Abcoude
M 812	Drachten
M 813	Ommen
M 823	Naarden
M 830	Sittard

Amphibious Forces

L 9530-35
L 9536-41

Auxiliary Ships

A 801	Pelikaan
A 832	Zuiderkruis
A 835	Poolster
A 836	Amsterdam
A 851	Cerberus
A 852	Argus
A 853	Nautilus
A 854	Hydra
A 872	Westgat
A 874	Linge
A 875	Regge
A 876	Hunze
A 877	Rotte
A 880	Bulgia
A 886	Cornelis Drebbel
A 887	Thetis
A 900	Mercuur
A 903	Zeefakkel
A 904	Buyskes
A 905	Blommendal
A 906	Tydeman
Y 8001	Van Speijk (old)
Y 8018	Breezand
Y 8019	Balgzand
Y 8050	Urania
Y 8055	Schelde
Y 8056	Wierbalg
Y 8057	Malzwin
Y 8058	Zuidwal
Y 8059	Westwal
Y 8500	Tax

SUBMARINES

Note: The Moray class is a private design by Rotterdam Drydock with the government giving limited financial support on condition that the company collaborates with developers of air independent systems (AIP). The old *Zeehond* hull is being used as a test platform for air independent propulsion by RDM with support from the Navy.

3 + 1 WALRUS CLASS

Name	No	Builders	Laid down	Launched	Commissioned
WALRUS	S 802	Rotterdamse Droogdok Mij, Rotterdam	11 Oct 1979	28 Oct 1985 (13 Sep 1989)	25 Mar 1992
ZEELEEUW	S 803	Rotterdamse Droogdok Mij, Rotterdam	24 Sep 1981	20 June 1987	25 Apr 1990
DOLFIJN	S 808	Rotterdamse Droogdok Mij, Rotterdam	12 June 1986	25 Apr 1990	29 Jan 1993
BRUINVIS	S 810	Rotterdamse Droogdok Mij, Rotterdam	14 Apr 1988	25 Apr 1992	Feb 1994

Displacement, tons: 1900 standard; 2465 surfaced; 2800 dived
Dimensions, feet (metres): 223.1 × 27.6 × 21.6 *(67.7 × 8.4 × 6.6)*
Main machinery: Diesel-electric; 3 SEMT-Pielstick 12 PA4 200 VG diesels; 6900 hp(m) *(5.07 MW)*; 3 alternators; 2.88 MW; 1 Holec motor; 6910 hp(m) *(5.1 MW)*; 1 shaft; 7-bladed propeller
Speed, knots: 13 surfaced; 20 dived
Range, miles: 10 000 at 9 kts snorting
Complement: 50 (7 officers)

Missiles: SSM: McDonnell Douglas Sub-Harpoon; active radar homing to 130 km *(70 nm)* at 0.9 Mach; warhead 227 kg.
Torpedoes: 4—21 in *(533 mm)* tubes. Honeywell Mk 48 Mod 4; wire-guided; active/passive homing to 38 km *(20.5 nm)* active at 55 kts; 50 km *(27 nm)* passive at 40 kts; warhead 267 kg and Honeywell NT 37D; wire-guided; active/passive homing to 20 km *(10.8 nm)* at 35 kts; warhead 150 kg; 20 torpedoes or missiles carried. Water-ram discharge gear.
Mines: 40 in lieu of torpedoes.
Countermeasures: ESM: Radar warning.
Fire control: Signaal SEWACO VIII action data automation. Signaal Gipsy data system.
Radars: Surface search: Signaal/Racal ZW 07; I band; range 29 km *(16 nm)* surfaced.
Sonars: Thomson Sintra TSM 2272 Eledone Octopus; hull-mounted; passive/active search and attack; medium frequency.
GEC Avionics Type 2026; towed array; passive search; very low frequency.
Acoustic Telemetry Fenelon; passive ranging.

Programmes: In the 1975 Navy Estimates money was set aside for design work on this class and a contract for the building of the first was signed 16 June 1979, the second was on 17 December 1979. In 1981 various changes to the design were made which resulted in a delay of 1-2 years. *Dolfijn* and *Bruinvis* ordered 16 August 1985; prefabrication started late 1985. Completion of *Walrus* delayed by serious fire 14 August 1986; hull undamaged but cabling and computers destroyed. *Walrus* re-launched 13 September 1989.
Structure: These are improved Zwaardvis class with similar dimensions and silhouettes except for X stern. Use of H T steel increases the diving depth by some 50 per cent. New Gipsy fire control and electronic command system fitted and automation reduces the crew from 65 to 50. Diving depth, 300 m *(984 ft)*.

ZEELEEUW   *10/1992, Campanera i Rovira*

ZEELEEUW   *10/1992, Camil Busquets i Vilanova*

2 ZWAARDVIS CLASS

Name	No	Builders	Laid down	Launched	Commissioned
ZWAARDVIS	S 806	Rotterdamse Droogdok Mij, Rotterdam	14 July 1966	2 July 1970	18 Aug 1972
TIJGERHAAI	S 807	Rotterdamse Droogdok Mij, Rotterdam	14 July 1966	25 May 1971	20 Oct 1972

Displacement, tons: 2350 surfaced; 2640 dived
Dimensions, feet (metres): 216.5 × 27.6 × 23.3 *(66 × 8.4 × 7.1)*
Main machinery: Diesel-electric; 3 Werkspoor RUB 215X12 diesels; 4200 hp(m) *(3.1 MW)*; 1 motor; 5100 hp(m) *(3.75 MW)*; 1 shaft
Speed, knots: 13 surfaced; 20 dived
Range, miles: 10 000 at 9 kts snorting
Complement: 67 (8 officers)

Missiles: SSM: McDonnell Douglas Sub-Harpoon; fitted for but not with.
Torpedoes: 6—21 in *(533 mm)* bow tubes. Honeywell Mk 48 Mod 4; wire-guided; active/passive homing to 38 km *(20.5 nm)* active at 55 kts; 50 km *(27 nm)* passive at 40 kts; warhead 267 kg and Honeywell NT 37D; wire-guided; active/passive homing to 20 km *(10.8 nm)* at 35 kts; warhead 150 kg; 20 torpedoes or missiles carried. Two torpedoes can be launched simultaneously.
Countermeasures: ESM: Radar warning.
Fire control: Signaal M8 digital system.
Radars: Surface search: RN Type 1001; I band.
Sonars: Thomson Sintra Eledone; hull-mounted; passive/active search and attack; medium frequency.
GEC Avionics Type 2026; towed array; passive search; very low frequency.

Programmes: In the 1964 Navy Estimates a first instalment was approved for the construction of two conventionally powered submarines of tear-drop design. Planned to pay off for sale in 1996.
Modernisation: Mid-life conversion carried out in 1988 *(Tijgerhaai)* and 1989-91 *(Zwaardvis)*. New Thomson Sintra Eledone sonar, Signaal fire control and GEC Avionics Type 2026 towed array plus other minor improvements including a quieter propulsion drive unit and shaft.
Structure: Diving depth, 200 m *(656 ft)*.

ZWAARDVIS   *2/1992, W Sartori*

FRIGATES

Note: It is planned to order two air defence frigates in 1996 in collaboration with Germany and Spain to an enlarged Karel Doorman design, and with a vertical launch Evolved Sea Sparrow SAM system.

2 TROMP CLASS

Name	No	Builders	Laid down	Launched	Commissioned
TROMP	F 801	Koninklijke Maatschappij De Schelde, Flushing	4 Aug 1971	2 June 1973	3 Oct 1975
DE RUYTER	F 806	Koninklijke Maatschappij De Schelde, Flushing	22 Dec 1971	9 Mar 1974	3 June 1976

Displacement, tons: 3665 standard; 4308 full load
Dimensions, feet (metres): 454 × 48.6 × 15.1 *(138.4 × 14.8 × 4.6)*
Main machinery: COGOG; 2 RR Olympus TM3B gas turbines; 50 880 hp *(37.9 MW)* sustained; 2 RR Tyne RM 1C gas turbines; 9900 hp *(7.4 MW)* sustained; 2 shafts
Speed, knots: 30. **Range, miles:** 5000 at 18 kts
Complement: 306 (34 officers)

Missiles: SSM: 8 McDonnell Douglas Harpoon (2 quad) launchers ❶; active radar homing to 130 km *(70 nm)* at 0.9 Mach; warhead 227 kg; 16 missiles.
SAM: 40 GDC Pomona Standard SM-1MR; Mk 13 Mod 4 launcher ❷; command guidance; semi-active radar homing to 46 km *(25 nm)* at 2 Mach.
Raytheon Sea Sparrow Mk 29 octuple launcher ❸; semi-active radar homing to 14.6 km *(8 nm)* at 2.5 Mach; warhead 39 kg; 16 missiles.
Guns: 2 Bofors 4.7 in *(120 mm)*/50 (twin) ❹; 85° elevation; 42 rounds/minute to 20 km *(10.8 nm)* anti-surface; 12 km *(6.5 nm)* anti-aircraft; weight of shell 24 kg.
Signaal SGE-30 Goalkeeper with GE 30 mm ❺; 7-barrelled; 4200 rounds/minute combined to 2 km.
2 Oerlikon 20 mm.
Torpedoes: 6—324 mm US Mk 32 (2 triple) tubes ❻. Honeywell Mk 46 Mod 5; anti-submarine; active/passive homing to 11 km *(5.9 nm)* at 40 kts; warhead 44 kg.
Countermeasures: Decoys: 2 Loral Hycor SRBOC ❼; IR flares and chaff.
ESM/ECM: Ramses; intercept and jammer.
Combat data systems: Signaal SEWACO I action data automation; Links 10 and 11. Scot SATCOM ❽.
Fire control: Signaal WM 25 for guns and missiles.
Radars: Air/surface search: Signaal MTTR/SPS 01 ❾; 3D; F band.
Navigation: Two Decca 1226; I band.
Fire control: Two Raytheon SPG 51C ❿; G/I band.
Signaal WM 25 ⓫; I/J band; range 46 km *(25 nm)*.
Sonars: CWE 610; hull-mounted; active search and attack; medium frequency.

Helicopters: 1 Westland SH-14B Lynx ⓬.

Programmes: First design allowance was voted for in 1967 estimates. The intention is to replace both ships towards the end of the century in collaboration with other European navies needing similar ships in the same timescale.
Modernisation: Modernisation plans cancelled in 1988 as an economy measure but partially resurrected in 1990.
Structure: Goalkeeper is fitted on the starboard side of the hangar roof.
Operational: Fitted as Flagships.

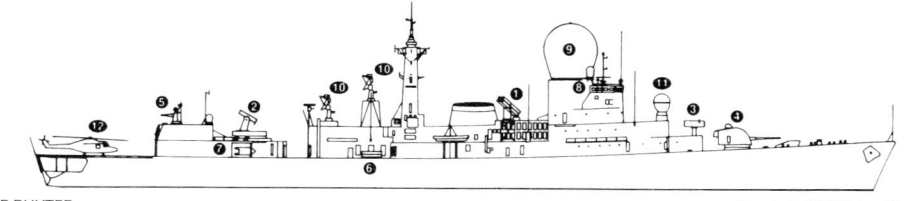

DE RUYTER *(Scale 1 : 1200), Ian Sturton*

TROMP *6/1992, Giorgio Arra*

DE RUYTER *10/1992, W Sartori*

Frigates / NETHERLANDS 431

2 JACOB VAN HEEMSKERCK CLASS

Name	No
JACOB VAN HEEMSKERCK	F 812
WITTE DE WITH	F 813

Builders	Laid down	Launched	Commissioned
Koninklijke Maatschappij De Schelde, Flushing	21 Jan 1981	5 Nov 1983	15 Jan 1986
Koninklijke Maatschappij De Schelde, Flushing	15 Dec 1981	25 Aug 1984	17 Sep 1986

Displacement, tons: 3750 full load approx
Dimensions, feet (metres): 428 × 47.9 × 14.1 (20.3 screws) *(130.5 × 14.6 × 4.3 (6.2))*
Main machinery: COGOG; 2 RR Olympus TM3B gas turbines; 50 880 hp *(37.9 MW)* sustained; 2 RR Tyne RM1C gas turbines; 9900 hp *(7.4 MW)* sustained; 2 shafts; cp props
Speed, knots: 30. **Range, miles:** 4700 at 16 kts on Tynes
Complement: 197 (23 officers)

Missiles: SSM: 8 McDonnell Douglas Harpoon (2 quad) launchers ❶; active radar homing to 130 km *(70 nm)* at 0.9 Mach; warhead 227 kg.
SAM: 40 GDC Pomona Standard SM-1MR; Mk 13 Mod 1 launcher ❷; command guidance; semi-active radar homing to 46 km *(25 nm)* at 2 Mach.
Raytheon Sea Sparrow Mk 29 octuple launcher ❸; semi-active radar homing to 14.6 km *(8 nm)* at 2.5 Mach; warhead 39 kg; 24 missiles.
Guns: 1 Signaal SGE-30 Goalkeeper ❹ with General Electric 30 mm 7-barrelled; 4200 rounds/minute combined to 2 km. 2 Oerlikon 20 mm.
Torpedoes: 4—324 mm US Mk 32 (2 twin) tubes ❺. Honeywell Mk 46 Mod 5; anti-submarine; active/passive homing to 11 km *(5.9 nm)* at 40 kts; warhead 44 kg.
Countermeasures: Decoys: 2 Loral Hycor Mk 36 SRBOC 6-tubed fixed quad launchers ❻; IR flares and chaff to 4 km *(2.2 nm)*.
ESM/ECM: Ramses; intercept and jammer.
Combat data systems: Signaal SEWACO VI action data automation; Link 11. SATCOM.
Radars: Air search: Signaal LW 08 ❼; D band; range 264 km *(145 nm)* for 2 m^2 target.
Air/surface search: Signaal DA 05 ❽; E/F band range 137 km *(75 nm)* for 2 m^2 target. To be replaced in refit by Signaal Smart; 3D.
Surface search: Signaal ZW 06 ❾; I band; range 26 km *(14 nm)*.
Fire control: Two Signaal STIR 240 ❿; I/J/K band; range 140 km *(76 nm)* for 1 m^2 target.
Signaal STIR 180 ⓫; I/J/K band.
Sonars: Westinghouse SQS 509; hull-mounted; active search and attack; medium frequency.

Programmes: Ordered as replacements for the two Kortenaer class frigates sold to Greece. Same hull and engines.
Operational: Air defence frigates with command facilities for a task group commander and his staff.

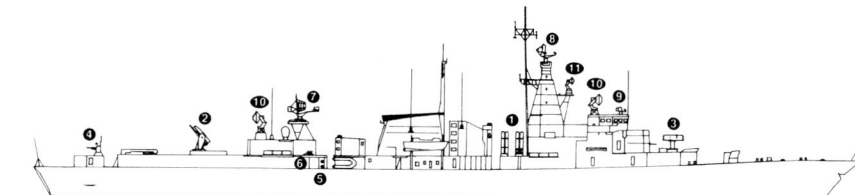
JACOB VAN HEEMSKERCK *(Scale 1 : 1200), Ian Sturton*

WITTE DE WITH *6/1992, Giorgio Arra*

7 KORTENAER CLASS

Name	No
KORTENAER	F 807
PIET HEYN	F 811
ABRAHAM CRIJNSSEN	F 816
PHILIPS VAN ALMONDE	F 823
BLOYS VAN TRESLONG	F 824
JAN VAN BRAKEL	F 825
PIETER FLORISZ (ex-*Willem van der Zaan*)	F 826

Builders	Laid down	Launched	Commissioned
Koninklijke Maatschappij De Schelde, Flushing	8 Apr 1975	18 Dec 1976	26 Oct 1978
Koninklijke Maatschappij De Schelde, Flushing	28 Apr 1977	3 June 1978	14 Apr 1981
Koninklijke Maatschappij De Schelde, Flushing	25 Oct 1978	16 May 1981	27 Jan 1983
Dok en Werfmaatschappij Wilton-Fijenoord	3 Oct 1977	11 Aug 1979	2 Dec 1981
Dok en Werfmaatschappij Wilton-Fijenoord	27 Apr 1978	15 Nov 1980	25 Nov 1982
Koninklijke Maatschappij De Schelde, Flushing	16 Nov 1979	16 May 1981	14 Apr 1983
Koninklijke Maatschappij De Schelde, Flushing	21 Jan 1981	8 May 1982	1 Oct 1983

Displacement, tons: 3050 standard; 3630 full load
Dimensions, feet (metres): 428 × 47.9 × 14.1; 20.3 (screws) *(130.5 × 14.6 × 4.3; 6.2)*
Main machinery: CODOG; 2 RR Olympus TM3B gas turbines; 50 880 hp *(37.9 MW)* sustained; 2 RR Tyne RM1C gas turbines; 9900 hp *(7.4 MW)* sustained; 2 shafts; cp props
Speed, knots: 30. **Range, miles:** 4700 at 16 kts on Tynes
Complement: 176 (18 officers) plus 24 spare berths

Missiles: SSM: 8 McDonnell Douglas Harpoon (2 quad) launchers ❶; active radar homing to 130 km *(70 nm)* at 0.9 Mach; warhead 227 kg.
SAM: Raytheon Sea Sparrow Mk 29 octuple launcher ❷; semi-active radar homing to 14.6 km *(8 nm)* at 2.5 Mach; warhead 39 kg; 24 missiles.
Guns: 1 OTO Melara 3 in *(76 mm)*/62 compact ❸; 85° elevation; 85 rounds/minute to 16 km *(8.6 nm)* anti-surface; 12 km *(6.5 nm)* anti-aircraft; weight of shell 6 kg. New 100 rounds/minute version to be fitted.
Signaal SGE-30 Goalkeeper with General Electric 30 mm ❹; 7-barrelled; 4200 rounds/minute combined to 2 km.
2 Oerlikon 20 mm.
Torpedoes: 4—324 mm US Mk 32 (2 twin) tubes ❺. Honeywell Mk 46 Mod 5; anti-submarine; active/passive homing to 11 km *(5.9 nm)* at 40 kts; warhead 44 kg.
Countermeasures: Decoys: 2 Loral Hycor SRBOC Mk 36 6-tubed launchers ❻; chaff distraction or centroid modes.
ESM/ECM: Ramses ❼; intercept and jammer.
Combat data systems: Signaal SEWACO II action data automation; Link 11. SATCOM.
Radars: Air search: Signaal LW 08 ❽; D band; range 264 km *(145 nm)* for 2 m^2 target.
Surface search: Signaal ZW 06 ❾; I band; range 26 km *(14 nm)*.
Fire control: Signaal STIR ❿; I/J band; range 140 km *(76 nm)* for 1 m^2 target.
Signaal WM 25 ⓫; I/J band; range 46 km *(25 nm)*.
Sonars: Westinghouse SQS 505 (F 807, 811 and 816); SQS 509 (F 823-F 826); bow-mounted; active search and attack; medium frequency.
Helicopters: 2 Westland SH-14B Lynx ⓬.

Modernisation: During refit in 1985-86 *Pieter Florisz* was adapted for a limited number of female crew (about 25); others similarly converted. Goalkeeper has replaced the 40 mm gun on the hangar roof. Plans to fit SMART fire control radars have been cancelled.

Structure: Although only one Lynx is carried there is hangar accommodation for two. TACTASS is not planned except that the last two ships had a temporary fit prior to the completion of the first of the Karel Doorman class. *Jan Van Brakel* had the trials SMART radar fitted on her hangar roof in 1990 with the control room in the hangar.

Sales: Two sold to Greece during construction, mid-1980 and mid-1981. *Bankert* to Greece in May 1993, *Callenburg* in April 1994 and *Van Kinsbergen* in February 1995. Sale agreed for all three on 11 November 1992, including refits by De Schelde, Flushing and the removal of Goalkeeper CIWS. Three more to be sold in 1995/96.

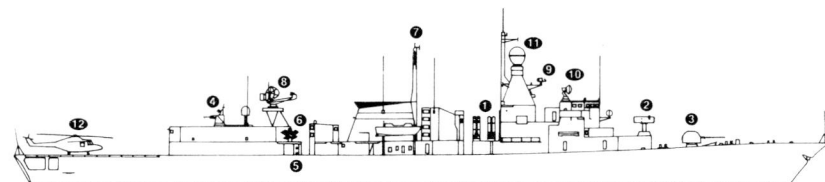
KORTENAER *(Scale 1 : 1200), Ian Sturton*

PIETER FLORISZ *5/1992, G Toremans*

432 NETHERLANDS / Frigates

4 + 4 KAREL DOORMAN CLASS

Name	No	Builders	Laid down	Launched	Commissioned
KAREL DOORMAN	F 827	Koninklijke Maatschappij De Schelde, Flushing	26 Feb 1985	20 Apr 1988	31 May 1991
WILLEM VAN DER ZAAN	F 829	Koninklijke Maatschappij De Schelde, Flushing	6 Nov 1985	21 Jan 1989	28 Nov 1991
TJERK HIDDES	F 830	Koninklijke Maatschappij De Schelde, Flushing	28 Oct 1986	9 Dec 1989	26 Feb 1993
VAN AMSTEL	F 831	Koninklijke Maatschappij De Schelde, Flushing	3 May 1988	19 May 1990	May 1993
ABRAHAM VAN DER HULST	F 832	Koninklijke Maatschappij De Schelde, Flushing	8 Feb 1989	7 Sep 1991	Dec 1993
VAN NES	F 833	Koninklijke Maatschappij De Schelde, Flushing	10 Jan 1990	16 May 1992	June 1994
VAN GALEN	F 834	Koninklijke Maatschappij De Schelde, Flushing	7 June 1990	21 Nov 1992	Dec 1994
VAN SPEIJK	F 828	Koninklijke Maatschappij De Schelde, Flushing	1 Oct 1991	Mar 1994	June 1995

Displacement, tons: 3320 full load
Dimensions, feet (metres): 401.1 × 47.2 × 14.1 *(122.3 × 14.4 × 4.3)*
Main machinery: CODOG; 2 RR Spey SM1C; 33 800 hp *(25.2 MW)* sustained (early ships of the class will initially only have SM1A gas generators and 30 800 hp *(23 MW)* sustained available); 2 Stork-Wärtsilä 12SW280 diesels; 8700 hp *(6.4 MW)* sustained; 2 shafts; cp props
Speed, knots: 30 (Speys); 21 (diesels). **Range, miles:** 5000 at 18 kts
Complement: 154 (16 officers) (accommodation for 163)

Missiles: SSM: 8 McDonnell Douglas Harpoon (2 quad) launchers ❶; active radar homing to 130 km *(70 nm)* at 0.9 Mach; warhead 227 kg.
SAM: Raytheon Sea Sparrow Mk 48 vertical launchers ❷; semi-active radar homing to 14.6 km *(8 nm)* at 2.5 Mach; warhead 39 kg; 16 missiles. Canisters mounted on port side of hangar.
Guns: 1—3 in *(76 mm)*/62 OTO Melara compact Mk 100 ❸; 85° elevation; 100 rounds/minute to 16 km *(8.6 nm)* anti-surface; 12 km *(6.5 nm)* anti-aircraft; weight of shell 6 kg. This is the latest version with an improved rate of fire.
1 Signaal SGE-30 Goalkeeper with General Electric 30 mm 7-barrelled ❹; 4200 rounds/minute combined to 2 km.
2 Oerlikon 20 mm; 55° elevation; 800 rounds/minute to 2 km.
Torpedoes: 4—324 mm US Mk 32 (2 twin) tubes (mounted inside the after superstructure) ❺. Honeywell Mk 46 Mod 5; anti-submarine; active/passive homing to 11 km *(5.9 nm)* at 40 kts; warhead 44 kg.
Countermeasures: Decoys: 2 Loral Hycor SRBOC 6-tubed fixed Mk 36 quad launchers; IR flares and chaff to 4 km *(2.2 nm)*.
ESM/ECM: Ramses; intercept and repeater jammers. Argo APECS II (includes AR 700 ESM) to be fitted in last four ships and retrofitted in remainder.
Combat data systems: Signaal SEWACO VII action data automation (upgraded from 1994); Links 11 and 16 in due course. SATCOM.
Radars: Air/surface search: Signaal SMART ❻; 3D; F band.
Air/surface search: Signaal LW 08 ❼; D band.
Surface search: Signaal ZW 06 ❽; I band.
Navigation: Racal Decca 1226; I band.
Fire control: Two Signaal STIR ❾; I/J/K band; range 140 km *(76 nm)* for 1 m² target.
Sonars: Signaal PHS 36; hull-mounted; active search and attack; medium frequency.
Thomson Sintra Anaconda DSBV 61; towed array; low frequency; to be fitted in last six ships on build and retrofitted to the remainder.

Helicopters: 1 Westland SH-14 Lynx ❿.

Programmes: This class is designed to be interoperable with the Kortenaer class frigates. Declaration of intent signed on 29 February 1984 although the contract was not signed until 29 June 1985 by which time the design had been completed. A further four ordered 10 April 1986. Because the trials ship *Van Speijk* is still operational, names have been shuffled to make the new *Van Speijk* the last of the class but she has retained her allocated pennant number.

Structure: The VLS SAM is similar to Canadian Halifax and Greek MEKO classes. The ship is designed to reduce radar and IR signatures and has extensive NBCD arrangements. Full automation and roll stabilisation fitted.
Operational: SEWACO VII(A) operational from January 1992.

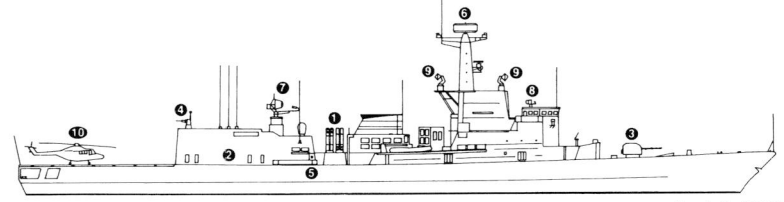

KAREL DOORMAN class *(Scale 1 : 1200), Ian Sturton*

VAN AMSTEL *2/1993, Maritime Photographic*

KAREL DOORMAN *6/1992, Royal Netherlands Navy*

SHIPBORNE AIRCRAFT

Numbers/Type: 22 Westland Lynx Mks 25/27/81.
Operational speed: 125 kts *(232 km/h)*.
Service ceiling: 12 500 ft *(3810 m)*.
Range: 320 nm *(590 km)*.
Role/Weapon systems: ASW, SAR and utility helicopter series all being converted to 14B type; Mk 25 (UH-14A) is shore-based; Mk 27/81 (SH-14B/C) embarked for ASW duties in escorts. Sensors: Search radar (Mk 25, Mk 28 and Mk 81), Alcatel DUAV-4 dipping sonar (Mk 27), AQS-81, MAD (Mk 81), Ferranti AWARE-3 ESM. Weapons: 2 × Mk 46 torpedoes or depth bombs (Mk 27 and Mk 81), unarmed (Mk 25).

LAND-BASED MARITIME AIRCRAFT

Numbers/Type: 2 Fokker F27 Maritime.
Operational speed: 250 kts *(463 km/h)*.
Service ceiling: 29 500 ft *(8990 m)*.
Range: 2700 nm *(5000 km)*.
Role/Weapon systems: Netherlands Antilles for ocean surveillance; operated by Air Force with naval observers. Sensors: APS-504 search radar, LAPADS processor. Weapons: ASW; 4 × Mk 46 torpedoes, 6 × underwing points. ASV; has provision for missiles.

Numbers/Type: 13 Lockheed P-3C/Update II Orion.
Operational speed: 410 kts *(760 km/h)*.
Service ceiling: 28 300 ft *(8625 m)*.
Range: 4000 nm *(7410 km)*.
Role/Weapon systems: Long-range MR and NATO area ocean surveillance, particularly for ASW/ASV operations. Sensors: APS-115 radar, AQS-81 MAD, AQA 7 processor, AQS-114 computer, IFF, ECM/ESM, sonobuoys. Weapons: ASW; 8 × Mk 46 torpedoes, depth bombs or mines. Underwing stations for Harpoon missiles for which procurement has been suspended.

LYNX *6/1992, Stefan Terzibaschitsch*

ORION *1992, J L M van der Burg*

MINE WARFARE FORCES

Note: As an alternative to building new minesweepers, it is planned to convert three Alkmaar class into Troika control ships and to build 14 Troika minesweeping systems.

15 ALKMAAR CLASS (TRIPARTITE TYPE) (MINEHUNTERS)

Name	No	Laid down	Launched	Commissioned
ALKMAAR	M 850	30 Jan 1979	18 May 1982	28 May 1983
DELFZYL	M 851	29 May 1980	29 Oct 1982	17 Aug 1983
DORDRECHT	M 852	5 Jan 1981	26 Feb 1983	16 Nov 1983
HAARLEM	M 853	16 June 1981	6 May 1983	12 Jan 1984
HARLINGEN	M 854	30 Nov 1981	9 July 1983	12 Apr 1984
SCHEVENINGEN	M 855	24 May 1982	2 Dec 1983	18 July 1984
MAASSLUIS	M 856	7 Nov 1982	5 May 1984	12 Dec 1984
MAKKUM	M 857	25 Feb 1983	27 Sep 1984	13 May 1985
MIDDELBURG	M 858	11 July 1983	23 Feb 1985	10 Dec 1986
HELLEVOETSLUIS	M 859	12 Dec 1983	18 July 1985	20 Feb 1987
SCHIEDAM	M 860	6 May 1984	20 Dec 1985	9 July 1986
URK	M 861	1 Oct 1984	2 May 1986	10 Dec 1986
ZIERIKZEE	M 862	25 Feb 1985	4 Oct 1986	7 May 1987
VLAARDINGEN	M 863	6 May 1986	4 Aug 1988	15 Mar 1989
WILLEMSTAD	M 864	3 Oct 1986	27 Jan 1989	20 Sep 1989

Displacement, tons: 562 standard; 595 full load
Dimensions, feet (metres): 168.9 × 29.2 × 8.5 *(51.5 × 8.9 × 2.6)*
Main machinery: 1 Brons-Werkspoor A-RUB 215X-12 diesel; 1860 hp(m) *(1.35 MW)* sustained; 1 shaft; Lips cp prop; 2 active rudders; 2 motors; 240 hp(m) *(179 kW)*; 2 bow thrusters
Speed, knots: 15 diesel; 7 electric. **Range, miles:** 3000 at 12 kts
Complement: 29-42 depending on task

Guns: 1 Giat 20 mm (an additional short range missile system may be added for patrol duties).
Countermeasures: MCM: 2 PAP 104 remote-controlled submersibles. Mechanical minesweeping gear and OD 3.
Combat data systems: Signaal Sewaco IX.
Radars: Navigation: Racal Decca TM 1229C; I band.
Sonars: Thomson Sintra DUBM 21A; hull-mounted; minehunting; 100 kHz (± 10 kHz).

Programmes: The two Indonesian ships ordered in 1985 took the place of M 863 and M 864 whose laying down was delayed as a result. This class is the Netherlands' part of a tripartite co-operative plan with Belgium and France for GRP hulled minehunters. The whole class built by van der Giessen-de Noord. Ships were launched virtually ready for trials.
Modernisation: If the new minesweeper project remains cancelled, the plan is to convert three of this class into Troika control ships and to improve the minehunting capability of four others.
Structure: A 5 ton container can be shipped, stored for varying tasks—research; patrol; extended diving; drone control.
Operational: Endurance, 15 days. Automatic radar navigation system. Automatic data processing and display. EVEC 20. Decca Hi-fix positioning system. Alcatel dynamic positioning system. Five of the class were to have been kept in reserve but all may be kept operational after 1993.
Sales: Two of a modified design to Indonesia, completed March 1988.

0 + (8) NEW MINESWEEPER (COASTAL)

Displacement, tons: 620 full load
Dimensions, feet (metres): 171.9 oa; 157.5 wl × 34.1 × 10.2 *(52.4; 48 × 10.4 × 3.1)*
Speed, knots: 15; 10 (sweeping). **Range, miles:** 3000 at 12 kts
Complement: 25 plus 5 spare

Guns: 1 DCN 20 mm/20.
Radars: Navigation: I band.

Programmes: Memorandum of Understanding signed 6 April 1989 for a joint Belgium/Netherlands minesweeper project. Design contract awarded November 1990 to van der Giessen-de Noord Marinebouw in a joint venture with Beliard Polyship NV, completed in August 1992. Orders of up to six vessels for Belgium, eight for the Netherlands and four for Portugal were expected but in a statement issued on 12 January 1993, the project was cancelled for the Netherlands Navy. This decision may be reviewed.
Operational: The requirement is to be able to sweep bottom mines which have sunk so far into soft sand that they are not detected by hunters.

6 DOKKUM CLASS (MINESWEEPERS—COASTAL)

NAALDWIJK M 809	**DRACHTEN** M 812	**NAARDEN** M 823
ABCOUDE M 810	**OMMEN** M 813	**SITTARD** M 830

Displacement, tons: 373 standard; 453 full load
Dimensions, feet (metres): 152.9 × 28.9 × 7.5 *(46.6 × 8.8 × 2.3)*
Main machinery: 2 Fijenoord MAN V64 diesels; 2500 hp(m) *(1.84 MW)*; 2 shafts
Speed, knots: 16. **Range, miles:** 2500 at 10 kts
Complement: 27-36 depending on task
Guns: 1 or 2 Oerlikon 20 mm (not in all).
Radars: Navigation: Racal Decca TM 1229C; I band.

Comment: 32 Western Union type coastal minesweepers were built in the Netherlands, 18 were under offshore procurement as the Dokkum class, with MAN engines. All launched in 1954-56 and completed in 1955-56. This class was subject to a fleet rehabilitation and modernisation programme completed by 1977 and a 'life prolonging' refit from the mid-1980s to 1991 for these last six. Included in the refit was additional accommodation in the form of a deckhouse. Five unmodernised vessels are stripped of parts and are to be scrapped in 1993. These ships are to remain in service until the Troika systems have been built. The ex-*Dokkum* is a trials ship.

URK *4/1992, Harald Carstens*

ABCOUDE *4/1992, Harald Carstens*

AMPHIBIOUS FORCES

0 + (1) AMPHIBIOUS TRANSPORT SHIP (LPD)

Displacement, tons: 9500 full load
Dimensions, feet (metres): 492.1 × 82 × 18.4 *(150 × 25 × 5.6)*
Main machinery: 2 diesels; 2 shafts
Speed, knots: 20. **Range, miles:** 6000 at 14 kts
Complement: 115 plus 12 spare
Military lift: 600 troops; 170 APCs or 33 MBTs. 3 LCVP and 2 LCU/LCM or 6 LCVP
Guns: 2 Signaal Goalkeeper 30 mm.
Helicopters: 6 NH 90 or equivalent; or 4 EH 101 or equivalent.

Comment: Collaborative project with Spain. Construction planned to start in 1994 with completion in 1996. Can be used to transport a fully equipped battalion of Marines. Docking facilities for landing craft and a two-spot helicopter flight deck. Alternative employment as an SAR ship for environmental and disaster relief tasks.

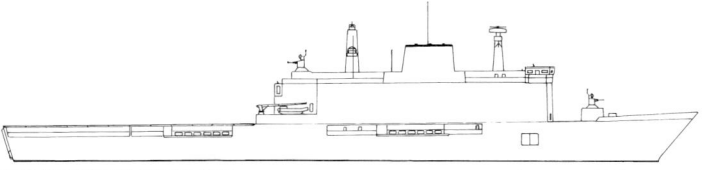

AMPHIBIOUS TRANSPORT SHIP   *(not to scale), Ian Sturton*

6 LCA Mk II

L 9530-9535

Displacement, tons: 17.5
Dimensions, feet (metres): 52.5 × 13.9 × 3.5 *(16 × 4.3 × 1.1)*
Main machinery: 1 DAF DKS 1160 M diesel; 300 hp(m) *(220 kW)* sustained; Schottel prop
Speed, knots: 11. **Range, miles:** 220 at 11 kts
Complement: 3
Military lift: 35 troops; 1 Land Rover or BV 202E Snowcat
Guns: 1 FN FAL 7.62 mm MG.
Radars: Navigation: Racal Decca 110; I band.

Comment: L 9530-9541 plus two extra ordered 27 October 1981 from Rijkswerf, Willemsoord and Schottel, Netherlands. First pair completed 1984, next three in 1985, last one in 1986. The rest were cancelled in favour of the Mk III design.

LCA 9531   *5/1989, Ralf Bendfeldt*

6 LCA Mk III

L 9536-9541

Displacement, tons: 30 full load
Dimensions, feet (metres): 55.4 × 15.7 × 3.6 *(16.9 × 4.8 × 1.1)*
Main machinery: 2 diesels; 750 hp(m) *(551 kW)*; 2 shafts
Speed, knots: 14 (full load); 16.5 (light). **Range, miles:** 200 at 12 kts
Complement: 3
Military lift: 34 troops or 7 tons or 2 Land Rovers or 1 Snowcat
Guns: 1—7.62 mm MG.
Radars: Navigation: Racal Decca; I band.

Comment: Ordered from van der Giessen-de Noord 10 December 1988. First one laid down 10 August 1989, commissioned 16 October 1990. Last one commissioned late 1992. These are an improvement over the Mk II type which did not come up to expectations.

L 9540   *9/1992, van Ginderen Collection*

SURVEY SHIPS

Note: There are also four survey boats 8901-8904 completed in 1989-90; dimensions 9.5 × 3.8 m; 1 Volvo Penta diesel of 170 hp(m) *(125 kW)*. The first two are carried by A 904 and A 905 respectively.

1 TYDEMAN CLASS (HYDROGRAPHIC/OCEANOGRAPHIC SHIP)

Name	No	Builders	Commissioned
TYDEMAN	A 906	Merwede, Hardinxveld, Giessendam	10 Nov 1976

Displacement, tons: 2977 full load
Dimensions, feet (metres): 295.9 × 47.2 × 15.7 *(90.2 × 14.4 × 4.8)*
Main machinery: Diesel-electric; 3 Stork-Werkspoor 8-FCHD-240 diesel generators; 3690 hp(m) *(2.71 MW)*; 1 motor; 2730 hp(m) *(2 MW)*; 1 shaft
 1 Paxman diesel; 485 hp(m) *(356 kW)*; 1 active rudder; 300 hp(m) *(220 kW)*; bow thruster; 450 hp(m) *(330 kW)*
Speed, knots: 15. **Range, miles:** 15 700 at 10.3 kts; 10 300 at 13.5 kts
Complement: 62 (8 officers) plus 15 scientists
Radars: Navigation: Racal Decca; I band.
Sonars: Atlas-Deco 10 echo-sounders with Edig digitisers. KAe Deso 25 replacements.
 Kelvin Hughes; hull-mounted; side-scan. Klein; towed; side-scan.
 Elac; bow-mounted; wreck search; trainable in sectors on either bow.
Helicopters: 1 Westland UH-14A Lynx.

Comment: Ordered in October 1974. Laid down 29 April 1975, launched 18 December 1975. Able to operate oceanographic cables down to 7000 m. Has six laboratories and two container spaces each for 20 ft standard container. Has forward working deck with wet-hall, midships and after working decks, one 10 ton crane, one 4 ton crane and frames. Diving facilities. Passive stabilisation tank. Decca Hi-fix 6; Digital PDP computer; COMPLOT plotting system. Normally operates in the Atlantic and between March 1991 and March 1992 tested a derivative of the Thomson Sintra DUBM 41 towed sonar for the detection of mines buried up to 2 m deep. Major refit from April to November 1992 by van der Giessen-de Noord.

TYDEMAN   *12/1992, van der Giessen-de Noord*

2 BUYSKES CLASS

Name	No	Builders	Commissioned
BUYSKES	A 904	Boele's Scheepswerven en Machinefabriek BV, Bolnes	9 Mar 1973
BLOMMENDAL	A 905	Boele's Scheepswerven en Machinefabriek BV, Bolnes	22 May 1973

Displacement, tons: 967 standard; 1033 full load
Dimensions, feet (metres): 196.6 × 36.4 × 12 *(60 × 11.1 × 3.7)*
Main machinery: Diesel-electric; 3 Paxman 12 RPH diesel generators; 2100 hp *(1.57 MW)*; 1 motor; 1400 hp(m) *(1.03 MW)*; 1 shaft
Speed, knots: 13.5. **Range, miles:** 3000 at 11.5 kts
Complement: 43 (6 officers)
Radars: Navigation: Racal Decca; I band.
Sonars: Side-scanning and wreck-search.

Comment: Both designed primarily for hydrographic work but have also limited oceanographic and meteorological capability. They operate mainly in the North Sea. A data logging system is installed as part of the automatic handling of hydrographic data. HYDRAUT logging system; wire-drags. Marconi Bathyscan swath sounders. Atlas Elektronik Deso 25 echo sounders. They carry two 22 ft survey launches capable of 15 kts and two work-boats normally used for sweeping. Major refits in 1988-89.

BLOMMENDAL   *11/1991, Harald Carstens*

SERVICE FORCES

0 + 1 AMSTERDAM CLASS (FAST COMBAT SUPPORT SHIP)

Name	No	Builders	Commissioned
AMSTERDAM	A 836	Merwede, Hardinxveld, Giessendam	Dec 1994

Displacement, tons: 17 040 full load
Dimensions, feet (metres): 544.6 × 72.2 × 26.2 *(166 × 22 × 8)*
Main machinery: 2 MAN 16V 40/45 diesels; 26 330 hp(m) *(19.36 MW)*; 1 shaft; cp prop
Speed, knots: 20. **Range, miles:** 13 440 at 20 kts
Complement: 160 (23 officers) including 24 aircrew
Cargo capacity: 6700 tons dieso; 1660 tons petrol; 500 tons solids
Guns: 2 Oerlikon 20 mm. 1 Goalkeeper 30 mm CIWS.
Countermeasures: Decoys: 4 chaff launchers.
ESM: radar warning.
Radars: 2 navigation; I band (includes helo control).
Helicopters: 4 Lynx or 2 NH 90.

Comment: NP/SP AOR 90 replacement for *Poolster* ordered 14 October 1991. Laid down 21 May 1992 and is scheduled to be launched in June 1993. Close co-operation between Dutch Nevesbu and Spanish Bazán has led to this design which has maintenance workshops as well as six alongside and Vertrep supply stations. Built to merchant ship standards but with military NBC damage control. Second of class required to replace *Zuiderkruis* after 2000. An identical ship is building for the Spanish Navy.

AMSTERDAM (model) *1991, Royal Netherlands Navy*

2 POOLSTER CLASS (FAST COMBAT SUPPORT SHIPS)

Name	No	Builders	Commissioned
ZUIDERKRUIS	A 832	Verolme Shipyards, Alblasserdam	27 June 1975
POOLSTER	A 835	Rotterdamse Droogdok Mij	10 Sep 1964

Displacement, tons: 16 800 (16 900, *Zuiderkruis*) full load
Measurement, tons: 10 000 dwt
Dimensions, feet (metres): 552.2 × 66.6 × 26.9 *(168.3 × 20.3 × 8.2)* (*Poolster*)
  556 × 66.6 × 27.6 *(169.6 × 20.3 × 8.4)* (*Zuiderkruis*)
Main machinery: 2 boilers; 2 turbines; 22 000 hp(m) *(16.2 MW)*; 1 shaft (*Poolster*)
  2 Stork-Werkspoor TM410 diesels; 21 000 hp(m) *(15.4 MW)*; 1 shaft (*Zuiderkruis*)
Speed, knots: 21
Complement: 200 (17 officers) (*Poolster*); 266 (17 officers) (*Zuiderkruis*)
Cargo capacity: 10 300 tons including 8-9000 tons oil fuel

Guns: 1 Signaal SGE-30 Goalkeeper with GE 30 mm 7-barrelled; 4200 rounds/minute combined to 2 km. Fitted for Gulf deployments in 1990-91.
  2 Bofors 40 mm (*Poolster*). 5 Oerlikon 20 mm (*Zuiderkruis*).
Countermeasures: Decoys: 2 Loral Hycor SRBOC Mk 36 fixed 6-barrelled launchers; IR flares and chaff.
ESM: Ferranti AWARE-4; radar warning.
Radars: Air/surface search: Racal Decca 2459; F/I band.
  Navigation: Two Racal Decca TM 1226C (*Zuiderkruis*); I band.
  Racal Decca TM 1229C (*Poolster*); I band.
Sonars: Signaal CWE 10 (*Poolster*); hull-mounted; active search; medium frequency.

Helicopters: 1 Westland UH-14A Lynx.

Programmes: *Poolster* laid down on 18 September 1962. Launched on 16 October 1963. *Zuiderkruis* laid down 16 July 1973, launched 15 October 1974, completed refit February 1981.
Structure: Helicopter deck aft. Funnel heightened by 4.5 m *(14.8 ft)*. Additional 20 mm guns, containerised Goalkeeper CIWS and SATCOM, fitted for operational deployments.
Operational: Capacity for five helicopters. Both ships carry A/S weapons for helicopters. Two fuelling stations each side for underway replenishment. *Poolster* offered for sale in 1993.

ZUIDERKRUIS (with Goalkeeper) *6/1992, Giorgio Arra*

POOLSTER *6/1992, Stefan Terzibaschitsch*

TRAINING SHIPS

Name	No	Builders	Commissioned
BULGIA	A 880 (ex-P 803)	Rijkswerf, Willemsoord	20 Sep 1954

Displacement, tons: 150 standard; 163 full load
Dimensions, feet (metres): 119.1 × 20.2 × 6.3 *(36.3 × 6.2 × 1.9)*
Main machinery: 2 Werkspoor RUB 612 diesels; 1050 hp(m) *(772 kW)*; 2 shafts
Speed, knots: 15. **Range, miles:** 1000 at 13 kts
Complement: 28
Radars: Navigation: Decca; I band.

Comment: Non-commissioned training tender to the Naval College since November 1986. Armament removed.

BULGIA *8/1991, van Ginderen Collection*

Name	No	Builders	Commissioned
ZEEFAKKEL	A 903	J & K Smit, Kinderdijk	16 Mar 1951

Displacement, tons: 355 standard; 384 full load
Dimensions, feet (metres): 149 × 24.6 × 7.2 *(45.4 × 7.5 × 2.2)*
Main machinery: 2 Smit-MAN diesels; 640 hp(m) *(470 kW)*; 2 shafts
Speed, knots: 12
Complement: 26
Radars: Navigation: Racal Decca; I band.

Comment: Laid down 28 November 1949, launched 21 July 1950. Former surveying vessel. Now used as local training ship at Den Helder. Re-engined 1980.

ZEEFAKKEL *6/1992, van Ginderen Collection*

Name	No	Builders	Commissioned
URANIA (ex-*Tromp*)	Y 8050	Haarlem	23 Apr 1938

Displacement, tons: 76
Dimensions, feet (metres): 78.4 × 17.4 × 10.5 *(23.9 × 5.3 × 3.2)*
Main machinery: 1 diesel; 65 hp(m) *(48 kW)*; 1 shaft
Speed, knots: 5 diesel; 10 sail
Complement: 17

Comment: Schooner used for training in seamanship.

URANIA *7/1990, Wright and Logan*

436 NETHERLANDS / Auxiliaries — Tugs

AUXILIARIES

Note: In addition to vessels listed below, non self-propelled craft include Y 8514, floating crane built in 1974 and about 40 others including tank-cleaning vessels, barges, berthing pontoons (Y 8594-8617), diving pontoons (Y 8579-92). Other small craft include general purpose harbour and dockyard craft (Y 8351-2) (Y 8200-03) (Y 8012), four diving craft attached to *Thetis* (Y 8579-82), seven targets (Y 8694-99, Y 8704), four small transports (Y 8343-46) and eight fuel lighters (Y 8347-52, Y 8536, Y 8538).

3 ACCOMMODATION SHIPS

Name	No
CORNELIS DREBBEL	A 886
THETIS	A 887
TAX	Y 8500

Displacement, tons: 775 *(Cornelis Drebbel)*; 800 *(Thetis)*
Dimensions, feet (metres): 206.7 × 38.7 × 3.6 *(63 × 11.8 × 1.1) (Cornelis Drebbel)*
223 × 39.4 × 5.3 *(68 × 12 × 1.6) (Thetis)*

Comment: *Cornelis Drebbel* built by Scheepswerf Voorwaarts at Hoogezand in 1971. Serves as accommodation vessel for crews of ships building and refitting at private yards in the Rotterdam area. *Thetis* built by Koninklijke Maatschappij De Schelde, Flushing; completed 14 March 1985 and commissioned 27 June 1985; accommodation for 106. Stationed at Den Oever, she provides harbour training for divers and underwater swimmers. *Tax* built in 1953 as a small cargo ship and converted in 1988.

1 SUBMARINE SUPPORT SHIP and TORPEDO TENDER

Name	No	Builders	Commissioned
MERCUUR	A 900	Koninklijke Maatschappij de Schelde	21 Aug 1987

Displacement, tons: 1400 full load
Dimensions, feet (metres): 212.6 × 39.4 × 14.1 *(64.8 × 12 × 4.3)*
Main machinery: 2 Brons 61-20/27 diesels; 1100 hp(m) *(808 kW)*; 2 shafts; bow thruster
Speed, knots: 14
Complement: 39
Guns: 2 Oerlikon 20 mm.
Torpedoes: 3—324 mm (triple) tubes. 1—21 in *(533 mm)* underwater tube.
Mines: Can lay mines.
Sonars: Hull-mounted; passive search.

Comment: Replacement for previous ship of same name. Ordered 13 June 1984. Laid down 6 November 1985. Floated out 25 October 1986. Can launch training and research torpedoes above and below the waterline. Services, maintains and recovers torpedoes.

MERCUUR   10/1992, Camil Busquets i Vilanova

1 SUPPORT SHIP

Name	No	Builders	Commissioned
PELIKAAN (ex-*Kilindoni*)	A 801	Vinholmen, Arendal	1984

Displacement, tons: 505 full load
Dimensions, feet (metres): 151.6 × 34.8 × 9.2 *(46.2 × 10.6 × 2.8)*
Main machinery: 2 Caterpillar 3412T diesels; 1080 hp *(806 kW)* sustained; 2 shafts
Speed, knots: 10
Complement: 15
Guns: 2—12.7 mm MGs.

Comment: Ex-oil platform supply ship acquired 28 May 1990 after being refitted in Curaçao. Has taken over from the deleted *Woerden* as tender and transport for marines in the Antilles. Capacity for 40 marines in five accommodation units.

PELIKAAN   11/1990, Hartmut Ehlers

2 SMALL FLOATING DOCKS

Y 8678   Y 8679

Comment: Built in 1950 and 1959 at Willemsoord. Of 420 and 450 tons capacity respectively.

1 EXPERIMENTAL SHIP

VAN SPEIJK (ex-*Dokkum*) Y 8001

Comment: For data see Dokkum class in Mine Warfare Forces. Weapon systems removed and converted by Wilton Fijenoord, Schiedam in November 1986 for testing fuels. Renamed because there has to be a *Van Speijk* in commission in the Navy.

VAN SPEIJK   6/1987, Hartmut Ehlers

4 CERBERUS CLASS (DIVING TENDERS)

Name	No	Builders	Commissioned
CERBERUS	A 851	Visser, Den Helder	28 Feb 1992
ARGUS	A 852	Visser, Den Helder	2 June 1992
NAUTILUS	A 853	Visser, Den Helder	18 Sep 1992
HYDRA	A 854	Visser, Den Helder	20 Nov 1992

Displacement, tons: 223 full load
Dimensions, feet (metres): 89.9 × 27.9 × 4.9 *(27.4 × 8.5 × 1.5)*
Main machinery: 2 Volvo Penta TMAD 122A diesels; 760 hp(m) *(560 kW)*; 2 shafts
Speed, knots: 12
Complement: 8 (2 officers)

Comment: Ordered 29 November 1990. Capable of maintaining 10 kts in sea state 3. Can handle a 2 ton load at 4 m from the ship's side. Have replaced the Triton class.

CERBERUS   3/1992, Royal Netherlands Navy

TUGS

Name	No	Builders	Commissioned
WESTGAT	A 872	Rijkswerf, Willemsoord	10 Jan 1968

Displacement, tons: 206
Dimensions, feet (metres): 89.2 × 23 × 7.7 *(27.2 × 7 × 2.3)*
Main machinery: 1 Bolnes diesel; 720 hp(m) *(529 kW)*; 1 shaft
Speed, knots: 12
Complement: 9
Guns: 2 Oerlikon 20 mm (not fitted).

Comment: Equipped with salvage pumps and firefighting equipment. Stationed at Den Helder. One of the class deleted in 1992.

WESTGAT   5/1990, J L M van der Burg

Name	No	Builders	Commissioned
LINGE	A 874	Delta SY, Sliedrecht	20 Feb 1987
REGGE	A 875	Delta SY, Sliedrecht	6 May 1987
HUNZE	A 876	Delta SY, Sliedrecht	20 Oct 1987
ROTTE	A 877	Delta SY, Sliedrecht	20 Oct 1987

Displacement, tons: 200 approx
Dimensions, feet (metres): 90.2 × 27.2 × 8.9 *(27.5 × 8.3 × 2.7)*
Main machinery: 2 Stork-Werkspoor diesel; 1600 hp(m) *(1.18 MW)*; 2 shafts
Speed, knots: 11
Complement: 7

Comment: Order placed in 1986. Based at Den Helder.

ROTTE *6/1992, G Toremans*

7 HARBOUR TUGS

BREEZAND Y 8018	SCHELDE Y 8055	ZUIDWAL Y 8058
BALGZAND Y 8019	WIERBALG Y 8056	WESTWAL Y 8059
	MALZWIN Y 8057	

Dimensions, feet (metres): 54.2 × 17.5 × 5.9 *(16.5 × 5.3 × 1.8)* (Y 8018/19); 35.4 × 12.5 × 4.3 *(10.8 × 3.8 × 1.3)* (remainder)
Main machinery: 2 diesels; 760 hp(m) *(559 kW)*; 2 shafts (Y 8018/19)
1 DAF diesel; 115 hp(m) *(85 kW)*; 1 shaft (remainder)

Comment: *Breezand* completed December 1989, *Balgzand* January 1990. Remainder completed December 1986 to February 1987. All built by Delta Shipyard.

BALGZAND *8/1992, van Ginderen Collection*

ROYAL NETHERLANDS ARMY

Note: In addition there are three patrol boats with a limited coastal capability and 15 vessels for inland waters.

1 TANK LANDING CRAFT

RV 40

Displacement, tons: 815
Dimensions, feet (metres): 150.3 × 31.2 × 8.2 *(45.8 × 9.5 × 2.5)*
Main machinery: 2 diesels; 654 hp(m) *(481 kW)*; 2 shafts
Speed, knots: 9.4
Complement: 4

Comment: Built by Grave BV and completed 22 November 1979.

RV 40 *1988, Royal Netherlands Army*

1 DIVING VESSEL

RV 50

Dimensions, feet (metres): 121.4 × 29.5 × 4.9 *(37 × 9 × 1.5)*
Main machinery: 2 diesels; 476 hp(m) *(350 kW)*; 2 shafts
Speed, knots: 9
Complement: 21
Radars: Navigation: AP Mk 4; I band.

Comment: Built by Vervako as a diving training ship. There is a moonpool aft with a 50 m diving bell, and a decompression chamber.

RV 50 *1990, Vervako*

COAST GUARD (KUSTWACHT)

Note: In 1987 many of the separate maritime services were merged to form a Coast Guard with its own distinctive colours. Included are some of the 70 police craft, 23 customs vessels and over 320 assorted craft of the Ministry of Transport and Public Works. Many of these vessels would come under naval control in an emergency.

TERSCHELLING *7/1992, van Ginderen Collection*

RP 20 (Police) *11/1990, J L M van der Burg*

NEW ZEALAND

Headquarters' Appointments

Chief of Defence Force:
　Vice Admiral S F Teagle, ADC
Chief of Naval Staff:
　Rear Admiral I Hunter
Deputy Chief of Naval Staff:
　Commodore K R Moen
Commodore Auckland:
　Commodore K F Wilson, LVO

Diplomatic Representation

Head of Defence Liaison Staff, London:
　Commodore J G Leonard
Naval Adviser, Canberra:
　Captain M N Franklin
Naval Technical Liaison Officer, London:
　Commander M I Louisson

Personnel

(a) 1993: 2300
(b) Reserve: 520 RNZNVR officers and ratings

Shore Establishments

Naval Staff: HMNZS Wakefield (Wellington)
Fleet Support: HMNZS Philomel (Auckland)
Training: HMNZS Tamaki (Auckland)
Communications: HMNZS Irirangi (Waiouru)
Ship Repair: HMNZ Dockyard (Auckland)

RNZNVR Divisions

Auckland: HMNZS *Ngapona*
Wellington: HMNZS *Olphert*
Christchurch: HMNZS *Pegasus*
Dunedin: HMNZS *Toroa*

Prefix to Ships' Names

HMNZS

Mercantile Marine

Lloyd's Register of Shipping:
　145 vessels of 252 318 tons gross

Strength of the Fleet

Type	Active (Reserve)	Building (Projected)
Frigates	4	2
Inshore Patrol Craft	4	—
Survey Vessels	3	—
Fleet Supply Ship	1	—
Military Sealift Ship	—	(1)
Research Vessel	1	—
Training Craft	1	—
Tugs	2	—
Diving Support Ship	1	—

DELETIONS

Light Forces

1991　*Pukaki, Rotoiti, Taupo, Hawea* (all for sale)

FRIGATES

4 BRITISH LEANDER CLASS

Name	No	Builders	Laid down	Launched	Commissioned
WAIKATO	F 55	Harland & Wolff Ltd, Belfast	10 Jan 1964	18 Feb 1965	16 Sep 1966
WELLINGTON (ex-HMS *Bacchante*)*	F 69	Vickers Armstrong Ltd, Newcastle	27 Oct 1966	29 Feb 1968	17 Oct 1969
SOUTHLAND (ex-HMS *Dido*)	F 104	Yarrow & Co Ltd, Scotstour	2 Dec 1959	22 Dec 1961	18 Sep 1963
CANTERBURY*	F 421	Yarrow Ltd, Clyde	12 Apr 1969	6 May 1970	22 Oct 1971

* Broad-beamed

Displacement, tons: 2580 standard; 3035 full load 2474 standard; 2945 full load (Broad-beamed)
Dimensions, feet (metres): 372 × 41; 43 (Broad-beamed) ×18 *(113.4 × 12.5; 13.1 × 5.5)*
Main machinery: 2 Babcock & Wilcox boilers; 550 psi *(38.7 kg/cm sq)*; 850°F *(454°C)*; 2 White-English Electric turbines; 30 000 hp *(22.4 MW)*; 2 shafts
Speed, knots: 28. **Range, miles:** 3000 at 15 kts; 5500 at 15 kts *(Wellington)*
Complement: 243 (16 officers) *(Waikato)*; 245 (15 officers) *(Canterbury)*; 257 (19 officers) *(Southland)*; 260 (19 officers) *(Wellington)*

Missiles: SAM: Short Bros Seacat GWS 22 quad launcher (2 quad in *Southland*) ❶; optical/radar guidance to 5 km *(2.7 nm)*; warhead 10 kg; 12 missiles.
Guns: 2 Vickers 4.5 in *(114 mm)*/45 Mk 6 (twin) (except *Southland*) ❷; 80° elevation; 20 rounds/minute to 19 km *(10.3 nm)* anti-surface; 6 km *(3.2 nm)* anti-aircraft; weight of shell 25 kg. 4 or 6 Browning 12.7 mm MGs.
2 Bofors 40 mm/60 Mk 9 *(Southland)* ❸; 80° elevation; 120 rounds/minute to 10 km *(5.4 nm)* anti-surface; 3 km *(1.6 nm)* anti-aircraft; weight of shell 0.89 kg.
Torpedoes: 6—324 mm US Mk 32 Mod 5 (2 triple) tubes ❹. Honeywell/Marconi Mk 46 Mod 2; anti-submarine; active/passive homing to 11 km *(5.9 nm)* at 40 kts; warhead 44 kg.
Countermeasures: Decoys: 2 Loral Hycor SRBOC Mk 36 6-barrelled trainable launchers (except *Waikato*). Graseby Type 182; towed torpedo decoy.
ESM: Phoenix (all). PST 1288 HVU *(Canterbury* and *Wellington)*.
Combat data systems: ADAWS 5 action data automation; Link 10 *(Southland)*. Plessey/Marconi Nautis F system fitted in *Wellington* and *Canterbury* in 1992-93.
Fire control: GWS 22 for Seacat. MRS 3 for 114 mm *(Waikato)*. RCA R-76C5 for 114 mm *(Wellington* and *Canterbury)*.
Radars: Air search: Marconi Type 965 AKE-1 *(Waikato)* ❺; A band.
Signaal LW08 *(Canterbury* and *Wellington)* ❻; D band; range 265 km *(145 nm)* for 2 m² target.

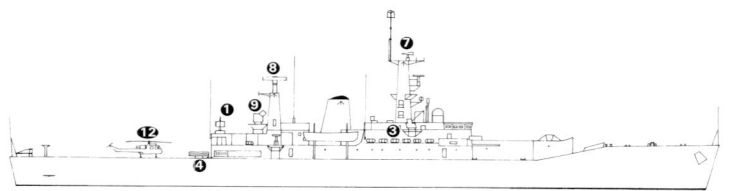
SOUTHLAND
(Scale 1 : 1200), Ian Sturton

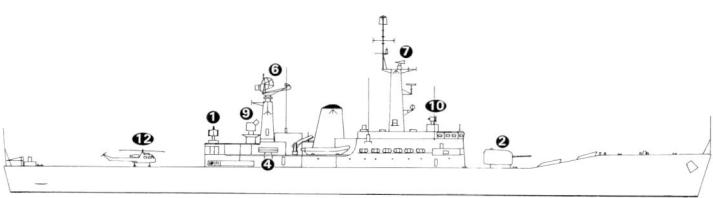
CANTERBURY
(Scale 1 : 1200), Ian Sturton

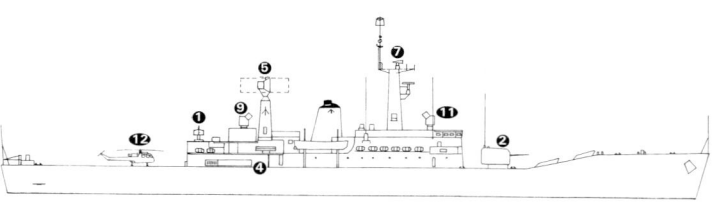
WAIKATO
(Scale 1 : 1200), Ian Sturton

WAIKATO
5/1990, 92 Wing RAAF

Frigates / NEW ZEALAND 439

SOUTHLAND
10/1989, RNZN

Air/surface search: Plessey Type 993 ❼ or Plessey Type 994 (*Southland*) ❽; E/F band.
Navigation: Kelvin Hughes Type 1006; I band.
Fire control: Plessey Type 904 ❾; I band (for Seacat). RCA TR 76 (*Wellington* and *Canterbury*) ❿ or Plessey 903 ⓫ (*Waikato*) (for 114 mm guns).
Sonars: Kelvin Hughes Type 162M; hull-mounted; bottom classification; 50 kHz.
Graseby Type 750 or Type 177 (*Waikato*); hull-mounted; active search and attack; medium frequency.
Ferranti FMS 15/2 TACTASS may be fitted in due course.

Helicopters: 1 Westland Wasp HAS 1 ⓬.

Programmes: *Waikato*, ordered on 14 June 1963, arrived in New Zealand in May 1967. *Canterbury* was ordered in August 1968, arrived in New Zealand in August 1972. *Wellington* was transferred on 1 October 1982, arriving in New Zealand December 1982. She immediately paid off into refit to become fully operational in 1986. *Southland* transferred on 18 July 1983. She then had a refit at Vosper Thornycroft, commissioned 21 December, sailing for New Zealand on completion.

Modernisation: *Wellington*'s 1984-85 refit programme included: internal rearrangement to provide extra fuel tanks, new RCA gun control system, replacement of A/S mortar by Mk 32 torpedo tubes, improvements to surface radar and new radar intercept system, flight deck enlarged and fitting of SRBOC chaff launcher. *Canterbury* modernisation in 1988-90 included new RCA gun fire control, new LW08 radar and ESM, fitting of SRBOC and an extension to her flight deck. *Southland* and *Waikato* completed limited refits in 1990 and 1991 respectively. Plessey Nautis combat system fitted in *Wellington* and *Canterbury* in 1992-93. LW08 radar fitted in *Wellington* in 1992.

Structure: Extensions fitted to funnel uptakes on *Waikato* and *Canterbury*.

Operational: *Waikato* has an enlarged hangar for Lynx helicopters. Reported that all ships are to be fitted with MUSL Stingray torpedoes and slimline towed sonar arrays in due course. The Ikara system, including the GWS 41 fire control director in *Southland* is non-operational.

CANTERBURY
10/1991, John Mortimer

0 + 2 ANZAC CLASS

Name	No	Builders	Laid down	Launched	Commissioned
—	—	Amecon	Feb 1993	Mar 1995	Feb 1997
—	—	Amecon	Feb 1995	Jan 1997	Nov 1998

Displacement, tons: 3600 full load
Dimensions, feet (metres): 387.1 oa; 357.6 wl × 48.6 × 14.3 *(118; 109 × 14.8 × 4.4)*
Main machinery: CODOG; 1 GE LM 2500 gas turbine; 30 172 hp *(22.5 MW)* sustained; 2 MTU 12V 1163 TB83 diesels; 8840 hp(m) *(6.5 MW)* sustained; 2 shafts; cp props
Speed, knots: 27. Range, miles: 6000 at 18 kts
Complement: 163

Missiles: SAM: Raytheon Sea Sparrow; Mk 41 Mod 5 octuple vertical launcher ❶.
Guns: 1 FMC 5 in *(127 mm)*/54 Mk 45 Mod 2 ❷.
Countermeasures: Decoys; G & D Aircraft GD 36 Mod 1 chaff launchers for SRBOC ❸.
ESM: Telefunken Telegon 10; intercept.
Combat data systems: NobelTech (BEAB) 9LV 453 Mk 3. Link 11.
Fire control: NobelTech 9LV 453 optronic director ❹. Raytheon CW Mk 73 (for SAM).
Radars: Air search: Raytheon SPS 49(V)8 ANZ ❺; C/D band.
Air/surface search: NobelTech 9LV 453 TIR (Ericsson Tx/Rx) ❻; G band.
Navigation: Atlas Elektronik 8600 ARPA; I band.
Fire control: NobelTech 9LV 453 ❼; J band.
Sonars: Thomson Sintra Spherion B; hull-mounted; active search and attack; medium frequency.

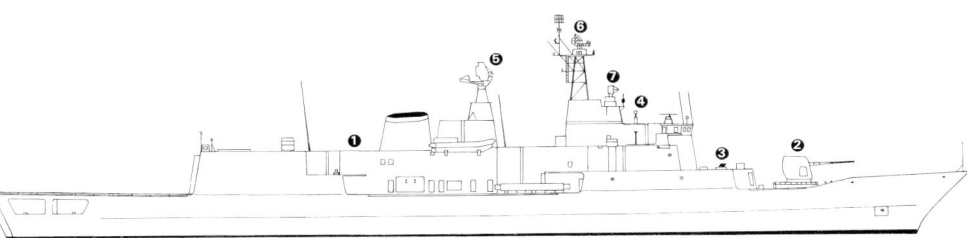

ANZAC
(Scale 1 : 900), Ian Sturton

Provision for Dowty FMS 15 towed array; passive; very low frequency.

Helicopters: 1 light ASW.

Programmes: Contract signed with Amecon consortium on 19 November 1989 to build eight Blohm & Voss-designed MEKO 200 ANZ frigates for Australia and two for New Zealand, which has an option for two more. Modules being constructed from 1992 at Newcastle, Australia and New Zealand, and shipped to Melbourne for final assembly. The two New Zealand ships will be second and fourth of the class to be completed.

Structure: The ships include space and weight provision for considerable enhancement including canister-launched SSM and ESM extensions. Mk 32 torpedo tubes will probably be fitted in New Zealand as soon as the ships are delivered. Signature suppression features are incorporated in the design. All steel construction. Fin stabilisers.

SHIPBORNE AIRCRAFT

Note: Replacement helicopters are urgently needed. Sensors are to be optimised for surface surveillance.

Numbers/Type: 7 Westland Wasp HAS Mk 1.
Operational speed: 96 kts *(177 km/h)*.
Service ceiling: 12 200 ft *(3720 m)*.
Range: 263 nm *(488 km)*.
Role/Weapon systems: ASW helicopter; low time aircraft procured from UK. Flown by Navy, maintained by Air Force. Were to have been paid off in 1992 but lives extended. Sensors: None. Weapons: ASW; 1 × Mk 46 torpedo or depth bomb.

WESTLAND WASP *1986, Paul Beaver*

LAND-BASED MARITIME AIRCRAFT

Numbers/Type: 6 Lockheed P-3K Orion.
Operational speed: 410 kts *(760 km/h)*.
Service ceiling: 28 300 ft *(8625 m)*.
Range: 4000 nm *(7410 km)*.
Role/Weapon systems: Long-range surveillance and ASW patrol; update 1981-84 and to Phase II standard 1988-92. Operated by RNZAF. Sensors: APS-134 radar, ASQ-10 MAD, AQH5/AQA1 processor, 3 AYK 14 computers, IFF, ESM, SQ 41/47/SSQ 46 sonobuoys. Weapons: ASW; 8 × torpedoes, depth bombs or mines, 10 × underwing stations for weapons.

LIGHT FORCES

4 MOA CLASS (INSHORE PATROL CRAFT)

Name	No	Builders	Commissioned
MOA	P 3553	Whangarei Engineering and Construction Co Ltd	28 Nov 1983
KIWI	P 3554	Whangarei Engineering and Construction Co Ltd	2 Sep 1984
WAKAKURA	P 3555	Whangarei Engineering and Construction Co Ltd	26 Mar 1985
HINAU	P 3556	Whangarei Engineering and Construction Co Ltd	4 Oct 1985

Displacement, tons: 91.5 standard; 105 full load
Dimensions, feet (metres): 88 × 20 × 7.2 *(26.8 × 6.1 × 2.2)*
Main machinery: 2 Cummins KT-1105M diesels; 710 hp *(530 kW)*; 2 shafts
Speed, knots: 12. **Range, miles:** 1000 at 11 kts
Complement: 18 (5 officers (4 training))
Guns: 1 Browning 12.7 mm MG.
Radars: Surface search: Racal Decca 916; I band.
Sonars: Sidescan *(Hinau)*; high frequency.

Comment: On 11 February 1982 the New Zealand Cabinet approved the construction of four inshore patrol craft. The four IPC are operated by the Reserve Divisions, *Moa* with *Toroa* (Dunedin), *Kiwi* with *Pegasus* (Christchurch), *Wakakura* with *Olphert* (Wellington), *Hinau* with *Ngapona* (Auckland). Same design as Inshore Survey and Training craft *Kahu* but with a modified internal layout. Procurement of an MCM system is being considered. Sidescan sonar was fitted to *Hinau* in 1992/93; the remainder to be fitted in 1994/95.

MOA *10/1991, Guy Toremans*

SURVEY VESSELS

Name	No	Builders	Commissioned
MONOWAI (ex-*Moana Roa*)	A 06	Grangemouth D. Y.	Aug 1960

Displacement, tons: 3903 full load
Dimensions, feet (metres): 298 × 46 × 17 *(90.8 × 14 × 5.2)*
Main machinery: 2 Clark-Sulzer 7-cyl diesels; 3640 hp(m) *(2.68 MW)*; 2 shafts; bow thruster
Speed, knots: 14. **Range, miles:** 12 000 at 12 kts
Complement: 136 (11 officers)
Guns: 2 Oerlikon 20 mm.
Radars: Navigation: Racal Decca 1290A/9; ARPA 1690S; I band.
Helicopters: 1 Wasp HAS Mk 1 (not always embarked).

Comment: Previously owned by the New Zealand Government department of Maori and Island Affairs and employed on the Cook Islands service. Taken over 1974 for conversion by Scott Lithgow which included an up-rating of the engines, provision of a helicopter deck and hangar and fitting of cp propellers and a bow thruster. Commissioned into RNZN 4 October 1977. Racal System 960 automated data acquisition and processing system (RNZN Hadlaps) fitted in 1991. New radar and communications equipment fitted during 1988 modernisation which included the installation of a reverse osmosis plant and a rigid hull inflatable boat. The ship is white with a yellow funnel. Inmarsat comms fitted.

MONOWAI *10/1991, John Mortimer*

Name	No	Builders	Commissioned
TAKAPU	A 07	Whangarei Engineering and Construction Co Ltd	8 July 1980
TARAPUNGA	A 08	Whangarei Engineering and Construction Co Ltd	9 Apr 1980

Displacement, tons: 91.5 standard; 104.9 full load
Dimensions, feet (metres): 88 × 20 × 7.2 *(26.8 × 6.1 × 2.2)*
Main machinery: 2 Cummins KT-1150M diesels; 710 hp *(530 kW)*; 2 shafts
Speed, knots: 12. **Range, miles:** 1000 at 12 kts
Complement: 11 (2 officers)
Radars: Navigation: Racal Decca; I band.

Comment: Equipment has been specifically designed to work with *Monowai*. Same hull design as Inshore Patrol and Training craft *Kahu* with modified internal layout. Survey equipment: Magnavox MX1102 satellite navigation; Atlas Deso 20 echo-sounders; Del Norte Trisponder position fixing. EG and G 135 *(Tarapunga)* and Klein 531T *(Takapu)* side scan sonars; fitted for but not with Decca Hi-Fix/6. Fitted with two Omega power control gearboxes for slow speed running. Racal System 960 (Hadlaps) fitted in 1991.

TARAPUNGA *10/1991, Guy Toremans*

SERVICE FORCES

Note: In addition to vessels listed below there are four 12 m sail training craft used for seamanship training: *Paea II, Mako II, Mango II, Haku II* (sail nos 6911-6914).

Name	No	Builders	Commissioned
ENDEAVOUR	A 11	Hyundai, South Korea	6 Apr 1988

Displacement, tons: 12 390 full load
Dimensions, feet (metres): 453.1 × 60 × 23 *(138.1 × 18.4 × 7.3)*
Main machinery: 1 MAN-Burmeister & Wain 12V32/36 diesel; 5780 hp(m) *(4.25 MW)* sustained; 1 shaft
Speed, knots: 14. **Range, miles:** 8000 at 14 kts
Complement: 30 (6 officers)
Cargo capacity: 7500 tons dieso; 100 tons Avcat; 100 tons water
Radars: Navigation: Racal Decca 1290A/9; ARPA 1690S; I band.
Helicopters: 1 Westland Wasp HAS Mk 1 (not always embarked).

Comment: Ordered July 1986, laid down April 1987 and launched 14 August 1987. Completion delayed by engine problems but arrived in New Zealand in May 1988. Two abeam RAS rigs (one QRC, one Probe) and one astern refuelling rig. Fitted with Inmarsat. Standard merchant design modified on building to provide a relatively inexpensive replenishment tanker.

ENDEAVOUR *10/1991, John Mortimer*

Service forces / NEW ZEALAND 441

MILITARY SEALIFT SHIP

Comment: Project Definition Study completed in Autumn 1989 for a logistic support ship to carry equipment and stores for the Army's Ready Reaction Force. The design solution produced by British Maritime Technology Defence Services seems to have been cancelled but after a second successive disaster in Samoa in 1991, the project has a new lease of life as a Sealift Ship for the Army as well as for disaster relief. The conversion of a commercially built ship looks likely in 1993/94.

1 RESEARCH VESSEL

Name	No	Builders	Commissioned
TUI (ex-USS *Charles H Davis*, T-AGOR 5)	A 05	Christy Corporation, Sturgeon Bay, Wis.	25 Jan 1963

Displacement, tons: 1432 full load
Dimensions, feet (metres): 208.9 × 40 × 15.3 *(63.7 × 12.2 × 4.7)*
Main machinery: Diesel-electric; 2 Caterpillar D 398B diesel generators; 1 twin motor; 1000 hp *(746 kW)*; 1 shaft; bow thruster; 175 hp *(130 kW)*
Speed, knots: 13. **Range, miles:** 14 800 at 12 kts
Complement: 45 (5 officers, 15 scientists)
Radars: Navigation: SPN 7A and LR 880; I band.

Comment: Oceanographic research ship. Laid down on 15 June 1961, launched on 30 June 1962. On loan from the USA since 10 August 1970. Commissioned in the RNZN on 11 September 1970. Operates for NZ Defence Scientific Establishment on acoustic research. Port after gallows removed—gallows at stern—cable reels on quarterdeck and amidships—light cable-laying gear over bow. Ferranti FMS 15/2 towed sonar array for trial 1989-91. Fitted with Inmarsat.

TUI   10/1991, John Mortimer

1 TRAINING VESSEL

Name	No	Builders	Commissioned
KAHU (ex-*Manawanui*)	A 04 (ex-A 09)	Whangarei Engineering and Construction Co Ltd	28 May 1979

Displacement, tons: 91.5 standard; 105 full load
Dimensions, feet (metres): 88 × 20 × 7.2 *(26.8 × 6.1 × 2.2)*
Main machinery: 2 Cummins KT-1150M diesels; 710 hp *(530 kW)*; 2 shafts
Speed, knots: 12. **Range, miles:** 1000 at 11 kts
Complement: 16
Radars: Navigation: Racal Decca 916; I band.

Comment: Same hull design as Inshore Survey Craft and Patrol Craft. Formerly a Diving Tender, now used for navigation and seamanship training.

KAHU   10/1991, Guy Toremans

1 DIVING TENDER

Name	No	Builders	Commissioned
MANAWANUI (ex-*Star Perseus*)	A 09	Cochrane, Selby	May 1979

Displacement, tons: 911 full load
Dimensions, feet (metres): 143 × 31.2 × 10.5 *(43.6 × 9.5 × 3.2)*
Main machinery: 2 Caterpillar diesels; 1130 hp *(843 kW)*; 2 shafts; bow thruster
Speed, knots: 10.7. **Range, miles:** 5000 at 10 kts
Complement: 24 (2 officers)

Comment: North Sea Oil Rig Diving support vessel commissioned into the RNZN on 5 April 1988. Completed conversion in December 1988 and has replaced the previous ship of the same name which proved to be too small for the role. Equipment includes two Phantom HDX remote-controlled submersibles, a decompression chamber (to 250 ft), wet diving bell and 13 ton crane. Fitted with Inmarsat.

MANAWANUI   10/1991, John Mortimer

ARATAKI (ex-*Aorangi*) A 10

Displacement, tons: 180 full load
Dimensions, feet (metres): 74.8 × 19 × 8.2 *(22.8 × 5.8 × 2.5)*
Main machinery: Ruston 6 ARM diesel; 1100 hp *(821 kW)*; 1 shaft; bow thruster
Speed, knots: 12

Comment: Bollard pull, 16.3 tons. Purchased in November 1984 from Timaru Harbour Board by the RNZFA to replace previous tug of same name. Based at Devonport, Auckland. May be replaced.

ARATAKI   10/1991, John Mortimer

WAITANGI

Displacement, tons: 410 full load
Dimensions, feet (metres): 105 × 28 × 14.6 *(32 × 8.5 × 4.5)*
Main machinery: 2 Veiten diesels; 1720 hp(m) *(1.3 MW)*; 2 shafts
Speed, knots: 12. **Range, miles:** 2500 at 12 kts
Complement: 4

Comment: Bollard pull, 21 tons. Leased from Northland Harbour Board and still wears NHB colours. Lease renewed in 1991.

WAITANGI   10/1991, van Ginderen Collection

NICARAGUA

Headquarters' Appointment

Head of Navy:
Major Manuel Rivas Guatemala

Personnel

1993: 800 officers and men

General

All craft operated by Marina de Guerra Sandinista. Pennant numbers: odd—Atlantic; even—Pacific.

Bases

Corinto, Puerto Cabezas, El Bluff, San Juan del Sur

Mercantile Marine

Lloyd's Register of Shipping:
25 vessels of 4064 tons gross

DELETIONS

1990 2 Kimjin class
1991 1 Zhuk class, 1 Sin Hung class

PATROL FORCES

3 Ex-SOVIET YEVGENYA CLASS (MINEHUNTERS—INSHORE)

501   508   510

Displacement, tons: 77 standard; 90 full load
Dimensions, feet (metres): 80.7 × 18 × 4.9 *(24.6 × 5.5 × 1.5)*
Main machinery: 2 Type 3-D-12 diesels; 600 hp(m) *(440 kW)* sustained; 2 shafts
Speed, knots: 11. Range, miles: 300 at 10 kts
Complement: 10
Guns: 2 USSR 25 mm/80 (twin).
Radars: Surface search/navigation: Don 2; I band.
Sonars: A small sonar is lifted over stern on crane.

Comment: Transferred in 1984 and 1986 via Algeria and Cuba. All four refitted in Cuba in 1987-88 but one then sank in the hurricane of 1989 and was subsequently scrapped. Have GRP hulls. Tripod mast. Used as patrol craft but none was seen at sea during 1992.

YEVGENYA 508   1989

4 Ex-SOVIET K8 CLASS (MINESWEEPING BOATS)

500   502   504   506

Displacement, tons: 26 full load
Dimensions, feet (metres): 55.4 × 10.5 × 3.9 *(16.9 × 3.2 × 1.2)*
Main machinery: 2 Type 3-D-6 diesels; 300 hp(m) *(220 kW)* sustained; 2 shafts
Speed, knots: 18. Range, miles: 300 at 10 kts
Complement: 6
Guns: 2 USSR 14.5 mm (twin) MGs.

Comment: Transferred in 1984. Built in Poland in late 1950s. Non-operational in 1992.

K8 502   1988

7 Ex-SOVIET ZHUK CLASS

304   305   307   309   311   315   317

Displacement, tons: 50 full load
Dimensions, feet (metres): 75.4 × 17 × 6.2 *(23 × 5.2 × 1.9)*
Main machinery: 2 Type M 50 diesels; 2200 hp(m) *(1.6 MW)* sustained; 2 shafts
Speed, knots: 30. Range, miles: 1100 at 15 kts
Complement: 17
Guns: 4 USSR 14.5 mm (2 twin) MGs.
Radars: Surface search: Spin Trough; I band.

Comment: First transferred April 1982, having previously been sent to Algeria in May 1981. Second transferred 24 July 1983, third in 1984, two more early 1986 and three in late 1986/early 1987 via Cuba. Two more of this class were transferred via Cuba in December 1989 to replace two sunk in the hurricane of October 1989. No more than three were seaworthy in 1992.

ZHUK 304   1988

8 Ex-NORTH KOREAN SIN HUNG CLASS

400-404   406   408-410

Displacement, tons: 40 full load
Dimensions, feet (metres): 72.2 × 11 × 5.5 *(22 × 3.4 × 1.7)*
Main machinery: 2 diesels; 2400 hp(m) *(1.76 MW)*; 2 shafts
Speed, knots: 40
Guns: 4 USSR 14.5 mm (2 twin) MGs.

Comment: Two transferred June 1984, one in August 1988, five in December 1988, and two in 1989. Torpedo tubes have been removed. Two deleted so far, one of which sank in the 1989 hurricane. About three operational in 1992.

SIN HUNG 404 and 406   1989

2 Ex-NORTH KOREAN KIMJIN CLASS

306   308

Displacement, tons: 25 full load
Dimensions, feet (metres): 66.6 × 11 × 5.5 *(20.3 × 3.4 × 1.7)*
Main machinery: 2 diesels; 2400 hp(m) *(1.76 MW)*; 2 shafts
Speed, knots: 42. Range, miles: 220 at 20 kts
Complement: 10
Guns: 4 USSR 14.5 mm (2 twin) MGs.

Comment: A smaller version of the Sin Hung class transferred in the early 1980s, causing some confusion over numbers. Non-operational in 1992.

2 Ex-ISRAEL DABUR CLASS

231   235

Displacement, tons: 39 full load
Dimensions, feet (metres): 64.9 × 18 × 5.8 *(19.8 × 5.5 × 1.8)*
Main machinery: 2 GM 12V-71TA; 840 hp *(626 kW)* sustained; 2 shafts
Speed, knots: 19. **Range, miles:** 450 at 13 kts
Complement: 6
Guns: 2 Oerlikon 20 mm. 2 Browning 12.7 mm (twin) MGs.

Comment: Delivered by Israel April 1978 (first pair), May 1978 (second pair). One lost by gunfire in 1985; a second was severely damaged in 1987 and has been deleted. Original armament may have been replaced by Soviet 14.5 mm MGs. Non-operational in 1992.

DABUR (Israel number)   1989

2 FRENCH VEDETTE TYPE

300   302

Displacement, tons: 57 full load
Dimensions, feet (metres): 92.5 × 17.1 × 5.2 *(28.2 × 5.2 × 1.6)*
Main machinery: 2 Poyaud 520 V12 M25 diesels; 1520 hp(m) *(1.12 MW)*; 2 shafts
Speed, knots: 24. **Range, miles:** 800 at 15 kts
Guns: 2 USSR 14.5 mm (twin) MGs.

Comment: Built by Ch N de l'Esterel. Ordered December 1981 and completed 24 June 1983. Oerlikon 20 mm replaced by Soviet MG. Both in service during 1992.

VEDETTE 300   1990

2 EL TUYACAN CLASS

301   303

Comment: 105 ft ex-transport craft taken over and used as Presidential yachts. Fitted with twin 37 mm/63 guns. Probably now hulks without propulsion.

EL TUYACAN 301   5/1988

NIGERIA

Headquarters' Appointments

Chief of the Naval Staff:
  Vice Admiral Dan-Preston Omatsola
Chief of Administration:
  Vice Admiral Babtunde Elegbede
Chief of Personnel:
  Rear Admiral J Ayinla
Chief of Logistics:
  Rear Admiral C O Kaja
Chief of Operations:
  Rear Admiral S O Oloko

Personnel

(a) 1993: 5200 (560 officers)
(b) Voluntary service

Bases

Apapa—Lagos: Western Naval Command; Dockyard (Wilmot Point, Victoria Island, Lagos)
Calabar: Eastern Naval Command (Naval schools at Lagos, Port Harcourt, Apapa (NNS *Quorra*) and Calabar)
Okemimi, Port Harcourt

Prefix to Ships' Names

NNS

Port Security Police

A separate force of 1600 officers and men.

Mercantile Marine

Lloyd's Register of Shipping:
  271 vessels of 503 680 tons gross

FRIGATES

1 MEKO TYPE 360

Name	No	Builders	Laid down	Launched	Commissioned
ARADU (ex-*Republic*)	F 89	Blohm & Voss, Hamburg	1 Dec 1978	25 Jan 1980	20 Feb 1982

Displacement, tons: 3360 full load
Dimensions, feet (metres): 412 × 49.2 × 19 (screws) *(125.6 × 15 × 5.8)*
Main machinery: CODOG; 2 RR Olympus TM3B gas turbines; 50 880 hp *(37.9 MW)* sustained; 2 MTU 20V 956 TB92 diesels; 10 420 hp(m) *(7.71 MW)* sustained; 2 shafts; 2 KaMeWa cp props
Speed, knots: 30.5. **Range, miles:** 6500 at 15 kts
Complement: 195 (26 officers) plus 35 midshipmen

Missiles: SSM: 8 OTO Melara/Matra Otomat Mk 1 ❶; active radar homing to 80 km *(43.2 nm)* at 0.9 Mach; warhead 210 kg.
SAM: Selenia Elsag Albatros octuple launcher ❷; 24 Aspide; semi-active radar homing to 13 km *(7 nm)* at 2.5 Mach; height envelope 15-5000 m *(49.2-16 405 ft)*; warhead 30 kg.
Guns: 1 OTO Melara 5 in *(127 mm)*/54 ❸; 85° elevation; 45 rounds/minute to 16 km *(8.7 nm)*; weight of shell 32 kg.
8 Breda Bofors 40 mm/70 (4 twin) ❹; 85° elevation; 300 rounds/minute to 12.5 km *(6.8 nm)* anti-surface; weight of shell 0.96 kg.
Torpedoes: 6—324 mm Plessey STWS-1B (2 triple) tubes ❺. 18 Whitehead A244S; anti-submarine; active/passive homing to 7 km *(3.8 nm)* at 33 kts; warhead 34 kg (shaped charge).
Depth charges: 1 rack.
Countermeasures: Decoys: 2 Breda 105 mm SCLAR 20-tubed trainable; chaff to 5 km *(2.7 nm)*; illuminants to 12 km *(6.6 nm)*.
ESM: Decca RDL-2; intercept.
ECM: RCM-2; jammer.
Combat data systems: Sewaco-BV action data automation.
Fire control: M20 series GFCS. Signaal Vesta ASW.
Radars: Air/surface search: Plessey AWS 5 ❻; E/F band; range 155 km *(85 nm)* for 4 m² target.
Navigation: Racal Decca 1226; I band.
Fire control: Signaal STIR ❼; I/J/K band; range 140 km *(76 nm)* for 1 m² target.
Signaal WM 25 ❽; I/J band; range 46 km *(25 nm)*.
IFF/SIF: Two Decca.
Sonars: Atlas Elektronik EA80; hull-mounted; active search and attack; medium frequency.

Helicopters: 1 Lynx Mk 89 ❾.

Programmes: Originally named *Republic*; renamed *Aradu* 1 November 1980.
Modernisation: Refit started at Wilmot Point, Lagos with Blohm & Voss assistance in 1991. In late 1992 the ship was still in dock with little work being done. No equipment changes have been reported.
Structure: This design shows the flexibility of the modular approach: the Argentinian Meko 360 ships have an all-gas turbine propulsion and two helicopters. This is the first class with containerised armament.
Operational: Had two groundings and a major collision in 1987.

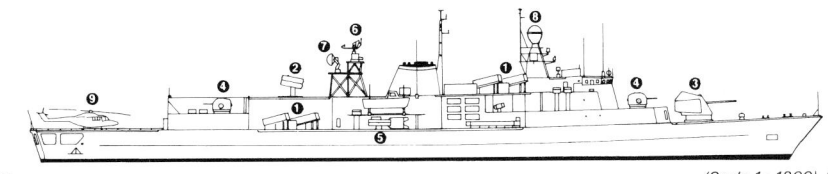

ARADU   (Scale 1 : 1200), Ian Sturton

ARADU   9/1987, Hartmut Ehlers

444 NIGERIA / Frigates — Corvettes

1 OBUMA CLASS

Name	No	Builders	Laid down	Launched	Commissioned
OBUMA (ex-*Nigeria*)	F 87	Wilton-Fijenoord NV, Netherlands	9 Apr 1964	12 Apr 1965	16 Sep 1965

Displacement, tons: 1724 standard; 2000 full load
Dimensions, feet (metres): 360.2 × 37 × 11.5 *(109.8 × 11.3 × 3.5)*
Main machinery: 4 MAN Burmeister & Wain V9V24/30B; 16 000 hp(m) *(11.8 MW)* sustained; 2 shafts
Speed, knots: 26. **Range, miles:** 3500 at 15 kts
Complement: 216

Guns: 2 Vickers 4 in *(102 mm)*/45 (twin); 80° elevation; 16 rounds/minute to 19 km *(10.4 nm)*; weight of shell 16 kg.
2 Bofors 40 mm/70 (fitted for but not with).
2 Oerlikon 20 mm.
Fire control: Optical director for 102 mm guns.
Radars: Surface search: Plessey AWS 4; E/F band; range 101 km *(55 nm)*.
Navigation: Decca; I band.

Helicopters: Platform for 1 Lynx Mk 89.

Programmes: Refitted at Birkenhead, 1973. Further refit completed at Schiedam October 1977.
Modernisation: Various plans to improve armament not yet realised. Squid A/S mortar non-operational and sonar removed.
Operational: Used as a training ship. Badly in need of a refit.

OBUMA   6/1983, Hartmut Ehlers

CORVETTES

Note: *Dorina* is a training hulk.

2 Mk 9 VOSPER THORNYCROFT TYPE

Name	No	Builders	Commissioned
ERINOMI	F 83	Vosper Thornycroft Ltd	29 Jan 1980
ENYIMIRI	F 84	Vosper Thornycroft Ltd	2 May 1980

Displacement, tons: 680 standard; 780 full load
Dimensions, feet (metres): 226 × 31.5 × 9.8 *(69 × 9.6 × 3)*
Main machinery: 4 MTU 20V 956 TB92 diesels; 22 140 hp(m) *(16.27 MW)* sustained; 2 shafts; 2 KaMeWa cp props
Speed, knots: 27. **Range, miles:** 2200 at 14 kts
Complement: 90 (including Flag Officer)

Missiles: SAM: Short Bros Seacat triple launcher ❶; optical/radar or TV guidance to 5 km *(2.7 nm)*; warhead 10 kg; 12 missiles.
Guns: 1 OTO Melara 3 in *(76 mm)*/62 Mod 6 compact ❷; 85° elevation; 85 rounds/minute to 16 km *(8.7 nm)*; weight of shell 6 kg.
1 Breda Bofors 40 mm/70 Type 350 ❸; 85° elevation; 300 rounds/minute to 12.5 km *(6.8 nm)*; weight of shell 0.96 kg.
2 Oerlikon 20 mm ❹; 50° elevation; 800 rounds/minute to 2 km.
A/S mortars: 1 Bofors 375 mm twin launcher ❺; range 1600 m or 3600 m (depending on type of projectile).
Countermeasures: ESM: Decca Cutlass; radar warning.
Fire control: Signaal WM 20 series.
Radars: Air/surface search: Plessey AWS 2 ❻; E/F band; range 110 km *(60 nm)*.
Navigation: Racal Decca TM 1226; I band.
Fire control: Signaal WM 24 ❼; I/J band; range 46 km *(25 nm)*.
Sonars: Plessey PMS 26; lightweight; hull-mounted; active search and attack; 10 kHz.

Programmes: Ordered from Vosper Thornycroft 22 April 1975.
Modernisation: Proposals for refits in Lagos submitted in 1991 but no progress so far.
Operational: Much of the armament is non-operational and both ships were reported as being unseaworthy in early 1993.

1 Mk 3 VOSPER THORNYCROFT TYPE

Name	No	Builders	Commissioned
OTOBO	F 82	Vosper Thornycroft	Nov 1972

Displacement, tons: 580 standard; 660 full load
Dimensions, feet (metres): 202 × 31 × 11.3 *(61.6 × 9.5 × 3.5)*
Main machinery: 2 MAN V8V24/30-B diesels; 8000 hp(m) *(5.88 MW)*; 2 shafts
Speed, knots: 22. **Range, miles:** 3000 at 14 kts
Complement: 67 (8 officers)

Guns: 1 OTO Melara 76 mm/62 or 1 Bofors 40 mm/70.
2 Bofors 40 mm/70 (aft).
Fire control: Naja optronic director. Selenia 1 PN 10 action data automation.
Radars: Air/surface search: Plessey AWS 1; E/F band; range 110 km *(60 nm)*.
Navigation: Racal Decca TM 1626; I band.

Programmes: Ordered on 28 March 1968. Refitted by Vosper Thornycroft 1975. Originally two of the class but both fell into disrepair and *Dorina* was disarmed in April 1987 (although still exists as a hulk).
Modernisation: Arrived Genoa 21 April 1988 for a two year refit by Fincantieri but this has been suspended by difficulties over payments and the ship was still there at the end of 1992.
Operational: Likely to be scrapped in 1993.

OTOBO   10/1992

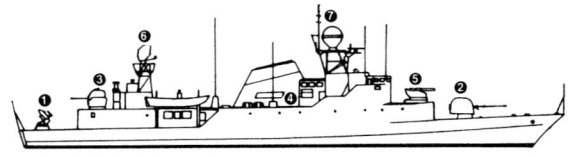

ERINOMI   *(Scale 1 : 900), Ian Sturton*

SHIPBORNE AIRCRAFT

Numbers/Type: 2 Westland Lynx Mk 89.
Operational speed: 125 kts *(232 km/h)*.
Service ceiling: 12 500 ft *(3810 m)*.
Range: 320 nm *(590 km)*.
Role/Weapon systems: Coastal patrol and ASW helicopter; embarked and shore-based for frigate ASW and SAR duties. Sensors: RCA 5000 radar. Weapons: ASW; 2 × 244/S torpedoes. ASV; 1 × 7.62 mm door-mounted machine gun.

LAND-BASED MARITIME AIRCRAFT

Numbers/Type: 18 Dornier Do 128-6MPA.
Operational speed: 165 kts *(305 km/h)*.
Service ceiling: 32 600 ft *(9335 m)*.
Range: 790 nm *(1460 km)*.
Role/Weapon systems: Coastal surveillance and EEZ protection duties; anti-smuggling tasks. Sensors: Weather radar, cameras. Weapons: Unarmed.

Numbers/Type: 3 Fokker F27 Maritime.
Operational speed: 250 kts *(463 km/h)*.
Service ceiling: 25 000 ft *(7620 m)*.
Range: 2700 nm *(5000 km)*.
Role/Weapon systems: Long-range MR and offshore surveillance of vital oil and fishing grounds Sensors: Search radar, MAD, provision for sonobuoys. Weapons: ASW; 2 × torpedoes, depth bombs or mines. ASV; 4 × 127 mm rockets.

Numbers/Type: 19 MBB BO 105C.
Operational speed: 113 kts *(210 km/h)*.
Service ceiling: 9845 ft *(3000 m)*.
Range: 407 nm *(754 km)*.
Role/Weapon systems: Onshore, coastal and inshore search and rescue helicopter; limited commando assault tasks and other fleet support duties. Sensors: None. Weapons: Unarmed but could be provided with machine gun or cannon pods.

ENYIMIRI   7/1985, Hartmut Ehlers

LIGHT FORCES

3 LÜRSSEN FPB-57 CLASS (FAST ATTACK CRAFT—MISSILE)

Name	No	Builders	Commissioned
EKPE	P 178	Lürssen, Vegesack	Aug 1980
DAMISA	P 179	Lürssen, Vegesack	Apr 1981
AGU	P 180	Lürssen, Vegesack	Apr 1981

Displacement, tons: 444 full load
Dimensions, feet (metres): 190.6 × 24.9 × 10.2 *(58.1 × 7.6 × 3.1)*
Main machinery: 4 MTU 16V 956 TB92 diesels; 17 700 hp(m) *(13 MW)* sustained; 2 shafts
Speed, knots: 42. **Range, miles:** 670 at 36 kts; 2000 at 16 kts
Complement: 40

Missiles: SSM: 4 OTO Melara/Matra Otomat Mk 1; active radar homing to 80 km *(43.2 nm)* at 0.9 Mach; warhead 210 kg.
Guns: 1 OTO Melara 3 in *(76 mm)*/62; 85° elevation; 60 rounds/minute to 16 km *(8.7 nm)*; weight of shell 6 kg.
2 Breda 40 mm/70 (twin); 85° elevation; 300 rounds/minute to 12.5 km *(6.8 nm)*; weight of shell 0.96 kg.
4 Emerson Electric 30 mm (2 twin); 80° elevation; 1200 rounds/minute combined to 6 km *(3.3 nm)*; weight of shell 0.35 kg.
Countermeasures: ESM: Decca RDL; radar intercept.
Radars: Surface search/navigation: Racal Decca TM 1226; I band.
Fire control: Signaal WM 28; I/J band; range 46 km *(25 nm)*.

Programmes: Ordered in late 1977. All three sailed in company for Nigeria on 21 August 1981 and completed major refit at building yard in February 1984.
Operational: Not regular sea-going but two of the class took part in the 1987 fleet exercise 'Odion'.

AGU (alongside DAMISA)　　　　　　　　　　　　11/1983, G Koop

4 BROOKE MARINE TYPE (LARGE PATROL CRAFT)

Name	No	Builders	Commissioned
MAKURDI	P 167	Brooke Marine, Lowestoft	14 Aug 1974
HADEJIA	P 168	Brooke Marine, Lowestoft	14 Aug 1974
JEBBA	P 171	Brooke Marine, Lowestoft	29 Apr 1977
OGUTA	P 172	Brooke Marine, Lowestoft	29 Apr 1977

Displacement, tons: 115 standard; 143 full load
Dimensions, feet (metres): 107 × 20 × 11.5 *(32.6 × 6.1 × 3.5)*
Main machinery: 2 Paxman Ventura 12CM diesels; 3000 hp *(2.24 MW)* sustained; 2 shafts
Speed, knots: 20.5
Complement: 21 (4 officers)
Guns: 4 Emerson Electric 30 mm (2 twin). 2 rocket flare launchers.
Radars: Surface search: Racal Decca TM 1226; I band.

Comment: First pair ordered in 1971. Second pair ordered 30 October 1974. Modifications to *Makurdi* and *Hadejia* were carried out by Brooke Marine in 1981-82. This included provision of new engines and Emerlec guns. The second pair similarly refitted in Nigeria.

HADEJIA　　　　　　　　　　　　　　　　　　　1982, Brooke Marine

6 DAMEN 1500 TYPE (COASTAL PATROL CRAFT)

P 227　P 228　P 229　P 230　P 231　P 232

Displacement, tons: 16 full load
Dimensions, feet (metres): 49.5 × 14.8 × 4.9 *(15.1 × 4.5 × 1.5)*
Main machinery: 2 MTU diesels; 2250 hp(m) *(1.65 MW)*; 2 shafts
Speed, knots: 34
Complement: 6
Guns: 1—7.62 mm MG.

Comment: Built by Damen, Netherlands. First three completed April 1986, second three June 1986. Aluminium hulls.

5 VAN MILL TYPE (COASTAL PATROL CRAFT)

P 215　P 216　P 217　P 218　P 219

Displacement, tons: 45 full load
Dimensions, feet (metres): 66.3 × 17.4 × 5.9 *(20.2 × 5.3 × 1.8)*
Main machinery: 3 Detroit 12V-71TA diesels; 1260 hp *(939 kW)* sustained; 3 shafts *(P 215-216)*
2 MTU diesels; 2200 hp(m) *(1.61 MW)*; 2 shafts *(P 217-220)*
Speed, knots: 35. **Range, miles:** 950 at 25 kts
Complement: 12 (2 officers)
Guns: 1 Rheinmetall 20 mm. 2—7.62 mm MGs.

Comment: Built by Van Mill, Netherlands. Completed between July 1985 and end 1986. Sixth of class given to Equatorial Guinea in June 1986.

3 COMBATTANTE IIIB CLASS (FAST ATTACK CRAFT—MISSILE)

Name	No	Builders	Commissioned
SIRI	P 181	CMN, Cherbourg	19 Feb 1981
AYAM	P 182	CMN, Cherbourg	11 June 1981
EKUN	P 183	CMN, Cherbourg	18 Sep 1981

Displacement, tons: 385 standard; 430 full load
Dimensions, feet (metres): 184 × 24.9 × 7 *(56.2 × 7.6 × 2.1)*
Main machinery: 4 MTU 16V 956 TB92 diesels; 17 700 hp(m) *(13 MW)* sustained; 2 shafts
Speed, knots: 41. **Range, miles:** 2000 at 15 kts
Complement: 42

Missiles: SSM: 4 Aerospatiale MM 38 Exocet; inertial cruise; active radar homing to 42 km *(23 nm)* at 0.9 Mach; warhead 165 kg; sea-skimmer.
Guns: 1 OTO Melara 3 in *(76 mm)*/62; 85° elevation; 60 rounds/minute to 16 km *(8.7 nm)*; weight of shell 6 kg.
2 Breda 40 mm/70 (twin); 85° elevation; 300 rounds/minute to 12.5 km *(6.8 nm)*; weight of shell 0.96 kg.
4 Emerson Electric 30 mm (2 twin); 80° elevation; 1200 rounds/minute combined to 6 km *(3.3 nm)*; weight of shell 0.35 kg.
Countermeasures: ESM: Decca RDL; radar intercept.
Fire control: Thomson-CSF Vega system. 2 CSEE Panda optical directors.
Radars: Air/surface search: Thomson-CSF Triton (TRS 3033); G band; range 33 km *(18 nm)* for 2 m² target.
Navigation: Racal Decca TM 1226; I band.
Fire control: Thomson-CSF Castor II (TRS 3203); I/J band; range 15 km *(8 nm)* for 1 m² target.

Programmes: Ordered in late 1977. Finally handed over in February 1982 after delays caused by financial problems.
Modernisation: Major refit and repairs carried out at Cherbourg from March to December 1991.

EKUN (*Siri* behind)　　　　　　　　　　　12/1985, Hartmut Ehlers

4 ABEKING AND RASMUSSEN TYPE (LARGE PATROL CRAFT)

Name	No	Builders	Commissioned
ARGUNGU	P 165	Abeking & Rasmussen	Aug 1973
YOLA	P 166	Abeking & Rasmussen	Aug 1973
BRAS	P 169	Abeking & Rasmussen	Mar 1976
EPE	P 170	Abeking & Rasmussen	Mar 1976

Displacement, tons: 90
Dimensions, feet (metres): 95.1 × 18 × 5.2 *(29 × 5.5 × 1.6)*
Main machinery: 2 MTU diesels; 2200 hp(m) *(1.62 MW)*; 2 shafts
Speed, knots: 20
Complement: 25
Guns: 4 Emerson Electric 30 mm (2 twin).
Radars: Surface search: Racal Decca TM 1229; I band.

Comment: *Yola* and *Bras* rearmed in 1978, the remainder in 1982.

YOLA　　　　　　　　　　　　　　　　　　　　8/1983, Hartmut Ehlers

446 NIGERIA / Light forces — Survey ships

6 SIMMONEAU 500 TYPE (COASTAL PATROL CRAFT)

P 233   P 234   P 235   P 236   P 237   P 238

Displacement, tons: 22 full load
Dimensions, feet (metres): 51.8 × 15.7 × 5.9 *(15.8 × 4.8 × 1.8)*
Main machinery: 2 MTU 6V 396 TC82 diesels; 1300 hp(m) *(956 kW)* sustained; 2 shafts
Speed, knots: 33. **Range, miles:** 375 at 25 kts
Complement: 6
Guns: 2—7.62 mm MGs (interchangeable with 20 mm if required).
Radars: Surface search: Racal Decca 976; I band.

Comment: First two commissioned October 1986, remainder by early 1987. Built by Simmoneau Fontenay-le-Comte, France. Aluminium hulls.

P 234   *1987, Simmoneau*

14 INTERMARINE TYPE (COASTAL PATROL CRAFT)

ABEOKUTA P 200	IKEJA P 205	MAIDUGURI P 210
AKURE P 201	ILORIN P 206	MINNA P 211
BAUCHI P 202	JOS P 207	OWERRI P 212
BENIN CITY P 203	KADUNA P 208	SOKOTO P 214
ENUGU P 204	KANO P 209	

Displacement, tons: 22 full load
Dimensions, feet (metres): 55.1 × 14.8 × 3.3 *(16.8 × 4.5 × 1)*
Main machinery: 2 MTU 8V 331 TC82 diesels; 1740 hp(m) *(1.28 MW)* sustained; 2 waterjets
Speed, knots: 32. **Range, miles:** 400 at 28 kts
Complement: 6
Guns: 1 Oerlikon 20 mm. 2—7.62 mm (twin) MGs.

Comment: GRP hulls. Last of class delivered April 1982. Built by Intermarine, Sazana, Italy. Most are not operational and are on cradles ashore as in the picture. P 213 sank in 1984.

ENUGU   *9/1987, Hartmut Ehlers*

4 ROTORK SEA TRUCKS

P 239   P 240   P 241   P 242

Dimensions, feet (metres): 47.6 × 14.4 × 2.9 *(14.5 × 4.4 × 0.9)*
Main machinery: 2 MTU diesels; 600 hp(m) *(441 kW)*; 2 shafts
Speed, knots: 20
Complement: 8
Guns: 1—7.62 mm MG.

Comment: Delivered in 1986. P 242 used for survey work.

ROTORK P 242   *12/1985, Hartmut Ehlers*

2 WATERCRAFT P-2000 TYPE (COASTAL PATROL CRAFT)

OKRIKA P 225   ABONNEMA P 226

Displacement, tons: 49 full load
Dimensions, feet (metres): 68.2 × 19 × 9.8 *(20.8 × 5.8 × 3)*
Main machinery: 2 MTU 8V 396 TB93 diesels; 2180 hp(m) *(1.6 MW)* sustained; 2 shafts
Speed, knots: 33. **Range, miles:** 660 at 22 kts
Guns: 1 Rheinmetall 20 mm. 2—7.62 mm MGs.

Comment: Delayed by Watercraft's insolvency until 1988. GRP hulls.

4 SWIFTSHIPS TYPE (COASTAL PATROL CRAFT)

ISEYIN P 221   AFIKTO P 223
ERUWA P 222   ABA P 224

Displacement, tons: 36 full load
Dimensions, feet (metres): 65.6 × 18.4 × 4.9 *(20 × 5.6 × 1.5)*
Main machinery: 2 MTU 8V 396 TB93 diesels; 2180 hp(m) *(1.6 MW)* sustained; 2 shafts
Speed, knots: 32. **Range, miles:** 500 at 18 kts
Complement: 6
Guns: 1 Rheinmetall 20 mm. 2—7.62 mm MGs.

Comment: Delivered by Swiftships, USA in 1986. Aluminium hulls.

MINE WARFARE FORCES

2 LERICI CLASS (MINEHUNTERS/SWEEPERS)

Name	No	Builders	Commissioned
OHUE	M 371	Intermarine SY, Italy	28 May 1987
MARABAI	M 372	Intermarine SY, Italy	25 Feb 1988

Displacement, tons: 540 full load
Dimensions, feet (metres): 167.3 × 31.5 × 9.2 *(51 × 9.6 × 2.8)*
Main machinery: 2 MTU 12V 396 TB83 diesels; 3120 hp(m) *(2.3 MW)* sustained; 2 waterjets
Speed, knots: 15.5. **Range, miles:** 2500 at 12 kts
Complement: 50 (5 officers)
Guns: 2 Emerson Electric 30 mm (twin); 80° elevation; 1200 rounds/minute combined to 6 km *(3.3 nm)*; weight of shell 0.35 kg.
2 Oerlikon 20 mm GAM-BO1.
Countermeasures: Fitted with 2 Pluto remote-controlled submersibles, Oropesa 'O' Mis 4 and Ibis V control system.
Radars: Navigation: Racal Decca 1226; I band.
Sonars: Thomson Sintra TSM 2022; hull-mounted; mine detection; high frequency.

Comment: *Ohue* ordered in April 1983 and *Marabai* in January 1986 with an option for a third which has not been taken up. *Ohue* laid down 23 July 1984 and launched 22 November 1985. *Marabai* laid down 11 March 1985, launched 6 June 1986. GRP hulls but, unlike Italian and Malaysian versions they do not have separate hydraulic minehunting propulsion. Carry Galeazzi 2-man decompression chambers. Endurance, 14 days.

OHUE   *7/1987, Marina Fraccaro*

SURVEY SHIP

Name	No	Builders	Commissioned
LANA	A 498	Brooke Marine, Lowestoft	15 July 1976

Displacement, tons: 800 standard; 1088 full load
Dimensions, feet (metres): 189 × 37.5 × 12 *(57.8 × 11.4 × 3.7)*
Main machinery: 4 Lister-Blackstone ERS-8M diesels; 2640 hp *(1.97 MW)*; 2 shafts
Speed, knots: 16. **Range, miles:** 4500 at 12 kts
Complement: 52 (12 officers)
Guns: 2 Oerlikon 20 mm.
Radars: Navigation: Racal Decca; I band.

Comment: Ordered in late 1973, laid down 5 April 1974, launched 4 March 1976. Sister to Bulldog class.

LANA   *8/1983, Hartmut Ehlers*

AMPHIBIOUS FORCES

2 FDR TYPE RO-RO 1300 (LSTs)

Name	No	Builders	Commissioned
AMBE	LST 1312	Howaldtswerke, Hamburg	Apr 1979
OFIOM	LST 1313	Howaldtswerke, Hamburg	July 1979

Displacement, tons: 1470 standard; 1860 full load
Dimensions, feet (metres): 285.4 × 45.9 × 7.5 *(87 × 14 × 2.3)*
Main machinery: 2 MTU 16V 956 TB92 diesels; 8850 hp(m) *(6.5 MW)* sustained; 2 shafts
Speed, knots: 17. **Range, miles:** 5000 at 10 kts
Complement: 56 (6 officers)
Military lift: 460 tons and 220 troops long haul; 540 troops or 1000 troops seated short haul; can carry 5—40 ton tanks
Guns: 1 Breda 40 mm/70; 85° elevation; 300 rounds/minute to 12.5 km *(6.8 nm)*; weight of shell 0.96 kg.
2 Oerlikon 20 mm.
Radars: Navigation: Racal Decca 1226; I band.

Comment: Ordered September 1976. Built to a design prepared for the FGN. Have a 19 m bow ramp and a 4 m stern ramp. Reported that *Ambe*'s bow ramp is welded shut. One of the class inadvertently grounded in 1992 and may not be recoverable.

AMBE   *5/1986, Michael D J Lennon*

SERVICE FORCES

Note: Two 46 ft pusher tugs delivered by Damen in 1986 for use in Lagos.

3 TUGS

Displacement, tons: 200
Dimensions, feet (metres): 90.5 × 25.5 × 11.3 *(27.6 × 7.8 × 3.5)*
Main machinery: 2 GM diesels; 2400 hp *(1.79 MW)*; 2 shafts
Speed, knots: 12.5

Comment: Built by Alblas (Krimpen A/D, Rijn). First launched 9 October 1981.

1 TUG

Name	No	Builders	Commissioned
COMMANDER APAYI JOE	A 499	SY de Wial BV, Asperen, Netherlands	Sep 1983

Displacement, tons: 310 full load
Dimensions, feet (metres): 76.1 × 23.6 × 9.5 *(23.2 × 7.2 × 2.9)*
Main machinery: 2 MAN diesels; 1510 hp(m) *(1.11 MW)*; 2 shafts

Comment: A second of class *Commander Rudolf* was not paid for and therefore not delivered.

COMMANDER APAYI JOE   *11/1983, Hartmut Ehlers*

2 TUGS

DOLPHIN MIRA   DOLPHIN RIMA

Comment: Based at Apapa.

1 TRAINING SHIP

Name	No	Builders	Commissioned
RUWAN YARO (ex-*Ogina Brereton*)	A 497	Van Lent, Netherlands	1976

Displacement, tons: 400 full load
Dimensions, feet (metres): 144.6 × 26.2 × 12.8 *(44.2 × 8 × 3.9)*
Main machinery: 2 Deutz BA12M528 diesels; 3000 hp(m) *(2.2 MW)*; 1 shaft; cp prop; bow thruster
Speed, knots: 17. **Range, miles:** 3000 at 15 kts
Complement: 42 (11 midshipmen)
Radars: Navigation: Racal Decca TM 1626; I band.

Comment: Originally built in 1975 as a yacht. Used as navigational training vessel.

RUWAN YARO   *12/1983, Hartmut Ehlers*

56 LAUNCHES

Comment: Includes 22 of 7 m, eight of 8 m, two 10 m personnel launches, fifteen 22 ft work boats and five 18 ft work boats, all by Fairey Allday Marine Ltd, UK and four 8.2 m whalers by Cheverton Work-Boats, UK.

POLICE CRAFT

Note: Mostly used to patrol Niger River and Lake Chad. In addition to the craft listed there are some 60 light launches and five small hovercraft, many of which are non-operational.

1 FAIREY TRACKER

Displacement, tons: 31
Dimensions, feet (metres): 63.1 × 16.3 × 4.8 *(19.3 × 5 × 1.5)*
Main machinery: 2 diesels; 1290 hp *(962 kW)*; 2 shafts
Speed, knots: 24. **Range, miles:** 650 at 20 kts
Complement: 11
Guns: 1 Oerlikon 20 mm.

Comment: Delivered February 1978 for fishery protection.

1 P 1200 TYPE (COASTAL PATROL CRAFT)

Displacement, tons: 9.5
Dimensions, feet (metres): 39 × 13.4 × 3.5 *(11.9 × 4.1 × 1.1)*
Main machinery: 2 Detroit 8V-71TA diesels; 460 hp *(343 kW)* sustained; 2 shafts
Speed, knots: 27. **Range, miles:** 240 at 25 kts

Comment: GRP hull. Delivered February 1981 by Watercraft Ltd, Shoreham, Sussex.

P 1200   *1981, Watercraft*

8 VOSPER THORNYCROFT TYPE (COASTAL PATROL CRAFT)

Displacement, tons: 15
Dimensions, feet (metres): 34 × 10 × 2.8 *(10.4 × 3.1 × 0.9)*
Main machinery: 2 diesels; 290 hp *(216 kW)*; 2 shafts
Speed, knots: 19
Complement: 6
Guns: 1—12.7 mm MG.

Comment: Ordered for Nigerian Police in March 1971, completed 1971-72. GRP hulls.

NORWAY

Headquarters' Appointments

Inspector General Royal Norwegian Navy:
  Rear Admiral K A Prytz
Commander Naval Material Command:
  Rear Admiral H F Neegaard
Chief of Naval Staff (Defence HQ):
  Commodore R H Christensen
Inspector of Coast Artillery:
  Commodore K M Aam
Commodore Coast Fleet and Sea Training:
  Commodore H K Svensholt

Diplomatic Representation

Defence Attaché in Bonn:
  Colonel Odd I Ruud (A)
Defence Attaché in Helsinki:
  Colonel Wegger Strømmen (A)
Defence Attaché in London:
  Colonel Per Johan Aunaas (A)
Defence Attaché in Moscow:
  Colonel Brynjar Nymo (A)
Defence Attaché in Paris:
  Colonel Per Harildstad (AF)
Defence Attaché in Stockholm:
  Captain Erik Langum
Defence Attaché in Washington and Ottawa:
  Lieutenant General Eyvind B Schibbye (AF)

Personnel

(a) 1993: 7500 officers and ratings (including 2000 Coast Artillery)
(b) 12-15 months' national service

Home Guard

Total of 90 000 men and women. The naval section mans some 400 craft.

Bases

Karl Johans Vern (Horten)—HQ Eastern District. Haakonsvern (Bergen)—HQ Western District and Major Base. Ramsund (Harstad) and Olavsvern (Tromsø). Laksevag—Submarine Repair and Maintenance

Air Force Squadrons (see *Shipborne* and *Land-based Aircraft* section)

Aircraft (Squadron)	Location	Duties
Sea King Mk 43 (330)	Bodø, Banak, Sola Ørland	SAR
Orion P3B (333)	Andøya	LRMP
Lynx (337)	Coast Guard vessels/ Bardufoss	MP
Bell UH-1D (719 & 720)	Bodø, Rygge	Army Transport

Prefix to Ships' Names

KNM (Naval)
K/V (Coast Guard)

Coast Artillery

Numerous coastal forts—all with co-ordinated radar stations and guns and some with torpedo tubes and/or controlled minefields. Some are also equipped with RB 70 SAM missiles and 120 mm guns.

Coast Guard

Inspector:
  Commodore T M Nikoliaisen

Founded April 1977 with operational command held by Norwegian Defence Command. Main bases at Sortland (North) and Haakonsvern (South).

Strength of the Fleet

Type	Active	Building (Projected)
Submarines—Coastal	12	—
Frigates	5	—
Fast Attack Craft—Missile	30	(12)
Minelayers	3	—
Minesweepers/Hunters	5	9
LCTs	5	—
Depot Ship	1	—
Auxiliaries and District Patrol Craft	21	—
Royal Yacht	1	—
Tugs	2	—
Coast Guard Vessels	13	—
Survey Vessels	8	1

Mercantile Marine

Lloyd's Register of Shipping:
  2499 vessels of 22 583 133 tons gross

DELETIONS

Submarines

1991	*Utsira* (old), *Utstein* (old)
1992	*Kaura, Kinn*

Corvettes

1992	*Sleipner, Aeger*

Light Forces

1990-91	*Sev, Hval, Laks, Knurr, Skrei, Hai, Lyr, Delfin*
1991-92	*Glimt, Arg, Brann, Tross, Traust, Brott, Odd, Rokk*

Minesweepers

1992	*Sira, Vosso, Glomma*

Amphibious Forces

1991	*Kvalsund, Raftsund*

Survey Vessels

1990	*Hydrograf*
1992	*Sjøvern, Sjøfalk, Sjøskvett, Sjørokk, Sjødrev, Sverdrup*

Coast Guard

1992	*Malene Østervold*

PENNANT LIST

Note: Ships and craft with three letters preceding their numbers are non-combatant naval district craft.

Submarines

S 300	Ula
S 301	Utsira
S 302	Utstein
S 303	Utvaer
S 304	Uthaug
S 305	Uredd
S 306	Skolpen
S 308	Stord
S 309	Svenner
S 314	Sklinna
S 318	Kobben
S 319	Kunna

Frigates and Corvettes

F 300	Oslo
F 301	Bergen
F 302	Trondheim
F 303	Stavanger
F 304	Narvik

Minesweepers/Hunter

M 313	Tana
M 314	Alta
M 331	Tista
M 332	Kvina
M 334	Utla
M 340	Oksøy
M 341	Karmøy
M 342	Maløy
M 343	Hinnøy
M 350	Alta
M 351	Otra
M 352	Rauma
M 353	Orkla
M 354	Glomma

Minelayers

N 51	Borgen
N 52	Vidar
N 53	Vale

Light Forces

P 358	Hessa
P 359	Vigra
P 961	Blink
P 963	Skjold
P 964	Trygg
P 965	Kjekk
P 966	Djerv
P 967	Skudd
P 969	Steil
P 972	Hvass
P 977	Brask
P 979	Gnist
P 980	Snögg
P 981	Rapp
P 982	Snar
P 983	Rask
P 984	Kvikk
P 985	Kjapp
P 986	Hauk
P 987	Ørn
P 988	Terne
P 989	Tjeld
P 990	Skarv
P 991	Teist
P 992	Jo
P 993	Lom
P 994	Stegg
P 995	Falk
P 996	Ravn
P 997	Gribb
P 998	Geir
P 999	Erle

Amphibious Forces

L 4502	Reinøysund
L 4503	Sørøysund
L 4504	Maursund
L 4505	Rotsund
L 4506	Borgsund

Auxiliaries

A 530	Horten
A 531	Sarpen
A 532	Draug
HSD 15	Krøttøy
N 533	Norge
NSD 35	Rotvaer
ØSD 1	Welding
ØSD 2	Wisting
ØSD 11	Oscarsborg
HSD 12	Garsøy
ØSD 14	Folden
ØSD 15	Nordkep
RSD 20	Foracs II
RSD 21	FKS I
RSD 22	Fjoly
RSD 23	Brimse
RSD 28	Rogin
TRSD 4	Karlsøy
TSD 5	Tautra
VSD 1	Vernøy
VSD 2	Kvarven
VSD 4	Torpen
VSD 7	Samson

Coast Guard

W 300	Nornen
W 301	Farm
W 302	Heimdal
W 312	Kim
W 314	Stålbas
W 315	Nordsjøbas
W 316	Volstad Jr.
W 317	Lafjord
W 318	Garpeskjaer
W 319	Grimsholm
W 320	Nordkapp
W 321	Senja
W 322	Andenes

SUBMARINES

6 ULA CLASS (TYPE P 6071 (Ex-210))

Name	No	Builders	Laid down	Launched	Commissioned
ULA	S 300	Thyssen Nordseewerke, Emden	29 Jan 1987	28 July 1988	27 Apr 1989
UREDD	S 305	Thyssen Nordseewerke, Emden	23 June 1988	22 Sep 1989	3 May 1990
UTVAER	S 303	Thyssen Nordseewerke, Emden	8 Dec 1988	19 Apr 1990	8 Nov 1990
UTHAUG	S 304	Thyssen Nordseewerke, Emden	15 June 1989	18 Oct 1990	7 May 1991
UTSTEIN	S 302	Thyssen Nordseewerke, Emden	6 Dec 1989	25 Apr 1991	14 Nov 1991
UTSIRA	S 301	Thyssen Nordseewerke, Emden	15 June 1990	21 Nov 1991	30 Apr 1992

Displacement, tons: 1040 surfaced; 1150 dived
Dimensions, feet (metres): 193.6 × 17.7 × 15.1 *(59 × 5.4 × 4.6)*
Main machinery: Diesel-electric; 2 MTU 16V 396 SB83 diesels; 2700 hp(m) *(1.98 MW)* sustained; 1 Siemens motor; 6000 hp(m) *(4.41 MW)*; 1 shaft
Speed, knots: 11 surfaced; 23 dived
Range, miles: 5000 at 8 kts
Complement: 18-20 (3 officers)

Torpedoes: 8—21 in *(533 mm)* bow tubes. 14 AEG DM 2A3 Seeal; dual purpose; wire-guided; active/passive homing to 28 km *(15 nm)* at 23 kts; 13 km *(7 nm)* at 35 kts; warhead 260 kg.
Countermeasures: ESM: Racal Sealion; radar warning.
Fire control: Kongsberg MSI-90(U); command and weapon control system.
Radars: Surface search: Kelvin Hughes 1007; I band.
Sonars: Atlas Elektronik CSU83; active/passive intercept search and attack; medium frequency.
Thomson Sintra; flank array; passive; low frequency.

Programmes: Contract signed on 30 September 1982. This was a joint West German/Norwegian effort known as Project 210 in Germany and is the most expensive ever undertaken by the Norwegian Navy. Although final assembly was at Thyssen a number of pressure hull sections were provided by Norway.
Structure: Diving depth, 250 m *(820 ft)*. The basic command and weapon control systems are Norwegian, the attack sonar is German but the flank array, based on piezoelectric polymer antenna technology, has been developed in France and substantially reduces flow noise. Calzoni Trident modular system of non-penetrating masts has been installed.

UTHAUG *6/1991, Stefan Terzibaschitsch*

UTSIRA *6/1992, van Ginderen Collection*

6 KOBBEN CLASS (TYPE 207)

Name	No	Builders	Laid down	Launched	Commissioned
KLINNA	S 314 (ex-S 305)	Rheinstahl-Nordseewerke, Emden	17 Aug 1965	21 Jan 1966	27 May 1966
SKOLPEN	S 306	Rheinstahl-Nordseewerke, Emden	1 Nov 1965	24 Mar 1966	17 Aug 1966
STORD	S 308	Rheinstahl-Nordseewerke, Emden	1 Apr 1966	2 Sep 1966	14 Feb 1967
SVENNER	S 309	Rheinstahl-Nordseewerke, Emden	8 Sep 1966	27 Jan 1967	12 June 1967
KOBBEN	S 318	Rheinstahl-Nordseewerke, Emden	9 Dec 1963	25 Apr 1964	17 Aug 1964
KUNNA	S 319	Rheinstahl-Nordseewerke, Emden	3 Mar 1964	16 July 1964	29 Oct 1964

Displacement, tons: 370; 459 (modernised) standard; 435; 524 (modernised) dived
Dimensions, feet (metres): 148.9 (155.5, modernised) × 15 × 14 *(45.4 (47.4) × 4.6 × 4.3)*
Main machinery: Diesel-electric; 2 MTU 12V 493 AZ80 GA31L diesels; 1200 hp(m) *(880 kW)* sustained; 1 motor; 1800 hp(m) *(1.32 MW)* sustained; 1 shaft
Speed, knots: 12 surfaced; 18 dived. **Range, miles:** 5000 at 8 kts (snorting)
Complement: 18 (17 Svenner) (5 officers)

Torpedoes: 8—21 in *(533 mm)* bow tubes. 8 mix of (a) FFV Type 61; anti-surface; wire-guided; passive homing to 25 km *(13.7 nm)* at 45 kts; warhead 240 kg and (b) Honeywell NT37C; dual purpose; wire-guided; active/passive homing to 20 km *(10.8 nm)* at 35 kts; warhead 150 kg.
Countermeasures: ESM: Argo radar warning.
Fire control: Kongsberg MSI-90(U) TFCS.
Radars: Surface search: Kelvin Hughes 1007; I band.
Sonars: Atlas Elektronik or Simrad; passive search and attack; medium/high frequency.

Programmes: It was announced in July 1959 that the USA and Norway would share equally the cost of these submarines. They are a development of IKL Type 205 (West German U4-U8) with increased diving depth. Kobben was the name of the first submarine in the Royal Norwegian Navy. Commissioned on 28 November 1909.
Modernisation: These six modernised at Urivale Shipyard, Bergen, to a similar standard to the three sold to Denmark including lengthening and new communications, navigation and fire control equipment. The remainder phased out with some taken on by the USN for trials. Modernisation completion programme was S 314 January 1989, S 306 October 1989, S 308 August 1990, S 318 May 1991, S 319 December 1991, S 309 April 1992.
Structure: Diving depth, 200 m *(650 ft)*. Svenner's second periscope for COs training operations is a metre longer.
Sales: Utvaer, Uthaug and Kya sold to Denmark and modernised to the same standard as the Norwegian programme. Kaura has also been sold to Denmark to be cannibalised to repair Saelen, which was flooded after conversion.

KOBBEN *5/1988, W Sartori*

FRIGATES

5 OSLO CLASS

Name	No	Builders	Laid down	Launched	Commissioned
OSLO	F 300	Marinens Hovedverft, Horten	1963	17 Jan 1964	29 Jan 1966
BERGEN	F 301	Marinens Hovedverft, Horten	1964	23 Aug 1965	15 June 1967
TRONDHEIM	F 302	Marinens Hovedverft, Horten	1963	4 Sep 1964	2 June 1966
STAVANGER	F 303	Marinens Hovedverft, Horten	1965	4 Feb 1966	1 Dec 1967
NARVIK	F 304	Marinens Hovedverft, Horten	1964	8 Jan 1965	30 Nov 1966

Displacement, tons: 1450 standard; 1745 full load
Dimensions, feet (metres): 317 × 36.8 × 18 (screws) *(96.6 × 11.2 × 5.5)*
Main machinery: 2 Babcock & Wilcox boilers; 600 psi *(42.18 kg/cm sq)*; 850°F *(454°C)*; 1 De Laval Ljungstrom PN20 turbine; 20 000 hp(m) *(14.7 MW)*; 1 shaft
Speed, knots: 25+. **Range, miles:** 4500 at 15 kts
Complement: 150 (11 officers)

Missiles: SSM: 4 Kongsberg Penguin Mk 2 ❶; IR homing to 27 km *(14.6 nm)* at 0.8 Mach; warhead 120 kg.
SAM: Raytheon NATO RIM-7M Sea Sparrow Mk 29 octuple launcher ❷; semi-active radar homing to 14.6 km *(8 nm)* at 2.5 Mach; warhead 39 kg; 24 cell magazine.
Guns: 2 US 3 in *(76 mm)*/50 Mk 33 (twin) ❸; 85° elevation; 50 rounds/minute to 12.8 km *(7 nm)*; weight of shell 6 kg.
1 Bofors 40 mm/70 ❹; 90° elevation; 300 rounds/minute to 12 km *(6.6 nm)*; weight of shell 0.96 kg
2 Rheinmetall 20 mm/20 (not in all); 55° elevation; 1000 rounds/minute to 2 km.
Torpedoes: 6—324 mm US Mk 32 (2 triple) tubes ❺. Marconi Stingray; anti-submarine; active/passive homing to 11 km *(5.9 nm)* at 45 kts; warhead 32 kg (shaped charge); depth to 750 m *(2460 ft)*.
A/S mortars: Kongsberg Terne III 6-tubed trainable ❻; range pattern from 400-5000 m; warhead 70 kg. Automatic reloading in 40 seconds.
Mines: Laying capability.
Countermeasures: Decoys: 2 chaff launchers.
ESM/ECM: Argo intercept and jammer.
Combat data systems: NFT MSI-3100 action data automation; capability for Link 11 and 14.
Fire control: Mk 91 MFCS. TVT 300 tracker ❼.
Radars: Air search: Thomson-CSF DRBV 22 ❽; D band; range 366 km *(200 nm)*.
Surface search: Racal Decca TM 1226 ❾; I band.
Fire control: NobelTech 9LV 200 Mk 2 ❿; I band (includes search).
Raytheon Mk 95 ⓫; I/J band (for Sea Sparrow).
Navigation: Decca; I band.
Sonars: Thomson Sintra/Simrad TSM 2633; combined hull and VDS; active search and attack; medium frequency.
Simrad Terne III; active attack; high frequency.

Programmes: Built under the five-year naval construction programme approved by the Norwegian Storting (Parliament) late in 1960. Although all the ships of this class were constructed in the Norwegian Naval Dockyard, half the cost was borne by Norway and the other half by the USA. The hull and propulsion design of these ships is based on that of the Dealey class destroyer escorts (now deleted) of the US Navy, but considerably modified to suit Norwegian requirements.

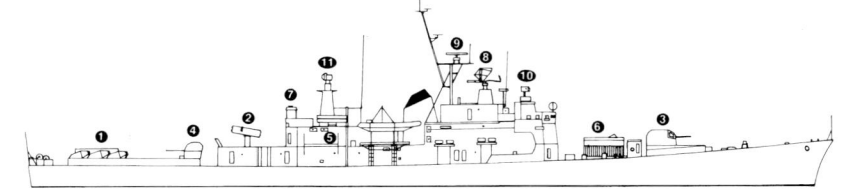

TRONDHEIM *(Scale 1 : 900), Ian Sturton*

NARVIK *1/1992, W Sartor*

Modernisation: All ships modernised with improvements in weapons control and habitability; new countermeasures equipment includes two chaff launchers; Spherion TSM-2633 sonar (with VDS) (a joint Thomson Sintra/Simrad-Subsea (Norway) project); the after 76 mm mounting replaced by a Bofors 40 mm/70; and MSI 3100 action data automation. Modernisation completion programme: F 302 30 November 1987, F 304 21 October 1988, F 303 5 June 1989, F 301 4 April 1990, F 300 1 February 1991.

BERGEN *7/1992, Maritime Photographic*

SHIPBORNE AIRCRAFT

Numbers/Type: 6 Westland Lynx Mk 86.
Operational speed: 125 kts *(232 km/h)*.
Service ceiling: 12 500 ft *(3810 m)*.
Range: 320 nm *(590 km)*.
Role/Weapon systems: Helicopter, operated by Air Force on behalf of the Coast Guard for fishery protection, offshore oil protection and SAR; embarked in CG vessels and shore-based. Sensors: Search radar, ESM. Weapons: Generally unarmed.

LYNX *11/1989, Westland*

LAND-BASED MARITIME AIRCRAFT

Numbers/Type: 2/4 Lockheed P-3B/C Orion.
Operational speed: 410 kts *(760 km/h)*.
Service ceiling: 28 300 ft *(8625 m)*.
Range: 4000 nm *(7410 km)*.
Role/Weapon systems: Long-range MR and oceanic surveillance duties in peacetime, with ASW added as a war role; P-3Bs used by Coast Guard. Sensors: APS-115 radar, ASQ-81 MAD, processor and computer, IFF, ECM/ESM, sonobuoys. Weapons: ASW; 8 MUSL Stingray torpedoes, depth bombs or mines. ASV; possible arming with Penguin missile.

Numbers/Type: 8/1/2 Westland Sea King Mk 43/43A/43B.
Operational speed: 125 kts *(232 km/h)*.
Service ceiling: 10 500 ft *(3200 m)*.
Range: 630 nm *(1165 km)*.
Role/Weapon systems: SAR, surface search and surveillance helicopter; supplemented by civil helicopters in wartime. Two 43B delivered in 1992; remainder to be updated to 43B standard. Sensors: MEL search radar; FLIR and dual radar when modernised. Weapons: Generally unarmed.

LIGHT FORCES

Note: 12 new FAC planned by 2000. Air cushion design of 125 tons capable of 52 kts.

14 HAUK CLASS (FAST ATTACK CRAFT—MISSILE)

Name	No	Builders (see Programmes)	Commissioned
HAUK	P 986	Bergens Mek Verksteder	17 Aug 1977
ØRN	P 987	Bergens Mek Verksteder	19 Jan 1979
TERNE	P 988	Bergens Mek Verksteder	13 Mar 1979
TJELD	P 989	Bergens Mek Verksteder	25 May 1979
SKARV	P 990	Bergens Mek Verksteder	17 July 1979
TEIST	P 991	Bergens Mek Verksteder	11 Sep 1979
JO	P 992	Bergens Mek Verksteder	1 Nov 1979
LOM	P 993	Bergens Mek Verksteder	15 Jan 1980
STEGG	P 994	Bergens Mek Verksteder	18 Mar 1980
FALK	P 995	Bergens Mek Verksteder	30 Apr 1980
RAVN	P 996	Westamarin A/S, Alta	20 May 1980
GRIBB	P 997	Westamarin A/S, Alta	10 July 1980
GEIR	P 998	Westamarin A/S, Alta	16 Sep 1980
ERLE	P 999	Westamarin A/S, Alta	10 Dec 1980

Displacement, tons: 120 standard; 148 full load
Dimensions, feet (metres): 120 × 20 × 5 *(36.5 × 6.1 × 1.5)*
Main machinery: 2 MTU 16V 538 TB92 diesels; 6820 hp(m) *(5 MW)* sustained; 2 shafts
Speed, knots: 32. **Range, miles:** 440 at 30 kts
Complement: 20

Missiles: SSM: 6 Kongsberg Penguin Mk 2; IR homing to 27 km *(14.6 nm)* at 0.8 Mach; warhead 120 kg. At least one boat reported as fitted with Mk 2 Mod 7 Penguin which has a range of 40 km *(21.6 nm)*.
SAM: Twin Simbad launcher for Matra Mistral being fitted from 1992.
Guns: 1 Bofors 40 mm/70; 90° elevation; 300 rounds/minute to 12 km *(6.6 nm)*; weight of shell 0.96 kg.
1 Rheinmetall 20 mm/20; 55° elevation; 1000 rounds/minute to 2 km.
Torpedoes: 2—21 in *(533 mm)* tubes. FFV Type 61; anti-surface; wire-guided; passive homing to 25 km *(13.7 nm)* at 45 kts; warhead 240 kg.
Fire control: Kongsberg MSI-80S TV optronic tracker and laser rangefinder.
Radars: Surface search/navigation: Two Racal Decca TM 1226; I band.
Sonars: Simrad; active search; high frequency.

Programmes: Ordered 12 June 1975.
Modernisation: Simbad twin launchers for SAM being fitted from 1992.
Structure: Very similar to Snøgg class with improved fire control.

FALK *3/1992, Jürg Kürsener*

SKARV *5/1992, Antonio Moreno*

10 STORM CLASS (FAST ATTACK CRAFT—MISSILE)

Name	No	Builders	Commissioned
BLINK	P 961	Bergens Mek. Verksteder	18 Dec 1965
SKJOLD	P 963	Westermoen, Mandal	1966
TRYGG	P 964	Bergens Mek Verksteder	1966
KJEKK	P 965	Bergens Mek Verksteder	1966
DJERV	P 966	Westermoen, Mandal	1966
SKUDD	P 967	Bergens Mek Verksteder	1966
STEIL	P 969	Westermoen, Mandal	1967
HVASS	P 972	Westermoen, Mandal	1967
BRASK	P 977	Bergens Mek Verksteder	1967
GNIST	P 979	Bergens Mek Verksteder	1968

Displacement, tons: 100 standard; 135 full load
Dimensions, feet (metres): 120 × 20 × 5 *(36.5 × 6.1 × 1.5)*
Main machinery: 2 MTU MB 16V 538 TB90 diesels; 6000 hp(m) *(4.41 MW)* sustained; 2 shafts
Speed, knots: 32
Complement: 19 (4 officers)

Missiles: SSM: 6 Kongsberg Penguin Mk 1; IR homing to 20 km *(10.8 nm)* at 0.7 Mach; warhead 120 kg.
Guns: 1 Bofors 3 in *(76 mm)*/50; 30° elevation; 30 rounds/minute to 13 km *(7 nm)* surface fire only; weight of shell 5.9 kg.
1 Bofors 40 mm/70; 90° elevation; 300 rounds/minute to 12 km *(6.6 nm)*; weight of shell 0.96 kg.
Fire control: TVT 300 optronic tracker and laser rangefinder.
Radars: Surface search: Racal Decca TM 1226; I band.
Fire control: Signaal WM 26; I/J band; range 46 km *(25 nm)*.

Programmes: Originally a class of 20. *Storm* (P 960) used as a trials vessel.
Modernisation: The introduction of Penguin surface-to-surface guided missile launchers started in 1970, in addition to originally designed armament, although all boats do not carry full complement at all times. Further modernisation of the surviving 10 of the class is intended and these may in due course also be fitted with Simbad twin launchers for SAM.
Structure: Depth charge rails can still be fitted. The optronic tracker is fitted aft of the mainmast.

TRYGG *5/1992, Antonio Moreno*

6 SNÖGG CLASS (FAST ATTACK CRAFT—MISSILE)

Name	No	Builders	Commissioned
SNÖGG (ex-Lyr)	P 980	Båtservice, Mandal	1970
RAPP	P 981	Båtservice, Mandal	1970
SNAR	P 982	Båtservice, Mandal	1970
RASK	P 983	Båtservice, Mandal	1971
KVIKK	P 984	Båtservice, Mandal	1971
KJAPP	P 985	Båtservice, Mandal	1971

Displacement, tons: 100 standard; 135 full load
Dimensions, feet (metres): 120 × 20 × 5 *(36.5 × 6.1 × 1.5)*
Main machinery: 2 MTU 16V 538 TB92 diesels; 6820 hp(m) *(5 MW)* sustained; 2 shafts
Speed, knots: 32
Complement: 19 (3 officers)

Missiles: SSM: 4 Kongsberg Penguin Mk 1; IR homing to 20 km *(10.8 nm)* at 0.7 Mach; warhead 120 kg.
Guns: 1 Bofors 40 mm/70; 90° elevation; 300 rounds/minute to 12 km *(6.6 nm)*; weight of shell 0.96 kg.
Torpedoes: 4—21 in *(533 mm)* tubes. FFV Type 61; anti-surface; wire-guided; passive homing to 25 km *(13.7 nm)* at 45 kts; warhead 240 kg.
Fire control: PEAB TORC1 system.
Radars: Surface search: Racal Decca 1626; I band.

Programmes: Steel hulled fast attack craft, started coming into service in 1970.
Modernisation: Modernisation of fire control and electronics to be done in due course and may include installation of a Simbad SAM twin launcher.
Structure: Hulls are similar to those of the Storm class.

KJAPP 5/1992, Antonio Moreno

NAVAL DISTRICT PATROL CRAFT

Note: A total of 58 vessels includes the coastal patrol craft below and the transports listed under Miscellaneous, and auxiliary craft attached to the Rogaland (R) and Oestlandet (O) naval districts. These include: *Oscarsborg* (ØSD 11), *Folden* (ØSD 14), *Nordkep* (ØSD 15), *Rogin* (RSD 28), *FKS I* (RSD 21), and *Foracs II* (RSD 20). Some of them carry a single 12.7 mm MG.

FOLDEN 1990, Royal Norwegian Navy

2 COASTAL PATROL CRAFT

Name	No	Builders	Commissioned
BRIMSE (ex-Tarva)	RSD 23 (ex-TSD 1)	Fjellstrand Yachts, Omastrand	1 Dec 1974
WELDING	ØSD 1	Fjellstrand Yachts, Omastrand	1 Nov 1974

Displacement, tons: 27.5
Dimensions, feet (metres): 53.3 × 17.3 × 3.8 *(16.3 × 5.3 × 1.2)*
Main machinery: 2 GM diesels; 800 hp *(597 kW)*; 2 shafts
Speed, knots: 15
Complement: 4
Guns: 1 Browning 12.7 mm MG.
Radars: Surface search: Racal Decca; I band.

Comment: All-welded aluminium hull. Non-combatant Naval District craft.

BRIMSE 10/1988, Royal Norwegian Navy

MINE WARFARE FORCES

2 VIDAR CLASS (COASTAL MINELAYERS)

Name	No	Builders	Commissioned
VIDAR	N 52	Mjellem and Karlsen, Bergen	21 Oct 1977
VALE	N 53	Mjellem and Karlsen, Bergen	10 Feb 1978

Displacement, tons: 1500 standard; 1673 full load
Dimensions, feet (metres): 212.6 × 39.4 × 13.1 *(64.8 × 12 × 4)*
Main machinery: 2 Wichmann 7AX diesels; 4200 hp(m) *(3.1 MW)*; 2 shafts; bow thruster; 425 hp(m) *(312 kW)*
Speed, knots: 15
Complement: 50

Guns: 2 Bofors 40 mm/70; 90° elevation; 300 rounds/minute to 12 km *(6.6 nm)*; weight of shell 0.96 kg.
Torpedoes: 6—324 mm US Mk 32 (2 triple) tubes. Probably Honeywell Mk 46; anti-submarine; active/passive homing to 11 km *(5.9 nm)* at 40 kts; warhead 44 kg.
Mines: 300-400 (dependent on type) on 3 decks with an automatic lift between. Loaded through hatches fwd and aft, each served by 2 cranes.
Radars: Surface search: Racal Decca TM 1226; I band.
Sonars: Simrad; hull-mounted; search and attack; medium/high frequency.

Programmes: Ordered 11 June 1975.
Operational: Versatile ships that can perform a number of roles in addition to minelaying.

VIDAR 8/1991, van Ginderen Collection

1 CONTROLLED MINELAYER

Name	No	Builders	Commissioned
BORGEN	N 51	Marinens Hovedverft, Horten	1961

Displacement, tons: 282 standard
Dimensions, feet (metres): 102.5 × 26.2 × 11 *(31.2 × 8 × 3.4)*
Main machinery: 2 GM 3-71 diesels; 660 hp *(492 kW)*; 2 Voith-Schneider props
Speed, knots: 9
Guns: 1 Rheinmetall 20 mm.
Mines: 2 rails.
Radars: Navigation: I band.

Comment: Launched 29 April 1960. Has two derricks used for mine placement. To be replaced in mid-1994 by a new construction dual purpose amphibious vessel.

BORGEN 1990, Royal Norwegian Navy

0 + 9 OKSØY/ALTA CLASS (MINEHUNTERS/SWEEPERS)

Name	No	Builders	Commissioned
Hunters			
OKSØY	M 340	Kvaerner Mandal	June 1993
KARMØY	M 341	Kvaerner Mandal	June 1994
MALØY	M 342	Kvaerner Mandal	Dec 1994
HINNØY	M 343	Kvaerner Mandal	Feb 1995
Sweepers			
ALTA	M 350	Kvaerner Mandal	May 1995
OTRA	M 351	Kvaerner Mandal	Nov 1995
RAUMA	M 352	Kvaerner Mandal	Feb 1996
ORKLA	M 353	Kvaerner Mandal	June 1996
GLOMMA	M 354	Kvaerner Mandal	Dec 1996

Displacement, tons: 367 full load
Dimensions, feet (metres): 181.1 × 44.6 × 7.5 (2.76 cushion) *(55.2 × 13.6 × 2.3 (0.84))*
Main machinery: 2 MTU 12V 396 TE84 diesels; 3700 hp(m) *(2.72 MW)* sustained; 2 Kvaerner Eureka waterjets; 2 MTU 8V 396 TE54 diesels; 1740 hp(m) *(1.28 MW/60 Hz)* sustained; lift engines
Speed, knots: 30. **Range, miles:** 1200 at 22 kts
Complement: 41 (14 officers)

Guns: 2 Rheinmetall 20 mm. 2—12.7 mm MGs.
Countermeasures: MCMV: 2 Pluto submersibles (minehunter); mechanical and influence sweeping equipment (minesweepers).
Radars: Navigation: 2 Racal Decca; I band.
Sonars: Thomson Sintra/Simrad TSM 2023N; hull-mounted (minehunters); high frequency. Simrad Subsea SA 950; hull-mounted (minesweepers); high frequency.

Programmes: Orders for nine placed with Kvaerner on 9 November 1989. Four will be minehunters, the remainder minesweepers. Option on a tenth of class will not be taken up. *Oksøy* launched on 8 March 1993.
Structure: Design developed by the Navy in Bergen with the Defence Research Institute and Norsk Veritas and uses an air-cushion created by the surface effect between two hulls. The hull is built of Fibre Reinforced Plastics (FRP) in sandwich configuration.
Operational: Simrad Albatross tactical system including mapping; Seatax/Racal mobile positioning system with GPS. The catamaran design is claimed to give higher transit speeds with lesser installed power than a traditional hull design. Other advantages are lower magnetic and acoustic signatures, more comfortable motion, clearer water for sonar operations, and less susceptibility to shock.
Opinion: There is some scepticism amongst international naval architects as to whether this design will live up to expectations. It is certainly a very bold choice by the Norwegian Navy.

OKSØY *4/1993, A Lervik/Forsvaret*

5 Ex-US ADJUTANT/SAUDA CLASS (MSC 60) (MINESWEEPERS—COASTAL)

Name	No	Builders	Commissioned
TANA (ex-*Roeselare* M 914, ex-*MSC 103*)	M 313	Hodgeson Bros, Gowdy & Stevens, Maine	Sep 1953
ALTA (ex-*Arlon* M 915, ex-*MSC 104*)	M 314	Hodgeson Bros, Gowdy & Stevens, Maine	Oct 1953
TISTA	M 331	Forende Båtbyggerier, Risör	27 Apr 1955
KVINA	M 332	Båtservice, Mandal	12 July 1955
UTLA	M 334	Båtservice, Mandal	15 Nov 1955

Displacement, tons: 333 standard; 384 full load
Dimensions, feet (metres): 144 × 28 × 8.5 *(44 × 8.5 × 2.6)*
Main machinery: 2 GM 8-268A diesels; 880 hp *(656 kW)*; 2 shafts
Speed, knots: 13.5. **Range, miles:** 2500 at 10 kts
Complement: 38; 39 *Tana*

Guns: 2 Rheinmetall 20 mm/20; 55° elevation; 1000 rounds/minute to 2 km.
Countermeasures: Thomson-CSF Ibis III minehunting system including 2 PAP 104 (*Tana* only).
Radars: Navigation: Racal Decca TM 1226; I band.
Sonars: UQS-1; hull-mounted; minehunting; high frequency. Plessey 193M (*Tana*).

Programmes: Five coastal minesweepers were built in Norway with US engines. *Alta* and *Tana* were taken over from the Royal Belgian Navy in 1966.
Modernisation: *Tana* converted as a minehunter in 1977. All have been given 20 mm guns.
Operational: To be replaced by the Alta class.

ALTA *5/1992, Wright & Logan*

AMPHIBIOUS FORCES

Note: Replacements in the late 1990s will have a minelaying capability.

5 REINØYSUND CLASS (LCTs)

Name	No	Builders	Commissioned
REINØYSUND	L 4502	Mjellem & Karlsen, Bergen	Jan 1972
SØRØYSUND	L 4503	Mjellem & Karlsen, Bergen	May 1972
MAURSUND	L 4504	Mjellem & Karlsen, Bergen	Sep 1972
ROTSUND	L 4505	Mjellem & Karlsen, Bergen	Nov 1972
BORGSUND	L 4506	Mjellem & Karlsen, Bergen	Feb 1973

Displacement, tons: 595 full load
Dimensions, feet (metres): 171 × 33.8 × 5.9 *(52.1 × 10.3 × 1.8)*
Main machinery: 2 MTU MD diesels; 1350 hp(m) *(992 kW)*; 2 shafts
Speed, knots: 11.5
Complement: 10 (2 officers)
Military lift: 7 tanks; 200 troops
Guns: 3 Rheinmetall 20 mm/20.

Comment: Same design as deleted Kvalsund class.

MAURSUND *3/1992, Jürg Kürsener*

BORGSUND *5/1991, Royal Norwegian Navy*

DEPOT SHIP

Name	No	Builders	Commissioned
HORTEN	A 530	A/S Horten Verft	Apr 1978

Displacement, tons: 2530
Dimensions, feet (metres): 287 × 42.6 × 16.4 *(87.5 × 13 × 5)*
Main machinery: 2 Wichmann 7AX diesels; 4200 hp(m) *(3.1 MW)*; 2 shafts; bow thruster
Speed, knots: 16.5
Complement: 86
Guns: 2 Bofors 40 mm/70.
Helicopters: Platform only.

Comment: Contract signed 30 March 1976. Laid down 28 January 1977; launched 12 August 1977. To serve both submarines and fast attack craft. Quarters for 45 extra and can cater for 190 extra.

HORTEN *8/1991, van Ginderen Collection*

AUXILIARIES

1 RESEARCH SHIP (AGI)

MARJATA

Measurement, tons: 1385 dwt
Dimensions, feet (metres): 193.2 × 36.1 × 15.4 *(58.9 × 11 × 4.7)*
Main machinery: 2 diesels; 2600 hp(m) *(1.91 MW)*; 2 shafts
Speed, knots: 15

Comment: Built by Mjellem and Karlsen in 1976. Has a white superstructure. Used as an AGI and for experimental work.

MARJATA 4/1980

2 DIVING TENDERS

Name	No	Builders	Commissioned
SARPEN	A 531	Nielsen, Harstad	1972
DRAUG	A 532	Nielsen, Harstad	1972

Displacement, tons: 250 full load
Dimensions, feet (metres): 95 × 22 × 8.2 *(29 × 6.8 × 2.5)*
Main machinery: 1 diesel; 530 hp(m) *(389 kW)*; 1 shaft
Speed, knots: 12

Comment: Small depot ships for frogmen and divers.

SARPEN 1992, Royal Norwegian Navy

1 GARSØY CLASS (COASTAL TRANSPORT)

Name	No	Builders	Commissioned
GARSØY	HSD 12	Eikefjord Marine	19 Aug 1988

Displacement, tons: 195 standard
Dimensions, feet (metres): 111.5 × 23 × 5.9 *(34 × 7 × 1.8)*
Main machinery: 2 MWM TBD604BV8 diesels; 2313 hp(m) *(1.7 MW)* sustained; 2 waterjets
Speed, knots: 27
Complement: 4
Cargo capacity: 80 passengers

Comment: GRP sandwich hull used as a trials craft for the SES MCMV design. Now used as a personnel transport and patrol craft. Second of class was cancelled in 1992.

GARSØY 8/1990, T J Gander

7 WISTING CLASS (COASTAL TRANSPORTS)

Name	No	Builders	Commissioned
TORPEN	VSD 4	Båtservice Verft, Mandal	15 Dec 1977
WISTING	ØSD 2	Voldnes Skipsverft, Fosnavåg	30 Jan 1978
TAUTRA	TSD 5	Båtservice Verft, Mandal	15 Feb 1978
ROTVAER	NSD 35	Båtservice Verft, Mandal	Mar 1978
FJØLØY	RSD 22 (ex-ØSD 5)	Voldnes Skipsverft, Fosnavåg	Apr 1978
KRØTTØY	HSD 15	Voldnes Skipsverft, Fosnavåg	June 1978
KARLSØY	TRSD 4	P Høivolds Mek Verksted	July 1978

Displacement, tons: 300 full load
Dimensions, feet (metres): 95.1 × 21.6 × 10 *(29 × 6.7 × 3.2)*
Main machinery: 1 MWM TBD6016K diesel; 530 hp(m) *(390 kW)*; 1 shaft; cp prop
Speed, knots: 11. Range, miles: 1200 at 10 kts
Complement: 6
Cargo capacity: 100 tons; 100 passengers
Guns: 1 Browning 12.7 mm MG.

Comment: Non-combatant Naval District ships. Not all have characteristics listed.

WISTING 6/1991, van Ginderen Collection

1 TORPEDO RECOVERY VESSEL

Name	No	Builders	Commissioned
VERNØY	VSD 1	Fjellstrand Aluminium Yachts, Omastrand	Oct 1978

Displacement, tons: 100
Dimensions, feet (metres): 102.9 × 22.5 × 6.5 *(31.3 × 6.8 × 2)*
Main machinery: 2 MWM diesels; 2 Schottel rudders
Speed, knots: 10+
Complement: 5

Comment: The vessel is fitted with equipment for oil pollution operations and firefighting. All-welded aluminium hull. Non-combatant Naval District craft.

VERNØY 1983, Royal Norwegian Navy

2 TRAINING VESSELS

Name	No	Builders	Commissioned
HESSA (ex-*Hitra*, ex-*Marsteinen*)	P 358	Fjellstrand, Omastrand	Jan 1978
VIGRA (ex-*Kvarven*)	P 359	Fjellstrand, Omastrand	July 1978

Displacement, tons: 39
Dimensions, feet (metres): 77 × 16.4 × 3.5 *(23.5 × 5 × 1.1)*
Main machinery: 2 GM diesels; 1800 hp *(1.34 MW)*; 2 shafts
Speed, knots: 20
Complement: 5
Guns: 1—12.7 mm Browning MG.

Comment: The vessels are designed for training students at the Royal Norwegian Naval Academy in navigation, manoeuvring and seamanship. All-welded aluminium hulls. Also equipped with an open bridge and a blind pilotage position below deck. 18 berths.

HESSA 1992, Royal Norwegian Navy

ROYAL YACHT

Name	No	Builders	Commissioned
NORGE (ex-*Philante*)	N 533	Camper & Nicholson's Ltd, Southampton	1937

Displacement, tons: 1786
Dimensions, feet (metres): 263 × 38 × 15.2 *(80.2 × 11.6 × 4.6)*
Main machinery: 2 Bergen KRMB-8 diesels; 4850 hp(m) *(3.6 MW)* sustained; 2 shafts
Speed, knots: 17

Comment: Built to the order of the late T O M Sopwith as an escort and store vessel for the yachts *Endeavour I* and *Endeavour II*. Launched on 17 February 1937. Served in the Royal Navy as an anti-submarine escort during the Second World War, after which she was purchased by the Norwegian people for King Haakon and reconditioned as a Royal Yacht at Southampton. Can accommodate about 50 people in addition to crew. Repaired after serious fire on 7 March 1985.

NORGE　　　　　　　　　　　　　　　　　　　　　　　8/1992, G Toremans

TUGS

Note: Ex-German tug *Saale* was acquired by a civilian company in 1992.

SAMSON VSD 7

Displacement, tons: 300
Dimensions, feet (metres): 87.3 × 26.2 × 10.5 *(26.6 × 8 × 3.2)*
Main machinery: 1 MWM diesel; 650 hp(m) *(478 kW)*; 1 shaft
Speed, knots: 10

Comment: Ex-West German built in 1938. Modified in 1978. Non-combatant Naval District craft.

SAMSON　　　　　　　　　　　　　　　　　　1981, Royal Norwegian Navy

KVARVEN (ex-*Oscar Tybring*) VSD 2

Displacement, tons: 97
Dimensions, feet (metres): 73.8 × 20.7 × 11.2 *(22.5 × 6.3 × 3.4)*
Main machinery: 1 Detroit V16-149T diesel; 1175 hp *(876 kW)* sustained; 1 shaft
Speed, knots: 11

Comment: Built in 1979 by Haugesund Slip. Acquired in 1988.

COAST GUARD

7 CHARTERED SHIPS

Name	No	Tonnage	Completion
KIM	W 312	493	1955
STÅLBAS	W 314	498	1955
NORDSJØBAS	W 315	814	1978
VOLSTAD JR	W 316	598	1950
LAFJORD	W 317	814	1978
GARPESKJAER	W 318	1122	1956
GRIMSHOLM	W 319	1189	1978

Comment: *Stålbas* and *Volstad Jr* chartered in 1977; *Lafjord*, *Nordsjøbas* and *Grimsholm* in 1980; *Garpeskjaer* in 1986 and *Kim* in 1991. All armed with one 40 mm/60 gun.

GARPESKJAER　　　　　　　　　　　　　　　　　8/1990, T J Gander

VOLSTAD JR　　　　　　　　　　　　　　　　　5/1992, Erik Laursen

3 NORDKAPP CLASS

Name	No	Builders	Commissioned
NORDKAPP	W 320	Bergens Mek Verksteder	25 Apr 1981
SENJA	W 321	Horten Verft	6 Mar 1981
ANDENES	W 322	Haugesund Mek Verksted	30 Jan 1982

Displacement, tons: 3240 full load
Dimensions, feet (metres): 346 × 47.9 × 16.1 *(105.5 × 14.6 × 4.9)*
Main machinery: 4 Wichmann 9AXAG diesels; 16 163 hp(m) *(11.9 MW)*; 2 shafts
Speed, knots: 23. **Range, miles:** 7500 at 15 kts
Complement: 52 (6 aircrew)

Missiles: SSM: Fitted for 6 Kongsberg Penguin II but not embarked.
Guns: 1 Bofors 57 mm/70 ❶; 75° elevation; 200 rounds/minute to 17 km *(9.3 nm)*; weight of shell 2.4 kg.
　4 Rheinmetall 20 mm/20 ❷; 55° elevation; 1000 rounds/minute to 2 km.
Torpedoes: 6—324 mm US Mk 32 (2 triple) tubes ❸. Honeywell Mk 46; anti-submarine; active/passive homing to 11 km *(5.9 nm)* at 40 kts; warhead 44 kg. Mountings only in peacetime.
Depth charges: 1 rack.
Countermeasures: Decoys: 2 chaff launchers.
Combat data systems: Navkis action data automation. SATCOM can be carried ❹.
Radars: Air/surface search: Plessey AWS 5 ❺; E/F band; range 155 km *(85 nm)* for 4 m² target.
Navigation: Two Racal Decca 1226; I band.
Fire control: Philips 9LV 200 Mk 2 ❻; J band.
Sonars: Simrad SS 105; hull-mounted; active search and attack; 14 kHz.

Helicopters: 1 Westland Lynx Mk 86 ❼.

Programmes: In November 1977 the Coast Guard budget was cut resulting in a reduction of the building programme from seven to three ships.
Structure: Strengthened for ice. Fitted for firefighting, anti-pollution work, all with two motor cutters and a Gemini-type dinghy. SATCOM fitted for Gulf deployment.
Operational: Bunks for 109. War complement increases to 76.

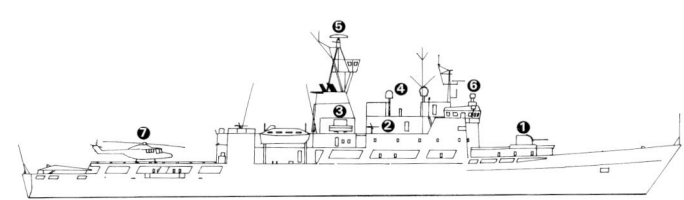

ANDENES　　　　　　　　　　　　　　　(Scale 1 : 1200), Ian Sturton

NORDKAPP　　　　　　　　　　　　　　　1992, Royal Norwegian Navy

Name	No	Builders	Commissioned
NORNEN	W 300	Mjellem & Karlsens, Bergen	1963

Displacement, tons: 1030
Dimensions, feet (metres): 201.8 × 32.8 × 15.8 *(61.5 × 10 × 4.8)*
Main machinery: 4 diesels; 3500 hp(m) *(2.57 MW)*; 1 shaft
Speed, knots: 17
Complement: 32
Guns: 1 Bofors 40 mm/70.

Comment: Launched 20 August 1962. Modernised in 1978 with increased tonnage.

Name	No	Builders	Commissioned
FARM	W 301	Ankerlokken Verft	1962
HEIMDAL	W 302	Bolsones Verft, Molde	1962

Measurement, tons: 600 gross
Dimensions, feet (metres): 177 × 26.2 × 16.1 *(54.3 × 8.2 × 4.9)*
Main machinery: 2 Wichmann 9ACAT diesels; 2400 hp(m) *(1.76 MW)*; 1 shaft; cp prop
Speed, knots: 16
Complement: 29
Guns: 1 Bofors 40 mm/70.

Comment: *Farm* modernised by Bergens Mekaniske Verksteder in 1979 and *Heimdal* by same firm ir 1980.

NORNEN   1988, Royal Norwegian Navy

FARM   6/1991, van Ginderen Collection

SURVEY VESSELS

Notes: (1) Under control of Ministry of Environment based at Stavanger.
(2) In addition *Sverdrup II* works for the Defence Research Establishment and a new vessel *Minerva* will be in service in late 1993.

Name	Displacement tons	Launched	Officers	Crew
LANCE	960	1978	7	8
SJØTROLL	80	1976	1	4
OLJEVERN 01	200	1978	2	6
OLJEVERN 02	200	1978	2	6
OLJEVERN 03	200	1978	2	6
OLJEVERN 04	200	1978	2	6
GEOFJORD	—	—	—	—

LANCE   10/1988, Gilbert Gyssels

OMAN

Senior Officers

Commander Royal Navy of Oman:
 Rear Admiral (Liwaa Bahry) H H Sayyid Shihab bin Tarik bin Taimur al Said
Chief of Staff:
 Commodore (Ameed) Hilal bin Mohammad bin Rashid al Rashdy
Commander Coast Guard:
 Captain (Aqeed Bahry) Hamdan bin Marhoon al Mamari
Commander Royal Yacht Squadron:
 Commodore (Ameed) J M Knapp

Bases

Qa'Adat Said Bin Sultan Albahria, Wudam (main base, dockyard and shiplift)
Mina Raysut (advanced naval base), Salalah
Jazirat Ghanam (advanced naval base), Musandam
Muaskar al Murtafa'a (headquarters)

Personnel

(a) 1993: 3600 officers and men
(b) Voluntary service

Future Plans

The main deficiency in this force is in the MCMV category and plans for a limited capability seem to have been postponed.

Mercantile Marine

Lloyd's Register of Shipping:
 26 vessels of 22 348 tons gross

PATROL SHIP

Name	No	Builders	Commissioned
AL MABRUKAH (ex-*Al Said*)	A 1	Brooke Marine, Lowestoft	1971

Displacement, tons: 900 full load
Dimensions, feet (metres): 203.4 × 35.1 × 9.8 *(62 × 10.7 × 3)*
Main machinery: 2 Paxman Valenta 12 CM diesels; 5000 hp *(3.73 MW)* sustained; 2 shafts
Speed, knots: 12
Complement: 39 (7 officers)
Guns: 1 Bofors 40 mm/70. 2 Oerlikon 20 mm A41A.
Countermeasures: Decoys: Wallop Barricade 18-barrelled chaff launcher.
ESM: Radar warning.
Radars: Surface search: Racal Decca TM 1226; I band.
Helicopters: Platform only.

Comment: Built by Brooke Marine, Lowestoft. Launched 7 April 1970 as a yacht for the Sultan of Oman. Carried on board is one Rotork landing craft. Converted to training ship/patrol ship in 1983 with enlarged helicopter deck.

AL MABRUKAH   1991, van Ginderen Collection

CORVETTES

0 + 2 MUHEET PROJECT TYPE 83

Name	No	Builders	Laid down	Launched	Commissioned
—	—	Vosper Thornycroft	23 Sep 1992	Sep 1994	Dec 1995
—	—	Vosper Thornycroft	Aug 1993	Aug 1995	Nov 1996

Displacement, tons: 1400 full load
Dimensions, feet (metres): 274.6 oa; 249.3 wl × 37.7 × 11.5 *(83.7; 76 × 11.5 × 3.5)*
Main machinery: CODAD; 4 Crossley Pielstick 16 PA6 V 280 STC; 28 160 hp(m) *(20.7 MW)* sustained; 2 shafts; cp props
Speed, knots: 25
Complement: 76 (14 officers)

Missiles: SSM: 8 Aerospatiale MM 40 Exocet ❶.
SAM: Thomson CSF Crotale NG octuple launcher ❷; 8 VT1 (no reloads).
Guns: 1 OTO Melara 3 in *(76 mm)*/62 Super Rapid ❸.
2 Oerlikon/BMARC 20 mm GAM-B01 ❹.
Countermeasures: Decoys: 2 Barricade chaff launchers ❺.
ESM/ECM: Thomson CSF DR 3000; intercept and jammer.
Combat data systems: Signaal SEWACO-FD with Thomson CSF TACTICOS; Link Y; SATCOM.
Fire control: Signaal STING optronic tracker ❻; two optical directors.
Radars: Air/surface search: Signaal MW 08 ❼; G band.

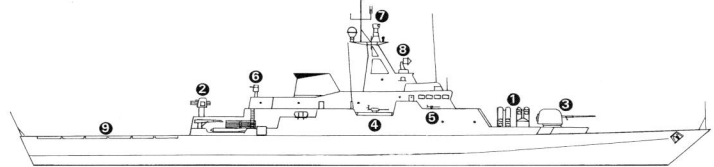

MUHEET PROJECT Type 83 *(Scale 1 : 900), Ian Sturton*

Fire control: Signaal STING ❽; I/J band.
Navigation: Kelvin Hughes 1007; I band.

Helicopters: Platform for 1 medium ❾.

Programmes: Vosper Thornycroft signed the contract on 5 April 1992.

Structure: The ship is based on the Vigilance class design. It is possible a bow sonar may be fitted. Also a towed array could replace the helicopter platform, although this is unlikely.
Opinion: The rapid progression from Dhow to high technology corvette has taken just 20 years. The effectiveness of these ships will depend on retaining close links with western technology.

LIGHT FORCES

Note: Project Mawj (Ocean Wave): tenders were returned for two 47.5 m attack craft on 28 September 1992. Orders are expected in 1993/94.

4 BROOKE MARINE TYPE (FAST ATTACK CRAFT—GUN)

Name	No	Builders	Commissioned
AL WAAFI	B 4	Brooke Marine, Lowestoft	24 Mar 1977
AL FULK	B 5	Brooke Marine, Lowestoft	24 Mar 1977
AL MUJAHID	B 6	Brooke Marine, Lowestoft	20 July 1977
AL JABBAR	B 7	Brooke Marine, Lowestoft	6 Oct 1977

Displacement, tons: 135 standard; 153 full load
Dimensions, feet (metres): 123 × 22.5 × 6 *(37.5 × 6.9 × 1.8)*
Main machinery: 2 Paxman 16YJCM diesels; 3000 hp *(2.24 MW)* sustained; 2 shafts
Speed, knots: 25. **Range, miles:** 3300 at 15 kts
Complement: 27 (3 officers)
Guns: 1 OTO Melara 3 in *(76 mm)*/62 compact; 85° elevation; 85 rounds/minute to 16 km *(8.7 nm)*; weight of shell 6 kg.
1 Oerlikon 20 mm. 2—7.62 mm MGs.
Fire control: Laurence Scott optical director and Sperry Sea Archer system.
Radars: Surface search/navigation: Racal Decca 1226; Racal Decca 1229; I band.

Comment: Ordered 26 April 1974. To be replaced in the 1990s.

4 VOSPER 25 METRE CLASS (INSHORE PATROL CRAFT)

Name	No	Builders	Commissioned
SEEB	B 20	Vosper Private, Singapore	15 Mar 1981
SHINAS	B 21	Vosper Private, Singapore	15 Mar 1981
SADH	B 22	Vosper Private, Singapore	15 Mar 1981
KHASSAB	B 23	Vosper Private, Singapore	15 Mar 1981

Displacement, tons: 60.7
Dimensions, feet (metres): 82.8 × 19 × 5.2 *(25 × 5.8 × 1.6)*
Main machinery: 2 MTU 12V 331 TC92 diesels; 2660 hp(m) *(1.96 MW)* sustained; 2 shafts
1 Cummins N-855M diesel for slow cruising; 189 hp *(141 kW)* sustained; 1 shaft
Speed, knots: 25; 8 (Cummins diesel). **Range, miles:** 750 at 14 kts
Complement: 13
Guns: 1 Oerlikon 20 mm. 2—7.62 mm (twin) MGs.

Comment: Arrived in Oman on 19 May 1981 having been ordered one month earlier. The craft were built on speculation and completed in 1980.

AL FULK *1989, Royal Navy of Oman*

KHASSAB *1989, Royal Navy of Oman*

AL WAAFI *10/1992, Hartmut Ehlers*

SHINAS *10/1992, Hartmut Ehlers*

4 PROVINCE CLASS (FAST ATTACK CRAFT—MISSILE)

Name	No	Builders	Commissioned
DHOFAR	B 10	Vosper Thornycroft	7 Aug 1982
AL SHARQIYAH	B 11	Vosper Thornycroft	5 Dec 1983
AL BAT'NAH	B 12	Vosper Thornycroft	18 Jan 1984
MUSSANDAM	B 14	Vosper Thornycroft	31 Mar 1989

Displacement, tons: 311 light; 394 full load
Dimensions, feet (metres): 186 × 26.9 × 7.9 *(56.7 × 8.2 × 2.4)*
Main machinery: 4 Paxman Valenta 18 CM diesels; 15 000 hp *(11.2 MW)* sustained; 4 shafts; auxiliary propulsion; 2 motors; 200 hp *(149 kW)*
Speed, knots: 38. **Range, miles:** 2000 at 18 kts
Complement: 45 (5 officers) plus 14 trainees

Missiles: SSM: 8 or 6 (B 10) Aerospatiale MM 40 Exocet; inertial cruise; active radar homing to 70 km *(40 nm)* at 0.9 Mach; warhead 165 kg; sea-skimmer.
Guns: 1 OTO Melara 3 in *(76 mm)*/62 compact; 85° elevation; 85 rounds/minute to 16 km *(8.7 nm)*; weight of shell 6 kg.
2 Breda 40 mm/70 (twin); 85° elevation; 300 rounds/minute to 12.5 km *(6.8 nm)*; weight of shell 0.96 kg.
2—12.7 mm MGs.
Countermeasures: Decoys: 2 Wallop Barricade fixed triple barrels; 4 modes of fire for chaff and IR deception.
ESM: Racal Cutlass; radar warning.
ECM: Scorpion; jammer.
Fire control: Sperry Sea Archer (B 10). Philips 9LV 307 (remainder).
Radars: Air/surface search: Plessey AWS 4 (B 10) or AWS 6 (remainder); E/F band.
Navigation: Racal Decca TM 1226C; I band.

Programmes: First ordered in 1980, launched 14 October 1981 and sailed from Portsmouth for Oman 21 October 1982. Two more ordered in January 1981 and sailed for Oman on 16 May 1984. Fourth ordered January 1986, launched 19 March 1988 and sailed for Oman 1 May 1989.
Structure: Similar to Kenyan Nyayo class.

DHOFAR (with 6 Exocet and AWS 4 radar) *1989, Royal Navy of Oman*

AL SHARQIYAH *10/1992, Hartmut Ehlers*

1 TYLER-VORTEX TYPE (INSHORE PATROL CRAFT)

Q 2

Dimensions, feet (metres): 42.7 × 11.8 × 4.6 *(13 × 3.6 × 1.4)*
Main machinery: 2 diesels; 1000 hp *(746 kW)*; 2 shafts
Speed, knots: 30
Guns: 1—12.7 mm MG.
Radars: Surface search: I band.

Comment: A quick reaction boat of Tyler-Vortex design. A second of class Q 1 was scrapped after grounding.

Q 2 *10/1992, Hartmut Ehlers*

AMPHIBIOUS FORCES

1 LANDING SHIP—LOGISTIC

Name	No	Builders	Commissioned
NASR AL BAHR	L 2	Brooke Marine, Lowestoft	6 Feb 1985

Displacement, tons: 2500 full load
Dimensions, feet (metres): 305 × 50.8 × 8.5 *(93 × 15.5 × 2.6)*
Main machinery: 2 Paxman Valenta 18 CM diesels; 7500 hp *(5.6 MW)* sustained; 2 shafts
Speed, knots: 16. **Range, miles:** 5000 at 15 kts
Complement: 81 (13 officers)
Military lift: 7 MBT or 400 tons cargo; 240 troops; 2 LCVPs
Guns: 4 Breda 40 mm/70 (2 twin). 2 Oerlikon 20 mm. 2—12.7 mm MGs.
Countermeasures: Decoys: Wallop Barricade double layer chaff launchers.
Fire control: PEAB 9LV 200 GFCS and CSEE Lynx optical sight.
Radars: Surface search/navigation: Two Racal Decca; I band.
Helicopters: Platform for Super Puma.

Comment: Ordered 18 May 1982. Launched 16 May 1984. Carries one 16 ton crane. Bow and stern ramps. Full naval command facilities. The forward ramp is of two sections measuring length 59 ft (when extended) × 16.5 ft breadth *(18 × 5 m)*, and the single section stern ramp measures 14 × 16.5 ft *(4.3 × 5 m)*. Both hatches can support a 60 ton tank. The tank deck side bulkheads extend 7.5 ft *(2.25 m)* above the upper deck between the forecastle and the forward end of the superstructure, and provide two hatch openings to the tank deck below. Positioned between the hatches is a two ton crane with athwartship travel.

NASR AL BAHR *10/1992, Hartmut Ehlers*

1 LANDING SHIP—LOGISTIC

Name	No	Builders	Commissioned
AL MUNASSIR	L 1	Brooke Marine, Lowestoft	31 Jan 1979

Displacement, tons: 2000
Dimensions, feet (metres): 276 × 49 × 7.3 *(84.1 × 14.9 × 2.3)*
Main machinery: 2 Mirrlees Blackstone ESL 8MGR diesels; 2440 hp *(1.82 MW)*; 2 shafts
Speed, knots: 12. **Range, miles:** 1000 at 12 kts
Complement: 45 (9 officers)
Military lift: 8 MBTs or 550 tons cargo; 188 troops; 2 Rotork LCPs
Radars: Navigation: Racal Decca TM 1229; I band.
Helicopters: Platform for 1 medium.

Comment: This ship is in reserve but is used for harbour training. Armament has been removed including the OTO Melara 76 mm gun.

AL MUNASSIR (disarmed) *10/1992, Hartmut Ehlers*

3 LCMs

Name	No	Builders	Commissioned
SABA AL BAHR	C 8	Vosper Private, Singapore	17 Sep 1981
AL DOGHAS	C 9	Vosper Private, Singapore	10 Jan 1983
AL TEMSAH	C 10	Vosper Private, Singapore	12 Feb 1983

Displacement, tons: 230 full load
Dimensions, feet (metres): 108.2 (83.6, C 8) × 24.3 × 4.3 *(33 (25.5) × 7.4 × 1.3)*
Main machinery: 2 Caterpillar 3408TA diesels; 1880 hp *(1.4 MW)* sustained; 2 shafts
Speed, knots: 8. **Range, miles:** 1400 at 8 kts
Complement: 11
Military lift: 100 tons

Comment: C 8 launched 30 June 1981. C 9 and C 10, similar but not identical ships, ordered 8 May 1982.

AL TEMSAH   *10/1992, Hartmut Ehlers*

2 LANDING CRAFT—UTILITY

Name	No	Builders	Commissioned
AL SANSOOR	C 4	Cheverton Ltd, Isle of Wight	Jan 1975
AL NEEMRAN	C 7	Lewis Offshore, Stornoway	1979

Displacement, tons: 130 full load (C 4)
Measurement, tons: 45 (C 4), 85 (C 7) dwt
Dimensions, feet (metres): 60 × 20 × 3.6 *(18.3 × 6.1 × 1.1)* (C 4)
  84 × 24 × 6 *(25.5 × 7.4 × 1.8)* (C 7)
Main machinery: 2 diesels; 300 hp *(220 kW)*; 2 shafts
Speed, knots: 7/8

Comment: *Al Sansoor* converted into a Tank Cleaning vessel in 1987 and strictly speaking is no longer an LCU.

AL SANSOOR   *1975, Roger Smith*

SUPPORT SHIPS

Notes: 1. There is a requirement for a 1500 ton Survey Ship similar to the British Roebuck class.
2. In addition to the listed vessels there are four 12 m Cheverton Workboats (W 41-W 44) and eight 8 m Workboats (W 4-W 11).

SUPPLY SHIP

Name	No	Builders	Commissioned
AL SULTANA	A 2	Conoship, Groningen	4 June 1975

Measurement, tons: 1380 dwt
Dimensions, feet (metres): 215.6 × 35 × 13.5 *(65.7 × 10.7 × 4.2)*
Main machinery: 1 Mirrlees Blackstone diesel; 1120 hp(m) *(835 kW)*; 1 shaft
Speed, knots: 11
Complement: 20

Comment: Major refit in 1992.

AL SULTANA   *1989, Royal Navy of Oman*

1 SURVEY CRAFT

AL RAHMANNIYA H 1

Displacement, tons: 23.6 full load
Dimensions, feet (metres): 50.8 × 13.1 × 4.3 *(15.5 × 4 × 1.3)*
Main machinery: 2 Volvo TMD120A diesels; 604 hp(m) *(444 kW)* sustained; 2 shafts
Speed, knots: 13.5. **Range, miles:** 500 at 12 kts

Comment: Built by Watercraft, Shoreham, England in 1980.

AL RAHMANNIYA   *1988, Royal Navy of Oman*

2 HARBOUR TUGS

T 2   T 3

Comment: Van Damen Pushy Cat 1500 type of 15 m acquired in 1990/91.

R 1   *10/1992, Hartmut Ehlers*

1 DIVING CRAFT

R 1

Comment: 13 m Rotork type acquired in 1991. Used as a diver's boat.

T 2   *10/1992, Hartmut Ehlers*

1 SAIL TRAINING SHIP

Name	No	Builders	Recommissioned
SHABAB OMAN (ex-*Captain Scott*)	S 1	Herd and Mackenzie, Buckie, Scotland	1979

Displacement, tons: 386
Dimensions, feet (metres): 144.3 × 27.9 × 15.1 *(44 × 8.5 × 4.6)*
Main machinery: 2 Caterpillar auxiliary diesels; 1 shaft
Complement: 20 (5 officers) plus 3 officers and 24 trainees

Comment: Topsail schooner taken over from Dulverton Trust in 1977 used for sail training for the young people of Oman.

SHABAB OMAN 12/1991, Giorgio Ghiglione

ROYAL YACHT SQUADRON

Note: There is also a Royal Dhow *Zinat Al Bihar*.

Name	No	Builders	Commissioned
AL SAID	—	Picchiotti SpA, Viareggio	1982

Displacement, tons: 3800 full load
Dimensions, feet (metres): 340.5 × 53.2 × 16.4 *(103.8 × 16.2 × 5)*
Main machinery: 2 GMT A 420.6 H diesels; 8400 hp(m) *(6.17 MW)* sustained; 2 shafts; cp props; bow thruster
Speed, knots: 18
Complement: 156 (16 officers)
Radars: Navigation: Decca TM 1226C; ACS 1230C; I band.

Comment: This ship is an independent command and not part of the Omani Navy. Fitted with helicopter deck and fin stabilisers. Carries three Puma C service launches and one Rotork beach landing craft.

AL SAID 1991, van Ginderen Collection

Name	No	Builders	Commissioned
FULK AL SALAMAH (ex-*Ghubat Al Salamah*)	L 3	Bremer-Vulkan	3 Apr 1987

Measurement, tons: 10 864 grt; 5186 net
Dimensions, feet (metres): 447.5 × 68.9 × 19.7 *(136.4 × 21 × 6)*
Main machinery: 4 Fincantieri GMT A 420.6 H diesels; 16 800 hp(m) *(12.35 MW)* sustained; 2 shafts
Speed, knots: 19.5
Helicopters: Up to 2 AS 332C Super Puma.

Comment: Support ship and transport with side doors for heavy loading. Part of the Royal Yacht Squadron.

FULK AL SALAMAH 8/1990, Maritime Photographic

ROYAL OMAN POLICE

Note: In addition to the vessels listed below there are several harbour craft including a Cheverton 8 m workboat *Zahra 24* and a fireboat pennant number 10.

3 CG 29 TYPE (COASTAL PATROL CRAFT)

HARAS VII   HARAS IX   HARAS X

Displacement, tons: 84
Dimensions, feet (metres): 94.8 × 17.7 × 4.3 *(28.9 × 5.4 × 1.3)*
Main machinery: 2 MTU 12V 331 TC92 diesels; 2660 hp(m) *(1.96 MW)* sustained; 2 shafts
Speed, knots: 25. **Range, miles:** 600 at 15 kts
Complement: 13
Guns: 2 Oerlikon 20 mm.

Comment: Built by Karlskrona Varvet. Commissioned in 1981-82. GRP Sandwich hulls.

HARAS X 10/1992, Hartmut Ehlers

1 P 1903 TYPE (COASTAL PATROL CRAFT)

HARAS VIII

Displacement, tons: 26
Dimensions, feet (metres): 63 × 15.7 × 5.2 *(19.2 × 4.8 × 1.6)*
Main machinery: 2 MTU 8V 331 TC92 diesels; 1770 hp(m) *(1.3 MW)*; 2 shafts
Speed, knots: 30. **Range, miles:** 1650 at 17 kts
Complement: 10
Guns: 2—12.7 mm MGs.

Comment: Built by Le Comte, Netherlands. Commissioned August 1981. Type 1903 Mk III.

HARAS VIII 10/1992, Hartmut Ehlers

1 CG 27 TYPE (COASTAL PATROL CRAFT)

HARAS VI

Displacement, tons: 53
Dimensions, feet (metres): 78.7 × 18 × 6.2 *(24 × 5.5 × 1.9)*
Main machinery: 2 MTU 12V 331 TC92 diesels; 2660 hp(m) *(1.96 MW)* sustained; 2 shafts
Speed, knots: 25
Complement: 11
Guns: 1 Oerlikon 20 mm.

Comment: Completed in 1980 by Karlskrona Varvet. GRP hull.

HARAS VI   *10/1992, Hartmut Ehlers*

5 VOSPER THORNYCROFT 75 ft TYPE (COASTAL PATROL CRAFT)

HARAS I-V

Displacement, tons: 50
Dimensions, feet (metres): 75 × 20 × 5.9 *(22.9 × 6.1 × 1.8)*
Main machinery: 2 Caterpillar D 348 diesels; 1450 hp *(1.08 MW)* sustained; 2 shafts
Speed, knots: 24.5. **Range, miles:** 600 at 20 kts; 1000 at 11 kts
Complement: 11
Guns: 1 Oerlikon 20 mm.

Comment: First four completed 22 December 1975 by Vosper Thornycroft. GRP hulls. *Haras V* commissioned November 1978.

HARAS II   *1984, N Overington*

1 P 2000 TYPE (COASTAL PATROL CRAFT)

DHEEB AL BAHAR I

Displacement, tons: 80
Dimensions, feet (metres): 68.2 × 19 × 5 *(20.8 × 5.8 × 1.5)*
Main machinery: 2 MTU 12V 396 TB93 diesels; 3260 hp(m) *(2.4 MW)* sustained; 2 shafts
Speed, knots: 40. **Range, miles:** 423 at 36 kts; 700 at 18 kts
Guns: 1—12.7 mm MG.
Radars: Surface search: Furuno 701; I band.

Comment: Delivered January 1985 by Watercraft Ltd, Shoreham, England. GRP hull. Carries SATNAV.

DHEEB AL BAHAR I (with *Dheeb Al Bahar II*)   *10/1992, Hartmut Ehlers*

2 D 59116 TYPE (COASTAL PATROL CRAFT)

DHEEB AL BAHAR II and III

Displacement, tons: 65
Dimensions, feet (metres): 75.5 × 17.1 × 3.9 *(23 × 5.2 × 1.2)*
Main machinery: 2 MTU 12V 396 TB93 diesels; 3260 hp(m) *(2.4 MW)* sustained; 2 shafts
Speed, knots: 36. **Range, miles:** 420 at 30 kts
Complement: 11
Guns: 1—12.7 mm MG.
Radars: Surface search: Furuno 711-2; Furuno 2400; I band.

Comment: Built by Yokohama Yacht Co, Japan. Commissioned in 1988.

DHEEB AL BAHAR II   *1988, Royal Oman Police*

3 WATERCRAFT TYPE and 2 EMSWORTH TYPE
(INSHORE PATROL CRAFT)

ZAHRA 14   ZAHRA 15   ZAHRA 17   ZAHRA 18   ZAHRA 21

Displacement, tons: 16; 18 (*Zahra 18* and *21*)
Dimensions, feet (metres): 45.6 × 14.1 × 4.6 *(13.9 × 4.3 × 1.4)*
    52.5 × 13.8 × 7.5 *(16 × 4.2 × 2.3)* (*Zahra 18* and *21*)
Main machinery: 2 Cummins VTA-903M diesels; 643 hp *(480 kW)*; 2 shafts
Speed, knots: 36. **Range, miles:** 510 at 22 kts
Complement: 5-6
Guns: 1 or 2—7.62 mm MGs.

Comment: *Zahra 14*, *15* and *17* built by Watercraft, Shoreham, England and completed in 1981. *Zahra 18* and *21* completed by Emsworth S B in 1987 to a different design.

ZAHRA 14 and 17   *10/1992, Hartmut Ehlers*

ZAHRA 18   *10/1992, Hartmut Ehlers*

4 LOGISTICS SUPPORT CRAFT

ZAHRA 16   ZAHRA 20   ZAHRA 22   ZAHRA 27

Displacement, tons: 13; 12 (*Zahra 20* and *22*)
Dimensions, feet (metres): 59 × 12.4 × 3.6 *(18 × 3.8 × 1.1)*
    52.5 × 12.5 × 3.6 *(16 × 3.8 × 1.1)* (*Zahra 20* and *22*)
Main machinery: 2 Volvo Penta AQD70D diesels; 430 hp(m) *(316 kW)* sustained; 2 shafts
Speed, knots: 20
Complement: 4
Guns: 2—7.62 mm MGs.

Comment: *Zahra 20* and *22* built by Le Comte, Netherlands. Commissioned 1981-82. Designed as landing craft. *Zahra 16* and *27* are Rotork types.

ZAHRA 20   10/1992, *Hartmut Ehlers*   ZAHRA 27   10/1992, *Hartmut Ehlers*

PAKISTAN

Headquarters' Appointments

Chief of the Naval Staff:
    Admiral Saeed M Khan, HI(M), S Bt
Vice Chief of Naval Staff:
    Vice Admiral Syed Iqtidar Hussain, HI(M), S Bt

Flag Officers

Commander, Karachi:
    Vice Admiral Khalid Mir, S Bt
Commander Pakistan Fleet:
    Rear Admiral Abaidullah Khan, SJ, SI(M)

Diplomatic Representation

Naval Adviser in London:
    Commodore M Jamil Akhtar, T Bt
Naval Attaché in Paris:
    Captain S T Naqvi
Naval Attaché in Washington:
    Captain Obaid Sadiq

Personnel

(a) 1993: 22 000 (2200 officers) including 743 (63 officers) seconded to the MSA
(b) Voluntary service

Bases

Karachi, Gwadar (shore base), Port Qasim

Prefix to Ships' Names

PNS

Maritime Security Agency

Set up in 1986 with four Shanghai II class and Fokker reconnaissance aircraft as its assets. Personnel in 1993: 743 (63 officers). Main purpose is to patrol the EEZ in co-operation with the Navy and the Army-manned Coast Guard. The obsolete destroyer *Badr* has been replaced as the HQ ship by *Nazim* (ex-*Tariq*), and Chinese-built Barkat class patrol craft have replaced the Shanghai IIs. A Norman Defender aircraft acquired in early 1993.

Marines

A Marine Commando Unit of about 150 men was formed at PNS Qasim, Karachi in 1991.

Strength of the Fleet

Type	Active (reserve)	Building
Submarines—Patrol	6	(3)
Submarines—40 tons	3	—
Destroyers	5 (1)	—
Frigates	10	—
Fast Attack Craft—Missile	8	—
Fast Attack Craft—Gun	9 (3)	—
Large Patrol Craft	1	—
Minehunters	1	2
Minesweepers—Coastal	2	—
Survey Vessel	1	—
Tankers	4	—
Tugs	8	—
Repair Ship	1	—
Auxiliaries	7	—
Customs Service	22	—
Coast Guard	5	—
Maritime Security Agency		
Destroyers	1	—
Large Patrol Craft	6	1

Mercantile Marine

Lloyd's Register of Shipping:
    73 vessels of 363 010 tons gross

DELETIONS

Destroyers

1992   *Shahjahan* (reserve)

Light Forces

1992   *HDF 01-04* (sold), *Lahore* (reserve), *Baluchistan* (reserve), *Kalat* (reserve)

Minesweepers

1992   *Mukhtar*

Auxiliaries

1991   *Bholu* (old), *Gama* (old)

Maritime Security Agency

1990   *Quetta, Sehwan*
1991   *Larkana, Sahiwal*

PENNANT LIST

Submarines

S 131	Hangor
S 132	Shushuk
S 133	Mangro
S 134	Ghazi
S 135	Hashmat
S 136	Hurmat

Destroyers

C 84	Babur
D 160	Alamgir
D 166	Taimur
D 167	Tughril
D 168	Tippu Sultan

Frigates

F 159	Tabuk
F 161	Badr
F 163	Khaibar
F 169	Hunain
F 262	Zulfiquar
F 263	Shamsher
F 264	Saif
F 265	Aslat
F 266	Harbah
F 267	Siqqat

Minesweepers

M 166	Munsif
M 167	Muhafiz (bldg)
M 160	Mahmood
M 164	Mujahid

Light Forces

P 140	Rajshahi
P 143	Mardan
P 144	Gilgit
P 145	Pishin
P 147	Sukkur
P 149	Bahawalpur
P 154	Bannu
P 159	Sind
P 161	Sarhad
P 197	Punjab
P 301-304	Huangfen class
P 1021	Haibat
P 1022	Jalalat
P 1023	Jurat
P 1024	Shujaat

Maritime Security Agency

D 156	Nazim
1060	Barkat
1061	Rehmat
1062	Nusrat
1063	Vehdat
1064	Sabqat
1065	Rafaqat

Service Forces

A 20	Moawin
A 21	Kalmat
A 40	Attock
A 41	Dacca
A 42	Madadgar
A 44	Bholu
A 45	Gama
A 46	Zum Zum
A 47	Nasr
A 49	Gwadar
A 260	Orwell

SUBMARINES

Note: Reported that an interest has been shown in acquiring a Chinese Han class SSN.

2 + (3) FRENCH AGOSTA CLASS

Name	No	Builders	Laid down	Launched	Commissioned
HASHMAT (ex-SAS *Astrant*)	S 135	Dubigeon Normandie, Nantes	15 Sep 1976	14 Dec 1977	17 Feb 1979
HURMAT (ex-SAS *Adventurous*)	S 136	Dubigeon Normandie, Nantes	18 Sep 1977	1 Dec 1978	18 Feb 1980

Displacement, tons: 1230 standard; 1490 surfaced; 1740 dived
Dimensions, feet (metres): 221.7 × 22.3 × 17.7 *(67.6 × 6.8 × 5.4)*
Main machinery: Diesel-electric; 2 SEMT-Pielstick 16 PA4 V 185 VG diesels; 3600 hp(m) *(2.65 MW)*; 2 Jeumont Schneider alternators; 1.7 MW; 1 motor; 4600 hp(m) *(3.4 MW)*; 1 cruising motor; 32 hp(m) *(23 kW)*; 1 shaft
Speed, knots: 12 surfaced; 20 dived
Range, miles: 8500 at 9 kts snorting; 350 at 3.5 kts dived
Complement: 54 (7 officers)

Missiles: SSM: McDonnell Douglas Sub Harpoon; active radar homing to 130 km *(70 nm)* at 0.9 Mach; warhead 227 kg.
Torpedoes: 4—21 in *(533 mm)* bow tubes. Up to 20 ECAN F17P; wire-guided; active/passive homing to 20 km *(10.8 nm)* at 40 kts; warhead 250 kg; water ram discharge gear.
Mines: Stonefish.
Countermeasures: ESM: ARUD; intercept and warning.
Radars: Surface search: Thomson-CSF DRUA 33; I band.
Sonars: Thomson Sintra DSUV 2H; passive search; medium frequency.
 DUUA 2A/2B; active/passive search and attack; 8 kHz active.
 DUUX 2A; hull-mounted; passive ranging.
 DUUA 1D; active; high frequency.

Programmes: Purchased in mid-1978 after United Nations' ban on arms sales to South Africa. *Hashmat* arrived Karachi 31 October 1979, *Hurmat* arrived 11 August 1980. A provisional order for three more of the class was reported in September 1992. If confirmed they will start entering service when released by the French Navy.
Structure: Diving depth, 300 m *(985 ft)*. Probably equipped with SSM in 1985 although there is some doubt about this.
Operational: Endurance, 45 days.

HASHMAT *1990, G Jacobs*

4 FRENCH DAPHNE CLASS

Name	No	Builders	Laid down	Launched	Commissioned
HANGOR	S 131	Arsenal de Brest	1 Dec 1967	28 June 1969	12 Jan 1970
SHUSHUK	S 132	C N Ciotat, Le Trait	1 Dec 1967	30 July 1969	12 Jan 1970
MANGRO	S 133	C N Ciotat, Le Trait	8 July 1968	7 Feb 1970	8 Aug 1970
GHAZI (ex-*Cachalote*)	S 134	Dubigeon, Normandie, Nantes	12 May 1967	23 Sep 1968	1 Oct 1969

Displacement, tons: 700 standard; 869 surfaced; 1043 dived
Dimensions, feet (metres): 189.6 × 22.3 × 15.1 *(57.8 × 6.8 × 4.6)*
Main machinery: Diesel-electric; 2 SEMT-Pielstick 12 PA4 V 185 diesels; 2450 hp(m) *(1.8 MW)*; 2 Jeumont Schneider alternators; 1.7 MW; 2 motors; 2600 hp(m) *(1.9 MW)*; 2 shafts
Speed, knots: 13 surfaced; 15.5 dived
Range, miles: 4500 at 5 kts
Complement: 45 (5 officers)

Missiles: SSM: McDonnell Douglas Sub Harpoon; active radar homing to 130 km *(70 nm)* at 0.9 Mach; warhead 227 kg.
Torpedoes: 12—21.7 in *(550 mm)* (8 bow, 4 stern). Probably 12 ECAN L5 Mod 3; dual purpose; active/passive homing to 9.5 km *(5.1 nm)* at 35 kts; warhead 150 kg; depth to 550 m *(1800 ft)*. No reloads.
Mines: Stonefish.
Countermeasures: ESM: ARUD; intercept and warning.
Radars: Surface search: Thomson-CSF DRUA 31; I band.
Sonars: Thomson Sintra DSUV 1; hull-mounted; passive search; medium frequency.
 DUUA 1; active/passive search and attack.

Programmes: The first three are the first submarines built for the Pakistan Navy. The Portuguese Daphne class *Cachalote* was bought by Pakistan in December 1975.
Structure: They are broadly similar to the submarines built in France for Portugal and South Africa and the submarines constructed to the Daphne design in Spain, but slightly modified internally to suit Pakistan requirements and naval conditions. Diving depth 300 m *(985 ft)*. SSM capability added in late 1980s.
Operational: *Hangor* in collision in September 1990 and badly damaged but back in service in 1992.

GHAZI *10/1991, G Jacobs*

3 MIDGET SUBMARINES

Displacement, tons: 40 surfaced; 70 dived
Dimensions, feet (metres): 75.5 × 13.1 *(23 × 4)*
Speed, knots: 11 surfaced; 6 dived
Range, miles: 1200 surfaced; 60 dived
Complement: 4

Comment: These are SX 756 of Italian Cosmos design and have replaced the SX 404 which were acquired in 1972. Diving depth of 100 m and can carry eight swimmers with two tons of explosives as well as two SDVs (swimmer delivery vehicles). Similar to the type in service in Colombia.

MIDGET SUBMARINE (Italian design) *10/1990, Hartmut Ehlers*

DESTROYERS

1 Ex-BRITISH COUNTY CLASS

Name	No	Builders	Laid down	Launched	Commissioned
BABUR (ex-HMS *London*)	C 84	Swan Hunter & Wigham Richardson, Wallsend	26 Feb 1960	7 Dec 1961	4 Nov 1963

Displacement, tons: 5440 standard; 6200 full load
Dimensions, feet (metres): 520.5 × 54 × 20.5 *(158.7 × 16.5 × 6.3)*
Main machinery: COSAG; 2 Babcock & Wilcox boilers; 700 psi *(49.2 kg/cm sq)*; 950°F *(510°C)*; 2 AEI turbines; 30 000 hp *(22.4 MW)*; 4 English Electric G6 gas turbines; 30 000 hp *(22.4 MW)*; 2 shafts
Speed, knots: 30
Complement: 470 (36 officers)

Missiles: SAM: 2 Short Bros Seacat GWS 22 quad launchers ❶; non-operational.
Guns: 4 Vickers 4.5 in *(114 mm)*/45 (2 twin) Mk 6 ❷; 80° elevation; 20 rounds/minute to 19 km *(10.4 nm)* anti-surface; 6 km *(3.3 nm)* anti-aircraft; weight of shell 25 kg.
  6 China 37 mm/63 (3 twin) ❸; 85° elevation; 180 rounds/minute to 8.5 km *(4.6 nm)*; weight of shell 1.42 kg.
  1 GE/GD 20 mm 6-barrelled Vulcan Phalanx Mk 15 ❹; 3000 rounds/minute combined to 1.5 km.
  8 ZSU 23 mm (2 quad) ❺; anti-aircraft.
Countermeasures: Decoys: 2 Knebworth Corvus 8-tubed trainable ❻; distraction or centroid chaff to 1 km.
  ESM/ECM: Argo APECS II includes AR 700 intercept plus jammer.
Fire control: MRS 3 for 4.5 in guns. SATCOM.
Radars: Air search: Marconi Type 965M (AKE-1 single aerial) ❼; A band.
  Admiralty Type 277M ❽; E band.
  Air/surface search: Marconi Type 992Q ❾; E/F band.
  Navigation: Decca 978; I band.
  Fire control: Sperry/Plessey Type 903 ❿; I band (for 4.5 in guns).
Sonars: Graseby Type 177; hull-mounted; active search and attack; 7-9 kHz.
  Type 176; passive search and torpedo warning.
  Type 162; active classification and attack.

Helicopters: 1 or 2 Sea King Mk 45 ⓫.

Programmes: Transferred after refit 24 March 1982 and sailed for Pakistan May 1982. Officially classed as a cruiser.
Modernisation: Seaslug removed in 1984 and the spaces converted into accommodation and classrooms for trainees. In 1988 the flight deck was extended aft and hangar enlarged to carry Sea King helicopters. At the same time two twin 37 mm guns replaced the Seacat directors (although the launchers remain in place) and a Vulcan Phalanx gun was fitted on the mounting once used by the 901 radar director. A third twin 37 mm is mounted on the quarterdeck and two quadruple 23 mm guns are on new sponsons at bridge level either side of the foremast. New EW equipment fitted.
Operational: Primarily used as the midshipmen training ship but

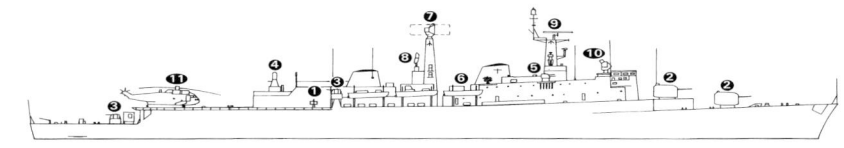

BABUR *(Scale 1 : 1500), Ian Sturton*

BABUR *1990, Pakistan Navy*

BABUR *8/1992, van Ginderen Collection*

BABUR *1991, Ships of the World*

Destroyers — Frigates / PAKISTAN   465

4 Ex-US GEARING (FRAM I) CLASS

Name	No	Builders	Laid down	Launched	Commissioned
ALAMGIR (ex-USS *Cone* DD 866)	D 160	Bethlehem, Staten Island	30 Nov 1944	10 May 1945	18 Aug 1945
TAIMUR (ex-USS *Epperson* DD 719)	D 166	Todd Pacific Shipyards	20 June 1945	29 Dec 1945	19 Mar 1949
TUGHRIL (ex-USS *Henderson* DD 785)	D 167	Todd Pacific Shipyards	27 Oct 1944	28 May 1945	4 Aug 1945
TIPPU SULTAN (ex-USS *Damato* DD 871)	D 168	Bethlehem, Staten Island	10 May 1945	21 Nov 1945	27 Apr 1946

Displacement, tons: 2425 standard; 3500 full load
Dimensions, feet (metres): 390.5 × 41.2 × 19 *(119 × 12.6 × 5.8)*
Main machinery: 4 Babcock & Wilcox boilers; 600 psi *(43.3 kg/cm sq)*; 850°F *(454°C)*; 2 GE turbines; 60 000 hp *(45 MW)*; 2 shafts
Speed, knots: 32. **Range, miles:** 4500 at 16 kts
Complement: 274 (27 officers)

Missiles: SSM: 6 McDonnell Douglas Harpoon (3 twin) launchers (not in D 168) ❶; active radar homing to 130 km *(70 nm)* at 0.9 Mach; warhead 227 kg.
A/S: Honeywell ASROC Mk 112 octuple launcher ❷; 8 reloads; inertial guidance to 1.6-10 km *(1-5.4 nm)*; payload Mk 46 torpedo.
Guns: 2 or 4 (D 168) US 5 in *(127 mm)*/38 (twin) Mk 38 ❸; 85° elevation; 15 rounds/minute to 17 km *(9.3 nm)* anti-surface; 11 km *(5.9 nm)* anti-aircraft; weight of shell 25 kg.
General Electric/General Dynamics 20 mm 6-barrelled Vulcan Phalanx Mk 15 ❹; 3000 rounds/minute combined to 1.5 km.
8—23 mm/87 (2 quad) ❺ (not in D 168).
Torpedoes: 6—324 mm US Mk 32 (2 triple) tubes ❻. Honeywell Mk 46; anti-submarine; active/passive homing to 11 km *(5.9 nm)* at 40 kts; warhead 44 kg.
Countermeasures: Decoys: 2 Plessey Shield 6-barrelled fixed launchers; chaff and IR flares in distraction, decoy or centroid modes.
ESM/ECM: Argo APECS II includes AR 700 intercept and jammer (not in D 168). WLR-1 (D 168).
Fire control: Mk 37 for 5 in guns. OE 2 SATCOM (not in D 168).
Radars: Air search: Lockheed SPS 40 ❼; E/F band; range 320 km *(175 nm)*.
Surface search: Raytheon/Sylvania ❽; SPS 10; G band.
Navigation: Racal Decca TM 1226; I band.
Fire control: Western Electric Mk 25 ❾; I/J band.
Sonars: Sangamo SQS 23D with Raytheon Solid State transmitters; hull-mounted; active search and attack; medium frequency.

Helicopters: Facilities for 1 SA 319B Alouette III seldom used ❿.

Programmes: First pair transferred 29 April 1977, second pair 30 September 1980. *Alamgir* on 1 October 1982.
Modernisation: *Alamgir*, *Taimur* and *Tughril* have all been modernised with Harpoon and Vulcan Phalanx fitted in place of Y gun turret, improved EW equipment and the addition of two 23 mm quadruple mountings at the base of the foremast.
Operational: Form 25 Destroyer Squadron. *Tughril* is able to launch Banshee target drones. *Tippu Sultan* is used as an alongside training ship. One of the class *Tariq* was converted to an MSA HQ ship in early 1990 (see MSA section). *Shahjahan* has been placed in 'reserve' and used to provide spares.

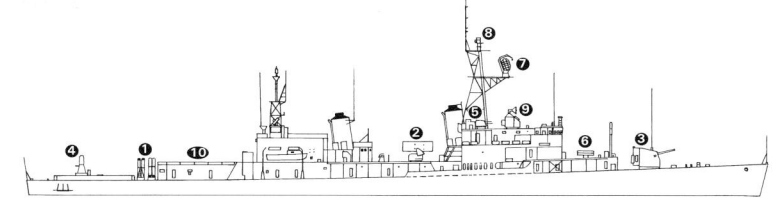

TUGHRIL   *(Scale 1 : 1200), Ian Sturton*

TUGHRIL   *10/1988, Gilbert Gyssels*

FRIGATES

Note: By early 1993 it appeared to be unlikely that any of the leases would be extended on the ex-US Brooke and Garcia class escorts, because of problems over the Pressler Amendment. It is probable that ex-British Type 21 and/or more Leander class will replace them.

2 Ex-BRITISH LEANDER CLASS

Name	No	Builders	Laid down	Launched	Commissioned
ZULFIQUAR (ex-HMS *Apollo*)	F 262	Yarrows, Glasgow	1 May 1969	15 Oct 1970	28 May 1972
SHAMSHER (ex-HMS *Diomede*)	F 263	Yarrows, Glasgow	30 Jan 1968	15 Apr 1969	2 Apr 1971

Displacement, tons: 2500 standard; 2962 full load
Dimensions, feet (metres): 360 wl; 372 oa × 43 × 14.8 (keel); 18 (screws) *(109.7; 113.4 × 13.1 × 4.5; 5.5)*
Main machinery: 2 Babcock & Wilcox boilers; 550 psi *(38.7 kg/cm sq)*; 850°F *(454°C)*; 2 White/English Electric turbines; 30 000 hp *(22.4 MW)*; 2 shafts
Speed, knots: 28. **Range, miles:** 4000 at 15 kts
Complement: 235 (15 officers)

Missiles: SAM: Short Bros Seacat GWS 22 quad launcher ❶; optical/radar guidance to 5 km *(2.7 nm)*; warhead 10 kg.
Guns: 2 Vickers 4.5 in *(114 mm)*/45 Mk 6 (twin) ❷; 80° elevation; 20 rounds/minute to 19 km *(10.3 nm)* anti-surface; 6 km *(3.3 nm)* anti-aircraft; weight of shell 25 kg.
2 Oerlikon 20 mm/70 ❸; 50° elevation; 800 rounds/minute to 2 km; weight of shell 0.24 kg.
1 Oerlikon/BMARC 20 mm GAM-BO1 (on after end of flight deck when fitted) ❹; 55° elevation; 1000 rounds/minute to 2 km.
A/S mortars: 3-barrelled UK MoD Mortar Mk 10 ❺; automatic loading; range 1 km; warhead 92 kg.
Countermeasures: Decoys: Graseby Type 182; towed torpedo decoy.
2 Vickers Corvus 8-barrelled trainable launchers ❻; chaff to 1 km.
ESM: UA-8/9/13; radar warning.
ECM: Type 668; jammer.
Fire control: MRS 3 system for 114 mm guns.
Radars: Air search: Marconi Type 966 ❼; A band; AKE-1; long range.
Surface search: Plessey Type 993 ❽; E/F band.
Navigation: Kelvin Hughes Type 1006; I band.
Fire control: Two Plessey Type 904 (for Seacat and 114 mm guns) ❾; I/J band.
Sonars: Kelvin Hughes Type 162M; hull-mounted; bottom classification; 50 kHz.
Graseby Type 170B; hull-mounted; active search and attack; 15 kHz.
Graseby Type 184P; hull-mounted; active search and attack; 6-9 kHz.

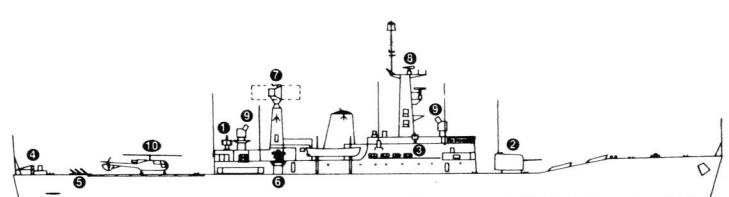

SHAMSHER   *(Scale 1 : 1200), Ian Sturton*

SHAMSHER   *10/1991, G Jacobs*

Helicopters: 1 SA 319B Alouette III ❿.

Programmes: Transferred 15 July 1988 (*Shamsher*) and 14 October 1988 (*Zulfiquar*). Both ships are from the Batch 3B broad-beamed group of this class.

Structure: No equipment changes made on transfer except the replacement of the Wasp helicopter by an Alouette III.
Operational: Both ships sailed for Pakistan in August and December 1988 respectively.

466 PAKISTAN / Frigates

4 Ex-US GARCIA CLASS

Name	No	Builders	Laid down	Launched	Commissioned
SAIF (ex-*Garcia*)	F 264 (ex-FF 1040)	Bethlehem Steel, San Francisco	16 Oct 1962	31 Oct 1963	21 Dec 1964
ASLAT (ex-*O'Callaghan*)	F 265 (ex-FF 1051)	Defoe Shipbuilding Co.	19 Feb 1964	20 Oct 1965	13 Jul 1968
HARBAH (ex-*Brumby*)	F 266 (ex-FF 1044)	Avondale Shipyard	1 Aug 1963	6 Jun 1964	5 Aug 1965
SIQQAT (ex-*Koelsch*)	F 267 (ex-FF 1049)	Defoe Shipbuilding Co.	19 Feb 1964	8 Jun 1965	10 Jun 1967

Displacement, tons: 2620 standard; 3403 full load
Dimensions, feet (metres): 414.5 × 44.2 × 24 sonar; 14.5 keel *(126.3 × 13.5 × 7.3; 4.4)*
Main machinery: 2 Foster-Wheeler boilers; 1200 psi *(83.4 kg/cm sq)*; 950°F *(510°C)*; 1 GE/Westinghouse turbine; 35 000 hp *(26 MW)*; 1 shaft
Speed, knots: 27.5. **Range, miles:** 4000 at 20 kts
Complement: 270 (18 officers)

Missiles: A/S: Honeywell ASROC Mk 116 octuple launcher ❶; inertial flight to 1.6-10 km *(1-5.5 nm)*: payload Mk 46 torpedo. *Aslat* and *Siqqat* have reload magazines.
Guns: 2 USN 5 in *(127 mm)*/38 Mk 30 ❷; 85° elevation; 15 rounds/minute to 17 km *(9.3 nm)*; weight of shell 25 kg.
Torpedoes: 6—324 mm Mk 32 (2 triple) tubes ❸; 14 Honeywell Mk 46; active/passive homing to 11 km *(6 nm)* at 40 kts; warhead 44 kg.
Countermeasures: Decoys: 2 Loral Hycor Mk 33 RBOC 6-barrelled chaff launchers. T-Mk 6 Fanfare; torpedo decoy system. Prairie/Masker hull noise/blade rate suppression.
ESM: WLR-6, radar warning.
ECM: ULQ-6, jammer.
Fire control: Mk 56 GFCS. Mk 114 ASW FCS. Mk 1 target designation system.
Radars: Air search: Lockheed SPS 40 ❹; E/F band; range 320 km *(175 nm)*.
Surface search: Raytheon SPS 10 ❺; G band.
Navigation: Marconi LN 66; I band.
Fire control: General Electric Mk 35 ❻; I/J band.
Tacan: SRN 15.
Sonars: EDO/General Electric SQS 26; bow-mounted; active search and attack; medium frequency.

Helicopters: Lamps I capable ❼.

Programmes: Four frigates leased from the US. *Saif* transferred 31 January 1989; *Aslat* 8 February 1989; *Harbah* 31 March 1989 and *Siqqat* on 31 May 1989. All arrived in Pakistan by the end of July 1989.
Operational: These ships are being paid off as the leases expire in 1993/94.

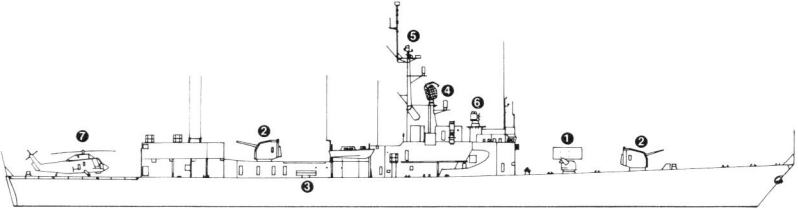

SAIF *(Scale 1 : 1200), Ian Sturton*

SAIF *8/1992, van Ginderen Collection*

SIQQAT *10/1991, G Jacobs*

SAIF *1990, Pakistan Navy*

Frigates — Land-based maritime aircraft / PAKISTAN

4 Ex-US BROOKE CLASS

Name	No	Builders	Laid down	Launched	Commissioned
BADR (ex-*Julius A Furer*)	F 161 (ex-FFG 6)	Bath Iron Works, Maine	12 Jul 1965	22 Jul 1966	11 Nov 1967
KHAIBAR (ex-*Brooke*)	F 163 (ex-FFG 1)	Lockheed Shipbuilding	10 Dec 1962	19 Jul 1963	3 Jun 1967
TABUK (ex-*Richard L Page*)	F 159 (ex-FFG 5)	Bath Iron Works, Maine	4 Jan 1965	4 Apr 1966	5 Aug 1967
HUNAIN (ex-*Talbot*)	F 169 (ex-FFG 4)	Bath Iron Works, Maine	4 May 1964	6 Jan 1966	22 Apr 1967

Displacement, tons: 2640 standard; 3426 full load
Dimensions, feet (metres): 414.5 × 44.2 × 24.2 sonar; 15 keel *(126.3 × 13.5 × 7.4; 4.6)*
Main machinery: 2 Foster-Wheeler boilers; 1200 psi *(83.4 kg/cm sq)*; 950°F *(510°C)*; 1 GE/Westinghouse turbine; 35 000 hp *(26 MW)*; 1 shaft
Speed, knots: 27.2. **Range, miles:** 4000 at 20 kts
Complement: 277 (17 officers)

Missiles: SAM: 16 GDC Standard MR-SM1 Block IV; Mk 22 Mod 0 launcher ❶; semi-active radar homing to 46 km *(25 nm)* at 2 Mach; height envelope 45.7-18 288 m *(150-60 000 ft)*.
A/S: Honeywell ASROC; Mk 116 octuple launcher ❷; inertial flight to 1.6-10 km *(1-5.5 nm)*; payload Mk 46 torpedo. All except *Harbah* have a reload magazine.
Guns: 1 USN 5 in *(127 mm)*/38 Mk 30 ❸; 85° elevation; 15 rounds/minute to 17 km *(9.3 nm)*; weight of shell 25 kg.
1 GE/GD 20 mm 6-barrelled Vulcan Phalanx Mk 15 (*Badr, Tabuk*).
Torpedoes: 6—324 mm Mk 32 (2 triple) tubes ❹. 14 Honeywell Mk 46; active/passive homing to 11 km *(6 nm)* at 40 kts; warhead 44 kg.
Countermeasures: Decoys: 4 Loral Hycor SRBOC 6-barrelled fixed Mk 36; IR flares and chaff to 4 km *(2.2 nm)*.
ESM/ECM: WLR-6, ULQ-6; radar warning and jammers.
Fire control: Mk 74 Mod 6 MFCS. Mk 56 Mod 43 GFCS. Mk 114 ASW FCS. Mk 4 Mod 2 weapon direction system.
Radars: Air search: Hughes SPS 52 ❺; 3D; E/F band; range 439 km *(240 nm)*.
Surface search: Raytheon SPS 10 ❻; G band.
Navigation: Marconi LN 66; I band.
Fire control: Raytheon SPG 51C ❼; G/I band (for SAM).
General Electric Mk 35 ❽; I/J band (for gun).
Tacan: SRN 15.
Sonars: EDO/General Electric SQS 26; bow-mounted; active search and attack; medium frequency.

Helicopters: Lamps I capable ❾.

Programmes: Four frigates leased from the US. Classified as Destroyers in the Pakistan Navy. *Badr* transferred 31 January 1989; *Khaibar* 8 February 1989; *Tabuk* 31 March 1989 and *Hunain* on 31 May 1989. All arrived in Pakistan by the end of July 1989.
Structure: Identical to ex-Garcia class except for the SAM missile system which replaced the second 5 in gun and different electronic equipment. The helicopter hangar is telescopic. *Tabuk* and *Badr* has a Vulcan Phalanx CIWS mounted on their flight decks.
Operational: These ships are being paid off as the leases expire

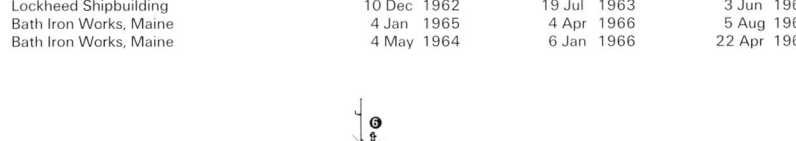
HARBAH *(Scale 1 : 1200), Ian Sturton*

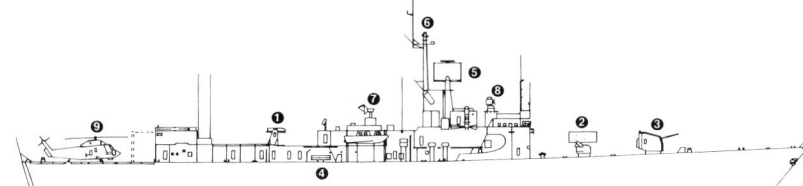
BADR (with Phalanx) *1990, Pakistan Navy*

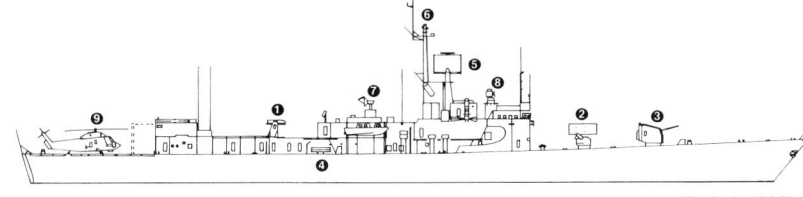
TABUK *1990, Pakistan Navy*

SHIPBORNE AIRCRAFT

Note: It is unlikely that Seasprite helicopters will be acquired. Alternatives include Lynx and Dauphin.

Numbers/Type: 4 Aerospatiale SA 319B Alouette III.
Operational speed: 113 kts *(210 km/h)*.
Service ceiling: 10 500 ft *(3200 m)*.
Range: 290 nm *(540 km)*.
Role/Weapon systems: Reconnaissance helicopter; one embarked in County class DLG and can be carried in the Frigates for reconnaissance, support and SAR. Sensors: Weather/search radar. Weapons: Generally unarmed.

SEA KING *1990, Pakistan Navy*

ALOUETTE III *1988*

Numbers/Type: 6 Westland Sea King Mk 45.
Operational speed: 125 kts *(232 km/h)*.
Service ceiling: 10 500 ft *(3200 m)*.
Range: 630 nm *(1165 km)*.
Role/Weapon systems: ASVW helicopter with all ASW gear removed. Sensors: MEL search radar. Weapons: ASW; none. ASV; 1 × AM 39 Exocet missile.

LAND-BASED MARITIME AIRCRAFT

Numbers/Type: 4 Breguet Atlantic 1.
Operational speed: 355 kts *(658 km/h)*.
Service ceiling: 32 800 ft *(10 000 m)*.
Range: 4855 nm *(8995 km)*.
Role/Weapon systems: Long-range MR/ASW cover for Arabian Sea; ex-French stock. Upgraded in 1992/93. Sensors: Thomson-CSF radar, ECM/ESM, MAD, sonobuoys. Weapons: ASW; 9 × Mk 46 or 244/S torpedoes, depth bombs, mines. ASV; 2 × AS 12 or AM 39 Exocet missiles.

Numbers/Type: (3) Lockheed P-3C Orion.
Operational speed: 410 kts *(760 km/h)*.
Service ceiling: 28 300 ft *(8625 m)*.
Range: 4000 nm *(7410 km)*.
Role/Weapon systems: Maritime reconnaissance aircraft ordered under US FMS policy for delivery by May 1991 but embargoed under the Pressler Amendment. Sensors and weapons to include Proteus acoustic processor and possibly air-launched Harpoon.

Numbers/Type: 5 AMD-BA Mirage 5.
Operational speed: 750 kts *(1390 km/h)*.
Service ceiling: 59 055 ft *(18 000 m)*.
Range: 740 nm *(1370 km)*.
Role/Weapon systems: Maritime strike aircraft operated by the Air Force. Sensors: Thomson-CSF radar. Weapons: ASVW; 2 × AM 39 Exocet; 2 × 30 mm DEFA.

Numbers/Type: 3 Fokker F27 MPA Friendship.
Operational speed: 250 kts *(463 km/h)*.
Service ceiling: 25 000 ft *(7620 m)*.
Range: 2700 nm *(5000 km)*.
Role/Weapon systems: Visual reconnaissance and coastal surveillance aircraft (ex-Airline) used by the Maritime Security Agency. Possibly one more to come. Sensors: Weather radar and visual means only. Weapons: Limited armament.

LIGHT FORCES

4 Ex-CHINESE HUANGFEN CLASS
(FAST ATTACK CRAFT—MISSILE)

P 301-P 304 (ex-*1025-1028*)

Displacement, tons: 171 standard; 205 full load
Dimensions, feet (metres): 110.2 × 24.9 × 8.9 *(33.6 × 7.6 × 2.7)*
Main machinery: 3 Type M 503 diesels; 8025 hp(m) *(5.4 MW)* sustained; 3 shafts
Speed, knots: 35. **Range, miles:** 800 at 30 kts
Complement: 28
Missiles: SSM: 4 Hai Ying 2 (C 201); active radar or IR homing to 95 km *(51 nm)* at 0.9 Mach; warhead 513 kg.
Guns: 4 Norinco 25 mm/80 (2 twin); 85° elevation; 270 rounds/minute to 3 km *(1.6 nm)*; weight of shell 0.34 kg.
Radars: Surface search/target indication: Square Tie; I band.

Comment: Transferred April 1984. Chinese version of the Soviet Osa II class.

P 303 (old number) *1989, Pakistan Navy*

4 Ex-CHINESE HEGU CLASS (FAST ATTACK CRAFT—MISSILE)

| HAIBAT P 1021 | JALALAT P 1022 | JURAT P 1023 | SHUJAAT P 1024 |

Displacement, tons: 68 standard; 79.2 full load
Dimensions, feet (metres): 88.6 × 20.7 × 4.3 *(27 × 6.3 × 1.3)*
Main machinery: 4 Type L-12V-180 diesels; 4800 hp(m) *(3.53 MW)*; 4 shafts
Speed, knots: 37.5. **Range, miles:** 400 at 30 kts
Complement: 17
Missiles: SSM: 2 SY 1; active radar or IR homing to 45 km *(24.3 nm)* at 0.9 Mach; warhead 513 kg.
Guns: 2 Norinco 25 mm/80 (twin); 85° elevation; 270 rounds/minute to 3 km *(1.6 nm)*; weight of shell 0.34 kg.
Radars: Surface search: Pot Head; I band.

Comment: Two transferred in May and two in October 1981. Steel hull version of Komar class.

JALALAT *1992, Pakistan Navy*

3 Ex-CHINESE HAINAN CLASS (FAST ATTACK CRAFT—GUN)

| SIND P 159 | SARHAD P 161 | PUNJAB P 197 |

Displacement, tons: 375 standard; 392 full load
Dimensions, feet (metres): 192.8 × 23.6 × 6 *(58.8 × 7.2 × 2.2)*
Main machinery: 4 PCR/Kolomna Type 9-D-8 diesels; 4000 hp(m) *(2.94 MW)* sustained; 4 shafts
Speed, knots: 30.5. **Range, miles:** 1300 at 15 kts
Complement: 70
Guns: 4 Norinco 57 mm/70 (2 twin); 85° elevation; 120 rounds/minute to 12 km *(6.5 nm)*; weight of shell 6.3 kg.
4 Norinco 25 mm/80 (2 twin); 85° elevation; 270 rounds/minute to 3 km *(1.6 nm)*; weight of shell 0.34 kg.
A/S mortars: 4 RBU 1200 5-tubed fixed; range 1200 m; warhead 34 kg.
Depth charges: 2 projectors; 2 racks.
Mines: Rails fitted.
Radars: Surface search: Pot Head; I band.
Sonars: Hull-mounted; active attack; high frequency.

Comment: First pair transferred mid-1976, second pair in April 1980. *Baluchistan* P 155 in reserve and used for spares.

PUNJAB *1990, Pakistan Navy*

6 Ex-CHINESE SHANGHAI II CLASS
(FAST ATTACK CRAFT—GUN)

| MARDAN P 143 | PISHIN P 145 | BAHAWALPUR P 149 |
| GILGIT P 144 | SUKKUR P 147 | BANNU P 154 |

Displacement, tons: 113 standard; 131 full load
Dimensions, feet (metres): 127.3 × 17.7 × 5.6 *(38.8 × 5.4 × 1.7)*
Main machinery: 2 Type L12-180 diesels; 2400 hp(m) *(1.76 MW)* (forward); 2 Type 12-D-6 diesels; 1820 hp(m) *(1.34 MW)* (aft); 4 shafts
Speed, knots: 30. **Range, miles:** 700 at 16.5 kts
Complement: 34
Guns: 4—37 mm/63 (2 twin). 4—25 mm/80 (2 twin).
Depth charges: 2 projectors; 8 weapons.
Mines: Fitted with mine rails for approx 10 mines.
Radars: Surface search: Skin Head; I band.

Comment: Acquired between 1972 and 1976. Four were transferred to the Maritime Security Agency in 1986 and scrapped in 1990. *Lahore* P 142 and *Kalat* P 156 are in reserve and used for spares.

GILGIT *1990, Pakistan Navy*

1 TOWN CLASS (LARGE PATROL CRAFT)

Name	No	Builders	Commissioned
RAJSHAHI	P 140	Brooke Marine	1965

Displacement, tons: 115 standard; 143 full load
Dimensions, feet (metres): 107 × 20 × 6.9 *(32.6 × 6.1 × 2.1)*
Main machinery: 2 MTU 12V 538 diesels; 3400 hp(m) *(2.5 MW)*; 2 shafts
Speed, knots: 24
Complement: 19
Guns: 2 Bofors 40 mm/70.

Comment: The last survivor in Pakistan of a class of four built by Brooke Marine in 1965. Steel hull and aluminium superstructure.

RAJSHAHI *1989, Pakistan Navy*

MARITIME SECURITY AGENCY

Notes: (i) All ships are painted white with a distinctive diagonal blue band and MSA on each side.
(ii) One 200 ton patrol craft reported building at Karachi in 1992.

1 Ex-US GEARING (FRAM 1) CLASS

Name	No	Builders	Commissioned
NAZIM (ex-*Tariq*, ex-*Wiltsie*)	D 156 (ex-D 165, ex-DD 716)	Federal SB & DD Co	12 Jan 1946

Comment: Transferred from the Navy on 25 January 1990 and has replaced the old *Badr* as the MSA Flagship. All details as for the Gearing class (see *Destroyers*) except that ASROC and Torpedo Tubes have been removed and there is a quadruple 14.5 mm gun mounting on each side of the foremast.

NAZIM *1991, Ships of the World*

6 CHINESE BARKAT CLASS (LARGE PATROL CRAFT)

Name	No	Builders	Commissioned
BARKAT	1060 (ex-P 60)	China Shipbuilding Corp	29 Dec 1989
REHMAT	1061 (ex-P 61)	China Shipbuilding Corp	29 Dec 1989
NUSRAT	1062 (ex-P 62)	China Shipbuilding Corp	13 June 1990
VEHDAT	1063 (ex-P 63)	China Shipbuilding Corp	13 June 1990
SABQAT	1064	China Shipbuilding Corp	Apr 1992
RAFAQAT	1065	China Shipbuilding Corp	Apr 1992

Displacement, tons: 435 full load
Dimensions, feet (metres): 190.3 × 24.9 × 7.5 *(58 × 7.6 × 2.3)*
Main machinery: 4 MTU 16V 396 TB93 diesels; 8720 hp(m) *(6.4 MW)* sustained; 4 shafts
Speed, knots: 27. **Range, miles:** 1500 at 12 kts
Complement: 50 (5 officers)
Guns: 2—37 mm/63 (twin); 4—25 mm/80 (2 twin).
Radars: Surface search: 2 Fujitsu Ops 9; I band.

Comment: Type P58A patrol craft built in China for the MSA. First two arrived in Karachi at the end of January 1990, second pair in August 1990. Third pair reported in April 1992.

BARKAT (old number)   *1990, CSSC*

MINE WARFARE FORCES

Note: There are also five inshore vessels used for harbour MCM operations. Numbers MSI 01, 02, 06-08.

2 Ex-US MSC 268 CLASS (MINESWEEPERS—COASTAL)

MAHMOOD (ex-*MSC 267*) M 160   **MUJAHID** (ex-*MSC 261*) M 164

Displacement, tons: 330 light; 390 full load
Dimensions, feet (metres): 144 × 27.9 × 8.5 *(43.9 × 8.5 × 2.6)*
Main machinery: 2 GM 8-268A diesels; 880 hp *(656 kW)*; 2 shafts
Speed, knots: 13.5. **Range, miles:** 3000 at 10.5 kts
Complement: 39
Guns: 4 USSR 23 mm (quad) or 1 Oerlikon 20 mm.
Radars: Navigation: Decca 45; I band.

Comment: Transferred to Pakistan by the USA under MAP. *Mahmood* in May 1957, *Mujahid* in November 1956. *Mujahid* paid off in 1990 but back in service in 1992.

MAHMOOD   *1991, Pakistan Navy*

1 + 2 FRENCH ERIDAN CLASS (MINEHUNTERS)

Name	No	Builders	Commissioned
MUNSIF (ex-*Sagittaire*)	M 166	Lorient Dockyard	27 July 1989
MUHAFIZ	M 167	Lorient Dockyard	1995
—	M 168	Lorient/Karachi	1996

Displacement, tons: 562 standard; 595 full load
Dimensions, feet (metres): 168.9 × 29.2 × 8.2 *(51.5 × 8.9 × 2.5)*
Main machinery: 1 Brons Werkspoor A-RUB 215X-12 diesel; 1860 hp(m) *(1.37 MW)* sustained; 1 shaft; Lips cp prop; Auxiliary propulsion; 2 motors; 240 hp(m) *(179 kW)*; 2 active rudders; 2 bow thrusters
Speed, knots: 15; 7 on auxiliary propulsion. **Range, miles:** 3000 at 12 kts
Complement: 46 (5 officers)
Guns: 1 GIAT 20F2 20 mm; 1—12.7 mm MG.
Countermeasures: MCM; 2 PAP 104 Mk 5 systems; mechanical sweep gear. AP-4 acoustic sweep.
Radars: Navigation: Racal Decca 1229; I band.
Sonars: Thomson Sintra DUBM 21B; hull-mounted; active; high frequency; 100 kHz (±10 kHz). Thomson Sintra TSM 2054 MCM towed array may be included.

Comment: Contract signed 17 January 1992. The first recommissioned into the Pakistan Navy on 24 September 1992 after active service in the Gulf in 1991. Sailed for Pakistan in November 1992. The second is building at Lorient Dockyard and the third hull will be shipped to Karachi for fitting out.

MUNSIF   *9/1992, B Sullivan*

OCEANOGRAPHIC SHIP

BEHR PAIMA

Measurement, tons: 1183 gross
Dimensions, feet (metres): 200.1 × 38.7 × 12.1 *(61 × 11.8 × 3.7)*
Main machinery: 2 Daihatsu diesels; 2000 hp(m) *(1.47 MW)*; 2 shafts
Speed, knots: 13.7
Complement: 84 (16 officers)

Comment: Ordered from Ishikawajima, Japan in November 1981. Laid down 16 February 1982, completed 17 December 1982. There is a second survey ship *Jatli* under civilian control.

BEHR PAIMA   *1989, G Jacobs*

TANKERS

1 Ex-US MISSION CLASS (AOR)

Name	No	Builders	Commissioned
DACCA (ex-USNS *Mission Santa Cruz* AO 132)	A 41	Marinship Corp, California	21 June 1944

Displacement, tons: 5730 light; 22 380 full load
Dimensions, feet (metres): 524 × 68 × 31 *(159.7 × 20.7 × 9.5)*
Main machinery: Turbo-electric; 2 Babcock & Wilcox boilers; 600 psi *(42.3 kg/cm sq)*; 825°F *(440°C)*; 2 GE turbo generators; 10 000 hp(m) *(7.46 MW)*; 1 motor; 1 shaft
Speed, knots: 16
Complement: 160 (15 officers)
Cargo capacity: 20 000 tons fuel
Guns: 3 Bofors 40 mm/60.

Comment: Transferred on loan to Pakistan under MDAP. Handed over from the USA on 17 January 1963 after being fitted with underway replenishment rigs on both sides. Purchased 31 May 1974.

DACCA   *1990, Pakistan Navy*

470 PAKISTAN / Tankers — Auxiliaries

1 CHINESE FUQING CLASS (AOR)

Name	No	Builders	Commissioned
NASR (ex-X-350)	A 47	Dalian Shipyard	27 Aug 1987

Displacement, tons: 7500 standard; 21 750 full load
Dimensions, feet (metres): 561 × 71.5 × 30.8 *(171 × 21.8 × 9.4)*
Main machinery: 1 Sulzer 8RLB66 diesel; 13 000 hp(m) *(9.56 MW)*; 1 shaft
Speed, knots: 18. **Range, miles:** 18 000 at 14 kts
Complement: 130 (during visit to Australia in October 1988 carried 373 (23 officers) including 100 cadets)
Cargo capacity: 10 550 tons fuel; 1000 tons dieso; 200 tons feed water; 200 tons drinking water
Radars: Navigation: Two Decca 1006; I band.
Helicopters: 1 SA 319B Alouette III.

Comment: Similar to Chinese ships of the same class. Two replenishment at sea positions on each side for liquids and one for solids.

NASR   10/1988, G Toremans

2 HARBOUR TANKERS

Name	No	Builders	Commissioned
GWADAR	A 49	Karachi Shipyard	1984
KALMAT	A 21	Karachi Shipyard	29 Aug 1992

Displacement, tons: 831 gross
Dimensions, feet (metres): 206 × 37.1 × 9.8 *(62.8 × 11.3 × 3)*
Main machinery: 1 Sulzer diesel; 550 hp(m) *(404 kW)*; 1 shaft
Speed, knots: 10

Comment: Second of class launched 6 June 1991. One used for oil and one for water.

GWADAR   1987

TUGS

Note: There are three more general purpose tugs plus two harbour tugs *Goga* and *Jhara*.

1 Ex-US CHEROKEE CLASS

Name	No	Builders	Commissioned
MADADGAR (ex-USS *Yuma* ATF 94)	A 42	Commercial Iron Works, Portland, Oregon	31 Aug 1943

Displacement, tons: 1235 standard; 1640 full load
Dimensions, feet (metres): 205 × 38.5 × 17 *(62.5 × 11.7 × 5.2)*
Main machinery: Diesel-electric; 4 GM 12-278 diesels; 4400 hp *(3.28 MW)*; 4 generators; 1 motor; 3000 hp *(2.24 MW)*; 1 shaft
Speed, knots: 16.5. **Range, miles:** 6500 at 16 kts
Complement: 85
Guns: 2 Bofors 40 mm (aft). 1 Oerlikon 20 mm (fwd).
Radars: Navigation: Decca 45; I band.

Comment: Ocean-going salvage tug. Transferred from the US Navy to the Pakistan Navy on 25 March 1959 under MDAP. Fitted with powerful pumps and other salvage equipment. Used for MCMV support and submarine rescue.

MADADGAR   1989, G Jacobs

2 COASTAL TUGS

Name	No	Builders	Commissioned
BHOLU	A 44	Giessendam Shipyard, Netherlands	Apr 1991
GAMA	A 45	Giessendam Shipyard, Netherlands	Apr 1991

Displacement, tons: 265 full load
Dimensions, feet (metres): 85.3 × 22.3 × 9.5 *(26 × 6.8 × 2.9)*
Main machinery: 2 Cummins KTA38-M diesels; 1836 hp *(1.26 MW)* sustained; 2 shafts
Speed, knots: 12
Complement: 6

Comment: Ordered from Damen in 1990. Have replaced the two old tugs of the same name and pennant numbers.

BHOLU   1991, Pakistan Navy

AUXILIARIES

1 AJAX CLASS (REPAIR SHIP)

Name	No	Builders	Commissioned
MOAWIN (ex-USS *Hector*)	A 20 (ex-AR 7)	Todd Shipyards, Los Angeles	7 Feb 1944

Displacement, tons: 9140 standard; 16 245 full load
Dimensions, feet (metres): 529.3 × 73.3 × 23.3 *(161.3 × 22.3 × 7.1)*
Main machinery: 4 Babcock & Wilcox boilers; 2 Allis-Chalmers turbines; 11 000 hp *(8.2 MW)*; 2 shafts
Speed, knots: 19.2. **Range, miles:** 18 000 at 12 kts
Complement: 841 (29 officers)
Guns: 4 Oerlikon 20 mm Mk 67.
Radars: Surface search: Raytheon SPS 10 series; G band.

Comment: Ex-US repair ship transferred 20 April 1989 and modernised at Subic Bay, Philippines. Should have recommissioned on 20 January 1990 but this was probably delayed until April 1990. May be moored permanently.

MOAWIN (with *Taimur* alongside)   8/1992, van Ginderen Collection

2 UTILITY CRAFT

427   428

Measurement, tons: 57 gross
Dimensions, feet (metres): 65.6 × 16.4 × 4.9 *(20 × 5 × 1.5)*
Main machinery: 2 Detroit 8V-71TI diesels; 1360 hp *(1 MW)*; 2 shafts
Speed, knots: 12

Comment: Built by Karachi Shipyard and completed in 1991.

1 SUPPLY TENDER

ORWELL   A 260

Comment: Patrol craft, supply tender and berthing hulk based at Gwadar.

2 WATER BARGES

ZUM ZUM A 46   ATTOCK A 40

Displacement, tons: 1200 full load
Dimensions, feet (metres): 177.2 × 32.3 × 15.1 *(54 × 9.8 × 4.6)*
Main machinery: 2 diesels; 800 hp(m) *(276 kW)*; 2 shafts
Speed, knots: 8
Cargo capacity: 550 tons
Guns: 2 Oerlikon 20 mm.

Comment: Built in Italy in 1957 under MDAP.

ATTOCK   1990

1 DEGAUSSING VESSEL

Displacement, tons: 250
Dimensions, feet (metres): 115.5 × 23 × 7.9 *(35.2 × 7 × 2.4)*
Main machinery: 1 diesel; 375 hp(m) *(276 kW)*; 1 shaft
Speed, knots: 10

Comment: Built at Karachi with French assistance 1981-82.

1 OIL BARGE

JANBAZ

Measurement, tons: 282 gross
Dimensions, feet (metres): 114.8 × 30.5 × 11.5 *(35 × 9.3 × 3.5)*
Main machinery: 2 Niigata diesels; 2 shafts

Comment: Built by Karachi Shipyard in 1990.

2 FLOATING DOCKS

PESHAWAR (ex-US *ARD 6*)   FD II

Comment: *Peshawar* transferred June 1961, 3000 tons lift. *FD II* built 1974, 1200 tons lift.

COAST GUARD AND CUSTOMS SERVICE

Note: Unlike the Maritime Security Agency which comes under the Defence Ministry, the official Coast Guard was set up in 1985 and is manned by the Army and answerable to the Ministry of the Interior.

1 SWALLOW CRAFT

SAIF

Displacement, tons: 30 full load
Dimensions, feet (metres): 65.6 × 14.4 × 4.3 *(20 × 4.4 × 1.3)*
Main machinery: 2 diesels; 1800 hp(m) *(1.3 MW)*; 2 shafts
Speed, knots: 27. **Range, miles:** 500 at 20 kts
Complement: 8
Guns: 2—12.7 mm MGs.

Comment: Built in South Korea in 1986.

22 CRESTITALIA 16.5 METRE CRAFT

P 551-568 (Customs)   SADD   SHABAZ   VAQAR   BURQ

Displacement, tons: 23
Dimensions, feet (metres): 54.1 × 17.1 × 2.9 *(16.5 × 5.2 × 0.9)*
Main machinery: 2 diesels; 1600 hp(m) *(1.18 MW)*; 2 shafts
Speed, knots: 30. **Range, miles:** 425 at 25 kts
Complement: 5
Guns: 1—14.5 mm MG.

Comment: Acquired 1979-80 from Crestitalia, Italy. The four named craft belong to the Coast Guard.

4 UNIFLITE 10 METRE CRAFT

Displacement, tons: 9
Dimensions, feet (metres): 32.2 × 11.5 × 2.6 *(9.8 × 3.5 × 0.8)*
Main machinery: 2 diesels; 550 hp(m) *(404 kW)*; 2 waterjets
Speed, knots: 30. **Range, miles:** 150 at 25 kts
Complement: 4
Guns: 3—12.7 mm (1 twin, 1 single) MGs.

Comment: Built by Uniflite, Washington in 1983. Customs craft.

PANAMA

Senior Appointment

Commander of the Navy:
Major Jose Rosas

General

A force which became a naval service in 1983 and is split between both coasts. Aircraft are all Air Force operated. During the US invasion in December 1989, half the fleet was sunk and most of the others damaged. In 1990 virtually all the officers were dismissed so recovery is going to take time. The US Coast Guard is assisting the re-training and is providing replacement patrol craft and a buoy tender. Much repair work was started in 1992 and some of the damaged vessels are being refitted.

Personnel

(a) 1993: 280
(b) Voluntary service

Bases

Flamenco Island

Mercantile Marine

Lloyd's Register of Shipping:
5217 ships of 49 629 986 tons gross

PATROL FORCES

Note: In addition to the vessels listed below, there are three Boston Whalers acquired in mid-1991 and one confiscated motor yacht. *Macho de Monte 2* back in service in 1992.

1 Ex-USCG POINT CLASS (LARGE PATROL CRAFT)

TRES DE NOVIEMBRE (ex-*Point Barrow*) P 204

Displacement, tons: 67 full load
Dimensions, feet (metres): 83 × 17.2 × 5.8 *(25.3 × 5.2 × 1.8)*
Main machinery: 2 Caterpillar diesels; 1600 hp *(1.19 MW)*; 2 shafts
Speed, knots: 23. **Range, miles:** 1500 at 8 kts
Complement: 10 (1 officer)
Guns: 2—12.7 mm MGs.
Radars: Navigation: Raytheon SPS 64; I band.

Comment: Built at Coast Guard Yard, Maryland in early 1960s. Transferred 7 June 1991.

POINT class (USCG colours)   *4/1992, van Ginderen Collection*

1 Ex-US MSB 29 CLASS (LARGE PATROL CRAFT/MINESWEEPER)

ex-*MSB 29*

Displacement, tons: 80 full load
Dimensions, feet (metres): 87 × 19 × 5.5 *(26.5 × 5.8 × 1.7)*
Main machinery: 2 Packard 2D850 diesels; 600 hp *(448 kW)*; 2 shafts
Speed, knots: 11
Complement: 11 (2 officers)
Guns: 1—12.7 mm MG.
Radars: Surface search: Raytheon 1900; I band.
Sonars: Hydroscan Mk 24; active; high frequency.

Comment: Built in 1954 as an enlarged MSB 5 design by John Trumpy, Annapolis. Paid off in 1992 and transferred to Panama in March 1993 after refit. Wooden hull.

Ex-MSB 29   *1986, US Navy*

2 VOSPER TYPE (LARGE PATROL CRAFT)

Name	No	Builders	Commissioned
PANQUIACO	P 301 (ex-GC 10)	Vospers, Portsmouth	Mar 1971
LIGIA ELENA	P 302 (ex-GC 11)	Vospers, Portsmouth	Mar 1971

Displacement, tons: 96 standard; 123 full load
Dimensions, feet (metres): 103 × 18.9 × 5.8 *(31.4 × 5.8 × 1.8)*
Main machinery: 2 Paxman 12YJCM diesels; 5000 hp *(3.73 MW)* sustained; 2 shafts
Speed, knots: 24
Complement: 23
Guns: 2 Oerlikon 20 mm.
Radars: Surface search: Decca 916; I band.

Comment: *Panquiaco* launched on 22 July 1970, *Ligia Elena* on 25 August 1970. Hull of welded mild steel and upperworks of welded or buck-bolted aluminium alloy. Vosper fin stabiliser equipment. Both vessels undergoing major repairs in a Panama shipyard from September 1992. Should be back in service in 1993.

PANQUIACO   1987

3 Ex-US MSB 5 CLASS
(COASTAL PATROL CRAFT/MINESWEEPERS)

ex-*MSB 25*   ex-*MSB 28*   ex-*MSB 41*

Displacement, tons: 44 full load
Dimensions, feet (metres): 57.2 × 15.5 × 4 *(17.4 × 4.7 × 1.2)*
Main machinery: 2 Packard 2D850 diesels; 600 hp *(448 kW)*; 2 shafts
Speed, knots: 12
Complement: 6
Guns: 1—12.7 mm MG.
Radars: Surface search: Raytheon 1900; I band.
Sonars: Hydroscan Mk 24; active; high frequency.

Comment: Built between 1952 and 1956. Served in the canal area until 1992 and were transferred to Panama in March 1993 after refits. Wooden hulls.

Ex-MSB 41   1988, Giorgio Arra

1 SWIFTSHIPS 65 ft TYPE (COASTAL PATROL CRAFT)

Name	No	Builders	Commissioned
COMANDANTE TORRIJOS	P 201 (ex-GC 16)	Swiftships Inc, USA	July 1982

Displacement, tons: 35 full load
Dimensions, feet (metres): 65 × 18.5 × 6 *(19.8 × 5.6 × 1.8)*
Main machinery: 2 Detroit 12V-71TA diesels; 840 hp *(627 kW)* sustained; 2 shafts
Speed, knots: 21
Complement: 8
Guns: 1—12.7 mm MG.
Radars: Surface search: Decca 110; I band.

Comment: Aluminium hull. Second of class sunk in 1989.

TORRIJOS   1988

SUPPORT FORCES

Note: There is also a support ship *Carlos Guzman Baules*, commissioned in March 1992.

1 Ex-US SUPPORT CRAFT

NAOS (ex-*Erline*) P 303 (ex-RV 821)

Displacement, tons: 120 full load
Dimensions, feet (metres): 105 × 20.7 × 5.9 *(32 × 6.3 × 1.8)*
Main machinery: 2 diesels; 2 shafts
Speed, knots: 10. **Range, miles:** 1100 at 10 kts

Comment: Built by Equitable, New Orleans in 1965. Served as a support/research craft at the US Underwater Systems establishment at Bermuda. Transferred in July 1992.

1 Ex-US WORK BOAT

FLAMENCO (ex-*Scheherazade*) P 304 (ex-WB 831)

Comment: Transferred to Panama 22 July 1992.

4 Ex-US LCM 8 CLASS

| COIBA | CEBACO | BASTIMENTO | SAN MIGUEL |

Displacement, tons: 118 full load
Dimensions, feet (metres): 73.5 × 21 × 5.2 *(22.4 × 6.4 × 1.6)*
Main machinery: 4 GM 6-71 diesels; 348 hp *(260 kW)* sustained; 2 shafts
Speed, knots: 10
Complement: 6

Comment: Used for patrol and logistic duties with converted superstructure and bows giving increased berthing, thereby extending endurance. Unarmed. Three transferred 1972, one deleted in 1986, two more acquired. Two badly damaged in December 1989 (one was sunk) but both have been salvaged and repaired.

LCM 8 (converted)   1989

LAND-BASED MARITIME AIRCRAFT

Numbers/Type: 4 CASA C-212 Aviocar.
Operational speed: 190 kts *(353 km/h)*.
Service ceiling: 24 000 ft *(7315 m)*.
Range: 1650 nm *(3055 km)*.
Role/Weapon systems: Coastal patrol aircraft for EEZ protection and anti-smuggling duties. Sensors: APS-128 radar, limited ESM. Weapons: ASW; 2 × Mk 44/46 torpedoes. ASV; 2 × rocket or machine gun pods.

Numbers/Type: 1 Pilatus Britten-Norman Islander.
Operational speed: 150 kts *(280 km/h)*.
Service ceiling: 18 900 ft *(5760 m)*.
Range: 1500 nm *(2775 km)*.
Role/Weapon systems: Coastal surveillance duties. Sensors: Search radar. Weapons: Unarmed.

PAPUA NEW GUINEA

Senior Officers

Commander Defence Forces:
Brigadier Robert Dadimo
Director Maritime Operations:
Lieutenant Colonel P Molean

Personnel

(a) 1993: 430
(b) Voluntary

Bases

Port Moresby (HQ PNGDF and PNGDF Landing Craft Base);
Lombrum (Manus) (being improved with Australian assistance)
Buka and Alotau (1 Pacific Forum Patrol Craft at each)

Prefix to Ships' Names

HMPNGS

Mercantile Marine

Lloyd's Register of Shipping:
87 vessels of 44 209 tons gross

DELETIONS

1990 *Aitape*
1992 *Madang*

PATROL FORCES

4 PACIFIC FORUM TYPE (LARGE PATROL CRAFT)

Name	No	Builders	Commissioned
TARANGAU	01	Australian Shipbuilding Industries	16 May 1987
DREGER	02	Australian Shipbuilding Industries	31 Oct 1987
SEEADLER	03	Australian Shipbuilding Industries	29 Oct 1988
BASILISK	04	Australian Shipbuilding Industries	1 July 1989

Displacement, tons: 162 full load
Dimensions, feet (metres): 103.3 × 26.6 × 6.9 *(31.5 × 8.1 × 2.1)*
Main machinery: 2 Caterpillar 3516TA diesels; 4400 hp *(3.3 MW)* sustained; 2 shafts
Speed, knots: 20. **Range, miles:** 2500 at 12 kts
Complement: 17 (3 officers)
Guns: 1 GAM-BO1 20 mm. 2—7.62 mm MGs.
Radars: Surface search: Furuno 1011; I band.

Comment: Contract awarded in 1985 to Australian Shipbuilding Industries (Hamilton Hill, West Australia) under Australian Defence co-operation. These are the first, third, sixth and seventh of the class and the only ones to be armed. Training and support provided by the Australian Navy. Others of the class belong to Vanuatu, Western Samoa, Solomon Islands, Cook Islands, Micronesia, Tonga and Marshall Islands.

DREGER *12/1990, James Goldrick*

2 LANDING CRAFT (LCH)

Name	No	Builders	Commissioned
SALAMAUA	31	Walkers Ltd, Maryborough	19 Oct 1973
BUNA	32	Walkers Ltd, Maryborough	7 Dec 1973

Displacement, tons: 310 light; 503 full load
Dimensions, feet (metres): 146 × 33 × 6.5 *(44.5 × 10.1 × 1.9)*
Main machinery: 2 GM diesels; 2 shafts
Speed, knots: 10. **Range, miles:** 3000 at 10 kts
Complement: 15 (2 officers)
Military lift: 150 tons approx
Guns: 2—12.7 mm MGs.
Radars: Navigation: Racal Decca RM 916; I band.

Comment: Underwent extensive refits 1985-86.

SALAMAUA *12/1990, James Goldrick*

1 TUG

HTS 503 (ex-RAN *503*)

Displacement, tons: 47.5
Dimensions, feet (metres): 50 × 15 × 3.6 *(15.2 × 4.6 × 1.1)*
Main machinery: 2 GM diesels; 340 hp *(250 kW)*; 2 shafts
Speed, knots: 9
Complement: 8

Comment: Built by Perrin Engineering, Brisbane 1972. Transferred 1974.

2 LANDING CRAFT (LCVP)

01   02

LCVP 01 *12/1990, James Goldrick*

LAND-BASED MARITIME AIRCRAFT

Numbers/Type: 6 GAF N22B Missionmaster.
Operational speed: 168 kts *(311 km/h)*.
Service ceiling: 21 000 ft *(6400 m)*.
Range: 730 nm *(1352 km)*.
Role/Weapon systems: Coastal surveillance and transport duties. Sensors: Search radar. Weapons: Unarmed.

GOVERNMENT CRAFT

1 BUOY TENDER

SEPURA

Displacement, tons: 944
Speed, knots: 12

Comment: Built by Sing Koon Seng Yard, Singapore. Completed 14 December 1982. Government owned, civilian manned.

SEPURA *1990, van Ginderen Collection*

4 LANDING CRAFT

BURTIDE   BURCREST   BURSEA   BURWAVE

Displacement, tons: 725 full load
Dimensions, feet (metres): 122 × 29.5 × 7.9 *(37.2 × 9 × 2.4)*
Main machinery: 2 Deutz MWM BA6M816 diesels; 930 hp(m) *(684 kW)* sustained; 2 shafts
Speed, knots: 9. **Range, miles:** 1800 at 9 kts
Complement: 18

Comment: Built at Sing Koon Seng Yard, Singapore. Completed April-September 1981. Government owned, civilian manned. Not part of PNGDF, but occasionally used by the Armed Forces. Can carry about 500 tons cargo.

2 PILOT/PATROL CRAFT

DAVARA   NANCY DANIEL

Comment: Pilot craft of 12 and 8.2 m built by FBM Marine and delivered in March 1989.

PARAGUAY

Headquarters' Appointments

Commander-in-Chief of the Navy:
  Vice Admiral Eduardo González Petit
Chief of the Naval Staff:
  Rear Admiral Flavio Alcibiades Abadie Gaona

Personnel

(a) 1993: 3680 including Coast Guard and 500 marines (50 per cent conscripts)
(b) 12 months' national service

Training

Specialist training is done with Argentina (Operation Sirena), Brazil (Operation Ninfa) and USA (Operation Unitas).

Bases

Base Naval de Bahia Negra (BNBN) (on upper Paraguay river)
Base Aeronaval de Pozo Hondo (BANPH) (on upper Pilcomayo river)
Base Naval de Saltos del Guaira (BNSG) (on upper Parana river)
Base Naval de Ciudad del Este (BNCE) (on Parana river)
Base Naval de Encarnacion (BNE) (on Parana river)
Base Naval de Ita-Piru (BNIP) (on Parana river)

Marine Corps

BIM 1 (COMIM). BIM 2 (Bahia Negra). BIM 3 (Cuartel Gral del Comando de la Armada). BIM 4 (Prefectura Gral Naval). BIM 5 (BNBN – BANPH – BNIP). BIM 8 (BNSG – BNCE – BNE).

Coast Guard

Prefectura General Naval

Prefix to Ships' Names

Type designators only used

Mercantile Marine

Lloyd's Register of Shipping:
  38 vessels of 35 232 tons gross

PATROL FORCES

2 RIVER DEFENCE VESSELS

Name	No	Builders	Commissioned
PARAGUAY	C 1	Odero, Genoa	May 1931
HUMAITA	C 2	Odero, Genoa	May 1931

Displacement, tons: 636 standard; 865 full load
Dimensions, feet (metres): 231 × 35 × 5.3 *(70 × 10.7 × 1.7)*
Main machinery: 2 boilers; 2 Parsons turbines; 3800 hp *(2.83 MW)*; 2 shafts
Speed, knots: 17. **Range, miles:** 1700 at 16 kts
Complement: 86
Guns: 4—4.7 in *(120 mm)*. 3—3 in *(76 mm)*. 2—40 mm. 2—20 mm *(Paraguay only)*.
Mines: 6.
Radars: Navigation *(Paraguay)*; I band.

Comment: Both refitted in 1975. Have 0.5 in side armour plating and 0.3 in on deck.

PARAGUAY *5/1991, Paraguay Navy*

1 ITAIPÚ CLASS (RIVER DEFENCE VESSEL)

Name	No	Builders	Commissioned
ITAIPÚ	P 05 (ex-P 2)	Arsenal de Marinha, Rio de Janeiro	2 Apr 1985

Displacement, tons: 365 full load
Dimensions, feet (metres): 151.9 × 27.9 × 4.6 *(46.3 × 8.5 × 1.4)*
Main machinery: 2 MAN V6V16/18TL diesels; 1920 hp(m) *(1.41 MW)*; 2 shafts
Speed, knots: 14. **Range, miles:** 6000 at 12 kts
Complement: 40 (9 officers)
Guns: 1 Bofors 40 mm/60. 2—81 mm mortars. 6—12.7 mm MGs.
Radars: Navigation: I band.
Helicopters: Platform for 1 HB 350B or equivalent.

Comment: Ordered late 1982. Launched 16 March 1984. Same as Brazilian Roraima class.

ITAIPÚ *6/1990, Paraguay Navy*

3 BOUCHARD CLASS (PATROL SHIPS)

Name	No	Builders	Commissioned
NANAWA (ex-*Bouchard* M 7)	P 02 (ex-P 01, ex-M 1)	Rio Santiago Naval Yard	27 Jan 1937
CAPITAN MEZA (ex-*Seaver* M 12)	P 03 (ex-P 02, ex-M 2)	Hansen, San Fernando	20 May 1939
TENIENTE FARINA (ex-*Py* M 10)	P 04 (ex-P 03, ex-M 3)	Rio Santiago Naval Yard	1 July 1939

Displacement, tons: 450 standard; 620 normal; 650 full load
Dimensions, feet (metres): 197 × 24 × 8.5 *(60 × 7.3 × 2.6)*
Main machinery: 2 sets MAN 2-stroke diesels; 2000 hp(m) *(1.47 MW)*; 2 shafts
Speed, knots: 16. **Range, miles:** 6000 at 12 kts
Complement: 70
Guns: 4 Bofors 40 mm/60 (2 twin). 2—12.7 mm MGs.
Mines: 1 rail.
Radars: Navigation: I band.

Comment: Former Argentinian minesweepers of the Bouchard class. Launched on 20 March 1936, 24 August 1938, 31 March 1938 respectively. Transferred from the Argentine Navy to the Paraguayan Navy; *Nanawa* commissioned 14 March 1964; *Teniente Farina* and *Capitan Meza*, 6 May 1968.

NANAWA *6/1990, Paraguay Navy*

1 RIVER PATROL CRAFT

Name	No	Builders	Commissioned
CAPITAN CABRAL (ex-*Triunfo*)	P 01 (ex-P 04, ex-A 1)	Werf-Conrad, Haarlem	1908

Displacement, tons: 180 standard; 206 full load
Dimensions, feet (metres): 107.2 × 23.5 × 9.8 *(32.7 × 7.2 × 3)*
Main machinery: 1 Caterpillar 3408 diesel; 360 hp *(269 kW)*; 1 shaft
Speed, knots: 9
Complement: 47
Guns: 1 Bofors 40 mm/60. 2 Oerlikon 20 mm. 2—12.7 mm MGs.

Comment: Former tug. Launched in 1907. Of wooden construction and with a single boiler and steam reciprocating engine. Stationed on Upper Paraña River and still in excellent condition. Vickers guns were replaced, and a diesel engine fitted by Arsenal de Marina in 1984.

CAPITAN CABRAL *6/1990, Paraguay Navy*

5 RIVER PATROL CRAFT

P 07   P 08   P 09   P 10   P 11

Displacement, tons: 18 full load
Dimensions, feet (metres): 48.2 × 10.2 × 4.6 *(14.7 × 3.1 × 1.4)*
Main machinery: 1 diesel; 200 hp(m) *(147 kW)*; 1 shaft
Speed, knots: 12
Complement: 4
Guns: 2—12.7 mm MGs.

Comment: Built by Arsenal de Marina, Paraguay. One launched in 1989, two in 1990 and two in 1991. More may be building.

P 08   *3/1991, Paraguay Navy*

6 TYPE 701 CLASS (RIVER PATROL CRAFT)

P 101   102   103   104   105   106

Displacement, tons: 15 full load
Dimensions, feet (metres): 42.5 × 12.8 × 3 *(13 × 3.9 × 0.9)*
Main machinery: 2 GM diesels; 500 hp *(373 kW)*; 2 shafts
Speed, knots: 20
Complement: 7
Guns: 2—12.7 mm MGs.

Comment: Built by Sewart Inc, Berwick. Transferred by USA, two in December 1967, three in September 1970 and one in March 1971.

P 104   *6/1992, Paraguay Navy*

Ex-US LSM 1 CLASS (CONVERTED TENDER)

Name	No	Builders	Commissioned
BOQUERON (ex-Argentinian Corrientes, ex-US LSM 86)	BC 1	Brown S B Co, Houston	13 Oct 1944

Displacement, tons: 1095 full load
Dimensions, feet (metres): 203.5 × 33.8 × 8 *(62 × 10.3 × 2.4)*
Main machinery: 2 Fairbanks-Morse 38D8-1/8-10 diesels; 3540 hp *(2.64 MW)*; 2 shafts
Speed, knots: 13. **Range, miles:** 4100 at 12 kts
Complement: 66
Guns: 2 Bofors 40 mm (twin). 4 Oerlikon 20 mm.
Helicopters: Platform for 1 medium support type.

Comment: Converted at Navyard, Buenos Aires during 1968. Transferred as a gift from Argentina 13 January 1972. Light Forces Tender with helicopter deck added aft.

BOQUERON   *1990, Paraguay Navy*

LAND-BASED MARITIME AIRCRAFT (FRONT LINE)

Numbers/Type: 5 Cessna U 206.
Operational speed: 167 kts *(309 km/h)*.
Service ceiling: 20 000 ft *(6100 m)*.
Range: 775 nm *(1435 km)*.
Role/Weapon systems: Fixed-wing MR for short-range operations. Sensors: Visual reconnaissance. Weapons: Unarmed.

Numbers/Type: 2 Helibras HB 350B Esquilo
Operational speed: 125 kts *(232 km/h)*.
Service ceiling: 10 000 ft *(3050 m)*.
Range: 390 nm *(720 km)*.
Role/Weapon systems: Support helicopter for riverine patrol craft. Delivered in July 1985.

AUXILIARIES

1 TRAINING SHIP/TRANSPORT

Name	No	Builders	Commissioned
GUARANI	—	Tomas Ruiz de Velasco, Bilbao	Feb 1968

Measurement, tons: 714 gross; 1047 dwt
Dimensions, feet (metres): 240.3 × 36.3 × 11.9 *(73.6 × 11.1 × 3.7)*
Main machinery: 1 MWM diesel; 1300 hp(m) *(956 kW)*; 1 shaft
Speed, knots: 13
Complement: 21
Cargo capacity: 1000 tons

Comment: Refitted in 1975 after a serious fire in the previous year off the coast of France. Used to spend most of her time acting as a freighter on the Asunción-Europe run, commercially operated for the Paraguayan Navy. Since 1991 she has only been used for river service Asunción-Montevideo.

GUARANI   *3/1988, van Ginderen Collection*

4 Ex-US TUGS

R 2   R 4   R 6   R 7

Displacement, tons: 70 full load
Dimensions, feet (metres): 65 × 16.4 × 7.5 *(19.8 × 5 × 2.3)*
Main machinery: 1 Caterpillar 3408 diesel; 360 hp *(269 kW)*; 1 shaft
Speed, knots: 9

Comment: Harbour tugs transferred under MAP in the 1960s and 1970s. Details given are for *R 4*. The others are smaller 20 ton vessels.

1 Ex-US YTL TUG

ANGOSTURA R 5 (ex-YTL 211)

Displacement, tons: 82 full load
Dimensions, feet (metres): 64 × 16.4 × 9.2 *(19.5 × 5 × 2.8)*
Main machinery: 1 Scania DSI 14 M03 diesel; 357 hp *(266 kW)*; 1 shaft
Speed, knots: 9

Comment: Built by Robert Jacob Inc in 1942. Sold to Paraguay 11 February 1977. Refitted at Arsenal de Marina in 1992.

ANGOSTURA   *4/1992, Paraguay Navy*

1 SURVEY VESSEL

LANCHA ECOGRAFA

Comment: Built in 1957. Displacement 50 tons with a crew of seven.

476 PARAGUAY / Auxiliaries — PERU / Introduction

1 RIVER TRANSPORT

TENIENTE HERREROS (ex-*Presidente Stroessner*) T 1

Displacement, tons: 150 full load
Dimensions, feet (metres): 124 × 29.5 × 7.2 *(37.8 × 9 × 2.2)*
Main machinery: 2 MWM diesels; 330 hp(m) *(243 kW)*
Speed, knots: 10
Military lift: 120 tons

Comment: Built by Arsenal de Marina in 1964.

2 Ex-US LCU 501 CLASS

BT 1 (ex-US *YFB 82*)   **BT 2** (ex-US *YFB 86*)

Displacement, tons: 309 full load
Main machinery: 3 Gray Marine 64 YTL diesels; 675 hp *(504 kW)*; 3 shafts
Speed, knots: 10
Military lift: 120 tons

Comment: Built in 1944 and converted in 1958-60. Leased by the USA in June 1970 and by sale 11 February 1977. Used as ferries.

TENIENTE HERREROS   *5/1991, Paraguay Navy*

BT 1   *1991, Paraguay Navy*

4 DREDGERS

Name	No	Displacement	Launched	Officers	Crew
ASUNCIÓN	RP 1	107 tons	1908	1	27
PROGRESO	D 1	140 tons	1907	2	28
DRAGA (ex-*Teniente O C Saguier*)	D 2	110 tons	1957	2	17
—	—	550 tons	1988	2	35

1 FLOATING DOCK

DF 1 (Ex-US *AFDL 26*)

Comment: Built 1944, leased March 1965. Purchased 11 February 1977. Lift 1000 tons.

PERU

Headquarters' Appointments

Commander of the Navy:
  Admiral Alfredo Arnaiz Ambrosiani
Chief of the Naval Staff:
  Vice Admiral Carlos Martinez Rogas
Chief of Naval Operations:
  Vice Admiral Guillerno Zariquiey Alegne
Flag Officer Commanding Marines:
  Rear Admiral Luis Monteverde

Personnel

(a) 1993: 25 000 (2500 officers)
(b) 2 years' national service

Bases and Organisation

Three areas:—Pacific Naval Force (HQ Callao), Amazon River Force (HQ Iquitos) and Lake Titicaca Patrol Force (HQ at Puno).
Callao—Main naval base; dockyard with shipbuilding capacity, 1 dry dock, 2 floating docks, 1 floating crane; training schools
Iquitos—River base for Amazon Flotilla; small building yard, repair facilities, floating dock
La Punta (naval academy), San Lorenzo (submarine base), Chimbote, Paita, Talara, Puno (Lake Titicaca), Madre de Dios (river base)

Marines

There is one brigade of 3000 men, armed with amphibious vehicles (twin Oerlikon, 88 mm rocket launchers) and armoured cars. Headquarters at Ancon. First Battalion—Guarnicion de Marina; Second Battalion—Guardia Chalaca.

Strength of the Fleet

Type	Active
Submarines—Patrol	10
Cruisers	1 (1)
Destroyers	6
Frigates	4
Fast Attack Craft—Missile	6
Patrol Craft	7
River Gunboats	4
Landing Ships	4
Transports	1
Tankers	9
Survey and Oceanographic Vessels	6
Tugs	11
Water Carriers	2
Hospital Craft	2
Torpedo Recovery Vessel	1
Floating Docks	5
Coast Guard	15

Prefix to Ships' Names

BAP (Buque Armada Peruana). PC (Coastal Patrol). PL (Lake Patrol). PP (Port Patrol). PF (River Patrol).

Coast Guard

A separate service set up in 1975 with a number of light forces transferred from the Navy.

Mercantile Marine

Lloyd's Register of Shipping:
  623 vessels of 498 541 tons gross

DELETIONS

Submarine

1990 *Angamos*

Destroyers

1990 *Bolognesi, Castilla*

Auxiliaries

1990 *Rodriguez, Navarro, Chuquito*
1991 *Independencia*

Coast Guard

1990 *Rio Canete, Rio Vitor, Rio Sama, Rio Zarumilla, Rio Reque*

PENNANT LIST

Submarines		Frigates		Amphibious Forces				Coast Guard	
SS 31	Casma	FM 51	Meliton Carvajal	DT 141	Paita	AH 172	Stiglich		
SS 32	Antofagasta	FM 52	Manuel Villavicencio	DT 142	Pisco	AH 175	Carrillo		
SS 33	Pisagua	FM 53	Montero	DT 143	Callao	AH 176	Melo		
SS 34	Chipana	FM 54	Mariategui	DT 144	Eten	ABH 302	Morona		
SS 35	Islay					ABH 306	Puno		
SS 36	Arica			**Auxiliaries**		ART 322	San Lorenzo		
SS 41	Dos de Mayo	**Light Forces**							
SS 42	Abtao			ACA 110	Mantilla				
SS 44	Iquique	CF 401	Marañon	ACA 111	Colayeras	**Coast Guard**			
SS 49	La Pedrera	CF 402	Ucayali	ACP 118	Noguera				
		CF 403	Amazonas	ACP 119	Gauden	PC 223	Rio Chira		
Cruisers		CF 404	Loreto	ARB 120	Mejia	PC 225	Rio Pativilca		
		CM 21	Velarde	ARB 121	Huerta	PC 227	Rio Locumba		
CH 81	Almirante Grau	CM 22	Santillana	ARB 123	Rios	PC 241	Rio Tumbes		
CH 84	Aguirre	CM 23	De los Heros	ARB 124	Franco	PC 242	Rio Piura		
		CM 24	Herrera	ARB 126	Duenas	PC 243	Rio Nepeña		
Destroyers		CM 25	Larrea	ARB 128	Olaya	PC 244	Rio Tambo		
		CM 26	Sanchez Carrillon	ARB 129	Selendon	PC 245	Rio Ocoña		
DM 73	Palacios	PF 272	Rio Manu	ATC 131	Ilo	PC 246	Rio Huarmey		
DM 74	Ferré	PF 273	Rio Inambari	ATP 150	Bayovar	PC 247	Rio Zaña		
DD 76	Quiñones	PF 274	Rio Tambopata	ATP 152	Talara	PP 230	La Punta		
DD 77	Villar	PL 290	Rio Ramis	ATP 156	Parinas	PP 232	Rio Santa		
DD 78	Galvez	PL 291	Rio Ilave	ATP 158	Zorritos	PP 233	Rio Majes		
DD 79	Diez Canseco	PL 292	Rio Azangaro	ATP 159	Lobitos	PP 235	Rio Viru		
		MP 147	Lagarto	AH 170	Unanue	PP 236	Rio Lurin		

SUBMARINES

1 Ex-US GUPPY 1A CLASS

Name	No	Builders	Laid down	Launched	Commissioned
LA PEDRERA (ex-*Pabellon de Pica*, ex-USS *Sea Poacher* SS 406)	SS 49	Portsmouth Navy Yard, USA	23 Feb 1944	20 May 1944	31 July 1944

Displacement, tons: 1870 standard; 2440 dived
Dimensions, feet (metres): 308 × 27 × 17 *(93.8 × 8.2 × 5.2)*
Main machinery: Diesel-electric; 4 Fairbanks-Morse 38D8-1/8-10 diesels; 6000 hp *(4.48 MW)*; 2 motors; 5600 hp *(4.2 MW)*; 2 shafts
Speed, knots: 17 surfaced; 15 dived
Range, miles: 8000 at 12 kts
Complement: 85

Torpedoes: 10—21 in *(533 mm)* (6 bow, 4 stern) tubes. Probably Westinghouse Mk 37 Type; typically active/passive homing to 8 km *(4.4 nm)* at 24 kts; warhead 150 kg.
Countermeasures: ESM: Radar warning.
Radars: Surface search: I band.
Sonars: EDO BQR 2B; passive search and attack; medium frequency.
Raytheon/EDO BQS 4; adds an active capability to BQR 2B.

Programmes: Modernised under the 1951 Guppy programme. Purchased by Peru on 1 July 1974. Ex-USS *Tench* (SS 417) purchased for spares in 1976. New batteries shipped in 1982.
Operational: Now used for alongside training. *Pacocha* (SS 48) sunk in 110 ft of water on 2 September 1988 after a surfaced collision with a Japanese fishing boat off Callao. Most of the crew were saved by free ascent. She was salvaged and cannibalised for spares.

GUPPY class (old number) *1986, Peruvian Navy*

6 TYPE 209 CLASS (TYPE 1200)

Name	No	Builders	Laid down	Launched	Commissioned
CASMA	SS 31	Howaldtswerke, Kiel	15 July 1977	31 Aug 1979	19 Dec 1980
ANTOFAGASTA	SS 32	Howaldtswerke, Kiel	3 Oct 1977	19 Dec 1979	20 Feb 1981
PISAGUA	SS 33	Howaldtswerke, Kiel	15 Aug 1978	19 Oct 1980	12 July 1983
CHIPANA	SS 34	Howaldtswerke, Kiel	1 Nov 1978	19 May 1981	20 Sep 1982
ISLAY	SS 35	Howaldtswerke, Kiel	15 Mar 1971	11 Oct 1973	29 Aug 1974
ARICA	SS 36	Howaldtswerke, Kiel	1 Nov 1971	5 Apr 1974	21 Jan 1975

Displacement, tons: 1185 surfaced; 1290 dived
Dimensions, feet (metres): 183.7 × 20.3 × 17.9 *(56 × 6.2 × 5.5)*
Main machinery: Diesel-electric; 4 MTU Siemens 12V 493 AZ80 GA31L diesels; 2400 hp(m) *(1.76 MW)* sustained; 4 Siemens alternators; 1.7 MW; 1 Siemens motor; 4600 hp(m) *(3.38 MW)* sustained; 1 shaft
Speed, knots: 11 surfaced/snorting; 21.5 dived
Range, miles: 240 at 8 kts
Complement: 35 (5 officers) *(Islay* and *Arica)*; 31 (others)

Torpedoes: 8—21 in *(533 mm)* tubes. 14 Whitehead A184; dual purpose; wire-guided; active/passive homing to 25 km *(13.7 nm)* at 24 kts; 17 km *(9.2 nm)* at 38 kts; warhead 250 kg. Swim-out discharge.

Countermeasures: ESM: Radar warning.
Fire control: Sepa Mk 3 or Signaal Sinbad M8/24 *(Casma* and *Antofagasta).*
Radars: Surface search: Thomson-CSF Calypso; I band.
Sonars: Atlas Elektronik CSU 3; active/passive search and attack; medium/high frequency.
Thomson Sintra DUUX 2C or Atlas Elektronik PRS 3; passive ranging.

Programmes: First pair ordered 1969. Two further boats ordered 12 August 1976 and two more ordered 21 March 1977. Designed by Ingenieurkontor, Lübeck for construction by Howaldtswerke, Kiel and sale by Ferrostaal, Essen all acting as a consortium.

Modernisation: Sepa Mk 3 fire control fitted progressively from 1986. A184 torpedoes supplied from 1990.
Structure: A single-hull design with two ballast tanks and forward and after trim tanks. Fitted with snort and remote machinery control. The single screw is slow revving, very high capacity batteries with GRP lead-acid cells and battery cooling—by Wilh Hagen and VARTA. Fitted with two periscopes and Omega receiver. Foreplanes retract. Diving depth, 250 m *(820 ft)*.
Operational: Endurance, 50 days. At least two are in reserve and may be sold.

CASMA *12/1986, G Jacobs*

3 ABTAO CLASS

Name	No	Builders	Laid down	Launched	Commissioned
DOS DE MAYO (ex-*Lobo*)	SS 41	General Dynamics (Electric Boat), Groton, Connecticut	12 May 1952	6 Feb 1954	14 June 1954
ABTAO (ex-*Tiburon*)	SS 42	General Dynamics (Electric Boat), Groton, Connecticut	12 May 1952	27 Oct 1953	20 Feb 1954
IQUIQUE (ex-*Merlin*)	SS 44	General Dynamics (Electric Boat), Groton, Connecticut	27 Oct 1955	5 Feb 1957	1 Oct 1957

Displacement, tons: 825 standard; 1400 dived
Dimensions, feet (metres): 243 × 22 × 14 *(74.1 × 6.7 × 4.3)*
Main machinery: Diesel-electric; 2 GM 12-278A diesels; 2400 hp *(1.8 MW)*; 2 motors; 2 shafts
Speed, knots: 16 surfaced; 10 dived
Range, miles: 5000 at 10 kts surfaced
Complement: 40

Guns: 1—5 in *(127 mm)*/25 *(Abtao* and *Dos de Mayo);* manual control; line of sight range.
Torpedoes: 6—21 in *(533 mm)* (4 bow, 2 stern) tubes. Probably Westinghouse Mk 37 Type; typically active/passive homing to 8 km *(4.4 nm)* at 24 kts; warhead 150 kg.
Countermeasures: ESM: Radar warning.
Radars: Surface search: I band.
Sonars: Thomson Sintra Eledone series; active/passive intercept search and attack; medium frequency.

Programmes: They are of modified US Mackerel class. Refitted at Groton as follows—*Dos de Mayo* and *Abtao* in 1965, *Iquique* in 1968. One deleted in 1990.
Modernisation: New batteries shipped in 1981. Since then engineering and electrical systems have been modernised and Eledone sonar fitted.

ABTAO (with 5 in gun) *1990, Peruvian Navy*

CRUISERS

2 Ex-NETHERLANDS DE RUYTER CLASS

Name	No	Builders	Laid down	Launched	Commissioned
ALMIRANTE GRAU (ex-HrMs *De Ruyter*)	CH 81	Wilton-Fijenoord, Schiedam	5 Sep 1939	24 Dec 1944	18 Nov 1953
AGUIRRE (ex-HrMs *De Zeven Provincien*)	CH 84	Rotterdamse Droogdok Maatschappij	19 May 1939	22 Aug 1950	17 Dec 1953

Displacement, tons: 9529 standard; 12 165 full load *(Grau)*
9850 standard; 12 250 full load *(Aguirre)*
Dimensions, feet (metres): 609 × 56.7 × 22
(185.6 × 17.3 × 6.7) (length 624.5 *(190.3) (Grau)*)
Flight deck, feet (metres): 115 × 56 *(35 × 17) (Aguirre)*
Main machinery: 4 Werkspoor-Yarrow boilers; 2 De Schelde-Parsons turbines; 85 000 hp *(62.5 MW)*; 2 shafts
Speed, knots: 32. **Range, miles:** 7000 at 12 kts
Complement: 953 (49 officers)

Missiles: SSM: 8 OTO Melara/Matra Otomat Teseo Mk 2 *(Grau* only) ❶; may be replaced by Exocets from the Daring class.
Guns: 8 Bofors 6 in *(152 mm)*/53 (4 twin) (4 in *Aguirre*) ❷; 60° elevation; 15 rounds/minute to 26 km *(14 nm)*; weight of shell 46 kg.
6 Bofors 57 mm/60 (3 twin) ❸ (these guns removed from *Grau*); 90° elevation; 130 rounds/minute to 14 km *(7.7 nm)*; weight of shell 2.6 kg.
6 Bofors 40 mm/70 (4 in *Aguirre*) ❹; 90° elevation; 300 rounds/minute to 12 km *(6.6 nm)*; weight of shell 0.96 kg. Removed from *Grau* during modernisation—reported still not back at the end of 1991.
Depth charges: 2 racks.
Countermeasures: Decoys: 2 Dagaie and 1 Sagaie chaff launchers *(Grau)*.
Combat data systems: Signaal Sewaco PE *(Grau)*.
Fire control: 2 Lirod 8 optronic directors *(Grau)* ❺.
Radars: Air search: Signaal LW 08 *(Grau)* ❻; D band. Signaal LW 02 *(Aguirre)* ❼; D band.
Surface search/target indication: Signaal DA 08 *(Grau)* ❽; E/F band. Signaal DA 02 *(Aguirre)* ❾; E/F band.
Navigation: Signaal ZW 03 *(Aguirre)*; I/J band. Racal Decca 1226 *(Grau)*; I band.
Fire control: Signaal WM25 *(Grau)* ❿; I/J band (for 6 in guns); range 46 km *(25 nm)*.
Two M45 *(Aguirre)* ⓫; I/J band. One M25 *(Aguirre)* ⓬; I/J band.
Signaal STIR *(Grau)* ⓭; I/J/K band; range 140 km *(76 nm)* for 1 m² target.
Sonars: CWC 10N; hull-mounted; active search.

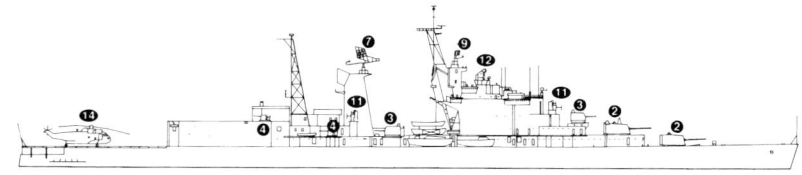

AGUIRRE (Scale 1 : 1800), Ian Sturton

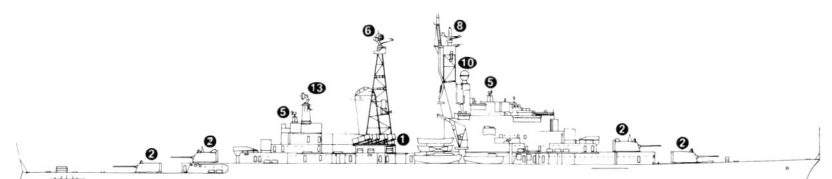

ALMIRANTE GRAU (Scale 1 : 1800), Ian Sturton

Helicopters: 3 Agusta ASH-3D Sea Kings *(Aguirre)* ⓮.

Programmes: *Grau* transferred by purchase 7 March 1973 and *Aguirre* bought August 1976. *Grau* commissioned in Peruvian Navy 23 May 1973. After sale *Aguirre* was taken in hand by her original builders for conversion to a helicopter cruiser. Conversion completed 31 October 1977. In 1986 *Aguirre* assumed the name *Almirante Grau* and the former *Almirante Grau* became *Proyecto 01*, while refitting in Amsterdam. Former names were resumed as soon as *Grau* started sea trials in November 1987.
Modernisation: *Grau* taken in hand for a two and a half year modernisation at Amsterdam Dry Dock Co in March 1985. This was to include reconditioning of mechanical and electrical engineering systems, fitting of SSM and SAM, replacement of electronics and fitting of one CSEE Sagaie and two Dagaie launchers. In 1986 financial constraints limited the work but Otomat missiles were fitted and much has been done to update sensors and fire control equipment. *Grau* sailed for Peru 23 January 1988 without her secondary gun armament, for the work to be completed at Sima Yard, Callao, but lack of funds has so far prevented this and there must be doubts about whether she will go to sea again. The plan is to fit the Exocet SSMs from the Daring class. *Aguirre* had her boilers retubed and underwent major refit completing in mid-1986.
Structure: *Aguirre* Terrier missile system replaced by hangar (67 × 54 ft) and flight deck built from midships to the stern. Second landing spot on hangar roof.
Operational: *Aguirre* helicopters carry AM 39 Exocet missiles.

AGUIRRE 198

ALMIRANTE GRAU 11/1987, J L M van der Bu...

DESTROYERS

2 Ex-BRITISH DARING CLASS

Name	No	Builders	Laid down	Launched	Commissioned
PALACIOS (ex-HMS *Diana*)	DM 73	Yarrow, Glasgow	3 Apr 1947	8 May 1952	29 Mar 1954
FERRÉ (ex-HMS *Decoy*)	DM 74	Yarrow, Glasgow	22 Sep 1946	29 Mar 1949	28 Apr 1953

Displacement, tons: 2800 standard; 3600 full load
Dimensions, feet (metres): 390 × 43 × 18 *(118.9 × 13.1 × 5.5)*
Main machinery: 2 Foster-Wheeler boilers; 650 psi *(45.7 kg/cm sq)*; 850°F *(454°C)*; 2 English Electric turbines; 54 000 hp *(40 MW)*; 2 shafts
Speed, knots: 32. **Range, miles:** 3000 at 20 kts
Complement: 297

Missiles: SSM: 8 Aerospatiale MM 38 Exocet ❶; inertial cruise; active radar homing to 42 km *(23 nm)* at 0.9 Mach; warhead 165 kg; sea-skimmer.
Guns: 6 (3 twin) *(Ferré)* ❷ or 4 (2 twin) *(Palacios)* Vickers 4.5 in *(114 mm)*/45 Mk 6; 80° elevation; 20 rounds/minute to 19 km *(10.4 nm)*; weight of shell 25 kg.
4 Breda 40 mm/70 (2 twin) ❸; 85° elevation; 300 rounds/minute to 12.5 km *(6.8 nm)*; weight of shell 0.96 kg.
Radars: Air/surface search: Plessey AWS 1 ❹; E/F band; range 110 km *(60 nm)*.
Navigation: Decca; I band.
Fire control: TSF forward; Signaal aft ❺; I/J band.

Helicopters: Platform only.

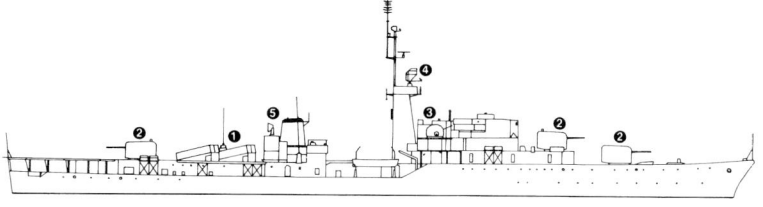

FERRÉ *(Scale 1 : 1200), Ian Sturton*

Programmes: Purchased by Peru in 1969 and refitted by Cammell Laird (Ship Repairers) Ltd, Birkenhead.
Structure: Two reconstructions took place in the 1970s in which *Palacios* had her X-turret replaced by a helicopter hangar (later removed) and both had helicopter platforms fitted over the quarter deck.

Operational: Both still operational but there are plans to sell them without Exocet missiles which may be fitted in *Almirante Grau*.

FERRÉ 2/1988

4 Ex-NETHERLANDS FRIESLAND CLASS

Name	No	Builders	Laid down	Launched	Commissioned
QUIÑONES (ex-HrMs *Limburg* DD 814)	DD 76	Koninklijke Maatschappij de Schelde, Flushing	28 Nov 1953	5 Sep 1955	31 Oct 1956
VILLAR (ex-HrMs *Amsterdam* DD 819)	DD 77	Nederlandse Dok en Scheepsbouw Mij, Amsterdam	26 Mar 1955	25 Aug 1956	10 Aug 1958
GALVEZ (ex-HrMs *Groningen* DD 813)	DD 78	Nederlandse Dok en Scheepsbouw Mij, Amsterdam	21 Feb 1952	9 Jan 1954	12 Sep 1956
DIEZ CANSECO (ex-HrMs *Rotterdam* DD 818)	DD 79	Rotterdamse Droogdok Mij, Rotterdam	7 Jan 1954	26 Jan 1956	28 Feb 1957

Displacement, tons: 2497 standard; 3070 full load
Dimensions, feet (metres): 380.5 × 38.5 × 17 *(116 × 11.7 × 5.2)*
Main machinery: 2 Babcock & Wilcox boilers; 550 psi *(38.7 kg/cm sq)*; 850°F *(454°C)*; 2 English Electric/Werkspoor geared turbines; 60 000 hp *(45 MW)*; 2 shafts
Speed, knots: 36. **Range, miles:** 4000 at 15 kts
Complement: 284

Guns: 4 Bofors 4.7 in *(120 mm)*/50 (2 twin) ❶; 85° elevation; 42 rounds/minute to 20 km *(10.8 nm)*; weight of shell 24 kg.
4 Bofors 40 mm/70 ❷; 90° elevation; 300 rounds/minute to 12 km *(6.6 nm)*; weight of shell 2.4 kg.
1—103 mm launcher for illuminants.
A/S mortars: 2 Bofors 375 mm 4-barrelled trainable launchers ❸; range 1600 m or 3600 m depending on weapon.
Depth charges: 2 racks.
Radars: Air search: Signaal LW 03 ❹; D band; range 219 km *(120 nm)* for 2 m² target.
Air/surface search: Signaal DA 05 ❺; E/F band; range 137 km *(75 nm)* for 2 m² target.

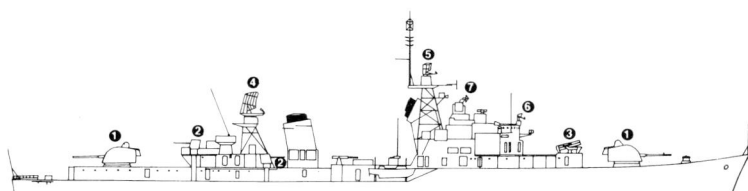

FRIESLAND class *(Scale 1 : 1200), Ian Sturton*

Surface search: Signaal ZW 06 ❻; I band.
Navigation: Racal Decca TM 1229; I band.
Fire control: Signaal M45 ❼; I/J band.
Sonars: Signaal CWE 10-N, PAE 1-N; hull-mounted; active search and attack; medium frequency.

Programmes: *Quiñones* recommissioned 27 June 1980, *Villar* 23 May 1980, *Galvez* 2 March 1981 and *Diez Canseco* 29 June 1981.

Modernisation: All of this class were to be modernised but plans were rejected as not being cost effective on ships of this age.
Operational: *Quiñones* and *Galvez* were in reserve but recommissioned in 1989. *Bolognesi* and *Castilla* have paid off but are still used for spare parts.

QUIÑONES 1987

FRIGATES

4 ITALIAN MODIFIED LUPO CLASS

Name	No	Builders	Laid down	Launched	Commissioned
MELITON CARVAJAL	FM 51	Fincantieri, Riva Trigoso	8 Aug 1974	17 Nov 1976	5 Feb 1979
MANUEL VILLAVICENCIO	FM 52	Fincantieri, Riva Trigoso	6 Oct 1976	7 Feb 1978	25 June 1979
MONTERO	FM 53	SIMA, Callao	Oct 1978	8 Oct 1982	25 July 1984
MARIATEGUI	FM 54	SIMA, Callao	1979	8 Oct 1984	10 Oct 1987

Displacement, tons: 2208 standard; 2500 full load
Dimensions, feet (metres): 371.3 × 37.1 × 12.1 *(113.2 × 11.3 × 3.7)*
Main machinery: CODOG; 2 GE/Fiat LM 2500 gas turbines; 50 000 hp *(37.3 MW)* sustained; 2 GMT A 230.20 M diesels; 8000 hp(m) *(5.88 MW)* sustained; 2 shafts; cp props
Speed, knots: 35. **Range, miles:** 3450 at 20.5 kts
Complement: 185 (20 officers)

Missiles: SSM: 8 OTO Melara/Matra Otomat Mk 2 (TG 1) ❶; active radar homing to 80 km *(43.2 nm)* at 0.9 Mach; warhead 210 kg; sea-skimmer for last 4 km *(2.2 nm)*.
SAM: Selenia Elsag Albatros octuple launcher ❷; 8 Aspide; semi-active radar homing to 13 km *(7 nm)* at 2.5 Mach; height envelope 15-5000 m *(49.2-16 405 ft)*; warhead 30 kg.
Guns: 1 OTO Melara 5 in *(127 mm)*/54 ❸; 85° elevation; 45 rounds/minute to 16 km *(8.7 nm)*; weight of shell 32 kg.
4 Breda 40 mm/70 (2 twin) ❹; 85° elevation; 300 rounds/minute to 12.5 km *(6.8 nm)*; weight of shell 0.96 kg.
Torpedoes: 6—324 mm ILAS (2 triple) tubes ❺. Probably Whitehead A244; anti-submarine; active/passive homing to 7 km *(3.8 nm)* at 33 kts; warhead 34 kg (shaped charge).
Countermeasures: Decoys: 2 Breda 105 mm SCLAR 20-barrelled trainable launchers ❻; multi-purpose; chaff to 5 km *(2.7 nm)*; illuminants to 12 km *(6.6 nm)*; HE bombardment.
ESM: Radar intercept.
Combat data systems: Selenia IPN-10 action data automation.
Fire control: 2 Elsag Mk 10 Argo with NA-21 directors. Dardo system for 40 mm.
Radars: Air search: Selenia RAN 10S ❼; E/F band; range 155 km *(85 nm)*.
Surface search: Selenia RAN 11LX ❽; D/I band; range 82 km *(45 nm)*.
Navigation: SMA 3 RM 20R; I band; range 73 km *(40 nm)*.
Fire control: Two RTN 10X ❾; I/J band.
Two RTN 20X ❿; I/J band; range 12.8 km *(7 nm)* (for Dardo).
Sonars: EDO 610E; hull-mounted; active search and attack; medium frequency.

Helicopters: 1 Agusta AB 212ASW ⓫.

Programmes: *Montero* and *Mariategui* were the first major warships to be built on the Pacific Coast of South America, although some equipment was provided by Fincantieri.

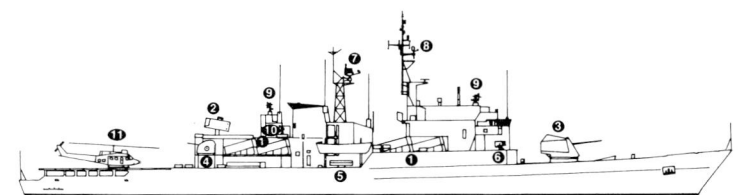

MONTERO

(Scale 1 : 1200), Ian Sturton

Structure: In the design for the pair built by Servicios Industriales de la Marina, Callao (SIMA) the two 40 mm guns are mounted higher and reloading of the Albatros is by hand not power. Also the hangar is fixed and the flight deck does not come flush to the stern of the ship.

MONTERO

5/1986, Lieutenant D M Stevens RAN

Operational: Helicopter provides an over-the-horizon targetting capability for SSM. HIFR facilities fitted in 1989 allow refuelling of Sea King helicopters.

SHIPBORNE AIRCRAFT

Note: 4 Agusta AB-412 assault, and 5 Agusta A-109K SAR helicopters to be delivered in 1993.

Numbers/Type: 3 Aerospatiale SA 316B Alouette III.
Operational speed: 113 kts *(210 km/h)*.
Service ceiling: 10 500 ft *(3200 m)*.
Range: 290 nm *(540 km)*.
Role/Weapon systems: ASW helicopter; used for liaison as well. Sensors: None. Weapons: ASW; 2 × Mk 44 torpedoes.

Numbers/Type: 5 Agusta AB 212ASW.
Operational speed: 106 kts *(196 km/h)*.
Service ceiling: 14 200 ft *(4330 m)*.
Range: 230 nm *(425 km)*.
Role/Weapon systems: ASW and surface search helicopter for smaller escorts. Sensors: Selenia search radar, Bendix ASQ-18 dipping sonar, ECM. Weapons: ASW; 2 × Mk 46 or 244/S torpedoes or depth bombs.

Numbers/Type: 8 Agusta-Sikorsky ASH-3D Sea King.
Operational speed: 120 kts *(222 km/h)*.
Service ceiling: 12 200 ft *(3720 m)*.
Range: 630 nm *(1165 km)*.
Role/Weapon systems: ASW helicopter; embarked in *Aguirre*. Sensors: Selenia search radar, ASQ-18 dipping sonar, sonobuoys. Weapons: ASW; 4 × Mk 46 or 244/S torpedoes or depth bombs or mines. ASV; 2 × AM 39 Exocet missiles.

LAND-BASED MARITIME AIRCRAFT (FRONT LINE)

Numbers/Type: 6 Beechcraft Super King Air 200T.
Operational speed: 282 kts *(523 km/h)*.
Service ceiling: 35 000 ft *(10 670 m)*.
Range: 2030 nm *(3756 km)*.
Role/Weapon systems: Coastal surveillance and EEZ patrol duties. Sensors: Search radar, cameras. Weapons: Unarmed.

Numbers/Type: 7/4 Grumman S-2E/G Tracker.
Operational speed: 130 kts *(241 km/h)*.
Service ceiling: 25 000 ft *(7620 m)*.
Range: 1350 nm *(2500 km)*.
Role/Weapon systems: ASW and coastal MR aircraft with limited ASV role. Sensors: Search radar, MAD, sonobuoys. Weapons: ASW; torpedoes, depth bombs and/or mines. ASV; 6 × 127 mm rockets.

LIGHT FORCES

6 PR-72P CLASS (FAST ATTACK CRAFT—MISSILE)

Name	No	Builders	Commissioned
VELARDE	CM 21	SFCN, France	25 July 1980
SANTILLANA	CM 22	SFCN, France	25 July 1980
DE LOS HEROS	CM 23	SFCN, France	17 Nov 1980
HERRERA	CM 24	SFCN, France	10 Feb 1981
LARREA	CM 25	SFCN, France	16 June 1981
SANCHEZ CARRILLON	CM 26	SFCN, France	14 Sep 1981

Displacement, tons: 470 standard; 560 full load
Dimensions, feet (metres): 210 × 27.4 × 5.2 *(64 × 8.4 × 2.6)*
Main machinery: 4 SACM AGO 240 V16 M7 diesels; 22 200 hp(m) *(16.32 MW)* sustained; 4 shafts
Speed, knots: 37. **Range, miles:** 2500 at 16 kts
Complement: 36 (accommodation for 46)

Missiles: SSM: 4 Aerospatiale MM 38 Exocet; inertial cruise; active radar homing to 42 km *(23 nm)* at 0.9 Mach; warhead 165 kg; sea-skimmer.
Guns: 1 OTO Melara 3 in *(76 mm)*/62; 85° elevation; 85 rounds/minute to 16 km *(8.7 nm)*; weight of shell 6 kg.
2 Breda 40 mm/70 (twin); 85° elevation; 300 rounds/minute to 12.5 km *(6.8 nm)*; weight of shell 0.96 kg.
Fire control: CSEE Panda director. Vega system.
Radars: Surface search: Thomson-CSF Triton; G band; range 33 km *(18 nm)* for 2 m² target.
Navigation: Racal Decca 1226; I band.
Fire control: Thomson-CSF/Castor II; I/J band; range 15 km *(8 nm)* for 1 m² target.

Programmes: Ordered late 1976 from SFCN, France. Hulls of *Velarde*, *De Los Heros*, *Larrea* sub-contracted to Lorient Naval Yard, the others being built at Villeneuve-la-Garenne. Classified as corvettes by Peruvian Navy. Launched—*Velarde*, 16 Sep 1978; *Santillana*, 11 Sep 1978; *De Los Heros*, 20 May 1979; *Herrera*, 16 Feb 1979; *Larrea*, 12 May 1979; *Sanchez Carrion*, 28 Jun 1979.

HERRERA

1987, Peruvian Navy

Light forces — Service forces / PERU 481

2 MARAÑON CLASS (RIVER GUNBOATS)

Name	No	Builders	Commissioned
MARAÑON	CF 401 (ex-CF 13)	John I Thornycroft & Co Ltd	July 1951
UCAYALI	CF 402 (ex-CF 14)	John I Thornycroft & Co Ltd	June 1951

Displacement, tons: 365 full load
Dimensions, feet (metres): 154.8 wl × 32 × 4 *(47.2 × 9.7 × 1.2)*
Main machinery: 2 British Polar M 441 diesels; 800 hp *(597 kW)*; 2 shafts
Speed, knots: 12. **Range, miles:** 6000 at 10 kts
Complement: 40 (4 officers)
Guns: 2—3 in *(76 mm)*/50. 1 Bofors 40 mm/60. 4 Oerlikon 20 mm (2 twin).

Comment: Ordered early in 1950 and both laid down in early 1951. Employed on police duties in Upper Amazon. Superstructure of aluminium alloy. Based at Iquitos.

MARAÑON (old number) *1987, Peruvian Navy*

2 LORETO CLASS (RIVER GUNBOATS)

Name	No	Builders	Commissioned
AMAZONAS	CF 403 (ex-CF 11)	Electric Boat Co, Groton	1935
LORETO	CF 404 (ex-CF 12)	Electric Boat Co, Groton	1935

Displacement, tons: 250 standard
Dimensions, feet (metres): 145 × 22 × 4 *(44.2 × 6.7 × 1.2)*
Main machinery: 2 diesels; 750 hp(m) *(551 kW)*; 2 shafts
Speed, knots: 15. **Range, miles:** 4000 at 10 kts
Complement: 35 (5 officers)
Guns: 2—3 in *(76 mm)*. 4 Bofors 40 mm/60. 1 Oerlikon 20 mm.

Comment: Launched in 1934. In Upper Amazon Flotilla.

LORETO (old number) *1987, Peruvian Navy*

3 LAKE PATROL CRAFT

Name	No	Builders	Commissioned
RIO RAMIS	PL 290	American SB&D, Miami	15 Sep 1982
RIO ILAVE	PL 291	American SB&D, Miami	20 Nov 1982
RIO AZANGARO	PL 292	American SB&D, Miami	4 Feb 1983

Displacement, tons: 5
Dimensions, feet (metres): 32.8 × 11.2 × 2.6 *(10 × 3.4 × 0.8)*
Main machinery: 2 Perkins diesels; 480 hp *(358 kW)*; 2 shafts
Speed, knots: 29. **Range, miles:** 450 at 28 kts
Complement: 4
Guns: 1—12.7 mm MG.

Comment: On Lake Titicaca. GRP hulls.

4 RIVER PATROL CRAFT

RIO MANU PF 272 RIO INAMBARI PF 273 RIO TAMBOPATA PF 274
LAGARTO MP 147

Comment: First three based at Madre de Dios. Commissioned in 1975. Armed with one MG and capable of 18 kts.

AMPHIBIOUS FORCES

Note: Reported that orders may be placed for up to three 300 ft LSLs to be locally built.

4 Ex-US TERREBONNE PARISH CLASS (LSTs)

Name	No	Builders	Commissioned
PAITA (ex-USS *Walworth County* LST 1164)	DT 141	Ingalls SB	26 Oct 1953
PISCO (ex-USS *Waldo County* LST 1163)	DT 142	Ingalls SB	17 Sep 1953
CALLAO (ex-USS *Washoe County* LST 1165)	DT 143	Ingalls SB	30 Nov 1953
ETEN (ex-USS *Traverse County* LST 1160)	DT 144	Bath Iron Works	19 Dec 1953

Displacement, tons: 2590 standard; 5800 full load
Dimensions, feet (metres): 384 × 55 × 17 *(117.1 × 16.8 × 5.2)*
Main machinery: 4 GM 16-278A diesels; 6000 hp *(4.48 MW)*; 2 shafts
Speed, knots: 15. **Range, miles:** 15 000 at 9 kts
Complement: 116
Military lift: 2000 tons; 395 troops
Guns: 6 Bofors 40 mm/60 (3 twin).
Radars: Surface search: Raytheon SPS 10; G band.
Navigation: I band.

Comment: All transferred on loan 7 August 1984, recommissioned 4 March 1985. Have small helicopter platform. Original 3 inch guns replaced by 40 mm. *Pisco* is non-operational providing spares for the others. Lease extended to 1994.

PAITA *9/1991, Giorgio Arra*

SERVICE FORCES

Note: All service forces may be used for commercial purposes if not required for naval use.

1 ILO CLASS (TRANSPORT)

Name	No	Builders	Commissioned
ILO	ATC 131	SIMA, Callao	Dec 1971

Displacement, tons: 18 400 full load
Measurement, tons: 13 000 dwt
Dimensions, feet (metres): 507.7 × 67.3 × 27.2 *(154.8 × 20.5 × 8.3)*
Main machinery: 1 Burmeister & Wain 6K47 diesel; 11 600 hp(m) *(8.53 MW)*; 1 shaft
Speed, knots: 15.6
Complement: 60
Cargo capacity: 13 000 tons

Comment: Sister ship *Rimac* is on permanent commercial charter.

ILO *12/1990, Hartmut Ehlers*

1 TALARA CLASS (REPLENISHMENT TANKER)

Name	No	Builders	Commissioned
TALARA	ATP 152	SIMA, Callao	23 Jan 1978

Displacement, tons: 30 000 full load
Measurement, tons: 25 000 dwt
Dimensions, feet (metres): 561.5 × 82 × 31.2 *(171.2 × 25 × 9.5)*
Main machinery: 2 Burmeister & Wain 6K47EF diesels; 12 000 hp(m) *(8.82 MW)*; 1 shaft
Speed, knots: 15.5
Cargo capacity: 35 662 cu m

Comment: Capable of underway replenishment at sea. *Talara* laid down 1975, launched 9 July 1976. *Bayovar* of this class laid down 9 July 1976, launched 18 July 1977 having been originally ordered by Petroperu (State Oil Company) and transferred to the Navy while building. Sold back to Petroperu in 1979 and renamed *Pavayacu*. A third, *Trompeteros*, of this class has been built for Petroperu.

482 PERU / Service forces — Survey and oceanographic vessels

1 PIMENTEL CLASS (REPLENISHMENT TANKER)

Name	No	Builders	Commissioned
PARINAS (ex-*Pimentel*)	ATP 156	SIMA, Callao	27 June 1969

Displacement, tons: 3434 light; 13 600 full load
Measurement, tons: 10 000 dwt
Dimensions, feet (metres): 410.9 × 63.1 × 26 *(125.3 × 19.2 × 7.9)*
Main machinery: 1 Burmeister & Wain Type 750 diesel; 5400 hp(m) *(3.97 MW)*; 1 shaft
Speed, knots: 14.5

Comment: Capable of underway replenishment at sea.

PARINAS   5/1986, Surgeon Lieutenant P J Buxton RN

1 FREIGHTING TANKER

Name	No	Builders	Commissioned
BAYOVAR (ex-*Loreto II*, ex-*St Vincent*)	ATP 150	Ch N de la Ciotat	1976

Displacement, tons: 15 175 light; 107 320 full load
Dimensions, feet (metres): 821.9 × 116.5 × 63.7 *(250.5 × 35.5 × 19.4)*
Main machinery: 1 Sulzer 7RND90 diesel; 20 300 hp(m) *(14.92 MW)*; 1 shaft
Speed, knots: 16

Comment: Launched in 1976. Acquired by Peruvian Navy from Peruvian civilian company in 1986. Sold in 1992 but chartered back until February 1994.

BAYOVAR   1986, Peruvian Navy

2 SECHURA CLASS (SUPPORT TANKERS)

Name	No	Builders	Commissioned
ZORRITOS	ATP 158	SIMA, Callao	1959
LOBITOS	ATP 159	SIMA, Callao	1966

Displacement, tons: 8700 full load
Measurement, tons: 4300 gross; 6000 dwt
Dimensions, feet (metres): 385 × 52 × 21.2 *(117.4 × 15.9 × 6.4)*
Main machinery: 1 Burmeister & Wain 562-VTF-115 diesels; 2400 hp(m) *(1.76 MW)*; 1 shaft
Speed, knots: 12
Radars: Navigation: Decca; I band.

Comment: Alongside at sea refuelling capability. 2 Scotch boilers with Thornycroft oil burners for cargo tank cleaning.

ZORRITOS   5/1986, Surgeon Lieutenant P J Buxton RN

4 HARBOUR TANKERS (FUEL/WATER)

MANTILLA ACA 110 (ex-US *YW 122*)   NOGUERA ACP 118 (ex-US *YO 221*)
COLAYERAS ACA 111 (ex-US *YW 128*)   GAUDEN ACP 119 (ex-US *YO 171*)

Displacement, tons: 1235 full load
Dimensions, feet (metres): 174 × 32 × 13.3 *(52.3 × 9.8 × 4.1)*
Main machinery: 1 GM diesel; 560 hp *(418 kW)*; 1 shaft
Speed, knots: 8
Cargo capacity: 200 000 gal

Comment: *YW 122* transferred to Peru July 1963; *YO 221* January 1975; *YO 171* 20 January 1981; *YW 128* 26 January 1985.

GAUDEN   1988, Peruvian Navy

SURVEY AND OCEANOGRAPHIC VESSELS

Note: Possible second hand purchase may be made in due course.

1 Ex-US SOTOYOMO CLASS

Name	No	Builders	Commissioned
UNANUE (ex-USS *Wateree* ATA 174)	AH 170	Levingston S B Co, Orange, Texas	20 July 1944

Displacement, tons: 534 standard; 860 full load
Dimensions, feet (metres): 143 × 33.9 × 13 *(43.6 × 10.3 × 4)*
Main machinery: Diesel-electric; 2 GM 12-278A diesels; 2200 hp *(1.64 MW)*; 2 generators; 1 motor; 1500 hp *(1.12 MW)*; 1 shaft
Speed, knots: 13
Complement: 31 (3 officers)

Comment: Former US auxiliary ocean tug. Laid down on 5 October 1943, launched on 18 November 1943. Purchased from the USA in November 1961 under MAP. Refitted in 1985 for operation in the Antarctic.

2 Ex-NETHERLANDS VAN STRAELEN CLASS

CARRILLO (ex-*van Hamel*) AH 175   MELO (ex-*van der Wel*) AH 176

Displacement, tons: 169 full load
Dimensions, feet (metres): 99.3 × 18.2 × 5.2 *(30.3 × 5.6 × 1.6)*
Main machinery: 2 Werkspoor diesels; 1100 hp(m) *(808 kW)*; 2 shafts
Speed, knots: 13
Complement: 17 (2 officers)

Comment: Both built as inshore minesweepers in Netherlands in 1960, 1961 respectively. Acquired 23 February 1985.

MELO   1989, Peruvian Navy

2 INSHORE SURVEY CRAFT

AH 173   AH 174

Displacement, tons: 23 *(AH 173)*; 53 *(AH 174)* full load
Dimensions, feet (metres): 64.9 × 17.1 × 3 *(19.8 × 5.2 × 0.9)* *(AH 174)*
Speed, knots: 13
Complement: 8 (2 officers) *(AH 174)*; 4 (1 officer) *(AH 173)*

Comment: *AH 173* launched in 1979. *AH 174* built at SIMA, Chimbote, commissioned 1982, and has a side scan sonar for plotting bottom contours.

1 INSHORE SURVEY CRAFT

STIGLICH (ex-*Rio Chillón*) AH 172

Displacement, tons: 43 full load
Dimensions, feet (metres): 61 × 17.3 × 5.6 *(18.6 × 5.3 × 1.7)*
Main machinery: 2 Detroit 12V-71TA diesels; 840 hp *(616 kW)* sustained; 2 shafts
Speed, knots: 25
Complement: 28 (2 officers)

Comment: Transferred from Coast Guard. Built by McLaren, Niteroi in 1981.

Tugs — Coast guard / PERU   483

1 Ex-US CHEROKEE CLASS

Name	No	Builders	Commissioned
RIOS (ex-USS *Pinto* ATF 90)	ARB 123	USA	1943

Displacement, tons: 1235 standard; 1640 full load
Dimensions, feet (metres): 205 × 38.5 × 17 *(62.5 × 11.7 × 5.2)*
Main machinery: Diesel-electric; 4 GM 12-278 diesels; 4400 hp *(3.28 MW)*; 4 generators; 1 motor; 3000 hp *(2.24 MW)*; 1 shaft
Speed, knots: 16.5. **Range, miles:** 6500 at 16 kts
Complement: 99

Comment: Transferred to Peru on loan in 1960, sold 17 May 1974. Fitted with powerful pumps and other salvage equipment.

Name	No	Builders	Commissioned
OLAYA	ARB 128	Ruhrorter, SW Duisburg	1967
SELENDON	ARB 129	Ruhrorter, SW Duisburg	1967

Measurement, tons: 80 gross
Dimensions, feet (metres): 61.3 × 20.3 × 7.4 *(18.7 × 6.2 × 2.3)*
Main machinery: 1 diesel; 600 hp(m) *(441 kW)*; 1 shaft
Speed, knots: 10

Name	No	Builders	Commissioned
FRANCO (ex-USS *Menewa* YTM 2)	ARB 124	S Bushey, Brooklyn, NY	1939

Displacement, tons: 132
Dimensions, feet (metres): 91 × 23 × 11 *(27.7 × 7 × 3.4)*
Main machinery: 1 diesel; 805 hp(m) *(592 kW)*; 1 shaft

Comment: Transferred March 1947.

7 HARBOUR TUGS

MEJIA ARB 120	180-181
HUERTA ARB 121	185-186
DUENAS ARB 126	

AUXILIARIES

Notes: (1) There is also *Duenas* (ex-USS Lapeer) built in 1943 and acquired in 1987.
(2) Names of other miscellaneous craft: *Neptuno, Jupiter, Robles, Tapuina, Sandoval, Andrade, Zambrano, Pucallpa.*

1 TORPEDO RECOVERY VESSEL

SAN LORENZO ART 322

Displacement, tons: 58 standard; 65 full load
Dimensions, feet (metres): 82.7 × 18.4 × 5.6 *(25.2 × 5.6 × 1.7)*
Main machinery: 2 MTU 8V 396 TC82 diesels; 1740 hp(m) *(1.28 MW)* sustained; 2 shafts
Speed, knots: 19. **Range, miles:** 500 at 15 kts
Complement: 9

Comment: Built by Lürssen/Burmeister. Shipped to Peru September 1981. Can carry four long or eight short torpedoes.

SAN LORENZO   1981, Lürssen Werft

1 RIVER HOSPITAL CRAFT

Name	No	Builders	Commissioned
MORONA	ABH 302	SIMA, Iquitos	1976

Displacement, tons: 150
Dimensions, feet (metres): 98.4 × 19.6 × 1.5 *(30 × 6 × 0.5)*
Speed, knots: 12

Comment: For service on Peruvian rivers. Two more projected but not built.

MORONA   1989, Peruvian Navy

1 LAKE HOSPITAL CRAFT

PUNO (ex-*Yapura*) ABH 306

Comment: Stationed on Lake Titicaca. Commissioned in 1873 at Cammell Laird, Birkenhead. 500 grt and has a diesel engine. Sadly the second of the class was finally paid off in 1990 after 119 years service.

5 FLOATING DOCKS

ADF 106-110

Displacement, tons: 1900 (*106*); 5200 (*107*); 600 (*108*); 18 000 (*109*); 4500 tons (*110*)

Comment: *106* (ex-US *AFDL 33*) transferred 1959; *107* (ex-US *ARD 8*) transferred 1961; *108* built in 1951; *109* built in 1979; *110* built in 1991.

2 WATER CARRIERS

ABA 330 (ex-091)   **ABA 332** (ex-113)

Comment: Built in Peru 1972. Attached to Amazon Flotilla. Capacity 800 tons water (330), 300 tons (332).

COAST GUARD

Note: Six 40 ft river patrol boats are being provided by the United States for drug interdiction patrols. Contract placed in late 1990.

5 LARGE PATROL CRAFT

Name	No	Builders	Commissioned
RIO NEPEÑA	PC 243	SIMA, Chimbote	1 Dec 1981
RIO TAMBO	PC 244	SIMA, Chimbote	1982
RIO OCOÑA	PC 245	SIMA, Chimbote	1983
RIO HUARMEY	PC 246	SIMA, Chimbote	1984
RIO ZAÑA	PC 247	SIMA, Chimbote	12 Feb 1985

Displacement, tons: 300 full load
Dimensions, feet (metres): 164 × 24.8 × 5.6 *(50 × 7.4 × 1.7)*
Main machinery: 4 Bazán MAN V8V diesels; 5640 hp(m) *(4.15 MW)*; 2 shafts
Speed, knots: 25. **Range, miles:** 3050 at 17 kts
Complement: 39
Guns: 1 Bofors 40 mm/60. 1 Oerlikon 20 mm.

Comment: Have aluminium alloy superstructures. The prototype craft was scrapped in 1990.

RIO TAMBO   1989, Peruvian Navy

2 VOSPER TYPE (LARGE PATROL CRAFT)

Name	No	Builders	Commissioned
RIO PATIVILCA	PC 225	Vosper Ltd, Portsmouth	1965
RIO LOCUMBA	PC 227	Vosper Ltd, Portsmouth	1965

Displacement, tons: 100 standard; 130 full load
Dimensions, feet (metres): 109.7 × 21 × 5.7 *(33.5 × 6.4 × 1.7)*
Main machinery: 2 Napier Deltic T38-37 diesels; 6200 hp *(4.62 MW)*; 2 shafts
Speed, knots: 30. **Range, miles:** 1100 at 15 kts
Complement: 25 (4 officers)
Guns: 2 Bofors 40 mm.

Comment: Of all-welded steel construction with aluminium upperworks. Equipped with Vosper roll damping fins, Decca Type 707 true motion radar, comprehensive radio, up-to-date navigation aids and air-conditioning. A twin rocket projector can be fitted forward instead of gun.

RIO LOCUMBA (old pennant number)   Peruvian Navy

484 PERU / Coast guard — PHILIPPINES / Introduction

1 US PGM 71 CLASS (LARGE PATROL CRAFT)

Name	No	Builders	Commissioned
RIO CHIRA (ex-US *PGM 111*)	PC 223 (ex-PC 12)	SIMA, Callao	June 1972

Displacement, tons: 130 standard; 147 full load
Dimensions, feet (metres): 101 × 21 × 6 *(30.8 × 6.4 × 1.8)*
Main machinery: 2 GM diesels; 1450 hp *(1.08 MW)*; 2 shafts
Speed, knots: 18.5. Range, miles: 1500 at 10 kts
Complement: 15
Guns: 1 Bofors 40 mm. 2 Oerlikon 20 mm. 2—12.7 mm MGs.

2 RIVER PATROL CRAFT

Name	No	Builders	Commissioned
RIO TUMBES	PC 241 (ex-P 251)	Viareggio, Italy	5 Sep 1960
RIO PIURA	PC 242 (ex-P 252)	Viareggio, Italy	5 Sep 1960

Displacement, tons: 37 full load
Dimensions, feet (metres): 65.7 × 17 × 3.2 *(20 × 5.2 × 1)*
Main machinery: 2 GM 8V-71 diesels; 460 hp *(344 kW)* sustained; 2 shafts
Speed, knots: 18
Guns: 2 Bofors 40 mm.

Comment: Ordered in 1959.

5 PORT PATROL CRAFT

LA PUNTA PP 230   RIO MAJES PP 233   RIO LURIN PP 236
RIO SANTA PP 232   RIO VIRU PP 235

Displacement, tons: 43 full load
Dimensions, feet (metres): 61 × 17.3 × 5.6 *(18.6 × 5.3 × 1.7)*
Main machinery: 2 GM 12V-71TA diesels; 840 hp *(616 kW)* sustained; 2 shafts
Speed, knots: 25
Guns: 2 Oerlikon 20 mm.

Comment: Built by McLaren, Niteroi in 1980-82. PP 231 transferred to the Navy as a survey craft. PP 234 wrecked in 1990.

RIO CHIRA   *1987, Peruvian Navy*

RIO PIURA   *1975, Peruvian Navy*

PHILIPPINES

Headquarters' Appointments

Flag Officer-in-Command:
  Rear Admiral Mariano J Dumancas, Jr
Chief of Naval Staff:
  Commodore Eduardo Domingo
Commander Fleet:
  Commodore Dario T Fajardo
Commandant Coast Guard:
  Commodore Carlos L Agustin
Commandant Marines:
  Brigadier Eduardo T Cabanlig

Diplomatic Representation

Defence Attaché in London:
  Colonel C P Garcia, Jr

Personnel

1993: (a) 22 158 (including 7744 marines and 3087 Coast Guard)
(b) 163 945 reserves

Organisation

The Navy is organised into three major commands: Fleet, Coast Guard and Marines. There are seven Naval Districts, eight Coast Guard Districts, within which there are 42 stations and 148 detachments. Coast Guard units are under operational control of Naval District commanders when conducting counter-insurgency operations. The Navy and the Coast Guard are interchangeable and often share duties, although it is reported that the Coast Guard may revert to civilian control in 1994.

Marine Corps

Marines comprise three Tactical Brigades, one Support Brigade, ten Tactical Battalions, one Support Battalion, one Service Support Battalion, one Security Battalion, and one Administrative Battalion deployed as follows: seven battalions in Metro Manilla, six in Mindanao, one in Palawan. Additionally, there are three Naval Construction Battalions plus twenty-six SEAL teams deployed in Naval Districts and other units of the Navy.

Naval Bases

Main: Cavite, Mactan (under construction).
Stations: Zamboanga, Poro, Cebu, Davao, Legaspi, Bonifacio.

Prefix to Ships' Names

BRP: Barko Republika Pilipinas

New Construction

By 1996 it is planned to acquire six FAC missile/gun, 35 PCF 70 class, two PSMH and four LSMs. An MCM programme of four vessels will begin in FY 1997. There are also intentions to build a frigate and three corvettes by the end of the century.

Mercantile Marine

Lloyd's Register of Shipping:
  1499 vessels of 8 448 711 tons gross

Strength of the Fleet (1 January 1993)

Type	Active	Building
Frigates	2	—
Corvettes	10	—
Fast Attack Craft	—	(6)
Large Patrol Craft	8	2 (3)
Coastal Patrol Craft	61	10 (17)
LST/LSV	8	2 (1)
LCM/LCU/RUC/LCVP	38	—
Command Ship	1	—
Repair Ship	1	—
Transport Vessels	2	—
Tankers	4	—
Buoy Tenders	4	—
Survey Ships	3	1
SAR Craft	2	—

DELETIONS

Frigates

1990   *Datu Siratuna*

Patrol Craft

1990   *Katapangan, Nueva Viscaya* (sunk)
1991   *PCF 304* (sunk)
1992   *Negros Oriental*

Amphibious Ships

1991   *Samar Oriental* (sunk), 1 LCM 6 (sunk)
1992   *Ilocos Norte, Tawi-Tawi*

Service Forces

1991   *Bataan, Narra, Explorer*

PENNANT LIST

Frigates

| PF 7 | Andres Bonifacio |
| PF 11 | Rajah Humabon |

Corvettes

PS 19	Miguel Malvar
PS 20	Magat Salamat
PS 22	Sultan Kudarat
PS 23	Datu Marikudo
PS 28	Cebu
PS 29	Negros Occidental
PS 31	Pangasinan
PS 32	Iloilo
PS 70	Quezon
PS 74	Rizal

Light Forces

PG 101	Kagitingan
PG 102	Bagong Silang
PG 104	Bagong Lakas
PG 140	Emilo Aguinaldo
PG 141	General Antonio Luna

Amphibious Forces

LT 57	Sierra Madre
LT 86	Zamboanga Del Sur
LT 87	South Cotobato
LT 501	Laguna
LT 504	Lanao Del Norte
LT 507	Benguet
LT 510	Northern Samar
LT 516	Kalinga Apayao
LC 550	Bacolod City
LC 551	Cagayan De Oro City

Service Forces

PS 21	Mount Samat
AT 25	Ang Pangulo
AW 33	Lake Buluan
AW 34	Lake Paoay
AE 72	Lake Taal
TP 77	Ang Pinuno
AE 78	Lake Buhi
AC 90	Mactan
AP 617	Yakal

Coast Guard

AE 46	Cape Bojeador
AE 59	Badjao
PG 61	Agusan
PG 62	Catanduanes
PG 63	Romblon
PG 64	Palawan
AE 71	Mangyan
AU 75	Bessang Pass
AE 79	Limasawa
AE 89	Kalinga
AU 100	Tirad Pass

FRIGATES

Note: *Rajah Lakandula*, paid off in 1988, is still afloat as an alongside HQ and depot ship where she is planned to remain until the end of the century.

1 Ex-US CANNON CLASS

Name	No	Builders	Laid down	Launched	Commissioned
RAJAH HUMABON (ex-*Hatsuhi* DE 263, ex-USS *Atherton* DE 169)	PF 11 (ex-PF 78)	Norfolk Navy Yard, Portsmouth, Va.	14 Jan 1943	27 May 1943	29 Aug 1943

Displacement, tons: 1390 standard; 1750 full load
Dimensions, feet (metres): 306 × 36.6 × 14 *(93.3 × 11.2 × 4.3)*
Main machinery: Diesel-electric; 4 GM 16-278A diesels; 6000 hp *(4.5 MW)*; 4 generators; 2 motors; 2 shafts
Speed, knots: 18. **Range, miles:** 10 800 at 12 kts
Complement: 165

Guns: 3 US 3 in *(76 mm)*/50 Mk 22; 85° elevation; 20 rounds/minute to 12 km *(6.6 nm)*; weight of shell 6 kg.
6 US/Bofors 40 mm/56 (3 twin); 45° elevation; 160 rounds/minute to 11 km *(5.9 nm)*; weight of shell 0.9 kg.
2 Oerlikon 20 mm/70; 50° elevation; 800 rounds/minute to 2 km.
A/S mortars: 1 manually loaded Hedgehog; range 350 m; warhead 26 kg; 24 rockets.
Depth charges: 8 K-gun Mk 6 projectors; range 160 m; warhead 150 kg; 1 rack.
Fire control: Mk 52 GFCS with Mk 51 rangefinder for 3 in guns. 3 Mk 51 Mod 2 GFCS for 40 mm.
Radars: Surface search: Raytheon SPS 5; G/H band; range 37 km *(20 nm)*.
Navigation: RCA/GE Mk 26; I band.
Sonars: SQS 17B; hull-mounted; active search and attack; medium/high frequency.

Programmes: *Hatsuhi* originally transferred by the USA to Japan 14 June 1955 and paid off June 1975 reverting to US Navy. Transferred to Philippines 23 December 1978. Towed to South Korea 1979 for overhaul and modernisation. Recommissioned 27 February 1980. A sister ship *Datu Kalantiaw* lost during Typhoon Clara 20 September 1981.

CANNON class (old number)   *1980*

1 Ex-US BARNEGAT CLASS

Name	No	Builders	Laid down	Launched	Commissioned
ANDRES BONIFACIO (ex-*Ly Thoung Kiet*, ex-USCG *Chincoteague*)	PF 7 (ex-WHEC 375)	Lake Washington Shipyard	23 July 1941	15 Apr 1942	12 Apr 1943

Displacement, tons: 2926 full load
Dimensions, feet (metres): 311.6 × 41.1 × 13.5 *(95 × 12.5 × 4.1)*
Main machinery: 4 Fairbanks-Morse 38D3-1 diesels; 6080 hp *(4.54 MW)*; 2 shafts
Speed, knots: 18
Complement: 180 (12 officers)

Guns: 1—5 in *(127 mm)*/38 Mod 70. 2—81 mm mortars.
2 Bofors 40 mm/60 Mk 3. 1 Oerlikon 20 mm/68. 4—12.7 mm MGs.
Fire control: Mk 52 Mod 3 (for 5 in gun).
Radars: Air search: SPA 34; E band.
Surface search: SPS 53; I band.
Navigation: SPN 29; I band.
Fire control: Mk 26; I band.
Helicopters: Platform for 1 light.

Programmes: Built as a sea plane tender for the US Navy. Transferred to the Coast Guard in 1946, then to the South Vietnamese Navy in 1971. Acquired by the Philippines as one of a class of four on 5 April 1976. In reserve in the late 1980s but brought back into service.
Structure: Fitted with a helicopter deck in the late 1980s.

ANDRES BONIFACIO   *1991, Philippine Navy*

CORVETTES

2 Ex-US AUK CLASS

Name	No	Builders	Commissioned
RIZAL (ex-USS *Murrelet* MSF 372)	PS 74 (ex-PS 69)	Savannah Machine & Foundry Co, Georgia	21 Aug 1945
QUEZON (ex-USS *Vigilance* MSF 324)	PS 70	Associated Shipbuilders, Seattle, Washington	28 Feb 1944

Displacement, tons: 1090 standard; 1250 full load
Dimensions, feet (metres): 221.2 × 32.2 × 10.8 *(67.4 × 9.8 × 3.3)*
Main machinery: Diesel-electric; 2 GM 12-278 diesels; 2200 hp *(1.64 MW)*; 2 generators; 2 motors; 2 shafts
Speed, knots: 18. **Range, miles:** 5700 at 16 kts
Complement: 80 (5 officers)

Guns: 1 US 3 in *(76 mm)*/50 Mk 26; 85° elevation; 20 rounds/minute to 12 km *(6.6 nm)*; weight of shell 6 kg.
4 US/Bofors 40 mm/56 (2 twin); 45° elevation; 160 rounds/minute to 11 km *(5.9 nm)*; weight of shell 0.9 kg.
4 Oerlikon 20 mm (2 twin); 50° elevation; 800 rounds/minute to 2 km.
Torpedoes: 3—324 mm US Mk 32 (triple) tubes. Probably Honeywell Mk 44; anti-submarine; active homing to 5.5 km *(3 nm)* at 30 kts; warhead 34 kg.
A/S mortars: 1 manually loaded Hedgehog; range 350 m; warhead 26 kg; 24 rockets.
Depth charges: 2 Mk 9 racks.
Radars: Surface search: Raytheon SPS 5C; G/H band; range 37 km *(20 nm)*.
Navigation: DAS 3; I band.
Sonars: SQS 17B; hull-mounted; active search and attack; high frequency.
Helicopters: Platform only.

Programmes: PS 74 transferred to the Philippines on 18 June 1965 and PS 70 on 19 August 1967.
Structure: Upon transfer the minesweeping gear was removed and a second 3 in gun fitted aft; additional anti-submarine weapons also fitted. PS 70 has bulwarks on iron deck to end of superstructure. Now have helicopter flight deck (but no facilities) in place of after 3 in gun. Both to be deleted in 1994.

QUEZON   *1976, Michael D J Lennon*

486 PHILIPPINES / Corvettes — Light forces

8 Ex-US PCE 827 CLASS

Name	No	Builders	Commissioned
MIGUEL MALVAR (ex-*Ngoc Hoi*, ex-USS *Brattleboro* PCER 852)	PS 19	Pullman Standard Car Co, Chicago	26 May 1944
MAGAT SALAMAT (ex-*Chi Lang II*, ex-USS *Gayety* MSF 239)	PS 20	Winslow Marine Co, Seattle	14 June 1944
SULTAN KUDARAT (ex-*Dong Da II*, ex-USS *Crestview* PCER 895)	PS 22	Willamette Iron & Steel Corporation, Portland	30 Oct 1943
DATU MARIKUDO (ex-*Van Kiep II*, ex-USS *Amherst* PCER 853)	PS 23	Pullman Standard Car Co, Chicago	16 June 1944
CEBU (ex-USS *PCE 881*)	PS 28	Albina E and M Works, Portland, Oregon	31 July 1944
NEGROS OCCIDENTAL (ex-USS *PCE 884*)	PS 29	Albina E and M Works, Portland, Oregon	30 Mar 1944
PANGASINAN (ex-USS *PCE 891*)	PS 31	Willamette Iron & Steel Corporation, Portland	15 June 1944
ILOILO (ex-USS *PCE 897*)	PS 32	Willamette Iron & Steel Corporation, Portland	6 Jan 1945

Displacement, tons: 640 standard; 914 full load
Dimensions, feet (metres): 184.5 × 33.1 × 9.5 *(56.3 × 10.1 × 2.9)*
Main machinery: 2 GM 12-278A diesels; 2200 hp *(1.64 MW)*; 2 shafts
Speed, knots: 15. **Range, miles:** 6600 at 11 kts
Complement: 85 (8 officers)

Guns: 1 US 3 in *(76 mm)*/50; 85° elevation; 20 rounds/minute to 12 km *(6.6 nm)*; weight of shell 6 kg.
2 to 6 US/Bofors 40 mm/56 (single or 1-3 twin); 45° elevation; 160 rounds/minute to 11 km *(5.9 nm)*; weight of shell 0.9 kg.
4 Oerlikon 20 mm/70; 50° elevation; 800 rounds/minute to 2 km.
Radars: Surface search: SPS 50 (PS 23). SPS 21D (PS 19). CRM-NIA-75 (PS 29, 31, 32). SPS 53A (PS 20).
Navigation: RCA SPN 18; I/J band.

Programmes: Five transferred to the Philippines in July 1948 (PS 28-32); PS 22 to South Vietnam from US Navy on 29 November 1961, PS 20 in April 1962, PS 19 on 11 July 1966, and PS 23 in June 1970. PS 19, 20 and 22 to Philippines November 1975 and PS 23 5 April 1976.
Modernisation: PS 19, 22, 31 and 32 refurbished in 1990-91, PS 23 and 28 in 1992, and the last pair in 1993 if funds are available.
Structure: First three were originally fitted as rescue ships (PCER). A/S equipment has now been removed or is inoperable. PS 20 has some minor structural differences having been built as an Admirable class MSF.

PANGASINAN 10/1989, Mel Back

CEBU 1991

LAND-BASED MARITIME AIRCRAFT

Note: In addition there are two L 4 training aircraft and one Cessna transport.

Numbers/Type: 5 PADC (Pilatus Britten-Norman) Islander.
Operational speed: 150 kts *(280 km/h)*.
Service ceiling: 18 900 ft *(5760 m)*.
Range: 1500 nm *(2775 km)*.
Role/Weapon systems: Short-range MR and SAR aircraft. Purchased at the rate of one per year up to 1992. Three more belonging to the Air Force are used for coastal surveillance. Sensors: Search radar, cameras. Weapons: Unarmed.

SHIPBORNE AIRCRAFT

Numbers/Type: 7 PADC (MBB) BO 105C.
Operational speed: 145 kts *(270 km/h)*.
Service ceiling: 17 000 ft *(5180 m)*.
Range: 355 nm *(657 km)*.
Role/Weapon systems: Sole shipborne helicopter; some shore-based for SAR; some commando support capability. Purchased at the rate of one per year up to 1992. Sensors: Some fitted with search radar. Weapons: Unarmed.

BO 105C 1990

LIGHT FORCES

Note: The Navy operates two Mk 1 (50 ft) and two Mk 3 (65 ft) coastal patrol craft. Details under identical craft operated by the Coast Guard.

0 + (3) CORMORAN CLASS (FAST ATTACK CRAFT—MISSILE)

Displacement, tons: 384 full load
Dimensions, feet (metres): 185.7 × 24.7 × 6.5 *(56.6 × 7.5 × 2)*
Main machinery: 3 Bazán-MTU 16V 956 TB91 diesels; 11 250 hp(m) *(8.27 MW)* sustained; 3 shafts
Speed, knots: 34
Complement: 32 (5 officers)
Missiles: SSM: 4 Aerospatiale Exocet MM 40.
Guns: 1 OTO Melara 76 mm/62. 2 Breda 40 mm/70 (twin).
Fire control: Alenia NA 21.

Comment: Contract signed with Bazán on 30 September 1991. First of class to be built at San Fernando, Spain and delivered by 1996, the other two to be built at Cavite Shipyard. The contract is subject to Spanish Government approval and financial support, as well as credit guarantees from weapon systems manufacturers. Construction had not started by early 1993.

CORMORAN (Spanish number) 1991

0 + (3) LAUNCESTON TYPE (FAST ATTACK CRAFT—GUN)

Displacement, tons: 396 full load
Dimensions, feet (metres): 187 × 27 × 8 *(57 × 8.2 × 2.4)*
Main machinery: 3 MTU 16V 956 TB91 diesels; 11 250 hp(m) *(8.27 MW)* sustained; 3 shafts; cp props
Speed, knots: 30. **Range, miles:** 3500 at 18 kts
Guns: 1 OTO Melara 76 mm/62. 2 Breda 40 mm/70 (twin) compact. 2 Oerlikon 25 mm.
Radars: Surface search/fire control: Signaal WM 22.

Comment: Agreement signed in April 1990 with Launceston Marine, Tasmania for six of the class. Negotiations were then taken over by the Australia Submarine Corporation (ASC) which signed a contract on 21 October 1991 to build three of the craft. The contract is subject to Australian Government approval and financial support, as well as credit guarantees from the weapons systems manufacturers. The plan is to build the vessels (or at least the first) at ASC Newcastle, which is the former Carrington Slipways, to be delivered by 1996. The propulsion details have changed since the original CODAG proposals.

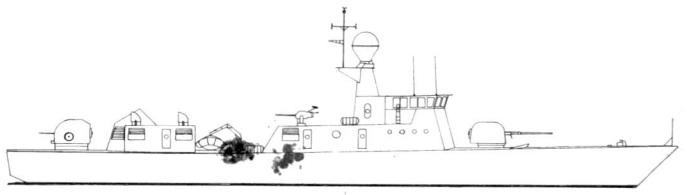

LAUNCESTON TYPE (not to scale), Ian Sturton

Light forces — Amphibious forces / PHILIPPINES   487

1 + 2 (3) AGUINALDO CLASS (LARGE PATROL CRAFT)

Name	No	Builders	Commissioned
EMILIO AGUINALDO	PG 140	Cavite, Sangley Point	21 Nov 1990
GENERAL ANTONIO LUNA	PG 141	Cavite, Sangley Point	1993

Displacement, tons: 279 full load
Dimensions, feet (metres): 144.4 × 24.3 × 5.2 *(44 × 7.4 × 1.6)*
Main machinery: 4 Detroit 12V-92TA diesels; 2040 hp *(1.52 MW)* sustained; 2 shafts
Speed, knots: 25. **Range, miles:** 1100 at 18 kts
Complement: 58 (6 officers)
Guns: 2 Bofors 40 mm/60. 2 Oerlikon 20 mm. 4—12.7 mm MGs.

Comment: First of class launched 23 June 1984 but only completed in 1990. Second launched in September 1992 and the keel laid of PG 142 in early 1993. The plan is one more every 18 months to a total of six. Steel hulls of similar design to *Tirad Pass* (see Coast Guard). The intention is to upgrade the armament in due course to include a SAM and an OTO Melara 76 mm/62 gun.

EMILIO AGUINALDO   *1992, Philippine Navy*

3 KAGITINGAN CLASS (LARGE PATROL CRAFT)

Name	No	Builders	Commissioned
KAGITINGAN	P 101	Hamelin SY, Germany	9 Feb 1979
BAGONG LAKAS	PG 104 (ex-P 102)	Hamelin SY, Germany	9 Feb 1979
BAGONG SILANG	PG 102 (ex-P 104)	Hamelin SY, Germany	1979

Displacement, tons: 132 full load
Dimensions, feet (metres): 100.3 × 18.6 × 5 *(30.6 × 5.7 × 1.5)*
Main machinery: 2 MTU MB 12V 493 TZ60 diesels; 1360 hp(m) *(1 MW)* sustained; 2 shafts
Speed, knots: 16
Guns: 4—20 mm (2 twin). 2—12.7 mm MGs.

Comment: Based at Cavite. P 103 paid off and used for spares.

8 + 10 (17) PCF 70 (HALTER) CLASS (COASTAL PATROL CRAFT)

DF 370-372   DF 374-378

Displacement, tons: 56 full load
Dimensions, feet (metres): 78 × 20 × 5.8 *(23.8 × 6.1 × 1.8)*
Main machinery: 2 Detroit 16V-92TAB diesels; 1380 hp *(1.03 MW)* sustained; 2 shafts
Speed, knots: 28. **Range, miles:** 1200 at 12 kts
Complement: 8 (1 officer)
Guns: 1 Breda 25 mm. 4—12.7 mm M2 MGs. 2—7.62 mm M60 MGs.
Radars: Surface search: Raytheon; I band.

Comment: First five ordered from Halter Marine in August 1989, a second batch of three in September 1990. Built at Equitable Shipyard, New Orleans. First completed in August 1990, second in December 1990 and then delivered at a rate of one about every three weeks. Ten more are programmed to be built in 1993/94 in the Philippines. The aim is for 35 craft divided into five squadrons each based on a support ship and spread through the archipelago. Built to Coast Guard standards with an aluminium hull and superstructure.

DF 370   *1992, Philippine Navy*

AMPHIBIOUS FORCES

0 + (1) CHINESE TYPE (LSV)

Displacement, tons: 1560 full load
Dimensions, feet (metres): 279.5 × 44 × 15.1 *(85.2 × 13.4 × 4.6)*
Main machinery: 2 diesels; 2 shafts
Speed, knots: 16
Complement: 45 (5 officers)

Comment: Contract signed in September 1991 with China Shipbuilding Corporation for one LSV with an option on a second. Subject to final approval which was reported as still not confirmed by early 1993. The original delivery date was given as 1994. It is probable that this contract was overtaken by the Frank S Besson class. To be built at Guangzhou shipyard.

8 Ex-US 1-511 and 512-1152 CLASSES (LSTs)

Name	No	Commissioned
ZAMBOANGA DEL SUR (ex-*Cam Ranh*, ex-USS *Marion County* LST 975)	LT 86	3 Feb 1945
SOUTH COTOBATO (ex-*Cotobato Del Sur*, ex-USS *Cayuga County* LST 529)	LT 87	28 Feb 1944
LAGUNA (ex-USNS *T-LST 230*)	LT 501	3 Nov 1943
LANAO DEL NORTE (ex-USNS *T-LST 566*)	LT 504	29 May 1944
BENGUET (ex-USNS *Davies County* T-LST 692)	LT 507	10 May 1944
SIERRA MADRE (ex-*Dumagat*, ex-*My Tho*, ex-USS *Harnett County*, AGP 821, ex-LST 821)	LT 57 (ex-AL 57)	14 Jan 1944
NORTHERN SAMAR (ex-*Samar Del Norte*, ex-USNS *Nansemond County* T-LST 1064)	LT 510	12 Mar 1945
KALINGA APAYAO (ex-*Can Tho*, ex-USS *Garrett County* AGP 786, ex-LST 786)	LT 516 (ex-AE 516)	28 Aug 1944

Displacement, tons: 1620 standard; 2472 beaching; 4080 full load
Dimensions, feet (metres): 328 × 50 × 14 *(100 × 15.2 × 4.3)*
Main machinery: 2 GM 12-567A diesels; 1800 hp *(1.34 MW)*; 2 shafts
Speed, knots: 10
Complement: Varies—approx 60 to 110 (depending upon employment)
Military lift: 2100 tons. 16 tanks or 10 tanks plus 200 troops

Guns: 6 US/Bofors 40 mm (2 twin, 2 single). 4 Oerlikon 20 mm (in refitted ships).
Radars: Navigation: SPS 53 (LT 87); RCA CR 107 or SPS 21D (remainder).

Programmes: LT 506 and 510 were transferred to Japan in April 1961 and thence to Philippines in 1975—remainder transferred from US Navy in 1976 with exception of LT 57 and LT 516 which were used as light craft repair ships in South Vietnam and have retained amphibious capability (transferred to Vietnam 1970 and to Philippines 1976, acquired by purchase 5 April 1976). LT 87 and LT 86 transferred (grant aid) 17 November 1975. LT 510 acquired by purchase 24 September 1977. LT 501 and 504 commissioned in Philippine Navy 8 August 1978 and LT 507 on 18 October 1978.
Modernisation: Several have had major refits including replacement of frames and plating as well as engines and electrics and provision for four 20 mm guns.
Structure: Some of the later ships have tripod masts, others have pole masts.
Operational: Many of these ships served as cargo ships in the western Pacific under the US Military Sealift Command (USNS/T-LST); they were civilian-manned by Korean and Japanese crews. The USNS ships lack troop accommodation and other amphibious warfare features. Some are used for general cargo work in Philippine service. Fourteen were deleted in 1989 and one more sunk in 1991. Two more paid off in 1992.

Ex-US LST 1072   *6/1988*

0 + 2 (1) FRANK S BESSON CLASS (LSV)

Name	No	Builders	Commissioned
BACOLOD CITY	LC 550	Moss Point Marine	June 1993
CAGAYAN DE ORO CITY	LC 551	Moss Point Marine	Sep 1993

Displacement, tons: 4265 full load
Dimensions, feet (metres): 272.8 × 60 × 12 *(83.1 × 18.3 × 3.7)*
Main machinery: 2 GM EMD 16-645E2 diesels; 3900 hp *(2.9 MW)* sustained; 2 shafts; bow thruster; 250 hp *(187 kW)*
Speed, knots: 11.6. **Range, miles:** 6000 at 11 kts
Complement: 30 (6 officers)
Military lift: 2280 tons (900 for amphibious operations) of vehicles, containers or cargo, plus 150 troops

Comment: Contract announced by Trinity Marine 3 April 1992 for two ships with an option on a third. Ro-Ro design with 10 500 sq ft of deck space for cargo. Capable of beaching with 4 ft over the ramp on a 1 : 30 offshore gradient with a 900 ton cargo. Similar to US Army vessels but with only a bow ramp. The stern ramp space is used for accommodation for 150 troops.

FRANK S BESSON (US colours)   *1988, Giorgio Arra*

488 PHILIPPINES / Amphibious forces — Service forces

38 Ex-US LCM/LCU

Comment: Ex-US minor landing craft mostly transferred in the mid-1970s. 11 LCM 6, six LCM 8, eight LCU, 11 RUC and two LCVP. More LCVP may be building at Cavite.

SERVICE FORCES

1 Ex-US ACHELOUS CLASS (REPAIR SHIPS)

Name	No	Commissioned
YAKAL (ex-USS *Satyr* ARL 23, ex-*LST 852*)	AP 617 (ex-AR 517)	20 Nov 1944

Displacement, tons: 4342 full load
Dimensions, feet (metres): 328 × 50 × 14 *(100 × 15.2 × 4.3)*
Main machinery: 2 GM 12-567A diesels; 1800 hp *(1.34 MW)*; 2 shafts
Speed, knots: 11.6
Complement: 220 approx
Guns: 4 US/Bofors 40 mm (quad). 10 Oerlikon 20 mm (5 twin).

Comment: Transferred to the Philippines on 24 January 1977 by sale. (Originally to South Vietnam 30 September 1971.) Converted during construction. Extensive machine shop, spare parts stowage, supplies, etc. Second of class paid off in 1992.

ACHELOUS class (old number)   *1968, Philippine Navy*

1 TRANSPORT VESSEL

Name	No	Builders	Commissioned
ANG PANGULO (ex-*The President*, ex-*Roxas*, ex-*Lapu-Lapu*)	AT 25 (ex-TP 777)	Ishikawajima, Japan	1959

Displacement, tons: 2239 standard; 2727 full load
Dimensions, feet (metres): 257.6 × 42.6 × 21 *(78.5 × 13 × 6.4)*
Main machinery: 2 Mitsui DE642/VBF diesels; 5000 hp(m) *(3.68 MW)*; 2 shafts
Speed, knots: 18. **Range, miles:** 6900 at 15 kts
Complement: 81 (8 officers)
Guns: 2 Oerlikon 20 mm/70 Mk 4 (twin).
Radars: Navigation: RCA CRMN-1A-75; I band.

Comment: Built as war reparation; launched in 1958. Was used as presidential yacht and command ship with accommodation for 50 passengers. Originally named *Lapu-Lapu* after the chief who killed Magellan; renamed *Roxas* on 9 October 1962 after the late Manuel Roxas, the first President of the Philippines Republic, renamed *The President* in 1967 and *Ang Pangulo* in 1975. One 15 ton crane. In early 1987 she was in Hong Kong with a full crew, having not returned to Cavite after the banishment of ex-President Marcos, but since then has been taken on as an attack transport.

ANG PANGULO   *1988, Gilbert Gyssels*

1 Ex-US ADMIRABLE CLASS (SUPPLY SHIP)

Name	No	Builders	Commissioned
MOUNT SAMAT (ex-*Santa Maria*, ex-*Pagasa*, ex-*APO 21*, ex-USS *Quest*, AM 281)	PS 21 (ex-TP 21)	Gulf Shipbuilding Corporation	25 Oct 1944

Displacement, tons: 650 standard; 945 full load
Dimensions, feet (metres): 184.5 × 33 × 9.8 *(56.3 × 10.1 × 3)*
Main machinery: 2 Cooper-Bessemer GSB8 diesels; 1710 hp *(1.28 MW)*; 2 shafts
Speed, knots: 15. **Range, miles:** 4500 at 14 kts
Complement: 67
Radars: Navigation: RCA CR-104; I/J band.

Comment: Former US Navy minesweeper (AM). Commissioned on 25 October 1944. Transferred to the Philippines in July 1948. Was used as presidential yacht and command ship but now is a humble supply vessel.

MOUNT SAMAT   *2/1982, G Jacobs*

1 Ex-US ALAMOSA CLASS (SUPPLY SHIP)

Name	No	Builders	Commissioned
MACTAN (ex-USCGC *Kukui* WAK 186, ex-USS *Colquitt* AK 174)	AC 90 (ex-TK 90)	Froemming Brothers, Milwaukee	22 Sep 1945

Displacement, tons: 2499 light; 7570 full load
Dimensions, feet (metres): 338.5 × 50 × 18 *(103.2 × 15.2 × 5.5)*
Main machinery: 1 Nordberg TSM-6 diesel; 1700 hp *(1.27 MW)*; 1 shaft
Speed, knots: 11.5
Complement: 85
Guns: 2—12.7 mm Mk 2 MG (twin).
Radars: Navigation: RCA CRMN 1A 75; I band.

Comment: Commissioned in US Navy on 22 September 1945; transferred to the US Coast Guard two days later. Subsequently served as Coast Guard supply ship in Pacific until transferred to Philippines on 1 March 1972 and by purchase 1 August 1980. Used to supply military posts and lighthouses in the Philippine archipelago. Carries one 30 ton, one 20 ton and six 5 ton cranes.

1 BATAAN CLASS (COMMAND SHIP)

Name	No	Builders	Commissioned
ANG PINUNO	TP 77	Vosper (Private) Ltd, Singapore	Dec 1975

Displacement, tons: 150 full load
Dimensions, feet (metres): 124.3 × 23.6 × 12.5 *(37.9 × 7.2 × 3.8)*
Main machinery: 3 MTU 12V 538 TB91 diesels; 4600 hp(m) *(3.38 MW)* sustained; 3 shafts
Speed, knots: 30
Complement: 32

Comment: Used as a command ship and has been used before 1986 as a presidential yacht. Sister ship *Bataan* deleted in 1991.

BATAAN   *1984, Gilbert Gyssels*

2 Ex-US YW TYPE (WATER CARRIERS)

LAKE BULUAN (ex-US *YW 111*, ex-*YW 33*) AW 33
LAKE PAOAY (ex-US *YW 130*, ex-*YW 34*) AW 34

Displacement, tons: 1237 full load
Dimensions, feet (metres): 174 × 32.7 × 13.2 *(53 × 10 × 4)*
Main machinery: 2 GM 8-278A diesels; 1500 hp *(1.12 MW)*; 2 shafts
Speed, knots: 7.5
Complement: 29
Cargo capacity: 200 000 gal
Guns: 2 Oerlikon 20 mm.

Comment: Basically similar to YOG type but adapted to carry fresh water. Transferred to the Philippines on 16 July 1975.

2 Ex-US YOG TYPE (TANKERS)

Name	No	Commissioned
LAKE BUHI (ex-US *YOG 73*)	AE 78 (ex-YO 78)	1944
LAKE TAAL (ex-US *YOG*)	AE 72 (ex-YO 72)	1945

Displacement, tons: 447 standard; 1400 full load
Dimensions, feet (metres): 174 × 32.7 × 13.2 *(53 × 10 × 4)*
Main machinery: 2 GM 8-278A diesels; 1500 hp *(1.12 MW)*; 2 shafts
Speed, knots: 8
Complement: 28
Cargo capacity: 6570 barrels dieso and gasoline
Guns: 2 Oerlikon 20 mm/70 Mk 4.

Comment: Former US Navy gasoline tankers. Transferred in July 1967 on loan and by purchase 5 March 1980.

Ex-US YO/YOG Type (old number)   *10/1977, Giorgio Arra*

1 RIVER UTILITY CRAFT

VO 163

Displacement, tons: 12 full load
Dimensions, feet (metres): 36 × 9.3 × 2.2 *(11 × 2.8 × 0.6)*
Main machinery: 2 Detroit diesels; 562 hp *(419 kW)*; 2 shafts
Speed, knots: 28
Guns: 1—12.7 mm MG. 1—7.62 mm MG.

Comment: Similar craft sunk in 1991.

4 Ex-US YTL 422 CLASS (TUGS)

IGOROT (ex-*YTL 572*) YQ 222
TAGBANUA (ex-*YTL 429*) YQ 223
ILONGOT (ex-*YTL 427*) YQ 225
TASADAY (ex-*YTL 425*) YQ 226

Displacement, tons: 71
Main machinery: 1 diesel; 240 hp *(179 kW)*; 1 shaft
Speed, knots: 10

Comment: Former US Navy 66 ft harbour tugs. *YTL 748* was to be transferred but sank on passage. YQ 225 and 226 acquired by sale 1 August 1980.

3 FLOATING DOCKS

YD 200 (ex-*AFDL 24*)   YD 204 (ex-*AFDL 20*)   YD 205 (ex-*AFDL 44*)

Comment: Floating steel dry docks built in the USA; all are former US Navy units with YD 200 transferred in July 1948, YD 204 in October 1961 (sale 1 August 1980) and YD 205 in September 1969. Capacities: YD 205, 2800 tons; YD 200 and YD 204, 1000 tons. In addition there are two floating cranes, YU 206 and YU 207, built in USA in 1944 and capable of lifting 30 tons.

SURVEY AND RESEARCH SHIPS

Notes: (a) Operated by Coast and Geodetic Survey of Ministry of National Defence.
(b) An 83 m hydrographic ship ordered in April 1990 from Japan.

Name	No	Builders	Commissioned
ARLUNUYA	—	Walkers, Maryborough, Australia	1964
ARINYA	—	Walkers, Maryborough, Australia	1962

Displacement, tons: 255 full load
Dimensions, feet (metres): 101 × 22 × 8 *(30.8 × 6.7 × 2.4)*
Main machinery: 2 GM 6-71 diesels; 348 hp *(260 kW)* sustained; 2 shafts
Speed, knots: 10
Complement: 33 (6 officers)

Comment: Survey ships of same design as Australian *Banks* and *Bass*.

ARLUNUYA TYPE (Australian number)   1983

1 SURVEY SHIP

Name	No	Builders	Commissioned
ATYIMBA	—	Walkers, Maryborough, Australia	1969

Displacement, tons: 611 standard; 686 full load
Dimensions, feet (metres): 161 × 33 × 12 *(49.1 × 10 × 3.7)*
Main machinery: 2 Paxman diesels; 1452 hp *(1.08 MW)*; 2 shafts
Speed, knots: 11. **Range, miles:** 5000 at 8 kts
Complement: 54 (8 officers)
Guns: 2 Oerlikon 20 mm.

Comment: Survey ship similar to HMAS *Flinders* with differences in displacement and use of davits aft instead of cranes. Guns may be removed.

ATYIMBA   1981, van Ginderen Collection

Service forces — Coast guard / PHILIPPINES 489

COAST GUARD

Notes: 1. Some of the PCF craft listed are manned by the Navy.
2. The Coast Guard also operates one LCM 6, one LCU, one LCVP and a River Utility Craft VU 463.

1 Ex-US COAST GUARD BALSAM CLASS (TENDER)

Name	No	Builders	Commissioned
KALINGA (ex-USCGC *Redbud*, WAGL 398, ex-USNS *Redbud*, T-AKL 398)	AE 89 (ex-AG 89)	Marine Iron & Shipbuilding Co, Duluth	2 May 1944

Displacement, tons: 950 standard; 1041 full load
Dimensions, feet (metres): 180 × 37 × 13 *(54.8 × 11.3 × 4)*
Main machinery: Diesel-electric; 2 Cooper-Bessemer GSB-8 diesels; 1710 hp *(1.28 MW)*; 2 generators; 1 motor; 1200 hp *(895 kW)*; 1 shaft
Speed, knots: 12. **Range, miles:** 3500 at 7 kts
Complement: 53
Guns: 2—12.7 mm MGs.
Radars: Navigation: Sperry SPS 53; I/J band.

Comment: Originally US Coast Guard buoy tender (WAGL 398). Transferred to US Navy on 25 March 1949 as AG 398 and then to the Philippine Navy 1 March 1972. One 20 ton derrick.

KALINGA   10/1977, Giorgio Arra

4 Ex-US ARMY FS 381 TYPE (BUOY TENDERS)

Name	No
CAPE BOJEADOR (ex-US Army *FS 203*)	AE 46 (ex-TK 46)
LIMASAWA (ex-USCGC *Nettle* WAK 129, ex-US Army *FS 169*)	AE 79 (ex-TK 79)
BADJAO (ex-Japanese, ex-US Army *FS 524*)	AE 59 (ex-AS 59)
MANGYAN (ex-Japanese, ex-US Army *FS 408*)	AE 71 (ex-AS 71)

Displacement, tons: 470 standard; 950 full load
Dimensions, feet (metres): 180 × 32 × 10 *(54.9 × 9.8 × 3)*
Main machinery: 2 GM 6-278A diesels; 1120 hp *(836 kW)*; 2 shafts
Speed, knots: 10. **Range, miles:** 4150 at 10 kts
Complement: 50
Cargo capacity: 400 tons
Guns: 12.7 mm (TK 79). 7.62 mm MGs (TK 79).
Radars: Navigation: RCA CRMN 1A 75; I band.

Comment: Former US Army freight and supply ships. First three are employed as tenders for buoys and lighthouses. Ex-*FS 408* transferred 24 September 1976 by sale. TK 79 acquired by sale 31 August 1978. One 5 ton derrick. TK 46 paid off in 1988 but was back in service in 1991 after a major overhaul.

LIMASAWA   1977, G Jacobs

2 LARGE PATROL CRAFT (SAR)

Name	No	Builders	Commissioned
TIRAD PASS	AU 100 (ex-SAR 100)	Sumidagawa, Japan	1974
BESSANG PASS	AU 75 (ex-SAR 99)	Sumidagawa, Japan	1974

Displacement, tons: 279 full load
Dimensions, feet (metres): 144.3 × 24.3 × 4.9 *(44 × 7.4 × 1.5)*
Main machinery: 2 diesels; 800 hp(m) *(588 kW)*; 2 shafts
Speed, knots: 27.5
Complement: 32
Guns: 4—12.7 mm (2 twin) MGs.

Comment: Paid for under Japanese war reparations. Similar type building for the Navy as the Aguinaldo class.

TIRAD PASS   1992, Phillippine Navy

490 PHILIPPINES / Coast guard — POLAND / Introduction

4 US PGM-39 CLASS (LARGE PATROL CRAFT)

Name	No	Builders	Commissioned
AGUSAN (ex-PGM 39)	PG 61	Tacoma Boatbuilding Co, Washington	Mar 1960
CATANDUANES (ex-PGM 40)	PG 62	Tacoma Boatbuilding Co, Washington	Mar 1960
ROMBLON (ex-PGM 41)	PG 63	Peterson Builders, Wisconsin	June 1960
PALAWAN (ex-PGM 42)	PG 64	Tacoma Boatbuilding Co, Washington	June 1960

Displacement, tons: 124 full load
Dimensions, feet (metres): 100.3 × 18.6 × 6.9 *(30.6 × 5.7 × 2.1)*
Main machinery: 2 MTU MB 12V 493 TY57 diesels; 2200 hp(m) *(1.6 MW)* sustained; 2 shafts
Speed, knots: 17. **Range, miles:** 1400 at 11 kts
Complement: 26-30
Guns: 2—20 mm. 2—12.7 mm MGs. 1—81 mm mortar.
Radars: Surface search: Alpelco DFR-12; I/J band.

Comment: Steel-hulled craft built under US military assistance programmes. Assigned US PGM-series numbers while under construction. Transferred upon completion. These craft are lengthened versions of the US Coast Guard 95 ft Cape class patrol boat design.

CATANDUANES   10/1977, Giorgio Arra

16 PCF 46 CLASS (COASTAL PATROL CRAFT)

DF 326	DB 411	DB 419	DB 429
DF 328	DB 413	DB 422	DB 431-435
DF 330-331	DB 417	DB 427	

Displacement, tons: 15 full load
Dimensions, feet (metres): 45.9 × 14.5 × 3.3 *(14 × 4.4 × 1)*
Main machinery: 2 Cummins diesels; 740 hp *(552 kW)*; 2 shafts
Speed, knots: 25. **Range, miles:** 1000 at 15 kts
Complement: 8
Guns: 2—12.7 mm MGs. 1—7.62 mm M60 MG.
Radars: Surface search: Kelvin Hughes 17; I band.

Comment: Survivors of a class built by De Havilland Marine, Sydney NSW between 20 November 1974 and 8 February 1975 (DF series). In August 1975 further craft of this design (DB series) were ordered from Marcelo Yard, Manila to be delivered 1976-78 at the rate of two per month. By the end of 1976, 25 more had been completed but a serious fire in the shipyard destroyed 14 new hulls and halted production. Some deleted.

PCF 46   1977, De Havilland

10 PCF 65 (SWIFT Mk 3) CLASS (COASTAL PATROL CRAFT)

DF 325-332   DF 353-354

Displacement, tons: 29 standard; 37 full load
Dimensions, feet (metres): 65 × 16 × 3.4 *(19.8 × 4.9 × 1)*
Main machinery: 3 GM 12V-71TI diesels; 840 hp *(616 kW)* sustained; 3 shafts
Speed, knots: 25
Complement: 8
Guns: 2—12.7 mm (twin) MGs. 2—7.62 mm MGs.
Radars: Surface search: Marconi Canada LN 66; I band.

Comment: Improved Swift type inshore patrol boats built by Sewart for the Philippine Navy. Delivered 1972-1976. *DF 353-354* belong to the Navy.

DF 352   1984, Gilbert Gyssels

15 PCF 50 (SWIFT Mk 1 and Mk 2) CLASS (COASTAL PATROL CRAFT)

DF 300-303   DF 305   DF 307-316

Displacement, tons: 22.5 full load
Dimensions, feet (metres): 50 × 13.6 × 4 *(15.2 × 4.1 × 1.2)* (Mk 1) 51.3 × 13.6 × 4 *(15.6 × 4.1 × 1.2)* (Mk 2)
Main machinery: 2 GM 12-71 diesels; 680 hp *(504 kW)* sustained; 2 shafts
Speed, knots: 28. **Range, miles:** 685 at 16 kts
Complement: 6
Guns: 2—12.7 mm (twin) MGs. 2 M-79 40 mm grenade launchers.
Radars: Surface search: Decca 202; I band.

Comment: Most built in the USA. Built for US military assistance programmes and transferred in the late 1960s. Some built in 1970 in the Philippines (ferro-concrete) with enlarged superstructure. *DF 303, 308, 309, 311* and *312* belong to the Navy.

DF 308   10/1977, Giorgio Arra

12 COAST GUARD CUTTERS

CGC 103	CGC 115
CGC 107	CGC 128-130
CGC 110	CGC 132-136

Displacement, tons: 13 full load
Dimensions, feet (metres): 40 × 13.6 × 3 *(12.2 × 4.1 × 0.9)*
Main machinery: 2 Detroit diesels; 560 hp *(418 kW)*; 2 shafts
Speed, knots: 28
Guns: 1—12.7 mm MG. 1—7.62 mm MG.

Comment: Built at Cavite Yard from 1984.

POLAND

Headquarters' Appointments

Commander-in-Chief:
 Rear Admiral Romuald Waga
Chief of the Naval Staff:
 Rear Admiral Ryszard Kukasik

Diplomatic Representation

Naval Attaché in London:
 Colonel K Cukierski

Personnel

(a) 1993: 19 110 (including 6000 conscripts, 4100 coastal defence)
(b) 18 months national service

Prefix to Ships' Names

ORP, standing for *Okręt Rzeczypospolitej Polskiej*

Strength of the Fleet

Type	Active	Building
Submarines—Patrol	3	—
Destroyer	1	—
Frigates	1	(4)
Corvettes	5	2
Fast Attack Craft—Missile	7	—
Large Patrol Craft	8	—
Coastal Patrol Craft	11	—
Minesweepers—Ocean	8	—
Minesweepers—Coastal	15	—
Minehunters (Coastal)	1	4
LCTs	6	—
LCUs	3	(9)
Surveying and Research Vessels	5	—
AGIs	2	—
Training Ships	6	—
Salvage Ships and Craft	7	—
Tankers	5	(3)
TRVs	2	—
Coastal Tugs	12	—
DGVs	3	—
Icebreaker	1	—

Maritime Frontier Guard (MOSG)

A para-naval force, subordinate to the Minister of the Interior, which could be integrated into the navy in a crisis.

Type	Active	Building
Fast Attack Craft (Gun)	3	—
Large Patrol Craft	7	—
Coastal Patrol Craft	12	—
Inshore Patrol Craft	29	—

Bases

Gdynia (3rd Flotilla), Hel (9th Flotilla), Swinoujscie (8th Flotilla), Kolobrzeg, Ustka, Gdansk (Frontier Guard)

Introduction — Submarines / POLAND

Coastal Defence

This branch is formed into several battalions with SS-C-3 missiles and a number of gun batteries covering approaches to naval bases and major commercial ports.

Mercantile Marine

Lloyd's Register of Shipping:
644 vessels of 3 162 140 tons gross

DELETIONS

Mine Warfare Forces

1990 *Los, Dzik, Rozmak, Foka, Mors, Rys, Zbik, Orlik, Krogulec, Czapla, Jastrzab*
1991 *Bizon, Bobr, Tur* (ex-AGI)

Amphibious Forces

1990 *Brda, San,* 5 Polnochny class, 14 Eichstaden class

1991 14 Polnochny class, 1 Eichstaden class
1992 *Glogow*

Support Ships

1991 *Z 5, Z 7,* 3 Goliat class (civilian)

Coast Guard

1990 *Orion, PVK 5*

PENNANT LIST

Submarines

291	Orzel
292	Wilk
293	Dzik

Destroyer

271	Warszawa

Frigate

240	Kaszub

Corvettes

421	Orkan
422	Piorun
423	Huragan
434	Gornik
435	Hutnik
436	Metalowiec
437	Rolnik

Light Forces

351	Grozny
352	Wytrwaly
353	Zreczny
354	Zwinny
355	Zwrotny
356	Zawziety
357	Nieugiety
358	Czujny
427	Puck
428	Ustka
429	Oksywie
430	Darlowo
431	Swinoujscie
432	Dziwnów
433	Wladyslawowo

Minesweepers

616	Kormoran
618	Albatros
619	Pelikan
620	Tukan
621	Flamingo
622	Rybitwa
623	Mewa
624	Czajka
630	Goplo
631	Gardno
632	Bukowo
633	Dabie
634	Jamno
635	Mielno
636	Wicko
637	Resko
638	Sarbsko
639	Necko
640	Naklo
641	Druzno
642	Hancza
643	Mamry

Amphibious Forces

811	Grunwald
821	Lublin
822	Gniezno
823	Krakow
824	Poznan
825	Torun

Survey Ships

261	Kopernik
262	Navigator
263	Hydrograf
265	Heweliusz
266	Arctowski

Auxiliaries

251	Wodnik
252	Gryf
711	Podchorazy
712	Kadet
713	Elew
281	Piast
282	Lech
R 11	Gniewko
R 12	Bolko
R 13	Semko
R 14	Zbyszko
R 15	Macko
K 18	Bryza

Maritime Frontier Guard

301	Gdynia
302	Szczecin
303	Elblag
304	Kolobrzeg
321	Fala
322	Szkwal
323	Zefir
324	Zorza
325	Tecza

SUBMARINES

1 Ex-SOVIET KILO CLASS (TYPE 877E)

ORZEL 291

Displacement, tons: 2325 surfaced; 3076 dived
Dimensions, feet (metres): 243.8 × 32.8 × 21.7 *(74.3 × 10 × 6.6)*
Main machinery: Diesel-electric; 2 diesels; 3650 hp(m) *(2.68 MW);* 2 generators; 1 motor; 5900 hp(m) *(4.34 MW);* 1 shaft
Speed, knots: 10 surfaced; 20 dived; 9 snorting
Range, miles: 6000 at 7 kts surfaced; 400 at 3 kts dived
Complement: 45

Torpedoes: 6—21 in *(533 mm)* tubes. 18 Soviet Type 53; dual purpose; pattern active/passive homing up to 20 km *(10.8 nm)* at up to 45 kts; warhead 400 kg.
Mines: 18 in lieu of torpedoes.
Countermeasures: ESM: Brick Group; radar warning; Quad Loop HF D/F.
Radars: Surface search: Snoop Tray; I band.
Sonars: Shark Teeth; hull-mounted; passive search and attack (some active capability); low/medium frequency.
Whale series; passive search; medium frequency.

Programmes: Built in Leningrad (Sudomekh), transferred 21 June 1986. This was the second transfer of this class, the first being to India and others have since gone to Romania and Algeria. It was expected that more than one would be acquired as part of an exchange deal with the USSR for Polish-built amphibious ships, but this class is considered too large for Baltic operations and subsequent transfers have been of the Foxtrot class.
Structure: A SAM system has been fitted in the fin of some of this class. Diving depth, 300 m *(985 ft).*

ORZEL

6/1992, A Smigielski

2 Ex-SOVIET FOXTROT CLASS (TYPE 641)

WILK 292   **DZIK** 293

Displacement, tons: 1952 surfaced; 2475 dived
Dimensions, feet (metres): 299.5 × 24.6 × 19.7 *(91.3 × 7.5 × 6)*
Main machinery: Diesel-electric; 3 Type 37-D diesels; 6000 hp(m) *(4.4 MW)*; 3 motors; 5400 hp(m) *(1 × 2700 and 2 × 1350) (3.97 MW)*; 3 shafts; 1 auxiliary motor; 140 hp(m) *(103 kW)*
Speed, knots: 16 surfaced; 15 dived; 9 snorting
Range, miles: 20 000 at 8 kts surfaced; 380 at 2 kts dived
Complement: 75

Torpedoes: 10—21 in *(533 mm)* (6 bow, 4 stern) tubes. 22 Type 53; dual purpose; pattern active/passive homing up to 20 km *(10.8 nm)* at up to 45 kts; warhead 400 kg or low yield nuclear.
Mines: 44 in lieu of torpedoes.
Countermeasures: ESM: Stop Light; radar warning.
Radars: Surface search: Snoop Tray; I band.
Sonars: Hull-mounted; passive/active search and attack; high frequency.

Programmes: *Wilk* commissioned 3 November 1987; *Dzik* on 10 December 1988. Both leased from the former USSR.
Structure: Diving depth, 250 m (820 ft).
Operational: The Polish Navy considers that this is about the largest practical size of submarine for Baltic operations. Both operational in 1992 and plans to return them have been shelved.

WILK   6/1992, A Smigielski

DESTROYER

1 Ex-SOVIET MODIFIED KASHIN CLASS (TYPE 61MP) (DDG)

WARSZAWA (ex-*Smely*) 271

Displacement, tons: 3950 standard; 4900 full load
Dimensions, feet (metres): 482.3 × 51.8 × 15.4 *(147 × 15.8 × 4.7)*
Main machinery: 4 gas turbines; 72 000 hp(m) *(53 MW)*; 2 shafts
Speed, knots: 35. **Range, miles:** 2600 at 30 kts
Complement: 280 (25 officers)

Missiles: SSM: 4 SS-N-2C Styx ❶; active radar or IR homing to 83 km *(45 nm)* at 0.9 Mach; warhead 513 kg; sea-skimmer at end of run; no reloads.
SAM: 2 SA-N-1 Goa twin launchers ❷; command guidance to 31.5 km *(17 nm)* at 2 Mach; warhead 60 kg; 32 missiles. Some SSM capability.
Guns: 4—3 in *(76 mm)*/60 (2 twin) ❸; 80° elevation; 90 rounds/minute to 15 km *(8 nm)*; weight of shell 6.8 kg.
4—30 mm/65; 6 barrels per mounting ❹; 85° elevation; 3000 rounds/minute combined to 2 km.
Torpedoes: 5—21 in *(533 mm)* (quin) tubes ❺. Soviet Type 53; dual purpose; pattern active/passive homing up to 20 km *(10.8 nm)* at up to 45 kts; warhead 400 kg.
A/S mortars: 2 RBU 6000 12-tubed trainable ❻; range 6000 m; warhead 31 kg; 120 rockets.
Countermeasures: Decoys: 4—16-tubed chaff launchers. 2 towed torpedo decoys.
ESM/ECM: 2 Bell Shroud. 2 Bell Squat.
Radars: Air/surface search: Big Net ❼; C band.
Head Net C; 3D; E band ❽; range 128 km *(70 nm)*.
Navigation: Two Palm Frond; I band.
Fire control: Two Peel Group ❾; H/I band (for SA-N-1). Two Bass Tilt ❿; H/I band (for 30 mm). Two Owl Screech ⓫; G band (for guns).
IFF: High Pole B.
Sonars: Hull-mounted; active search and attack; medium frequency.
VDS; active search; medium frequency.

Helicopters: Platform for 1 Haze.

Programmes: Built at Nikolaev in 1969 and converted in the mid-1970s. Transferred to the Polish Navy on 9 January 1988 at the port of Oksywie after a lengthy refit in St Petersburg.
Structure: No changes were made to the armament before the transfer.
Operational: The Flagship of the Polish Navy.

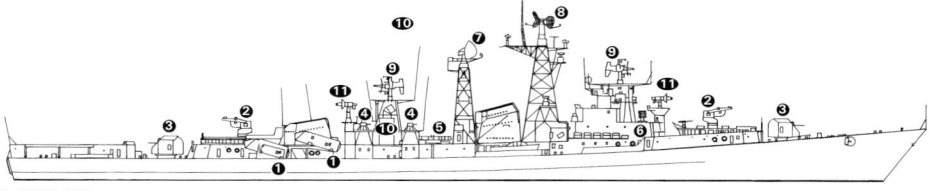

WARSZAWA   (Scale 1 : 1200), Ian Sturton

WARSZAWA   5/1992, Stefan Terzibaschitsch

WARSZAWA   4/1992, Antonio Moreno

FRIGATE

1 + (4) KASZUB CLASS (TYPE 620)

Name	No	Builders	Laid down	Launched	Commissioned
KASZUB	240	Stocznia Polnocna, Gdansk	11 May 1985	4 Oct 1986	23 Nov 1988

Displacement, tons: 1051 standard; 1183 full load
Dimensions, feet (metres): 270 × 32.8 × 10.2 *(82.3 × 10 × 3.1)*
Main machinery: CODAD; 4 Cegielski-Sulzen AS 16V 25/30 diesels; 16 900 hp(m) *(12.42 MW)*; 2 shafts
Speed, knots: 26. **Range, miles:** 2000 at 18 kts
Complement: 87

Missiles: SAM: 2 SA-N-5 quad launchers ❶; IR homing to 10 km *(5.5 nm)* at 1.5 Mach.
Guns: 1 USSR 3 in *(76 mm)*/66 ❷; 85° elevation; 120 rounds/minute to 15 km *(8 nm)*; weight of shell 7 kg.
6 USSR 23 mm (3 twin) ❸; to be replaced by 30 mm/65 AK 630.
Torpedoes: 4—21 in *(533 mm)* (2 twin) tubes ❹.
A/S mortars: 2 RBU 6000 12-tubed trainable ❺; range 6000 m; warhead 31 kg; 120 rockets.
Depth charges: 2 rails.
Countermeasures: 2 chaff launchers ❻.
Radars: Air/surface search: Strut Curve ❼; F band.
Surface search: Tamirio RN 231 ❽; I band.
IFF: Square Head.

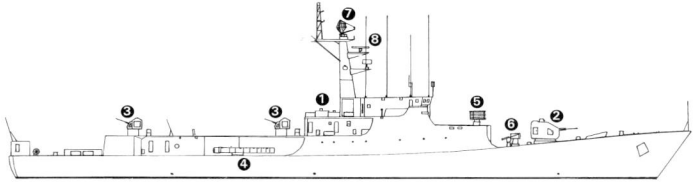

KASZUB *(Scale 1 : 900), Ian Sturton*

Sonars: Stern-mounted dipping type mounted on the transom; active; high frequency.

Programmes: Second of class cancelled in 1989 but consideration is now being given to a class of four more ships based on the Kaszub hull and specialised for anti-submarine warfare.
Structure: Design appears to be based on Grisha class but with many alterations. The 76 mm gun was fitted in late 1991. The 23 mm guns are to be replaced by Gatlings in due course. There is also space for a fire control director on the bridge roof.
Operational: Finally achieved operational status in 1990. Based at Hel with the Border Guard in 1990 but returned to the Navy in 1991.

KASZUB 5/1992, W Sartori

CORVETTES

4 SOVIET TARANTUL I CLASS (TYPE 1241)

Name	No	Builders	Commissioned
GORNIK	434	Volodyarski Yard	Dec 1983
HUTNIK	435	Volodyarski Yard	Apr 1984
METALOWIEC	436	Volodyarski Yard	Jan 1988
ROLNIK	437	Volodyarski Yard	Jan 1989

Displacement, tons: 455 full load
Dimensions, feet (metres): 184.1 × 37.7 × 8.2 *(56.1 × 11.5 × 2.5)*
Main machinery: COGOG; 2 Type NK-12MV gas turbines; 20 400 hp(m) *(15 MW)* sustained; 2 gas turbines with reversible gearbox; 8000 hp(m) *(5.88 MW)*; 2 shafts
Speed, knots: 35. **Range, miles:** 2300 at 18 kts
Complement: 34 (5 officers)

Missiles: SSM: 4 SS-N-2C Styx (2 twin) launchers; active radar or IR homing to 83 km *(45 nm)* at 0.9 Mach; warhead 513 kg; sea-skimmer in terminal flight.
SAM: SA-N-5 Grail quad launcher; manual aiming; IR homing to 6 km *(3.2 nm)* at 1.5 Mach; warhead 1.5 kg.
Guns: 1—3 in *(76 mm)*/60 automatic; 85° elevation; 120 rounds/minute to 15 km *(8 nm)*; weight of shell 7 kg.
2—30 mm/65 6-barrelled type; 85° elevation; 3000 rounds/minute combined to 2 km.
Countermeasures: Decoys: 2 chaff launchers.
Radars: Air/surface search: Plank Shave; E band.
Navigation: Krivach; I band.
Fire control: Bass Tilt; H/I band.
IFF: Square Head.

Programmes: Plans to take two more from the former GDR stock have been cancelled.
Structure: Similar to others of the class exported to India, Yemen and Romania.

1 + 2 SASSNITZ CLASS (TYPE 151)

Name	No	Builders	Commissioned
ORKAN	421	Peenewerft/Gdansk	18 Sep 1992
PIORUN	422	Peenewerft/Gdansk	1993
HURAGAN	423	Peenewerft/Gdansk	1993

Displacement, tons: 333 standard; 361 full load
Dimensions, feet (metres): 160.4 oa; 147.6 wl × 28.5 × 7.2 *(48.9; 45 × 8.7 × 2.2)*
Main machinery: 3 Type M 520T diesels; 14 670 hp(m) *(10.78 MW)* sustained; 3 shafts
Speed, knots: 36. **Range, miles:** 1530 at 14 kts
Complement: 34 (6 officers)

Missiles: SSM: 8 (2 quad) launchers Type 152; missiles to be fitted in due course.
SAM: SA-N-5 Grail quad launcher; manual aiming; IR homing to 6 km *(3.2 nm)* at 1.5 Mach; warhead 1.5 kg.
Guns: 1 USSR 3 in *(76 mm)*/66 AK 176; 85° elevation; 120 rounds/minute to 15 km *(8 nm)*; weight of shell 7 kg.
1—30 mm/65 ADG 630; 6 barrels; 3000 rounds/minute combined to 2 km.
Countermeasures: Decoys: 8—12-tubed chaff and IR launchers.
Radars: Air/surface search: NUR-27XA; E/F band.
Fire control: Bass Tilt; H/I band.
Navigation: SRN 443; I band.
IFF: Square Head; Salt Pot.

Programmes: Originally six of this former GDR Sassnitz class were to be built at Peenewerft for Poland. The future of the programme is uncertain but so far three units have been acquired for completion at Stocznia Polnocna Gdansk. Programme delayed by lack of funds.
Structure: The prototype vessel had two quadruple SSM launchers with an Exocet type (SS-N-25) of missile and the plan is to fit eight SSM in due course. Plank Shave radar has been replaced by a Polish set. Unlike the German Coast Guard vessels of the same class, these ships have retained three engines.

ROLNIK 5/1992, Stefan Terzibaschitsch

ORKAN 10/1992, Polish Navy

SHIPBORNE AIRCRAFT

Numbers/Type: 12/4 Mil Mi-14PL/PS Haze A.
Operational speed: 120 kts *(222 km/h)*.
Service ceiling: 15 000 ft *(4570 m)*.
Range: 240 nm *(445 km)*.
Role/Weapon systems: PL for ASW, PS for SAR. PL operates in co-operation with surface units; supported by 12 Mi-2 Hoplite helicopters in same unit. Can be carried in *Warszawa*. Sensors: Search radar, MAD, sonobuoys. Weapons: ASV; internal torpedoes, depth bombs and mines.

HAZE A   9/1992, van Ginderen Collection

LAND-BASED MARITIME AIRCRAFT (FRONT LINE)

Note: In addition there are eight AN-28 patrol and 10 TS-11R reconnaissance aircraft.

Numbers/Type: 10 PZL Swidnik W-3 Sokol.
Operational speed: 119 kts *(220 km/h)*.
Service ceiling: 15 256 ft *(4650 m)*.
Range: 335 nm *(620 km)*.
Role/Weapon systems: Planned to replace the Haze in due course. Total of 18 planned for SAR (Anaconda version).

SOKOL ANACONDA   1992, Swidnik

LIGHT FORCES

7 Ex-SOVIET OSA I CLASS (TYPE 205)
(FAST ATTACK CRAFT—MISSILE)

PUCK 427	OKSYWIE 429	SWINOUJSCIE 431	WLADYSLAWOWO 433
USTKA 428	DARLOWO 430	DZIWNÓW 432	

Displacement, tons: 171 standard; 210 full load
Dimensions, feet (metres): 126.6 × 24.9 × 8.8 *(38.6 × 7.6 × 2.7)*
Main machinery: 3 Type M 503A diesels; 8025 hp(m) *(5.9 MW)* sustained; 3 shafts
Speed, knots: 35. **Range, miles:** 800 at 30 kts
Complement: 30
Missiles: SSM: 4 SS-N-2A Styx; active radar or IR homing to 46 km *(25 nm)* at 0.9 Mach; warhead 513 kg.
Guns: 4—30 mm/65 (2 twin) automatic; 85° elevation; 500 rounds/minute to 5 km *(2.7 nm)*; weight of shell 0.54 kg.
Radars: Surface search: Square Tie; I band; range 73 km *(40 nm)*.
Fire control: Drum Tilt; H/I band.

Programmes: All date from early to mid-1960s and are running out of operational life.
Structure: Pennant numbers are carried on side-boards on the bridge. By the end of 1992 four (423, 425, 426 and 424) had been converted to Frontier Guard ships with SSM and after gun removed and the forward gun replaced by a twin 25 mm 2M3M. More may be converted.

DARLOWO   8/1992

8 MODIFIED OBLUZE CLASS (TYPE 912M)
(LARGE PATROL CRAFT)

GROZNY 351	ZRECZNY 353	ZWROTNY 355	NIEUGIETY 357
WYTRWALY 352	ZWINNY 354	ZAWZIETY 356	CZUJNY 358

Displacement, tons: 237 full load
Dimensions, feet (metres): 135.5 × 20.7 × 6.6 *(41.3 × 6.3 × 2)*
Main machinery: 2 Type 40D diesels; 4400 hp(m) *(3.23 MW)* sustained; 2 shafts
Speed, knots: 24. **Range, miles:** 600 at 18 kts
Complement: 28
Guns: 4—30 mm/65 (2 twin).
Depth charges: 2 racks.
Radars: Surface search: Tamirio RN 231; I band.
Fire control: Drum Tilt; H/I band.
IFF: Two Square Head. High Pole.
Sonars: Hull-mounted; active attack; high frequency.

Comment: Modified Obluze class. Completed 1969-72 at the Naval Shipyard, Gdynia.

ZWROTNY   8/1983, Ralf Bendfeldt

11 PILICA CLASS (TYPE 918) (COASTAL PATROL CRAFT)

166-176

Displacement, tons: 87 full load
Dimensions, feet (metres): 95.1 × 18.4 × 4.6 *(29 × 5.6 × 1.4)*
Main machinery: 3 diesels; 3600 hp(m) *(2.65 MW)*; 3 shafts
Speed, knots: 30
Complement: 15
Guns: 2—23 mm/87 (twin).
Torpedoes: 2—21 in *(533 mm)* tubes; anti-surface.
Radars: Surface search: Tamirio RN 231; I band.
Sonars: Dipping VDS aft.

Comment: Built in Poland since 1973. Based at Kolobrzeg and Gdansk. First batch of five, without torpedo tubes are part of the Maritime Frontier Guard.

PILICA 170   3/1992, Erik Laursen

MINE WARFARE FORCES

8 KROGULEC CLASS (TYPE 206F) (MINESWEEPERS—OCEAN)

Name	No	Builders	Commissioned
KORMORAN	616	Stocznia, Gdynia	1963
ALBATROS	618	Stocznia, Gdynia	1964
PELIKAN	619	Stocznia, Gdynia	1965
TUKAN	620	Stocznia, Gdynia	1966
FLAMINGO	621	Stocznia, Gdynia	1966
RYBITWA	622	Stocznia, Gdynia	1966
MEWA	623	Stocznia, Gdynia	1967
CZAJKA	624	Stocznia, Gdynia	1967

Displacement, tons: 474 full load
Dimensions, feet (metres): 190.9 × 25.3 × 6.9 *(58.2 × 7.7 × 2.1)*
Main machinery: 2 Fiat A-230S diesels; 3750 hp(m) *(2.76 MW)*; 2 shafts
Speed, knots: 18. **Range, miles:** 2000 at 17 kts
Complement: 48 (6 officers)
Guns: 6—25 mm/60 (3 twin) or 4—23 mm (2 twin) and 2—25 mm/60 (twin).
Depth charges: 2 racks.
Mines: 2 rails.
Radars: Surface search: Tamirio RN 231; I band.
Sonars: Hull-mounted; minehunting; high frequency.

Comment: Project 206F. Armament varies with some having 23 mm guns aft instead of the 25 mm guns. Four deleted so far.

FLAMINGO   8/1992

13 GOPLO (NOTEC) CLASS (TYPE 207P) (MINESWEEPERS—COASTAL)

GOPLO 630	JAMNO 634	SARBSKO 638	HANCZA 642
GARDNO 631	MIELNO 635	NECKO 639	
BUKOWO 632	WICKO 636	NAKLO 640	
DABIE 633	RESKO 637	DRUZNO 641	

Displacement, tons: 208 standard; 225 full load
Dimensions, feet (metres): 125.7 × 23.6 × 5.9 *(38.3 × 7.2 × 1.8)*
Main machinery: 2 M 40-1A diesels; 1874 hp(m) *(1.38 MW)*; 2 shafts
Speed, knots: 14. **Range, miles:** 1100 at 9 kts
Complement: 24 (4 officers)
Guns: 2 Wrobel ZU-23-2M 23 mm (twin).
Radars: Navigation: Tamirio RN 231; I band.

Comment: *Goplo* launched April 1981 as an experimental prototype numbered 207D. Built at about one per year, with the last one completing in January 1992. The 23 mm guns have replaced the original 25 mm. GRP hulls. Some carry divers for minehunting work.

RESKO 5/1992, MoD Bonn

NAKLO 10/1992, Erik Laursen

1 + 4 MAMRY (NOTEC II) CLASS (TYPE 207M) (MINEHUNTERS—COASTAL)

Name	No	Builders	Commissioned
MAMRY	643	Naval Shipyard, Gdynia	25 Sep 1992
WIGRY	644	Naval Shipyard, Gdynia	1993

Displacement, tons: 262 full load
Dimensions, feet (metres): 142.7 × 25.3 × 5.9 *(43.5 × 7.7 × 1.8)*
Main machinery: 2 diesels; 1605 hp(m) *(1.18 MW)*; 2 shafts; 2 auxiliary motors; 816 hp(m) *(60 kW)*
Speed, knots: 13
Complement: 24 (4 officers)
Guns: 2 Wrobel ZU-23-2MR 23 mm (twin).
Radars: Navigation: I band.
Sonars: Atlas Elektronik; active search; high frequency.

Comment: This is a minehunter variant of the Goplo class designed to deal with magnetic and acoustic mines. Five of the class are planned. *Wigry* launched 28 November 1992.

2 LENIWKA CLASS (TYPE 410S) (MINESWEEPERS—COASTAL)

625 626

Displacement, tons: 245 full load
Dimensions, feet (metres): 84.6 × 23.6 × 8.9 *(25.8 × 7.2 × 2.7)*
Main machinery: 1 Puck-Sulzer 6AL20/24 diesel; 570 hp(m) *(420 kW)*; 1 shaft
Speed, knots: 11. **Range, miles:** 3100 at 8 kts

Comment: Project 410S modified stern trawlers built at Ustka Shipyard in 1982/83. Sweeping is done by using strung-out charges. The ships can carry 40 tons of cargo or 40 people.

LENIWKA 625 9/1992, Hartmut Ehlers

AMPHIBIOUS FORCES

Note: The following ships and craft plus a number of civilian Ro-ro ships are for use by the 7th Coastal Defence Brigade (ex-Sea Landing Division) (5000 men) based in the Gdansk area.

1 MODIFIED POLNOCHNY C CLASS (TYPE 776) (LCTs)

Name	No	Builders	Commissioned
GRUNWALD	811	Stocznia Polnocna	1973

Displacement, tons: 1253 full load
Dimensions, feet (metres): 246.1 × 31.5 × 7.5 *(75 × 9.6 × 2.3)*
Main machinery: 2 Type 40-D diesels; 4400 hp(m) *(3.2 MW)* sustained; 2 shafts
Speed, knots: 19. **Range, miles:** 1000 at 18 kts
Complement: 45 plus 54 flag staff
Military lift: 2 light trucks
Guns: 2 or 4—30 mm (1 or 2 twin). 2—140 mm rocket launchers.
Radars: Navigation: Don 2; I band.
Fire control: Drum Tilt; H/I band.
IFF: Square Head. High Pole.

Comment: A modified Group C ship converted to an amphibious command vessel. Command and electronic equipment fitted on the vehicle deck leaving a small area behind the bow doors for two light trucks or jeeps. The remainder of this class have been deleted.

GRUNWALD 9/1992, van Ginderen Collection

5 LUBLIN CLASS (TYPE 767) (LCT/MINELAYER)

Name	No	Builders	Launched	Commissioned
LUBLIN	821	Stocznia Polnocna, Gdansk	12 July 1988	12 Oct 1989
GNIEZNO	822	Stocznia Polnocna, Gdansk	7 Dec 1988	23 Feb 1990
KRAKOW	823	Stocznia Polnocna, Gdansk	7 Mar 1989	27 June 1990
POZNAN	824	Stocznia Polnocna, Gdansk	5 Jan 1990	8 Mar 1991
TORUN	825	Stocznia Polnocna, Gdansk	8 June 1990	24 May 1991

Displacement, tons: 1089 standard; 1745 full load
Dimensions, feet (metres): 313 × 35.4 × 6.6 *(95.4 × 10.8 × 2)*
Main machinery: 3 Cegielski 6ATL25D diesels; 5390 hp(m) *(3.96 MW)* sustained; 3 shafts
Speed, knots: 16. **Range, miles:** 1400 at 16 kts
Complement: 37 (5 officers)
Military lift: 5 MBT or 9 APC or 7 amphibious tanks. 135 troops plus equipment
Missiles: SAM: 2—72 mm Strela 2M launchers on each gun mounting.
Guns: 8—23 mm (4 twin).
Depth charges: 9 throwers for counter-mining.
Mines: 50-134.
Countermeasures: Decoys: 2 chaff launchers.
Radars: 2 navigation: SRN 7455 and SRN 433XTA; I band.

Comment: Designed with a through deck from bow to stern and can be used as minelayers as well as for amphibious landings. Folding bow and stern ramps and a stern anchor are fitted. The ship has a pressurised citadel for NBC defence and an upper deck washdown system.

GNIEZNO 9/1992, Hartmut Ehlers

LUBLIN 1992, MoD Bonn

3 + (9) DEBA CLASS (TYPE 716) (LCU)

851   852   853

Displacement, tons: 176 full load
Dimensions, feet (metres): 122 × 23.3 × 5.6 *(37.2 × 7.1 × 1.7)*
Main machinery: 3 Type M 401A diesels; 3000 hp(m) *(2.2 MW)*; 3 shafts
Speed, knots: 20. **Range, miles:** 430 at 16 kts
Complement: 10
Military lift: 2 small tanks or 3 vehicles up to 15 tons or 50 troops
Guns: 2—23 mm (twin).

Comment: Built at Navy Yard, Gdynia. First one commissioned 16 June 1988, second in 1990 and third in 1991. The plan was to build 12 but the programme was suspended through lack of funds. The intention is to start again when money is available. Can carry up to six launchers for strung-out charges.

DEBA 851   *1992, Polish Navy*

INTELLIGENCE VESSELS

2 MODIFIED MOMA CLASS (TYPE 863) (AGIs)

NAVIGATOR 262   **HYDROGRAF** 263

Displacement, tons: 1680 full load
Dimensions, feet (metres): 240.5 × 39.4 × 12.8 *(73.3 × 12 × 3.9)*
Main machinery: 2 Zgoda-Sulzer 6TD48 diesels; 3300 hp(m) *(2.43 MW)* sustained; 2 shafts
Speed, knots: 17. **Range, miles:** 9000 at 12 kts
Complement: 65 (10 officers)

Comment: Built by Stocznia Polnocna in Gdansk and commissioned June 1975. Much altered in the upperworks and unrecognisable as Momas. The fo'c'sle in *Hydrograf* is longer than in *Navigator* and one deck higher. Both fitted for but not with two twin 25 mm gun mountings. Forward radomes replaced by a cylindrical type and after ones removed on both ships in 1987.

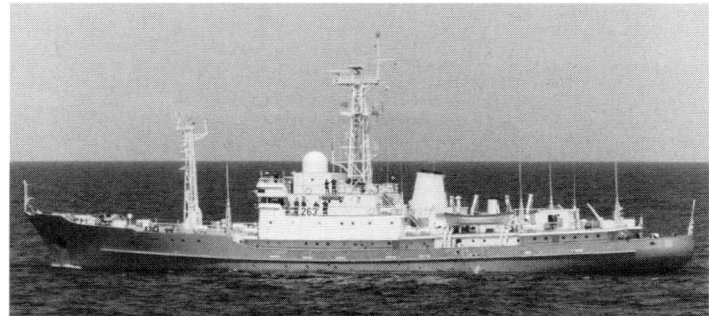

HYDROGRAF   *1992*

TRAINING SHIPS

Note: There is a 498 ton Type B79 sailing sloop *Iskra* 253 which was built in 1982 by Stocznia Gdanska and has a complement of 40 cadets. The much larger *Dar Mlodziezy* is civilian owned and operated but also takes naval personnel for training.

ISKRA   *4/1992, Giorgio Ghiglione*

2 WODNIK CLASS (TYPE 888)

WODNIK 251   **GRYF** 252

Displacement, tons: 1697 standard; 1820 full load
Dimensions, feet (metres): 234.3 × 38.1 × 12.8 *(71.4 × 11.6 × 3.9)*
Main machinery: 2 Zgoda-Sulzer 6TD48 diesels; 3300 hp(m) *(2.43 MW)* sustained; 2 shafts
Speed, knots: 16. **Range, miles:** 7200 at 11 kts
Complement: 75 plus 101 midshipmen
Guns: 4—30 mm (2 twin). 4—23 mm (2 twin).
Radars: Navigation: Two RN 231; I band.
Fire control: Drum Tilt; H/I band.

Comment: Type 888 built by Stocznia Polnocna in Gdansk. *Wodnik* launched November 1975, *Gryf* March 1976. Sisters to former GDR *Wilhelm Pieck* and two Soviet ships. *Wodnik* converted to a hospital ship (150 beds) in 1990 for deployment to the Gulf. Armament removed as part of the conversion but restored in 1992. *Wodnik* has a helicopter platform.

WODNIK (guns restored)   *5/1992, Maritime Photographic*

GRYF   *5/1992, H M Steele*

4 BRYZA CLASS (TYPE OS-1)

BRYZA K 18   **PODCHORAZY** 711   **KADET** 712   **ELEW** 713

Displacement, tons: 180 (167, *Bryza*) full load
Dimensions, feet (metres): 98.4 × 22.9 × 6.4 *(30 × 7 × 2)*
Main machinery: 2 Wola diesels; 300 hp(m) *(220 kW)*; 2 shafts
Speed, knots: 10. **Range, miles:** 1100 at 10 kts
Complement: 11 plus 26 cadets
Radars: Navigation: Two RN 231; I band.

Comment: *Podchorazy* commissioned 30 November 1974, *Elew* 5 March 1975 and *Kadet* July 1975. All built by Stocznia Wista, Gdansk. *Bryza* has a lighter superstructure than remainder.

BRYZA   *4/1989, Marek Twardowski*

ELEW   *11/1990, Marek Twardowski*

SURVEYING AND RESEARCH VESSELS

2 MODIFIED FINIK 2 CLASS (TYPE 874)

HEWELIUSZ 265   **ARCTOWSKI** 266

Displacement, tons: 1135 full load
Dimensions, feet (metres): 202.1 × 36.7 × 10.8 *(61.6 × 11.2 × 3.3)*
Main machinery: 2 Cegielski-Sulzer 6AL25/30 diesels; 1920 hp(m) *(1.4 MW)*; 2 auxiliary motors; 204 hp(m) *(150 kW)*; 2 shafts; cp props; bow thruster
Speed, knots: 13. **Range, miles:** 3000 at 13 kts
Complement: 55 (10 officers)

Comment: Built at Stocznia Polnocna, Gdansk and both commissioned 27 November 1982. Sister ships to Soviet class which were built in Poland, except that *Heweliusz* and *Arctowski* have been modified and have no buoy handling equipment. Two sister ships, *Zodiak* and *Planeta*, are civilian operated.

ARCTOWSKI   8/1992

1 MOMA CLASS (TYPE 861K)

KOPERNIK 261

Displacement, tons: 1240 standard; 1580 full load
Dimensions, feet (metres): 240.5 × 36.8 × 12.8 *(73.3 × 11.2 × 3.9)*
Main machinery: 2 Zgoda-Sulzer 6TD48 diesels; 3300 hp(m) *(2.43 MW)* sustained; 2 shafts
Speed, knots: 17. **Range, miles:** 9000 at 12 kts
Complement: 41 (8 officers) plus 40 scientists

Comment: Built by Stocznia Polnocna, Gdansk and commissioned 20 February 1971. Forward crane removed in 1983.

KOPERNIK   1992, Polish Navy

2 KHK 121 CLASS

K 20   K 21

Displacement, tons: 12.3 standard
Dimensions, feet (metres): 29.5 × 9.8 × 2.6 *(9 × 3 × 0.8)*
Main machinery: 2 diesels; 800 hp(m) *(588 kW)*; 2 shafts
Speed, knots: 8. **Range, miles:** 85 at 8 kts
Complement: 18

Comment: Survey craft built by Stocznia Rzeczna, Wroclawska in 1989-90.

TANKERS

4 MOSKIT CLASS (TYPE B 199)

KRAB Z 3   MEDUZA Z 8   SLIMAK Z 9   Z 5

Displacement, tons: 1200 full load
Dimensions, feet (metres): 189.3 × 31.2 × 11.2 *(57.7 × 9.5 × 3.4)*
Main machinery: 2 Sulzer diesels; 850 hp(m) *(625 kW)*; 2 shafts
Speed, knots: 11. **Range, miles:** 1200 at 10 kts
Complement: 18
Cargo capacity: 656 tons
Guns: 4—25 mm (2 twin).

Comment: Built in Poland in 1971-72 by Stocznia Rzeczna, Wroclawska. First two carry oil, the other two water. Names are unofficial.

KRAB   10/1992, Erik Laursen

1 BALTYK CLASS (TYPE ZP 1200)

Name	No	Builders	Commissioned
BALTYK	Z 1	Naval Shipyard, Gdynia	11 Mar 1991

Displacement, tons: 2918 standard; 2974 full load
Dimensions, feet (metres): 278.2 × 43 × 15.4 *(84.8 × 13.1 × 4.7)*
Main machinery: 2 Cegielski diesels; 4025 hp(m) *(2.96 MW)*; 2 shafts
Speed, knots: 15. **Range, miles:** 4250 at 12 kts
Guns: 2 Wrobel 23 mm.

Comment: Beam replenishment stations, one each side. First of a projected class of four, of which the others have been cancelled.

BALTYK   1992, Polish Navy

1 TYPE 500

Z 6

Displacement, tons: 625 full load
Dimensions, feet (metres): 138.5 × 23 × 10.2 *(42.2 × 7 × 3.1)*
Main machinery: 1 Wola diesel; 300 hp(m) *(220 kW)*; 1 shaft
Speed, knots: 8. **Range, miles:** 500 at 8 kts
Complement: 14
Cargo capacity: 385 tons
Guns: 4—25 mm (2 twin).

Comment: Built in 1961 at Gdansk for coastal service. Two others deleted.

Z 6   1990, Polish Navy

TORPEDO RECOVERY VESSELS

2 KORMORAN CLASS

K 8   K 11

Displacement, tons: 149 full load
Dimensions, feet (metres): 114.8 × 19.7 × 5.2 *(35 × 6 × 1.6)*
Main machinery: 2 Type M 50F5 diesels; 2400 hp(m) *(1.76 MW)*; 2 shafts
Speed, knots: 21. **Range, miles:** 550 at 15 kts
Complement: 18
Guns: 2—25 mm (twin).

Comment: Built at Naval Shipyard, Gdynia in 1970.

K 8   1992, Polish Navy

TUGS

Note: In addition there are a number of small berthing tugs with M numbers.

2 GOLIAT CLASS (TYPE 667R)

H 16   H 18

Displacement, tons: 150 full load
Dimensions, feet (metres): 70.2 × 20 × 8.5 *(21.4 × 6.1 × 2.6)*
Main machinery: 1 8NVD 36 diesel; 300 hp(m) *(221 kW)*; 1 shaft
Speed, knots: 12

Comment: Built at Gdynia in the 1960s. Remainder of class sold for civilian use in 1991.

H 18   9/1992, Hartmut Ehlers

5 H 900 and 2 H 800 CLASSES

H 3, 4, 5, 6, 7   H 1, 2

Displacement, tons: 218 full load
Dimensions, feet (metres): 84 × 22.3 × 11.5 *(25.6 × 6.8 × 3.5)*
Main machinery: 1 Cegielski-Sulzer 6AL20/24H diesel; 935 hp(m) *(687 kW)*; 1 shaft
Speed, knots: 10
Complement: 17

Comment: Similar designs. *H 1* and *H 2* built in 1970, the remainder in the early 1980s. Have fire-fighting capability.

H 4   9/1992, Hartmut Ehlers

3 MOTYL CLASS (TYPE 1500)

H 12, 19, 20

Displacement, tons: 439 full load
Dimensions, feet (metres): 103.7 × 27.6 × 11.5 *(31.6 × 8.4 × 3.5)*
Main machinery: 1 Sulzer 5TD48 diesel; 1500 hp(m) *(1.1 MW)*; 1 shaft
Speed, knots: 12. Range, miles: 1500 at 12 kts
Complement: 22

Comment: Built at Gdansk in 1964.

H 19   1973

DEGAUSSING VESSELS

3 MROWKA CLASS (TYPE B 208)

WRONA SD 11   **RYS** SD 12   SD 13

Displacement, tons: 600 full load
Dimensions, feet (metres): 145.3 × 26.6 × 7.5 *(44.3 × 8.1 × 2.3)*
Main machinery: 1 diesel; 335 hp(m) *(246 kW)*; 1 shaft
Speed, knots: 9.5
Guns: 1—25 mm (not in all).

Comment: A class of DGVs. Completed in 1971-72 by Naval Yard, Gdynia. Names are unofficial.

SD 13   1992, Polish Navy

SALVAGE SHIPS

2 PIAST CLASS (TYPE 570)

Name	No	Builders	Commissioned
PIAST	281	Stocznia Polnocna, Gdansk	26 Jan 1974
LECH	282	Stocznia Polnocna, Gdansk	30 Nov 1974

Displacement, tons: 1732 full load
Dimensions, feet (metres): 238.5 × 38.1 × 13.1 *(72.7 × 11.6 × 4)*
Main machinery: 2 Zgoda-Sulzer 6TD48 diesels; 3300 hp(m) *(2.43 MW)* sustained; 2 shafts
Speed, knots: 15. Range, miles: 3000 at 12 kts
Complement: 52 (6 officers) plus 15 spare
Guns: 8—25 mm (4 twin) (can be fitted).

Comment: Basically a Moma class hull with towing and firefighting capabilities. Ice-strengthened hulls. Wartime role as hospital ships. Carry three-man diving bells capable of 100 m depth and a decompression chamber.

PIAST   5/1991, Fotoflite

3 PLUSKWA CLASS (TYPE R-30)

Name	No	Builders	Commissioned
GNIEWKO	R 11	Navy Yard, Gdynia	25 July 1981
BOLKO	R 12	Navy Yard, Gdynia	7 Nov 1982
SEMKO	R 13	Navy Yard, Gdynia	9 May 1987

Displacement, tons: 365 full load
Dimensions, feet (metres): 105 × 29.2 × 10.2 *(32 × 8.9 × 3.1)*
Main machinery: 1 Cegielski-Sulzer diesel; 1470 hp(m) *(1.08 MW)*; 1 shaft
Speed, knots: 12. Range, miles: 4000 at 7 kts

Comment: Rescue tugs.

BOLKO   9/1992, Hartmut Ehler

2 ZBYSZKO CLASS (TYPE B 823)

Name	No	Builders	Commissioned
ZBYSZKO	R 14	Uskta Shipyard	Sep 1991
MACKO	R 15	Uskta Shipyard	Dec 1991

Displacement, tons: 380 full load
Dimensions, feet (metres): 114.8 × 26.2 × 9.8 *(35 × 8 × 3)*
Main machinery: 1 Sulzer 6AL20/24D; 750 hp(m) *(551 kW)*; 1 shaft
Speed, knots: 11. **Range, miles:** 3000 at 10 kts
Radars: Navigation: SRN 402X; I band.

Comment: Type B-823 ordered 30 May 1988. Carries a decompression chamber and two divers. Mobile gantry crane on the stern.

1 ICEBREAKER

PERKUN

Measurement, tons: 1152 gross; 272 net
Dimensions, feet (metres): 185 × 46 × — *(56.5 × 14 × —)*
Main machinery: Diesel-electric; 4 diesel generators; 3680 hp(m) *(2.7 MW)*; 4 motors; 3000 hp(m) *(2.2 MW)*; 2 shafts
Speed, knots: 10

Comment: Built by P K Harris and Sons Ltd, Appledore, Devon in 1963. Civilian owned, naval operated and manned.

MARITIME FRONTIER GUARD (MOSG)

Note: MOSG (Morski Oddzial Strazy Graniczna). Vessels have blue hulls with red and yellow striped insignia. Superstructures are painted white.

2 KAPER CLASS (TYPE SKS-40) (LARGE PATROL CRAFT)

KAPER I 311   **KAPER II** 312

Displacement, tons: 470 full load
Dimensions, feet (metres): 139.4 × 27.6 × 9.2 *(42.5 × 8.4 × 2.8)*
Main machinery: 2 Sulzer 8ATL25/30 diesels; 4720 hp(m) *(3.47 MW)*; 2 shafts
Speed, knots: 17. **Range, miles:** 2800 at 14 kts
Complement: 11 plus 7 spare
Radars: Surface search: E/F band.
Navigation: I band.

Comment: *Kaper I* completed at Wisla Yard, Gdansk in January 1991, *Kaper II* in November 1991. Have fish finding sonars fitted. Used for Fishery Protection. More may be built.

KAPER I   1992 MOSG

4 Ex-SOVIET OSA I CLASS (TYPE 205) (FAST ATTACK CRAFT—GUN)

GDYNIA 301 (ex-423)	ELBLAG 303 (ex-426)
SZCZECIN 302 (ex-425)	KOLOBRZEG 304 (ex-424)

Comment: Three transferred from the Navy in 1991 and one in 1992. Details under *Light Forces* except that all armament and fire control radar has been removed, leaving only a twin 25 mm 2M3M gun forward.

ELBLAG   1992 MOSG

5 OBLUZE CLASS (TYPE 912) (LARGE PATROL CRAFT)

FALA 321	ZEFIR 323	TECZA 325
SZKWAL 322	ZORZA 324	

Displacement, tons: 250 full load
Dimensions, feet (metres): 135.5 × 21.3 × 7 *(41.3 × 6.5 × 2.1)*
Main machinery: 2 diesels; 4400 hp(m) *(3.23 MW)* sustained; 2 shafts
Speed, knots: 24
Complement: 34
Guns: 4—30 mm (2 twin). Some have after mounting removed.
Depth charges: 2 internal racks.
Radars: Surface search: Tamirio RN 231; I band.
Sonars: Hull-mounted; active attack; high frequency.

Comment: Built at Gdynia in 1965-66.

SZKWAL   1992, MOSG

12 WISLOKA CLASS (TYPE 90) (COASTAL PATROL CRAFT)

SG 141-152

Displacement, tons: 45 full load
Dimensions, feet (metres): 69.6 × 12.8 × 4.6 *(21.1 × 3.9 × 1.4)*
Main machinery: 2 Wola ZM diesels; 1000 hp(m) *(735 kW)*; 2 shafts
Speed, knots: 18. **Range, miles:** 300 at 18 kts
Complement: 9
Guns: 2—14.5 mm MGs (in some). 1—12.7 mm MG and 1 ZM rocket launcher (in others).

Comment: Built at Wisla Shipyard, Gdansk between 1973 and 1977.

SG 148   9/1992, Hartmut Ehlers

5 PILICA CLASS (TYPE 918) (COASTAL PATROL CRAFT)

SG 161-165

Displacement, tons: 85 full load
Dimensions, feet (metres): 95.1 × 18.4 × 4.3 *(29 × 5.6 × 1.3)*
Main machinery: 3 diesels; 3600 hp(m) *(2.65 MW)*; 3 shafts
Speed, knots: 30
Complement: 15
Guns: 2—23 mm/87 (twin).
Radars: Surface search: Tamiro RN 231; I band.

Comment: Same as naval craft but without the torpedo tubes and sonar. Built in the 1970s.

SG 165   9/1992, Hartmut Ehlers

SG 161   1992 MOSG

500 POLAND / Maritime frontier guard (MOSG) — PORTUGAL / Introduction

5 SZKWAL CLASS (TYPE S-12) (INSHORE PATROL CRAFT)

SG 111-115

Dimensions, feet (metres): 38.4 × 15.1 × 3 *(11.7 × 4.6 × 0.9)*
Main machinery: 2 diesels; 2000 hp(m) *(1.47 MW)*; 2 shafts
Speed, knots: 38
Complement: 4
Guns: 1—7.62 mm MG.
Radars: Surface search: I band.

Comment: Built at Wisla, Gdansk between 1986 and 1990. Fast pursuit boats possibly taken over from the Police. There may be up to 14 of this class but some are still used by the Police.

INSHORE PATROL CRAFT

Comment: There are at least two other classes of harbour patrol craft with numbers in the SG 008 and SG 125 series. Overall numbers not known.

SG 113   *9/1992, Hartmut Ehlers*

SG 008   *9/1992, Hartmut Ehlers*

PORTUGAL

Headquarters' Appointments

Chief of Naval Staff:
  Admiral António Carlos Fuzeta da Ponte
Vice Chief of Naval Staff:
  Vice Admiral Fernando Manuel Palla Machado da Silva
Continental Naval Commander:
  Vice Admiral Narciso Augusto do Carmo Duro
Azores Naval Commander:
  Vice Admiral Jose Malheiro Garcia
Madeira Naval Commander:
  Captain Raul Trincalhetas Janes Semedo
Marine Corps Commander:
  Captain Francisco Isidoro Montes de Oliveira Monteiro
Submarine Squadron Commander:
  Captain Adolfo Esteves Sousa

Diplomatic Representation

Naval Attaché in London:
  Commander Rui Cardoso de Telles Palhinha
Naval Attaché in Paris, Brussels and Hague:
  Commander José Manuel de Oliveira Alves Correia
Naval Attaché in Washington, Ottawa and NLR SACLANT:
  Captain Jose Luis Lopes Celestino da Silva
Defence Attaché in Bissau, Dakar and Conakry:
  Commander Antonio Joao Carreiro e Silva

Personnel

(a) 1993: 15 000 (1700 officers) including 2800 marines
(b) 12 months national service

Strength of the Fleet

Type	Active (Reserve)	Building (Projected)
Submarines (Patrol)	3	—
Frigates	17	—
Large Patrol Craft	15	—
Coastal/River Patrol Craft	9	—
Minesweepers	—	(4)
LCTs	3	—
LCMs	9	—
Survey Ships and Craft	9	—
Replenishment Tankers	2	—
Logistic Support Ship	1	—
Diving Tender	1	—
Sail Training Ships	4	—
Tugs	2	—
Harbour Tankers	3	—
Buoy Tender	1	—

Prefix to Ships' Names

NRP

Bases

Main Base: Lisbon—Alfeite
Dockyard: Arsenal do Alfeite
Fleet Support: Porto, Portimão, Funchal, Ponta Delgada
Air Base: Montigo (Lisbon)

Mercantile Marine

Lloyd's Register of Shipping:
  332 vessels of 717 733 tons gross

DELETIONS

Patrol Forces

1991   Atria, Lagoa, Rosario
1992   São Roque

PENNANT LIST

Submarines

S 163	Albacora
S 164	Barracuda
S 166	Delfim

Frigates

F 330	Vasco da Gama
F 331	Alvares Cabral
F 332	Corte Real
F 471	Antonio Enes
F 475	João Coutinho
F 476	Jacinto Candido
F 477	Gen Pereira d'Eça
F 480	Comandante João Belo
F 481	Comandante Hermenegildo Capelo
F 482	Comandante Roberto Ivens
F 483	Comandante Sacadura Cabral
F 484	Augusto de Castilho
F 485	Honorio Barreto
F 486	Baptista de Andrade
F 487	João Roby
F 488	Afonso Cerqueira
F 489	Oliveira E Carmo

Light Forces

P 370	Rio Minho
P 1140	Cacine
P 1141	Cunene
P 1142	Mandovi
P 1143	Rovuma
P 1144	Cuanza
P 1145	Geba
P 1146	Zaire
P 1147	Zambeze
P 1148	Dom Aleixo
P 1149	Dom Jeremias
P 1150	Argos
P 1151	Dragão
P 1152	Escorpião
P 1153	Cassiopeia
P 1154	Hidra
P 1160	Limpopo
P 1161	Save
P 1162	Albatroz
P 1163	Açor
P 1164	Andorinha
P 1165	Aguia
P 1167	Cisne
UAM 630	Condor

Amphibious Forces

LDG 201	Bombarda
LDG 202	Alabarda
LDG 203	Bacamarte

LDM 119-121
LDM 406, 418, 420-423

Service Forces

A 520	Sagres
A 521	Schultz Xavier
A 527	Almeida Carvalho
A 5201	Vega
A 5203	Andromeda
A 5204	Polar
A 5205	Auriga
A 5206	São Gabriel
A 5207	Ribeira Grande
A 5208	São Miguel
A 5210	Berrio

SUBMARINES

3 FRENCH DAPHNE CLASS

Name	No	Builders	Laid down	Launched	Commissioned
ALBACORA	S 163	Dubigeon-Normandie, Nantes	6 Sep 1965	13 Oct 1966	1 Oct 1967
BARRACUDA	S 164	Dubigeon-Normandie, Nantes	19 Oct 1965	24 Apr 1967	4 May 1968
DELFIM	S 166	Dubigeon-Normandie, Nantes	14 May 1967	23 Sep 1968	1 Oct 1969

Displacement, tons: 869 surfaced; 1043 dived
Dimensions, feet (metres): 189.6 × 22.3 × 15.1 *(57.8 × 6.8 × 4.6)*
Main machinery: Diesel-electric; 2 SEMT-Pielstick 12 PA4 V 185 diesels; 2450 hp(m) *(1.8 MW)*; 2 Jeumont Schneider alternators; 1.7 MW; 2 motors; 2600 hp(m) *(1.9 MW)*; 2 shafts
Speed, knots: 13.5 surfaced; 16 dived
Range, miles: 2710 at 12.5 kts surfaced; 2130 at 10 kts snorting
Complement: 55 (6 officers)

Torpedoes: 12—21.7 in *(550 mm)* (8 bow, 4 stern) tubes. ECAN E14/15; anti-surface; passive homing to 12 km *(6.6 nm)* at 25 kts; warhead 300 kg or ECAN L3; anti-submarine; active homing to 5.5 km *(3 nm)* at 25 kts; warhead 200 kg. No reloads.
Countermeasures: ESM: ARUR; radar warning.
Fire control: DLT D3 torpedo control.
Radars: Surface search: Kelvin Hughes KH 1007; I band.
Sonars: Thomson Sintra DSUV 2; passive search and attack; medium frequency.
DUUA 2; active search and attack; 8.4 kHz.

Programmes: Basically similar to the French Daphne type, but slightly modified to suit Portuguese requirements. Replacements needed but plans have been postponed in favour of minehunters, possibly to the end of the decade.
Modernisation: Similar to French Daphne class but without the external modification to the hull. New radar fitted in 1993/94.
Structure: Diving depth, 300 m *(984 ft)*. Crushing depth, 575 m *(1885 ft)*.
Sales: *Cachalote* transferred to Pakistan as *Ghazi* in 1975.

ALBACORA   *4/1992, G Toremans*

FRIGATES

3 VASCO DA GAMA CLASS

Name	No	Builders	Laid down	Launched	Commissioned
VASCO DA GAMA	F 330	Blohm & Voss, Hamburg	1 Feb 1989	26 Jan 1989	18 Jan 1991
ALVARES CABRAL	F 331	Howaldtswerke, Kiel	2 June 1989	6 June 1990	24 May 1991
CORTE REAL	F 332	Howaldtswerke, Kiel	24 Nov 1989	6 June 1990	22 Nov 1991

Displacement, tons: 2700 standard; 3300 full load
Dimensions, feet (metres): 380.3 oa; 357.6 pp × 48.7 × 20 *(115.9; 109 × 14.8 × 6.1)*
Main machinery: CODOG; 2 GE LM 2500 gas turbines; 53 000 hp *(39.5 MW)* sustained; 2 MTU 12V 1163 TB83 diesels; 8840 hp(m) *(6.5 MW)*; 2 shafts; cp props
Speed, knots: 32 gas; 20 diesel. **Range, miles:** 4900 at 18 kts; 9600 at 12 kts
Complement: 182 (23 officers) (including air crew of 16 (4 officers)) plus 16 Flag Staff

Missiles: SSM: 8 McDonnell Douglas Harpoon (2 quad) launchers ❶; active radar homing to 130 km *(70 nm)* at 0.9 Mach; warhead 227 kg.
SAM: Raytheon Sea Sparrow Mk 29 Mod 1 octuple launcher ❷; semi-active radar homing to 14.6 km *(8 nm)* at 2.5 Mach; warhead 39 kg. Space left for VLS Sea Sparrow ❸.
Guns: 1 Creusot Loire 3.9 in *(100 mm)*/55 Mod 68 CADAM ❹; 80° elevation; 60 rounds/minute to 17 km *(9 nm)* anti-surface; 8 km *(4.4 nm)* anti-aircraft; weight of shell 13.5 kg.
1 General Electric/General Dynamics Vulcan Phalanx 20 mm Mk 15 Mod 11 ❺; 6 barrels per mounting; 3000 rounds/minute combined to 1.5 km.
Torpedoes: 6—324 mm US Mk 32 (2 triple) tubes ❻. Honeywell Mk 46 Mod 5; anti-submarine; active/passive homing to 11 km *(5.9 nm)* at 40 kts; warhead 44 kg.
Countermeasures: Decoys: 2 Loral Hycor Mk 36 SRBOC 6-barrelled chaff launchers ❼.
SLQ 25 Nixie; towed torpedo decoy.
ESM/ECM: Argo AR 700/APECS II; intercept and jammer.
Combat data systems: Signaal SEWACO action data automation with STACOS tactical command; Link 11 and 14. SATCOMs (from 1994).
Fire control: SWG 1A(V) for SSM. Vesta Helo transponder with data link for OTHT.
Radars: Air search: Signaal MW 08 (derived from Smart 3D) ❽; 3D; G band.
Air/surface search: Signaal DA 08 (fitted with IFF Mk 12 Mod 4) ❾; F band.
Navigation: Kelvin Hughes Type 1007; I band.
Fire control: 2 Signaal STIR ❿; I/J/K band; range 140 km *(76 nm)* for 1 m² target.
Sonars: Computing Devices (Canada) SQS 510(V); hull-mounted; active search and attack; medium frequency.

Helicopters: 2 Super Sea Lynx Mk 95 ⓫.

Programmes: The contract for all three was signed on 25 July 1986. These are Meko 200 type ordered from a consortium of builders. As well as Portugal, which is bearing 40 per cent of the cost, assistance has been given by Germany and NATO with some missile, CIWS and torpedo systems being provided by the USA.
Structure: All-steel construction. Stabilisers fitted. Full RAS facilities. Space has been left for a sonar towed array and for VLS Sea Sparrow.
Operational: Designed primarily as ASW ships.

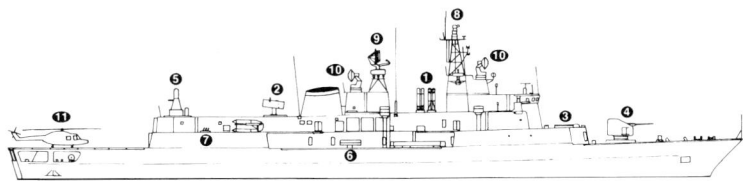

VASCO DA GAMA   *(Scale 1 : 1200), Ian Sturton*

ALVARES CABRAL   *7/1992, G Toremans*

VASCO DA GAMA   *7/1992, G Toremans*

502 PORTUGAL / Frigates

4 COMANDANTE JOÃO BELO CLASS

Name	No	Builders	Laid down	Launched	Commissioned
COMANDANTE JOÃO BELO	F 480	At et Ch de Nantes	6 Sep 1965	22 Mar 1966	1 July 1967
COMANDANTE HERMENEGILDO CAPELO	F 481	At et Ch de Nantes	13 May 1966	29 Nov 1966	26 Apr 1968
COMANDANTE ROBERTO IVENS	F 482	At et Ch de Nantes	13 Dec 1966	8 Aug 1967	23 Nov 1968
COMANDANTE SACADURA CABRAL	F 483	At et Ch de Nantes	18 Aug 1967	15 Mar 1968	25 July 1969

Displacement, tons: 1750 standard; 2250 full load
Dimensions, feet (metres): 336.9 × 38.4 × 14.4 *(102.7 × 11.7 × 4.4)*
Main machinery: 4 SEMT-Pielstick 12 PC2.2 V 400 diesels; 16 000 hp(m) *(11.8 MW)* sustained; 2 shafts
Speed, knots: 25. **Range, miles:** 7500 at 15 kts
Complement: 201 (15 officers)

Guns: 3 Creusot Loire 3.9 in *(100 mm)*/55 Mod 1953 ❶; 80° elevation; 60 rounds/minute to 17 km *(9 nm)* anti-surface; 8 km *(4.4 nm)* anti-aircraft; weight of shell 13.5 kg.
2 Bofors 40 mm/60 ❷; 90° elevation; 300 rounds/minute to 12 km *(6.6 nm)*; weight of shell 0.89 kg.
Torpedoes: 6—21.7 in *(550 mm)* (2 triple) tubes ❸ or 6—324 mm US Mk 32 Mod 5 (2 triple) tubes (after modernisation); ECAN L3 being replaced by Honeywell Mk 46 Mod 5 (after modernisation).
A/S mortars: 1 Mortier 305 mm 4-barrelled ❹; automatic loading; range 2700 m; warhead 227 kg. To be removed during modernisation.
Countermeasures: Decoys: 2 Loral Hycor Mk 36 SRBOC 6-barrelled chaff launchers.
SLQ-25 Nixie; towed torpedo decoy.
ESM: ARBR-10 or Argo 700 DF (after modernisation); radar warning.
Fire control: C T Analogique. Sagem DMA optical director.
Radars: Air search: Thomson-CSF DRBV 22A ❺; D band; range 366 km *(200 nm)*.
Surface search: Thomson-CSF DRBV 50 ❻; G band; range 29 km *(16 nm)*.
Navigation: Kelvin Hughes KH 1007; I band.
Fire control: Thomson-CSF DRBC 31D ❼; I band.
Sonars: CDC SQS 510 (after modernisation); hull-mounted; active search and attack; medium frequency.
Thomson Sintra DUBA 3A; hull-mounted; active search; high frequency.

Modernisation: Modernisation of external communications, sensors and electronics completed 1987-90. Chaff launchers installed in 1989. In 1993-96 the hull sonar is being replaced, torpedo tubes updated, the A/S mortar removed, towed torpedo decoy installed and ESM equipment changed. It is also planned to add a combat data system with Link 11 compatible with the Vasco da Gama class. The plan to have one or both after guns replaced either by flight deck and hangar for helicopter or by SSM has been shelved but X turret is to be removed.

Structure: They are generally similar to the French Commandant Rivière class.
Operational: Designed for tropical service but being modernised primarily for the ASW role.

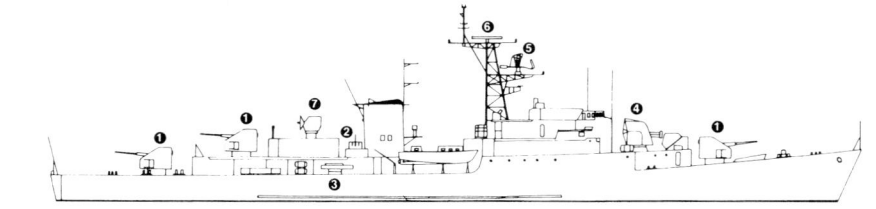
COMANDANTE JOÃO BELO class *(Scale 1 : 900), Ian Sturton*

COMANDANTE ROBERTO IVENS *10/1992, C D Yaylali*

COMANDANTE ROBERTO IVENS *11/1991, Hartmut Ehlers*

4 BAPTISTA DE ANDRADE CLASS

Name	No	Builders	Laid down	Launched	Commissioned
BAPTISTA DE ANDRADE	F 486	Empresa Nacional Bazán, Cartagena	1 Sep 1972	13 Mar 1973	19 Nov 1974
JOÃO ROBY	F 487	Empresa Nacional Bazán, Cartagena	1 Dec 1972	3 June 1973	18 Mar 1975
AFONSO CERQUEIRA	F 488	Empresa Nacional Bazán, Cartagena	10 Mar 1973	6 Oct 1973	26 June 1975
OLIVEIRA E CARMO	F 489	Empresa Nacional Bazán, Cartagena	1 June 1973	22 Feb 1974	28 Oct 1975

Displacement, tons: 1203 standard; 1380 full load
Dimensions, feet (metres): 277.5 × 33.8 × 10.2 *(84.6 × 10.3 × 3.1)*
Main machinery: 2 OEW Pielstick 12 PC2.2 V 400 diesels; 12 000 hp(m) *(8.82 MW)* sustained; 2 shafts
Speed, knots: 22. **Range, miles:** 5900 at 18 kts
Complement: 122 (11 officers) plus marine detachment

Guns: 1 Creusot Loire 3.9 in *(100 mm)*/55 Mod 1968 ❶; 80° elevation; 80 rounds/minute to 17 km *(9 nm)* anti-surface; 8 km *(4.4 nm)* anti-aircraft; weight of shell 13.5 kg.
2 Bofors 40 mm/70 ❷; 90° elevation; 300 rounds/minute to 12 km *(6.6 nm)*; weight of shell 0.96 kg.
Torpedoes: 6—324 mm US Mk 32 (2 triple) tubes ❸. Honeywell Mk 46; anti-submarine; active/passive homing to 11 km *(5.9 nm)* at 40 kts; warhead 44 kg.
Fire control: Vega GFCS.
Radars: Air/surface search: Plessey AWS 2 ❹; E/F band; range 110 km *(60 nm)*.
Navigation: Decca RM 316P; I band.
Fire control: Thomson-CSF Pollux ❺; I/J band; range 31 km *(17 nm)* for 2 m² target.
Sonars: Thomson Sintra Diodon; hull-mounted; active search and attack; 11, 12 or 13 kHz.

Helicopters: Platform for 1 Lynx.

Modernisation: Planned programme to include PDMS Sea Sparrow and SSM has been shelved although space and weight allowance is available for two SSM. Communications equipment updated 1988-91.

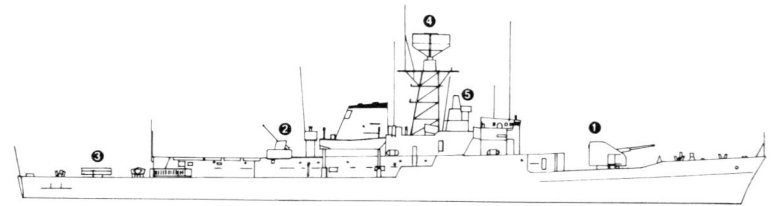
BAPTISTA DE ANDRADE *(Scale 1 : 900), Ian Sturton*

JOÃO ROBY *3/1991, van Ginderen Collection*

6 JOÃO COUTINHO CLASS

Name	No	Builders	Laid down	Launched	Commissioned
ANTONIO ENES	F 471	Empresa Nacional Bazán, Cartagena	10 Apr 1968	16 Aug 1969	18 June 1971
JOÃO COUTINHO	F 475	Blohm & Voss AG, Hamburg	24 Dec 1968	2 May 1969	28 Feb 1970
JACINTO CANDIDO	F 476	Blohm & Voss AG, Hamburg	10 Feb 1969	16 June 1969	29 May 1970
GENERAL PEREIRA D'EÇA	F 477	Blohm & Voss AG, Hamburg	21 Apr 1969	26 July 1969	10 Oct 1970
AUGUSTO DE CASTILHO	F 484	Empresa Nacional Bazán, Cartagena	15 Oct 1968	4 July 1969	14 Nov 1970
HONORIO BARRETO	F 485	Empresa Nacional Bazán, Cartagena	20 Feb 1968	11 Apr 1970	15 Apr 1971

Displacement, tons: 1203 standard; 1380 full load
Dimensions, feet (metres): 277.5 × 33.8 × 10.8 *(84.6 × 10.3 × 3.3)*
Main machinery: 2 OEW Pielstick 12 PC2.2 V 400 diesels; 12 000 hp(m) *(8.82 MW)* sustained; 2 shafts
Speed, knots: 22. **Range, miles:** 5900 at 18 kts
Complement: 77 (9 officers)

Guns: 2 US 3 in *(76 mm)*/50 (twin) Mk 33 ❶; 85° elevation; 50 rounds/minute to 12.8 km *(7 nm)*; weight of shell 6 kg.
2 Bofors 40 mm/60 (twin) ❷; 90° elevation; 300 rounds/minute to 12 km *(6.6 nm)*; weight of shell 0.89 kg.
Fire control: Mk 51 GFCS for 40 mm. Mk 63 for 76 mm.
Radars: Air/surface search: Kelvin Hughes ❸; I band.
Navigation: Racal Decca RM 1226C; I band.
Fire control: Western Electric SPG 34 ❹; I/J band.

Modernisation: A programme for this class to include SSM and PDMS has been shelved. In 1989-91 the main radar was updated and JATCOMS installed. Also fitted with SIFICAP which is a Fishery Protection data exchange system by satellite to the main database ashore.
Structure: Helicopter platform only.
Operational: A/S equipment no longer operational and laid apart on shore. Crew reduced by 23 as a result.

JOÃO COUTINHO *(Scale 1 : 900), Ian Sturton*

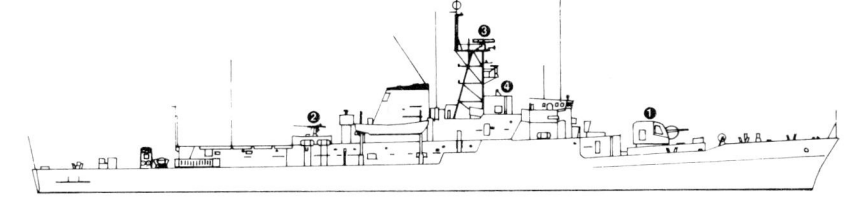

AUGUSTO DE CASTILHO *1/1991, Harald Carstens*

SHIPBORNE AIRCRAFT

Numbers/Type: 5 Westland Super Navy Lynx Mk 95.
Operational speed: 125 kts *(231 km/h)*.
Service ceiling: 12 000 ft *(3660 m)*.
Range: 320 nm *(593 km)*.
Role/Weapon systems: Ordered 2 November 1990 for MEKO 200 frigates; operational in September 1993. Sensors: Bendix 1500 radar; AQS-18 dipping sonar; Racal RNS 252 data link. Weapons: Mk 46 torpedoes.

SUPER LYNX *11/1989, Westlands*

LAND-BASED MARITIME AIRCRAFT

(All Air Force manned)

Numbers/Type: 12 Aerospatiale SA 330C Puma.
Operational speed: 151 kts *(280 km/h)*.
Service ceiling: 15 090 ft *(4600 m)*.
Range: 343 nm *(635 km)*.
Role/Weapon systems: For SAR and surface search. Sensors: Omera search radar. Weapons: Unarmed except for pintle-mounted machine guns.

Numbers/Type: 6 CASA C-212 Aviocar.
Operational speed: 190 kts *(353 km/h)*.
Service ceiling: 24 000 ft *(7315 m)*.
Range: 1650 nm *(3055 km)*.
Role/Weapon systems: Short-range SAR support and transport operations. Sensors: Search radar and MAD. Weapons: Unarmed.

Numbers/Type: 5 Lockheed C-130H Hercules.
Operational speed: 325 kts *(602 km/h)*.
Service ceiling: 33 000 ft *(10 060 m)*.
Range: 4250 nm *(7880 km)*.
Role/Weapon systems: MR is a secondary role for the Air Force transport aircraft assigned to NATO. Sensors: Search radar. Weapons: Unarmed.

Numbers/Type: 6 Lockheed P-3B Orion.
Operational speed: 410 kts *(760 km/h)*.
Service ceiling: 28 300 ft *(8625 m)*.
Range: 4000 nm *(7410 km)*.
Role/Weapon systems: Long-range surveillance and ASW patrol aircraft; acquired with NATO funding from RAAF update programme and modernised by Lockheed starting in 1987. Progress is slow. Sensors: APS-115 radar, ASQ-81 MAD, AQS-901 sonobuoy processor, AQS-114 computer, IFF, ECM/ESM. Weapons: ASW; 8 × Mk 46 torpedoes, depth bombs or mines; ASV; 10 × underwing stations for ASMs.

LIGHT FORCES

Note: Up to 12 offshore patrol vessels are required. Orders may be placed from 1996.

10 CACINE CLASS (LARGE PATROL CRAFT)

Name	No	Builders	Commissioned
CACINE	P 1140	Arsenal do Alfeite	May 1969
CUNENE	P 1141	Arsenal do Alfeite	June 1969
MANDOVI	P 1142	Arsenal do Alfeite	Sep 1969
ROVUMA	P 1143	Arsenal do Alfeite	Nov 1969
CUANZA	P 1144	Estaleiros Navais do Mondego	May 1969
GEBA	P 1145	Estaleiros Navais do Mondego	May 1970
ZAIRE	P 1146	Estaleiros Navais do Mondego	Nov 1970
ZAMBEZE	P 1147	Estaleiros Navais do Mondego	Jan 1971
LIMPOPO	P 1160	Arsenal do Alfeite	Apr 1973
SAVE	P 1161	Arsenal do Alfeite	May 1973

Displacement, tons: 292.5 standard; 310 full load
Dimensions, feet (metres): 144 × 25.2 × 7.1 *(44 × 7.7 × 2.2)*
Main machinery: 2 MTU 12V 538 TB80 diesels; 3750 hp(m) *(2.76 MW)* sustained; 2 shafts
Speed, knots: 20. **Range, miles:** 4400 at 12 kts
Complement: 33 (3 officers)
Guns: 1 Bofors 40 mm/60. 1 Oerlikon 20 mm/65.
Radars: Surface search: Kelvin Hughes Type 1007; I/J band.

Comment: Originally mounted a second Bofors aft but most have been removed as has the 37 mm rocket launcher. Have SIFICAP satellite data handling system for Fishery Protection duties.

CUANZA *5/1992, van Ginderen Collection*

ROVUMA *6/1992, Erik Laursen*

504 PORTUGAL / Light forces — Mine warfare forces

5 ARGOS CLASS (COASTAL PATROL CRAFT)

Name	No	Builders	Commissioned
ARGOS	P 1150	Arsenal do Alfeite	2 July 1991
DRAGÃO	P 1151	Arsenal do Alfeite	18 Oct 1991
ESCORPIÃO	P 1152	Arsenal do Alfeite	26 Nov 1991
CASSIOPEIA	P 1153	Conafi	11 Nov 1991
HIDRA	P 1154	Conafi	18 Dec 1991

Displacement, tons: 84 standard; 94 full load
Dimensions, feet (metres): 89.2 × 19.4 × 4.6 *(27.2 × 5.9 × 1.4)*
Main machinery: 2 MTU 12V 396 TE84 diesels; 3700 hp(m) *(2.73 MW)* sustained; 2 shafts
Speed, knots: 28. **Range, miles:** 1350 at 15 kts; 200 at 28 kts
Complement: 9 (1 officer)
Guns: 2—12.7 mm MGs.
Radars: Navigation: Furuno 1505 DA; I band.

Comment: Ordered in 1989 and 50 per cent funded by the EC. Capable of full speed operation up to sea state 3.

ARGOS 1991, Arsenal do Alfeite

2 DOM ALEIXO CLASS (COASTAL PATROL CRAFT)

Name	No	Builders	Commissioned
DOM ALEIXO	P 1148	S Jacinto Aveiro	7 Dec 1967
DOM JEREMIAS	P 1149 (ex-A 5202)	S Jacinto Aveiro	22 Dec 1967

Displacement, tons: 62.6 standard; 67.7 full load
Dimensions, feet (metres): 82.1 × 17 × 5.2 *(25 × 5.2 × 1.6)*
Main machinery: 2 Cummins diesels; 1270 hp *(947 kW)*; 2 shafts
Speed, knots: 16
Complement: 10 (2 officers)
Gun: 1 Oerlikon 20 mm/65.
Radars: Surface search: Decca 303; I band.

Comment: *Dom Jeremias* has been used as a survey craft but reverted to being a patrol craft in 1989.

DOM JEREMIAS 3/1991, van Ginderen Collection

6 ALBATROZ CLASS (COASTAL PATROL CRAFT)

Name	No	Builders	Commissioned
ALBATROZ	P 1162	Arsenal do Alfeite	9 Dec 1974
AÇOR	P 1163	Arsenal do Alfeite	9 Dec 1974
ANDORINHA	P 1164	Arsenal do Alfeite	20 Dec 1974
AGUIA	P 1165	Arsenal do Alfeite	28 Feb 1975
CISNE	P 1167	Arsenal do Alfeite	31 Mar 1976
CONDOR	UAM 630 (ex-P 1166)	Arsenal do Alfeite	23 Apr 1975

Displacement, tons: 45 full load
Dimensions, feet (metres): 77.4 × 18.4 × 5.2 *(23.6 × 5.6 × 1.6)*
Main machinery: 2 Cummins diesels; 1100 hp *(820 kW)*; 2 shafts
Speed, knots: 20. **Range, miles:** 2500 at 12 kts
Complement: 8 (1 officer)
Guns: 1 Oerlikon 20 mm/65. 2—12.7 mm MGs.
Radars: Surface search: Decca RM 316P; I band.

Comment: *Condor* is now used for harbour patrol duties.

ANDORINHA 1992, Portuguese Navy

1 RIO MINHO CLASS (RIVER PATROL CRAFT)

Name	No	Builders	Commissioned
RIO MINHO	P 370	Arsenal do Alfeite	1 Aug 1991

Displacement, tons: 72 full load
Dimensions, feet (metres): 73.5 × 19.7 × 2.6 *(22.4 × 6 × 0.8)*
Main machinery: 2 KHD-Deutz diesels; 664 hp(m) *(488 kW)*; 2 Schottel pump jets
Speed, knots: 9.5. **Range, miles:** 420 at 7 kts
Complement: 8 (1 officer)
Guns: 1—7.62 mm MG.
Radars: Navigation: Furuno FR 1505DA; I band.

Comment: River patrol craft which has replaced *Atria* on the River Minho.

RIO MINHO 1991, Arsenal do Alfeite

MINE WARFARE FORCES

0 + (4) NEW MINESWEEPER (COASTAL)

Displacement, tons: 620 full load
Dimensions, feet (metres): 171.9 oa; 157.5 wl × 34.1 × 10.2 *(52.4; 48 × 10.4 × 3.1)*
Speed, knots: 15; 10 (sweeping). **Range, miles:** 3000 at 12 kts
Complement: 25 plus 5 spare

Guns: 1 DCN 20 mm/20.
Radars: Navigation: I band.

Programmes: Memorandum of Understanding signed 6 April 1989 for a joint Belgium/Netherlands minesweeper project. Design contract awarded November 1990 to van der Giessen-de Noord Marinebouw in a joint venture with Beliard Polyship NV, completed in August 1992 when Portugal joined the project. Orders of up to six vessels for Belgium, eight for the Netherlands and four for Portugal were expected in 1993 but impending cancellation by the Netherlands is likely to delay progress. This project has been given a higher priority than replacement submarines by the Portuguese Chief of Defence.
Operational: The ship is to be equipped with a newly developed magnetic sweeping gear, 'Sterne M', by Thomson Sintra. This development, ordered by the joint navies, is based upon the concept of 'target simulation' and consists of six bodies, towed in array, each carrying two coils. By automatically computed coil settings a simulated ship's signature is generated without any assumption concerning the mine itself. In addition, proven acoustic and mechanic sweeping capabilities are installed. The requirement is to be able to sweep bottom mines which have sunk so far into soft sand that they are not detected by hunters.

AMPHIBIOUS FORCES

3 BOMBARDA CLASS LDG (LCT)

Name	No	Builders	Commissioned
BOMBARDA	LDG 201	Estaleiros Navais do Mondego	1969
ALABARDA	LDG 202	Estaleiros Navais do Mondego	1970
BACAMARTE	LDG 203	Arsenal do Alfeite	1985

Displacement, tons: 652 full load
Dimensions, feet (metres): 184.3 × 38.7 × 6.2 *(56.2 × 11.8 × 1.9)*
Main machinery: 2 MTU MB diesels; 910 hp(m) *(669 kW)*; 2 shafts
Speed, knots: 9.5. **Range, miles:** 2600 at 9 kts
Complement: 21 (3 officers)
Military lift: 350 tons
Guns: 2 Oerlikon 20 mm.
Radars: Navigation: Decca RM 316P; I band.

Comment: Similar to French EDIC.

BACAMARTE 4/1992, Hartmut Ehlers

6 LDM 400 CLASS (LCM)

LDM 406	LDM 420	LDM 422
LDM 418	LDM 421	LDM 423

Displacement, tons: 48 full load
Dimensions, feet (metres): 58.3 × 15.8 × 3.3 *(17.3 × 4.8 × 1)*
Main machinery: 2 Cummins diesels; 400 hp *(298 kW)*; 2 shafts
Speed, knots: 10

Comment: Built 1967-68.

LDM 421 3/1992, van Ginderen Collection

3 LDM 100 CLASS (LCM)

LDM 119	LDM 120	LDM 121

Displacement, tons: 50 full load
Dimensions, feet (metres): 50 × 14.4 × 3.6 *(15.3 × 4.4 × 1.1)*
Main machinery: 2 GM diesels; 450 hp *(336 kW)*; 2 shafts
Speed, knots: 9

Comment: All built at the Estaleiros Navais do Mondego in 1965.

SURVEY SHIPS

Note: A sister ship is needed for *Almeida Carvalho* to aid work on behalf of Portuguese-speaking African countries. An ex-US Robert D Conrad class is a possibility.

1 Ex-US KELLAR CLASS

Name	No	Builders	Commissioned
ALMEIDA CARVALHO (ex-USNS *Kellar*, T-AGS 25)	A 527	Marietta Shipbuilding Co	31 Jan 1969

Displacement, tons: 1297 standard; 1400 full load
Dimensions, feet (metres): 209 × 37.1 × 15.1 *(63.7 × 11.3 × 4.6)*
Main machinery: Diesel-electric; 2 Caterpillar diesel generators; 1 motor; 1300 hp *(970 kW)*; 1 shaft
Speed, knots: 15. **Range, miles:** 1200 at 14 kts
Complement: 47 (7 officers)
Radars: Surface search: Kelvin Hughes Type 1007; I band.
Navigation: Racal Decca TM 829; I band.

Comment: Leased from the US Navy on 21 January 1972. Transferred finally in 1988.

ALMEIDA CARVALHO 1986, Portuguese Navy

2 ANDROMEDA CLASS

Name	No	Builders	Commissioned
ANDROMEDA	A 5203	Arsenal do Alfeite	1 Feb 1987
AURIGA	A 5205	Arsenal do Alfeite	1 July 1987

Displacement, tons: 230 full load
Dimensions, feet (metres): 103.3 × 25.4 × 8.2 *(31.5 × 7.7 × 2.5)*
Main machinery: 1 MTU 12V 396 TC62 diesel; 1200 hp(m) *(880 kW)* sustained; 1 shaft
Speed, knots: 12. **Range, miles:** 1980 at 10 kts
Complement: 17 (3 officers)
Radars: Navigation: Decca RM 914C; I band.

Comment: Both ordered in January 1984. *Auriga* has a research submarine ROV Phantom S2 and a Klein side scan sonar.

ANDROMEDA 1987, Arsenal do Alfeite

6 SURVEY CRAFT

CORAL UAM 801	ACTINIA UAM 803	FISALIA UAM 805
ATLANTA (ex-*Hidra*) UAM 802	SICANDRA UAM 804	SAVEL UAM 830

Comment: 801 and 802 are of 36 tons and were launched in 1980. 803 to 805 are converted fishing vessels (803 of 90 tons, 804 of 70 tons) of different designs mostly used as lighthouse tenders. 830 is of 7 tons and was built by Conafi in 1992/93.

FISALIA 4/1992, Hartmut Ehlers

SERVICE FORCES

3 HARBOUR TANKERS

ODELEITE UAM 301
ODIVELAS UAM 302
OEIRAS UAM 303 (ex-BC 3, ex-YO 3)

Comment: Cargo capacity: First two, 674 tons; *Oeiras*, 924 tons. Two to be placed in reserve in 1993 as a result of a new fuel delivery system installed at the Alfeite naval base.

OEIRAS 5/1987, Hartmut Ehlers

506 PORTUGAL / Service forces

1 Ex-UK ROVER CLASS (REPLENISHMENT TANKER)

Name	No	Builders	Commissioned
BERRIO (ex-*Blue Rover*)	A 5210 (ex-A 270)	Swan Hunter	15 July 1970

Displacement, tons: 4700 light; 11 522 full load
Dimensions, feet (metres): 461 × 63 × 24 *(140.6 × 19.2 × 7.3)*
Main machinery: 2 SEMT-Pielstick 16PA4 185 diesels; 5344 hp(m) *(3.93 MW)*; 1 shaft; cp prop; bow thruster
Speed, knots: 19. **Range, miles:** 15 000 at 15 kts
Complement: 49
Cargo capacity: 6600 tons fuel
Guns: 2 Oerlikon 20 mm.
Countermeasures: Decoys: 2 Vickers Corvus launchers. 2 Plessey Shield launchers. 1 Graseby Type 182; towed torpedo decoy.
Radars: Navigation: Kelvin Hughes Type 1006; I band.
Helicopters: Platform for 1 medium.

Comment: Transfered 31 March 1993. Small fleet tanker designed to replenish fuel, fresh water, limited dry cargo and refrigerated stores under all conditions while under way. No hangar but helicopter landing platform is served by a stores lift, to enable stores to be transferred at sea by 'vertical lift'. Capable of HIFR.

BERRIO (British colours)   *12/1990, Gilbert Gyssels*

1 REPLENISHMENT TANKER

Name	No	Builders	Commissioned
SÃO GABRIEL	A 5206	Estaleiros de Viana do Castelo	27 Mar 1963

Displacement, tons: 14 200 full load
Measurement, tons: 9854 gross; 9000 dwt
Dimensions, feet (metres): 479 × 59.8 × 26.2 *(146 × 18.2 × 8)*
Main machinery: 2 boilers; 1 Pametrada turbine; 9500 hp *(7.1 MW)*; 1 shaft
Speed, knots: 17. **Range, miles:** 6000 at 15 kts
Complement: 99 (11 officers)
Radars: Air search: Westinghouse SPS 6C; D band.
Navigation: Racal Decca RM 1226C; I band. Racal Decca RMS 1230C; E/F band.

Comment: Two replenishment at sea stations on each side and one Vertrep from helicopter platform aft. Probably to be paid off in 1993.

SÃO GABRIEL   *6/1989, Gilbert Gyssels*

1 LOGISTIC SUPPORT SHIP

Name	No	Builders	Commissioned
SÃO MIGUEL (ex-*Cabo Verde*)	A 5208	Howaldtswerke, Kiel	1962

Displacement, tons: 8290 full load
Measurement, tons: 5456 dwt
Dimensions, feet (metres): 354.6 × 51.2 × 24.7 *(108 × 15.6 × 7.5)*
Main machinery: 1 MAN K62 60/105C diesel; 4000 hp(m) *(2.94 MW)*; 1 shaft
Speed, knots: 15
Complement: 57 (8 officers)
Radars: Navigation: Kelvin Hughes 1600. Kelvin Hughes 18/12; I band.

Comment: Merchant ship purchased and commissioned in the Navy on 8 November 1985. Plans to install helicopter deck and fit facilities for troops and equipment have been shelved. Used to supply allied forces in the Gulf in early 1991. Now used for resupply of Azores and Madeira islands. To be paid off in 1993.

SÃO MIGUEL   *4/1992, Hartmut Ehlers*

1 SÃO ROQUE CLASS (Ex-MINESWEEPER)

Name	No	Builders	Commissioned
RIBEIRA GRANDE	A 5207 (ex-M 402)	CUF Shipyard, Lisbon	8 Feb 1957

Displacement, tons: 394.4 standard; 451.9 full load
Dimensions, feet (metres): 153 × 27.7 × 8.2 *(46.3 × 8.5 × 2.5)*
Main machinery: 2 Mirrlees JVSS-12 diesels; 2500 hp *(1.87 MW)*; 2 shafts
Speed, knots: 15. **Range, miles:** 2400 at 12 kts
Complement: 46 (3 officers)
Guns: 1 Oerlikon 20 mm/65.
Radars: Navigation: I band.

Comment: Same style as British Ton class coastal minesweepers. 40 mm gun removed 1972, as was the minesweeping gear. Neither the equipment nor the trained personnel are available for mine warfare operations. This ship has replaced *São Roque* as the diver support vessel in 1993.

SÃO ROQUE class (old number)   *3/1991, van Ginderen Collection*

1 TRAINING SHIP

Name	No	Builders	Commissioned
SAGRES (ex-*Guanabara*, ex-*Albert Leo Schlageter*)	A 520	Blohm & Voss, Hamburg	10 Feb 1938

Displacement, tons: 1725 standard; 1940 full load
Dimensions, feet (metres): 231 wl; 295.2 oa × 39.4 × 17 *(70.4; 90 × 12 × 5.2)*
Main machinery: 2 MTU 12V 183 TE92 auxiliary diesels; 1 shaft
Speed, knots: 10.5. **Range, miles:** 5450 at 7.5 kts on diesel
Complement: 162 (12 officers)

Comment: Former German sail training ship launched 30 October 1937. Sister of US Coast Guard training ship *Eagle* (ex-German *Horst Wessel*) and Soviet *Tovarisch* (ex-German *Gorch Fock*). Taken by the USA as a reparation after the Second World War in 1945 and sold to Brazil in 1948. Purchased from Brazil and commissioned in the Portuguese Navy on 2 February 1962 at Rio de Janeiro and renamed *Sagres*. Sail area, 20 793 sq ft. Height of main-mast, 142 ft. Phased refits 1987-88 and again in 1991-92 which included new engines, improved accommodation, a hydraulic crane and updated navigation equipment.

SAGRES   *4/1992, Hartmut Ehlers*

1 TRAINING SHIP

Name	No	Builders	Commissioned
CREOULA	UAM 201	Lisbon Shipyard	1937

Displacement, tons: 818 standard; 1055 full load
Dimensions, feet (metres): 221.1 × 32.5 × 13.8 *(67.4 × 9.9 × 4.2)*
Main machinery: 1 MTU 8V 183 TE92 auxiliary diesel; 1 shaft

Comment: Ex-deep sea sail fishing ship used off the coast of Newfoundland for 36 years. Bought by Fishing Department in 1976 to turn into a museum ship but because she was still seaworthy it was decided to convert her to a training ship. Recommissioned in the Navy in 1987. Refit completed in 1992 including a new engine and improved accommodation.

CREOULA   *9/1991, van Ginderen Collection*

1 BUOY TENDER (RIVER)

Name	No	Builders	Commissioned
GUIA	UAM 676	S Jacinto, Aveiro	30 Jan 1985

Displacement, tons: 70
Dimensions, feet (metres): 72.2 × 25.9 × 7.2 *(22 × 7.9 × 2.2)*
Main machinery: 1 Deutz MWM SBA6M816 diesel; 465 hp(m) *(342 kW)* sustained; Schottel Navigator prop
Speed, knots: 8.5 (3.5 on auxiliary engine)

GUIA   *3/1991, van Ginderen Collection*

1 OCEAN TUG

Name	No	Builders	Commissioned
SCHULTZ XAVIER	A 521	Alfeite Naval Yard	14 July 1972

Displacement, tons: 900
Dimensions, feet (metres): 184 × 33 × 12.5 *(56 × 10 × 3.8)*
Main machinery: 2 diesels; 2400 hp(m) *(1.76 MW)*; 2 shafts
Speed, knots: 14.5. **Range, miles:** 3000 at 12.5 kts
Complement: 54 (4 officers)

SCHULTZ XAVIER   *3/1991, van Ginderen Collection*

2 TRAINING YACHTS

VEGA (ex-*Arreda*) A 5201   POLAR (ex-*Anne Linde*) A 5204

Displacement, tons: 70 (60, *Vega*)
Dimensions, feet (metres): 75 × 16 × 8.2 *(22.9 × 4.9 × 2.5)* (*Polar*)
65 × 14.1 × 8.2 *(19.8 × 4.3 × 2.5)* (*Vega*)

HARBOUR PATROL CRAFT AND FERRIES

SURRIADA UAM 602	**BONANCA** UAM 612	**TUFAO** UAM 639
MARETA UAM 605	**MAR CHAO** UAM 613	**VASCAO** UAM 912
MARESIA UAM 608	**LEVANTE** UAM 631	**ZEZERE** UAM 913
BOLINA UAM 611	**VENTANTE** UAM 636	

Displacement, tons: 9
Dimensions, feet (metres): 39 × 11.8 × 3.3 *(11.8 × 3.6 × 1)*
Main machinery: 2 Volvo Penta diesels; 426 hp(m) *(313 kW)*; 2 shafts
Speed, knots: 20
Complement: 4

Comment: Large numbers of harbour craft of similar characteristics to those listed. 912 and 913 are ferries. Some have *Marinha* on the side, others of the same type have *Guarda Fiscal*. Two new classes of fast patrol boats are planned for the *Guarda Fiscal* from 1993 onwards and the first eight were ordered from Bazán in 1992. Up to 24 craft are required to assist in controlling drug runners.

MAR CHAO   *3/1992, van Ginderen Collection*

ZEZERE   *4/1992, Hartmut Ehlers*

VENTANTE   *4/1992, van Ginderen Collection*

QATAR

Senior Appointment

Commander Naval Force:
Colonel Said Al Suweidi

Personnel

(a) 1993: 700 officers and men (including Marine Police)
(b) Voluntary service

Bases

Doha (main); Halul Island (secondary)

Mercantile Marine

Lloyd's Register of Shipping:
65 vessels of 423 705 tons gross

PATROL FORCES

0 + 4 VITA CLASS (FAST ATTACK CRAFT—MISSILE)

Displacement, tons: 376 full load
Dimensions, feet (metres): 185.7 × 29.5 × 7.5 *(56.3 × 9 × 2.3)*
Main machinery: 4 MTU 20V 538 TB93 diesels; 15 020 hp(m) *(11 MW)* sustained; 4 shafts
Speed, knots: 35
Complement: 47 (7 officers)

Missiles: SSM: 4 or 8 Aerospatiale MM 40 Exocet ❶.
SAM: Matra Sadral sextuple launcher for Mistral ❷.
Guns: 1 OTO Melara 76 mm/62 Super Rapid ❸.
1 Signaal Goalkeeper 30 mm ❹ or Thomson-CSF Crotale. 2—12.7 mm MGs.
Countermeasures: Decoys: CSEE Dagaie for chaff ❺.
ESM: Thomson-CSF DR 3000S; intercept.
ECM: Dassault ARBB 33; jammer.
Combat data systems: Signaal SEWACO FD with Thomson-CSF TACTICOS; Link Y.
Fire control: Signaal STING optronic director. IRSCAN electro-optical tracker ❻.
Radars: Air/surface search ❼; E/F band.
Navigation: I band.
Fire control: Signaal STING ❽; I/J band.

Programmes: Order announced on 4 June 1992 by Vosper Thornycroft. First of class laid down in late 1992 for delivery in 1996.
Structure: Described as a Vita design derivative. There are few officially released details so some of the dimensions and weapon systems listed are subject to change.

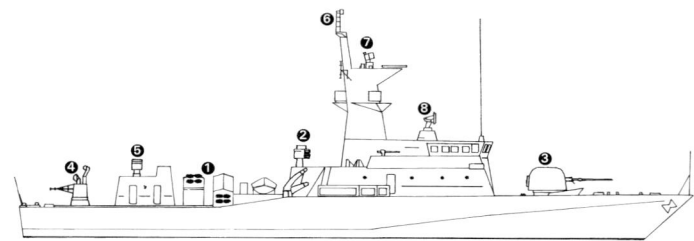

VITA *(not to scale), Ian Sturton*

3 COMBATTANTE III M CLASS (FAST ATTACK CRAFT—MISSILE)

Name	No	Builders	Commissioned
DAMSAH	Q 01	CMN, Cherbourg	10 Nov 1982
AL GHARIYAH	Q 02	CMN, Cherbourg	10 Feb 1983
RBIGAH	Q 03	CMN, Cherbourg	11 May 1983

Displacement, tons: 345 standard; 395 full load
Dimensions, feet (metres): 183.7 × 26.9 × 7.2 *(56 × 8.2 × 2.2)*
Main machinery: 4 MTU 20V 538 TB93 diesels; 15 020 hp(m) *(11 MW)* sustained; 4 shafts
Speed, knots: 38.5. **Range, miles:** 2000 at 15 kts
Complement: 41 (6 officers)

Missiles: SSM: 8 Aerospatiale MM 40 Exocet; inertial cruise; active radar homing to 70 km *(40 nm)* at 0.9 Mach; warhead 165 kg; sea-skimmer.
Guns: 1 OTO Melara 3 in *(76 mm)*/62; 85° elevation; 60 rounds/minute to 16 km *(8.7 nm)*; weight of shell 6 kg.
2 Breda 40 mm/70 (twin); 85° elevation; 300 rounds/minute to 12.5 km *(6.8 nm)*; weight of shell 0.96 kg.
4 Oerlikon 30 mm/75 (2 twin); 85° elevation; 650 rounds/minute to 10 km *(5.5 nm)*; weight of shell 1 kg or 0.36 kg.
Countermeasures: Decoys: CSEE Dagaie trainable single launcher; 6 containers; IR flares and chaff; H/J band.
ESM/ECM: Racal Cutlass/Cygnus.
Fire control: Vega system. 2 CSEE Naja directors.
Radars: Surface search: Thomson-CSF Triton; G band.
Navigation: Racal Decca 1226; I band.
Fire control: Thomson-CSF Castor II; I/J band; range 15 km *(8 nm)* for 1 m² target.

Programmes: Ordered in 1980 and launched in 1982. All arrived at Doha July 1983.

DAMSAH *1984, N Overington*

6 VOSPER THORNYCROFT TYPE (LARGE PATROL CRAFT)

Name	No	Builders	Commissioned
BARZAN	Q 11	Vosper Thornycroft Ltd	13 Jan 1975
HWAR	Q 12	Vosper Thornycroft Ltd	30 Apr 1975
THAT ASSUARI	Q 13	Vosper Thornycroft Ltd	3 Oct 1975
AL WUSAIL	Q 14	Vosper Thornycroft Ltd	28 Oct 1975
FATEH-AL-KHAIR	Q 15	Vosper Thornycroft Ltd	22 Jan 1976
TARIQ	Q 16	Vosper Thornycroft Ltd	1 Mar 1976

Displacement, tons: 120 full load
Dimensions, feet (metres): 110 × 21 × 5.5 *(33.5 × 6.4 × 1.6)*
Main machinery: 2 Paxman Valenta 16CM diesels; 6703 hp(m) *(5 MW)* sustained; 2 shafts
Speed, knots: 27
Complement: 25
Guns: 4 Oerlikon 30 mm/75 (2 twin).
Radars: Surface search: Racal Decca; I band.

Comment: Ordered in 1972-73. Replacements are needed and funds were allocated in 1992.

AL WUSAIL *1984*

6 DAMEN POLYCAT 1450 CLASS (COASTAL PATROL CRAFT)

Q 31-36

Displacement, tons: 18 full load
Dimensions, feet (metres): 47.6 × 15.4 × 4.9 *(14.5 × 4.7 × 2.1)*
Main machinery: 2 Detroit 12V-71TA diesels; 840 hp *(627 kW)* sustained; 2 shafts
Speed, knots: 26
Complement: 11
Guns: 1 Oerlikon 20 mm.
Radars: Navigation: Racal Decca; I band.

Comment: Delivered February-May 1980. May have been transferred to the Marine Police.

Q 33 *3/1980, Damen SY*

25 FAIREY MARINE SPEAR CLASS (COASTAL PATROL CRAFT)

Q 71-Q 95

Displacement, tons: 4.3
Dimensions, feet (metres): 29.8 × 9 × 2.8 *(9.1 × 2.8 × 0.9)*
Main machinery: 2 diesels; 290 hp *(216 kW)*; 2 shafts
Speed, knots: 26
Complement: 4
Guns: 3—7.62 mm MGs.

Comment: First seven ordered early 1974 and delivered June 1974 to February 1975. Contract for further five signed December 1975. Third contract for three fulfilled with delivery of two on 30 June 1975 and one on 14 July 1975. Fourth order for 10 (four Mk 1, six Mk 2) received October 1976 and delivery effected April 1977. These craft belong to the Navy, not the Police.

MISCELLANEOUS

Note: There are a number of amphibious craft including an LCT *Rabha* of 160 ft *(48.8 m)* with a capacity for three tanks and 110 troops, acquired in 1986-87. Also four Rotork craft and 30 Sea Jeeps in 1985. It is not clear how many of the smaller craft are for civilian use.

LAND-BASED MARITIME AIRCRAFT

Numbers/Type: 7 Westland Commando Mk 3.
Operational speed: 125 kts *(230 km/h)*.
Service ceiling: 10 500 ft *(3200 m)*.
Range: 630 nm *(1165 km)*.
Role/Weapon systems: Form No 8 Anti-surface Vessel Squadron for coastal surveillance and anti-shipping operations. Sensors: MEL ARI 5955 radar. Weapons: ASV; 1 × AM 39 Exocet ASM, carried by two helicopters only; general purpose machine guns carried; door-mounted.

MARINE POLICE

2 KEITH NELSON TYPE (COASTAL PATROL CRAFT)

Displacement, tons: 13
Dimensions, feet (metres): 44 × 12.3 × 3.8 *(13.5 × 3.8 × 1.1)*
Main machinery: 2 Caterpillar diesels; 800 hp *(597 kW)*; 2 shafts
Speed, knots: 26
Complement: 6
Guns: 1—12.7 mm MG. 2—7.62 mm MGs.

Comment: The third of this group has been converted into a pilot cutter.

KEITH NELSON TYPE 9/1990

4 CRESTITALIA MV-45 CLASS (COASTAL PATROL CRAFT)

Displacement, tons: 17 full load
Dimensions, feet (metres): 47.6 × 12.5 × 2.6 *(14.5 × 3.8 × 0.8)*
Main machinery: 2 diesels; 1270 hp(m) *(933 kW)*; 2 shafts
Speed, knots: 32. **Range, miles:** 275 at 29 kts
Complement: 6
Guns: 1 Oerlikon 20 mm. 2—7.62 mm MGs.

Comment: Built by Crestitalia and delivered in mid-1989. GRP construction.

MV-45 1989, Crestitalia

5 WATERCRAFT P 1200 TYPE (COASTAL PATROL CRAFT)

Displacement, tons: 12.7
Dimensions, feet (metres): 39 × 13.4 × 3.6 *(11.9 × 4.1 × 1.1)*
Main machinery: 2 Wizeman Mercedes 400 diesels; 660 hp(m) *(485 kW)*; 2 shafts
Speed, knots: 29
Complement: 4
Guns: 2—7.62 mm MGs.

Comment: Built by Watercraft, Shoreham, England in 1980. Two have been deleted.

2 FAIREY MARINE INTERCEPTOR CLASS (ASSAULT CRAFT)

Displacement, tons: 1.25
Dimensions, feet (metres): 25 × 8 × 2.5 *(7.9 × 2.4 × 0.8)*
Main machinery: 2 Johnson outboard motors; 270 hp *(201 kW)*
Speed, knots: 35. **Range, miles:** 150 at 30 kts
Complement: 3
Military lift: 10 troops

Comment: Delivered 28 November 1975. GRP catamaran hull. In rescue role carry a number of life rafts.

ROMANIA

General

Up to the overthrow of President Ceausescu in December 1989 the Fleet was undermanned and seldom went to sea mostly because sailors were used for civilian tasks. At the end of 1990 it was reported that due to financial problems work had stopped on all new construction and major refits, but there was more activity in 1991 and in August 1992 a Naval Review was held.

Headquarters' Appointments

Commander-in-Chief of the Navy:
  Vice Admiral Gheorghe Anghelescu

Personnel

1993: 7000 regulars plus 9500 conscripts.

Bases

Black Sea—Mangalia (HQ and Training); Constanta (Coastal Defence and Naval Aviation)
Danube—Giurgiu (HQ), Sulina, Galati, Dulcea

Strength of the Fleet

Type	Active
Submarine	1
Destroyer	1
Frigates	5
Corvettes/Monitor	11
Fast Attack Craft (Missile)	6
Fast Attack Craft (Gun and Patrol)	27
Fast Attack Craft (Torpedo)	42
River Patrol Craft	22
Minelayer/MCM Support	2
Minesweepers (Coastal and River)	29
Training Ship	1
Logistic Support Ships	2
Oceanographic Ships	2
Tugs	14
Auxiliaries	10

Mercantile Marine

Lloyd's Register of Shipping:
  439 vessels of 3 266 168 tons gross

DELETIONS

Light Forces

1990 2 Kronshtadt class, 9 SM 165 class, 5 SD 200 class,

Minesweepers

1990-92 12 T 301 class

SUBMARINES

1 Ex-SOVIET KILO CLASS (TYPE 877E)

DELFINUL 521

Displacement, tons: 2325 surfaced; 3076 dived
Dimensions, feet (metres): 243.8 × 32.8 × 21.7 *(74.3 × 10 × 6.6)*
Main machinery: Diesel-electric; 2 diesels; 3650 hp(m) *(2.68 MW)*; 2 generators; 1 motor; 5900 hp(m) *(4.34 MW)*; 1 shaft
Speed, knots: 10 surfaced; 20 dived; 9 snorting
Range, miles: 6000 at 7 kts surfaced; 400 at 3 kts dived
Complement: 45

Torpedoes: 6—21 in *(533 mm)* tubes. 18 Soviet Type 53; pattern active/passive homing up to 20 km *(10.8 nm)* at up to 45 kts; warhead 400 kg.
Mines: 36 in lieu of torpedoes.
Countermeasures: ESM: Brick Group; radar warning. Quad Loop D/F.
Radars: Surface search: Snoop Tray; I band.
Sonars: Shark Teeth; hull-mounted; passive search and attack; medium frequency.
  Mouse Roar; active attack; high frequency.

DELFINUL 5/1990

Programmes: Transferred in December 1986. Second one planned but funds not available.
Structure: Diving depth, 240 m *(785 ft)*.
Operational: Very rarely goes to sea.

DESTROYER

1 MUNTENIA CLASS

Name	No	Builders	Laid down	Launched	Commissioned
MARASESTI (ex-*Muntenia*)	—	Mangalia Shipyard	1979	1982	5 Aug 1985

Displacement, tons: 6000 full load
Dimensions, feet (metres): 485.6 × 48.6 × 23 *(148 × 14.8 × 7)*
Main machinery: COGOG; 4 gas turbines; 94 000 hp(m) *(69 MW)*; 2 shafts
Speed, knots: 32

Missiles: SSM: 8 SS-N-2C Styx ❶; active radar or IR homing to 83 km *(45 nm)* at 0.9 Mach; warhead 513 kg.
Guns: 4 USSR 3 in *(76 mm)*/60 (2 twin) ❷; 80° elevation; 90 rounds/minute to 15 km *(8 nm)*; weight of shell 6.8 kg.
8 USSR 30 mm/65 (4 twin) ❸; 85° elevation; 500 rounds/minute to 4 km *(2.2 nm)*; weight of shell 0.54 kg.
Torpedoes: 6—21 in *(533 mm)* (2 triple) tubes ❹. Probably Soviet Type 53; pattern active/passive homing up to 20 km *(10.8 nm)* at up to 45 kts; warhead 400 kg.
A/S mortars: 2 RBU 6000 ❺; 12 tubed trainable; range 6000 m; warhead 31 kg.
Radars: Air/surface search: Strut Curve ❻; F band; range 110 km *(60 nm)* for 2 m² target.
Fire control: Two Drum Tilt ❼; H/I band.
Hawk Screech ❽; I band; range 27 km *(15 nm)* (for guns).
Navigation: Spin Trough; I band.
IFF: High Pole B.
Sonars: Hull-mounted; active search and attack; medium frequency.

Helicopters: 3 IAR-316 Alouette III type ❾.

Modernisation: Attempts have been made to modernise some of the electronic equipment. Also topweight problems have been addressed by reducing the height of the mast structures and lowering the Styx missile launchers by one deck. Probably fitted with SA-N-5 SAM launchers. RBU 6000 has replaced the RBU 1200.
Structure: A distinctive Romanian design.
Operational: Deactivated in June 1988 due to manpower and fuel shortages but modernisation work was done from 1990 to 1992 and sea trials started in mid-1992.

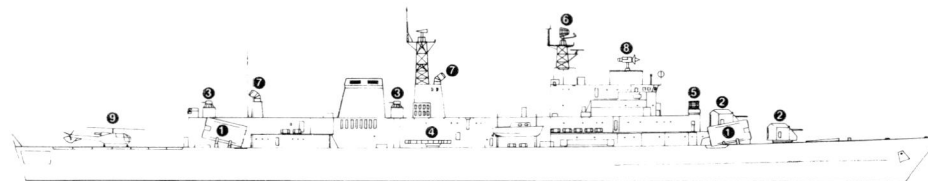
MARASESTI (modernised) *(Scale 1 : 1200), Ian Sturton*

MARASESTI *1991, Romanian Navy*

FRIGATES

5 TETAL CLASS

260   261   262   263   264

Displacement, tons: 1800 full load
Dimensions, feet (metres): 312 × 37.7 × 9.8 *(95 × 11.5 × 3)*
Main machinery: 2 diesels; 2 shafts
Speed, knots: 25
Complement: 98

Guns: 2 or 4 USSR 3 in *(76 mm)*/60 (1 or 2 twin) ❶; 80° elevation; 90 rounds/minute to 15 km *(8 nm)*; weight of shell 6.8 kg.
4 USSR 30 mm/65 (2 twin) ❷; 85° elevation; 500 rounds/minute to 4 km *(2.2 nm)*; weight of shell 0.54 kg.
2—14.5 mm MGs.
Torpedoes: 2—21 in *(533 mm)* (twin) tubes ❸. Soviet Type 53; pattern active/passive homing up to 20 km *(10.8 nm)* at up to 45 kts; warhead 400 kg.
A/S mortars: 2 RBU 2500 16-tubed trainable ❹; range 2500 m; warhead 21 kg.
Countermeasures: ESM: 2 Watch Dog; radar warning.
Radars: Air/surface search: Strut Curve ❺; F band.
Fire control: Drum Tilt ❻; H/I band (for 30 mm). Hawk Screech ❼; I band (for 76 mm).
Sonars: Hull-mounted; active search and attack; medium frequency.

Helicopters: Platform only (in *264*).

Programmes: Built at Mangalia. First commissioned 1983, second in 1984, third in 1985, fourth in 1987 and fifth in 1990. Programme probably continues as there have been unconfirmed reports of frigate building activity at Mangalia.
Structure: Probably a modified Soviet Koni design. At least one of the class *(264)* has a helicopter platform in place of the after 76 mm gun.

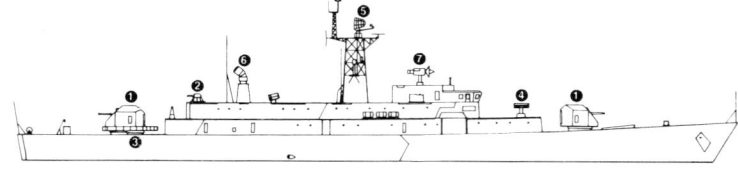
TETAL class *(Scale 1 : 900), Ian Sturton*

TETAL 261 *1991, Romanian Navy*

CORVETTES

3 Ex-SOVIET TARANTUL I CLASS (TYPE 1241)

| PESCARUSUL 189 | LASTUNUL 190 | ZBORUL 191 |

Displacement, tons: 385 standard; 450 full load
Dimensions, feet (metres): 184.1 × 37.7 × 8.2 *(56.1 × 11.5 × 2.5)*
Main machinery: CODOG; 2 Type NK-12MV gas turbines; 20 400 hp(m) *(15 MW)* sustained; 2 diesels; 8000 hp(m) *(5.88 MW)*; 2 shafts
Speed, knots: 36. **Range, miles:** 2000 at 20 kts; 400 at 36 kts
Complement: 41 (5 officers)

Missiles: 4 SS-N-2C Styx (2 twin); active radar or IR homing to 83 km *(45 nm)* at 0.9 Mach; warhead 513 kg.
Guns: 1 USSR 3 in *(76 mm)*/60; 85° elevation; 120 rounds/minute to 15 km *(8 nm)*; weight of shell 7 kg.
2—30 mm/65 AK 630; 6 barrels per mounting; 3000 rounds/minute to 20 km.
Countermeasures: 2—16 barrelled chaff launchers.
ESM: 2 Watch Dog; radar intercept.
Fire control: Hood Wink optronic director.
Radars: Air/surface search: Plank Shave; E band.
Fire control: Bass Tilt; H/I band.
Navigation: Spin Trough; I band.
IFF: Square Head. High Pole.

Programmes: Built at Petrovsky in 1985. First one transferred in December 1990, two more in February 1992.
Structure: Export version similar to those built for Poland, India, Yemen and former GDR.

TARANTUL I   *1991, Stefan Terzibaschitsch*

3 Ex-SOVIET POTI CLASS

| 31 | 32 | 33 |

Displacement, tons: 400 full load
Dimensions, feet (metres): 196.8 × 26.2 × 6.6 *(60 × 8 × 2)*
Main machinery: CODAG; 2 gas turbines; 30 000 hp(m) *(22 MW)*; 2 Type M 503A diesels; 5350 hp(m) *(3.91 MW)* sustained; 2 shafts
Speed, knots: 38. **Range, miles:** 4500 at 10 kts; 500 at 37 kts
Complement: 78

Guns: 2 USSR 57 mm/80 (twin); 85° elevation; 120 rounds/minute to 6 km *(3.3 nm)*; weight of shell 2.8 kg.
Torpedoes: 2—21 in *(533 mm)* (twin) tubes. Soviet Type 53.
A/S mortars: 2 RBU 2500 16-tubed trainable; range 2500 m; warhead 21 kg.
Radars: Air/surface search: Strut Curve; F band; range 110 km *(60 nm)* for 2 m² target.
Navigation: Spin Trough; I band.
Fire control: Muff Cob; G/H band.
IFF: High Pole B.
Sonars: Hull-mounted; active search and attack; medium/high frequency.

Programmes: Transferred from the USSR in 1970.

4 Ex-GERMAN M 40 CLASS (Ex-MINESWEEPERS)

| DEMOCRATIA 13 | DESROBIREA 15 |
| DESCATUSARIA 14 | DREPTATEA 16 |

Displacement, tons: 543 standard; 775 full load
Dimensions, feet (metres): 206.5 × 28 × 7.5 *(62.3 × 8.5 × 2.3)*
Main machinery: 2 diesels; 12 400 hp(m) *(9.11 MW)*; 2 shafts
Speed, knots: 17. **Range, miles:** 1200 at 15 kts
Complement: 80

Guns: 4—37 mm (2 twin). 2—12.7 mm MGs.
A/S mortars: 2 RBU 1200 5-tubed fixed; range 1200 m; warhead 34 kg.
Mines: 2 rails.
Radars: Navigation: Don 2; I band.

Comment: German M Boote design—designed as coal-burning minesweepers. Built at Galata. Converted to oil in 1951. The appearance of this class has been changed drastically during recent refits. Referred to locally as Corvettes. All minesweeping gear and the single 37 mm gun removed. A small helicopter platform has been fitted aft.

DREPTATEA   *1991, Romanian Navy*

MONITOR

Note: There are unconfirmed reports of up to five Brutar II class in commission.

1 BRUTAR CLASS (RIVER MONITOR)

96

Displacement, tons: 400 full load
Dimensions, feet (metres): 141.1 × 26.2 × 4.9 *(43 × 8 × 1.5)*
Guns: 1—100 mm (in tank turret). 4—14.5 mm (2 twin) MGs. 1—122 mm BM-21 40-barrelled rocket launcher.
Mines: Has laying capability.

Comment: Completed in 1984. Belongs to Danube Flotilla.

SHIPBORNE AIRCRAFT

Numbers/Type: 6 IAR 316 Alouette III.
Operational speed: 113 kts *(210 km/h)*.
Service ceiling: 10 500 ft *(3200 m)*.
Range: 290 nm *(540 km)*.
Role/Weapon systems: ASW helicopter. Status uncertain. Sensors: Nose-mounted search radar(?) Weapons: ASW; 2 × lightweight torpedoes.

LAND-BASED MARITIME AIRCRAFT

Numbers/Type: 5 Mil Mi-14P Haze A.
Operational speed: 124 kts *(230 km/h)*.
Service ceiling: 15 000 ft *(4570 m)*.
Range: 432 nm *(800 km)*.
Role/Weapon systems: Medium range ASW helicopter; used to support Soviet and coastal naval forces in Black Sea. Sensors: Search radar, dipping sonar, MAD, sonobuoys. Weapons: ASW; internally stored torpedoes, depth mines and bombs.

POTI 33   *1991, Romanian Navy*

512 ROMANIA / Light forces

LIGHT FORCES

Note: It is reported that one Kronshtadt class patrol craft was still operational in 1991.

6 Ex-SOVIET OSA I CLASS (TYPE 205)
(FAST ATTACK CRAFT—MISSILE)

194-199

Displacement, tons: 171 standard; 210 full load
Dimensions, feet (metres): 126.6 × 24.9 × 8.8 *(38.6 × 7.6 × 2.7)*
Main machinery: 3 Type M 503A diesels; 8025 hp *(5.9 MW)* sustained; 3 shafts
Speed, knots: 35. **Range, miles:** 400 at 34 kts
Complement: 30

Missiles: SSM: 4 SS-N-2 Styx; active radar or IR homing to 46 km *(25 nm)* at 0.9 Mach; warhead 513 kg.
Guns: 4 USSR 30 mm/65 (2 twin); 85° elevation; 500 rounds/minute to 5 km *(2.7 nm)*; weight of shell 0.54 kg.
Radars: Surface search: Square Tie; I band.
Fire control: Drum Tilt; H/I band.
IFF: High Pole. Square Head.

Programmes: Six transferred by the USSR in 1964. One deleted in error in 1988.

OSA 199   *1991, Romanian Navy*

27 CHINESE SHANGHAI CLASS
(FAST ATTACK CRAFT—GUN and PATROL)

20-40   41-44   VENUS   SATURN

Displacement, tons: 113 standard; 131 full load
Dimensions, feet (metres): 127.3 × 17.7 × 5.6 *(38.8 × 5.4 × 1.7)*
Main machinery: 2 L12-180 diesels (forward); 2400 hp(m) *(1.76 MW)*; 2 L12-180Z diesels (aft); 1820 hp(m) *(1.34 MW)*; 4 shafts
Speed, knots: 30. **Range, miles:** 700 at 17 kts
Complement: 34

Guns: 4 China 37 mm/63 (2 twin) *(20-40)*; 85° elevation; 180 rounds/minute to 8.5 km *(4.6 nm)*; weight of shell 1.42 kg.
1 China 37 mm/63 *(41-44)*. 4—14.5 mm MGs *(41-44)*.
A/S mortars: 2 RBU 1200 5-tubed fixed *(41-44)*; range 1200 m; warhead 34 kg.
Depth charges: 2 racks *(41-44)*.
Radars: Surface search: Don 2; I band.
Sonars: Hull-mounted; active attack; high frequency *(41-44)*.

Programmes: Built at Mangalia since 1973 in a programme of about two a year (which is now complete) with the exception of 22, 24 and 25 which were imported from China. V numbers have been removed.
Structure: Three variants of the Shanghai class of which the *41-44* were a new departure and the two named craft differ greatly in their bridge superstructure. The 57 mm gun has been replaced by a second twin 37 mm in the *20-40* type.
Operational: *20-40* serve with Border Guard, *41-44* are used for anti-submarine patrols and *Venus* and *Saturn* are Harbour Security craft. Some may be non-operational.

SHANGHAI 29   *1991, Romanian Navy*

29 CHINESE HUCHUAN CLASS
(FAST ATTACK CRAFT—TORPEDO)

51-77   MARS   JUPITER

Displacement, tons: 39 standard; 45 full load
Dimensions, feet (metres): 71.5 × 20.7 oa; 11.8 hull × 3.3 *(21.8 × 6.3; 3.6 × 1)*
Main machinery: 3 Type M 50 diesels; 3000 hp(m) *(2.4 MW)* sustained; 3 shafts
Speed, knots: 50 foilborne. **Range, miles:** 500 at 30 kts
Complement: 11
Guns: 4—14.5 mm (2 twin) MGs.
Torpedoes: 2—21 in *(533 mm)* tubes; anti-surface.

Comment: Hydrofoils of the same class as the Chinese which were started in 1956. Three imported from China. Remainder locally built at Dobreta SY, Turnu in a programme of about two a year which started 1973-74 and is now complete. *Mars* and *Jupiter* have no torpedo tubes and are without foils. V numbers deleted. Some may be non-operational.

HUCHUAN 51   *1988*

13 EPITROP CLASS (FAST ATTACK CRAFT—TORPEDO)

200-212

Displacement, tons: 215 full load
Dimensions, feet (metres): 120.7 × 24.9 × 5.9 *(36.8 × 7.6 × 1.8)*
Main machinery: 3 Type M 503A diesels; 8025 hp *(5.9 MW)* sustained; 3 shafts
Speed, knots: 36. **Range, miles:** 500 at 35 kts
Guns: 4—30 mm/65 (2 twin).
Torpedoes: 4—21 in *(533 mm)* tubes; anti-surface.
Radars: Surface search: Pot Drum; H/I band.
Fire control: Drum Tilt; H/I band.
IFF: High Pole A.

Comment: First reported in 1981. Built in Mangalia. Based on the Osa class hull.

EPITROP 210   *1991, Romanian Navy*

18 MONITORS (RIVER PATROL CRAFT)

76-93

Displacement, tons: 85
Dimensions, feet (metres): 105 × 16 × 3 *(32 × 4.8 × 0.9)*
Main machinery: 2 diesels; 1200 hp(m) *(882 kW)*; 2 shafts
Speed, knots: 17
Complement: 25
Guns: 1—85 mm. 4—14.5 mm (2 twin). 2—81 mm mortars.

Comment: Built in Dulcea Shipyard from 1973 in a programme of about two a year. Belong to Danube Flotilla.

RIVER MONITOR 76

4 RIVER PATROL CRAFT

14-17

Displacement, tons: 40
Dimensions, feet (metres): 52.5 × 14.4 × 4 *(16 × 4.4 × 1.2)*
Main machinery: 2 Type 3-D-12 diesels; 600 hp(m) *(440 kW)* sustained; 2 shafts
Speed, knots: 18
Complement: 10
Guns: 1—20 mm. 1—7.9 mm MG.

Comment: Steel-hulled craft built at Galata in 1954. Belong to Danube Flotilla. Obsolescent and four paid off in 1988.

RIVER PATROL CRAFT 17

Mine warfare forces — Training ship / ROMANIA

MINE WARFARE FORCES

Note: Reported that two Nestin class were ordered from Yugoslavia in 1990.

2 COSAR CLASS (MINELAYER/MCM SUPPORT SHIPS)

271   274

Displacement, tons: 1500 full load
Dimensions, feet (metres): 259.1 × 34.8 × 11.8 *(79 × 10.6 × 3.6)*
Main machinery: 2 diesels; 2 shafts
Speed, knots: 18
Complement: 75
Guns: 1—57 mm. 4—30 mm/65 (2 twin). 4—14.5 mm (2 twin) MGs.
A/S mortars: 2 RBU 1200 5-tubed fixed; range 1200 m; warhead 34 kg.
Mines: 200 approx.
Countermeasures: ESM: Watch Dog; radar warning.
Radars: Air/surface search: Strut Curve; F band; range 110 km *(60 nm)* for 2 m^2 target.
Navigation: Don 2; I band.
Fire control: Muff Cob; G/H band. Drum Tilt; H/I band.
Sonars: Hull-mounted; active search; high frequency.

Comment: Completed in 1980 and 1982. *271* has a helicopter platform, but *274* has a crane on the after deck.

COSAR 271   *1991, Romanian Navy*

4 MUSCA CLASS (MINESWEEPERS—COASTAL)

21-24

Displacement, tons: 660 full load
Dimensions, feet (metres): 171.3 × 31.2 × 9.2 *(52.2 × 9.5 × 2.8)*
Main machinery: 2 diesels; 2 shafts
Speed, knots: 14
Guns: 4—30 mm/65 (2 twin). 16—14.5 mm (4 quad).
A/S mortars: 2 RBU 1200 5-tubed fixed; range 1200 m; warhead 34 kg.
Mines: 50.
Radars: Surface search: Krivach; I band.
Fire control: Drum Tilt; H/I band.

Comment: Built at Mangalia at the rate of about one a year from 1986 to 1990.

MUSCA 24   *1991, Romanian Navy*

25 RIVER MINESWEEPERS

VD 141-165

Displacement, tons: 65 full load
Dimensions, feet (metres): 85.3 × 13.1 × 2.6 *(26 × 4 × 0.8)*
Main machinery: 2 Type M 50 diesels; 2200 hp(m) *(1.6 MW)* sustained; 2 shafts
Speed, knots: 18
Guns: 4—14.5 mm (2 twin) MGs.
Mines: Have laying capacity.

Comment: Built in Romania from 1975 onwards and may still be building.

MINESWEEPER 144   *1979*

OCEANOGRAPHIC SHIPS

2 AGOR

GRIGORE ANTIPA   EMIL RACOVITA

Displacement, tons: 1500 full load
Dimensions, feet (metres): 259.1 × 34.8 × 11.8 *(79 × 10.6 × 3.6)*
Main machinery: 2 diesels; 2 shafts
Speed, knots: 18
Complement: 75

Comment: Same hull as Cosar class. First in service in 1980, second in 1984. Large davits aft for launching submersible. One may have the number 278.

GRIGORE ANTIPA   *1991, Romanian Navy*

LOGISTIC SUPPORT SHIPS

2 CROITOR CLASS

CONSTANTA 281   **MIDIA** 283

Displacement, tons: 3500 full load
Dimensions, feet (metres): 354.3 × 44.3 × 12.5 *(108 × 13.5 × 3.8)*
Main machinery: 2 diesels; 2 shafts
Speed, knots: 14
Missiles: SAM: 2 SA-N-5 Grail quad launchers; manual aiming; IR homing to 6 km *(3.2 nm)* at 1.5 Mach; warhead 1.5 kg.
Guns: 2—57 mm/70 (twin). 4—30 mm/65 (2 twin). 4—14.5 mm (2 twin) MGs.
A/S mortars: 2 RBU 1200 5-tubed fixed; range 1200 m; warhead 34 kg.
Radars: Air/surface search: Strut Curve; F band; range 110 km *(60 nm)* for 2 m^2 target.
Navigation: Krivach; I band.
Fire control: Muff Cob; G/H band. Drum Tilt; H/I band.
Helicopters: 1 IAR-316 Alouette III type.

Comment: Reported in service in 1981 (281) and 1984 (283). These ships are a scaled down version of Soviet Don class. Forward crane for ammunition replenishment. Some ASW escort capability.

MIDIA   *6/1992, Giorgio Ghiglione*

TRAINING SHIP

Note: *Neptun* belongs to the Merchant Navy.

Name	No	Builders	Commissioned
MIRCEA	—	Blohm & Voss, Hamburg	29 Mar 1939

Displacement, tons: 1604
Dimensions, feet (metres): 206; 266.4 (with bowsprit) × 39.3 × 16.5 *(62.8; 81.2 × 12 × 5.2)*
Main machinery: Auxiliary MAN diesel; 500 hp(m) *(367 kW)*; 1 shaft
Speed, knots: 6
Complement: 83 plus 140 midshipmen for training

Comment: Refitted at Hamburg in 1966. Sail area, 5739 sq m *(18 830 sq ft)*.

MIRCEA   *7/1980, Marius Bar*

514 ROMANIA / Tugs — Auxiliaries

TUGS

2 ROSLAVL CLASS

VITEAZUL 101   **VOINICUL** 116

Displacement, tons: 450 full load
Dimensions, feet (metres): 135 × 29.5 × 10.8 *(41.2 × 9 × 3.3)*
Main machinery: Diesel-electric; 2 diesel generators; 1 motor; 1200 hp(m) *(882 kW)*; 1 shaft
Speed, knots: 13
Complement: 28

Comment: Built in Galata shipyard 1953-54.

ROSLAVL class   *10/1992, Per Kornefeldt*

12 HARBOUR TUGS

SRS 571-573, 576-577, 583-584, 675
MM 132-133, 136-137

AUXILIARIES

1 Ex-FRENCH FRIPONNE CLASS

STIHI (ex-*Mignonne*) 113

Displacement, tons: 440 full load
Dimensions, feet (metres): 200.1 × 23 × 8.2 *(61 × 7 × 2.5)*
Main machinery: 2 Sulzer diesels; 1800 hp(m) *(1.32 MW)*; 2 shafts
Speed, knots: 12. Range, miles: 3000 at 10 kts
Complement: 50
Guns: 1—37 mm. 4—14.5 mm (2 twin) MGs.
A/S mortars: 2 RBU 1200 5-tubed fixed; range 1200 m; warhead 34 kg.
Radars: Navigation: Two sets.
Sonars: Hull-mounted; active attack; high frequency.

Comment: Originally built at Brest and Lorient in 1916-17 as a minesweeper. The armament listed above reflects the latest conversion which also included a smoother bridge form. Second of class probably deleted in the late 1980s.

3 BRAILA CLASS (RIVER TRANSPORTS)

415   419   420

Displacement, tons: 240 full load
Dimensions, feet (metres): 124.7 × 28.2 × 3.3 *(38 × 8.6 × 1)*
Main machinery: 2 diesels; 2 shafts
Speed, knots: 4

Comment: Very old and used by civilian as well as naval authorities.

BRAILA 419   *1987*

3 COASTAL TANKERS

TM 530   TM 531   TM 532

Displacement, tons: 1300 full load
Dimensions, feet (metres): 196.8 × 30.2 × 13.4 *(60 × 9.2 × 4.1)*
Main machinery: 1 diesel; 600 hp(m) *(441 kW)*; 1 shaft
Speed, knots: 10
Cargo capacity: 800 tons
Guns: 1—37 mm. 2—12.7 mm MGs.

Comment: Completed between 1971 and 1973.

3 ACCOMMODATION BARGES

OLTUL   IALOMITA   SIRETUL

3 FIRE FLOATS

AUTOMATICE   ELECTRONICA   ENERGERICA

Displacement, tons: 160 full load
Dimensions, feet (metres): 124.6 × 18 × 4.6 *(38 × 5.5 × 1.4)*
Main machinery: 2 diesel; 2 shafts
Speed, knots: 12

Comment: Reported that *Electronica* has an additional AGI role.

STIHI   *1991, Romanian Navy*

RUSSIA AND ASSOCIATED STATES

Headquarters' Appointments

Commander-in-Chief and Deputy Minister of Defence:
    Admiral F N Gromov
1st Deputy Commander-in-Chief:
    Admiral I V Kasatonov
Chief of Main Naval Staff:
    Admiral V Y Selivanov
1st Deputy Chief of the Main Naval Staff:
    Vice Admiral V Y Lyaschenko
Deputy Commander-in-Chief (Operational Training):
    Vice Admiral A V Gorbunov
Deputy Commander-in-Chief (Repair and Armaments):
    Vice Admiral G N Gurinov
Deputy Commander-in-Chief (Technical Readiness and New Construction):
    Vice Admiral V P Yeremin
Commander-in-Chief (Main Ship Repair):
    Admiral Y Churikov
Commander of Naval Aviation:
    Colonel General V P Potapov
1st Deputy Commander Naval Aviation:
    Lieutenant General V V Budeyev
Chief of Navigation and Oceanography:
    Vice Admiral Y I Zheglov
Commander, Coastal Defence Forces:
    Lieutenant General I S Skuratov

Northern Fleet
Commander:
    Admiral O A Yerofeyev
Deputy Commander (Combat Training):
    Vice Admiral V A Poroshin
Commander Naval Aviation:
    Lieutenant General V Deyneka
Deputy Commander (Rear Services):
    Rear Admiral V N Dobushev

Pacific
Commander:
    Admiral G N Gurinov
1st Deputy Commander:
    Vice Admiral A G Oleynik
Chief of Staff:
    Vice Admiral V I Kalabin
Commander Naval Aviation:
    Lieutenant General V V Akporisov
Deputy Commander (Combat Training):
    Vice Admiral B F Prikhodko
Deputy Commander (Rear Services):
    Rear Admiral A N Loiko
Commander, Indian Ocean Squadron:
    Vice Admiral V N Sergeyev

Black Sea
Commander:
    Vice Admiral E D Baltin
1st Deputy Commander and Acting Commander:
    Vice Admiral V P Larionov
Chief of Staff:
    Vice Admiral A Manchenko
Deputy Commander (Rear Services):
    Vice Admiral L A Vasiliev
Commander Naval Aviation:
    Major General N N Fadeyev
Commander Mediterranean Squadron:
    Vice Admiral P G Svyatashov

Baltic
Commander:
    Vice Admiral V G Yegorov
Chief of Staff:
    Vice Admiral V V Grishanov
Commander Naval Aviation:
    Lieutenant General V Proskurin
Deputy Commander (Combat Training):
    Vice Admiral Y I Chebanov
Deputy Commander (Rear Services):
    Vice Admiral I I Ryabinin

Caspian Flotilla
Commander:
    Rear Admiral B M Zinin

Personnel

(a) 1993: 350 000 officers and ratings (Afloat, 120 000; Naval Aviation, 70 000; Training, 40 000; Naval Infantry 17 000 (one Brigade for each Fleet); Coastal Defence, 14 000; Shore Support, 90 000; Communications, 4000) plus 22 000 Maritime Border Guard
(b) Approximately 30 per cent volunteers (officers and senior ratings)—remainder two years' national service (18 months if ashore) since 1991 (or three years if volunteered)
(c) Deployed: Northern 89 000, Baltic 75 000, Black Sea 78 000, Pacific 88 000, elsewhere 20 000.

Associated States

The Soviet Union was dissolved in December 1991. In 1992 a Commonwealth of Independent States was formed from the Republics of the former Union, but without the Baltic States. The two major Fleets in the North and Pacific are wholly Russian based. In the Baltic the Russian flotilla had withdrawn from the former East German and Polish ports by 1993 but still retained some vessels in the Baltic republics which are also forming their own Coast Guards (see Estonia, Latvia and Lithuanian sections). The Caspian flotilla has divided with about one third going to Azerbaijan, and in the Black Sea an uneasy coalition has been formed between Russia, Georgia and Ukraine until 1995.

Main Bases (Russian unless indicated otherwise)

North: Severomorsk (HQ), Motovsky Gulf, Polyarny, Severodvinsk, Gremika
Baltic: Kaliningrad (HQ), St Petersburg, Kronshtadt, Baltiysk
Black Sea: Sevastopol (HQ) (Crimea), Tuapse, Poti (Georgia), Balaklava (Crimea), Odessa (Ukraine), Nikolayev (Ukraine), Novorssiysk
Caspian: Astrakhan (HQ), Baku (Azerbaijan)
Pacific: Vladivostok (HQ), Sovetskaya Gavan, Magadan, Petropavlovsk, Komsomolsk

Pennant Numbers

The Navy has changes of pennant numbers as a matter of routine every three years and when ships change fleet. The last major overall change of numbers took place in May 1990 and therefore may change again in May 1993. Such a list has therefore been omitted in this section as it is of little use identifying ships over any lengthy period.

Class Names

Some Russian class names differ from those allocated by NATO. In such cases the Russian name is placed in brackets after the NATO name.

Building Programme

Submarines
SSGN—Oscar class at one a year.
SSN—Akula class at one or two a year.
One Sierra fitting out.
SS—Kilo class at two or three a year.
Production in 1992 included three nuclear submarines and three diesel submarines including export models.

Aircraft Carriers
One Kuznetsov class fitting out.

Cruisers
Fourth Kirov fitting out. Fourth Slava fitting out.

Destroyers
Two Sovremenny class fitting out, more building.
One Udaloy II class fitting out.

Frigates
First Neustrashimy on trials, two building.
Grisha V class continues.
Gepard class, building.

Light Forces
Tarantul III class continues.
Tarantul class continues for export.
Pauk class continues for export.
Zhuk class coastal patrol craft continue, some for export.
Svetlyak class continues.

Mine Warfare Forces
Natya class continues for export.
Sonya class (MSC) continues including for export.
Lida class (MSI) building.

Air Cushion Vehicles
Pomornik and Tsaplya classes continue.

Auxiliaries
Sorum class ocean tugs continue.
Antonov class cargo ships continue.

Strength of the Fleet

Type	Active (Reserve)	Building
Submarines (SSBN)	54	—
Submarines (SSGN)	30	2
Submarines (SSG)	7	—
Submarines (SSN)	65 (7)	6
Submarines (SS)	69	7
Auxiliary Submarines (SSA(N))	16	—
Aircraft Carriers (CV)	4	1
Helicopter Cruisers (CHG)	1	—
Battle Cruisers (CGN)	3	1
Cruisers (CG)	20	1
Destroyers (DDG)	36	4
Frigates (FFG)	32	2
Frigates (FF)	109	5
Corvettes (Missile)	66	2
Patrol Ships/Radar Pickets	5	—
Fast Attack Craft (Missile)	38	—
Hydrofoils (Missile)	17	—
Fast Attack Craft (Patrol)	148	5
Fast Attack Craft (Hydrofoil)	44	—
Coastal Patrol Craft	32	—
River Patrol Craft	119	—
Minelayers	3	—
Minehunters—Ocean	2	—
Minesweepers—Ocean	73	—
Minesweepers—Coastal	97	2
Minesweepers—Inshore	68	6
Minesweeping Boats	15	—
LPDs	3	—
LSTs	40	—
LSMs	32	—
Hovercraft	62	2
Depot, Support and Repair Ships	79	—
Intelligence Collectors (AGI)	52 (6)	—
Survey Ships	85 + 42 civilian	—
Oceanographic Research Ships	41 + 62 civilian	—
Missile Range Ships	11	—
Space Associated Ships	0 + 6 civilian	—
Training Ships	12	—
Cable Ships	13	—
Replenishment Tankers	28	—
Support Tankers	17+	—
Special Tankers	13	—
Hospital Ships	5	—
Salvage and Mooring Vessels	49	—
Submarine Rescue Ships	18	—
Transports and Cargo Ships	64+	—
Icebreakers (Nuclear)	0 + 7 civilian	1
Icebreakers	7 + 63 civilian	—

Mercantile Marine

Lloyd's Register of Shipping:
    4543 vessels of 15 632 698 tons gross

Fleet Disposition on 1 January 1993

Type	Northern	Baltic	Black Sea and Caspian	Pacific
SSBN	33	—	—	21
SSGN	20	—	—	10
SSG	—	5	2	—
SSN	44	—	—	18
SS	26	16	9	23
SSAN, SSA	10	1	3	2
CV	3	—	—	1
CHG	—	—	1	—
CGN	2	—	—	1
CG	6	1	7	6
DDG	14	4	7	11
FFG	7	9	6	10
FF and FFL	33	14	22	23
FAC(M), Missile Corvettes and Hydrofoils (Missile)	9	42	32	36
FAC(P), Patrol Craft	16	126	102	98
MCM Forces	44	73	74	67
LPD	1	—	—	2
LST	7	9	9	13
LSM	6	6	16	4
Hovercraft	5	15	22	20
Depot, Repair and Support Ships	26	11	14	28
Underway Replenishment Ships	7	3	7	11
Support Tankers	8	3	5	2

DELETIONS

Note: Some of the ships listed are still theoretically 'in reserve' but none will go to sea again and a realistic scrapping policy continues with the aim of having 65 per cent of operational ships less than 20 years old. The average age of the ships deleted between 1988 and 1993 is 27 years.

Submarines

1989-90	12 Golf II (SSB), 1 Golf V (SSB), 5 Echo I (SSN), 32 Whiskey (SS), 2 Zulu IV (SS)
1990-91	3 Yankee I (SSBN), 1 Hotel III (SSBN), 1 Papa (SSGN), 1 Charlie (SSGN), 11 Echo II (SSGN), 1 Juliett (SSG), 11 November (SSN), 7 Hotel II (SSN/QN), 34 Whiskey (SS)
1991	1 Yankee I (SSBN), 1 Yankee II (SSBN), 2 Charlie I (SSGN), 3 Echo II (SSGN), 1 Victor I (SSN), 3 Juliett (SSG), 2 Mod Golf (SSQ), 15 Foxtrot (SS), 18 Whiskey (SS)
1992	4 Yankee I (SSBN), 1 Delta I (SSBN), 1 Charlie II (SSGN), 3 Charlie I (SSGN), 5 Echo II (SSGN), 7 Juliett (SSG), 10 Foxtrot (SS)

Aircraft Carriers

1992	*Ulyanovsk, Minsk, Leningrad*

Cruisers

1990-91	1 Kresta I (*Sevastopol*), 1 Kynda (*Varyag*), 3 Sverdlov (CC and CL)
1991	2 Kresta I (*V. A. Drozd, Vladivostok*)
1992	3 Kresta II (*Kronstadt, A Nakhimov, A Isachenkov*), 1 Kynda (*Grozny*)

Destroyers

1989-90	3 Mod Kildin (DDG), 4 Kanin (DDG), 7 Sam Kotlin (DDG), 11 Kotlin (DD), 9 Skory (DD)
1990-91	2 Kashin (DDG)
1991	3 Kashin (DDG)
1992	3 Kashin (DDG)

Frigates

1990-91	15 Riga, 3 Mirka, 5 Petya
1991-92	5 Riga, 7 Mirka, 5 Petya
1992	1 Krivak I (FFG), 3 Grisha I, 2 Grisha III (to Lithuania), 5 Riga, 3 Mirka II

Corvettes (Missile)

1992	3 Matka, 4 Osa I, 5 Osa II

Patrol Ships/Craft

1990	1 Purga, 3 T 43/PGR
1991	12 T 58/PGF
1992	2 Zhuk, 2 Yaz, 3 Vosh, 16 Schmel, 4 TR 40

Fast Attack Craft

1990-91	25 Osa, 2 Turya, 9 Poti, 6 SO 1, 1 Sarancha
1991-92	8 Osa, 3 Shershen, 29 Poti; 3 SO 1, 5 Stenka
1992	6 Poti
1993	2 Turya (to Lithuania), 3 SO 1, 6 Stenka (to Azerbaijan)

Mine Warfare Vessels

1990-91	2 Yurka, 10 Vanya, 1 Sasha, 10 TR 40, 15 K 8, 10 T 43
1991-92	12 Yurka, 10 T 43, 2 Zhenya, 20 Vanya, 3 Ilyusha, 1 Olya
1992	2 Natya I, 1 T 43, 4 Vanya, 1 Sasha

Amphibious Forces

1990-91	7 Polnochny
1991-92	15 SMB 1
1992	2 Alligator

Hovercraft

1990-91	12 Gus, 1 Aist, 1 Lebed
1991	10 Gus
1992	3 Lebed

AGIs

1990-91	3 Okean
1991	4 Mirny, 2 Lentra

Survey and Research Ships

1992	5 Melitopol, *Otto Schmidt* (sold), *A I Voeykov, Arnold Veimer* (to Estonia), *Rudolf Samoylovich* (to Lithuania)

Support Ships and Tankers

1990	2 Komsomol, 2 Muna
1990-91	2 MP 6, 5 Dnepr, 1 Oskol, *Feolent*
1991	1 Ugra, *Polyarnik, Indiga, Ural, Ishim*
1992	1 Ugra, 1 Don, 1 Amur I, 1 Altay, 8 Khobi, 5 Neptun, 2 Valday, 1 Chulym, 10 Lentra, 1 MP 6, 4 Khabarov, 1 Vikhr (to Syria), 1 Sekstan, 5 Okhtensky

Space Associated Ships

1990-91	*Kosmonaut Komarov*, 4 Morzhovets
1991	*Nevelsky*, 5 Telnovsk, *Petr Lebedev, Sergey Vavilov, Chukotka*

Icebreaker

1990	*Lenin*

NAVAL AVIATION

Overall totals: 1500 (some in storage) front-line and training aircraft in early 1993.

Tactical deployment: A total of 180 strike/bombers (Badger, Backfire and Blinder), 360 fighter/fighter bombers (Fencer, Flogger, Fulcrum, Frogfoot and Fitter).
Deployed as follows: Northern 80, Baltic 180, Black Sea 50, Pacific 50.

Tactical support deployment: A total of 120 fixed wing (Badger tankers; Bear D, Badger, Coot, Cub, Blinder and Fencer reconnaissance and electronic warfare).
Deployed as follows: Northern 30, Baltic 30, Black Sea 25, Pacific 35.
A total of 25 rotary wing (Hormone reconnaissance).
Deployed as follows: Northern 5, Baltic 5, Black Sea 5, Pacific 10.

Anti-submarine warfare deployment: A total of 190 fixed wing (Bear F, May, Mail).
Deployed as follows: Northern 80, Baltic 20, Black Sea 30, Pacific 60.
A total of 240 rotary wing (Helix A, Hormone A, Haze A).
Deployed as follows: Northern 60, Baltic 30, Black Sea 70, Pacific 80.

Mine warfare deployment: A total of 40 (Haze B).

Transport/training deployment: A total of 330 (includes about 15 Flanker B and 10 Fulcrum).
Deployed as follows: Northern 80, Baltic 90, Black Sea 80, Pacific 80.

Ex-Air Force: In 1990-91 about 680 Air Force aircraft (including Fencers, Floggers, Fulcrums, Fitters and Frogfoots) were transferred to naval air bases. All aircraft that can be embarked in carriers are not subject to CFE restrictions. Some of these aircraft have been transferred to the independent Republics.

TORPEDOES

Note: There are several torpedo types in service. The following table lists broad characteristics.

Type/Designator	Diameter/Length	Role	Launch Platform	Propulsion	Speed/Range	Guidance	Warhead	Remarks
40	40 cm/4.5 m	ASW	1. Submarine 2. Escorts	Electric	40 kts/15 km (8.1 nm)	Active/passive	100 kg	
45	45 cm/3.9 m	ASW	1. Helicopter 2. SS-N-16	Electric	30 kts/15 km (8.1 nm)	Active/passive	100 kg	
SAET-60	53 cm/7.8 m	Anti-ship	1. Submarine 2. Surface ship	Electric	40 kts/15 km (8.1 nm)	Passive	400 kg	Low yield nuclear variant available
53-65	53 cm/7.8 m	Anti-ship	1. Submarine 2. Surface ship	Turbine	50 kts/25 km (13.8 nm)	Passive/wake	300 kg	Low yield nuclear variant available
ET80-67	53 cm/7.8 m	ASW	1. Submarine 2. Surface ship	Electric	40 kts/15 km (8.1 nm)	Active/passive	300 kg	May be wire-guided
E53-72	53 cm/4.7 m	ASW	1. Aircraft 2. SS-N-14	Electric	40 kts/15 km (8.1 nm)	Active/passive	150 kg	
65	65 cm/10 m	Anti-ship	1. Submarine (Akula, Sierra, Victor III)	Turbine	50 kts/50 km (27.5 nm)	Wake	900 kg	Low yield nuclear variant available

SUBMARINES

Strategic Missile Submarines

Note: In the late 1960s the SS-N-8 was first tested and this was fitted in the Delta I class in 1972 and subsequently the Delta II in 1975. In the latter half of the 1970s the SS-N-18 appeared in the Delta III class and comes in three versions. Mod 1 and Mod 3 have three and seven MIRV respectively. Mod 2 has a single RV. In early 1980 a new type of solid-fuelled SLBM, SS-N-20, was tested. This is larger than SS-N-18, carries a seven to ten MIRV head and is in the Typhoon class.
In 1983 testing of SS-N-23 began; this missile is carried in the Delta IV class. Operational in 1986 with seven to ten MIRV. With both Delta IV and Typhoon programmes terminated a new class of SSBN is expected in due course to maintain an operational force of about 25 hulls on a one for one replacement basis. If this plan is maintained, the first of the new class will not be in service until all the remaining Yankee, Delta I and Delta II submarines have paid off. However, at least two types of new ballistic missile are being developed and may be retrofitted to existing classes, as well as being available for new classes, including possibly a Delta IV variant.
In addition to the ballistic missiles a sea-launched cruise missile (SLCM), the SS-N-21, is operational. Its primary role is nuclear strike against land targets. Its size is compatible with submarine torpedo tubes and it is probably carried in all modern classes of SSN. A larger missile of this type, SS-NX-24, was under test in 1989/90 in a modified Yankee SSN but this programme has been abandoned.

6 TYPHOON CLASS (SSBN)

Displacement, tons: 21 500 surfaced; 26 500 dived
Dimensions, feet (metres): 562.7 oa; 541.3 wl × 80.7 × 42.7 *(171.5; 165 × 24.6 × 13)*
Main machinery: Nuclear; 2 PWR; 320 MW; 2 turbines; 81 600 hp(m) *(60 MW)*; 2 shafts; shrouded props
Speed, knots: 26 dived; 19 surfaced
Complement: 175 (55 officers). 2 crews

Missiles: SLBM: 20 SS-N-20 Sturgeon; three-stage solid fuel rocket; stellar inertial guidance to 8300 km *(4500 nm)*; warhead nuclear 6-9 MIRV each of 100 kT; CEP 500 m. 2 missiles fired from the first of class in 15 seconds. Being modified to take an improved version of the Sturgeon (SS-N-24/26) which has improved accuracy.
SAM: There are suggestions that this class may have a SAM capability.
A/S: SS-N-15 fired from 21 in *(533 mm)* tubes; inertial flight to 37 km *(20 nm)*; warhead nuclear 200 kT.
SS-N-16 fired from 25.6 in *(650 mm)* tubes; inertial flight to 120 km *(65 nm)*; payload Type 45 torpedo; active/passive homing to 15 km *(8.1 nm)* at 30 kts; warhead 100 kg. There is also a 16B version with a nuclear warhead.
Torpedoes: 2—21 in *(533 mm)* and 4—25.6 in *(650 mm)* tubes. Type 53; dual purpose; pattern active/passive homing up to 20 km *(10.8 nm)* at up to 45 kts; warhead 400 kg or low yield nuclear and Type 65; anti-surface; pattern active/passive wake homing to 50 km *(27.5 nm)* at 50 kts; warhead 900 kg or low yield nuclear. The weapon load includes a combination of 36 torpedoes and A/S missiles.
Mines: Could be carried in lieu of torpedoes.
Countermeasures: ESM: Rim Hat; radar warning. Park Lamp D/F.
Radars: Surface search: Snoop Pair; I/J band.
Sonars: Shark Gill; hull-mounted; passive/active search and attack; low/medium frequency.
Mouse Roar; hull-mounted; active attack; high frequency.

Programmes: This is the largest type of submarine ever built. The first was begun in 1977 and launched at Severodvinsk in September 1980 (in service 1982) and the second in September 1982 entering service in late 1983. The third was commissioned in late 1984, the fourth followed a year later, the fifth in 1987 and the sixth in 1989. Statements by senior officers indicate disenchantment with these very large submarines and no more of this class are to be completed. One is called *Miskiy Komsomolets*.
Modernisation: The class is being modernised to take an SS-N-20 follow-on missile which has improved accuracy.
Structure: Two separate 8.5 m diameter hulls covered by a single outer free-flood hull with anechoic Cluster Guard tiles plus separate 6 m diameter pressure-tight compartments in the fin and fore-ends. There is a large separation between the outer and inner hulls along the sides. The unique features of Typhoon are her enormous size and the fact that the missile tubes are mounted forward of the fin. The positioning of the launch tubes means a fully integrated weapons area in the bow section leaving space abaft the fin for the provision of two nuclear reactors, one in each hull—probably needed to achieve a reasonable speed with this huge hull. The fin configuration indicates a designed capability to break through ice cover possibly up to 3 m thick; the retractable forward hydroplanes, the rounded hull and the shape of the fin are all related to under-ice operations. Diving depth, 1000 ft *(300 m)*.
Operational: Strategic targets are within range from anywhere in the world. Two VLF/ELF communication buoys are fitted. VLF navigation system for under-ice operations. Pert Spring SATCOM mast, Cod Eye radiometric sextant and Kremmny 2 IFF. All are based in the Northern Fleet.

TYPHOON *1991, S Breyer*

TYPHOON *5/1991*

TYPHOON *1992*

TYPHOON *1990*

518 RUSSIA / Submarines

7 DELTA IV (DELFIN) CLASS (SSBN)

Displacement, tons: 10 750 surfaced; 12 150 dived
Dimensions, feet (metres): 544.6 oa; 518.4 wl × 39.4 × 28.5 *(166; 158 × 12 × 8.7)*
Main machinery: Nuclear; 2 PWR; 160 MW; 2 turbines; 37 400 hp(m) *(27.5 MW)* 2 shafts
Speed, knots: 24 dived; 19 surfaced
Complement: 130

Missiles: SLBM: 16 SS-N-23 Skiff; three-stage liquid fuel rocket; stellar inertial guidance to 8300 km *(4500 nm)*; warhead nuclear 10 MIRV each of 100 kT; CEP 500 m. Same diameter as SS-N-18 but longer.
Torpedoes: 4—21 in *(533 mm)* and 2—25.6 in *(650 mm)* tubes. Type 53; dual purpose; pattern active/passive homing up to 20 km *(10.8 nm)* at up to 45 kts; warhead 400 kg or low yield nuclear and Type 65; anti-surface; pattern active/passive wake homing to 50 km *(27.5 nm)* at 50 kts; warhead 900 kg or low yield nuclear. Total of 18 weapons.
Countermeasures: ESM: Brick Pulp/Group; radar warning. Park Lamp D/F.
Radars: Surface search: Snoop Tray; I band.
Sonars: Shark Gill; hull-mounted; passive/active search and attack; low/medium frequency.
Mouse Roar; hull-mounted; active attack; high frequency.

Programmes: First of class launched February 1984 and commissioned later that year. All built at Severodvinsk and launched at the rate of about one per year. This programme completed in late 1990. A follow-on class is expected in the mid-1990s.
Structure: A slim fitting is sited on the after fin which is reminiscent of a similar tube in one of the November class in the early 1980s. This may be a form of dispenser for a buoyant communications wire aerial. The other distinguishing feature, apart from the size being greater than Delta III, is the pressure-tight fitting on the after end of the missile tube housing, which may be a TV camera to monitor communications buoy and wire retrieval operations. Also there are two 650 mm torpedo tubes. Diving depth, 1000 ft *(300 m)*. The outer casing has a continuous acoustic coating.
Operational: Two VLF/ELF communication buoys. Navigation systems include SATNAV, SINS, Cod Eye. Pert Spring SATCOM. A modified and more accurate version of SS-N-23 was tested at sea in 1988 bringing the CEP down from 900 m to 500 m. All based in the Northern Fleet.

DELTA IV 1992

DELTA IV 1992

14 DELTA III (KALMAR) CLASS (SSBN)

Displacement, tons: 10 000 surfaced; 11 700 dived
Dimensions, feet (metres): 524.9 oa; 498.7 wl × 39.4 × 28.5 *(160; 152 × 12 × 8.7)*
Main machinery: Nuclear; 2 PWR; 160 MW; 2 turbines; 37 400 hp(m) *(27.5 MW)* 2 shafts
Speed, knots: 24 dived; 19 surfaced
Complement: 130

Missiles: SLBM: 16 SS-N-18 Stingray; two stage liquid fuel rocket with post boost vehicle (PBV); stellar inertial guidance; 3 variants:
Mod 1; range 6500 km *(3500 nm)*; warhead nuclear 3 MIRV each of 200 kT; CEP 900 m.
Mod 2; range 8000 km *(4320 nm)*; warhead nuclear 450 kT; CEP 900 m.
Mod 3; range 6500 km *(3500 nm)*; warhead nuclear 7 MIRV 100 kT; CEP 900 m.
Mods 1 and 3 are the first MIRV SLBMs in Soviet service. SS-N-23 retrofitted in some (see Delta IV for details).
Torpedoes: 6—21 in *(533 mm)* tubes. 18 Type 53; dual purpose; pattern active/passive homing to 20 km *(10.8 nm)* at up to 45 kts; warhead 400 kg or low yield nuclear.
Countermeasures: ESM: Brick Pulp/Group; radar warning. Park Lamp D/F.
Radars: Surface search: Snoop Tray; I band.
Sonars: Shark Teeth; hull-mounted; passive/active search and attack; low/medium frequency.
Mouse Roar; hull-mounted; active attack; high frequency.

Programmes: Built at Severodvinsk 402. Completed 1976-1982.
Modernisation: SS-N-23 Skiff has been retrofitted in some of this class.
Structure: The missile casing is higher than in Delta II class to accommodate SS-N-18 missiles which are longer than the SS-N-8 of the Delta II class. The outer casing has a continuous 'acoustic' coating. Diving depth, 1000 ft *(300 m)*.
Operational: ELF/VLF communications with floating aerial and buoy; UHF and SHF aerials. Navigation equipment includes Cod Eye radiometric sextant, SATNAV, SINS and Omega. Pert Spring SATCOM. Kremmny 2 IFF. Nine of the class are based in the Pacific and five in the Northern Fleet.

DELTA III 1990

DELTA III 1991

4 DELTA II (NURENA-M) CLASS (SSBN)

Displacement, tons: 9700 surfaced; 11 300 dived
Dimensions, feet (metres): 508.4 oa; 498.7 wl × 39.4 × 28.5 *(155; 152 × 12 × 8.7)*
Main machinery: Nuclear; 2 PWR; 160 MW; 2 turbines; 37 400 hp(m) *(27.5 MW)*; 2 shafts
Speed, knots: 24 dived; 19 surfaced
Complement: 130

Missiles: SLBM: 16 SS-N-8 Sawfly; 2-stage liquid fuel rocket; stellar inertial guidance; 2 variants:
  Mod 1; range 7800 km *(4210 nm)*; warhead nuclear 1.2 MT; CEP 400 m.
  Mod 2; range 9100 km *(4910 nm)*; warhead nuclear 2 MIRV each of 800 kT; CEP 400 m.
Torpedoes: 6—21 in *(533 mm)* bow tubes. 18 Type 53; dual purpose; pattern active/passive homing up to 20 km *(10.8 nm)* at up to 45 kts; warhead 400 kg or low yield nuclear.
Countermeasures: ESM: Brick Pulp/Group; radar warning.
Radars: Surface search: Snoop Tray; I band.
Sonars: Shark Teeth; hull-mounted; passive/active search and attack; low/medium frequency.
  Mouse Roar; hull-mounted; active attack; high frequency.

Programmes: Building yard—Severodvinsk. First appeared in 1976. Further construction cancelled with the advent of SS-N-18 and the Delta III class.
Structure: A larger edition of Delta I designed to carry four extra missile tubes and suffering a speed reduction as a result. Has a straight run on the after part of the missile casing. The outer casing has a continuous 'acoustic' coating. Diving depth, 1000 ft *(300 m)*.
Operational: ELF/VLF communications with floating aerial and buoy; UHF and SHF aerials. Navigation equipment includes SATNAV, SINS, Omega, Cod Eye radiometric sextant. Pert Spring SATCOM. Kremmny 2 IFF. All based in the Northern Fleet.

DELTA II   1992

17 DELTA I (NURENA) CLASS (SSBN)

Displacement, tons: 8700 surfaced; 10 200 dived
Dimensions, feet (metres): 459.3 oa; 446.2 wl × 39.4 × 28.5 *(140; 136 × 12 × 8.7)*
Main machinery: Nuclear; 2 PWR; 160 MW; 2 turbines; 37 400 hp(m) *(27.5 MW)*; 2 shafts
Speed, knots: 25 dived; 19 surfaced
Complement: 120

Missiles: SLBM: 12—SS-N-8 Sawfly; 2-stage liquid fuel rocket; stellar inertial guidance; 2 variants:
  Mod 1; range 7800 km *(4210 nm)*; warhead nuclear 1.2 MT; CEP 400 m.
  Mod 2; range 9100 km *(4910 nm)*; warhead nuclear 2 MIRV each of 800 kT; CEP 400 m.
Torpedoes: 6—21 in *(533 mm)* bow tubes. 18 Type 53; dual purpose; pattern active/passive homing up to 20 km *(10.8 nm)* at up to 45 kts; warhead 400 kg or low yield nuclear.
Countermeasures: ESM: Brick Pulp/Group; radar warning. Park Lamp D/F.
Radars: Surface search: Snoop Tray; I band.
Sonars: Shark Teeth; hull-mounted; passive/active search and attack; low/medium frequency.
  Mouse Roar; hull-mounted; active attack; high frequency.

Programmes: The first of this class, an advance on the Yankee class SSBNs, was laid down at Severodvinsk in 1969 and completed in 1972. Programme completed 1972-77. Building yards—Severodvinsk 402 (10) and Komsomolsk (8).
Structure: The longer-range SS-N-8 missiles are of greater length than the SS-N-6s and, as this length cannot be accommodated below the keel, they stand several feet proud of the after-casing. At the same time the need to compensate for the additional top-weight would seem to be the reason for the reduction to 12 missiles in this class. The outer casing has a continuous 'acoustic' coating. Diving depth, 1000 ft *(300 m)*.
Operational: ELF/VLF communications with floating aerial and buoy; UHF and SHF aerials. Cod Eye radiometric sextant.

DELTA I   1990

Kremmny 2 IFF. In common with all the Delta class variations, this submarine is ill-designed for under-ice operations. Eight based in the North, nine in the Pacific. First of this class paid off in 1992 from the Northern Fleet.

6 YANKEE I CLASS (SSBN)

Displacement, tons: 8000 surfaced; 9450 dived
Dimensions, feet (metres): 426.4 × 38 × 26.2 *(130 × 11.6 × 8)*
Main machinery: Nuclear; 2 PWR; 160 MW; 2 turbines; 37 400 hp(m) *(27.5 MW)*; 2 shafts
Speed, knots: 26.5 dived; 20 surfaced
Complement: 120

Missiles: SLBM: 16 SS-N-6 Serb; single-stage liquid fuel rocket; inertial guidance; 2 variants:
  Mod 1; range 2400 km *(1300 nm)*; warhead nuclear 1 MT; CEP 1300 m.
  Mod 3; range 3000 km *(1620 nm)*; warhead 2 MRV each of 500 kT; CEP 1300 m.
  Launch rate for a full salvo is reported as less than 2 minutes.
Torpedoes: 6—21 in *(533 mm)* tubes. 18 Type 53; dual purpose; pattern active/passive homing up to 20 km *(10.8 nm)* at up to 45 kts; warhead 400 kg or low yield nuclear.
Countermeasures: ESM: Brick Group; radar warning. Park Lamp D/F.
Radars: Surface search: Snoop Tray; I band.
Sonars: Shark Teeth; hull-mounted; passive/active search and attack; low/medium frequency.
  Mouse Roar; hull-mounted; active attack; high frequency

Programmes: The first of the class was laid down in 1963-64 and delivered late 1967 and the programme then accelerated with output rising to six to eight a year in the period around 1970. The last one was completed in 1974. Construction took place at Severodvinsk 402 (first laid down in 1965) and Komsomolsk. The original deployment of this class was to the eastern seaboard of the US giving a coverage at least as far as the Mississippi. Increase in numbers allowed a Pacific patrol to be established off California in 1971 providing coverage from the western seaboard to the eastern side of the Rockies. In the last 15 years some of this class had their missile tubes

YANKEE I   1990

removed to remain within SALT 1 limits (see entries under SSGN, SSN and SSAN).
Structure: Design is similar to USS *Ethan Allen* (now deleted) with vertical tubes in two rows of eight and fin-mounted foreplanes; the first time the Navy had used this arrangement. The outer casing has a continuous 'acoustic' coating. Diving depth, 1000 ft *(300 m)*.
Operational: Fitted for ELF communications with floating aerial and VLF buoy. VHF and SHF aerials. Navigation equipment includes SATNAV, SINS, Omega and Cod Eye radiometric sextant. Pert Spring SATCOM. Kremmny 2 IFF. One Yankee I sank in Western Atlantic after an internal explosion 6 October 1986 while patrolling 600 miles north of Bermuda. The single Yankee II paid off in 1991. In early 1993 three were in the Northern Fleet and three in the Pacific. All are expected to be withdrawn from service by 1994.

Cruise Missile Submarines

Note: The Echo II nuclears and the conventional Juliett class were built over the same period (1961-68), armed with eight and four SS-N-3A missiles respectively as a counter to the threat of the US carriers with their nuclear strike capability. The SS-N-3As were replaced by SS-N-12 in about 14 of the Echo II class. By 1968 both production lines had stopped when the first Charlie class appeared with underwater launch capability for its SS-N-7 missiles. The problem which had faced all the earlier boats, that of having to surface to launch, had been overcome. An improved design of Charlie I (Charlie II) and the single unit of the Papa class (since deleted) appeared in the early 1970s with SS-N-9 missiles to be followed by the launch of the giant Oscar in 1980 with 24 SS-N-19 supersonic missiles.

The arrival of SS-N-21, a sea launched land attack cruise missile with an estimated range of 1600 nm and a tube-launch capability for all modern classes of SSN, changed the balance of cruise missile submarines. A larger land attack missile, SS-NX-24 was fitted in a converted Yankee class for trials in 1989 but this programme was abandoned in 1991.

All these submarines with the exception of Echo II and Juliett classes are coated with Cluster Guard anechoic tiles. All are capable of laying mines from their torpedo tubes.

8 + 2 OSCAR II (ANTYEY) and 2 OSCAR I (GRANIT) CLASSES (SSGN)

Displacement, tons: 10 200 surfaced; 12 500 dived (Oscar I); 10 700 surfaced; 13 500 dived (Oscar II)
Dimensions, feet (metres): 469.2; 505.2 (Oscar II) × 59.7 × 29.5 *(143; 154 × 18.2 × 9)*
Main machinery: Nuclear; 2 PWR; 200 MW; 2 turbines; 75 000 hp(m) *(55 MW)*; 2 shafts; 2 spinners
Speed, knots: 30; 28 (Oscar II) dived; 19 surfaced
Complement: 135

Missiles: SSM: 24 SS-N-19 Shipwreck (improved SS-N-12 with lower flight profile); inertial with command update guidance; active radar homing to 20-550 km *(10.8-300 nm)* at 1.6 Mach; warhead 750 kg HE or nuclear.
A/S: SS-N-15 fired from 21 in *(533 mm)* tubes; inertial flight to 37 km *(20 nm)*; warhead nuclear 200 kT.
SS-N-16 fired from 25.6 in *(650 mm)* tubes; inertial flight to 120 km *(65 nm)*; payload Type 45 torpedo; active passive homing to 15 km *(8.1 nm)* at 40 kts; warhead 100 kg. There is also a 16B version with a nuclear warhead.
Torpedoes: 4—21 in *(533 mm)* and 4—25.6 in *(650 mm)* tubes. Type 53; dual purpose; pattern active/passive homing up to 20 km *(10.8 nm)* at up to 45 kts; warhead 400 kg or low yield nuclear and Type 65; anti-surface; pattern active/passive wake homing to 50 km *(27.5 nm)* at 50 kts; warhead 900 kg or low yield nuclear. Total of 24 weapons including tube-launched A/S missiles.
Countermeasures: ESM: Bald Head/Rim Hat; radar warning. Park Lamp D/F.
Fire control: Punch Bowl for third party targeting.
Radars: Surface search: Snoop Head/Pair; I band.
Sonars: Shark Gill; hull-mounted; passive/active search and attack; low/medium frequency.
Mouse Roar; hull-mounted; active attack; high frequency.

Programmes: First Oscar I class laid down at Severodvinsk in 1978 and launched in Spring 1980. Second completed in 1982. The first Oscar II completed in 1985, a second in 1986, a third in 1988, a fourth in 1989, two more in 1990, one in 1991 and one in 1992. Still building at one a year.
Structure: SSM missile tubes are in banks of 12 either side and external to the 8.5 m diameter pressure hull; they are inclined at 40° with one hatch covering each pair, the whole resulting in the very large beam. The position of the missile tubes provides a large gap of some 3 m between the outer and inner hulls. The Oscar II has a hull lengthened by 36.1 ft *(11 m)* and an increased displacement of 1400 tons, presumably the result of some deficiency found in first of class trials, which could not have been corrected in time to change hull number two. Alternatively it could have something to do with incorporating an SS-N-24 weapon system in due course. Diving depth, 1000 ft *(300 m)*.
Operational: ELF/VLF communications buoy. All but the first of class have a tube on the rudder fin as in Delta IV which may be used for dispensing a VLF floating aerial. Pert Spring SATCOM. Based in both Northern and Pacific Fleets.

OSCAR II   7/1992

OSCAR II   7/1992

OSCAR II   1990

OSCAR I

5 CHARLIE II CLASS (SSGN)

Displacement, tons: 4500 surfaced; 5550 dived
Dimensions, feet (metres): 334.6 oa; 324.8 wl × 32.5 × 25.6 *(102; 99 × 9.9 × 7.8)*
Main machinery: Nuclear; 1 PWR; 65 MW; 1 turbine; 20 000 hp(m) *(15 MW)*; 1 shaft
Speed, knots: 25 dived; 15 surfaced
Complement: 90

Missiles: SSM: 8 SS-N-9 Siren; IR and active radar homing to 110 km *(60 nm)* at 0.9 Mach; warhead nuclear 250 kT or HE 500 kg.
A/S: SS-N-15 fired from 21 in *(533 mm)* tubes; inertial flight to 37 km *(20 nm)*; warhead nuclear 200 kT.
Torpedoes: 6—21 in *(533 mm)* tubes. Type 53; dual purpose; pattern active/passive homing up to 20 km *(10.8 nm)* at up to 45 kts; warhead 400 kg or low yield nuclear. Total of 14 tube-launched weapons.
Countermeasures: ESM: Stop Light and Brick Group; radar warning. Park Lamp D/F.
Radars: Surface search: Snoop Tray; I band.
Sonars: Shark Fin; hull-mounted; passive/active search and attack; low/medium frequency.
Mouse Roar; hull-mounted; active attack; high frequency.

Programmes: Six built at Gorky from 1973-80.
Structure: Enlarged Charlie class. The extra length is probably required for the additional fire control equipment for the longer range SS-N-9 missiles. The general remarks for Charlie I apply to this class; the platform on the fin is fitted in the majority of the six boats as well as the platform aft. Diving depth, 1000 ft *(300 m)*.
Operational: VLF communications buoy. Pert Spring SATCOM. Kremmny 2 IFF. All based in the Northern Fleet. One paid off in 1992.

CHARLIE II 7/1992

5 CHARLIE I CLASS (SSGN)

Displacement, tons: 4000 surfaced; 5000 dived
Dimensions, feet (metres): 308.3 oa; 295.3 wl × 32.5 × 24.6 *(94; 90 × 9.9 × 7.5)*
Main machinery: Nuclear; 1 PWR; 65 MW; 1 turbine; 15 000 hp(m) *(11 MW)*; 1 shaft; 2 spinners
Speed, knots: 26 dived; 15 surfaced
Complement: 100

Missiles: SSM: 8 SS-N-7; active radar homing to 64 km *(35 nm)* at 0.9 Mach; warhead nuclear 200 kT or HE 500 kg. The 8 SSM tubes are mounted outside the pressure hull with tube doors which hinge upwards.
A/S: SS-N-15 fired from 21 in *(533 mm)* tubes; inertial flight to 37 km *(20 nm)*; warhead nuclear 200 kT.
Torpedoes: 6—21 in *(533 mm)* bow tubes. Type 53; dual purpose; pattern active/passive homing up to 20 km *(10.8 nm)* at up to 45 kts; warhead 400 kg or low yield nuclear. Total of 14 tube-launched weapons.
Countermeasures: ESM: Stop Light and Brick Group; radar warning. Park Lamp D/F.
Radars: Surface search: Snoop Tray; I band.
Sonars: Shark Fin; hull-mounted; passive/active search and attack; low/medium frequency.

Programmes: A class of 12 cruise missile submarines built at Gorky 1967-72.
Structure: The first Soviet SSGNs capable of launching SSMs without having to surface. Although similar in some respects to the Victor class, visible differences include the bulge at the bow, the almost vertical drop of the forward end of the fin, a slightly lower after casing and a different arrangement of free-flood holes in the casing. Some of this class have a raised platform around the forward part of the fin as well as a similar addition around the stern fin. This may be designed to smooth the flow of water in these areas. There is single improved reactor design vice the two in the Victor class resulting in a loss of some five knots. Diving depth, 1000 ft *(300 m)*.
Operational: All are based in the Pacific. One sank off Petropavlovsk in June 1983 and was subsequently salvaged but scrapped in 1987. The class is being paid off.
Sales: One on lease to India in January 1988 and returned for scrapping in January 1991. There are no plans to lease a second.

CHARLIE I 1986

CHARLIE I 1986

9 ECHO II CLASS (SSGN)

Displacement, tons: 4800 surfaced; 5800 dived
Dimensions, feet (metres): 390.4 × 30.2 × 22.6 *(119 × 9.2 × 6.9)*
Main machinery: Nuclear; 2 PWR, 17 500 hp(m) *(13 MW)*; 2 turbines; 30 000 hp(m) *(22 MW)*; 2 shafts
Speed, knots: 24 dived; 18 surfaced
Complement: 90

Missiles: SSM: Either 8 SS-N-12 Sandbox (in 7 of the class); inertial guidance with command update; active radar homing to 550 km *(300 nm)* at 1.7 + Mach; warhead nuclear 350 kT or HE 1000 kg; altitude 10 668 m *(35 000 ft)* or 8 SS-N-3C Shaddock (in 2 of the class); command guidance; active radar or IR homing to 460 km *(250 nm)* at 1.1 Mach; warhead nuclear 350 kT or HE 1000 kg.
Torpedoes: 6—21 in *(533 mm)* bow tubes. Type 53; dual purpose; pattern active/passive homing up to 20 km *(10.8 nm)* at up to 45 kts; warhead 400 kg or low yield nuclear.
4—16 in *(406 mm)* stern tubes. Type 40; anti-submarine; active/passive homing up to 15 km *(8 nm)* at up to 40 kts; warhead 100-150 kg. Total of 20 torpedoes carried.
Countermeasures: ESM: Stop Light and Brick Pulp or Squid Head; radar warning. Quad Loop D/F.
Radars: Surface search: Snoop Tray/Snoop Slab; I band.
Fire control: Front Piece/Front Door; F band (for SS-N-3A mid-course guidance).
Sonars: Hull-mounted; passive/active search and attack; medium frequency.

Programmes: The decision to produce this class may have been due to the availability of building ways because of a break in SSBN production between the Hotel and Yankee classes in the first half of the 1960s, the development of the SS-N-3A cruise missile with an anti-ship capability and the need to counter the threat from Western strike carriers. Built at Severodvinsk and Komsomolsk between 1961 and 1967.
Structure: SS-N-3A guidance radar is housed in the forward section of fin which opens outward. In SS-N-12 boats a large radome Punch Bowl, used for satellite missile targeting, is housed in the fin and raised like any other mast. At the after end of the fin there is a hinged communications aerial which stows in a depression in the casing. There is no acoustic coating. Diving depth, 650 ft *(200 m)*.

ECHO II   1992

Operational: The submarine needs to be fully surfaced for about 20 minutes to launch all its missiles. After an accident to the reactor primary cooling system in June 1989, it was announced that the H, E and N classes would be prematurely retired. This is happening with great rapidity and the remainder of the class seem likely to be deleted by the end of 1993. Based in the Northern and Pacific Fleets. One acts as a mother ship for the X-Ray class trials submarine.

1 YANKEE CLASS (conversion) (SSGN)
(see also Yankee Notch class in *Attack Submarine* section)

Displacement, tons: 13 650 dived
Dimensions, feet (metres): 501.8 × 49.2 × 26.2 *(153 × 15 × 8)*
Main machinery: Nuclear; 2 PWR; 160 MW; 2 turbines; 37 400 hp(m) *(27.5 MW)*; 2 shafts
Speed, knots: 22 dived
Complement: 120

Missiles: SLCM: 12 SS-NX-24; inertial guidance; terrain following to 4000 km *(2200 nm)* at 2 Mach; warhead nuclear 1 MT. 6 tubes are sited on either side abaft the fin, inclined and built in outside the pressure hull.
Torpedoes: 6—21 in *(533 mm)* bow tubes. Type 53; dual purpose; pattern active/passive homing up to 20 km *(10.8 nm)* at up to 45 kts; warhead 400 kg or low yield nuclear.
Countermeasures: ESM: Brick Pulp; radar warning.
Radars: Surface search: Snoop Tray; I band.
Sonars: Shark Fin; hull-mounted; passive/active search and attack; low/medium frequency.

Programmes: Completed conversion in 1983 as the trials submarine for SSN-X-24, a new long-range SLCM. Trials were cancelled in 1991 but the submarine remains operational presumably in the hope of resumption at some future date. Others of the Yankee class ex-SSBNs have been modified as SSNs and to carry SS-N-21 torpedo tube-launched SLCMs, and also as SSANs.
Structure: A lengthened section of some 23 m added in place of original SLBM tubes. The configuration of the SLCM launchers has also increased the beam dimensions and the fin is rounder in appearance. Diving depth, 1000 ft *(300 m)*.

7 JULIETT CLASS (SSG)

Displacement, tons: 3150 surfaced; 3850 dived
Dimensions, feet (metres): 285.4 × 32.8 × 23 *(87 × 10 × 7)*
Main machinery: Direct drive or diesel-electric; 2 Type D-43 diesels; 4000 hp(m) *(2.94 MW)*; 2 motors; 4000 hp(m) *(2.94 MW)*; 2 shafts
Speed, knots: 19 surfaced; 11 dived; 8 snorting
Range, miles: 9000 at 8 kts snorting
Complement: 79

Missiles: SSM: 4 SS-N-12 Sandbox; inertial guidance with command update; active radar homing to 550 km *(300 nm)* at 1.7 Mach; warhead nuclear 350 kT or HE 1000 kg; altitude 10 668 m *(35 000 ft)* or 4 SS-N-3C Shaddock; command guidance; active radar or IR homing to 460 km *(250 nm)* at 1.1 Mach; warhead nuclear 350 kT or HE 1000 kg. The tubes elevate to 20°.
Torpedoes: 6—21 in *(533 mm)* bow tubes. 18 Type 53; dual purpose; pattern active/passive homing up to 20 km *(10.8 nm)* at up to 45 kts; warhead 400 kg or low yield nuclear.
4—15.7 in *(400 mm)* stern tubes; 4 Type 40; active/passive homing to 15 km *(8.1 nm)* at 40 kts; warhead 100 kg.
Countermeasures: ESM: Stop Light; radar warning. Quad Loop D/F.
Radars: Surface search: Snoop Slab; I band.
Fire control: Front Door; F band (for SSM mid-course guidance).
Sonars: Pike Jaw; hull-mounted; passive/active search and attack; medium/high frequency.

Programmes: Completed between 1961 and 1968 at Gorky and was the logical continuation of the Whiskey class conversions.
Structure: The massive casing and four missile launchers either end of the long, fairly low fin make this an unmistakable class. At least one has the large Punch Bowl radome in the fin similar to Echo II. This is a receiver for satellite targeting information for an SS-N-12 retrofit. Diving depth, 650 ft *(200 m)*.
Operational: There are suggestions that silver zinc batteries are installed. This would give an increased dived endurance. In 1980-81 three were transferred from the Northern Fleet to the Baltic Fleet, probably establishing a pattern of patrols in that area. Two more were transferred in 1989 but operational patrols have now stopped and the class began paying off in 1990. Two are based in the Black Sea.

JULIETT   1988

524 RUSSIA / Submarines

Attack Submarines

Note: The use of nuclear power for marine propulsion was developed from 1950 onwards, the first submarine reactor being put in hand in 1953 probably about the same time as a larger reactor for the icebreaker *Lenin* was under construction.

No prototype was produced before series production of the November class began and this was also true for the Victor class which followed after a four year pause in 1967. Since the early November class provided sea experience of this new form of submarine some years of redesign were therefore available before the first Victor was laid down. The ability to produce hydrodynamically advanced hull forms was further proved by the efficiency of the Victor and her near sister the Charlie. Five years after the first Victor came the Victor II, an enlarged edition whose increase in size may be due to the fitting of the new tube-launched ASW system, SS-N-15, probably similar to the Subroc of the US Navy. This again was followed six years later by the Victor III, slightly longer than the Victor II.

The Alfa class was a new concept of attack submarine built in 1970-83 with a length/beam ratio very different from its predecessors, much improved propulsion plant with high speeds and a very deep diving depth. This was probably an extended research and development project with a limited production run. Some of this technology was reflected in the Mike and Sierra classes which appeared in 1983. The Akula class which is a more traditional design successor of the Victor III class, appeared first in 1984 and by 1993 was the only class in series production, with the last Sierra fitting out. A new generation SSN is expected towards the end of the century. The single Mike was sunk in an accident in April 1989 and subsequent Soviet official statements indicated a diving depth of 1000 m with a titanium-reinforced hull and the use of explosive charges to blow main ballast tanks at great depths. An attempt is being made to salvage the Mike but there are problems with funding the operation.

A significant change in the capability of the fleet submarines has resulted from the introduction of SS-N-21, a tube-launched land attack cruise missile with a 1600 nm range. The stern pod on the rudder of the Victor III, Sierra, Akula and one converted Yankee is a towed array dispenser which has taken several years to become operational, and may not be very effective.

The last of the November class paid off in mid-1991. All Fleet submarines are coated with Cluster Guard anechoic tiles. All submarines are capable of laying mines from their torpedo tubes. Newer classes are increasingly being fitted with environmental sensors for measuring discontinuities caused by the passage of a submarine in deep water.

10 + 5 AKULA (BARS) CLASS (SSN)

Displacement, tons: 7500 surfaced; 9100 dived
Dimensions, feet (metres): 360.1 oa; 337.9 wl × 45.9 × 34.1 *(110; 103 × 14 × 10.4)*
Main machinery: Nuclear; 2 PWR; 200 MW; 2 turbines; 47 600 hp(m) *(35 MW)*; 1 shaft; 2 spinners
Speed, knots: 32 dived; 18 surfaced
Complement: 90 approx

Missiles: SLCM: SS-N-21 Sampson fired from 21 in *(533 mm)* tubes; land-attack; inertial/terrain following to 3000 km *(1620 nm)* at 0.7 Mach; warhead nuclear 200 kT. CEP 150 m. Probably flies at a height of about 200 m.
A/S: SS-N-15 fired from 21 in *(533 mm)* tubes; inertial flight to 37 km *(20 nm)*; warhead nuclear 200 kT.
SS-N-16 fired from 25.6 in *(650 mm)* tubes; inertial flight to 120 km *(65 nm)*; payload Type 45 torpedo; warhead 100 kg. There is also a 16B version with a nuclear warhead.
Torpedoes: 4—21 in *(533 mm)* and 4—25.6 in *(650 mm)* tubes. Type 53; dual purpose; pattern active/passive homing up to 20 km *(10.8 nm)* at up to 45 kts; warhead 400 kg or low yield nuclear and Type 65; anti-surface; pattern active/passive wake homing to 50 km *(27.5 nm)* at 50 kts; warhead 900 kg or low yield nuclear. Tube liners can be used to reduce 25.6 in tubes to 21 in.
Countermeasures: ESM: Rim Hat; radar warning. Park Lamp D/F.
Radars: Surface search: Snoop Pair with back-to-back aerials on same mast as ESM.
Sonars: Shark Gill; hull-mounted; passive/active search and attack; low/medium frequency.
Mouse Roar; hull-mounted; active attack; high frequency.

Programmes: First of class launched July 1984 at Komsomolsk and operational at the end of 1985. The class is in series production at Severodvinsk with a construction rate of one or two per year. The fifth or sixth and subsequent hulls are sometimes referred to as the Akula II class. There are no dimensional changes but better sensors and improved acoustic quieting have been reported. The most recent to be commissioned was named *Leopard* and joined the Northern Fleet on 15 January 1993.
Structure: The very long fin is particularly notable. Has the same broad hull as Sierra and has reduced radiated noise levels by comparison with Victor III of which she is the traditional follow-on design. A number of prominent water environment sensors have begun to appear on the fin leading edge and on the forward casing. These are similar to devices tested on a Hotel II class from the early 1980s. The engineering standards around the bridge and casing are noticeably to a higher quality than other classes. Diving depth, 1300 ft *(400 m)*.
Operational: A multi-role SSN following the Victor III class. Pert Spring SATCOM. Based in both Northern and Pacific Fleets.

AKULA I 1992

AKULA II 1992

AKULA I 1992

2 + 1 SIERRA II (BARACUDA II) CLASS (SSN)

Displacement, tons: 7200 surfaced; 8200 dived
Dimensions, feet (metres): 364.2 × 46.6 × 28.9 *(111 × 14.2 × 8.8)*
Main machinery: Nuclear; 2 PWR; 200 MW; 2 turbo alternators; 95 000 hp(m) *(70 MW)*; 1 shaft; 2 spinners
Speed, knots: 32 dived; 18 surfaced
Complement: 100 approx

Missiles: SLCM: SS-N-21 Sampson fired from 21 in *(533 mm)* tubes; land-attack; inertial/terrain following to 3000 km *(1620 nm)* at 0.7 Mach; warhead nuclear 200 kT. CEP 150 m. Probably flies at a height of about 200 m.
A/S: SS-N-15 fired from 21 in *(533 mm)* tubes; inertial flight to 37 km *(20 nm)*; warhead nuclear 200 kT.
SS-N-16 fired from 25.6 in *(650 mm)* tubes; inertial flight to 120 km *(65 nm)*; payload Type 45 torpedo; warhead 100 kg. There is also a 16B version with a nuclear warhead.
Torpedoes: 8—25.6 in *(650 mm)* tubes. Type 53; dual purpose; pattern active/passive homing up to 20 km *(10.8 nm)* at up to 45 kts; warhead 400 kg or low yield nuclear and Type 65; anti-surface; pattern active/passive wake homing to 50 km *(27.5 nm)* at 50 kts; warhead 900 kg or low yield nuclear. Tube liners are used for 21 in *(533 mm)* weapons. A typical load might include 10 Type 53 and 12 Type 65. Carrying missiles would reduce this torpedo load.
Mines: Up to 50 or 60 in lieu of torpedoes.
Countermeasures: ESM: Rim Hat; radar warning. Park Lamp D/F.
Radars: Surface search: Snoop Pair with back-to-back ESM aerial.
Sonars: Shark Gill; hull-mounted; passive/active search and attack; low/medium frequency.
Mouse Roar; hull-mounted; active attack; high frequency.

Programmes: First launched in July 1989 and on trials in 1990. Second launched July 1992 and in service in 1993. A fifth of class has probably either been scrapped or construction has stopped until funds are again available.
Structure: A follow-on class to the Sierra I. Apart from larger overall dimensions the Sierra II has a longer fin by some 16.5 ft *(5 m)* and an almost flat surface at the leading edge. The towed communications buoy has been recessed. A ten point environmental sensor is fitted at the front end of the fin. The stand-off distance between hulls is considerable and has obvious advantages for radiated noise reduction and damage resistance. Diving depth, 2100 ft *(650 m)*.
Operational: Pert Spring SATCOM.

SIERRA II — 1992

SIERRA II — 1992

2 SIERRA I (BARACUDA I) CLASS (SSN)

Displacement, tons: 7000 surfaced; 7900 dived
Dimensions, feet (metres): 351 × 41 × 28.9 *(107 × 12.5 × 8.8)*
Main machinery: Nuclear; 2 PWR; 200 MW; 2 turbo alternators; 95 000 hp(m) *(70 MW)*; 1 shaft; 2 spinners
Speed, knots: 34 dived; 18 surfaced
Complement: 100 approx

Missiles: SLCM: SS-N-21 Sampson fired from 21 in *(533 mm)* tubes; land-attack; inertial/terrain following to 3000 km *(1620 nm)* at 0.7 Mach; warhead nuclear 200 kT. CEP 150 m. Probably flies at a height of about 200 m.
A/S: SS-N-15 fired from 21 in *(533 mm)* tubes; inertial flight to 37 km *(20 nm)*; warhead nuclear 200 kT.
SS-N-16 fired from 25.6 in *(650 mm)* tubes; inertial flight to 120 km *(65 nm)*; payload Type 45 torpedo; warhead 100 kg. There is also a 16B version with a nuclear warhead.
Torpedoes: 8—25.6 in *(650 mm)* tubes. Type 53; dual purpose; pattern active/passive homing up to 20 km *(10.8 nm)* at up to 45 kts; warhead 400 kg or low yield nuclear and Type 65; anti-surface; pattern active/passive wake homing to 50 km *(27.5 nm)* at 50 kts; warhead 900 kg or low yield nuclear. Tube liners are used for 21 in *(533 mm)* weapons. A typical load might include 10 Type 53 and 12 Type 65. Carrying missiles would reduce this torpedo load.
Mines: Up to 50 or 60 in lieu of torpedoes.
Countermeasures: ESM: Rim Hat; radar warning. Park Lamp D/F.
Radars: Surface search: Snoop Pair with back-to-back ESM aerial.
Sonars: Shark Gill; hull-mounted; passive/active search and attack; low/medium frequency.
Mouse Roar; hull-mounted; active attack; high frequency.

Programmes: First launched in August 1983 at Gorky, and fitted out at Severodvinsk. In service for trials in late 1984. Second launched July 1986 and on trials in early 1987.
Structure: Probably similar to the late Mike in having a strengthened hull which would make it much more expensive than Akula and a logical successor to the Alfa class. The pod on the after fin is larger than that in Victor III. The stand-off distance between hulls is considerable and has obvious advantages for radiated noise reduction and damage resistance. The second unit picture shows the V-shaped casing on the port side of the fin which covers the releasable escape chamber. This submarine also has a bulbous casing at the after end of the fin for a towed communications buoy. Diving depth, 2100 ft *(650 m)*.
Operational: Pert Spring SATCOM.

SIERRA I (Unit 2)   1989

SIERRA I (Unit 1)   1984

1 + 4 (RESERVE) ALFA (ALPHA) CLASS (SSN)

Displacement, tons: 2700 surfaced; 3600 dived
Dimensions, feet (metres): 267.4 oa; 246.1 wl × 31.2 × 24.6 *(81.5; 75 × 9.5 × 7.5)*
Main machinery: Nuclear; 2 PWR; 170 MW; 2 turbo alternators; 50 000 hp(m) *(37 MW)*; 1 shaft; 2 spinners
Speed, knots: 40 dived; 20 surfaced
Complement: 40

Missiles: A/S: SS-N-15 fired from 21 in *(533 mm)* tubes; inertial flight to 37 km *(20 nm)*; warhead nuclear 200 kT.
Torpedoes: 6—21 in *(533 mm)* fwd tubes. Type 53; dual purpose; pattern active/passive homing up to 20 km *(10.8 nm)* at up to 45 kts; warhead 400 kg or low yield nuclear. Can carry 20 torpedoes or a mixed equivalent load.
Mines: Up to 40 in lieu of torpedoes.
Countermeasures: ESM: Bald Head and Brick Group; radar warning. Park Lamp D/F.
Radars: Surface search: Snoop Head (on same mast as ESM); I band.
Sonars: Shark Gill; hull-mounted; passive/active search and attack; low/medium frequency.
Mouse Roar; hull-mounted; active attack; high frequency.

Programmes: The first of this class was laid down in mid-1960s and completed in 1970 at Sudomekh, Leningrad. The building time was very long in comparison with normal programmes and it seems most likely that this was a prototype. This boat was scrapped in 1974. Six more were then built between 1979 and 1983 at Sudomekh and Severodvinsk.
Structure: The reduction of the length combined with the high speed indicates considerable progress in hydrodynamic design and laminar flow techniques. A greater diving depth, down to 2500 ft *(700 m)* has been achieved by use of titanium alloy for the hull. This also results in a much reduced magnetic signature. The sound profile of this class is, however, high, reflecting the fact that this is a design now over 25 years old. All these submarines may have minor variations, possibly to study future designs now at sea in the Sierra class and to be incorporated in future classes.
Operational: Small complement indicates a high level of automation. Navigation systems include SINS, SATNAV, Loran and Omega. High levels of speed dependent noise, much quieter when slow. One was scrapped in 1988 and a second recommissioned in late 1989 as a trials boat, having been in refit for five years. The rest of the class were in reserve as an economy measure in 1992/93 and may in due course be scrapped.

ALFA   5/1990

26 VICTOR III (KEFAL III) CLASS (SSN)

Displacement, tons: 4850 surfaced; 6300 dived
Dimensions, feet (metres): 351.1 × 34.8 × 24.3 *(107 × 10.6 × 7.4)*
Main machinery: Nuclear; 2 PWR; 130 MW; 2 turbines; 30 000 hp(m) *(22 MW)*; 1 shaft; 2 spinners
Speed, knots: 30 dived; 18 surfaced
Complement: 70 (17 officers)

Missiles: SLCM: SS-N-21 Sampson fired from 21 in *(533 mm)* tubes; land-attack; inertial/terrain following to 3000 km *(1620 nm)* at 0.7 Mach; warhead nuclear 200 kT. CEP 150 m. Probably flies at a height of about 200 m.
A/S: SS-N-15 fired from 21 in *(533 mm)* tubes; inertial flight to 37 km *(20 nm)*; warhead nuclear 200 kT.
SS-N-16 A/B fired from 25.6 in *(650 mm)* tubes; inertial flight to 120 km *(65 nm)*; payload Type 45 torpedo; warhead 100 kg. There is also a 16B version with a nuclear warhead.
Torpedoes: 2—21 in *(533 mm)* and 4—25.6 in *(650 mm)* tubes. Type 53; dual purpose; pattern active/passive homing up to 20 km *(10.8 nm)* at up to 45 kts; warhead 400 kg or low yield nuclear and Type 65; anti-surface; pattern active/passive wake homing to 50 km *(27.5 nm)* at 50 kts; warhead 900 kg or low yield nuclear. Can carry up to 24 torpedoes. Liners can be used to reduce 25.6 in tubes to 21 in.
Mines: Can carry 36 in lieu of torpedoes.
Countermeasures: ESM: Brick Group (Brick Spit and Brick Pulp); radar warning. Park Lamp D/F.
Radars: Surface search: Snoop Tray; I band.
Sonars: Shark Gill; hull-mounted; passive/active search and attack; low/medium frequency.
Mouse Roar; hull-mounted; active attack; high frequency.

Programmes: An improvement on Victor II, the first of class being completed at Komsomolsk in 1978. With construction also being carried out at Admiralty Yard, Leningrad, there was a very rapid building programme up to the end of 1984. Since then construction continued only at Leningrad and at a rate of about one per year which terminated in 1991. The last of the class completed sea trials in late 1992.
Structure: The streamlined pod on the stern fin is now described as a towed sonar array dispenser. Water environment sensors are being mounted at the front of the fin and on the forward casing as in the Akula and Sierra classes. One of the class has the trials SS-N-21 SLCM mounted on the forward casing. Diving depth, 1000 ft *(300 m)*.
Operational: VLF communications buoy. VHF/UHF aerials. Navigation equipment includes SINS and SATNAV. Pert Spring SATCOM. Kremmny 2 IFF. Much improved acoustic quietening puts the radiated noise levels at the upper limits of the USN Los Angeles class. Based in Northern and Pacific Fleets.

VICTOR III (sensors at front of the fin)   6/1992

VICTOR III   6/1992

7 VICTOR II (KEFAL II) CLASS (SSN)

Displacement, tons: 4700 surfaced; 5800 dived
Dimensions, feet (metres): 337.9 oa; 315 wl × 34.8 × 24.3 *(103; 96 × 10.6 × 7.4)*
Main machinery: Nuclear; 2 PWR; 130 MW; 2 turbines; 30 000 hp(m) *(22 MW)*; 1 shaft; 2 spinners
Speed, knots: 30 dived; 18 surfaced
Complement: 70 (17 officers)

Missiles: A/S: SS-N-15 fired from 21 in *(533 mm)* tubes; inertial flight to 37 km *(20 nm)*; warhead nuclear 200 kT.
SS-N-16 A/B fired from 25.6 in *(650 mm)* tubes; inertial flight to 120 km *(65 nm)*; payload Type 45 torpedo; warhead 100 kg. There is also a 16B version with a nuclear warhead.
Torpedoes: 2—21 in *(533 mm)* and 4—25.6 in *(650 mm)* tubes. Type 53; dual purpose; pattern active/passive homing up to 20 km *(10.8 nm)* at up to 45 kts; warhead 400 kg or low yield nuclear and Type 65; anti-surface; pattern active/passive wake homing to 50 km *(27.5 nm)* at 50 kts; warhead 900 kg or low yield nuclear. Can carry up to 24 torpedoes.
Mines: Up to 48 in lieu of torpedoes.
Countermeasures: ESM: Brick Group (Brick Spit and Brick Pulp); radar warning. Park Lamp D/F.
Radars: Surface search: Snoop Tray; I band.
Sonars: Shark Teeth; hull-mounted; passive/active search and attack; low/medium frequency.
Mouse Roar; hull-mounted; active attack; high frequency.

Programmes: First appeared in 1972, class completed 1978. Built at Admiralty Yard, Leningrad and Gorky.
Structure: An enlarged Victor I design, 9 m longer to provide more space for torpedo stowage. Diving depth, 1000 ft *(300 m)* approx.
Operational: VLF communications buoy. VHF and UHF aerials. Navigation equipment includes SINS and SATNAV. Kremmny 2 IFF. All based in the Northern Fleet.

VICTOR II 6/1992

14 VICTOR I (KEFAL I) CLASS (SSN)

Displacement, tons: 4400 surfaced; 5300 dived
Dimensions, feet (metres): 308.4 oa; 282.2 wl × 34.4 × 24 *(94; 86 × 10.5 × 7.3)*
Main machinery: Nuclear; 2 PWR; 130 MW; 2 turbines; 30 000 hp(m) *(22 MW)*; 1 shaft; 2 spinners
Speed, knots: 32 dived; 18 surfaced
Complement: 70 (17 officers)

Missiles: A/S: SS-N-15 fired from 21 in *(533 mm)* tubes; inertial flight to 37 km *(20 nm)*; warhead nuclear 200 kT.
Torpedoes: 6—21 in *(533 mm)* bow tubes. Type 53; dual purpose; pattern active/passive homing up to 20 km *(10.8 nm)* at up to 45 kts; warhead 400 kg or low yield nuclear. Can carry up to 24 torpedoes.
Mines: In lieu of torpedoes.
Countermeasures: ESM: Brick Group; radar warning. Park Lamp D/F.
Radars: Surface search: Snoop Tray; I band.
Sonars: Shark Teeth; hull-mounted; passive/active search and attack; low/medium frequency.
Mouse Roar; hull-mounted; active attack; high frequency.

Programmes: The first of class laid down in 1965 entering service in 1967-68—class completed 1974 at a building rate of two per year. Superseded by the Victor II programme. Built at Admiralty Yard, Leningrad.
Structure: This was the first Soviet submarine with an Albacore hull-form and a new reactor system, a new generation design shared by the Charlie class. Is of double-hulled form but, unlike Charlie, has two reactors giving an enhanced speed. Diving depth, 1000 ft *(300 m)* approx.
Operational: The majority is deployed with the Northern Fleet, although two are with the Pacific Fleet. Becoming unreliable and of the original 16 units at least two have been withdrawn from service, one as a result of a reactor refuelling accident in August 1985.

VICTOR I 1991

3 YANKEE NOTCH CLASS (SSN, ex-SSBN)

Displacement, tons: 8500 surfaced; 10 300 dived
Dimensions, feet (metres): 464.2 × 38.1 × 26.6 *(141.5 × 11.6 × 8.1)*
Main machinery: Nuclear; 2 PWR; 160 MW; 2 turbines; 37 400 hp(m) *(27.5 MW)*; 2 shafts
Speed, knots: 26 dived; 16 surfaced
Complement: 120

Missiles: SLCM: 35 approx SS-N-21 Sampson fired from 21 in *(533 mm)* tubes; land attack; inertial/terrain following to 3000 km *(1620 nm)* at 0.7 Mach; warhead nuclear 200 kT. CEP 150 m. Probably flies at a height of about 200 m.
Torpedoes: 6—21 in *(533 mm)* tubes; Type 53; dual purpose; pattern active/passive homing up to 20 km *(10.8 nm)* at up to 45 kts; warhead 400 kg or low yield nuclear.
Countermeasures: ESM: Brick Group; radar warning. Park Lamp D/F.
Radars: Surface search: Snoop Tray; I band.
Sonars: Shark Gill; hull-mounted; passive/active search and attack; low/medium frequency.
Mouse Roar; hull-mounted; active attack; high frequency.

Programmes: The SALT limits of 62 SSBNs and 950 SLBMs were adhered to by the Soviet Navy and this resulted in the conversion of Yankee class as well as the deleted Hotel and Golf classes. The Yankee conversion to SSN was first seen in 1983. The conversion takes about two years and it seemed to be the intention to convert about 10 of the class until the programme fell victim to financial cuts in 1989-90. See also *Auxiliary Submarine* section.
Structure: In spite of the removal of the ballistic missile section the overall length of the hull has increased by 39.4 ft *(12 m)* with the insertion of a 'notch waisted' central section. This new section houses three tubes amidships on each side and it is likely that the magazine holds up to 20 SS-N-21s or additional torpedoes and mines. There may also have been a rearrangement of torpedo tubes to include some at 26.5 in *(650 mm)*. Diving depth, 1000 ft *(300 m)*.

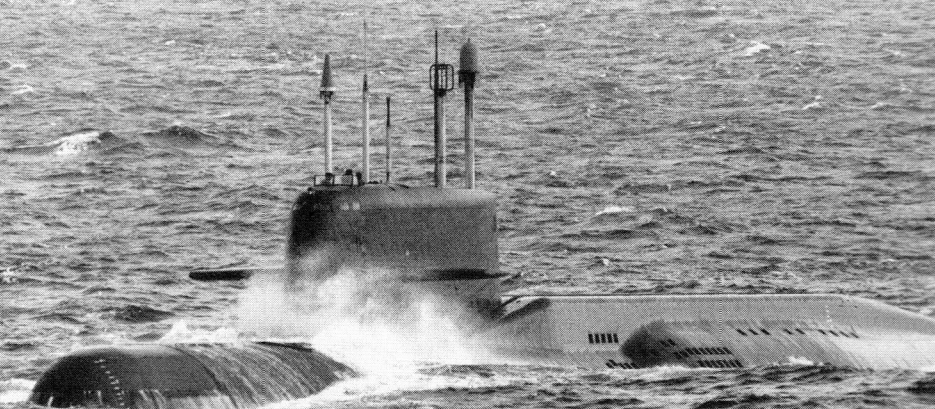

YANKEE NOTCH 1990

Patrol Submarines

Note: The Foxtrot class was built from 1958-71 with 62 completed for the Soviet Navy, and a further 17, last in 1983, for client countries. In 1972 came the Tango class, with a total of 18, produced at the rate of two a year. The Kilo class, built at Komsomolsk, appeared in the late 1970s and was initially produced at the rate of one a year. This rate increased with production at Gorky and St Petersburg. The latter two yards are most concerned with exports, the first clients being Poland, Romania, India, Algeria and Iran. Non-nuclear submarine construction will continue, probably with a follow-on to the Kilo class as its 1970s technology has severe limitations by modern Western standards. In addition certain specialised submarines have been built—the four Bravo class target boats in the late 1960s, the two India class rescue submarines and the single Lima research submarine in the late 1970s, Beluga in 1987 and others.

Kilo and Tango classes are coated with Cluster Guard anechoic tiles and both have a minelaying capability from their torpedo tubes. In 1992 a Tango was fitted with a towed array.

21 + 7 KILO (GRANAY) CLASS (TYPE 877E) (SS)

Displacement, tons: 2325 surfaced; 3076 dived
Dimensions, feet (metres): 243.8 × 32.8 × 21.7 *(74.3 × 10 × 6.6)*
Main machinery: Diesel-electric; 2 diesels; 3650 hp(m) *(2.68 MW)*; 2 generators; 1 motor; 5900 hp(m) *(4.34 MW)*; 1 shaft
Speed, knots: 20 dived; 10 surfaced
Range, miles: 6000 at 7 kts surfaced; 400 at 3 kts dived.
Complement: 45

Torpedoes: 6—21 in *(533 mm)* tubes. 18 Type 53; dual purpose; pattern active/passive homing up to 20 km *(10.8 nm)* at up to 45 kts; warhead 400 kg or low yield nuclear.
Mines: In lieu of torpedoes.
Countermeasures: ESM: Squid Head or Brick Pulp; radar warning. Quad Loop D/F.
Radars: Surface search: Snoop Tray; I band.
Sonars: Shark Teeth; hull-mounted; passive/active search and attack; medium frequency.
Mouse Roar; hull-mounted; active attack; high frequency.

Programmes: First launched in 1979 at Komsomolsk. Construction is taking place at St Petersburg as well as at Komsomolsk. The building rate at the beginning of 1993 was about three a year, Soviet numbers depending on the export rate.
Structure: Has a better hull form than the Foxtrot or Tango but is still fairly basic by comparison with modern Western designs. Diving depth, 1000 ft *(300 m)*.
Operational: There is evidence of trials carried out with a SAM launcher fitted on the fin. Probably SA-N-8; IR homing from 600 m to 6000 m; warhead 2 kg.

KILO (with anechoic tiles) 6/1992

Sales: The Kilo programme replaced the Foxtrot export stream and the class has so far been exported to Poland (one), Romania (one), India (eight), Algeria (two) and Iran (one). Further transfers are expected to Iran, and Syria is also expected to become a customer.

KILO 6/1992

18 TANGO CLASS (SS)

Displacement, tons: 3000 surfaced; 3800 dived
Dimensions, feet (metres): 298.6 × 29.9 × 23.6 *(91 × 9.1 × 7.2)*
Main machinery: Diesel-electric; 3 diesels; 5475 hp(m) *(4 MW)*; 3 motors; 6256 hp(m) *(4.6 MW)*; 3 shafts
Speed, knots: 13 surfaced; 16 dived
Complement: 62

Torpedoes: 8—21 in *(533 mm)* (6 bow, 2 stern) tubes. Type 53; dual purpose; pattern active/passive homing up to 20 km *(10.8 nm)* at up to 45 kts; warhead 400 kg or low yield nuclear.
Mines: In lieu of torpedoes.
Countermeasures: ESM: Squid Head or Stop Light; radar warning. Quad Loop D/F.
Radars: Surface search: Snoop Tray; I band.
Sonars: Shark Teeth; hull-mounted; passive/active search and attack; medium frequency. There is a large array mounted above the torpedo tubes as well as a bow-mounted dome.

Programmes: This class was first seen at the Sevastopol Review in July 1973 and, immediately succeeding the Foxtrot class, showed a continuing commitment to non-nuclear-propelled boats. The building rate rose to two a year at Gorky and the programme finished in 1982.
Structure: There is a marked increase in the internal capacity of the hull which has most likely been used to improve battery capacity, habitability and weapon load compared with Foxtrot. Diving depth, 1000 ft *(300 m)*. The casing and fin have a continuous acoustic coating. One Northern Fleet unit was fitted with a towed array stern tube and a reel mounted in the casing forward of the fin in 1992.
Operational: Long-range operational capability as shown by deployments to the Mediterranean and to West Africa. All except one is based in the Northern Fleet with refits at Kronstadt in the Baltic. One of the class is in the Black Sea.

TANGO (with towed array) 8/1992

30 FOXTROT CLASS (TYPE 641) (SS)

Displacement, tons: 1952 surfaced; 2475 dived
Dimensions, feet (metres): 299.5 × 24.6 × 19.7 *(91.3 × 7.5 × 6)*
Main machinery: Diesel-electric; 3 Type 37-D diesels; 6000 hp(m) *(4.4 MW)*; 3 motors (1 × 2700 and 2 × 1350); 5400 hp(m) *(3.97 MW)*; 3 shafts; 1 auxiliary motor; 140 hp(m) *(103 kW)*
Speed, knots: 16 surfaced; 15 dived; 9 snorting
Range, miles: 20 000 at 8 kts surfaced; 380 at 2 kts dived
Complement: 75

Torpedoes: 10—21 in *(533 mm)* (6 bow, 4 stern) tubes. 22 Type 53; dual purpose; pattern active/passive homing up to 20 km *(10.8 nm)* at up to 45 kts; warhead 400 kg or low yield nuclear.
Mines: 44 in lieu of torpedoes.
Countermeasures: ESM: Stop Light; radar warning. Quad Loop D/F.
Radars: Surface search: Snoop Tray or Snoop Plate; I band.
Sonars: Herkules/Feniks; hull-mounted; passive/active search and attack; high frequency.

Programmes: Built between 1958 and 1971 at Sudomekh. Production continued until 1984 for transfer to other countries ie Cuba, India, Libya. A follow-on of the Zulu class. Only 60 out of a total programme of 160 were completed as the changeover to nuclear boats took effect. A most successful class which has been deployed worldwide, forming the bulk of the submarine force in the Mediterranean in the 1960s and 1970s.
Operational: This class is now progressively being withdrawn from front-line service, with Northern Fleet units being redeployed to the Baltic and Black Sea. Diving depth was 820 ft *(250 m)* but this is reducing with age.
Sales: All new construction (except those for Poland): Cuba: One in February 1979, one in March 1980, one in February 1984. India: One in April 1968, one in March 1969, one in November 1969, one in February 1970, one in November 1973, one in December 1973, one in October 1974, one in February 1975. Libya: One in December 1976, two in February 1978, one in February 1981, one in January 1982 and one in February 1983. One to Poland in 1987 and a second in 1988.

FOXTROT

Auxiliary Submarines

Note: In addition to those listed there is also an Alfa class SSN used for trials, and an elderly Romeo class diesel submarine with two large experimental torpedo type tubes fitted on the casing at the bow.

1 YANKEE POD and 1 YANKEE STRETCH CLASS (SSAN, ex-SSBN)

Displacement, tons: 9800 surfaced
Dimensions, feet (metres): 440.6 × 38 × 26.6 *(134.3 × 11.6 × 8.1)*
Main machinery: Nuclear; 2 PWR; 160 MW; 2 turbines; 37 400 hp(m) *(27.5 MW)*; 2 shafts
Speed, knots: 26 dived; 20 surfaced
Complement: 120

Comment: As well as the Yankee SSGN and Yankee Notch SSN conversions, two other hulls have been converted for research and development roles. The dimensions given are for the so-called Yankee Pod which has been used as a trials platform for the towed array pod on the stern since about 1984. There are also two prominent bulges either side of the fin. The other conversion is a Yankee Stretch which has a lengthened central section extending the hull to some 525 ft *(160 m)* and is used for unspecified underwater research which may include submarine rescue operations. The Yankee Pod probably has the same torpedo armament as the standard Yankee class. Based in the Northern Fleet.

YANKEE POD   1989

2 UNIFORM CLASS (SSAN)

Displacement, tons: 1390 dived
Dimensions, feet (metres): 226.4 × 23 × 17 *(69 × 7 × 5.2)*
Speed, knots: 10 surfaced

Comment: Appear to be research and development nuclear powered submarines. The first launched at Sudomekh, St Petersburg in November 1982 and entered service in July 1983. The second launched April 1988 and in service November 1989. There are very deep diving submarines based in the Northern Fleet.

UNIFORM   1992

1 LIMA CLASS (SSA)

Displacement, tons: 1700 surfaced; 2100 dived
Dimensions, feet (metres): 282.2 × 25.9 × 23 *(86 × 7.9 × 7)*
Main machinery: Diesel-electric; 2 diesels; 1 motor; 2500 hp(m) *(1.8 MW)*; 1 shaft
Speed, knots: 12 surfaced; 12 dived
Complement: 70
Radars: Navigation: Snoop Tray; I band.
Sonars: Hull-mounted; passive/active search and attack; high frequency.

Comment: Built at Sudomekh Yard and launched in August 1978. A bulge at the forward end of the fin is similar to that used for the German Balkon sonar in the early 1940s but could be a tower for exit/re-entry trials. The most conspicuous feature is that some of the masts are non-retractable. Returned to St Petersburg from the Black Sea to start refit in 1990.

LIMA   1990

1 BELUGA CLASS (SSA)

Displacement, tons: 1900 dived
Dimensions, feet (metres): 213.3 × 28.5 × 19.7 *(65 × 8.7 × 6)*
Main machinery: 1 motor; 5440 hp *(4 MW)*; 1 shaft
Speed, knots: 10 surfaced; 22 dived

Comment: Built at St Petersburg, launched in 1985 and completed in February 1987. A single experimental unit with a fin similar to the Alfa class. Stated by the Russians to be for marine biological research and probably used for hydrodynamic tests including hull forms, propulsors and boundary layer control methods. One report suggests there is no power source other than main batteries and therefore the submarine has to return alongside to recharge. It seems more likely that an AIP system is involved. Unarmed but there is probably a standard Snoop Tray radar, Brick Group ESM and Shark Teeth and Mouse Roar sonars. Based in the Black Sea.

BELUGA *10/1991*

1 PALTUS CLASS (SSAN) and 1 X-RAY CLASS (SSA)

Displacement, tons: 520 dived
Dimensions, feet (metres): 154.2 × 13.1 × 13.1 *(47 × 4 × 4)*

Comment: Details given are for the X-Ray which is a very small research submarine built at Sudomekh Yard, St Petersburg in 1984. Originally thought to be nuclear powered. Based in the Northern Fleet and probably associated with deep diving seabed operations associated with an Echo II SSGN. Paltus is of a similar size and was launched at Sudomekh in April 1991. Probably nuclear powered and is associated with the Yankee Stretch SSAN.

2 LOSOS (PYRANJA) CLASS (SSA)

Dimensions, feet (metres): 95.8 × 16.4 × 12.8 *(29.2 × 5 × 3.9)*
Main machinery: 1 diesel generator; 160 kW; 1 motor; 82 hp(m) *(60 kW)*; 1 shaft
Speed, knots: 6.5. **Range, miles:** 1000 at 4 kts
Complement: 4

Comment: Built at St Petersburg and launched in mid-1986. Based at Kronstadt and claimed by Sweden to be the type of submarine responsible for violating Swedish territorial waters. Can carry up to 6 divers or torpedoes or mines. There are two outboard pressurised containers for special equipment, and two outboard tubes for mines or torpedoes. The main battery has a capacity of 1200 kilowatt hours. Radar can be fitted. Capable of diving to 200 m.

LOSOS *1992, Pressens Bild/Press Association*

2 INDIA CLASS (SSA)

Displacement, tons: 4000 surfaced; 4800 dived
Dimensions, feet (metres): 354.3 oa; 344.5 wl × 32.8 × 23 *(108; 105 × 10 × 7)*
Main machinery: 2 diesels; 3800 hp(m) *(2.79 MW)*; 2 motors; 3000 hp *(2 MW)*; 2 shafts; bow thruster
Speed, knots: 15 surfaced; 10 dived

Countermeasures: ESM: Stop Light/Squid Head; radar warning. Quad Loop D/F.
Radars: Navigation: Snoop Tray; I band.
Sonars: Hull-mounted; passive/active search; high frequency.

Programmes: Built at Komsomolsk. First launched in 1975, second in 1979.
Structure: Designed for rescue work and carry two 12.1 m DSRVs on the after casing. The overall silhouette is similar to Delta class SSBNs. Both DSRVs have access hatches in the hull and probably have an operating depth of about 2000 m, although this would be reduced to 600-700 m for actual submarine rescue operations. It seems unlikely that these submarines carry any armament.
Operational: One is in service in the Pacific and one in the Northern Fleet.

INDIA with DSRVs *7/1987*

4 BRAVO CLASS (TARGET SUBMARINES)

Displacement, tons: 2250 surfaced; 2750 dived
Dimensions, feet (metres): 239.5 oa; 219.8 wl × 32.1 × 26.2 *(73; 67 × 9.8 × 8)*
Main machinery: Diesel-electric; 2 diesels; 3970 hp(m) *(2.9 MW)*; 2 generators; 1 motor; 5900 hp(m) *(4.34 MW)*; 1 shaft
Speed, knots: 14 dived
Complement: 60

Torpedoes: 6—21 in *(533 mm)* bow tubes. Type 53; dual purpose; pattern active/passive homing up to 20 km *(10.8 nm)* at up to 45 kts; warhead 400 kg or low yield nuclear.
Countermeasures: ESM: Brick Group; radar warning.
Radars: Navigation: Snoop Tray; I band.
Sonars: Hull-mounted; passive; medium frequency and active search and attack; high frequency.

Programmes: Completed at Komsomolsk 1967-70.
Structure: The beam-to-length ratio is larger than normal in a diesel submarine which would account in part for the large displacement for a comparatively short hull. Diving depth 1000 ft *(300 m)*.
Operational: These four submarines are in the Black Sea and Pacific Fleets and act as 'padded targets' for ASW exercises and weapon firings. One of the Pacific Fleet units may be in reserve.

BRAVO *1986*

AIRCRAFT CARRIERS

Note: Work on the *Ulyanovsk* stopped in March 1992 when the ship was within a few months of being launched. She has now been dismantled for sale as scrap, which puts an end to Russian naval plans for a nuclear powered, steam catapult aircraft carrier for the foreseeable future.

1 + 1 KUZNETSOV CLASS (CV)

Name	Builders	Laid down	Launched	Commissioned
ADMIRAL KUZNETSOV (ex-*Tbilisi*, ex-*Leonid Brezhnev*)	Nikolayev South	22 Feb 1983	5 Dec 1985	21 Jan 1991
VARYAG (ex-*Riga*)	Nikolayev South	8 Dec 1985	28 Nov 1988	—

Displacement, tons: 55 000 standard; 67 500 full load
Dimensions, feet (metres): 999 oa; 918.6 wl × 229.7 oa; 121.4 wl × 34.4 *(304.5; 280 × 70; 37 × 10.5)*
Flight deck, feet (metres): 999 × 229.7 *(304.5 × 70)*
Main machinery: 8 boilers; 4 turbines; 200 000 hp(m) *(147 MW)*; 4 shafts
Speed, knots: 30
Complement: 1700 (200 officers)

Missiles: SSM: 12 SS-N-19 Shipwreck launchers (flush mounted) ❶; inertial guidance with command update; active radar homing to 20-450 km *(10.8-243 nm)* at Mach 1.6; warhead 500 kT nuclear or 750 kg HE.
SAM: 4 SA-N-9 sextuple vertical launchers (192 missiles) ❷; command guidance and active radar homing to 12 km *(6.6 nm)* at 2 Mach; warhead 15 kg.
SAM/Guns: 8 CADS-N-1 ❸; each has a twin 30 mm Gatling combined with 8 SA-N-11 and Hot Flash/Hot Spot fire control radar/optronic director. Laser beam riding guidance for missiles to 8 km *(4.4 nm)*; 4500 rounds/minute combined to 2 km (for guns).
Guns: 6—30 mm/65 ❹ AK 630; 6 barrels per mounting; 85° elevation; 3000 rounds/minute combined to 2 km. Probably controlled by Hot Flash/Hot Spot on CADS-N-1.
A/S mortars: 2 RBU 12 000 ❺; range 12 000 m; warhead 80 kg.
Countermeasures: Decoys: chaff launchers.
ESM/ECM: 2 Bell Crown. 2 Bell Push. 8 Foot Ball. 2 Wine Flask. 2 Flat Track.
Fire control: 4 Tin Man optronic trackers. 2 Punch Bowl SATCOM data link ❻. 2 Low Ball SATNAV ❼.
Radars: Air search: Sky Watch; four Planar phased arrays ❽; 3D.
Air/surface search: Top Plate ❾; D/E band.
Surface search: Two Strut Pair ❿; F band.
Navigation: Three Palm Frond; I band.
Fire control: Four Cross Sword (for SAM) ⓫.
Aircraft control: Fly Trap B; G/H band.
Tacan: Cake Stand ⓬.
IFF: Four Watch Guard.
Sonars: Horse Jaw; hull-mounted; active search and attack; medium/low frequency.

Fixed wing aircraft: 12 Su-27B2 Flanker; 12 MiG-29 Fulcrum or 12 Su-25 Frogfoot (see *Shipborne Aircraft* section).
Helicopters: 15 Ka-27 Helix. 3 Ka-29 Helix AEW.

ADMIRAL KUZNETSOV *12/1991*

Programmes: This is a logical continuation of the Kiev class and a basic component of a task force including the nuclear-propelled Kirov class battle cruisers. *Varyag* was between 70 and 80 per cent complete by early 1993 and still fitting out slowly. The Russian Navy wants her and rumours of sales in 1992 to China or India have been premature. Nonetheless the future is uncertain. Names were changed in 1990 because the Navy was unhappy about ships being called after the cities of independent republics. The full name of *Kuznetsov* is *Admiral Flota Sovietskogo Sojuza Kuznetsov*.

Structure: The hangar is approximately 610 × 98 × 25 ft and can hold up to 18 Flanker or 25 Fulcrum aircraft. There are two starboard side lifts, a ski-jump of 12° and an angled deck of 7°. There are four arrester wires. The SSM system is in the centre of the flight deck forward with flush deck covers. The class has some 16.5 m of freeboard (13 m in *Kiev*). There is no Bass Tilt radar and the ADG guns are probably controlled by CADS-N-1 fire control system.

Operational: AEW, ASW and reconnaissance tasks undertaken by Helix helicopters. Three varieties of fixed wing aircraft (Su-27 Flanker, Su-25 Frogfoot and MiG-29 Fulcrum) have conducted extensive deck landings. The aircraft complement listed is based on the number which might be embarked for peacetime operations but the Russians claim a top limit of sixty. With Forger taken out of service, the preferred fixed wing aircraft is the Flanker. Hokum helicopters may supplement Helix in due course.

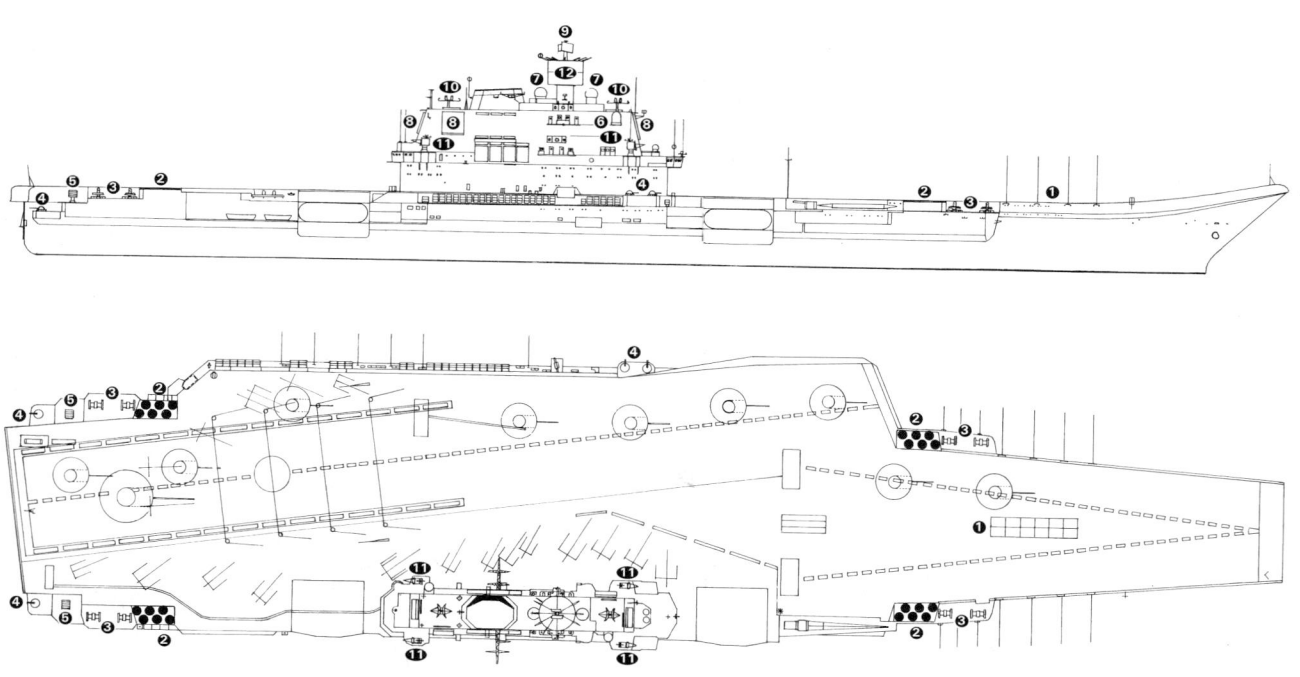

ADMIRAL KUZNETSOV

(Scale 1 : 1800), Ian Sturton

Aircraft carriers / RUSSIA

ADMIRAL KUZNETSOV 1992

ADMIRAL KUZNETSOV 1992

ADMIRAL KUZNETSOV 12/1991

ADMIRAL KUZNETSOV 12/1991

2 KIEV CLASS (CVG)

Name	Builders	Laid down	Launched	Commissioned
KIEV	Nikolayev South (Nosenko, 444)	July 1970	27 Dec 1972	May 1975
NOVOROSSIYSK	Nikolayev South (Nosenko, 444)	Oct 1975	4 Dec 1978	Aug 1982

Displacement, tons: 40 500 full load
Dimensions, feet (metres): 899 oa; 818.6 wl × 154.8 oa; 107.3 wl × 32.8 (screws) *(274; 249.5 × 47.2; 32.7 × 10)*
Flight deck, feet (metres): 620 × 68 *(189 × 20.7)*
Main machinery: 8 boilers; 4 turbines; 200 000 hp(m) *(147 MW)*; 4 shafts
Speed, knots: 32. **Range, miles:** 13 500 at 18 kts; 4000 at 31 kts
Complement: 1200 plus aircrew

Missiles: SSM: 8 SS-N-12 Sandbox (4 twin) launchers ❶; inertial guidance with command update; active radar homing to 550 km *(300 nm)* at 1.7 Mach; warhead nuclear 350 kT or HE 1000 kg; 16 reloads.
SAM: 2 SA-N-3B Goblet twin launchers ❷; semi-active radar homing to 55 km *(30 nm)* at 2.5 Mach; warhead 80 kg; altitude 91.4-22 860 m *(300-75 000 ft)*; 72 missiles.
2 SA-N-4 Gecko twin launchers *(Kiev)* ❸; semi-active radar homing to 15 km *(8 nm)* at 2.5 Mach; warhead 50 kg; altitude 9.1-3048 m *(30-10 000 ft)*; 40 missiles.
4 SA-N-9 sextuple vertical launchers *(Novorossiysk)*; command guidance; active radar homing to 12 km *(6.6 nm)* at 2 Mach; warhead 15 kg; altitude 3.4-12 192 m *(10-40 000 ft)*; 96 missiles.
A/S: SUW-N-1 twin launcher ❹; FRAS-1; inertial flight to 29 km *(16 nm)*; warhead nuclear 5 kT.
Guns: 4—3 in *(76 mm)*/60 (2 twin) ❺; 80° elevation; 90 rounds/minute to 15 km *(8 nm)*; weight of shell 6.8 kg.
8—30 mm/65 ❻; 6 barrels per mounting; 85° elevation; 3000 rounds/minute combined to 2 km.
Torpedoes: 10—21 in *(533 mm)* (2 quin). Type 53; dual purpose; pattern active/passive homing up to 20 km *(10.8 nm)* at up to 45 kts; warhead 400 kg or low yield nuclear.
A/S mortars: 2 RBU 6000 12-tubed trainable ❼; range 6000 m; warhead 31 kg.
Countermeasures: Decoys: 2 twin chaff launchers. Towed torpedo decoy.
ESM/ECM: 8 Side Globe *(Kiev)*. 4 Rum Tub. 2 Bell Bash. 4 Bell Nip *(Novorossiysk)*. 2 Cage Pot *(Kiev)*.
Fire control: 4 Tin Man optronic trackers (5 in *Novorossiysk*). Punch Bowl SATCOM for SSM data link. *Novorossiysk* has more VHF systems.
Radars: Air search: Top Sail ❽; 3D; D band; range 555 km *(300 nm)*.
Two Strut Pair *(Novorossiysk)*; F band.
Air/surface search: Top Steer ❾; 3D; D/E band.
Navigation: Don Kay; I band. Two Palm Frond (three in *Novorossiysk*); I band. Shot Dome; I band.
Fire control: Trap Door (for SS-N-12) ❿. Two Head Light C ⓫; E band (for SA-N-3). Two Pop Group *(Kiev)* ⓬; F/H/I band (for SA-N-4). Two Owl Screech ⓭; G band (for 76 mm). Four Bass Tilt ⓮; H/I band (for Gatlings). Four Cross Sword (for SA-N-9) *(Novorossiysk)*.
Aircraft control: Top Knot; G/H band.
IFF: High Pole A and B *(Kiev)*. Salt Pot A and B *(Novorossiysk)*. Square Head.
Sonars: Moose Jaw and Bull Horn or Horse Jaw *(Novorossiysk)*; hull-mounted; active search and attack; low/medium frequency.
Mare Tail or Horse Tail; VDS; active search; medium frequency.

Fixed wing aircraft: 12 VSTOL ⓯; (see *Operational*).
Helicopters: 19 Ka-25 Hormone A or Ka-27 Helix (ASW); 2 Ka-25 Hormone B (OTHT) ⓰.

Programmes: Although originally classified as *protivolodochny kreyser* meaning anti-submarine cruiser, this class is now classified as *takticheskoye avianosny kreyser* meaning tactical aircraft-carrying cruiser.
Structure: Flight deck has a 4½ degree angle and two lifts, one larger one abaft the island and a smaller one amidships abreast the bridge. Six spots are provided with a seventh at the forward tip of the flight deck. A larger spot amidships aft is for VSTOL. The layout varies in *Novorossiysk*.
Operational: The ageing Forger was withdrawn from service in 1992 which means no fixed wing capability, unless Freestyle development continues. The task of this class is primarily to act as the focus for task group operations making use of the excellent command, control and communications equipment. The third of class *Minsk* was sold for scrap in 1992 because propulsion system damage put her beyond economical repair. *Kiev* is to be deleted in 1993 and may be used for spares to keep *Gorshkov* operational. *Novorossiysk* needs new boilers.

KIEV   1992

KIEV   1989

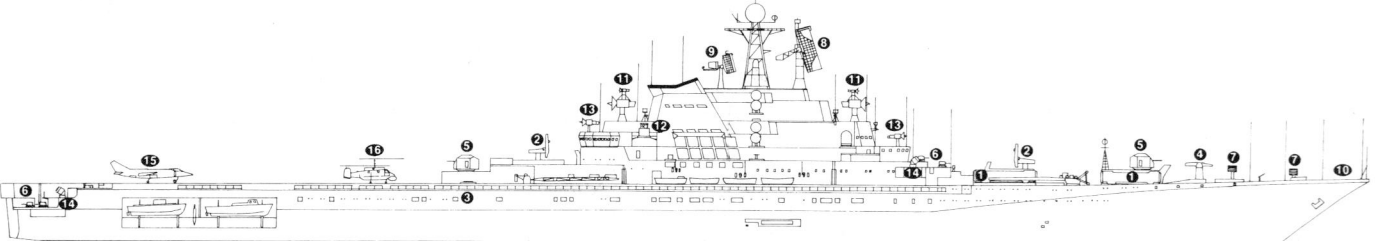

KIEV   (Scale 1 : 1500), Ian Sturton

Aircraft carriers / RUSSIA

1 MODIFIED KIEV CLASS (CVG)

Name	Builders	Laid down	Launched	Commissioned
ADMIRAL GORSHKOV (ex-*Baku*)	Nikolayev South (Nosenko, 444)	Dec 1978	17 Apr 1982	Jan 1987

Displacement, tons: 40 500 full load
Dimensions, feet (metres): 899 oa; 818.6 wl × 167.3 oa; 107.3 wl × 32.8 (screws) *(274; 249.5 × 51; 32.7 × 10)*
Flight deck, feet (metres): 640 × 68 *(195 × 20.7)*
Main machinery: 8 boilers; 4 turbines; 200 000 hp(m) *(147 MW)*; 4 shafts
Speed, knots: 32. **Range, miles:** 13 500 at 18 kts; 4000 at 31 kts
Complement: 1200 plus aircrew

Missiles: SSM: 12 SS-N-12 Sandbox (6 twin) launchers ❶; inertial guidance with command update; active radar homing to 550 km *(300 nm)* at 1.7 Mach; warhead nuclear 350 kT or HE 1000 kg; 24 reloads.
SAM: 4 SA-N-9 sextuple vertical launchers ❷; command guidance; active radar homing to 12 km *(6.6 nm)* at 2 Mach; warhead 15 kg; altitude 3.4-12 192 m *(10-40 000 ft)*; 24 magazines; 192 missiles.
Guns: 2—3.9 in *(100 mm)*/70 ❸; 80° elevation; 80 rounds/minute to 15 km *(8.2 nm)*; weight of shell 16 kg.
8—30 mm/65 ❹; 6 barrels per mounting; 85° elevation; 3000 rounds/minute combined to 2 km.
A/S mortars: 2 RBU 12 000 ❺; 10 tubes per launcher; range 12 000 m; warhead 80 kg.
Countermeasures: Decoys: 2 twin chaff launchers. Towed torpedo decoy.
ESM/ECM: 4 Wine Flask; 8 Foot Ball; 4 Bell Nip; 4 Bell Thump. 2 Cage Pot.
Fire control: 3 Tin Man optronic trackers ❻. 2 Punch Bowl SATCOM for SSM data link. 2 Low Ball SATNAV. 1 Bob Tail.
Radars: Air search: Sky Watch; 4 Planar phased array ❼; 3D.
Air/surface search: Plate Steer ❽; E band.
Surface search: Two Strut Pair ❾; F band.
Navigation: Three Palm Frond; I band.
Fire control: Trap Door (for SS-N-12) ❿. Kite Screech ⓫; H/I/K band (for 100 mm). Four Bass Tilt ⓬; H/I band (for Gatlings). Four Cross Sword ⓭ (for SA-N-9).
Aircraft control: Fly Trap; G/H band. Cake Stand ⓮.
IFF: 2 Salt Pot A and B. 1 Long Head.
Sonars: Horse Jaw; hull-mounted; active search and attack; low/medium frequency.
Horse Tail; VDS; active search; medium frequency.

Fixed wing aircraft: 12 VSTOL ⓯; (see *Operational*).
Helicopters: 19 Ka-27 Helix A ⓰; 3 Ka-25 Hormone B (OTHT).

Programmes: The fourth and last of the Kiev class much delayed by the planar radar development. Full name is *Admiral Flota Sovietskogo Sojuza Gorshkov*.
Structure: Major differences with *Kiev* include 12 SSMs, 2—100 mm guns, 24 SA-N-9 magazines, planar 3D radar and a 30.5 × 19.7 ft *(9 × 6 m)* cupola at the top of the mast. The *Kiev's* torpedo armament has been removed. Many of these innovations have been incorporated in *Kuznetsov*.

ADMIRAL GORSHKOV 11/1990

Operational: *Gorshkov* is based in the Northern Fleet. The Sky Watch radar should allow full control of the air battle when it finally becomes operational. As with the Kiev class, the withdrawal of Forger aircraft from service in 1992 has reduced the ship to a Helicopter Carrier unless Freestyle development continues.

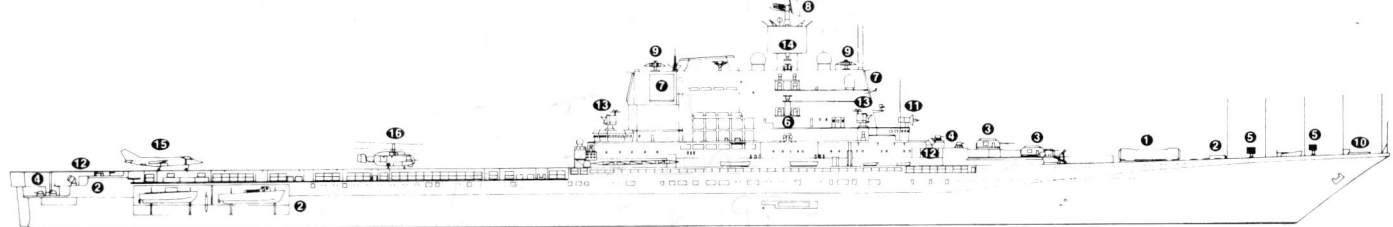

ADMIRAL GORSHKOV (Scale 1 : 1500), Ian Sturton

ADMIRAL GORSHKOV 6/1989

BATTLE CRUISERS

3 + 1 KIROV CLASS

Name	Builders	Laid down	Launched	Commissioned
ADMIRAL USHAKOV (ex-*Kirov*)	Baltic Yard 189, Leningrad	June 1973	26 Dec 1977	July 1980
ADMIRAL LAZAREV (ex-*Frunze*)	Baltic Yard 189, Leningrad	26 Dec 1977	23 May 1981	Nov 1983
ADMIRAL NAKHIMOV (ex-*Kalinin*)	Baltic Yard 189, Leningrad	May 1983	26 Apr 1986	Oct 1988
PYOTR VELIKIY (ex-*Yuri Andropov*)	Baltic Yard 189, St Petersburg	Apr 1986	29 Apr 1989	1993

Displacement, tons: 19 000 standard; 24 300 full load
Dimensions, feet (metres): 826.8; 754.6 wl × 93.5 × 29.5 *(252; 230 × 28.5 × 9.1)*
Main machinery: Nuclear; 2 PWR; 2 oil-fired boilers; 2 turbines; 108 800 hp(m) *(80 MW)*; 2 shafts
Speed, knots: 30. **Range, miles:** 14 000 at 30 kts
Complement: 692 (82 officers)

Missiles: SSM: 20 SS-N-19 Shipwreck (improved SS-N-12 with lower flight profile) ❶; inertial guidance with command update; active radar homing to 20-450 km *(10.8-243 nm)* at 1.6 Mach; warhead 350 kT nuclear or 750 kg HE; no reloads.
SAM: 12 SA-N-6 Grumble vertical launchers ❷; 8 rounds per launcher; command guidance; semi-active radar homing to 100 km *(54 nm)*; warhead 90 kg (or nuclear?); altitude 27 432 m *(90 000 ft)*.
2 SA-N-4 twin launchers ❸; semi-active radar homing to 15 km *(8 nm)* at 2.5 Mach; warhead 50 kg; altitude 9.1-3048 m *(30-10 000 ft)*; 40 missiles.
2 SA-N-9 octuple vertical launchers (not in *Kirov*) ❹; command guidance; active radar homing to 12 km *(6.6 nm)* at 2 Mach; warhead 15 kg; altitude 3.4-12 192 m *(10-40 000 ft)*; 128 missiles.
SAM/Guns: 6 CADS-N-1 (*Nakhimov*) ❼; each has a twin 30 mm Gatling combined with 8 SA-N-11 and Hot Flash/Hot Spot fire control radar/optronic director. Laser beam riding guidance for missiles to 8 km *(4.4 nm)*; 4500 rounds/minute combined to 2 km (for guns).
A/S: 1 twin SS-N-14 Silex launcher (*Ushakov*) ❹; command guidance to 55 km *(30 nm)* at 0.95 Mach; payload nuclear or Type 53 torpedo; active/passive homing to 15 km *(8.1 nm)* at 40 kts; warhead 150 kg; 14 missiles. SSM version; range 35 km *(19 nm)*; warhead 500 kg.
SS-N-15 (not in *Ushakov*); inertial flight to 120 km *(65 nm)*; payload Type 45 torpedo or nuclear warhead; fired from fixed torpedo tubes behind shutters in the superstructure.
Guns: 2—3.9 in *(100 mm)*/70 (*Ushakov*) ❺; 80° elevation; 80 rounds/minute to 15 km *(8.2 nm)*; weight of shell 16 kg.
2—130 mm/70 (twin) (not in *Ushakov*) ❺; 85° elevation; 35/45 rounds/minute to 29 km *(16 nm)*; weight of shell 27 kg.
8—30 mm/65 (*Ushakov* and *Lazarev*) ❻; 6 barrels per mounting; 85° elevation; 3000 rounds/minute combined to 2 km. *Lazarev* guns controlled by CADS-N-1 system.
Torpedoes: 10—21 in *(533 mm)* (2 quin). Type 53; dual purpose; pattern active/passive homing up to 20 km *(10.8 nm)* at up to 45 kts; warhead 400 kg or low yield nuclear. Mounted in the hull adjacent to the RBU 1000s on both quarters. Fixed tubes behind shutters (not in *Ushakov*) can fire either SS-N-15 (see *Missiles A/S*) or Type 45 torpedoes.
A/S mortars: 1 RBU 6000 12-tubed trainable fwd (*Kirov* and *Frunze*) ❽; range 6000 m; warhead 31 kg.
1 RBU 12 000 (*Lazarev*) ❾; 10 tubes per launcher; range 12 000 m; warhead 80 kg.
2 RBU 1000 6-tubed aft ❿; range 1000 m; warhead 55 kg.
Countermeasures: Decoys: 2 twin 150 mm chaff launchers. Towed torpedo decoy.
ESM/ECM: 8 Side Globe (*Ushakov*). 8 Foot Ball (not in *Ushakov*). 4 Rum Tub (*Ushakov*). 4 Wine Flask (not in *Ushakov*). 8 Bell Bash. 4 Bell Nip.
Fire control: 4 Tin Man optronic trackers. 2 Punch Bowl SATCOM ⓫. 4 Low Ball SATNAV.
Radars: Air search: Top Pair (Top Sail + Big Net) ⓬; 3D; C/D band; range 366 km *(200 nm)* for bomber, 183 km *(100 nm)* for 2 m² target.
Air/surface search: Top Steer ⓭ (Top Plate in *Lazarev*) ⓮; 3D; D/E band.
Navigation: Three Palm Frond; I band.
Fire control: Two Eye Bowl (*Ushakov* only) ⓯; F band (for SS-N-14). Cross Dome (not in *Ushakov*) ⓰; E/F band (for SA-N-9). Two Top Dome ⓱; J band (for SA-N-6). Two Pop Group, F/H/I band (for SA-N-4) ⓲. Kite Screech ⓳; H/I/K band (for main guns). Four Bass Tilt ⓴; H/I band (for Gatlings (not in *Lazarev*)).
Aircraft control: Flyscreen A (*Ushakov*) or B; I band.
IFF: Salt Pot A and B.
Tacan: 2 Round House B.
Sonars: Horse Jaw; hull-mounted; active search and attack; low/medium frequency.
Horse Tail; VDS; active search; medium frequency. Depth to 150-200 m *(492.1-656.2 ft)* depending on speed.

Helicopters: 3 Ka-25 Hormone ㉑ or Ka-27 Helix ㉒.

Programmes: Type name is *atomny raketny kreyser* meaning nuclear-powered missile cruiser. In 1989-90 Baltic Yard started to build eight Kronstadt Ro-Ro ships for civilian use, which confirmed statements that only four Kirovs are to be built. All re-named in 1992. *Pyotr Velikiy* (Peter the Great) is making very slow progress to completion.
Structure: The first surface warships with nuclear propulsion. In addition to the nuclear plant a unique maritime combination with an auxiliary oil-fuelled system has been installed. This provides a superheat capability, boosting the normal steam output by some 50 per cent. The SS-N-19 tubes are set at an angle of about 45 degrees. *Lazarev* and subsequent ships of the class have a modified superstructure and armament although the SS-N-19 and SA-N-6 missile fits are the same. *Lazarev* has an SA-N-9 octuple launcher in place of *Ushakov*'s SS-N-14 and another one aft in place of 4—30 mm guns which have been moved to a lengthened after deckhouse. *Nakhimov* has CADS-N-1 with a central fire control radar on six mountings, each of which has two cannon and eight missile launchers. Two are mounted either side of the SS-N-19 forward and four on the after superstructure. All except *Ushakov* have the same A/S system as the frigate *Neustrashimy* with fixed torpedo tubes in ports behind shutters in the superstructure for firing SS-N-15 or Type 45 torpedoes. These ships are reported as carrying about 500 SAM of different types.
Operational: The CIWS in *Nakhimov* is an attempt further to improve inadequate hard-kill air defences in *Ushakov*, following the installation of SA-N-9 in *Lazarev*. Over-the-horizon targeting for SS-N-19 provided by SATCOM or Hormone B helicopter. *Ushakov* and *Nakhimov* are in the Northern Fleet, *Lazarev* in the Pacific and *Pyotr Velikiy* may start sea trials in the Baltic in 1993. As the support for a strike carrier or as the focus of a task force including the Slava, Kara, Krivak and Ivan Rogov classes with support from *Berezina* or *Boris Chilikin*, they would form a formidable intervention force, with VTOL and helicopter aircraft as well as a full outfit of missiles and guns.

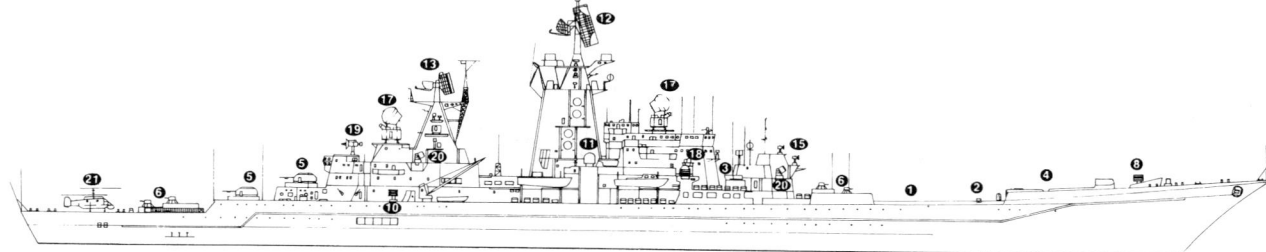

ADMIRAL USHAKOV *(Scale 1 : 1500), Ian Sturton*

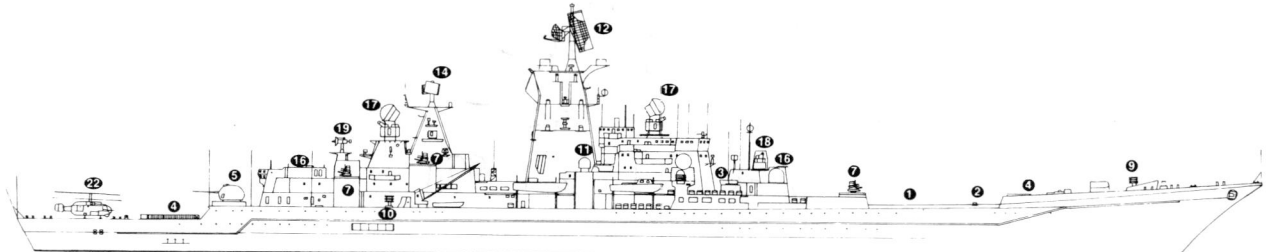

ADMIRAL NAKHIMOV *(Scale 1 : 1500), Ian Sturton*

ADMIRAL NAKHIMOV

ADMIRAL NAKHIMOV 5/1990

ADMIRAL NAKHIMOV 5/1990

ADMIRAL USHAKOV 6/1990

HELICOPTER CRUISERS

1 MOSKVA CLASS (CHG)

Name	Builders	Laid down	Launched	Commissioned
MOSKVA	Nikolayev South	1963	1965	May 1967

Displacement, tons: 14 900 standard; 17 500 full load
Dimensions, feet (metres): 626.6 oa; 587.3 wl × 115.5 oa; 75.5 wl × 28.5 *(191 oa; 179 wl × 34; 23 × 8.7)*
Flight deck, feet (metres): 265.7 × 111.5 *(81 × 34)*
Main machinery: 4 boilers; 2 turbines; 100 000 hp(m) *(73.5 MW)*; 2 shafts
Speed, knots: 31. **Range, miles:** 9000 at 18 kts; 4500 at 29 kts
Complement: 840 plus aircrew

Missiles: SAM: 2 SA-N-3 Goblet twin launchers ❶; semi-active radar homing to 55 km *(30 nm)* at 2.5 Mach; warhead 80 kg; altitude 91.4-22 860 m *(300-75 000 ft)*; 48 missiles.
A/S: SUW-N-1 twin launcher ❷; 18 Fras 1A or 1B; inertial flight to 29 km *(16 nm)*; warhead nuclear 5 kT or Type 45 torpedo.
Guns: 4—57 mm/80 (2 twin) ❸; 85° elevation; 120 rounds/minute to 6 km *(3.3 nm)*; weight of shell 2.8 kg.
A/S mortars: 2 RBU 6000 12-tubed trainable ❹; range 6000 m; warhead 31 kg.
Countermeasures: Decoys: 2 twin chaff launchers.
ESM/ECM: 8 Side Globe. 2 Bell Clout. 2 Bell Slam. 2 Bell Tap. 2 Top Hat
Fire control: 2 Tee Plinth and 3 Tilt Pot optronic directors.
Radars: Air search: Top Sail ❺; 3D; D band; range 555 km *(300 nm)*.
Head Net C ❻; E band; range 128 km *(70 nm)*.
Surface search: Two Don 2; I band.
Fire control: Two Head Light A ❼; F/G/H band (for SA-N-3). Two Muff Cob ❽; G/H band (for 57 mm).
IFF: 2 High Pole.
Sonars: Moose Jaw; hull-mounted; active search and attack; medium/low frequency.
Mare Tail; VDS ❾; active search; medium frequency.

Helicopters: 14 Ka-25 Hormone A ASW ❿.

Programmes: Type name is *protivolodochny kreyser* meaning anti-submarine cruiser.
Structure: In early 1973 *Moskva* was seen with a landing pad on the after end of the flight deck for flight tests of VTOL aircraft. Since removed. Main hangar, 67 × 25 m *(219.8 × 82 ft)*. There is also a small hangar 41 × 12 m *(134.5 × 39.4 ft)* in the superstructure. Two 10 ton lifts. Has Bell Crown data link antennas.
Operational: General purpose capability including command, air defence and ASW. Based in the Black Sea and kept in service in a Flagship role. Sister ship *Leningrad* was scrapped in 1992.

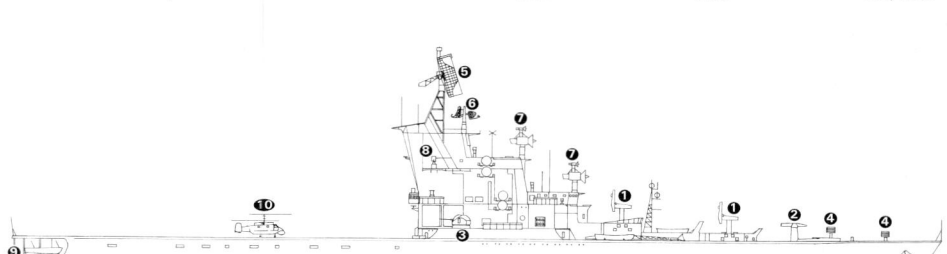

MOSKVA *(Scale 1 : 1500), Ian Sturton*

MOSKVA *4/1992, van Ginderen Collection*

CRUISERS

7 KRESTA II CLASS (CG)

Name	Builders	Laid down	Launched	Commissioned
ADMIRAL ISAKOV	Zhdanov, Leningrad	June 1966	Dec 1968	Sep 1970
ADMIRAL MAKAROV	Zhdanov, Leningrad	Mar 1968	Apr 1970	June 1972
KHABAROVSK (ex-*Marshal Voroshilov*)	Zhdanov, Leningrad	Jan 1969	Nov 1970	May 1973
ADMIRAL OKTYABRSKY	Zhdanov, Leningrad	May 1969	June 1971	Sep 1973
MARSHAL TIMOSHENKO	Zhdanov, Leningrad	June 1971	Oct 1973	Aug 1975
VASILY CHAPAYEV	Zhdanov, Leningrad	Feb 1972	Jan 1975	Sep 1976
ADMIRAL YUMASHEV	Zhdanov, Leningrad	Nov 1973	Oct 1976	Oct 1977

Displacement, tons: 6400 standard; 7850 full load
Dimensions, feet (metres): 519.9 × 55.4 × 19.7 *(158.5 × 16.9 × 6)*
Main machinery: 4 boilers; 2 turbines; 110 000 hp(m) *(80.85 MW)*; 2 shafts
Speed, knots: 35. **Range, miles:** 10 500 at 14 kts; 2400 at 32 kts
Complement: 400

Missiles: SAM: 2 SA-N-3 Goblet twin launchers ❶; semi-active radar homing to 55 km *(30 nm)* at 2.5 Mach; warhead 80 kg; altitude 91.4-22 860 m *(300-75 000 ft)*; 48 missiles.
A/S: 2 SS-N-14 Silex quad launchers ❷; command guidance to 55 km *(30 nm)* at 0.95 Mach; payload nuclear or Type E53 torpedo; active/passive homing to 15 km *(8.1 nm)* at 40 kts; warhead 150 kg. SSM version; range 35 km *(19 nm)*; warhead 500 kg.
Guns: 4—57 mm/80 (2 twin) ❸; 85° elevation; 120 rounds/minute to 6 km *(3.3 nm)*; weight of shell 2.8 kg.
4—30 mm/65 ❹; 6 barrels per mounting; 85° elevation; 3000 rounds/minute combined to 2 km.
Torpedoes: 10—21 in *(533 mm)* (2 quin) ❺. Type 53; dual purpose; pattern active/passive homing up to 20 km *(10.8 nm)* at up to 45 kts; warhead 400 kg or low yield nuclear.
A/S mortars: 2 RBU 6000 12-tubed trainable ❻; range 6000 m; warhead 31 kg.
2 RBU 1000 6-tubed ❼; range 1000 m; warhead 55 kg.
Countermeasures: Decoys: 2 twin chaff launchers.
ESM/ECM: 8 Side Globe. 2 Bell Slam. 1 Bell Clout. 2 Bell Tap. 2 Bell Crown.
Fire control: 2 Tee Plinth optronic directors.
Radars: Air search: Top Sail ❽; 3D; D band; range 555 km *(300 nm)*.
Air/surface search: Head Net C ❾; 3D; E band; range 128 km *(70 nm)*.
Navigation: Two Don Kay; I band or Two Palm Frond; I band.
Fire control: Two Head Light A (aft), B (forward) or C ❿; F/G/H band (for SA-N-3 and SS-N-14). Two Muff Cob ⓫; G/H band (for 57 mm). Two Bass Tilt (not in hulls 1-4) ⓬; H/I band (for 30 mm).
IFF: High Pole A and B.
Sonars: Bull Nose; hull-mounted; active search and attack; medium frequency.

Helicopters: 1 Ka-25 Hormone A ⓭.

Programmes: Type name is *bolshoy protivolodochny korabl*, meaning large anti-submarine ship.
Structure: The design was developed from that of the Kresta I class, but with the SS-N-14 replacing the SS-N-3 the role has been changed from that of surface warfare for Kresta I to ASW for Kresta II although the SS-N-14 probably has an anti-surface ship capability. At the same time the substitution of SA-N-3 for SA-N-1 improved Kresta II class's air defence capability. Fin stabilisers. Hulls 8-10 have an additional deck-house abaft the bridge and between the four 30 mm mounts. The helicopter is raised to flight deck level by a lift.
Operational: Three scrapped in 1992 and *Isakov*, *Makarov* and *Yumashev* are expected to follow in 1993 as an economy measure. *Marshal Timoshenko* has been in Kronstadt dockyard since August 1987.

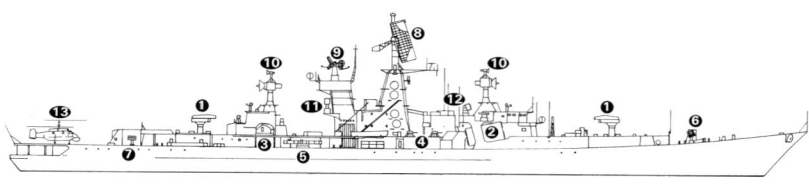

KRESTA II *(Scale 1 : 1500), Ian Sturton*

KRESTA II *1/1992*

1 KRESTA I CLASS (CG)

Name	Builders	Laid down	Launched	Commissioned
ADMIRAL ZOZULYA	Zhdanov, Leningrad	Sep 1964	Oct 1965	Mar 1967

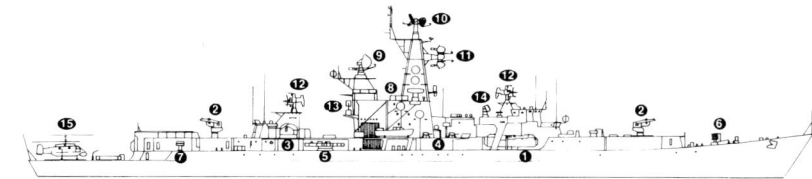

ADMIRAL ZOZULYA (Scale 1: 1500), Ian Sturton

Displacement, tons: 6140 standard; 7700 full load
Dimensions, feet (metres): 510 × 55.7 × 19.7 *(155.5 × 17 × 6)*
Main machinery: 4 boilers; 2 turbines; 110 000 hp(m) *(80.85 MW)*; 2 shafts
Speed, knots: 35. **Range, miles:** 10 500 at 14 kts; 2400 at 32 kts
Complement: 360

Missiles: SSM: 4 SS-N-3B Sepal (2 twin) launchers ❶; command guidance; active radar homing to 460 km *(250 nm)* at 1.1 Mach; warhead nuclear 350 kT or HE 1000 kg; no reloads.
SAM: 2 SA-N-1 Goa twin launchers ❷; command guidance to 31.5 km *(17 nm)* at 2 Mach; warhead 60 kg; altitude 91.4-22 860 m *(300-75 000 ft)*; 32 missiles.
Guns: 4—57 mm/80 (2 twin) ❸; 85° elevation; 120 rounds/minute to 6 km *(3.3 nm)*; weight of shell 2.8 kg.
4—30 mm/65 AK 630 ❹; 6 barrels per mounting; 3000 rounds/minute to 2 km.
Torpedoes: 10—21 in *(533 mm)* (2 quin) ❺. Type 53; dual purpose; pattern active/passive homing up to 20 km *(10.8 nm)* at up to 45 kts; warhead 400 kg or low yield nuclear.
A/S mortars: 2 RBU 6000 12-tubed trainable ❻; range 6000 m; warhead 31 kg.
2 RBU 1000 6-tubed ❼; range 1000 m; warhead 55 kg.
Countermeasures: Decoys: 2 twin chaff launchers.
ESM/ECM: 8 Side Globe. Bell Clout. 2 Bell Slam. 2 Bell Tap. 2 Bell Strike. 2 Bell Crown.
Fire control: 2 Tee Plinth optronic directors ❽.
Radars: Air search: Big Net ❾; C band; range 183 km *(100 nm)* for 2 m^2 target.
Air/surface search; Head Net C ❿; 3D; E band; range 128 km *(70 nm)*.
Navigation: Two Palm Frond; I band.
Fire control: Scoop Pair ⓫; E band (for SS-N-3). Two Peel Group ⓬; H/I band (for SA-N-1). Two Muff Cob ⓭; G/H band (for 57 mm). Two Bass Tilt ⓮; H/I band (for 30 mm).
IFF: High Pole B.
Sonars: Herkules; hull-mounted; active search and attack; medium frequency.

Helicopters: 1 Ka-25 Hormone B ⓯.

Programmes: Designed for surface warfare, the successor to the Kynda class. Type name *bolshoy protivolodochny korabl*, meaning large anti-submarine ship. Changed in 1977-78 to *raketny kreyser*, meaning missile cruiser.
Modernisation: 30 mm guns and fire control radars were added during refit at Kronstadt from 1985 to November 1991.
Structure: Provided with a helicopter landing deck and hangar aft. This gives an enhanced carried-on-board target-location facility for the SS-N-3B system. The Kresta I was therefore the first missile cruiser free to operate alone and without targeting assistance from shore-based aircraft.
Operational: Baltic Fleet Flagship. The remainder of the class have been paid off.

ADMIRAL ZOZULYA 6/1992

2 KYNDA CLASS (CG)

Name	Builders	Laid down	Launched	Commissioned
ADMIRAL FOKIN	Zhdanov, Leningrad	Dec 1960	Nov 1961	May 1963
ADMIRAL GOLOVKO	Zhdanov, Leningrad	Dec 1961	Nov 1962	June 1963

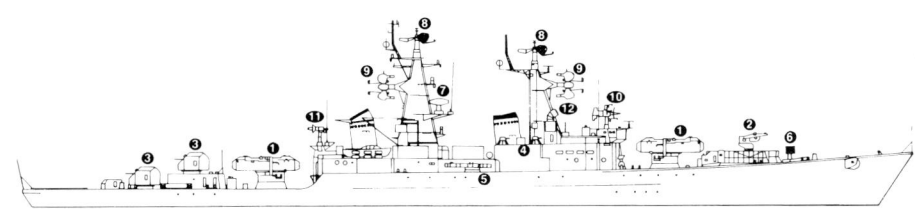

ADMIRAL GOLOVKO (Scale 1: 1200), Ian Sturton

Displacement, tons: 4400 standard; 5550 full load
Dimensions, feet (metres): 465.8 × 51.8 × 17.4 *(142 × 15.8 × 5.3)*
Main machinery: 4 boilers; 2 turbines; 110 000 hp(m) *(80.85 MW)*; 2 shafts
Speed, knots: 34. **Range, miles:** 6000 at 14.5 kts; 1500 at 34 kts
Complement: 329 (25 officers)

Missiles: SSM: 8 SS-N-3B Sepal (2 quad) launchers ❶; inertial guidance; active radar homing to 460 km *(250 nm)* at 1.1 Mach; warhead nuclear 350 kT or HE 1000 kg; 8 reloads.
SAM: SA-N-1 Goa twin launcher ❷; command guidance to 31.5 km *(17 nm)* at 2 Mach; warhead 60 kg; altitude 91.4-22 860 m *(300-75 000 ft)*; 16 missiles. Some SSM capability.
Guns: 4—3 in *(76 mm)*/60 (2 twin) ❸; 80° elevation; 90 rounds/minute to 15 km *(8 nm)*; weight of shell 6.8 kg.
4—30 mm/65 ❹; 6 barrels per mounting; 85° elevation; 3000 rounds/minute combined to 2 km.
Torpedoes: 6—21 in *(533 mm)* (2 triple) ❺. Type 53; dual purpose; pattern active/passive homing up to 20 km *(10.8 nm)* at up to 45 kts; warhead 400 kg or low yield nuclear.
A/S mortars: 2 RBU 6000 12-tubed trainable ❻; range 6000 m; warhead 31 kg.
Countermeasures: ESM/ECM: 4 Top Hat. Bell Clout. Bell Tap. Bell Slam.
Fire control: 2 Tee Plinth; 2 Plinth Net ❼ (not *Admiral Golovko*) optronic directors.
Radars: Air search: Two Head Net A ❽ *(Admiral Golovko)* or Head Net A and Head Net C *(Admiral Fokin)*; E band.
Surface search and Navigation: Two Don 2; I band.
Fire control: Two Scoop Pair ❾; E band (for SS-N-3B). Peel Group ❿; H/I band (for SS-N-1). Owl Screech ⓫; G band (for 76 mm). Two Bass Tilt ⓬; H/I band (for 30 mm).
IFF: High Pole B.
Sonars: Herkules; hull-mounted; active search and attack; medium frequency.

Helicopters: Platform only.

Programmes: This class was designed for surface warfare and was the first class of missile cruisers built. The role made it the successor of the Sverdlov class. Type name is *raketny kreyser* meaning missile cruiser.
Modernisation: Modernised in the early 1980s, including the installation of a Head Net C radar in place of Head Net A *(Fokin)*, the four 30 mm Gatling mounts with two associated Bass Tilt radars and a twin level deckhouse abaft the forward funnel.
Operational: This class showed at an early stage the Soviet ability to match radar availability to weapons systems. The duplicated aerials provide not only a capability for separate target engagement but also provide a reserve in the event of damage. *Fokin* based in the Pacific and *Golovko* in the Black Sea. One deleted in 1990, one in 1992.

KYNDA 7/1985

540 RUSSIA / Cruisers

3 + 1 SLAVA CLASS (CG)

Name	Builders	Laid down	Launched	Commissioned
SLAVA	Nikolayev North (61 Kommuna)	1976	1979	Aug 1982
MARSHAL USTINOV	Nikolayev North (61 Kommuna)	1978	1982	Apr 1986
CHERVONA UKRAINA	Nikolayev North (61 Kommuna)	1979	1983	Jan 1990
ADMIRAL LOBOV	Nikolayev North (61 Kommuna)	1984	Aug 1990	—

Displacement, tons: 9800 standard; 11 200 full load
Dimensions, feet (metres): 610.2 × 68.2 × 24.9 *(186 × 20.8 × 7.6)*
Main machinery: COGAG; 4 gas turbines; 108 800 hp(m) *(80 MW)*; 2 gas turbines; 13 600 hp(m) *(10 MW)*; 2 shafts
Speed, knots: 32. **Range, miles:** 2500 at 30 kts; 6000 at 15 kts
Complement: 454 (38 officers)

Missiles: SSM: 16 SS-N-12 (8 twin) launchers ❶; inertial guidance with command update; active radar homing to 550 km *(300 nm)* at 1.7 Mach; warhead nuclear 350 kT or HE 1000 kg.
SAM: 8 SA-N-6 Grumble vertical launchers ❷; 8 rounds per launcher; command guidance; semi-active radar homing to 100 km *(54 nm)*; warhead 90 kg (or nuclear?); altitude 27 432 m *(90 000 ft)*.
2 SA-N-4 Gecko twin launchers ❸; semi-active radar homing to 15 km *(8 nm)* at 2.5 Mach; warhead 50 kg; altitude 9.1-3048 m *(30-10 000 ft)*; 40 missiles.
Guns: 2—130 mm/70 (twin) ❹; 35/45 rounds/minute to 29 km *(16 nm)*; weight of shell 27 kg.
6—30 mm/65; 6 barrels per mounting; 85° elevation; 3000 rounds/minute to 2 km.
Torpedoes: 10—21 in *(533 mm)* (2 quin) ❺. Type 53; dual purpose; pattern active/passive homing up to 20 km *(10.8 nm)* at up to 45 kts; warhead 400 kg or low yield nuclear.
A/S mortars: 2 RBU 6000 12-tubed trainable ❻; range 6000 m; warhead 31 kg.
Countermeasures: Decoys: 2 twin 12-tubed chaff launchers.
ESM/ECM: 8 Side Globe. 4 Rum Tub. Bell series. IR surveillance.
Fire control: 2 Tee Plinth and 3 Tilt Pot optronic directors. 2 Punch Bowl satellite data receiving/targeting systems.
Radars: Air search: Top Pair (Top Sail + Big Net) ❼; 3D; C/D band; range 366 km *(200 nm)* for bomber, 183 km *(100 nm)* for 2 m² target.
Air/surface search: Top Steer ❽ or Top Plate *(Ukraina)*; 3D; D/E band.
Navigation: Three Palm Frond; I band.
Fire control: Front Door ❾; F band (for SS-N-12). Top Dome ❿; J band (for SA-N-6). Two Pop Group ⓫; F/H/I band (for SA-N-4). Three Bass Tilt ⓬; H/I band (for Gatlings). Kite Screech ⓭; H/I/K band (for 130 mm).
IFF: Salt Pot A and B. 2 Long Head.
Sonars: Bull Horn; hull-mounted; active search and attack; low/medium frequency.
Mare Tail; VDS; active search; medium frequency.

Helicopters: 1 Ka-25 Hormone B ⓮.

Programmes: Building at the same yard that built the Kara class. This is a smaller edition of the dual-purpose surface warfare/ASW *Kirov*, designed as a conventionally powered back-up for that class. *Admiral Lobov* is the last of the class and was 75 per cent complete in early 1993. Her future is uncertain.
Structure: The notable gap abaft the twin funnels (SA-N-6 area) is traversed by a large crane which stows between the funnels. The hangar is recessed below the flight deck with an inclined ramp. The torpedo tubes are behind shutters in the hull below the Top Dome radar director aft.
Operational: The SA-N-6 system effectiveness is diminished by having only one radar director. Over-the-horizon targeting for SS-N-12 provided by Hormone or SATCOM. *Slava* is based in the Black Sea Fleet, *Marshal Ustinov* deployed to the Northern Fleet on a permanent basis in March 1987. *Chervona Ukraina* started sea trials in August 1989 and transferred to the Pacific in October 1990.

MARSHAL USTINOV   7/1991, Giorgio Arra

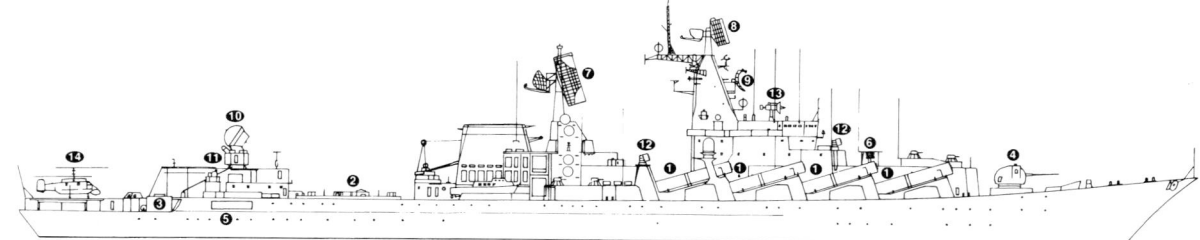
SLAVA   (Scale 1 : 1200), Ian Sturton

CHERVONA UKRAINA (with Top Plate)   10/1990, 92 Wing RAAF

7 KARA CLASS (CG)

Name	Builders	Laid down	Launched	Commissioned
NIKOLAYEV	Nikolayev North (61 Kommuna)	Jan 1969	Feb 1970	Sep 1971
OCHAKOV	Nikolayev North (61 Kommuna)	Mar 1970	June 1971	Mar 1973
KERCH	Nikolayev North (61 Kommuna)	June 1971	July 1972	Sep 1974
AZOV	Nikolayev North (61 Kommuna)	Aug 1972	Sep 1973	Nov 1975
PETROPAVLOVSK	Nikolayev North (61 Kommuna)	Nov 1973	Dec 1974	Nov 1976
TASHKENT	Nikolayev North (61 Kommuna)	Jan 1975	Oct 1975	Nov 1977
VLADIVOSTOK (ex-*Tallinn*)	Nikolayev North (61 Kommuna)	Dec 1975	Mar 1977	Apr 1980

Displacement, tons: 8000 standard; 9900 full load
Dimensions, feet (metres): 568 × 61 × 22 *(173.2 × 18.6 × 6.7)*
Main machinery: COGAG; 4 gas turbines; 108 800 hp(m) *(80 MW)*; 2 gas turbines; 13 600 hp(m) *(10 MW)*; 2 shafts
Speed, knots: 34. **Range, miles:** 9000 at 15 kts cruising turbines; 3000 at 32 kts
Complement: 540 (30 officers)

Missiles: SAM: 2 SA-N-3 Goblet twin launchers (1 launcher in *Azov*) ❶; semi-active radar homing to 55 km *(30 nm)* at 2.5 Mach; warhead 80 kg; altitude 91.4-22 860 m *(300- 75 000 ft)*; 72 missiles.
6 SA-N-6 Grumble vertical launchers (*Azov* only); 4 rounds per launcher; command guidance; semi-active radar homing to 100 km *(54 nm)*; warhead 90 kg (or nuclear?); altitude 27 432 m *(90 000 ft)*.
2 SA-N-4 Gecko twin launchers (twin either side of mast) ❷; semi-active radar homing to 15 km *(8 nm)* at 2.5 Mach; warhead 50 kg; altitude 9.1-3048 m *(30-10 000 ft)*; 40 missiles.
A/S: 2 SS-N-14 Silex quad launchers ❸; command guidance to 55 km *(30 nm)* at 0.95 Mach; payload nuclear or Type E53 torpedo; active/passive homing to 15 km *(8.1 nm)* at 40 kts; warhead 150 kg. SSM version; range 35 km *(19 nm)*; warhead 500 kg.
In addition to the Kresta II armament of eight tubes for the SS-N-14 A/S system (probably with a surface-to-surface capability) and the pair of twin launchers for SA-N-3 system with Goblet missiles, Kara class mounts the SA-N-4 system in 2 silos, either side of the mast. The SA-N-3 system has only 2 loading doors per launcher and a larger launching arm. This might indicate an SSM capability for the SA-N-3. *Azov* was the trials ship for the new SA-N-6 SAM system designed for subsequent classes. This replaces the after SA-N-3, after RBUs and torpedo tubes of a standard Kara.
Guns: 4—3 in *(76 mm)*/60 (2 twin) ❹; 80° elevation; 90 rounds/ minute to 15 km *(8 nm)*; weight of shell 6.8 kg.
4—30 mm/65 ❺; 6 barrels per mounting; 85° elevation; 3000 rounds/minute combined to 2 km.
The siting of both main and secondary armament on either beams in the waist follows the precedent of both Kresta classes, although the weight of the main armament is increased.
Torpedoes: 10 or 4—21 in *(533 mm)* (2 quin) (2 twin in *Azov*) ❻. Type 53; dual purpose; pattern active/passive homing up to 20 km *(10.8 nm)* at up to 45 kts; warhead 400 kg or low yield nuclear.
A/S mortars: 2 RBU 6000 12-tubed trainable ❼; range 6000 m; warhead 31 kg.
2 RBU 1000 6-tubed (aft) (not in *Petropavlovsk*) ❽; range 1000 m; warhead 55 kg.
Countermeasures: Decoys: 2 twin chaff launchers. 1 BAT-1 torpedo decoy.
ESM/ECM: 8 Side Globe. 2 Bell Slam. 1 Bell Clout and 2 Bell Tap (in *Nikolayev* and *Ochakov*). 4 Rum Tub (fitted on mainmast in *Kerch*).

KERCH (with Flat Screen) *3/1990*

Fire control: 2 Tee Plinth (*Azov*) and 4 Tilt Pot optronic directors.
Radars: Air search: Top Sail ❾; 3D; D band; or Flat Screen; E/F band.
Air/surface search: Head Net C ❿; 3D; E band; range 128 km *(70 nm)*.
Navigation: Two Don Kay (not in *Nikolayev*); I band. Two Palm Frond (*Nikolayev* only); I band. Don 2 (not in *Azov*); I band.
Fire control: Two Head Light B or C (one in *Azov*) ⓫; F/G/H band (for SA-N-3 and SS-N-14). Two Pop Group ⓬; F/H/I band (for SA-N-4). Top Dome (aft in *Azov* in place of one Head Light C); J band (for SA-N-6). Two Owl Screech ⓭; G band (for 76 mm). Two Bass Tilt ⓮; H/I band (for 30 mm).
Tacan: Fly Screen A (not in all). Two Round House (*Petropavlovsk*).
IFF: High Pole A. High Pole B. Salt Pot/Square Head (*Nikolayev*).
Sonars: Bull Nose; hull-mounted; active search and attack; low/ medium frequency.
Mare Tail; VDS ⓯; active search; medium frequency.

Helicopters: 1 Ka-25 Hormone A ⓰.

Programmes: Apart from the specialised Moskva class this was the first class of large cruisers to join the Soviet Navy since the Sverdlov class—designed specifically for ASW. *Nikolayev* although commissioned in 1971 was first seen out of area when she entered the Mediterranean from the Black Sea on 2 March 1973. Type name is *bolshoy protivolodochny korabl*, meaning large anti-submarine ship.
Modernisation: The Flat Screen air search radar, first seen in *Kerch*, is expected to be retrofitted in all of the class. *Nikolayev* and *Tashkent* have been in dockyard refits in the Black Sea since July 1987.
Structure: *Azov* is of a modified design as the SA-N-6 trials ship and emerged from the Black Sea only in June 1986. All are fitted with stabilisers. *Petropavlovsk* has a higher hangar with two Round House Tacan on each side. The helicopter is raised to flight deck level by a lift in all of the class.

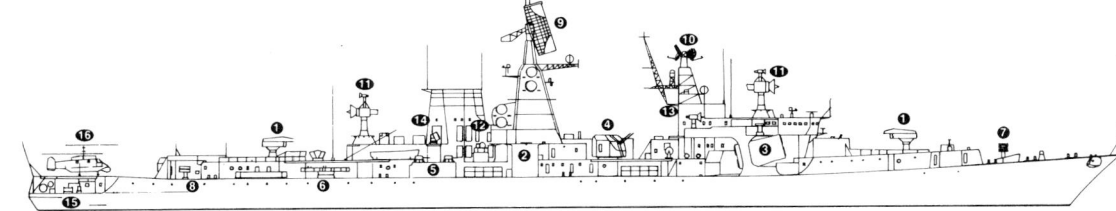

KARA class *(Scale 1 : 1200), Ian Sturton*

AZOV (with Top Dome and one Head Light) *6/1990*

542 RUSSIA / Destroyers

DESTROYERS
0 + 1 UDALOY II CLASS (DDG)

Name	Builders	Laid down	Launched	Commissioned
—	Yantar, Kaliningrad 820	1989	12 Dec 1992	1994

Displacement, tons: 8900 full load
Dimensions, feet (metres): 536.4 × 63.3 × 24.6 (163.5 × 19.3 × 7.5)
Main machinery: COGAG; 4 gas turbines; 2 shafts
Speed, knots: 30. **Range, miles:** 6000 at 20 kts
Complement: 250

Missiles: SSM: 4 SS-N-22 Sunburn ❶.
SAM: 8 SA-N-9 vertical launchers ❷.
SAM/Guns: 2 CADS-N-1 ❸; each with twin 30 mm Gatling; combined with 8 SA-N-11.
Guns: 2—130 mm/70 (twin) ❹.
Torpedoes: 10—21 in (533 mm) (2 quin tubes) ❺.
A/S mortars: 2 RBU 6000 ❻.
Radars: Air Search: Strut Pair ❼. Top Plate ❽.
Surface Search: Palm Frond ❾.
Fire Control: Band Stand ❿. 2 Cross Sword ⓫. Kite Screech ⓬.
CCA: Fly Screen B ⓭.

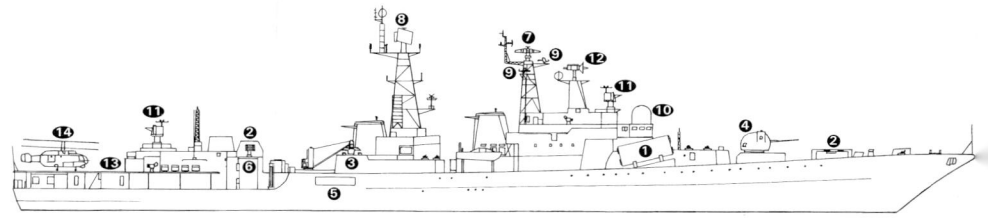

UDALOY II

(not to scale) Ian Sturton

Helicopters: 2 Ka-27 Helix A ⓮.

Programmes: Follow-on class from the Udaloys. Progress is very slow and only one of the class may be completed.

Structure: Similar size to the Udaloy and has the same propulsion machinery. Improved combination of weapon systems owing something to both the Sovremenny and the Neustrashimy classes.

12 UDALOY CLASS (DDG)

Name	Builders	Laid down	Launched	Commissioned
UDALOY	Yantar, Kaliningrad 820	1978	Feb 1980	Nov 1980
VITSE-ADMIRAL KULAKOV	Zhdanov Yard, Leningrad 190	1978	Apr 1980	Sep 1981
MARSHAL VASILEVSKY	Zhdanov Yard, Leningrad 190	1979	Jan 1982	June 1983
ADMIRAL ZAKHAROV	Yantar, Kaliningrad 820	1979	Nov 1982	Oct 1983
ADMIRAL SPIRIDONOV	Zhdanov Yard, Leningrad 190	1981	Nov 1983	Sep 1984
ADMIRAL TRIBUTS	Yantar, Kaliningrad 820	1980	Apr 1983	Aug 1985
MARSHAL SHAPOSHNIKOV	Yantar, Kaliningrad 820	1983	Jan 1985	Oct 1985
SIMFEROPOL (ex-Marshal Buokenny)	Yantar, Kaliningrad 820	1983	Feb 1985	Dec 1986
ADMIRAL LEVCHENKO	Yantar, Kaliningrad 820	1982	Mar 1985	Jan 1988
ADMIRAL VINOGRADOV	Yantar, Kaliningrad 820	1985	June 1987	Oct 1988
ADMIRAL KHARLAMOV	Yantar, Kaliningrad 820	1985	June 1988	Sep 1989
ADMIRAL PANTELEYEV	Yantar, Kaliningrad 820	1987	Feb 1990	July 1991

Displacement, tons: 6700 standard; 8700 full load
Dimensions, feet (metres): 536.4 × 63.3 × 24.6 (163.5 × 19.3 × 7.5)
Flight deck, feet (metres): 65.6 × 59 (20 × 18)
Main machinery: COGAG; 2 gas turbines; 55 500 hp(m) (40.8 MW); 2 gas turbines; 13 600 hp(m) (10 MW); 2 shafts
Speed, knots: 30. **Range, miles:** 2600 at 30 kts; 6000 at 20 kts
Complement: 249 (29 officers)

Missiles: SAM: 8 SA-N-9 vertical launchers ❶; command guidance; active radar homing to 12 km (6.6 nm) at 2 Mach; warhead 15 kg; altitude 3.4-12 192 m (10-40 000 ft); 64 missiles. Probably 4 channels of fire.
The launchers are set into the ships' structures with 6 ft diameter cover plates—four on the fo'c'sle, two between the torpedo tubes and two at the forward end of the after deckhouse between the RBUs.
A/S: 2 SS-N-14 Silex quad launchers ❷; command guidance to 55 km (30 nm) at 0.95 Mach; payload nuclear or Type E53 torpedo; active/passive homing to 15 km (8.1 nm) at 40 kts; warhead 150 kg. SSM version; range 35 km (19 nm); warhead 500 kg.
Guns: 2—3.9 in (100 mm)/70 ❸; 80° elevation; 80 rounds/minute to 15 km (8.2 nm); weight of shell 16 kg.
4—30 mm/65 ❹; 6 barrels per mounting; 85° elevation; 3000 rounds/minute combined to 2 km.
Torpedoes: 8—21 in (533 mm) (2 quad) tubes ❺. Type 53; dual purpose; pattern active/passive homing up to 20 km (10.8 nm) at up to 45 kts; warhead 400 kg or low yield nuclear.
A/S mortars: 2 RBU 6000 12-tubed trainable ❻; range 6000 m; warhead 31 kg.
Mines: Rails for 30 mines.
Countermeasures: Decoys: 8 ten-barrelled chaff launchers. US Masker type noise reduction.
ESM/ECM: 2 Bell Shroud. 2 Bell Squat. 4 Foot Ball (not in all).
Radars: Air search: One or two (Udaloy and Kulakov) Strut Pair ❼; F band.
Top Plate (not Udaloy and Kulakov) ❽; 3D/ D/E band.
Surface search: Three Palm Frond ❾; I band.
Fire Control: Two Eye Bowl ❿; F band (for SS-N-14). Two Cross Sword ⓫ (for SA-N-9). Kite Screech ⓬; H/I/K band (for 100 mm guns). Two Bass Tilt ⓭; H/I/K band (for 30 mm guns).
IFF: Salt Pot A and B.
Tacan: Two Round House.
CCA: Fly Screen B (by starboard hangar) ⓮.
Sonars: Horse Jaw; hull-mounted; active search and attack; low/medium frequency.
Horse Tail; VDS; active search; medium frequency.

Helicopters: 2 Ka-27 Helix A ⓯.

Programmes: Successor to Kresta II class but based on Krivak class design. Type name is *bolshoy protivolodochny korabl* meaning large anti-submarine ship.
Structure: The two hangars are set side by side with inclined elevating ramps to the flight deck. Has pre-wetting NBCD equipment and replenishment at sea gear. Initially SA-N-9 was not operational and the first three of the class commissioned without the Cross Sword fire control radars. There also seemed to be a shortage of Strut Pair radars and numbers three to seven initially had no air search radar on their foremasts on commissioning. These deficiencies are slowly being made good. Active stabilisers are fitted. The chaff launchers are fitted on both sides of the foremast and inboard of the torpedo tubes.
Operational: A general purpose ship with the emphasis on ASW and complementary to Sovremenny class. Good sea-keeping and endurance have been reported. Based as follows: Northern Fleet—*Udaloy, Vasilevsky, Simferopol, Kharlamov* and *Levchenko*; Pacific Fleet—*Zakharov, Spiridonov, Tributs, Shaposhnikov, Panteleyev* and *Vinogradov. Kulakov* returned to the Baltic from the Northern Fleet in 1992. *Admiral Zakharov* may be beyond economical repair after a fire in March 1992.

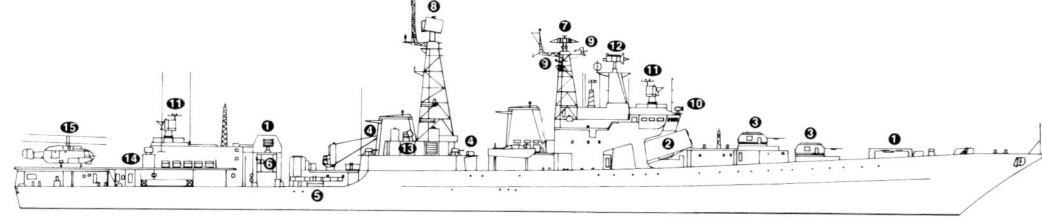

ADMIRAL SPIRIDONOV

(Scale 1 : 1200), Ian Sturton

MARSHAL SHAPOSHNIKOV

3/1992

16 + 3 SOVREMENNY CLASS (DDG)

Name	Builders	Laid down	Launched	Commissioned
SOVREMENNY	Zhdanov Yard, Leningrad	1977	Nov 1978	Aug 1980
OTCHYANNY	Zhdanov Yard, Leningrad	1977	Apr 1980	May 1982
OTLICHNNY	Zhdanov Yard, Leningrad	1978	Apr 1981	May 1983
OSMOTRITELNY	Zhdanov Yard, Leningrad	1979	Apr 1982	June 1984
BEZUPRECHNY	Zhdanov Yard, Leningrad	1980	Aug 1983	June 1985
BOYEVOY	Zhdanov Yard, Leningrad	1981	Aug 1984	June 1986
STOYKY	Zhdanov Yard, Leningrad	1982	Aug 1985	Sep 1986
OKRYLENNY	Zhdanov Yard, Leningrad	1983	June 1986	Sep 1987
BURNY	Zhdanov Yard, Leningrad	1984	Feb 1987	Aug 1988
GREMYASHCHY	Zhdanov Yard, Leningrad	1984	June 1987	Nov 1988
BYSTRY	Zhdanov Yard, Leningrad	1985	Dec 1987	Feb 1989
RASTOROPNY	Zhdanov Yard, Leningrad	1986	June 1988	Dec 1989
BEZBOYAZNENNY	Zhdanov Yard, Leningrad	1986	Mar 1989	Sep 1990
BEZUDERZHNY	Zhdanov Yard, Leningrad	1987	Oct 1990	Feb 1991
BESPOKOINY	Zhdanov Yard, Leningrad	1987	June 1990	Nov 1991
NASTOYCHIVY	North Yard, St Petersburg	1987	June 1991	Nov 1992
—	North Yard, St Petersburg	1988	Dec 1991	1993
—	North Yard, St Petersburg	1988	1993	1994
—	North Yard, St Petersburg	1989	1994	1995

Displacement, tons: 6500 standard; 7300 full load
Dimensions, feet (metres): 511.8 × 56.8 × 21.3 (156 × 17.3 × 6.5)
Main machinery: 4 boilers; 2 turbines; 102 000 hp(m) (75 MW); 2 shafts; bow thruster
Speed, knots: 32. **Range, miles:** 2400 at 32 kts; 6500 at 20 kts; 14 000 at 14 kts
Complement: 296 (25 officers)

Missiles: SSM: 8 SS-N-22 Sunburn (2 quad) launchers ❶; active radar homing to 110 km (60 nm) at 2.5 Mach; warhead nuclear or HE; sea-skimmer. Modified missile has a range of 160 km (87 nm).
SAM: 2 SA-N-7 Gadfly ❷; command/semi-active radar and IR homing to 28 km (15 nm) at 3 Mach; warhead 54 kg; altitude 30.4-14 020 (100-46 000 ft); 44 missiles. Multiple channels of fire.
Guns: 4—130 mm/70 (2 twin) ❸; 85° elevation; 35/45 rounds/minute to 29.5 km (16 nm); weight of shell 27 kg.
4—30 mm/65 ADG 630 ❹; 6 barrels per mounting; 85° elevation; 3000 rounds/minute combined to 2 km.
Torpedoes: 4—21 in (533 mm) (2 twin) tubes ❺. Type 53; dual purpose; pattern active/passive homing up to 20 km (10.8 nm) at up to 45 kts; warhead 400 kg or low yield nuclear.
A/S mortars: 2 RBU 1000 6-barrelled ❻; range 1000 m; warhead 55 kg; 120 rockets carried.
Mines: Have mine rails for up to 40.
Countermeasures: Decoys: 8 ten-barrelled chaff launchers.
ESM/ECM: 4 Foot Ball (some variations including 2 Bell Shroud and 2 Bell Squat).
Fire control: 1 Squeeze Box optronic director and laser rangefinder ❼. 2 Shot Dome.
Radars: Air search: Top Steer (in first three). Plate Steer (in 4th and 5th ships). Top Plate (remainder) ❽; 3D; D/E band.
Surface search: Three Palm Frond ❾; I band.
Fire control: Band Stand ❿; D/E/F band (for SS-N-22). Six Front Dome ⓫; F band (for SA-N-7). Kite Screech ⓬; H/I/K band (for 130 mm guns). Two Bass Tilt ⓭; H/I band (for 30 mm guns).
IFF: Salt Pot A and B. High Pole A and B. Long Head.
Tacan: Two Light Bulb.
Sonars: Bull Horn and Steer Hide; hull-mounted; active search and attack; medium frequency.

Helicopters: 1 Ka-25 Hormone B or Ka-27 Helix ⓮.

Programmes: Built at the same yard as the Kresta II class. Zhdanov was renamed North Yard in 1989. Type name is *eskadrenny minonosets* meaning destroyer. Building rate has slowed down to about one a year.

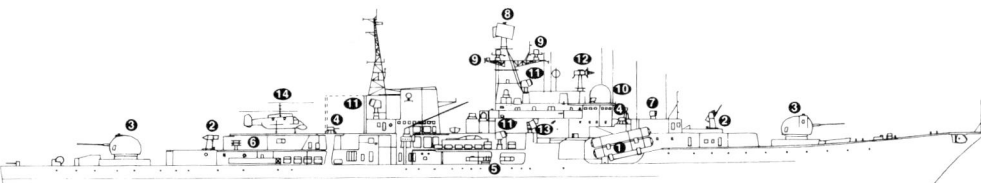

BOYEVOY (Scale 1 : 1200), Ian Sturton

Structure: Telescopic hangar. The fully automatic 130 mm gun was first seen in 1976. Chaff launchers are fitted on both sides of the foremast and either side of the after SAM launcher.
Operational: A specialist surface warfare ship complementing the ASW-capable Udaloy class. Based as follows: Northern Fleet—Sovremenny, Otchyanny, Otlichnny, Bezuprechny, Okrylenny, Gremyashchy, Rastoropny and Bezuderzhny. Pacific Fleet—Osmotritelny, Boyevoy, Stoyky, Burny, Bystry and Bezboyaznenny. Bespokoiny started trials in the Baltic in early 1992, Nastoychivy in November 1992.

BEZUDERZHNY 1/1992

BEZUPRECHNY (with Plate Steer) 7/1990, W Sartori

544 RUSSIA / Destroyers

6 KASHIN and 2 MODIFIED KASHIN CLASSES (TYPE 61MP) (DDG)

KRASNY-KAVKAZ	OBRAZTSOVY	SKORY	SMYSHLENNY*
KRASNY-KRYM	SDERZHANNY*	SMETLIVY	SPOSOBNY

* Modified

Displacement, tons: 3500 standard; 4750 full load (Kashin)
3950 standard; 4900 full load (mod Kashin)
Dimensions, feet (metres): 472.4 (482.3 mod) × 51.8 × 15.4 *(144 (147) × 15.8 × 4.7)*
Main machinery: COGAG; 4 gas turbines; 72 000 hp(m) *(52.9 MW)*; 2 shafts
Speed, knots: 35. **Range, miles:** 4000 at 20 kts; 2600 at 30 kts
Complement: 280 (20 officers, unmodified), (25 officers, modified).

Missiles: SSM: 4 SS-N-2C Styx (modified ships) ❶; active radar or IR homing to 83 km *(45 nm)* at 0.9 Mach; warhead 513 kg; sea-skimmer at end of run; no reloads.
  SAM: 2 SA-N-1 Goa twin launchers ❷; command guidance to 31.5 km *(17 nm)* at 2 Mach; warhead 60 kg; altitude 91.4-22 860 m *(300-75 000 ft)*; 32 missiles. Some SSM capability.
Guns: 4—3 in *(76 mm)*/60 (2 twin) ❸; 80° elevation; 90 rounds/minute to 15 km *(8 nm)*; weight of shell 6.8 kg.
  4—30 mm/65 (modified ships) ❹; 6 barrels per mounting; 85° elevation; 3000 rounds/minute combined to 2 km.
Torpedoes: 5—21 in *(533 mm)* (quin) tubes ❺. Type 53; dual purpose; pattern active/passive homing up to 20 km *(10.8 nm)* at up to 45 kts; warhead 400 kg or low yield nuclear.
A/S mortars: 2 RBU 6000 12-tubed trainable ❻; range 6000 m; warhead 31 kg; 120 rockets.
  2 RBU 1000 6-tubed (not in modified ships) ❼; range 1000 m; warhead 55 kg.
Mines: Laying capability (unmodified only) for up to 20.
Countermeasures: Decoys: 4—16-tubed chaff launchers (modified ships). 2 towed torpedo decoys.
ESM/ECM: 2 Bell Shroud. 2 Bell Squat (modified ships). 2 Watch Dog (remainder).
Fire control: 3 Tee Plinth and 4 Tilt Pot optronic directors.
Radars: Air/surface search: Head Net C ❽; 3D; E band; (except *Obraztsovy*).
  Big Net ❾; C band (except *Obraztsovy*).
  Two Head Net A ❿; E band *(Obraztsovy)*.
  Navigation: Two Don 2/Don Kay/Palm Frond; I band.
  Fire control: Two Peel Group ⓫; H/I band (for SA-N-1). Two Owl Screech ⓬; G band (for guns). Two Bass Tilt (modified ships) ⓭; H/I band (for 30 mm).
IFF: High Pole B (Modified ships).
Sonars: Bull Horn or Bull Nose; hull-mounted; active search and attack; medium frequency.
  Mare Tail; VDS (modified ships plus *Smetlivy* and *Sposobny*); search; medium frequency.

Helicopters: Platform only ⓮.

Programmes: The first class of warships in the world to rely entirely on gas-turbine propulsion. These ships were delivered from 1962 to 1972 from the Zhdanov Yard, Leningrad *(Obraztsovy)* (1965) and the remainder from the 61 Kommuna (North) Yard, Nikolayev (1962-72). *Sderzhanny*, last of the class, was the only one to be built to the modified design, *Smyshlenny* was converted after completion. Type name is *bolshoy protivolodochny korabl*, meaning large anti-submarine ship.
Modernisation: In order to bring this class up to date with SSM and VDS a conversion programme was started in 1972 to the same pattern as set in *Sderzhanny*. This conversion consisted of lengthening the hull by 10 ft *(3 m)*, shipping four SS-N-2 (C) launchers (SSM), four Gatling close range weapons, a VDS under a new stern helicopter platform and removing the after RBUs. All but two of the modified ships have been paid off.
Operational: One sank in the Black Sea in 1974. The class is now being paid off at the rate of about three a year. *Smetlivy* and *Sposobny* have been in refit in the Black Sea since 1987.
Sales: Additional ships of a modified design built for India. First transferred September 1980, the second in June 1982, the third in 1983, the fourth in August 1986 and the fifth and last in January 1988. All are fitted with helicopter hangars. *Smely* transferred to Poland 9 January 1988.

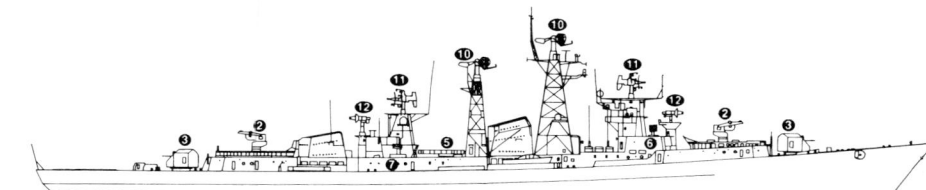
KRASNY-KRYM
(Scale 1 : 1200), Ian Sturton

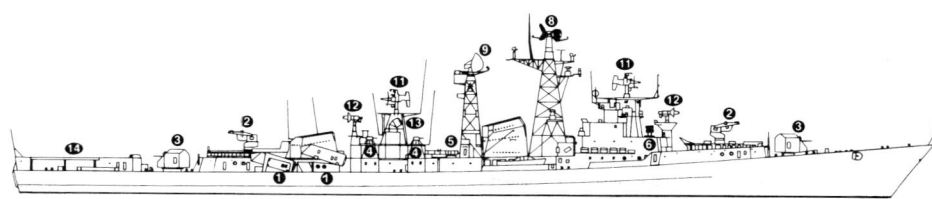
SMYSHLENNY
(Scale 1 : 1200), Ian Sturton

KRASNY-KRYM
6/1991, van Ginderen Collection

SKORY
4/1992, van Ginderen Collection

SDERZHANNY (modified)
6/1992, van Ginderen Collection

Frigates / RUSSIA

Note: In addition to the Gepard class, Russian industry is also advertising a new corvette. This is a ship of 1560 tons and 86 m in length, powered by two diesels for a speed of 25 knots.

FRIGATES

Designed by the Northern Design Bureau for export it is equipped with SS-N-25 SSM, SA-N-4 SAM, 76 mm gun, 4 single torpedo tubes and a Helix helicopter. A prototype may be built as a demonstrater.

1 + 2 NEUSTRASHIMY CLASS (FFG)

Name	Builders	Laid down	Launched	Commissioned
NEUSTRASHIMY	Yantar, Kaliningrad	Apr 1986	May 1988	24 Jan 1993
—	Yantar, Kaliningrad	May 1988	May 1991	1994
—	Yantar, Kaliningrad	Sep 1990	Aug 1992	1995

Displacement, tons: 4100 full load
Dimensions, feet (metres): 423.2 oa; 403.5 wl × 50.9 × 15.7 *(129; 123 × 15.5 × 4.8)*
Main machinery: COGAG; 4 gas turbines; 68 000 hp(m) *(50 MW)*; 2 shafts
Speed, knots: 32
Complement: 200
Missiles: SSM: 8 SS-N-25 ❶ active radar homing to 130 km *(70.2 nm)* at 0.9 Mach; warhead 145 kg; sea-skimmer.
SAM: 4 SA-N-9 sextuple vertical launchers ❷; command guidance; active radar homing to 12 km *(6.6 nm)* at 2 Mach; warhead 15 kg.
SAM/Guns: 2 CADS-N-1 ❸; each has a twin 30 mm Gatling combined with 8 SA-N-11 and Hot Flash/Hot Spot fire control radar/optronic director. Laser beam guidance for missiles to 8 km *(4.4 nm)*; 4500 rounds/minute (combined) to 2 km (for guns).
A/S: SS-N-15 type; inertial flight to 120 km *(65 nm)*; payload Type 45 torpedo or nuclear warhead; fired from torpedo tubes.
Guns: 1—3.9 in *(100 mm)*/70 ❹; 80° elevation; 80 rounds/minute to 15 km *(8.2 nm)*; weight of shell 16 kg.
Torpedoes: 6—21 in *(533 mm)* tubes combined with A/S launcher ❺; can fire SS-N-15 missiles or anti-submarine torpedoes.
A/S mortars: 1 RBU 12 000 ❻; 10-tubed trainable; range 12 000 m; warhead 80 kg.
Mines: 2 rails.
Countermeasures: Decoys: 2—10-barrelled chaff launchers.
ESM/ECM: Intercept and jammers. 2 Bell Crown; 2 Foot Ball; 2 Half Hat; 3 Cage Flask.
Radars: Air/surface search: Top Plate ❼; 3D; D/E band.
Navigation: 2 Palm Frond; I band.
Fire control: Cross Dome ❽ (for SAM); E/F band. Kite Screech ❾ (for SSM and guns); I band.
IFF: 2 Salt Pot.
Sonars: Bull Nose; hull-mounted; active search and attack.
Steer Hide VDS ❿ or towed sonar array.
Helicopters: 1 Ka-27 Helix ⓫.

Programmes: The last naval (as opposed to Border Guard) Krivak class frigate commissioned in 1981 and a follow-on class has been expected for some time. The first of class started sea trials in the Baltic in December 1990. Build rate appears to be about one a year but as the third of class was launched with sections of hull blanked off it is possible it may be completed at St Petersburg.
Structure: This ship is slightly larger than the Krivak and has a helicopter which is a standard part of the armament of modern Western frigates. There are three horizontal launchers at main deck level on each side of the ship, angled at 18° from forward. These double up for A/S missiles of the submarine-launched SS-N-15 type and normal torpedoes. Similar launchers are behind shutters in the last three of the Kirov class. The helicopter deck extends across the full width of the ship. The after funnel is unusually flush decked.

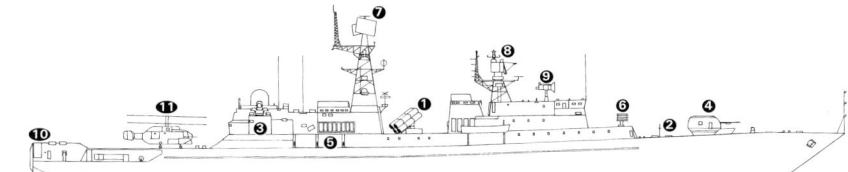

NEUSTRASHIMY *(Scale 1 : 1200), Ian Sturton*

NEUSTRASHIMY *3/1991, MoD Bonn*

NEUSTRASHIMY *3/1991, MoD Bonn*

546 RUSSIA / Frigates

20 KRIVAK I (FFG), 11 KRIVAK II (FFG) and 9 KRIVAK III (BUREVESTNIK) CLASSES (FF)

KRIVAK I (Kaliningrad)	KRIVAK I (Zhdanov, Leningrad*) (Kamysh-Burun (Kerch))	KRIVAK II (Kaliningrad)	KRIVAK III (Zaliv (Kerch))
BDITELNY	LENINGRADSKY KOMSOMOLETS*	BESSMENNY	MENZHINSKY
BODRY	LETUCHY*	GORDELIVY	DZERZHINSKY
DRUZHNY	PYLKY*	GROMKY	OREL (ex-Imeni XXVII Sezda KPSS)
RAZUMNY	RETIVY*	GROZYASHCHY	IMENI LXX LETIYA VCHK-KGB
SILNY	ZADORNY*	NEUKROTIMY (ex-Komsomolets Litvii)	IMENI LXX LETIYA POGRANVOYSK
STOROZHEVOY	ZHARKY*	PYTLIVY	KEDROV
SVIREPY	BEZZAVETNY	RAZITELNY	VOROVSKY
	BEZUKORIZNENNY	REVNOSTNY	HETMAN DOROSENKO
	DOSTOYNY	REZKY	HETMAN PETR SAGADACHNY
	DOBLESTNY	REZVY	
	DEYATELNY	RYANNY	
	LADNY		
	PORYVISTY		

Displacement, tons: 3100 standard; 3600 full load
Dimensions, feet (metres): 405.2 × 46.9 × 16.4 *(123.5 × 14.3 × 5)*
Main machinery: COGAG; 2 gas turbines; 55 500 hp(m) *(40.8 MW)*; 2 gas turbines; 13 600 hp(m) *(10 MW)*; 2 shafts
Speed, knots: 32. **Range, miles:** 4600 at 20 kts; 1600 at 30 kts
Complement: 180 (18 officers)

Missiles: SSM: 8 SS-N-25 (2 quad) ❶; (Krivak I after modernisation); active radar homing to 130 km *(70.2 nm)* at 0.9 Mach; warhead 145 kg; sea-skimmer.
  SAM: 2 SA-N-4 Gecko twin launchers (1 in Krivak III) ❷; semi-active radar homing to 15 km *(8 nm)* at 2.5 Mach; warhead 50 kg; altitude 9.1-3048 m *(30-10 000 ft)*; 40 missiles (20 in Krivak III). The launcher retracts into the mounting for stowage and protection, rising to fire and retracting to reload. The two mountings are forward of the bridge and abaft the funnel.
A/S: SS-N-14 Silex quad launcher (not in Krivak III) ❸; command guidance to 55 km *(30 nm)* at 0.95 Mach; payload nuclear or Type E53 torpedo; active/passive homing to 15 km *(8.1 nm)* at 40 kts; warhead 150 kg. SSM version; range 35 km *(19 nm)*; warhead 500 kg.
Guns: 4—3 in *(76 mm)*/60 (2 twin) (Krivak I) ❹; 80° elevation; 90 rounds/minute to 15 km *(8 nm)*; weight of shell 6.8 kg.
  2—3.9 in *(100 mm)*/70 (Krivak II) (1 in Krivak III) ❺; 80° elevation; 80 rounds/minute to 15 km *(8.2 nm)*; weight of shell 16 kg.
  2—30 mm/65 (Krivak III) ❻; 6 barrels per mounting; 3000 rounds/minute combined to 2 km.
Torpedoes: 8—21 in *(533 mm)* (2 quad) tubes ❼. Type 53; dual purpose; pattern active/passive homing up to 20 km *(10.8 nm)* at up to 45 kts; warhead 400 kg or low yield nuclear.
A/S mortars: 2 RBU 6000 12-tubed trainable ❽; (not in modernised Krivak I); range 6000 m; warhead 31 kg.
Mines: Capacity for 20.
Countermeasures: Decoys: 4 chaff launchers (16 tubes per launcher) or 10 (10 tubes per launcher). Towed torpedo decoy.
ESM/ECM: 2 Bell Shroud. 2 Bell Squat.
Radars: Air search: Head Net C ❾; 3D; E band; range 128 km *(70 nm)*. Top Plate *(Imeni XXVII* and later and some Krivak I after modernisation) ❿.
  Surface search: Don Kay or Palm Frond or Don 2 or Spin Trough ⓫; I band.
  Peel Cone ⓬; I band (Krivak III).
  Fire control: Two Eye Bowl (not in Krivak III) ⓭; F band (for SS-N-14). Two Pop Group (one in Krivak III) ⓮; F/H/I band (for SA-N-4). Owl Screech (Krivak I) ⓯; G band. Kite Screech (Krivak II and III) ⓰; H/I/K band. Bass Tilt (Krivak III) ⓱; H/I band.
IFF: High Pole B. Salt Pot (Krivak III).
Sonars: Bull Nose; hull-mounted; active search and attack; medium frequency.
  Mare Tail or Steer Hide *(Zharky, Bditelny, Leningradsky Komsomolets* and other Krivak Is after modernisation); VDS ⓲; active search; medium frequency.

Helicopters: 1 Ka-25 Hormone or Ka-27 Helix (Krivak III) ⓳.

Programmes: The Krivak I class built from 1969-1981, Krivak II from 1976-81 and Krivak III from 1984-1992. Type name was originally *bolshoy protivolodochny korabl*, meaning large anti-submarine ship. Changed in 1977-78 to *storozhevoy korabl* meaning escort ship. Most of the Krivak III names seem certain to be changed. The last pair have been given Ukrainian names.
Modernisation: Krivak Is are being modernised with SS-N-25 quadruple launchers replacing RBU mountings forward of the bridge. Top Plate radar is replacing Head Net and a more modern VDS is also being fitted.
Structure: Krivak II class has X-gun mounted higher and the break to the quarter-deck further aft apart from other variations noted. Krivak III class built for the former KGB but now under naval control. The removal of SS-N-14 and one SA-N-4 mounting compensates for the addition of a hangar and flight deck.
Operational: First Krivak I paid off in 1992 in the Pacific.

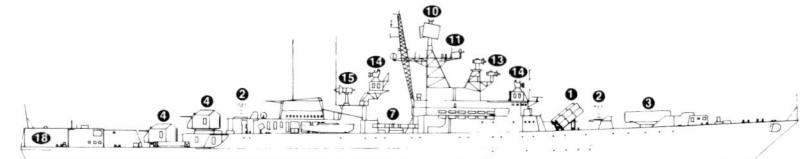
KRIVAK I (mod) *(Scale 1 : 1200), Ian Sturton*

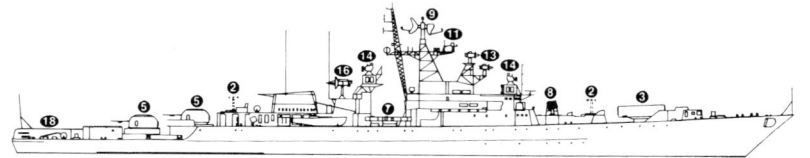
KRIVAK II *(Scale 1 : 1200), Ian Sturton*

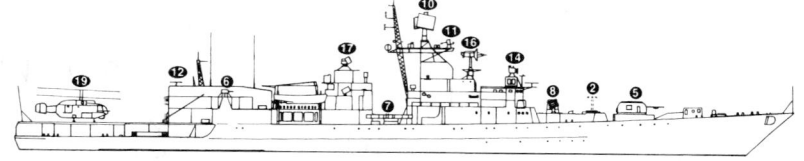
KRIVAK III *(Scale 1 : 1200), Ian Sturton*

NEUKROTIMY (II) *6/1991, Harald Carstens*

DRUZHNY (I) *3/1992, MoD Bonn*

LENINGRADSKY KOMSOMOLETS (I)   10/1991
(with SS-N-25 rails, Top Plate radar and Steer Hide VDS)

BDITELNY (I)   6/1991, Guy Toremans
(with Head Net radar and Mare Tail VDS)

PYTLIVY (II)   3/1992

OROVSKY (III) (with Top Plate)   10/1991

548 RUSSIA / Frigates

12 GRISHA I, 12 GRISHA II, 28 GRISHA III and 29 + 3 GRISHA V (ALBATROS) CLASSES (FFL)

AMETYST, BRILLIANT, IZUMRUD, PREDANNY, IZMAIL, DNEPR, RESITELNY, PRIMERNY, RUBIN, SAPFIR, ZHEMCHUG, PROVORNY
(All Grisha II class (Border Guard))

Displacement, tons: 950 standard; 1200 full load
Dimensions, feet (metres): 236.2 × 32.8 × 12.1 *(72 × 10 × 3.7)*
Main machinery: CODAG; 1 gas turbine; 15 000 hp(m) *(11 MW)*; 2 diesels; 16 000 hp(m) *(11.8 MW)*; 3 shafts
Speed, knots: 30. **Range, miles:** 4500 at 10 kts; 1750 at 22 kts diesels; 950 at 27 kts
Complement: 70 (Grisha III); 60 (Grisha I)

Missiles: SAM: SA-N-4 Gecko twin launcher (Grisha I, III and V classes) ❶; semi-active radar homing to 15 km *(8 nm)* at 2.5 Mach; warhead 50 kg; altitude 9.1-3048 m *(30-10 000 ft)*; 20 missiles (see *Structure* for SA-N-9).
Guns: 2—57 mm/80 (twin) (2 twin in Grisha II class) ❷; 85° elevation; 120 rounds/minute to 6 km *(3.3 nm)*; weight of shell 2.8 kg.
1—3 in *(76 mm)*/60 (Grisha V) ❸; 85° elevation; 120 rounds/minute to 15 km *(8 nm)*; weight of shell 7 kg.
1—30 mm/65 (Grisha III and V classes) ❹; 6 barrels; 85° elevation; 3000 rounds/minute combined to 2 km.
Torpedoes: 4—21 in *(533 mm)* (2 twin) tubes ❺. Type 53; dual purpose; pattern active/passive homing up to 20 km *(10.8 nm)* at up to 45 kts; warhead 400 kg or low yield nuclear.
A/S mortars: 2 RBU 6000 12-tubed trainable ❻; range 6000 m; warhead 31 kg. (Only 1 in Grisha Vs).
Depth charges: 2 racks (12).
Mines: Capacity for 18 in lieu of depth charges.
Countermeasures: ESM: 2 Watch Dog. 1—10-barrelled chaff launcher (Grisha V).
Radars: Air/surface search: Strut Curve (Strut Pair in early Grisha Vs) ❼; F band; range 110 km *(60 nm)* for 2 m² target.
Half Plate Bravo (in later Grisha Vs); E/F band.
Navigation: Don 2; I band.
Fire control: Pop Group (Grisha I, III and V) ❽; F/H/I band (for SA-N-4). Muff Cob (except in Grisha III and V) ❾; G/H band (for 57 mm). Bass Tilt (Grisha III and V) ❿; H/I band (for 57/76 mm and 30 mm).
IFF: High Pole A or B. Square Head. Salt Pot.
Sonars: Hull-mounted; active search and attack; high/medium frequency.
VDS ⓫; active search; high frequency. Similar to Hormone helicopter dipping sonar.

Programmes: Grisha I series production 1968-75; Grisha II 1973-84; Grisha III 1973-85; Grisha V 1982 onwards. All were built or are building at Kiev, Kharbarovsk and Zelenodolsk except Grisha II which were only built at Zelenodolsk. Type name is *maly protivolodochny korabl* meaning small anti-submarine ship (Grisha I, III and V) or *pogranichny storozhevoy korabl* meaning border patrol ship (Grisha II).
Structure: SA-N-4 launcher mounted on the fo'c'sle in all but Grisha II. This is replaced by a second twin 57 mm in Grisha II class. Grisha III class has Muff Cob radar removed, Bass Tilt and 30 mm ADG (fitted aft), and Rad-haz screen removed from abaft funnel as a result of removal of Muff Cob. Grisha V is similar to Grisha III with the after twin 57 mm mounting replaced by a single Tarantul type 76 mm gun. One Grisha III in the Black Sea was modified as the trials unit for the SA-N-9/Cross Swords SAM system in the early 1980s and is sometimes known as Grisha IV.

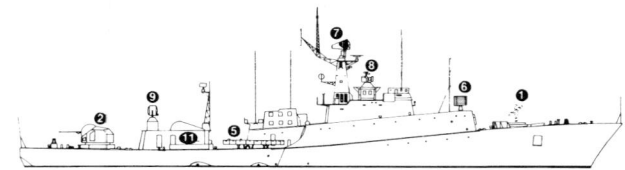
GRISHA I *(Scale 1 : 900), Ian Sturton*

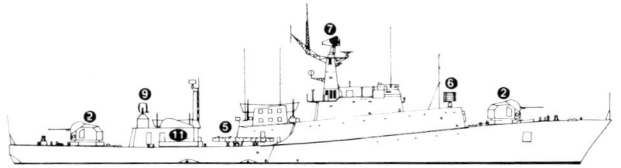
GRISHA II *(Scale 1 : 900), Ian Sturton*

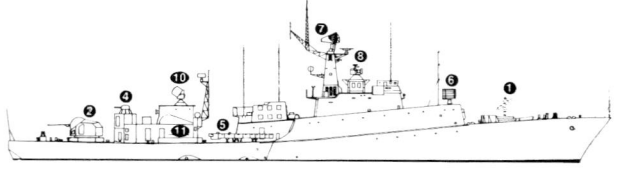
GRISHA III *(Scale 1 : 900), Ian Sturton*

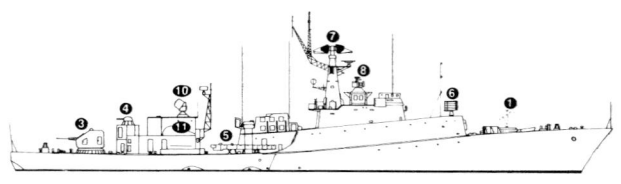
GRISHA V *(Scale 1 : 900), Ian Sturton*

Operational: Grisha II and six Grisha III are Border Guard ships and have names. Some Grisha III and V may have 2 SA-N-5 launchers. Grisha I are beginning to pay off.
Sales: Two Grisha III to Lithuania in November 1992.

GRISHA I 5/1990

GRISHA III 7/1991

GRISHA II 7/1992

GRISHA V 3/199

Frigates / RUSSIA 549

1 + 2 GEPARD CLASS (FFG)

Displacement, tons: 1900 full load
Dimensions, feet (metres): 334.6 × 44.6 × 14.4
  (102 × 13.6 × 4.4)
Main machinery: CODOG; 2 gas turbines; 2 diesels; 2 shafts; cp props
Speed, knots: 26 (18 on diesels). **Range, miles:** 3500 at 18 kts
Complement: 110 plus 21 spare

Missiles: SSM: 8 SS-N-25 (2 quad) ❶; IR or radar homing to 130 km *(70.2 nm)* at 0.9 Mach; warhead 145 kg; sea-skimmer.
  SAM: 1 SA-N-4 Gecko twin launcher ❷; semi-active radar homing to 15 km *(8 nm)* at 2.5 Mach; warhead 50 kg.
Guns: 1—3 in *(76 mm)*/60 ❸; 85° elevation; 120 rounds/minute to 15 km *(8 nm)*; weight of shell 7 kg.
  2—30 mm/65 ADG 630 ❹; 6 barrels per mounting; 85° elevation; 3000 rounds/minute combined to 2 km.
Torpedoes: 4—21 in *(533 mm)* (2 twin) tubes ❺. Type 53; dual purpose; pattern active/passive homing up to 20 km *(10.8 nm)* at up to 45 kts; warhead 400 kg.
A/S mortars: 1 RBU 6000 12-tubed trainable ❻; range 6000 m; warhead 31 kg.
Mines: 2 rails.
Countermeasures: Decoys: 4 chaff launchers.
  ESM/ECM: Intercept and jammers.
Radars: Air/surface search: Cross Dome ❼; E/F band.
  Band Stand ❽; D/E/F band.
  Fire control: Bass Tilt ❾; H/I band (for guns and SSM). Pop Group ❿; F/H/I band (for SAM).
  Navigation: Palm Frond; I band.
Sonars: Hull-mounted; active search and attack; medium frequency.
  VDS ⓫; active search and attack; medium frequency.

Programmes: Successor to the Koni class being built at Zelenodolsk. First of class trials in 1993. Available for export.
Structure: A logical development of existing light frigate classes with the addition of SS-N-25. Stealth features are claimed and the ship has roll stabilisers and air-conditioned spaces.

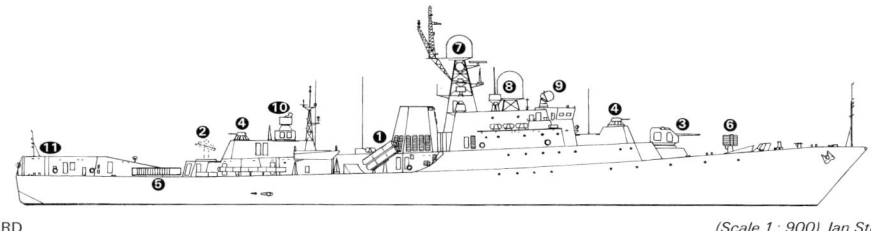

GEPARD   *(Scale 1 : 900), Ian Sturton*

GEPARD (artist's impression)   1/1993

12 PARCHIM II CLASS (FFL)

Displacement, tons: 769 standard; 1200 full load
Dimensions, feet (metres): 246.7 × 32.2 × 14.4
  (75.2 × 9.8 × 4.4)
Main machinery: 3 Type M 504A diesels; 10 812 hp(m) *(7.95 MW)* sustained; 3 shafts
Speed, knots: 28
Complement: 60

Missiles: SAM: 2 SA-N-5 Grail quad launchers ❶; manual aiming; IR homing to 6 km *(3.2 nm)* at 1.5 Mach; altitude to 2500 m *(8000 ft)*; warhead 1.5 kg.
Guns: 1—3 in *(76 mm)*/66 ❷; 85° elevation; 120 rounds/minute to 15 km *(8 nm)*; weight of shell 7 kg.
  1—30 mm/65 ❸; 6 barrels; 85° elevation; 3000 rounds/minute combined to 2 km.
Torpedoes: 4—21 in *(533 mm)* (2 twin) tubes ❹. Type 53; dual purpose.
A/S mortars: 2 RBU 6000 12-tubed trainable ❺; range 6000 m; warhead 31 kg.
Depth charges: 2 racks.
Mines: Rails fitted.
Countermeasures: Decoys: 2—16 barrelled chaff launchers.
  ESM: 2 Watch Dog.
Radars: Air/surface search: Cross Dome ❻; E/F band.
  Navigation: TSR 333; I band.
  Fire control: Bass Tilt ❼; H/I band.
Sonars: Hull-mounted; active search and attack; medium frequency.
  Helicopter type VDS; high frequency.

Programmes: Built in the GDR at Peenewerft, Wolgast for the Soviet Navy. First one commissioned 19 December 1986 and the last on 6 April 1990.
Structure: Similar design to the ex-GDR Parchim I class but some armament differences.
Operational: All operate in the Baltic.

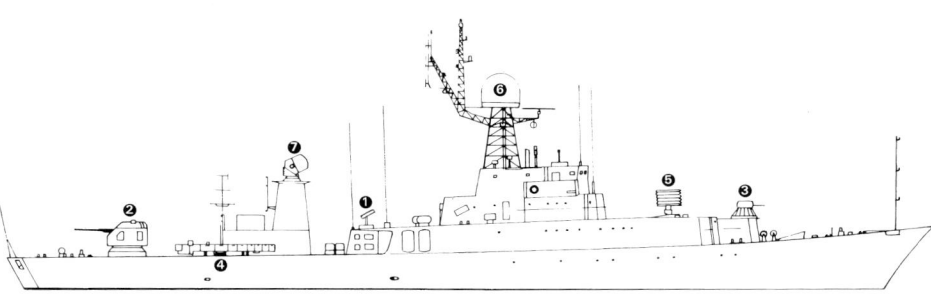

PARCHIM II   *(Scale 1 : 600), Ian Sturton*

PARCHIM II   1992

1 PETYA I, 4 MODIFIED PETYA I, 8 PETYA II and 1 MODIFIED PETYA II CLASSES (FFL)

Displacement, tons: 950 standard; 1180 full load
Dimensions, feet (metres): 268.3 (270.6, Mod Petya II) × 29.9 × 9.5 *(81.8 (82.5) × 9.1 × 2.9)*
Main machinery: CODAG; 2 gas turbines; 30 000 hp(m) *(22 MW)*; 1 Type 61V-3 diesel; 5400 hp(m) *(3.97 MW)* sustained (centre shaft); 3 shafts
Speed, knots: 32. **Range, miles:** 4870 at 10 kts; 450 at 29 kts
Complement: 98

Guns: 4—3 in *(76 mm)*/60 (2 twin); (1 twin in some Mod Petya I); 80° elevation; 90 rounds/minute to 15 km *(8 nm)*; weight of shell 6.8 kg.
Torpedoes: 10 (Petya II) or 5 (remainder) 16 in *(406 mm)* (2 or 1 quin) tubes. Type 40; anti-submarine; active/passive homing to 15 km *(8.1 nm)* at 40 kts; warhead 100 kg.
A/S mortars: 4 (Petya I) or 2 (Mod Petya I) RBU 2500 16-tubed trainable; range 2500 m; warhead 21 kg.
 2 RBU 6000 12-tubed trainable (Petya II and Mod Petya II); range 6000 m; warhead 31 kg.
Depth charges: 2 racks (not in Mod Petya II and some Mod Petya I).
Mines: Capacity for 22 (not in Mod Petya I).
Countermeasures: ESM: 2 Watch Dog; radar warning.
Radars: Air/surface search: Slim Net (Petya I); E/F band.
 Strut Curve (Petya II); F band; range 110 km *(60 nm)* for 2 m² target.
 Navigation: Neptun or Don 2 (Petya I); I band. Don 2 (Mod Petya I and II); I band.
 Fire control: Hawk Screech; I band; range 27 km *(15 nm)*.
 IFF: Two Square Head (Petya I). High Pole B (Petya I and II).
Sonars: Hull-mounted; active search and attack; high/medium frequency.
 VDS (in some); active search; high frequency.

Programmes: The first ship was built in 1960-61 at Kaliningrad. Construction continued there and at Komsomolsk until about 1970.
Structure: Petya I—the basic hull and armament.
 Mod Petya I—carry towed sonar in a deckhouse on the stern. One has a towed acoustic sensor in the open with no deckhouse. One has a deckhouse abaft the funnel replacing the quintuple torpedo tube mounting and a reel and winch on the stern similar to a towed array, while another has a deckhouse smaller than the remainder on the stern.
 Petya II—extra quin torpedo tubes vice after RBUs.
 Mod Petya II—first seen in 1978. After torpedo tubes removed and with a deckhouse built abaft the after 3 in *(76 mm)* gun to contain the towed trials equipment. There is a space either side for mine rails.
Operational: Numbers represent operational hulls in early 1993. More are being scrapped. One Petya II 'defected' to Ukraine in July 1992; two more were under Azerbaijan control from November 1992.
Sales: Petya III (sales version)—ten to India, two to Syria and two to Vietnam December 1978. Some of these have been deleted including one Indian ship which sank in 1990. These export versions are on Petya II hulls but fitted with one triple 21 in *(533 mm)* torpedo tube mounting in place of the two 16 in *(406 mm)* mountings and four RBU 2500s in place of two RBU 6000s. In addition other Petya II of Soviet type have been transferred: to Ethiopia—one in July 1983, second in March 1984, and to Vietnam—two in December 1983 and one in December 1984.

Mod PETYA I 6/1989

PETYA II 9/1991

SHIPBORNE AIRCRAFT

Note: All Yak-38 Forger aircraft have been taken out of service.

Numbers/Type: 125 Kamov Ka-25 Hormone.
Operational speed: 119 kts *(220 km/h)*.
Service ceiling: 11 500 ft *(3500 m)*.
Range: 350 nm *(650 km)*.
Role/Weapon systems: First Soviet successful shipborne ASW helicopter (being replaced by 'Helix'). 'A' version for ASW, 'B' for recce (called REB) and 'C' for utility; 25 Ka-25B versions reported. Sensors: Puff Ball search radar, dipping sonar, sonobuoys, MAD, ECM (A), EW equipment and Big Bulge search radar (B), Radar only (C). Weapons: ASW; 2 × torpedoes, nuclear or conventional depth bombs (A). ASV; 2 or 4 × missiles or rocket launchers (A).

Numbers/Type: 5 Kamov Ka-34 Hokum.
Operational speed: 189 kts *(350 km/h)*.
Service ceiling: 20 175 ft *(6150 m)*.
Range: 135 nm *(250 km)*.
Role/Weapon systems: Possible amphibious assault role still being evaluated. Full production started in 1991.

HORMONE 8/1992

HOKUM 1992

Numbers/Type: 170 Kamov Ka-27/Ka-29 Helix A/B.
Operational speed: 135 kts *(250 km/h)*.
Service ceiling: 19 685 ft *(6000 m)*.
Range: 432 nm *(800 km)*.
Role/Weapon systems: ASW helicopter; successor to 'Hormone' with greater ASW potential; three versions—'A' for ASW, 'B' for assault, 'C' for SAR/utility; deployed to surface ships and some shore stations. Sensors: Search radar, dipping sonar, sonobuoys, MAD, ECM. Weapons: ASW; 3 × torpedoes, nuclear or conventional depth bombs or mines. Assault type: 2 UV-57 rocket pods (2 × 32).

HELIX *8/1992*

Numbers/Type: 15/5 Sukhoi Su-27 Flanker B/D.
Operational speed: 1345 kts *(2500 km/h)*.
Service ceiling: 59 000 ft *(18 000 m)*.
Range: 2160 + nm *(4000 km)*.
Role/Weapon systems: Fleet air defence fighter. Sensors: Track-while-scan pulse Doppler radar, IR scanner. Weapons: 1 × 30 mm cannon, 10 × AAMs (AA-10, AA-11, AA-8, AA-9), 1 × ASM.

FLANKER *8/1992, Linda Jackson*

Numbers/Type: 85 Sukhoi Su-25UD Frogfoot B.
Operational speed: 526 kts *(975 km/h)*.
Service ceiling: 22 965 ft *(7000 m)*.
Range: 675 nm *(1250 km)*.
Role/Weapon systems: Two seater ground attack aircraft used for deck trials in the carrier *Kuznetsov* but not considered a likely candidate for the normal air wing complement.

Numbers/Type: 10 Mikoyan MiG-29 Fulcrum D.
Operational speed: 1320 kts *(2450 km/h)*.
Service ceiling: 56 000 ft *(17 000 m)*.
Range: 1130 nm *(2100 km)*.
Role/Weapon systems: Fleet air defence fighter or ground attack. Sensors: pulse Doppler radar, IR scanner, laser rangefinder. Weapons: 1 × 30 mm cannon, 6 × AA-10 and/or AA-11, 2 × ASM.

FULCRUM *8/1992, Linda Jackson*

Numbers/Type: 40 Mil Mi-14BT Haze B.
Operational speed: 124 kts *(230 km/h)*.
Service ceiling: 15 000 ft *(4570 m)*.
Range: 432 nm *(800 km)*.
Role/Weapon systems: Minesweeping and possible minelaying helicopter; seen in action in Red Sea in 1985. Sensors: Search radar, sweep gear. Weapons: Unarmed.

HAZE *6/1989*

Numbers/Type: 1 Yakovlev Yak-41 Freestyle.
Operational speed: 984 kts *(1800 km/h)*.
Service ceiling: 49 200 ft *(15 000 m)*.
Range: 1150 nm *(2100 km)*.
Role/Weapon systems: Follow-on to the Forger. STOVL development which has run into problems and may even be cancelled. Much may depend on the future of the Russian aircraft carriers.

FREESTYLE *8/1991*

LAND-BASED MARITIME AIRCRAFT (FRONT LINE)

Notes: 1. The numbers listed below do not include some 680 Fencer, Flogger, Fitter, Fulcrum and Frogfoot aircraft transferred from the Air Force in 1989-91 to naval bases apparently to place them outside CFE arms reduction negotiations. Some transferred to the independent Republics in 1992.
2. All Mi-8 Hip aircraft out of service by late 1992.

Numbers/Type: 100 Beriev Be-12 Mail.
Operational speed: 328 kts *(608 km/h)*.
Service ceiling: 37 000 ft *(11 280 m)*.
Range: 4050 nm *(7500 km)*.
Role/Weapon systems: Long-range ASW/MR amphibian in arctic waters, Baltic and Black Sea areas; to be replaced by mid-1990s. Sensors: Search/weather radar, sonobuoys, MAD, EW. Weapons: ASW; 5 tons of depth bombs, mines or torpedoes, nuclear-capable. ASV; limited missile and rocket armament.

Numbers/Type: 3 Ilyushin Il-20 Coot A.
Operational speed: 364 kts *(675 km/h)*.
Service ceiling: 32 800 ft *(10 000 m)*.
Range: 3508 nm *(6500 km)*.
Role/Weapon systems: Long-range Elint and MR for naval forces' intelligence gathering, especially in European waters. Sensors: SLAR, weather radar, cameras, Elint equipment. Weapons: Unarmed.

MAIL *5/1992*

552 RUSSIA / Land-based maritime aircraft (front line) — Light missile forces

Numbers/Type: 45 Ilyushin Il-38 May.
Operational speed: 347 kts (645 km/h).
Service ceiling: 32 800 ft (10 000 m).
Range: 3887 nm (7200 km).
Role/Weapon systems: Long-range MR and ASW over Atlantic, Indian and Mediterranean Sea areas. Sensors: Wet Eye search/weather radar, MAD, sonobuoys. Weapons: ASW; internal storage for 6 tons weapons.

MAY 5/1992

Numbers/Type: 8 Antonov An-12 Cub ('Cub B/C/D') ('Cub C/D' ECM/ASW).
Operational speed: 419 kts (777 km/h).
Service ceiling: 33 500 ft (10 200 m).
Range: 3075 nm (5700 km).
Role/Weapon systems: Used either for intelligence gathering (B) or electronic warfare (C, D); is versatile with long range; operated by and for all Soviet Fleets and in support of client states. Sensors: Search/weather radar, 3 × EW blisters (B), tail-mounted EW/Elint equipment in addition (C/D). Weapons: Self-defence; 2 × 23 mm cannon (B and D only).

Numbers/Type: 70 Mil Mi-14PL/BT/PS Haze A/C.
Operational speed: 124 kts (230 km/h).
Service ceiling: 15 000 ft (4570 m).
Range: 432 nm (800 km).
Role/Weapon systems: ASW (A) and assault (C) helicopters for medium-range operations. Sensors: Search radar, dipping sonar, sonobuoys, MAD, EW (A only). Weapons: ASW; 4 × torpedoes, nuclear or conventional depth bombs or mines (A); self-defence weapons (B).

Numbers/Type: 150 Sukhoi Su-17 Fitter C/D.
Operational speed: Mach 2.09.
Service ceiling: 59 050 ft (18 000 m).
Range: 700 nm (1300 km).
Role/Weapon systems: Anti-ship and support strike aircraft. Sensors: Attack radar, ECM. Weapons: ASV; 2 × 30 mm cannon and 3.5 tons of underwing stores, including rockets and missiles. Self-defence; can mount AAMs.

Numbers/Type: 20 Tupolev Tu-22 Blinder.
Operational speed: 800 kts (1480 km/h).
Service ceiling: 60 000 ft (18 300 m).
Range: 3100 nm (5740 km).
Role/Weapon systems: Limited number in service for Fleet reconnaissance, intelligence gathering and EW tasks, especially from Kola bases. Sensors: Short Horn search/attack radar, EW, cameras. Weapons: ASV; 'iron' bombs or stand-off weapons. Self-defence; 1 × 23 mm cannon.

Numbers/Type: 170 Tupolev Tu-22 M Backfire B/C.
Operational speed: Mach 2.0.
Service ceiling: 60 000 ft (18 300 m).
Range: 5000 nm (9260 km).
Role/Weapon systems: Medium-range nuclear/conventional strike against CVBG and other groups; reconnaissance in peacetime. Sensors: Down Beat search/Fan Tail attack radars, EW. Weapons: ASV; 12 tons of 'iron' bombs or stand-off missiles including 'Kitchen'. Self-defence; 2 × 23 mm cannon.

Numbers/Type: 180 Tupolev Tu-16 Badger.
Operational speed: 535 kts (992 km/h).
Service ceiling: 40 350 ft (12 300 m).
Range: 2605 nm (4800 km).
Role/Weapon systems: Medium-range operations over most oceans in the strike/attack role. Other variants include reconnaissance, tanker and electronic warfare support role. Sensors: Puff Ball or Short Horn search/weather radar, EW. Weapons: Self-defence; 2 × 23 mm cannon. ASV; 2 × 'Kangaroo' or 'Kitchen' ASMs or 9 tons of nuclear/conventional bombs.

BADGER 8/1992

Numbers/Type: 105 Tupolev Tu-95/Tu-142 Bear D/F/J.
Operational speed: 500 kts (925 km/h).
Service ceiling: 60 000 ft (18 300 m).
Range: 6775 nm (12 550 km).
Role/Weapon systems: Multi-mission long-range aircraft (reconnaissance, ASW and communications variants); seen over all oceans of the world, in increased numbers. Sensors: Big Bulge and Short Horn search radars, ECM (D); search radar, sonobuoys, ECM, MAD (F), ELINT systems (J). Weapons: ASW; various torpedoes, depth bombs and/or mines (F). ASV; none (D), (J). Self-defence; some have 2 × 23 mm or more cannon.

BEAR 8/1992

Numbers/Type: 65 Sukhoi Su-24 Fencer A/C/D.
Operational speed: Mach 1.15.
Service ceiling: 57 400 ft (17 500 m).
Range: 650 nm (1050 km).
Role/Weapon systems: Maritime reconnaissance and strike. Sensors: Radar and ECM. Weapons: 30 mm Gatling gun; various ASM missiles and bombs; some have 23 mm cannon.

Numbers/Type: 16 Beriev Be-42 Albatross.
Operational speed: 431 kts (800 km/h).
Service ceiling: 42 980 ft (13 100 m).
Range: 2700 nm (5000 km).
Role/Weapon systems: Multi-role amphibian capable of nine hour patrols. Could replace the Mail in due course.

LIGHT MISSILE FORCES

2 DERGACH (SIVUCH) CLASS
(FAST ATTACK CRAFT—MISSILE
AIR CUSHION VESSEL)

Displacement, tons: 750 full load
Dimensions, feet (metres): 211.6 × 55.8 × 7.9 (64.5 × 17 × 2.4)
Main machinery: 2 gas turbines; 2 diesels; 2 props on retractable pods
Speed, knots: 40+
Range, miles: 2000 (hull), 500 (air cushion)
Complement: 60

Missiles: SSM: 8 SS-N-22 (2 quad) Sunburn launchers ❶; active radar homing to 110 km (60 nm) at 2.5 Mach; warhead nuclear or HE; sea-skimmer.
SAM: SA-N-4 Gecko twin launcher ❷; semi-active radar homing to 15 km (8 nm) at 2.5 Mach; warhead 50 kg; 20 missiles.
Guns: 1—3 in (76 mm)/60 ❸; 85° elevation; 120 rounds/minute to 7 km (3.8 nm); weight of shell 16 kg.
2—30 mm/65 AK 630 ❹; 6 barrels per mounting; 3000 rounds/minute combined to 2 km.
Countermeasures: Decoys: 2—10-barrelled launchers.
ESM/ECM: 2 Foot Ball A.
Fire control: 2 Light Bulb data link ❺.
Radars: Air/surface search: Band Stand ❻; D/E/F band.
Surface search: Cross Dome ❼; E/F band.
Fire control: Bass Tilt ❽; H/I band (for guns).
Pop Group ❾; F/H/I band (for SAM).
IFF: Square Head. Salt Pot.

Programmes: Built at Zelenodolsk; first one launched in 1987, second in 1992. Classified as a PGGA (Guided Missile Patrol Air Cushion Vessels).
Structure: Twin hulled surface effect design.
Operational: Based in the Black Sea at Sevastopol.

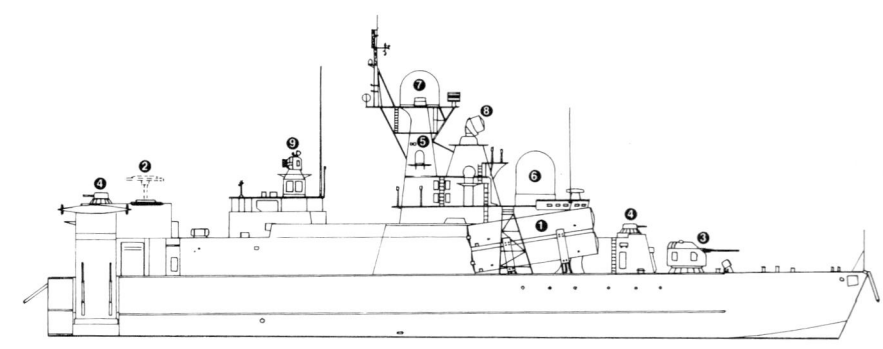

SIVUCH (Scale 1 : 600), Ian Sturton

SIVUCH 5/1990

16 NANUCHKA I, 18 NANUCHKA III and 1 NANUCHKA IV (BURYA) CLASSES (MISSILE CORVETTES)

Nanuchka I: GRAD RADUGA SUVAL STORM TAIFUN ZYKLON METL ZARNITSA GROM MOLNIJA MUSSON + 5
Nanuchka III: METEOR ZYB TUCHA PRILIV BURUN URAGAN LIVEN + 11
Nanuchka IV: NAKAT

Displacement, tons: 850 full load
Dimensions, feet (metres): 194.5 × 38.7 × 8.5 *(59.3 × 11.8 × 2.6)*
Main machinery: 3 Type M 507 diesels; 21 600 hp(m) *(15.9 MW)* sustained; 3 shafts
Speed, knots: 36. **Range, miles:** 2500 at 12 kts; 900 at 31 kts
Complement: 42 (7 officers)

Missiles: SSM: 6 SS-N-9 Siren (2 triple) launchers ❶; command guidance and IR and active radar homing to 110 km *(60 nm)* at 0.9 Mach; warhead nuclear 250 kT or HE 500 kg. Nanuchka IV has 2 sextuple launchers for a possible improved version of SS-N-9 or a new longer range missile.
SAM: SA-N-4 Gecko twin launcher ❷; semi-active radar homing to 15 km *(8 nm)* at 2.5 Mach; warhead 50 kg; altitude 9.1-3048 m *(30-10 000 ft)*; 20 missiles. Some anti-surface capability.
Guns: 2—57 mm/80 (twin) (Nanuchka I) ❸; 85° elevation; 120 rounds/minute to 6 km *(3.3 nm)*; weight of shell 2.8 kg.
1—3 in *(76 mm)*/60 (Nanuchka III and IV) ❹; 85° elevation; 120 rounds/minute to 7 km *(3.8 nm)*; weight of shell 7 kg.
1—30 mm/65 (Nanuchka III and IV) ❺; 6 barrels; 3000 rounds/minute combined to 2 km.
Countermeasures: Decoys: 2—16 or 10 (Nanuchka III) barrelled chaff launchers ❻.
ESM: Bell Tap or other Bell series. 4 radomes.
Fire control: Two Fish Bowl or Light Bulb (data links).
Radars: Air/surface search: Band Stand (also associated with SS-N-9 fire control) ❼; D/E/F band. Plank Shave in later Nanuchka III units.
Surface search: Peel Pair ❽; I band (in early units).
Fire control: Muff Cob (Nanuchka I) ❾; G/H band. Bass Tilt (Nanuchka III) ❿; H/I band. Pop Group ⓫; F/H/I band (for SA-N-4).
IFF: High Pole. Square Head. Spar Stump.

Programmes: Built from 1969 onwards at Petrovsky, Leningrad and in the Pacific (Nanuchka III only). Nanuchka III, first seen in 1978. Nanuchka IV completed in 1987 as a trials ship. Programme terminated when *Liven* was commissioned in November 1991. A follow-on class is expected. Type name is *maly raketny korabl* meaning small missile ship.
Structure: The Nanuchka IV is similar in detail to Nanuchka III except that she is the trials vehicle for a possible 300 km range version of SS-N-9 or its successor.
Operational: Probably mainly intended for deployment in coastal waters although formerly deployed in the Mediterranean (in groups of two or three), North Sea and Pacific. One more Nanuchka I in reserve.
Sales: Three of a modified version of Nanuchka I (Nanuchka II) with four SS-N-2B missiles have been supplied to India in 1977-78, three to Algeria in 1980-82, one to Libya in 1981, a second in February 1983, a third in February 1984 and a fourth in September 1985.

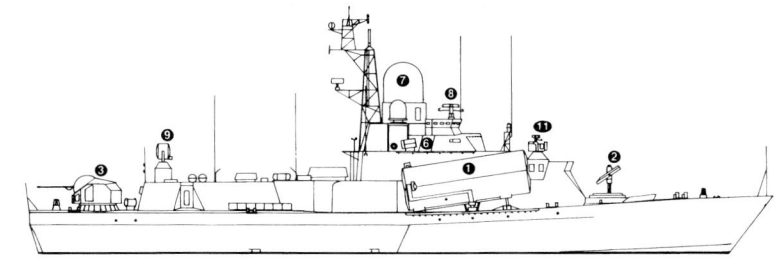

NANUCHKA I *(Scale 1 : 600), Ian Sturton*

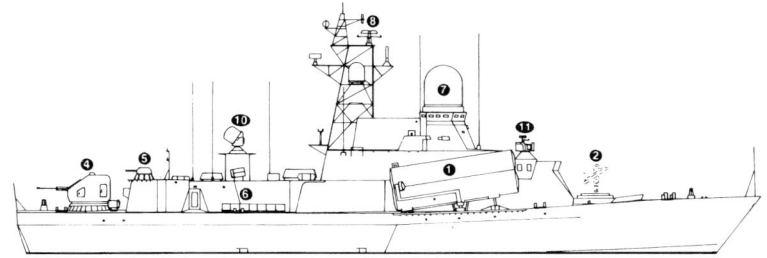

NANUCHKA III *(Scale 1 : 600), Ian Sturton*

NANUCHKA IV (2 sextuple launchers) 5/1990

NANUCHKA I 4/1992, van Ginderen Collection

NANUCHKA III 8/1992

2 TARANTUL I, 18 TARANTUL II and 22 + 2 TARANTUL III (MOLNIYA) CLASSES (TYPE 1241) (MISSILE CORVETTES)

Displacement, tons: 385 standard; 455 full load
Dimensions, feet (metres): 184.1 × 37.7 × 8.2 *(56.1 × 11.5 × 2.5)*
Main machinery: COGOG; 2 Nikolayev Type DR 77 gas turbines; 16 016 hp(m) *(11.77 MW)* sustained; 2 Nikolayev Type DR 76 gas turbines with reversible gearboxes; 4993 hp(m) *(3.67 MW)* sustained; 2 shafts or CODOG with 2 diesels; 8000 hp(m) *(5.88 MW)*; replacing second pair of gas turbines
Speed, knots: 36. **Range, miles:** 400 at 36 kts; 2000 at 20 kts
Complement: 34 (5 officers)

Missiles: SSM: 4 SS-N-2C/D Styx (2 twin) launchers (Tarantul I and Tarantul II); active radar or IR homing to 83 km *(45 nm)* at 0.9 Mach; warhead 513 kg; sea-skimmer at end of run.
4 SS-N-22 (2 twin) launchers (Tarantul III); active radar homing to 110 km *(60 nm)* at 2.5 Mach; warhead nuclear or HE; sea-skimmer. Modified version in one of the class.
SAM: SA-N-5 Grail quad launcher; manual aiming; IR homing to 6 km *(3.2 nm)* at 1.5 Mach; altitude to 2500 m *(8000 ft)*; warhead 1.5 kg.
SAM/Guns: 1 CADS-N-1 (one Tarantul II only); twin 30 mm Gatling combined with 8 SA-N-11 and Hot Flash/Hot Spot fire control radar/optronic director; laser beam guidance for missiles to 8 km *(4.4 nm)*; 4500 rounds/minute combined to 2 km (for guns).
Guns: 1—3 in *(76 mm)*/60; 85° elevation; 120 rounds/minute to 15 km *(8 nm)*; weight of shell 7 kg.
2—30 mm/65; 6 barrels per mounting; 3000 rounds/minute to 2 km.
Countermeasures: Decoys: 2—16 or 10 (Tarantul III) barrelled chaff launchers.
ESM: 2 Foot Ball, 2 Half Hat (in some).
Fire control: Hood Wink optronic director. Light Bulb data link.
Radars: Air/surface search: Plank Shave (Tarantul I); I band. Band Stand (with Plank Shave) (Tarantul II and III); E band.
Navigation: Spin Trough; I band.
Fire control: Bass Tilt; H/I band.
IFF: Square Head. High Pole.

Programmes: The first Tarantul I was completed in 1978 at Petrovsky, Leningrad. A single experimental Tarantul III with four SS-N-22 was completed at Petrovsky in 1981. Tarantul II were built at Kolpino, Petrovsky, Leningrad and in the Pacific in 1980-86. A second Tarantul I without Band Stand is retained to train foreign crews. Current production is of Tarantul III class for Russia and Tarantul I for export. Type name is *raketny kater* meaning missile cutter.
Modernisation: One Tarantul III is serving as a trials platform for a modified version of SS-N-22 possibly with a longer range; the missile is distinguished by end caps on the launcher doors. A Tarantul II is serving as a trials platform for the CADS-N-1 air defence system in the Black Sea.
Structure: Basically same hull as Pauk class without 2 m extension for sonar.
Sales: Tarantul I class—one to Poland 28 December 1983, second in April 1984, third in March 1988 and fourth in January 1989. One to GDR in September 1984, second in December 1984, third in September 1985, fourth in January 1986 and fifth in November 1986 (all deleted or sold including one which is doing trials with the US Navy). One to India in April 1987, second in January 1988, third in December 1988, fourth in November 1989 and fifth in January 1990. Two to Yemen in November 1990 and January 1991. One to Romania in December 1990, two more in February 1992. One Tarantul II to Bulgaria in March 1990.

TARANTUL I   7/1992, Jürg Kürsener

TARANTUL II   5/1991

TARANTUL III   9/1991, MoD Bonn

13 MATKA CLASS
(FAST ATTACK CRAFT—MISSILE HYDROFOIL)

Displacement, tons: 225 standard; 260 full load
Dimensions, feet (metres): 129.9 × 24.9 (41 over foils) × 6.9 (13.1 over foils) *(39.6 × 7.6 (12.5) × 2.1 (4))*
Main machinery: 3 Type M 504 diesels; 10 800 hp(m) *(7.94 MW)* sustained; 3 shafts
Speed, knots: 40. **Range, miles:** 600 at 35 kts foilborne; 1500 at 14 kts hullborne
Complement: 33

Missiles: SSM: 2 SS-N-2C Styx; active radar or IR homing to 83 km *(45 nm)* at 0.9 Mach; warhead 513 kg; sea-skimmer at end of run.
8 SS-N-25 (in one of the class); radar homing to 130 km *(70.2 nm)* at 0.9 Mach; warhead 145 kg; sea-skimmer.
Guns: 1—3 in *(76 mm)*/60; 85° elevation; 120 rounds/minute to 15 km *(8 nm)*; weight of shell 7 kg.
1—30 mm/65 AK 630; 6 barrels per mounting; 3000 rounds/minute to 2 km.
Countermeasures: Decoys: 2—16-barrelled chaff launchers.
ESM: Radar warning.
Radars: Air/surface search: Plank Shave; E band.
Navigation: Cheese Cake; I band.
Fire control: Bass Tilt; H/I band.
IFF: High Pole B or Salt Pot B and Square Head.

Programmes: In early 1978 the first of class was seen. Built at Kolpino Yard, Leningrad. Production stopped in 1983 being superseded by Tarantul class. Type name is *raketny kater* meaning missile cutter.
Structure: Similar hull to the Osa class with similar single hydrofoil system to Turya class. The combination has produced a better sea-boat than the Osa class. One of the class is the trials craft for the SS-N-25 first seen in 1988 in the German prototype Sassnitz class but removed when the GDR was reunited with Germany. Also being fitted in modernised Krivak Is, Neustrashimy and Udaloy II classes.
Operational: Based in the Baltic and Black Seas. Some may be fitted with quadruple SA-N-5 systems. Three deleted in 1992.

MATKA   1990

14 OSA I (TYPE 205) and 15 OSA II CLASSES
(FAST ATTACK CRAFT—MISSILE)

Displacement, tons: 210 (245, Osa II) full load
Dimensions, feet (metres): 126.6 × 24.9 × 8.8 *(38.6 × 7.6 × 2.7)*
Main machinery: 3 Type M 503A diesels; 8025 hp(m) *(5.9 MW)* sustained; 3 shafts (Osa I)
3 Type M 504 diesels; 10 800 hp(m) *(7.94 MW)* sustained; 3 shafts (Osa II)
Speed, knots: 35 (Osa I); 37 (Osa II). **Range, miles:** 400 at 34 kts (Osa I); 500 at 35 kts (Osa II)
Complement: 30

Missiles: SSM: 4 SS-N-2A/B (Osa I); 4 SS-N-2B/C (Osa II); active radar or IR homing to 46 km *(25 nm)* at 0.9 Mach; warhead 513 kg. C has a range of 83 km *(45 nm)* and is a sea-skimmer at end of run.
SAM: SA-N-5 Grail quad launcher (some Osa II); manual aiming; IR homing to 6 km *(3.2 nm)* at 1.5 Mach; altitude to 2500 m *(8000 ft)*; warhead 1.5 kg.
Guns: 4—30 mm/65 (2 twin); 85° elevation; 500 rounds/minute to 5 km *(2.7 nm)*; weight of shell 0.54 kg.
Radars: Surface search/fire control: Square Tie; I band.
Fire control: Drum Tilt; H/I band.
IFF: High Pole A or B. Square Head.

Programmes: Osa I class built in first half of the 1960s and Osa II class in the latter half at a number of yards. Type name is *raketny kater* meaning missile cutter.
Structure: This class was a revolution in naval shipbuilding leading to a whole generation of fast missile patrol craft being built worldwide.
Operational: Although confined by their size and range to coastal operations the lethality and accuracy of the Styx missile were first proved by the sinking of the Israeli destroyer *Eilat* on 21 October 1967 by an Egyptian Komar class vessel. Nine deleted in 1988-89, 25 in 1990, eight in 1991 and nine in 1992.
Sales: Osa I: Algeria (three), Bulgaria (three), Cuba (five), Egypt (12—eight remaining), East Germany (15), India (eight), Iraq (four), North Korea (eight), Poland (14), Romania (six), Syria (six), Yugoslavia (10).
Osa II: Algeria (nine), Angola (six), Bulgaria (three), Cuba (13), Ethiopia (four), Finland (four), India (eight), Iraq (eight), Libya (12), Somalia (two), Syria (10—six remaining), North Yemen (two) (subsequently returned), South Yemen (eight), Vietnam (eight). Many of both types have been deleted.

OSA I   7/1991

OSA II   1992, MoD Bonn

PATROL SHIPS

2/3 T 58 PGF/PGR CLASS

Displacement, tons: 790 standard; 860 full load
Dimensions, feet (metres): 229.9 × 29.5 × 7.9 *(70.1 × 9 × 2.4)*
Main machinery: 2 diesels; 4000 hp(m) *(2.94 MW)*; 2 shafts
Speed, knots: 17. **Range, miles:** 2500 at 13 kts
Complement: 82

Guns: 4—57 mm/70 (2 twin); 90° elevation; 120 rounds/minute to 8 km *(4.4 nm)*; weight of shell 2.8 kg.
  2—25 mm/80 (2 twin) (in some); 85° elevation; 270 rounds/minute to 3 km *(1.6 nm)*; weight of shell 0.34 kg.
A/S mortars: 2 RBU 1200 5-tubed fixed; range 1200 m; warhead 34 kg (in PGF type).
Depth charges: 2 projectors.
Countermeasures: ESM: 2 Watch Dog.
Radars: Air search: Big Net; C band (PGR type).
  Surface search: Spin Trough or Strut Curve; I band.
  Navigation: One or two Don 2; I band.
  Fire control: Muff Cob; G/H band.
IFF: Two Square Head. High Pole A or B.
Sonars: Tamir 11; hull-mounted; active search and attack; high frequency.

Programmes: Built from 1957 to 1963, conversion to patrol ships in about 1975 with sweep winches, magnetic sweep cable reel and stern davit retained but without associated minesweeping gear. Originally fleet minesweepers with steel hulls. Of this class 16 were completed as submarine rescue ships with armament and sweeping gear removed, see later page (Valday class).
Modernisation: Three converted to radar pickets with Big Net radar in late 1970s and early 1980s. These ships had the A/S systems removed and have two SA-N-5 quad launchers fitted.
Operational: From a total of 18 in 1988, these are the survivors in early 1993.

T 58/PGR 5/1990

LIGHT FORCES

32 PAUK I CLASS (FAST ATTACK CRAFT—PATROL)

Displacement, tons: 440 full load
Dimensions, feet (metres): 195.2 × 33.5 × 10.8 *(59.5 × 10.2 × 3.3)*
Main machinery: 2 Type M 507 diesels; 14 400 hp(m) *(10.6 MW)* sustained; 2 shafts
Speed, knots: 32. **Range, miles:** 2200 at 18 kts
Complement: 32

Missiles: SAM: SA-N-5 Grail quad launcher; manual aiming; IR homing to 6 km *(3.2 nm)* at 1.5 Mach; altitude to 2500 m *(8000 ft)*; warhead 1.5 kg; 8 missiles.
Guns: 1—3 in *(76 mm)*/60; 85° elevation; 120 rounds/minute to 15 km *(8 nm)*; weight of shell 7 kg.
  1—30 mm/65 AK 630; 6 barrels; 3000 rounds/minute combined to 2 km.
Torpedoes: 4—16 in *(406 mm)* tubes. Type 40; anti-submarine; active/passive homing up to 15 km *(8 nm)* at up to 40 kts; warhead 100-150 kg.
A/S mortars: 2 RBU 1200 5-tubed fixed; range 1200 m; warhead 34 kg.
Depth charges: 2 racks (12).
Countermeasures: Decoys: 2—16-barrelled chaff launchers.
  ESM: Radar warning.
Radars: Air/surface search: Peel Cone; E band.
  Surface search: Kivach; I band.
  Fire control: Bass Tilt; H/I band.
Sonars: Rat Tail; VDS (mounted on transom); active attack; high frequency.

Programmes: First laid down in 1977 and completed in 1979. Replacement for Poti class. In series production at Yaroslavl in the Black Sea and at Vladivostok until 1988 when the Sveltyak class took over. Type name is *maly protivolodochny korabl* meaning small anti-submarine ship. Overall numbers slightly reduced from previous assessments.
Structure: This appears to be an ASW version of the Tarantul class having the same hull form with a 1.8 m extension for dipping sonar. First three of class have a lower bridge than successors.
Operational: 25 of the craft are operated by the Border Guard.
Sales: A modified version (Pauk II) with a longer superstructure, two twin 533 mm torpedo tubes and a radome similar to the Parchim class is building for export. First one to India in March 1989, second in January 1990, third in December 1990 and fourth in February 1991. One Pauk I to Bulgaria in September 1989 and a second in December 1990.

PAUK I 8/1992

27 TURYA CLASS (FAST ATTACK CRAFT—TORPEDO HYDROFOIL)

Displacement, tons: 190 standard; 250 full load
Dimensions, feet (metres): 129.9 × 24.9 (41 over foils) × 5.9 (13.1 over foils)
  (39.6 × 7.6 (12.5) × 1.8 (4))
Main machinery: 3 Type M 504 diesels; 10 800 hp(m) *(7.94 MW)* sustained; 3 shafts
Speed, knots: 40 foilborne. **Range, miles:** 600 at 35 kts foilborne; 1450 at 14 kts hullborne
Complement: 30

Guns: 2—57 mm/80 (twin, aft); 85° elevation; 120 rounds/minute to 6 km *(3.3 nm)*; weight of shell 2.8 kg.
  2—25 mm/80 (twin, fwd); 85° elevation; 270 rounds/minute to 3 km *(1.6 nm)*; weight of shell 0.34 kg.
  1—14.5 mm MG.
Torpedoes: 4—21 in *(533 mm)* tubes. Type 53; dual purpose; pattern active/passive homing up to 20 km *(10.8 nm)* at up to 45 kts; warhead 400 kg or low yield nuclear.
Depth charges: 1 rack.
Radars: Surface search: Pot Drum; H/I band.
  Fire control: Muff Cob; G/H band.
IFF: High Pole B. Square Head.
Sonars: VDS; active search and attack; high frequency. Similar to Hormone dipping sonar. This sonar is not fitted in most export versions.

Programmes: The second class of hydrofoil with single foil forward (after Matka class). Has a naval orientation rather than the earlier Pchela class of the Border Guard. Entered service from 1972 to 1978—built at Petrovsky, Kolpino, Leningrad and Vladivostok. Basically Osa hull. Type name is *torpedny kater* meaning torpedo cutter. Production ended in 1987.
Sales: Two to Cuba 9 February 1979, two in February 1980, two in February 1981, two in January 1983 and one in November 1983; one to Ethiopia in early 1985 and one in March 1986; one to Kampuchea in mid-1984 and one in early 1985; one to Seychelles in April 1986 (no tubes or sonar); two to Vietnam in mid-1984, one in late 1984 and two in early 1986. Two to be transferred to Lithuania in 1993.

TURYA 8/1988, van Ginderen Collection

3 BABOCHKA (SOKOL) CLASS (FAST ATTACK CRAFT—PATROL HYDROFOIL)

Displacement, tons: 400 full load
Dimensions, feet (metres): 164 × 27.9 (33.5 over foils) × 13.1 (19.4 foils)
  (50 × 8.5 (10.2) × 4 (5.9))
Main machinery: CODOG; 3 Type NK-12M gas turbines; 23 046 hp(m) *(16.95 MW)* sustained; 2 diesels; 3 shafts
Speed, knots: 45
Complement: 45

Guns: 1—3 in *(76 mm)*/60 (in one only); 85° elevation; 120 rounds/minute to 15 km *(8 nm)*; weight of shell 7 kg.
  2—30 mm/65 AK 630; 6 barrels per mounting; 3000 rounds/minute combined to 2 km.
Torpedoes: 8—16 in *(406 mm)* (2 quad) tubes. Type 40; anti-submarine; active/passive homing up to 15 km *(8 nm)* at up to 40 kts; warhead 100-150 kg.
Countermeasures: Decoys: 2—16-barrelled chaff launchers.
  ESM: Radar warning.
Radars: Surface search: Peel Cone; E band.
  Navigation: Don 2; I band.
  Fire control: Bass Tilt; H/I band.
Sonars: Dipping sonar.

Programmes: First sighted 1977 in the Black Sea. Probably used for research and development. Two more of a modified type were completed in 1986 and 1987.
Structure: Features include a hydrofoil arrangement with a single fixed foil forward, large gas turbine exhausts aft, and trainable torpedo mountings forward.

BABOCHKA 1991

556 RUSSIA / Light forces

10 + 5 SVETLYAK CLASS (FAST ATTACK CRAFT—PATROL)

Displacement, tons: 450 full load
Dimensions, feet (metres): 164 × 29.5 × 11.5 *(50 × 9 × 3.5)*
Main machinery: 2 diesels; 20 000 hp(m) *(14.7 MW)*; 2 shafts
Speed, knots: 30
Complement: 55
Missiles: SAM: SA-N-5 Grail quad launcher; manual aiming; IR homing to 6 km *(3.2 nm)* at 1.5 Mach; warhead 1.5 kg.
Guns: 1—3 in *(76 mm)*/60; 85° elevation; 120 rounds/minute to 15 km *(8 nm)*; weight of shell 7 kg.
1—30 mm/65 AK 630; 6 barrels; 3000 rounds/minute combined to 2 km.
Torpedoes: 2—16 in *(406 mm)* tubes; Type 40; anti-submarine; active/passive homing up to 15 km *(8 nm)* at up to 40 kts; warhead 100-150 kg.
Radars: Air/surface search: Peel Cone; E band.
Fire control: Bass Tilt; H/I band.
IFF: High Pole B; Square Head.

Comment: A class of attack craft for the Border Guard building at Vladivostok, St Petersburg and Yaroslavl. It complements the Pauks in the Pacific in place of the less seaworthy Muravey class. Series production after first of class trials in 1989, has risen to about three a year.

SVETLYAK *12/1989, G Jacobs*

14 MURAVEY CLASS
(FAST ATTACK CRAFT—PATROL HYDROFOIL)

Displacement, tons: 180 standard; 230 full load
Dimensions, feet (metres): 126.6 × 24.9 × 6.2; 14.4 (foils) *(38.6 × 7.6 × 1.9; 4.4)*
Main machinery: 2 gas turbines; 8000 hp(m) *(5.88 MW)*; 2 shafts
Speed, knots: 40. **Range, miles:** 950 at 28 kts
Guns: 1—3 in *(76 mm)*/60; 85° elevation; 120 rounds/minute to 15 km *(8 nm)*; weight of shell 7 kg.
1—30 mm/65 AK 630; 6 barrels; 3000 rounds/minute combined to 2 km.
Torpedoes: 2—16 in *(406 mm)* tubes; Type 40; anti-submarine; active/passive homing up to 15 km *(8 nm)* at up to 40 kts; warhead 100-150 kg.
Depth charges: 6.
Radars: Surface search: Peel Cone; E band.
Fire control: Bass Tilt; H/I band.
IFF: High Pole B; Square Head.
Sonars: VDS: active attack; high frequency; dipping sonar.

Comment: Built at Feodosya. First seen in 1983. Programme terminated in 1988 in favour of the Mukha class. Assigned to Border Guard.

MURAVEY *1/1989, MoD Bonn*

MURAVEY *9/1992*

2 MUKHA CLASS (FAST ATTACK CRAFT—PATROL HYDROFOIL)

Displacement, tons: 400 full load
Dimensions, feet (metres): 164 × 27.9 × 9.2 *(50 × 8.5 × 2.8)*
Main machinery: 2 gas turbines; 2 shafts
Speed, knots: 45
Complement: 45

Guns: 1—3 in *(76 mm)*/60; 85° elevation; 120 rounds/minute to 7 km *(3.8 nm)*; weight of shell 16 kg.
1—30 mm/65 AK 630; 6 barrels; 3000 rounds/minute combined to 2 km.
Torpedoes: 8—16 in *(406 mm)* tubes (2 quad); Type 40; anti-submarine; active/passive homing up to 15 km *(8 nm)* at up to 40 kts; warhead 100-150 kg.
Radars: Surface search: Peel Cone; E band.
Fire control: Bass Tilt; H/I band.
IFF: High Pole B. Square Head.

Programmes: Built at Feodosiya and first seen in 1987. Only two of the class completed and there may be no series production.
Structure: Looks like a development of *Babochka* with two sets of torpedo tubes mounted aft.
Operational: Based in the Black Sea.

MUKHA *1990, S Breyer*

104 STENKA CLASS (FAST ATTACK CRAFT—PATROL)

Displacement, tons: 170 standard; 210 full load
Dimensions, feet (metres): 127.9 × 25.6 × 5.9 *(39 × 7.8 × 1.8)*
Main machinery: 3 Type M 503A diesels; 10 125 hp(m) *(7.44 MW)* sustained; 3 shafts
Speed, knots: 36. **Range, miles:** 800 at 24 kts; 500 at 35 kts
Complement: 30
Guns: 4—30 mm/65 (2 twin).
Torpedoes: 4—16 in *(406 mm)* tubes.
Depth charges: 2 racks.
Radars: Surface search: Pot Drum or Peel Cone; H/I or E band.
Fire control: Drum Tilt; H/I band.
IFF: High Pole. 2 Square Head.
Sonars: VDS; high frequency; Hormone type dipping sonar.

Comment: Based on the hull design of the Osa class. Construction started in 1967 and continued at a rate of about five a year at Petrovsky, Leningrad and Vladivostok for the Border Guard. Programme terminated in 1989 at a total of 133 hulls. Type name is *pogranichny storozhevoy korabl* meaning border patrol ship. Some are beginning to be paid off.
Transfers include: Cuba, two in February 1985 and one in August 1985. Four to Cambodia, in October 1985 and November 1987. Six transferred to Azerbaijan control in November 1992.

STENKA *3/1992, Hartmut Ehlers*

32 ZHUK CLASS (COASTAL PATROL CRAFT)

Displacement, tons: 50 full load
Dimensions, feet (metres): 75.4 × 17 × 6.2 *(23 × 5.2 × 1.9)*
Main machinery: 2 Type M 50 diesels; 2200 hp(m) *(1.6 MW)* sustained; 2 shafts
Speed, knots: 30. **Range, miles:** 1100 at 15 kts
Complement: 17
Guns: 2—14.5 mm (twin, fwd) MGs. 1—12.7 mm (aft) MG.
Radars: Surface search: Spin Trough; I band.

Comment: Under construction since 1970. Building at three to eight a year mostly for export. Manned by the Border Guard. Export versions have twin (over/under) 14.5 mm aft.
Transfers: Algeria (one in 1981), Angola (one in 1977), Benin (four in 1978-80), Bulgaria (five in 1977), Cape Verde (one in 1980), Cuba (40 in 1971-88), Equatorial Guinea (three in 1974-75), Ethiopia (two in October 1982 and two in June 1990), Guinea (two in July 1987), Iraq (five in 1974-75), Kampuchea (three in 1985-87), Mauritius (two in January 1990), Mozambique (five in 1978-80), Nicaragua (eight in 1982-86), Seychelles (one in 1981, one in October 1982), Somalia (one in 1974), Syria (six in 1981-84), Vietnam (nine in 1978-88 (at least one passed on to Cambodia, five in 1990), North Yemen (five in 1978-87), South Yemen (two in 1975). Some have been deleted.

ZHUK *5/1991*

RIVER PATROL CRAFT

Note: Attached to Black Sea and Pacific Fleets for operations on the Danube, Amur and Usuri Rivers, and to the Caspian Flotilla. Belong to the Maritime Border Guard.

19 YAZ CLASS

Displacement, tons: 400 full load
Dimensions, feet (metres): 180.4 × 29.5 × 4.9 *(55 × 9 × 1.5)*
Main machinery: 2 diesels; 2 shafts
Speed, knots: 15. **Range, miles:** 1000 at 10 kts
Complement: 60
Guns: 2—115 mm tank guns (TB 62). Twin barrel rocket launcher on after deckhouse.
2—30 mm/65 AK 630; 6 barrels per mounting.
Mines: Laying capability.
Radars: Surface search: Square Tie; I band.
Fire control: Bass Tilt; H/I band.
Navigation: Don 2; I band.
IFF: High Pole B. Square Head.

Comment: First entered service in Amur Flotilla 1978. Building on Pacific coast until 1987.

YAZ 2/1991, A Pavlov

10 PIYAVKA CLASS

Displacement, tons: 150 full load
Dimensions, feet (metres): 126.3 × 20.7 × 2.9 *(38.5 × 6.3 × 0.9)*
Main machinery: 2 diesels; 2 shafts
Speed, knots: 14
Guns: 1—30 mm/65 AK 630; 6 barrels. 2—14.5 mm (twin) MG.

Comment: Built at Khabarovsk from 1979 to 1984. Amur Flotilla.

7 VOSH CLASS

Displacement, tons: 190 full load
Dimensions, feet (metres): 140.1 × 20.7 × 3.3 *(42 × 6.3 × 1)*
Main machinery: 2 diesels; 2 shafts
Speed, knots: 18
Guns: 1—3 in *(76 mm)*/48 (tank turret). 1—30 mm/65 AK 630.
Countermeasures: 1 twin barrel decoy launcher.

Comment: Built in Pacific yards 1980-84.

VOSH 1991

2 TR 40 CLASS

Displacement, tons: 70 full load
Dimensions, feet (metres): 91.2 × 13.1 × 3.6 *(27.8 × 4 × 1.1)*
Main machinery: 2 diesels; 600 hp(m) *(440 kW)*; 2 shafts
Speed, knots: 17. **Range, miles:** 500 at 10 kts
Guns: 2—25 mm/70 (twin). 2—14.5 mm (twin) MGs.

Comment: This last pair are likely to be scrapped in 1993.

TR 40 1990

80 SHMEL CLASS

Displacement, tons: 85 full load
Dimensions, feet (metres): 91.8 × 14.1 × 3.6 *(28 × 4.3 × 1.1)*
Main machinery: 2 Type M 50 diesels; 2200 hp(m) *(1.6 MW)* sustained; 2 shafts
Speed, knots: 22. **Range, miles:** 600 at 12 kts
Complement: 12
Guns: 1—3 in *(76 mm)*/48 (tank turret). 2—25 mm/70 (twin) (later ships). 2—14.5 mm (twin) MGs (earlier ships). 5—7.62 mm MGs. 1 BP 6 rocket launcher; 18 barrels.
Mines: Can lay 9.
Radars: Surface search: Spin Trough; I band.

Comment: Completed at Kerch and Khabarovsk 1967-74. Some of the later ships also mount one or two multi-barrelled rocket launchers amidships. The 7.62 mm guns fire through embrasures in the superstructure with one mounted on the 76 mm. Can be carried on land transport. Type name is *artillerisky kater* meaning artillery cutter. Some have been scrapped.
Transfers: Four to Cambodia (1984-85).

SHMEL 1991

1 COMMAND SHIP

SSV-10

Displacement, tons: 340 full load
Dimensions, feet (metres): 129.3 × 23 × 3.9 *(39.4 × 7 × 1.2)*
Speed, knots: 12
Guns: 2—40 mm saluting guns. 6—14.5 mm MGs (3 twin).

Comment: Support ship on the Danube for the river patrols. Built in 1940.

SSV-10 6/1991, van Ginderen Collection

558 RUSSIA / Mine warfare forces

MINE WARFARE FORCES

Note: Some 40-50 craft of various dimensions, some with cable reels, some self-propelled and unmanned, some towed and unmanned are reported including the 8 m Kater and Volga unmanned mine-clearance craft. Some are attached to the Polnochny (MCM) ships, others may be used for wide deployment of magnetic sweeps. Both Mi-8 'Hip' and Mi-14 'Haze B' helicopters have carried out what may be acoustic and magnetic sweeping with small craft of the Volga type towed by a cable.

MINE CLEARANCE SWEEPS   *1990*

2 GORYA CLASS (MINEHUNTERS—OCEAN)

ZHELEZNYAKOV   + 1

Displacement, tons: 1130 full load
Dimensions, feet (metres): 216.5 oa; 200.1 wl × 36.1 × 10.8 *(66; 61 × 11 × 3.3)*
Main machinery: 2 diesels; 5000 hp(m) *(3.7 MW)*; 2 shafts
Speed, knots: 17
Complement: 80

Missiles: 2 SA-N-5 Grail quad launchers; IR homing to 6 km *(3.2 nm)* at 1.5 Mach; warhead 1.5 kg.
Guns: 1—3 in *(76 mm)*/60; 85° elevation; 120 rounds/minute to 15 km *(8 nm)*; weight of shell 7 kg.
  1—30 mm/65 AK 630; 6 barrels; 3000 rounds/minute to 2 km.
Countermeasures: Decoys: 2—16-barrelled chaff launchers.
ESM: Cross Loop; Long Fold.
Radars: Surface search: Palm Frond; I band.
  Navigation: Nayada; I band.
  Fire control: Bass Tilt; H/I band.
IFF: Salt Pot C. 2 Square Head.
Sonars: Hull-mounted; active search; high frequency.

Programmes: Both completed at Kolpino Yard, Leningrad, first in late 1986 and second in 1991.
Structure: Appears to carry mechanical, magnetic and acoustic sweep gear and may have accurate positional fixing equipment. A remote-controlled submersible is housed behind the sliding doors in the superstructure below the ADG gun mounting.
Operational: *Zheleznyakov* is conducting trials and training in the Black Sea. The second of class conducted sea trials in 1992 and has remained in the Baltic.

ZHELEZNYAKOV   *8/1989*

4 POLNOCHNY A (TYPE 770) and B (TYPE 771) CLASSES

Comment: Four of this class of LSMs (see *Amphibious Warfare* section for details) have been converted to carry large counter-mining charges on long chutes discharging over the stern on either side. These charges are laid in lines using a radio-controlled MCM craft to tow the charges into position before detonation. In one case these craft are carried on davits amidships and the remainder carry them on chutes aft.

POLNOCHNY B (MCM)   *1984, JMSDF*

33 NATYA I and 1 NATYA II (MINER) CLASSES (MINESWEEPERS—OCEAN)

DIZELIST	MINER	STARSHKIY	SNAYPR
ELEKTRIK	MOTORIST	SIGNALSHIK	TURBINIST
POLEMETCHIK	RULEVOY	ZAPAL	ZENITCHIK
RADIST	DOBROTAY	ZARYAD	ARTILLERIST
NAVODCHIK	PARAYAN	TRAL	+ 15

Displacement, tons: 770 full load
Dimensions, feet (metres): 200.1 × 31.8 × 8.9 *(61 × 9.7 × 2.7)*
Main machinery: 2 Type M 504 diesels; 7200 hp(m) *(5.3 MW)* sustained; 2 shafts
Speed, knots: 19. **Range, miles:** 4000 at 10 kts
Complement: 65

Missiles: SAM: 2 SA-N-5 Grail quad launchers (in some); manual aiming; IR homing to 6 km *(3.2 nm)* at 1.5 Mach; altitude to 2500 m *(8000 ft)*; warhead 1.5 kg; 16 missiles.
Guns: 4—30 mm/65 (2 twin); 85° elevation; 500 rounds/minute to 5 km *(2.7 nm)*; weight of shell 0.54 kg or 2—30 mm/65 AK 630; 6 barrels per mounting; 3000 rounds/minute combined to 2 km.
  4—25 mm/80 (2 twin) (Natya I); 85° elevation; 270 rounds/minute to 3 km *(1.6 nm)*; weight of shell 0.34 kg.
A/S mortars: 2 RBU 1200 5-tubed fixed (Natya I); range 1200 m; warhead 34 kg.
Mines: 10.
Countermeasures: MCM: Capable of magnetic, acoustic and mechanical sweeping.
Radars: Surface search: Don 2 or Low Trough; I band.
  Fire control: Drum Tilt; H/I band (not in all).
IFF: Two Square Head. High Pole B.
Sonars: Hull-mounted; active minehunting; high frequency.

Programmes: First reported in 1970, as successor to the Yurka class. Built at Kolpino and Khabarovsk. Construction for Soviet Navy ended in 1980 with Natya II although Natya I building continues for export. Type name is *morskoy tralshchik* meaning seagoing minesweeper.
Structure: Some have hydraulic gantries aft. Have aluminium/steel alloy hulls. Natya II was built without minesweeping gear to make way for a lengthened superstructure, the transom has been cut away amidships to take a 5 ft sheave. This is believed to be a minehunting version for research and development. Some have Gatling 30 mm guns and a different radar configuration without Drum Tilt.
Operational: Usually operate in home waters but have deployed to the Mediterranean, Indian Ocean and West Africa.
Sales: India (two in 1978, two in 1979, two in 1980, one in August 1986, two in 1987, three in 1988). Libya (two in 1981, two in February 1983, one in August 1983, one in January 1984, one in January 1985, one in October 1986). Syria (one in 1985). Yemen (two in 1991).

NATYA I   *8/1992*

NATYA I   *6/1992*

NATYA II   *5/1986, US Navy*

Mine warfare forces / RUSSIA

3 ALESHA CLASS (MINELAYERS)

PRIPYAT   VYCHEGDA   PECHORA

Displacement, tons: 3860 full load
Dimensions, feet (metres): 324.8 × 44.3 × 17.7 *(99 × 13.5 × 5.4)*
Main machinery: 4 diesels; 30 000 hp(m) *(22.4 MW)*; 2 shafts
Speed, knots: 24. **Range, miles:** 4000 at 16 kts
Complement: 150
Guns: 4—45 mm/70 (quad, fwd).
Mines: 400.
Radars: Surface search: Strut Curve; F band.
Navigation: Don 2; I band.
Fire control: Muff Cob; G/H band.
IFF: High Pole B.

Comment: In service since 1967. Fitted with four mine tracks to provide stern launchings. Also have a capability in general support role. Can act as netlayers. Type name is *zagraditel minny* meaning minelayer and the Russian name is the Alyosha Popovich class. One in each of the Northern, Pacific and Black Sea Fleets. *Vychegda* sighted in the Pacific in 1991 with Elint vans fitted forward of the bridge. Fitted with Army surplus guns.

VYCHEGDA   *12/1989, G Jacobs*

30 YURKA CLASS (MINESWEEPERS—OCEAN)

GAFEL   EVGENIY NIKONOV   MAZLOV
NAVODCHIK   SEMEN ROSAL   + 25

Displacement, tons: 460 full load
Dimensions, feet (metres): 171.9 × 30.8 × 8.5 *(52.4 × 9.4 × 2.6)*
Main machinery: 2 Type M 503 diesels; 5350 hp(m) *(3.91 MW)* sustained; 2 shafts
Speed, knots: 17. **Range, miles:** 1500 at 12 kts
Complement: 60

Missiles: SAM: 2 SA-N-5 Grail quad launchers (in some); manual aiming; IR homing to 6 km *(3.2 nm)* at 1.5 Mach; altitude to 2500 m *(8000 ft)*; warhead 1.5 kg; 16 missiles.
Guns: 4—30 mm/65 (2 twin); 85° elevation; 500 rounds/minute to 5 km *(2.7 nm)*; weight of shell 0.54 kg.
Mines: 10.
Countermeasures: Fitted for wire, magnetic and acoustic sweeping.
ESM: Watch Dog.
Radars: Surface search: Don 2 or Spin Trough; I band.
Fire control: Drum Tilt; H/I band.
IFF: Two Square Head. High Pole B.
Sonars: Hull-mounted; active minehunting; high frequency.

Programmes: A class of medium fleet minesweepers with aluminium/steel alloy hull. Completed from 1963 to 1972 at Kolpino and Khabarovsk. Type name is *morskoy tralshchik* meaning seagoing minesweeper.
Operational: One sank in the Black Sea after an explosion in August 1989. Being scrapped at about 10 per year.
Sales: Four to Egypt (1969), two to Vietnam (1979).

YURKA   *7/1992*

1 BALTIKA CLASS (MINESWEEPER—COASTAL)

Displacement, tons: 210 full load
Dimensions, feet (metres): 83.3 × 22.3 × 10.8 *(25.4 × 6.8 × 3.3)*
Main machinery: 1 ChISP 18/22 diesel; 300 hp(m) *(220 kW)*; 1 shaft; cp prop
Speed, knots: 9. **Range, miles:** 1400 at 9 kts
Complement: 10
Guns: 2—14.5 mm MGs (twin).
Radars: Navigation: Spin Trough; I band.

Comment: A trawler acquired in 1983 and converted for some form of MCM operations probably to test the feasibility of rapid conversion of trawlers to the minesweeping role.

9 T 43 CLASS (MINESWEEPERS—OCEAN)

Displacement, tons: 500 standard; 580 (600 for 60 m ships) full load
Dimensions, feet (metres): 190.2 × 27.6 × 6.9 *(58 × 8.4 × 2.1)* (older units)
  196.8 × 27.6 × 7.5 *(60 × 8.4 × 2.3)* (in later ships)
Main machinery: 2 Kolomna Type 9-D-8 diesels; 2000 hp(m) *(1.47 MW)* sustained; 2 shafts
Speed, knots: 15. **Range, miles:** 3000 at 10 kts; 2000 at 14 kts
Complement: 65

Guns: 4—37 mm/63 (2 twin); 85° elevation; 160 rounds/minute to 9 km *(5 nm)*; weight of shell 0.7 kg.
  2 or 4—14.5 mm (1 or 2 twin) MGs.
Depth charges: 2 projectors.
Mines: 16.
Radars: Surface search: Ball End; E/F band.
Navigation: Don 2 or Spin Trough; I band.
IFF: Square Head. High Pole A.
Sonars: Hull-mounted; active minehunting; high frequency.

Programmes: Built in 1948-57 in shipyards throughout the Soviet Union. A number of this class was converted into radar pickets. Of the 200+ hulls built a number were also used as diving ships, tenders and so on as well as a number employed as patrol ships. Type name is *morskoy tralshchik* meaning seagoing minesweeper.
Structure: Steel hulls. The later version *(60 m long)* carries the additional four 25 mm guns and has a double-level type bridge instead of the straight-up type in earlier ships.
Operational: Seven of the class are in the Caspian Sea.
Sales: Algeria (two), Albania (two), Bulgaria (three), China (two), Egypt (seven), Indonesia (six), Iraq (two), Syria (two), 12 built in Poland for Polish Navy; one converted to a radar picket in late 1970s. Many of these had the 58 m hull and double-level bridges.

T 43   *1981*

2 ANDRYUSHA (TOPAZ) CLASS
(MINESWEEPERS—COASTAL SPECIAL)

ALTAYSKIY   ESTONIY

Displacement, tons: 380 full load
Dimensions, feet (metres): 154.2 × 27.9 × 6.5 *(47 × 8.5 × 2)*
Main machinery: 2 diesels; 2200 hp(m) *(1.6 MW)*; 2 shafts
Speed, knots: 15. **Range, miles:** 3000 at 10 kts
Complement: 40
Guns: None.
Radars: Surface search: Spin Trough or Don 2; I band.
IFF: High Pole B.

Comment: First entered service in 1975. Probably built at Kolpino. Specially designed, possibly with GRP hulls, for deep water magnetic sweeping. Possibly carry a gas turbine generator. May be trials ships as no more have been built and one has been paid off.

ALTAYSKIY   *9/1984, G Jacobs*

2 PELIKAN CLASS ACV (MINESWEEPER—INSHORE)

Displacement, tons: 115
Dimensions, feet (metres): 98.4 × 42.7 *(30 × 13)*
Speed, knots: 55
Guns: 1—30 mm/65 AK 630.
Radars: Navigation: Shot Dome; I band.
IFF: Salt Pot.

Comment: Air cushion vehicles built at Feodosiya and commissioned in 1985-86. Experimental craft to investigate the application of hovercraft for the mine countermeasures role. The programme is reported as unsuccessful and no more are to be built. One of the pair may have been wrecked in 1990.

560 RUSSIA / Mine warfare forces

75 + 2 SONYA CLASS (MINESWEEPERS—HUNTERS/COASTAL)

Displacement, tons: 400 full load
Dimensions, feet (metres): 157.4 × 28.9 × 6.6 *(48 × 8.8 × 2)*
Main machinery: 2 Kolomna Type 9-D-8 diesels; 2000 hp(m) *(1.47 MW)* sustained; 2 shafts
Speed, knots: 15. **Range, miles:** 3000 at 10 kts
Complement: 43
Missiles: SAM: 2 quad SA-N-5 launchers (in some).
Guns: 2—30 mm/65 AK 630 or 2—30 mm/65 (twin) and 2—25 mm/80 (twin).
Mines: 8.
Radars: Surface search: Don 2; I band.
IFF: Two Square Head. High Pole B.

Comment: Wooden hull with GRP sheath. Still in series production at about two a year in western yards and at Ulis (Pacific). First reported 1973. Type name is *bazovy tralshchik* meaning base minesweeper. Some have two twin 30 mm Gatling guns, others one 30 mm/65 (twin) plus one 25 mm (twin).
Transfers: Bulgaria, four in 1981-85. Cuba, four in 1980-85. Syria, one in 1986. Vietnam, one in February 1987, one in February 1988, one in July 1989 and one in February 1990. Yemen, one in February 1991.

SONYA (new guns)   *5/1990, MoD Bonn*

SONYA (old guns)   *1991, Ships of the World*

16 VANYA and 3 MODIFIED VANYA CLASSES
(MINESWEEPERS—HUNTERS/COASTAL)

Displacement, tons: 250 full load
Dimensions, feet (metres): 131.2 × 23.9 × 5.9 *(40 × 7.3 × 1.8)*
Main machinery: 2 Kolomna Type 9-D-8 diesels; 2000 hp(m) *(1.47 MW)* sustained; 2 shafts
Speed, knots: 16. **Range, miles:** 1400 at 14 kts; 2400 at 10 kts
Complement: 30
Guns: 2—30 mm/65 (twin). 2—25 mm/80 (twin) (in conversions in place of 30 mm).
Mines: 8 (12 in Vanya II).
Radars: Surface search: Don 2. Don Kay (in conversions).
IFF: Square Head (unmodified). High Pole B.

Comment: A coastal class with wooden hulls of a type suitable for series production built from 1961-73. The normal Vanya class can act as minehunters. Three have been modified with superstructure extended forward, with 25 mm mounting on fo'c'sle in place of 30 mm, lattice mast at break amidships and two boats stowed on quarterdeck. Guidance ships for Ilyusha class. Type name is *bazovy tralshchik* meaning base minesweeper. Twelve deleted in 1988-89, ten in 1990, twenty in 1991 and four in 1992. Remainder in reserve.
Transfers: Six to Bulgaria (1970-85), two to Syria (1973) and one to Vietnam (November 1986).

VANYA (under tow)   *6/1992*

45 YEVGENYA CLASS (MINEHUNTERS—INSHORE)

Displacement, tons: 77 standard; 90 full load
Dimensions, feet (metres): 80.7 × 18 × 4.9 *(24.6 × 5.5 × 1.5)*
Main machinery: 2 Type 3-D-12 diesels; 600 hp(m) *(440 kW)* sustained; 2 shafts
Speed, knots: 11. **Range, miles:** 300 at 10 kts
Complement: 10
Guns: 2—14.5 mm (twin) MGs or 2—25 mm/80 (twin) (in some later ships).
Radars: Surface search: Spin Trough; I band.
IFF: High Pole.
Sonars: A small sonar is lifted over stern on crane; a TV system may also be used.

Comment: GRP hulls. Production started in 1967 and completed in 1988 at Kolpino. Type name is *reydny tralshchik* meaning roadstead minesweeper.
Transfers: Two to Angola (September 1987), three to Bulgaria (1976-77), 10 to Cuba (1977-82), six to India (1983-84), three to Iraq (1975), three to Mozambique (1985-86), eight to Nicaragua (1984-88), five to Syria (1978-86), three to North Yemen (May 1982-November 1987), three to Vietnam (December 1986-November 1987), three to South Yemen in March 1990.

YEVGENYA   *1991*

8 + 4 LIDA CLASS (MINEHUNTERS—INSHORE)

Displacement, tons: 110 full load
Dimensions, feet (metres): 101.7 × 20.3 × 5.2 *(31 × 6.2 × 1.6)*
Main machinery: 2 diesels; 400 hp(m) *(294 kW)*; 2 shafts
Speed, knots: 11
Complement: 10
Guns: 2—25 mm/80 (twin).
Radars: Surface search: I band.

Comment: A follow-on to the Yevgenya class started construction in 1989 at Kolpino Yard, Leningrad. Similar in appearance to Yevgenya. Building rate is about three a year.

LIDAs   *1991*

3 + 2 TANYA CLASS (MINESWEEPERS—INSHORE)

Displacement, tons: 73 full load
Dimensions, feet (metres): 87 × 13 × 5 *(26.5 × 4 × 1.5)*
Main machinery: 1 diesel; 270 hp(m) *(200 kW)*; 1 shaft
Speed, knots: 10
Radars: Surface search: Spin Trough; I band.

Comment: Built at Kolpino Yard. First operational in 1987, second and third in 1989/90. Probably replacing the Ilyusha class as radio-controlled drones.

TANYA   *1991*

7 ILYUSHA CLASS (MINESWEEPERS—INSHORE)

Displacement, tons: 85 full load
Dimensions, feet (metres): 86.6 × 19.4 × 4.6 *(26.4 × 5.9 × 1.4)*
Main machinery: 2 diesels; 500 hp(m) *(367 kW)*; 2 shafts
Speed, knots: 12. **Range, miles:** 300 at 10 kts
Complement: 10
Radars: Navigation: Spin Trough; I band.

Comment: First reported in 1966. Large foremast carrying electronic arrays. Capable of operating unmanned and radio controlled. (See Vanya class.) Three left in the Baltic and four in the Black Sea; the remainder scrapped.

OLYA　　　　　　　　　　　　　　　　　　　　　　　　　　　　　　　　8/1991, MoD Bonn

15 K 8 CLASS (MINESWEEPING BOATS)

Displacement, tons: 26 full load
Dimensions, feet (metres): 55.4 × 10.5 × 3.9 *(16.9 × 3.2 × 1.2)*
Main machinery: 2 Type 3-D-6 diesels; 300 hp(m) *(220 kW)* sustained; 2 shafts
Speed, knots: 18. **Range, miles:** 300 at 10 kts
Complement: 6
Guns: 2—14.5 mm (twin) MGs.

Comment: Built in Poland between 1954-59. Being deleted. Over half in reserve.
　　　　Transfers: Two to Egypt (late 1960s), four to Nicaragua (1984), five to Vietnam (October 1980).

ILYUSHA　　　　　　　　　　　　　　　　　　　　　　　　　　　　　　　　　　　　　1980

3 OLYA CLASS (MINESWEEPERS—INSHORE)

Displacement, tons: 66 full load
Dimensions, feet (metres): 74.8 × 14.8 × 4.6 *(22.8 × 4.5 × 1.4)*
Main machinery: 2 Type 3-D-12 diesels; 600 hp(m) *(440 kW)* sustained; 2 shafts
Speed, knots: 12. **Range, miles:** 500 at 10 kts
Complement: 15
Guns: 2—25 mm/80 (twin).
Radars: Surface search: Spin Trough; I band.

Comment: Built in mid-1970s. Type name is *reydny tralshchik* meaning roadstead minesweeper. One deleted in 1988-89 and one in 1991. Remainder based in the Baltic. Two to Bulgaria in mid-1970s.

K 8

AMPHIBIOUS FORCES

12 ALLIGATOR CLASS (LSTs)

Type 1	Type 2	Type 3	Type 4
KRIMSKY KOMSOMOLETS	SERGEY LAZO	ALEKSANDR TORTSEV	NIKOLAY FILCHENKOV
TOMSKY KOMSOMOLETS	BDK-69	PETR ILICHEV	NIKOLAY VILKOV
VORONEZHSKY KOMSOMOLETS		50 LET SHEFTSVA VLKSM	
KOMSOMOLETS KARELY		ILYA AZAROV	

Displacement, tons: 3400 standard; 4700 full load
Dimensions, feet (metres): 370.7 × 50.8 × 14.7
　(113 × 15.5 × 4.5)
Main machinery: 2 diesels; 9000 hp(m) *(6.6 MW)*; 2 shafts
Speed, knots: 18. **Range, miles:** 10 000 at 15 kts
Complement: 100
Military lift: 300 troops; 1700 tons including about 20 tanks and various trucks; 40 AFVs

Missiles: SAM: 3 SA-N-5 Grail twin launchers with 24 missiles in all ships except *Komsomolets Karely*, *Sergey Lazo* and *Donetsky Shakhter*.
　2 SA-N-5 Grail twin launchers *(Petr Ilichev)*; manual aiming; IR homing to 6 km *(3.2 nm)* at 1.5 Mach; altitude to 2500 m *(8000 ft)*; warhead 1.5 kg; 16 missiles.
Guns: 2—57 mm/70 (twin); 85° elevation; 120 rounds/minute to 8 km *(4.4 nm)*; weight of shell 2.8 kg.
　4—25 mm/80 (2 twin) (Type 4); 85° elevation; 270 rounds/minute to 3 km *(1.6 nm)*; weight of shell 0.34 kg.
　1—122 mm BM-21; 2 × 20-barrelled rocket launchers (in last seven); range 9 km *(5 nm)*.
Fire control: 1 Squeeze Box optronic director (Types 3 and 4).
Radars: Surface search: Two Don 2 or Don 2 and Spin Trough (in two Type 1); I band.
　Don 2 *(Krimsky Komsomolets)*; I band.

Programmes: First ship commissioned in 1966 at Kaliningrad. Last of class completed in 1976. Type name is *bolshoy desantny korabl* meaning large landing ship.
Structure: These ships have ramps on the bow and stern. There are four variations of rig. In Type 1 two cranes are carried—other types have only one crane. In Type 3 the bridge structure has been raised and a forward deck house has been added to accommodate shore bombardment rocket launchers. Type 4 is similar to Type 3 with the addition of two twin 25 mm gun mountings on centre-line abaft the bridge superstructure. As well as a tank deck 300 ft long stretching right across the hull there are two smaller deck areas and a hold.
Operational: In the 1980s the class operated regularly off West Africa, in the Mediterranean and in the Indian Ocean, usually with Naval Infantry units embarked. Two of the Type 3s were deleted in 1992.

NIKOLAY FILCHENKOV (Type 4)　　　　　　　　　　　　　　　　　　　　　　　7/1991

SERGEY LAZO (Type 2)　　　　　　　　　　　　　　　　　　　　　　　1991, Ships of the V

562 RUSSIA / Amphibious forces

3 IVAN ROGOV CLASS (LPDs)

IVAN ROGOV   ALEKSANDR NIKOLAEV   MITROFAN MOSKALENKO

Displacement, tons: 12 600 full load
Dimensions, feet (metres): 518.2 × 80.2 × 21.2 (27.8 flooded) *(158 × 24.5 × 6.5 (8.5))*
Main machinery: 2 gas turbines; 48 000 hp(m) *(35.3 MW)*; 2 shafts
Speed, knots: 25. **Range, miles:** 4000 at 18 kts
Complement: 250
Military lift: 522 troops (battalion); 20 tanks or equivalent weight of APCs and trucks; 2 Lebed class ACVs and 1 Ondatra class LCM in docking bay

Missiles: SAM: SA-N-4 Gecko twin launcher ❶; semi-active radar homing to 15 km *(8 nm)* at 2.5 Mach; warhead 50 kg; altitude 9.1-3048 m *(30-10 000 ft)*; 20 missiles.
2 SA-N-5 Grail quad launchers; manual aiming; IR homing to 6 km *(3.2 nm)* at 1.5 Mach; warhead 1.5 kg.
Guns: 2—3 in *(76 mm)*/60 (twin) ❷; 80° elevation; 60 rounds/minute to 15 km *(8 nm)*; weight of shell 6.8 kg.
1—122 mm BM-21 (naval); 2 × 20-barrelled rocket launcher; range 9 km *(5 nm)*.
4—30 mm/65 AK 630 ❸; 6 barrels per mounting; 3000 rounds/minute combined to 2 km.
Countermeasures: Decoys: 4—10-barrelled chaff launchers.
ESM: 2 Bell Squat. 2 Bell Shroud.
Fire control: 2 Squeeze Box optronic directors ❹.
Radars: Air/surface search: Head Net C (first two); Half Plate (third) ❺; 3D; E band.
Navigation: 2 Don Kay or 2 Palm Frond; I band.
Fire control: Owl Screech ❻; G band (for 76 mm). Two Bass Tilt ❼; H/I band (for 30 mm). Pop Group ❽; F/H/I band (for SA-N-4).
CCA: Fly Screen ❾; I band.
IFF: High Pole B. Salt Pot B.
Tacan: 2 Round House ❿.

Helicopters: 4 Ka-29 Helix B ⓫.

Programmes: First launched in July 1977 having been built at Kaliningrad. Second launched April 1982; third launched in July 1989 and completed trials in March 1991. No more are to be built. Type name is *bolshoy desantny korabl* meaning large landing ship.
Structure: Has bow ramp with beaching capability leading from a tank deck 200 ft long and 45 ft wide. Stern doors open into a docking bay 250 ft long and 45 ft wide. A helicopter spot forward has a flying-control station and the after helicopter deck and hangar is similarly fitted. Helicopters can enter the hangar from both front and rear. Positions arranged on main superstructure for replenishment of both fuel and solids.
Operational: The first long-range, long endurance assault capability acquired by the Soviet Navy. First two are based in the Pacific and the last one in the Northern Fleet.

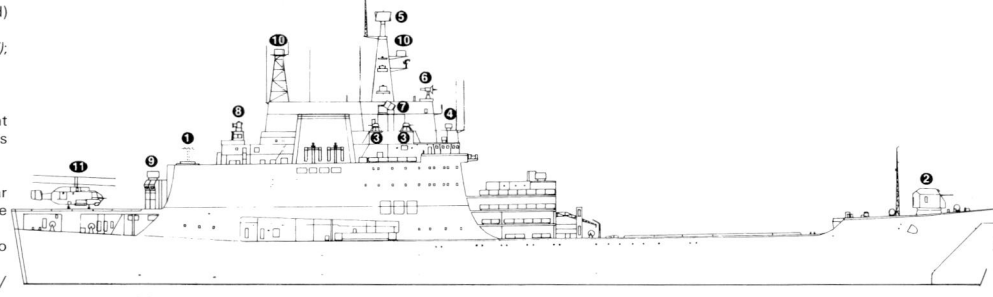
MITROFAN MOSKALENKO   *(Scale 1 : 1200), Ian Sturton*

MITROFAN MOSKALENKO   *10/1992*

25 ROPUCHA I and 3 ROPUCHA II CLASSES (TYPE B 23) (LSTs)

ALEKSANDR SHABALIN   KONSTANTIN OLSHANSKIY   TSESAR KUNIKOV   BOBRUISK

Displacement, tons: 4080 full load
Dimensions, feet (metres): 369.1 × 49.2 × 12.1 *(112.5 × 15 × 3.7)*
Main machinery: 2 Zgoda-Sulzer 16ZVB40/48 diesels; 19 230 hp(m) *(14.14 MW)* sustained; 2 shafts
Speed, knots: 17.5. **Range, miles:** 3500 at 16 kts; 6000 at 12 kts
Complement: 98
Military lift: 10 MBT plus 190 troops or 24 AFVs plus 170 troops or mines

Missiles: SAM: 4 SA-N-5 Grail quad launchers (in at least two ships); manual aiming; IR homing to 6 km *(3.2 nm)* at 1.5 Mach; altitude to 2500 m *(8000 ft)*; warhead 1.5 kg; 32 missiles.
Guns: 4—57 mm/80 (2 twin) (Ropucha I); 85° elevation; 120 rounds/minute to 6 km *(3.3 nm)*; weight of shell 2.8 kg.
1—76 mm/60 (Ropucha II); 2—30 mm/65 AK 630 (Ropucha II).
2—122 mm BM-21 (naval) (in some). 2 × 20-barrelled rocket launchers; range 9 km *(5 nm)*.
Mines: 92 contact type.
Fire Control: 2 Squeeze Box optronic directors.
Radars: Air/surface search: Strut Curve or Cross Dome (Ropucha II); F band.
Navigation: Don 2 or Kivach; I band.
Fire control: Muff Cob (Ropucha I); G/H band.
Bass Tilt (Ropucha II); H/I band.
IFF: Two High Pole A or Salt Pot A.

Programmes: Ropucha Is completed at Gdansk, Poland in two spells from 1974-78 (12 ships) and 1980-88. Ropucha IIs started building in 1987 with the first one commissioning in May 1990. The third and last of the class completed in January 1992. Type name is *bolshoy desantny korabl* meaning large landing ship.
Structure: A 'roll-on-roll-off' design with a tank deck running the whole length of the ship. All have very minor differences in appearance. These ships have a higher troop-to-vehicle ratio than the Alligator class. At least five of the class have rocket launchers at the after end of the forecastle. The second type have a 76 mm gun forward in place of one twin 57 mm and an ADG aft instead of the second. Radar and EW suites are also different. The after mast has been replaced by a solid extension to the superstructure. One Ropucha II has a masthead radome possibly with a Positive E radar underneath it.
Operational: Distributed between the four Fleets. Only four appear to show names.
Sales: One to South Yemen in 1979, returned to Russia in late 1991.

ROPUCHA II (with 76 mm gun and 30 mm ADGs)   *10/1992*

ROPUCHA I (with 57 mm guns)   *10/1992*

32 POLNOCHNY CLASS (13 GROUP A (TYPE 770), 16 GROUP B (TYPE 771), 3 GROUP C (TYPE 773)) (LSMs)

Displacement, tons: 750 standard; 800 full load (Group A)
780 standard; 834 full load (Group B)
1120 standard; 1150 full load (Group C)
Dimensions, feet (metres): 239.5 × 27.9 × 5.8
(73 × 8.5 × 1.8) (Group A)
246.1 × 31.5 × 7.5 *(75 × 9.6 × 2.3)* (Group B)
266.7 × 31.8 × 7.9 *(81.3 × 9.7 × 2.4)* (Group C)
Main machinery: 2 Kolomna Type 40-D diesels; 4400 hp(m) *(3.2 MW)* sustained; 2 shafts
Speed, knots: 19; 18 (Group C). **Range, miles:** 1000 at 18 kts (Groups A and B); 900 at 17 kts (Group C); 2000 at 12 kts (Group C)
Complement: 40-42
Military lift: 180 troops; 350 tons including 6 tanks

Missiles: SAM: 2 SA-N-5 Grail quad launchers (Group A); manual aiming; IR homing to 6 km *(3.2 nm)* at 1.5 Mach; altitude to 2500 m *(8000 ft)*; warhead 1.5 kg; 16 missiles.
4 SA-N-5 Grail quad launchers (Groups B and C); manual aiming; IR homing to 6 km *(3.2 nm)* at 1.5 Mach; altitude to 2500 m *(8000 ft)*; warhead 1.5 kg; 32 missiles.
Guns: 2—30 mm (twin) (in one ship) (Group A).
2 or 4—30 mm (1 or 2 twin) (Group B). 4—30 mm (2 twin) (Group C).
2—140 mm rocket launchers (Groups A, B and C); 18 barrels.
Fire control: PED-1 system.
Radars: Surface search: Spin Trough; I band.
Fire control: Drum Tilt; H/I band (for 30 mm guns).
IFF: High Pole A. Square Head.

Programmes: All Soviet ships built in Poland, Group A in 1963-68, Group B in 1968-70 and Group C in 1970-74. Many of Group A are unarmed. Group D are export models for Iraq, Libya and India built later than the others. Soviet type name is *stredny desantny korabl* meaning medium landing ship. Another four of the class (probably from Group B) have been converted for MCM operations (see *Mine Warfare* section).
Structure: Have bow ramps only. Tank decks vary considerably in size between groups—Group A, 36.9 × 5.2 m *(120 × 17 ft)*;

POLNOCHNY A *1991, MoD Bonn*

Group B, 45.7 × 5.2 m *(150 × 17 ft)*; Group C, 53.3 × 6.7 m *(175 × 22 ft)*. Group D have a helicopter landing platform amidships.
Operational: Many of the earlier units are being paid off.
Sales: From Navy: Algeria (one), Angola (three), Bulgaria (two), Cuba (two), Egypt (three), Ethiopia (two), Somalia (one), Syria (three), Vietnam (three), Yemen (three). All Type A or B. From Poland: India (eight), Indonesia (one), Iraq (four), Libya (four). All Type D. Of these some have been deleted. In addition 23 built for the Polish Navy, most of which have been scrapped.

POLNOCHNY C *4/1992*

9 VYDRA CLASS (LCUs)

Displacement, tons: 550 full load
Dimensions, feet (metres): 179.7 × 25.3 × 6.6 *(54.8 × 7.7 × 2)*
Main machinery: 2 Type 3-D-12 diesels; 600 hp(m) *(440 kW)* sustained; 2 shafts
Speed, knots: 12. **Range, miles:** 2500 at 10 kts
Complement: 20
Military lift: 3 MBTs or 200 tons or 100 troops
Radars: Navigation: Don 2; I band.

Comment: Built from 1967-69 to a German MFP design. No armament. Transfers: 19 to Bulgaria, 10 to Egypt. Some employed as YF transports.

14 ONDATRA CLASS (LCMs)

Displacement, tons: 145 full load
Dimensions, feet (metres): 78.7 × 16.4 × 4.9 *(24 × 5 × 1.5)*
Main machinery: 1 diesel; 300 hp(m) *(220 kW)*
Speed, knots: 10. **Range, miles:** 500 at 5 kts
Military lift: 1 MBT

Comment: First completed in 1979—associated with *Ivan Rogov*. Tank deck of 45 × 13 ft.

VYDRA *8/1980, MoD*

ONDATRA *4/1979, MoD*

AMPHIBIOUS CRAFT (AIR CUSHION VEHICLES)

Notes: (a) Fuller details appear in the latest edition of *Jane's High-Speed Marine Craft and Air-Cushion Vehicles.*
(b) Pelikan class is included under *Mine Warfare Forces.*

7 POMORNIK CLASS

Displacement, tons: 370 full load
Dimensions, feet (metres): 189 × 70.5 *(57.6 × 21.5)*
Main machinery: 5 Type NK-12MV gas turbines (2 for lift, 23 672 hp(m) *(17.4 MW)* nominal; 3 for drive, 35 508 hp(m) *(26.1 MW)* nominal
Speed, knots: 63
Complement: 40
Military lift: 3 MBT or 10 APC plus 1 Infantry Company
Missiles: SAM: 2 SA-N-5 Grail quad launchers; manual aiming; IR homing to 6 km *(3.2 nm)* at 1.5 Mach; altitude to 2500 m *(8000 ft)*; warhead 1.5 kg.
Guns: 2—30 mm/65 AK 630; 6 barrels per mounting; 3000 rounds/minute combined to 2 km. 2 retractable 122 mm rocket launchers (not in first of class).
Fire control: Quad Look (modified Squeeze Box) optronic director.
Radars: Air/surface search: Kivach II or Cross Dome; I band.
Fire control: Bass Tilt; H/I band.
IFF: Salt Pot A/B; High Pole A.

Comment: First of class delivered 1986. Produced at St Petersburg and at Feodosiya. Probable total of seven for Russia with more building for export. Bow and stern ramps for ro-ro working. The three Black Sea units have a different radar. The other four are in the Baltic.

POMORNIK (with Cross Dome) 1991

POMORNIK (with Kivach II and rocket launchers raised) 1992, S S Breyer

18 AIST (DZHEYRAN) CLASS

Displacement, tons: 275 full load
Dimensions, feet (metres): 155.2 × 58.4 *(47.3 × 17.8)*
Main machinery: 2 Type NK-12M gas turbines driving four axial lift fans and four propeller units for propulsion; 19 200 hp(m) *(14.1 MW)* nominal
Speed, knots: 70. **Range, miles:** 120 at 50 kts
Complement: 10
Military lift: 80 tons or 4 light tanks plus 50 troops or 2 medium tanks plus 200 troops or 3 APCs plus 100 troops
Guns: 4—30 mm/65 (2 twin) AK 630; 6 barrels per mounting; 3000 rounds/minute combined to 2 km.
Radars: Surface search: Kivach; I band.
Fire control: Drum Tilt; H/I band.
IFF: High Pole B. Square Head.

Comment: First produced at Leningrad in 1970, subsequent production at rate of about six every four years. The first large hovercraft for naval use. Similar to British SR. N4. Type name is *maly desantny korabl na vozdushnoy podushke* meaning small ACV. Modifications have been done to the original engines and some units have been reported carrying two SA-N-5 quadruple SAM systems and chaff launchers. One scrapped in the Baltic in 1988.

AIST 10/1992, Hartmut Ehlers

9 + 2 TSAPLYA CLASS

Displacement, tons: 115 full load
Dimensions, feet (metres): 102.4 × 42.6 *(31.2 × 13)*
Main machinery: 2 gas turbines; 8000 hp(m) *(5.88 MW)*; 2 shafts
Speed, knots: 70
Complement: 6
Military lift: 1 MBT plus 80 troops or 25 tons plus 160 troops
Guns: 2—30 mm/65 AK 630. 8—14.5 mm MGs (4 twin).

Comment: Prototype built at Feodosiya entered service in 1982, second in 1987, and then at about one a year. Follow-on to the Lebed class and to replace the Gus class. Embarked in Ivan Rogov class.

TSAPLYA 1989

16 LEBED (KALMAR) CLASS

Displacement, tons: 87 full load
Dimensions, feet (metres): 80.1 × 36.7 *(24.4 × 11.2)*
Main machinery: 2 Ivchenko AI-20K gas turbines for lift and propulsion; 8000 hp(m) *(5.88 MW)*
Speed, knots: 50. **Range, miles:** 100 at 50 kts
Complement: 6 (2 officers)
Military lift: 2 light tanks or 40 tons cargo or 120 troops
Guns: 2—30 mm (twin) MGs.
Radars: Navigation: Kivach; I band.

Comment: First entered service 1975. At least two can be carried in Ivan Rogov class. Have a bow ramp with gun on starboard side and the bridge to port. Three scrapped in 1992. The Russian name for the class is shared with the Delta III SSBN.

LEBED 9/1991

2 UTENOK CLASS

Displacement, tons: 70 full load
Dimensions, feet (metres): 75.4 × 36.1 *(23 × 11)*
Main machinery: 1 gas turbine; 530 hp(m) *(390 kW)*; 2 airscrews
Speed, knots: 65
Military lift: 1 MBT or 24 tons.
Guns: 2—30 mm/65 (twin).

Comment: Completed at Feodosiya in 1980-81.

10 GUS (SKAT) CLASS

Displacement, tons: 27 full load
Dimensions, feet (metres): 67.6 × 24 *(20.6 × 7.3)*
Main machinery: 2 TVD-10 marine gas turbines; 1560 hp(m) *(1.15 MW)* (propulsion); 1 TVD-10 marine gas turbine; 780 hp(m) *(573 kW)* (lift)
Speed, knots: 60. **Range, miles:** 230 at 43 kts; 185 at 50 kts
Complement: 6
Military lift: 70 tons or 25 troops and equipment

Comment: Completed 1969-1974. This is a naval version of a passenger carrying design *(Skate)*. Built for Naval Infantry. Deployed to all fleets except Northern. Rapidly being scrapped.

GUS 9/1981, Royal Danish Navy

1 UTKA (LON) and 2 ORLAN (ORLENOK) CLASSES
(WING-IN-GROUND EFFECT CRAFT)

Displacement, tons: 125 full load
Dimensions, feet (metres): 190.3 × 103.3 *(58 × 31.5)*
Main machinery: 1 NK-12 gas turbine; 12 000 hp(m) *(8.82 MW)* (propulsion); 2 NK-8 gas turbines (lift)
Speed, knots: 250. **Range, miles:** 1200 at 250 kts
Complement: 5
Military lift: 28 tons or 150 troops with equipment

Comment: Details given are for the Orlan class which is an amphibious transporter. This type of craft takes advantage of the lift created between a wide wing and the ground at low altitude. On take-off the forward engines are angled down to generate initial lift. The first experimental craft dates back to the 1960s followed by two prototypes completed in 1982. *Utka* is 246 ft *(75 m)* in length and has a wing span of 134.5 ft *(41 m)*. Weight is 400 tons and it is thought to have an operational radius of 1000 nm flying at an altitude of 5 m. There are eight turbofan engines and the craft is armed with six SS-N-22 anti-ship missiles. In service in 1989. This was an ambitious programme which is reported to have failed mainly because of corrosion problems associated with flying so close to the sea. All these craft are probably for sale. At least one crashed during testing and a second was scrapped after an accident in the Black Sea in August 1992.

ORLAN 1990

SUPPORT AND DEPOT SHIPS

5 UGRA CLASS (SUBMARINE DEPOT SHIPS)

IVAN KOLYSHKIN   IVAN KUCHERENKO   IVAN VAKHRAMEEV   TOBOL   VOLGA

Displacement, tons: 6750 standard; 9650 full load
Dimensions, feet (metres): 462.6 × 57.7 × 23 *(141 × 17.6 × 7)*
Main machinery: Diesel-electric; 4 Kolomna Type 2-D-42 diesel generators; 2 motors; 8000 hp(m) *(5.88 MW)*; 2 shafts
Speed, knots: 17. **Range, miles:** 21 000 at 10 kts; 9500 at 16 kts
Complement: 450

Missiles: SAM: 2 SA-N-5 Grail quad launchers; manual aiming; IR homing to 6 km *(3.2 nm)* at 1.5 Mach; altitude to 2500 m *(8000 ft)*; warhead 1.5 kg; 16 missiles (in some ships).
Guns: 8—57 mm/70 (4 twin).
Countermeasures: ESM: 2 Watch Dog.
Radars: Air/surface search: Strut Curve; F band.
Navigation: Two Don 2; I band.
Fire control: Two Muff Cob; G/H band.
IFF: Two Square Head. High Pole B.

Helicopters: Platform (hangar in *Ivan Kolyshkin*).

Programmes: Built at Nikolayev from 1962 to 1970. Type name is *plavuchaya baza* meaning floating base.
Structure: Improved versions of the Don class with the superstructure stretching aft to the funnel. Equipped with workshops. Provided with a helicopter platform and, in *Ivan Kolyshkin* (last of class), a hangar. Has mooring points in hull about 100 ft apart, and has baggage ports for coastal craft and submarines. Two 10 ton and two 5 ton cranes. *Volga* and some others have lattice mainmast with Vee Cone HF antenna.

Operational: Two scrapped in 1991. The last pair of this class were completed as training ships (*Borodino* and *Gangut*). *Tobol* to be sold in 1993.
Sales: *Amba*, (sixth of class) which has 76 mm guns, was transferred to India in 1969.

IVAN KOLYSHKIN (with hangar) 1988

5 DON (BATOOR) CLASS (SUBMARINE DEPOT SHIPS)

FEDOR VIDYAYEV   KAMCHATSKY KOMSOMOLETS (ex-*Mikhail Tukhachevsky*)   MAGOMET GADZHIEV
VIKTOR KOTELNIKOV   MAGADANSKY KOMSOMOLETS

Displacement, tons: 5100 standard; 6850 full load
Dimensions, feet (metres): 459.3 × 57.7 × 17.7 *(140 × 17.6 × 5.4)*
Main machinery: Diesel-electric; 4 diesel generators; 2 motors; 8000 hp(m) *(5.88 MW)*; 2 shafts
Speed, knots: 17. **Range, miles:** 21 000 at 10 kts; 9500 at 16 kts
Complement: 300 plus 450 submariners

Guns: 4—3.9 in *(100 mm)*/56 (2 in *Viktor Kotelnikov*, none mounted in *Magadansky Komsomolets*).
8—57 mm/70 (4 twin).
8—25 mm/80 (4 twin) (mounted in *K. Komsomolets* and *Fedor Vidyayev*).
Countermeasures: ESM: 2 Watch Dog.
Radars: Surface search: Slim Net; E/F band. Strut Curve (in some); F band.
Navigation: Two Don 2; I band. Snoop Plate (in some); I band.
Fire control: Two Hawk Screech (not in *M. Komsomolets*); I band.
IFF: Two Square Head. High Pole A.

Helicopters: Platform (*Magadansky Komsomolets* and *Viktor Kotelnikov*).

Programmes: Originally seven ships were built in 1957 to 1962, all in Nikolayev. Type name is *plavuchaya baza* meaning floating base.
Structure: Have a 100 ton bow lift and two 10 ton and two 5 ton cranes.
Operational: Used as Flagships. Vee Cone fitted in *Fedor Vidyayev* for long-range communications. One scrapped in the Black Sea in 1991.
Sales: One to Indonesia in 1962.

VIKTOR KOTELNIKOV 11/1990

566 RUSSIA / Support and depot ships

1 ALEKSANDR BRYKIN CLASS (MISSILE SUPPORT SHIP)

ALEKSANDR BRYKIN

Displacement, tons: 14 350 full load
Dimensions, feet (metres): 511.8 × 76.1 × 26.2 *(156 × 23.2 × 8)*
Main machinery: Diesel-electric; 2 diesel generators; 1 motor; 26 000 hp(m) *(19 MW)*; 1 shaft; bow thruster
Speed, knots: 16
Complement: 140
Missiles: SAM: 4 SA-N-5 Grail quad launchers; manual aiming; IR homing to 6 km *(3.2 nm)* at 1.5 Mach; altitude to 2500 m *(8000 ft)*; warhead 1.5 kg.
Guns: 4—30 mm/65 AK 630.
Countermeasures: ESM: 2 Bell Shroud; 2 Bell Squat.
Radars: Surface search: Half Plate Alpha; E/F band.
Navigation: 2 Nayhda; I band.
Fire control: Two Bass Tilt; H/I band.
IFF: Salt Pot. Longhead.

Comment: Completed in Leningrad in 1986. A missile supply ship for submarine ballistic missiles including SS-N-20, carried in the Typhoon class. A 75 ton crane plumbs 16 vertical storage holds forward of the funnel. Transferred to Northern Fleet in 1987.

ALEKSANDR BRYKIN 5/1987

3 AMGA CLASS (MISSILE SUPPORT SHIPS)

AMGA   VETLUGA   DAUGAVA

Displacement, tons: 5750 *(Amga)*, 6100 *(Vetluga)*, 6400 *(Daugava)* full load
Dimensions, feet (metres): 334.6 × 59 × 14.8 *(102 × 18 × 4.5)* *(Amga)* (see *Comment*)
Main machinery: 2 diesels; 9000 hp(m) *(6.6 MW)*; 2 shafts
Speed, knots: 16. **Range, miles:** 4500 at 14 kts
Complement: 210
Guns: 4—25 mm/80 (2 twin).
Radars: Surface search: Strut Curve; F band; range 110 km *(60 nm)* for 2 m² target.
Navigation: Don 2; I band.
IFF: High Pole B.

Comment: Built at Gorkiy. Ships with similar duties to the Lama class. Fitted with a large 55 ton crane forward and thus capable of handling much larger missiles than their predecessors. Each ship has a different length and type of crane to handle later types of missiles. Designed for servicing submarines, particularly those armed with SS-N-6, 8 and 18 missiles. First appeared in December 1972, the second *Vetluga* (6 m longer than *Amga*) in 1976 and third *Daugava* (11 m longer than *Amga*) in 1981. *Amga* in the North, *Vetluga* and *Daugava* in the Pacific.

DAUGAVA 10/1981, MoD

2 PINEGA CLASS (NUCLEAR SUBMARINE SUPPORT SHIPS)

AMUR   PINEGA

Displacement, tons: 6500 full load
Dimensions, feet (metres): 393.7 × 55.8 × 18 *(120 × 17 × 5.5)*
Main machinery: 2 diesels; 6800 hp(m) *(5 MW)*; 2 shafts
Speed, knots: 16
Complement: 100

Comment: Built at Vyborg. *Amur* completed in 1986 and went to the Northern Fleet. *Pinega* completed in 1987 and transferred to the Pacific in 1989.

PM 74 1990

2 MODIFIED ANDIZHAN CLASS (MISSILE SUPPORT SHIPS)

VENTA   VILYUY

Displacement, tons: 6700 full load
Dimensions, feet (metres): 341.1 × 47.2 × 21.6 *(104 × 14.4 × 6.6)*
Main machinery: 2 diesels; 2500 hp(m) *(1.84 MW)*; 2 shafts
Speed, knots: 14. **Range, miles:** 6000 at 13 kts
Complement: 60
Radars: Navigation: Don 2; I band.
IFF: Square Head. High Pole.

Comment: Cargo ships built in late 1950s at Rostock. Converted to support ships 1974-75. Have one main crane forward, two smaller cranes aft and a helicopter platform. Can carry 10 SS-N-9 missiles as well as 20 SA-N-3. Type name is *voyenny transport* meaning military transport. *Venta* in the Pacific, *Vilyuy* in the Black Sea.

PINEGA 10/1991, G Jacobs

3 MALINA CLASS (NUCLEAR SUBMARINE SUPPORT SHIPS)

PM 63   PM 74   PM 12

Displacement, tons: 10 500 full load
Dimensions, feet (metres): 449.5 × 68.9 × 18.4 *(137 × 21 × 5.6)*
Main machinery: 4 gas turbines; 60 000 hp(m) *(44 MW)*; 2 shafts
Speed, knots: 17
Complement: 260
Radars: Navigation: Two Palm Frond; I band.

Comment: Built at Nikolayev. First deployed to the Northern Fleet in October 1984, second to Pacific in 1986, and third to the Northern Fleet in 1991. Designed to support nuclear-powered submarines and surface ships. Carry two 15 ton cranes.

VENTA 1980

7 LAMA CLASS (MISSILE SUPPORT SHIPS)

GENERAL RYABAKOV (877)   918   872   873   874   + 2

Displacement, tons: 4600 full load
Dimensions, feet (metres): 370 × 49.2 × 14.4 *(112.8 × 15 × 4.4)*
Main machinery: 2 diesels; 4800 hp(m) *(3 MW)*; 2 shafts
Speed, knots: 14. Range, miles: 6000 at 10 kts
Complement: 200
Missiles: SAM: 4 SA-N-5 Grail quad launchers *(General Ryabakov, Voronesh, PM 131 and PM 154)*; manual aiming; IR homing to 6 km *(3.2 nm)* at 1.5 Mach; altitude to 2500 m *(8000 ft)*; warhead 1.5 kg.
Guns: 4 or 8—57 mm/70 (quad, on the fo'c'sle or 2 or 4 twin) *(PM 44 and PM 131)*.
  4—25 mm/80 *(PM 44 and PM 131)*.
Radars: Surface search: Slim Net; E/F band *(Voronesh, PM 44 and PM 154)* or Strut Curve (remainder); F band.
Navigation: Don 2; I band.
Fire control: Two Hawk Screech or Owl Screech *(PM 44)*; I band or Muff Cob; G/H band.
IFF: Two Square Head. High Pole A.

Comment: Built between 1963 and 1972 at Nikolayev with seventh ship in 1979. The engines are sited aft to allow for a very large and high hangar or hold amidships for carrying missiles or weapons' spares for submarines, surface ships and missile craft. This is about 12 ft high above the main deck. There are doors at the forward end with rails leading in and a raised turntable gantry or 20 ton travelling cranes for armament supply. Variations in armament may reflect differences in missile stowage. The well-deck is about 40 ft long, enough for most missiles to fit horizontally before being lifted for loading. There are several differences in midships superstructure in these ships, those specifically designed for missile craft having a longer missile store, two 10 ton cranes and a shorter forward well-deck. Type name is *plavuchaya masterskaya* meaning floating workshop. PM numbers have been removed. *918* and *872* are in the North; *873, 874* and *877* in the Black Sea; the other pair are in the Pacific.

LAMA 872   6/1989

23 AMUR I and 5 AMUR II CLASS (REPAIR SHIPS)

AMUR I
PM 9, PM 10, PM 37, PM 49, PM 56, PM 75, PM 138, PM 161, PM 163
5, 15, 30, 34, 40, 52, 64, 73, 81, 82, 129, 139, 140, 156
AMUR II
59, 69, 86, 92, 97

Displacement, tons: 5500 full load
Dimensions, feet (metres): 400.3 × 55.8 × 16.7 *(122 × 17 × 5.1)*
Main machinery: 1 diesel; 3000 hp(m) *(2.2 MW)*; 1 shaft
Speed, knots: 12. Range, miles: 13 000 at 8 kts
Complement: 145
Radars: Navigation: Don 2; I band.

Comment: Amur I class general purpose depot and repair ships completed 1968-83 in Szczecin, Poland. Successors to the Oskol class. Carry two 5 ton cranes and have accommodation for 200 from ships alongside. Amur II class similar in design. Built at Szczecin 1983-85. *PM 94* scrapped in the Baltic in 1992.

PM 138 (Amur I)   1992

PM 97 (Amur II)   9/1991, G Jacobs

11 OSKOL CLASS (REPAIR SHIPS)

PM 2, PM 24, PM 26, PM 42, PM 147, PM 148
20, 21, 51, 68, 146

Displacement, tons: 2550 (3500, Oskol IV) full load
Dimensions, feet (metres): 300.1 × 40 × 13.1 *(91.5 × 12.2 × 4)*
Main machinery: 2 diesels; 2500 hp(m) *(1.84 MW)*; 1 shaft
Speed, knots: 12. Range, miles: 8000 at 10 kts
Complement: 100
Radars: Navigation: Don 2; I band.
IFF: High Pole.

Comment: Four series: Oskol I class, well-decked hull, no armament; Oskol II class, well-decked hull, open promenade deck aft and twin 14.5 mm MGs forward; Oskol III class, well-decked hull, armed with two 57 mm guns (one twin forward) and four 25 mm guns (2 twin aft); Oskol IV class, flush-decked hull with no armament and a bridge one deck higher than other types. General purpose tenders and repair ships with one or two 3.5 ton cranes. Built from 1963 to 1970 in Poland. Type name is *plavuchaya masterskaya* meaning floating workshop. *PM 21* to South Yemen in 1988 but may have been returned, in which case there are 12 in the class.

OSKOL III PM 24 (with twin 57 mm gun)   4/1991

4 TOMBA CLASS (SUPPORT SHIPS)

244, 254, 348, 357

Displacement, tons: 5200 full load
Dimensions, feet (metres): 351 × 55.8 × 16.4 *(107 × 17 × 5)*
Main machinery: Diesel-electric; 3 diesel generators; 1 motor; 5500 hp(m) *(4 MW)*; 1 shaft
Speed, knots: 18. Range, miles: 7000 at 14 kts
Complement: 50
Radars: Navigation: Don 2 and Spin Trough; I band.
IFF: High Pole B.

Comment: First completed 1974. *254* deployed in Northern Fleet, *244* in the Baltic and *348* and *357* in the Pacific. There is a donkey funnel on fo'c'sle. Two 3 ton cranes. Type name is *elektrostantsiye nalivatelnoye sudno* meaning electricity supply ship.

TOMBA   10/1982

8 VYTEGRALES CLASS

APSHERON (ex-*Vagales*)   **DONBAS** (ex-*Vostok 4*)
BASKUNCHAK (ex-*Kirishi*)   **SEVAN** (ex-*Siverles*)
DAURIYA (ex-*Vyborgles*)   **TAMAN** (ex-*Suzdal*)
DIKSON (ex-*Vostok 3*)   **YAMAL** (ex-*Tosnoles*)

Displacement, tons: 6150 full load
Dimensions, feet (metres): 400.3 × 55.1 × 22.3 *(122.1 × 16.8 × 6.8)*
Main machinery: 1 Burmeister & Wain 950VTBF diesel; 5200 hp(m) *(3.82 MW)*; 1 shaft
Speed, knots: 15
Complement: 150
Radars: Air search: Big Net; C band *(Donbas only)*.
Navigation: Two Don 2; I band.
Helicopters: 1 Ka-25 'Hormone C'.

Comment: Standard timber carriers of a class of 27. These eight ships were modified for naval use in 1966-68 with helicopter flight deck. Built at Zhdanov Yard, Leningrad between 1963 and 1966. *Sevan* and *Taman* fitted as squadron Flagships in support of Indian Ocean detachments. Variations exist between ships of this class; *Baskunchak* and *Dauriya* have a deckhouse over the aft hold and *Donbas* has a large air-search radar aerial on the central mast. All have two Vee Cone communications aerials. The first of class, completed in 1962, was originally *Vytegrales*, but this was later changed to *Kosmonaut Pavel Belyayev* and, with three other ships of this class, converted to Space Support Ships. Four others *(Borovichi* etc) received a different conversion for the same purpose. *Dikson* which is a trials ship was laid up in 1992. The eight civilian-manned ships together with these eight naval ships are often incorrectly called Vostok or Baskunchak class.

BASKUNCHAK   5/1992, van Ginderen Collection

BARRACKS SHIPS
8 BOLVA 1, 30 BOLVA 2 and 10 BOLVA 3 CLASSES

Displacement, tons: 6500
Dimensions, feet (metres): 560.9 × 45.9 × 9.8 *(110 × 14 × 3)*
Cargo capacity: 350-400 tons

Comment: All built by Valmet Oy, Helsinki between 1960-74. Used for accommodation of ships' companies during refit etc. The Bolva 2 and 3 have a helicopter pad. Have alongside berthing facilities for about 400. Have no means of propulsion but can be steered. In addition there are several other types of Barracks Ships including five ex-Atrek class depot ships as well as converted merchant ships and large barges.

INTELLIGENCE COLLECTORS (AGIs)

Notes: (a) About half of the AGIs are fitted with SA-N-5 (Grail).
(b) SSV in pennant numbers of some AGIs is a contraction of *sudno svyazy* meaning communications vessel.
(c) GS in pennant numbers of some AGIs is a contraction of *gidrograficheskoye sudno* meaning survey ship.
(d) One Keyla class *(Ritsa)* converted to AGI in 1987. Details under Keyla class.
(e) Since 1991 activity has been largely confined to an area from the Baltic approaches to the Mediterranean, and occasional excursions to the South China Seas.

7 VISHNYA CLASS (TYPE 864)

SSV 169, SSV 175, SSV 201, SSV 208, SSV 231, SSV 520, SSV 535

Displacement, tons: 3470 full load
Dimensions, feet (metres): 309.7 × 47.9 × 14.8 *(94.4 × 14.6 × 4.5)*
Main machinery: 2 Zgoda 12AV25/30 diesels; 4406 hp(m) *(3.24 MW)* sustained; 2 auxiliary electric motors; 286 hp(m) *(210 kW)*; 2 shafts; cp props
Speed, knots: 16. Range, miles: 7000 at 14 kts
Complement: 146
Missiles: SAM: 2 SA-N-5 Grail quad launchers; manual aiming; IR homing to 6 km *(3.2 nm)* at 1.5 Mach; altitude to 2500 m *(8000 ft)*; warhead 1.5 kg.
Guns: 2—30 mm/65 AK 630; 6 barrels per mounting. 2—72 mm four-tubed rocket launchers.

Comment: Built in Poland. First of class entered service in July 1986, the last had completed by July 1988. *SSV 169, 231* and *520* based in the Baltic, *SSV 175* and *201* in the Black Sea and *SSV 208* and *535* in the Pacific. NBC pressurised citadels. Ice-strengthened hulls.

SSV 231   6/1991, Foto Flite

SSV 175   10/1992

4 BALZAM CLASS

SSV 80   SSV 493   SSV 516   SSV 571

Displacement, tons: 4000 standard; 5400 full load
Dimensions, feet (metres): 344.5 × 50.9 × 16.4 *(105 × 15.5 × 5)*
Main machinery: 2 diesels; 18 000 hp(m) *(13.2 MW)*; 2 shafts
Speed, knots: 20. Range, miles: 7000 at 16 kts
Complement: 200
Missiles: SAM: 2 SA-N-5 Grail quad launchers; manual aiming; IR homing to 6 km *(3.2 nm)* at 1.5 Mach; altitude to 2500 m *(8000 ft)*; warhead 1.5 kg; 16 missiles.
Guns: 1—30 mm/65 AK 630; 6 barrels per mounting.

Comment: All built at Kaliningrad. First of class completed in 1980, second in 1981, third in 1984 and last in 1987. Notable for twin radomes. The first class of AGI to be armed. *SSV 80* and *493* based in Pacific, the other two in the Northern Fleet.

SSV 493   10/1991, G Jacobs

6 PRIMORYE CLASS

ZABAYKALYE SSV 464	ZAKARPATYE SSV 502
PRIMORYE SSV 465	KRYM SSV 590
ZAPOROZHYE SSV 501	KAVKAZ SSV 591

Displacement, tons: 3400 standard; 5000 full load
Dimensions, feet (metres): 278 × 46 × 23 *(84.7 × 14 × 7)*
Main machinery: 2 diesels; 2000 hp(m) *(1.47 MW)*; 2 shafts
Speed, knots: 12. Range, miles: 10 000 at 10 kts
Complement: 120
Missiles: SAM: 2 SA-N-5 Grail quad launchers (SSV 464, 501 and 591); manual aiming; IR homing to 6 km *(3.2 nm)* at 1.5 Mach; altitude to 2500 m *(8000 ft)*; warhead 1.5 kg; 16 missiles. SSV 590 has 1 launcher.

Comment: The first custom-built class of AGIs and the first to have an onboard analysis capability. First unit built 1968-70 to the same hull design as the Mayakovsky class of stern trawlers. Mast arrangements and electronic fits vary between ships. SSV 464 and 465 in the Pacific, 501 and 502 in the North and 590 and 591 in the Black Sea. SSV 501 has a Mad Hack active phased array radar for the collection of missile related data and telemetry.

KAVKAZ   11/1989

ZAKARPATYE   1986, US Navy

ZAPOROZHYE   5/1992

PRIMORYE   9/1992, Hachiro Naka

3 NIKOLAY ZUBOV CLASS

GAVRIL SARYCHEV (mod) SSV 468 **KHARITON LAPTEV** (mod) SSV 503
SEMEN CHELYUSKIN SSV 469

Displacement, tons: 2674 standard; 3021 full load
Dimensions, feet (metres): 294.2 × 42.7 × 15 *(89.7 × 13 × 4.6)*
Main machinery: 2 Zgoda 8TD48 diesels; 4400 hp(m) *(3.23 MW)* sustained; 2 shafts
Speed, knots: 16.5. **Range, miles:** 11 000 at 14 kts
Complement: 85
Missiles: SAM: 3 SA-N-5 Grail quad launchers (SSV 468 and 469); manual aiming; IR homing to 6 km *(3.2 nm)* at 1.5 Mach; altitude to 2500 m *(8000 ft)*; warhead 1.5 kg; 24 missiles.

Comment: Built in Poland. Similar class operates as research ships. SSV 468 and SSV 503 now have additional superstructure and a flush deck from bow to stern. Operational in 1965. SSV 468 and 469 in the Pacific, 503 in the Northern Fleet.

SEMEN CHELYUSKIN   *8/1991, G Jacobs*

1 MODIFIED PAMIR CLASS

PELENG (ex-*Arban*) SSV 477

Displacement, tons: 1443 standard; 2240 full load
Dimensions, feet (metres): 256 × 42 × 13.5 *(78 × 12.8 × 4.1)*
Main machinery: 2 MAN Giot 40/60 diesels; 4200 hp(m) *(3.1 MW)*; 2 shafts; cp props
Speed, knots: 18. **Range, miles:** 21 000 at 12 kts
Complement: 60
Missiles: SAM: 3 SA-N-5 Grail quad launchers; manual aiming; IR homing to 6 km *(3.2 nm)* at 1.5 Mach; altitude to 2500 m *(8000 ft)*; warhead 1.5 kg; 24 missiles.

Comment: Built in Sweden 1959-60. Originally a salvage tug and has higher deckhouse abaft bridge than other ships of class. Converted to AGI by 1965. Based in the Pacific.

PELENG   *1985*

9 MOMA CLASS

EKVATOR   **SSV 472** (ex-*Ilmen*) (mod)   **SSV 509** (ex-*Pelorus*) (mod)
YUPITER (mod)   **SSV 474** (ex-*Vega*) (mod)   **SSV 512** (ex-*Arkhipelag*) (mod)
KILDIN (mod)   **SSV 506** (ex-*Nakhodka*)   **SSV 514** (ex-*Seliger*) (mod)

Displacement, tons: 1240 standard; 1600 full load
Dimensions, feet (metres): 240.5 × 36.8 × 12.8 *(73.3 × 11.2 × 3.9)*
Main machinery: 2 Zgoda-Sulzer 6TD48 diesels; 3300 hp(m) *(2.43 MW)* sustained; 2 shafts
Speed, knots: 17. **Range, miles:** 9000 at 11 kts
Complement: 85
Missiles: SAM: 2 SA-N-5 Grail quad launchers (SSV 472, 474, 514, *Kildin* and *Yupiter*); manual aiming; IR homing to 6 km *(3.2 nm)* at 1.5 Mach; altitude to 2500 m *(8000 ft)*; warhead 1.5 kg; 16 missiles.

Comment: The six modernised versions have a foremast in the fore well-deck and a new, low superstructure before the bridge. Non-modernised ships retain their cranes in the forward well-deck. Similar class operates as survey ships. Built at Gdansk, Poland between 1968-72. *SSV 472* and *474* in the Pacific, named ships in the Black Sea, remainder Northern Fleet.

SSV 512   *7/1992*

YUPITER   *1986, US Navy*

EKVATOR   *5/1991*

4 ALPINIST CLASS

GS 7 (mod)   **GS 8**   **GS 19** (mod)   **GS 39** (mod)

Displacement, tons: 1260 full load
Dimensions, feet (metres): 177.1 × 34.4 × 13.1 *(54 × 10.5 × 4)*
Main machinery: 1 SKL 8 NVD 48 A2U diesel; 1320 hp(m) *(970 kW)* sustained; 1 shaft; bow thruster
Speed, knots: 13. **Range, miles:** 7000 at 13 kts
Complement: 50
Missiles: SAM: 1 SA-N-5 Grail quad launcher *(GS 39)*; manual aiming; IR homing to 6 km *(3.2 nm)* at 1.5 Mach; altitude to 2500 m *(8000 ft)*; warhead 1.5 kg.

Comment: Similar to Alpinist stern-trawlers which have been built at about 10 a year at the Leninskaya Kuznitsa yard at Kiev and at the Volvograd shipyard. These AGIs could come from either yard. In 1987 and 1988 *GS 7, GS 39* and *GS 19* forecastle was extended further aft and the electronics fit upgraded. *GS 7* and *GS 8* in the Pacific, the other two in the Baltic.

GS 19   *6/1990, Foto Flite*

GS 39   *5/1989, Hartmut Ehlers*

8 MAYAK CLASS

KHERSONES	GS 239
KURS	GS 242
KURSOGRAF	GIRORULEVOY
LADOGA	ANEROID

Displacement, tons: 914 full load
Dimensions, feet (metres): 178.1 × 30.5 × 11.8 *(54.3 × 9.3 × 3.6)*
Main machinery: 1 SKL 8 NVD 48 2U diesel; 880 hp(m) *(647 kW)* sustained; 1 shaft
Speed, knots: 16. **Range, miles:** 9500 at 7.5 kts
Complement: 75
Missiles: SAM: 2 SA-N-5 Grail quad launchers (in all except *GS 239, Girorulevoy* and *Khersones*); manual aiming; IR homing to 6 km *(3.2 nm)* at 1.5 Mach; altitude to 2500 m *(8000 ft)*; warhead 1.5 kg; 16 missiles.
Guns: 4—14.5 mm (2 twin) MGs (*Kursograf* only).

Comment: Built in the USSR from 1965. All ships except *Aneroid* have had additional accommodation built on the well-deck. The port side of the superstructure is enclosed while the starboard is open. *Kursograf* and *Aneroid* are in the Pacific, *GS 239, Kurs* and *Ladoga* in the Black Sea and remainder in the Baltic. More ships of the class are in the *Transports* section.

12 OKEAN CLASS

ALIDADA*	KRENOMETR	REPITER
BAROGRAF	LINZA (mod)*	TEODOLIT
DEFLEKTOR	LOTLIN (mod)*	TRAVERZ
EKHOLOT	REDUKTOR (mod)*	ZOND (mod)*

* No missiles

Displacement, tons: 750 full load
Dimensions, feet (metres): 167.3 × 28.9 × 12.1 *(51 × 8.8 × 3.7)*
Main machinery: 1 diesel; 540 hp(m) *(397 kW)*; 1 shaft
Speed, knots: 13. **Range, miles:** 7900 at 11 kts
Complement: 70
Missiles: SAM: 2 SA-N-5 Grail quad launchers (in some ships); manual aiming; IR homing to 6 km *(3.2 nm)* at 1.5 Mach; altitude to 2500 m *(8000 ft)*; warhead 1.5 kg; 16 missiles.

Comment: Built in East Germany from 1959 to mid-1960s. Have the same unbalanced superstructure with the port side closed in and the starboard side open as in the Mayak class, although there are many variations. Modified ships have additional accommodation on the well-deck. Three of the class scrapped in 1990-91. *Alidada* in the Black Sea, *Barograf* and *Deflektor* in the Pacific, *Lotlin, Reduktor* and *Zond* in the Baltic, and the remainder in Northern Fleet. Baltic Fleet units were active in 1992, some of the others may be about to be scrapped.

KHERSONES 9/1992

LOTLIN (mod) 10/1992

KURS 5/1990

LINZA (mod) 5/1989

GS 242 5/1991

REDUKTOR (mod) 10/1992

4 LENTRA CLASS

GS 41 GS 43 (mod) GS 55 GS 59

Displacement, tons: 250 standard; 480 (600, *GS 43* and *55*) full load
Dimensions, feet (metres): 128.6 × 24.3 × 9.2 *(39.2 × 7.4 × 2.8)*
  141.7 × 24.9 × 9.5 *(43.2 × 7.6 × 2.9)* (*GS 43* and *55*)
Main machinery: 1 diesel; 330 hp(m) *(243 kW)* (450 hp(m) *(331 kW)* in *GS 43* and *55*); 1 shaft
Speed, knots: 11. **Range, miles:** 6000 at 9 kts
Complement: 35; 45 (*GS 43* and *55*)

Comment: Built in USSR and East Germany *(GS 59)* 1957-63. Mainly employed in-area in the Pacific Fleet *(GS 59)*, the remainder in the Black Sea. Two of the class deleted in 1991, remainder were not active in 1992.

LENTRA   3/1988

NAVAL RESEARCH SHIPS

Note: Research submarines are listed at the end of the Submarine section.

2 SIBIRIYAKOV CLASS (TYPE 865)

SIBIRIYAKOV   ROMAULD MUKLEVITCH

Displacement, tons: 3422 full load
Dimensions, feet (metres): 281.2 × 49.2 × 16.4 *(85.7 × 15 × 5)*
Main machinery: 2 Zgoda 12 ASV 25D diesels; 6528 hp(m) *(4.8 MW)* sustained; 2 6AL 20D auxiliary diesels; 1142 hp(m) *(840 kW)*; 2 shafts; cp props
Speed, knots: 14. **Range, miles:** 11 000 at 14 kts
Complement: 58 plus 12 scientists
Guns: 1—30 mm (not carried).
Radars: 2 navigation: I band.

Comment: Built in Danzig 1990-92. Has a pressurised citadel for NBC defence, and a degaussing installation. Six separate laboratories for hydrographic and geophysical research.

SIBIRIYAKOV   1992

6 AKADEMIK KRYLOV CLASS

ADMIRAL VLADIMIRSKY   IVAN KRUZENSHTERN   LEONID DEMIN
AKADEMIK KRYLOV   LEONID SOBOLEV   MIKHAIL KRUPSKY

Displacement, tons: 9100 full load
Dimensions, feet (metres): 482.3 × 60.7 × 20.3 *(147 × 18.5 × 6.2)*
Main machinery: 2 diesels; 14 500 hp(m) *(10.7 MW)*; 2 shafts
Speed, knots: 20. **Range, miles:** 23 000 at 15 kts
Complement: 90
Radars: Navigation: Two Don 2; I band.
Helicopters: 1 Hormone.

Comment: Built in Szczecin 1974-79. Carry two survey launches and have 26 laboratories. *Krupsky* has a large radome abaft the foremast.

AKADEMIK KRYLOV   1992

4 ABKHAZIYA CLASS

ABKHAZIYA   ADZHARIYA   BASHKIRIYA   MOLDAVIA

Displacement, tons: 7500 full load
Dimensions, feet (metres): 409.2 × 56 × 21.1 *(124.8 × 17.1 × 6.4)*
Main machinery: 2 MAN K62 57/80 diesels; 10 500 hp(m) *(7.72 MW)*; 2 shafts; 2 bow thrusters
Speed, knots: 17. **Range, miles:** 20 000 at 16 kts
Complement: 105
Helicopters: 1 Hormone (not normally carried).

Comment: Built by Mathias Thesen Werft at Wismar. A modified Akademik Kurchatov class. Fitted telescopic hangar aft. Completed: 1971, *Abkhaziya*; 1972, *Adzhariya*; 1973, other two. Two survey launches are usually embarked. Vee Cone communications. Endurance, 60 days.

ADZHARIYA   3/1990

3 POLYUS CLASS (KOVEL TYPE)

BAYKAL (mod)   BALKHASH (mod)   POLYUS

Displacement, tons: 6700 full load
Measurement, tons: 3897 gross; 1195 net
Dimensions, feet (metres): 365.8 × 46.2 × 20.7 *(111.6 × 14.1 × 6.3)*
Main machinery: Diesel-electric; 4 diesel generators; 1 motor; 3000 hp(m) *(2.2 MW)* (*Polyus*), 3700 hp(m) *(2.72 MW)* (remainder); 1 shaft
Speed, knots: 14. **Range, miles:** 25 000 at 12 kts
Complement: 120

Comment: These ships are a part of the Andizhan class of some 45 ships. They were converted while building by Schiffswerft Neptun of Rostock. *Polyus* in 1962 and the other two in 1964. Oceanographic research ships. First two ships have modified superstructure with two king-posts on the fo'c'sle and several A-frame davits down each side.

BAYKAL   7/1989, G Jacobs

1 MODIFIED DOBRYNYA NIKITICH CLASS

VLADIMIR KAVRAYSKY

Displacement, tons: 3900 full load
Dimensions, feet (metres): 239.4 × 59.4 × 20 *(73 × 18.1 × 6.1)*
Main machinery: Diesel-electric; 3 Type 13-D-100 diesel generators; 2 motors; 5400 hp(m) *(3.97 MW)*; 2 shafts
Speed, knots: 14. **Range, miles:** 8000 at 13 kts
Complement: 60

Comment: One of a numerous class of icebreakers built at Leningrad since the early 1960s and built for polar research in 1970. Has helicopter deck aft, 8 ton crane on the after well-deck and two 3 ton derricks. Carries a survey launch. Has nine laboratories.

VLADIMIR KAVRAYSKY   1982

572 RUSSIA / Naval research ships — Naval survey ships

8 NIKOLAY ZUBOV CLASS

ALEKSEY CHIRIKOV	FADDEY BELLINSGAUSEN	SEMEN DEZHNEV
ANDREY VILKITSKY	FEDOR LITKE	VASILY GOLOVNIN
BORIS DAVIDOV	NIKOLAY ZUBOV	

Displacement, tons: 2674 standard; 3021 full load
Dimensions, feet (metres): 294.2 × 42.7 × 15 *(89.7 × 13 × 4.6)*
Main machinery: 2 Zgoda-Sulzer 8TD48 diesels; 4400 hp(m) *(3.23 MW)* sustained; 2 shafts
Speed, knots: 16.5. **Range, miles:** 11 000 at 14 kts
Complement: 50

Comment: Oceanographic research ships built at Szczecin Shipyard, Poland in 1964-68. Also employed on navigational, sonar and radar trials. Have nine laboratories and small deck aft for hydromet-balloon work. Carry two to four survey launches. Ships of same class act as AGIs. The whole class varies marginally in appearance from ship to ship.

BORIS DAVIDOV   8/1992

18 YUG CLASS

V ADM VORONTSOV (ex-*Briz*)	MANGYSHLAK	PLUTON	TAYGA
DONUZLAV	MARSHAL GELOVANI	SENEZH	VIZIR
GALS	NIKOLAY MATUSEVICH	STRELETS	ZODIAK
GIDROLOG	PEGAS	STVOR	SSV 704
GORIZONT	PERSEY		(ex-*SSV 328*)

Displacement, tons: 2500 full load
Dimensions, feet (metres): 270.6 × 44.3 × 13.1 *(82.5 × 13.5 × 4)*
Main machinery: 2 Zgoda-Sulzer Type 6TD48 diesels; 3300 hp(m) *(2.43 MW)* sustained; 2 auxiliary motors; 272 hp(m) *(200 kW)*; 2 shafts; cp props; bow thruster; 300 hp *(220 kW)*
Speed, knots: 15. **Range, miles:** 9000 at 12 kts
Complement: 46 (8 officers) plus 20 scientists
Guns: 6—25 mm/80 (3 twin) (fitted for but not with).

Comment: Built at Northern Shipyard, Gdansk 1977-83. Have a 4 ton davit at the stern and two survey craft. *Zodiak* has a large gantry aft. Others have minor variations around the stern area. *704* was converted in 1989 and now serves in the Northern Fleet as an AGI.

PERSEY   7/1992

1 MOD SORUM CLASS

OS 572

Displacement, tons: 1660 full load
Dimensions, feet (metres): 190.2 × 41.3 × 15.1 *(58 × 12.6 × 4.6)*
Main machinery: Diesel-electric; 2 type 5-2-DW2 diesel generators; 1 motor; 2000 hp(m) *(1.47 MW)*; 1 shaft
Speed, knots: 14. **Range, miles:** 6750 at 13 kts
Complement: 35
Radars: Navigation: Two Nayada; I band.

Comment: A Sorum class tug built in 1987 and converted for acoustic trials. The built-up stern houses a winch and cable drum for a lengthy acoustic array which is deployed through the stern doors.

OS 572   1988, CHOD Norway

NAVAL SURVEY SHIPS

Note: These ships are reported available for commercial work but none was observed in 1992.

20 MOMA CLASS (+9 AGIs)

ALTAIR	ARKTIKA	KOLGUEV (mod)	OKEAN
ANADYR	ASKOLD	KRILON	RIBACHI (mod)
ANDROMEDA	BEREZAN	LIMAN	SEVER
ANTARES	CHELEKEN	MARS	TAYMYR
ANTARKTYDA	ELTON	MORZHOVETS	ZAPOLYARYE

Displacement, tons: 1550 full load
Dimensions, feet (metres): 240.5 × 36.8 × 12.8 *(73.3 × 11.2 × 3.9)*
Main machinery: 2 Zgoda-Sulzer 6TD48 diesels; 3300 hp(m) *(2.43 MW)* sustained; 2 shafts; cp props
Speed, knots: 17. **Range, miles:** 9000 at 11 kts
Complement: 55
Radars: Navigation: Two Don 2; I band.
IFF: High Pole A.

Comment: Built in Poland from 1967 to 1972. Some of the class are particularly active in ASW research associated operations. Four laboratories. One survey launch and a 7 ton crane. *Rybachi* has no crane but has an additional deckhouse forward and is classed as an experimental auxiliary. She also carries two twin 12.7 mm MG mountings and two SA-N-5 launchers. Ships of this class serve in the Bulgarian, Polish and Yugoslav navies.

CHELEKEN   9/1992, van Ginderen Collection

RIBACHI (mod)   2/1992

13 SAMARA CLASS

AZIMUT	GLUBOMER	TROPIK
DEVIATOR	GRADUS	VOSTOK
GIGROMETR	KOMPAS	VAYGACH (mod)
MOSKOVSKY UNIVERSITET	PAMYAT MERKURYIA	ZENIT
(ex-*Gorizont*) (mod)	RUMB	

Displacement, tons: 1000 standard; 1270 full load
Dimensions, feet (metres): 193.5 × 34.4 × 12.5 *(59 × 10.5 × 3.8)*
Main machinery: 2 Zgoda-Sulzer Type 6TD48 diesels; 3300 hp(m) *(2.43 MW)* sustained; 2 shafts; cp props
Speed, knots: 15. **Range, miles:** 6200 at 10 kts
Complement: 45

Comment: Built at Gdansk, Poland 1962-64 for hydrographic surveying and research. Have laboratories and one survey launch and a 5 ton crane. *Vaygach* has additional accommodation around the base of the crane. *Moskovsky Universitet* is subordinated to the Academy of Sciences and has an extended superstructure forward and no crane.

PAMYAT MERKURYIA   4/1992, van Ginderen Collection

24 FINIK CLASS (TYPE 872)

GS 44, 47, 84, 86, 87, 260, 265, 270, 272, 278, 296, 297, 301, 388, 392, 397-405

Displacement, tons: 1200 full load
Dimensions, feet (metres): 201.1 × 35.4 × 10.8 *(61.3 × 10.8 × 3.3)*
Main machinery: 2 Cegielski-Sulzer 6AL25/30 diesels; 1920 hp(m) *(1.4 MW)*; auxiliary propulsion; 2 motors; 204 hp(m) *(150 kW)*; 2 shafts; cp props; bow thruster
Speed, knots: 13. **Range, miles:** 3000 at 13 kts
Complement: 26 (5 officers) plus 9 scientists

Comment: Improved Biya class. Built at Northern Shipyard, Poland 1978-83. Fitted with 7 ton crane for buoy handling. Can carry two self-propelled pontoons and a boat on well-deck. Ships of same class serve in the Polish Navy.

FINIK 265   1991

14 BIYA CLASS

GS 182, 193, 194, 198, 200, 202, 204, 206, 210, 212, 214, 271, 273, 275

Displacement, tons: 750 full load
Dimensions, feet (metres): 180.4 × 32.1 × 8.5 *(55 × 9.8 × 2.6)*
Main machinery: 2 diesels; 1200 hp(m) *(882 kW)*; 2 shafts; cp props
Speed, knots: 13. **Range, miles:** 4700 at 11 kts
Complement: 25
Radars: Navigation: Don 2; I band.

Comment: Built in Poland 1972-76. With laboratory and one survey launch and a 5 ton crane. Transfers: One to Cuba in November 1980 (from Poland); one to Cape Verde in 1979.

GS 271   3/1991, van Ginderen Collection

12 KAMENKA CLASS

GS 66, 74, 78, 82, 107, 108 (ex-*Vernier*), 113 (ex-*Belbeck*), 118, 199 (ex-*Sima*), 207, 211, ASTRONOM (mod)

Displacement, tons: 700 full load
Dimensions, feet (metres): 175.5 × 29.8 × 8.5 *(53.5 × 9.1 × 2.6)*
Main machinery: 2 diesels; 1800 hp(m) *(1.32 MW)*; 2 shafts; cp props
Speed, knots: 14. **Range, miles:** 4000 at 10 kts
Complement: 25
Radars: Navigation: Don 2; I band.
IFF: High Pole.

Comment: Built in Poland 1968-72. A 5 ton crane forward. They do not carry a survey launch but have facilities for handling and stowing buoys. In *Astronom* the deckhouse below the crane is twice the length of that in other ships of the class.

GS 107   6/1984

2 VINOGRAD CLASS

GS 525   GS 526

Displacement, tons: 1000
Dimensions, feet (metres): 164 × 34.4 × 6.6 *(50 × 10.5 × 2)*
Main machinery: 2 diesels; 2 motors; 1200 hp(m) *(882 kW)*; 2 trainable props
Speed, knots: 11.5
Complement: 30

Comment: Built by Rauma-Repola 1985-87 as hydrographic research ships.

NYRYAT 1 and 2 CLASSES

Comment: A number of these 120 and 55 ton classes (see *Auxiliaries* section for details) were built for inshore survey work using Nyryat hull and machinery. They carry GPB pennant numbers which are also used in the 7 ton survey launches carried in the larger ships.

CIVILIAN RESEARCH SHIPS

Notes: (a) There are some 200 ships ranging downward from 3200 tons engaged on fishery research worldwide. The larger ships are of the Mayakovsky, Tropik, Atlantik, Leskov and Luchegorsk classes of 3200-2400 tons. Two of the Mayakovsky class carry submersibles. Research ships (also tugs, cargo ships, training ships) operating on behalf of the fishery ministries carry a form of pennant number. This usually consists of two letters followed by four numbers. The first letter indicates the port or area where the vessel is based, the second, the type of vessel and the numerals indicate a specific ship and are usually allocated consecutively to a particular class.
(b) In addition to the classes listed below there are several more, although some are converted trawler designs. New classes include Iscatel II and Svetlomar which are for civilian use.
(c) Some classes are not included because they are associated only with geophysical research. These include Bavenit, Tropik, Pulkovsky Meridian, Agat, Akademik Orbeli and Zarya.
(d) Activity since 1991 has been resource related with the Academy of Science ships looking for contract work. The Atlantic is the major operating area, with some ships being used to carry cargo or even to relay fishing crews.

Known letter allocations:

1st Letter		2nd Letter	
A/M	Murmansk	A	Fish factory
B	Novorossiysk	B/b	Large ST/FF
K	Kaliningrad	H	Tanker
L	Klaypeda	M	Fish factory-mother ship
M	Vladivostok	R	Fish carrier (small)
R	Riga	T	Fish carrier (large)
Q	Kerch/Sevastopol	Y	Tugs, rescue ship, icebreakers
C	Korsakov	X	Cargo ship
		G	Large stern trawler
		W	Tuna factory ship

1 A A KRYLOV and 2 A N ANDREYEV CLASSES

AKADEMIK ALEKSEY KRYLOV   AKADEMIK NIKOLAY ANDREYEV
AKADEMIK BORIS KONSTANTINOV

Displacement, tons: 9920 full load
Dimensions, feet (metres): 406.7 × 55.8 × 23 *(124 × 17 × 7)*
Main machinery: 2 Type 58-D-6R diesels; 9000 hp(m) *(6.6 MW)*; 2 shafts; cp props
Speed, knots: 16. **Range, miles:** 10 000 at 16 kts
Complement: 117 plus 32 scientists *(Krylov)*; 90 plus 40 scientists (remainder)

Comment: Built at Nikolayev, *Krylov* for the Institute of Shipbuilding, *Andreyev* and *Konstantinov* for the Institute of Acoustics. *Krylov* carries a submersible in an internal compartment with doors in the port side and sailed on her maiden voyage in December 1982. *Andreyev* entered service in October 1986 and *Konstantinov* in March 1989; they have a different superstructure shape from *Krylov*. *Konstantinov* has a large stern door for streaming towed devices and with *Andreyev* has replaced the two Lebedev class ships for oceanographic acoustic research.

AKADEMIK NIKOLAY ANDREYEV   10/1992, van Ginderen Collection

AKADEMIK ALEKSEY KRYLOV (Research Submarine)   9/1990, Harald Carstens

574 RUSSIA / Civilian research ships

2 AKADEMIK SERGEI VAVILOV CLASS

AKADEMIK SERGEI VAVILOV   **AKADEMIK IOFFE**

Displacement, tons: 6600 full load
Dimensions, feet (metres): 383.9 × 59.7 × 19.4 *(117 × 18.2 × 5.9)*
Main machinery: 2 SEMT-Pielstick diesels; 7000 hp(m) *(15.15 MW)*; 2 shafts; cp props; bow thruster
Speed, knots: 15. **Range, miles:** 20 000 at 14 kts
Complement: 128

Comment: Built by Hollming, Rauma, Finland for hydrophysical/biological/chemical research. *Vavilov* launched on 16 December 1986 and completed 17 February 1988; *Ioffe* launched on 29 August 1987 and completed sea trials in February 1989. Low speed manoeuvrability is achieved by an Aquamatic propulsion unit aft and bow thruster forward. *Ioffe* has two rigid sails which stow horizontally on the superstructure. The sails minimise self noise during acoustic research operations. Both have extensive acoustic trials equipment including multi-beam echo sounders and low frequency sidescan sonars. Sonar transducers are compact and ice resistant. It was reported in 1991 that *Ioffe* is to be converted to a ferry.

AKADEMIK SERGEI VAVILOV   *10/1992, Hartmut Ehlers*

AKADEMIK IOFFE   *6/1992*

3 VITYAZ CLASS

AKADEMIK ALEKSANDR NESMEYANOV   **VITYAZ**
AKADEMIK ALEKSANDR VINOGRADOV

Displacement, tons: 6000 full load
Dimensions, feet (metres): 364.1 × 54.5 × 18.7 *(111 × 16.6 × 5.7)*
Main machinery: 2 Zgoda-Sulzer 6ZL140/48 diesels; 6500 hp(m) *(4.78 MW)*; 2 shafts; cp props
Speed, knots: 17. **Range, miles:** 16 000 at 16 kts
Complement: 60 plus 65 scientists

Comment: Built in Poland. First completed in 1981, second in 1982 and third in 1983. Operate for Academy of Scientists. Capabilities for a wide range of oceanographical and meteorological studies and have excellent diver support facilities. Carry Argus submersible; 8 tons displacement; diving to 600 m *(1968.6 ft)* with endurance of eight hours; has a complement of three. *Vityaz* based at Novorossiysk, *A A Nesmeyanov* and *A A Vinogradov* at Vladivostok.

AKADEMIK ALEXANDR VINOGRADOV   *12/1991, 92 Wing RAAF*

1 AKADEMIK M KELDYSH CLASS

AKADEMIK MSTISLAV KELDYSH

Displacement, tons: 5500
Dimensions, feet (metres): 400.2 × 59 × 19.7 *(122 × 18 × 6)*
Main machinery: 4 Wärtsilä Vasa 824TS diesels; 5820 hp(m) *(3.88 MW)*; 2 shafts; bow thruster
Speed, knots: 16
Complement: 50 plus 80 scientists

Comment: Built by Hollming Yard, Rauma, Finland. Commissioned December 1980. One of the most sophisticated oceanographic research ships in the world. Under the Academy of Sciences. Has 17 laboratories and can carry two MIR manned submersibles which can dive to 6000 m *(19 686 ft)*. Two garage structures have been added aft of the funnel. Fitted with a rotatable stern propulser. Based at Kaliningrad. Treasure hunting for Mexico in 1993.

AKADEMIK MSTISLAV KELDYSH   *8/1988, Gilbert Gyssels*

1 AKADEMIK FEDOROV CLASS

AKADEMIK FEDOROV

Measurement, tons: 7600 dwt; 10 000 gross
Dimensions, feet (metres): 462.6 × 77 × 28 *(141 × 23.5 × 8.5)*
Main machinery: Diesel-electric; 2 Wärtsilä diesel generators; 18 700 hp(m) *(13.74 MW)*; 1 motor; 1 shaft
Speed, knots: 16
Complement: 90 plus 160 scientists
Helicopters: 1 Mi-8 Hip.

Comment: Built by Rauma-Repola, Finland and completed 10 September 1987 as a Polar Research and Support Ship. Comes under the Arctic and Antarctic Research Institute and is used for servicing Antarctic bases. Ice-strengthened and has a transverse omni-thruster. To replace *Mikhail Somov* in due course.

AKADEMIK FEDOROV   *8/1991, Peter Humphries*

1 KOLOMNA CLASS

MIKHAIL LOMONOSOV

Displacement, tons: 5470 full load
Measurement, tons: 3897 gross; 1195 net
Dimensions, feet (metres): 336 × 47.2 × 22 *(102.5 × 14.4 × 6.7)*
Main machinery: 1 Liebknecht reciprocating engine; 2450 ihp(m) *(1.8 MW)*; 1 shaft
Speed, knots: 13

Comment: Built by Neptun, Rostock, in 1957 from the hull of a freighter of the Kolomna class. Operated for the Academy of Sciences by Ukraine Institute of Oceanology, Black Sea. Equipped with 16 laboratories.

MIKHAIL LOMONOSOV   *9/1986, van Ginderen Collection*

1 AMGUEMA CLASS

MIKHAIL SOMOV

Displacement, tons: 15 100 full load
Measurement, tons: 8445 dwt; 7714 gross; 3113 net
Dimensions, feet (metres): 436.4 × 62.3 × 28.2 *(133 × 19 × 8.6)*
Main machinery: Diesel-electric; 4 diesel generators; 2 motors; 7200 hp(m) *(5.3 MW)*; 2 shafts
Speed, knots: 15
Complement: 58
Radars: Navigation: Two Don 2; I band.
Helicopters: Platform only.

Comment: Built at Kherson SY 1975. Ice-strengthened. Operates under Arctic and Antarctic Research Institute for research duties and Antarctic support. To be replaced by *Akademik Fedorov* in due course.

MIKHAIL SOMOV 4/1992, Robert Pabst

7 AKADEMIK KURCHATOV CLASS

AKADEMIK KOROLEV DMITRY MENDELEYEV
AKADEMIK KURCHATOV PROFESSOR ZUBOV
AKADEMIK SHIRSHOV PROFESSOR VIEZE
AKADEMIK VERNADSKY

Displacement, tons: 6681 full load
Measurement, tons: 1986 dwt; 5460 gross; 1387 net
Dimensions, feet (metres): 400.3-406.8 × 56.1 × 15 *(122.1-124.1 × 17.1 × 4.6)*
Main machinery: 2 Halberstadt-MAN 6KZ57/60 diesels; 8000 hp(m) *(5.88 MW)*; 2 shafts; 2 bow thrusters; 360 hp(m) *(264 kW)*
Speed, knots: 20. **Range, miles:** 20 000 at 18 kts

Comment: All built by Mathias Thesen Werft at Wismar, East Germany between 1966 and 1968. All have a hull of the same design as the Mikhail Kalinin class of merchant vessels. There are variations in mast and aerial rig. *Professor Vieze* is similar to *A Shirshov* while *A Kurchatov*, *A Vernadsky* and *D Mendeleyev* are the same. *Kurchatov* and *Mendeleyev* have launched submersibles from a specially fitted crane.
Employment: Hydromet (Vladivostok): *A Korolev, A Shirshov*. Institute of Oceanology (Baltic): *A Kurchatov*. Institute of Oceanology (Vladivostok): *D Mendeleyev*. Ukraine Institute of Oceanology: *A Vernadsky*. Hydromet (Baltic): *P Vieze, P Zubov*.

DMITRY MENDELEYEV 6/1992

IZUMRUD

Displacement, tons: 5170 full load
Measurement, tons: 3862 gross; 465 net
Dimensions, feet (metres): 326 × 46 × 15.5 *(99.4 × 14 × 4.7)*
Main machinery: Diesel-electric; 4 diesel generators; 1 motor; 1 shaft
Speed, knots: 13.8

Comment: A research ship built in 1970 at Nikolayev. Used for structural and material tests. Owned by Ministry of Shipping. Operated by Naval Institute of Shipbuilding, Black Sea.

IZUMRUD 6/1992

9 PASSAT CLASS (B 88 TYPE)

ERNST KRENKEL (ex-*Vikhr*) OKEAN PRILIV
GEORGY USHAKOV (ex-*Schkval*) PASSAT VIKTOR BUGAYEV (ex-*Poriv*)
MUSSON PRIBOY VOLNA

Displacement, tons: 4145 full load
Measurement, tons: 3280 (3311, *E Krenkel* and *V Bugayev*) gross
Dimensions, feet (metres): 318.5 × 45.6 × 15.4 *(97.1 × 13.9 × 4.7)*
 328 × 48.5 × 15.4 *(100 × 14.8 × 4.7)* (*E Krenkel* and *V Bugayev*)
Main machinery: 2 Cegielski Sulzer diesels; 4800 hp(m) *(3.53 MW)*; 2 shafts
Speed, knots: 16
Complement: 110

Comment: Hydromet ships built at Szczecin, Poland. 1968: *Musson, Passat, Volna*; 1969: *Okean, Priboy*; 1970: *Priliv*; 1971: *G Ushakov, E Krenkel, V Bugayev*. Most are based in the Black Sea and are claimed by Ukraine but *Okean, Priboy*, and *Priliv* are at Vladivostok.

MUSSON 3/1993, C. D. Yaylali

9 AKADEMIK FERSMAN CLASS (B 93 TYPE)

AKADEMIK FERSMAN AKADEMIK LAZAREV AKADEMIK NAMYOTKIN
AKADEMIK SHATSKY ZEPHYR (ex-*Akademik* AKADEMIK KREPS
AKADEMIK SELSKIY   *Gubkin*) SIROCCO (ex-*Akademik*
 AKADEMIK NALIVKIN   *Nemchinov*)

Displacement, tons: 3500 full load
Dimensions, feet (metres): 269 × 49.2 × 16.4 *(82 × 15 × 5)*
Main machinery: 1 Sulzer diesel; 4200 hp(m) *(3.1 MW)*; 1 Kort nozzle
Speed, knots: 15. **Range, miles:** 12 000 at 15 kts
Complement: 65

Comment: First pair completed at Szczecin, Poland in 1986, next five in 1987 and last two in 1988. Three more ordered in August 1988 but may not have been completed. Fitted for gravimetric and geophysical research with towed seismic array and bow thruster. Ice-strengthened. *Shatsky* and *Nemchinov* are working under contract for Western geophysical research companies and have been renamed. *Shatsky* has a helo deck aft.

AKADEMIK SHATSKY (helo deck) 7/1992

SIROCCO 5/1992

576 RUSSIA / Civilian research ships

9 AKADEMIK SHULEYKIN CLASS

AKADEMIK GAMBURTSEV*	PROFESSOR GOLITSYN*
AKADEMIK SHULEYKIN	PROFESSOR KHROMOV
AKADEMIK SHOKALSKY	PROFESSOR PAVEL MOLCHANOV
GEOLOG DIMITRI NALIVKIN*	PROFESSOR MULTANOVSKY
	PROFESSOR POLSHKOV*

* Second group

Displacement, tons: 2000 (first four); 2554 (second five)
Dimensions, feet (metres): 236.2 × 42.6 × 15.4 *(72 × 13 × 4.7)* (first four)
 244.3 × 48.3 × 14.8 *(74.5 × 14.7 × 4.5)* (second five)
Main machinery: 2 Gorkiy G-74 diesels; 3060 hp(m) *(2.25 MW)*; 2 shafts (first four)
 2 SEMT-Pielstick 6 PC2.5 L 400 diesels; 7020 hp(m) *(5.16 MW)* sustained; 2 shafts (second five)
Speed, knots: 14
Complement: 70 (including scientists)

Comment: Built by Laivateollisuus, Turku, Finland. Ice-strengthened. First two entered service in 1982, next pair in 1983. *A Shuleykin* based at St Petersburg, *A Shokalsky* at Vladivostok, *Professor P Molchanov* at Murmansk, *Professor Khromov* in Pacific, *Professor Multanovsky* at St Petersburg. All hydromet ships work for Hydromet Service. Four more built for Academy of Sciences and Ministry of Geology. Completion December 1983 to October 1984. *Nalivkin* has a Qubit TRAC IV integrated navigation and data logging system for work in the Norwegian Sea under contract to a Western company. Tenth of class *Arnold Veimer* belongs to Estonia.

PROFESSOR POLSHKOV 5/1992

7 VADIM POPOV CLASS

VADIM POPOV	VASILIY LOMINADZE
VIKTOR BUINITSKIY	IGOR MAKSIMOV
PAVEL GORDIYENKO	VLADIMIR PARSHIN
	IVAN PETROV

Displacement, tons: 927 full load
Dimensions, feet (metres): 164 × 33 × 12 *(49.9 × 10 × 3.6)*
Main machinery: 1 diesel; 1340 hp(m) *(985 kW)*; 1 shaft
Speed, knots: 13
Complement: 35

Comment: Small hydromet ships built at Laivateollisuus, Turku, the first of which entered service 6 October 1986. *Buinitskiy* is based at Murmansk, *Lominadze* in the Caspian, and three others are based in the Pacific. *Ivan Petrov* was the last to enter service, in 1991.

VLADIMIR PARSHIN 6/1992

3 ALEKSEY MARYSHEV CLASS

ALEKSEY MARYSHEV   GRIGORY MIKHEYEV   PETR KOTSOV

Comment: Built by Hollming, Rauma, Finland in 1990/91. Ice-strengthened, designed for survey work on the Arctic Coast and in the Siberian rivers. Owned by the Ministry of Transport. Of 1763 gross tons. So far used only for carrying timber.

ALEKSEY MARYSHEV 7/1992, Erik Laursen

4 AKADEMIK BORIS PETROV CLASS

AKADEMIK BORIS PETROV	AKADEMIK M A LAVRENTYEV
AKADEMIK N STRAKHOV	AKADEMIK OPARIN

Displacement, tons: 2550 full load
Dimensions, feet (metres): 247.6 × 48.2 × 15.4 *(75.5 × 14.7 × 4.7)*
Main machinery: 2 Russkiy SEMT-Pielstick 6 PC2.5 L 400 diesels; 7020 hp(m) *(5.16 MW)* sustained; 1 shaft; cp prop
Speed, knots: 15
Complement: 74
Radars: Navigation: Okean; I band. Don; I band.

Comment: Built by Hollming, Finland. Data similar to second group of Akademik Shuleykin class. *Petrov* and *Lavrentyev* completed June and October 1984, *Strakhov* on 14 May 1985 and *Oparin* launched 1 February 1985. May be used for sea-bed coring as part of programme of geophysical and hydrophysical research for Academy of Sciences.

AKADEMIK N STRAKHOV 7/1988, Gilbert Gyssels

21 VALERIAN URYVAYEV CLASS

CHAYVO	POISK
DALNIE ZELENTSY	PROFESSOR FEDYINSKY
ELM	VALERIAN URYVAYEV*
GEOFIZIK	VEKTOR
ISKATEL	ISSLEDOVATEL
VLADIMIR OBRUCHEV	LEV TITOV*
VSEVOLOD BEREZKIN*	MODUL
VULKANOLOG	MORSKOY GEOFIZIK
VYACHESLAV FROLOV*	ZOND
YAKOV GAKKEL*	PROFESSOR GAGARINSKY
KERN	

* Hydromet ships.

Displacement, tons: 1050 full load
Measurement, tons: 350 dwt; 697 gross; 85 net
Dimensions, feet (metres): 180.1 × 31.2 × 13.1 *(54.9 × 9.5 × 4)*
Main machinery: 1 Deutz diesel; 850 hp(m) *(625 kW)*; 1 shaft
Speed, knots: 12
Complement: 40 plus 12 scientists

Comment: Built at Khabarovsk between 1974 and 1990. One of the class transferred to Lithuania in 1992.
 Bases: Murmansk; *V Berezkin, D Zelentsy, Chayvo, Geofizik, Kern.* Baltic; *L Titov.* Black Sea *Modul, Vektor, Issledovatel, Y Gakkel.* Caspian; *Elm.* Pacific; Remainder.
 Tasks: Hydromet; *D Zelentsy, Elm,* Marine Biology; *Modul, Vektor,* Hydro-acoustics; *Issledovatel* General Oceanography; Remainder, geology and geophysics.

VEKTOR 10/1990

LEV TITOV 1/1991, van Ginderen Collection

3 MODIFIED ALPINIST CLASS

GIDROBIOLOG   GIDRONAVT   RIFT

Displacement, tons: 1140 full load
Dimensions, feet (metres): 177.1 × 34.4 × 13.1 *(54 × 10.5 × 4)*
Main machinery: 1 SKL 8 NVD 48 A-2U diesel; 1320 hp(m) *(970 kW)* sustained; 1 shaft; cp prop
Speed, knots: 13. **Range, miles:** 7000 at 13 kts
Complement: 26 plus 12 scientists

Comment: Of the same stern-trawler design as the Alpinist AGIs. Modified to carry and operate a manned submersible (*Rift*—Pisces; others—Argus) from the gantry crane. Completed 1982-83.

RIFT   1987

19 DMITRY OVSTYN CLASS

DMITRY LAPTEV	PROFESSOR BOGOROV
DMITRY OVSTYN	PROFESSOR KURENTSOV
DMITRY STERLEGOV	PROFESSOR SHTOKMAN
E TOLL	PROFESSOR VODYANITSKY
FEDOR MATISEN	SERGEY KRAKOV
GEORGY MAKSIMOV	STEFAN MALYGIN
IVAN KIREYEV	VALERIAN ALBANOV
NIKOLAI KOLOMEYTSEV	V SUKHOTSKY
NIKOLAI YEVGENOV	YAKOV SMIRNITSKY
PAVEL BASHMAKOV	

Displacement, tons: 1800 full load
Dimensions, feet (metres): 220 × 39 × 15 *(67.1 × 11.9 × 4.6)*
Main machinery: 1 Deutz RBV6M 358 diesel; 2200 hp(m) *(1.62 MW)*; 1 shaft; bow thruster
Speed, knots: 16. **Range, miles:** 9000 at 13.5 kts
Complement: 52 (including 20 scientists)
Radars: Navigation: Okean or Don 2 or Decca 626; I band.

Comment: Built by Laivateollisuus, Åbo, Finland except *P Bogorov* at Turku, Finland. Fitted with eight laboratories. Employed largely on geological research oceanographic work and survey in the Arctic. Completed between 1974 and 1978. Average time from launch to completion, seven months. Owned by Ministry of Merchant Marine except for the four Professors which are subordinated to the Academy of Sciences. Have ice-strengthened bows.

PROFESSOR VODYANITSKY   6/1992

NAVAL MISSILE RANGE SHIPS

Note: A Vytegrales class converted merchant ship *Yablonya* has been used for R & D work since 1989.

2 DESNA CLASS

CHAZHMA (ex-*Dangara*)   CHUMIKAN (ex-*Dolgeschtschelje*)

Displacement, tons: 5300 light; 13 600 full load
Dimensions, feet (metres): 457.7 × 59 × 25.9 *(139.6 × 18 × 7.9)*
Main machinery: 1 MAN diesel; 5200 hp(m) *(3.8 MW)*; 1 shaft
Speed, knots: 15. **Range, miles:** 20 000 at 13 kts
Complement: 240
Countermeasures: ESM: 2 Watch Dog; radar warning.
Radars: Missile tracker: Ship Globe.
  Air search: Head Net B; E band.
  Navigation: Don 2; I band.
Helicopters: 1 Ka-25 'Hormone C'.

Comment: Formerly bulk ore-carriers of the Dshankoy class (7265 tons gross) built at Warnemunde. Range Instrumentation Ships. Active since 1963. Based in the Pacific. Two Vee Cone communications aerials.

CHAZHMA   7/1989, G Jacobs

2 SIBIR CLASS

SAKHALIN   SPASSK (ex-*Suchan*)

Displacement, tons: 7400 full load
Dimensions, feet (metres): 354 × 49.2 × 20 *(108 × 15 × 6.1)*
Main machinery: 2 boilers; Compound reciprocating engine; 2500 ihp(m) *(1.84 MW)*; 1 shaft
Speed, knots: 12. **Range, miles:** 9800 at 12 kts
Complement: 200
Radars: Air search: Head Net C; E band.
  Three smaller trackers forward of the bridge.
  Navigation: Two Don 2; I band.
Helicopters: 1 Ka-25 'Hormone C' (no hangar).

Comment: Converted bulk ore-carriers employed as Missile Range Ships in the Pacific. *Sakhalin* has three radomes forward and aft. Launched in 1957-59. Formerly freighters of the Polish B 31 type (Donbas class). One of the class *Sibir* deleted in 1990 and *Chukotka* in 1991.

SIBIR class   1/1991, 92 Wing RAAF

3 MARSHAL NEDELIN CLASS

MARSHAL NEDELIN   MARSHAL KRYLOV   AKADEMIK NICOLAI PILYUGIN

Displacement, tons: 24 000 full load
Dimensions, feet (metres): 695.5 × 88.9 × 25.3 *(212 × 27.1 × 7.7)*
Main machinery: 2 gas turbines; 54 000 hp(m) *(40 MW)*; 2 shafts
Speed, knots: 20. **Range, miles:** 22 000 at 16 kts
Complement: 500
Radars: Air search: Strut Pair *(Nedelin)*; Top Plate *(Krylov)*.
  Navigation: Three Palm Frond; I band.
Helicopter control: Fly Screen B; I band.
Space trackers: End Tray (balloons). Quad Leaf. Three Quad Wedge. Four smaller aerials.
Tacan: Two Round House.
Helicopters: 2-4 Ka-32 'Helix C'.

Comment: First completed at Admiralty Yard, Leningrad in 1983, second in 1989 and third in 1993. Fitted with a variety of space and missile associated electronic systems. Fitted for but not with six twin 30 mm/65 ADG guns and three Bass Tilt fire control radars. Naval subordinated, the task is monitoring missile tests with a war time role of command ship. The Ship Globe radome is for SATCOM. The third ship of the class works for the Academy of Sciences under civilian control.

MARSHAL NEDELIN   3/1992

2 KAMCHATKA CLASS (AG)

KAMCHATKA SSV 391   **SLAVUTICH** SSV 679

Displacement, tons: 6000 full load
Dimensions, feet (metres): 350.1 × 52.5 × 19.7 *(106.7 × 16 × 6)*
Main machinery: 2 diesels; 6100 hp(m) *(4.5 MW)*; 2 shafts
Speed, knots: 16
Complement: 178
Missiles: SAM: 2 SA-N-5 Grail quad launchers; manual aiming; IR homing to 6 km *(3.2 nm)* at 1.5 Mach; altitude to 2500 m *(8000 ft)*; warhead 1.5 kg.
Guns: 2—30 mm/65 AK 630. 6 barrels per mounting.
Radars: Navigation: 3 Palm Frond; 2 Shot Dome; I band.
CCA: Fly Screen; I band.
Tacan: 2 Round House.
Helicopters: 2 Ka-25 'Hormone C'.

Comment: *Kamchatka* launched at Nikolayev in August 1985, started trials in the Black Sea in September 1987 and then sailed for the Pacific at the end of the year. AGE stands for Auxiliary General Experimental. Pennant number indicates intelligence collection and as the large tower could house an acoustic device for lowering below the hull, this ship is most probably involved in VLF bi-static sonar trials similar to the type being tested in major Western navies. *Slavutich* was laid down in 1988 and commissioned in a still uncompleted state as the Ukrainian Flagship on 28 July 1992. The ship is similar to *Kamchatka* but had no tower on commissioning.

KAMCHATKA   11/1987

1 KAPUSTA CLASS

URAL SSV 33

Displacement, tons: 36 000 full load
Dimensions, feet (metres): 866.1 × 98.1 × 31.5 *(264 × 29.9 × 9.6)*
Main machinery: CONAS; nuclear; 2 PWR; 2 boilers; 4 turbines; 75 000 hp(m) *(55 MW)*; 4 shafts
Speed, knots: 27
Complement: 940
Missiles: SAM: 4 SA-N-10 mountings each with 4 IR-guided missiles derived from SA-16.
Guns: 2—3 in *(76 mm)*/60. 4—30 mm/65 AK 630. 8—14.5 mm (4 twin) MGs.
Countermeasures: ESM: Trawl Net; 2 Soup Cup; Cage Box; Cake Tin.
Fire control: 4 Tin Man and 4 Spot Pot optronic directors.
Radars: Air search: Top Plate; 3D; D/E band.
Air/surface search: 4 Mad Hack planar arrays.
Navigation: 3 Palm Frond; I band.
Fire control: Two Bass Tilt. Six Owl Perch (missile telemetry and tracking).
CCA: Fly Screen B.
Tacan: Two Round House.
IFF: 1 Long Head; 2 Salt Pot.
Sonars: Hull-mounted active/passive sonar; medium frequency.
Helicopters: 1 or 2 Ka-27 'Helix D'.

Comment: Laid down in May 1981 and launched in May 1983 at Baltic Yard, Leningrad. Did trials in the Baltic in 1987 and 1988, commissioning in August 1989 and sailing for the Pacific in September 1989. Has an extensive space associated electronic fit including Ship Globe (satellite tracking) and 1 Quad Leaf, 2 Low Ball and Punch Bowl for SATCOMs. Naval manned and heavily armed, the official description is *sudno suyazyy* meaning communications ship. As well as being a missile range control ship and having an intelligence gathering role monitoring other countries' missile tests, it also has obvious potential as a Flagship. The fourth planar array is mounted horizontally on the deck aft and to starboard of the midship's mast. Probable Kirov class hull. There is some doubt about the name.

URAL   9/1989, 92 Wing RAAF

URAL   8/1989

CIVILIAN SPACE ASSOCIATED SHIPS

Note: Not used for space related activity during 1992.

1 GAGARIN CLASS

KOSMONAUT YURY GAGARIN

Displacement, tons: 53 500
Measurement, tons: 32 291 gross; 5247 net
Dimensions, feet (metres): 760 × 101.7 × 30.2 *(232 × 31 × 9.2)*
Main machinery: 2 boilers; 2 turbines; 19 000 hp(m) *(14 MW)*; 1 shaft; bow and stern thrusters
Speed, knots: 17
Radars: Navigation: Don Kay and Okean; I band.

Comment: Design based on the Sofia or Akhtyuba (ex-Hanoi) class steam tanker. Built at Leningrad by Baltic SB & Eng Works in 1970, completed in 1971. Used for investigation into conditions in the upper atmosphere, and the control of space vehicles. She is the largest research vessel. Communications fit includes two Ship Shell (the largest dishes), two Ship Bowl, four Quad Ring and two Vee Cone (alongside funnel). With all four aerials vertical and facing forward she experiences a loss in speed of 2 kts. Based in Black Sea.

KOSMONAUT YURY GAGARIN   8/1989

1 KOROLEV CLASS

AKADEMIK SERGEY KOROLEV

Displacement, tons: 21 250
Measurement, tons: 17 114 gross; 2158 net
Dimensions, feet (metres): 596.6 × 82 × 25.9 *(181.9 × 25 × 7.9)*
Main machinery: 1 Bryansk Burmeister & Wain diesel; 12 000 hp(m) *(8.8 MW)*; 1 shaft
Speed, knots: 17
Radars: Navigation: Two Don Kay; I band.

Comment: Built at Chernomorsky Shipyard, Nikolayev in 1970, completing in 1971. Space associated communications include four Quad Rings, two Ship Bowl and one Ship Globe. Based in the Pacific Fleet.

AKADEMIK SERGEY KOROLEV   3/1989

4 KOSMONAUT VLADISLAV VOLKOV CLASS

KOSMONAUT VLADISLAV VOLKOV   **KOSMONAUT PAVEL BELYAYEV**
KOSMONAUT GEORGY DOBROVOLSKY   **KOSMONAUT VIKTOR PATSAYEV**

Displacement, tons: 8920 full load
Dimensions, feet (metres): 400.3 × 55.1 × 22.3 *(122.1 × 16.8 × 6.8)*
Main machinery: 1 Bryansk Burmeister & Wain diesel; 5200 hp(m) *(3.82 MW)*; 1 shaft
Speed, knots: 15
Radars: Navigation: Don 2; I band.

Comment: Former freighters of Vytegrales class rebuilt as space associated research ships at Leningrad 1977-78. Space associated communications include one Quad Spring and three smaller aerials. Have Kite Screech fire control radars.

KOSMONAUT VLADISLAV VOLKOV   11/1990, Harald Carstens

TRAINING SHIPS

Note: In addition to the naval training ships listed here a considerable fleet of other training ships, mainly mercantile marine, may be encountered. These are mainly in the 300-400 ft bracket.
Names: *Equator, Gorizont, Meridian, Professor Anichkov, P Khlyustin, P Kudrevich, P Minyayev, P Pavlenko, P Rybaltovsky, P Shchyogolev, P Ukhov, P Yushchenko.*

3 SMOLNY CLASS (AXT)

KHASAN   PEREKOP   SMOLNY

Displacement, tons: 9150 full load
Dimensions, feet (metres): 452.8 × 53.1 × 21.3 *(138 × 16.2 × 6.5)*
Main machinery: 2 diesels; 15 000 hp(m) *(11 MW)*; 2 shafts
Speed, knots: 20. **Range, miles:** 12 000 at 15 kts
Complement: 150 plus 350 cadets
Guns: 4—3 in *(76 mm)*/60 (2 twin). 4—30 mm/65 (2 twin).
A/S mortars: 2 RBU 2500.
Countermeasures: ESM: 2 Watch Dog; radar warning.
Radars: Air/surface search: Head Net C; 3D; E band; range 128 km *(70 nm).*
Navigation: Four Don 2; I band. Don Kay *(Perekop)*; I band.
Fire control: Owl Screech; G band. Drum Tilt; H/I band.
IFF: Two High Pole A. Square Head.
Sonars: Hull-mounted; active search and attack; medium frequency.

Comment: Built at Szczecin, Poland. *Smolny* completed in 1976, *Perekop* in 1977 and *Khasan* in 1978. Have considerable combatant potential. *Khasan* collided with and sank a Turkish Kartal class FAC in the Bosphorus in October 1985.

PEREKOP   8/1992

KHASAN   7/1992

2 UGRA II CLASS (AXT)

BORODINO   GANGUT

Displacement, tons: 6750 standard; 7000 full load
Dimensions, feet (metres): 462.6 × 57.7 × 23 *(141 × 17.6 × 7)*
Main machinery: Diesel-electric; 4 Kolomna Type 2-D-42 diesel generators; 2 motors; 8000 hp(m) *(5.88 MW)*; 2 shafts
Speed, knots: 17. **Range, miles:** 21 000 at 10 kts; 9500 at 16 kts
Complement: 250 plus 400 instructors and trainees
Missiles: SAM: 2 SA-N-5 Grail quad launchers; manual aiming; IR homing to 6 km *(3.2 nm)* at 1.5 Mach; altitude to 2500 m *(8000 ft)*; warhead 1.5 kg.
Guns: 8—57 mm/70 (4 twin).
Radars: Air/surface search: Strut Curve; F band; range 110 km *(60 nm)* for 2 m² target.
Navigation: Three Don 2; I band.
Fire control: Two Muff Cob; G/H band.
IFF: Two Square Head. One High Pole B.
Sonars: Hull-mounted; active search; medium frequency (for training).

Comment: These are the last two of this class built, the remainder being submarine depot ships. Built at Nikolayev in 1971-72. Have large deckhouse aft in place of helicopter deck. No bow lift. One 10 ton and two 3.2 ton cranes.

2 WODNIK II CLASS (AXT)

LUGA   OKA

Displacement, tons: 1820 full load
Dimensions, feet (metres): 234.3 × 38.1 × 12.8 *(71.4 × 11.6 × 3.9)*
Main machinery: 2 Zgoda-Sulzer 6TD48 diesels; 3600 hp(m) *(2.65 MW)* sustained; 2 shafts; cp props
Speed, knots: 17. **Range, miles:** 7200 at 11 kts
Complement: 60 plus 100 instructors and cadets
Radars: Navigation: Two Don 2; I band.
IFF: High Pole A.

Comment: Built at Gdansk, Poland in 1976-77. Of same general design as Polish ships with an extra deck in the bridge and a larger superstructure. No armament.

OKA   1984

5 SAIL TRAINING SHIPS

MIR   DRUZJBA   KHERSONES   PALLADA   +1

Measurement, tons: 2996 gross
Dimensions, feet (metres): 346.1 × 45.9 × 19.7 *(105.5 × 14 × 6)*
Main machinery: 1 Sulzer 8AL20/24 diesel; 1500 hp(m) *(1.1 MW)*; 1 shaft
Speed, knots: 17
Complement: 55 plus 144 cadets

Comment: Three masted ship rig. Ordered from Stocznia Gdansk in July 1985. First launched 30 December 1986, second 31 March 1987, third 10 June 1988, fourth 30 July 1989. One more building. Not all are naval manned.

PALLADA   2/1992, 92 Wing RAAF

GANGUT   6/1992

CABLE SHIPS

8 KLASMA CLASS

DONETS	INGUL*	INGURI	KATUN
TAVDA	TSNA	YANA*	ZEYA

*Type I

Displacement, tons: 6000 standard; 6900 full load
Measurement, tons: 3400 dwt; 5786 gross
Dimensions, feet (metres): 427.8 × 52.5 × 19 *(130.5 × 16 × 5.8)*
Main machinery: Diesel-electric; 5 Wärtsilä Sulzer 624TS diesel generators (4 in *Ingul* and *Yana*); 5000 hp(m) *(3.68 MW)*; 2 motors; 2150 hp(m) *(1.58 MW)*; 2 shafts
Speed, knots: 14. **Range, miles:** 12 000 at 14 kts
Complement: 85
Radars: Navigation: Two Don 2; I band.

Comment: *Ingul* and *Yana* were built by Wärtsilä, Helsingforsvarvet, Finland in 1962; *Donets* and *Tsna* at the Wärtsilä, Åbovarvet in 1968-69; *Zeya* in 1970. *Donets*, *Tsna* and *Zeya* are of slightly modified design. *Tavda* completed 1977; *Inguri* in 1978. All are ice-strengthened and can carry 1650 miles of cable. Type II can be distinguished by gantry right aft.

TAVDA 3/1992

TSNA 5/1987

3 EMBA I and 2 EMBA II CLASSES

Group I: **EMBA, NEPRYADVA, SETUN**
Group II: **BIRIUSA, KEMJ**

Displacement, tons: 2050 full load (Group I); 2400 (Group II)
Dimensions, feet (metres): 249 × 41.3 × 9.8 *(75.9 × 12.6 × 3)* (Group I)
282.4 × 41.3 × 9.9 *(86.1 × 12.6 × 3)* (Group II)
Main machinery: Diesel-electric; 2 Wärtsilä Vasa 6R22 diesel alternators; 2350 kVA 60 Hz; 2 motors; 1360 hp(m) *(1 MW)*; 2 shafts (Group I)
2 Wärtsilä Vasa 8R22 diesel alternators; 3090 kVA 60 Hz; 2 motors; 2180 hp(m) *(1.6 MW)*; 2 shafts (Group II)
The two turnable propulsion units can be inclined to the ship's path giving, with a bow thruster, improved turning movement
Speed, knots: 11
Complement: 40
Radars: Navigation: Two Spin Trough; I band.

Comment: *Emba* completed by Wärtsilä in 1980, second pair in 1981. Designed for shallow water cable-laying. Carry 380 tons of cable. Order placed with Wärtsilä in January 1985 for two larger (Group II) ships; *Biriusa* delivered 4 July 1986 and *Kemj* on 23 October 1986. Can lay about 600 tons of cable. Designed for use off Vladivostok but also capable of operations in inland waterways.

SETUN (Emba I) 1981, Wärtsilä

KEMJ (Emba II) 1986, Wärtsilä

SERVICE FORCES

1 BEREZINA CLASS (REPLENISHMENT SHIP)

BEREZINA

Displacement, tons: 35 000 full load
Dimensions, feet (metres): 695.5 × 85.3 × 38.7 *(212 × 26 × 11.8)*
Main machinery: 2 diesels; 47 500 hp(m) *(35 MW)*; 2 shafts
Speed, knots: 22. **Range, miles:** 15 000 at 16 kts
Complement: 600
Cargo capacity: Approx 16 000 tons fuel (including Avgas); 2000 tons provisions; 500 tons fresh water

Missiles: SAM - SA-N-4 Gecko twin launcher (abaft funnel); semi-active radar homing to 15 km *(8 nm)* at 2.5 Mach; warhead 50 kg; altitude 9.1-3048 m *(30-10 000 ft)*; 20 missiles.
Guns: 4—57 mm/80 (2 twin); 85° elevation; 120 rounds/minute to 6 km *(3.3 nm)*; weight of shell 2.8 kg.
4—30 mm/65; 6 barrels per mounting; 3000 rounds/minute combined to 2 km.
A/S mortars: 2 RBU 1000 6-tubed; range 1000 m; warhead 55 kg
Countermeasures: Decoys: 2—16-barrelled Chaff launchers.
ESM: 2 Bell series.
Radars: Air/surface search: Strut Curve; F band; range 110 km *(60 nm)* for 2 m² target.
Navigation: Two Don Kay; I band. Two Don 2; I band.
Fire control: Pop Group; F/H/I band (for SA-N-4). Muff Cob; G/H band (for 57 mm). Two Bass Tilt; H/I band (for 30 mm).
IFF: Two High Pole B. Two Square Head.
Sonars: Hull-mounted; active search and attack; medium frequency.

Helicopters: 2 Ka-25 'Hormone C'.

Programmes: Laid down in 1973; launched in 1975. Built at Nikolayev (61 Kommuna) and completed in 1977.
Structure: Two storing gantries (apparently with moving high-points); four 10 ton cranes and one other; liquid fuelling gantry (amidships); stern refuelling. The weight of her armament is notable in comparison with Western practice. This is the first replenishment ship to be fitted with SAM missiles and Gatling guns as well as carrying helicopters and mounting RBUs. This gives her a considerable AA capability and, if the helicopters have an ASW as well as Vertrep role, some self-sufficiency in anti-submarine operations. This is the only ship to site the RBU 1000 forward of the bridge.
Operational: Can replenish two ships at a time or refuel three. Based in the Black Sea and rarely deploys even to the Mediterranean.

BEREZINA 8/1991

6 BORIS CHILIKIN CLASS (REPLENISHMENT SHIPS)

BORIS BUTOMA	GENRICH GASANOV
BORIS CHILIKIN	IVAN BUBNOV
DNESTR	VLADIMIR KOLECHITSKY

Displacement, tons: 23 400 full load
Dimensions, feet (metres): 531.5 × 70.2 × 33.8 *(162.1 × 21.4 × 10.3)*
Main machinery: 1 diesel; 9600 hp(m) *(7 MW)*; 1 shaft
Speed, knots: 17. **Range, miles:** 10 000 at 16 kts
Complement: 75 (without armament)
Cargo capacity: 13 000 tons oil fuel and dieso; 400 tons ammunition; 400 tons spares; 400 tons victualling stores; 500 tons fresh water

Guns: 4—57 mm/80 (2 twin). Most are fitted for but not with the guns.
Radars: Air/surface search/fire control: Strut Curve (fitted for but not with).
Muff Cob (fitted for but not with).
Navigation: Two Don Kay (plus Don 2 in *V Kolechitsky*); I band.
IFF: High Pole B.

Programmes: Based on the Veliky Oktyabr merchant ship tanker design, *Boris Chilikin* was built at the Baltic Yard, Leningrad completing in 1971. Last of class *Boris Butoma* completed in 1978.
Structure: This is the only class of purpose-built underway fleet replenishment ships for the supply of both liquids and solids. The removal of both fire control radar and armament is in contrast to the considerable weight of such items carried in *Berezina*. Although most operate in merchant navy paint schemes, all wear naval ensigns.
Operational: Earlier ships can supply solids on both sides forward. Later ships supply solids to starboard, liquids to port forward. All can supply liquids either side aft and astern. *Dnestr* and *Gasanov* are based in the North, *Bubnov* in the Black Sea, *Butoma* and *Kolechitsky* in the Pacific.

DNESTR   7/1991

4 DUBNA CLASS (REPLENISHMENT TANKERS)

DUBNA	PECHENGA
IRKUT	SVENTA

Displacement, tons: 11 500 full load
Dimensions, feet (metres): 426.4 × 65.6 × 23.6 *(130 × 20 × 7.2)*
Main machinery: 1 Russkiy 8DRPH23/230 diesel; 6000 hp(m) *(4.4 MW)*; 1 shaft
Speed, knots: 16. **Range, miles:** 7000 at 16 kts
Complement: 70

Cargo capacity: 7000 tons fuel; 300 tons fresh water; 1500 tons stores
Radars: Navigation: One or two Don 2; I band.

Programmes: *Dubna* completed 1974, *Irkut* December 1975, both at Rauma-Repola, Finland. *Pechenga* commissioned end 1978, *Sventa* completed April 1979.

Structure: Have 1 ton replenishment stations forward. Normally painted in merchant navy colours.
Operational: Can refuel on either beam and astern. *Dubna* in North, *Sventa* in Black Sea, remainder in Pacific.

DUBNA   8/1992

5 MOD ALTAY CLASS (REPLENISHMENT TANKERS)

| ELNYA | ILIM | KOLA | PRUT | YEGORLIK |

Displacement, tons: 7250 full load
Dimensions, feet (metres): 348 × 51 × 22 *(106.2 × 15.5 × 6.7)*
Main machinery: 1 Burmeister & Wain BM550VTBN110 diesel; 3200 hp(m) *(2.35 MW)*; 1 shaft
Speed, knots: 14. **Range, miles:** 8600 at 12 kts
Complement: 60
Cargo capacity: 4400 tons oil fuel
Radars: Navigation: Two Don 2; I band.

Comment: Built from 1967-72 by Rauma-Repola, Finland. All modified for alongside replenishment. This class is part of 38 ships, being the third group of Rauma types built in Finland in 1967. Some have armament fittings similar to the Uda class with 25 mm guns. A sixth of the class *Izhora* sunk in Vladivostok after an explosion in July 1991.

3 OLEKMA CLASS (REPLENISHMENT TANKERS)

| OLEKMA (mod) | IMAN | ZOLOTOY ROG |

Displacement, tons: 4000 standard; 6700 full load
Dimensions, feet (metres): 344.5 × 47.9 × 22 *(105.1 × 14.6 × 6.7)*
Main machinery: 1 Burmeister & Wain diesel; 2900 hp(m) *(2.13 MW)*; 1 shaft
Speed, knots: 14. **Range, miles:** 8000 at 14 kts
Complement: 40
Cargo capacity: 4500 tons oil fuel
Radars: Navigation: Don 2 and Spin Trough; I band.

Comment: Part of the second group of 34 tankers built by Rauma-Repola, Finland between 1960 and 1966. *Olekma* is modified for replenishment with refuelling rig abaft the bridge as well as astern refuelling. The other two can only refuel astern. *Zolotoy Rog* has a square sided funnel.

ELNYA   2/1992

OLEKMA   10/1992

582　RUSSIA / Service forces

3 MOD KAZBEK CLASS (REPLENISHMENT TANKERS)

ALATYR　　　DESNA　　　VOLKHOV

Displacement, tons: 16 250 full load
Measurement, tons: 12 000 dwt; 8230 gross; 3942 net
Dimensions, feet (metres): 477.2 × 62.9 × 26.9 *(145.5 × 19.2 × 8.2)*
Main machinery: 1 Russkiy Dizel diesel; 4000 hp(m) *(2.94 MW)*; 1 shaft
Speed, knots: 15. **Range, miles:** 18 000 at 12 kts
Complement: 46
Cargo capacity: 10 500 tons oil fuel
Radars: Navigation: Two Don 2; I band.
IFF: High Pole A.

Comment: Former Leningrad class merchant fleet tankers taken over by the Navy. Built at Leningrad and Nikolayev from 1951 to 1961. Eight others—*Karl Marx, Kazbek, Dzerzhinsk, Grodno, Cheboksary, Liepaya, Zhitomir* and *Buguzuslan*—have acted in support of naval operations. The original class numbered 64. All three now modified for alongside replenishment. The naval ships of this class can be distinguished by the A-frame before the bridge, the two forward kingposts and the cat-walks. Due to be scrapped.

DESNA　　　　　　　　　　　　　　　　　　　　　　　5/1992

6 UDA CLASS (REPLENISHMENT TANKERS)

DUNAY (mod)　**KOIDA**　**LENA** (mod)　**TEREK** (mod)　**VISHERA** (mod)
SHEKSNA (mod)

Displacement, tons: 5500 standard; 7110 full load
Dimensions, feet (metres): 400.3 × 51.8 × 20.3 *(122.1 × 15.8 × 6.2)*
Main machinery: 2 diesels; 9000 hp(m) *(6.6 MW)*; 2 shafts
Speed, knots: 17. **Range, miles:** 4000 at 15 kts
Complement: 85
Cargo capacity: 3000 tons oil fuel
Guns: Positions for 8—57 mm/70 (2 quad); 6—25 mm/80 (3 twin) (landed in peacetime).
Radars: Navigation: Two Don 2; I band.
Fire control: Two Muff Cob (when guns are fitted); G/H band.
IFF: High Pole A.

Comment: All have a beam replenishment capability. May retain fitting for a quadruple 57 mm or three twin 25 mm guns. Built in 1961-67. *Koida* was first Soviet ship refitted in Greek Orion shipyard. Modified ships have a second A-frame amidships thus providing two alongside refuelling positions. Three transferred to Indonesia 1963-64 and since deleted. One deleted in error in 1991.

VISHERA　　　　　　　　　　　　　　　　　　　　　　6/1992

2 KALININGRADNEFT CLASS (SUPPORT TANKERS)

ARGUN　　　VYAZMA

Displacement, tons: 8600 full load
Dimensions, feet (metres): 380.5 × 56 × 21 *(116 × 17 × 6.5)*
Main machinery: 1 Russkiy Burmeister & Wain 5DKRP50/110-2 diesel; 3850 hp(m) *(2.83 MW)*; 1 shaft
Speed, knots: 14. **Range, miles:** 5000 at 14 kts
Complement: 32
Cargo capacity: 5400 tons oil fuel and other liquids
Radars: Navigation: Okean; I band.

Comment: Built by Rauma-Repola, Finland in 1982. Can refuel alongside or astern. At least an additional 20 of this class operate with the fishing fleets.

ARGUN　　　　　　　　　　　　　　　　　11/1991, G Jacobs

1 SOFYA CLASS (SUPPORT TANKER)

AKHTYUBA (ex-*Hanoi*)

Displacement, tons: 62 600 full load
Dimensions, feet (metres): 757.9 × 100.4 × 38 *(231.2 × 30.6 × 11.6)*
Main machinery: 2 boilers; 1 turbine; 21 000 hp(m) *(15.4 MW)*; 1 shaft
Speed, knots: 17. **Range, miles:** 10 000 at 17 kts
Complement: 75
Cargo capacity: 45 000 tons oil fuel.
Radars: Navigation: Two Don 2; I band.

Comment: Built as the merchant tanker *Hanoi* in 1963 at Leningrad, she was taken over by the Navy in 1969 and renamed *Akhtyuba*. The hull type was used in the construction of the space associated ship *Kosmonaut Yury Gagarin*. Astern refuelling. Active in the South China Sea.

AKHTYUBA　　　　　　　　　　　　　　　9/1991, 92 Wing RAAF

2 NERCHA CLASS (SUPPORT TANKERS)

NARA　　　KLYAZMA

Displacement, tons: 1850 full load
Dimensions, feet (metres): 208.3 × 33 × 14.1 *(63.5 × 10.1 × 4.3)*
Main machinery: 1 diesel; 1000 hp(m) *(735 kW)*; 1 shaft
Speed, knots: 11. **Range, miles:** 2000 at 10 kts
Complement: 25
Cargo capacity: 700 tons oil fuel
Radars: Navigation: Don 2; I band.

Comment: Built in Finland 1952-55 as part of class of 12. Renamed in naval service. Have astern refuelling capability. Strengthened for ice.

4 KONDA CLASS (SUPPORT TANKERS)

KONDA　　　ROSSOSH　　　SOYANA　　　YAKHROMA

Displacement, tons: 2090 full load
Dimensions, feet (metres): 226.3 × 33 × 14.1 *(69 × 10.1 × 4.3)*
Main machinery: 1 diesel; 1600 hp(m) *(1.18 MW)*; 1 shaft
Speed, knots: 12. **Range, miles:** 2200 at 11.5 kts
Complement: 36
Cargo capacity: 1000 tons oil fuel
Radars: Navigation: Don 2; I band. Spin Trough; I band.

Comment: Originally of the Iskra class of merchant tankers built in 1955. Have a stern refuelling capability. Icebreaker bow.

KONDA　　　　　　　　　　　　　　　　　　　　　　　5/1990

5 KHOBI CLASS (SUPPORT TANKERS)

CHEREMSHAN　　ORSHA　　SEIMA　　SOSVA　　SYSOLA

Displacement, tons: 700 light; 1500 full load
Dimensions, feet (metres): 206.6 × 33 × 14.8 *(63 × 10.1 × 4.5)*
Main machinery: 2 diesels; 1600 hp(m) *(1.18 MW)*; 2 shafts
Speed, knots: 13. **Range, miles:** 2500 at 12 kts
Complement: 35 (4 officers)
Cargo capacity: 500 tons oil fuel
Radars: Navigation: Don 2 and Spin Trough; I band.

Comment: Built from 1957 to 1959. Survivors of a class of 25. Can refuel while being towed. Now being deleted. Transfers: Two to Albania; one to Hungary (deleted); three to Indonesia (two deleted).

KHOBI (Indonesian number)　　　　　　　　6/1991, 92 Wing RAAF

1 IRTYSH CLASS (SUPPORT TANKER)

NARVA

Displacement, tons: 1700 full load
Dimensions, feet (metres): 224.7 × 34.1 × 14.1 *(68.5 × 10.4 × 4.3)*
Main machinery: 1 diesel; 880 hp(m) *(647 kW)*; 1 shaft
Speed, knots: 12. Range, miles: 2000 at 10 kts
Complement: 40
Cargo capacity: 1170 tons oil fuel
Radars: Navigation: Neptun or Spin Trough; I band.

NARVA   *11/1985, van Ginderen Collection*

2 BASKUNCHAK CLASS (SUPPORT TANKERS)

| IVAN GOLUBETS | SOVIETSKY POGRANICHNIK |

Displacement, tons: 2280 full load
Dimensions, feet (metres): 272.6 × 39.4 × 15.7 *(83.1 × 12 × 4.8)*
Main machinery: 1 Bryansk Type 8DR34/61VI diesel; 2000 hp(m) *(1.47 MW)*; 1 shaft
Speed, knots: 13. Range, miles: 5000 at 12 kts
Complement: 30
Cargo capacity: 1500 tons oil fuel

Comment: Last of a large class. These two support Border Guard units in the Pacific.

SOVIETSKY POGRANICHNIK   *11/1991, G Jacobs*

TOPLIVO SERIES (HARBOUR TANKERS)

Comment: There are three versions under this name. Toplivo 1, built in Poland, are of 420 tons full load and 34.4 m long. Toplivo 2, some of which were built in Egypt but the majority in the USSR, are of 1200 tons full load and 53 m long. Toplivo 3, built in the USSR, are of 1300 tons full load and 52.7 m long with a very different appearance from Toplivo 2. These ships are used in many bases for the transport of all forms of liquids.

TOPLIVO 3   *5/1992, van Ginderen Collection*

7 VALA CLASS (SPECIAL TANKERS)

| VALA | TNT 11 | TNT 27 | 12 | 19 | 25 | 29 |

Displacement, tons: 2030 full load
Dimensions, feet (metres): 239.8 × 42.3 × 15.7 *(73.1 × 12.9 × 4.8)*
Main machinery: 1 diesel; 1000 hp(m) *(735 kW)*; 1 shaft
Speed, knots: 14. Range, miles: 2000 at 11 kts
Complement: 30
Guns: 4—14.5 mm (2 twin) MGs (in some).
Radars: Navigation: Spin Trough; I band.

Comment: Completed 1964-71. Used for transporting radiological liquids and nuclear waste.

VALA class   *9/1978*

6 LUZA CLASS (SPECIAL TANKERS)

| ALAMBAI | BARGUZIN | KAMA |
| ARAGVI | DON | SELENGA |

Displacement, tons: 1900 full load
Dimensions, feet (metres): 205 × 35.1 × 14.1 *(62.5 × 10.7 × 4.3)*
Main machinery: 1 diesel; 1000 hp(m) *(735 kW)*; 1 shaft
Speed, knots: 12. Range, miles: 2000 at 11 kts
Complement: 60
Radars: Navigation: Don 2; I band. Spin Trough; I band.
IFF: High Pole B.

Comment: Completed at Kolpino 1962-70. Used for transporting special liquids such as missile fuel.

DON   *8/1991, van Ginderen Collection*

HOSPITAL SHIPS

Note: The 9885 ton passenger liner *Mikhail Bulgakov* (ex-*Mikhail Suslov*) was converted to a hospital ship in a Polish shipyard in mid-1989.

4 OB CLASS (AH)

| OB | YENISEI | SVIR | IRTYSH |

Displacement, tons: 11 300 full load
Dimensions, feet (metres): 499.7 × 63.6 × 20.5 *(152.3 × 19.4 × 6.3)*
Main machinery: 2 Zgoda-Sulzer 12ZV40/48; 15 600 hp(m) *(11.47 MW)* sustained; 2 shafts; cp props
Speed, knots: 19. Range, miles: 10 000 at 18 kts
Complement: 124 plus 83 medical staff
Radars: Navigation: Three Don 2; I band.
IFF: High Pole A.
Helicopters: 1 Ka-25 'Hormone C'.

Comment: Built at Szczecin, Poland. *Ob* completed in 1980 and transferred to the Pacific in September 1980. *Yenisei* completed 1981 and is based in the Black Sea. *Svir* completed in early 1989 and transferred to the Northern Fleet in September 1989. *Irtysh* completed in June 1990, was stationed in the Gulf in 1990-91 and is now based in the Pacific. A fifth of the class was cancelled. Have 100 beds and seven operating theatres. The first purpose-built hospital ships in the Navy, a programme which may have been prompted by the use of several merchant ships off Angola for Cuban casualties in the 'war of liberation.' NBC pressurised citadel. Ship stabilisation system. Decompression chamber.

SVIR   *7/1992*

SALVAGE, RESCUE AND MOORING VESSELS

4 MIKHAIL RUDNITSKY CLASS (ARS)

| MIKHAIL RUDNITSKY | GEORGY KOZMIN | GEORGY TITOV | SAYANY |

Displacement, tons: 10 700 full load
Dimensions, feet (metres): 427.4 × 56.7 × 23.9 *(130.3 × 17.3 × 7.3)*
Main machinery: 1 S5DKRN62/140-3 diesel; 6100 hp(m) *(4.48 MW)*; 1 shaft
Speed, knots: 16. Range, miles: 12 000 at 15.5 kts
Complement: 70
Radars: Navigation: Palm Frond; Nayada; I band.

Comment: Built at Vyborg, based on Moskva Pionier class merchant ship hull. First completed 1979, second in 1980, third in 1983 and fourth in 1984. Fly flag of Salvage and Rescue Service. Have two 40 ton and one 20 ton lift with cable fairleads forward and aft. This lift capability would be adequate for handling small submersibles, one of which is carried in the centre hold. *Sayany* is also described as a research ship. *Rudnitsky* based in the Black Sea, *Titov* in the Northern Fleet and the other two in the Pacific.

MIKHAIL RUDNITSKY   *5/1991*

584 RUSSIA / Salvage, rescue and mooring vessels

2 PAMIR CLASS

AGATAN   ALDAN

Displacement, tons: 2050 full load
Dimensions, feet (metres): 256 × 42 × 13.5 *(78 × 12.8 × 4.1)*
Main machinery: 2 MAN G10V40/60 diesels; 4200 hp(m) *(3.1 MW)*; 2 shafts; cp props
Speed, knots: 17. **Range, miles:** 15 000 at 17 kts
Complement: 77
Radars: Navigation: Two Don 2; I band.
IFF: High Pole A.

Comment: Salvage tugs built at AB Gävle Varv, Sweden in 1959-60. Equipped with one 10 ton and two 1.5 ton derricks, powerful pumps, air compressors, diving gear, recompression chambers, firefighting apparatus and electric generators. Have rather less cluttered bridge area than the two of this class converted to AGIs. Both based in the North.

ALDAN   2/1983

4 INGUL CLASS

PAMIR   MASHUK   ALATAU   KARABAKH

Displacement, tons: 4050 full load
Dimensions, feet (metres): 304.4 × 50.5 × 19 *(92.8 × 15.4 × 5.8)*
Main machinery: 2 Type 58-D-4R diesels; 6000 hp(m) *(4.4 MW)*; 2 shafts; cp props
Speed, knots: 20. **Range, miles:** 9000 at 19 kts
Complement: 35 plus salvage party of 18
Guns: Positions for 2—57 mm/70 (twin) and 4—25 mm/80 (2 twin) (not fitted).
Radars: Navigation: Two Palm Frond; I band.
IFF: High Pole. Square Head.

Comment: Built at Admiralty Yard, Leningrad in 1975-84. NATO class-name the same as one of the Klasma class cable-ships. Naval-manned arctic salvage and rescue tugs. Two more, *Yaguar* (Murmansk) and *Bars* (Vladivostok), operate with the merchant fleet. Carry salvage pumps, diving and firefighting gear as well as a high-line for transfer of personnel. *Pamir* and *Karabakh* in the North, the other pair in the Pacific.

MASHUK   4/1990, Ships of the World

4 SLIVA CLASS

SB 406   SB 408   SB 921   SHAKHTER SB 922

Displacement, tons: 3050 full load
Dimensions, feet (metres): 227 × 50.5 × 16.7 *(69.2 × 15.4 × 5.1)*
Main machinery: 2 Russkiy SEMT-Pielstick 6 PC2.5 L 400 diesels; 7020 hp(m) *(5.2 MW)* sustained; 2 shafts; cp props; bow thruster
Speed, knots: 16
Complement: 43 plus 10 salvage party
Radars: Navigation: Nayada; I band.

Comment: Built at Rauma-Repola, Finland. *SB 406* completed 20 February 1984. *SB 408* completed 5 June 1984. Second pair ordered 1984 *SB 921* completed 5 July 1985 and *SB 922* on 20 December 1985. *SB 922* named *Shakhter* in 1989.

SB 406   9/1992

8 KASHTAN CLASS (BUOY TENDERS)

KIL 926   KIL 143   KIL 164   KIL 498
KIL 927   KIL 158   KIL 140   KIL 168

Displacement, tons: 4600 full load
Dimensions, feet (metres): 313.3 × 56.4 × 16.4 *(95.5 × 17.2 × 5)*
Main machinery: 4 Wärtsilä diesels; 29 000 hp(m) *(2.31 MW)*; 2 shafts
Speed, knots: 13.5
Complement: 51 plus 20 spare berths
Radars: Navigation: Nayada; I band.

Comment: Enlarged Sura class built at the Neptun Shipyard, Rostock. Ordered 29 August 1986; *926* handed over in June 1988 and is in the Baltic; *927* to the Pacific in July 1989; *143* to the North in July 1989; *158* to the Black Sea in November 1989; *164* to the North in January 1990; *140* to the Baltic in May 1990; *498* to the Pacific in November 1990 and *168* to the Pacific in mid-1991. Lifting capacity: one 130 ton lifting frame, one 100 ton derrick, one 12.5 ton crane and one 10 ton derrick.

KIL 140   6/1992, Bernd Fischer

10 SURA CLASS (BUOY TENDERS)

KIL 1, 2, 21, 22, 25, 27, 29, 31, 32, 33

Displacement, tons: 2370 standard; 3150 full load
Dimensions, feet (metres): 285.4 × 48.6 × 16.4 *(87 × 14.8 × 5)*
Main machinery: Diesel-electric; 4 diesel generators; 2 motors; 2240 hp(m) *(1.65 MW)*; 2 shafts
Speed, knots: 12. **Range, miles:** 2000 at 11 kts
Complement: 40
Cargo capacity: 900 tons cargo; 300 tons fuel for transfer
Radars: Navigation: Two Don 2; I band.

Comment: Heavy lift ships built as mooring and buoy tenders at Rostock in East Germany between 1965 and 1976. Lifting capacity: one 65 ton derrick and one 65 ton stern cage. Have been seen to carry 12 m DSRVs.

KIL 29   3/1992, Erik Laursen

9 KATUN I and 2 KATUN II CLASSES
(SALVAGE AND RESCUE TUGS)

Katun I: PZHS 96, 98, 123, 124, 209, 273, 279, 282, 551
Katun II: PZHS 64, 92

Displacement, tons: 920 full load
Dimensions, feet (metres): 205.3 × 33.1 × 11.5 *(62 × 10.1 × 3.5)* (Katun I)
Main machinery: 2 diesels; 5000 hp(m) *(3.68 MW)*; 2 shafts
Speed, knots: 17. **Range, miles:** 2000 at 17 kts
Complement: 30
Radars: Navigation: Spin Trough or Kivach (Katun II); I band.
IFF: High Pole A.

Comment: Katun I built in USSR 1970-78. Equipped for firefighting and rescue. PZHS 64 and 92, both Katun II, were completed in 1982—3 m *(9.8 ft)* longer than Katun I with an extra bridge level and lattice masts. Some may have a PDS prefix to their pennant numbers.

KATUN 123   8/1991, van Ginderen Collection

2 OREL CLASS (SALVAGE TUGS)

SB 38   SB 43

Displacement, tons: 1750 full load
Dimensions, feet (metres): 201.2 × 39.2 × 14.8 *(61.4 × 12 × 4.5)*
Main machinery: 1 MAN G5Z 52/70 diesel; 1700 hp(m) *(1.25 MW)*; 1 shaft
Speed, knots: 15. **Range, miles:** 14 000 at 13.5 kts
Complement: 40
Radars: Navigation: Two Don 2; I band.

Comment: Class of salvage and rescue tugs normally operated by Ministry of Fisheries with the fishing fleets. Naval manned with sick bay and recompression chamber. Built in Finland in late 1950s and early 1960s. Ice-strengthened.

SB 38   10/1988

4 NEPTUN CLASS

KIL 6, 9, 15, 17

Displacement, tons: 1240 full load
Dimensions, feet (metres): 187.9 × 37.4 × 10.8 *(57.3 × 11.4 × 3.3)*
Main machinery: 2 boilers; 2 steam reciprocating engines; 1000 ihp(m) *(735 kW)*; 2 shafts
Speed, knots: 12. **Range, miles:** 1000 at 10 kts
Complement: 28

Comment: Mooring tenders similar to Western boom defence vessels. Built in 1957-60 by Neptun, Rostock. Have a crane of 75 tons lifting capacity on the bow. Several of the class scrapped since 1989.

NEPTUN   1973

SUBMARINE RESCUE SHIPS

2 ELBRUS CLASS

ELBRUS   ALAGEZ

Displacement, tons: 19 000 standard; 22 500 full load
Dimensions, feet (metres): 562.7 × 80.4 × 27.9 *(171.5 × 24.5 × 8.5)*
Main machinery: Diesel-electric; 4 diesel generators; 2 motors; 24 500 hp(m) *(18 MW)*; 2 shafts
Speed, knots: 17. **Range, miles:** 14 500 at 15 kts
Complement: 420
Guns: 4—30 mm/65 (2 twin).
Radars: Navigation: Don 2 and two Don Kay; I band.
Helicopters: 1 Ka-25 Hormone C.

Comment: Very large submarine rescue and salvage ships with icebreaking capability, possibly in view of under-ice capability of some SSBNs. Built at Nikolayev. First seen 1981. Second one completed 1989. Can carry two submersibles in store abaft the funnel which are launched from telescopic gantries. *Elbrus* is based in the Black Sea, *Alagez* in the Pacific. A third of class reported launched in 1992 and taken over by Ukraine.

ALAGEZ   9/1991, G Jacobs

1 NEPA CLASS

KARPATY

Displacement, tons: 6100 full load
Dimensions, feet (metres): 424.9 × 62 × 21 *(129.5 × 18.9 × 6.4)*
Main machinery: Diesel-electric; 4 diesel generators; 2 motors; 8000 hp(m) *(5.88 MW)*; 2 shafts
Speed, knots: 16. **Range, miles:** 8000 at 14 kts
Complement: 270
Radars: Navigation: Two Don 2; I band.
IFF: High Pole B.

Comment: Completed 1968 at Nikolayev. Submarine rescue and salvage ship with a special high stern which extends out over the water for rescue manoeuvres. Has two 750 ton lifts which can work in tandem. Also one 100 ton lift, one 60 ton derrick and two 10 ton derricks. Carries a rescue bell, two submersibles and a number of recompression chambers. Based in the Baltic since November 1988.

KARPATY   1972, A Nubert

7 PRUT CLASS

ALTAY	BESHTAU	VLADIMIR TREFOLEV	ZHIGULI
SS 21	EPRON (ex-SS 26)	SS 83	

Displacement, tons: 2120 standard; 2800 full load
Dimensions, feet (metres): 295.9 × 46.9 × 18 *(90.2 × 14.3 × 5.5)*
Main machinery: Diesel-electric; 4 diesel generators; 2 motors; 10 000 hp(m) *(7.35 MW)*; 2 shafts
Speed, knots: 20. **Range, miles:** 9000 at 16 kts
Complement: 130
Guns: 4—57 mm/70 (2 quad) (not fitted).
Radars: Navigation: Two Don 2; I band.
Sonars: Tamir; hull-mounted; active search; high frequency.

Comment: Large rescue vessels. Built 1960-66. Carry two heavy duty derricks, submersible recompression chambers, rescue chambers and bells. Four marker buoys stowed abaft mainmast. All except *Altay* and *Zhiguli* have been modernised with quadruped foremasts and smaller marker buoys. One scrapped in 1987.

EPRON   6/1991, van Ginderen Collection

8 VALDAY CLASS (Ex-T 58 CLASS)

KAZBEK	KHIBINY	VALDAY	ZANGEZUR	PULKOVO (ex-SS 38)
SS 30, 35, 47				

Displacement, tons: 725 standard; 930 full load
Dimensions, feet (metres): 236.2 × 29.5 × 9.9 *(72 × 9 × 3)*
Main machinery: 2 diesels; 4000 hp(m) *(2.94 MW)*; 2 shafts
Speed, knots: 17. **Range, miles:** 2500 at 12 kts
Complement: 100
Radars: Navigation: Don; I band.
IFF: High Pole, Square Head or Dead Duck.
Sonars: Tamir; hull-mounted; active search; high frequency.

Comment: Basically of similar design to that of the T 58 class fleet minesweepers, but they were completed as emergency salvage vessels and submarine rescue ships at Leningrad in 1961-62. Equipped with diving bell, recompression chamber and emergency medical ward. Have stern lift of 10 tons and rescue chamber aft. One transferred to India (*Nistar* ex-SS 48) in 1971. Two scrapped in 1990 and two more in 1992.

VALDAY SS 30   3/1992, Hartmut Ehlers

TRANSPORTS

1 MARINA TSVETAYEVA CLASS (TYPE B 961)

MARINA TSVETAYEVA

Measurement, tons: 1500 gross
Dimensions, feet (metres): 291.3 × 56.4 × 16.4 *(88.8 × 17.2 × 5)*
Main machinery: 1 Zgoda-Sulzer 6ZL40/48 diesel; 4350 hp(m) *(3.2 MW)*; 1 shaft
Speed, knots: 14. **Range, miles:** 2000 at 14 kts
Complement: 34

Comment: Built at Stocznia Gdynia in 1990/91. Capable of taking up to 240 troops. Based in the Pacific. More of the class may be built for offshore supply tasks.

MARINA TSVETAYEVA   7/1991, 92 Wing RAAF

1 ANADYR CLASS

ANADYR

Displacement, tons: 27 000 full load
Dimensions, feet (metres): 741.5 × 98.4 × 21.3 *(226 × 30 × 6.5)*
Main machinery: 4 Wärtsilä Vasa 16V32 diesels; 32 200 hp(m) *(23.7 MW)* sustained; 2 shafts
Speed, knots: 20
Complement: 70
Cargo capacity: 10 500 tons
Radars: Navigation: Two Spin Trough; I band.
Helicopters: 2 medium.

Comment: Ro-flo ship built at Wärtsilä, Finland and completed in 1988. Handed over to the Navy and transferred to the Pacific via the Northern Sea route in August 1990. The ship's well-deck is 150 m in length.

ANADYR   10/1991, G Jacobs

1 ANGARA CLASS

ANGARA (ex-*Hela*)

Displacement, tons: 2520 full load
Dimensions, feet (metres): 327.4 × 41.7 × 13.5 *(99.8 × 12.7 × 4.1)*
Main machinery: 2 MAN diesels; 8360 hp(m) *(6.14 MW)*; 2 shafts
Speed, knots: 19. **Range, miles:** 2000 at 15 kts
Complement: 224
Radars: Navigation: Spin Trough; I band

Comment: Acts as a yacht for the Commander-in-Chief of the Navy. Stationed in the Black Sea. Built by Stülcken of Hamburg and launched 29 December 1938. Passed to USSR as partial reparation. Refit in Greece in 1983. Little change seen except improved electronics.

ANGARA   5/1990, S Breyer

1 AMGUEMA CLASS

YAUZA

Displacement, tons: 15 000 full load
Dimensions, feet (metres): 436.4 × 62.3 × 29.7 *(133 × 19 × 9)*
Main machinery: Diesel-electric; 4 diesel generators; 1 motor; 7200 hp(m) *(5.29 MW)*; 1 shaft
Speed, knots: 16. **Range, miles:** 7000 at 15 kts
Cargo capacity: 6500 tons
Radars: Navigation: Two Don 2; I band.

Comment: Built in Kherson in 1974. Ice-strengthened. Similar class operates in merchant fleet. Based in the Northern Fleet.

YAUZA   1985

2 ANDIZAN CLASS

ONDA   POSYET

Displacement, tons: 6550 full load
Dimensions, feet (metres): 341.1 × 47.6 × 21.7 *(104 × 14.5 × 6.6)*
Main machinery: 2 diesels; 2500 hp(m) *(1.84 MW)*; 1 shaft
Speed, knots: 14. **Range, miles:** 6000 at 13 kts
Complement: 43
Cargo capacity: 4000 tons
Radars: Navigation: Don 2; I band.

Comment: Part of a class of about 50 merchant ships, built at Neptun, Rostock 1960-61. *Onda* in the North, *Posyet* in the Pacific.

ONDA   7/1987

1 KALININ CLASS

KUBAN (ex-*Nadeshda-Krupskaya*)

Displacement, tons: 6400 full load
Dimensions, feet (metres): 401 × 52.5 × 16.4 *(122.2 × 16 × 5)*
Main machinery: 2 MAN diesels; 8000 hp(m) *(5.88 MW)*; 2 shafts
Speed, knots: 17. **Range, miles:** 8200 at 17 kts
Complement: 120 plus 350 passengers
Cargo capacity: 1000 tons
Radars: Navigation: Two Don 2; I band.

Comment: Built in 1958 by Mathias Thesen Werft, Wismar, East Germany. Part of Mikhail Kalinin class of merchant ships originally to have been 24 ships of which only 19 were completed 1958-64. Name changed on transfer to naval service. In the 1980s was employed under naval command as personnel support ship for the Mediterranean Squadron.

KUBAN   1987, Selçuk Emre

Transports / RUSSIA 587

10 ANTONOV CLASS

NEON ANTONOV	NIKOLAY SIPYAGIN	NICOLAY STARSHINOV
IVAN LEDNEV	VICTOR DENISON	IVAN SUDTSOV
DVINA	MIKHAIL KONOVALOV	SERGEY SUDETSKY
IRBIT		

Displacement, tons: 5600 full load
Dimensions, feet (metres): 311.7 × 48.2 × 21.3 *(95 × 14.7 × 6.5)*
Main machinery: 2 diesels; 7000 hp(m) *(5.15 MW)*; 2 shafts
Speed, knots: 17. Range, miles: 8500 at 13 kts
Complement: 40
Capacity: 2500 tons
Missiles: SAM: 2 SA-N-5 Grail twin launchers; manual aiming; IR homing to 6 km *(3.2 nm)* at 1.5 Mach; altitude to 2500 m *(8000 ft)*; warhead 1.5 kg.
Guns: 2—30 mm/65 (twin). 4—14.5 mm (2 twin) MGs.
Radars: Navigation: Don Kay; Spin Trough; I band.

Comment: Ten of the class built at Nikolayev in 1975-early 1980s. All but *Irbit* (Pacific Fleet) and *Dvina* (Northern Fleet) operated by the Border Guard in the Pacific. Have two small landing craft aft. Armament is not normally mounted.

SERGEY SUDETSKY   1/1992, van Ginderen Collection

4 PARTIZAN CLASS

PECHORA	TURGAY	UFA	V ADM FOMIN (ex-*Pinega*) (mod)

Displacement, tons: 2150 full load
Dimensions, feet (metres): 291.3 × 42.3 × 16.4 *(88.8 × 12.9 × 5)*
Main machinery: 1 Sulzer diesel; 2080 hp(m) *(1.53 MW)*; 1 shaft
Speed, knots: 13. Range, miles: 4000 at 12 kts
Complement: 35
Cargo capacity: 3150 tons
Radars: Navigation: Don 2 or Palm Frond; I band.

Comment: Built at Turnu Severin SY, Romania 1975-76. Have two 10 ton and one 20 ton derricks. Basically small container ships with 20 similar in merchant fleet. *Fomin* is an ammunition transport and is armed with SA-N-5 missiles and two twin MG mountings.

PECHORA   9/1988

10 KEYLA CLASS

MEZEN	ONEGA	PONOI
RITSA (AGI)	TERIBERKA	TULOMA
VERTSA	UNZA	USSURY
VERUSLAN		

Displacement, tons: 2440 full load
Dimensions, feet (metres): 257.5 × 34.8 × 14.8 *(78.5 × 10.6 × 4.5)*
Main machinery: 1 diesel; 1000 hp(m) *(735 kW)*; 1 shaft
Speed, knots: 14. Range, miles: 3000 at 11 kts
Complement: 26
Cargo capacity: 1195 tons
Radars: Navigation: Spin Trough or Neptun (plus Don 2 in some); I band.

Comment: Built 1959-61 in Budapest. Cargo ships. *Ritsa* has a deckhouse forward of the bridge, several communications type aerials, and has been used for intelligence gathering. *Teriberka* and *Ussury*, of original design, have one 15 ton and six 2.5 ton derricks. The remainder have one 10 ton and six 5 ton derricks.

PONOI   9/1991, G Jacobs

13 MUNA CLASS

VTR 28, 48, 81-86, 91-94, 148

Displacement, tons: 690 full load
Dimensions, feet (metres): 165 × 26.9 × 9.5 *(50.3 × 8.2 × 2.9)*
Main machinery: 1 diesel; 300 hp(m) *(220 kW)*; 1 shaft
Speed, knots: 10. Range, miles: 3000 at 10 kts
Complement: 40
Radars: Navigation: Two Spin Trough; I band.

Comment: Torpedo and ammunition transports with large crane amidships. Most have VTR prefix to their pennant numbers. Some act as experimental ships.

MUNA   8/1991, G Jacobs

8 MAYAK CLASS

BUZULUK, ISHIM, LAMA, MIUS, NEMAN, RIONI, ULMA, VYTEGRA

Displacement, tons: 920 full load
Dimensions, feet (metres): 178.1 × 30.5 × 11.8 *(54.3 × 9.3 × 3.6)*
Main machinery: 1 diesel; 1000 hp(m) *(735 kW)*; 1 shaft
Speed, knots: 12. Range, miles: 11 000 at 11 kts
Cargo capacity: 240 tons refrigerated stores
Radars: Navigation: Spin Trough; I Band.

Comment: Converted trawlers. Refrigerated stores ships.

LAMA   7/1992

2 MP 4 CLASS

VTR 294   VTR 295

Displacement, tons: 790 full load
Dimensions, feet (metres): 183.7 × 26.2 × 9.2 *(56 × 8 × 2.8)*
Main machinery: 1 diesel; 650 hp(m) *(478 kW)*; 1 shaft
Speed, knots: 10. Range, miles: 1500 at 8 kts
Complement: 40
Guns: 4—25 mm/80 (2 twin).
Radars: Navigation: Don 2; I band.
IFF: High Pole A.

Comment: Ex-amphibious craft with four 3 ton derricks. Based in the Northern Fleet.

MP 4 class   1979, USN

4 TELNOVSK CLASS

BUROVESTNIK, LAG, VTR 73, VTR 74 (ex-*Jan Kreuks*)

Displacement, tons: 1680 full load
Dimensions, feet (metres): 229.6 × 32.8 × 13.1 *(70 × 10 × 4)*
Main machinery: 2 diesels; 800 hp(m) *(588 kW)*; 2 shafts
Speed, knots: 11. Range, miles: 3000 at 10 kts
Complement: 28
Cargo capacity: 1000 tons
Radars: Navigation: Don 2; I band.

Comment: Light freighters built at Budapest 1949-57. *Burovestnik* operates with the Border Guard in the Pacific. Six sister ships serve as naval survey vessels. Two 10 ton and four 2 ton derricks.

4 MP 6 CLASS

| BIRA | VOLOGDA | IRGIZ | + 1 |

Displacement, tons: 2130 full load
Dimensions, feet (metres): 246 × 37.1 × 14.4 *(75 × 11.3 × 4.4)*
Main machinery: 2 diesels; 800 hp(m) *(588 kW)*; 2 shafts
Speed, knots: 11. **Range, miles:** 3000 at 10 kts
Cargo capacity: 1000 tons
Guns: 6—37 mm/63 (3 twin) (not always fitted).
Radars: Navigation: Don 2 and Spin Trough; I band.

Comment: Ex-amphibious craft. Bow doors now welded shut. One 10 ton derrick on some; six 2.5 ton derricks in all. Two of the class are used as ammunition transports.

BIRA 3/1992, Hartmut Ehlers

4 KHABAROV CLASS

VTR 13, 15, 109, 124

Displacement, tons: 650 full load
Dimensions, feet (metres): 152.5 × 26.2 × 9.2 *(46.5 × 8 × 2.8)*
Main machinery: 2 diesels; 650 hp(m) *(480 kW)*; 2 shafts
Speed, knots: 10. **Range, miles:** 1130 at 10 kts
Complement: 40
Cargo capacity: 400 tons
Guns: 2—14.5 mm (twin) MGs.
Radars: Navigation: Don 2 or Spin Trough; I band.

Comment: Built in USSR in 1950s and similar to the Shalanda class. Four 1.5 ton derricks. Being scrapped.

KHABAROV 3/1991, Erik Laursen

TORPEDO OPERATING/PATROL AND TARGET CRAFT

4 POTOK CLASS (TORPEDO EXPERIMENTAL SHIPS)

| OS-100 | OS-138 | OS-145 | OS-225 |

Displacement, tons: 850 full load
Dimensions, feet (metres): 236.5 × 30.8 × 8.2 *(72.1 × 9.4 × 2.5)*
Main machinery: 2 diesels; 4000 hp(m) *(2.94 MW)*; 2 shafts
Speed, knots: 17. **Range, miles:** 2500 at 12 kts
Torpedoes: 1—21 in *(533 mm)* tube. 1—16 in *(406 mm)* tube.

Comment: Used for torpedo trials in Black Sea. Torpedo tubes fitted on fo'c'sle with large recovery crane aft. Built since 1977. Type name is *opytnoye sudno* meaning experimental ship. Two scrapped in 1988-89.

OS-225 1978

20 SHELON CLASS

Displacement, tons: 270 full load
Dimensions, feet (metres): 150.9 × 19.7 × 6.6 *(46 × 6 × 2)*
Main machinery: 2 diesels; 10 000 hp(m) *(7.35 MW)*; 2 shafts
Speed, knots: 26
Complement: 20
Radars: Navigation: Spin Trough or Kivach; I band.

Comment: Built 1978-84. Built-in weapon recovery ramp aft.

SHELON 5/1992

70 POLUCHAT I, II and III CLASSES

Displacement, tons: 70 standard; 100 full load
Dimensions, feet (metres): 97.1 × 19 × 4.8 *(29.6 × 5.8 × 1.5)*
Main machinery: 2 M 50 diesels; 2200 hp(m) *(1.6 MW)* sustained; 2 shafts
Speed, knots: 20. **Range, miles:** 1500 at 10 kts
Complement: 15
Guns: 2—14.5 mm (twin) MGs (in some).
Radars: Navigation: Spin Trough; I band.

Comment: Employed as specialised or dual purpose torpedo recovery vessels and/or patrol boats. They have a stern slipway. Several exported as patrol craft. Some used by the Border Guard. Transfers: Algeria, Angola, Congo (3), Ethiopia (1), Guinea-Bissau, India, Indonesia (3), Iraq (2), Mozambique, Somalia (6), Syria, Tanzania, Vietnam (5), North Yemen (2), South Yemen. Many deleted.

POLUCHAT III 6/1989

16 OSA I CLASS (TYPE 205)

Comment: Details as in Light Forces (Osa) but with no armament. Half used as control craft and remainder as target vessels. Control craft use Square Tie radar while the targets carry radar reflectors and heat generators. In addition there is a large number of immobile target barges fitted with infra-red sources and radar reflectors as well as a number of P 6 class.

OSA Target 5/1990

BARGE Target 5/1992

AUXILIARIES

Note: Large numbers of assorted types and classes are employed on experimental work.

4 KOMANDOR CLASS

KOMANDOR   **SHKIPER GYEK**   **HERLUF BIDSTRUP**   **+1**

Displacement, tons: 2435 full load
Dimensions, feet (metres): 289.7 × 44.6 × 15.4 *(88.3 × 13.6 × 4.7)*
Main machinery: 2 Russkiy SEMT-Pielstick 6 PC2.5 L 400 diesels; 7020 hp(m) *(5.2 MW)* sustained; 1 shaft; bow thruster; 1500 hp(m) *(1.1 MW)*
Speed, knots: 19. **Range, miles:** 7000 at 19 kts
Complement: 42
Radars: Navigation: Furuno; I band.
Helicopters: 2 Helix type for SAR.

Comment: Built by Danyard A/S for the Ministry of Fisheries. Contract signed in December 1987 and the ships were completed between August 1989 and April 1990. The hull is ice strengthened. The helicopter deck has a lift serving the double hangar below. There are considerable command and control facilities and these vessels have obvious military potential.

HERLUF BIDSTRUP   5/1992, 92 Wing RAAF

16 ONEGA CLASS

| GKS 52 | SFP 95 | SFP 173 | SFP 224 | SFP 240 | GKS 244 | SFP 283 | GKS 286 |
| SFP 295 | SFP 322 | SFP 340 | SFP 372 | SFP 511 | SFP 542 | SFP 562 | SFP 177 |

Displacement, tons: 2150 full load
Dimensions, feet (metres): 265.7 × 36 × 13.7 *(81 × 11 × 4.2)*
Main machinery: 2 gas turbines; 8000 hp(m) *(5.88 MW)*; 1 shaft
Speed, knots: 20
Complement: 45
Radars: Navigation: Neptun or Spin Trough; I band.

Comment: First seen in September 1973. Helicopter platform but no hangar in earlier ships of the class but in later hulls the space is taken up with more laboratory accommodation. Used as hydroacoustic monitoring ships.

SFP 173   5/1991

18 T 43 CLASS

GKS 11, 12-24, 26, 37, 45, 62

Comment: Details under *Mine Warfare Forces*. Fitted with davits aft for laying hydroacoustic buoys for measuring ships' noise signatures. Unarmed but can carry one 37 mm/63 on fo'c'sle.

GKS 17   4/1992, van Ginderen Collection

PO 2 and NYRYAT 2 CLASSES

Displacement, tons: 56 full load
Dimensions, feet (metres): 70.5 × 11.5 × 3.3 *(21.5 × 3.5 × 1)*
Main machinery: 1 Type 3-D-12 diesel; 300 hp(m) *(220 kW)* sustained; 1 shaft
Speed, knots: 12
Complement: 8
Guns: Some carry 1—12.7 mm MG on the fo'c'sle.

Comment: This 1950s design of hull and machinery has been used for a wide and diverse number of adaptations. Steel hull. Nyryat 2 have the same characteristics but are used as diving tenders and inshore survey craft.
Transfers: Albania, Bulgaria, Cuba, Guinea, Iraq. Many deleted.

NYRYAT 2   3/1992

NYRYAT I CLASS

Displacement, tons: 120 full load
Dimensions, feet (metres): 93 × 18 × 5.5 *(28.4 × 5.5 × 1.7)*
Main machinery: 1 diesel; 450 hp(m) *(331 kW)*; 1 shaft
Speed, knots: 12.5. **Range, miles:** 1500 at 10 kts
Complement: 15
Guns: 1—12.7 mm MG (in some).

Comment: Built from 1955. Can operate as patrol craft or diving tenders with recompression chamber. Similar hull and propulsion used for inshore survey craft. Some have BGK, VM or GBP numbers.
Transfers: Albania, Algeria, Cuba, Egypt, Iraq, North Yemen. Many deleted.

NYRYAT I   3/1992

8 PETRUSHKA CLASS

MIERNYK   **ORSON**   **+ 6**

Displacement, tons: 335 full load
Dimensions, feet (metres): 129.3 × 27.6 × 7.2 *(39.4 × 8.4 × 2.2)*
Main machinery: 2 Wola H12 diesels; 756 hp(m) *(556 kW)*; 2 shafts
Speed, knots: 11. **Range, miles:** 1000 at 11 kts
Complement: 13 plus 30 cadets

Comment: Training vessels built in Poland; first one commissioned in 1989. Used for seamanship and navigation training.

PETRUSHKA 317   2/1991, MoD Bonn

590 RUSSIA / Auxiliaries — Water carriers

1 DALDYN CLASS

DALDYN

Displacement, tons: 360
Dimensions, feet (metres): 103.6 × 23.9 × 9.2 *(31.7 × 7.3 × 2.8)*
Main machinery: 1 SKL 6 VD 36/24-1U diesel; 305 hp(m) *(224 kW)* sustained; 1 shaft
Speed, knots: 9
Complement: 13

Comment: First seen in May 1973. Of Kareliya class trawler design with a high bridge. Used for MCM trials.

DALDYN   1973

12 YELVA CLASS

VM 143, 146, 154, 266, 268, 413, 414, 416, 420, 425, 907, 909

Displacement, tons: 300 full load
Dimensions, feet (metres): 134.2 × 26.2 × 6.6 *(40.9 × 8 × 2)*
Main machinery: 2 Type 3-D-12A diesels; 630 hp(m) *(463 kW)* sustained; 2 shafts
Speed, knots: 12.5
Complement: 30
Radars: Navigation: Spin Trough; I band.

Comment: Diving tenders built in early 1970s. Carry a 1 ton crane and diving bell. Some have submersible recompression chamber. Ice-strengthened. One to Cuba 1973, one to Libya 1977.

YELVA 413   7/1992, van Ginderen Collection

FIRE/PATROL CRAFT

Note: In addition there are many specialised firefighting vessels.

9 IVA CLASS

PZHK 415, 1514, 1544, 1547, 1859   +4

Displacement, tons: 320 full load
Dimensions, feet (metres): 119.8 × 25.6 × 7.2 *(36.5 × 7.8 × 2.2)*
Main machinery: 2 diesels; 1040 hp(m) *(764 kW)*; 2 shafts
Speed, knots: 12.5
Complement: 20

Comment: Carry four water monitors. Completed in 1984-86. Can be used for patrol/towage.

IVA 415   5/1990

14 VIKHR CLASS (TYPE B 98)

Displacement, tons: 2300 full load
Dimensions, feet (metres): 237.2 × 46.9 × 15.1 *(72.3 × 14.3 × 4.6)*
Main machinery: 2 Cegielski-Sulzer 16AV25/30 diesels; 5875 hp(m) *(4.32 MW)*; 2 shafts; cp props; 2 side thrusters; 1006 hp(m) *(740 kW)*
Speed, knots: 16. Range, miles: 2500 at 12 kts
Complement: 26 plus 8 for SAR

Comment: Built at Northern Shipyard, Gdansk from 1983 to 1987. Ice-strengthened hulls. One to Syria in 1992.

VIKHR 4   1988

40 POZHARNY I CLASS

Displacement, tons: 180 full load
Dimensions, feet (metres): 114.5 × 20 × 6 *(34.9 × 6.1 × 1.8)*
Main machinery: 2 Type M 50 diesels; 2200 hp(m) *(1.6 MW)* sustained; 2 shafts
Speed, knots: 10
Guns: 4—12.7 mm (2 twin) MGs (in some).

Comment: Built in the mid-1950s. Harbour fire boats but can be used for patrol duties. One transferred to Iraq.

POZHARNY I   9/1992, Hartmut Ehlers

WATER CARRIERS

13 VODA CLASS

ABAKAN, SURA
MVT 6, 9, 10, 16, 17, 18, 20, 21, 24, 134, 138

Displacement, tons: 3000 full load
Dimensions, feet (metres): 267.3 × 37.7 × 13.2 *(81.5 × 11.5 × 4)*
Main machinery: 2 diesels; 1600 hp(m) *(1.18 MW)*; 2 shafts
Speed, knots: 12. Range, miles: 3000 at 10 kts
Complement: 40
Cargo capacity: 1500 tons
Radars: Navigation: Don 2; Spin Trough; I band.
IFF: High Pole A.

Comment: Built in 1956 onwards. No armament. Some lack the catwalk forward of the bridge. Astern replenishment only. One deleted in 1992.

SURA   6/1992

Water carriers — Icebreakers / RUSSIA

2 MANYCH CLASS (WATER TANKERS)

MANYCH   TAGIL

Displacement, tons: 7700 full load
Dimensions, feet (metres): 380.5 × 51.5 × 23 *(116 × 15.7 × 7)*
Main machinery: 2 diesels; 9000 hp(m) *(6.6 MW)*; 2 shafts
Speed, knots: 18. **Range, miles:** 7500 at 16 kts
Complement: 90
Cargo capacity: 4400 tons
Guns: 4—57 mm/70 (2 twin) (not normally fitted).
Radars: Air/surface search: Strut Curve; F band.
Navigation: Two Don Kay; I band.
Fire control: Two Muff Cob (not in *Tagil*); G/H band.
IFF: High Pole B.

Comment: Completed 1972 and 1976 in Vyborg. The high point on the single gantry is very similar to that on *Boris Chilikin*'s third gantry. Both ships in use as distilled water-carriers with armament removed. Have underway abeam replenishment capability.

MANYCH   2/1990

DEGAUSSING SHIPS (ADG)

22 PELYM CLASS

SR 26	SR 70	SR 111	SR 179	SR 180	SR 191	SR 203
SR 215	SR 218	SR 221	SR 222	SR 233	SR 241	SR 276
SR 280	SR 281	SR 407	SR 409	SR 455	+3	

Displacement, tons: 1370 full load
Dimensions, feet (metres): 214.8 × 38 × 11.2 *(65.5 × 11.6 × 3.4)*
Main machinery: 2 diesels; 2400 hp(m) *(1.76 MW)*; 2 shafts
Speed, knots: 14. **Range, miles:** 4500 at 13 kts
Complement: 70

Comment: First completed in 1971. Earlier ships have stump mast on funnel, later ships a tripod main mast and a platform deck extending to the stern. Type name is *sudno razmagnichivanya* meaning degaussing ship. One to Cuba 1982.

PELYM SR 409   5/1979

5 KHABAROV CLASS

KHABAROV   SR 164   +3

Displacement, tons: 650 full load
Dimensions, feet (metres): 152.5 × 26.2 × 9.2 *(46.5 × 8 × 2.8)*
Main machinery: 2 diesels; 650 hp(m) *(480 kW)*; 2 shafts
Speed, knots: 10. **Range, miles:** 1130 at 10 kts
Complement: 30

Comment: Steel-hulled built in USSR in 1950s. Prominent deckhouse and stern anchors. Same class listed under *Transports*.

30 SEKSTAN CLASS

Displacement, tons: 528 full load
Dimensions, feet (metres): 136.2 × 29.9 × 9.8 *(41.5 × 9.1 × 3)*
Main machinery: 1 diesel; 400 hp(m) *(294 kW)*; 1 shaft
Speed, knots: 10

Comment: Most have SR numbers in the 100 series.

19 BEREZA CLASS

SR 28	SR 59	SR 74	SR 120	SR 137	SR 188	SR 216
SR 245	SR 370	SR 478	SR 479	SR 541	SR 548	SR 568
SR 569	SR 570	SR 936	SR 938	SR 939		

Displacement, tons: 1850 standard; 2051 full load
Dimensions, feet (metres): 228 × 45.3 × 13.1 *(69.5 × 13.8 × 4)*
Main machinery: 2 Zgoda-Sulzer 8AL25/30 diesels; 2938 hp(m) *(2.16 MW)* sustained
Speed, knots: 14. **Range, miles:** 1000 at 14 kts
Complement: 48
Radars: Navigation: Kivach; I band.

Comment: First completed in Poland in 1984. One transferred to Bulgaria in 1988. Still building in Poland. Have NBC citadels and three laboratories.

BEREZA SR 668 (with submarine)   10/1991, van Ginderen Collection

KORALL CLASS

Displacement, tons: 620 full load
Dimensions, feet (metres): 140.4 × 29.9 × 11.4 *(42.8 × 9.1 × 3.5)*
Main machinery: 1 diesel; 400 hp(m) *(294 kW)*; 1 shaft
Speed, knots: 10

Comment: Modified schooners fitted with deperming equipment. Numbers not known.

ICEBREAKERS

Notes: All these ships are operated by Ministry of Merchant Marine and civilian manned except for the seven Dobrynya Nikitich class shown as being naval manned. All are an indispensable part of many naval operations not only in the Baltic, Northern and Pacific Fleet areas but also on rivers, lakes and canals.

3 MUDYUG CLASS

Name	Builders	Commissioned
MUDYUG	Wärtsilä, Helsinki	29 Oct 1982
MAGADAN	Wärtsilä, Helsinki	29 Dec 1982
DIKSON	Wärtsilä, Helsinki	17 Mar 1983

Displacement, tons: 6210; 7775 *(Mudyug)*
Dimensions, feet (metres): 290.7 × 69.6 × 19.7 *(88.6 × 21.2 × 6)*
365.5 × 72.8 × 21.3 *(111.4 × 22.2 × 6.5) (Mudyug)*
Main machinery: 4 Wärtsilä Vasa 8R32 diesels; 16 100 hp(m) *(11.83 MW)* sustained; 2 shafts; cp props
Speed, knots: 16.5. **Range, miles:** 15 000 at 16 kts
Complement: 43
Radars: Navigation: Okean and Nyada; I band.

Comment: Ordered on 3 April 1980 and all launched 16 April 1982. For use in Barents Sea, the Baltic and the Sea of Okhotsk. Fitted with Wärtsilä bubbling gear. *Mudyug* fitted with a new ice-breaking bow and longer stern by Thyssen-Nordseewerke, Emden. This means a power saving of about 65 per cent when breaking ice. Completed 30 October 1986.

MUDYUG (modified)   1992

DIKSON   8/1989

592 RUSSIA / Icebreakers

2 TAMYR CLASS

TAMYR   VAYGACH

Displacement, tons: 23 500 full load
Dimensions, feet (metres): 492 × 93.8 × 26.2 *(150 × 28.6 × 8)*
Main machinery: Nuclear; 2 PWR; 3 turbines; 52 000 hp(m) *(38 MW)*; 3 shafts
Speed, knots: 18.5
Complement: 138 plus 12 spare bunks
Radars: Navigation: 3 Okean; I band.
Helicopters: 1 Ka-32 Helix C.

Comment: Ordered from Wärtsilä, Helsinki 12 November 1984; first launched 10 April 1987, second 26 February 1988. *Tamyr* handed over 7 April 1988 and *Vaygach* 8 March 1989. Both ships had to spend over a year in the Baltic Yard, Leningrad for installation of nuclear reactors. The design is a combined Finnish/Soviet effort, the requirement being for comparatively shallow draught ships to operate in Siberian estuaries in temperatures down to –50°C. *Tamyr* joined the Northern Fleet in July 1989, *Vaygach* in late 1990.

TAMYR   8/1991, Bryan Hird

5 + 1 ARKTIKA CLASS

Name	Builders	Commissioned
ARKTIKA	Baltic Yard, Leningrad	Dec 1974
SIBIR	Baltic Yard, Leningrad	Nov 1977
ROSSIYA	Baltic Yard, Leningrad	Feb 1986
SOVETSKIY SOYUZ	Baltic Yard, Leningrad	Jan 1990
YAMAL (ex-*Oktyabryskaya Revolutsiya*)	Baltic Yard, Leningrad	Oct 1992
URAL	Baltic Yard, Leningrad	1996

Displacement, tons: 19 300 standard; 23 460 full load
Dimensions, feet (metres): 485.4 × 98.4 × 36.4 *(148 × 30 × 11.1)*
Main machinery: Nuclear; 2 PWR; 3 turbines; 67 500 hp(m) *(49.6 MW)*; 3 shafts
Speed, knots: 22
Complement: 144 (49 officers)
Guns: 4—3 in *(76 mm)*/60 (2 twin) (fitted for but not with). 2—30 mm/65 AK 630.
Radars: Air/surface search: Head Net C (first two); Flat Screen (remainder); 3D; E band.
Navigation: Don 2 or Palm Frond; I band.
Helicopters: 2 Ka-32 Helix C.

Comment: *Arktika* launched 1972, *Sibir* 1976, *Rossiya* November 1983, *Sovetskiy Soyuz* 31 October 1986, *Yamal* in October 1989. *Ural* laid down in October 1989. *Arktika* was renamed *L I Brezhnev* in 1982 but reverted to original name in 1986. Can be fitted with guns and fire control radars. Some superstructure differences between the first two and the newer ships. The purpose of these ships is to extend the Arctic passage navigational season beyond the present June to October period, but according to a former Captain of *Arktika* the ships would need twice the power to achieve this aim, and it is reported that *Ural* may have an increased power output of 90 000 bhp. 2.3 m ice can be broken at 3 kts and ridges up to 8 m have been broken. Double hull construction with water ballast. The outer hull is 55 mm thick at ice levels, with the cast steel prow 2 m thick at its strongest point.

SOVETSKIY SOYUZ   7/1992

ROSSIYA   7/1992

3 YERMAK CLASS

Name	Builders	Commissioned
YERMAK	Wärtsilä, Helsinki	30 June 1974
ADMIRAL MAKAROV	Wärtsilä, Helsinki	2 June 1975
KRASIN	Wärtsilä, Helsinki	28 Apr 1976

Displacement, tons: 20 241 full load
Dimensions, feet (metres): 442.8 × 85.3 × 36.1 *(135 × 26 × 11)*
Main machinery: Diesel-electric; 9 Wärtsilä-Sulzer 12ZH40/48 diesels; 41 400 hp(m) *(30.4 MW)*; 9 Oy Strömberg Ab generators; 3 Strömberg motors; 36 000 hp(m) *(26.5 MW)*; 3 shafts
Speed, knots: 19.5. **Range, miles:** 40 000 at 15 kts
Complement: 118 plus 28 spare berths
Radars: Navigation: Okean and Don 2; I band.
Helicopters: Platform only.

Comment: Ordered on 29 April 1970 from Wärtsilä Shipyard, Helsinki, for delivery in 1974, 1975 and 1976. These are the first vessels to be fitted with Wärtsilä mixed-flow air-bubbling system to decrease friction between hull and ice. *Yermak* launched 7 September 1973. *A Makarov* launched 26 April 1974. *Krasin* launched 18 April 1975. Can maintain 2 kts in 6 ft ice.
There is also a former icebreaker built in 1917 called *Krasin* which is still afloat and occasionally goes to sea.

KRASIN   3/1992

5 MOSKVA CLASS

Name	Builders	Commissioned
KIEV	Wärtsilä, Helsinki	Dec 1965
LENINGRAD	Wärtsilä, Helsinki	1960
MOSKVA	Wärtsilä, Helsinki	1959
MURMANSK	Wärtsilä, Helsinki	May 1968
VLADIVOSTOK	Wärtsilä, Helsinki	Apr 1969

Displacement, tons: 13 290 standard; 15 360 full load
Dimensions, feet (metres): 400.7 × 80.3 × 34.5 *(122.2 × 24.5 × 10.5)*
Main machinery: Diesel-electric; 8 Wärtsilä-Sulzer 9MH51 diesels; 8 generators; 26 000 hp(m) *(19.1 MW)* (*Murmansk* and *Vladivostok*); 22 000 hp(m) *(16.2 MW)* (remainder); 1 motor (centre shaft); 11 000 hp(m) *(8.1 MW)*; 2 motors (wing shafts); 5500 hp(m) *(4 MW)*; 3 shafts
Speed, knots: 18. **Range, miles:** 20 000 at 14 kts
Complement: 100
Helicopters: 2 Ka-32 Helix C.

Comment: Built by Wärtsilä Shipyard, Helsinki. *Moskva* was launched on 10 January 1959; *Leningrad* on 24 October 1959; *Murmansk* on 14 July 1967 and *Vladivostok* on 28 May 1968. Designed to stay at sea for a year without returning to base. The concave embrasure in the ship's stern is a housing for the bow of a following vessel when additional power is required. *Moskva* has four pumps which can move 480 tons of water from one side to the other in two minutes to rock the icebreaker and wrench her free of thick ice. Becoming increasingly unreliable and may soon start to be scrapped.

LENINGRAD   3/1992

4 KAPITAN SOROKIN CLASS

Name	Builders	Commissioned
KAPITAN SOROKIN (mod)	Wärtsilä, Helsinki	14 July 1977
KAPITAN NIKOLAYEV	Wärtsilä, Helsinki	31 Jan 1978
KAPITAN DRANITSYN	Wärtsilä, Helsinki	2 Dec 1980
KAPITAN KHLEBNIKOV	Wärtsilä, Helsinki	1 Dec 1981

Displacement, tons: 14 917 full load; 17 150 (conversion) full load
Dimensions, feet (metres): 424.5; 463.9 (conversion) × 86.9; 102 (conversion) × 27.9 *(129.4; 141.4 × 26.5; 31.1 × 8.5)*
Main machinery: Diesel-electric; 6 Wärtsilä-Sulzer 9ZL40/48 diesels; 24 800 hp(m) *(18.2 MW)*; 6 alternators; 22 000 hp(m) *(16.2 MW)*; 3 motors; 3 shafts
Speed, knots: 19. **Range, miles:** 10 500 at 16 kts
Complement: 76 (16 spare berths)
Helicopters: Platform only.

Comment: Shallow draught polar icebreakers fitted with Wärtsilä bubbling system. Fitted with single cabins (except spare berths), sauna, swimming pool, gymnasium, library, cinema and hospital. They are used for North Siberian operations in shallow deltas at ambient temperatures down to −50°C. As a result of *Mudyug's* successful conversion, the first two of this class are being given similar treatment with major extensions to bow and stern. *Sorokin* completed 18 November 1990 at Thyssen-Nordseewerke, Emden. *Nikolayev* is planned to be similarly converted in due course. After conversion the hull is 17 per cent wider, has an increased displacement of 15 per cent and, as well as cutting a wider channel, has an icebreaking performance increased by 48 per cent to 2.15 m thick.

KAPITAN SOROKIN (modified)   7/1992

KAPITAN KHLEBNIKOV   11/1992, Robert Pabst

21 DOBRYNYA NIKITICH CLASS

AFANASY NIKITIN (ex-*Ledokol 2*) (1962)
BURAN (1966)*
DOBRYNYA NIKITICH (1960)*
FEDOR LITKE (1970)
GEORGY SEDOV (1967)**
ILYA MUROMETS (1966)*
IVAN MOSKVITIN (1971)
IVAN KRUZENSHTERN (ex-*Ledokol 6*)(1964)
KHARITON LAPTEV (ex-*Ledokol 3*) (1962)
P PAKHTUSOV (1966)**
PERESVET (1969)*
YURY LISYANSKY (ex-*Ledokol 9*) (1965)
PURGA (1961)*
SADKO (1968)*
SEMEN CHELYUSKIN (ex-*Ledokol 8*) (1965)
SEMEN DEZHNEV (1971)
VASILY POYARKOV (ex-*Ledokol 4*) (1963)
VLADIMIR RUSANOV (ex-*Ledokol 7*)(1964)
VYUGA (1961)*
(ex-*Ledokol 5*) (1963)
YEROFEI KHABAROV
PLUG (1961)
* Naval manned.
** Occasionally used for hydrographic work in the Arctic.

Displacement, tons: 2995 full load
Measurement, tons: 2254 gross; 1118 dwt; 50 net
Dimensions, feet (metres): 222.1 × 59.4 × 20 *(67.7 × 18.1 × 6.1)*
Main machinery: Diesel-electric; 3 Type 13-D-100 diesel generators; 3 motors; 5400 hp(m) *(4 MW)*; 3 shafts (1 fwd, 2 aft)
Speed, knots: 14.5. **Range, miles:** 5500 at 12 kts
Complement: 45
Guns: 2—57 mm/70 (twin). 2—37 mm/63 (fitted for but not with in *Dobrynya Nikitich* and *Vyuga*). 2—25 mm/80 (twin) *(Sadko)* (fitted for but not with in remainder). Non-naval ships unarmed.
Radars: Navigation: Two Don 2; I band.

Comment: All built at Admiralty Yard, Leningrad between 1960 (first ship, *Dobrynya Nikitich*) and 1971 (last ship, *Semen Dezhnev*). Divided between the Baltic, Black Sea and Pacific. One scrapped in 1989.

AFANASY NIKITIN   7/1992

3 KAPITAN BELOUSOV CLASS

Name	Builders	Commissioned
KAPITAN BELOUSOV	Wärtsilä, Helsinki	1955
KAPITAN MELEKHOV	Wärtsilä, Helsinki	1957
KAPITAN VORONIN	Wärtsilä, Helsinki	1956

Displacement, tons: 4375-4415 standard; 5350 full load
Dimensions, feet (metres): 273 × 63.7 × 23 *(83.3 × 19.4 × 7)*
Main machinery: Diesel-electric; 6 Polar diesel generators; 4 motors; 10 500 hp(m) *(7.72 MW)*; 4 shafts (2 fwd, 2 aft)
Speed, knots: 14.9. **Range, miles:** 10 000 at 14 kts
Complement: 75

Comment: *K Belousov* launched 1954, *K Voronin* 1955 and *K Melekhov* 19 October 1956. Used for harbour ice clearance.

KAPITAN BELOUSOV   1970, Michael D J Lennon

6 KAPITAN CHECHKIN CLASS

Name	Builders	Commissioned
KAPITAN CHECHKIN	Wärtsilä, Helsinki	6 Nov 1977
KAPITAN PLAKHIN	Wärtsilä, Helsinki	30 Dec 1977
KAPITAN CHADAYEV	Wärtsilä, Helsinki	7 Apr 1978
KAPITAN KRUTOV	Wärtsilä, Helsinki	6 June 1978
KAPITAN BUKAYEV	Wärtsilä, Helsinki	29 Sep 1978
KAPITAN ZARUBIN	Wärtsilä, Helsinki	10 Nov 1978

Displacement, tons: 2240 full load
Dimensions, feet (metres): 254.5 × 53.5 × 10.7 *(77.6 × 16.3 × 3.3)*
Main machinery: Diesel-electric; 3 Wärtsilä Vasa 12V22 diesel generators; 6.3 MW sustained; 3 motors; 3877 hp(m) *(2.85 MW)*; 3 shafts
Speed, knots: 14
Complement: 28

Comment: Ordered 16 May 1975. *K Chechkin* launched 29 April 1977; *K Plakhin*, 8 August 1977; *K Chadayev*, 13 October 1977; *K Krutov*, 11 January 1978; *K Bukayev*, in 1978. Designed for service on Volga-Baltic waterways and Siberian rivers. Fitted with three rudders, air-bubbling system and an automatic lowering system for masts, radar and aerials.

KAPITAN CHADAYEV (operating bubbling equipment)   1978, Wärtsilä

8 KAPITAN YEVDOKIMOV CLASS

Name	Builders	Commissioned
KAPITAN YEVDOKIMOV	Wärtsilä, Helsinki	31 Mar 1983
KAPITAN BABICHEV	Wärtsilä, Helsinki	30 June 1983
KAPITAN CHUDINOV	Wärtsilä, Helsinki	9 Sep 1983
KAPITAN BORODKIN	Wärtsilä, Helsinki	18 Nov 1983
AVRAMIY ZAVENYAGIN (ex-*Kapitan Krylov*)	Wärtsilä, Helsinki	1 Dec 1983
KAPITAN METSAYK	Wärtsilä, Helsinki	21 Aug 1984
KAPITAN DEMIDOV	Wärtsilä, Helsinki	22 Nov 1984
KAPITAN MOSHKIN	Wärtsilä, Helsinki	14 May 1986

Displacement, tons: 2150 full load
Dimensions, feet (metres): 250.9 × 54.4 × 8.2 *(76.5 × 16.6 × 2.5)*
Main machinery: Diesel-electric; 3 Wärtsilä Vasa 12V22 diesel generators; 6.3 kVA 60 Hz; 4 Strömberg motors; 5170 hp(m) *(3.8 MW)*; 4 shafts
Speed, knots: 13.5
Complement: 25

Comment: Contract for first seven signed in December 1980 for completion by 1984. One more ordered in 1983. This design is unique, having a draught shallower than any previous icebreaker. Designed for service in temperatures of −50°C on Siberian rivers and deltas.

KAPITAN YEVDOKIMOV   1990, van Ginderen Collection

594 RUSSIA / Icebreakers — Tugs

3 KAPITAN IZMAYLOV CLASS

Name	Builders	Commissioned
KAPITAN M IZMAYLOV	Wärtsilä, Helsinki	15 June 1976
KAPITAN KOSOLAPOV	Wärtsilä, Helsinki	14 July 1976
KAPITAN A RADZABOV	Wärtsilä, Helsinki	5 Oct 1976

Displacement, tons: 2045 full load
Dimensions, feet (metres): 185.3 × 51.5 × 13.8 *(56.5 × 15.7 × 4.2)*
Main machinery: Diesel-electric; 4 Wärtsilä Vasa 824TS diesel generators; 5820 hp(m) *(3.83 MW)*; 2 Strömberg motors; 3400 hp(m) *(2.5 MW)*; 2 shafts
Speed, knots: 13. **Range, miles:** 5000 at 12 kts
Complement: 25
Radars: Navigation: Low Trough; I band.

Comment: Contract signed with Wärtsilä, Helsinki on 22 March 1974 for the building of these three icebreakers for delivery in 1976. All fitted with Wärtsilä air-bubbling system. *K Izmaylov* launched 11 December 1975; *K Kosolapov*, 13 February 1976; *K Radzabov*, 9 March 1976.

7 STROPTIVY CLASS

Name	Builders	Commissioned
STROPTIVY	Wärtsilä, Helsinki	30 Nov 1979
STAKHANOVETS	Wärtsilä, Helsinki	29 Feb 1980
SIBIRSKY	Wärtsilä, Helsinki	2 July 1980
SPRAVEDLIVY	Wärtsilä, Helsinki	1982
SUVOROVETS	Wärtsilä, Helsinki	1982
FOBOS	Wärtsilä, Helsinki	29 Apr 1983
DEYMOS	Wärtsilä, Helsinki	31 May 1983

Displacement, tons: 4200 full load
Dimensions, feet (metres): 238.5 × 59 × 21.3 *(72.7 × 18 × 6.5)*
Main machinery: 2 Wärtsilä SEMT-Pielstick 6 PC2.5 L 400 diesels; 7020 hp(m) *(5.2 MW)* sustained; 2 shafts; cp props; bow thruster
Speed, knots: 15
Complement: 40 plus 12 spare berths

Comment: Designed as icebreaking salvage vessels, serving in support of Arctic fishing fleets. Can carry out repair, firefighting, salvage and towing. Have two 5 ton and two 3 ton cranes, four foam generators, a diving centre with oxy-acetylene equipment, TV monitors and a hospital.

KAPITAN A RADZABOV 7/1986, Ralf Bendfeldt

STAKHANOVETS 10/1991, van Ginderen Collection

ARMED ICEBREAKERS

8 IVAN SUSANIN CLASS

AISBERG
DUNAY
IMENI XXVI SYEZDA KPSS
IVAN SUSANIN
NEVA
RUSLAN
VOLGA
IMENI XXV SYEZDA KPSS

Displacement, tons: 2720 full load
Dimensions, feet (metres): 229.7 × 59.4 × 21 *(70 × 18.1 × 6.4)*
Main machinery: Diesel-electric; 3 Type 13-D-150 diesel generators; 3 motors; 5400 hp(m) *(4 MW)*; 3 shafts (1 fwd, 2 aft)
Speed, knots: 14.5. **Range, miles:** 5500 at 12.5 kts
Guns: 2—3 in *(76 mm)*/60 (twin). 2—30 mm/65 AK 630 (not in all).
Radars: Surface search: Strut Curve; F band.
Navigation: 2 Don Kay; I band.
Fire control: Hawk Screech; I band.
Helicopters: Platform only.

Comment: Generally similar to Dobrynya Nikitich class though larger with a tripod mast and different superstructure. Operated by the Border Guard. Armament sometimes removed.

AISBERG 8/1991, Bryan Hird

TUGS

Note: SB means *Spasatelny Buksir* or Salvage Tug. MB means *Morskoy Buksir* or Seagoing Tug.

2 BAKLAZHAN CLASS

NIKOLAI CHIKER SB 131   **FEODOR KRYLOV** SB 135

Displacement, tons: 7000 full load
Dimensions, feet (metres): 324.8 × 64 × 23.6 *(99 × 19.5 × 7.2)*
Main machinery: 4 Wärtsilä Vasa 12V32 diesels; 24 160 hp(m) *(17.76 MW)*; 2 shafts; bow thruster; 1360 hp(m) *(1 MW)*
Speed, knots: 18. **Range, miles:** 11 000 at 16 kts
Complement: 51 plus 20 spare berths
Radars: Navigation: Nyada; I band.

Comment: Built by Hollming (Rauma), Helsinki and completed 12 April 1989 and 30 June 1989 respectively. These are the largest salvage tugs in the world with a 250 ton bollard pull on each of two towing winches with a third 60 ton winch. The crew includes two divers and there are two decompression chambers. Four firefighting foam/water guns are fitted on the bridge/mast. Designed to operate in extreme temperatures.

NIKOLAI CHIKER 10/1991

4 NEFTEGAZ CLASS

| ALEKSEY KORTUNOV | ILGA | UMKA | KALAR |

Displacement, tons: 2800 full load
Dimensions, feet (metres): 267.4 × 53.5 × 14.8 *(81.5 × 16.3 × 4.5)*
Main machinery: 2 Sulzer diesels; 7200 hp(m) *(5.29 MW)*; 2 shafts; bow thruster
Speed, knots: 15
Complement: 25

Comment: Built by Warski, Szczecin in 1983. Can carry 600 tons cargo or be used as a tug or for firefighting. These naval units are mostly used in a range monitoring role.

KALAR *4/1992, 92 Wing RAAF*

13 GORYN CLASS

MB 15	MB 36	MB 119	SB 522 (ex-*MB 62*)	SB 931 (ex-*MB 18*)
MB 32	MB 38	SB 365 (ex-*MB 29*)	SB 523 (ex-*MB 64*)	
MB 35	MB 105	SB 521 (ex-*MB 61*)	SB 524 (ex-*MB 108*)	

Displacement, tons: 2240 standard; 2600 full load
Dimensions, feet (metres): 208.3 × 46.9 × 16.7 *(63.5 × 14.3 × 5.1)*
Main machinery: 2 Russkiy SEMT-Pielstick 6 PC2.5 L 400 diesels; 7020 hp(m) *(5.2 MW)* sustained; 2 shafts; cp props; bow thruster
Speed, knots: 15
Complement: 43 plus 16 spare berths
Radars: Navigation: Two Don 2; I band.

Comment: Built by Rauma-Repola 1977-83. Have sick-bay. First ships have goal-post mast with 10 ton and 5 ton derricks and bollard pull of 35 tons. Remainder have an A-frame mast with a 15 ton crane and bollard pull of 45 tons. SB number indicates a 'rescue' tug. Four in the North, five in the Pacific, two each in Black and Baltic Seas.

MB 15 (with goalposts) *5/1990*

GORYN SB 523 *12/1992*

39 SORUM CLASS

AMUR	PRIMORYE	MB 4	MB 31	MB 147
BREST	SAKHALIN	MB 6	MB 37	MB 148
BUG	URAL	MB 13	MB 56	MB 196
BURYA	VICTOR KINGSEPP	MB 19	MB 58	MB 236
CHUKOTKA	YAN BERZIN	MB 25	MB 61	MB 304
KAMCHATKA	YENISEY	MB 26	MB 76	MB 307
KARELIA	ZABAYKALYE	MB 28	MB 99	
LADOGA	ZAPOLARYE	MB 30	MB 110	
NEMAN				

Displacement, tons: 1660 full load
Dimensions, feet (metres): 190.2 × 41.3 × 15.1 *(58 × 12.6 × 4.6)*
Main machinery: Diesel-electric; 2 Type 5-2-DW2 diesel generators; 2900 hp(m) *(2.13 MW)*; 1 motor; 2000 hp(m) *(1.47 MW)*; 1 shaft
Speed, knots: 14. **Range, miles:** 3500 at 13 kts
Complement: 35
Guns: 4—30 mm/65 (2 twin) (all fitted for, but only Border Guard ships carry them).
Radars: Navigation: Two Don 2 or Nayada; I band.
IFF: High Pole B.

Comment: A class of ocean tugs with firefighting and diving capability. Named ships are used as patrol vessels and are Border Guard operated. Built in Yaroslavl and Oktyabskoye since 1973 to a similar design used for Ministry of Fisheries rescue tugs.

LADOGA *8/1992*

45 OKHTENSKY CLASS

| LOKSA | ORION | SATURN |
| NEPTUN | POCHETNY | TYULEN |

Displacement, tons: 930 full load
Dimensions, feet (metres): 156.1 × 34 × 13.4 *(47.6 × 10.4 × 4.1)*
Main machinery: Diesel-electric; 2 BM diesel generators; 1 motor; 1500 hp(m) *(1.1 MW)*; 1 shaft
Speed, knots: 13. **Range, miles:** 8000 at 7 kts; 6000 at 13 kts
Complement: 40
Guns: 2—57 mm/70 (twin) or 2—25 mm/80 (twin) (Border Guard only).
Radars: Navigation: One or two Don 2 or Spin Trough; I band.
IFF: High Pole B.

Comment: Ocean-going salvage and rescue tugs. First completed 1958. Fitted with powerful pumps and other apparatus for salvage. The six named ships are manned by the Border Guard and are armed; others have either SB or MB numbers. Some being scrapped in 1992/93.

OKHTENSKY *5/1992, van Ginderen Collection*

16 ZENIT CLASS

Displacement, tons: 800 full load
Dimensions, feet (metres): 157.1 × 32.8 × 15.3 *(47.9 × 10 × 4.3)*
Main machinery: 2 boilers; 1 steam reciprocating engine; 800 ihp(m) *(588 kW)*; 1 shaft
Speed, knots: 11. **Range, miles:** 10 000 at 8 kts
Complement: 25
Radars: Navigation: Don 2; I band.

Comment: Have icebreaking capability. Survivors in the navy of a large class of naval and merchant tugs built by Wärtsilä in 1950s.

ZENIT *1991, van Ginderen Collection*

10 ROSLAVL CLASS

MB 50, MB 94, MB 95, MB 102, MB 125, MB 145-147, SB 41, SB 46

Displacement, tons: 750 full load
Dimensions, feet (metres): 146 × 31.2 × 10.8 *(44.5 × 9.5 × 3.3)*
Main machinery: Diesel-electric; 2 diesel generators; 1 motor; 1200 hp(m) *(882 kW)*; 1 shaft
Speed, knots: 12. **Range, miles:** 6000 at 11 kts
Complement: 30
Radars: Navigation: Don 2; I band.

Comment: First completed in 1953. Some of the same class are in the merchant fleet.

MB 94   3/1992, Hartmut Ehlers

BERTHING TUGS

Displacement, tons: 350 full load
Dimensions, feet (metres): 114.1 × 27.9 × 9.2 *(34.8 × 8.5 × 2.8)*
Main machinery: 1 diesel; 1 shaft
Speed, knots: 11

Comment: Large numbers built in 1970s by Edgar Andre, Magdeburg, East Germany. All originally numbered MB 70 *et seq.* Some renamed.

SCHOLLE CLASS (HARBOUR TUGS)

Displacement, tons: 189 full load
Dimensions, feet (metres): 98.4 × 21.3 × 9.8 *(30 × 6.5 × 3)*
Main machinery: 1 RGDV 148 K10 diesel; 1 shaft
Speed, knots: 10

Comment: Very numerous class built in East Germany in 1964.

SCHOLLE   5/1992, van Ginderen Collection

TUGUR CLASS (HARBOUR TUGS)

Displacement, tons: 300 full load
Dimensions, feet (metres): 100.7 × 25.3 × 7.5 *(30.7 × 7.7 × 2.3)*
Main machinery: 2 boilers; 1 steam reciprocating engine; 500 ihp(m) *(367 kW)*; 1 shaft
Speed, knots: 10

Comment: Numerous class (over 200 built) with tall funnel built in 1950s in Finland. Two transferred to Albania.

TUGUR   3/1991, Erik Laursen

50 SIDEHOLE 1 and 2 CLASSES (HARBOUR TUGS)

Displacement, tons: 183 (Sidehole 1); 197 (Sidehole 2)
Dimensions, feet (metres): 80 × 23 × 6.9 *(24.4 × 7 × 2.1)*
Main machinery: 2 diesels; 600 hp(m) *(441 kW)* (Sidehole 1), 900 hp(m) *(661 kW)* (Sidehole 2); 2 shafts
Speed, knots: 9 (Sidehole 1); 10 (Sidehole 2)
Complement: 12
Radars: Navigation: Spin Trough; I band.

Comment: Built at Leningrad in 1960s (Sidehole 1) and 1970s (Sidehole 2). About 20 are Sidehole 2s. There are a large number of other tugs in naval and commercial service.

SIDEHOLE 2   4/1992

FLOATING DOCKS and ANCILLARIES

Note: In addition to the docks there are also numerous floating cranes—the largest having a lift of 1500 tons—and many floating workshops, either purpose built or converted.

2 LARGE FLOATING DOCKS

PD 41   PD 50

Displacement, tons: 80 000
Dimensions, feet (metres): 1082.4 × 232.9 (inertial beam) × 49.2 (over blocks) *(330 × 71 × 15)* (PD 41)
1000.4 × 226.3 (inertial beam) × 49.2 (over blocks) *(305 × 69 × 15)* (PD 50)
Complement: 175

Comment: Amongst the largest independently supported dry docks in the world. *PD 41* built by Ishikawajima Heavy Industries, Japan and towed to Vladivostok in October 1978. *PD 50* built by Götaverken Arendal, Sweden. Two 30 ton cranes *(PD 41)* and two 50 ton *(PD 50)*.

FLOATING DOCK   3/1992

150 FLOATING DOCKS

Comment: There is a dock of some 35-40 000 tons capacity in Vladivostok in addition to the 80 000 ton dock above. At least six of 30 000 tons capacity have been built in Yugoslavia and another six of about 28 000 tons capacity have been delivered from Sweden. The 20 or so various types of docks which are in use throughout the Soviet naval bases may total about 150 of which about half have a capacity of 5000 tons to 25 000 tons.

FLOATING DOCK   10/1989

MARITIME BORDER GUARD

Note: The Border Guard operates a considerable fleet of warships which would be integrated with naval operations in a crisis. Formerly run by the KGB, the force came under the Ministry of Defence in October 1991 and some of the vessels will be devolved to the individual Republics with coastal regions. The OOB of this group on 1 January 1993 is listed here for convenience—details of the classes are in the sections preceding.

Frigates
7 Krivak III class
12 Grisha II class
6 Grisha III class
Light Forces
112 Stenka class
14 Muravey class
30 Zhuk class
7 Svetlyak class
18 Sorum class
5 Okhtensky class

Patrol Ships
25 Pauk class

River Monitors
10 Piyavka class
8 Vosh class
20 Yaz class
96 Schmel class

Armed Icebreakers
8 Ivan Susanin class

Support Forces
8 Antonov class
3 Khabarov class
1 Telnovsk class
2 Baskunchak class

PO 2   *1991, van Ginderen Collection*

ST KITTS-NEVIS

Senior Appointments

Commissioner of Police:
Stanley V Franks
Commanding Officer:
Inspector Ivor Blake

Base

Basseterre

Personnel

1993: 35

Mercantile Marine

Lloyd's Register of Shipping:
1 vessel of 300 tons

PATROL FORCES

1 SWIFTSHIPS 110 ft PATROL CRAFT

STALWART C 253

Displacement, tons: 99.1 normal
Dimensions, feet (metres): 116.5 × 25 × 7 *(35.5 × 7.6 × 2.1)*
Main machinery: 4 Detroit 12V-71TA diesels; 1680 hp *(1.25 MW)* sustained; 4 shafts
Speed, knots: 21. **Range, miles:** 1800 at 15 kts
Complement: 11
Guns: 2—12.7 mm MGs. 2—7.62 mm MGs.

Comment: Built by Swiftships, Morgan City, and delivered August 1985. Aluminium alloy hull and superstructure.

STALWART   *4/1992, van Ginderen Collection*

1 FAIREY MARINE SPEAR CLASS

RANGER I

Displacement, tons: 4.3 full load
Dimensions, feet (metres): 29.8 × 9.5 × 2.8 *(9.1 × 2.8 × 0.9)*
Main machinery: 2 Ford Mermaid diesels; 360 hp *(268 kW)*; 2 shafts
Speed, knots: 30
Complement: 2
Guns: Mountings for 2—7.62 mm MGs.

Comment: Ordered for the police in June 1974—delivered 10 September 1974. Refitted 1986.

RANGER I   *1992, St Kitts-Nevis Police*

2 BOSTON WHALERS

ROVER I C 087   **ROVER II** C 088

Displacement, tons: 3 full load
Dimensions, feet (metres): 22 × 7.5 × 2 *(6.7 × 2.3 × 0.6)*
Main machinery: 1 Johnson outboard; 223 hp *(166 kW)*
Speed, knots: 35. **Range, miles:** 70 at 35 kts
Complement: 2

Comment: Delivered in May 1988.

ROVER I   *1990, St Kitts-Nevis Police*

ST LUCIA

Senior Appointments

Comptroller of Customs and Excise:
M J Scholar
Coast Guard Commander:
Lieutenant Commander Mike Critchley RN

Base

Castries

Personnel

1993: 10

Mercantile Marine

Lloyd's Register of Shipping:
7 vessels of 1891 tons gross

DELETION

1990   *Vigilant I*

PATROL FORCES

1 SWIFT 65 ft CLASS

DEFENDER P 02

Displacement, tons: 42 full load
Dimensions, feet (metres): 64.9 × 18.4 × 6.6 *(19.8 × 5.6 × 2)*
Main machinery: 2 Detroit 12V-71 diesels; 680 hp *(507 kW)* sustained; 2 shafts
Speed, knots: 22. Range, miles: 1200 at 18 kts
Complement: 5

Comment: Ordered from Swiftships, Morgan City in November 1983. Completed 1985. Similar to craft supplied to Antigua and Dominica.

1 PATROL CRAFT

VIGILANT II P 06

Displacement, tons: 5 full load
Dimensions, feet (metres): 29 × 10 × 2.4 *(8.8 × 3.1 × 0.7)*
Main machinery: 2 Volvo Turbo diesels; 400 hp(m) *(294 kW)*; 2 shafts
Speed, knots: 30

Comment: Completed in May 1990 by Phoenix Marine Enterprises, Hialeah, Florida. Has replaced *Vigilant I*.

VIGILANT II   *1990, St Lucia CG*

2 BOSTON WHALERS

P 03   P 04

Displacement, tons: 3
Dimensions, feet (metres): 22 × 6.8 × 2 *(6.7 × 2 × 0.6)*
Main machinery: 1 V6-2500CC Johnson outboard
Speed, knots: 36

Comment: Acquired in July 1988.

DEFENDER   *1/1992, A Sheldon Duplaix*

ST VINCENT AND THE GRENADINES

Senior Appointments

Commissioner of Police:
  Randolph Toussaint, OBE, LVO
Coast Guard Commander:
  Lieutenant Commander C E Jagger, RN

Base

Calliaqua

Personnel

1993: 47

Mercantile Marine

Lloyd's Register of Shipping:
  881 vessels of 4 380 956 tons gross

1 SWIFTSHIPS 120 ft PATROL CRAFT

CAPTAIN MULZAC SVG 01

Displacement, tons: 101
Dimensions, feet (metres): 120 × 25 × 7 *(36.6 × 7.6 × 2.1)*
Main machinery: 4 Detroit 12V-71TA diesels; 1360 hp *(1.01 MW)* sustained; 4 shafts
Speed, knots: 21. Range, miles: 1800 at 15 kts
Complement: 13
Guns: 2—12.7 mm MGs. 2—7.62 mm MGs.
Radars: Surface search: Furuno 1411 Mk II; I/J band.

Comment: Built by Swiftships, Morgan City and delivered in June 1987.

1 VOSPER THORNYCROFT 75 ft PATROL CRAFT

GEORGE McINTOSH SVG 05

Displacement, tons: 70
Dimensions, feet (metres): 75 × 19.5 × 8 *(22.9 × 6 × 2.4)*
Main machinery: 2 Caterpillar D 348 diesels; 1450 hp *(1.08 MW)* sustained; 2 shafts
Speed, knots: 24.5. Range, miles: 1000 at 11 kts; 600 at 20 kts
Complement: 11
Guns: 1 Oerlikon 20 mm.
Radars: Surface search: Furuno 1411 Mk III; I/J band.

Comment: Handed over 23 March 1981. GRP hull.

GEORGE McINTOSH   *1992, St Vincent Coastguard*

2 BUHLER TYPE (PATROL CRAFT)

LARIKAI SVG 06   **BRIGHTON** SVG 07

Displacement, tons: 6 full load
Dimensions, feet (metres): 27 × 6.8 × 2.4 *(8.2 × 2.1 × .73)*
Main machinery: 2 outboard engines; 2 props
Speed, knots: 23

Comment: Locally built by Buhler's Yachts Ltd. Converted to outboard engines in 1990-91.

BRIGHTON   *1991, St Vincent Coastguard*

CAPTAIN MULZAC   *1992, St Vincent Coastguard*

SAUDI ARABIA

Senior Appointments

Chief of Naval Staff:
  Vice Admiral Talal Salem Al Mofadhi
Director of Coast Guard:
  Captain Al Jumayha

Personnel

(a) 1993: 11 400 officers and men (including 1200 marines)
(b) Voluntary service

Bases

Naval HQ: Riyadh
Main bases: Jiddah, Al Jubail, Aziziah (Coast Guard)
Minor bases (Naval and Coast Guard): Ras Tanura, Al Dammam, Yanbo, Ras al-Mishab, Al Wajh, Al Qatif, Haqi, Al Sharmah, Qizan

Command and Control

The United States is providing an update of C^3 capabilities during the period 1991-95, including a commercial datalink to improve interoperability.

Strength of the Fleet

Type	Active	Building
Frigates	4	(3)
Corvettes—Missile	4	—
Fast Attack Craft—Missile	9	—
Fast Attack Craft—Torpedo	2 (1)	—
Patrol Craft	57	—
Minehunters	2	1 (3)
Minesweepers—Coastal	4	—
Replenishment Tankers	2	—
LCMs	4	—
LCUs	4	—
Tugs	14	—
Royal Yacht	1	—
Hydrofoil	1	—

Coast Guard

Fast Attack Craft—Missile	2
Large Patrol Craft	8
Coastal Patrol Craft	38
Hovercraft	31
Inshore Patrol Craft	653
Royal Yachts	2
Training Ships	2
Tankers	3
Firefighting Craft	3
Tugs	3

Coast Guard

Part of the Frontier Force under the Minister of the Interior. 5400 officers and men in January 1993. It is not always clear which ships belong to the Navy and which to the Coast Guard.

Mercantile Marine

Lloyd's Register of Shipping:
  301 vessels of 1 016 127 tons gross

DELETION

Patrol Forces

1990 Riyadh

SUBMARINES

Note: Orders for patrol submarines are unlikely until mid-1990s although training is being done in France and Pakistan. It has been reported that up to two midget submarines of 225 tons and six KSS-1 class have been acquired from South Korea in an Agreement reached in July 1989.

FRIGATES

4 TYPE F 2000S

Name	No	Builders	Laid down	Launched	Commissioned
MADINA	702	Lorient (DTCN)	15 Oct 1981	23 Apr 1983	4 Jan 1985
HOFOUF	704	CNIM, Seyne-sur-Mer	14 June 1982	24 June 1983	31 Oct 1985
ABHA	706	CNIM, Seyne-sur-Mer	7 Dec 1982	23 Dec 1983	4 Apr 1986
TAIF	708	CNIM, Seyne-sur-Mer	1 Mar 1983	25 May 1984	29 Aug 1986

Displacement, tons: 2000 standard; 2870 full load
Dimensions, feet (metres): 377.3 × 41 × 16 (sonar) *(115 × 12.5 × 4.9)*
Main machinery: 4 SEMT-Pielstick 16 PA6 280 BTC diesels; 38 400 hp(m) *(28 MW)* sustained; 2 shafts
Speed, knots: 30. **Range, miles:** 8000 at 15 kts; 6500 at 18 kts
Complement: 179 (15 officers)

Missiles: SSM: 8 OTO Melara/Matra Otomat Mk 2 (2 quad) ❶; active radar homing to 160 km *(86.4 nm)* at 0.9 Mach; warhead 210 kg; sea-skimmer for last 4 km *(2.2 nm)*. ERATO system allows mid-course guidance by ship's helicopter.
SAM: Thomson-CSF Crotale Naval octuple launcher ❷; command line of sight guidance; radar/IR homing to 13 km *(7 nm)* at 2.4 Mach; warhead 14 kg; 26 missiles.
Guns: 1 Creusot Loire 3.9 in *(100 mm)*/55 compact ❸; 80° elevation; 20/45/90 rounds/minute to 17 km *(9.3 nm)* anti-surface; 6 km *(3.3 nm)* anti-aircraft; weight of shell 13.5 kg.
4 Breda 40 mm/70 (2 twin) ❹; 85° elevation; 300 rounds/minute to 12.5 km *(6.8 nm)*; weight of shell 0.96 kg.
Torpedoes: 4—21 in *(533 mm)* tubes ❺. ECAN F17P; anti-submarine; wire-guided; active/passive homing to 20 km *(10.8 nm)* at 40 kts; warhead 250 kg.
Countermeasures: Decoys: CSEE Dagaie double trainable mounting ❻; IR flares and chaff; H/J band.
ESM: Thomson-CSF DR 4000; intercept; HF/DF.
ECM: Janet; jammer.
Combat data systems: Thomson-CSF TAVITAC (Senit 6) action data automation; capability for Link 11.
Fire control: Vega system. 3 CSEE Naja optronic directors. DLT for torpedoes.
Radars: Air/surface search/IFF: Thomson-CSF Sea Tiger (DRBV 15) ❼; E/F band; range 110 km *(60 nm)* for 2 m² target.
Navigation: Racal Decca TM 1226; I band.
Fire control: Thomson-CSF Castor IIB ❽; I/J band; range 15 km *(8 nm)* for 1 m² target.
Thomson-CSF DRBC 32 ❾; I/J band (for SAM).
Sonars: Thomson Sintra Diodon TSM 2630; hull-mounted; active search and attack with integrated Sorel VDS ❿; 11, 12 or 13 kHz.

Helicopters: 1 SA 365F Dauphin 2 ⓫.

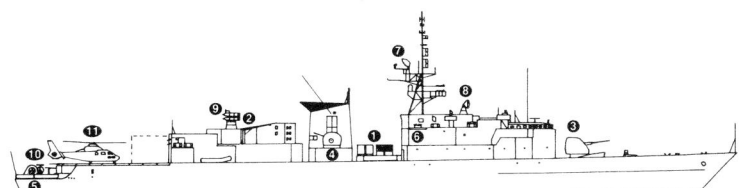

MADINA (Scale 1 : 1200), Ian Sturton

ABHA 4/1988, A Sheldon Duplaix

Programmes: Ordered in 1980, the major part of the Sawari contract. Agreement for France to provide supplies and technical help.
Structure: Fitted with Snach/Saphir folding fin stabilisers.

Operational: Navigation: CSEE Sylosat. Helicopter can provide mid-course guidance for SSM. All based at Jiddah. Only a few weeks a year are spent at sea.

TAIF 9/1989, G Jacobs

SAUDI ARABIA / Frigates — Land-based maritime aircraft

0 + (3) IMPROVED LA FAYETTE CLASS

Displacement, tons: 3700 full load
Dimensions, feet (metres): 423.2 × 50.5 × 13.5 *(129 × 15.4 × 4.1)*
Main machinery: 4 SEMT-Pielstick 16 PA6 280 BTC diesels; 35 200 hp(m) *(25.87 MW)* sustained; 2 shafts
Speed, knots: 28
Complement: 160

Missiles: SSM: 8 Aerospatiale MM 40 Exocet ❶.
SAM: 16 Aster 15 SAAM VLS ❷ or Crotale NG octuple launcher.
2 Matra Sadral sextuple launchers ❸; Mistral.
Guns: 1 Creusot Loire 3.9 in *(100 mm)*/55 compact ❹.
2 Emerlec 30 mm (twin) ❺.
Torpedoes: 4 fixed 324 mm tubes (2 twin) ❻; Murene.
Countermeasures: Decoys: 2 Dagaie Mk 2 launchers ❼; chaff and IR flares.
ESM/ECM: Intercept and jammer.
Combat data systems: Thomson-CSF TAVITAC. Syracuse SATCOM ❽.
Fire control: Vega system; NAJIR optronic director ❾.
Radars: Air/surface search: Thomson-CSF DRBV 26C ❿; D band.
Fire control: Castor II ⓫; I band.
Arabel ⓬ for SAAM.

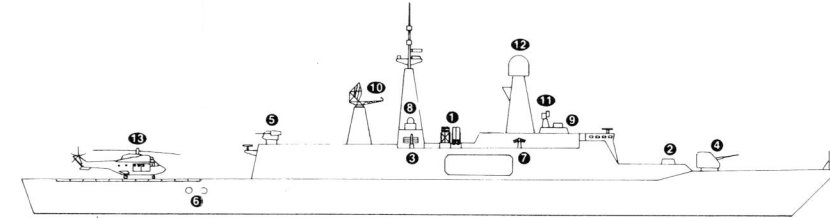

IMPROVED LA FAYETTE class *(Scale 1 : 1200), Ian Sturton*

Navigation: 2 Racal Decca (one for helo control); I band.
Sonars: Thomson Sintra Spherion; hull-mounted active search and attack; medium frequency.
Helicopters: 2 SA 365F Dauphin 2 ⓭.

Programmes: An outline agreement (accord cadre) was signed on 11 June 1989 for three French *La Fayette* type frigates to be built at Lorient Naval Yard. The plan was for the first of class to start sea trials in 1995 with the others following at 18 month intervals. The programme was still under evaluation in early 1993.
Structure: Details shown above represent the outline plan and there will probably be some changes.
Operational: Main role is air defence.

CORVETTES

4 MISSILE CORVETTES

Name	No	Builders	Laid down	Launched	Commissioned
BADR	612	Tacoma Boatbuilding Co, Tacoma	6 Oct 1979	26 Jan 1980	30 Nov 1980
AL YARMOOK	614	Tacoma Boatbuilding Co, Tacoma	3 Jan 1980	13 May 1980	18 May 1981
HITTEEN	616	Tacoma Boatbuilding Co, Tacoma	19 May 1980	5 Sep 1980	3 Oct 1981
TABUK	618	Tacoma Boatbuilding Co, Tacoma	22 Sep 1980	18 June 1981	10 Jan 1983

Displacement, tons: 870 standard; 1038 full load
Dimensions, feet (metres): 245 × 31.5 × 8.9 *(74.7 × 9.6 × 2.7)*
Main machinery: CODOG; 1 GE LM 2500 gas turbine; 23 000 hp *(17.2 MW)* sustained; 2 MTU 12V 652 TB91 diesels; 3470 hp(m) *(2.55 MW)* sustained; 2 shafts; cp props
Speed, knots: 30 gas; 20 diesels. **Range, miles:** 4000 at 20 kts
Complement: 58 (7 officers)

Missiles: SSM: 8 McDonnell Douglas Harpoon (2 quad) launchers ❶; active radar homing to 130 km *(70 nm)* at 0.9 Mach; warhead 227 kg.
Guns: 1 FMC/OTO Melara 3 in *(76 mm)*/62 Mk 75 Mod 0 ❷; 85° elevation; 85 rounds/minute to 16 km *(8.7 nm)*; weight of shell 6 kg.
1 General Electric/General Dynamics 20 mm 6-barrelled Vulcan Phalanx ❸; 3000 rounds/minute combined to 2 km.
2 Oerlikon 20 mm/80 ❹; 55° elevation; 800 rounds/minute to 2 km anti-aircraft.
1—81 mm mortar. 2—40 mm Mk 19 grenade launchers.
Torpedoes: 6—324 mm US Mk 32 (2 triple) tubes ❺. Honeywell Mk 46; anti-submarine; active/passive homing to 11 km *(5.9 nm)* at 40 kts; warhead 44 kg.
Countermeasures: Decoys: 2 Loral Hycor SRBOC 6-barrelled fixed Mk 36 ❻; IR flares and chaff to 4 km *(2.2 nm)*.
ESM: SLQ 32(V)1 ❼; intercept.
Fire control: Mk 24 optical director ❽. Mk 309 for torpedoes.
Radars: Air search: Lockheed SPS 40B ❾; E/F band; range 320 km *(175 nm)*.
Surface search: ISC Cardion SPS 55 ❿; I/J band.
Fire control: Sperry Mk 92 ⓫; I/J band.
Sonars: Raytheon SQS 56 (DE 1164); hull-mounted; active search and attack; medium frequency.

Modernisation: A five year programme started in 1988.
Structure: Fitted with fin stabilisers.
Operational: All based at Al Jubail on the east coast.

BADR *(Scale 1 : 600), Ian Sturton*

BADR *1989, van Ginderen Collection*

SHIPBORNE AIRCRAFT

Numbers/Type: 20 Aerospatiale SA 365F Dauphin 2.
Operational speed: 140 kts *(260 km/h)*.
Service ceiling: 15 000 ft *(4575 m)*.
Range: 410 nm *(758 km)*.
Role/Weapon systems: ASV/ASW helicopter; procured for initial embarked naval aviation force; systems developed jointly with France; surface search/attack is the primary role. Sensors: Thomson-CSF Agrion 15, Crouzet MAD. Weapons: ASV; 4 × AS/15TT missiles. ASW; 2 Mk 46 torpedoes.

LAND-BASED MARITIME AIRCRAFT

Note: 6 P3C Orion may be acquired in due course.

Numbers/Type: 21 Aerospatiale AS 332SC Super Puma.
Operational speed: 150 kts *(280 km/h)*.
Service ceiling: 15 090 ft *(4600 m)*.
Range: 335 nm *(620 km)*.
Role/Weapon systems: Two delivered in August 1989 then one per month to a total of 21 by the end of 1990. Sensors: Twelve have Omera search radar. Weapons: Nine have GIAT 20 mm cannon; twelve have AM39 Exocet or Sea Eagle ASM.

Numbers/Type: 4 Aerospatiale SA 365N Dauphin 2.
Operational speed: 140 kts *(260 km/h)*.
Service ceiling: 15 000 ft *(4575 m)*.
Range: 410 nm *(758 km)*.
Role/Weapon systems: Overwater SAR and limited surface search helicopter. Sensors: Omera ORB 32 search radar. Weapons: Unarmed.

DAUPHIN 2

LIGHT FORCES

9 FAST ATTACK CRAFT (MISSILE)

Name	No	Builders	Commissioned
AL SIDDIQ	511	Peterson Builders, Wisconsin	15 Dec 1980
AL FAROUQ	513	Peterson Builders, Wisconsin	22 June 1981
ABDUL AZIZ	515	Peterson Builders, Wisconsin	3 Sep 1981
FAISAL	517	Peterson Builders, Wisconsin	23 Nov 1981
KAHLID	519	Peterson Builders, Wisconsin	11 Jan 1982
AMYR	521	Peterson Builders, Wisconsin	21 June 1982
TARIQ	523	Peterson Builders, Wisconsin	11 Aug 1982
OQBAH	525	Peterson Builders, Wisconsin	18 Oct 1982
ABU OBAIDAH	527	Peterson Builders, Wisconsin	6 Dec 1982

Displacement, tons: 425 standard; 478 full load
Dimensions, feet (metres): 190.5 × 26.5 × 6.6 *(58.1 × 8.1 × 2)*
Main machinery: CODOG; 1 GE LM 2500 gas turbine; 23 000 hp *(17.2 MW)* sustained; 2 MTU 12V 652 TB91 diesels; 3470 hp(m) *(2.55 MW)* sustained; 2 shafts; cp props
Speed, knots: 38 gas; 25 diesel. **Range, miles:** 2900 at 14 kts
Complement: 38 (5 officers)

Missiles: SSM: 4 McDonnell Douglas Harpoon (2 twin) launchers; active radar homing to 130 km *(70 nm)* at 0.9 Mach; warhead 227 kg.
Guns: 1 FMC/OTO Melara 3 in *(76 mm)*/62 Mk 75 Mod 0; 85° elevation; 85 rounds/minute to 16 km *(8.7 nm)*; weight of shell 6 kg.
  1 General Electric/General Dynamics 20 mm 6-barrelled Vulcan Phalanx; 3000 rounds/minute combined to 2 km.
  2 Oerlikon 20 mm/80; 55° elevation; 800 rounds/minute to 2 km anti-aircraft.
  2—81 mm mortars. 2—40 mm Mk 19 grenade launchers.
Countermeasures: Decoys: 2 Loral Hycor SRBOC 6-barrelled fixed Mk 36; IR flares and chaff to 4 km *(2.2 nm)*.
ESM: SLQ 32(V)1; intercept.
Fire control: Mk 92 mod 5 GFCS.
Radars: Surface search: ISC Cardion SPS 55; I/J band.
Fire control: Sperry Mk 92; I/J band.

Modernisation: There is a planned modernisation programme but the Gulf conflict caused it to be postponed.
Operational: *Amyr* and *Tariq* operate from Jiddah, the remainder are based at Al Jubail.

AL SIDDIQ *1992, G Toremans*

3 FDR JAGUAR CLASS (FAST ATTACK CRAFT—TORPEDO)

Name	No	Builders	Commissioned
DAMMAM	90 (ex-190)	Lürssen, Vegesack	1969
KHABAR	50 (ex-192)	Lürssen, Vegesack	1969
MACCAH	10 (ex-194)	Lürssen, Vegesack	1969

Displacement, tons: 160 standard; 190 full load
Dimensions, feet (metres): 139.4 × 23 × 7.9 *(42.5 × 7 × 2.4)*
Main machinery: 4 Maybach 16-cyl diesels; 12 000 hp(m) *(8.82 MW)*; 4 shafts
Speed, knots: 42. **Range, miles:** 1000 at 30 kts
Complement: 33 (3 officers)
Guns: 2 Bofors 40 mm/70; 90° elevation; 300 rounds/minute to 12 km *(6.6 nm)*; weight of shell 0.96 kg.
Torpedoes: 4—21 in *(533 mm)* tubes; anti-surface.

Comment: Refitted by Lürssen Werft, West Germany in 1976. Two are used for training, mostly alongside, and one is in reserve. All based at Al Jubail.

JAGUAR class *1989*

17 HALTER TYPE (COASTAL PATROL CRAFT)

Displacement, tons: 56 full load
Dimensions, feet (metres): 78 × 20 × 5.8 *(23.8 × 6.1 × 1.8)*
Main machinery: 2 Detroit 16V-92TAB diesels; 1380 hp *(1.03 MW)* sustained; 2 shafts
Speed, knots: 28. **Range, miles:** 1200 at 12 kts
Complement: 8 (2 officers)
Guns: 2—12.7 mm MGs. 2—7.62 mm MGs (can be carried).

Comment: Ordered from Halter Marine 17th February 1991. Last delivered in late 1992. Same type for Philippines, Ecuador and Panama. These may be Coast Guard craft.

HALTER TYPE *8/1990, Trinity Marine*

40 SIMMONEAU 51 TYPE (INSHORE PATROL CRAFT)

Displacement, tons: 22
Dimensions, feet (metres): 51.8 × 15.7 × 5.9 *(15.8 × 4.8 × 1.8)*
Main machinery: 2 outboards; 2400 hp(m) *(1.76 MW)*
Speed, knots: 33. **Range, miles:** 375 at 25 kts
Guns: 1 GIAT 20 mm. 2—7.62 mm MGs.
Radars: Surface search: Furuno; I band.

Comment: First 20 ordered in June 1988 and delivered in 1989-90. A second batch of 20 ordered in 1991. Used by naval commandos. These craft were also reported as Panhards.

SIMMONEAU TYPE *1989, Simmoneau Marine*

MINE WARFARE FORCES

2 + 1 (3) SANDOWN CLASS (MINEHUNTERS—COASTAL)

Name	No	Builders	Launched	Commissioned
AL JAWF	420	Vosper Thornycroft	2 Aug 1989	12 Dec 1991
SHAQRA	422	Vosper Thornycroft	15 May 1991	7 Feb 1993
AL KHARJ	424	Vosper Thornycroft	8 Feb 1993	1994
ONAIZAH	426	Vosper Thornycroft	—	—
AL RASS	428	Vosper Thornycroft	—	—
AL BAHAN	430	Vosper Thornycroft	—	—

Displacement, tons: 450 standard; 480 full load
Dimensions, feet (metres): 172.9 × 34.4 × 6.9 *(52.7 × 10.5 × 2.1)*
Main machinery: 2 Paxman 6RP200E diesels; 1500 hp *(1.12 MW)* sustained; Voith-Schneider propulsion; 2 shafts; 2 Schottel bow thrusters
Speed, knots: 13 diesels; 6 electric drive. **Range, miles:** 3000 at 12 kts
Complement: 34 (7 officers) plus 6 spare berths
Guns: 2 Emmerson Electric 30 mm (twin); 80° elevation; 1200 rounds/minute combined to 6 km *(3.3 nm)*; weight of shell 0.35 kg.
Countermeasures: Decoys: Chaff launcher.
MCM: ECA mine disposal system; 2 PAP 104 Mk 5.
Combat data systems: Plessey Nautis M action data automation.
Fire control: Contraves TMEO optronic director.
Radars: Navigation: Kelvin Hughes Type 1007; I band.
Sonars: Plessey/MUSL Type 2093; VDS; high frequency.

Comment: Three ordered 2 November 1988 from Vosper Thornycroft with option for three more. *Al Kharj* laid down September 1990. GRP hull. Combines vectored thrust units with bow thrusters and Remote Controlled Mine Disposal System (RCMDS). Some of the hulls have been reallocated from the RN production line.

SHAQRA *4/1992, H M Steele*

AL JAWF *3/1993, Maritime Photographic*

602　SAUDI ARABIA / Mine warfare forces — Royal yacht squadron

4 MSC 322 CLASS (MINESWEEPERS/HUNTERS—COASTAL)

Name	No	Builders	Commissioned
ADDRIYAH	MSC 412	Peterson Builders, Wisconsin	6 July 1978
AL QUYSUMAH	MSC 414	Peterson Builders, Wisconsin	15 Aug 1978
AL WADEEAH	MSC 416	Peterson Builders, Wisconsin	7 Sep 1979
SAFWA	MSC 418	Peterson Builders, Wisconsin	2 Oct 1979

Displacement, tons: 320 standard; 407 full load
Dimensions, feet (metres): 153 × 26.9 × 8.2 *(46.6 × 8.2 × 2.5)*
Main machinery: 2 Waukesha L1616 diesels; 1200 hp *(895 kW)*; 2 shafts
Speed, knots: 13
Complement: 39 (4 officers)
Guns: 1 Oerlikon 20 mm.
Radars: Surface warning: ISC Cardion SPS 55; I/J band.
Sonars: GE SQQ 14; VDS; active minehunting; high frequency.

Comment: Ordered on 30 September 1975 under the International Logistics Programme. Wooden structure.
Fitted with fin stabilisers, wire and magnetic sweeps and also for minehunting. *Addriyah* based at Jiddah, the remainder at Al Jubail.

2 MOD DURANCE CLASS (REPLENISHMENT SHIPS)

Name	No	Builders	Commissioned
BORAIDA	902	C du N et de la Méditerranée, La Ciotat	29 Feb 1984
YUNBOU	904	C du N et de la Méditerranée, La Ciotat	29 Aug 1985

Displacement, tons: 10 500
Dimensions, feet (metres): 442.9 × 61.3 × 22.9 *(135 × 18.7 × 7)*
Main machinery: 2 SEMT-Pielstick 14 PC2.5 V 400 diesels; 18 200 hp(m) *(13.4 MW)* sustained; 2 shafts; cp props
Speed, knots: 20.5. **Range, miles:** 7000 at 15 kts
Complement: 129 plus 11 trainees
Cargo capacity: 4350 tons diesel; 350 tons AVCAT; 140 tons fresh water; 100 tons victuals; 100 tons ammunition; 70 tons spares

Guns: 4 Breda Bofors 40 mm/70 (2 twin); 85° elevation; 300 rounds/minute to 12.5 km *(6.8 nm)*; weight of shell 0.96 kg.
Fire control: 2 CSEE Naja optronic directors. 2 CSEE Lynx optical sights.
Radars: Navigation: Two sets; I band.

Helicopters: 2 SA 365 F Dauphin or 1 AS 332SC Super Puma.

Programmes: Contract signed October 1980 as part of Sawari programme.
Structure: Refuelling positions: Two alongside, one astern.
Operational: Also serve as training ships and as depot and maintenance ships. Helicopters can have ASM or ASW armament. Both based at Jiddah.

SAFWA　　　　　　　　　　　　　　　　　　　　　　　　　*1984, van Ginderen Collection*

AMPHIBIOUS FORCES

Notes: 1. Four ex-German LCMs have been scrapped.
2. Two LSTs may be bought as troop carriers for Naval Infantry.

4 Ex-US LCU 1610 TYPE

AL QIAQ (ex-*SA 310*) 212　　　　　AL ULA (ex-*SA 312*) 216
AL SULAYEL (ex-*SA 311*) 214　　　AFIF (ex-*SA 313*) 218

Displacement, tons: 200 light; 375 full load
Dimensions, feet (metres): 134.9 × 29 × 6.1 *(41.1 × 8.8 × 1.9)*
Main machinery: 4 GM diesels; 1000 hp *(746 kW)*; 2 Kort nozzles
Speed, knots: 11. **Range, miles:** 1200 at 8 kts
Complement: 14 (2 officers)
Military lift: 170 tons; 20 troops
Guns: 2—12.7 mm MGs.
Radars: Surface search: Marconi LN 66; I band.

Comment: Built by Newport Shipyard, Rhode Island. Transferred June/July 1976. Based at Al Jubail.

4 US LCM 6 TYPE

DHEBA 220　　　　　　　　　　　　AL LEETH 224
UMLUS 222　　　　　　　　　　　　AL QUONFETHA 226

Displacement, tons: 62 full load
Dimensions, feet (metres): 56.2 × 14 × 3.9 *(17.1 × 4.3 × 1.2)*
Main machinery: 2 GM diesels; 450 hp *(336 kW)*; 2 shafts
Speed, knots: 9. **Range, miles:** 130 at 9 kts
Complement: 5
Military lift: 34 tons or 80 troops
Guns: 2—40 mm grenade launchers.

Comment: Four transferred July 1977 and four in July 1980. The first four have been cannibalised for spares. Based at Jiddah.

BORAIDA　　　　　　　　　　　　　　　　　　　　　　　　　*11/1987, G Toremans*

8 HARBOUR TUGS (ATB)

RADHWA 1-6, 14-15

Measurement, tons: 350 gross
Dimensions, feet (metres): 118 × 42 × 15 *(35.9 × 12.8 × 4.6)*
Main machinery: 2 Fuji 8L32X diesels; 6250 hp(m) *(4.6 MW)* sustained; 2 shafts
Speed, knots: 15

Comment: Builders Hitachi Robin DY, Singapore (for 1-3), Jonker and Stans, Netherlands (4-6) and Damen, Netherlands (14-15). All commissioned between 1981 and 1983.

2 Ex-US YTB TYPE (HARBOUR TUGS)

TUWAIG (ex-*YTB 837*) 111　　　　DAREEN (ex-*YTB 838*) 112

Displacement, tons: 350 full load
Dimensions, feet (metres): 109 × 30 × 13.8 *(31.1 × 9.8 × 4.5)*
Main machinery: 2 diesels; 2000 hp *(1.49 MW)*; 2 shafts
Speed, knots: 12
Complement: 12
Guns: 2 Oerlikon 20 mm.

Comment: Transferred by US Navy 15 October 1975. Used mostly to aid weapons firing exercises. *Tuwaig* based at Al Jubail, *Dareen* at Damman.

YTB TYPE (US colours)　　　　　　　　　　　　　　　　　　*9/1992, Jürg Kürsener*

SERVICE FORCES

1 SALVAGE TUG (ARS)

JIDDAH 13

Displacement, tons: 350
Dimensions, feet (metres): 112.8 × — × — *(34.4 × — × —)*
Main machinery: 2 diesels; 800 hp(m) *(588 kW)*; 2 shafts
Speed, knots: 12

Comment: Built at Hayashikane, Shimonoseki. Laid down 19 August 1977.

3 OCEAN TUGS (ATA)

RADHWA 12, 16, 17

Displacement, tons: 680
Dimensions, feet (metres): 142.7 × 44.9 × 18.4 *(43.5 × 13.7 × 5.6)*
Main machinery: 2 Fuji diesels; 5600 hp(m) *(4.12 MW)*; 2 shafts
Range, miles: 12

Comment: First launched 16 October 1982, second 17 May 1983 and third 24 June 1983.

ROYAL YACHT SQUADRON

1 ROYAL YACHT

Name	No	Builders	Commissioned
AL RIYADH	—	Van Lent (de Kaag), Netherlands	Jan 1978

Displacement, tons: 670 full load
Dimensions, feet (metres): 228 × 34.4 × 10.8 *(69.5 × 10.5 × 3.3)*
Main machinery: 2 MTU 16V 956 TB91 diesels; 7500 hp(m) *(5.51 MW)* sustained; 2 shafts; Schottel bow thruster
Speed, knots: 26
Complement: 26 (accommodation for 18 passengers)
Radars: Navigation: Decca 1216 and Decca 916; I band.

Comment: Ordered 12 December 1975. Laid down 6 May 1976. Launched 17 December 1977. Fittings include helicopter pad, sauna, swimming pool, hospital with intensive care unit. Steel hull fitted with stabilisers. Based at Damman.

1 PEGASUS CLASS (HYDROFOIL)

Displacement, tons: 115 full load
Dimensions, feet (metres): 89.9 × 29.9 × 6.2 *(27.4 × 9.1 × 1.9)*
Main machinery: 2 Allison 501-KF20A gas turbines; 8660 hp *(6.46 MW)* sustained; 2 waterjets (foilborne); 2 Detroit 8V92 diesels; 606 hp *(452 kW)* sustained; 2 shafts (hullborne)
Speed, knots: 46. **Range, miles:** 890 at 42 kts
Guns: 2 General Electric 20 mm Sea Vulcan.

Comment: Ordered in 1984 from Boeing, Seattle; delivered in August 1985. Mostly used as a tender to the Royal Yacht.

COAST GUARD

2 SEA GUARD CLASS (FAST ATTACK CRAFT—MISSILE)

AL RIYADH   + 1

Displacement, tons: 53 standard
Dimensions, feet (metres): 73.8 × 18.4 × 5.6 *(22.5 × 5.6 × 1.7)*
Main machinery: 2 MTU 12V 331 TC92 diesels; 2920 hp(m) *(21.46 MW)*; 2 shafts
Speed, knots: 35
Complement: 10
Missiles: SSM: 2 Aerospatiale AS 15TT (twin); radar guidance to 15 km *(8.1 nm)* at 0.8 Mach; warhead 30 kg; sea-skimmer.
Guns: 2—12.7 mm MGs.
Radars: Surface search: Racal Decca; I band.
Fire control: Thomson-CSF Agrion; J band.

Comment: Built by Simonneau Marine and delivered by SOFREMA in April 1992. Aluminium construction. Both based at Jiddah.

AL RIYADH   *1992, Simonneau Marine*

AL RIYADH   *1992, Aerospatiale*

LARGE PATROL CRAFT

ADR   YARMOUK

Displacement, tons: 65 full load
Dimensions, feet (metres): 95.1 × 22 × 4.9 *(29 × 6.7 × 1.5)*
Main machinery: 2 GM 16V-149 diesels; 2 shafts
Speed, knots: 25. **Range, miles:** 1000 at 22 kts
Complement: 17
Guns: 2—12.7 mm MGs.
Radars: Surface search: Racal Decca RM 1690; I band.

Comment: Built by Bayerische, Germany in the 1970s. Aluminium hulls. Both based at Aziziah.

4 LARGE PATROL CRAFT

AL JOUF 351   TURAIF 352   HAIL 353   NAJRAN 354

Displacement, tons: 210 full load
Dimensions, feet (metres): 126.6 × 26.2 × 6.2 *(38.6 × 8 × 1.9)*
Main machinery: 3 MTU 16 V 538 TB93 diesels; 11 265 hp(m) *(8.28 MW)* sustained; 3 shafts
Speed, knots: 38. **Range, miles:** 1700 at 15 kts
Complement: 20
Guns: 2 Oerlikon GAM-BO1 20 mm. 2—12.7 mm MGs.
Radars: Surface search: Racal S 1690; I band.
Navigation: Racal RM 1290A; I band.

Comment: Ordered on 18 October 1987 from Blohm & Voss. First two completed 15 June 1989; second pair 20 August 1989. Steel hulls with aluminium superstructure. *Hail* and *Najran* based at Jiddah in the Red Sea and the others at Aziziah.

AL JOUF   *6/1989, Blohm & Voss*

2 LARGE PATROL CRAFT

AL JUBATEL   SALWA

Displacement, tons: 95 full load
Dimensions, feet (metres): 86 × 19 × 6.9 *(26.2 × 5.8 × 2.1)*
Main machinery: 2 MTU 16V 396 TB94 diesels; 5800 hp(m) *(4.26 MW)* sustained; 2 shafts
Speed, knots: 34. **Range, miles:** 1100 at 25 kts
Complement: 12
Guns: 1 Oerlikon/GAM-BO1 20 mm. 2—12.7 mm MGs.
Radars: Surface search: Racal Decca AC 1290; I band.

Comment: Built by Abeking & Rasmussen, completed in April 1987. Smaller version of Turkish SAR 33 Type. One based at Jizan and one at Al Wajh.

AL JUBATEL   *1987, Abeking and Rasmussen*

25 SKORPION CLASS (COASTAL PATROL CRAFT)

139-164

Displacement, tons: 33 full load
Dimensions, feet (metres): 55.8 × 16.1 × 4.6 *(17 × 4.9 × 1.4)*
Main machinery: 2 Detroit 12V-71TA diesels; 840 hp *(627 kW)* sustained; 2 shafts
Speed, knots: 25. **Range, miles:** 200 at 20 kts
Complement: 7
Guns: 2—7.62 mm MGs.
Radars: Surface search: Decca 914C; I band.

Comment: Twenty built by Bayerische SY, Erlenbach am Main. 139-148 shipped to Jiddah in October 1979. Last 10 built by Arminias Werft, Bodenwerder in 1980. Some deleted. Spread around all six Coast Guard bases.

SKORPION 144   *10/1979, van Ginderen Collection*

604 SAUDI ARABIA / Coast guard

1 COASTAL PATROL CRAFT

Displacement, tons: 72 full load
Dimensions, feet (metres): 69.9 × 19 × 5.2 *(21.3 × 5.8 × 1.6)*
Main machinery: 2 Deutz SBF 12M 716 diesels; 724 hp(m) *(532 kW)*; 2 shafts
Speed, knots: 12
Guns: 1—12.7 mm MG.
Radars: Surface search: Decca 110; I band.

Comment: Built by Whittingham and Mitchell in the 1970s. Steel hull. Based at Jiddah.

12 RAPIER CLASS (COASTAL PATROL CRAFT)

127-138

Displacement, tons: 26 full load
Dimensions, feet (metres): 50 × 15.1 × 4.6 *(15.2 × 4.6 × 1.4)*
Main machinery: 2 Detroit 12V-71TA diesels; 840 hp *(627 kW)* sustained; 2 shafts
Speed, knots: 28. **Range, miles:** 290 at 24 kts
Complement: 9 (1 officer)
Guns: 2—7.62 mm MGs.
Radars: Surface search: Decca 101; I band.

Comment: Three completed 1976, remainder in 1977 by Halter Marine, New Orleans. Steel hulls. Three based at Jiddah, five at Al Wajh, four at Aziziah.

7 SR N6 Mod 4 HOVERCRAFT

Displacement, tons: 10.9 normal
Dimensions, feet (metres): 48.5 × 23 × 3.9 (skirt) *(14.8 × 7 × 1.2)*
Main machinery: 1 Rolls-Royce Gnome 1050 gas turbine; 900 hp *(671 kW)* sustained
Speed, knots: 60. **Range, miles:** 170 at 54 kts
Complement: 3
Military lift: 20 troops plus 5 tons equipment
Guns: 1—7.62 mm MG.

Comment: First eight acquired from British Hovercraft Corporation, between February and December 1970. Eight more ordered in 1980 of which two delivered in 1981, four in 1982 and two in 1983. First nine have been scrapped.

SR N6 Hovercraft   11/1981, G S Long

8 SR N6 Mod 8 HOVERCRAFT

Displacement, tons: 17 normal
Dimensions, feet (metres): 60 × 27.9 × 5.2 *(18.3 × 8.5 × 1.6)*
Main machinery: 1 RR Gnome 1060 gas turbine; 1060 hp *(791 kW)*
Speed, knots: 55
Military lift: 30 troops plus equipment
Guns: 1—7.62 mm MG.

Comment: Acquired in the mid-1980s from the British Hovercraft Corporation. Five based at Aziziah, three at Jiddah.

16 SLINGSBY SAH 2200 HOVERCRAFT

Dimensions, feet (metres): 34.8 × 13.8 *(10.6 × 4.2)*
Main machinery: 1 Deutz BF6L913C diesel; 190 hp(m) *(140 kW)* sustained; lift and propulsion
Speed, knots: 40. **Range, miles:** 500 at 40 kts
Military lift: 2.2 tons or 24 troops
Guns: 1—7.62 mm MG.

Comment: First three supplied in 1990. Final total could be up to 30 for coastal defence and oil rig protection. Have Kevlar armour.

SLINGSBY 2200   1991

653 INSHORE PATROL CRAFT

Number	Builder/Type	Date	Speed
4	Lambro, Greece, 14 m	1974	12
8	LCVP, 14 m	1970s	8
10	Cytra, Germany, 12.8 m	1970s	38
2	Enforcer, USA, 9.4 m	1980s	30
30	Simonneau SM 331, 9.3 m	1992	40
60	Boston Whalers, 8.3 m	1980s	30
50	Cytra, Greece, 6.5 m	1970s	30
8	Catamarans, 6.4 m	1977	30
475	Task Force Boats, 5.25 m	1976	20
4	Viper, 5.1 m	1980s	25
2	Cobra, 3.9 m	1984	40

Comment: Many are based at Jiddah with the rest spread around the other bases. Most are armed with MGs and the larger craft have I band radars.

SIMONNEAU SM 331   1992, Simonneau Marine

MISCELLANEOUS

1 ROYAL YACHT

Name	No	Builders	Commissioned
ABDUL AZIZ	—	Halsingør Waerft, Denmark	12 June 1984

Displacement, tons: 5000 full load
Measurement, tons: 1450 dwt
Dimensions, feet (metres): 482.2 × 59.2 × 16.1 *(147 × 18 × 4.9)*
Main machinery: 2 Lindholmen-Pielstick 12 PC2.5 V diesels; 15 600 hp(m) *(11.47 MW)* sustained; 2 shafts
Speed, knots: 22.5
Complement: 65 plus 4 Royal berths and 60 spare
Helicopters: 1 Bell 206B JetRanger type.

Comment: Completed March 1983 for subsequent fitting out at Vosper's Ship Repairers, Southampton. Helicopter hangar set in hull forward of bridge—covers extend laterally to form pad Swimming pool. Stern ramp leading to garage. Based at Jiddah.

ABDUL AZIZ   6/1984, W Sartor

1 ROYAL YACHT

AL DERYAH

Displacement, tons: 112 full load
Dimensions, feet (metres): 91.2 × 20 × 6.9 *(27.8 × 6.1 × 2.1)*
Main machinery: 2 MTU 16V 92 diesels; 2 shafts
Speed, knots: 16. **Range, miles:** 550 at 14 kts
Radars: Navigation: Decca 370; I band.

Comment: Based at Aziziah.

1 TRAINING SHIP

TABBOUK

Displacement, tons: 585 full load
Dimensions, feet (metres): 196.8 × 32.8 × 5.8 *(60 × 10 × 1.8)*
Main machinery: 2 MTU MD 16V 538 TB80 diesels; 5000 hp(m) *(3.68 MW)* sustained; 2 shafts
Speed, knots: 20. **Range, miles:** 3500 at 12 kts
Complement: 24 plus 36 trainees
Guns: 1 Oerlikon GAM-BO1 20 mm.
Radars: Surface search: Racal Decca TM 1226; I band.
Navigation: Racal Decca 2690BT; I band.

Comment: Built by Bayerische, Germany and commissioned 1 December 1977. Based at Jiddah.

Coast guard / SAUDI ARABIA — Light forces / SENEGAL   605

1 TRAINING YACHT

AL TAIF

Displacement, tons: 75 full load
Dimensions, feet (metres): 70.2 × 19 × 5.6 *(21.4 × 5.8 × 1.7)*
Main machinery: 2 Deutz SBF 12M 716 diesels; 2 shafts
Speed, knots: 15
Radars: Navigation: Decca 101; I band.

Comment: Based at Jiddah.

3 HARBOUR TUGS

Displacement, tons: 210 full load
Dimensions, feet (metres): 84.3 × 23.6 × 9.5 *(25.7 × 7.2 × 2.9)*
Main machinery: 1 Deutz SBA 16M 816 diesel; 1 shaft
Speed, knots: 13. Range, miles: 1200 at 12 kts

Comment: Two based at Jiddah and one at Aziziah.

3 SMALL TANKERS

AL FORAT   **DAJLAH**   **AL NIL**

Displacement, tons: 233 full load
Dimensions, feet (metres): 94.2 × 21.3 × 6.9 *(28.7 × 6.5 × 2.1)*
Main machinery: 2 Caterpillar D343 diesels; 2 shafts
Speed, knots: 12. Range, miles: 500 at 12 kts
Radars: Navigation: Decca 110; I band.

Comment: *Al Nil* based at Aziziah, the others at Jiddah.

4 FIREFIGHTING CRAFT

JUBAIL   **JIDDAH**   **DAMMAM**   **AZIZIAH**

Displacement, tons: 82 full load
Dimensions, feet (metres): 80.4 × 24.9 × 7.5 *(24.5 × 7.6 × 2.3)*
Main machinery: 2 GM 16V 92; 2 shafts
Speed, knots: 19. Range, miles: 350 at 14 kts

Comment: Built by Brooke Marine in 1979. Two based at Jiddah, two at Aziziah.

SENEGAL

Political

On 1 February 1982 the two countries of Senegal and The Gambia united to form the confederation of Senegambia, which included merging the armed forces. Confederation was cancelled on 30 September 1989 and the forces again became national and independent of each other.

Head of Navy:
  Captain Alexandre Diam

Personnel

(a) 1993: 700 officers and men
(b) 2 years' conscript service

Bases

Dakar, Casamance

Mercantile Marine

Lloyd's Register of Shipping:
  183 vessels of 50 084 tons gross

LIGHT FORCES

1 IMPROVED OSPREY 55 CLASS

Name	No	Builders	Commissioned
FOUTA	—	Danyard A/S, Fredrikshavn	1 June 1987

Displacement, tons: 470 full load
Dimensions, feet (metres): 180.5 × 33.8 × 8.5 *(55 × 10.3 × 2.6)*
Main machinery: 2 MAN Burmeister & Wain Alpha 12V23/30-DVO diesels; 4400 hp(m) *(3.23 MW)* sustained; 2 shafts; cp props
Speed, knots: 20. Range, miles: 4000 at 16 kts
Complement: 38 (4 officers) plus 8 spare berths
Guns: 1 Hispano Suiza 30 mm.
Radars: Surface search: Furuno FR 1411; I band.
Navigation: Furuno FR 1221; I band.

Comment: Ordered in 1985. Intended for patrolling the EEZ rather than as a warship, hence the modest armament. A 25 knot rigid inflatable boat can be launched from a stern ramp which has a protective hinged door. Similar vessels built for Morocco and Greece.

FOUTA   *1992, Ships of the World*

3 P 48 CLASS (LARGE PATROL CRAFT)

Name	No	Builders	Commissioned
SAINT LOUIS	—	SFCN, Villeneuve-la-Garenne	1 Mar 1971
POPENGUINE	—	SFCN, Villeneuve-la-Garenne	10 Aug 1974
PODOR	—	SFCN, Villeneuve-la-Garenne	13 July 1977

Displacement, tons: 250 full load
Dimensions, feet (metres): 156 × 23.3 × 8.1 *(47.5 × 7.1 × 2.5)*
Main machinery: 2 SACM AGO V12 CZSHR diesels; 4340 hp(m) *(3.2 MW)*; 2 shafts
Speed, knots: 23. Range, miles: 2000 at 16 kts
Complement: 33 (3 officers)
Guns: 2 Bofors 40 mm/70.

Comment: Sisters to *Malaika* of Madagascar, *Le Vigilant* and *Le Valeureux* of Ivory Coast and Bizerte class of Tunisian Navy. *Podor* ordered August 1975.

48 class   *1989, van Ginderen Collection*

3 INTERCEPTOR CLASS (COASTAL PATROL CRAFT)

Name	No	Builders	Commissioned
SÉNÉGAL II	—	Les Bateaux Turbec Ltd, Sainte Catherine, Canada	Feb 1979
SINE-SALOUM II	—	Les Bateaux Turbec Ltd, Sainte Catherine, Canada	16 Nov 1979
CASAMANCE II	—	Les Bateaux Turbec Ltd, Sainte Catherine, Canada	Aug 1979

Displacement, tons: 62 full load
Dimensions, feet (metres): 86.9 × 19.3 × 5.2 *(26.5 × 5.8 × 1.6)*
Main machinery: 2 diesels; 2700 hp *(2.01 MW)*; 2 shafts
Speed, knots: 32.5
Guns: 2 Oerlikon 20 mm.

Comment: Used for EEZ patrol. Doubtful operational status.

CASAMANCE II   *9/1979, van Ginderen Collection*

2 FAIREY MARINE TRACKER 2 CLASS (COASTAL PATROL CRAFT)

Name	No	Builders	Commissioned
CHALLENGE	P 3	Fairey Marine, UK	1978
CHAMPION	P 4	Fairey Marine, UK	1978

Displacement, tons: 34
Dimensions, feet (metres): 65.7 × 17 × 4.8 *(20 × 5.2 × 1.5)*
Main machinery: 2 Detroit 12V-71TA diesels; 820 hp *(612 kW)* sustained; 2 shafts
Speed, knots: 24. Range, miles: 650 at 20 kts
Complement: 11
Guns: 1 Oerlikon 20 mm. 2—7.62 mm MGs.
Radars: Surface search: Racal Decca; I band.

Comment: Hull and superstructure of GRP. Air-conditioned accommodation. The third of the class belongs to Gambia.

TRACKER 2 class (Gambia number)   *1/1990, E Grove*

606 SENEGAL / Light forces — Customs service

1 PR 72M CLASS

Name	No	Builders	Commissioned
NJAMBUUR	P 773	SFCN, Villeneuve-la-Garenne	1983

Displacement, tons: 375 standard; 451 full load
Dimensions, feet (metres): 192.5 × 24.9 × 7.2 *(58.7 × 7.6 × 2.2)*
Main machinery: 4 SACM AGO 195 V16 RVR diesels; 11 760 hp(m) *(8.64 MW)* sustained; 4 shafts
Speed, knots: 29. **Range, miles:** 2500 at 16 kts
Complement: 39 plus 7 passengers
Guns: 2 OTO Melara 3 in *(76 mm)* compact.
  2 Oerlikon 20 mm F2.
Fire control: 2 CSEE Naja optronic directors.
Radars: Surface search: Racal Decca 1226; I band

Comment: Ordered in 1979. Completed September 1981 for shipping of armament at Lorient.

NJAMBUUR 1983

LAND-BASED MARITIME AIRCRAFT

Note: In addition there are six F27-400M aircraft.

Numbers/Type: 1 de Havilland Canada DHC-6 Twin Otter.
Operational speed: 168 kts *(311 km/h)*.
Service ceiling: 23 200 ft *(7070 m)*.
Range: 1460 nm *(2705 km)*.
Role/Weapon systems: MR for coastal surveillance but effectiveness limited. Backed up by a French Navy Breguet Atlantique based at Dakar. Sensors: Search radar. Weapons: Unarmed.

AMPHIBIOUS FORCES

1 FRENCH EDIC 700 CLASS (LCT)

Name	No	Builders	Commissioned
KARABANE	841	SFCN, Villeneuve-la-Garenne	30 Jan 1987

Displacement, tons: 736 full load
Dimensions, feet (metres): 193.5 × 39 × 5.6 *(59 × 11.9 × 1.7)*
Main machinery: 2 SACM MGO 175 V12 ASH diesels; 1200 hp(m) *(882 kW)* sustained; 2 shafts
Speed, knots: 12. **Range, miles:** 1800 at 10 kts
Complement: 18 (33 spare billets)
Military lift: 12 trucks; 340 tons equipment
Guns: Fitted for 2 Oerlikon 20 mm.

Comment: Ordered May 1985, delivered 23 June 1986. Replaced similar LCT *Damour*.

EDIC 700 1991, G Toremans

2 Ex-US LCM 6 CLASS

DIOU LOULOU (ex-6723)   DIOMBOS (ex-6733)

Displacement, tons: 62 full load
Dimensions, feet (metres): 56.2 × 14 × 3.9 *(17.1 × 4.3 × 1.2)*
Main machinery: 2 Gray Marine 64 HN9 diesels; 330 hp *(264 kW)*; 2 shafts
Speed, knots: 10
Military lift: 34 tons or 80 troops

Comment: Transferred to Senegal July 1968.

1 Ex-FRENCH EDIC CLASS (LCT)

LA FALEME (ex-9095)

Displacement, tons: 670 full load
Dimensions, feet (metres): 193.5 × 39.2 × 4.5 *(59 × 12 × 1.3)*
Main machinery: 2 SACM MGO diesels; 1000 hp(m) *(735 kW)*; 2 shafts
Speed, knots: 8. **Range, miles:** 1800 at 8 kts
Complement: 16
Military lift: 10 trucks or 5 LCPs
Guns: 2 Oerlikon 20 mm.

Comment: Launched 7 April 1958. Transferred to Senegal 1 July 1974.

EDIC (old number) 1985

MISCELLANEOUS

1 TENDER

CRAME JEAN (ex-*Raymond Sarr*)

Comment: An 18 ton fishing boat used as training craft since 1979.

2 TUGS

IBIS   AIGRETTE

Displacement, tons: 56
Dimensions, feet (metres): 60.4 × 18.7 × 8.2 *(18.4 × 5.7 × 2.5)*
Main machinery: 1 SACM Poyaud diesel; 250 hp(m) *(184 kW)*; 1 shaft
Speed, knots: 9. **Range, miles:** 1700 at 9 kts

Comment: Lent by France.

CUSTOMS SERVICE

2 TYPE DS-01 (COASTAL PATROL CRAFT)

Displacement, tons: 22
Dimensions, feet (metres): 52.5 × 15.1 × 7.5 *(16 × 4.6 × 2.3)*
Main machinery: 2 GM diesels; 970 hp *(724 kW)*; 2 shafts
Speed, knots: 20
Complement: 8
Guns: 1—12.7 mm MG.

Comment: Ordered A T Celaya, Bilbao March 1981. Delivered 9 February 1982.

4 LVI 85 S CLASS

DJIBRIL   N'DIAYE   GORÉE   DJILOR

Displacement, tons: 3.4
Speed, knots: 18

Comment: Ordered from Aresa, Barcelona and delivered in mid-1987 after long delays.

ARESA patrol craft 1980, Ares

SEYCHELLES

Senior Appointment	Base	Personnel	Mercantile Marine
Commander of the Navy: Major Paul Hodoul	Port Victoria, Mahé	1993: 200 officers and men	*Lloyd's Register of Shipping:* 9 vessels of 4465 tons gross

PATROL CRAFT

1 Ex-SOVIET TURYA CLASS

ZOROASTER

Displacement, tons: 190 standard; 250 full load
Dimensions, feet (metres): 129.9 × 24.9 × 5.9 *(39.6 × 7.6 × 1.8)*
Main machinery: 3 Type M 504 diesels; 10 800 hp *(7.94 MW)* sustained; 3 shafts
Speed, knots: 18. **Range, miles:** 1450 at 14 kts
Complement: 30
Guns: 2—57 mm/70 (twin). 2—25 mm/80 (twin).
Depth charges: 1 rack.
Radars: Surface search: Pot Drum; H/I band.
Fire control: Muff Cob; G/H band.
Sonars: Helicopter type VDS; active search and attack; high frequency.

Comment: Craft presented by USSR 21 June 1986. Same as Turya class except torpedo tubes and hydrofoils removed. Seychelles crew trained in USSR. Russian Commanding Officer and Executive Officer returned to USSR in August 1986. The retention of the sonar is unusual in the export version as is the removal of the hydrofoils. Non-operational in 1992.

ZOROASTER 1988

1 TYPE FPB 42 (LARGE PATROL CRAFT)

Name	No	Builders	Commissioned
ANDROMACHE	— (ex-605)	Picchiotti, Viareggio	10 Jan 1983

Displacement, tons: 268 full load
Dimensions, feet (metres): 137.8 × 26 × 8.2 *(41.8 × 8 × 2.5)*
Main machinery: 2 Paxman Valenta 16 CM diesels; 6650 hp *(5 MW)* sustained; 2 shafts
Speed, knots: 26. **Range, miles:** 3000 at 16 kts
Complement: 22 (3 officers)
Guns: 1 Oerlikon 25 mm. 2—7.62 mm MGs.
Radars: Navigation: Furuno; I band.

Comment: Ordered from Inma, La Spezia in November 1981. Pennant numbers no longer worn. A second of class reported ordered in 1991.

ANDROMACHE 1988, PDFS

1 Ex-FRENCH SIRIUS CLASS (LARGE PATROL CRAFT)

TOPAZ (ex-*Croix du Sud*)

Displacement, tons: 440 full load
Dimensions, feet (metres): 152 × 28 × 8.2 *(46.4 × 8.6 × 2.5)*
Main machinery: 2 SEMT-Pielstick diesels; 2000 hp(m) *(1.47 MW)*; 2 shafts
Speed, knots: 15. **Range, miles:** 3000 at 10 kts
Complement: 38
Guns: 1 Bofors 40 mm/60. 1 Oerlikon 20 mm.

Comment: Ex-French minesweeper built in 1956 and transferred without sweep gear in January 1979. Paid off in 1987 but brought back into service in late 1990. Not in good repair.

2 Ex-SOVIET ZHUK CLASS (COASTAL PATROL CRAFT)

CONSTANT   FORTUNE

Displacement, tons: 50 full load
Dimensions, feet (metres): 75.4 × 17 × 6.2 *(23 × 5.2 × 1.9)*
Main machinery: 2 Type M 50 diesels; 2200 hp *(1.6 MW)* sustained; 2 shafts
Speed, knots: 30. **Range, miles:** 1100 at 15 kts
Complement: 17
Guns: 4—14.5 mm (2 twin) MGs.
Radars: Surface search: Furuno; I band.

Comment: Transferred from Black Sea on 11 October 1981 and 6 November 1982.

CONSTANT 1990

1 COASTAL PATROL CRAFT

JUNON

Displacement, tons: 40 approx
Dimensions, feet (metres): 60 × — × — *(18.3 × — × —)*
Main machinery: 2 GM diesels; 1040 hp *(746 kW)*; 2 shafts
Speed, knots: 26. **Range, miles:** 1000 at 22 kts

Comment: Built by Tyler, UK in 1980.

JUNON 1989, PDFS

1 LANDING CRAFT (TANK)

Name	No	Builders	Commissioned
CINQ JUIN	—	La Perrière, France	11 Jan 1979

Displacement, tons: 855 full load
Dimensions, feet (metres): 186.8 × 38 × 6 *(56.9 × 11.6 × 1.9)*
Main machinery: 2 Poyaud A12 150M diesels; 880 hp(m) *(647 kW)*; 2 shafts
Speed, knots: 9. **Range, miles:** 2000 at 8 kts
Military lift: 300 tons plus 1 LCP

Comment: Ordered 12 December 1977. Although government-owned, this ship is commercially operated except for occasional exercises.

CINQ JUIN 1986, PDFS

LAND-BASED MARITIME AIRCRAFT

Numbers/Type: 2 HAL (Aerospatiale) Chetak (Alouette III).
Operational speed: 113 kts *(210 km/h)*.
Service ceiling: 10 500 ft *(3200 m)*.
Range: 290 nm *(540 km)*.
Role/Weapon systems: Support helicopter; used for police and anti-smuggler patrols. Sensors: None. Weapons: 2 × 7.62 mm machine guns can be fitted.

Numbers/Type: 1 Pilatus Britten-Norman Maritime Defender.
Operational speed: 150 kts *(280 km/h)*.
Service ceiling: 18 900 ft *(5760 m)*.
Range: 1500 nm *(2775 km)*.
Role/Weapon systems: Coastal surveillance and surface search aircraft. Sensors: Search radar. Weapons: Provision for rockets or guns.

SIERRA LEONE

Senior Appointment

Commander of Navy:
Lieutenant Commander Alimany Sasay

Personnel

(a) 1993: 140 officers and men
(b) Voluntary service

Base

Freetown

Mercantile Marine

Lloyd's Register of Shipping:
62 vessels of 25 569 tons gross

DELETIONS

1992 *Maritime Protector* (charter ended), *Pompoli, Gulama, Kailondo*

PATROL FORCES

2 SHANGHAI II CLASS (FAST ATTACK CRAFT—GUN)

MOA   NAIMBANA

Displacement, tons: 113 standard; 131 full load
Dimensions, feet (metres): 127.3 × 17.7 × 5.6 *(38.8 × 5.4 × 1.7)*
Main machinery: 2 Type L12-180 diesels; 2400 hp(m) *(1.76 MW)* (forward); 2 Type L12-180Z diesels; 1820 hp(m) *(1.34 MW)* (aft); 4 shafts
Speed, knots: 30. **Range, miles:** 700 at 16.5 kts
Complement: 34
Guns: 2 China 37 mm/63 (twin); 85° elevation; 180 rounds/minute to 8.5 km *(4.6 nm)*; weight of shell 1.42 kg.
4 USSR 25 mm/60 (2 twin); 85° elevation; 270 rounds/minute to 3 km *(1.6 nm)* anti-aircraft; weight of shell 0.34 kg.
Mines: Mine rails can be fitted for 10 mines.
Radars: Surface search: Skin Head or Pot Head; I band.

Comment: Delivered in March 1987. Chinese technicians were loaned for maintenance work and training. These craft only have one twin 37 mm gun (forward) vice two in Chinese craft. One was serviceable in early 1993, but not reliable.

SHANGHAI II   *1990*

1 HALMATIC CLASS (INSHORE PATROL CRAFT)

Displacement, tons: 13.5 full load
Dimensions, feet (metres): 40.3 × 11.2 × 3.3 *(12.3 × 3.4 × 1)*
Main machinery: 2 Volvo Penta TAMD70E diesels; 418 hp *(307 kW)* sustained; 2 shafts
Speed, knots: 23
Guns: Can carry 1—7.62 mm MG.

Comment: Built by Halmatic, UK in 1987. Used mainly for Pilot duties and non-operational in early 1993.

1 SWIFT 105 FT CLASS (LARGE PATROL CRAFT)

FARANDUGU

Displacement, tons: 103 full load
Dimensions, feet (metres): 105 × 22 × 7 *(31.5 × 6.7 × 2.1)*
Main machinery: 4 MTU 12V 331 TC92 diesels; 5320 hp(m) *(3.92 MW)* sustained; 4 shafts
Speed, knots: 25. **Range, miles:** 1200 at 12 kts
Complement: 19
Guns: 2—12.7 mm MGs. 2—7.62 mm MGs.

Comment: Laid down under FMS funding by Swiftships in October 1987 and delivered in December 1989. In early 1993 this was the only fully operational vessel.

SWIFT 105 FT   *1991*

2 CAT 900S CLASS (INSHORE PATROL CRAFT)

Displacement, tons: 7.4 full load
Dimensions, feet (metres): 34.1 × 9.5 × 2.6 *(10.4 × 2.9 × 0.8)*
Main machinery: 2 Volvo Penta TAMD41A diesels; 400 hp(m) *(294 kW)* maximum; 2 shafts
Speed, knots: 30
Complement: 4

Comment: Built by Cougar Holdings Ltd, Hamble and completed in May 1988. Catamaran hulls. Both unserviceable by 1992.

SINGAPORE

Headquarters' Appointment

Chief of the Navy:
Commodore Kwek Siew Jin

Personnel

(a) 1993: 4500 officers and men including 1800 conscripts
(b) National Service: two and a quarter years for Corporals and above; two years for the remainder
(c) 4500 reservists

Base

Pulau Brani, Tuas (Jurong) (by 1994)

Prefix to Ships' Names

RSS

Organisation

First Flotilla: Squadrons 188 (six Victory), 185 (six Lürssen), 182 (six Vosper Type A and B)
Third Flotilla: Squadrons 191 (five LSTs), 194 *(Mercury* and *Jupiter)*, 195 (LCVPs), 192 and 193 (Civil Reserve)
Coastal Patrol Squadrons (COPAS): 183 and 186 (8 Swift, 12 IPC)
Naval Logistics Command

Maritime Air

The navy has no separate air arm but the Air Force has Grumman E 2C Hawkeyes (see *Land-based Maritime Aircraft* section) and several reconnaissance aircraft. In addition the Air Force has more than 50 A4 Skyhawks, (possibly with Harpoon when modernised), and eight F16 A/B. There is a requirement for up to eight maritime patrol aircraft.

Mercantile Marine

Lloyd's Register of Shipping:
946 vessels of 9 247 352 tons gross

Strength of the Fleet

Type	Active	Building (Projected)
Missile Corvettes	6	—
Fast Attack Craft—Missile	6	—
Fast Attack Craft—Gun	6	(6)
Coastal Patrol Craft	8 (4)	—
Inshore Patrol Craft	12	—
Minesweepers—Coastal	—	4
LSTs/LSL	5 (1)	—
LCMs	8	—
LHC	1	—
Training Ships	1	—
Diving Support Vessels	2	—

DELETIONS

1990 *Utara, Jupiter* (old)
1991 *Panglima*
1993 *4 Swift Class (to Police)*

MISSILE CORVETTES

6 VICTORY CLASS

Name	No	Builders	Launched	Commissioned
VICTORY	P 88	Lürssen Werft, Bremen	8 June 1988	18 Aug 1990
VALOUR	P 89	Singapore SB and Marine	10 Dec 1988	18 Aug 1990
VIGILANCE	P 90	Singapore SB and Marine	27 Apr 1989	18 Aug 1990
VALIANT	P 91	Singapore SB and Marine	22 July 1989	25 May 1991
VIGOUR	P 92	Singapore SB and Marine	1 Dec 1989	25 May 1991
VENGEANCE	P 93	Singapore SB and Marine	23 Feb 1990	25 May 1991

Displacement, tons: 550 full load
Dimensions, feet (metres): 204.7 oa; 190.3 wl × 27.9 × 10.2 *(62.4; 58 × 8.5 × 3.1)*
Main machinery: 4 MTU 16V 538 TB93 diesels; 15 020 hp(m) *(11 MW)* sustained; 4 shafts
Speed, knots: 35. **Range, miles:** 4000 at 18 kts
Complement: 49 (8 officers)

Missiles: SSM: 8 McDonnell Douglas Harpoon; active radar homing to 130 km *(70 nm)* at 0.9 Mach; warhead 227 kg.
  SAM: Rafael Barak I to be fitted in 1993/94.
Guns: 1 OTO Melara 3 in *(76 mm)*/62 Super Rapid; 85° elevation; 120 rounds/minute to 16 km *(8.7 nm)*; weight of shell 6 kg.
Torpedoes: 6—324 mm Whitehead B 515 (2 triple) tubes. Whitehead A 244S; anti-submarine; active/passive homing to 7 km *(3.8 nm)* at 33 kts; warhead 34 kg (shaped charge).
Countermeasures: Decoys: Plessey Shield chaff launcher.
ESM/ECM: Rafael RAN 1101 intercept and jammer.
Fire control: BEAB 9LV 200 Mk 3
Radars: Surface search: Ericsson/Radamec Sea Giraffe 150HC; G/H band.
  Navigation: Racal Decca; I band.
  Fire control: Bofors Electronic 9LV 200; I/J band.
Sonars: EDO 780; VDS; active search and attack; 13, 7 or 5 kHz.

Programmes: Ordered in June 1986 to a Lürssen MGB 62 design similar to Bahrain and UAE vessels.
Structure: Close range armament is to include Barak I CIWS which may start being installed in 1992. Reported but not confirmed that a Sewaco combat data system is fitted. Trials are being done on stabilisers to try and improve roll characteristics. It is possible that the mast may have to be rebuilt and reduced in size.
Operational: Form Squadron 188.

VIGOUR
10/1991, John Mortimer

LIGHT FORCES

Note: Six new construction FAC(G) to replace Vosper Type. Contracts to be placed in 1993. Vessels are to be 45-55 m in length and be armed with Harpoon/Gabriel SSM, 76 mm guns and torpedo tubes.

6 LÜRSSEN FPB 45 CLASS (FAST ATTACK CRAFT—MISSILE)

Name	No	Builders	Commissioned
SEA WOLF	P 76	Lürssen Werft, Vegesack	1972
SEA LION	P 77	Lürssen Werft, Vegesack	1972
SEA DRAGON	P 78	Singapore SBEC	1974
SEA TIGER	P 79	Singapore SBEC	1974
SEA HAWK	P 80	Singapore SBEC	1975
SEA SCORPION	P 81	Singapore SBEC	29 Feb 1976

Displacement, tons: 226 standard; 254 full load
Dimensions, feet (metres): 147.3 × 23 × 7.5 *(44.9 × 7 × 2.3)*
Main machinery: 4 MTU 16V 538 TB92 diesels; 13 640 hp(m) *(10 MW)* sustained; 4 shafts
Speed, knots: 38. **Range, miles:** 950 at 30 kts; 1800 at 15 kts
Complement: 36 (6 officers)

Missiles: SSM: 4 McDonnell Douglas Harpoon (2 twin); active radar homing to 130 km *(70 nm)* at 0.9 Mach; warhead 227 kg.
  2 IAI Gabriel I launchers; radar or optical guidance; semi-active radar homing to 20 km *(10.8 nm)* at 0.7 Mach; warhead 75 kg.
Guns: 1 Bofors 57 mm/70 (not in all); 75° elevation; 200 rounds/minute to 17 km *(9.3 nm)*; weight of shell 2.4 kg.
  1 Bofors 40 mm/70; 90° elevation; 300 rounds/minute to 12 km *(6.6 nm)*; weight of shell 0.96 kg.
Countermeasures: Decoys: 4 Mk 36 SRBOC chaff launchers.
ESM/ECM: Racal intercept and jammer.
Radars: Surface search: Racal Decca; I band.
  Fire control: Signaal WM 28/5; I/J band; range 46 km *(25 nm)*.

Programmes: Designed by Lürssen Werft which built the first pair.
Modernisation: *Sea Hawk* was the first to complete refit in January 1988 with two sets of twin Harpoon launchers replacing the triple Gabriel launcher. The remainder were converted by December 1990 with the exception of *Sea Wolf* which finished refit in Spring 1991. ECM equipment has also been fitted on a taller mast. SATCOM and GPS installed. The Bofors 40 mm gun may be replaced with a Matra Simbad SAM launcher if trials are successful.

SEA HAWK
4/1990, 92 Wing RAAF

3 VOSPER TYPE A (FAST ATTACK CRAFT—GUN)

Name	No	Builders	Commissioned
INDEPENDENCE	P 69	Vosper Thornycroft Ltd, Gosport	8 July 1970
FREEDOM	P 70	Vosper Thornycroft Private Ltd, Singapore	11 Jan 1971
JUSTICE	P 72	Vosper Thornycroft Private Ltd, Singapore	23 Apr 1971

Displacement, tons: 112 standard; 142 full load
Dimensions, feet (metres): 109.6 × 21 × 5.6 *(33.5 × 6.4 × 1.8)*
Main machinery: 2 MTU MD 16V 538 TB90 diesels; 3580 hp(m) *(2.63 MW)* sustained; 2 shafts
Speed, knots: 32. **Range, miles:** 1100 at 14 kts
Complement: 19-22 (3 officers)
Guns: 1 Bofors 40 mm/70 fwd; 90° elevation; 300 rounds/minute to 12 km *(6.6 nm)*; weight of shell 0.96 kg.
  1 Oerlikon 20 mm/80 aft; 55° elevation; 800 rounds/minute to 2 km.
Radars: Surface search: Racal Decca; I band.
  Navigation: Decca 626; I band.

Comment: Ordered on 21 May 1968. To be replaced by new class in 1995/96.

JUSTICE
4/1990, 92 Wing RAAF

610 SINGAPORE / Light forces — Amphibious forces

3 VOSPER TYPE B (FAST ATTACK CRAFT—GUN)

Name	No	Builders	Commissioned
SOVEREIGNTY	P 71	Vosper Thornycroft Ltd, Gosport	Feb 1971
DARING	P 73	Vosper Thornycroft Private Ltd, Singapore	18 Sep 1971
DAUNTLESS	P 74	Vosper Thornycroft Private Ltd, Singapore	July 1971

Displacement, tons: 112 standard; 142 full load
Dimensions, feet (metres): 109.6 × 21 × 5.6 *(33.5 × 6.4 × 1.8)*
Main machinery: 2 MTU MD 16V 538 TB90 diesels; 3580 hp(m) *(2.63 MW)* sustained; 2 shafts
Speed, knots: 32. **Range, miles:** 1000 at 14 kts
Complement: 19 (3 officers)
Guns: 1 Bofors 3 in *(76 mm)*/50; 30° elevation; 30 rounds/minute to 13 km *(7 nm)* surface fire only; weight of shell 5.9 kg.
  1 Oerlikon 20 mm/80; 55° elevation; 800 rounds/minute to 2 km.
Radars: Surface search: Racal Decca; I band.
  Fire control: Signaal WM 26; I/J band; range 46 km *(25 nm)*.

Comment: Steel hulls of round bilge form. Aluminium alloy superstructure. To be replaced in 1995/96.

DARING 5/1992, G Toremans

12 SWIFT CLASS (COASTAL PATROL CRAFT)

SWIFT KNIGHT P 11	SWIFT COMBATANT P 18
SWIFT LANCER P 12	SWIFT CHALLENGER P 19
SWIFT SWORDSMAN P 14	SWIFT CAVALIER P 20
SWIFT WARRIOR P 15	SWIFT CONQUEROR P 21
SWIFT ARCHER P 16	SWIFT CENTURION P 22
SWIFT WARLORD P 17	SWIFT CHIEFTAIN P 23

Displacement, tons: 45.7 full load
Dimensions, feet (metres): 74.5 × 20.3 × 5.2 *(22.7 × 6.2 × 1.6)*
Main machinery: 2 Deutz BA16M816 diesels; 2680 hp(m) *(1.96 MW)* sustained; 2 shafts
Speed, knots: 32. **Range, miles:** 550 at 20 kts; 900 at 10 kts
Complement: 12 (3 officers)
Guns: 1 Oerlikon 20 mm. 2—7.62 mm MGs.
Radars: Surface search: Decca 1226; I band.

Comment: Delivered by Singapore SBEC 20 October 1981. Fitted for but not with two Gabriel SSMs. P12, P14, P16 and P18 transferred to the Police on 15 February 1993.

SWIFT CHALLENGER 5/1992, G Toremans

12 INSHORE PATROL CRAFT

FB 31-42

Displacement, tons: 20 full load
Dimensions, feet (metres): 47.6 × 13.8 × 3.6 *(14.5 × 4.2 × 1.1)*
Main machinery: 2 MTU 12V 183 TC91 diesels; 1200 hp(m) *(882 kW)*; 2 Hamilton waterjets
Speed, knots: 30
Complement: 4
Guns: 1—7.62 mm MG.
Radars: Surface search: Racal Decca; I band.

Comment: Built by Singapore SBEC and delivered in 1990/91. Based at Brani.

FB 42 1991, Singapore Shipbuilding and Engineering

LAND-BASED MARITIME AIRCRAFT

Note: A squadron of four Fokker F50 Maritime Enforcer II aircraft to be formed in 1994.

Numbers/Type: 4 Grumman E-2C Hawkeye.
Operational speed: 323 kts *(598 km/h)*.
Service ceiling: 30 800 ft *(9390 m)*.
Range: 1000 nm *(1850 km)*.
Role/Weapon systems: Delivered in 1987 for surveillance of shipping in sea areas around Singapore and South China Sea; understood to have priority assistance from US Government. Sensors: APS-125 radar; data link for SSM targeting; later aircraft will have APS-138 radar. Weapons: Unarmed.

MINE WARFARE FORCES

0 + 4 LANDSORT CLASS (MINEHUNTERS)

Displacement, tons: 360 full load
Dimensions, feet (metres): 155.8 × 31.5 × 7.3 *(47.5 × 9.6 × 2.2)*
Main machinery: 4 diesels; 1500 hp(m) *(1.11 MW)*; 2 Voith Schneider props
Speed, knots: 15. **Range, miles:** 2000 at 12 kts
Complement: 26 (8 officers)
Guns: 1 Bofors 40 mm/70.
Fire control: Thomson-CSF TSM 2061 tactical system.
Radars: Navigation: I band.
Sonars: Thomson-CSF TSM 2022; hull-mounted; minehunting; high frequency.

Comment: Kockums/Karlskrona design selected in 1991. GRP hulls. All to be delivered by 1995. First one is being built in Sweden; the remainder to be fitted out in Singapore Shipbuilders yard at Benoi Basin starting in 1993. Two PAP ROVs to be carried.

LANDSORT (Swedish colours) 1988, G Toremans

AMPHIBIOUS FORCES

1 Ex-BRITISH SIR LANCELOT CLASS (LSL)

Name	No	Builders	Commissioned
— (ex-*Sir Lancelot*)	— (ex-L 3029)	Fairfield, Glasgow	16 Jan 1964

Displacement, tons: 3270 light; 5674 full load
Dimensions, feet (metres): 412.1 × 59.8 × 13 *(125.6 × 18.2 × 4)*
Main machinery: 2 Mirrlees 10-ALSSDM diesels; 9400 hp *(7.01 MW)*; 2 shafts; bow thruster
Speed, knots: 17. **Range, miles:** 8000 at 15 kts
Complement: 65
Military lift: 340 troops (534 hard lying); 16 MBTs; 34 mixed vehicles; 120 tons POL; 30 tons ammunition; 1—20 ton crane; 2—4.5 ton cranes.
Guns: 2 Bofors 40 mm/70. 2—12.7 mm MGs.
Radars: Navigation: Kelvin Hughes Type 1006; I band.
Helicopters: Platform for 2 medium.

Comment: Paid off from the British Navy in 1989 and used commercially for survey work. Acquired by Singapore in late 1992 and being refitted to upgrade accommodation and fit 40 mm guns. Fitted for bow and stern loading with drive-through facilities and deck-to-deck ramps. Facilities provided for onboard maintenance of vehicles and for laying out pontoon equipment. Mexeflote self-propelled floating platforms can be strapped one on each side. Carries 850 tons oil fuel.

LSL (British colours) 1988

5 Ex-US 511-1152 CLASS (LSTs)

Name	No	Builders	Commissioned
ENDURANCE (ex-USS Holmes County LST 836)	L 201 (ex-A 82)	American Bridge Co	25 Nov 1944
EXCELLENCE (ex-US LST 629)	L 202 (ex-A 81)	Chicago Bridge & Iron Co	28 July 1944
INTREPID (ex-US LST 579)	L 203 (ex-A 83)	Missouri Valley B and I Co	21 July 1944
RESOLUTION (ex-US LST 649)	L 204 (ex-A 84)	Chicago Bridge & Iron Co	26 Oct 1944
PERSISTENCE (ex-US LST 613)	L 205 (ex-A 85)	Chicago Bridge & Iron Co	19 May 1944

Displacement, tons: 1653 light; 4100-4150 full load (modernised)
Dimensions, feet (metres): 328 × 50 × 14 (100 × 15.2 × 4.3)
Main machinery: 2 GM 12-567ATL diesels; 1800 hp (1.34 MW); 2 shafts
Speed, knots: 11.6. **Range, miles:** 19 000 at 10.5 kts
Complement: 120 (15 officers)
Military lift: 1500 tons general; 500 tons beaching; 440 m² tank deck; 500 m² main deck storage; can carry 125 troops on long haul; 2—5 ton cranes; 2 LCVPs on davits
Guns: 1 or 3 (Endurance) Bofors 40 mm/60; 80° elevation; 120 rounds/minute to 10 km (5.5 nm); weight of shell 0.89 kg.
2—7.62 mm MGs.
Radars: Navigation: Decca 626; I band.
IFF: UPX 12.

Helicopters: Platform only.

Programmes: Endurance loaned from the US Navy on 1 July 1971 and bought on 5 December 1975. Remainder transferred 4 June 1976. One of the class Perseverence has been cannibalised for spares.
Modernisation: This class has been modernised since 1977. This includes new electrics, new communications, an enclosed bridge and updated command facilities. A goal-post derrick has been fitted forward of the bridge (except in Endurance) and the lattice mast replaced by a pole mast. Excellence has a helicopter pad aft, others have a landing spot amidships. Most have been re-engined and service life extensions continue.
Operational: Used as Command ships and in support of the Army. Resolution is in reserve and may be paid off in 1993.

ENDURANCE 10/1991, John Mortimer

EXCELLENCE (with helo platform aft) 5/1990, G Toremans

4 RPL TYPE (LCM)

RPL 60 RPL 61 RPL 62 RPL 63

Displacement, tons: 151
Dimensions, feet (metres): 120.4 × 28 × 5.9 (36.7 × 8.5 × 1.8)
Main machinery: 2 MAN D2540MLE diesels; 860 hp(m) (632 kW); 2 Schottel props
Speed, knots: 10.7
Complement: 6
Military lift: 2 tanks or 450 troops or 110 tons cargo (fuel or stores)

Comment: First pair built at North Shipyard Point, second pair by Singapore SBEC. First two launched August 1985, next two in October 1985. Cargo deck 86.9 × 21.6 ft (26.5 × 6.6 m). Bow ramp suitable for beaching.

RPL 61 1/1989, Hartmut Ehlers

4 AYER CHAWAN CLASS (LCM)

AYER CHAWAN RPL 54 AYER MERBAN RPL 55 RPL 56 RPL 57

Displacement, tons: 60 light; 150 full load
Dimensions, feet (metres): 88.5 × 22 × 4 (27 × 6.9 × 1.2)
Main machinery: 2 diesels; 650 hp(m) (478 kW); 2 shafts
Speed, knots: 10. **Range, miles:** 300 at 10 kts
Complement: 9
Military lift: 40 tons general or 20 tons fuel or 1 medium tank.

Comment: Built by Vosper Thornycroft Private Ltd, Singapore 1968-69.

AYER CHAWAN 1/1989, Hartmut Ehlers

LANDING CRAFT (LCVP)

EP series

Displacement, tons: 4 full load
Dimensions, feet (metres): 44.6 × 12.1 × 2 (13.6 × 3.7 × 0.6)
Main machinery: 2 MAN D2866 LE diesels; 816 hp(m) (600 kW); 2 Hamilton 362 waterjets
Speed, knots: 20. **Range, miles:** 100 at 20 kts
Complement: 2
Military lift: 4 tons

Comment: Fast Craft, Equipment and Personnel (FCEP), built by Singapore SBEC, are used to transport troops around the Singapore archipelago. They have a single bow ramp and can carry a rifle platoon. More than 100 are in service and more of a stretched version FCU (fast craft utility) are being built. Form part of 195 Squadron.

LCVPs 9/1992, van Ginderen Collection

1 TIGER 40 HOVERCRAFT (LHC)

Displacement, tons: 12
Dimensions, feet (metres): 54.1 × 19.7 (16.5 × 6)
Main machinery: 4 Deutz diesels; 760 hp(m) (559 kW) (for lift and propulsion)
Speed, knots: 35. **Range, miles:** 175 at 35 kts
Military lift: 30 troops or 2.6 tons equipment
Guns: 2—12.7 mm MGs.

Comment: Delivered by Singapore SBEC in 1987 for trials as a logistic support craft. More may be ordered.

TIGER 40 class 3/1987, Singapore Shipbuilding and Engineering

450 ASSAULT CRAFT

Dimensions, feet (metres): 17.7 × 5.9 × 2.3 (5.4 × 1.8 × 0.7)
Main machinery: 1 outboard; 50 hp(m) (37 kW)
Speed, knots: 12
Military lift: 12 troops

Comment: Built by Singapore SBEC. Manportable craft which can carry a section of troops in the rivers and creeks surrounding Singapore island.

SUPPORT SHIPS

1 Ex-US BLUEBIRD CLASS (DIVING SUPPORT VESSEL)

Name	No	Builders	Commissioned
MERCURY (ex-USS *Whippoorwill* MSC 207)	M 101	Bellingham S Y	20 Oct 1955

Displacement, tons: 365 standard; 408 full load
Dimensions, feet (metres): 144 × 28 × 8.2 *(43.9 × 8.5 × 2.5)*
Main machinery: 2 GM 8-268A diesels; 880 hp *(656 kW)*; 2 shafts
Speed, knots: 12. **Range, miles:** 2500 at 10 kts
Complement: 39 (4 officers)
Guns: 1 Oerlikon 20 mm.
Radars: Navigation: Racal Decca; I band.
Sonars: UQS 1; hull-mounted; active minehunting; high frequency.

Comment: Transferred by sale 5 December 1975. Wooden hulled former minesweeper now acts as a platform for diving and salvage operations as part of 194 Squadron. Also used for target towing.

MERCURY   10/1992, John Mortimer

1 DIVING SUPPORT VESSEL

Name	No	Builders	Commissioned
JUPITER	A 102	Singapore SBEC	June 1990

Displacement, tons: 170 full load
Dimensions, feet (metres): 117.5 × 23.3 × 7.5 *(35.8 × 7.1 × 2.3)*
Main machinery: 2 Deutz MWM TBD234V12 diesels; 1360 hp(m) *(1 MW)* sustained; 2 shafts; bow thruster
Speed, knots: 14. **Range, miles:** 200 at 14 kts
Complement: 33 (5 officers)
Guns: 1 Oerlikon 20 mm.
Radars: Navigation: Racal Decca; I band.

Comment: Designed for underwater search and salvage operations and built to German naval standards. Secondary role of surveying. Equipped with a precise navigation system, towed sidescan sonar, and a remotely operated vehicle (ROV). The ship's diving support equipment comprises two high pressure compressors, a two-man decompression chamber, a rubber dinghy with 40 hp outboard motor and a 1.5 ton SWL crane.

JUPITER   9/1991, G Toremans

1 TRAINING SHIP

Name	No	Builders	Commissioned
ENDEAVOUR	P 75	Schiffswerft Oberwinter, Germany	30 Sep 1970

Displacement, tons: 250 full load
Dimensions, feet (metres): 135 × 25 × 8 *(40.9 × 7.6 × 2.4)*
Main machinery: 2 MTU MD diesels; 2600 hp(m) *(1.91 MW)*; 2 shafts
Speed, knots: 20. **Range, miles:** 800 at 8 kts
Complement: 24
Guns: 2 Oerlikon 20 mm.
Radars: Navigation: Racal Decca; I band.

Comment: Training ship for divers.

ENDEAVOUR   1976, Singapore Navy

POLICE PATROL CRAFT

Note: 4 Swift Class transferred from the Navy in February 1993.

24 PATROL CRAFT

PX 10-33

Displacement, tons: 11
Dimensions, feet (metres): 37 × 10.5 × 1.6 *(11 × 3.2 × 0.5)*
Main machinery: 2 MTU diesels; 770 hp(m) *(566 kW)*; 2 shafts
Speed, knots: 30

Comment: Completed 1981 by Sembawang SY.

PX 14   6/1990, F Sadek

23 PATROL CRAFT

PT 1-23

Displacement, tons: 20 full load
Dimensions, feet (metres): 47.6 × 13.8 × 3.9 *(14.5 × 4.2 × 1.2)*
Main machinery: 2 MAN D2542MLE diesels; 1076 hp(m) *(791 kW)*; or MTU 12V 183 TC91 diesels; 1200 hp(m) *(882 kW)* maximum; 2 shafts
Speed, knots: 30. **Range, miles:** 310 at 22 kts
Complement: 4 plus 8 spare berths
Guns: 1—7.62 mm MG.

Comment: First 13 completed by Singapore SBEC between January and August 1984, two more completed February 1987 and eight more (including two Command Boats) in 1989. Of aluminium construction. Four more operated by Customs and Excise. There are differences in the deck houses between earlier and later vessels.

PT 13   1984, Singapore Shipbuilding and Engineering

34 PATROL CRAFT

PC 32-51   PC 52-65

Comment: First 20 were of 21.3 ft *(6.5 m)*, 35 kt craft from Vosper Thornycroft Private Ltd, built in 1978-79. Second series built in the 1980s. Some used by the Navy. All have twin Johnson outboard engines.

PC 61   4/1990, F Sadek

PILOT and CUSTOMS CRAFT

Note: Customs Craft include CE 1-4 and CE 5-8, the latter being sisters to PT 1 Police Craft. Pilot craft have GP numbers and include GP 40-57 built in 1989-90 by Cheoy Lee, Kowloon.

CE 2   1/1989, Hartmut Ehlers

SOLOMON ISLANDS

Control

Tulagi is operated by the Department of Fisheries. SIPV Lata and Savo are operated by the maritime wing of the Royal Solomon Islands Police Force.

Senior Officer

Commissioner of Police:
F Soaks

Personnel

1993: 30 (6 officers)

Prefix to Ships' Names

RSIPV

Mercantile Marine

Lloyd's Register of Shipping:
33 vessels of 7739 tons gross

DELETION

1989 1 LCU

PATROL FORCES

2 PACIFIC FORUM TYPE

Name	No	Builders	Commissioned
LATA	03	Australian Shipbuilding Industries	3 Sep 1988
AUKI	04	Australian Shipbuilding Industries	2 Nov 1991

Displacement, tons: 162 full load
Dimensions, feet (metres): 103.3 × 26.6 × 6.9 *(31.5 × 8.1 × 2.1)*
Main machinery: 2 Caterpillar 3516TA diesels; 4400 hp *(3.28 MW)* sustained; 2 shafts
Speed, knots: 20. **Range, miles:** 2500 at 12 kts
Complement: 14 (1 officer)
Guns: 3—12.7 mm MGs (not always mounted).
Radars: Surface search: Furuno 1011; I band.

Comment: Built under the Australian Defence Co-operation Programme. Training, operational and technical assistance provided by the Royal Australian Navy. Aluminium construction. Nominal endurance of 10 days.

LATA   5/1992, van Ginderen Collection

2 LANDING CRAFT

LIGOMO 3   ULUSAGE

Measurement, tons: 105 dwt
Main machinery: 2 diesels; 2 shafts
Speed, knots: 9

Comment: Built by Carpenter BY, Suva in 1981. 27 m in length.

2 TUGS

SOLOMAN ATU   SOLOMAN KARIQUA

Comment: Acquired in 1981. 140 tons and capable of 9 kts.

1 PATROL CRAFT

SAVO 02

Dimensions, feet (metres): 82 × 25.8 × 6.2 *(25 × 7.9 × 1.9)*
Main machinery: 2 Caterpillar 3516TA diesels; 4400 hp *(3.28 MW)* sustained; 2 shafts
Speed, knots: 36. **Range, miles:** 3000 at 12 kts

Comment: Built by ASI, Western Australia in 1984 as a prototype for the Pacific Forum class.

SAVO   5/1992, van Ginderen Collection

1 CARPENTARIA CLASS

TULAGI 01

Displacement, tons: 27 full load
Dimensions, feet (metres): 51.5 × 15.7 × 4.3 *(15.7 × 4.8 × 1.3)*
Main machinery: 2 Detroit 12V-71TA diesels; 840 hp *(626 kW)* sustained; 2 shafts
Speed, knots: 28. **Range, miles:** 950 at 18 kts
Complement: 10
Guns: 1—7.62 mm MG.
Radars: Surface search: Racal Decca; I band.

Comment: Built by De Havilland Marine, Homebush Bay, Australia. Launched December 1978. Arrived Solomon Islands 4 May 1979.

TULAGI   1984, van Ginderen Collection

SOMALIA

General

After the revolution in January 1991, the Navy effectively ceased to exist. The only vessels which were not sunk were one Polnochny LST and four Mol class attack craft. All were ransacked with every fixture and fitting removed by mid-1991, and two of the Mol class sank in 1992.

Bases

Berbera, Mogadishu and Kismayu

Mercantile Marine

Lloyd's Register of Shipping:
28 vessels of 17 340 tons gross

SOUTH AFRICA

Headquarters' Appointments

Chief of the Navy:
Vice Admiral R C Simpson-Anderson
Chief of Naval Support:
Rear Admiral H J M Trainer
Chief of Naval Operations:
Rear Admiral J F Retief

Personnel

(a) 1993: 4200
(b) Voluntary service plus 12 months' compulsory national service and 720 days' camps

Prefix to Ships' Names

SAS (South African Ship/Suid Afrikaanse Skip)

Bases

Pretoria: Headquarters and Command Centre
Durban: Attack Craft
Simonstown: Remainder of the Fleet
Saldanha Bay (basic training), Gordon's Bay (officer training).

Marine Corps

The Marine Branch was re-established in 1979 after its earlier stand-down in 1957. Disbanded again in 1990 as part of the defence cuts.

Future Construction

In December 1990 the Navy reported that six of its original nine Minister class FACs were currently in service, and that the operational life of the craft was expected to end around 2000. The plan was to replace the FACs by corvettes, carrying a medium helicopter, which would have restored the Navy's surface ASW capability. In August 1991 further government funding cuts forced the Navy to abandon plans to build four armed 2000 ton corvettes. Cancellation has meant that the Minister class will have to serve at least five years longer than expected, up to 2005, and a replacement programme must start in the mid-1990s if the Navy is to remain a viable force.

Mercantile Marine

Lloyd's Register of Shipping:
219 vessels of 336 715 tons gross

DELETIONS

Frigates

1990 *President Pretorius* (reserve), *President Steyn* (sunk)

SUBMARINES

3 FRENCH DAPHNE CLASS

Name	No	Builders	Laid down	Launched	Commissioned
MARIA VAN RIEBEECK	S 97	Dubigeon—Normandie, Nantes-Chantenay	14 Mar 1968	18 Mar 1969	22 June 1970
EMILY HOBHOUSE	S 98	Dubigeon—Normandie, Nantes-Chantenay	18 Nov 1968	24 Oct 1969	25 Jan 1971
JOHANNA VAN DER MERWE	S 99	Dubigeon—Normandie, Nantes-Chantenay	24 Apr 1969	21 July 1970	21 July 1971

Displacement, tons: 869 surfaced; 1043 dived
Dimensions, feet (metres): 189.6 × 22.3 × 15.1 *(57.8 × 6.8 × 4.6)*
Main machinery: Diesel-electric; 2 SEMT-Pielstick 12 PA4 V 185 diesels; 2450 hp(m) *(1.8 MW)*; 2 Jeumont Schneider alternators; 1.7 MW; 2 motors; 2600 hp(m) *(1.9 MW)*; 2 shafts
Speed, knots: 13.5 surfaced; 16 dived
Range, miles: 4500 at 5 kts snorting; 2700 at 12.5 kts surfaced
Complement: 47 (6 officers)

Torpedoes: 12—21.7 in *(550 mm)* (8 bow, 4 stern) tubes. ECAN E15; dual purpose; passive homing to 12 km *(6.6 nm)* at 25 kts; warhead 300 kg; or ECAN L4/L5 to 9.5 km *(5.1 nm)*. No reloads.
Countermeasures: ESM: ARUD; radar warning.
Fire control: Trivetts-UEC weapon control system.
Radars: Surface search: Thomson-CSF Calypso II; I band; range 31 km *(17 nm)* for 10 m² target.
Sonars: Thomson Sintra DUUA 2; hull-mounted; active/passive search and attack; 8.4 kHz active.
Thomson Sintra DUUX 2; passive range finding.
Thomson Sintra DSUV 2; passive search; medium frequency.

Programmes: First submarines ordered for the South African Navy. Armscor are conducting a feasibility study into the local construction of additional submarines by Dorbyl Shipbuilders, Durban. Design would be similar to German S 209 class.

Modernisation: Weapon systems upgrading (including sonar) as well as improved habitability as part of a mid-life improvement programme. *Emily Hobhouse* completed in July 1988, *Van der Merwe* in late 1990.

Structure: French Daphne design, similar to those built in France for that country, Pakistan and Portugal and also built in Spain. Diving depth, 300 m *(985 ft)*.

MARIA VAN RIEBEECK 10/1992, Robert Pabst

LIGHT FORCES

9 MINISTER CLASS (FAST ATTACK CRAFT—MISSILE)

Name	No	Builders	Commissioned
JAN SMUTS	P 1561	Haifa Shipyard	18 July 1977
P W BOTHA	P 1562	Haifa Shipyard	2 Dec 1977
FREDERIC CRESSWELL	P 1563	Haifa Shipyard	6 Apr 1978
JIM FOUCHÉ	P 1564	Sandock Austral, Durban	22 Dec 1978
FRANS ERASMUS	P 1565	Sandock Austral, Durban	27 July 1979
OSWALD PIROW	P 1566	Sandock Austral, Durban	4 Mar 1980
HENDRIK MENTZ	P 1567	Sandock Austral, Durban	11 Feb 1983
KOBIE COETSEE	P 1568	Sandock Austral, Durban	11 Feb 1983
MAGNUS MALAN	P 1569	Sandock Austral, Durban	4 July 1986

Displacement, tons: 430 full load
Dimensions, feet (metres): 204 × 25 × 8 *(62.2 × 7.8 × 2.4)*
Main machinery: 4 Maybach MTU 16V 965 TB91 diesels; 15 000 hp(m) *(11 MW)* sustained; 4 shafts
Speed, knots: 32. **Range, miles:** 1500 at 30 kts; 3600+ at economical speed
Complement: 47 (7 officers)

Missiles: SSM: 8 Skerpioen; active radar or optical guidance; semi-active radar homing to 36 km *(19.4 nm)* at 0.7 Mach; warhead 75 kg. Another pair may be mounted. Skerpioen is an Israeli Gabriel II built under licence in South Africa.
Guns: 2 OTO Melara 3 in *(76 mm)*/62 compact; 85° elevation; 85 rounds/minute to 16 km *(8.7 nm)*; weight of shell 6 kg; 500 rounds per gun.
2 Oerlikon 20 mm. 2—12.7 mm MGs.
Countermeasures: Decoys: 4 launchers for chaff.
ESM: Elta; radar warning.
Combat data systems: Mini action data automation with Link.
Radars: Air/surface search: Thomson-CSF Triton; G band; range 33 km *(18 nm)* for 2 m² target.
Fire control: Selenia RTN 10X; I/J band; range 40 km *(22 nm)*.

Programmes: Contract signed with Israel in late 1974 for this class, similar to Saar 4 class. Three built in Haifa and reached South Africa in July 1978. The ninth craft launched late March 1986. Three more improved vessels of this class were ordered but subsequently cancelled. The last of the class was finally christened in March 1992.
Modernisation: *P W Botha* recommissioned 3 November 1986 after modernisation; *Kobie Coetsee* in July 1988; *Oswald Pirow* in May 1989. The cancellation of the corvette replacements in 1991 has led to the expansion of the upgrade programme into a major ship-life extension. This includes a new communications refit, improvements to sensors, a third-generation target designation assembly, a computer-assisted action information system served by data links, improvements to fire control, a complete overhaul of the Skorpioen missiles, and a new engine room monitoring system.

OSWALD PIROW 3/1992, Peter Humphries

P W BOTHA 1/1993, Peter Humphries

SHIPBORNE AIRCRAFT

Note: Super Frelon and Wasp helicopters paid off in 1990.

Numbers/Type: 10 Aerospatiale SA 330E/H/J Puma.
Operational speed: 139 kts *(258 km/h)*.
Service ceiling: 15 750 ft *(4800 m)*.
Range: 297 nm *(550 km)*.
Role/Weapon systems: Support helicopter; allocated by SAAF for naval duties and can be embarked in both AORs and in *Agulhas*. Sensors: Doppler navigation, some with search radar. Weapons: Unarmed but can mount Armscor 30 mm Ratler.

LAND-BASED MARITIME AIRCRAFT

Note: Albatross aircraft were withdrawn from service in 1990.

Numbers/Type: 20 Douglas Turbodaks.
Operational speed: 161 kts *(298 km/h)*.
Service ceiling: 24 000 ft *(7315 m)*.
Range: 1390 nm *(2575 km)*.
Role/Weapon systems: A number of Dakotas are being converted for MR/SAR and other tasks. Additional fuel tanks extend the range to 2620 nm *(4800 km)*. Sensors: Search radar and navigation aids. Weapons: Unarmed.

MINE WARFARE FORCES

4 BRITISH TON CLASS (MINESWEEPERS)

Name	No	Builders	Commissioned
KIMBERLEY (ex-HMS *Stratton*)	M 1210	Dorset Yacht Co	1958
WALVISBAAI (ex-HMS *Packington*)	M 1214	Harland & Wolff, Belfast	1959
EAST LONDON (ex-HMS *Chilton*)	M 1215	Cook Welton and Gemmell	1958
WINDHOEK	M 1498	Thornycroft, Southampton	1959

Displacement, tons: 360 standard; 440 full load
Dimensions, feet (metres): 153 × 28.9 × 8.2 *(46.6 × 8.8 × 2.5)*
Main machinery: 2 Paxman Deltic 18A-7A diesels; 3000 hp *(2.24 MW)*; 2 shafts
Speed, knots: 15. **Range, miles:** 2300 at 13 kts
Complement: 27
Guns: 1 Bofors 40 mm/60; 80° elevation; 120 rounds/minute to 10 km *(5.5 nm)*; weight of shell 0.89 kg.
 2 Oerlikon 20 mm. 2—7.62 mm MGs.
Radars: Navigation: Racal Decca; I band.

Comment: The last four survivors of a class of 10. Six were paid off in 1987 because of a shortage of trained personnel. Major modernisation started in 1991 with a new MCM control system and renewal of decks and frames. *Kimberley* converted to minehunter 1977-78 but has now reverted to minesweeping duties.

WINDHOEK *4/1992, Peter Humphries*

4 RIVER CLASS (COASTAL MINEHUNTERS)

UMKOMAAS   UMHLOTI   UMZIMKULU   UMGENI

Displacement, tons: 380 full load
Dimensions, feet (metres): 157.5 × 27.9 × 7.5 *(48 × 8.5 × 2.3)*
Main machinery: 2 MTU diesels; 4500 hp(m) *(3.3 MW)*; 2 shafts
Speed, knots: 15
Complement: 37 (7 officers)
Guns: 1 Oerlikon 20 mm. 2—12.7 mm MGs.
Countermeasures: MCM: 2 PAP remote-controlled submersibles.
Radars: Navigation: Decca; I band.
Sonars: Klein VDS; sidescan; high frequency.

Comment: Completed by Sandock Austral, Durban. The design derived from the German Schütze class. First one reported to have commissioned 13 January 1981. Wooden hulls. Minehunting gear was mostly taken from the deleted Ton class. Reported that DUBM 21 hull-mounted sonar was fitted on build but this is apparently incorrect. Four more are to be built in due course to replace the surviving Ton class.

UMKOMAAS *10/1992, Robert Pabst*

SURVEY SHIP

Note: A trawler *Margit Rye* was bought in 1989 from Denmark and used as an AGS. Laid up in 1992.

Name	No	Builders	Commissioned
PROTEA	A 324	Yarrow (Shipbuilders) Ltd	23 May 1972

Displacement, tons: 2733 full load
Dimensions, feet (metres): 260.1 × 49.1 × 15.6 *(79.3 × 15 × 4.7)*
Main machinery: Diesel-electric; 3 Paxman 12YJCM diesels; 3840 hp *(2.68 MW)* sustained; 3 generators; 1 motor; 2000 hp *(1.49 MW)*; 1 shaft; cp prop; bow thruster
Speed, knots: 14. **Range, miles:** 12 000 at 11 kts
Complement: 114 (10 officers)
Helicopters: 1 Alouette III.

Comment: Laid down 20 July 1970. Launched 14 July 1971. RN Hecla class equipped for hydrographic survey with limited facilities for the collection of oceanographical data and for this purpose fitted with special communications equipment, naval surveying gear, survey launches and facilities for helicopter operations. Hull strengthened for navigation in ice and fitted with a passive roll stabilisation system.

PROTEA *5/1992, Giorgio Ghiglione*

FLEET REPLENISHMENT SHIPS

Name	No	Builders	Commissioned
TAFELBERG (ex-*Annam*)	A 243	Nakskovs Skibsvaerft, Denmark	1959

Displacement, tons: 27 000 full load
Measurement, tons: 12 500 gross; 18 980 dwt
Dimensions, feet (metres): 559.8 × 72.1 × 30.2 *(170.6 × 21.9 × 9.2)*
Main machinery: 1 Burmeister & Wain diesel; 8420 hp(m) *(6.19 MW)*; 1 shaft
Speed, knots: 15.5
Complement: 100 plus 60 midshipmen
Military lift: 1000 troops plus 6 Delta 80 LCUs
Guns: 2 Bofors 40 mm. 2 Oerlikon 20 mm.
Helicopters: 2 SA 330H/J Puma.

Comment: Built as Danish East Asiatic Co tanker. Launched on 20 June 1958. Purchased by the Navy in 1965. Accommodation rehabilitated by Barens Shipbuilding & Engineering Co, Durban with extra accommodation, air-conditioning, re-wiring for additional equipment, new upper RAS (replenishment at sea) deck to contain gantries, re-fuelling pipes. Remainder of conversion by James Brown & Hamer, Durban. A helicopter flight deck was added aft during refit in 1975. One fuel and one stores replenishment station each side. During a major refit 1983-84 armament was added and the flight deck, hangar and sick-bay were enlarged with additional accommodation. A major engine problem in 1992 has kept her alongside and the ship is to be scrapped in 1993, the crew transferring to *Juvent*. Refitted again in 1991 with facilities for 60 midshipmen.

TAFELBERG *4/1992, Peter Humphries*

Name	No	Builders	Commissioned
Ex-JUVENT	—	Kherson Shipyard	Mar 1992

Displacement, tons: 21 025 full load
Dimensions, feet (metres): 545.6 × 75.5 × 29.5 *(166.3 × 23 × 9)*
Main machinery: 1 diesel; 1 shaft
Speed, knots: 17. **Range, Miles:** 8000 at 15 kts
Helicopters: 1 SA 330H/J Puma.

Comment: Russian arctic supply ship acquired in early 1993 to replace *Tafelberg*. Has a hangar and flight deck aft, and a side Ro-Ro ramp. After an initial refit, the ship is to be operated for a short time before full conversion at Simonstown to meet naval requirements.

SOUTH AFRICA / Fleet replenishment ships — Air sea rescue launches

Name	No	Builders	Commissioned
DRAKENSBERG	A 301	Sandock Austral, Durban	11 Nov 1987

Displacement, tons: 6000 light; 12 500 full load
Dimensions, feet (metres): 482.3 × 64 × 25.9 *(147 × 19.5 × 7.9)*
Main machinery: 2 diesels; 16 320 hp(m) *(12 MW)*; 1 shaft; cp prop; bow thruster
Speed, knots: 20+
Complement: 96 (10 officers)
Cargo capacity: 5500 tons fuel; 750 tons ammunition and dry stores; 2 Delta 80 LCUs
Guns: 4 Oerlikon 20 mm.
Helicopters: 2 SA 330H/J Puma.

Comment: The largest ship built in South Africa and the first naval vessel to be completely designed in that country. In addition to her replenishment role she is employed on SAR, patrol and surveillance with a considerable potential for disaster relief. Laid down in August 1984 and launched 24 April 1986. Two abeam positions and astern fuelling, jackstay and vertrep. Two helicopter landing spots. Can be used as a mother ship for small craft and for troop transport and commando insertion operations.

DRAKENSBERG 1/1993, Robert Pabst

DRAKENSBERG 7/1991, van Ginderen Collection

TORPEDO RECOVERY VESSEL

Name	No	Builders	Commissioned
FLEUR	P 3148	Dorman Long, Durban	3 Dec 1969

Displacement, tons: 220 standard; 257 full load
Dimensions, feet (metres): 121.5 × 27.5 × 11.1 *(37 × 8.4 × 3.4)*
Main machinery: 2 Paxman 6YJCM diesels; 1400 hp *(1.04 MW)* sustained; 2 shafts
Speed, knots: 14
Complement: 22 (4 officers)
Radars: Navigation: Decca; I band.

Comment: Combined torpedo recovery vessel and diving tender with recompression chamber.

FLEUR 11/1992, Robert Pabst

HARBOUR PATROL VESSELS

8 DELTA 80 CLASS (LCU)

Displacement, tons: 5.5 full load
Dimensions, feet (metres): 27.2 × 10.2 × 3 *(8.3 × 3.1 × 0.9)*
Main machinery: 2 outboards; 350 hp *(261 kW)*
Speed, knots: 37. **Range, miles:** 150 at 35 kts
Complement: 5

Comment: Six can be carried in *Tafelberg* and two in *Drakensberg*.

3 TYPE T 2212 COASTGUARD CRAFT

Displacement, tons: 23 full load
Dimensions, feet (metres): 72.2 × 23 × 3 *(22 × 7 × 0.9)*
Main machinery: 2 ADE 444 TI 12V diesels; 2000 hp *(1.5 MW)*; 2 Castoldi waterjets
Speed, knots: 37. **Range, miles:** 530 at 30 kts
Complement: 4 (1 officer)
Guns: 1 MG-151 20 mm. 6—107 mm mortars.
Fire control: Hesis optical director.
Radars: Surface search: I band.

Comment: Twin hulled catamarans of GRP sandwich construction. Built by T Craft International, Cape Town. Capable of carrying up to 15 people. First three ordered in mid-1991.

COASTGUARD 1991, T Craft International

30 NAMACURRA TYPE

Y 1501-1530

Displacement, tons: 5 full load
Dimensions, feet (metres): 29.5 × 9 × 2.8 *(9 × 2.7 × 0.8)*
Complement: 4
Guns: 1—12.7 mm MG. 2—7.62 mm MGs.
Depth charges: 1 rack.

Comment: Built in South Africa in 1980-81. Can be transported by road.

NAMACURRA 12/1981, South African Navy

AIR SEA RESCUE LAUNCHES

1 FAIREY MARINE TRACKER CLASS

P 1555

Displacement, tons: 26
Dimensions, feet (metres): 64 × 16 × 5 *(19.5 × 4.9 × 1.5)*
Main machinery: 2 GM diesels; 1120 hp *(836 kW)*; 2 shafts
Speed, knots: 28. **Range, miles:** 650 at 18 kts
Complement: 11

Comment: Built by Groves and Gutteridge, Cowes and commissioned in 1973.

1 KRÖGERWERFT TYPE

P 1551

Displacement, tons: 82 full load
Dimensions, feet (metres): 96 × 19 × 4 *(29.3 × 5.8 × 1.2)*
Main machinery: 2 MTU MD diesels; 4480 hp(m) *(3.29 MW)*; 2 shafts
Speed, knots: 30. **Range, miles:** 1000 at 30 kts
Complement: 12

Comment: Built by Krögerwerft, Rendsburg and commissioned in 1961. Can carry a 12.7 mm MG. Sister ship was wrecked in Saldanha Bay in 1988.

P 1551 4/1992, Robert Pabst

TUGS

DE MIST

Displacement, tons: 275
Dimensions, feet (metres): 111.5 × 29.5 × 9.8 *(34 × 9 × 3)*
Main machinery: 2 Lister-Blackstone diesels; 2400 hp *(1.79 MW)*; 2 Voith-Schneider props
Speed, knots: 12

Comment: Completed by Dorman Long, Durban in December 1978.

DE NEYS

Displacement, tons: 170
Dimensions, feet (metres): 94 × 26.5 × 15.7 *(28.7 × 8.7 × 4.8)*
Main machinery: 2 Lister-Blackstone diesels; 1216 hp *(907 kW)*; 2 Voith-Schneider props
Speed, knots: 9
Complement: 10

Comment: Built by Globe Engineering, Cape Town and commissioned 23 July 1969.

DE NOORDE

Displacement, tons: 180
Dimensions, feet (metres): 104.5 × 25 × 15 *(31.9 × 7.6 × 4.6)*
Main machinery: 2 Lister-Blackstone diesels; 1216 hp *(907 kW)*; 2 Voith-Schneider props
Speed, knots: 8
Complement: 10

Comment: Built by Globe Engineering, Cape Town and commissioned in December 1961.

DEPARTMENT OF TRANSPORT

1 ANTARCTIC SURVEY AND SUPPLY VESSEL

S A AGULHAS

Measurement, tons: 5353 gross
Dimensions, feet (metres): 358.3 × 59 × 19 *(109.2 × 18 × 5.8)*
Main machinery: 2 Mirrlees-Blackstone K6 major diesels; 6600 hp *(4.49 MW)*; 1 shaft; bow and stern thrusters
Speed, knots: 14. **Range, miles:** 8200 at 14 kts
Complement: 40 plus 92 spare berths
Radars: Navigation: Racal Decca; I band.
Helicopters: 2 SA 330J Puma.

Comment: Built by Mitsubishi, Shimonoseki and commissioned 31 January 1978. Red hull and white superstructure. Civilian manned. Major refit March to October 1992; 25 ton crane moved forward, transverse thrusters and roll damping fitted, improved navigation and communications equipment. A hinged hatch has been fitted at the stern to recover towed equipment. All scientific spaces improved.

DE NEYS   3/1992, Peter Humphries

S A AGULHAS   10/1992, Robert Pabst

SPAIN

Headquarters' Appointments

Chief of the Defence Staff:
  Admiral Gonzalo Rodriguez Martin-Granizo
Chief of the Naval Staff:
  Admiral Carlos Vila Miranda
Second Chief of the Naval Staff:
  Vice Admiral Eduardo Liberal Lucini
Chief of Fleet Support:
  Admiral José Maria Gurucharri Martinez

Commands

Commander-in-Chief of the Fleet:
  Admiral Pedro Regalado Aznar
Commander-in-Chief, Cantabrian Zone:
  Admiral Francisco J Lopez de Arenosa Diaz
Commander-in-Chief, Straits Zone:
  Vice Admiral José Antonio Serrano Punyed
Commander-in-Chief, Mediterranean Zone:
  Admiral Miguel J Garcia de Lomas Ristori
Commander-in-Chief, Canarias Zone:
  Vice Admiral José E Delgado Manzanares
Commander-in-Chief, Central Zone:
  Vice Admiral Justino Antón Pérez-Pardo
Commandant General, Marines:
  Major General José Manuel Estévez Ons

Diplomatic Representation

Naval Attaché in Bonn:
  Commander Miguel Angel Castillo Cuervo-Arango
Naval Attaché in Brasilia:
  Commander José Luis Gamboa Ballester
Naval Attaché in Buenos Aires:
  Commander Francisco J Fontán Suances
Naval Attaché in Lisbon:
  Captain Luis Molina Sainz-Diez
Naval Attaché in London:
  Captain José Maria Pascual del Río
Naval Attaché in Paris:
  Commander Antonio M Ugarte de la Azuela
Naval Attaché in Rome:
  Commander Santiago Zárate y López de Roda
Naval Attaché in Santiago:
  Captain Santiago Gibert Crespo
Naval Attaché in Washington:
  Captain Miguel Fernández Fernández
Naval Attaché in The Hague:
  Captain Carlos Rodriguez Casau
Naval Attaché in Morocco:
  Commander Ramón López Alemanij

Personnel

(a) 1993: 29 300 (2700 officers) plus 8500 civilians
    Marine Corps: 6200 (470 officers)
(b) 9 months' national service

Bases

Ferrol: Cantabrian Zone HQ—Ferrol arsenal, support centre at La Graña, naval school at Marín, Pontevedra, electronics school at Vigo, Pontevedra
Cadiz: Straits Zone HQ—La Carraca arsenal, fleet command HQ and naval air base at Rota, amphibious base at Puntales, Tarifa small ships' base
Cartagena: Mediterranean Zone HQ—Cartagena arsenal, underwater weapons and divers school at La Algameca; support base at Mahón, Minorca and at Porto Pi, Majorca, submarine weapons schools at La Algameca and Porto Pi base, Majorca
Las Palmas: Canaries Zone HQ—Las Palmas arsenal

Naval Air Service (see *Shipborne Aircraft* section)

Type	Escuadrilla
AB 212ASW (with AS-12 missiles)	3
Twin Comanche ⎱	4
Cessna Citation ⎰	
Sikorsky SH-3D/G Sea King (with AS-12 missiles) ⎱	5
Sikorsky SH-3E Sea King (AEW) ⎰	
Hughes 500M (Training)	6
Matador AV-8A (Harrier) ⎱	8
Matador TAV-8A (Harrier) ⎰	
EAV-8B Bravo	9
Sikorsky SH-60B Seahawk	10

Marine Corps

This consists of four 'Tercios' (intermediate between a Regiment and a Brigade) based at Ferrol, Cartagena and Cádiz (two). Two Groups (intermediate between a Battalion and a Regiment) are based in Madrid and Las Palmas (Canary Islands). These Tercios and Groups are charged with the protection of their naval bases and establishments.
The Tercio de Armada is based at San Fernando, Cádiz and is the landing force available for immediate embarkation. The Tercio de Armada, brigade-sized, consists of two landing battalions plus a special operations unit (UOE) of 170 men, a support logistic battalion, a communications company, a tank company (with 17 M-48E and one M-88 recovery vehicle, plus 17 Scorpion light tanks), one amphibious tractors company (19 LVT-7 in three versions, possibly to be replaced by the VMA Pegaso 8331), one artillery battalion (six M109A2 with six M-992 ammunition vehicles, 12 towed OTO Melara 105 mm L14 howitzers), one anti-tank company with 12 TOW and 16/18 Dragon missile launchers. Infantry support weapons include 106 mm M40 recoilless rifles, 120, 81 and 60 mm ECIA mortars, Instalaza 90 mm and LAWS 72 mm anti-tank rocket launchers, Rasura infantry locating radars. Also armoured Pegaso BLR-400 infantry carriers (not in Tercio de Armada) and Pegaso 3550 three ton amphibious trucks.
There are plans for a Fuerza de Intervencion Rápida (FIR). This would include Marines and Group Delta amphibious ships.

Guardia Civil del Mar

Started operations in 1992. For details, see end of section.

Fleet Deployment

1. Flota
   (a) Grupo Aeronaval Alfa: (based at Rota)
       Principe de Asturias with appropriate escorts
   (b) Escuadrillas de Escoltas:
       21st Squadron; 6 Descubierta class (based at Cartagena)
       31st Squadron; 5 Baleares class (based at Ferrol)
       41st Squadron; 4 Santa Maria class (based at Rota)
   (c) Grupo Anfibio Delta: (based at Puntales, Cádiz)
       All Amphibious Forces
   (d) Fuerza de Medidas contra Minas: (based at Cartagena from September 1990)
       8 MSCs and 4 MSOs
   (e) Flotilla de Submarinos: (based at Cartagena)
       All submarines
2. Support units, Cantabrian Zone:
   1 Ocean Tug, 2 Water-boats, 8 Tugs, 4 Patrol Ships, 5 Large Patrol Craft, 7 Coastal Patrol Craft, 10 Inshore Patrol Craft, 1 Inshore/River Patrol Launch, 3 Sail Training Ships, 5 Training Craft
3. Support units, Straits Zone:
   6 Oceanographic Ships, 1 Sail Training Ship, 8 Fast Attack Craft, 1 Transport, 1 Ocean Tug, 7 Tugs, 2 Water-boats, 13 Coastal Patrol Craft, 6 Inshore Patrol Craft
4. Support units, Mediterranean Zone:
   4 Fast Attack Craft, 1 Boom Defence Vessel, 1 Water-boat, 1 Large Patrol Craft, 2 Inshore/River Patrol Launch, 11 Coastal Patrol Craft, 14 Inshore Patrol Craft, 7 Tugs, 1 Frogman Support Ship
5. Support units, Canaries Zone:
   1 Water-boat, 2 Ocean Tugs, 4 Large Patrol Craft, 7 Coastal Patrol Craft, 2 Tugs

Mercantile Marine

Lloyd's Register of Shipping:
  2190 vessels of 3 224 604 tons gross

618 SPAIN / Introduction — Submarines

Strength of the Fleet

Type	Active	Building (Planned)
Submarines—Patrol	8	(4)
Aircraft Carrier	1	—
Frigates	15	2 (4)
Corvettes	4	—
Offshore Patrol Vessels	4	—
Fast Attack Craft—Missile/Gun	13	(1)
Large Patrol Craft	14	—
Coastal Patrol Craft	37	—
Inshore Patrol Craft	30	—
Attack Transports	2	—
LPDs	—	(2)
LSTs	2	—
LCTs	3	—
LCU/LCM/LCP	55	—
Hovercraft	1	—
Minesweepers	12	(4)
Minehunters	—	4
Survey Ships	8	—
Replenishment Tankers	1	1
Harbour Tankers	11	—
Transport	1	—
Training Ships	9	—
Tugs (Ocean, Coastal and Harbour)	39	—

DELETIONS

Destroyers

1991 *Gravina, Blas de Lezo*
1992 *Méndez Núñez, Lángara*

Offshore Patrol Vessels

1991 *Princesa, Nautilus*
1992 *Atrevida, Villa de Bilbao*

Amphibious Forces

1990 *Conde del Venadito*

Light Forces

1990 *Sálvora, P 103, P 126, P 236-237*

Support Ships

1990 *Azor*
1991 *Y 234* (tanker)
1992 *Y 322, Y 332, Y 112, Y 233, Y 136*

PENNANT LIST

Submarines

S 61	Delfin
S 62	Tonina
S 63	Marsopa
S 64	Narval
S 71	Galerna
S 72	Siroco
S 73	Mistral
S 74	Tramontana

Aircraft Carriers

R 11	Principe de Asturias

Frigates

F 31	Descubierta
F 32	Diana
F 33	Infanta Elena
F 34	Infanta Cristina
F 35	Cazadora
F 36	Vencedora
F 71	Baleares
F 72	Andalucia
F 73	Cataluña
F 74	Asturias
F 75	Extremadura
F 81	Santa Maria
F 82	Victoria
F 83	Numancia
F 84	Reina Sofía
F 85	Navarra (bldg)
F 86	Canarias (bldg)

Offshore Patrol Vessels

P 71	Serviola
P 72	Centinela
P 73	Vigia
P 74	Atalaya

Light Forces

P 01	Lazaga
P 02	Alsedo
P 03	Cadarso
P 04	Villamil
P 05	Bonifaz
P 06	Recalde
P 11	Barceló
P 12	Laya
P 13	Javier Quiroga
P 14	Ordóñez
P 15	Acevedo
P 16	Cándido Pérez
P 21	Anaga
P 22	Tagomago
P 23	Marola
P 24	Mouro
P 25	Grosa
P 26	Medas
P 27	Izaro
P 28	Tabarca
P 29	Deva
P 30	Bergantin
P 31	Conejera
P 32	Dragonera
P 33	Espalmador
P 34	Alcanada
P 41	Cormoran
P 51	Nalón
P 52	Ulla
P 54	Turia
P 61	Chilreu
P 81	Toralla
P 82	Formentor
P 201	Cabo Fradera

Amphibious Forces

L 11	Velasco
L 12	Martin Alvarez
L 21	Castilla
L 22	Aragón

Mine Warfare Forces

M 21	Júcar
M 22	Ebro
M 23	Duero
M 24	Tajo
M 25	Genil
M 26	Odiel
M 27	Sil
M 28	Miño
M 41	Guadalete
M 42	Guadalmedina
M 43	Guadalquivir
M 44	Guadiana

Survey Ships

A 21	Castor
A 22	Pollux
A 23	Antares
A 24	Rigel
A 31	Malaspina
A 32	Tofiño
A 33	Hesperides
A 111	Alerta

Service Forces

A 01	Contramaestre Casado
A 11	Mar del Norte
A 12	Poseidón
A 13	Ciclope
A 41	Cartagena
A 42	Cádiz
A 43	Ferrol
A 51	Mahón
A 52	Las Palmas
A 61	Contramaestre Castelló
A 62	Maquinista Mácias
A 63	Torpedista Hernández
A 64	Fogonero Bañobre
A 65	Marinero Jarana
A 66	Condestable Zaragoza
A 71	Juan Sebastian de Elcano
A 72	Arosa
A 73	Hispania
A 74	La Graciosa
A 81	Guardiamarina Barrutia
A 82	Guardiamarina Salas
A 83	Guardiamarina Godínez
A 84	Guardiamarina Rull
A 85	Guardiamarina Chereguini
A 101	Mar Caribe
A 102	Mar Rojo
Y 381	Sanson
Y 562	Nereida
Y 563	Proserpina

SUBMARINES

Note: Four Scorpene class (S 80) are planned to start construction in 1999. Being developed with DCN, France. Probably about 2000 tons and 300 m with a complement of 35.

4 DELFIN CLASS (FRENCH DAPHNE)

Name	No	Builders	Laid down	Launched	Commissioned
DELFIN	S 61	Bazán, Cartagena	13 Aug 1968	25 Mar 1972	3 May 1973
TONINA	S 62	Bazán, Cartagena	2 Mar 1970	3 Oct 1972	10 July 1973
MARSOPA	S 63	Bazán, Cartagena	19 Mar 1971	15 Mar 1974	12 Apr 1975
NARVAL	S 64	Bazán, Cartagena	24 Apr 1972	14 Dec 1974	22 Nov 1975

Displacement, tons: 869 surfaced; 1043 dived
Dimensions, feet (metres): 189.6 × 22.3 × 15.1 *(57.8 × 6.8 × 4.6)*
Main machinery: Diesel-electric; 2 SEMT-Pielstick 12 PA4 V 185 diesels; 2450 hp(m) *(1.8 MW)*; 2 Jeumont Schneider alternators; 1.7 MW; 2 motors; 2600 hp(m) *(1.9 MW)*; 2 shafts
Speed, knots: 13.2 surfaced; 15.5 dived
Range, miles: 4300 snorting at 7.5 kts; 2710 surfaced at 12.5 kts
Complement: 47 (6 officers)
Torpedoes: 12—21.7 in *(550 mm)* (8 bow, 4 stern) tubes. 12 combination of (a) ECAN L5 Mod 3/4; dual purpose; active/passive homing to 9.5 km *(5.1 nm)* at 35 kts; warhead 150 kg; depth to 550 m *(1800 ft)*.
(b) ECAN F17 Mod 2; wire-guided; active/passive homing to 20 km *(10.8 nm)* at 40 kts; warhead 250 kg; depth 600 m *(1970 ft)*.
Mines: 12 in lieu of torpedoes.
Countermeasures: ESM: THORN EMI Manta; radar warning.
Radars: Surface search: Thomson-CSF DRUA 31 or 33A; I band.
Sonars: Thomson Sintra DSUV 22; passive search and attack; medium frequency.
Thomson Sintra DUUA 2A; active search and attack; 8 or 8.4 kHz active.

Programmes: First pair ordered 26 December 1966 and second pair in March 1970. Identical to the French Daphne class and built with extensive French assistance.
Modernisation: The class has been taken in hand since 1983 for modernisation of sonar (DUUA 2A for DUUA 1), updating of fire control and torpedo handling. It is possible that torpedo tubes were also linered to 21 in *(533 mm)*. Last one completed at the end of 1988. ESM updated in 1990-91.
Structure: Diving depth, 300 m *(984 ft)*.

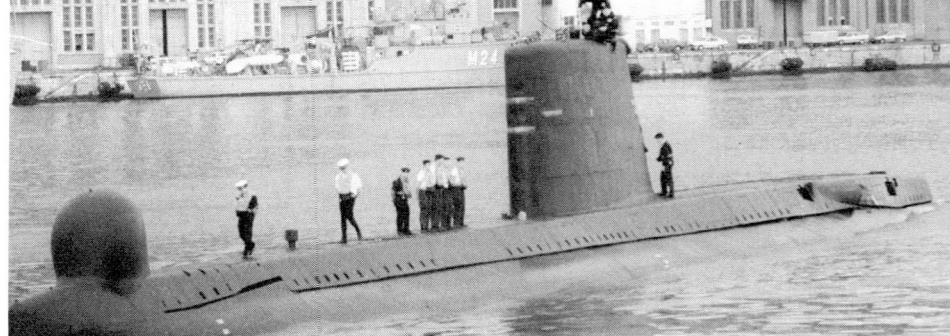

NARVAL — 6/1992, Diego Quevedo

4 GALERNA CLASS (FRENCH AGOSTA)

Name	No	Builders	Laid down	Launched	Commissioned
GALERNA	S 71	Bazán, Cartagena	5 Sep 1977	5 Dec 1981	22 Jan 1983
SIROCO	S 72	Bazán, Cartagena	27 Nov 1978	13 Nov 1982	5 Dec 1983
MISTRAL	S 73	Bazán, Cartagena	30 May 1980	14 Nov 1983	5 June 1985
TRAMONTANA	S 74	Bazán, Cartagena	10 Dec 1981	30 Nov 1984	27 Jan 1986

Displacement, tons: 1490 surfaced; 1740 dived
Dimensions, feet (metres): 221.7 × 22.3 × 17.7 *(67.6 × 6.8 × 5.4)*
Main machinery: Diesel-electric; 2 SEMT-Pielstick 16 PA4 V 185 VG diesels; 3600 hp(m) *(2.7 MW)*; 2 Jeumont Schneider alternators; 1.7 MW; 1 motor; 4600 hp(m) *(3.4 MW)*; 1 cruising motor; 32 hp(m) *(23 kW)*; 1 shaft
Speed, knots: 12 surfaced; 20 dived; 17.5 sustained
Range, miles: 8500 snorting at 9 kts; 350 dived on cruising motor at 3.5 kts
Complement: 54 (6 officers)

Missiles: SSM: Probably Aerospatiale SM 39 Exocet; active radar homing to 50 km *(27 nm)* at 0.9 Mach; warhead 165 kg. Each missile carried in lieu of 1 torpedo.
Torpedoes: 4—21 in *(533 mm)* tubes. 20 combination of (a) ECAN L5 Mod 3/4; dual purpose; active/passive homing to 9.5 km *(5.1 nm)* at 35 kts; warhead 150 kg; depth to 550 m *(1800 ft)*.
(b) ECAN F17 Mod 2; wire-guided; active/passive homing to 20 km *(10.8 nm)* at 40 kts; warhead 250 kg; depth 600 m *(1970 ft)*.
Mines: 19 can be carried if torpedo load is reduced to 9.
Countermeasures: ESM: THORN EMI Manta; radar warning.
Radars: Surface search: Thomson-CSF DRUA 33C; I band.
Sonars: Thomson Sintra DSUV 22; passive search and attack; medium frequency.
Thomson Sintra DUUA 2A/2B; active search and attack; 8 or 8.4 kHz active.
DUUX 2A (S 71-72) or DUUX-5 (S 73-74); passive; range finding. Eledone; intercept.
Thomson Sintra DSUV-62 towed passive array (S 72-73); trials in 1991.

Programmes: First two ordered 9 May 1975 and second pair 29 June 1977. Built with some French advice. About 67 per cent of equipment and structure from Spanish sources.
Modernisation: All to be modernised by the mid-1990s with new attack periscopes, towed array sonars, new ESM and IR enhanced periscopes. New main batteries to be installed with central control monitoring. *Galerna* is the first to start the update in 1993.
Structure: Diving depth, 300 m *(984 ft)*.
Operational: Endurance, 45 days.

GALERNA   7/1992, Diego Quevedo

MISTRAL   7/1992, Diego Quevedo

SIROCO   2/1993, Diego Quevedo

AIRCRAFT CARRIER

Name	No	Builders	Laid down	Launched	Commissioned
PRINCIPE DE ASTURIAS (ex-*Almirante Carrero Blanco*)	R 11	Bazán, Ferrol	8 Oct 1979	22 May 1982	30 May 1988

Displacement, tons: 16 700 full load
Dimensions, feet (metres): 642.7 oa; 615.2 pp × 79.7 × 30.8 *(195.9; 187.5 × 24.3 × 9.4)*
Flight deck, feet (metres): 575.1 × 95.1 *(175.3 × 29)*
Main machinery: 2 GE LM 2500 gas turbines; 46 400 hp *(34.61 MW)* sustained; 1 shaft; cp prop; 2 motors; 1600 hp(m) *(1.18 MW)*; retractable prop
Speed, knots: 26 (4.5 on motors). **Range, miles:** 6500 at 20 kts
Complement: 555 (90 officers) plus 208 (Flag Staff (7 officers) and Air Group)

Guns: 4 Bazán Meroka 12-barrelled 20 mm/120 ❶; 85° elevation; 3600 rounds/minute combined to 2 km.
2 Rheinmetall 37 mm saluting guns.
Countermeasures: Decoys: 4 Loral Hycor SRBOC 6-barrelled fixed Mk 36; IR flares and chaff to 4 km *(2.2 nm)*.
SLQ 25 Nixie; towed torpedo decoy.
US Prairie/Masker; hull noise/blade rate suppression.
ESM/ECM: Elettronica Nettunel; intercept and jammers.

Combat data systems: Tritan Digital Command and Control System NTDS; Links 11 and 14. Saturn SATCOM ❷.
Fire control: Four Selenia directors (for Meroka). Radamec 2000 series.
Radars: Air search: Hughes SPS 52 C/D ❸; 3D; E/F band; range 439 km *(240 nm)*.
Surface search: ISC Cardion SPS 55 ❹; I/J band.
Aircraft control: ITT SPN 35 A ❺; J band.
Fire control: Four Selenia RAN 12L ❻; I/J band (for Meroka).
RTN 11L/X; I/J band; missile warning.

Fixed wing aircraft: 6-12 AV 8B Bravo (see *Shipborne Aircraft* section).
Helicopters: 6-10 SH-3 Sea Kings; 2-4 AB 212ASW/EW; 2 SH-60B Seahawks.

Programmes: Ordered on 29 June 1977. Associated US firms were Gibbs and Cox, Dixencast, Bath Iron Works and Sperry SM. Commissioning delays caused by changes to command and control systems and the addition of a Flag Bridge.
Modernisation: After two years service some modifications were made to the port after side of the island, to improve briefing rooms and provide sheltered parking space for FD vehicles. Also improved accommodation has been added on for six officers and 50 specialist ratings.
Structure: Based on US Navy Sea Control Ship design. 12 degree ski-jump of 46.5 m. Two flight deck lifts, one right aft. Two LCVPs carried. Two pairs of fin stabilisers. The hangar is 24 748 sq ft *(2300 m²)*. The Battle Group Commander occupies the lower bridge. Two saluting guns have been mounted on the port quarter.
Operational: Three Sea Kings have Searchwater AEW radar. Aircraft complement could be increased to 37 (parking on deck) in an emergency but maximum operational number is 24. A typical air wing includes 10 Matador IIs and 10 Sea Hawks/Sea Kings (including two AEW). Ship is based at Rota.

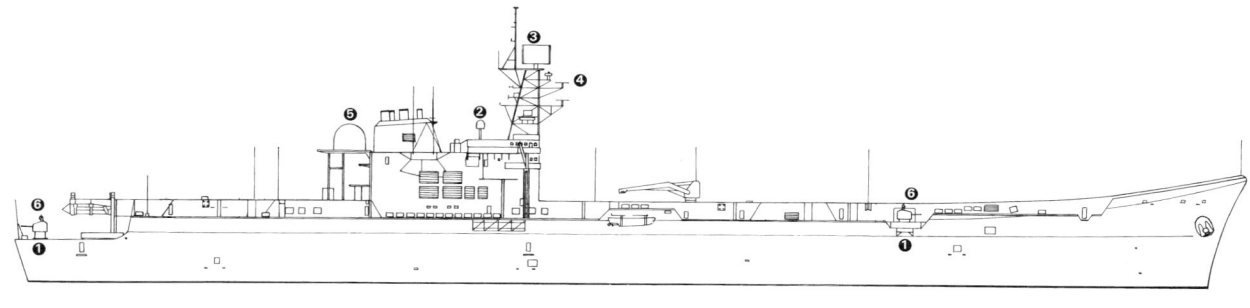

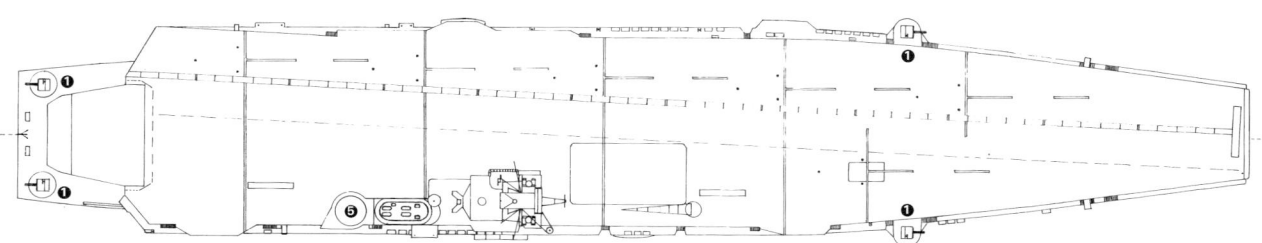

PRINCIPE DE ASTURIAS *(Scale 1 : 1200), Ian Sturton*

PRINCIPE DE ASTURIAS *4/1992, A Campanera i Rovira*

PRINCIPE DE ASTURIAS *5/1992, F Gámez*

Frigates

0 + (4) F 100 CLASS

Displacement, tons: 4400 full load
Dimensions, feet (metres): 419.3 × 50.9 × 15.4 *(127.8 × 15.5 × 4.7)*
Main machinery: CODOG; 2 gas turbines; 2 diesels; 2 shafts; cp props
Speed, knots: 28. **Range, miles:** 4500 at 18 kts
Complement: 200

Missiles: SSM: 8 McDonnell Douglas Harpoon ❶.
SAM: Aster or Evolved Sea Sparrow; VLS ❷.
Guns: 1 FMC 5 in *(127 mm)*/54 Mk 45 ❸.
2 Bazán 20 mm/120 Meroka ❹; possibly including a SAM combination.
Torpedoes: 4 fixed tubes ❺.
Countermeasures: Decoys: 4 chaff launchers ❻. ESM/ECM.
Combat data systems: Link. SATCOM ❼.
Fire control: 2 optronic directors.
Radars: Air search ❽.
Surface search ❾.
Fire control ❿.
Sonars: Hull-mounted; active search and attack; medium frequency. Possible active towed sonar.

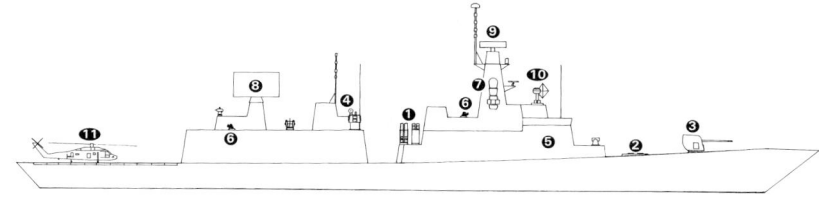

F 100 *(Scale 1 : 1200), Ian Sturton*

Helicopters: 1 LAMPS III ⓫.

Programmes: Project definition from September 1992 to February 1994. First ship to be laid down in 1995 for completion in late 1999. Possible collaboration with the Netherlands.

Structure: The VLS system is to have four channels of fire. Stealth features are to be an important part of the design. Many of the weapon systems details are still to be decided.

4 + 2 SANTA MARÍA CLASS

Name	No	Builders	Laid down	Launched	Commissioned
SANTA MARÍA	F 81	Bazán, Ferrol	23 May 1982	24 Nov 1984	12 Oct 1986
VICTORIA	F 82	Bazán, Ferrol	16 Aug 1983	23 July 1986	11 Nov 1987
NUMANCIA	F 83	Bazán, Ferrol	8 Jan 1986	30 Jan 1987	8 Nov 1988
REINA SOFÍA (ex-*América*)	F 84	Bazán, Ferrol	12 Dec 1987	19 July 1989	18 Oct 1990
NAVARRA	F 85	Bazán, Ferrol	15 Apr 1991	23 Oct 1992	Feb 1995
CANARIAS	F 86	Bazán, Ferrol	15 Apr 1992	Aug 1993	Oct 1995

Displacement, tons: 3610 standard; 4017 full load
Dimensions, feet (metres): 451.2 × 46.9 × 24.6 *(137.7 × 14.3 × 7.5)*
Main machinery: 2 GE LM 2500 gas turbines; 41 000 hp *(30.59 MW)* sustained; 1 shaft; cp prop; 2 motors; 1600 hp(m) *(1.18 MW)*; 1 retractable prop
Speed, knots: 29; 4.5 on auxiliary. **Range, miles:** 4500 at 20 kts
Complement: 223 (13 officers)

Missiles: SSM: 8 McDonnell Douglas Harpoon; active radar homing to 130 km *(70 nm)* at 0.9 Mach; warhead 227 kg.
SAM: 32 GDC Pomona Standard SM-1MR; Mk 13 Mod 4 launcher ❶; command guidance; semi-active radar homing to 46 km *(25 nm)* at 2 Mach.
Both missile systems share a common magazine.
Guns: 1 OTO Melara 3 in *(76 mm)*/62 ❷; 85° elevation; 85 rounds/minute to 16 km *(8.7 nm)*; weight of shell 6 kg.
1 Bazán 20 mm/120 12-barrelled Meroka ❸; 85° elevation; 3600 rounds/minute combined to 2 km.
Torpedoes: 6—324 mm US Mk 32 (2 triple) tubes ❹. Honeywell Mk 46 Mod 5; anti-submarine; active/passive homing to 11 km *(5.9 nm)* at 40 kts; warhead 44 kg.
Countermeasures: Decoys: 2 Loral Hycor SRBOC 6-barrelled fixed Mk 37 Mod 1 ❺; IR flares and chaff to 4 km *(2.2 nm)*.
Prairie/Masker: hull noise/blade rate suppression.
SLQ 25 Nixie; torpedo decoy.
ESM/ECM: Elettronica Nettunel or Mk 3000 (F 84-86); intercept and jammer.
Combat data systems: IPN 10 action data automation; Link 11. SSQ 28 LAMPS III helo data link. Saturn SATCOM ❻.
Fire control: Mk 92 Mod 2 (Mod 6 with CORT in F 85 and 86).
Radars: Air search: Raytheon SPS 49 or 52 (F 85-86) ❼; C/D band; range 457 km *(250 nm)*.
Surface search: Raytheon SPS 55 or Signaal ZW 06 (F 85-86) ❽; I band.
Navigation: Raytheon 1650/9; I/J band.
Fire control: RCA Mk 92 Mod 2/6 (F 81-84) ❾; I/J band. 1 or 2 (F 85-86) Signaal STIR ❿; I/J band.
Selenia RAN 30L/X (RAN 12L + RAN 30X) ⓫; I band (for Meroka). Sperry VPS 2 ⓬ (for Meroka).
Tacan: URN-25.
Sonars: Raytheon SQS 56 (DE 1160); hull-mounted; active search and attack; medium frequency.
Gould SQR 19; tactical towed array (TACTASS); passive; very low frequency.

Helicopters: 2 Sikorsky S-70L Seahawk ⓭ (only one normally embarked).

Programmes: Three ordered 29 June 1977. The execution of this programme was delayed due to the emphasis placed on the carrier construction. The fourth ship was ordered on 19 June 1986, and numbers five and six on 26 December 1989. The original plan to build four more has been shelved and the last two have been delayed by a shortage of funds.
Modernisation: All are being modified with a combined RAN 12L and RAN 30X fire control radar for Meroka. The combined system is called RAN 30L/X.

Structure: Based on the US FFG 7 Oliver Perry class although broader in the beam and therefore able to carry more topweight. Fin stabilisers fitted. RAST helicopter handling system. *Navarra* and *Canarias* have an indigenous combat data system thereby increasing national inputs to 75 per cent. They also have improved search and fire control radars.

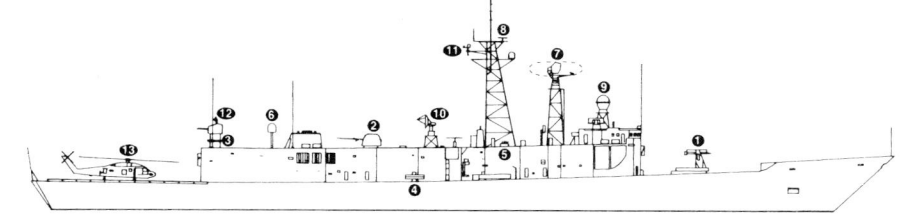

SANTA MARÍA *(Scale 1 : 1200), Ian Sturton*

SANTA MARÍA *8/1992, F Gámez*

VICTORIA *7/1992, F Gámez*

5 BALEARES (F 70) CLASS

Name	No	Builders	Laid down	Launched	Commissioned
BALEARES	F 71	Bazán, Ferrol	31 Oct 1968	20 Aug 1970	24 Sep 1973
ANDALUCÍA	F 72	Bazán, Ferrol	2 July 1969	30 Mar 1971	23 May 1974
CATALUÑA	F 73	Bazán, Ferrol	20 Aug 1970	3 Nov 1971	16 Jan 1975
ASTURIAS	F 74	Bazán, Ferrol	30 Mar 1971	13 May 1972	2 Dec 1975
EXTREMADURA	F 75	Bazán, Ferrol	3 Nov 1971	21 Nov 1972	10 Nov 1976

Displacement, tons: 3350 standard; 4177 full load
Dimensions, feet (metres): 438 × 46.9 × 15.4; 25.6 (sonar) *(133.6 × 14.3 × 4.7; 7.8)*
Main machinery: 2 Combustion Engineering V2M boilers; 1200 psi *(84.4 kg/cm sq)*; 950°F *(510°C)*; 1 Westinghouse turbine; 35 000 hp(m) *(25.7 MW)*; 1 shaft
Speed, knots: 28. **Range, miles:** 4500 at 20 kts
Complement: 256 (15 officers)

Missiles: SSM: 8 McDonnell Douglas Harpoon (4 normally carried) ❶; active radar homing to 130 km *(70 nm)* at 0.9 Mach; warhead 227 kg.
SAM: 16 GDC Pomona Standard SM-1MR; Mk 22 Mod 0 launcher ❷; command guidance; semi-active radar homing to 46 km *(25 nm)* at 2 Mach.
A/S: Honeywell ASROC Mk 112 octuple launcher ❸; 8 reloads; inertial guidance to 1.6-10 km *(1-5.4 nm)*; payload Mk 46 torpedo.
Guns: 1 FMC 5 in *(127 mm)*/54 Mk 42 Mod 9 ❹; dual purpose; 85° elevation; 20-40 rounds/minute to 24 km *(13 nm)* anti-surface; 14 km *(7.7 nm)* anti-aircraft; weight of shell 32 kg; 600 rounds in magazine.
2 Bazán 20 mm/120 12-barrelled Meroka ❺; 85° elevation; 3600 rounds/minute combined to 2 km.
Torpedoes: 4—324 mm US Mk 32 fixed tubes (fitted internally and angled at 45 degrees) ❻. Honeywell Mk 46 Mod 5; anti-submarine; active/passive homing to 11 km *(5.9 nm)* at 40 kts; warhead 44 kg.
2—484 mm US Mk 25 stern tubes ❼. Westinghouse Mk 37; anti-submarine; wire-guided; active/passive homing to 8 km *(4.4 nm)* at 24 kts; warhead 150 kg. Total of 41 torpedoes of all types carried.
Countermeasures: Decoys: 4 Loral Hycor SRBOC Mk 36 6-barrelled chaff launchers.
ESM: Ceselsa Deneb; intercept.
ECM: Ceselsa Canopus; jammer.
Combat data systems: Tritan 1 action data automation; Link 11. Saturn SATCOM ❽.
Fire control: Mk 68 GFCS (2 channels of fire). Mk 74 missile system with Mk 73 director. Mk 114 torpedo control.
Radars: Air search: Hughes SPS 52A ❾; 3D; E/F band; range 439 km *(240 nm)*.
Surface search: Raytheon SPS 10 ❿; G band.
Navigation: Raytheon Marine Pathfinder; I/J band.
Fire control: Western Electric SPG 53B ⓫; I/J band (for Mk 68). Raytheon SPG 51C ⓬; G/I band (for Mk 73).
Selenia RAN 12L ⓭; I band (for Meroka). 2 Sperry VPS 2 ⓮ (for Meroka).
Tacan: SRN 15A.
Sonars: Raytheon SQS 56 (DE 1160); hull-mounted; active search and attack; medium frequency.
EDO SQS 35V; VDS; active search and attack; medium frequency.

Programmes: This class resulted from a very close co-operation between Spain and the USA. Programme was approved 17 November 1964, technical support agreement with USA being signed 31 March 1966. US Navy supplied weapons and sensors. Major hull sections, turbines and gearboxes made at El Ferrol, superstructures at Alicante, boilers, distilling plants and propellers at Cadiz.
Modernisation: The mid-life update programme was done in two stages; all had completed the first stage by the end of 1987 and *Asturias* was the first to be fully modernised in 1988; *Extremadura* completed in May 1989, *Cataluña* in early 1990, *Baleares* in July 1990 and *Andalucía* in February 1991. Changes included the fitting of two Meroka 20 mm CIWS, Link 11, Tritan data control, Deneb passive EW systems, four Mk 36 SRBOC chaff launchers and replacing SQS 23 with DE 1160 sonar.
Structure: Generally similar to US Navy's Knox class although they differ in the missile system, Mk 25 torpedo tubes and lack of helicopter facilities.

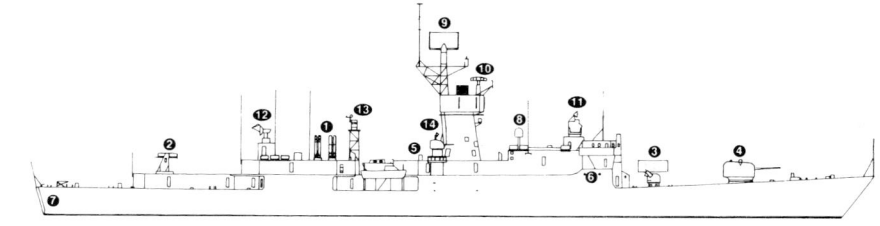

BALEARES (Scale 1 : 1200), Ian Sturton

CATALUÑA 3/1992, C D Yaylali

EXTREMADURA 5/1991, H M Steele

Frigates — Offshore patrol vessels / SPAIN

6 DESCUBIERTA CLASS

Name	No	Builders	Laid down	Launched	Commissioned
DESCUBIERTA	F 31	Bazán, Cartagena	16 Nov 1974	8 July 1975	18 Nov 1978
DIANA	F 32	Bazán, Cartagena	8 July 1975	26 Jan 1976	30 June 1979
INFANTA ELENA	F 33	Bazán, Cartagena	26 Jan 1976	14 Sep 1976	12 Apr 1980
INFANTA CRISTINA	F 34	Bazán, Cartagena	11 Sep 1976	25 Apr 1977	24 Nov 1980
CAZADORA	F 35	Bazán, Ferrol	14 Dec 1977	17 Oct 1978	20 July 1982
VENCEDORA	F 36	Bazán, Ferrol	1 June 1978	27 Apr 1979	18 Mar 1983

Displacement, tons: 1233 standard; 1482 full load
Dimensions, feet (metres): 291.3 × 34 × 12.5
(88.8 × 10.4 × 3.8)
Main machinery: 4 MTU-Bazán 16V 956 TB91 diesels; 15 000 hp(m) *(11 MW)* sustained; 2 shafts; cp props
Speed, knots: 25. **Range, miles:** 4000 at 18 kts; 7500 at 12 kts
Complement: 118 (10 officers) plus 30 marines

Missiles: SSM: 8 McDonnell Douglas Harpoon (2 quad) launchers ❶; active radar homing to 130 km *(70 nm)* at 0.9 Mach; warhead 227 kg. Normally only 2 pairs are embarked.
SAM: Selenia Albatros octuple launcher ❷; 24 Raytheon Sea Sparrow; semi-active radar homing to 14.6 km *(8 nm)* at 2.5 Mach; height envelope 15-5000 m *(49.2-16 405 ft)*; warhead 39 kg.
Guns: 1 OTO Melara 3 in *(76 mm)*/62 compact ❸; 85° elevation; 85 rounds/minute to 16 km *(8.7 nm)*; weight of shell 6 kg.
1 or 2 Bofors 40 mm/70 ❹; 85° elevation; 300 rounds/minute to 12.5 km *(6.8 nm)*; weight of shell 0.96 kg.
1 Bazán 20 mm/120 12-barrelled Meroka; 85° elevation; 3600 rounds/minute combined to 2 km. Replacing one 40 mm gun in due course.
Torpedoes: 6—324 mm US Mk 32 (2 triple) tubes ❺. Honeywell Mk 46 Mod 5; anti-submarine; active/passive homing to 11 km *(5.9 nm)* at 40 kts; warhead 44 kg.
A/S mortars: 1 Bofors 375 mm twin-barrelled trainable ❻; automatic loading; range 3600 m.
Countermeasures: Decoys: 2 Loral Hycor SRBOC 6-barrelled Mk 36 for chaff and IR flares.
US Prairie Masker; blade rate suppression.
ESM/ECM: Elettronica SpA 'Beta'; intercept and jammer.
Combat data systems: SEWACO action data automation; Link 11 being fitted. Saturn SATCOM ❼.
Fire control: Signaal WM 22/41 or WM 25; GM 101.
Radars: Air/surface search: Signaal DA 05/2 ❽; E/F band; range 137 km *(75 nm)* for 2 m² target.
Navigation: Signaal ZW 06 ❾; I band.
Fire control: Signaal WM 22/41 or WM 25 system ❿; I/J band; range 46 km *(25 nm)*.
Selenia RAN 12L; I band and Sperry VPS 2 (to be fitted with Meroka).
Sonars: Raytheon 1160B; hull-mounted; active search and attack; medium frequency. VDS may be added.

Programmes: Officially rated as Corvettes. *Diana* (tenth of the name) originates with the galley *Diana* of 1570. Infanta Elena and Cristina are the daughters of King Juan Carlos. Approval for second four ships given on 21 May 1976. First four ordered 7 December 1973 (83 per cent Spanish ship construction components) and four more from Bazán, Ferrol on 25 May 1976.
Modernisation: The 40 mm gun aft of the mainmast is planned to be replaced by Meroka with associated fire control radars. SRBOC chaff launchers fitted and EW equipment updated. Link 11 added. WM 25 fire control system being updated in four of the class by 1995.
Structure: Original Portuguese 'João Coutinho' design by Comodoro de Oliveira PN developed by Blohm & Voss and considerably modified by Bazán including use of Y-shaped funnel. Harpoon fitted between bridge and funnel. Noise reduction measures include Masker fitted to shafts, propellers (five types tested) under trial for four years, auxiliary gas turbine generator fitted on upper deck for use during passive sonar search, all main and auxiliary diesels sound-mounted. Fully stabilised. Automatic computerised engine and alternator control; two independent engine rooms; normal running on two diesels.
Sales: F 37 and F 38 sold to Egypt prior to completion. One to Morocco in 1983.

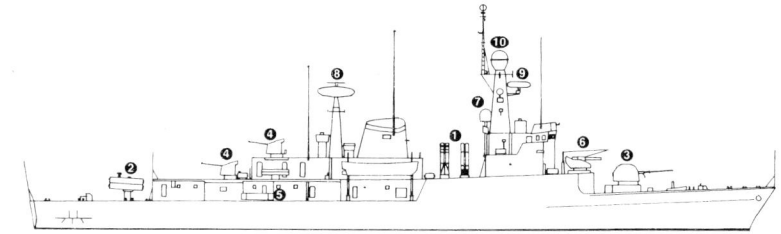

DESCUBIERTA *(Scale 1 : 900), Ian Sturton*

DIANA *7/1992, Diego Quevedo*

OFFSHORE PATROL VESSELS

4 SERVIOLA CLASS

Name	No	Builders	Laid down	Launched	Commissioned
SERVIOLA	P 71	Bazán, Ferrol	17 Oct 1989	10 May 1990	22 Mar 1991
CENTINELA	P 72	Bazán, Ferrol	12 Dec 1989	30 Mar 1990	24 Sep 1991
VIGIA	P 73	Bazán, Ferrol	30 Oct 1990	12 Apr 1991	24 Mar 1992
ATALAYA	P 74	Bazán, Ferrol	14 Dec 1990	22 Nov 1991	29 June 1992

Displacement, tons: 836 standard; 1106 full load
Dimensions, feet (metres): 225.4; 206.7 pp × 34 × 11
(68.7; 63 × 10.4 × 3.4)
Main machinery: 2 MTU-Bazán 16V 956 TB91 diesels; 7500 hp(m) *(5.5 MW)* sustained; 2 shafts
Speed, knots: 19. **Range, miles:** 8000 at 12 kts
Complement: 42 (8 officers) plus 6 spare berths

Guns: 1 US 3 in *(76 mm)*/50 Mk 27; 85° elevation; 20 rounds/minute to 12 km *(6.6 nm)*; weight of shell 6 kg (see *Structure*).
2—12.7 mm MGs.
Fire control: Bazán Alcor optronic director. Hispano mini combat system.
Radars: Surface search: Racal Decca 2459; I band.
Navigation: Racal Decca ARPA 2690 BT; I band.

Helicopters: 1 AB-212.

Programmes: Project B215 ordered from Bazán, Ferrol in late 1988. Patrulleros de Altura have replaced the Atrevida class. The larger Milano design was rejected as being too expensive.
Structure: A modified Halcón class design similar to ships produced for Argentina and Mexico. Full helicopter facilities enabling operation in up to Sea State 4 using non-retractable stabilisers. Three firefighting pumps. The guns are old stock refurbished but could be replaced by an OTO Melara 76 mm/62 or a Bofors 40 mm/70 Model 600. Other equipment fits could include four Harpoon SSM, Meroka CIWS, Sea Sparrow SAM or a Bofors 375 mm ASW rocket launcher.
Operational: For EEZ patrol only. May carry some female crew. *Vigia* and *Atalaya* are based at Cadiz, *Serviola* at Ferrol and *Centinela* at Las Palmas.

SERVIOLA *5/1992, Giorgio Arra*

SHIPBORNE AIRCRAFT

Numbers/Type: 11 BAe/McDonnell Douglas EAV-8B Bravo (Harrier II).
Operational speed: 562 kts *(1041 km/h).*
Service ceiling: Not available.
Range: 480 nm *(889 km).*
Role/Weapon systems: Delivered in 1987-88 for the new aircraft carrier. The plan is to update them to AV-8B Harrier Plus standard with APG-65 radar plus FLIR by 1994-95. Sensors: No radar (a letter of intent for the APG-65 multi-mode radar was signed in 1988). ECM: ALQ 164. Weapons: Strike; 2 × 25 mm GAU-12/U cannon, 2 or 4 × AIM-9L Sidewinder, 2 or 4 × AGM-65E Maverick; up to 16 GP bombs.

BRAVO 5/1992, F Gámez

Numbers/Type: 7 BAe/McDonnell Douglas AV-8S Matador (Harrier).
Operational speed: 640 kts *(1186 km/h).*
Service ceiling: 51 200 ft *(15 600 m).*
Range: 800 nm *(1480 km).*
Role/Weapon systems: AV-8S supplied via US and formed for strike/reconnaissance role with one squadron. Sensors: None. Weapons: Strike; 2 × 30 mm Aden cannon, 2 × AIM-9 Sidewinder or 20 mm/127 mm rockets and 'iron' bombs.

MATADOR 8/1991, Camil Busquets i Vilanova

Numbers/Type: 9 Sikorsky SH-3D/G Sea King.
Operational speed: 118 kts *(219 km/h).*
Service ceiling: 14 700 ft *(4480 m).*
Range: 542 nm *(1005 km).*
Role/Weapon systems: Medium ASW helicopter from aircraft carrier; surface search and SAR are secondary roles. Modernisation in 1989 included new sonars, Doppler radars and IFF. Sensors: APS-124 search radar, Bendix AQS-13F dipping sonar, sonobuoys. Weapons: ASW; 4 × Mk 46 torpedoes or depth bombs. ASV; 4 Aerospatiale AS 12 wire-guided missiles.

SEA KING 4/1992, Diego Quevedo

Numbers/Type: 3 Sikorsky SH-3D Sea King AEW.
Operational speed: 110 kts *(204 km/h).*
Service ceiling: 14 700 ft *(4480 m).*
Range: 542 nm *(1005 km).*
Role/Weapon systems: Three Sea King helicopters were taken in hand in 1986 for conversion to AEW role to provide organic cover; first entered service August 1987. Three more may be converted in due course. Sensors: Thorn-EMI Searchwater radar, ESM. Weapons: Unarmed.

SEA KING AEW 5/1992, A Campanera i Rovira

Numbers/Type: 6 Sikorsky SH-70L Seahawk (LAMPS III).
Operational speed: 135 kts *(249 km/h).*
Service ceiling: 10 000 ft *(3050 m).*
Range: 600 nm *(1110 km).*
Role/Weapon systems: ASW helicopter; delivery in 1988-89 for new FFG 7 frigates. Four more to be acquired in due course. Sensors: Search radar, sonobuoys, ECM/ESM. Weapons: ASW; 2 × Mk 46 torpedoes or depth bombs. ASV; ASM being considered.

SEAHAWK 7/1992, Camil Busquets i Vilanova

Numbers/Type: 10 Agusta AB 212ASW.
Operational speed: 106 kts *(196 km/h).*
Service ceiling: 14 200 ft *(4330 m).*
Range: 230 nm *(426 km).*
Role/Weapon systems: ASW and surface search; four are equipped for Fleet ECM support and six for Assault operations with the Amphibious Brigade. Sensors: Selenia search radar, Bendix dipping sonar, Elmer ECM. Weapons: ASW; 2 × Mk 46 torpedoes or 4 × depth bombs. ASV; 4 × Aerospatiale AS 12 wire-guided missiles.

AB 212 5/1992, A Campanera i Rovira

Numbers/Type: 10 Hughes 500MD/ASW.
Operational speed: 110 kts *(204 km/h).*
Service ceiling: 10 000 ft *(3050 m).*
Range: 203 nm *(376 km).*
Role/Weapon systems: Weapons carrier helicopter for ASW operations, with MAD detection capability; used for training; secondary role is SAR and surface search. Sensors: Some have search radar, MAD. Weapons: ASW; 1 × Mk 46 torpedo or depth bomb.

HUGHES 500 5/1992, A Campanera i Rovira

LAND-BASED MARITIME AIRCRAFT (FRONT LINE)

Numbers/Type: 10 Aerospatiale AS 332M Super Puma.
Operational speed: 151 kts *(279 km/h).*
Service ceiling: 15 090 ft *(4600 m).*
Range: 335 nm *(620 km).*
Role/Weapon systems: Limited search and SAR helicopter operated by Air Force. Sensors: Search radar. Weapons: Unarmed.

Numbers/Type: 7 CASA C-212 Aviocar.
Operational speed: 190 kts *(353 km/h).*
Service ceiling: 24 000 ft *(7315 m).*
Range: 1650 nm *(3055 km).*
Role/Weapon systems: Mediterranean and Atlantic surveillance is carried out by detached flights for the Air Force; SAR is secondary role. Sensors: APS-128 radar, MAD, sonobuoys and ESM. Weapons: ASW; Mk 46 torpedoes or depth bombs. ASV; 2 × rockets or machine gun pods.

Numbers/Type: 6 CASA/Nurtanio CN-235.
Operational speed: 240 kts *(445 km/h).*
Service ceiling: 26 600 ft *(8110 m).*
Range: 669 nm *(1240 km).*
Role/Weapon systems: Air Force operated; 21 of the type used for transport tasks. Programme to be completed by 1993. Medium-range maritime patrol for surface surveillance and possible ASV/ASW; Sensors: Search radar: Litton AN/APS 504; MAD; acoustic processors; sonobuoys. Weapons suite to be selected.

Numbers/Type: 3 Fokker F27 Maritime.
Operational speed: 250 kts *(463 km/h).*
Service ceiling: 29 500 ft *(8990 m).*
Range: 2700 nm *(5000 km).*
Role/Weapon systems: Canaries and offshore patrol by Air Force. Sensors: APS-504 search radar, cameras. Weapons: ASW; torpedoes or depth bombs. ASV; possible conversion for missiles under consideration.

Numbers/Type: 2/5 Lockheed P-3A/B Orion.
Operational speed: 410 kts *(760 km/h).*
Service ceiling: 28 300 ft *(8625 m).*
Range: 4000 nm *(7410 km).*
Role/Weapon systems: Air Force operation for long-range MR/ASW; P-3A supplemented in 1988 by P-3B Orions from Norway after Lockheed modernisation. All to be further upgraded with APS 134 radar, FLIR, ALR 66 V(3) ESM and AQS 81 MAD by 1995. Sensors: Search radar, MAD, ECM/ESM, 87 × sonobuoys. Weapons: ASW; 8 × torpedoes or depth bombs internally; 10 × underwing stations. ASV; 4 × Harpoon or 127 mm rockets.

LIGHT FORCES

0 + (1) BES-50 CLASS (SURFACE EFFECT SHIP—MISSILE)

Displacement, tons: 360 full load
Dimensions, feet (metres): 180.4 oa; 158.1 pp × 47.6 × 3.9 (with lift) *(55; 48.2 × 14.5 × 1.2)*
Main machinery: 2 Allison 570-KF gas turbines (for propulsion); 13 080 hp *(9.75 MW)* sustained; 2 KaMeWa waterjets
4 MTU 6V 396 TB83 diesels (for lift); 3120 hp(m) *(2.3 MW)* sustained
Speed, knots: 50. **Range, miles:** 800 at 50 kts; 2000 at 12 kts
Complement: 30 (6 officers)
Missiles: SSM: 8 McDonnell Douglas Harpoon.
Guns: 2 Bazán/Bofors 40 mm/70.
Countermeasures: Decoys: 1 chaff launcher. ESM.
Fire control: 2 optronic directors.
Radars: Air/surface search.
Navigation.
Helicopters: 1 S-70L Seahawk.

Comment: Surface effect ship planned to be built by Bazán-Chaconsa based on the experimental BES-16 platform which started trials in June 1988. If the Navy decides to go ahead the first ship should be in service in the mid-1990s and 6000 million pesetas have been allocated for research and development between 1989 and 1993. The programme has been held up by budget problems in 1991 and may be cancelled in 1993. BES-16 has a displacement of 14 tons; dimensions, 55.1 × 17.7 × 2.5 ft (lifted) *(16.8 × 5.4 × 0.75 m);* two Isotta Fraschini diesels generating 900 hp(m) *(662 kW)* and two Macchi-Castoldi waterjets. The cushion is generated by two MWM diesels (220 hp(m) *(162 kW))* and the craft has a speed of 38 kts. BES (*Buque de Efecto de Superficie*).

BES-50 (model)   *1989, Bazán*

BES-16   *3/1993, Diego Quevedo*

6 LAZAGA CLASS (FAST ATTACK CRAFT—MISSILE)

Name	No	Builders	Commissioned
LAZAGA	P 01	Lürssen, Vegesack	16 July 1975
ALSEDO	P 02	Bazán, La Carraca	28 Feb 1977
CADARSO	P 03	Bazán, La Carraca	10 July 1976
VILLAMIL	P 04	Bazán, La Carraca	26 Apr 1977
BONIFAZ	P 05	Bazán, La Carraca	11 July 1977
RECALDE	P 06	Bazán, La Carraca	17 Dec 1977

Displacement, tons: 275 standard; 393 full load
Dimensions, feet (metres): 190.6 × 24.9 × 8.5 *(58.1 × 7.6 × 2.6)*
Main machinery: 2 MTU-Bazán 16V 956 TB91 diesels; 7500 hp(m) *(5.5 MW)* sustained; 2 shafts
Speed, knots: 28. **Range, miles:** 6100 at 17 kts
Complement: 30 (4 officers)

Guns: 1 OTO Melara 3 in *(76 mm)*/62 compact; 85° elevation; 85 rounds/minute to 16 km *(8.7 nm)*; weight of shell 6 kg.
1 Breda 40 mm/70 (not always carried).
2 Oerlikon 20 mm/85; 55° elevation; 800 rounds/minute to 2 km.
Torpedoes: Fitted for but not with 6—324 mm US Mk 31 (2 triple) tubes.
Depth charges: Fitted for 2 racks.
Countermeasures: ESM: Radar intercept.
Fire control: CSEE optical director.
Radars: Surface search/fire control: Signaal WM 22/41; I/J band.
Navigation: Raytheon TM 1620/6X; I/J band.
Sonars: Fitted for—hull-mounted; active attack; high frequency.

Programmes: Ordered in 1972, primarily for Fishery Protection duties. Although all are operated by the Navy half the cost is being borne by the Ministry of Commerce.
Modernisation: Fire control radars to be modernised by Signaal by 1995.
Structure: Of similar hull form to Israeli Reshef class and to S-143 class of West Germany and of basic Lürssen Type 57 design but with only two engines. A mast which is abaft and higher than the radome has been fitted in some of the class, probably for ESM. The plan was to fit SSMs but this is unlikely to happen.
Operational: Meroka CIWS trials were carried out in P 03. At least one of the class may be fitted with the ASW equipment. Portable containers with EW equipment are sometimes embarked. Most of these equipments are carried at the expense of the 40 mm gun. It is reported that all may be put in reserve in mid-1993.

VILLAMIL (no 40 mm gun)   *5/1992, Camil Busquets i Vilanova*

RECALDE (no ESM mast)   *10/1992, Diego Quevedo*

1 CORMORAN CLASS (FAST ATTACK CRAFT—GUN)

Name	No	Builders	Commissioned
CORMORAN	P 41 (ex-P 53)	Bazán, San Fernando	27 Oct 1989

Displacement, tons: 374 full load
Dimensions, feet (metres): 185.7 × 24.7 × 6.5 *(56.6 × 7.5 × 2)*
Main machinery: 3 MTU-Bazán 16V 956 TB91 diesels; 11 250 hp(m) *(8.27 MW)* sustained; 3 shafts
Speed, knots: 34
Complement: 32 (5 officers)
Guns: 1 Bofors 40/70 SP 48; 1 Oerlikon 20 mm.
Fire control: Alcor C modular system.
Radars: Surface search: I band.

Comment: Launched as a private venture and demonstrator in October 1985; taken over by the Navy in October 1989 but not purchased, and may be reclaimed by Bazán if a buyer is found. The design is able to carry SSMs and a 76 mm/62 gun but has commissioned with a second-hand Bofors taken from a deleted ship. Based at Cadiz and is used as a testbed as well as for Straits patrols. More being built for sale.

CORMORAN   *4/1992, van Ginderen Collection*

626 SPAIN / Light forces

1 PESCALONSO CLASS (LARGE PATROL CRAFT)

Name	No	Builders	Commissioned
CHILREU (ex-Pescalonso 2)	P 61	Gijon Naval Yard	30 Mar 1992

Displacement, tons: 1157 full load
Dimensions, feet (metres): 222.4 × 36.1 × 15.4 *(67.8 × 11 × 4.7)*
Main machinery: 1 MAK 6M-453K diesel; 2460 hp(m) *(1.81 MW)* sustained; 1 shaft
Speed, knots: 13. **Range, miles:** 1500 at 12 kts
Complement: 25
Guns: 1—12.7 mm MG.

Comment: Probably built in 1987 and purchased by the Fisheries Department for the Navy to use as a Fishery Protection vessel based at Ferrol. Former stern ramp trawler. Inmarsat fitted.

6 BARCELÓ CLASS (FAST ATTACK CRAFT—GUN)

Name	No	Builders	Commissioned
BARCELÓ	P 11	Lürssen, Vegesack	20 Mar 1976
LAYA	P 12	Bazán, La Carraca	23 Dec 1976
JAVIER QUIROGA	P 13	Bazán, La Carraca	4 Apr 1977
ORDÓÑEZ	P 14	Bazán, La Carraca	7 June 1977
ACEVEDO	P 15	Bazán, La Carraca	14 July 1977
CÁNDIDO PÉREZ	P 16	Bazán, La Carraca	25 Nov 1977

Displacement, tons: 134 full load
Dimensions, feet (metres): 118.7 × 19 × 6.2 *(36.2 × 5.8 × 1.9)*
Main machinery: 2 MTU-Bazán MD 16V 538 TB90 diesels; 6000 hp(m) *(4.41 MW)* sustained; 2 shafts
Speed, knots: 36. **Range, miles:** 1200 at 17 kts
Complement: 19 (3 officers)
Guns: 1 Breda 40 mm/70. 1 Oerlikon 20 mm/85. 2—12.7 mm MGs.
Torpedoes: Fitted for 2—21 in *(533 mm)* tubes.
Fire control: CSEE optical director.
Radars: Surface search: Raytheon 1220/6XB; I/J band.

Comment: Ordered 5 December 1973. All manned by the Navy although the cost is being borne by the Ministry of Commerce. Of Lürssen TNC 36 design. Reported as able to take two or four surface-to-surface missiles instead of 20 mm gun and torpedo tubes. All may be transferred to the Guardia Civil del Mar in 1993.

ORDÓÑEZ   7/1992, Diego Quevedo

3 ADJUTANT CLASS (LARGE PATROL CRAFT)

Name	No	Builders	Commissioned
NALÓN (ex-MSC 139)	P 51	S Coast SY, Calif	16 Feb 1954
ULLA (ex-MSC 265)	P 52	Adams YY, Mass	24 July 1956
TURIA (ex-MSC 130)	P 54	Hildebrand DD, NY	1 June 1959

Displacement, tons: 384 full load
Dimensions, feet (metres): 144 × 28 × 8.2 *(43.9 × 8.5 × 2.5)*
Main machinery: 2 GM 8-268A diesels; 880 hp *(656 kW)*; 2 shafts
Speed, knots: 14. **Range, miles:** 2700 at 12 kts
Complement: 39 (3 officers)
Guns: 2 Oerlikon 20 mm (twin).
Radars: Surface search: Racal Decca RM 914; I band.
Navigation: Furuno; I band.

Comment: These ships were transferred from the Mine Warfare Forces in 1980 for patrol duties. All minesweeping gear removed. A boat launching derrick is mounted aft.

NALÓN   7/1990, Maritime Photographic

4 CONEJERA CLASS (COASTAL PATROL CRAFT)

Name	No	Builders	Commissioned
CONEJERA	P 31	Bazán, Ferrol	31 Dec 1981
DRAGONERA	P 32	Bazán, Ferrol	31 Dec 1981
ESPALMADOR	P 33	Bazán, Ferrol	10 May 1982
ALCANADA	P 34	Bazán, Ferrol	10 May 1982

Displacement, tons: 85 full load
Dimensions, feet (metres): 106.6 × 17.4 × 4.6 *(32.2 × 5.3 × 1.4)*
Main machinery: 2 MTU-Bazán MA 16V 362 SB80 diesels; 2450 hp(m) *(1.8 MW)*; 2 shafts
Speed, knots: 25. **Range, miles:** 1200 at 15 kts
Complement: 12
Guns: 1 Oerlikon 20 mm Mk 10. 1—12.7 mm MG.

Comment: Ordered in 1978, funded jointly by the Navy and the Ministry of Commerce. Naval manned.

CONEJERA   7/1992, Camil Busquets i Vilanova

10 ANAGA CLASS (LARGE PATROL CRAFT)

Name	No	Builders	Commissioned
ANAGA	P 21	Bazán, La Carraca	14 Oct 1980
TAGOMAGO	P 22	Bazán, La Carraca	30 Jan 1981
MAROLA	P 23	Bazán, La Carraca	4 June 1981
MOURO	P 24	Bazán, La Carraca	14 July 1981
GROSA	P 25	Bazán, La Carraca	15 Sep 1981
MEDAS	P 26	Bazán, La Carraca	16 Oct 1981
IZARO	P 27	Bazán, La Carraca	9 Dec 1981
TABARCA	P 28	Bazán, La Carraca	30 Dec 1981
DEVA	P 29	Bazán, La Carraca	3 June 1982
BERGANTIN	P 30	Bazán, La Carraca	28 July 1982

Displacement, tons: 296.5 standard; 350 full load
Dimensions, feet (metres): 145.6 × 21.6 × 8.2 *(44.4 × 6.6 × 2.5)*
Main machinery: 1 MTU-Bazán 16V 956 SB90 diesel; 4000 hp(m) *(2.94 MW)* sustained; 1 shaft; cp prop
Speed, knots: 22. **Range, miles:** 4000 at 13 kts
Complement: 25 (3 officers)
Guns: 1 FMC 3 in *(76 mm)*/50 Mk 22. 1 Oerlikon 20 mm Mk 10. 2—7.62 mm MGs.
Radars: Surface search: 1 Racal Decca 1226; I band.
Navigation: Sperry; I band.

Comment: Ordered from Bazán, Cádiz on 22 July 1978. For fishery and EEZ patrol duties. Rescue and firefighting capability.

DEVA   9/1992, Diego Quevedo

2 TORALLA CLASS (COASTAL PATROL CRAFT)

Name	No	Builders	Commissioned
TORALLA	P 81	Viudes, Barcelona	27 Feb 1987
FORMENTOR	P 82	Viudes, Barcelona	23 June 1988

Displacement, tons: 56 standard; 77 full load
Dimensions, feet (metres): 93.5 × 21.3 × 5.9 *(28.5 × 6.5 × 1.8)*
Main machinery: 2 MTU-Bazán 8V 396 TB93 diesels; 2100 hp(m) *(1.54 MW)* sustained; 2 shafts
Speed, knots: 20. **Range, miles:** 1000 at 12 kts
Complement: 13
Guns: 1 Browning 12.7 mm MG.
Radars: Surface search: Racal Decca RM 1070; I band.
Navigation: Racal Decca RM 270; I band.

Comment: Wooden hull with GRP sheath.

FORMENTOR   8/1992, F Gámez

Light forces / SPAIN 627

3 USCG TYPE (COASTAL PATROL CRAFT)

No	Builders	Commissioned
P 311 (ex-PAS 11, ex-LAS 1, ex-LAS 10)	Bazán, Cartagena	26 Apr 1965
P 312 (ex-PAS 12, ex-LAS 2, ex-LAS 20)	Bazán, Cartagena	4 May 1965
P 313 (ex-PAS 13, ex-LAS 3, ex-LAS 30)	Bazán, Cartagena	3 Sep 1965

Displacement, tons: 49 standard; 62 full load
Dimensions, feet (metres): 83.3 × 14.8 × 6.6 *(25.4 × 4.5 × 2)*
Main machinery: 2 diesels; 800 hp(m) *(588 kW)*; 2 shafts
Speed, knots: 15
Complement: 10
Guns: 1 Oerlikon 20 mm. 2—7.62 mm MGs.
Radars: Navigation: Decca; I band.

Comment: All launched 1964. Of wooden hull construction. Former anti-submarine craft which have had all ASW equipment removed. To be paid off in mid-1993.

P 312 *7/1992, Diego Quevedo*

22 P 101 CLASS (COASTAL PATROL CRAFT)

P 101-102   P 104-123

Displacement, tons: 18.5 standard; 20.8 full load
Dimensions, feet (metres): 44.9 × 14.4 × 4.3 *(13.7 × 4.4 × 1.3)*
Main machinery: 2 Baudouin-Interdiesel DNP-350; 768 hp(m) *(564 kW)*; 2 shafts
Speed, knots: 23.3. **Range, miles:** 430 at 18 kts
Complement: 6
Guns: 1—12.7 mm MG.
Radars: Surface search: Decca 110; I band.

Comment: Ordered under the programme agreed 13 May 1977, funded jointly by the Navy and the Ministry of Commerce. Built to the Aresa LVC 160 design by Aresa, Arenys de Mar, Barcelona. GRP hull. All completed by early 1980 except *P 121* in February 1981 and *P 122* and *123* in 1983. *P 122* and *123* have supercharged engines giving a 25 per cent increase in power and a speed of 27 kts. *P 103* deleted in 1990. *P 115* may be scrapped after a fire.

P 119 *8/1992, F Gámez*

5 P 231 CLASS (COASTAL PATROL CRAFT)

P 231-235

Displacement, tons: 18 full load
Dimensions, feet (metres): 46 × 15.4 × 3.3 *(14 × 4.7 × 1)*
Main machinery: 2 Gray Marine diesels; 450 hp *(336 kW)*; 2 shafts
Speed, knots: 13
Complement: 8
Guns: 2—7.62 mm (twin) MGs.

Comment: Laid down 1964 by Bazán, La Carraca. Wooden hulled. Originally LPI-1 etc. All completed February-March 1965 to USCG design.

P 233 *9/1987, Camil Busquets i Vilanova*

1 COASTAL PATROL CRAFT

P 124 (ex-*PVC 21*, ex-*V 33*)

Displacement, tons: 23 full load
Dimensions, feet (metres): 52.5 × 14.1 × 3.3 *(16 × 4.3 × 1)*
Main machinery: 2 MAN D2542MTE diesels; 1100 hp(m) *(808 kW)*; 2 shafts
Speed, knots: 24. **Range, miles:** 700 at 18 kts
Complement: 6
Guns: 1 Browning 12.7 mm MG.
Radars: Surface search: Decca 110; I band.

Comment: Built by Viudes, Barcelona to Bazán 16 m design with GRP hull in 1977. Painted white.

P 124 *7/1992, Camil Busquets i Vilanova*

1 INSHORE/RIVER PATROL LAUNCH

Name	No	Builders	Commissioned
CABO FRADERA	P 201	Bazán, La Carraca	25 Feb 1963

Displacement, tons: 21
Dimensions, feet (metres): 58.3 × 13.8 × 3 *(17.8 × 4.2 × 0.9)*
Speed, knots: 10
Complement: 9
Guns: 1—7.62 mm MG

Comment: Based at Tuy on River Minho for border patrol with Portugal.

CABO FRADERA *1987, Royal Spanish Navy*

29 P 202 CLASS (INSHORE PATROL CRAFT)

P 202-230 (ex-*PVI 1-18* and ex-*PVI 110-130*)

Displacement, tons: 4.8 full load
Dimensions, feet (metres): 29.2 × 10.2 × 2.3 *(8.9 × 3.1 × 0.7)*
Main machinery: 2 Ebro MH 58 diesels; 180 hp(m) *(132 kW)* sustained; 2 shafts
Speed, knots: 18. **Range, miles:** 120 at 18 kts
Complement: 4
Guns: 1—7.62 mm MG.
Radars: Navigation: Decca 60 for 10 craft based in northern ports.

Comment: A class of 30 craft ordered from Rodman, Vigo under the programme agreed 13 May 1977, funded jointly by the Navy and the Ministry of Commerce. All completed 1978-79. GRP hull. Ex-PVI 19 destroyed by terrorists in 1984 in San Sebastian (before new pennant number system was introduced). *P 205* attacked in August 1990 and another one in February 1991 but both have been repaired.

P 218 *7/1992, Diego Quevedo*

628 SPAIN / Amphibious forces

AMPHIBIOUS FORCES

Note: There are also a number of elderly LCPs used for various tasks listed under *Miscellaneous*.

0 + (2) AMPHIBIOUS TRANSPORT SHIP (LPD)

Displacement, tons: 9500 full load
Dimensions, feet (metres): 492.1 × 82 × 18.4 *(150 × 25 × 5.6)*
Main machinery: 2 diesels, 2 shafts
Speed, knots: 20. **Range, miles:** 6000 at 14 kts
Complement: 115 plus 12 spare
Military lift: 600 fully equipped troops or 170 APCs or 33 MBTs. 3 LCVPs and 2 LCUs/LCMs or 6 LCVPs in docking well
Guns: 2 Meroka CIWS.
Helicopters: 6 NH-90 or 4 EH-101.

Comment: Originally started as a national project by the Netherlands. In 1990 the ATS was seen as a possible solution to fulfil the requirements for a new LPD. Joint project definition study announced in July 1991. The ship will be able to transport a fully equipped battalion of 600 marines providing a built-in dock for landing craft and a helicopter flight deck for debarkation in offshore conditions. Alternatively the ship can also be used as a general logistic support ship for both military and civil operations, including environmental and disaster relief tasks. Construction is planned to start in January 1995 for commissioning in mid-1998. No dates are available for the second of class.

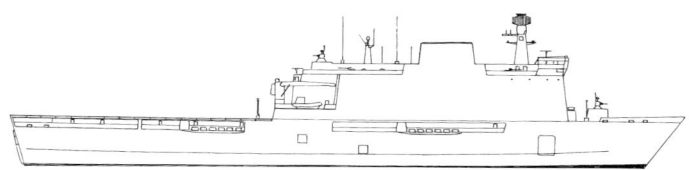

ATS *(not to scale), Ian Sturton*

2 Ex-US PAUL REVERE CLASS (ATTACK TRANSPORTS)

Name	No	Builders	Commissioned
CASTILLA (ex-*Diamond Mariner*, ex-USS *Paul Revere* LPA 248)	L 21 (ex-TA 12)	New York SB	3 Sep 1958
ARAGÓN (ex-*Prairie Mariner*, ex-USS *Francis Marion* LPA 249)	L 22	New York SB	6 July 1961

Displacement, tons: 10 709 light; 16 315 (L 21), 16 573 (L 22) full load
Dimensions, feet (metres): 563.5 × 76 × 27 *(171.8 × 23.1 × 8.2)*
Main machinery: 2 Foster-Wheeler boilers; 600 psi *(42.3 kg/cm sq)*; 870°F *(467°C)*; 1 GE turbine; 22 000 hp *(16.4 MW)*; 1 shaft
Speed, knots: 22. **Range, miles:** 17 000 at 14 kts
Complement: 610 (L 21), 660 (L 22) (35 officers)
Military lift: 1657 troops; 7 LCM 6s (161-167 for L 21 and 261-267 for L 22); 5 LCVPs; 3 LCPs

Guns: 8 US 3 in *(76 mm)*/50 (4 twin); 85° elevation; 50 rounds/minute to 12.8 km *(7 nm)*; weight of shell 6 kg.
Countermeasures: Decoys: Loral Hycor SRBOC Mk 36 chaff launcher.
ESM: WLR1; radar intercept. ECM: ULQ 6; jammer.
Radars: Air search: RCA SPS 12 (L 21); D band; range 119 km *(65 nm)*.
Lockheed SPS 40 (L 22); E/F band; range 320 km *(175 nm)*.
Surface search: Raytheon SPS 10; G band.
Fire control: Four SPG 50 or SPG 34; I/J band.

Helicopters: Platform for 1 AS 332 Super Puma type.

Programmes: Originally C4-S-1 cargo vessels converted to APAs. L 21 by Todd Shipyard, San Pedro and L 22 by Bethlehem, Baltimore. Designated LPAs in 1969. L 21 transferred 17 January 1980 by sale, L 22 11 July 1980.
Operational: *Aragón* is the Flagship for Amphibious Command.

ARAGÓN *1/1993, Diego Quevedo*

2 Ex-US TERREBONNE PARISH CLASS (LSTs)

Name	No	Builders	Commissioned
VELASCO (ex-USS *Terrebonne Parish* LST 1156)	L 11	Bath Iron Works	21 Nov 1952
MARTIN ALVAREZ (ex-USS *Wexford County* LST 1168)	L 12	Christy Corporation	15 June 1954

Displacement, tons: 2590 standard; 5800 full load
Dimensions, feet (metres): 384 × 55 × 17 *(117.1 × 16.8 × 5.2)*
Main machinery: 4 General Motors 16-278A diesels; 6000 hp *(4.48 MW)*; 2 shafts
Speed, knots: 15. **Range, miles:** 15 000 at 9 kts
Complement: 153 (395 troops)
Military lift: 395 troops; 10 Mk 48 tanks or 17 LVTPs; 3 LCVPs; 1 LCP

Guns: 6 US 3 in *(76 mm)*/50 (3 twin).
Fire control: 2 Mk 63 GFCS.
Radars: Surface search: Racal Decca TM 1229; I band.
Navigation: Decca; I band.
Fire control: Two Western Electric SPG 34; I/J band.

Programmes: Both transferred on 29 October 1971. Purchased on 17 May 1978.

TERREBONNE PARISH class (old number) *1/1990, F Gámez*

3 SPANISH LCTs

A 06-A 08

Displacement, tons: 279 standard; 665 full load
Dimensions, feet (metres): 193.5 × 39 × 4.3 *(59 × 11.9 × 1.3)*
Main machinery: 2 MTU-Bazán MA 6 R 362 SB70 diesels; 1120 hp(m) *(823 kW)*; 2 shafts
Speed, knots: 9.5. **Range, miles:** 1500 at 9 kts
Complement: 23
Military lift: 300 tons; 35 troops
Guns: 2—12.7 mm MGs. 1—81 mm mortar.
Radars: Navigation: Decca; I band.

Comment: Built by Bazán, La Carraca and commissioned in December 1966. Rated as logistic craft.

A 08 *5/1992, van Ginderen Collection*

2 Ex-US LCUs

L 71 (ex-*LCU 11*, ex-*LCU 1*, ex-*LCU 1471*)
L 72 (ex-*LCU 12*, ex-*LCU 2*, ex-*LCU 1491*)

Displacement, tons: 354 full load
Dimensions, feet (metres): 119.7 × 31.5 × 5.2 *(36.5 × 9.6 × 1.6)*
Main machinery: 3 Gray Marine 64 YTL diesels; 675 hp *(504 kW)*; 3 shafts
Speed, knots: 7.6
Complement: 14
Military lift: 160 tons

Comment: Transferred June 1972. Purchased August 1976.

L 71 *1990, Royal Spanish Navy*

8 LCM 8

L 81-86 (ex-*LCM 81-86*, ex-*E 81-86*)   **L 87-88**

Displacement, tons: 113 full load
Dimensions, feet (metres): 74.5 × 21.7 × 5.9 *(22.7 × 6.6 × 1.8)*
Main machinery: 4 GM 6-71 diesels; 696 hp *(519 kW)* sustained; 2 shafts
Speed, knots: 11
Complement: 5

Comment: First six ordered from Oxnard, California in 1974. Assembled in Spain. Commissioned in July-September 1975. Two more built by Bazán, San Fernando, and completed in early 1989.

L 82 *10/1989, Camil Busquets i Vilanova*

43 LANDING CRAFT

Comment: Apart from those used for divers there are 14 LCM 6, 20 LCVP and 9 LCP. Ten of the LCM 6, eight of the LCVPs and most of the LCPs were built in Spanish Shipyards 1986-88.

1 HOVERCRAFT

VCA 36

Displacement, tons: 36 full load
Dimensions, feet (metres): 82.7 × 37.4 × 31.2 (height) *(25.2 × 11.4 × 9.5)*
Main machinery: 2 Textron-Lycoming TF-25 gas turbines; 5000 hp *(3.73 MW)* sustained
Speed, knots: 60. **Range, miles:** 145 at 45 kts
Complement: 3
Military lift: 14 tons or 70 troops and 3 Land Rovers or 1 Scorpion light tank
Sonars: French helicopter type for trials; VDS; high frequency.

Comment: Built by Chaconsa, Mercia as an evolution of the VCA 3 design. Operational in 1988. More may be ordered in due course to fulfill tactical and logistic requirements.

VCA 36   *6/1988, Camil Busquets i Vilanova*

MINE WARFARE FORCES

0 + 4 CME CLASS (MODIFIED SANDOWN) (MINEHUNTERS)

Displacement, tons: 530 full load
Dimensions, feet (metres): 177.2 oa; 167.3 wl × 32.8 × 7.2 *(54; 51 × 10 × 2.2)*
Main machinery: 2 MTU-Bazán diesels; 1523 hp(m) *(1.12 MW)*; 2 shafts
Speed, knots: 14. **Range, miles:** 2000 at 12 kts
Complement: 40 (7 officers)
Guns: 1 Oerlikon 20 mm.
Radars: Navigation: I band.

Comment: On 4 July 1989 a technology transfer contract was signed with Vosper Thornycroft to allow Bazán to design a new MCM vessel based on the Sandown class. Minehunting system will be by FABA-Bazán with Inisel. The ships will have an SAES ROV and either the British 2093 sonar or the SQQ 32 developed for the US Osprey class. The programme is uncertain but the official plan in early 1993 was to start building the first of class at Cartagena in June 1994 with the fourth completing in March 1999. Final requirement is for eight of the class.

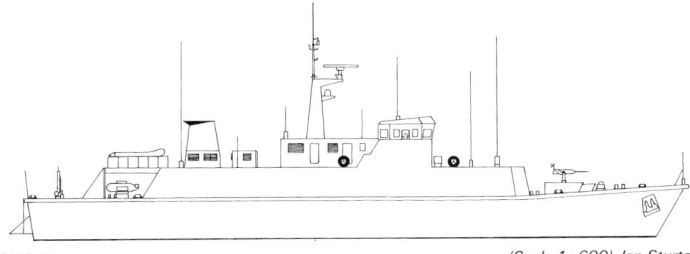

CME class   *(Scale 1 : 600), Ian Sturton*

4 Ex-US AGGRESSIVE CLASS (MINESWEEPERS—OCEAN)

Name	No	Builders	Commissioned
GUADALETE (ex-USS *Dynamic* MSO 432)	M 41	Colbert BW, Stockton, Calif	15 Dec 1953
GUADALMEDINA (ex-USS *Pivot* MSO 463)	M 42	Wilmington BW, Calif	12 July 1954
GUADALQUIVIR (ex-USS *Persistant* MSO 491)	M 43	Tacoma, Washington	3 Feb 1956
GUADIANA (ex-USS *Vigor* MSO 473)	M 44	Burgess Boat Co, Manitowoc	8 Nov 1954

Displacement, tons: 804-840 full load
Dimensions, feet (metres): 172.5 × 35 × 14.1 *(52.6 × 10.7 × 4.3)*
Main machinery: 4 Packard ID-1700 diesels; 2280 hp *(1.7 MW)*; 2 shafts; cp props
Speed, knots: 14. **Range, miles:** 3000 at 10 kts
Complement: 74 (6 officers)

Guns: 2 Oerlikon 20 mm (twin).
Countermeasures: Pluto ROVs in some.
Radars: Surface search: Raytheon SPS 5C; G/H band; range 37 km *(20 nm)*.
Navigation: Decca; I band.
Sonars: General Electric SQQ 14; VDS; active minehunting; high frequency.

Programmes: The first three were transferred and commissioned on 1 July 1971. The fourth ship was delivered 4 April 1972. All purchased August 1974. To be paid off when new MCMVs commission.
Modernisation: Completed in 1984-86 to extend service lives. At least two Pluto ROVs acquired in 1989 in order to gain experience while the new MCMVs are being built.

GUADIANA   *9/1992, Diego Quevedo*

8 Ex-US ADJUTANT, REDWING and MSC 268 CLASSES
(MINESWEEPERS—COASTAL)

Name	No	Builders	Commissioned
JÚCAR (ex-*MSC 220*)	M 21	Bellingham SY	22 June 1956
EBRO (ex-*MSC 269*)	M 22	Bellingham SY	19 Dec 1958
DUERO (ex-*Spoonbill* MSC 202)	M 23	Tampa Marine Corporation	16 June 1959
TAJO (ex-*MSC 287*)	M 24	Tampa Marine Corporation	9 July 1959
GENIL (ex-*MSC 279*)	M 25	Tacoma, Seattle	11 Sep 1959
ODIEL (ex-*MSC 288*)	M 26	Tampa Marine Corporation	9 Oct 1959
SIL (ex-*Redwing* MSC 200)	M 27	Tampa Marine Corporation	16 Jan 1959
MIÑO (ex-*MSC 266*)	M 28	Adams YY, Mass	25 Oct 1956

Displacement, tons: 355 standard; 384 full load
Dimensions, feet (metres): 144 × 28 × 8.2 *(43.9 × 8.5 × 2.5)*
Main machinery: 2 GM 8-268A diesels; 880 hp *(656 kW)*; 2 shafts
Speed, knots: 14. **Range, miles:** 2700 at 10 kts
Complement: 39 (3 officers)
Guns: 2 Oerlikon 20 mm (twin).
Radars: Navigation: Decca TM 626 or RM 914; I band.
Sonars: UQS 1; active minehunting; high frequency.

Comment: Wooden hulled. Two sub-types: M 22, M 24, M 25 and M 26 with no mainmast but crane abreast the funnel. M 21, M 23, M 27 and M 28 have derrick on mainmast. Three others of the class transferred to Patrol Ship duties in 1980.

SIL   *9/1992, Diego Quevedo*

GENIL   *9/1992, Diego Quevedo*

SURVEY AND RESEARCH SHIPS

1 Ex-GERMAN DARSS CLASS (AGI)

Name	No	Builders	Launched
ALERTA (ex-*Jasmund*)	A 111	Peenewerft, Wolgast	27 Feb 1982

Displacement, tons: 2292 full load
Dimensions, feet (metres): 250.3 × 39.7 × 13.8 *(76.3 × 12.1 × 4.2)*
Main machinery: 1 Kolomna Type 40-DM diesel; 2200 hp(m) *(1.6 MW)* sustained; 1 shaft; cp prop
Speed, knots: 12. **Range, miles:** 1000 at 12 kts
Complement: 60
Guns: Fitted for 3 twin 25 mm/70.
Radars: Air/surface search: E/F band.
Navigation: I band.

Comment: Former GDR depot ship converted to an AGI, with additional accommodation replacing much of the storage capacity. Was to have transferred to Ecuador in 1991 but the sale was cancelled. Commissioned in the Spanish Navy on 6 December 1992 and sailed from Wilhelmshaven for a refit at Las Palmas prior to being based at Cartagena and used as an AGI. New armament and sensors after refit.

ALERTA
3/1993, Diaz Lorenzo

1 RESEARCH SHIP

Name	No	Builders	Commissioned
HESPÉRIDES (ex-*Mar Antártico*)	A 33	Bazán, Cartagena	16 May 1991

Displacement, tons: 2738 full load
Dimensions, feet (metres): 270.7; 255.2 × 46.9 × 14.8 *(82.5; 77.8 × 14.3 × 4.5)*
Main machinery: Diesel-electric; 4 MAN-Bazán 14V20/27 diesels; 6860 hp(m) *(5 MW)* sustained; 4 generators; 2 AEG motors; 3800 hp(m) *(2.8 MW)*; 1 shaft; bow and stern thrusters; 350 hp(m) *(257 kW)* each
Speed, knots: 15. **Range, miles:** 12 000 at 13 kts
Complement: 39 (9 officers) plus 30 scientists
Radars: Surface search: Racal/Hispano ARPA 2690; I band.
Navigation: Racal 2690 ACS; F band.
Helicopters: AB 212 or similar.

Comment: Ordered in July 1988 from Bazán, Cartagena, by the Ministry of Education and Science. Laid down in 1989, launched 12 March 1990. Has 330 sq m of laboratories, Simbad ice sonar, navigation radars and GPS. Dome in keel houses several sensors. Ice strengthened hull capable of breaking first year ice up to 45 cm at 5 kts. The main task is to support the Spanish base at Livingston Island, Antarctica replacing the tug *Las Palmas*. Manned and operated by the Navy. Has a red hull, foremast and funnels and a telescopic hangar.

HESPÉRIDES
7/1992, Diego Quevedo

2 MALASPINA CLASS (OCEANOGRAPHIC SHIPS)

Name	No	Builders	Commissioned
MALASPINA	A 31	Bazán, La Carraca	21 Feb 1975
TOFIÑO	A 32	Bazán, La Carraca	23 Apr 1975

Displacement, tons: 820 standard; 1090 full load
Dimensions, feet (metres): 188.9 × 38.4 × 12.8 *(57.6 × 11.7 × 3.9)*
Main machinery: 2 San Carlos MWM TbRHS-345-61 diesels; 3600 hp(m) *(2.64 MW)*; 2 shafts; cp props
Speed, knots: 15. **Range, miles:** 4000 at 12 kts; 3140 at 14.5 kts
Complement: 63 (9 officers)
Guns: 2 Oerlikon 20 mm.
Radars: Navigation: Raytheon 1220/6XB; I/J band.

Comment: Ordered mid-1972. Both named after their immediate predecessors. Developed from British Bulldog class. Fitted with two Atlas DESO-10 AN 1021 (280-1400 m) echo-sounders, retractable Burnett 538-2 sonar for deep sounding, Egg Mark B side-scan sonar, Raydist DR-S navigation system, Hewlett Packard 2100A computer inserted into Magnavox Transit satellite navigation system, active rudder with fixed pitch auxiliary propeller. *Malaspina* used for a NATO evaluation of a Ship's Laser Inertial Navigation System (SLINS) produced by British Aerospace.

TOFIÑO
8/1992, F Gámez

4 CASTOR CLASS

Name	No	Builders	Commissioned
CASTOR	A 21 (ex-H 4)	Bazán, La Carraca	10 Nov 1966
POLLUX	A 22 (ex-H 5)	Bazán, La Carraca	6 Dec 1966
ANTARES	A 23	Bazán, La Carraca	21 Nov 1974
RIGEL	A 24	Bazán, La Carraca	21 Nov 1974

Displacement, tons: 327 standard; 355 full load
Dimensions, feet (metres): 125.9 × 24.9 × 10.2 *(38.4 × 7.6 × 3.1)*
Main machinery: 1 Sulzer 4TD36 diesel; 720 hp(m) *(530 kW)*; 1 shaft
Speed, knots: 11.5. **Range, miles:** 3620 at 8 kts
Complement: 36 (4 officers)
Radars: Navigation: Raytheon 1620; I/J band.

Comment: Fitted with Raydist, Omega and digital presentation of data. A 21 and 22 have gaps in the gunwhale aft for Oropesa sweep. In A 23 and 24 this is a full run to the stern.

CASTOR
10/1992, Diego Quevedo

SERVICE FORCES

Note: *Campeón* is a civilian tanker owned by CAMPSA and chartered as required. Fitted for one beam and one stern RAS station. 14 862 grt, 166 m in length and with a top speed of 14.5 kts.

0 + 1 AOR 90 CLASS (ZUIDERKRUIS TYPE)
(FLEET LOGISTIC TANKER)

Name	No	Builders	Commissioned
MAR DEL SUR (?)	—	Bazán, Ferrol	June 1995

Displacement, tons: 17 045 full load
Dimensions, feet (metres): 544.6 × 72.2 × 26.2 *(166 × 22 × 8)*
Main machinery: Diesel-electric; 2 Bazán MAN 16V40/45 diesels; 24 000 hp(m) *(17.6 MW)* sustained; 1 motor; 1 shaft; cp prop
Speed, knots: 20. **Range, miles:** 13 440 at 20 kts
Complement: 136 plus 24 aircrew plus 20 spare
Cargo capacity: 6815 tons dieso; 1660 tons petrol; 500 tons solids
Guns: 2 Bazán 20 mm/120 Meroka CIWS. 2 Oerlikon 20 mm/90.
Countermeasures: Decoys: 4 chaff launchers.
ESM/ECM: Aldebaran intercept and jammer.
Radars: 2 navigation/helo control; I band.
Helicopters: 3 SH-3D Sea King size.

Comment: The Bazán design AP 21 was rejected in favour of this joint Netherlands/Spain design based on *Zuiderkruis*. Ordered on 26 December 1991. To be laid down in June 1993 which is two years later than planned. Scheduled launch June 1994. She will replace the discarded *Teide* as a carrier group support ship. Two supply stations each side for both liquids and solids. Stern refuelling. Two Vertrep supply stations and workshops for aircraft maintenance. Medical facilities. Built to merchant ship standards with military NBC. Accommodation for up to 50 female crew members. The name is provisional.

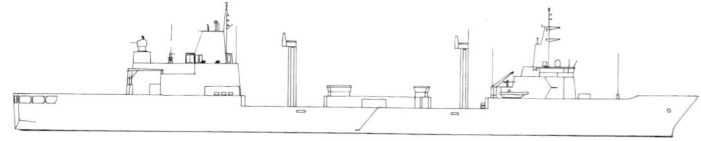

MAR DEL SUR
(not to scale), Ian Sturton

1 TRANSPORT

Name	No	Builders	Commissioned
CONTRAMAESTRE CASADO (ex-*Thanasis-K*, ex-*Fortuna Reefer*, ex-*Bonzo*, ex-*Bajamar*, ex-*Leeward Islands*)	A 01	Eriksberg-Göteborg, Sweden	15 Dec 1982

Displacement, tons: 5300 full load
Dimensions, feet (metres): 343.4 × 46.9 × 29.2 *(104.7 × 14.3 × 8.9)*
Main machinery: 1 Burmeister & Wain diesel; 3600 hp(m) *(2.65 MW)*; 1 shaft
Speed, knots: 16. **Range, miles:** 8000 at 15 kts
Complement: 72
Guns: 2 Oerlikon 20 mm.

Comment: Built in the 1950s. Impounded as smuggler. Delivered after conversion 6 December 1983. Has a helicopter deck.

CONTRAMAESTRE CASADO　　　　　　　　　　　　　　4/1992, van Ginderen Collection

1 FLEET TANKER

Name	No	Builders	Commissioned
MAR DEL NORTE	A 11	Bazán, Ferrol	3 June 1991

Displacement, tons: 13 380 full load
Dimensions, feet (metres): 403.9 oa; 377.3 wl × 64 × 25.9 *(123.1; 115 × 19.5 × 7.9)*
Main machinery: 1 MAN-Bazán 18V40/50A; 11 247 hp(m) *(8.27 MW)* sustained; 1 shaft
Speed, knots: 16. **Range, miles:** 10 000 at 15 kts
Complement: 80 (11 officers)
Cargo capacity: 7498 tons dieso; 1746 tons JP-5; 120 tons deck cargo
Guns: 2—7.62 mm MGs.
Radars: Surface search: Racal Decca 2459; I/F band.
Navigation: Racal Decca ARPA 2690/9; I band.
Helicopters: 1 AB 212 or similar.

Comment: Ordered 30 December 1988. Laid down 16 November 1989 and launched 3 October 1990. The deletion of the *Teide* has left a serious deficiency in the Fleet's at sea replenishment capability which is to be restored in due course by the new Zuiderkruis type of logistic tanker. In addition, and as a stop gap, this tanker is being built at one third of the cost of the larger support ship. It will have two Vertrep stations and a platform for a Sea King size helicopter. Replenishment stations on both sides and one astern. Provision for Meroka CIWS behind the bridge and four chaff launchers as well as ESM. Has a small hospital.

MAR DEL NORTE　　　　　　　　　　　　　　　　　　7/1992, Diego Quevedo

MAR DEL NORTE　　　　　　　　　　　　　　　　　　5/1992, A Campanera i Rovira

10 HARBOUR TANKERS

No	Displacement, tons	Dimensions, metres	Builders	Commissioned
Y 231	524	34 × 7 × 2.9	Bazán, Cádiz	1981
Y 232	830	42.8 × 8.4 × 3.1	Bazán, Cádiz	1981
Y 235	510	37.8 × 6.6 × 3	Bazán, Ferrol	1959
Y 236	200	28 × 5.2 × 1.9	Bazán, Ferrol	1959
Y 237	344	34.3 × 6.2 × 2.5	Bazán, Cádiz	1965
Y 251	200	28 × 5.2 × 1.9	Bazán, Ferrol	1959
Y 252	337	34.3 × 6.2 × 2.5	Bazán, Cádiz	1965
Y 253	337	34.3 × 6.2 × 2.5	Bazán, Cádiz	1965
Y 254	214.7	24.5 × 5.5 × 2.2	Bazán, Cádiz	1981
Y 255	524	34 × 7 × 2.9	Bazán, Cádiz	1981

TRAINING SHIPS

4 SAIL TRAINING SHIPS

Name	No	Builders	Commissioned
JUAN SEBASTIÁN DE ELCANO	A 71	Echevarrieta, Cadiz	28 Feb 1928
AROSA	A 72	—	1 Apr 1981
HISPANIA	A 73	Barracuda SY, Palma	25 July 1988
LA GRACIOSA (ex-*Deja Vu*)	A 74	—	30 June 1988

Displacement, tons: 3420 standard; 3656 full load
Dimensions, feet (metres): 269.2 pp; 308.5 oa × 43.3 × 24.6 *(82; 94.1 × 13.2 × 7.5)*
Main machinery: 1 Deutz MWM RBV 6M diesel; 1500 hp(m) *(1.1 MW)*; 1 shaft
Speed, knots: 8.5. **Range, miles:** 10 000 at 9.5 kts
Complement: 332
Guns: 2—37 mm saluting guns.
Radars: Navigation: Two Decca TM 626; I band.

Comment: Details are for A 71 which is a four masted top-sail schooner—near sister of Chilean *Esmeralda*. Named after the first circumnavigator of the world (1519-22) who succeeded to the command of the expedition led by Magellan after the latter's death. Laid down 24 November 1925. Launched on 5 March 1927. Carries 230 tons oil fuel. Engine replaced in 1992. She may be kept in service until 2027. The other three are a ketch (A 72) and two schooners (38 tons and 24.5 m in length) used by the Naval School.

JUAN SEBASTIAN DE ELCANO　　　　　　　　　　　　1/1992, F Gámez

5 TRAINING CRAFT

Name	No	Builders	Commissioned
GUARDIAMARINA BARRUTIA	A 81	Cartagena	14 Sep 1982
GUARDIAMARINA SALAS	A 82	Cartagena	10 May 1983
GUARDIAMARINA GODINEZ	A 83	Cartagena	4 July 1984
GUARDIAMARINA RULL	A 84	Cartagena	11 June 1984
GUARDIAMARINA CHEREGUINI	A 85	Cartagena	11 June 1984

Displacement, tons: 56
Dimensions, feet (metres): 62 × 16.7 × 5.2 *(18.9 × 5.1 × 1.6)*
Speed, knots: 13
Complement: 15; 22 (A 81)
Radars: Navigation: Halcon 948; I band.

Comment: Tenders to Naval School. A 81 has an operations centre.

GUARDIAMARINA BARRUTIA　　　　　　　　　　　　1987, Royal Spanish Navy

BOOM DEFENCE VESSELS

Y 611 (ex-*YBPN 01*)　　　　Y 361-362　　　　Y 364-365

Displacement, tons: 51.1
Dimensions, feet (metres): 73.1 × 28.5 × 2.6 *(22.3 × 8.7 × 0.8)*

Comment: *Y 611* is a gate vessel. Delivered 1960. Unpropelled. *Y 361-362* are net laying barges, *Y 364-365* are tugs for gate vessel and barges.

632 SPAIN / Boom defence vessels — Tugs

Name	No	Builders	Commissioned
CÍCLOPE	A 13 (ex-AC 01, ex-CR 1, ex-G 6)	Penhoët, France	29 July 1955

Displacement, tons: 750.5 full load
Dimensions, feet (metres): 151.9 × 33.5 × 13.8 *(46.3 × 10.2 × 4.2)*
Main machinery: Diesel-electric; 2 diesel generators; 1 motor; 1600 hp(m) *(1.18 MW)*; 1 shaft
Speed, knots: 14. **Range, miles:** 5200 at 12 kts
Complement: 40
Guns: 1 Bofors 40 mm/60. 4 Oerlikon 20 mm.

Comment: US off-shore order. Transferred from the USA in 1955 under MDAP. Sister ship of French Cigale class (deleted). Based at Cartagena.

CÍCLOPE *11/1992, Diego Quevedo*

TUGS

2 LOGISTIC SUPPORT TUGS

Name	No	Builders	Commissioned
MAR CARIBE (ex-*Amatista*)	A 101	Duro Felguera, Gijon	24 Mar 1975
MAR ROJO (ex-*Amapola*)	A 102	Duro Felguera, Gijon	24 Mar 1975

Displacement, tons: 1860 full load
Dimensions, feet (metres): 176.4 × 38.8 × 14.8 *(53.8 × 11.8 × 4.5)*
Main machinery: 2 Echevarria-Burmeister & Wain 18V23HU diesels; 4860 hp(m) *(3.57 MW)*; 2 shafts; bow thruster
Speed, knots: 13.5. **Range, miles:** 6000 at 10 kts
Complement: 44

Comment: Two offshore oil rig support tugs were acquired and commissioned into the Navy 14 December 1988. Bollard pull, 80 tons. Mar Rojo converted as a diver support vessel completing in January 1991. A Vosma submergence vehicle is to be replaced by a DSRV. She has a dynamic positioning system and carries a sidescan mine detection high frequency sonar. Mar Caribe works with Amphibious Forces.

MAR CARIBE *1/1993, Diego Quevedo*

2 COASTAL TUGS

Y 116 (ex-*YRR 21*, ex-*71*)   Y 117 (ex-*YRR 22*, ex-*72*)

Displacement, tons: 422 full load
Dimensions, feet (metres): 91.8 × 26.2 × 12.5 *(28 × 8 × 3.8)*
Main machinery: 1 diesel; 1500 hp *(1.1 MW)*; 1 shaft
Speed, knots: 12.4. **Range, miles:** 3000 at 10 kts

Comment: Built by Bazán, Ferrol. Commissioned 10 April and 1 June 1981 respectively.

Y 116 *10/1992, Camil Busquets i Vilanova*

2 OCEAN TUGS

Name	No	Builders	Commissioned
MAHÓN	A 51	Astilleros Atlántico, Santander	1978
LAS PALMAS	A 52	Astilleros Atlántico, Santander	1978

Displacement, tons: 1437 full load
Dimensions, feet (metres): 134.5 × 38.1 × 18 *(41 × 11.6 × 5.5)*
Main machinery: 2 AESA/Sulzer 16ASV25/30 diesels; 7744 hp(m) *(5.69 MW)*; 2 shafts
Speed, knots: 13. **Range, miles:** 27 000 at 12 kts (A 52)
Complement: 33 (8 officers) plus 45 scientists
Guns: 2—12.7 mm MGs.

Comment: Built for Compania Hispano Americana de Offshore SA as *Circos* (A 51) and *Somiedo*. Commissioned in the Navy 30 July 1981. Las Palmas converted in 1988 for Polar Research Ship duties in Antarctica with an ice strengthened bow, an enlarged bridge and two containers aft for laboratories. With the commissioning of *Hesperides*, the ship is based at Las Palmas and is being used as a tug.

MAHÓN *2/1992, Giorgio Arra*

4 OCEAN TUGS

Name	No	Builders	Commissioned
POSEIDÓN	A 12 (ex-*AS 01*, ex-*RA 6*)	Bazán, La Carraca	8 Aug 1964
CARTAGENA (ex-*Valen*)	A 41 (ex-*RA 1*)	Bazán, Cartagena	9 July 1955
CÁDIZ	A 42 (ex-*AR 44*, ex-*RA 4*)	Bazán, La Carraca	25 Mar 1964
FERROL	A 43 (ex-*AR 45*, ex-*RA 5*)	Bazán, La Carraca	11 Apr 1964

Displacement, tons: 951 standard; 1069 full load
Dimensions, feet (metres): 183.5 × 32.8 × 13.1 *(55.9 × 10 × 4)*
Main machinery: 2 Sulzer diesels; 3200 hp *(2.53 MW)*; 1 shaft; cp prop
Speed, knots: 15. **Range, miles:** 4640 at 14 kts
Complement: 49; 60 (A 12)
Guns: 2 or 4 Oerlikon 20 mm (twin).
Radars: Navigation: Decca TM 626; I band.

Comment: A 12 acts as a frogman support ship and submarine SAR vessel at Cartagena and carries a 300 m/6 h bathyscaphe. Some superstructure differences in all of the class.

CÁDIZ *4/1992, van Ginderen Collection*

CARTAGENA *2/1993, Diego Quevedo*

29 COASTAL and HARBOUR TUGS

No	Displacement tonnes (full load)	HP/speed	Commissioned
Y 111, Y 114	227	800/10	1963
Y 113	217	1400/12	1965
Y 115	216	1500/12	1967
Y 118, Y 121-123	236	1560/14	1989-91
Y 119 (ex-*Punta Amer*)	260	1750/12	1973
Y 120 (ex-*Punta Roca*)	260	1750/12	1973
Y 131-135, Y 137-140	70	200/8	1965-67
Y 141-142	229	800/11	1981
Y 143	133	600/10	1961
Y 144-145	195	2030/11	1983
Y 146	173	829/10	1983
Y 147	87	400/10	1987
Y 171-173	10	440/11	1982 (171) 1985 (172-3)

Comment: Y 143 has a troop carrying capability. Y 171-173 are pusher tugs for submarines. Y 118, Y 119-123 have Voith Schneider propulsion.

Y 118 — 1988, Bazán

WATER CARRIERS

CONTRAMAESTRE CASTELLÓ A 61 (ex-*AA 06*, ex-*A 6*)

Displacement, tons: 1811 full load
Dimensions, feet (metres): 210.3 × 31.5 × 15.7 *(64.1 × 9.6 × 4.8)*
Main machinery: 1 boiler; 1 reciprocating engine; 800 ihp(m) *(588 kW)*; 1 shaft
Speed, knots: 9
Complement: 27
Cargo capacity: 1000 tons
Guns: 2—12.7 mm MGs.

Comment: Commissioned 30 January 1952. Ocean-going.

CONTRAMAESTRE CASTELLÓ — 1987, Royal Spanish Navy

MAQUINISTA MACÍAS A 62 (ex-*AA 21*, ex-*A 9*)
TORPEDISTA HERNÁNDEZ A 63 (ex-*AA 22*, ex-*A 10*)
FOGONERO BAÑOBRE A 64 (ex-*AA 23*, ex-*A 11*)

Displacement, tons: 575 full load
Dimensions, feet (metres): 146.9 × 24.9 × 9.8 *(44.8 × 7.6 × 3)*
Main machinery: 1 diesel; 700 hp(m) *(514 kW)*; 1 shaft
Speed, knots: 9. **Range, miles:** 1000 at 8 kts
Complement: 17
Cargo capacity: 350 tons

Comment: Built at Bazán, La Carraca. Commissioned 24 January 1963. All ocean-going.

TORPEDISTA HERNÁNDEZ — 4/1992, Diego Quevedo

MARINERO JARANA A 65 (ex-*AA 31*)

Displacement, tons: 527 full load
Dimensions, feet (metres): 123 × 23 × 9.8 *(37.5 × 7 × 3)*
Main machinery: 1 diesel; 600 hp(m) *(441 kW)*; 1 shaft
Speed, knots: 10.8
Complement: 13
Cargo capacity: 300 tons

Comment: Built by Bazán, Cádiz. Similar to Y 231 and Y 255 (harbour tankers). Commissioned 16 March 1981.

MARINERO JARANA — 1987, Royal Spanish Navy

CONDESTABLE ZARAGOZA A 66 (ex-*AA 41*)

Displacement, tons: 892 full load
Dimensions, feet (metres): 152.2 × 27.6 × 11.2 *(46.4 × 8.4 × 3.4)*
Main machinery: 1 diesel; 700 hp(m) *(515 kW)*; 1 shaft
Speed, knots: 10.8
Complement: 16
Cargo capacity: 600 tons

Comment: Built by Bazán, Cádiz. Commissioned 16 October 1981.

CONDESTABLE ZARAGOZA — 1990, Royal Spanish Navy

Y 271-273 (ex-*YA 01-03*, ex-*AB 01-03*)

Displacement, tons: 320 (Y 271-2); 344 (Y 273)
Dimensions, feet (metres): 112.5 × 20.3 × 8.2 *(34.3 × 6.2 × 2.5)*
Main machinery: 1 diesel; 280 hp(m) *(206 kW)*; 1 shaft
Speed, knots: 9.7
Complement: 8
Cargo capacity: 200 tons

Comment: Harbour water-boats. Commissioned 1959. Similar to tankers Y 237, 252 and 253.

MISCELLANEOUS

3 DIVING SUPPORT VESSELS

NEREIDA Y 562 (ex-*YBZ 11*)   **Y 565** (ex-*YBZ 31*)
PROSERPINA Y 563 (ex-*YBZ 12*)

Displacement, tons: 103.5
Dimensions, feet (metres): 70.5 × 19.2 × 9.5 *(21.5 × 5.9 × 2.9)*
Main machinery: 1 Sulzer diesel; 200 hp(m) *(147 kW)*; 1 shaft
Speed, knots: 9

Comment: Built by Bazán, Cartagena. Frogmen support craft.

PROSERPINA — 2/1993, Diego Quevedo

634 SPAIN / Miscellaneous — Salvage and anti-pollution

35 HARBOUR CRAFT

| Y 501-513 | Y 531-535 | Y 572-578 |
| Y 517-518 | Y 538-540 | Y 580-584 |

Displacement, tons: 8-13.7
Speed, knots: 7-17

Comment: Some used as divers boats, others as harbour ferries.

Y 575   7/1992, Diego Quevedo

1 MINE TRANSPORT CRAFT

YTM 352

Displacement, tons: 178 full load
Dimensions, feet (metres): 101.4 × 21.7 × 9.8 *(30.9 × 6.6 × 3)*
Speed, knots: 7
Complement: 8
Mines: 50.

Comment: Built by Bazán 1961. Transports torpedoes and mines and, in emergency, can act as a minelayer.

5 FLOATING CRANES

SANSÓN Y 381   Y 382-384   Y 385

Displacement, tons: 589 (Y 381); 490 (Y 384); 470 (Y 382-3); 272 (Y 385)
Dimensions, feet (metres): 102.4 × 54.1 × 10.5 *(31.2 × 16.5 × 3.2)* (Y 381)
   73.8 × 45.9 × 9.8 *(22.5 × 14 × 3)* (Y 382-4)
   62.3 × 38.4 × 7.9 *(19 × 11.7 × 2.4)* (Y 385)
Military lift: 100 tons (Y 381); 30 tons (Y 382-4); 15 tons (Y 385)

Comment: Based at Cartagena, Ferrol and La Carraca. Completed 1929 (Y 381), 1953-56 remainder. Y 386 deleted in 1990.

1 SUCTION DREDGER

Y 441 (ex-*YDR 11*)

Comment: Can dredge to 8 m. Built in 1981 by IHC, Netherlands. Operates at La Carraca.

1 BARRACK SHIP

Y 601 (ex-*YCFN 01*)

Comment: Former US LSM of 1094 tons. Built in 1944. Based at Ferrol.

36 BARGES

Comment: Have Y numbers. 200 series carry fuel, 300 for ammunition and general stores. 400 for anti-pollution. Four deleted in 1991 and replaced by Y 421-425. Three deleted in 1992.

Y 423   8/1992, Diego Quevedo

GUARDIA CIVIL DEL MAR

Note: Created by Royal decree on 22 February 1991. Bases at La Coruña, Santander, Barcelona, Murcia and Algeciras. Personnel strength 1526 (39 officers). The force takes over the anti-terrorist role and some general patrol duties as a peacetime paramilitary organisation coming under the Ministry of Defence in war. Order of battle to include:
(a) 11 Coastal Patrol Craft (PA)
(b) 37 Inshore Patrol Craft (PM)
(c) 39 Harbour Patrol Craft (PL)
(d) Light helicopters.
All vessels are to be armed. Full strength will take about five years to achieve.

BO 105   8/1992, F Gámez

10 RODMAN TYPE (INSHORE PATROL CRAFT—PM)

Displacement, tons: 15.7 full load
Dimensions, feet (metres): 54.1 × 12.5 × 2.3 *(16.5 × 3.8 × 0.7)*
Main machinery: 2 Bazán/MAN D2848-LXE diesels; 1360 hp(m) *(1 MW)*; 2 Hamilton waterjets
Speed, knots: 40
Complement: 7
Guns: 1—12.7 mm MG.
Radars: Surface search: I band.

Comment: GRP hulls built by Rodman, Vigo. First five in service in 1992.

RODMAN TYPE   5/1992, Camil Busquets i Vilanova

SALVAGE AND ANTI-POLLUTION

Note: A new service under the direction of the Merchant Marine, but may come under a future Coast Guard service in due course. Up to 11 salvage tugs and 11 fast launches (Salvamar). Distinctive red hulls and superstructures with a white diagonal marking on the hull.

SAINT CHARLES   12/1992, Camil Busquets i Vilanova

CUSTOMS SERVICE

Note: All carry ADUANAS on ships' sides. Craft of all types were painted black with a white diagonal stripe in 1990/91. In addition to the listed vessels there are a number of fast boats. Some of the larger vessels are armed with machine guns. There are also four CASA C-212 maritime patrol aircraft and four helicopters.

Name	Displacement tons (full load)	HP/speed	Commissioned
ÁGUILA	80	2700/29	1974
ALBATROS 2 and 3	83	2700/29	1964-69
ALCA 1 and 3	22	2000/45	1987-88
ALCAVARÁN 1-5	85	3920/28	1984-87
ALCOTÁN 2	95	3200/23	—
CÁRABO	57	1350/16	1977
COLIMBO	26	640/20	—
GAVILÁN 1, AGUILUCHO	63	2700/28	1975-76
GAVILÁN 2-4	65	3200/30	1983-87
HALCÓN 2-3	68	3200/28	1980-83
HJ 1, HJ 3-13	20	2000/50	1986
VA 2-5	23	1400/27	1985
CORMORÁN	22	2970/65	1990
CONDOR I	125	5200/30	1991
CONDOR 2	160	1300/15	—
CONDOR 3 (Depot Ship)	1600	2700/14	1991
COUGAR CAT (2100) 1-2	50	3480/42	1992

ALCAVARÁN 5 *7/1992, Camil Busquets i Vilanova*

SRI LANKA

Headquarters' Appointment

Commander of the Navy:
Rear Admiral Damr Samarasekera

Formation

The Royal Ceylon Navy was formed on 9 December 1950 when the Navy Act was proclaimed. Called the Sri Lanka Navy since Republic Day 22 May 1972.

Personnel

(a) 1993: 9850 (740 officers)
(b) Voluntary service
(c) SLVNF: 1020 (102 officers)
(d) Naval reservists: 100 (12 officers)

General

The Tamil insurgency in Sri Lanka had a major impact on the naval programme. The main area of maritime importance is the Palk Strait between India and the primarily Tamil area of northern Sri Lanka. This area has many small creeks—the main requirement is the support of shallow draught fast craft, a very different task from EEZ patrols.

Bases

Naval Base at Trincomalee was expanded in 1988-89 programme.
Other bases at Karainagar, Colombo, Welisara, Tangalle, and Kalpitiya.
There are four Area Commands—North, South, East and West.

Prefix to Ships' Names

SLNS. Pennant numbers changed on 1 November 1987.

Strength of the Fleet

Type	Active	Building
Command Ships/Tenders	4	—
Fast Attack Craft—Gun	23	(2)
Offshore Patrol Vessels	2	—
Coastal Patrol Craft	19	4
Inshore Patrol Craft	34	(10)
Landing Craft	3	—
FPCs	2	—

Mercantile Marine

Lloyd's Register of Shipping:
66 vessels of 303 932 tons gross

DELETIONS

1990 P 236
1991 *Balawatha*, P 150
1992 *Kandula* (sunk)

COMMAND SHIPS

Name	No	Builders	Commissioned
ABHEETHA (ex-*Carinia*)	P 714	Chung Wah SB & Eng Co Ltd	9 Aug 1984
EDITHARA (ex-*Francesca*)	P 715	Singapore Slipway Co	9 Aug 1984
WICKRAMA (ex-*Delicia*)	P 716	Chung Wah SB & Eng Co Ltd	9 Aug 1984

Displacement, tons: 2628 full load
Dimensions, feet (metres): 249.7 × 56.1 × 12.5 *(76.1 × 17.1 × 3.8)*
Main machinery: 2 Deutz SBA12M525 diesels; 3000 hp(m) *(2.2 MW)*; 2 shafts
Speed, knots: 12. **Range, miles:** 6000 at 10 kts
Complement: 50
Guns: 2 China 25 mm/60 (twin) Type 61; 85° elevation; 270 rounds/minute to 3 km *(1.6 nm)*; weight of shell 0.34 kg.
8 China 14.5 mm/93 (4 twin) MGs.
Radars: Surface search: Selesmar/Selescan; I band.
Navigation: Furuno; I band.

Comment: Former Ro-Ro ships built 1976-77 and used as command and HQ ships for Light Forces. Classified as Surveillance Command Ships. Dates given are commissioning dates in the Navy. Have a 30 ton crane.

A 516 *1986, Sri Lanka Navy*

LIGHT FORCES

2 OFFSHORE PATROL VESSELS (OPV)

Name	No	Builders	Commissioned
JAYESAGARA	P 601	Colombo Dockyard	9 Dec 1983
SAGARAWARDENE	P 602	Colombo Dockyard	6 Apr 1984

Displacement, tons: 330 full load
Dimensions, feet (metres): 130.5 × 23 × 7 *(39.8 × 7 × 2.1)*
Main machinery: 2 MAN 8L20/27 diesels; 2 180 hp(m) *(1.6 MW)* sustained; 2 shafts
Speed, knots: 15. **Range, miles:** 3000 at 11 kts
Complement: 52 (4 officers)
Guns: 2 China 25 mm/80 (twin). 2 China 14.5 mm (twin) MGs.

Comment: Ordered from Colombo Dockyard on 31 December 1981. P 601 launched 26 May 1983, P 602 launched 20 November 1983.

EDITHARA *1992, Sri Lanka Navy*

A 516 (ex-*Kota Rukun*, ex-*Mercury Cove*, ex-*Tjimanuk*)

Displacement, tons: 6300 full load
Dimensions, feet (metres): 326.4 × 51.2 × 22.6 *(99.5 × 15.6 × 6.9)*
Main machinery: 1 NV Werkspoor 6-cyl diesel; 3600 hp(m) *(2.64 MW)*; 1 shaft
Speed, knots: 13. **Range, miles:** 12 000 at 8 kts
Complement: 50
Guns: 1—12.7 mm MG.
Radars: Surface search: Decca 110; I band.
Navigation: Furuno FR 1011; I band.

Comment: Launched in 1959 at Gorinchem Shipyard and acquired from Pacific International Lines in 1986. 3350 grt. Classified as a Command Tender.

JAYESAGARA *5/1990, John Mortimer*

5 SOORAYA CLASS (FAST ATTACK CRAFT—GUN)

SOORAYA P 310 (ex-P 3140)	JAGATHA P 315 (ex-P 3145)
WEERAYA P 311 (ex-P 3141)	RAKSHAKA P 316 (ex-P 3146)
RANAKAMEE P 312 (ex-P 3142)	

Displacement, tons: 113 standard; 131 full load
Dimensions, feet (metres): 127.3 × 17.7 × 5.2 *(38.8 × 5.4 × 1.6)*
Main machinery: 2 Type L12-180 diesels; 2400 hp(m) *(1.76 MW)* (forward); 2 Type L12-180Z; 1820 hp(m) *(1.34 MW)* (aft); 4 shafts
Speed, knots: 29. **Range, miles:** 700 at 16 kts
Complement: 34
Guns: 2 China 37 mm/63 (twin). 4 China 25 mm/80 (2 twin abaft the bridge). 2 China 14.5 mm (twin) MG.
Depth charges: 8.
Radars: Surface search: Skin Head; I band; range 37 km *(20 nm)*.
Navigation: Furuno 825 D; I band.

Comment: Ex-Shanghai II class, the first pair transferred by China in February 1972, the second pair in July 1972, one in December 1972 and two more on 30 November 1980. One deleted in 1991. *Weeraya*, and possibly others, have the alternative gun arrangement of a twin 14.5 mm forward and the 37 mm right aft.

SOORAYA   *1992, Sri Lanka Navy*

3 + (2) RANA CLASS (FAST ATTACK CRAFT—GUN)

RANASURU P 320	RANAWIRU P 321	RANARISI P 322

Displacement, tons: 150 full load
Dimensions, feet (metres): 134.5 × 17.7 × 5.2 *(41 × 5.4 × 1.6)*
Main machinery: 4 diesels; 4800 hp(m) *(3.53 MW)*; 4 shafts
Speed, knots: 29. **Range, miles:** 750 at 16 kts
Complement: 28 (4 officers)
Guns: 2 China 37 mm/63 (twin) Type 76. 4 China 14.5 mm (twin) Type 69.
Radars: Surface search: Racal Decca; I band.

Comment: Modified Shanghai II class acquired from China in September 1991 and commissioned in November 1991. More powerful engines than the Sooraya class; automatic guns and improved habitability. Two more may be acquired.

RANASURU   *1992, Sri Lanka Navy*

6 ISRAELI DVORA CLASS (FAST ATTACK CRAFT—GUN)

P 453-P 458

Displacement, tons: 47 full load
Dimensions, feet (metres): 70.8 × 18 × 5.8 *(21.6 × 5.5 × 1.8)*
Main machinery: 2 MTU 12V 331 TC81 diesels; 2605 hp(m) *(1.91 MW)* sustained; 2 shafts
Speed, knots: 36. **Range, miles:** 1200 at 17 kts
Complement: 12
Guns: 2 Oerlikon 20 mm. 2—12.7 mm MGs.
Radars: Surface search: Decca 926; I band.

Comment: First pair transferred early 1984, next four in October 1986. Built by Israeli Aircraft Industries.

P 456   *1992, Sri Lanka Navy*

6 ISRAELI SUPER DVORA CLASS (FAST ATTACK CRAFT—GUN)

P 463-P 468

Displacement, tons: 54 full load
Dimensions, feet (metres): 73.5 × 18 × 5.8 *(22.4 × 5.5 × 1.8)*
Main machinery: 2 MTU 12V 396 TB93 diesels; 3260 hp(m) *(2.4 MW)* sustained; 2 shafts
Speed, knots: 46. **Range, miles:** 1200 at 17 kts
Complement: 12
Guns: 2 Oerlikon 20 mm. 2—12.7 mm MGs.
Radars: Surface search: Decca 926; I band.

Comment: Ordered from Israeli Aircraft Industries in October 1986 and delivered in 1987/88. A more powerful version of the Dvora class.

P 464   *1992, Sri Lanka Navy*

3 SOUTH KOREAN KILLER CLASS (FAST ATTACK CRAFT—GUN)

P 473-P 475

Displacement, tons: 56 full load
Dimensions, feet (metres): 75.5 × 17.7 × 5.9 *(23 × 5.4 × 1.8)*
Main machinery: 2 MTU 396 TB93 diesels; 3260 hp(m) *(2.4 MW)* sustained; 2 shafts
Speed, knots: 40
Complement: 12
Guns: 2 Oerlikon 20 mm. 2—12.7 mm MGs.
Radars: Surface search: Racal Decca; I band.

Comment: Built by Korea SB and Eng, Buson. All commissioned February 1988.

P 473   *1992, Sri Lanka Navy*

10 COASTAL PATROL CRAFT

P 231-P 235   P 241-P 245

Displacement, tons: 40 full load
Dimensions, feet (metres): 66 × 18 × 7 *(20 × 5.5 × 2.1)*
Main machinery: 2 Detroit 12V-71TA diesels; 840 hp *(626 kW)* sustained; 2 shafts
Speed, knots: 22. **Range, miles:** 1500 at 14 kts
Complement: 10
Guns: 2 Oerlikon 20 mm (24 series). 2—12.7 mm MGs (23 series).

Comment: Ordered from Colombo DY June 1976 (first pair). First six commissioned 1980-81, last five in 1982-83. All craft refitted 1988-89 except *P 236* which was deleted in June 1990.

P 234   *1992, Sri Lanka Navy*

4 COASTAL PATROL CRAFT

P 201-P 202   P 211   P 214

Displacement, tons: 21 full load
Dimensions, feet (metres): 46.6 × 12.8 × 3.3 *(14.2 × 3.9 × 1)*
Main machinery: 2 Detroit 8V-71TA diesels; 460 hp *(343 kW)*; 2 shafts
Speed, knots: 20. **Range, miles:** 450 at 14 kts
Complement: 6
Guns: 2—12.7 mm MGs.
Radars: Surface search: I band.

Comment: Built by Colombo DY and commissioned in 1982-83 *(P 201-P 202)*, June 1986 *(P 211* and *P 214)*.

P 201   *1986, Sri Lanka Navy*

0 + 4 SIMONNEAU SM 500 CLASS (COASTAL PATROL CRAFT)

Displacement, tons: 22 full load
Dimensions, feet (metres): 51.8 × 15.1 × 5.9 *(15.8 × 4.6 × 1.8)*
Main machinery: 2 diesels; 1600 hp(m) *(1.18 MW)*; 2 shafts
Speed, knots: 30
Complement: 6
Guns: 1 Oerlikon 20 mm. 1—7.62 mm MG.
Radars: Surface search: I band.

Comment: Ordered from Simonneau Marine in October 1992. Two to be built in France, two in Sri Lanka.

SIMONNEAU SM 500 (old number)   *1992, Simonneau Marine*

5 COASTAL PATROL CRAFT

P 221-P 225 (ex-*P 421-425*)

Displacement, tons: 22 full load
Dimensions, feet (metres): 55.9 × 14.8 × 3.9 *(17 × 4.5 × 1.2)*
Main machinery: 2 Detroit 8V-71TA diesels; 460 hp *(343 kW)*; 2 shafts
Speed, knots: 23. **Range, miles:** 1000 at 12 kts
Complement: 7
Guns: 1—12.7 mm MG.

Comment: Used for general patrol duties. Built by Cheverton Workboats, UK and commissioned in 1977.

P 224   *1992, Sri Lanka Navy*

9 COUGAR CLASS (INSHORE PATROL CRAFT)

P 101-109

Displacement, tons: 7.4 full load
Dimensions, feet (metres): 34.1 × 9.5 × 2.6 *(10.4 × 2.9 × 0.8)*
Main machinery: 2 Sabre diesels; 500 hp *(373 kW)*; 2 shafts
Speed, knots: 30
Complement: 4
Guns: 1—12.7 mm MG.

Comment: First ordered in 1984 for trials, order for remainder placed in 1985. Operate from Command Ships.

P 106   *1992, Sri Lanka Navy*

2 + (10) INSHORE PATROL CRAFT

P 151-152

Displacement, tons: 9
Dimensions, feet (metres): 9.8 × 12.1 × 1.6 *(3 × 3.7 × 0.5)*
Main machinery: 2 Cummins 6BTA5.9-M2; 584 hp *(436 kW)* sustained; 2 waterjets
Speed, knots: 33. **Range, miles:** 330 at 25 kts
Complement: 5
Guns: 1—12.7 mm MG.

Comment: Built by TAOS Yacht Company, Colombo, and delivered in 1991. Ten more may be acquired.

P 151   *1991, Sri Lanka Navy*

13 INSHORE PATROL CRAFT

P 111-P 123

Displacement, tons: 5
Dimensions, feet (metres): 44 × 9.8 × 1.6 *(13.4 × 3 × 0.5)*
Main machinery: 2 Yamaha D 343 diesels; 730 hp(m) *(544 kW)* sustained; 2 shafts
Speed, knots: 26
Complement: 5
Guns: 1—12.7 mm MG.

Comment: Built by Consolidated Marine Engineers, Sri Lanka. First nine delivered in 1988; four more in 1992. Operate from Command Ships.

P 111   *1992, Sri Lanka Navy*

10 INSHORE PATROL CRAFT

P 140-149

Displacement, tons: 3.5
Dimensions, feet (metres): 42 × 8 × 1.6 *(12.8 × 2.4 × 0.5)*
Main machinery: 2 outboard motors; 280 hp *(209 kW)*
Speed, knots: 30
Complement: 4

Comment: Acquired in 1988. Similar to *P 111* but with outboard engines. *P 150* was mined and sunk in August 1991.

P 150   *1989, Sri Lanka Navy*

AMPHIBIOUS FORCES

Note: There are plans for an assault force of Marines in due course. Reports of possible transfers of Russian Alligator or Vydra class landing ships have not been confirmed.

2 LANDING CRAFT (LCM)

Name	No	Builders	Commissioned
PABBATHA	L 838 (ex-A 538)	Vospers, Singapore	21 Dec 1987
RANAGAJA (ex-*Gajasingha*)	L 839	Colombo Dockyard	15 Nov 1991

Displacement, tons: 268 full load
Dimensions, feet (metres): 108.3 × 26 × 4.9 *(33 × 8 × 1.5)*
Main machinery: 2 Caterpillar diesels; 1524 hp *(1.14 MW)*; 2 shafts
Speed, knots: 8. **Range, miles:** 1800 at 8 kts
Complement: 12 (2 officers)
Guns: 4 China 25 mm/80 (2 twin) *(Ranagaja)*. 2 Oerlikon 20 mm (remainder). 2—12.7 mm MGs.

Comment: Two built in 1983 and acquired in October 1985. Third of the class taken over by the Navy in September 1991. More may be built. *Kandula* sank in October 1992 and was salvaged in mid-December. The plan is to refurbish her, but there must be doubts about the feasibility of doing this successfully after the ship has been underwater for two months.

RANAGAJA   *10/1991, Sri Lanka Navy*

2 FAST PERSONNEL CARRIERS (FPC)

Name	No	Builders	Commissioned
HANSAYA	A 540 (ex-*Offshore Pioneer*)	Sing Koon Seng, Singapore	20 Dec 1987
LIHINIYA	A 541 (ex-*Offshore Pride*)	Sing Koon Seng, Singapore	20 Dec 1987

Displacement, tons: 154 full load
Dimensions, feet (metres): 98.4 × 36.8 × 7.7 *(30 × 11.2 × 2.3)*
Main machinery: 2 MTU diesels; 2 shafts
Speed, knots: 30
Complement: 12 (2 officers)
Cargo capacity: 60 tons; 120 troops
Guns: 1 Oerlikon 20 mm. 2—12.7 mm MGs.

Comment: Acquired in January 1986 from Aluminium Shipbuilders. Catamaran hulls used for fast transport.

LIHINIYA   *1992, Sri Lanka Navy*

1 CHINESE YUNNAN CLASS (LCU)

L 820

Displacement, tons: 128 full load
Dimensions, feet (metres): 93.8 × 17.7 × 4.6 *(28.6 × 5.4 × 1.4)*
Main machinery: 2 diesels; 600 hp(m) *(441 kW)*; 2 shafts
Speed, knots: 12. **Range, miles:** 500 at 10 kts
Complement: 12 (2 officers)
Military lift: 46 tons
Guns: 2—12.7 mm MGs.

Comment: Acquired from China in May 1991.

L 820   *1992, Sri Lanka Navy*

SUDAN

Headquarters' Appointment

Commander (Navy):
Brigadier Abbas Al-Sayyid Uthman

Personnel

(a) 1993: 500 officers and men
(b) Voluntary service

Establishment

The Navy was established in 1962 to operate on the Red Sea coast and on the River Nile.

Bases

Flamingo Bay for Red Sea operations with a separate riverine unit on the Nile based at Khartoum.

General

The overall standard of operational efficiency has suffered from lack of maintenance and spare parts and auxiliaries have drifted into total disrepair. Also reported are an ex-Tanker used for training, a Water Tanker (PB 6) and an unarmed Survey Ship (PB 35). More patrol craft may be acquired from China or Iran.

Mercantile Marine

Lloyd's Register of Shipping:
16 vessels of 45 445 tons gross

LIGHT FORCES

2 Ex-IRANIAN COASTAL PATROL CRAFT

KADIR (ex-*Shahpar*) 129   **KARARI** (ex-*Shahram*) 130

Displacement, tons: 70 full load
Dimensions, feet (metres): 75.2 × 16.5 × 6 *(22.9 × 5 × 1.8)*
Main machinery: 2 MTU diesels; 2200 hp(m) *(1.62 MW)*; 2 shafts
Speed, knots: 27
Complement: 19 (3 officers)
Guns: 1 Oerlikon 20 mm.

Comment: Built for Iran by Abeking & Rasmussen in 1970. Transferred to Iranian Coast Guard 1975 and to Sudan later that year. *Sheikan* (128) has been cannibalised for spares but may be refurbished with Iranian assistance. Armaments could also be upgraded.

KADIR   2/1990

4 YUGOSLAV TYPE 15 (INSHORE PATROL CRAFT)

KURMUK 502   **QAYSAN** 503   **RUMBEK** 504   **MAYOM** 505

Displacement, tons: 19.5 full load
Dimensions, feet (metres): 55.4 × 12.8 × 2.3 *(16.9 × 3.9 × 0.7)*
Main machinery: 2 diesels; 330 hp(m) *(243 kW)*; 2 shafts
Speed, knots: 16. **Range, miles:** 160 at 12 kts
Complement: 6
Guns: 1 Oerlikon 20 mm; 2—7.62 mm MGs.
Radars: Surface search: I band.

Comment: Delivered by Yugoslavia on 18 May 1989 for operations on the White Nile.

KURMUK   1989, G Jacobs

4 Ex-IRANIAN SEWART PATROL CRAFT

MAROUB 1161   **SALAK** 1163
FIJAB 1162   **HALOTE** 1164

Displacement, tons: 9.1 full load
Dimensions, feet (metres): 40 × 12.1 × 3.3 *(12.2 × 3.7 × 1)*
Main machinery: 2 GM diesels; 348 hp *(260 kW)*; 2 shafts
Speed, knots: 31
Complement: 6
Guns: 1—12.7 mm MG.

Comment: Transferred by Iranian Coast Guard in 1975. At least three were operational in 1992.

LAND-BASED MARITIME AIRCRAFT

Numbers/Type: 2 CASA C-212 Aviocar.
Operational speed: 190 kts *(353 km/h)*.
Service ceiling: 24 000 ft *(7315 m)*.
Range: 1650 nm *(3055 km)*.
Role/Weapon systems: Limited capability over the Red Sea; no real combat role. Sensors: Search radar. Weapons: Unarmed.

SUPPLY SHIPS

Note: Five river supply craft, probably LCM type, were delivered in 1991 and are based at Kosti. Used for transporting ammunition, petrol and supplies. Of Yugoslav design but may have been assembled in Sudan.

2 Ex-YUGOSLAV DTM 221 CLASS (LCUs)

SOBAT 221   **DINDER** 222

Displacement, tons: 410
Dimensions, feet (metres): 155.1 × 21 × 7.5 *(47.3 × 6.4 × 2.3)*
Speed, knots: 9
Complement: 15
Guns: 1 Oerlikon 20 mm. 2—12.7 mm MGs.

Comment: Transferred during 1969. Probably immobile hulks.

SURINAM

Personnel	Base	Mercantile Marine
1993: 240 officers and men	Paramaribo	*Lloyd's Register of Shipping:* 24 vessels of 12 876 tons gross

PATROL FORCES

Note: Four ex-German Kondor I class minesweepers were reported as being bought in 1992. Confirmation of payment had not been made by early 1993 and the ships were still in German ports. An option to buy patrol craft from the same source was cancelled.

3 LARGE PATROL CRAFT

P 401-P 403 (ex-*S 401-403*)

Displacement, tons: 140 full load
Dimensions, feet (metres): 105 × 21.3 × 5.5 *(32 × 6.5 × 1.7)*
Main machinery: 2 Paxman 12YHCM diesels; 2110 hp *(1.57 MW)*; 2 shafts
Speed, knots: 17.5. **Range, miles:** 1200 at 13.5 kts
Complement: 15
Guns: 2 Bofors 40 mm. 2—7.62 mm MGs.
Radars: Surface search: Decca 110; I band.

Comment: Built by De Vries, Aalsmeer, Netherlands and commissioned in 1976-77. This design has far greater speed and armament potential but Surinam apparently opted for the scaled-down version.

2 SURVEY CRAFT

COEROENI   **LITANI**

Comment: *Coeroeni* of 80 tons launched in 1962; *Litani* of 70 tons launched in 1958. Both craft are owned by the Ministry of Economic Affairs and manned by the Navy.

2 COASTAL PATROL CRAFT

C 301   **C 303**

Displacement, tons: 65
Dimensions, feet (metres): 72.2 × 15.5 × 7.6 *(22 × 4.7 × 2.3)*
Main machinery: 2 Dorman 8JT diesels; 560 hp *(418 kW)*; 2 shafts
Speed, knots: 13.5. **Range, miles:** 650 at 13 kts
Complement: 8
Guns: 1—12.7 mm MG. 2—7.62 mm MGs.
Radars: Surface search: Decca 110; I band.

Comment: Three ordered April 1975 from Schottel, Netherlands. Commissioned in 1976. *C 302* cannibalised for spares.

P 403   1988

C 301   1980, Surinam Ministry

640 SURINAM / Patrol forces — SWEDEN / Introduction

3 RIVER PATROL CRAFT

Name	No	Builders	Commissioned
BAHADOER	RP 201	Schottel, Netherlands	Dec 1975
FAJABLOW	RP 202	Schottel, Netherlands	Dec 1975
KORANGON	RP 203	Schottel, Netherlands	Feb 1976

Displacement, tons: 15
Dimensions, feet (metres): 41.4 × 12.5 × 3.6 *(12.6 × 3.8 × 1.1)*
Main machinery: 1 Dorman 8JT diesel; 280 hp *(209 kW)*; 1 shaft
Speed, knots: 14. **Range, miles:** 350 at 10 kts
Complement: 4
Guns: 1—12.7 mm MG.

Comment: Ordered December 1974.

LAND-BASED MARITIME AIRCRAFT

Numbers/Type: 4 Pilatus Britten-Norman BN-2A Maritime Defender.
Operational speed: 150 kts *(280 km/h)*.
Service ceiling: 18 900 ft *(5760 m)*.
Range: 1500 nm *(2775 km)*.
Role/Weapon systems: Flown by Air Force for coastal patrol. **Sensors:** Lightweight search radar.
Weapons: Unarmed.

KORANGON   *1980, Surinam Ministry*

SWEDEN

Headquarters' Appointments

Chief of the Defence Staff:
  General Bengt Gustafsson
Commander-in-Chief:
  Vice Admiral Dick Börjesson
Chief of Naval Material Department:
  Rear Admiral Torbjörn Hultman

Senior Command

Commander-in-Chief of Coastal Fleet:
  Rear Admiral Sten Swedlund

Diplomatic Representation

Defence Attaché in London:
  Commodore Gustaf Taube
Naval Attaché in Moscow:
  Captain Magnus Haglund
Naval Attaché in Washington:
  Captain Bjorn Ljunggren
Defence Attaché in Canberra:
  Commander Nils Bruzelius
Naval Attaché in Bonn:
  Captain Lars Norrsell

Pennant Numbers

Numbers are not displayed on major patrol craft.

Coastal Artillery

Being re-organised into six amphibious battalions of 800 men in each. Each battalion to have 35 Combatboat 90, 13 Combatboat 90E, four Trossbåt, 26 section vessels and 19 canoes. The plan is to form one battalion per year having started in 1991. All Coastal Artillery vessels are fully integrated with the Navy and are therefore not shown as a separate section.

Personnel

(a) 1992: 9150 officers and men of Navy and Coastal Artillery made up of 3100 regulars and 6050 national servicemen
(b) 10-17¼ months' national service

Strength of the Fleet

Type	Active (Reserve)	Building (Planned)
Submarines—Patrol	12	3
Missile Corvettes	6	—
Fast Attack Craft—Missile	28	—
Coastal Patrol Craft	7	—
Inshore Patrol Craft	21	4
Experimental Patrol Craft	1	—
Minelayers	3	—
MCM Support Ship	1	—
Minelayers—Coastal	9	—
Minelayers—Small	22	—
Minesweepers/Hunters—Coastal	10	—
Minesweepers—Inshore	14	—
Sonobuoy Craft	4	—
LCMs	22	(4)
LCUs	79	—
LCAs	42	(59)
Mine Transports	2	—
Survey Ships	3	—
Electronic Surveillance Ship	1	—
Transport Ships	1	—
Tankers—Support	2	—
Divers Support Ship	1	—
Tugs	20	—
Salvage Ship	1	—
Sail Training Ships	2	—
Icebreakers	7	—
TRVs	3	—
Water Boats	2	—
Coast Guard	130 (approx)	16

Bases

Muskö (Stockholm), Karlskrona.
Minor bases at Härnösand and Göteborg.

Mercantile Marine

Lloyd's Register of Shipping:
  664 vessels of 3 081 166 tons gross

DELETIONS

Submarines

1989-90 Delfinen, Nordkaparen (museum ship), Springaren, Vargen

Light Forces

1990 Tjurko
1992 Rörö, Arild, Viken, Marstrand
1993 Ornö

Mine Warfare Forces

1990 Skaftö
1992 Fårösund

Amphibious Forces

1992 Ane, Balder, Loke, Ring
1993 Sleipner (old)

Miscellaneous

1993 Belos (old)

PENNANT LIST

Corvettes

K 11	Stockholm
K 12	Malmö
K 21	Göteborg
K 22	Gälve
K 23	Kalmar
K 24	Sundsvall

Light Forces

P 151	Hugin
P 152	Munin
P 153	Magne
P 154	Mode
P 155	Vale
P 156	Vidar
P 157	Mjölner
P 158	Mysing
P 159	Kaparen
P 160	Väktaren
P 161	Snapphanen
P 162	Spejaren
P 163	Styrbjörn
P 164	Starkodder
P 165	Tordön
P 166	Tirfing
R 131	Norrköping
R 132	Nynäshamn
R 133	Norrtälje
R 134	Varberg
R 135	Västerås
R 136	Västervik
R 137	Umeå
R 138	Piteå
R 139	Luleå
R 140	Halmstad
R 141	Strömstad
R 142	Ystad
V 05	Öregrund
V 06	Slite
V 08	Lysekil
V 09	Dalarö
V 10	Sandhamn
V 11	Osthammar
V 150	Jägaren
61-77	CPC
SVK 1	Svärdet
SVK 2	Spjutet
SVK 3	Pilen
SVK 4	Bågen

Mine Warfare Forces

M 02	Älvsborg
M 03	Visborg
M 04	Carlskrona
M 21-22	IMS
M 24-25	IMS
M 31	Gåssten
M 32	Norsten
M 33	Viksten
M 43	Hisingen
M 44	Blackan
M 45	Dämman
M 46	Galten
M 47	Gillöga
M 48	Rödlöga
M 49	Svartlöga
M 57	Arkö
M 67	Nämdö
M 68	Blidö
M 71	Landsort
M 72	Arholma
M 73	Koster
M 74	Kullen
M 75	Vinga
M 76	Ven
M 77	Ulvön
MUL 11	Kalvsund
MUL 12	Arkosund
MUL 13	Kalmarsund
MUL 14	Alnösund
MUL 15	Grundsund
MUL 17	Skramsösund
MUL 18	Öresund
MUL 19	Barösund
MUL 20	Furusund
501-516	Small Minelayers
1879-1834	Small Minelayers
B 01	Ejdern
B 02	Krickan
B 03	Svärten
B 04	Viggen

Service Forces

A 201	Orion
A 214	Belos III
A 217	Fryken
A 228	Brännaren
A 229	Eldaren
A 236	Fällaren
A 237	Minören
A 241	Urd
A 242	Skuld
A 246	Hägern
A 247	Pelikanen
A 248	Pingvinen
A 251	Achilles
A 252	Ajax
A 253	Hermes
A 256	Sigrun
A 261	Utö
A 262	Skredsvik
A 313	Meranda
A 322	Heros
A 323	Hercules
A 324	Hera
A 326	Hebe
A 327	Passopp
A 330	Atlas
A 341	ATB 1
A 342	ATB 2
A 701-705	Tugs
A 751-756	Tugs
S 01	Gladan
S 02	Falken

SUBMARINES

Notes: (a) A rescue vehicle, *Urf (Ubåts Räddnings Farkost)* of 52 tons with a diving depth of 1500 ft *(460 m)* was launched 17 April 1978. Similar to US Navy DSRV she has a capacity for 25 men on each dive.
(b) R-2 (Mala class) acquired from Yugoslavia in 1985. This is a two-man craft with a laden weight of 1400 kg, 4.9 × 1.4 m, and a 4.5 kW electric motor. With a lead-acid battery the performance is 4.4 kts for 18 n miles and 3.7 kts for 23 n miles. Has aluminium and plexiglass hull. Can carry 250 kg of limpet mines. With a silver-zinc battery the performance is much improved. Diving depth 30 m normal, 60 m maximum. R-1 deleted in 1990.
(c) A midget submarine *Spiggen II* was launched on 19 June 1990. Displacing 14 tons dived she has Volvo Penta diesel, a submerged speed of 5 kts, and a diving depth of 100 m. Dimensions, 11 × 1.7 × 1.4 m. She is used as a 'target' for ASW training and has an endurance of 14 days.

SPIGGEN II *1991, Royal Swedish Navy*

0 + 3 GOTLAND (A 19) CLASS

Name	No	Builders	Laid down	Launched	Commissioned
GOTLAND	—	Kockums, Malmö	20 Nov 1992	Dec 1994	1997
UPPLAND	—	Kockums, Malmö	1993	Jan 1996	1998
HALLAND	—	Kockums, Malmö	1994	Sep 1996	1999

Displacement, tons: 1240 surfaced; 1490 dived
Dimensions, feet (metres): 183.7 × 19.7 × 18.4 *(56 × 6 × 5.6)*
Main machinery: Diesel-electric; 2 MTU diesels; 1 Kockums Stirling AIP system; 1 motor; 1 shaft
Speed, knots: 11 surfaced; 20 dived
Complement: 27

Torpedoes: 4—21 in *(533 mm)* tubes; 12 FFV Type 613.
 2—15.75 in *(400 mm)* tubes; 6 Swedish Ordnance Type 432.
Mines: Capability for 50 mines in external containers.
Countermeasures: ESM: Argo 700A; radar warning.
Fire control: NobelTech data automation.
Radars: Navigation: I band.
Sonars: Atlas Elektronik; hull-mounted; passive search and attack; medium frequency.

Programmes: In October 1986 a research contract was awarded to Kockums for a design to replace the A 12 class in the mid-1990s. Ordered on 28 March 1990.
Structure: The design has been developed on the basis of the Type A 17 series but this class will be the first to be built with Air Independent propulsion as part of the design. Details are not yet known but three 75 kW Stirling engines of the type fitted in *Näcken* have been reported, as has one 600 kW V12 version.

GOTLAND (model) *1991, Kockums*

4 VÄSTERGÖTLAND (A 17) CLASS

Name	No	Builders	Laid down	Launched	Commissioned
VÄSTERGÖTLAND	—	Kockums, Malmö	10 Jan 1983	17 Sep 1986	27 Nov 1987
HÄLSINGLAND	—	Kockums, Malmö	1 Jan 1984	31 Aug 1987	20 Oct 1988
SÖDERMANLAND	—	Kockums, Malmö	1985	12 Apr 1988	21 Apr 1989
ÖSTERGÖTLAND	—	Kockums, Malmö	1986	9 Dec 1988	10 Jan 1990

Displacement, tons: 1070 surfaced; 1143 dived
Dimensions, feet (metres): 159.1 × 20 × 18.4 *(48.5 × 6.1 × 5.6)*
Main machinery: Diesel-electric; 2 Hedemora V12A/15 diesels; 2200 hp(m) *(1.62 MW)*; 1 Jeumont Schneider motor; 1800 hp(m) *(1.32 MW)*; 1 shaft
Speed, knots: 11 surfaced; 20 dived
Complement: 27 (5 officers)

Torpedoes: 6—21 in *(533 mm)* tubes. 12 FFV Type 613; anti-surface; wire-guided; passive homing to 15 km *(8.2 nm)* at 45 kts; warhead 240 kg. Swim-out discharge.
 3—15.75 in *(400 mm)* tubes. 6 FFV Type 431; anti-submarine; wire-guided; active/passive homing to 20 km *(10.8 nm)* at 25 kts; warhead 45 kg shaped charge or a small charge anti-intruder version is available.
Mines: Capability for 22 mines in external removable containers. Not fitted.
Countermeasures: ESM: Argo; radar warning.
Fire control: Ericsson IPS-17 data automation.
Radars: Navigation: Terma; I band.
Sonars: Atlas Elektronik CSU83; hull-mounted; passive search and attack; medium frequency.

Programmes: Design contract awarded to Kockums, Malmö on 17 April 1978. Contract for construction of these boats signed 8 December 1981. Kockums built midship section and carried out final assembly while Karlskrona built bow and stern sections. Have replaced the Draken class.
Structure: Single hulled with an X type rudder/after hydroplane design. Reported that SSM were considered but rejected as non-cost-effective weapons in the context of submarine operations in the Baltic. May be back fitted with Stirling engines in due course.

VÄSTERGÖTLAND *6/1992, Maritime Photographic*

3 NÄCKEN (A 14) CLASS

Name	No	Builders	Laid down	Launched	Commissioned
NÄCKEN	—	Kockums, Malmö	Nov 1972	17 Apr 1978	25 Apr 1980
NAJAD	—	Kockums, Malmö/Karlskronavarvet	Sep 1973	6 Dec 1978	26 June 1981
NEPTUN	—	Kockums, Malmö	Mar 1974	13 Aug 1979	5 Dec 1980

Displacement, tons: 1015 surfaced; 1085 dived
Dimensions, feet (metres): 162.4 (182.1, *Näcken*) × 18.7 × 18 *(49.5 (55.5) × 5.7 × 5.5)*
Main machinery: Diesel-electric; 1 MTU 16V 652 MB80 diesel; 1730 hp(m) *(1.27 MW)*; 2 Stirling V4-275R engines (*Näcken*); 150 kW; 1 Jeumont Schneider motor; 1800 hp(m) *(1.32 MW)*; 1 shaft
Speed, knots: 12 surfaced; 20 dived
Complement: 27 (5 officers)

Torpedoes: 6—21 in *(533 mm)* tubes. 8 FFV Type 613; anti-surface; wire-guided; passive homing to 15 km *(8.2 nm)* at 45 kts; warhead 250 kg.
2—15.75 in *(400 mm)* tubes. 4 FFV Type 431; anti-submarine; wire-guided; active/passive homing to 20 km *(10.8 nm)* at 25 kts; warhead 45 kg shaped charge.
Mines: Minelaying capability including an external girdle of 48 mines.
Countermeasures: ESM: Argo; radar warning.
Fire control: Ericsson A1 with 2 Censor 932 computers for data processing.
Radars: Navigation: Terma; I band.
Sonars: Thomson Sintra; hull-mounted; passive search and attack; medium frequency.

Modernisation: *Näcken* was taken in hand by Kockums in November 1987 for the installation of a closed-circuit Tillma Stirling diesel which provides non-nuclear propulsion without requiring access to the atmosphere. This involved the ship being lengthened by 6 m and she was relaunched on 6 September 1988. The new section which is neutrally buoyant contains the Stirling generators, two LOX supply tanks and control systems. The other two of the class will not be similarly modified. There are plans to update all of the class with new fire control systems, torpedo tube automation and new sonars, to extend service lives into the next century.
Structure: The very high beam to length ratio is notable in this hull design. Has large bow-mounted sonar. Main accommodation space is abaft the control room with machinery spaces right aft. A central computer provides both attack information and data on main machinery. Single periscope. Diving depth 300 m *(984 ft)*.
Operational: The Stirling engine is primarily for slow submerged speed patrolling without much use of battery power. Liquid oxygen (LOX) provides the combustible air. Exhaust products dissolve in water. It is claimed that fully submerged endurance is possible up to 14 days. Trials started on 23 November 1988 and the submarine returned to operational service on 11 April 1989.

NACKEN 4/1992, Erik Laursen

NÄCKEN 4/1992, Erik Laursen

5 SJÖORMEN (A 12) CLASS

Name	No	Builders	Laid down	Launched	Commissioned
SJÖORMEN	—	Kockums, Malmö	1965	25 Jan 1967	31 July 1968
SJÖLEJONET	—	Kockums, Malmö	1966	29 June 1967	16 Dec 1968
SJÖHUNDEN	—	Kockums, Malmö	1966	21 Mar 1968	25 June 1969
SJÖBJÖRNEN	—	Karlskronavarvet	1967	6 Aug 1968	28 Feb 1969
SJÖHÄSTEN	—	Karlskronavarvet	1966	9 Jan 1968	15 Sep 1969

Displacement, tons: 1130 surfaced; 1210 dived
Dimensions, feet (metres): 167.3 × 20 × 19 *(51 × 6.1 × 5.8)*
Main machinery: Diesel-electric; 2 Hedemora-Pielstick V12A/A2/15 diesels; 2200 hp(m) *(1.62 MW)*; 1 ASEA motor; 1500 hp(m) *(1.1 MW)*; 1 shaft
Speed, knots: 12 surfaced; 20 dived
Complement: 23 (7 officers)

Torpedoes: 4—21 in *(533 mm)* bow tubes. 10 FFV Type 613; anti-surface; wire-guided; passive homing to 15 km *(8.2 nm)* at 45 kts; warhead 250 kg.
2—15.75 in *(400 mm)* tubes. 4 FFV Type 431; anti-submarine; wire-guided; active/passive homing to 20 km *(10.8 nm)* at 25 kts; warhead 45 kg shaped charge.
Mines: Minelaying capability.
Fire control: Ericsson A1 system.
Radars: Navigation: Terma; I band.
Sonars: Plessey Hydra; hull-mounted; passive search and attack; medium frequency.

Modernisation: *Sjölejonet* and *Sjöhunden* modernised with Näcken type electronics to extend life into the late 1990s. All of the class are being given Plessey sonars (replacing Atlas Elektronik CSU 3) which are similar to RN Type 2074.
Structure: Albacore hull. Twin-decked. Diving depth, 150 m *(492 ft)*.
Operational: Endurance, three weeks. The three unmodernised boats will be replaced in the late 1990s by the Gotland class.

SJÖHÄSTEN 6/1991, Erik Laursen

MISSILE CORVETTES

2 STOCKHOLM CLASS

Name	No	Builders	Laid down	Launched	Commissioned
STOCKHOLM	K 11	Karlskronavarvet	1 Aug 1982	24 Aug 1984	22 Feb 1985
MALMÖ	K 12	Karlskronavarvet	14 Mar 1983	22 Mar 1985	10 May 1985

Displacement, tons: 310 standard; 335 full load
Dimensions, feet (metres): 164 × 22.3 × 6.2 *(50 × 6.8 × 1.9)*
Main machinery: CODAG; 1 GM/Allison 570-KF gas turbine; 6540 hp(m) *(4.74 MW)* sustained; 2 MTU 16V 396 TB93 diesels; 4200 hp(m) *(3.1 MW)* sustained; 3 shafts
Speed, knots: 32 gas; 20 diesel
Complement: 30

Missiles: SSM: 8 Saab RBS 15 (4 twin) launchers ❶; inertial guidance; active radar homing to 70 km *(37.8 nm)* at 0.8 Mach; warhead 150 kg.
Guns: 1 Bofors 57 mm/70 Mk 2 ❷; 75° elevation; 220 rounds/minute to 17 km *(9.3 nm)*; weight of shell 2.4 kg.
1 Bofors 40 mm/70 ❸; 85° elevation; 300 rounds/minute to 12.5 km *(6.8 nm)*; weight of shell 0.96 kg.
Torpedoes: 2—21 in *(533 mm)* tubes ❹. FFV Type 613; wire-guided; passive homing to 15 km *(8.2 nm)* at 45 kts; warhead 240 kg. Up to 4 more 21 in *(533 mm)* can be fitted in lieu of missiles or 4—15.75 in *(400 mm)* tubes; Swedish Ordnance Type 43 or Whitehead A 244/S Mod 2.
A/S mortars: 4 Saab Elma LLS-920 9-tubed launchers ❺; range 300 m; warhead 4.2 kg shaped charge. IR/chaff decoys.
Depth charges: On mine rails.
Mines: Minelaying capability.
Countermeasures: Decoys: 2 Philips Philax fixed launchers; 4 magazines each holding 36 IR/chaff grenades; fired in groups of nine. A/S mortars have also been adapted to fire IR/chaff decoys.
ESM: Saab-Scania Argo; radar intercept.
Combat data systems: Ericsson MARIL 880; data link.
Fire control: Philips 9LV 300 GFCS including a 9LV 100 optronic director ❻.
Radars: Air/surface search: Ericsson Sea Giraffe 50HC ❼; G band.
Navigation: Terma PN 612; I band.
Fire control: Philips 9LV 200 Mk 3 ❽; J band.
Sonars: Simrad SA 950; hull-mounted; active attack.
Thomson Sintra TSM 2642 Salmon ❾; VDS; search; medium frequency.

Programmes: Orders placed in September 1981. Developed from Spica II class.
Operational: Some flexibility in weapon fit depending on mission. Trials have been done with a Plessey COMTASS towed passive sonar array. The Elma LLS-920 system is designed to surface a submarine even if it does not sink it.

STOCKHOLM *(Scale 1 : 600), Ian Sturton*

STOCKHOLM *4/1991, Antonio Moreno*

4 GÖTEBORG CLASS

Name	No	Builders	Laid down	Launched	Commissioned
GÖTEBORG	K 21	Karlskronavarvet	10 Feb 1986	14 Apr 1989	15 Feb 1990
GÄLVE	K 22	Karlskronavarvet	Sep 1988	23 Mar 1990	1 Feb 1991
KALMAR	K 23	Karlskronavarvet	Sep 1988	1 Nov 1990	1 Sep 1991
SUNDSVALL	K 24	Karlskronavarvet	Mar 1989	29 Nov 1991	Apr 1993

Displacement, tons: 300 standard; 399 full load
Dimensions, feet (metres): 187 × 26.2 × 6.6 *(57 × 8 × 2)*
Main machinery: 3 MTU 16V 396 TB94 diesels; 8700 hp(m) *(6.4 MW)* sustained; KaMeWa 80562-6 waterjets
Speed, knots: 32+
Complement: 36 (7 officers) plus 4 spare berths

Missiles: SSM: 8 Saab RBS 15 (4 twin) launchers ❶; inertial guidance; active radar homing to 70 km *(37.8 nm)* at 0.8 Mach; warhead 150 kg.
Guns: 1 Bofors 57 mm/70 Mk 2 ❷; 75° elevation; 220 rounds/minute to 17 km *(9.3 nm)*; weight of shell 2.4 kg.
1 Bofors 40 mm/70 (or Bofors Sea Trinity) ❸; 85° elevation; 330 rounds/minute to 12.5 km *(6.8 nm)*; weight of shell 0.96 kg.
Torpedoes: 4—15.75 in *(400 mm)* tubes ❹. Swedish Ordnance Type 43/45; anti-submarine.
A/S mortars: 4 Saab Elma LLS-920 9-tubed launchers ❺; range 300 m; warhead 4.2 kg shaped charge. IR/chaff decoys.
Depth charges: On mine rails.
Mines: Minelaying capability.
Countermeasures: Decoys: 4 Philips Philax fixed launchers; IR flares and chaff grenades. A/S mortars have also been adapted to fire IR/chaff decoys.
ESM/ECM: NobelTech/THORN EMI; intercept and jammer.
Combat data systems: NobelTech 9LV Mk 3.
Fire control: Two Bofors Electronics 9LV 200 Mk 3 Sea Viking optronic directors ❼. Bofors Electronics 9LV 450 GFCS. RC1-400 MFCS. 9AU-300 ASW control system. Bofors 9EW 400 EW control.
Radars: Air/surface search: Ericsson Sea Giraffe 150 HC ❻; G/H band.
Navigation: Terma PN 612; I-band.
Fire control: Two Bofors Electronics 9GR 400 ❼; I/J band.
Sonars: Thomson Sintra TSM 2643 Salmon ❽; VDS; active search; medium frequency.
Simrad SA 950; hull-mounted; active attack.

Programmes: Ordered 1 December 1985 as replacements for Spica I class.
Structure: Efforts have been made to reduce radar and IR signatures. A Bofors Sea Trinity gun has replaced the 40 mm/70 in one of the class for trials.

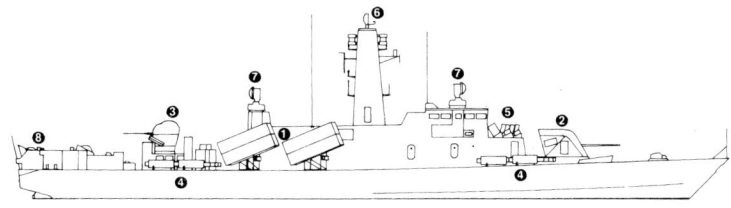

GÖTEBORG *(Scale 1 : 600), Ian Sturton*

KALMAR *8/1992, Erik Laursen*

LAND-BASED MARITIME AIRCRAFT

Numbers/Type: 10 Agusta-Bell 206A JetRanger (HKP-6B).
Operational speed: 115 kts *(213 km/h)*.
Service ceiling: 13 500 ft *(4115 m)*.
Range: 368 nm *(682 km)*.
Role/Weapon systems: Primarily operated in a liaison and training role and for secondary ASW, SAR and surface search helicopter operations. Weapons: ASW; 4 × Type 11 or 45 depth bombs.

Numbers/Type: 7 Boeing 107-II-5/7 Kawasaki KV 107-II. All to HKP-4B/C standard.
Operational speed: 137 kts *(254 km/h)*.
Service ceiling: 8500 ft *(2590 m)*.
Range: 300 nm *(555 km)*.
Role/Weapon systems: ASW and surface search helicopter; updated with new avionics, TM2D engines, BEAB Omera radar PS 864, data link for SSM targeting, MARIL 920 combat information system, updated Thomson Sintra DUAV-4 dipping sonar; life prolonged until 2000. Sensors: BEAB Omera radar, Thomson Sintra DUAV-4 dipping sonar. Weapons: ASW; 6 × Type 11/51 depth bombs and/or 2 × Type 42 or Type 43/45 torpedoes.

Numbers/Type: 24 Saab-Scania SH 37 Viggen.
Operational speed: 726 kts *(1345 km/h)*.
Service ceiling: 50 000 ft *(15 240 m)*.
Range: 1080 nm *(1975 km)*.
Role/Weapon systems: Operated by Air Force; to cover the Baltic approaches; peacetime EEZ surveillance assisted by air data camera. Sensors: Ericsson UAP-1023 radar, 1 × recce pod, 1 × camera pod, 1 × ECM pod, 1 × chaff/jammer pod. Weapons: Attack; 2 × Saab RB04 bombs + 2 × Saab RB05 ASV missiles. MR; 2 × RB24 air-to-air missiles. Total warload is 6 tons.

Numbers/Type: 1 CASA C-212 Aviocar.
Operational speed: 190 kts *(353 km/h)*.
Service ceiling: 24 000 ft *(7315 m)*.
Range: 1650 nm *(3055 km)*.
Role/Weapon systems: For ASW and surface surveillance. Sensors: Omera radar, Sonobuoys/Lofar, CDC sonobuoy processor, FLIR, data link. Coastguard variants also in service. Weapons: ASW; depth charges.

LIGHT FORCES

12 NORRKÖPING CLASS (FAST ATTACK CRAFT—MISSILE)

Name	No	Builders	Commissioned
NORRKÖPING	R 131	Karlskronavarvet	11 May 1973
NYNÄSHAMN	R 132	Karlskronavarvet	28 Sep 1973
NORRTÄLJE	R 133	Karlskronavarvet	1 Feb 1974
VARBERG	R 134	Karlskronavarvet	14 June 1974
VÄSTERÅS	R 135	Karlskronavarvet	25 Oct 1974
VÄSTERVIK	R 136	Karlskronavarvet	15 Jan 1975
UMEÅ	R 137	Karlskronavarvet	7 May 1975
PITEÅ	R 138	Karlskronavarvet	12 Sep 1975
LULEÅ	R 139	Karlskronavarvet	28 Nov 1975
HALMSTAD	R 140	Karlskronavarvet	9 Apr 1976
STRÖMSTAD	R 141	Karlskronavarvet	24 Sep 1976
YSTAD	R 142	Karlskronavarvet	10 Jan 1976

Displacement, tons: 190 standard; 230 full load
Dimensions, feet (metres): 143 × 23.3 × 7.4 *(43.6 × 7.1 × 2.4)*
Main machinery: 3 RR Proteus gas turbines; 12 750 hp *(9.5 MW)* sustained; 3 shafts
Speed, knots: 40.5
Complement: 27 (7 officers)

Missiles: SSM: 8 Saab RBS 15; active radar homing to 70 km *(37.8 nm)* at 0.8 Mach; warhead 150 kg.
Guns: 1 Bofors 57 mm/70 Mk 1; 75° elevation; 200 rounds/minute to 17 km *(9.3 nm)*; weight of shell 2.4 kg. 8 launchers for 57 mm illuminants on side of mounting.
Torpedoes: 6—21 in *(533 mm)* tubes (2-6 can be fitted at the expense of missile armament); Swedish Ordnance Type 613; anti-surface; wire-guided passive homing to 15 km *(8.2 nm)* at 45 kts; warhead 240 kg.
Mines: Minelaying capability.
Countermeasures: Decoys: 2 Philips Philax fixed launchers; IR flares and chaff. A/S mortars can also fire chaff/IR decoys.
ESM: Saab Scania EWS 905; radar intercept.
Combat data systems: MARIL 880 data link.
Radars: Air/surface search: Ericsson Sea Giraffe 50HC; G/H band.
Fire control: Philips 9LV 200 Mk 1; J band.

Modernisation: Programme included missile launchers, new fire control equipment, modernised electronics and new 57 mm guns. A/S mortars removed. All completed by late 1984. Six of the craft are planned to get new engines, and some weapon systems upgrading including sonobuoy processors AQS 924/928, to keep them in service until 2010.
Structure: Similar to the original Spica class from which they were developed.
Operational: Six of the craft may be fitted with GEC Avionics AQS 924 or the more modern AQS 928 sonobuoy processing equipment.

UMEÅ (with 2 SSM and 4 Torpedoes) *4/1989, Antonio Moreno*

1 JÄGAREN CLASS (COASTAL PATROL CRAFT)

Name	No	Builders	Commissioned
JÄGAREN	V 150	Bergens MV, Norway	24 Nov 1972

Displacement, tons: 120 standard; 150 full load
Dimensions, feet (metres): 120 × 20.7 × 5.6 *(36.6 × 6.3 × 1.7)*
Main machinery: 2 Cummins KTA50-M; 2500 hp *(1.87 MW)* sustained; 2 shafts
Speed, knots: 20
Complement: 15
Guns: 1 Bofors 40 mm/70.
Mines: Minelaying capability.
Radars: Surface search.

Comment: The prototype for the Hugin class but was not fitted with missiles, and up to 1988 was used for training and testing. In 1988 new engines were installed and the craft recommissioned for patrol duties. Has no torpedo tubes, fire control radar, ESM or sonar.

STRÖMSTAD (with 4 SSM and 2 Torpedoes) *8/1990, Gilbert Gyssels*

JÄGAREN *8/1991, Maritime Photographic*

1 + 6 TAPPER CLASS (COASTAL ARTILLERY)

TAPPER 81	HÄNDIG 84	MODIG 86
DJÄRV 82	TRYGG 85	HURTIG 87
DRISTIG 83		

Displacement, tons: 60 full load
Dimensions, feet (metres): 71.9 × 17.7 × 4.9 *(21.9 × 5.4 × 1.5)*
Main machinery: 2 MWM TBD 234 V16 diesels; 2090 hp(m) *(1.56 MW)*; 2 shafts
Speed, knots: 25
Complement: 9
Guns: 2—12.7 mm MGs.
A/S mortars: 4 Elma grenade launchers.
Depth charges: 8 racks.
Mines: 1 rail.
Radars: Surface search: 2 Racal Decca; I band.
Sonars: Simrad; active search; high frequency.

Comment: Type 80 ordered from Djupviksvarvet in early 1992, for delivery between February 1993 and December 1995.

NORRKÖPING *1/1993, van Ginderen Collection*

Light forces / SWEDEN

16 HUGIN CLASS (FAST ATTACK CRAFT—MISSILE)

Name	No	Builders	Commissioned
HUGIN	P 151	Bergens MV, Norway	3 July 1978
MUNIN	P 152	Bergens MV, Norway	3 July 1978
MAGNE	P 153	Bergens MV, Norway	12 Oct 1978
MODE	P 154	Westamarin, Norway	12 Jan 1979
VALE	P 155	Westamarin, Norway	26 Apr 1979
VIDAR	P 156	Westamarin, Norway	10 Aug 1979
MJÖLNER	P 157	Westamarin, Norway	25 Oct 1979
MYSING	P 158	Westamarin, Norway	14 Feb 1980
KAPAREN	P 159	Bergens MV, Norway	7 Aug 1980
VÄKTAREN	P 160	Bergens MV, Norway	19 Sep 1980
SNAPPHANEN	P 161	Bergens MV, Norway	14 Jan 1980
SPEJAREN	P 162	Bergens MV, Norway	21 Mar 1980
STYRBJÖRN	P 163	Bergens MV, Norway	15 June 1980
STARKODDER	P 164	Bergens MV, Norway	24 Aug 1981
TORDÖN	P 165	Bergens MV, Norway	26 Oct 1981
TIRFING	P 166	Bergens MV, Norway	23 Jan 1982

Displacement, tons: 120 standard; 150 or 170 full load (after modernisation)
Dimensions, feet (metres): 120 × 20.7 × 5.6 *(36.6 × 6.3 × 1.7)*
Main machinery: 2 MTU 16V 396 TB94 (after modernisation) or 20V 672 TY90 diesels; 5800 hp(m) *(4.26 MW)* sustained; 2 shafts; 2 hydraulic motors for slow speed propulsion (after modernisation)
Speed, knots: 36
Complement: 22 (3 officers)

Missiles: SSM: 6 Kongsberg Penguin Mk 2; IR homing to 27 km *(14.6 nm)* at 0.8 Mach; warhead 120 kg.
Guns: 1 Bofors 57 mm/70 Mk 1; 75° elevation; 200 rounds/minute to 17 km *(9.3 nm)*; weight of shell 2.4 kg. 57 mm illuminant launchers on either side of mounting.
A/S mortars: 4 Saab Elma 9-tubed launchers; range 300 m; warhead 4.2 kg shaped charge.
Depth charges: 2 racks.
Mines: 24. Mine-rails extend from after end of bridge superstructure with an extension over the stern. Use of these would mean the removal of any missiles.
Countermeasures: Decoys: The A/S mortars can fire IR/chaff decoys.
ESM: Saab Scania EWS 905; radar intercept.
Radars: Surface search: Skanter 16 in Mk 009; I band.
Fire control: Philips 9LV 200 Mk 2; J band.
Sonars: Simrad SA 950 (after modernisation) or SQ 3D/SF; hull-mounted; active attack; high frequency.
Simrad ST 570 VDS (in some); active; high frequency.

Programmes: In the early 1970s it was decided to build fast attack craft similar to the Norwegian Hauk class. Prototype *Jägaren* underwent extensive trials and, on 15 May 1975, an order for a further 11 was placed.
Modernisation: Half life modernisation is being done to eight of the class between 1991 and 1994. *Kaparen* and *Tordön* completed by early 1993. The update includes new engines with improved loiter capability and new sonars.

SNAPPHANEN (with VDS)   *4/1991, Hartmut Ehlers*

MUNIN   *10/1992, van Ginderen Collection*

3 DALARÖ CLASS (COASTAL PATROL CRAFT)

Name	No	Builders	Commissioned
DALARÖ	V 09	Djupviksvarvet	21 Sep 1984
SANDHAMN	V 10	Djupviksvarvet	5 Dec 1984
ÖSTHAMMAR	V 11	Djupviksvarvet	1 Mar 1985

Displacement, tons: 50
Dimensions, feet (metres): 76.8 × 16.7 × 3.6 *(23.4 × 5.1 × 1.1)*
Main machinery: 2 MTU 8V 396 TB83 diesels; 2100 hp(m) *(1.54 MW)* sustained; 2 shafts
Speed, knots: 30
Complement: 7 (3 officers)
Guns: 1 Bofors 40 mm/70. 2—7.62 mm MGs.
Mines: Rails fitted.
Radars: Surface search: Terma 610; I band.

Comment: Ordered 28 February 1983 for anti-intruder patrols instead of conversion of further Skanör class.

ÖSTHAMMAR   *1991, Royal Swedish Navy*

3 SKANÖR CLASS (COASTAL PATROL CRAFT)

Name	No	Builders	Recommissioned
ÖREGRUND	V 05 (ex-T 47)	Naval Dockyard, Stockholm	1 Feb 1983
SLITE	V 06 (ex-T 48)	Naval Dockyard, Stockholm	15 Apr 1983
LYSEKIL	V 08 (ex-T 52)	Naval Dockyard, Stockholm	13 June 1983

Displacement, tons: 25 standard
Dimensions, feet (metres): 75.5 × 19.4 × 3.9 *(23 × 5.9 × 1.2)*
Main machinery: 2 MTU 8V 396 TB83 diesels; 2100 hp(m) *(1.54 MW)* sustained; 2 shafts
Speed, knots: 25
Complement: 12
Guns: 1 Bofors 40 mm/70. 1—12 rail 57 mm illuminant launcher.
Mines: Up to 10 (or depth charges).
Radars: Surface search: Skanter 009; I band.

Comment: These craft were originally three of the eight of the T 42 class which first commissioned in 1957-59. Converted having their torpedo tubes removed and their petrol engines replaced by diesels. First two deleted in early 1989, next three in 1992.

LYSEKIL   *8/1989, Erik Laursen*

4 SVK CLASS (INSHORE PATROL CRAFT)

SVÄRDET SVK 1 (ex-*TV 228*)   PILEN SVK 3 (ex-*TV 230*)
SPJUTET SVK 2 (ex-*TV 226*)   BÅGEN SVK 4 (ex-*TV 234*)

Displacement, tons: 12
Dimensions, feet (metres): 45.9 × 11.1 × 3.3 *(14 × 3.4 × 1)*
Speed, knots: 10
Guns: 1 Oerlikon 20 mm (not always carried).

Comment: *Svärdet*, *Spjutet* and *Pilen* completed 1954-57. *Bågen* completed 1960 is slightly larger at 15.2 × 3.6 × 1.2 m. All belong to Sjövärnskåren (SVK) which is the Swedish Naval Reserve Association and are used for navigational training.

SVÄRDET   *1989, Royal Swedish Navy*

646 SWEDEN / Light forces — Mine warfare forces

17 INSHORE PATROL CRAFT (COASTAL ARTILLERY)

TORSKÄR 61	ÖRSKÄR 66	HOJSKÄR 70	BREDSKÄR 74
VÄDERSKÄR 62	VITASKÄR 67	GETORSKÄR 71	SPRÄNGSKÄR 75
EKESKÄR 63	ALTARSKÄR 68	FLAGGSKÄR 72	HAMNSKÄR 76
SKIFTESKÄR 64	ÄGGSKÄR 69	HÄRADOSKÄR 73	HUVUDSKÄR 77
GRÅSKÄR 65			

Displacement, tons: 30 full load
Dimensions, feet (metres): 69.2 × 15 × 4.3 *(21.1 × 4.6 × 1.3)*
Main machinery: 3 diesels; 3 shafts
Speed, knots: 18 *(61-67)*; 22 *(68-77)*
Guns: 1 Oerlikon 20 mm.
Depth charges: Carried in all of the class.
Radars: Surface search: Decca RM 914; I band.

Comment: These are operated by the Coastal Artillery. The 60 series launched in 1960-61 and 70 series in 1966-67. Modernised in the 1980s with a tripod mast and radar mounted over the bridge. Now called Type 72.

73 (older type)   8/1990, Gilbert Gyssels

EKESKÄR (after conversion)   9/1991, van Ginderen Collection

1 EXPERIMENTAL PATROL CRAFT (SES)

SMYGE

Displacement, tons: 140 full load
Dimensions, feet (metres): 99.7 oa; 88.6 wl × 37.4 × 6.2; 2.3 on cushion *(30.4; 27 × 11.4 × 1.9; 0.7)*
Main machinery: 2 MTU 16V 396 TB94 diesels (drive); 5080 hp(m) *(3.73 MW)* sustained; 2 KaMeWa waterjets
2 Scania DSI14 diesels (lift); 796 hp(m) *(585 kW)* sustained
Speed, knots: 40+
Complement: 14 (6 officers)
Missiles: SSM: 2 RBS 15 retractable mountings.
Guns: 1 Sea Trinity 40 mm CIWS; stealth cupola.
Torpedoes: Type 42; anti-submarine; wire-guided from covered stern tubes.
Mines: Rails or mine countermeasure equipment.
Radars: Air/surface search: Elevating mast.
Sonars: VDS or light towed array.

Comment: A surface effect experimental craft launched 14 March 1991 incorporating a high degree of stealth technology. GRP sandwich construction with Kevlar protection. Evaluation and trials in the period 1991-93 as a basis for the design of future attack craft.

SMYGE   1991, Royal Swedish Navy

MINE WARFARE FORCES

Note: A transportable COOP system was ordered in 1991. The unit can be shifted from one ship to another and comprises a container, processing module and tactical display, an underwater positioning system, sonar, double Eagle ROV and mine disposal charge and a Type 432 torpedo. Optimised for shallow water surveillance and can be used in conjunction with other MCM systems. The primary role is the detection and destruction of mines.

1 CARLSKRONA CLASS (MINELAYER)

Name	No	Builders	Commissioned
CARLSKRONA	M 04	Karlskronavarvet	11 Jan 1982

Displacement, tons: 3300 standard; 3550 full load
Dimensions, feet (metres): 346.7 × 49.9 × 13.1 *(105.7 × 15.2 × 4)*
Main machinery: 4 Nohab F212 D825 diesels; 10 560 hp(m) *(7.76 MW)*; 2 shafts; cp props
Speed, knots: 20
Complement: 50 plus 136 trainees. Requires 118 as operational minelayer.
Guns: 2 Bofors 57 mm/70. 2 Bofors 40 mm/70. 6—103 mm (2 triple) launchers for illuminants.
Mines: Can lay 105.
Countermeasures: 2 Philips Philax chaff/IR launchers.
Radars: Air/surface search: Ericsson Sea Giraffe 50HC; G/H band.
Surface search: Raytheon; E/F band.
Fire control: Two Philips 9LV 200 Mk 2; I/J band.
Sonars: Simrad SQ 3D/SF; hull-mounted; active search; high frequency.
Helicopters: Platform only.

Comment: Ordered 25 November 1977, laid down in sections late 1979 and launched 28 June 1980 at the same time as Karlskrona celebrated its tercentenary. Midshipmen's Training Ship as well as a minelayer; also a 'padded' target for exercise torpedoes. Name is an older form of Karlskrona.

CARLSKRONA   6/1992, van Ginderen Collection

2 ÄLVSBORG CLASS (MINELAYERS)

Name	No	Builders	Commissioned
ÄLVSBORG	M 02	Karlskronavarvet	6 Apr 1971
VISBORG	M 03	Karlskronavarvet	6 Feb 1976

Displacement, tons: 2500 standard; 2660 full load *(Älvsborg)*
2400 standard; 2650 full load *(Visborg)*
Dimensions, feet (metres): 303.1 × 48.2 × 13.2 *(92.4 × 14.7 × 4)*
Main machinery: 2 Nohab-Polar diesels; 4200 hp(m) *(3.1 MW)*; 1 shaft
Speed, knots: 16
Complement: 95 (accommodation for 205 submariners in Älvsborg—158 Admiral's staff in Visborg)
Guns: 3 Bofors 40 mm/70. 6—103 mm (2 triple) launchers for illuminants.
Mines: 300.
Countermeasures: 2 Philips Philax chaff/IR launchers.
Radars: Surface search: Raytheon; E/F band.
Fire control: Philips 9LV 200 Mk 2; I/J band.
Helicopters: Platform only.

Comment: Älvsborg was ordered in 1968 and launched on 11 November 1969; acts as a submarine depot ship. Visborg, laid down on 16 October 1973 and launched 22 January 1975 also acts as Command Ship for C-in-C Coastal Fleet. A Bofors Sea Trinity CIWS was to replace one of the 40 mm/70 guns for trials in Älvsborg but this was cancelled in 1992.

ALVSBORG   1/1993, van Ginderen Collection

VISBORG   8/1992, Maritime Photographic

Mine warfare forces / SWEDEN 647

1 MCM SUPPORT SHIP

Name	No	Builders	Commissioned
UTÖ (ex-*Smit Manila*, ex-*Seaford* ex-*Seaforth Challenger*)	A 261	Drypool, Selby	1974

Displacement, tons: 1100 full load
Dimensions, feet (metres): 182.1 × 40.4 × 14.1 *(55.5 × 12.3 × 4.3)*
Main machinery: 1 diesel; 5000 hp(m) *(3.68 MW)*; 1 shaft
Speed, knots: 12
Complement: 32
Guns: 2 Oerlikon 20 mm.

Comment: Ex-supply ship converted by Pan United Ltd, Singapore and recommissioned in April 1989 replacing *Thule*.

UTÖ   6/1989, van Ginderen Collection

1 FURUSUND CLASS (COASTAL MINELAYER)

FURUSUND MUL 20

Displacement, tons: 155 standard; 216 full load
Dimensions, feet (metres): 106.9 × 26.9 × 7.5 *(32.6 × 8.2 × 2.3)*
Main machinery: Diesel-electric; 2 Scania GAS 1 diesel generators; 2 motors; 416 hp(m) *(306 kW)*; 2 shafts
Speed, knots: 11.5
Complement: 24
Guns: 1 Oerlikon 20 mm. 2—7.62 mm MGs.
Mines: 22 tons.
Radars: Navigation: Racal Decca 1226; I band.

Comment: Built for Coastal Artillery by ASI Verken, Åmål. *Furusund* launched 16 December 1982, completed 10 October 1983. Plans for three more abandoned.

FURUSUND   1984, Royal Swedish Navy

7 ARKÖSUND CLASS (COASTAL MINELAYERS)

ARKÖSUND MUL 12   GRUNDSUND MUL 15   ÖRESUND MUL 18
KALMARSUND MUL 13   SKRAMSÖSUND MUL 17   BARÖSUND MUL 19
ALNÖSUND MUL 14

Displacement, tons: 200 standard; 245 full load
Dimensions, feet (metres): 102.3 × 24.3 × 10.2 *(31.2 × 7.4 × 3.1)*
Main machinery: Diesel-electric; 2 Nohab/Scania diesel generators; 2 motors; 460 hp(m) *(338 kW)*; 2 shafts
Speed, knots: 10.5
Guns: 1 Bofors 40 mm/60; on platform aft of the funnel.
Mines: 26 tons.
Radars: Navigation: Racal Decca 1226; I band.

Comment: All completed by 1954-1957. Operated by Coastal Artillery. One scrapped in 1992 and *Skramsösund* has been reclassified as an auxiliary.

ALNÖSUND   6/1989, T J Gander

1 COASTAL MINELAYER

KALVSUND MUL 11

Displacement, tons: 200 full load
Dimensions, feet (metres): 98.4 × 23.6 × 11.8 *(30 × 7.2 × 3.6)*
Main machinery: 2 MAN Atlas diesels; 300 hp(m) *(221 kW)*; 2 shafts
Speed, knots: 10
Guns: 2 Oerlikon 20 mm.
Mines: 21 tons.

Comment: Commissioned in 1947. Operated by Coastal Artillery. To be reclassified as an auxiliary in 1993.

KALVSUND   11/1991, van Ginderen Collection

16 SMALL MINELAYERS

501-516

Displacement, tons: 15
Dimensions, feet (metres): 47.9 × 13.8 × 2.9 *(14.6 × 4.2 × 0.9)*
Main machinery: 2 diesels; 2 shafts
Speed, knots: 14
Complement: 7
Mines: 12.

Comment: Ordered in 1969. Mines are laid from single traps on either beam. Operated by Coastal Artillery.

510   9/1990, van Ginderen Collection

3 ARKÖ CLASS (MINESWEEPERS—COASTAL)

Name	No	Builders	Commissioned
ARKÖ	M 57	Karlskronavarvet	1958
NÄMDÖ	M 67	Karlskronavarvet	1964
BLIDÖ	M 68	Hälsingborg	1964

Displacement, tons: 285 standard; 300 full load
Dimensions, feet (metres): 145.6 × 24.6 × 9.9 *(44.4 × 7.5 × 3)*
Main machinery: 2 MTU MB 12V 493 TZ60 diesels; 1360 hp(m) *(1 MW)* sustained; 2 shafts
Speed, knots: 14
Complement: 25
Guns: 1 Bofors 40 mm/70 Mod 48.

Comment: Of wooden construction. There is a small difference in the deck-line between *Arkö* and the remainder. The RBS 70 missiles have been removed.

NÄMDÖ   8/1990, Gilbert Gyssels

648 SWEDEN / Mine warfare forces

6 SMALL MINELAYERS

1879-1884

Displacement, tons: 2.5
Speed, knots: 20

Comment: Ordered from Farösünd on 27 November 1982. Completed July 1983-January 1984 for Coastal Artillery. Waterjet propulsion.

7 LANDSORT CLASS (MINEHUNTERS)

Name	No	Builders	Commissioned
LANDSORT	M 71	Karlskronavarvet	19 Apr 1984
ARHOLMA	M 72	Karlskronavarvet	23 Nov 1984
KOSTER	M 73	Karlskronavarvet	30 May 1986
KULLEN	M 74	Karlskronavarvet	28 Nov 1986
VINGA	M 75	Karlskronavarvet	27 Nov 1987
VEN	M 76	Karlskronavarvet	12 Dec 1988
ULVÖN	M 77	Karlskronavarvet	9 Oct 1992

Displacement, tons: 270 standard; 360 full load
Dimensions, feet (metres): 155.8 × 31.5 × 7.3 *(47.5 × 9.6 × 2.2)*
Main machinery: 4 Saab-Scania DSI14 diesels; 1592 hp(m) *(1.17 MW)* sustained; coupled in pairs to 2 Voith Schneider props
Speed, knots: 15. Range, miles: 2000 at 12 kts
Complement: 29 (12 officers) plus 4 spare berths

Guns: 1 Bofors 40 mm/70 Mod 48; 85° elevation; 300 rounds/minute to 12.5 km *(6.8 nm)*; weight of shell 0.96 kg. Bofors Sea Trinity CIWS trial carried out in *Vinga* (fitted in place of 40 mm/70).
2—7.62 mm MGs.
A/S mortars: 4 Saab Elma 9-tubed launchers; range 300 m; warhead 4.2 kg shaped charge.
Countermeasures: Decoys: 2 Philips Philax fixed launchers can be carried with 4 magazines each holding 36 grenades; IR/chaff.
MCM: This class is fitted for mechanical sweeps for moored mines as well as magnetic and acoustic sweeps. In addition it is possible to operate 2—15 ton unmanned catamaran magnetic and acoustic sweepers (59 × 20 ft *(18 × 6 m)*); these have SAM numbers. Fitted with 2 Sutec Sea Owl or Double Eagle remote controlled units with 600 m tether and capable of 350 m depth.
Fire control: Philips 9LV 100 optronic director. Philips 9 MJ 400 minehunting system.
Radars: Navigation: Thomson-CSF Terma; I band.
Sonars: Thomson-CSF TSM-2022; Racal Decca 'Mains' control system; hull-mounted; minehunting; high frequency.

Programmes: The first two of this class ordered in early 1981. Second four in 1984 and the seventh in 1989. *Landsort* launched 2 November 1982, *Arholma* 2 August 1984, *Koster* 16 January 1986, *Kullen* 15 August 1986, *Vinga* 14 August 1987, *Ven* 10 August 1988, and *Ulvön* in 1992. The projected eighth of the class has been cancelled.
Structure: The GRP mould for the hull has been available for several years and has been used for the Coast Guard Kbv 171 class.
Operational: The integrated navigation and action data automation system has been developed by Philips and Racal Decca.
Sales: SAM 3 and SAM 5 sold to the United States Navy in February 1991.

ARHOLMA   *10/1990, Per Kornefeldt*

SAM 02   *1990, van Ginderen Collection*

4 EJDERN CLASS (SONOBUOY CRAFT)

EJDERN B 01	SVÄRTEN B 03
KRICKAN B 02	VIGGEN B 04

Displacement, tons: 36 full load
Dimensions, feet (metres): 65.6 × 15.7 × 4.3 *(20 × 4.8 × 1.3)*
Main machinery: 2 Volvo Penta TAMD122 diesels; 366 hp(m) *(269 kW)* sustained; 2 shafts
Speed, knots: 15
Complement: 9
Guns: 1—12.7 mm MG.

Comment: Built by Djupviksvarvet and completed in 1991. GRP hulls. Classified as mine warfare vessels. Used for laying and monitoring long sonar arrays.

3 GILLÖGA CLASS (MINESWEEPERS—INSHORE)

GILLÖGA M 47	RÖDLÖGA M 48	SVARTLÖGA M 49

Displacement, tons: 110 standard; 135 full load
Dimensions, feet (metres): 72.2 × 21.3 × 11.5 *(22 × 6.5 × 3.5)*
Main machinery: 1 diesel; 380 hp(m) *(279 kW)*; 1 shaft
Speed, knots: 9
Guns: 1 Oerlikon 20 mm.

Comment: Built in 1964. Trawler type.

SVARTLÖGA   *9/1985, Gilbert Gyssels*

4 HISINGEN CLASS (MINESWEEPERS—INSHORE)

HISINGEN M 43	BLACKAN M 44
DÄMMAN M 45	GALTEN M 46

Displacement, tons: 130 standard; 150 full load
Dimensions, feet (metres): 78.7 × 21.3 × 11.5 *(24 × 6.5 × 3.5)*
Main machinery: 1 diesel; 380 hp(m) *(279 kW)*; 1 shaft
Speed, knots: 9
Guns: 1 Oerlikon 20 mm.

Comment: Built in 1960. Trawler type. Now used as diver support ships for mine clearance.

GALTEN   *8/1987, Gilbert Gyssels*

3 GÅSSTEN CLASS (MINESWEEPERS—INSHORE)

Name	No	Builders	Commissioned
GÅSSTEN	M 31	Knippla Skeppsvarv	16 Nov 1973
NORSTEN	M 32	Hellevikstrands Skeppsvarv	12 Oct 1973
VIKSTEN	M 33	Karlskronavarvet	20 June 1974

Displacement, tons: 120 standard; 135 full load
Dimensions, feet (metres): 78.7 × 21.3 × 11.5 *(24 × 6.5 × 3.5)*
Main machinery: 1 diesel; 460 hp(m) *(338 kW)*; 1 shaft
Speed, knots: 11
Guns: 1 Oerlikon 20 mm.

Comment: Ordered 1972. *Viksten* built of GRP, as a forerunner to new minehunters building at Karlskrona. Others have wooden hulls. These are repeat Hisingen class.

NORSTEN   *8/1985, Gunnar Olsen*

4 M 15 CLASS (MINESWEEPERS—INSHORE)

M 21   M 22   M 24   M 25

Displacement, tons: 70 standard
Dimensions, feet (metres): 90.9 × 16.5 × 4.6 *(27.7 × 5 × 1.4)*
Main machinery: 2 diesels; 320 hp(m) *(235 kW)* sustained; 2 shafts
Speed, knots: 12
Complement: 10

Comment: All launched in 1941 and now used as platforms for mine clearance divers. M 20 of this class was re-rated as tender and renamed *Skuld* (see *Tenders* section). Four deleted in 1989.

M 15 class   8/1985, Gunnar Olsen

2 MINE TRANSPORTS

FÄLLAREN A 236   MINÖREN A 237

Displacement, tons: 170 full load
Dimensions, feet (metres): 97 × 20.3 × 7.2 *(31.8 × 6.2 × 2.2)*
Main machinery: 2 diesels; 240 hp(m) *(176 kW)*; 2 shafts
Speed, knots: 9
Mines: Have minelaying capability.

Comment: Built in 1941 and 1940 respectively. Mahogany hulls.

FÄLLAREN   1987, Royal Swedish Navy

AMPHIBIOUS FORCES

Note: The deleted Ane class LCMs are to be replaced.

3 LCMs

Name	No	Builders	Commissioned
BORE	—	Åsigeverken	1967
GRIM	—	Åsigeverken	1961
HEIMDAL	—	Åsigeverken	1967

Displacement, tons: 340 full load
Dimensions, feet (metres): 124 × 28.2 × 8.5 *(37.8 × 8.6 × 2.6)*
Main machinery: 2 diesels; 800 hp(m) *(588 kW)*; 2 shafts
Speed, knots: 12
Military lift: 325 troops
Guns: 2 Oerlikon 20 mm.

Comment: Launched in 1961 *(Grim)* and other two in 1966. Operated by Coastal Artillery and used to transport guns.

BORE   5/1990, Hartmut Ehlers

24 LCAs

Displacement, tons: 6 full load
Dimensions, feet (metres): 30.8 × 10.5 × 1.6 *(9.4 × 3.2 × 0.5)*
Speed, knots: 20-25

Comment: Built between 1965 and 1973. Operated by Coastal Artillery.

LCA 352   8/1990, Gilbert Gyssels

18 + 59 (30) COMBATBOAT 90H RAIDING CRAFT

801-818

Displacement, tons: 19 full load
Dimensions, feet (metres): 52.2 × 12.5 × 2.6 *(15.9 × 3.8 × 0.8)*
Main machinery: 2 SAAB Scania DSI14 diesels; 1100 hp(m) *(808 kW) (801)*; 1250 hp(m) *(919 kW)* (remainder); 2 Alumina waterjets
Speed, knots: 35
Complement: 3
Military lift: 20 troops plus equipment or 2.8 tons
Missiles: SSM: Rockwell RBS 17 Hellfire; semi-active laser guidance to 5 km *(3 nm)* at 1.0 Mach; warhead 8 kg.
Guns: 3—12.7 mm MG.
Mines: 4 (or 6 depth charges).
Radars: Navigation: Racal Decca; RD 360 or Furuno 8050; I band.

Comment: The first two are prototypes ordered in January 1988 and built at Dockstavarvet in 1989. 12 more built in 1991/92. 63 more ordered from Dockstavarvet and Gotlands Varv in mid-January 1992, with an option for 30 more. The building period for the ordered boats will take up to 1995. This craft has a large hatch forward to aid disembarkation. *802* has a 26° deadrise, *801* and the remainder have 20°. All carry four six-man inflatable rafts. The Aden 30 mm gun fitted in one of the prototypes has been replaced by a standard fit of 3—12.7 mm MGs.

COMBATBOAT 803   6/1992, Maritime Photographic

2 LCMs

SKAGUL   SLEIPNER (ex-Årdal)

Displacement, tons: 275 standard *(Skagul)*; 450 standard *(Sleipner)*
Dimensions, feet (metres): 116.4 × 27.9 × 9.5 *(35.5 × 8.5 × 2.9) (Skagul)*
164 × 36.1 × 9.8 *(50 × 11 × 3) (Sleipner)*
Main machinery: 2 diesels; 2 shafts
Speed, knots: 11
Military lift: 100 tons

Comment: *Skagul* built by Hammarbyverken in 1960. *Sleipner* replaced the second of class in 1992 (taking the same name) having been bought from Norway where she commissioned in 1982. Both are Ro-Ro ferries.

SKAGUL   1981, Royal Swedish Navy

650 SWEDEN / Amphibious forces — Icebreakers

17 LCMs

603, 604, 606-612, 651-658

Displacement, tons: 55 full load
Dimensions, feet (metres): 68.9 × 19.7 × 4.9 *(21 × 6 × 1.5)*
Main machinery: 2 diesels; 340 hp(m) *(250 kW)*; 2 shafts
Speed, knots: 10
Military lift: 30 tons

Comment: Operated by Navy and Coastal Artillery. Completed from 1980-88. Equipped with Schottel system. Classified as Trossbåt (support boat). Built by Djupviksvarvet.

LCM 657   8/1992, Erik Laursen

79 LCUs

210-288

Displacement, tons: 31 full load
Dimensions, feet (metres): 70.2 × 13.8 × 4.2 *(21.4 × 4.2 × 1.3)*
Main machinery: 3 diesels; 600 hp(m) *(441 kW)*; 3 shafts
Speed, knots: 18
Military lift: 40 tons; 40 troops
Guns: 3 to 8—6.5 mm MGs (277-279). 1 Oerlikon 20 mm (remainder).
Mines: Minelaying capability (280-288 only).

Comment: 210-276 completed 1960-76; 277-279 in 1976, 280-284 in 1976-77 and 285-288 in 1986-87.

LCU 271   8/1992, Maritime Photographic

ICEBREAKERS

1 ODEN CLASS

Name	No	Builders	Commissioned
ODEN	—	Gotaverken Arendal, Göteborg	29 Jan 1989

Displacement, tons: 12 900 full load
Dimensions, feet (metres): 352.4 × 102 × 27.9 *(107.4 × 31.1 × 8.5)*
Main machinery: 4 Sulzer ZAL40S8L diesels; 23 940 hp(m) *(17.6 MW)* sustained; 2 shafts; cp props
Speed, knots: 17. **Range, miles:** 30 000 at 13 kts
Complement: 32 plus 17 spare berths
Guns: 4 Bofors 40 mm/70 can be fitted.

Comment: Ordered in February 1987, laid down 19 October 1987, launched 25 August 1988. Can break 1.8 m thick ice at 3 kts. Towing winch aft with a pull of 150 tons. Helicopter platform 73.5 × 57.4 ft *(22.4 × 17.5 m)*. The main hull is only 25 m wide but the full width is at the bow. Also equipped as a minelayer. Second of class may be ordered in due course and is to be called *Thule*.

ODEN   8/1992, Erik Laursen

3 ATLE CLASS

Name	No	Builders	Commissioned
ATLE	—	Wärtsilä, Helsinki	21 Oct 1974
FREJ	—	Wärtsilä, Helsinki	30 Sep 1975
YMER	—	Wärtsilä, Helsinki	25 Oct 1977

Displacement, tons: 7900 standard; 9500 full load
Dimensions, feet (metres): 343.1 × 78.1 × 23.9 *(104.6 × 23.8 × 7.3)*
Main machinery: 5 Wärtsilä-Pielstick diesels; 22 000 hp(m) *(16.2 MW)*; 4 Strömberg motors; 22 000 hp(m) *(16.2 MW)*; 4 shafts (2 fwd, 2 aft)
Speed, knots: 19
Complement: 54 (16 officers)
Guns: 4 Bofors 40 mm/70 (not all always embarked).
Helicopters: 2 light.

Comment: Similar to Finnish Urho class.

ATLE and YMER   8/1992, Maritime Photographic

Name	No	Builders	Commissioned
NJORD	—	Wärtsilä, Helsinki	8 Oct 1969

Displacement, tons: 5150 standard; 5686 full load
Dimensions, feet (metres): 283.8 × 69.5 × 22.6 *(86.5 × 21.2 × 6.9)*
Main machinery: Diesel-electric; 4 Wärtsilä diesel generators; 4 motors; 12 000 hp(m) *(8.82 MW)*; 4 shafts (2 fwd, 2 aft)
Speed, knots: 18
Guns: 4 Bofors 40 mm/70 (not all always embarked).
Helicopters: 1 light.

Comment: Near sister ship of *Tor*.

NJORD   6/1988, A Sheldon Duplaix

Name	No	Builders	Commissioned
TOR	—	Wärtsilä, Crichton-Vulcan Yard, Turku	31 Jan 1964

Displacement, tons: 5290 full load
Dimensions, feet (metres): 277.2 × 66.9 × 20.3 *(84.5 × 20.4 × 6.2)*
Main machinery: Diesel-electric; 4 Wärtsilä diesel generators; 4 motors; 12 000 hp(m) *(8.82 MW)*; 4 shafts (2 fwd, 2 aft)
Speed, knots: 18
Guns: 4 Bofors 40 mm/70 (not all always embarked).
Helicopters: 1 light.

Comment: Towed to Sandvikens Skeppsdocka, Helsingfors, for completion. A near sister to *Tarmo* built for Finland.

TOR   1986, Royal Swedish Navy

Icebreakers — Service forces / SWEDEN   651

Name	No	Builders	Commissioned
ALE	—	Wärtsilä, Helsinki	19 Dec 1973

Displacement, tons: 1550
Dimensions, feet (metres): 154.2 × 42.6 × 16.4 *(47 × 13 × 5)*
Main machinery: 2 diesels; 4750 hp(m) *(3.49 MW)*; 2 shafts
Speed, knots: 14
Complement: 32 (8 officers)
Guns: 1 Bofors 40 mm/70 (not embarked).

Comment: Built for operations on Lake Vänern. Also used for surveying.

ALE   7/1990, A Sheldon Duplaix

SURVEY SHIPS

Notes: (1) Owned by the National Maritime Administration but manned and operated by the Navy.
(2) There is a research ship *Argos*. Civilian manned and owned by the National Board of Fisheries. A second civilian ship *Ocean Surveyor* belongs to the Geological Investigation.

JOHAN NORDENANKAR

Displacement, tons: 2000
Dimensions, feet (metres): 239.5 × 45.9 × 12.5 *(73 × 14 × 3.8)*
Main machinery: 2 diesels; 4000 hp(m) *(2.94 MW)*; 1 shaft
Speed, knots: 15
Complement: 64 (14 officers)
Helicopters: Platform only.

Comment: Ordered from Falkenbergsvarvet in 1977. Commissioned 1 July 1980. Carries eight survey boats.

JOHAN NORDENANKAR   1980, Maritime Defence

NILS STRÖMCRONA

Displacement, tons: 175 standard
Dimensions, feet (metres): 95.1 × 32.8 × 5.2 *(29 × 10 × 1.6)*
Main machinery: 4 Saab Scania DSI14 diesels; 1592 hp(m) *(1.17 MW)* sustained; 2 shafts
Speed, knots: 12
Complement: 14 (5 officers)

Comment: Completed 28 June 1985. Of catamaran construction—each hull of 3.9 m made of aluminium.

NILS STRÖMCRONA   1986, Ove Hagström

JACOB HÄGG

Displacement, tons: 131 standard; 160 full load
Dimensions, feet (metres): 119.8 × 24.6 × 5.6 *(36.5 × 7.5 × 1.7)*
Main machinery: 4 Saab Scania DSI14 diesels; 1592 hp(m) *(1.17 MW)* sustained; 2 shafts
Speed, knots: 16
Complement: 13 (5 officers)

Comment: Laid down April 1982. Launched 12 March 1983. Completed 16 May 1983. Aluminium hull.

JACOB HÄGG   1988, Royal Swedish Navy

SERVICE FORCES

1 ELECTRONIC SURVEILLANCE SHIP

Name	No	Builders	Commissioned
ORION	A 201	Karlskronavarvet	7 June 1984

Displacement, tons: 1400 full load
Dimensions, feet (metres): 201.1 × 32.8 × 9.8 *(61.3 × 10 × 3)*
Main machinery: 2 Hedemora V8A diesels; 1800 hp(m) *(1.32 MW)* sustained; 2 shafts; cp props
Speed, knots: 15
Complement: 35

Comment: Ordered 23 April 1982. Laid down 28 June 1982. Launched 30 November 1983.

ORION   10/1990, van Ginderen Collection

1 OIL TANKER

Name	No	Builders	Commissioned
BRÄNNAREN	A 228	West Germany	1965

Displacement, tons: 655 standard; 857 full load
Dimensions, feet (metres): 203.4 × 28.2 × 12.1 *(62 × 8.6 × 3.7)*
Main machinery: 1 MAN 6MU51 diesel; 800 hp(m) *(588 kW)*; 1 shaft
Speed, knots: 11
Cargo capacity: 777 tons oil fuel

Comment: Ex-West German merchant tanker *Indio* purchased early 1972.

BRÄNNAREN   1991, Royal Swedish Navy

652 SWEDEN / Service forces

1 DIVER SUPPORT SHIP

SKREDSVIK (ex-*Kbv 172*)   A 262 (ex-M 70)

Comment: Details as for Kbv 171 in *Coast Guard* section. Transferred from the Coast Guard in 1991 and used as a Diver Support ship after a refit from October 1992 to February 1993. Will be employed for Command and Control in war.

SKREDSVIK (old number)   *6/1991, Erik Laursen*

2 BUOY TENDERS

BALTICA   **SCANDICA**

Displacement, tons: 450
Dimensions, feet (metres): 177.1 × 39.4 × 16.4 *(54 × 12 × 5)*
Speed, knots: 15

Comment: Completed in 1982-83.

1 SALVAGE SHIP

Name	No	Builders	Recommissioned
BELOS III (ex-*Energy Supporter*)	A 214	De Hoop, Netherlands	Nov 1992

Measurement, tons: 5096 grt
Dimensions, feet (metres): 344.2 × 59.1 × 16.7 *(104.9 × 18 × 5.1)*
Main machinery: 5 MAN 9ASL 25/30 diesel alternators; 8.15 MW; 2 motors; 5110 hp(m) *(3.76 MW)*; 2 shafts
Speed, knots: 14

Comment: Bought from Midland and Scottish Resources in mid-1992 and arrived in Sweden in November 1992. Replaced the previous ship of the same name which paid off in April 1993. Ice strengthened hull and fitted with a helicopter platform.

BELOS III (old name)   *1992, Royal Swedish Navy*

2 SAIL TRAINING SHIPS

Name	No	Builders	Commissioned
GLADAN	S 01	Naval Dockyard, Stockholm	1947
FALKEN	S 02	Naval Dockyard, Stockholm	1947

Displacement, tons: 225 standard
Dimensions, feet (metres): 112.8 × 23.6 × 13.8 *(34.4 × 7.2 × 4.2)*
Main machinery: 1 diesel; 120 hp(m) *(88 kW)*; 1 shaft

Comment: Sail training ships. Two masted schooners. Sail area, 512 sq m. Both have had major overhauls in 1986-88 in which all technical systems have been replaced.

FALKEN   *7/1990, Maritime Photographic*

2 TORPEDO AND MISSILE RECOVERY VESSELS

Name	No	Builders	Commissioned
PELIKANEN	A 247	Djupviksvarvet	26 Sep 1963
PINGVINEN	A 248	Lundevarv-Ooverkstads	14 Mar 1975

Displacement, tons: 191 full load
Dimensions, feet (metres): 108.2 × 19 × 7.2 *(33 × 5.8 × 2 2)*
Main machinery: 2 MTU MB diesels; 1040 hp(m) *(764 kW)*; 2 shafts
Speed, knots: 14

Comment: Torpedo recovery and rocket trials vessels. A 247 has her bridge superstructure forward instead of aft and only has one mast which is abaft the bridge.

PINGVINEN   *11/1991, van Ginderen Collection*

1 TORPEDO TRANSPORT

HÄGERN A 246

Displacement, tons: 50 standard; 58 full load
Dimensions, feet (metres): 95.1 × 16.4 × 5.9 *(29 × 5 × 1.8)*
Main machinery: 2 diesels; 480 hp(m) *(353 kW)*; 2 shafts
Speed, knots: 10

Comment: Launched in 1951.

HÄGERN   *8/1990, Gilbert Gyssels*

1 + 1 (23) COASTAL ARTILLERY SUPPORT VESSEL (TROSSBÄT)

Displacement, tons: 45 full load
Dimensions, feet (metres): 75.5 × 17.7 × 4.6 *(23 × 5.4 × 1.4)*
Main machinery: 2 Saab Scania DSI14 diesels; 796 hp(m) *(586 kW)* sustained; 2 Alumina waterjets
Speed, knots: 15
Complement: 3
Guns: 1 — 12.7 mm MG

Comment: Prototype Trossbät built at Holms Shipyard in 1991 and capable of carrying 15 tons of deck cargo and nine tons internal cargo or 17 troops plus mines. Aluminium hull with a bow ramp. Some ice capability. A second prototype is to be delivered in late 1993 with a view to series production, starting at the end of 1994.

TROSSBÄT   *5/1991, Per Kornefeldt*

Service forces — Tugs / SWEDEN   653

3 TENDERS

SIGRUN A 256

Displacement, tons: 256 standard
Dimensions, feet (metres): 105 × 22.3 × 10.5 *(32 × 6.8 × 3.2)*
Main machinery: 1 diesel; 320 hp(m) *(235 kW)*; 1 shaft
Speed, knots: 11

Comment: Launched in 1961. Laundry ship.

URD (ex-*Capella*) A 241

Displacement, tons: 63 standard; 90 full load
Dimensions, feet (metres): 73.8 × 18.3 × 9.2 *(22.5 × 5.6 × 2.8)*
Main machinery: 1 diesel; 200 hp(m) *(147 kW)*; 1 shaft
Speed, knots: 8

Comment: Experimental vessel added to the official list in 1970. Launched in 1929.

SKULD (ex-*M 20*) A 242

Displacement, tons: 70 standard
Dimensions, feet (metres): 90.9 × 16.5 × 4.6 *(27.7 × 5 × 1.4)*
Main machinery: 2 diesels; 410 hp(m) *(301 kW)*; 2 shafts
Speed, knots: 12

Comment: Former inshore minesweeper of the M 15 class. Launched in 1941.

SKULD   *6/1992, Maritime Photographic*

2 AMMUNITION TRANSPORTS

ATB 1 A 341   **ATB 2** A 342

Displacement, tons: 70
Dimensions, feet (metres): 99.7 × 19.7 × 6.6 *(30.4 × 6 × 2)*
Speed, knots: 10
Cargo capacity: 100 tons

ATB 1   *8/1986, van Ginderen Collection*

TUGS

ACHILLES A 251   **AJAX** A 252

Displacement, tons: 450
Dimensions, feet (metres): 108.2 × 28.9 × 15.1 *(33 × 8.8 × 4.6)*
Main machinery: 1 diesel; 1650 hp(m) *(1.2 MW)*; 1 shaft
Speed, knots: 12

Comment: *Achilles* was launched in 1962 and *Ajax* in 1963. Both are icebreaking tugs.

ACHILLES   *4/1991, Hartmut Ehlers*

HERMES A 253   **HEROS** A 322

Displacement, tons: 185 standard; 215 full load
Dimensions, feet (metres): 80.5 × 22.6 × 13.1 *(24.5 × 6.9 × 4)*
Main machinery: 1 diesel; 600 hp(m) *(441 kW)*; 1 shaft
Speed, knots: 11

Comment: Launched 1953-57. Icebreaking tugs.

HERMES   *1990, van Ginderen Collection*

HERCULES A 323   **HERA** A 324

Displacement, tons: 127 full load
Dimensions, feet (metres): 65.3 × 21.3 × 12.5 *(19.9 × 6.5 × 3.8)*
Main machinery: 1 diesel; 615 hp(m) *(452 kW)*; 1 shaft
Speed, knots: 10.5

Comment: Launched 1969 and 1971. Icebreaking tugs.

HERA   *8/1990, Gilbert Gyssels*

A 701-705, 751-756

Displacement, tons: 42 full load
Dimensions, feet (metres): 50.9 × 16.4 × 8.9 *(15.5 × 5 × 2.7)*
Main machinery: 1 diesel; 1 shaft
Speed, knots: 9.5

Comment: Can carry 40 people. Icebreaking tugs. 701-703 used by Coastal Artillery.

A 755   *8/1990, Gilbert Gyssels*

HEBE A 326   **PASSOPP** A 327   **ATLAS** A 330

Displacement, tons: 35; 25 *(Passopp)*
Speed, knots: 9

Comment: *Passopp* built in 1957; *Hebe* in 1969; *Atlas* in 1975.

WATER CARRIERS

1 WATER TANKER

Name	No	Builders	Commissioned
ELDAREN (ex-*Brotank*)	A 229	Asiverken, Åmål	1959

Measurement, tons: 320 dwt
Dimensions, feet (metres): 122 × 21.3 × 9.5 *(37.2 × 6.5 × 2.9)*
Main machinery: 1 Volvo-Penta diesel; 300 hp(m) *(220 kW)*; 1 shaft
Speed, knots: 9
Cargo capacity: 300 tons oil fuel; 10 tons water

Comment: Civilian tanker purchased from A F Karlsson in 1980.

ELDAREN *8/1992, Erik Laursen*

FRYKEN A 217   **MERANDA** A 313

Displacement, tons: 307 standard
Dimensions, feet (metres): 111.5 × 19.7 × 9.5 *(34 × 6 × 2.9)*
Main machinery: 1 diesel; 370 hp(m) *(272 kW)*; 1 shaft
Speed, knots: 10
Cargo capacity: 200 tons

Comment: Naval construction water carriers built in 1960-61.

FRYKEN *1976, Royal Swedish Navy*

COAST GUARD

(KUSTBEVAKNING)

Establishment: Established in 1638, and for 350 years was a part of the Swedish Customs administration. From 1 July 1988 the Coast Guard became an independent civilian authority with a Board supervised by the Ministry of Defence. Organised in four regions with a central Headquarters.

Duties: Responsible for civilian surveillance of Swedish waters, fishery zone and continental shelf. Supervises and enforces fishing regulations, customs, dumping and pollution regulations, environmental protection and traffic regulations. Also concerned with prevention of drug running and forms part of the Swedish search and rescue organisation.

Headquarters Appointments

Director General:
  Leif H Sjöström
Chief of Operations:
  Staffan Kvarnström

Personnel: 1993: 585

Aircraft: One Cessna 337. Three CASA 212.

Ships: Tv pennant numbers replaced by Kbv in 1988 but the Kbv is not displayed. Vessels are unarmed and have two distinctive yellow diagonal stripes on blue painted hulls. Superstructures are painted white.

Deletions

1991 *Kbv 172* (sold to Navy)
1992 *Kbv 257* (to Estonia)
1993 *Kbv 244* (to Latvia), *Kbv 245* (to Lithuania)

1 KBV 181 CLASS

Kbv 181

Displacement, tons: 800 approx
Dimensions, feet (metres): 183.7 × 33.5 × 15.1 *(56 × 10.2 × 4.6)*
Main machinery: 2 diesels; 3755 hp(m) *(2.76 MW)*; 2 shafts
Speed, knots: 16
Complement: 12
Guns: 1 Oerlikon 20 mm (if required).
Radars: Navigation: Racal Decca; I band.
Sonars: Simrad Subsea; active search; high frequency.

Comment: Ordered from Rauma Shipyards in August 1989 and built at Uusikaupunki. Commissioned 30 November 1990. Unarmed in peacetime. Equipped as a Command vessel for SAR and anti-pollution operations. All-steel construction similar to Finnish *Tursas*. Has replaced *Kbv 172*.

Kbv 181 *1992, Swedish Coast Guard*

1 KBV 171 CLASS

Kbv 171

Displacement, tons: 335 standard; 375 full load
Dimensions, feet (metres): 164 × 27.9 × 7.9 *(50 × 8.5 × 2.4)*
Main machinery: 2 Hedemora V16A diesels; 4500 hp(m) *(3.3 MW)*; 2 shafts
Speed, knots: 20. **Range, miles:** 3000 at 12 kts
Complement: 9
Gun: 1 Oerlikon 20 mm (if required).
Mines: Has mining capability.
Radars: Navigation: Two Racal Decca; I band.
Sonars: Simrad Subsea; active search; high frequency.
Helicopters: Platform for 1 light.

Comment: Ordered from Karlskronavarvet in 1978 and completed in 1980. GRP hull identical to Landsort class for the Navy. Sister ship *Kbv 172* replaced by *181* and sold to the Navy as a Diver support ship.

Kbv 171 *8/1992, Erik Laursen*

5 KBV 101 CLASS

Kbv 101-105

Displacement, tons: 50-53 full load
Dimensions, feet (metres): 87.6 × 16.4 × 3.6 *(26.7 × 5 × 1.1)*
Main machinery: 2 Cummins KTA38-M diesels; 2120 hp *(1.56 MW)*; 2 shafts
Speed, knots: 20. **Range, miles:** 1000 at 15 kts
Complement: 8 (accommodation for 16)
Sonars: Hull-mounted; active search; high frequency.

Comment: Built 1969-73 at Djupviksvarvet. Class A cutters. All-welded aluminium hull and upperworks. Equipped for salvage divers. Modernised with new diesels, a new bridge and new electronics completed in 1988.

Kbv 101 *1992, Royal Swedish Navy*

10 KBV 281 CLASS (CLASS B)

Kbv 281-290

Displacement, tons: 36-39 full load
Dimensions, feet (metres): 68.9 × 16.4 × 3 *(21 × 5 × 0.9)*
Main machinery: 2 Cummins KTA38-M diesels; 2120 hp *(1.56 MW)*; 2 shafts
Speed, knots: 27
Complement: 5

Comment: Built by Djupviksvarvet and delivered at one a year from 1979. Last one commissioned 6 December 1990. Aluminium hulls.

Kbv 287   1992, Royal Swedish Navy

8 KBV 271 CLASS (CLASS C)

Kbv 271-278

Displacement, tons: 18-20 full load
Dimensions, feet (metres): 63 × 13.1 × 4.3 *(19.2 × 4 × 1.3)*
Main machinery: 2 Volvo Penta TAMD120A diesels; 366 hp(m) *(269 kW)* sustained; 2 shafts
Speed, knots: 22
Complement: 5

Comment: Built 1974-77. Aluminium hulls.

Kbv 274   1992, Royal Swedish Navy

COAST GUARD PATROL CRAFT (SMALL)

Number	Comment
Kbv 238, 240-250, 255-261	17 ton aluminium hulls built 1961-72. Class D.
Kbv 301-315	38 kts. Building 1993-97.
Kbv 314, 317-8, 321, 341 365-6, 368-9, 371-3 381-5, 389, 391-4	Fast patrol craft built 1962-88.
Kbv 602, 661-2, 644-5	'Gemini' type built 1971-88.
Kbv 801, 804-8	Ice craft built 1965-72.

Comment: Kbv 257 transferred to Estonia in April 1992. Kbv 244 and 245 to Latvia and Lithuania respectively in February/March 1993.

Kbv 250   8/1992, Erik Laursen

POLLUTION CONTROL CRAFT

Number	Displacement (tons)	Comment
Kbv 041-4	70-76	Steel hulled. Class B sea trucks built 1972-1983 by Lunde SY. Complement includes salvage divers.
045-51	235-340	
Kbv 02-03	190-300	Steel hulled support ships. Class A built 1971-76 by Lunde SY. Complement includes salvage divers. Kbv 02 is an older modernised vessel.
Kbv 04	450	Built by Lunde SY in 1978. Carries salvage divers
Kbv 010	400	15 kts. Built by Lunde SY 1985. Sea Truck.
Kbv 020-23	30 (60 Kbv 020)	Aluminium catamaran hulls. Class D.
Kbv 0701-0712	6	Skerry boats. Class E built since 1979.
Kbv 081-099	1	Work boats. GRP on aluminium hulls. Class K built 1971-79.

Kbv 010   1992, Royal Swedish Navy

Kbv 022   6/1992, Per Kornefeldt

Kbv 048   3/1992, Per Kornefeldt

SWITZERLAND

Diplomatic Representation

Defence Attaché in London:
Major General G de Loës

General

The patrol boats are manned by the Army and split between Lakes Constance, Geneva and Maggiore; one company to each.

Mercantile Marine

Lloyd's Register of Shipping:
24 vessels of 348 700 tons gross

PATROL FORCES

11 AQUARIUS CLASS (Patrouillenboot 80)

ANTARES, AQUARIUS, CASTOR, MARS, ORION, PERSEUS, POLLUX, SATURN, SIRIUS, URANUS, VENUS

Displacement, tons: 5.2
Dimensions, feet (metres): 35.1 × 10.8 × 3 *(10.7 × 3.3 × 0.9)*
Main machinery: 2 Volvo Penta AQ260A petrol engines; 520 hp(m) *(382 kW)* maximum; 2 shafts
Speed, knots: 32.5
Complement: 8
Guns: 2—12.7 mm MGs.
Radars: Surface search: I band.

Comment: Builders Müller AG, Spiez. GRP hulls, wooden superstructure. *Aquarius* commissioned in 1978, *Pollux* in 1984, the remainder in 1981.

6 RELIANCE TYPE

Comment: Standard 11 m craft ordered in March 1991 for the Police. Built by Reliance Workboats, Laverstock.

MARS

1991, Aldo Fraccaroli

SYRIA

Headquarters' Appointments

Commander-in-Chief Navy:
Vice Admiral Tayyara
Chief of Staff:
Vice Admiral Kassiem Mahummed Baydoun
Director of Naval Operations:
Commodore Muhammad Hamud

Personnel

(a) 1993: 4000 officers and men (2500 reserves)
(b) 18 months' national service

Pennant Numbers

Side numbers are not displayed.

Bases

Latakia, Tartous, Al-Mina-al-Bayca, Baniyas

Mercantile Marine

Lloyd's Register of Shipping:
94 vessels of 129 651 tons gross

DELETIONS

1990   2 Osa Is

SUBMARINES

Note: There continue to be rumours of impending Kilo class replacements for the Romeos.

3 Ex-SOVIET ROMEO CLASS

Displacement, tons: 1475 surfaced; 1830 dived
Dimensions, feet (metres): 251.3 × 22 × 16.1 *(76.6 × 6.7 × 4.9)*
Main machinery: Diesel-electric; 2 Type 37-D diesels; 4000 hp(m) *(2.94 MW)*; 2 motors; 2700 hp(m) *(1.98 MW)*; 2 creep motors; 2 shafts
Speed, knots: 16 surfaced; 13 dived
Range, miles: 9000 at 9 kts surfaced
Complement: 54

Torpedoes: 8—21 in *(533 mm)* (6 bow, 2 stern) tubes. 14 Type 53; dual purpose; pattern active/passive homing up to 20 km *(10.8 nm)* at up to 45 kts; warhead 400 kg.
Mines: 28 in lieu of torpedoes.
Countermeasures: ESM: Stop Light; radar warning.
Radars: Surface search: Snoop Tray; I band.
Sonars: Hercules/Feniks; hull-mounted; passive/active search and attack; medium/high frequency.

Programmes: First pair sailed for Tartous in November 1985 under Soviet flag and transferred to Syrian flag after training period in July 1986. Third transferred December 1986. These are unlikely to be new construction and would therefore have been completed about 1961 and badly need replacements.
Operational: One ex-Soviet Whiskey class submarine transferred from the Black Sea in November 1985 and acts as an alongside charging platform. All based at Tartous and seldom go to sea.

ROMEO

1987

FRIGATES

2 Ex-SOVIET PETYA III CLASS

1/508 (ex-*12*)   **AL HIRASA** 2/508 (ex-*14*)

Displacement, tons: 950 standard; 1180 full load
Dimensions, feet (metres): 268.3 × 29.9 × 9.5 *(81.8 × 9.1 × 2.9)*
Main machinery: CODAG; 2 gas turbines; 30 000 hp(m) *(22 MW)*; 1 Type 61V-3 diesel; 5400 hp(m) *(3.97 MW)* sustained (centre shaft); 3 shafts
Speed, knots: 32. **Range, miles:** 4870 at 10 kts; 450 at 29 kts
Complement: 98 (8 officers)

Guns: 4—3 in *(76 mm)*/60 (2 twin) ❶; 80° elevation; 90 rounds/minute to 15 km *(8 nm)*; weight of shell 6.8 kg.
Torpedoes: 3—21 in *(533 mm)* (triple) tubes ❷. Soviet Type 53; dual purpose; pattern active/passive homing up to 20 km *(10.8 nm)* at up to 45 kts; warhead 400 kg or low yield nuclear.
A/S mortars: 4 RBU 2500 16-tubed trainable ❸; range 2500 m; warhead 21 kg.
Depth charges: 2 racks.
Mines: Can carry 22.
Radars: Surface search: Slim Net ❹; E/F band.
Navigation: Don 2; I band.
Fire control: Hawk Screech ❺; I band; range 27 km *(15 nm)*.
IFF: High Pole B. Two Square Head.
Sonars: Hull-mounted; active search and attack; high frequency.

Programmes: Transferred by the USSR in July 1975 and March 1975.
Operational: Based at Tartous.

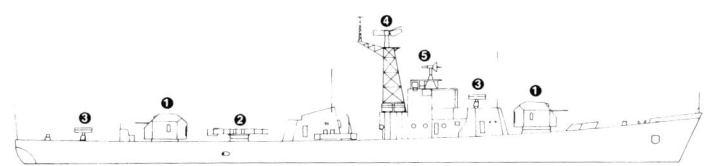

PETYA class   *(Scale 1 : 900), Ian Sturton*

AL HIRASA   *7/1975, MoD*

LAND-BASED MARITIME AIRCRAFT

Numbers/Type: 20/3 Mil Mi-14P Haze A/C.
Operational speed: 124 kts *(230 km/h)*.
Service ceiling: 15 000 ft *(4570 m)*.
Range: 432 nm *(800 km)*.
Role/Weapon systems: Medium-range ASW helicopter. Sensors: Search radar, dipping sonar, MAD, sonobuoys. Weapons: ASW; internally stored torpedoes, depth mines and bombs.

Numbers/Type: 4 Kamov Ka-27 Helix.
Operational speed: 135 kts *(250 km/h)*.
Service ceiling: 19 685 ft *(6000 m)*.
Range: 432 nm *(800 km)*.
Role/Weapon systems: ASW helicopter. All delivered in February 1990. Sensors: Search radar, dipping sonar, sonobuoys, MAD, ECM. Weapons: ASW; 3 torpedoes, depth bombs, mines.

LIGHT FORCES

Notes: (a) There is still one ex-Soviet P6 class (No 75) based at Tartous and two Hamelin class 37 m patrol craft based at Latakia.
(b) Second-hand purchase of Nanuchka class is a possibility in due course.

4 Ex-SOVIET OSA I (TYPE 205) and 10 OSA II CLASSES (FAST ATTACK CRAFT—MISSILE)

23-26 (Osa I); **31-40** (Osa II)

Displacement, tons: 210 (245 Osa II) full load
Dimensions, feet (metres): 126.6 × 24.9 × 8.8 *(38.6 × 7.6 × 2.7)*
Main machinery: 3 Type M 503A diesels; 8025 hp(m) *(5.9 MW)* sustained; 3 shafts (Osa I)
3 Type M 504 diesels; 10 800 hp(m) *(9.94 MW)* sustained; 3 shafts (Osa II)
Speed, knots: 35 (Osa I); 37 (Osa II). **Range, miles:** 400 at 34 kts (Osa I); 500 at 35 kts (Osa II)
Complement: 30

Missiles: SSM: 4 SS-N-2A Styx (Osa I); active radar or IR homing to 46 km *(25 nm)* at 0.9 Mach; warhead 513 kg.
4 SS-N-2C (Osa II); active radar or IR homing to 83 km *(43 nm)* at 0.9 Mach; warhead 513 kg; sea-skimmer at end of run.
Guns: 4—30 mm/65 (2 twin, 1 fwd, 1 aft); 85° elevation; 500 rounds/minute to 5 km *(2.7 nm)*; weight of shell 0.54 kg.
Radars: Surface search: Square Tie; I band; range 73 km *(40 nm)* or limits of radar horizon.
Fire control: Drum Tilt; H/I band.
IFF: Two Square Head. High Pole A or B.

Programmes: Osa I class delivered as follows: December 1972 (two), October 1973 (three), November 1973 (one), December 1973 (three). Osa II class delivered: September 1978 (one), October 1978 (one), October 1979 (two), November 1979 (two), August 1982 (one), September 1982 (one) and May 1984 (two). Some have already been deleted; more may follow soon.
Structure: Two of the Osa IIs are modified (Nos 39 and 40).
Operational: Osa Is based at Tartous; Osa IIs at Latakia.

5 Ex-SOVIET KOMAR CLASS (FAST ATTACK CRAFT—MISSILE)

42-46

Displacement, tons: 85 full load
Dimensions, feet (metres): 88.6 × 20.7 × 4.3 *(27 × 6.3 × 1.3)*
Main machinery: 4 Type M 50 diesels; 4400 hp(m) *(3.2 MW)* sustained; 4 shafts
Speed, knots: 37. **Range, miles:** 400 at 30 kts
Complement: 19

Missiles: SSM: 2 SSN-2A Styx; active radar or IR homing to 46 km *(25 nm)* at 0.9 Mach; warhead 513 kg.
Guns: 2—25 mm/80 (twin); 85° elevation; 270 rounds/minute to 3 km *(1.6 nm)*; weight of shell 0.34 kg.
Radars: Surface search: Square Tie; I band.
Fire control: Drum Tilt; H/I band.

Programmes: Acquired in May 1974. Laid up in 1987 but refitted and operational again in 1990.
Operational: Based at Al-Mina-al-Bayda.

8 Ex-SOVIET ZHUK CLASS (COASTAL PATROL CRAFT)

1-8

Displacement, tons: 50 full load
Dimensions, feet (metres): 75.4 × 17 × 6.2 *(23 × 5.2 × 1.9)*
Main machinery: 2 Type M 50 diesels; 2200 hp(m) *(1.6 MW)* sustained; 2 shafts
Speed, knots: 30. **Range, miles:** 1100 at 15 kts
Complement: 17
Guns: 4—14.5 mm (2 twin) MGs.
Radars: Surface search: Spin Trough; I band.

Comment: Three transferred from Black Sea in August 1981, three on 25 December 1984 and two more in the late 1980s. All based at Tartous.

OSA II (old number)   *1987*

ZHUK (Yemen colours)   *1989*

658 SYRIA / Amphibious forces — Mine warfare forces

AMPHIBIOUS FORCES

3 Ex-SOVIET POLNOCHNY B CLASS (TYPE 771) (LSM)

1/114   2/114   3/114

Displacement, tons: 760 standard; 834 full load
Dimensions, feet (metres): 246.1 × 31.5 × 7.5 *(75 × 9.6 × 2.3)*
Main machinery: 2 Kolomna Type 40-D diesels; 4400 hp(m) *(3.2 MW)* sustained; 2 shafts
Speed, knots: 19. Range, miles: 1500 at 15 kts
Complement: 40
Military lift: 180 troops; 350 tons cargo
Guns: 4—30 mm/65 (2 twin); 85° elevation; 500 rounds/minute to 5 km *(2.7 nm)*; weight of shell 0.54 kg.
 2—140 mm rocket launchers; 18 barrels per launcher; range 9 km *(5 nm)*.
Radars: Surface search: Spin Trough; I band.
Fire control: Drum Tilt; H/I band.

Comment: First transferred January 1984, two in February 1985 from Black Sea. All based at Tartous.

POLNOCHNY B   1988

MINE WARFARE FORCES

1 Ex-SOVIET NATYA CLASS

642

Displacement, tons: 770 full load
Dimensions, feet (metres): 200.1 × 31.8 × 8.9 *(61 × 9.7 × 2.7)*
Main machinery: 2 Type 504 diesels; 7200 hp(m) *(5.3 MW)* sustained; 2 shafts
Speed, knots: 19. Range, miles: 4000 at 10 kts
Complement: 65
Missiles: SAM: 2 SA-N-5 Grail quad launchers; manual aiming; IR homing to 6 km *(3.2 nm)* at 1.5 Mach; altitude to 2500 m *(8000 ft)*; warhead 1.5 kg; 16 missiles.
Guns: 4—30 mm/65 (2 twin). 4—25 mm/80 (2 twin).
A/S mortars: 2 RBU 1200 5-tubed fixed; range 1200 m; warhead 34 kg.
Mines: 10.
Radars: Surface search: Don 2; I band.
Fire control: Drum Tilt; H/I band.

Comment: Arrived in Tartous January 1985. Has had sweeping gear removed and acts as a patrol ship. Based at Tartous.

NATYA Class (old number)   1991

2 Ex-SOVIET VANYA CLASS (MINESWEEPERS—COASTAL)

KADISIA 775   YARMUK 776

Displacement, tons: 200 standard; 250 full load
Dimensions, feet (metres): 131.2 × 23.9 × 5.9 *(40 × 7.3 × 1.8)*
Main machinery: 2 Kolomna Type 9-D-8 diesels; 2000 hp(m) *(1.47 MW)* sustained; 2 shafts
Speed, knots: 16. Range, miles: 1400 at 14 kts
Complement: 30
Guns: 2—30 mm/65 (twin).
Mines: Can carry 8.
Radars: Surface search: Don 2; I band.
IFF: Square Head. High Pole B.

Comment: Transferred January 1973. Probably only one is still operational. Based at Tartous.

---

1 Ex-SOVIET T 43 CLASS (MINESWEEPER—OCEAN)

HITTIN 504

Displacement, tons: 500 standard; 580 full load
Dimensions, feet (metres): 190.2 × 27.6 × 6.9 *(58 × 8.4 × 2.1)*
Main machinery: 2 Kolomna Type 9-D-8 diesels; 2000 hp(m) *(1.47 MW)* sustained; 2 shafts
Speed, knots: 15. Range, miles: 3000 at 10 kts
Complement: 65
Guns: 2—37 mm/63 (twin). 8—14.5 mm MGs (4 twin).
Mines: Can carry 16.
Radars: Surface search: Ball End; E/F band.
Navigation: Don 2; I band.
IFF: Square Head. High Pole A.

Comment: Two transferred in 1959. The second of this class was sunk in the Israeli October 1973 war.

T 43 class (old number)   1985, van Ginderen Collection

1 Ex-SOVIET SONYA CLASS

532

Displacement, tons: 400 full load
Dimensions, feet (metres): 157.4 × 28.9 × 6.6 *(48 × 8.8 × 2)*
Main machinery: 2 Kolomna Type 9-D-8 diesels; 2000 hp(m) *(1.47 MW)* sustained; 2 shafts
Speed, knots: 15. Range, miles: 3000 at 10 kts
Complement: 43
Guns: 2—30 mm/65 (twin) or 2—30 mm/65 AK 630. 2—25 mm/80 (twin).
Mines: 5.
Radars: Surface search: Don 2; I band.
IFF: Two Square Head. One High Pole B.

Comment: Wooden hull. Made passage from Black Sea in December 1985, transferred January 1986. Based at Tartous.

SONYA (old number)   4/1992, van Ginderen Collection

5 Ex-SOVIET YEVGENYA CLASS (MINESWEEPERS—INSHORE)

4/507-8/507

Displacement, tons: 77 standard; 90 full load
Dimensions, feet (metres): 80.7 × 18 × 4.9 *(24.6 × 5.5 × 1.5)*
Main machinery: 2 Type 3-D-12 diesels; 600 hp(m) *(444 kW)*; 2 shafts
Speed, knots: 11. Range, miles: 300 at 10 kts
Complement: 10
Guns: 2—14.5 mm (twin) MGs (first pair). 2—25 mm/80 (twin) (second pair).
Radars: Surface search: Spin Trough; I band.
IFF: High Pole.

Comment: First transferred 1978, two in 1985 and two in 1986. Second pair by Ro-flow from Baltic in February 1985 being new construction with tripod mast. The first two may be non-operational. All based at Tartous.

YEVGENYA class (old number)   1991

SUPPORT SHIPS

1 Ex-SOVIET SEKSTAN CLASS

SR 153

Displacement, tons: 400 full load
Dimensions, feet (metres): 133.8 × 30.5 × 14.1 *(40.8 × 9.3 × 4.3)*
Main machinery: 1 diesel; 400 hp(m) *(2.94 MW)*; 1 shaft
Speed, knots: 11. Range, miles: 1000 at 11 kts
Complement: 24
Cargo capacity: 115 tons

Comment: Initially probably belonged to and was used by the Soviet Mediterranean Squadron. At some stage transferred to the Syrian Navy.

1 Ex-RUSSIAN VIKHR CLASS (TYPE B 98)

Displacement, tons: 2300 full load
Dimensions, feet (metres): 237.2 × 46.9 × 15.1 *(72.3 × 14.3 × 4.6)*
Main machinery: 2 Cegielski-Sulzer 16AV25/30 diesels; 5875 hp(m) *(4.32 MW)*; 2 shafts; cp props; 2 side thrusters; 1006 hp(m) *(740 kW)*
Speed, knots: 16. Range, miles: 2500 at 12 kts
Complement: 26 plus 8 salvage team

Comment: Specialist salvage vessel built at North Shipyard, Gdansk in the mid-1980s and delivered to Syria in May 1992. Ice strengthened hull. Capable of carrying 50 survivors.

1 Ex-SOVIET POLUCHAT CLASS

Displacement, tons: 70 standard; 100 full load
Dimensions, feet (metres): 97.1 × 19 × 4.8 *(29.6 × 5.8 × 1.5)*
Main machinery: 2 Type M 50 diesels; 2200 hp(m) *(1.6 MW)* sustained; 2 shafts
Speed, knots: 20. Range, miles: 1500 at 10 kts
Complement: 15
Guns: 2—14.5 mm (twin) MGs.
Radars: Surface search: Spin Trough; I band.

Comment: Used as divers' base-ship. Transferred September 1967. Based at Al-Mina-al-Bayda.

3 SURVEY LAUNCHES

Dimensions, feet (metres): 32.2 × 11.2 × 3 *(9.8 × 3.4 × 0.9)*
Main machinery: 2 Volvo Penta diesels; 310 hp(m) *(228 kW)*; 2 shafts
Speed, knots: 25
Complement: 4

Comment: Completed 1986 at Arcor, La Teste, France. GRP hulls.

1 TRAINING SHIP

AL ASSAD

Displacement, tons: 3500 full load
Dimensions, feet (metres): 344.5 × 56.4 × 13.1 *(105 × 17.2 × 4)*
Main machinery: 2 diesels; 2 shafts
Speed, knots: 16. Range, miles: 12 500 at 15 kts
Complement: 56 plus 140 cadets

Comment: Built in Polnocny Shipyard, Gdansk and launched 18 February 1987. Delivered in late 1988. Ro-Ro design used as a naval training ship. Unarmed. Based at Latakia.

AL ASSAD   6/1990, Selçuk Emre

7 ROTORK SEA TRUCKS

Dimensions, feet (metres): 47.6 × 14.4 × 2.9 *(14.5 × 4.4 × 0.9)*
Main machinery: 2 diesels; 600 hp(m) *(441 kW)*; 2 shafts
Speed, knots: 20
Complement: 8
Guns: 1—7.62 mm MG.

Comment: Light logistic craft delivered in 1980.

TAIWAN

Headquarters' Appointments

Chief of the General Staff:
 Admiral Ho-Chien Liu
Commander-in-Chief:
 Admiral Ming-Yao Chuang
Deputy Commanders-in-Chief:
 Vice Admiral Li-Chung Cheng
 Vice Admiral Ming-Kao Lee
Commandant of Marine Corps:
 Lieutenant General Kuo-Nan Cheng
Director of Political Warfare:
 Vice Admiral Wei Ouyang

Senior Flag Officers

Fleet Commander:
 Vice Admiral Li-Ming Chi
Director of Logistics:
 Vice Admiral Te-An Han
Commander of ASW:
 Vice Admiral Tse-Fong Wu

Personnel

(a) 1993: 31 000 (and 32 500 reserves) in Navy, 35 000 (and 35 000 reserves) in Marine Corps
(b) 2 years' conscript service

Bases

Tsoying: HQ First Naval District (Southern Taiwan, Pratas and Spratly). Main Base, HQ of Fleet Command, Naval Aviation Group and Marine Corps. Base of southern patrol and transport squadrons. Officers and ratings training, Naval Academy, Naval Shipyard.
Kao-hsiung: Naval Shipyard.
Makung (Pescadores): HQ Second Naval District (Pescadores, Quemoy and Wu Ch'iu). Base for attack squadrons. Naval Shipyard and Training facilities.
Keelung: HQ Third Naval District (Northern Taiwan and Matsu group). Base of northern patrol and transport squadrons. Naval Shipyard.
Minor bases at Suao, Hualien, Tamshui, Hsinchu, Wuchi, Anping and Kenting.

Commands

1. Fleet Commander commands two destroyer squadrons, one patrol squadron, one fast attack squadron, one mine warfare squadron, one amphibious squadron, one coastal patrol group, one helicopter group, and one submarine unit.
2. Logistic Commander commands one support ships squadron and one rescue group.
3. Anti-submarine Warfare (ASW) Command co-ordinates the surface, underwater, and air patrol to hunt down hostile submarines off Taiwan. The TF62 and Amphibious Command were deleted in 1991.
4. A land-based naval anti-ship missile Command is under naval operational control. Equipped with SSM Hsiung Feng II, this Command has forward deployment at off-shore islets of Quemoy, Matsu, WuChiu, and Pescadores along the mainland Chinese coast.

Marine Corps

Two divisions, the 66th and 99th are supported by one amphibious regiment and one logistics regiment. Equipped with M-116, M-733, LARC-5, LVTP5 personnel carriers and LVTH6 armour tractors. Based at Tsoying and in southern Taiwan with detachments at Pratas and Spratley Islands in the South China Sea.

Strength of the Fleet

Type	Active	Building/Transfer (Planned)
Submarines	4	(16)
Destroyers	22	—
Frigates	12	16 (18)
Corvettes	1	(10)
Fast Attack Craft (Missile)	52	(12)
Coastal Patrol Craft	80	—
Coastal Minesweepers/Hunters	15	2 (6)
Minesweeping Boats	9	—
LSD	1	—
Landing Ships (LST and LSM)	19 (6)	—
LCUs	54	1
LCMs	250	—
Minor Landing Craft	150	—
Combat Support Ship	1	—
Repair Ship	1	—
Transports	10	—
Salvage Ship	1	—
Support Tankers	4	—
AGI	1	—
Tugs	12	—
Floating Docks	5	—
Customs	13+	(18)

Maritime Security Police

Comes under the Minister of the Interior but its numerous patrol boats are integrated with the Navy for operational purposes.

Pennant Numbers

Pennant numbers were changed in early 1987.

Mercantile Marine

Lloyd's Register of Shipping:
 649 vessels of 6 103 581 tons gross

DELETIONS

Destroyers

1993 Heng Yang, Yuen Yang

Frigates

1992 Wen Shan, Tai Shan

Corvettes

1992 Wu Sheng, Chu Yung

Light Forces

1990 PTC 35-36

Amphibious Forces

1990 Chung Cheng

Mine Warfare Forces

1992 Yung Ching, Yung Fu

Survey Ships

1991 Lien Chang, Bien Dou
1992 Chiu Lien

PENNANT LIST

Submarines

736	Hai Shih
793	Hai Lung
795	Hai Hu
791	Hai Pao

Destroyers

903	Hua Yang
906	Huei Yang
907	Fu Yang
908	Kwei Yang
909	Chiang Yang
911	Dang Yang
912	Chien Yang
914	Lo Yang
915	Han Yang
917	Nan Yang
918	An Yang
919	Kun Yang
920	Lai Yang
921	Liao Yang
923	Chen Yang
924	Kai Yang
925	Te Yang
926	Shao Yang
927	Yun Yang
928	Cheng Yang
929	Chao Yang
930	Lao Yang

Frigates

815	Tien Shan
827	Tai Yuan
832	Yu Shan
833	Hua Shan
835	Fu Shan
836	Lu Shan
837	Shou Shan
843	Chung Shan
932	Chin Yang
933	Fong Yang
934	Feng Yang
1101	Cheng Kung
1103	Cheng Ho (bldg)
1105	Chi Kuang (bldg)
1106	Yueh Fei (bldg)
1107	Tzu-I (bldg)
1108	Pan Chao (bldg)
1109	Chang Chien (bldg)
1110	Tien Tan (bldg)

Corvettes

| 867 | Ping Jin |

Light Forces

| 601 | Lung Chiang |
| 602 | Sui Chang |

Amphibious Forces

192	Cheng Hai
201	Chung Hai
203	Chung Ting
204	Chung Hsing
205	Chung Chien
206	Chung Chi
208	Chung Shun
209	Chung Lien
210	Chung Yung
216	Chung Kuang
217	Chung Suo
219	Kao Hsiung
221	Chung Chuan
222	Chung Sheng
223	Chung Fu
225	Chung Chiang
226	Chung Chih
227	Chung Ming
228	Chung Shu
229	Chung Wan
230	Chung Pang
231	Chung Yeh
401	Ho Chi
402	Ho Huei
403	Ho Yao
404	Ho Deng
405	Ho Feng
406	Ho Chao
407	Ho Teng
481	Ho Shun
482	Ho Tsung
484	Ho Chung
485	Ho Cheng
486	Ho Shan
488	Ho Chuan
489	Ho Seng
490	Ho Meng
491	Ho Mou
492	Ho Shou
493	Ho Chun
494	Ho Yung
495	Ho Chien
496	Mei Lo
637	Mei Chin
649	Mei Ping
659	Mei Sung
694	Ho Chie
SB 1	

Mine Warfare Forces

| 423 | Yung Chou |

Service Forces

441	Yung Cheng
449	Yung An
457	Yung Ju
462	Yung Sui
469	Yung Lo
476	Yung Shan
479	Yung Nien
485	Yung Jen
488	Yung Hsin
497	Yung Chi
324	Ta Hu
505	Chang Pei
507	Hsin Lung
515	Lung Chuan
518	Yun Tai
521	Yu Tai
522	Tai Hu
523	Yuen Feng
525	Wu Kang
530	Wu Yi
AKL 359	Yung Kang
AP 520	Tai Wu
AOG 512	Wan Shou

Tugs

AFDL 1	Hay Tan
AFDL 2	Kim Men
AFDL 3	Han Jih
ARD 5	Fo Wu 5
ARD 6	Fo Wu 6
ATA 357	Ta Sueh
ATA 367	Ta Teng
ATA 395	Ta Peng
ATF 542	Ta Han
ATF 548	Ta Tung

SUBMARINES

Notes: (a) There are plans to acquire up to 16 patrol submarines in the 1990s. In January 1993 the export of German built hulls was blocked by the Federal Security Council. In February 1992 the Netherlands Government also refused permission to build in Dutch shipyards but the project was still being reviewed in early 1993, with the possibility of supplying technology and some non-strategic components. There is also mention of French SSNs.
(b) A Maschinebau Gabler, German-built Tows 64 DGK/300 class midget submarine was acquired in the early 1980s. Weight, 14 tons; length, 22.6 ft *(6.9 m)*; speed, 3 kts submerged and a diving depth of 300 m. Further craft based on this commercial prototype may have been built locally for military purposes although this is not confirmed.

2 NETHERLANDS HAI LUNG CLASS

Name	No	Builders	Laid down	Launched	Commissioned
HAI LUNG	793	Wilton Fijenoord	1982	6 Oct 1986	9 Oct 1987
HAI HU	795	Wilton Fijenoord	1982	20 Dec 1986	9 Apr 1988

Displacement, tons: 2376 surfaced; 2660 dived
Dimensions, feet (metres): 219.6 × 27.6 × 22 *(66.9 × 8.4 × 6.7)*
Main machinery: Diesel-electric; 3 Bronswerk D-RUB 215-12 diesels; 4050 hp(m) *(3 MW)*; 3 alternators; 2.7 MW; 1 Holec motor; 5100 hp(m) *(3.74 MW)*; 1 shaft
Speed, knots: 12 surfaced; 20 dived
Range, miles: 10 000 at 9 kts surfaced
Complement: 67 (8 officers)

Torpedoes: 6—21 in *(533 mm)* bow tubes. 28 AEG SUT; dual purpose; wire-guided; active/passive homing to 12 km *(6.6 nm)* at 35 kts; warhead 250 kg.
Countermeasures: ESM: Signaal Rapids; radar warning.
Fire control: Sinbads M Combat System.
Radars: Surface search: Signaal ZW 06; I band.
Sonars: Signaal SIASS-Z; hull-mounted; passive/active intercept search and attack; low/medium frequency.
Fitted for but not with towed passive array.

Programmes: Order signed with Wilton Fijenoord in September 1981 for these submarines with variations from the standard Zwaardvis design. Construction was delayed by the financial difficulties of the builders but was resumed in 1983. Sea trials of *Hai Lung* in March 1987 and *Hai Hu* in January 1988 and both submarines were shipped out on board a heavy dock vessel. The names mean *Sea Dragon* and *Sea Tiger*.
Structure: Two 196-cell batteries. The four horns on the forward casing are Signaal sonar intercept transducers. Torpedoes manufactured under licence in Indonesia.
Operational: Hsiung Feng 2 submerged launch SSMs are planned to be part of the weapons load but a torpedo-launched version has not yet been developed.

HAI LUNG *10/1991, Dr Chien Chung*

2 Ex-US GUPPY II TYPE

Name	No	Builders	Laid down	Launched	Commissioned
HAI SHIH (ex-USS *Cutlass* SS 478)	736 (ex-SS 91)	Portsmouth Navy Yard	22 July 1944	5 Nov 1944	17 Mar 1945
HAI PAO (ex-USS *Tusk* SS 426)	791 (ex-SS 92)	Federal SB & DD Co, Kearney, New Jersey	23 Aug 1943	8 July 1945	11 Apr 1946

Displacement, tons: 1870 standard; 2420 dived
Dimensions, feet (metres): 307.5 × 27.2 × 18 *(93.7 × 8.3 × 5.5)*
Main machinery: Diesel-electric; 3 Fairbanks-Morse diesels; 4500 hp *(3.3 MW)*; 2 Elliott motors; 5400 hp *(4 MW)*; 2 shafts
Speed, knots: 18 surfaced; 15 dived
Range, miles: 8000 at 12 kts surfaced
Complement: 75 (7 officers)

Torpedoes: 10—21 in *(533 mm)* (6 fwd, 4 aft) tubes. Probably US Mk 37 or AEG SUT; dual purpose.
Countermeasures: ESM: WLR-1/3; radar warning.
Radars: Surface search: US SS 2; I band.
Sonars: EDO BQR 2B; hull-mounted; passive search and attack; medium frequency.
Raytheon/EDO BQS 4C; adds active capability to BQR 2B.
Thomson Sintra DUUG 1B; passive ranging.

Programmes: Originally fleet-type submarines of the US Navy's Tench class; extensively modernised under the Guppy II programme. *Hai Shih* transferred in April 1973 and *Hai Pao* in October the same year.
Structure: Four 126-cell batteries. After 45 years in service diving depth will be very limited.
Operational: Used for anti-submarine training exercises.

HAI PAO *8/1990, DTM*

Destroyers / TAIWAN

DESTROYERS

6 Ex-US GEARING (WU CHIN I and II CONVERSIONS) (FRAM I and II) CLASS

Name	No	Builders	Laid down	Launched	Commissioned
*FU YANG (ex-USS *Ernest G Small* DD 838)(FRAM II)	907	Bath Iron Works Corporation	30 Jan 1945	14 June 1945	21 Aug 1945
**DANG YANG (ex-USS *Lloyd Thomas* DD 764) (FRAM II)	911	Bethlehem Steel, San Francisco	26 Mar 1944	5 Oct 1945	21 Mar 1947
**HAN YANG (ex-USS *Herbert J Thomas* DD 833)	915	Bath Iron Works Corporation	30 Oct 1944	25 Mar 1945	29 May 1945
**LAI YANG (ex-USS *Leonard F Mason* DD 852)	920	Bethlehem (Quincy)	8 June 1945	4 Jan 1946	28 June 1946
**KAI YANG (ex-USS *Richard B Anderson* DD 786)	924	Todd Pacific SY, Seattle, Washington	1 Dec 1944	7 July 1945	26 Oct 1945
*SHAO YANG (ex-USS *Hawkins* DD 873)	926	Consolidated Steel Corporation	14 May 1944	7 Oct 1944	10 Feb 1945

* Wu Chin I   ** Wu Chin II

Displacement, tons: 2425 standard; 3500 approx full load
Dimensions, feet (metres): 390.5 × 41.2 × 19 *(119 × 12.6 × 5.8)*
Main machinery: 4 Babcock & Wilcox boilers; 600 psi *(43.3 kg/cm sq)*; 850°F *(454°C)*; 2 GE turbines; 60 000 hp *(45 MW)*; 2 shafts
Speed, knots: 32.5. **Range, miles:** 5800 at 15 kts
Complement: 275 approx

Missiles: SSM: 5 Hsiung Feng I or II (1 triple ❶, 2 single ❷); radar or optical guidance (HFI); inertial guidance and active radar or IR homing (HF II) to 36 km *(19.4 nm)* (I) or 60 km *(32.4 nm)* (II) at 0.7 Mach (I) and 0.85 Mach (II); warhead 75 kg.
1 Sea Chapparal quad launcher ❸; Sidewinder missile; IR homing to 3 km *(1.6 nm)* supersonic; warhead 5 kg; 16 reloads.
A/S: Honeywell ASROC Mk 112 octuple launcher ❹ *(Shao Yang)*; inertial guidance to 1.6-10 km *(1-5.4 nm)*; payload Mk 46 torpedo.
Guns: 2 or 4 USN 5 in *(127 mm)*/38 (1 or 2 twin) Mk 38 ❺; 85° elevation; 15 rounds/minute to 17 km *(9.3 nm)*; weight of shell 25 kg.
1 OTO Melara 3 in *(76 mm)*/62 ❻; 85° elevation; 85 rounds/minute to 16 km *(8.7 nm)*; weight of shell 6 kg.
2 or 4 Bofors 40 mm/70 (2 single or 2 twin) ❼. 4 or 6—12.7 mm MGs.
Torpedoes: 6—324 mm US Mk 32 (2 triple) tubes ❽. Honeywell Mk 46; anti-submarine; active/passive homing to 11 km *(5.9 nm)* at 40 kts; warhead 44 kg.
Countermeasures: Decoys: 4 Kung Fen 6 16-tubed chaff launchers.
Mk T-6 Fanfare torpedo decoy.
ESM/ECM: ULQ-6 jammers and WLR-1 and WLR-3 passive warning receivers or Chang Feng II combined intercept and jammers.
Combat data systems: Elbit; action data automation (Wu Chin II). SATCOM in some.
Fire control: Honeywell H 930 with 2 RCA HR 76 directors for SSM. Mk 37 GFCS with Kollmorgen electro-optical sight ❾ for 127 mm or IAI Galileo optronic director Mk 114 system (for ASROC).
Radars: Air search: Lockheed SPS 40 ❿; E/F band or Westinghouse SPS 29 ⓫; B/C band.
Surface search: Raytheon SPS 10/SPS 58 ⓬; G band or Israeli Elta 1040 ⓭ (Wu Chin II).
Fire control: Western Electric Mk 25 ⓮ or Selenia RTN-10X ⓯ (Wu Chin II); I/J band.
Two RCA HR 76 ❻; I/J band (for SSM and guns).
Tacan: SRN 15.
Sonars: Atlas Elektronik DSQS-21CZ *(Fu Yang* and *Dang Yang)* or Raytheon SQS 23H; hull-mounted; active search and attack; medium frequency.

Helicopters: 1 McDonnell Douglas 500MD ⓱.

Programmes: *Fu Yang* transferred 5 February 1971; *Dang Yang*, 12 October 1972; *Han Yang*, 6 May 1974; *Lai Yang*, 20 April 1973; *Kai Yang*, 10 June 1977 by sale; *Shao Yang*, 10 March 1978.
Modernisation: All ships have been modernised:
(a) Wu Chin I: Installation of SSM and Honeywell H 930 Mod 1 fire control system with twin lattice masts topped by HR 76 directors in *Fu Yang* and *Shao Yang*. Developed by Honeywell and Chung-Shan Institute. Can track eight targets simultaneously and attack three with a 20 second response time.
(b) Wu Chin II: *Han Yang, Lai Yang, Kai Yang* and *Dang Yang* separately upgraded with the Elbit Naval Tactical Command and Control System. Developed by IAI, Israel and Chung-Shan Institute. Can track up to 12 targets simultaneously and attack three with a 20 second response time. Each ship also received an OTO Melara 76 mm gun, two Bofors 40 mm/70 single mounts, a quad Sea Chapparal SAM launcher and five (two single and one triple) Hsiung Feng I missile launchers. An RTN-10X on a lattice mast and an Officine Galileo optronic director replaced the Mk 37 fire control director on the bridge.

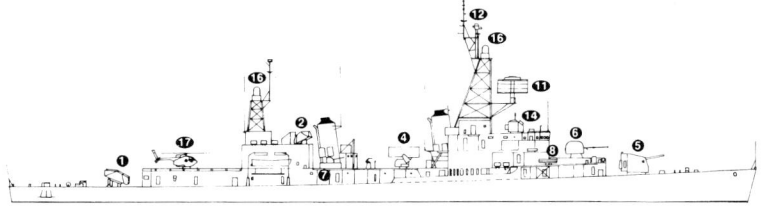
FU YANG *(Scale 1 : 1200), Ian Sturton*

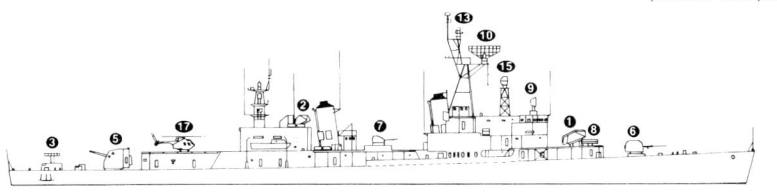
SHAO YANG *(Scale 1 : 1200), Ian Sturton*

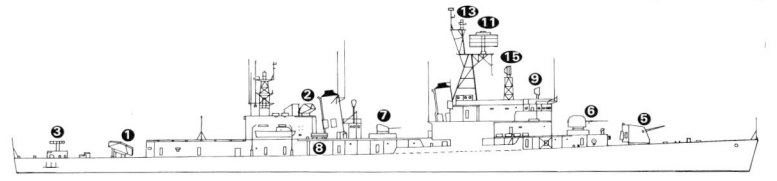
DANG YANG *(Scale 1 : 1200), Ian Sturton*

KAI YANG *(Scale 1 : 1200), Ian Sturton*

KAI YANG *6/1992, van Ginderen Collection*

The SPS-10 surface search radar was replaced by an Elta EL-1040. *Dang Yang* is unique in having her OTO Melara in 'A' position, triple Hsiung Fengs in 'B' position and a twin 5 in mount aft. All the others have a twin 5 in, in 'A', OTO Melara in 'B' and triple Hsiung Fengs aft.
Operational: *Fu Yang* is the Fleet Flagship.

SHAO YANG *6/1990*

8 Ex-US GEARING (WU CHIN III CONVERSION) (FRAM I) CLASS

Name	No	Builders	Laid down	Launched	Commissioned
CHIEN YANG (ex-USS *James E Kyes* DD 787)	912	Todd Pacific SY, Seattle, Washington	27 Dec 1944	4 Aug 1945	8 Feb 1946
LIAO YANG (ex-USS *Hanson* DD 832)	921	Bath Iron Works Corporation	7 Oct 1944	11 Mar 1945	11 May 1945
CHEN YANG (ex-USS *Hollister* DD 788)	923	Todd Pacific SY, Seattle, Washington	18 Jan 1945	9 Oct 1945	26 Mar 1946
TE YANG (ex-USS *Sarsfield* DD 837)	925	Bath Iron Works Corporation	15 Jan 1945	27 May 1945	31 July 1945
YUN YANG (ex-USS *Johnston* DD 821)	927	Consolidated Steel Corporation	6 May 1945	19 Oct 1945	10 Oct 1946
SHEN YANG (ex-USS *Power* DD 839)	928	Bath Iron Works Corporation	26 Feb 1945	30 June 1945	13 Sep 1945
CHAO YANG (ex-USS *Hamner* DD 718)	929	Federal SB and DD Co	5 Apr 1945	24 Nov 1945	11 July 1946
LAO YANG (ex-USS *Shelton* DD 790)	930	Todd Pacific SY, Seattle, Washington	31 May 1945	8 Mar 1946	21 June 1946

Displacement, tons: 2425 standard; 3500 approx full load
Dimensions, feet (metres): 390.5 × 41.2 × 19 *(119 × 12.6 × 5.8)*
Main machinery: 4 Babcock & Wilcox boilers; 600 psi *(43.3 kg/cm sq)*; 850°F *(454°C)*; 2 GE turbines; 60 000 hp *(45 MW)*; 2 shafts
Speed, knots: 32.5. **Range, miles:** 5800 at 15 kts
Complement: 275 approx

Missiles: SAM: 10 General Dynamics Standard SM1-MR (2 triple ❶; 2 twin ❷); command guidance; semi-active radar homing to 46 km *(25 nm)* at 2 Mach.
A/S: Honeywell ASROC Mk 112 octuple launcher ❸; inertial guidance to 1.6-10 km *(1-5.4 nm)*; payload Mk 46 torpedo.
Guns: 1 OTO Melara 3 in *(76 mm)*/62 ❹; 85° elevation; 85 rounds/minute to 16 km *(8.7 nm)*; weight of shell 6 kg.
1 GE/GD 20 mm Vulcan Phalanx Block 1 6-barrelled Mk 15 ❺; 3000 rounds/minute combined to 1.5 km.
4 Bofors 40 mm/70 (2 single or 2 twin) ❻. 4 or 6—12.7 mm MGs.
Torpedoes: 6—324 mm US Mk 32 (2 triple) tubes ❼. Honeywell Mk 46; anti-submarine; active/passive homing to 11 km *(5.9 nm)* at 40 kts; warhead 44 kg.
Countermeasures: Decoys: 4 Kung Fen 6 16-tubed chaff launchers.
Mk T-6 Fanfare torpedo decoy.
ESM/ECM: Chang Feng III (Hughes SLQ 17) intercept and jammers.
Fire control: Honeywell H 930 MFCS Mk 114 system (for ASROC).
Radars: Air search: Signaal DA-08 (with DA 05 aerial) ❽; E/F band.
Surface search: Raytheon SPS 10/SPS 58 ❾; G band.
Fire control: Signaal STIR ❿; I/J band (for Standard and 76 mm).
Westinghouse W-160 ⓫; I band (for Bofors).
Tacan: SRN 15.
Sonars: Raytheon SQS 23 H; hull-mounted; active search and attack; medium frequency.

Helicopters: 1 McDonnell Douglas 500MD ⓬.

Programmes: *Chien Yang* transferred 18 April 1973; *Liao Yang*, 18 April 1973; *Te Yang* and *Chen Yang*, 1 October 1977 by sale; *Yun Yang*, December 1980; *Shen Yang* by sale 27 February 1981; *Chao Yang* and *Lao Yang* by sale 3 March 1983.
Modernisation: All ships converted to area air defence ships under the Wu Chin III programme. This upgrade involved the installation of the H 930 Modular Combat System (MCS) with a Signaal DA-08 air search radar (employing a lightweight DA-05 antenna) and a Signaal STIR missile control radar directing 10 box-launched Standard SM-1 surface-to-air missiles (two twin in 'B' position, two triple facing either beam aft). The system can track 24 targets simultaneously and attack four with an eight second response time. An OTO Melara 76 mm is fitted to 'A' position, one Bofors 40 mm/70 is mounted forward of the seaboat on the starboard side, one abaft the ASROC magazine on the port side and a Mk 15 Block 1 Phalanx CIWS is aft between two banks of Standard launchers. A Westinghouse W-160 is mounted on a lattice mast on the hangar to control the Bofors. The amidships ASROC launcher is retained, its Mk 114 fire control system is integrated with the H 930 MCS via a digital-analogue interface. The SQS-23 sonar has also been upgraded to the H standard using a Raytheon solid-state transmitter. The Chang Feng III EW system was developed jointly by Taiwan's Chung-Shan Institute of Science and Technology (CSIST) with the assistance of Hughes. The Chang Feng III employs phased-array antennas which resemble those of the Hughes SLQ-17, it is capable of both deception and noise jamming.

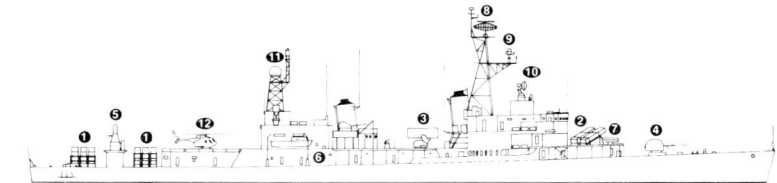
LIAO YANG (Wu Chin III) *(Scale 1 : 1200), Ian Sturton*

TE YANG *5/1992, Peter Humphries*

CHAO YANG *6/1992*

LIAO YANG *1989, IDR*

Destroyers / TAIWAN 663

2 Ex-US ALLEN M SUMNER CLASS

Name	No	Builders	Laid down	Launched	Commissioned
HUA YANG (ex-USS *Bristol* DD 857)	903	Bethlehem Steel, San Pedro	5 May 1944	29 Oct 1944	17 Mar 1945
*HUEI YANG (ex-USS *English* DD 696)	906	Federal SB & DD Co	19 Oct 1943	27 Feb 1944	4 May 1944

* Wu Chin I

Displacement, tons: 2200 standard; 3320 full load
Dimensions, feet (metres): 376.6 × 40.9 × 19 *(114.8 × 12.4 × 5.8)*
Main machinery: 4 Babcock & Wilcox boilers; 600 psi *(43.3 kg/cm sq)*; 850°F *(454°C)*; 2 GE or Westinghouse turbines; 60 000 hp *(45 MW)*; 2 shafts
Speed, knots: 34. **Range, miles:** 1000 at 32 kts
Complement: 275

Missiles: SSM: 5 or 6 Hsiung Feng I (2 triple or 1 triple, 2 single in *Huei Yang*) ❶; radar or optical guidance to 36 km *(19.4 nm)* at 0.7 Mach; warhead 75 kg.
SAM: 1 Sea Chapparal quad launcher ❷; Sidewinder missile; IR homing to 3 km *(1.6 nm)* supersonic; warhead 5 kg; 16 reloads.
Guns: 4 USN 5 in *(127 mm)*/38 (2 twin) Mk 38 ❸; 85° elevation; 15 rounds/minute to 17 km *(9.3 nm)*; weight of shell 25 kg.
1 OTO Melara 3 in *(76 mm)*/62 ❹ *(Huei Yang)*.
4 Bofors 40 mm/70 (2 twin) ❺.
Several 20 mm and 12.7 mm MGs. Secondary armament varies.
Torpedoes: 6—324 mm US Mk 32 (2 triple) tubes ❻. Honeywell Mk 46; anti-submarine; active/passive homing to 11 km *(5.9 nm)* at 40 kts; warhead 44 kg.
A/S mortars: 2 Mk 10 24-tubed fixed Hedgehogs ❼; range 350 m; warhead 26 kg.
Depth charges: 1 rack in some ships; 9 weapons.
Countermeasures: Decoys: 4 Kung Fen 6 16-barrelled chaff launchers.
ECM/ESM: Argo 680/681; intercept and jammer.
Fire control: Galileo optronic director or Honeywell H 930 with two RCA HR 76 directors *(Huei Yang)*.
Radars: Air search: Lockheed SPS 40 ❽; D band; range 146 km *(80 nm)* against fighter aircraft.
Surface search: Raytheon SPS 10 ❾; G band.
Fire control: Selenia RTN 10X ❿; I/J band or two RCA HR 76 *(Huei Yang)* ⓫; I/J band.
Sonars: EDO SQS 29; hull-mounted; active search and attack; medium frequency.

Programmes: *Hua Yang* transferred 9 December 1969; *Huei Yang*, 11 August 1970.
Modernisation: Unmodified on transfer. *Hua Yang* had most of its weapons and sensors updated under the Tien Shi (Angel) modification programme. This included the addition of Hsiung Feng SSM and Sea Chapparal SAM. *Huei Yang* was modified under the Wu Chin I programme and have 76 mm OTO Melara guns fitted in 'B' position.
Operational: Two of the class scrapped in 1993; last two to follow in 1994.

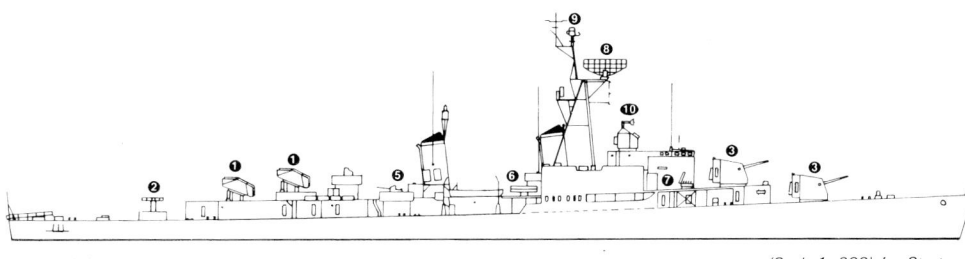

HUA YANG *(Scale 1 : 900), Ian Sturton*

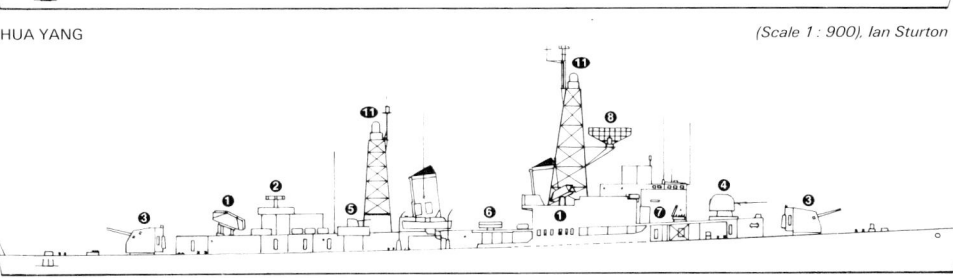

HUEI YANG

HUEI YANG *1990, Ships of the World*

2 Ex-US ALLEN M SUMNER (FRAM II) CLASS

Name	No	Builders	Laid down	Launched	Commissioned
LO YANG (ex-USS *Taussig* DD 746)	914	Bethlehem Steel, Staten Island	30 Aug 1943	25 Jan 1944	20 May 1944
NAN YANG (ex-USS *John W Thomas* DD 760)	917	Bethlehem Steel, San Francisco	21 Nov 1944	30 Sep 1944	11 Oct 1945

Displacement, tons: 2200 standard; 3320 full load
Dimensions, feet (metres): 376.6 × 40.9 × 19 *(114.8 × 12.4 × 5.8)*
Main machinery: 4 Babcock & Wilcox boilers; 600 psi *(43.3 kg/cm sq)*; 850°F *(454°C)*; 2 GE or Westinghouse geared turbines; 60 000 hp *(45 MW)*; 2 shafts
Speed, knots: 34. **Range, miles:** 1000 at 32 kts
Complement: 275 approx

Missiles: SSM: 5 Hsiung Feng I (1 triple ❶ and 2 single ❷); radar or optical guidance to 36 km *(19.4 nm)* at 0.7 Mach; warhead 75 kg.
SAM: 1 Sea Chaparral quad launcher ❸; Sidewinder missile; IR homing to 3 km *(1.6 nm)* supersonic; warhead 5 kg; 16 reloads.
Guns: 2 USN 5 in *(127 mm)*/38 (twin) Mk 38 ❹; 85° elevation; 15 rounds/minute to 17 km *(9.3 nm)*; weight of shell 25 kg.
1 OTO Melara 3 in *(76 mm)*/62 ❺; 85° elevation; 85 rounds/minute to 16 km *(8.7 nm)*; weight of shell 6 kg.
2 Bofors 40 mm/70 ❻. 4—12.7 mm MGs.
Torpedoes: 6—324 mm US Mk 32 (2 triple) tubes ❼. Honeywell Mk 46; anti-submarine; active/passive homing to 11 km *(5.9 nm)* at 40 kts; warhead 44 kg.
A/S mortars: 2 Mk 10 24-tubed fixed Hedgehogs ❽; range 350 m; warhead 26 kg.
Countermeasures: Decoys: 4 Kung Fen 6 16-barrelled chaff launchers.
ESM/ECM: Argo AR 680/681; intercept and jammer.
Fire control: Honeywell H 930 for SSM. Mk 37 GFCS with Kollmorgen electro-optical sight ❾ for 127 mm.
Radars: Air search: Westinghouse SPS 29 or SPS 37 ❿; B/C band; range 457 km *(250 nm)*.
Air/surface search: Raytheon SPS 10/SPS 58 ⓫; D band.
Fire control: Two RCA HR 76 ⓬; I/J band (for SSM and guns).
Tacan: SRN-15.
Sonars: EDO SQS 29; hull-mounted; active search and attack; medium frequency.
Helicopters: 1 McDonnell Douglas 500MD ⓭.

Programmes: Both ships transferred 6 May 1974.
Modernisation: Under the Wu Chin I modification programme the same weapon system changes were made as in the Gearing class.
Structure: Both ships have latticed masts. *Lo Yang* has the single SSM launchers on the signal deck on either side of the foremast; its Starboard Bofors abreast the forward funnel and the Port Bofors abreast the after funnel. *Nan Yang* has both Bofors abreast the after funnel.

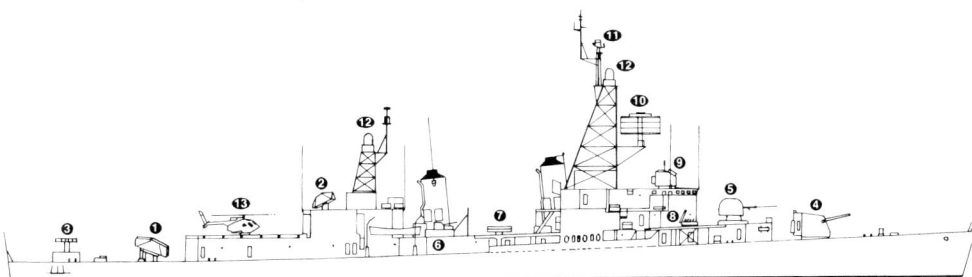

NAN YANG *(Scale 1 : 900), Ian Sturton*

NAN YANG *1985, DTM (Raymond Cheung)*

664 TAIWAN / Destroyers — Frigates

4 Ex-US FLETCHER CLASS

Name	No
KWEI YANG (ex-USS *Twining* DD 540)	908
CHIANG YANG (ex-USS *Mullany* DD 528)	909
AN YANG (ex-USS *Kimberly* DD 521)	918
KUN YANG (ex-USS *Yarnall* DD 541)	919

Builders	Laid down	Launched	Commissioned
Bethlehem Steel, San Francisco	20 Nov 1942	11 July 1943	1 Dec 1943
Bethlehem Steel, San Francisco	15 Jan 1942	12 Oct 1942	23 Apr 1943
Bethlehem Steel, Staten Island	27 July 1942	4 Feb 1943	22 May 1943
Bethlehem Steel, San Francisco	5 Dec 1942	25 July 1943	30 Dec 1943

Displacement, tons: 2100 standard; 3050 full load
Dimensions, feet (metres): 376.5 × 39.5 × 18 *(114.8 × 12 × 5.5)*
Main machinery: 4 Babcock & Wilcox boilers; 600 psi *(43.3 kg/cm sq)*; 850°F *(454°C)*; 2 GE/Allis Chalmers/Westinghouse turbines; 60 000 hp *(45 MW)*; 2 shafts
Speed, knots: 35. **Range, miles:** 3750 at 14 kts
Complement: 261 *(Kwei Yang)*; 279 *(Chiang Yang)*; 270 (remainder)

Missiles: SSM: 5 Hsiung Feng I (1 triple ❶ and 2 single ❷); radar or optical guidance to 36 km *(19.4 nm)* at 0.7 Mach; warhead 75 kg.
SAM: 1 Sea Chaparral quad launcher ❸; Sidewinder missile; IR homing to 3 km *(1.6 nm)* supersonic; warhead 5 kg; 16 reloads.
Guns: 2 USN 5 in *(127 mm)*/38 Mk 30 ❹; 85° elevation; 15 rounds/minute to 17 km *(9.3 nm)*; weight of shell 25 kg. Some may still have 3-5 in *(127 mm)* instead of the 76 mm.
1 OTO Melara 3 in *(76 mm)*/62 ❺; 85° elevation; 85 rounds/minute to 16 km *(8.8 nm)*; weight of shell 6 kg.
Torpedoes: 6—324 mm US Mk 32 (2 triple) tubes ❻. Honeywell Mk 46; anti-submarine; active/passive homing to 11 km *(5.9 nm)* at 40 kts; warhead 44 kg.
A/S mortars: 2 Mk 10 24-tubed fixed Hedgehogs ❼; range 350 m; warhead 26 kg.
Depth charges: 1 rack.
Mines: 1 rail.
Countermeasures: Decoys: 4 Kung Fen 6 16-barrelled chaff launchers.
ESM/ECM: Argo 680/681; intercept and jammer.
Fire control: Honeywell H 930 for SSM. Mk 37 GFCS with Kollmorgen electro-optical sight ❽ for 127 mm.
Radars: Air search: Lockheed SPS 40 ❾; E/F band.
Air/surface search: Westinghouse SPS 58 ❿; D band.
Fire control: Two RCA HR 76 ⓫; I/J band (for SSM and guns).
Sonars: Atlas Elektronik DSQS-21CZ; hull-mounted; active search and attack; medium frequency.

Programmes: *Kwei Yang* transferred 16 August 1971 (sale); *Chiang Yang*, 6 October 1971 (sale); *An Yang*, 2 June 1967; *Kun Yang*, 10 June 1968. *Kun Yang* and *An Yang* purchased 25 January 1974.
Modernisation: Armaments modernised under the Wu Chin I programme. *Kun Yang* can act as a minelayer.
Operational: Because of the state of the hulls, time spent at sea is very limited. All will be scrapped when the second batch of three Knox class are transferred in 1994/95.

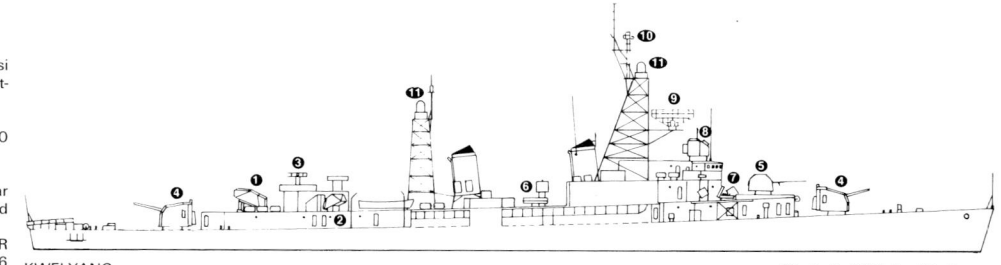

KWEI YANG *(Scale 1 : 900), Ian Sturton*

CHIANG YANG *4/1991, DTM*

FRIGATES

1 + 5 CHENG KUNG CLASS (KWANG HUA PROJECT) (FLIGHT I)

Name	No
CHENG KUNG	1101
CHENG HO	1103
CHI KUANG	1105
YUEH FEI	1106
TZU-I	1107
PAN CHAO	1108

Builders	Laid down	Launched	Commissioned
China SB Corporation, Keelung	7 Jan 1990	5 Oct 1991	May 1993
China SB Corporation, Keelung	21 Dec 1990	15 Oct 1992	Apr 1994
China SB Corporation, Keelung	Oct 1991	1993	Mar 1995
China SB Corporation, Keelung	Dec 1992	1994	Feb 1996
China SB Corporation, Keelung	1993	1995	Jan 1997
China SB Corporation, Keelung	1994	1996	Dec 1997

Displacement, tons: 2750 light; 4105 full load
Dimensions, feet (metres): 453 × 45 × 14.8; 24.5 (sonar) *(138.1 × 13.7 × 4.5; 7.5)*
Main machinery: 2 GE LM 2500 gas turbines; 41 000 hp *(30.59 MW)* sustained; 1 shaft; cp prop
2 auxiliary retractable props; 650 hp *(484 kW)*
Speed, knots: 29. **Range, miles:** 4500 at 20 kts
Complement: 206 (13 officers) including 19 aircrew

Missiles: SSM: 8 Hsiung Feng II ❶ (2 quad); inertial guidance; active radar or IR homing to 60 km *(32.4 nm)* at 0.85 Mach; warhead 75 kg.
SAM: 40 GDC Standard SM1-MR; Mk 13 launcher ❷; command guidance; semi-active radar homing to 46 km *(25 nm)* at 2 Mach.
Guns: 1 OTO Melara 76 mm/62 Mk 75 ❸; 85° elevation; 85 rounds/minute to 16 km *(8.7 nm)*; weight of shell 6 kg.
2 Bofors 40 mm/70 ❹. 4—12.7 mm MGs.
1 GE/GD 20 mm/76 Vulcan Phalanx 6-barrelled Mk 15 ❺; 3000 rounds/minute combined to 1.5 km.
Torpedoes: 6—324 mm Mk 32 (2 triple) tubes ❻. Honeywell Mk 46 Mod 5; anti-submarine; active/passive homing to 11 km *(5.9 nm)* at 40 kts; warhead 44 kg.
Countermeasures: Decoys: 4 Kung Fen 6 chaff launchers or locally produced version of RBOC (114 mm).
ESM/ECM: Chang Feng IV (locally produced version of SLQ 32(V)2 with Sidekick); combined radar warning and jammers.
Combat data systems: SYS-2(V)2 action data automation with UYK 43 computer. Ta Chen link (from *Chi Kuang* onwards).
Fire control: Unisys Mk 92 Mod 6. Mk 114 Mod 4 weapon direction system. Mk 114 ASW. 2 Mk 24 optical directors. Mk 309 TFCS.
Radars: Air search: Raytheon SPS 49(V)2 ❼; C/D band.
Surface search: ISC Cardion SPS 55 ❽ or Raytheon Chang Bai; I/J band.
Fire control: USN UD 417 STIR ❾; I/J band.
Signaal WM 28 ❿; I/J band.
Sonars: Raytheon SQS 56; hull-mounted; active search and attack; medium frequency.
SQR 18A; passive towed array (from *Chi Kuang* onwards).

Helicopters: 2 Sikorsky S-70C(M) ⓫ or Kamen SH-2F LAMPS I (only 1 to be embarked).

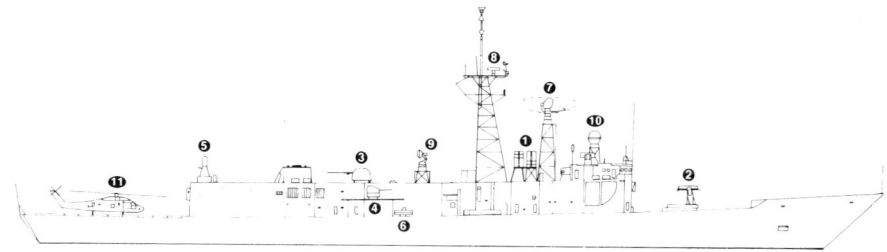

CHENG KUNG *(Scale 1 : 1200), Ian Sturton*

CHENG KUNG *8/1992, van Ginderen Collection*

Programmes: First two ordered 8 May 1989. The first six of the class are known as Flight I. Named after Chinese generals and warriors. Reports that the first planned Flight II ship *Chang Chien* may become a seventh Flight I are not confirmed.

Structure: Similar to the USS *Ingraham*. RAST helicopter haul down. The area between the mast had to be strengthened to take the Hsiung Feng II missiles.

Frigates / TAIWAN

0 + 2 (8) PFG-2 CLASS (KWANG HUA PROJECT) (FLIGHT II)

Name	No	Builders	Laid down	Launched	Commissioned
CHANG CHIEN	1109	China SB Corporation, Keelung	1995	1997	Nov 1998
TIEN TAN	1110	China SB Corporation, Keelung	1996	1998	Oct 1999

Displacement, tons: 4300 full load
Dimensions, feet (metres): 470 × 45 × 14.8; 24.5 (sonar) *(143.3 × 13.7 × 4.5; 7.5)*
Main machinery: 2 GE LM 2500 gas turbines; 41 000 hp *(30.59 MW)* sustained; 1 shaft; cp prop; 2 auxiliary props
Speed, knots: 29
Missiles: SSM: 8 Hsiung Feng II (2 quad) ❶.
SAM: Mk 41 VLS ❷; Tien Kung or Standard SM-2 (32 cells).
Guns: 1 OTO Melara 76 mm/62 Mk 75 ❸.
2 GE/GD 20 mm/76 6-barrelled Vulcan Phalanx ❹.
Torpedoes: 6—324 mm Mk 32 (2 triple) tubes ❺; Honeywell Mk 46 Mod 5.
Radars: Air search: GE/RCA ADAR-2N; E/F band; phased arrays ❻.
Fire control: 2 USN UD 417 STIR ❼.
Helicopters: 1 Sikorsky S-70C(M)1 ❽ or Kaman SH-2F LAMPS I.

Programmes: Flight II of the PFG-2 class project. If more time is needed because of revised instructions to potential contractors, *Chang Chien* may become the seventh Flight I ship. The last four will be Flight III.
Structure: Several design and equipment options are not yet finalised and the details listed could change. Modifications to Flight I include adding 17 ft to the hull forward of the bridge. The 76 mm gun mounted in 'A' position. A 32-cell Mk 41 VLS will replace the Mk 13 launcher and a second Phalanx will be added on a step forward of the bridge. The starboard hangar may be replaced by four Mk 41 VLS cells sub-divided into 16 with the Martin Marrietta Quad-pack. The superstructure will be cut down amidships, the CIC will be moved from the superstructure down into the hull. There will be a backup CIC aft of the main CIC as survivability measure (made possible by the modular nature of the combat system). A phased array radar system similar to the SPY-1 will be fitted, the two competing are the GE/RCA ADAR-2N and the Raytheon C-MAR. Two STIRs will provide target illumination. Hughes is offering the MCS-2000 combat data system while Raytheon has a licensed produced version of the Plessey Nautis-F. In the break in the superstructure amidships, eight Hsiung Feng II launchers will be fitted with options for either Bofors guns or ASW missiles.

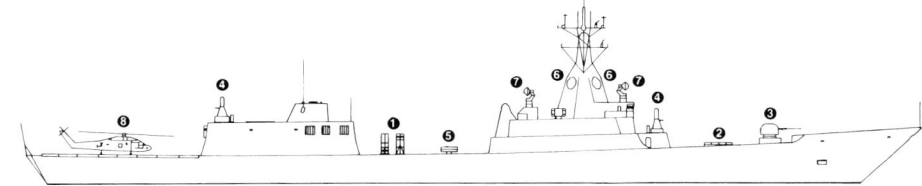
PFG-2 (FLIGHT II)   *(Scale 1 : 1200), Ian Sturton*

1 RUDDEROW, 2 Ex-US CHARLES LAWRENCE and 5 CROSLEY CLASSES

Name	No	Builders	Laid down	Launched	Commissioned
TIEN SHAN (ex-USS *Kleinsmith* APD 134/DE 718)	815 (ex-615)	Defoe SB Co, Bay City, Michigan	1944	27 Jan 1945	12 June 1945
**TAI YUAN (ex-USS *Ridley* DE 579)	827 (ex-959)	Bethlehem SB Co, Higham, Mass	1943	29 Dec 1943	13 Mar 1944
YU SHAN (ex-USS *Kinzer* APD 91/DE 232)	832 (ex-826)	Charleston Navy Yard, South Carolina	1943	9 Dec 1943	1 Nov 1944
HUA SHAN (ex-USS *Donald W Wolf* APD 129/DE 713)	833 (ex-854)	Defoe SB Co, Bay City, Michigan	1944	22 July 1944	13 Apr 1945
FU SHAN (ex-USS *Truxton* APD 98/DE 282)	835 (ex-838)	Charleston Navy Yard, South Carolina	1943	9 Mar 1944	9 July 1944
*LU SHAN (ex-USS *Bull* APD 78/DE 693)	836 (ex-821)	Defoe SB Co, Bay City, Michigan	1942	25 Mar 1943	12 Aug 1943
SHOU SHAN (ex-USS *Kline* APD 120/DE 687)	837 (ex-893)	Bethlehem, Quincy, Mass	1944	27 June 1944	18 Oct 1944
*CHUNG SHAN (ex-USS *Blessman* APD 48/DE 69)	843 (ex-845)	Bethlehem SB Co, Higham, Mass	1943	19 June 1943	19 Sep 1943

* Charles Lawrence class   ** Rudderow class

Displacement, tons: 1680 standard; 2130 full load
Dimensions, feet (metres): 306 × 37 × 12.6 *(93.3 × 11.3 × 3.8)*
Main machinery: Turbo-electric; 2 Foster-Wheeler boilers; 435 psi *(30.6 kg/cm sq)*; 750°F *(399°C)*; 2 GE turbo generators; 12 000 hp *(9 MW)*; 2 motors; 2 shafts
Speed, knots: 23.6. **Range, miles:** 5000 at 15 kts
Complement: 200
Military lift: 160 troops, commandos or frogmen
Guns: 4 or 6 Bofors 40 mm/56 (2 or 3 twin); 45° elevation; 160 rounds/minute to 11 km *(5.9 nm)*; weight of shell 0.9 kg.
4—20 mm (2 twin) (4 twin in *Hua Shan*).
Fire control: Mk 51 GFCS.
Radars: Surface search: Raytheon SPS 5 (in most); G/H band; SPS 6C (in *Tai Yuan*); D band.
Navigation: Decca 707 (in some); I band.
Fire control: RCA/GE Mk 26; I/J band.
Sonars: Hull-mounted; active attack; high frequency.

Programmes: *Yu Shan* transferred April 1962; *Hua Shan*, May 1965; *Fu Shan*, March 1966; *Lu Shan*, August 1966; *Shou Shan*, March 1966; *Chung Shan*, July 1967; *Tien Shan*, June 1967; *Tai Yuan* July 1968. All began as destroyer escorts (DE), but converted during construction or after completion to high-speed transports.
Modernisation: All ships were refitted with a second 5 in gun aft (since removed). One twin 40 mm gun mount forward of bridge and two twin mounts amidships.
Structure: Charles Lawrence class (APD 37-86) class has high bridge; Crosley class (APD 87 and above) has low bridge. Radars and fire control equipment vary. Davits amidships can hold four LCVP-type landing craft but ships usually carry only one each. Rudderow class (*Tai Yuan*) has a tripod mast and platforms below the bridge for 20 mm guns.
Operational: Sea Chaparral SAM and 5 inch gun systems removed as only the lighter guns are needed for fishery patrol duties. *Wen Shan* and *Tai Shan* used for spares but the remainder were all operational in early 1993.

CHUNG SHAN   *8/1990, ROC Navy*

TAI YUAN   *1992, Ships of the World*

666 TAIWAN / Frigates

3 + 3 Ex-US KNOX CLASS

Name	No	Builders	Laid down	Launched	Commissioned	Recommissioned
CHIN YANG (ex-*Robert E Peary*)	932 (ex-FF 1073)	Lockheed Shipbuilding	20 Dec 1970	23 June 1971	23 Sep 1972	7 Aug 1992
FONG YANG (ex-*Brewton*)	933 (ex-FF 1086)	Avondale Shipyards	2 Oct 1970	24 July 1971	8 July 1972	23 July 1992
FENG YANG (ex-*Kirk*)	934 (ex-FF 1087)	Avondale Shipyards	4 Dec 1970	25 Sep 1971	9 Sep 1972	Aug 1993
— (ex-*Bagley*)	935 (ex-FF 1069)	Lockheed Shipbuilding	22 Sep 1970	24 Apr 1971	6 May 1972	1995

Displacement, tons: 3011 standard; 3877 (932, 935), 4260 (933, 934) full load
Dimensions, feet (metres): 439.6 × 46.8 × 15; 24.8 (sonar) *(134 × 14.3 × 4.6; 7.8)*
Main machinery: 2 Combustion Engineering/Babcock & Wilcox boilers; 1200 psi *(84.4 kg/cm sq)*; 950°F *(510°C)*; 1 turbine; 35 000 hp *(26 MW)*; 1 shaft
Speed, knots: 27. **Range, miles:** 4000 at 22 kts on 1 boiler
Complement: 288 (17 officers)

Missiles: SSM: 8 McDonnell Douglas Harpoon; active radar homing to 130 km *(70 nm)* at 0.9 Mach; warhead 227 kg.
A/S: Honeywell ASROC Mk 16 octuple launcher with reload system (has 2 cells modified to fire Harpoon) ❶; inertial guidance to 1.6-10 km *(1-5.4 nm)*; payload Mk 46 Mod 5 Neartip.
Guns: 1 FMC 5 in *(127 mm)*/54 Mk 42 Mod 9 ❷; 85° elevation; 20-40 rounds/minute to 24 km *(13 nm)* anti-surface; 14 km *(7.7 nm)* anti-aircraft; weight of shell 32 kg.
1 General Electric/General Dynamics 20 mm/76 6-barrelled Mk 15 Vulcan Phalanx ❸; 3000 rounds/minute combined to 1.5 km.
Torpedoes: 4—324 mm Mk 32 (2 twin) fixed tubes ❹. 22 Honeywell Mk 46 Mod 5; anti-submarine; active/passive homing to 11 km *(5.9 nm)* at 40 kts; warhead 44 kg.
Countermeasures: Decoys: 2 Loral Hycor SRBOC 6-barrelled fixed Mk 36 ❺; IR flares and chaff to 4 km *(2.2 nm)*. T Mk-6 Fanfare/SLQ-25 Nixie; torpedo decoy. Prairie Masker hull and blade rate noise suppression.
ESM/ECM: SLQ 32(V)2 ❻; radar warning. Sidekick modification adds jammer and deception system.

Combat data systems: Link 14 receive only. FFISTS (Frigate Integrated Shipboard Tactical System).
Fire control: SWG-1A Harpoon LCS. Mk 68 GFCS. Mk 114 ASW FCS. Mk 1 target designation system. SRQ-4 for LAMPS I.
Radars: Air search: Lockheed SPS 40B ❼; E/F band; range 320 km *(175 nm)*.
Surface search: Raytheon SPS 10 or Norden SPS 67 ❽; G band.
Navigation: Marconi LN 66; I band.
Fire control: Western Electric SPG 53A/D/F ❾; I/J band.
Tacan: SRN 15. IFF: UPX-12.
Sonars: EDO/General Electric SQS 26 CX; bow-mounted; active search and attack; medium frequency.
EDO SQS 35; independent VDS.
EDO SQR 18A(V)1; passive towed array.

Helicopters: 1 SH-2F LAMPS I ❿.

Programmes: First three (or four) are to be in service and based in Taiwan by August 1993. Second batch scheduled for early 1995.
Structure: ASROC-torpedo reloading capability (note slanting face of bridge structure immediately behind ASROC). Four Mk 32 torpedo tubes are fixed in the midships structure, two to a side, angled out at 45 degrees. The arrangement provides improved loading capability over exposed triple Mk 32 torpedo tubes. A 4000 lb lightweight anchor is fitted on the port side and an 8000 lb anchor fits into the after section of the sonar.

CHIN YANG *(Scale 1 : 1200), Ian Sturton*

FENG YANG (US Colours) *8/1992, Giorgio Arra*

0 + 6 (10) FRENCH LA FAYETTE CLASS (KWANG HUA PROJECT II)

Name	No	Builders	Laid down	Launched	Commissioned
—	—	Lorient Dockyard/China SB Corporation	1 Feb 1992	Mar 1996	1997

Displacement, tons: 3500 full load
Dimensions, feet (metres): 410.1 × 50.5 × 13.1 *(125 × 15.4 × 4)*
Main machinery: CODAD; 4 diesels; 2 shafts
Speed, knots: 25. **Range, miles:** 7000 at 12 kts
Complement: 134 (15 officers) plus 25 spare

Missiles: SSM: 8 Hsiung Feng II (2 quad).
Guns: 1 OTO Melara 76 mm/62 Mk 35.
2 GE/GD 20 mm/76 6-barrelled Vulcan Phalanx.
Countermeasures: Decoys: 2 CSEE Dagaie chaff launchers.
Combat data systems: Thomson-CSF Tavitac 2000.
Fire control: CSEE Najir optronic director.

Helicopters: 1 Sikorsky S-70C(M)1 or Kamen SH-2F.

Programmes: Sale of up to 16 of the class authorised by the French Government in August 1991. Contract for the first six signed with Thomson-CSF in early 1992, to be manufactured in France and assembled by China SB Corporation at Kaohsiung in Taiwan. Second batch of 10 to be built by China SB Corporation.
Structure: Construction details are for the French design but the equipment listed has already been selected. Much of the remaining electronic systems are to be provided by Thomson-CSF but it is not clear how many are to be fitted before the hulls are transferred to Taiwan. It is reported but not confirmed that VLS SAM will also be included, as will a Thomson Sintra/BAe/Sema active towed sonar.

LA FAYETTE (French artist's impression) *1990, DCN*

SHIPBORNE AIRCRAFT

Numbers/Type: 12 Kaman SH-2F Seasprite (LAMPS I).
Operational speed: 130 kts *(241 km/h)*.
Service ceiling: 22 500 ft *(6860 m)*.
Range: 367 nm *(679 km)*.
Role/Weapon systems: ASW and OTHT helicopter; to transfer in August 1993. In LAMPS I programme, acts as ASW information relay for surface ships. Sensors: LN-66HP radar, ALR-66 ESM, ASN-123 tactical navigation, ASQ-81(V)2 MAD, AAQ-16 night vision system; ARR-57 sonobuoy receivers; 15 sonobuoys. Weapons: ASW; 2 × Mk 46 torpedoes, 8 × Mk 25 smoke markers. ASV; 1 Penguin; 1—7.62 mm MG M60.

Numbers/Type: 10 Hughes 500MD/ASW.
Operational speed: 110 kts *(204 km/h)*.
Service ceiling: 16 000 ft *(4880 m)*.
Range: 203 nm *(376 km)*.
Role/Weapon systems: Short-range ASW helicopter with limited surface search capability. Sensors: Search radar, Texas Instruments MAD. Weapons: ASW; 1 × Mk 46 torpedo or 2 × depth bombs. ASV; Could carry machine gun pods.

HUGHES 500 MD   *1990, Dr Chien Chung*

Numbers/Type: 10 Sikorsky S-70C(M)1.
Operational speed: 145 kts *(269 km/h)*.
Service ceiling: 19 000 ft *(5790 m)*.
Range: 324 nm *(600 km)*.
Role/Weapon systems: Delivered in 1991. This is a variant of the SH-60B and will become seaborne with the first Cheng Kung and La Fayette class frigates. Another 14 S-70B/C SAR and assault aircraft belong to the Air Force. Sensors: APS 143 search radar; ALR 606 ESM; ARR 84 sonobuoy receiver with ASN 150 data link; dipping sonar. Weapons: ASW; 2 × Mk 46 torpedoes or 2 × Mk 64 depth bombs. ASV; Could carry ASM.

SIKORSKY 70 C(M)   *1992, D Hughes*

LAND-BASED MARITIME AIRCRAFT

Note: Albatross aircraft replaced by Air Force Sikorsky S-70B/C for SAR.

Numbers/Type: 32 Grumman S-2E/T (Turbo) Trackers.
Operational speed: 130 kts *(241 km/h)*.
Service ceiling: 25 000 ft *(7620 m)*.
Range: 1350 nm *(2500 km)*.
Role/Weapon systems: Patrol and ASW tasks undertaken by Air Force-manned Trackers, which come under naval control; all updated with turboprop engines and new sensors by 1994. Based at Pintung. Seeking P-3C Orion as replacement. Sensors: APS 504 search radar, ESM, MAD, AAS 40 FLIR, SSQ-41B, SSQ-47B sonobuoys; AQS 902F sonobuoy processor; ASN 150 data link. Weapons: ASW; 4 × Mk 44 torpedoes, Mk 54 depth charges or Mk 64 depth bombs or mines. ASV; 6 × 127 mm rockets.

TRACKER   *1992, D Hughes*

CORVETTES

Note: Ten 1250 ton corvettes (PCEG) are planned to be equipped with Hsiung Feng II SSM. First pair to be acquired from a European shipbuilder and the remainder constructed locally.

1 Ex-US AUK CLASS

Name	No	Builders	Commissioned
PING JIN	867	American SB Co,	16 Nov 1942
(ex-USS *Steady* MSF 118)		Cleveland, Ohio	

Displacement, tons: 890 standard; 1250 full load
Dimensions, feet (metres): 221.2 × 32.2 × 10.8 *(67.4 × 9.8 × 3.3)*
Main machinery: Diesel-electric; 2 GM 12-278A diesels; 2200 hp *(1.64 MW)*; 2 shafts
Speed, knots: 18
Complement: 80
Guns: 4 Bofors 40 mm/56 (2 twin). 4 Oerlikon 20 mm (2 twin).
Radars: Surface search: Raytheon SPS 5; G/H band; range 37 km *(20 nm)*.

Comment: Transferred March 1968. The last survivor stripped of all heavy armament and used for limited fishery protection duties. Two others of the class became non-operational in 1992.

AUK (old number)   *1980*

LIGHT FORCES

Note: Twelve 300 ton craft are planned. First two to be acquired from European shipbuilders and remainder constructed locally.

2 LUNG CHIANG CLASS (FAST ATTACK CRAFT—MISSILE)

Name	No	Builders	Commissioned
LUNG CHIANG	601 (ex-PGG 581)	Tacoma Boatbuilding, Wa	15 May 1978
SUI CHIANG	602 (ex-PGG 582)	China SB Corporation, Kaohsiung	1982

Displacement, tons: 218 standard; 250 full load
Dimensions, feet (metres): 164.5 × 23.1 × 7.5 *(50.2 × 7.3 × 2.3)*
Main machinery: CODAG; 3 Avco Lycoming TF-40A gas turbines; 12 000 hp *(8.95 MW)* sustained; 3 Detroit 12V-149TI diesels; 2736 hp *(2.04 MW)* sustained; 3 shafts; cp props
Speed, knots: 20 kts diesels; 40 kts gas. **Range, miles:** 2700 at 12 kts on 1 diesel; 1900 at 20 kts; 700 at 40 kts
Complement: 34 (5 officers)

Missiles: SSM: 4 Hsiung Feng I; radar or optical guidance to 36 km *(19.4 nm)* at 0.7 Mach; warhead 75 kg.
Guns: 1 OTO Melara 3 in *(76 mm)*/62; 85° elevation; 60 rounds/minute to 16 km *(8.7 nm)*; weight of shell 6 kg.
2 Emerlec 30 mm (twin). 2—12.7 mm MGs.
Countermeasures: Decoys: 4 chaff launchers.
Combat data systems: IPN 10 action data automation.
Fire control: NA 10 Mod 0 GFCS. Honeywell H 930 Mod 2 MFCS (602).
Radars: Surface/air search: Selenia RAN 11 L/X; D/I band; range 82 km *(45 nm)*.
Fire control: RCA HR 76; I/J band (for SSM) (602).
Navigation: SPS 58(A); I band.

Programmes: Similar to the US Patrol Ship Multi-Mission Mk 5 (PSMM Mk 5). Second of class was built to an improved design. A much larger number of this class was intended, all to be armed with Harpoon. However, the US ban on export of Harpoon to Taiwan coupled with the high cost and doubts about seaworthiness caused the cancellation of this programme.
Structure: Fin stabilisers were fitted to help correct the poor sea keeping qualities of the design. Hsiung Feng missiles are mounted aft. *Sui Chiang* has a large lattice mast for the HR 76 radar. Both have had engine room fires caused by overheating in GT gearboxes.

PSMM Mk 5

15 TYPE 42 (COASTAL PATROL CRAFT)

PB 60-74

Displacement, tons: 10.5
Main machinery: 2 diesels; 2 shafts
Speed, knots: 40
Guns: 1 Bofors 40 mm/60.

Comment: Built in late 1960s and early 1970s in Taiwan.

668 TAIWAN / Light forces — Amphibious forces

50 HAI OU CLASS (FAST ATTACK CRAFT—MISSILE)

FABG 1-50

Displacement, tons: 47 full load
Dimensions, feet (metres): 70.8 × 18 × 3.3 *(21.6 × 5.5 × 1)*
Main machinery: 2 MTU 12V 331 TC82 diesels; 2605 hp(m) *(1.92 MW)* sustained; 2 shafts
Speed, knots: 36. **Range, miles:** 700 at 32 kts
Complement: 10

Missiles: SSM: 2 Hsiung Feng I; radar or optical guidance to 36 km *(19.4 nm)* at 0.7 Mach; warhead 75 kg.
Guns: 1 Oerlikon 20 mm. 2—12.7 mm MGs.
Countermeasures: Decoys: 4 Israeli AV2 chaff launchers.
Fire control: Kollmorgen Mk 35 optical director.
Radars: Surface search: Marconi LN 66; I band.
Fire control: RCA R76 C5; I band; range 40 km *(22 nm)* for 1 m² target.

Programmes: This design was developed by Sun Yat Sen Scientific Research Institute from the basic Israeli Dvora plans. Built by China SB Corporation (Tsoying SY), Kaohsiung.
Structure: Aluminium alloy hulls. The first series had a solid mast and the missiles were nearer the stern. Second series changed to a lattice mast and moved the missiles further forward allowing room for 1—20 mm gun right aft.
Operational: The prototype reached 45 kts on trials (probably without 20 mm gun). These craft often carry shoulder launched SAMs. Based at Makung, Pescadores where they form the Hai Chiao squadron. One task is to provide exercise high speed targets in shallow waters.

FABG 17 *8/1989, ROC Navy*

22 PCL TYPE (COASTAL PATROL CRAFT)

PCL 1-22

Displacement, tons: 143 full load
Dimensions, feet (metres): 105 × 29.5 × 5.9 *(32 × 9 × 1.8)*
Main machinery: 3 MTU 12V 396 TB93 diesels; 4890 hp(m) *(3.6 MW)* sustained; 3 shafts
Speed, knots: 40
Complement: 16 (3 officers)
Guns: 1 Bofors 40 mm/60. 2—12.7 mm MGs.
Depth charges: 2 racks.
Radars: Surface search: Decca; I band.
Sonars: Hull-mounted; active search and attack; high frequency.

Comment: Built to Vosper QAF design by China SB Corporation, Kaohsiung in 1987-90. They are used mainly for harbour defence against midget submarines and frogmen and also for Fishery protection tasks.

PCL *1990, DTM*

16 COASTAL PATROL CRAFT

Displacement, tons: 30 approx
Main machinery: 2 diesels; 2 waterjets
Speed, knots: 25
Guns: 1 Bofors 40 mm/60.

Comment: Small patrol boats designated PB. Constructed in Taiwan with the first of a reported 10 craft completed about 1971. These are believed the first warships of indigenous Taiwan construction.

PB 1

7 PBC 5501 TYPE (COASTAL PATROL CRAFT)

PBC 5501-5507

Displacement, tons: 100 full load
Dimensions, feet (metres): 90 × 28.6 × 6 *(27.4 × 8.7 × 1.8)*
Main machinery: 2 diesels; 2 shafts
Speed, knots: 30
Guns: 2—12.7 mm MGs (aft).
Radars: Surface search: Decca; I band.

Comment: Built by China SB Corporation, Kaohsiung 1989-91. For Fishery patrol and counter-insurgency tasks.

PBC 5506 and 5507 *1/1992, Dr Chien Chung*

26 PBC 3501 TYPE (COASTAL PATROL CRAFT)

PBC 3501-3526

Displacement, tons: 55 full load
Dimensions, feet (metres): 68.9 × 15.7 × 3.3 *(21 × 4.8 × 1)*
Main machinery: 2 Detroit 16V-92TA diesels; 1380 hp *(1.03 MW)* sustained; 2 shafts
Speed, knots: 35
Complement: 8
Guns: 2—12.7 mm MGs.
Radars: Surface search: Decca; I band.

Comment: Building at China SB Corporation, Kaohsiung, from 1990 after the first of class had been constructed in Singapore by Vosper QAF. Form the bulk of the Coastal Patrol Squadron for Fishery protection.

PBC 3521 *1991, Dr Chien Chung*

AMPHIBIOUS FORCES

4 Ex-US LSM 1 CLASS

Name	No
MEI LO (ex-USS *LSM 362*)	637 (ex-*LSM 356*)
MEI CHIN (ex-USS *LSM 155*)	649 (ex-*LSM 341*)
MEI PING (ex-USS *LSM 471*)	659 (ex-*LSM 353*)
MEI SUNG (ex-USS *LSM 431*)	694 (ex-*LSM 347*)

Displacement, tons: 1095 full load
Dimensions, feet (metres): 203.5 × 34.2 × 8.3 *(62.1 × 10.4 × 2.5)*
Main machinery: 2 Fairbanks Morse 38D8-1/8-10 diesels; 3540 hp *(2.64 MW)* sustained (637 and 659); 4 GM 16-278A diesels; 3000 hp *(2.24 MW)* (649 and 694); 2 shafts
Speed, knots: 13. **Range, miles:** 2500 at 12 kts
Complement: 65-75
Guns: 2 Bofors 40 mm/56 (twin). 4 or 8 Oerlikon 20 mm (4 single or 4 twin).
Radars: Surface search: SO 8; I band.

Comment: All built in 1945. *Mei Chin* and *Mei Sung* transferred 1946, *Mei Ping* in 1956 and *Mei Lo* in 1962. Rebuilt in Taiwan and bear little resemblance to 1970s photographs.

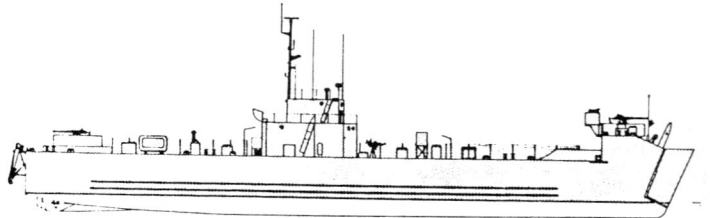

LSM 1 class (modernised) *1988*

Amphibious forces / TAIWAN   669

1 Ex-US CABILDO CLASS (LSD)

Name	No	Builders	Commissioned
CHENG HAI	192	Gulf SB Co, Chickasaw,	29 Jan 1946
(ex-USS *Fort Marion* LSD 22)	(ex-618)	Alabama	

Displacement, tons: 4790 standard; 9078 full load
Dimensions, feet (metres): 457.8 × 72.2 × 18 *(139.6 × 22 × 5.5)*
Main machinery: 2 boilers; 435 psi *(30.6 kg/cm sq)*; 740°F *(393°C)*; 2 turbines; 7000 hp *(5.22 MW)*; 2 shafts
Speed, knots: 15.4. **Range, miles:** 8000 at 15 kts
Complement: 316
Military lift: 3 LCUs or 18 LCMs or 32 LVTs in docking well
Missiles: SAM: 1 Sea Chaparral quadruple launcher.
Guns: 12 Bofors 40 mm/56 (2 quad, 2 twin).
Fire control: US Mk 26 Mod 4.
Radars: Surface search: Raytheon SPS 5; G/H band.
Navigation: Marconi LN 66; I band.

Comment: Launched on 22 May 1945, modernised in 1960 and transferred to Taiwan on 15 April 1977. Docking well is 392 × 44 ft with a redundant helicopter platform over well. SAM system fitted forward in 1989.

CHENG HAI   2/1988

20 Ex-US LST 1-510 and 511-1152 CLASSES

Name	No
CHUNG HAI (ex-USS *LST 755*)	201 (ex-697)
CHUNG TING (ex-USS *LST 537*)	203 (ex-673)
CHUNG HSING (ex-USS *LST 557*)	204 (ex-684)
CHUNG CHIEN (ex-USS *LST 716*)	205 (ex-679)
CHUNG CHI (ex-USS *LST 1017*)	206 (ex-626)
CHUNG SHUN (ex-USS *LST 732*)	208 (ex-624)
CHUNG LIEN (ex-USS *LST 1050*)	209 (ex-691)
CHUNG YUNG (ex-USS *LST 574*)	210 (ex-657)
CHUNG KUANG (ex-USS *LST 503*)	216 (ex-646)
CHUNG SUO (ex-USS *Bradley County* LST 400)	217 (ex-667)
CHUNG CHUAN (ex-*LST 1030*)	221 (ex-651)
CHUNG SHENG (ex-*LST 211*, ex-USS *LSTH 1033*)	222 (ex-686)
CHUNG FU (ex-USS *Iron County* LST 840)	223 (ex-619)
CHUNG CHIANG (ex-USS *San Bernardino County* LST 1110)	225 (ex-635)
CHUNG CHIH (ex-USS *Sagadahoc County* LST 1091)	226 (ex-655)
CHUNG MING (ex-USS *Sweetwater County* LST 1152)	227 (ex-681)
CHUNG SHU (ex-USS *LST 520*)	228 (ex-642)
CHUNG WAN (ex-USS *LST 535*)	229 (ex-654)
CHUNG PANG (ex-USS *LST 578*)	230 (ex-629)
CHUNG YEH (ex-USS *Sublette County* LST 1144)	231 (ex-699)

Displacement, tons: 1653 standard; 4080 (3640, 1-510 class) full load
Dimensions, feet (metres): 328 × 50 × 14 *(100 × 15.2 × 4.3)*
Main machinery: 2 GM 12-567A diesels; 1800 hp *(1.34 MW)*; 2 shafts
Speed, knots: 11.6. **Range, miles:** 15 000 at 10 kts
Complement: Varies—100-125 in most ships
Guns: Varies—up to 10 Bofors 40 mm/56 (2 twin, 6 single) with some modernised ships rearmed with 2 USN 3 in *(76 mm)*/50 and 6—40 mm (3 twin).
Several Oerlikon 20 mm (twin or single).
Radars: Navigation: US SO 1, 2 or 8; I band.

Comment: Constructed between 1943 and 1945. These ships have been rebuilt in Taiwan. Six transferred 1946; two in 1947; one in 1948; eight in 1958; one in 1959; two in 1960; one in 1961. Some have davits forward and aft. Pennant numbers have reverted to those used in the 1960s. One deleted in 1990. The midships deck is occasionally used as a helicopter platform. Six were in reserve in late 1992.

CHUNG YUNG   1990, Dr Chien Chung

1 Ex-US LST 511-1152 CLASS (FLAGSHIP) (AGC)

Name	No	Builders	Commissioned
KAO HSIUNG (ex-*Chung Hai*,	219 (ex-663)	Dravo Corporation,	26 Apr 1944
ex-USS *Dukes County* LST 735)		Neville Island, Penn	

Displacement, tons: 1653 standard; 3675 full load
Dimensions, feet (metres): 328 × 50 × 14 *(100 × 15.2 × 4.3)*
Main machinery: 2 GM 12-567A diesels; 1800 hp *(1.34 MW)*; 2 shafts
Speed, knots: 11.6. **Range, miles:** 11 200 at 10 kts
Complement: 195
Guns: 10 Bofors 40 mm/56 (5 twin).
Radars: Air search: RCA SPS 12; D band; range 119 km *(65 nm)*.
Surface search: Raytheon SPS 10; G band.

Comment: Launched on 11 March 1944. Transferred to Taiwan in May 1957 for service as an LST. Converted to a flagship for amphibious operations and renamed and redesignated (AGC) in 1964. Purchased November 1974. Note lattice mast above bridge structure, modified bridge levels, and antenna mountings on main deck. Redesignated as Command and Control Ship LCC 1.

KAO HSIUNG (old pennant number)   1968

22 Ex-US LCU 501 and LCU 1466 CLASSES

Name	No	Name	No
HO CHI (ex-*LCU 1212*)	401	HO CHENG (ex-*LCU 1145*)	486
HO HUEI (ex-*LCU 1218*)	402	HO SHAN (ex-*LCU 1596*)	488
HO YAO (ex-*LCU 1244*)	403	HO CHUAN (ex-*LCU 1597*)	489
HO DENG (ex-*LCU 1367*)	404	HO SENG (ex-*LCU 1598*)	490
HO FENG (ex-*LCU 1397*)	405	HO MENG (ex-*LCU 1599*)	491
HO CHAO (ex-*LCU 1429*)	406	HO MOU (ex-*LCU 1600*)	492
HO TENG (ex-*LCU 1452*)	407	HO SHOU (ex-*LCU 1601*)	493
HO SHUN (ex-*LCU 892*)	481	HO CHUN (ex-*LCU 1225*)	494
HO TSUNG (ex-*LCU 1213*)	482	HO YUNG (ex-*LCU 1271*)	495
HO CHUNG (ex-*LCU 849*)	484	HO CHIEN (ex-*LCU 1278*)	496
HO CHANG (ex-*LCU 512*)	485	HO CHIE (ex-*LCU 700*)	SB 1

LCU 501 Class (401-486, 494-496, SB 1)

Displacement, tons: 158 light; 309 full load
Dimensions, feet (metres): 119 × 32.7 × 5 *(36.3 × 10 × 1.5)*
Main machinery: 3 GM 6-71 diesels; 522 hp *(390 kW)* sustained; 3 shafts
Speed, knots: 10
Complement: 10-25
Guns: 2 Oerlikon 20 mm. Some also may have 2—12.7 mm MGs.

LCU 1466 Class (488-493)

Displacement, tons: 180 light; 360 full load
Dimensions, feet (metres): 119 × 34 × 6 *(36.3 × 10.4 × 1.8)*
Main machinery: 3 Gray Marine 64 YTL diesels; 675 hp *(504 kW)*; 3 shafts
Speed, knots: 10
Complement: 15-25
Guns: 3 Oerlikon 20 mm. Some may also have 2—12.7 mm MGs.

Comment: The LCU 501 series were built in the USA during the Second World War; initially designated LCT(6) series. The six of LCU 1466 series built by Ishikawajima Heavy Industries Co, Tokyo, Japan, for transfer to Taiwan; completed in March 1955. All originally numbered in 200-series; subsequently changed to 400-series.
Transfers: 401-407: November/December 1959 (acquired outright 3 April 1978). SB1, 494-496: January/February 1958. Remainder: 1946-48.

LCU 489   1991

250 US LCM(6) CLASS

Displacement, tons: 57 full load
Dimensions, feet (metres): 56.4 × 13.8 × 3.9 *(17.2 × 4.2 × 1.2)*
Main machinery: 2 diesels; 450 hp *(336 kW)*; 2 shafts
Speed, knots: 9
Military lift: 34 tons
Guns: 1—12.7 mm MG.

Comment: Some built in the US, some in Taiwan.

2 + 1 TAIWAN TYPE LCU

LCU 497-498

Comment: Locally built versions of US types.

LCU 498 *10/1992, Dr Chien Chung*

150 LCVPs and ASSAULT CRAFT

Comment: Some ex-US, and some built in Taiwan. Most are armed with one or two 7.62 mm MGs.

TYPE 272 *1989, DTM (Raymond Cheung)*

MINE WARFARE FORCES

11 Ex-US ADJUTANT and MSC 268 CLASSES (MINESWEEPERS—COASTAL)

Name	No	Builders	Commissioned
YUNG CHOU (ex-US *MSC 278*)	423	USA	July 1959
YUNG CHENG (ex-*Maaseik*, ex-US *MSC 78*)	441	USA	July 1953
YUNG AN (ex-US *MSC 123*)	449	USA	June 1955
YUNG JU (ex-US *MSC 300*)	457	USA	Apr 1965
YUNG SUI (ex-*Diksmuiden*, ex-US *MSC 65*)	462	USA	Feb 1954
YUNG LO (ex-US *MSC 306*)	469	USA	Apr 1966
YUNG SHAN (ex-*Lier*, ex-US *MSC 63*)	476	USA	July 1953
YUNG NIEN (ex-US *MSC 277*)	479	USA	May 1959
YUNG JEN (ex-*St Niklaas*, ex-US *MSC 64*)	485	USA	Feb 1954
YUNG HSIN (ex-US *MSC 302*)	488	USA	Mar 1965
YUNG CHI (ex-*Charleroi*, ex-US *MSC 152*)	497	USA	Feb 1954

Displacement, tons: 375 full load
Dimensions, feet (metres): 144 × 27.9 × 8 *(43.9 × 8.5 × 2.4)*
Main machinery: 2 GM 8-268A diesels; 880 hp *(656 kW)*; 2 shafts
Speed, knots: 13. **Range, miles:** 2500 at 12 kts
Complement: 35
Guns: 2 Oerlikon 20 mm (twin).
Radars: Navigation: Decca 707; I band.
Sonars: UQS 1; hull-mounted; minehunting; high frequency.

Comment: Non-magnetic, wood-hulled minesweepers built in the USA specifically for transfer to allied navies. Seven originally built for Belgium and transferred to Taiwan November 1969. The remainder transferred directly from USA on completion. All are of similar design; the ex-Belgian ships have a small boom aft on a pole mast. All refitted 1984-86. Reported that only four of the class have operational sonars, and all are in poor condition. Two deleted in 1992.

ADJUTANT class (old number)

4 + 2 (6) MWV 50 CLASS (MINEHUNTERS—COASTAL)

EXPLORER I-IV

Displacement, tons: 500 full load
Dimensions, feet (metres): 163.1 × 28.5 × 10.2 *(49.7 × 8.7 × 3.1)*
Main machinery: 2 MTU 8V 396 TB93 diesels; 2180 hp(m) *(1.6 MW)* sustained; 2 shafts
Speed, knots: 14
Complement: 45 (5 officers)
Guns: 1 Bofors 40 mm/60 or Oerlikon 20 mm.
Radars: Navigation: I band.
Sonars: Simrad SA 950; hull-mounted; active minehunting; high frequency.

Comment: Built for the Chinese Petroleum Corporation by Abeking & Rasmussen at Lemwerder, Germany. First four delivered in 1991 as offshore oil rig support ships and then converted for minehunting in Taiwan. Armament is uncertain. It is reported that Thomson-CSF MCM system is fitted and that a Pluto ROV is carried. Up to eight more of the class may be built with two more reported building in 1993 in Taiwan.

MWV 50 *1990, van Ginderen Collection*

EXPLORER III *1992, Dr Chien Chung*

1 MINESWEEPING BOAT

MSB 12 (ex-US *MSB 4*)

Displacement, tons: 39 full load
Dimensions, feet (metres): 57.1 × 15.1 × 3.9 *(17.4 × 4.6 × 1.2)*
Main engines: 2 diesels; 1200 hp *(895 kW)*; 2 shafts
Speed, knots: 12
Complement: 6

Comment: Former US Army minesweeping boat; assigned hull number MSB 4 in US Navy and transferred to Taiwan in December 1961.

8 MINESWEEPING LAUNCHES

| MSML 1 | MSML 5 | MSML 7 | MSML 11 |
| MSML 3 | MSML 6 | MSML 8 | MSML 12 |

Comment: These 50 ft minesweeping launches originally built in the USA as personnel transports in 1944-45 were transferred to Taiwan in March 1961. Have wooden hulls and must be near the end of their lives.

SERVICE FORCES

1 Ex-US DIVER CLASS (SALVAGE SHIP)

Name	No	Builders	Commissioned
TA HU (ex-USS *Grapple* ARS 7)	324	Basalt Rock Co, USA	16 Dec 1943

Displacement, tons: 1557 standard; 1745 full load
Dimensions, feet (metres): 213.5 × 39 × 15 *(65.1 × 11.9 × 4.6)*
Main machinery: Diesel-electric; 4 Cooper Bessemer GSB-8 diesels; 3420 hp *(2.55 MW)*; 2 generators; 2 motors; 2 shafts
Speed, knots: 14. **Range, miles:** 8500 at 13 kts
Complement: 85
Guns: 2 Oerlikon 20 mm.
Radars: Navigation: SPS-53; I band.

Comment: Fitted for salvage, towing and compressed-air diving. Transferred 1 December 1977 by sale.

Service forces / TAIWAN 671

1 COMBAT SUPPORT SHIP (AOE)

Name	No	Builders	Launched	Commissioned
WU YI	530	China SB Corporation, Keelung	4 Mar 1989	23 June 1990

Displacement, tons: 7700 light; 17 000 full load
Dimensions, feet (metres): 531.8 × 72.2 × 28 *(162.1 × 22 × 8.6)*
Main machinery: 2 MAN 14-cyl diesels; 25 000 hp(m) *(18.37 MW)*; 2 shafts
Speed, knots: 21. **Range, miles:** 9200 at 10 kts
Cargo capacity: 9300 tons
Missiles: SAM: 1 Sea Chaparral quad launcher.
Guns: 2 Bofors 40 mm/70. 2 Oerlikon 20 mm GAM-CO1.
Countermeasures: Decoys: 2 chaff launchers.
ESM: Radar warning.
Radars: 2 navigation; I band.
Helicopters: Platform for 2 CH-47 or 2 S-70C(M)1.

Comment: Largest unit built so far for the Taiwanese Navy. Design assisted by the United Shipping Design Center in the USA. Beam replenishment rigs on both sides. SAM system on forecastle, 40 mm guns aft of the funnels. Helicopter deck at the stern. Although this is a major step forward in fleet support at sea, more than one of these ships will be needed.

WU YI *6/1992, Robert Pabst*

1 Ex-US AMPHION CLASS (REPAIR SHIP)

Name	No	Builders	Commissioned
YU TAI (ex-USS *Cadmus* AR 14)	521	Tampa Shipbuilding Co, Tampa, Florida	23 Apr 1946

Displacement, tons: 7826 standard; 14 490 full load
Dimensions, feet (metres): 492 × 70 × 27.5 *(150.1 × 21.3 × 8.4)*
Main machinery: 2 Foster-Wheeler boilers; 435 psi *(30.6 kg/cm sq)*; 720°F *(382°C)*; 2 Westinghouse turbines; 8560 hp *(6.4 MW)*; 1 shaft
Speed, knots: 16.5
Complement: 920
Guns: 1 USN 5 in *(127 mm)*/38. 6 Bofors 40 mm/56 (3 twin).
Radars: Surface search: Raytheon SPS 5; G/H band; range 37 km *(20 nm)*.

Comment: Transferred to Taiwan on 31 January 1974. Fitted with SATCOM and carries up to three LCVPs.

YU TAI *6/1989, van Ginderen Collection*

1 Ex-US ACHELOUS CLASS (TRANSPORT)

Name	No	Builders	Commissioned
TAI WU (ex-*Sung Shan* ARL 336, ex-USS *Agenor* ARL 3, ex-*LST 490*)	AP 520	Kaiser Co, Vancouver, Washington	20 Aug 1943

Displacement, tons: 1625 light; 4100 full load
Dimensions, feet (metres): 328 × 50 × 14 *(100 × 15.2 × 4.3)*
Main machinery: 2 GM 12-567A diesels; 1800 hp *(1.34 MW)*; 2 shafts
Speed, knots: 11.6
Complement: 100
Military lift: 600 troops
Guns: 8 Bofors 40 mm/56 (2 quad).

Comment: Begun for the US Navy as an LST, completed as a repair ship for landing craft (ARL). Launched on 3 April 1943. Transferred to France in 1951 for service in Indo-China; subsequently returned to USA and retransferred to Taiwan on 15 September 1957. Employed as a repair ship (ARL 336, subsequently ARL 236) until converted in Japan in 1973-74 to troop transport. Fully air-conditioned.

TAI WU (as repair ship) (old pennant number)

2 YUEN FENG CLASS (ATTACK TRANSPORTS)

Name	No	Builders	Commissioned
YUEN FENG	523	Taiwan Shipbuilding Co, Keelung	1983
—	524	Taiwan Shipbuilding Co, Keelung	1984

Displacement, tons: 4500 full load
Dimensions, feet (metres): 360.9 × 59.1 × 18 *(110 × 18 × 5.5)*
Main machinery: 1 diesel; 1 shaft
Speed, knots: 18
Guns: 1 Bofors 40 mm/70. 2 Oerlikon 20 mm.

Comment: Can carry between 500 and 800 troops in air-conditioned accommodation.

YUEN FENG *7/1985, L J Lamb*

5 WU KANG CLASS (ATTACK TRANSPORTS) (AK)

Name	No	Builders	Commissioned
WU KANG	525	China SB Corporation, Keelung	Feb 1985
—	526	China SB Corporation, Keelung	1987
—	527	China SB Corporation, Keelung	1989
—	528	China SB Corporation, Keelung	1991
—	529	China SB Corporation, Keelung	1993

Displacement, tons: 3040 full load
Dimensions, feet (metres): 331.3 × 55.8 × 16.4 *(101 × 17 × 5)*
Main machinery: 2 diesels; 2 shafts; bow thruster
Speed, knots: 20
Missiles: SAM: 1 Sea Chaparral quad launcher.
Guns: 3 Bofors 40 mm/70.

Comment: With a helicopter platform, stern docking facility and davits for 4 LCVP, the design resembles an LPD. Used mostly for supplying garrisons in offshore islands, and on the Spratly and Pratas islands in the South China Sea. SAM launcher is mounted aft of the foremast.

WU KANG *1985, DTM*

AK 526 *10/1992, Dr Chien Chung*

1 Ex-US MARK CLASS (AGI)

Name	No	Builders	Commissioned
YUNG KANG (ex-USS *Mark* AKL 12, ex-*AG 143*, ex-US Army *FS 214*)	AKL 359	Higgins	21 Dec 1944

Displacement, tons: 900 full load
Dimensions, feet (metres): 180.1 × 32.2 × 10.2 *(54.9 × 9.8 × 3.1)*
Main machinery: 2 GM 6-278A diesels; 1120 hp *(836 kW)*; 2 shafts
Speed, knots: 12. **Range, miles:** 4000 at 11 kts
Complement: 37
Guns: 2 Oerlikon 20 mm.

Comment: Built as a small cargo ship (freight and supply) for the US Army. Transferred to US Navy on 30 September 1947; operated in South-east Asia from 1963 until transferred to Taiwan on 1 June 1971 and by sale 19 May 1976. Acts as AGI.

672 TAIWAN / Service forces — Customs service

2 TAI HU CLASS (TRANSPORTS)

Name	No	Builders	Commissioned
TAI HU (ex-*Ling Yuen*)	522	Taiwan Shipbuilding Co, Keelung	15 Aug 1975
YUN TAI	518	Taiwan Shipbuilding Co, Keelung	1985

Measurement, tons: 2510 dwt; 3040 gross
Dimensions, feet (metres): 328.7 × 47.9 × 16.4 *(100.2 × 14.6 × 5)*
Main machinery: 1—6-cyl diesel; 1 shaft
Complement: 55
Military lift: 500 troops
Guns: 2 Oerlikon 20 mm. 2—12.7 mm MGs.

Comment: Designed by Chinese First Naval Shipyard at Tsoying. *Tai Hu* launched 27 January 1975.

YUN TAI   *7/1985, L J Lamb*

1 JAPANESE TYPE (SUPPORT TANKER)

Name	No	Builders	Commissioned
WAN SHOU	AOG 512	Ujina Shipbuilding Co, Hiroshima, Japan	1 Nov 1969

Displacement, tons: 1049 light; 4150 full load
Dimensions, feet (metres): 283.8 × 54 × 18 *(86.5 × 16.5 × 5.5)*
Main machinery: 1 diesel; 2100 hp(m) *(1.54 MW)*; 1 shaft
Speed, knots: 13
Complement: 70
Cargo capacity: 73 600 gal fuel; 62 000 gal water
Guns: 2 Bofors 40 mm/56. 2 Oerlikon 20 mm.

Comment: Employed in resupply of offshore islands.

WAN SHOU   *1984, L J Lamb*

3 Ex-US PATAPSCO CLASS (SUPPORT TANKERS)

Name	No	Builders	Commissioned
CHANG PEI (ex-USS *Pecatonica* AOG 57)	505	Cargill, Inc, Savage, Minnesota	28 Nov 1945
HSIN LUNG (ex-USS *Elkhorn* AOG 7)	507	Cargill, Inc, Savage, Minnesota	12 Feb 1944
LUNG CHUAN (ex-HMNZS *Endeavour*, ex-USS *Namakagon* AOG 53)	515	Cargill, Inc, Savage, Minnesota	10 May 1945

Displacement, tons: 1850 light; 4335 full load
Dimensions, feet (metres): 310.8 × 48.5 × 15.7 *(94.8 × 14.8 × 4.8)*
Main machinery: 2 GM 16-278A diesels; 3000 hp *(2.24 MW)*; 2 shafts
Speed, knots: 14. **Range, miles:** 7000 at 12 kts
Complement: 124
Cargo capacity: 2000 tons
Guns: 1 USN 3 in *(76 mm)*/50. 2 Bofors 40 mm/60.
Radars: Surface search: Raytheon SPS 21 *(Chang Pei)*; G/H band.

Comment: *Chang Pei* was launched on 17 March 1945 and transferred to Taiwan on 24 April 1961. The ex-USS *Namakagon* was launched on 4 November 1944 and transferred to New Zealand on 5 October 1962 for use as an Antarctic resupply ship; strengthened for polar operations and renamed *Endeavour;* returned to the US Navy on 29 June 1971 and retransferred to Taiwan the same date. *Hsin Lung* was launched on 15 May 1943 and was transferred to Taiwan on 1 July 1972. All three transferred by sale 19 May 1976.

LUNG CHUAN   *2/1988*

TUGS

4 Ex-US CHEROKEE CLASS

Name	No	Builders	Commissioned
TA HAN (ex-USS *Tawakoni*)	ATF 542	United Engineering Co	14 Sep 1944
TA TUNG (ex-USS *Chickasaw*)	ATF 548	United Engineering Co	4 Feb 1943
— (ex-USS *Wenatchee*)	ARS 552	Charleston SB & DD	7 Sep 1944
— (ex-USS *Achomawi*)	ATF 563	United Engineering Co	10 Sep 1944

Displacement, tons: 1235 standard; 1731 full load
Dimensions, feet (metres): 205 × 38.5 × 17 *(62.5 × 11.7 × 5.2)*
Main machinery: Diesel-electric; 4 GM 12-278 diesels; 4400 hp *(3.28 MW)*; 4 generators; 1 motor; 3000 hp *(2.24 MW)*; 1 shaft
Speed, knots: 15. **Range, miles:** 6000 at 14 kts
Complement: 85
Guns: 1 USN 3 in *(76 mm)*/50. Several 12.7 mm MGs.

Comment: *Ta Tung* transferred to Taiwan in January 1966 and by sale 19 May 1976, *Ta Han* by sale 1 August 1978. Three more transferred in 1990 but one was immediately cannibalised for spares. *Ta Wan* was sunk as a target in 1988.

ATF 563   *2/1988*

3 Ex-US SOTOYOMO CLASS

Name	No	Builders	Commissioned
TA SUEH (ex-USS *Tonkawa* ATA 176)	ATA 357	Levingston SB Co, Orange, Texas	19 Aug 1944
TA TENG (ex-USS *Cahokia* ATA 186)	ATA 367	Levingston SB Co, Orange, Texas	24 Nov 1944
TA PENG (ex-USS *Mahopac* ATA 196)	ATA 395	Levingston SB Co, Orange, Texas	21 Dec 1944

Displacement, tons: 435 standard; 860 full load
Dimensions, feet (metres): 143 × 33.9 × 13 *(43.6 × 10.3 × 4)*
Main machinery: Diesel-electric; 2 GM 12-278A diesels; 2200 hp *(1.64 MW)*; 2 generators; 1 motor, 1500 hp *(1.12 MW)*; 1 shaft
Speed, knots: 13
Guns: 1 USN 3 in *(76 mm)*/50. Several 12.7 mm MGs.

Comment: *Ta Sueh* transferred to Taiwan in April 1962. *Ta Teng* assigned briefly to US Air Force in 1971 until transferred to Taiwan on 14 April 1972. *Ta Peng* transferred on 1 July 1971. Latter two by sale 19 May 1976. A fourth tug of this class served as a surveying ship but has been scrapped.

4 Ex-US ARMY TUGS

YTL 9 (ex-US Army *ST 2004*)   YTL 12 (ex-USN *YTL 584*)
YTL 11 (ex-USN *YTL 454*)   YTL 14 (ex-USN *YTL 585*)

Comment: One diesel and 8 kts.

5 Ex-US FLOATING DOCKS

HAY TAN (ex-USN *AFDL 36*) AFDL 1   **FO WU 5** (ex-USN *ARD 9*) ARD 5
KIM MEN (ex-USN *AFDL 5*) AFDL 2   **FO WU 6** (ex-USS *Windsor* ARD 22) ARD 6
HAN JIH (ex-USN *AFDL 34*) AFDL 3

Comment: Former US Navy floating dry docks. *Hay Tan* transferred in March 1947, *Kim Men* in January 1948, *Han Jih* in July 1959, *Fo Wu 5* in June 1971, *Fo Wu 6* in June 1971. *Fo Wu 6* by sale 19 May 1976 and *Fo Wu 5* on 12 January 1977.

CUSTOMS SERVICE

Notes: 1. Director General De-Ho Jan.
2. Eighteen 500 ton patrol vessels authorised in October 1992 for acquisition.

1 HSUN HSING CLASS (COASTAL PATROL CRAFT)

HSUN HSING

Displacement, tons: 239 full load
Dimensions, feet (metres): 146 × 24.6 × 5.8 *(44.5 × 7.5 × 1.7)*
Main machinery: 3 MTU 16V 396 TB93 diesels; 6540 hp(m) *(4.81 MW)* sustained; 3 shafts

Comment: Built by China SB Corporation and delivered 15 December 1986.

2 TACOMA TYPE (LARGE PATROL CRAFT)

HO HSING   **WEI HSING**

Displacement, tons: 1795 full load
Dimensions, feet (metres): 270 × 38.1 × 13.1 *(82.3 × 11.6 × 4)*
Main machinery: 2 MTU 16V 1163 TB93 diesels; 13 310 hp(m) *(9.78 MW)* sustained; 2 shafts
Speed, knots: 22. **Range, miles:** 7000 at 16 kts
Complement: 80 (18 officers)

Comment: Built by the China SB Corporation, Keelung, to a Tacoma design and delivered in 1992. Four high speed interceptor boats are carried on individual davits.

HO HSING   *1992*

2 PAO HSING CLASS (COASTAL PATROL CRAFT)

PAO HSING   **CHIN HSING**

Displacement, tons: 550 full load
Dimensions, feet (metres): 189.6 × 25.6 × 6.9 *(57.8 × 7.8 × 2.1)*
Main machinery: 2 MAN 12V25/30 diesels; 7183 hp(m) *(5.28 MW)* sustained; 2 shafts
Speed, knots: 20
Complement: 40
Guns: 1 Bofors 40 mm/56. 2 Oerlikon 20 mm.

Comment: First delivered 20 May 1980; second 23 May 1985. Built by Keelung yard of China SB Corporation.

CHIN HSING   *2/1988*

2 COASTAL PATROL CRAFT

MOU HSING   **FU HSING**

Displacement, tons: 1163 full load
Dimensions, feet (metres): 214.6 × 31.5 × 10.5 *(65.4 × 9.6 × 3.2)*
Main machinery: 2 MTU 16V 538 TB93 diesels; 7510 hp(m) *(5.52 MW)* sustained; 2 shafts
Speed, knots: 28
Complement: 54

Comment: Ordered from Wilton Fijenoord in September 1986, and commissioned 14 June 1988.

MOU HSING   *5/1988, Wilton Fijenoord*

1 YUN HSING CLASS (COASTAL PATROL CRAFT)

YUN HSING

Displacement, tons: 900 full load
Dimensions, feet (metres): 213.3 × 32.8 × 9.5 *(65 × 10 × 2.9)*
Main machinery: 2 MAN 12V 25/30 diesels; 7183 hp(m) *(5.28 MW)*; 2 shafts

Comment: Built by China SB Corporation and delivered 28 December 1987.

YUN HSING   *6/1988*

3 HAI PING CLASS (INSHORE PATROL CRAFT)

HAI PING   **HAI AN**   **HAI CHENG**

Displacement, tons: 63 full load
Dimensions, feet (metres): 85.3 × 18.4 × 3.6 *(26 × 5.6 × 1.1)*
Main machinery: 2 MTU 8V 331 TC81 diesels; 1740 hp(m) *(1.28 MW)* sustained; 2 shafts
Speed, knots: 28
Complement: 18

Comment: Built by China SB Corporation, Keelung and delivered 28 February, 18 April and 8 June 1979 respectively.

HAI PING   *1989*

2 HALTER TYPE (INSHORE PATROL CRAFT)

Displacement, tons: 70
Dimensions, feet (metres): 78.7 × 18.4 × 4.9 *(24 × 5.6 × 1.5)*
Main machinery: 2 Detroit 12V-71TA diesels; 840 hp *(627 kW)* 2sustained; 2 shafts
Speed, knots: 19

Comment: Purchased in 1977. Steel hulls.

MARITIME SECURITY POLICE

Note: Set up in 1990, the 800-man Maritime Police has two squadrons of coastal patrol vessels for its duties of anti-smuggling, anti-insurgence, and fishery patrol. First squadron, homebased at Tamshui, has three detachments stationed at Hualien, Suao, and Whchi; the second squadron, homebased at Kaohsiung, has another three detachments stationed at Anping, Makung, and Kaohsiung. They operate 20 60-ft patrol boats (PP-601 to 607; PP-801 to 813), six 50-ft patrol boats (PP-501 to 506), and 12 inshore M-4 speedboats (PP-301 to 312). In addition, ocean-going fishery control ships, including one 800-tonner, two 400-tonners, one 200-tonner, and one 100-tonner, will be commissioned in 1993. All these units except PP-300 series, are armed with MGs and up to 40 mm AA.

POLICE 601   *1989, DTM*

TANZANIA

Senior Appointment

Chief of Navy:
  Brigadier Ligate G Sande

General

In 1992 approximately one in five craft was operational. There is a small Coastguard Service (KMKM), based on Zanzibar, which uses small boats for anti-smuggling patrols.

Personnel

(a) 1993: 1050
(b) Voluntary service

Bases

Dar Es Salaam, Zanzibar, Mwanza (Lake Victoria). Mtwara (Lake Victoria).

Mercantile Marine

Lloyd's Register of Shipping:
  43 vessels of 40 662 tons gross

DELETIONS

1990 *Araka, Salaam*
1991 *Utafiti, Rafiki, Uhuru*

PATROL FORCES

Note: There is a Police Marine Unit which operates two ex-Chinese Yuchai LSMs. There is also a survey craft TG 5 which is non-operational.

8 Ex-CHINESE SHANGHAI II CLASS (FAST ATTACK CRAFT—GUN)

JW 9861-9868

Displacement, tons: 131 full load
Dimensions, feet (metres): 127.3 × 17.7 × 5.6 *(38.8 × 5.4 × 1.7)*
Main machinery: 2 Type L12-180 diesels; 2400 hp(m) *(1.76 MW)* (forward); 2 Type 12-D-6 diesels; 1820 hp(m) *(1.34 MW)* (aft); 4 shafts
Speed, knots: 30. Range, miles: 700 at 16.5 kts
Complement: 34
Guns: 4—37 mm/63 (2 twin). 4—25 mm/80 (2 twin).
Radars: Surface search: Skin Head; I band.

Comment: Six transferred by the People's Republic of China in 1971-72, two more in June 1992. Only the last two are fully operational.

4 Ex-CHINESE HUCHUAN CLASS
(FAST ATTACK CRAFT—TORPEDO)

JW 9841-9844

Displacement, tons: 39 standard; 45.8 full load
Dimensions, feet (metres): 71.5 × 20.7 oa × 11.8 (hullborne) *(21.8 × 6.3 × 3.6)*
Main machinery: 3 Type M 50 diesels; 3300 hp(m) *(2.4 MW)* sustained; 3 shafts
Speed, knots: 50. Range, miles: 500 at 20 kts
Complement: 11
Guns: 2—14.5 mm (twin) MGs.
Torpedoes: 2—21 in *(533 mm)* tubes. Probably Soviet Type 53.
Radars: Surface search: Skin Head; I band.

Comment: Transferred 1975. After a major effort in 1992, these craft are in reasonable repair.

4 Ex-CHINESE YULIN CLASS (LAKE PATROL CRAFT)

Displacement, tons: 9.8 full load
Dimensions, feet (metres): 42.6 × 9.5 × 3.5 *(13 × 2.9 × 1.1)*
Main machinery: 1 PRC Type 12150 diesel; 300 hp(m) *(221 kW)*; 1 shaft
Speed, knots: 24
Complement: 10
Guns: 2—14.5 mm (twin) MGs. 2—12.7 mm (twin) MGs.

Comment: Transferred late 1966. Based on Victoria Nyanza. One operational in early 1993.

5 Ex-NORTH KOREAN KIMJIN CLASS (COASTAL PATROL CRAFT)

YU CHAI   SCHALBE   + 3

Displacement, tons: 25 full load
Dimensions, feet (metres): 66.6 × 11 × 5.5 *(20.3 × 3.4 × 1.7)*
Main machinery: 2 Type M 50 diesels; 2200 hp(m) *(1.6 MW)* sustained; 2 shafts
Speed, knots: 42. Range, miles: 220 at 20 kts
Complement: 10
Guns: 4—14.5 mm (2 twin) MGs.

Comment: Two delivered in September 1987, three more in September 1988. Same type to Nicaragua. One or possibly two operational in early 1993.

4 VOSPER THORNYCROFT 75ft TYPE (COASTAL PATROL CRAFT)

Displacement, tons: 70 full load
Dimensions, feet (metres): 75 × 19.5 × 8 *(22.9 × 6 × 2.4)*
Main machinery: 2 diesels; 1840 hp *(1.37 MW)*; 2 shafts
Speed, knots: 24.5. Range, miles: 800 at 20 kts
Complement: 11
Guns: 2 Oerlikon 20 mm

Comment: First pair delivered 6 July 1973, second pair 1974. Used for anti-smuggling patrols off Zanzibar.

SHANGHAI II (old number)   1992

VOSPER THORNYCROFT 75ft Type   1984, N Overington

THAILAND

Headquarters' Appointments

Commander-in-Chief of the Navy:
  Admiral Vichet Karunyavanij
Deputy Commander-in-Chief:
  Admiral Songsit Kittipeerachol
Assistant Commander-in-Chief:
  Admiral Prachet Siridej
Chief of Staff:
  Admiral Surawut Maharom
Deputy Chief-of-Staff:
  Vice Admiral Matra Ampaipast
Commander-in-Chief, Fleet:
  Admiral Santiparb Moo-Ming
Deputy Commander-in-Chief, Fleet:
  Vice Admiral Vinai Nayananonda
Chief of Staff, Fleet:
  Vice Admiral Chaichit Ratanapol

Diplomatic Representation

Naval Attaché in London:
  Captain Suchart Kolasastraseni
Naval Attaché in Washington:
  Captain Vati Sribhadung
Naval Attaché in Bonn:
  Captain Daweesak Somabha
Naval Attaché in Paris:
  Captain Werapon Waranon
Naval Attaché in Canberra:
  Captain Wichai Juthapakdeeprasert
Naval Attaché in Madrid:
  Captain Amorntep Na-Bangchang

Personnel

(a) 1993: Navy, 62 000 including Naval Air Arm, Marines and Coastal Defence Command
(b) 2 years' national service

Organisation

First naval area command (East Thai Gulf)
Second naval area command (West Thai Gulf)
Third naval area command (Andaman Sea)
First air wing (U-Tapao)
Second air wing (Songkhla)

Bases

Bangkok, Sattahip, Songkhla, Phang-Nga (west coast)

Prefix to Ships' Names

HTMS

Strength of the Fleet

Type	Active	Building (Projected)
Helicopter Carrier	—	1
Frigates	10	2 (2)
Corvettes	5	—
Fast Attack Craft (Missile)	6	—
Fast Attack Craft (Gun)	3	—
Large Patrol Craft	19	—
Coastal Patrol Craft	35	—
River Patrol Craft	60+	—
MCM Support Ship	1	—
Minehunters	2	—
Coastal Minesweepers	3	—
MSBs	5	—
LSTs	6	—
LSMs	2	—
LCG	1	—
LSIL	1	—
Hovercraft	3	—
LCUs	9	—
Landing Craft	40	—
Survey Vessels	5	—
Replenishment Ship	—	(1)
Oil Tankers	5	—
Water Tanker	1	—
Tugs	4	2
Training Ships	2	—
Marine Police Craft	125	—

Marine Corps

Currently consists of two Divisions including an amphibious assault battalion. In 1993 personnel strength is about 20 500, although the establishment figure is 25 000.

Coast Guard

A trial coastal unit of one frigate, eight patrol craft and four aircraft was established on 1 April 1989. The Coast Guard Squadron was officially authorised on 29 September 1992 when the eight patrol craft were increased to 11. Armed Sea Rangers in converted Fishing Vessels are being used to counter pirates.

Coastal Defence Command

This unit was rapidly expanded to the 1992 two Division level after the government charged the RTN with the responsibility of defending the entire Eastern Seaboard Development Project on the east coast of the Gulf of Thailand in 1988. Equipment includes 155 mm and 130 mm guns for coastal defence, 76 mm, 40 mm, 37 mm, 20 mm guns and PL-9B SAM for air defence.

Marine Police

Acts as a Coast Guard in inshore waters with some 62 armed patrol craft and another 63 equipped with small arms only.

Future Plans

Plans to acquire submarines still under consideration. Potential submarine officers have been trained in the Netherlands. A new dockyard is planned at Sattahip, with facilities for large vessels.

Mercantile Marine

Lloyd's Register of Shipping:
  351 vessels of 798 099 tons gross

DELETIONS

Light Forces

1992 *Sarasin, Phali*

Mine Warfare Forces

1992 *Tadindang*

Amphibious Forces

1990 *Phai*

Service Forces

1990 *Prong, Kled Keo*

HELICOPTER CARRIER

0 + 1 CHAKRI NARUEBET CLASS

Name	No
CHAKRI NARUEBET	911

Builders	Laid down	Launched	Commissioned
Bazán, Ferrol	1994	1996	1997

Displacement, tons: 11 485 full load
Dimensions, feet (metres): 599.1 oa; 538.4 wl × 100.1 oa; 73.8 wl × 20.3 *(182.6; 164.1 × 30.5; 22.5 × 6.2)*
Flight deck, feet (metres): 572.8 × 100.1 *(174.6 × 30.5)*
Main machinery: CODOG; 2 GE LM 2500 gas turbines; 44 250 hp *(33 MW)* sustained; 2 MTU 16V 1163 TB91 diesels; 11 193 hp(m) *(8.2 MW)*; 2 shafts; cp props
Speed, knots: 27; 16 (diesels). **Range, miles:** 10 000 at 12 kts
Complement: 455 (62 officers) plus 146 aircrew plus 4 (Royal family)
Missiles: SAM: 1 Mk 41 LCHR 8 cell VLS launcher; Sea Sparrow missiles.
Guns: 4 CIWS. 2—30 mm.
Countermeasures: Decoys: 4 chaff launchers. ESM/ECM.
Radars: Air search. Surface search. Aircraft control.
Fixed wing aircraft: STOVL capable.
Helicopters: 14 Sea King; Chinook capable.

Programmes: An initial contract for a 7800 ton vessel with Bremer Vulcan was cancelled on 22 July 1991 and replaced on 27 March 1992 with a government to government contract for a larger ship to be built by Bazán. Confirmation of the design and the order is expected in about April 1993.
Structure: Similar to Spanish *Principe de Asturias*. 12° ski jump and two 20 ton aircraft lifts. Weapon systems still to be confirmed and may be fitted in Thailand after delivery. Hangar can take up 10 Sea Harrier or Sea King sized aircraft.
Operational: Main tasks are SAR co-ordination and EEZ surveillance. Secondary role is air support for all maritime operations.

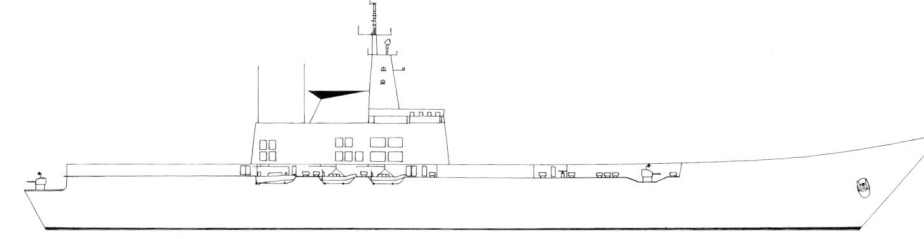

CHAKRI NARUEBET   (Scale 1 : 1500), Ian Sturton

CHAKRI NARUEBET (model)   1992, Bazán

FRIGATES

4 + (2) CHAO PHRAYA CLASS (TYPES 053 HT and 053 HT (H)) (FFG)

Name	No	Builders	Laid down	Launched	Commissioned
CHAO PHRAYA	455	Hudong SY, Shanghai	1989	24 June 1990	5 Apr 1991
BANGPAKONG	456	Hudong SY, Shanghai	1989	25 July 1990	20 July 1991
KRABURI	457	Hudong SY, Shanghai	1990	28 Dec 1990	16 Jan 1992
SAIBURI	458	Hudong SY, Shanghai	1990	27 Aug 1991	4 Aug 1992

Displacement, tons: 1676 standard; 1924 full load
Dimensions, feet (metres): 338.5 × 37.1 × 10.2 *(103.2 × 11.3 × 3.1)*
Main machinery: 4 MTU 20V 1163 TB83 diesels; 29 440 hp(m) *(21.6 MW)* sustained; 2 shafts; cp props
Speed, knots: 30. **Range, miles:** 3500 at 18 kts
Complement: 168 (22 officers)

Missiles: SSM: 8 Ying Ji (Eagle Strike) (C-801) ❶; active radar/IR homing to 85 km *(45.9 nm)* at 0.9 Mach; warhead 165 kg; sea-skimmer. This is the extended range version.
SAM: 1 HQ-61 launcher for PL-9 to be fitted in due course.
Guns: 2 (457 and 458) or 4 China 100 mm/56 (1 or 2 twin) ❷; 85° elevation; 25 rounds/minute to 22 km *(12 nm)*; weight of shell 15.9 kg.
8 China 37 mm/76 (4 twin) H/PJ 76 A ❸; 85° elevation; 180 rounds/minute to 8.5 km *(4.6 nm)* anti-aircraft; weight of shell 1.42 kg.
A/S mortars: 2 RBU 1200 (China Type 86) 5-tubed fixed launchers ❹; range 1200 m.
Depth charges: 2 BMB racks.
Countermeasures: Decoys: 2 China Type 945 GPJ 26-barrelled chaff launchers.
ESM: China Type 923(1); intercept.
ECM: China Type 981(3); jammer.
Combat data systems: China Type ZKJ-3 action data automation.
Radars: Air/surface search: China Type 354 Eye Shield ❺; E band.
Surface search/fire control: China Type 352C Square Tie ❻; I band (for SSM).
Fire control: China Type 343 Sun Visor ❼; I band (for 100 mm). China Type 341 Rice Lamp ❽; I band (for 37 mm).
Navigation: Racal Decca 1290 A/D ARPA; I band.
IFF: Type 651.
Sonars: China Type SJD-5A; hull-mounted; active search and attack; medium frequency.

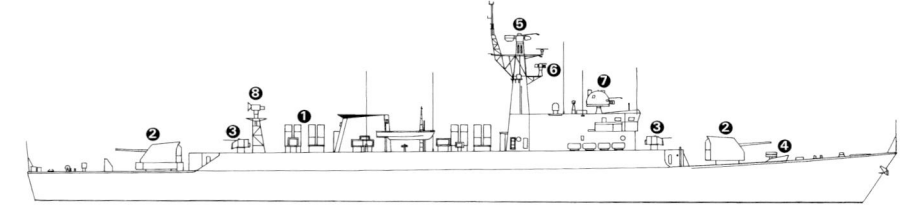

CHAO PHRAYA *(Scale 1 : 900), Ian Sturton*

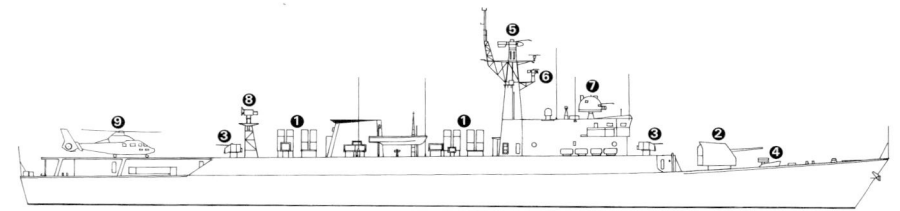

KRABURI *(Scale 1 : 900), Ian Sturton*

Helicopters: 1 Kaman SH-2F Seasprite (457 and 458) ❾ in due course. Bell 212 are embarked as an interim measure.

Programmes: Contract signed 18 July 1988 for four modified Jianghu class ships to be built by the China State SB Corporation (CSSC). Two more improved 053 HT (H) type are to be built in Thailand with initial work beginning in 1993.
Structure: Thailand would have preferred only the hulls but China insisted on full armament. Two of the ships are the Type III variant with 100 mm guns, fore and aft, and the other two are a variation of the Type II with a helicopter platform replacing the after 100 mm gun. German communication equipment fitted.
Operational: On arrival in Thailand each ship was docked to make good poor shipbuilding standards, and improve damage control capabilities.

CHAO PHRAYA *4/1992, 92 Wing RAAF*

KRABURI *3/1992, 92 Wing RAAF*

Frigates / THAILAND

0 + 2 NARESUAN CLASS (TYPE 25T) (FFG)

Name	No	Builders	Laid down	Launched	Commissioned
NARESUAN	621	Zhonghua SY, Shanghai	1991	July 1993	1995
TAKSIN	622	Zhonghua SY, Shanghai	1991	Apr 1994	1995

Displacement, tons: 2500 standard; 2980 full load
Dimensions, feet (metres): 393.7 × 42.7 × 12.5 *(120 × 13 × 3.8)*
Main machinery: CODOG; 2 GE LM 2500 gas turbines; 55 000 hp *(41 MW)* sustained; 2 MTU 20 V 1163 TB83 diesels; 14 730 hp(m) *(10.84 MW)* sustained; 2 shafts; cp props
Speed, knots: 32. **Range, miles:** 4000 at 18 kts
Complement: 150

Missiles: SSM: 8 McDonnell Douglas Harpoon (2 quad) launchers ❶.
SAM: Mk 41 LCHR 8 cell VLS launcher ❷ Sea Sparrow missiles.
Guns: 1 FMC 5 in *(127 mm)*/54 Mk 45 Mod 2 ❸.
4 China 37 mm/76 (2 twin) H/PJ 76 A ❹.
Torpedoes: 6—324 mm Mk 32 Mod 5 (2 triple) tubes ❺. Honeywell Mk 46.
Countermeasures: Decoys: China Type 945 GPJ 26-barrelled launchers ❻; chaff and IR.
ESM/ECM: Mirage EW System.
Fire control: 1 JM-83H Optical Director ❼.
Radars: Air search: Signaal LW 08 ❽; D band.
Surface search: China Type 360 ❾.
Navigation: Two Raytheon SPS 64(V)5; I band.
Fire control: Two Signaal STIR ❿; I/J/K band (for SSM and 127 mm).
China 374 G ⓫ (for 37 mm).
Sonars: China SJD-7; hull-mounted; active search and attack; medium frequency.

Helicopters: 1 Kamen SH-2F Seasprite ⓬.

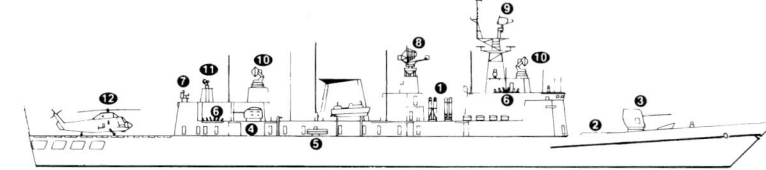

NARESUAN *(Scale 1 : 1200), Ian Sturton*

Programmes: Contract signed 21 September 1989 for construction of two ships by the China State SB Corporation (CSSC) with delivery in 1994. US and European weapon systems are to be fitted after delivery in Thailand. By early 1993 the programme had slipped by 12 months.
Structure: Jointly designed by the Royal Thai Navy and China State Shipbuilding Corporation (CSSC). This is a new design incorporating much Western machinery and equipment and will be more formidable than the four Type 053 class.

NARESUAN (model) *1991, Royal Thai Navy*

1 YARROW TYPE (FF)

Name	No	Builders	Laid down	Launched	Commissioned
MAKUT RAJAKUMARN	7	Yarrow (Shipbuilders)	11 Jan 1970	18 Nov 1971	7 May 1973

Displacement, tons: 1650 standard; 1900 full load
Dimensions, feet (metres): 320 × 36 × 18.1 *(97.6 × 11 × 5.5)*
Main machinery: CODOG; 1 RR Olympus TBM 3B gas turbine; 22 500 hp *(16.8 MW)* sustained; 1 Crossley-SEMT Pielstick 12 PC2.2 V 400 diesel; 6000 hp(m) *(4.4 MW)* sustained; 2 shafts
Speed, knots: 26 gas; 18 diesel. **Range, miles:** 5000 at 18 kts; 1200 at 26 kts
Complement: 140 (16 officers)

Guns: 2 Vickers 4.5 in *(114 mm)*/55 Mk 8 ❶; 55° elevation; 25 rounds/minute to 22 km *(12 nm)* anti-surface; 6 km *(3.3 nm)* anti-aircraft; weight of shell 21 kg.
2 Bofors 40 mm/60 ❷; 80° elevation; 120 rounds/minute to 10 km *(5.5 nm)*; weight of shell 0.89 kg.
Depth charges: 1 rack.
Countermeasures: ESM: Racal UA 3; radar warning. FH-4; D/F.
Combat data systems: Signaal Sewaco TH action data automation.
Radars: Air/surface search: Signaal DA 05 ❸; E/F band; range 137 km *(75 nm)* for 2 m² target.
Navigation: Signaal ZW 06; I band.
Fire control: Signaal WM 22 series ❹; I/J band; range 46 km *(25 nm)*.
Sonars: Atlas Elektronik DSQS 21C; hull-mounted; active search and attack; medium frequency.

Programmes: Ordered on 21 August 1969 as a general purpose frigate.
Modernisation: A severe fire in February 1984 resulted in extensive work including replacement of the Olympus gas turbine, a new ER control room and central electric switchboard. Further modifications included the removal of Limbo mortar, Seacat SAM system and the installation of new electronics. Plans to fit SSM, Sea Sparrow SAM system or CIWS, and torpedo tubes, have been shelved.
Operational: The ship is largely automated with a consequent saving in complement, and has been most successful in service. Will lose its Flagship role to one of the Chinese-built frigates and will then become a training ship.

MAKUT RAJAKUMARN *(Scale 1 : 900), Ian Sturton*

MAKUT RAJAKUMARN *1991, Royal Thai Navy*

678 THAILAND / Frigates

2 US PF 103 CLASS

Name	No
TAPI	5
KHIRIRAT	6

Builders	Laid down	Launched	Commissioned
American S B Co, Toledo, Ohio	1 July 1970	17 Oct 1970	19 Nov 1971
Norfolk S B & D D Co	18 Feb 1972	2 June 1973	10 Aug 1974

Displacement, tons: 885 standard; 1172 full load
Dimensions, feet (metres): 275 × 33 × 10; 14.1 (sonar) *(83.8 × 10 × 3; 4.3)*
Main machinery: 2 Fairbanks-Morse 38TD8-1/8-9 diesels; 5250 hp *(3.9 MW)* sustained; 2 shafts
Speed, knots: 20. **Range, miles:** 2400 at 18 kts
Complement: 135 (15 officers)

Guns: 1 OTO Melara 3 in *(76 mm)*/62 compact ❶; 85° elevation; 85 rounds/minute to 16 km *(8.7 nm)* anti-surface; 12 km *(6.6 nm)* anti-aircraft; weight of shell 6 kg.
  1 Bofors 40 mm/70 ❷; 85° elevation; 300 rounds/minute to 12.5 km *(6.8 nm)*; weight of shell 0.96 kg.
  2 Oerlikon 20 mm ❸. 2—12.7 mm MGs.
Torpedoes: 6—324 mm US Mk 32 (2 triple) tubes ❹. Honeywell Mk 46; anti-submarine; active/passive homing to 11 km *(5.9 nm)* at 40 kts; warhead 44 kg.
Depth charges: 1 rack.
Combat data systems: Signaal Sewaco TH.
Radars: Air/surface search: Signaal LW 04 ❺; E/F band; range 137 km *(75 nm)* for 2 m² target.
  Surface search: Raytheon SPS 53E ❻; I band.
  Fire control: Signaal WM 22-61 ❼; I/J band; range 46 km *(25 nm)*.
IFF: UPX-23.

TAPI (Scale 1 : 900), Ian Sturton

Sonars: Atlas Elektronik DSQS 21C; hull-mounted; active search and attack; medium frequency.

Programmes: *Tapi* was ordered on 27 June 1969. *Khirirat* was ordered on 25 June 1971.
Modernisation: *Tapi* completed 1983 and *Khirirat* in 1987. This included new gunnery and radars and a slight heightening of the funnel. Further modernisation in 1988-89 mainly to external and internal communications.
Structure: Of similar design to the Iranian ships of the Bayandor class.

KHIRIRAT 4/1992, 92 Wing RAAF

2 Ex-US TACOMA CLASS

Name	No
TACHIN (ex-USS *Glendale* PF 36)	1
PRASAE (ex-USS *Gallup* PF 47)	2

Builders	Laid down	Launched	Commissioned
Consolidated Steel Corporation, Los Angeles	6 Apr 1943	28 May 1943	1 Oct 1943
Consolidated Steel Corporation, Los Angeles	18 Aug 1943	17 Sep 1943	29 Feb 1944

Displacement, tons: 1430 standard; 2454 full load
Dimensions, feet (metres): 304 × 37.5 × 12.5 *(92.7 × 11.4 × 4.1)*
Main machinery: 2 boilers; 2 reciprocating engines; 5500 ihp *(4.1 MW)*; 2 shafts
Speed, knots: 18. **Range, miles:** 7200 at 12 kts; 5400 at 15 kts
Complement: 214 (13 officers)

Guns: 3 USN 3 in *(76 mm)*/50; 85° elevation; 20 rounds/minute to 12 km *(6.6 nm)*; weight of shell 6 kg.
  2 Bofors 40 mm/60; 80° elevation; 120 rounds/minute to 10 km *(5.5 nm)*; weight of shell 0.89 kg.
  9 Oerlikon 20 mm/70; 800 rounds/minute to 2 km.
Torpedoes: 6—324 mm US Mk 32 (2 triple) tubes; anti-submarine.
A/S mortars: 1 Mk 10 multi-barrelled fixed Hedgehog; range 350 m; warhead 26 kg; 24 rockets.
Depth charges: 8 projectors; 2 racks.
Radars: Air search: Westinghouse SPS 6; D band; range 146 km *(80 nm)* against fighter aircraft.
  Surface search: Raytheon SPS 5 *(Tachin)*; G/H band. Raytheon SPS 10 *(Prasae)*; G/H band.
  Navigation: Decca; I band.
  Fire control: Mk 51; I/J band.
IFF: UPX 12B.

PRASAE 1/1991, Royal Thai Navy

Sonars: EDO SQS 17B; hull-mounted; active search and attack; medium/high frequency.

Programmes: Delivered to the Royal Thai Navy on 29 October 1951. The last active survivors of the US equivalent of the British and Canadian River class.
Operational: Used in Training Squadron but one has been transferred to Coastguard duties.

Frigates — Corvettes / THAILAND 679

1 Ex-US CANNON CLASS

Name	No	Builders	Laid down	Launched	Commissioned
PIN KLAO (ex-USS *Hemminger* DE 746)	3 (ex-1)	Western Pipe & Steel Co	1943	12 Sep 1943	30 May 1944

Displacement, tons: 1240 standard; 1930 full load
Dimensions, feet (metres): 306 × 36.7 × 14 *(93.3 × 11.2 × 4.3)*
Main machinery: Diesel-electric; 4 GM 16-278A diesels; 6000 hp *(4.5 MW)*; 4 generators; 2 motors; 2 shafts
Speed, knots: 20. **Range, miles:** 10 800 at 12 kts; 6700 at 19 kts
Complement: 192 (14 officers)

Guns: 3 USN 3 in *(76 mm)*/50 Mk 22; 85° elevation; 20 rounds/minute to 12 km *(6.6 nm)*; weight of shell 6 kg.
 6 Bofors 40 mm/60 (3 twin); 80° elevation; 120 rounds/minute to 10 km *(5.5 nm)*; weight of shell 0.89 kg.
Torpedoes: 6—324 mm US Mk 32 (2 triple) tubes; anti-submarine.
A/S mortars: 1 Mk 10 multi-barrelled fixed Hedgehog; range 350 m; warhead 26 kg; 24 rockets.
Depth charges: 8 projectors; 2 racks.
Countermeasures: ESM: WLR-1; radar warning.
Fire control: Mk 52 radar GFCS for 3 in guns. Mk 63 radar GFCS for aft gun only. 2 Mk 51 optical GFCS for 40 mm.
Radars: Air/surface search: Raytheon SPS 5; G/H band.
 Navigation: Raytheon SPS 21; G/H band.
 Fire control: Western Electric Mk 34; I/J band.
 RCA/General Electric Mk 26; I/J band.
IFF: SLR 1.
Sonars: SQS 11; hull-mounted; active attack; high frequency.

Programmes: Transferred from US Navy to Royal Thai Navy at New York Navy Shipyard in July 1959 under MDAP and by sale 6 June 1975.
Modernisation: The three 21 in torpedo tubes were removed and the four 20 mm guns were replaced by four 40 mm. The six A/S torpedo tubes were fitted in 1966.
Operational: Used mostly as an alongside training ship.

PIN KLAO   3/1991, 92 Wing RAAF

CORVETTES

2 RATTANAKOSIN CLASS (MISSILE CORVETTES)

Name	No	Builders	Laid down	Launched	Commissioned
RATTANAKOSIN	1	Tacoma Boatbuilders, Washington	6 Feb 1984	11 Mar 1986	26 Sep 1986
SUKHOTHAI	2	Tacoma Boatbuilders, Washington	26 Mar 1984	20 July 1986	10 June 1987

Displacement, tons: 960 full load
Dimensions, feet (metres): 252 × 31.5 × 8 *(76.8 × 9.6 × 2.4)*
Main machinery: 2 MTU 20V 1163 TB83 diesels; 14 730 hp(m) *(10.83 MW)* sustained; 2 shafts
Speed, knots: 26. **Range, miles:** 3000 at 16 kts
Complement: 87 (15 officers) plus Flag Staff

Missiles: SSM: 8 McDonnell Douglas Harpoon (2 quad) launchers ❶; active radar homing to 130 km *(70 nm)* at 0.9 Mach; warhead 227 kg (84A) or 258 kg (84B/C).
 SAM: Selenia Elsag Albatros octuple launcher ❷; 24 Aspide; semi-active radar homing to 13 km *(7 nm)* at 2.5 Mach; height envelope 15-5000 m *(49.2-16 405 ft)*; warhead 30 kg.
Guns: 1 OTO Melara 3 in *(76 mm)*/62 ❸; 85° elevation; 60 rounds/minute to 16 km *(8.7 nm)*; weight of shell 6 kg.
 2 Breda 40 mm/70 (twin) ❹; 85° elevation; 300 rounds/minute to 12.5 km *(6.8 nm)*; weight of shell 0.96 kg.
 2 Oerlikon 20 mm ❺; 55° elevation; 800 rounds/minute to 2 km.
Torpedoes: 6—324 mm US Mk 32 (2 triple) tubes ❻. MUSL Stingray; active/passive homing to 11 km *(5.9 nm)* at 45 kts; warhead 35 kg (shaped charge); depth to 750 m *(2460 ft)*.
Countermeasures: Decoys: CSEE Dagaie 6 or 10-tubed trainable; IR flares and chaff; H-J band.
 ESM: Elettronica; intercept.
Fire control: Signaal Sewaco TH action data automation. Lirod 8 optronic director ❼.
Radars: Air/surface search: Signaal DA 05 ❽; E/F band; range 137 km *(75 nm)* for 2 m² target.
 Surface search: Signaal ZW 06 ❾; I band.
 Navigation: Decca 1226; I band.
 Fire control: Signaal WM 25/41 ❿; I/J band; range 46 km *(25 nm)*.
Sonars: Atlas Elektronik DSQS 21C; hull-mounted; active search and attack; medium frequency.

Programmes: Contract signed with Tacoma on 9 May 1983. Intentions to build a third were overtaken by the Vosper corvettes. First laid down 6 February 1984, launched 11 March 1986; second laid down 26 March 1984, launched 20 July 1986.
Structure: Similar design to missile corvettes built for Saudi Arabia five years earlier. Space for Phalanx aft of the Harpoon launchers.

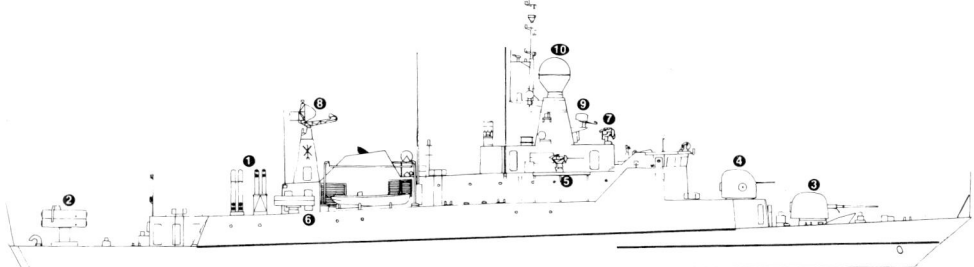

RATTANAKOSIN   (Scale 1 : 600), Ian Sturton

RATTANAKOSIN   1992, Ships of the World

680 THAILAND / Corvettes — Light forces

3 KHAMRONSIN CLASS (ASW CORVETTES)

Name	No	Builders	Laid down	Launched	Commissioned
KHAMRONSIN	1	Ital Thai Marine, Bangkok	15 Mar 1988	15 Aug 1989	29 July 1992
THAYANCHON	2	Ital Thai Marine, Bangkok	20 Apr 1988	7 Dec 1989	5 Sep 1992
LONGLOM	3	Bangkok Naval Dockyard	15 Mar 1988	8 Aug 1989	2 Oct 1992

Displacement, tons: 475 half load
Dimensions, feet (metres): 203.4 oa; 186 wl × 26.9 × 8.2 *(62; 56.7 × 8.2 × 2.5)*
Main machinery: 2 MTU 12V 1163 TB93; 9980 hp(m) *(7.34 MW)* sustained; 2 KaMeWa cp props
Speed, knots: 25. **Range, miles:** 2500 at 15 kts
Complement: 57 (6 officers)

Guns: 1 OTO Melara 76 mm/62 Mod 7; 85° elevation; 60 rounds/minute to 16 km *(8.7 nm)*; weight of shell 6 kg.
2 Breda 30 mm/70 (twin); 85° elevation; 800 rounds/minute to 12.5 km *(6.8 nm)*; weight of shell 0.37 kg.
Torpedoes: 6 Plessey PMW 49A (2 triple) launchers; MUSL Stingray; active/passive homing to 11 km *(6 nm)* at 45 kts; warhead 35 kg shaped charge.
Combat data systems: Plessey Nautis P action data automation.
Fire control: British Aerospace Sea Archer 1A Mod 2 optronic GFCS.
Radars: Air/surface search: Plessey AWS 4; E/F band; range 101 km *(55 nm)*.
Sonars: Atlas Elektronik DSQS-21C; hull-mounted; active search and attack; medium frequency.

Programmes: Contract signed on 29 September 1987 with Ital Thai Marine of Bangkok for the construction of two ASW corvettes and for technical assistance with a third to be built in Bangkok Naval Dockyard. A fourth of the class with a different superstructure and less armament was ordered by the Police in September 1989. There are no plans for any more of the class.
Structure: The vessels are based on a Vosper Thornycroft Province class 56 m design stretched by increasing the frame spacing along the whole length of the hull. Depth charge racks and mine rails may be added.

KHAMRONSIN   1991, Royal Thai Navy

SHIPBORNE AIRCRAFT

Note: Six medium size helicopters are to be ordered in 1993. Plans to acquire Kamen Seasprite are still under consideration but not Z-9A Haitun helicopters.

Numbers/Type: 7 Bell 212.
Operational speed: 100 kts *(185 km/h)*.
Service ceiling: 13 200 ft *(4025 m)*.
Range: 200 nm *(370 km)*.
Role/Weapon systems: Commando assault and general support. Mostly based ashore but operate from Normed class and 053 HT (H) frigates. Weapons: Pintle-mounted M60 machine guns.

BELL 212   1992, Royal Thai Navy

LAND-BASED MARITIME AIRCRAFT (FRONT LINE)

Note: Three P-3B Orion (with Harpoon) are to be acquired in 1993. There are also unconfirmed plans for up to 30 A7-E Corsair aircraft to be delivered from the US Navy. Cessna transports and UH-1H utility helicopters are in service in the support role.

Numbers/Type: 4 Bell 214ST.
Operational speed: 130 kts *(241 km/h)*.
Service ceiling: 10 000 ft *(3050 m)*.
Range: 450 nm *(834 km)*.
Role/Weapon systems: VIP and general support duties. Weapons: Pintle-mounted M60 machine guns.

Numbers/Type: 3/2 Fokker F27 Maritime 200/400.
Operational speed: 250 kts *(463 km/h)*.
Service ceiling: 2500 ft *(7620 m)*.
Range: 2700 nm *(5000 km)*.
Role/Weapon systems: Increased coastal surveillance and response is provided, including ASW and ASV action. Sensors: APS-504 search radar, Bendix weather radar, ESM and MAD equipment. Weapons: ASW; 4 × Mk 46 or Stingray torpedoes or depth bombs or mines. ASV; 2 × Harpoon ASM.

Numbers/Type: 5 GAF Searchmaster B (Nomad).
Operational speed: 168 kts *(311 km/h)*.
Service ceiling: 21 000 ft *(6400 m)*.
Range: 730 nm *(1352 km)*.
Role/Weapon systems: Short-range MR for EEZ protection and anti-smuggling operations. Sensors: Search radar, cameras. Weapons: Unarmed.

Numbers/Type: 8 Grumman S-2F Tracker.
Operational speed: 130 kts *(241 km/h)*.
Service ceiling: 25 000 ft *(7620 m)*.
Range: 1350 nm *(2500 km)*.
Role/Weapon systems: MR and ASW operations, with limited ASV capability; now being supplemented by F27. Turbo conversion being considered but is unlikely because of airframe condition. Sensors: Search radar, ESM, MAD. Weapons: ASW; 4 × Mk 46 torpedoes, depth bombs, mines. ASV; 6 × 127 mm rockets.

Numbers/Type: 3 Dornier 228.
Operational speed: 200 kts *(370 km/h)*.
Service ceiling: 28 000 ft *(8535 m)*.
Range: 940 nm *(1740 km)*.
Role/Weapon systems: Coastal surveillance and EEZ protection. Acquired in 1991.

LIGHT FORCES

Note: About 150 small patrol boats belong to the Naval Riverine Squadron.

3 RATCHARIT CLASS (FAST ATTACK CRAFT—MISSILE)

Name	No	Builders	Commissioned
RATCHARIT	4	C N Breda (Venezia)	10 Aug 1979
WITTHAYAKHOM	5	C N Breda (Venezia)	12 Nov 1979
UDOMDET	6	C N Breda (Venezia)	21 Feb 1980

Displacement, tons: 235 standard; 270 full load
Dimensions, feet (metres): 163.4 × 24.6 × 7.5 *(49.8 × 7.5 × 2.3)*
Main machinery: 3 MTU MD 20 V 538 TB91 diesels; 11 520 hp(m) *(8.47 MW)* sustained; 3 shafts
Speed, knots: 37. **Range, miles:** 2000 at 15 kts
Complement: 45 (7 officers)

Missiles: SSM: 4 Aerospatiale MM 38 Exocet; inertial cruise; active radar homing to 42 km *(23 nm)* at 0.9 Mach; warhead 165 kg; sea-skimmer.
Guns: 1 OTO Melara 3 in *(76 mm)*/62 compact; 85° elevation; 85 rounds/minute to 16 km *(8.7 nm)* anti-surface; 12 km *(6.6 nm)* anti-aircraft; weight of shell 6 kg.
1 Bofors 40 mm/70; 85° elevation; 300 rounds/minute to 12.5 km *(6.8 nm)*; weight of shell 0.96 kg.
Countermeasures: ESM: Radar warning.
Radars: Surface search: Decca; I band.
Fire control: Signaal WM 25; I/J band; range 46 km *(25 nm)*.

Programmes: Ordered June 1976. *Ratcharit* launched 30 July 1978, *Witthayakhom* 2 September 1978 and *Udomdet* 28 September 1978.
Structure: Standard Breda BMB 230 design.

WITTHAYAKHOM   1/1991

12 Ex-US SWIFT CLASS (COASTAL PATROL CRAFT)

T 21-29   T 210-212

Displacement, tons: 20 standard; 22 full load
Dimensions, feet (metres): 50 × 13 × 3.5 *(15.2 × 4 × 1.1)*
Main machinery: 2 diesels; 480 hp *(358 kW)*; 2 shafts
Speed, knots: 25
Complement: 5
Guns: 2—81 mm mortars. 2—12.7 mm MGs.

Comment: Transferred from US Navy from 1967 to 1975.

T 27   10/1989, S Tabusa

3 PRABPARAPAK CLASS (FAST ATTACK CRAFT—MISSILE)

Name	No	Builders	Commissioned
PRABPARAPAK	1	Singapore SBEC	28 July 1976
HANHAK SATTRU	2	Singapore SBEC	6 Nov 1976
SUPHAIRIN	3	Singapore SBEC	1 Feb 1977

Displacement, tons: 224 standard; 268 full load
Dimensions, feet (metres): 149 × 24.3 × 7.5 *(45.4 × 7.4 × 2.3)*
Main machinery: 4 MTU 16V 538 TB92 diesels; 13 640 hp(m) *(10 MW)* sustained; 4 shafts
Speed, knots: 40. **Range, miles:** 2000 at 15 kts; 750 at 37 kts
Complement: 41 (5 officers)
Missiles: SSM: 5 IAI Gabriel I (1 triple, 2 single) launchers; radar or optical guidance; semi-active radar homing to 20 km *(10.8 nm)* at 0.7 Mach; warhead 75 kg.
Guns: 1 Bofors 57 mm/70; 75° elevation; 200 rounds/minute to 17 km *(9.3 nm)*; weight of shell 2.4 kg. 8 rocket illuminant launchers on either side of 57 mm gun.
1 Bofors 40 mm/70; 90° elevation; 300 rounds/minute to 12 km *(6.6 nm)*; weight of shell 2.4 kg.
Countermeasures: ESM: Radar intercept.
Radars: Surface search: Kelvin Hughes Type 17; I band.
Fire control: Signaal WM 28/5 series; I/J band.

Programmes: Ordered June 1973. Built under licence from Lürssen. Launch dates—*Prabparapak* 29 July 1975, *Hanhak Sattru* 28 October 1975, *Suphairin* 20 February 1976.
Structure: Same design as Lürssen standard 45 m class built for Singapore. Normally only three Gabriel SSM are carried.

PRABPARAPAK   *1/1991, Royal Thai Navy*

6 SATTAHIP CLASS (LARGE PATROL CRAFT)

Name	No	Builders	Commissioned
SATTAHIP	4	Ital Thai (Samutprakarn) Ltd	16 Sep 1983
KLONGYAI	5	Ital Thai (Samutprakarn) Ltd	7 May 1984
TAKBAI	6	Ital Thai (Samutprakarn) Ltd	18 July 1984
KANTANG	7	Ital Thai (Samutprakarn) Ltd	14 Oct 1985
THEPHA	8	Ital Thai (Samutprakarn) Ltd	17 Apr 1986
TAIMUANG	9	Ital Thai (Samutprakarn) Ltd	17 Apr 1986

Displacement, tons: 270 standard; 300 full load
Dimensions, feet (metres): 164.5 × 23.9 × 5.9 *(50.1 × 7.3 × 1.8)*
Main machinery: 2 MTU 16V 538 TB92 diesels; 6820 hp(m) *(5 MW)* sustained; 2 shafts
Speed, knots: 22. **Range, miles:** 2500 at 15 kts
Complement: 56
Guns: 2 USN 3 in *(76 mm)*/50 Mk 26 (in three of the class) or 1 OTO Melara 3 in *(76 mm)*/62 and 1 Bofors 40 mm/70 (in three of the class). 2 Oerlikon 20 mm. 2—12.7 mm MGs.
Fire control: NA 18 optronic director (in three ships).
Radars: Surface search: Decca; I band.

Comment: First four ordered 9 September 1981, *Thepha* on 27 December 1983 and *Taimuang* on 31 August 1984.

TAKBAI (with OTO Melara gun)   *1992, Royal Thai Navy*

THEPHA (with US guns)   *1992, Royal Thai Navy*

3 CHON BURI CLASS (FAST ATTACK CRAFT—GUN)

Name	No	Builders	Commissioned
CHON BURI	1	C N Breda (Venezia) Mestre	22 Feb 1983
SONGKHLA	2	C N Breda (Venezia) Mestre	15 July 1983
PHUKET	3	C N Breda (Venezia) Mestre	13 Jan 1984

Displacement, tons: 450 full load
Dimensions, feet (metres): 198 × 29 × 15 *(60.4 × 8.8 × 4.5)*
Main machinery: 3 MTU 20V 538 TB92 diesels; 12 795 hp(m) *(9.4 MW)* sustained; 3 shafts; cp props
Speed, knots: 30. **Range, miles:** 2500 at 18 kts; 900 at 30 kts
Complement: 41 (6 officers)
Guns: 2 OTO Melara 3 in *(76 mm)*/62. 2 Breda 40 mm/70 (twin).
Countermeasures: Decoys: 4 Hycor Mk 135 chaff launchers.
ESM: Radar intercept.
Fire control: Lirod 8 optronic director.
Radars: Surface search: Signaal ZW 06; I band.
Fire control: Signaal WM 22/61; I/J band; range 46 km *(25 nm)*.

Comment: Ordered in 1979 (first pair) and 1981. Laid down—*Chon Buri* 15 August 1981 (launched 29 November 1982), *Songkhla* 15 September 1981, *Phuket* 15 December 1981 (launched 3 February 1983). Steel hulls, alloy superstructure. Can be adapted to carry surface-to-surface missiles.

SONGKHLA   *1992, Royal Thai Navy*

3 Ex-US PC 461 CLASS (LARGE PATROL CRAFT)

SUKRIP (ex-*PC 1218*) PC 5   TONGPLIU (ex-*PC 616*) PC 6   LIULOM (ex-*PC 1253*) PC 7

Displacement, tons: 280 standard; 450 full load
Dimensions, feet (metres): 173.7 × 23 × 8.9 *(52.9 × 7 × 2.7)*
Main machinery: 2 diesels; 2880 hp *(2.15 MW)* or 2560 hp *(1.91 MW)* (*Sukrip*); 2 shafts
Speed, knots: 20. **Range, miles:** 5000 at 10 kts
Complement: 62-71
Guns: 1 USN 3 in *(76 mm)*/50. 1 Bofors 40 mm/60. 5 Oerlikon 20 mm.
Torpedoes: 2—324 mm US Mk 32 tubes; anti-submarine.
A/S mortars: 1 Mk 22 Mousetrap.
Radars: Surface search: Raytheon SPS 35 (1500B) or SPS 21D (PC5); I band.

Comment: Launched in 1941-43 as US PCs. Transferred between March 1947 and December 1952.

TONGPLIU   *1992, Royal Thai Navy*

10 Ex-US PGM 71 CLASS (LARGE PATROL CRAFT)

T 11-19   T 110

Displacement, tons: 130 standard; 147 full load
Dimensions, feet (metres): 101 × 21 × 6 *(30.8 × 6.4 × 1.9)*
Main machinery: 2 GM diesels; 1800 hp *(1.34 MW)*; 2 shafts
Speed, knots: 18.5. **Range, miles:** 1500 at 10 kts
Complement: 30
Guns: 1 Bofors 40 mm/60. 1 Oerlikon 20 mm. 2—12.7 mm MGs.
In some craft the 20 mm gun has been replaced by an 81 mm mortar/12.7 mm combined mounting aft.
Radars: Surface search: Decca 303 *(T 11* and *12)* or Decca 202 (remainder); I band.

Comment: Built by Peterson Inc between 1966 and 1970.

T 18   *1992, Royal Thai Navy*

9 T 91 CLASS (COASTAL PATROL CRAFT)

T 91-99

Displacement, tons: 87.5 (T 91), 130 (remainder) standard
Dimensions, feet (metres): 104.3 × 17.5 × 5.5 *(31.8 × 5.3 × 1.7)* (T 91)
  118 × 18.7 × 4.9 *(36 × 5.7 × 1.5)* (remainder)
Main machinery: 2 MTU 12V 538 TB81/82 diesels; 3300 hp(m) *(2.43 MW)*/4430 hp(m) *(3.26 MW)* sustained; 2 shafts
Speed, knots: 25. **Range, miles:** 700 at 21 kts
Complement: 21; 23 (T 93-94); 25 (T 99)
Guns: 2 Bofors 40 mm/60. 1—12.7 mm MG (see *Comment*).
Fire control: Sea Archer 1A optronic director (T 99 only).
Radars: Surface search: Raytheon SPS 35 (1500B); I band.

Comment: Built by Royal Thai Naval Dockyard, Bangkok. T 91 commissioned in 1965; T 92-93 in 1973; T 94-98 between 1981 and 1984; T 99 in 1987. T 91 has an extended upperworks and a 20 mm gun in place of the after 40 mm. T 99 has a single Bofors 40/70, one Oerlikon 20 mm and two MGs. There may be other armament variations in the group T 94-98. Major refits from 1983-86 for earlier vessels of the class.

T 97   5/1991, Royal Thai Navy

14 T 213 CLASS (COASTAL PATROL CRAFT)

T 213-226   T 227-230

Displacement, tons: 35 standard
Dimensions, feet (metres): 64 × 17.5 × 5 *(19.5 × 5.3 × 1.5)*
Main machinery: 2 MTU diesels; 715 hp(m) *(526 kW)*; 2 shafts
Speed, knots: 25
Complement: 8
Guns: 1 Oerlikon 20 mm. 1—81 mm mortar with 12.7 mm MG.

Comment: Built by Ital Thai Marine Ltd. Commissioned—T 213-215, 29 August 1980; T 216-218, 26 March 1981; T 219-223, 16 September 1981; T 224, 19 November 1982; T 225 and T 226, 28 March 1984; T 227-230 in 1990/91. Of alloy construction. Used for fishery patrol and coastal control duties.

T 221   1992, Royal Thai Navy

1 HYSUCAT 18 HYDROFOIL (RIVER PATROL CRAFT)

T 231

Displacement, tons: 39
Dimensions, feet (metres): 60 × 21.6 (hull) × 5.9 *(18.3 × 6.6 × 1.6)*
Main machinery: 2 MWM Type diesels; 1640 hp(m) *(1.2 MW)*; 2 shafts
Speed, knots: 36
Complement: 10
Guns: 1 Oerlikon 20 mm.

Comment: Designed by Technautic in association with Lürssen. Ordered in 1984 and started trials in December 1986. GRP hull for hydrofoil-supported catamarans. Reported that the Thai Navy was not happy with the trials results and the plan for a class of 12 was cancelled. Gatling gun replaced in 1988 and the associated fire control equipment removed.

HYSUCAT 231   11/1988, Trevor Brown

3 Ex-US RPC CLASS (RIVER PATROL CRAFT)

Displacement, tons: 13 full load
Dimensions, feet (metres): 35.8 × 10.5 × 3.3 *(10.9 × 3.2 × 1)*
Main machinery: 2 Gray diesels; 450 hp *(335 kW)*; 2 shafts
Speed, knots: 14
Complement: 6
Guns: 4—12.7 mm MGs.

Comment: Transferred in 1967. Employed on Mekong River.

FPC class   1989

37 Ex-US PBR Mk II (RIVER PATROL CRAFT)

11-19, 110-132   +5

Displacement, tons: 8 full load
Dimensions, feet (metres): 32.1 × 11.5 × 2.3 *(9.8 × 3.5 × 0.7)*
Main machinery: 2 Detroit diesels; 430 hp *(321 kW)*; 2 Jacuzzi waterjets
Speed, knots: 25. **Range, miles:** 150 at 23 kts
Complement: 4
Guns: 2—12.7 mm (twin) MGs. 2—6.72 mm MGs. 1—60 mm mortar.

Comment: Transferred from 1967-73. Employed on Mekong River. Reported to be getting old and maximum speed has been virtually halved. All belong to the Riverine Squadron.

PBR Mk II   1991, Royal Thai Navy

100 + ASSAULT BOATS (AB)

Displacement, tons: 0.4 full load
Dimensions, feet (metres): 16.4 × 6.2 × 1.3 *(5 × 1.9 × 0.4)*
Speed, knots: 24
Guns: 1—7.62 mm MG.

Comment: Part of the Riverine Squadron with the PBRs and two PCFs.

ASSAULT BOAT   1991, Royal Thai Navy

MINE WARFARE FORCES

Note: Purchase of further Lürssen types is unlikely because of cost and reported problems with the minehunting system. Acquisition of inshore minehunters is being considered; possibly eight Chinese Type 312 drones which can be controlled from shore.

1 MCM SUPPORT SHIP

Name	No	Builders	Commissioned
THALANG	1	Bangkok Dock Co Ltd	4 Aug 1980

Displacement, tons: 1000 standard
Dimensions, feet (metres): 185.5 × 33 × 10 *(55.7 × 10 × 3.1)*
Main machinery: 2 MTU diesels; 1310 hp(m) *(963 kW)*; 2 shafts
Speed, knots: 12
Complement: 77
Guns: 1 Bofors 40 mm/70. 2 Oerlikon 20 mm. 2—12.7 mm MGs.
Radars: Surface search: Racal Decca 1226; I band.

Comment: Has minesweeping capability. Two 3 ton cranes provided for change of minesweeping gear in MSCs—four sets carried. Design by Ferrostaal, Essen.

THALANG　　　　　　　　　　　　　　　　　　　　　　　　1981, Royal Thai Navy

2 BANG RACHAN CLASS (MINEHUNTERS/SWEEPERS)

Name	No	Builders	Commissioned
BANG RACHAN	2	Lürssen Vegesack	29 Apr 1987
NONGSARAI	3	Lürssen Vegesack	17 Nov 1987

Displacement, tons: 444 full load
Dimensions, feet (metres): 161.1 × 30.5 × 8.2 *(49.1 × 9.3 × 2.5)*
Main machinery: 2 MTU 12V 396 TB83 diesels; 3120 hp(m) *(2.3 MW)* sustained; 2 shafts; KaMeWa cp props
 Auxiliary propulsion; 1 motor
Speed, knots: 17; 7 (electric motor). **Range, miles:** 3100 at 12 kts
Complement: 30
Guns: 3 Oerlikon GAM-BO1 20 mm.
Countermeasures: MCM: MWS 80R minehunting system. Acoustic, magnetic and mechanical sweeps.
 2 Gaymarine Pluto 15 remote controlled submersibles.
Radars: Navigation: 2 Atlas Elektronik 8600 ARPA; I band.
Sonars: Atlas Elektronik DSQS-11H; hull-mounted; minehunting; high frequency.

Comment: First ordered from Lürssen late 1984, arrived Bangkok 22 October 1987. Second ordered 5 August 1985 and arrived in Bangkok May 1988. There have been reports of problems with the minehunting systems, and that more of the class are not being considered. Amagnetic steel frames and deckhouses, wooden hull. Motorola Miniranger MRS III precise navigation system. Draeger decompression chamber.

BANG RACHAN　　　　　　　　　　　　　　　　　　　　　1992, Royal Thai Navy

5 Ex-US MSBs

MLMS 6-10

Displacement, tons: 25 full load
Dimensions, feet (metres): 50.2 × 13.1 × 3 *(15.3 × 4 × 0.9)*
Main machinery: 1 Gray Marine 64 HN9 diesel; 165 hp *(123 kW)*; 1 shaft
Speed, knots: 8
Complement: 10
Guns: 2—7.62 mm MGs.

Comment: Three transferred in October 1963 and two in 1964. Wooden hulled, converted from small motor launches. Operated on Chao Phraya river.

3 US BLUEBIRD CLASS (MINESWEEPERS—COASTAL)

Name	No	Builders	Commissioned
LADYA (ex-US *MSC 297*)	5	Peterson Builders Inc, Sturgeon Bay, Wisconsin	14 Dec 1963
BANGKEO (ex-US *MSC 303*)	6	Dorchester S B Corporation, Camden	9 July 1965
DONCHEDI (ex-US *MSC 313*)	8	Peterson Builders Inc, Sturgeon Bay, Wisconsin	17 Sep 1965

Displacement, tons: 317 standard; 384 full load
Dimensions, feet (metres): 145.3 × 27 × 8.5 *(44.3 × 8.2 × 2.6)*
Main machinery: 2 GM 8-268 diesels; 880 hp *(656 kW)*; 2 shafts
Speed, knots: 13. **Range, miles:** 2750 at 12 kts
Complement: 43 (7 officers)
Guns: 2 Oerlikon 20 mm/80 (twin).
Countermeasures: MCM: US Mk 4 (V). Mk 6. US Type Q2 magnetic.
Radars: Navigation: Decca TM 707; I band.
IFF: UPX 5 *(Ladya)*. UPX 12 (rest).
Sonars: UQS 1; hull-mounted; minehunting; high frequency.

Comment: Constructed for Thailand. One paid off in 1992 and the last three are now in limited operational service.

DONCHEDI　　　　　　　　　　　　　　　　　　　　　　　　1/1991

AMPHIBIOUS FORCES

2 NORMED CLASS (LSTs)

Name	No	Builders	Commissioned
SICHANG	LST 6	Ital Thai	9 Oct 1987
SURIN	LST 7	Bangkok Dock Co Ltd	16 Dec 1988

Displacement, tons: 3540 standard; 4235 full load
Dimensions, feet (metres): 337.8 × 51.5 × 11.5 *(103 × 15.7 × 3.5)*
Main machinery: 2 MTU 20V 1163 TB82 diesels; 11 000 hp(m) *(8.1 MW)* sustained; 2 shafts
Speed, knots: 16. **Range, miles:** 7000 at 12 kts
Complement: 129
Military lift: 348 troops; 14 tanks or 12 APCs or 850 tons cargo; 3 LCVP; 1 LCPL
Guns: 1 Bofors 40 mm/70. 2 Oerlikon GAM-CO1 20 mm. 2—12.7 mm MGs. 1—81 mm mortar.
Fire control: 2 Sea Archer Mk 1A optronic directors.
Radars: Navigation: Decca; I band.
Helicopters: Platform for 2 Bell 212.

Comment: First ordered 31 August 1984 to a Chantier du Nord (Normed) design. Second ordered from Bangkok Dock Co Ltd, to a modified design (possibly 31.2 ft *(9.5 m)* longer and with MWM diesels). The largest naval ships yet built in Thailand. First launched in April 1987, second in early 1988. Have bow doors and a 17 m ramp.

SICHANG　　　　　　　　　　　　　　　　　　　　　　　　　1/1991

684 THAILAND / Amphibious forces

4 Ex-US 511-1152 CLASS (LSTs)

Name	No	Builders	Commissioned
CHANG (ex-USS *Lincoln County* LST 898)	LST 2	Dravo Corporation	29 Dec 1944
PANGAN (ex-USS *Stark County* LST 1134)	LST 3	Chicago Bridge and Iron Co, Ill.	7 Apr 1945
LANTA (ex-USS *Stone County* LST 1141)	LST 4	Chicago Bridge and Iron Co, Ill.	9 May 1945
PRATHONG (ex-USS *Dodge County* LST 722)	LST 5	Jefferson B & M Co, Ind.	13 Sep 1944

Displacement, tons: 1650 standard; 3640/4145 full load
Dimensions, feet (metres): 328 × 50 × 14 *(100 × 15.2 × 4.4)*
Main machinery: 2 GM 12-567A diesels; 1800 hp *(1.34 MW)*; 2 shafts
Speed, knots: 11.5. **Range, miles:** 9500 at 9 kts
Complement: 80; 157 (war)
Military lift: 1230 tons max; 815 tons beaching
Guns: 8 Bofors 40 mm/60 (2 twin, 4 single). 2—12.7 mm MGs *(Chang)*. 2 Oerlikon 20 mm/80 (others).
Fire control: 2 Mk 51 GFCS. 2 optical systems.
Radars: Surface search: Raytheon SPS 10 *(Pangan)*; G band.
Navigation: Raytheon; I/J band.

Comment: *Chang*, transferred to Thailand in August 1962. *Pangan* was transferred on 16 May 1966, *Lanta* on 15 August 1973 (by sale 1 March 1979) and *Prathong* on 17 December 1975. *Chang* has a reinforced bow and waterline. *Lanta*, *Prathong* and *Chang* have mobile crane on well deck. All have tripod mast.

PRATHONG 1/1991

2 Ex-US LSM 1 CLASS

Name	No	Builders	Commissioned
KUT (ex-USS *LSM 338*)	LSM 1	Pullman Std Car Co, Chicago	10 Jan 1945
KRAM (ex-USS *LSM 469*)	LSM 3	Brown S B Co, Houston, Texas	17 Mar 1945

Displacement, tons: 743 standard; 1107 full load
Dimensions, feet (metres): 203.5 × 34.5 × 9.9 *(62 × 10.5 × 3)*
Main machinery: 2 Fairbanks-Morse 38D8-1/8-10 diesels; 3540 hp *(2.64 MW)* sustained; 2 shafts
Speed, knots: 12.5. **Range, miles:** 4500 at 12.5 kts
Complement: 91 (6 officers)
Military lift: 452 tons beaching; 50 troops with vehicles
Guns: 2 Bofors 40 mm/60 Mk 3 (twin). 4 Oerlikon 20 mm/70.
Fire control: Mk 51 Mod 2 optical director *(Kram)*.
Radars: Surface search: Raytheon SPS 5 *(Kram)*; G/H band.
Navigation: Raytheon 1500 B; I band.

Comment: Former US landing ships of the LCM, later LSM (Medium Landing Ship) type. *Kram* was transferred to Thailand under MAP at Seattle, Washington, on 25 May 1962, *Kut* in October 1946. One deleted in 1990.

KUT 1/1991

2 Ex-US LSIL 351 CLASS

PRAB LSIL 1   SATAKUT (ex-*LSIL 739*) LSIL 2

Displacement, tons: 230 standard; 399 full load
Dimensions, feet (metres): 157 × 23 × 6 *(47.9 × 7 × 1.8)*
Main machinery: 4 GM diesels; 2320 bhp *(1.73 MW)*; 2 shafts
Speed, knots: 15. **Range, miles:** 5600 at 12.5 kts
Complement: 49 (7 officers)
Military lift: 101 tons or 76 troops
Guns: 1 Bofors 40 mm/60. 4 Oerlikon 20 mm/70.
Radars: Surface search: Raytheon SPS 35 (1500B); I band.

Comment: Built in 1944-45—transferred May 1947. *Prab* has been refitted and is back in commission.

PRAB 8/1991

1 Ex-US LCG TYPE

NAKHA (ex-USS *LSSL 102*) LSSL 3

Displacement, tons: 233 standard; 393 full load
Dimensions, feet (metres): 158.1 × 23.6 × 6.2 *(48.2 × 7.2 × 1.9)*
Main machinery: 2 GM diesels; 1320 hp *(985 kW)*; 2 shafts
Speed, knots: 15. **Range, miles:** 5000 at 6 kts
Complement: 60
Guns: 1 USN 3 in *(76 mm)*/50. 4 Bofors 40 mm/60 (2 twin). 4 Oerlikon 20 mm/70 (2 twin). 6—81 mm mortars. 2—12.7 mm MGs.
Radars: Navigation: Raytheon 1500 B; I band.

Comment: Built by Commercial Ironworks, Oregon in 1945. Transferred in 1966. Acquired when Japan returned her to the USA.

NAKHA

4 THONG KAEO CLASS (LCUs)

Name	No	Builders	Commissioned
THONG KAEO	7	Bangkok Dock Co Ltd	23 Dec 1982
THONG LANG	8	Bangkok Dock Co Ltd	19 Apr 1983
WANG NOK	9	Bangkok Dock Co Ltd	16 Sep 1983
WANG NAI	10	Bangkok Dock Co Ltd	11 Nov 1983

Displacement, tons: 193 standard; 396 full load
Dimensions, feet (metres): 134.5 × 29.5 × 6.9 *(41 × 9 × 2.1)*
Main machinery: 2 GM 16V-71 diesels; 1400 hp *(1.04 MW)*; 2 shafts
Speed, knots: 10. **Range, miles:** 1200 at 10 kts
Complement: 31 (3 officers)
Military lift: 3 lorries; 150 tons equipment
Guns: 2 Oerlikon 20 mm. 2—7.62 mm MGs.

Comment: Ordered in 1980. A fifth ship of the class was abandoned.

WANG NOK 1/1991, Royal Thai Navy

3 GRIFFON 1000 TD HOVERCRAFT

Dimensions, feet (metres): 27.6 × 12.5 *(8.4 × 3.8)*
Main machinery: 1 Deutz BF6L913C diesel; 190 hp(m) *(140 kW)*
Speed, knots: 33. **Range, miles:** 200 at 27 kts
Cargo capacity: 1000 kg plus 9 troops

Comment: Acquired in mid-1990 from Griffon Hovercraft. Although having an obvious amphibious capability they are also to be used for rescue and flood control.

GRIFFON HOVERCRAFT 1990, Griffon

5 Ex-US 501 CLASS (LCUs)

MATAPHON LCU 1	ADANG LCU 3	TALIBONG LCU 6
RAWI LCU 2	PHETRA LCU 4	

Displacement, tons: 145 standard; 330 full load
Dimensions, feet (metres): 120.4 × 32 × 4 *(36.7 × 9.8 × 1.2)*
Main machinery: 3 Gray Marine 65 diesels; 675 hp *(503 kW)*; 3 shafts
Speed, knots: 10. **Range, miles:** 650 at 8 kts
Complement: 13
Military lift: 150 tons or 3-4 tanks or 250 troops
Guns: 2 Oerlikon 20 mm/80.

Comment: Transferred 1946-47. Employed as transport ferries.

TALIBONG *8/1991*

24 Ex-US LCM 6

14-16, 61-68, 71-78, 81-82, 85-87

Displacement, tons: 56 full load
Main machinery: 2 Gray Marine 64 HN9 diesels; 330 hp *(264 kW)*; 2 shafts
Speed, knots: 9
Complement: 5
Military lift: 34 tons

Comment: First 21 delivered 1965-69.

12 Ex-US LCVP

L 51-59, 510-512

Displacement, tons: 12
Main machinery: 1 diesel; 225 hp *(168 kW)*; 1 shaft
Speed, knots: 9
Military lift: 40 troops

Comment: Six transferred in 1953, remainder in 1963.

4 LCAs

L 40-43

Displacement, tons: 10 full load
Dimensions, feet (metres): 39.4 × 9.8 × 3.3 *(12 × 3 × 1)*
Main machinery: 2 Chrysler diesels; 2 Castoldi Mod 06 waterjets
Speed, knots: 25
Military lift: 35 troops

Comment: Built in Thailand in 1984. Fibreglass hull with bow ramp.

TRAINING SHIPS

1 Ex-BRITISH ALGERINE CLASS

Name	No	Builders	Commissioned
PHOSAMTON (ex-HMS *Minstrel*)	MSF 1	Redfern Construction Co	1945

Displacement, tons: 1040 standard; 1335 full load
Dimensions, feet (metres): 225 × 35.5 × 11.5 *(68.6 × 10.8 × 3.5)*
Main machinery: 2 boilers; 2 reciprocating engines; 2000 ihp *(1.49 MW)*; 2 shafts
Speed, knots: 16. **Range, miles:** 4000 at 10 kts
Complement: 103
Guns: 1 Vickers 4 in *(102 mm)*/45. 1 Bofors 40 mm/60. 2 Oerlikon 20 mm.
Radars: Navigation: Decca Type 974; I band.

Comment: Transferred in April 1947. Received engineering overhaul in 1984. Minesweeping gear replaced by a deckhouse to increase training space.

PHOSAMTON *1/1991, Royal Thai Navy*

Name	No	Builders	Commissioned
MAEKLONG	3	Uraga Dock Co, Japan	June 1937

Displacement, tons: 1400 standard; 2000 full load
Dimensions, feet (metres): 269 × 34 × 10.5 *(82 × 10.4 × 3.2)*
Main machinery: 2 boilers; 2 reciprocating engines; 2500 ihp *(1.87 MW)*; 2 shafts
Speed, knots: 14. **Range, miles:** 8000 at 12 kts
Complement: 155 as training ship
Guns: 4 USN 3 in *(76 mm)*/50. 3 Bofors 40 mm/60. 3 Oerlikon 20 mm.

Comment: The four 18 in torpedo tubes were removed to provide more training space.

MAEKLONG *3/1991, 92 Wing RAAF*

OCEANOGRAPHIC AND SURVEY SHIPS

Note: There is also a civilian research vessel *Chulab Horn* which completed in 1986.

Name	No	Builders	Commissioned
SUK	—	Bangkok Dock Co Ltd	3 Mar 1982

Displacement, tons: 1450 standard; 1526 full load
Dimensions, feet (metres): 206.3 × 36.1 × 13.4 *(62.9 × 11 × 4.1)*
Main machinery: 2 MTU diesels; 2400 hp(m) *(1.76 MW)*; 2 shafts
Speed, knots: 15
Complement: 86 (20 officers)
Guns: 2 Oerlikon 20 mm. 2—7.62 mm MGs.

Comment: Laid down 27 August 1979, launched 8 September 1981. Designed for oceanographic and survey duties.

SUK *5/1988, van Ginderen Collection*

Name	No	Builders	Commissioned
CHANTHARA	AGS 11	Lürssen Werft	1961

Displacement, tons: 870 standard; 996 full load
Dimensions, feet (metres): 229.2 × 34.5 × 10 *(69.9 × 10.5 × 3)*
Main machinery: 2 KHD diesels; 1090 hp(m) *(801 kW)*; 2 shafts
Speed, knots: 13.25. **Range, miles:** 10 000 at 10 kts
Complement: 68 (8 officers)
Guns: 1 Bofors 40 mm/60. 1 Oerlikon 20 mm.

Comment: Laid down on 27 September 1960. Launched on 17 December 1960.

CHANTHARA *1/1991*

686 THAILAND / Oceanographic and survey ships — Miscellaneous

Name	No	Builders	Commissioned
SURIYA	—	Bangkok Dock Co Ltd	14 May 1979

Displacement, tons: 690 full load
Dimensions, feet (metres): 177.8 × 33.5 × 10.2 *(54.2 × 10.2 × 3.1)*
Main machinery: 2 MTU diesels; 1310 hp(m) *(963 kW)*; 2 shafts; bow thruster; 135 hp(m) *(99 kW)*
Speed, knots: 12
Complement: 60 (12 officers)
Guns: 2 Oerlikon 20 mm.

Comment: Mostly used to service navigational aids.

SURIYA   *5/1990, 92 Wing RAAF*

2 OCEANOGRAPHIC VESSELS

II   III

Displacement, tons: 90 full load
Dimensions, feet (metres): 91.9 × 18 × 4.9 *(28 × 5.5 × 1.5)*
Main machinery: 1 diesel; 1 shaft
Speed, knots: 12
Complement: 11 (2 officers)

Comment: *II* launched in 1955 by Lürssen, Vegesack and *III* in 1972.

SERVICE FORCES

Note: A replenishment-at-sea ship is to be ordered in 1993 for delivery in 1995/96. The design is for a vessel of about 22 000 tons with a capacity for 9000 tons of fuel, water, ammunition and stores.

3 HARBOUR TANKERS

PROET YO 9   **CHIK** YO 10   **SAMED** YO 11

Displacement, tons: 360 standard; 485 full load
Dimensions, feet (metres): 122.7 × 19.7 × 8.7 *(37.4 × 6 × 2.7)*
Main machinery: 1 GM 8-268A diesel; 500 hp(m) *(368 kW)*; 1 shaft
Speed, knots: 9
Cargo capacity: 210 tons

Comment: Built by Bangkok Naval Dockyard. *Proet* commissioned 27 January 1967, remainder the same year. All three vessels are identical.

SAMED   *8/1991*

1 HARBOUR TANKER

SAMUI (ex-USS *YOG 60*) YO 4

Displacement, tons: 422 standard
Dimensions, feet (metres): 174.5 × 32 × 15 *(53.2 × 9.7 × 4.6)*
Main machinery: 2 diesels; 600 hp *(448 kW)*; 2 shafts
Speed, knots: 8
Complement: 29
Guns: 2 Oerlikon 20 mm.

Comment: Deleted in error in 1990.

SAMUI (alongside CHANG)   *8/1991*

1 REPLENISHMENT TANKER

CHULA   2

Displacement, tons: 2000 full load
Measurement, tons: 960 dwt
Dimensions, feet (metres): 219.8 × 31.2 × 14.4 *(67 × 9.5 × 4.4)*
Main machinery: 2 MTU 12V 396 TC62 diesels; 2400 hp(m) *(1.76 MW)* sustained; 2 shafts
Speed, knots: 14
Complement: 39 (7 officers)
Cargo capacity: 800 tons oil fuel
Guns: 2 Oerlikon 20 mm.
Radars: Navigation: Decca; I band.

Comment: Launched on 24 September 1980 by Singapore Slipway and Engineering Company. Fitted with SATNAV. Replenishment is done by a hose handling crane boom.

CHULA   *1992, Royal Thai Navy*

1 WATER CARRIER

Name	No	Builders	Commissioned
CHUANG	YW 5	Royal Thai Naval Dockyard, Bangkok	1965

Displacement, tons: 305 standard; 485 full load
Dimensions, feet (metres): 136 × 24.6 × 10 *(42 × 7.5 × 3.1)*
Main machinery: 1 GM diesel; 500 hp *(373 kW)*; 1 shaft
Speed, knots: 11
Complement: 29

Comment: Launched on 14 January 1965.

CHUANG   *8/1991*

MISCELLANEOUS

VISUD SAKORN

Comment: Naval manned and looks like a VIP yacht. Training ship of the Merchant Marine Training Centre, run by the Harbour Department.

VISUD SAKORN   *10/1987*

TUGS

0 + 2 HARBOUR TUGS

Displacement, tons: 300 standard
Dimensions, feet (metres): 82 × 27.9 × 7.9 (25 × 8.5 × 2.4)
Main machinery: 2 Caterpillar 3512 DITA diesels; 2 Aquamaster US 901 props
Speed, knots: 10
Complement: 6

Comment: Contract signed 23 September 1992 for local construction at Thonburi Naval dockyard. Commissioning scheduled for December 1993.

RIN ATA 5   **RANG** ATA 6

Displacement, tons: 350 standard
Dimensions, feet (metres): 106 × 29.9 × 15.2 (32.3 × 9 × 4.6)
Main machinery: 1 MWM TBD441V/12K diesel; 2100 hp(m) (1.54 MW); 1 shaft
Speed, knots: 12. Range, miles: 1000 at 10 kts
Complement: 19

Comment: Launched 12 and 14 June 1980 at Singapore Marine Shipyard. Both commissioned 5 March 1981.

RANG   1992, Royal Thai Navy

2 Ex-US YTL 422 CLASS

KLUENG BADEN YTL 2   **MARN VICHAI** YTL 3

Displacement, tons: 63 standard
Dimensions, feet (metres): 64.7 × 16.5 × 6 (19.7 × 5 × 1.8)
Main machinery: 1 diesel; 240 hp (179 kW); 1 shaft
Speed, knots: 8

Comment: Bought from Canada 1953.

MARN VICHAI   1992, Royal Thai Navy

ROYAL THAI MARINE POLICE

1 VOSPER THORNYCROFT TYPE (LARGE PATROL CRAFT)

SRINAKARIN 1804

Displacement, tons: 630 full load
Dimensions, feet (metres): 203.4 × 26.9 × 8.2 (62 × 8.2 × 2.5)
Main machinery: 2 Deutz MWM BV16M628 diesels; 9524 hp(m) (7 MW) sustained; 2 shafts; KaMeWa cp props
Speed, knots: 25. Range, miles: 2500 at 15 kts
Complement: 45
Guns: 1 Oerlikon 30 mm. 2 Oerlikon 20 mm (twin).

Comment: Ordered in September 1989 from Ital Thai Marine. Same hull as the Khamronsin class corvettes for the Navy but much more lightly armed. Delivered in April 1992.

SRINAKARIN   1992, Marine Police

2 HAMELN TYPE (LARGE PATROL CRAFT)

DAMRONG RACHANUPHAT 1802   **LOPBURI RAMAS** 1803

Displacement, tons: 430 full load
Dimensions, feet (metres): 186 × 26.6 × 8 (56.7 × 8.1 × 2.4)
Main machinery: 2 MTU diesels; 4400 hp(m) (3.23 MW); 2 shafts
Speed, knots: 23
Complement: 45
Guns: 1 USN 3 in (76 mm)/50. 2 Oerlikon 20 mm (twin).

Comment: Delivered by Schiffwerft Hameln, Germany, on 3 January 1969 and 10 December 1972 respectively.

LOPBURI RAMAS   1992, Marine Police

2 SUMIDAGAWA TYPE (COASTAL PATROL CRAFT)

CHASANYABADEE 1101   **PHROMYOTHEE** 1103

Displacement, tons: 130 full load
Dimensions, feet (metres): 111.5 × 19 × 9.1 (34 × 5.8 × 2.8)
Main machinery: 3 Ikegai diesels; 4050 hp(m) (2.98 MW); 3 shafts
Speed, knots: 32
Complement: 23
Guns: 2—12.7 mm MGs.

Comment: Commissioned in August 1972 and May 1973 respectively.

PHROMYOTHEE   1990, Marine Police

1 YOKOHAMA TYPE (COASTAL PATROL CRAFT)

CHAWENGSAK SONGKRAM 1102

Displacement, tons: 190 full load
Dimensions, feet (metres): 116.5 × 23 × 11.5 (35.5 × 7 × 3.5)
Main machinery: 4 Ikegai diesels; 5400 hp(m) (3.79 MW); 2 shafts
Speed, knots: 32
Complement: 23
Guns: 2 Oerlikon 20 mm.

Comment: Commissioned 13 April 1973.

CHAWENGSAK SONGKRAM   1990, Marine Police

1 ITAL THAI MARINE TYPE (COASTAL PATROL CRAFT)

SRIYANONT 901

Displacement, tons: 52 full load
Dimensions, feet (metres): 90 × 16 × 6.5 (27.4 × 4.9 × 2)
Main machinery: 2 Deutz BA16M816 diesels; 2680 hp(m) (1.97 MW) sustained; 2 shafts
Speed, knots: 23
Complement: 14
Guns: 1 Oerlikon 20 mm. 2—7.62 mm MGs.

Comment: Commissioned 12 June 1986.

SRIYANONT   1990, Marine Police

THAILAND / Royal Thai marine police

3 HALTER TYPE (COASTAL PATROL CRAFT)

PHRAONGKAMROP 807
PICHARNPHOLAKIT 808
RAMINTHRA 809

Displacement, tons: 34 full load
Dimensions, feet (metres): 65 × 17 × 8.3 *(19.8 × 5.2 × 2.5)*
Main machinery: 3 Detroit 12V-71TA diesels; 1020 hp(m) *(761 kW)* sustained; 3 shafts
Speed, knots: 25
Complement: 14
Guns: 1 Oerlikon 20 mm. 2—7.62 mm MGs.

Comment: Delivered by Halter Marine, New Orleans, and all commissioned on 9 March 1969. Aluminium hulls.

PICHARNPHOLAKIT   1990, Marine Police

3 TECHNAUTIC TYPE (COASTAL PATROL CRAFT)

810-812

Displacement, tons: 50 full load
Dimensions, feet (metres): 88.6 × 19.4 × 6.2 *(27 × 5.9 × 1.9)*
Main machinery: 3 Isotta Fraschini diesels; 2500 hp(m) *(1.84 MW)*; 3 hydrojets
Speed, knots: 27
Guns: 1 Oerlikon 20 mm. 2—7.62 mm MGs.

Comment: Delivered by Technautic, Bangkok in 1984.

812   1990, Marine Police

5 ITAL THAI MARINE TYPE (COASTAL PATROL CRAFT)

625-629

Displacement, tons: 42 full load
Dimensions, feet (metres): 64 × 17.5 × 5 *(19.5 × 5.3 × 1.5)*
Main machinery: 2 MAN D2842LE diesels; 1350 hp(m) *(992 kW)* sustained; 2 shafts
Speed, knots: 27
Guns: 1—12.7 mm MG.

Comment: Built in Bangkok 1987-90. Aluminium hulls.

ITAL THAI 625   1990, Marine Police

17 TECHNAUTIC TYPE (COASTAL PATROL CRAFT)

608-624

Displacement, tons: 30 full load
Dimensions, feet (metres): 60 × 16 × 2.9 *(18.3 × 4.9 × 0.9)*
Main machinery: 2 Isotta Fraschini ID 36 SS 8V diesels; 1760 hp(m) *(1.29 MW)* sustained; 2 hydrojets
Speed, knots: 27
Guns: 1—12.7 mm MG.

Comment: Built from 1983 to 1987 in Bangkok.

TECHNAUTIC 614   1990, Marine Police

2 MARSUN TYPE

539-540

Displacement, tons: 30 full load
Dimensions, feet (metres): 57 × 16 × 3 *(17.4 × 4.9 × 0.9)*
Main machinery: 2 Detroit 12V-71TA diesels; 840 hp *(627 kW)* sustained; 2 shafts
Speed, knots: 25
Complement: 8
Guns: 1—12.7 mm MG.

Comment: Built in Thailand. Both commissioned 26 March 1986.

MARSUN 540   1990, Marine Police

26 SUMIDAGAWA TYPE (RIVER PATROL CRAFT)

513-538

Displacement, tons: 18 full load
Dimensions, feet (metres): 54.1 × 12.5 × 2.3 *(16.5 × 3.8 × 0.7)*
Main machinery: 2 Cummins diesels; 800 hp *(597 kW)*; 2 shafts
Speed, knots: 23
Guns: 1—12.7 mm MG.

Comment: First 21 built by Sumidagawa, last five by Captain Co, Thailand 1978-79.

SUMIDAGAWA 530   1990, Marine Police

24 CAMCRAFT TYPE (RIVER PATROL CRAFT)

415-440

Displacement, tons: 13 full load
Dimensions, feet (metres): 40 × 12 × 3.2 *(12.2 × 3.7 × 1)*
Main machinery: 2 Detroit diesels; 540 hp *(403 kW)*; 2 shafts
Speed, knots: 25

Comment: Delivered by Camcraft, Louisiana. Aluminium hulls.

38 RIVER PATROL CRAFT

Displacement, tons: 5 full load
Dimensions, feet (metres): 37 × 11 × 6 *(11.3 × 3.4 × 1.8)*
Speed, knots: 25

Comment: Numbers in the 300 series.

RIVER PATROL CRAFT 339   *1990, Marine Police*

TYPHOON BOATS

Comment: Rigid inflatables acquired from Task Force Boats in 1990-91. Two Johnson outboard motors, 450 hp *(336 kW)*; speed 50 kts light or 40 kts with 12 men embarked.

CAMCRAFT 434   *1990, Marine Police*

TOGO

Senior Officer
Commanding Officer, Navy:
  Commander Lucien Laval

Personnel
(a) 1993: 115
(b) Voluntary service

Base
Lome

Mercantile Marine
Lloyd's Register of Shipping:
  8 vessels of 12 191 tons gross

PATROL FORCES

2 COASTAL PATROL CRAFT

Name	No	Builders	Commissioned
KARA	P 761	Chantiers Navals de l'Esterel, Cannes	1976
MONO	P 762	Chantiers Navals de l'Esterel, Cannes	1976

Displacement, tons: 80 full load
Dimensions, feet (metres): 105 × 19 × 5.3 *(32 × 5.8 × 1.6)*
Main machinery: 2 MTU MB 12V 493 TY60 diesels; 2000 hp(m) *(1.47 MW)* sustained; 2 shafts
Speed, knots: 30. Range, miles: 1500 at 15 kts
Complement: 17 (1 officer)
Missiles: SSM: Aerospatiale SS 12M; wire-guided to 5 km *(3 nm)* subsonic; warhead 30 kg.
Guns: 1 Bofors 40 mm/70 (aft). 1 Oerlikon 20 mm.
Radars: Surface search: Decca 916; I band; range 88 km *(48 nm)*.

Comment: Both craft in good condition.

KARA   *1990*

TONGA

Headquarters' Appointments
Commander Tongan Defence Services:
  Lieutenant Colonel F Tupou
Commanding Officer Maritime Force:
  Lieutenant P Matoto

Base
Touliki Base, Nuku'alofa

Mercantile Marine
Lloyd's Register of Shipping:
  15 vessels of 10 872 tons gross

DELETIONS

1991   *Tufou, Koula*
1992   *Siliva, Fangailifuka, 'Alo-i-talau*

PATROL FORCES

3 PACIFIC FORUM TYPE (LARGE PATROL CRAFT)

Name	No	Builders	Commissioned
NEIAFU	P 201	Australian Shipbuilding Industries	28 Oct 1989
PANGAI	P 202	Australian Shipbuilding Industries	30 June 1990
SAVEA	P 203	Australian Shipbuilding Industries	23 Mar 1991

Displacement, tons: 162 full load
Dimensions, feet (metres): 103.3 × 26.6 × 6.9 *(31.5 × 8.1 × 2.1)*
Main machinery: 2 Caterpillar 3516TA diesels; 2820 hp *(2.1 MW)* sustained; 2 shafts
Speed, knots: 20. Range, miles: 2500 at 12 kts
Complement: 17 (3 officers)
Radars: Surface search: Furuno 1101; I band.

Comment: Part of the Pacific Forum Australia Defence co-operation. First laid down 30 January 1989, second 2 October 1989, third February 1990. Capable of mounting a 20 mm gun or MGs. *Savea* has an oceanographic survey capability.

SAVEA   *10/1991, John Mortimer*

1 LCM

Name	No	Builders	Commissioned
LATE (ex-Australian Army LCM 8 *1057*)	C 315	North Queensland Eng Ltd, Cairns	1 Sep 1982

Displacement, tons: 116 full load
Dimensions, feet (metres): 73.5 × 21 × 3.3 *(22.4 × 6.4 × 1)*
Main machinery: 2 Detroit 12V-71 diesels; 680 hp *(507 kW)* sustained; 2 shafts
Speed, knots: 10. **Range, miles:** 480 at 10 kts
Military lift: 60 tons
Radars: Surface search: Koden MD 305; I band.

Comment: Acquired from the Australian Army.

1 ROYAL YACHT

TITILUPE

Comment: 34 ft *(10.4 m)* long and has a speed of 8 kts. GRP displacement hull. Also used as auxiliary patrol craft.

LATE

1992, Tonga Maritime Force

TRINIDAD AND TOBAGO

COAST GUARD

Headquarters' Appointments

Chief of Defence Staff:
Brigadier Ralph Brown, ED
Commanding Officer, Coast Guard:
Commander Anthony Franklin, HBM, ED

General

On 30 June 1989 all former Police craft were handed over to the Coast Guard and re-named.

Aircraft

The Coast Guard operates a single Cessna 402B for surveillance. This aircraft can be backed by Air Division helicopters when necessary.

Personnel

(a) 1993: 655 (45 officers)
(b) Voluntary service

Bases

Staubles Bay (HQ)
Hart's Cut, Tobago, Port Fortin (all established in 1989)
Piarco (Air station), Cedros

Prefix to Ships' Names

T. T. S.

Mercantile Marine

Lloyd's Register of Shipping:
53 vessels of 25 522 tons gross

DELETIONS

1990 *Mathura*
1991 *Fort Chacon*
1992 *Buccoo Reef*

PATROL FORCES

2 TYPE CG 40 (LARGE PATROL CRAFT)

Name	No	Builders	Commissioned
BARRACUDA	CG 5	Karlskronavarvet	15 June 1980
CASCADURA	CG 6	Karlskronavarvet	15 June 1980

Displacement, tons: 210 full load
Dimensions, feet (metres): 133.2 × 21.9 × 5.2 *(40.6 × 6.7 × 1.6)*
Main machinery: 2 Paxman Valenta 16 CM diesels; 6700 hp *(5 MW)* sustained; 2 shafts
Speed, knots: 30. **Range, miles:** 3000 at 15 kts
Complement: 25
Guns: 1 Bofors 40 mm/70. 1 Oerlikon 20 mm.
Radars: Surface search: Racal Decca 1226; I band.

Comment: Ordered in Sweden mid-1978. Laid down early 1979. Fitted with foam-cannon oil pollution equipment and for oceanographic and hydrographic work. Nine spare berths. The hull is similar to Swedish Spica class but with the bridge amidships. One refitted in 1988, the other in 1989.

MORUGA

1985, Trinidad and Tobago Coast Guard

2 WASP 20 METRE CLASS (COASTAL PATROL CRAFT)

Name	No	Builders	Commissioned
KAIRI (ex-*Sea Bird*)	CG 31	W A Souter, Cowes	Dec 1982
MORIAH (ex-*Sea Dog*)	CG 32	W A Souter, Cowes	Dec 1982

Displacement, tons: 32 full load
Dimensions, feet (metres): 65.8 × 16.5 × 5 *(20.1 × 5 × 1.5)*
Main machinery: 2 GM Stewart and Stevenson diesels; 2400 hp *(1.79 MW)*; 2 shafts
Speed, knots: 30. **Range, miles:** 450 at 30 kts
Complement: 6 (2 officers)
Guns: 2—7.62 mm MGs.
Radars: Navigation: Decca 150; I band.

Comment: Ordered late 1981. Aluminium alloy hull. Transferred from the Police in June 1989.

CASCADURA

1990, Trinidad and Tobago Coast Guard

4 SOUTER WASP 17 METRE CLASS (COASTAL PATROL CRAFT)

Name	No	Builders	Commissioned
PLYMOUTH	CG 27	W A Souter, Cowes	27 Aug 1982
CARONI	CG 28	W A Souter, Cowes	27 Aug 1982
GALEOTA	CG 29	W A Souter, Cowes	27 Aug 1982
MORUGA	CG 30	W A Souter, Cowes	27 Aug 1982

Displacement, tons: 19.3
Dimensions, feet (metres): 55.1 × 13.8 × 4.6 *(16.8 × 4.2 × 1.4)*
Main machinery: 2 GM Stewart and Stevenson 8V-92MTAB diesels; 1470 hp *(1.1 MW)* maximum; 2 shafts
Speed, knots: 32. **Range, miles:** 500 at 18 kts
Complement: 7 (2 officers)
Guns: 1—7.62 mm MG.
Radars: Surface search: Decca 150; I band.

Comment: GRP hulls. There have been reliability problems.

MORIAH

1989, Trinidad and Tobago Coast Guard

Patrol forces / **TRINIDAD AND TOBAGO** 691

1 WASP 17 METRE CLASS (COASTAL PATROL CRAFT)

Name	No	Builders	Commissioned
CEDROS (ex-*Sea Erne*)	CG 35	W A Souter, Cowes	1984

Displacement, tons: 19.3 full load
Dimensions, feet (metres): 55.1 × 13.8 × 4.6 *(16.8 × 4.2 × 1.4)*
Main machinery: 2 GM Stewart and Stevenson 8V-92MTAB diesels; 1470 hp *(1.1 MW)* maximum; 2 shafts
Speed, knots: 25
Complement: 7
Radars: Navigation: Decca 150; I band.

Comment: Transferred from Police in June 1989.

1 COASTAL PATROL CRAFT

Name	No	Builders	Commissioned
CARENAGE (ex-*Sea Dragon*)	CG 37	Watercraft, Shoreham	1980

Displacement, tons: 14.9 full load
Dimensions, feet (metres): 45 × 14.1 × 4 *(13.7 × 4.3 × 1.2)*
Main machinery: 2 GM 8V-92 diesels; 606 hp *(452 kW)* sustained; 2 shafts
Speed, knots: 23.5. **Range, miles:** 360 at 18 kts
Complement: 4
Guns: 2—7.62 mm MGs.

Comment: GRP hull. Transferred from Police in June 1989.

CARENAGE   *1989, Trinidad and Tobago Coast Guard*

CEDROS   *1989, Trinidad and Tobago Coast Guard*

2 BOWEN CLASS (FAST INTERCEPTOR CRAFT)

CG 001   CG 002

Comment: 31 ft fast patrol boats acquired with US funds in May 1991. Capable of 40 kts.

1 SWORD CLASS (COASTAL PATROL CRAFT)

Name	No	Builders	Commissioned
MATELOT (ex-*Sea Skorpion*)	CG 33	Sea Ark Marine	May 1979

Displacement, tons: 15.5 full load
Dimensions, feet (metres): 44.9 × 13.4 × 4.3 *(13.7 × 4.1 × 1.3)*
Main machinery: 2 GM diesels; 850 hp *(634 kW)*; 2 shafts
Speed, knots: 28. **Range, miles:** 500 at 20 kts
Complement: 6
Guns: 1—7.62 mm MG.

Comment: Two transferred from the Police in June 1989, one scrapped in 1990.

CG 001   *1991, Trinidad and Tobago Coast Guard*

8 AUXILIARY VESSELS

NAPARIMA (ex-*CG 26*) A 01   REHAB A 05   RELAY A 08
EL TUCUCHE (ex-*CG 25*) A 02   REDEEM (ex-*Cocrico*) A 06 REVIEW (ex-*Egret*) A 09
REFORM A 04   RECOVER (ex-*Semp*) A 07

Comment: A variety of craft some of which transferred from Police duties in June 1989 and used for Port Services.

MATELOT   *1989, Trinidad and Tobago Coast Guard*

1 SURVEY CRAFT

MERIDAN

Comment: 75 tons displacement craft launched in 1985. Has a complement of five (two officers).

1 COASTAL SUPPORT CRAFT

SPEYSIDE (ex-*Sea Hawk*)   CG 36

Displacement, tons: 12 full load
Dimensions, feet (metres): 36 × 13 × 4 *(10.9 × 3.9 × 1.2)*
Main machinery: 2 GM diesels; 460 hp *(343 kW)*; 2 shafts
Speed, knots: 22. **Range, miles:** 400 at 20 kts

Comment: Built by Tugs and Lighters Ltd, Port of Spain. Transferred from Police in June 1989.

REFORM   *1989, Trinidad and Tobago Coast Guard*

TUNISIA

Headquarters' Appointment	Bases	Personnel	Mercantile Marine
Chief of Naval Staff: Capitaine Chadli Cherif	Sfax, Bizerte, La Goulette, Kelibia	(a) 1993: 4500 officers and men (including 700 conscripts) (b) 1 year's national service	*Lloyd's Register of Shipping:* 77 vessels of 279 914 tons gross

FRIGATE

1 Ex-US SAVAGE CLASS

Name	No	Builders	Laid down	Launched	Commissioned
INKADH (ex-*Président Bourguiba*, ex-USS *Thomas J Gary* DER 326, ex-*DE 326*)	E 7	Consolidated Steel Corporation, Texas	15 June 1943	21 Aug 1943	27 Nov 1943

Displacement, tons: 1200 standard; 1490 full load
Dimensions, feet (metres): 306 × 35 × 14 *(93.3 × 10.7 × 4.3)*
Main machinery: 4 Fairbanks-Morse 38D8-1/8-10 diesels; 7000 hp *(5.2 MW)* sustained; 2 shafts
Speed, knots: 19. **Range, miles:** 12 000 at 11 kts
Complement: 169

Guns: 2—3 in *(76 mm)*/50; 85° elevation; 20 rounds/minute to 12 km *(6.6 nm)*; weight of shell 6 kg.
 2 Oerlikon 20 mm/80; 800 rounds/minute to 2 km.
Torpedoes: 6—324 mm US Mk 32 (2 triple) tubes. Honeywell Mk 44; anti-submarine; active homing to 5.5 km *(3 nm)* at 30 kts; warhead 34 kg.
Fire control: Mk 63 GFCS. Mk 51 Mod 2 GFCS.
Radars: Air search: Westinghouse SPS 29; B/C band; range 457 km *(250 nm)*.
 Surface search: Raytheon SPS 10; G band.
 Fire control: Western Electric Mk 34; I/J band.
Sonars: EDO SQS 29; hull-mounted; active search and attack; medium/high frequency.

Programmes: Completed as Edsall class DE. Converted to Radar Picket Savage class in 1958. Transferred 27 October 1973.
Operational: Used for training but non-operational as a warship and is likely to be replaced by *Salambo* in 1993.

INKADH
7/1989, van Ginderen Collection

LIGHT FORCES

3 COMBATTANTE III M CLASS (FAST ATTACK CRAFT—MISSILE)

Name	No	Builders	Commissioned
LA GALITÉ	501	CMN, Cherbourg	27 Feb 1985
TUNIS	502	CMN, Cherbourg	27 Mar 1985
CARTHAGE	503	CMN, Cherbourg	29 Apr 1985

Displacement, tons: 345 standard; 425 full load
Dimensions, feet (metres): 183.7 × 26.9 × 7.2 *(56 × 8.2 × 2.2)*
Main engines: 4 MTU 20V538 TB93 diesels; 18 740 hp(m) *(13.8 MW)* sustained; 4 shafts
Speed, knots: 38.5. **Range, miles:** 700 at 33 kts; 2800 at 10 kts
Complement: 35

Missiles: SSM: 8 Aerospatiale MM 40 Exocet (2 quad) launchers; inertial cruise; active radar homing to 70 km *(40 nm)* at 0.9 Mach; warhead 165 kg; sea-skimmer.
Guns: 1 OTO Melara 3 in *(76 mm)*/62; 85° elevation; 55-65 rounds/minute to 16 km *(8.7 nm)*; weight of shell 6 kg.
 2 Breda 40 mm/70 (twin); 85° elevation; 300 rounds/minute to 12.5 km *(6.8 nm)*; weight of shell 0.96 kg.
 4 Oerlikon 30 mm/75 (2 twin); 85° elevation; 650 rounds/minute to 10 km *(5.5 nm)*; weight of shell 1 kg or 0.36 kg.
Countermeasures: Decoys: 1 CSEE Dagaie trainable launcher; IR flares and chaff.
 ESM: Radar warning.
Combat data systems: Tavitac action data automation.
Fire control: 2 CSEE Naja optronic directors for 30 mm. Thomson-CSF Vega II for SSM, 76 mm and 40 mm.
Radars: Air/surface search: Thomson-CSF Triton S; G band; range 33 km *(18 nm)* for 2 m² target.
 Fire control: Thomson-CSF Castor II; I/J band; range 31 km *(17 nm)* for 2 m² target.

Programmes: Ordered in 1981.
Operational: One CSEE Sylosat navigation system.

TUNIS
6/1992, van Ginderen Collection

0 + 3 CHINESE HULUDAO CLASS (TYPE 206) (FAST ATTACK CRAFT—PATROL)

Displacement, tons: 180 full load
Dimensions, feet (metres): 147.6 × 21 × 5.6 *(45 × 6.4 × 1.7)*
Main machinery: 3 MWM TBD604BV12 diesels; 5204 hp(m) *(3.82 MW)* sustained; 3 shafts
Speed, knots: 29. **Range, miles:** 1000 at 15 kts
Complement: 24 (6 officers)
Guns: 4 China 14.5 mm Type 82 (2 twin); 85° elevation; 600 rounds/minute to 7 km *(3.8 nm)*; weight of shell 1.42 kg.

Comment: First three of a possible six to be transferred in 1993. Built at Wuxi Shipyard starting in 1988 and is a smaller version of the Pakistan Barkat class. Armament is not confirmed.

HULUDAO
1991, CSSC

2 Ex-CHINESE SHANGHAI II CLASS (FAST ATTACK CRAFT—GUN)

GAFSAH P 305   **AMILCAR** P 306

Displacement, tons: 113 standard; 131 full load
Dimensions, feet (metres): 127.3 × 17.7 × 5.6 *(38.8 × 5.4 × 1.7)*
Main machinery: 4 MTU 8V 331 TC92 diesels; 3540 hp(m) *(2.6 MW)* sustained; 4 shafts
Speed, knots: 30. **Range, miles:** 700 at 16.5 kts
Complement: 34
Guns: 4—37 mm/63 (2 twin). 4—25 mm/80 (2 twin).
Radars: Surface search: Skin Head; I band; range 37 km *(20 nm)*.

Comment: Transferred 2 April 1977. Two others transferred in 1973, since deleted. Engine change completed December 1984 by the Navy at Socomena shipyards, Bizerte.

SHANGHAI II
1984

2 VOSPER THORNYCROFT TYPE (FAST ATTACK CRAFT—PATROL)

Name	No	Builders	Commissioned
TAZARKA	P 205	Vosper Thornycroft	27 Oct 1977
MENZEL BOURGUIBA	P 206	Vosper Thornycroft	27 Oct 1977

Displacement, tons: 125 full load
Dimensions, feet (metres): 103 × 19.5 × 5.5 *(31.4 × 5.9 × 1.7)*
Main machinery: 2 MTU diesels; 4000 hp(m) *(2.94 MW)*; 2 shafts
Speed, knots: 27. **Range, miles:** 1500 at 15 kts
Complement: 24
Guns: 2 Oerlikon 20 mm.
Radars: Surface search: Decca 916; I band; range 88 km *(48 nm)*.

Comment: Ordered 9 September 1975. *Tazarka* laid down 23 March 1976 and launched 19 July 1976.

MENZEL BOURGUIBA *1989*

3 P 48 CLASS (LARGE PATROL CRAFT)

Name	No	Builders	Commissioned
BIZERTE	P 301	SFCN, Villeneuve-la-Garenne	10 July 1970
HORRIA (ex-*Liberté*)	P 302	SFCN, Villeneuve-la-Garenne	Oct 1970
MONASTIR	P 304	SFCN, Villeneuve-la-Garenne	25 Mar 1975

Displacement, tons: 250 full load
Dimensions, feet (metres): 157.5 × 23.3 × 7.5 *(48 × 7.1 × 2.3)*
Main machinery: 2 MTU 16V 652 TB81 diesels; 4600 hp(m) *(3.4 MW)* sustained; 2 shafts
Speed, knots: 20. **Range, miles:** 2000 at 16 kts
Complement: 34 (4 officers)
Missiles: SSM: 8 Aerospatiale SS 12M; wire-guided to 5.5 km *(3 nm)* subsonic; warhead 30 kg.
Guns: 2 Bofors 40 mm/70. 2—12.7 mm MGs.
Radars: Surface search: Thomson-CSF DRBN 31; I band.

Comment: First pair ordered in 1968, third in August 1973.

P 48 class *1972*

4 COASTAL PATROL CRAFT

Name	No	Builders	Commissioned
ISTIKLAL (ex-*VC 11, P 761*)	P 201	Ch Navals de l'Esterel	Apr 1957
JOUMHOURIA	P 202	Ch Navals de l'Esterel	Jan 1961
AL JALA	P 203	Ch Navals de l'Esterel	Nov 1963
REMADA	P 204	Ch Navals de l'Esterel	July 1967

Displacement, tons: 60 standard; 80 full load
Dimensions, feet (metres): 104 × 19 × 5.3 *(31.5 × 5.8 × 1.6)*
Main machinery: 2 MTU MB 12V 493 TY70 diesels; 2200 hp(m) *(1.62 MW)* sustained; 2 shafts
Speed, knots: 30. **Range, miles:** 1500 at 15 kts
Complement: 17 (3 officers)
Guns: 2 Oerlikon 20 mm.

Comment: *Istiklal* transferred from France March 1959. Wooden hulls. Doubtful operational status.

AL JALA *1989*

6 COASTAL PATROL CRAFT

V 101-106

Displacement, tons: 38 full load
Dimensions, feet (metres): 83 × 15.6 × 4.2 *(25 × 4.8 × 1.3)*
Main machinery: 2 Detroit 12V-71TA diesels; 840 hp *(627 kW)* sustained; 2 shafts
Speed, knots: 23. **Range, miles:** 900 at 15 kts
Complement: 11
Guns: 1 Oerlikon 20 mm.

Comment: Built by Chantiers Navals de l'Esterel and commissioned in 1961-63. Two further craft of the same design (*Sabaq el Bahr* T 2 and *Jaouel el Bahr* T 1) but unarmed were transferred to the Fisheries Administration in 1971—same builders. Doubtful operational status.

V 101 *10/1984, van Ginderen Collection*

TRAINING/SURVEY SHIPS

1 Ex-US ROBERT D CONRAD CLASS

Name	No	Builders	Commissioned
N O SALAMBO (ex-*De Stiguer*)	— (ex-T-AGOR 12)	Northwest Iron Works, Portland	28 Feb 1969

Displacement, tons: 1370 full load
Dimensions, feet (metres): 208.9 × 40 × 15.3 *(63.7 × 12.2 × 4.7)*
Main machinery: Diesel-electric; 2 Cummins diesel generators; 1 motor; 1000 hp *(746 kW)*; 1 shaft; bow thruster
Speed, knots: 13. **Range, miles:** 12 000 at 12 kts
Complement: 40
Radars: Navigation: TM 1650/6X; I band.

Comment: Transferred on 23 October 1992. Built as an oceanographic research ship. Special features include a 10 ton boom, and a gas turbine for quiet propulsion up to 6 kts. Probably to be used for training replacing *Inkadh*.

N O SALAMBO (old name) *5/1989, Giorgio Arra*

1 GUESETTE CLASS

Displacement, tons: 8.5 full load
Dimensions, feet (metres): 36.1 × 12.5 × 3.6 *(11 × 3.8 × 1.1)*
Main machinery: 1 Perkins diesel; 1 shaft
Speed, knots: 10
Complement: 6

Comment: French built survey launch acquired in 1992.

COAST GUARD

10 COASTAL PATROL CRAFT

ASSAD BIN FOURAT   +9

Displacement, tons: 32 full load
Dimensions, feet (metres): 67.3 × 15.4 × 4.3 *(20.5 × 4.7 × 1.3)*
Main machinery: 2 diesels; 1000 hp(m) *(735 kW)*; 2 shafts
Speed, knots: 28. **Range, miles:** 500 at 20 kts
Complement: 8
Guns: 1—12.7 mm MG.

Comment: First one built by Socomena, Bizerte with assistance from South Korea, and completed March 1986. Nine more started building in 1991.

4 INSHORE PATROL CRAFT

GABES   KELIBIA
JERBA   TABARK

Displacement, tons: 12
Dimensions, feet (metres): 42.3 × 12.5 × 3 *(12.9 × 3.8 × 0.9)*
Main machinery: 2 diesels; 800 hp(m) *(588 kW)*; 2 shafts
Speed, knots: 38. **Range, miles:** 250 at 15 kts
Complement: 6
Guns: 2—12.7 mm MGs.

Comment: Built by SBCN, Loctudy in 1988-89.

4 Ex-GERMAN KONDOR I CLASS

RAS EL BLAD (ex-*Demmin*)   **RAS AJDIR** (ex-*Malchin*)
RAS MAAMOURA (ex-*Templin*)   **RAS ED DREK** (ex-*Altentreptow*)

Displacement, tons: 377 full load
Dimensions, feet (metres): 170.3 × 23.3 × 7.2 *(51.9 × 7.1 × 2.2)*
Main machinery: 2 Russki/Kolomna 40DM; 4408 hp(m) *(3.24 MW)* sustained; 2 shafts
Speed, knots: 20
Complement: 24
Guns: 2—25 mm (twin) can be carried.
Radars: Navigation: I band.

Comment: Former GDR minesweepers built at Peenewerft, Wolgast in 1969-71 and transferred in May 1992. In German service they were fitted with a twin 25 mm gun and a hull-mounted sonar. Ships of the same class acquired by Malta and Guinea Bissau.

5 Ex-GERMAN BREMSE CLASS

SBEITLA (ex-*G 32*)   **UTIQUE** (ex-*G 37*)   **SELEUTA** (ex-*G 39*)
BULLARIJIA (ex-*G 36*)   **UERKOUANE** (ex-*G 38*)

Displacement, tons: 42 full load
Dimensions, feet (metres): 74.1 × 15.4 × 3.6 *(22.6 × 4.7 × 1.1)*
Main machinery: 2 DM 6VD 18/5 AL-1 diesels; 1020 hp(m) *(750 kW)*; 2 shafts
Speed, knots: 14
Complement: 6
Guns: 2—14.5 mm (twin) MGs can be carried.
Radars: Navigation: TSR 333; I band.

Comment: Built in 1971-72 for the ex-GDR GBK. Transferred in May 1992. Others of the class sold to Malta and Jordan.

RAS MAAMOURA   *6/1992, Diego Quevedo*

UTIQUE (GDR number)   *4/1991, Hartmut Ehlers*

TURKEY

Headquarters' Appointments

Commander-in-Chief, Turkish Naval Forces:
  Admiral Vural Bayazit
Chief of Naval Staff:
  Vice Admiral Salim Dervisoglu

Senior Commands

Fleet Commander (Gölcük):
  Admiral Guven Erkaya
Comsarnorth (Istanbul):
  Vice Admiral Turhan Ozer
Comsarsouth (Izmir):
  Vice Admiral Cetin Ersari
Comiststrait (Istanbul):
  Rear Admiral Kemal Tok
Comcanstrait (Çanakkale):
  Rear Admiral Orhun Ozdemir
Combasetraining (Karamürsel):
  Vice Admiral Ilhami Erdil
Comeageanzone (Izmir):
  Rear Admiral A Yuksel Onel
Commedzone (Mersin):
  Rear Admiral Tanel Uzunay
Comebaseiskenderun (Iskenderun):
  Rear Admiral Aytekin Ersan
Combasegölcük (Gölcük):
  Rear Admiral Erdal Baykal
Comblackzone (Ereğli):
  Rear Admiral Hüseyin Saglam
Comseaguard (Coast Guard) (Ankara):
  Rear Admiral Niyazi Ulusoy
Comsuracgrup (Gölcük):
  Rear Admiral Ekmel Totrakan
Comsabğrup (Gölcük):
  Rear Admiral Dogan Haçipoglu
Comminesgrup (Gölcük):
  Rear Admiral Bulent Alpkaya
Comamphibigrup (Foça-Izmir):
  Rear Admiral Aydin Canel
Comfastgrup (Istanbul):
  Rear Admiral Saim Ergun

Diplomatic Representation

Naval Attaché in Athens:
  Captain Zafer Demirel
Naval Attaché in Bonn:
  Captain Levent Gungor
Naval Attaché in London:
  Captain Ramis Akdemir
Naval Attaché in Moscow:
  Rear Admiral Erol Adayener
Naval Attaché in Paris:
  Commander Reha Erzi
Naval Attaché in Rome:
  Lieutenant Commander Baha Eren
Naval Attaché in Tokyo:
  Captain Feridun Giray
Naval Attaché in Washington:
  Captain Eser Sahan

Personnel

(a) 1993: 59 800 officers and ratings including 900 Naval Air Arm (reserves 70 000)
  (see additional Marines)
(b) 18 months' national service

Bases

Headquarters: Ankara
Main Naval Base: Gölcük
Istanbul, Izmir, Foça, Erdek
Ereğli, Büyükdere, Aksas, Karamürsel (Training), Çanakkale, Iskenderun, Mersin
Dockyards: Gölcük, Taşkizak (Istanbul)

Strength of the Fleet (including Coast Guard)

Type	Active	Building (Planned)
Submarines—Patrol	15	2 (4)
Destroyers	12	—
Frigates	8	4
Fast Attack Craft—Missile	16	2 (6)
Fast Attack Craft—Gun	1	—
Fast Attack Craft—Torpedo	2	—
Large Patrol Craft	23	—
Coastal Patrol Craft	5	—
Minelayer—Large	1	—
Minelayers—Coastal	4	—
Minelayers—Tenders	2	—
Minesweepers/Hunters—Coasta	22	(6)
Minesweepers—Inshore	4	—
Minehunting Tenders	8	—
LSTs	7	1
LCTs	35	2
LCUs	2	—
LCMs	22	—
Survey Vessels	4	—
Depot/Training Ships	5	—
Fleet Replenishment Tanker	1	—
Support Tankers	5	—
Harbour Tankers	3	—
Water Tankers	10	—
Repair Ships	2	—
Transports—Large and small	40	—
Salvage Ships	3	—
Boom Defence Vessels	4	—
Net Vessels	2 (5)	—
Tugs	51	—
Coast Guard	58	(14)

Marines

Total: 4000
One brigade of HQ company, three infantry battalions, one artillery battalion, support units.

Coast Guard (Sahil Güvenlik)

Formed in July 1982 from the naval wing of the Jandarma. Prefix J replaced by SG and paint scheme is very light grey with a diagonal stripe forward. About 1000 officers and men. Some craft are permanently based in North Cyprus.

Mercantile Marine

Lloyd's Register of Shipping:
  880 vessels of 4 186 083 tons gross

DELETIONS

Destroyers

1992   *Muavenet*

Mine Warfare Forces

1990   *Dalgiç 1*

Amphibious Forces

1991   4 EDIC, 8 LCM 8, 7 LCUs
1992   1 LCM 8, 3 LCUs

Service Forces

1992   *Cephane 3, Kanarya, Bekirdere, Gonca, Turgut Alp, Acar*

PENNANT LIST

Submarines

S 333	Ikinci Inönü
S 335	Burakreis
S 336	Muratreis
S 338	Uluçalireis
S 340	Çerbe
S 341	Çanakkale
S 342	Hizirreis
S 343	Pirireis
S 346	Birinci Inönü
S 347	Atilay
S 348	Saldiray
S 349	Batiray
S 350	Yildiray
S 351	Doğanay
S 352	Dolunay
S 353	Preveze
S 354	Sakarya

Destroyers

D 345	Yücetepe
D 346	Alcitepe
D 347	Anittepe
D 348	Savaştepe
D 349	Kiliç Ali Paşa
D 350	Piyale Paşa
D 351	M Fevzi Çakmak
D 352	Gayret
D 353	Adatepe
D 354	Kocatepe
D 356	Zafer

Frigates

D 358	Berk
D 359	Peyk
D 360	Gelibolu
D 361	Gemlik
F 240	Yavuz
F 241	Turgutreis
F 242	Fatih
F 243	Yildirim
F 244	Barbaros
F 245	Orucreis

Mine Warfare Forces (Layers)

N 101	Mordogan
N 104	Mersin
N 105	Mürefte
N 110	Nusret
N 115	Mehmetcik

Mine Warfare Forces (Sweepers)

M 500	Foça
M 501	Fethiye
M 502	Fatsa
M 503	Finike
M 507	Seymen
M 508	Selçuk
M 509	Seyhan
M 510	Samsun
M 511	Sinop
M 512	Surmene
M 513	Seddülbahir
M 514	Silifke
M 515	Saros
M 516	Sigacik
M 517	Sapanca
M 518	Sariyer
M 520	Karamürsel
M 521	Kerempe
M 522	Kilimli
M 523	Kozlu
M 524	Kuşadasi
M 525	Kemer
P 530	Trabzon
P 531	Terme
P 532	Tirebolu
A 601	Tekirdağ
P 312-19	MTB 2-9

Amphibious Forces

L 401	Ertuğrul
L 402	Serdar
NL 120	Bayraktar
NL 121	Sancaktar
NL 122	Çakabey
NL 123	Sarucabey
NL 124	Karamürselbey
NL 125	Osman Gazi

Light Forces

P 111	Sultanhisar
P 112	Demirhisar
P 113	Yarhisar
P 114	Akhisar
P 115	Sivrihisar
P 116	Koçhisar
P 140	Girne
P 145	Caner Gönyeli
P 321	Denizkusu
P 322	Atmaca
P 323	Sahin
P 324	Kartal
P 326	Pelikan
P 327	Albatros
P 328	Şimşek
P 329	Kasirga
P 333	Mizrak
P 335	Kalkan
P 339	Bora
P 340	Dogan
P 341	Marti
P 342	Tayfun
P 343	Volkan
P 344	Rüzgar
P 345	Poyraz
P 346	Gurbet
P 347	Firtina
P 348	Yildiz
P 349	Karayel
P 121-136	AB 21-36
P 141-144	LS 9-12

Service Forces

A 570	Taşkizak
A 571	Yüzbaşi Tolunay
A 572	Albay Hakki Burak
A 573	Binbasi Saadettin Gürçan
A 574	Öncü
A 575	Inebolu
A 576	Derya
A 577	Sokullu Mehmet Paşa
A 579	Cezayirli Gazi Hasan Paşa
A 580	Akar
A 581	Onaran
A 582	Basaran
A 583	Akbas
A 584	Kurtaran
A 585	Akin
A 586	Ülkü
A 587	Gazal
A 588	Umur Bey
A 589	Isin
A 590	Yunus
A 591	Sarköy
A 592	Karadeniz Ereglisi
A 593	Eceabat
A 594	Çubuklu
A 596	Ulubat
A 597	Van
A 598	Söğüt
A 599	Önder
A 600	Kavak
P 301	AG 1 (BDV)
P 304	AG 4 (BDV)
P 305	AG 5 (BDV)
P 306	AG 6 (BDV)

Auxiliaries

All have Y numbers (four figure numbers reduced to three in 1991)

SUBMARINES

Note: In addition to those listed below, three old submarines are moored at Gölcük as accommodation ships.

0 + 2 + 2 (2) TYPE 209 CLASS (TYPE 1400)

Name	No	Builders	Laid down	Launched	Commissioned
PREVEZE	S 353	Gölcük, Kocaeli	12 Sep 1989	1993	1994
SAKARYA	S 354	Gölcük, Kocaeli	1 Feb 1990	1994	1995

Displacement, tons: 1454 surfaced; 1586 dived
Dimensions, feet (metres): 203.4 × 20.3 × 18 *(62 × 6.2 × 5.5)*
Main machinery: Diesel-electric; 4 MTU 12V 396 SB83 diesels; 3800 hp(m) *(2.8 MW)* sustained; 4 alternators; 1 Siemens motor; 4000 hp(m) *(3.38 MW)* sustained; 1 shaft
Speed, knots: 15 surfaced/snorting; 21.5 dived
Range, miles: 8200 at 8 kts surfaced; 400 at 4 kts dived
Complement: 30

Missiles: SSM: McDonnell Douglas Sub Harpoon.
Torpedoes: 8—21 in *(533 mm)* bow tubes. MUSL Tigerfish Mk 24 Mod 2. Total of 14 torpedoes and missiles.
Countermeasures: ESM: Racal Porpoise; radar warning.
Fire control: Atlas Elektronik system.
Radars: Surface search; I band.
Sonars: Atlas Elektronik; passive/active search and attack; medium/high frequency.

Programmes: Order for first two signed in Ankara on 17 November 1987. Being built with HDW assistance. Prefabrication started in March 1989. Tenders for second pair invited in late 1992.
Structure: Diving depth, 280 m *(820 ft)*. Kollmorgen masts.
Operational: Endurance, 50 days.

6 TYPE 209 CLASS (TYPE 1200)

Name	No	Builders	Laid down	Launched	Commissioned
ATILAY	S 347	Howaldtswerke, Kiel	1 Dec 1972	23 Oct 1974	23 July 1975
SALDIRAY	S 348	Howaldtswerke, Kiel	2 Jan 1973	14 Feb 1975	21 Oct 1976
BATIRAY	S 349	Howaldtswerke, Kiel	1 June 1975	24 Oct 1977	20 July 1978
YILDIRAY	S 350	Gölcük, Izmit	1 May 1976	20 July 1979	20 July 1981
DOĞANAY	S 351	Gölcük, Izmit	21 Mar 1980	16 Nov 1983	16 Nov 1985
DOLUNAY	S 352	Gölcük, Izmit	9 Mar 1981	22 July 1988	21 July 1989

Displacement, tons: 980 surfaced; 1185 dived
Dimensions, feet (metres): 200.8 × 20.3 × 17.9 *(61.2 × 6.2 × 5.5)*
Main machinery: Diesel-electric; 4 MTU 12V 493 AZ80 GA31L diesels; 2400 hp(m) *(1.76 MW)* sustained; 4 alternators; 1.7 MW; 1 Siemens motor; 4600 hp(m) *(3.38 MW)* sustained; 1 shaft
Speed, knots: 11 surfaced; 22 dived
Range, miles: 7500 at 8 kts surfaced
Complement: 33 (6 officers)

Torpedoes: 8—21 in *(533 mm)* tubes. 14 AEG SST 4; wire-guided; active/passive homing to 28 km *(15.3 nm)* at 23 kts; 12 km *(6.6 nm)* at 35 kts; warhead 260 kg. Swim-out discharge.
Countermeasures: ESM: Thomson-CSF DR 2000; radar warning.
Fire control: Signaal M8 (S 347-348). Sinbads (remainder).
Radars: Surface search: S 63B; I band.
Sonars: Atlas Elektronik CSU 3; hull-mounted; passive/active search and attack; medium/high frequency.

Programmes: Designed by Ingenieurkontor, Lübeck for construction by Howaldtswerke, Kiel and sale by Ferrostaal, Essen, all acting as a consortium. Last three built in Turkey with assistance given by Howaldtswerke.
Modernisation: Fire control system to be updated starting with the first pair. Possibly by Atlas Elektronik to Preveze class standards.
Structure: A single-hull design with two ballast tanks and forward and after trim tanks. Fitted with snort and remote machinery control. The single screw is slow revving. Very high capacity batteries with GRP lead-acid cells and battery cooling—by Wilh Hagen. Active and passive sonar, sonar detection equipment, sound ranging gear and underwater telephone. Fitted with two periscopes, radar and Omega receiver. Fore-planes retract. Diving depth, 250 m *(820 ft)*.
Operational: Endurance, 50 days.

DOLUNAY   12/1991, Selim San

696 TURKEY / Submarines

2 Ex-US GUPPY III CLASS

Name	No	Builders	Laid down	Launched	Commissioned
ÇANAKKALE (ex-USS *Cobbler* SS 344)	S 341	Electric Boat Co	3 Apr 1944	1 Apr 1945	8 Aug 1945
IKINCI INÖNÜ (ex-USS *Corporal* SS 346)	S 333	Electric Boat Co	27 Apr 1944	10 June 1945	9 Nov 1945

Displacement, tons: 1975 standard; 2450 dived
Dimensions, feet (metres): 326.5 × 27 × 17 *(99.5 × 8.2 × 5.2)*
Main machinery: Diesel-electric; 4 GM 16-278A diesels; 6000 hp *(4.41 MW)*; 2 motors; 5600 hp *(4.2 MW)*; 2 shafts
Speed, knots: 17.5 surfaced; 15 dived
Range, miles: 10 000 at 10 kts surfaced
Complement: 86 (8 officers)

Torpedoes: 10—21 in *(533 mm)* (6 bow, 4 stern) tubes; 24 US Mk 37 torpedoes.
Mines: 40 in lieu of torpedoes.
Radars: Surface search: SS 2A; I band.
Sonars: EDO BQR 2B; hull-mounted; passive search and attack; medium frequency.
Sperry/Raytheon BQG 4; passive ranging.

Programmes: Transferred 21 November 1973.
Operational: Diving probably restricted to periscope depth.

IKINCI INÖNÜ   *10/1987, Selim San*

5 Ex-US GUPPY IIA CLASS

Name	No	Builders	Laid down	Launched	Commissioned
BURAKREIS (ex-USS *Seafox* SS 402)	S 335	Portsmouth Navy Yard	2 Nov 1943	28 Mar 1944	13 June 1944
MURATREIS (ex-USS *Razorback* SS 394)	S 336	Portsmouth Navy Yard	9 Sep 1943	27 Jan 1944	3 Apr 1944
ULUÇALIREIS (ex-USS *Thornback* SS 418)	S 338	Portsmouth Navy Yard	5 Apr 1944	7 July 1944	13 Oct 1944
ÇERBE (ex-USS *Trutta* SS 421)	S 340	Portsmouth Navy Yard	22 Dec 1943	22 May 1944	16 Nov 1944
BIRINCI INÖNÜ (ex-USS *Threadfin* SS 410)	S 346	Portsmouth Navy Yard	18 Mar 1944	26 June 1944	30 Aug 1944

Displacement, tons: 1848 surfaced; 2440 dived
Dimensions, feet (metres): 306 × 27 × 17 *(93.2 × 8.2 × 5.2)*
Main machinery: Diesel-electric; 3 Fairbanks-Morse 38D8-1/8-10 diesels; 4500 hp *(3.4 MW)*; 2 motors; 4800 hp *(3.6 MW)*; 2 shafts
Speed, knots: 17 surfaced; 14-15 dived
Range, miles: 12 000 at 10 kts surfaced
Complement: 82 (8 officers)

Torpedoes: 10—21 in *(533 mm)* (6 bow, 4 stern) tubes; 24 US Mk 37 torpedoes.
Mines: 40 in lieu of torpedoes.
Fire control: Mk 106 TFCS.
Radars: Surface search: SS 2A; I band.
Sonars: EDO BQR 2B; hull-mounted; passive search and attack; medium frequency.
EDO BQS 4; adds active capability to BQR 2B.
Sperry/Raytheon BQG 3; passive ranging.

ÇERBE   *10/1985, Selim San*

Programmes: Transfers: S 335 December 1970, S 336 17 November 1970, S 340 June 1972, S 338 24 August 1973 and S 346 15 August 1973.

Structure: Çerbe is the only Guppy class submarine still in commission to retain the original low bridge which becomes unpleasantly wet during surface passages in heavy seas.
Operational: Diving probably restricted to periscope depth.

ULUÇALIREIS   *6/1990, Selim San*

2 Ex-US TANG CLASS

Name	No	Builders	Laid down	Launched	Commissioned
HIZIRREIS (ex-USS *Gudgeon* SS 567)	S 342	Portsmouth Navy Yard	20 May 1950	11 June 1952	21 Nov 1952
PIRIREIS (ex-USS *Tang* SS 563)	S 343	Portsmouth Navy Yard	18 Apr 1949	Apr 1951	25 Oct 1951

Displacement, tons: 2100 surfaced; 2700 dived
Dimensions, feet (metres): 287 × 27.3 × 19 *(87.4 × 8.3 × 5.8)*
Main machinery: Diesel-electric; 3 Fairbanks-Morse 38D8-1/8-10 diesels; 4500 hp *(3.4 MW)*; 2 motors; 5600 hp *(4.2 MW)*; 2 shafts
Speed, knots: 16 surfaced; 16 dived
Range, miles: 7600 at 15 kts surfaced

Complement: 87 (8 officers)

Torpedoes: 8—21 in *(533 mm)* (6 fwd, 2 aft) tubes. Mixed load including Westinghouse Mk 37 (aft tubes); active/passive homing to 8 km *(4.4 nm)* at 24 kts; warhead 150 kg.
Mines: In lieu of torpedoes.
Fire control: Mk 106 torpedo FCS.
Radars: Surface search: Fairchild BPS 12; I band.

Sonars: EDO BQR 2B; hull-mounted; passive search and attack; medium frequency.
EDO BQS 4; adds active capability to BQR 2B.
Sperry/Raytheon BQG 4; passive ranging.

Programmes: S 343 transferred by lease January 1980—commissioned 21 March 1980. S 342 transferred by lease 30 September 1983. Both finally purchased in June 1987.

PIRIREIS   *7/1989, Selçuk Emre*

DESTROYERS

8 Ex-US GEARING (FRAM I and II) CLASS

Name	No	Builders	Laid down	Launched	Commissioned
YÜCETEPE (ex-USS *Orleck* DD 886)	D 345	Consolidated Steel Corporation	28 Nov 1944	12 May 1945	15 Sep 1945
SAVAŞTEPE (ex-USS *Meredith* DD 890)	D 348	Consolidated Steel Corporation	27 Jan 1945	28 June 1945	31 Dec 1945
KILIÇ ALI PAŞA (ex-USS *Robert H. McCard* DD 822)	D 349	Consolidated Steel Corporation	26 June 1945	9 Nov 1945	26 Oct 1946
PIYALE PAŞA (ex-USS *Fiske* DD 842)	D 350	Bath Iron Works	9 Apr 1945	8 Sep 1945	28 Nov 1945
M FEVZI ÇAKMAK (ex-USS *Charles H Roan* DD 853)	D 351	Bethlehem Steel Corporation, Quincy	27 Sep 1944	15 May 1945	12 Sep 1946
GAYRET (ex-USS *Eversole* DD 789)	D 352	Todd Pacific Shipyard	28 Feb 1945	8 Jan 1946	10 July 1946
ADATEPE (ex-USS *Forrest Royal* DD 872)	D 353	Bethlehem Steel Corporation, Staten Island	6 Aug 1945	17 Jan 1946	28 June 1946
*KOCATEPE (ex-USS *Norris* DD 859)	D 354	Bethlehem Steel Corporation, San Pedro	29 June 1944	25 Feb 1945	9 June 1945

* FRAM II conversion

Displacement, tons: 2425 standard; 3500 full load
Dimensions, feet (metres): 390.5 × 41.2 × 19 *(119 × 12.6 × 5.8)*
Main machinery: 4 Babcock & Wilcox boilers; 600 psi *(43.3 kg/cm sq)*; 850°F *(454°C)*; 2 GE turbines; 60 000 hp *(45 MW)*; 2 shafts
Speed, knots: 32.5. **Range, miles:** 5800 at 15 kts; 2400 at 25 kts
Complement: 275 (15 officers)

Missiles: SSM: McDonnell Douglas Harpoon ❶ (DD 351-352); active radar homing to 130 km *(70 nm)* at 0.9 Mach; warhead 227 kg.
A/S: Honeywell ASROC Mk 112 octuple launcher (FRAM I) ❷; inertial guidance to 1.6-10 km *(1-5.4 nm)*; payload Mk 46 torpedo.
Guns: 4 USN 5 in *(127 mm)*/38 (2 twin) Mk 38 ❸; 85° elevation; 15 rounds/minute to 17 km *(9.3 nm)*; weight of shell 25 kg. In A and Y positions in all except D 348 which has them in A and B.
2 or 4 Bofors 40 mm/56 (1 twin mounting fwd in D 353, 2 twin mountings midships in D 354, none in D 345) ❹; 45° elevation; 160 rounds/minute to 11 km *(5.9 nm)*; weight of shell 0.9 kg.
2 or 4 Oerlikon 35 mm/90 (twin) ❺ (2 twin in D 351-352); 85° elevation; 550 rounds/minute to 6 km *(3.3 nm)*; weight of shell 1.55 kg. In B and X positions in D 351-352; remainder have a single mounting in X position except D 348 which has it in Y and D 345 in B.
Torpedoes: 6—324 mm US Mk 32 (2 triple) tubes ❻. Honeywell Mk 46; anti-submarine; active/passive homing to 11 km *(5.9 nm)* at 40 kts; warhead 44 kg.
A/S mortars: 1 Mk 15 Hedgehog 24-rocket launcher (FRAM II) ❼; range 350 m; warhead 26 kg.
Depth charges: 1 rack (9).
Countermeasures: Decoys: 2 or 4 20-barrelled Breda 105 mm SCLAR Mk 2 or SRBOC chaff launchers.
ESM: WLR-1 and WLR-3; radar warning.
ECM: ULQ 6; jammer.
Fire control: GFCS Mk 37 for 127 mm. 1 or 2 Mk 51 for 40 mm.
Radars: Air search: Lockheed SPS 40 ❽; E/F band; range 320 km *(175 nm)*.
Surface search: Raytheon SPS 10 ❾; G band.
Navigation: Racal Decca; I band.
Fire control: Western Electric Mk 25 ❿; I/J band.
Sonars: Sangamo SQS 23; hull-mounted; active search and attack; medium frequency.

Programmes: D 354 is FRAM II conversion—remainder FRAM I. Transfers to Turkey took place on 27 March 1971 (D 353), 11 July 1973 (D 352) and 21 September 1973 (D 351). D 353 purchased 15 February 1973 and D 354 7 July 1974. D 349 and D 350 leased 5 June 1980, D 348 commissioned in the Turkish Navy on 20 July 1981. D 345 commissioned 30 March 1983. Ex-USS *McKean* DD 784 purchased for spares 25 November 1982. D 345, 349 and 350 purchased outright in June 1987.
Modernisation: Plans to install SAM systems in some of the class have been cancelled but *Kocatepe* may be fitted with Sea Zenith CIWS in due course.
Structure: All were built with a DASH helicopter platform and hangar but only D 345 and D 348 retain a flight deck uncluttered by guns.

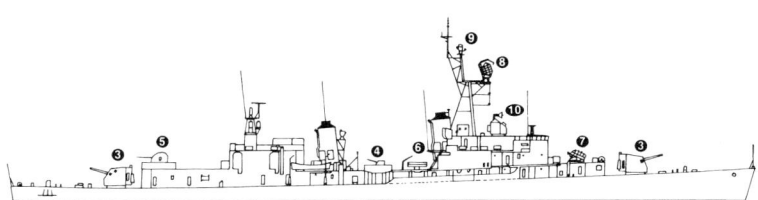
KOCATEPE *(Scale 1 : 1200), Ian Sturton*

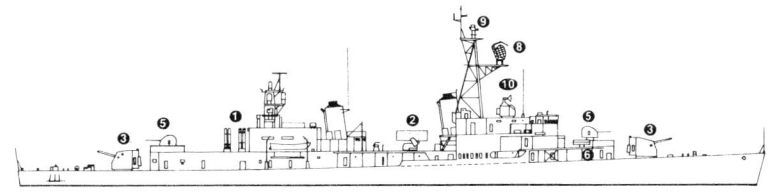
GAYRET *(Scale 1 : 1200), Ian Sturton*

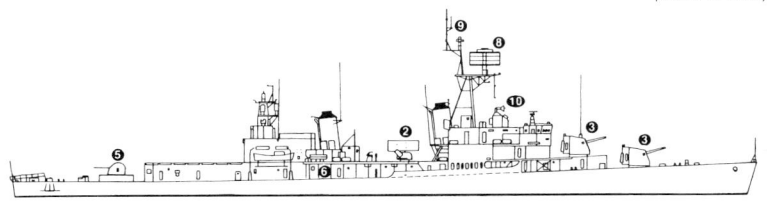
SAVASTEPE *(Scale 1 : 1200), Ian Sturton*

SAVASTEPE *8/1992, C D Yaylali*

GAYRET *10/1991, Selim San*

KOCATEPE *8/1992, C D Yaylali*

KILIÇ ALI PASA *8/1992, C D Yaylali*

698 TURKEY / Destroyers

2 Ex-US CARPENTER (FRAM I) CLASS

Name	No	Builders	Laid down	Launched	Commissioned
ALCITEPE (ex-USS *Robert A Owens* DD 827)	D 346	Bath Iron Works, Maine	29 Oct 1945	15 July 1946	5 Nov 1949
ANITTEPE (ex-USS *Carpenter* DD 825)	D 347	Consolidated Steel, Texas	30 July 1945	30 Dec 1945	15 Dec 1949

Displacement, tons: 2425 standard; 3540 full load
Dimensions, feet (metres): 390.5 × 41 × 20.9 *(119 × 12.5 × 6.4)*
Main machinery: 4 Babcock & Wilcox boilers; 600 psi *(43.3 kg/cm sq)*; 850°F *(454°C)*; 2 GE turbines; 60 000 hp *(45 MW)*; 2 shafts
Speed, knots: 33. **Range, miles:** 6000 at 12 kts
Complement: 275 (15 officers)

Missiles: A/S: Honeywell ASROC Mk 112 octuple launcher ❶; inertial guidance to 1.6-10 km *(1-5.4 nm)*; payload Mk 46 torpedo.
Guns: 2—5 in *(127 mm)*/38 (twin) Mk 38 ❷; 85° elevation; 15 rounds/minute to 17 km *(9.3 nm)*; weight of shell 25 kg.
2—3 in *(76 mm)*/50 twin ❸; 85° elevation; 50 rounds/minute to 12.8 km *(7 nm)*; weight of shell 6 kg.
2 Oerlikon 35 mm/90 (twin) ❹; 85° elevation; 550 rounds/minute to 6 km *(3.3 nm)*; weight of shell 1.55 kg.
Torpedoes: 6—324 mm US Mk 32 (2 triple) tubes ❺. Honeywell Mk 46; anti-submarine; active/passive homing to 11 km *(5.9 nm)* at 40 kts; warhead 44 kg.
Depth charges: 1 rack (9).
Countermeasures: ESM: WLR-1; radar warning.
ECM: ULQ-6; jammer.
Fire control: Mk 56 GFCS. Mk 114 ASW FCS. Mk 1 target designation system.
Radars: Air search: Lockheed SPS 40 ❻; E/F band; range 320 km *(175 nm)*.
Surface search: Raytheon SPS 10 ❼; G band.
Fire control: General Electric Mk 35 ❽; I/J band.
Sonars: Sangamo SQS 23; hull-mounted; active search and attack; medium frequency.

Helicopters: 1 AB 212ASW ❾.

Programmes: D 347 transferred 1981, D 346 in 1982. Both purchased outright in June 1987.
Modernisation: Plans to fit a SAM system have been suspended.
Structure: A Gearing design with an ASW bias. Can handle but not house AB 212ASW helicopters.

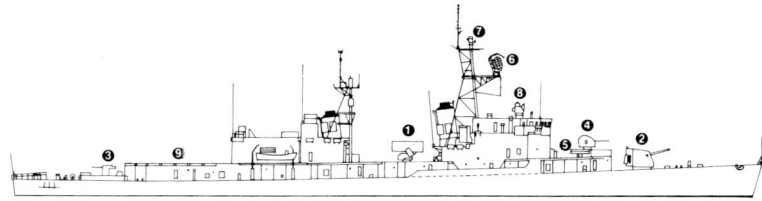

ALCITEPE (Scale 1 : 1200), Ian Sturton

ANITTEPE 1990, Camil Busquets i Vilanova

1 Ex-US ALLEN M SUMNER (FRAM II) CLASS

Name	No	Builders	Laid down	Launched	Commissioned
ZAFER (ex-USS *Hugh Purvis* DD 709)	D 356	Federal S B and D D Co	23 May 1944	17 Dec 1944	1 Mar 1945

Displacement, tons: 2200 standard; 3320 full load
Dimensions, feet (metres): 376.5 × 40.9 × 19 *(114.8 × 12.5 × 5.8)*
Main machinery: 4 Babcock & Wilcox boilers; 600 psi *(43.3 kg/cm sq)*; 850°F *(454°C)*; 2 GE turbines; 60 000 hp *(45 MW)*; 2 shafts
Speed, knots: 34. **Range, miles:** 4600 at 15 kts
Complement: 275 (15 officers)

Guns: 6 USN 5 in *(127 mm)*/38 (3 twin) Mk 38 ❶; 85° elevation; 15 rounds/minute to 17 km *(9.3 nm)*; weight of shell 25 kg.
4 Bofors 40 mm/56 (2 twin) ❷; 45° elevation; 160 rounds/minute to 11 km *(5.9 nm)*; weight of shell 0.9 kg.
2 Oerlikon 35 mm/90 (twin) ❸; 85° elevation; 550 rounds/minute to 6 km *(3.3 nm)*; weight of shell 1.55 kg.
Torpedoes: 6—324 mm US Mk 32 (2 triple) tubes ❹. Honeywell Mk 46; anti-submarine; active/passive homing to 11 km *(5.9 nm)* at 40 kts; warhead 44 kg.
A/S mortars: 2 Mk 15 Hedgehog 24-rocket launchers ❺; range 350 m; warhead 26 kg.
Depth charges: 1 rack (9).
Countermeasures: Decoys: 2 multi-barrelled chaff launchers.
ESM: WLR 1; radar warning. ECM: ULQ 6; jammer.
Fire control: Mk 37 GFCS for 127 mm. 2 Mk 51 GFCS for 40 mm.
Radars: Air search: Westinghouse SPS 37 ❻; B/C band; range 556 km *(300 nm)*.
Surface search: Raytheon SPS 10 ❼; G band.
Fire control: Western Electric Mk 25 ❽; I/J band.
Sonars: Sangamo SQS 29 series; hull-mounted; active search and attack; high frequency.

Programmes: Allen M Sumner class of modified FRAM II having been used as a US Navy trials ship for planar passive sonar. Purchased 15 February 1973.
Structure: 35 mm gun mounting on former helicopter platform. There is an extra deckhouse in X position.

ZAFER (Scale 1 : 900), Ian Sturton

ZAFER 7/1992, C D Yaylali

FRIGATES

Note: In late 1992 the US Navy offered to lease three Knox class frigates, *T C Hart* (FF 1092), *Capadanno* (FF 1093) and *Reasoner* (FF 1063), and recommended a fourth *Elmer Montgomery* (FF 1082) be transferred on a grant basis under the Foreign Assistance Act. The latter ship is probably to replace the destroyer *Muavenet* taken out of service after being damaged by the accidental firing of a Sea Sparrow missile from the USS *Saratoga*. If the transfers go ahead the first ship is expected to recommission after refit sometime in 1994.

4 YAVUZ CLASS (MEKO 200 TYPE)

Name	No	Builders	Laid down	Launched	Commissioned
YAVUZ	F 240	Blohm & Voss, Hamburg	30 May 1985	7 Nov 1985	17 July 1987
TURGUTREIS (ex-*Turgut*)	F 241	Howaldtswerke, Kiel	20 May 1985	30 May 1986	4 Feb 1988
FATIH	F 242	Gölcük, Izmit	1 Jan 1986	24 Apr 1987	22 July 1988
YILDIRIM	F 243	Gölcük, Izmit	24 Apr 1987	22 July 1988	21 July 1989

Displacement, tons: 2500 standard; 2784 full load
Dimensions, feet (metres): 362.4 × 46.6 × 13.5 *(110.5 × 14.2 × 4.1)*
Main machinery: CODAD; 4 MTU 20V 1163 TB93 diesels; 33 300 hp(m) *(24.5 MW)* sustained; 2 shafts; cp props
Speed, knots: 27. **Range, miles:** 4100 at 18 kts
Complement: 180 (24 officers)

Missiles: SSM: 8 McDonnell Douglas Harpoon (2 quad) launchers ❶; active radar homing to 130 km *(70 nm)* at 0.9 Mach; warhead 227 kg.
SAM: Raytheon Sea Sparrow Mk 29 octuple launcher ❷; 24 Selenia Elsag Aspide; semi-active radar homing to 13 km *(7 nm)* at 2.5 Mach; warhead 39 kg.
Guns: 1 FMC 5 in *(127 mm)*/54 Mk 45 Mod 1 ❸; 65° elevation; 20 rounds/minute to 23 km *(12.6 nm)* anti-surface; 15 km *(8.2 nm)* anti-aircraft; weight of shell 32 kg.
3 Oerlikon-Contraves 25 mm Sea Zenith ❹; 4 barrels per mounting; 127° elevation; 3400 rounds/minute combined to 2 km.
Torpedoes: 6—324 mm Mk 32 (2 triple) tubes ❺. Honeywell Mk 46; anti-submarine; active/passive homing to 11 km *(5.9 nm)* at 40 kts; warhead 44 kg.
Countermeasures: Decoys: 2 Loral Hycor 6-tubed fixed Mk 36 Mod 1 SRBOC ❻; IR flares and chaff to 4 km *(2.2 nm)*.
Nixie SLQ 25; towed torpedo decoy.
ESM/ECM: Signaal Rapids/Ramses; intercept and jammer.
Combat data systems: Signaal STACOS-TU; action data automation; Link 11. WSC 3V(7) SATCOMs.
Fire control: 2 Siemens Albis optronic directors.
Radars: Air search: Signaal DA 08 ❼; F band.
Air/surface search: Plessey AWS 6 Dolphin ❽; G band.
Fire control: Signaal STIR ❾; I/J/K band (for SAM); range 140 km *(76 nm)* for 1 m² target.
Signaal WM 25 ❿; I/J band (for SSM and 127 mm); range 46 km *(25 nm)*.
Two Contraves Seaguard ⓫; I/J band (for 25 mm).
Tacan: URN 25. IFF Mk XII.
Sonars: Raytheon SQS 56 (DE 1160); hull-mounted; active search and attack; medium frequency.

Helicopters: 1 AB 212ASW ⓬.

YAVUZ *(Scale 1 : 900), Ian Sturton*

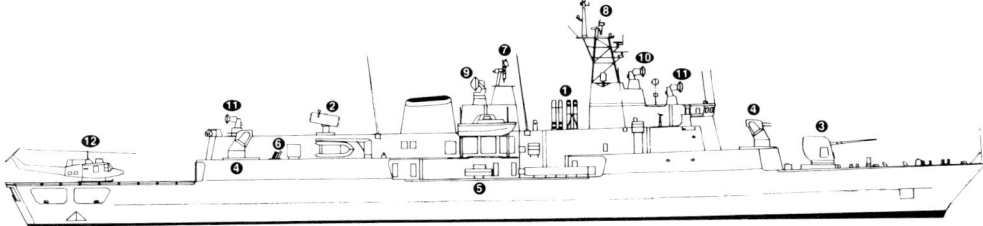

TURGUTREIS *6/1992, Giorgio Ghiglione*

Programmes: Ordered 29 December 1982 with builders and Thyssen Rheinstahl Technik of Dusseldorf. Meko 200 type similar to Portuguese frigates. *Turgutreis* was renamed on 14 February 1988. A second batch of two ships are sufficiently different to merit a separate entry.
Operational: Helicopter has Sea Skua anti-ship missiles.

0 + 4 BARBAROS CLASS (MODIFIED MEKO 200 TYPE)

Name	No	Builders	Laid down	Launched	Commissioned
BARBAROS	F 244	Blohm & Voss, Hamburg	18 Mar 1993	May 1994	Mar 1995
ORUCREIS	F 245	Gölcük, Kocaeli	Sep 1993	Nov 1994	Mar 1996
—	F 246	Blohm & Voss, Hamburg	1994	1996	1997
—	F 247	Gölcük, Kocaeli	1994	1997	1998

Displacement, tons: 3350 full load
Dimensions, feet (metres): 383.5 × 48.6 × 14.1 *(116.9 × 14.8 × 4.3)*
Main machinery: CODOG; 2 GE LM 2500 gas turbines; 60 000 hp *(44.76 MW)* sustained; 2 MTU 16V 1163 TB83 diesels; 11 780 hp(m) *(8.67 MW)* sustained; 2 shafts; cp props
Speed, knots: 32. **Range, miles:** 4100 at 18 kts
Complement: 180 (24 officers)

Missiles: SSM: 8 McDonnell Douglas Harpoon (2 quad) launchers ❶; active radar homing to 130 km *(70 nm)* at 0.9 Mach; warhead 227 kg.
SAM: Raytheon Sea Sparrow Mk 29 octuple launcher ❷; 24 Selenia Elsag Aspide; semi-active radar homing to 13 km *(7 nm)* at 2.5 Mach; warhead 39 kg. To be fitted for but not with VLS Mk 41 in F 244 and 245; to be fitted on build in F 246 and F 247.
Guns: 1 FMC 5 in *(127 mm)*/54 Mk 45 Mod 2 ❸; 65° elevation; 20 rounds/minute to 23 km *(12.6 nm)* anti-surface; 15 km *(8.2 nm)* anti-aircraft; weight of shell 32 kg.
3 Oerlikon-Contraves 25 mm Sea Zenith ❹; 4 barrels per mounting; 127° elevation; 3400 rounds/minute combined to 2 km.
Torpedoes: 6—324 mm Mk 32 (2 triple) tubes ❺. Honeywell Mk 46; anti-submarine; active/passive homing to 11 km *(5.9 nm)* at 40 kts; warhead 44 kg.
Countermeasures: Decoys: 2 Loral Hycor 6-tubed fixed Mk 36 Mod 1 SRBOC ❻; IR flares and chaff to 4 km *(2.2 nm)*.
Nixie SLQ 25; towed torpedo decoy.
ESM/ECM: Racal Cutlass/Cygnus; intercept and jammer.
Combat data systems: Thomson-CSF/Signaal TACTICOS; Link 11. WSC 3V(7) SATCOMs.
Fire control: 2 Siemens Albis optronic directors.
Radars: Air search: Siemens/Plessey AWS 9 ❼; 3D; E/F band.
Air/surface search: Plessey AWS 6 Dolphin ❽; G band.
Fire control: Signaal STIR ❾; I/J/K band (for SAM); range 140 km *(76 nm)* for 1 m² target.
Contraves TMX ❿; I/J band (for SSM and 127 mm).
Two Contraves Seaguard ⓫; I/J band (for 25 mm).
Tacan: URN 25. IFF Mk XII.
Sonars: Raytheon SQS 56 (DE 1160); hull-mounted; active search and attack; medium frequency.

Helicopters: 1 AB 212ASW ⓬.

Programmes: First pair ordered 19 January 1990, second pair 14 December 1992. Programme started 5 November 1991 with construction commencing in June 1992 in Germany and December 1992 in Turkey.

BARBAROS *(Scale 1 : 900), Ian Sturton*

BARBAROS (artist's impression) *1991, Blohm & Voss*

Structure: An improvement on the Yavuz class. Mk 29 Sea Sparrow launchers will still be fitted in the first two, while the second pair will have Mk 41 VLS, which will then be retrofitted in the first two in due course. The ships will be longer and have CODOG propulsion for a higher top speed. Other differences include a full command system, improved radars, better NBCD and air-conditioning.
Operational: Helicopter has Sea Skua anti-ship missiles. The first pair will probably be used as Flagships.

700 TURKEY / Frigates

2 KÖLN CLASS

Name	No	Builders	Laid down	Launched	Commissioned
GELIBOLU (ex-*Gazi Osman Pasa*) (ex-*Karlsruhe* F 223)	D 360	H C Stulcken Sohn, Hamburg	15 Dec 1958	24 Oct 1959	15 Dec 1962
GEMLIK (ex-*Emden* F 221)	D 361	H C Stulcken Sohn, Hamburg	15 Apr 1958	21 Mar 1959	24 Oct 1961

Displacement, tons: 2100 standard; 2700 full load
Dimensions, feet (metres): 360.5 × 36.1 × 16.7 (sonar) *(109.9 × 11 × 5.1)*
Main machinery: CODAG; 2 Brown Boveri gas turbines; 24 000 hp(m) *(17.7 MW)*; 4 MAN 16-cyl diesels; 12 000 hp(m) *(8.8 MW)*; 2 shafts; cp props
Speed, knots: 28; 18 diesels. **Range, miles:** 920 at 28 kts; 3000 at 18 kts
Complement: 210 (17 officers)

Guns: 2 Creusot Loire 3.9 in *(100 mm)*/55 Mod 53 ❶; 80° elevation; 60-80 rounds/minute to 17 km *(9.3 nm)*; weight of shell 13.5 kg.
6 Bofors 40 mm/70 (2 twin ❷, 2 single ❸); 85° elevation to 12 km *(6.6 nm)*; weight of shell 0.96 kg.
Torpedoes: 4—21 in *(533 mm)* tubes ❹; anti-submarine.
A/S mortars: 2 Bofors 375 mm 4-tubed trainable ❺; range 1600 m or 3600 m depending on weapon; 72 carried.
Depth charges: 2 racks (12).
Mines: Can carry 80.
Countermeasures: Decoys: 2 multi-barrelled chaff launchers.
ESM: Radar intercept.
Radars: Air/surface search: Signaal DA 08 ❻; F band; range 204 km *(110 nm)* for 2 m² target.
Navigation: Kelvin Hughes; I band.
Fire control: Two Signaal M 44 ❼; I/J band (for 100 mm).
Signaal M 45 ❽; I/J band (for 40 mm).
Sonars: PAE/CWE; hull-mounted; active search and attack; high/medium frequency.

Programmes: First two transferred by West German Navy. *Gelibolu* commissioned 28 March 1983; *Gemlik*, 23 September 1983. The last two of this class, ex-FGN *Lübeck* and *Braunschweig* were also bought in December 1988 and June 1989 respectively to be used to provide spares for the other two.
Operational: An engine fire in *Gemlik* in 1989 led to speculation that she might be replaced by one of the others, but this did not happen.

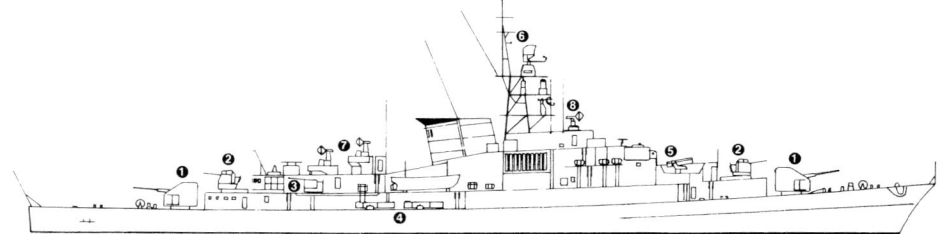
GELIBOLU (Scale 1 : 1200), Ian Sturton

GELIBOLU 10/1992, C D Yaylali

2 BERK CLASS

Name	No	Builders	Laid down	Launched	Commissioned
BERK	D 358	Gölcük Naval Yard	9 Mar 1967	25 June 1971	12 July 1972
PEYK	D 359	Gölcük Naval Yard	18 Jan 1968	7 June 1972	24 July 1975

Displacement, tons: 1450 standard; 1950 full load
Dimensions, feet (metres): 311.7 × 38.7 × 18.1 *(95 × 11.8 × 5.5)*
Main machinery: 4 Fiat-Tosi Type 3-016-RSS diesels; 24 000 hp(m) *(17.7 MW)*; 1 shaft
Speed, knots: 25

Guns: 4 USN 3 in *(76 mm)*/50 (2 twin) ❶; 85° elevation; 50 rounds/minute to 12.8 km *(7 nm)*; weight of shell 6 kg.
Torpedoes: 6—324 mm US Mk 32 (2 triple) tubes ❷. Honeywell Mk 46; anti-submarine; active/passive homing to 11 km *(5.9 nm)* at 40 kts; warhead 44 kg.
A/S mortars: 2 Mk 11 Hedgehog 24-rocket launchers ❸; range 350 m; warhead 26 kg.
Depth charges: 1 rack.
Countermeasures: ESM: WLR 1; radar warning.
Fire control: 2 Mk 63 GFCS.
Radars: Air search: Lockheed SPS 40 ❹; E/F band; range 320 km *(175 nm)*.
Surface search: Raytheon SPS 10 ❺; G band.
Navigation: Racal Decca; I band.
Fire control: Two Western Electric Mk 34 ❻; I/J band (for guns).
Sonars: Sangamo SQS 29/31 series; hull-mounted; active search and attack; high frequency.

Helicopters: Platform only for AB 212ASW ❼.

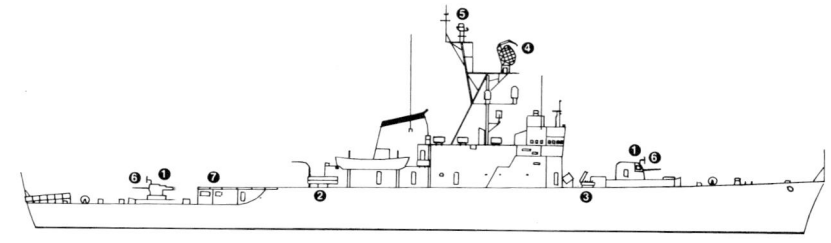
BERK (Scale 1 : 900), Ian Sturton

Programmes: First major warships built in Turkey. Both are named after famous ships of the Ottoman Navy.
Structure: Of modified US Claud Jones design (now Indonesian Samadikun class).

BERK 1/1989, Hartmut Ehlers

SHIPBORNE AIRCRAFT

Numbers/Type: 12 Agusta AB 212ASW.
Operational speed: 106 kts *(196 km/h).*
Service ceiling: 14 200 ft *(4330 m).*
Range: 230 nm *(426 km).*
Role/Weapon systems: ASV/ASW helicopter with recently updated systems. Sensors: Ferranti Sea Spray Mk 3 radar, ECM/ESM, MAD, Bendix ASQ-18 dipping sonar. Weapons: ASW; 2 × Mk 46 or 244/S torpedoes. AVS; 2 × Sea Skua missiles.

AB 212 *1988, Turkish Navy*

LAND-BASED MARITIME AIRCRAFT

Note: The plan is to acquire P3 Orion aircraft from the US in 1993/94.

Numbers/Type: 8/15/18 Grumman S-2A/2E/2F Tracker.
Operational speed: 130 kts *(241 km/h).*
Service ceiling: 2500 ft *(7620 m).*
Range: 1350 nm *(2500 km).*
Role/Weapon systems: Air Force manned for ASW and MR operations in Black and Mediterranean Seas; 18 updated in past but in need of replacement. Sensors: Search radar, ESM, MAD. Weapons: ASW; 4 × Mk 46 torpedoes, depth bombs or mines. ASV; 6 × 127 mm rockets.

TRACKER *1991*

LIGHT FORCES

0 + 2 + 3 (3) YILDIZ CLASS (FAST ATTACK CRAFT—MISSILE)

Name	No	Builders	Commissioned
YILDIZ	P 348	Taskizak Yard, Istanbul	1994
KARAYEL	P 349	Taskizak Yard, Istanbul	1995

Displacement, tons: 436 full load
Dimensions, feet (metres): 190.6 × 25 × 8.8 *(58.1 × 7.6 × 2.7)*
Main machinery: 4 MTU 16V 956 TB92 diesels; 17 700 hp(m) *(13 MW)* sustained; 4 shafts
Speed, knots: 38. **Range, miles:** 1050 at 30 kts
Complement: 45 (6 officers)

Missiles: SSM: 8 McDonnell Douglas Harpoon (2 quad) launchers; active radar homing to 130 km *(70 nm)* at 0.9 Mach; warhead 227 kg.
Guns: 1 OTO Melara 3 in *(76 mm)*/62 compact; 85° elevation; 85 rounds/minute to 16 km *(8.7 nm)* anti-surface; 12 km *(6.6 nm)* anti-aircraft; weight of shell 6 kg.
2 Oerlikon 35 mm/90 (twin); 85° elevation; 550 rounds/minute to 6 km *(3.3 nm)*; weight of shell 1.55 kg.
Countermeasures: Decoys: 2 SRBOC chaff launchers.
ESM/ECM: Racal Cutlass.
Combat data systems: Signaal/Thomson-CSF TACTICOS.
Fire control: LIOD optronic director; Vesta helo data link.
Radars: Surface search: Siemens Plessey AW 6 Dolphin; G band.
Fire control: Oerlikon/Contraves TMX; I/J band.

Programmes: First pair ordered in June 1991. Three more authorised in early 1993, to be ordered later in the year.
Structure: Dogan class hull with much improved weapon systems.

YILDIZ (model) *1991, C D Yaylali*

8 DOGAN CLASS (FAST ATTACK CRAFT—MISSILE)

Name	No	Builders	Commissioned
DOĞAN	P 340	Lürssen, Vegesack	15 June 1977
MARTI	P 341	Taşkizak Yard, Istanbul	28 July 1978
TAYFUN	P 342	Taşkizak Yard, Istanbul	19 July 1979
VOLKAN	P 343	Taşkizak Yard, Istanbul	25 July 1980
RÜZGAR	P 344	Taşkizak Yard, Istanbul	17 Dec 1984
POYRAZ	P 345	Taşkizak Yard, Istanbul	7 Feb 1986
GURBET	P 346	Taşkizak Yard, Istanbul	22 July 1988
FIRTINA	P 347	Taşkizak Yard, Istanbul	23 Oct 1988

Displacement, tons: 436 full load
Dimensions, feet (metres): 190.6 × 25 × 8.8 *(58.1 × 7.6 × 2.7)*
Main machinery: 4 MTU 16V 956 TB92 diesels; 17 700 hp(m) *(13 MW)* sustained; 4 shafts
Speed, knots: 38. **Range, miles:** 1050 at 30 kts
Complement: 38 (5 officers)

Missiles: SSM: 8 McDonnell Douglas Harpoon (2 quad) launchers; active radar homing to 130 km *(70 nm)* at 0.9 Mach; warhead 227 kg.
Guns: 1 OTO Melara 3 in *(76 mm)*/62 compact; 85° elevation; 85 rounds/minute to 16 km *(8.7 nm)* anti-surface; 12 km *(6.6 nm)* anti-aircraft; weight of shell 6 kg.
2 Oerlikon 35 mm/90 (twin); 85° elevation; 550 rounds/minute to 6 km *(3.3 nm)*; weight of shell 1.55 kg.
Countermeasures: Decoys: 2 multi-barrelled chaff launchers.
ESM: MEL Susie; radar warning.
Radars: Surface search: Racal Decca 1226; I band.
Fire control: Signaal WM 28/41; I/J band; range 46 km *(25 nm).*

Programmes: First ordered 3 August 1973 to a Lürssen FPB 57 design. Successor class being built using the same hull and propulsion.
Structure: Aluminium superstructure; steel hulls.

POYRAZ *6/1992, Selim San*

8 KARTAL CLASS (FAST ATTACK CRAFT—MISSILE)

Name	No	Builders	Commissioned
DENIZKUSU	P 321 (ex-*P 336*)	Lürssen, Vegesack	1967
ATMACA	P 322 (ex-*P 335*)	Lürssen, Vegesack	1967
SAHIN	P 323 (ex-*P 334*)	Lürssen, Vegesack	1967
KARTAL	P 324 (ex-*P 333*)	Lürssen, Vegesack	1967
PELIKAN	P 326	Lürssen, Vegesack	1968
ALBATROS	P 327 (ex-*P 325*)	Lürssen, Vegesack	1968
ŞIMŞEK	P 328 (ex-*P 332*)	Lürssen, Vegesack	1968
KASIRGA	P 329 (ex-*P 338*)	Lürssen, Vegesack	1967

Displacement, tons: 160 standard; 190 full load
Dimensions, feet (metres): 139.4 × 23 × 7.9 *(42.5 × 7 × 2.4)*
Main machinery: 4 MTU MD 16V 538 TB90 diesels; 12 000 hp(m) *(8.82 MW)* sustained; 4 shafts
Speed, knots: 42. **Range, miles:** 500 at 40 kts
Complement: 39

Missiles: SSM: 2 or 4 Kongsberg Penguin Mk 2; IR homing to 27 km *(14.6 nm)* at 0.8 Mach; warhead 120 kg.
Guns: 2 Bofors 40 mm/70; 90° elevation; 300 rounds/minute to 12 km *(6.6 nm)*; weight of shell 0.96 kg.
Torpedoes: 2—21 in *(533 mm)* tubes; anti-surface.
Mines: Can carry 4.
Radars: Surface search: Racal Decca 1226; I band.

Structure: Similar design to the Jaguar class.
Operational: *Meltem* sunk in collision with Soviet naval training ship *Khasan* in Bosphorus in 1985. Subsequently salvaged but beyond repair.

ALBATROS *1/1989, Hartmut Ehlers*

702 TURKEY / Light forces

2 Ex-GERMAN JAGUAR CLASS (FAST ATTACK CRAFT—TORPEDO)

Name	No	Builders	Commissioned
MIZRAK (ex-*Häher* P 6087)	P 333	Lürssen, Vegesack	1962
KALKAN (ex-*Wolf* P 6062)	P 335	Lürssen, Vegesack	1959

Displacement, tons: 160 standard; 190 full load
Dimensions, feet (metres): 139.4 × 23 × 7.9 *(42.5 × 7 × 2.4)*
Main machinery: 4 MTU 16V 538 TB90 diesels; 12 000 hp *(8.82 MW)* sustained; 4 shafts
Speed, knots: 42. **Range, miles:** 500 at 40 kts
Complement: 39
Guns: 2 Bofors 40 mm/70; 90° elevation; 300 rounds/minute to 12 km *(6.6 nm)*; weight of shell 0.96 kg.
Torpedoes: 4—21 in *(533 mm)* tubes (2 tubes can be removed to embark 4 mines).
Mines: Up to 4.

Comment: In late 1975-early 1976 seven Jaguar class were transferred by West Germany to Turkey. In addition three more were transferred for spare parts. Two deleted 1982, one in 1987 and two in 1988.

MIZRAK *1/1989, Hartmut Ehlers*

1 GIRNE CLASS (FAST ATTACK CRAFT—GUN)

Name	No	Builders	Commissioned
GIRNE	P 140	Taşkizak Naval Yard	30 July 1976

Displacement, tons: 341 standard; 399 full load
Dimensions, feet (metres): 190.6 × 24.9 × 9.2 *(58.1 × 7.6 × 2.8)*
Main machinery: 2 MTU 16V 956 SB90 diesels; 8000 hp(m) *(5.9 MW)* sustained; 2 shafts
Speed, knots: 36. **Range, miles:** 4200 at 16 kts
Complement: 30 (3 officers)
Guns: 2 Bofors 40 mm/70. 2 Oerlikon 20 mm.
A/S mortars: 2 Mk 20 Mousetrap 4-rocket launchers; range 200 m; warhead 50 kg.
Depth charges: 2 projectors; 2 racks.
Fire control: CSEE Naja optronic director.
Radars: Surface search: Racal Decca; I band.
Sonars: MS 25; hull-mounted; active attack; high frequency.

Comment: Unsuccessful prototype of an ASW patrol boat on a Lürssen 57 hull.

GIRNE *1988, Turkish Navy*

1 Ex-US ASHEVILLE CLASS (LARGE PATROL CRAFT)

Name	No	Builders	Commissioned
BORA (ex-USS *Surprise* PG 97)	P 339	Petersons, Wisconsin	17 Oct 1969

Displacement, tons: 225 standard; 245 full load
Dimensions, feet (metres): 164.5 × 23.8 × 9.5 *(50.1 × 7.3 × 2.9)*
Main machinery: CODAG; 1 GE LM 1500 gas turbine; 13 300 hp *(9.92 MW)*; 2 Cummins VT12-875M diesels; 1450 hp *(1.08 MW)*; 2 shafts
Speed, knots: 40 gas; 16 diesels. **Range, miles:** 320 at 38 kts
Complement: 25
Guns: 1 USN 3 in *(76 mm)*/50 Mk 34; 85° elevation; 50 rounds/minute to 12.8 km *(7 nm)*; weight of shell 6 kg.
1 Bofors 40 mm/56 Mk 10. 4—12.7 mm (2 twin) MGs.
Fire control: Mk 63 GFCS.
Radars: Surface search: Sperry SPS 53; I/J band.
Fire control: Western Electric SPG 50; I/J band.

Comment: This vessel belongs to the largest Patrol Type built by the US Navy since the Second World War and the first of that Navy to have gas turbines. Transferred to Turkey on 28 February 1973 on loan and purchased outright in June 1987.

BORA *8/1988, Selçuk Emre*

6 Ex-US PC 1638 CLASS (LARGE PATROL CRAFT)

Name	No	Builders	Commissioned
SULTANHISAR (ex-*PC 1638*)	P 111	Gunderson Bros Engineering Co, Portland, Oregon	May 1964
DEMIRHISAR (ex-*PC 1639*)	P 112	Gunderson Bros Engineering Co, Portland, Oregon	Apr 1965
YARHISAR (ex-*PC 1640*)	P 113	Gunderson Bros Engineering Co, Portland, Oregon	Sep 1964
AKHISAR (ex-*PC 1641*)	P 114	Gunderson Bros Engineering Co, Portland, Oregon	Dec 1964
SIVRIHISAR (ex-*PC 1642*)	P 115	Gunderson Bros Engineering Co, Portland, Oregon	June 1965
KOÇHISAR (ex-*PC 1643*)	P 116	Gölcük Dockyard, Turkey	July 1965

Displacement, tons: 325 standard; 477 full load
Dimensions, feet (metres): 173.7 × 23 × 10.2 *(53 × 7 × 3.1)*
Main machinery: 2 Fairbanks-Morse diesels; 2800 hp *(2.09 MW)*; 2 shafts
Speed, knots: 19. **Range, miles:** 6000 at 10 kts
Complement: 65 (5 officers)
Guns: 1 Bofors 40 mm/60. 4 Oerlikon 20 mm (2 twin).
A/S mortars: 1 Mk 15 trainable Hedgehog 24-rocket launcher; range 350 m; warhead 26 kg.
Depth charges: 4 projectors; 1 rack (9).
Radars: Surface search: Decca 707; I band.
Sonars: EDO SQS 17A; hull-mounted; active attack; high frequency.

YARHISAR *1/1990, Selim San*

12 LARGE PATROL CRAFT

AB 25-AB 36 P 125-P 136 (ex-P 1225-P 1236)

Displacement, tons: 170 full load
Dimensions, feet (metres): 132 × 21 × 5.5 *(40.2 × 6.4 × 1.7)*
Main machinery: 4 SACM-AGO V16CSHR diesels; 9600 hp(m) *(7.06 MW)*
2 cruise diesels; 300 hp(m) *(220 kW)*; 2 shafts
Speed, knots: 22
Guns: 1 or 2 Bofors 40 mm/70 (in some).
1 Oerlikon 20 mm (in those with 1—40 mm). 2—12.7 mm MGs.
A/S mortars: 1 Mk 20 Mousetrap 4-rocket launcher; range 200 m; warhead 50 kg.
Depth charges: 1 rack.
Sonars: Hull-mounted; active search and attack; high frequency.

Comment: Built at Taşkizak Naval Yard and commissioned between 1967 and 1970. Pennant numbers changed in 1991.

AB 31 *6/1992, Selim San*

4 US PGM 71 CLASS (LARGE PATROL CRAFT)

AB 21-AB 24 (ex-*PGM 104-PGM 108*) P 121-P 124 (ex-P 1221-P 1224)

Displacement, tons: 130 standard; 147 full load
Dimensions, feet (metres): 101 × 21 × 7 *(30.8 × 6.4 × 2.1)*
Main machinery: GM diesels; 2 shafts
Speed, knots: 18.5. **Range, miles:** 1500 at 10 kts
Complement: 15
Guns: 1 Bofors 40 mm/60. 4 Oerlikon 20 mm (2 twin). 1—7.62 mm MG.
A/S mortars: 2 Mk 22 Mousetrap 8-rocket launchers; range 200 m; warhead 50 kg.
Depth charges: 2 racks (4).
Radars: Surface search: Raytheon; I band.
Sonars: EDO SQS 17A; hull-mounted; active attack; high frequency.

Comment: Built by Peterson, Sturgeon Bay and commissioned 1967-68. Transferred almost immediately after completion. Pennant numbers changed in 1991.

AB 23 (old number) *5/1990, A Sheldon Duplaix*

4 Ex-US COAST GUARD TYPE (COASTAL PATROL CRAFT)

LS 9-LS 12   P 141-P 144   (ex-P 1209-P 1212)

Displacement, tons: 63 standard
Dimensions, feet (metres): 83 × 14 × 5 *(25.3 × 4.3 × 1.6)*
Main machinery: 2 Cummins diesels; 1100 hp *(820 kW)*; 2 shafts
Speed, knots: 20
Complement: 15
Guns: 1 Oerlikon 20 mm.
A/S mortars: 2 Mk 20 Mousetrap 8-rocket launchers; range 200 m; warhead 50 kg.
Radars: Surface search: I band.
Sonars: Hull-mounted; active attack; high frequency.

Comment: Transferred on 25 June 1953. All built by US Coast Guard Yard, Curtis Bay, Maryland. Pennant numbers changed in 1991.

LS 12 (old number)   *1986, Selçuk Emre*

1 COASTAL PATROL CRAFT

CANER GÖNYELI   P 145

Displacement, tons: 56 full load
Dimensions, feet (metres): 87.6 × 15.4 × 5.6 *(26.7 × 4.7 × 1.7)*
Main machinery: 2 diesels; 1250 hp(m) *(918 kW)*; 2 shafts
Speed, knots: 19
Guns: 2 Oerlikon 20 mm.

Comment: Based in North Cyprus.

CANER GÖNYELI   *1990, Turkish Navy*

MINE WARFARE FORCES

Notes: (a) Options for new construction include a Tripartite type for local production under protocol arrangement with the Netherlands, an Abeking & Rasmussen design or a Spanish CME class. Four Simrad Subsea minehunting sonars acquired in 1989. The plan is to order six of the class with eight more to follow in due course. The operational requirement is to be able to classify and neutralise all ground and moored mines to a depth of 200 m. Tenders called for in April 1991. Bids submitted in October 1991 and were still being received in late 1992. Initial order delayed to 1993/94.
(b) Minelayers: see *Bayraktar, Sancaktar, Çakabey, Sarucabey* and *Karamürselbey* under Amphibious Forces

1 MINELAYER

Name	No	Builders	Commissioned
NUSRET	N 110 (ex-N 108)	Frederikshavn Dockyard, Denmark	16 Sep 1964

Displacement, tons: 1880 standard
Dimensions, feet (metres): 252.7 × 41 × 11 *(77 × 12.6 × 3.4)*
Main machinery: 2 GM EMD 16-567 diesels; 2800 hp *(2.1 MW)*; 2 shafts; cp props
Speed, knots: 18
Complement: 146
Guns: 4 USN 3 in *(76 mm)* (2 twin) Mk 33; 85° elevation; 50 rounds/minute to 12.8 km *(7 nm)*; weight of shell 6 kg.
Mines: 400.
Fire control: 2 Mk 63 GFCS.
Radars: Air/surface search: Selenia RAN 7S; E/F band; range 165 km *(90 nm)*.
Navigation: I band.
Fire control: Western Electric Mk 34; I/J band.

Comment: Laid down in 1962, launched in 1964. Similar to Danish Falster class.

NUSRET   *1986, Selçuk Emre*

3 Ex-US MODIFIED LSM 1 CLASS (COASTAL MINELAYERS)

Name	No	Builders	Commissioned
MORDOĞAN (ex-US *LSM 484*, ex-*MMC 11*)	N 101	Brown S B Co, Texas	15 Apr 1945
MERSIN (ex-US *LSM 494*, ex-*MMC 13*)	N 104	Brown S B Co, Texas	8 May 1945
MÜREFTE (ex-US *LSM 492*, ex-*MMC 14*)	N 105	Brown S B Co, Texas	1 May 1945

Displacement, tons: 743 standard; 1100 full load
Dimensions, feet (metres): 203.2 × 34.5 × 8.5 *(61.9 × 10.5 × 2.6)*
Main machinery: 2 GM 16-278A diesels; 3000 hp *(2.24 MW)*; 2 shafts
Speed, knots: 12. **Range, miles:** 2500 at 12 kts
Complement: 89
Guns: 6 Bofors 40 mm/60 (3 twin). 6 Oerlikon 20 mm.
Mines: 400.

Comment: Ex-US Landing Ships Medium. All launched in 1945, converted into coastal minelayers by the US Navy in 1952 and taken over by the Turkish Navy (LSM 484 and 490) and the Norwegian Navy (LSM 492) in October 1952 under MAP. LSM 492 *(Vale)* was retransferred to the Turkish Navy on 1 November 1960 at Bergen, Norway.

MORDOĞAN   *5/1990, A Sheldon Duplaix*

1 Ex-US YMP TYPE (COASTAL MINELAYER)

Name	No	Builders	Commissioned
MEHMETCIK (ex-US *YMP 3*)	N 115	Higgins Inc, New Orleans	1958

Displacement, tons: 540 full load
Dimensions, feet (metres): 130 × 35 × 6 *(39.6 × 10.7 × 1.9)*
Main machinery: 2 GM 6-71 diesels; 348 hp *(260 kW)* sustained; 2 shafts
Speed, knots: 10
Complement: 22

Comment: Former US motor mine planter. Steel hulled. Transferred under MAP in 1958. For harbour defence. Soon to be deleted.

MEHMETCIK   *9/1991, Erik Laursen*

12 Ex-US ADJUTANT, MSC 268 and MSC 294 CLASSES (MINESWEEPERS—COASTAL)

SEYMEN (ex-*MSC 131*) M 507		SEDDULBAHIR (ex-*MSC 272*) M 513	
SELÇUK (ex-*MSC 124*) M 508		SILIFKE (ex-USS *MSC 304*) M 514	
SEYHAN (ex-*MSC 142*) M 509		SAROS (ex-USS *MSC 305*) M 515	
SAMSUN (ex-USS *MSC 268*) M 510		SIGACIK (ex-USS *MSC 311*) M 516	
SINOP (ex-USS *MSC 270*) M 511		SAPANCA (ex-USS *MSC 312*) M 517	
SURMENE (ex-USS *MSC 271*) M 512		SARIYER (ex-USS *MSC 315*) M 518	

Displacement, tons: 320 standard; 370 full load
Dimensions, feet (metres): 141 × 26 × 8.3 *(43 × 8 × 2.6)*
Main machinery: 4 GM 6-71 diesels; 696 hp *(519 kW)* sustained; 2 shafts (MSC 268 class)
2 Waukesha L 1616 diesels; 1200 hp *(895 kW)*; 2 shafts (MSC 294 class)
Speed, knots: 14. **Range, miles:** 2500 at 10 kts
Complement: 38 (4 officers)
Guns: 2 Oerlikon 20 mm (twin).
Radars: Navigation: Decca; I band.
Sonars: UQS-1D; hull-mounted mine search; high frequency.

Comment: Built 1955-59 (M 507-M 513) and 1965-67 (M 514-M 518). Transferred on 19 November 1970, 24 March 1970, 24 March 1970, 30 September 1958, February 1959, 27 March 1959, May 1959, September 1965, February 1966, June 1965, 26 July 1965, 8 September 1967, respectively. M 508 and M 509 were transferred from France (via the USA) and M 507 from Belgium (via the USA). Height of funnels and bridge arrangements vary.

SELÇUK   *7/1991, Selim San*

704 TURKEY / Mine warfare forces — Amphibious forces

2 MINELAYER TENDERS

SAMANDIRA 1 Y 131 (ex-Y 1148)   **SAMANDIRA 2** Y 132 (ex-Y 1149)

Displacement, tons: 72 full load
Dimensions, feet (metres): 64.3 × 18.7 × 5.9 *(19.6 × 5.7 × 1.8)*
Main machinery: 1 Gray Marine 64 HN9 diesel; 225 hp *(168 kW)*; 1 shaft
Speed, knots: 10
Complement: 8

Comment: Acquired in 1959. Used for laying and recovering mine distribution boxes.

SAMANDIRA 2   9/1991, Erik Laursen

4 Ex-CANADIAN MCB TYPE (MINESWEEPERS/PATROL VESSELS)

TRABZON (ex-HMCS *Gaspe*)   **TIREBOLU** (ex-HMCS *Comax*)
P 530 (ex-M 530)   P 532 (ex-M 532)
TERME (ex-HMCS *Trinity*)   **TEKIRDAG** (ex-HMCS *Ungava*)
P 531 (ex-M 531)   A 601 (ex-M 533)

Displacement, tons: 370 standard; 470 full load
Dimensions, feet (metres): 164 × 30.2 × 9.2 *(50 × 9.2 × 2.8)*
Main machinery: 2 GM 12-278A diesels; 2200 hp *(1.64 MW)*; 2 shafts
Speed, knots: 15. **Range, miles:** 4500 at 11 kts
Complement: 35 (4 officers)
Guns: 1 Bofors 40 mm/60. 2—12.7 mm MGs.

Comment: Sailed from Sydney, Nova Scotia, to Turkey on 19 May 1958. Built by Davie S B Co 1951-53. Of similar type to British Ton class. *Tekirdag* has been fitted with ECM pods abaft mast. Pennant numbers changed in 1991 reflecting use of three as patrol ships and one as an auxiliary.

TERME (old number)   10/1989, Hartmut Ehlers

6 Ex-GERMAN VEGESACK CLASS (MINESWEEPERS—COASTAL)

Name	No	Builders	Commissioned
KARAMÜRSEL (ex-*Worms* M 1253)	M 520	Amiot, Cherbourg	30 Apr 1960
KEREMPE (ex-*Detmold* M 1252)	M 521	Amiot, Cherbourg	20 Feb 1960
KILIMLI (ex-*Siegen* M 1254)	M 522	Amiot, Cherbourg	9 July 1960
KOZLU (ex-*Hameln* M 1251)	M 523	Amiot, Cherbourg	15 Oct 1959
KUŞADASI (ex-*Vegesack* M 1250)	M 524	Amiot, Cherbourg	19 Sep 1959
KEMER (ex-*Passau* M 1255)	M 525	Amiot, Cherbourg	15 Oct 1960

Displacement, tons: 362 standard; 378 full load
Dimensions, feet (metres): 155.1 × 28.2 × 9.5 *(47.3 × 8.6 × 2.9)*
Main machinery: 2 MTU MB diesels; 1500 hp(m) *(1.1 MW)*; 2 shafts; cp props
Speed, knots: 15
Complement: 40
Guns: 2 Oerlikon 20 mm (twin).
Radars: Navigation: Decca; I band.

Comment: Of similar class to French *Mercure*. M 520-524 transferred by West Germany to Turkey late 1975-early 1976. M 525 transferred 1979 and refitted 1980 at Taşkizak. M 520 converted for trials July 1986-1987.

KARAMÜRSEL   9/1992, B Sullivan

4 Ex-US CAPE CLASS (MINESWEEPERS—INSHORE)

Name	No	Builders	Commissioned
FOÇA (ex-*MSI 15*)	M 500	Peterson, Wisconsin	Aug 1967
FETHIYE (ex-*MSI 16*)	M 501	Peterson, Wisconsin	Aug 1967
FATSA (ex-*MSI 17*)	M 502	Peterson, Wisconsin	Sep 1967
FINIKE (ex-*MSI 18*)	M 503	Peterson, Wisconsin	Nov 1967

Displacement, tons: 180 standard; 235 full load
Dimensions, feet (metres): 111.9 × 23.5 × 7.9 *(34 × 7.1 × 2.4)*
Main machinery: 4 GM 6-71 diesels; 696 hp *(520 kW)* sustained; 2 shafts
Speed, knots: 13. **Range, miles:** 900 at 11 kts
Complement: 30
Guns: 1—12.7 mm MG.

Comment: Built in USA and transferred under MAP at Boston, Massachusetts, August-December 1967.

FATSA   9/1990, Selim San

8 MINEHUNTING TENDERS

DALGIÇ 2 (ex-*MTB 2*) P 312	MTB 5 P 315	MTB 8 P 318
MTB 3 P 313	MTB 6 P 316	MTB 9 P 319
MTB 4 P 314	MTB 7 P 317	

Displacement, tons: 70 standard
Dimensions, feet (metres): 71.5 × 13.8 × 8.5 *(21.8 × 4.2 × 2.6)*
Main machinery: 2 diesels; 2000 hp(m) *(1.47 MW)*; 2 shafts
Speed, knots: 20
Guns: 1 Oerlikon 20 mm or 1—12.7 mm MG (aft) (in some).

Comment: All launched in 1942. Now employed as minehunting base ships (P 313-319) and diver support craft (P 312).

MTB 9   9/1991, Erik Laursen

AMPHIBIOUS FORCES

Note: The prefix 'Ç' for smaller amphibious vessels stands for 'Çikartma Gemisi' (landing vessel) and indicates that the craft are earmarked for national rather than NATO control.

0 + 1 OSMAN GAZI CLASS (LST)

Name	No	Builders	Commissioned
OSMAN GAZI	NL 125	Taşkizak Yard, Istanbul	Mar 1994

Displacement, tons: 3773 full load
Dimensions, feet (metres): 344.5 × 52.8 × 15.7 *(105 × 16.1 × 4.8)*
Main machinery: 2 MTU 12V 1163 TB73 diesels; 8800 hp(m) *(6.47 MW)*; 2 shafts
Speed, knots: 17. **Range, miles:** 4000 at 15 kts
Military lift: 900 troops; 15 tanks; 4 LCVPs
Guns: 3 Bofors 40 mm/70; 2 Oerlikon 35 mm/90 (twin).
Helicopters: Platform for one large.

Comment: Laid down 7 July 1989, launched 20 July 1990. Full NBCD protection. Equipped with a support weapons co-ordination centre to control amphibious operations. The ship has about a 50 per cent increase in military lift capacity compared with the Sarucabey class. Second of class cancelled in 1991 and *Osman Gazi* has been badly delayed.

OSMAN GAZI   9/1991, Erik Laursen

Amphibious forces / TURKEY 705

2 Ex-US TERREBONNE PARISH CLASS (LSTs)

Name	No	Builders	Commissioned
ERTUĞRUL (ex-USS *Windham County* LST 1170)	L 401	Christy Corporation	15 Dec 1954
SERDAR (ex-USS *Westchester County* LST 1167)	L 402	Christy Corporation	10 Mar 1954

Displacement, tons: 2590 light; 5800 full load
Dimensions, feet (metres): 384 × 55 × 17 *(117.1 × 16.8 × 5.2)*
Main machinery: 4 GM 16-278A diesels; 6000 hp *(4.48 MW)*; 2 shafts; cp props
Speed, knots: 15
Complement: 116
Military lift: 395 troops; 2200 tons cargo; 4 LCVPs
Guns: 6 USN 3 in *(76 mm)*/50 (3 twin).
Fire control: 2 Mk 63 GFCS.
Radars: Surface search: Raytheon SPS 21; G/H band; range 22 km *(12 nm)*.
Fire control: Two Western Electric Mk 34; I/J band.

Comment: Transferred by USA June 1973 (L 401) and 27 August 1974 (L 402) on loan. Purchased outright in 1988.

ERTUĞRUL   *1990, Turkish Navy*

2 Ex-US 512-1152 CLASS (LSTs)

Name	No	Commissioned
BAYRAKTAR (ex-FDR *Bottrop*, ex-USS *Saline County* LST 1101)	NL 120 (ex-N-111, ex-A 579, ex-L 403)	26 Jan 1945
SANCAKTAR (ex-FDR *Bochum*, ex-USS *Rice County* LST 1089)	NL 121 (ex-N-112, ex-A 580, ex-L 404)	14 Mar 1945

Displacement, tons: 1653 standard; 4080 full load
Dimensions, feet (metres): 328 × 50 × 14 *(100 × 15.2 × 4.3)*
Main machinery: 2 GM 12-567A diesels; 1800 hp *(1.34 MW)*; 2 shafts; cp props
Speed, knots: 11. **Range, miles:** 15 000 at 9 kts
Complement: 125
Guns: 6 Bofors 40 mm/70 (2 twin, 2 single).
Mines: 4 rails.
Radars: Navigation: Kelvin Hughes; I band.

Comment: Transferred to West Germany in 1961 and thence to Turkey on 13 December 1972. Converted into minelayers in West Germany 1962-64. Minelaying gear removed 1974-75 and replaced in 1979. Now dual purpose ships.

BAYRAKTAR   *1990, Turkish Navy*

1 ÇAKABEY CLASS (LST)

Name	No	Builders	Commissioned
ÇAKABEY	NL 122 (ex-L 405)	Taşkizak Naval Yard	25 July 1980

Displacement, tons: 1600
Dimensions, feet (metres): 253.5 × 39.4 × 7.5 *(77.3 × 12 × 2.3)*
Main machinery: 3 diesels; 4320 hp *(3.2 MW)*; 3 shafts
Speed, knots: 14
Military lift: 400 troops; 9 tanks; 10 jeeps; 2 LCVPs
Guns: 4 Bofors 40 mm/60 (2 twin). 4 Oerlikon 20 mm (2 twin).
Mines: 150 in lieu of amphibious load.
Radars: Navigation: Racal Decca; I band.
Helicopters: Platform only.

Comment: Launched 30 June 1977. Dual purpose minelayer.

ÇAKABEY   *2/1987, Selçuk Emre*

2 SARUCABEY CLASS (LSTs)

Name	No	Builders	Commissioned
SARUCABEY	NL 123	Taşkizak Naval Yard	26 July 1984
KARAMÜRSELBEY	NL 124	Taşkizak Naval Yard	27 July 1985

Displacement, tons: 2600 full load
Dimensions, feet (metres): 301.8 × 45.9 × 7.5 *(92 × 14 × 2.3)*
Main machinery: 3 diesels; 4320 hp *(3.2 MW)*; 3 shafts
Speed, knots: 14
Military lift: 600 troops; 11 tanks; 12 jeeps; 2 LCVPs
Guns: 3 Bofors 40 mm/70. 4 Oerlikon 20 mm (2 twin).
Mines: 150 in lieu of amphibious lift.
Radars: Navigation: Racal Decca; I band.
Helicopters: Platform only.

Comment: *Sarucabey* is an enlarged Çakabey design more suitable for naval requirements. First one launched 30 July 1981, second 26 July 1984. Dual purpose minelayers.

KARAMÜRSELBEY   *1989, Selçuk Emre*

8 EDIC TYPE (LCTs)

Ç 108, 110, 112-114, 116-118

Displacement, tons: 580 full load
Dimensions, feet (metres): 186.9 × 39.4 × 4.6 *(57 × 12 × 1.4)*
Main machinery: 3 GM 6-71 diesels; 522 hp *(390 kW)* sustained; 3 shafts
Speed, knots: 8.5. **Range, miles:** 600 at 10 kts
Complement: 15
Military lift: 100 troops; up to 5 tanks
Guns: 2 Oerlikon 20 mm. 2—12.7 mm MGs.

Comment: Built at Gölcük Naval Shipyard 1966-73. French EDIC type. Four scrapped in 1991.

EDIC Type (old number)   *1987*

27 + 2 LCTs

Ç 119-129, 132-135, 137-147, 151-153

Displacement, tons: 600 full load
Dimensions, feet (metres): 195.5 × 38 × 4.6 *(59.6 × 11.6 × 1.4)*
Main machinery: 3 GM 6-71 diesels; 522 hp *(390 kW)* sustained; 3 shafts (119-138) or 3 MTU diesels; 900 hp(m) *(662 kW)*; 3 shafts (139-147)
Speed, knots: 8.5. **Range, miles:** 600 at 8 kts
Complement: 15
Military lift: 100 troops; 5 tanks
Guns: 2 Oerlikon 20 mm. 2—12.7 mm MGs.

Comment: Follow-on to the Ç 107 type started building in 1977. Ç 130 and Ç 131 transferred to Libya January 1980 and Ç 136 sunk in 1985. The delivery rate was about two per year from the Taşkizak and Gölcük yards until 1987. Two launched in July 1987 and commissioned in mid-1991. One more completed in 1992 with two others fitting out at Taşkizak. Dimensions given are for Ç 139 onwards, earlier craft are 3.6 m shorter and have less freeboard.

Ç 120   *10/1991, Harald Carstens*

Ç 141   *6/1986, Hartmut Ehlers*

706 TURKEY / Amphibious forces — Service forces

2 LCUs

Ç 213-214

Displacement, tons: 320 light; 405 full load
Dimensions, feet (metres): 142 × 28 × 5.7 *(43.3 × 8.5 × 1.7)*
Main machinery: 2 GM 6-71 diesels; 348 hp *(260 kW)* sustained; 2 shafts
Speed, knots: 10
Guns: 2 Oerlikon 20 mm.

Comment: Built by Taşkizak, Istanbul 1965-66. Seven scrapped in 1991, three more in 1992.

Ç 206 (old number) 9/1988, Selçuk Emre

22 LCM 8 TYPE

Ç 302-303, 305, 308-309, 312-314, 316, 318-319, 321-331

Displacement, tons: 58 light; 113 full load
Dimensions, feet (metres): 72 × 20.5 × 4.8 *(22 × 6.3 × 1.4)*
Main machinery: 2 GM 6-71 diesels; 348 hp *(260 kW)* sustained; 2 shafts
Speed, knots: 9.5
Complement: 9
Guns: 1—12.7 mm MG.

Comment: Built by Taşkizak, Istanbul in 1965-66. Eight scrapped in 1991, one more in 1992.

Ç 308 10/1989, Hartmut Ehlers

SURVEY SHIPS

Name	No	Builders	Commissioned
YUNUS (ex-*Alster*, ex-*Mellum*)	A 590 (ex-A 50)	Unterweser, Bremen	21 Mar 1961

Displacement, tons: 1497 full load
Dimensions, feet (metres): 275.5 × 34.4 × 18.4 *(84 × 10.5 × 5.6)*
Main machinery: 1 Deutz diesel; 1800 hp(m) *(1.32 MW)*; 1 shaft
Speed, knots: 15
Complement: 90

Comment: Ex-trawler, purchased by West German Navy in 1965. Conversion at Blohm & Voss and commissioned for naval service on 19 October 1971. Transferred in February 1989. Continues to be used as an AGI.

YUNUS 10/1991, Selim San

Name	No	Builders	Commissioned
ÇUBUKLU (ex-*Y 1251*)	A 594	Gölcük	July 1984

Displacement, tons: 680 full load
Dimensions, feet (metres): 132.8 × 31.5 × 10.5 *(40.5 × 9.6 × 3.2)*
Main machinery: 1 MWM diesel; 820 hp(m) *(603 kW)*; 1 shaft; cp prop
Speed, knots: 11
Complement: 31 (5 officers)
Guns: 2 Oerlikon 20 mm.

Comment: Launched 17 November 1983. Qubit advanced integrated navigation and data processing system fitted in 1991.

ÇUBUKLU 7/1990, Selçuk Emre

MESAHA 1 Y 35 (ex-Y 1221)   MESAHA 2 Y 36 (ex-Y 1222)

Displacement, tons: 45 full load
Dimensions, feet (metres): 52.2 × 14.8 × 4.3 *(15.9 × 4.5 × 1.3)*
Main machinery: 2 GM diesels; 330 hp *(246 kW)*; 2 shafts
Speed, knots: 10. **Range, miles:** 600 at 10 kts
Complement: 8

Comment: Built in 1966. Former US Sounding Boats. Similar to Brazil Paraibano class. Pennant numbers changed in 1991.

MESAHA 1 6/1992, C D Yaylali

SERVICE FORCES

1 Ex-US DIXIE CLASS (DEPOT SHIP)

Name	No	Builders	Commissioned
DERYA (ex-USS *Piedmont* AD 17)	A 576	Tampa Shipbuilding Co	5 Jan 1944

Displacement, tons: 9450 standard; 18 000 full load
Dimensions, feet (metres): 530.5 × 73.2 × 25.6 *(161.7 × 22.3 × 7.8)*
Main machinery: 4 Babcock & Wilcox boilers; 400 psi *(28.4 kg/cm sq)*; 720°F *(382°C)*; 2 Allis Chalmers turbines; 12 000 hp *(8.95 MW)*; 2 shafts
Speed, knots: 18.2. **Range, miles:** 12 000 at 12 kts
Complement: 120
Guns: 3 Bofors 40 mm/70. 8 Oerlikon 20 mm.
Radars: Surface search: Raytheon SPS 10; G band.
Helicopters: Platform only.

Comment: Modernised to service destroyers with ASROC, helicopters and modern electronics. Transferred on loan at Norfolk, Virginia October 1982. Commissioned in Turkish Navy 28 March 1983. Purchased outright in June 1987.

DERYA 3/1988, Hartmut Ehlers

2 Ex-GERMAN RHEIN CLASS (TRAINING SHIPS)

Name	No	Builders	Commissioned
SOKULLU MEHMET PAŞA (ex-*Isar*)	A 577	Blohm & Voss	25 Jan 1964
CEZAYIRLI GAZI HASAN PAŞA (ex-*Ruhr*)	A 579	Schliekerwerft, Hamburg	2 May 1964

Displacement, tons: 2370 standard; 2940 full load
Dimensions, feet (metres): 322.1 × 38.8 × 14.4 *(98.2 × 11.8 × 4.4)*
Main machinery: 6 MTU MD diesels; 14 400 hp(m) *(10.58 MW)*; 2 shafts
Speed, knots: 20.5. **Range, miles:** 1625 at 15 kts
Complement: 110/125 (accommodation for 200)
Guns: 2 Creusot Loire 3.9 in *(100 mm)*/55. 4 Bofors 40 mm/60.
Radars: Surface search: Signaal DA 02; E/F band.
Fire control: Two Signaal M 45; I/J band.

Comment: A 579, transferred 18 July 1975, commissioned in Turkish Navy 16 January 1977 after major refit. A 577 transferred 30 September 1982, commissioned 28 March 1983.

SOKULLU MEHMET PAŞA 7/1992, W Sartori

2 Ex-GERMAN ANGELN CLASS (DEPOT SHIPS)

Name	No	Builders	Commissioned
ÜLKÜ (ex-Angeln)	A 586	A C de Bretagne	20 Jan 1955
UMUR BEY (ex-Dithmarschen)	A 588	A C de Bretagne	17 Nov 1955

Displacement, tons: 4190 full load
Dimensions, feet (metres): 296.9 × 43.6 × 20.3 (90.5 × 13.3 × 6.2)
Main machinery: 2 SEMT-Pielstick diesels; 3000 hp(m) (2.2 MW); 1 shaft
Speed, knots: 17. **Range, miles:** 3660 at 15 kts
Complement: 57
Cargo capacity: 2670 tons
Guns: 2 Bofors 40 mm/60 (aft). 2 Oerlikon 20 mm.

Comment: Ex-cargo ships bought by West Germany in 1959. Transferred 22 March 1972 and December 1975. A 588 employed as submarine depot ship and A 586 as light forces depot ship.

UMUR BEY   4/1986, Hartmut Ehlers

1 FLEET REPLENISHMENT TANKER

Name	No	Builders	Commissioned
AKAR	A 580	Gölcük Naval DY	24 Apr 1987

Displacement, tons: 19 350 full load
Dimensions, feet (metres): 475.9 × 74.8 × 27.6 (145.1 × 22.8 × 8.4)
Main machinery: 1 diesel; 6500 hp(m) (4.78 MW); 1 shaft
Speed, knots: 15
Complement: 329
Cargo capacity: 6000 tons oil fuel
Guns: 2—3 in (76 mm)/50 (twin). 2 Bofors 40 mm/70.
Fire control: Mk 63; GFCS.
Helicopters: Platform only.

Comment: Launched 17 November 1983. Helicopter flight deck aft. There is a requirement for a second ship.

AKAR   9/1991, Nikolaus Sifferlinger

1 SUPPORT TANKER

Name	No	Builders	Commissioned
TAŞKIZAK	A 570	Taşkizak Naval DY, Istanbul	25 July 1984

Displacement, tons: 1440
Dimensions, feet (metres): 211.9 × 30.8 × 11.5 (64.6 × 9.4 × 3.5)
Main machinery: 1 diesel; 1400 hp(m) (1.03 MW); 1 shaft
Speed, knots: 13
Complement: 57
Cargo capacity: 800 tons
Guns: 1 Bofors 40 mm/70. 2 Oerlikon 20 mm.

Comment: Laid down 20 July 1983.

TAŞKIZAK (Dogan class in background)   5/1990, A Sheldon Duplaix

1 SUPPORT TANKER

Name	No	Builders	Commissioned
YÜZBAŞI TOLUNAY	A 571	Taşkizak Naval DY, Istanbul	1951

Displacement, tons: 2500 standard; 3500 full load
Dimensions, feet (metres): 260 × 41 × 19.5 (79 × 12.4 × 5.9)
Main machinery: 2 Atlas-Polar diesels; 1920 hp(m) (1.41 MW); 2 shafts
Speed, knots: 14
Guns: 2 Bofors 40 mm/70 (not always embarked).

Comment: Launched on 22 August 1950. Beam and stern replenishment facilities.

YÜZBAŞI TOLUNAY   2/1992, C D Yaylali

1 SUPPORT TANKER

Name	No	Builders	Commissioned
ALBAY HAKKI BURAK	A 572	Gölcük Naval DY	1965

Displacement, tons: 3800 full load
Dimensions, feet (metres): 274.7 × 40.2 × 18 (83.7 × 12.3 × 5.5)
Main machinery: Diesel-electric; 4 GM 16-567A diesels; 5600 hp (4.12 MW); 4 generators; 2 motors; 4400 hp (3.28 MW); 2 shafts
Speed, knots: 16
Complement: 88
Cargo capacity: 1900 tons oil fuel approx
Guns: 2 Bofors 40 mm/60 (not always fitted).

ALBAY HAKKI BURAK   3/1988, Hartmut Ehlers

1 SUPPORT TANKER

Name	No	Builders	Commissioned
BINBAŞI SAADETTIN GÜRÇAN	A 573	Taşkizak Naval DY, Istanbul	1970

Displacement, tons: 1505 standard; 4460 full load
Dimensions, feet (metres): 294.2 × 38.7 × 17.7 (89.7 × 11.8 × 5.4)
Main machinery: Diesel-electric; 4 GM 16-567A diesels; 5600 hp (4.12 MW); 4 generators; 2 motors; 4400 hp (3.28 MW); 2 shafts
Speed, knots: 16
Guns: 1—3 in (76 mm)/62. 2 Oerlikon 20 mm.

BINBAŞI SAADETTIN GÜRÇAN   1987, Selçuk Emre

3 HARBOUR TANKERS

H 500, H 501, H 502   Y 140-Y 142 (ex-Y 1231-1233)

Displacement, tons: 300
Dimensions, feet (metres): 110.2 × 27.9 × 5.9 (33.6 × 8.5 × 1.8)
Main machinery: 1 diesel; 225 hp(m) (165 kW); 1 shaft
Speed, knots: 11
Cargo capacity: 150 tons

Comment: Sisters of water tankers of Pinar series. Built at Taşkizak in early 1970s. Pennant numbers changed in 1991.

H 501 (old number)   3/1990, Selim San

708 TURKEY / Service forces

1 Ex-GERMAN SUPPORT TANKER

Name	No	Builders	Commissioned
INEBOLU (ex-*Bodensee* A 1406, ex-*Unkas*)	A 575	Lindenau, Kiel	26 Mar 1959

Displacement, tons: 1840 full load
Measurement, tons: 1238 dwt
Dimensions, feet (metres): 219.8 × 32.1 × 14.1 *(67 × 9.8 × 4.3)*
Main machinery: 1 MAK diesel; 1050 hp(m) *(772 kW)*; 1 shaft
Speed, knots: 12
Complement: 26
Cargo capacity: 1230 tons
Guns: 2 Oerlikon 20 mm (on bridge).

Comment: Launched 19 November 1955. Of Bodensee class. Transferred September 1977 at Wilhelmshavn, under West German military aid programme. Has replenishment capability.

INEBOLU *4/1986, Hartmut Ehlers*

2 Ex-US REPAIR SHIPS

Name	No	Builders	Commissioned
ONARAN (ex-*Alecto* AGP 14, ex-*LST 558*)	A 581	Missouri Valley Bridge & Iron Co	8 Feb 1945
BAŞARAN (ex-*Patroclus* ARL 19, ex-*LST 955*)	A 582	Bethlehem Hingham Shipyard	13 Nov 1944

Displacement, tons: 1625 standard; 4080 full load
Dimensions, feet (metres): 328 × 50 × 14 *(100 × 15.2 × 4.4)*
Main machinery: 2 GM 12-278A diesels; 2200 hp *(1.64 MW)*; 2 shafts
Speed, knots: 11. **Range, miles:** 9000 at 9 kts
Complement: 80
Guns: 8 Bofors 40 mm/60 (2 quad). 8 Oerlikon 20 mm.

Comment: Former US repair ship and MTB tender, respectively, of the LST type. A 582 was launched on 22 October 1944, A 581 on 14 April 1944. Acquired from the USA in November 1952 and May 1948, respectively.

BAŞARAN *1986, Selçuk Emre*

1 Ex-US DIVER CLASS (SALVAGE SHIP)

Name	No	Builders	Commissioned
IŞIN (ex-USS *Safeguard* ARS 25)	A 589	Basalt Rock Co, Napa, California	31 Oct 1944

Displacement, tons: 1530 standard; 1970 full load
Dimensions, feet (metres): 213.5 × 41 × 13 *(65.1 × 12.5 × 4)*
Main machinery: Diesel-electric; 4 Cooper-Bessemer GSB-8 diesels; 3420 hp *(2.55 MW)*; 4 generators; 2 motors; 2 shafts
Speed, knots: 14.8
Complement: 110
Guns: 2 Oerlikon 20 mm.

Comment: Transferred 28 September 1979 and purchased outright in June 1987.

IŞIN *5/1990, A Sheldon Duplaix*

1 Ex-US CHANTICLEER CLASS (SUBMARINE RESCUE SHIP)

Name	No	Builders	Commissioned
AKIN (ex-USS *Greenlet* ASR 10)	A 585	Moore S B & D D Co	29 May 1943

Displacement, tons: 1653 standard; 2321 full load
Dimensions, feet (metres): 251.5 × 44 × 16 *(76.7 × 13.4 × 4.9)*
Main machinery: Diesel-electric; 4 Alco 539 diesels; 3532 hp *(2.63 MW)*; 4 generators; 1 motor; 1 shaft
Speed, knots: 15
Complement: 85
Guns: 1 Bofors 40 mm/60. 4 Oerlikon 20 mm (twin).

Comment: Transferred 12 June 1970 and purchased 15 February 1973. Carries a Diving Bell.

AKIN *9/1991, Erik Laursen*

1 Ex-US BLUEBIRD CLASS (SUBMARINE RESCUE SHIP)

KURTARAN (ex-USS *Bluebird* ASR 19, ex-*Yurak* AT 165) A 584

Displacement, tons: 1294 standard; 1675 full load
Dimensions, feet (metres): 205 × 38.5 × 11 *(62.5 × 12.2 × 3.5)*
Main machinery: Diesel-electric; 4 GM 12-278A diesels; 4400 hp *(3.28 MW)*; 4 generators; 1 motor; 3000 hp *(2.24 MW)*; 1 shaft
Speed, knots: 16
Complement: 100
Guns: 1 USN 3 in *(76 mm)*/50. 2 Oerlikon 20 mm.

Comment: Former salvage tug adapted as a submarine rescue vessel in 1947. Transferred from the US Navy on 15 August 1950. Carries a Diving Bell.

KURTARAN *4/1992, C D Yaylali*

3 TRANSPORTS

SARKÖY A 591 (ex-Y 1156)   KARADENIZ EREĞLISI A 592 (ex-Y 1157)
ECEABAT A 593 (ex-Y 1165)

Displacement, tons: 820 full load
Dimensions, feet (metres): 166.3 × 26.2 × 9.2 *(50.7 × 8 × 2.8)*
Main machinery: 1 diesel; 1440 hp *(1.06 MW)*; 1 shaft
Speed, knots: 10
Cargo capacity: 300 tons
Guns: 1 Oerlikon 20 mm.

Comment: Funnel-aft coaster type. *Sarköy* has a wireless mast at after end of the superstructure. Pennant numbers changed in 1991. Fourth of class *Kanarya* scrapped in 1992.

KANARYA (old number) *12/1987, Selçuk Emre*

1 AMMUNITION TRANSPORT

CEPHANE 2 Y 97 (ex-Y 1195)

Comment: Pennant number changed in 1991.

CEPHANE 2 (old number) 1980, Stüdyo Oskar, Gölcük

2 BARRACK SHIPS

NAŞIT ÖNGEREN (ex-US *APL 47*) Y 38 (ex-Y 1204)
BINBAŞI NETIN SÜLÜS (ex-US *APL 53*) Y 39 (ex-Y 1205)

Comment: Ex-US barrack ships transferred on lease: Y 1204 in October 1972 and Y 1205 on 6 December 1974. Y 1204 based at Ereğli and Y 1205 at Gölcük. Purchased outright June 1987. Pennant numbers changed in 1991.

36 SMALL TRANSPORTS

SALOPA 1-15 Y 21-35 (ex-Y 1031-1045)
LAYTER 1-4 and **6-7** Y 101-104 and Y 106-107
AZIZIYE (ex-Y 1016)
PONTON 1-7 (ex-Y 1061-1067)
ISCI TASITI 1-4 Y 44-47 (ex-Y 1096, Y 1097, Y 1110, Y 1102)
ARSLAN Y 75 (ex-Y 1112)
GOLCUK Y 50
YAKIT Y 139

Comment: Of varying size and appearance. Pennant numbers changed in 1991.

SALOPA 9/1991, Erik Laursen

2 WATER TANKERS

SÖGÜT (ex-FGR *FW 2*) A 598 (ex-Y 1217)   **KAVAK** (ex-German *FW 4*) A 600

Displacement, tons: 626 full load
Dimensions, feet (metres): 144.4 × 25.6 × 8.2 *(44.1 × 7.8 × 2.5)*
Main machinery: 1 MWM diesel; 230 hp(m) *(169 kW)*; 1 shaft
Speed, knots: 9.5
Cargo capacity: 340 tons

Comment: *Sögüt* transferred by West Germany 3 December 1975. Pennant number changed in 1991. *Kavak* transferred from Germany 12 April 1991.

SÖGÜT (old number) 11/1985, Bernd Langensiepen

2 WATER TANKERS

VAN A 597 (ex-Y 1208)   **ULUBAT** A 596 (ex-Y 1209)

Displacement, tons: 1200 full load
Dimensions, feet (metres): 174.2 × 29.5 × 9.8 *(53.1 × 9 × 3)*
Main machinery: 1 diesel; 650 hp(m) *(478 kW)*; 1 shaft
Speed, knots: 14
Cargo capacity: 700 tons
Guns: 1 Oerlikon 20 mm.

Comment: Two small tankers built in 1968-70 at Gölcük Dockyard. Pennant numbers changed in 1991.

VAN 9/1991, Selim San

6 WATER TANKERS

PINAR 1-6 Y 111-Y 116 (ex-Y 1211-Y 1216)

Displacement, tons: 300
Dimensions, feet (metres): 110.2 × 27.9 × 5.9 *(33.6 × 8.5 × 1.8)*
Main machinery: 1 GM diesel; 225 hp *(168 kW)*; 1 shaft
Speed, knots: 11
Cargo capacity: 150 tons

Comment: Built by Taşkizak Naval Yard. Details given for last four, sisters to harbour tankers H 500-502. First pair differ from these particulars and are individually different. *Pinar 1* (launched 1938) of 490 tons displacement with one 240 hp *(179 kW)* diesel, and *Pinar 2* built in 1958 of 1300 tons full load, 167.3 × 27.9 ft *(51 × 8.5 m)*.

PINAR 5 (old number) 10/1988, Selim San

BOOM DEFENCE VESSELS

Name	No	Builders	Commissioned
AG 6 (ex-USS *AN 93*, ex-Netherlands *Cerberus* A 895)	P 306	Bethlehem Steel Corporation, Staten Island	10 Nov 1952

Displacement, tons: 780 standard; 855 full load
Dimensions, feet (metres): 165 × 33 × 10 *(50.3 × 10.1 × 3)*
Main machinery: Diesel-electric; 2 GM 8-268A diesels; 880 hp *(656 kW)*; 2 generators; 1 motor; 1 shaft
Speed, knots: 12.8. Range, miles: 5200 at 12 kts
Complement: 48
Guns: 1 USN 3 in *(76 mm)*/50. 4 Oerlikon 20 mm.

Comment: Netlayer. Transferred from USA to Netherlands in December 1952. Used first as a boom defence vessel and latterly as salvage and diving tender since 1961 but retained her net-laying capacity. Handed back to US Navy on 17 September 1970 but immediately turned over to the Turkish Navy under grant aid.

AG 6 5/1990, A Sheldon Duplaix

710 TURKEY / Boom defence vessels — Tugs

Name	No	Builders	Commissioned
AG 5 (ex-AN 104)	P 305	Kröger, Rendsburg	5 Feb 1961

Displacement, tons: 680 standard; 960 full load
Dimensions, feet (metres): 173.8 × 35 × 13.5 *(53 × 10.7 × 4.1)*
Main machinery: 1 MAN G7V40/60 diesel; 1470 hp(m) *(1.08 MW)*; 1 shaft
Speed, knots: 12. **Range, miles:** 6500 at 11 kts
Complement: 49
Guns: 1 Bofors 40 mm/60. 3 Oerlikon 20 mm.

Comment: Netlayer P 305 built in US off-shore programme for Turkey.

AG 5   *5/1987, van Ginderen Collection*

Name	No	Builders	Commissioned
AG 4 (ex-USS *Larch*, ex-AN 21)	P 304	American S B Co, Cleveland	13 Dec 1941

Displacement, tons: 560 standard; 805 full load
Dimensions, feet (metres): 163 × 30.5 × 10.5 *(49.7 × 9.3 × 3.2)*
Main machinery: Diesel-electric; 2 diesels; 800 hp *(597 kW)*; 2 generators; 1 motor; 1 shaft
Speed, knots: 12
Complement: 48
Guns: 1—3 in *(76 mm)*. 4 Oerlikon 20 mm.

Comment: Former US netlayer of the Aloe class. Acquired in May 1946.

AG 4   *5/1982, Hartmut Ehlers*

1 BAR CLASS

Name	No	Builders	Commissioned
AG 1 (ex-HMS *Barbarian*)	P 301	Blyth S B Co	16 Apr 1938

Displacement, tons: 750 standard; 1000 full load
Dimensions, feet (metres): 173.8 × 32.2 × 9.5 *(52.9 × 9.8 × 2.9)*
Main machinery: 1 diesel; 1 shaft
Speed, knots: 11.5. **Range, miles:** 3100 at 10 kts
Complement: 32
Guns: 4 Oerlikon 20 mm.

Comment: Former British boom defence vessel. Re-engined in 1960s.

AG 1   *6/1980, Selçuk Emre*

2 NET TENDERS/DAN LAYERS

ŞAMANDIRA MOTORU 11-12   Y 91-Y 92

Comment: Five more of the class laid up in reserve.

TUGS

1 Ex-US CHEROKEE CLASS

GAZAL (ex-USS *Sioux* ATF 75) A 587

Displacement, tons: 1235 standard; 1675 full load
Dimensions, feet (metres): 205 × 38.5 × 17 *(62.5 × 11.7 × 5.2)*
Main machinery: Diesel-electric; 4 GM 12-278 diesels; 4400 hp *(3.28 MW)*; 4 generators; 1 motor; 3000 hp *(2.24 MW)*; 1 shaft
Speed, knots: 16. **Range, miles:** 15 000 at 8 kts
Complement: 85
Guns: 1 USN 3 in *(76 mm)*/50. 2 Oerlikon 20 mm.

Comment: Transferred 30 October 1972. Purchased 15 August 1973. Can be used for salvage.

GAZAL   *3/1988, Hartmut Ehlers*

1 Ex-US ARMY TYPE

AKBAŞ A 583 (ex-Y 1119)

Displacement, tons: 971
Dimensions, feet (metres): 146.6 × 33.5 × 14.1 *(44.7 × 10.2 × 4.3)*
Speed, knots: 12
Guns: 2 Oerlikon 20 mm.

Comment: Based at Gölcük. Pennant number changed in 1991.

AKBAŞ (old number)   *1990, Turkish Navy*

1 OCEAN TUG

DARICA Y 578 (ex-Y 1125)

Displacement, tons: 750 full load
Dimensions, feet (metres): 134.2 × 32.2 × 12.8 *(40.9 × 9.8 × 3.9)*
Main machinery: 2 ABC diesels; 4000 hp *(2.94 MW)*; 2 shafts
Speed, knots: 14. **Range, miles:** 2500 at 14 kts

Comment: Built at Taşkizak Naval Yard and commissioned 20 July 1990. Equipped for firefighting and as a torpedo tender. Pennant number changed in 1991.

DARICA (old number)   *1987, Selçuk Emre*

Tugs — Auxiliaries / TURKEY   711

2 COASTAL TUGS

ÖNCÜ A 574 (ex-Y 1120)   **ÖNDER** A 599 (ex-Y 1124)

Displacement, tons: 500
Dimensions, feet (metres): 131.2 × 29.9 × 13.1 *(40 × 9.1 × 4)*
Main machinery: 1 diesel; 1 shaft
Speed, knots: 12
Guns: 2 Oerlikon 20 mm (twin).

Comment: Transferred by USA under MAP. Y 1124 based at Ereğli supporting submarines operating in the Black Sea and towing targets. Y 1120 at Izmir.

ÖNDER (old number)   10/1989, Hartmut Ehlers

8 COASTAL/HARBOUR TUGS

Name	No	Displacement, tons/ Speed, knots	Commissioned
SÖNDÜREN	Y 51 (ex-Y 1117)	128/12	1954
KUVVET	Y 53 (ex-Y 1122)	390/10	1962
DOGANARSLAN	Y 52 (ex-Y 1123)	—	1985
ÖZGEN	Y 56 (ex-Y 1128)	—	1987
ATIL	Y 55 (ex-Y 1132)	300/10	1962
ERSEN BAYRAK	Y 64 (ex-Y 1134)	30/9	1946
KUDRET	Y 54 (ex-Y 1229)	128/12	1957
KEPEZ	Y 57	—	1992

DOGANARSLAN (old number)   10/1989, Hartmut Ehlers

38 PUSHER TUGS

KATIR 1-38

Comment: From Katir 36, new design.

KATIR 38   10/1989, Hartmut Ehlers

12 FLOATING DOCKS/CRANES

HAVUZ 1 Y 121 (ex-Y 1081)
16 000 tons lift.

HAVUZ 2 Y 122 (ex-Y 1082)
12 000 tons lift.

HAVUZ 3 Y 123 (ex-Y 1083) (ex-US AFDL)
2500 tons lift.
3500 tons lift.

HAVUZ 4 Y 124 (ex-Y 1084)
4500 tons lift.
700 tons lift.

HAVUZ 5 Y 125 (ex-Y 1085)
400 tons lift.

HAVUZ 6 Y 126 (ex-Y 1086)
3000 tons lift.

HAVUZ 7 Y 127 (ex-Y 1087) (ex-US ARD 12)

HAVUZ 8-10 Y 128-130 (ex-Y 1088-1090)

ALGARNA 3   Y 60 (ex-Y 1021)   **LEVENT** Y 59 (ex-Y 1022)

Comment: *Havuz 7* transferred November 1971 by lease; purchased outright in June 1987. *Algarna* and *Levent* are ex-US floating cranes.

AUXILIARIES

14 UTILITY CRAFT

MAVNA 1-4   (ex-Y 1181-1184)   **MAVNA 7-13**   (ex-Y 1187-1193)
MAVNA 14-16   (ex-Y 1198-1200)

MAVNA 9 (old number)   10/1989, Hartmut Ehlers

1 Ex-GERMAN TORPEDO RETRIEVER (TRV)

Ex-TF 107   (ex-Y 873)

Comment: Transferred 4 September 1989. Built in 1966 of approximately 56 tons.

TRV (old number)   7/1987, Gilbert Gyssels

3 TORPEDO RETRIEVERS (TRV)

TORPITO TENDERI Y 95 (ex-Y 1051)   **TAKIP** Y 98 (ex-Y 1052)   **AHMET ERSOY** Y 99 (ex-Y 1102)

TAKIP (old number)   6/1986, Selçuk Emre

712 TURKEY / Auxiliaries — Coast Guard (Sahil Güvenlik)

2 FLAG OFFICERS' YACHTS

HALAS Y 66 (ex-Y 1089)   **GÜL** Y 76 (ex-Y 1103)

Comment: Pennant numbers not displayed.

FLAG OFFICER YACHT   6/1983, F Örgünsür

COAST GUARD (SAHIL GÜVENLIK)

Notes: 1. Tenders out to local shipyards for fourteen 200 ton patrol vessels. Orders expected in 1993.
2. At least three patrol craft are permanently based in North Cyprus.

8 KW 15 CLASS (LARGE PATROL CRAFT)

SG 12-16, 18-20

Displacement, tons: 70 full load
Dimensions, feet (metres): 94.8 × 15.4 × 4.6 *(28.9 × 4.7 × 1.4)*
Main machinery: 2 MTU diesels; 2000 hp(m) *(1.47 MW)*; 2 shafts
Speed, knots: 25. **Range, miles:** 1500 at 19 kts
Complement: 15
Guns: 1 Bofors 40 mm/60. 2 Oerlikon 20 mm.

Comment: Built by Schweers, Bardenfleth. Commissioned 1961-62.

SG 14   10/1991, Harald Carstens

14 LARGE PATROL CRAFT

SG 21-34

Displacement, tons: 170 full load
Dimensions, feet (metres): 132 × 21 × 5.5 *(40.2 × 6.4 × 1.7)*
131.2 × 21.3 × 4.9 *(40 × 6.5 × 1.5)* (SG 30-34)
Main machinery: 2 SACM AGO 195 V16 CSHR diesels; 4800 hp(m) *(3.53 MW)*
2 cruise diesels; 300 hp(m) *(220 kW)*; 2 shafts
Speed, knots: 22
Guns: 1 or 2 Bofors 40 mm/60. 2—12.7 mm MGs.

Comment: SG 21 and 22 built by Gölcük Naval Yard, remainder by Taşkizak Naval Yard. SG 34 commissioned in 1977, remainder 1968-71. SG 30-34 have minor modifications—knuckle at bow, radar stirrup on bridge and MG on superstructure sponsons. These are similar craft to the 12 listed under Light Forces for the Navy.

SG 22   9/1990, Selçuk Emre

10 SAR 33 TYPE (LARGE PATROL CRAFT)

SG 61-70

Displacement, tons: 140 standard; 170 full load
Dimensions, feet (metres): 108.3 × 28.3 × 9.7 *(33 × 8.6 × 3)*
Main machinery: 3 SACM AGO 195 V16 CSHR diesels; 7200 hp(m) *(5.29 MW)*; 3 shafts; cp props
Speed, knots: 40. **Range, miles:** 450 at 35 kts; 1000 at 20 kts
Complement: 24
Guns: 1 Bofors 40 mm/60. 2—7.62 mm MGs.
Radars: Surface search: Racal Decca; I band.

Comment: Prototype ordered from Abeking & Rasmussen, Lemwerder in May 1976. The remainder were built at Taşkizak Naval Yard, Istanbul between 1979 and 1981. Fourteen of this class were to have been transferred to Libya but the order was cancelled. Two delivered to Saudi Arabia.

SG 66   9/1992, C D Yaylali

4 SAR 35 TYPE (LARGE PATROL CRAFT)

SG 71-74

Displacement, tons: 210 full load
Dimensions, feet (metres): 120 × 28.3 × 6.2 *(36.6 × 8.6 × 1.9)*
Main machinery: 3 SACM AGO 195 V16 CSHR diesels; 7200 hp(m) *(5.29 MW)*; 3 shafts
Speed, knots: 40. **Range, miles:** 450 at 35 kts; 1000 at 20 kts
Complement: 24
Guns: 1 Bofors 40 mm/70. 2—7.62 mm MGs.
Radars: Surface search: Racal Decca; I band.

Comment: A slightly enlarged version of SAR 33 Type built by Taşkizak Shipyard between 1985 and 1987.

SG 74   10/1989, Hartmut Ehlers

9 COASTAL PATROL CRAFT

SG 41-47, 49, 50

Displacement, tons: 19 full load
Dimensions, feet (metres): 45.9 × 13.8 × 3.6 *(14 × 4.2 × 1.1)*
Main machinery: 2 diesels; 450 hp *(335 kW)*; 2 shafts
Speed, knots: 13
Complement: 5
Guns: 2—7.62 mm (twin) MGs.

Comment: Transferred in the 1950s. Former US Mk 5 45 ft craft built in Second World War. Some have radar on forward edge of bridge, whilst SG 41 has circular scuttles in place of square ports. Similar to Spanish P 231-P 235.

SG 44   6/1991, Mike Foster

1 INSHORE PATROL CRAFT

RAIF DENKTAS

Displacement, tons: 10 full load
Dimensions, feet (metres): 38 × 11.5 × 2.4 *(11.6 × 3.5 × 0.7)*
Main machinery: 2 Volvo Aquamatic AQ 200F petrol engines; 400 hp(m) *(294 kW)*; 2 shafts
Speed, knots: 28. **Range, miles:** 250 at 25 kts
Complement: 6
Guns: 1—12.7 mm MG.
Radars: Surface search: Raytheon; I band.

Comment: Built by Protekson, Istanbul. Transferred to North Cyprus 23 September 1988. Can be equipped with a rocket launcher.

RAIF DENKTAS   9/1988, Selçuk Emre

8 COASTAL PATROL CRAFT

SG 51-56   SG 102-103

Displacement, tons: 25 full load
Dimensions, feet (metres): 47.9 × 11.5 × 3.6 *(14.6 × 3.5 × 1.1)*
Main machinery: 2 diesels; 700 hp(m) *(514 kW)*; 2 shafts
Speed, knots: 18
Complement: 6
Guns: 1—12.7 mm MG or 1 Breda-Oerlikon 25 mm *(SG 102-103)*.

Comment: First three built at Taşkizak Shipyard and commissioned 20 July 1990. Three more laid down in mid-1990 and commissioned in 1991. *SG 102* and *103* were built for North Cyprus and have been based there since August 1990 and July 1991 respectively. Both these craft were given a heavier gun in 1992.

SG 52   *10/1991, Harald Carstens*

SG 102   *8/1990, Selçuk Emre*

2 TRANSPORT CRAFT

SG 104-105

Comment: Small utility craft which sometimes carry two 12.7 mm MGs.

SG 104   *10/1989, Hartmut Ehlers*

2 HARBOUR PATROL CRAFT

SG 1-2

Comment: High speed patrol boats for anti-smuggling duties.

SG 2   *7/1991, Selim San*

TURKS AND CAICOS

General

An Island Police Force funded by the UK Government.

Mercantile Marine

Lloyd's Register of Shipping:
13 vessels of 3533 tons gross

1 DAGGER CLASS (PATROL CRAFT)

Displacement, tons: 8
Dimensions, feet (metres): 39.7 × 11.2 × 3.6 *(12.1 × 3.4 × 1.1)*
Main machinery: 2 Perkins T6.3544M diesels; 330 hp *(246 kW)* sustained; 2 shafts
Speed, knots: 24. **Range, miles:** 540 at 20 kts
Guns: 1—7.62 mm MG.

Comment: Completed by Fairey Marine in June 1986. GRP hull.

1 HALMATIC M160 CLASS (PATROL CRAFT)

SEA QUEST

Displacement, tons: 18.5 light
Dimensions, feet (metres): 52.5 × 15.4 × 4.6 *(16 × 4.7 × 1.4)*
Main machinery: 2 Detroit 6V-92TA diesels; 520 hp *(388 kW)* sustained; 2 shafts
Speed, knots: 27. **Range, miles:** 500 at 17 kts
Complement: 8

Comment: Built by Halmatic, Havant and delivered on 22 December 1989. Similar craft acquired by the Virgin Islands, Montserrat and Anguilla. Has a rigid inflatable boat on the stern launched by a gravity davit.

SEA QUEST   *9/1989, Gilbert Gyssels*

UGANDA

Headquarters' Appointment

Commander, Army Marine Unit:
Captain Saleh Agondoa

Personnel

1993: 400

Bases

HQ: Fort Bell
Entebbe, Sese Isles, Gaba, Jinja, Majinji, Bukakata (all on Lake Victoria).

Mercantile Marine

Lloyd's Register of Shipping:
2 vessels of 3394 tons gross

PATROL FORCES

6 YUGOSLAV AL8K TYPE

Displacement, tons: 6.3 full load
Dimensions, feet (metres): 36.6 × 12.3 × 1.5 *(11.2 × 3.7 × 0.5)*
Main machinery: 2 diesels; 300 hp(m) *(220 kW)*; 2 shafts
Speed, knots: 25
Complement: 3
Guns: 1—12.7 mm MG.

Comment: Acquired in September 1988. Aluminium hulls. Designed for patrol work on rivers and lakes.

LAKE PATROL CRAFT   *1989*

714 UGANDA / Patrol forces — UAE / Light forces

2 Ex-NORTH KOREAN KIMJIN CLASS

Displacement, tons: 25 full load
Dimensions, feet (metres): 66.6 × 11 × 5.5 *(20.3 × 3.4 × 1.7)*
Main machinery: 2 diesels; 2400 hp(m) *(1.76 MW)*; 2 shafts
Speed, knots: 42. **Range, miles:** 220 at 20 kts
Complement: 10
Guns: 4—14.5 mm (2 twin) MGs.

Comment: Transferred in the early 1980s. One is for use by the President.

14 GRP PATROL CRAFT

Comment: These are fast motor boats used on the minor lakes and waterways. Some are armed with 7.62 mm MGs.

UKRAINE

Headquarters' Appointments

Commander of the Navy:
   Rear Admiral Boris Kozhin
Chief of Naval Border Guard:
   Rear Admiral Boris Ryabov

Bases

Sevastopol (HQ), Odessa, Nikolayev

General

A Maritime Border Guard of some 40 minor Black Sea Fleet units was formed in early 1992. On 21 July a Petya II (815) class light frigate 'defected' from the Russian Navy, and this was immediately followed on 28 July by the commissioning of the *Slavutich*, a second of the Kamchatka class, as the new Flagship of the Navy. On 3 August 1992 a joint agreement signed by Russia and Ukraine, in theory put a stop to further Ukrainian acquisitions by declaring that all Black Sea Fleet units would be jointly operated by the two states until 1995, by which time the division of the Fleet would be agreed. However in December 1992 the Commander of the Ukrainian Navy was talking about a Navy of 40 000 men, the possession of a new patrol craft and Pomornik class hovercraft, and plans to refit submarines and upgrade naval aviation. He expected to receive a guided missile cruiser and several patrol ships in the near future. In early 1993 some Black Sea Fleet units were flying a combined Russian/Ukrainian ensign. Details of all Black Sea Fleet ships are listed in the section headed Russia and Associated States.

UNITED ARAB EMIRATES

Headquarters' Appointments

Commander, Naval Forces:
   Brigadier Hazza Sultan Al Darmaki
Commander, Coast Guard:
   Brigadier Saif Al Shaafar

General

This federation of the former Trucial States (Abu Dhabi, Ajman, Dubai, Fujairah, Ras al Khaimah, Sharjah, Umm al Qaiwan) was formed under a provisional constitution in 1971 with a new constitution coming into effect on 2 December 1976.
Following a decision of the UAE Supreme Defence Council on 6 May 1976 the armed forces of the member states were unified and the organisation of the UAE Armed Forces was furthered by decisions taken on 1 February 1978.

Personnel

(a) 1993: 1980 (145 officers)
(b) Voluntary service

Bases

Taweela (main base) between Abu Dhabi and Dubai.
Dalma and Mina Zayed (Abu Dhabi),
Mina Rashid and Mina Jebel Ali (Dubai),
Mina Saqr (Ras al Khaimah), Mina Sultan (Sharjah),
Khor Fakkan (Sharjah-East Coast).

Mercantile Marine

Lloyd's Register of Shipping:
   276 vessels of 928 720 tons gross

MISSILE CORVETTES

2 LÜRSSEN 62 TYPE

Name	No	Builders	Commissioned
MURAY JIP	P 6501	Lürssen, Bremen	Nov 1990
DAS	P 6502	Lürssen, Bremen	Jan 1991

Displacement, tons: 630 full load
Dimensions, feet (metres): 206.7 × 30.5 × 8.2 *(63 × 9.3 × 2.5)*
Main machinery: 4 MTU 16V 538 TB92 diesels; 13 640 hp(m) *(10 MW)* sustained; 4 shafts
Speed, knots: 32. **Range, miles:** 4000 at 16 kts
Complement: 43

Missiles: SSM: 4 Aerospatiale MM 40 Exocet; inertial cruise; active radar homing to 70 km *(40 nm)* at 0.9 Mach; warhead 165 kg; sea-skimmer.
   SAM: Thomson-CSF modified Crotale Navale octuple launcher; radar guidance; IR homing to 13 km *(7 nm)* at 2.4 Mach; warhead 14 kg.
Guns: 1 OTO Melara 3 in *(76 mm)*/62 Super Rapid; 85° elevation; 120 rounds/minute to 16 km *(8.7 nm)*; weight of shell 6 kg.
   1 Signaal Goalkeeper with GE 30 mm 7-barrelled; 4200 rounds/minute combined to 2 km.
Countermeasures: Decoys: Dagaie launcher; IR flares and chaff.
ESM/ECM: Racal Cutlass/Cygnus; intercept/jammer.
Radars: Air/surface search: Bofors Ericsson Sea Giraffe 50HC; G band.
   Navigation: Racal Decca 1226; I band.
   Fire control: Bofors Electronic 9LV 331; J band (for gun and SSM).
      Thomson-CSF DRBV 51C; J band (for Crotale).
Helicopters: 1 Aerospatiale Alouette SA 316.

Programmes: Ordered in late 1986. Similar vessels to Bahrain craft. Delivery in late 1991. One more may be ordered.
Structure: Lürssen design adapted for the particular conditions of the Gulf. This class has good air defence and a considerable anti-ship capability if the helicopter also carries anti-surface missiles.

DAS   *4/1991, Harald Carstens*

LIGHT FORCES

Note: Six fast patrol craft ordered from Halmatic in June 1992. To be used for Special Forces.

3 KEITH NELSON TYPE (COASTAL PATROL CRAFT)

Name	No	Builders	Commissioned
KAWKAB	P 561	Keith Nelson, Bembridge	7 Mar 1969
THOABAN	P 562	Keith Nelson, Bembridge	7 Mar 1969
BANI YAS	P 563	Keith Nelson, Bembridge	27 Dec 1969

Displacement, tons: 32 standard; 38 full load
Dimensions, feet (metres): 57 × 16.5 × 4.5 *(17.4 × 5 × 1.4)*
Main machinery: 2 Caterpillar diesels; 750 hp *(560 kW)*; 2 shafts
Speed, knots: 19. **Range, miles:** 445 at 15 kts
Complement: 11 (2 officers)
Guns: 2 Oerlikon 20 mm.
Radars: Surface search: Racal Decca TM 1626; I band.

Comment: Of glass fibre hull construction. Originally operated by Abu Dhabi.

MURAY JIP   *6/1990, van Ginderen Collection*

BANI YAS   *11/1976, UAE Armed Forces*

Light forces — Service forces / UAE   715

2 MUBARRAZ CLASS (FAST ATTACK CRAFT—MISSILE)

Name	No	Builders	Commissioned
MUBARRAZ	P 4401	Lürssen, Bremen	Aug 1990
MAKASIB	P 4402	Lürssen, Bremen	Aug 1990

Displacement, tons: 260 full load
Dimensions, feet (metres): 147.3 × 23 × 7.2 *(44.9 × 7 × 2.2)*
Main machinery: 2 MTU 20V 538 TB93 diesels; 9370 hp(m) *(6.9 MW)* sustained; 2 shafts
Speed, knots: 40. **Range, miles:** 500 at 38 kts
Complement: 40 (5 officers)

Missiles: SSM: 4 Aerospatiale MM 40 Exocet; inertial cruise; active radar homing to 70 km *(40 nm)* at 0.9 Mach; warhead 165 kg; sea-skimmer.
  SAM: 1 Matra Sadral sextuple launcher; Mistral; IR homing to 4 km *(2.2 nm)*; warhead 3 kg.
Guns: 1 OTO Melara 3 in *(76 mm)*/62 Super Rapid; 85° elevation; 120 rounds/minute to 16 km *(8.7 nm)*; weight of shell 6 kg.
Countermeasures: Decoys: Dagaie launchers; IR flares and chaff.
ESM/ECM: Racal Cutlass/Cygnus; intercept/jammer.
Fire control: CSEE Najir optronic director (for SAM).
Radars: Air/surface search: Bofors Ericsson Sea Giraffe 50HC; G band.
  Navigation: Racal Decca 1226; I band.
  Fire control: Bofors Electronic 9LV 331; J band (for gun and SSM).

Programmes: Ordered in late 1986 from Lürssen Werft at the same time as the two Type 62 vessels. Possibly one more to follow.
Structure: This is a modified FPB 38 design, with the first export version of Matra Sadral.

MAKASIB   *9/1990, Foto Flite*

6 LÜRSSEN TNC 45 CLASS (FAST ATTACK CRAFT—MISSILE)

Name	No	Builders	Commissioned
BAN YAS	P 4501	Lürssen Vegesack	Nov 1980
MARBAN	P 4502	Lürssen Vegesack	Nov 1980
RODQM	P 4503	Lürssen Vegesack	July 1981
SHAHEEN	P 4504	Lürssen Vegesack	July 1981
SAGAR	P 4505	Lürssen Vegesack	Sep 1981
TARIF	P 4506	Lürssen Vegesack	Sep 1981

Displacement, tons: 260 full load
Dimensions, feet (metres): 147.3 × 23 × 8.2 *(44.9 × 7 × 2.5)*
Main machinery: 4 MTU 16V 538 TB92 diesels; 13 640 hp(m) *(10 MW)* sustained; 4 shafts
Speed, knots: 40. **Range, miles:** 500 at 38 kts
Complement: 40 (5 officers)

Missiles: SSM: 4 Aerospatiale MM 40 Exocet; inertial cruise; active radar homing to 70 km *(40 nm)* at 0.9 Mach; warhead 165 kg; sea-skimmer.
Guns: 1 OTO Melara 3 in *(76 mm)*/62; 85° elevation; 60 rounds/minute to 16 km *(8.7 nm)*; weight of shell 6 kg.
  2 Breda 40 mm/70 (twin); 85° elevation; 300 rounds/minute to 12.5 km *(6.8 nm)*; weight of shell 0.96 kg.
  2—7.62 mm MGs.
Countermeasures: Decoys: 1 CSEE trainable Dagaie; IR flares and chaff; H-J band.
ESM/ECM: Racal Cutlass/Cygnus; intercept/jammer.
Fire control: 1 CSEE Panda director for 40 mm. PEAB low light USFA IR and TV tracker.
Radars: Surface search: Bofors Ericsson Sea Giraffe 50HC; G band.
  Navigation: Racal Decca TM 1226; I band.
  Fire control: Philips 9LV 200 Mk 2; J band.

Programmes: Ordered in late 1977. First two shipped in September 1980 and four more in Summer 1981. This class was the first to be fitted with MM40.
Structure: Modified FPB 38 design.

SAGAR   *5/1987*

6 VOSPER THORNYCROFT TYPE (LARGE PATROL CRAFT)

Name	No	Builders	Commissioned
ARDHANA	P 1101	Vosper Thornycroft	24 June 1975
ZURARA	P 1102	Vosper Thornycroft	14 Aug 1975
MURBAN	P 1103	Vosper Thornycroft	16 Sep 1975
AL GHULLAN	P 1104	Vosper Thornycroft	16 Sep 1975
RADOOM	P 1105	Vosper Thornycroft	1 July 1976
GHANADHAH	P 1106	Vosper Thornycroft	1 July 1976

Displacement, tons: 110 standard; 175 full load
Dimensions, feet (metres): 110 × 21 × 6.6 *(33.5 × 6.4 × 2)*
Main machinery: 2 Paxman 12CM diesels; 5000 hp *(3.73 MW)* sustained; 2 shafts
Speed, knots: 30. **Range, miles:** 1800 at 14 kts
Complement: 26
Guns: 2 Oerlikon/BMARC 30 mm/75 A32 (twin); 85° elevation; 650 rounds/minute to 10 km *(5.5 nm)*; weight of shell 1 kg or 0.36 kg.
  1 Oerlikon/BMARC 20 mm/80 A41A; 800 rounds/minute to 2 km.
  2—51 mm projectors for illuminants.
Radars: Surface search: Racal Decca TM 1626; I band.

Comment: A class of round bilge steel hull craft. P 1101-2 and P 1105-6 transported by heavy-lift ships. P 1103 and P 1104 were sailed out. Originally operated by Abu Dhabi.

AL GHULLAN   *11/1987*

SERVICE FORCES

2 CHEVERTON TYPE (TENDERS)

A 271   A 272

Displacement, tons: 3.3 full load
Dimensions, feet (metres): 27 × 9 × 2.7 *(8.2 × 2.7 × 0.8)*
Main machinery: 1 Lister RMW3 diesel; 150 hp *(112 kW)*; 1 shaft
Speed, knots: 8

Comment: Built of GRP. Acquired from Chevertons, Cowes, Isle of Wight in 1975 by Abu Dhabi. A272 has a 2 ton hoist.

2 + 2 VOSPER QAF TYPE LANDING CRAFT (LCT)

JANANAH   DAYYINAH

Measurement, tons: 350 dwt
Dimensions, feet (metres): 177.2 × — × — *(54 × — × —)*

Comment: Built by Argos Shipyard, Singapore. Both completed December 1988. Can carry four medium tanks. Two more reported ordered in June 1990.

1 LSL

AL FEYI

Displacement, tons: 650 full load
Dimensions, feet (metres): 164 × 36.1 × 9.2 *(50 × 11 × 2.8)*
Main machinery: 2 diesels; 1248 hp *(931 kW)*; 2 shafts
Speed, knots: 11. **Range, miles:** 1800 at 11 kts
Complement: 10

Comment: Built by Siong Huat, Singapore; completed 4 August 1987.

1 M/V 100 TYPE DIVING TENDER

D 1051

Displacement, tons: 100 full load
Dimensions, feet (metres): 103 × 22.6 × 3.6 *(31.4 × 6.9 × 1.1)*
Main machinery: 2 MTU 12V 396 TB93 diesels; 3260 hp(m) *(2.4 MW)* sustained; 2 waterjets
Speed, knots: 26. **Range, miles:** 390 at 24 kts
Complement: 6

Comment: Ordered from Crestitalia end 1985 for Abu Dhabi and delivered in July 1987. GRP hull. Used primarily for mine clearance but also for diving training, salvage and SAR. Fitted with a decompression chamber and diving bell. Reports of a second of class are not confirmed. Lengthened version of Italian *Alcide Pedretti*.

D 1051   *1987, Crestitalia*

716 UAE / Service forces — Coast Guard craft

1 LCM

GHAGHA II

Displacement, tons: 100 full load
Dimensions, feet (metres): 131.2 × 32.8 × 3.3 *(40 × 10 × 1)*
Main machinery: 2 diesels; 730 hp *(544 kW)*; 2 shafts
Speed, knots: 9
Complement: 6

Comment: Built by Siong Huat, Singapore; launched 17 April 1987.

1 SUPPORT CRAFT

BARACUDA

Displacement, tons: 1400 full load
Dimensions, feet (metres): 190 × 39.4 × 13.1 *(57.9 × 12 × 4)*
Main machinery: 2 Ruston 12RKC diesels; 6200 hp *(4.6 MW)* sustained; 2 shafts
Speed, knots: 12

Comment: Completed June 1983 by Singapore Slipway Co.

1 TUG

ANNAD A 3501

Displacement, tons: 795 full load
Dimensions, feet (metres): 114.8 × 32.2 × 13.8 *(35 × 9.8 × 4.2)*
Main machinery: 2 Caterpillar 3606TA diesels; 4180 hp *(3.12 MW)* sustained; 2 shafts; bow thruster
Speed, knots: 14. **Range, miles:** 2500 at 14 kts
Complement: 14 (3 officers)

Comment: Built by Dunston, Hessle, and completed in April 1989. Bollard pull, 55 tons. Equipped for SAR.

SHIPBORNE AIRCRAFT

Numbers/Type: 6 Aerospatiale SA 316/319S Alouette.
Operational speed: 113 kts *(210 km/h)*.
Service ceiling: 10 500 ft *(3200 m)*.
Range: 290 nm *(540 km)*.
Role/Weapon systems: Reconnaissance and general purpose helicopters. Sensors: radar. Weapons: To be fitted with ASV weapons.

LAND-BASED MARITIME AIRCRAFT

Numbers/Type: 4 Aerospatiale AS 332F Super Puma.
Operational speed: 150 kts *(280 km/h)*.
Service ceiling: 15 090 ft *(4600 m)*.
Range: 335 nm *(620 km)*.
Role/Weapon systems: Anti-ship and transport helicopter with limited ASV role; utility role widely used. Sensors: Omera ORB 30 radar. Weapons: ASV; 1 × AM 39 Exocet. ASM; depth bombs.

Numbers/Type: 2 Pilatus Britten-Norman Maritime Defender.
Operational speed: 150 kts *(280 km/h)*.
Service ceiling: 18 900 ft *(5760 m)*.
Range: 1500 nm *(2775 km)*.
Role/Weapon systems: Coastal patrol and surveillance aircraft. Sensors: Nose-mounted search radar, underwing searchlight. Weapons: Underwing rocket and gun pods.

COAST GUARD CRAFT

Note: Under control of Minister of Interior. In addition to the vessels listed below there are a number of Customs and Police launches including three Swedish Boghammar 13 m craft of the same type used by Iran and delivered in 1985, two Baglietto police launches acquired in 1988, about 10 elderly Dhafeer and Spear class of 12 and 9 m respectively, and two Halmatic Arun class Pilot craft delivered in 1990/91; some of these launches carry light machine guns.

5 CAMCRAFT 77 ft (COASTAL PATROL CRAFT)

753-757

Displacement, tons: 70 full load
Dimensions, feet (metres): 76.8 × 18 × 4.9 *(23.4 × 5.5 × 1.5)*
Main machinery: 2 GM 12V-71TA diesels; 840 hp *(627 kW)* sustained; 2 shafts
Speed, knots: 25
Guns: 2 Lawrence Scott 20 mm (not always embarked).

Comment: Completed 1975 by Camcraft, New Orleans. To be replaced by three 59 ft speedboats ordered in 1992 and capable of 45 kts.

CAMCRAFT 757   6/1990

1 POSILIPO TYPE (COASTAL PATROL CRAFT)

Displacement, tons: 35.5 full load
Dimensions, feet (metres): 64.9 × 19.68 × 3.9 *(19.8 × 6 × 1.2)*
Main machinery: 2 MTU 6V 396 TB93 diesels; 1630 hp(m) *(1.2 MW)* sustained; 2 shafts
Speed, knots: 24
Gun: 1 Oerlikon 20 mm.

Comment: Built by Posilipo, Italy and commissioned on 24 November 1984 in the Abu Dhabi Coast Guard. GRP hull.

16 CAMCRAFT 65 ft (COASTAL PATROL CRAFT)

Displacement, tons: 50
Dimensions, feet (metres): 65 × 18 × 5 *(19.8 × 5.5 × 1.5)*
Main machinery: 2 MTU 6V 396 TB93 diesels; 1630 hp(m) *(1.2 MW)* sustained; 2 shafts (in 14) 2 Detroit 8V-92TA diesels; 700 hp *(522 kW)* sustained; 2 shafts (in 2)
Speed, knots: 25
Guns: 1 Oerlikon 20 mm.

Comment: Ordered in 1978.

CAMCRAFT 65 ft   1987, UAE Coast Guard

6 BAGLIETTO GC 23 TYPE (COASTAL PATROL CRAFT)

758   +5

Displacement, tons: 50.7 full load
Dimensions, feet (metres): 78.7 × 18 × 3 *(24 × 5.5 × 0.9)*
Main machinery: 2 MTU 12V 396 TB93 diesels; 3260 hp(m) *(2.4 MW)* sustained; 2 KaMeWa waterjets
Speed, knots: 43. **Range, miles:** 700 at 20 kts
Complement: 9
Guns: 1 Oerlikon 20 mm. 2—7.62 mm MGs.

Comment: Built by Baglietto, Varazze. First two completed in March and May 1986, second pair in July 1987 and two more in 1988. All were delivered to UAE Coast Guard in Dubai.

BAGLIETTO   1987, UAE Coast Guard

10 WATERCRAFT 45 ft (COASTAL PATROL CRAFT)

Displacement, tons: 25 full load
Dimensions, feet (metres): 45 × 14.1 × 4.6 *(13.7 × 4.3 × 1.4)*
Main machinery: 2 MAN D2542 diesels; 1300 hp(m) *(956 kW)*; 2 shafts
Speed, knots: 26. **Range, miles:** 380 at 18 kts
Complement: 5
Guns: Mounts for 2—7.62 mm MGs.

Comment: Ordered from Watercraft, UK in February 1982. Delivery in early 1983.

WATERCRAFT 45 ft   1984, UAE Coast Guard

38 HARBOUR PATROL CRAFT

Comment: The latest are 10 Shark 33 built by Shaali Marine, Dubai and delivered in 1993. The remainder are a mixture of Baracuda 30 ft and FPB 22 ft classes. All are powered by twin outboard engines and most carry a 7.62 mm MG.

2 DIVING TENDERS

Displacement, tons: 8.8
Main machinery: 2 Volvo Penta diesels; 2 shafts
Speed, knots: 11

Comment: FPB 512 Rotork design. Completed May 1981 for Abu Dhabi.

UNITED KINGDOM

Admiralty Board

Chief of the Naval Staff and First Sea Lord:
  Admiral Sir Benjamin Bathurst, GCB
Chief of Naval Personnel and Second Sea Lord:
  Vice Admiral Sir Michael Layard, KCB, CBE
Controller of the Navy:
  Admiral Sir Kenneth Eaton, KCB
Chief of Fleet Support:
  Vice Admiral Sir Neville Purvis, KCB
Assistant Chief of the Naval Staff:
  Rear Admiral P C Abbott

Commanders-in-Chief

Commander-in-Chief, Fleet:
  Admiral Sir Hugo White, KCB, CBE
Commander-in-Chief, Naval Home Command:
  Admiral Sir John Kerr, KCB

Flag Officers

Flag Officer, Submarines:
  Vice Admiral R T Frere
Flag Officer, Surface Flotilla:
  Rear Admiral M C Boyce, OBE
Flag Officer, Naval Aviation:
  Rear Admiral I D G Garnett
Commander, UK Task Group:
  Rear Admiral M P Gretton
Flag Officer, Sea Training:
  Rear Admiral J G Tolhurst
Commander British Forces, Gibraltar:
  Rear Admiral J T Sanders, OBE
Flag Officer, Plymouth:
  Vice Admiral Sir Roy Newman, KCB
Flag Officer, Portsmouth:
  Rear Admiral D K Bawtree
Flag Officer, Scotland and Northern Ireland:
  Vice Admiral C C Morgan
Hydrographer of the Navy:
  Rear Admiral J A L Myres
Commodore Minor War Vessels Flotilla:
  Commodore C J Freeman
Commodore Royal Fleet Auxiliaries:
  Commodore R M Thorn

Headquarters Royal Marines

Commandant-General, Royal Marines:
  Lieutenant General R J Ross, CB, OBE
Major General, Royal Marines:
  Major General A M Keeling, CBE

Fleet Disposition

Submarine Flotilla (3rd and 10th to become 1st Squadron 1 Oct 1993)
2nd Squadron (*Defiance*, Devonport) 7 Fleet submarines, 4 Patrol submarines
3rd Squadron (*Neptune*, Faslane) 6 Fleet submarines
10th Squadron (*Neptune*, Faslane) 4 Strategic submarines

Surface Flotilla
1st Frigate Squadron (Devonport) Type 22 Batch 2
2nd Frigate Squadron (Devonport) Type 22 Batches 1 and 3
3rd Destroyer Squadron (Portsmouth) Type 42
4th Frigate Squadron (Devonport) Type 21
5th Destroyer Squadron (Portsmouth) Type 42
6th Frigate Squadron (Devonport) Type 23

MCM Flotilla
1st Squadron (Rosyth), 2nd Squadron (Portsmouth)
3rd Squadron (Rosyth), 4th Squadron (Rosyth)
Fishery Protection Squadron (Rosyth), 10th Squadron (RNR)

Surveying Flotilla (Devonport)
2 Ocean and 4 Coastal Survey Ships

Diplomatic Representation

Naval Attaché in Athens:
  Captain J J Pearson
Naval Attaché in Beijing:
  Captain A B P Armstrong
Naval Attaché in Bonn:
  Captain R St J S Bishop
Naval Attaché in Brasilia:
  Captain J R Luard
Naval Adviser in Bridgetown:
  Captain R F Shercliffe
Naval Attaché in Cairo:
  Commander P G Blanchford
Defence Adviser in Canberra:
  Commodore B J Adams
Defence Attaché in Caracas (and Santo Domingo):
  Captain R L Perrett
Defence Attaché in Copenhagen:
  Commander R Kirkwood
Naval Attaché in The Hague:
  Captain H W Rickard
Naval Attaché in Islamabad:
  Commander D A Scott
Assistant Defence Adviser in Kuala Lumpur:
  Lieutenant Commander C C Williams
Defence Attaché in Lisbon:
  Commander P M Jones
Naval Attaché in Madrid:
  Captain J Gozzard
Defence Attaché in Manila:
  Colonel J P Clough, RM
Defence Attaché in Montevideo:
  Captain R A Highton
Naval Attaché in Moscow:
  Captain J M Dobson
Naval Adviser in Nassau (and Georgetown and Port of Spain):
  Captain A J S Taylor
Naval Adviser in New Delhi:
  Captain P N Galloway
Naval Attaché in Oslo:
  Commander G S Pearson, OBE
Naval Adviser in Ottawa:
  Captain R A Baller
Naval Attaché in Paris:
  Captain M A Johnson
Naval Attaché in Riyadh:
  Commander T Waddington
Naval Attaché in Rome:
  Captain K F Read
Defence Attaché in Santiago:
  Captain R A Rowley, OBE
Naval Attaché in Tokyo:
  Captain A P Masterson-Smith
Naval Attaché in Washington:
  Rear Admiral A P Hoddinott, OBE

Royal Marines Operational Units

HQ 3 Commando Brigade RM; 40 Commando RM; 42 Commando RM; 45 Commando Group (RM/Army); 3 Commando Brigade Air Squadron RM; Commando Logistic Regiment RM (RN/RM/Army); 3 Commando Brigade HQ and Signal Squadron RM including Air Defence Troop RM (Javelin), EW Troop RM, Tactical Air Command Posts RM (3 regular, 1 reserve); 539 Assault Squadron RM (landing craft and raiding craft), including 2 Raiding Troop RMR (raiding craft); Brigade Patrol Troop (reconnaissance); Special Boat Service RM; Comacchio Group RM (security); T Company RMR; 29 Commando Regiment RA (Army); 59 Independent Commando Squadron RE (Army); 289 Commando Battery RA (Volunteers); 131 Independent Squadron RE (Volunteers).

Bases

Northwood (*Warrior*); C-in-C Fleet; FO Submarines
Portsmouth; C-in-C Navhome; HQ Royal Marines; FO Portsmouth; FO Surface Flotilla
Devonport; FO Plymouth
Rosyth; FO Scotland and Northern Ireland
Portland; FO Sea Training
Faslane (*Neptune*); Commodore Clyde
Gibraltar; CBF Gibraltar
Hong Kong (*Tamar*); Captain-in-Charge

Personnel (including Royal Marines)

(a) 1 January 1993: 60 970 (RN 53 600; RM 7370)
(b) Volunteer Reserves: RN 4565; RM 1185
(c) Regular Reserves: RN 17 400; RM 2150
(d) RNXS: 2700

Strength of the Fleet—1 June 1993

Type	Active (Reserve)	Building (Projected)
SSBNs	4	3
Submarines—Attack	13	(6)
Submarines—Patrol	5	—
Aircraft Carriers	2 (1)	—
Destroyers	12 (1)	—
Frigates	24 (1)	7 (10)
Assault Ships (LPDs)	1 (1)	(2)
Helicopter Carrier (LPH)	—	(1)
LSLs (RFA)	5	—
LCLs (RCT)	2	—
LCRs (RCT)	9	—
LCVPs	21	—
LCUs	12	(4)
RPLs	3	—
Offshore Patrol Vessels	9	—
Patrol Craft/Training Craft	6/14	—
Minehunters/Minesweepers	20	1 (7)
Minesweepers—Coastal	10 (2)	—
Repair/Maintenance Ship (RFA)	1	—
Survey Ships	2	(2)
Coastal Survey Ships	4	—
Antarctic Patrol Ship	1	—
Training Ships	2	—
Royal Yacht	1	—
Large Fleet Tankers (RFA)	3	(3)
Support Tankers (RFA)	4	—
Small Fleet Tankers (RFA)	2	—
Coastal Tankers (RMAS)	4	—
Aviation Training Ship (RFA)	1	—
Fleet Replenishment Ships (RFA)	4 (1)	—
SMVs and PMLs	8	—
Trials Ships (RMAS)	2	—
TRVs (RMAS)	5	—
Armament Carriers (RMAS)	1 (1)	—
Water Carriers (RMAS)	5	—
Ocean Tugs	3	—
Harbour Tugs	49	—
Range Support Vessels (RMAS)	15	—
Submarine Support Vessels (RMAS)	6	1
Aviation Support Craft (RMAS)	11	—
Tenders (RMAS)	50	—
RNXS Craft	14	—
DG Vessels	1 (1)	—
Sea Cadet Corps Vessels	8	—
Target Vessels	3	—
Royal Corps of Transport	24	—

Mercantile Marine

Lloyd's Register of Shipping:
  1747 vessels of 6 016 868 tons gross

Fleet Air Arm Squadron (see *Shipborne Aircraft* section)

F/W Aircraft	Role	Deployment	Squadron no
Sea Harrier	FRS	*Invincible*	800
Sea Harrier	FRS	*Ark Royal*	801
Sea Harrier	Aircrew Training	Yeovilton, *Heron*	899
Jetstream	Aircrew Training	Culdrose, *Seahawk*	750

Helicopters	Role	Deployment	Squadron no.
Sea King AEW 2	Aircrew Training	Culdrose	849 HQ
Sea King AEW 2	AEW	*Invincible*	849 A flight
Sea King AEW 2	AEW	*Ark Royal*	849 B flight
Sea King HAS 5	ASW	*Invincible*	814
Sea King HAS 5	ASW	*Ark Royal*	820
Sea King HAS 5	ASW	RFAs	826
Sea King HAS 6	ASW	Prestwick, *Gannet*	819
Sea King HAS 5	Aircrew Training	Culdrose, *Seahawk*	810
Sea King HAS 5	Aircrew Training	Culdrose, *Seahawk*	706
Sea King HC 4	Commando Assault	Yeovilton, *Heron*	845
Sea King HC 4	Commando Assault	Yeovilton, *Heron*	846
Sea King HC 4	Aircrew Training	Yeovilton, *Heron*	707
Sea King HAS 5	SAR	Culdrose, *Seahawk*	771
Sea King HC 4	SAR	Portland, *Osprey*	772
Lynx HAS 3	ASUW/ASW	Portland, *Osprey*	815
Lynx HAS 3	Aircrew Training	Portland, *Osprey*	702
Gazelle HT 2	Aircrew Training	Culdrose, *Seahawk*	705

Note: Training and Liaison aircraft not listed under the *Shipborne* or *Land-based Aircraft* sections include five Sea Harrier T4N/T4, 31 Gazelle HT 2, 20 Jetstream, 16 Chipmunk, 26 Hunter, 16 Falcon 20 (under contract).

DELETIONS

Note: Those ships not shown as sold or broken up are awaiting disposal.

Submarines

- 1990 *Warspite*
- 1991 *Onyx* (sold), *Odin* (bu), *Onslaught* (bu), *Conqueror*, *Churchill*
- 1992 *Swiftsure*, *Courageous*, *Otter*, *Otus* (sold), *Ocelot* (museum), *Osiris* (sold), *Revenge*
- 1993 *Oracle*, *Opportune*

Frigates

- 1990 *Plymouth* (museum), *Achilles* (sold to Chile), *Naiad* (sunk), *Phoebe*
- 1991 *Danae* (sold to Ecuador), *Penelope* (sold to Ecuador), *Arethusa* (sunk), *Cleopatra*, *Minerva*, *Jupiter*, *Hermione*, *Charybdis*
- 1992 *Sirius*, *Argonaut*, *Juno*, *Ariadne* (sold to Chile)
- 1993 *Amazon*, *Ambuscade*, *Arrow*

Destroyers

- 1991 *Bristol* (immobile tender)

MCM Vessels

- 1990 *Walkerton* (sold), *Cuxton* (bu), *Brereton*, *Hubberston* (bu), *Bronington* (museum)
- 1991 *Gavinton* (bu), *Kirkliston* (bu), *Upton* (sold), *Soberton*, *Kedleston* (bu)
- 1992 *Iveston*, *Kellington* (both reserve)

Patrol Vessels

- 1991 *Sandpiper* (sold), *Peterel* (sold), *Cormorant* (sold), *Hart* (sold)
- 1992 *Attacker*, *Hunter*, *Striker* (all sold to Lebanon), *Sentinel*, *Fencer* (sold), *Chaser* (sold), *Endurance* (old) (sold)

Survey Ship and Craft

- 1990 *Fox* (sold), *Hecate*
- 1991 *Fawn* (sold), *Yarmouth Navigator* (sold)

Service Forces

- 1990 *Dolwen* (sold), *Engadine* (sold), *Denmead*, *Manly*, *Mentor*, *Millbrook*
- 1991 *Bembridge* (sold), *Lofoten* (sold), *Stalker* (sold), *Garganey* (sold), *Tidespring* (sold), *Challenger*, *Kinbrace*, *Mandarin*, *Crystal* (sold), *Torrid* (sold), *Goldeneye* (sold), *Green Rover* (sold to Indonesia)
- 1992 *Throsk* (sold), *Waterside* (sold) (both to Ecuador), *Regent*, *Oilstone*, *Oilfield*, *Whitehead*, *Watershed*, *Criccieth*, *Froxfield*, *Glencoe*, *Sultan Venturer* (old)
- 1993 *Blue Rover* (sold to Portugal), *Grey Rover*

Tugs

- 1991 *Dorothy* (sold)

PENNANT LIST

Note: Numbers are not displayed on Submarines or some RMAS craft.

Aircraft Carriers

R 05	Invincible
R 06	Illustrious
R 07	Ark Royal

Destroyers

D 86	Birmingham
D 87	Newcastle
D 88	Glasgow
D 89	Exeter
D 90	Southampton
D 91	Nottingham
D 92	Liverpool
D 95	Manchester
D 96	Gloucester
D 97	Edinburgh
D 98	York
D 108	Cardiff

Frigates

F 57	Andromeda
F 71	Scylla
F 85	Cumberland
F 86	Campbeltown
F 87	Chatham
F 88	Broadsword
F 89	Battleaxe
F 90	Brilliant
F 91	Brazen
F 92	Boxer
F 93	Beaver
F 94	Brave
F 95	London
F 96	Sheffield
F 98	Coventry
F 99	Cornwall
F 171	Active
F 174	Alacrity
F 185	Avenger
F 229	Lancaster
F 230	Norfolk
F 231	Argyll
F 233	Marlborough
F 234	Iron Duke
F 235	Monmouth
F 236	Montrose
F 237	Westminster
F 238	Northumberland
F 239	Richmond
F 240	Somerset
F 241	Grafton
F 242	Sutherland

Assault Ships

L 10	Fearless
L 11	Intrepid

Logistic Landing Ships and LCTs

L 105	Arromanches
L 106	Antwerp
L 107	Andalsnes
L 108	Abbeville
L 109	Akyab
L 110	Aachen
L 111	Arezzo
L 112	Agheila
L 113	Audemer
L 3004	Sir Bedivere
L 3005	Sir Galahad
L 3027	Sir Geraint
L 3036	Sir Percivale
L 3505	Sir Tristram
L 4001	Ardennes
L 4003	Arakan

LCMs (RCT)

RPL 05	Eden
RPL 06	Forth
RPL 12	Medway

Minesweepers/Minehunters

M 29	Brecon
M 30	Ledbury
M 31	Cattistock
M 32	Cottesmore
M 33	Brocklesby
M 34	Middleton
M 35	Dulverton
M 36	Bicester
M 37	Chiddingfold
M 38	Atherstone
M 39	Hurworth
M 40	Berkeley
M 41	Quorn
M 101	Sandown
M 102	Inverness
M 103	Cromer
M 104	Walney
M 105	Bridport
M 1114	Brinton
M 1116	Wilton (training)
M 1166	Nurton
M 1181	Sheraton
M 2003	Waveney
M 2004	Carron
M 2005	Dovey
M 2006	Helford
M 2007	Humber
M 2008	Blackwater
M 2009	Itchen
M 2010	Helmsdale
M 2011	Orwell
M 2012	Ribble
M 2013	Spey
M 2014	Arun

Light Forces/Patrol Ships

P 239	Peacock
P 240	Plover
P 241	Starling
P 258	Leeds Castle
P 259	Redpole
P 260	Kingfisher
P 261	Cygnet
P 264	Archer
P 265	Dumbarton Castle
P 270	Biter
P 272	Smiter
P 273	Pursuer
P 277	Anglesey
P 278	Alderney
P 279	Blazer
P 280	Dasher
P 291	Puncher
P 292	Charger
P 293	Ranger
P 294	Trumpeter
P 295	Jersey
P 297	Guernsey
P 298	Shetland
P 299	Orkney
P 300	Lindisfarne

Support Ships and Auxiliaries

A 00	Britannia
A 72	Cameron
A 81	Brambleleaf
A 83	Melton
A 84	Menai
A 86	Gleaner
A 87	Meon
A 91	Milford
A 100	Beddgelert
A 106	Alsatian
A 107	Messina
A 109	Bayleaf
A 110	Orangeleaf
A 111	Oakleaf
A 112	Felicity
A 114	Magnet
A 115	Lodestone
A 122	Olwen
A 123	Olna
A 124	Olmeda
A 126	Cairn
A 127	Torrent
A 129	Dalmatian
A 130	Roebuck
A 132	Diligence
A 133	Hecla
A 135	Argus
A 138	Herald
A 140	Tornado
A 141	Torch
A 142	Tormentor
A 143	Toreador
A 146	Waterman
A 147	Frances
A 148	Fiona
A 149	Florence
A 150	Genevieve
A 152	Georgina
A 153	Example
A 154	Explorer
A 155	Deerhound
A 156	Daphne
A 157	Loyal Helper
A 158	Supporter
A 159	Loyal Watcher
A 160	Loyal Volunteer
A 161	Loyal Mediator
A 162	Elkhound
A 163	Express
A 164	Goosander
A 165	Pochard
A 166	Kathleen
A 167	Exploit
A 168	Labrador
A 170	Kitty
A 171	Endurance
A 172	Lesley
A 174	Lilah
A 175	Mary
A 177	Edith
A 178	Husky
A 180	Mastiff
A 181	Irene
A 182	Saluki
A 183	Isabel
A 185	Salmoor
A 186	Salmaster
A 187	Salmaid
A 188	Pointer
A 189	Setter
A 190	Joan
A 193	Joyce
A 196	Gwendoline
A 197	Sealyham
A 198	Helen
A 199	Myrtle
A 201	Spaniel
A 202	Nancy
A 205	Norah
A 207	Llandovery
A 208	Lamlash
A 211	Lechlade
A 216	Bee
A 220	Loyal Moderator
A 221	Forceful
A 222	Nimble
A 223	Powerful
A 224	Adept
A 225	Bustler
A 226	Capable
A 227	Careful
A 228	Faithful
A 229	Cricket
A 230	Cockchafer
A 231	Dexterous
A 232	Adamant
A 239	Gnat
A 250	Sheepdog
A 251	Lydford
A 253	Ladybird
A 254	Sultan Venturer
A 263	Cicala
A 271	Gold Rover
A 272	Scarab
A 273	Black Rover
A 274	Ettrick
A 277	Elsing
A 285	Auricula
A 308	Ilchester
A 309	Instow
A 311	Ironbridge
A 317	Bulldog
A 318	Ixworth
A 319	Beagle
A 326	Foxhound
A 327	Basset
A 328	Collie
A 330	Corgi
A 341	Fotherby
A 344	Impulse
A 345	Impetus
A 348	Felsted
A 353	Elkstone
A 355	Epworth
A 361	Roysterer
A 365	Fulbeck
A 366	Robust
A 367	Newton
A 368	Warden
A 378	Kinterbury
A 381	Cricklade
A 382	Arrochar
A 383	Appleby (SCC)
A 385	Fort Grange
A 386	Fort Austin
A 387	Fort Victoria
A 388	Fort George
A 389	Clovelly
A 393	Dunster
A 394	Fintry
A 402	Grasmere
A 480	Resource
A 488	Cromarty
A 490	Dornoch
A 502	Rollicker
A 1766	Headcorn
A 1767	Hever
A 1768	Harlech
A 1769	Hambledon
A 1770	Loyal Chancellor
A 1771	Loyal Proctor
A 1772	Holmwood
A 1773	Horning

Auxiliaries

Y 01	Petard
Y 02	Falconet
Y 10	Aberdovey (SCC)
Y 11	Abinger (SCC)
Y 13	Alnmouth (SCC)
Y 17	Waterfall
Y 19	Waterspout
Y 21	Oilpress
Y 23	Oilwell
Y 25	Oilbird
Y 26	Oilman
Y 30	Watercourse
Y 31	Waterfowl
Y 32	Moorhen
Y 33	Moorfowl

SUBMARINES
Strategic Missile Submarines (SSBN)

0 + 4 VANGUARD CLASS (SSBN)

Name	No	Builders	Laid down	Launched	Commissioned
VANGUARD	S 28	Vickers Shipbuilding & Engineering, Barrow-in-Furness	3 Sep 1986	4 Mar 1992	1993
VICTORIOUS	S 29	Vickers Shipbuilding & Engineering, Barrow-in-Furness	3 Dec 1987	1993	1994
VIGILANT	S 30	Vickers Shipbuilding & Engineering, Barrow-in-Furness	16 Feb 1991	1994	1995
VALIANT (?)	S 31	Vickers Shipbuilding & Engineering, Barrow-in-Furness	1 Feb 1993	1996	1997

Displacement, tons: 16 000 dived
Dimensions, feet (metres): 491.8 × 42 × 39.4 *(149.9 × 12.8 × 12)*
Main machinery: Nuclear; 1 RR PWR 2; 2 turbines; 27 500 hp *(20.5 MW)*; 1 shaft; pump jet propulsor; 1 auxiliary retractable propulsion motor; 2 diesel alternators; 2700 hp *(2 MW)*
Speed, knots: 25 dived approx
Complement: 135 (2 crews)

Missiles: SLBM: 16 Lockheed Trident 2 (D5) three stage solid fuel rocket; stellar inertial guidance to 12 000 km *(6500 nm)*; thermonuclear warhead of 8 MIRV of 150 kT; cep 90 m. The D5 can carry up to 12 MIRV but each submarine carries a maximum of 128 warheads (of UK manufacture).
Torpedoes: 4—21 in *(533 mm)* tubes. Marconi Spearfish; dual purpose; wire-guided; active/passive homing to 65 km *(35 nm)* at 60 kts; warhead directed energy. Marconi Tigerfish Mk 24 Mod 2; wire-guided; active/passive homing to 13 km *(7 nm)* at 35 kts active; 29 km *(15.7 nm)* at 24 kts passive; warhead 134 kg.
Countermeasures: Decoys: 2 SSE Mk 10 launchers.
ESM: Racal UAP 3; passive intercept.
Combat data systems: Dowty Sema SMCS.
Fire control: Dowty tactical control system.
Radars: Navigation: Kelvin Hughes Type 1007; I band.
Sonars: Marconi/Plessey Type 2054 composite multi-frequency hull-mounted sonar suite plus Marconi/Ferranti Type 2046 towed array.

Programmes: On 15 July 1980 the government announced its intention to procure from the United States the Trident I weapon system, comprising the C4 ballistic missile and supporting systems for a force of new British missile launching submarines to replace the present Polaris-equipped force in the 1990s. On 11 March 1982 it was announced that the government had opted to procure the improved Trident II weapon system, with the D5 missile, to be deployed in a force of four submarines, in the mid-1990s. *Vanguard* ordered 30 April 1986; *Victorious* 6 October 1987; *Vigilant* 13 November 1990 and the last one 7 July 1992. The original programme anticipated ordering one per year for the first three years so there has been much stretching out of the building programme.
Structure: Refit and recore interval is anticipated at eight to nine years. The outer surface of the submarine is covered with conformal anechoic noise reduction coatings. An optronic mast is a new feature. The limits placed on warhead numbers leaves spare capacity within the Trident system. This capacity is available for a non-strategic warhead variant, if one is developed.

VANGUARD 12/1992

Operational: After some early problems there were three successful submerged launched firings of the D5 missile from USS *Tennessee* in December 1989 and the missile was first deployed operationally in March 1990. *Vanguard* started sea trials in October 1992; first operational patrol is planned for late 1994.

Opinion: Because the funding for Trident has come mainly from the naval share of the defence budget, it has had a detrimental effect on the equipment programmes for the rest of the Fleet. Annual expenditure remains at a high level until at least the mid-1990s. The stretching out of the building programme and the extended development programme of the follow-on SSN to the Trafalgar class, means some increase in estimated building costs.

VANGUARD 12/1992

3 RESOLUTION CLASS (SSBN)

Name	No	Builders	Laid down	Launched	Commissioned
RESOLUTION	S 22	Vickers Shipbuilding & Engineering, Barrow-in-Furness	26 Feb 1964	15 Sep 1966	2 Oct 1967
REPULSE	S 23	Vickers Shipbuilding & Engineering, Barrow-in-Furness	12 Mar 1965	4 Nov 1967	28 Sep 1968
RENOWN	S 26	Cammell Laird, Birkenhead	25 June 1964	25 Feb 1967	15 Nov 1968

Displacement, tons: 7600 surfaced; 8500 dived
Dimensions, feet (metres): 425 × 33 × 30 *(129.5 × 10.1 × 9.1)*
Main machinery: Nuclear; 1 RR PWR 1; 2 English Electric turbines; 15 000 hp *(11.2 MW)*; 1 shaft; 2 diesel alternators; 2200 hp *(1.64 MW)*; 1 motor for emergency drive; 1 auxiliary retractable prop
Speed, knots: 20 surfaced; 25 dived
Complement: 143 (13 officers) (2 crews)

Missiles: SLBM: 16 Lockheed Polaris A3 two stage solid fuel rocket; inertial guidance to 4630 km *(2500 nm)*; each missile carries 3 MRV heads each of 200 kT; Chevaline nuclear warheads (fitted in *Renown* 1982, *Resolution* 1984, *Repulse* 1986, *Revenge* 1988); cep 900 m.
Torpedoes: 6—21 in *(533 mm)* bow tubes. Marconi Tigerfish Mk 24 Mod 2; wire-guided; active/passive homing to 13 km *(7 nm)* at 35 kts active; 29 km *(15.7 nm)* at 24 kts passive; warhead 134 kg.
Countermeasures: Decoys: 2 SSDE launchers.
ESM: MEL UA 11/12; passive intercept.
Combat data systems: Gresham/Dowty DCB data handling system.
Fire control: Dowty tactical control system.
Radars: Navigation: Kelvin Hughes Type 1006; I band.
Sonars: Plessey Type 2001; hull-mounted; active/passive; low frequency.
BAe Type 2007; hull-mounted; flank array; passive; long range; low frequency.
Ferranti Type 2046; towed array; passive search; very low frequency.
Thomson Sintra Type 2019 PARIS (to be replaced by THORN EMI Type 2082); passive intercept and ranging.

Programmes: In February 1963 it was stated that it was intended to order four or five 7000 ton nuclear powered submarines, each to carry 16 Polaris missiles, and it was planned that the first would be on patrol in 1968. Their hulls and machinery would be of British design. As well as building two submarines Vickers (Shipbuilding) would give lead yard service to the builder of the other two. Four Polaris submarines were in fact ordered in May 1963. The plan to build a fifth Polaris submarine was cancelled on 15 February 1965. Britain's first SSBN, *Resolution,* put to sea on 22 June 1967.
Modernisation: The Chevaline warheads were substituted for the original Polaris missile payloads in a rolling programme between 1982 and 1988. The warhead is similar but it is supported by 'a variety of penetration aids' to overcome anti-ballistic missile (ABM) defences.

RESOLUTION   1992

Operational: Since early 1969 there has been at least one of these submarines at immediate readiness to fire its intercontinental ballistic missiles. Each submarine, which has accommodation for 19 officers and 135 ratings, is manned on a two-crew basis, in order to get maximum operational time at sea. It has been reported that the Polaris stockpile is some 70 missiles with 45-50 warheads. *Revenge* paid off earlier than expected in May 1992 and the others will decommission sequentially as the Vanguard class enters service.

REPULSE   1992

Attack Submarines (SSN)

Note: As pennant numbers are never displayed and rarely used class lists are in order of completion.

7 + (6) TRAFALGAR CLASS (SSN)

Name	No	Builders	Laid down	Launched	Commissioned
TRAFALGAR	S 107	Vickers Shipbuilding & Engineering, Barrow-in-Furness	1979	1 July 1981	27 May 1983
TURBULENT	S 87	Vickers Shipbuilding & Engineering, Barrow-in-Furness	1980	1 Dec 1982	28 Apr 1984
TIRELESS	S 88	Vickers Shipbuilding & Engineering, Barrow-in-Furness	1981	17 Mar 1984	5 Oct 1985
TORBAY	S 90	Vickers Shipbuilding & Engineering, Barrow-in-Furness	1982	8 Mar 1985	7 Feb 1987
TRENCHANT	S 91	Vickers Shipbuilding & Engineering, Barrow-in-Furness	1984	3 Nov 1986	14 Jan 1989
TALENT	S 92	Vickers Shipbuilding & Engineering, Barrow-in-Furness	1986	15 Apr 1988	12 May 1990
TRIUMPH	S 93	Vickers Shipbuilding & Engineering, Barrow-in-Furness	1987	16 Feb 1991	12 Oct 1991

Displacement, tons: 4700; 5400 (Batch 2) surfaced; 5208; 5900 (Batch 2) dived
Dimensions, feet (metres): 280.1; 293.3 (Batch 2) × 32.1 × 31.2 *(85.4; 89.4 × 9.8 × 9.5)*
Main machinery: Nuclear; 1 RR PWR 1; PWR 2 (Batch 2); 2 GEC turbines; 15 000 hp *(11.2 MW)*; 1 shaft; pump jet propulsor; 2 Paxman diesel alternators; 2800 hp *(2.09 MW)*; 1 motor for emergency drive; 1 auxiliary retractable prop
Speed, knots: 32 dived
Complement: 97 (12 officers)

Missiles: SSM: McDonnell Douglas UGM-84B Sub-Harpoon; active radar homing to 130 km *(70 nm)* at 0.9 Mach; warhead 227 kg.
Torpedoes: 5—21 in *(533 mm)* bow tubes. Marconi Spearfish; wire-guided; active/passive homing to 65 km *(35 nm)* at 60 kts; warhead directed energy. Marconi Tigerfish Mk 24 Mod 2; wire-guided; active/passive homing to 13 km *(7 nm)* at 35 kts active; 29 km *(15.7 nm)* at 24 kts passive; warhead 134 kg; 20 reloads.
Mines: Can be carried in lieu of torpedoes.
Countermeasures: Decoys: 2 SSE Mk 8 launchers.
ESM: Racal UAC/CXA (being upgraded to UAP); passive intercept.
Combat data systems: Ferranti/Gresham/Dowty DCB/DCG tactical data handling system. Dowty Sema SMCS after refit.
Fire control: Dowty tactical control system.
Radars: Navigation: Kelvin Hughes Type 1006 or Type 1007; I band.
Sonars: BAe Type 2007 AC or Marconi 2072; hull-mounted; flank array; passive; low frequency.
Plessey Type 2020 or Marconi/Plessey 2074; hull-mounted; passive/active search and attack; low frequency.
GEC Avionics Type 2026 or Ferranti Type 2046 or Marconi/Plessey 2057; towed array; passive search; very low frequency.
Thomson Sintra Type 2019 PARIS or THORN EMI 2082; passive intercept and ranging.
Marconi Type 2077; short range classification (to be fitted).

Programmes: The first of an improved class of Fleet Submarines was ordered in September 1977. *Turbulent* ordered 28 July 1978; *Tireless* 5 July 1979; *Torbay* 26 June 1981; *Trenchant* 22 March 1983; *Talent* 10 September 1984; *Triumph* 3 January 1986. An improved version of the class is planned to be ordered in early 1995 with an in service date of 2001, which is some 10 years after the last of the Batch 1s.
Modernisation: Trials have been done on Sonar Type 2057 which has a reelable wet end for the towed array sonar. *Turbulent* has a hump on the after casing under which there is a small winch. Type 1006 radar is to be replaced by Type 1007. All to be updated with Type 2076 sonar systems, integrated with SMCS and countermeasures. Sonar 2076 replaces 2074, 2046 and 2082. This update also includes Marconi Type 2077, short range classification sonar. Batch 2 is planned to incorporate the PWR 2 reactor and all those weapon systems improvements going in to Batch 1.
Structure: Designed to be considerably quieter than previous submarines. The pressure hull and outer surfaces are covered with conformal anechoic noise reduction coatings. Other improvements include speed and endurance. Retractable forward hydroplanes and strengthened fins for under ice operations. Diving depth in excess of 300 m *(985 ft)*.
Operational: *Trafalgar* was the trials submarine for Spearfish which started full production in 1992. All of the class belong to the Second Submarine Squadron based at Devonport.

TORBAY 7/1992

TRIUMPH 8/1992, Giorgio Arra

TIRELESS (at North Pole) 5/1991

5 SWIFTSURE CLASS (SSN)

Name	No	Builders	Laid down	Launched	Commissioned
SOVEREIGN	S 108	Vickers Shipbuilding & Engineering, Barrow-in-Furness	18 Sep 1970	17 Feb 1973	11 July 1974
SUPERB	S 109	Vickers Shipbuilding & Engineering, Barrow-in-Furness	16 Mar 1972	30 Nov 1974	13 Nov 1976
SCEPTRE	S 104	Vickers Shipbuilding & Engineering, Barrow-in-Furness	19 Feb 1974	20 Nov 1976	14 Feb 1978
SPARTAN	S 105	Vickers Shipbuilding & Engineering, Barrow-in-Furness	26 Apr 1976	7 Apr 1978	22 Sep 1979
SPLENDID	S 106	Vickers Shipbuilding & Engineering, Barrow-in-Furness	23 Nov 1977	5 Oct 1979	21 Mar 1981

Displacement, tons: 4000 light; 4400 standard; 4900 dived
Dimensions, feet (metres): 272 × 32.3 × 28 *(82.9 × 9.8 × 8.5)*
Main machinery: Nuclear; 1 RR PWR 1; 2 GEC turbines; 15 000 hp *(11.2 MW)*; 1 shaft; pump jet propulsor; 1 Paxman diesel alternator; 1900 hp *(1.42 MW)*; 1 motor for emergency drive; 1 auxiliary retractable prop
Speed, knots: 30+ dived
Complement: 116 (13 officers)

Missiles: SSM: McDonnell Douglas UGM-84B Sub-Harpoon; active radar homing to 130 km *(70 nm)* at 0.9 Mach; warhead 227 kg.
Torpedoes: 5—21 in *(533 mm)* bow tubes. Marconi Tigerfish Mk 24 Mod 2; wire-guided; active/passive homing to 13 km *(7 nm)* at 35 kts active; 29 km *(15.7 nm)* at 24 kts passive; warhead 134 kg; 20 reloads. Individual reloading of torpedoes in 15 seconds. To be replaced by Spearfish in mid-1990s.
Mines: Can be carried in lieu of torpedoes.
Countermeasures: Decoys: 2 SSE Mk 6 launchers.
ESM: Racal UAC (being upgraded to UAP); passive intercept.
Combat data systems: Ferranti/Gresham/Dowty DCB/DCG tactical data handling system. Dowty Sema SMCS after refit.
Radars: Navigation: Kelvin Hughes Type 1006; I band.
Sonars: AUWE Type 2001 or Plessey Type 2020 or Marconi/Plessey Type 2074; hull-mounted; active/passive search and attack; low frequency.
BAC Type 2007; hull-mounted; flank array; passive; low frequency.
Ferranti Type 2046; towed array; passive search; very low frequency.
Thomson Sintra Type 2019 PARIS; passive intercept and ranging (to be replaced by 2082 in due course).
Marconi Type 2077; short range classification (to be fitted).

Programmes: *Sovereign* ordered 16 May 1969; *Superb*, 20 May 1970; *Sceptre*, 1 Nov 1971; *Spartan*, 7 Feb 1973; *Splendid*, 26 May 1976.
Modernisation: *Sceptre* finished refit in 1987, *Spartan* in 1989, and *Splendid* in 1993, each fitted with a PWR 1 Core Z giving a 12 year life cycle although refits/refuel cycles will remain at eight to nine year intervals. Other improvements include acoustic elastomeric tiles, new sonar 2020 processing equipment and improved decoys. Marconi Type 2077, short range classification sonar is also to be fitted. Others of the class to follow some with Marconi/Plessey 2074 sonar instead of 2020 to replace Type 2001. Spearfish torpedoes are also to be carried in due course.
Structure: Compared with the Valiant class submarines these are slightly shorter with a fuller form, the fore-planes set further forward, one less torpedo tube and with a deeper diving depth and faster. The pressure hull in the Swiftsure class maintains its diameter for much greater length than previous classes. Control gear by MacTaggart, Scott & Co Ltd for: attack and search periscopes, snort induction and exhaust, radar and ESM masts, ALK buoy. The forward hydroplanes house within the casing.
Operational: All belong to the Third (First after 1 October 1993) Submarine Squadron based at Faslane. As a result of budget cuts *Swiftsure* paid off in 1992 after less than 20 years' service.

SUPERB　　1991

SPLENDID　　1992

1 VALIANT CLASS (SSN)

Name	No	Builders	Laid down	Launched	Commissioned
VALIANT	S 102	Vickers Shipbuilding & Engineering, Barrow-in-Furness	22 Jan 1962	3 Dec 1963	18 July 1966

Displacement, tons: 4000 light; 4300 standard; 4800 dived
Dimensions, feet (metres): 285 × 33.2 × 27.5 *(86.9 × 10.1 × 8.4)*
Main machinery: Nuclear; 1 RR PWR 1; 2 English Electric turbines; 15 000 hp *(11.2 MW)*; 1 shaft; 2 diesel alternators; 2200 hp *(1.64 MW)*; 1 motor for emergency drive; 1 auxiliary retractable prop
Speed, knots: 28 dived
Complement: 116 (13 officers)

Missiles: SSM: McDonnell Douglas UGM-84B Sub-Harpoon; active radar homing to 130 km *(70 nm)* at 0.9 Mach; warhead 227 kg.
Torpedoes: 6—21 in *(533 mm)* bow tubes. Marconi Tigerfish Mk 24 Mod 2; wire-guided; active/passive homing to 13 km *(7 nm)* at 35 kts active; 29 km *(15.7 nm)* at 24 kts passive; warhead 134 kg; 26 reloads. Individual reloading in 15 seconds.
Mines: Can be carried in lieu of torpedoes.
Countermeasures: ESM: Type UAL; radar warning.
Combat data systems: Gresham/Dowty DCB/DCG tactical data handling system.
Radars: Navigation: Kelvin Hughes Type 1006; I band.
Sonars: Plessey Type 2001; hull-mounted; active/passive search and attack; low frequency.
Ferranti Type 2046; towed array; passive search: very low frequency.
Thomson Sintra Type 2019 PARIS; passive intercept and ranging.

VALIANT *1992*

Operational: The first of a class of five and the last to survive the cutbacks in overall SSN numbers. To be paid off in early 1994.

Patrol Submarines (SS)

4 UPHOLDER CLASS (TYPE 2400) (SS)

Name	No	Builders	Start date	Launched	Commissioned
UPHOLDER	S 40	Vickers Shipbuilding & Engineering, Barrow-in-Furness	Nov 1983	2 Dec 1986	9 June 1990
UNSEEN	S 41	Cammell Laird, Birkenhead (VSEL)	Jan 1986	14 Nov 1989	7 June 1991
URSULA	S 42	Cammell Laird, Birkenhead (VSEL)	Aug 1987	28 Feb 1991	8 May 1992
UNICORN	S 43	Cammell Laird, Birkenhead (VSEL)	Feb 1989	16 Apr 1992	25 June 1993

Displacement, tons: 2168 surfaced; 2455 dived
Dimensions, feet (metres): 230.6 × 25 × 17.7 *(70.3 × 7.6 × 5.5)*
Main machinery: Diesel-electric; 2 Paxman Valenta 16SZ diesels; 3620 hp *(2.7 MW)* sustained; 2 GEC alternators; 2.8 MW; 1 GEC motor; 5400 hp *(4 MW)*; 1 shaft
Speed, knots: 12 surfaced; 20 dived; 12 snorting.
Range, miles: 8000 at 8 kts snorting
Complement: 47 (7 officers)

Missiles: SSM: McDonnell Douglas UGM-84B Sub-Harpoon; active radar homing to 130 km *(70 nm)* at 0.9 Mach; warhead 227 kg.
Torpedoes: 6—21 in *(533 mm)* bow tubes. Marconi Tigerfish Mk 24 Mod 2; wire-guided; active/passive homing to 13 km *(7 nm)* at 35 kts active; 29 km *(15.7 nm)* at 24 kts passive; warhead 134 kg; 12 reloads. Spearfish in due course. Air turbine pump discharge.
Mines: M Mk 5 carried in lieu of torpedoes.
Countermeasures: Decoys: 2 SSE launchers.
ESM: Racal Type UAC (being updated to UAP); passive intercept.
Combat data systems: Ferranti-Gresham-Lion DCC tactical data handling system.
Radars: Navigation: Kelvin Hughes Type 1007; I band.
Sonars: Thomson Sintra Type 2040; hull-mounted; passive search and intercept; medium frequency.
BAe Type 2007; flank array; passive; low frequency.
GEC Avionics Type 2026 or Type 2046; towed array; passive search; very low frequency.
Paramax Type 2041; passive ranging.

Programmes: The need for the provision of a new class of non-nuclear submarines was acknowledged in the late 1970s and in 1979 the Type 2400 design was first revealed. First boat ordered from Vickers SEL, 2 November 1983. Further three ordered on 2 January 1986. Plans for more of the class were dropped in 1990 as part of a cost cutting exercise designed to reduce the diesel submarine strength to four by the mid-1990s. Refit interval is anticipated at seven and a half years.
Modernisation: Sonar suite Type 2076 may be fitted in due course in place of the cancelled Type 2075.
Structure: Single skinned NQ1 high tensile steel hull, tear dropped shape 9:1 ratio, five man lock-out chamber in fin. This is the first time that the Valenta diesel has been fitted in submarines. Fitted with elastomeric acoustic tiles. Diving depth, greater than 200 m *(650 ft)*.
Operational: Endurance, 49 days stores and 90 hours at 3 kts dived. Problems with the torpedo tube discharge system have been rectified; *Upholder* in 1992, *Unseen* and *Ursula* in 1993, *Unicorn* before commissioning. All based at Devonport as part of the Second Squadron. The whole class may be sold or placed in reserve as a budget saving expedient.

UPHOLDER *2/1992*

1 OBERON CLASS (SS)

Name	No	Builders	Laid down	Launched	Commissioned
OPOSSUM	S 19	Cammell Laird, Birkenhead	21 Dec 1961	23 May 1963	5 June 1964

Displacement, tons: 1610 standard; 2030 surfaced; 2410 dived
Dimensions, feet (metres): 295.2 × 26.5 × 18 *(90 × 8.1 × 5.5)*
Main machinery: Diesel-electric; 2 ASR 16 VVS-ASR1 diesels; 3680 hp *(2.74 MW)*; 2 AEI motors; 6000 hp *(4.48 MW)*; 2 shafts
Speed, knots: 12 surfaced; 17 dived; 10 snorting.
Range, miles: 9000 at 12 kts surfaced
Complement: 69 (7 officers)

Torpedoes: 6—21 in *(533 mm)* bow tubes. Marconi Tigerfish Mk 24 Mod 2; wire-guided; active/passive homing to 13 km *(7 nm)* at 35 kts active; 29 km *(15.7 nm)* at 24 kts passive; warhead 134 kg; 20 torpedoes.
Mines: Can be carried in lieu of torpedoes.
Countermeasures: Decoys: 2 SSE Mk 4.
ESM: MEL Manta UAL; radar warning.
Fire control: Ferranti DCH tactical data handling system. Dual channel fire control.
Radars: Navigation: Kelvin Hughes Type 1006; I band.
Sonars: Plessey Type 2051; hull-mounted; passive/active search and attack; medium frequency.
BAC Type 2007; hull-mounted; flank array; passive; long-range; low frequency.
US Type 2024; clip-on towed array.

Modernisation: The Triton sonar modernisation programme was completed in 1989.
Structure: Before and abaft the bridge the superstructure is mainly of glass fibre laminate. Diving depth, 200 m *(650 ft)*.

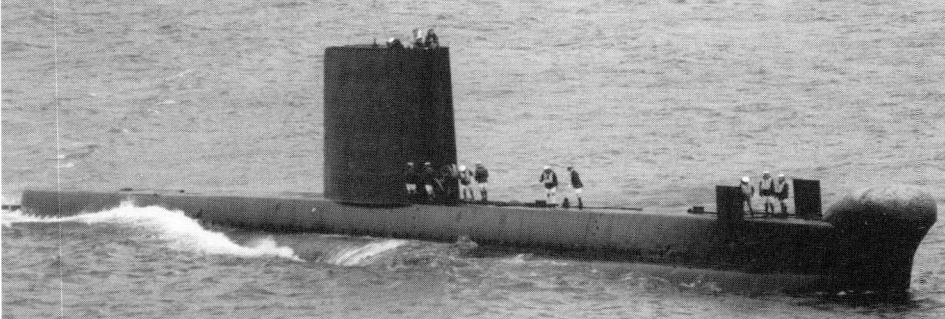

OPOSSUM *10/1992, Giorgio Arra*

Operational: The last survivor of the class planned to pay off in late 1993.
Sales: A total of 14 of this class were sold abroad, six to Australia, three to Canada, three to Brazil and two to Chile.

724 UK (NAVY) / Aircraft carriers

AIRCRAFT CARRIERS

3 INVINCIBLE CLASS (CVSG)

Name	No	Builders	Laid down	Launched	Commissioned
INVINCIBLE	R 05	Vickers Shipbuilding & Engineering, Barrow-in-Furness	20 July 1973	3 May 1977	11 July 1980
ILLUSTRIOUS	R 06	Swan Hunter Shipbuilders, Wallsend	7 Oct 1976	1 Dec 1978	20 June 1982
ARK ROYAL	R 07	Swan Hunter Shipbuilders, Wallsend	14 Dec 1978	2 June 1981	1 Nov 1985

Displacement, tons: 20 600 full load
Dimensions, feet (metres): 685.8 oa; 632 wl × 118 oa; 90 wl × 26 (screws)
(209.1; 192.6 × 36; 27.5 × 8)
Flight deck, feet (metres): 550 × 44.3 *(167.8 × 13.5)*
Main machinery: COGAG; 4 RR Olympus TM3B gas turbines; 97 200 hp *(72.5 MW)* sustained; 2 shafts
Speed, knots: 28. **Range, miles:** 5000 at 18 kts
Complement: 685 (60 officers) plus 366 (80 officers) aircrew

Missiles: SAM: British Aerospace Sea Dart twin launcher ❶; radar/semi-active radar guidance to 40 km *(21.5 nm)* at Mach 2; height envelope 100-18 300 m *(328-60 042 ft)*; 36 missiles; limited anti-ship capability.
Guns: 3 General Electric/General Dynamics 20 mm Mk 15 Vulcan Phalanx (R 07) ❷; 6 barrels per launcher; 3000 rounds/minute combined to 1.5 km.
3 Signaal/General Electric 30 mm 7-barrelled Gatling Goalkeeper (R 05 and R 06) ❸; 4200 rounds/minute to 1.5 km.
2 Oerlikon/BMARC 20 mm GAM-BO1 ❹; 55° elevation; 1000 rounds/minute to 2 km.
Countermeasures: Decoys: 2 Vickers Corvus 8-tubed trainable launchers (not in R 05); chaff to 1 km or 2 Loral Hycor SRBOC 6-tubed fixed Mk 36 launchers ❺; IR flares and chaff to 4 km *(2.2 nm)* max (in R 05).
2 THORN EMI Sea Gnat dispensers. Prairie Masker noise suppression system.
ESM: MEL UAA 2 or UAF (R 06); intercept.
ECM: THORN EMI Type 675(2); jammer.
Combat data systems: ADAWS 10 (with ADIMP in due course) action data automation; Links 10, 11 and 14. US OE-82 VHF SATCOM. SCOT communications ❻; Link 16 in due course. Marisat.
Fire control: GWS 30 for SAM.
Radars: Air search: Marconi/Signaal Type 1022 ❼; D band; range 265 km *(145 nm)*.
Surface search: Marconi Type 992R ❽ (R 07); or Plessey Type 996(2) ❾ (R 05 and 06); E/F band.
Navigation: Two Kelvin Hughes Type 1006 (R 05 and 07); Type 1007 (R 06); I band.
Fire control: Two Marconi Type 909 ❿; I/J band.
Sonars: Plessey Type 2016; hull-mounted; active search and attack.

Fixed wing aircraft: 9 British Aerospace Sea Harrier FRS 1 (see *Shipborne Aircraft* section) ⓫.
Helicopters: Up to 9 Westland Sea King HAS 6 ⓬; 3 Westland Sea King AEW 2.

Programmes: The first of class, the result of many compromises, was ordered from Vickers on 17 April 1973. The order for the second ship was placed on 14 May 1976, the third in December 1978.

Modernisation: In January 1989 R 05 completed a 27 month modernisation which included a 12° ski ramp, space and support facilities for at least 21 aircraft (Sea Harriers, Sea King AEW and ASW helicopters), three Goalkeeper systems, Sonar 2016, Seagnat decoys, 996 radar, Flag and Command facilities to R 07 standards and accommodation for an additional 120 aircrew and Flag Staff. In August 1991 R 06 started a similar 30 month modernisation to bring her to the same standard, but with additional command and weapon system improvements to those listed for R 05. Plans to fit four lightweight Seawolf launchers were cancelled as an economy measure in 1991. Contract placed in early 1991 to redesign the flight deck lifts.
Structure: The design allows for an open fo'c'sle head and a slightly angled deck which allows the Sea Dart launcher to be set almost amidships. In 1976-77 an amendment was incorporated to allow for the transport and landing of an RM Commando. The forward end of the flight deck (ski-ramp of 12°) allows STOVL aircraft of greater all-up weight to operate more efficiently.
Operational: The role of this class, apart from its primary task of providing a command, control and communications facility, is the operation of both helicopters and STOVL aircraft. Provision has been made for sufficiently large lifts and hangars to accommodate the next generation of both these aircraft. Only two of the class are in commission at any one time, the third either being in refit or stand-by. *Illustrious* is planned to replace *Ark Royal* in 1994.

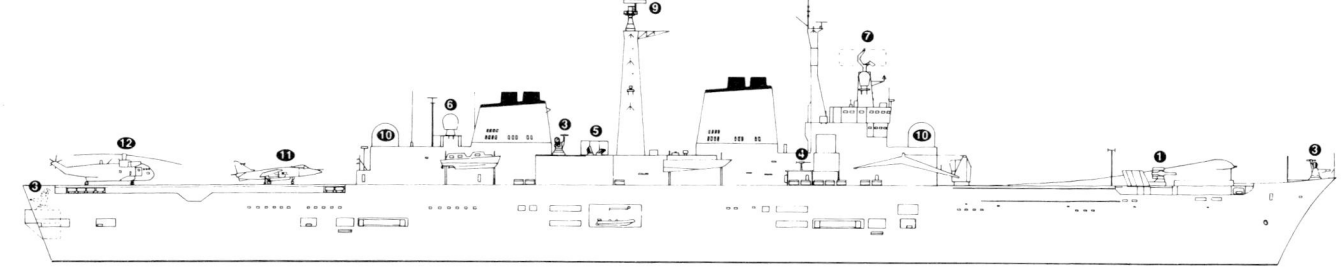

INVINCIBLE *(Scale 1 : 1200), Ian Sturton*

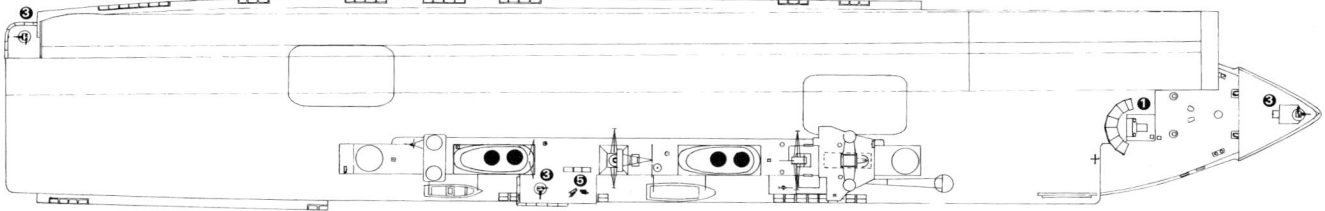

INVINCIBLE *(Scale 1 : 1200), Ian Sturton*

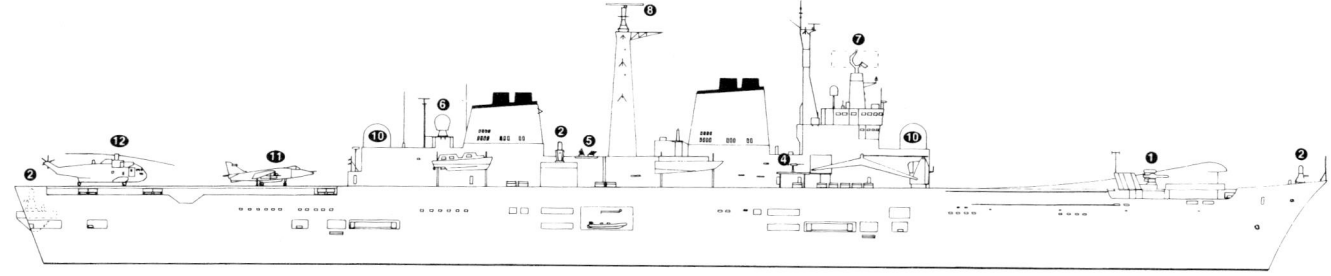

ARK ROYAL *(Scale 1 : 1200), Ian Sturton*

ARK ROYAL 10/1992

INVINCIBLE 7/1992

Aircraft carriers / UK (NAVY) 725

INVINCIBLE 7/1992, Hachiro Nakai

INVINCIBLE 11/1992, H M Steele

ARK ROYAL 2/1991

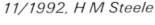

INVINCIBLE 11/1992, H M Steele

DESTROYERS

Note: *Bristol* (D 23) has replaced *Kent* as an immobile tender used for training in Portsmouth Harbour.

12 TYPE 42

Batch 1

Name	No	Builders	Laid down	Launched	Commissioned
BIRMINGHAM	D 86	Cammell Laird, Birkenhead	28 Mar 1972	30 July 1973	3 Dec 1976
NEWCASTLE	D 87	Swan Hunter Shipbuilders, Wallsend-on-Tyne	21 Feb 1973	24 Apr 1975	23 Mar 1978
GLASGOW	D 88	Swan Hunter Shipbuilders, Wallsend-on-Tyne	16 Apr 1974	14 Apr 1976	24 May 1979
CARDIFF	D 108	Vickers Shipbuilding & Engineering, Barrow-in-Furness	6 Nov 1972	22 Feb 1974	24 Sep 1979

Batch 2

Name	No	Builders	Laid down	Launched	Commissioned
EXETER	D 89	Swan Hunter Shipbuilders, Wallsend-on-Tyne	22 July 1976	25 Apr 1978	19 Sep 1980
SOUTHAMPTON	D 90	Vosper Thornycroft, Woolston	21 Oct 1976	29 Jan 1979	31 Oct 1981
NOTTINGHAM	D 91	Vosper Thornycroft, Woolston	6 Feb 1978	18 Feb 1980	14 Apr 1983
LIVERPOOL	D 92	Cammell Laird, Birkenhead	5 July 1978	25 Sep 1980	1 July 1982

Displacement, tons: 3500 standard; 4100 full load
Dimensions, feet (metres): 412 oa; 392 wl × 47 × 19 (screws) *(125; 119.5 × 14.3 × 5.8)*
Main machinery: COGOG; 2 RR Olympus TM3B gas turbines; 50 000 hp *(37.3 MW)* sustained; 2 RR Tyne RM1C gas turbines (cruising); 9900 hp *(7.4 MW)* sustained; 2 shafts; cp props
Speed, knots: 29. **Range, miles:** 4000 at 18 kts
Complement: 253 (24 officers) (accommodation for 312)

Missiles: SAM: British Aerospace Sea Dart twin launcher ❶; radar/semi-active radar guidance to 40 km *(21.5 nm)* at 2 Mach; height envelope 100-18 300 m *(328-60 042 ft)*; 22 missiles; limited anti-ship capability.
Guns: 1 Vickers 4.5 in *(114 mm)*/55 Mk 8 ❷; 55° elevation; 25 rounds/minute to 22 km *(11.9 nm)* anti-surface; 6 km *(3.3 nm)* anti-aircraft; weight of shell 21 kg.
2 or 4 Oerlikon/BMARC 20 mm GAM-BO1 ❸ and ❹; 55° elevation; 1000 rounds/minute to 2 km.
2 Oerlikon 20 mm Mk 7A ❹ (in those with only 2 BMARC); 50° elevation; 800 rounds/minute to 2 km; weight of shell 0.24 kg.
2 General Electric/General Dynamics 20 mm Vulcan Phalanx Mk 15 ❺; 6 barrels per launcher; 3000 rounds/minute combined to 1.5 km.
Torpedoes: 6—324 mm Plessey STWS Mk 3 (2 triple) tubes ❻. Fitted for, but not with. Batch 2 may be equipped from 1996.
Countermeasures: Decoys: 2 Vickers Corvus 8-tubed trainable launchers or 2 Marconi Sea Gnat (Batch 2 and D 87) ❼; chaff and IR flares.
2 Loral Hycor SRBOC 6-tubed fixed Mk 36 launchers ❽ (in D 86, 88 and 108); IR flares and chaff to 4 km *(2.2 nm)*.
Graseby Type 182; towed torpedo decoy.
ESM: MEL UAA-2; intercept.
ECM: Type 670; being replaced by Type 675(2) (Batch 2); jammer.
Combat data systems: ADAWS 7 action data automation. 2 Marconi SCOT SATCOMs ❾; Links 10, 11 and 14. Marisat. Link 16 in due course.
Fire control: GWS 30 Mod 2 (for SAM); GSA 1 secondary system. Radamec 2100 series optronic surveillance system.
Radars: Air search: Marconi/Signaal Type 1022 ❿; D band; range 265 km *(145 nm)*.
Surface search: Plessey Type 996 ⓫ or Plessey Type 992 (D 86); E/F band.
Navigation: Kelvin Hughes Type 1006; I band.

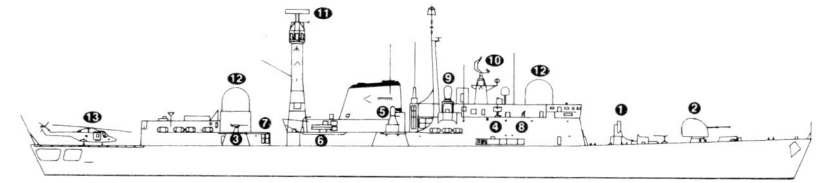

EXETER (Batch 2)   *(Scale 1 : 1200), Ian Sturton*

Fire control: Two Marconi Type 909 ⓬; or 9091; I/J band.
Sonars: Ferranti Type 2050 or Plessey Type 2016; hull-mounted; active search and attack; medium frequency.
Kelvin Hughes Type 162M; hull-mounted; bottom classification; 50 kHz.

Helicopters: 1 Westland Lynx HAS 3 ⓭.

EXETER   *10/1992, Maritime Photographic*

NOTTINGHAM   *7/1992, C & S Taylor*

CARDIFF   *3/1992, Wright & Logan*

Destroyers / UK (NAVY)

Batch 3

Name	No	Builders	Laid down	Launched	Commissioned
MANCHESTER	D 95	Vickers Shipbuilding & Engineering, Barrow-in-Furness	19 May 1978	24 Nov 1980	16 Dec 1982
GLOUCESTER	D 96	Vosper Thornycroft, Woolston	29 Oct 1979	2 Nov 1982	11 Sep 1985
EDINBURGH	D 97	Cammell Laird, Birkenhead	8 Sep 1980	14 Apr 1983	17 Dec 1985
YORK	D 98	Swan Hunter Shipbuilders, Wallsend-on-Tyne	18 Jan 1980	21 June 1982	9 Aug 1985

Displacement, tons: 3500 standard; 4675 full load
Dimensions, feet (metres): 462.8 oa; 434 wl × 49 × 19 (screws) *(141.1; 132.3 × 14.9 × 5.8)*
Main machinery: COGOG; 2 RR Olympus TM3B gas turbines; 43 000 hp *(32 MW)* sustained; 2 RR Tyne RM1C gas turbines (cruising); 10 680 hp *(8 MW)* sustained; 2 shafts; cp props
Speed, knots: 30+. **Range, miles:** 4000 at 18 kts
Complement: 301 (26 officers)

Missiles: SAM: British Aerospace Sea Dart twin launcher ❶; radar/semi-active radar guidance to 40 km *(21 nm)*; warhead HE; 22 missiles; limited anti-ship capability.
Guns: 1 Vickers 4.5 in *(114 mm)*/55 Mk 8 ❷; 55° elevation; 25 rounds/minute to 22 km *(11.9 nm)* anti-surface; 6 km *(3.3 nm)* anti-aircraft; weight of shell 21 kg.
2 Oerlikon/BMARC 20 mm GAM-BO1 ❸; 55° elevation; 1000 rounds/minute to 2 km.
2 Oerlikon 20 mm Mk 7A ❹; 50° elevation; 800 rounds/minute to 2 km; weight of shell 0.24 kg.
2 BMARC 30 mm ❺ (temporary mountings in D 97).
1 or 2 General Electric/General Dynamics 20 mm Vulcan Phalanx Mk 15 ❻; 6 barrels per launcher; 3000 rounds/minute combined to 1.5 km. See *Modernisation* comment.
Torpedoes: 6—324 mm STWS Mk 2 (2 triple) tubes ❼. Marconi Stingray; active/passive homing to 11 km *(5.9 nm)* at 45 kts; warhead 35 kg.
Countermeasures: Decoys: 2 Vickers Corvus 8-tubed trainable launchers (D 95) or 2 Marconi Sea Gnat ❽; chaff and IR flares.
2 Loral Hycor SRBOC 6-tubed fixed Mk 36 launchers; IR flares and chaff to 4 km *(2.2 nm)* (in some).
Graseby Type 182; towed torpedo decoy.
ESM: MEL UAA-2; intercept.
ECM: Type 670 being replaced by Type 675(2); jammer.
Combat data systems: ADAWS 8 (with ADIMP) action data automation. Marconi SCOT SATCOM ❾; Links 10, 11 and 14. Marisat. Link 16 in due course.
Fire control: GWS 30 Mod 2 (for SAM); GSA 1 secondary system. Radamec 2100 series optronic surveillance system.
Radars: Air search: Marconi/Signaal Type 1022 ❿; D band; range 265 km *(145 nm)*.
Air/surface search: Marconi Type 992R or Plessey Type 996 ⓫; E/F band.
Navigation: Kelvin Hughes Type 1006; I band.
Fire control: Two Marconi Type 909 ⓬ or 909 Mod 1; I/J band.
Sonars: Ferranti Type 2050 or Plessey Type 2016; hull-mounted; active search and attack.
Kelvin Hughes Type 162M; hull-mounted; bottom classification; 50 kHz.

Helicopters: 1 Westland Lynx HAS 3 ⓭.

Batches 1, 2 and 3

Programmes: Designed to provide area air defence for a task force. In order to provide space for improved weapon systems and to improve speed and seakeeping a radical change was made to this class. The completion of later ships was delayed to allow for some modifications resulting from experience in the Falklands' campaign (1982).
Modernisation: Vulcan Phalanx replaced 30 mm guns 1987-89. All are receiving Plessey Type 996 radar in place of Type 992, and Type 909(1) fire control radars with improved Tx/Rx circuits. STWS Mk 3 may replace the obsolete Mk 1 in Batch 2. D 97 had a partial conversion completing in 1990 with the Phalanx moved forward and a protective visor fitted around the bow of the ship. As a temporary measure 30 mm guns were placed where Seawolf launchers would have been fitted. That modification was cancelled in 1991 and D 97 will revert to the standard armament in due course. All Batch 3 ships are having a command system update starting with D 95 in 1992.
Structure: All have two pairs of stabilisers and twin rudders. Advantages of gas turbine propulsion include ability to reach maximum speed with great rapidity, reduction in space and weight and 25 per cent reduction in technical manpower. The stretched Batch 3 have been fitted with a strengthening beam on each side which increases displacement by 50 tons and width by 2 feet.
Operational: The helicopter carries the Sea Skua air-to-surface weapon for use against lightly defended surface ship targets. Ships may be fitted with DEC laser dazzle sight and additional decoy flare launchers on operational deployments.

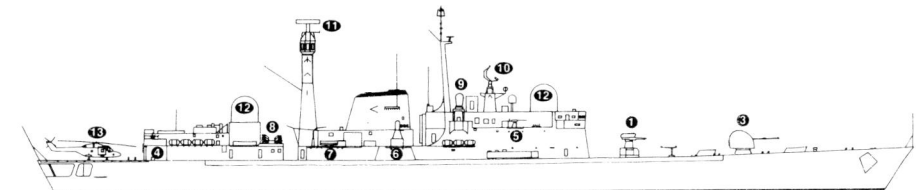

GLOUCESTER *(Scale 1 : 1200), Ian Sturton*

YORK *7/1992, Maritime Photographic*

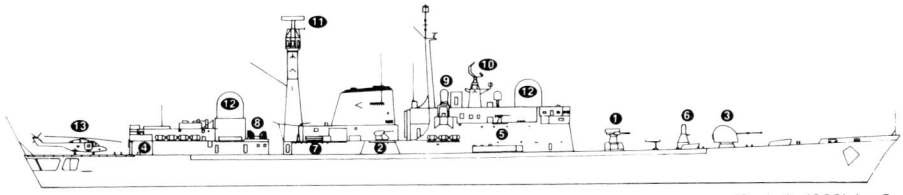

EDINBURGH *(Scale 1 : 1200), Ian Sturton*

MANCHESTER *2/1993, Maritime Photographic*

728 UK (NAVY) / Destroyers — Frigates

0 + (12) ANGLO-FRENCH NEW GENERATION TYPE

Displacement, tons: 6200 approx
Dimensions, feet (metres): 472.1 × 61.7 × 15.7 *(143.9 × 18.8 × 4.8)*
Main machinery: CODLAG; 2 gas turbines; 4 diesels; 2 motors; 2 shafts
Speed, knots: 30. **Range, miles:** 6000 at 18 kts
Complement: 200 plus 35 spare

Missiles: SSM: 8 (2 quad) or VLS ❶.
  SAM: Aster VLS ❷ PAMS (principal AAW missile system).
Guns: 1—100/114 mm ❸; anti-surface.
  2—30 mm ❹. 2 ILMS (inner layer missile system) ❺.
Torpedoes: 4 (2 twin) fixed launchers ❻.
Countermeasures: Decoys: Chaff/IR flare launchers. Torpedo defence system.
Combat data systems: Link 16 included.
Radars: Air/surface search ❼.
  Surveillance/fire control ❽; multi-function.
Sonars: Type 2050; hull-mounted; active search and attack; medium frequency.

Helicopters: 1 EH 101 Merlin ❾.

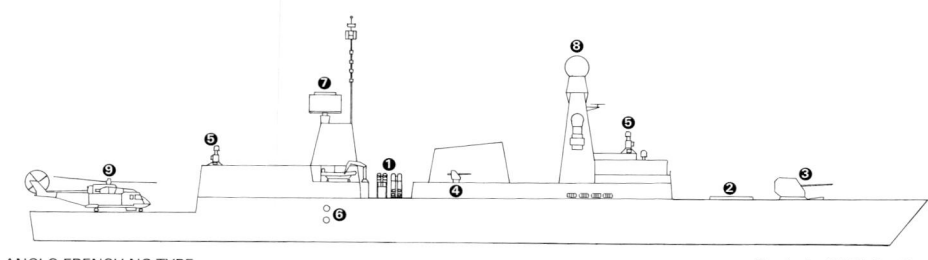

ANGLO-FRENCH NG TYPE *(Scale 1 : 1200), Ian Sturton*

Programmes: Bilateral project for a new AAW ship with the possibility of Italian participation. Warship design contract expected in late 1994 for first order in 1996 and an in service date of 2002.

Structure: Details given are speculative and the drawing should be compared with the same entry in the French section.

ANGLO-FRENCH NG TYPE (artist's impression) *1993*

FRIGATES

2 LEANDER (BATCH 3A) CLASS

Name	No	Builders	Laid down	Launched	Commissioned	Conversion completed
ANDROMEDA	F 57	HM Dockyard, Portsmouth	25 May 1966	24 May 1967	2 Dec 1968	16 Dec 1980
SCYLLA	F 71	HM Dockyard, Devonport	17 May 1967	8 Aug 1968	12 Feb 1970	7 Dec 1984

Displacement, tons: 2500 standard; 2962 full load
Dimensions, feet (metres): 372 oa; 360 wl × 43 × 14.8 (keel); 18 (screws) *(113.4; 109.7 × 13.1 × 4.5; 5.5)*
Main machinery: 2 Babcock & Wilcox boilers; 550 psi *(38.7 kg/cm sq)*; 850°F *(454°C)*; 2 White/English Electric turbines; 30 000 hp *(22.4 MW)*; 2 shafts
Speed, knots: 28. **Range, miles:** 4000 at 15 kts
Complement: 260 (19 officers)

Missiles: SSM: 4 Aerospatiale MM 38 Exocet ❶; inertial cruise; active radar homing to 42 km *(23 nm)* at 0.9 Mach; warhead 165 kg.
  SAM: British Aerospace 6-barrelled Seawolf GWS 25 Mod 0 ❷; command line of sight (CLOS) radar/TV tracking to 5 km *(2.7 nm)* at 2+ Mach; warhead 14 kg; 32 canisters.
Guns: 2 Oerlikon/BMARC 20 mm GAM-B01 ❸; 50° elevation; 800 rounds/minute to 2 km; weight of shell 0.24 kg.
  2 Oerlikon 20 mm Mk 7A; 50° elevation; 800 rounds/minute to 2 km; weight of shell 0.24 kg.
Torpedoes: 6—324 mm Mk 32 STWS 2 (2 triple) tubes ❹. Marconi Stingray; active/passive homing to 11 km *(5.9 nm)* at 45 kts; warhead 35 kg.
Countermeasures: Decoys: Graseby Type 182; towed torpedo decoy.
  2 Vickers Corvus 8-barrelled trainable launchers ❺; chaff to 1 km.
ESM: UAA-1; intercept.

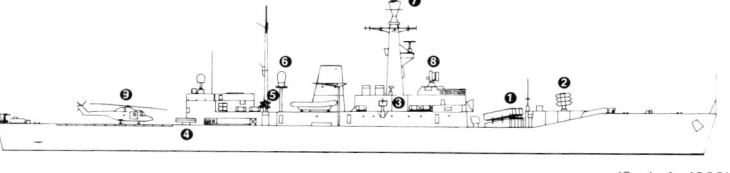

ANDROMEDA *(Scale 1 : 1200), Ian Sturton*

ECM: Type 670; jammer.
Combat data systems: CAAIS action data automation. SCOT SATCOM ❻; Link 10 and 14 (receive).
Fire control: GWS 50.
Radars: Air/surface search: Marconi Type 967/968 ❼; D/E band.
  Navigation: Kelvin Hughes Type 1006; I band.
  Fire control: Marconi Type 910 ❽ I/J band (for Seawolf).
Sonars: Plessey Type 2016; hull-mounted; active search and attack; medium frequency.
  Kelvin Hughes Type 162M; hull-mounted; bottom classification; 50 kHz.

Helicopters: 1 Westland Lynx HAS 3 ❾.

Programmes: The last survivors of an original class of 26 ships.
Modernisation: Batch 3A conversion included the provision of four Exocet launchers, the Seawolf SAM system, improved sonar, Lynx helicopter, modern EW equipment and STWS torpedo tubes. At the same time the 114 mm turret, Seacat and Limbo were removed.
Operational: *Andromeda* is scheduled to be put in a state of extended readiness from June 1993 and pays off in 1994. *Scylla* pays off in late 1993.
Sales: *Bacchante* and *Dido* to New Zealand, the former on 1 October 1982 and *Dido* on 18 July 1983. *Apollo* and *Diomede* to Pakistan in 1988. *Achilles* to Chile in September 1990 followed by *Ariadne* in 1992. *Danae* and *Penelope* to Ecuador in 1991.

SCYLLA *9/1992, C & S Taylor*

6 + 7 + (10) DUKE CLASS (TYPE 23)

Name	No	Builders	Laid down	Launched	Commissioned
NORFOLK	F 230	Yarrow Shipbuilders, Glasgow	14 Dec 1985	10 July 1987	1 June 1990
ARGYLL	F 231	Yarrow Shipbuilders, Glasgow	20 Mar 1987	8 Apr 1989	31 May 1991
LANCASTER	F 229 (ex-F 232)	Yarrow Shipbuilders, Glasgow	18 Dec 1987	24 May 1990	1 May 1992
MARLBOROUGH	F 233	Swan Hunter Shipbuilders, Wallsend-on-Tyne	22 Oct 1987	21 Jan 1989	14 June 1991
IRON DUKE	F 234	Yarrow Shipbuilders, Glasgow	12 Dec 1988	2 Mar 1991	20 May 1993
MONMOUTH	F 235	Yarrow Shipbuilders, Glasgow	1 June 1989	23 Nov 1991	Oct 1993
MONTROSE	F 236	Yarrow Shipbuilders, Glasgow	1 Nov 1989	31 July 1992	May 1994
WESTMINSTER	F 237	Swan Hunter Shipbuilders, Wallsend-on-Tyne	18 Jan 1991	4 Feb 1992	Dec 1993
NORTHUMBERLAND	F 238	Swan Hunter Shipbuilders, Wallsend-on-Tyne	4 Apr 1991	4 Apr 1992	May 1994
RICHMOND	F 239	Swan Hunter Shipbuilders, Wallsend-on-Tyne	16 Feb 1992	6 Apr 1993	Dec 1994
SOMERSET	F 240	Yarrow Shipbuilders, Glasgow	12 Oct 1992	1995	1996
GRAFTON	F 241	Yarrow Shipbuilders, Glasgow	13 May 1993	1995	1997
SUTHERLAND	F 242	Yarrow Shipbuilders, Glasgow	14 Oct 1993	1996	1997

Displacement, tons: 3500 standard; 4200 full load
Dimensions, feet (metres): 436.2 × 52.8 × 18 (screws); 24 (sonar) *(133 × 16.1 × 5.5; 7.3)*
Main machinery: CODLAG; 2 RR Spey SM1A (F 229-F 236) or SM1C (F 237 onwards) gas turbines; 31 100 hp *(23.2 MW)* sustained; 4 Paxman 12YJCM diesels; 8100 hp *(6 MW)*; 2 GEC motors; 4000 hp *(3 MW)*; 2 shafts
Speed, knots: 28; 15 on diesel-electric. **Range, miles:** 7800 miles at 15 kts
Complement: 174 (12 officers) (accommodation for 185 (16 officers))
Missiles: SSM: 8 McDonnell Douglas Harpoon (2 quad) launchers ❶; active radar homing to 130 km *(70 nm)* at 0.9 Mach; warhead 227 kg (84C).
  SAM: British Aerospace Seawolf GWS 26 Mod 1 VLS ❷; command line of sight (CLOS) radar/TV tracking to 6 km *(3.3 nm)* at 2.5 Mach; warhead 14 kg; 32 canisters.
Guns: 1 Vickers 4.5 in *(114 mm)*/55 Mk 8 ❸; 55° elevation; 25 rounds/minute to 22 km *(11.9 nm)* anti-surface; 6 km *(3.3 nm)* anti-aircraft; weight of shell 21 kg.
  2 Oerlikon/DES 30 mm/75 Mk 1 ❹; 80° elevation; 650 rounds/minute to 10 km *(5.4 nm)* anti-surface, 3 km *(1.6 nm)* anti-aircraft; weight of shell 0.36 kg.
Torpedoes: 4 Cray Marine 324 mm fixed (2 twin) tubes ❺. Marconi Stingray; active/passive homing to 11 km *(5.9 nm)* at 45 kts; warhead 35 kg (shaped charge); depth to 750 m *(2460 ft)*. Automatic reload in 9 minutes.
Countermeasures: Decoys: 4 Marconi Sea Gnat 6-barrelled fixed launchers ❻; for chaff and IR flares.
  Type 182; towed torpedo decoy.
ESM: Racal UAF-1 Cutlass ❼; intercept. THORN EMI UAT (F 237 onwards and then retrofit if funds are available).
ECM: Type 675(2) or Racal Scorpion; jammer.
Combat data systems: Dowty Sema SSCS action data automation (see *Structure* comment); Links 11, 14 and 16 in due course. Marconi SCOT 1D SATCOMs ❽.
Fire control: BAe GSA 8B/GPEOD optronic director ❾. GWS 60 (for SSM). GWS 26 (for SAM).
Radars: Air/surface search: Plessey Type 996(I) ❿; 3D; E/F band.
  Navigation: Kelvin Hughes Type 1007; I band.
  Fire control: Two Marconi Type 911 ⓫; I/Ku band.
Sonars: Ferranti/Thomson Sintra Type 2050; bow-mounted; active search and attack.
  Dowty Type 2031Z; towed array; passive search; very low frequency. To be replaced by Marconi/Plessey 2057 in due course. One ship to be fitted with Type 2081 active low frequency VDS in due course; others may be back fitted.
Helicopters: 1 Westland Lynx HAS 3 (1 EH 101 Merlin, later) ⓬.

Programmes: The first of this class was ordered from Yarrows on 29 October 1984. Next three in September 1986, with four more out to tender in October 1987 but only three ordered in July 1988. Again four out to tender in late 1988 and only three ordered 19 December 1989. Long lead items for another six ordered in 1990 but contracts were not placed until 23 January 1992 when three more were ordered. Planned final total is 23 at the present rate of less than two per year is unlikely to be reached. F 229 pennant number changed because 232 was considered unlucky as it is the RN report form number for collisions and groundings.
Structure: Incorporates stealth technology to minimise acoustic, magnetic, radar and IR signatures. The design includes a 7° slope to all vertical surfaces, rounded edges, reduction of IR emissions and a hull bubble system to reduce radiated noise. The combined diesel electric and GT propulsion system provides quiet motive power during towed sonar operations. The SM1C engines although capable of 41 MW of power combined are constrained by output into the gearbox. A CIWS gun is not fitted but a possible extension by 7 m at some stage in the building programme would allow one or two Goalkeeper to be carried and increase Seawolf magazine capacity. The first seven ships of the class lack fully automated co-ordination of all weapons and sensors. SSCS software Phase I has been installed in *Westminster* on build and is to be retrofitted in earlier ships. Subsequent Phases are being fitted on build to all the later ships.
Operational: The ship is capable of carrying out all weapon systems functions without the SSCS Combat Data System. The problem is that in multi-threat situations command speed of response will in theory be much slower. F 233 carrying out a trial of a Dowty track management system (TMS) which uses a form of artificial intelligence.

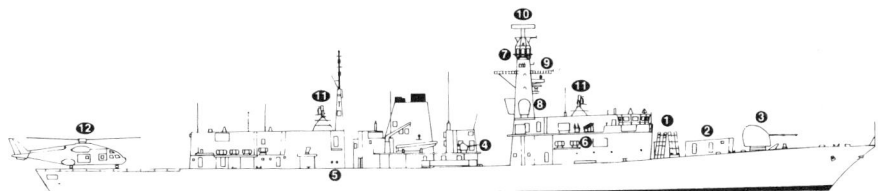

NORFOLK *(Scale 1 : 1200), Ian Sturton*

IRON DUKE *3/1993, Maritime Photographic*

NORFOLK *11/1992, H M Steele*

14 BROADSWORD CLASS (TYPE 22)

Batch 1

Name	No	Builders	Laid down	Launched	Commissioned
BROADSWORD	F 88	Yarrow Shipbuilders, Glasgow	7 Feb 1975	12 May 1976	3 May 1979
BATTLEAXE	F 89	Yarrow Shipbuilders, Glasgow	4 Feb 1976	18 May 1977	28 Mar 1980
BRILLIANT	F 90	Yarrow Shipbuilders, Glasgow	25 Mar 1977	15 Dec 1978	15 May 1981
BRAZEN	F 91	Yarrow Shipbuilders, Glasgow	18 Aug 1978	4 Mar 1980	2 July 1982

Batch 2

Name	No	Builders	Laid down	Launched	Commissioned
BOXER	F 92	Yarrow Shipbuilders, Glasgow	1 Nov 1979	17 June 1981	14 Jan 1984
BEAVER	F 93	Yarrow Shipbuilders, Glasgow	20 June 1980	8 May 1982	18 Dec 1984
BRAVE	F 94	Yarrow Shipbuilders, Glasgow	24 May 1982	19 Nov 1983	4 July 1986
LONDON (ex-*Bloodhound*)	F 95	Yarrow Shipbuilders, Glasgow	7 Feb 1983	27 Oct 1984	5 June 1987
SHEFFIELD	F 96	Swan Hunter Shipbuilders, Wallsend-or-Tyne	29 Mar 1984	26 Mar 1986	26 July 1988
COVENTRY	F 98	Swan Hunter Shipbuilders, Wallsend-or-Tyne	29 Mar 1984	8 Apr 1986	14 Oct 1988

Displacement, tons: 3500 standard; 4400 full load (Batch 1) 4100 standard; 4800 full load (Batch 2)
Dimensions, feet (metres): 430 oa; 410 wl × 48.5 × 19.9 (screws) *(131.2; 125 × 14.8 × 6)* (Batch 1) 485.8 oa × 48.5 × 21 (screws) *(145 × 14.8 × 6.4)* (F 92-93) 480.5 × 48.5 × 21 *(146.5 × 14.8 × 6.4)* (F 94-96 and 98)
Main machinery: COGOG; 2 RR Olympus TM3B gas turbines; 50 000 hp *(37.3 MW)* sustained or 2 RR Spey SM1C (F 94); 41 630 hp *(31 MW)* sustained; 2 RR Tyne RM1C gas turbines; 9900 hp *(7.4 MW)* sustained; 2 shafts; cp props
Speed, knots: 30; 18 on Tynes. **Range, miles:** 4500 at 18 kts on Tynes
Complement: 222 (17 officers) plus 65 officers under training (Batch 1) 273 (30 officers) (accommodation for 296) (Batch 2)

Missiles: SSM: 4 Aerospatiale MM 38 Exocet ❶; inertial cruise; active radar homing to 42 km *(23 nm)* at 0.9 Mach; warhead 165 kg; sea-skimmer.
SAM: 2 British Aerospace 6-barrelled Seawolf GWS 25 Mod 0 or Mod 4 (except F 94-96 and 98) ❷; command line of sight (CLOS) TV/radar tracking to 5 km *(2.7 nm)* at 2+ Mach; warhead 14 kg; 32 rounds. Being upgraded to Mod 4 with improved radar and optronics.
2 British Aerospace Seawolf GWS 25 Mod 3 (F 94-96 and 98) ❷; has a Type 911 tracker with a second radar channel instead of TV.
Guns: 4 Oerlikon/BMARC GCM-A03 30 mm/75 (2 twin) ❸; 80° elevation; 650 rounds/minute to 10 km *(5.5 nm)*; weight of shell 0.36 kg.
2 Oerlikon/BMARC 20 mm GAM-BO1 ❹; 55° elevation; 1000 rounds/minute to 2 km.
Torpedoes: 6—324 mm Plessey STWS Mk 2 (2 triple) tubes ❺. Marconi Stingray; active/passive homing to 11 km *(5.9 nm)* at 45 kts; warhead 35 kg.
Countermeasures: Decoys: 2 Plessey Shield 12-tubed launchers ❻; IR flares and chaff to 4 km *(2.2 nm)*.
4 Marconi Sea Gnat 6-barrelled fixed launchers.
Graseby Type 182; towed torpedo decoy.
ESM: MEL UAA-2; intercept.
ECM: Type 670; jammers.
Combat data systems: Ferranti CACS 1 (Batch 2); Links 11 and 14; CAAIS (Batch 1); Links 10 and 14 (receive); action data automation. Marconi SCOT SATCOM ❼. Marisat.
Fire control: GWS 25 Mod 0 or 4 (for SAM) (except F 94-96 and 98); GWS 25 Mod 3 (for SAM) (F 94-96 and 98); GWS 50.
Radars: Air/surface search: Marconi Type 967/968 (Type 967M in F 94) ❽; D/E band.
Navigation: Kelvin Hughes Type 1006 or Type 1007; I band.
Fire control: Two Marconi Type 911 or Type 910 (in Mod 0 ships) ❾; I/Ku band (for Seawolf).
Sonars: Plessey Type 2016 or Ferranti/Thomson Sintra Type 2050; hull-mounted; search and attack.
Dowty Type 2031Z (Batch 2 only); towed array; passive search; very low frequency.
Helicopters: 2 Westland Lynx HAS 3 (in all) ❿; or 1 Westland Sea King HAS 5 (or EH 101 Merlin) (F 94-96 and 98).

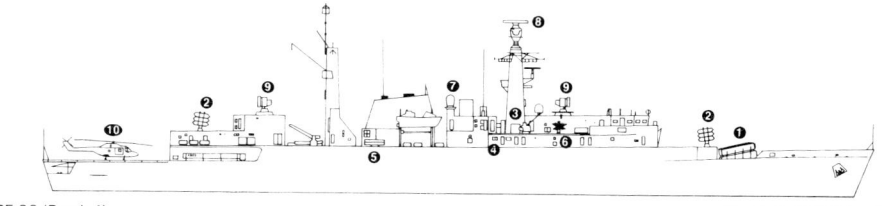

TYPE 22 (Batch 1) *(Scale 1 : 1200), Ian Sturton*

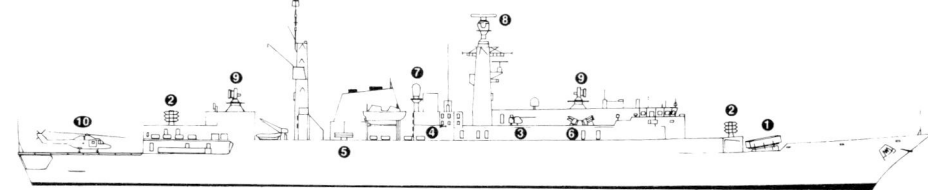

TYPE 22 (Batch 2) *(Scale 1 : 1200), Ian Sturton*

BRILLIANT *6/1992, Maritime Photographic*

BOXER *9/1992, Bill McBride, RAN*

Frigates / UK (NAVY) 731

Batch 3 Name	No	Builders	Laid down	Launched	Commissioned
CORNWALL	F 99	Yarrow Shipbuilders, Glasgow	14 Dec 1983	14 Oct 1985	23 Apr 1988
CUMBERLAND	F 85	Yarrow Shipbuilders, Glasgow	12 Oct 1984	21 June 1986	10 June 1989
CAMPBELTOWN	F 86	Cammell Laird, Birkenhead	4 Dec 1985	7 Oct 1987	27 May 1989
CHATHAM	F 87	Swan Hunter Shipbuilders, Wallsend-on-Tyne	12 May 1986	20 Jan 1988	4 May 1990

Displacement, tons: 4200 standard; 4900 full load
Dimensions, feet (metres): 485.9 × 48.5 × 21 *(148.1 × 14.8 × 6.4)*
Main machinery: COGOG; 2 RR Spey SM1A gas turbines; 29 500 hp *(22 MW)* sustained; 2 RR Tyne RM3C gas turbines; 10 680 hp *(8 MW)* sustained; 2 shafts; cp props
Speed, knots: 30; 18 on Tynes. **Range, miles:** 4500 at 18 kts on Tynes
Complement: 250 (31 officers) (accommodation for 301)

Missiles: SSM: 8 McDonnell Douglas Harpoon Block 1C (2 quad) launchers ❶; pre-programmed; active radar homing to 130 km *(70 nm)* at 0.9 Mach; warhead 227 kg.
SAM: 2 British Aerospace Seawolf GWS 25 Mod 3 ❷; command line of sight (CLOS) with 2 channel radar tracking to 5 km *(2.7 nm)* at 2+ Mach; warhead 14 kg.
Guns: 1 Vickers 4.5 in *(114 mm)*/55 Mk 8 ❸; 55° elevation; 25 rounds/minute to 22 km *(11.9 nm)* anti-surface; 6 km *(3.3 nm)* anti-aircraft; weight of shell 21 kg.
1 Signaal/General Electric 30 mm 7-barrelled Goalkeeper ❹; 4200 rounds/minute combined to 1.5 km.
2 DES/Oerlikon 30 mm/75 ❺; 80° elevation; 650 rounds/minute to 10 km *(5.5 nm)*; weight of shell 0.36 kg.
Torpedoes: 6—324 mm Plessey STWS Mk 2 (2 triple) tubes ❻. Marconi Stingray; active/passive homing to 11 km *(5.9 nm)* at 45 kts; warhead 35 kg.
Countermeasures: Decoys: 4 Marconi Sea Gnat 6-barrelled fixed launchers ❼; electronic decoy with jammer.
Graseby Type 182; towed torpedo decoy.
ESM: MEL UAA-2; intercept.
ECM: Type 670 or Type 675(2); jammer.
Combat data systems: CACS 5 action data automation; Links 11 and 14. 2 Marconi SCOT SATCOMs ❽. ICS-3 integrated comms. Marisat.
Fire control: 2 BAe GSA 8A Sea Archer optronic directors with TV and IR imaging and laser rangefinders ❾. GWS 60. GWS 25 Mod 3 (for SAM).
Radars: Air/surface search: Marconi Type 967/968 ❿; D/E band.
Navigation: Kelvin Hughes Type 1006 or Type 1007; I band.
Fire control: Two Marconi Type 911 ⓫; I/Ku band (for Seawolf).
Sonars: Plessey Type 2016; hull-mounted; active search and attack. Being replaced by Ferranti Type 2050.
Dowty Type 2031; towed array; passive search; very low frequency.

Helicopters: 2 Westland Lynx HAS 3; or 1 Westland Sea King HAS 5 ⓬ (or EH 101 Merlin).

Batches 1, 2 and 3

Programmes: Originally planned as successors to the Leander class. Order for the first of class, *Broadsword*, was placed on 8 February 1974.
Modernisation: Rolls Royce Spey SM1C engines (operational in F 94 in early 1990) give greater power and may be back fitted in due course. Seawolf GWS 25 will be progressively upgraded to Mod 4 standard in all Mod 0 ships. Sonar 2016 is being replaced by Sonar 2050 and Bofors 40 mm/60 in Batch 1 and 2 have been replaced by Oerlikon 30 mm guns. EW fit is being updated. CAAIS combat data system in Batch 1 is overdue for replacement by CACS-1, but the update may be cancelled by lack of funds.

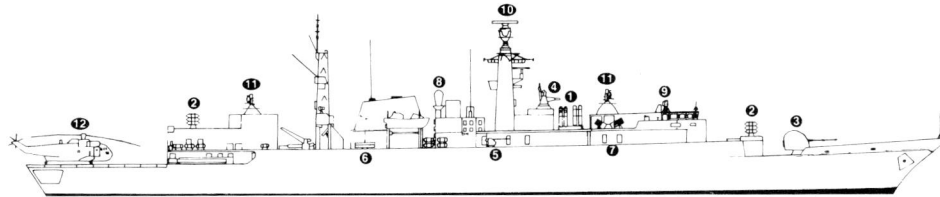

TYPE 22 (Batch 3) *(Scale 1 : 1200), Ian Sturton*

CUMBERLAND *12/1992, Harald Carstens*

CHATHAM *3/1992, G Toremans*

Structure: Funnel in *Brilliant* and later ships was smoother, slimmer and shorter than in first two in build but *Broadsword* and *Battleaxe* have been modified and are now the same. Last four Batch 2 and all Batch 3 have enlarged flight decks to take Sea King or EH 101 Merlin helicopters. Batch 1 have modified accommodation to take 65 officers under training.

Operational: This class is primarily designed for ASW operations and is capable of acting as OTC. Batch 3 have facilities for Flag and staff. Batch 1 used as training ships. One Lynx normally embarked for peacetime operations. Ships have been fitted with DEC laser dazzle device on operational deployments. Batch 2: 1st Frigate Squadron. Batch 1 and Batch 3: 2nd Frigate Squadron.

CORNWALL *4/1992, Giorgio Arra*

732 UK (NAVY) / Frigates — Shipborne aircraft

3 AMAZON CLASS (TYPE 21)

Name	No	Builders	Laid down	Launched	Commissioned
ACTIVE	F 171	Vosper Thornycroft, Woolston	23 July 1971	23 Nov 1972	17 June 1977
ALACRITY	F 174	Yarrow Shipbuilders, Glasgow	5 Mar 1973	18 Sep 1974	2 July 1977
AVENGER	F 185	Yarrow Shipbuilders, Glasgow	30 Oct 1974	20 Nov 1975	19 July 1978

Displacement, tons: 3100 standard; 3600 full load
Dimensions, feet (metres): 384 oa; 360 wl × 41.7 × 19.5 (screws) *(117; 109.7 × 12.7 × 5.9)*
Main machinery: COGOG; 2 RR Olympus TM3B gas turbines; 50 000 hp *(37.3 MW)* sustained; 2 RR Tyne RM1C gas turbines (cruising); 9900 hp *(7.4 MW)* sustained; 2 shafts; cp props
Speed, knots: 30; 18 on Tynes. **Range, miles:** 4000 at 17 kts; 1200 at 30 kts
Complement: 175 (13 officers) (accommodation for 192)

Missiles: SSM: 4 Aerospatiale MM 38 Exocet ❶; inertial cruise; active radar homing to 42 km *(23 nm)* at 0.9 Mach; warhead 165 kg; sea-skimmer.
SAM: Short Bros Seacat GWS 24 quad launcher ❷; optical/radar guidance to 5 km *(2.7 nm)*; warhead 10 kg; sea-skimmer modification.
Guns: 1 Vickers 4.5 in *(114 mm)*/55 Mk 8 ❸; 55° elevation; 25 rounds/minute to 22 km *(11.9 nm)* anti-surface; 6 km *(3.3 nm)* anti-aircraft; weight of shell 21 kg.
2 or 4 Oerlikon 20 mm Mk 7A ❹; 50° elevation; 800 rounds/minute to 2 km; weight of shell 0.24 kg.
Torpedoes: 6—324 mm Plessey STWS Mk 2 (2 triple) tubes ❺. Marconi Stingray; active/passive homing to 11 km *(5.9 nm)* at 45 kts; warhead 35 kg (shaped charge); depth to 750 m *(2460 ft)*. Only in *Alacrity* and *Active*; *Avenger* has a second pair of 20 mm guns in lieu.
Countermeasures: Decoys: Graseby Type 182; towed torpedo decoy.
2 Vickers Corvus 8-tubed trainable launchers ❻; chaff to 1 km.
ESM: MEL UAA-1; intercept.
Combat data systems: CAAIS combat data system with Ferranti FM 1600B computers. Marconi SCOT SATCOMs ❼; Links 10 and 14 (receive).
Fire control: Ferranti WSA-4 digital fire control system for gun and Seacat. GWS 50.
Radars: Air/surface search: Marconi Type 992R ❽; E/F band.
Navigation: Kelvin Hughes Type 1006; I band.
Fire control: Two Selenia Type 912 ❾; I/J band; range 40 km *(22 nm)*.
Sonars: Graseby Type 184P; hull-mounted; active search and attack.
Kelvin Hughes Type 162M; hull-mounted; bottom classification; 50 kHz.

Helicopters: 1 Westland Lynx HAS 3 ❿.

Programmes: A contract was awarded to Vosper Thornycroft on 27 February 1968 for the design of a patrol frigate to be prepared in full collaboration with Yarrow Ltd. This was the first custom built gas turbine frigate (designed and constructed as such from the keel up, as opposed to conversion) and the first RN warship designed by commercial firms for many years.
Modernisation: During service life, GWS 50 Exocet, SCOT, STWS Mk 1 and Lynx helicopter facilities added. With the removal from service of all STWS Mk 1, only two of the class were fitted with Mk 2 in lieu.
Structure: Due to cracking in the upper deck structure large strengthening pieces have been fixed to the ships' side at the top of the steel hull as shown in the illustration. The addition of permanent ballast to improve stability has increased displacement by about 350 tons. Further hull modifications to reduce noise and vibration started in 1988 and completed in 1992.
Operational: Form 4th Frigate Squadron (leader, *Active*). Three of the class paid off in mid-1993 and one more goes in 1994.
Sales: The whole class may be bought by Pakistan.

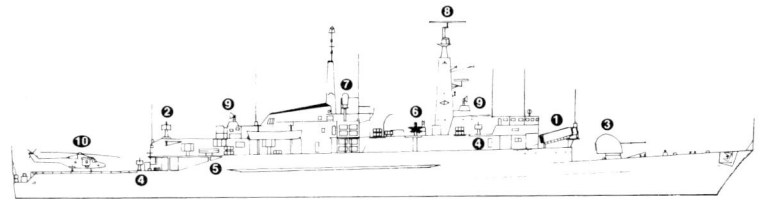

ALACRITY *(Scale 1 : 1200), Ian Sturton*

ALACRITY *11/1991, Giorgio Arra*

SHIPBORNE AIRCRAFT

Numbers/Type: 39/10 British Aerospace Sea Harrier FRS 1/FRS 2.
Operational speed: 640 kts *(1186 km/h)*.
Service ceiling: 51 200 ft *(15 600 m)*.
Range: 800 nm *(1480 km)*.
Role/Weapon systems: Air defence, reconnaissance and maritime attack; update for 31 aircraft by 1994 to FRS 2 Standard plus 10 new FRS 2 aircraft. Sensors: Blue Fox or Blue Vixen (FRS 2) radar, RWR, cameras. IFF Mk II from 1995. Weapons: ASV; 2 × Sea Eagle missiles. Strike; 2 × 30 mm cannon and 1000 lb bombs. AD; 4 × AIM-9L Sidewinder or AIM-120 AMRAAM (FRS 2); 2 × 30 mm Aden cannon.

SEA HARRIER *9/1992, H M Steele*

Numbers/Type: 80 Westland Lynx HAS 3.
Operational speed: 120 kts *(222 km/h)*.
Service ceiling: 10 000 ft *(3048 m)*.
Range: 320 nm *(593 km)*.
Role/Weapon systems: Primarily anti-surface helicopter with short-range ASW capability; embarked in all modern RN escorts; Royal Marines operate anti-armour/reconnaissance version (Lynx AH 1); planned update with centralised tactical system, Sea Owl passive identification system and MAD (Lynx HAS 8) to be fitted from 1994. Sensors: Ferranti Sea Spray Mk 1 radar, 'Orange Crop' ESM, chaff and flare dispenser. Weapons: ASW; 2 × Stingray torpedoes or Mk 11 depth bombs. ASV; 4 × Sea Skua missiles; 2—12.7 mm MG pods.

LYNX HAS 3 *9/1992, H M Steele*

LYNX HAS 8 *1992*

Numbers/Type: 76 Westland Sea King HAS 5/6.
Operational speed: 112 kts *(207 km/h)*.
Service ceiling: 10 000 ft *(3050 m)*.
Range: 500 nm *(925 km)*.
Role/Weapon systems: Embarked and shore-based medium ASW helicopter in front-line and training squadron service; used as active/passive screen force and provides RN's principal airborne ASW assets; Mk 6 entered service in June 1989. Sensors: MEL Sea Searcher radar, 'Orange Crop' ESM, Ferranti 2069 (HAS 6) replacing Type 195M dipping sonar, combined sonar processor AQS 902G-DS Mk 6 replacing 902C. Weapons: ASW; 4 × Stingray torpedoes or Mk 11 depth bombs.

SEA KING HAS 6   *10/1992, Maritime Photographic*

Numbers/Type: 10 Westland Sea King AEW 2.
Operational speed: 110 kts *(204 km/h)*.
Service ceiling: 10 000 ft *(3050 m)*.
Range: 660 nm *(1220 km)*.
Role/Weapon systems: Primarily used for airborne early warning organic to the Fleet, with EW, surface search and OTHT secondary roles; modified from ASW version. Improved radar, IFF Mk II and Link 16 to be fitted from 1995. Sensors: Searchwater AEW radar, 'Orange Crop' ESM, 'Jubilee Guardsmen' IFF. Weapons: Unarmed.

SEA KING AEW 2   *10/1992, Maritime Photographic*

Numbers/Type: 36 Westland Sea King HC4.
Operational speed: 112 kts *(208 km/h)*.
Service ceiling: 10 000 ft *(3050 m)*.
Range: 664 nm *(1230 km)*.
Role/Weapon systems: Commando support and re-supply helicopter; capable of carrying most RM Commando Force equipment underslung. Expected to remain in service to 2010. Sensors: None. Weapons: Can fit 7.62 mm GPMG or similar, missile armament abandoned.

SEA KING HC4   *9/1992, Maritime Photographic*

Numbers/Type: 12 Westland Gazelle AH Mk 1.
Operational speed: 142 kts *(264 km/h)*.
Service ceiling: 9350 ft *(2850 m)*.
Range: 361 nm *(670 km)*.
Role/Weapon systems: Observation with 3 Commando Brigade Air Squadron, Royal Marines. Sensors: None. Weapons: Normally unarmed.

GAZELLE   *1989*

Numbers/Type: 6 Westland Lynx AH Mk 1.
Operational speed: 140 kts *(259 km/h)*.
Service ceiling: 10 600 ft *(3230 m)*.
Range: 340 nm *(630 km)*.
Role/Weapon systems: Military general purpose and anti-tank with 3 Commando Brigade Air Squadron, Royal Marines. Sensors: None. Weapons: Up to 8 Hughes TOW anti-tank missiles.

LYNX AH Mk 1   *1989*

Numbers/Type: 1 Westland/Agusta EH 101 Merlin.
Operational speed: 160 kts *(296 km/h)*.
Service ceiling: 15 000 ft *(4572 m)*.
Range: 550 nm *(1019 km)*.
Role/Weapon systems: Primary anti-submarine role with secondary anti-surface and troop carrying capabilities. Contract for 44 signed 9 October 1991 for delivery from 1996. Sensors: Ferranti Blue Kestrel radar, Ferranti Flash dipping sonar, sonobuoy acoustic processor AQS-903, Racal Orange Reaper ESM, ECM. Weapons: ASW; 4 Stingray torpedoes or Mk 11 depth bombs. ASV; 4 Sea Skua or replacement, capability for guidance of ship-launched SSM.

MERLIN   *1991*

LAND-BASED MARITIME AIRCRAFT (FRONT LINE)

Numbers/Type: 26 Hawker Siddeley Nimrod MR 2/2P.
Operational speed: 500 kts *(926 km/h)*.
Service ceiling: 42 000 ft *(12 800 m)*.
Range: 5000 nm *(9265 km)*.
Role/Weapon systems: Primarily ASW but with ASV, OTHT and control potential at long range from shore bases; peacetime duties include SAR, EEZ protection, maritime surveillance. Sensors: THORN EMI Searchwater radar, ECM, ESM, cameras, MAD, sonobuoys, AQS-901 processor. Weapons: ASW; 6.1 tons of Mk 44/46 or Stingray torpedoes or depth bombs or mines. ASV; 4 × Harpoon missiles. Self-defence; 4 × AIM-9L Sidewinder.

Numbers/Type: 7 Boeing E-3D Sentry AWAC.
Operational speed: 460 kts *(853 km/h)*.
Service ceiling: 30 000 ft *(9145 m)*.
Range: 870 nm *(1610 km)*.
Role/Weapon systems: Air defence early warning aircraft with secondary role to provide coastal AEW for the Fleet; six hours endurance at the range given above. Sensors: Westinghouse APY-2 surveillance radar, Bendix weather radar, Mk XII IFF, Yellow Gate, ESM, ECM. Weapons: Unarmed.

734 UK (NAVY) / Mine warfare forces

MINE WARFARE FORCES

13 HUNT CLASS (MINESWEEPERS/MINEHUNTERS—COASTAL)

Name	No	Builders	Commissioned
BRECON	M 29	Vosper Thornycroft, Woolston	21 Mar 1980
LEDBURY	M 30	Vosper Thornycroft, Woolston	11 June 1981
CATTISTOCK	M 31	Vosper Thornycroft, Woolston	16 June 1982
COTTESMORE	M 32	Yarrow Shipbuilders, Glasgow	24 June 1983
BROCKLESBY	M 33	Vosper Thornycroft, Woolston	3 Feb 1983
MIDDLETON	M 34	Yarrow Shipbuilders, Glasgow	15 Aug 1984
DULVERTON	M 35	Vosper Thornycroft, Woolston	4 Nov 1983
BICESTER	M 36	Vosper Thornycroft, Woolston	20 Mar 1986
CHIDDINGFOLD	M 37	Vosper Thornycroft, Woolston	10 Aug 1984
ATHERSTONE	M 38	Vosper Thornycroft, Woolston	30 Jan 1987
HURWORTH	M 39	Vosper Thornycroft, Woolston	2 July 1985
BERKELEY	M 40	Vosper Thornycroft, Woolston	14 Jan 1988
QUORN	M 41	Vosper Thornycroft, Woolston	21 Apr 1989

Displacement, tons: 615 light; 750 full load
Dimensions, feet (metres): 187 wl; 197 oa × 32.8 × 9.5 (keel); 11.2 (screws) *(57; 60 × 10 × 2.9; 3.4)*
Main machinery: 2 Ruston-Paxman 9-59K Deltic diesels; 1900 hp *(1.42 MW)*; 1 Deltic Type 9-55B diesel for pulse generator and auxiliary drive; 780 hp *(582 kW)*; 2 shafts; bow thruster
Speed, knots: 15 diesels; 8 hydraulic drive. **Range, miles:** 1500 at 12 kts
Complement: 45 (6 officers)

Guns: 1 Oerlikon/BMARC 30 mm/75 DS 30B; 65° elevation; 650 rounds/minute to 10 km *(5.4 nm)* anti-surface; 3 km *(1.6 nm)* anti-aircraft; weight of shell 0.36 kg. Replaced Bofors 40 mm.
2 Oerlikon/BMARC 20 mm GAM-CO1 (enhancement); 55° elevation; 900 rounds/minute to 2 km.
2—7.62 mm MGs.
Countermeasures: Decoys: 2 Wallop Barricade (enhancement); 6 sets of triple barrels.
2 Irvin Replica RF; passive decoys.
ESM: MEL Matilda E (enhancement); Marconi Mentor A (in some).
Combat data systems: CAAIS DBA 4 action data automation.
Radars: Navigation: Kelvin Hughes Type 1006; I band.
Sonars: Plessey Type 193M or 193M Mod 1; hull-mounted; minehunting; 100/300 kHz.
Mil Cross mine avoidance sonar; hull-mounted; active; high frequency.
Type 2059 addition to track PAP 104/105.

Programmes: A class of MCM Vessels combining both hunting and sweeping capabilities.
Modernisation: Ten PAP 105 were acquired in 1988-89 to replace the 104s. They have a range of 600 m *(1968 ft)* down to 300 m *(984 ft)* depth and a speed of 6 kts; weight 700 kg. 30 mm gun has replaced the Bofors 40 mm. Racal Mk 53 navigation system ordered in August 1990 for all ships. Mid-life update planned to include VDS sonar, Nautis command system and a replacement PAP or mine disposal UUV.
Structure: Hulls of GRP.
Operational: Two PAP 104/105 remotely controlled submersibles, MS 14 magnetic loop, Sperry MSSA Mk 1 Towed Acoustic Generator and conventional Mk 8 Oropesa sweeps. For operational deployments fitted with enhanced weapons systems, Inmarsat SATCOMs and some have the SCARAB remote control floating mine towing device which helps the safe destruction of moored mines once they have been cut from their moorings.

ORWELL (RNR)   2/1992, G Toremans

BLACKWATER (RN)   2/1993, Maritime Photographic

BRECON   4/1992, W Sartori

12 RIVER CLASS (MINESWEEPERS—COASTAL)

Name	No	Builders	Commissioned
WAVENEY	M 2003	Richards Ltd (L)	12 July 1984
CARRON	M 2004	Richards Ltd (GY)	29 Sep 1984
DOVEY	M 2005	Richards Ltd (GY)	30 Mar 1985
HELFORD	M 2006	Richards Ltd (L)	May 1985
HUMBER	M 2007	Richards Ltd (L)	7 June 1985
BLACKWATER	M 2008	Richards Ltd (GY)	5 July 1985
ITCHEN	M 2009	Richards Ltd (L)	12 Oct 1985
HELMSDALE	M 2010	Richards Ltd (L)	1 Mar 1986
ORWELL	M 2011	Richards Ltd (GY)	27 Nov 1985
RIBBLE	M 2012	Richards Ltd (GY)	19 Feb 1986
SPEY	M 2013	Richards Ltd (L)	4 Apr 1986
ARUN	M 2014	Richards Ltd (L)	29 Aug 1986

Displacement, tons: 890 full load
Dimensions, feet (metres): 156 × 34.5 × 9.5 *(47.5 × 10.5 × 2.9)*
Main machinery: 2 Ruston 6RKC diesels; 3100 hp *(2.3 MW)* sustained; 2 shafts
Speed, knots: 14. **Range, miles:** 4500 at 10 kts
Complement: 30 (7 officers)

Guns: 1 Bofors 40 mm/60 Mk 3; 80° elevation; 120 rounds/minute to 10 km *(5.4 nm)* anti-surface; 3 km *(1.6 nm)* anti-aircraft; weight of shell 0.89 kg.
Radars: Navigation: Two Racal Decca TM 1226C; I band.

Programmes: First four ordered 23 September 1982. All built at Lowestoft and Great Yarmouth. Three more planned to be built for Fishery Protection Squadron to replace Ton class but the requirement was cancelled in 1990.
Structure: Steel hulled for deep team sweeping. There have been problems with upper-deck corrosion in some ships. 40 mm guns may be replaced by 30 mm.
Operational: BAJ Wire Sweep Mk 9 EDATS fitted. RNR 10th MCM Squadron: *Waveney* (South Wales); *Carron* (Severn); *Dovey* (Clyde); *Helford* (Ulster); *Itchen* (Solent); *Orwell* (Tyne); *Humber* (Mersey); *Spey* (Forth); *Arun* (Sussex); *Blackwater* (Coastal Division RN); *Helmsdale* and *Ribble* in reserve. London Division is having to share with other RNR sea training centres.

3 TON CLASS (COASTAL MINEHUNTERS)

Name	No	Builders	Commissioned
BRINTON	M 1114	Cook Welton and Gemmell	4 Mar 1954
NURTON	M 1166	Harland & Wolff, Belfast	21 Aug 1957
SHERATON	M 1181	White's Shipyard, Southampton	24 Aug 1956

Displacement, tons: 360 standard; 440 full load
Dimensions, feet (metres): 153 × 28.9 × 8.2 *(46.6 × 8.8 × 2.5)*
Main machinery: 2 Paxman Deltic 18A-7A diesels; 3000 hp *(2.24 MW)*; 2 shafts
Speed, knots: 15. **Range, miles:** 2500 at 12 kts
Complement: 38 (5 officers)

Guns: 1 Bofors 40 mm/60 Mk 3; 80° elevation; 120 rounds/minute to 10 km *(5.4 nm)* anti-surface; 3 km *(1.6 nm)* anti-aircraft; weight of shell 0.89 kg.
3 FN 7.62 mm MGs.
2 Oerlikon 20 mm (on deployment); 50° elevation; 800 rounds/minute to 2 km; weight of shell 0.24 kg.
Countermeasures: Decoys: Plessey Shield 12-tubed chaff launcher.
Radars: Navigation: Kelvin Hughes Type 1006; I band.
Sonars: Plessey Type 193M; hull-mounted; minehunting; 100/300 kHz.

Programmes: The survivors of a class of 118 built between 1953 and 1960, largely as a result of lessons from the Korean War. John I Thornycroft & Co Ltd, Southampton was the lead yard.
Structure: These ships have double mahogany hull on aluminium frames and incorporate a considerable amount of non-magnetic material. All have active rudders.
Operational: *Sheraton* and *Brinton* are part of the Third MCM Squadron and *Nurton* is in Northern Ireland. Two more of the class *Kellington* and *Iveston* are being kept in a state of reduced readiness and may not finally be scrapped until 1995/96. *Brinton* pays off in late 1993.
Sales: Argentina (six in 1968), Australia (six in 1962), Ghana (one in 1964), India (four in 1956), Ireland (three in 1971), Malaysia (seven in 1960-68), South Africa (ten in 1958-59). Many deleted.

SHERATON   2/1992, Wright & Logan

4 + 1 (5) SANDOWN CLASS (MINEHUNTERS)

Name	No	Builders	Launched	Commissioned
SANDOWN	M 101	Vosper Thornycroft, Woolston	16 Apr 1988	9 June 1989
INVERNESS	M 102	Vosper Thornycroft, Woolston	27 Feb 1990	24 Jan 1991
CROMER	M 103	Vosper Thornycroft, Woolston	6 Oct 1990	7 Apr 1992
WALNEY	M 104	Vosper Thornycroft, Woolston	25 Nov 1991	20 Feb 1993
BRIDPORT	M 105	Vosper Thornycroft, Woolston	30 July 1992	Sep 1993

Displacement, tons: 450 standard; 484 full load
Dimensions, feet (metres): 172.2 × 34.4 × 7.5 *(52.5 × 10.5 × 2.3)*
Main machinery: 2 Paxman Valenta 6RP200E diesels; 1500 hp *(1.12 MW)* sustained; Voith-Schneider propulsion; 2 shafts; 2 Schottel bow thrusters
Speed, knots: 13 diesels; 6.5 electric drive. **Range, miles:** 3000 at 12 kts
Complement: 34 (5 officers) plus 6 spare berths

Guns: 1 Oerlikon/DES 30 mm/75 DS 30B; 65° elevation; 650 rounds/minute to 10 km *(5.4 nm)* anti-surface; 3 km *(1.6 nm)* anti-aircraft; weight of shell 0.36 kg.
Countermeasures: Decoys: 2 Wallop Barricade (to be fitted for deployment).
Combat data systems: Plessey Nautis M action data automation.
Radars: Navigation: Kelvin Hughes Type 1007; I band.
Sonars: Marconi Type 2093; VDS; VLF-VHF multi-function with five arrays; mine search and classification.

Programmes: A class designed for hunting and destroying mines and for operating in deep and exposed waters. Complements the Hunt and River classes. On 9 January 1984 the Vosper Thornycroft design for this class was approved. First one ordered August 1985, laid down 2 February 1987. Four further ships ordered 23 July 1987. A second batch were to have been ordered in 1990 but these were deferred in 1991. A new order is expected to go to tender in 1993 with an order for five in 1994. The latest revised total is for a class of 12.

Structure: GRP hull. Combines vectored thrust units with bow thrusters and Remote Control Mine Disposal System (RCMDS). The sonar is deployed from a well in the hull.
Operational: ECA mine disposal system, two PAP 104 Mk 5. These craft can carry two mine wire cutters, a charge of 100 kg and a manipulator with TV/projector. Control cables are either 1000 m (high capacity) or 2000 m (low capacity) and the craft can dive to 300 m at 6 kts with an endurance of 5 × 20 minute missions. Racal Hyperfix. Decca Navigation Mk 21. Allocation: All to 3rd MCM Squadron.
Sales: Three plus an option of three more to Saudi Arabia. Short listed for Australia in early 1993. GRP technology transfer to Spain.

CROMER   *6/1992, Maritime Photographic*

CROMER   *6/1992, C & S Taylor*

AMPHIBIOUS WARFARE FORCES

Note: Further amphibious ships and craft covered in RFA and RCT sections. These include a Helicopter Support Ship, five LSLs, two LCLs and nine LCTs.

0 + (1) HELICOPTER CARRIER (LPH)

Displacement, tons: 17 000 full load
Dimensions, feet (metres): 623.4 × 111.5 × 23 *(190 × 34 × 7)*
Flight deck, feet (metres): 590 × 111.5 *(180 × 34)*
Main machinery: 2 diesels; 2 shafts
Speed, knots: 18. **Range, miles:** 8000 at 18 kts
Complement: 250 plus 170 aircrew plus 480 Marines
Military lift: 4 LCVP (on davits); 430 Marines plus vehicles and equipment

Guns: Oerlikon/BMARC 30 mm/75 GCM. Oerlikon/BMARC 20 mm GAM.
Countermeasures: ESM/ECM.
Radars: Air/surface search.
Helicopters: 12 Sea King or equivalent.

Programmes: In 1987 five joint venture consortia were invited to prepare tenders. Three tenders submitted in July 1989 by Swan Hunter/Ferranti International Signal/CAP, Tyne Shiprepairers/Sea Containers/Racal Marine Systems; and Vickers Shipbuilding and Engineering/Cammel Laird with Three Keys Marine. These tenders were then allowed to lapse and a further invitation for designs was issued in early 1992. Swan Hunter and VSEL responded in October 1992. If this project survives defence cutbacks, an order might be placed in 1993/94 with a projected in service date of 1997.
Structure: The details listed are illustrative of the sort of size of vessel required either as a new construction or a merchant conversion. The deck would be strong enough to take Chinook helicopters. Six landing and six parking spots are required for the aircraft. Armament to consist of light guns only.
Operational: The LPH is to provide a helicopter lift and assault capability. The prime role of the vessel will be embarking, supporting and operating a squadron of helicopters (currently Westland Sea King HC4) and carrying most of a Royal Marine Commando including vehicles, arms and ammunition. A second of class is preferred to meet the operational requirement but linkage with the new LPDs gives a single unit more credibility than it would have without the LPDs.

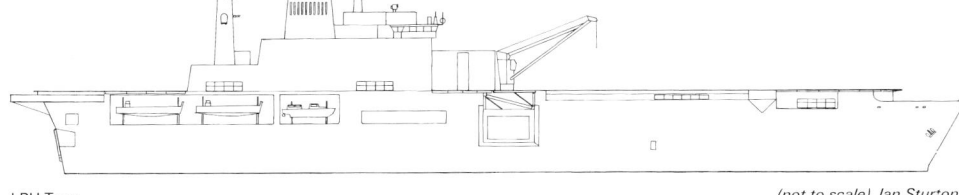

LPH Type   *(not to scale), Ian Sturton*

736 UK (NAVY) / Amphibious warfare forces

2 ASSAULT SHIPS (LPD)

Name	No	Builders	Laid down	Launched	Commissioned
FEARLESS	L 10	Harland & Wolff, Belfast	25 July 1962	19 Dec 1963	25 Nov 1965
INTREPID	L 11	John Brown, Clydebank	19 Dec 1962	25 June 1964	11 Mar 1967

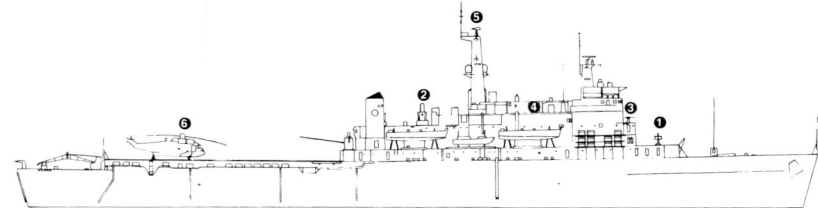

FEARLESS (Scale 1 : 1500), Ian Sturton

FEARLESS 8/1992, H M Steele

Displacement, tons: 11 060 standard; 12 120 full load; 16 950 dock flooded
Dimensions, feet (metres): 500 wl; 520 oa × 80 × 20.5 (32 flooded) *(152.4; 158.5 × 24.4 × 6.2 (9.8))*
Main machinery: 2 Babcock & Wilcox boilers; 550 psi *(38.66 kg/cm sq)*; 850°F *(454°C)*; 2 English Electric turbines; 22 000 hp *(16.4 MW)*; 2 shafts

Speed, knots: 21. **Range, miles:** 5000 at 20 kts
Complement: 550 (50 officers) plus 22 (3 officers) air group plus 88 (3 officers) RM
Military lift: 380-400 troops; overload 1000 troops; 15 MBTs; 7—3 ton trucks; 20¼ ton trucks (specimen load)
Landing craft: 4 LCU Mk 9 (dock); 4 LCVP Mk 3 (davits)

Missiles: SAM: 2 Shorts Seacat GWS 20 quad launchers ❶; optical guidance to 5 km *(2.7 nm)*.
Guns: 2 GE/GD 20 mm Mk 15 Vulcan Phalanx (L10) ❷; 6 barrels per launcher; 3000 rounds/minute combined to 1.5 km.
4 Oerlikon/BMARC 30 mm/75 GCM-AO3 (2 twin) (L 11); 80° elevation; 650 rounds/minute to 10 km *(5.4 nm)* anti-surface; 3 km *(1.6 nm)* anti-aircraft; weight of shell 0.36 kg.
2 Oerlikon/BMARC 20 mm GAM-BO1 ❸; 55° elevation; 1000 rounds/minute to 2 km.
Countermeasures: Decoys: 2 Vickers Corvus 8-tubed trainable launchers (L 11) or 4 Sea Gnat 6-barrelled fixed launchers for chaff and IR flares (L 10) ❹.
ESM: Marconi Mentor A; radar warning.
Combat data systems: Plessey Nautis M (L 10).
Fire control: GWS 20 optical directors for Seacat.
Radars: Surface search: Plessey Type 994 ❺; E/F band.
Navigation: Kelvin Hughes Type 1006; I band.

Helicopters: Platform for up to 4 Westland Sea King HC 4 ❻.

Programmes: In 1981 their impending deletion was announced—*Intrepid* in 1982 and *Fearless* in 1984. In February 1982 it was reported that they were to be reprieved, a fortunate decision in view of the vital part played by both in the 1982 Falklands' campaign.
Modernisation: *Intrepid* refitted 1984-85. *Fearless* completed a two year refit in November 1990 and has been fitted with two Vulcan Phalanx 20 mm gun mountings and new decoy launchers. Masthead height has been increased by 12 ft.
Structure: The two funnels are staggered across the beam of the ship. Landing craft are floated through the open stern by flooding compartments of the ship and lowering her in the water. They are able to deploy tanks, vehicles and men and have seakeeping qualities much superior to those of tank landing ships as well as greater speed and range. The helicopter platform is also the deckhead of the dock and has two landing spots.
Operational: Each ship is fitted out as a Naval Assault Group/Brigade Headquarters with an Assault Operations Room from which naval and military personnel can mount and control the progress of an assault operation. *Intrepid* is in reserve until her planned replacement commissions when she will be scrapped.

FEARLESS 4/1992, W Sartori

0 + (2) ASSAULT SHIPS (LPD)

Displacement, tons: 13 500 full load
Dimensions, feet (metres): 551 oa; 507.4 wl × 86.9 × 23 *(168; 154.7 × 26.5 × 7)*
Main machinery: Diesel or diesel-electric; 2 shafts
Speed, knots: 18
Complement: 320
Military lift: 300 troops; overload 600 troops; 70 support vehicles; 4 LCU (dock); 4 LCVP (davits)

Guns: CIWS supported by portable close range weapons.
Countermeasures: Decoys and ESM/ECM.
Combat data systems: GEC/Marconi command support.
Radars: Air/surface search. Fire control.

Helicopters: Platform for 2 medium.

Programmes: After surveys had shown that *Intrepid* could not again be refurbished, a decision was taken in mid-1991 to replace both existing LPDs by similar ships. Project definition studies by YARD Ltd completed in December 1992. Government statements indicate an intention to invite tenders for the first of class in 1993 with a projected in service date of 1998. The second would follow two years later.

Structure: The illustrative design shown in the drawing has emerged from project definition. Two helicopter landing spots. Substantial command and control facilities will be included.

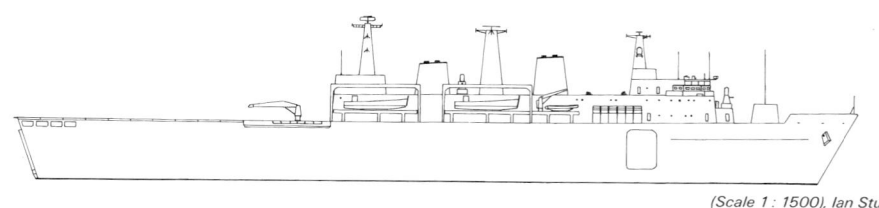

LPD (Scale 1 : 1500), Ian Sturton

12 LCU Mk 9

L 702   L 704-711   L 713-715

Displacement, tons: 89 light; 160 full load
Dimensions, feet (metres): 90.2 × 21.5 × 5 *(27.5 × 6.8 × 1.6)*
Main machinery: 2 Paxman or Dorman diesels; 474 hp *(354 kW)* sustained; 2 shafts; Kort nozzles
Speed, knots: 10
Military lift: 1 MBT or 70 tons of vehicles/stores

Comment: Operated by the Royal Marines. Four in each LPD. To be augmented by a new generation LCA of hovercraft design.

L 711   8/1992, Maritime Photographic

0 + (4) LCA (HOVERCRAFT)

Dimensions, feet (metres): 27.6 × 12.5 *(8.4 × 3.8)*
Main machinery: 1 diesel; 320 hp *(239 kW)*
Speed, knots: 25. **Range, miles:** 300 at 25 kts
Military lift: 16 troops plus equipment or 2 tons

Comment: Tenders returned in December 1992 and an order is expected in 1993. Capable of being embarked in an LCU. Speed indicated is at sea state 3 with a full load.

21 LCVP Mk 4

LCVPs 8031, 8401-8420

Displacement, tons: 9.7 light; 16 full load
Dimensions, feet (metres): 43.8 × 10.9 × 2.8 *(13.4 × 3.3 × 0.8)*
Main machinery: 2 Perkins T6.3544 diesels; 290 hp *(216 kW)*; 2 shafts
Speed, knots: 16 (light)
Complement: 3
Military lift: 20 Arctic equipped troops or 4 tons

Comment: Built by Souters and McTays. Introduced into service in 1986 as a replacement for the LCVP Mk 3. Fitted with removable arctic canopies across welldeck. Operated by the Royal Marines. *LCVPs 8402, 8409, 8419* and *8420* built for the Royal Corps of Transport. These serve in rotation between the Falklands and UK.

LCVP Mk 4   8/1992, H M Steele

3 TYPES OF SMALL CRAFT

Rigid Inflatable Boat Osborne Arctic 22

Comment: Of 1.4 tons and 7.2 m *(23.5 ft)*; twin 140 hp *(104 kW)* or Suzuki outboard motors; 40+ kts; range 30 nm (normal tanks); carry 15 troops or 2475 lbs stores. GRP hull, deck and command console with 20 in diameter neoprene tube.

Rigid Inflatable Boat Osborne Pacific 22

Comment: 2.25 tons and 6.8 m *(22.2 ft)*; Ford Mermaid 4-cyl; turbocharged diesel 155 hp *(115.6 kW)* max; 26 kts; range 85 nm; carry 15 troops or 2475 lbs stores. Construction similar to Arctic 22.

Rigid raiding craft

Comment: 0.87 tons and 5.2 m *(17.2 ft)*; powered by 140 hp *(104 kW)* or Suzuki outboard; 30+ kts fully laden; range 50 nm; carry coxswain plus 8 troops or 2000 lbs of equipment. This type is being replaced by a 6.5 m *(21.3 ft)*; powered by either a single or twin 140 hp *(104 kW)* outboard; carry 10 troops plus 1500 lbs of equipment. First eight delivered in December 1992, 16 more in 1993.

PACIFIC 22   1989

RRC   8/1992, H M Steele

ROYAL YACHT

Name	No	Builders	Laid down	Launched	Commissioned
BRITANNIA	A 00	John Brown, Clydebank	July 1952	16 Apr 1953	14 Jan 1954

Displacement, tons: 3990 light; 4961 full load
Measurement, tons: 5769 gross
Dimensions, feet (metres): 412.2 × 55 × 17 *(125.7 × 16.8 × 5.2)*
Main machinery: 2 boilers; 2 turbines; 12 000 hp *(8.95 MW)*; 2 shafts
Speed, knots: 21; 22.5 trials. **Range, miles:** 2800 at 20 kts; 3200 at 18 kts; 3675 at 14 kts
Complement: 277 (21 officers)
Radars: Navigation: Two Kelvin Hughes Type 1006; I band.

Comment: Designed for use by Her Majesty The Queen in peacetime as the Royal Yacht but can be converted as a medium sized naval hospital ship. Construction conformed to mercantile practice. Fitted with Denny-Brown single fin stabilisers to reduce roll in bad weather from 20 to 6 degrees. To pass under the bridges of the St. Lawrence Seaway when she visited Canada, the top 20 ft of her mainmast and the radio aerial on her foremast were hinged in November 1958 so that they could be lowered as required. 1984 refit included conversion to diesel fuel. SATNAV fitted. Further refit carried out at Devonport 1986-87 which has extended her life by 10-15 years. Oil fuel, 330 tons (510 with auxiliary fuel tanks). Ranges given are without auxiliary fuel tanks. Complement may be reduced to around 225.

BRITANNIA   6/1992, BRNC

PATROL SHIPS

1 ANTARCTIC PATROL SHIP

Name	No	Builders	Commissioned
ENDURANCE	A 171	Ulstein Hatlo, Norway	21 Nov 1991
(ex-*Polar Circle*)	(ex-A 176)		

Displacement, tons: 6500 full load
Dimensions, feet (metres): 298.6 × 57.4 × 21.3 *(91 × 17.9 × 6.5)*
Main machinery: 2 Bergen BRM8 diesels; 8160 hp(m) *(6 MW)* sustained; 1 shaft; cp prop; bow and stern thrusters
Speed, knots: 15. **Range, miles:** 6500 at 12 kts
Complement: 112 (15 officers) plus 14 Royal Marines
Radars: Surface search: Furuno; E/F band.
Navigation: Kelvin Hughes Type 1006; I band.
Helicopters: 2 Westland Lynx HAS 3.

Comment: Leased initially in late 1991 and then bought outright in early 1992 as support ship and guard vessel for the British Antarctic Survey. Hull is painted red. Inmarsat and SATCOM fitted. Main machinery is resiliently mounted. Ice strengthened hull capable of breaking one metre thick ice at 3 kts. Accommodation is to standards previously unknown in the Royal Navy. Name and pennant number changed during refit in mid-1992.

ENDURANCE   *11/1992, Maritime Photographic*

2 CASTLE CLASS (OFFSHORE PATROL VESSELS Mk 2)

Name	No	Builders	Commissioned
LEEDS CASTLE	P 258	Hall Russell, Aberdeen	27 Oct 1981
DUMBARTON CASTLE	P 265	Hall Russell, Aberdeen	26 Mar 1982

Displacement, tons: 1427 full load
Dimensions, feet (metres): 265.7 × 37.7 × 11.8 *(81 × 11.5 × 3.6)*
Main machinery: 2 Ruston 12RKC diesels; 5640 hp *(4.21 MW)* sustained; 2 shafts; cp props
Speed, knots: 19.5. **Range, miles:** 10 000 at 12 kts
Complement: 45 (6 officers) plus austerity accommodation for 25 Royal Marines
Guns: 1 DES/Lawrence Scott Mk 1 30 mm/75; 80° elevation; 650 rounds/minute to 10 km *(5.4 nm)*; weight of shell 0.36 kg.
Mines: Can lay mines.
Countermeasures: Decoys: 2 Plessey Shield chaff launchers.
Combat data systems: Racal CANE DEA-3 action data automation.
Fire control: Radamec 2000 series optronic director.
Radars: Surface search: Plessey Type 944 (P 265); E/F band.
Navigation: Kelvin Hughes Type 1006; I band.
Helicopters: Platform for operating Westland Sea King.

Comment: Started as a private venture. Ordered 8 August 1980. *Leeds Castle* launched 29 October 1980; *Dumbarton Castle* 3 June 1981. Design includes an ability to lay mines. Inmarsat commercial SATCOM terminals fitted. Two Avon Sea Rider high speed craft are embarked. *Dumbarton Castle* is the South Atlantic patrol ship until 1994. *Leeds Castle* belongs to the Fishery Protection Squadron Offshore Division.

LEEDS CASTLE   *8/1992, H M Steele*

7 ISLAND CLASS (OFFSHORE PATROL VESSELS)

Name	No	Builders	Commissioned
ANGLESEY	P 277	Hall Russell, Aberdeen	1 June 1979
ALDERNEY	P 278	Hall Russell, Aberdeen	6 Oct 1979
JERSEY	P 295	Hall Russell, Aberdeen	15 Oct 1976
GUERNSEY	P 297	Hall Russell, Aberdeen	28 Oct 1977
SHETLAND	P 298	Hall Russell, Aberdeen	14 July 1977
ORKNEY	P 299	Hall Russell, Aberdeen	25 Feb 1977
LINDISFARNE	P 300	Hall Russell, Aberdeen	3 Mar 1978

Displacement, tons: 925 standard; 1260 full load
Dimensions, feet (metres): 176 wl; 195.3 oa × 36 × 15 *(53.7; 59.5 × 11 × 4.5)*
Main machinery: 2 Ruston 12RKC diesels; 5640 hp *(4.21 MW)* sustained; 1 shaft
Speed, knots: 16.5. **Range, miles:** 7000 at 12 kts
Complement: 39

Guns: 1 Bofors 40 mm Mk 3. 1 DES/Oerlikon 30 mm/75 Mk 1 (P 297). 2 FN 7.62 mm MGs.
Countermeasures: ESM: Orange Crop; intercept.
Combat data systems: Racal CANE DEA-1 action data automation.
Radars: Navigation: Kelvin Hughes Type 1006; I band.

Programmes: Order for first five announced 11 February 1975. Order placed 2 July 1975. Two more of class ordered 21 October 1977.
Structure: The earlier ships of this class were retrofitted and the remainder built with enlarged bilge keels to damp down their motion in heavy weather. Fitted with stabilisers and water ballast arrangement.
Operational: Operate as the Offshore Division of the Fishery Protection Squadron. Can carry small RM detachment and two Avon Sea Rider semi-rigid craft with 85 hp motor, for boarding.

GUERNSEY   *6/1992, H M Steele*

TRAINING SHIPS

1 DARTMOUTH TRAINING SHIP

Name	No	Builders	Commissioned
WILTON	M 1116	Vosper Thornycroft, Woolston	14 July 1973

Displacement, tons: 450 full load
Dimensions, feet (metres): 145 wl; 153 oa × 29.2 × 8.5 *(44.2; 46.3 × 8.9 × 2.5)*
Main machinery: 2 Napier Deltic 18-7A diesels; 3000 hp *(2.24 MW)*; 2 shafts
Speed, knots: 16. **Range, miles:** 2300 at 13 kts
Complement: 37 (5 officers)
Guns: 1 Bofors 40 mm Mk 7; 90° elevation; 300 rounds/minute to 12 km *(6.5 nm)* anti-surface; 4 km *(2.2 nm)* anti-aircraft; weight of shell 0.96 kg.
Radars: Navigation: Kelvin Hughes Type 975; I/J band.
Sonars: Plessey Type 193M; hull-mounted; high frequency.

Comment: The world's first GRP warship. Laid down 7 August 1970 and launched on 18 January 1972. Similar to the Ton class minesweepers and fitted with reconditioned machinery and equipment from the scrapped *Derriton*. Twin active rudders. Used for seamanship and navigation training at the Naval College, Dartmouth. All minesweeping gear removed and a classroom has been built on the stern.

WILTON   *6/1992*

1 NAVIGATION TRAINING VESSEL

NORTHELLA

Comment: Having been taken up from trade in April 1982 to act as an auxiliary minesweeper in Falklands campaign (with four others) she was returned to her owners then taken up from trade again in October 1983 to act as target vessel. In 1985 became navigational training ship. Based at Portsmouth and now painted grey. She flies a Blue Ensign and is on charter until 1994 with NP 1020 embarked.

NORTHELLA   *2/1993, Maritime Photographic*

LIGHT FORCES

3 PEACOCK CLASS (LARGE PATROL CRAFT)

Name	No	Builders	Commissioned
PEACOCK	P 239	Hall Russell, Aberdeen	14 July 1984
PLOVER	P 240	Hall Russell, Aberdeen	20 July 1984
STARLING	P 241	Hall Russell, Aberdeen	10 Aug 1984

Displacement, tons: 690 full load
Dimensions, feet (metres): 204.1 × 32.8 × 8.9 *(62.6 × 10 × 2.7)*
Main machinery: 2 Crossley Pielstick 18 PA6 V 280 diesels; 14 000 hp(m) *(10.6 MW)* sustained; 2 shafts; 1 retractable Schottel prop; 181 hp *(135 kW)*
Speed, knots: 25. **Range, miles:** 2500 at 17 kts
Complement: 31 (6 officers) plus 7 spare berths
Guns: 1—3 in *(76 mm)*/62 OTO Melara compact; 85° elevation; 85 rounds/minute to 16 km *(8.6 nm)* anti-surface; 12 km *(6.5 nm)* anti-aircraft; weight of shell 6 kg.
4 FN 7.62 mm MGs.
Fire control: British Aerospace Sea Archer for 76 mm gun.
Radars: Navigation: Kelvin Hughes Type 1006; I band.

Comment: This class replaced the elderly Ton class in Hong Kong, the colony's government paying 75 per cent of the cost. All ordered 30 June 1981. *Peacock* launched 1 December 1982, *Plover* on 12 April 1983, *Starling* on 11 September 1983. All sailed for Hong Kong September 1984-July 1985. Carry two Sea Riders and a Fast Pursuit craft. Have telescopic cranes, loiter drive and replenishment at sea equipment. *Swallow* and *Swift* sold to Ireland 21 November 1988. The remainder are planned to remain in Hong Kong until 1997.

PLOVER 12/1992

2 BIRD and 1 SEAL CLASS (LARGE PATROL CRAFT)

Name	No	Builders	Commissioned
REDPOLE (ex-*Sea Otter*)	P 259	Brooke Marine, Lowestoft	4 Aug 1967
KINGFISHER	P 260	Dunston, Hessle	8 Oct 1975
CYGNET	P 261	Dunston, Hessle	8 July 1976

Displacement, tons: 194 (218, P 259) full load
Dimensions, feet (metres): 120 × 23.6 × 6.5 *(36.6 × 7.2 × 2)*
Main machinery: 2 Paxman 16YJCM diesels; 4200 hp *(3.13 MW)*; 2 shafts
Speed, knots: 21. **Range, miles:** 2000 at 14 kts
Complement: 28 (3 officers, 10 RM)
Guns: 2 FN 7.62 mm MGs.

Comment: *Kingfisher* launched 20 September 1974; *Cygnet* 6 October 1975; *Redpole* transferred by RAF March 1985. *Kingfisher* and *Redpole* completed extended refits in 1986; *Cygnet* in 1987. Bird class based on the Seal class RAF rescue launches with some improvement to seakeeping qualities by cutting down topweight. All deployed to Northern Ireland.

KINGFISHER 1990

14 ARCHER CLASS (TRAINING and PATROL CRAFT)

ARCHER P 264	DASHER P 280	EXAMPLE A153 (RNXS)
BITER P 270	PUNCHER P 291	EXPLORER A 154 (RNXS)
SMITER P 272	CHARGER P 292	EXPRESS A 163 (RNXS)
PURSUER P 273	RANGER P 293	EXPLOIT A 167 (RNXS)
BLAZER P 279	TRUMPETER P 294	

Displacement, tons: 49 full load
Dimensions, feet (metres): 68.2 × 19 × 5.9 *(20.8 × 5.8 × 1.8)*
Main machinery: 2 RR CV 12 M800T; 1590 hp *(1.19 MW)*; 2 shafts
Speed, knots: 22. **Range, miles:** 550 at 15 kts
Complement: 10-14
Guns: 1 Oerlikon 20 mm (can be fitted).
Radars: Navigation: Racal Decca 1216; I band.

Comment: Ordered from Watercraft Ltd, Shoreham. *Commissioning dates: Archer,* August 1985; *Example,* September 1985; *Explorer,* January 1986; *Biter* and *Smiter,* February 1986. The remaining nine were incomplete when Watercraft went into liquidation in 1986 and were towed to Portsmouth for completion by Vosper Thornycroft. Commissioning dates (all 1988): *Pursuer,* February; *Blazer,* March; *Express* and *Dasher,* May; *Charger,* June; *Puncher,* July; *Exploit,* August; *Ranger* and *Trumpeter,* September. Initially allocated for RNR training but under used in that role and now employed: *Ranger* and *Trumpeter* as Gibraltar guard ships; remainder University Naval Units (URNU)—*Puncher* (London), *Blazer* (Southampton), *Smiter* (Glasgow), *Charger* (Liverpool), *Dasher* (Bristol), *Archer* (Aberdeen), *Pursuer* (Sussex) and *Biter* (Manchester and Salford). Similar craft building for the Indian Coast Guard.

ARCHER 7/1992, Maritime Photographic

EXPLORER (RNXS) 11/1991, Maritime Photographic

COASTAL SURVEY VESSELS

1 ROEBUCK CLASS

Name	No	Builders	Commissioned
ROEBUCK	A 130	Brooke Marine, Lowestoft	3 Oct 1986

Displacement, tons: 1059 light, 1431 full load
Dimensions, feet (metres): 210 × 42.6 × 13 *(63.9 × 13 × 4)*
Main machinery: 4 Mirrlees Blackstone ESL8 Mk 1 diesels; 3040 hp *(2.27 MW)*; 2 shafts; cp props
Speed, knots: 15. **Range, miles:** 4000 at 10 kts
Complement: 46 (6 officers)

Comment: Designed for hydrographic surveys to full modern standards on UK continental shelf. Passive tank stabiliser; Hyperfix and transponder position fixing systems; Type 2033BB hull mounted, high definition, sector scanning sonar. Qubit SIPS I integrated navigation and survey system. Air-conditioned. Carries two 9 m surveying motor boats and one 4.5 m RIB.

ROEBUCK (with survey craft on davits) 5/1990, Gilbert Gyssels

UK (NAVY) / Coastal survey vessels — UK (RFA) / Introduction

Name	No	Builders	Commissioned
GLEANER	A 86	Emsworth Shipyard	5 Dec 1983

Displacement, tons: 22 full load
Dimensions, feet (metres): 48.6 × 15.4 × 4.3 *(14.8 × 4.7 × 1.3)*
Main machinery: 2 RR diesels; 524 hp *(391 kW)*; 1 Perkins 4-236 diesel; 72 hp *(54 kW)*; 3 shafts
Speed, knots: 14 diesels; 7 centre shaft only
Complement: 5 plus 1 spare bunk

Comment: This craft is prefixed HMSML—HM Survey Motor Launch.

GLEANER　　　　　　　　　　　　　　　　　　　　　　10/1987, W Sartori

SURVEY SHIPS

Notes: 1. In addition to the ships listed below some work is done by chartered vessels with Naval Parties embarked. These include *Proud Seahorse* (of MFV type) which operates for the Hydrographer with Naval Party 1016 embarked and *Marine Explorer* with Naval Party 1008.
2. The acquisition of two Hydrographic Survey vessels is projected for the mid-1990s. An invitation to tender designs was raised in July 1992. Possibilities include converted merchant hulls and Fleet Auxiliary status with a Naval Party embarked. The ships could be dual roled as MCMV tenders during deployments abroad. The requirement includes tasking for 320 days a year and the ability to maintain 13 kts in sea state 5.

1 IMPROVED HECLA CLASS

Name	No	Builders	Commissioned
HERALD	A 138	Robb Caledon, Leith	31 Oct 1974

Displacement, tons: 2000 standard; 2945 full load
Dimensions, feet (metres): 259.1 × 49.2 × 16 *(79 × 15.4 × 4.9)*
Main machinery: Diesel-electric; 3 Paxman 12YJCZ diesels; 3600 hp *(2.68 MW)* sustained; 3 generators; 1 motor; 2000 hp *(1.49 MW)*; 1 shaft; bow thruster
Speed, knots: 14. **Range, miles:** 12 000 at 11 kts
Complement: 128 (12 officers)
Guns: 2 Oerlikon 20 mm (can be fitted).
Radars: Navigation: Kelvin Hughes Type 1006; I band.
Helicopters: 1 Westland Lynx HAS 3.

Comment: A later version of the Hecla class design. Laid down 9 November 1972. Launched 4 October 1973. Fitted with Hydroplot Satellite navigation system, computerised data logging, gravimeter, magnetometer, sonars, echo-sounders, an oceanographic winch, passive stabilisation tank and two 35 ft surveying motor-boats. Completed refit in January 1988 with a strengthened and extended flight deck for Lynx. Conducted trials of Scarab remote controlled mine clearance device. Works in the North Norwegian Sea when not required as an MCM support ship.

1 HECLA CLASS

Name	No	Builders	Commissioned
HECLA	A 133	Yarrow Shipbuilders, Blythswood	9 June 1965

Displacement, tons: 1915 light; 2733 full load
Measurement, tons: 2898 gross
Dimensions, feet (metres): 260.1 × 49.1 × 15.4 *(79.3 × 15 × 4.7)*
Main machinery: Diesel-electric; 3 Paxman 12YJCZ diesels; 3600 hp *(2.68 MW)* sustained; 3 generators; 1 motor; 2000 hp *(1.49 MW)*; 1 shaft; bow thruster
Speed, knots: 14. **Range, miles:** 12 000 at 11 kts
Complement: 115 (13 officers) plus 6 scientists
Guns: 2 Oerlikon 20 mm (can be fitted).
Radars: Navigation: Kelvin Hughes Type 1006; I band.
Helicopters: 1 Westland Lynx HAS 3.

Comment: The first Royal Navy ship to be designed with a combined oceanographical and hydrographic role. Of merchant ship design and similar in many respects to the Royal Research ship *Discovery*. The fore end of the superstructure incorporates a Land Rover garage and the after end a helicopter hangar with adjacent flight deck. Equipped with chartroom, drawing office and photographic studio; two laboratories, dry and wet; electrical, engineering and shipwright workshops, large storerooms, two 9 m surveying motor-boats and an oceanographic winch. Air-conditioned throughout. Converted in 1990/91 to the same standard as *Herald* for MCM support ship duties with an extended flight deck and a recompression chamber for clearance divers. One of the class sold to Indonesia in 1986, a second paid off in 1990.

HECLA　　　　　　　　　　　　　　　　　　　　　　10/1991, D & B Teague

2 BULLDOG CLASS

Name	No	Builders	Commissioned
BULLDOG	A 317	Brooke Marine, Lowestoft	21 Mar 1968
BEAGLE	A 319	Brooke Marine, Lowestoft	9 May 1968

Displacement, tons: 800 standard; 1088 full load
Dimensions, feet (metres): 189 × 36.8 × 12 *(57.6 × 11.2 × 3.7)*
Main machinery: 4 Lister-Blackstone ERS8M diesels; 2640 hp *(1.97 MW)*; 2 shafts; cp props
Speed, knots: 15. **Range, miles:** 4500 at 12 kts
Complement: 39 (5 officers)
Guns: Fitted for 2 Oerlikon 20 mm.

Comment: Originally designed for duty overseas, working in pairs although normally now employed in home waters. Built to commercial standards. Fitted with passive tank stabiliser, precision ranging radar, Hyper Fix system, automatic steering. Qubit SIPS II integrated navigation and survey system being fitted in 1990. This allows chart processing in real time as the data is acquired. Air-conditioned throughout. Carry 9 m surveying motor-boat. *Bulldog* completed refit including new radar and UHF in early 1985. *Fox* sold in early 1989 and *Fawn* in 1991.

HERALD　　　　　　　　　　　　　　　　　　　　　3/1991, David Warren

BEAGLE (with 20 mm gun)　　　　　　　　　11/1990, van Ginderen Collection

ROYAL FLEET AUXILIARY SERVICE

Headquarters' Appointment

RFA Type Commander:
Commodore R M Thorn

Personnel

1993: 2400 UK personnel (reducing to 2050 by 1994); 33 Hong Kong Chinese

General

The Royal Fleet Auxiliary Service is a civilian manned fleet under the command of the Commander in Chief Fleet from 1 April 1993. Its main task is to supply warships at sea with fuel, food, stores and ammunition. It also provides aviation platforms, amphibious support for the Navy and Marines and sea transport for Army units. All ships take part in operational sea training. An order in council on 30 November 1989 changed the status of the RFA service to government-owned vessels on non-commercial service.

Ships taken up from Trade (1 April 1993)

The following ships taken up from trade: *Proud Seahorse* and *Marine Explorer* operate in home waters under the Hydrographer; *Northella* in service for navigational training. *Oil Mariner* (supply), *St Brandan* (ferry), *Indomitable* (tug), all operate in the Falkland Islands; *Maersk Ascension* and *Maersk Gannet* as tankers to Ascension Island; *St Angus* as Gulf supply ship.

LARGE FLEET TANKERS (AO)

Note: There is an urgent requirement to replace these ships with modern medium Fleet tankers (AO). These will probably be to a commercial design with an in service date of 1997.

3 OL CLASS (AO)

Name	No	Builders	Launched	Commissioned
OLWEN	A 122	Hawthorn Leslie, Hebburn-on-Tyne	10 July 1964	21 June 1965
OLNA	A 123	Hawthorn Leslie, Hebburn-on-Tyne	28 July 1965	1 Apr 1966
OLMEDA	A 124	Swan Hunter Shipbuilders, Wallsend-on-Tyne	19 Nov 1964	18 Oct 1965

Displacement, tons: 10 890 light; 36 000 full load
Measurement, tons: 25 100 dwt; 18 600 gross
Dimensions, feet (metres): 648 × 84 × 36.4 *(197.5 × 25.6 × 11.1)*
Main machinery: 2 Babcock & Wilcox boilers; 750 psi *(52.75 kg/cm sq)*; 950°F *(510°C)*; Pametrada turbines; 26 500 hp *(19.77 MW)*; 1 shaft
Speed, knots: 20
Complement: 95 RFA (accommodation for 40 RN)
Cargo capacity: 16 000 tons diesel; 125 tons lub oil; 2750 tons Avcat; 375 tons fresh water
Guns: 2 Oerlikon 20 mm. 2—7.62 mm MGs.
Countermeasures: 2 Corvus chaff launchers.
Radars: Surface search and Navigation: 2 Racal Decca; I band.
Helicopters: 2 Westland Sea King HAS 5.

Comment: Designed for underway replenishment both alongside and astern (fuel only) or by helicopter. Specially strengthened for operations in ice, fully air-conditioned. *Olna* has a transverse bow thrust unit for improved manoeuvrability in confined waters and an improved design of replenishment-at-sea systems. Inmarsat SATCOM system fitted. Hangar accommodation for two helicopters port side of funnel.

OLMEDA — *10/1992, Maritime Photographic*

SUPPORT TANKERS (AOT)

1 OAKLEAF CLASS (AOT)

Name	No	Builders	Commissioned	Recommissioned
OAKLEAF (ex-*Oktania*)	A 111	Uddevalla, Sweden	1981	14 Aug 1986

Displacement, tons: 49 648 full load
Measurement, tons: 37 328 dwt
Dimensions, feet (metres): 570 × 105.6 × 36.7 *(173.7 × 32.2 × 11.2)*
Main machinery: 1 Burmeister & Wain 4L80MCE diesel; 10 800 hp(m) *(7.96 MW)* sustained; 1 shaft; cp prop; bow and stern thrusters
Speed, knots: 14
Complement: 36
Cargo capacity: 40 000 cu m fuel
Guns: 2 Oerlikon 20 mm. 2—7.62 mm MGs.
Countermeasures: 2 Plessey Shield chaff launchers can be fitted.

Comment: Acquired in July 1985 and converted by Falmouth Ship Repairers to include full RAS rig and extra accommodation. Handed over on completion and renamed. Ice strengthened hull. Marisat fitted.

OAKLEAF — *1/1993, Maritime Photographic*

3 APPLELEAF CLASS (AOT)

Name	No	Builders	Launched	Commissioned
BRAMBLELEAF (ex-*Hudson Cavalier*)	A 81	Cammell Laird, Birkenhead	22 Jan 1976	3 Mar 1980
BAYLEAF	A 109	Cammell Laird, Birkenhead	27 Oct 1981	26 Mar 1982
ORANGELEAF (ex-*Balder London*, ex-*Hudson Progress*)	A 110	Cammell Laird, Birkenhead	—	2 May 1984

Displacement, tons: 37 747 full load (A 109-110); 40 870 (A 81)
Measurement, tons: 20 761 gross; 11 573 net; 29 999 dwt
Dimensions, feet (metres): 560 × 85 × 36.1 *(170.7 × 25.9 × 11)*
Main machinery: 2 Pielstick 14 PC2.2 V 400 diesels; 14 000 hp(m) *(10.29 MW)* sustained; 1 shaft
Speed, knots: 15.5; 16.3 (A 109)
Complement: 60 (20 officers)
Cargo capacity: 22 000 cu m dieso; 3800 cu m Avcat
Guns: 2 Oerlikon 20 mm (amidships in *Orangeleaf*). 4—7.62 mm MGs.
Countermeasures: Decoys: 2 Vickers Corvus launchers or 2 Plessey Shield launchers.

Comment: *Brambleleaf* chartered in 1979-80 and converted, completing Autumn 1979. Part of a four-ship order cancelled by Hudson Fuel and Shipping Co, but completed by the shipbuilders, being the only mercantile order then in hand. *Bayleaf* built under commercial contract to be chartered by MoD. *Orangeleaf* started major refit September 1985 to fit RAS capability and extra accommodation. *Appleleaf* leased to Australia in September 1989 for five years.

ORANGELEAF — *6/1992, Giorgio Arra*

SMALL FLEET TANKERS (AOL)

2 ROVER CLASS

Name	No	Builders	Commissioned
GOLD ROVER	A 271	Swan Hunter Shipbuilders, Wallsend-on-Tyne	22 Mar 1974
BLACK ROVER	A 273	Swan Hunter Shipbuilders, Wallsend-on-Tyne	23 Aug 1974

Displacement, tons: 4700 light; 11 522 full load
Measurement, tons: 6692 (A 271, 273), 6822 (remainder) dwt; 7510 gross; 3185 net
Dimensions, feet (metres): 461 × 63 × 24 *(140.6 × 19.2 × 7.3)*
Main machinery: 2 SEMT-Pielstick 16 PA4 185 diesels; 5344 hp(m) *(3.93 MW)*; 1 shaft; cp prop; bow thruster
Speed, knots: 19. **Range, miles:** 15 000 at 15 kts
Complement: 49 (A 268, 269-270); 54 (A 271, 273)
Cargo capacity: 6600 tons fuel
Guns: 2 Oerlikon 20 mm. 2—7.62 mm MGs.
Countermeasures: Decoys: 2 Vickers Corvus launchers. 2 Plessey Shield launchers.
1 Graseby Type 182; towed torpedo decoy.
Radars: Navigation: Racal Decca 52690 ARPA; Racal Decca 1690; I band.
Helicopters: Platform for Westland Sea King HAS 5 or HC 4.

Comment: Small fleet tankers designed to replenish HM ships at sea with fuel, fresh water, limited dry cargo and refrigerated stores under all conditions while under way. No hangar but helicopter landing platform is served by a stores lift, to enable stores to be transferred at sea by 'vertical lift'. Capable of HIFR. Siting of SATCOM aerial varies. One employed on training duties at Portland. *Green Rover* sold in 1991 to Indonesia. *Blue Rover* and *Grey Rover* paid off in early 1993; *Blue Rover* to Portugal in March 1993, *Grey Rover* may follow her.

BLACK ROVER *7/1992, G Toremans*

FLEET REPLENISHMENT SHIPS

2 FORT VICTORIA CLASS (AOR(H))

Name	No	Builders	Laid down	Launched	Commissioned
FORT VICTORIA	A 387	Harland & Wolff/Cammell Laird	4 Apr 1988	12 June 1990	Dec 1993
FORT GEORGE	A 388	Swan Hunter Shipbuilders, Wallsend-on-Tyne	9 Mar 1989	1 Mar 1991	Sep 1993

Displacement, tons: 32 300 full load
Dimensions, feet (metres): 667.7 oa; 607 wl × 99.7 × 32 *(203.5; 185 × 30.4 × 9.8)*
Main machinery: 2 Crossley SEMT-Pielstick 16 PC 2.6 V 400 diesels; 23 904 hp(m) *(17.57 MW)* sustained; 2 shafts
Speed, knots: 20
Complement: 126 (34 officers) RFA plus 32 (1 officer) RN plus 122 (29 officers) aircrew
Cargo capacity: 12 505 cu m liquids; 6234 cu m solids

Guns: 4 Lawrence Scott 30 mm/75 Mk 1. 2 Signaal 30 mm Goalkeeper may be fitted in due course.
Countermeasures: Decoys: 4 Plessey Shield 6-barrelled chaff/IR launchers. Graseby Type 182; towed torpedo decoy.
ESM: Marconi UAG Mentor; intercept.
Combat data systems: Dowty Sema SSCS in due course; Scot SATCOM.
Radars: Air search: Plessey Type 996; 3D; E/F band.
Fire control: Two Marconi Type 911; I/Ku band.
Navigation: Kelvin Hughes Type 1007; I band.

Helicopters: 3 Westland Sea King/Merlin helicopters.

Programmes: The requirement for these ships is to provide fuel and stores support to the Fleet at sea. *Fort Victoria* ordered 23 April 1986 and *Fort George* on 18 December 1987. *Fort Victoria* delayed by damage during building and entered Cammell Laird Shipyard for post sea trials completion in July 1992. The original plan for six of this class has been progressively eroded and the requirement for more AORs is being reviewed in 1993.
Structure: Four dual purpose abeam replenishment rigs for simultaneous transfer of liquids and solids. Stern refuelling. Repair facilities for Merlin helicopters. The plan to fit Seawolf GWS 26 VLS is likely to be abandoned in favour of Goalkeeper CIWS.
Operational: Two helicopter spots. There is a requirement to provide an emergency landing facility for Sea Harriers.

FORT GEORGE *1/1993, Swan Hunter*

2 FORT GRANGE CLASS (AFS(H))

Name	No	Builders	Launched	Commissioned
FORT GRANGE	A 385	Scott-Lithgow, Greenock	9 Dec 1976	6 Apr 1978
FORT AUSTIN	A 386	Scott-Lithgow, Greenock	9 Mar 1978	11 May 1979

Displacement, tons: 23 384 full load
Measurement, tons: 8300 dwt
Dimensions, feet (metres): 603 × 79 × 28.2 *(183.9 × 24.1 × 8.6)*
Main machinery: 1 Sulzer RND90 diesel; 23 200 hp(m) *(17.05 MW)*; 1 shaft; bow thruster
Speed, knots: 22. **Range, miles:** 10 000 at 20 kts
Complement: 127 RFA plus 45 RN plus 36 RNSTS (civilian supply staff)
Cargo capacity: 3500 tons armament, naval and victualling stores in 4 holds of 12 800 cu m
Guns: 2 Oerlikon GAM-BO3 20 mm. 4—12.7 mm MGs.
Countermeasures: 2 Vickers Corvus 8-barrelled launchers (upper bridge).
Radars: Navigation: Kelvin Hughes Type 1006; I band.
Helicopters: 4 Westland Sea King.

Comment: Ordered in November 1971. Fitted with a helicopter flight-deck and hangar, thus allowing not only for vertical replenishment but also a base for Force ASW helicopters. ASW stores for helicopters carried on board. Emergency flight deck on the hangar roof. There are six cranes, three of 10 tons lift and three of 5 tons.

FORT AUSTIN *11/1992, G Toremans*

1 REGENT CLASS (AFS(H))

Name	No	Builders	Launched	Commissioned
RESOURCE	A 480	Scotts Shipbuilding, Greenock	11 Feb 1966	16 May 1967

Displacement, tons: 13 590 light; 22 890 full load
Measurement, tons: 18 029 gross; 9300 dwt
Dimensions, feet (metres): 640 × 77.2 × 28.5 (195.1 × 23.5 × 8.7)
Main machinery: 2 Foster-Wheeler boilers; 2 AEI turbines; 20 000 hp (14.92 MW); 1 shaft
Speed, knots: 20. **Range, miles:** 12 000 at 18 kts
Complement: 134 RFA plus 37 RNSTS
Guns: 2 Oerlikon 20 mm (can be fitted). 2—12.7 mm MGs.
Countermeasures: Decoys: 2 Corvus chaff launchers.
Radars: Navigation: Two Kelvin Hughes; I band.

Comment: Ordered on 24 January 1963. Lifts for armaments and stores, seven advanced replenishment rigs and helicopter platforms for transferring loads at sea. A number of the seven holds are temperature controlled to increase cargo storage life. Helicopter not carried but hangar and full flight deck facilities are fitted although the hangar is not big enough for Sea King sized aircraft. Designed from the outset as a Fleet Replenishment Ship. Air-conditioned. *Regent* paid off in December 1992; *Resource* may be maintained in a lower state of operational readiness.

REGENT class (old number)   10/1992, Maritime Photographic

REPAIR/MAINTENANCE SHIP

1 STENA TYPE (FORWARD REPAIR SHIP)

Name	No	Builders	Commissioned
DILIGENCE (ex-*Stena Inspector*)	A 132	Oresundsvarvet AB, Landskrona, Sweden	1981

Displacement, tons: 10 765 full load
Measurement, tons: 6550 gross; 4939 dwt
Dimensions, feet (metres): 367.5 × 67.3 × 22.3 (112 × 20.5 × 6.8)
Flight deck, feet (metres): 83 × 83 (25.4 × 25.4)
Main machinery: Diesel-electric; 5 V16 Nohab-Polar diesel generators; 2650 kW; 4 NEBB motors; 6000 hp(m) (4.41 MW); 1 shaft; KaMeWa cp prop; 2 KaMeWa bow tunnel thrusters; 3000 hp(m) (2.2 MW); 2 azimuth thrusters (aft); 3000 hp(m) (2.2 MW)
Speed, knots: 12. **Range, miles:** 5000 at 12 kts
Complement: 41 RFA plus 80 RN (accommodation for 147 plus 55 temporary)
Cargo capacity: Long-jib crane SWL 5 tons; max lift, 40 tons

Guns: 4 Oerlikon 20 mm. 4—12.5 mm MGs.
Countermeasures: Decoys: 4 Plessey Shield 6-tubed launchers.

Helicopters: Facilities for up to Boeing Chinook HC 1 (medium lift) size.

Programmes: *Stena Inspector* was designed originally as a Multi-purpose Support Vessel for North Sea oil operations, and completed in January 1981. Chartered on 25 May 1982 for use as a fleet repair ship during the Falklands' campaign. Purchased from Stena (UK) Line in October 1983, and converted for use as Forward Repair Ship in the South Atlantic (Falkland Islands). Conversion by Clyde Dock Engineering Ltd, Govan from 12 November 1983 to 29 February 1984; accepted into RFA service on 12 March 1984. Naval Party 2010 embarked.
Modernisation: Following items added during conversion: large workshop for hull and machinery repairs (in well-deck); accommodation for naval Junior Rates (new accommodation block); accommodation for crew of conventional submarine (in place of Saturation Diving System); extensive craneage facilities; overside supply of electrical power, water, fuel, steam, air, to ships alongside; large naval store (in place of cement tanks); armament and magazines; Naval Communications System; decompression chamber.
Structure: Four 5 ton anchors for 4-point mooring system. Strengthened for operations in ice (Ice Class 1A). Köngsberg Albatross Positioning System has been retained in full. Uses bow and stern thrusters and main propeller to maintain a selected position to within a few metres, up to Beaufort Force 9. Controlled by Kongsberg KS 500 computers.
Operational: Deployed to the Gulf in August 1987. Back on station in the Falkland Islands in 1989 and then to the Gulf in September 1990, returning to the UK in December 1992 after nearly three years continuous service overseas.

DILIGENCE   12/1992, Maritime Photographic

AVIATION TRAINING SHIP

Name	No	Builders	Commissioned	Recommissioned
ARGUS (ex-*Contender Bezant*)	A 135	CNR Breda, Venice, Italy	1981	1 June 1988

Displacement, tons: 18 280 standard; 26 421 full load
Measurement, tons: 9965 dwt
Dimensions, feet (metres): 574.5 × 99.7 × 27 (175.1 × 30.4 × 8.2)
Main machinery: 2 Lindholmen SEMT-Pielstick 18 PC2.5 V 400 diesels; 23 400 hp(m) (17.2 MW) sustained; 2 shafts
Speed, knots: 18. **Range, miles:** 20 000 at 19 kts
Complement: 79 RFA plus 39 permanent RN plus 137 RN aircrew
Cargo capacity: 3300 tons dieso; 1100 tons aviation fuel

Guns: 4 BMARC 30 mm Mk 1. 4—12.7 mm MGs.
Countermeasures: Decoys: 2 Sea Gnat chaff launchers. Graseby Type 182; torpedo decoy.
ESM: THORN EMI Guardian; radar warning.
Combat data systems: Racal CANE DEB-1 data automation. Inmarsat SATCOM communications. Marisat.
Radars: Air search: Type 994 MTI; E/F band.
Air/surface search: Kelvin Hughes Type 1006; I band.
Navigation: Racal Decca Type 994; I band.

Fixed wing aircraft: Provision to transport 12 British Aerospace Sea Harrier FRS 1.
Helicopters: 6 Westland Sea King HAS 5 or similar.

Programmes: Ro-ro container ship whose conversion for her new task was begun by Harland and Wolff in March 1984 and completed on 3 March 1988. Purchase price approx £18 million; conversion approx £45 million which included full contractor responsibility for equipment, trials and setting to work. Relieved *Engadine* in early 1989.
Structure: Uses former ro-ro deck as hangar with four sliding WT doors able to operate at a speed of 10 m per minute. Can replenish other ships underway. One lift port midships, one abaft funnel. Domestic facilities are very limited if she is to be used in the Command support role. Flight deck is 372.4 ft (113.5 m) long and has a 5 ft thick concrete layer on its lower side. First RFA to be fitted with a command system.
Operational: Not as heavily armed as *Fort Victoria* but similar 'advantage' is being taken of the cost effectiveness of mixed civilian and naval manning. Deployed to the Gulf in the 1990/91 as a Primary Casualty Receiving Ship (PCRS) with the hangar converted into hospital accommodation.

ARGUS   6/1992, Maritime Photographic

LANDING SHIPS (LOGISTIC) (LSLs)

Name	No	Builders	Laid down	Launched	Commissioned
SIR BEDIVERE	L 3004	Hawthorn Leslie, Hebburn-on-Tyne	Oct 1965	20 July 1966	18 May 1967
SIR GERAINT	L 3027	Alex Stephen, Glasgow	June 1965	26 Jan 1967	12 July 1967
SIR PERCIVALE	L 3036	Hawthorn Leslie, Hebburn-on-Tyne	Apr 1966	4 Oct 1967	23 Mar 1968
SIR TRISTRAM	L 3505	Hawthorn Leslie, Hebburn-on-Tyne	Feb 1966	12 Dec 1966	14 Sep 1967

Displacement, tons: 3270 light; 5674 full load
  5800 full load *(Sir Tristram)*
Dimensions, feet (metres): 412.1; 441.1 *(Sir Tristram)* × 59.8 × 13 *(125.6; 134.4 × 18.2 × 4)*
Main machinery: 2 Mirrlees 10-ALSSDM diesels; 9400 hp *(7.01 MW)*; 2 shafts; bow thruster
Speed, knots: 17. **Range, miles:** 8000 at 15 kts
Complement: 65 (21 officers); 50 *(Sir Tristram)*
Military lift: 340 troops (534 hard lying); 16 MBTs; 34 mixed vehicles; 120 tons POL; 30 tons ammunition; 1—20 ton crane; 2—4.5 ton cranes. *Sir Tristram* has increased capacity for 20 helicopters (11 tank deck and 9 vehicle deck)
Guns: 2 Oerlikon 20 mm. 2—12.7 mm MGs.
Countermeasures: Decoys: 2 Corvus chaff launchers.
Radars: Navigation: Kelvin Hughes Type 1006; I band.
Helicopters: Platforms to operate Gazelle AH 1 or Lynx AH 1/7.

Comment: Fitted for bow and stern loading with drive-through facilities and deck-to-deck ramps. Facilities provided for onboard maintenance of vehicles and for laying out pontoon equipment. Mexeflote self-propelled floating platforms can be strapped one on each side. Carries 850 tons oil fuel. On 8 June 1982 *Sir Tristram* was severely damaged off the Falkland Islands. Tyne Shiprepairers were given a contract to repair and modify her. This included lengthening by 29 ft, an enlarged flight deck capable of taking Chinooks and a new bridge. The aluminium superstructure was replaced by steel and the provision of new communications, an EMR, SATCOM, new navigation systems and helicopter control radar greatly increase her effectiveness. Completed 9 October 1985. The first three are to be modernised to the same standard as *Sir Tristram* with SLEPs, the first one being scheduled to start in late 1993. All deployed to the Gulf in 1991 with additional 20 mm guns, decoy systems and navigation equipment.

SIR BEDIVERE 8/1992, H M Steele

Name	No	Builders	Laid down	Launched	Commissioned
SIR GALAHAD	L 3005	Swan Hunter Shipbuilders, Wallsend-on-Tyne	12 May 1985	13 Dec 1986	25 Nov 1987

Displacement, tons: 8585 full load
Measurement, tons: 3080 dwt
Dimensions, feet (metres): 461 × 64 × 14.1 *(140.5 × 19.5 × 4.3)*
Main machinery: 2 Mirrlees Blackstone diesels; 13 320 hp *(9.94 MW)*; 2 shafts; cp props
Speed, knots: 18. **Range, miles:** 13 000 at 15 kts
Complement: 49 (17 officers)
Military lift: 343 troops (537 hard-lying); 18 MBT; 20 mixed vehicles; ammunition, fuel and stores
Guns: 2 Oerlikon 20 mm GAM-BO3. 2—12.7 mm MGs.
Countermeasures: Decoys: 4 Plessey Shield launchers.
Combat data systems: Racal CANE data automation.
Radars: Navigation: Kelvin Hughes Type 1006; I band.
Helicopters: 1 Westland Sea King HC 4.

Comment: Ordered on 6 September 1984 as a replacement for *Sir Galahad*, sunk as a war grave after air attack at Bluff Cove, Falkland Islands on 8 June 1982. Has bow and stern ramps with a visor bow gate. One 25 ton crane and three smaller ones. Mexeflote pontoons can be attached on both sides of the hull superstructure.

SIR GALAHAD 11/1991, Maritime Photographic

ROYAL MARITIME AUXILIARY SERVICE

SALVAGE AND MOORING VESSELS

Note: Scarab (Insect class tender) with bow sheave acts as mooring vessel at Pembroke Dock. Cricket (no bow sheave) acts as mooring vessel in the Clyde.

3 SAL CLASS

Name	No	Builders	Commissioned
SALMOOR	A 185	Hall Russell, Aberdeen	12 Nov 1985
SALMASTER	A 186	Hall Russell, Aberdeen	10 Apr 1986
SALMAID	A 187	Hall Russell, Aberdeen	28 Oct 1986

Displacement, tons: 1605 light; 2225 full load
Dimensions, feet (metres): 253 × 48.9 × 12.5 *(77 × 14.9 × 3.8)*
Main machinery: 2 Ruston 8RKC diesels; 4000 hp *(2.98 MW)* sustained; 1 shaft
Speed, knots: 15
Complement: 17 (4 officers) plus 27 spare billets

Comment: Ordered on 23 January 1984. *Salmoor* on Clyde, *Salmaster* at Rosyth, *Salmaid* at Devonport. Lift, 400 tons; 200 tons on horns. Can carry submersibles including LR 5.

SALMAID 11/1992, Maritime Photograhic

2 WILD DUCK CLASS

Name	No	Builders	Commissioned
GOOSANDER	A 164	Robb Caledon, Leith	10 Sep 1973
POCHARD	A 165	Robb Caledon, Leith	11 Dec 1973

Displacement, tons: 692 light; 1648 full load
Dimensions, feet (metres): 197.6 × 40.5 × 13.8 *(60.2 × 12.2 × 4.2)*
Main machinery: 1 Paxman diesel; 750 hp *(560 kW)*; 1 shaft; cp prop
Speed, knots: 10. **Range, miles:** 3000 at 10 kts
Complement: 23

Comment: Capable of laying out and servicing the heaviest moorings used by the Fleet and also maintaining booms for harbour defence. Heavy lifting equipment enables a wide range of salvage operations to be performed, especially in harbour clearance work. The special heavy winches have an ability for tidal lifts over the apron of 200 tons. *Goosander* is based on the Clyde; *Pochard* in reserve at Portsmouth.

GOOSANDER 1991, RMAS

3 MOORHEN CLASS

Name	No	Builders	Commissioned
MOORHEN	Y 32	McTay, Bromborough	Apr 1989
MOORFOWL	Y 33	McTay, Bromborough	May 1989
CAMERON	A 72	Dunston, Hessle	Sep 1991

Displacement, tons: 530 full load
Dimensions, feet (metres): 106 × 37.7 × 6.6 *(32.3 × 11.5 × 2)*
Main machinery: 2 Cummins KT19-M diesels; 730 hp *(545 kW)* sustained; 2 Aquamasters
Speed, knots: 8
Complement: 10 (2 officers)

Comment: Classified as powered mooring lighters. The whole ship can be worked from a 'flying bridge' which is constructed over a through deck. Day mess for five divers. *Moorhen* at Portsmouth, *Moorfowl* at Devonport. *Cameron* works for DRA (Maritime) and is modified as a trials support vessel.

MOORHEN 11/1992, Maritime Photographic

COASTAL TANKERS

4 OILPRESS CLASS

Name	No	Builders	Commissioned
OILPRESS	Y 21	Appledore Ferguson SB	1969
OILWELL	Y 23	Appledore Ferguson SB	1969
OILBIRD	Y 25	Appledore Ferguson SB	1969
OILMAN	Y 26	Appledore Ferguson SB	1969

Displacement, tons: 280 standard; 530 full load
Dimensions, feet (metres): 139.5 × 30 × 8.3 *(42.5 × 9 × 2.5)*
Main machinery: 1 Lister-Blackstone ES6 diesel; 405 hp *(302 kW)*; 1 shaft
Speed, knots: 9
Complement: 8
Cargo capacity: 250 tons dieso

Comment: Ordered on 10 May 1967. Two deleted in 1992.

OILPRESS 2/1986, A Denholm

TRIALS SHIPS

Note: A Shock Trials Vessel, *STV 02*, was completed 14 June 1981 by Scotts Shipbuilding, Greenock.

Name	No	Builders	Commissioned
NEWTON	A 367	Scott-Lithgow, Greenock	17 June 1976

Displacement, tons: 3140 light; 4652 full load
Dimensions, feet (metres): 323.5 × 53 × 18.5 *(98.6 × 16 × 5.7)*
Main machinery: Diesel-electric; 3 Mirrlees-Blackstone diesel generators; 4350 hp *(3.25 MW)*; 1 GEC motor; 2040 hp *(1.52 MW)*; Kort nozzle; bow thruster
Speed, knots: 14. **Range, miles:** 5000 at 14 kts
Complement: 64 including 12 scientists

Comment: Passive tank stabilisation. Prime duty sonar propagation trials. Can serve as cable-layer with large cable tanks. Special winch system. Low noise level electric propulsion system. Based at Plymouth.

NEWTON 1990, van Ginderen Collection

Name	No	Builders	Commissioned
AURICULA	A 285	Appledore Ferguson SB	6 Nov 1980

Displacement, tons: 940 light; 1118 full load
Dimensions, feet (metres): 170.5 × 36 × 11.8 *(52 × 11 × 3.6)*
Main machinery: 2 Mirrlees-Blackstone diesels; 1300 hp *(970 kW)*; 2 shafts; bow thruster
Speed, knots: 12
Complement: 32 (7 officers, 10 trials party)

Comment: Sonar trials and experimental ship. Based at Portland.

AURICULA 1/1992, van Ginderen Collection

TORPEDO RECOVERY VESSELS

4 TORNADO CLASS

TORNADO A 140 TORMENTOR A 142
TORCH A 141 TOREADOR A 143

Displacement, tons: 698 full load
Dimensions, feet (metres): 154.5 × 31.3 × 11.3 *(47.1 × 9.6 × 3.4)*
Main machinery: 2 Mirrlees-Blackstone ESL8 MCR diesels; 2200 hp *(1.64 MW)*; 2 shafts
Speed, knots: 14. **Range, miles:** 3000 at 14 kts
Complement: 14

Comment: Ordered from Hall Russell, Aberdeen on 1 July 1977 and launched in 1979-80. *Torch* based at Portland, *Tormentor* at Plymouth, others in the Clyde.

TORMENTOR 1/1993, Maritime Photographic

746 UK (RMAS) / Torpedo recovery vessels — Tugs

Name	No	Builders	Commissioned
TORRENT	A 127	Cleland SB, Wallsend-on-Tyne	10 Sep 1971

Displacement, tons: 550 gross
Dimensions, feet (metres): 162 × 31 × 11.5 *(49.4 × 9.5 × 3.5)*
Main machinery: 2 Paxman diesels; 700 hp *(522 kW)*; 2 shafts
Speed, knots: 10
Complement: 18

Comment: Has a stern ramp for torpedo recovery—can carry 22 torpedoes in hold and 10 on deck. Based at Kyle of Loch Alsh.

TORRENT *1991, RMAS*

ARMAMENT STORE CARRIERS (AKF and ASL)

Name	No	Builders	Commissioned
KINTERBURY	A 378	Appledore Ferguson SB	Nov 1980
ARROCHAR (ex-*St George*)	A 382	Appledore Ferguson SB	July 1981

Displacement, tons: 2207 full load
Measurement, tons: 1150 dwt
Dimensions, feet (metres): 231.2 × 39 × 15 *(70.5 × 11.9 × 4.6)*
Main machinery: 2 Mirrlees-Blackstone diesels; 3000 hp *(2.24 MW)*; 1 shaft
Speed, knots: 14.5. **Range, miles:** 4000 at 11 kts
Complement: 24 (8 officers)

Comment: Carry armament stores in two holds. Internal arrangements of *Arrochar* differ and she is classified as an Armament Ship Logistic (ASL). Twin cranes in the well-deck. *Arrochar* transferred from the RCT on 7 November 1988.

ARROCHAR *1/1992, Gilbert Gyssels*

WATER CARRIERS

5 WATER CLASS

Name	No	Builders	Commissioned
WATERFALL	Y 17	Drypool Engineering & Drydock Co, Hull	1967
WATERSPOUT	Y 19	Drypool Engineering & Drydock Co, Hull	1967
WATERCOURSE	Y 30	Drypool Engineering & Drydock Co, Hull	1974
WATERFOWL	Y 31	Drypool Engineering & Drydock Co, Hull	1974
WATERMAN	A 146	Dunston, Hessle	1978

Measurement, tons: 285 gross
Dimensions, feet (metres): 131.5 × 24.8 × 8 *(40.1 × 7.5 × 2.4)*
Main machinery: 1 Lister-Blackstone ERS8 MCR diesel; 660 hp *(492 kW)*; 1 shaft
Speed, knots: 11
Complement: 8

Comment: Y 19 after deckhouse extended forward. A 146 is a modified ship, having a store-carrying capability and, like Y 31 has a deckhouse forward of the bridge. *Waterfall* based in the Clyde and used as a Salvage Training Vessel. One deleted in 1991 and one in 1992.

WATERCOURSE *1/1993, Maritime Photographic*

TUGS

Notes: 1. Appearance of RMAS tugs—black hull with white line, buff upperworks, buff funnel with black top. The blue band on the funnel varies between ports.
2. Two submarine tugs are included under *Submarine Support Vessels*.

3 OCEAN TUGS

Name	No	Builders	Commissioned
ROYSTERER	A 361	C D Holmes, Beverley, Humberside	26 Apr 1972
ROBUST	A 366	C D Holmes, Beverley, Humberside	6 Apr 1974
ROLLICKER	A 502	C D Holmes, Beverley, Humberside	6 Mar 1973

Displacement, tons: 1630 full load
Dimensions, feet (metres): 178 × 40.3 × 21 *(54.3 × 12.3 × 6.4)*
Main machinery: 2 Mirrlees KMR 6 diesels; 4500 hp *(3.36 MW)*; 2 shafts; cp props
Speed, knots: 15. **Range, miles:** 12 500 at 12 kts
Complement: 28 (salvage party—10 RN officers and ratings)

Comment: Nominal bollard pull, 50 tons. Designed principally for salvage and long-range towage but can be used for general harbour duties, which *Robust* undertakes at Devonport. *Roysterer* based on Clyde, *Rollicker* at Portsmouth.

ROLLICKER *2/1993, Maritime Photographic*

9 ADEPT CLASS (TUTT)

FORCEFUL A 221	ADEPT A 224	CAREFUL A 227
NIMBLE A 222	BUSTLER A 225	FAITHFUL A 228
POWERFUL A 223	CAPABLE A 226	DEXTEROUS A 231

Displacement, tons: 450
Dimensions, feet (metres): 127.3 × 30.8 × 11.2 *(38.8 × 9.4 × 3.4)*
Main machinery: 2 Ruston 6RKC diesels; 3000 hp *(2.24 MW)* sustained; 2 Voith-Schneider props
Speed, knots: 12
Complement: 10

Comment: 'Twin unit tractor tugs' (TUTT). First four ordered from Richard Dunston (Hessle) on 22 February 1979 and next five on 8 February 1984. Primarily for harbour work with coastal towing capability. Nominal bollard pull, 27.5 tons. *Adept* accepted 28 October 1980, *Bustler* 15 April 1981, *Capable* 11 September 1981, *Careful* 12 March 1982, *Forceful* 18 March 1985, *Nimble* 25 June 1985, *Powerful* 30 October 1985, *Faithful* 21 December 1985, *Dexterous* 23 April 1986. *Adept* at Portland, *Powerful* and *Bustler* at Portsmouth, *Forceful*, *Faithful* and *Careful* at Plymouth, *Nimble* and *Dexterous* at Rosyth, *Capable* at Gibraltar.

BUSTLER *1/1993, Maritime Photographic*

2 MODIFIED GIRL CLASS

DAPHNE A 156   EDITH A 177

Displacement, tons: 138 standard
Dimensions, feet (metres): 61 × 16.4 × 7.2 *(18.6 × 5 × 2.2)*
Main machinery: 1 diesel; 495 hp *(396 kW)*; 1 shaft
Speed, knots: 10
Complement: 6

Comment: *Edith* at Gibraltar. Both built by Dunstons. Completed 1971-72. Nominal bollard pull, 6.5 tons.

Modified GIRL class *4/1986, Michael D J Lennon*

18 DOG CLASS (16 TUGS + 2 RANGE TRIALS VESSELS)

ALSATIAN A 106	HUSKY A 178	SPANIEL A 201
CAIRN A 126	MASTIFF A 180	SHEEPDOG A 250
DALMATIAN A 129	SALUKI A 182	FOXHOUND (ex-*Boxer*) A 326
DEERHOUND A 155	POINTER A 188	BASSET (ex-*Beagle*) A 327
ELKHOUND A 162	SETTER A 189	COLLIE A 328
LABRADOR A 168	SEALYHAM A 197	CORGI A 330

Displacement, tons: 248 full load
Dimensions, feet (metres): 94 × 24.5 × 12 *(28.7 × 7.5 × 3.7)*
Main machinery: 2 Lister-Blackstone ERS8 MCR diesels; 1320 hp *(985 kW)*; 2 shafts
Speed, knots: 10. **Range, miles:** 2236 at 10 kts
Complement: 7

Comment: Harbour berthing tugs. *Sealyham* at Gibraltar. Nominal bollard pull, 17.5 tons. Completed 1962-72. *Cairn* and *Collie* operate at Kyle of Loch Alsh as Range trials vessels and have had towing gear removed. Appearance varies considerably, some with mast, some with curved upper-bridge work, some with flat monkey-island. The class needs replacing as a priority.

DALMATIAN   4/1992, Maritime Photographic

12 TRITON CLASS

KATHLEEN A 166	LILAH A 174	ISABEL A 183	MYRTLE A 199
KITTY A 170	MARY A 175	JOAN A 190	NANCY A 202
LESLEY A 172	IRENE A 181	JOYCE A 193	NORAH A 205

Displacement, tons: 107.5 standard
Dimensions, feet (metres): 57.7 × 18 × 7.9 *(17.6 × 5.5 × 2.4)*
Main machinery: 1 diesel; 330 hp *(264 kW)*; 1 shaft
Speed, knots: 7.5
Complement: 4

Comment: All completed by August 1974 by Dunstons. 'Water-tractors' with small wheelhouse and adjoining funnel. Later vessels have masts stepped abaft wheelhouse. Voith-Schneider vertical axis propellers. Nominal bollard pull, 3 tons. Order for two more in 1990 was cancelled.

KITTY   11/1991, W Sartori

8 FELICITY CLASS

FELICITY A 112	FLORENCE A 149	GWENDOLINE A 196
FRANCES A 147	GENEVIEVE A 150	HELEN A 198
FIONA A 148	GEORGINA A 152	

Displacement, tons: 144 full load
Dimensions, feet (metres): 70 × 21 × 9.8 *(21.5 × 6.4 × 3)*
Main machinery: 1 Mirrlees-Blackstone ESM8 diesel; 615 hp *(459 kW)*; 1 Voith-Schneider cp prop
Speed, knots: 10
Complement: 4

Comment: First five completed 1973. A 112 built by Dunstons and remainder by Hancocks. A 147, 149 and 150 ordered early 1979 from Richard Dunston (Thorne) and completed by end 1980. Nominal bollard pull, 5.7 tons.

HELEN   6/1992, Maritime Photographic

RANGE SUPPORT VESSELS

WARDEN A 368

Displacement, tons: 900 full load
Dimensions, feet (metres): 159.4 × 34.4 × 8.2 *(48.6 × 10.5 × 2.5)*
Main machinery: 2 Ruston 8RKC diesels; 4000 hp *(2.98 MW)* sustained; 1 shaft
Speed, knots: 15
Complement: 11 (4 officers)
Radars: Navigation: Racal Decca RM 1250; I band.
Sonars: Dowty 2053; high frequency.

Comment: Built by Richards, Lowestoft and completed in November 1989. In service at Pembroke Dock.

WARDEN   7/1991, van Ginderen Collection

FALCONET (ex-*Alfred Herring V C*)   **PETARD** (ex-*Michael Murphy V C*)
Y 02 (ex-Y 497)   Y 01 (ex-519)

Displacement, tons: 70 full load
Dimensions, feet (metres): 77.7 × 18 × 4.9 *(23.7 × 5.5 × 1.5)*
Main engines: 2 Paxman 8 CM diesels; 2000 hp *(1.49 MW)* sustained; 2 shafts
Speed, knots: 20

Comment: Range Safety Craft built by James and Stone, Brightlingsea. Similar design to Spitfire class. Transferred from the RCT on 30 September 1988. *Falconet* commissioned 1978 serves at the Royal Artillery missile range in the Outer Hebrides; *Petard* commissioned 1983 serves at Pendine range, South Wales.

PETARD   9/1987, Michael D J Lennon

RSC 7713 (ex-*Samuel Morley VC*)	RSC 7820 (ex-*Richard Masters VC*)
RSC 7821 (ex-*Joseph Hughes GC*)	RSC 7822 (ex-*James Dalton VC*)
RSC 8125 (ex-*Sir Paul Travers*)	RSC 8128 (ex-*Sir Reginald Kerr*)
RSC 8126 (ex-*Sir Cecil Smith*)	RSC 8129 (ex-*Sir Humfrey Gale*)
RSC 8487 (ex-*Geoffrey Rackman GC*)	RSC 8488 (ex-*Walter Cleal GC*)
RSC 8489 (ex-*Sir Evan Gibb*)	

Displacement, tons: 20.2
Dimensions, feet (metres): 49.2 × 14.9 × 4.3 *(15 × 4.6 × 1.3)*
Main machinery: 2 RR C8M 410 diesels; 820 hp *(612 kW)*; 2 shafts
Speed, knots: 22. **Range, miles:** 300 at 20 kts
Complement: 3

Comment: Range Safety Craft of the Honours and Sirs classes, built by Fairey Marine, A R P Whitstable and Halmatic. All completed 1982-86. Transferred from the RCT on 30 September 1988. A 13th vessel *Sir William Roe* is based in Cyprus and has remained with the RCT. Based at Whitehaven, Pembroke Dock, Hebrides, Dover and Portland. Now known only by their pennant numbers. 8124 went aground off Portland in December 1992 and was a write-off.

RSC 7820   6/1991, Maritime Photographic

SUBMARINE SUPPORT VESSELS

2 SUBMARINE BERTHING TUGS

Name	No	Builders	Completed
IMPULSE	A 344	Dunston, Hessle	11 Mar 1993
IMPETUS	A 345	Dunston, Hessle	June 1993

Displacement, tons: 530 full load
Dimensions, feet (metres): 106.7 × 34.2 × 11.5 *(32.5 × 10.4 × 3.5)*
Main machinery: 2 W H Allen 8S12 diesels; 3400 hp *(2.54 MW)* sustained; 2 Aquamaster Azimuth thrusters; 1 Jastrom bow thruster
Speed, knots: 12
Complement: 6

Comment: Ordered 28 January 1992 for submarine berthing duties. There are two 10 ton hydraulic winches forward and aft with break capacities of 110 tons. Designed for one man control from the bridge with all round vision and a comprehensive Navaids fit. *Impulse* launched 10 December 1992; *Impetus* 9 February 1993.

IMPULSE (artist's impression)　　　　　　　　　　　　　　　　　　1992

3 TOWED ARRAY TENDERS

Dimensions, feet (metres): 65.9 × 19.7 × 7.9 *(20.1 × 6 × 2.4)*
Main machinery: 2 Perkins diesels; 400 hp *(298 kW)*; 2 Kort nozzles
Speed, knots: 12
Complement: 8

Comment: Used for transporting clip-on towed arrays from submarine bases at Faslane, Portsmouth and Devonport. Naval manned.

TARV　　　　　　　　　　　　　　　　　　　　　　　　　7/1988, W Sartori

1 SUBMARINE TENDER

Name	No	Builders	Commissioned
ADAMANT	A 232	FBM, Cowes	18 Jan 1993

Dimensions, feet (metres): 101 × 25.6 × 3.6 *(30.8 × 7.8 × 1.1)*
Main machinery: 2 Cummins KTA 19M2 diesels; 2 waterjets
Speed, knots: 23. **Range, miles:** 250 at 22 kts
Complement: 5 plus 36 passengers

Comment: Twin-hulled support ship ordered in 1991 and launched 8 October 1992. Used for personnel and stores transfers in the Firth of Clyde. In addition to the passengers, half a ton of cargo can be carried. Capable of top speed up to sea state 3 and able to transit safely up to sea state 6.

ADAMANT　　　　　　　　　　　　　　　　　　　　　　12/1992, FBM

AVIATION SUPPORT CRAFT

Note: On 1 February 1991 vessels of the Royal Air Force Maritime Section were transferred to the RMAS. Operation by James Fisher & Son continued until 1 April 1993 when the contract was taken over by Vosper Thornycroft. The vessels are based at Plymouth, Invergordon, Holyhead and Great Yarmouth.

2 SEAL CLASS (LRRSC)

Name	No	Builders	Commissioned
SEAL	5000	Brooke Marine, Lowestoft	Aug 1967
SEAGULL	5001	Fairmile Construction, Berwick-on-Tweed	1970

Displacement, tons: 159 full load
Dimensions, feet (metres): 120.3 × 23.5 × 6.5 *(36.6 × 7.2 × 2)*
Main machinery: 2 Paxman 16YJCM diesels; 4000 hp *(2.98 MW)* sustained; 2 shafts
Speed, knots: 21
Complement: 9

Comment: Long range recovery and support craft (LRRSC). All welded steel hull. Aluminium alloy superstructure. Used for weapon recovery, target towing, search and rescue. Both at Invergordon.

SEAL　　　　　　　　　　　　　　　　　　　　8/1984, Michael D J Lennon

6 SPITFIRE CLASS (RTTL Mk 3)

Name	No	Builders	Commissioned
SPITFIRE	4000	James and Stone, Brightlingsea	1972
HALIFAX	4003	James and Stone, Brightlingsea	1977
HAMPDEN	4004	James and Stone, Brightlingsea	1980
HURRICANE	4005	James and Stone, Brightlingsea	1980
LANCASTER	4006	James and Stone, Brightlingsea	1981
WELLINGTON	4007	James and Stone, Brightlingsea	1981

Displacement, tons: 70.2 full load
Dimensions, feet (metres): 78.7 × 18 × 4.9 *(24.1 × 5.5 × 1.5)*
Main machinery: 2 Paxman 8YJCM diesels; 2000 hp *(1.49 MW)* sustained; 2 shafts
Speed, knots: 22
Complement: 6

Comment: Rescue target towing launches (RTTL). All welded steel hulls; aluminium alloy superstructure. *Spitfire* has twin funnels, remainder none. Invergordon, *Hurricane*; Great Yarmouth, *Hampden, Lancaster, Wellington*; Plymouth, *Spitfire, Halifax*.

HAMPDEN　　　　　　　　　　　　　　　　8/1987, Michael D J Lennon

3 PINNACES 1300 SERIES

1374, 1389, 1392

Displacement, tons: 28.3
Dimensions, feet (metres): 63 × 15.5 × 5 *(19.2 × 4.7 × 1.5)*
Main machinery: 2 RR C6 diesels; 190 hp *(142 kW)*; 2 shafts
Speed, knots: 13
Complement: 5
Guns: 1—12.7 mm MG.

Comment: Hard chine, wooden hulls. Built by Groves and Gutteridge, Robertsons (Dunoon) and Dorset Yacht Co (Poole) in 1955-65. Of 5 ton cargo capacity. *1392* and *1374* at Holyhead; *1389* at Plymouth. Two deleted in 1992.

1300 Series (old number)　　　　　　　　　　5/1991, van Ginderen Collection

FLEET TENDERS

7 INSECT CLASS

BEE A 216	CRICKET A 229	SCARAB A 272
CICALA A 263	GNAT A 239	
COCKCHAFER A 230	LADYBIRD A 253	

Displacement, tons: 475 full load
Dimensions, feet (metres): 111.8 × 28 × 11 *(34.1 × 8.5 × 3.4)*
Main machinery: 1 Lister-Blackstone ERS8 MCR diesel; 660 hp *(492 kW)*; 1 shaft
Speed, knots: 11.3. **Range, miles:** 3000 at 10 kts
Complement: 7

Comment: First three built as stores carriers, three as armament carriers and *Scarab* as mooring vessel capable of lifting 10 tons over the bows. All commissioned between 1970 and 1973. *Cricket* acts as a mooring vessel in the Clyde while *Gnat* and *Ladybird* operate as armament carriers with a red funnel band. *Bee* and *Cicala* have an armament capability. Of 200 ton cargo capacity and 2 ton crane.

BEE   *9/1990, Maritime Photographic*

4 DIVING TENDERS

ILCHESTER A 308	IRONBRIDGE* A 311
INSTOW A 309	IXWORTH* A 318
*RN manned	

Displacement, tons: 143
Dimensions, feet (metres): 80 × 21 × 6.6 *(24.1 × 6.4 × 2)*
Main machinery: 2 Gray Marine diesels; 450 hp *(336 kW)*; 2 shafts
Speed, knots: 12
Complement: 6

Comment: Similar to Clovelly class. Built by Gregson Ltd, Blyth and commissioned in 1974.

INSTOW   *8/1989, Wright & Logan*

8 LOYAL CLASS (RNXS)

LOYAL HELPER A 157	LOYAL MEDIATOR A 161
SUPPORTER (ex-*Loyal Supporter*) A 158	LOYAL MODERATOR A 220
LOYAL WATCHER A 159	LOYAL CHANCELLOR A 1770
LOYAL VOLUNTEER A 160	LOYAL PROCTOR A 1771

Displacement, tons: 143
Dimensions, feet (metres): 80 × 21 × 6.6 *(24.1 × 6.4 × 2)*
Main machinery: 1 Lister-Blackstone ERS4 MCR diesel; 320 hp *(239 kW)*; 1 shaft
Speed, knots: 10.5
Complement: 6 (1 officer)

Comment: *Loyal Helper* completed 10 February 1978 and last four later in 1978. (See also Coastal Training Craft). Bases: Portsmouth Command: *Loyal Mediator*. Plymouth Command: *Loyal Moderator* (Pembroke Dock), *Loyal Watcher* (Birkenhead), *Loyal Chancellor* (Plymouth). Scotland Command: *Loyal Volunteer*, *Loyal Proctor*, *Supporter* (Belfast), *Loyal Helper* (Rosyth).

LOYAL HELPER   *7/1990, Gilbert Gyssels*

25 CLOVELLY CLASS

CLOVELLY A 389	FELSTED A 348	HOLMWOOD A 1772
CRICKLADE A 381	FINTRY A 394	HORNING A 1773
CROMARTY A 488	FOTHERBY A 341	LAMLASH A 208
DORNOCH A 490	FULBECK A 365	LECHLADE A 211
DUNSTER A 393	GRASMERE A 402	LLANDOVERY A 207
ELKSTONE A 353	HAMBLEDON A 1769	LYDFORD (ex-*Loyal Governor*, ex-*Alert*) A 251
ELSING* A 277	HARLECH A 1768	
EPWORTH A 355	HEADCORN A 1766	SULTAN VENTURER* (ex-*Meavy*, ex-*Loyal Factor*, ex-*Vigilant*) A 254
ETTRICK** A 274	HEVER A 1767	
*RN **RNR		

Displacement, tons: 143 full load
Dimensions, feet (metres): 80 × 21 × 6.6 *(24.4 × 6.4 × 2)*
Main machinery: 1 Lister-Blackstone ERS4 MCR diesel; 320 hp *(239 kW)*; 1 shaft
Speed, knots: 10.3. **Range, miles:** 600 at 10 kts
Complement: 4
Cargo capacity: 36 tons

Comment: All fleet tenders of an improved Aberdovey class commissioned 1970-74. *Elsing* and *Ettrick* at Gibraltar (Royal Navy manned), used for patrol duties. Three based at Falmouth operating with Culdrose helicopters *(Clovelly, Hever, Headcorn)*. Can be used for varying tasks—cargo, passenger, training, diving *(Dornoch* and *Fotherby)*. *Lydford* at Portland. *Sultan Venturer* replaced the Aberdovey class of the same name in 1992 and serves as a tender to *Sultan*. Listed in alphabetical order.

DORNOCH   *12/1991, G Toremans*

5 MANLY CLASS

MELTON A 83	MEON A 87	MESSINA A 107
MENAI A 84	MILFORD A 91	

Displacement, tons: 143 full load
Dimensions, feet (metres): 80 × 21 × 6.6 *(24.4 × 6.4 × 2)*
Main machinery: 1 Lister-Blackstone ESR4 MCR diesel; 320 hp *(239 kW)*; 1 shaft
Speed, knots: 10
Complement: 6 (1 officer)

Comment: All built by Richard Dunston, Hessle. Details similar to Clovelly class but with larger deck-house. All completed by early 1983. *Messina*, attached to Royal Marines, Poole for navigational training and remainder RMAS. Three of the class used for training at *Raleigh* have been paid off.

MEON   *6/1990, van Ginderen Collection*

1 FBM CATAMARAN CLASS

Displacement, tons: 21 full load
Dimensions, feet (metres): 51.8 × 18 × 4.9 *(15.8 × 5.5 × 1.5)*
Main machinery: 2 Mermaid Turbo 4 diesels; 280 hp *(209 kW)*; 2 shafts
Speed, knots: 13. **Range, miles:** 400 at 10 kts
Complement: 2

Comment: Built by FBM Marine. Can carry 30 passengers or 2 tons stores. First of a new construction type designed to replace some of the older harbour launches.

FBM Type   *9/1990, Maritime Photographic*

TARGET VESSELS

BULLSEYE (ex-*Tokio*), **MAGPIE** (ex-*Hondo*), **TARGE** (ex-*Erimo*)

Measurement, tons: 273 gross; 91 net
Dimensions, feet (metres): 117.8 × 25.3 × 12.1 *(35.9 × 7.7 × 3.7)*
Main machinery: 1 Mirrlees diesel; 700 hp *(522 kW)*; 1 shaft
Speed, knots: 12
Complement: 2 (on passage only)

Comment: Built by Goole Shipbuilding Co in 1961-62. Side trawlers acquired in June 1982 and January 1984 *(Targe)*. These are employed as radio controlled targets at Portland. Naval manned.

MAGPIE 7/1987, Michael D J Lennon

DEGAUSSING VESSELS

2 MAGNET CLASS

MAGNET A 114   LODESTONE A 115

Displacement, tons: 955 full load
Dimensions, feet (metres): 179.7 × 37.4 × 9.8 *(54.8 × 11.4 × 3)*
Main machinery: 2 Mirrlees-Blackstone ESL6 MCR diesels; 1650 hp *(1.23 MW)*; 2 shafts
Speed, knots: 14. Range, miles: 1750 at 12 kts
Complement: 15

Comment: The pair replaced the three Ham class, *Magnet* based at Portsmouth (in reserve) and *Lodestone* at Greenock. Built by Cleland S B Co Ltd, Wallsend 1979-80.

LODESTONE 2/1993, Maritime Photographic

AUXILIARY TRAINING VESSELS

5 ABERDOVEY CLASS

APPLEBY A 383   ABINGER Y 11   BEDDGELERT A 100
ALNMOUTH Y 13   ABERDOVEY Y 10

Displacement, tons: 117.5 full load
Dimensions, feet (metres): 79.8 × 18 × 5.5 *(24 × 5.5 × 1.7)*
Main machinery: 1 Lister-Blackstone ERS4 MCR diesel; 320 hp *(239 kW)*; 1 shaft
Speed, knots: 10.5. Range, miles: 700 at 10 kts
Complement: 3

Comment: Commissioned in the mid-1960s as multi-purpose stores carriers (25 tons) or passengers (200). Four of the class have been modified with Sampson posts removed and improved accommodation. These are allocated to Sea Cadet Corps: *Aberdovey* (southern area based at Portsmouth); *Abinger* (eastern area based at Grimsby); *Appleby* (south-west area based at Bristol); *Alnmouth* (north-west area based at Liverpool). *Beddgelert* is a tender to *Caroline* at Belfast.

ABINGER 8/1991, Maurice Bell

4 SEA CADET CORPS VESSELS

Comment: As well as the Aberdovey class above, there are three MFVs and one ex-IMS used by the SCC: MFV 15 (northern area based at Rosyth); MFV 96 (London); MFV 816 (Gravesend); IMS *Pagham* (Stranraer). All these vessels are in constant use.

MFV 9/1991, Maritime Photographic

OLIVER TWIST   URIAH HEEP

Comment: Ex-RCT General Service Launches of 20 tons. Two RNR tenders—*Oliver Twist* (London); *Uriah Heep* (Bristol).

ROYAL CORPS OF TRANSPORT

Note: Four LCVPs are listed in the RN section.

2 LOGISTIC LANDING CRAFT (LCLs) (HMAV)

Name	No	Builders	Commissioned
ARDENNES	L 4001	Brooke Marine, Lowestoft	1977
ARAKAN	L 4003	Brooke Marine, Lowestoft	1978

Displacement, tons: 1146 light; 1733 full load
Dimensions, feet (metres): 236.8 × 49.3 × 15 *(72.2 × 15 × 4.6)*
Main machinery: 2 Mirrlees-Blackstone ESL8 MCR diesels; 2200 hp *(1.64 MW)*; 2 shafts
Speed, knots: 10.3. Range, miles: 4000 at 10 kts
Complement: 35 (4 officers) plus 34 troops
Military lift: 350 tons stores or 36 ISO containers; 5 MBTs or 11—8 ton trucks

Comment: Both ordered in October 1974. 150 tons dieso fuel.

ARAKAN 5/1992, van Ginderen Collection

1—15 METRE RANGE SAFETY CRAFT

SIR WILLIAM ROE 8127

Comment: Built by Halmatic in 1985. Details under RMAS 'Range Support Vessels'. The sole RCT survivor of a class of 13 of which 12 were transferred to the RMAS on 30 September 1988. Based in Cyprus.

9 RAMPED CRAFT, LOGISTIC (RCLs)

Name	No	Builders	Commissioned
ARROMANCHES	L 105	Brooke Marine, Lowestoft	31 July 1981
ANTWERP	L 106	Brooke Marine, Lowestoft	14 Aug 1981
ANDALSNES	L 107	James and Stone, Brightlingsea	22 May 1984
ABBEVILLE	L 108	James and Stone, Brightlingsea	9 Nov 1984
AKYAB	L 109	James and Stone, Brightlingsea	15 Dec 1984
AACHEN	L 110	James and Stone, Brightlingsea	12 Feb 1987
AREZZO	L 111	James and Stone, Brightlingsea	26 Mar 1987
AGHEILA	L 112	James and Stone, Brightlingsea	12 June 1987
AUDEMER	L 113	James and Stone, Brightlingsea	21 Aug 1987

Displacement, tons: 290 full load
Dimensions, feet (metres): 109.2 × 27.2 × 4.9 *(33.3 × 8.3 × 1.5)*
Main machinery: 2 Dorman 8JTCWM diesels; 504 hp *(376 kW)* sustained; 2 shafts
Speed, knots: 10
Complement: 6 (2 NCOs)

Comment: *Arromanches* and *Antwerp* based in Cyprus; *Andalsnes, Abbeville* and *Akyab* in Hong Kong.

AGHEILA   1/1993, Maritime Photographic

3 AVON CLASS

EDEN RPL 05   **FORTH** RPL 06   **MEDWAY** RPL 12

Displacement, tons: 100 full load approx
Dimensions, feet (metres): 72.2 × 20.5 × 5.5 *(22 × 6.2 × 1.7)*
Main machinery: 2 diesels; 870 hp *(649 kW)*; 2 shafts
Speed, knots: 9
Complement: 6

Comment: Ramped Powered Lighters (RPL) manned by RCT and available for short coastal hauls. Built by White and Saunders-Roe, Isle of Wight in 1961-67. All assigned to Belize (one normally in refit in UK).

EDEN   3/1987, Michael D J Lennon

4 WORK BOATS Mk II

BREAM WB 03   **PERCH** WB 06
ROACH WB 05   **MILL REEF** WB 08

Displacement, tons: 19
Dimensions, feet (metres): 47 *(14.3)* long
Speed, knots: 8

Comment: First three built 1966-71; last one built in 1987. Can be handled by LSLs.

PERCH   6/1987, Michael D J Lennon

SCOTTISH FISHERY PROTECTION AGENCY

Notes: (1) In addition to the ships listed below *Scotia* is used for research by the Department of Fisheries.
(2) Two Cessna Caravan II aircraft with Seaspray 2000 radars ordered in 1991.

SULISKER   **VIGILANT**   **NORNA**

Displacement, tons: 1652 full load
Dimensions, feet (metres): 233.9 × 38 × 15.7 *(71.3 × 11.6 × 4.8)*
Main machinery: 2 Ruston 6AT350 diesels; 6000 hp *(4.48 MW)* sustained *(Norna)*; 2 Ruston 12RKC diesels; 6000 hp *(4.48 MW)* sustained; 2 shafts; cp props; bow thruster; 450 hp *(336 kW)*
Speed, knots: 18. **Range, miles:** 7000 at 14 kts
Complement: 26 (7 officers) plus 6 spare bunks

Comment: Built by Appledore Ferguson SB. Fitted with 450 bhp bow thruster and helicopter platform. *Sulisker* completed 1981, *Vigilant* completed June 1982. Third ship of this class (although not identical) launched 11 September 1987 by Richards, Lowestoft and completed in June 1988. *Corystes* of this class was built for the Ministry of Agriculture and Fisheries in London.

SULISKER   6/1987, A Denholm

WESTRA

Displacement, tons: 778 light; 1285 full load
Measurement, tons: 942 gross
Dimensions, feet (metres): 195.3 × 35 × 14.4 *(59.6 × 10.7 × 4.4)*
Main machinery: 2 British Polar SP112VS-F diesels; 4200 hp *(3.13 MW)*; 1 shaft
Speed, knots: 15.5
Complement: 28

Comment: Built in 1975 by Hall Russell, Aberdeen. Near sister to RN Island class.

WESTRA   7/1982, van Ginderen Collection

MOIDART   **MORVEN**

Displacement, tons: 44 full load
Dimensions, feet (metres): 65 *(19.8)* long
Main machinery: 3 Detroit 8V-92TA diesels; 1050 hp *(783 kW)* sustained; 3 shafts
Speed, knots: 20
Complement: 5

Comment: Cheverton patrol craft completed April 1983. GRP hull.

MOIDART   1/1984, A Denholm

SKUA   **OSPREY**

Displacement, tons: 6 full load
Dimensions, feet (metres): 38 × 12.1 × 3.9 *(11.6 × 3.7 × 1.2)*
Main machinery: 2 Sabre 212 diesels; 424 hp *(316 kW)*; 2 shafts
Speed, knots: 28
Complement: 3

Comment: Pacific 38 class built by Osborne Marine in 1987-88. Dimensions given include the inflatable flotation collar.

HM CUSTOMS

Note: The Customs and Excise (Marine Branch) of HM Treasury operates a considerable number of craft around the UK: two Brooke Marine 33 m craft *(Searcher, Seeker)*; three FBM Marine 26 m craft *(Vigilant, Valiant* and *Venturous)* two Fairey Marine 20 m craft *(Safeguard* and *Swift)*; five Cheverton 8.2 m craft *(Avocet, Bittern, Courser, Diver* and *Egret)*; plus 59 small craft ranging from 4 m Seariders to 10 m harbour launches. None of these vessels is armed. A fourth V class is building at Rosyth and is planned to be in service in 1994.

TRINITY HOUSE

Note: A number of vessels of varying types—offshore support craft and lighthouse tenders—may be met throughout the waters of the UK.

VALIANT   6/1992, Maritime Photographic

THV PATRICIA   7/1990, Wright & Logan

BOXER   1992

UNITED STATES OF AMERICA

Headquarters' Appointments

Chief of Naval Operations:
  Admiral Frank B Kelso II
Vice Chief of Naval Operations:
  Admiral Stanley R Arthur
Director, Naval Nuclear Propulsion Programme, Naval Sea Systems Command:
  Admiral Bruce DeMars
US Representative to the NATO Military Committee:
  Admiral William D Smith
Commander, Military Sealift Command:
  Vice Admiral Michael P Kalleres
Commander, Naval Air Systems Command:
  Vice Admiral William C Bowes
Commander, Naval Sea Systems Command:
  Vice Admiral Kenneth C Malley
Commander, Space and Naval Warfare Systems Command:
  Rear Admiral Walter H Cantrell

Commanders-in-Chief

Commander-in-Chief, Atlantic Command and NATO Supreme Allied Commander, Atlantic:
  Admiral Paul D Miller
Commander-in-Chief, Pacific Command:
  Admiral Charles R Larson
Commander-in-Chief, Atlantic Fleet:
  Admiral Henry H Mauz Jr
Commander-in-Chief, Pacific Fleet:
  Admiral Robert J Kelly
Commander-in-Chief, Naval Forces, Europe, and NATO Forces, Southern Europe:
  Admiral Jeremy M Boorda
Commander-in-Chief, Central Command:
  General Joseph P Hoar (Marines)

Flag Officers (Central Area)

Commander, US Naval Forces, Central Command and Middle East Force:
  Vice Admiral Douglas J Katz
Commander, US Naval Forces, Central Command (Rear):
  Rear Admiral David N Rogers

Flag Officers (Atlantic Area)

Commander, Second Fleet, Atlantic Fleet and Striking Fleet, Atlantic:
  Vice Admiral William J Flanagan Jr
Commander, Naval Surface Force, Atlantic Fleet:
  Vice Admiral Joseph P Reason
Commander, Sixth Fleet and Striking and Support Forces, Southern Europe:
  Vice Admiral Thomas J Lopez
Commander, Submarine Force, Atlantic Fleet and Submarine Allied Command, Atlantic:
  Vice Admiral Henry G Chiles Jnr
Deputy Commander-in-Chief, Naval Forces, Europe:
  Vice Admiral Edward W Clexton Jnr
Commander, Naval Air Force, Atlantic Fleet:
  Vice Admiral Anthony A Less
Commander, Fleet Air, Keflavik and US Defense Force, Iceland:
  Rear Admiral Michael D Haskins
Commander, South Atlantic Force, Atlantic Fleet:
  Rear Admiral Theodore C Lockhart
Commander, Mine Warfare Command:
  Rear Admiral John D Pearson
Commander, Joint Task Force Four:
  Rear Admiral George N Gee

Flag Officers (Pacific Area)

Commander, Seventh Fleet, Pacific Fleet:
  Vice Admiral Timothy W Wright
Commander, Naval Surface Force, Pacific Fleet:
  Vice Admiral David B Robinson
Commander, Third Fleet, Pacific Fleet:
  Vice Admiral Jerry L Unruh
Commander, Naval Air Force, Pacific Fleet:
  Vice Admiral Edwin R Kohn Jnr
Commander, US Naval Forces, Japan:
  Rear Admiral Jesse J Hernandez
Commander, Submarine Force, Pacific Fleet:
  Rear Admiral Henry C McKinney
Commander, US Naval Forces, Korea:
  Rear Admiral William W Mathis

Marine Corps

Commandant:
  General Carl E Mundy Jnr
Assistant Commandant:
  General Walter E Boomer
Commander, Fleet Marine Force, Atlantic:
  Lieutenant General William M Keys
Commander, Fleet Marine Force, Pacific:
  Lieutenant General Henry C Stackpole III

Territorial Seas

On 27 December 1988, the United States claimed territorial seas were extended from three to 12 nautical miles. The USA now exercises sovereignty over waters, seabed and airspace out to 12 nautical miles. This extension also applies to the Commonwealth of Puerto Rico, Guam, American Samoa, the US Virgin Islands, the Commonwealth of the Northern Mariana Islands and any other territory or possession over which the USA exercises sovereignty.
The USA continues to recognise the right of all ships to conduct innocent passage and, in the case of international straits, the right of all ships and aircraft to conduct transit passage through its territorial sea.

Personnel

	31 Jan 1991	1 Jan 1992	1 Jan 1993
Navy			
Officers	76 894	72 392	70 777
Midshipmen	4368	4273	4336
Enlisted	532 516	505 174	478 051
Marine Corps			
Officers	20 605	19 753	18 980
Enlisted	179 643	174 287	166 059

Mercantile Marine

Lloyd's Register of Shipping:
  5736 vessels of 18 228 300 tons gross

Strength of the Fleet (1993)

Type	Active (NRF)	Building (Projected) + Conversion/SLEP
SHIPS OF THE FLEET		
Strategic Missile Submarines		
SSBN (Ballistic Missile Submarines) (nuclear-powered)	21	5
Attack Submarines		
SSN Submarines (nuclear-powered)	87	12 (1)
Aircraft Carriers		
CVN Multi-purpose Aircraft Carriers (nuclear-powered)	6	2 + 1
CV Multi-purpose Aircraft Carriers (conventionally powered)	6	+ 1
Cruisers		
CGN Guided Missile Cruisers (nuclear-powered)	9	—
CG Guided Missile Cruisers	41	4
Destroyers		
DDG Guided Missile Destroyers	7	15 (13)
DD Destroyers	31	—
Frigates		
FFG Guided Missile Frigates	35 (16)	—
FF Frigates	— (8)	—
Light Forces		
PHM Guided Missile Patrol Combatants	6	—
PC Coastal Patrol Craft	4	9
Amphibious Warfare Ships		
LCC Amphibious Command Ships	2	—
LHA Amphibious Assault Ships (general purpose)	5	—
LHD Amphibious Assault Ships (multi-purpose)	3	3
LKA Amphibious Cargo Ships	3	—
LPD Amphibious Transport Docks	11	—
LPH Amphibious Assault Ships (helicopter)	5	—
LSD Dock Landing Ships	13	4
LST Tank Landing Ships	13 (3)	—
LX Amphibious Ships	—	— (12)
Mine Warfare Ships		
MCM Mine Countermeasures Ships	10	4
MSO Minesweepers (Ocean)	1 (4)	—
MHC Minehunters (Coastal)	1	9 (2)
Auxiliary Ships		
AD Destroyer Tenders	8	—
AE Ammunition Ships	12	—
AFS Combat Stores Ships	5	—
AGF Miscellaneous Command Ships	2	—
AGSS Auxiliary Research Submarine	1	—
AO Oilers	5	—
AOE Fast Combat Support Ships	4	4
AOR Replenishment Oilers	5	—
AR Repair Ships	1	—
ARL Repair Ship Small	1	—
ARS Salvage Ships	8 (2)	—
AS Submarine Tenders	9	—
ASR Submarine Rescue Ships	2	—
ATS Salvage and Rescue Ships	3	—
AVT Training Carrier	1	—
NAVAL RESERVE FORCE		
FFT Frigates	8	—
FFG Guided Missile Frigates	16	—
LST Tank Landing Ships	3	—
MSO Minesweepers (Ocean)	4	—
ARS Salvage Ships	2	—
MILITARY SEALIFT COMMAND INVENTORY		
STRATEGIC SEALIFT (Active)		
Ocean Transportation Ships		
TAO/TAOT Oilers, Tankers	19	—
Ro-Ro, Freighters, Tankers	As required	—
Prepositioning Ships		
TAK/TAKB/TAKF Cargo Ships	9	—
TAOT Tankers	2	—
TAK Maritime Prepositioning Ships (MPS)	13	—
Naval Fleet Auxiliary Force		
TAO Oilers	12	6
TAFS Combat Stores Ships	5	—
TATF Fleet Ocean Tugs	7	—
TAGOS Ocean Surveillance Ships	18	1 (1)
TAK-FBM Fleet Ballistic Missile Ships	1	—
TAE Ammunition Ship	1	—
STRATEGIC SEALIFT (Reserve)		
Fast Sealift Ships		
TAKR Fast Sealift Ships (MPS)	8	—
Aviation Support Ships		
TAVB Aviation Support Ships (MPS)	2	—
Hospital Ships		
TAH Hospital Ships	2	—

USA / Introduction

Type	Active (NRF)	Building (Projected) + Conversion/SLEP	Type	Active (NRF)	Building (Projected) + Conversion/SLEP
Ready Reserve Force			**SPECIAL MISSION SUPPORT SHIPS**		
TAK/TAKR Cargo Ships (break bulk)	48	—	TAGM Missile Range Instrumentation Ships	3	—
TAKR Roll-on/Roll-off Ships	17	12	TAGOR Oceanographic Research Ships	1 (5 loan)	1
TACS Crain Ships	9	—	TAGS Surveying Ships	9	3
TAKR Heavy Lift Ships	3	—	TAG Navigation Research Ship	1	—
TAK Barge Carriers	4	—	TAG Acoustic Research Ship	1	—
TAOT/TAOG Product Carriers	13	—	TARC/TAK Cable Repairing Ships	2	—
TAP Troop Carriers	2	—			

Special Notes

To provide similar information to that included in other major navies' Deployment Tables the fleet assignment (abbreviated 'F/S') status of each ship in the US Navy has been included. The assignment appears in a column immediately to the right of the commissioning date. In the case of the Floating Dry Dock section this system is not used. The following abbreviations are used to indicate fleet assignments:

AA	active Atlantic Fleet
Active	active under charter with MSC
AR	in reserve Out of Commission, Atlantic Fleet
ASA	active In Service, Atlantic Fleet
ASR	in reserve Out of Service, Atlantic Fleet
Bldg	building
CONV	ship undergoing conversion
LOAN	ship or craft loaned to another government, or non-government agency, but US Navy retains title and the ship or craft is on the NVR
MAR	in reserve Out of Commission, Atlantic Fleet and laid up in the temporary custody of the Maritime Administration
MPR	same as 'MAR', but applies to the Pacific Fleet
NRF	assigned to the Naval Reserve Force (ships so assigned are listed in a special table for major warships and amphibious ships)
Ord	the contract for the construction of the ship has been let, but actual construction has not yet begun
PA	active Pacific Fleet
PR	in reserve Out of Commission, Pacific Fleet
Proj	ship is scheduled for construction at some time in the immediate future
PSA	active In Service, Pacific Fleet
PSR	in reserve Out of Service, Pacific Fleet
ROS	reduced Operating Status
TAA	active Military Sealift Command, Atlantic Fleet
TAR	in Ready Reserve, Military Sealift Command, Atlantic Fleet
TPA	active Military Sealift Command, Pacific Fleet
TPR	in Ready Reserve, Military Sealift Command, Pacific Fleet
TWWR	active Military Sealift Command, World-wide Routes

Ship Status Definitions

In Commission: as a rule any ship, except a Service Craft, that is active, is in commission. The ship has a Commanding Officer and flies a commissioning pennant. 'Commissioning date' as used in this section means the date of being 'in commission' rather than 'completion' or 'acceptance into service' as used in some other navies.

In Service: all service craft (dry docks and with classifications that start with 'Y'), with the exception of *Constitution*, that are active, are 'in service'. The ship has an Officer-in-Charge and does not fly a commissioning pennant.

Ships 'in reserve, out of commission' or 'in reserve, out of service' are put in a state of preservation for future service. Depending on the size of the ship or craft, a ship in 'mothballs' usually takes from 30 days to nearly a year to restore to full operational service. The above status definitions do not apply to the Military Sealift Command.

Approved Fiscal Year 1992 Programme

Shipbuilding

		Appropriations (US$ million)
1	Seawolf class SSN (SSN 23)	1903.2
5	Arleigh Burke class DDG (DDG 68-72)	3974.6
3	Osprey class MHC (MHC 58-60)	313.4
1	Supply class AOE (partial funding)	199.1
2	AGOR/TAGS Oceanographic Research Ships	108.7
18	Landing Craft, Air Cushion	383.9
	National Defense Sealift Fund	600.0

Note: 1 Whidbey Island CV class (LSD 52) authorised but not funded

Approved Fiscal Year 1993 Programme

Shipbuilding

		Appropriations (US$ million)
4	Arleigh Burke class DDG (DDG 73-76)	3244.4
1	Wasp class LHD (LHD 6) (partial funding)	303.1
1	Whidbey Island CV class LSD (LSD 52)	298.1
2	Osprey class MHC (MHC 11-12)	234.6
1	Supply class AOE (AOE 9)	298.1
	Carrier Replacement Programme (Advance Procurement)	829.4
	National Defense Sealift Fund	613.4

Notes: 1. Congress authorised the expenditure of $1200 million for construction of LHD 6, but funded only $303.1 million. The balance of the funding is included in the FY 1994 budget.
2. The construction of LSD 52 was authorised in the FY 1992 budget, but no funds were provided for construction. This action provides funding for construction.
3. $500 million was included in the FY 1992 budget for construction of the fourth ship of the AOE-6 class. Subsequently, $300 million of that sum was rescinded, and restored in FY 1993.
4. Funding for construction of sealift ships is incorporated into the National Defense Sealift Fund which now includes $2.643 million. Contracts for conversion and for new construction ships are expected in FY 1993. This fund is controlled by the Department of Defense.

Proposed Fiscal Year 1994 Programme

Shipbuilding

		Appropriations (US$ million)
3	Arleigh Burke class DDG (DDG 77-79)	2642.8
1	Wasp class LHD (LHD 6)	893.8
2	AGOR/TAGS Oceanographic Research Ships	110.0
1	Mine Warfare Command Ship Conversion (MCS(C))	124.2

Note: There is not a long range programme. FY 1995-99 Future Years Defense Programme is planned for February 1994.

Naval Aviation

US Naval Aviation is scaling down to an active inventory of 4990 aircraft, with approximately 25 per cent of these being operated by the Marine Corps. The principal naval aviation organisations are 11 carrier air wings, 18 maritime patrol squadrons, and three Marine aircraft wings. In addition the Naval Reserve and the Marine Corps Reserve operate four fighter squadrons, eight fighter/attack squadrons, four attack squadrons and 13 maritime patrol squadrons, plus various helicopter and transport units.

Fighter Attack: 22 Naval and 14 Marine Corps squadrons with F/A-18 Hornets. 21 Navy Squadrons for F-14 Tomcats.
Attack: 11 Navy squadrons with A-6E Intruders. 8 Marine squadrons with AV-8B Harriers.
Airborne Early Warning: 12 Navy squadrons with E-2C Hawkeye.
Electronic Warfare: 11 Navy and 4 Marine squadrons with EA-6B Prowler.
Anti-Submarine: 11 Navy squadrons with S-3A/B Viking.
Maritime Patrol: 18 Navy squadrons with P-3B/C Orion.
Helicopter Anti-Submarine: 29 Navy squadrons with SH-3G/H Sea King, SH-2 LAMPS I, SH-60B and SH-60F LAMPS III.
Helicopter Mine Countermeasures: 3 Navy squadrons with MH-53E Sea Dragons.
Helicopter Support: 7 Navy squadrons with UH-46D/E Sea Knight and CH-53E Super Stallions.
Electronic Reconnaissance: 3 Navy squadrons with EP-3E Orion and 2 with ES-3A Viking.
Communications Relay: 2 Navy squadrons with E-6A aircraft.
Helicopter Gunship: 6 Marine squadrons with AH-1T/W SuperCobra.
Helicopter Transport: 24 Marine squadrons with CH-46D/E Sea Knight, and CH-53D Sea Stallion/CH-53E Super Stallion.

Aircraft Procurement Plan FY 1993-94

	93	94
AV-8B	—	4
EA-6B	3	—
F/A-18C/D	36	36
CH/MH-53E	20	12
AH-1W	12	12
SH-60B	12	7
SH-60F	9	8
T-45TS	12	12
HH-60H	7	9

Note: FY 1995-99 will be in the Future Years Defense Programme (FYDP) planned for February 1994.

Naval Special Warfare

SEAL (Sea Air Land) teams are manned at a nominal 10 platoons per team, with 30 platoons on each coast based at Coronado and Norfolk, Virginia. Assigned directly to CinC US Special Operations Command, platoons are allocated to theatre commanders during operational deployments.

Bases

Naval Air Stations and Air Facilities

NAS Adak, AK; NAS Alameda, CA; NAF China Lake, CA; NAF El Centro, CA; NAS Los Alamitos, CA; NAS Miramar; NAS Lemoore, CA; NAS Moffett Field (San Jose), CA; NAS Point Mugu, CA; NAS North Island (San Diego), CA; NAF Andrews, Washington DC; NAS Cecil Field (Jacksonville), FL; NAS Jacksonville, FL; NAS Key West, FL; NAS Whiting Field (Milton), FL; NAS Saufley Field (Pensacola), FL; NAS Pensacola, FL; NAS Mayport, FL; NAS Atlanta (Marietta), GA; NAS Glenview, Ill; NAS Barbers Point (Oahu), HI; NAS New Orleans, LA; NAS Brunswick, ME; NAS Memphis (Millington), TN; NAS Patuxent River, MD; NAS South Weymouth, MA; NAF Detroit, MI; NAS Meridian, MS; NAS Fallon, NV; NAS Lakehurst, NJ; NAF Warminster, PA; NAS Willow Grove, PA; NAS Memphis (Millington), TN; NAS Chase Field (Beeville), TX; NAS Corpus Christi, TX; NAS Dallas, TX; NAS Kingsville, TX; NAS Norfolk, VA; NAS Oceana, VA; NAS Whidbey Island (Oak Harbor), WA; NAF Lajes, Azores; NAS Bermuda; NAS Guantanamo Bay, Cuba; NAF Naples, NAS Sigonella (Sicily), Italy; NAF Atsugi, Japan; NAS Agana, Guam; NAF Okinawa; NAS Diego Garcia.

Naval Stations and Naval Bases (22)

Yokosuka, Japan; Midway Is; Adak, AK; Pearl Harbor, HI; Treasure Is, San Francisco, CA; San Diego, CA; Coronado, San Diego, CA (Amphibs); Long Beach, CA; Mayport, FL; Roosevelt Roads, Puerto Rico; Guantanamo Bay, Cuba; Charleston, SC; Norfolk, VA; Little Creek, Norfolk, VA (Amphibs); Philadelphia, PA; New London, CT (Submarines); Newport, RI; Argentia, Newfoundland; Keflavik, Iceland; Rota, Spain; Naples, Italy; Staten Island, NY.

Strategic Missile Submarine Bases (3)

Charleston, SC; Bangor, WA (West Coast Trident base); Kings Bay, GA (East Coast Trident base)

Navy Yard (1)

Washington, DC (MSC Headquarters) (administration and historical activities).

Naval Shipyards (8)

Pearl Harbor, HI; Puget Sound, Bremerton, WA; Mare Is, Vallejo, CA; Charleston, SC; Norfolk, VA; Philadelphia, PA; Portsmouth, NH (located in Kittery, ME); Long Beach, CA.

Naval Ship Repair Facilities (3)

Yokosuka, Japan; Apra Harbor, Guam; Lumut, Singapore.

Marine Corps Air Stations and Helicopter Facilities (10)

MCAS: Beaufort, SC; El Toro (Santa Ana), CA; Yuma, AZ; Kaneohe Bay, Oahu, HI; Quantico, VA; Cherry Point, NC; Iwakuni, Honshu, Japan; New River (Jacksonville), NC.
MCHF: Tustin, CA; Futema, Okinawa.

Marine Corps Bases (5)

Camp Pendleton, CA; Twentynine Palms, CA; Camp H M Smith (Oahu), HI; Camp Lejeune, NC; Camp Smedley D Butler (Kawasaki), Okinawa, Japan.

CLASSIFICATION OF NAVAL SHIPS AND SERVICE CRAFT

COMBATANT SHIPS

WARSHIPS
Aircraft Carriers:
Aircraft Carrier	CV
Aircraft Carrier (nuclear propulsion)	CVN

Surface Combatants:
Guided Missile Cruiser	CG
Guided Missile Cruiser (nuclear propulsion)	CGN
Destroyer	DD
Guided Missile Destroyer	DDG
Frigate	FF
Guided Missile Frigate	FFG

Patrol Combatants:
Patrol Combatant Missile (hydrofoil)	PHM

Submarines:
Ballistic Missile Submarine (nuclear propulsion)	SSBN
Attack Submarine (nuclear propulsion)	SSN
Auxiliary Submarine	SSAG

AMPHIBIOUS WARFARE SHIPS
Amphibious Command Ship	LCC
Amphibious Assault Ship (multi-purpose)	LHA/LHD
Amphibious Cargo Ship	LKA
Amphibious Transport Dock	LPD
Amphibious Assault Ship (helicopter)	LPH
Dock Landing Ship	LSD
Logistic Support Vessel (Army)	LSV
Tank Landing Ship	LST

MINE WARFARE SHIPS
Mine Countermeasures Ship	MCM
Minehunter Coastal	MHC
Minesweeper Ocean	MSO
Minesweeping Boats	MSB

COMBATANT CRAFT

AMPHIBIOUS WARFARE CRAFT
Landing Craft, Air Cushion	LCAC
Landing Craft, Mechanised	LCM
Landing Craft, Personnel, Large	LCPL
Landing Craft, Utility	LCU
Landing Craft, Vehicle, Personnel	LCVP
Light Seal Support Craft	LSSC
Amphibious Warping Tug	LWT
Medium Seal Support Craft	MSSC
Swimmer Delivery Vehicle	SDV
Side Loading Warping Tug	SLWT
Special Warfare Craft, Light	SWCL
Special Warfare Craft, Medium	SWCM

MINE WARFARE CRAFT
Minesweeping Boat	MSB
Minesweeping, Drone	MSD

PATROL CRAFT
Mini-Armored Troop Carrier	ATC
Patrol Boat (Coastal)	PB(C)
River Patrol Boat	PBR
Patrol Craft	PC
Patrol Craft (fast)	PCF
Patrol Craft (Coastal)	PCC

AUXILIARY SHIPS
Destroyer Tender	AD
Ammunition Ship	AE
Combat Store Ship	AFS
Miscellaneous	AG
Deep Submergence Support Ship	AGDS
Hydrofoil Research Ship	AGEH
Miscellaneous Command Ship	AGF
Missile Range Instrumentation Ship	AGM
Oceanographic Research Ship	AGOR
Ocean Surveillance Ship	AGOS
Patrol Craft Tender	AGP
Surveying Ship	AGS
Auxiliary Research Submarine	AGSS
Hospital Ship	AH
Cargo Ship	AK
Vehicle Cargo Ship	AKR
Auxiliary Lighter	ALS
Oiler	AO
Fast Combat Support Ship	AOE
Gasoline Tanker	AOG
Replenishment Oiler	AOR
Transport Oiler	AOT
Transport	AP
Self-Propelled Barracks Ship	APB
Repair Ship	AR
Cable Repairing Ship	ARC
Repair Ship, Small	ARL
Salvage Ship	ARS
Submarine Tender	AS
Submarine Rescue Ship	ASR
Auxiliary Ocean Tug	ATA
Fleet Ocean Tug	ATF
Salvage and Rescue Ship	ATS
Guided Missile Ship	AVM
Auxiliary Aircraft Landing Training Ship	AVT

SERVICE CRAFT
Large Auxiliary Floating Dry Dock (non self-propelled)	AFDB
Small Auxiliary Floating Dry Dock (non self-propelled)	AFDL
Medium Auxiliary Floating Dry Dock (non self-propelled)	AFDM
Barracks Craft (non self-propelled)	APL
Auxiliary Repair Dry Dock (non self-propelled)	ARD
Medium Auxiliary Repair Dry Dock (non self-propelled)	ARDM
Deep Submergence Rescue Vehicle	DSRV
Deep Submergence Vehicle	DSV
Harbour Security Boats	HSB
Unclassified Miscellaneous	IX
Submersible Research Vehicle	NR
Miscellaneous Auxiliary (self-propelled)	YAG
Open Lighter (non self-propelled)	YC
Car Float (non self-propelled)	YCF
Aircraft Transportation Lighter (non self-propelled)	YCV
Floating Crane (non self-propelled)	YD
Diving Tender (non self-propelled)	YDT
Covered Lighter (self-propelled)	YF
Ferry Boat or Launch (self-propelled)	YFB
Yard Floating Dry Dock (non self-propelled)	YFD
Covered Lighter (non self-propelled)	YFN
Large Covered Lighter (non self-propelled)	YFNB
Dry Dock Companion Craft (non self-propelled)	YFND
Lighter (special purpose) (non self-propelled)	YFNX
Floating Power Barge (non self-propelled)	YFP
Refrigerated Covered Lighter (self-propelled)	YFR
Refrigerated Covered Lighter (non self-propelled)	YFRN
Covered Lighter (range tender) (self-propelled)	YFRT
Harbor Utility Craft (self-propelled)	YFU
Garbage Lighter (self-propelled)	YG
Garbage Lighter (non self-propelled)	YGN
Salvage Lift Craft, Heavy (non self-propelled)	YHLC
Dredge (self-propelled)	YM
Salvage Lift Craft, Medium (non self-propelled)	YMLC
Gate Craft (non self-propelled)	YNG
Fuel Oil Barge (self-propelled)	YO
Gasoline Barge (self-propelled)	YOG
Gasoline Barge (non self-propelled)	YOGN
Fuel Oil Barge (non self-propelled)	YON
Oil Storage Barge (non self-propelled)	YOS
Patrol Craft (self-propelled)	YP
Floating Pile Driver (non self-propelled)	YPD
Floating Workshop (non self-propelled)	YR
Repair and Berthing Barge (non self-propelled)	YRB
Repair, Berthing and Messing Barge (non self-propelled)	YRBM
Floating Dry Dock Workshop (hull) (non self-propelled)	YRDH
Floating Dry Dock Workshop (machine) (non self-propelled)	YRDM
Radiological Repair Barge (non self-propelled)	YRR
Salvage Craft Tender (non self-propelled)	YRST
Seaplane Wrecking Derrick (self-propelled)	YSD
Sludge Removal Barge (non self-propelled)	YSR
Large Harbour Tug	YTB
Small Harbour Tug	YTL
Medium Harbour Tug	YTM
Water Barge (self-propelled)	YW
Water Barge (non self-propelled)	YWN

Letter prefixes to classification symbols may be added for further identification. E: prototype ship in an experimental or developmental status. T: assigned to Military Sealift Command. F: being built for a foreign government. X: often added to existing classifications to indicate a new class whose characteristics have not been defined. N: denotes nuclear propulsion when used as last letter of ship symbol.

Classification Of Maritime Administration

Ship Designs

The US Maritime Administration is a Division of the US Department of Transportation. All US flag merchant vessels are built under the jurisdiction of the US Maritime Administration and are assigned Maritime Administration design classifications. These classifications consist of three groups of letters and numbers. A number of US Naval Auxiliaries were originally built to Maritime Administration specifications and were designed during construction or after the ship was completed. It should be noted that the Maritime Administration acts as a 'ship broker' for the US Government and does not build ships for itself. The Maritime Administration generally oversees the operation and administration of the US Merchant Marine.

Merchant Ship Design Classifications

Length in feet at load water line

Type	1	2	3	4
C Cargo	¶3C400	400-450	450-500	500-550
P Passenger	¶3C500	500-600	600-700	700-800
N Coastal Cargo	¶3C200	200-250	250-300	300-350
R Refrigerated Cargo	¶3C400	400-450	450-500	500-550
S Special (Navy)	¶3C200	200-300	300-400	400-500
T Tanker	¶3C450	450-500	500-550	550-600

Type of propulsion; number of propellers and passengers

	Single screw		Twin screw	
Passengers	1/12	13+	1/12	13+
Power				
Steam	S	S1	ST	S2
Motor (Diesel)	M	M1	MT	M2
Turbo-Electric	SE	SE1	SET	SE2

Example: C4-S-B1. C4: Cargo Ship between 500 and 550 ft long; S: steam powered; B1: 1st variation ('1') of the original design ('B'). If the third group of letters and numbers read BV1 instead of B1, the translation of the code would be, the 1st variation ('1') of the 22nd modification ('V') of the original design ('B').

Electronic Equipment Classification

The 'AN' nomenclature was designed so that a common designation could be used for Army, Navy and Air Force equipment. The system indicator 'AN' does not mean that the Army, Navy and Air Force use the equipment, but means that the type number was assigned in the 'AN' system.

'AN' nomenclature is assigned to complete sets of equipment and major components of military design; groups of articles of either commercial or military design which are grouped for military purposes; major articles of military design which are not part of or used with a set; and commercial articles when nomenclature will not facilitate military identification and/or procedures. 'AN' nomenclature is not assigned to articles catalogued commercially except as stated above; minor components of military design for which other adequate means of identification are available; small parts such as capacitors and resistors; and articles having other adequate identification in joint military specifications. Nomenclature assignments remain unchanged regardless of later installation and/or application.

Installation

A	Airborne (installed and operated in aircraft).
B	Underwater mobile, submarine.
C	Air transportable (inactivated, do not use).
D	Pilotless carrier.
F	Fixed.
G	Ground, general ground use (includes two or more ground-type installations).
K	Amphibious.
M	Ground, mobile (installed as operating unit in a vehicle which has no function other than transporting the equipment).
P	Pack or portable (animal or man).
S	Water surface craft.
T	Ground, transportable.
U	General utility (includes two or more general installation classes, airborne, shipboard, and ground).
V	Ground, vehicular (installed in vehicle designed for functions other than carrying electronic equipment, etc, such as tanks).
W	Water surface and underwater.

Type of Equipment

A Invisible light, heat radiation.
B Pigeon.
C Carrier.
D Radiac.
E Nupac.
F Photographic.
G Telegraph or teletype.
I Interphone and public address.
J Electromechanical or inertial wire covered.
K Telemetering.
L Countermeasures.
M Meteorological.
N Sound in air.
P Radar.
Q Sonar and underwater sound.
R Radio.
S Special types, magnetic, etc., or combinations of types.
T Telephone (wire).
V Visual and visible light.
W Armament (peculiar to armament, not otherwise covered).
X Facsimile or television.
Y Data processing.

Purpose

A Auxiliary assemblies (not complete operating sets used with or part of two or more sets or sets series).
B Bombing.
C Communications (receiving and transmitting).
D Direction finder, reconnaissance and/or surveillance.
E Ejection and/or release.
G Fire-control or searchlight directing.
H Recording and/or reproducing (graphic meteorological and sound).
K Computing.
L Searchlight control (inactivated, use G).
M Maintenance and test assemblies (including tools).
N Navigational aids (including altimeters, beacons, compasses, racons, depth sounding, approach, and landing).
P Reproducing (inactivated, do not use).
Q Special, or combination of purposes.
R Receiving, passive detecting.
S Detecting and/or range and bearing, search.
T Transmitting.
W Automatic flight or remote control.
X Identification and recognition.

Example: AN/URD-4A. AN: 'AN' System; U: General Utility; R: Radio; D: Direction Finder, Reconnaissance, and/or Surveillance; 4: Model Number; A: Modification Letter.

Major Commercial Shipyards

Avondale Industries, New Orleans, Louisiana
Avondale Gulfport, Gulfport, Mississippi
Bath Iron Works, Bath, Maine
Bethlehem Steel, Sparrows Point, Maryland
Bollinger Machine Shop and Shipyard, Lockport, Louisiana
Derecktor Shipyards, Middletown, Rhode Island
General Dynamics Corporation, Electric Boat Division, Groton, Connecticut
Halter Marine Inc, Moss Point, Mississippi
Ingalls Shipbuilding, Pascagoula, Mississippi
Intermarine USA, Savannah, Georgia
Marinette Marine, Marinette, Wisconsin
McDermott Shipyards, Morgan City, Louisiana
National Steel & Shipbuilding Company, San Diego, California
Newport News Shipbuilding Company, Newport News, Virginia
Peterson Builders Incorporated, Sturgeon Bay, Wisconsin
Tampa Shipyards, Tampa, Florida
Textron Marine Systems, New Orleans, Louisiana

Note: All the above yards have engaged in naval shipbuilding, overhaul, or modernisation except for the General Dynamics/Electric Boat yard which is engaged only in submarine work. Newport News is the only US shipyard capable of building nuclear-powered aircraft carriers.

Ships Scheduled for Delivery during FY 1993 (22)

Fleet Ballistic Missile Submarine: *Nebraska* (SSBN 739).
Attack Submarines: *Springfield* (SSN 761), *Columbus* (SSN 762).
Cruisers: *Vicksburg* (CG 69), *Lake Erie* (CG 70), *Cape St George* (CG 71), *Vella Gulf* (CG 72).
Guided Missile Destroyers: *John Barry* (DDG 52), *John Paul Jones* (DDG 53).
Amphibious Assault Ship: *Kearsage* (LHD 3).
Mine Countermeasures Ships: *Warrior* (MCM 10), *Gladiator* (MCM 11), *Ardent* (MCM 12).
Coastal Minehunter: *Osprey* (MHC 51).
Oceanographic Survey Ship: *Waters* (TAGS 45).
Oilers: *Tippecanoe* (TAO 199), *Guadalupe* (TAO 200).
Ocean Surveillance Ships: *Effective* (TAGOS 21), *Loyal* (TAGOS 22).
Coastal Patrol Craft: *Tempest* (PC 2), *Hurricane* (PC 3).
Combat Support Ship: *Supply* (AOE 6).

CONVERSIONS (2):
Aircraft Carrier: *Constellation* (CV 64).
Fleet Oiler (Jumbo): *Platte* (AO(J) 186).

Ships Scheduled for Delivery during FY 1994 (26)

Fleet Ballistic Missile Submarine: *Rhode Island* (SSBN 740).
Attack Submarines: *Santa Fe* (SSN 763), *Montpelier* (SSN 765), *Charlotte* (SSN 766).
Cruiser: *Port Royal* (CG 73).
Guided Missile Destroyers: *Curtis Wilber* (DDG 54), *Stout* (DDG 55), *John S McCain* (DDG 56), *Mischer* (DDG 57), *Laboon* (DDG 58).
Mine Countermeasures Ships: *Dextrous* (MCM 13), *Chief* (MCM 14).
Coastal Minehunters: *Heron* (MHC 52), *Pelican* (MHC 53).
Ocean Surveillance Ship (SURTASS): *Impeccable* (TAGOS 23).
Oilers: *Benjamin Isherwood* (TAO 191), *Henry Eckford* (TAO 192), *Yukon* (TAO 202).
Coastal Patrol Boats: *Monsoon* (PC 4), *Typhoon* (PC 5), *Sirocco* (PC 6), *Squall* (PC 7), *Zephyr* (PC 8), *Chinook* (PC 9), *Firebolt* (PC 10).
Combat Support Ship: *Rainier* (AOE 7).

Major Warships Taken Out of Service mid-1990 to mid-1993

SSBN
1990 *James Monroe, Henry Clay, Lafayette, Daniel Webster* (training ship)
1991 *Lewis and Clark, George C Marshall*
1992 *Alexander Hamilton, Ulysses S Grant, George Washington, Carver, Will Rodgers, James Madison, Henry L Stimson*
1993 *Woodrow Wilson, Tecumseh, Benjamin Franklin, Francis Scott Key*

SSN
1990 *Plunger, Shark, Barb, Jack, Skipjack, Skulpin*
1991 *Permit, Tinosa, Guardfish, Haddo, Lapon, Guitarro, Queenfish, Sea Devil*
1992 *John Marshall, Gato, Haddock, Flasher, Greenling, Ray*

SS
1990 *Blueback*

CV
1990 *Coral Sea*
1991 *Midway, Lexington*
1993 *Ranger*

BB
1990 *Iowa*
1991 *Wisconsin, New Jersey*
1992 *Missouri*

DDG
1990 *Dewey, Joseph Strauss* (to Greece), *John King, Lawrence, Byrd, Barney, Towers, Conyngham, Cochrane, Hoel*
1991 *Luce, King, Sampson, Tattnall, William V Pratt, Preble, Lynde McCormick, Robison, Buchanan, Semmes* (to Greece), *Benjamin Stoddert*
1992 *Charles F Adams, Dahlgren, Goldsborough, Waddell* (to Greece), *Berkeley* (to Greece)
1993 *MacDonough*

FF/FFG
1990 *Bronstein, McCloy, Glover* (to MSC)
1991 *Roark, Gray, Hepburn, Meyerkord, W S Sims, Lang, Patterson, Bagley, Badger, Blakely, Barbey, Miller, Valdez*
1992 *Knox, Connole, Rathburne, Whipple, Reasoner, Stein, Francis Hammond, Vreeland* (to Greece), *Downes, Robert E Peary* (to Taiwan), *Harold E Holt, Trippe* (to Greece), *Paul, Aylwin, Brewton* (to Taiwan), *Pharris*
1993 *Kirk* (to Taiwan), *Lockwood, Marvin Shields, Fanning, Ouellet, Elmer Montgomery, Cook, Thomas C Hart, Capodanno*

LSD/LPD/LST
1990 *Alamo* (Brazil)
1991 *Raleigh*
1992 *Vancouver, Barbour County, Newport, Charleston*
1993 *Manitowoc, Sumter, Saint Louis, Iwo Jima, Okinawa*

MSO/MSB
1990 *Fearless, Illusive, Inflict, Pluck, Esteem*
1991 *Adroit, Engage, Enhance, Impervious, Leader*
1992 *Constant, Excel, Exploit, Fortify*, 7 MSBs

Auxiliaries
1990 *Robert D Conrad* (AGOR), *Mispillion* (AO)
1991 *Vulcan* (AR), *Fulton* (AS), *Petrel* (ASR), *Florikan* (ASR), *Lynch* (AGOR), *H H Hess* (AGS), *Mississinewa* (AO), *Hassayampa* (AO), *Truckee* (AO), *Navasota* (AO), *Passumpsic* (AO), *Pawcatuck* (AO), *Waccamaw* (AO), *Neptune* (ARC)
1992 *Prairie* (AD), *Concord* (AFS) (to MSC), *Wichita* (AOR), *Milwaukee* (AOR), *Preserver* (ARS), *Orion* (AS), *Proteus* (AS), *Pigeon* (ASR), *Sunbird* (ASR), *Paiute* (ATF), *Papago* (ATF), *Vanguard* (AG), *Rigel* (AF), *Destiguer* (AGOR) (to Tunisia), *Thomas Washington* (AGOR) (to Chile), *S P Lee* (AG) (to Mexico), *Adventurous* (AGOS) (to NOAA)
1993 *Mars* (AFS) (to MSC), *Point Loma* (AGDS), *Glover* (AGFF), *Stalwart* (AGOS), *Contender* (AGOS), *Indomitable* (AGOS), *Chauvenet* (AGS), *Harkness* (AGS), *Marshfield* (AK), *Neosho* (AO), *Kawishiwi* (AO), *Ponchatoula* (AO)

HULL NUMBERS

Note: Ships in reserve not included.

SUBMARINES

Ballistic Missile Submarines

James Madison class
SSBN 629 Daniel Boone
SSBN 630 John C Calhoun
SSBN 632 Von Steuben
SSBN 633 Casimir Pulaski
SSBN 634 Stonewall Jackson

Benjamin Franklin class
SSBN 641 Simon Bolivar
SSBN 643 George Bancroft
SSBN 658 Mariano G Vallejo

Ohio class
SSBN 726 Ohio
SSBN 727 Michigan
SSBN 728 Florida
SSBN 729 Georgia
SSBN 730 Henry M Jackson
SSBN 731 Alabama
SSBN 732 Alaska
SSBN 733 Nevada
SSBN 734 Tennessee
SSBN 735 Pennsylvania
SSBN 736 West Virginia
SSBN 737 Kentucky
SSBN 738 Maryland
SSBN 739 Nebraska
SSBN 740 Rhode Island
SSBN 741 Maine
SSBN 742 Wyoming
SSBN 743 Louisiana

Attack Submarines

Benjamin Franklin class
SSN 642 Kamehameha
SSN 645 James K Polk

Seawolf class
SSN 21 Seawolf
SSN 22 Connecticut

Sturgeon class
SSN 637 Sturgeon
SSN 638 Whale
SSN 639 Tautog
SSN 646 Grayling
SSN 647 Pogy
SSN 648 Aspro
SSN 649 Sunfish
SSN 650 Pargo
SSN 652 Puffer
SSN 660 Sand Lance
SSN 662 Gurnard
SSN 663 Hammerhead
SSN 666 Hawkbill
SSN 667 Bergall
SSN 668 Spadefish
SSN 669 Seahorse
SSN 670 Finback
SSN 672 Pintado
SSN 673 Flying Fish
SSN 674 Trepang
SSN 675 Bluefish
SSN 676 Billfish
SSN 677 Drum
SSN 678 Archerfish
SSN 679 Silversides
SSN 680 William H Bates
SSN 681 Batfish
SSN 682 Tunny
SSN 683 Parche
SSN 684 Cavalla
SSN 686 L Mendel Rivers
SSN 687 Richard B Russell

Narwhal class
SSN 671 Narwhal

Los Angeles class
SSN 688 Los Angeles
SSN 689 Baton Rouge
SSN 690 Philadelphia
SSN 691 Memphis
SSN 692 Omaha
SSN 693 Cincinnati
SSN 694 Groton
SSN 695 Birmingham
SSN 696 New York City
SSN 697 Indianapolis
SSN 698 Bremerton
SSN 699 Jacksonville
SSN 700 Dallas
SSN 701 La Jolla
SSN 702 Phoenix
SSN 703 Boston
SSN 704 Baltimore
SSN 705 City of Corpus Christi
SSN 706 Albuquerque
SSN 707 Portsmouth
SSN 708 Minneapolis—Saint Paul
SSN 709 Hyman G Rickover
SSN 710 Augusta
SSN 711 San Francisco
SSN 712 Atlanta
SSN 713 Houston
SSN 714 Norfolk
SSN 715 Buffalo

Introduction / USA

SSN 716 Salt Lake City
SSN 717 Olympia
SSN 718 Honolulu
SSN 719 Providence
SSN 720 Pittsburgh
SSN 721 Chicago
SSN 722 Key West
SSN 723 Oklahoma City
SSN 724 Louisville
SSN 725 Helena
SSN 750 Newport News
SSN 751 San Juan
SSN 752 Pasadena
SSN 753 Albany
SSN 754 Topeka
SSN 755 Miami
SSN 756 Scranton
SSN 757 Alexandria
SSN 758 Asheville
SSN 759 Jefferson City
SSN 760 Annapolis
SSN 761 Springfield
SSN 762 Columbus
SSN 763 Santa Fe
SSN 764 Boise
SSN 765 Montpelier
SSN 766 Charlotte
SSN 767 Hampton
SSN 768 Hartford
SSN 769 Toledo
SSN 770 Tucson
SSN 771 Columbia
SSN 772 Greeneville
SSN 773 Cheyenne

SURFACE COMBATANTS

Aircraft Carriers

Forrestal class
AVT 59 Forrestal
CV 60 Saratoga
CV 62 Independence

Kitty Hawk class
CV 63 Kitty Hawk
CV 64 Constellation
CV 66 America

John F Kennedy class
CV 67 John F Kennedy

Enterprise class
CVN 65 Enterprise

Nimitz class
CVN 68 Nimitz
CVN 69 Dwight D Eisenhower
CVN 70 Carl Vinson
CVN 71 Theodore Roosevelt
CVN 72 Abraham Lincoln
CVN 73 George Washington
CVN 74 John C Stennis
CVN 75 United States

Cruisers

Leahy class
CG 16 Leahy
CG 17 Harry E Yarnell
CG 18 Worden
CG 19 Dale
CG 20 Richmond K Turner
CG 21 Gridley
CG 22 England
CG 23 Halsey
CG 24 Reeves

Belknap class
CG 26 Belknap
CG 27 Josephus Daniels
CG 28 Wainwright
CG 29 Jouett
CG 30 Horne
CG 31 Sterett
CG 32 William H Standley
CG 33 Fox
CG 34 Biddle

Ticonderoga class
CG 47 Ticonderoga
CG 48 Yorktown
CG 49 Vincennes
CG 50 Valley Forge
CG 51 Thomas S Gates
CG 52 Bunker Hill
CG 53 Mobile Bay
CG 54 Antietam
CG 55 Leyte Gulf
CG 56 San Jacinto
CG 57 Lake Champlain
CG 58 Philippine Sea
CG 59 Princeton
CG 60 Normandy
CG 61 Monterey
CG 62 Chancellorsville
CG 63 Cowpens
CG 64 Gettysburg
CG 65 Chosin
CG 66 Hue City
CG 67 Shiloh
CG 68 Anzio
CG 69 Vicksburg
CG 70 Lake Erie
CG 71 Cape St George
CG 72 Vella Gulf
CG 73 Port Royal

Long Beach class
CGN 9 Long Beach

Bainbridge class
CGN 25 Bainbridge

Truxtun class
CGN 35 Truxtun

California class
CGN 36 California
CGN 37 South Carolina

Virginia class
CGN 38 Virginia
CGN 39 Texas
CGN 40 Mississippi
CGN 41 Arkansas

Destroyers

Spruance class
DD 963 Spruance
DD 964 Paul F Foster
DD 965 Kinkaid
DD 966 Hewitt
DD 967 Elliott
DD 968 Arthur W Radford
DD 969 Peterson
DD 970 Caron
DD 971 David R Ray
DD 972 Oldendorf
DD 973 John Young
DD 974 Comte de Grasse
DD 975 O'Brien
DD 976 Merrill
DD 977 Briscoe
DD 978 Stump
DD 979 Conolly
DD 980 Moosbrugger
DD 981 John Hancock
DD 982 Nicholson
DD 983 John Rodgers
DD 984 Leftwich
DD 985 Cushing
DD 986 Harry W Hill
DD 987 O'Bannon
DD 988 Thorn
DD 989 Deyo
DD 990 Ingersoll
DD 991 Fife
DD 992 Fletcher
DD 997 Hayler

Coontz class
DDG 42 Mahan

Arleigh Burke class
DDG 51 Arleigh Burke
DDG 52 Barry
DDG 53 John Paul Jones
DDG 54 Curtis Wilbur
DDG 55 Stout
DDG 56 John S McCain
DDG 57 Mitscher
DDG 58 Laboon
DDG 59 Russell
DDG 60 Paul Hamilton
DDG 61 Ramage
DDG 62 Fitzgerald
DDG 63 Stethem
DDG 64 Carney
DDG 65 Benfold
DDG 66 Gonzalez
DDG 67 Cole
DDG 68 Hopper
DDG 69 Milius

Kidd class
DDG 993 Kidd
DDG 994 Callaghan
DDG 995 Scott
DDG 996 Chandler

Frigates

Knox class
FFT 1078 Joseph Hewes
FFT 1079 Bowen
FFT 1084 McCandless
FFT 1085 Donald B Beary
FFT 1089 Jesse L Brown
FFT 1090 Ainsworth
FFT 1095 Truett
FFT 1097 Moinester

Oliver Hazard Perry class
FFG 7 Oliver Hazard Perry
FFG 8 McInerney
FFG 9 Wadsworth
FFG 10 Duncan
FFG 11 Clark
FFG 12 George Philip
FFG 13 Samuel Eliot Morison
FFG 14 John H Sides
FFG 15 Estocin
FFG 16 Clifton Sprague
FFG 19 John A Moore
FFG 20 Antrim
FFG 21 Flatley
FFG 22 Fahrion
FFG 23 Lewis B Puller
FFG 24 Jack Williams
FFG 25 Copeland
FFG 26 Gallery
FFG 27 Mahlon S Tisdale
FFG 28 Boone
FFG 29 Stephen W Groves
FFG 30 Reid
FFG 31 Stark
FFG 32 John L Hall
FFG 33 Jarrett
FFG 34 Aubrey Fitch
FFG 36 Underwood
FFG 37 Crommelin
FFG 38 Curts
FFG 39 Doyle
FFG 40 Halyburton
FFG 41 McClusky
FFG 42 Klakring
FFG 43 Thach
FFG 45 De Wert
FFG 46 Rentz
FFG 47 Nicholas
FFG 48 Vandegrift
FFG 49 Robert G Bradley
FFG 50 Taylor
FFG 51 Gary
FFG 52 Carr
FFG 53 Hawes
FFG 54 Ford
FFG 55 Elrod
FFG 56 Simpson
FFG 57 Reuben James
FFG 58 Samuel B Roberts
FFG 59 Kauffman
FFG 60 Rodney M Davis
FFG 61 Ingraham

Hydrofoil Missile Ships

Pegasus class
PHM 1 Pegasus
PHM 2 Hercules
PHM 3 Taurus
PHM 4 Aquila
PHM 5 Aries
PHM 6 Gemini

Coastal Patrol Craft

Cyclone class
PC 1 Cyclone
PC 2 Tempest
PC 3 Hurricane
PC 4 Monsoon
PC 5 Typhoon
PC 6 Sirocco
PC 7 Squall
PC 8 Zephyr

AMPHIBIOUS WARFARE SHIPS

Amphibious Assault Ships

Wasp class
LHD 1 Wasp
LHD 2 Essex
LHD 3 Kearsage
LHD 4 Boxer
LHD 5 Bataan
LHD 6 Bonhomme Richard

Tarawa class
LHA 1 Tarawa
LHA 2 Saipan
LHA 3 Belleau Wood
LHA 4 Nassau
LHA 5 Peleliu

Iwo Jima class
LPH 7 Guadalcanal
LPH 9 Guam
LPH 10 Tripoli
LPH 11 New Orleans
LPH 12 Inchon

Amphibious Transport Docks

Austin class
LPD 4 Austin
LPD 5 Ogden
LPD 6 Duluth
LPD 7 Cleveland
LPD 8 Dubuque
LPD 9 Denver
LPD 10 Juneau
LPD 12 Shreveport
LPD 13 Nashville
LPD 14 Trenton
LPD 15 Ponce

Amphibious Cargo Ships

Charleston class
LKA 114 Durham
LKA 115 Mobile
LKA 117 El Paso

Anchorage class
LSD 36 Anchorage
LSD 37 Portland
LSD 38 Pensacola
LSD 39 Mount Vernon
LSD 40 Fort Fisher

Whidbey Island class
LSD 41 Whidbey Island
LSD 42 Germantown
LSD 43 Fort McHenry
LSD 44 Gunston Hall
LSD 45 Comstock
LSD 46 Tortuga
LSD 47 Rushmore
LSD 48 Ashland
LSD 49 Harpers Ferry
LSD 50 Carter Hall
LSD 51 Oak Hill

Tank Landing Ships

Newport class
LST 1182 Fresno
LST 1183 Peoria
LST 1184 Frederick
LST 1185 Schenectady
LST 1186 Cayuga
LST 1187 Tuscaloosa
LST 1188 Saginaw
LST 1189 San Bernardino
LST 1190 Boulder
LST 1191 Racine
LST 1192 Spartanburg County
LST 1193 Fairfax County
LST 1194 La Moure County
LST 1196 Harlan County
LST 1197 Barnstable County
LST 1198 Bristol County

Amphibious Command Ships

Blue Ridge class
LCC 19 Blue Ridge
LCC 20 Mount Whitney

MINE WARFARE SHIPS

Ocean Minesweepers

Aggressive class
MSO 441 Exultant
MSO 455 Implicit
MSO 488 Conquest
MSO 489 Gallant
MSO 492 Pledge

Acme class
MSO 511 Affray

Mine Countermeasures Ships

Avenger class
MCM 1 Avenger
MCM 2 Defender
MCM 3 Sentry
MCM 4 Champion
MCM 5 Guardian
MCM 6 Devastator
MCM 7 Patriot
MCM 8 Scout
MCM 9 Pioneer
MCM 10 Warrior
MCM 11 Gladiator
MCM 12 Ardent
MCM 13 Dextrous
MCM 14 Chief

Osprey class
MHC 51 Osprey
MHC 52 Heron
MHC 53 Pelican
MHC 54 Robin
MHC 55 Oriole
MHC 56 Kingfisher
MHC 57 Cormorant
MHC 58 Black Hawk
MHC 59 Falcon
MHC 60 Cardinal

UNDERWAY REPLENISHMENT SHIPS

Ammunition Ships

Suribachi class
AE 21 Suribachi
AE 22 Mauna Kea

Nitro class
AE 23 Nitro
AE 24 Pyro
AE 25 Haleakala

Kilauea class
AE 27 Butte
AE 28 Santa Barbara
AE 29 Mount Hood
AE 32 Flint
AE 33 Shasta
AE 34 Mount Baker
AE 35 Kiska

Combat Stores Ships

Mars class
AFS 2 Sylvania
AFS 3 Niagara Falls
AFS 4 White Plains
AFS 6 San Diego
AFS 7 San Jose

Fleet Oilers

Cimarron class
- AO 177 Cimarron
- AO 178 Monongahela
- AO 179 Merrimack
- AO 180 Willamette
- AO 186 Platte

Fast Combat Support Ships

Sacramento class
- AOE 1 Sacramento
- AOE 2 Camden
- AOE 3 Seattle
- AOE 4 Detroit

Supply class
- AOE 6 Supply
- AOE 7 Rainier
- AOE 8 Arctic
- AOE 10 Bridge

Replenishment Oilers

Wichita class
- AOR 3 Kansas City
- AOR 4 Savannah
- AOR 5 Wabash
- AOR 6 Kalamazoo
- AOR 7 Roanoke

MATERIAL SUPPORT SHIPS

Destroyer Tenders

Dixie class
- AD 18 Sierra
- AD 19 Yosemite

Samuel Gompers class
- AD 37 Samuel Gompers
- AD 38 Puget Sound

Yellowstone class
- AD 41 Yellowstone
- AD 42 Acadia
- AD 43 Cape Cod
- AD 44 Shenandoah

Repair Ship

Vulcan class
- AR 8 Jason

Submarine Tenders

Hunley class
- AS 31 Hunley
- AS 32 Holland

Simon Lake class
- AS 33 Simon Lake
- AS 34 Canopus

Spear class
- AS 36 L Y Spear
- AS 37 Dixon

Emory S Land class
- AS 39 Emory S Land
- AS 40 Frank Cable
- AS 41 McKee

Salvage Ships

Bolster class
- ARS 8 Preserver
- ARS 38 Bolster
- ARS 39 Conserver
- ARS 40 Hoist
- ARS 41 Opportune
- ARS 42 Reclaimer
- ARS 43 Recovery

Safeguard class
- ARS 50 Safeguard
- ARS 51 Grasp
- ARS 52 Salvor
- ARS 53 Grapple

Edenton class
- ATS 1 Edenton
- ATS 2 Beaufort
- ATS 3 Brunswick

Submarine Rescue Ships

Chanticleer class
- ASR 13 Kittiwake

Pigeon class
- ASR 22 Ortolan

SHIPS WITH MISCELLANEOUS MISSIONS

Miscellaneous Flagships

Raleigh and Austin classes
- AGF 3 La Salle
- AGF 11 Coronado

Auxiliary Research Submarine

Dolphin class
- AGSS 555 Dolphin

SHIPS OF THE MILITARY SEALIFT COMMAND

(These ships, when operational, are manned by civilian crews, and carry the prefix 'T' before their normal Hull Numbers)

NAVAL FLEET AUXILIARY FORCE

Fleet Ballistic Missile Support Ship

- TAK 286 Vega

Ammunition Ship

- TAE 26 Kilauea

Combat Stores Ships

- TAFS 1 Mars
- TAFS 5 Concord
- TAFS 8 Sirius
- TAFS 9 Spica
- TAFS 10 Saturn

Oilers

Henry J Kaiser class
- TAO 187 Henry J Kaiser
- TAO 188 Joshua Humphreys
- TAO 189 John Lenthall
- TAO 190 Andrew J Higgins
- TAO 191 Benjamin Isherwood
- TAO 192 Henry Eckford
- TAO 193 Walter S Diehl
- TAO 194 John Ericsson
- TAO 195 Leroy Grumman
- TAO 196 Kanawha
- TAO 197 Pecos
- TAO 198 Big Horn
- TAO 199 Tippicanoe
- TAO 200 Guadalupe
- TAO 201 Patuxent
- TAO 202 Yukon
- TAO 203 Laramie
- TAO 204 Rappahannock

Fleet Ocean Tugs

Powhatan class
- TATF 166 Powhatan
- TATF 167 Narragansett
- TATF 168 Catawba
- TATF 169 Navajo
- TATF 170 Mohawk
- TATF 171 Sioux
- TATF 172 Apache

Ocean Surveillance Ships

- TAGOS 3 Vindicator
- TAGOS 4 Triumph
- TAGOS 5 Assurance
- TAGOS 6 Persistent
- TAGOS 8 Prevail
- TAGOS 9 Assertive
- TAGOS 10 Invincible
- TAGOS 11 Audacious
- TAGOS 12 Bold
- TAGOS 14 Worthy
- TAGOS 15 Titan
- TAGOS 16 Capable
- TAGOS 17 Intrepid
- TAGOS 18 Relentless

Ocean Surveillance Ships (SWATH)

- TAGOS 19 Victorious
- TAGOS 20 Able
- TAGOS 21 Effective
- TAGOS 22 Loyal
- TAGOS 23 Impeccable
- TAGOS 24 Integrity

STRATEGIC SEALIFT (Active)

Maritime Prepositioning Ships (MPS)

(These 13 ships are divided into three squadrons and are almost constantly underway. Each squadron contains the equipment and 30 days of supplies for a marine amphibious brigade.)

- TAK 3000 Cpl Louis J Hauge Jr
- TAK 3001 Pfc William B Baugh
- TAK 3002 Pfc James Anderson Jr
- TAK 3003 1st Lt Alexander Bonnyman
- TAK 3004 Pvt Franklin J Phillips
- TAK 3005 Sgt Matej Kocak
- TAK 3006 Pfc Eugene A Obregon
- TAK 3007 Maj Stephen W Pless
- TAK 3008 2nd Lt John P Bobo
- TAK 3009 Pfc Dewayne T Williams
- TAK 3010 1st Lt Baldomero Lopez
- TAK 3011 1st Lt Jack Lummus
- TAK 3012 Staff Sgt William R Button

Prepositioning (PREPO) Ships

Lash
- TAKB 924 Jeb Stuart
- TAK 2043 American Kestrel
- TAK 2046 Austral Rainbow
- TAK 2049 Green Valley
- TAK 2064 Green Harbour

Freighters
- TAK 322 Buffalo Soldier
- TAK 323 American Merlin
- TAK 2062 American Cormorant
- — Strong Virginian

Tankers
- TAOT 181 Potomac
- TAOT 5075 American Osprey

Ocean Transportation Ships

Additional ships come and go as needed to meet MSC commitments. Types of vessel include Ro-Ro, Freighters, Tankers and Combination ships.

Tankers
- TAOT 168 Sealift Pacific
- TAOT 169 Sealift Arabian Sea
- TAOT 170 Sealift South China Sea
- TAOT 171 Sealift Indian Ocean
- TAOT 172 Sealift Atlantic
- TAOT 173 Sealift Mediterranean
- TAOT 174 Sealift Caribbean
- TAOT 175 Sealift Arctic
- TAOT 176 Sealift Antarctic

- TAOT 1121 Gus W Darnell
- TAOT 1122 Paul Buck
- TAOT 1123 Samuel L Cobb
- TAOT 1124 Richard G Matthieson
- TAOT 1125 Lawrence H Gianella

STRATEGIC SEALIFT (Reserve)

Fast Sealift Ships

(These ships are maintained in a high state of readiness for deployment with equipment for a full Army division, but have only skeleton crews except when assigned to specific missions.)

- TAKR 287 Algol
- TAKR 288 Bellatrix
- TAKR 289 Denebola
- TAKR 290 Pollux
- TAKR 291 Altair
- TAKR 292 Regulus
- TAKR 293 Capella
- TAKR 294 Antares

Aviation Support Ships

- TAVB 3 Wright
- TAVB 4 Curtiss

Hospital Ships

- TAH 19 Mercy
- TAH 20 Comfort

SPECIAL MISSION SUPPORT SHIPS

Missile Range Instrumentation Ships

- TAGM 20 Redstone
- TAGM 22 Range Sentinel
- TAGM 23 Observation Island

Oceanographic Research Ships

(Note: Those on loan are not MSC ships)

- TAGOR 13 Bartlett
- AGOR 14 Melville (loan)
- AGOR 15 Knorr (loan)
- AGOR 21 Gyre (loan)
- AGOR 22 Moana Wave (loan)
- AGOR 23 Thomas G Thompson (loan)
- AGOR 24 Revelle (bldg)
- TAG 195 Hayes

Surveying Ships

- TAGS 26 Silas Bent
- TAGS 27 Kane
- TAGS 33 Wilkes
- TAGS 34 Wyman
- TAGS 39 Maury
- TAGS 40 Tanner
- TAGS 45 Waters
- TAGS 51 John McDonnell
- TAGS 52 Littlehales
- TAGS 60 Pathfinder
- TAGS 61 Sumner

Navigation Research Ship

- TAG 194 Vanguard

Cable Repair Ships

- TARC 6 Albert J Myer
- TARC 7 Zeus

Ready Reserve Force (RRF)

(See pages 818/819.)

SUBMARINES

Strategic Missile Submarines (SSBN)

Notes: 1. Trident: The Trident fitted SSBN force provides the principle US strategic deterrent. Land and air based systems have been sharply reduced since 1991. The current treaty which is being considered for ratification is the Strategic Arms Reduction Treaty (START). The second treaty resulting from the Washington Summit Agreement of June 1992 is called START II. If ratified, START will limit to eight the number of re-entry bodies (RBs) attributed to each SSBN launch tube associated with the Trident I (C4) and the Trident II (D5) missiles. Under START II the total number of SLBM RBs is limited first to 2160 and then to 1750, with the reductions to be accomplished in two stages. This limit will be achieved by declaring launch tubes aboard SSBNs as attributed with a certain number of RBs. This tube limit must be uniform for each weapon system and/or for each coast. The whole force comes under the US Strategic Command Headquarters at Offutt Air Force Base, Nebraska. Submarines are essentially in constant communications, and speed of response is equivalent to that of ground-based silos. Trident missile accuracy is as good as ground-based systems and the warhead has a 50 per cent higher yield than the most lethal ICBM.
2. Strategic Cruise Missiles: A canister version of the Tomahawk SLCM is carried in submarines. This is an underwater-launched weapon with ram-jet propulsion which can deliver nuclear warheads to a range of approximately 2500 km *(1400 nm)*. A shorter range version of the weapon with a conventional warhead has a land attack capability of 900 km *(485 nm)* which is increased by more than 30 per cent in the Block III version approved for production in early 1992. The strategic cruise missile has a low-level, terrain-following flight path over land, much like that of a manned bomber in contrast to the ballistic trajectory of a Polaris/Poseidon/Trident missile. In September 1991 all nuclear capable Tomahawks were removed from both submarines and surface ships.
3. Names: When the Polaris submarine programme was initiated, ballistic missile submarines were named after 'distinguished Americans who were known for their devotion to freedom'. Included as 'Americans' were Latin American and Hawaiian leaders, and several Europeans who supported the American fight for independence. In 1976 the SSBN name source was changed to States of the Union, although an exception was made in September 1983 when the selected name of SSBN 730 was changed from *Rhode Island* to *Henry M Jackson*. Jackson was a long time Senator from the State of Washington, a presidential candidate in 1976 and one of the most vigorous and outspoken advocates of a strong national defence.

13 + 5 OHIO CLASS (SSBN)

Name	No	Builders	Launched	Commissioned	F/S
OHIO	SSBN 726	General Dynamics (Electric Boat Div)	7 Apr 1979	11 Nov 1981	PA
MICHIGAN	SSBN 727	General Dynamics (Electric Boat Div)	26 Apr 1980	11 Sep 1982	PA
FLORIDA	SSBN 728	General Dynamics (Electric Boat Div)	14 Nov 1981	18 June 1983	PA
GEORGIA	SSBN 729	General Dynamics (Electric Boat Div)	6 Nov 1982	11 Feb 1984	PA
HENRY M JACKSON	SSBN 730	General Dynamics (Electric Boat Div)	15 Oct 1983	6 Oct 1984	PA
ALABAMA	SSBN 731	General Dynamics (Electric Boat Div)	19 May 1984	25 May 1985	PA
ALASKA	SSBN 732	General Dynamics (Electric Boat Div)	12 Jan 1985	25 Jan 1986	PA
NEVADA	SSBN 733	General Dynamics (Electric Boat Div)	14 Sep 1985	16 Aug 1986	PA
TENNESSEE	SSBN 734	General Dynamics (Electric Boat Div)	13 Dec 1986	17 Dec 1988	AA
PENNSYLVANIA	SSBN 735	General Dynamics (Electric Boat Div)	23 Apr 1988	9 Sep 1989	AA
WEST VIRGINIA	SSBN 736	General Dynamics (Electric Boat Div)	14 Oct 1989	20 Oct 1990	AA
KENTUCKY	SSBN 737	General Dynamics (Electric Boat Div)	11 Aug 1990	13 July 1991	AA
MARYLAND	SSBN 738	General Dynamics (Electric Boat Div)	10 Aug 1991	13 June 1992	AA
NEBRASKA	SSBN 739	General Dynamics (Electric Boat Div)	15 Aug 1992	July 1993	Bldg/AA
RHODE ISLAND	SSBN 740	General Dynamics (Electric Boat Div)	July 1993	July 1994	Bldg
MAINE	SSBN 741	General Dynamics (Electric Boat Div)	July 1994	July 1995	Bldg
WYOMING	SSBN 742	General Dynamics (Electric Boat Div)	July 1995	Aug 1996	Bldg
LOUISIANA	SSBN 743	General Dynamics (Electric Boat Div)	Sep 1996	Aug 1997	Bldg

Displacement, tons: 16 600 surfaced; 18 750 dived
Dimensions, feet (metres): 560 × 42 × 36.4 *(170.7 × 12.8 × 11.1)*
Main machinery: Nuclear; 1 GE PWR S8G; 2 turbines; 60 000 hp *(44.8 MW)*; 1 shaft; 1 Magnetek auxiliary prop motor; 325 hp *(242 kW)*
Speed, knots: 20+ dived
Complement: 155 (14 officers in first 6, 15 in remainder)

Missiles: SLBM: 24 Lockheed Trident I (C4) (726-733); stellar inertial guidance to 7400 km *(4000 nm)*; thermonuclear warhead of 8 MIRV of 100 kT or 6 MARV of 100 kT; CEP 450 m. The Mk 500 MARV (Manoeuvring Re-entry Vehicle) is under development to demonstrate its compatibility with the Trident I missile. This re-entry vehicle is intended to evade ABM interceptor missiles.
24 Lockheed Trident II (D5) (734 onwards); stellar inertial guidance to 12 000 km *(6500 nm)*; thermonuclear warhead of 12 MIRV of 150 kT or 7 MARV of 300-475 kT; CEP 90 m. See note on START at head of section.
Torpedoes: 4—21 in *(533 mm)* Mk 68 bow tubes. Gould Mk 48; wire-guided (option); active/passive homing to 50 km *(27 nm)*/38 km *(21 nm)* at 40/55 kts; warhead 267 kg; depth to 900 m *(2950 ft)*.
Countermeasures: Decoys: 8 launchers for Emerson Electric Mk 2; torpedo decoy.
ESM: WLR-8(V)5; intercept.
Combat data systems: CCS Mk 2 Mod 3 with UYK 43/UYK 44 computers.
Fire control: Mk 118 digital torpedo fire control system. Mk 98 missile control system.
Radars: Surface search/navigation/fire control: BPS 15A; I/J band.
Sonars: IBM BQQ 6; passive search.
Raytheon BQS 13; spherical array for BQQ 6.
Ametek BQS 15; active/passive for close contacts; high frequency.
Western Electric BQR 15 (with BQQ 9 signal processor); passive towed array.
Raytheon BQR 19; active for navigation; high frequency.

Programmes: The 'date laid down' column has been deleted in this case as being irrelevant because there is a great amount of pre-fabrication before the various sections are joined on the building ways. The lead submarine was contracted to the Electric Boat Division of the General Dynamics Corp (Groton, Connecticut) on 25 July 1974. Newport News Shipbuilding failed in its bid to win a contract for construction of the FY 1987 ship and has not bid on later ships.
Structure: The size of the Trident submarine is dictated primarily by the 24 vertically launched Trident missiles and the larger reactor plant to drive the ship. The reactor has a nuclear core life of about nine years between refuellings. Diving depth is 300 m *(984 ft)*.
Operational: The Extremely Low Frequency (ELF) communications system became operational in 1986 at Michigan and in 1991 at Wisconsin enabling SSBNs to receive signals at greater depths and higher speeds than before although the data rate of ELF is much less than VLF. Each submarine has two Mk 2 Ship's Inertial Navigation Systems.
Pacific Fleet units with C4 missiles are based at Bangor, Washington, while the D5 submarines in the Atlantic Fleet are based at King's Bay, Georgia. The base structure permits bringing in ships of the Ohio class after 70 days at sea, accomplishing necessary, and sometimes very significant, voyage repairs, and sending them back to sea in 25 days. That schedule allows keeping these ships at sea, from commissioning to decommissioning, 66% of the time, including shipyard overhauls. The latter will be at nine year intervals. After two failed tests of the D-5 missile at sea early in 1989, modifications were made leading to eight successful tests from *Tennessee* and her first operational deployment started in March 1990. The original plan to retrofit D-5 missiles into the first eight of the class may not go ahead unless the threat posed by Russian strategic forces is revived.

WEST VIRGINIA 10/1991, Giorgio Arra

WEST VIRGINIA 10/1991, Giorgio Arra

10 BENJAMIN FRANKLIN and JAMES MADISON CLASSES (SSBN and SSN)

Name	No	Builders	Laid down	Launched	Commissioned	F/S
DANIEL BOONE	SSBN 629	Mare Island Naval Shipyard	6 Feb 1962	22 June 1963	23 Apr 1964	AA
JOHN C CALHOUN	SSBN 630	Newport News Shipbuilding & D D Co	4 June 1962	22 June 1963	15 Sep 1964	AA
VON STEUBEN	SSBN 632	Newport News Shipbuilding & D D Co	4 Sep 1962	18 Oct 1963	30 Sep 1964	AA
CASIMIR PULASKI	SSBN 633	General Dynamics (Electric Boat Div)	12 Jan 1963	1 Feb 1964	14 Aug 1964	AA
STONEWALL JACKSON	SSBN 634	Mare Island Naval Shipyard	4 July 1962	30 Nov 1963	26 Aug 1964	AA
SIMON BOLIVAR	SSBN 641	Newport News Shipbuilding & D D Co	17 Apr 1963	22 Aug 1964	29 Oct 1965	AA
KAMEHAMEHA*	SSN (ex-SSBN) 642	Mare Island Naval Shipyard	2 May 1963	16 Jan 1965	10 Dec 1965	AA
GEORGE BANCROFT	SSBN 643	General Dynamics (Electric Boat Div)	24 Aug 1963	20 Mar 1965	22 Jan 1966	AA
JAMES K POLK*	SSN (ex-SSBN) 645	General Dynamics (Electric Boat Div)	23 Nov 1963	22 May 1965	16 Apr 1966	AA
MARIANO G VALLEJO	SSBN 658	Mare Island Naval Shipyard	7 July 1964	23 Oct 1965	16 Dec 1966	AA

* SSN conversions

Displacement, tons: 7330 surfaced; 8250 dived
Dimensions, feet (metres): 425 × 33 × 31.5 (129.5 × 10.1 × 9.6)
Main machinery: Nuclear; 1 Westinghouse PWR S5W; 2 turbines; 15 000 hp (11.2 MW); 1 shaft; 1 Magnetek auxiliary prop motor; 325 hp (242 kW)
Speed, knots: 18 surfaced; 25 dived
Complement: 143 (13 officers)

Missiles: SLBM: 16 Lockheed Trident I (C4) (in 8 of the class); stellar inertial guidance to 7400 km (4000 nm); thermonuclear warhead of 8 MIRV of 100 kT or 6 MARV of 100 kT; CEP 450 m.
Torpedoes: 4—21 in (533 mm) Mk 65 bow tubes. Gould Mk 48; wire-guided (option); active/passive homing to 50 km (27 nm)/38 km (21 nm) at 40/55 kts; warhead 267 kg; depth to 900 m (2950 ft).
Countermeasures: Decoys: Emerson Electric Mk 2; torpedo decoy.
ESM: WLR-8; intercept.
Fire control: Mk 113 Mod 9 torpedo fire control system. Mk 88 missile control system.
Radars: Surface search/navigation/fire control: BPS 11A or BPS 15; I/J band.
Sonars: EDO BQR 7; passive search.
Western Electric; BQR 15; passive towed array.
Raytheon BQR 19; active for navigation; high frequency.
Honeywell BQR 21 (Dimus); passive array.
Raytheon BQS 4; active search and classification.

Programmes: In early 1986, on commissioning of *Alaska* SSBN 732, *Sam Rayburn* had her missile tubes plugged in order to keep within limits of the SALT agreement and has converted to a 'moored nuclear reactor training submarine'. Since then the earlier ships of the class have decommissioned at the rate of two to three per year, a process which rapidly accelerated from 1991 with all Poseidon submarines withdrawn from operational patrols. *Daniel Webster* has joined *Sam Rayburn* as a second moored training ship.
Modernisation: The first eight submarines of this class were fitted with the Polaris A-2 missile (1500 nm range) and the next 23 with the Polaris A-3 missile (2500 nm range). All were then fitted with Poseidon between 1970 and 1977. Between 24 September 1978 and 10 December 1982 twelve were converted to launch Trident I missiles. The conversion included minor modifications to the launcher and to the ballasting of the submarine to accommodate the greater weight of the Trident missile as well as extensive modifications to the installed fire control, instrumentation and missile checkout subsystems to support the increased sophistication of the longer range missile. Two of the class *Kamehameha* and *James K Polk* are being converted to drydock shelters (DDS) SSNs. They are being equipped for special operations, supporting SEALs.
Structure: All have diesel-electric stand-by machinery, snorts, and 'outboard' auxiliary propeller for emergency use. Diving depth is approx 300 m (984 ft).
Operational: Trident-fitted SSBNs are based in Charleston, SC. The last eight of these submarines will continue to conduct strategic deterrent patrols at sea until 1994. In a phased schedule between now and then, they will offload missiles, combine crews, and start ship inactivation. Two crews continue to remain necessary while the SSBNs are conducting operations at sea to allow adequate time for training, schooling, and leave for both crews. Some of the inactivated ships linger on in the Navy List because of overloaded decommissioning facilities. The two SSN conversions are replacing *John Marshall* and *Sam Houston*.

BENJAMIN FRANKLIN class 5/1992, Giorgio Arra

BENJAMIN FRANKLIN class 5/1992, Giorgio Arra

Attack Submarines (SSN)

Notes: 1. **Building programme:** The attack submarine force is entirely nuclear. The last remaining diesel-electric submarine paid off in May 1990. The current SSN building programme was thrown into disarray by the proposal to terminate the Seawolf programme, and to advance the design work on the follow-on Centurion class. On the basis of money already spent, it was decided in July 1992 to proceed with the second Seawolf and the same argument may save the third of the class. With the last of the Los Angeles hulls scheduled for completion in 1996 and the last Trident submarine in 1997, there is obvious concern over the possible loss of one of the two nuclear submarine building yards.
The Centurion design is based on a capability of about 75% of Seawolf. Studies have included a modular concept with common propulsion and different weapon systems sections to be decided on build. To control unit costs, size has to be sacrificed, which means compromising on stealth characteristics and weapons capacity. If a successful compromise cannot be agreed, there is danger of an imposed solution based on an improved Los Angeles design.
2. **Ancillary programmes:** These include thin-line towed arrays with greatly enhanced detection capability, special hull treatments which improve detection capability against quieter targets, the Mk 48 advanced capability (ADCAP) torpedo, improved Tomahawk missiles, offboard sensors and decoys.
3. **Deep submergence vehicles:** The Deep Submergence Vehicles (DSV), including the nuclear-propelled *NR-1*, are rated as Service Craft and are listed at the end of the 'Special Vessels' section following the MSC section.
4. **Swimmer-Seal Delivery Vehicles (SDVs):** About 15 two-man and six-man mini submarines are in service for naval commando units. These SDVs have a speed of six kts and can be carried by suitably modified SSNs. A new design ASDS (Advanced Swimmer Delivery System) with electric propulsion is out to tender in 1993. These will be mini submarines capable of carrying four men from a mother submarine to a hostile shore.
5. **Unmanned Undersea Vehicles (UUVs):** Two prototype vessels started tests in Spring 1990 and a third in late 1991. The prototype is 36 ft long and has a diameter of 3 ft 8 in, while the second has a titanium hull. The mission payload is housed in an internal pressure hull. The propulsion motor is free flooding and develops about 12 hp from two battery sections. The first set of operational trials are expected to complete in about mid-1993 followed by launch and control experiments using *Memphis* (SSN 691) as the mother ship. The UUV is capable of remote-control from either submarine or surface ship. Roles are limitless but remote sensing and acoustic deception are two obvious front runners.
6. **Autonomous Undersea Vehicles (AUVs):** Early research work is being done with the aim of producing torpedo-launched remote-controlled vehicles for a range of tasks including surveillance, communications and mine warfare.

0 + 2 (1) SEAWOLF CLASS (SSN)

Name	No	Builders	Start date	Launched	Commissioned
SEAWOLF	SSN 21	General Dynamics (Electric Boat Div)	25 Oct 1989	Jan 1995	May 1996
CONNECTICUT	SSN 22	General Dynamics (Electric Boat Div)	9 Sep 1992	Mar 1997	Aug 1998

Displacement, tons: 7460 surfaced; 9137 dived
Dimensions, feet (metres): 353 × 42.3 × 35.8 *(107.6 × 12.9 × 10.9)*
Main machinery: Nuclear; 1 GE PWR S6W; 2 turbines; 52 000 hp *(38.8 MW)*; 1 shaft; pumpjet propulsor; 1 Westinghouse secondary propulsion submerged motor
Speed, knots: 35 dived
Complement: 133 (12 officers)

Missiles: SLCM: 12 GDC Tomahawk.
SSM: Tomahawk; Harpoon.
Torpedoes: 8—26 in *(660 mm)* tubes (external measurement is 30 in *(762 mm)*); Mk 48 ADCAP (added capability). Total of about 50 tube-launched missiles and torpedoes.
Mines: In lieu of torpedoes.
Countermeasures: Decoys: torpedo decoys.
ESM: WLQ-4(V)1; intercept.
Combat data systems: General Electric BSY-1 system with UYK 44 computers.
Fire control: Raytheon Mk 2 FCS
Sonars: BQQ 5D suite; TB-16 and TB-23 towed arrays. One surveillance; one tactical.

Programmes: First of class ordered on 9 January 1989; second of class on 3 May 1991. Third funded in FY 1992. In January 1992 it was proposed that funding for the second and third would be rescinded and long-lead work was suspended on 14 February, starting again for *Connecticut* on 17 June. Delays in *Seawolf* construction programme have been caused by pressure hull welding problems.
Structure: The modular design has more weapons, a higher tactical speed, better sonars and an ASW mission effectiveness 'three times better than the improved Los Angeles class' according to the Navy. It is estimated that over a billion dollars has been allocated for research and development including $365 million for the S6W reactor system. Full acoustic cladding will be fitted. There are no external weapons (as in the improved Los Angeles class). Emphasis has been put on sub-ice capabilities including retractable bow planes. Diving depth, 2000 ft *(610 m)* approx.
Operational: A quoted 'silent' speed of 20 kts. Other operational advantages include greater manoeuvrability and space for subsequent weapon systems development.
Opinion: This submarine was intended to restore the level of acoustic advantage (in the one to one nuclear submarine engagement against the Russians) which the USN has enjoyed for the last three decades. At the same time the larger capacity of the magazine will enhance overall effectiveness in a number of other roles. The decision to discontinue building this one very expensive design has happened sooner than expected but was the inevitable result of falling defence budgets, technical problems and a perception of a diminishing Russian threat.

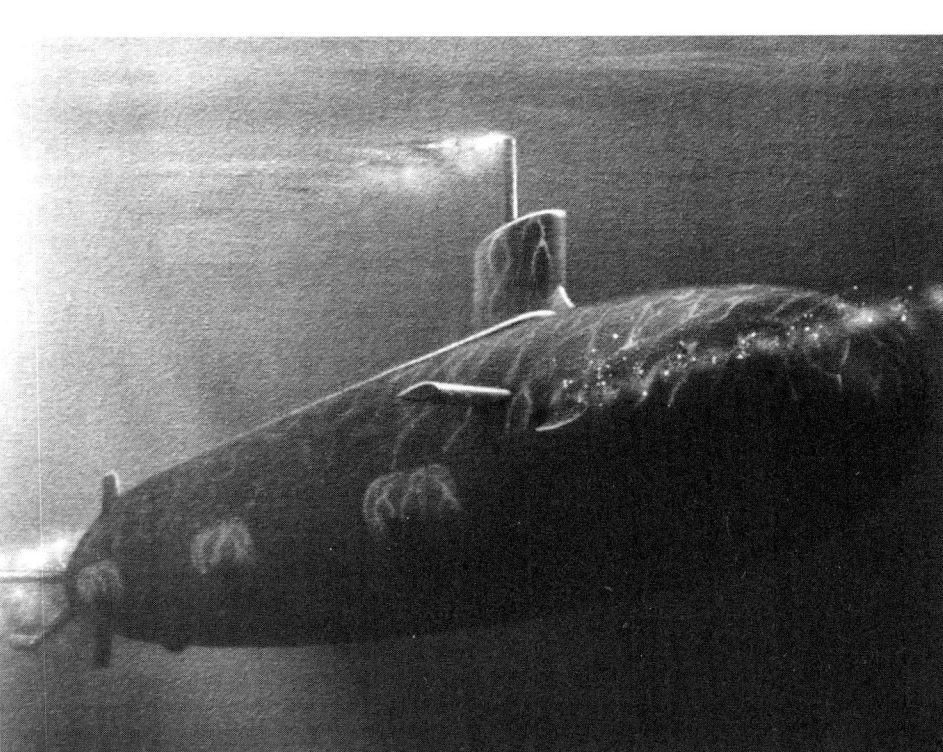

SEAWOLF (artist's impression) *1989, General Dynamics*

SEAWOLF (model) *1989, David Merriman, D & E Miniatures*

52 + 10 LOS ANGELES CLASS (SSN)

Name	No	Builders	Laid down	Launched	Commissioned	F/S
LOS ANGELES	SSN 688	Newport News S B & D D Co	8 Jan 1972	6 Apr 1974	13 Nov 1976	PA
BATON ROUGE	SSN 689	Newport News S B & D D Co	18 Nov 1972	26 Apr 1975	25 June 1977	AA
PHILADELPHIA	SSN 690	General Dynamics (Electric Boat Div)	12 Aug 1972	19 Oct 1974	25 June 1977	AA
MEMPHIS	SSN 691	Newport News S B & D D Co	23 June 1973	3 Apr 1976	17 Dec 1977	AA
OMAHA	SSN 692	General Dynamics (Electric Boat Div)	27 Jan 1973	21 Feb 1976	11 Mar 1978	PA
CINCINNATI	SSN 693	Newport News S B & D D Co	6 Apr 1974	19 Feb 1977	10 June 1978	AA
GROTON	SSN 694	General Dynamics (Electric Boat Div)	3 Aug 1973	9 Oct 1976	8 July 1978	AA
BIRMINGHAM	SSN 695	Newport News S B & D D Co	26 Apr 1975	29 Oct 1977	16 Dec 1978	AA
NEW YORK CITY	SSN 696	General Dynamics (Electric Boat Div)	15 Dec 1973	18 June 1977	3 Mar 1979	PA
INDIANAPOLIS	SSN 697	General Dynamics (Electric Boat Div)	19 Oct 1974	30 July 1977	5 Jan 1980	PA
BREMERTON	SSN 698	General Dynamics (Electric Boat Div)	8 May 1976	22 July 1978	14 Mar 1981	PA
JACKSONVILLE	SSN 699	General Dynamics (Electric Boat Div)	21 Feb 1976	18 Nov 1978	16 May 1981	AA
DALLAS	SSN 700	General Dynamics (Electric Boat Div)	9 Oct 1976	28 Apr 1979	18 July 1981	AA
LA JOLLA	SSN 701	General Dynamics (Electric Boat Div)	16 Oct 1976	11 Aug 1979	24 Oct 1981	PA
PHOENIX	SSN 702	General Dynamics (Electric Boat Div)	30 July 1977	8 Dec 1979	19 Dec 1981	AA
BOSTON	SSN 703	General Dynamics (Electric Boat Div)	11 Aug 1978	19 Apr 1980	30 Jan 1982	AA
BALTIMORE	SSN 704	General Dynamics (Electric Boat Div)	21 May 1979	13 Dec 1980	24 July 1982	AA
CITY OF CORPUS CHRISTI	SSN 705	General Dynamics (Electric Boat Div)	4 Sep 1979	25 Apr 1981	8 Jan 1983	AA
ALBUQUERQUE	SSN 706	General Dynamics (Electric Boat Div)	27 Dec 1979	13 Mar 1982	21 May 1983	AA
PORTSMOUTH	SSN 707	General Dynamics (Electric Boat Div)	8 May 1980	18 Sep 1982	1 Oct 1983	AA
MINNEAPOLIS-SAINT PAUL	SSN 708	General Dynamics (Electric Boat Div)	30 Jan 1981	19 Mar 1983	10 Mar 1984	AA
HYMAN G RICKOVER	SSN 709	General Dynamics (Electric Boat Div)	24 July 1981	27 Aug 1983	21 July 1984	AA
AUGUSTA	SSN 710	General Dynamics (Electric Boat Div)	1 Apr 1982	21 Jan 1984	19 Jan 1985	AA
SAN FRANCISCO	SSN 711	Newport News S B and D D Co	26 May 1977	27 Oct 1979	24 Apr 1981	PA
ATLANTA	SSN 712	Newport News S B and D D Co	17 Aug 1978	16 Aug 1980	6 Mar 1982	AA
HOUSTON	SSN 713	Newport News S B and D D Co	29 Jan 1979	21 Mar 1981	25 Sep 1982	PA
NORFOLK	SSN 714	Newport News S B and D D Co	1 Aug 1979	31 Oct 1981	21 May 1983	AA
BUFFALO	SSN 715	Newport News S B and D D Co	25 Jan 1980	8 May 1982	5 Nov 1983	PA
SALT LAKE CITY	SSN 716	Newport News S B and D D Co	26 Aug 1980	16 Oct 1982	12 May 1984	PA
OLYMPIA	SSN 717	Newport News S B and D D Co	31 Mar 1981	30 Apr 1983	17 Nov 1984	PA
HONOLULU	SSN 718	Newport News S B and D D Co	10 Nov 1981	24 Sep 1983	6 July 1985	PA
PROVIDENCE	SSN 719	General Dynamics (Electric Boat Div)	14 Oct 1982	4 Aug 1984	27 Aug 1985	AA
PITTSBURGH	SSN 720	General Dynamics (Electric Boat Div)	15 Apr 1983	8 Dec 1984	23 Nov 1985	AA
CHICAGO	SSN 721	Newport News S B & D D Co	5 Jan 1983	13 Oct 1984	27 Sep 1986	PA
KEY WEST	SSN 722	Newport News S B & D D Co	6 July 1983	20 July 1985	12 Sep 1987	PA
OKLAHOMA CITY	SSN 723	Newport News S B & D D Co	4 Jan 1984	2 Nov 1985	9 June 1988	AA
LOUISVILLE	SSN 724	General Dynamics (Electric Boat Div)	16 Sep 1984	14 Dec 1985	8 Nov 1986	PA
HELENA	SSN 725	General Dynamics (Electric Boat Div)	28 Mar 1985	28 June 1986	11 July 1987	PA
NEWPORT NEWS	SSN 750	Newport News S B & D D Co	3 Mar 1984	15 Mar 1986	3 June 1989	AA
SAN JUAN	SSN 751	General Dynamics (Electric Boat Div)	16 Aug 1985	6 Dec 1986	6 Aug 1988	AA
PASADENA	SSN 752	General Dynamics (Electric Boat Div)	20 Dec 1985	12 Sep 1987	11 Feb 1989	PA
ALBANY	SSN 753	Newport News S B & D D Co	22 Apr 1985	13 June 1987	7 Apr 1990	AA
TOPEKA	SSN 754	General Dynamics (Electric Boat Div)	13 May 1986	23 Jan 1988	21 Oct 1989	PA
MIAMI	SSN 755	General Dynamics (Electric Boat Div)	24 Oct 1986	12 Nov 1988	30 June 1990	AA
SCRANTON	SSN 756	Newport News S B & D D Co	29 June 1986	3 July 1989	26 Jan 1991	AA
ALEXANDRIA	SSN 757	General Dynamics (Electric Boat Div)	19 June 1987	23 June 1990	29 June 1991	AA
ASHEVILLE	SSN 758	Newport News S B & D D Co	1 Jan 1987	24 Feb 1990	28 Sep 1991	PA
JEFFERSON CITY	SSN 759	Newport News S B & D D Co	21 Sep 1987	17 Aug 1990	30 Jan 1992	AA
ANNAPOLIS	SSN 760	General Dynamics (Electric Boat Div)	15 June 1988	18 May 1991	11 Apr 1992	AA
SPRINGFIELD	SSN 761	General Dynamics (Electric Boat Div)	29 Jan 1990	4 Jan 1992	4 Jan 1993	PA
COLUMBUS	SSN 762	General Dynamics (Electric Boat Div)	7 Jan 1991	1 Aug 1992	July 1993	Bldg/AA
SANTA FE	SSN 763	General Dynamics (Electric Boat Div)	9 July 1991	12 Dec 1992	Dec 1993	Bldg
BOISE	SSN 764	Newport News S B & D D Co	25 Aug 1988	23 Mar 1991	7 Nov 1992	AA
MONTPELIER	SSN 765	Newport News S B & D D Co	19 May 1989	23 Aug 1991	13 Mar 1993	AA
CHARLOTTE	SSN 766	Newport News S B & D D Co	17 Aug 1990	3 Oct 1992	Aug 1994	Bldg
HAMPTON	SSN 767	Newport News S B & D D Co	2 Mar 1990	3 Apr 1992	Nov 1993	Bldg
HARTFORD	SSN 768	General Dynamics (Electric Boat Div)	27 Apr 1992	Dec 1993	Dec 1994	Bldg
TOLEDO	SSN 769	Newport News S B & D D Co	6 May 1991	Aug 1993	Feb 1995	Bldg
TUCSON	SSN 770	Newport News S B & D D Co	15 Aug 1991	Mar 1994	Aug 1995	Bldg
COLUMBIA	SSN 771	General Dynamics (Electric Boat Div)	24 Apr 1993	Dec 1994	Feb 1996	Bldg
GREENEVILLE	SSN 772	Newport News S B & D D Co	28 Feb 1992	Sep 1994	Feb 1996	Bldg
CHEYENNE	SSN 773	Newport News S B & D D Co	6 July 1992	Apr 1995	Aug 1996	Bldg

Displacement, tons: 6080 standard; 6927 dived
Dimensions, feet (metres): 362 × 33 × 32.3 *(110.3 × 10.1 × 9.9)*
Main machinery: Nuclear; 1 GE PWR S6G; 2 turbines; 35 000 hp *(26 MW)*; 1 shaft; 1 Magnetek auxiliary prop motor; 325 hp *(242 kW)*
Speed, knots: 32 dived
Complement: 133 (13 officers)

Missiles: SLCM: GDC Tomahawk (TLAM-N); land attack; Tercom aided inertial navigation system (TAINS) to 2500 km *(1400 nm)* at 0.7 Mach; altitude 15-100 m; nuclear warhead 200 kT; CEP 80 m. There are also two versions (TLAM-C/D) with either a single 454 kg HE warhead or a single warhead with submunitions; range 900 km *(485 nm)*; CEP 10 m. Nuclear warheads are not normally carried. Block III missiles, approved for production in 1992, increases TLAM-C ranges by more than 30%.
SSM: GDC Tomahawk (TASM); anti-ship; inertial guidance; active radar/anti-radiation homing to 460 km *(250 nm)* at 0.7 Mach; warhead 454 kg.
From SSN 719 onwards all are equipped with the Vertical Launch System, which places 12 launch tubes external to the pressure hull behind the BQQ 5 spherical array forward.
McDonnell Douglas Harpoon; active radar homing to 130 km *(70 nm)* at 0.9 Mach; warhead 227 kg.
Torpedoes: 4—21 in *(533 mm)* tubes midships. Gould Mk 48; wire-guided (option); active/passive homing to 50 km *(27 nm)*/38 km *(21 nm)* at 40/55 kts; warhead 267 kg; depth to 900 m *(2950 ft)*. ADCAP first carried in 1990. Air Turbine Pump discharge.
Total of 26 weapons can be tube-launched, for example—8 Tomahawk, 4 Harpoon, 14 torpedoes.
Mines: Can lay Mk 67 Mobile and Mk 60 Captor mines.
Countermeasures: Decoys: Emerson Electric Mk 2; torpedo decoy.
ESM: BRD-7; direction finding. WLR-12; radar warning. WLR-9A; intercept. WLR-1H (in 771-773).
Combat data systems: CCS Mk 1 (being replaced by Mk 2) (688-750) with UYK 7 computers; IBM BSY-1 (751-773) with UYK 43/UYK 44 computers.
Fire control: Mk 113 Mod 10 torpedo fire control system fitted in SSN 688-699 (being replaced by Mk 117) and Mk 117 in later submarines.
Radars: Surface search/navigation/fire control: Sperry BPS 15 A; I/J band.
Sonars: IBM BQQ 5A(V)1 (being updated to BQQ 5D/E); passive/active search and attack; low frequency.
BQR 23/25 (being replaced by TB-23/29 thin line array during overhauls); passive towed array.
Ametek BQS 15; active close-range including ice detection; high frequency.
MIDAS (mine and ice detection avoidance system) (SSN 751 onwards); high frequency.
Raytheon SADS-TG active detection system (being retrofitted).

Programmes: Various major improvement programmes and updating design changes caused programme delays in the late 1980s, not helped by a long strike at the Electric Boat Division. Future commissioning dates are very speculative. From SSN 751 onwards the class is prefixed by an 'I' for 'improved'. Programme terminates at 62 hulls.
Modernisation: Mk 117 TFCS is being back fitted in earlier submarines of the class.
Structure: Every effort has been made to improve sound quieting and from SSN 751 onwards the class have acoustic tile cladding to augment the 'mammalian' skin which up to then had been the standard USN outer casing coating. Also from SSN 751 the forward hydro planes are fitted forward instead of on the fin. The planes are retractable mainly for surfacing through ice. The S6G reactor is a modified version of the D2G type fitted in *Bainbridge* and *Truxtun*. The towed sonar array is stowed in a blister on the side of the casing. Reactor core life between refuellings is estimated at 10 years. Diving depth is 450 m *(1475 ft)*. *Memphis* was withdrawn from active service in late 1989 to become an interim research platform for advanced submarine technology. Up to now these trials have not involved major changes to the submarine but tests started in September 1990 for optronic non-hull penetrating masts and a major overhaul in 1993 will include installation of a large diameter tube for testing UUVs and large torpedoes. Subsequently an after casing hangar will be fitted for housing larger UUVs and towed arrays. *Augusta* is the trials platform for the BQG-5D wide aperture array passive sonar system which may be built into the last three and retrofitted in others of the class. Various staged design improvements have added some 220 tons to the class displacement between 668 and 773.
Operational: Increased emphasis on the ability to operate under the Arctic ice has led to improvements in ice detection sensors, navigation and communications equipment as well as strengthening the sail and placing the sailplanes forward in later units of the class. *Norfolk* fired the first ADCAP torpedo on 23 July 1988 and sank the destroyer *Jonas K Ingram*. Ten of the class took part in the war with Iraq in 1991 and two fired Tomahawk from the eastern Mediterranean. Normally eight Tomahawk missiles are carried internally (in addition to the external tubes in 719 onwards) but this load can be increased depending on the mission. Subroc phased out in 1990. Nuclear weapons disembarked but still available.

MEMPHIS
5/1992, Giorgio Arra

ANNAPOLIS   9/1992, Giorgio Arra

SAN JUAN   4/1992, Giorgio Arra

PHILADELPHIA   7/1992, Maritime Photographic

NORFOLK   5/1992, Giorgio Arra

32 STURGEON CLASS (SSN)

Name	No	Builders	Laid down	Launched	Commissioned	F/S
STURGEON	SSN 637	General Dynamics (Electric Boat Div)	10 Aug 1963	26 Feb 1966	3 Mar 1967	AA
WHALE	SSN 638	General Dynamics (Quincy)	27 May 1964	14 Oct 1966	12 Oct 1968	AA
TAUTOG	SSN 639	Ingalls Shipbuilding Corp	27 Jan 1964	15 Apr 1967	17 Aug 1968	PA
GRAYLING	SSN 646	Portsmouth Naval Shipyard	12 May 1964	22 June 1967	11 Oct 1969	AA
POGY	SSN 647	Ingalls Shipbuilding Corp	4 May 1964	3 June 1967	15 May 1971	PA
ASPRO	SSN 648	Ingalls Shipbuilding Corp	23 Nov 1964	29 Nov 1967	20 Feb 1969	PA
SUNFISH	SSN 649	General Dynamics (Quincy)	15 Jan 1965	14 Oct 1966	15 Mar 1969	AA
PARGO	SSN 650	General Dynamics (Electric Boat Div)	3 June 1964	17 Sep 1966	5 Jan 1968	AA
PUFFER	SSN 652	Ingalls Shipbuilding Corp	8 Feb 1965	30 Mar 1968	9 Aug 1969	PA
SAND LANCE	SSN 660	Portsmouth Naval Shipyard	15 Jan 1965	11 Nov 1969	25 Sep 1971	AA
GURNARD	SSN 662	San Francisco NSY (Mare Island)	22 Dec 1964	20 May 1967	6 Dec 1968	PA
HAMMERHEAD	SSN 663	Newport News S B & D D Co	29 Nov 1965	14 Apr 1967	28 June 1968	AA
HAWKBILL	SSN 666	San Francisco NSY (Mare Island)	12 Sep 1966	12 Apr 1969	4 Feb 1971	PA
BERGALL	SSN 667	General Dynamics (Electric Boat Div)	16 Apr 1966	17 Feb 1968	13 June 1969	AA
SPADEFISH	SSN 668	Newport News S B & D D Co	21 Dec 1966	15 May 1968	14 Aug 1969	AA
SEAHORSE	SSN 669	General Dynamics (Electric Boat Div)	13 Aug 1966	15 June 1968	19 Sep 1969	AA
FINBACK	SSN 670	Newport News S B & D D Co	26 June 1967	7 Dec 1968	4 Feb 1970	AA
PINTADO	SSN 672	San Francisco NSY (Mare Island)	27 Oct 1967	16 Aug 1969	11 Sep 1971	PA
FLYING FISH	SSN 673	General Dynamics (Electric Boat Div)	30 June 1967	17 May 1969	29 Apr 1970	AA
TREPANG	SSN 674	General Dynamics (Electric Boat Div)	28 Oct 1967	27 Sep 1969	14 Aug 1970	AA
BLUEFISH	SSN 675	General Dynamics (Electric Boat Div)	13 Mar 1968	10 Jan 1970	8 Jan 1971	AA
BILLFISH	SSN 676	General Dynamics (Electric Boat Div)	20 Sep 1968	1 May 1970	12 Mar 1971	AA
DRUM	SSN 677	San Francisco NSY (Mare Island)	20 Aug 1968	23 May 1970	15 Apr 1972	PA
ARCHERFISH	SSN 678	General Dynamics (Electric Boat Div)	19 June 1969	16 Jan 1971	17 Dec 1971	AA
SILVERSIDES	SSN 679	General Dynamics (Electric Boat Div)	13 Oct 1969	4 June 1971	5 May 1972	AA
WILLIAM H BATES (ex-*Redfish*)	SSN 680	Ingalls Shipbuilding (Litton)	4 Aug 1969	11 Dec 1971	5 May 1973	PA
BATFISH	SSN 681	General Dynamics (Electric Boat Div)	9 Feb 1970	9 Oct 1971	1 Sep 1972	AA
TUNNY	SSN 682	Ingalls Shipbuilding (Litton)	22 May 1970	10 June 1972	26 Jan 1974	PA
PARCHE	SSN 683	Ingalls Shipbuilding (Litton)	10 Dec 1970	13 Jan 1973	17 Aug 1974	PA
CAVALLA	SSN 684	General Dynamics (Electric Boat Div)	4 June 1970	19 Feb 1972	9 Feb 1973	PA
L MENDEL RIVERS	SSN 686	Newport News S B & D D Co	26 June 1971	2 June 1973	1 Feb 1975	AA
RICHARD B RUSSELL	SSN 687	Newport News S B & D D Co	19 Oct 1971	12 Jan 1974	16 Aug 1975	PA

Displacement, tons: 4250; 4460 standard; 4780; 4960 dived (see *Structure*)
Dimensions, feet (metres): 302.2; 292 × 31.8 × 28.9 *(92.1; 89 × 9.7 × 8.8)* (see *Structure*)
Main machinery: Nuclear; 1 Westinghouse PWR S5W; 2 turbines; 15 000 hp *(11.2 MW)*; 1 shaft
Speed, knots: 15 surfaced; 30 dived
Complement: 107 (12 officers)

Missiles: SLCM: GDC Tomahawk (TLAM-N); land attack; Tercom aided inertial navigation system (TAINS) to 2500 km *(1400 nm)* at 0.7 Mach; altitude 15-100 m; nuclear warhead 200 kT; CEP 80 m. There are also two versions (TLAM-C/D) with either a single 454 kg HE warhead or a single warhead with submunitions; range 900 km *(485 nm)*; CEP 10 m.
Nuclear warheads are not normally carried. TLAM-C Block III missiles with increased ranges of more than 30% may be embarked in due course.
SSM: GDC Tomahawk (TASM); anti-ship; inertial guidance; active radar/anti-radiation homing to 460 km *(250 nm)* at 0.7 Mach; warhead 454 kg.
McDonnell Douglas Harpoon; active radar homing to 130 km *(70 nm)* at 0.9 Mach; warhead 227 kg (84A) or 258 kg (84B/C).
Torpedoes: 4—21 in *(533 mm)* Mk 63 tubes midships. Gould Mk 48; wire-guided (option); active/passive homing to 50 km *(27 nm)*/38 km *(21 nm)* at 40/55 kts; warhead 267 kg; depth to 900 m *(2950 ft)*.
Total of 23 weapons, for example 4 Harpoon, 4 Tomahawk and 15 torpedoes. Up to 8 Tomahawk can be carried in most of the class in place of other weapons.
Mines: Mk 67 Mobile and Mk 60 Captor can be carried.
Countermeasures: Decoys: Emerson Electric Mk 2; torpedo decoy.
ESM: WLQ-4; radar warning.
Fire control: Mk 117 torpedo fire control system.
Radars: Surface search/navigation/fire control: Sperry BPS 15 or Raytheon BPS 14; I/J band.
Sonars: IBM BQQ 5 (SSN 678 onwards) or Raytheon BQQ 2; passive/active search and attack; low frequency.
EDO BQS 8 or Raytheon BQS 14A; ice detection; high frequency.
Raytheon BQS 13; active/passive array.
BQR 15; towed array; passive search; very low frequency.

Structure: Sail height is 20 ft 6 in above deck. Sail-mounted diving planes rotate to vertical for breaking through ice when surfacing in arctic regions. SSN 678-684, 686 and 687 are 10 ft longer than remainder of class to accommodate BQQ 5 sonar and electronic gear. Under FY 1982 programme *Cavalla* was converted at Pearl Harbor in August-December 1982 to have a secondary amphibious assault role by carrying a Swimmer Delivery Vehicle (SDV). *Archerfish, Silversides, Tunny* and *L Mendel Rivers* are similarly equipped. *William H Bates, Hawkbill, Pintado, Richard B Russell, Billfish* and others have been modified to carry and support the Navy's Deep Submergence Rescue Vehicles (DSRV). See section on Deep Submergence Vehicles for additional DSRV details. *Silversides* and *Richard B Russell* carry Bustle prototype communications buoy in container abaft the sail. Diving depth is 400 m *(1320 ft)*. Acoustic tiles are fitted and some of the class have anechoic coatings.
Operational: Operational life was expected to be 30 years but many have been decommissioned early and more will follow as a result of defence cutbacks. Subroc phased out in 1990. Nuclear warheads are not carried. *Sturgeon, Aspro, Pargo, Gurnard, Hammerhead* and *Silverside* are to pay off in 1993/94.

RICHARD B RUSSELL (with DSRV and Bustle) *1987, Giorgio Arra*

SILVERSIDES (with SDV) *3/1992, Giorgio Arra*

SEAHORSE *8/1992, Giorgio Arra*

1 NARWHAL CLASS (SSN)

Name	No	Builders	Laid down	Launched	Commissioned	F/S
NARWHAL	SSN 671	General Dynamics (Electric Boat Div)	17 Jan 1966	9 Sep 1967	12 July 1969	AA

Displacement, tons: 5284 standard; 5830 dived
Dimensions, feet (metres): 314.6 × 37.7 × 27 *(95.9 × 11.5 × 8.2)*
Main machinery: Nuclear; 1 GE PWR S5G; 2 turbines; 17 000 hp *(12.7 MW)*; 1 shaft
Speed, knots: 20 surfaced; 25 dived
Complement: 129 (13 officers)

Missiles: SSM: 8 GDC Tomahawk (TASM); anti-ship; inertial guidance; active radar/anti-radiation homing to 460 km *(250 nm)* at 0.7 Mach; warhead 454 kg. 4 McDonnell Douglas Harpoon; active radar homing to 130 km *(70 nm)* at 0.9 Mach; warhead 227 kg.
Torpedoes: 4—21 in *(533 mm)* tubes midships. Gould Mk 48; wire-guided (option); active/passive homing to 50 km *(27 nm)*/38 km *(21 nm)* at 40/55 kts; warhead 227 kg; depth to 900 m *(2950 ft)*.
Countermeasures: Decoys: Emerson Electric Mk 2; torpedo decoy.
ESM: WLQ-4; radar warning.
Fire control: Mk 117 torpedo fire control system. Fitted with WSC-3 satellite communications transceiver.
Radars: Surface search/navigation/fire control: Raytheon BPS 14; I/J band.
Sonars: IBM BQQ 5; passive/active search and attack; low frequency.
EDO BQS 8; upward-looking for ice detection; high frequency.

Programmes: Authorised in FY 1964.

Structure: *Narwhal* is similar to the Sturgeon class submarines in hull design but is fitted with the prototype sea-going S5G natural circulation reactor plant. The natural circulation reactor 'offers promise of increased reactor plant reliability, simplicity, and noise reduction due to the elimination of the need for large reactor coolant pumps and associated electrical and control equipment by taking maximum advantage of natural convection to circulate the reactor coolant.'

NARWHAL
3/1987, Michael D J Lennon

AIRCRAFT CARRIERS

Notes: 1. Air Wings: Air wing composition depends on the operational task, but is based on a normal complement of two fighter squadrons of 20 F-14 Tomcats, two light attack squadrons of 20 F/A-18 Hornets, two medium attack squadrons of 20 A-6E Intruders (including some tanker KA-6D aircraft depending on availability), one ASW squadron of five S-3A Viking aircraft, one detachment of five EA-6B Prowler electronic-warfare aircraft, five E-2C Hawkeye early-warning/control aircraft and one ASW squadron of eight SH-60F Seahawk which are replacing the SH-3G/H Sea King helicopters. A Power Projection Airwing is being introduced in 1993. This replaces four Intruders by four Hornets, and reduces to four both the Prowler and Hawkeye numbers. Marine fighter/attack squadrons operate alongside Navy air wings. Budget constraints and shortages of aircraft may limit numbers embarked. See *Shipborne Aircraft* section for details of aircraft.

2. Service Life Extension Programme (SLEP): The SLEP programme was initiated in 1979. *Saratoga, Forrestal, Independence, Kitty Hawk* and *Constellation* have completed, but from 1993 extended overhauls have replaced SLEPs. The principal objective of SLEP was to extend the service life of aircraft carriers an additional 15 years, providing a reliable, logistically supportable platform capable of operating all current and future fleet aircraft. While the major thrust of SLEP was repair and life enhancement, warfighting improvements are incorporated to keep pace with the aircraft carrier modernisation baseline. SLEP included complete overhaul of propulsion, auxiliary, and launch systems; upgrade of aircraft recovery equipment; extensive structure, tank, and piping repair, and installation of updated sensors, weapons systems, and electronic suites. On earlier SLEP ships this included installation of Vulcan Phalanx close-in weapons system (CIWS), NATO Sea Sparrow missile system, SPS 49 radar, and F/A-18 Hornet capability. In future overhauls, carriers, if already equipped with these systems, will receive modernisation to current standards incorporating improved NTDS, SPS 48E, TAS Mk 23 radar, new ASW systems and Raytheon SLQ-32(V)4 combined EW intercept and jammer.

ABRAHAM LINCOLN
7/1991, 92 Wing RAAF

766 USA / Aircraft carriers

6 + 2 NIMITZ CLASS (CVN)

Name	No	Builders	Laid down	Launched	Commissioned	F/S
NIMITZ	CVN 68	Newport News Shipbuilding & Dry Dock Co	22 June 1968	13 May 1972	3 May 1975	PA
DWIGHT D EISENHOWER	CVN 69	Newport News Shipbuilding & Dry Dock Co	15 Aug 1970	11 Oct 1975	18 Oct 1977	AA
CARL VINSON	CVN 70	Newport News Shipbuilding & Dry Dock Co	11 Oct 1975	15 Mar 1980	13 Mar 1982	PA
THEODORE ROOSEVELT	CVN 71	Newport News Shipbuilding & Dry Dock Co	13 Oct 1981	27 Oct 1984	25 Oct 1986	AA
ABRAHAM LINCOLN	CVN 72	Newport News Shipbuilding & Dry Dock Co	3 Nov 1984	13 Feb 1988	11 Nov 1989	PA
GEORGE WASHINGTON	CVN 73	Newport News Shipbuilding & Dry Dock Co	25 Aug 1986	21 July 1990	4 July 1992	AA
JOHN C STENNIS	CVN 74	Newport News Shipbuilding & Dry Dock Co	13 Mar 1991	Nov 1993	June 1996	Bldg
UNITED STATES	CVN 75	Newport News Shipbuilding & Dry Dock Co	Nov 1993	Mar 1996	June 1998	Bldg

Displacement, tons: 72 916 (CVN 68-70), 73 973 (CVN 71) light; 91 487 (CVN 68-70), 96 386 (CVN 71), 102 000 (CVN 72-73) full load
Dimensions, feet (metres): 1040 pp; 1092 × 134 × 37 (CVN 68-70); 38.7 (CVN 71); 39 (CVN 72-73)
(317; 332.9 × 40.8 × 11.3; 11.8; 11.9)
Flight deck, feet (metres): 1092; 779.8 (angled) × 252
(332.9; 237.7 × 76.8)
Main machinery: Nuclear; 2 GE PWR A4W/A1G; 4 turbines; 260 000 hp *(194 MW)*; 4 emergency diesels; 10 720 hp *(8 MW)*; 4 shafts
Speed, knots: 30+
Complement: 3184 (203 officers); 2800 aircrew (366 officers); Flag 70 (25 officers)

Missiles: SAM: 3 Raytheon GMLS Mk 29 octuple launchers; NATO Sea Sparrow; semi-active radar homing to 14.6 km *(8 nm)* at 2.5 Mach; warhead 39 kg.
Guns: 4 General Electric/General Dynamics 20 mm Vulcan Phalanx 6-barrelled Mk 15 (3 in CVN 68 and 69); 3000 rounds/minute (or 4500 in Block 1) combined to 1.5 km.
Countermeasures: Decoys: 4 Loral Hycor SRBOC 6-barrelled fixed Mk 36; IR flares and chaff to 4 km *(2.2 nm)*. SSTDS (torpedo defence system). SLQ 36 Nixie (Phase I).
ESM/ECM: SLQ-32(V)4 (in CVN 73); SLQ 29 (WLR 8 radar warning and SLQ 17AV jammer and deception system). Being replaced by SLQ-32(V)4.
Combat data systems: NTDS/ACDS naval tactical and advanced combat direction systems; Links 4A, 11 and 14. Link 16 in due course. JOTS, POST, CVIC, TESS UMM-1(V)1, SSQ-82. SATCOMS SRR-1, WSC-3 (UHF), WSC-6 (SHF), USC-38 (EHF) (from 1992).
Fire control: 3 Mk 91 Mod 1 MFCS directors (part of the NSSMS Mk 57 SAM system).
Radars: Air search: ITT SPS 48E; 3D; E/F band; range 402 km *(220 nm)*.
Raytheon SPS 49(V)5; C/D band; range 457 km *(250 nm)*.
Hughes Mk 23 TAS; D band.
Surface search: Norden SPS 67V; G band.
CCA: SPN 41, 2 SPN 42 (CVN 68-70), SPN 43B, SPN 44, 2 SPN 46 (CVN 71-73); J/K/E/F band.
Navigation: Raytheon SPS 64(V)9; I/J band.
Fire control: Six Mk 95; I/J band (for SAM).
Tacan: URN 25.

Fixed wing aircraft: Notional air wing including: 20 F14 Tomcat; 20 F/A-18 Hornet; 6 EA-6B Prowler; 20 A-6E Intruders (includes some KA-6D tankers); 5 E-2C Hawkeye; 5 S-3A/B Viking. Power Projection Airwing substitutes 4 more Hornets for 4 Intruders and reduces Prowlers and Hawkeyes by one each.
Helicopters: 8 SH-3G/H Sea King or SH-60F Seahawk.

Programmes: *Nimitz* was authorised in FY 1967, *Dwight D Eisenhower* in FY 1970, *Carl Vinson* in FY 1974, *Theodore Roosevelt* in FY 1980 and *Abraham Lincoln* and *George Washington* in FY 1983. Construction contracts for the last two were awarded in June 1988. The builder is the only US shipyard capable of constructing large, nuclear-propelled surface warships. The FY 1993 ship construction budget shows lead items for CVN 76 which is expected to be included in the FY 1995 programme.
Structure: Damage control measures include sides with system of full and empty compartments (full compartments can contain aviation fuel), approximately 2.5 in Kevlar plating over certain areas of side shell, box protection over magazine and machinery spaces. Aviation facilities include four lifts, two at the forward end of the flight deck, one to starboard abaft the island and one to port at the stern. There are four steam catapults (C13-1) and four (or three) Mk 7 Mod 3 arrester wires. Launch rate is one every 20 seconds. The hangar can hold less than half the full aircraft complement, deckhead is 25.6 ft. Aviation fuel, 9000 tons. Tactical Flag Command Centre for Flagship role.
Operational: Multi-mission role of 'attack/ASW'. From CVN 70 onwards ships have an A/S control centre and A/S facilities; CVN 68 and 69 will be back fitted. Endurance of 16 days for aviation fuel (steady flying). 13 years' theoretical life for nuclear reactors (CVN 68-70); 15 years' (CVN 71-73); 800 000 to 1 million miles between refuellings. Trials started in December 1992 in CVN 71 with 600 Marines embarked, including six CH-53D and four UH-1N helicopters, which displaced two squadrons of fixed wing aircraft.

GEORGE WASHINGTON 10/1992, Giorgio Arra

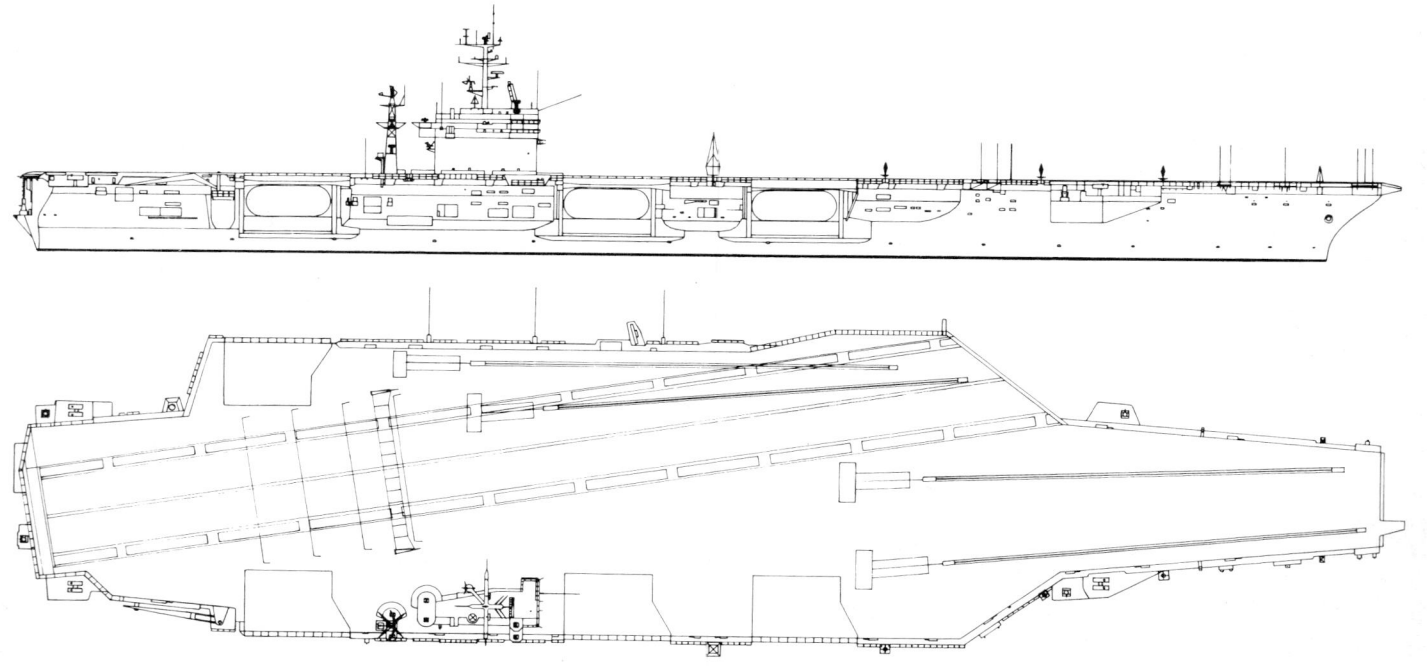

CARL VINSON (Scale 1 : 1800), Ian Sturton

GEORGE WASHINGTON *10/1992, Giorgio Arra*

THEODORE ROOSEVELT *10/1992, Giorgio Arra*

DWIGHT D EISENHOWER *8/1992, Giorgio Arra*

GEORGE WASHINGTON *11/1992, Newport News Shipbuilding*

4 KITTY HAWK and JOHN F KENNEDY CLASSES (CV)

Name	No	Builders	Laid down	Launched	Commissioned	F/S
KITTY HAWK	CV 63	New York Shipbuilding Corp, Camden, NJ	27 Dec 1956	21 May 1960	29 Apr 1961	PA
CONSTELLATION	CV 64	New York Naval Shipyard	14 Sep 1957	8 Oct 1960	27 Oct 1961	SLEP/PA
AMERICA	CV 66	Newport News Shipbuilding & Dry Dock Co	9 Jan 1961	1 Feb 1964	23 Jan 1965	AA
JOHN F KENNEDY	CV 67	Newport News Shipbuilding & Dry Dock Co	22 Oct 1964	27 May 1967	7 Sep 1968	AA

Displacement, tons: 60 100 standard; 81 123 full load (CV 63)
60 100 standard; 81 773 full load (CV 64)
60 300 standard; 79 724 full load (CV 66)
61 000 standard; 80 941 full load (CV 67)
Dimensions, feet (metres): 1062.5 (CV 63); 1072.5 (CV 64); 1047.5 (CV 66); 1052 (CV 67) × 130 × 37.4
(323.6; 326.9; 319.3; 320.6 × 39.6 × 11.4)
Flight deck, feet (metres): 1046 × 252 *(318.8 × 76.8)*
Main machinery: 8 Foster-Wheeler boilers; 1200 psi *(83.4 kg/cm sq)*; 950°F *(510°C)*; 4 Westinghouse turbines; 280 000 hp *(209 MW)*; 4 shafts
Speed, knots: 32. **Range, miles:** 4000 at 30 kts; 12 000 at 20 kts
Complement: 2930 (155 officers); aircrew 2480 (320 officers) (except CV 67); aircrew 2279 (329 officers) (CV 67); Flag 70 (25 officers)

Missiles: SAM: 3 Raytheon GMLS Mk 29 octuple launchers; NATO Sea Sparrow; semi-active radar homing to 14.6 km *(8 nm)* at 2.5 Mach; warhead 39 kg.
Guns: 3 General Electric/General Dynamics 20 mm Vulcan Phalanx 6-barrelled Mk 15; 3000 rounds/minute (or 4500 in Block 1) combined to 1.5 km.
Countermeasures: Decoys: 4 Loral Hycor SRBOC 6-barrelled fixed Mk 36; IR flares and chaff to 4 km *(2.2 nm)*. SSTDS (Surface Ship Torpedo Defence System). SLQ-36 Nixie (Phase I).
ESM/ECM: SLQ-32(V)4 (in CV 63 and 64) to be retrofitted in all. SLQ 29 (WLR 8 and SLQ 17) in CV 66; SLQ 17 and SLQ 26 in CV 67; WLR 3, WLR 11; combined radar warning, jammer and deception system.
Combat data systems: NTDS/ACDS naval tactical and advanced combat direction systems; Links 4A, 11 and 14. Link 16 in due course. JOTS, POST, CVIC, TESS UMM-1(V)1, SSQ-82. SATCOMS SRR-1, WSC-3 (UHF), WSC-6 (SHF), USC-38 (EHF) (from 1992).
Fire control: 3 Mk 91 MFCS directors (part of NSSMS Mk 57 SAM system).
Radars: Air search: ITT SPS 48C/E; 3D; E/F band; range 402 km *(220 nm)*.
Raytheon SPS 49(V)5; C/D band; range 457 km *(250 nm)*.
Hughes Mk 23 TAS; D band.
Surface search: Raytheon SPS 10F or Norden SPS 67; G band.
CCA: SPN 41, SPN 43A; SPN 44; 2 SPN 46; J/K/E/F band.
Navigation: Raytheon SPN 64(V)9; I band.
Fire control: 6 Mk 95; I/J band (for SAM).
Tacan: URN 25.
Sonars: Fitted for SQS 23 (CV 66-67).

Fixed wing aircraft: Notional air wing including: 20 F14 Tomcat; 20 F/A-18 Hornet; 4 EA-6B Prowler; 14 A-6E Intruders (includes some KA-6D tankers); 4 E-2C Hawkeye; 5 S-3A/B Viking. Power Projection Airwing substitutes 4 more Hornets for 4 Intruders and reduces Prowlers and Hawkeyes by one each.
Helicopters: 8 SH-3G/H Sea King or SH-60F Seahawk.

Programmes: *Kitty Hawk* was authorised in FY 1956, *Constellation* in FY 1957, *America* in FY 1961, and *John F Kennedy* in FY 1963. *America* is due to pay off in 1996.
Modernisation: Service Life Extension Programme (SLEP): *Kitty Hawk* completed in February 1991 and *Constellation* in December 1992. $113 million was funded in the FY 1991 budget for procurement of materials to be used in the 'complex overhaul' of *Kennedy*, which is scheduled to start in September 1993 subject to operational tasking.
Structure: These ships were built to an improved Forrestal design and are easily recognised by their island structure being set farther aft than the superstructure in the four Forrestal class ships. They have two deck-edge lifts forward of the superstructure, a third lift aft of the structure, and the port-side lift on the after quarter. This arrangement considerably improves flight deck operations. Four C13 steam catapults (with one C13-1 in *America* and *Kennedy*) and four arrester wires. *John F Kennedy*

KENNEDY
9/1992, Maritime Photographic

and *America* have stern anchors as well as bow anchors because of their planned bow sonar domes. All have a small radar mast abaft the island. The island is painted black between flight deck and bridge to mask jet exhaust stains. Aviation fuel of 5882 tons are carried.

KENNEDY
9/1992, Maritime Photographic

Aircraft carriers / USA 769

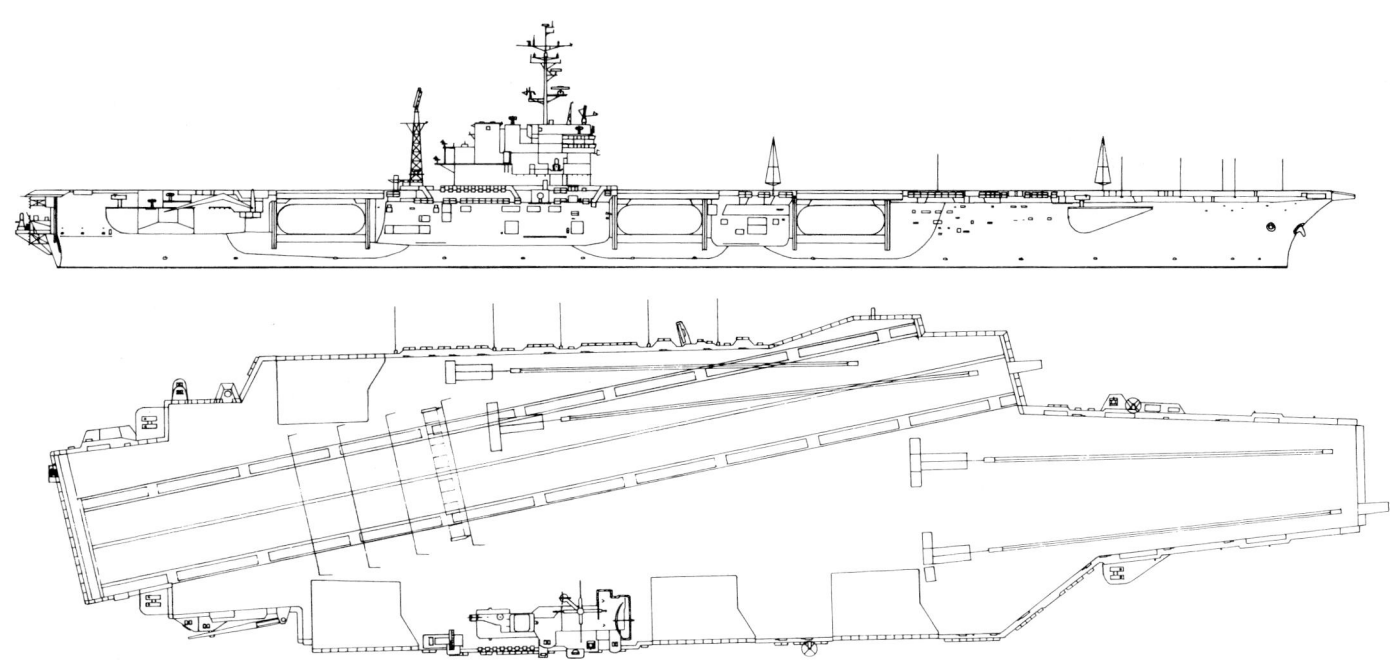

AMERICA *(Scale 1 : 1800), Ian Sturton*

AMERICA *9/1991, Maritime Photographic*

AMERICA *10/1991, H M Steele*

770 USA / Aircraft carriers

3 FORRESTAL CLASS (2 CV and 1 AVT)

Name	No	Builders	Laid down	Launched	Commissioned	F/S
FORRESTAL	AVT 59	Newport News S B & D D Co	14 July 1952	11 Dec 1954	1 Oct 1955	AA
SARATOGA	CV 60	New York Naval Shipyard	16 Dec 1952	8 Oct 1955	14 Apr 1956	AA
INDEPENDENCE	CV 62	New York Naval Shipyard	1 July 1955	6 June 1958	10 Jan 1959	PA

Displacement, tons: 59 060 (AVT 59 and CV 60), 60 000 (CV 62) standard;
79 250 (AVT 59), 80 383 (CV 60), 80 643 (CV 62) full load
Dimensions, feet (metres): 1086 (AVT 59); 1063 (CV 60); 1071 (CV 62) × 130 × 37 *(331; 324; 326.4 × 39.6 × 11.3)*
Flight deck, feet (metres): 1047 × 250.3 (AVT 59 and CV 60); 270 (CV 62) *(319.1 × 76.3; 82.3)*
Main machinery: 8 Babcock & Wilcox boilers; 600 psi *(41.7 kg/cm sq)* (AVT 59); 1200 psi *(83.4 kg/cm sq)* (remainder); 950°F *(510°C)*; 4 Westinghouse turbines; 260 000 hp *(194 MW)* (AVT 59); 280 000 hp *(209 MW)* (remainder); 4 shafts
Speed, knots: 33. **Range, miles:** 8000 at 20 kts; 4000 at 30 kts
Complement: 2900 (154 officers); aircrew 2279 (329 officers); Flag 70 (25 officers)

Missiles: SAM: 2 (AVT 59) or 3 Raytheon GMLS Mk 29 octuple launchers; NATO Sea Sparrow; semi-active radar homing to 14.6 km *(8 nm)* at 2.5 Mach; warhead 39 kg.
Guns: 3 General Electric/General Dynamics 20 mm Vulcan Phalanx 6-barrelled Mk 15; 3000 rounds/minute (or 4500 in Block 1) combined to 1.5 km.
Countermeasures: Decoys: 4 Loral Hycor SRBOC 6-barrelled fixed Mk 36; IR flares and chaff to 4 km *(2.2 nm)*. SSTDS (Surface Ship Torpedo Defence System). SLQ-36 Nixie (Phase I).
ESM/ECM: SLQ-32(V)3 (CV 62). SLQ-32(V)4 (AVT 59 and CV 60); combined radar warning, jammer and deception systems.
Combat data systems: NTDS/ACDS naval tactical and advanced combat direction systems; Links 4A, 11 and 14. Link 16 in due course. JOTS, POST, CVIC, TESS UMM-1(V)1, SSQ-82. SATCOMS SRR-1, WSC-3 (UHF), WSC-6 (SHF), USC-38 (EHF) (from 1992).
Fire control: 2 or 3 Mk 91 Mod 3 MFCS directors (part of NSSMS Mk 57 SAM system).
Radars: Air search: ITT SPS 48C; 3D; E/F band; range 402 km *(220 nm)*.
Raytheon SPS 49(V)5; C/D band; range 457 km *(250 nm)*.
Hughes Mk 23 TAS; D band.
Surface search: Norden SPS 67; G band.
CCA: SPN 41, 2 SPN 42, SPN 43A, SPN 44; J/K/E/F band.
Navigation: Raytheon SPN 64(V)9; I band.
Fire control: 4 or 6 Mk 95 (for SAM); I/J band.
Tacan: URN 25.

Fixed wing aircraft: Notional air wing (not in AVT 59) including: 20 F-14; 20 F/A 18; 20 A-6E (includes some KA-6D tankers); 4 EA-6B; 5 S-3A/B; 4 E-2C. Power Projection Airwing substitutes 4 more Hornets for 4 Intruders and reduces Prowlers and Hawkeyes by one each.
Helicopters: 8 SH-3H Sea King or SH-60F Seahawk.

Programmes: *Forrestal* was the world's first aircraft carrier built after the Second World War. The *Forrestal* design drew heavily from the aircraft carrier *United States* (CVA 58) which was cancelled immediately after being laid down in April 1949. *Forrestal* was authorised in FY 1952, *Saratoga* followed in FY 1953 and *Independence* in FY 1955.
Modernisation: Service Life Extension Programme (SLEP): The Navy's aircraft carrier Service Life Extension Programme (SLEP) began with three ships of the *Forrestal* class. *Saratoga* from October 1980 to February 1983, *Forrestal* January 1983 to 20 May 1985, and *Independence* April 1985 to May 1988.

INDEPENDENCE 2/1993, Hachiro Nakai

FORRESTAL (as AVT) 2/1992, Giorgio Arra

The four after 5 in guns were removed from *Forrestal* late in 1967 and a single BPDMS launcher for Sea Sparrow missiles was installed forward on the starboard side. Two Mk 25 BPDMS launchers fitted in *Independence* in 1973 with the subsequent removal of all 5 in guns, *Saratoga* in 1974, *Forrestal* in 1976. These have been replaced by three Mk 29 GMLS launchers during SLEP.
Structure: The Forrestal class ships were the first aircraft carriers designed and built specifically to operate jet-propelled aircraft. *Forrestal* was redesigned early in construction to incorporate British-developed angled flight deck and steam catapults. These were the first US aircraft carriers built with an enclosed bow area to improve seaworthiness. Other features include armoured flight deck and advanced underwater protection and internal compartmentation to reduce effects of conventional and nuclear attack. Mast configurations differ. Funnel height of *Forrestal* and *Independence* increased by 10 ft in 1980. Aviation facilities include four 72 × 50 ft *(21.9 × 15.2 m)* lifts with capacity of 99 000 lb (45 tons), four steam catapults (2 C7 and 2 C 11 in AVT 59 and CV 60 and 4 C 13 in CV 62) and four arrester wires. During SLEP the port forward elevator in *Independence* was moved to the port quarter. Aviation fuel, 5500 tons.
Operational: *Independence* is based in Yokosuka, Japan. *Forrestal* was reclassified as the training carrier (AVT) in February 1992. *Ranger* paid off in 1993, *Saratoga* or *Forrestal* may be decommissioned early as a budget saving measure.

INDEPENDENCE 11/1990, 92 Wing RAAF

Aircraft carriers / USA

FORRESTAL (Scale 1 : 1800), Ian Sturton

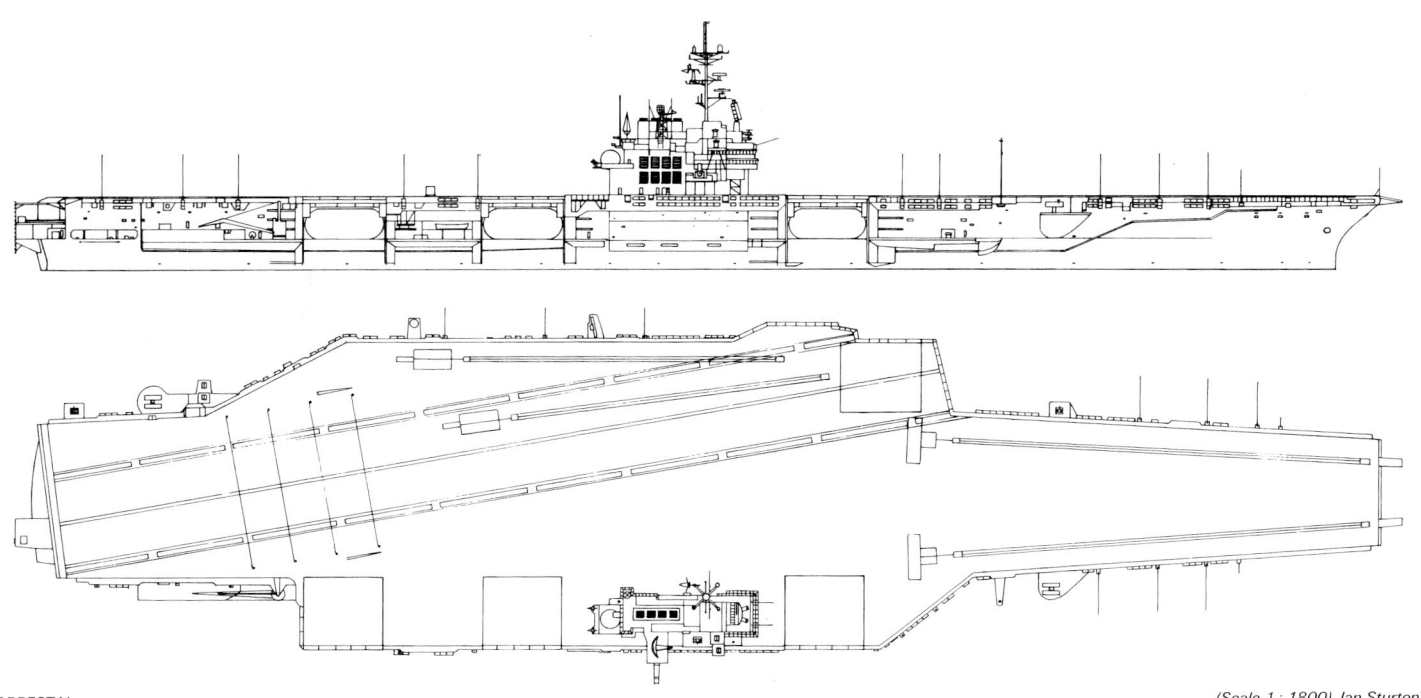
SARATOGA 3/1991, Giorgio Arra

INDEPENDENCE 11/1990, 92 Wing RAAF

1 ENTERPRISE CLASS (CVN)

Name	No	Builders	Laid down	Launched	Commissioned	F/S
ENTERPRISE	CVN 65	Newport News Shipbuilding & Dry Dock Co	4 Feb 1958	24 Sep 1960	25 Nov 1961	Conv

Displacement, tons: 73 502 light; 75 700 standard; 93 970 full load
Dimensions, feet (metres): 1123 × 133 × 39 *(342.3 × 40.5 × 11.9)*
Flight deck, feet (metres): 1088 × 252 *(331.6 × 76.8)*
Main machinery: Nuclear; 8 Westinghouse PWR A2W; 4 Westinghouse turbines; 280 000 hp *(209 MW)*; 4 emergency diesels; 10 720 hp *(8 MW)*; 4 shafts
Speed, knots: 33
Complement: 3215 (171 officers); 2480 aircrew (358 officers); Flag 70 (25 officers)

Missiles: SAM: 3 Raytheon GMLS Mk 29 octuple launchers; NATO Sea Sparrow; semi-active radar homing to 14.6 km *(8 nm)* at 2.5 Mach; warhead 39 kg.
Guns: 3 General Electric/General Dynamics 20 mm Vulcan Phalanx 6-barrelled Mk 15; 3000 rounds/minute (or 4500 in Block 1) combined to 1.5 km.
Countermeasures: Decoys: 4 Loral Hycor SRBOC 6-barrelled fixed Mk 36; IR flares and chaff to 4 km *(2.2 nm)*. SSTDS (Surface Ship Torpedo Defence System). SLQ-36 Nixie (Phase I).
ESM/ECM: SLQ 32(V)4; radar warning; jammer and deception system.
Combat data systems: NTDS/ACDS naval tactical and advanced combat direction systems; Links 4A, 11 and 14. Link 16 in due course. JOTS, POST, CVIC, TESS UMM-1(V)1, SSQ-82. SATCOMS SRR-1, WSC-3 (UHF), WSC-6 (SHF), USC-38 (EHF).
Fire control: 3 Mk 91 Mod 1 MFCS directors (part of NSSMS Mk 57 SAM system).
Radars: Air search: ITT SPS 48E; 3D; E/F band; range 402 km *(220 nm)*.
Raytheon SPS 49(V)5; C/D band; range 457 km *(250 nm)*.
Hughes Mk 23 TAS; D band.
Surface search: Norden SPS 67; G band.
CCA: SPN 41, SPN 43A; SPN 44; 2 SPN 46; J/K/E/F band.
Navigation: Raytheon SPS 64(V)9; I/J band.
Fire control: Six SPG 95; I/J band (for SAM).
Tacan: URN 25.

Fixed wing aircraft: Notional air wing including: 20 F14 Tomcat; 20 F/A-18 Hornet; 5 EA-6B Prowler; 20 A-6E Intruders (includes some KA-6D tankers); 5 E-2C Hawkeye; 5 S-3A/B Viking. Power Projection Airwing substitutes 4 more Hornets for 4 Intruders and reduces Prowlers and Hawkeyes by one each.
Helicopters: 8 SH-3G/H Sea King or SH-60F Seahawk.

Programmes: Authorised in FY 1958 and launched only 31 months after her keel was laid down. Underwent a refit/overhaul at Puget Sound Naval SY, Bremerton, Washington from January 1979 to March 1982. $1.4 billion provided in FY 1990 budget for a 42 month 'complex overhaul' including refuelling, which is the CVN equivalent of SLEP. This started at Newport News in early 1991 and is scheduled to complete in May 1994.
Modernisation: *Enterprise* was completed without any armament in an effort to hold down construction costs. Space for Terrier missile system was provided. Mk 25 Sea Sparrow BPDMS subsequently was installed in later 1967 and this has been replaced by first two and then three Mk 29 and supplemented with three 20 mm Mk 15 CIWS. A re-shaping of the island took place in her 1979-82 refit. This included the removal of the mast and dome (which carried obsolete ECM gear) which were replaced with a mast similar to that of the Nimitz class. The 'billboards' of the SPS 32 and 33 radars were removed and replaced by the antennas of SPS 48C and 49 radars on the new mast. Planned improvements during current overhaul include SPS 48E and Mk 23 TAS air search radars, SPN 46 (vice SPN 42) precision approach and landing radar and improved C^3 and EW systems.
Structure: Built to a modified Forrestal class design. *Enterprise* was the world's second nuclear powered warship (the cruiser *Long Beach* was completed a few months earlier). The first of the eight reactors installed achieved initial criticality on 2 December 1960, shortly after the carrier was launched. After three years of operation during which she steamed more than 207 000 miles, *Enterprise* was refuelled from November 1964 to July 1965. Her second set of cores provided about 300 000 miles steaming. The eight cores initially installed cost $64 million; the second set cost about $20 million. Refuelled again in 1970 the third set of cores lasted for eight years until replaced in 1979-82 overhaul. There are two reactors for each of the ship's four shafts. The eight reactors feed 32 heat exchangers. Aviation facilities include four deck edge lifts, two forward and one each side abaft the island. There are four 295 ft C 13 Mod 1 catapults. Hangars cover 216 000 sq ft with 25 ft deck head. Aviation fuel, 8500 tons.
Operational: 12 days' aviation fuel for intensive flying.

ENTERPRISE
9/1992, Stefan Terzibaschitsch

ENTERPRISE
3/1990, Giorgio Arra

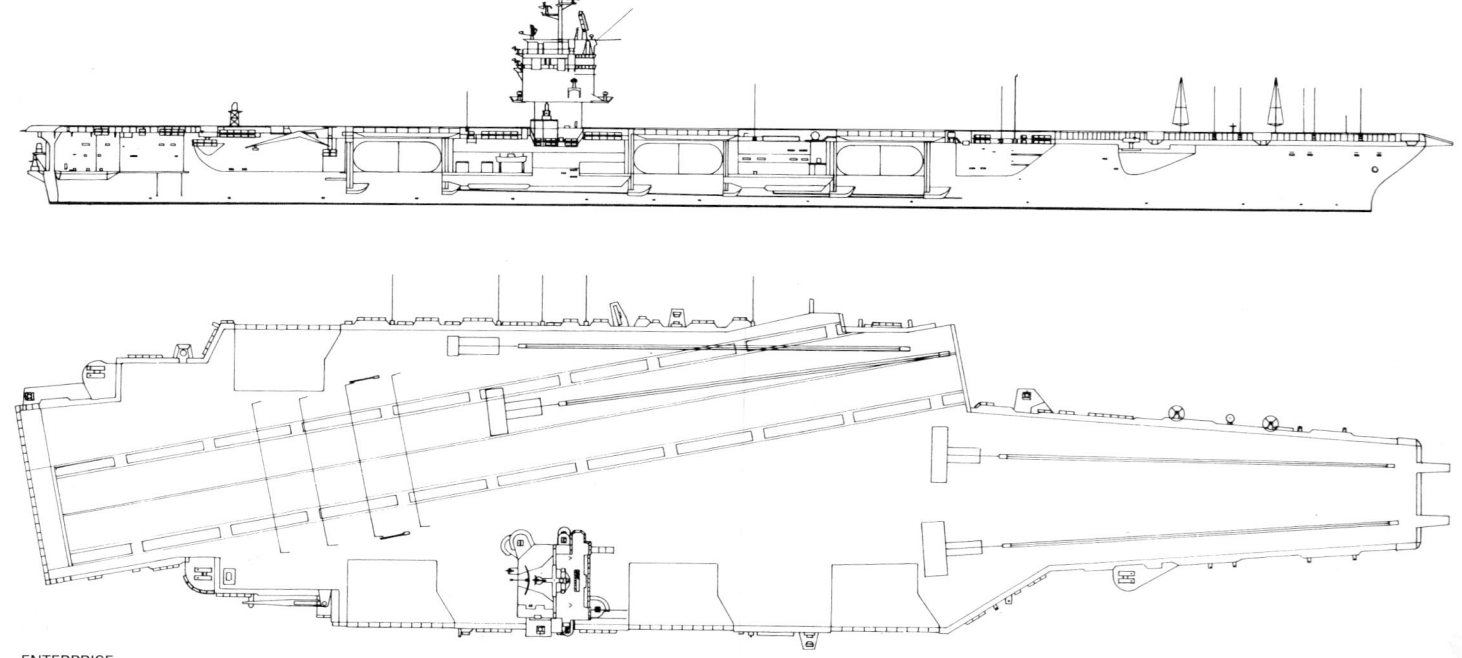

ENTERPRISE
(Scale 1 : 1800), Ian Sturton

CRUISERS

Notes: (a) The Virginia, California, Belknap and Leahy class cruisers, and Kidd class destroyers, have either received or are receiving the New Threat Upgrade (NTU) modernisation. This includes Standard SM-2 missiles where appropriate, updated air/surface search and fire control radars, improved weapons direction and missile fire control systems and the SYS-2 Integrated Automatic Target Detection and Tracking system (IADT). Where appropriate Mk 10 and Mk 26 missile launchers are also being converted from analog to digital systems. The original timetable for these changes ran from FY 1986 to FY 1991, but budget constraints have delayed completion of the work into FY 1996 at least.
(b) Navstar GPS (SRN-24) is being fitted in all major warships. As well as being an incomparable aid to navigation, this system has marked implications in combat data exchange and third party targeting for long-range weapon systems.

4 VIRGINIA CLASS: GUIDED MISSILE CRUISERS (CGN)

Name	No	Builders	Laid down	Launched	Commissioned	F/S
VIRGINIA	CGN 38	Newport News S B and D D Co	19 Aug 1972	14 Dec 1974	11 Sep 1976	AA
TEXAS	CGN 39	Newport News S B and D D Co	18 Aug 1973	9 Aug 1975	10 Sep 1977	PA
MISSISSIPPI	CGN 40	Newport News S B and D D Co	22 Feb 1975	31 July 1976	5 Aug 1978	AA
ARKANSAS	CGN 41	Newport News S B and D D Co	17 Jan 1977	21 Oct 1978	18 Oct 1980	PA

Displacement, tons: 8623 light; 11 300 full load
Dimensions, feet (metres): 585 × 63 × 31.5 (sonar) *(178.3 × 19.2 × 9.6)*
Main machinery: Nuclear; 2 GE PWR D2G; 2 turbines; 70 000 hp *(52 MW)*; 2 shafts
Speed, knots: 30+
Complement: 558-624 (38-45 officers)

Missiles: SLCM/SSM: 8 GDC Tomahawk (2 quad) ❶; combination of (a) land attack; TAINS (Tercom aided navigation system) to 2500 km *(1400 nm)* at 0.7 Mach; altitude 15-100 m *(49.2-328.1 ft)*; warhead nuclear 200 kT (TLAM-N); CEP 80 m; or warhead 454 kg (TLAM-C) or submunitions (TLAM-D); range 1300 km *(700 nm)*; CEP 10 m. Nuclear warheads are not normally carried. Range increased by over 30% in TLAM-C Batch III which started production in 1992.
(b) anti-ship (TASM); inertial guidance; active radar and anti-radiation homing to 460 km *(250 nm)* at 0.7 Mach; warhead 454 kg.
8 McDonnell Douglas Harpoon (2 quad) ❷; active radar homing to 130 km *(70 nm)* at 0.9 Mach; warhead 227 kg.
SAM: GDC Standard SM-2MR; command/inertial guidance; semi-active radar homing to 73 km *(40 nm)* at 2 Mach.
A/S: Honeywell ASROC; inertial guidance to 1.6-10 km *(1-5.4 nm)*; payload Mk 46 Mod 5 Neartip or Mk 50 in due course. SAM and A/S missiles are fired from 2 twin GMLS Mk 26 launchers supplied by a total of 68 weapons ❸.
Guns: 2 FMC 5 in *(127 mm)*/54 Mk 45 Mod 0 ❹; 65° elevation; 20 rounds/minute to 23 km *(12.6 nm)* anti-surface; 15 km *(8.2 nm)* anti-aircraft; weight of shell 32 kg.
2 General Electric/General Dynamics 20 mm Vulcan Phalanx 6-barrelled Mk 15 ❺; 3000 rounds/minute (or 4500 in Block 1) combined to 1.5 kg.
4—12.7 mm MGs.
Torpedoes: 6—324 mm Mk 32 (2 triple) tubes ❻. Honeywell Mk 46 Mod 5; anti-submarine; active/passive homing to 11 km *(5.9 nm)* at 40 kts; warhead 44 kg. To be replaced by Mk 50 in due course.
Countermeasures: Decoys: 4 Loral Hycor SRBOC 6-barrelled fixed Mk 36 ❼; IR flares and chaff to 4 km *(2.2 nm)*. T Mk 6 Fanfare or SLQ-26 Nixie; torpedo decoy system.
ESM/ECM: SLQ 32V(3); combined radar warning, jammer and deception system. OUTBOARD II (CGN 38 only).
Combat data systems: NTDS with Links 4A, 11, 14 and 16 in due course. SATCOM ❽ SRR-1; WSC-3 (UHF); USC 38 (EHF) (from 1992).
Fire control: SWG-2 Tomahawk WCS. SWG-1A Harpoon LCS. 1 Mk 74 MFCS. 1 digital Mk 116 ASW FCS. 1 Mk 86 Mod 5 GFCS for forward missile channel and gun fire. SYS-2(V)1 IADT.
Radars: Air search: ITT SPS 48C or 48D/E (NTU) ❾; 3D; E/F band; range 402 km *(220 nm)*.
Lockheed SPS 40B ❿ or Raytheon SPS 49(V)5 (NTU); C/D band.
Surface search: ISC Cardion SPS 55 ⓫; I/J band.
Navigation: Raytheon SPS 64(V)9; I/J band.
Fire control: Two SPG 51D ⓬; G/I band.
SPG 60D ⓭; I/J band. SPQ 9A ⓮; I/J band.
Tacan: URN 25. IFF Mk XII AIMS UPX 29.
Sonars: EDO/GE SQS 53A; bow-mounted; active search and attack; medium frequency. Based on SQS 26 but with digital computers.

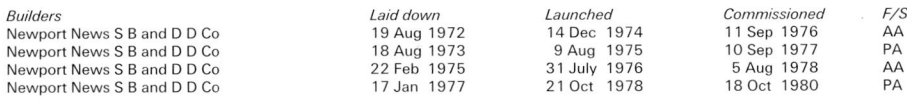

VIRGINIA *(Scale 1 : 1500), Ian Sturton*

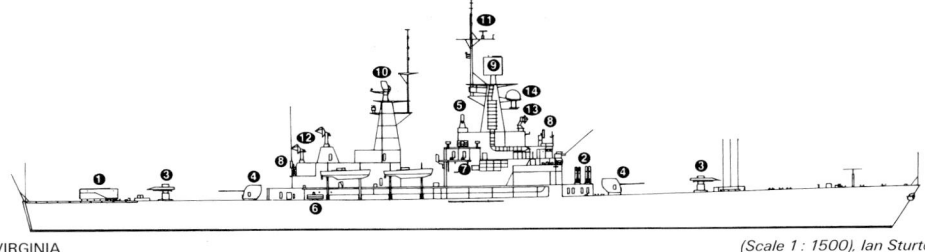

VIRGINIA *9/1992, Maritime Photographic*

Programmes: *Virginia* was authorised in FY 1970, *Texas* in FY 1971, *Mississippi* in FY 1972, and *Arkansas* in FY 1975. Originally classified as guided missile frigates (DLGN); subsequently reclassified as guided missile cruisers (CGN) on 30 June 1975.
Modernisation: Standard SM-1MR replaced by SM-2MR using Block II missiles to counter current and projected anti-ship cruise missile threats at extended ranges in the presence of severe enemy electronic countermeasures. Production systems were deployed in all guided missile cruisers and in DDG 993 class destroyers in FY 1988. The initial phase of fleet introduction of SM-2 in a Tartar ship was completed in May 1986 in *Virginia*. Tomahawk fitted in two armoured box launchers in all of the class at the expense of the helicopter capability. *Mississippi* and *Arkansas* have completed NTU; *Virginia* was underway in early 1993 and *Texas* is scheduled for FY 1994. This includes upgrading the Mk 74 MFCS and SPG 51D radars, improving the Mk 26 launchers, replacing SPS 40B radar by Raytheon SPS 49 and improving SPS 48, plus IADT SYS-2(V)2 (Integrated Automatic Detection and Track). The programme has been delayed by cuts in the defence budget.
Structure: The principal differences between the Virginia and California classes are the provision of improvements to anti-air warfare capability, electronic warfare equipment, and anti-submarine fire control system. The deletion of the separate ASROC Mk 16 launcher permitted the Virginia class to be 11 ft shorter.

ARKANSAS *10/1991, Scott Connolly, RAN*

774 USA / Cruisers

1 TRUXTUN CLASS: GUIDED MISSILE CRUISER (CGN)

Name	No	Builders	Laid down	Launched	Commissioned	F/S
TRUXTUN	CGN 35	New York SB Corp (Camden, New Jersey)	17 June 1963	19 Dec 1964	27 May 1967	PA

Displacement, tons: 8322 light; 9127 full load
Dimensions, feet (metres): 564 × 58 × 31 (sonar) *(171.9 × 17.7 × 9.4)*
Main machinery: Nuclear; 2 GE PWR D2G; 2 turbines; 70 000 hp *(52 MW)*; 2 shafts
Speed, knots: 30
Complement: 561 (39 officers); Flag 18 (6 officers)

Missiles: SSM: 8 McDonnell Douglas Harpoon (2 quad) launchers ❶; active radar homing to 130 km *(70 nm)* at 0.9 Mach; warhead 227 kg.
SAM: 40 GDC Standard SM-2ER Block 2; command/inertial guidance; semi-active radar homing to 137 km *(75 nm)* at 2.5 Mach.
A/S: 20 Honeywell ASROC; inertial guidance to 1.6-10 km *(1-5.4 nm)*; payload Mk 46 Mod 5 Neartip. 1 twin Mk 10 Mod 16 launcher for SAM and ASROC ❷.
Guns: 1 FMC 5 in *(127 mm)*/54 Mk 42 Mod 10 ❸; 85° elevation; 20-40 rounds/minute to 24 km *(13.1 nm)* anti-surface; 14 km *(7.7 nm)* anti-aircraft; weight of shell 32 kg.
2 General Electric/General Dynamics 20 mm Vulcan Phalanx 6-barrelled Mk 15 ❹; 3000 rounds/minute (or 4500 in Block 1) combined to 1.5 km.
4—12.7 mm MGs.
Torpedoes: 4—324 mm Mk 32 (2 twin) fixed tubes. Honeywell Mk 46 Mod 5; anti-submarine; active/passive homing to 11 km *(5.9 nm)* at 40 kts; warhead 44 kg.
Countermeasures: Decoys: 4 Loral Hycor SRBOC 6-barrelled fixed Mk 36; IR flares and chaff to 4 km *(2.2 nm)*. SLQ-25 Nixie; towed torpedo decoy.
ESM/ECM: SLQ 32(V)3; combined radar warning, jammer and deception system. WLR-1; radar warning.
Combat data systems: NTDS with Links 4A, 11 and 14. SATCOM SRR-1, WSC-3 (UHF).
Fire control: SWG-1A Harpoon LCS. 2 Mk 76 Mod 6 MFCS. 1 Mk 68 GFCS. 1 Mk 14 weapon direction system. Mk 111 ASW FCS. SYS-2(V)2 IADT.
Radars: Air search: ITT SPS 48E ❺; 3D; E/F band; range 402 km *(220 nm)*.
Raytheon SPS 49(V)5 ❻; C/D band; range 457 km *(250 nm)*.
Surface search: Norden SPS 67 ❼; G band.
Navigation: Marconi LN 66; I band.
Fire control: SPG 53F ❽; I/J band. Two SPG 55C ❾; G/H band.
Tacan: URN 25. IFF Mk 12 AIMS.
Sonars: EDO/GE SQS 26 AXR; bow-mounted; active search and attack; medium frequency.

Helicopters: 1 SH-2F Sea Sprite ❿.

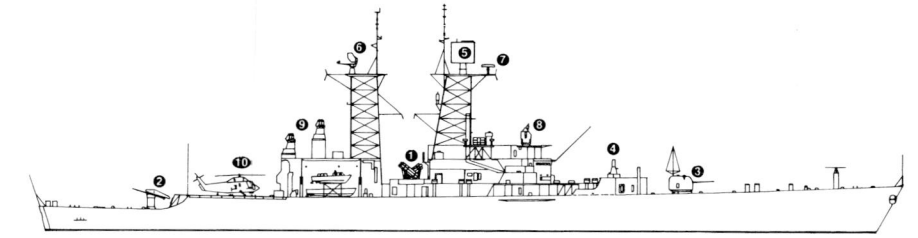
TRUXTUN *(Scale 1 : 1500), Ian Sturton*

TRUXTUN *6/1990, G Salmeri, RAN*

Programmes: *Truxtun* was the US Navy's fourth nuclear-powered surface warship. The Navy had requested seven oil-burning frigates in the FY 1962 shipbuilding programme; Congress authorised seven ships, but stipulated that one ship must be nuclear powered. Originally classified as a guided missile frigate (DLGN); subsequently reclassified as a guided missile cruiser (CGN) on 30 June 1975. *Truxtun* is the fifth ship to be named after Commodore Thomas Truxtun (sic) who commanded the frigate *Constellation* (38 guns) in her successful encounter with the French frigate *L'Insurgente* (44) in 1799.
Structure: Although the *Truxtun* design is adapted from the Belknap class, the nuclear ship's gun-missile launcher arrangement is reversed from the non-nuclear ships.
Operational: Now planned to be paid off in FY 1994.

1 BAINBRIDGE CLASS: GUIDED MISSILE CRUISER (CGN)

Name	No	Builders	Laid down	Launched	Commissioned	F/S
BAINBRIDGE	CGN 25	Bethlehem Steel Co, Quincy, Mass	15 May 1959	15 Apr 1961	6 Oct 1962	AA

Displacement, tons: 7804 light; 8592 full load
Dimensions, feet (metres): 565 × 57.9 × 31.2 (sonar) *(172.3 × 17.6 × 9.5)*
Main machinery: Nuclear; 2 GE PWR D2G; 2 turbines; 70 000 hp *(52 MW)*; 2 shafts
Speed, knots: 30
Complement: 558 (42 officers); Flag 18 (6 officers)

Missiles: SSM: 8 McDonnell Douglas Harpoon (2 quad) launchers ❶; active radar homing to 130 km *(70 nm)* at 0.9 Mach; warhead 227 kg.
SAM: 80 GDC Standard SM-2ER; 2 twin Mk 10 launchers (Mod 13 fwd, Mod 14 aft) ❷; command/inertial guidance; semi-active radar homing to 137 km *(75 nm)* at 2.5 Mach.
A/S: Honeywell ASROC Mk 16 octuple launcher ❸; inertial guidance to 1.6-10 km *(1-5.4 nm)*; payload Mk 46 Mod 5 Neartip.
Guns: 2 General Electric/General Dynamics 20 mm Vulcan Phalanx 6-barrelled Mk 15 ❹; 3000 rounds/minute (or 4500 in Block 1) combined to 1.5 km.
4—12.7 mm MGs.
Torpedoes: 6—324 mm Mk 32 (2 triple) tubes ❺. Honeywell Mk 46; anti-submarine; active/passive homing to 11 km *(5.9 nm)* at 40 kts; warhead 44 kg.
Countermeasures: Decoys: 4 Loral Hycor SRBOC 6-barrelled fixed Mk 36; IR flares and chaff to 4 km *(2.2 nm)*. T-Mk 6-Fanfare; towed torpedo decoy.
ESM/ECM: SLQ 32V(3); combined radar warning, jammer and deception system. WLR-1; radar warning.
Combat data systems: NTDS with Links 4A, 11 and 14. SATCOM SRR-1, WSC-3 (UHF).
Fire control: SWG-1A Harpoon LCS. 2 Mk 76 MFCS. 1 Mk 14 weapons direction system. Mk 111 ASW FCS.
Radars: Air search: ITT SPS 48C ❻; 3D; E/F band; range 402 km *(220 nm)*.
Raytheon SPS 49(V)5 ❼; C/D band; range 457 km *(250 nm)*.
Surface search: Norden SPS 67 ❽; G band.
Fire control: Four Sperry SPG 55C ❾; G/H band; range 51 km *(28 nm)*.
Navigation: Raytheon SPS 64(V)9; I band.
Tacan: URN 25. IFF Mk XV.
Sonars: Sperry SQQ 23; bow-mounted; active search and attack; medium frequency.
BQR-20A sonar receiver.

Helicopters: Platform for Sea King but no hangar.

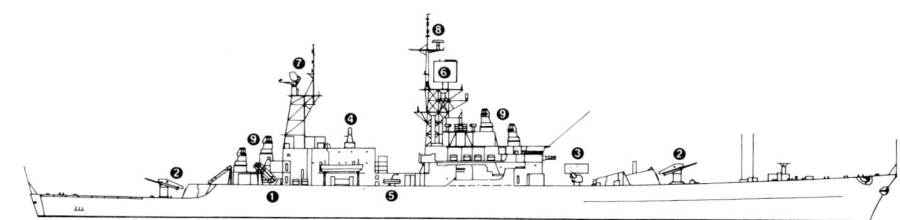
BAINBRIDGE *(Scale 1 : 1500), Ian Sturton*

BAINBRIDGE *9/1990, W Sartori*

Programmes: *Bainbridge* was the US Navy's third nuclear-powered surface warship (after the cruiser *Long Beach* and the aircraft carrier *Enterprise*). Originally classified as a guided missile frigate (DLGN); reclassified as a guided missile cruiser (CGN) on 30 June 1975.
Modernisation: *Bainbridge* underwent an Anti-Air Warfare (AAW) modernisation at the Puget Sound Naval Shipyard from 30 June 1974 to 24 September 1976. The ship was fitted with the Naval Tactical Data System (NTDS) and improved guidance capability for missiles. Four 3 in twin gun mountings were removed. Further improvements during 1983/85 refit, including Phalanx 20 mm, upgrading of SAM, SRBOC fit and replacement radars and ESM.
Operational: Now planned to be paid off in FY 1995 although she may cease to be operational some time before then.

1 LONG BEACH CLASS: GUIDED MISSILE CRUISER (CGN)

Name	No	Builders	Laid down	Launched	Commissioned	F/S
LONG BEACH	CGN 9 (ex-CGN 160, CLGN 160)	Bethlehem Steel Co, Quincy, Mass	2 Dec 1957	14 July 1959	9 Sep 1961	PA

Displacement, tons: 15 540 light; 17 525 full load
Dimensions, feet (metres): 721.2 × 73.2 × 29.7 (sonar) *(219.9 × 22.3 × 9.1)*
Main machinery: Nuclear; 2 Westinghouse PWR C1W; 2 GE turbines; 80 000 hp *(60 MW)*; 2 shafts
Speed, knots: 30
Complement: 958 (65 officers); Flag 68 (10 officers); marines 45 (1 officer)

Missiles: SLCM/SSM: 8 GDC Tomahawk (2 quad) ❶; combination of (a) land attack; TAINS (Tercom aided navigation system) to 2500 km *(1400 nm)* at 0.7 Mach; altitude 15-100 m *(49.2-328.1 ft)*; warhead nuclear 200 kT (TLAM-N); CEP 80 m; or warhead 454 kg (TLAM-C) or submunitions (TLAM-D); range 1300 km *(700 nm)*; CEP 10 m. Nuclear warheads are not normally carried. Range increased by 30% in TLAM-C Block III which started production in 1992.
(b) anti-ship (TASM); inertial guidance; active radar and anti-radiation homing to 460 km *(250 nm)* at 0.7 Mach; warhead 454 kg.
8 McDonnell Douglas Harpoon (2 quad) ❷; active radar homing to 130 km *(70 nm)* at 0.9 Mach; warhead 227 kg.
SAM: 120 GDC Standard SM-2ER; 2 twin Mk 10 launchers (Mod 11 forward, Mod 12 aft) ❸; command/inertial guidance; semi-active radar homing to 137 km *(75 nm)* at 2.5 Mach.
A/S: Honeywell ASROC Mk 16 octuple launcher ❹; inertial guidance to 1.6-10 km *(1-5.4 nm)*; payload Mk 46 Mod 5 Near-tip/Mk 50.
Guns: 2 USN 5 in *(127 mm)*/38 Mk 30 ❺; 85° elevation; 15 rounds/minute to 17 km *(9.3 nm)* anti-surface; 11 km *(5.9 nm)* anti-aircraft; weight of shell 25 kg. Completed with an all-missile armament. 2 single 5 in mounts were fitted during 1962-63.
2 General Electric/General Dynamics 20 mm Vulcan Phalanx 6-barrelled Mk 15 ❻; 3000 rounds/minute (or 4500 in Block 1) combined to 1.5 km.
4—12.7 mm MGs.
Torpedoes: 6—324 mm Mk 32 (2 triple) tubes ❼. Honeywell Mk 46; anti-submarine; active/passive homing to 11 km *(5.9 nm)* at 40 kts; warhead 44 kg. To be replaced by Mk 50 in due course.
Countermeasures: Decoys: 4 Loral Hycor SRBOC 6-barrelled fixed Mk 36; IR flares and chaff to 4 km *(2.2 nm)*. SLQ-25 Nixie; towed torpedo decoy.

ESM/ECM: SLQ 32V(3); combined radar warning, jammer and deception system. OUTBOARD I. SAR-8 IRSDT (Infra-Red Search, Detection and Track) in due course.
Combat data systems: NTDS with Links 4A, 11 14 and 16 in due course. SATCOM SRR-1, WSC-3 (UHF), USC-38 (EHF) (from 1993).
Fire control: SWG-2 Tomahawk WCS. SWG-1 Harpoon LCS. 4 Mk 76 Mod 2 MFCS. 2 Mk 56 GFCS. 1 Mk 14 weapon direction system. Mk 111 ASW. SYS 1(V)1 IADT.
Radars: Air search: ITT SPS 48C ❽; 3D; E/F band; range 402 km *(220 nm)*.
Raytheon SPS 49(V)3 ❾; C/D band; range 457 km *(250 nm)*.
Surface search: Norden SPS 67 ❿; G band.
Navigation: Marconi LN 66; I band.
Fire control: Four SPG 55D ⓫; G/H band.
Two General Electric Mk 35 Mod 2 ⓬; I/J band.
Tacan: URN 25. IFF Mk XII AIMS UPX-29.
Sonars: Sperry SQQ 23B pair; hull-mounted; active search and attack; medium frequency.

Helicopters: Platform but no facilities.

Programmes: *Long Beach* was the first ship to be designed as a cruiser for the USA after the end of the Second World War. She is the world's first nuclear-powered surface warship and the first warship to have a guided missile main battery. Authorised in FY 1957 and first got underway on nuclear power on 5 July 1961. Ordered as a guided missile light cruiser (CLGN 160) reclassified as a guided missile cruiser (CGN 160) early in 1957 and renumbered (CGN 9) on 1 July 1957. The original plan was to install Polaris missiles.
Modernisation: As a result of the 1976 cancellation of the planned fitting of AEGIS *Long Beach* underwent a mid-life modernisation 1980-83. This included updating of missile systems, restoration of the missile radars, the SPS 32 and 33 air search replaced by SPS 48 and 49 systems, replacement of the ship's computer and modernisation of the communications system. Tomahawk box launchers have since been added. New Threat Update, planned to start in 1993, has been shelved.
Structure: Initially planned at about 7800 tons (standard) to test the feasibility of a nuclear-powered surface warship. Early in 1956 her displacement was increased to 11 000 tons and a second SAM missile launcher was added. A Talos missile launcher (now removed) was also added which, with other features, further increased the displacement.
Operational: Scheduled to become the first nuclear-powered surface ship to pay off, probably in 1994.

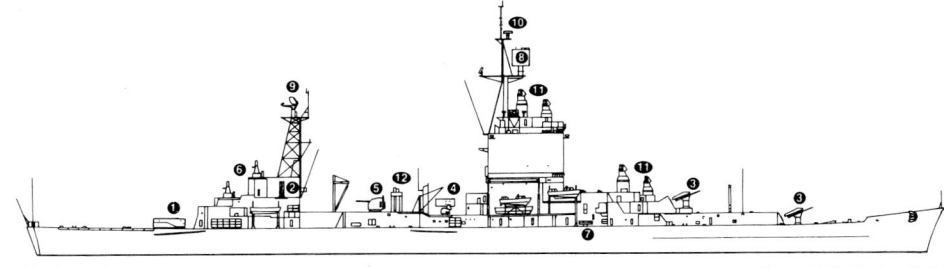

LONG BEACH *(Scale 1 : 1800), Ian Sturton*

LONG BEACH

10/1991, 92 Wing RAAF

23 + 4 TICONDEROGA CLASS: GUIDED MISSILE CRUISERS (CG—AEGIS)

Name	No	Builder/Programme	Laid down	Launched	Commissioned	F/S
TICONDEROGA	CG 47 (ex-DDG 47)	Ingalls Shipbuilding	21 Jan 1980	25 Apr 1981	22 Jan 1983	AA
YORKTOWN	CG 48	Ingalls Shipbuilding	19 Oct 1981	17 Jan 1983	4 July 1984	AA
VINCENNES	CG 49	Ingalls Shipbuilding	20 Oct 1982	14 Jan 1984	6 July 1985	PA
VALLEY FORGE	CG 50	Ingalls Shipbuilding	14 Apr 1983	23 June 1984	18 Jan 1986	PA
THOMAS S GATES	CG 51	Bath Iron Works	31 Aug 1984	14 Dec 1985	22 Aug 1987	PA
BUNKER HILL	CG 52	Ingalls Shipbuilding	11 Jan 1984	11 Mar 1985	20 Sep 1986	PA
MOBILE BAY	CG 53	Ingalls Shipbuilding	6 June 1984	22 Aug 1985	21 Feb 1987	PA
ANTIETAM	CG 54	Ingalls Shipbuilding	15 Nov 1984	14 Feb 1986	6 June 1987	PA
LEYTE GULF	CG 55	Ingalls Shipbuilding	18 Mar 1985	20 June 1986	26 Sep 1987	AA
SAN JACINTO	CG 56	Ingalls Shipbuilding	24 July 1985	14 Nov 1986	23 Jan 1988	AA
LAKE CHAMPLAIN	CG 57	Ingalls Shipbuilding	3 Mar 1986	3 Apr 1987	12 Aug 1988	PA
PHILIPPINE SEA	CG 58	Bath Iron Works	8 May 1986	12 July 1987	18 Mar 1989	AA
PRINCETON	CG 59	Ingalls Shipbuilding	15 Oct 1986	2 Oct 1987	11 Feb 1989	PA
NORMANDY	CG 60	Bath Iron Works	7 Apr 1987	19 Mar 1988	9 Dec 1989	AA
MONTEREY	CG 61	Bath Iron Works	19 Aug 1987	23 Oct 1988	16 June 1990	AA
CHANCELLORSVILLE	CG 62	Ingalls Shipbuilding	24 June 1987	15 July 1988	4 Nov 1989	PA
COWPENS	CG 63	Bath Iron Works	23 Dec 1987	11 Mar 1989	9 Mar 1991	PA
GETTYSBURG	CG 64	Bath Iron Works	17 Aug 1988	22 July 1989	22 June 1991	AA
CHOSIN	CG 65	Ingalls Shipbuilding	22 July 1988	1 Sep 1989	12 Jan 1991	PA
HUE CITY	CG 66	Ingalls Shipbuilding	20 Feb 1989	1 June 1990	14 Sep 1991	AA
SHILOH	CG 67	Bath Iron Works	1 Aug 1989	8 Sep 1990	2 July 1992	PA
ANZIO	CG 68	Ingalls Shipbuilding	21 Aug 1989	2 Nov 1990	2 May 1992	AA
VICKSBURG	CG 69	Ingalls Shipbuilding	30 May 1990	2 Aug 1991	14 Nov 1992	AA
LAKE ERIE	CG 70	Bath Iron Works	6 Mar 1990	13 July 1991	July 1993	Bldg
CAPE ST GEORGE	CG 71	Ingalls Shipbuilding	19 Nov 1990	10 Jan 1992	June 1993	Bldg
VELLA GULF	CG 72	Ingalls Shipbuilding	22 Apr 1991	13 June 1992	Sep 1993	Bldg
PORT ROYAL	CG 73	Ingalls Shipbuilding	20 Nov 1991	14 Nov 1992	Apr 1994	Bldg

Displacement, tons: 7015 light; 9590 (CG 47-48); 9407 (CG 49-51); 9466 (remainder) full load
Dimensions, feet (metres): 567 × 55 × 31 (sonar) *(172.8 × 16.8 × 9.5)*
Main machinery: 4 GE LM 2500 gas turbines; 86 000 hp *(64.16 MW)* sustained; 2 shafts; cp props
Speed, knots: 30+. **Range, miles:** 6000 at 20 kts
Complement: 358 (24 officers); accommodation for 405 total

Missiles: SLCM/SSM: GDC Tomahawk (CG 52 onwards); combination of (a) land attack; TAINS (Tercom aided navigation system) to 2500 km *(1400 nm)* at 0.7 Mach; altitude 15-100 m *(49.2-328.1 ft)*; warhead nuclear 200 kT (TLAM-N); CEP 80 m; or warhead 454 kg (TLAM-C) or submunitions (TLAM-D); range 1300 km *(700 nm)*; CEP 10 m. Nuclear warheads are not normally carried. Range increased by 30% in TLAM-C Block III which started production in 1992.
(b) anti-ship (TASM); inertial guidance; active radar and anti-radiation homing to 460 km *(250 nm)* at 0.7 Mach; warhead 454 kg.
8 McDonnell Douglas Harpoon (2 quad) ❶; active radar homing to 130 km *(70 nm)* at 0.9 Mach; warhead 227 kg. Extended range SLAM can be fired from modified Harpoon canisters.
SAM: 68 (CG 47-51); 122 (CG 52 onwards) GDC Standard SM-2MR; command/inertial guidance; semi-active radar homing to 73 km *(40 nm)* at 2 Mach.
A/S: 20 Honeywell ASROC; inertial guidance to 1.6-10 km *(1-5.4 nm)*; payload Mk 46 Mod 5 Neartip/Mk 50.
SAM and A/S missiles are fired from 2 twin Mk 26 Mod 5 launchers ❷ (CG 47-51) and 2 Mk 41 Mod 0 vertical launchers ❸ (61 missiles per launcher) (CG 52 onwards). Tomahawk is carried in CG 52 onwards with 8 missiles in each VLS launcher and 12 missiles in the magazines. Operational evaluation of VLS continues in conjunction with operational evaluation of Tomahawk. Vertical launch ASROC will be back fitted when available.
Guns: 2 FMC 5 in *(127 mm)*/54 Mk 45 (Mod 0 (CG 47-50); Mod 1 (CG 51 onwards)) ❹; 65° elevation; 20 rounds/minute to 23 km *(12.6 nm)* anti-surface; weight of shell 32 kg.
2 General Electric/General Dynamics 20 mm/76 Vulcan Phalanx 6-barrelled Mk 15 ❺; 3000 rounds/minute (4500 in Block 1) combined to 1.5 km.
4—12.7 mm MGs.
Torpedoes: 6—324 mm Mk 32 (2 triple) tubes (fitted in the ship's side aft) ❻. 36 Honeywell Mk 46 Mod 5; anti-submarine; active/passive homing to 11 km *(5.9 nm)* at 40 kts; warhead 44 kg. To be replaced by Mk 50 in due course.
Countermeasures: Decoys: 4 or 6 Loral Hycor SRBOC 6-barrelled fixed Mk 36 ❼; IR flares and chaff to 4 km *(2.2 nm)*. SLQ-25 Nixie; towed torpedo decoy.
ESM/ECM: Raytheon SLQ 32V(3) ❽; combined radar warning, jammer and deception system.
Combat data systems: NTDS with Links 4A, 11, 14 and 16 in due course. SATCOM SRR-1, WSC-3 (UHF), USC-38 (EHF) (from 1992). UYK 7 and 20 computers (CG 47-58); UYK 43/44 (CG 59 onwards). SQQ 28 for LAMPS sonobuoy data link ❾.
Fire control: SWG-3 Tomahawk WCS. SWG-1A Harpoon LCS. Aegis Mk 7 Mod 2 multi-target tracking with Mk 99 MFCS (includes 4 Mk 80 illuminator directors); has at least 12 channels of fire. Singer Librascope Mk 116 Mod 6 (53B) or 7 (53C) FCS for ASW. Lockheed Mk 86 Mod 9 GFCS.
Radars: Air search/fire control: RCA SPY 1A phased arrays ❿; 3D; E/F band (CG 47-58).
Raytheon SPY 1B phased arrays ⓫; 3D; E/F band (CG 59 on).
Air search: Raytheon SPS 49(V)7 ⓬; C/D band; range 457 km *(250 nm)*.
Surface search: ISC Cardion SPS 55 ⓭; I/J band.
Navigation: Marconi LN 66 (CG 47-48); I band.
Raytheon SPS 64(V)9 (remainder); I band.
Fire control: Lockheed SPQ 9A ⓮; I/J band; range 37 km *(20 nm)*.
Four Raytheon/RCA SPG 62 ⓯; I/J band.
Tacan: URN 25. IFF Mk XII AIMS UPX-29.
Sonars: General Electric/Hughes SQS 53A/B (CG 47-55); bow-mounted; active search and attack; medium frequency.
Gould SQR 19 (CG 54-55); passive towed array (TACTAS).
Gould/Raytheon SQQ 89(V)3 (CG 56 onwards); combines hull-mounted active SQS 53B (CG 56-67) or SQS 53C (CG 68-73) and passive towed array SQR 19.

Helicopters: 2 SH-60B Seahawk LAMPS III ⓰; 2 SH-2F LAMPS I (CG 47-48) ⓱.

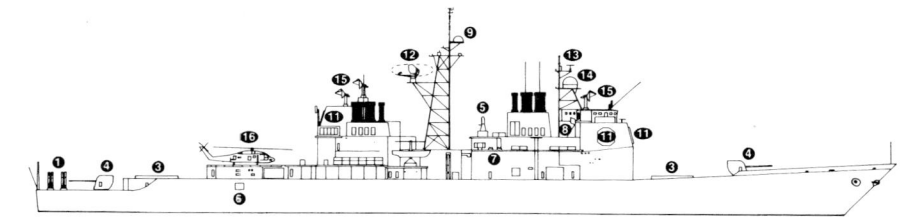
BUNKER HILL *(Scale 1 : 1500), Ian Sturton*

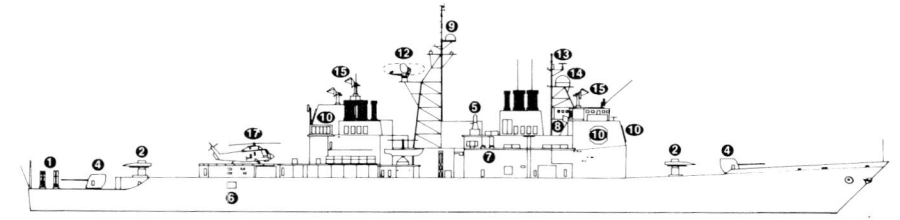
TICONDEROGA *(Scale 1 : 1500), Ian Sturton*

SHILOH *8/1992, Giorgio Arra*

Programmes: In finally approving the FY 1988 ship construction budget, Congress elected to authorise and fund the remaining five cruisers in the 27-ship programme. That decision stemmed from the delays being encountered in the construction of *Arleigh Burke* by Bath Iron Works, and the realisation that the Navy was in no position at that time to award further contracts for construction of more DDG 51s.
Modernisation: Long Range Improvement Programme: In order to include the latest in technology in these ships, four baselines were planned and five have evolved. *Ticonderoga*, equipped with LAMPS I, represents Baseline 0. Baseline I starts with *Vincennes* equipped with LAMPS III, RAST haul down flight deck system and Block 2 Standard missiles. Baseline II, beginning with *Bunker Hill*, adds Tomahawk, and the Vertical Launch System. Baseline III starting with *San Jacinto* adds the SQQ 89 sonar. Baseline IV, beginning with *Princeton* (CG 59), incorporates the advanced AN/SPY 1B radar on UYQ-21 displays and includes the upgraded computers UYK-43/44. According to the Navy, this method of upgrading ship capabilities provides the best available combat system to the fleet while reducing operation and support costs. *Lake Champlain* fired the first SLAM missile from a Harpoon canister in June 1990; the extended range SSM was controlled in terminal flight by a LAMPS III helicopter.
Structure: The Ticonderoga class design is a modification of the Spruance class. The same basic hull is used, with the same gas turbine propulsion plant although the overall length is slightly increased. The design includes Kevlar armour to protect vital spaces. No stabilisers. *Vincennes* and later ships have a lighter tripod mainmast vice the square quadruped of the first two.

Operational: *Yorktown* provided the air-intercept support for Navy fighters intercepting the Egyptian airliner carrying the hijackers of the cruise ship *Achille Lauro* from Egypt to Tunisia. In March and April of 1986, *Yorktown* and *Vincennes* were focal points of the successful operations in the Gulf of Sidra which led to the sinking of two Libyan patrol boats and of the strike by carrier-based Navy aircraft and shore-based F-111s against Libyan missile sites and other targets. *Vincennes* was again in the news with the misidentification and shooting down of an airliner during a surface engagement with Iranian gunboats in 1988. The report of that incident describes the Aegis system as having performed as designed, and the sensor data collected was accurate but 'it should be appreciated that Aegis is not capable of identifying the type of aircraft being tracked. Ships of the class were again active in directing the air defence of the northern Gulf during the Iraq war in early 1991. *Princeton* was damaged by a mine; repairs were completed in December 1991. Seven of the class fired Tomahawk missiles and another of the class fired again in January 1993 at a nuclear weapons plant in Iraq. Aegis's major advantages are the extended range of its sensors, its fast reaction time, the capacity to track many targets at once, its ability to send this information automatically to other units, and its data displays which combine sensor information with other inputs. Because of its long-range radar, it gives operators additional time to react, to gather data, and to make considered judgements. Operating close to land, these advantages can be eroded. Two of the class are based at Yokosuka, Japan.

THOMAS S GATES *1/1992, Giorgio Arra*

TICONDEROGA *6/1992, Giorgio Arra*

ANZIO *3/1992, Ingalls Shipbuilding*

MOBILE BAY *5/1992, John Mortimer*

VALLEY FORGE *8/1992, Hachiro Nakai*

778 USA / Cruisers

9 BELKNAP CLASS: GUIDED MISSILE CRUISERS (CG)

Name	No	Builders	Laid down	Launched	Commissioned	F/S
BELKNAP	CG 26	Bath Iron Works Corporation	5 Feb 1962	20 July 1963	7 Nov 1964	AA
JOSEPHUS DANIELS	CG 27	Bath Iron Works Corporation	23 Apr 1962	2 Dec 1963	8 May 1965	AA
WAINWRIGHT	CG 28	Bath Iron Works Corporation	2 July 1962	25 Apr 1964	8 Jan 1966	AA
JOUETT	CG 29	Puget Sound Naval Shipyard	25 Sep 1962	30 June 1964	3 Dec 1966	PA
HORNE	CG 30	San Francisco Naval Shipyard	12 Dec 1962	30 Oct 1964	15 Apr 1967	PA
STERETT	CG 31	Puget Sound Naval Shipyard	25 Sep 1962	30 June 1964	8 Apr 1967	PA
WILLIAM H STANDLEY	CG 32	Bath Iron Works Corporation	29 July 1963	19 Dec 1964	9 July 1966	PA
FOX	CG 33	Todd Shipyard Corporation	15 Jan 1963	21 Nov 1964	8 May 1966	PA
BIDDLE	CG 34	Bath Iron Works Corporation	9 Dec 1963	2 July 1965	21 Jan 1967	AA

Displacement, tons: 6570 standard; 8200 full load (CG 27-28); 8065 (CG 29-33); 8250 (CG 34); 8575 (CG 26)
Dimensions, feet (metres): 547 × 54.8 × 28.8 (sonar) *(166.7 × 16.7 × 8.8)*
Main machinery: 4 Babcock & Wilcox/Combustion Engineering boilers; 1200 psi *(84.4 kg/cm sq)*; 950°F *(510°C)*; 2 GE/De Laval/Allis Chalmers turbines; 85 000 hp *(63 MW)*; 2 shafts
Speed, knots: 32.5. **Range, miles:** 8000 at 14 kts; 2500 at 30 kts
Complement: 479 (26 officers); Flag 18 (6 officers); Flag 111 (30 officers) (CG 26)

Missiles: SSM: 8 McDonnell Douglas Harpoon (2 quad) launchers ❶; active radar homing to 130 km *(70 nm)* at 0.9 Mach; warhead 227 kg.
SAM: 40 GDC Standard SM-2ER; combined/inertial guidance; semi-active radar homing to 137 km *(75 nm)* at 2.5 Mach.
A/S: 20 Honeywell ASROC; inertial guidance to 1.6-10 km *(1-5.4 nm)*; payload Mk 46 Mod 5 Neartip/Mk 50. 1 twin Mk 10 Mod 15 launcher for SAM and ASROC ❷.
Guns: 1 FMC 5 in *(127 mm)*/54 Mk 42 Mod 10 ❸; 85° elevation; 20-40 rounds/minute to 24 km *(13.1 nm)* anti-surface; 14 km *(7.7 nm)* anti-aircraft; weight of shell 32 kg.
2 General Electric/General Dynamics 20 mm Vulcan Phalanx 6-barrelled Mk 15 ❹; 3000 rounds/minute (4500 in Block 1) combined to 1.5 km.
Torpedoes: 6—324 mm Mk 32 (2 triple) tubes ❺. 18 Honeywell Mk 46 Mod 5; anti-submarine; active/passive homing to 11 km *(5.9 nm)* at 40 kts; warhead 44 kg. To be replaced by Mk 50 in due course.
Countermeasures: Decoys: 4 Loral Hycor SRBOC 6-barrelled fixed Mk 36; IR flares and chaff to 4 km *(2.2 nm)*. SLQ 25 Nixie; torpedo decoy.
ESM/ECM: SLQ 32(V)3; combined radar warning, jammer and deception system. OUTBOARD II (CG 27-29 and 32-34).
Combat data systems: NTDS with Links 4A, 11, 14 and 16 in due course. SATCOM SRR-1, WSC-3 (UHF); WSC-6 (SHF) (CG 26); USC-38 (EHF) (from 1992).
Fire control: SWG-1 Harpoon LCS. 2 Mk 76 Mod 9 MFCS. Mk 68 GFCS. Mk 14 weapon direction system (Mk 7 in CG26). Mk 114 ASW fire control system (Mk 116 in CG 26). SYS 2(V)1/2 IADT.
Radars: Air search: ITT SPS 48E (C in CG26) ❻; 3D; E/F band; range 402 km *(220 nm)*.
Raytheon SPS 49(V)3/5 ❼; C/D band.
Surface search: Norden SPS 67 ❽; G band.
Navigation: Marconi LN 66; I band.
Fire control: Western Electric SPG 53F ❾; I/J band.
Two Sperry/RCA SPG 55D ❿; G/H band; range 51 km *(28 nm)* (for Standard).
Tacan: URN 25. IFF Mk XII AIMS UPX-29.
Sonars: EDO SQS 26BX; General Electric/Hughes SQS 53C (CG 26); bow-mounted; active search and attack; medium/low frequency.

Helicopters: 1 SH-2F LAMPS I ⓫ (no hangar in *Belknap*).

Programmes: Authorised as guided missile frigates; first three in FY 1961, remainder in FY 1962. Reclassified as CGs on 30 June 1975.
Modernisation: *Belknap* was severely damaged in a collision with the carrier *John F Kennedy* (CV 67) on 22 November 1975 near Sicily. Repair and modernisation began 9 January 1978. Included Flag accommodation in front of the bridge and the hangar converted for additional accommodation. Recommissioned 10 May 1980. *Belknap*, *Wainwright*, *Horne* and *Sterett* all had the Tactical Flag Command Centre fitted in 1983-85. All except *Belknap* have received the New Threat Upgrade modernisation which includes SPS 48E radar, Mk 14 WDS and SYS 2 automated action data system, integrated with SPS 49 radar.
Structure: Distinctive in having their single missile launcher forward and 5 in gun mount aft. This arrangement allowed missile stowage in the larger bow section and provided space aft of the superstructure for a helicopter hangar and platform. Harpoon is forward of Phalanx on the port side, with this arrangement reversed on the starboard side.
Operational: *Belknap* is Sixth Fleet Flagship. *Wainwright* was the SM-2ER trials ship.

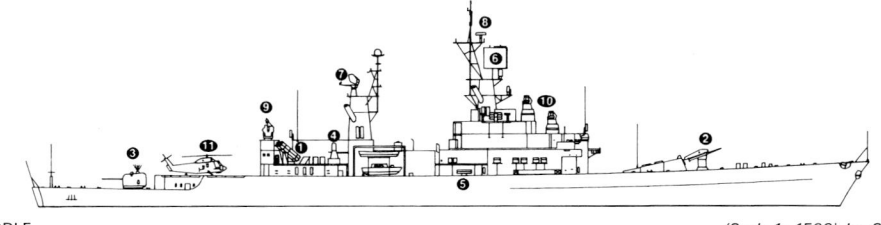
BIDDLE *(Scale 1: 1500), Ian Sturton*

BIDDLE *7/1992, Giorgio Ghiglione*

WAINWRIGHT *9/1992, Giorgio Arra*

BIDDLE *3/1991, Giorgio Arra*

BELKNAP *10/1991, C D Yaylali*

9 LEAHY CLASS: GUIDED MISSILE CRUISERS (CG)

Name	No	Builders	Laid down	Launched	Commissioned	F/S
LEAHY	CG 16	Bath Iron Works Corporation	3 Dec 1959	1 July 1961	4 Aug 1962	PA
HARRY E YARNELL	CG 17	Bath Iron Works Corporation	31 May 1960	9 Dec 1961	2 Feb 1963	AA
WORDEN	CG 18	Bath Iron Works Corporation	19 Sep 1960	2 June 1962	3 Aug 1963	PA
DALE	CG 19	New York S B Corporation	6 Sep 1960	28 July 1962	23 Nov 1963	AA
RICHMOND K TURNER	CG 20	New York S B Corporation	9 Jan 1961	6 Apr 1963	13 June 1964	AA
GRIDLEY	CG 21	Puget Sound Bridge & Dry Dock Co	15 July 1960	31 July 1961	25 May 1963	PA
ENGLAND	CG 22	Todd Shipyards Corporation	4 Oct 1960	6 Mar 1962	7 Dec 1963	PA
HALSEY	CG 23	San Francisco Naval Shipyard	26 Aug 1960	15 Jan 1962	20 July 1963	PA
REEVES	CG 24	Puget Sound Naval Shipyard	1 July 1960	12 May 1962	15 May 1964	PA

Displacement, tons: 4650 light; 5670 standard; 8203 full load
Dimensions, feet (metres): 533 × 54.9 × 24.8 (sonar) *(162.5 × 16.6 × 7.6)*
Main machinery: 4 boilers (Babcock & Wilcox in CG 16-20, Foster-Wheeler in CG 21-24); 1200 psi *(84.4 kg/cm sq)*; 950°F *(510°C)*; 2 GE/De Laval/Allis Chalmers turbines; 85 000 hp *(63 MW)*; 2 shafts
Speed, knots: 32.7. **Range, miles:** 8000 at 20 kts; 2500 at 30 kts
Complement: 423 (26 officers); Flag 18 (6 officers)

Missiles: SSM: 8 McDonnell Douglas Harpoon (2 quad) launchers ❶; active radar homing to 130 km *(70 nm)* at 0.9 Mach; warhead 227 kg.
SAM: 80 GDC Standard SM-2ER; 2 twin Mk 10 launchers (Mod 13 fwd, Mod 14 aft) ❷; command/inertial guidance; semi-active radar homing to 137 km *(75 nm)* at 2.5 Mach.
A/S: Honeywell ASROC Mk 16 octuple launcher ❸; inertial guidance to 1.6-10 km *(1-5.4 nm)*; payload Mk 46 Mod 5 Near-tip/Mk 50.
Guns: 2 General Electric/General Dynamics 20 mm Vulcan Phalanx 6-barrelled Mk 15 ❹; 3000 rounds/minute (4500 in Block 1) combined to 1.5 km.
4—12.7 mm MGs.
Torpedoes: 6—324 mm Mk 32 (2 triple) tubes ❺. Honeywell Mk 46 Mod 5; anti-submarine; active/passive homing to 11 km *(5.9 nm)* at 40 kts; warhead 44 kg. To be replaced by Mk 50 in due course.
Countermeasures: Decoys: 6 Loral Hycor SRBOC 6-barrelled fixed Mk 36; IR flares and chaff to 4 km *(2.2 nm)*. T-Mk 6 Fanfare/SLQ 25 Nixie; towed torpedo decoy. NATO Sea Gnat. SSQ-95 AEB. SLQ 39/49 chaff buoy/expendables.
ESM/ECM: SLQ 32(V)3; combined radar warning, jammer and deception system.
Combat data systems: NTDS with Links 4A, 11, 14 and 16 in due course. SATCOM SRR-1, WSC-3 (UHF), USC-38 (EHF) (from 1992).
Fire control: SWG-1A Harpoon LCS. Mk 76 MFCS. Mk 14 weapon direction system. Mk 114 ASW FCS. SYS-2(V)2 IADT.
Radars: Air search: ITT SPS 48 E ❻; 3D; E/F band; range 402 km *(220 nm)*.
Raytheon SPS 49(V)3/5 ❼; C/D band; range 457 km *(250 nm)*.
Surface search: Raytheon SPS 10F or Norden SPS 67 ❽; G band.
Navigation: Raytheon SPS 64(V)9; I band.
Fire control: Four Sperry/RCA SPG 55C ❾; G/H band; range 51 km *(28 nm)*.
Tacan: URN 25. IFF Mk XV.
Sonars: Sperry SQQ 23 pair (CG 17); bow-mounted; active search and attack; medium frequency.
Sangamo SQS 23B (remainder); active search and attack; medium frequency.

Helicopters: Platform only with limited facilities.

Programmes: First three authorised in FY 1958 and remainder in FY 1959. Reclassified as guided missile cruisers (CG) on 30 June 1975.
Modernisation: Modernised between 1967 and 1972 to improve their Anti-Air Warfare (AAW) capabilities. 76 mm guns were removed and superstructure enlarged to provide space for additional electronic equipment, including NTDS; improved Tacan fitted and improved guidance system for SAM missiles installed, and larger ship's service turbo generators provided. New Threat Upgrade modernisation completed in all of the class 1987-91; this included SPS 48E radar, updating the Mk 10 launchers and Mk 76 MFCS and improving the SPG 55 fire control radars.

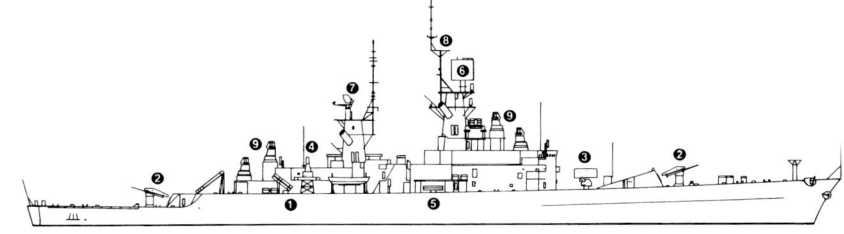

LEAHY *(Scale 1 : 1500), Ian Sturton*

LEAHY *9/1992, Stefan Terzibaschitsch*

ENGLAND *2/1992, Hachiro Nakai*

Structure: Distinctive in having twin missile launchers forward and aft with ASROC launcher between the forward missile launcher and bridge on main deck level.

Operational: 'Double-end' missile cruisers especially designed to screen fast carrier task forces. Six to be paid off in 1994.

HARRY E YARNELL *7/1992, H M Steele*

USA / Cruisers — Destroyers

2 CALIFORNIA CLASS: GUIDED MISSILE CRUISERS (CGN)

Name	No	Builders	Laid down	Launched	Commissioned	F/S
CALIFORNIA	CGN 36	Newport News S B and D D Co	23 Jan 1970	22 Sep 1971	16 Feb 1974	PA
SOUTH CAROLINA	CGN 37	Newport News S B and D D Co	1 Dec 1970	1 July 1972	25 Jan 1975	AA

Displacement, tons: 8706 light; 9561 standard; 10 450 full load (9473, CGN 37)
Dimensions, feet (metres): 596 × 61 × 31.5 (sonar) *(181.7 × 18.6 × 9.6)*
Main machinery: Nuclear; 2 GE PWR D2G; 2 turbines; 70 000 hp *(52 MW)*; 2 shafts
Speed, knots: 30+
Complement: 603 (44 officers)

Missiles: SSM: 8 McDonnell Douglas Harpoon (2 quad) launchers ❶; active radar homing to 130 km *(70 nm)* at 0.9 Mach; warhead 227 kg.
SAM: 80 GDC Standard SM-2MR; 2 Mk 13 Mod 7 launchers ❷; command/inertial guidance; semi-active radar homing to 73 km *(40 nm)* at 2 Mach.
A/S: Honeywell ASROC Mk 16 octuple launcher ❸; inertial guidance to 1.6-10 km *(1-5.4 nm)*; Mk 46 Mod 5 Neartip/Mk 50; 24 weapons carried.
Guns: 2 FMC 5 in *(127 mm)*/54 Mk 45 Mod 0 ❹; 65° elevation; 20 rounds/minute to 23 km *(12.6 nm)* anti-surface; 15 km *(8.2 nm)* anti-aircraft; weight of shell 32 kg.
2 General Electric/General Dynamics 20 mm Vulcan Phalanx 6-barrelled Mk 15 ❺; 3000 rounds/minute (or 4500 in Block 1) combined to 1.5 km.
4—12.7 mm MGs.
Torpedoes: 4—324 mm Mk 32 (2 twin) fixed tubes. Honeywell Mk 46 Mod 5; anti-submarine; active/passive homing to 11 km *(5.9 nm)* at 40 kts; warhead 44 kg. To be replaced by Mk 50 in due course.
Countermeasures: Decoys: 4 Loral Hycor SRBOC 6-barrelled fixed Mk 36; IR flares and chaff to 4 km *(2.2 nm)*. SLQ-25; torpedo decoy system.
ESM/ECM: SLQ 32(V)3; combined radar warning, jammer and deception system. OUTBOARD.
Combat data systems: NTDS with Links 4A, 11, 14 and 16 in due course. SATCOM SRR-1, WSC-3 (UHF), USC 38 (EHF) (from 1992).
Fire control: SWG-1A Harpoon LCS. 2 Mk 74 MFCS Mod 2. 1 Mk 86 Mod 3 GFCS. 1 Mk 14 weapon direction system. 1 Mk 114 ASW FCS. SYS-2(V)2 IADT.
Radars: Air search: ITT SPS 48E ❻; 3D; E/F band; range 402 km *(220 nm)*.
Raytheon SPS 49(V)5 ❼; C/D band.
Surface search: Norden SPS 67 ❽; G band.
Navigation: Marconi LN 66; I/J band.
Fire control: Four SPG 51D ❾; G/I band.
SPG 60D ❿; I/J band. SPQ 9A ⓫; I/J band.
Tacan: URN 25.
Sonars: EDO/GE SQS 26 CX; bow-mounted; active search and attack; medium frequency.

Helicopters: Platform only.

CALIFORNIA *(Scale 1 : 1500), Ian Sturton*

SOUTH CAROLINA *3/1991, Giorgio Arra*

Programmes: *California* was authorised in FY 1967 and *South Carolina* in FY 1968. Originally classified as guided missile destroyers (DLGN); subsequently reclassified as guided missile cruisers (CGN) on 30 June 1975.
Modernisation: It was planned to fit Tomahawk missiles but the project was cancelled due to topweight constraints. Both have completed the New Threat Upgrade modernisation. This included Standard SM-2 missiles, upgrading the Mk 74 MFCS and SPG 51D radars, replacing SPS 40B radar by SPS 49, upgrading SPS 48 radar, fitting the Mk 14 weapon direction system and the SYS(V)2 IADT.
Structure: Harpoon missiles are in two quadruple sets with the midships launcher facing to starboard and the aft launcher to port.

DESTROYERS

Note: One Forrest Sherman class *Decatur* (DDG 31) is being refurbished with a full ship self-defence system to act as a live target in 1994. All systems will be operated by remote control.

1 COONTZ CLASS: GUIDED MISSILE DESTROYER (DDG)

Name	No	Builders	Laid down	Launched	Commissioned	F/S
MAHAN	DDG 42 (ex-DLG 11)	San Francisco Naval Shipyard	31 July 1957	7 Oct 1959	25 Aug 1960	AA

Displacement, tons: 4580 standard; 6150 full load
Dimensions, feet (metres): 512.5 × 52.5 × 15; 23.4 sonar *(156.3 × 16 × 4.6; 7.1)*
Main machinery: 4 Foster-Wheeler/Babcock & Wilcox boilers; 1200 psi *(84.4 kg/cm sq)*, 950°F *(510°C)*; 2 De Laval/Allis Chalmers turbines; 85 000 hp *(63 MW)*; 2 shafts
Speed, knots: 33. **Range, miles:** 5000 at 20 kts; 1500 at 30 kts
Complement: 402 (25 officers)

Missiles: SSM: 8 McDonnell Douglas Harpoon (2 quad) launchers ❶; active radar homing to 130 km *(70 nm)* at 0.9 Mach; warhead 227 kg.
SAM: 40 GDC Standard SM-2ER; twin Mk 10 Mod 0 launcher ❷; command/inertial guidance; semi-active radar homing to 137 km *(75 nm)* at 2.5 Mach.
A/S: Honeywell ASROC Mk 16 octuple launcher ❸; inertial guidance to 1.6-10 km *(1-5.4 nm)*; payload Mk 46 Mod 5 Neartip.
Guns: 1 FMC 5 in *(127 mm)*/54 Mk 42 Mod 10 ❹; 85° elevation; 20-40 rounds/minute to 24 km *(13 nm)*; weight of shell 32 kg.
4—12.7 mm MGs.
Torpedoes: 6—324 mm Mk 32 (2 triple) tubes ❺. Honeywell Mk 46; anti-submarine; active/passive homing to 11 km *(5.9 nm)* at 40 kts; warhead 44 kg.
Countermeasures: Decoys: 4 Loral Hycor SRBOC 6-barrelled fixed Mk 36; IR flares and chaff to 4 km *(2.2 nm)*. T Mk 6 Fanfare; torpedo decoy.
ESM/ECM: SLQ 32(V)3; combined radar warning, jammer and deception system.
Combat data systems: NTDS with Links 11 and 14 (receive only). SATCOM SRR-1, WSC-3 (UHF).
Fire control: SWG-1 Harpoon LCS. 1 Mk 76 MFCS. Mk 68 GFCS. Mk 14 WDS. Mk 111 ASW FCS. SYS-2(V)2 IADT.
Radars: Air search: ITT SPS 48E ❻; 3D; E/F band; range 402 km *(220 nm)*.
Raytheon SPS 49(V)2 ❼ ((V)5 in DDG 42); C/D band; range 457 km *(250 nm)*.
Surface search: Raytheon SPS 10B ❽; G band.
Navigation: Marconi LN 66; I/J band.
Fire control: Western Electric SPG 53A ❾; I/J band.
Two Sperry/RCA SPG 55B ❿; G/H band; range 51 km *(28 nm)* (for Standard).
Tacan: URN 25. IFF Mk XII AIMS UPX-29.
Sonars: Sperry SQQ 23A PAIR; hull-mounted; active search and attack; medium frequency.

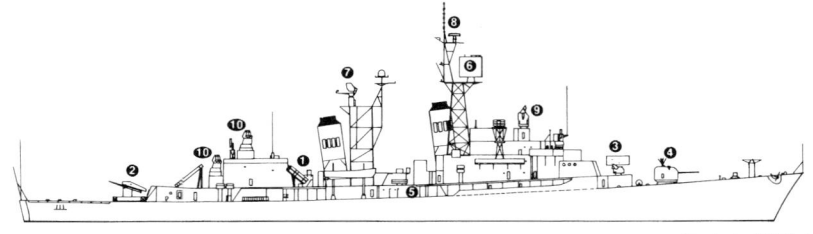

MAHAN *(Scale 1 : 1500), Ian Sturton*

MAHAN *2/1990, Giorgio Arra*

Helicopters: Platform and limited support capability only.

Modernisation: *Mahan* was trials ship for the New Threat Upgrade (NTU) system which included SPS 48E (3D radar), SPS 49(V)5 (2D radar), SYS 2 computerised AIO system and Standard SM-2ER missiles.
Operational: The last of the class and likely to pay off in 1993.

0 + (4) ARLEIGH BURKE CLASS (FLIGHT IIA): GUIDED MISSILE DESTROYERS (AEGIS) (DDG)

Displacement, tons: 9217 full load
Dimensions, feet (metres): 509.5 × 66.9 × 20.7; 32.7 (sonar) *(155.3 × 20.4 × 6.3; 9.9)*
Main machinery: 4 GE LM 2500-30 gas turbines; 105 000 hp *(78.33 MW)* sustained; 2 shafts; cp props
Speed, knots: 32. **Range, miles:** 4400 at 20 kts
Complement: 380 (32 officers)

Missiles: SLCM/SSM: Tomahawk.
SAM: Standard SM-2ER (Block IV).
  Evolved Sea Sparrow CIWS.
A/S: ASROC.
  2 Vertical Launch Systems for Tomahawk, Standard, Sea Sparrow and ASROC. 32 cells forward, 64 cells aft ❶.
Guns: 1—5 in *(127 mm)*/54 ❷.
Torpedoes: 6—324 mm Mk 32 (2 triple) tubes ❸.
Countermeasures: Decoys: 2 chaff launchers ❹.
ESM/ECM: SLQ 32(V)3 ❺; intercept and jammer.
Combat data systems: Includes JTIDS, Tactical Information Exchange System (TADIX B) and Tactical Data Information Link (TADIL J).
Radars: Air search/fire control: SPY 1D phased arrays ❻ with Track Initiation Processor.
  Surface search: SPS 67(V) ❼.
  Fire control: 3 SPG 62 ❽.
Sonars: SQS 53C; hull-mounted; active search and attack; medium frequency.
  Kingfisher; hull-mounted mine detection; active; high frequency.

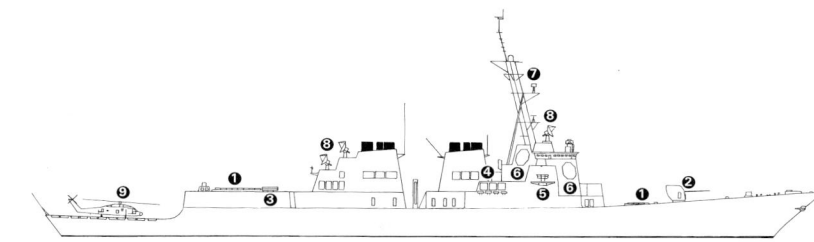

ARLEIGH BURKE FLIGHT IIA *(Scale 1 : 1200), Ian Sturton*

Helicopters: 2 SH-60B/F LAMPS III ❾.

Programmes: First ship of this revised Arleigh Burke class design is scheduled to be DDG 77 which should be authorised in the FY 1994 budget.
Structure: The upgrade from Flight II includes two hangars for embarked helicopters and an extended transom to increase the size of a RAST fitted flight deck at the expense of SQR 19 TACTAS. Vertical launchers are increased at each end by three cells and will be able to fire the agile Evolved Sea Sparrow missile which replaces Phalanx. Harpoon may be fitted for, but not with. Other changes include the Kingfisher minehunting sonar, a reconfiguration of the SPY-1D arrays and the inclusion of a Track Initiation Processor in the Aegis radar system. Use of fibre optic technology should reduce weight and improve reliability. The line drawing shows the ship as configured in early 1993, no doubt there are more changes to come. The At Sea Missile Handling System has been deleted.

4 KIDD CLASS: GUIDED MISSILE DESTROYERS (DDG)

Name	No	Builders	Laid down	Launched	Commissioned	F/S
KIDD (ex-Iranian *Kouroosh*)	DDG 993 (ex-US DD 993)	Ingalls Shipbuilding Corp	26 June 1978	11 Aug 1979	27 June 1981	AA
CALLAGHAN (ex-Iranian *Daryush*)	DDG 994 (ex-US DD 994)	Ingalls Shipbuilding Corp	23 Oct 1978	1 Dec 1979	29 Aug 1981	PA
SCOTT (ex-Iranian *Nader*)	DDG 995 (ex-US DD 995, ex-US DD 996)	Ingalls Shipbuilding Corp	12 Feb 1979	1 Mar 1980	24 Oct 1981	AA
CHANDLER (ex-Iranian *Anoushirvan*)	DDG 996 (ex-US DD 996, ex-US DD 998)	Ingalls Shipbuilding Corp	7 May 1979	24 May 1980	13 Mar 1982	PA

Displacement, tons: 6950 light; 9574 full load
Dimensions, feet (metres): 563.3 × 55 × 20; 33 sonar *(171.7 × 16.8 × 6.2; 10)*
Main machinery: 4 GE LM 2500 gas turbines; 86 000 hp *(64.16 MW)* sustained; 2 shafts
Speed, knots: 33. **Range, miles:** 3300 at 30 kts; 6000 at 20 kts; 8000 at 17 kts
Complement: 339 (20 officers)

Missiles: SSM: 8 McDonnell Douglas Harpoon (2 quad) launchers ❶; active radar homing to 130 km *(70 nm)* at 0.9 Mach; warhead 227 kg.
  SAM: 52 GDC Standard SM-2MR; command/inertial guidance; semi-active radar homing to 73 km *(40 nm)* at 2 Mach.
  A/S: 16 Honeywell ASROC; inertial guidance to 1.6-10 km *(1-5.4 nm)*; payload Mk 46 Mod 5 Neartip/Mk 50. 2 twin Mk 26 (Mod 3 and Mod 4) launchers for Standard and ASROC ❷; missiles are split between 2 magazines.
Guns: 2 FMC 5 in *(127 mm)*/54 Mk 45 Mod 0 ❸; 65° elevation; 20 rounds/minute to 23 km *(12.6 nm)*; weight of shell 32 kg plus SALGP (Semi-Active Laser-Guided Projectiles).
  2 General Electric/General Dynamics 20 mm Vulcan Phalanx 6-barrelled Mk 15 ❹; 3000 rounds/minute (4500 in Block 1) combined to 1.5 km.
  4—12.7 mm MGs.
Torpedoes: 6—324 mm Mk 32 (2 triple) tubes ❺. Honeywell Mk 46; anti-submarine; active/passive homing to 11 km *(5.9 nm)* at 40 kts; warhead 44 kg. To be replaced by Mk 50 in due course. Torpedoes fired from inside the hull under the hangar.
Countermeasures: Decoys: 4 Loral Hycor SRBOC 6-barrelled fixed Mk 36; IR flares and chaff to 4 km *(2.2 nm)*. SLQ 25 Nixie; torpedo decoy.
ESM/ECM: SLQ 32(V)2; radar warning. Sidekick modification adds jammer and deception system.
Combat data systems: NTDS with Links 4A, 11, 14 and 16 in due course. SATCOM SRR-1, WSC-3 (UHF); USC-38 (EHF) (from 1992).
Fire control: SWG-1A Harpoon LCS. 2 Mk 74 MFCS. Mk 86 Mod 5 GFCS. Mk 116 FCS for ASW. Mk 14 WDS. SYS 2(V)2 IADT. SRQ-4 for LAMPS III. 4 SYR 3393 for SAM mid-course guidance.
Radars: Air search: ITT SPS 48E ❻; 3D; E/F band; range 402 km *(220 nm)*.
  Raytheon SPS 49(V)5 ❼; C/D band.
  Surface search: ISC Cardion SPS 55 ❽; I/J band.
  Navigation: Raytheon SPS 64; I/J band.
  Fire control: Two SPG 51D ❾, 1 SPG 60 ❿, 1 SPQ 9A ⓫; G/I/J band.
  Tacan: URN 25. IFF Mk XII AIMS UPX-29.
Sonars: General Electric/Hughes SQS 53A; bow-mounted; search and attack; medium frequency. To receive SQS 53C on completion of evaluation.
  Gould SQR 19 (TACTAS); passive towed array (may be fitted).

Helicopters: 2 SH-2F LAMPS I ⓬ or 1 SH-60 LAMPS III.

Programmes: On 25 July 1979 the US Navy took over the contracts of four destroyers originally ordered by the Iranian Government in 1974.
Modernisation: Between 1988 and 1990 all received the New Threat Upgrade modernisation with updated Mk 74 MFCS for SM-2MR and SPG 51D radars, SPS 49(V)5 and Mk 14 weapon direction system.
Structure: The modular concept has been used extensively to facilitate construction and modernisation. Displacement could be up to 1000 tons over design because of the addition of Kevlar armour. Excellent air conditioning because of original Iranian requirements. NTU has led to a rearrangement of the mainmast and repositioning of SPS 48 and the SPG 60 aerials, in order to make room for the SPS 49.
Operational: These ships are optimised for general warfare instead of anti-submarine warfare as are the Spruance class, and the ability to fire SM-2MR allows them to support Aegis cruisers, if necessary allowing Aegis to control the missiles. The addition of SPS 49 markedly improves air picture compilation capability.

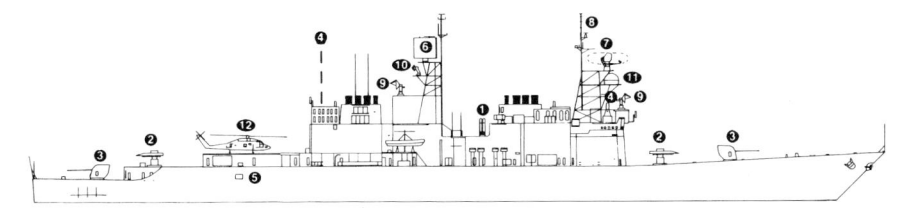

SCOTT *(Scale 1 : 1500), Ian Sturton*

CALLAGHAN *6/1992, A Campanera i Rovira*

SCOTT *7/1992, Jürg Kürsenor*

31 SPRUANCE CLASS: DESTROYERS (DD)

Name	No	Builders	Laid down	Launched	Commissioned	F/S
SPRUANCE	DD 963	Ingalls Shipbuilding Corporation	17 Nov 1972	10 Nov 1973	20 Sep 1975	AA
PAUL F FOSTER	DD 964	Ingalls Shipbuilding Corporation	6 Feb 1973	23 Feb 1974	21 Feb 1976	PA
KINKAID	DD 965	Ingalls Shipbuilding Corporation	19 Apr 1973	25 May 1974	10 July 1976	PA
HEWITT	DD 966	Ingalls Shipbuilding Corporation	23 July 1973	24 Aug 1974	25 Sep 1976	PA
ELLIOTT	DD 967	Ingalls Shipbuilding Corporation	15 Oct 1973	19 Dec 1974	22 Jan 1976	PA
ARTHUR W RADFORD	DD 968	Ingalls Shipbuilding Corporation	14 Jan 1974	1 Mar 1975	16 Apr 1977	AA
PETERSON	DD 969	Ingalls Shipbuilding Corporation	29 Apr 1974	21 June 1975	9 July 1977	AA
CARON	DD 970	Ingalls Shipbuilding Corporation	1 July 1974	24 June 1975	1 Oct 1977	AA
DAVID R RAY	DD 971	Ingalls Shipbuilding Corporation	23 Sep 1974	23 Aug 1975	19 Nov 1977	PA
OLDENDORF	DD 972	Ingalls Shipbuilding Corporation	27 Dec 1974	21 Oct 1975	4 Mar 1978	PA
JOHN YOUNG	DD 973	Ingalls Shipbuilding Corporation	17 Feb 1975	7 Feb 1976	20 May 1978	PA
COMTE DE GRASSE	DD 974	Ingalls Shipbuilding Corporation	4 Apr 1975	26 Mar 1976	5 Aug 1978	AA
O'BRIEN	DD 975	Ingalls Shipbuilding Corporation	9 May 1975	8 July 1976	3 Dec 1977	PA
MERRILL	DD 976	Ingalls Shipbuilding Corporation	16 June 1975	1 Sep 1976	11 Mar 1978	PA
BRISCOE	DD 977	Ingalls Shipbuilding Corporation	21 July 1975	15 Dec 1976	3 June 1978	AA
STUMP	DD 978	Ingalls Shipbuilding Corporation	25 Aug 1975	29 Jan 1977	19 Aug 1978	AA
CONOLLY	DD 979	Ingalls Shipbuilding Corporation	29 Sep 1975	19 Feb 1977	14 Oct 1978	AA
MOOSBRUGGER	DD 980	Ingalls Shipbuilding Corporation	3 Nov 1975	23 July 1977	16 Dec 1978	AA
JOHN HANCOCK	DD 981	Ingalls Shipbuilding Corporation	16 Jan 1976	29 Oct 1977	1 Mar 1979	AA
NICHOLSON	DD 982	Ingalls Shipbuilding Corporation	20 Feb 1976	11 Nov 1977	12 May 1979	AA
JOHN RODGERS	DD 983	Ingalls Shipbuilding Corporation	12 Aug 1976	25 Feb 1978	14 July 1979	AA
LEFTWICH	DD 984	Ingalls Shipbuilding Corporation	12 Nov 1976	8 Apr 1978	25 Aug 1979	PA
CUSHING	DD 985	Ingalls Shipbuilding Corporation	27 Dec 1976	17 June 1978	21 Sep 1979	PA
HARRY W HILL	DD 986	Ingalls Shipbuilding Corporation	3 Jan 1977	10 Aug 1978	17 Nov 1979	PA
O'BANNON	DD 987	Ingalls Shipbuilding Corporation	21 Feb 1977	25 Sep 1978	15 Dec 1979	AA
THORN	DD 988	Ingalls Shipbuilding Corporation	29 Aug 1977	14 Nov 1978	16 Feb 1980	AA
DEYO	DD 989	Ingalls Shipbuilding Corporation	14 Oct 1977	27 Jan 1979	22 Mar 1980	AA
INGERSOLL	DD 990	Ingalls Shipbuilding Corporation	5 Dec 1977	10 Mar 1979	12 Apr 1980	PA
FIFE	DD 991	Ingalls Shipbuilding Corporation	6 Mar 1978	1 May 1979	31 May 1980	PA
FLETCHER	DD 992	Ingalls Shipbuilding Corporation	24 Apr 1978	16 June 1979	12 July 1980	PA
HAYLER	DD 997	Ingalls Shipbuilding Corporation	20 Oct 1980	27 Mar 1982	5 Mar 1983	AA

Displacement, tons: 5770 light; 8040 full load
Dimensions, feet (metres): 563.2 × 55.1 × 19; 29 (sonar) *(171.7 × 16.8 × 5.8; 8.8)*
Main machinery: 4 GE LM 2500 gas turbines; 86 000 hp *(64.16 MW)* sustained; 2 shafts; cp props
Speed, knots: 33. **Range, miles:** 6000 at 20 kts
Complement: 319-339 (20 officers)

Missiles: SLCM/SSM: GDC Tomahawk ❶; combination of (a) land attack; TAINS (Tercom aided navigational system) to 2500 km *(1400 nm)* at 0.7 Mach; altitude 15-100 m *(49.2-328.1 ft)*; warhead nuclear 200 kT (TLAM-N); CEP 80 m; or warhead 454 kg (TLAM-C) or submunitions (TLAM-D); range 1300 km *(700 nm)*; CEP 10 m. Nuclear warheads not normally carried. Range increased by 30% in TLAM-C Batch III which started production in 1992.
(b) anti-ship (TASM); active radar/anti-radiation homing to 460 km *(250 nm)* at 0.7 Mach; warhead 454 kg.
8 fitted on the forecastle in 2 Mk 44 armoured box launchers in DD 974, 976, 979, 983-984, 989-990. Remainder being fitted with the Mk 41 Mod 0 VLS ❷ with one 61 missile magazine combining 45 Tomahawk and ultimately ASROC.
8 McDonnell Douglas Harpoon (2 quad) ❸; active radar homing to 130 km *(70 nm)* at 0.9 Mach; warhead 227 kg.
SAM: Raytheon GMLS Mk 29 octuple launcher ❹; 24 Sea Sparrow; semi-active radar homing to 14.6 km *(8 nm)* at 2.5 Mach; warhead 39 kg.
GDC RAM quadruple launcher (DD 971); passive IR/anti-radiation homing to 9.6 km *(5.2 nm)* at 2 Mach; warhead 9.1 kg. To be fitted in others from FY 1994. Fitted starboard side right aft.
A/S: 24 Honeywell ASROC Mk 16 octuple launcher with Mk 112 reload system ❺ (not in VLS fitted ships); inertial guidance to 1.6-10 km *(1-5.5 nm)*; payload Mk 46 Mod 5 Neartip/Mk 50.

Guns: 2 FMC 5 in *(127 mm)*/54 Mk 45 Mod 0/1 ❻; 65° elevation; 20 rounds/minute to 23 km *(12.6 nm)* anti-surface; 15 km *(8.2 nm)* anti-aircraft; weight of shell 32 kg. SALGP (Semi-Active Laser-Guided Projectile).
2 General Electric/General Dynamics 20 mm/76 6-barrelled Mk 15 Vulcan Phalanx ❼; 3000 rounds/minute (4500 in Batch 1) combined to 1.5 km.
4—12.7 mm MGs.
Torpedoes: 6—324 mm Mk 32 (2 triple) tubes ❽. 14 Honeywell Mk 46; anti-submarine; active/passive homing to 11 km *(5.9 nm)* at 40 kts; warhead 44 kg. To be replaced by Mk 50 in due course. The tubes are inside the superstructure to facilitate maintenance and reloading. Torpedoes are fired through side ports.
Countermeasures: Decoys: 4 Loral Hycor SRBOC 6-barrelled fixed Mk 36 ❾; IR flares and chaff to 4 km *(2.2 nm)*.
SLQ 25 Nixie; torpedo decoy. Prairie/Masker hull/blade rate noise suppression system.
ESM/ECM: SLQ 32(V)2 ❿; radar warning. Sidekick modification adds jammer and deception system. WLR-1 (in some). OUTBOARD (in some).
Combat data systems: NTDS with Links 11 and 14. SATCOMS ⓫ SRR-1, WSC-3 (UHF), USC-38 (EHF) (in DD 971; others to be fitted from 1992). SQQ 28 for LAMPS data link.
Fire control: SWG-3 Tomahawk WCS. SWG-1A Harpoon LCS. Mk 116 Mod 7 FCS ASW. Mk 86 Mod 3 GFCS. Mk 91 MFCS. SRQ-4 LAMPS III. SAR-8 IR director (DD 965).
Radars: Air search: Lockheed SPS 40B/C/D (not in DD 997) ⓬; E/F band; range 320 km *(175 nm)*.
Raytheon SPS 49V (DD 997); C/D band; range 457 km *(250 nm)*.
Hughes Mk 23 TAS; D band.
Surface search: ISC Cardion SPS 55 ⓭; I/J band.
Navigation: Marconi LN 66 or SPS 53; I band. Raytheon SPS 64(V)9 to be fitted.

Fire control: Lockheed SPG 60 ⓮; I/J band.
Lockheed SPQ 9A ⓯; I/J band; range 37 km *(20 nm)*.
Raytheon Mk 95 ⓰; I/J band (for SAM).
Tacan: URN 20 or URN 25 (D 997). IFF Mk XII AIMS UPX-25.
Sonars: SQQ 89(V)6 including GE/Hughes SQS 53B/C; bow-mounted; active search and attack; medium frequency; and Gould SQR 19 (TACTASS); passive towed array. Some ships still have SQR 15 but these are being replaced. All except DDs 988-990 will have the full SQQ 89 system by 1994.

Helicopters: 1 SH-60B LAMPS III ⓱ or 1 SH-2F LAMPS I.

Programmes: Funds approved between FY 1970 and FY 1978.
Modernisation: Beginning with FY 1986 overhauls, major improvements have been made. These include the installation of VLS, upgrading of EW to SLQ 32V(2) plus sidekick; LAMPS III and the recovery, assist, secure and traverse system (RAST), the Halon 1301 firefighting system and anti-missile and target acquisition systems. VLS Mk 41 ships are capable of launching Standard SM-2MR for control by Aegis fitted vessels. Seventeen of the class converted to VLS by early 1993 and the goal is to convert all of them by the end of the century. One of the class is being used to test the development model of RAIDS (rapid anti-ship missile integrated defence system).
Structure: Extensive use of the modular concept has been used to facilitate construction and block modernisation. There is a high level of automation. These were the first large US warships to employ gas turbine propulsion and advanced self-noise reduction features. Kevlar internal coating in all vital spaces.
Operational: Three of the class are based at Yokosuka, Japan. Eleven took part in the war with Iraq in 1991. *Fife* with 58 firings was the most prolific launcher of Tomahawk missiles. Three of the class again fired missiles into Iraq in January 1993.

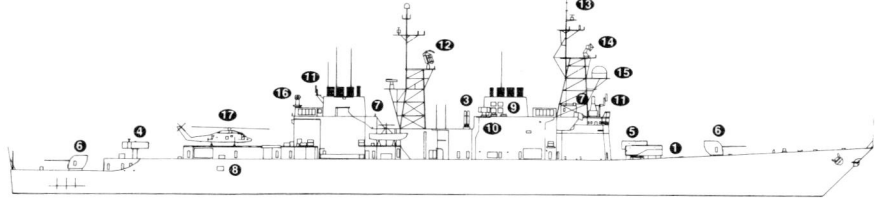

MERRILL *(Scale 1 : 1500), Ian Sturton*

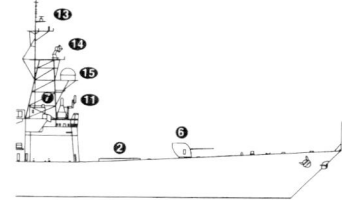

SPRUANCE *(Scale 1 : 1500), Ian Sturton*

MERRILL (with box Tomahawk)

7/1991, 92 Wing RAAF

O'BRIEN (with VLS) *10/1991, Giorgio Arra*

JOHN RODGERS *6/1992, Giorgio Arra*

NICHOLSON *5/1992, G Toremans*

MOOSBRUGGER *3/1992, Giorgio Arra*

784 USA / Destroyers

2 + 15 (9) ARLEIGH BURKE CLASS (FLIGHTS I and II): GUIDED MISSILE DESTROYERS (AEGIS) (DDG)

Name	No	Builders	Laid down	Launched	Commissioned	F/S
ARLEIGH BURKE	DDG 51	Bath Iron Works, Maine	6 Dec 1988	16 Sep 1989	4 July 1991	AA
BARRY (ex-*John Barry*)	DDG 52	Ingalls Shipbuilding	26 Feb 1990	10 May 1991	12 Dec 1992	AA
JOHN PAUL JONES	DDG 53	Bath Iron Works, Maine	8 Aug 1990	26 Oct 1991	Dec 1993	Bldg
CURTIS WILBUR	DDG 54	Bath Iron Works, Maine	12 Mar 1992	16 May 1992	Oct 1993	Bldg
STOUT	DDG 55	Ingalls Shipbuilding	8 Aug 1991	16 Oct 1992	Feb 1994	Bldg
JOHN S McCAIN	DDG 56	Bath Iron Works, Maine	3 Sep 1991	26 Sep 1992	Mar 1994	Bldg
MITSCHER	DDG 57	Ingalls Shipbuilding	12 Feb 1992	May 1993	July 1994	Bldg
LABOON	DDG 58	Bath Iron Works, Maine	23 Mar 1992	May 1993	Aug 1994	Bldg
RUSSELL	DDG 59	Ingalls Shipbuilding	27 July 1992	Oct 1993	Jan 1995	Bldg
PAUL HAMILTON	DDG 60	Bath Iron Works, Maine	25 Aug 1992	July 1993	Dec 1994	Bldg
RAMAGE	DDG 61	Ingalls Shipbuilding	4 Jan 1993	Feb 1994	Apr 1995	Bldg
FITZGERALD	DDG 62	Bath Iron Works, Maine	9 Feb 1993	Dec 1993	May 1995	Bldg
STETHEM	DDG 63	Ingalls Shipbuilding	May 1993	June 1994	July 1995	Bldg
CARNEY	DDG 64	Bath Iron Works, Maine	Aug 1993	June 1994	Oct 1995	Bldg
BENFOLD	DDG 65	Ingalls Shipbuilding	Sep 1993	Nov 1994	Dec 1995	Bldg
GONZALEZ	DDG 66	Ingalls Shipbuilding	Jan 1994	Nov 1994	Apr 1996	Bldg
COLE	DDG 67	Bath Iron Works, Maine	Feb 1994	Apr 1995	June 1996	Bldg
HOPPER	DDG 68	Ingalls Shipbuilding	July 1994	May 1995	Oct 1996	Ord
MILIUS	DDG 69	Ingalls Shipbuilding	Aug 1994	Sep 1995	Nov 1997	Ord
—	DDG 70	Ingalls Shipbuilding	Jan 1995	Nov 1995	Apr 1997	Ord
—	DDG 71	Bath Iron Works, Maine	Jan 1995	Feb 1996	Apr 1997	Ord
—	DDG 72	Bath Iron Works, Maine	July 1995	May 1996	Oct 1997	Ord
—	DDG 73-76	Authorised FY 1993	—	—	—	Proj

Displacement, tons: 8315; 9033 (from DDG 72) full load
Dimensions, feet (metres): 504.5 × 66.9 × 20.7; 32.7 (sonar) *(153.8 × 20.4 × 6.3; 9.9)*
Main machinery: 4 GE LM 2500 gas turbines; 105 000 hp *(78.33 MW)* sustained; 2 shafts; cp props
Speed, knots: 32. **Range, miles:** 4400 at 20 kts
Complement: 303 (23 officers) plus 38 spare

Missiles: SLCM/SSM: 56 GDC Tomahawk; combination of (a) land attack; TAINS (Tercom aided navigation system) to 2500 km *(1400 nm)* at 0.7 Mach; altitude 15-100 m *(49.2-328.1 ft)*; warhead nuclear 200 kT (TLAM-N); CEP 80 m; or warhead 454 kg (TLAM-C) or submunitions (TLAM-D); range 1300 km *(700 nm)*; CEP 10 m. Nuclear warheads not normally carried. Range increased by 30% in TLAM-C Block III which started production in 1992.
(b) anti-ship (TASM); inertial guidance; active radar and anti-radiation; homing to 460 km *(250 nm)* at 0.7 Mach; warhead 454 kg.
8 McDonnell Douglas Harpoon (2 quad) ❶; active radar homing to 130 km *(70 nm)* at 0.9 Mach; warhead 227 kg.
SAM: GDC Standard SM-2MR Block 4; command/inertial guidance; semi-active radar homing to 73 km *(40 nm)* at 2 Mach. Extended range from DDG 72 onwards.
A/S: Honeywell ASROC; inertial guidance to 1.6-10 km *(1-5.4 nm)*; payload Mk 46 Mod 5 Neartip/Mk 50.
2 Martin Marietta Mk 41 (Mod 0 forward, Mod 1 aft) Vertical Launch Systems (VLS) for Tomahawk, Standard and ASROC ❷; 2 magazines; 29 missiles fwd, 61 aft. Mod 2 from DDG 59 onwards.
Guns: 1 FMC 5 in *(127 mm)*/54 Mk 45 Mod 1 or 2 ❸; 65° elevation; 20 rounds/minute to 23 km *(12.6 nm)*; weight of shell 32 kg. No anti-aircraft capability.
2 General Electric/General Dynamics 20 mm Vulcan Phalanx 6-barrelled Mk 15 ❹; 3000 rounds/minute (4500 in Block 1) combined to 1.5 km.
Torpedoes: 6—324 mm Mk 32 Mod 14 (2 triple) tubes ❺. Honeywell Mk 46 Mod 5; anti-submarine; active/passive homing to 11 km *(5.9 nm)* at 40 kts; warhead 44 kg. To be replaced by Mk 50 in due course.
Countermeasures: Decoys: 2 Loral Hycor SRBOC 6-barrelled fixed Mk 36 Mod 12 ❻; IR flares and chaff to 4 km *(2.2 nm)*. SLQ 25 Nixie; torpedo decoy. NATO Sea Gnat. SLQ-95 AEB. SLQ-39 chaff buoy.
ESM/ECM: Raytheon SLQ 32(V)2 ❼ or (V)3; radar warning. Sidekick modification adds jammer and deception system to (V)2. Combat DF (from DDG 72).
Combat data systems: NTDS Mod 5 with Links 4A, 11, 14 and 16 (from DDG 72). SATCOM SRR-1, WSC-3 (UHF), USC-38 (EHF) (from 1992). SQQ 28 for LAMPS processor data link. TADIX B Tactical Information Exchange System (from DDG 72).
Fire control: SWG-3 Tomahawk WCS. SWG-1A Harpoon LCS. Aegis multi-target tracking with Mk 99 Mod 3 MFCS and three Mk 80 illuminators. GWS 34 Mod 0 GFCS (includes Mk 160 Mod 4 computing system and Kollmorgen optronic sight). Singer Librascope Mk 116 Mod 7 FCS for ASW. SAR-8 IR surveillance system to be fitted in due course.
Radars: Air search/fire control: RCA SPY 1D phased arrays ❽; 3D; E/F band.
Surface search: Norden SPS 67(V)3 ❾; G band.
Navigation: Raytheon SPS 64(V)9; I band.
Fire control: Three Raytheon/RCA SPG 62 ❿; I/J band.
Tacan: URN 25 ⓫. IFF Mk XII AIMS UPX-29.
Sonars: Gould/Raytheon/GE SQQ 89(V)6; combines SQS 53C; hull-mounted; active search and attack with SQR 19 passive towed array (TACTAS) (and SRQ-4 LAMPS III shipboard terminal); medium frequency.

Helicopters: Platform and facilities to fuel and rearm LAMPS III SH 60B/F helicopters ⓬.

Programmes: Designed as replacements for the Adams and Coontz classes of guided missile destroyers. First ship authorised in FY 1985. Order rate is projected at three or four per year up to a total of 49. The first 21 are Flight 1 and the next five are planned to be Flight II. See separate entry for Flight IIA.
Structure: The ship, except for the aluminium funnels, is constructed of steel. 70 tons of Kevlar armour provided to protect vital spaces. This is the first class of US Navy warship designed with a 'collective protection system for defense against the fall-out associated with NBC Warfare'. The ship's crew are protected by double air-locked hatches, fewer accesses to the weatherdecks and positive pressurisation of the interior of the ship to keep out contaminants. All incoming air is filtered and more reliance placed on recirculating air inside the ship. All accommodation compartments have sprinkler systems. Stealth technology includes angled surfaces and rounded edges to reduce radar signature and IR signature suppression.

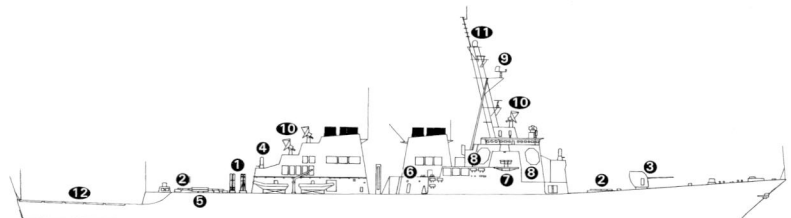

ARLEIGH BURKE *(Scale 1 : 1200), Ian Sturton*

BARRY *8/1992, Ingalls Shipbuilding*

ARLEIGH BURKE *2/1992, Giorgio Arra*

The Ops room is below the waterline and electronics are EMP hardened. The original upright mast design has been changed possibly to increase separation between electronic systems and the forward funnel. Differences in Flight II starting with DDG 72 include Link 16, SLQ 32(V)3 EW suite, extended range SAM missiles and improved tactical information exchange systems.

Opinion: The obvious deficiency in a ship of this size is the lack of its own helicopter and this has been recognised in the bringing forward of modifications proposed for later ships of the class. Regardless of attempts at role specialisation the modern warship's usage over its full life means that the ubiquitous helicopter receives more operational tasking than any other weapon system.

FRIGATES

8 KNOX CLASS: FRIGATES (FFT)

Name	No	Builders	Laid down	Launched	Commissioned	F/S
JOSEPH HEWES	FFT 1078	Avondale Shipyards	15 May 1969	7 Mar 1970	24 Apr 1971	NRF
BOWEN	FFT 1079	Avondale Shipyards	11 July 1969	2 May 1970	22 May 1971	NRF
McCANDLESS	FFT 1084	Avondale Shipyards	4 June 1970	20 Mar 1971	18 Mar 1972	NRF
DONALD B BEARY	FFT 1085	Avondale Shipyards	24 July 1970	22 May 1971	22 July 1972	NRF
JESSE L BROWN	FFT 1089	Avondale Shipyards	8 Apr 1971	18 Mar 1972	17 Feb 1973	NRF
AINSWORTH	FFT 1090	Avondale Shipyards	11 June 1971	15 Apr 1972	31 Mar 1973	NRF
TRUETT	FFT 1095	Avondale Shipyards	27 Apr 1972	3 Feb 1973	1 June 1974	NRF
MOINESTER	FFT 1097	Avondale Shipyards	25 Aug 1972	12 May 1973	2 Nov 1974	NRF

Displacement, tons: 3011 standard; 4260 full load
Dimensions, feet (metres): 439.6 × 46.8 × 15; 24.8 (sonar) *(134 × 14.3 × 4.6; 7.8)*
Main machinery: 2 Combustion Engineering/Babcock & Wilcox boilers; 1200 psi *(84.4 kg/cm sq)*; 950°F *(510°C)*; 1 turbine; 35 000 hp *(26 MW)*; 1 shaft
Speed, knots: 27. **Range, miles:** 4000 at 22 kts on 1 boiler
Complement: 288 (17 officers)

Missiles: SSM: 8 McDonnell Douglas Harpoon; active radar homing to 130 km *(70 nm)* at 0.9 Mach; warhead 227 kg.
A/S: Honeywell ASROC Mk 16 octuple launcher with reload system (has 2 cells modified to fire Harpoon) ❶; inertial guidance to 1.6-10 km *(1-5.4 nm)*; payload Mk 46 Mod 5 Neartip/Mk 50.
Guns: 1 FMC 5 in *(127 mm)*/54 Mk 42 Mod 9 ❷; 85° elevation; 20-40 rounds/minute to 24 km *(13 nm)* anti-surface; 14 km *(7.7 nm)* anti-aircraft; weight of shell 32 kg.
1 General Electric/General Dynamics 20 mm/76 6-barrelled Mk 15 Vulcan Phalanx ❸; 3000 rounds/minute combined to 1.5 km.
Torpedoes: 4—324 mm Mk 32 (2 twin) fixed tubes ❹. 22 Honeywell Mk 46 Mod 5; anti-submarine; active/passive homing to 11 km *(5.9 nm)* at 40 kts; warhead 44 kg.
Countermeasures: Decoys: 2 Loral Hycor SRBOC 6-barrelled fixed Mk 36 ❺; IR flares and chaff to 4 km *(2.2 nm)*. T Mk-6 Fanfare/SLQ-25 Nixie; torpedo decoy. Prairie Masker hull and blade rate noise suppression.
ESM/ECM: SLQ 32(V)2 ❻; radar warning. Sidekick modification adds jammer and deception system.
Combat data systems: Link 14 receive only. SATCOM ❼ SRR-1, WSC-3 (UHF). FFISTS (Frigate Integrated Shipboard Tactical Systems) (see *Modernisation*).
Fire control: SWG-1A Harpoon LCS. Mk 68 GFCS. Mk 114 ASW FCS. Mk 1 target designation system. MMS target acquisition sight (for mines, small craft and low flying aircraft). SRQ-4 for LAMPS I.
Radars: Air search: Lockheed SPS 40B ❽; E/F band; range 320 km *(175 nm)*.
Surface search: Raytheon SPS 10 or Norden SPS 67 ❾; G band.
Navigation: Marconi LN 66; I band.
Fire control: Western Electric SPG 53A/D/F ❿; I/J band.
Tacan: SRN 15. IFF: UPX-12.
Sonars: EDO/General Electric SQS 26 CX; bow-mounted; active search and attack; medium frequency.
EDO SQR 18A(V)1; passive towed array; very low frequency.

Helicopters: 1 SH-2F LAMPS I ⓫.

Modernisation: Designed to operate the now-discarded DASH unmanned helicopter. From FY 1972 to FY 1976 they were modified to accommodate the Light Airborne Multi-Purpose System (LAMPS) and the SH-2F Seasprite anti-submarine helicopter; hangar and flight deck are enlarged. In 1979 a programme was initiated to fit 3.5 ft bow bulwarks and spray strakes to all ships of the class adding 9.1 tons to the displacement. Sea Sparrow SAM replaced by Phalanx 1982-88. FFISTS is a poor man's combat system using desktop computers to integrate ASW data from Link and from ships' sonars.
Structure: Improved ASROC-torpedo reloading capability (note slanting face of bridge structure immediately behind ASROC). Four Mk 32 torpedo tubes are fixed in the midships structure, two to a side, angled out at 45 degrees. The arrangement provides improved loading capability over exposed triple Mk 32 torpedo tubes. A 4000 lb lightweight anchor is fitted on the port side and an 8000 lb anchor fits into the after section of the sonar dome.
Operational: Each ship is designated as a training platform (FFT) for its own selected reserve crew and four additional crews designated as the nucleus of reactivation crews for the decommissioned ships of the class. In theory the laid up ships can be reactivated within 180 days. SQS 35 sonar deactivated in 1992. This scheme is planned to terminate in FY 1994 as a result of further defence cuts.
Sales: FF 1056, 1068 and 1075 to Greece in mid-1992; FF 1073 and 1086 to Taiwan in mid-1992 and 1087 in mid-1993. Four more have been offered to Turkey, FF 1092, 1093, 1063 and 1082, the last of these on a grant basis. Apart from 1082 all the other transfers, and proposed transfers, are leases.

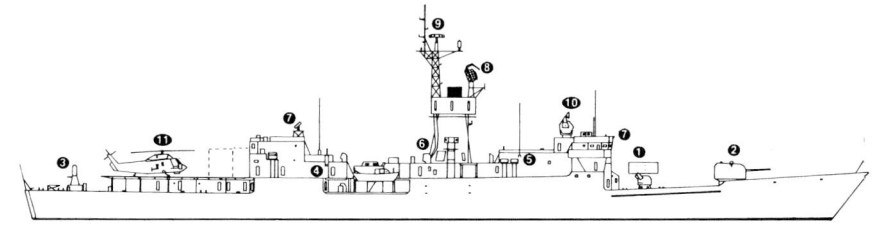

KNOX class *(Scale 1 : 1200), Ian Sturton*

BOWEN *9/1992, Maritime Photographic*

BOWEN *9/1992, Maritime Photographic*

Major Combatant Naval Reserve Force Training Ships

Name/Hull No	NRF Homeport	Assignment	Name/Hull No	NRF Homeport	Assignment
OLIVER HAZARD PERRY (FFG 7)	New York, NY	May 1984	FAHRION (FFG 22)	Charleston, SC	Sep 1988
WADSWORTH (FFG 9)	Long Beach, CA	June 1985	LEWIS B PULLER (FFG 23)	Long Beach, CA	June 1987
DUNCAN (FFG 10)	Long Beach, CA	Jan 1984	COPELAND (FFG 25)	San Diego, CA	July 1988
CLARK (FFG 11)	Boston, MA	Sep 1985	MAHLON S TISDALE (FFG 27)	San Diego, CA	July 1988
GEORGE PHILIP (FFG 12)	Long Beach, CA	Jan 1986	JOSEPH HEWES (FFT 1078)	Ingleside, TX	Dec 1991
SAMUEL ELIOT MORISON (FFG 13)	Charleston, SC	June 1986	BOWEN (FFT 1079)	New York, NY	Dec 1991
JOHN H SIDES (FFG 14)	Long Beach, CA	Aug 1986	McCANDLESS (FFT 1084)	Ingleside, TX	Dec 1991
ESTOCIN (FFG 15)	Newport, RI	Sep 1986	DONALD B BEARY (FFT 1085)	New York, NY	Dec 1991
CLIFTON SPRAGUE (FFG 16)	New York, NY	Aug 1984	JESSE L BROWN (FFT 1089)	Mobile, AL	Dec 1991
JOHN A MOORE (FFG 19)	Long Beach, CA	Jan 1987	AINSWORTH (FFT 1090)	New York, NY	Dec 1991
ANTRIM (FFG 20)	Mobile, AL	Jan 1987	TRUETT (FFT 1095)	Ingleside, TX	Dec 1991
FLATLEY (FFG 21)	Mobile, AL	Nov 1987	MOINESTER (FFT 1097)	Mobile, AL	Dec 1991

51 OLIVER HAZARD PERRY CLASS: GUIDED MISSILE FRIGATES (FFG)

Name	No	Builders	Laid down	Launched	Commissioned	F/S
OLIVER HAZARD PERRY	FFG 7 (ex-PF 109)	Bath Iron Works, Bath, Maine	12 June 1975	25 Sep 1976	17 Dec 1977	NRF
McINERNEY	FFG 8	Bath Iron Works, Bath, Maine	7 Nov 1977	4 Nov 1978	19 Nov 1979	AA
WADSWORTH	FFG 9	Todd Shipyards Corporation, San Pedro	13 July 1977	29 July 1978	28 Feb 1980	NRF
DUNCAN	FFG 10	Todd Shipyards Corporation, Seattle	29 Apr 1977	1 Mar 1978	15 May 1980	NRF
CLARK	FFG 11	Bath Iron Works, Bath, Maine	17 July 1978	24 Mar 1979	9 May 1980	NRF
GEORGE PHILIP	FFG 12	Todd Shipyards Corporation, San Pedro	14 Dec 1977	16 Dec 1978	10 Oct 1980	NRF
SAMUEL ELIOT MORISON	FFG 13	Bath Iron Works, Bath, Maine	4 Dec 1978	14 July 1979	11 Oct 1980	NRF
JOHN H SIDES	FFG 14	Todd Shipyards Corporation, San Pedro	7 Aug 1978	19 May 1979	30 May 1981	NRF
ESTOCIN	FFG 15	Bath Iron Works, Bath, Maine	2 Apr 1979	3 Nov 1979	10 Jan 1981	NRF
CLIFTON SPRAGUE	FFG 16	Bath Iron Works, Bath, Maine	30 Sep 1979	16 Feb 1980	21 Mar 1981	NRF
JOHN A MOORE	FFG 19	Todd Shipyards Corporation, San Pedro	19 Dec 1978	20 Oct 1979	14 Nov 1981	NRF
ANTRIM	FFG 20	Todd Shipyards Corporation, Seattle	21 June 1978	27 Mar 1979	26 Sep 1981	NRF
FLATLEY	FFG 21	Bath Iron Works, Bath, Maine	13 Nov 1979	15 May 1980	20 June 1981	NRF
FAHRION	FFG 22	Todd Shipyards Corporation, Seattle	1 Dec 1978	24 Aug 1979	16 Jan 1982	NRF
LEWIS B PULLER	FFG 23	Todd Shipyards Corporation, San Pedro	23 May 1979	15 Mar 1980	17 Apr 1982	NRF
JACK WILLIAMS	FFG 24	Bath Iron Works, Bath, Maine	25 Feb 1980	30 Aug 1980	19 Sep 1981	AA
COPELAND	FFG 25	Todd Shipyards Corporation, San Pedro	24 Oct 1979	26 July 1980	7 Aug 1982	NRF
GALLERY	FFG 26	Bath Iron Works, Bath, Maine	17 May 1980	20 Dec 1980	5 Dec 1981	AA
MAHLON S TISDALE	FFG 27	Todd Shipyards Corporation, San Pedro	19 Mar 1980	7 Feb 1981	27 Nov 1982	NRF
BOONE	FFG 28	Todd Shipyards Corporation, Seattle	27 Mar 1979	16 Jan 1980	15 May 1982	AA
STEPHEN W GROVES	FFG 29	Bath Iron Works, Bath, Maine	16 Sep 1980	4 Apr 1981	17 Apr 1982	AA
REID	FFG 30	Todd Shipyards Corporation, San Pedro	8 Oct 1980	27 June 1981	19 Feb 1983	PA
STARK	FFG 31	Todd Shipyards Corporation, Seattle	24 Aug 1979	30 May 1980	23 Oct 1982	AA
JOHN L HALL	FFG 32	Bath Iron Works, Bath, Maine	5 Jan 1981	24 July 1981	26 June 1982	AA
JARRETT	FFG 33	Todd Shipyards Corporation, San Pedro	11 Feb 1981	17 Oct 1981	2 July 1983	PA
AUBREY FITCH	FFG 34	Bath Iron Works, Bath, Maine	10 Apr 1981	17 Oct 1981	9 Oct 1982	AA
UNDERWOOD	FFG 36	Bath Iron Works, Bath, Maine	3 Aug 1981	6 Feb 1982	29 Jan 1983	AA
CROMMELIN	FFG 37	Todd Shipyards Corporation, Seattle	30 May 1980	1 July 1981	18 June 1983	PA
CURTS	FFG 38	Todd Shipyards Corporation, San Pedro	1 July 1981	6 Mar 1982	8 Oct 1983	PA
DOYLE	FFG 39	Bath Iron Works, Bath, Maine	16 Nov 1981	22 May 1982	21 May 1983	AA
HALYBURTON	FFG 40	Todd Shipyards Corporation, Seattle	26 Sep 1980	15 Oct 1981	7 Jan 1984	AA
McCLUSKY	FFG 41	Todd Shipyards Corporation, San Pedro	21 Oct 1981	18 Sep 1982	10 Dec 1983	PA
KLAKRING	FFG 42	Bath Iron Works, Bath, Maine	19 Feb 1982	18 Sep 1982	20 Aug 1983	AA
THACH	FFG 43	Todd Shipyards Corporation, San Pedro	10 Mar 1982	18 Dec 1982	17 Mar 1984	PA
De WERT	FFG 45	Bath Iron Works, Bath, Maine	14 June 1982	18 Dec 1982	19 Nov 1983	AA
RENTZ	FFG 46	Todd Shipyards Corporation, San Pedro	18 Sep 1982	16 July 1983	30 June 1984	PA
NICHOLAS	FFG 47	Bath Iron Works, Bath, Maine	27 Sep 1982	23 Apr 1983	10 Mar 1984	AA
VANDEGRIFT	FFG 48	Todd Shipyards Corporation, Seattle	13 Oct 1981	15 Oct 1982	24 Nov 1984	PA
ROBERT G BRADLEY	FFG 49	Bath Iron Works, Bath, Maine	28 Dec 1982	13 Aug 1983	11 Aug 1984	AA
TAYLOR	FFG 50	Bath Iron Works, Bath, Maine	5 May 1983	5 Nov 1983	1 Dec 1984	AA
GARY	FFG 51	Todd Shipyards Corporation, San Pedro	18 Dec 1982	19 Nov 1983	17 Nov 1984	PA
CARR	FFG 52	Todd Shipyards Corporation, Seattle	26 Mar 1982	26 Feb 1983	27 July 1985	AA
HAWES	FFG 53	Bath Iron Works, Bath, Maine	22 Aug 1983	18 Feb 1984	9 Feb 1985	AA
FORD	FFG 54	Todd Shipyards Corporation, San Pedro	16 July 1983	23 June 1984	29 June 1985	PA
ELROD	FFG 55	Bath Iron Works, Bath, Maine	21 Nov 1983	12 May 1984	18 May 1985	AA
SIMPSON	FFG 56	Bath Iron Works, Bath, Maine	27 Feb 1984	21 Aug 1984	10 Aug 1985	AA
REUBEN JAMES	FFG 57	Todd Shipyards Corporation, San Pedro	19 Nov 1983	8 Feb 1985	22 Mar 1986	PA
SAMUEL B ROBERTS	FFG 58	Bath Iron Works, Bath, Maine	21 May 1984	8 Dec 1984	12 Apr 1986	AA
KAUFFMAN	FFG 59	Bath Iron Works, Bath, Maine	8 Apr 1985	29 Mar 1986	28 Feb 1987	AA
RODNEY M DAVIS	FFG 60	Todd Shipyards Corporation, San Pedro	8 Feb 1985	11 Jan 1986	9 May 1987	PA
INGRAHAM	FFG 61	Todd Shipyards Corporation, San Pedro	30 Mar 1987	25 June 1988	5 Aug 1989	PA

Displacement, tons: 2750 light; 3638; 4100 (FFG 8, 36-61) full load
Dimensions, feet (metres): 445; 453 (FFG 8, 36-61) × 45 × 14.8; 24.5 (sonar) *(135.6; 138.1 × 13.7 × 4.5; 7.5)*
Main machinery: 2 GE LM 2500 gas turbines; 41 000 hp *(30.59 MW)* sustained; 1 shaft; cp prop
2 auxiliary retractable props; 650 hp *(484 kW)*
Speed, knots: 29. **Range, miles:** 4500 at 20 kts
Complement: 206 (13 officers) including 19 aircrew

Missiles: SSM: 4 McDonnell Douglas Harpoon; active radar homing to 130 km *(70 nm)* at 0.9 Mach; warhead 227 kg.
SAM: 36 GDC Standard SM-1MR; command guidance; semi-active radar homing to 46 km *(25 nm)* at 2 Mach.
1 Mk 13 Mod 4 launcher for both SSM and SAM missiles ❶.
Guns: 1 OTO Melara 3 in *(76 mm)*/62 Mk 75 ❷; 85° elevation; 85 rounds/minute to 16 km *(8.7 nm)* anti-surface; 12 km *(6.6 nm)* anti-aircraft; weight of shell 6 kg.
1 General Electric/General Dynamics 20 mm/76 6-barrelled Mk 15 Vulcan Phalanx ❸; 3000 rounds/minute (4500 in Block 1) combined to 1.5 km.
4—12.7 mm MGs. McDonnell Douglas 25 mm Mk 38 guns can be fitted.
Torpedoes: 6—324 mm Mk 32 (2 triple) tubes ❹. 24 Honeywell Mk 46; anti-submarine; active/passive homing to 11 km *(5.9 nm)* at 40 kts; warhead 44 kg. To be replaced by Mk 50 in due course.
Countermeasures: Decoys: 2 Loral Hycor SRBOC 6-barrelled fixed Mk 36 ❺; IR flares and chaff to 4 km *(2.2 nm)*.
T—Mk-6 Fanfare/SLQ-25 Nixie; torpedo decoy.
ESM/ECM: SLQ 32(V)2 ❻; radar warning. Sidekick modification adds jammer and deception system.
Combat data systems: NTDS with Link 11 and 14. Link 14 only (NRF ships). SATCOM ❼ SRR-1, WSC-3 (UHF). SQQ 28 for LAMPS data link.
Fire control: SWG-1 Harpoon LCS. Mk 92 (Mod 4 or Mod 6 (FFG 61 and during modernisation in others of the class)), WCS with CAS (Combined Antenna System). The Mk 92 is the US version of the Signaal WM-28 system. Mk 13 weapon direction system. 2 Mk 24 optical directors. SYS 2(V)2 IADT (FFG 61 and during modernisation in others of the class). SRQ-4 for LAMPS III, SKR-4A for LAMPS I.
Radars: Air search: Raytheon SPS 49(V)4 or 5 (FFG 61 and during modernisation of others) ❽; C/D band; range 457 km *(250 nm)*.
Surface search: ISC Cardion SPS 55 ❾; I band.
Fire control: Lockheed STIR (modified SPG 60) ❿; I/J band; range 110 km *(60 nm)*.
Sperry Mk 92 (Signaal WM 28) ⓫; I/J band.
Tacan: URN 25. IFF Mk XII AIMS UPX-29.
Sonars: Raytheon SQS 56 or SQS 53B; hull-mounted; active search and attack; medium frequency.
Gould SQR 19; passive towed array. A few SQR 18A still fitted to ships assigned to the NRF.
SQQ 89(V)2 (SQS 53B and SQR 19) (in FFG 36-61 and retrofitted in all except 14 of the class by 1994).

Helicopters: 2 SH-2F LAMPS I or 2 SH-60B LAMPS III ⓬ (FFG 8, 36-61). 3 Canadair CL 227 (FFG 39) (see *Operational*).

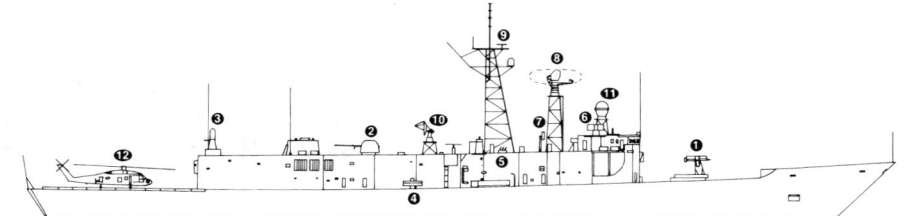

FFG 7 class (modified)   *(Scale 1 : 1200), Ian Sturton*

INGRAHAM   *7/1992, Per Kornefeldt*

Programmes: They are follow-on ships to the large number of frigates (formerly DE) built in the 1960s and early 1970s, with the later ships emphasising anti-ship/aircraft/missile capabilities while the previous classes were oriented primarily against submarines (eg, larger SQS 26 sonar and ASROC). The lead ship (FFG 7) was authorised in FY 1973. On 31 January 1984 the first of this class transferred to the Naval Reserve Force. Since then 15 more have transferred. NRF ships have about 75 reservists in their complement.
Modernisation: To accommodate the helicopter landing system (RAST), the overall length of the ship was increased by 8 ft *(2.4 m)* by increasing the angle of the ship's transom, between the waterline and the fantail, from virtually straight up to a 45° angle outwards. LAMPS III support facilities and RAST were fitted in all ships authorised from FFG 36 onwards, during construction. Thirty three of this class are able to operate, land and maintain LAMPS III while the remainder can operate this aircraft without landing facilities. *Ingraham* has much improved Combat Data and Fire Control equipment which was retrofitted in five ships by early 1993, with seven more to follow.
Structure: The original single hangar has been changed to two adjacent hangars. Provided with 19 mm Kevlar armour protection over vital spaces. 25 mm guns can be fitted for some operational deployments.
Operational: Ships of this class were the first Navy experience in implementing a design-to-cost acquisition concept. Many of their limitations were manifest during the intense fires which resulted from *Stark* (FFG 31) being struck by two Exocet missiles in the Persian Gulf 17 May 1987. Since then there have been many improvements in firefighting and damage control doctrine and procedures and equipment to deal with residual missile propellant-induced fires. *Stark* was once again operational in August 1988. On 14 April 1988, *Samuel B Roberts* (FFG 58), was mined in the Gulf. *Roberts* was able to reach Bahrain using the auxiliary propulsion motor. She was repaired at Bath Iron Works returning to the fleet in November 1989. Fourteen ships of the class were active in the war with Iraq in 1991. *Doyle* is the trials ship for the Sentinel MAVUS unmanned rotary wing air vehicle. This machine can carry either TV or IR cameras, or an ECM decoy system or a communications relay. Other payloads include synthetic aperture radar or Elint and Sigint equipment.
Sales: Australia has bought four of the class and has built two more. Spain has four completed and is building two more. Taiwan is building six or seven.

CURTS
10/1992, S Poynton, RAN

McCLUSKY
4/1992, 92 Wing RAAF

788 USA / Shipborne aircraft (front line)

SHIPBORNE AIRCRAFT (FRONT LINE)

Numbers/Type: 619 McDonnell Douglas F/A-18A/B/C/D Hornet.
Operational speed: 1032 kts (1910 km/h).
Service ceiling: 50 000 ft (15 240 m).
Range: 1000 nm (1850 km).
Role/Weapon systems: Strike interdictor for USN/USMC air groups; total procurement of at least 800 expected. Some are used for EW support with ALQ-167 jammers. Sensors: ESM: ALQ 165 ASPJ (18C/D), APG-65 radar, AAS-38 FLIR, ASQ-173 tracker. Weapons: ASV; 4 × Harpoon or SLAM missiles. Strike; up to 7.7 tons of 'iron' bombs. AD; 1 × 20 mm Vulcan cannon, 9 × AIM-7/ AIM-9 missiles. Typical ASV load might include 20 mm gun, 7.7 ton bombs, 2 AIM-9 missiles. Typical AAW load might include 20 mm gun, 4 AIM-7, 2 AIM-9 missiles. 18C/D includes AMRAAM and Maverick capability.

HORNET *9/1992, Maritime Photographic*

Numbers/Type: 436 Grumman F-14A/A Plus/D Tomcat.
Operational speed: 1342 kts (2485 km/h).
Service ceiling: 56 000 ft (17 070 m).
Range: 1735 nm (3220 km).
Role/Weapon systems: Standard fleet fighter aircraft for long-range air defence of task groups; undergoing phased improvements; F-14D flew in early 1988 with in service date of 1990. Sensors: AWG-9 or APG-71 (D type) radar, ALQ-126 jammer, ASN-92 nav or ASN-139 (D type), ALR-45 or ALR-67 (D type) RWR; IRST and JTIDS (D type). Weapons: AD; 1 × 20 mm cannon, 6 × AIM-54 Phoenix; HARM and Harpoon/SLAM to be added. CAP; 1 × 20 mm cannon, 4 × Phoenix, 2 × AIM-7M, 2 × AIM-9M. Recce; 1 × 20 mm cannon, 2 × AIM-7M, 2 × AIM-9M.

TOMCAT *9/1992, Maritime Photographic*

TOMCAT *1989*

Numbers/Type: 189/1/24 McDonnell Douglas/British Aerospace AV-8B/AV-8B Plus/TAV-8B Harrier II.
Operational speed: 562 kts (1041 km/h).
Service ceiling: 50 000 ft (15 240 m).
Range: 800 nm (1480 km).
Role/Weapon systems: Close support for USMC operational from 1985. A total of 28 AV-8B Plus delivery scheduled to start in June 1993. Sensors: FLIR, laser designator and ECM; APG-65 radar (AV-8B Plus). Weapons: Strike; up to 4.2 tons of 'iron' bombs or Paveway II LGM, AGM-62 Walleye or AGM-65 Maverick. Self-defence; 1 × GAU-12/U 25 mm cannon and 4 × AIM-9L Sidewinder.

HARRIER II *1/1991, Ingalls Shipbuilding*

Numbers/Type: 22/314 Grumman KA-6D/A-6E Intruder.
Operational speed: 560 kts (1037 km/h).
Service ceiling: 42 400 ft (12 925 m).
Range: 2818 nm (5222 km).
Role/Weapon systems: All weather strike and armed reconnaissance role; 290 aircraft are being progressively updated. KA-6D is the tanker version. Sensors: APQ-148 or 156 search/attack radar, RWR, ECM. Weapons: ASV; 24 × Harpoon and nuclear weapons, 12 × Mk 36 mines. Strike; up to 8.2 tons of underwing stores. Self-defence; 4 × AIM-9 Sidewinder or 2 AIM-120 AMRAAM or 2 AIM-7M Sparrow. Systems Weapons Improvements Programme (SWIP) includes HARM, Maverick and Skipper missiles.

INTRUDER *1990, US Navy*

Numbers/Type: 39 McDonnell Douglas A-4M Skyhawk.
Operational speed: 560 kts (1038 km/h).
Service ceiling: 45 000 ft (13 780 m).
Range: 1060 nm (1963 km).
Role/Weapon systems: Ageing but important strike potential for USMC maintained for reserves; about 150 training versions in service. Sensors: Attack radar, ECM. Weapons: Strike; up to 1.6 tons fuselage and 3 tons underwing. AD; 2 × 20 mm cannon, 4 × AIM-7 or 9s.

SKYHAWK *1989, Hughes Aircraft*

Numbers/Type: 127 Lockheed S-3A/3B/ES-3A Viking.
Operational speed: 450 kts (834 km/h).
Service ceiling: 35 000 ft (10 670 m).
Range: 2000 nm (3706 km).
Role/Weapon systems: Standard ASW/ASV aircraft; works in concert with towed array escorts; possible replacement from 1996 by Osprey tilt-rotor; first S-3B flew in 1987; conversion to B type at the rate of about 30 a year to complete in 1994; 16 being converted to ELINT configuration (ES-3A), to replace obsolete EA-3B for combined EW and targeting. First one flew in January 1992. Link 11 fitted. Sensors: APS-137(V)1 radar; APN-200 radar, FLIR, MAD, ASQ-81(V)1, 60 × sonobuoys; ESM: ALR-76; ECM ALE 47; ALE 39 chaff. Weapons: ASW; 4 × Mk 54 depth charges, 4 × Mk 46 (or Mk 50) torpedoes. ASV; 2 × Harpoon Block 1C; mines.

VIKING *1987, US Navy*

Numbers/Type: 130 Grumman EA-6B Prowler.
Operational speed: 566 kts (1048 km/h).
Service ceiling: 41 200 ft (12 550 m).
Range: 955 nm (1769 km).
Role/Weapon systems: EW and jamming aircraft to accompanying strikes and armed reconnaissance; being uprated to ADVCAP with new engines and ECM. Sensors: APS-130 radar; ALQ-99F, ALQ-149 (ADVCAP) jammers. Weapons: HARM anti-radiation missile capable.

PROWLER *10/1990, US Navy*

Numbers/Type: 109 Grumman E-2C Hawkeye.
Operational speed: 323 kts *(598 km/h).*
Service ceiling: 30 800 ft *(9390 m).*
Range: 1000 nm *(1850 km).*
Role/Weapon systems: Used for direction of AD and strike operations; being ordered at about six a year to a planned total of 147. Sensors: ESM: ALR-73 PDS, ALQ-108; Airborne tactical data system with Links 4A and 11, APS-125 radar, later aircraft have APS-138/139 radar. Weapons: Unarmed.

HAWKEYE *1989, US Navy*

Numbers/Type: 187 Sikorsky SH-60B/F Seahawk (LAMPS III).
Operational speed: 135 kts *(250 km/h).*
Service ceiling: 10 000 ft *(3050 m).*
Range: 600 nm *(1110 km).*
Role/Weapon systems: LAMPS III air vehicle for medium-range ASW and for ASV; total of 204 (60B) and 175 (60F) planned at a rate of about 12 each per year; operated from DDH and FFH class escorts; non-autonomous; SH-60F is derived model to replace Sea King; entered service 1989; Link 11 fitted. Sensors: APS-124 search radar, FLIR, ASQ-811(V) MAD, 25 sonobuoys (Difar or Dicass (60F)), LLTV. AQS-13F dipping sonar (60F) (to be replaced by ALFS in due course). Weapons: ASW; 2/3 × Mk 46/Mk 50 torpedoes or depth bombs. ASV; 1 × Penguin Mk 2 Mod 7 missile (in 28 aircraft for Oliver Perry frigates from 1992); 1—7.62 mm MG M60.

SEAHAWK *1991*

Numbers/Type: 68/20 Kaman SH-2F/G Seasprite (LAMPS I).
Operational speed: 130 kts *(241 km/h).*
Service ceiling: 22 500 ft *(6860 m).*
Range: 367 nm *(679 km).*
Role/Weapon systems: ASW and OTHT helicopter; second production run ended in 1987; in LAMPS I programme, acts as ASW information relay for surface ships. Six SH-2G were new build, 14 more converted by 1993 with improved engines, avionics and sensor processing. 30 more to be converted in due course. Sensors: LN-66HP radar, ALR-66 ESM, ASN-123 tactical nav, ASQ-81(V)2 MAD, AAQ-16 night vision system; ARR-57 sonobuoy receivers; 15 sonobuoys. For the Gulf War in 1991, additional EW equipment included AAQ-34 FLIR, ALE-37 chaff, ALQ 144 IR counter, plus DLQ 3B video data link. A DEMON mine detection system was also fitted. Weapons: ASW; 2 × Mk 46 (or Mk 50) torpedoes, 8 × Mk 25 smoke markers, 1 depth bomb. ASV: 1 Penguin; 1—7.62 mm MG M60.

SEASPRITE *6/1992, Antonio Moreno*

Numbers/Type: 130 Sikorsky SH-3G/H Sea King.
Operational speed: 144 kts *(267 km/h).*
Service ceiling: 12 200 ft *(3720 m).*
Range: 630 nm *(1166 km).*
Role/Weapon systems: Carrier battle group inner zone ASW; also used for liaison and SAR tasks. Being replaced by SH-60F. Sensors: AN/APS-24 search radar, Bendix AQS-13 dipping sonar, Texas Instruments ASQ-81(V)2 MAD, 25 sonobuoys. Weapons: ASW; 2 × Mk 46/Mk 50 torpedoes or depth bombs or mines.

SEA KING *9/1992, Maritime Photographic*

Numbers/Type: 47/29/13 Boeing HH-46D/CH-46D/E/UH-46D/E Sea Knight.
Operational speed: 137 kts *(254 km/h).*
Service ceiling: 8500 ft *(2590 m).*
Range: 180 nm *(338 km).*
Role/Weapon systems: Support/assault (USMC) for 18 Marines and re-supply (USN) helicopter respectively. Can lift 1.3 tons or 4.5 tons in a cargo net or sling. Sensors: None. Weapons: Unarmed.

SEA KNIGHT CH-46 *10/1992, Maritime Photographic*

Numbers/Type: 75 Sikorsky CH-53E Super Stallion.
Operational speed: 170 kts *(315 km/h).*
Service ceiling: 18 500 ft *(5640 m).*
Range: 230 nm *(425 km).*
Role/Weapon systems: Uprated, three-engined version of Sea Stallion with support (USN) and transport (USMC) roles. Total of about 200 aircraft planned. Carries 56 Marines. Sensors: None. Weapons: Up to 3 × 12.7 mm machine guns.

SUPER STALLION *1990, US Navy*

790 USA / Shipborne aircraft (front line) — Land-based maritime aircraft (front line)

Numbers/Type: 75 Sikorsky CH-53D Sea Stallion.
Operational speed: 150 kts *(278 km/h)*.
Service ceiling: 21 000 ft *(6400 m)*.
Range: 540 nm *(1000 km)*.
Role/Weapon systems: Assault, support and transport helicopters; can carry 38 Marines. Sensors: None. Weapons: Up to 3 × 12.7 mm machine guns.

SEA DRAGON MCM SLEDGE *7/1992, Jürg Kürsener*

Numbers/Type: 118 Bell AH-1W Super Cobra.
Operational speed: 149 kts *(277 km/h)*.
Service ceiling: 12 200 ft *(3718 m)*.
Range: 317 nm *(587 km)*.
Role/Weapon systems: Close support helicopter; uprated and improved version, with own air defence capability; being procured at about 12 a year. Sensors: NTS (laser and FLIR nightsight) to be retrofitted from 1993 at the rate of 24 aircraft per year. Weapons: Strike/assault; 1 or 3 × 20 mm cannon, 8 × TOW or Hellfire missiles, gun and grenade pods. Self-defence; 2 × AIM-9L Sidewinder missiles.

SEA STALLION *11/1991, A Campanera i Rovira*

Numbers/Type: 29 Sikorsky MH-53E Sea Dragon.
Operational speed: 170 kts *(315 km/h)*.
Service ceiling: 18 500 ft *(5640 m)*.
Range: 1000 nm *(1850 km)*.
Role/Weapon systems: Three-engined AMCM helicopter similar to Super Stallion; total of about 60 planned; tows ALQ-166 MCM sweep equipment; self-deployed if necessary. Sensors: AQS-14 or AQS-20 dipping sonar being fitted. Weapons: 2 × 12.7 mm guns for self-defence.

SUPER COBRA *1984, Bell Helicopters*

Numbers/Type: 115 Bell UH-1N Iroquois. Twin Huey
Operational speed: 110 kts *(204 km/h)*.
Service ceiling: 15 000 ft *(4570 m)*.
Range: 250 nm *(463 km)*.
Role/Weapon systems: Support and logistics helicopter for USMC operations afloat and ashore. Can carry 16 Marines. Sensors: None. Weapons: Can be armed with 7.62 mm machine guns.

SEA DRAGON *1991*

TWIN HUEY *1990, Bell Helicopters*

LAND-BASED MARITIME AIRCRAFT (FRONT LINE)

Numbers/Type: 251 Lockheed P-3C Orion.
Operational speed: 411 kts *(761 km/h)*.
Service ceiling: 28 300 ft *(8625 m)*.
Range: 4000 nm *(7410 km)*.
Role/Weapon systems: 144 in operational squadrons deployed worldwide in support of US Naval operations; primarily ASW; update III conversions to 138 airframes; update IV with tactical ESM cancelled. Remainder of P-3Bs have been allocated to the Naval Reserves. Sensors: APS-115 search radar or APS 137(V)5 to be fitted in 68 aircraft, ASQ-81 MAD, up to 100 × sonobuoys, FLIR, cameras, AXR-13 LLTV, ALR 66 or ALQ 78 ESM. Weapons: ASW; 4 × Mk 44/46 torpedoes or 2 × Mk 101 nuclear depth bombs (not carried). ASV; 4 × Harpoon, 6 × Mk 55/56 mines.

Numbers/Type: 13 Lockheed EP-3E Orion.
Operational speed: 411 kts *(761 km/h)*.
Service ceiling: 28 300 ft *(8625 m)*.
Range: 4000 nm *(7410 km)*.
Role/Weapon systems: Electronic warfare and intelligence gathering aircraft. Sensors: EW equipment including AN/ALR-60, AN/ALQ-76, AN/ALQ-78, AN/ALQ-108 and AN/ASQ-114. Weapons: Unarmed.

Numbers/Type: 16 Boeing E-6A Hermes/TACAMO.
Operational speed: 455 kts *(842 km/h)*.
Service ceiling: 42 000 ft *(12 800 m)*.
Range: 6350 nm *(11 760 km)*.
Role/Weapon systems: First flew in February 1987 and has replaced EC-130Q. EMP hardened against nuclear bursts. Sensors: Supports Trident Fleet radio communications. Weapons: Unarmed.

TACAMO *1989, Boeing*

AMPHIBIOUS WARFARE FORCES

Notes: 1. Additional capacity is provided by the maritime pre-positioning ships (see listing at end of *Military Sealift Command* section) which are either new construction or conversions of relatively new commercial ships. One squadron is maintained on station in the Atlantic, a second at Guam, and a third at Diego Garcia. Each carries equipment to support a Marine Expeditionary Force. Ships of the latter two squadrons were the first to arrive at Saudi Arabian ports after the build-up of US forces in the Middle East was ordered in late 1990. The Diego Garcia squadron was also involved in late 1992 providing equipment for US forces in Somalia.

Other operations in 1992 included assistance to the thousands left homeless after Hurricane Andrew in south Florida, after Hurricane Iniki in the Hawaiian island of Kauai, and after six typhoons, including Omar, in Guam. Amphibious ships were offshore near Mogadishu in early 1993, and were poised for action in the Adriatic.

2. **Minesweeping:** Several of the larger amphibious ships have been used as operating bases for minesweeping helicopters in the absence of a 'mother ship' for such aircraft. *Inchon* is planned to become a dedicated support ship by 1996.

0 + (12) LX MULTI-PURPOSE AMPHIBIOUS SHIPS

Displacement, tons: 23 000 full load
Dimensions, feet (metres): 684 × 101 × 21 *(208.5 × 30.8 × 6.4)*
Main machinery: 4 diesels; 2 shafts
Speed, knots: 22
Complement: 495
Military lift: 900 troops; LCACs

Helicopters: CH-46 Sea Knight, CH-53 Sea Stallion.

Programmes: The LX programme was approved by the Defense Acquisition Board on 11 January 1993. The ship has entered the preliminary design phase. It is intended to replace four classes of amphibious ships: LPD 4s, LSTs, LKAs and LSD 36s. The lead-ship contract award is planned for FY 1996 with delivery in FY 2002. In 1998, and in each year thereafter, two ship contracts are to be awarded. With the exception of the first ship, it is anticipated that 55-60 months will be required between contract award and delivery. Twelve ships are planned.

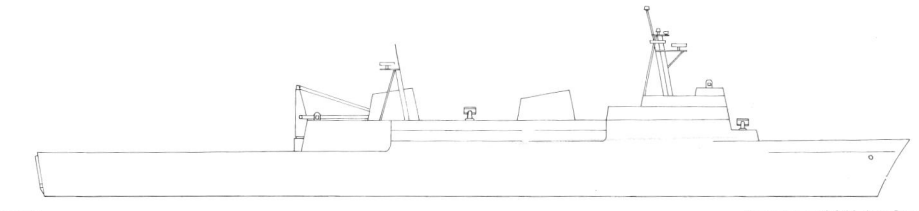

LX 90 *(Scale 1 : 1800), Ian Sturton*

Structure: This is an LPD-type vessel required to load, transport and offload troops, heavy vehicles, helicopters, landing craft, amphibious vehicles and both dry and liquid cargo. It will not have the flag configuration of LPDs, the over-the-side heavy lift capability of LKAs, or the ability to offload over the beach via causeways of LSTs. Otherwise, it will have most of the remaining capabilities of these four classes of ships.

2 BLUE RIDGE CLASS: AMPHIBIOUS COMMAND SHIPS (LCC)

Name	No	Builders	Laid down	Launched	Commissioned	F/S
BLUE RIDGE	LCC 19	Philadelphia Naval Shipyard	27 Feb 1967	4 Jan 1969	14 Nov 1970	PA
MOUNT WHITNEY	LCC 20	Newport News Shipbuilding & Dry Dock Co	8 Jan 1969	8 Jan 1970	16 Jan 1971	AA

Displacement, tons: 16 790 light; 18 372 full load *(Blue Ridge)* 16 100 light; 18 646 full load *(Mount Whitney)*
Dimensions, feet (metres): 636.5 × 107.9 × 28.9 *(194 × 32.9 × 8.8)*
Main machinery: 2 Foster-Wheeler boilers; 600 psi *(42.3 kg/cm sq)*; 870°F *(467°C)*; 1 GE turbine; 22 000 hp *(16.4 MW)*; 1 shaft
Speed, knots: 23. **Range, miles:** 13 000 at 16 kts
Complement: 821 (43 officers); Flag 170-190
Military lift: 700 troops; 3 LCPs; 2 LCVPs

Missiles: SAM: 2 Raytheon GMLS Mk 25 Mod 1 octuple launchers ❶; 16 Sea Sparrow; semi-active radar homing to 14.6 km *(8 nm)* at 2.5 Mach; warhead 39 kg.
Guns: 4 USN 3 in *(76 mm)*/50 (2 twin) Mk 33 ❷; 85° elevation; 50 rounds/minute to 12.8 km *(7 nm)*; weight of shell 6 kg. Antennas and their supports severely restrict firing arcs of guns.
2 General Electric/General Dynamics 20 mm/76 6-barrelled Vulcan Phalanx Mk 15 ❸; 3000 rounds/minute (4500 in Block 1) combined to 1.5 km.
Countermeasures: Decoys: 4 Loral Hycor SRBOC 6-barrelled fixed Mk 36; IR flares and chaff to 4 km *(2.2 nm)*. SLQ-25 Nixie; torpedo decoy.
ESM/ECM: SLQ 32(V)3; combined radar intercept, jammer and deception system.
Combat data systems: NTDS with Links 4A, 11, 14 and 16 in due course. Amphibious Command Information System (ACIS), and Naval Intelligence Processing System (NIPS). SATCOMS ❹; SSR-1, WSC-3 (UHF), WSC-6 (SHF), USC-38 (EHF) (from 1992), SMQ-6 receiver.
Fire control: 2 Mk 115 MFCS. No GFCS.
Radars: Air search: ITT SPS 48C ❺; 3D; E/F band; range 402 km *(220 nm)*.
Lockheed SPS 40C ❻; E/F band; range 320 km *(175 nm)*.
Hughes Mk 23 TAS; D band (to be fitted).
Surface search: Raytheon SPS 65(V)1 ❼; G band.
Navigation: Marconi LN 66; Raytheon SPS 64(V)9; I band.
Fire control: Two Mk 51; I/J band (for SAM).
Tacan: URN 20/25. IFF: Mk XII AIMS UPX-29.

Helicopters: 1 utility can be carried.

BLUE RIDGE *(Scale 1 : 1800), Ian Sturton*

Programmes: Authorised in FY 1965 and 1966. Originally designated Amphibious Force Flagships (AGC); redesignated Amphibious Command Ships (LCC) on 1 January 1969.
Modernisation: Modernisation completed FY 1987 although the Mk 23 TAS radar may be fitted in due course.
Structure: General hull design and machinery arrangement are similar to the Iwo Jima class assault ships.
Operational: These are large amphibious force command ships of post-Second World War design. They can provide integrated command and control facilities for sea, air and land commanders in amphibious operations. *Blue Ridge* is the Seventh Fleet flagship, based at Yokosuka, Japan. *Mount Whitney* serves as flagship Second Fleet, based at Norfolk, Virginia.

MOUNT WHITNEY *9/1992, Maritime Photographic*

3 + 3 WASP CLASS: AMPHIBIOUS ASSAULT SHIP (multi-purpose) (LHD)

Name	No	Builders	Laid down	Launched	Commissioned	F/S
WASP	LHD 1	Ingalls Shipbuilding	30 May 1985	4 Aug 1987	29 July 1989	AA
ESSEX	LHD 2	Ingalls Shipbuilding	20 Mar 1989	4 Jan 1991	17 Oct 1992	PA
KEARSARGE	LHD 3	Ingalls Shipbuilding	6 Feb 1990	26 Mar 1992	May 1993	AA
BOXER	LHD 4	Ingalls Shipbuilding	8 Apr 1991	Aug 1993	Dec 1994	Bldg/PA
BATAAN	LHD 5	Ingalls Shipbuilding	25 Apr 1995	Mar 1996	May 1997	Ord
BONHOMME RICHARD	LHD 6	Ingalls Shipbuilding	—	—	—	Ord

Displacement, tons: 28 233 light; 40 532 full load
Dimensions, feet (metres): 844 oa; 788 wl × 140.1 oa; 106 wl × 26.6 *(257.3; 240.2 × 42.7; 32.3 × 8.1)*
Flight deck, feet (metres): 819 × 106 *(249.6 × 32.3)*
Main machinery: 2 Combustion Engineering boilers; 600 psi *(42.3 kg/cm sq)*; 900°F *(482°C)*; 2 Westinghouse turbines; 70 000 hp *(52.2 MW)*; 2 shafts
Speed, knots: 22. **Range, miles:** 9500 at 18 kts
Complement: 1077 (98 officers)
Military lift: 2074 troops; 12 LCM 6s or 3 LCACs; 1232 tons aviation fuel; 4 LCPL

Missiles: SAM: 2 Raytheon GMLS Mk 29 octuple launchers ❶; 16 Sea Sparrow; semi-active radar homing to 14.6 km *(8 nm)* at 2.5 Mach; warhead 39 kg. 1 launcher located aft, on a transom that overhangs the stern, and a second on a raised deck forward of the superstructure.
Guns: 3 General Electric/General Dynamics 20 mm 6-barrelled Vulcan Phalanx Mk 15 ❷; 3000 rounds/minute (4500 in Batch 1) combined to 1.5 km. One fitted on each quarter and one aft of the NSSMS launcher on the island.
8—12.7 mm MGs.
Countermeasures: Decoys: 4 or 6 Loral Hycor SRBOC 6-barrelled fixed Mk 36; IR flares and chaff to 4 km *(2.2 nm)*. SLQ 25 Nixie; acoustic torpedo decoy system. NATO Sea Gnat. SLQ-49 chaff buoys. AEB SSQ-95.
ESM/ECM: SLQ 32(V)3; combined radar warning, jammer and deception system.
Combat data systems: Integrated Tactical Amphibious Warfare Data System (ITAWDS) and Marine Tactical Amphibious C² System (MTACCS). Links 4A, 11 (modified), 14 and 16 in due course. SATCOMS ❸ SSR-1, WSC-3 (UHF), USC-38 (EHF) (from 1992). SMQ-11 Metsat.
Fire control: 2 Mk 91 MFCS. SYS-2(V)3 IADT.
Radars: Air search: Hughes SPS 52C ❹ (LHD 1); 3D; E/F band; range 439 km *(240 nm)*.
ITT SPS 48E (except LHD 1); 3D; E/F band; range 402 km *(220 nm)*.
Raytheon SPS 49(V)9 ❺; C/D band; range 457 km *(250 nm)*.
Hughes Mk 23 TAS ❻; D band.
Surface search: Norden SPS 67 ❼; G band.
Navigation: SPS 64(V)9; I band.
CCA: SPN 35A and SPN 43B.
Fire control: 2 Mk 95; I/J band.
Tacan: URN 25. IFF: CIS Mk XV UPX-29.

Fixed wing aircraft: 6-8 AV-8B Harriers or up to 20 in secondary role.
Helicopters: Capacity for 42 CH-46E Sea Knight but has the capability to support: AH-1W Super Cobra, CH-53E Super Stallion, CH-53D Sea Stallion, UH-1N Twin Huey, AH-1T Sea Cobra, and SH-60B Seahawk helicopters.

Programmes: Fifth of the class ordered 20 December 1991. Although an LHD was not included in the FY 1993 budget, Congress took the unusual action of authorising the expenditure of $1.2 billion for a sixth, but providing only $300 million in funding, enough to get it under a construction contract. The balance of the funding will have to be included in future Navy shipbuilding budgets.
Structure: Two aircraft elevators, one to starboard and aft of the 'island' and one to port amidships; both fold for Panama canal transits. The well deck is 267 × 50 ft and can accommodate up to three Amphibious Air-Cushion Vehicles (LCAC). The flight deck has nine helicopter landing spots. Cargo capacity is 101 000 cu ft total with an additional 20 000 sq ft to accomodate vehicles. Vehicle storage is available for five M1 tanks, 25 LAVs, eight M 198 guns, 68 trucks, 10 logistic vehicles and several service vehicles. The bridge is two decks lower than that of an LHA, command, control and communication spaces having been moved inside the hull to avoid 'cheap kill' damage. Fitted with a 600-bed capacity hospital and six operating rooms. HY-100 steel covers the flight deck. Nine 32 ft monorail trains each carrying 6000 lbs, deliver material to the well deck at 6.8 mph.
Operational: A typical complement of aircraft would be a mix of 30 helicopters and six to eight Harriers (AV-8B). In the secondary role as a sea control ship the most likely mix is 20 AV-8B Harriers and four to six SH-60B Seahawk helicopters.

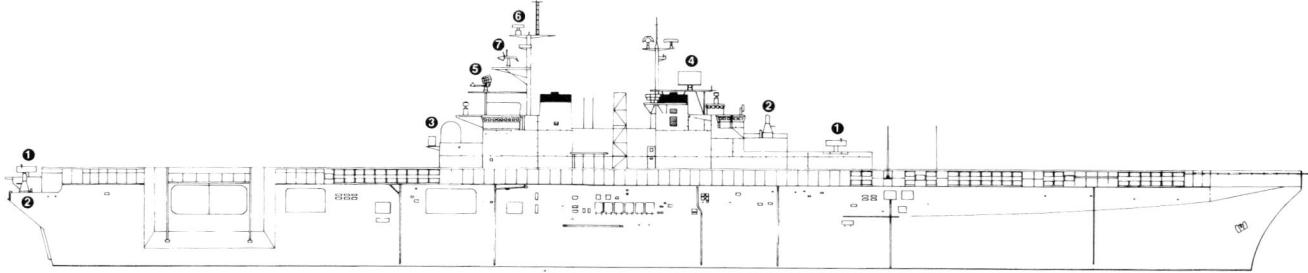

WASP   *(Scale 1 : 1500), Ian Sturton*

WASP   *1992, US Navy*

KEARSARGE   *5/1992, Ingalls Shipbuilding*

ESSEX   *3/1992, Ingalls Shipbuilding*

5 TARAWA CLASS: AMPHIBIOUS ASSAULT SHIPS (multi-purpose) (LHA)

Name	No	Builders	Erection of First Module	Launched	Commissioned	F/S
TARAWA	LHA 1	Ingalls Shipbuilding	15 Nov 1971	1 Dec 1973	29 May 1976	PA
SAIPAN	LHA 2	Ingalls Shipbuilding	21 July 1972	18 July 1974	15 Oct 1977	AA
BELLEAU WOOD	LHA 3	Ingalls Shipbuilding	5 Mar 1973	11 Apr 1977	23 Sep 1978	PA
NASSAU	LHA 4	Ingalls Shipbuilding	13 Aug 1973	21 Jan 1978	28 July 1979	AA
PELELIU (ex-*Da Nang*)	LHA 5	Ingalls Shipbuilding	12 Nov 1976	25 Nov 1978	3 May 1980	PA

Displacement, tons: 39 967 full load
Dimensions, feet (metres): 834 × 131.9 × 25.9 *(254.2 × 40.2 × 7.9)*
Flight deck, feet (metres): 820 × 118.1 *(250 × 36)*
Main machinery: 2 Combustion Engineering boilers; 600 psi *(42.3 kg/cm sq)*; 900°F *(482°C)*; 2 Westinghouse turbines; 70 000 hp *(52.2 MW)*; 2 shafts; bow thruster; 900 hp *(670 kW)*
Speed, knots: 24. **Range, miles:** 10 000 at 20 kts
Complement: 930 (56 officers)
Military lift: 1703 troops; 4 LCU 1610 type or 2 LCU and 2 LCM 8 or 17 LCM 6 or 45 LVT tractors; 1200 tons aviation fuel. 1 LCAC may be embarked. 4 LCPL

Missiles: SAM: 2 GDC RAM; passive IR/anti-radiation homing to 9.6 km *(5.2 nm)* at 2 Mach; warhead 9.1 kg (being fitted).
Guns: 2 FMC 5 in *(127 mm)*/54 Mk 45 Mod 1 ❶; 65° elevation; 20 rounds/minute to 23 km *(12.6 nm)* anti-surface; 15 km *(8.2 nm)* anti-aircraft; weight of shell 32 kg.
6 Mk 242 25 mm automatic cannons.
2 General Electric/General Dynamics 20 mm/76 6-barrelled Vulcan Phalanx Mk 15 ❷; 3000 rounds/minute (4500 in Block 1) combined to 1.5 km.
Countermeasures: Decoys: 4 Loral Hycor SRBOC 6-barrelled fixed Mk 36; IR flares and chaff to 4 km *(2.2 nm)*.
SLQ 25 Nixie; acoustic torpedo decoy system. NATO Sea Gnat.
SLQ-49 chaff buoys. AEB SSQ-95.
ESM/ECM: SLQ 32V(3); combined radar intercept, jammer and deception system.
Combat data systems: Integrated Tactical Amphibious Warfare Data System (ITAWDS) to provide computerised support in control of helicopters and aircraft, shipboard weapons and sensors, navigation, landing craft control, and electronic warfare. Links 4A, 11, 14 and 16 in due course. SATCOM SRR-1, WSC-3 (UHF), USC-38 (EHF) (LHA 2 and 4). SMQ-11 Metsat.
Fire control: Mk 86 Mod 4 GFCS. 2 optronic directors.
Radars: Air search: Hughes SPS 52C ❸; 3D; E/F band; range 439 km *(240 nm)*.
Lockheed SPS 40B/C/D ❹; E/F band; range 320 km *(175 nm)*.
Hughes Mk 23 TAS; D band.
Surface search: Raytheon SPS 67 ❺; G band.
Navigation: Raytheon SPS 64(V)9; I band.
CCA: SPN 35A; SPN 43B.
Fire control: Lockheed SPG 60 ❻; I/J band.
Lockheed SPQ 9A ❼; I/J band; range 37 km *(20 nm)*.
Tacan: URN 25. IFF: CIS Mk XV.

Fixed wing aircraft: Harrier AV-8B VSTOL aircraft in place of some helicopters as required.
Helicopters: 19 CH-53D Sea Stallion or 26 CH-46D/E Sea Knight.

Programmes: Originally intended to be a class of nine ships. LHA1 was authorised in FY 1969, LHA 2 and LHA 3 in FY 1970 and LHA 4 and LHA 5 in FY 1971.
Modernisation: Two Vulcan Phalanx CIWS replaced the GMLS Mk 25 Sea Sparrow launchers. Programme completed in early 1991. RAM launchers being fitted, first in LHA 5 in late 1992. Mk 23 TAS target acquisition radar fitted in LHA 3 and 5 in 1992, LHA 4 in 1993 and the last pair in 1994.
Structure: Beneath the full-length flight deck are two half-length hangar decks, the two being connected by an elevator amidships on the port side and a stern lift; beneath the after elevator is a floodable docking well measuring 268 ft in length and 78 ft in width which is capable of accommodating four LCU 1610 type landing craft. Also included is a large garage for trucks and AFVs and troop berthing for a reinforced battalion. 33 730 sq ft available for vehicles and 116 900 cu ft for palletted stores. Extensive medical facilities including operating rooms, X-ray room, hospital ward, isolation ward, laboratories, pharmacy, dental operating room and medical store rooms.
Operational: The flight deck can operate a maximum of nine CH-53D Sea Stallion or 12 CH-46D/E Sea Knight helicopters or a mix of these and other helicopters. With some additional modifications, ships of this class can effectively operate AV-8B aircraft. The normal mix of aircraft allows for six AV-8Bs. The optimum aircraft configuration for this class is dependent upon assigned missions. Unmanned Reconnaissance Vehicles (URVs) can be operated. *Belleau Wood* is based at Sasebo, Japan.

NASSAU

4/1992, W Sartori

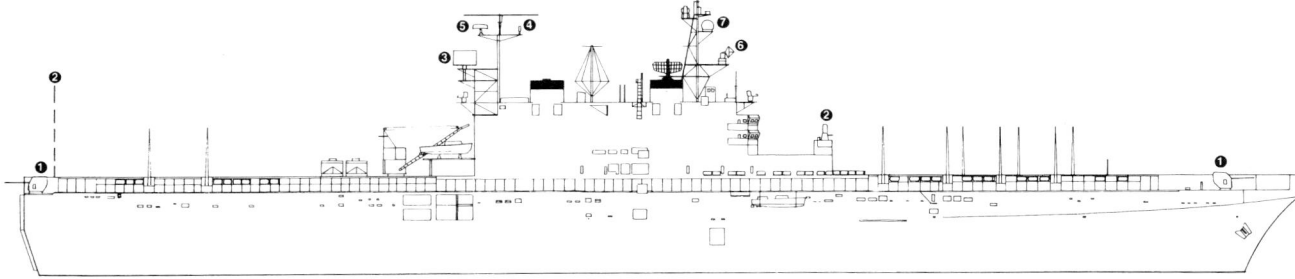

TARAWA

(Scale 1 : 1500), Ian Sturton

TARAWA

6/1991, 92 Wing RAAF

5 IWO JIMA CLASS: AMPHIBIOUS ASSAULT SHIPS (LPH)

Name	No	Builders	Laid down	Launched	Commissioned	F/S
GUADALCANAL	LPH 7	Philadelphia Naval Shipyard	1 Sep 1961	16 Mar 1963	20 July 1963	AA
GUAM	LPH 9	Philadelphia Naval Shipyard	15 Nov 1962	22 Aug 1964	16 Jan 1965	AA
TRIPOLI	LPH 10	Ingalls Shipbuilding Corp	15 June 1964	31 July 1965	6 Aug 1966	PA
NEW ORLEANS	LPH 11	Philadelphia Naval Shipyard	1 Mar 1966	3 Feb 1968	16 Nov 1968	PA
INCHON	LPH 12	Ingalls Shipbuilding Corp	8 Apr 1968	24 May 1969	20 June 1970	AA

Displacement, tons: 11 250 light; 18 300 full load
Dimensions, feet (metres): 602.3 × 104 × 31.7 *(183.7 × 31.7 × 9.7)*
Flight deck, feet (metres): 602.3 × 104 *(183.7 × 31.7)*
Main machinery: 2 Babcock & Wilcox/Combustion Engineering boilers; 600 psi *(42.3 kg/cm sq)*; 900°F *(482°C)*; 1 De Laval/GE/Westinghouse turbine; 23 000 hp *(17.2 MW)*; 1 shaft
Speed, knots: 23. **Range, miles:** 10 000 at 20 kts
Complement: 686 (48 officers)
Military lift: 1746 troops (144 officers); 1500 tons aviation fuel; 2 LCPL

Missiles: SAM: 2 Raytheon GMLS Mk 25 octuple launchers ❶; Sea Sparrow; semi-active radar homing to 14.6 km *(8 nm)* at 2.5 Mach; warhead 39 kg. 1 launcher forward of island structure and 1 on the port quarter.
Guns: 4 USN 3 in *(76 mm)*/50 (2 twin) Mk 33 ❷; 85° elevation; 50 rounds/minute to 12.8 km *(7 nm)*; weight of shell 6 kg.
2 General Electric/General Dynamics 20 mm 6-barrelled Vulcan Phalanx Mk 15 ❸; 3000 rounds/minute (4500 in Batch 1) combined to 1.5 km.
Up to 8—12.7 mm MGs.
Countermeasures: Decoys: 4 Loral Hycor SRBOC 6-barrelled fixed Mk 36; IR flares and chaff to 4 km *(2.2 nm)*.
ESM/ECM: SLQ 32(V)3; combined radar warning, jammer and deception system.
Combat data systems: SATCOM ❹ SRR-1, WSC-3 (UHF).
Fire control: Mk 115 MFCS. 2 Mk 71 directors.
Radars: Air search: Westinghouse SPS 58 ❺; 3D; D band.
Lockheed SPS 40 ❻; E/F band; range 320 km *(175 nm)*.
Surface search: Raytheon SPS 10 ❼; G band.
CCA: SPN 35 and SPN 43.
Navigation: Marconi LN 66; I band.
Fire control: Two Mk 51; I/J band.
Tacan: URN 25. IFF: Mk XII UPX-29.

Fixed wing aircraft: 4 AV-8B Harriers in place of some helicopters.
Helicopters: Capacity for 20 CH-46D/E Sea Knight or 11 CH-53D Sea Stallion.

Programmes: *Guam* was modified late in 1971 and began operations in January 1972 as an interim sea control ship; she reverted to the amphibious role in 1974 but kept 12 AV-8As on board. All are being replaced by the Wasp class. The first two paid off in 1992 and 1993 respectively.
Structure: Two deck-edge lifts, one to port opposite the bridge and one to starboard aft of island. Full hangars are provided; no arresting wires or catapults. Two small elevators carry cargo from holds to flight deck. Stowage of 4300 sq ft for vehicles and 37 400 cu ft for palletted stores. Fitted with extensive medical facilities including operating room, X-ray room, hospital ward, isolation ward, laboratory, pharmacy, dental operating room, and medical store rooms.
Operational: The flight decks provide for simultaneous take off or landing of seven CH-46 Sea Knight or four CH-53 Sea Stallion helicopters during normal operations. Can operate AV-8Bs following modifications to refine day/night capability. Each LPH can carry a Marine battalion landing team, its guns, vehicles, and equipment, plus a reinforced squadron of transport helicopters and various support personnel. All have been used on many occasions as platforms for airborne minesweeping operations. *Tripoli* was damaged by a mine in the Gulf in 1991 but was operational again within a few weeks. She was the principal support ship for the Somalian operation in December 1992. *Inchon* is to be converted to a mine warfare command and support ship by 1996. *Guadalcanal* is to pay off in 1994.

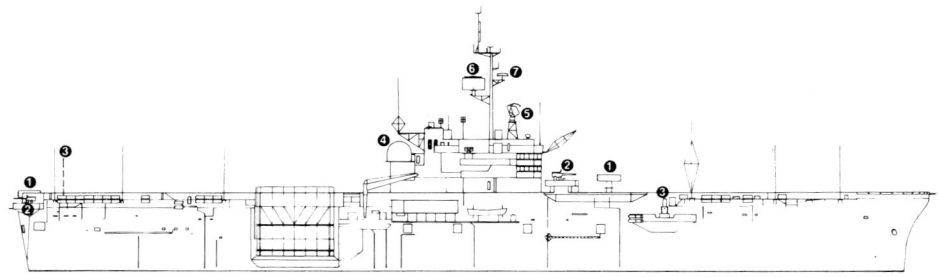

IWO JIMA *(Scale 1 : 1500), Ian Sturton*

TRIPOLI *10/1991, Giorgio Arra*

GUAM *9/1992, Stefan Terzibaschitsch*

TRIPOLI *1/1993, van Ginderen Collection*

Amphibious warfare forces / USA 795

11 AUSTIN CLASS: AMPHIBIOUS TRANSPORT DOCKS (LPD)

Name	No	Builders	Laid down	Launched	Commissioned	F/S
AUSTIN	LPD 4	New York Naval Shipyard	4 Feb 1963	27 June 1964	6 Feb 1965	AA
OGDEN	LPD 5	New York Naval Shipyard	4 Feb 1963	27 June 1964	19 June 1965	PA
DULUTH	LPD 6	New York Naval Shipyard	18 Dec 1963	14 Aug 1965	18 Dec 1965	PA
CLEVELAND	LPD 7	Ingalls Shipbuilding Corp	30 Nov 1964	7 May 1966	21 Apr 1967	PA
DUBUQUE	LPD 8	Ingalls Shipbuilding Corp	25 Jan 1965	6 Aug 1966	1 Sep 1967	PA
DENVER	LPD 9	Lockheed SB & Construction Co	7 Feb 1964	23 Jan 1965	26 Oct 1968	PA
JUNEAU	LPD 10	Lockheed SB & Construction Co	23 Jan 1965	12 Feb 1966	12 July 1969	PA
SHREVEPORT	LPD 12	Lockheed SB & Construction Co	27 Dec 1965	25 Oct 1966	12 Dec 1970	AA
NASHVILLE	LPD 13	Lockheed SB & Construction Co	14 Mar 1966	7 Oct 1967	14 Feb 1970	AA
TRENTON	LPD 14	Lockheed SB & Construction Co	8 Aug 1966	3 Aug 1968	6 Mar 1971	AA
PONCE	LPD 15	Lockheed SB & Construction Co	31 Oct 1966	20 May 1970	10 July 1971	AA

Displacement, tons: 9130 light; 16 500-17 244 full load
Dimensions, feet (metres): 570 × 100 (84 hull) × 23 *(173.8 × 30.5 (25.6) × 7)*
Main machinery: 2 Foster-Wheeler boilers (Babcock & Wilcox in LPD 5 and 12); 600 psi *(42.3 kg/cm sq)*; 870°F *(467°C)*; 2 De Laval turbines; 24 000 hp *(18 MW)*; 2 shafts
Speed, knots: 21. **Range, miles:** 7700 at 20 kts.
Complement: 420 (24 officers); Flag 90 (in LPD 7-13)
Military lift: 930 troops (840 only in LPD 7-13); 9 LCM 6s or 4 LCM 8s or 2 LCAC or 20 LVTs. 4 LCPL/LCVP

Guns: 2 or 4 USN 3 in *(76 mm)*/50 (1 or 2 twin) Mk 33 ❶; 85° elevation; 50 rounds/minute to 12.8 km *(7 nm)*; weight of shell 6 kg. Local control only.
2 General Electric/General Dynamics 20 mm/76 6-barrelled Vulcan Phalanx Mk 15 ❷; 3000 rounds/minute (4500 in Block 1) combined to 1.5 km. Being fitted in FY 1988-93 during maintenance periods.
Countermeasures: Decoys: 4 Loral Hycor SRBOC 6-barrelled Mk 36; IR flares and chaff to 4 km *(2.2 nm)*.
ESM: SLQ 32(V)1; intercept. May be updated to (V)2.
Combat data systems: SATCOM SRR-1, WSC-3 (UHF).
Radars: Air search: Lockheed SPS 40B/C ❸; E/F band; range 320 km *(175 nm)*.
Surface search: Raytheon SPS 10F or Norden SPS 67 ❹; G band.
Navigation: Marconi LN 66; I band.
Tacan: URN 25. IFF: Mk XII UPX-29.

Helicopters: Up to 6 CH-46D/E Sea Knight can be carried. Hangar for only 1 light (not in LPD 4).

Programmes: LPD 4-6 were authorised in the FY 1962 new construction programme, LPD 7-10 in FY 1963, LPD 12 and 13 in FY 1964, LPD 14 and LPD 15 in FY 1965. LPD 16 was cancelled.
Modernisation: Planned SLEPs cancelled. Modernisation being carried out in normal maintenance periods from FY 1987. This includes fitting two Phalanx, SPS 67 radar replacing SPS 10 and updating EW capability.
Structure: Enlarged versions of the earlier Raleigh class (now paid off). LPD 7-13 have an additional bridge and are fitted as flagships. One small telescopic hangar. There are structural variations in the positions of guns and electronic equipment in different ships of the class. Flight deck is 168 ft *(51.2 m)* in length. Well deck 394 × 50 ft *(120.1 × 15.2 m)*. This design is the model for the LX class to start building in the mid-1990s.
Operational: A typical operational load might include one Seahawk, two Sea Knight, two Twin Huey, four Sea Cobra helicopters and one patrol boat armed with two 20 mm guns. Eight of the class were involved in the war with Iraq in 1991.

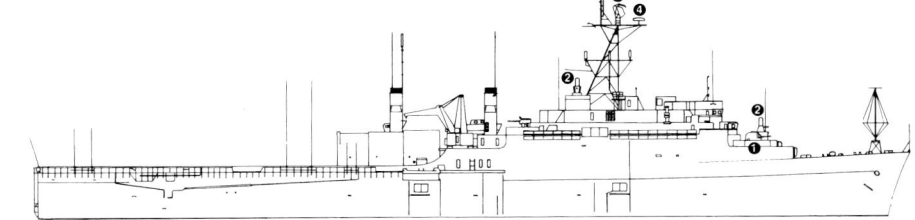

NASHVILLE (Scale 1 : 1500), Ian Sturton

JUNEAU (high bridge) 9/1992, Stefan Terzibaschitsch

OGDEN (low bridge) 10/1992, S Poynton, RAN

796 USA / Amphibious warfare forces

8 WHIDBEY ISLAND and 0 + 4 HARPERS FERRY CLASSES: DOCK LANDING SHIPS (LSD and LSD-CV)

Name	No	Builders	Laid down	Launched	Commissioned	F/S
WHIDBEY ISLAND	LSD 41	Lockheed SB & Construction Co	4 Aug 1981	10 June 1983	9 Feb 1985	AA
GERMANTOWN	LSD 42	Lockheed SB & Construction Co	5 Aug 1982	29 June 1984	8 Feb 1986	PA
FORT McHENRY	LSD 43	Lockheed SB & Construction Co	10 June 1983	1 Feb 1986	8 Aug 1987	PA
GUNSTON HALL	LSD 44	Avondale Industries	26 May 1986	27 June 1987	22 Apr 1989	AA
COMSTOCK	LSD 45	Avondale Industries	27 Oct 1986	16 Jan 1988	3 Feb 1990	PA
TORTUGA	LSD 46	Avondale Industries	23 Mar 1987	15 Sep 1988	17 Nov 1990	AA
RUSHMORE	LSD 47	Avondale Industries	9 Nov 1987	6 May 1989	1 June 1991	PA
ASHLAND	LSD 48	Avondale Industries	4 Apr 1988	11 Nov 1989	9 May 1992	AA
HARPERS FERRY	LSD 49	Avondale Industries	15 Apr 1991	16 Jan 1993	Aug 1994	Bldg
CARTER HALL	LSD 50	Avondale Industries	8 Nov 1991	Oct 1993	Mar 1995	Bldg
OAK HILL	LSD 51	Avondale Industries	21 Sep 1992	Mar 1993	May 1995	Bldg
—	LSD 52	Avondale Industries	—	—	—	Ord

Displacement, tons: 11 125 light; 15 726 (LSD 41-48), 16 740 (LSD 49 onwards) full load
Dimensions, feet (metres): 609 × 84 × 20.5 *(185.6 × 25.6 × 6.3)*
Main machinery: 4 Colt SEMT-Pielstick 16 PC2.5 V 400 diesels; 37 440 hp(m) *(27.5 MW)* sustained; 2 shafts; cp props
Speed, knots: 22. **Range, miles:** 8000 at 18 kts
Complement: 340 (21 officers)
Military lift: 450 troops; 2 (CV) or 4 LCACs (Amphibious Air Cushion Vehicles), or 9 (CV) or 21 LCM 6, or 1 (CV) or 3 LCUs, or 64 LVTs. 2 LCPL
Cargo capacity: 5000 cu ft for marine cargo, 12 500 sq ft for vehicles (including four preloaded LCACs in the well deck). The 'cargo version' has 67 600 cu ft for marine cargo, 20 200 sq ft for vehicles but only two LCACs. Aviation fuel, 90 tons.

Guns: 2 General Electric/General Dynamics 20 mm/76 6-barrelled Vulcan Phalanx Mk 15 ❶; 3000 rounds/minute (4500 in Block 1) combined to 1.5 km.
2 Mk 68 Mod 1 20 mm. 8—12.7 mm MGs. 2 Mk 88 25 mm Bushmaster (LSD 47 and 48 vice the 20 mm guns).
Countermeasures: Decoys: 4 Loral Hycor SRBOC 6-barrelled Mk 36; IR flares and chaff to 4 km *(2.2 nm)*.
ESM: SLQ 32(V)1; intercept. May be updated to (V)2.
Combat data systems: SATCOM SRR-1, WSC-3 (UHF). SSDS (in LSD 41) (see *Modernisation*).
Radars: Air search: Raytheon SPS 49V ❷; C/D band.
Surface search: Norden SPS 67V ❸; G band.
Navigation: Raytheon SPS 64(V)9; I/J band.
Tacan: URN 25. **IFF:** Mk XII UPX-29.

Helicopters: Platform only for 2 CH-53 series Stallion.

Programmes: Originally it was planned to construct six ships of this class as replacements for the Thomaston class LSDs. Eventually, the level of Whidbey Island class ships was established at eight, with five additional cargo-carrying variants of that class to be built to provide increased cargo-carrying capability. The first cargo variant, LSD 49, was authorised and funded in the FY 1988 budget; LSD 50 in FY 1989 and LSD 51 in FY 1991. The fourth was authorised in FY 1992 and although Congress failed to provide funds, the ship was included in the FY 1993 budget.
Modernisation: The SSDS (ship self-defence system) is being fitted in LSD 41 for trials in late 1993. The system integrates and controls SPS 49, SLQ-32, SAR-8 IR directors (if fitted) and Phalanx (or RAM if fitted). The aim is to improve response times to anti-ship cruise missiles in non-Aegis ships.

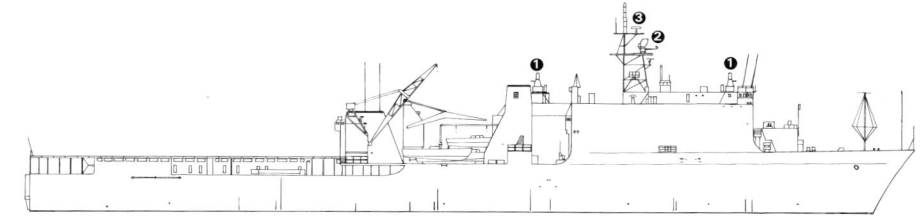

WHIDBEY ISLAND *(Scale 1 : 1500), Ian Sturton*

GERMANTOWN *9/1992, Stefan Terzibaschitsch*

Structure: Based on the earlier Anchorage class. One 60 and one 20 ton crane. Well deck measures 440 × 50 ft *(134.1 × 15.2 m)* in the LSD but is shorter in the Cargo Variant (CV). The cargo version is a minimum modification to the LSD 41 design. Changes in that design include additional air-conditioning, piping and hull structure; the forward Phalanx is lower down and there is only one crane. There is approximately 90% commonality between the two ships.
Operational: LSD 42 is based at Sasebo.

5 ANCHORAGE CLASS: DOCK LANDING SHIPS (LSD)

Name	No	Builders	Laid down	Launched	Commissioned	F/S
ANCHORAGE	LSD 36	Ingalls Shipbuilding Corp	13 Mar 1967	5 May 1968	15 Mar 1969	PA
PORTLAND	LSD 37	General Dynamics, Quincy, Mass	21 Sep 1967	20 Dec 1969	3 Oct 1970	AA
PENSACOLA	LSD 38	General Dynamics, Quincy, Mass	12 Mar 1969	11 July 1970	27 Mar 1971	AA
MOUNT VERNON	LSD 39	General Dynamics, Quincy, Mass	29 Jan 1970	17 Apr 1971	13 May 1972	PA
FORT FISHER	LSD 40	General Dynamics, Quincy, Mass	15 July 1970	22 Apr 1972	9 Dec 1972	PA

Displacement, tons: 8600 light; 13 700 full load
Dimensions, feet (metres): 553.3 × 84 × 20 *(168.6 × 25.6 × 6)*
Main machinery: 2 Foster-Wheeler boilers (Combustion Engineering in LSD 36); 600 psi *(42.3 kg/cm sq)*; 870°F *(467°C)*; 2 De Laval turbines; 24 000 hp *(18 MW)*; 2 shafts
Speed, knots: 22. **Range, miles:** 14 800 at 12 kts
Complement: 374 (24 officers)
Military lift: 366 troops (18 officers); 3 LCUs or 3 LCACs or 18 LCM 6 or 9 LCM 8 or 50 LVTs; 1 LCM 6 on deck; 2 LCPLs and 1 LCVP on davits. Aviation fuel, 90 tons

Guns: 4 USN 3 in *(76 mm)*/50 (2 twin) Mk 33 ❶; 85° elevation; 50 rounds/minute to 12.8 km *(7 nm)*; weight of shell 6 kg. Local control only.
2 General Electric/General Dynamics 20 mm/76 6-barrelled Vulcan Phalanx Mk 15 ❷; 3000 rounds/minute combined to 1.5 km.
Countermeasures: Decoys: 4 Loral Hycor SRBOC 6-barrelled Mk 36; IR flares and chaff to 4 km *(2.2 nm)*.
ESM: SLQ 32(V)1; intercept. May be updated to (V)2.
Combat data systems: SATCOM SRR-1, WSC-3 (UHF).
Radars: Air search: Lockheed SPS 40 ❸; E/F band; range 320 km *(175 nm)*.
Surface search: Raytheon SPS 10 ❹; G band.
Navigation: Marconi LN 66; I band.

Helicopters: Platform only.

Structure: Helicopter platform aft with docking well partially open; helicopter platform can be removed. Docking well approximately 430 × 50 ft *(131.1 × 15.2 m)*. Two 50 ton capacity cranes.
Operational: Four of the class were involved in the war with Iraq in 1991.

ANCHORAGE *(Scale 1 : 1500), Ian Sturton*

PENSACOLA *4/1992, Gilbert Gyssels*

Amphibious warfare forces / USA   797

16 NEWPORT CLASS: TANK LANDING SHIPS (LST)

Name	No	Builders	Laid down	Launched	Commissioned	F/S
FRESNO	LST 1182	National Steel & SB Co, San Diego, California	16 Dec 1967	28 Sep 1968	22 Nov 1969	NRF
PEORIA	LST 1183	National Steel & SB Co, San Diego, California	22 Feb 1968	23 Nov 1968	21 Feb 1970	PA
FREDERICK	LST 1184	National Steel & SB Co, San Diego, California	13 Apr 1968	8 Mar 1969	11 Apr 1970	PA
SCHENECTADY	LST 1185	National Steel & SB Co, San Diego, California	2 Aug 1968	24 May 1969	13 June 1970	PA
CAYUGA	LST 1186	National Steel & SB Co, San Diego, California	28 Sep 1968	12 July 1969	8 Aug 1970	PA
TUSCALOOSA	LST 1187	National Steel & SB Co, San Diego, California	23 Nov 1968	6 Sep 1969	24 Oct 1970	PA
SAGINAW	LST 1188	National Steel & SB Co, San Diego, California	24 May 1969	7 Feb 1970	23 Jan 1971	AA
SAN BERNARDINO	LST 1189	National Steel & SB Co, San Diego, California	12 July 1969	28 Mar 1970	27 Mar 1971	PA
BOULDER	LST 1190	National Steel & SB Co, San Diego, California	6 Sep 1969	22 May 1970	4 June 1971	NRF
RACINE	LST 1191	National Steel & SB Co, San Diego, California	13 Dec 1969	15 Aug 1970	9 July 1971	NRF
SPARTANBURG COUNTY	LST 1192	National Steel & SB Co, San Diego, California	7 Feb 1970	11 Nov 1970	1 Sep 1971	AA
FAIRFAX COUNTY	LST 1193	National Steel & SB Co, San Diego, California	28 Mar 1970	19 Dec 1970	16 Oct 1971	AA
LA MOURE COUNTY	LST 1194	National Steel & SB Co, San Diego, California	22 May 1970	13 Feb 1971	18 Dec 1971	AA
HARLAN COUNTY	LST 1196	National Steel & SB Co, San Diego, California	7 Nov 1970	24 July 1971	8 Apr 1972	AA
BARNSTABLE COUNTY	LST 1197	National Steel & SB Co, San Diego, California	19 Dec 1970	2 Oct 1971	27 May 1972	AA
BRISTOL COUNTY	LST 1198	National Steel & SB Co, San Diego, California	13 Feb 1971	4 Dec 1971	5 Aug 1972	PA

Displacement, tons: 4975 light; 8450 full load
Dimensions, feet (metres): 522.3 (hull) × 69.5 × 17.5 (aft) *(159.2 × 21.2 × 5.3)*
Main machinery: 6 ARCO 16-251 diesels; 16 500 hp *(12.3 MW)* sustained; 2 shafts; cp props; bow thruster
Speed, knots: 20. **Range, miles:** 2500 at 14 kts
Complement: 257 (13 officers)
Military lift: 400 troops (20 officers); 500 tons vehicles; 3 LCVPs and 1 LCPL on davits

Guns: 4 USN 3 in *(76 mm)*/50 (2 twin) Mk 33; 85° elevation; 50 rounds/minute to 12.8 km *(7 nm)*; weight of shell 6 kg. Local control only.
  1 General Electric/General Dynamics 20 mm Vulcan Phalanx Mk 15 (being fitted on bridge roof).
Combat data systems: SATCOM SRR-1, WSC-3 (UHF).
Radars: Surface search: Raytheon SPS 10F; G band. Being replaced by SPS 67 in FY 1990-93.
  Navigation: Marconi LN 66 (LST 1183, 1184, 1186, 1187, 1196, 1197); I band.
  Raytheon CRP 3100 Pathfinder (LST 1188, 1192-94); I/J band.

Helicopters: Platform only.

Programmes: *Boulder* (LST 1190) was assigned to the NRF on 1 December 1980, *Racine* (LST 1191) on 15 January 1981 and *Fresno* (LST 1182) on 30 September 1990.
Modernisation: Phalanx CIWS is being fitted on the bridge roof in some of the class.
Structure: The hull form required to achieve 20 kts would not permit bow doors, thus these ships unload by a 112 ft ramp over their bow. The ramp is supported by twin derrick arms. A ramp just forward of the superstructure connects the lower tank deck with the main deck and a vehicle passage through the superstructure provides access to the parking area amidships. A stern gate to the tank deck permits unloading of amphibious tractors into the water, or unloading of other vehicles into an LCU or on to a pier. Vehicle stowage covers 19 000 sq ft. Length over derrick arms is 562 ft *(171.3 m)*; full load draught is 11.5 ft forward and 17.5 ft aft. Bow thruster fitted to hold position offshore while unloading amphibious tractors.
Operational: They operate with 20 knot amphibious squadrons to transport tanks, other heavy vehicles, engineering equipment, and supplies which cannot be readily landed by helicopters or landing craft. ESM equipment fitted in some. Fourteen of the class were involved in the war with Iraq in 1991. One deleted in early 1992, three more by mid-1993 and four in 1994. *San Bernardino* is based at Sasebo, Japan.

PEORIA (ramp extended)   9/1992, Stefan Terzibaschitsch

HARLAN COUNTY (with Mexeflotes)   2/1992, F Sadek

3 CHARLESTON CLASS: AMPHIBIOUS CARGO SHIPS (LKA)

Name	No	Builders	Commissioned	F/S
DURHAM	LKA 114	Newport News SB & DD Co	24 May 1969	PA
MOBILE	LKA 115	Newport News SB & DD Co	29 Sep 1969	PA
EL PASO	LKA 117	Newport News SB & DD Co	17 Jan 1970	AA

Displacement, tons: 10 000 light; 20 700 full load
Dimensions, feet (metres): 575.5 × 62 × 25.5 *(175.4 × 18.9 × 7.7)*
Main machinery: 2 Combustion Engineering boilers; 600 psi *(42.3 kg/cm sq)*; 870°F *(467°C)*; 1 Westinghouse turbine; 19 250 hp *(14.4 MW)*; 1 shaft
Speed, knots: 20. **Range, miles:** 9600 at 16 kts
Complement: 356 (22 officers)
Military lift: 362 troops (25 officers). 4 LCM 8, 5 LCM 6, 2 LCPL

Guns: 2 or 6 USN 3 in *(76 mm)*/50 (1 or 3 twin) Mk 33; 85° elevation; 50 rounds/minute to 12.8 km *(7 nm)*; weight of shell 6 kg. Local control only.
  2 General Electric/General Dynamics 20 mm Vulcan Phalanx Mk 15 (instead of 2 twin 76 mm).
Countermeasures: Decoys: 2 MBA Loral Hycor SRBOC 6-barrelled fixed Mk 36; IR flares and chaff to 4 km *(2.2 nm)*.
ESM: SLQ 32(V)1; intercept. May be upgraded to (V)2.
Combat data systems: SATCOM SRR-1, WSC-3 (UHF).
Radars: Surface search: Raytheon SPS 10F; G band.
  SPS 67 (fitted in FY 1989-92).
  Navigation: Marconi LN 66; I band.
Tacan: IFF: Mk XII.

Helicopters: Platform only.

Programmes: Originally designated Attack Cargo Ship (AKA), redesignated Amphibious Cargo Ships on 1 January 1969.
Structure: Designed specifically for the attack cargo ship role for amphibious operations. Design includes two heavy-lift cranes with a 78.4 ton capacity, two 40 ton capacity booms, and eight 15 ton capacity booms. These are among the first US Navy ships with a fully automated main propulsion plant. Control of plant is from bridge or central machinery space console. This automation permitted a 45 man reduction in complement. Phalanx have replaced two of the 76 mm guns in some of the class.
Operational: Being paid off.

DURHAM   3/1991, 92 Wing RAAF

LANDING CRAFT

60 + 24 LANDING CRAFT AIR-CUSHION (LCAC)

Displacement, tons: 87.2 light; 170-182 full load
Dimensions, feet (metres): 88 oa (on cushion) (81 between hard structures) × 47 beam (on cushion) (43 beam hard structure) × 2.9 draught (off cushion) *(26.8 (24.7) × 14.3 (13.1) × 0.9)*
Main machinery: 4 Avco-Lycoming TF-40B gas turbines; 2 for propulsion and 2 for lift; 16 000 hp *(12 MW)* sustained; 2 shrouded reversible pitch airscrews (propulsion); 4 double entry fans, centrifugal or mixed flow (lift)
Speed, knots: 40 (loaded). **Range, miles:** 300 at 35 kts; 200 at 40 kts
Complement: 5
Military lift: 24 troops; 1 MBT or 60-75 tons

Guns: 2—12.7 mm MGs.
Radars: Navigation: Marconi LN 66; I band.

Programmes: Being built by Textron Marine Systems and Avondale Gulfport, the latter yard having been purchased from Lockheed Shipbuilding. 33 funded FY 1982-86, 15 in FY 1989, 12 in each of FY 1990 and 1991. In FY 1992 Congress authorised 12 but then provided funds for 24 although only the 12 authorised are to be built, for a total of 84.
Structure: Incorporates the best attributes of the JEFF(A) and JEFF(B) learned from over five years of testing the two prototypes. Bow ramp 28.8 ft, stern ramp 15 ft. Cargo space capacity is 1809 sq ft. Noise and dust levels are high and if disabled the craft is not easy to tow. Spray suppressors have been added to the skirt to reduce interference with the driver's vision.
Operational: Ship classes capable of carrying the LCAC are Wasp (three), Tarawa (one), Anchorage (four), Austin (two), Whidbey (four) and Modified Whidbey (two). MCMV role is being evaluated as a secondary priority to the amphibious commitment. According to the USMC the craft can cross 70 per cent of the world's coastlines compared to about 15 per cent for conventional landing craft. Some limitations in very rough seas. Shore bases on each coast at Little Creek, Virginia and Camp Pendleton, California. Some were used in the Gulf in 1991 to recapture an Iraq-held island which belonged to Kuwait. They were also used for relief operations in Bangladesh, and in landing Marines in Somalia in December 1992. Performance and reliability have exceeded expectations.

LCAC 34 — *9/1992, Stefan Terzibaschitsch*

LCAC 38 — *9/1992, Stefan Terzibaschitsch*

5 FRANK S BESSON CLASS: LOGISTIC SUPPORT VESSELS (LSV-ARMY)

Name	No	Builders	Completed
GENERAL FRANK S BESSON JR	LSV 1	Moss Point Marine, Mississippi	18 Dec 1987
CW 3 HAROLD C CLINGER	LSV 2	Moss Point Marine, Mississippi	20 Feb 1988
GENERAL BREHON B SOMERVELL	LSV 3	Moss Point Marine, Mississippi	2 Apr 1988
LT GENERAL WILLIAM B BUNKER	LSV 4	Moss Point Marine, Mississippi	18 May 1988
MAJOR GENERAL CHARLES P GROSS	LSV 5	Moss Point Marine, Mississippi	30 Apr 1991

Displacement, tons: 4265 full load
Dimensions, feet (metres): 272.8 × 60 × 12 *(83.1 × 18.3 × 3.7)*
Main machinery: 2 GM EMD 16-645E2 diesels; 3900 hp *(2.9 MW)* sustained; 2 shafts
Speed, knots: 11.6. **Range, miles:** 6000 at 11 kts
Complement: 30 (6 officers)
Military lift: 2280 tons of vehicles, containers or general cargo

Comment: Army owned Ro-ro design with 10 500 sq ft of deck space for cargo. Capable of beaching with 4 ft over the ramp on a 1:30 offshore gradient with a payload of 900 tons of cargo. Two of the class building for the Philippines Navy in 1993.

GENERAL FRANK S BESSON — *1988, Giorgio Arra*

35 + 5 LCU 2001 CLASS: UTILITY LANDING CRAFT (LCU-ARMY)

LCU 2001-2035

Displacement, tons: 1102 full load
Dimensions, feet (metres): 173.8 × 42 × 8.5 *(53 × 12.8 × 2.6)*
Main machinery: 2 Cummins KTA50-M diesels; 2500 hp *(1.87 MW)* sustained; 2 shafts; bow thruster
Speed, knots: 11.5. **Range, miles:** 4500 at 11.5 kts
Complement: 13 (2 officers)
Military lift: 350 tons
Radars: Navigation: Two Raytheon SPS 64; I band.

Comment: Order placed with Avondale by US Army 11 June 1986 for 25 craft with an option on 15 more. First one completed 21 February 1990 by Moss Point Marine. Building rate about 12 a year. The 2001 series have names, some of which duplicate naval ships. These are the first ships to be built to an Army specification.

LCU 2006 — *7/1990, Giorgio Arra*

37 LCU 1600 CLASS: UTILITY LANDING CRAFT (LCU-ARMY and NAVY)

Displacement, tons: 200 light; 375 (437, LCU 1680-81) full load
Dimensions, feet (metres): 134.9 × 29 × 6.1 *(41.1 × 8.8 × 1.9)*
Main machinery: 4 Detroit 6-71 diesels; 696 hp *(519 kW)* sustained; 2 shafts; Kort nozzles
2 Detroit 12V-71 diesels (LCU 1621, 1680-1681); 680 hp *(508 kW)* sustained; 2 shafts; Kort nozzles
Speed, knots: 11. **Range, miles:** 1200 at 8 kts
Complement: 14 (2 officers)
Military lift: 170 tons; 3 M103 (64 tons) or M48 (48 tons) tanks or 350 troops
Guns: 2—12.7 mm MGs.
Radars: Navigation: LN 66 or SPS-53; I band.

Comment: Improved steel hulled landing craft, larger than previous series. Versatile craft used for a variety of tasks. Pennant numbers are in the 1600 series. Most were built between the mid-1960s and mid-1980s. There are no plans for more of this type. At least three converted as ASDV 1-3, 1 and 3 based in San Diego and 2 in Little Creek. LCU 1641 carries a chute over a cutaway stern and is apparently used as a mine recovery tender at Charleston, South Carolina.

LCU 1635 — *7/1992, Per Kornefeldt*

74 + 12 MECHANISED LANDING CRAFT: LCM 8 TYPE

Displacement, tons: 105 full load (aluminium)
Dimensions, feet (metres): 73.7 × 21 × 5.2 *(22.5 × 6.4 × 1.6)*
Main machinery: 2 Detroit 6-71 diesels; 348 hp *(260 kW)* sustained or 2 Detroit 12V-71 diesels; 680 hp *(508 kW)* sustained; 2 shafts
Speed, knots: 12. **Range, miles:** 190 at 9 kts full load
Complement: 5
Military lift: 180 tons or 1 M48 or 1 M60 tank or 200 troops

Comment: Naval craft are Mk 7 all-aluminium new construction types for use in amphibious ships. 12 more included in the FY 1992 budget. Older welded steel types are used by the Army and can only lift 60 tons. Also operated in large numbers by the US Army.

LCM 8 — *9/1991, Giorgio Arra*

Landing craft — Mine warfare forces / USA 799

72 MECHANISED LANDING CRAFT: LCM 6 TYPE

Displacement, tons: 64 full load
Dimensions, feet (metres): 56.2 × 14 × 3.9 *(17.1 × 4.3 × 1.2)*
Main machinery: 2 Detroit 6-71 diesels; 348 hp *(260 kW)* sustained or 2 Detroit 8V-71 diesels; 460 hp *(344 kW)* sustained; 2 shafts
Speed, knots: 9. **Range, miles:** 130 at 9 kts
Complement: 5
Military lift: 34 tons or 80 troops

Comment: Welded-steel construction. Used for various utility tasks.

160 + 7 LANDING CRAFT PERSONNEL (LCPL)

Displacement, tons: 11 full load
Dimensions, feet (metres): 36 × 12.1 × 3.8 *(11 × 3.7 × 1.2)*
Main machinery: 1 GM 8V-71TI diesel; 425 hp *(317 kW)* sustained; 1 shaft
Speed, knots: 20. **Range, miles:** 150 at 20 kts
Complement: 3
Military lift: 17 troops

Comment: There are 12 Mk 11, 140 Mk 12 and eight Mk 13. Details given are for the Mk 13 of GRP construction, ordered from Bollinger Shipyard in FY 1989 and delivered in 1991. For use as control craft and carried aboard LHA, LPD, LSD and LST classes. A further seven were ordered from Peterson in October 1992.

LCPL 4/1991, Bollinger

NAVAL RESERVE FORCE AMPHIBIOUS WARFARE TRAINING SHIPS

Name/Hull No	NRF Homeport	Assignment
BOULDER (LST 1190)	Little Creek, VA	1 Dec 1980
RACINE (LST 1191)	San Diego, CA	15 Jan 1981
FRESNO (LST 1182)	Long Beach, CA	30 Sep 1990

LCM 6 9/1986, Giorgio Arra

MINE WARFARE FORCES

Notes: (1) The use of LCACs for MCM duties is being evaluated.
(2) There are no surface minelayers. Mining is done by carrier-based aircraft, land-based patrol aircraft and submarines. US Air Force B-52s also have a minelaying capability.
(3) NRF ships are manned by composite active/reserve crews.
(4) Two SAM unmanned sweepers (*Gerry* (SAM 03) and *Peggy* (SAM 05)) were acquired from Sweden in February 1991 and are still being evaluated. Details under Swedish Landsort class.
(5) MH-53E Sea Stallion helicopters are deployed in amphibious assault ships for mine countermeasures operations.
(6) The Acme class Ocean Minesweeper *Affray* (MSO 511) may be retained in service until FY 1996.
(7) The LPH *Inchon* is to be converted as a Command and Support Ship by 1996.

10 + 4 AVENGER CLASS: MINE COUNTERMEASURES VESSELS (MCM)

Name	No	Builders	Laid down	Launched	Commissioned	F/S
AVENGER	MCM 1	Peterson Builders Inc, Sturgeon Bay, Wisc	3 June 1983	15 June 1985	12 Sep 1987	AA
DEFENDER	MCM 2	Marinette Marine Corp, Marinette, Wisc	1 Dec 1983	4 Apr 1987	30 Sep 1989	AA
SENTRY	MCM 3	Peterson Builders Inc, Sturgeon Bay, Wisc	8 Oct 1984	20 Sep 1986	2 Sep 1989	AA
CHAMPION	MCM 4	Marinette Marine Corp, Marinette, Wisc	28 June 1984	15 Apr 1989	31 Jan 1991	PA
GUARDIAN	MCM 5	Peterson Builders Inc, Sturgeon Bay, Wisc	8 May 1985	20 June 1987	16 Dec 1989	AA
DEVASTATOR	MCM 6	Peterson Builders Inc, Sturgeon Bay, Wisc	9 Feb 1987	11 June 1988	6 Oct 1990	AA
PATRIOT	MCM 7	Marinette Marine Corp, Marinette, Wisc	31 Mar 1987	15 May 1990	18 Oct 1991	AA
SCOUT	MCM 8	Peterson Builders Inc, Sturgeon Bay, Wisc	8 June 1987	20 May 1989	15 Dec 1990	AA
PIONEER	MCM 9	Peterson Builders Inc, Sturgeon Bay, Wisc	5 June 1989	25 Aug 1990	7 Dec 1992	AA
WARRIOR	MCM 10	Peterson Builders Inc, Sturgeon Bay, Wisc	25 Sep 1989	8 Dec 1990	3 Apr 1993	AA
GLADIATOR	MCM 11	Peterson Builders Inc, Sturgeon Bay, Wisc	7 July 1990	29 June 1991	June 1993	Bldg
ARDENT	MCM 12	Peterson Builders Inc, Sturgeon Bay, Wisc	22 Oct 1990	16 Nov 1991	Aug 1993	Bldg
DEXTROUS	MCM 13	Peterson Builders Inc, Sturgeon Bay, Wisc	11 Mar 1991	20 June 1992	Nov 1993	Bldg
CHIEF	MCM 14	Peterson Builders Inc, Sturgeon Bay, Wisc	19 Aug 1991	June 1993	July 1994	Bldg

Displacement, tons: 1312 full load
Dimensions, feet (metres): 224 × 39 × 12.2 *(68.3 × 11.9 × 3.7)*
Main machinery: 4 Waukesha L-1616 diesels (MCM 1-2); 2400 hp(m) *(1.76 MW)* sustained; 2 shafts; 1 omni-thruster hydrojet; 350 hp *(257 kW)*
4 Isotta Fraschini ID 36 SS 6V AM diesels (MCM 3 onwards); 2400 hp(m) *(1.76 MW)* sustained; 2 motors; 400 hp(m) *(294 kW)* for hovering; 2 shafts; 1 omni-thruster hydrojet; 350 hp *(257 kW)*
Speed, knots: 13.5
Complement: 81 (6 officers)

Guns: 2—12.7 mm Mk 26 MGs.
Countermeasures: MCM: 2 SLQ-48; ROV mine neutralisation system, capable of 6 kts (1500 m cable with cutter and countermining charge). SLQ 37(V)2; magnetic/acoustic influence sweep equipment. Oropesa Type O Size 1; mechanical sweep. EDO ALQ 166 magnetic minesweeping vehicle to be provided when available.
Combat data systems: SATCOM SRR-1; WSC-3 (UHF). Nautis (M) (in later units) includes Paramax SYQ 13 command system and SSN 2 PINS.
Radars: Surface search: ISC Cardion SPS 55; I/J band.
Sonars: General Electric SQQ 30 or SQQ 32 (Raytheon/Thomson Sintra SQQ 32 in MCM 10 onwards and being retrofitted); VDS; active minehunting; high frequency.

Programmes: The contract for the prototype MCM was awarded in June 1982; MCM 2 in May 1983; MCM 3-5 in December 1983; MCM 6-8 in August 1986. MCM 9 was funded in the FY 1985 programme and MCM 10-11 in the FY 1986 programme; however, contracts for their construction were not awarded until January 1989. The last three were funded in FY 1990.
Structure: The hull is constructed of oak, Douglas fir and Alaskan cedar, with a thin coating of fibreglass on the outside, to permit taking advantage of wood's low magnetic signature. A problem of engine rotation on the Waukesha diesels in MCM 1-2 was resolved; however, those engines have been replaced in the rest of the class by low magnetic engines manufactured by Isotta-Fraschini of Milan, Italy. Fitted with SSN2(V) precise integrated navigation system (PINS).
Operational: *Avenger* fitted with the SQQ 32 for Gulf operations in 1991 and all of the class are to be retrofitted. The plan is for all to be based at Ingleside, Texas, but this may prove to be too expensive an option.

DEFENDER 3/1992, Giorgio Arra

800 USA / Mine warfare forces

1 + 9 + 2 OSPREY CLASS (MINEHUNTERS COASTAL) (MHC)

Name	No	Builders	Launched	Commissioned	F/S
OSPREY	MHC 51	Intermarine, Savannah	23 Mar 1991	May 1993	Bldg/AA
HERON	MHC 52	Intermarine, Savannah	21 Mar 1992	Oct 1993	Bldg
PELICAN	MHC 53	Avondale Industries	27 Feb 1993	Mar 1994	Bldg
ROBIN	MHC 54	Avondale Industries	31 Mar 1993	Oct 1994	Bldg
ORIOLE	MHC 55	Intermarine, Savannah	May 1993	Sep 1994	Bldg
KINGFISHER	MHC 56	Avondale Industries	Oct 1993	Mar 1995	Bldg
CORMORANT	MHC 57	Avondale Industries	May 1994	July 1995	Bldg
BLACK HAWK	MHC 58	Intermarine, Savannah	Mar 1994	Sep 1995	Bldg
FALCON	MHC 59	Intermarine, Savannah	June 1994	Nov 1995	Bldg
CARDINAL	MHC 60	Intermarine, Savannah	Sep 1994	Jan 1996	Bldg
—	MHC 61-62	Approved FY 1993 programme	—	—	Proj

Displacement, tons: 918 full load
Dimensions, feet (metres): 188 × 35.9 × 9.5 *(57.3 × 11 × 2.9)*
Main machinery: 2 Isotta Fraschini ID 36 SS 8V AM diesels; 1600 hp(m) *(1.18 MW)* sustained; 2 Voith Schneider props; 2 hydraulic motors; 360 hp(m) *(265 kW)*
Speed, knots: 12. **Range, miles:** 1500 at 12 kts
Complement: 51 (4 officers)

Guns: 2—12.7 mm MGs.
Countermeasures: MCM: Both mechanical and modular influence sweep systems being developed independently of ship construction programme. SLQ-48 ROV mine neutralisation system.
Combat data systems: Unisys integrated control system.
Radars: Navigation: Raytheon SPS 64; I band.
Sonars: Raytheon/Thomson Sintra SQQ 32; VDS; active minehunting; high frequency.

Programmes: A project to construct 17 MSH was cancelled in mid-1986 because the design, based on a surface effect ship, failed shock testing. A design contract for Lerici class mine hunters was then awarded in August 1986 followed by a construction contract in May 1987 for the lead ship of the class. Intermarine Sarzana established Intermarine USA and purchased Sayler Marine Corporation in Savannah, Georgia. On 2 October 1989 Avondale, Gulfport was named as the second construction source. Twelve of the class are to be built but plans for a lengthened version have been shelved. Engine modifications in *Osprey* have delayed completion. Intermarine has an option on the last pair.
Structure: Construction is of heavy GRP throughout hull, decks and bulkheads, with frames eliminated. Main machinery is mounted on vibration dampers. SQQ 32 is deployed from a central well forward. The hydraulic motors are used for slow speed propulsion.

OSPREY 12/1992, Intermarine

5 AGGRESSIVE CLASS: OCEAN MINESWEEPERS (MSO)

Name	No	Builders	Launched	Commissioned	F/S
EXULTANT*	MSO 441	Higgins, New Orleans	6 June 1953	22 June 1954	AA
IMPLICIT	MSO 455	Wilmington Boat	1 Aug 1953	10 Mar 1954	NRF
CONQUEST*	MSO 488	Martinac, Tacoma	20 May 1954	20 July 1955	NRF
GALLANT	MSO 489	Martinac, Tacoma	4 June 1954	14 Sep 1955	NRF
PLEDGE	MSO 492	Martinac, Tacoma	20 July 1955	20 Apr 1956	NRF

* Modernised

Displacement, tons: 720 standard; 780 full load
Dimensions, feet (metres): 172.5 × 35.1 × 14.1 *(52.6 × 10.7 × 4.3)*
Main machinery: 4 Packard ID-1700 diesels (Waukesha in modernised ships); 2280 hp *(1.7 MW)*; 2 shafts; cp props
Speed, knots: 14. **Range, miles:** 3000 at 10 kts
Complement: 86 (7 officers); 39 (3 officers) plus 47 (4 officers) reserves in NRF ships

Guns: 2—12.7 mm MGs.
Combat data systems: SATCOM SRR-1.
Radars: Navigation: Sperry SPS 53L; I/J band.
Sonars: General Electric SQQ 14; VDS; active minehunting; high frequency.

Programmes: Built on the basis of mine warfare experience in the Korean War (1950-53); 58 built for US service and 35 transferred on completion to NATO navies. All surviving ships were built in private shipyards. Initially designated as minesweepers (AM); reclassified as ocean minesweepers (MSO) in February 1955. Originally fitted with UQS 1 mine detecting sonar.
Modernisation: Some MSOs were modernised during the mid-1960s. The modernisation provided improvements in mine detection, engines, communications, and habitability: four Waukesha Motor Co diesel engines installed (plus two or three diesel generators for sweep gear), SQQ 14 sonar with mine classification as well as detection capability provided, guns removed, habitability improved, and advanced communications equipment fitted; bridge structure in modernised ships extended around mast and aft to funnel.
Structure: Wooden hulls. Diesel engines are fabricated of non-magnetic stainless steel alloy.
Operational: Many have paid off; the remainder will decommission by 1994. *Exultant* was reported as paid off in 1991 but re-emerged in 1992.
Sales: Ships of this class were transferred to the navies of Belgium, France, Italy, Netherlands and Spain; many of them have been deleted.

GALLANT 1992, van Ginderen Collection

1 ACME CLASS: OCEAN MINESWEEPER (MSO)

Name	No	Launched	Commissioned	F/S
AFFRAY	MSO 511	18 Dec 1956	8 Dec 1958	NRF

Displacement, tons: 633 light; 924 full load
Dimensions, feet (metres): 173 × 35 × 14 *(52.7 × 10.7 × 4.3)*
Main machinery: 4 Packard ID-1700 diesels; 2280 hp *(1.7 MW)*; 2 shafts; cp props
Speed, knots: 15. **Range, miles:** 3000 at 10 kts
Complement: 44 (7 officers) plus 37 (4 officers) reserves
Countermeasures: MCM: Acoustic; A Mk 2, Mk 4, Mk 6, Magnetic; M Mk 5, Mk 6, Mk 7. Wire; Orepesa No 1.
Radars: Navigation: Sperry SPS 53L; I/J band
Sonars General Electric SQQ 14; VDS; active minehunting; high frequency

Comment: Built by Frank L Sample, Jr, Inc, Boothbay Harbor, Maine. Was to have paid off in 1993 but may now stay in service until 1996.

AFFRAY 4/1988, Giorgio Arra

HARBOUR DEFENCE PROJECT (COOP)

10 YP 654 CLASS + 5 HATTERAS and WESTPORT CLASS

Displacement, tons: 68 full load
Dimensions, feet (metres): 80.4 × 18.8 × 5.3 *(24.5 × 5.7 × 1.6)*
Main machinery: 4 GM diesels; 660 hp *(492 kW)*; 2 shafts
Speed, knots: 13. **Range, miles:** 400 at 12 kts
Complement: 9
Radars: Navigation: Raytheon 1220; I band.

Comment: Details given are for the YP class. The COOP programme came into being at a time when USN mine warfare assets were at a low point, and it was expected that the use of converted patrol boats, craft captured from drug smugglers, and fishing boats could provide a useful mine countermeasures force in and around US harbours. It was estimated that the force might number in excess of 80 craft dispersed in 22 ports. Unfortunately, few of the captured drug smuggling boats proved usable and enhancing the capabilities of patrol craft (YPs) and fishing boats proved to be difficult. Also the Navy embarked upon a major construction programme of mine countermeasures vessels, and as a result the COOP programme was sharply reduced from the original concept. The Navy had planned to eliminate the programme at the end of FY 1992, but Congress both authorised and appropriated funds for another year's operation. Currently, the Navy is examining alternative future mission and employment options for COOP as a deployable asset in support of littoral warfare. In early 1993 there were COOPMINEUNITS in 14 ports (two in Seattle)-11 on the east and Gulf coasts, three on the west coast, and one in Hawaii-to which are assigned 10 former YPs and five Hatteras and Westport craft. No craft is assigned to the unit in Hawaii. Four crews comprised of nine Reservists each are assigned to each craft.

CT 6 4/1991, Giorgio Arra

LIGHT FORCES

Notes: 1. The FY 1993 small craft plan includes 4 × 78 ft PCFs and 12 × 42 ft PCCs. The PCFs are SEAL delivery craft which must be air transportable and usable on rivers with existing techniques and equipment. Top speed required is 50 kts. Contracts are expected in 1993/94.
2. There are large numbers of RIBs in service. 70 more are included in the FY 1993/94 planned acquisition list.

4 + 9 CYCLONE CLASS (COASTAL PATROL CRAFT) (PC)

CYCLONE PC 1	SIROCCO PC 6	FIREBOLT PC 10
TEMPEST PC 2	SQUALL PC 7	WHIRLWIND PC 11
HURRICANE PC 3	ZEPHYR PC 8	THUNDERBOLT PC 12
MONSOON PC 4	CHINOOK PC 9	— PC 13
TYPHOON PC 5		

Displacement, tons: 328 full load
Dimensions, feet (metres): 170.6 × 24.9 × 7.2 *(52 × 7.6 × 2.2)*
Main machinery: 4 Paxman Valenta 16RP200 diesels; 13 400 hp *(10 MW)*; 4 shafts
Speed, knots: 35. **Range, miles:** 2500 at 12 kts
Complement: 39 (4 officers) including 8 Marines or SEALs
Missiles: SAM: 1 sextuple Stinger mounting to be fitted in due course.
Guns: 2—25 mm Mk 38. 2 M60 12.7 mm MGs. 2—40 mm Mk 19 grenade launchers (MG and grenade launchers are interchangeable).
Countermeasures: Decoys: 2 Mk 52 chaff launchers.
Fire control: Marconi VISTAR IM 405 IR system.
Radars: Surface search: I band.

Comment: Contract awarded for eight in August 1990 and five more in July 1991. Building at Bollinger Shipyard, Louisiana. The design is based on the Vosper Thornycroft Ramadan class modified to meet US Navy requirements. Shoulder-launched Stinger SAM may be carried. The craft have a slow speed loiter capability. *Cyclone* commissioned 24 October 1992, then one every two months to early 1995. The plan is to operate them in pairs with a 12 man maintenance team in two trucks ashore. Based at Norfolk, VA and San Diego, CA. The names of the last five are not confirmed.

CYCLONE 1992, Boilinger

12 PATROL BOATS—Mk III (9) and Mk IV (3) Series (PB)

Displacement, tons: 31.5 light; 41.25 full load
Dimensions, feet (metres): 65 × 18 × 5.9 *(19.8 × 5.5 × 1.8)*
Main machinery: 3 Detroit 8V-71 diesels; 690 hp *(515 kW)* sustained (Mk III); 3 Detroit 8V-92; 909 hp *(670 kW)* sustained (Mk IV); 3 shafts
Speed, knots: 28. **Range, miles:** 450 at 26 kts
Complement: 9 (1 officer)
Guns: 2—25 mm Mk 38. 2—12.7 mm MGs. 1—81 mm mortar. 1—40 mm Mk 19 grenade launcher.

Comment: The PB series was developed as replacements for the Swift type inshore patrol craft (PCF). Mk III built by Peterson, Wisconsin in the mid-1970s and Mk IV by Atlantic Marine, Florida in 1985-86. The Mk III design has the pilot house offset to starboard to provide space on port side for installation of additional weapons. Armaments can vary with combinations of guns, MGs and mortars. Used by the Special Boat Units. Active in the Gulf, one of them being involved with the capture of the *Iran Ajr* minelayer on 22 September 1987. Two delivered to Columbia in 1990. The three Mk IV are extended by 3 ft in length, based in Panama and may be transferred.

PB Mk III 4/1991, Giorgio Arra

802 USA / Light forces

6 PATROL COMBATANTS MISSILE (HYDROFOIL) (PHM)

Name	No	Builders	Commissioned	F/S
PEGASUS	PHM 1	Boeing Co, Seattle	9 July 1977	AA
HERCULES	PHM 2	Boeing Co, Seattle	15 Jan 1983	AA
TAURUS	PHM 3	Boeing Co, Seattle	10 Oct 1981	AA
AQUILA	PHM 4	Boeing Co, Seattle	26 June 1982	AA
ARIES	PHM 5	Boeing Co, Seattle	11 Sep 1982	AA
GEMINI	PHM 6	Boeing Co, Seattle	13 Nov 1982	AA

Displacement, tons: 239.6 full load
Dimensions, feet (metres): 132.9 oa × 28.2 hull; 47.5 (foils) × 23.2 (foils extended) *(40.5 × 8.6; 14.5 × 7.1)*
145.3 oa × 28.2 hull × 7.5 (foils retracted) *(44.3 × 8.6 × 2.3)*
Main machinery: 1 GE LM 2500 gas turbine (foilborne); 19 500 hp *(14.55 MW)* sustained; 2 Aerojet waterjets
2 MTU 8V 331 TC81 diesels (hullborne); 1600 hp(m) *(1.18 MW)* sustained; 2 waterjets
Speed, knots: 40 foils; 10 hullborne. **Range, miles:** 1700 at 9 kts; 700 at 40 kts
Complement: 25 (5 officers) plus 5 (1 officer) Coast Guard for drug patrols

Missiles: SSM: 8 McDonnell Douglas Harpoon; active radar homing to 130 km *(70 nm)* at 0.9 Mach; warhead 227 kg.
Guns: 1 OTO Melara 3 in *(76 mm)*/62 Mk 75; 85° elevation; 85 rounds/minute to 16 km *(8.7 nm)*; weight of shell 6 kg.
Countermeasures: Decoys: 2 Loral Hycor RBOC Mk 34; IR flares and chaff to 4 km *(2.2 nm)*.
ESM/ECM: TAC Mk 105 (ALR 66 in PHM 6).
Combat data systems: SATCOM SSR-1; WSC-3 (UHF).
Fire control: SWG-1A(V)4 ship command launch and control systems replacing SWG-1(V)4.
Radars: Surface search: Raytheon SPS 64; I band (PHM 2 has APS-137).
Fire control: Signaal WM 28 *(Pegasus)*; Mk 92 (remainder); I/J band.

Programmes: *Pegasus* made her first foilborne trip on 25 February 1975 but the programme was cancelled in February 1977 leaving only *Pegasus* to serve as a High Speed Test Vehicle. In August 1977 after heavy Congressional pressure, the Secretary of Defense released the funds appropriated to complete the six ship programme. The designation PHM originally was for Patrol Hydrofoil-Missile; reclassified Patrol Combatant Missile (Hydrofoil) on 30 June 1975.
Structure: The PHM design was developed in conjunction with the Italian and West German navies in an effort to produce a small combatant that would be universally acceptable to NATO navies with minor modifications.
Operational: All based at Key West. Operations are conducted off the Yucatan peninsula and off bases at Guantanamo Bay (Cuba) and Roosevelt Roads (Puerto Rico). Because of high operating costs, all are scheduled to pay off by March 1994.

PEGASUS   10/1992, Giorgio Arra

31 RIVER PATROL BOATS Mk II Series (PBR)

Displacement, tons: 8.9 full load
Dimensions, feet (metres): 32 × 11 × 2.6 *(9.8 × 3.4 × 0.8)*
Main machinery: 2 GM 6V-53 diesels; 296 hp *(221 kW)*; 2 Jacuzzi waterjets
Speed, knots: 24. **Range, miles:** 150 at 22 kts
Complement: 4 or 5
Guns: 3—12.7 mm MGs (twin mount fwd, single aft). 1—40 mm Mk 19 grenade launcher.
1—60 mm mortar (in some boats).
Radars: Navigation: Raytheon 1900; I band.

Comment: Fibreglass hull river patrol boats. Approximately 500 built 1967-73; most transferred to South Vietnam and some to Thailand. Used for Reserve training.

PBR Mk II   1988, Giorgio Arra

6 STINGER CLASS (RIVER PATROL BOATS)

Displacement, tons: 7.4 full load
Dimensions, feet (metres): 35 × 9.3 × 2.2 *(10.6 × 2.8 × 0.6)*
Main machinery: 2 Cummins 6BTA5.9-M2 diesels; 600 hp *(448 kW)* maximum; 2 Hamilton waterjets
Speed, knots: 38. **Range, miles:** 250 at 26 kts
Complement: 4
Military lift: 10 troops
Guns: 2 or 4—12.7 mm MGs (2 single or 2 twin) or 2—40 mm Mk 19 grenade launchers; 2—7.62 mm MGs.
Radars: Navigation: Raytheon 1900; I band.

Comment: Riverine assault craft ordered for the Marines from SeaArk Marine 5 May 1990 and delivered less than three months later on 1 August 1990. Aluminium hulls which can be transported by road each on its own trailer. Being evaluated in transport, fire support and reconnaissance roles. See note under *Light Forces* heading.

STINGER   7/1990, SeaArk

22 MINI ARMOURED TROOP CARRIERS (ATC)

Displacement, tons: 14.8 full load
Dimensions, feet (metres): 36 × 12.7 × 3.5 *(11 × 3.9 × 1.1)*
Main machinery: 2 GM 8V-53 diesels; 566 hp *(422 kW)*; 2 Jacuzzi 14YS waterjets
Speed, knots: 28. **Range, miles:** 37 at 28 kts
Complement: 2
Military lift: 20 troops
Guns: 4—12.7 mm MGs. 1—40 mm Mk 19 grenade launcher.

Comment: Built by Sewart, Louisiana 1972-73. A small troop carrier for riverine and SEAL operations; aluminium hull; ceramic armour. Draught 1 ft when underway at high speed. Used by Special Boat Forces of the NRF.

MINI ATC   1987, Giorgio Arra

85 PORT SECURITY CRAFT

Displacement, tons: 3.9 full load
Dimensions, feet (metres): 24 × 8 × 3.3 *(7.3 × 2.4 × 1)*
Main machinery: 1 Volvo Penta AQAD41A diesel; 200 hp(m) *(149 kW)* maximum; Type 290 outdrive
Speed, knots: 22
Complement: 2
Guns: 1—7.62 mm MG.

Comment: Built by Peterson, Wisconsin and delivered between 29 February 1988 and 12 May 1989 in batches of 50, 25 and 10. Used for protecting naval installations, ports, harbours and anchorages. In addition there are large numbers of other small craft used in similar roles.

PORT SECURITY CRAFT   1/1988, Peterson

AUXILIARY SHIPS

Notes: 1. The Auxiliary Ships of the US Navy are usually divided into two broad categories, underway replenishment ships (UNREP) and fleet support ships. UNREP ships carry out the direct support of deployed forces in the forward area of operations.
Most US Navy replenishment ships are fitted with helicopter platforms to allow the transfer of supplies by vertical replenishment (VERTREP). Helicopters are carried specifically for this purpose by the ammunition ships (AE), the combat store ships (AFS), the fast combat support ships (AOE), and replenishment oilers (AOR). Carrier-based helicopters are sometimes employed in this role.
Planned UNREP ship force levels provide a wartime capability to support deployed carrier and amphibious task groups in up to four or five locations simultaneously. This plan is based on the availability of some storage depots on foreign territory, and the use of Military Sealift Ships to carry fuels, munitions, and the stores from the USA or overseas sources for transfer to UNREP ships in overseas areas.

Some 16 to 18 UNREP ships are normally forward deployed in the Mediterranean, Western Pacific and Indian Ocean areas in support of the 6th and 7th Fleets, respectively. During the build up to the war with Iraq in 1991, more than 30 ships were involved.
Fleet support ships provide primarily maintenance and related towing and salvage services at advanced bases and at ports in the USA. These ships normally do not provide fuel, munitions, or other supplies except when ships are alongside for maintenance. Most fleet support ships operate from bases in the USA.
2. Some underway replenishment ships and fleet support ships are Navy manned and armed, but an increasing number are operated by the Military Sealift Command (MSC) with civilian crews and unarmed. The latter ships have T-prefix before their designations and are listed in the next section.

6 YELLOWSTONE and SAMUEL GOMPERS CLASSES: DESTROYER TENDERS (AD)

Name	No	Builders	Commissioned	F/S
SAMUEL GOMPERS	AD 37	Puget Sound SY, Bremerton	1 July 1967	PA
PUGET SOUND	AD 38	Puget Sound SY, Bremerton	27 Apr 1968	AA
YELLOWSTONE	AD 41	National Steel, San Diego	31 May 1980	AA
ACADIA	AD 42	National Steel, San Diego	6 June 1981	PA
CAPE COD	AD 43	National Steel, San Diego	17 Apr 1982	PA
SHENANDOAH	AD 44	National Steel, San Diego	17 Dec 1983	AA

Displacement, tons: 20 500 (20 224, AD 41-44) full load
Dimensions, feet (metres): 644 × 85 × 22.5 *(196.3 × 25.9 × 6.9)* (AD 37-38)
   641.8 × 85 × 22.5 *(195.6 × 25.9 × 6.9)* (AD 41-44)
Main machinery: 2 Combustion Engineering boilers; 620 psi *(43.6 kg/cm sq)*; 860°F *(462°C)*; 1 De Laval turbine; 20 000 hp *(14.9 MW)*; 1 shaft
Speed, knots: 20
Complement: 1681 including 4 officers and 96 enlisted women
Guns: 4—20 mm Mk 67 (AD 37-38). 2—20 mm Mk 67 (AD 41-44).
   2—40 mm Mk 14 MGs. 2—40 mm saluting guns (AD 37-38).
Radars: Surface search: Raytheon SPS 10; G band.
Navigation: Marconi LN 66; I band.
Helicopters: Platform for 1 utility.

Comment: The first US destroyer tenders of post-Second World War design. Also have facilities for servicing nuclear power plants. Services can be provided simultaneously to six guided-missile destroyers moored alongside. Basic hull design similar to L Y Spear and Simon Lake submarine tenders. Two 30 ton capacity cranes. *Puget Sound* has a hangar. All have WSC-3 (UHF) SATCOM.

CAPE COD   10/1991, Giorgio Arra

2 DIXIE CLASS: DESTROYER TENDERS (AD)

Name	No	Builders	Commissioned	F/S
SIERRA	AD 18	Tampa Shipbuilding Co, Florida	20 Mar 1944	AA
YOSEMITE	AD 19	Tampa Shipbuilding Co, Florida	25 Mar 1944	AA

Displacement, tons: 9876 light; 17 430-18 400 full load
Dimensions, feet (metres): 530.5 × 73.3 × 25.5 *(161.7 × 22.3 × 7.8)*
Main machinery: 4 Babcock & Wilcox boilers; 400 psi *(28.4 kg/cm sq)*; 720°F *(382°C)*; 2 Allis Chalmers turbines; 12 000 hp *(8.95 MW)*; 2 shafts
Speed, knots: 18.2. **Range, miles:** 12 200 at 12 kts
Complement: 872 (32 officers)
Guns: 4—20 mm Mk 67. 2—40 mm saluting guns.
Radars: Surface search: Raytheon SPS 10 series; G band.
Navigation: Marconi LN 66; I band.
Helicopters: Platform only.

Comment: Both fitted as flagships. Modernised under the FRAM II programme to service destroyers fitted with ASROC, improved electronics, helicopters, etc. Two or three 5 in guns and eight 40 mm guns removed during modernisation. Two 20 ton cranes. One of the class is in service with the Turkish Navy. Both to pay off in 1993/94.

YOSEMITE   3/1991, Giorgio Arra

7 KILAUEA CLASS: AMMUNITION SHIPS (AE)

Name	No	Builders	Commissioned	F/S
BUTTE	AE 27	General Dynamics Corp, Quincy, Mass	14 Dec 1968	AA
SANTA BARBARA	AE 28	Bethlehem Steel Corp, Sparrows Pt, Md	11 July 1970	AA
MOUNT HOOD	AE 29	Bethlehem Steel Corp, Sparrows Pt, Md	1 May 1971	PA
FLINT	AE 32	Ingalls SB Corp, Pascagoula, Miss	20 Nov 1971	PA
SHASTA	AE 33	Ingalls SB Corp, Pascagoula, Miss	26 Feb 1972	PA
MOUNT BAKER	AE 34	Ingalls SB Corp, Pascagoula, Miss	22 July 1972	AA
KISKA	AE 35	Ingalls SB Corp, Pascagoula, Miss	16 Dec 1972	PA

Displacement, tons: 9340 light; 19 940 full load
Dimensions, feet (metres): 564 × 81 × 28 *(171.9 × 24.7 × 8.5)*
Main machinery: 3 Foster-Wheeler boilers; 600 psi *(42.3 kg/cm sq)*; 870°F *(467°C)*; 1 GE turbine; 22 000 hp *(16.4 MW)*; 1 shaft
Speed, knots: 20. **Range, miles:** 10 000 at 18 kts
Complement: 383 (17 officers)
Guns: 4 USN 3 in *(76 mm)*/50 (2 twin) Mk 33. Twin closed mounts forward and twin open mounts aft, between funnel and after booms. Local control only.
   2 General Electric/General Dynamics 20 mm Vulcan Phalanx.
Countermeasures: Decoys: 2 Loral Hycor SRBOC 6-barrelled Mk 36; IR flares and chaff.
ESM: SLQ 32(V)1; intercept.
Radars: Surface search: Raytheon SPS 10F; G band.
Navigation: Marconi LN 66; I band.
Tacan: URN 25.
Helicopters: 2 UH-46E Sea Knight (cargo normally embarked).

Comment: FAST replenishment system. Vulcan Phalanx is now fitted in all. Another of the class, *Kilauea*, disarmed and transferred to MSC 1 October 1980 and is renumbered TAE 26.

FLINT   3/1991, Scott Connolly, RAN

5 MARS CLASS: COMBAT STORE SHIPS (AFS)

Name	No	Builders	Commissioned	F/S
SYLVANIA	AFS 2	National Steel and SB Co, San Diego	11 July 1964	AA
NIAGARA FALLS	AFS 3	National Steel and SB Co, San Diego	29 Apr 1967	PA
WHITE PLAINS	AFS 4	National Steel and SB Co, San Diego	23 Nov 1968	PA
SAN DIEGO	AFS 6	National Steel and SB Co, San Diego	24 May 1969	AA
SAN JOSE	AFS 7	National Steel and SB Co, San Diego	23 Oct 1970	AA

Displacement, tons: 9200 light; 15 900-18 663 full load
Dimensions, feet (metres): 581 × 79 × 24 *(177.1 × 24.1 × 7.3)*
Main machinery: 3 Babcock & Wilcox boilers; 580 psi *(40.8 kg/cm sq)*; 825°F *(440°C)*; 1 De Laval turbine (Westinghouse in AFS 6); 22 000 hp *(16.4 MW)*; 1 shaft
Speed, knots: 20. **Range, miles:** 10 000 at 18 kts
Complement: 428 (25 officers)
Cargo capacity: 2625 tons dry stores; 1300 tons refrigerated stores (varies with specific loadings)
Guns: 4 USN 3 in *(76 mm)*/50 (2 twin) Mk 33. Local control only.
   2 General Electric/General Dynamics 20 mm Vulcan Phalanx Mk 15.
Countermeasures: Decoys: 2 Loral Hycor SRBOC 6-barrelled Mk 36; IR flares and chaff to 4 km *(2.2 nm)*.
ESM: SLQ 32(V)1; intercept.
Radars: Surface search: Raytheon SPS 10 series; G band.
Navigation: Marconi LN 66.
Tacan: URN 25.
Helicopters: 2 UH-46E Sea Knight normally assigned.

Comment: 'M' frames replace conventional king posts and booms, which are equipped with automatic tensioning devices. Armament has been modified. As well as the provisions listed above these ships carry comprehensive inventories of aviation and spare parts of all types for the Fleet. Phalanx placements vary in different ships of the class. Two of the class were disarmed and transferred to the MSC on 15 October 1992 and 1 February 1993 respectively. Four others are planned to follow. AFS 3 and 4 grounded at Guam in a typhoon in August 1992.

SAN DIEGO   3/1992, Giorgio Arra

804 USA / Auxiliary ships

5 SURIBACHI and NITRO CLASSES: AMMUNITION SHIPS (AE)

Name	No	Builders	Commissioned	F/S
SURIBACHI	AE 21	Bethlehem Steel Corp, Sparrows Pt, Md	17 Nov 1956	AA
MAUNA KEA	AE 22	Bethlehem Steel Corp, Sparrows Pt, Md	30 Mar 1957	PA
NITRO	AE 23	Bethlehem Steel Corp, Sparrows Pt, Md	1 May 1959	AA
PYRO	AE 24	Bethlehem Steel Corp, Sparrows Pt, Md	24 July 1959	PA
HALEAKALA	AE 25	Bethlehem Steel Corp, Sparrows Pt, Md	3 Nov 1959	PA

Displacement, tons: 7470 light; 10 000 standard; 15 500 full load (AE 21-22) 15 900 standard; 16 083 full load (remainder)
Dimensions, feet (metres): 502 × 72 × 29 (153 × 21.9 × 8.8) (AE 21-22)
512 × 72 × 29 (156.1 × 21.9 × 8.8) (remainder)
Main machinery: 2 Combustion Engineering boilers; 625 psi (43.9 kg/cm sq); 850°F (454°C); 1 Bethlehem turbine; 16 000 hp (11.9 MW); 1 shaft
Speed, knots: 20.6; 18 (AE 21-22)
Complement: 312 (18 officers)
Guns: 4 USN 3 in (76 mm)/50 (2 twin) Mk 33. Local control only.
Countermeasures: Decoys: 2 Loral Hycor SRBOC 6-barrelled Mk 36; IR flares and chaff (not in all).
ESM: SLQ 32(V)1; intercept (not in all).
Radars: Surface search: Raytheon SPS 10; G band.
Navigation: Marconi LN 66; I band.
Helicopters: Platform only.

Comment: All five ships were modernised in 1960s, being fitted with high-speed transfer equipment, three holds configured for stowage of missiles and helicopter platform fitted aft (two after twin 3 in gun mounts removed). Arrangements of twin 3 in gun mounts differ, some ships have them in tandem and others side-by-side. *Mauna Kea* fitted with mine rails for trials in 1984. *Mauna Kea* to NRF 1 October 1979 and *Pyro* 1 September 1980. Both returned to active fleet on 1 January 1982 and 1 June 1982 respectively. No plans for replacement reflected in five year shipbuilding forecast.

MAUNA KEA   6/1990, Vic Jeffery

1 CONVERTED RALEIGH CLASS: MISCELLANEOUS COMMAND SHIP (AGF)

Name	No	Builders	Commissioned	F/S
LA SALLE	AGF 3 (ex-LPD 3)	New York Naval Shipyard	22 Feb 1964	AA

Displacement, tons: 9670 light; 14 650 full load
Dimensions, feet (metres): 519.7 × 84 × 21 (158.4 × 25.6 × 6.4)
Main machinery: 2 Babcock & Wilcox boilers; 600 psi (42.2 kg/cm sq); 870°F (467°C); 2 De Laval turbines; 24 000 hp (17.9 MW); 2 shafts
Speed, knots: 20. **Range, miles:** 9600 at 16 kts
Complement: 440 (25 officers) plus 59 Flag Staff (12 officers)
Guns: 4 USN 3 in (76 mm)/50 (2 twin) Mk 33. Local control only.
2 General Electric/General Dynamics 20 mm Vulcan Phalanx Mk 15.
2—40 mm saluting guns.
Countermeasures: Decoys: 4 Loral Hycor SRBOC Mk 36; chaff and IR flares.
ESM: SLQ 32(V)2; WLR-1; intercept.
Radars: Air search: Lockheed SPS 40; E/F band; range 320 km (175 nm).
Surface search: Raytheon SPS 10D; G band.
Navigation: Marconi LN 66; I band.
Tacan: URN 25.
Helicopters: 1 light.

Comment: A former amphibious transport dock (LPD) of the Raleigh class. Authorised in FY 1961. She served as an amphibious ship until 1972 and still retains an amphibious assault capability. Converted in 1972 at Philadelphia Navy Yard. Flag command and communications facilities installed; additional air-conditioning fitted; painted white to help retard heat of Persian Gulf area. Helicopter hangar installed on the port side of the flight deck. Deck landing spots for heavy helicopters. Reclassified as a flagship and designated AGF 3 on 1 July 1972 keeping previous '3' hull number. Serves as flagship for the US Commander, Middle East Force, operating in the Persian Gulf, Arabian Sea and Indian Ocean. A comprehensive communications fit includes WSC-6.

LA SALLE   1983, Giorgio Arra

1 CONVERTED AUSTIN CLASS: MISCELLANEOUS COMMAND SHIP (AGF)

Name	No	Builders	Commissioned	F/S
CORONADO	AGF 11 (ex-LPD 11)	Lockheed SB & Construction Co	23 May 1970	PA

Displacement, tons: 11 482 light; 16 912 full load
Dimensions, feet (metres): 570 × 100 × 23 (173.8 × 30.5 × 7)
Main machinery: 2 Foster-Wheeler boilers; 600 psi (42.2 kg/cm sq); 870°F (467°C); 2 De Laval turbines; 24 000 hp (17.9 MW); 2 shafts
Speed, knots: 21. **Range, miles:** 7700 at 20 kts
Complement: 516 (25 officers) plus 120 Flag Staff
Guns: 2 USN 3 in (76 mm)/50 (twin) Mk 33. Local control only.
2 General Electric/General Dynamics 20 mm Vulcan Phalanx Mk 15. 2—12.7 mm MGs.
Countermeasures: Decoys: 4 Loral Hycor SRBOC 6-barrelled Mk 36; IR flares and chaff.
ESM: SLQ 32V(2); WLR-1; intercept.
Radars: Air search: Lockheed SPS 40C; E/F band; range 320 km (175 nm).
Surface search: Raytheon SPS 10F; G band.
Navigation: Marconi LN 66; I band.
Tacan: URN 25.
Helicopters: 2 Light.

Comment: A former LPD of the Austin class. Authorised in FY 1964. She retains an amphibious assault capability. Converted in late 1980 as a temporary replacement for *La Salle* (AGF 3), as flagship, US Commander, Middle East Force, so *La Salle* could be overhauled. When *Coronado* was relieved by *La Salle* in early 1983, it was planned for her to be reconverted back to an LPD. Due to the shortage of fleet flagships, however, she will continue in the flagship role for the foreseeable future. When relieved by *Belknap* as Sixth Fleet flagship in July 1986, she deployed to the Pacific to become the flagship of the Third Fleet then in Hawaii. She is now based at San Diego. Comprehensive communications fit includes WSC-6 on a lattice mast fitted in 1987. At the same time a sponson built out over the port side increased the overall width of the ship by some 15 ft.

CORONADO   1988, Giorgio Arra

5 JUMBOISED CIMARRON CLASS: OILERS (AO)

Name	No	Builders	Commissioned	F/S
CIMARRON	AO 177	Avondale SY	10 Jan 1981	PA
MONONGAHELA	AO 178	Avondale SY	5 Sep 1981	AA
MERRIMACK	AO 179	Avondale SY	14 Nov 1981	AA
WILLAMETTE	AO 180	Avondale SY	18 Dec 1982	PA
PLATTE	AO 186	Avondale SY	16 Apr 1983	AA

Displacement, tons: 8210 light; 37 870 full load
Dimensions, feet (metres): 708.5 × 88 × 35 (216 × 26.8 × 10.7)
Main machinery: 2 Combustion Engineering boilers; 600 psi (42.2 kg/cm sq); 850°F (454°C); 1 turbine; 24 000 hp (17.9 MW); 1 shaft
Speed, knots: 19
Complement: 135 (12 officers) plus 90 spare berths
Cargo capacity: 180 000 barrels of fuel
Guns: 2 General Electric/General Dynamics 20 mm Vulcan Phalanx Mk 15.
Countermeasures: Decoys: Loral Hycor SRBOC 6-barrelled Mk 36; IR flares and chaff to 4 km (2.2 nm).
SLQ Nixie; towed torpedo decoy.
ESM: SLQ 32(V)1; intercept.
Radars: Surface search: ISC Cardion SPS 55 (AO 177-179); I/J band.
Raytheon SPS 10B (AO 180 and 186); G band.
Navigation: Marconi LN 66; I band.
Helicopters: Platform only.

Comment: Significantly smaller than the previous Neosho class (now in MSC), these ships were originally 'sized' to provide two complete refuellings of a fossil-fuelled aircraft carrier and six to eight accompanying destroyers. All five ships of the class have been 'jumboised', thus increasing their capacities from 120 000 bbls to 180 000 bbls and improving underway replenishment capabilities. Funding for the first 'jumboisation' was provided in FY 1987, second in FY 1988, third and fourth in FY 1989, and fifth in FY 1990. All completed with new mid-body sections by the end of 1992. The class may be transferred to the MSC in due course.

MONONGAHELA   2/1992, G Toremans

Auxiliary ships / USA   805

1 DOLPHIN CLASS (AGSS)

Name	No	Builders	Commissioned	F/S
DOLPHIN	AGSS 555	Portsmouth Naval Shipyard	17 Aug 1968	PA

Displacement, tons: 800 standard; 930 full load
Dimensions, feet (metres): 152 × 19.3 × 18 *(46.3 × 5.9 × 5.5)*
Main machinery: Diesel-electric; 2 Detroit 12V-71 diesels; 840 hp *(616 kW)* sustained; 2 generators; 1 motor; 1 shaft
  Fitted with 330 cell silver-zinc battery
Speed, knots: 15+ dived
Complement: 37 (4 officers) plus 4-7 scientists
Radars: Navigation: Sperry SPS 53 portable; I/J band.
Sonars: Ametek BQS 15; active close-range detection; high frequency.
  EDO BQR 2; passive search; low frequency.
  Acoustic arrays towed at up to 4000 ft astern.

Comment: Authorised in FY 1961; laid down 9 November 1962 and launched 8 June 1968 after delays caused by changes in mission. Has a constant diameter cylindrical pressure hull approximately 15 ft in outer diameter closed at both ends with hemispherical heads. Pressure hull fabricated of HY-80 steel with aluminium and fibreglass used in secondary structures to reduce weight. No conventional hydroplanes are mounted, improved rudder design and other features provide manoeuvring control and hovering capability. Fitted for deep-ocean sonar and oceanographic research. She is highly automated and has three computer-operated systems, a safety system, hovering system, and one that is classified. The digital-computer submarine safety system monitors equipment and provides data on closed-circuit television screens; malfunctions in equipment set off an alarm and if they are not corrected within the prescribed time the system, unless overridden by an operator, automatically brings the submarine to the surface. There are several research stations for scientists and she is fitted to take water samples down to her operating depth. Assigned to Submarine Development Group 1 at San Diego. Designed for deep diving operations. Submerged endurance is approximately 24 hours with an at-sea endurance of 14 days.

0 + 4(2) SUPPLY CLASS: FAST COMBAT SUPPORT SHIPS (AOE)

Name	No	Builders	Commissioned
SUPPLY	AOE 6	National Steel & SB	July 1993
RAINIER (ex-*Paul Hamilton*)	AOE 7	National Steel & SB	Apr 1994
ARCTIC	AOE 8	National Steel & SB	Nov 1994
BRIDGE	AOE 10	National Steel & SB	Sep 1997

Displacement, tons: 19 700 light; 48 800 full load
Dimensions, feet (metres): 753.7 × 107 × 38 *(229.7 × 32.6 × 11.6)*
Main machinery: 4 GE LM 2500 gas turbines; 105 000 hp *(78.33 MW)* sustained; 2 shafts
Speed, knots: 25
Complement: Accommodation for 667 (40 officers)
Cargo capacity: 156 000 barrels of fuel; 1800 tons ammunition; 400 tons refrigerated cargo; 250 tons general cargo; 20 000 gallons water
Missiles: SAM: Raytheon GMLS Mk 29 octuple launcher; NATO Sea Sparrow.
Guns: 2 General Electric/General Dynamics 20 mm Vulcan Phalanx Mk 15.
  2 Hughes 25 mm Mk 88. 4—12.7 mm MGs.
Countermeasures: Decoys: 4 Loral Hycor SRBOC 6-barrelled Mk 36; IR flares and chaff. Nixie torpedo decoy.
ESM/ECM: SLQ 32(V)3; combined intercept and jammer.
Fire control: Mk 91 MFCS.
Radars: Air search: Hughes Mk 23 TAS; D band.
  Air/surface search: Norden SPS 67; G band.
  Navigation: Raytheon SPS 64(V)9; I band.
  Fire control: 2 Raytheon Mk 95; I/J band.
Tacan: URN 25.
Helicopters: 3 UH-46E Sea Knight.

Comment: To augment underway replenishment capability. Construction of *Supply* started in June 1988 and the second and third in August 1989 and July 1990 respectively. Funds for fourth of class were rescinded in FY 1992 but restored in FY 1993. The aim was one ship per carrier air group but after the fourth there are only two more projected . *Supply* was launched on 6 October 1990 and started sea trials in March 1993. *Rainier* launched 28 September 1991, *Arctic* 11 December 1992. The ships have six RAS stations, four 10 ton cargo booms and two Vertrep positions.

SUPPLY   *2/1993, National Steel & Shipbuilding Company*

RAINIER   *9/1992, Stefan Terzibaschitsch*

4 SACRAMENTO CLASS: FAST COMBAT SUPPORT SHIPS (AOE)

Name	No	Builders	Commissioned	F/S
SACRAMENTO	AOE 1	Puget Sound SY	14 Mar 1964	PA
CAMDEN	AOE 2	New York SB, Camden	1 Apr 1967	PA
SEATTLE	AOE 3	Puget Sound SY	5 Apr 1969	AA
DETROIT	AOE 4	Puget Sound SY	28 Mar 1970	AA

Displacement, tons: 19 200 light; 51 400-53 600 full load
Dimensions, feet (metres): 793 × 107 × 39.3 *(241.7 × 32.6 × 12)*
Main machinery: 4 Combustion Engineering boilers; 600 psi *(42.2 kg/cm sq)*; 900°F *(480°C)*; 2 GE turbines; 100 000 hp *(76.4 MW)*; 2 shafts
Speed, knots: 26. **Range, miles:** 6000 at 25 kts; 10 000 at 17 kts
Complement: 601 (24 officers)
Cargo capacity: 177 000 barrels of fuel; 2150 tons munitions; 500 tons dry stores; 250 tons refrigerated stores
Missiles: SAM: Raytheon NATO Sea Sparrow Mk 29 octuple launcher.
Guns: 2 General Electric/General Dynamics 20 mm Vulcan Phalanx Mk 15. 4—12.7 mm MGs.
Countermeasures: Decoys: Loral Hycor SRBOC 6-barrelled Mk 36; IR flares and chaff to 4 km *(2.2 nm)*.
ESM/ECM: SLQ 32(V)3; combined intercept and jammer.
Fire control: Mk 91 Mod 1 MFCS.
Radars: Air search: Lockheed SPS 40 series, Westinghouse SPS 58A (AOE 1 and 2), SPS 58A only (AOE 4); E/F and D band (SPS 58). Hughes Mk 23 TAS (AOE 3); D band.
  Surface search: Raytheon SPS 10F; G band.
  Navigation: Marconi LN 66; I band.
  Fire control: 2 Raytheon Mk 95; I/J band (for SAM).
Tacan: URN 25.
Helicopters: 2 UH-46E Sea Knight normally assigned.

Comment: Designed to provide rapid replenishment at sea of petroleum, munitions, provisions, and fleet freight. Fitted with large hangar for vertical replenishment operations (VERTREP). These ships can be distinguished from the smaller Wichita class replenishment oilers by their larger superstructures and funnel, helicopter deck at lower level, and hangar structure aft of funnel. *Camden* is being used as the trials ship for improved replenishment at sea equipment.

SACRAMENTO   *9/1992, Stefan Terzibaschitsch*

5 WICHITA CLASS: REPLENISHMENT OILERS (AOR)

Name	No	Builders	Commissioned	F/S
KANSAS CITY	AOR 3	General Dynamics, Quincy	6 June 1970	PA
SAVANNAH	AOR 4	General Dynamics, Quincy	5 Dec 1970	AA
WABASH	AOR 5	General Dynamics, Quincy	20 Nov 1971	PA
KALAMAZOO	AOR 6	General Dynamics, Quincy	11 Aug 1973	AA
ROANOKE	AOR 7	National Steel & SB, San Diego	30 Oct 1976	PA

Displacement, tons: 13 000 light; 41 350 full load
Dimensions, feet (metres): 659 × 96 × 33.3 *(200.9 × 29.3 × 10.2)*
Main machinery: 3 Foster-Wheeler boilers; 615 psi *(43.3 kg/cm sq)*; 851°F *(454°C)*; 2 GE turbines; 32 000 hp *(23.9 MW)*; 2 shafts
Speed, knots: 20. **Range, miles:** 6500 at 19 kts; 10 000 at 16 kts
Complement: 454 (20 officers)
Cargo capacity: 160 000 barrels of fuel; 600 tons munitions; 200 tons dry stores; 100 tons refrigerated stores
Missiles: SAM: Raytheon NATO Sea Sparrow Mk 29 octuple launcher.
Guns: 2 General Electric/General Dynamics 20 mm Vulcan Phalanx Mk 15. 2 or 4 Oerlikon 20 mm may also be carried.
Countermeasures: Decoys: 4 Loral Hycor SRBOC 6-barrelled Mk 36; IR flares and chaff to 4 km *(2.2 nm)*.
ESM/ECM: SLQ 32(V)3 (being fitted to replace WLR 6).
Fire control: 1 Mk 91 MFCS.
Radars: Air search: Hughes Mk 23 TAS; D band.
  Surface search: Raytheon SPS 10F; G band.
  Navigation: Marconi LN 66; I band.
  Fire control: 2 Mk 76; I/J band. Raytheon Mk 95; I/J band.
Tacan: URN 25 or SRN 15.
Helicopters: 2 UH-46E Sea Knight can be embarked.

Comment: Designed to provide rapid replenishment at sea of petroleum and munitions with a limited capacity for provision and fleet freight. Fitted with helicopter platform and internal arrangement for vertical replenishment operations (VERTREP). Hangars were added after the main gun armament was removed. Two paid off in FY 1993.

WABASH   *8/1992, Hachiro Nakai*

806 USA / Auxiliary ships

1 VULCAN CLASS: REPAIR SHIP (AR)

Name	No	Builders	Commissioned	F/S
JASON	AR 8 (ex-ARH 1)	Los Angeles SB & DD Corp	19 June 1944	PA

Displacement, tons: 9140 standard; 16 380 full load
Dimensions, feet (metres): 529.3 × 73.3 × 23.3 *(161.3 × 22.3 × 7.1)*
Main machinery: 4 Babcock & Wilcox boilers; 400 psi *(28.2 kg/cm sq)*; 720°F *(382°C)*; 2 Allis Chalmers turbines; 11 535 hp *(8.6 MW)*; 2 shafts
Speed, knots: 19.2. **Range, miles:** 18 000 at 12 kts
Complement: 841 (29 officers)
Guns: 4 Oerlikon 20 mm Mk 67.
Radars: Surface search: Raytheon SPS 10 series; G band.
Navigation: Marconi LN 66; I band.

Comment: Carry equipment to undertake repairs of every description. *Jason*, originally designated ARH 1 and rated as heavy hull repair ship, was reclassified AR 8 on 9 September 1957. Deployed to the Gulf for the war with Iraq in 1991. AR 7 transferred to Pakistan in 1989.

JASON *9/1992, Stefan Terzibaschitsch*

6 BOLSTER CLASS: SALVAGE SHIPS (ARS)

Name	No	Builders	Commissioned	F/S
BOLSTER	ARS 38	Basalt Rock Co, Napa, Calif	1 May 1945	NRF
CONSERVER	ARS 39	Basalt Rock Co, Napa, Calif	9 June 1945	PA
HOIST	ARS 40	Basalt Rock Co, Napa, Calif	21 July 1945	AA
OPPORTUNE	ARS 41	Basalt Rock Co, Napa, Calif	5 Oct 1945	AA
RECLAIMER	ARS 42	Basalt Rock Co, Napa, Calif	20 Dec 1945	NRF
RECOVERY	ARS 43	Basalt Rock Co, Napa, Calif	15 May 1946	AA

Displacement, tons: 1530 standard; 2045 full load
Dimensions, feet (metres): 213.5 × 44 (41, ARS 38) × 13 *(65.1 × 13.4 (12.5) × 4)*
Main machinery: Diesel-electric; 4 Cooper-Bessemer GSB-8 diesels; 2736 hp *(2.04 MW)* sustained; 4 generators; or 2 Caterpillar D 399 in ARS 38, 39, 42; 2250 hp *(1.67 MW)* sustained; 2 generators; 2 shafts
Speed, knots: 14.8. **Range, miles:** 9000 at 14 kts; 20 000 at 7 kts
Complement: 103 (6 officers)
Guns: 2 Oerlikon 20 mm Mk 68 (Mk 67 in ARS 39 and 41).
Radars: Surface search: Raytheon SPS 10; G band or Sperry SPS 53; I/J band.
Navigation: Marconi LN 66; I band.

Comment: Equipped with compressed air diving equipment and 10 ton and 20 ton booms. Bollard pull 30 tons. All have SATCOM receivers.

RECOVERY *4/1991, Giorgio Arra*

4 SAFEGUARD CLASS: SALVAGE SHIPS (ARS)

Name	No	Builders	Commissioned	F/S
SAFEGUARD	ARS 50	Peterson Builders Inc, Sturgeon Bay, Wisc	16 Aug 1985	PA
GRASP	ARS 51	Peterson Builders Inc, Sturgeon Bay, Wisc	14 Dec 1985	AA
SALVOR	ARS 52	Peterson Builders Inc, Sturgeon Bay, Wisc	14 June 1986	PA
GRAPPLE	ARS 53	Peterson Builders Inc, Sturgeon Bay, Wisc	15 Nov 1986	AA

Displacement, tons: 2880 full load
Dimensions, feet (metres): 255 × 51 × 17 *(77.7 × 15.5 × 5.2)*
Main machinery: 4 Caterpillar diesels; 4200 hp *(3.13 MW)*; 2 shafts; cp Kort nozzle props; bow thruster; 500 hp *(373 kW)*
Speed, knots: 14. **Range, miles:** 8000 at 12 kts
Complement: 90 (6 officers)
Guns: 2 Oerlikon 20 mm Mk 67.
Radars: Navigation: ISC Cardion SPS 55; I/J band.

Comment: Prototype approved in FY 1981, two in FY 1982 and one in FY 1983. The procurement of the fifth ARS was dropped on instructions from Congress. *Safeguard* launched 12 November 1983, *Grasp* 21 April 1984, *Salvor* 28 July 1984 and *Grapple* 8 December 1984. This class is essentially an updated Bolster class ARS which required only a moderate amount of development effort, primarily to satisfy new standards of habitability, galley, messing, medical and storeroom areas. The design follows conventional commercial and Navy design criteria. Equipped with recompression chamber. Bollard pull, 65.5 tons. Using beach extraction equipment the pull increases to 360 tons. 150 ton deadlift.

GRAPPLE *5/1991, W Sartori*

5 L Y SPEAR and EMORY S LAND CLASS: SUBMARINE TENDERS (AS)

Name	No	Builders	Commissioned	F/S
L Y SPEAR	AS 36	General Dynamics Corp, Quincy	28 Feb 1970	AA
DIXON	AS 37	General Dynamics Corp, Quincy	7 Aug 1971	PA
EMORY S LAND	AS 39	Lockheed SB & Cons Co, Seattle	7 July 1979	AA
FRANK CABLE	AS 40	Lockheed SB & Cons Co, Seattle	5 Feb 1980	AA
McKEE	AS 41	Lockheed SB & Cons Co, Seattle	15 Aug 1981	PA

Displacement, tons: 13 000 standard (13 840, later ships); 22 640 (AS 36 and AS 37); 23 493 (AS 39-41) full load
Dimensions, feet (metres): 643.8 × 85 × 28.5 *(196.2 × 25.9 × 8.7)*
Main machinery: 2 Foster-Wheeler boilers; 620 psi *(43.6 kg/cm sq)*; 860°F *(462°C)*; 1 GE turbine; 20 000 hp *(14.9 MW)*; 1 shaft
Speed, knots: 20. **Range, miles:** 10 000 at 12 kts
Complement: 535 (52 officers) plus Flag Staff 69 (25 officers) (AS 39-41)
Guns: 4 Oerlikon 20 mm Mk 67.
Radars: Navigation: Raytheon SPS 10 (AS 36, 37); G band.
ISC Cardion SPS 55 (others); I/J band.
Helicopters: Platform only.

Comment: The first US submarine tenders designed specifically for servicing nuclear-propelled attack submarines. Basic hull design similar to Samuel Gompers and Simon Lake classes tenders. Each ship can simultaneously provide services to four submarines moored alongside. AS 39 and later ships (Emory S Land class) are especially configured to support SSN 688 class submarines. Carry one 30 ton crane and two 5 ton mobile cranes. Have a 23 bed sick bay.

L Y SPEAR *7/1992, Jürg Kürsener*

Auxiliary ships / USA 807

2 SIMON LAKE CLASS: SUBMARINE TENDERS (AS)

Name	No	Builders	Commissioned	F/S
SIMON LAKE	AS 33	Puget Sound Naval Shipyard	7 Nov 1964	AA
CANOPUS	AS 34	Ingalls SB Co, Pascagoula	4 Nov 1965	AA

Displacement, tons: 19 934 (AS 33); 21 089 (AS 34) full load
Dimensions, feet (metres): 643.7 × 85 × 30 *(196.2 × 25.9 × 9.1)*
Main machinery: 2 Combustion Engineering boilers; 620 psi *(43.6 kg/cm sq)*; 860°F *(462°C)*; 1 De Laval turbine; 20 000 hp *(14.9 MW)*; 1 shaft
Speed, knots: 20. **Range, miles:** 7600 at 18 kts
Complement: 915 (58 officers) (AS 33); 660 (56 officers) (AS 34)
Guns: 4 USN 3 in *(76 mm)*/50 (twin) Mk 33. Local control only.
Radars: Surface search: Raytheon SPS 10; G band.
Navigation: Marconi LN 66; I band.
Helicopters: Platform only.

Comment: Designed to service fleet ballistic missile submarines (SSBN), with three submarines alongside being supported simultaneously. Carry two 30 ton cranes and four 5 ton mobile cranes. Capable of handling all existing submarine ballistic missiles.

SIMON LAKE   6/1990, van Ginderen Collection

2 HUNLEY CLASS: SUBMARINE TENDERS (AS)

Name	No	Builders	Commissioned	F/S
HUNLEY	AS 31	Newport News SB & DD Co	16 June 1962	AA
HOLLAND	AS 32	Ingalls SB Co, Pascagoula	7 Sep 1963	PA

Displacement, tons: 10 500 standard; 19 820 full load
Dimensions, feet (metres): 599 × 83 × 27 *(182.6 × 25.3 × 8.2)*
Main machinery: Diesel-electric; 6 Fairbanks-Morse 38D-1/8-12 diesel generators; 8.7 MW sustained; 1 motor; 1 shaft
Speed, knots: 19. **Range, miles:** 10 000 at 12 kts
Complement: 612/658 (54 officers)
Guns: 4 Oerlikon 20 mm.
Radars: Surface search: Raytheon SPS 10; G band.
Navigation: Marconi LN 66; I band.
Helicopters: Platform only.

Comment: The first US submarine tenders of post-Second World War construction; they are designed to provide repair and supply services to fleet ballistic missile submarines (SSBN). Have 52 separate workshops to provide complete support. Both ships originally fitted with a 32 ton capacity hammerhead crane; subsequently refitted with two amidships cranes as in Simon Lake class. Capable of handling all existing submarine ballistic missiles. Hunley is to pay off by 1994.

HOLLAND   5/1991, Louis Amsterdam

1 PIGEON CLASS: SUBMARINE RESCUE SHIP (ASR)

Name	No	Builders	Commissioned	F/S
ORTOLAN	ASR 22	Alabama DD & SB Co, Mobile	14 July 1973	AA

Displacement, tons: 3411 standard; 4570 full load
Dimensions, feet (metres): 251 × 86 (see *Comment*) × 21.3 *(76.5 × 26.2 × 6.5)*
Main machinery: 4 Alco diesels; 6000 hp *(4.48 MW)*; 2 shafts; 2 bow thrusters to be fitted
Speed, knots: 15. **Range, miles:** 8500 at 13 kts
Complement: 195 (9 officers); includes 24 (4 officers) for the submersibles; Flag 14 (4 officers)
Guns: 2 Oerlikon 20 mm Mk 68.
Radars: Surface search: Sperry SPS 53; I/J band.
Navigation: Marconi LN 66; I band.
Sonars: SQQ-25; hull-mounted; precision 3D system for tracking submersibles; high frequency.
Helicopters: Platform only.

Comment: Tasks include (1) surface support for the Deep Submergence Rescue Vehicles (DSRV), (2) rescue employing the existing McCann rescue chamber, (3) major deep-sea diving support and (4) operational control for salvage operations. Capable of transporting, servicing, lowering, and raising two Deep Submergence Rescue Vehicles (DSRV) (see section on Deep Submergence Vehicles). Designed with catamaran hull, the first ocean-going catamaran ship to be built for the US Navy with the exception of TAG *Hayes* of the MSC, since Robert Fulton's steam gunboat *Demologos* of 1812. Each of the twin hulls is 251 ft long and 26 ft wide. The well between the hulls is 34 ft across, giving the ASR a maximum beam of 86 ft. The Mk II Deep Diving System supports conventional or saturation divers operating at depths to 850 ft. The system consists of two recompression chambers and two personnel transfer capsules to transport divers between the ship and ocean floor. Fitted for helium-oxygen diving. One of the class decommissioned in FY 1993.

ORTOLAN   8/1992, Giorgio Arra

2 CHANTICLEER CLASS: SUBMARINE RESCUE SHIPS (ASR)

Name	No	Builders	Commissioned	F/S
KITTIWAKE	ASR 13	Savannah Machine & Foundry Co	18 July 1946	AA

Displacement, tons: 1653 standard; 2320 full load
Dimensions, feet (metres): 251.5 × 44 × 16 *(76.7 × 13.4 × 4.9)*
Main machinery: Diesel-electric; 4 GM diesels; 3000 hp *(2.24 MW)*; 4 generators; 1 motor; 1 shaft
Speed, knots: 15
Complement: 103 (7 officers)
Guns: 2 Oerlikon 20 mm Mk 68.
Radars: Surface search: Sperry SPS 53; I/J band.

Comment: Equipped with powerful pumps, heavy air compressors, and rescue chambers for submarine salvage and rescue operations. Fitted for helium-oxygen diving. Underwater communications equipped. Former US Navy submarine rescue ships transferred to the navies of Brazil and Turkey.

KITTIWAKE   4/1991, Giorgio Arra

3 EDENTON CLASS: SALVAGE AND RESCUE SHIPS (ATS)

Name	No	Builders	Commissioned	F/S
EDENTON	ATS 1	Brooke Marine, Lowestoft, England	23 Jan 1971	AA
BEAUFORT	ATS 2	Brooke Marine, Lowestoft, England	22 Jan 1972	PA
BRUNSWICK	ATS 3	Brooke Marine, Lowestoft, England	19 Dec 1972	PA

Displacement, tons: 2929 full load
Dimensions, feet (metres): 282.6 × 50 × 15.1 *(86.1 × 15.2 × 4.6)*
Main machinery: 4 Paxman 12YJCM diesels; 6000 hp *(4.48 MW)* sustained; 2 shafts; cp props; bow thruster
Speed, knots: 16. **Range, miles:** 10 000 at 13 kts
Complement: 129 (7 officers)
Guns: 2 Oerlikon 20 mm Mk 68 (ATS 2 and 3). 2 Oerlikon 20 mm (twin) Mk 24 (ATS 1).
Radars: Navigation: Sperry SPS 53; I/J band.

Comment: Capable of (1) ocean towing, (2) supporting diver operations to depths of 850 ft, (3) lifting submerged objects weighing as much as 600 000 lb from a depth of 120 ft by static tidal lift or 30 000 lb by dynamic lift, (4) fighting ship fires. Fitted with 10 ton capacity crane forward and 20 ton capacity crane aft. ATS 1 was authorised in FY 1966; ATS 2 and ATS 3 in FY 1967. Three follow-on ships of this class were cancelled. Classification changed from salvage tug (ATS) to salvage and rescue ship (ATS) on 16 February 1971. Can carry the air-transportable Mk 1 Deep Diving System which can support four divers working in two-man shifts at depths to 850 ft. The system consists of a double-chamber recompression chamber and a personnel transfer capsule to transport divers between the ship and ocean floor. The ships' organic diving capability is compressed air only.

BEAUFORT   6/1991, 92 Wing RAAF

808 USA / Auxiliary ships — Floating dry docks

NAVAL RESERVE AUXILIARY SHIPS

Name/Hull No.	NR Homeport	Date Entered NRF
BOLSTER (ARS 38)	Long Beach, CA	June 1983
RECLAIMER (ARS 42)	Pearl Harbor, HI	Sep 1986

FLOATING DRY DOCKS

Note: The US Navy operates a number of floating dry docks to supplement dry dock facilities at major naval activities, to support fleet ballistic missile submarines (SSBN) at advanced bases, and to provide repair capabilities in forward combat areas.

The larger floating dry docks are made sectional to facilitate movement overseas and to render them self docking. The ARD-type docks have the forward end of their docking well closed by a structure resembling the bow of a ship to facilitate towing. Berthing facilities, repair shops, and machinery are housed in sides of larger docks. None is self-propelled.

Each section of the AFDB docks has a lifting capacity of about 10 000 tons and is 256 × 80 ft, with wing walls 83 ft high; the wing walls, which contain compartments, fold down when the sections are towed.

There are plans to seek funding for large floating docks.

LARGE AUXILIARY FLOATING DRY DOCKS (AFDB)

Name/No	Completed	Capacity (tons)	Construction*	Status
ARTISAN (AFDB 1)	1943	90 000	Steel (4)	Pearl Harbor (B-E), inactive
AFDB 2	1944	90 000	Steel (10)	Pearl Harbor (B-E), inactive
MACHINIST (AFDB 8)	1979	25 000	Steel (1)	Hawaii

* Figures in brackets indicate the number of sections of each dock remaining.

AFDB   6/1990, van Ginderen collection

MEDIUM AUXILIARY FLOATING DRY DOCKS (AFDM)

Name/No	Completed	Capacity (tons)	Construction	Status
AFDM 2 (ex-YFD 4)	1942	15 000	Steel (3)	Commercial Lease, Halter Marine, Beaumont, TX
AFDM 3 (ex-YFD 6)	1943	15 000	Steel (3)	Commercial lease, Todd SY, New Orleans
RESOURCEFUL (AFDM 5) (ex-YFD 21)	1943	15 000	Steel (3)	Active, Diego Garcia
COMPETENT (AFDM 6) (ex-YFD 62)	1944	15 000	Steel (3)	Active, Pearl Harbor
SUSTAIN (AFDM 7) (ex-YFD 63)	1945	15 000	Steel (3)	Active, Norfolk, Va. Two sections in reserve at James River
RICHLAND (AFDM 8) (ex-YFD 64)	1944	15 000	Steel (3)	Active, Guam, Marianas
RESOLUTE (AFDM 10)	1945	15 000	Steel (3)	Active, Norfolk, Va
STEADFAST (AFDM 14) (ex-YFD 71)	1945	14 000	Steel (3)	Active, San Diego

STEADFAST   9/1992, Stefan Terzibaschitsch

SMALL AUXILIARY FLOATING DRY DOCKS (AFDL)

Name/No	Completed	Capacity (tons)	Construction	Status
DYNAMIC (AFDL 6)	1944	1000	Steel	Little Creek, Virginia
ADEPT (AFDL 23)	1944	1900	Steel	Guam
UNDAUNTED (AFDL 25)	1944	499	Steel	Guantanamo Bay, Cuba
RELIANCE (AFDL 47)	1946	6500	Steel	Commercial lease, Deytens, South Carolina, 15 May 1991
DILIGENCE (AFDL 48)	—	—	Concrete	Commercial lease, South West Marine, San Diego

Sales: AFDL 1 to Dominican Republic; 4, Brazil; 5, Taiwan; 11, Kampuchea; 20, Philippines; 22, Vietnam; 24, Philippines; 26, Paraguay; 28, Mexico; 33, Peru; 34 and 36, Taiwan; 39, Brazil; 44, Philippines.

DYNAMIC   6/1986, Giorgio Arra

AUXILIARY REPAIR DRY DOCKS and MEDIUM AUXILIARY REPAIR DRY DOCKS (ARD and ARDM)

Name/No	Completed	Capacity (tons)	Construction	Status
WATERFORD (ARD 5)	1942	3500	Steel	New London, Connecticut
SAN ONOFRE (ARD 30)	1944	3500	Steel	San Diego, Calif
OAK RIDGE (ARDM 1) (ex-ARD 19)	1944	8000	Steel	Kings Bay, Georgia
ENDURANCE (ARDM 3) (ex-ARD 18)	1944	8000	Steel	Charleston, South Carolina
SHIPPINGPORT (ARDM 4)	1979	10 000	Steel	New London, Connecticut
ARCO (ARDM 5)	1986	7800	Steel	San Diego Naval Station

Sales: ARD 2 to Mexico; 6, Pakistan; 8, Peru; 9, Taiwan; 11, Mexico; 12, Turkey; 13, Venezuela; 14, Brazil; 15, Mexico; 17, Ecuador; 22 *(Windsor)*, Taiwan; 23, Argentina; 24, Ecuador; 25, Chile; 28, Colombia; 29, Iran; 32, Chile.

SAN ONOFRE   9/1992, Stefan Terzibaschitsch

YARD FLOATING DRY DOCKS (YFD)

Name/No	Completed	Capacity (tons)	Construction	Status
YFD 54	1943	5000	Wood	Commercial lease, Todd Pacific SY, Seattle
YFD 68	1945	14 000	Steel (3)	Commercial lease, Todd Pacific SY, San Pedro
YFD 69	1945	14 000	Steel (3)	Commercial lease, Port of Portland, Oregon
YFD 70	1945	14 000	Steel (3)	Commercial lease, Todd Pacific SY, Seattle
YFD 83 (ex-AFDL 31)	1943	1000	Steel	US Coast Guard loan since Jan 1947

UNCLASSIFIED MISCELLANEOUS (IX)

Notes: (1) In addition to the vessels listed below it is planned to use one of the ex-Forrest Sherman class, *Decatur* as a platform for high energy laser trials in 1994.
(2) IX 502, 503, 504, 507 and 510 are barrack ships of mid-1940s vintage.
(3) IX 512 and 516 are barges used as Trident missile training simulators and IX 509 is a research barge.
(4) IX 513 *(Empress II)* was taken out of service in 1993.

Name	No	Under Way	F/S
CONSTITUTION	— (ex-IX 21)	22 July 1798	AA

Displacement, tons: 2200
Dimensions, feet (metres): 175.2 × 45 × 20 *(53.4 × 13.7 × 6.1)*
Speed, knots: 12 under sail
Complement: 49 (2 officers)

Comment: The oldest ship remaining on the Navy List. *Constitution* is one of the six frigates authorised by act of Congress on 27 March 1794. After rehabilitation was formerly placed in commission 1 July 1931. Served as Flagship of the First Naval District until 1 October 1977 when she was transferred to the control of the Director of Naval History, Department of the Navy. She is usually taken out every year into Boston Harbor and 'turned around' so her masts and spars will weather evenly. Overhauled at the former Boston Naval Shipyard from April 1973 to early 1975 to 'spruce her up' for the American Bicentennial. Refitted again from September 1992 to October 1993. This includes sonic testing of the ship's hull to detect rot in the wood, and radiography and ultrasonic testing of fastenings.

CONSTITUTION   7/1992, van Ginderen Collection

IX 506 (ex-YFU 82)

Displacement, tons: 375 full load
Dimensions, feet (metres): 119 × 34 × 6 *(36.3 × 10.4 × 1.8)*
Main machinery: 4 GM 6-71 diesels; 696 hp *(519 kW)* sustained; 2 shafts
Speed, knots: 10
Complement: 12 (2 officers)

Comment: Reclassified 1 April 1978 for Naval Oceanographic Systems Center and fitted with a triple 324 mm torpedo tube mounting in the bows.

IX 506   5/1986, Giorgio Arra

Name	No	Builders	Commissioned	F/S
ORCA	IX 508 (ex-LCU 1618)	Gunderson Bros, Portland	1959	PSA

Comment: For general characteristics, see under LCU 1610 class in the *Amphibious Warfare* section. Conversion and overhaul in 1977 included installation of a bow thruster, a bridge and pilot house, and a hangar type enclosed storage area in the well deck, for the support of the Center's recovery vehicles CURV I and CURV II and installation of a crane. Reclassified as IX on 1 December 1979. Assigned to the Naval Ocean Systems Center, San Diego, California for trials with NAVSTAR GPS.

ORCA   4/1988, Giorgio Arra

Name	Builders	Commissioned
IX 514 (ex-YFU 79)	Pacific Coast Eng, Alameda	1968

Displacement, tons: 380 full load
Dimensions, feet (metres): 125 × 36 × 7.5 *(38.1 × 10.9 × 2.3)*
Main machinery: 4 GM 6-71 diesels; 696 hp *(519 kW)* sustained; 2 shafts
Speed, knots: 8

Comment: Harbour utility craft converted in 1986 with a flight deck covering two thirds of the vessel and a new bridge and flight control position at the forward end. Used for basic helicopter flight training at Pensacola, Florida.

1 SURFACE EFFECT SHIP (SES)

Name	Builders	Commissioned
IX 515 (SES-200) (ex-USCG *Dorado*)	Bell Halter, New Orleans	Feb 1979

Displacement, tons: 243 full load
Dimensions, feet (metres): 159.1 × 42.6 × 6; 3 on cushion *(48.5 × 13 × 1.8; 0.9)*
Main machinery: 2 MTU 16V 396 TB94 diesels (propulsion); 5800 hp(m) *(4.26 MW)* sustained; 2 KaMeWa waterjets
2 MTU 6V 396 TB83 diesels (lift); 1560 hp(m) *(1.15 MW)* sustained
Speed, knots: 45. **Range, miles:** 2950 at 30 kts
Complement: 22 (2 officers)

Comment: Transferred to Coast Guard operational control for joint Navy/Coast Guard trials, she was commissioned as USCG *Dorado* (WSES 1). After the conclusion of successful trials, which led to the Coast Guard ordering three more for duty in the Caribbean Sea (see Coast Guard Sea Bird class for details), she was decommissioned on 15 December 1981 and returned to the Navy. After 10 months (December 1981 to August 1982) modification at the Bell-Halter yard, New Orleans, which included the addition of a 50 ft *(15.2 m)* mid-section, she was returned to service 24 September 1982. The mid-section was added to increase the cushion length-to-beam ratio which leads to higher speeds. From January-June 1986, IX 515, carried out a series of trials in European waters in conjunction with NATO navies and in August-September 1986 in Canadian waters. In 1990 she was fitted with more powerful MTU diesels driving KaMeWa waterjets and new lift engines.
The IX 515 is a water-borne, air-supported craft with catamaran-style rigid sidewalls. It uses a cushion of air trapped between the sidewalls and flexible bow and stern seals to lift a large part of the hull clear of the water to reduce drag. A portion of the sidewall remains in the water to aid in stability and manoeuvrability. Modifications to the advanced ride control system were made in 1988 and 1989. Under operational control of Carderock Division, Naval Surface Warfare Center (formerly David Taylor Research Center), and based at Special Trials Unit Detachment, Naval Air Station, Patuxent River, MD. Will continue to serve as a high performance test platform for Navy HM&E and weapon system development programmes, and as operational demonstrator for an advanced naval vehicle hullform.

IX 515   2/1990, Giorgio Arra

SERVICE CRAFT

Note: As of January 1993, the US Navy had 897 active and about 50 inactive service craft, primarily small craft, on the US Naval Vessel Register. A majority of them provide services to the fleet in various harbours and ports. Other are ocean going ships such as *Elk River* that provide services to the fleet in the research area. Only the self-propelled craft and relics are listed in the Register. The non self-propelled craft, such as floating cranes and dredgers are not included. Most of the service craft are rated as 'active, in service', but a few are rated as 'in commission'. In addition there are over 3000 craft rated as 'floating equipment'.

Name	No	Builders	Commissioned	F/S
MONOB I	YAG 61 (ex-IX 309, ex-YW 87)	Zenith Dredge Co	Nov 1943	ASA

Displacement, tons: 440 light; 1390 full load
Dimensions, feet (metres): 191.9 × 33.1 × 15.7 *(58.5 × 10.1 × 4.8)*
Main machinery: 1 Caterpillar D 398 diesel; 850 hp *(634 kW)*; 1 shaft
Speed, knots: 9

Comment: *Monob I* is a mobile listening barge converted from a self-propelled water barge. Built in 1943 and completed conversion for acoustic research in May 1969. Conducts research for the Naval Mine Defence Laboratory, Panama City, Florida. Designation changed from IX 309 to YAG 61 on 1 July 1970. Planned to be replaced by TAG and TAGOS ships.

MONOB I 7/1988, Giorgio Arra

Name	No	Builders	Commissioned	F/S
DEER ISLAND	YAG 62	Halter Marine	1962	ASA

Displacement, tons: 400 full load
Dimensions, feet (metres): 120.1 × 27.9 × 6.9 *(36.6 × 8.5 × 2.1)*
Speed, knots: 10
Complement: 20

Comment: Acquired for use in tests in sound quieting for surface vessels. Based at Port Everglades, Florida. Put on the Naval Vessel Register on 15 March 1982. Planned to be replaced by TAG and TAGOS ships.

DEER ISLAND 5/1992, Giorgio Arra

3 FERRYBOATS (YFB)

Comment: 390 ton ferryboats built in the late 1960s and used to transport personnel and vehicles in large harbours; self-propelled. YFB 83, 88 and 89 are active, three others are inactive.

11 DIVING TENDERS (YDT)

Comment: Tenders used to support shallow-water diving operations. Of 1940s vintage are *Phoebus* YDT 14 (ex-YF 294), and *Suitland* YDT 15 (ex-YF 336). There is also a non self-propelled vessel *Tom O'Malley* YDT 16 (ex-YFNB 43). More recent acquisitions include eight Peterson Dive Boats with portable standardised diving systems delivered between November 1989 and August 1990. The boats are 50 ft in length, displace some 42 tons and are capable of 9 knots on two diesels. The Diving Module has its own diesel generator.

DIVING TENDER 11/1990, Peterson Builders

2 HARBOUR UTILITY CRAFT LCU TYPE (YFU)

YFU 83   YFU 91 (ex-LCU 1608)

Comment: Former utility landing craft employed primarily as harbour and coastal cargo craft (see section on Landing Craft for basic characteristics).

YFU 91 7/1991, Giorgio Arra

8 FUEL OIL BARGES (YO)

YO 47 (reserve), **129, 203, 220, 223-225, 230**—active

Comment: Small liquid fuel carriers intended to fuel ships where no pierside fuelling facilities are available, self-propelled; seven active, one in reserve. In addition there are 51 non self-propelled (YON).

YO 203 9/1992, Stefan Terzibaschitsch

5 GASOLINE BARGES (YOG)

YOG 58 (reserve), **78, 88,** 93 (reserve), **196**

Comment: Similar to the fuel barges (YO), but carry about 950 tons of gasoline and aviation fuels; self-propelled; three are active and two in reserve. In addition there are 12 non self-propelled (YOGN).

YOG 88 4/1988, Giorgio Arra

Service craft / USA 811

29 PATROL CRAFT (YP)

YP 676-705

Displacement, tons: 167 full load
Dimensions, feet (metres): 108 × 24 × 5.9 *(32.9 × 7.3 × 1.8)*
Main machinery: 2 Detroit 12V-71 diesels; 680 hp *(507 kW)* sustained; 2 shafts
Speed, knots: 13.3. **Range, miles:** 1500 at 12 kts
Complement: 6 (2 officers) plus 24 midshipmen
Radars: Navigation: I band.

Comment: Built in the 1980s by Peterson Builders and Marinette Marine, both in Wisconsin. Used for instruction in seamanship and navigation at the US Naval Academy, Annapolis, MD, and Naval Officer Candidate School and Surface Warfare Officers School, both at Newport, RI. Some earlier versions converted for mine countermeasures operations and assigned to the COOP project (see *Mine Warfare Forces*).

YP 683   9/1992, Maritime Photographic

76 LARGE HARBOUR TUGS (YTB)

Name	Hull	Name	Hull
EDENSHAW	YTB 752	OPELIKA	YTB 798
OSHKOSH	YTB 757	NATCHITOCHES	YTB 799
PADUCAH	YTB 758	PALATKA	YTB 801
BOGALUSA	YTB 759	CHERAW	YTB 802
NATICK	YTB 760	NANTICOKE	YTB 803
OTTUMWA	YTB 761	AHOSKIE	YTB 804
TUSCUMBIA	YTB 762	OCALA	YTB 805
MUSKEGON	YTB 763	TUSKEGEE	YTB 806
MISHAWAKA	YTB 764	MASSAPEQUA	YTB 807
OKMULGEE	YTB 765	WENATCHEE	YTB 808
WAPAKONETA	YTB 766	AGAWAM	YTB 809
APALACHICOLA	YTB 767	ANOKA	YTB 810
ARCATA	YTB 768	HOUMA	YTB 811
CHESANING	YTB 769	ACCONAC	YTB 812
DAHLONEGA	YTB 770	POUGHKEEPSIE	YTB 813
KEOKUK	YTB 771	WAXAHATCHIE	YTB 814
NASHUA	YTB 774	NEODESHA	YTB 815
WAUWATOSA	YTB 775	CAMPTI	YTB 816
WEEHAWKEN	YTB 776	HYANNIS	YTB 817
NOGALES	YTB 777	MECOSTA	YTB 818
APOPKA	YTB 778	IUKA	YTB 819
MANHATTAN	YTB 779	WANAMASSA	YTB 820
SAUGUS	YTB 780	TONTOGANY	YTB 821
NIANTIC	YTB 781	PAWHUSKA	YTB 822
MANISTEE	YTB 782	CANONCHET	YTB 823
REDWING	YTB 783	SANTAQUIN	YTB 824
KALISPELL	YTB 784	WATHENA	YTB 825
WINNEMUCCA	YTB 785	WASHTUCNA	YTB 826
KITTANNING	YTB 787	CHETEK	YTB 827
WAPATO	YTB 788	CATAHECASSA	YTB 828
TOMAHAWK	YTB 789	METACOM	YTB 829
MENOMINEE	YTB 790	PUSHMATAHA	YTB 830
MARINETTE	YTB 791	DEKANAWIDA	YTB 831
ANTIGO	YTB 792	PETALESHARO	YTB 832
PIQUA	YTB 793	SHABONEE	YTB 833
MANDAN	YTB 794	NEWGAGON	YTB 834
KETCHIKAN	YTB 795	SKENANDOA	YTB 835
SACO	YTB 796	POKAGON	YTB 836
TAMAQUA	YTB 797		

Displacement, tons: 356 full load
Dimensions, feet (metres): 109 × 30 × 13.8 *(33.2 × 9.1 × 4.2)*
Main machinery: 2 Fairbanks-Morse 38D8-1/8-12 diesels; 7000 hp *(5.2 MW)* sustained; 2 shafts
Speed, knots: 12. **Range, miles:** 2000 at 12 kts
Complement: 10-12

Comment: Built between 1959 and 1975. Two transferred to Saudi Arabia in 1975. In future tugs will be provided by contractors and numbers are being reduced.

WATHENA   9/1992, Maritime Photographic

4 TORPEDO TRIALS CRAFT (YTT)

CAPE FLATTERY YTT 9	DISCOVERY BAY YTT 11
BATTLE POINT YTT 10	AGATE PASS YTT 12

Displacement, tons: 1168 full load
Dimensions, feet (metres): 186.5 × 40 × 10.5 *(56.9 × 12.2 × 3.2)*
Main machinery: 1 Cummins KTA50-M diesel; 1250 hp *(932 kW)* sustained; 1 shaft; 1 bow thruster; 400 hp *(298 kW)*; 2 stern thrusters; 600 hp *(448 kW)*
Speed, knots: 11. **Range, miles:** 1000 at 10 kts
Complement: 31 plus 9 spare berths

Comment: Built by McDermott Shipyard, Morgan City, and delivered in 1990-91. Fitted with two 21 in Mk 59 and three (one triple) 12.75 in Mk 32 Mod 5 torpedo tubes. These vessels have replaced the YFRT covered lighters for torpedo trials and development. Underwater recovery vessels SORD 4, TROV and CURV.

CAPE FLATTERY   1990, McDermott Shipyard

31 TORPEDO RETRIEVERS (TR and TWR)

Comment: Four different types spread around the Fleet bases and at AUTEC.

TWR 1   6/1989, Giorgio Arra

TWR 821   3/1992, Giorgio Arra

TWR 3   4/1991, Giorgio Arra

RESEARCH AND EXPERIMENTAL SHIPS

Note: There are many naval associated research vessels which are civilian manned and not carried on the US Naval Vessel Register. In addition civilian ships are leased for short periods to support a particular research project or trial.

SEACON (missile retriever)   10/1992, Giorgio Arra

ATHENA   4/1991, Giorgio Arra

3 ASHEVILLE CLASS

ATHENA (ex-*Chehalis*)   **ATHENA II** (ex-*Grand Rapids*)   **LAUREN** (ex-*Douglas*)

Displacement, tons: 245 full load
Dimensions, feet (metres): 164.5 × 23.8 × 9.5 *(50.1 × 7.3 × 2.9)*
Main machinery: CODOG; 1 GE LM 1500 gas turbine; 12 500 hp *(9.3 MW)*; 2 Cummins VT 12-875 diesels; 1450 hp *(1.07 MW)*; 2 shafts
Speed, knots: 16. **Range, miles:** 1700 at 16 kts
Complement: 22

Comment: All built 1969-71. Work for the Ships Research and Development centre, Carderock. Disarmed except *Lauren* which has maintained its military appearance.

LAUREN   11/1991, Giorgio Arra

MILITARY SEALIFT COMMAND (MSC)

Notes: (1) The US Navy's Military Sealift Command has the responsibility for providing sealift for all components of the Department of Defense. In 1990-91, the US response to the Iraqi invasion of Kuwait resulted in MSC having to use almost all of its available and usable sealift and support ship assets to move military equipment to the Middle East and to provide maintenance and medical support to US forces transported to that area.

This mobilisation and supply effort included the activation of all eight fast sealift ships (former SL-7s) and 79 of the 96 ships in the Ready Reserve Force at the time of the invasion, including all 17 Ro-Ros in the RRF. It required the movement of two Maritime Prepositioning Ship squadrons (nine ships loaded with equipment for two Marine Expeditionary Brigades) from Guam and Diego Garcia to Saudi Arabia and of the Afloat Prepositioning Force (12 ships loaded with equipment for the Army and the Air Force). Later the third Maritime Prepositioning Ship squadron was moved from the Atlantic to the combat area. The two hospital ships were sailed immediately to the Middle East, as were the two aviation support ships. With usable MSC assets exhausted, MSC began chartering ships, both US flag and foreign, and by the end of 1991 a total of 127 US flag and 293 foreign ships had been chartered. At the start of the war with Iraq on 17 January 1991, MSC had delivered 1.7 million short tons of cargo to Saudi Arabia, had another half million tons underway, and had delivered 3.9 million tons of POL. In all, more than 2.5 million short tons of cargo and 6.1 million tons of POL were moved to the Middle East.

To meet manning requirements for all of the ships activated more than 3000 merchant seamen were hired by the Maritime Administration at MSC's request. Difficulties were encountered in finding enough qualified personnel to man the steam propulsion plants which were predominant in the RRF.

This operation focused attention on a number of basic US sealift problems:
(a) There was a shortage of Ro-Ros, the types of ships most needed to handle military rolling stock.
(b) Over the years, insufficient funds had been made available to properly maintain RRF ships and have them ready for emergencies. As a consequence, many could not be activated.
(c) There are not enough fast sealift ships available. The United States only has eight, and seven of these (one broke down on its initial voyage) were operated at a tempo that caused maintenance problems. Those seven ships carried nine per cent of the cargo moved to and from the Middle East. Six of the class were again active in late 1992/93 to move equipment and supplies to Somalia.

(2) In January 1992, a Mobility Requirements Study calling for DoD to acquire at least 20 large medium-speed (24 kts) roll-on/roll-off ships was submitted to Congress. These were defined as having 35 302 m^2 of total capacity, with 27 870 m^2 available for prepositioning. $1.8 billion already had been appropriated for construction and conversion of such ships. The funding was increased by another $600 million which was included in the FY 1993 defence budget. Contracts for engineering designs for new construction were awarded in November 1992 to seven shipyards, with award of multiple detail design and construction contracts for the first six ships anticipated in May 1993. There are options for additional ships from 1994 to 1997. Additionally, contracts for engineering design for conversion of existing ships were awarded in October 1992 to five US shipyards, with multiple contracts for acquisition, detail design, and conversion anticipated in September 1993. The shipyard(s) will procure ships if its proposal wins a contract for detail design and conversion work. Conversions would range in scope from jumboising to enlarging deckhouses to renewing engines. As a result of Congressional limitations, up to a maximum of five foreign-built ships may be converted.
(3) Other MSC ships such as ocean surveillance vessels, research ships, and scientific support ships continue their routine operations. At the beginning of 1993 a total of 20 ships was assigned to special mission support, and 41 to MSC's fleet auxiliary force. This section also lists six AGORs which are not part of the MSC.
(4) MSC headquarters are in the Washington Navy Yard. The organisation is commanded by a vice admiral, and its four principal area commands by captains.
(5) No ship of the Military Sealift Command is armed in peacetime.
(6) Military Sealift Command nucleus ships are assigned standard US Navy hull designations with the added prefix 'T'. Funnels have black, grey, blue and gold horizontal bands.
(7) On 1 October 1987, the transportation elements of the three services were merged into the US Transportation Command, a unified command with headquarters at Scott AFB, Illinois, and reporting directly to the Joint Chiefs of Staff. Commander USTRANSCOM (Military Sealift Command, Military Airlift Command, and Military Traffic Management Command) has exercised fiscal and operational control of all three components since mid-1992.

1 KILAUEA CLASS: AMMUNITION SHIP (AE)

Name	No	Commissioned	F/S
KILAUEA	T-AE 26	10 Aug 1968	TPA

Comment: Transferred to MSC for activation and operation 1 October 1980. Ship underwent a civilian modification (CIVMOD) overhaul during which extensive superstructure work was accomplished in the living spaces. All gear from station seven was removed. Main armament was taken out. *Kilauea* has 7 UNREP stations operational: 4 port, 3 stbd and has been outfitted with a commercial type satellite navigation equipment. For particulars refer to Kilauea class in Auxiliaries section. Complement is 120 civilians and 67 naval personnel (for communications equipment and helicopter handling).

2 MARS CLASS: COMBAT STORE SHIPS (AFS)

Name	No	Builders	Commissioned	F/S
CONCORD	T-AFS 5	National Steel & SB Co, San Diego	27 Nov 1968	TPA
MARS	T-AFS 1	National Steel & SB Co, San Diego	21 Dec 1963	TPA

Comment: *Concord* transferred to MSC on 15 October 1992 after disarming and conversion to a civilian crew of 135. *Mars* followed on 1 February 1993. For details see Mars class in *Auxiliaries* section. Four more of the class are scheduled to be similarly converted.

KILAUEA   10/1989, L/S P Steele RAN

CONCORD   10/1992, A Sheldon Duplaix

3 Ex-BRITISH LYNESS CLASS: COMBAT STORES SHIP (AFS)

Name	No	Builders	Commissioned	F/S
SIRIUS (ex-RFA *Lyness*)	T-AFS 8	Swan Hunter & Wigham Richardson Ltd, Wallsend-on-Tyne	22 Dec 1966	TAA
SPICA (ex-RFA *Tarbatness*)	T-AFS 9	Swan Hunter & Wigham Richardson Ltd, Wallsend-on-Tyne	21 Mar 1967	TPA
SATURN (ex-RFA *Stromness*)	T-AFS 10	Swan Hunter & Wigham Richardson Ltd, Wallsend-on-Tyne	10 Aug 1967	TAA

Displacement, tons: 9010 light; 16 792 full load
Measurement, tons: 7782 dwt; 12 359 gross; 4744 net
Dimensions, feet (metres): 524 × 72 × 22 *(159.7 × 22 × 6.7)*
Main machinery: 1 Wallsend-Sulzer 8RD76 diesel; 11 520 hp *(8.59 MW)*; 1 shaft
Speed, knots: 18. **Range, miles:** 12 000 at 16 kts
Complement: 116 (with a Navy contingent of 18 (1 officer))
Cargo capacity: 8313 cu m dry; 3921 cu m frozen
Helicopters: 2 UH-46E Sea Knight.

Comment: Lifts and mobile appliances for handling stores internally, and a new replenishment at sea system and a helicopter landing platform for transferring loads at sea. A feature of the ship is the use of closed-circuit television to monitor the movement of stores. Air-conditioned. After a period of charter *Sirius* was purchased on 1 March 1982, *Spica* on 30 September 1982 and *Saturn* on 1 October 1983.

SPICA
1/1992, 92 Wing RAAF

1 HAYES CLASS: ACOUSTIC RESEARCH SHIP (AG)

Name	No	Builders	Completed	F/S
HAYES	T-AG 195 (ex-AGOR 16)	Todd Shipyards, Seattle	21 July 1971	TAA

Displacement, tons: 4037 full load
Dimensions, feet (metres): 256.5 × 75 (see *Comment*) × 22 *(78.2 × 22.9 × 6.7)*
Main machinery: Diesel-electric; 2 Caterpillar 3516TA diesels; 3620 hp *(2.7 MW)* sustained; 2 generators; 2 Westinghouse motors; 2400 hp *(1.79 MW)*; 2 auxiliary diesels (for creep speed); 330 hp *(246 kW)*; 2 shafts; cp props
Speed, knots: 10. **Range, miles:** 2000 at 10 kts
Complement: 74 (10 officers) including scientists
Radars: Navigation: Raytheon TM 1650/6X and TM 1660/12S; I band.

Comment: *Hayes* is one of two classes of US naval ships to have a catamaran hull, the other being the ASR 21 class submarine rescue ship. Laid down 12 November 1969; launched 2 July 1970. To Ready Reserve 10 June 1983 and transferred to James River (Maritime Administration) for lay-up in 1984 having been too costly to operate. Under FY 1986 programme being converted to Acoustic Research Ship (AG) in place of *Monob I* (YAG 61); reclassified T-AG 195 and completed in early 1992 after five years work in two shipyards. Mission is to transport, deploy and retrieve acoustic arrays, to conduct acoustic surveys in support of the submarine noise reduction programme and to carry out acoustic testing. Catamaran hull design provides large deck working area, centre well for operating equipment at great depths, and removes laboratory areas from main propulsion machinery. Each hull is 246 ft long and 24 ft wide (maximum). There are three 36 in diameter instrument wells in addition to the main centre well.

HAYES
2/1992

1 CONVERTED HASKELL CLASS: MISSILE RANGE INSTRUMENTATION SHIP (AGM)

Name	No	Builders	Commissioned	F/S
RANGE SENTINEL (ex-*Sherburne*)	T-AGM 22 (ex-APA 205)	Permanente Metals Corp, Richmond, Calif	20 Sep 1944	TAA

Displacement, tons: 8853 light; 12 170 full load
Dimensions, feet (metres): 455 × 62 × 26 *(138.7 × 18.9 × 7.9)*
Main machinery: 2 Combustion Engineering boilers; 525 psi *(37 kg/cm sq)*; 750°F *(399°C)*; 1 Westinghouse turbine; 8500 hp *(6.34 MW)*; 1 shaft
Speed, knots: 17.7. **Range, miles:** 12 000 at 15 kts
Complement: 81 civilian (15 officers, 12 technical personnel); 43 naval (3 officers)
Radars: Navigation: Raytheon TM 1650/6X and TM 1660/12S; I band.

Comment: Former attack transport (APA) converted specifically to serve as a range instrumentation ship in support of the Fleet Ballistic Missile (FBM) programme. Maritime Administration VC2-S-AP5 type. Reclassified AGM 22 on 16 April 1969 and renamed *Range Sentinel* on 26 April 1971. In Maritime Administration reserve from 1 October 1958 until 22 October 1969. Converted from October 1969 to October 1971; placed in service as T-AGM 22 on 14 October 1971. Has telemetry and missile tracking equipment.

RANGE SENTINEL
11/1989, Giorgio Arra

1 CONVERTED COMPASS ISLAND CLASS: MISSILE RANGE INSTRUMENTATION SHIP (AGM)

Name	No	Builders	Commissioned	F/S
OBSERVATION ISLAND (ex-*Empire State Mariner*)	T-AGM 23 (ex-AG 154, ex-YAG 57)	New York SB Corp, NJ	5 Dec 1958	TPA

Displacement, tons: 13 060 light; 17 015 full load
Dimensions, feet (metres): 564 × 76 × 25 *(171.6 × 23.2 × 7.6)*
Main machinery: 2 Foster-Wheeler boilers; 600 psi *(42.3 kg/cm sq)*; 875°F *(467°C)*; 1 GE turbine; 19 250 hp *(14.36 MW)*; 1 shaft
Speed, knots: 20. **Range, miles:** 17 000 at 15 kts
Complement: 143 civilian (20 officers, 60-65 technicians)
Missiles: SLBM: She fired the first ship-launched Polaris missile at sea on 27 August 1959. Refitted to fire the improved Poseidon missile in 1969 and launched the first Poseidon test missile fired afloat on 16 December 1969.
AS mortars: X
Radars: Navigation: Raytheon 1650/9X and 1660/12S; I band.

Comment: Built as a Mariner class merchant ship (C4-S-A1 type); launched on 15 August 1953; acquired by the Navy on 10 September 1956 for use as a Fleet Ballistic Missile (FBM) test ship. Converted at Norfolk Naval Shipyard. In reserve from September 1972. On 18 August 1977, *Observation Island* was re-acquired by the US Navy from the Maritime Administration and transferred to the Military Sealift Command. Reclassified AGM 23 on 1 May 1979. Converted to Missile Range Instrumentation Ship from July 1979-April 1981 at Maryland SB and DD Co to carry an Air Force shipborne phased-array radar system (Cobra Judy) for collection of data on foreign ballistic missile tests. Operated by the Navy for the US Air Force Intelligence command, Patrick Air Force Base, Florida.

OBSERVATION ISLAND
1992, MSC

814 USA / Military sealift command (MSC)

2 CONVERTED MISSION CLASS:
MISSILE RANGE INSTRUMENTATION SHIP (AGM)
AND NAVIGATION RESEARCH SHIP (AG)

Name	No	Builders	Completed	F/S
REDSTONE (ex-*Johnstown*, ex-*Mission de Pala*)	T-AGM 20 (ex-AO 114)	Marine Ship Corp, Sausalito, Calif	22 Apr 1944	TAA
VANGUARD (ex-*Muscle Shoals*, ex-*Mission San Fernando*)	T-AG 194 (ex-AGM 19, ex-AO 122)	Marine Ship Corp, Sausalito, Calif	29 Feb 1944	TAA

Displacement, tons: 13 882 light; 24 710 full load
Dimensions, feet (metres): 595 × 75 × 25 *(181.4 × 22.9 × 7.6)*
Main machinery: Turbo-electric; 2 Babcock & Wilcox boilers; 600 psi *(42.3 kg/cm sq)*; 825°F *(440°C)*; Westinghouse turbo-generators; 10 000 hp *(7.46 MW)*; 1 motor; 1 shaft
Speed, knots: 14. **Range, miles:** 25 000 at 13 kts
Complement: 165 civilian (20 officers, 80 technical personnel) *(Redstone)*
Radars: Navigation: Raytheon TM 1650/9X and TM 1660/12S; I band.

Comment: Maritime Administration T2-SE-A2 type. *Redstone* was converted in 1964-66 to serve as mid-ocean communications and tracking ship in support of the Apollo manned lunar flights. Converted to range instrumentation ship by General Dynamics Corp, Quincy Division, Massachusetts; was cut in half and a 72 ft mid-section was inserted, increasing length, beam, and displacement; approximately 450 tons of electronic equipment installed for support of lunar flight operations, including communications and tracking systems; balloon hangar and platform fitted aft. Operated for the US Air Force 45th Space Wing, Patrick Air Force Base, Florida.
Vanguard supports sponsor programmes in navigation research by providing a platform for testing fleet ballistic missile guidance and missile systems. Reclassified as AG 194 in September 1980. Is under operational control of Director, Strategic Systems Program and is currently manned by 45 crew members and 18 DIRSSP personnel; ship can accommodate 91 crew members and 113 other personnel.

REDSTONE   *1/1990, Giorgio Arra*

VANGUARD   *5/1992, Giorgio Arra*

2 MELVILLE CLASS: OCEANOGRAPHIC RESEARCH SHIPS (AGOR)

Name	No	Builders	Completed	F/S
MELVILLE	AGOR 14	Defoe SB Co, Bay City, Mich	27 Aug 1969	Loan
KNORR	AGOR 15	Defoe SB Co, Bay City, Mich	14 Jan 1970	Loan

Displacement, tons: 2670 full load
Dimensions, feet (metres): 278.9 × 46.3 × 15.1 *(85 × 14.1 × 4.6)*
Main machinery: Diesel-electric; 4 diesel generators; 3 motors; 3000 hp *(2.24 MW)*; 3 shafts (2 aft, 1 fwd)
Speed, knots: 14. **Range, miles:** 12 000 at 12 kts
Complement: 58 (9 officers) plus 33 scientists

Comment: *Melville* operated by Scripps Institution of Oceanography and *Knorr* by Woods Hole Oceanography Institution for the Office of Naval Research, under technical control of the Oceanographer of the Navy. These ships are not part of the MSC. Fitted with internal wells for lowering equipment, underwater lights and observation ports. Facilities for handling small research submersibles. Problems with the propulsion system have led to major modifications including electric drive (vice the original mechanical) and the insertion of a 34 ft central section increasing the displacement from the original 1915 tons and allowing better accommodation and improved laboratory spaces. The forward propeller is retractable. These ships are highly manoeuvrable for precise position keeping.

MELVILLE   *1986, Giorgio Arra*

1 ROBERT D CONRAD CLASS:
OCEANOGRAPHIC RESEARCH SHIP (AGOR)

Name	No	Builders	Completed	F/S
BARTLETT	T-AGOR 13	Northwest Marine Iron Works, Portland, Oregon	31 Mar 1969	TAA

Displacement, tons: 1200 light; 1370 full load
Dimensions, feet (metres): 208.9 × 40 × 15.3 *(63.7 × 12.2 × 4.7)*
Main machinery: Diesel-electric; 2 Caterpillar D 378 diesel generators; 1 motor; 1000 hp *(746 kW)*; 1 shaft; bow thruster
Speed, knots: 13.5. **Range, miles:** 12 000 at 12 kts
Complement: 41 (9 officers, 15 scientists)
Radars: Navigation: TM 1660/12S; I band.

Comment: The survivor of a class of ships designed and built by the US Navy for oceanographic research. Fitted with instrumentation and laboratories to measure gravity and magnetism, water temperature, sound transmission in water, and the profile of the ocean floor. Special features include 10 ton capacity boom and winches for handling over-the-side equipment; bow thruster; 620 hp gas turbine (housed in funnel structure) for providing 'quiet' power when conducting experiments; can propel the ship at 6.5 kts.
Ships of this class are in service with Brazil, Mexico, New Zealand, Chile and Tunisia. The last pair transferred in 1992.

BARTLETT   *12/1991, Giorgio Arra*

2 GYRE CLASS: OCEANOGRAPHIC RESEARCH SHIPS (AGOR)

Name	No	Builders	Completed	F/S
GYRE	AGOR 21	Halter Marine Service, New Orleans	14 Nov 1973	Loan
MOANA WAVE	AGOR 22	Halter Marine Service, New Orleans	16 Jan 1974	Loan

Displacement, tons: 1427 (AGOR 21), 1853 (AGOR 22) full load
Dimensions, feet (metres): 174 × 36 × 13 *(53 × 11 × 4)* (AGOR 21) 210 × 36 × 13 *(64 × 11 × 4)* (AGOR 22)
Main machinery: 2 Caterpillar diesels; 1700 hp *(1.27 MW)*; 2 shafts; cp props; bow thruster; 150 hp *(112 kW)*
Speed, knots: 11.5. **Range, miles:** 12 000 at 10 kts
Complement: 13 plus 19 scientists

Comment: Based on a commercial ship design. Open deck aft provides space for equipment vans to permit rapid change of mission capabilities. Single hard-chine hulls. *Moana Wave* was lengthened in 1984 and fitted with a laboratory at the stern. They are assigned for operation to Texas A & M University and the University of Hawaii, respectively and are not MSC ships.

MOANA WAVE   *1991, van Ginderen Collection*

Military sealift command (MSC) / USA 815

1 + 1 OCEANOGRAPHIC RESEARCH SHIPS (AGOR)

Name	No	Builders	In Service	F/S
THOMAS G THOMPSON (ex-*Ewing*)	AGOR-23	Halter Marine, Moss Point	July 1992	Loan
REVELLE	AGOR-24	Halter Marine, Moss Point	Jan 1996	Bldg

Displacement, tons: 3251 full load
Dimensions, feet (metres): 274 oa; 246.8 wl × 52.5 × 19 *(83.5; 75.2 × 16 × 5.6)*
Main machinery: Diesel-electric; 6 diesel generators; 6.65 MW (3 × 1.5 MW and 3 × 715 kW); 2 motors; 2 shafts; bow thruster; 1140 hp *(850 kW)*
Speed, knots: 15. **Range, miles:** 8000 at 12 kts
Complement: 20 plus 30 scientists plus 20 spare berths
Sonars: Atlas Elektronik Hydrographic.

Comment: *Thomas G Thompson* is the first of a new class of oceanographic research vessels capable of operating worldwide in all seasons and suitable for use by navy laboratories, contractors and academic institutions; laid down 23 March 1989, launched 27 July 1990 and delivered 8 July 1991. Dynamic positioning system enables station to be held within 300 ft of a point. 4000 sq ft of laboratories. Loaned to the University of Washington and sponsored by the Chief of Naval Research, these ships are not part of the MSC. Ships in this series may be of different hull designs and will be able to meet changing oceanographic requirements for general, year-round, worldwide research. This will include launching, towing and recovering a variety of equipment. The ships will also be involved in hydrographic data collection. The second ship of the class was authorised in FY 1992 and ordered in January 1993.

THOMAS G THOMPSON 7/1991, Halter Marine

14 STALWART CLASS: OCEAN SURVEILLANCE SHIPS (AGOS)

Name	No	Laid down		Completed		F/S
VINDICATOR	T-AGOS 3	14 Apr	1983	20 Nov	1984	TAA
TRIUMPH	T-AGOS 4	3 Jan	1984	19 Feb	1985	TPA
ASSURANCE	T-AGOS 5	16 Apr	1984	1 May	1985	TPA
PERSISTENT	T-AGOS 6	22 Oct	1984	14 Aug	1985	TAA
PREVAIL	T-AGOS 8	13 Mar	1985	5 Mar	1986	TAA
ASSERTIVE	T-AGOS 9	30 July	1985	12 Sep	1986	TPA
INVINCIBLE	T-AGOS 10	8 Nov	1985	30 Jan	1987	TAA
AUDACIOUS (ex-*Dauntless*)	T-AGOS 11	29 Feb	1986	18 June	1989	TPA
BOLD (ex-*Vigorous*)	T-AGOS 12	13 June	1988	20 Oct	1989	TAA
WORTHY	T-AGOS 14	3 Apr	1986	7 Apr	1989	TAA
TITAN	T-AGOS 15	30 Oct	1986	8 Mar	1989	TPA
CAPABLE	T-AGOS 16	17 Oct	1987	8 July	1989	TAA
TENACIOUS (ex-*Intrepid*)	T-AGOS 17	26 Feb	1988	8 Nov	1989	TPA
RELENTLESS	T-AGOS 18	22 Apr	1988	8 Mar	1990	TAA

Displacement, tons: 2262 full load
Dimensions, feet (metres): 224 × 43 × 14.9 *(68.3 × 13.1 × 4.5)*
Main machinery: Diesel-electric; 4 Caterpillar D 398B diesel generators; 3200 hp *(2.39 MW)*; 2 motors; 1600 hp *(1.2 MW)*; 2 shafts; bow thruster; 550 hp *(410 kW)*
Speed, knots: 11; 3 when towing. **Range, miles:** 4000 at 11 kts; 6450 at 3 kts
Complement: 30-33 (9 officers) (21 civilian manning, 9-12 Navy contingent)
Radars: Navigation: Two Raytheon; I band.
Sonars: UQQ2 SURTASS; towed array; passive surveillance.

Comment: This programme has been completed after several rocky years stemming from the financial difficulties of Tacoma Boatbuilding Co, which built the first eight ships but initially was unable to complete T-AGOS 9-12 before filing for bankruptcy. Halter Marine built T-AGOS 13-18. The ships are operated and maintained by civilian contractors. SURTASS is a linear array of 8575 ft *(2614 m)* deployed on a 6000 ft *(1829 m)* tow cable and neutrally buoyant. The array can operate at depths between 500 and 1500 ft. Information from the array is relayed via WSC-6 (SHF) SATCOM link to shore. Patrols are of 60-90 days duration which even with passive tank stabilisation is a long time to wallow around at 3 kts. Many of the COs are retired USN Captains. Because of the diminished operational requirement, the whole class are being decommissioned/re-employed at the rate of three per year. *Worthy*, *Capable* and *Relentless* are being converted for drug interdiction activities. *Capable* started conversion in January 1993. *Adventurous* transferred to NOAA in 1992. Up to six more may follow. *Contender* given to the Merchant Marine Academy as a training ship.

BOLD 10/1992, Giorgio Arra

4 VICTORIOUS CLASS: OCEAN SURVEILLANCE SHIPS (AGOS)

Name	No	Builders	Completed	F/S
VICTORIOUS	T-AGOS 19	McDermott Marine	5 Sep 1991	TPA
ABLE	T-AGOS 20	McDermott Marine	24 July 1992	TAA
EFFECTIVE	T-AGOS 21	McDermott Marine	30 Nov 1992	TPA
LOYAL	T-AGOS 22	McDermott Marine	June 1993	TAA

Displacement, tons: 3396 full load
Dimensions, feet (metres): 234.5 × 93.6 × 24.8 *(71.5 × 28.5 × 7.6)*
Main machinery: Diesel-electric; 4 Caterpillar 3512TA diesels; 5440 hp *(4 MW)* sustained; 2 GE motors; 3200 hp *(2.39 MW)*; 2 shafts; 2 bow thrusters; 2400 hp *(1.79 MW)*
Speed, knots: 16; 3 when towing
Complement: 34 (22 civilian, 12 Navy)
Radars: Navigation: Two Raytheon; I band.
Sonars: UQQ 2 SURTASS; towed array; passive surveillance.

Comment: All of SWATH design because of its greater stability at slow speeds in high latitudes under adverse weather conditions. A contract for the first SWATH ship, T-AGOS 19, was awarded in November 1986, and options for the next three were exercised in October 1988. Same WSC-6 communications, links and operating procedures as the Stalwart class.

VICTORIOUS 8/1992, P Campbell

ABLE 9/1992, Stefan Terzibaschitsch

0 + 1 (1) IMPECCABLE CLASS: OCEAN SURVEILLANCE SHIPS (AGOS)

Name	No	Builders	Completed	F/S
IMPECCABLE	T-AGOS 23	Tampa Shipyard	May 1994	Bldg
INTEGRITY	T-AGOS 24	—	—	Proj

Displacement, tons: 5370 full load
Dimensions, feet (metres): 281.5 × 95.8 × 26 *(85.8 × 29.2 × 7.9)*
Main machinery: Diesel-electric; 3 GM EMD 12-645F7B diesel generators; 5.48 MW *(60 Hz)* sustained; 2 Westinghouse motors; 5000 hp *(3.73 MW)*; 2 shafts; 2 omni-thruster hydrojets; 1800 hp *(1.34 MW)*
Speed, knots: 12; 3 when towing
Complement: 45 (26 civilian, 19 Navy)

Comment: Hull form based on that of *Victorious*. Acoustic systems should include an active low frequency towed array, which has a series of modules each of which houses two high powered transducers. These can be used with either mono or bi-static receivers. First of the class included in FY 1990 budget but a contract was not awarded until March 1991. A second of class was approved in FY 1992 but no contract is to be given until the first of class has been tested.

IMPECCABLE (artist's impression) 1991, Tampa Shipyard

816 USA / Military sealift command (MSC)

4 SILAS BENT and WILKES CLASSES: SURVEYING SHIPS (AGS)

Name	No	Builders	Completed	F/S
SILAS BENT	T-AGS 26	American SB Co, Lorain	23 July 1965	TPA
KANE	T-AGS 27	Christy Corp, Sturgeon Bay	19 May 1967	TAA
WILKES	T-AGS 33	Defoe SB Co, Bay City, Mich	28 June 1971	TAA
WYMAN	T-AGS 34	Defoe SB Co, Bay City, Mich	3 Nov 1971	TAA

Displacement, tons: 2550-2843 full load
Dimensions, feet (metres): 285.3 × 48 × 15.1 *(87 × 14.6 × 4.6)*
Main machinery: Diesel-electric; 2 Alco diesel generators; 1 Westinghouse/GE motor; 3600 hp *(2.69 MW)*; 1 shaft; bow thruster; 350 hp *(261 kW)*
Speed, knots: 15. **Range, miles:** 8000 at 13 kts
Complement: 37 (12 officers) plus 28 scientists
Radars: Navigation: RM 1650/9X and TM 1660/12S *(Silas Bent)*; I band.

Comment: Designed specifically for surveying operations. Bow propulsion unit for precise manoeuvrability and station keeping. All ships in commission operated for the Oceanographer of the Navy under technical control of the Naval Oceanographic Office.

WYMAN *3/1991, Giorgio Arra*

2 MAURY CLASS: SURVEYING SHIPS (AGS)

Name	No	Builders	Completed	F/S
MAURY	T-AGS 39	Bethlehem, Sparrows Point	31 Mar 1989	TAA
TANNER	T-AGS 40	Bethlehem, Sparrows Point	27 Aug 1990	TAA

Displacement, tons: 16 074 full load
Dimensions, feet (metres): 500; 462.1 wl × 72 × 30 *(152.4; 140.8 × 22 × 9.1)*
Main machinery: 2 Transamerica De Laval R5-V16 Enterprise diesels; 27 240 hp *(20.4 MW)* sustained; 1 shaft
Speed, knots: 20. **Range, miles:** 12 000 at 20 kts
Complement: 108 (56 civilian, 52 Navy) plus 20 scientists

Comment: The first such ships to be constructed in many years. Both ordered 25 June 1985. *Maury* laid down 29 July 1986 and *Tanner* 22 October 1986. They have replaced *Bowditch* (T-AGS 21) and *Dutton* (T-AGS 22) and are operated by MSC for the Oceanographer of the Navy under technical control of the Naval Oceanographic Office. Fitted with SQN-17 bottom topography survey system and other acoustic systems including 2 BQN-3 narrow-beam for surveying purposes. In-service dates delayed by main machinery installation problems. Almost half the displacement is water ballast to provide sufficient draft for the sonar.

TANNER *12/1990, Harald Carstens*

1 WATERS CLASS: SURVEYING SHIP (AGS)

Name	No	Builders	Completed	F/S
WATERS	T-AGS 45	Avondale Industries	June 1993	Bldg/TPA

Displacement, tons: 12 208 full load
Dimensions, feet (metres): 455 × 68.9 × 21 *(138.7 × 21 × 6.4)*
Main machinery: Diesel-electric; 5 GM EMD diesels; 2 Westinghouse motors; 6800 hp *(15.07 MW)*; 2 shafts
Speed, knots: 13. **Range, miles:** 6500 at 12 kts
Complement: 89 (37 officers) plus 6 spare

Comment: Ordered 4 April 1990. Laid down 16 May 1991 and launched 6 June 1992. Supports the Integrated Underwater Surveillance System. Planned to conduct oceanographic and acoustic surveys. The ship carries a remote-controlled submersible.

WATERS (artist's impression) *1990, Avondale*

2 JOHN McDONNELL CLASS: SURVEYING SHIPS (AGS)

Name	No	Builders	Completed	F/S
JOHN McDONNELL	T-AGS 51	Halter Marine, Moss Point	Nov 1992	TAA
LITTLEHALES	T-AGS 52	Halter Marine, Moss Point	Jan 1993	PAA

Displacement, tons: 2054 full load
Dimensions, feet (metres): 208 × 45 × 14 *(63.4 × 13.7 × 4.3)*
Main machinery: 1 GM EMD 12-645E6 diesel; 2550 hp *(1.9 MW)* sustained; 1 auxiliary diesel; 230 hp *(172 kW)*; 1 shaft
Speed, knots: 12. **Range, miles:** 13 800 at 12 kts
Complement: 22 plus 11 scientists

Comment: Laid down on 3 August 1989 and 25 October 1989 respectively. *McDonnell* launched 15 August 1990 and delivered 16 December 1991; *Littlehales* launched 14 February 1991 and delivered 10 January 1992. Have replaced *Chauvenet* and *Harkness*. Carry 34 ft survey launches for data collection in coastal regions with depths between 10 and 600 m and in deep water to 4000 m. A small diesel is used for propulsion at towing speeds of up to 6 kts.

JOHN McDONNELL *1/1992, Halter Marine*

0 + 3 PATHFINDER CLASS: SURVEYING SHIPS (AGS)

Name	No	Builders	Completed
PATHFINDER	T-AGS 60	Halter Marine, Moss Point	Dec 1994
SUMNER	T-AGS 61	Halter Marine, Moss Point	May 1995
—	T-AGS 62	Halter Marine, Moss Point	Jan 1996

Displacement, tons: 4762 full load
Dimensions, feet (metres): 328.5 × 58 × 18 *(100.1 × 17.7 × 5.5)*
Main machinery: Diesel-electric; 6 diesel generators; 2 motors; 6000 hp *(4.48 MW)*; 2 shafts; bow thruster
Speed, knots: 16. **Range, miles:** 12 000 at 12 kts
Complement: 60

Comment: Contract awarded in January 1991 for two ships with an option for a third which was taken up in June 1992. *Pathfinder* laid down 20 January 1993. Replacements for Robert D Conrad class. *Sumner* may be equipped for Arctic operations.

PATHFINDER (artist's impression) *1992, Trinity Marine*

1 CONVERTED C3-S-33a TYPE: CARGO SHIP (AK)

Name	No	Completed	F/S
VEGA (ex-SS *Bay*, ex-*Mormacbay*)	T-AK 286	14 Oct 1960	TAA

Displacement, tons: 15 404 full load
Measurement, tons: 6590 gross
Dimensions, feet (metres): 483.3 × 68 × 28.5 *(147.2 × 20.7 × 8.7)*
Main machinery: 2 Combustion Engineering boilers; 615 psi *(43.3 kg/cm sq)*; 850°F *(457°C)*; 1 GE turbine; 12 100 hp *(9 MW)*; 1 shaft
Speed, knots: 19. **Range, miles:** 14 000 at 18 kts
Complement: 67 plus 7 man naval contingent

Comment: Built by Sun Shipbuilding and Drydock Co, Chester, Pennsylvania for the Moore-McCormack Lines. *Vega* was acquired in October 1981 and was converted to an FBM Support Ship. Capable of carrying 16 Trident missiles; equipped with eight 10-ton capacity booms, four 5-ton capacity booms and one 75-ton capacity boom. Deployed with MSC Atlantic Fleet in July 1983.

VEGA *1986, Giorgio Arra*

Military sealift command (MSC) / USA   817

12 + 6 HENRY J KAISER CLASS: OILERS (AO)

Name	No	Builders	Laid down	Completed	F/S
HENRY J KAISER	T-AO 187	Avondale	22 Aug 1984	19 Dec 1986	TAA
JOSHUA HUMPHREYS	T-AO 188	Avondale	17 Dec 1984	2 Apr 1987	TAA
JOHN LENTHALL	T-AO 189	Avondale	15 July 1985	2 June 1987	TAA
ANDREW J HIGGINS	T-AO 190	Avondale	21 Nov 1985	20 Oct 1987	TPA
BENJAMIN ISHERWOOD	T-AO 191	Penn Ship/Tampa	12 July 1986	Sep 1993	Bldg/TPA
HENRY ECKFORD	T-AO 192	Penn Ship/Tampa	22 Jan 1987	Apr 1994	Bldg/TPA
WALTER S DIEHL	T-AO 193	Avondale	8 July 1986	13 Sep 1988	TPA
JOHN ERICSSON	T-AO 194	Avondale	15 Mar 1989	18 Mar 1991	TPA
LEROY GRUMMAN	T-AO 195	Avondale	7 June 1987	2 Aug 1989	TAA
KANAWHA	T-AO 196	Avondale	13 July 1989	6 Dec 1991	TAA
PECOS	T-AO 197	Avondale	17 Feb 1988	6 July 1990	TPA
BIG HORN	T-AO 198	Avondale	9 Oct 1989	31 July 1992	TAA
TIPPECANOE	T-AO 199	Avondale	19 Nov 1990	26 Mar 1993	TPA
GUADALUPE	T-AO 200	Avondale	9 July 1990	26 Oct 1992	TPA
PATUXENT	T-AO 201	Avondale	21 Oct 1991	June 1994	Bldg/TAA
YUKON	T-AO 202	Avondale	13 May 1991	Dec 1995	Bldg/TPA
LARAMIE	T-AO 203	Avondale	12 Nov 1992	Apr 1996	Bldg/TAA
RAPPAHANNOCK	T-AO 204	Avondale	14 Mar 1992	Nov 1995	Bldg/TPA

Displacement, tons: 40 700 full load
Dimensions, feet (metres): 677.5 × 97.5 × 35 *(206.5 × 29.7 × 10.7)*
Main machinery: 2 Colt-Pielstick 10 PC4.2 V 570 diesels; 34 422 hp(m) *(24.3 MW)* sustained; 2 shafts
Speed, knots: 20. **Range, miles:** 6000 at 18 kts
Complement: 95 civilian (20 officers); 21 naval (1 officer)
Cargo capacity: 180 000 barrels of fuel oil
Guns: 1 Vulcan Phalanx CIWS (fitted for).
Countermeasures: Decoys: SLQ-25 Nixie; towed torpedo decoy.
Helicopters: Platform only.

Comment: Construction of the class was delayed initially by design difficulties, and by excessive vibration at high speeds and other problems encountered in the first ship of the class. The two ships being constructed by Penn Ship are being completed by Tampa Shipyards after Penn Ship went bankrupt and shut down. As the ships had sat idle for months, much refurbishing was necessary. Funding for the final five ships in the programme was provided in FY 1989. The ships are fitted for Vulcan Phalanx CIWS. There are stations on both sides for underway replenishment of fuel and solids. Fitted with integrated electrical auxiliary propulsion. The last three have been delayed by the decision to fit double hulls to meet the requirements of the Oil Pollution Act of 1990. This modification increases construction time from 32 to 42 months and will reduce cargo capacity by 15 per cent.

HENRY J KAISER   7/1992, F Sadek

JOSHUA HUMPHREYS (with *Abraham Lincoln*)   2/1992, G Toremans

2 MERCY CLASS: HOSPITAL SHIPS (AH)

Name	No	Builders	Completed	F/S
MERCY (ex-SS *Worth*)	T-AH 19	National Steel and SB Co, San Diego	1976	ROS
COMFORT (ex-SS *Rose City*)	T-AH 20	National Steel and SB Co, San Diego	1976	ROS

Displacement, tons: 69 360 full load
Measurement, tons: 54 367 gross; 35 958 net
Dimensions, feet (metres): 894 × 105.6 × 32.8 *(272.6 × 32.2 × 10)*
Main machinery: 2 boilers; 2 GE turbines; 24 500 hp *(18.3 MW)*; 2 shafts
Speed, knots: 16.5. **Range, miles:** 12 500 at 15 kts
Complement: 68 civilian crew; 820 naval medical staff; 372 naval support staff; 15 naval communications staff
Radars: Navigation: SPS 67; I band.
Tacan: URN 25.
Helicopters: Platform only.

Comment: Plans to convert SS *United States* were dropped in favour of converting these two San Clemente class tankers. Contracts awarded to National Steel & Shipbuilding in 1983. Conversion of T-AH 19 was begun in 1984 and that of T-AH 20 in 1985. *Mercy* was commissioned 19 December 1986; *Comfort* on 30 November 1987. *Mercy* berthed at Oakland, CA, in a reduced operating status; *Comfort* at Baltimore. Each ship has 1000 beds, 12 operating theatres, laboratories, pharmacies, dental, radiology and optometry departments, physical-therapy and burn-care units and radiological services. Both deployed in the Gulf in 1990-91 with full medical staffs mostly drawn from naval hospitals on both US coasts.

MERCY   3/1991, 92 Wing RAAF

5—T 5 TYPE: TRANSPORT OILERS (AOT)

Name	No	Builders	Commissioned
GUS W DARNELL	T-AOT 1121	American SB Co, Tampa, Fla	11 Sep 1985
PAUL BUCK	T-AOT 1122	American SB Co, Tampa, Fla	11 Sep 1985
SAMUEL L COBB	T-AOT 1123	American SB Co, Tampa, Fla	15 Nov 1985
RICHARD G MATTHIESON	T-AOT 1124	American SB Co, Tampa, Fla	18 Feb 1986
LAWRENCE H GIANELLA	T-AOT 1125	American SB Co, Tampa, Fla	22 Apr 1986

Displacement, tons: 39 000 full load
Dimensions, feet (metres): 615 × 90 × 34 *(187.5 × 27.4 × 10.4)*
Main machinery: 1 Sulzer 5RTA76 diesel; 18 400 hp(m) *(13.52 MW)* sustained; 1 shaft
Speed, knots: 16. **Range, miles:** 12 000 at 16 kts
Complement: 23 (9 officers)
Cargo capacity: 238 400 barrels of oil fuel

Comment: Built for Ocean Carriers Inc, Houston, Texas specifically for long term time charter to the Military Sealift Command (20 years) as Ocean Transportation ships. The last two are able to rig underway replenishment gear.

SAMUEL L COBB   3/1988, Giorgio Arra

9 SEALIFT CLASS: TRANSPORT OILERS (AOT, ex-AO)

Name	No	Builders	Completed	F/S
SEALIFT PACIFIC	T-AOT 168	Todd Shipyards	14 Aug 1974	TWWR
SEALIFT ARABIAN SEA	T-AOT 169	Todd Shipyards	6 May 1975	TWWR
SEALIFT CHINA SEA	T-AOT 170	Todd Shipyards	9 May 1975	TWWR
SEALIFT INDIAN OCEAN	T-AOT 171	Todd Shipyards	29 Aug 1975	TWWR
SEALIFT ATLANTIC	T-AOT 172	Bath Iron Works	26 Aug 1974	TWWR
SEALIFT MEDITERRANEAN	T-AOT 173	Bath Iron Works	6 Nov 1974	TWWR
SEALIFT CARIBBEAN	T-AOT 174	Bath Iron Works	10 Feb 1975	TWWR
SEALIFT ARCTIC	T-AOT 175	Bath Iron Works	22 May 1975	TWWR
SEALIFT ANTARCTIC	T-AOT 176	Bath Iron Works	1 Aug 1975	TWWR

Displacement, tons: 34 100 full load
Measurement, tons: 27 300 dwt
Dimensions, feet (metres): 587 × 84 × 34.6 *(178.9 × 25.6 × 10.6)*
Main machinery: 2 Colt-Pielstick 14 PC2 V 400 diesels; 14 000 hp(m) *(10.3 MW)* sustained; 1 shaft; cp prop; bow thruster
Speed, knots: 16. **Range, miles:** 7500 at 16 kts
Complement: 24 (9 officers) plus 2 Maritime Academy cadets
Cargo capacity: 185 000 barrels of oil fuel

Comment: Built specially for long term-charter by the Military Sealift Command. Operated for MSC as Ocean Transportation Ships under charter by Marine Transport Lines Inc. Automated engine room. All reclassified T-AOT on 30 September 1978.

SEALIFT ATLANTIC   7/1992, Per Kornefeldt

MISCELLANEOUS OCEAN TRANSPORTATION SHIPS

Comment: In addition to the AOTs listed in the Sealift and T Type classes, there are a number of ships of varying types under charter to the MSC. Numbers and names are constantly changing.

MERCURY (MSC charter) 8/1991, 92 Wing RAAF

1 ZEUS CLASS: CABLE REPAIRING SHIP (ARC)

Name	No	Builders	Completed	F/S
ZEUS	T-ARC 7	National Steel and SB Co, San Diego	19 Mar 1984	TPA

Displacement, tons: 8370 light; 14 157 full load
Dimensions, feet (metres): 502.5 × 73 × 25 *(153.2 × 22.3 × 7.6)*
Main machinery: Diesel-electric; 5 GM EMD 20-645F7B diesel generators; 14.32 MW sustained; 2 motors; 2 shafts; cp props; bow thrusters (forward and aft)
Speed, knots: 15.8. **Range, miles:** 10 000 at 15 kts
Complement: 126 (88 civilians, 6 Navy, 32 scientists)

Comment: Ordered 7 August 1979. Remotely manned engineering room controlled from the bridge.

ZEUS 4/1991, Giorgio Arra

1 NEPTUNE CLASS: CABLE REPAIRING SHIP (ARC)

Name	No	Builders	Commissioned	F/S
ALBERT J MYER	T-ARC 6	Pusey & Jones Corp, Wilmington, Del	13 May 1963	TPA

Displacement, tons: 8500 full load
Dimensions, feet (metres): 369 × 47 × 27 *(112.5 × 14.3 × 8.2)*
Main machinery: Diesel-electric; 4 GE diesel generators; 2 motors; 4000 hp *(2.98 MW)*; 2 shafts
Speed, knots: 14. **Range, miles:** 10 000 at 13 kts
Complement: 92 civilian (16 officers, 18 scientists)
Radars: Navigation: RM 1650/6X *(Myer)*; I band.

Comment: Built as an S3-S2-BP1 type cable ship for the Maritime Administration. *Albert J Myer* acquired from US Army on 18 September 1963. Fitted with electric cable handling machinery (in place of steam equipment) and precision navigation equipment. Rebuilt at Bethlehem Steel Co, Key Highway Division, Baltimore from March 1978 to May 1980. Modernisation included stripping the superstructure down to the main deck, gutting the hull, replacing the entire propulsion system, the wiring and piping and replacing the decks and superstructure with aluminium where possible. Sister ship *Neptune* in reserve from October 1991.

ALBERT J MYER 4/1990, Giorgio Arra

7 POWHATAN CLASS: FLEET OCEAN TUGS (ATF)

Name	No	Laid down	Completed	F/S
POWHATAN	T-ATF 166	30 Sep 1976	15 June 1979	TAA
NARRAGANSETT	T-ATF 167	5 May 1977	9 Nov 1979	TPA
CATAWBA	T-ATF 168	14 Dec 1977	28 May 1980	TPA
NAVAJO	T-ATF 169	14 Dec 1977	13 June 1980	TPA
MOHAWK	T-ATF 170	22 Mar 1979	16 Oct 1980	TAA
SIOUX	T-ATF 171	22 Mar 1979	1 May 1981	TPA
APACHE	T-ATF 172	22 Mar 1979	30 July 1981	TAA

Displacement, tons: 2260 full load
Dimensions, feet (metres): 240.2 × 42 × 15 *(73.2 × 12.8 × 4.6)*
Main machinery: 2 GM EMD 20-645F7B diesels; 5.73 MW sustained; 2 shafts; Kort nozzles (except in *Powhatan* and one other); cp props; bow thruster; 300 hp *(224 kW)*
Speed, knots: 14.5. **Range, miles:** 10 000 at 13 kts
Complement: 23 (17 civilians, 6 naval communications technicians)
Guns: Space provided to fit 2—20 mm and 2—12.7 mm MGs in war.

Comment: Built at Marinette Marine Corp, Wisconsin patterned after commercial off-shore supply ship design. Originally intended as successors to the Cherokee and Abnaki class ATFs. However, procurement was halted at seven ships with no more planned. All transferred to MSC upon completion. 10 ton capacity crane and a bollard pull of at least 54 tons. A 'deck grid' is fitted aft which contains 1 in bolt receptacles spaced 24 in apart. This allows for the bolting down of a wide variety of portable equipment. There are two GPH fire-pumps supplying three fire monitors with up to 2200 gallons of foam per minute. A deep module can be embarked to support naval salvage teams.

SIOUX 4/1992, 92 Wing RAAF

AUXILIARY SEALIFT SHIPS: READY RESERVE FORCE (RRF)

Note: Due to the lack of sealift capability within both the US Navy and US Merchant Marine, a programme was initiated in the early 1980s to create a Ready Reserve Force (RRF) of ships that could be made available quickly for military sealift operations without disrupting routine commerce. Now included in the RRF are auxiliary crane ships, roll-on/roll-off, break bulk, heavy lift, barge carriers, POL product tankers, and troopships. Most of these are normally maintained in a laid-up status at three principal sites: James River, VA (East); Beaumont, TX (Gulf); and Suisun Bay, CA (West). However, in early 1993 more than half the force was either at sea or dispersed among 17 other ports. The responsibility for maintenance and upkeep was transferred from the Military Sealift Command to the Maritime Administration in FY 1989, but they remain under operational control of MSC. More than three-quarters of the force was employed during Desert Shield/Storm in 1990/91, transporting equipment to the Middle East before and during the war, and returning it to the United States at the conclusion of hostilities. MSC hopes to increase the numbers of Ro-Ros by purchasing them through MARAD. The long-range goal for the RRF is 140 ships. RRF ships have red, white and blue funnel markings. All have had additional navigation and communications equipment fitted.

9 AUXILIARY CRANE SHIPS

KEYSTONE STATE TACS 1
GEM STATE TACS 2
GRAND CANYON STATE TACS 3
GOPHER STATE TACS 4
FLICKERTAIL STATE TACS 5
CORNHUSKER STATE TACS 6
DIAMOND STATE TACS 7
EQUALITY STATE TACS 8
GREEN MOUNTAIN STATE TACS 9

Comment: See *MPS* section for details.

13 PRODUCT TANKERS

MOUNT WASHINGTON TAOT 169
PETERSBURG TAOT 9101
AMERICAN OSPREY TAOT 5075
POTOMAC TAOT 181
SHOSHONE TAOT 151
CHESAPEAKE TAOT 5084
NODAWAY TAOG 78
ALATNA TAOG 81
CHATTAHOOCHEE TAOG 82
AMERICAN EXPLORER TAOT 165
MISSION BUENAVENTURA TAOT 1012
MISSION CAPISTRANO TAOT 5005
MOUNT VERNON TAOT 5083

48 BREAK BULK SHIPS

CAPE CATAWBA TAK 5074	GULF SHIPPER TAK 2035
LAKE TAK 5016	BANNER TAK 5008
PRIDE TAK 5017	DEL MONTE TAK 5049
SCAN TAK 5018	DEL VALLE TAK 5050
SOUTHERN CROSS TAK 285	DEL VIENTO TAK 5026
CAPE CANAVERAL TAK 5040	COURIER TAK 5019
CAPE CANSO TAK 5037	PIONEER COMMANDER TAK 2016
CAPE CHALMERS TAK 5036	PIONEER CONTRACTOR TAK 2018
CAPE COD TAK 5041	PIONEER CRUSADER TAK 2019
CAPE CLEAR TAK 5039	BUYER TAK 2033
CAPE CARTHAGE TAK 5042	CALIFORNIA TAK 5029
CAPE CATOCHE TAK 5043	SANTA ANA TAK 5022
CAPE JOHNSON TAK 5075	CAPE GIBSON TAK 5051
CAPE JUBY TAK 5077	CAPE GIRARDEAU TAK 2039
CAPE ALAVA TAK 5012	NORTHERN LIGHT TAKR 284
CAPE ALEXANDER TAK 5010	AGENT TAK 5015
CAPE ANN TAK 5009	AMBASSADOR TAK 5007
CAPE ARCHWAY TAK 5011	CAPE BON TAK 5059
CAPE AVINOF TAK 5013	ADVENTURER TAK 5005
CAPE NOME TAK 1014	AIDE TAK 5006
GULF BANKER TAK 5044	CAPE BORDA TAK 5058
GULF FARMER TAK 5045	CAPE BOVER TAK 5057
GULF MERCHANT TAK 5046	CAPE BLANCO TAK 5060
GULF TRADER TAK 2036	CAPE BRETON TAKR 5056

GULF TRADER *4/1992, 92 Wing RAAF*

17 + 12 RO-RO SHIPS

ADM WM H CALLAGHAN TAKR 1001	CAPE EDMONT TAKR 5069
CAPE HENRY TAKR 5067	CAPE LAMBERT TAKR 5077
CAPE HORN TAKR 5068	CAPE LOBOS TAKR 5078
CAPE HUDSON TAKR 5066	CAPE INSCRIPTION TAKR 5076
CAPE DOMINGO TAKR 5053	CAPE ISABEL TAKR 5062
CAPE DIAMOND TAKR 5055	JUPITER TAKR 11
CAPE DECISION TAKR 5054	COMET TAKR 7
CAPE DOUGLAS TAKR 5052	METEOR TAKR 9
CAPE DUCATO TAKR 5051	

Comment: In addition to the listed ships 12 more, acquired in December 1992, are to be brought up to RRF standards. Names are *Santos, Lyra, Cygnus, Mercury, Saudi Riyadh, Saudi Makkah, G&C Admiral, American Eagle, Hual Trader, Hual Transporter, Taabot Italia* and *Mezzario Britannia*. Some of these names may be changed.

CAPE HENRY *7/1992, Jürg Kürsener*

9 MISCELLANEOUS SHIPS

Barge carriers	Troopships	Heavy lift ships
CAPE FAREWELL TAK 5073	EMPIRE STATE TAP 1001	CAPE MOHICAN TAKR 5065
CAPE FLATTERY TAK 5070	PATRIOT STATE TAP 1000	CAPE MAY TAKR 5063
CAPE FLORIDA TAK 5071		CAPE MENDOCINO TAKR 5064
AUSTRAL LIGHTNING TAK 5061		

CAPE MENDOCINO *9/1992, Stefan Terzibaschitsch*

AFLOAT PREPOSITIONING FORCE (PREPO)

Notes: 1. In order to improve US capability to deploy its forces rapidly to any area of conflict, and especially to South-West Asia, and to enhance the readiness of existing forces, the Carter Administration created a force comprising elements of all three services and named it the Rapid Deployment Joint Task Force (RDJTF). Initially composed of seven Military Sealift Command ships, it was first deployed to Diego Garcia in July 1980. For a time it was expanded to 17 ships; it carried tactical equipment, ammunition, POL, and supplies to sustain combat operations until reinforcements could be shipped from the USA. Thirteen ships were converted or built as part of the Maritime Prepositioning Ship programme (MPS) (see following section), and one five-ship squadron of MPS ships was based at Diego Garcia in 1985. On 7 August 1990, the PREPO force consisted of 11 ships. All 11 of these were deployed to Saudi Arabia in 1990 when the military reinforcement began and were among the first arrivals in the build-up of American forces.
2. The PREPO ships carry Army, Navy and Air Force equipment and supplies. Commander, Maritime Prepositioning Squadron Two controls MPS and PREPO ships at Deigo Garcia. Commander, MSC Mediterranean controls *Buffalo Soldier* (TAK 322) and *American Merlin* (TAK 323). In addition, a tanker shuttles in and out of the force. In 1992, this ship was the *Lawrence H Gianella* (TAOT 1125).
3. In early 1993, the 11 ships listed below were deployed.

2 LASH TYPE: CARGO SHIPS, BARGE (AKB)

Name	No	Builders	Completed	F/S
GREEN VALLEY	T-AK 2049	Avondale Shipyards	Feb 1975	PREPO
GREEN HARBOR	T-AK 2064	Avondale Shipyards	Feb 1974	PREPO

Displacement, tons: 62 314 full load
Measurement, tons: 32 278 gross; 46 152 dwt
Dimensions, feet (metres): 893.3 × 100 × 60 *(272.3 × 30.5 × 18.3)*
Main machinery: 2 Combustion Engineering boilers; 1100 psi *(77.3 kg/cm sq)*; 2 De Laval turbines; 32 000 hp *(23.9 MW)*; 1 shaft
Speed, knots: 22. **Range, miles:** 15 000 at 20 kts
Complement: 32
Cargo capacity: 1 691 500 cu ft (in 85 bales)

Comment: *Green Valley* acquired on 31 January 1992 and *Green Harbor* 20 October 1985. Stationed at Diego Garcia. Owned and operated by Central Gulf Lines.

GREEN VALLEY *7/1991, van Ginderen Collection*

2 LASH TYPE: CARGO SHIPS, BARGE (AKB)

Name	No	Builders	Completed	F/S
AUSTRAL RAINBOW (ex-*China Bear*)	TAK 2046	Avondale Shipyards	1972	PREPO
AMERICAN KESTREL	TAK 2043	Avondale Shipyards	1974	PREPO

Measurement, tons: 26 406 gross; 39 277 dwt
Dimensions, feet (metres): 820 × 100 × 40.7 *(249.9 × 30.4 × 12.4)*
Speed, knots: 19+
Complement: 33
Cargo capacity: 1 663 248 cu ft (77 bales)

Comment: *Austral Rainbow* re-acquired 26 May 1987. Owned and operated by Central Gulf Lines and stationed at Diego Garcia. *American Kestrel* acquired 20 June 1988. Owned by Kestrel Shipbuilding and operated by Osprey Ship Management. Stationed at Diego Garcia.

1 FLOAT-ON/FLOAT-OFF TYPE CARGO SHIP, SEMI-SUBMERSIBLE (AKF)

Name	No	Builders	Completed	F/S
AMERICAN CORMORANT (ex-*Ferncarrier*)	T-AK 2062	Eriksbergs Mekaniska Verkstads AB	Sep 1974	PREPO

Displacement, tons: 69 555 full load
Measurement, tons: 10 196 gross; 47 230 dwt
Dimensions, feet (metres): 738 × 135 × 35.1 *(225 × 41.1 × 10.7)*
Main machinery: 1 Eriksberg/Burmeister & Wain 10K84EF diesel; 19 900 hp(m) *(14.6 MW)*; 1 shaft; 2 thrusters; 3000 hp(m) *(2.2 MW)*
Speed, knots: 16. **Range, miles:** 23 700 at 13 kts
Complement: 21
Cargo capacity: 10 000 barrels of fuel; 44 000 tons deck cargo

Comment: Converted in 1982. Acquired on time charter 25 November 1985. Owned by Cormorant Shipbuilding and operated by Osprey Ship Management. Cargo includes Army watercraft and port support equipment. Rated as a heavy lift ship and stationed at Diego Garcia.

AMERICAN CORMORANT *8/1989, W Sartori*

820 USA / Afloat prepositioning force (PREPO) — Maritime prepositioning ship (MPS) programme

1 TANKER TYPE: TRANSPORT OILER (AOT)

Name	No	Builders	Commissioned	F/S
POTOMAC	TAOT 181	Sun Shipbuilding	Jan 1957	PREPO

Displacement, tons: 34 700 full load
Dimensions, feet (metres): 614.5 × 83.5 × 33.7 *(187.3 × 25.5 × 10.3)*
Main machinery: 2 boilers; 2 turbines; 20 460 hp *(15.3 MW)*; 2 shafts
Speed, knots: 18
Complement: 49
Cargo capacity: 1 069 700 cu ft liquids; 30 400 cu ft solids

Comment: Acquired in 1991. Operated by American Foreign Steamship and owned by MARAD.

1 LASH TYPE: CARGO SHIP, BARGE (TAKB)

Name	No	Builders	Completed	F/S
JEB STUART (ex-*Atlantic Forest*)	TAKB 924	Sumitomo Shipbuilding	1969	PREPO

Displacement, tons: 66 629 full load
Dimensions, feet (metres): 857 × 106 × 40 *(261.2 × 32.3 × 12.2)*
Speed, knots: 17
Complement: 27
Cargo capacity: 1 683 191 cu ft

Comment: Acquired 8 December 1992 for Army PREPO and assigned to Diego Garcia. Owned and operated by Waterman Steamship Company.

2 RO-RO CONTAINERS: CARGO SHIPS (TAK)

Name	No	Builders	Completed	F/S
AMERICAN MERLIN (ex-*CGM Utrillo*)	TAK 323	Chantiers Navigation de la Ciotat	1978	MED PREPO
BUFFALO SOLDIER (ex-*CGM Monet*)	TAK 322	Chantiers Navigation de la Ciotat	1978	MED PREPO

Displacement, tons: 40 357 full load
Dimensions, feet (metres): 670 × 87 × 34.5 *(204.2 × 26.5 × 10.5)*
Speed, knots: 16
Complement: 23
Cargo capacity: 1 517 447 cu ft

Comment: Reflagged French Government Line ships. *American Merlin* owned by American Automar and operated by American Ship Management. *Buffalo Soldier* owned and operated by Red River Shipping.

1 RO-RO CONTAINER: CARGO SHIP (TAK)

Name	No	Builders	Completed	F/S
STRONG VIRGINIA (ex-*Saint Magnus*)	—	Bremer-Vegesach, Germany	1984	PREPO

Displacement, tons: 31 390 full load
Dimensions, feet (metres): 512 × 105 × 29.6 *(156.1 × 32 × 9)*
Speed, knots: 16.5
Complement: 33
Cargo capacity: 855 859 cu ft

Comment: Reflagged Antigua/Barbuda flag with heavy lift capability. Stationed at Diego Garcia with Navy fleet hospital aboard. Owned and operated by Van Ommeren Shipping Inc.

1 TANKER TYPE: TRANSPORT OILER (TAOT)

Name	No	Builders	Completed	F/S
AMERICAN OSPREY	TAOT 5075	Bethlehem Steel, MD	1958	PREPO

Displacement, tons: 44 840 full load
Dimensions, feet (metres): 661.1 × 89.9 × 36.1 *(201.5 × 27.4 × 11)*
Main machinery: 2 Combustion Engineering boilers; 2 Bethlehem turbines; 15 000 hp *(11.19 MW)*; 1 shaft
Speed, knots: 17. **Range, miles:** 14 000 at 17 kts
Complement: 37
Cargo capacity: 268 000 bbls fuel oil

Comment: Acquired by MARAD in 1984 and operated by American Foreign Steamship. Ship has been fitted with the Offshore Petroleum Discharge System.

AMERICAN OSPREY   8/1990, Giorgio Arra

MARITIME PREPOSITIONING SHIP (MPS) PROGRAMME

Notes: (1) The Navy has been able to achieve a notable increase in its lift capability by the construction of five ships and the conversion of eight others. These are now divided into three squadrons, each of which contains the equipment for one Marine Expeditionary Brigade (MEB). Lift capability can also be augmented by the eight Algol class fast logistics ships. These amphibious elements are supported by two maintenance aviation support ships, nine crane ships and two hospital ships. The maintenance aviation support ships and the hospital ships are maintained in a reduced operating status and the crane ships as a part of the Ready Reserve Force.

(2) With the ending of Marine Expeditionary Brigades (MEB), each MPS squadron supports a Marine Expeditionary Force (MEF) up to brigade level. Squadron 1 supports MEF II, Squadron 2 supports MEF I and Squadron 3 supports MEF III.
(3) Strictly speaking, only the 13 T-AKs are MPS ships but it is convenient to place the details of fast sealift ships, aviation support ships and crane ships in this section.

5 CPL LOUIS J HAUGE, JR CLASS: VEHICLE CARGO SHIPS (T-AK)

Name	No	Builders	Completed	F/S
CPL LOUIS J HAUGE, JR (ex-MV *Estelle Maersk*)	T-AK 3000	Odense Staalskibsvaerft A/S, Lindo	Oct 1979	Sqn 2
PFC WILLIAM B BAUGH (ex-MV *Eleo Maersk*)	T-AK 3001	Odense Staalskibsvaerft A/S, Lindo	Apr 1979	Sqn 2
PFC JAMES ANDERSON, JR (ex-MV *Emma Maersk*)	T-AK 3002	Odense Staalskibsvaerft A/S, Lindo	July 1979	Sqn 2
1st LT ALEX BONNYMAN (ex-MV *Emilie Maersk*)	T-AK 3003	Odense Staalskibsvaerft A/S, Lindo	Jan 1980	Sqn 2
PVT FRANKLIN J PHILLIPS (ex-*Pvt Harry Fisher*, ex-MV *Evelyn Maersk*)	T-AK 3004	Odense Staalskibsvaerft A/S, Lindo	Apr 1980	Sqn 2

Displacement, tons: 46 552 full load
Dimensions, feet (metres): 755 × 90 × 37.1 *(230 × 27.4 × 11.3)*
Main machinery: 1 Sulzer 7RND76M diesel; 16 800 hp(m) *(12.35 MW)*; 1 shaft
Speed, knots: 17.5. **Range, miles:** 10 800 at 16 kts
Complement: 27 plus 10 technicians
Cargo capacity: Containers, 361; Ro-ro, 121 595 sq ft; JP-5 bbls, 17 128; DF-2 bbls, 10 642; Mogas bbls, 3865; stable water, 2022; cranes, 3 twin 30 ton; 92 831 cu ft breakbulk
Helicopters: Platform only.

Comment: Converted from five Maersk Line ships by Bethlehem Steel, Sparrow Point, MD; T-AK 3000, 3002 and 3004 delivered 7 September 1984, 26 March 1985 and 24 September 1985 respectively and by Bethlehem Steel, Beaumont, TX; T-AK 3001 and 3003 delivered 12 September 1985 and 30 October 1985 respectively. Conversion work included the addition of 157 ft *(47.9 m)* amidships.

3 SGT MATEJ KOCAK CLASS: VEHICLE CARGO SHIPS (T-AK)

Name	No	Builders	Completed	F/S
SGT MATEJ KOCAK (ex-SS *John B Waterman*)	T-AK 3005	Pennsylvania SB Co, Chester, Pa	Mar 1981	Sqn 1
PFC EUGENE A OBREGON (ex-SS *Thomas Heywood*)	T-AK 3006	Pennsylvania SB Co, Chester, Pa	Nov 1982	Sqn 1
MAJ STEPHEN W PLESS (ex-SS *Charles Carroll*)	T-AK 3007	General Dynamics Corp, Quincy, Mass	Mar 1983	Sqn 1

Displacement, tons: 48 754 full load
Dimensions, feet (metres): 821 × 105.6 × 32.3 *(250.2 × 32.2 × 9.8)*
Main machinery: 2 boilers; 2 GE turbines; 30 000 hp *(22.4 MW)*; 1 shaft
Speed, knots: 20. **Range, miles:** 13 000 at 20 kts
Complement: 29 plus 10 technicians
Cargo capacity: Containers, 532; Ro-ro, 152 236 sq ft; JP-5 bbls, 20 290; DF-2 bbls, 12 355; Mogas bbls, 3717; stable water, 2189; cranes, 2 twin 50 ton and 1–30 ton gantry
Helicopters: Platform only.

Comment: Converted from three Waterman Line ships by National Steel and Shipbuilding, San Diego. Delivery dates T-AK 3005, 1 October 1984; T-AK 3006, 16 January 1985; T-AK 3007, 15 May 1985. Conversion work included the addition of 157 ft *(47.9 m)* amidships.

LOUIS J HAUGE   1/1991, van Ginderen Collection

MATEJ KOCAK   6/1991, Giorgio Arra

5 2nd LT JOHN P BOBO CLASS: VEHICLE CARGO SHIPS (T-AK)

Name	No	Builders	Completed	F/S
2nd LT JOHN P BOBO	T-AK 3008	General Dynamics Corp, Quincy, Mass	14 Feb 1985	Sqn 1
PFC DEWAYNE T WILLIAMS	T-AK 3009	General Dynamics Corp, Quincy, Mass	6 June 1985	Sqn 3
1st LT BALDOMERO LOPEZ	T-AK 3010	General Dynamics Corp, Quincy, Mass	20 Nov 1985	Sqn 3
1st LT JACK LUMMUS	T-AK 3011	General Dynamics Corp, Quincy, Mass	6 Mar 1986	Sqn 3
SGT WILLIAM R BUTTON	T-AK 3012	General Dynamics Corp, Quincy, Mass	27 May 1986	Sqn 3

Displacement, tons: 44 330 full load
Dimensions, feet (metres): 675.2 × 105.5 × 29.6 *(205.8 × 32.2 × 9)*
Main machinery: 2 Stork Werkspoor 18TM410 diesels; 27 000 hp(m) *(19.84 MW)* sustained; 1 shaft; bow thruster; 1000 hp *(746 kW)*
Speed, knots: 18. **Range, miles:** 12 840 at 18 kts
Complement: 30 plus 10 technicians
Cargo capacity: Containers, 530; Ro-ro, 152 185 sq ft; JP-5 bbls, 20 776; DF-2 bbls, 13 334; Mogas bbls, 4880; stable water, 2357; cranes, 1 single and 2 twin 39 ton
Helicopters: Platform only.

Comment: Operated by American Overseas Marine on a long charter. Each squadron supports a Marine Expeditionary Force.

JACK LUMMUS   9/1991, Giorgio Arra

8 ALGOL CLASS: VEHICLE CARGO SHIPS (T-AKR)

Name	No	Builders	Delivered
ALGOL (ex-SS *Sea-Land Exchange*)	T-AKR 287	Rotterdamsche DD Mij NV, Rotterdam	7 May 1973
BELLATRIX (ex-SS *Sea-Land Trade*)	T-AKR 288	Rheinstahl Nordseewerke, Emden, West Germany	6 Apr 1973
DENEBOLA (ex-SS *Sea-Land Resource*)	T-AKR 289	Rotterdamsche DD Mij NV, Rotterdam	4 Dec 1973
POLLUX (ex-SS *Sea-Land Market*)	T-AKR 290	A G Weser, Bremen, West Germany	20 Sep 1973
ALTAIR (ex-SS *Sea-Land Finance*)	T-AKR 291	Rheinstahl Nordseewerke, Emden, West Germany	17 Sep 1973
REGULUS (ex-SS *Sea-Land Commerce*)	T-AKR 292	A G Weser, Bremen, West Germany	30 Mar 1973
CAPELLA (ex-SS *Sea-Land McLean*)	T-AKR 293	Rotterdamsche DD Mij NV, Rotterdam	4 Oct 1972
ANTARES (ex-SS *Sea-Land Galloway*)	T-AKR 294	A G Weser, Bremen, West Germany	27 Sep 1972

Displacement, tons: 55 355 full load
Measurement, tons: 25 389 net; 27 051-28 095 dwt
Dimensions, feet (metres): 946.2 × 106 × 34.8 *(288.4 × 32.3 × 10.6)*
Main machinery: 2 Foster-Wheeler boilers; 875 psi *(61.6 kg/cm sq)*; 950°F *(510°C)*; 2 GE MST-19 steam turbines; 120 000 hp *(89.5 MW)*; 2 shafts
Speed, knots: 30. **Range, miles:** 12 200 at 27 kts
Complement: 42 (as merchant ship); 24 (minimum)
Helicopters: Platform only.

Comment: All originally built as container-ships for Sea-Land Services Inc, Port Elizabeth, New Jersey but reported as using too much fuel to be cost effective as merchant ships. Six ships of this class were approved for acquisition in FY 1981 and the remaining two in FY 1982. The purchase price included 4000 containers and 800 container chassis for use in container ship configuration. All eight converted to Vehicle Cargo Ships (AKR). Conversion included the addition of roll-on/roll-off features. The area between the forward and after superstructures allows for a helicopter flight deck and hangar. The capacities are as follows: (square feet) enclosed roll-on/roll-off and helo hangar 114 000—128 000, flight deck 32 000 and light vehicle roll-on/roll-off aft 17 500. In addition to one roll-on/roll-off ramp port and starboard, twin 35-ton pedestal cranes are installed between the deckhouses and twin 50-ton cranes are installed aft to facilitate lift-on/lift-off cargo operations. 93 per cent of an army mechanised division can be lifted using all eight ships.
Seven of the class (*Antares* broke down) moved some nine per cent of all cargo transported between the US and Saudi Arabia during and after the war with Iraq and six were activated for the Somalian operation in December 1992. All are based in Atlantic and Gulf of Mexico ports. They will probably be augmented by 25 kt diesel propelled ships which will be cheaper to build and maintain.

DENEBOLA   7/1992, Jürg Kürsener

Maritime prepositioning ship (MPS) programme / USA

2 T-AVB 3 CLASS: MAINTENANCE AVIATION/SUPPORT SHIPS (T-AVB)

Name	No	Builders	Completed
WRIGHT (ex-SS *Young America*)	T-AVB 3	Ingalls SB Corp, Pascagoula, Miss	1970
CURTISS (ex-SS *Great Republic*)	T-AVB 4	Ingalls SB Corp, Pascagoula, Miss	1969

Displacement, tons: 23 872 full load
Measurement, tons: 11 757 gross; 6850 net; 15 946 dwt
Dimensions, feet (metres): 602 × 90.2 × 29.8 *(183.5 × 27.5 × 9.1)*
Main machinery: 2 Combustion Engineering boilers; 2 GE turbines; 30 000 hp *(22.4 MW)*; 1 shaft
Speed, knots: 23. **Range, miles:** 9000 at 22 kts
Complement: 41 crew and 1 Aircraft Maintenance Detachment totalling 366 men

Comment: To further reinforce the capabilities of the Maritime Prepositioning Ship programme, conversion of two ro-ro ships into maintenance aviation support ships was approved in FY 1985 and FY 1986. *Wright* was completed 14 May 1986, *Curtiss* 18 August 1987. Both conversions took place at Todd Shipyards, Galveston, Texas. Each ship has side ports and three decks aft of the bridge superstructure and has the capability to load the vans and equipment of a Marine Aviation Intermediate Maintenance Activity. The ships' mission is to service aircraft until their containerised units can be offloaded. They can then revert to a standard sealift role if required. Maritime Administration hull design is C5-S-78a. They are maintained by MARAD in the RRF.

WRIGHT   10/1991, 92 Wing RAAF

9 KEYSTONE STATE CLASS: AUXILIARY CRANE SHIPS (T-ACS)

Name	No	Builders	Conversion Completed
KEYSTONE STATE (ex-SS *President Harrison*)	T-ACS 1	Defoe SB Co, Bay City	1984
GEM STATE (ex-SS *President Monroe*)	T-ACS 2	Defoe SB Co, Bay City	1985
GRAND CANYON STATE (ex-SS *President Polk*)	T-ACS 3	Dillingham S R, Portland	1986
GOPHER STATE (ex-*Export Leader*)	T-ACS 4	Norshipco, Norfolk	Oct 1987
FLICKERTAIL STATE (ex-*Export Lightning*)	T-ACS 5	Norshipco, Norfolk	Dec 1987
CORNHUSKER STATE (ex-*Staghound*)	T-ACS 6	Norshipco, Norfolk	Mar 1988
DIAMOND STATE (ex-*President Truman*)	T-ACS 7	Tampa SY	Jan 1989
EQUALITY STATE (ex-*American Banker*)	T-ACS 8	Tampa SY	May 1989
GREEN MOUNTAIN STATE (ex-*American Altair*)	T-ACS 9	Norshipco, Norfolk	Sep 1990

Displacement, tons: 31 500 full load
Dimensions, feet (metres): 668.6 × 76.1 × 33.5 *(203.8 × 23.2 × 10.2)*
Main machinery: 2 boilers; 2 GE turbines; 19 250 hp *(14.4 MW)*; 1 shaft
Speed, knots: 20. **Range, miles:** 13 000 at 20 kts
Complement: 89
Cargo capacity: 300+ standard containers

Comment: Auxiliary crane ships are container ships to which have been added up to three twin boom pedestal cranes which will lift containerised or other cargo from itself or adjacent vessels and deposit it on a pier or into lighterage. Since a significant portion of the US merchant fleet is composed of non-self sustaining container ships lacking integral cranes, thus needing a fully developed port to unload, a requirement exists for crane ships that can unload others in areas of the world which have very simple, damaged or no developed port facilities. Funds provided in the FY 1988 budget for conversion of T-ACS 9 and 10 were transferred to other Navy SCN accounts. Funding for T-ACS 9 was then taken from Maritime Administration budgets. The 10th ship was cancelled in 1991. There are minor dimensional differences between ships of the class. Five of the ships were deployed to the Gulf in 1990-91 but the excellent Saudi harbour facilities meant that dockside cranes were available to unload cargoes, so their particular talents were not required other than as standard cargo ships.

DIAMOND STATE   4/1992, 92 Wing RAAF

DEEP SUBMERGENCE VEHICLES

(Included in US Naval Vessel Register)

Note: The US Navy acquired its first deep submergence vehicle with the purchase in 1958 of the bathyscope *Trieste*, designed and constructed by Professor Auguste Piccard.
Trieste reached a record depth of 35 800 ft *(10 910 m)* in the Challenger Deep off the Marianas on 23 January 1960, being piloted by Lieutenant Don Walsh, USN, and Jacques Piccard (son of Auguste). Rebuilt and designated *Trieste II*. Transferred to Naval museum of Underwater Warfare, Keyport Washington.

After the loss of *Thresher* (SSN 593) in 1963 the US Navy initiated an extensive deep submergence programme that led to construction of two Deep Submergence Rescue Vehicles (DSRV).
Several of these deep submergence vehicles and other craft and support ships are operated by Submarine Development Group One at San Diego, California. The Group is a major operational command that includes advanced diving equipment; divers trained in 'saturation' techniques; the DSVs *Turtle*, *Sea Cliff*, DSRV-1, DSRV-2; the submarine *Dolphin* (AGSS 555); several submarine rescue ships. Two unmanned vessels CURV (Cable Controlled Underwater Remote Vehicle) and ATV (Advanced Tethered Vehicle) made test dives to 20 000 ft *(1800 m)* in late 1990.

1 NUCLEAR-POWERED OCEAN ENGINEERING AND RESEARCH VEHICLE

Name	Builders	In service	F/S
NR 1	General Dynamics (Electric Boat Div)	27 Oct 1969	ASA

Displacement, tons: 380 surfaced; 700 dived
Dimensions, feet (metres): 147 × 12.4 × 14.6 *(44.8 × 3.8 × 4.5)*
Main machinery: Nuclear; 1 PWR; 1 turbo-alternator; 2 motors (external to the hull); 2 props; 4 ducted thrusters (2 vertical, 2 horizontal)
Complement: 7 (2 officers, 2 scientists)

Comment: NR 1 was built primarily to serve as a test platform for a small nuclear propulsion plant; however, the craft additionally provides an advanced deep submergence ocean engineering and research capability. She was the only Naval deep submergence vehicle to be used in the recovery of the wreckage of the space shuttle *Challenger* January-April 1986.
Laid down on 10 June 1967; launched on 25 January 1969. Commanded by an officer-in-charge vice commanding officer. First nuclear-propelled service craft. Refitted with a new bow which extended her length by 9.6 ft, and new sonars and cameras.
The NR 1 is fitted with wheels beneath the hull to permit 'bottom crawling' and she is fitted with external lights, external television cameras, a remote-controlled manipulator, and various recovery devices. No periscopes, but fixed television mast. Diving depth, 2600 ft *(800 m)*. A surface 'mother' ship is required to support her.

2 DEEP SUBMERGENCE RESCUE VEHICLES

Name	No	Builders	In service	F/S
MYSTIC	DSRV 1	Lockheed Missiles and Space Co,	7 Aug 1971	PSA
AVALON	DSRV 2	Sunnyvale, Calif	28 July 1972	ASA

Displacement, tons: 30 surfaced; 38 dived
Dimensions, feet (metres): 49.2 × 8 *(15 × 2.4)*
Main machinery: Electric motors; silver/zinc batteries; 1 prop (movable control shroud); 4 ducted thrusters (2 fwd, 2 aft)
Speed, knots: 4. **Range, miles:** 24 at 3 kts
Complement: 4 (pilot, co-pilot, 2 rescue sphere operators) plus 24 rescued men
Sonars: Search and navigational sonar, and closed-circuit television (supplemented by optical devices) are installed in the DSRV to determine the exact location of a disabled submarine within a given area and for pinpointing the submarine's escape hatches. Side-looking sonar can be fitted for search missions.

Comment: The DSRV is intended to provide a quick-reaction world-wide, all-weather capability for the rescue of survivors in a disabled submarine. Transportable by road, aircraft (in C 141 and C 5 jet cargo aircraft), surface ship (*Ortolan* (ASR 22) submarine rescue ship), and specially modified SSNs.
The carrying submarine will launch and recover the DSRV while submerged and, if necessary, while under ice. A total of six DSRVs were planned, but only two were funded. They alternate their duties every two months.
The outer hull is constructed of formed fibreglass. Within this outer hull are three interconnected spheres which form the main pressure capsule. Each sphere is 7.5 ft in diameter and is constructed of HY-140 steel. The forward sphere contains the vehicle's control equipment and is manned by the pilot and co-pilot, the centre and after spheres accommodate 24 passengers and a third crewman. Under the DSRV's centre sphere is a hemispherical protrusion or 'skirt' which seals over the disabled submarine's hatch. During the mating operation the skirt is pumped dry to enable personnel to transfer. Operating depth, 1525 m *(5000 ft)*. Names are not 'official'. Both have been upgraded with modern electronics and navigation systems.

AVALON   *12/1985, Giorgio Arra*

2 DEEP SUBMERGENCE VEHICLES: MODIFIED ALVIN TYPE

Name	No	Builders	F/S
TURTLE (ex-*Autec II*)	DSV 3	General Dynamics (Electric Boat Div)	PA
SEA CLIFF (ex-*Autec I*)	DSV 4	General Dynamics (Electric Boat Div)	PSA

Displacement, tons: 26 full load
Dimensions, feet (metres): 26 × 10 *(7.9 × 3.1)* (DSV 3); 31 × 12 *(9.5 × 3.7)* (DSV 4)
Main machinery: Electric motors; 1 prop (trainable); 2 thrusters (trainable)
Speed, knots: 2.5. **Range, miles:** 24 at 2 kts
Complement: 3 (pilot, co-pilot, observer)

Comment: Intended for deep submergence research and work tasks. Launched on 11 December 1968 and placed in service on 1 June 1971. In 1979-80 *Turtle* was overhauled and upgraded for operations to 10 000 feet. In 1983-84 *Sea Cliff* provided with titanium sphere giving a depth capability of 20 000 feet. *Sea Cliff* reached a depth of 20 000 feet 10 March 1985. Both vessels have been upgraded with improved cameras, lighting and navigation systems. Twin-arm manipulator fitted. Silver/zinc batteries. Operating depth 3050 m *(10 000 ft)* for DSV 3 and 6100 m *(20 000 ft)* for DSV 4.

NR 1   *1986, US Navy*

1 DEEP SUBMERGENCE VEHICLE: ALVIN TYPE

Name	No	Builders	F/S
ALVIN	DSV 2	General Mills Inc, Minneapolis, Minn	PSA

Displacement, tons: 18 full load
Dimensions, feet (metres): 22.5 × 8.5 *(6.9 × 2.6)*
Main machinery: 6 brushless DC motors; 6 thrusters; 2 vertical-motion thrusters (located near the centre of gravity); 2 horizontally (near stern) (1 directed athwartships, 1 directed longitudinally); 2 on rotatable shaft near stern for vertical or longitudinal motion
Speed, knots: 1.5. **Range, miles:** 6-10 at 1 kt
Complement: 3 (1 pilot, 2 observers)

Comment: *Alvin* was built for operation by the Woods Hole Oceanographic Institution for the Office of Naval Research. Original configuration had an operating depth of 6000 ft. Named for Allyn C Vine of Woods Hole Oceanographic Institution. *Alvin* accidentally sank in 5051 ft of water on 16 October 1968; subsequently raised in August 1969; refurbished 1970-71 in original configuration. Placed in service on Navy List 1 June 1971. Subsequently refitted with titanium pressure sphere to provide increased depth capability and again operational in November 1973. Currently leased to Wood's Hole. She has three banks of lead acid batteries, 120 and 30 volt DC systems with 72 KHW capacity. Operating depth, 4000 m *(13 120 ft)*.

TURTLE   *7/1988, W Donko*

1 MOTHER SHIP

LANEY CHOUEST

Measurement, tons: 497 grt
Dimensions, feet (metres): 233.9 × 49.9 × 14.1 *(71.3 × 15.2 × 4.3)*
Main machinery: 3 GM/EMD 16-710G7 diesels; 9210 hp *(6.87 MW)*; 3 shafts
Speed, knots: 16
Complement: 24

Comment: Acts as the mother ship to the DSVs.

LANEY CHOUEST (tender) 5/1991, Stefan Terzibaschitsch

COAST GUARD

Senior Officers

Commandant:
  Admiral J William Kime
Vice-Commandant:
  Vice Admiral Robert T Nelson
Chief of Staff:
  Rear Admiral Robert E Kramek
Commander, Atlantic Area:
  Vice Admiral Paul A Welling
Commander, Pacific Area:
  Vice Admiral Martin H Daniell

Establishment

The United States Coast Guard was established by an Act of Congress approved 28 January 1915, which consolidated the Revenue Cutter Service (founded in 1790) and the Life Saving Service (founded in 1848). The act of establishment stated the Coast Guard "shall be a military service and a branch of the armed forces of the USA at all times. The Coast Guard shall be a service in the Treasury Department except when operating as a service in the Navy".
Congress further legislated that in time of national emergency or when the President so directs, the Coast Guard operates as a part of the Navy. Some ships of the Coast Guard did operate as a part of the Navy during the First and Second World Wars and the Vietnam War.
The Lighthouse Service (founded in 1789) was transferred to the Coast Guard on 1 July 1939 and the Bureau of Navigation and Steamboat Inspection on 28 February 1942.
The Coast Guard was transferred to the newly established Department of Transportation on 1 April 1967.

Personnel

1 Jan 1993: 5823 officers, 1535 warrant officers,
30 910 enlisted men, 903 cadets,
159 Public Health Service personnel,
10 576 reserves (1600 officers).

Missions

The current missions of the Coast Guard are to (1) enforce or assist in the enforcement of applicable Federal laws upon the high seas and waters subject to the jurisdiction of the USA including environmental protection; (2) administer all Federal laws regarding safety of life and property on the high seas and on waters subject to the jurisdiction of the USA, except those laws specifically entrusted to other Federal agencies; (3) develop, establish, maintain, operate, and conduct aids to maritime navigation, ocean stations, icebreaking activities, oceanographic research, and rescue facilities; and (4) maintain a state of readiness to function as a specialised service in the Navy when so directed by the President.

Cutter Strength

All Coast Guard vessels over 65 ft in length and that have adequate crew accommodation are referred to as 'cutters'. All names are preceded by USCG. The first two digits of the hull number for all Coast Guard vessels under 100 ft in length indicates the approximate length overall.
Approximately 2000 standard and non-standard boats are in service ranging in size from 11 ft skiffs to 55 ft aids-to-navigation craft.

Category/Classification		Active	Building
Cutters			
WHEC	High Endurance Cutters	12	—
WMEC	Medium Endurance Cutters	35	—
Icebreakers			
WAGB	Icebreakers	3	(1)
WTGB	Icebreaking Tugs	9	—
Patrol Craft			
WSES	Surface Effect Craft	3	—
WPB	Patrol Craft, Large	91	—

Training Cutter			
WIX	Training Cutter	1	—
Buoy Tenders			
WLB	Buoy Tenders, Seagoing	27	1 (4)
WLM	Buoy Tenders, Coastal	11	—
WLI	Buoy Tenders, Inland	6	—
WLR	Buoy Tenders, River	18	—
Construction Tenders			
WLIC	Construction Tenders, Inland	16	—
Harbour Tugs			
WYTL	Harbour Tugs, Small	14	—
SAR Craft		2000+	—

DELETIONS

Medium Endurance Cutters

1990 *Clover, Evergreen*
1991 *Chilula, Cherokee*

Patrol Craft

1990 *Cape Cross* (Micronesia), *Cape George* (Micronesia), *Cape Carter* (Mexico), *Cape Higgon* (Uruguay), *Cape Horn* (Uruguay), *Cape Corwin* (Micronesia)
1991 *Cape Hatteras* (Mexico), *Point Hope* (Costa Rica), *Point Verde* (Mexico), *Point Herron* (Mexico), *Point Roberts, Point Judith* (Venezuela), *Point Barrow* (Panama), *Point Charles, Point Knoll* (Venezuela)
1992 *Point Thatcher, Point Brown, Point Harris*

Tenders

1990 *Mesquite, Dogwood, Lantana*
1991 *Fir, Salvia*
1993 *Blackhaw*

HIGH ENDURANCE CUTTERS

CHASE 7/1992, Per Kornefeldt

824   USA (COAST GUARD) / High endurance cutters — Medium endurance cutters

12 HAMILTON and HERO CLASSES (WHEC)

Name	No	Builders	Laid down	Launched	Commissioned	F/S
HAMILTON	WHEC 715	Avondale Shipyards Inc, New Orleans, Louisiana	Jan 1965	18 Dec 1965	20 Feb 1967	PA
DALLAS	WHEC 716	Avondale Shipyards Inc, New Orleans, Louisiana	7 Feb 1966	1 Oct 1966	1 Oct 1967	AA
MELLON	WHEC 717	Avondale Shipyards Inc, New Orleans, Louisiana	25 July 1966	11 Feb 1967	22 Dec 1967	PA
CHASE	WHEC 718	Avondale Shipyards Inc, New Orleans, Louisiana	27 Oct 1966	20 May 1967	1 Mar 1968	PA
BOUTWELL	WHEC 719	Avondale Shipyards Inc, New Orleans, Louisiana	5 Dec 1966	17 June 1967	14 June 1968	PA
SHERMAN	WHEC 720	Avondale Shipyards Inc, New Orleans, Louisiana	23 Jan 1967	23 Sep 1967	23 Aug 1968	PA
GALLATIN	WHEC 721	Avondale Shipyards Inc, New Orleans, Louisiana	27 Feb 1967	18 Nov 1967	20 Dec 1968	AA
MORGENTHAU	WHEC 722	Avondale Shipyards Inc, New Orleans, Louisiana	17 July 1967	10 Feb 1968	14 Feb 1969	PA
RUSH	WHEC 723	Avondale Shipyards Inc, New Orleans, Louisiana	23 Oct 1967	16 Nov 1968	3 July 1969	PA
MUNRO	WHEC 724	Avondale Shipyards Inc, New Orleans, Louisiana	18 Feb 1970	5 Dec 1970	10 Sep 1971	PA
JARVIS	WHEC 725	Avondale Shipyards Inc, New Orleans, Louisiana	9 Sep 1970	24 Apr 1971	30 Dec 1971	PA
MIDGETT	WHEC 726	Avondale Shipyards Inc, New Orleans, Louisiana	5 Apr 1971	4 Sep 1971	17 Mar 1972	PA

Displacement, tons: 3050 full load
Dimensions, feet (metres): 378 × 42.8 × 20 (sonar)
(115.2 × 13.1 × 6.1)
Flight deck, feet (metres): 88 × 40 (26.8 × 12.2)
Main machinery: CODOG; 2 Pratt & Whitney FT4A-6 gas turbines; 36 000 hp (26.86 MW); 2 Fairbanks-Morse 38TD8-1/8-12 diesels; 7000 hp (5.22 MW) sustained; 2 shafts; cp props; retractable bow propulsor; 350 hp (261 kW)
Speed, knots: 29. **Range, miles:** 14 000 at 11 kts diesels; 2400 at 29 kts gas
Complement: 179 (21 officers)

Missiles: SSM: 8 McDonnell Douglas Harpoon ❶; active radar homing to 130 km (70 nm) at 0.9 mach; warhead 227 kg. Not in all and being removed.
Guns: 1 OTO Melara 3 in (76 mm)/62 Mk 75 Compact ❷; 85° elevation; 85 rounds/minute to 16 km (8.7 nm) anti-surface; 12 km (6.6 nm) anti-aircraft; weight of shell 6 kg.
2 Aerospace 20 mm/80 Mk 67 or 2 McDonnell Douglas 25 mm/87 Mk 38 (being retrofitted). 4—12.7 mm MGs.
1 GE/GD 20 mm Vulcan Phalanx 6 barrelled Mk 15 ❸; 3000 rounds/minute combined to 1.5 km. Not in all.
Torpedoes: 6—324 mm Mk 32 (2 triple) tubes ❹. Honeywell Mk 46; anti-submarine; active/passive homing to 11 km (5.9 nm) at 40 kts; warhead 44 kg (being removed).
Countermeasures: Decoys: 2 Loral Hycor SRBOC 6-barrelled fixed Mk 36; IR flares and chaff.
ESM: WLR-1C, WLR-3; radar warning.
Combat data systems: SCCS (to be fitted to all by 1996) includes OTCIXS satellite link.
Fire control: Mk 92 Mod 1 GFCS. Mk 309 ASW (being removed).
Radars: Air search: Lockheed SPS 40B ❺; D/E band.
Surface search: Raytheon SPS 64(V)6 ❻; I band.
Fire control: Sperry Mk 92 ❼; I/J band.
Tacan: URN 25.

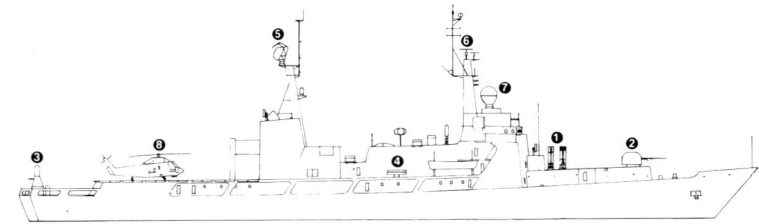

HAMILTON

(Scale 1 : 1200), Ian Sturton

Sonars: EDO SQS 38; hull-mounted; active search and attack; medium frequency (being removed).

Helicopters: 1 HH-65A or LAMPS I ❽.

Programmes: In the Autumn of 1977 Gallatin and Morgenthau were the first of the Coast Guard ships to have women assigned as permanent members of the crew.
Modernisation: FRAM programme for all 12 ships in this class from October 1985 to October 1992. Work included standardising the engineering plants, improving the clutching systems, replacing SPS 29 air-search radar with SPS 40 radar and replacing the Mk 56 fire control system and 5 in/38 gun mount with the Mk 92 system and a single 76 mm OTO Melara Compact gun. In addition Harpoon and Phalanx CIWS fitted to five of the class by 1992. The flight deck and other aircraft facilities upgraded to handle the LAMPS I helicopter including a telescopic hangar. URN 25 Tacan added along with the SQR 4 and SQR 17 sonobuoy receiving set and passive acoustic analysis systems. SRBOC chaff launchers are also fitted but not improved ESM which has been shelved along with towed array sonar. All sonar and ASW equipment is being removed in 1993/94. 25 mm Mk 38 guns are replacing the 20 mm Mk 67. Shipboard Command and Control System (SCCS) is to be fitted to all of the class by 1996; Hamilton and Dallas fitted by late 1992.
Structure: These ships have clipper bows, twin funnels enclosing a helicopter hangar, helicopter platform aft. All are fitted with elaborate communications equipment. Superstructure is largely of aluminium construction. Bridge control of manoeuvring is by aircraft-type joystick rather than wheel. Engine and propeller pitch consoles are located in wheelhouse and at bridge wing stations as well as engine room control booth.
Operational: Mellon fired the first Harpoon missile to be fitted in this class on 16 January 1990. Ten of the class are based in the Pacific, leaving only two on the East Coast. In July 1992 a decision was made to remove all missiles, sonar and ASW equipment.

MEDIUM ENDURANCE CUTTERS

13 FAMOUS CUTTER CLASS (WMEC)

Name	No	Builders	Laid down	Launched	Commissioned	F/S
BEAR	WMEC 901	Tacoma Boatbuilding Co, Tacoma	23 Aug 1979	25 Sep 1980	4 Feb 1983	AA
TAMPA	WMEC 902	Tacoma Boatbuilding Co, Tacoma	3 Apr 1980	19 Mar 1981	16 Mar 1984	AA
HARRIET LANE	WMEC 903	Tacoma Boatbuilding Co, Tacoma	15 Oct 1980	6 Feb 1982	20 Sep 1984	AA
NORTHLAND	WMEC 904	Tacoma Boatbuilding Co, Tacoma	9 Apr 1981	7 May 1982	17 Dec 1984	AA
SPENCER	WMEC 905	Robert E Derecktor Corp, Middletown, RI	26 June 1982	17 Apr 1984	28 June 1986	AA
SENECA	WMEC 906	Robert E Derecktor Corp, Middletown, RI	16 Sep 1982	17 Apr 1984	4 May 1987	AA
ESCANABA	WMEC 907	Robert E Derecktor Corp, Middletown, RI	1 Apr 1983	6 Feb 1985	27 Aug 1987	AA
TAHOMA	WMEC 908	Robert E Derecktor Corp, Middletown, RI	28 June 1983	6 Feb 1985	6 Apr 1988	AA
CAMPBELL	WMEC 909	Robert E Derecktor Corp, Middletown, RI	10 Aug 1984	29 Apr 1986	19 Aug 1988	AA
THETIS	WMEC 910	Robert E Derecktor Corp, Middletown, RI	24 Aug 1984	29 Apr 1986	30 June 1989	AA
FORWARD	WMEC 911	Robert E Derecktor Corp, Middletown, RI	11 July 1986	22 Aug 1987	4 Aug 1990	AA
LEGARE	WMEC 912	Robert E Derecktor Corp, Middletown, RI	11 July 1986	22 Aug 1987	4 Aug 1990	AA
MOHAWK	WMEC 913	Robert E Derecktor Corp, Middletown, RI	15 Mar 1987	5 May 1988	20 Mar 1991	AA

Displacement, tons: 1780 full load
Dimensions, feet (metres): 270 × 38 × 13.5
(82.3 × 11.6 × 4.1)
Main machinery: 2 Alco 18V-251 diesels; 7290 hp (5.44 MW) sustained; 2 shafts; cp props
Speed, knots: 19.5. **Range, miles:** 9500 at 13 kts, 3850 at 19.5 kts
Complement: 100 (14 officers) plus 16 aircrew when LAMPS is embarked

Guns: 1 OTO Melara 3 in (76 mm)/62 Mk 75 ❶; 85° elevation; 85 rounds/minute to 16 km (8.7 nm) anti-surface; 12 km (6.6 nm) anti-aircraft; weight of shell 6 kg.
2—12.7 mm MGs and/or 2—40 mm Mk 19 grenade launchers ❷.
Countermeasures: Decoys: 2 Loral Hycor SRBOC 6-barrelled fixed Mk 36; IR flares and chaff.
ESM/ECM: SLQ 32(V)2; radar intercept.
Combat data systems: Sperry COMDAC. OTCIXS satellite link (being fitted).
Radars: Surface search: Raytheon SPS 64(V) ❸; I band.
Fire control: Sperry Mk 92 Mod 1 ❹; I/J band.
Tacan: URN 25.

Helicopters: 1 HH-65A ❺ or LAMPS I or 1 LAMPS III.

Programmes: This class has replaced the Campbell class and other medium and high endurance cutters. The contract for construction of WMEC 905-913 was originally awarded to Tacoma Boatbuilding Co on 29 August 1980. However, under lawsuit from the Robert E Derecktor Corp, Middletown, Rhode Island, the contract to Tacoma was determined by a US District Court to be invalid and was awarded to Robert E Derecktor Corp on 15 January 1981. The cutters WMEC 901-902 were authorised in FY 1977, WMEC 903-904 in FY 1978, WMEC 905-906 in FY 1979, WMEC 907-909 in FY 1980, WMEC 910 in FY 1981, and WMEC 911-913 in FY 1982. Confusion over commissioning dates has arisen in the past because ships are placed 'in service' on leaving the builder but not commissioned until all defects have been rectified.
Modernisation: OTCIXS satellite link being fitted from 1992.

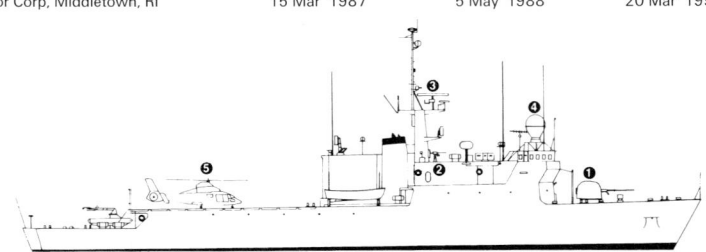

BEAR

(Scale 1 : 900), Ian Sturton

BEAR

9/1992, Maritime Photographic

Structure: They are the only medium endurance cutters with a helicopter hangar (which is telescopic) and the first cutters with automated command and control centre. Fin stabilisers fitted. Thetis has been fitted with the French DCN Talon landing and hold down helicopter system, which in due course is to be retrofitted to all helicopter capable cutters. Plans to fit SSM and/or CIWS have been abandoned as has towed array sonar.

Operational: No A/S weapons other than those carried by helicopter. Bases are at Portsmouth, New Bedford, Key West and Boston. Reported to be very lively in heavy seas perhaps because the length to beam ratio is unusually small for ships required to operate in Atlantic conditions.

Medium endurance cutters / USA (COAST GUARD) 825

16 RELIANCE CLASS (WMEC)

Name	No	Builders	Commissioned	MMA completion	F/S
RELIANCE	WMEC 615	Todd Shipyards	20 June 1964	Jan 1989	AA (Newcastle)
DILIGENCE	WMEC 616	Todd Shipyards	26 Aug 1964	Mar 1992	AA (Wilmington)
VIGILANT	WMEC 617	Todd Shipyards	3 Oct 1964	Aug 1990	AA (Cape Canaveral)
ACTIVE	WMEC 618	Christy Corp	17 Sep 1966	Feb 1987	PA (Port Angeles)
CONFIDENCE	WMEC 619	Coast Guard Yard, Baltimore	19 Feb 1966	June 1988	AA (Cape Canaveral)
RESOLUTE	WMEC 620	Coast Guard Yard, Baltimore	8 Dec 1966	Nov 1995	PA (Astoria)
VALIANT	WMEC 621	American Shipbuilding Co	28 Oct 1967	May 1993	AA (Miami)
COURAGEOUS	WMEC 622	American Shipbuilding Co	10 Apr 1968	Mar 1990	AA (Panama City)
STEADFAST	WMEC 623	American Shipbuilding Co	25 Sep 1968	Nov 1993	PA (Astoria)
DAUNTLESS	WMEC 624	American Shipbuilding Co	10 June 1968	Nov 1994	MMA/AA (Galveston)
VENTUROUS	WMEC 625	American Shipbuilding Co	16 Aug 1968	May 1995	MMA/PA (St Petersburg)
DEPENDABLE	WMEC 626	American Shipbuilding Co	22 Nov 1968	May 1996	AA (Galveston)
VIGOROUS	WMEC 627	American Shipbuilding Co	2 May 1969	Nov 1992	AA (Cape May)
DURABLE	WMEC 628	Coast Guard Yard, Baltimore	8 Dec 1967	Jan 1989	AA (St Petersburg)
DECISIVE	WMEC 629	Coast Guard Yard, Baltimore	23 Aug 1968	Nov 1996	AA (St Petersburg)
ALERT	WMEC 630	Coast Guard Yard, Baltimore	4 Aug 1969	May 1994	AA (Astoria)

Displacement, tons: 950 standard; 1007 (1129 after MMA) full load (WMEC 620-630)
970 (1110 after MMA) full load (WMEC 618, 619)
Dimensions, feet (metres): 210.5 × 34 × 10.5 (64.2 × 10.4 × 3.2)
Main machinery: 2 Alco 16V-251 diesels; 6480 hp (4.83 MW) sustained; 2 shafts; cp props
Speed, knots: 18. **Range, miles:** 6100 at 14 kts; 2700 at 18 kts
Complement: 74 (12 officers)

Guns: 1 McDonnell Douglas 25 mm/87 Mk 38; 55° elevation; 200 rounds/minute to 6.8 km (3.4 nm) replacing the 3 in (76 mm)/50. 2—12.7 mm MGs.
Radars: Surface search: 2 Raytheon SPS 64(V); I band.

Helicopters: 1 HH-65A embarked as required.

Modernisation: All 16 cutters have undergone or will undergo a Major Maintenance Availability (MMA) which takes approximately 18 months. The exhausts for main engines, ship service generators and boilers are run in a new vertical funnel which reduces flight deck size. Scheduled completion dates are listed above but future dates are at best only estimates. 76 mm guns are being replaced by 25 mm Mk 38.
Structure: Designed for search and rescue duties. Design features include 360 degree visibility from bridge; helicopter flight deck (no hangar); and engine exhaust vent at stern in place of conventional funnel which is being built during MMA. Capable of towing ships up to 10 000 tons. Air-conditioned throughout except engine room; high degree of habitability.
Operational: Normally operate within 500 miles of the coast. All these cutters are active with the exception of those decommissioned for an MMA. Primary roles are SAR, law-enforcement and defence operations. Vessels up to 10 000 tons can be towed.

DAUNTLESS (before MMA) 10/1992, Giorgio Arra

COURAGEOUS (after MMA) 4/1991, Giorgio Arra

1 CHEROKEE CLASS (WMEC)

Name	No	Builders	USN Comm.	F/S
TAMAROA (ex-Zuni)	WMEC 166 (ex-WAT 166, ATF 95)	Commercial Iron Works, Portland, Oregon	9 Oct 1943	AA

Displacement, tons: 1731 full load
Dimensions, feet (metres): 205 × 38.5 × 17 (62.5 × 11.7 × 5.2)
Main machinery: Diesel-electric; 4 GM 12-278A diesels; 4400 hp (3.28 MW); 4 generators; 1 motor; 3000 hp (2.24 MW); 1 shaft
Speed, knots: 16.2. **Range, miles:** 6500 at 16 kts
Complement: 72 (7 officers)
Guns: 1 McDonnell Douglas 25 mm/87 Mk 38 (to be fitted).
Radars: Navigation: Raytheon SPS 64; I band.

Comment: The one remaining cutter of this class was transferred from the Navy to the Coast Guard on loan in 1946 and permanently transferred in 1969. Classification was changed to WMEC in 1968. The 3 in gun has been landed and is to be replaced by a 25 mm Mk 38.

TAMAROA 9/1990, Gilbert Gyssels

3 DIVER CLASS (WMEC)

Name	No	Builders	USN Comm.	F/S
ACUSHNET (ex-USS *Shackle*)	WMEC 167 (ex-WAGO 167, ex-WAT 167, ex-ARS 9)	Basalt Rock Co, Napa, California	5 Feb 1944	PA
YOCONA (ex-USS *Seize*)	WMEC 168 (ex-WAT 168, ex-ARS 26)	Basalt Rock Co, Napa, California	3 Nov 1944	PA
ESCAPE	WMEC 6 (ex-ARS 6)	Basalt Rock Co, Napa, California	20 Nov 1943	AA

Displacement, tons: 1557 standard; 1745 full load
Dimensions, feet (metres): 213.5 × 39 × 15 *(65.1 × 11.9 × 4.6)*
Main machinery: 4 Cooper-Bessemer GSB-8 *(Yocona)*, 4 Caterpillar D 399 diesels; 4500 hp *(3.36 MW)* sustained *(Escape)*, 4 Fairbanks-Morse *(Acushnet)* diesels; 3000 hp *(2.24 MW)*; 2 shafts
Speed, knots: 15.5. **Range, miles:** 9000 at 15 kts
Complement: 64 (7 officers) *(Acushnet)*; 72 (7 officers) *(Yocona)*
Radars: Navigation: 2 Raytheon SPS 64; I band.

Comment: Large, steel-hulled salvage ships transferred from the Navy to the Coast Guard and employed in tug and oceanographic duties. *Acushnet* modified for handling environmental data buoys and reclassified WAGO in 1968 and reclassified WMEC in 1980; *Yocona* reverted to WMEC in 1968. *Escape* transferred on loan from USN on 4 December 1980. Refitted at Curtis Bay Yard in 1980-81. Major renovation work completed on *Acushnet* in 1983 will enable her to continue operating through 1997. Plans to replace *Yocona* have been delayed.

ACUSHNET *5/1989, Giorgio Arra*

ESCAPE (twin masts) *7/1990, Giorgio Arra*

1 STORIS CLASS (WMEC)

Name	No	Builders	Commissioned	F/S
STORIS (ex-*Eskimo*)	WMEC 38 (ex-WAGB 38, ex-WAGL 38)	Toledo Shipbuilding Co, Ohio	30 Sep 1942	PA

Displacement, tons: 1715 standard; 1925 full load
Dimensions, feet (metres): 230 × 43 × 15 *(70.1 × 13.1 × 4.6)*
Main machinery: Diesel-electric; 3 GM EMD diesel generators; 1 motor; 3000 hp *(2.24 MW)*; 1 shaft
Speed, knots: 14. **Range, miles:** 22 000 at 8 kts; 12 000 at 14 kts
Complement: 106 (10 officers)
Guns: 1 USN 3 in *(76 mm)*/50.
Radars: Navigation: Raytheon SPS 64; I band.

Comment: Laid down on 14 July 1941; launched on 4 April 1942 as ice patrol tender. Strengthened for ice navigation and sometimes employed as icebreaker. Employed in Alaskan service for search, rescue and law enforcement. *Storis* completed a major maintenance availability in June 1986, during which her main engines were replaced with EMD diesels and her living quarters expanded.

STORIS *1983, USCG*

5 AEROSTAT SHIPS (ARMY)

Name	Builders	Completed	F/S
ATLANTIC SENTRY	Steiner Marine, Alabama	1986	AA (Key West)
CARIBBEAN SENTRY	Halter Marine, Louisiana	1987	AA (Key West)
GULF SENTRY	Halter Marine, Louisiana	1984	AA (Miami)
PACIFIC SENTRY	Halter Marine, Louisiana	1983	AA (Miami)
WINDWARD SENTRY	McDermott, Louisiana	1979	AA (Key West)

Displacement, tons: 2140 full load
Dimensions, feet (metres): 192 × 44 × 15.1 *(58.5 × 13.4 × 4.6)*
Main machinery: 2 GM EMD 16-645E6 diesels; 3900 hp *(2.91 MW)*; 2 shafts
Speed, knots: 12. **Range, miles:** 7000 at 10 kts
Complement: 10 civilian plus 9 Army

Comment: There are some minor differences between these ships which have been either purchased or leased between April 1987 and November 1989. Each consists of a Mobile Aerostat Platform (MAP) with installed mooring system, a helium-filled aerostat with APS-143(V)2 or APS 128 attached radar, and radar, communications, and computer consoles in the MAP operations centre. Their mission is to provide continuous traffic-surveillance information to other law-enforcement units for the purpose of interdicting drug-trafficking and alien vessels. SBAs normally work in conjunction with Coast Guard cutters and patrol boats but successful operations have also been conducted with other US and foreign naval resources. They are operated throughout the Caribbean Sea, the Gulf of Mexico, and the Straits of Florida, and particularly in choke points between major islands where target vessels must pass. The aerostats are 109 ft long and 37 ft in diameter; their operational altitude is zero to 2500 ft. The first system was first tested and evaluated in 1984. Four of the five systems are operational at any given time. At sea endurance is 31 days. Transferred to the Army in 1992.

CARIBBEAN SENTRY with AEROSTAT *1/1990, Giorgio Arra*

SHIPBORNE AIRCRAFT

Numbers/Type: 96 Aerospatiale HH 65A Dolphin.
Operational speed: 165 kts *(300 km/h)*.
Service ceiling: 11 810 ft *(3600 m)*.
Range: 400 nm *(741 km)*.
Role/Weapon systems: Short-range rescue and recovery (SRR) helicopter. 80 aircraft are operational. Sensors: Bendix RDR 1500 radar and Collins mission management system. Weapons: Unarmed.

DOLPHIN *1989, USCG*

LAND-BASED MARITIME AIRCRAFT (FRONT LINE)

Note: In February 1993 there were in addition three CH-3Es on loan from the Air Force and two RG-8A single-engined reconnaissance aircraft. Four P-3B Orions are used for AEW by US Customs.

Numbers/Type: 41 AMD-BA HU-25A/B/C Guardian Falcon.
Operational speed: 420 kts *(774 km/h)*.
Service ceiling: 42 000 ft *(12 800 m)*.
Range: 1940 nm *(3594 km)*.
Role/Weapon systems: Medium-range maritime reconnaissance role. 31 are operational. Sensors: Weather/search radar. Weapons: Unarmed.

Numbers/Type: 31 Lockheed HC-130H/V.
Operational speed: 325 kts *(602 km/h)*.
Service ceiling: 33 000 ft *(10 060 m)*.
Range: 4250 nm *(7876 km)*.
Role/Weapon systems: Long-range maritime reconnaissance role; further orders expected. 26 are operational. Sensors: Weather/search radar; APS 137 or APS 125 (in V conversion). Weapons: Unarmed.

Numbers/Type: 32 Sikorsky HH-60J Jay Hawk.
Operational speed: 180 kts *(333 km/h).*
Service ceiling: 17 200 ft *(5240 m).*
Range: 350 nm *(648 km).*
Role/Weapon systems: Coast Guard version of Seahawk, first flew in 1988, replacing HH-3F in MRR role. Total of 40 ordered, all to be delivered by 1995. Sensors: Bendix weather/search radar. Weapons: Unarmed.

JAY HAWK   *1992, Sikorsky*

ICEBREAKERS

0 + (1) NEWCON TYPE (WAGB)

HEALY   WAGB 20

Comment: In response to the 1984 Interagency Polar Icebreaker Requirements Study and Congressional mandate, approval was given for the construction of a new icebreaker as a replacement for two Wind class which were then decommissioned in 1988. However, no action was taken to provide funds for the new ship until Congress surprisingly appropriated $329 million for inclusion in the Navy's FY 1991 ship construction budget. Proposals were sought for the new ship in 1992, but their estimated costs exceeded available funds. The scheduled date for a new design contract is 23 July 1993 with a construction order in May 1994. Characteristics now include a ship of less than 400 ft in length and 32 ft draft. Range is to be 16 000 nm at not less than 12.5 kts, with an endurance of 180 days. Two helicopters to be carried. Crew size less than 100. Icebreaking capability of not less than 4.5 ft at 3 kts.

2 POLAR CLASS (WAGB)

Name	No	Builders	Commissioned	F/S
POLAR STAR	WAGB 10	Lockheed Shipbuilding Co, Seattle, Washington	19 Jan 1976	PA
POLAR SEA	WAGB 11	Lockheed Shipbuilding Co, Seattle, Washington	23 Feb 1978	PA

Displacement, tons: 13 190 full load
Dimensions, feet (metres): 399 × 86 × 32 *(121.6 × 26.2 × 9.8)*
Main machinery: CODLAG; 3 Pratt & Whitney FT4A-12 gas turbines; 60 000 hp *(44.76 MW)* sustained; 6 Alco 16V-251/Westinghouse diesel generators; 21 000 hp *(15.66 MW)* sustained; 3 Westinghouse DC motors; 18 000 hp *(13.42 MW)* sustained; 3 Philadelphia 75 VMGS gears; 20 000 hp *(14.9 MW)* sustained; 3 shafts; cp props
Speed, knots: 18. **Range, miles:** 28 275 at 13 kts
Complement: 142 (15 officers) plus 33 scientists and 12 aircrew
Guns: 2—12.7 mm MGs.
Radars: Navigation: Raytheon SPS 64; I band.
Helicopters: 2 HH-65A.

Comment: These ships are the first icebreakers built for US service since *Glacier* was constructed two decades earlier. Both are based at Seattle, WA. At a continuous speed of 3 kts, they can break ice 6 ft *(1.8 m)* thick, and by ramming can break 21 ft *(6.4 m)* pack. Conventional icebreaker hull form with 'White' cutaway bow configuration and well-rounded body sections to prevent being trapped in ice. The ice belt is 1.75 in thick supported by framing at 16 in centres. Three heeling systems assist icebreaking and ship extraction. Two 15 ton capacity cranes fitted aft; one 3 ton capacity crane fitted forward. Two over-the-side oceanographic winches, one over-the-side trawl/core winch. Deck fixtures for scientific research, and research laboratories provided for arctic and oceanographic research. Between 1986-92, science facilities were upgraded including habitability, lab spaces and winch capabilities.

POLAR STAR   *9/1991, W Sartori*

POLAR SEA   *8/1992, H M Steele*

1 MACKINAW CLASS (WAGB)

Name	No	Builders	Commissioned	F/S
MACKINAW	WAGB 83	Toledo Shipbuilding Co, Ohio	20 Dec 1944	GLA

Displacement, tons: 5252
Dimensions, feet (metres): 290 × 74 × 19 *(88.4 × 22.6 × 5.8)*
Main machinery: Diesel-electric; 6 Fairbanks-Morse 38D8-1/8-12 diesel generators; 8.7 MW sustained; Elliot electric drive; 10 000 hp *(7.46 MW)*; 3 shafts (1 fwd, 2 aft)
Speed, knots: 18.7. **Range, miles:** 41 000 at 11.5 kts; 10 000 at 18.7 kts
Complement: 74 (8 officers)
Radars: Navigation: Raytheon SPS 64; I band.

Comment: Specially designed and constructed for service as icebreaker on the Great Lakes. Equipped with two 5 ton capacity cranes. Clear area for helicopter is provided on the quarterdeck, the aircraft being called for from shore Coast Guard station. Scheduled to be paid off in FY 1988 as a means of helping the Coast Guard cope with severe budget cuts but pressure from members of Congress from states bordering the Great Lakes, where *Mackinaw* operates, resulted in her being placed in an 'In Commission, Special' status. Operational again in Spring 1988. A safety and survivability overhaul is being done around operations from 1992-94.

MACKINAW   *1983, USCG*

9 BAY CLASS (TUGS—WGTB)

Name	No	Laid down	Commissioned	F/S
KATMAI BAY	WTGB 101	7 Nov 1977	8 Jan 1979	GLA
BRISTOL BAY	WTGB 102	13 Feb 1978	5 Apr 1979	GLA
MOBILE BAY	WTGB 103	13 Feb 1978	6 May 1979	GLA
BISCAYNE BAY	WTGB 104	29 Aug 1978	8 Dec 1979	GLA
NEAH BAY	WTGB 105	6 Aug 1979	18 Aug 1980	GLA
MORRO BAY	WTGB 106	6 Aug 1979	25 Jan 1981	AA
PENOBSCOT BAY	WTGB 107	24 July 1983	4 Sep 1984	AA
THUNDER BAY	WTGB 108	20 July 1984	29 Dec 1985	AA
STURGEON BAY	WTGB 109	9 July 1986	20 Aug 1988	AA

Displacement, tons: 662 full load
Dimensions, feet (metres): 140 × 37.6 × 12.5 *(42.7 × 11.4 × 3.8)*
Main machinery: Diesel-electric; 2 Fairbanks-Morse 38D8-1/8-10 diesel generators; 2.4 MW sustained; Westinghouse electric drive; 2500 hp *(1.87 MW)*; 1 shaft
Speed, knots: 14.7. **Range, miles:** 4000 at 12 kts
Complement: 17 (3 officers)
Radars: Navigation: Raytheon SPS 64; I band.

Comment: The size, manoeuvrability and other operational characteristics of these vessels are tailored for operations in harbours and other restricted waters and for fulfilling present and anticipated multi-mission requirements. All units are ice strengthened for operation on the Great Lakes, coastal waters and in rivers and can break 24 in of ice continuously and up to 8 ft by ramming. A self contained portable bubbler van and system reduces hull friction. First six built at Tacoma Boatbuilding, Tacoma. WTGB 107-109 built in Tacoma by Bay City Marine, San Diego. *Bristol Bay* and *Mobile Bay* have had their bows reinforced to push the two aids-to-navigation barges on the Great Lakes.

PENOBSCOT BAY   *6/1991, Giorgio Arra*

USA (COAST GUARD) / Patrol craft

PATROL CRAFT

Note: Heritage class programme cancelled on 25 November 1991. The first of class *Leopold* is unlikely to be completed. The cause of the cancellation was attributed to changing requirements and availability of more ships as a result of Soviet decline. It was also reported that there were concerns about the design. A smaller patrol craft is now being considered.

49 ISLAND CLASS (WPB)

Name	No	Home Port	Commissioned
FARALLON	WPB 1301	Miami, FL	15 Nov 1985
MANITOU	WPB 1302	Miami, FL	24 Jan 1986
MATAGORDA	WPB 1303	Miami, FL	28 Feb 1986
MAUI	WPB 1304	Miami, FL	24 Mar 1986
MONHEGAN	WPB 1305	Roosevelt Roads, PR	11 Apr 1986
NUNIVAK	WPB 1306	Roosevelt Roads, PR	2 May 1986
OCRACOKE	WPB 1307	Roosevelt Roads, PR	23 May 1986
VASHON	WPB 1308	Roosevelt Roads, PR	13 June 1986
AQUIDNECK	WPB 1309	Portsmouth, VA	25 July 1986
MUSTANG	WPB 1310	Seward, AK	29 Aug 1986
NAUSHON	WPB 1311	Ketchikan, AK	3 Oct 1986
SANIBEL	WPB 1312	Rockland, ME	14 Nov 1986
EDISTO	WPB 1313	Crescent City, CA	7 Jan 1987
SAPELO	WPB 1314	Eureka, CA	24 Feb 1987
MATINICUS	WPB 1315	Cape May, NJ	16 Apr 1987
NANTUCKET	WPB 1316	Roosevelt Roads, PR	4 June 1987
ATTU	WPB 1317	San Juan, PR	6 Feb 1988
BARANOF	WPB 1318	Miami, FL	12 Mar 1988
CHANDELEUR	WPB 1319	Miami, FL	16 Apr 1988
CHINCOTEAGUE	WPB 1320	Mobile, AL	21 May 1988
CUSHING	WPB 1321	Mobile, AL	25 June 1988
CUTTYHUNK	WPB 1322	Port Angeles, WA	30 July 1988
DRUMMOND	WPB 1323	Port Canaveral, FL	3 Sep 1988
KEY LARGO	WPB 1324	Savannah, GA	8 Oct 1988
METOMPKIN	WPB 1325	Charleston, SC	12 Nov 1988
MONOMOY	WPB 1326	Woods Hole, MA	17 Dec 1988
ORCAS	WPB 1327	Coos Bay, OR	21 Jan 1989
PADRE	WPB 1328	Key West, FL	25 Feb 1989
SITKINAK	WPB 1329	Key West, FL	1 Apr 1989
TYBEE	WPB 1330	San Diego, CA	5 May 1989
WASHINGTON	WPB 1331	Honolulu, HI	9 June 1989
WRANGELL	WPB 1332	Sandy Hook, NJ	9 July 1989
ADAK	WPB 1333	Sandy Hook, NJ	18 Aug 1989
LIBERTY	WPB 1334	Auke Bay, AK	22 Sep 1989
ANACAPA	WPB 1335	Petersburg, AK	27 Oct 1989
KISKA	WPB 1336	Hilo, HI	1 Dec 1989
ASSATEAGUE	WPB 1337	Honolulu, HI	5 Jan 1990
GRAND ISLE	WPB 1338	Gloucester, MA	19 Feb 1991
KEY BISCAYNE	WPB 1339	Corpus Christi, TX	12 Mar 1991
JEFFERSON ISLAND	WPB 1340	South Portland, ME	9 Apr 1991
KODIAK ISLAND	WPB 1341	Panama City, FL	14 May 1991
LONG ISLAND	WPB 1342	Monterey, CA	18 June 1991
BAINBRIDGE ISLAND	WPB 1343	Sandy Hook, NJ	16 July 1991
BLOCK ISLAND	WPB 1344	Atlantic Beach, NC	27 Aug 1991
STATEN ISLAND	WPB 1345	Atlantic Beach, NC	1 Oct 1991
ROANOKE ISLAND	WPB 1346	Homer, AK	5 Nov 1991
PEA ISLAND	WPB 1347	Mayport, FL	10 Dec 1991
KNIGHT ISLAND	WPB 1348	Freeport, TX	14 Jan 1992
GALVESTON ISLAND	WPB 1349	Apra Harbor, Guam	25 Feb 1992

Displacement, tons: 162 (A series); 154 (B and C series) full load
Dimensions, feet (metres): 110 × 21 × 7.3 *(33.5 × 6.4 × 2.2)*
Main machinery: 2 Paxman Valenta diesels (A and B series); 5800 hp *(4.3 MW)*; 2 Caterpillar diesels (C series); 5400 hp *(4.03 MW)*; 2 shafts
Speed, knots: 29. **Range, miles:** 3600 at 12 kts
Complement: 16 (2 officers)
Guns: 1 Oerlikon 20 mm Mk 16 or 1 McDonnell Douglas 25 mm/87 Mk 38. 2—12.7 mm M60 MGs.
Radars: Navigation: Raytheon SPS 64V; I band.

Comment: All built by the Bollinger Machine Shop and Shipyard at Lockport, Louisiana. The design is based upon the 110 ft patrol craft built by Vosper Thornycroft, UK, which are currently serving in Venezuela, Qatar, Abu Dhabi and Singapore, but modified to meet Coast Guard needs. Vosper Thornycroft supplied design support, stabilisers, propellers, and steering gear. All are having 25 mm Mk 38 guns installed. Batches: A 1301-1316, B 1317-1337, C 1338-1349. Batch C had their allocated names changed prior to completion in 1991/92.

FARALLON 10/1992, Maritime Photographic

BARANOF 4/1992, Giorgio Arra

3 SEA BIRD CLASS (SURFACE EFFECT SHIPS—WSES)

Name	No	Builders	Commissioned	F/S
SEA HAWK	WSES 2	Bell Halter Inc, New Orleans, La	16 Oct 1982	AA
SHEARWATER	WSES 3	Bell Halter Inc, New Orleans, La	16 Oct 1982	AA
PETREL	WSES 4	Bell Halter Inc, New Orleans, La	17 June 1983	AA

Displacement, tons: 150 full load
Dimensions, feet (metres): 110 × 39 × 8.3 *(33.5 × 11.9 × 2.5)*
Main machinery: 2 Detroit 16V-149TI diesels (propulsion); 2322 hp *(1.73 MW)* sustained; 2 shafts; cp prop; 2 Detroit 8V-92TA diesels (lift); 700 hp *(522 kW)* sustained; 2 centrifugal fans (lift); 736 hp *(549 kW)*
Speed, knots: 30+. **Range, miles:** 1500 at 23 kts
Complement: 17 (1 officer)
Guns: 2—12.7 mm MGs.
Radars: Navigation: 2 Decca 914; I band.

Comment: Modified units of the surface effect ship constructed in the late 1970s which in 1981, after extensive testing by the Navy, was transferred to the Coast Guard and became the *Dorado* (WSES 1). All three are based in Key West and their high speed and shallow draft make them ideal for drug-interdiction and law-enforcement missions in the Caribbean basin. Designed primarily for law-enforcement and search and rescue missions. Design includes welded marine aluminium alloy 5086 hull with a catamaran configuration that consists of two side hulls with a connecting deck. The bow and stern have flexible seals to contain an air cushion. Each craft is supported by cushion lift as well as hydrostatic and hydrodynamic lift on the sidewalls. The bow seal consists of eight fingers, each of which is attached to the underside of the centre hull. The stern seal consists of three inflated lobes. During the early years of operation, vibration was a major concern; however, that problem has been corrected and they have become sufficiently reliable to exceed by far their planned operating hours. There are no plans to build more of them.

SEA HAWK 4/1990, Giorgio Arra

42 POINT CLASS (WPB)

Name	No	F/S	Name	No	F/S
A Series			POINT HANNON	82355	AA
POINT SWIFT	82312	AA	POINT FRANCIS	82356	AA
			POINT HURON	82357	AA
C Series			POINT STUART	82358	PA
POINT HIGHLAND	82333	AA	POINT STEELE	82359	AA
POINT LEDGE	82334	AA	POINT WINSLOW	82360	PA
POINT COUNTESS	82335	PA	POINT NOWELL	82363	AA
POINT GLASS	82336	AA	POINT WHITEHORN	82364	AA
POINT DIVIDE	82337	PA	POINT TURNER	82365	AA
POINT BRIDGE	82338	PA	POINT LOBOS	82366	AA
POINT CHICO	82339	PA	POINT WARDE	82368	AA
POINT BATAN	82340	AA	POINT HEYER	82369	PA
POINT LOOKOUT	82341	AA	POINT RICHMOND	82370	AA
POINT BAKER	82342	AA			
POINT WELLS	82343	AA	D Series		
POINT ESTERO	82344	AA	POINT BARNES	82371	AA
POINT ARENA	82346	AA	POINT BROWER	82372	PA
POINT BONITA	82347	AA	POINT CAMDEN	82373	PA
POINT SPENCER	82349	AA	POINT CARREW	82374	PA
POINT FRANKLIN	82350	AA	POINT DORAN	82375	AA
POINT BENNETT	82351	PA	POINT HOBART	82377	PA
POINT SAL	82352	AA	POINT JACKSON	82378	AA
POINT MONROE	82353	AA	POINT MARTIN	82379	AA
POINT EVANS	82354	PA			

Displacement, tons: 67 (A series); 66 (C series); 69 (D series) full load
Dimensions, feet (metres): 83 × 17.2 × 5.8 *(25.3 × 5.2 × 1.8)*
Main machinery: 2 Cummins or Caterpillar diesels; 1600 hp *(1.19 MW)*; 2 shafts
Speed, knots: 23.5; 22.6 (D series). **Range, miles:** 1500 at 8 kts; 1200 at 8 kts (D series)
Complement: 10 (1 officer)
Guns: 2—12.7 mm MGs.
Radars: Navigation: Raytheon SPS 64; I band.

Comment: Steel-hulled craft with aluminium superstructures designed for patrol and search and rescue. A series built 1960-61; C series in 1961-67, and D series in 1970. Some of the cutters operate with an officer assigned, the rest with all-enlisted crews. Twenty-six of the 'A' and 'B' series were transferred to South Vietnam in 1969-70. Some of the remaining cutters are being re-engined with Caterpillar engines. Some of the class are now in service with navies of Costa Rica, Panama, Mexico and Venezuela. *Point Baker* deleted in error in 1991.

POINT BROWER 10/1991, Giorgio Arra

SEAGOING TENDERS

0 + 1 (4) JUNIPER CLASS (BUOY TENDERS—WLB)

Displacement, tons: 2000 full load
Dimensions, feet (metres): 225 × 46 × 13 *(68.6 × 14 × 4)*
Main machinery: 2 diesels; 6200 hp *(4.6 MW)*; 1 shaft; bow and stern thrusters
Speed, knots: 15
Complement: 40 (6 officers)
Guns: 1—25 mm/87 Mk 38.
Radars: Surface search: I band.

Comment: In January 1993, the Coast Guard awarded Marinette Marine of Marinette, WI, a contract to construct the first of a new class of seagoing buoy tenders, with an option for four more. Construction of the first of class is scheduled to start in 1994, with delivery in 1995. The class is named after the first *Juniper*, which was built in 1940 and decommissioned in 1975. Capable of breaking 14 in of ice at 3 kts or a minimum of 3 ft by ramming.

27 BALSAM CLASS (BUOY TENDERS—WLB)

Name	No	Launched	F/S	Name	No	Launched	F/S
A Series				C Series			
COWSLIP	WLB 277	1942	AA	BASSWOOD	WLB 388	1944	AA
GENTIAN	WLB 290	1942	AA	BITTERSWEET	WLB 389	1944	AA
LAUREL	WLB 291	1942	AA	BRAMBLE	WLB 392	1944	GLA
SORREL	WLB 296	1943	AA	FIREBUSH	WLB 393	1944	PA
CITRUS	WMEC 300	1943	PA	HORNBEAM	WLB 394	1944	AA
CONIFER	WLB 301	1943	PA	IRIS	WLB 395	1944	PA
MADRONA	WLB 302	1943	AA	MALLOW	WLB 396	1944	PA
				MARIPOSA	WLB 397	1944	GLA
B Series				SASSAFRAS	WLB 401	1944	PA
IRONWOOD	WLB 297	1943	PA	SEDGE	WLB 402	1944	PA
BUTTONWOOD	WLB 306	1943	PA	SPAR	WLB 403	1944	AA
PLANETREE	WLB 307	1943	PA	SUNDEW	WLB 404	1944	GLA
PAPAW	WLB 308	1943	AR	SWEETBRIER	WLB 405	1944	PA
SWEETGUM	WLB 309	1943	AR	ACACIA	WLB 406	1944	GLA
				WOODRUSH	WLB 407	1944	PA

Displacement, tons: 757 standard; 1034 full load
Dimensions, feet (metres): 180 × 37 × 12 *(54.9 × 11.3 × 3.8)*
Main machinery: Diesel-electric; 2 diesels; 1402 hp *(1.06 MW)*; 1 motor; 1200 hp *(895 kW)*; 1 shaft; bow thruster (except in 307, 309, 388, 395 and 396)
Speed, knots: 13
Complement: 53 (6 officers)
Guns: 2—12.7 mm MGs (except 392, 397, 406 and 404).
Radars: Navigation: Raytheon SPS 64; I band.

Comment: Seagoing buoy tenders. *Ironwood* built by Coast Guard Yard at Curtis Bay, Maryland; others by Marine Iron & Shipbuilding Co, Duluth, Minnesota, or Zenith Dredge Co, Duluth, Minnesota. Completed 1943-45. All have 20 ton capacity booms.
Modernisation and Service Life Extension Programmes: *Cowslip, Gentian, Conifer, Sorrel, Madrona, Laurel, Papaw, Sweetgum* and *Buttonwood* have completed an 18 month SLEP. Work included replacement of main engines, improvement of electronics, navigation and weight-handling systems, and improved habitability. *Ironwood, Bittersweet, Bramble, Firebush, Hornbeam, Mariposa, Sassafras, Sedge, Spar, Sundew, Sweetbrier, Acacia* and *Woodrush* all underwent major renovation in the mid- to late 1970s which was not as extensive as the current SLEPs. However, in the 1988-91 period all of these cutters received same main engines as those installed in cutters receiving SLEP. The last 20 mm guns removed in 1993. *Citrus* deleted in error in 1990 retains her WMEC markings.

PAPAW   6/1992, Giorgio Arra

COASTAL TENDERS

5 RED CLASS (BUOY TENDERS—WLM)

Name	No	Launched	F/S	Name	No	Launched	F/S
RED WOOD	WLM 685	1964	AA	RED CEDAR	WLM 688	1970	AA
RED BEECH	WLM 686	1964	AA	RED OAK	WLM 689	1971	AA
RED BIRCH	WLM 687	1965	AA				

Displacement, tons: 471 standard; 536 full load
Dimensions, feet (metres): 157 × 33 × 6 *(47.9 × 10.1 × 1.8)*
Main machinery: 2 diesels; 1800 hp *(1.34 MW)*; 2 shafts; cp props; bow thruster
Speed, knots: 12.8. **Range, miles:** 2248 at 11.6 kts
Complement: 31 (4 officers)

Comment: All built by Coast Guard Yard, Curtis Bay, Maryland. Steel hulls strengthened for light icebreaking. Steering and engine controls on each bridge wing as well as in pilot house. Living spaces are air-conditioned. Fitted with 10 ton capacity boom.

RED OAK   8/1987, van Ginderen Collection

6 WHITE SUMAC CLASS (BUOY TENDERS—WLM)

Name	No	F/S	Name	No	F/S
WHITE SUMAC	WLM 540	AA	WHITE HEATH	WLM 545	AA
WHITE LUPINE	WLM 546	AA	WHITE HOLLY	WLM 543	AA
WHITE PINE	WLM 547	AA	WHITE SAGE	WLM 544	AA

Displacement, tons: 435 standard; 485 full load
Dimensions, feet (metres): 133 × 31 × 9 *(40.5 × 9.5 × 2.7)*
Main machinery: 2 Caterpillar diesels; 600 hp *(448 kW)*; 2 shafts
Speed, knots: 9.8
Complement: 24 (1 officer)

Comment: All launched in 1943. All six ships are former US Navy YFs, adapted for the Coast Guard. Fitted with 10 ton capacity boom.

WHITE SUMAC   1/1992, Giorgio Arra

BUOY TENDERS (RIVER) (WLR)

Notes: (1) All are based on rivers of USA especially the Mississippi and the Missouri and its tributaries.
(2) Two ATON (aids to navigation) barges completed in 1991/92 by Marinette Marine. For use on the Great Lakes in conjunction with icebreaker tugs *Bristol Bay* and *Mobile Bay*.

ATON I and Buoy Tender   1991, Marinette Marine

KANKAKEE WLR 75500   **GREENBRIAR** WLR 75501

Displacement, tons: 161 full load
Dimensions, feet (metres): 75.1 × 24 × 4.9 *(22.9 × 7.3 × 1.5)*
Main machinery: 2 Caterpillar 3412T diesels; 1006 hp *(750 kW)* sustained; 2 shafts
Speed, knots: 12. **Range, miles:** 600 at 12 kts
Complement: 13

Comment: *Kankakee* completed by Avondale 27 February 1990, and *Greenbriar* 12 April 1990. Have replaced *Dogwood* and *Lantana*. More of the class are planned.

OUACHITA	WLR 65501	SCIOTO	WLR 65504
CIMARRON	WLR 65502	OSAGE	WLR 65505
OBION	WLR 65503	SANGAMON	WLR 65506

Displacement, tons: 146 full load
Dimensions, feet (metres): 65.6 × 21 × 5 *(20 × 6.4 × 1.5)*
Main machinery: 2 Caterpillar diesels; 660 hp *(492 kW)*; 2 shafts
Speed, knots: 12.5
Complement: 10

Comment: Built in 1960-62.

830 USA (COAST GUARD) / Buoy tenders (river) (WLR) — Construction tenders (inland) (WLIC)

SUMAC WLR 311

Displacement, tons: 423 full load
Dimensions, feet (metres): 115 × 30 × 6 *(35.1 × 9.1 × 1.8)*
Main machinery: 3 Caterpillar D 379 diesels; 1644 hp *(1.23 MW)*; 3 shafts
Speed, knots: 10.6
Complement: 22

Comment: Built in 1943. Scheduled for replacement in 1993.

GASCONADE	WLR 75401	KICKAPOO	WLR 75406
MUSKINGUM	WLR 75402	KANAWHA	WLR 75407
WYACONDA	WLR 75403	PATOKA	WLR 75408
CHIPPEWA	WLR 75404	CHENA	WLR 75409
CHEYENNE	WLR 75405		

Displacement, tons: 150 full load
Dimensions, feet (metres): 75 × 22 × 4 *(22.9 × 6.7 × 1.2)*
Main machinery: 2 Caterpillar diesels; 660 hp *(492 kW)*; 2 shafts
Speed, knots: 10.8
Complement: 12

Comment: Built 1964-71.

Buoy Tender 6/1991, Giorgio Arra

BUOY TENDERS (INLAND—WLI)

Name	No	F/S	Name	No	F/S
BLUEBELL	WLI 313	PA	BUCKTHORN	WLI 642	GLA

Displacement, tons: 226 (174 *Bluebell*) full load
Dimensions, feet (metres): 100 × 24 × 5 *(30.5 × 7.3 × 1.5)* (*Buckthorn* draught 4 *(1.2)*)
Main machinery: 2 Caterpillar diesels; 600 hp *(448 kW)*; 2 shafts
Speed, knots: 11.9; 10.5 (*Bluebell*)
Complement: 14 (1 officer); 15 (*Bluebell*)

Comment: *Bluebell* completed 1945, and *Buckthorn* in 1963.

BUCKTHORN 2/1989, van Ginderen Collection

Name	No	F/S	Name	No	F/S
BLACKBERRY	WLI 65303	AA	BAYBERRY	WLI 65400	PA
CHOKEBERRY	WLI 65304	AA	ELDERBERRY	WLI 65401	PA

Displacement, tons: 68 full load
Dimensions, feet (metres): 65 × 17 × 4 *(19.8 × 5.2 × 1.2)*
Main machinery: 2 GM diesels (various); 2 shafts
Speed, knots: 11
Complement: 5

Comment: First two completed in 1946, second two in 1954.

BAYBERRY 1983, USCG

SAIL TRAINING CUTTER

1 EAGLE CLASS (WIX)

Name	No	Builders	F/S
EAGLE (ex-*Horst Wessel*)	WIX 327	Blohm & Voss, Hamburg	AA

Displacement, tons: 1784 full load
Dimensions, feet (metres): 231 wl; 293.6 oa × 39.4 × 16.1 *(70.4; 89.5 × 12 × 4.9)*
Main machinery: 1 Caterpillar D 399 auxiliary diesel; 1125 hp *(839 kW)* sustained; 1 shaft
Speed, knots: 10.5; 18 sail. **Range, miles:** 5450 at 7.5 kts diesel only
Complement: 245 (19 officers, 180 cadets)
Radars: Navigation: Raytheon SPS 64; I band.

Comment: Former German training ship. Launched on 13 June 1936. Taken by the USA as part of reparations after the Second World War for employment in US Coast Guard Practice Squadron. Taken over at Bremerhaven in January 1946; arrived at home port of New London, Connecticut, in July 1946. (Sister ship *Albert Leo Schlageter* was also taken by the USA in 1945 but was sold to Brazil in 1948 and re-sold to Portugal in 1962. Another ship of similar design, *Gorch Fock*, transferred to the USSR in 1946 and survives as *Tovarisch*). *Eagle* was extensively overhauled 1981-82. When the Coast Guard added the orange-and-blue marking stripes to cutters in the 1960s *Eagle* was exempted because of their effect on her graceful lines; however, in early 1976 the stripes and words 'Coast Guard' were added in time for the July 1976 Operation Sail in New York harbour. During the Coast Guard's year-long bicentennial celebration, which ended 4 August 1990, *Eagle* visited each of the 10 ports where the original revenue cutters were home-ported: Baltimore, MD; New London, CT; Washington, NC; Savannah, GA; Philadelphia, PA; Newburyport, MA; Portsmouth, NH; Charleston, SC; New York, NY; and Hampton, VA.
Fore and main masts 150.3 ft *(45.8 m)*; mizzen 132 ft *(40.2 m)*; sail area, 25 351 sq ft.

EAGLE and CONDOR (the old and the new) 1991

CONSTRUCTION TENDERS (INLAND) (WLIC)

Note: All, although operating on inland waters, are administered by the Atlantic Area.

4 PAMLICO CLASS

Name	No	F/S	Name	No	F/S
PAMLICO	WLIC 800	AA	KENNEBEC	WLIC 802	AA
HUDSON	WLIC 801	AA	SAGINAW	WLIC 803	AA

Displacement, tons: 459 full load
Dimensions, feet (metres): 160.9 × 30 × 4 *(49 × 9.1 × 1.2)*
Main machinery: 2 Caterpillar diesels; 1000 hp *(746 kW)*; 2 shafts
Speed, knots: 11.5
Complement: 15 (1 officer)

Comment: Completed in 1976 at the Coast Guard Yard, Curtis Bay, Maryland. These ships maintain structures and buoys in bay areas along the Atlantic and Gulf coasts.

HUDSON 12/1989, Giorgio Arra

3 COSMOS CLASS

Name	No	F/S	Name	No	F/S
RAMBLER	WLIC 298	AA	PRIMROSE	WLIC 316	AA
SMILAX	WLIC 315	AA			

Displacement, tons: 178 full load
Dimensions, feet (metres): 100 × 24 × 5 *(30.5 × 7.3 × 1.5)*
Main machinery: 2 Caterpillar D 353 diesels; 425 hp *(317 kW)* sustained; 2 shafts
Speed, knots: 10.5
Complement: 15 (1 officer)

Comment: Completed in 1944. *Primrose* fitted with pile driver. Primary areas of operation are intercoastal waters from Virginia to Georgia.

PRIMROSE 7/1990, van Ginderen Collection

9 ANVIL/CLAMP CLASSES

Name	No	F/S	Name	No	F/S	Name	No	F/S
ANVIL	WLIC 75301	AA	MALLET	WLIC 75304	AA	WEDGE	WLIC 75307	AA
HAMMER	WLIC 75302	AA	VISE	WLIC 75305	AA	HATCHET	WLIC 75309	AA
SLEDGE	WLIC 75303	AA	CLAMP	WLIC 75306	AA	AXE	WLIC 75310	AA

Displacement, tons: 140 full load
Dimensions, feet (metres): 75 (76—WLIC 75306-75310) × 22 × 4 *(22.9 (23.2) × 6.7 × 1.2)*
Main machinery: 2 Caterpillar diesels; 660 hp *(492 kW)*; 2 shafts
Speed, knots: 10
Complement: 13 (1 officer in *Mallet, Sledge* and *Vise*)

Comment: Completed 1962-65. Primary areas of operation are intercoastal waters from Texas to New Jersey.

SLEDGE 7/1988, W Donko

HARBOUR TUGS

14 65 ft CLASS (WYTL)

CAPSTAN WYTL 65601	CATENARY WYTL 65606	LINE WYTL 65611
CHOCK WYTL 65602	BRIDLE WYTL 65607	WIRE WYTL 65612
SWIVEL WYTL 65603	PENDANT WYTL 65608	BOLLARD WYTL 65614
TACKLE WYTL 65604	SHACKLE WYTL 65609	CLEAT WYTL 65615
TOWLINE WYTL 65605	HAWSER WYTL 65610	

Displacement, tons: 72 full load
Dimensions, feet (metres): 65 × 19 × 7 *(19.8 × 5.8 × 2.1)*
Main machinery: 1 diesel; 400 hp *(298 kW)*; 1 shaft
Speed, knots: 10
Complement: 10

Comment: Built from 1961 to 1967. All active in the Atlantic Fleet.

WIRE 2/1992, van Ginderen Collection

1450 + RESCUE AND UTILITY CRAFT

Note: There are a large number of utility craft of several different types.

UTILITY CRAFT 5/1992, Giorgio Arra

FERRY 6/1990, Giorgio Arra

6 + (90) MOTOR LIFEBOATS

Displacement, tons: 20 full load
Dimensions, feet (metres): 47.9 × 14 × 1.8 *(14.6 × 4.3 × 0.5)*
Main machinery: 2 diesels; 850 hp *(634 kW)*; 2 shafts
Speed, knots: 27. **Range, miles:** 250 at 27 kts
Complement: 4

Comment: Built by Textron Marine, New Orleans. The first completed trials in mid-1991 when five more were ordered. Final numbers will be up to 100 to replace the aging fleet of 44 ft lifeboats. Aluminium hulls, self-righting with a 9000 lb bollard pull and a towing capability of 150 tons. Primarily a lifeboat but it has a multi-mission capability.

MOTOR LIFEBOAT 1992, USCG

NATIONAL OCEANIC AND ATMOSPHERIC ADMINISTRATION

Command

Director, NOAA Corps Operations:
  Rear Admiral Sigmund R Petersen
Director, Charting and Geodetic Services:
  Rear Admiral J Austin Yeager
Deputy Director, NOAA Corps Operations:
  Rear Admiral William L Stubblefield
Director, Atlantic Marine Center:
  Rear Admiral Freddie L Jeffries
Director, Pacific Marine Center:
  Rear Admiral John C Albright
Director Aircraft Operations Center:
  Rear Admiral Francis D Moran

Establishment

The Survey of the Coast was established by an act of the US Congress on February 10, 1807. In 1834 the organisation was renamed the US Coast Survey, and in 1878, the Coast and Geodetic Survey. In 1917 the Commissioned Officer Corps was established to provide a pool of sea-going scientists and engineers to command and operate the vessels of the Coast and Geodetic Survey, lead field parties, and manage research and engineering programs. The Coast and Geodetic Survey was made a component of the Environmental Science Services Administration in the US Department of Commerce on July 13, 1965. In October 1970, the Environmental Science Services Administration was reorganised and renamed the National Oceanic and Atmospheric Administration (NOAA). The Coast and Geodetic Survey was incorporated into NOAA as the National Ocean Survey, with its jurisdiction expanded to include functions of the US Lake Survey (formerly a part of the US Army Corps of Engineers), the US Coast Guard's national Data Buoy Development Project, and the US Navy's National Oceanographic Instrumentation Center. The Commissioned Officer Corps was renamed the NOAA Corps.

Missions

The office of NOAA Corps Operations is responsible to the US Department of Commerce. NOAA's research vessels conduct operations in hydrography, bathymetry, oceanography, atmospheric research, fisheries surveys and research, and related programmes in living and non-living marine resources. Larger research vessels operate in international waters; smaller vessels operate primarily in Atlantic and Pacific coastal waters, in the Gulfs of Mexico and Alaska, and in the US Lakes. The Office of NOAA also conducts diving operations and operates fixed-wing and rotary-wing aircraft for reconnaissance, oceanographic and atmospheric research, and to support aerial mapping and charting.
NOAA is the largest component of the US Department of Commerce, with a diverse set of responsibilities in environmental science. These responsibilities include the Office of NOAA Corps Operations, the National Ocean Service, the National Weather Service, the National Marine Fisheries Service, the National Environmental Satellite, Data, and Information Service, and the Office of Oceanic and Atmospheric Research.

Ships

The following ships may be met with at sea. All are painted white with two-tone blue bands on the funnels and buff masts.
Oceanographic Survey Ships: *Researcher, Oceanographer, Surveyor, Malcolm Baldrige.*
Hydrographic Survey Ships: *Fairweather, Rainier, Mt. Mitchell.*
Coastal Survey Ships: *McArthur, Davidson, Whiting, Pierce.*
Coastal Vessels: *Rude, Heck, Ferrel.*
Fisheries Assessment: *Millar Freeman, Oregon II, Chapman, Albatros IV, Townsend Cromwell, David Jorden, Delaware II, John N Cobb, Murre II*
One Stalwart class TAGOS ship *(Adventurous)* was acquired on 1 June 1992. Six more are planned to follow in due course.

Personnel

The National Ocean Survey has approximately 400 commissioned officers and 12 000 civil service personnel. NOAA commissioned officers frequently serve with the military and may be transferred for hostilities.

Bases

Major: Norfolk, Va and Seattle, Wa.
Minor: Woods Hole, Mass; Pascagoula, Miss; Miami, Fla; La Jolla, Calif; Honolulu, Haw.

MT MITCHELL   9/1992, Stefan Terzibaschitsch

WHITING   9/1992, Stefan Terzibaschitsch

ADVENTUROUS   9/1992, Maritime Photographic

URUGUAY

Headquarters' Appointment

Commander-in-Chief of the Navy:
Vice Admiral James Coates

Diplomatic Representation

Naval Attaché in London:
Captain Julian Valdez

Personnel

(a) 1993: 4320 (including Marines, Air Arm and Prefectura)
(b) Voluntary service

Prefectura Naval (PNN)

Established in 1981 primarily for harbour security and coastline guard duties. In 1991 it was integrated with the Navy but some patrol craft still retain Prefectura markings.

Bases

Montevideo: Main naval base with two dry docks and a slipway at Punta Lobos
La Paloma: Naval station Ernesto Motto
Paysandu: River base

Marines

Cuerpo de Fusileros Navales consisting of 550 men in three units of 150 plus command company of 100.

Prefix to Ships' Names

ROU

Mercantile Marine

Lloyd's Register of Shipping:
93 vessels of 128 238 tons gross

DELETIONS

Frigates

1990 *Uruguay* (old)
1991 *18 de Julio*

Patrol Craft

1990 *Rio Negro* (old)

Support Ship

1991 *Vanguardia* (old)

FRIGATES

3 Ex-FRENCH COMMANDANT RIVIÈRE CLASS

Name	No	Builders	Laid down	Launched	Commissioned	Recommissioned
URUGUAY (ex-*Commandant Bourdais*)	1	Lorient Naval Dockyard	Apr 1959	15 Apr 1961	10 Mar 1962	20 Aug 1990
GENERAL ARTIGAS (ex-*Victor Schoelcher*)	2	Lorient Naval Dockyard	Oct 1957	11 Oct 1958	15 Oct 1962	9 Jan 1989
MONTEVIDEO (ex-*Amiral Charner*)	3 (ex-4)	Lorient Naval Dockyard	Nov 1958	12 Mar 1960	14 Dec 1962	28 Jan 1991

Displacement, tons: 1750 standard; 2250 full load
Dimensions, feet (metres): 336.9 × 38.4 × 14.1 *(102.7 × 11.7 × 4.3)*
Main machinery: 4 SEMT-Pielstick 12 PC series diesels; 16 000 hp(m) *(11.8 MW)*; 2 shafts
Speed, knots: 25. **Range, miles:** 7500 at 15 kts
Complement: 159 (9 officers)

Missiles: SSM: 4 Aerospatiale MM 38 Exocet ❶; active radar homing to 42 km *(23 nm)* at 0.9 Mach; warhead 165 kg; sea-skimmer.
Guns: 2 DCN 3.9 in *(100 mm)*/55 Mod 1953 automatic ❷; dual purpose; 80° elevation; 60 rounds/minute to 17 km *(9 nm)* anti-surface; 8 km *(4.4 nm)* anti-aircraft; weight of shell 13.5 kg.
2 Hispano Suiza 30 mm/70 ❸; 83° elevation; 600 rounds/minute to 8.5 km *(4.8 nm)* anti-aircraft.
Torpedoes: 6—21.7 in *(550 mm)* (2 triple) tubes ❹ ECAN L3; anti-submarine; active homing to 5.5 km *(3 nm)* at 25 kts; warhead 200 kg; depth to 300 m *(985 ft)*.
A/S mortars: 1 Mortier 305 mm 4-barrelled launcher ❺; automatic loading; range 2700 m; warhead 227 kg.
Countermeasures: ESM: ARBR 16; radar warning.
Fire control: C T Analogique. Sagem DMAA optical director.
Radars: Air/surface search: Thomson-CSF DRBV 22A ❻; D band.
Navigation: Racal Decca 1226 ❼; I band.
Fire control: Thomson-CSF DRBC 32C ❽; I band.
Sonars: EDO SQS 17; hull-mounted; active search; medium frequency.
Thomson Sintra DUBA 3; active attack; high frequency.

Programmes: First one bought through SOFMA on 30 September 1988, second pair 14 March 1990. All refitted before transfer.
Structure: Exocet and Dagaie removed before transfer but SSM casings were retained and missiles restored in 1991/92.
Operational: Can carry a Flag Officer and staff. In French service this class sometimes embarked up to 80 soldiers and two LCPs.

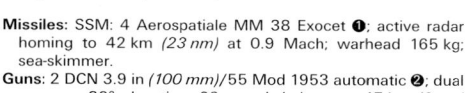

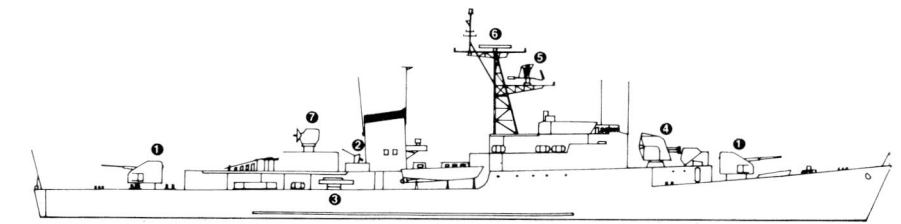

MONTEVIDEO *(Scale 1 : 900), Ian Sturton*

URUGUAY *4/1992, Hartmut Ehlers*

MONTEVIDEO *3/1992*

LAND-BASED MARITIME AIRCRAFT (FRONT LINE)

Note: In addition there are also four helicopters (one Sikorsky CH-34A, one Bell 47G and two Westland Wessex) and four fixed wing aircraft (three Cessna C-182 and one Piper Seneca).

Numbers/Type: 1/2/2 Beechcraft Super King Air 200T/T34B/T34C.
Operational speed: 282 kts *(523 km/h)*.
Service ceiling: 35 000 ft *(10 670 m)*.
Range: 2030 nm *(3756 km)*.
Role/Weapon systems: Used for coastal patrol and protection operations, as well as transport. Sensors: Search radar. Weapons: Unarmed.

Numbers/Type: 3 Grumman S-3G Tracker.
Operational speed: 130 kts *(241 km/h)*.
Service ceiling: 25 000 ft *(7620 m)*.
Range: 1350 nm *(2500 km)*.
Role/Weapon systems: ASW and surface search with recently improved systems. Sensors: Search radar, MAD, sonobuoys. Weapons: ASW; torpedoes, depth bombs or mines. ASV; rockets underwing.

LIGHT FORCES

3 VIGILANTE CLASS (LARGE PATROL CRAFT)

Name	No	Builders	Commissioned
25 de AGOSTO	5	CMN, Cherbourg	25 Mar 1981
15 de NOVIEMBRE	6	CMN, Cherbourg	25 Mar 1981
COMODORO COÉ	7	CMN, Cherbourg	25 Mar 1981

Displacement, tons: 190 full load
Dimensions, feet (metres): 137 × 22.4 × 5.2 *(41.8 × 6.8 × 1.6)*
Main machinery: 2 MTU 12V 538 TB91 diesels; 4600 hp(m) *(3.4 MW)* sustained; 2 shafts
Speed, knots: 28. Range, miles: 2400 at 15 kts
Complement: 28 (5 officers)
Gun: 1 Bofors 40 mm/70.
Fire control: CSEE Naja optronic director.
Radars: Surface search: Racal Decca TM 1226C; I band.

Comment: Ordered in 1979. Steel hull. First launched 16 October 1980, second 11 December 1980 and third 27 January 1981. Offered for sale in 1992 but remaining in the Navy until sold.

COMODORO COÉ *4/1992, Hartmut Ehlers*

2 Ex-US CAPE CLASS (LARGE PATROL CRAFT)

Name	No	Builders	Commissioned
COLONIA (ex-*Cape Higgon*)	10	Coast Guard Yard, Curtis Bay	14 Oct 1953
RIO NEGRO (ex-*Cape Horn*)	11	Coast Guard Yard, Curtis Bay	3 Sep 1958

Displacement, tons: 98 standard; 148 full load
Dimensions, feet (metres): 95 × 20.2 × 6.6 *(28.9 × 6.2 × 2)*
Main machinery: 2 GM 16V-149TI diesels; 2322 hp *(1.73 MW)* sustained; 2 shafts
Speed, knots: 20. Range, miles: 2500 at 10 kts
Complement: 14 (1 officer)
Guns: 2—12.7 mm MGs.
Radars: Navigation: Raytheon SPS 64; I band.

Comment: Designed for port security and search and rescue. Steel hulled. During modernisation in 1974 received new engines, electronics, and deck equipment, had superstructure modified or replaced, and had habitability improved. Transferred from the US Coast Guard in January 1990. Both based at Paysandu.

COLONIA *1/1990, Giorgio Arra*

1 LARGE PATROL CRAFT

Name	No	Builders	Commissioned
SALTO	14 (ex-GS 24, ex-PR 2)	Cantieri Navali Riuniti, Ancona	1936

Displacement, tons: 150 standard; 180 full load
Dimensions, feet (metres): 137 × 18 × 10 *(41.8 × 5.5 × 3.1)*
Main machinery: 2 GM diesels; 1000 hp *(746 kW)*; 2 shafts
Speed, knots: 17. Range, miles: 4000 at 10 kts
Complement: 26
Guns: 1 Bofors 40 mm/70.

Comment: She also acts as a survey vessel. Based at Paysandu.

SALTO *1988, Uruguayan Navy*

1 COASTAL PATROL CRAFT

Name	No	Builders	Commissioned
PAYSANDU	12 (ex-PR 12)	Sewart, USA	1968

Displacement, tons: 60 full load
Dimensions, feet (metres): 83 × 18 × 6 *(25.3 × 5.5 × 1.8)*
Main machinery: 2 GM 16V-71 diesels; 811 hp *(605 kW)* sustained; 2 shafts
Speed, knots: 22. Range, miles: 800 at 20 kts
Complement: 8
Guns: 3—12.7 mm MGs.
Radars: Surface search: Raytheon 1500B; I band.

Comment: Formerly incorrectly listed under Coast Guard. Based at Paysandu.

MINE WARFARE FORCES

4 Ex-GERMAN KONDOR II CLASS (MINESWEEPERS—COASTAL)

Name	No	Builders	Recommissioned
TEMERARIO (ex-*Riesa*)	31	Peenewerft, Wolgast	11 Oct 1991
VALIENTE (ex-*Eilenburg*)	32	Peenewerft, Wolgast	11 Oct 1991
FORTUNA (ex-*Bernau*)	33	Peenewerft, Wolgast	11 Oct 1991
AUDAZ (ex-*Eisleben*)	34	Peenewerft, Wolgast	11 Oct 1991

Displacement, tons: 414 standard
Dimensions, feet (metres): 186 × 24.6 × 7.9 *(56.7 × 7.5 × 2.4)*
Main machinery: 2 Russki/Kolomna Type 40DM diesels; 4408 hp(m) *(3.24 MW)* sustained; 2 shafts; cp props
Speed, knots: 21
Complement: 40
Guns: Twin 25 mm guns removed on transfer. To be replaced by 40 mm.
Mines: 2 rails.
Radars: Surface search: TSR 333; I band.

Comment: Built between 1970 and 1978 and belonged to the former GDR Navy. Transferred in October 1991 without armament. Minesweeping gear retained including MSG-3 variable depth sweep device.

VALIENTE *6/1992, Uruguayan Navy*

RESEARCH VESSEL

1 Ex-US AUK CLASS

Name	No	Builders	Commissioned
COMANDANTE PEDRO CAMPBELL (ex-USS *Chickadee*, MSF 59)	24 (ex-4, ex-MS 31, ex-MSF 1)	Defoe B & M Works	9 Nov 1942

Displacement, tons: 1090 standard; 1250 full load
Dimensions, feet (metres): 221.2 × 32.2 × 10.8 *(67.5 × 9.8 × 3.3)*
Main machinery: Diesel-electric; 4 Alco 539 diesels; 3532 hp *(2.63 MW)*; 4 generators; 2 motors; 2 shafts
Speed, knots: 18. **Range, miles:** 4300 at 10 kts
Complement: 105

Comment: Former US fleet minesweeper. Launched on 20 July 1942. Transferred on loan and commissioned at San Diego on 18 August 1966. Purchased 15 August 1976. Sweeping gear removed and classified as a corvette. Refitted again at Montevideo naval yard in 1988-89 and then recommissioned for Antarctic service without armament. Now classified as a 'Buque Cientifico' and has a red hull. To be relieved by *Vanguardia* and will probably be scrapped in late 1993.

COMANDANTE PEDRO CAMPBELL 4/1992, Hartmut Ehlers

SAIL TRAINING SHIP

Name	No	Builders	Commissioned
CAPITAN MIRANDA	20 (ex-GS 10)	Sociedad Espanola de Construccion Naval, Matagorda, Cadiz	1930

Displacement, tons: 516 standard; 527 full load
Dimensions, feet (metres): 179 × 26 × 10.5 *(54.6 × 7.9 × 3.2)*
Main machinery: 1 GM diesel; 600 hp *(448 kW)*; 1 shaft
Speed, knots: 11
Complement: 49

Comment: Originally a diesel-driven survey ship with pronounced clipper bow. Converted for service as a three-masted schooner, commissioning as cadet training ship in 1978.

CAPITAN MIRANDA 4/1992, Giorgio Ghiglione

SALVAGE VESSELS

1 Ex-GERMAN PIAST CLASS

Name	No	Builders	Commissioned
VANGUARDIA (ex-*Otto Von Guericke*)	26 (ex-A 441)	Danzig, Poland	1977

Displacement, tons: 1732 full load
Dimensions, feet (metres): 240 × 39.4 × 13.1 *(73.2 × 12 × 4)*
Main machinery: 2 Zgoda diesels; 3800 hp(m) *(2.79 MW)*; 2 shafts
Speed, knots: 16. **Range, miles:** 3000 at 12 kts
Radars: Navigation: TSR 333; I band.

Comment: Acquired from Germany in October 1991 and sailed from Rostock in January 1992 after a refit at Neptun-Warnow Werft. Carries extensive towing and firefighting equipment plus a diving bell forward of the bridge. Armed with four 25 mm twin guns when in service with the former GDR Navy.

VANGUARDIA 10/1991, Reinhard Kramer

1 Ex-US COHOES CLASS

Name	No	Builders	Commissioned
HURACAN (ex-USS *Nahant* AN 83)	25 (ex-AM 25, ex-BT 30)	Commercial Ironworks, Portland, Oregon	24 Aug 1945

Displacement, tons: 650 standard; 855 full load
Dimensions, feet (metres): 168.5 × 33.8 × 11.7 *(51.4 × 10.3 × 3.6)*
Main machinery: Diesel-electric; 2 Busch-Sulzer 539 diesels; 1500 hp *(1.12 MW)*; 2 generators; 1 motor; 1 shaft
Speed, knots: 11.5
Complement: 48
Guns: 3 Oerlikon 20 mm.

Comment: Former US netlayer, transferred 15 October 1968 for salvage services carrying divers and underwater swimmers. In 1954 diving equipment and a recompression chamber were installed. Commissioned in Uruguayan Navy 7 April 1969.

HURACAN 1987, Uruguayan Navy

AMPHIBIOUS CRAFT

4 LCM 6 CLASS

LD 40-43

Displacement, tons: 24 light; 57 full load
Dimensions, feet (metres): 56.1 × 14.1 × 3.9 *(17.1 × 4.3 × 1.2)*
Main machinery: 2 Gray Marine 64 HN9 diesels; 330 hp *(264 kW)*; 2 shafts
Speed, knots: 9. **Range, miles:** 130 at 9 kts
Complement: 5
Military lift: 30 tons

Comment: Transferred on lease October 1972. *LD 43* is subordinate to the Fleet Air Arm Flying School at Lago del Sauce.

LD 41 4/1992, Hartmut Ehlers

836 URUGUAY / Amphibious craft — Support ships

2 LCVPs

LD 44-45

Displacement, tons: 15 full load
Dimensions, feet (metres): 46.5 × 11.6 × 2.7 *(14.1 × 3.5 × 0.8)*
Main machinery: 1 GM 4-71 diesel; 115 hp *(86 kW)* sustained; 1 shaft
Speed, knots: 9. **Range, miles:** 580 at 9 kts
Military lift: 10 tons

Comment: Built at Naval Shipyard, Montevideo and completed 1981.

LD 45   4/1992, Hartmut Ehlers

TANKER

Name	No	Builders	Commissioned
PRESIDENTE RIVERA (ex-M/V *Viking Harrier*)	—	Uddevallavarvet AB	2 July 1981

Measurement, tons: 42 235 gross; 87 325 dwt
Dimensions, feet (metres): 750 × 139.1 × 44.3 *(228.6 × 42.4 × 13.5)*
Main machinery: 1 MAN Burmeister & Wain diesel; 15 800 hp(m) *(11.6 MW)*; 1 shaft
Speed, knots: 15

Comment: Purchased in September 1987 and handed over in January 1988. Chartered to ANCAP (state oil company). Offered for sale in 1992.

PRESIDENTE RIVERA   2/1991, van Ginderen Collection

SUPPORT SHIPS

SIRIUS 21

Displacement, tons: 290 full load
Dimensions, feet (metres): 115.1 × 32.8 × 5.9 *(35.1 × 10 × 1.8)*
Main machinery: 2 Detroit 12V-71TA diesels; 840 hp *(626 kW)* sustained; 2 shafts
Speed, knots: 11
Complement: 15

Comment: Buoy tender built at Montevideo Naval Yard and completed in 1988. Endurance, five days.

SIRIUS   4/1992, Hartmut Ehlers

1 SOTOYOMO CLASS

Name	No	Builders	Commissioned
SAN JOSÉ (ex-*Lautaro*)	22 (ex-USS ATA 122, ex-62)	Levingstone SB Co	10 June 1943

Displacement, tons: 860 full load
Dimensions, feet (metres): 143 × 33.9 × 13 *(43.6 × 10.3 × 4)*
Main machinery: Diesel-electric; 2 GM 12-278A diesels; 2200 hp *(1.64 MW)*; 2 generators; 1 motor; 1500 hp *(1.12 MW)*; 1 shaft
Speed, knots: 13. **Range, miles:** 16 500 at 12 kts
Complement: 49 (3 officers)
Guns: 1 USN 3 in *(76 mm)*/50 Mk 26.
Radars: Navigation: Decca 505; I band.

Comment: Originally an ocean rescue tug in USN service but was reclassified as a patrol vessel on transfer to the Chilean Navy. Paid off in 1990 and recommissioned in the Uruguay Navy on 17 May 1991.

SAN JOSÉ   5/1991, Uruguayan Navy

BANCO ORTIZ (ex-*Zingst*, ex-*Elbe*)   27 (ex-7, ex-Y 1655)

Displacement, tons: 261 full load
Dimensions, feet (metres): 100 × 26.6 × 10.8 *(30.5 × 8.1 × 3.3)*
Main machinery: 1 R6 DV 148 diesel; 1 shaft
Speed, knots: 10

Comment: Ex-GDR Type 270 coastal tug acquired in October 1991.

BANCO ORTIZ   4/1992, Hartmut Ehlers

3 COASTGUARD PATROL CRAFT

70-72

Comment: The Prefectura is part of the Navy but some patrol craft retain Prefectura markings.

PREFECTURA 70   4/1992, Hartmut Ehlers

VANUATU

Senior Officer

Commissioner of Police:
W D Saul

General

Originally the New Hebrides. Achieved independence on 30 July 1980, having previously been under Franco-British condominium. The Marine Police are based at Vita (capital) on Efate Island.

Mercantile Marine

Lloyd's Register of Shipping:
280 vessels of 2 154 913 tons gross

PATROL FORCES

1 PACIFIC FORUM PATROL CRAFT

Name	No	Builders	Commissioned
TUKORO	—	Australian Shipbuilding Industries	13 June 1987

Displacement, tons: 165 full load
Dimensions, feet (metres): 103.3 × 26.6 × 6.9 *(31.5 × 8.1 × 2.1)*
Main machinery: 2 Caterpillar 3516TA diesels; 4400 hp *(3.28 MW)* sustained; 2 shafts
Speed, knots: 18. **Range, miles:** 2500 at 12 kts
Complement: 18 (3 officers)
Guns: Can carry 1—20 mm and 2—12.7 mm MGs, but will probably remain unarmed.
Radars: Navigation: Furuno 1011; I band.

Comment: Under the Defence Co-operation Programme Australia has provided one Patrol Craft to the Vanuatu Government. Training and operational and technical assistance is also given by the Royal Australian Navy. Ordered 13 September 1985.

TUKORO
10/1991, Guy Toremans

VENEZUELA

Headquarters' Appointments

Commander General of the Navy (Chief of Naval Operations):
Vice Admiral Ignacio Peña Cimarro
Deputy Chief of Naval Operations:
Vice Admiral Julian Mauco Quinta
Chief of Naval Staff:
Rear Admiral Hector Gerardô Pacheco Moreno

Diplomatic Representation

Naval Attaché in London:
Captain N A Eljuri

Personnel

(a) 1993: 14 200 officers and men including 5200 Marine Corps
(b) 2 years national service

Marines

Two operational Commands—Western and Eastern. The Marines consist of four Battalion Groups—UTC 1 *Libertador Simón Bolívar*, at Maiquetía; UTC 2 *General Rafael Urdaneta*, at Puerto Cabello; UTC 3 *Mariscal José Antonio de Sucre*, at Carúpano and UTC 4 *General Francisco de Miranda*, at Punto Fijo—the existing battalions having been re-designated 'Unidades Tácticas de Combate'; an Amphibious Vehicles Unit—the Unidad de Tanques Anfíbios *Capitán de Corbeta Miguel Ponce Lugo*, a Mixed Artillery Group, an Engineer Unit; a Signals Unit; a Transport Unit and one regiment of Naval Police. There is also the Comando Ribereno de Infantería de Marina *General Frank Rísquez Irribaren*, a paracommando unit and a unit of frogmen commandos.

Coast Guard

Formed in August 1982 as a para-naval force under the command of a Rear Admiral. With headquarters at La Guaira its primary task is the surveillance of the 200 mile Exclusive Economic Zone. Naval control.

National Guard

The Fuerzas Armadas de Cooperacion, generally known as the National Guard, is a paramilitary organisation, currently 17 000 strong. It is concerned, among other things, with customs and internal security—the Maritime Wing operates Coastal and Inshore Patrol Craft.

Bases

Caracas: Main HQ. La Carlota Naval Air Station.
Puerto Cabello: Contralmirante Agustin Armario Main Naval Base, Naval Air Station Command, Naval Schools and Dockyard.
Punto Fijo: Mariscal Falcón Base for Fast Attack Craft.
La Guaira: Small Naval Base (Naval Academy).
Maracaibo: Teniente de Navio Pedro Lucas Urribarri Base for Coast Guard Squadron.
La Banquilla: Secondary Coast Guard Base.
La Tortuga, Los Testigos Islands and Aves de Sotavento: Minor Coast Guard Bases.
Ciudad Bolivar (Orinoco River): HQ Fluvial Command.

Fleet Organisation

The fleet is split into 'Type' squadrons—all the frigates together (except GC 11 and 12) and the same for submarines, light and amphibious forces. Service Craft Squadron composed of T 44 and BE 11, and Coast Guard Squadron includes GC 11 and 12, RA 33 and BO 11. The Fast Attack Squadron of the Constitución class is subordinate to the Fleet Command. There is also a River Forces (Fluvial) Command subordinate to the Marines.

New Construction

Long term plans include two further submarines, four MCM vessels, two LSMs and a replenishment tanker. Current financial problems continue to cause delays in construction and modernisation programmes.

Mercantile Marine

Lloyd's Register of Shipping:
271 vessels of 916 409 tons gross

Strength of the Fleet

Type	Active	Building (Planned)
Submarines, Patrol	2	—
Frigates	6	—
Fast Attack Craft—Missile/Gun	6	—
LSTs	5	—
LCUs	2	—
LCVPs	12	—
Transport	1	—
Survey Vessels	3	—
Coast Guard Craft	26	(4)
Sail Training Ship	1	—
National Guard CPC	100 approx	—

DELETIONS

1990 *Picua, Felipe Larrazabal, Fernando Gomez*

SUBMARINES

Note: The Guppy II *Picua* is used for harbour training. Plans to acquire an ex-USN Barbel class have probably been shelved.

2 TYPE 209 CLASS (TYPE 1300)

Name	No	Builders	Laid down	Launched	Commissioned
SABALO	S 31 (ex-S 21)	Howaldtswerke, Kiel	2 May 1973	1 July 1975	6 Aug 1976
CARIBE	S 32 (ex-S 22)	Howaldtswerke, Kiel	1 Aug 1973	6 Nov 1975	11 Mar 1977

Displacement, tons: 1285 surfaced; 1600 dived
Dimensions, feet (metres): 200.1 × 20.3 × 18 *(61.2 × 6.2 × 5.5)*
Main machinery: Diesel-electric; 4 MTU 12V 493 AZ80 GA31L diesels; 2400 hp(m) *(1.76 MW)* sustained; 4 alternators; 1.7 MW; 1 Siemens motor; 4600 hp(m) *(3.38 MW)* sustained; 1 shaft
Speed, knots: 10 surfaced; 22 dived
Range, miles: 7500 at 10 kts surfaced
Complement: 33 (5 officers)
Torpedoes: 8—21 in *(533 mm)* bow tubes. Combination of (a) AEG SST 4; anti-surface; wire-guided; active/passive homing to 12 km *(6.6 nm)* at 35 kts or 28 km *(15.3 nm)* at 23 kts; warhead 260 kg and (b) Westinghouse Mk 37; anti-submarine; wire-guided; active/passive homing to 8 km *(4.4 nm)* at 24 kts; warhead 150 kg. 14 torpedoes carried. Swim-out discharge. May be replaced by Marconi Tigerfish.
Countermeasures: ESM: Radar warning.
Fire control: Atlas Elektronik TFCS.
Radars: Surface search: Thomson-CSF Calypso C61/63; I band; range 31 km *(17 nm)* for 10 m² target.
Sonars: Atlas Elektronik; hull-mounted; passive/active search and attack; medium frequency.
Thomson Sintra DUUX 2; passive ranging.

Programmes: Type 209, IK81 designed by Ingenieurkontor Lübeck for construction by Howaldtswerke, Kiel and sale by Ferrostaal, Essen, all acting as a consortium. Both refitted at Kiel in 1981 and 1984 respectively. There are plans for two more of the class.
Modernisation: Being carried out by HDW at Kiel. *Sabalo* started in April 1990 and left in late 1992 without fully completing the refit. *Caribe* still docked in Kiel in early 1993 awaiting payment. The hull is slightly lengthened and new engines, fire control, sonar and attack periscopes fitted.
Structure: A single-hull design with two main ballast tanks and forward and after trim tanks. The additional length is due to the new sonar dome similar to German Type 206 system. Fitted with snort and remote machinery control. Slow revving single screw. Very high capacity batteries with GRP lead-acid cells and battery-cooling. Diving depth 250 m *(820 ft)*.
Operational: Endurance, 50 days patrol.

SABALO
1990, HDW

838 VENEZUELA / Frigates — Amphibious forces

FRIGATES
6 MODIFIED LUPO CLASS

Name	No	Builders	Laid down	Launched	Commissioned
MARISCAL SUCRE	F 21	Fincantieri, Riva Trigoso	19 Nov 1976	28 Sep 1978	10 May 1980
ALMIRANTE BRIÓN	F 22	Fincantieri, Riva Trigoso	June 1977	22 Feb 1979	7 Mar 1981
GENERAL URDANETA	F 23	Fincantieri, Riva Trigoso	23 Jan 1978	23 Mar 1979	8 Aug 1981
GENERAL SOUBLETTE	F 24	Fincantieri, Riva Trigoso	26 Aug 1978	4 Jan 1980	5 Dec 1981
GENERAL SALOM	F 25	Fincantieri, Riva Trigoso	7 Nov 1978	13 Jan 1980	3 Apr 1982
ALMIRANTE GARCIA (ex-*José Felix Ribas*)	F 26	Fincantieri, Riva Trigoso	21 Aug 1979	4 Oct 1980	30 July 1982

Displacement, tons: 2208 standard; 2520 full load
Dimensions, feet (metres): 371.3 × 37.1 × 12.1 *(113.2 × 11.3 × 3.7)*
Main machinery: CODOG; 2 Fiat/GE LM 2500 gas turbines; 50 000 hp *(37.3 MW)* sustained; 2 GMT A230.20M diesels; 8000 hp(m) *(5.97 MW)* sustained; 2 shafts; cp props
Speed, knots: 35; 21 on diesels. **Range, miles:** 5000 at 15 kts
Complement: 185

Missiles: SSM: 8 OTO Melara/Matra Otomat Teseo Mk 2 TG1 ❶; active radar homing to 80 km *(43.2 nm)* at 0.9 Mach; warhead 210 kg; sea-skimmer for last 4 km *(2.2 nm)*.
SAM: Selenia Elsag Albatros octuple launcher ❷; 8 Aspide; semi-active radar homing to 13 km *(7 nm)* at 2.5 Mach; height envelope 15-5000 m *(49.2-16 405 ft)*; warhead 30 kg.
Guns: 1 OTO Melara 5 in *(127 mm)*/54 ❸; 85° elevation; 45 rounds/minute to 16 km *(8.7 nm)*; weight of shell 32 kg.
4 Breda 40 mm/70 (2 twin) ❹; 85° elevation; 300 rounds/minute to 12.5 km *(6.8 nm)*; weight of shell 0.96 kg.
Torpedoes: 6—324 mm ILAS 3 (2 triple) tubes ❺. Whitehead A 244S; anti-submarine; active/passive homing to 7 km *(3.8 nm)* at 33 kts; warhead 34 kg (shaped charge).
Countermeasures: Decoys: 2 Breda 105 mm SCLAR 20-barrelled trainable ❻; chaff to 5 km *(2.7 nm)*; illuminants to 12 km *(6.6 nm)*. Can be used for HE bombardment.
ESM: Sperry Marine Guardian Star or Elisra; intercept.
Fire control: Selenia IPN 10 action data automation. 2 Elsag NA 10 MFCS. 2 Dardo GFCS for 40 mm.
Radars: Air/surface search: Selenia RAN 10S ❼; E/F band; range 155 km *(85 nm)*.
Surface search: SMA SPQ/2F; I band; range 73 km *(40 nm)*.
Fire control: Two Selenia Orion 10XP ❽; I/J band.
Two Selenia RTN 20X ❾; I/J band; range 15 km *(8 nm)* (for Dardo).
Tacan: SRN 15A.
Sonars: EDO SQS 29 (Mod 610E); hull-mounted; active search and attack; medium frequency.

Helicopters: 1 AB 212ASW ❿.

MARISCAL SUCRE *(Scale 1 : 900), Ian Sturton*

Programmes: All ordered on 24 October 1975. Similar to ships in the Italian and Peruvian navies.
Modernisation: The first two of the class were scheduled to start a refit by Litton's Ingalls Shipyard in September 1992 but this has probably been further delayed. New communications, EW and data link equipment to be fitted. The helicopter is also to be upgraded.
Structure: Fixed hangar means no space for Aspide reloads. Fully stabilised.

ALMIRANTE BRIÓN *7/1989*

SHIPBORNE AIRCRAFT

Numbers/Type: 5 Agusta AB 212ASW.
Operational speed: 106 kts *(196 km/h)*.
Service ceiling: 14 200 ft *(4330 m)*.
Range: 230 nm *(426 km)*.
Role/Weapon systems: ASW helicopter with secondary ASV role; has ECM/EW potential. Sensors: APS-705 search radar, Bendix ASQ-18A dipping sonar. Weapons: ASW; 2 × Mk 46 or A244/S torpedoes or depth bombs. ASV; 2 × Marte anti-ship missiles.

LAND-BASED MARITIME AIRCRAFT

Numbers/Type: 1 CASA C-212 S 3 Aviocar.
Operational speed: 190 kts *(353 km/h)*.
Service ceiling: 24 000 ft *(7315 m)*.
Range: 1650 nm *(3055 km)*.
Role/Weapon systems: Medium-range MR and coastal protection aircraft; limited armed action. Eight additional aircraft reported ordered in mid-1990 to replace the Trackers and to provide two Communications aircraft. Sensors: APS-128 radar. Weapons: ASW; depth bombs. ASV; gun and rocket pods.

Numbers/Type: 6 Grumman S-2E Tracker.
Operational speed: 130 kts *(241 km/h)*.
Service ceiling: 25 000 ft *(7620 m)*.
Range: 1350 nm *(2500 km)*.
Role/Weapon systems: ASW, surface search and armed MR in Caribbean Sea. Plans to update engines have been abandoned. Sensors: Search radar, MAD, 32 × sonobuoys. Weapons: ASW; internally carried torpedoes, depth bombs and/or mines. ASV; 6 × 127 mm rockets.

Numbers/Type: 3 Agusta ASH-3H Sea King.
Operational speed: 120 kts *(222 km/h)*.
Service ceiling: 12 200 ft *(3720 m)*.
Range: 630 nm *(1165 km)*.
Role/Weapon systems: Medium ASW support. Sensors: Selenia MM/APS-705 chin-mounted search radar, limited ESM. Weapons: ASW, 4 × Mk 46 or A244/S torpedoes or 4 × depth bombs, or combination. ASV; 2 × Marte anti-ship missiles.

AMPHIBIOUS FORCES

Note: In addition there are 11 LCVPs built in 1976.

4 CAPANA CLASS (TANK LANDING SHIPS)

Name	No	Builders	Commissioned
CAPANA	T 61	Korea Tacoma Marine	24 July 1984
ESEQUIBO	T 62	Korea Tacoma Marine	24 July 1984
GOAJIRA	T 63	Korea Tacoma Marine	20 Nov 1984
LOS LLANOS	T 64	Korea Tacoma Marine	20 Nov 1984

Displacement, tons: 4070 full load
Dimensions, feet (metres): 343.8 × 50.5 × 9.8 *(104.8 × 15.4 × 3)*
Main machinery: 2 diesels; 7200 hp(m) *(5.3 MW)*; 2 shafts
Speed, knots: 14. **Range, miles:** 5600 at 11 kts
Complement: 117 (13 officers)
Cargo capacity: 202 troops; 1600 tons cargo; 4 LCVPs
Guns: 2 Breda 40 mm/70 (twin). 2 Oerlikon 20 mm GAM-BO1.
Fire control: Selenia NA 18/V; optronic director.
Helicopters: Platform only.

Comment: Ordered in August 1982. Version III of Korea Tacoma Alligator type. Each has a 50 ton tank turntable and a lift between decks. Similar to Indonesian LSTs.

CAPANA *1990*

1 Ex-US TERREBONNE PARISH CLASS (LST)

Name	No	Builders	Commissioned
AMAZONAS (ex-USS Vernon County LST 1161)	T 51 (ex-T 21)	Ingalls Shipbuilding Corp	1953

Displacement, tons: 2590 light; 5800 full load
Dimensions, feet (metres): 384 oa × 55 × 17 *(117.4 × 16.8 × 3.7)*
Main machinery: 4 GM 16-278A diesels; 6000 hp *(4.48 MW)*; 2 shafts; cp props
Speed, knots: 15. **Range, miles:** 6000 at 12 kts
Complement: 116
Military lift: 395 troops; 2000 tons cargo; 4 LCVPs
Guns: 6 USN 3 in *(76 mm)*/50 (3 twin).
Fire control: 2 Mk 63 GFCS.
Radars: Surface search: Racal Decca; I band.
Fire control: Two Western Electric Mk 34; I/J band.

Comment: Built 1952-53. Transferred on loan 29 June 1973. Purchased 1977. Recommissioned following repairs after grounding 6 August 1980.

2 LCUs

Name	No	Builders	Commissioned
MARGARITA	T 71	Swiftships Inc, Morgan City	Jan 1984
LA ORCHILA	T 72	Swiftships Inc, Morgan City	May 1984

Displacement, tons: 390 full load
Dimensions, feet (metres): 129.9 × 36.1 × 5.9 *(39.6 × 11 × 1.8)*
Main machinery: 2 Detroit 16V-149 diesels; 1800 hp *(1.34 MW)* sustained; 2 shafts
Speed, knots: 13. **Range, miles:** 1500 at 10 kts
Complement: 26 (4 officers)
Military lift: 150 tons cargo; 100 tons fuel
Guns: 3—12.7 mm MGs.

Comment: Both serve in River Command. Reported that four or more are planned in due course. Have a 15 ton crane.

AMAZONAS
1990, van Ginderen Collection

MARGARITA (with MANAURE alongside)
1989, Venezuelan Navy

LIGHT FORCES

Note: Plans for new patrol craft have been delayed by priority being given to modernisation programme.

6 CONSTITUCIÓN CLASS (FAST ATTACK CRAFT—MISSILE AND GUN)

Name	No	Builders	Laid down	Launched	Commissioned
CONSTITUCIÓN	PC 11	Vosper Thornycroft	Jan 1973	1 June 1973	16 Aug 1974
FEDERACIÓN	PC 12	Vosper Thornycroft	Aug 1973	26 Feb 1974	25 Mar 1975
INDEPENDENCIA	PC 13	Vosper Thornycroft	Feb 1973	24 July 1973	20 Sep 1974
LIBERTAD	PC 14	Vosper Thornycroft	Sep 1973	5 Mar 1974	12 June 1975
PATRIA	PC 15	Vosper Thornycroft	Mar 1973	27 Sep 1973	9 Jan 1975
VICTORIA	PC 16	Vosper Thornycroft	Mar 1974	3 Sep 1974	22 Sep 1975

Displacement, tons: 170 full load
Dimensions, feet (metres): 121 × 23.3 × 6 *(36.9 × 7.1 × 1.8)*
Main machinery: 2 MTU MD 16V 538 TB90 diesels; 6000 hp(m) *(4.4 MW)* sustained; 2 shafts
Speed, knots: 31. **Range, miles:** 1350 at 16 kts
Complement: 20 (4 officers)

Missiles: SSM: 2 OTO Melara/Matra Otomat Teseo Mk 2 TG1 *(Federación, Libertad* and *Victoria)*; active radar homing to 80 km *(43.2 nm)* at 0.9 Mach; warhead 210 kg; sea-skimmer.
Guns: 1 OTO Melara 3 in *(76 mm)*/62 compact *(Constitución, Independencia* and *Patria)*; 85° elevation; 85 rounds/minute to 16 km *(8.7 nm)*; weight of shell 6 kg.
1 Breda 30 mm/70 *(Federación, Libertad* and *Victoria)*; 85° elevation; 800 rounds/minute; weight of shell 0.37 kg.
Fire control: Elsag NA 10 Mod 1 GFCS (gunships). Alenia Elsag Medusa optronic director (missile ships).
Radars: Surface search: SPQ 2D.
Fire control: Selenia RTN 10X (in 76 mm ships); I/J band.

Programmes: Transferred from the Navy in 1983 to the Coast Guard but now back again with Fleet Command.
Modernisation: All were to have been modernised with the three gun FACs being fitted with Harpoon SSM in place of the 76 mm and Harpoon replacing Otomat in the other three. It is possible that this may not now happen if the Harpoon missiles are to be used for shore-based coastal defence. Single Breda 30 mm guns were acquired in 1989 and have replaced the 40 mm guns in the missile craft.

FEDERACIÓN
7/1990, Venezuelan Navy

7/1990, Venezuelan Navy

840 VENEZUELA / Service forces — Coast Guard

SERVICE FORCES

Notes: (1) A fleet tanker is to be acquired as soon as possible.
(2) A Torpedo Recovery Vessel was ordered from Maracaibo in 1989.

1 LOGISTIC SUPPORT SHIP

Name	No	Builders	Commissioned
PUERTO CABELLO (ex-M/V *Sierra Nevada*)	T 44	Drammen Slip & Verk, Drammen	1972

Displacement, tons: 13 500 full load
Measurement, tons: 6682 gross; 9218 dwt
Dimensions, feet (metres): 461.3 × 59 × 29.5 *(140.6 × 18 × 9)*
Main machinery: 1 Sulzer diesel; 13 200 hp(m) *(9.7 MW)*; 1 shaft
Speed, knots: 22.5

Comment: Commissioned in the Navy 22 May 1986. Former refrigerated cargo ship.

PUERTO CABELLO 5/1991, Giorgio Arra

SAIL TRAINING SHIP

Name	No	Builders	Commissioned
SIMON BOLIVAR	BE 11	A T Celaya, Bilbao	6 Aug 1980

Displacement, tons: 1260 full load
Measurement, tons: 934 gross
Dimensions, feet (metres): 270.6 × 34.8 × 14.4 *(82.5 × 10.6 × 4.4)*
Main machinery: 1 Detroit 12V-149T diesel; 875 hp *(652 kW)* sustained; 1 shaft
Speed, knots: 10
Complement: 195 (17 officers, 76 ratings, 18 midshipwomen, 84 midshipmen)

Comment: Ordered in 1978. Launched 21 November 1979. Three-masted barque; near sister to *Guayas* (Ecuador). Sail area (23 sails), 1650 m². Highest mast, 131.2 ft *(40 m)*.

SIMON BOLIVAR 4/1992, van Ginderen Collection

SURVEY VESSELS

Name	No	Builders	Commissioned
PUNTA BRAVA	BO 11	Bazán, Cartagena	14 Mar 1991

Displacement, tons: 1170 full load
Dimensions, feet (metres): 202.4 × 39 × 12.1 *(61.7 × 11.9 × 3.7)*
Main machinery: 2 Bazán-MAN 7L20/27 diesels; 2500 hp(m) *(1.84 MW)*; 2 shafts
Speed, knots: 13. **Range, miles:** 8000 at 13 kts
Complement: 49 (6 officers) plus 6 scientists
Radars: Navigation: ARPA; I band.

Comment: Ordered in September 1988 and launched 9 March 1990. Developed from the Spanish Malaspina class. A multi-purpose ship for oceanography, marine resource evaluation, geophysical and biological research. Equipped with Qubit hydrographic system. Carries two survey launches. EW equipment is to be fitted.

PUNTA BRAVA 1991, Bazán

Name	No	Builders	Commissioned
PENINSULA DE ARAYA (ex-*Gabriela*)	LH 11 (ex-P 119)	Abeking & Rasmussen, Lemwerder	5 Feb 1974
PENINSULA DE PARAGUANA (ex-*Lely*)	LH 12 (ex-P 121)	Abeking & Rasmussen, Lemwerder	7 Feb 1974

Displacement, tons: 90 full load
Dimensions, feet (metres): 88.6 × 18.4 × 4.9 *(27 × 5.6 × 1.5)*
Main machinery: 2 MTU diesels; 2300 hp(m) *(1.69 MW)*; 2 shafts
Speed, knots: 20
Complement: 9 (1 officer)

Comment: LH 12 laid down 28 May 1973, launched 12 December 1973 and LH 11 laid down 10 March 1973, launched 29 November 1973. Acquired in September 1986 from the Instituto de Canalizaciones.

COAST GUARD

Note: Plans for new offshore patrol ships have been delayed by lack of funds.

2 ALMIRANTE CLEMENTE CLASS

Name	No	Builders	Commissioned
ALMIRANTE CLEMENTE	GC 11	Ansaldo, Leghorn	1956
GENERAL JOSÉ TRINIDAD MORAN	GC 12	Ansaldo, Leghorn	1956

Displacement, tons: 1300 standard; 1500 full load
Dimensions, feet (metres): 325.1 × 35.5 × 12.2 *(99.1 × 10.8 × 3.7)*
Main machinery: 2 GMT 16-645E7C diesels; 6080 hp(m) *(4.47 MW)* sustained; 2 shafts
Speed, knots: 22. **Range, miles:** 3500 at 15 kts
Complement: 162 (12 officers)

Guns: 2 OTO Melara 3 in *(76 mm)*/62 compact; 85 ° elevation; 85 rounds/minute to 16 km *(8.7 nm)*; weight of shell 6 kg.
2 Breda 40 mm/70 (twin); 85° elevation; 300 rounds/minute to 12.5 km *(6.8 nm)*; weight of shell 0.96 kg.
Torpedoes: 6—324 mm ILAS 3 (2 triple) tubes. Whitehead A 244S; anti-submarine; active/passive homing to 7 km *(3.8 nm)* at 33 kts; warhead 34 kg (shaped charge).
Fire control: Elsag NA 10 GFCS.
Radars: Air search: Plessey AWS 4; D band.
Surface search: Racal Decca 1226; I band.
Fire control: Selenia RTN 10X; I/J band; range 40 km *(22 nm)*.
Sonars: Plessey PMS 26; hull-mounted; active search and attack; 10 kHz.

Programmes: Survivors of a class of six ordered in 1953. Both laid down 5 May 1954 and launched 12 December 1954.
Modernisation: Both ships were refitted by Cammell Laird/Plessey group in April 1968. 4 in guns replaced by 76 mm OTO Melara compact. Both refitted again in Italy in 1983-85, prior to transfer to Coast Guard duties.
Structure: Fitted with Denny-Brown fin stabilisers and air-conditioned throughout the living and command spaces.
Operational: Navigation, SATNAV fitted. Oil fuel, 350 tons.

ALMIRANTE CLEMENTE 1989, Venezuelan Navy

1 Ex-US CHEROKEE CLASS

Name	No	Builders	Commissioned
MIGUEL RODRIGUEZ (ex-USS *Salinan* ATF 161)	RA 33 (ex-R 23)	Charleston SB and DD Co	9 Nov 1945

Displacement, tons: 1235 standard; 1675 full load
Dimensions, feet (metres): 205 × 38.5 × 17 *(62.5 × 11.7 × 5.2)*
Main machinery: Diesel-electric; 4 GM 16-278A diesels; 4400 hp *(3.28 MW)*; 4 generators; 1 motor; 3000 hp *(2.24 MW)*; 1 shaft
Speed, knots: 15. **Range, miles:** 7000 at 15 kts.
Complement: 85
Guns: 1 USN 3 in *(76 mm)*/50 *(Felipe Larrazábal)*.
Radars: Navigation: Sperry SPS 53; I/J band.

Comment: Acquired on 1 Septe

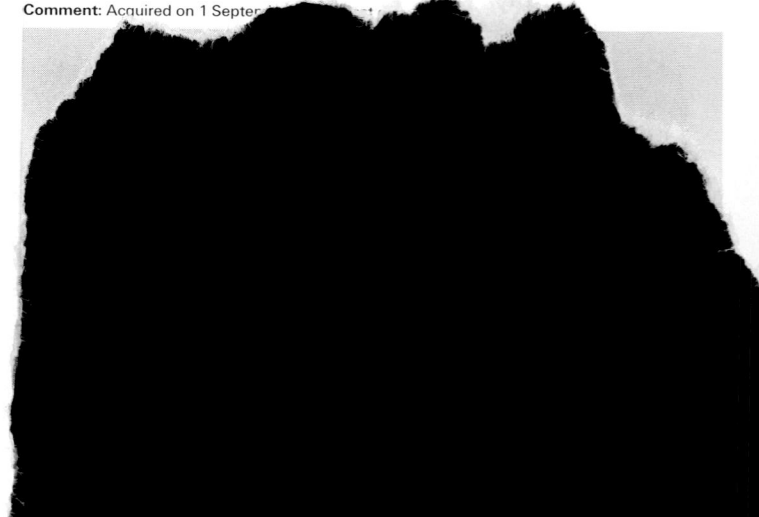

2 Ex-US POINT CLASS

PETREL (ex-*Point Knoll*) PG 31 **ALCATRAZ** (ex-*Point Judith*) PG 32

Displacement, tons: 66 full load
Dimensions, feet (metres): 83 × 17.2 × 5.8 *(25.3 × 5.2 × 1.8)*
Main machinery: 2 Caterpillar diesels; 1600 hp *(1.19 MW)*; 2 shafts
Speed, knots: 23.5. Range, miles: 1500 at 8 kts
Complement: 10 (1 officer)

Comment: *Petrel* transferred on 11 September 1991, and *Alcatraz* on 20 December 1991. The 12.7 mm MGs in US service may be upgraded. Eight more of the class may be acquired.

2 UTILITY CRAFT

LOS TAQUES LG 11 **LOS CAYOS** LG 12

Comment: Former trawlers; displacement, 300 tons. Commissioned 15 May 1981 and 17 July 1984 respectively. Used for salvage and SAR tasks.

LOS CAYOS *1989, Venezuelan Navy*

POINT class (USCG colours) *1988, Giorgio Arra*

6 RIVER CRAFT

ANACOCO LF 11	ATURES LF 13	EL AMPARO LA 01
MANAIPO LF 12	MAIPURES LF 14	YOPITO LC 01

Comment: *El Amparo* is an ambulance launch similar to PF 31.

8 RIVER PATROL CRAFT

Name	No	Displacement (tons)	Speed (kts)
MANAURE	PF 21	18	15
MARA	PF 22	18	15
GUAICAIPURO	PF 23	14	15
TAMANACO	PF 24	14	15
TEREPAIMA	PF 31	3	45
TIUNA	PF 32	3	45
YARACUY	PF 33	3	45
SOROCAIMA	PF 34	3	45

Comment: All have a complement of five and are armed with one 12.7 mm MG. See picture of *Margarita* with *Manaure* alongside.

7 INSHORE PATROL CRAFT

POLARIS LG 21	RIGEL LG 23	ANTARES LG 25	ALTAIR LG 27
SPICA LG 22	ALDEBARAN LG 24	CANOPUS LG 26	

Displacement, tons: 5 full load
Dimensions, feet (metres): 32.8 × 8.5 × 2.6 *(10 × 2.6 × 0.8)*
Main machinery: 2 diesels; 400 hp(m) *(294 kW)*; 2 shafts
Speed, knots: 45. Range, miles: 140 at 45 kts
Complement: 4

Comment: Acquired in 1987 from Cougar Marine, Hamble.

NATIONAL GUARD

(FUERZAS ARMADAS DE COOPERACION)

Note: Up to about 100 patrol craft in total including River Launches and undecked District Craft. Only about half were operational in early 1993.

22 ITALIAN TYPE A (COASTAL PATROL CRAFT)

Name	No	Name	No
RIO ORINOCO	A 7414	RIO CAPANAPARO	A 7425
RIO CUYUNI	A 7415	RIO YURUARI	A 7426
RIO VENTUARI	A 7416	RIO CAURA	A 7427
RIO CAPARO	A 7417	RIO MOTATAN	A 7628
RIO TOCUYO	A 7418	RIO GRITA	A 7629
RIO VENAMO	A 7419	RIO YURUAN	A 7630
RIO LIMON	A 7420	RIO BOCONO	A 7631
RIO SAN JUAN	A 7421	RIO NEVERI	A 7632
RIO TURBIO	A 7422	RIO CARONI	A 7633
RIO TORBES	A 7423	RIO GUANARE	A 7634
RIO ESCALANTE	A 7424	RIO GUAINIA	A 7635

Italian built (A 7414, A 7416-A 7424)

Displacement, tons: 48 full load
Dimensions, feet (metres): 75.4 × 19 × 8.5 *(23 × 5.8 × 2.6)*
Main machinery: 2 MTU 12V 493 TY70 diesels; 2200 hp(m) *(1.62 MW)* sustained; 2 shafts
Speed, knots: 30. Range, miles: 500 at 25 kts
Complement: 8
Guns: 1—12.7 mm MG.
Radars: Navigation: FR 24; I band.

Comment: First ordered in May 1973 from INMA, La Spezia and delivered from 1974 onwards.

Venezuelan built (A 7415, A 7425-A 7635)

Displacement, tons: 43 full load
Dimensions, feet (metres): 76.8 × 16.1 × 10.2 *(23.4 × 4.9 × 3.1)*
Main machinery: 2 GM 12V 92 TI diesels; 2040 hp *(1.52 kW)* sustained; 2 shafts
Speed, knots: 30. Range, miles: 1000 at 25 kts
Complement: 12
Guns: 1—12.7 mm MG.
Radars: Navigation: FR 711; I band.

Comment: Ordered from Dianca, Puerto Cabello.

2 VENEZUELAN TYPE

RIO ALTAGRACIA A 6704 **RIO MANZANARES** A 6705

Dimensions, feet (metres): 49.2 × 12.5 × 6.2 *(15 × 3.8 × 1.9)*
Main machinery: 1 Type 4B-316 diesel; 1 shaft
Speed, knots: 12. Range, miles: 140 at 12 kts
Complement: 6
Radars: Navigation: FR 10; I band.

12 PUNTA CLASS

Name	No	Name	No
PUNTA BARIMA	A 8201	PUNTA MACOYA	A 8307
PUNTA MOSQUITO	A 8202	PUNTA MORON	A 8308
PUNTA MULATOS	A 8203	PUNTA UNARE	A 8309
PUNTA PERRET	A 8204	PUNTA BALLENA	A 8310
PUNTA CARDON	A 8205	PUNTA MACURO	A 8311
PUNTA PLAYA	A 8206	PUNTA MARIUSA	A 8312

Displacement, tons: 15 full load
Dimensions, feet (metres): 43 × 13.4 × 3.9 *(13.1 × 4.1 × 1.2)*
Main machinery: 2 Detroit 12V-92TA diesels; 1020 hp *(761 kW)* sustained; 2 shafts
Speed, knots: 28. Range, miles: 390 at 25 kts
Complement: 4
Guns: 2—12.7 mm MGs.
Radars: Navigation: Raytheon; I band.

Comment: Ordered 24 January 1984. Built by Bertram Yacht, Miami, Florida. Aluminium hulls. Completed from July-December 1984.

RIO GUANARE *1989*

PUNTA class (alongside RIO GUANARE) *1989*

12 PROTECTOR CLASS

Name	No	Name	No
RIO ARAUCA II	B 8421	RIO SARARE	B 8427
RIO CATATUMBO II	B 8422	RIO URIBANTE	B 8428
RIO APURE II	B 8423	RIO SINARUCO	B 8429
RIO NEGRO II	B 8424	RIO ICABARU	B 8430
RIO META II	B 8425	RIO GUARICO II	B 8431
RIO PORTUGUESA II	B 8426	RIO YARACUY	B 8432

Displacement, tons: 15 full load
Dimensions, feet (metres): 43.6 × 14.8 × 3.9 *(13.3 × 4.5 × 1.2)*
Main machinery: 2 Detroit 8V-92TA diesels; 750 hp *(560 kW)* sustained; 2 shafts
Speed, knots: 28. **Range, miles:** 600 at 25 kts
Complement: 4
Guns: 2—12.7 mm MGs.

Comment: Built by SeaArk Marine, Monticello and commissioned in 1987.

PROTECTOR class　　　　　　　　　　　　　　　　　　　　　　　　*1987, SeaArk*

10 LAGO CLASS (RIVER PATROL CRAFT)

Name	No	Name	No
LAGO 1	A 6901	RIO CHAMA	A 7919
LAGO 2	A 6902	RIO CARIBE	A 7920
LAGO 3	A 6903	RIO TUY	A 7921
LAGO 4	A 6904	MANATI	A 7929
RIO CABRIALES	A 7918	GOAIGOAZA	A 8223

Displacement, tons: 1.5 full load
Dimensions, feet (metres): 20.7 × 7.9 × 1 *(6.3 × 2.4 × 0.3)*
Main machinery: 2 Evinrude outboard petrol engines; 230 hp *(172 kW)*
Speed, knots: 30. **Range, miles:** 120 at 15 kts
Complement: 4
Guns: 1—12.7 mm MG.
Radars: Navigation: FR 10.

Comment: Built by SeaArk Marine, Monticello. All delivered 6 August 1984. The last pair are classified as Yachts.

15 SEA ARK TYPE (RIVER PATROL CRAFT)

Displacement, tons: 0.5
Dimensions, feet (metres): 18 × 6.9 × 0.7 *(5.5 × 2.1 × 0.2)*
Main machinery: 1 OMC outboard
Speed, knots: 30. **Range, miles:** 75 at 15 kts
Complement: 4
Guns: 1—12.7 mm MG.

Comment: Ordered from SeaArk Marine, Monticello. Completed May-August 1984. Aluminium hull.

VIETNAM

Headquarters' Appointment

Chief of Naval Forces:
Vice Admiral Hoang Hau Thai

Personnel

(a) 1993: 9000 regulars
(b) Additional conscripts on three to four year term (about 3000)
(c) 27 000 naval infantry

Strength of the Fleet

From 1978 to 1990 the USSR transferred a number of ships and craft as well as providing fuel in return for the use of Cam-Ranh Bay naval base. From 1 January 1991 the relationship became formal with further transfers only available at market prices. Many of the ex-US naval ships have now been deleted either by sale or scrap. The resultant order of battle is now composed of vessels most of which can lay some claim to operational availability. There are many others still alongside in naval bases either as hulks or providing spares for the operational units.

Bases

Cam Ranh Bay, Cân Tho, Hai Phong, Hue, Da Nang, Hanoi.

Pennant numbers

Appear to change frequently.

Mercantile Marine

Lloyd's Register of Shipping:
230 vessels of 562 581 tons gross

FRIGATES

5 Ex-SOVIET PETYA CLASS

HQ 09, 11 (Type III)　　HQ 13, 15, 17 (Type II)

Displacement, tons: 950 standard; 1180 full load
Dimensions, feet (metres): 268.3 × 29.9 × 9.5 *(81.8 × 9.1 × 2.9)*
Main machinery: CODAG; 2 gas turbines; 30 000 hp(m) *(22 MW)*; 1 Type 61V-3 diesel; 5400 hp(m) *(3.97 MW)* sustained; centre shaft; 3 shafts
Speed, knots: 32. **Range, miles:** 4870 at 10 kts; 450 at 29 kts
Complement: 98

Guns: 4 USSR 3 in *(76 mm)*/60 (2 twin); 80° elevation; 90 rounds/minute to 15 km *(8 nm)*; weight of shell 6.8 kg.
Torpedoes: 3—21 in *(533 mm)* (triple) tubes (Petya III). Soviet Type 53; dual purpose; pattern active/passive homing up to 20 km *(10.8 nm)* at up to 45 kts; warhead 400 kg.
10—16 in *(406 mm)* (2 quin) tubes (Petya II). Soviet Type 40; anti-submarine; active/passive homing up to 15 km *(8 nm)* at up to 40 kts; warhead 100-150 kg.
A/S mortars: 4 RBU 6000 12-tubed trainable (Petya II); range 6000 m; warhead 31 kg.
4 RBU 2500 16-tubed trainable (Petya III); range 2500 m; warhead 21 kg.
Depth charges: 2 racks.
Mines: Can carry 22.
Countermeasures: ESM: 2 Watch Dog; radar warning.
Radars: Air/surface search: Strut Curve; F band; range 110 km *(60 nm)* for 2 m² target.
Navigation: Don 2; I band.
Fire control: Hawk Screech; I band.
IFF: High Pole B. Two Square Head.
Sonars: Hull-mounted; active attack; high frequency.

Programmes: Two Petya III (export version) transferred in December 1978 and three Petya IIs, two in December 1983 and one in December 1984.
Structure: The Petya IIIs have the same hulls as the Petya IIs but are fitted with one triple 21 in *(533 mm)* torpedo launcher in place of the two 16 in *(406 mm)* quintuple tubes and have four RBU 2500s in place of two RBU 6000s.

1 Ex-US SAVAGE CLASS

Name	No	Builders	Commissioned
DAI KY	HQ 03	Consolidated Steel Corporation, Orange, Texas	25 Jan 1944
(ex-*Tran Khanh Du*, ex-USS *Forster* DER 334)			

Displacement, tons: 1590 standard; 1850 full load
Dimensions, feet (metres): 306 × 36.6 × 14 *(93.3 × 11.2 × 4.3)*
Main machinery: 4 Fairbanks-Morse 38D8-1/8-10 diesels; 7080 hp *(5.28 MW)* sustained; 2 shafts
Speed, knots: 21. **Range, miles:** 10 000 at 15 kts
Complement: 170 approx

Missiles: SAM: 2 SA-N-5 Grail quad launchers; manual aiming; IR homing to 6 km *(3.2 nm)* at 1.5 Mach; altitude to 2500 m *(8000 ft)*; warhead 1.5 kg.
Guns: 2 USN 3 in *(76 mm)*/50; 85° elevation; 20 rounds/minute to 12 km *(6.6 nm)*; weight of shell 6 kg.
Torpedoes: 6—324 mm US Mk 32 (2 triple) tubes.
A/S mortars: 1 Mk 15 Hedgehog.
Depth charges: 1 rack.
Fire control: Mk 63 GFCS (fwd). Mk 51 GFCS (aft).
Radars: Air search: Westinghouse SPS 28; B/C band.
Surface search: Raytheon SPS 10; G band.
Fire control: Western Electric Mk 34; I/J band.
Sonars: SQS 29; hull-mounted; active attack; high frequency.

Programmes: Former US Navy destroyer escort of the FMR design group. Transferred to South Vietnamese Navy on 25 September 1971. Was in overhaul at time of occupation of South Vietnam and was written off by the USN as 'Transferred to Vietnam' 30 April 1975.
Operational: Used as a training ship.

PETYA II　　　　　　　　　　　　　　　　　　　　　　　　　　　　*1989*

SAVAGE (Tunisian colours)　　　　　　　　　　　*1989, van Ginderen Collection*

Frigates — Light forces / VIETNAM

1 Ex-US BARNEGAT CLASS

Name	No	Builders	Commissioned
PHAM NGU LAO (ex-USCG *Absecon* WHEC 374, ex-*WAVP 23*)	HQ 01	Lake Washington S. Y.	28 Jan 1943

Displacement, tons: 1766 standard; 2800 full load
Dimensions, feet (metres): 310.8 × 41.1 × 13.5 *(94.7 × 12.5 × 4.1)*
Main machinery: 2 Fairbanks-Morse 38D8-1/8-10 diesels; 3540 hp *(2.64 MW)* sustained; 2 shafts
Speed, knots: 18. **Range, miles:** 20 000 at 12 kts
Complement: 200 approx

Missiles: SSM: 2 SS-N-2A Styx; active radar or IR homing to 46 km *(25 nm)* at 0.9 Mach; warhead 513 kg.
SAM: 2 SA-N-5 Grail quad launchers; manual aiming; IR homing to 6 km *(3.2 nm)* at 1.5 Mach; altitude to 2500 m *(8000 ft)*; warhead 1.5 kg.
Guns: 1 USN 5 in *(127 mm)*/38; 85° elevation; 15 rounds/minute to 17 km *(9.3 nm)*; weight of shell 25 kg.
3—37 mm/63. 4—25 mm (2 twin).
2—81 mm mortars.
Radars: Surface search: Raytheon SPS 21; G/H band; range 22 km *(12 nm)*.
Fire control: RCA/GE Mk 26; I/J band.

Programmes: Last of a group built as seaplane tenders for the US Navy. Transferred to US Coast Guard in 1948, initially on loan designated WAVP and then on permanent transfer, subsequently redesignated as high endurance cutter (WHEC). Transferred from US Coast Guard to South Vietnamese Navy in 1971.
Modernisation: SSMs mounted aft and close range armament fitted in the mid-1980s.

CORVETTES

2 Ex-US ADMIRABLE CLASS

Name	No	Launched
— (ex-USS *Prowess* IX 305, ex-MSF 280, ex-*Ha Hoi*)	HQ 07	17 Feb 1944
— (ex-USS *Sentry*, ex-MSF 299)	HQ 13	30 May 1944

Displacement, tons: 650 standard; 945 full load
Dimensions, feet (metres): 184.5 × 33 × 9.75 *(56.3 × 10 × 3)*
Main machinery: 2 Cooper-Bessemer GSB-8 diesels; 1710 hp *(1.28 MW)*; 2 shafts
Speed, knots: 14
Complement: 80 approx
Guns: 2 China 57 mm/70 (twin). 2—37 mm/63. Up to 8 Oerlikon 20 mm (4 twin).
Radars: Surface search: Sperry SPS 53; I band.

Comment: Former US Navy minesweepers of the Admirable class (originally designated AM). Built by Gulf SB Corp, Chicasaw, Alabama. Transferred to South Vietnam in 1970. Minesweeping equipment has been removed. Written off by the USN as 'Transferred to Vietnam' 30 April 1975. One employed in patrol and escort roles. Second ship probably non-operational.

BARNEGAT (Italian colours) *1991, van Ginderen Collection*

ADMIRABLE (Dominican Republic colours) *1990, Hartmut Ehlers*

LAND-BASED MARITIME AIRCRAFT

Numbers/Type: 5 Mil Mi-4 Hound B.
Operational speed: 113 kts *(210 km/h)*.
Service ceiling: 18 000 ft *(5500 m)*.
Range: 216 nm *(400 km)*.
Role/Weapon systems: Limited value ASW helicopter with primary support and assault roles. Sensors: Possible search radar and sonobuoys. Weapons: 4 × torpedoes or mines, light machine guns.

Numbers/Type: 5 Kamov Ka-27/Ka-29 Helix A.
Operational speed: 135 kts *(250 km/h)*.
Service ceiling: 19 685 ft *(6000 m)*.
Range: 432 nm *(800 km)*.
Role/Weapon systems: ASW helicopter; successor to Hormone with greater ASW potential. Sensors: Search radar, dipping sonar, MAD, ECM. Weapons: ASW; 3 × torpedoes, depth bombs or mines.

Numbers/Type: 8 Kamov Ka-25 Hormone A.
Operational speed: 119 kts *(220 km/h)*.
Service ceiling: 11 500 ft *(3500 m)*.
Range: 350 nm *(650 km)*.
Role/Weapon systems: Sensors: Search radar, dipping sonar, MAD, ECM, EW equipment and search radar. Weapons: ASW; 2 × torpedoes, depth bombs. ASV; 2 or 4 × missiles or rocket launchers.

Numbers/Type: 4 Beriev Be-12 Mail.
Operational speed: 328 kts *(608 km/h)*.
Service ceiling: 37 000 ft *(11 280 m)*.
Range: 4050 nm *(7500 km)*.
Role/Weapon systems: Long-range ASW/MR amphibian. Sensors: Search/weather radar, MAD, EW. Weapons: ASW; 5 tons of depth bombs, mines or torpedoes. ASV; limited missile and rocket armament.

LIGHT FORCES

Note: In addition to the craft listed below there are eight ex-Chinese Shanghai II class and 14 ex-Chinese Shantou class of doubtful operational status.

8 Ex-SOVIET OSA II CLASS (FAST ATTACK CRAFT—MISSILE)

Displacement, tons: 245 full load
Dimensions, feet (metres): 126.6 × 24.9 × 8.8 *(38.6 × 7.6 × 2.7)*
Main machinery: 3 Type M 504 diesels; 10 800 hp(m) *(7.94 MW)* sustained; 3 shafts
Speed, knots: 37. **Range, miles:** 500 at 35 kts
Complement: 30
Missiles: SSM: 4 SS-N-2B Styx; active radar or IR homing to 46 km *(25 nm)* at 0.9 Mach; warhead 513 kg.
Guns: 4 USSR 30 mm/65 (2 twin); 85° elevation; 500 rounds/minute to 5 km *(2.7 nm)*; weight of shell 0.54 kg.
Radars: Surface search: Square Tie; I band.
Fire control: Drum Tilt; H/I band.
IFF: High Pole. Two Square Head.

Comment: Transferred: two in October 1979, two in September 1980, two in November 1980 and two in February 1981.

16 Ex-SOVIET SHERSHEN CLASS (FAST ATTACK CRAFT—TORPEDO)

Displacement, tons: 145 standard; 170 full load
Dimensions, feet (metres): 113.8 × 22 × 4.9 *(34.7 × 6.7 × 1.5)*
Main machinery: 3 Type 503A diesels; 8025 hp(m) *(5.9 MW)* sustained; 3 shafts
Speed, knots: 45. **Range, miles:** 850 at 30 kts; 460 at 42 kts
Complement: 23
Missiles: SAM: 1 SA-N-5 Grail quad launcher; manual aiming; IR homing to 6 km *(3.2 nm)* at 1.5 Mach; altitude to 2500 m *(8000 ft)*; warhead 1.5 kg.
Guns: 4 USSR 30 mm/65 (2 twin); 85° elevation; 500 rounds/minute to 5 km *(2.7 nm)*; weight of shell 0.54 kg.
Torpedoes: 4—21 in *(533 mm)* tubes (not in all). Soviet Type 53.
Depth charges: 2 racks (12).
Mines: Can carry 6.
Radars: Surface search: Pot Drum; H/I band.
Fire control: Drum Tilt; H/I band.
IFF: High Pole A. Square Head.

Comment: Transferred: two in 1973, two in April 1979 (without torpedo tubes), two in September 1979, two in August 1980, two in October 1980, two in January 1983 and four in June 1983.

OSA II (Russian number) *1987, G Jacobs*

SHERSHEN *1987*

5 Ex-SOVIET TURYA CLASS (FAST ATTACK CRAFT—TORPEDO, HYDROFOIL)

Displacement, tons: 190 standard; 250 full load
Dimensions, feet (metres): 129.9 × 29.9 (41 over foils) × 5.9 (13.1 over foils) *(39.6 × 7.6 (12.5) × 1.8 (4))*
Main machinery: 3 Type M 504 diesels; 10 800 hp(m) *(7.94 MW)* sustained; 3 shafts
Speed, knots: 40. **Range, miles:** 600 at 35 kts foilborne; 1450 at 14 kts hullborne
Complement: 30
Guns: 2 USSR 57 mm/70 (twin, aft); 90° elevation; 120 rounds/minute to 8 km *(4.4 nm)*; weight of shell 2.8 kg.
2 USSR 25 mm/80 (twin, fwd); 85° elevation; 270 rounds/minute to 3 km *(1.6 nm)*; weight of shell 0.34 kg.
Torpedoes: 4—21 in *(533 mm)* tubes (not in all). Soviet Type 53.
Depth charges: 2 racks.
Radars: Surface search: Pot Drum; H/I band.
Fire control: Muff Cob; G/H band.
IFF: High Pole B. Square Head.
Sonars: Helicopter (not in all); VDS; high frequency.

Comment: Transferred: two in mid-1984, one in late 1984 and two in January 1986. Two of the five do not have torpedo tubes or sonar.

TURYA (without torpedo tubes)   1988

8 Ex-SOVIET SO 1 CLASS (LARGE PATROL CRAFT)

Displacement, tons: 170 standard; 215 full load
Dimensions, feet (metres): 137.8 × 19.7 × 5.9 *(42 × 6 × 1.8)*
Main machinery: 3 Kolomna Type 40-D diesels; 6600 hp(m) *(4.8 MW)* sustained; 3 shafts
Speed, knots: 28. **Range, miles:** 1100 at 13 kts; 350 at 28 kts
Complement: 31
Guns: 4 USSR 25 mm/80 (2 twin); 85° elevation; 270 rounds/minute to 3 km *(1.6 nm)*; weight of shell 0.34 kg.
A/S mortars: 4 RBU 1200 5-tubed fixed; range 1200 m; warhead 34 kg.
Depth charges: 2 racks (24).
Mines: 10.
Radars: Surface search: Pot Head; I band.
IFF: High Pole A. Dead Duck.

Comment: Transferred: two in March 1980, two in September 1980, two in May 1981, and two in September 1983. Four more of this class were transferred in 1960-63 but have been deleted.

SO 1   1984

2 Ex-SOVIET PO 2 CLASS (COASTAL PATROL CRAFT)

Displacement, tons: 55 full load
Dimensions, feet (metres): 82 × 16.7 × 5.6 *(25 × 5.1 × 1.7)*
Main machinery: 1 Type 3-D-12 diesel; 300 hp(m) *(220 kW)* sustained; 1 shaft
Speed, knots: 12
Complement: 8
Guns: 2 USSR 25 mm/80.

Comment: Two transferred in 1977, two in February 1980, one in October 1981, one in 1982 and four in 1983. Four deleted 1983-84, four more in 1986-87.

PO 2   1990

3 Ex-US PGM 71 CLASS (LARGE PATROL CRAFT)

Displacement, tons: 142 full load
Dimensions, feet (metres): 101 × 21.3 × 7.5 *(30.8 × 6.5 × 2.3)*
Main machinery: 2 GM 6-71 diesels; 1392 hp(m) *(1.04 MW)* sustained; 2 shafts
Speed, knots: 17. **Range, miles:** 1000 at 17 kts
Complement: 30
Guns: 1 Bofors 40 mm/56. 4 Oerlikon 20 mm.

Comment: Ten transferred to South Vietnam 1963-67. Three deleted in 1988-89, four more in 1990-91. Probably non-operational.

11 Ex-SOVIET ZHUK CLASS (FAST ATTACK CRAFT—PATROL)

Displacement, tons: 50 full load
Dimensions, feet (metres): 75.4 × 17 × 6.2 *(23 × 5.2 × 1.9)*
Main machinery: 2 Type M 50 diesels; 2200 hp(m) *(1.6 MW)* sustained; 2 shafts
Speed, knots: 30. **Range, miles:** 1100 at 15 kts
Complement: 17
Guns: 4—14.5 mm (2 twin) MGs.

Comment: Transferred: three in 1978, three in November 1979, three in February 1986, two in January 1990 and three in August 1990. So far three have been deleted, a further four are of doubtful operational status.

ZHUK   1989

2 Ex-SOVIET POLUCHAT CLASS (COASTAL PATROL CRAFT)

Displacement, tons: 100 full load
Dimensions, feet (metres): 97.1 × 19 × 4.8 *(29.6 × 5.8 × 1.5)*
Main machinery: 2 Type M 50 diesels; 2200 hp(m) *(1.6 MW)* sustained; 2 shafts
Speed, knots: 20. **Range, miles:** 1500 at 10 kts
Complement: 15
Guns: 2—12.7 mm MGs.
Radars: Navigation: Spin Trough; I band.

Comment: Both transferred in January 1990. Can be used as torpedo recovery vessels.

POLUCHAT (Russian colours)   1992, Hachiro Nakai

AMPHIBIOUS FORCES

3 Ex-SOVIET POLNOCHNY CLASS (TYPE 771) (LSM)

HQ 511   HQ 512   HQ 513

Displacement, tons: 760 standard; 834 full load
Dimensions, feet (metres): 246.1 × 31.5 × 7.5 *(75 × 9.6 × 2.3)*
Main machinery: 3 Kolomna Type 40-D diesels; 4400 hp(m) *(3.2 MW)* sustained; 3 shafts
Speed, knots: 19
Complement: 40
Guns: 2 or 4 USSR 30 mm/65 (1 or 2 twin). 2—140 mm rocket launchers.
Radars: Surface search: Don 2 or Spin Trough; I band.
Fire control: Drum Tilt; H/I band.

Comment: Transfers: one in May 1979 (B), one in November 1979 (A) and one in February 1980 (B). Details as for Polnochny B class.

POLNOCHNY B   1989

1 Ex-US LST 1-510 and 2 Ex-US LST 511-1152 CLASSES

QUI NONH (ex-USS *Bulloch County* LST 509)   HQ 502
VUNG TAU (ex-USS *Cochino County* LST 603)   HQ 503
DA NANG (ex-USS *Maricopa County* LST 938)   HQ 505

Displacement, tons: 2366 beaching; 4080 full load
Dimensions, feet (metres): 328 × 50 × 14 *(100 × 15.2 × 4.3)*
Main machinery: 2 GM 12-567A diesels; 1800 hp *(1.34 MW)*; 2 shafts
Speed, knots: 11. **Range, miles:** 6000 at 10 kts
Complement: 110

Comment: Built in 1943-44. Transferred to South Vietnam in mid-1960s.

DA NANG   1988, G Jacobs

12 Ex-SOVIET T 4 CLASS (LCUs)

Displacement, tons: 93 full load
Dimensions, feet (metres): 65.3 × 18.4 × 4.6 *(19.9 × 5.6 × 1.4)*
Main machinery: 2 diesels; 316 hp(m) *(232 kW)*; 2 shafts
Speed, knots: 10
Complement: 4

Comment: Transfers: ten in 1967, five in 1969, all of which were probably sunk. Twelve more in 1979.

24 Ex-US LANDING CRAFT (LCM and LCU)

Comment: It is reported that at the beginning of 1992 there were still some seven LCUs, 14 LCM 8 and LCM 6, and three LCVPs remaining of the 180 minor landing craft left behind by the US in 1975.

MINE WARFARE FORCES

2 LIENYUN CLASS (MINESWEEPERS—COASTAL)

Displacement, tons: 400 full load
Dimensions, feet (metres): 131.2 × 26.2 × 11.5 *(40 × 8 × 3.5)*
Main machinery: 1 diesel; 400 hp(m) *(294 kW)*; 1 shaft
Speed, knots: 8
Guns: 2—12.7 mm MGs.

Comment: Acquired from China. Trawler type with a minesweeping winch and davits aft.

2 Ex-SOVIET YURKA CLASS (MINESWEEPER—OCEAN)

HQ 851   HQ 852

Displacement, tons: 460 full load
Dimensions, feet (metres): 171.9 × 30.8 × 8.5 *(52.4 × 9.4 × 2.6)*
Main machinery: 2 Type M 503 diesels; 5350 hp(m) *(3.91 MW)* sustained; 2 shafts
Speed, knots: 17. **Range, miles:** 1500 at 12 kts
Complement: 60
Guns: 4 USSR 30 mm/65 (2 twin); 500 rounds/minute to 5 km *(2.7 nm)*; weight of shell 0.54 kg.
Mines: 10.
Radars: Surface search: Don 2; I band.
Fire control: Drum Tilt; H/I band.
Sonars: Hull-mounted; active minehunting; high frequency.

Comment: Transferred December 1979. Steel-hulled, built in early 1970s.

YURKA (Russian colours)   1991, van Ginderen Collection

4 SOVIET SONYA CLASS (MINESWEEPER/HUNTER—COASTAL)

Displacement, tons: 400 full load
Dimensions, feet (metres): 157.4 × 28.9 × 6.6 *(48 × 8.8 × 2)*
Main machinery: 2 Kolomna 9-D-8 diesels; 2000 hp(m) *(1.47 MW)* sustained; 2 shafts
Speed, knots: 15. **Range, miles:** 3000 at 10 kts
Complement: 43
Guns: 2 USSR 30 mm/65 AK 630. 2—25 mm/80 (twin).
Mines: 5.
Radars: Surface search: Don 2; I band.

Comment: First one transferred 16 February 1987, second in February 1988, third in July 1989, fourth in March 1990.

SONYA   11/1991, G Jacobs

2 YEVGENYA CLASS (MINEHUNTER—INSHORE)

Displacement, tons: 90 full load
Dimensions, feet (metres): 80.7 × 18 × 4.9 *(24.6 × 5.5 × 1.5)*
Main machinery: 2 Type 3-D-12 diesels; 600 hp(m) *(440 kW)* sustained; 2 shafts
Speed, knots: 11. **Range, miles:** 300 at 10 kts
Complement: 10
Guns: 2 USSR 25 mm/80 (twin).
Radars: Surface search: Spin Trough; I band.

Comment: First transferred in October 1979; two in December 1986. One deleted in 1990.

5 Ex-SOVIET K 8 CLASS (MINESWEEPING BOATS)

Displacement, tons: 26 full load
Dimensions, feet (metres): 55.4 × 10.5 × 2.6 *(16.9 × 3.2 × 0.8)*
Main machinery: 2 Type 3-D-6 diesels; 300 hp(m) *(220 kW)* sustained; 2 shafts
Speed, knots: 18
Complement: 6
Guns: 2—14.5 mm (twin) MGs.

Comment: Transferred in October 1980.

VIETNAM — Miscellaneous

MISCELLANEOUS

Notes: (a) In addition to the vessels listed below there are two YOG 5 fuel lighters, two floating cranes and two ex-Soviet unarmed Nyryat 2 diving tenders.
(b) Small numbers of ex-US Riverine craft have been refitted with Soviet engines and are still operational with Soviet weapons.
(c) A diving support vessel *(Hai Son)* of 881 tons and 50 m in length was completed by Korea Tacoma, Masan in March 1990. This ship may not be naval.

1 Ex-SOVIET KAMENKA CLASS (SURVEY SHIP)

Displacement, tons: 705 full load
Dimensions, feet (metres): 175.5 × 29.8 × 8.5 *(53.5 × 9.1 × 2.6)*
Main machinery: 2 diesels; 1800 hp(m) *(1.32 MW)*; 2 shafts; cp props
Speed, knots: 14. **Range, miles:** 4000 at 10 kts
Complement: 25
Radars: Navigation: Don 2; I band.

Comment: Transferred December 1979 having been built in Poland in 1971.

2 Ex-SOVIET FLOATING DOCKS

Comment: One has a lift capacity of 8500 tons. Transferred August 1983. Second one *(Khersson)* has a lift capacity of 4500 tons and was supplied in 1988.

12 Ex-CHINESE SL CLASS TRANSPORTS AND 4 TANKERS

Comment: These are ships of between 200 and 550 tons used for coastal transport having been left over from the Vietnam war. Most were delivered in the late 1960s. The tankers have a cargo capacity of 400 tons of fuel oil. All are armed with 12.7 mm MGs.

KAMENKA (Russian colours) 1984

HQ 671 (SL class) 12/1988, G Jacobs

VIRGIN ISLANDS

Headquarters' Appointment
Commissioner of Police:
 J B Rutherford

Base
Road Town, Tortola

Mercantile Marine
Lloyd's Register of Shipping:
 1 vessels of 170 tons gross

1 HALMATIC M 140 PATROL CRAFT

ST URSULA

Displacement, tons: 17 full load
Dimensions, feet (metres): 50.6 × 12.8 × 3.9 *(15.4 × 3.9 × 1.2)*
Main machinery: 2 Detroit 6V-92TA diesels; 520 hp *(388 kW)* sustained; 2 shafts
Speed, knots: 23. **Range, miles:** 300 at 20 kts
Complement: 6
Guns: 2—7.62 mm MG.

Comment: Built by Halmatic with funds provided by the UK and commissioned 4 July 1988. Large davit aft for rapid launch and recovery of a rigid inflatable boat.

2 SEA RIDER DINGHIES

Comment: Model SR5M, built by Avon, with 70 hp *(52 kW)* Yamaha and 65 hp *(48.5 kW)* Evinrude outboard engines. Acquired in 1986.

ST URSULA 1988, Halmatic

WESTERN SAMOA

General
After 48 years of New Zealand occupation, mandate and trusteeship, Western Samoa achieved independence in 1962.

Base
Apia

Mercantile Marine
Lloyd's Register of Shipping:
 7 vessels of 6253 tons gross

1 PACIFIC FORUM PATROL CRAFT

NAFANUA

Displacement, tons: 165 full load
Dimensions, feet (metres): 103.3 × 26.6 × 6.9 *(31.5 × 8.1 × 2.1)*
Main machinery: 2 Caterpillar 3516TA diesels; 4400 hp *(3.28 MW)* sustained; 2 shafts
Speed, knots: 20. **Range, miles:** 2500 at 12 kts
Complement: 17 (3 officers)
Guns: Can carry 1 Oerlikon 20 mm and 2—7.62 mm MGs.
Radars: Surface search: Furuno 1011; I band.

Comment: Under the Defence Co-operation Programme Australia has provided an Australian Shipbuilding Industries (ASI) 315 Patrol Boat to the Western Samoan Government. Training, operational and technical assistance is being provided by the Royal Australian Navy. Ordered 3 October 1985, commissioned 5 March 1988.

1 LCU

LADY SAMOA II

Comment: Built by Yokohama Yacht Co and launched 28 July 1988.

NAFANUA 10/1991, John Mortimer

YEMEN

General

In May 1990 the north and south Yemen republics were again reunited. Many ships of the Ethiopian Navy took refuge in Yemeni ports during 1991. An agreement was reached in mid-1992 to return these ships.

Headquarters' Appointments

Commander Naval Forces:
Colonel Ali Qasim Talib
Chief of Staff
Lieutenant Colonel Abdul Karim Muharram

Personnel

(a) 1993: 2500 (including 500 Marines)
(b) 2 years' national service

Bases

Main: Aden, Hodeida
Secondary: Mukalla, Perim, Socotra

Mercantile Marine

Lloyd's Register of Shipping:
40 vessels of 16 924 tons gross

DELETIONS

1991 *Ropucha 139* (returned Russia), 1 Oskol II class (returned Russia)

LIGHT FORCES

Notes: (a) Two ex-Soviet Mol class occasionally reported, but both belong to Ethiopia.
(b) Two ex-Soviet SO 1 class (*402* and *619*) may still be just operational.

2 SOVIET TARANTUL I CLASS (TYPE 1241) (MISSILE CORVETTE)

971   976

Displacement, tons: 385 standard; 580 full load
Dimensions, feet (metres): 184.1 × 37.7 × 8.2 *(56.1 × 11.5 × 2.5)*
Main machinery: COGOG; 2 Nikolayev Type DR 77 gas turbines; 16 016 hp(m) *(11.77 MW)* sustained; 2 Nikolayev Type DR 76 gas turbines with reversible gearboxes; 4993 hp(m) *(3.67 MW)* sustained; 2 shafts
Speed, knots: 36. **Range, miles:** 400 at 36 kts; 2000 at 20 kts
Complement: 50

Missiles: SSM: 4 SS-N-2C Styx (2 twin) launchers; active radar or IR homing to 83 km *(45 nm)* at 0.9 Mach; warhead 513 kg; sea-skimmer at end of run.
SAM: SA-N-5 Grail quad launcher; manual aiming; IR homing to 10 km *(5.4 nm)* at 1.5 Mach; altitude to 2500 m *(8000 ft)*; warhead 1.1 kg.
Guns: 1—3 in *(76 mm)*/60; 85° elevation; 120 rounds/minute to 7 km *(3.8 nm)*; weight of shell 7 kg.
2—30 mm/65 AK 630; 6 barrels per mounting; 3000 rounds/minute to 2 km.
Countermeasures: Decoys: 2—16-barrelled chaff launchers.
ESM: 2 receivers.
Fire control: Hood Wink optronic director.
Radars: Air/surface search: Plank Shave (also for missile control); E band.
Navigation: Spin Trough; I band.
Fire control: Bass Tilt; H/I band.
IFF: Square Head. High Pole.

Programmes: First one delivered in November 1990, second in January 1991. This is the standard export version.

TARANTUL 971   *1991, US Navy*

6 Ex-SOVIET OSA II CLASS (FAST ATTACK CRAFT—MISSILE)

116-121

Displacement, tons: 245 full load
Dimensions, feet (metres): 126.6 × 24.9 × 8.8 *(38.6 × 7.6 × 2.7)*
Main machinery: 3 Type M 504 diesels; 10 800 hp(m) *(7.94 MW)* sustained; 3 shafts
Speed, knots: 37. **Range, miles:** 500 at 35 kts
Complement: 30
Missiles: SSM: 4 SS-N-2B Styx; active radar or IR homing to 46 km *(25 nm)* at 0.9 Mach; warhead 513 kg.
Guns: 4 USSR 30 mm/65 (2 twin); 85° elevation; 500 rounds/minute to 5 km *(2.7 nm)*; weight of shell 0.54 kg.
Radars: Surface search: Square Tie; I band.
Fire control: Drum Tilt; H/I band.

Comment: Transferred: one in February 1979, one in March 1979, two in January 1980, one in December 1980, one in January 1982, one on 24 February 1983 and one in September 1983. Two (*122* and *123*) were sunk in 1987.

OSA II   *1986*

3 BROADSWORD CLASS (COASTAL PATROL CRAFT)

26 SEPTEMBER 141   RAMADAN 142   SANA'A 143

Displacement, tons: 90.5 standard; 110 full load
Dimensions, feet (metres): 105 × 20.4 × 6.3 *(32 × 6.2 × 1.9)*
Main machinery: 2 GM 16V-149TI diesels; 2322 hp *(1.73 MW)* sustained; 2 shafts
Speed, knots: 32
Complement: 14
Guns: 2 USSR 25 mm/80 (twin). 2—14.5 mm (twin) MGs. 2—12.7 mm MGs.
Radars: Surface search: Decca 914; I band.

Comment: Acquired in 1978 from Halter Marine, New Orleans. Guns added after delivery. Still used for offshore patrol but in poor repair.

RAMADAN   *1987*

5 Ex-SOVIET ZHUK CLASS (FAST ATTACK CRAFT—PATROL)

400   500   600   700   800

Displacement, tons: 50 full load
Dimensions, feet (metres): 75.4 × 17 × 6.2 *(23 × 5.2 × 1.9)*
Main machinery: 2 Type M 50 diesels; 2200 hp(m) *(1.6 MW)* sustained; 2 shafts
Speed, knots: 30. **Range, miles:** 1100 at 15 kts
Complement: 17
Guns: 4—14.5 mm (2 twin) MGs.
Radars: Surface search: Spin Trough; I band.

Comment: Two delivered in December 1984 and three in January 1987. Earlier transfers have been deleted.

ZHUK   *3/1990*

AMPHIBIOUS FORCES

2 Ex-SOVIET T 4 CLASS (LCVP)

134   135

Displacement, tons: 70 full load
Dimensions, feet (metres): 62.3 × 14 × 3.3 *(19 × 4.3 × 1)*
Main machinery: 2 diesels; 316 hp(m) *(232 kW)*; 2 shafts
Speed, knots: 10. **Range, miles:** 1500 at 10 kts
Complement: 4

Comment: Three transferred in November 1970 and two in December 1981. First three deleted.

2 Ex-SOVIET POLNOCHNY A CLASS (TYPE 770) (LCT)

AL WUDIA 136   **SIRA** 137

Displacement, tons: 750 standard; 800 full load
Dimensions, feet (metres): 239.3 × 27.9 × 5.8 *(73 × 8.5 × 1.8)*
Main machinery: 2 Kolomna Type 40-D diesels; 4400 hp(m) *(3.2 MW)* sustained; 2 shafts
Speed, knots: 19. **Range, miles:** 1000 at 18 kts
Complement: 40
Military lift: 100 troops; 6 tanks
Guns: 2 USSR 30 mm/65 (twin). 2—18-barrelled 140 mm rocket launchers.

Comment: Transferred in August 1973 (two) and July 1977. *138* burnt out in March 1986.

SIRA   7/1986, van Ginderen Collection

2 Ex-SOVIET ONDATRA CLASS (LCUs)

13   14

Displacement, tons: 145 full load
Dimensions, feet (metres): 78.7 × 16.4 × 4.9 *(24 × 5 × 1.5)*
Main machinery: 1 diesel; 300 hp(m) *(221 kW)*; 1 shaft
Speed, knots: 10. **Range, miles:** 500 at 5 kts
Complement: 4
Military lift: 1 MBT

Comment: Transferred January 1983.

ONDATRA 14   1990

MINE WARFARE FORCES

2 SOVIET NATYA CLASS (MINESWEEPERS—OCEAN)

634   641

Displacement, tons: 770 full load
Dimensions, feet (metres): 200.1 × 31.8 × 8.9 *(61 × 9.7 × 2.7)*
Main machinery: 2 Type M 504 diesels; 7200 hp(m) *(5.3 MW)* sustained; 2 shafts
Speed, knots: 19. **Range, miles:** 4000 at 10 kts
Complement: 65
Guns: 4—30 mm/65 (2 twin); 85° elevation; 500 rounds/minute to 5 km *(2.7 nm)*; weight of shell 0.54 kg.
4—25 mm/80 (2 twin); 270 rounds/minute to 3 km *(1.6 nm)*; weight of shell 0.34 kg.
A/S mortars: 2 RBU 1200 five-tubed fixed launchers; range 1200 m; warhead 34 kg.
Mines: 10
Radars: Surface search: Don 2; I band.
Sonars: Hull-mounted; active minehunting; high frequency.

Comment: First one transferred in February 1991, second in October 1991.

NATYA 634   10/1991, Foto Flite

1 SOVIET SONYA CLASS (MINESWEEPER—COASTAL)

441

Displacement, tons: 400 full load
Dimensions, feet (metres): 157.4 × 28.9 × 6.6 *(48 × 8.8 × 2)*
Main machinery: 2 Kolomna 9-D-8 diesels; 2000 hp(m) *(1.47 MW)* sustained; 2 shafts
Speed, knots: 15. **Range, miles:** 3000 at 10 kts
Complement: 43

Guns: 2—30 mm/65 (twin); 85° elevation; 500 rounds/minute to 5 km *(2.7 nm)*; weight of shell 0.54 kg.
2—25 mm/80 (twin); 85° elevation; 270 rounds/minute to 3 km *(1.6 nm)*.
Mines: 8.
Radars: Surface search: Don 2; I band.

Programmes: Delivered in January 1991. There was some early confusion as to whether this ship had been delivered to Ethiopia or Yemen.

SONYA (Russian colours)   1991, Ships of the World

6 Ex-SOVIET YEVGENYA CLASS (MINEHUNTERS—INSHORE)

11   12   15   +3

Displacement, tons: 77 standard; 90 full load
Dimensions, feet (metres): 80.7 × 18 × 4.9 *(24.6 × 5.5 × 1.5)*
Main machinery: 2 Type 3-D-12 diesels; 600 hp(m) *(440 kW)* sustained; 2 shafts
Speed, knots: 11. **Range, miles:** 300 at 10 kts
Complement: 10
Guns: 2—25 mm/80 (twin) or 2—14.5 mm (twin) MGs.
Radars: Navigation: Spin Trough; I band.
IFF: High Pole.
Sonars: Small transducer lifted over stern on crane.

Comment: GRP hulls. Two transferred in May 1982, third in November 1987, and three more in March 1990.

SERVICE FORCES

Notes: (a) A 4500 ton Floating Dock was provided by the USSR.
(b) A 14 m Hydrographic craft acquired from Cougar Marine in 1988.

2 TOPLIVO CLASS

135   140

Displacement, tons: 1300
Dimensions, feet (metres): 172.9 × 27.2 × 12.5 *(52.7 × 8.3 × 3.8)*
Main machinery: 2 diesels; 2 shafts
Speed, knots: 10

Comment: Two small harbour tankers acquired in the early 1980s. *135* carries water, *140* oil.

TOPLIVO   1990, van Ginderen Collection

CUSTOMS SERVICE

2 SHABWAH CLASS (TUGS)

SHABWAH   AL MAHRAH

Comment: 225 grt; built by McTay Marine, Bromborough and launched 14 November 1986 and 6 January 1987. Both delivered in May 1987.

1 FAIREY MARINE TRACKER 2 CLASS (COASTAL PATROL CRAFT)

1034

Displacement, tons: 31 full load
Dimensions, feet (metres): 63.1 × 16.3 × 4.8 *(19.3 × 5 × 1.5)*
Main machinery: 2 MTU 8V 331 TC92 diesels; 1770 hp(m) *(1.3 MW)* sustained; 2 shafts
Speed, knots: 29. **Range, miles:** 650 at 22 kts
Complement: 11
Gun: 1 Oerlikon 20 mm.

Comment: Delivered 1979. Four destroyed in the civil war in January 1986.

3 FAIREY MARINE SPEAR CLASS (COASTAL PATROL CRAFT)

Displacement, tons: 4.5 full load
Dimensions, feet (metres): 29.8 × 9.2 × 2.6 *(9.1 × 2.8 × 0.8)*
Main machinery: 2 Perkins diesels; 290 hp *(216 kW)*; 2 shafts
Speed, knots: 25
Guns: 3—7.62 mm MGs.

Comment: Three delivered 30 September 1975, one in 1978. One acts as Navy Commander's barge; one deleted in 1986.

YUGOSLAVIA

Headquarters' Appointments

Commander-in-Chief:
Vice Admiral Nikola Ercegovic
Chief of Staff:
Vice Admiral Fridrih Moreti
Commander Boka Naval Sector:
Captain Milan Zec

Personnel

1993: 9000 approx

General

In spite of losing most of its former major naval facilities to Croatia, the Federal Navy in early 1993 was still about 80 per cent operational. The command is now almost wholly Serbian and bases in the Bay of Cattaro, although lacking an adequate support infrastructure, have been improved.

Bases and Organisation

Headquarters: Kumbor
Main bases: Tivat, Bar, Djenovic

Strength of the Fleet

Type	Active (Reserve)
Submarines—Patrol	5
Midget Submarines	6
Frigates	4
Corvettes	2
Fast Attack Craft—Missile	13
Fast Attack Craft—Torpedo	12
Fast Attack Craft—Patrol	5 (4)
Large Patrol Craft	7
River Patrol Craft	11
Minehunters/sweepers	(3)
Minesweepers—Inshore	5 (3)
River Minesweepers	16
LCTs/Minelayers	13
LCUs/LCVPs	18
Training Ships	1
Survey Craft	7
HQ Ships	2
Tankers	2
Transports	9

Mercantile Marine

Lloyd's Register of Shipping:
12 vessels of 2780 tons gross

DELETIONS

Light Forces

1990 *Marijan*
1991 *Mukos* (sunk), *Sibenic* (Croatia), 2 Osa I (Croatia), 2 Shershen (Croatia)

Minesweepers

1991 *Olib* (Croatia)
1992 *Vukov Klanac*, 1 Type M 117

Amphibious Vessels

1991 4 MFPD-3 Type (Croatia), 1 DSM 501 Type (Croatia), 3 Type 22 (Croatia), 4 Type 21 (Croatia), 12 Type 11
1992 2 Type 21 (sunk)

Auxiliaries

1991 *Andrija Mohorovicic* (Croatia), *Spasilac* (Croatia), *PN 25* (Croatia), *PO 51* (Croatia), *Alga* (Croatia)
1992 *Jadran*

SUBMARINES

Note: One Una and two Mala class are probably in Croatian hands.

2 SAVA CLASS (PATROL SUBMARINES)

Name	No	Builders	Laid down	Launched	Commissioned
SAVA	831	S and DE Factory, Split	1975	1977	1978
DRAVA	832	S and DE Factory, Split	1978	1980	1981

Displacement, tons: 830 surfaced; 960 dived
Dimensions, feet (metres): 182.7 × 23.6 × 16.7 *(55.7 × 7.2 × 5.1)*
Main machinery: Diesel-electric; 2 Sulzer diesels; 1600 hp(m) *(1.18 MW)*; 2 generators; 1 MW; 1 motor; 1560 hp(m) *(1.15 MW)*; 1 shaft
Speed, knots: 10 surfaced; 16 dived
Complement: 27

Torpedoes: 6—21 in *(533 mm)* bow tubes. 10 Soviet Type 53 or Swedish TP 61.
Mines: 20 in lieu of torpedoes.
Countermeasures: ESM: Stop Light; radar warning.
Radars: Surface search: Snoop Group; I band.
Sonars: Atlas Elektronik PRS3; hull-mounted; passive ranging; medium frequency.

Structure: An improved version of the Heroj class. Diving depth, 300 m *(980 ft)*. Probably built with Soviet electronic equipment and armament. Possible Thomson Sintra active/passive sonar and unconfirmed reports of Swedish torpedoes. Both operational in early 1993.

DRAVA *1988, Yugoslav Navy*

3 HEROJ CLASS (PATROL SUBMARINES)

Name	No	Builders	Laid down	Launched	Commissioned
HEROJ	821	Uljanik Shipyard, Pula	1964	1967	1968
JUNAK	822	S and DE Factory, Split	1965	1968	1969
USKOK	823	Uljanik Shipyard, Pula	1966	1969	1970

Displacement, tons: 1170 surfaced; 1350 dived
Dimensions, feet (metres): 210 × 23.6 × 16.7 *(64 × 7.2 × 5.1)*
Main machinery: Diesel-electric; 2 Sulzer diesels; 1600 hp(m) *(1.18 MW)*; 2 generators; 1 MW; 1 motor; 1560 hp(m) *(1.15 MW)*; 1 shaft
Speed, knots: 10 surfaced; 16 dived
Range, miles: 4100 at 10 kts dived and snorting
Complement: 35

Torpedoes: 6—21 in *(533 mm)* bow tubes. 10 Soviet Type 53.
Mines: 20 in lieu of torpedoes.
Countermeasures: ESM: Stop Light; radar warning.
Radars: Surface search: Snoop Group; I band.
Sonars: Atlas Elektronik PRS3; hull-mounted; passive ranging; medium frequency.

Structure: Have mainly Soviet electronic equipment and armament. Diving depth 300 m *(980 ft)*.
Operational: Two operational in early 1993, with one in reserve providing spares.

HEROJ *1982*

6 UNA CLASS (MIDGET SUBMARINES)

TISA 911	UNA 912	ZETA 913
SOCA 914	KUPA 915	VARDAR 916

Displacement, tons: 76 surfaced; 88 dived
Dimensions, feet (metres): 61.7 × 9 × 8.2 *(18.8 × 2.7 × 2.5)*
Main machinery: 2 motors; 68 hp(m) *(50 kW)*; 1 shaft
Speed, knots: 6 surfaced; 8 dived
Range, miles: 200 at 4 kts
Complement: 6
Sonars: Atlas Elektronik; passive/active search; high frequency.

Comment: Building yard, Split. First of class commissioned May 1985; last two in 1989. Exit/re-entry capability with mining capacity. Can carry six combat swimmers, plus four Swimmer Delivery Vehicles (SDV) and limpet mines. Diving depth: 105 m *(345 ft)*. Batteries can only be charged from shore or from a depot ship. One of the class probably in Croatian hands.

UNA *1987*

2 R-2 MALA CLASS (TWO-MAN SWIMMER DELIVERY VEHICLES)

Displacement, tons: 1.4
Dimensions, feet (metres): 16.1 × 4.6 × 4.3 *(4.9 × 1.4 × 1.3)*
Main machinery: 1 motor; 4.5 hp(m) *(3.3 kW)*; 1 shaft
Speed, knots: 4.4
Range, miles: 18 at 4.4 kts; 23 at 3.7 kts
Complement: 2
Mines: 250 kg of limpet mines.

Comment: This is a free-flood craft with the main motor, battery, navigation-pod and electronic equipment housed in separate watertight cylinders. Instrumentation includes aircraft type gyro-compass, magnetic compass, depth gauge (with 0-100 m scale), echo sounder, sonar and two searchlights. Constructed of light aluminium and plexiglass, it is fitted with fore and after-hydroplanes, the tail being a conventional cruciform with a single rudder abaft the screw. Large perspex windows give a good all-round view. Operating depth, 60 m *(196.9 ft)*, maximum. A number of these craft have been sold to Russia. Six transferred to Libya. Sweden has also taken delivery of both two and one-man versions of this type. Two more of the class were probably captured by Croatia.

Note: Yugoslavia also reported to operate a number of R-1 'wet chariots'. Can be transported in submarine torpedo tubes. Crewed by one man. Propulsion 1 kW electric motor; 24 v silver-zinc batteries. Normal operating depth 60 m *(196.9 ft)*. Range 6 nm at 3 kts. Weight 145 kg. Dimensions 12.2 × 3.45 × 0.8 ft *(3.72 × 1.05 × 0.26 m)*.

R-2 with Swedish NACKEN *12/1988, Gilbert Gyssels*

FRIGATES

2 SPLIT and 2 KOTOR CLASSES

— (ex-*Split*) 31 ZAGREB (ex-*Kopar*) 32
KOTOR 33 PULA 34

Displacement, tons: 1700 standard; 1900 full load
Dimensions, feet (metres): 317.3 × 42 × 13.7 *(96.7 × 12.8 × 4.2)*
Main machinery: CODAG; 1 gas turbine; 18 000 hp(m) *(13.2 MW)*; 2 Russki B-68 diesels; 15 820 hp(m) *(11.63 MW)* sustained (31 and 32); 2 SEMT-Pielstick 12 PA6 280 diesels; 9600 hp(m) *(7.1 MW)* sustained (33 and 34); 3 shafts
Speed, knots: 27 gas; 22 diesel. **Range, miles:** 1800 at 14 kts
Complement: 110

Missiles: SSM: 4 SS-N-2C Styx ❶; active radar or IR homing to 83 km *(45 nm)* at 0.9 Mach; warhead 513 kg; sea-skimmer at end of run. May be replaced by RBS-15 in due course.
SAM: SA-N-4 Gecko twin launcher ❷; semi-active radar homing to 15 km *(8 nm)* at 2.5 Mach; height envelope 9-3048 m *(29.5-10 000 ft)*; warhead 50 kg.
Guns: 4 USSR 3 in *(76 mm)*/60 (2 twin) (1 mounting only in VPB 33 and 34) ❸; 80° elevation; 90 rounds/minute to 15 km *(8 nm)*; weight of shell 6.8 kg.
4 USSR 30 mm/65 (2 twin) ❹; 85° elevation; 500 rounds/minute to 5 km *(2.7 nm)*; weight of shell 0.54 kg.
Torpedoes: 6—324 mm (2 triple) tubes ❺ (VPB 33 and 34 only). Whitehead A 244; anti-submarine; active passive homing to 6 km *(3.3 nm)* at 30 kts; warhead 34 kg.
A/S mortars: 2 RBU 6000 12-barrelled trainable ❻; range 6000 m; warhead 31 kg.
Mines: Can lay mines.
Countermeasures: Decoys: 2 Wallop Barricade double layer chaff launchers.
Radars: Air/surface search: Strut Curve ❼; F band; range 110 km *(60 nm)* for 2 m² target.
Navigation: Don 2 (VPB 31 and 32); I band. Palm Frond (VPB 33 and 34); I band.
Fire control: Owl Screech ❽; G band (VPB 31 and 32). PEAB 9LV200 ❾; I band (VPB 33 and 34) (for 76 mm and SSM).
Drum Tilt ❿; H/I band (for 30 mm).
Pop Group ⓫; F/H/I band (for SAM).
IFF: High Pole; two Square Head.
Sonars: Hull-mounted; active search and attack; medium frequency.

Programmes: First two transferred from the USSR 10 March 1980 and 5 December 1982. Second pair built under licence in Uljanic and Tito SYs, respectively. Both completed in mid-1988. Type name, VPB (Veliki Patrolni Brod).

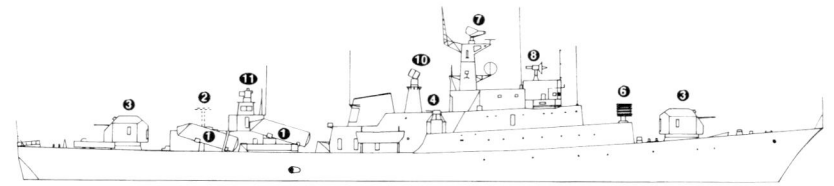

ZAGREB *(Scale 1 : 900), Ian Sturton*

ZAGREB *1989, Yugoslav Navy*

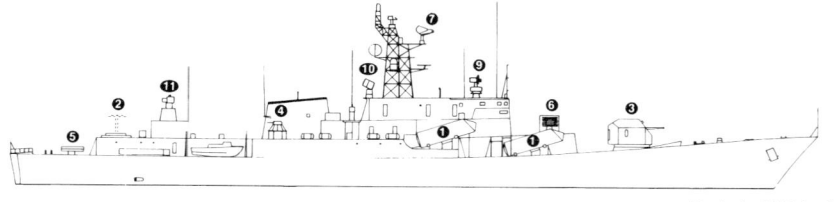

KOTOR *(Scale 1 : 900), Ian Sturton*

Structure: Although the hulls are identical to the Koni class there are some equipment, and considerable structural differences between the Soviet and Yugoslav built ships. The two ex-Soviet ships have the SS-N-2C missiles aft of midships and facing aft. The second pair have the same missiles level with the forward end of the bridge facing forward. The Yugoslav built ships probably have the same gas turbine engines as the other pair but there are different diesels. Two triple torpedo tubes replace the after 76 mm gun mounting and there is a different arrangement of the bridge superstructure which is similar to the training frigates sold to Iraq and Indonesia.

Operational: In spite of damage to one of the class in 1991, all were operational in early 1993.

KOTOR *1989, Yugoslav Navy*

CORVETTES

2 MORNAR CLASS

Name	No	Builders	Commissioned
MORNAR	551	Tito SY, Kraljevica	10 Sep 1959
BORAČ	552	Tito SY, Kraljevica	1965

Displacement, tons: 330 standard; 430 full load
Dimensions, feet (metres): 174.8 × 23 × 6.6 *(53.3 × 7 × 2)*
Main machinery: 4 SEMT-Pielstick PA1 175 diesels; 3240 hp(m) *(2.38 MW)*; 2 shafts
Speed, knots: 20. **Range, miles:** 3000 at 12 kts; 2000 at 15 kts
Complement: 60

Guns: 2 Bofors 40 mm/60. 2 Hispano 20 mm.
A/S mortars: 4 RBU 1200.
Depth charges: 2 projectors; 2 racks.
Countermeasures: 2 Wallop Barricade double layer chaff launchers.
Radars: Surface search: Decca 45; I band.
Sonars: Hull-mounted; active attack; high frequency.

Comment: The design is an improved version of that of *Udarnik*. Type name, Patrolni Brod. Modernised in 1970-73 at Naval repair yard, Sava Kovacevic, Tivat, Gulf of Cattaro. Probably non-operational in early 1993.

MORNAR   10/1990, Eric Grove

LAND-BASED MARITIME AIRCRAFT

Notes: 1. Operational numbers of aircraft are uncertain but there are probably about 20 including some Mi-14 Haze.
2. The Air Force has a naval brigade with about 50 Galeb/Jastreb fighter bombers, 15 Orao reconnaissance, and four CL-215 amphibians.

Numbers/Type: 5 Kamov Ka-25 Hormone A.
Operational speed: 104 kts *(193 km/h)*.
Service ceiling: 11 500 ft *(3500 m)*.
Range: 217 nm *(400 km)*.
Role/Weapon systems: ASW within Yugoslavian waters in support of submarine flotilla. Sensors: Search radar, MAD, dipping sonar, sonobuoys. Weapons: ASW; 2 × torpedoes or depth bombs. ASV; 4 × locally produced wire-guided missiles.

Numbers/Type: 10 Mil Mi-8 Hip C.
Operational speed: 112 kts *(225 km/h)*.
Service ceiling: 14 760 ft *(4500 m)*.
Range: 251 nm *(465 km)*.
Role/Weapon systems: Coastal patrol and support helicopter for harbour protection and coastal patrol; supported by air force Aerospatiale SA 341/2 Gazelles from time to time. Sensors: Cameras only. Weapons: Self-defence; 1 × 27 mm cannon. Strike; up to 192 × 68 mm rockets or gun pods, 6 × locally produced wire-guided missiles.

Numbers/Type: 3 Kamov Ka-28 Helix A.
Operational speed: 110 kts *(204 km/h)*.
Service ceiling: 12 000 ft *(3658 m)*.
Range: 270 nm *(500 km)*.
Role/Weapon systems: ASW within territorial waters, to supplement and replace Ka-25. Sensors: Search radar, MAD, dipping sonar, sonobuoys. Weapons: ASW only; 2 × torpedoes or depth bombs.

LIGHT FORCES

8 Ex-SOVIET OSA I CLASS (TYPE 205)
(FAST ATTACK CRAFT—MISSILE)

VLADO BAGAT 302	NIKOLA MARTINOVIĆ 306
PETAR DRAPŠIN 303	JOSIP MAŽAR SOSA 307
STEVAN FILIPOVIĆ STEVA 304	KARLO ROJC 308
ŽIKICA JOVANOVIĆ-ŠPANAC 305	FRANČ ROZMAN-STANE 309

Displacement, tons: 171 standard; 210 full load
Dimensions, feet (metres): 126.6 × 24.9 × 8.8 *(38.6 × 7.6 × 2.7)*
Main machinery: 3 Type M 503A diesels; 8025 hp(m) *(5.9 MW)* sustained; 3 shafts
Speed, knots: 35. **Range, miles:** 400 at 34 kts
Complement: 30 (4 officers)

Missiles: SSM: 4 SS-N-2A Styx; active radar or IR homing to 46 km *(25 nm)* at 0.9 Mach; warhead 513 kg.
Guns: 4 USSR 30 mm/65 (2 twin); 85° elevation; 500 rounds/minute to 5 km *(2.7 nm)*; weight of shell 0.54 kg.
Radars: Surface search: Square Tie; I band.
Fire control: Drum Tilt; H/I band.
IFF: High Pole. 2 Square Head.

Programmes: Transferred in the late 1960s. Named after war heroes. Type name, Raketni Čamac. There is some doubt over the alignment of names and pennant numbers
Operational: Two more of the class held by Croatia. At least three were non-operational, providing spares for the others in early 1993.

FRANČ ROZMAN-STANE   1982, Yugoslav Navy

5 KONČAR CLASS (TYPE 240) (FAST ATTACK CRAFT—MISSILE)

Name	No	Builders	Commissioned
RADE KONČAR	401	Tito SY, Kraljevica	Apr 1977
RAMIZ SADIKU	403	Tito SY, Kraljevica	Aug 1978
HASAN ZAHIROVIČ-LACA	404	Tito SY, Kraljevica	Dec 1978
ORCE NIKOLOV	405	Tito SY, Kraljevica	Aug 1979
ANTE BANINA	406	Tito SY, Kraljevica	Nov 1980

Displacement, tons: 242 full load
Dimensions, feet (metres): 147.6 × 27.6 × 8.2 *(45 × 8.4 × 2.5)*
Main machinery: CODAG; 2 RR Proteus gas turbines; 7200 hp *(5.37 MW)* sustained; 2 MTU 20V 538 TB92 diesels; 8530 hp(m) *(6.27 MW)* sustained; 4 shafts
Speed, knots: 39. **Range, miles:** 500 at 35 kts; 880 at 23 kts (diesels)
Complement: 30 (5 officers)

Missiles: SSM: 2 SS-N-2B Styx; active radar or IR homing to 46 km *(25 nm)* at 0.9 Mach; warhead 513 kg. May be replaced by RBS-15 in due course.
Guns: 1 or 2 Bofors 57 mm/70; 75° elevation; 200 rounds/minute to 17 km *(9.3 nm)*; weight of shell 2.4 kg.
128 mm rocket launcher for illuminants.
2—30 mm/65 (twin) may be fitted in place of the after 57 mm.
Countermeasures: Wallop Barricade double layer chaff launcher.
Fire control: PEAB 9LV 200 GFCS
Radars: Surface search: Decca 1226; I band.
Fire control: Philips TAB; I/J band.

Programmes: Type name, Raketna Topovnjaca.
Structure: Aluminium superstructure. Designed by the Naval Shipping Institute in Zagreb based on Swedish Spica class with bridge amidships like Malaysian boats. The after 57 mm gun is replaced by a twin 30 mm mounting in some of the class.
Operational: 402 was taken by Croatia and one of these five was either badly damaged or sunk. Probably only three of the class were operational in early 1993.

RADE KONČAR   1986

6 TYPE 20 (RIVER PATROL CRAFT)

PC 211-216

Displacement, tons: 55 standard
Dimensions, feet (metres): 71.5 × 17 × 3.9 *(21.8 × 5.3 × 1.2)*
Main machinery: 2 diesels; 1156 hp(m) *(850 kW)*; 2 shafts
Speed, knots: 16. **Range, miles:** 200 at 15 kts
Complement: 10
Guns: 2 Oerlikon 20 mm.
Radars: Surface search: Decca 110; I band.

Comment: Completed since 1984. Steel hull with GRP superstructure.

TYPE 20   1988, Yugoslav Navy

852 YUGOSLAVIA / Light forces — Mine warfare forces

12 Ex-SOVIET SHERSHEN CLASS (TYPE 201)
(FAST ATTACK CRAFT—TORPEDO)

PIONIR 211	**KORNAT** 217
PARTIZAN 212	**BIOKOVAC** 218
PROLETER 213	**CRVENA ZVEZDA** 220
TOPCIDER 214	**PARTIZAN II** 221
IVAN 215	**NAPREDAK** 223
JADRAN 216	**PIONIR II** 224

Displacement, tons: 145 standard; 170 full load
Dimensions, feet (metres): 113.8 × 22.3 × 4.9 *(34.7 × 6.7 × 1.5)*
Main machinery: 3 Type M 503A diesels; 8025 hp(m) *(5.9 MW)* sustained; 3 shafts
Speed, knots: 45. **Range, miles:** 850 at 30 kts
Complement: 23
Guns: 4 USSR 30 mm/65 (2 twin); 85° elevation; 500 rounds/minute to 5 km *(2.7 nm)*; weight of shell 0.54 kg.
Torpedoes: 4—21 in *(533 mm)* tubes. Soviet Type 53.
Mines: 6.
Radars: Surface search: Pot Head; I band.
Fire control: Drum Tilt; H/I band.
IFF: High Pole. Square Head

Comment: Three craft acquired from USSR. Remainder built under licence by Tito Shipyard, Kraljevica between 1966 and 1971. Named after partisan craft of the Second World War. Type name, Torpedni Čamac. One more held by Croatia; a second was captured but damaged beyond repair. Of these 12, at least two were providing spares for the others in early 1993.

PARTIZAN   *1988, Yugoslav Navy*

9 MIRNA CLASS (TYPE 140) (FAST ATTACK CRAFT—PATROL)

BIOKOVO 171	**UČKA** 174	**KOSMAJ** 178
POHORJE 172	**GRMEČ** 175	**ZELENGORA** 179
KOPRIVNIK 173	**FRUŠKA GORA** 177	**KOZOLO** 181

Displacement, tons: 120 full load
Dimensions, feet (metres): 104.9 × 22 × 7.5 *(32 × 6.7 × 2.3)*
Main machinery: 2 SEMT-Pielstick 12 PA4 200 VGDS diesels; 5292 hp(m) *(3.89 MW)* sustained; 2 shafts
Speed, knots: 30. **Range, miles:** 400 at 20 kts
Complement: 19 (3 officers)
Missiles: SAM: 1 SA-N-5 Grail quad mounting; manual aiming; IR homing to 6 km *(3.2 nm)* at 1.5 Mach; altitude to 2500 m *(8000 ft)*; warhead 1.5 kg.
Guns: 1 Bofors 40 mm/70. 1 Oerlikon 20 mm. 2—128 mm illuminant launchers.
Depth charges: 8 rails.

Comment: Builders, Kraljevica Yard. Commissioned 1981-85. A most unusual feature of this design is the fitting of an electric outboard motor giving a speed of up to 6 kts. One sunk possibly by a limpet mine in November 1991. Two held by Croatia. Probably fewer than five were operational in early 1993.

POHORJE   *1988, Yugoslav Navy*

7 TYPE 131 (LARGE PATROL CRAFT)

Displacement, tons: 85 standard; 120 full load
Dimensions, feet (metres): 91.9 × 14.8 × 8.3 *(28 × 4.5 × 2.5)*
Main machinery: 2 MTU MB 12V 493 TY7 diesels; 2200 hp(m) *(1.62 MW)* sustained; 2 shafts
Speed, knots: 22
Guns: 6 Hispano-Suiza 20 mm (2 triple).
Radars: Surface search: Kelvin Hughes; I band.

Comment: Built at Trogir SY between 1965 and 1968. Type name, Patrolni Čamac. Two sold to Malta in March 1982.

TYPE 131   *1982, Yugoslav Navy*

5 BOTICA CLASS (TYPE 16) (RIVER PATROL CRAFT)

PC 301-304, 306

Displacement, tons: 23 full load
Dimensions, feet (metres): 55.8 × 11.8 × 2.8 *(17 × 3.6 × 0.8)*
Main machinery: 2 diesels; 464 hp(m) *(340 kW)*; 2 shafts
Speed, knots: 15
Complement: 7
Military lift: 3 tons
Guns: 1 Oerlikon 20 mm. 7—7.62 mm MGs.
Radars: Surface search: Decca 110; I band.

Comment: Can carry up to 30 troops. May be in reserve.

TYPE 16 (model)   *1988, Yugoslav Navy*

12 TYPE 15 (RIVER PATROL CRAFT)

Displacement, tons: 19.5 full load
Dimensions, feet (metres): 55.4 × 12.8 × 2.3 *(16.9 × 3.9 × 0.7)*
Main machinery: 2 diesels; 330 hp(m) *(242 kW)*; 2 shafts
Speed, knots: 16. **Range, miles:** 160 at 12 kts
Complement: 6
Guns: 1 Oerlikon 20 mm; 2—7.62 mm MGs.
Radars: Surface search: Racal Decca 110; I band.

Comment: Built in Yugoslavia in the late 1980s for use in shallow water. Steel hulls with GRP superstructure. Four air conditioned craft were delivered to Sudan on 18 May 1989.

TYPE 15   *1989, Yugoslav Navy*

MINE WARFARE FORCES

5 TYPE M 117 CLASS (MINESWEEPERS—INSHORE)

M 117-121

Displacement, tons: 131 full load
Dimensions, feet (metres): 98.4 × 18 × 4.9 *(30 × 5.5 × 1.5)*
Main machinery: 2 GM diesels; 1000 hp *(746 kW)*; 2 shafts
Speed, knots: 12
Complement: 25
Guns: 1 Bofors 40 mm/60. 2—12.7 mm MGs.

Comment: Built in Yugoslavia 1966-68. M 117 used for surveying. One deleted in 1992.

3 VUKOV KLANAC CLASS (MINESWEEPERS/HUNTERS)

Name	No	Builders	Commissioned
PODGORA (ex-Smeli)	M 152 (ex-D 26)	A Normand, France	Sep 1957
BLITVENICA* (ex-Slobodni)	M 153 (ex-D 27)	A Normand, France	Sep 1957
GRADAC (ex-Snazni)	M 161	Mali Losinj SY, Yugoslavia	1960

*Hunter

Displacement, tons: 365 standard; 424 full load
Dimensions, feet (metres): 152 × 28 × 8.2 (46.4 × 8.6 × 2.5)
Main machinery: 2 SEMT-Pielstick PA1 175 diesels; 1620 hp(m) (1.19 MW); 2 shafts
Speed, knots: 15. **Range, miles:** 3000 at 10 kts
Complement: 40
Guns: 2 Oerlikon 20 mm.
Countermeasures: MCMV: PAP 104 (minehunters); remote-controlled submersibles.
Radars: Navigation: Thomson-CSF DRBN 30; I band.
Sonars: Plessey Type 193M (minehunters); hull-mounted; active minehunting; high frequency.

Comment: The first three were built as US 'off-shore' orders. *Gradac* (ex-*Snazni*) was built in Yugoslavia in 1960 with French assistance. *Blitvenica* converted to minehunter in 1980-81. Decca Hi-fix. *Vukov Klanac* had her upper deck extensively damaged in November 1991 and was scrapped. All probably non-operational.

BLITVENICA 1988, Yugoslav Navy

3 BRITISH HAM CLASS (MINESWEEPERS—INSHORE)

MLJ M 141 **BRSEČ** M 142 **IZ** M 144

Displacement, tons: 120 standard; 159 full load
Dimensions, feet (metres): 106.5 × 21.3 × 5.5 (32.5 × 6.5 × 1.7)
Main machinery: 2 Paxman YHAXM diesels; 1100 hp (821 kW); 2 shafts
Speed, knots: 14. **Range, miles:** 2000 at 9 kts
Complement: 22
Guns: 2 Oerlikon 20 mm (twin).

Comment: Built in Yugoslavia 1964-66 under the US Military Aid Programme. Wooden hulls. All probably non-operational. One more acquired by Croatia.

HAM 1988, Yugoslav Navy

7 NESTIN CLASS (RIVER MINESWEEPERS)

Name	No	Builders	Commissioned
NESTIN	M 331	Brodotehnika, Belgrade	20 Dec 1975
MOTAJICA	M 332	Brodotehnika, Belgrade	18 Dec 1976
BELEGIŠ	M 333	Brodotehnika, Belgrade	1976
BOCUT	M 334	Brodotehnika, Belgrade	1979
VUČEDOL	M 335	Brodotehnika, Belgrade	1979
DJERDAR	M 336	Brodotehnika, Belgrade	1980
PANONSKO MORE	M 337	Brodotehnika, Belgrade	1980

Displacement, tons: 65 full load
Dimensions, feet (metres): 88.6 × 21.7 × 5.2 (27 × 6.3 × 1.6)
Main machinery: 2 diesels; 520 hp(m) (382 kW); 2 shafts
Speed, knots: 15. **Range, miles:** 860 at 11 kts
Complement: 17
Guns: 5 Hispano 20 mm (triple fwd, 2 single aft).
Mines: 24 can be carried.
Countermeasures: MCMV: Magnetic, acoustic and explosive sweeping gear.
Radars: Surface search: Racal Decca 1226; I band.

Comment: Eight transferred to Hungary and three to Iraq.

MOTAJICA 1982, Yugoslav Navy

9 TYPE M 301 CLASS (RIVER MINESWEEPERS)

M 314, 317-324

Displacement, tons: 38
Speed, knots: 12
Guns: 2 Oerlikon 20 mm.
Radars: Surface search: Racal Decca; I band.

Comment: All launched in 1951-53. Serve on the Danube. Have minelaying capability. Probably all non-operational.

M 301 TYPE 1982, Yugoslav Navy

AMPHIBIOUS FORCES

1 SILBA CLASS (LCT/MINELAYER)

Name	No	Builders	Commissioned
SILBA	DBM 241	Brodosplit Shipyard, Split	1990

Displacement, tons: 880 full load
Dimensions, feet (metres): 163.1 oa; 144 wl × 33.5 × 8.5 (49.7; 43.9 × 10.2 × 2.6)
Main machinery: 2 Alpha 10V23L-VO diesels; 3100 hp(m) (2.28 MW) sustained; 2 shafts; cp props
Speed, knots: 12. **Range, miles:** 1200 at 12 kts
Complement: 33 (3 officers)
Military lift: 460 tons or 6 medium tanks or 7 APCs or 4—130 mm guns plus towing vehicles or 300 troops with equipment
Missiles: SAM: 1 SA-N-5 Grail quad mounting.
Guns: 4—30 mm/65 (2 twin) AK 230.
 4—20 mm M75 (quad). 2—128 mm illuminant launchers.
Mines: 94 Type SAG-1.
Radars: Surface search: I band.

Comment: Ro-Ro design with bow and stern ramps. Can be used for minelaying, transporting weapons or equipment and troops. A second of class was launched in July 1992 for the Croatian Navy.

SILBA 1990, Yugoslav Navy

10 MFPD-3 TYPE + 2 DSM 501 TYPE (LCTs/MINELAYERS)

Displacement, tons: 410 full load
Dimensions, feet (metres): 155.1 × 21 × 7.5 (47.3 × 6.4 × 2.3)
Main machinery: 3 Gray Marine 64 HN9 diesels; 495 hp (369 kW); 3 shafts
Speed, knots: 9
Complement: 15
Military lift: 200 troops or 3 heavy tanks
Guns: 2—20 mm (twin).
Mines: Can carry 100.

Comment: Unlike other tank landing craft in that the centre part of the bow drops to form a ramp down which the tanks go ashore, the vertical section of the bow being articulated to form outer end of ramp. Built in Yugoslavia. Can also act as minelayers. Two sold to Sudan in 1969. DTM (Desantni Tenkonosac/Minopolagac means landing ship tank/minelayer). Five of the class held by Croatia.

MFPD-3 TYPE 1989, Yugoslav Navy

854   YUGOSLAVIA / Amphibious forces — Headquarters ships

9 TYPE 22 (LCUs)

DJC 624-632

Displacement, tons: 48 full load
Dimensions, feet (metres): 73.2 × 15.7 × 3.3 *(22.3 × 4.8 × 1)*
Main engines: 2 MTU diesels; 1740 hp(m) *(1.28 MW)*; 2 waterjets
Speed, knots: 35. Range, miles: 320 at 22 kts
Complement: 8
Military lift: 40 troops or 15 tons cargo
Guns: 2—20 mm M71.
Radars: Navigation: Decca 101; I band.

Comment: Built of polyester and glass fibre. Last one completed in 1987. Three held by Croatia.

DJC 627   *1989, Yugoslav Navy*

6 TYPE 21 (LCUs)

DJC 601-631 series

Displacement, tons: 32 full load
Dimensions, feet (metres): 69.9 × 15.7 × 5.2 *(21.3 × 4.8 × 1.6)*
Main machinery: 1 diesel; 1450 hp(m) *(1.07 MW)*; 1 shaft
Speed, knots: 23. Range, miles: 320 at 22 kts
Complement: 6
Military lift: 6 tons
Guns: 1—20 mm M71.

Comment: The survivors of a class of 30 built between 1976 and 1979. Four held by Croatia. Two sunk in 1991. Numbers are uncertain.

DJC 607   *1989, Yugoslav Navy*

3 TYPE 11 (LCVP)

Displacement, tons: 10 full load
Dimensions, feet (metres): 37 × 10.2 × 1.6 *(11.3 × 3.1 × 0.5)*
Main machinery: 2 diesels; 2 waterjets
Speed, knots: 23. Range, miles: 100 at 15 kts
Complement: 2
Military lift: 4.8 tons of equipment or troops
Guns: 1—7.62 mm MG.
Radars: Navigation: I band.

Comment: GRP construction building from 1986. Many sunk or damaged.

LCVP TYPE 11   *1990, Yugoslav Navy*

TRAINING SHIP

1 GALEB CLASS

Name	No	Builders	Commissioned
GALEB (ex-*Kuchuk*, ex-*Ramb III*, ex-German *Kiebitz*)	M 11	Ansaldo, Genoa	1939

Displacement, tons: 5182 standard
Measurement, tons: 3667 gross
Dimensions, feet (metres): 384.8 × 51.2 × 18.4 *(117.3 × 15.6 × 5.6)*
Main machinery: 2 Burmeister & Wain diesels; 7200 hp(m) *(5.29 MW)*; 2 shafts
Speed, knots: 17. Range, miles: 20 000 at 16 kts
Guns: 4—40 mm/56.
Mines: Capacity not known.

Comment: Ex-Italian. Launched 6 March 1938. Sunk as an auxiliary cruiser in 1944, refloated and reconstructed in 1952. Serves as Fleet Flagship, Presidential Yacht and training ship. Former armament was four 3.5 in, four 40 mm and 24—20 mm (six quadruple) guns but these guns were landed in the mid-1960s and replacements only mounted several years later. Classified as a minelayer. Operational in early 1993.

GALEB   *7/1989, A Sheldon Duplaix*

HEADQUARTERS SHIPS

Notes: (1) Previously reported *Sabac* is not part of the Yugoslav Navy.
(2) Two Presidential yachts are manned by the Navy. Now used as supply craft.

2 Presidential Yachts   *1990, Florian Jentsch*

KOZARA PB 30

Displacement, tons: 695 full load
Dimensions, feet (metres): 219.8 × 31.2 × 4.6 *(67 × 9.5 × 1.4)*
Main machinery: 2 Deutz RV6M545 diesels; 800 hp(m) *(588 kW)*; 2 shafts
Speed, knots: 12

Comment: Former Presidential Yacht on Danube. Built in Austria in 1940. Acts as Flagship of the river flotilla.

KOZARA   *1982, Yugoslav Navy*

VIS PB 25

Displacement, tons: 680 full load
Dimensions, feet (metres): 187 × 27.9 × 11.5 *(57 × 8.5 × 3.5)*
Main machinery: 2 diesels; 2000 hp(m) *(1.47 MW)*; 2 shafts
Speed, knots: 17
Guns: 1 Bofors 40 mm/60. 2 Oerlikon 20 mm.

Comment: Built in 1956. Serves as the Command ship of the Federal Navy.

VIS   1987

SURVEY CRAFT

Note: The Moma class survey ship is held by Croatia.

7 SURVEY CRAFT

Comment: *PH 123* of 115 tons and a complement of 21; *BH 11* and *BH 12* of 70 tons, complement 12; and *BH 1* and *BH 2* of 30 tons, complement 5; *CH 1* and *CH 2* of 4.5 tons, complement 3.

PH 123   1991, van Ginderen Collection

SERVICE FORCES

3 LUBIN CLASS (AKL)

LUBIN PO 91   **UGOR** PO 92   **KIT** PO 93

Displacement, tons: 860 full load
Dimensions, feet (metres): 190.9 × 36 × 9.2 *(58.2 × 11 × 2.8)*
Main machinery: 2 diesels; 3500 hp(m) *(2.57 MW)*; 2 shafts; cp props
Speed, knots: 16. **Range, miles:** 1500 at 16 kts.
Complement: 43
Military lift: 150 troops; 6 tanks
Guns: 1 Bofors 40 mm/70. 4—20 mm M75 (quad). 128 mm rocket launcher for illuminants.

Comment: Fitted with bow doors and two upper-deck cranes. Roll-on/roll-off cargo ships built in the 1950s and employed by the Navy usually as ammunition transports. PO (Pomocni Oruzar or auxiliary ammunition ship).

KIT   1987, Yugoslav Navy

2 HARBOUR TANKERS

PN 20   **PN 21**

Displacement, tons: 430 full load
Dimensions, feet (metres): 151 × 23.6 × 10.2 *(46 × 7.2 × 3.1)*
Main machinery: 1 diesel; 300 hp(m) *(220 kW)*; 1 shaft
Speed, knots: 7

Comment: Built at Split in mid-1950s. The last survivors of the class. One more held by Croatia.

4 PT 82 CLASS (AKL)

PT 82   **PT 83**   **PT 86**   **PT 87**

Displacement, tons: 58 full load
Dimensions, feet (metres): 67.3 × 14.8 × 3.7 *(20.5 × 4.5 × 1.4)*
Main machinery: 2 diesels; 304 hp(m) *(223 kW)*; 2 shafts
Speed, knots: 12. **Range, miles:** 400 at 10 kts
Complement: 6
Cargo capacity: 15 tons or 70 troops with equipment
Guns: 2—20 mm M71 (can be fitted).

Comment: Completed in 1987. General purpose transport craft.

PT 83   1989, Yugoslav Navy

2 PT 71 TYPE

MEDUZA PT 71   **JASTOG** PT 72

Displacement, tons: 310 standard; 428 full load
Dimensions, feet (metres): 152.2 × 23.6 × 17.1 *(46.4 × 7.2 × 5.2)*
Main machinery: 1 Burmeister & Wain diesel; 300 hp(m) *(220 kW)*; 1 shaft
Speed, knots: 7

Comment: Built in 1953.

JASTOG   1982, Yugoslav Navy

4 COASTAL TUGS

PR 36-39

Displacement, tons: 550 full load
Dimensions, feet (metres): 105 × 26.2 × 16.4 *(32 × 8 × 5)*
Speed, knots: 11

Comment: Built at Split in 1950s. Type name, PR (Pomorski Remorker). One held by Croatia in early 1992.

COASTAL TUG   1988, Yugoslav Navy

856 YUGOSLAVIA / Service forces — ZAIRE / Patrol forces

1 DEGAUSSING VESSEL

36

Displacement, tons: 110 standard
Dimensions, feet (metres): 105.6 × 23.3 × 3.9 *(32.2 × 7.1 × 1.2)*
Main machinery: 1 diesel; 528 hp(m) *(388 kW)*; 1 shaft
Speed, knots: 10. Range, miles: 660 at 10 kts
Complement: 20
Guns: 2—20 mm M71.

Comment: Used to degauss River vessels up to a length of 50 m.

TENDERS

Displacement, tons: 51 full load
Dimensions, feet (metres): 69 × 14.8 × 4.6 *(21 × 4.5 × 1.4)*
Main machinery: 2 diesels; 304 hp(m) *(224 kW)*; 2 shafts
Speed, knots: 12
Guns: 2—20 mm M71 can be carried.
Radars: Navigation: Decca; I band.

Comment: A number of tenders which, as transports, can carry 130 people or 15 tons of cargo and also act as diving tenders.

36   1987, Yugoslav Navy

TENDER   10/1990, Eric Grove

ZAIRE

Personnel

(a) 1993: 2000 officers and men (including 600 marines)
(b) Voluntary service

Bases

Matadi, Boma, Banana

Mercantile Marine

Lloyd's Register of Shipping:
27 vessels of 28 074 tons gross

DELETIONS

1990 2 Shanghai II class, 1 Swift class

PATROL FORCES

Note: Six TB 40 and 20 TB 11PA patrol craft were ordered from North Korea in 1989 but none have been delivered due to lack of funds.

2 Ex-CHINESE SHANGHAI II CLASS (FAST ATTACK CRAFT—GUN)

106   +1

Displacement, tons: 113 standard; 131 full load
Dimensions, feet (metres): 127.3 × 17.7 × 5.6 *(38.8 × 5.4 × 1.7)*
Main machinery: 2 Type L12-180 diesels; 2400 hp(m) *(1.76 MW)* forward; 2 Type L12-180Z diesels; 1820 hp(m) *(1.34 MW)* aft; 4 shafts
Speed, knots: 30. Range, miles: 700 at 17 kts
Complement: 34
Guns: 4—37 mm/65 (2 twin). 4—25 mm/80 (2 twin).

Comment: First four delivered in 1976-78. All were thought to be beyond repair by 1985 but two of the four were patched up and two replacements were delivered in February 1987. Two sunk at moorings in mid-1990.

4 SWIFTSHIPS (COASTAL PATROL CRAFT)

KIALA   LUADIA   KANITSHA   MBOKO

Displacement, tons: 19 full load
Dimensions, feet (metres): 51.2 × 13.5 × 3.6 *(15.6 × 4.1 × 1.1)*
Main machinery: 2 GM 12V-71 diesels; 680 hp *(507 kW)* sustained; 2 shafts
Speed, knots: 25. Range, miles: 400 at 24 kts
Complement: 12
Guns: 6—12.7 mm MGs.

Comment: Built by Swiftships, Morgan City, in 1971. Doubtful operational status and two have already been deleted.

SHANGHAI II 106   1988, Gilbert Gyssels

8 ARCOA 25 CLASS (PATROL CRAFT)

Displacement, tons: 2 full load
Dimensions, feet (metres): 24.6 × 9.8 × 2.6 *(7.5 × 3 × 0.8)*
Main machinery: 2 Baudouin diesels; 320 hp(m) *(235 kW)*; 2 shafts
Speed, knots: 30

Comment: Twenty-nine ordered in 1974 in France and delivered by Arcoa. MG mountings forward and aft. Fourteen more delivered 1980-81. Eight were still serviceable at the end of 1990.

Indexes

COUNTRY ABBREVIATIONS

Alb	Albania
Alg	Algeria
Ana	Anguilla
Ang	Angola
Ant	Antigua and Barbuda
Arg	Argentina
Aus	Austria
Aust	Australia
Az	Azerbaijan
Ban	Bangladesh
Bar	Barbados
Bel	Belgium
Ben	Benin
Bhm	Bahamas
Bhr	Bahrain
Blz	Belize
Bmd	Bermuda
Bol	Bolivia
Bru	Brunei
Brz	Brazil
Bul	Bulgaria
Bur	Burma
Cam	Cameroon
Can	Canada
Chi	Chile
CI	Cook Islands
Cmb	Cambodia
Col	Colombia
Com	Comoro Islands
Con	Congo
CPR	China, People's Republic
CpV	Cape Verde
CR	Costa Rica
Cro	Croatia
Cub	Cuba
Cypr	Cyprus (Republic)
Den	Denmark
Dji	Djibouti
Dom	Dominica
DPRK	Korea, Democratic People's Republic (North)
DR	Dominican Republic
Ecu	Ecuador
Egy	Egypt
EIS	El Salvador
EqG	Equatorial Guinea
Eth	Ethiopia and Eritrea
Est	Estonia
Fae	Faeroes
Fij	Fiji
FI	Falkland Islands
Fin	Finland
Fra	France
Gab	Gabon
Gam	The Gambia
GB	Guinea-Bissau
Ger	Germany
Geo	Georgia
Gha	Ghana
Gn	Guinea
Gra	Grenada
Gre	Greece
Gua	Guatemala
Guy	Guyana
Hai	Haiti
HK	Hong Kong
Hon	Honduras
Hun	Hungary
IC	Ivory Coast
Ice	Iceland
Ind	India
Indo	Indonesia
Iran	Iran
Iraq	Iraq
Ire	Ireland
Isr	Israel
Ita	Italy
Jam	Jamaica
Jor	Jordan
Jpn	Japan
Ken	Kenya
Kwt	Kuwait
Lat	Latvia
Lbr	Liberia
Lby	Libya
Leb	Lebanon
Lit	Lithuania
Mad	Madagascar
Mex	Mexico
MI	Marshall Islands
Mic	Micronesia
Mld	Maldive Islands
Mlt	Malta
Mlw	Malawi
Mly	Malaysia
Mnt	Montserrat
Mor	Morocco
Moz	Mozambique
Mrt	Mauritius
Mtn	Mauritania
Nam	Namibia
NATO	NATO
Nic	Nicaragua
Nig	Nigeria
Nld	Netherlands
Nor	Norway
NZ	New Zealand
Omn	Oman
Pak	Pakistan
Pan	Panama
Par	Paraguay
Per	Peru
Plp	Philippines
PNG	Papua New Guinea
Pol	Poland
Por	Portugal
Qat	Qatar
RoC	Taiwan
RoK	Korea, Republic (South)
Rom	Romania
Rus	Russia and Associated States
SA	South Africa
Sab	Sabah
SAr	Saudi Arabia
Sen	Senegal
Sey	Seychelles
Sin	Singapore
SL	Sierra Leone
Sol	Solomon Islands
Spn	Spain
Sri	Sri Lanka
StK	St Kitts
StL	St Lucia
StV	St Vincent and the Grenadines
Sud	Sudan
Sur	Surinam
Swe	Sweden
Swi	Switzerland
Syr	Syria
Tan	Tanzania
TC	Turks and Caicos
Tld	Thailand
Tog	Togo
Ton	Tonga
TT	Trinidad and Tobago
Tun	Tunisia
Tur	Turkey
UAE	United Arab Emirates
Uga	Uganda
UK	United Kingdom
Uru	Uruguay
USA	United States of America
Van	Vanuatu
Ven	Venezuela
VI	Virgin Islands
Vtn	Vietnam
WS	Western Samoa
Yem	Yemen
Yug	Yugoslavia
Zai	Zaire

Named Ships

† denotes secondary reference is in text or note.

1st Lt Alex Bonnyman (USA) 820
1st Lt Baldomero Lopez (USA) .. 821
1st Lt Jack Lummus (USA) 821
2nd Lt John P Bobo (USA) 821
3 de Noviembre (Ecu) 174
5 de Augusto (Ecu) 174
5 July (CpV) 102
8 de Octubre (Col) 142
9 de Octubre (Ecu) 174
10 de Agosto (Ecu) 174
15 de Enero (Gua) .... 266†
15 de Noviembre (Uru) 834
21 de Febrero (Ecu) 174
24 de Mayo (Ecu) 174
25 de Agosto (Uru) 834
25 de Julio (Ecu) 174
26 September (Yem) 847
27 de Octubre (Col) 142
27 de Octubre (Ecu) 174
50 Let Sheftsva Vlksm (Rus) 561

A

A 06–A 08 (Spn) 628
A 15, 16, 42, 43 (Ger) 248
A 33, A34, A35 (Lby) 400
A 71, A 72 (Ind) 290
A 82 (Iraq) 315
A 271, A 272 (UAE) 715
A 502 (Eth) 187
A 516 (Sri) 635
A 584–A 587 (Ban) 45
A 641 (Alg) 7
A 701-705, 751-756 (Swe) 653
A F Dufour (Bel) 49
Aachen (UK) 751
AB 21-24, AB 25-36 (Tur) 702
AB 1050-53, 1055-6, 1058-67 (Aust) 33
ABA 330, ABA 332 (Per) 483
Aba (Nig) 446
Abaco (Bhm) 36
Abakan (Rus) 590
Abbeville (UK) 751
Abcoude (Nld) 433
Abdul Aziz (fast attack craft) (SAr) 601
Abdul Aziz (Royal Yacht) (SAr) ... 604
Abdul Halim Perdana Kusuma (Indo) 294
Abdul Rahman Al Fadel (Bhr) 38
Abdullah (Jor) 375
Abeille Bretagne (Fra) 227
Abeille Flandre (Fra) 227
Abeille Languedoc (Fra) 227
Abeokuta (Nig) 446
Aberdovey (UK) 750
Abha (SAr) 599
Abhay (Ind) 284
Abheetha (Sri) 635
Abinger (UK) 750
Abkhaziya (Rus) 571
Able (USA) 815
Abonnema (Nig) 446
Abou Abdallah El Ayachi (Mor) .. 426
Abraham Crijnssen (Nld) 431
Abraham Lincoln (USA) 766
Abraham van der Hulst (Nld) 432
Abrolhos (Brz) 62
Abtao (Per) 477
Abu Bakr (Ban) 41
Abu El Ghoson (Egy) 181
Abu Obaidah (SAr) 601
Abu Qir (Egy) 177
Abukuma (Abukuma class) (Jpn) 353
Abukuma (Bihoro class) (Jpn) 367
Acacia (USA) 829
Acadia (USA) 803
Acadian (Can) 91
Acara (Brz) .... 67†
Acchileus (Gre) 265
Acconac (USA) 811
Acevedo (Spn) 626
Acharné (Fra) 226
Achéron (Fra) 218
Acheron (Ger) 240
Achilles (Swe) 653
Achimota (Gha) 252
Achziv (Isr) 320
Aconcagua (Chi) 113
Aconit (Fra) 206
Açor (Por) 504
Actif (Fra) 226
Actinia (Por) 505
Active (UK) 732
Active (USA) 825
Acushnet (USA) 826
Ad Dakhla (Mor) 426
Adak (USA) 828
Adamant (UK) 748
Adamastos (Gre) 265
Adang (Tld) 685
Adatepe (Tur) 697
Addriyah (SAr) 602
Adelaide (Aust) 25
Adept (UK) 746
Adept (USA) 808
ADF 106–ADF 110 (Per) 483
ADG 40 (Cub) 153
Adhara II (Arg) 21
Aditya (Ind) 289
Adm Wm H Callaghan (USA) ... 819†
Admiral Branimir Ormanov (Bul) .. 73
Admiral Fokin (Rus) 539
Admiral Golovko (Rus) 539
Admiral Gorshkov (Rus) 535
Admiral Isakov (Rus) 538
Admiral Kharlamov (Rus) 542
Admiral Kuznetsov (Rus) .... 532, 533, 535†
Admiral Lazarev (Rus) 536
Admiral Levchenko (Rus) 542
Admiral Lobov (Rus) 540
Admiral Makarov (Kresta class) (Rus) 538
Admiral Makarov (Yermak class) (Rus) 592
Admiral Nakhimov (Rus) ... 536, 537
Admiral Oktyabrsky (Rus) 538
Admiral Panteleyev (Rus) 542
Admiral Spiridonov (Rus) 542
Admiral Tributs (Rus) 542
Admiral Ushakov (Rus) 536, 537
Admiral Vinogradov (Rus) 542
Admiral Vladimirsky (Rus) 571
Admiral Yumashev (Rus) 538
Admiral Zakharov (Rus) 542
Admiral Zozulya (Rus) 539
ADRI XXXI–ADRI LVIII (Indo) 304
Advance (Aust) .... 28†
Adventurer (USA) .... 819†
Adversus (Can) 91
Adzhariya (Rus) 571
Aedon (Gre) 262
Aegeon (Gre) 256
Aegeus (Gre) 265
Aegir (Ice) 275
Aesche (Ger) 239
Afanasy Nikitin (Rus) 593
AFDB 2 (USA) 808
AFDM 2, 3 (USA) 808
Affray (USA) .... 799†, 801
Afif (SAr) 602
Afikto (Nig) 446
Afonso Cerqueira (Por) 502
Afonso Pena (Brz) 68
AG 1, 4, 5 (Tur) 710
AG 6 (Tur) 709
Agaral (Ind) 290
Agatan (Rus) 584
Agate Pass (USA) 811
Agawam (USA) 811
Agdlek(Den) 160
Agent (USA) .... 819†
Äggskaur (Swe) 646
Agheila (UK) 751
Agnadeen (Iraq) 314
Agnes 200 (Fra) .... 221†
Agosta (Fra) 203
Agpa (Den) 160
Agray (Ind) 284
Agu (Nig) 445
Aguascalientes (Mex) 422
Aguia (Por) 504
Aguila (Chi) 110
Aguila (Spn) 635
Aguilucho (Spn) 635
Aguirre (Per) 478
Agulha (Brz) .... 67†
Agusan (Plp) 490
AH 173, AH 174 (Per) 482
Ahalya Bai (Ind) 291
Ahmad El Fateh (Bhr) 38
Ahmed Es Sakali (Mor) 426
Ahmed Yani (Indo) 294
Ahmet Ersoy (Tur) 711
Ahoskie (USA) 811
Ahrenshoop (Ger) 249
Aias (Gre) 265
Aida IV (Egy) .... 181†
Aide (USA) .... 819†
Aigeo (Gre) .... 262†
Aigle (Fra) 218
Aigli (Gre) 262
Aigrette (Sen) 606
Aiguière (Fra) 227
Ailette (Fra) 227
Aina Vao Vao (Mad) .... 216†, 401
Ainsworth (USA) .... 785†, 785
Air Condor (Aust) 34
Air Eagle (Aust) 34
Air Hawk (Aust) 34
Airisto (Fin) 196
Airone (Ita) .... 329†
Aisberg (Rus) 594
Aisling (Ire) 316
Aiyar Lulin (Bur) 78
Aiyar Mai (Bur) 78
Aiyar Maung (Bur) 78
Aiyar Minthamee (Bur) 78
Aiyar Minthar (Bur) 78
Ajak (Indo) 298
Ajax (Swe) 653
Ajay (Ind) 284
Ajeera (Bhr) 38
AK 1, 3 (Ger) 243
AK 2, 5, 6 (Ger) 246
Aka (Iraq) 315
Akademik M A Lavrentyev (Rus) 576
Akademik Aleksandr Nesmeyanov (Rus) 574
Akademik Aleksandr Vinogradov (Rus) 574
Akademik Aleksey Krylov (Rus) . 573
Akademik Boris Konstantinov (Rus) 573
Akademik Boris Petrov (Rus) 576
Akademik Fedorov (Rus) . 574, 575†
Akademik Fersman (Rus) 575
Akademik Gubkin (Rus) 550
Akademik Gumburtsev (Rus) 576
Akademik Ioffe (Rus) 574
Akademik Korolev (Rus) 575
Akademik Kreps (Rus) 575
Akademik Krylov (Rus) 571
Akademik Kurchatov (Rus) 575
Akademik Lazarev (Rus) 575
Akademik Mstislav Keldysh (Rus) 574
Akademik N Strakhov (Rus) 576
Akademik Nalivkin (Rus) 575
Akademik Namyotkin (Rus) 575
Akademik Nicolai Pilyugin (Rus) 577
Akademik Nikolay Andreyev (Rus) 573
Akademik Oparin (Rus) 576
Akademik Selskiy (Rus) 575
Akademik Sergei Vavilov (Rus) .. 574
Akademik Sergey Korolev (Rus) 578
Akademik Shatsky (Rus) 575
Akademik Shirshov (Rus) 575
Akademik Shokalsky (Rus) 576
Akademik Shuleykin (Rus) 576
Akademik Vernadsky (Rus) 575
Akagi (Jpn) 368
Akar (Tur) 707
Akashi (AGS) (Jpn) 363

858 INDEXES/Named Ships

Akashi (HS) (Jpn) 372
Akbaş (Tur) 710
Akdu (Egy) 181
Akhisar (Tur) 702
Akhtyuba (Rus) 582
Akigumo (Murakumo class) (Jpn) 369
Akigumo (Yamagumo class) (Jpn) 351
Akin (Tur) 708
Akishio (Jpn) 344
Akizuki (ASU) (Jpn) 359
Akizuki (PC) (Jpn) 369
Akka Devi (Ind) 291
Akko (Isr) 319
Akshay (Ind) 284
Aktion (Gre) 261
Akuna (Aust) 34
Akure (Nig) 446
Akyab (UK) 751
Al Agami (Egy) 181
Al Ahad (Lby) 395
Al Ahweirif (Lby) 400
Al Assad (Syr) 659
Al Badr (Lby) 395
Al Bahan (SAr) 601
Al Baida (Lby) 398
Al Bat'nah (Omn) 458
Al Bitar (Lby) 398
Al Deryah (SAr) 604
Al Dikhila (Egy) 181
Al Doghas (Omn) 459
Al Faisal (Jor) 374
Al Farouq (SAr) 601
Al Fateh (Lby) 395†
Al Feyi (UAE) 715
Al Fikah (Lby) 398
Al Forat (SAr) 605
Al Fulk (Omn) 457
Al Ghariyah (Qat) 508
Al Ghullan (UAE) 715
Al Hady (Egy) 180
Al Hakim (Egy) 180
Al Hamza (Jor) 374
Al Hani (Lby) 396
Al Hashim (Jor) 374
Al Hirasa (Syr) 657
Al Hunain (Lby) 395
Al Hussan (Jor) 375
Al Hussein (Jor) 375
Al Isar (Lby) 398
Al Iskandarani (Egy) 181
Al Jabbar (Omn) 457
Al Jabiri (Bhr) 38
Al Jala (Tun) 693
Al Jarim (Bhr) 38
Al Jasrah (Bhr) 38
Al Jawf (SAr) 601
Al Jouf (SAr) 603
Al Jubatel (SAr) 603
Al Katum (Lby) 398
Al Keriat (Lby) 400
Al Kharj (SAr) 601
Al Khyber (Lby) 395
Al Kousser (Egy) 181†
Al Leeth (SAr) 602
Al Mabrukah (Omn) 456
Al Mahrah (Yem) 848
Al Manama (Bhr) 38
Al Manoud (Lby) 400
Al Mathur (Lby) 398
Al Meks (Egy) 181
Al Mitraqa (Lby) 395
Al Mosha (Lby) 398
Al Muharraq (Lürssen) (Bhr) 38
Al Muharraq (Wasp) (Bhr) 38
Al Mujahid (Omn) 457
Al Munassir (Omn) 458
Al Munjed (Lby) 399
Al Nabha (Lby) 398
Al Neemran (Omn) 459
Al Nil (SAr) 605
Al Nour (Egy) 180
Al Qatar (Egy) 180
Al Qiaq (SAr) 602
Al Qirdabiyah (Lby) 396
Al Quonfetha (SAr) 602
Al Quysumah (SAr) 602
Al Rafia (Egy) 180
Al Rahmanniya (Omn) 459
Al Rass (SAr) 601
Al Riffa (Bhr) 37
Al Riyadh (SAr) 602
Al Ruha (Lby) 398
Al Sadad (Lby) 398
Al Saddam (Egy) 180
Al Safhra (Lby) 398
Al Said (Omn) 460
Al Sakab (Lby) 398
Al Salam (Egy) 180
Al Sanbouk (Kwt) 392
Al Sansoor (Omn) 459
Al Sharqiyah (Omn) 458
Al Siddiq (SAr) 601
Al Sulayel (SAr) 602
Al Sultana (Omn) 459
Al Tabkah (Lby) 400
Al Taif (SAr) 605
Al Taweelah (Bhr) 38
Al Temsah (Omn) 459
Al Tiyar (Lby) 398
Al Ula (SAr) 602
Al Waafi (Omn) 457
Al Wadeeah (SAr) 602
Al Wakil (Egy) 180
Al Wudia (Yem) 848
Al Wusail (Qat) 508
Al Yarmook (SAr) 600
Al Zahraa (Iraq) 314
Al Zuara (Lby) 398
Alabama (USA) 759
Alabarda (Por) 505
Alacalufe (Chi) 112
Alacrity (UK) 732
Alagez (Rus) 585
Alagoas (Brz) 56
Alambai (Rus) 583
Alamgir (Pak) 465
Alaska (USA) 759, 760†
Alatau (Rus) 584
Alatna (USA) 818†
Alatyr (Rus) 582
Albacora (DR) 169†
Albacora (Por) 501
Albacore (Fra) 227
Albany (USA) 762
Albardão (Brz) 62
Albatros IV (USA) 832†
Albatros (Fra) 217
Albatros (Ger) 238
Albatros (Pol) 494
Albatros (Tur) 701
Albatros 2, 3 (Spn) 635
Albatroz (Brz) 66
Albatroz (Por) 504
Albay Hakki Burak (Tur) 707
Albert J Myer (USA) 818
Alborz (Iran) 307
Albuquerque (Col) 141
Albuquerque (USA) 762
Alca 1, 3 (Spn) 635
Alcanada (Spn) 626
Alcaraván 1-5 (Spn) 635
Alcatraz (Ven) 841
Alcide Pedretti (Ita) 334, 715†
Alcione (Ita) 329†
Alcitepe (Tur) 698
Alcotán 2 (Spn) 635
Alcyon (Fra) 227
Aldan (Rus) 584
Aldebaran (Den) 161
Aldebarán (DR) 168
Aldebaran (Ven) 841
Alderney (UK) 738
Ale (Swe) 651
Alejandro de Humbolt (Mex) 420
Aleksandr Brykin (Rus) 566
Aleksandr Nikolaev (Rus) 562
Aleksandr Shabalin (Rus) 562
Aleksandr Tortsev (Rus) 561
Aleksey Chirikov (Rus) 572
Aleksey Kortunov (Rus) 595
Aleksey Maryshev (Rus) 576
Alençon (Fra) 218
Alert (Can) 98
Alert (USA) 825
Alerta (Spn) 630
Alexander of Cresswell (Aust) 33†
Alexandria (USA) 762
Alfange (ex-) (Ang) 9
Alferez Sobral (Arg) 16
Alfonso Vargas (Col) 142
Alfred Needler (Can) 102
Alga (Cro) 150
Algarna 1 (Tur) 711
Alghero (Ita) 331
Algol (USA) 821
Algonquin (Can) 84
Ali Haider (Ban) 41
Alidada (Rus) 570
Alidade (Alg) 7
Alioth (Gua) 267
Aliseo (Ita) 327
Aliya (Isr) 318
Alk (Ger) 238
Alkmaar (Nld) 433
Alkor (Ger) 251
Alkyon (Gre) 262
Alleppey (Ind) 288
Alliance (NATO) 428
Alloro (Ita) 331†, 336
Almamy Bocar Biro Barry (Gn) 268
Almeida Carvalho (Por) 505
Almirante Alvaro Alberto (Brz) 63
Almirante Brión (Ven) 838
Almirante Brown (Arg) 12
Almirante Câmara (Brz) 63
Almirante Clemente (Ven) 840
Almirante Garcia (Ven) 838
Almirante Gastão Motta (Brz) 66
Almirante Graça Aranha (Brz) 63
Almirante Grau (Bol) 53
Almirante Grau (Per) 478, 479†
Almirante Guilhem (Brz) 67
Almirante Guillobel (Brz) 67
Almirante Hess (Brz) 68
Almirante Irizar (Arg) 18
Almirante Jeronimo Gonçalves (Brz) 68
Almirante Jorge Montt (Chi) 111
Almirante Padilla (Col) 140
Almirante Riveros (Chi) 104
Almirante Schieck (Brz) 68
Almirante Williams (Chi) 104
Alnmouth (UK) 750
Alnösund (Swe) 647
Alor Star (Mly) 409
Alphée (Fra) 223
Alpino (Ita) 326
Alsatian (UK) 747
Alsedo (Spn) 625
Alsfeld (Ger) 250
Alster (Ger) 244
Alta (Alta class) (Nor) 453
Alta (Sauda class) (Nor) 453
Altair (Mex) 420
Altair (Rus) 572
Altair (USA) 821
Altair (Ven) 841
Altar (Ecu) 174
Altarskaur (Swe) 646
Altay (Rus) 585
Altayskiy (Rus) 559
Alte Liebe (Ger) 251†
Altmark (Ger) 242
Alu Alu (Mly) 408
Alumine (Arg) 21
Alvand (Iran) 307
Alvares Cabral (Por) 501
Alvin (USA) 822
Älvsborg (Swe) 646
AM 4-8, AM 11-23 (Mex) 420
AM 6, 7, 8 (Ger) 246
AM 11–AM 25 (Mex) 419
AM 215–AM 220 (Aust) 34
Amagiri (Jpn) 348
Aman (Kwt) 391
Amapá (Brz) 61
Amar (Mrt) 414
Amatsukaze (Jpn) 352
Amazonas (Ecu) 173
Amazonas (Per) 481
Amazonas (Ven) 839
Amba (Ind) 289
Ambassador (USA) 819†
Ambe (Nig) 447
Ambuda (Ind) 290
America (USA) 768, 769
American Cormorant (USA) 819
American Eagle (USA) 819†
American Explorer (USA) 818†
American Kestrel (USA) 819
American Merlin (USA) 819†, 820
American Osprey (USA) 818†, 820
Amerigo Vespucci (Ita) 336
Améthyste (Fra) 202
Ametyst (Rus) 548
Amga (Rus) 566
Amilcar (Tun) 692
Amini (Ind) 282
Amir (Iran) 311
Amira Rama (Egy) 181
Amiral Courbet (Fra) 213
Ammersee (Ger) 242
Ammiraglio Magnaghi (Ita) 333
Amphitrite (Gre) 254
Amrit Kaur (Ind) 291
Amrum (Ger) 247
Amsterdam (Nld) 425
Amur (Pinega class) (Rus) 566
Amur (Sorum class) (Rus) 595
Amvrakia (Gre) 261
Amyot d'Inville (Fra) 212
Amyr (SAr) 601
An Dong (RoK) 385
An Yang (RoC) 664
An Yang (RoK) 385
Anacapa (USA) 828
Anacoco (Ven) 841
Anadyr (Anadyr class) (Rus) 586
Anadyr (Moma class) (Rus) 572
Anaga (Spn) 626
Anami (Jpn) 368
Anand (Ind) 290
Anchorage (USA) 796
Andalsnes (UK) 751
Andalucía (Spn) 622
Andenes (Nor) 455
Andenne (Bel) 50
Andorinha (Por) 504
Andrade (Per) 483†
Andres Bonifacio (Plp) 485
Andres Quintana Roo (Mex) 419
Andrew J Higgins (USA) 817
Andrey Vilkitsky (Rus) 572
Andrija Mohorovičić (Cro) 150
Andromache (Sey) 607
Andromeda (Den) 161
Andromeda (Gre) 259
Andromeda (Por) 505
Andromeda (Rus) 572
Andromeda (UK) 728
Andromède (Fra) 218
Andros (Bhm) 36
Androth (Ind) 282
Aneroid (Rus) 570
Ang Pangulo (Plp) 488
Ang Pinuno (Plp) 488
Angamos (Chi) 111
Angara (Rus) 586
Angela (Ger) 251†
Anglesey (UK) 738
Angostura (Brz) 61
Angostura (Par) 475
Anhatomirim (Brz) 62
Anittepe (Tur) 698
Anjadip (Ind) 282
Ann Harvey (Can) 94
Annad (UAE) 716
Annapolis (Can) 86
Annapolis (USA) 762, 763
Annie Besant (Ind) 291
Anoka (USA) 811
Anqing (CPR) 122
Anshun (CPR) 120
Antaios (Gre) 265
Antar (Egy) 181
Antares (Brz) 62
Antares (Bul) 73
Antares (Den) 161
Antares (Mex) 420
Antares (Rus) 572
Antares (Spn) 630
Antares (Swi) 656
Antares (USA) 821
Antares (Ven) 841
Antarktyda (Rus) 572
Ante Banina (Yug) 851
Anteo (Ita) 336
Anthiploiarhos Laskos (Gre) 258
Anthipoploiarhos Anninos (Gre) 259
Anthipoploiarhos Kostakos (Gre) 258
Anticosti (Can) 90
Antietam (USA) 776
Antigo (USA) 811
Antiopi (Gre) 262
Antioquia (Col) 140
Antizana (Ecu) 174
Antofagasta (Per) 477
Antonio Enes (Por) 503
Antonio Joao (Brz) 67†
Antonio Zara (Ita) 340
Antrim (USA) 785†, 786
Antuco (Chi) 112
Antwerp (UK) 751
Anvil (USA) 831
Anzac (Aust) 27
Anzio (USA) 776, 777
Aoife (Ire) 316
Aokumo (Jpn) 351
Apache (USA) 818
Apalachicola (USA) 811
Apollo (Den) 161
Apopka (USA) 811
Apostolis (Gre) 255
Appleby (UK) 750
Appleleaf (UK) 31†, 741†
Apsheron (Rus) 567
Apu (Fin) 193
Aquarius (Swi) 656
Aquidneck (USA) 828
Aquila (USA) 802
Aquiles (Chi) 110
AR 15 (Mex) 422
Ara (Fra) 226
Araçatuba (Brz) 62
Arachthos (Gre) 264
Aradu (Nig) 443
Arago (Fra) 219
Aragón (Spn) 628
Aragosta (Ita) 336
Aragvi (Rus) 583
Arakan (UK) 750
Aramis (Fra) 224
Aranda (Fin) 196
Aras (Iran) 312
Arashio (Jpn) 344
Arataki (NZ) 441
Aratú (Brz) 62
Arau (Mly) 409
Arauca (Col) 141
Araucano (Chi) 111
Arcata (USA) 811
Archer (UK) 739
Archerfish (USA) 764
Arco (USA) 808
Arctic (USA) 805
Arctowski (Pol) 497
Ardennes (UK) 750
Ardent (Aust) 28
Ardent (USA) 799
Ardhana (UAE) 715
Ardito (Ita) 325
Arenque (Brz) 67†
Arethousa (Gre) 263
Arezzo (UK) 751
Argentina (Brz) 67†
Argos (Por) 504
Argos (Swe) 651†
Argun (Rus) 582
Argungu (Nig) 445
Argus (Aust) 32
Argus (Brz) 63
Argus (Nld) 436
Argus (UK) 743
Argyll (UK) 729
Arholma (Swe) 648
Ariadni (Gre) 263
Arica (Per) 477
Ariel (Fra) 223
Aries (Den) 161
Aries (USA) 802
Arinya (Plp) 489
Aris (Gre) 263
Arjun (Ind) 290
Ark Royal (UK) 724, 725
Arkansas (USA) 773
Arkö (Swe) 647
Arkosund (Swe) 647
Arktika (Arktika class) (Rus) 592
Arktika (Moma class) (Rus) 572
Arleigh Burke (USA) 784
Arlunuya (Plp) 489
Armatolos (Gre) 258
Armen (Fra) 226
Arnala (Ind) 282
Arnold Veimer (Est) 185, 576†
Arosa (Spn) 631
Arrafiq (Mor) 426
Arrernte (Aust) 27
Arrochar (UK) 746
Arrojado (Brz) 67
Arromanches (UK) 751
Arslan (Tur) 709
Arthur W Radford (USA) 782
Artigliere (Ita) 328
Artillerist (Rus) 558
Artisan (USA) 808
Aruana (Brz) 67†
Arun (Indo) 302
Arun (UK) 734
Ary Parreiras (Brz) 65
Asagiri (Asagiri class) (Jpn) 348
Asagiri (Murakumo class) (Jpn) 369
Asagumo (Murakumo class) (Jpn) 369
Asagumo (Yamagumo class) (Jpn) 351
Asakaze (Jpn) 350
Asayuki (Jpn) 349
Ashdod (Isr) 320
Asheville (USA) 762
Ashitaka (Jpn) 369
Ashizuri (Jpn) 366
Ashkelon (Isr) 320
Ashland (USA) 796
Askar (Bhr) 39
Askeri (Fin) 195
Askø (Den) 162
Askold (Rus) 572
Aslat (Pak) 466
Asoyuki (Jpn) 370
Aspirante Isaza (Chi) 108
Aspirante Jose V Razcon (Mex) 419
Aspirante Morel (Chi) 108
Aspirante Nascimento (Brz) 66
Aspro (USA) 764
Assa (Mor) 427
Assad Al Bihar (Lby) 397
Assad Al Hudud (Lby) 397
Assad Al Khali (Lby) 397
Assad Bin Fourat (Tun) 693
Assad El Tougour (Lby) 397
Assateague (USA) 828
Assertive (USA) 815
Assiniboine (Can) 88†
Assiout (Egy) 180
Assurance (USA) 815
Aster (Bel) 48
Astice (Ita) 336
Astore (Ita) 333
Astravahini (Ind) 290
Astronauta Franklin Chang (CR) 146
Astronom (Rus) 573
Asturias (Spn) 622
ASU 81–ASU 85 (Jpn) 362
Asunción (Par) 476
Aswan (Egy) 180
Atahualpa (Ecu) 173
Atair (Ger) 251
Atalaia (Brz) 62
Atalanti (Gre) 262
Atalaya (Spn) 623
ATB 1, ATB 2 (Swe) 653
Athabaskan (Can) 84
Athena, Athena II (USA) 812
Atherstone (UK) 734
Athos (Fra) 224
Atil (Tur) 711
Atilay (Tur) 695
Atiya (Bul) 74
Atlanta (Por) 505
Atlanta (USA) 762
Atlante (Ita) 338
Atlantic Sentry (USA) 826
Atlantico (Ang) 8
Atlantis (Ger) 240
Atlas (Brz) 68†
Atlas (Gre) 265
Atlas (Swe) 653
Atle (Swe) 650
Atmaca (Tur) 701
Atrak (Iran) 312
Atromitos (Gre) 265
Atsmout (Isr) 318
Atsumi (Jpn) 356
Attock (Pak) 471
Attu (USA) 828
Atum (Brz) 67†
Atún (DR) 169
Atures (Ven) 841
Atyimba (Plp) 30†, 489
Aubrey Fitch (USA) 786
Audace (Ita) 325
Audacious (USA) 815
Audaz (Uru) 834
Audemer (UK) 751
Auerbach (Ger) 240
Augsburg (Ger) 235
Augusta (USA) 762
Augusto de Castilho (Por) 503
Auk (HK) 272
Auki (Sol) 613
Aures (Alg) 8
Auricula (UK) 745
Auriga (Por) 505
Aurora Australis (Aust) 30†
Auster (Ger) 239
Austin (USA) 795
Austin Smith (Bhm) 36
Austral Lightning (USA) 819†
Austral Rainbow (USA) 819
Automatice (Rom) 514
Auxiliar (Bol) 53
Avalon (USA) 822
Avenger (UK) 732
Avenger (USA) 799
Aviere (Ita) 328
Avila (Bel) 51
Avocet (Can) 99
Avocet (UK) 752†
Avra (Gre) 262
Avramiy Zavenyagin (Rus) 593
Avvayar (Ind) 291
Awagiri (Jpn) 369
Awaji (Jpn) 367
Aware (Aust) 28
Awashima (Jpn) 358
AWB 400–AWB 445 (Aust) 33
AWL 304 (Aust) 33
Axe (USA) 831
Axios (Gre) 263
Ayabane (Jpn) 373
Ayam (Nig) 445
Ayase (Jpn) 354
Ayeda (Egy) 181
Ayer Chawan (Sin) 611
Ayer Merban (Sin) 611
Azadi (Iran) 308
Azimut (Rus) 572
Aziziah (SAr) 605
Aziziye (Tur) 709
Azopardo (Arg) 19
Azov (Rus) 541
Azuma (Jpn) 360
Azumanche (Gua) 266

B

B 03, 11, 30 *et al* (Ger) 246
B 5-7, B 9-13 (Pol) 499
B-015 (Cub) 154
Baagø (Den) 162
Babr (Iran) 306
Babur (Pak) 464
Bacamarte (Por) 505
Bacolod City (Plp) 487
Bad Bevensen (Ger) 240
Bad Bramstedt (Ger) 250
Bad Rappenau (Ger) 240
Badek (Mly) 406
Badik (Indo) 297
Badjao (Plp) 489
Badr (Egy) 178
Badr (Pak) 467
Badr (FFL) (SAr) 600
Badr (PV) (SAr) 603
Bågen (Swe) 645
Bagong Lakas (Plp) 487
Bagong Silang (Plp) 487
Bahadoer (Sur) 640
Bahasha Shaeed (Ban) 44†
Bahawalpur (Pak) 468
Bahia Blanca (Arg) 20
Bahia Cupica (Col) 143
Bahia Honda (Col) 143
Bahia Malaga (Col) 143
Bahia Portete (Col) 143
Bahia San Blas (Arg) 17
Bahia Solano (Col) 143
Bahia Utria (Col) 143
Bahiana (Brz) 61
Bahram (Iran) 309
Bainbridge (USA) 762†, 774
Bainbridge Island (USA) 828
Baja (Hun) 274
Bajrang (Ind) 290
Bakassi (Cam) 81
Balaban (Ban) 45†
Balder (Den) 164
Baldur (Ice) 275
Baleares (Spn) 622
Balgzand (Nld) 437
Balikpapan (Aust) 30
Balikpapan (Indo) 302
Balkhash (Rus) 571
Ballarat (Aust) 27
Balny (Fra) 211
Balong (Mly) 408
Balqees (Iraq) 314
Balram (Ind) 290
Balshil (Ind) 290
Baltica (Swe) 652
Baltimore (USA) 762
Baltrum (Ger) 247
Baltyk (Pol) 497

Named Ships/INDEXES 859

Baluchistan (Pak) 468†
Bambu (Ita) 331
Bamfield (Can) 99
Ban Yas (UAE) 715
Banco Ortiz (Uru) 836
Bandar Abbas (Iran) 311
Bandicoot (Aust) 29
Bang Rachan (Tld) 683
Bangkeo (Tld) 683
Bangpakong (Tld) 676
Bani Yas (UAE) 714
Banks (Aust) 30
Banner (USA) 819†
Bannu (Pak) 468
Bant (Ger) 244
Baptista de Andrade (Por) 502
Baracuda (UAE) 716
Baradero (Arg) 16
Baranof (USA) 828
Barão de Teffé (Brz) 62
Barbara (Ger) 245
Barbara (Ita) 334
Barbaros (Tur) 699
Barceló (Spn) 626
Barguzin (Rus) 583
Bark (Lby) 397
Barkat (Ban) 44†
Barkat (Pak) 469
Barnstable County (USA) 797
Barograf (Rus) 570
Barösund (Swe) 647
Barracuda (Gua) 267
Barracuda (Mrt) 414
Barracuda (Por) 501
Barracuda (TT) 690
Barrangueras (Arg) 16
Barroso Pereira (Brz) 65
Barry (USA) 784
Bars (Rus) 583†
Barsemeister Brehme (Ger) 251†
Barsø (Den) 160
Bartlett (Can) 96
Bartlett (USA) 814
Barunajaya I, II, III (Indo) 301
Barzan (Qat) 508
Başaran (Tur) 708
Basento (Ita) 337
Bashkiriya (Rus) 571
Basilisk (PNG) 473
Baskunchak (Rus) 567
Bassein (Ind) 288
Basset (UK) 747
Basswood (USA) 829
Bastimento (Pan) 472
Bat Sheva (Isr) 320
Bataan (USA) 792
Batfish (USA) 764
Batiray (Tur) 695
Baton Rouge (USA) 762
Battle Point (USA) 811
Battleaxe (UK) 730, 731†
Bauchi (Nig) 446
Baunen (Den) 162
Baung (Mly) 406
Bayandor (Iran) 307
Bayberry (USA) 830
Bayern (Brandenburg class) (Ger) 236
Bayern (Hamburg class) (Ger) 234
Bayfield (Can) 101
Baykal (Rus) 571
Bayleaf (UK) 741
Bayonet (Aust) 28†
Bayovar (Per) 482
Bayraktar (Tur) 703†, 705
Bayreuth (Ger) 250
Bayu (Mly) 409
BC 1000–BC 9000 series (Indo) 303, 304
Bditelni (Bul) 72
Bditelny (Rus) 546, 547
BDK-69 (Rus) 561
Beagle (UK) 740
Bear (USA) 824
Beata (DR) 169†
Beaufort (USA) 807
Beaver (Aust) 33
Beaver (UK) 730
Beddgelert (UK) 750
Bedi (Ind) 288
Bee (UK) 749
Behr Paima (Pak) 469
Belati (Indo) 303
Belawkas (Mly) 408
Beledau (Mly) 406
Belegiš (Yug) 853
Belgica (Bel) 50
Belian (Mly) 408
Bélier (Fra) 225
Belknap (USA) 778, 804†
Bellatrix (Chi) 113
Bellatrix (DR) 168
Bellatrix (USA) 821
Belleau Wood (USA) 793
Bellis (Bel) 48
Belmonte (Brz) 64
Belos (Swe) 652
Benalla (Aust) 30
Bendeharu (Bru) 69
Bendigo (Aust) 28
Benfold (USA) 784
Bengali (Fra) 226
Benguela (Nam) 427†
Benguet (Plp) 487
Benin City (Nig) 446
Benina (Lby) 398
Benjamin Isherwood (USA) 817
Bentara (Mly) 409
Berezan (Rus) 572
Berezina (Rus) 536†, 580, 581†
Bergall (USA) 764
Bergantin (Spn) 626
Bergen (Nor) 450
Berk (Tur) 700
Berkeley (UK) 734
Berrio (Por) 506
Berry (new) (Fra) 221†
Berry (old) (Fra) 222
Bersagliere (Ita) 328
Bervang (Indo) 297
Beshtau (Rus) 585
Beskytteren (Den) 157
Bespokoiny (Rus) 543
Bessang Pass (Plp) 489
Bessmenny (Rus) 546
Betano (Aust) 30
Betelgeuse (Den) 161
Betelgeuse (DR) 168
Betika (Cam) 82
Bévéziers (Fra) 203
Bezboyaznenny (Rus) 543
Bezstrashni (Bul) 72
Bezuderzhny (Rus) 543
Bezukoriznenny (Rus) 546
Bezuprechny (Rus) 543
Bezzavetny (Rus) 546
BG 6, BG 7 (Ger) 250
Bhatkal (Ind) 288
Bhavnagar (Ind) 288
Bholu (Pak) 470
Bi Bong (RoK) 388
Bibundi (Cam) 82
Bicester (UK) 734
Bickerton (Can) 99†, 99
Biddle (USA) 778
Biduk (Indo) 302
Big Horn (USA) 817
Bigliani (Ita) 340
Bihoro (Jpn) 367
Bij (Bel) 51
Bille (Den) 160
Billfish (USA) 764
Bima Samudera 1 (Indo) 298
Bimbia (Cam) 82†
Bimlipitan (Ind) 288
Bin Hai (CPR) 133
Binbaşi Netin Sülüs (Tur) 709
Binbaşi Saadettin Gürçan (Tur) 707
Binz (Ger) 249
Biokovak (Yug) 852
Biokovo (Yug) 852
Bira (Rus) 588
Birinci İnönü (Tur) 696
Biriusa (Rus) 580
Birknack (Ger) 251†
Birmingham (UK) 726
Birmingham (USA) 762
Biscayne Bay (USA) 827
Bishkhali (Ban) 43
Bison (Fra) 225
Biter (UK) 739
Bitol (Gua) 266
Bittern (Can) 99
Bittern (UK) 752†
Bittersweet (USA) 829
Bizerte (Tun) 693
Black Hawk (USA) 800
Black Rover (UK) 742
Blackan (Swe) 648
Blackberry (USA) 830
Blackwater (UK) 734
Blanca Estela (Chi) 110†
Blanco Encalada (Chi) 105
Blazer (UK) 739
Blidö (Swe) 647
Blink (Nor) 451
Blitvenica (Yug) 853
Block Island (USA) 828
Blommendal (Nld) 434
Bloys van Treslong (Nld) 431
Blue Heron (Bmd) 52
Blue Ridge (USA) 791
Bluebell (USA) 830
Bluefish (USA) 764
Bluethroat (Can) 91†
Bobruisk (Rus) 562
Bodri (Bul) 71
Bodry (Rus) 546
Bogalusa (USA) 811
Bogra (Ban) 43
Bohechio (DR) 169
Bois Rond Tonnerre (Hai) 270
Boise (USA) 762
Bold (USA) 815
Bolina (Por) 507
Bolko (Pol) 498
Bollard (USA) 831
Bolognesi (Per) 479†
Bolster (USA) 806, 808
Boltenhagen (Ger) 249
Bombarda (Por) 505
Bonanca (Por) 507
Bonhomme Richard (USA) 792
Bonifaz (Spn) 625
Bonite (Fra) 226
Bonito (DR) 169†
Bocne (USA) 786
Boongaree (Aust) 34
Bopa (Den) 161
Boqueron (Par) 475
Bora (Tur) 702
Borač (Yug) 851
Boraida (SAr) 602
Borby (Ger) 243
Borda (Fra) 219
Börde (Ger) 242
Bore (Swe) 649
Borgen (Nor) 452
Borgsund (Nor) 453
Boris Butoma (Rus) 581
Boris Chilikin (Rus) 536†, 581, 591†
Boris Davidov (Rus) 572
Bormida (Ita) 337
Borodino (Rus) 565†, 579
Boronia (Aust) 33
Boston (USA) 762
Bosut (Yug) 853
Bottsand (Ger) 247
Bougainville (Fra) 199†, 216
Boulder (USA) 797, 799†
Boushehr (Iran) 311
Boutwell (USA) 824
Bouzagza (Alg) 8
Bowditch (USA) 816†
Bowen (USA) 785†, 785
Boxer (UK) 730
Boxer (USA) 792
Boyaca (Col) 140
Boyevoy (Rus) 543
Bradano (Ita) 337
Bramble (USA) 829
Brambleleaf (UK) 741
Brandenburg (Ger) 236
Brännaren (Swe) 651
Bras (Nig) 445
Brasil (Brz) 65†, 66
Brask (Nor) 451
Brave (UK) 730
Brazen (UK) 730
Bream (UK) 751
Brecon (UK) 734
Bredal (Den) 160
Bredskaur (Swe) 646
Bredstedt (Ger) 249
Breezand (Nld) 437
Breitgrund (Ger) 244
Brekele (Brz) 66
Bremen (Ger) 235
Bremen 2, Bremen 3 (Ger) 251†
Bremerhaven (Ger) 251†
Bremerton (USA) 762
Brenta (Ita) 337
Brest (Rus) 595
Breydel (Bel) 49
Bridge (USA) 805
Bridle (USA) 831
Bridport (UK) 735
Brigaden (Den) 161
Brigadier Jose Maria de la Vega Gonzalez (Mex) 417
Brighton (StV) 598
Brilliant (Rus) 548
Brilliant (UK) 730, 731†
Brimse (Nor) 452
Brinton (UK) 734
Brisbane (Aust) 24
Briscoe (USA) 782
Bristol (UK) 726†
Bristol Bay (USA) 827, 829†
Bristol County (USA) 797
Britannia (UK) 737
Briz (Bul) 72
Broadsword (UK) 730, 731†
Brocklesby (UK) 734
Brolga (Aust) 29
Bromo (Indo) 303
Bronzewing (Aust) 32
Brseč (Yug) 853
Brufut (Gam) 230
Bruinvis (Nld) 429
Brunei (Aust) 30
Bruno Gregoretti (Ita) 339†
Bruno Illing (Ger) 251†
Bruno Racua (Bol) 53
Brunswick (Ger) 251†
Brunswick (USA) 807
Bryza (Pol) 496
BT 1, BT 2 (Par) 476
Bu Chon (RoK) 385
Buckthorn (USA) 830
Budstikken (Den) 162
Buenos Aires (Pilot Craft) (Arg) 21
Buenos Aires (PV) (Arg) 20
Buffalo (USA) 762
Buffalo Soldier (USA) 819†, 820
Buffle (Fra) 225
Bug (Rus) 595
Buguzuslan (Rus) 582†
Buk Han (RoK) 388
Bukhansan (RoK) 390
Bukowo (Pol) 495
Bulgia (Nld) 435
Bullarijia (Tun) 694
Bulldog (UK) 740
Bullseye (UK) 750
Bulsar (Ind) 288
Bums (Ger) 246
Buna (PNG) 473
Bunbury (Aust) 28
Bunker Hill (USA) 776
Burakreis (Tur) 696
Buran (Rus) 593
Burcrest (PNG) 473
Burgeo (Can) 99
Burin (Can) 99
Burny (Rus) 543
Burong Nuri (Bru) 69
Burovestnik (Rus) 587
Burq (Pak) 471
Bursea (PNG) 473
Burtide (PNG) 473
Burujulasad (Indo) 301
Burun (Rus) 553
Burwave (PNG) 473
Burya (Bul) 72
Burya (Rus) 595
Busan (RoK) 384
Bussard (Ger) 238
Bustler (UK) 746
Butte (USA) 803
Buttonwood (USA) 829
Buyer (USA) 819†
Buyskes (Nld) 434
Buzuluk (Rus) 587
Bystry (Rus) 543

C

C 01–C 08 (Ind) 292
Ç 108 and series, Ç 119 and series (Tur) 705
Ç 213-214, Ç 302 and series (Tur) 706
C 301, C 303 (Sur) 639
C G C Albert Porte (Lbr) 395
Cabo Blanco (CR) 147
Cabo Bojeador (Plp) 489
Cabo Branco (Brz) 64†
Cabo Calcanhar (Brz) 64†
Cabo Catoche (Mex) 419
Cabo Corrientes (Arg) 20
Cabo Corrientes (Mex) 419
Cabo Corzo (Mex) 419
Cabo Fradera (Spn) 627
Cabo Frio (Brz) 64†
Cabo de Hornos (Arg) 17
Cabo Odger (Chi) 112
Cabo Orange (Brz) 64†
Cabo San Antonio (Arg) 16
Cabo Schram (Brz) 67
Cabo Velas (CR) 147
Caboclo (Brz) 61
Cacine (Por) 503
Cadarso (Spn) 625
Cadete Virgilio Uribe Robles (Mex) 417
Cádiz (Spn) 632
Cagayan de Oro City (Plp) 487
Caio Duilio (Ita) 332†
Cairn (UK) 747
Çakabey (Tur) 703†, 705
Cakra (Indo) 293
Calchaqui (Arg) 18
Caldas (Col) 140
Calderas (DR) 167
Calgary (Can) 85
Calibio (Col) 142
Calicuchima (Ecu) 173
California (USA) 780, 819†
Calima (Col) 144
Callaghan (USA) 781
Callao (Per) 481
Calliope (Fra) 218
Calmar (Fra) 223
Cambiaso (DR) 167
Camboriú (Brz) 60
Camden (USA) 805
Cameron (UK) 745
Camocim (Brz) 64
Campbell (USA) 824
Campbeltown (UK) 731
Campeche (Mex) 419
Campéon (Spn) 630†
Campos Salles (Brz) 68†
Campti (USA) 811
Çanakkale (Tur) 696
Canal Beagle (Arg) 17
Canal de Beagle (Arg) 20
Canal Emilio Mitre (Arg) 21
Canarias (Spn) 621
Canberra (Aust) 25
Cándido Pérez (Spn) 626
Caner Gönyeli (Tur) 154†, 703
Cannanore (Ind) 288
Canonchet (USA) 811
Canopus (Brz) 63
Canopus (DR) 168
Canopus (Mrt) 414
Canopus (USA) 807
Canopus (Ven) 841
Canterbury (NZ) 438-9
Caonabo (DR) 169
Cap aux Meules (Can) 99
Cap Goélands (Can) 99
Capable (UK) 746
Capable (USA) 815
Capadanno (USA) 699†
Capana (Ven) 838
Capayan (Arg) 18
Cape Alava (USA) 819†
Cape Alexander (USA) 819†
Cape Ann (USA) 819†
Cape Archway (USA) 819†
Cape Avinof (USA) 819†
Cape Blanco (USA) 819†
Cape Bon (USA) 819†
Cape Borda (USA) 819†
Cape Bover (USA) 819†
Cape Breton (USA) 819†
Cape Canaveral (USA) 819†
Cape Canso (USA) 819†
Cape Carthage (USA) 819†
Cape Catawba (USA) 819†
Cape Catoche (USA) 819†
Cape Chalmers (USA) 819†
Cape Clear (USA) 819†
Cape Cod (USA) 803, 819†
Cape Decision (USA) 819†
Cape Diamond (USA) 819†
Cape Domingo (USA) 819†
Cape Douglas (USA) 819†
Cape Ducato (USA) 819†
Cape Edmont (USA) 819†
Cape Farewell (USA) 819†
Cape Flattery (USA) 811, 819†
Cape Florida (USA) 819†
Cape Gibson (USA) 819†
Cape Girardeau (USA) 819†
Cape Henry (USA) 819†
Cape Horn (USA) 819†
Cape Hudson (USA) 819†
Cape Hurd (Can) 99
Cape Inscription (USA) 819†
Cape Isabel (USA) 819†
Cape Johnson (USA) 819†
Cape Juby (USA) 819†
Cape Lambert (USA) 819†
Cape Lobos (USA) 819†
Cape May (USA) 819†
Cape Mendocino (USA) 819†
Cape Mohican (USA) 819†
Cape Nome (USA) 819†
Cape Roger (Can) 101
Cape St George (USA) 776
Capella (DR) 168
Capella (Mrt) 414
Capella (USA) 821
Capitan Alsina (DR) 168
Capitan Alvaro Ruiz (Col) 144
Capitan Beotegui (DR) 169
Capitan Cabral (Par) 474
Capitan Castro (Col) 144
Capitan de Fragata Pedro Sáinz de Baranda Borreyro (Mex) 417
Capitán de Navio Blas Godinez Brito (Mex) 417
Capitán de Navio Sebastian Jose Holzinger (Mex) 417
Capitan Meza (Par) 474
Capitan Miranda (Uru) 835
Capitan Olo Pantoja (Cub) 153†
Capitan R D Binney (Col) 142
Capitan Rigoberto Giraldo (Col) 144
Capitan Vladimir Valek (Col) 144
Caprera (Ita) 334
Capri (Ita) 334
Capstan (USA) 831
Captain Mulzac (StV) 598
Captor (Can) 91
Carabiniere (Ita) 326
Cárabo (Spn) 635
Caratasca (Hon) 271†
Caravelas (Brz) 64
Cardiel (Arg) 21
Cardiff (UK) 726
Cardinal (USA) 800
Careful (UK) 746
Carenage (TT) 691
Carey (DR) 169†
Cariari (CR) 147
Caribbean Sentry (USA) 826
Caribe (Ven) 837
Caribou Isle (Can) 97
Carina (Den) 161
Carite (DR) 169
Carl Fr Gauss (Ger) 251
Carl Vinson (USA) 766
Carlos Alban (Col) 144
Carlos Chagas (Brz) 65
Carlos Galindo (Col) 142
Carlos Guzman Baules (Pan) 472†
Carlskrona (Swe) 646
Carmen (Hon) 271†
Carney (USA) 784
Caroly (Ita) 336
Caron (USA) 782
Caroni (TT) 690
Carr (USA) 786
Carrillo (Per) 482
Carron (UK) 734
Cartagena (Spn) 632
Carter Hall (USA) 796
Carteria (Gre) 258
Carthage (Tun) 692
Casabianca (Fra) 202
Casamance II (Sen) 605
Cascade (Fra) 227
Cascadura (TT) 690
Casimir Pulaski (USA) 760
Casma (Chi) 108
Casma (Per) 477
Caspana (Chi) 113
Cassard (Fra) 208
Cassiopea (Ita) 330
Cassiopée (Fra) 218
Cassiopeia (Den) 161
Cassiopeia (Por) 504
Castagno (Ita) 332
Castelhanos (Brz) 63
Castilla (Per) 479†
Castilla (Spn) 628
Castillo y Rada (Col) 144†
Castor (Aust) 34
Castor (Chi) 113
Castor (Mrt) 414
Castor (Spn) 630
Castor (Swi) 656
Catahecassa (USA) 811
Cataluña (Spn) 622
Catanduanes (Plp) 490
Catawba (USA) 818
Catenary (USA) 831
Cattistock (UK) 734
Cau-Cau (Chi) 113
Caupolican (Chi) 111†
Cavaglia (Ita) 340
Cavalla (USA) 764
Cayacca (DR) 169
Cayambe (Ecu) 174
Cayuga (USA) 797
Cazadora (Spn) 623
CE series (Sin) 612†
Ceará (Brz) 60, 67†
Cebaco (Pan) 472
Cebu (Plp) 486
Cedro (Ita) 332
Cedros (TT) 691
Celurit (Indo) 303
Centaure (Fra) 225
Centauro (Bol) 53
Centinela (Spn) 623
Cephane 2, 3 (Tur) 709
Çerbe (Tur) 696
Cerberus (Nld) 436
Cérès (Fra) 218
Ceres (HK) 273
Cessnock (Aust) 28
Cetina (Cro) 149
Cezayirli Gazi Hasan Pasca (Tur) 706
CG 001, CG 002 (TT) 691
CG 039, 045, 086 (Can) 100
CG 091-092, 101-103, 121-123, (Jam) 342
CG 119 (Can) 99
CGC 103, 110, 128 *et al* (Plp) 490
CGR 100 (Can) 99
CHA 8, 14, 17, 19, 23-38 (Fra) 227
Chacabuco (Chi) 109
Chacal (Fra) 225
Chaco (Arg) 17
Chadmo (Chi) 113
Chah Bahar (Iran) 311
Chakra (Ind) 277†
Chakri Naruebet (Tld) 675
Chaleur (Can) 91
Challenge (Sen) 605
Chamak (Ind) 286
Chamelecon (Hon) 270
Chamois (Fra) 199†, 221
Champion (Sen) 605
Champion (USA) 799
Champlain (Fra) 216, 426†
Chancellorsville (USA) 776
Chand Bibi (Ind) 291
Chandeleur (USA) 828
Chandler (USA) 781
Chang (Tld) 684
Chang Bogo (RoK) 381
Chang Chien (RoC) 664†, 665
Chang De (CPR) 120
Chang Pei (RoC) 672
Chang Won (RoK) 389
Changsha (CPR) 118
Changxingdao (CPR) 129
Changzhi (CPR) 120
Chanthara (Tld) 685
Chao Phraya (Tld) 676
Chao Yang (RoC) 662
Chapal (Ind) 286
Chapman (USA) 832†
Charag (Ind) 286
Charak (Iran) 311
Charger (UK) 739
Charlemagne Perrault (Hai) 270
Charles de Gaulle (Fra) 204, 205†
Charlotte (USA) 762
Charlotte of Cerberus (Aust) 33†
Charlottetown (Can) 85
Chasanyabadee (Tld) 687
Chase (USA) 824
Chataigner (Fra) 226
Chatak (Ind) 286
Chatham (UK) 731
Chattahoochee (USA) 818†
Chauvenet (USA) 816†
Chawengsak Songkram (Tld) 687
Chayvo (Rus) 576
Chazhma (Rus) 577

860 INDEXES/Named Ships

Che Ju (RoK) 384
Cheboksary (Rus) 582†
Chebucto (Can) 101
Cheetah (Ind) 287
Cheleken (Rus) 572
Chen Yang (RoC) 662
Chena (USA) 830
Chêne (Fra) 226
Cheng Hai (RoC) 669
Cheng Ho (RoC) 664
Cheng Kung (RoC) 664
Chengdu (CPR) 119
Cheradi (Ita) 337†
Cheraw (USA) 811
Cheremshan (Rus) 582
Chervona Ukraina (Rus) 540
Chesaning (USA) 811
Chesapeake (USA) 818†
Chetek (USA) 811
Chevreuil (Fra) 221
Cheyenne (Coastguard) (USA) 830
Cheyenne (Los Angeles class) (USA) 762
Chi Kuang (RoC) 664
Chiang Yang (RoC) 664
Chiapas (Mex) 423
Chicago (USA) 762
Chichijima (Jpn) 358
Chiddingfold (UK) 734
Chidori (Jpn) 374
Chief (USA) 799
Chien Yang (RoC) 662
Chignecto (Can) 91
Chihuahua (Mex) 416
Chik (Tld) 687
Chikala (Mlw) 402
Chikugo (Bihoro class) (Jpn) 367
Chikugo (Chikugo class) (Jpn) 354
Chikuma (Jpn) 353
Chikuzen (Jpn) 365
Chilreu (Spn) 626
Chimborazo (Ecu) 174
Chimera (Ita) 329
Chimère (Fra) 225
Chin Hsing (RoC) 673
Chin Yang (RoC) 666
Chincoteague (USA) 828
Chinook (USA) 801
Chioggia (Ita) 331
Chios (Gre) 260
Chipana (Chi) 108
Chipana (Per) 477
Chippewa (USA) 830
Chiquillan (Arg) 18
Chiroo (Iran) 311
Chitose (Jpn) 354, 367
Chiyoda (Jpn) 360
Chock (USA) 831
Chokai (Jpn) 366
Chokeberry (USA) 830
Choluteca (Hon) 270
Chon An (RoK) 385
Chon Buri (Tld) 681
Chon Nam (RoK) 384
Chongmingdao (CPR) 129
Chongoing (CPR) 118
Choong Seong-Ho Numbers One, Two, Three (DPRK) 380†
Choshuenco (Chi) 112
Chosin (USA) 776
Chuang (Tld) 687
Chubut (Arg) 17
Chukotka (Rus) 595
Chula (Tld) 687
Chulab Horn (Tld) 685†
Chulmasan (RoK) 390
Chulupi (Arg) 18
Chumikan (Rus) 577
Chun Jee (RoK) 388
Chung Buk (RoK) 382
Chung Chi (RoC) 669
Chung Chiang (RoC) 669
Chung Chien (RoC) 669
Chung Chih (RoC) 669
Chung Chuan (RoC) 669
Chung Fu (RoC) 669
Chung Hai (RoC) 669
Chung Hsing (RoC) 669
Chung Ju (Hang class) (RoK) 385
Chung Ju (Ulsan class) (RoK) 384
Chung Kuang (RoC) 669
Chung Lien (RoC) 669
Chung Ming (RoC) 669
Chung Nam (RoK) 384
Chung Pang (RoC) 669
Chung Shan (RoC) 665
Chung Sheng (RoC) 669
Chung Shu (RoC) 669
Chung Shun (RoC) 669
Chung Suo (RoC) 669
Chung Ting (RoC) 669
Chung Wan (RoC) 669
Chung Yeh (RoC) 669
Chung Yung (RoC) 669
Ch'ungnam (RoK) 389
Ciara (Ire) 316
Cicala (UK) 749
Ciclope (Ita) 338
Ciclope (Spn) 632
Cidade de Natal (Brz) 68
Cigogne (Fra) 226
Cimarron (Jumboised Cimarron class) (USA) 804
Cimarron (tender) (USA) 829
Cincinnati (USA) 762
Cinq Juin (Sey) 607
Circé (Fra) 218
Cirujano Videla (Chi) 113
Cisne (Por) 504
Cisne Branco (Brz) 66
Cista Velika (Cro) 149
Citrus (USA) 829
City of Corpus Christi (USA) 762
CL 01-04, 66-67 *et al* (Jpn) 370
Clamp (USA) 831
Clark (USA) 785†, 786
Clark's Harbour (Can) 99
Cleat (USA) 831
Clemenceau (Fra) . 196†, 204†, 205
Cleveland (USA) 795
Clifton Sprague (USA) 785†, 786
Clio (Fra) 218
Clorinda (Arg) 16
Clovelly (UK) 749
Coahuila (Mex) 416
Cochin (Ind) 290
Cochrane (Chi) 105
Cockchafer (UK) 749
Coconut Queen (Aust) 33†
Coeroeni (Sur) 639
Coiba (Pan) 472
Cojinoa (DR) 169†
Colayeras (Per) 482
Cole (USA) 784
Colhue (Arg) 21
Colhue Huapi (Arg) 21
Colibri (Fra) 226
Colimbo (Spn) 635
Collie (UK) 747
Collins (Aust) 23
Colo Colo (Chi) 112
Colonel Djoue Dabany (Gab) 229
Colonia (Uru) 834
Columbia (Can) 87†
Columbia (USA) 762
Columbus (USA) 762
Comandante Arandia (Bol) 53
Comandante Didier (Brz) 67
Comandante General Irigoyen (Arg) 15
Comandante Hermenegildo Capelo (Por) 502
Comandante João Belo (Por) 502
Comandante Manhães (Brz) 64
Comandante Marroig (Brz) 67
Comandante Pedro Campbell (Uru) 835
Comandante Roberto Ivens (Por) 502
Comandante Sacadura Cabral (Por) 502
Comandante Torrijos (Pan) 472
Comandante Varella (Brz) 64
Comando (Bol) 53
Comet (USA) 819†
Cometa (Lat) 393
Comfort (USA) 817
Commandant Azouggarh (Mor) . 425
Commandant Birot (Fra) 212
Commandant Blaison (Fra) 212
Commandant Bory (Fra) 211
Commandant Bouan (Fra) 212
Commandant Boutouba (Mor) 425
Commandant Ducuing (Fra) 212
Commandant El Harty (Mor) 425
Commandant l'Herminier (Fra) 212
Commandant de Pimodan (Fra) . 212
Commander Apayi Joe (Nig) 447
Commander Marshall (Bar) 46
Commander Rudolf (Nig) 447†
Comodoro Carlos Castillo Bretón Barrero (Mex) 417
Comodoro Coé (Uru) 834
Comodoro Manuel Azueta Perillos (Mex) 417
Comodoro Rivadavia (Arg) 17
Comodoro Somellera (Arg) 16
Competent (USA) 808
Comstock (USA) 796
Comte de Grasse (USA) 782
Concepción del Uruguay (Arg) 16
Concord (USA) 812
Condell (Chi) 106
Condestable Zaragoza (Spn) 633
Condor (Ita) 333
Condor (Por) 504
Condor 1, 2, 3 (Spn) 635
Conejera (Spn) 626
Confidence (USA) 825
Conifer (USA) 829
Connecticut (USA) 761
Conolly (USA) 782
Conquest (USA) 800
Conserver (USA) 806
Constant (Sey) 607
Constanta (Rom) 513
Constellation (USA) 765†, 768
Constitución (Ven) 839
Constituição (Brz) 57
Constitution (USA) 809
Contraalmirante Angel Ortiz Monasterio (Mex) 417
Contralmirante Bell Salter (Col) . 142
Contramaestre Casado (Spn) 631
Contramaestre Castelló (Spn) 633
Contramaestre Micalvi (Chi) 108
Contramaestre Ortiz (Chi) 108
Copahue (Chi) 112
Copeland (USA) 785†, 786
Copiapo (Chi) 113
Cora (Mex) 422
Coral (Por) 505
Coralline (Fra) 224
Corcovado (Chi) 112
Corgi (UK) 747
Cormier (Fra) 226
Cormoran (Arg) 17
Cormoran (Cormoran class) (Spn) 625
Cormoraan (customs) (Spn) 635
Cormorant (Can) 89
Cormorant (USA) 800
Cornelis Drebbel (Nld) 436
Cornhusker State (USA) .. 818†, 821
Cornwall (UK) 731
Coronado (USA) 804
Corrubia (Ita) 340
Corsair (Ger) 244†
Corsaro II (Ita) 336
Corte Real (Por) 501
Cortés (Chi) 111†
Corystes (UK) 751†
Cotopaxi (Ecu) 174
Cottesmore (UK) 734
Cougar Cat (Spn) 635
Courageous (USA) 825
Courier (USA) 819†
Courser (UK) 752†
Covadonga (Chi) 108
Cove Isle (Can) 97
Coventry (UK) 730
Cowichan (Can) 91
Cowpens (USA) 776
Cowslip (USA) 829
CP series (Ita) 339†
CP 1000–CP 1005 (Leb) 394
Cpl Louis J Hauge Jr (USA) 820
Crame Jean (Sen) 606
Creidne (Ire) 316†
Creoula (Por) 507
Cricket (UK) 744†, 749
Cricklade (UK) 749
Cristobal Colon (Mex) 423
Cristoforo Colombo II (Ita) 336
Crocus (Bel) 48
Croix du Sud (Fra) 218
Cromarty (UK) 749
Cromer (UK) 735
Crommelin (USA) 786
Crossbow (Can) 92
Crotone (Ita) 331
Crux (Den) 161
Crvena Zvezda (Yug) 852
CTM 2, 3, 9, 12 *et al* (Fra) 217
Cuanza (Por) 503
Cuauhtemoc (Mex) 422
Çubuklu (Tur) 706
Cuddalore (Ind) 288
Cuenca (Ecu) 172
Cuitlahuac (Mex) 415
Cumberland (UK) 731
Cundrik (Indo) 303
Cunene (Por) 503
Currawong (Aust) 32
Curtis Wilbur (USA) 784
Curtiss (USA) 821
Curts (USA) 786, 787
CURV I, II (USA) 809†
Cushing (Island class) (USA) 829
Cushing (Spruance class) (USA) 782
Custódio de Mello (Brz) 65
Cuttyhunk (USA) 828
Cuxhaven (Ger) 239
CW 3 Harold C Clinger (USA) 798
Cybèle (Fra) 218
Cyclone (USA) 801
Cygne (Fra) 226
Cygnet (UK) 739
Cygnus (Can) 101
Cygnus (USA) 819†
Czajka (Pol) 494
Czujny (Pol) 494

D

D 01, 03-05, 11-15, 17-19 (Mex) 418
D 01–D 18 (Mor) 426
D 1051 (UAE) 715
Da Nang (Vtn) 845
Dabie (Pol) 495
Dacca (Pak) 469
Dachs (Ger) 237
Dae Chon (Rok) 385
Dae Gu (RoK) 383
Dafni (Gre) 262
Dagushan (CPR) 130
Dahlonega (USA) 811
Dai Ky (Vtn) 842
Daio (Jpn) 366
Dajlah (SAr) 605
Dalarö (Swe) 645
Daldyn (Rus) 590
Dale (USA) 779
Dalgiç 2 (Tur) 704
Dalian (CPR) 118
Dallas (Hamilton class) (USA) 824
Dallas (Los Angeles class) (USA) 762
Dalmatian (UK) 747
Dalnie Zelentsy (Rus) 576
Damavand (Iran) 306
Damisa (Nig) 445
Dammam (firefighting craft) (SAr) 605
Dammam (Jaguar class) (SAr) 601
Dämman (Swe) 648
Damour (Leb) 394
Damrong Rachanuphat (Tld) 687
Damsah (Qat) 508
Damuan (Bru) 68
Danaide (Ita) 329
Danaos (Gre) 265
Danbjørn (Den) 164
Dandong (CPR) 120
Dang Yang (RoC) 661
Dangriga (Blz) 51
Daniel Boone (USA) 760
Daniel Webster (USA) 760†
Dannebrog (Den) 164
Dante Novaro (Ita) 339†
Daoud Ben Aicha (Mor) 426
Daphne (UK) 746
Daqahliya (Egy) 180
Dar Mlodziezy (Pol) 496†
Dareen (SAr) 602
Darica (Tur) 710
Daring (Sin) 610
Darlowo (Pol) 494
Darshak (Ban) 44
Darwin (Aust) 25
Das (UAE) 714
Dasher (UK) 739
Dat Assawari (Lby) 396
Datteln (Ger) 240
Datu Marikudo (Plp) 486
Daugava (Rus) 566
Dauntless (Sin) 610
Dauntless (USA) 825
Dauriya (Rus) 567
Davara (PNG) 473
David F (Ire) 316†
David Jorden (USA) 832†
David R Ray (USA) 782
David Tucker (Bhm) 36
Davidson (USA) 832†
Dayer (Iran) 311
Dayyinah (UAE) 715
Dazhi (CPR) 129
De Brouwer (Bel) 49
De Grasse (Fra) 209
De los Heros (Per) 480
De Mist (SA) 617
De Neys (SA) 617
De Noorde (SA) 617
De Ruyter (Nld) 430
De Wert (USA) 786
Decatur (USA) 780†, 809†
Dechaineux (Aust) 23
Decisive (USA) 825
Deepak (Ind) 289
Deer Island (USA) 810
Deerhound (UK) 747
Defender (HK) 272
Defender (StL) 598
Defender (USA) 799
Defensora (Brz) 57
Deflektor (Rus) 570
Deirdre (Ire) 316
Dekanawida (USA) 811
Del Monte (USA) 819†
Del Valle (USA) 819†
Del Viento (USA) 819†
Delaware II (USA) 832†
Delfim (Por) 501
Delfin (Arg) 19
Delfin (Spn) 618
Delfinul (Rom) 509
Delfzyl (Nld) 433
Delhi (Ind) 280
Delvar (Iran) 311
Demirhisar (Tur) 702
Democratia (Rom) 511
Deneb (Ger) 251
Denebola (USA) 821
Denizkusu (Tur) 701
Denti (Fra) 222
D'Entrecasteaux (Fra) 219
Denver (USA) 795
Dependable (USA) 825
Dera'a 1, 3, 4, 5 (Bhr) 39
Dera'a 2, 6, 7, 8 (Bhr) 38
Derwent (Aust) 26
Derya (Tur) 706
Des Groseilliers (Can) 93
Descatusaria (Rom) 511
Descubierta (Spn) 623
Desna (Rus) 582
Desrobirea (Rom) 511
D'Estienne d'Orves (Fra) 212
Detector (HK) 272
Detroit (USA) 805
Détroyat (Fra) 212
Deva (Spn) 626
Devastator (USA) 799
Deviator (Rus) 572
Dewa Kembar (Indo) 300
Dewarutji (Indo) 303
Dexterous (UK) 746
Dexterous (USA) 799
Deyatelny (Rus) 546
Deymos (Rus) 594
Deyo (USA) 782
DF 1 (Par) 476
DF 300 series (Plp) 490
DF 370-372, DF 374-378 (Plp) . 487
DF 400 series (Plp) 490
Dheba (SAr) 602
Dheeb Al Bahar I, II, III (Omn) 461
Dhofar (Omn) 458
Diamant (Fra) 202†
Diamond State (USA) 818†, 821
Diana (Ger) 240
Diana (Spn) 623
Dianthus (Bel) 48
Diez Canseco (Per) 479
Dikson (Mudyug class) (Rus) 591
Dikson (Vytegrales class) (Rus) .. 567
Dili (Indo) 299
Diligence (UK) 743
Diligence (dry dock) (USA) 808
Diligence (Reliance class) (USA) 825
Dilim (Iran) 311
Dillingen (Ger) 240
Dilos (Gre) 260
Dimiter A Dimitrov (Bul) 74
Dinder (Sud) 639
Diombos (Sen) 606
Diopos Antoniou (Gre) 259
Diou Loulou (Sen) 606
Discovery (UK) 740†
Discovery Bay (Jam) 341
Discovery Bay (USA) 811
Dithmarchen (Ger) 251†
Diver (UK) 752†
Dixon (USA) 806
Dizelist (Rus) 558
Djaurv (Swe) 644
DJC 601-631 series, 624-632 (Yug) 854
Djebel Chinoise (Alg) 5
Djerdar (Yug) 853
Djerv (Nor) 451
Djibril (Sen) 606
Djilor (Sen) 606
Djurdjura (Alg) 8
DKN 504-513, 908-916 (Indo) . 304
Dmitry Laptev (Rus) 577
Dmitry Mendeleyev (Rus) 575
Dmitry Ovstyn (Rus) 577
Dmitry Sterlegov (Rus) 577
Dnepr (Rus) 548
Dnestr (Rus) 581
D. N. O. G. (Brz) 67
Do Bong (RoK) 389
Doblestny (Rus) 546
Dobrotay (Rus) 558
Dobrotich Bul) 72
Dobrynya Nikitich (Rus) 593
Doğan (Tur) 701
Doganarslan (Tur) 711
Doğanay (Tur) 695
Dogwood (USA) 829†
Doirani (Gre) 265
Dokkum (Nld) 433†
Dolfijn (Nld) 429
Dolphin (Ang) 9
Dolphin (Aust) 33
Dolphin (Iran) 312
Dolphin (USA) 805, 822†
Dolphin Mira (Nig) 447
Dolphin Rima (Nig) 447
Dolunay (Tur) 695
Dom Aleixo (Por) 504
Dom Jeremias (Por) 504
Dommel (Ger) 238
Don (Rus) 583
Donald B Beary (USA) 785†, 785
Donau (Elbe class) (Ger) 241
Donau (Rhein class) (Ger) 238†, 241
Donbas (Rus) 567
Donchedi (Tld) 683
Donets (Rus) 580
Dong Geon Ae Gook-Ho (DPRK) 380†
Dong Hae (RoK) 385
Dong Hae-Ho (DPRK) 380†
Dong Qin (CPR) 136
Dongchuan (CPR) 119
Donghae 101, 102 (DPRK) 380
Dongyun (CPR) 136
Donna Margarita (CR) 147
Donuzlav (Rus) 572
Dorade (Alg) 8
Dorado (Arg) 20
Dorang (Indo) 298
Dordanda (Ban) 42
Dordrecht (Nld) 433
Dore (Indo) 299
Dorina (Nig) 444†
Doris (Fra) 203
Doris (Gre) 263
Dornoch (UK) 749
Dos de Mayo (Per) 477
Dostoyny (Rus) 546
Dovey (UK) 734
Doxa (Gre) 258
Doyle (USA) 786
Dr Gondim (Brz) 67†
Dr Jamot (Cam) 82†
Drachten (Nld) 433
Draga (Par) 476
Dragão (Por) 504
Dragonera (Spn) 626
Drakensberg (SA) 616†, 616
Drankse (Ger) 248
Draug (Nor) 454
Drava (Yug) 849
Dreger (PNG) 473
Drejø (Den) 160
Dreptatea (Rom) 511
Driade (Ita) 329
Dristig (Swe) 644
Drogou (Fra) 212
Drum (USA) 764
Drummond (Arg) 13
Drummond (USA) 828
Druzhny (Rus) 546
Druzjba (Rus) 579
Druzki (Bul) 70
Druzno (Pol) 495
Dryade (Fra) 223
DSRV-1, DSRV-2 (USA) 822†
Dubbo (Aust) 28
Dubhe (Den) 161
Dubna (Rus) 581
Dubuque (USA) 795
Duderstadt (Ger) 250
Duenas (Per) 483†, 483
Duero (Spn) 629
Dugong (Aust) 33
Duguay-Trouin (Fra) 209
Duluth (USA) 795
Dulverton (UK) 734
Dumbarton Castle (UK) 738
Dumit (Can) 97
Dumont d'Urville (Fra) 216
Dunafoldvar (Hun) 274
Dunagiri (Ind) 282
Dunaújváros (Hun) 274
Dunay (Ivan Susanin class) (Rus) 594
Dunay (Uda class) (Rus) 582
Duncan (USA) 785†, 786
Dundurn (Can) 89
Dungun (Mly) 408
Dunster (UK) 749
Dupleix (Fra) 207
Duque de Caxais (Brz) 60
Duquesne (Fra) 209
Durable (USA) 825
Durance (Fra) 220
Durango (Mex) 421
Duranta (Ban) 42
Durbar (Ban) 42
Durdam (Ban) 42
Durdanta (Ban) 42
Durdharsha (Ban) 42
Düren (Ger) 239
Durham (USA) 797
Durjoy (Ban) 42
Durnibar (Ban) 42
Durvedya (Ban) 42
Dutton (USA) 816†
Duyong (Mly) 407
Dvina (Rus) 587
Dwight D Eisenhower (USA) 766, 767
Dynamic (USA) 808
Dzata (Gha) 252
Dzerzhinsk (Rus) 582†
Dzerzhinsky (Rus) 546
Dzik (Pol) 492
Dziwnow (Pol) 494

E

E 277, E 321 (CPR) 125
E E Prince (Can) 102
E Panagopoulos 2, 3 (Gre) 260
E Toll (Rus) 577
Eagle (USA) 506†, 830
Ean Al Gazala (Lby) 397
Ean Zara (Lby) 397
Earl Grey (Can) 95
East London (SA) 615
Ébène (Fra) 226
Ebro (Spn) 629
Eceabat (Tur) 708
Echigo (Jpn) 365
Echizen (Jpn) 367
Eckaloo (Can) 97†, 98
Eden (UK) 751
Edenshaw (USA) 811
Edenton (USA) 807
Edinburgh (UK) 727
Edisto (USA) 828
Edith (UK) 746
Edithara (Sri) 635
EDM 1, 2, 3, 4 (Arg) 16
EDVP 30–EDVP 37 (Arg) 16
Edward Cornwallis (Can) 94
Edward Williams (Bhm) 36
Effective (USA) 815
Efficace (Fra) 226

Named Ships/INDEXES 861

Eglantine (Fra) 225
Egret (UK) 752†
Eider (Fra) 226
EIG series (Ita) 339†
Eilath (Isr) 319
Eisbar (Ger) 248
Eisvogel (Ger) 248
Eithne (Ire) 315
Ejdern (Swe) 648
Ekeskaur (Swe) 646
Ekholot (Rus) 570
Ekpe (Nig) 445
Ekstati Vinarov (Bul) 72
Ekster (Bel) 51
Ekun (Nig) 445
Ekvator (Rus) 569
El Aigh (Mor) 426
El Akid (Mor) 425
El Amparo (Ven) 841
El Bachir (Mor) 425
El Beig (Mtn) 413
El Djari (Alg) 6
El Essahir (Mor) 425
El Fateh (Egy) 176
El Hahiq (Mor) 425
El Hamiss (Mor) 425
El Haris (Mor) 425
El Horriya (Egy) 181
El Idrissi (Alg) 7
El Jail (Mor) 425
El Kaced (Mor) 426
El Kadessaya (Egy) 178
El Karib (Mor) 425
El Kechef (Alg) 6
El Khafir (Mor) 425
El Khattabi (Mor) 425
El Kinz (Mtn) 413
El Kobayat (Lby) 399
El Maher (Mor) 425
El Majid (Mor) 425
El Mikdam (Mor) 425
El Mourakeb (Alg) 6
El Moutarid (Alg) 6
El Nasr (Mtn) 413
El Nasser (Egy) 176
El Oro (Ecu) 171
El Paso (USA) 797
El Rassed (Alg) 6
El Suez (Egy) 177
El Tawfiq (Mor) 425
El Temsah (Lby) 400
El Tucuche (TT) 691
El Vaiz (Mtn) 413
El Wacil (Mor) 425
El Yadekh (Alg) 6
El Yarmouk (Egy) 178
Élan (Fra) 221
Elbe (Ger) 241
Elbjørn (Den) 165
Elblag (Pol) 499
Elbrus (Rus) 585
Eldaren (Swe) 654
Elderberry (USA) 830
Electronica (Rom) 514
Eleftheria (Gre) 258
Elektrik (Rus) 558
Eleuthera (Bhm) 36
Elew (Pol) 496
Elfe (Fra) 223
Elicura (Chi) 109
Elk River (USA) 810†
Elkhound (UK) 747
Elkstone (UK) 749
Ellerbek (Ger) 248
Elli (Gre) 256
Elliott (USA) 782
Elm (Rus) 576
Elmer Montgomery (USA) 699†
Elnya (Rus) 581
Elrod (USA) 786
Elsing (UK) 749
Elster (Ger) 238
Elton (Rus) 572
Emba (Rus) 580
Embrun (Fra) 227
Emden (Bremen class) (Ger) 235
Emden (customs) (Ger) 251†
Emer (Ire) 316
Emeraude (Fra) 202
Emil Racovita (Rom) 513
Emilio Aguinaldo (Plp) 487
Emily Hobhouse (SA) 614
Emory S Land (USA) 806
Empire State (USA) 819†
Empress II (USA) 809†
Endeavor (DR) 169
Endeavour (Can) 91
Endeavour (NZ) 440
Endeavour (Sin) 612
Endeavour I, II (Nor) 455†
Endurance (Sin) 611
Endurance (UK) 738†
Endurance (USA) 808
Energerica (Rom) 514
England (USA) 779
Engoulevant (Fra) 226
Enø (Den) 162
Enoshima (Jpn) 358
Enrico Dandolo (Ita) 322
Enrico Toti (Ita) 322
Enriquillo (DR) 169
Ensdorf (Ger) 240
Enseigne de Vaisseau Henry (Fra) 211
Enseigne de Vaisseau Jacoubet (Fra) 212
Enterprise (Mly) 408
Enterprise (USA) 772
Enugu (Nig) 446
Enyimiri (Nig) 444
EP series (Sin) 611, 612
Epe (Nig) 445
Épée (Fra) 228
Epirus (Gre) 257
Epron (Rus) 585
Epworth (UK) 749
Equality State (USA) 818†, 821
Equator (Rus) 579†
Érable (Fra) 226
Éridan (Fra) 218
Erimo (Jpn) 366
Erinomi (Nig) 444
Erle (Nor) 451
Ernst Krenkel (Rus) 575
Erraced (Mor) 426
Errachiq (Mor) 425
Erraid (Mor) 426
Ersen Bayrak (Tur) 711
Ertuğrul (Tur) 705
Eruwa (Nig) 446
Esan (Jpn) 366
Escanaba (USA) 824
Escape (USA) 826
Eschwege (Ger) 250
Escorpião (Por) 504
Escuintla (Gua) 267
Esequibo (Ven) 838
Esmeralda (Chi) 110, 631†
Esmeraldas (Ecu) 171
Espadon (Alg) 8
Espalmador (Spn) 626
Espartana (Col) 142
Esperanza (Arg) 21
Espero (Ita) 327
Espirito Santo (Brz) 56
Espora (Arg) 14
Essaid (Mor) 426
Essaouira (Mor) 426†
Essex (USA) 792
Esteban Baca Calderon (Mex) 419
Estocin (USA) 785†, 786
Estoniy (Rus) 559
Etajima (Jpn) 358
Etchebarne (Brz) 67†
Eten (Per) 481
Etomo (Jpn) 366
Ettrick (UK) 749
Euro (Ita) 327
Evagoras (Cypr) 155
Eversand (Ger) 247
Evgeniy Nikonov (Rus) 559
Evros (Gre) 264
Evrotas (Gre) 264
Example (UK) 739
Excellence (Bar) 46
Excellence (Sin) 611
Exeter (UK) 726
Exploit (UK) 739
Explorer (UK) 739
Explorer I-IV (RoC) 670
Express (UK) 739
Extremadura (Spn) 622
Exultant (USA) 800
Exuma (Bhm) 36

F

F Bovesse (Bel) 49
F C G Smith (Can) 101
FABG 1-50 (RoC) 668
Faddey Bellinggausen (Rus) 572
Faedra (Gre) 262
Faenø (Den) 162
Fagnano (Arg) 21
Fahrion (USA) 785†, 786
Fainleog (Ire) 316†
Fairfax County (USA) 797
Fairweather (USA) 832†
Faisal (SAr) 601
Faithful (Bmd) 52†
Faithful (UK) 746
Fajablow (Sur) 640
Fala (Pol) 499
Falakhon (Iran) 308
Falcon (USA) 800
Falcone (Ita) 333
Falconet (UK) 747
Falk (Nor) 451
Falke (Ger) 238
Falken (Swe) 652
Falkland Desire (Fl) 187
Falkland Protector (Fl) 187
Falkner (Arg) 21
Fällaren (Swe) 649
Falshöft (Ger) 251†
Falster (Den) 162
Fanantenana (Mad) 401
Farallon (USA) 828
Farandugu (Lbr) 394
Farandugu (SL) 608
Farfadet (Fra) 225
Farm (Nor) 456
Farncomb (Aust) 23
Farø (Den) 160
Faroleiro Areas (Brz) 63
Faroleiro Mário Seixas (Brz) 63
Faroleiro Nascimento (Brz) 63
Farwa (Lby) 398
Fatahillah (Indo) 293
Fateh-Al-Khair (Qat) 508
Fatih (Tur) 699
Fatsa (Tur) 704
Faune (Fra) 223
Fauvette (Fra) 226
Faysal (Jor) 374
FB 31-42 (Sin) 610
FD II (Pak) 471
Fearless (UK) 736
Fecia di Cossato (Ita) 322
Federación (Ven) 839
Fedor Litke (Dobrynya class) (Rus) 593
Fedor Litke (Nikolay Zobov class) (Rus) 572
Fedor Matisen (Rus) 577
Fedor Vidyayev (Rus) 129†, 565
Fehmarn (Ger) 247, 251†
Felicity (UK) 747
Felinto Perry (Brz) 64, 65†
Felix Romero (Mex) 419
Felstead (UK) 749
Feng Yang (RoC) 666
Fenice (Ita) 329
Fennica (Fin) 193
Fenrick Sturrup (Bhm) 36
Feodor Chiker (Rus) 594
Fernando M Lizardi (Mex) 419
Ferré (Per) 479
Ferrel (USA) 832†
Ferrol (Spn) 632
Fethiye (Tur) 704
Fiachdubh (Ire) 316†
Fife (USA) 782
Fiherenga (Mad) 401
Fijab (Sud) 639
Filogonio Hichamón (Col) 143
Finback (USA) 764
Finike (Tur) 704
Fintry (UK) 749
Fiona (UK) 747
Firebird (Can) 92
Firebolt (USA) 801
Firebrand (Can) 92
Firebush (USA) 829
Firtina (Tur) 701
Fisalia (Por) 505
Fitzgerald (USA) 784
Fjøløy (Nor) 454
FKS I (Nor) 452†
Flaggskaur (Swe) 646
Flamenco (Pan) 472
Flamingo (Pol) 494
Flatley (USA) 785†, 786
Fleesensee (Ger) 242
Fletcher (USA) 782
Fleur (SA) 616
Flickertail State (USA) 818†, 821
Flinders (Aust) 30, 489†
Flint (USA) 803
Floreál (Fra) 210
Florence (UK) 747
Florida (USA) 759
Flunder (Ger) 239
Flying Fish (USA) 764
Flyvefisken (Den) 159
FMB 163 (Eth) 186
Fo Wu 5, 6 (RoC) 672
Fobos (Rus) 594
Foça (Tur) 704
Foch (Fra) 204†, 205
Fogonero Bañobre (Spn) 633
Föhr (Ger) 247
Folden (Nor) 452†
Fong Yang (RoC) 666
Fontana (Arg) 21
Foracs II (Nor) 452†
Forceful (UK) 746
Ford (USA) 786
Formentor (Spn) 626
Formion (Gre) 254
Formosa (Arg) 17
Forrestal (USA) 765†, 770, 771
Fort Austin (UK) 742
Fort Charles (Jam) 341
Fort Charlotte (Bhm) 37
Fort Fincastle (Bhm) 36
Fort Fisher (USA) 796
Fort George (UK) 742
Fort Grange (UK) 742
Fort McHenry (USA) 796
Fort Montague (Bhm) 37
Fort Steele (Can) 90
Fort Victoria (UK) 742, 743†
Forte de Coimbra (Brz) 61
Forth (UK) 751
Fortuna (Uru) 834
Fortuna I, II (Arg) 18†
Fortune (Sey) 607
Forward (USA) 824
Fotherby (UK) 749
Foudre (Fra) 215
Fouta (Sen) 605
Fox (USA) 778
Foxhound (UK) 747
Franč Rozman-Stane (Yug) 851
Frances (UK) 747
Francesco Mimbelli (Ita) 326
Francis Garnier (Fra) 216
Francisco de Gurruchaga (Arg) 15
Francisco J Mujica (Mex) 419
Francisco Zarco (Mex) 418
Franco (Per) 483
Frank Cable (USA) 806
Frankenthal (Ger) 240
Franklin (Aust) 30†
Frans Erasmus (SA) 614
Fraser (Can) 88
Frauenlob (Ger) 240
Frederic Cresswell (SA) 614
Frederick (USA) 797
Fredericton (Can) 85
Freedom (Sin) 609
Frehel (Fra) 226
Freiburg (Ger) 242
Frej (Swe) 650
Fremantle (Aust) 28
Fréne (Fra) 226
Fresia (Chi) 108
Fresno (USA) 797, 799†
Frettchen (Ger) 237
Friendship of Leeuwin (Aust) 33†
Frithjof (Ger) 250
Fritz Hagale (Col) 142
Frontin (Brz) 58
Fruška Gora (Yug) 852
Fryken (Swe) 654
FTB 111 (Eth) 186
Fu Hsing (RoC) 673
Fu Shan (RoC) 665
Fu Yang (RoC) 661
Fuchs (Ger) 238
Fuchsia (Bel) 48
Fuji (Jpn) 367
Fukue (Jpn) 359
Fulbeck (UK) 749
Fulk Al Salamah (Omn) 460
Fundy (Can) 91
Furusund (Swe) 647
Fushimi (Jpn) 361
Futalaufquen (Arg) 21
Futami (Jpn) 362
FW 1, 5 (Ger) 243
Fyen (Den) 162

G

G&C Admiral (USA) 819†
G, GL series (Ita) 339†
G Truffaut (Bel) 49
Gabes (Tun) 693
Gabinga (Aust) 34
Gaeta (Ita) 331
Gafel (Rus) 559
Gafsah (Tun) 692
Gaj (Ind) 290
Gal (Isr) 317
Galeb (Yug) 854
Galeota (TT) 690
Galerna (Spn) 619
Gallant (USA) 800
Gallatin (USA) 824
Gallery (USA) 786
Gals (Rus) 572
Galten (Swe) 648
Galvarino (Chi) 112
Gälve (Swe) 643
Galveston Island (USA) 828
Galvez (Chi) 111†
Galvez (Per) 479
Gama (Pak) 470
Ganas (Mly) 405
Ganga (Ind) 281
Ganga Devi (Ind) 291
Gangut (Rus) 565†, 579
Gannet (HK) 272
Ganni Bonnici (Mlt) 411
Ganyang (Mly) 405
Gapeau (Fra) 221
Gardno (Pol) 495
Gardouneh (Iran) 308
Garnele (Ger) 239
Garonne (Fra) 219
Garpeskjaer (Nor) 455
Garsøy (Nor) 454
Gary (USA) 786
Garyounis (Lby) 400
Gasconade (USA) 830
Gåssten (Swe) 648
Gastão Moutinho (Brz) 64†, 65
Gatineau (Can) 87
Gauden (Per) 482
Gauss (Ger) 251
Gave (Fra) 227
Gavilán 1, 2, 3, 4 (Spn) 635
Gavril Sarychev (Rus) 569
Gawler (Aust) 28
Gayret (Tur) 697
Gazal (Tur) 710
Gazelle (Fra) 221
Gazzana Priaroggia (Ita) 322
GC 6, 7, 8, 10, 11 (EIS) 183
GC 48-61, 88-95, *et al* (Arg) 20
GC 100, 112-4, 231-3 *et al* (Alg) 7
Gdynia (Pol) 499
Geba (Por) 503
Geelong (Aust) 28
Gefests (Lat) 393
Gefion (Ger) 240
Geier (Ger) 238
Geir (Nor) 451
Gelibolu (Tur) 700
Gelinotte (Fra) 226
Gelso (Ita) 332
Gem State (USA) 818†, 821
Gemini (Den) 161
Gemini (USA) 802
Gemlik (Tur) 700
Gempita (Mly) 405
Genaveh (Iran) 312
General Antonio Luna (Plp) 487
Général d'Armée Ba Oumar (Gab) 229
General Artigas (Uru) 833
General Banzer (Brz) 53†
General Baquedano (Chi) 106
General Belgrano (Bol) 53
General Brehon B Somervell (USA) 798
General Felipe B Berriozabal (Mex) 417
General Frank S Besson Jr (USA) 798
General Ignacio Zaragoza (Mex) 419
General Josea Trinidad Moran (Ven) 840
General Nazaire Boulingui (Gab) 229
General Pando (Bol) 53
General Pereira d'Ecca (Por) 503
General Ryabakov (Rus) 567
General Salom (Ven) 838
General Soublette (Ven) 838
General Urdaneta (Ven) 838
Genevieve (UK) 747
Genil (Spn) 629
Genkai (Jpn) 366
Genna (Ita) 339†
Geno (Iran) 312

ANTI MISSILE
ELECTRONIC WARFARE
CHOSEN BY
16 NAVIES
ALL OVER
THE WORLD

CENTROID EFFECT SEDUCTION

DAGAIE
A GREAT
SUCCESS

SEDUCTION
DISTRACTION

DECOYS DESIGNED AND PRODUCED BY ETIENNE LACROIX DEFENSE

BP 213 - 31601 MURET Cedex France. ✆ 61 56 65 00 - Télex : 531478F LACART - Fax : 61 51 42 77

Official trade title : Etienne LACROIX - Tous artifices SA.

862 INDEXES/Named Ships

Genrich Gasanov (Rus) ... 581
Gentian (USA) ... 829
Geofizik (Rus) ... 576
Geofjord (Nor) ... 456
Geolog Dimitri Nalivkin (Rus) ... 576
George Bancroft (USA) ... 760
George McIntosh (StV) ... 598
George Philip (USA) ... 785†, 786
George R Pearkes (Can) ... 94
George Washington (USA) ... 766, 767
Georges Leygues (Fra) ... 207
Georgia (USA) ... 759
Georgina (UK) ... 747
Georgy Kozmin (Rus) ... 583
Georgy Maksimov (Rus) ... 577
Georgy Sedov (Rus) ... 593
Georgy Titov (Rus) ... 583
Georgy Ushakov (Rus) ... 575
Geoula (Isr) ... 318
Gepard (Ger) ... 237
Geraldton (Aust) ... 28
Germantown (USA) ... 796
Germinal (Fra) ... 210
Gerry (USA) ... 799†
Getorskaur (Swe) ... 646
Gettysburg (USA) ... 776
GFA 1-6 (Fra) ... 227
GGS 185-6, 500-3, *et al* (Ita) ... 338
Ghagha II (UAE) ... 716
Ghanadhah (UAE) ... 715
Gharbiya (Egy) ... 180
Gharial (Ind) ... 287
Ghazi (Pak) ... 463, 501†
Gheppio (Ita) ... 333
Ghorpad (Ind) ... 287
Gian Maria Paolini (Ita) ... 339†
Gidrobiolog (Rus) ... 577
Gidrolog (Rus) ... 572
Gidronavt (Rus) ... 577
Gigante (Ita) ... 338
Gigas (Gre) ... 265
Gigrometr (Rus) ... 572
Gilgit (Pak) ... 468
Gillöga (Swe) ... 648
Ginga (Jpn) ... 373
Giorgio Cini (Ita) ... 339†
Girelle (Fra) ... 227
Girne (Tur) ... 702
Girorulevoy (Rus) ... 570
Giudice (Ita) ... 340
Giuliano Prini (Ita) ... 322
Giuseppe Garibaldi (Ita) ... 323, 335†
Giuseppe Mazzini (Ita) ... 323†
Giza (Egy) ... 180
GKS 52, 244, 286 (Onega) (Rus) ... 589
GKS series (T 43) (Rus) ... 589
Gladan (Swe) ... 652
Gladiator (USA) ... 799
Gladstone (Aust) ... 28
Glaive (Fra) ... 228
Glasgow (UK) ... 726
Glavkos (Gre) ... 254
Gleaner (UK) ... 740
Glenbrook (Can) ... 92
Glendale (Can) ... 92
Glendyne (Can) ... 92
Glenevis (Can) ... 92
Glenside (Can) ... 92
Glenten (Den) ... 159
Globe (Nam) ... 427†
Glomma (Nor) ... 453
Gloria (Col) ... 144
Gloucester (UK) ... 727
GLS 501, 502 (Ita) ... 336†
Glubomer (Rus) ... 572
Glücksburg (Ger) ... 242
Glückstadt (Ger) ... 251†
Glycine (Fra) ... 225†
Gnat (UK) ... 749
Gniewko (Pol) ... 498
Gniezno (Pol) ... 495
Gnist (Nor) ... 451
GO series (Ita) ... 339
Goaigoaza (Ven) ... 842
Goajira (Ven) ... 838
Goascoran (Hon) ... 270
Godavari (Ind) ... 281
Godetia (Bel) ... 50
Goéland (Fra) ... 226
Goga (Pak) ... 470†
Goiana (Brz) ... 61
Golcuk (Tur) ... 709
Gold Rover (UK) ... 742
Golfinho (Ang) ... 8
Golfo San Matias (Arg) ... 20
Golok (Indo) ... 303
Gomati (Ind) ... 281
Gomez Roca (Arg) ... 14
Gonjur (Gam) ... 230
Gonzalez (USA) ... 784
Goosander (UK) ... 745
Gopher State (USA) ... 818†, 821
Goplo (Pol) ... 495
Gorch Fock (Ger) ... 246
Gordelivy (Rus) ... 546
Gordon Reid (Can) ... 98
Gorée (Sen) ... 606
Gorgona (Col) ... 143
Gorgona (Ita) ... 334
Gorizont (training ship) (Rus) ... 579†
Gorizont (Yug class) (Rus) ... 572
Gornik (Pol) ... 493
Gorz (Iran) ... 308
Göteborg (Swe) ... 643
Gotland (Swe) ... 641
Goto (Jpn) ... 366
Göttingen (Ger) ... 239
GP series (Sin) ... 612†
Graciosa (Moz) ... 427†
Grad (Rus) ... 553
Gradac (Yug) ... 853
Gradus (Rus) ... 572
Grafton (UK) ... 729
Grajaú (Brz) ... 61
Grampus (Aust) ... 33
Granatiere (Ita) ... 328
Grand Batanga (Cam) ... 82
Grand Canyon State (USA) ... 818†, 821
Grand Duc (Fra) ... 226
Grand Isle (USA) ... 828
Granville (Arg) ... 13
Grapple (USA) ... 806
Grauskar (Swe) ... 646
Grasmere (UK) ... 749
Grasp (USA) ... 806
Graúna (Brz) ... 61
Gray Seal (Ire) ... 316†
Grayling (USA) ... 764
Grèbe (Fra) ... 217
Grecale (Ita) ... 327
Green Harbour (USA) ... 819
Green Mountain State (USA) ... 818†, 821
Green Valley (USA) ... 819
Greenbriar (USA) ... 829
Greeneville (USA) ... 762
Gregori (Hon) ... 271†
Greif (Ger) ... 238
Gremyashchy (Rus) ... 543
Grenfell (Can) ... 98†
Gribb (Nor) ... 451
Gribben (Den) ... 159
Gridley (USA) ... 779
Griep (Ger) ... 245
Griffon (Can) ... 94
Griffon (Fra) ... 222†
Grifone (Ita) ... 333
Grigore Antipa (Rom) ... 513
Grigory Mikheyev (Rus) ... 576
Grim (Swe) ... 649
Grimsholm (Nor) ... 455
Grmeč (Yug) ... 852
Grodno (Rus) ... 582†
Grom (Rus) ... 553
Grömitz (Ger) ... 240
Gromky (Rus) ... 546
Grønsund (Den) ... 163
Grosa (Spn) ... 626
Groton (USA) ... 762
Grozny (Pol) ... 494
Grozyashchy (Rus) ... 546
Grum (Bul) ... 72
Grumete Bolados (Chi) ... 109
Grumete Bravo (Chi) ... 109
Grumete Campos (Chi) ... 109
Grumete Diaz (Chi) ... 109
Grumete Salinas (Chi) ... 109
Grumete Tellez (Chi) ... 109
Grundsund (Swe) ... 647
Grunwald (Pol) ... 495
Gryf (Pol) ... 496
GS series (Alpinist) (Rus) ... 569
GS series (Biya, Finik, Kamenka) (Rus) ... 573
GS series (Lentra) (Rus) ... 571
GS 239, 242 (Mayak) (Rus) ... 574
GS 525, 526 (Vinograd) (Rus) ... 573
Guul (Tur) ... 712
Guacanagarix (DR) ... 169
Guacolda (Chi) ... 108
Guadalcanal (USA) ... 794
Guadalete (Spn) ... 629
Guadalmedina (Spn) ... 629
Guadalquivir (Spn) ... 629
Guadalupe (USA) ... 817
Guadiana (Spn) ... 629
Guaiba (Brz) ... 61
Guaicaipuro (Ven) ... 841
Guairia (Brz) ... 67†
Guajará (Brz) ... 61
Guale (Chi) ... 113
Guam (USA) ... 794
Guama (Cub) ... 153
Guanajuato (Mex) ... 418
Guaporé (Brz) ... 61
Guarani (Par) ... 475
Guarapari (Brz) ... 60
Guarda Marinha Brito (Brz) ... 66
Guarda Marinha Jensen (Brz) ... 66
Guardiamarina Barrutia (Spn) ... 631
Guardiamarina Chereguini (Spn) ... 631
Guardiamarina Godinez (Spn) ... 631
Guardiamarina Rull (Spn) ... 631
Guardiamarina Salas (Spn) ... 631
Guardian (HK) ... 272
Guardian (USA) ... 799
Guardian Brito (Chi) ... 111
Guayaquil (Ecu) ... 172
Guayas (Ecu) ... 173, 840†
Guaymuras (Hon) ... 270
Gucumaz (Gua) ... 266
Guépard (Fra) ... 225
Guernsey (UK) ... 738
Guerrico (Arg) ... 13
Guglielmo Marconi (Ita) ... 322
Guia (Por) ... 507
Guilin (CPR) ... 118
Guillermo Prieto (Mex) ... 418
Guldar (Ind) ... 287
Gulf Banker (USA) ... 819†
Gulf Farmer (USA) ... 819†
Gulf Merchant (USA) ... 819†
Gulf Sentry (USA) ... 826
Gulf Shipper (USA) ... 819†
Gulf Trader (USA) ... 819†
Gull (HK) ... 272
Gull Isle (Can) ... 97
Gumantong (Mly) ... 409
Gumi (RoK) ... 389
Gunnar Seidenfaden (Den) ... 166
Gunnar Thorson (Den) ... 166
Gunston Hall (USA) ... 796
Gurbet (Tur) ... 701
Gurnard (USA) ... 764
Gurupá (Brz) ... 61
Gurupi (Brz) ... 61
Gus W Darnell (USA) ... 817
Gustav Meyer (Ger) ... 251†
Gwadar (Pak) ... 470
Gwendoline (UK) ... 747
Gyre (USA) ... 814

H

H 1, H 12, H 16 *et al* (Pol) ... 498
H 11 (Ger) ... 247
H 93–H 96 (Cub) ... 153
H 500, 501, 502 (Tur) ... 707
Ha Dong (RoK) ... 387
Haamoon (Iran) ... 312
Haarlem (Nld) ... 433
Habbakhatun (Ind) ... 291
Habicht (Albatros class) (Ger) ... 238
Habicht (police craft) (Ger) ... 251†
Hachijyo (Jpn) ... 358
Hadejia (Nig) ... 445
Hae Gum Gang-Ho (DPRK) ... 380†
Hägern (Swe) ... 652
Hahajima (Jpn) ... 358
Häher (Ger) ... 238
Hai 521 (CPR) ... 134
Hai An (RoC) ... 673
Hai Cheng (RoC) ... 673
Hai Dzu 745, 746 (CPR) ... 136
Hai Dzu 950, 951 *et al* (CPR) ... 135
Hai Hu (RoC) ... 660†, 660
Hai Lao 456, 520, 523, 666 (CPR) ... 130
Hai Leng L191, L201 (CPR) ... 135
Hai Lung (RoC) ... 660†, 660
Hai Pao (RoC) ... 660
Hai Ping (RoC) ... 673
Hai Sheng 701, 702, 623 (CPR) ... 134
Hai Shih (RoC) ... 660
Hai Shui 412, 555, 608 *et al* (CPR) ... 135
Hai Son (Vtn) ... 846†
Hai Wu (CPR) ... 130
Hai Yang 01, 02 (CPR) ... 134
Hai Yun L 790, L 794 (CPR) ... 135
Haibat (Pak) ... 468
Haifa (Isr) ... 319
Haijiu (CPR) ... 135
Haijui 403, 512 (CPR) ... 130
Haikou (CPR) ... 119
Hail (SAr) ... 603
Haito 210, 319, 403, T147 *et al* (CPR) ... 137
Haitse 502, 583, 601 (CPR) ... 133
Haiyun 126, 300, 315, 318 (CPR) ... 135
Hajar Dewantara (Indo) ... 313†
Hajen (Den) ... 159
Haku II (NZ) ... 440†
Hakuni (Fin) ... 194
Hakuun (Jpn) ... 373
Halas (Tur) ... 712
Halcon 2-3 (Spn) ... 635
Haleakala (USA) ... 804
Halifax (Can) ... 85
Halifax (UK) ... 748
Halland (Swe) ... 641
Hallef (Chi) ... 112
Halli (Fin) ... 196
Halmstad (Swe) ... 644
Halote (Sud) ... 639
Halsey (USA) ... 779
Hälsingland (Swe) ... 641
Halyburton (USA) ... 786
Hamagiri (Asagiri class) (Jpn) ... 348
Hamagiri (Hamagiri class) (Jpn) ... 370
Hamana (Jpn) ... 361
Hamanami (Jpn) ... 370
Hamashio (Jpn) ... 372
Hamashio (Yuushio class) (Jpn) ... 344
Hamayuki (Hatsuyuki class) (Jpn) ... 349
Hamayuki (Murakumo class) (Jpn) ... 369
Hamazuki (Jpn) ... 369
Hambledon (UK) ... 749
Hamburg (Customs Service) (Ger) ... 251†
Hamburg (Hamburg class) (Ger) ... 234
Hameenmaa (Fin) ... 192
Hameln (Ger) ... 240
Hamilton (USA) ... 824
Hammer (Den) ... 160
Hammer (USA) ... 831
Hammerhead (USA) ... 764
Hamnskaur (Swe) ... 646
Hampden (UK) ... 748
Hampton (USA) ... 762
Han (Jor) ... 374
Han Jih (RoC) ... 672
Han Kang (RoK) ... 390
Han Yang (RoC) ... 661
Hanayuki (Jpn) ... 369
Hancza (Pol) ... 495
Handalan (Mly) ... 405
Haundig (Swe) ... 644
Hang Tuah (Mly) ... 404
Hangor (Pak) ... 463
Hanhak Sattru (Tld) ... 681
Hankoniemi (Fin) ... 194
Hansa (Fin) ... 193†
Hansaya (Sri) ... 638
Hanse (Ger) ... 251†
Haouz (Mor) ... 427
Hauradoskaur (Swe) ... 646
Harambee (Ken) ... 376
Haras I-V, Haras VI (Omn) ... 461
Haras VII–Haras X (Omn) ... 460
Harbah (Pak) ... 466
Hari-Rud (Iran) ... 312
Harima (Jpn) ... 362
Harimau Akar (Mly) ... 408
Harimau Belang (Mly) ... 408
Harimau Bintang (Mly) ... 408
Harimau Kumbang (Mly) ... 408
Harischi (Iran) ... 310
Harkness (USA) ... 816†
Harlan County (USA) ... 797
Harlech (UK) ... 749
Harlingen (Nld) ... 433
Harp (Can) ... 99
Harpers Ferry (USA) ... 796
Harriet Lane (USA) ... 824
Harry E Yarnell (USA) ... 779
Harry W Hill (USA) ... 782
Hartford (USA) ... 762
Harun (Fin) ... 195
Haruna (Jpn) ... 347
Harushio (Jpn) ... 344
Haruyuki (Jpn) ... 349
Haruzuki (Jpn) ... 370
Hasan Zahirovič-Laca (Yug) ... 851
Hasanuddin (Indo) ... 295
Hasayu (Jor) ... 374
Hashira (Jpn) ... 358
Hashmat (Pak) ... 463
Hatagumo (Jpn) ... 369
Hatakaze (Jpn) ... 345
Hatchet (USA) ... 831
Hateruma (Jpn) ... 366
Hatsushima (Jpn) ... 358
Hatsuyuki (Jpn) ... 349
Hauk (Nor) ... 451
Hauki (Fin) ... 194
Haukipää (Fin) ... 196
Havkatten (Den) ... 159
Havouri (Fin) ... 194
Havuz 1–Havuz 7 (Tur) ... 711
Hawar (Bhr) ... 37
Hawes (USA) ... 786
Hawkbill (USA) ... 764
Hawser (USA) ... 831
Hay Tan (RoC) ... 672
Hayagiri (Jpn) ... 370
Hayagumo (Jpn) ... 369
Hayanami (Jpn) ... 370
Hayase (Jpn) ... 357
Hayashio (Harushio class) (Jpn) ... 344
Hayashio (Iseshio class) (Jpn) ... 372
Hayate (Jpn) ... 374
Hayatomo (Jpn) ... 372
Hayes (USA) ... 807†, 813
Hayler (USA) ... 782
Headcorn (UK) ... 749
Healy (USA) ... 827
Hebe (Swe) ... 653
Heck (USA) ... 832†
Hecla (UK) ... 740
Hefei (CPR) ... 118
Heimdal (Nor) ... 456
Heimdal (Swe) ... 649
Heincke (Ger) ... 250
Heinz Roggenkamp (Ger) ... 245
Helen (UK) ... 747
Helena (USA) ... 762
Helford (UK) ... 734
Helgoland (Customs Service) (Ger) ... 251†
Helgoland (Helgoland class) (Ger) ... 247
Helgoland (Police launch) (Ger) ... 251†
Hellevoetsluis (Nld) ... 433
Helmsand (Ger) ... 244
Helmsdale (UK) ... 734
Helsinki (Fin) ... 190
Hendijan (Iran) ... 312
Hendrik Mentz (SA) ... 614
Hengam (Iran) ... 310
Henri Christophe (Hai) ... 269
Henry M Jackson (USA) ... 758†, 759
Henry Eckford (USA) ... 817
Henry J Kaiser (USA) ... 817
Henry Larsen (Can) ... 94
Heppens (Ger) ... 248
Hera (Swe) ... 653
Heraklis (Gre) ... 264
Herald (UK) ... 740
Hercules (Arg) ... 13
Hercules (Den) ... 161
Hercules (DR) ... 169
Hercules (Swe) ... 653
Hercules (USA) ... 802
Heriberto Jara Corona (Mex) ... 419
Hering (Ger) ... 239
Herluf Bidstrup (Rus) ... 589
Hermelin (Ger) ... 237
Hermenegildo Galeana (Mex) ... 418
Hermes (Swe) ... 653
Hermis (Gre) ... 262
Hermod (Den) ... 164
Hernando Gutierrez (Col) ... 143
Heroina (Arg) ... 12
Heroj (Yug) ... 849
Heron (USA) ... 800
Heron I, II, III (Bmd) ... 52
Heros (Swe) ... 653
Herrera (Per) ... 480
Herten (Ger) ... 240
Hespérides (Spn) ... 630, 632†
Hesperos (Gre) ... 259
Hessa (Nor) ... 454
Hetman Dorosenko (Rus) ... 546
Hetman Petr Sagadachny (Rus) ... 546
Hêtre (Fra) ... 226
Hettein (Egy) ... 178
Hetz (Isr) ... 318
Hevea (Fra) ... 226
Hever (UK) ... 749
Heweliusz (Pol) ... 497
Hewitt (USA) ... 782
Hibiki (Jpn) ... 362
Hibueras (Hon) ... 270
Hidra (Por) ... 504
Hiei (Jpn) ... 347
Hiev (Ger) ... 245
Hijau (Mly) ... 409
Hikoshima (Jpn) ... 358
Hila (Fin) ... 195
Himeshima (Jpn) ... 358
Himgiri (Ind) ... 282
Hinau (NZ) ... 440
Hinda (Con) ... 145
Hinnøy (Nor) ... 453
Hirmand (Iran) ... 312
Hiromine (Jpn) ... 368
Hirsala (Fin) ... 194
Hiryu (Jpn) ... 371
Hisingen (Swe) ... 648
Hispania (Spn) ... 631
Hitachi (Jpn) ... 367
Hitteen (SAr) ... 600
Hittin (Syr) ... 658
Hiyodori (Jpn) ... 362
Hizirreis (Tur) ... 696
HJ 1, HJ 3-13 (Spn) ... 635
Hjortø (Den) ... 162
Ho Chang (RoC) ... 669
Ho Chao (RoC) ... 669
Ho Cheng (RoC) ... 669
Ho Chi (RoC) ... 669
Ho Chie (RoC) ... 669
Ho Chien (RoC) ... 669
Ho Chuan (RoC) ... 669
Ho Chun (RoC) ... 669
Ho Chung (RoC) ... 669
Ho Deng (RoC) ... 669
Ho Feng (RoC) ... 669
Ho Hsing (RoC) ... 673
Ho Huei (RoC) ... 669
Ho Meng (RoC) ... 669
Ho Mou (RoC) ... 669
Ho Seng (RoC) ... 669
Ho Shan (RoC) ... 669
Ho Shou (RoC) ... 669
Ho Shun (RoC) ... 669
Ho Teng (RoC) ... 669
Ho Tsung (RoC) ... 669
Ho Yao (RoC) ... 669
Ho Yung (RoC) ... 669
Hobart (Aust) ... 24
Hodna (Alg) ... 8
Hofouf (SAr) ... 599
Hoggar (Alg) ... 8
Hohwacht (Ger) ... 251†
Hoist (USA) ... 806
Hojskaur (Swe) ... 646
Hokuto (Jpn) ... 373
Holger Danske (Den) ... 161
Holland (USA) ... 807
Holland Bay (Jam) ... 341
Holmwood (UK) ... 749
Holnis (Ger) ... 241
Homburg (Ger) ... 240
Hommel (Bel) ... 51
Honduras (Hon) ... 270
Honolulu (USA) ... 762
Honorio Barreto (Por) ... 503
Hood (Can) ... 99
Hopper (USA) ... 784
Hornbeam (USA) ... 829
Horne (USA) ... 778
Horning (UK) ... 749
Horobetsu (Jpn) ... 367
Horria (Tun) ... 693
Horten (Nor) ... 453
Hos Durg (Ind) ... 285
Houma (USA) ... 811
Houri (Guy) ... 269
Houston (USA) ... 762
Houtskär (Fin) ... 194
Houun (Jpn) ... 373
HQ 07, HQ 13 (Vtn) ... 843
HQ 09, 11, 13, 15, 17 (Vtn) ... 842
HQ 502, 503, 505, 511-513 (Vtn) ... 845
HQ 851, 852 (Vtn) ... 845
Hrvatska Kostajnica (Cro) ... 149
Hsad Dan (Bur) ... 79
Hsiang Yan Hung 1 (CPR) ... 133†
Hsin Lung (RoC) ... 672
HSPC 1-2 (Ml) ... 413
Hsun 701 (CPR) ... 133
Hsun Hsing (RoC) ... 672
HTS 503 (PNG) ... 473
Hu Hang Biao No 3 (CPR) ... 130†
Hu Hang CE Nos 11-15 (CPR) ... 130†
Hua Shan (RoC) ... 665
Hua Yang (RoC) ... 663
Huainan (CPR) ... 122
Hual Trader (USA) ... 819†
Hual Transporter (USA) ... 819†
Hualcopo (Ecu) ... 172
Huancavilca (Ecu) ... 170
Huangshi (CPR) ... 121
Huarpe (Arg) ... 18
Huascar (Chi) ... 111†
Huasteco (Mex) ... 421
Huayin (CPR) ... 120
Huayuankou (CPR) ... 127†
Hudson (Can) ... 101
Hudson (USA) ... 830
Hue City (USA) ... 776
Huechulafquen (Arg) ... 21
Huei Yang (RoC) ... 663
Huerta (Per) ... 483
Hugin (Den) ... 164
Hugin (Swe) ... 645
Huian (CPR) ... 129†
Huitfeld (Den) ... 160
Hulubalang (Mly) ... 409
Humaitá (Brz) ... 54
Humaita (Par) ... 474
Humber (UK) ... 734
Humberto Cortes (Col) ... 142
Hummer (Ger) ... 239
Hunain (Pak) ... 467
Hunley (USA) ... 807
Hunze (Nld) ... 437
Huracan (Uru) ... 835
Huragan (Pol) ... 493
Hurja (Fin) ... 191
Hurmat (Pak) ... 463
Huron (Can) ... 84
Hurricane (UK) ... 748
Hurricane (USA) ... 801
Hurtig (Swe) ... 644
Hurworth (UK) ... 734
Husky (UK) ... 747
Hutnik (Pol) ... 493
Huvudskaur (Swe) ... 646
Hvass (Nor) ... 451
Hvidbjørnen (Den) ... 158
Hvidsten (Den) ... 161
Hwa San (RoK) ... 388
Hwar (Qat) ... 508
Hyäne (Ger) ... 237
Hyannis (USA) ... 811
Hyatt (Chi) ... 104
Hydra (Gre) ... 256
Hydra (Nld) ... 436
Hydrograf (Pol) ... 496
Hylje (Fin) ... 196
Hyman G Rickover (USA) ... 762
Hyperion (Gre) ... 264

I

I Karavoyiannos Theophilopoulos (Gre) ... 264
Ialomita (Rom) ... 514
Iason (Gre) ... 264
Ibis (Sen) ... 606
Ibn Al Farat (Lby) ... 399
Ibn Al Hadrami (Lby) ... 399
Ibn Al Idrisi (Lby) ... 399
Ibn Harissa (Lby) ... 399
Ibn Khaldoum (Iraq) ... 296†
Ibn Marjid (Iraq) ... 313
Ibn Marwan (Lby) ... 399
Ibn Ouf (Lby) ... 399
Ibn Umayaa (Lby) ... 399
Ibuki (Jpn) ... 369
Icebird (Aust) ... 30†
Ieshima (Jpn) ... 358
Igaraparana (Col) ... 144
Ignacio L Vallarta (Mex) ... 418

Named Ships/INDEXES 863

Ignacio de la Llave (Mex) 418
Ignacio Lopez Rayon (Mex) 419
Ignacio Manuel Altamirano (Mex) 418
Ignacio Mariscal (Mex) 419
Ignacio Ramirez (Mex) 419
Igor Maksimov (Rus) 576
Igorot (Plp) 489
Iguacu (Brz) 67†
Iguatemi (Brz) 61
Ihlen Raso (CpV) 102
Ikaria (Jason and 511 classes) (Gre) 260
Ikeja (Nig) 446
Ikinci Inönü (Tur) 696
Ilchester (UK) 749
Ile des Barques (Can) 97
Ile d'Oléron (Fra) 221
Ile Saint-Ours (Can) 97
Ilga (Rus) 595
Ilim (Rus) 581
Illustrious (UK) 724
Ilo (Per) 481
Iloilo (Plp) 486
Ilongot (Plp) 489
Ilorin (Nig) 446
Ilya Azarov (Rus) 561
Ilya Muromets (Rus) 593
Iman (Rus) 581
Imeni XXV, XXVI Syezda KPSS (Rus) 594
Imeni LXX Letiya VCHK-KGB (Rus) 546
Imeni LXX Letiya Pogranvoysk (Rus) 546
Impavido (Brz) 67
Impeccable (USA) 815
Imperial Marinheiro (Brz) 61
Impetus (UK) 748
Implicit (USA) 800
Impulse (UK) 748
Inagua (Bhm) 36
Inasa (Jpn) 368
Inazuma (Jpn) 374
Inchon (RoK) 383
Inchon (USA) 794, 799†
Indaw (Bur) 75
Independence (Sin) 609
Independence (USA) 765†, 770, 771
Independência (Brz) 57
Indépendencia (DR) 167
Independencia (Ven) 839
Independiente (Col) 140
Indianapolis (USA) 762
Indio (Swe) 651†
Indomable (Col) 139
Indomita (Arg) 16
Indomitable (UK) 740†
Inebolu (Tur) 708
Infanta Cristina (Spn) 623
Infanta Elena (Spn) 623
Ing Gumuchio (Bol) 53
Ing Palacios (Bol) 53
Ingeniero Mery (Chi) 112
Ingeniero White (Arg) 20
Ingersoll (USA) 782
Ingraham (USA) 664†, 786
Ingul (Rus) 580
Inguri (Rus) 580
Inhaúma (Brz) 58
Inirida (Col) 144
Inkadh (Tun) 692
Inma (Bur) 75
Inouse (Gre) 260
Instow (UK) 749
Integrity (USA) 815
Interbunker (Bur) 79
Inti (Bol) 53
Intishat (Egy) 181†
Intrepid (Sin) 611
Intrepid (UK) 736†, 736
Intrepida (Arg) 16
Intrepide (Gn) 267
Intrepido (Brz) 67
Intrepido (Col) 139
Inttisar (Kwt) 391
Inverness (UK) 735
Investigator (Ind) 288
Invincible (UK) 724, 725
Invincible (USA) 815
Inya (Bur) 75
Ionmeto I, Ionmeto II (Ml) 413
Ipoploiarhos Arliotis (Gre) 259
Ipoploiarhos Batsis (Gre) 259
Ipoploiarhos Daniolos (Gre) 260
Ipoploiarhos Deyiannis (Gre) 258
Ipoploiarhos Grigoropoulos (Gre) 260
Ipoploiarhos Konidis (Gre) 259
Ipoploiarhos Krystalidis (Gre) 260
Ipoploiarhos Mikonios (Gre) 258
Ipoploiarhos Roussen (Gre) 260
Ipoploiarhos Troupakis (Gre) 258
Ipswich (Aust) 28
Iquique (Chi) 108
Iquique (Per) 477
Iran Ajr (Iran) 801†
Iran Asir (Iran) 310
Iran Ghaydr (Iran) 310
Irbit (Rus) 587
Irene (UK) 747
Iris (Bel) 48
Iris (Fra) 217†
Iris (USA) 829
Irkut (Rus) 581
Iron Duke (UK) 729
Ironbridge (UK) 749
Ironwood (USA) 829
Iroquois (Can) 84
Irtysh (Rus) 583
Isabel (UK) 747
Isard (Fra) 221
Isazu (Jpn) 367
Isbjørn (Den) 164
Isci Tasiti 1-4 (Tur) 709
Isenami (Jpn) 370
Iseshio (Jpn) 372
Iseyin (Nig) 446
Iseyuki (Jpn) 369
Ishikari (Bihoro class) (Jpn) 367
Ishikari (Ishikari class) (Jpn) 353†, 354
Ishim (Rus) 587
Işin (Tur) 708
Iskar (Bul) 72
Iskatel (Rus) 576
Iskra (Pol) 496†
Isku (Fin) 191
Isla Azteca (Mex) 423
Isla de Bioko (EqG) 184
Isla del Carmen (Mex) 423
Isla del Coco (CR) 146
Isla de la Juventud (Cub) 153
Isla de la Plata (Ecu) 173
Isla Puna (Ecu) 173
Isla Uvita (CR) 147
Islay (Per) 477
Isle Rouge (Can) 99
Isluga (Chi) 113
Isonami (Jpn) 369
Isoshi (Jpn) 372
Isoshigi (Jpn) 374
Isoshio (Jpn) 372
Isoyuki (Jpn) 349
Isozuki (Jpn) 369
Issledovatel (Rus) 576
Istiklal (Tun) 693
Istiqlal (Kwt) 392
Isuzu (Jpn) 367
Itacurussá (Brz) 64
Itaipú (Par) 474
Itapoa (Brz) 66
Itapura (Brz) 67†
Itati II (Arg) 18†
Itchen (UK) 734
Iterez (Bol) 53
Iuka (USA) 811
Ivan (Yug) 852
Ivan Bubnov (Rus) 581
Ivan Golubets (Rus) 583
Ivan Kireyev (Rus) 577
Ivan Kolyshkin (Rus) 565
Ivan Kruzenshtern (Akademik Krylov class) (Rus) 571
Ivan Kruzenshtern (Dobrynya class) (Rus) 593
Ivan Kucherenko (Rus) 565
Ivan Lednev (Rus) 587
Ivan Moskvitin (Rus) 593
Ivan Odtejev (Rus) 562
Ivan Petrov (Rus) 576
Ivan Rogov (Rus) 562, 563†
Ivan Sudtsov (Rus) 587
Ivan Susanin (Rus) 594
Ivan Vakhrameev (Rus) 565
Iwai (Jpn) 358
Iwaki (Jpn) 366
Iwase (Jpn) 354
IX 506, 514, 515 *et al* (USA) 809†, 809
Ixworth (UK) 749
Iz (Yug) 853
Izaro (Spn) 626
Izhora (Rus) 581†
Izmail (Rus) 548
Izu (Jpn) 365
Izumrud (Grisha class) (Rus) 548
Izumrud (research ship) (Rus) 575

J

J 120 (CPR) 138
J 304 (CPR) 129
J 503, J 504 (CPR) 130
J Chavez Suarez (Bol) 53
J E Bernier (Can) 95
J E Van Haverbeke (Bel) 49
J G Repsold (Ger) 251†
J T C Ramsey (Bar) 46
Jacana II (Brz) 66
Jaceguay (Brz) 58
Jacinto Candido (Por) 503
Jack Williams (USA) 786
Jacksonville (USA) 762
Jacmin (RoK) 391
Jacob Hägg (Swe) 651
Jacob van Heemskerck (Nld) 431
Jacques Cartier (Fra) 216
Jadran (Yug) 852
Jägaren (Swe) 644
Jagatha (Sri) 636
Jaguar (Fra) 225
Jaguar (Ger) 238
Jaime Gomez (Col) 142
Jalalat (Pak) 468
Jalanidhi (Indo) 301
James K Polk (USA) 760
James Sinclair (Can) 101
Jamhuri (Ken) 376
Jamie Rook (Col) 142
Jamno (Pol) 495
Jamuna (Ban) 43
Jamuna (Ind) 288
Jan Bart (Bel) 51†
Jan Smuts (SA) 614
Jan van Brakel (Nld) 431
Jananah (UAE) 715
Janbaz (Pak) 471
Janequeo (Chi) 112
Jaouel el Bahr (Tun) 693†
Jarrett (USA) 786
Jarvis (USA) 824
Jason (USA) 806
Jastog (Yug) 855
Jastreb (Cro) 149
Jatli (Pak) 469†
Jato (Gam) 230
Javier Quiroga (Spn) 626
Jaya Wijaya (Indo) 301
Jayesagara (Sri) 635
Je Chon (RoK) 385
Jean Bart (Fra) 208
Jean Moulin (Fra) 212
Jean de Vienne (Fra) 207
Jeanne d'Arc (Fra) 206, 210†
Jeb Stuart (USA) 820
Jebba (Nig) 445
Jebel Antar (Alg) 8
Jebel Handa (Alg) 8
Jefferson City (USA) 762
Jefferson Island (USA) 828
Jens Vaever (Den) 165
Jeon Buk (RoK) 382
Jeon Ju (RoK) 382
Jerai (Lerici class) (Mly) 406
Jerai (Vosper class) (Mly) 409
Jerba (Tun) 693
Jernih (Mly) 408
Jerong (Mly) 406
Jersey (UK) 738
Jervis Bay (Aust) 31†, 31
Jesse L Brown (USA) 785†, 785
Jesus Gonzalez Ortega (Mex) 418
Jetstream (HK) 272
Jhara (Pak) 470†
Ji Di Hao (CPR) 130
Jian (CPR) 120
Jida (Bhr) 39
Jiddah (firefighting craft) (SAr) 605
Jiddah (tug) (SAr) 602
Jija Bai (Ind) 291
Jim Fouchea (SA) 614
Jin Hae (RoK) 385
Jin Hang Biao No.1 (CPR) 130†
Jin Hang CE Nos 1 and 2 (CPR) 130†
Jin Ju (RoK) 385
Jinan (CPR) 118
Jinhua (CPR) 120
Jintsu (Jpn) 353
Jishou (CPR) 120
Jiujiang (CPR) 120
Jo (Nor) 451
Joan (UK) 747
Joato Coutinho (Por) 503
Joato Roby (Por) 502
Joe Mann (Aust) 33
Johan Nordenankar (Swe) 651
Johanna van der Merwe (SA) 614
John A Moore (USA) 785†, 786
John C Calhoun (USA) 760
John C Stennis (USA) 766
John Cabot (Can) 93
John Ericsson (USA) 817
John F Kennedy (USA) 768, 778†
John H Sides (USA) 785†, 786
John Hancock (USA) 782
John Jacobson (Can) 98
John L Hall (USA) 786
John Lenthall (USA) 817
John McDonnell (USA) 816
John Marshall (USA) 760†
John N Cobb (USA) 832†
John P Tully (Can) 101
John Paul Jones (USA) 784
John Rodgers (USA) 782, 783
John S McCain (USA) 784
John Young (USA) 782
Johore Bahru (Mly) 409
Jonas (Ger) 246†
Jos (Nig) 446
Jose Maria del Castillo Velasco (Mex) 419
Jose Maria Izazaga (Mex) 419
Jose Maria Mata (Mex) 419
Jose Maria Palas (Col) 141
Jose Natividad Macias (Mex) 419
Josefa Ortiz de Dominguez (Mex) 419
Joseph Hewes (USA) 785†, 785
Josephus Daniels (USA) 778
Joshua Humphreys (USA) 817
Josip Mazhkar Sosa (Yug) 851
Josuea Alvarez (Col) 144
Jouett (USA) 778
Joumhouria (Tun) 693
Joyce (UK) 747
Juan Aldama (Mex) 418
Juan Antonio de la Fuente (Mex) 419
Juan Bautista Morales (Mex) 419
Juan Lucio (Col) 142
Juan N Alvares (Mex) 418
Juan Sebastián de Elcano (Spn) 110†, 631
Juang (Mly) 409
Jubail (SAr) 605
Juacar (Spn) 629
Juist (Ger) 247
Jules Verne (Fra) 220
Julian Apaza (Bol) 53
Juliana (Hon) 271†
Julio de Noronha (Brz) 58
Junak (Yug) 849
Juneau (USA) 795
Juniper (USA) 829†
Junon (Fra) 203
Junon (Sey) 607
Jupiter (Bul) 74
Jupiter (Den) 161
Jupiter (Per) 483†
Jupiter (Rom) 512
Jupiter (Sin) 612
Jupiter (USA) 819†
Jurat (Pak) 468
Jurel (DR) 169
Justice (Sin) 609
Juvent (ex-) (SA) 615
JW 9841-9844, 9861-9868 (Tan) 674
Jyuu-Go (Jpn) 359
Jyuu-Ichi-Go (Jpn) 359
Jyuu-Ni-Go (Jpn) 359

K

K1, K 7, K 14 (Pol) 499
K 8, K 11, K 20, K 21 (Pol) 497
K 200, 427, 943 *et al* (CPR) 133
K 420, 982, 983 (CPR) 134
Kabashima (Jpn) 367
Kader (Alg) 7
Kadet (Pol) 496
Kadir (Sud) 639
Kadisia (Syr) 658
Kadmath (Ind) 282
Kadmos (Gre) 265
Kaduna (Nig) 446
Kae Bong (RoK) 388
Kagitingan (Plp) 487
Kahlid (SAr) 601
Kahu (NZ) 440†, 441
Kai Yang (RoC) 661
Kaibil Balam (Gua) 266
Kaifeng (CPR) 118, 120
Kaio (Jpn) 373
Kairi (TT) 690
Kairyu (Jpn) 371
Kaivan (Iran) 308
Kaiyo (Jpn) 372
Kaiyuan (CPR) 119
Kajava (Fin) 198
Kakap (Indo) 297
Kakinada (Ind) 288
Kala 1-Kala 6 (Fin) 194
Kalaat Beni Hammad (Alg) 6
Kalaat Beni Rached (Alg) 6
Kalamazoo (USA) 805
Kalar (Rus) 595
Kalat (Iran) 312
Kalat (Pak) 468†
Kalinga (Plp) 489
Kalinga Apayao (Plp) 487
Kalispell (USA) 811
Kalkan (Tur) 702
Kalkgrund (Ger) 244
Kalla (Fin) 196
Kallanpää (Fin) 196
Kalliroe (Gre) 265
Kalmar (Swe) 643
Kalmarsund (Swe) 647
Kalmat (Pak) 470
Kalvsund (Swe) 647
Kama (Rus) 583
Kaman (Iran) 308
Kamchatka (Kamchatka class) (Rus) 578
Kamchatka (Sorum class) (Rus) 595
Kamchatsky Komsomolets (Rus) 565
Kamehameha (USA) 760
Kamishima (Hatsushima class) (Jpn) 358
Kamishima (Kunashiri class) (Jpn) 367
Kamla Devi (Ind) 291
Kampela 1, 2, 3 (Fin) 194
Kamui (Jpn) 369
Kan (CPR) 132
Kan Keong (RoK) 387
Kanaris (Gre) 255
Kanarya (Tur) 708†
Kanawha (CG tender) (USA) 830
Kanawha (Henry Kaiser class) (USA) 817
Kane (USA) 816
Kang Reung (RoK) 385
Kang Won (RoK) 382
Kangan (Iran) 311
Kangwon (RoK) 389
Kanitsha (Zai) 856
Kankakee (USA) 829
Kano (Jpn) 367
Kano (Nig) 446
Kansas City (USA) 805
Kantang (Tld) 681
Kao Hsiung (RoC) 669
Kapak (Indo) 303
Kaparen (Swe) 645
Kaper I, Kaper II (Pol) 499
Kapitan A Radzabov (Rus) 594
Kapitan M Izmaylov (Rus) 594
Kapitan Babichev (Rus) 593
Kapitan Belousov (Rus) 593
Kapitan Borodkin (Rus) 593
Kapitan Bukayev (Rus) 593
Kapitan Chadayev (Rus) 593
Kapitan Chechkin (Rus) 593
Kapitan Chudinov (Rus) 593
Kapitan Demidov (Rus) 593
Kapitan Dimiter Dobrev (Bul) 74
Kapitan Dranitsyn (Rus) 593
Kapitan Khlebnikov (Rus) 593
Kapitan Kosolapov (Rus) 594
Kapitan Krutov (Rus) 593
Kapitan Melekhov (Rus) 593
Kapitan Metsayk (Rus) 593
Kapitan Moshkin (Rus) 593
Kapitan Nikolayev (Rus) 593
Kapitan Plakhin (Rus) 593
Kapitan Sorokin (Rus) 593
Kapitan Voronin (Rus) 593
Kapitan Yevdokimov (Rus) 593
Kapitan Zarubin (Rus) 593
Kara (Tog) 689
Karabakh (Rus) 584
Karabane (Sen) 606
Karadeniz Ereğlisi (Tur) 708
Karamürsel (Tur) 704
Karamürselbey (Tur) 703†, 705
Karanj (Ind) 277
Karari (Sud) 639
Karatsu (Jpn) 368
Karayel (Tur) 701
Karel Doorman (Nld) 432
Karel Satsuitubun (Indo) 294
Karelia (Rus) 595
Karimata (Indo) 302
Karimundsa (Indo) 302
Karir (Egy) 182
Karjala (Fin) 189
Karkas (Iran) 310
Karl Marx (Rus) 582†
Karlo Rojc (Yug) 851
Karlsøy (Nor) 454
Karlsruhe (Ger) 235
Karmøy (Nor) 453
Karnaphuli (Ban) 42
Karpaty (Rus) 585
Kartal (Tur) 701
Karthala (Com) 145
Karwar (Ind) 288
Kasirga (Tur) 701
Kastoria (Gre) 265
Kasturi (Mly) 404
Kaszub (Pol) 493
Kathleen (UK) 747
Katir 1-Katir 38 (Tur) 711
Katmai Bay (USA) 827
Katori (Shiretoko class) (Jpn) 366
Katori (training ship) (Jpn) 359†, 360
Katsonis (Gre) 253
Katsura (Jpn) 367
Katsuragi (Jpn) 368
Katsuren (Jpn) 374
Katun (Rus) 580
Kauffman (USA) 786
Kaura (Den) 156, 449†
Kavak (Tur) 709
Kavkaz (Rus) 568
Kawagiri (Jpn) 369
Kawkab (UAE) 714
Kawlan (Lby) 398
Kazbek (Rus) 582†, 585
Kbv series (Swe) 654, 655
Ke Xue Yihao 1, 2 (CPR) 131
Kearsage (USA) 792
Kedrov (Rus) 546
Kegon (Jpn) 371
Kekrops (Gre) 265
Kelang (Mly) 409
Kelefstis Stamou (Gre) 259
Kelewang (Mly) 406
Kelibia (Tun) 693
Kemaindera (Bru) 69
Kemer (Tur) 704
Kemj (Rus) 580
Kempong (Mly) 408
Kennebec (USA) 830
Kentouros (Gre) 259
Kentucky (USA) 759
Keokuk (USA) 811
Kepah (Mly) 408
Kepez (Tur) 711
Kerama (Jpn) 372
Kerambit (Mly) 406
Kerapu (Indo) 297
Kerch (Rus) 541
Kerempe (Tur) 704
Kereon (Fra) 226
Keris (Indo) 297
Kerkini (Gre) 265
Kern (Rus) 576
Kesari (Ind) 287
Keshet (Isr) 318
Ketam (Mly) 408
Ketchikan (USA) 811
Kewol (Aust) 34
Kexueyihao 1 and 2 (CPR) 131
Key Biscayne (USA) 828
Key Largo (USA) 828
Key West (USA) 762
Keystone State (USA) 818†, 821
Khabar (SAr) 601
Khabarov (Rus) 591
Khabarovsk (Rus) 538
Khadang (Iran) 308
Khadem (Ban) 44
Khafra (Egy) 182
Khaibar (Pak) 467
Khamronsin (Tld) 680
Khan Jahan Ali (Ban) 44
Khanjar (Ind) 283
Khanjar (Iran) 308
Kharg (Iran) 311
Khariton Laptev (Dobrynya Nikitich class) (Rus) 593
Khariton Laptev (Nikolay Zubov class) (Rus) 569
Khasan (Rus) 579
Khassab (Omn) 457
Khawla (Iraq) 314
Khersones (Mayak class) (Rus) 570
Khersones (sailing ship) (Rus) 579
Khersson (Vtn) 846†
Khibiny (Rus) 585
Khirirat (Tld) 678
Khoufan (Egy) 182
Khukri (Ind) 283
Khyber (Egy) 178
Kim (Nor) 455
Ki Hajar Dewantara (Indo) 296
Ki Rin (RoK) 388
Kiala (Zai) 856
Kichli (Gre) 262
Kickapoo (USA) 830
Kidd (USA) 781
Kidon (Isr) 318
Kiel (Ger) 251†
Kiev (Kiev class) (Rus) 534
Kiev (Moskva class) (Rus) 592
Kihu (Fin) 198
Kiiski 1-7 (Fin) 193
Kiisla (Fin) 197
Kiklops (Gre) 265
Kikuchi (Jpn) 367
Kikuzuki (Jpn) 350
KIL series (Kashtan, Sura) (Rus) 584
KIL series (Neptun) (Rus) 585
Kilauea (USA) 803†, 812
Kildin (Rus) 569
Kiliç Ali Pasca (Tur) 697
Kilimli (Tur) 704
Kim Chon (RoK) 385
Kim Men (RoC) 672
Kimberley (SA) 615
Kimitahi (Chi) 113
Kimon (Cypr) 155
Kimon (Gre) 254
Kinabalu (Mly) 406
King (Arg) 15
King Chi (HK) 272
King Chung (HK) 272
King Dai (HK) 272
King Hau (HK) 272
King Kan (HK) 272
King Kwan (HK) 272
King Lai (HK) 272
King Lim (HK) 272
King Mei (HK) 272
King Shun (HK) 272
King Tai (HK) 272
King Tak (HK) 272
King Yan (HK) 272
King Yee (HK) 272
King Yung (HK) 272
Kingfisher (UK) 739
Kingfisher (USA) 800
Kinkaid (USA) 782
Kinterbury (UK) 746
Kinugasa (Jpn) 374
Kirch (Ind) 283
Kirishima (Jpn) 368
Kiro (Fij) 188
Kirpan (Ind) 283
Kish (Iran) 312
Kiska (Island class) (USA) 828
Kiska (Kilauea class) (USA) 803
Kissa (Gre) 262
Kit (Yug) 855
Kitagumo (Jpn) 369
Kitakami (Jpn) 360
Kithera (Gre) 261
Kithnos (Gre) 261
Kittanning (USA) 811
Kittiwake (USA) 807

864 INDEXES/Named Ships

Kittur Chinnama (Ind) 291
Kitty (UK) 747
Kitty Hawk (USA) 765†, 768
Kiwi (NZ) 440
Kiyonami (Jpn) 370
Kiyotaki (Jpn) 371
Kiyozuki (Jpn) 370
Kjapp (USA) 452
Kjekk (Nor) 451
Klakring (USA) 786
Klio (Gre) 262
Klongyai (Tld) 681
Klueng Baden (Tld) 687
Knechtsand (Ger) 248
Kniepsand (Ger) 251†
Knight Island (USA) 828
Knorr (USA) 814
Knossos (Gre) 260
Knurrhahn (Ger) 243
Ko Hung (RoK) 387
Ko Mun (RoK) 388
Kobben (Nor) 449
Kobie Coetsee (SA) 614
Koblenz (Ger) 239
Kocatepe (Tur) 697
Kochab (Gua) 267
Koçhisar (Tur) 702
Kodiak Island (USA) 828
Koida (Rus) 582
Kojima (Jpn) 365
Kola (Rus) 581
Kolguev (Rus) 572
Köln (Ger) 235
Kolobrzeg (Pol) 499
Kölpinsee (Ger) 242†
Komandor (Rus) 589
Komayuki (Jpn) 369
Komemiut (Isr) 318
Komet (Ger) 251
Kompas (Rus) 572
Komsomolets Karely (Rus) 561
Konarak (Iran) 312
Konda (Rus) 582
Kondo (Ben) 52
Kondor (Ger) 238
Kongo (Jpn) 346
Kongou (Jpn) 368
Konkan (Ind) 288
Konrad Meisel (Ger) 251†
Konstantin Olshanskiy (Rus) 562
Konstanz (Ger) 239
Kontio (Fin) 193
Koos (Ger) 248
Kootenay (Can) 87
Kopernik (Pol) 497
Koprivnik (Yug) 852
Kora (Ind) 283
Koraaga (Aust) 29
Koralle (Ger) 239
Korangon (Sur) 640
Kormoran (Ger) 238
Kormoran (Pol) 494
Kornat (Yug) 852
Korrigan (Fra) 223
Kortenaer (Nld) 431
Kos (Gre) 260
Koshiki (Jpn) 366
Kosmaj (Yug) 852
Kosmonaut Georgy Dobrovolsky (Rus) 578
Kosmonaut Pavel Belyayev (Rus) 567†, 578
Kosmonaut Viktor Patsayev (Rus) 578
Kosmonaut Vladislav Volkov (Rus) 578
Kosmonaut Yury Gagarin (Rus) 578, 582†
Koster (Swe) 648
Kota Bahru (Mly) 409
Kotka (Fin) 190
Kotobiki (Jpn) 371
Kotor (Yug) 850
Kountouriotis (Gre) 255
Kozara (Yug) 854
Kozhikoda (Ind) 288
Kozlu (Tur) 704
Kozolo (Yug) 852
Krab (Pol) 497
Krabbe (Ger) 239
Krabri (Bul) 72
Kraburi (Tld) 676
Krakow (Pol) 495
Kralj Petar Kresimir IV (Cro) 148
Kram (Tld) 684
Kranich (Ger) 248
Krasin (Rus) 592†, 592
Krasny-Kavkaz (Rus) 544
Krasny-Krym (Rus) 544
Krekel (Bel) 51
Krenometr (Rus) 570
Krickan (Swe) 648
Krieger (Den) 160
Kriezis (Gre) 255
Krill (Ger) 239
Krilon (Rus) 572
Krimsky Komsomolets (Rus) 561
Kris (Mly) 406
Kriti (Gre) 260
Kronsort (Ger) 244
Krøttøy (Nor) 454
Krym (Rus) 568
Ku Yong (RoK) 389
Kuala Bengkoka (Mly) 410
Kuala Kangsar (Mly) 409
Kuala Trengganu (Mly) 409
Kuban (Rus) 586
Kuching (Mly) 409
Kudaka (Jpn) 366
Kudret (Tur) 711
Kuha 21-26 (Fin) 192
Kühlungsborn (Ger) 249
Kujang (Indo) 303
Kukulkán (Gua) 266
Kula (Fij) 188†
Kullen (Swe) 648
Kulmbach (Ger) 240
Kum Kok (RoK) 387
Kum San (RoK) 387
Kuma (Jpn) 367
Kumano (Chikugo class) (Jpn) 354
Kumano (Takatori class) (Jpn) 367
Kumbhir (Ind) 287

Kun San (RoK) 385
Kun Yang (RoC) 664
Kunashiri (Jpn) 367
Kunigami (Jpn) 366
Kunimi (Jpn) 369
Kunisaki (Jpn) 366
Kunming (CPR) 119
Kunna (Nor) 449
Kupa (Yug) 850
Kupang (Indo) 299
Kupang (Mly) 408
Kurama (Hidaka class) (Jpn) 369
Kurama (Shirane class) (Jpn) 347
Kureren (Den) 162
Kurihama (Akashi class) (Jpn) 372
Kurihama (Kurihama class) (Jpn) 363
Kurita (Jpn) 370
Kurki (Fin) 197
Kurmuk (Sud) 639
Kurobe (Bihoro class) (Jpn) 367
Kurobe (Kurobe class) (Jpn) 360
Kuroshio (Iseshio class) (Jpn) 372
Kuroshio (Uzushio class) (Jpn) 345
Kurs (Rus) 570
Kursograf (Rus) 570
Kursura (Ind) 277
Kurt Burkowitz (Ger) 251†
Kurtaran (Tur) 708
Kurushima (Jpn) 372
Kuşadasi (Tur) 704
Kustaanmiekka (Fin) 194
Kuthar (Ind) 283
Kuvvet (Tur) 711
Kuwano (Jpn) 367
Kuzuryu (Jpn) 367
Kvarven (Nor) 455
Kvikk (Nor) 452
Kvina (Nor) 453
KW 15-18, 20 (Ger) 247
Kwan Myong (RoK) 385
Kwang Ju (RoK) 382
Kwei Yang (RoC) 664
Kyklon (Gre) 259
Kyknos (Gre) 259
Kyong Buk (RoK) 384
Kyong Ju (RoK) 385
Kyong Ki (RoK) 382
Kyuu-Go (Jpn) 359

L

L 35-37, L 40 (Ind) 287
L 40-43, 51-59, 510-12 (Tld) 685
L 71-72, L 81-88 (Spn) 628
L 700 series (UK) 737
L 820 (Sri) 638
L 9051, 9070, 9096 et al (Fra) 216
L 9061, 9062 (Fra) 214
L 9530-9535, L 9536-9541 (Nld) 434
L Mendel Rivers (USA) 764
LCM 1-LCM 5 (Mly) 406
LCM 701-LCM 710 (Bur) 78
LCP 1-LCP 15 (Mly) 406
LCT 101-LCT 104 (Ban) 45
LCU 1-LCU 4 (Mly) 407
LCU 497-498 (RoC) 670
LCU 2001-2035 (USA) 798
LCVP 011, 012, 013 (Ban) 45
LCVP 8000 series (USA) 737
LD 40-43 (Uru) 835
LD 44-45 (Uru) 836
LDM 119-121, 406 and series (Por) 505
Le Fort (Fra) 226
Le Foudroyant (Fra) 201
Le Téméraire (Fra) 201
Le Terrible (Fra) 201
Le Tonnant (Fra) 201
Le Triomphant (Fra) 201
Le Valeureux (IC) 340, 605†
Le Vigilant (IC) 340, 605†
Leahy (USA) 779
Leandro Valle (Mex) 418
Lech (Pol) 498
Lechlade (UK) 749
Ledang (Mly) 406
Ledbury (UK) 734
Leeds Castle (UK) 738
Leftwich (USA) 782
Legare (USA) 824
Lekir (Mly) 404
Lelaps (Gre) 259
Lembing (Mly) 406
Lena (Rus) 582
Leningrad (CHG) (Rus) 538†
Leningrad (icebreaker) (Rus) 592
Leningradsky Komsomolets (Rus) 546, 547
Leon Guzman (Mex) 419
Leona Vicario (Mex) 419
Leonard J Cowley (Can) 100
Leonardo da Vinci (Ita) 322
Leonid Demin (Rus) 571
Leonid Sobolev (Rus) 571
Léopard (Fra) 225
Leopard (Ger) 238
Leopard (Rus) 524†
Leopold (USA) 828†
Lerici (Ita) 331
Leroy Grumman (USA) 817
Les Maloango (Con) 145
Les Trois Glorieuses (Con) 145
Lesbos (Gre) 260
Leslie (UK) 747
L'Espérance (Fra) 219
Leticia (Col) 141
L'Étoile (Fra) 225
Letuchy (Rus) 546
Letyashti (Bul) 72
Leucoton (Chi) 112
Levante (Por) 507
Levanzo (Ita) 337
Levent (Tur) 711
Levuka (Fij) 188
Lewis B Puller (USA) 785†, 786
Leyte Gulf (USA) 776
LF 91-LF 96 (Ecu) 172
Liao Yang (RoC) 662

Lakshadweep (Ind) 290
Lakshmi Bai (Ind) 291
Lama (Rus) 587
Lamine Sadji Kaba (Gn) 267
Lamlash (UK) 749
Lampo Batang (Indo) 303
Lana (Nig) 446
Lanao del Norte (Plp) 487
Lancaster (Duke class) (UK) 729
Lancaster (Spitfire class) (UK) 748
Lance (Nor) 456
Lancha Ecografa (Par) 475
Landsort (Swe) 648
Laney Chouest (USA) 823
Lang Hindek (Mly) 408
Lang Hitam (Mly) 408
Lang Kangok (Mly) 408
Lang Kuik (Mly) 408
Lang Lebah (Mly) 408
Lang Malam (Mly) 408
Lang Siput (Mly) 408
Lang Tiram (Mly) 408
Langeness (Ger) 248
Langeoog (Ger) 247
Langevin (Fra) 228
Languste (Ger) 239
Lanta (Tld) 684
Lantana (USA) 829†
Lao Yang (RoC) 662
Lapérouse (Fra) 219
Laplace (Fra) 219
Lapwing (Ana) 9
Larak (Iran) 310
Laramie (USA) 817
L'Ardent (IC) 340
Lardier (Fra) 226
Larikai (StV) 598
Larrea (Per) 480
Las Guasimas (Cub) 153†
Las Palmas (Spn) 630†, 632
Lastunul (Rom) 511
Lata (Sol) 613
Late (Ton) 690
Latorre (Chi) 105
Latouche-Tréville (Fra) 207
Lauca (Chi) 113
Laurel (USA) 829
Lauren (USA) 812
Lautaro (Chi) 112
Lautoka (Fij) 188
Lavan (Iran) 310
L'Aventurière II (Fra) 221†
Lawrence H Gianella (USA) 817, 819†
Lawrenceville (Can) 92
Laxen (Den) 159
Laya (Spn) 626
Layter 1-6 (Tur) 709
Lazaga (Spn) 625

Libeccio (Ita) 327
Liberal (Brz) 57
Liberation (Bel) 49
Liberta (Ant) 9
Libertad (Arg) 18
Libertad (DR) 167
Libertad (Ven) 839
Libertador (Bol) 53
Liberty (USA) 828
Libra (Ita) 330
Liepaya (Rus) 582†
Lieutenant Colonel Errhamani (Mor) 424
Lieutenant Malghagh (Mor) 426
Lieutenant de Vaisseau Lavallée (Fra) 212
Lieutenant de Vaisseau le Hénaff (Fra) 212
Ligia Elena (Pan) 472
Ligomo 3 (Sol) 613
Lihiniya (Sri) 638
Lilah (UK) 747
Liman (Rus) 572
Limasawa (Plp) 489
Limnos (Can) 101
Limnos (Gre) 256
Limpopo (Por) 503
Lindau (Ger) 239
Lindisfarne (UK) 738
L'Indomptable (Fra) 201
Lindormen (Den) 163
Lindos (Gre) 260
Line (USA) 831
L'Inflexible (Fra) 201
Linge (Nld) 437
Linssi (Fin) 196
L'Intrépide (IC) 340
Linza (Rus) 570
Lion (Fra) 225
Lipari (Ita) 334
Listerville (Can) 92
Litani (Sur) 639
Litoral (Bol) 53
Littlehales (USA) 816
Liulom (Tld) 681
Liven (Rus) 553
Liverpool (UK) 726
Llaima (Chi) 112
Llandovery (UK) 749
Lo Yang (RoC) 663
Loa (Chi) 113
Lobelia (Bel) 48
Lobitos (Per) 482
Lodestone (UK) 750
LOF 1-LOF 6 (EIS) 183
Lohi (Fin) 195
Lohm (Fin) 195
Loire (Fra) 219
Loja (Ecu) 171
Lokki (Fin) 198
Loksa (Rus) 595
Lom (Nor) 451
Lommen (Den) 159
London (UK) 730
Long Beach (USA) 772†, 775
Long Island (USA) 828
Longlom (Tld) 680
Lopburi Ramas (Tld) 687
Loreley (Ger) 240
Loreto (Per) 481
Loriot (Fra) 226
Los Angeles (USA) 762
Los Cayos (Ven) 841
Los Galapagos (Ecu) 171
Los Llanos (Ven) 838
Los Rios (Ecu) 171
Los Taques (Ven) 841
Lossen (Den) 163
Lotlin (Rus) 570
Louis M Lauzier (Can) 101
Louis S St Laurent (Can) 93, 94†
Louisbourg (Can) 99
Louisiana (USA) 759
Louisville (USA) 762
Löwe (Ger) 238
Loyal (USA) 815
Loyal Chancellor (UK) 749
Loyal Helper (UK) 749
Loyal Mediator (UK) 749
Loyal Moderator (UK) 749
Loyal Proctor (UK) 749
Loyal Volunteer (UK) 749
Loyal Watcher (UK) 749
LP 1, 2, 3, (Ger) 243
LP 03 series, LP 04 series (EIS) 183
LS series (Jpn) 373
LS 9-LS 12 (Tur) 703
LS 11201 and series (Arg) 19†
Lt General William B Bunker (USA) 798
LTC 1036, 1037 (Eth) 186
LTC 1038 (Eth) 187
Lu Shan (RoC) 665
Luadia (Zai) 856
Lübeck (Ger) 235
Lubin (Yug) 855
Lublin (Pol) 495
Luchs (Ger) 238
Luga (Rus) 579
Luhu (CPR) 117
Luigi Durand de la Penne (Ita) 326
Luis Manuel Rojas (Mex) 419
Luleam (UK) 644
Luna (Den) 161
Lunden (Ger) 161
Lüneburg (Ger) 242
Lung Chiang (RoC) 667
Lung Chuan (RoC) 672
Luperon (DR) 168
Lupo (Ita) 328
Lütje Horn (Ger) 248
Lütjens (Ger) 234
Lutteur (Fra) 226
Lydford (UK) 749
Lynch (Arg) 20
Lynch (Chi) 106
Lynx (Fra) 225
Lyø (Den) 162
Lyra (Den) 161
Lyra (USA) 819†
Lyre (Fra) 218
Lysekil (Swe) 645

M

M 5, M 12, M 25 et al (Pol) 499
M 21, 22, 24, 25 (Swe) 649
M 117-121 (Yug) 852
M 314, 317-324 (Yug) 853
M Fevzi Cakmak (Tur) 697
MA 1, 2, 3 (Ger) 243
Maassluis (Nld) 433
McArthur (USA) 832†
Maccah (SAr) 601
McCandless (USA) 785†, 785
McClusky (USA) 786, 787
Machinist (USA) 808
Macho de Monte 2 (Pan) 471†
McInerney (USA) 786
McKee (USA) 806
Mackinaw (USA) 827
Macko (Pol) 499
Macreuse (Fra) 226
Mactan (Plp) 488
Madadgar (Pak) 470
Madarako (Ken) 375†, 376
Madina (SAr) 599
Madrona (USA) 829
Madryn (Arg) 20
Maeklong (Tld) 685
Maersk Ascension (UK) 740†
Maersk Gannet (UK) 740†
Maestrale (Ita) 327
Magadan (Rus) 591
Magadansky Komsomolets (Rus) 565
Magar (Ind) 287
Magat Salamat (Plp) 486
Magdala (Ind) 287
Magne (Swe) 645
Magnet (UK) 750
Magnus Malan (SA) 614
Magomed Gadzhiev (Rus) 565
Magpie (UK) 750
Mahamiru (Mly) 406
Mahan (USA) 780
Maharajalela (Bru) 69
Maharajalela (Mly) 409
Maharajasetia (Mly) 409
Mahawangsa (Mly) 407
Mahé (Ind) 287
Mahish (Ind) 287
Mahkota (Mly) 409
Mahlon S Tisdale (USA) 785†, 786
Mahmood (Pak) 469
Mahnavi-Hamraz (Iran) 309
Mahnavi-Taheri (Iran) 309
Mahnavi-Vahedi (Iran) 309
Mahón (Spn) 632
Mahvan (Iran) 308
Maiduguri (Nig) 446
Main (Elbe class) (Ger) 241
Main (Rhein class) (Ger) 241
Maine (USA) 759
Maipo (Chi) 19
Maipures (Ven) 841
Maipuri (Guy) 269
Mairy (Hon) 271†
Maito (Fra) 199†, 226
Maj Stephen W Pless (USA) 820
Majang (Indo) 303
Major General Charles P Gross (USA) 798
Makar (Ind) 288
Makasib (UAE) 715
Makedonia (Gre) 257
Makigumo (Akizuki class) (Jpn) 369
Makigumo (Yamagumo class) (Jpn) 359
Makkum (Nld) 433
Mako II (NZ) 440†
Makrelen (Den) 159
Makurdi (Nig) 445
Makut Rajakumarn (Tld) 677
Malabar (Fra) 225
Malahayati (Indo) 293
Malaika (Mad) 401, 605†
Malaspina (Spn) 630
Malcolm Baldrige (USA) 832†
Mallard (Can) 99
Mallcu (Bol) 53
Mallet (USA) 831
Mallow (USA) 829
Malmö (Swe) 643
Malpe (Ind) 287
Malpelo (Col) 143
Malvan (Ind) 287
Maløy (Nor) 453
Malzwin (Nld) 437
Mamba (Ken) 375
Mamry (Pol) 495
Manabi (Ecu) 171
Manacasias (Col) 144
Manaipo (Ven) 841
Manatee Bay (Jam) 341
Manati (Ven) 842
Manaure (Ven) 841
Manawanui (NZ) 441
Manchester (UK) 727
Mandan (USA) 811
Mandau (Indo) 297
Mandorlo (Ita) 332
Mandovi (Por) 503
Mandubi (Arg) 20
Mandume (Ang) 8
Manga (Gab) 229
Mangala (Ind) 287
Mangalore (Ind) 287
Mangkasa (Mly) 408
Mango (Ita) 331
Mango II (NZ) 440†
Mangro (Pak) 463
Manguier (Fra) 226
Manini (Fra) 199†, 226
Manistee (USA) 811
Manitou (USA) 828
Manø (Den) 162
Manta (Ecu) 172
Mantilla (Arg) 19
Mantilla (Col) 143†
Mantilla (Per) 482
Manuel Crescencio Rejon (Mex) 419

Named Ships/INDEXES 865

Manuel Doblado (Mex) 418
Manuel Gutierrez Zamora (Mex) 418
Manuel Lara (Col) 143†
Manuel Villavicencio (Per) 480
Manuela Saenz (Col) 142
Manuripi (Bol) 53
Manych (Rus) 591
Manzanillo (Mex) 421
Maoming (CPR) 120
Maquinista Macías (Spn) 633
Mar Caribe (Spn) 632
Mar Chao (Por) 507
Mar del Norte (Spn) 17†, 631
Mar del Plata (Arg) 20
Mar Rojo (Spn) 632
Mar del Sur (Spn) 630
Mara (Ven) 841
Marabai (Nig) 446
Marabout (Fra) 226
Marañon (Per) 481
Marasesti (Rom) 510
Marban (UAE) 715
Marburg (Ger) 239
Marcilio Dias (Brz) 56
Mardan (Pak) 468
Marder (Ger) 238
Maresia (Por) 507
Mareta (Por) 507
Margarita (Ven) 839
Margarita Maza de Juarez (Mex) 419
Margherita (Mly) 409
Margit Rye (SA) 615†
Maria Paolina (NATO) 428†
Maria van Riebeeck (SA) 614
Mariano Escobedo (Mex) 418
Mariano G Vallejo (USA) 760
Mariategui (Per) 480
Marie Miljø (Den) 165
Marien N'Gouabi (Con) 145
Marikh (Mly) 405
Marina Tsvetayeva (Rus) 586
Marine Explorer (UK) 740†
Marinero Fuentealba (Chi) 112
Marinero Guterierrez (Chi) 112
Marinero Jarana (Spn) 633
Marinette (USA) 811
Mario L Pendo (Arg) 21
Mario Marino (Ita) 334
Mariposa (USA) 829
Mariscal Cruz (Bol) 53
Mariscal Santa Cruz (Bol) 53
Mariscal Sucre (Ven) 838
Mariz E Barros (Brz) 56
Marjata (Nor) 454
Marlborough (UK) 729
Marlin (Bhm) 36
Marlin (Mrt) 414
Marn Vichai (Tld) 687
Marne (Fra) 220
Maroa (Fra) 199†, 226
Marola (Mad) 401
Marola (Spn) 626
Maronnier (Fra) 226
Maroub (Sud) 639
Mars (Ind) 288†
Mars (Rom) 512
Mars (Rus) 572
Mars (Swi) 656
Mars (USA) 812
Marshal Gelovani (Rus) 572
Marshal Krylov (Rus) 577
Marshal Nedelin (Rus) 577
Marshal Shaposhnikov (Rus) 542
Marshal Timoshenko (Rus) 538
Marshal Ustinov (Rus) 540
Marshal Vasilevsky (Rus) 542
Marsopa (Spn) 618
Marsouin (Alg) 8
Martadinata (Indo) 295
Martha Kristina Tiyahahu (Indo) 295
Martha L Black (Can) 94
Marti (Tur) 701
Martin (Can) 100†
Martin Alvarez (Spn) 628
Martin Garcia (Arg) 20
Martin Pêcheur (Fra) 226
Martinet (Fra) 226
Mary (UK) 747
Mary Hichens (Can) 98
Maryland (USA) 759
Marysville (Can) 92
Maryut Atbarah (Egy) 181
Masan (RoK) 384
Mascardi (Arg) 21
Mascarin (Fra) 219†
Mashtan (Bhr) 39
Mashu (Jpn) 366
Mashuk (Rus) 584
Massapequa (USA) 811
Mastiff (UK) 747
Mataco (Arg) 18
Matagorda (USA) 828
Matanga (Ind) 290
Mataphon (Tld) 685
Matelot (TT) 691
Matias de Cordova (Mex) 419
Matinicus (USA) 828
Matsunami (Jpn) 369
Matsushima (Jpn) 366
Matsuyuki (Jpn) 349
Matthew (Can) 101
Maui (USA) 828
Maule (Chi) 113
Maulin (Chi) 113
Maumee (USA) 17†
Mauna Kea (USA) 804
Maursund (Nor) 453
Maury (USA) 816
Mavna 1-4, 7-16 (Tur) 711
Max Paredes (Bol) 53
Max Waldeck (Ger) 251†
Maxwell (Can) 101
Maya (Mex) 421
Mayo (Mex) 423
Mayom (Sud) 639
Mayor Jaime Arias (Col) 143
Mazatenango (Gua) 267
Mazatlan (Mex) 423
Mazlov (Rus) 559
MB series (Goryn, Sorum classes) (Rus) 595
MB series (Roslavl) (Rus) 596
Mbcko (Zai) 856
MCC 1101–MCC 1104 (Ita) 338
Mearim (Brz) 61
Mecklenburg-Vorpommern (Ger) 236
Mecosta (USA) 811
Medardo Monzon (Col) 141
Medas (Spn) 626
Medusa (Ger) 240
Meduza (Pol) 497
Meduza (Yug) 855
Medway (UK) 751
Meen (Ind) 288
Meerkatze (Ger) 250
Meersburg (Ger) 233†, 242
Meghna (Ban) 43
Mehmetcik (Tur) 703
Mei Chin (RoC) 668
Mei Lo (RoC) 668
Mei Ping (RoC) 668
Mei Sung (RoC) 668
Meiyo (Jpn) 372
Mejia (Per) 483
Melbourne (Aust) 25
Melchor Ocampo (Mex) 418
Meleban (Mly) 408
Mélèze (Fra) 226
Meliton Carvajal (Per) 480
Mella (DR) 167
Mellon (USA) 824
Mellum (Ger) 251†
Melo (Per) 482
Melton (UK) 749
Melville (Dom) 166
Mélusine (Fra) 223
Melville (USA) 814
Memphis (USA) 761†, 762
MEN 212, 215, 216 (Ita) 335
Mena II (Aust) 34
Menab (Iran) 312
Menai (UK) 749
Menominee (USA) 811
Menzel Bourguiba (Tun) 693
Menzhinsky (Rus) 546
Meon (UK) 749
Meranda (Swe) 654
Merawa (Lby) 398
Mercury (HK) 273
Mercury (Sin) 612
Mercury (USA) 819†
Mercuur (Nld) 436
Mercy (USA) 817
Merguro (Jpn) 362†
Meridan (TT) 691
Meridian (Rus) 579†
Merisier (Fra) 226
Merle (Fra) 226
Merlin (Fra) 223
Mermaid (Aust) 30
Mero (Gua) 267
Mérou (Fra) 227
Merrickville (Can) 92
Merrill (USA) 782
Merrimack (USA) 804
Mersin (Tur) 703
Mersuji (Mly) 408
Mesaha 1, 2 (Tur) 706
Mésange (Fra) 226
Mesh (Ind) 288
Messina (UK) 749
Mestre João dos Santos (Brz) 63
Metacom (USA) 811
Metalowiec (Pol) 493
Meteor (Ger) 251
Meteor (Rus) 553
Meteor (USA) 819†
Meteoro (Chi) 111
Metl (Rus) 553
Metompkin (USA) 828
Mette Miljø (Den) 165
Meuse (Fra) 220
Mewa (Pol) 494
Mezen (Rus) 587
Mezzario Britannia (USA) 819†
MFV 15, 96, 816 (UK) 750†
MFV 66 (Ban) 45
MGB 102, 110 (Bur) 77
Miami (USA) 762
Michelle Fiorillo (Ita) 339†
Michigan (USA) 759
Micronesia (Mic) 423
Middelburg (Nld) 433
Middleton (UK) 734
Midgett (USA) 824
Midhur (Ind) 287
Midia (Rom) 513
Mielno (Pol) 495
Miernyk (Rus) 589
Mifgav (Isr) 319
Miguel Malvar (Plp) 486
Miguel Ramos Arizpe (Mex) 419
Miguel Rodriguez (Ven) 840
Mihashi (Jpn) 368
Mikhail Bulgakov (Rus) 583†
Mikhail Konovalov (Rus) 587
Mikhail Krupsky (Rus) 571
Mikhail Lomonosov (Rus) 574
Mikhail Rudnitsky (Rus) 583
Mikhail Somov (Rus) 574†, 575
Mikula (Can) 100
Mikuma (Jpn) 354
Milazzo (Ita) 331
Milford (UK) 749
Milius (USA) 784
Miljø 101, 102 (Den) 165
Mill Reef (UK) 751
Millar Freeman (USA) 832†
Milos (Gre) 261
Mimer (Den) 164
Minabe (Jpn) 367
Minas Gerais (Brz) 55
Minden (Ger) 239
Minegumo (Minegumo class) (Jpn) 351
Minegumo (Shikinami class) (Jpn) 370
Miner (Rus) 558
Minerva (Ger) 240
Minerva (Ita) 329
Minerva (Nor) 456†
Mineyuki (Jpn) 349
Ministro Zenteno (Chi) 106
Mink (Can) 100†
Minna (Nig) 446
Minneapolis-St Paul (USA) 762
Miño (Spn) 629
Minoo (Jpn) 371
Minören (Swe) 649
Minos (Gre) 265
Minsk (Rus) 534†
Mir (Rus) 579
Miramichi (Can) 91
Mircea (Rom) 513
Mirto (Ita) 331†, 333†, 333
Misasa (Jpn) 368
Mishawaka (USA) 811
Miskinaw (Can) 97
Miskiy Komsomolets (Rus) 517†
Mission Bonaventura (USA) 818†
Mission Capistrano (USA) 818†
Mississippi (USA) 773
Mistral (Spn) 619
Misurata (Lby) 398
Mitar Acev (Cro) 148
Mithun (Ind) 288
Mitilo (Ita) 336
Mitrofan Moskalenko (Rus) 562
Mitscher (USA) 784
Mittelgrund (Ger) 244
Mitu (Col) 144
Miura (Izu class) (Jpn) 365
Miura (Miura class) (Jpn) 356
Mius (Rus) 587
Mivtach (Isr) 319
Mixteco (Mex) 423
Miyajima (Jpn) 358
Miyake (Kunashiri class) (Jpn) 367
Miyake (Takami class) (Jpn) 361
Miyato (Jpn) 361
Miyazuki (Jpn) 369
Mizan (Indo) 303
Miznag (Isr) 319
Mizrak (Tur) 702
Mizuho (Jpn) 365
Mizunangi (Jpn) 374
Mjölner (Swe) 645
Mlj (Yug) 853
MLMS 6-10 (Tld) 683
MM 132-133, 136-137 (Rom) 514
Moa (NZ) 440
Moa (SL) 608
Moana Wave (USA) 814
Moawin (Pak) 470
Mobile (USA) 797
Mobile Bay (Bay class) (USA) 827, 829†
Mobile Bay (Ticonderoga class) (USA) 776, 777
MOC 1201–MOC 1205 (Ita) 337
Mochishio (Jpn) 344
Mochizuki (Jpn) 370
Mochizuki (Takatsuki class) (Jpn) 350
Mocovi (Arg) 18
Mode (Swe) 645
Modig (Swe) 644
Modul (Rus) 576
Møen (Den) 162
Mogam (Iran) 312
Mogano (Ita) 331
Mohawk (Famous Cutter class) (USA) 824
Mohawk (Powhatan class) (USA) 818
Moidart (UK) 751
Moineau (Fra) 226
Moinester (USA) 785†, 785
Mok Po (RoK) 385
Moldavia (Rus) 571
Mölders (Ger) 234
Moledet (Isr) 318
Mollymawk (Aust) 32
Molnija (Rus) 553
Monastir (Tun) 693
Monge (Fra) 221
Monginsidi (Indo) 295
Monhegan (USA) 828
Monmouth (UK) 729
Mono (Tog) 689
Monob I (USA) 810, 813†
Monomoy (USA) 828
Monongahela (USA) 804
Monowai (NZ) 440†, 440
Monsoon (USA) 801
Mont Arreh (Dji) 166
Montcalm (Fra) 207
Monterey (USA) 776
Montero (Per) 480
Montevideo (Uru) 833
Montmagny (Can) 96
Montpelier (USA) 762
Montreal (Can) 85
Montrose (UK) 729
Moorfowl (UK) 745
Moorhen (UK) 745
Moosbrugger (USA) 782, 783
Moran Valverde (Ecu) 171
Morcoyan (Arg) 18
Mordoğan (Tur) 703
Moresby (Aust) 30
Moresby (Can) 90
Morgane (Fra) 223
Morgenthau (USA) 824
Moriah (TT) 690
Mornar (Yug) 851
Morona (Per) 483
Moroshima (Jpn) 358
Morro Bay (USA) 827
Morrosquillo (Col) 143
Morskoy Geofizik (Rus) 576
Moruga (TT) 690
Morven (UK) 751
Morzhovets (Rus) 572
Mosel (Ger) 241
Moses (Ger) 244†
Moskovsky Universitet (Rus) 572
Moskva (icebreaker) (Rus) 592
Moskva (Moskva class) (Rus) 538
Motajica (Yug) 853
Motobu (Atsumi class) (Jpn) 356
Motobu (Shiretoko class) (Jpn) 366
Motorist (Rus) 558
Motoura (Jpn) 367
Mou Hsing (RoC) 673
Mouette (Fra) 226
Mount Baker (USA) 803
Mount Hood (USA) 803
Mount Samat (Plp) 488
Mount Vernon (USA) 796, 818†
Mount Washington (USA) 818†
Mount Whitney (USA) 791
Mourad Rais (Alg) 5
Mouro (Spn) 626
Moussa Ali (Dji) 166
MRF 1, MRF 2 (Den) 163
MSA 4 (Den) 164
MSB 12 (RoC) 670
MSI 01, 02, 06-8 (Pak) 469
MSML 1, 3, 5-8, 11-12 (RoC) 670
MT 1 (Ger) 246
Mt Mitchell (USA) 832†
MTB 3-9 (Tur) 704
MTM 217-227, 542-556 (Ita) 335
MTP 96-107, 9726 *et al* (Ita) 335
Muavenet (Tur) 699†
Mubarraz (UAE) 715
Mudyug (Rus) 591, 593†
Muhafiz (Pak) 469
Muhammed (Jor) 374
Mujahid (Pak) 469
Mujoulqinaku (Alb) 3
Mulkae 72, 73, 75-8 (RoK) 388
Mulki (Ind) 287
Mulniya (Bul) 72
Multatuli (Indo) 301
Mungo (Cam) 82†
Munin (Den) 165
Munin (Swe) 645
Munro (USA) 824
Munsif (Pak) 469
Murakumo (Minegumo class) (Jpn) 351
Murakumo (Murakumo class) (Jpn) 369
Muratreis (Tur) 696
Murature (Arg) 15
Muray Jip (UAE) 714
Murban (UAE) 715
Mürefte (Tur) 703
Murena (Ita) 334, 336†
Murène (Alg) 8
Murmansk (Rus) 592
Muroto (cable layer) (Jpn) 361
Muroto (Erimo class) (Jpn) 366
Murotsu (Jpn) 362
Murre II (USA) 832†
Mursu (Fin) 194
Muschel (Ger) 239
Muskegon (USA) 811
Muskingum (USA) 830
Muskrat (Can) 100†
Mussa Ben Nussair (Iraq) 312
Mussandam (Omn) 458
Musson (Nanuchka class) (Rus) 553
Musson (Passat class) (Rus) 575
Mustang (USA) 828
Musters (Arg) 21
Musytari (Mly) 405
Mutiara (Mly) 407
Mutilla (Chi) 112
Mutin (Fra) 225
Mutsuki (Jpn) 370
Muzuki (Jpn) 362
MVT series (Rus) 590
Myojo (Jpn) 373
Myosotis (Bel) 48
Myrtle (UK) 747
Mysing (Swe) 645
Mysore (Ind) 280
Mystic (USA) 822

N

N 1121, 3215, 4301 *et al* (CPR) 125
N I Vaptsarov (Bul) 74
N O Salambo (Tun) 692†, 693
Naaldwijk (Nld) 433
Naantali (Fin) 190
Naarden (Nld) 433
Nacaome (Hon) 270
Nachi (Jpn) 371
Näcken (Swe) 642
Nadashio (Jpn) 344
Nadezhda (Bul) 70
Nafanua (WS) 846
Nafkratoussa (Gre) 261
Naftilos (Gre) 262
Nagakyay (Bur) 75
Nagatzuki (Jpn) 350
Naghdi (Iran) 307
Nagozuki (Jpn) 369
Nahid (Iran) 309
Nahidik (Can) 97
Nahuel Huapi (Arg) 21
Naiade (Fra) 223
Naiki Devi (Ind) 291
Naimbana (SL) 608
Najad (Swe) 642
Najim Al Zaffer (Egy) 176
Najran (SAr) 603
Nakat (Rus) 553
Nakha (Tld) 684
Naklo (Pol) 495
Nala (Indo) 293
Nalón (Spn) 626
Nam Won (RoK) 385
Nam Yang (RoK) 387
Namao (Can) 96
Nämdö (Swe) 647
Nan Hai (CPR) 133
Nan Yang (RoC) 663
Nan Yun (CPR) 135
Nanawa (Par) 474
Nanchang (CPR) 118
Nanchong (CPR) 119
Nancy (UK) 747
Nancy Bet (Isr) 316†
Nancy Daniel (PNG) 473
Nanggala (Indo) 293
Nanjing (CPR) 118
Nanning (CPR) 118
Nanping (CPR) 120
Nanryu (Jpn) 371
Nanticoke (USA) 811
Nantong (CPR) 120
Nantucket (USA) 828
Naos (Pan) 472
Naparima (TT) 691
Napo (Ecu) 173
Naporisti (Bul) 72
Napredak (Yug) 852
Nara (Rus) 582
Narcis (Bel) 48
Naresuan (Tld) 677
Narhvalen (Den) 156
Narragansett (USA) 818
Narushima (Jpn) 358
Narva (Rus) 583
Narval (Spn) 618
Narvik (Fra) 222
Narvik (Nor) 450
Narwhal (Can) 95
Narwhal (USA) 765
Nashua (USA) 811
Nashville (USA) 795
Nasr (Pak) 470
Nasr Al Bahr (Omn) 6†, 458
Nassau (USA) 793
Nastoychivy (Rus) 543
Natchitoches (USA) 811
Natick (USA) 811
Natori (Jpn) 368
Natsugiri (Jpn) 370
Natsugumo (Minegumo class) (Jpn) 351
Natsugumo (Murakumo class) (Jpn) 369
Natsushio (Jpn) 344
Natsuzuki (Jpn) 369
Natuna (Indo) 302
Naushon (USA) 828
Nautilus (Ger) 240
Nautilus (Nld) 436
Navajo (USA) 818
Navarra (Spn) 621
Navigator (Pol) 496
Navmachos (Gre) 258
Navodchik (Natya class) (Rus) 558
Navodchik (Rus) 559
Nawarat (Bur) 75
Naxos (Gre) 261
Nazario Sauro (Ita) 322
Nazim (Pak) 462†, 468
N'Diaye (Sen) 606
Neah Bay (USA) 827
Nearchos (Gre) 254
Nebraska (USA) 759
Necko (Pol) 495
Negros Occidental (Plp) 486
Neiafu (Ton) 689
Nele (Bel) 51†
Neman (Mayak class) (Rus) 587
Neman (Sorum class) (Rus) 595
Nemuro (Jpn) 356
Neodesha (USA) 811
Neon Antonov (Rus) 587
Nepomuceno Peña (Col) 142
Nepryadva (Rus) 580
Neptun (Rom) 513†
Neptun (Rus) 595
Neptun (Swe) 642
Neptune (USA) 818†
Neptuno (DR) 168
Neptuno (Per) 483†
Ner Darchau (Ger) 251†
Nereida (Spn) 633
Nereide (Fra) 223
Nereus (Gre) 254
Nerz (Ger) 237
Nestin (Yug) 853
Nestor (Gre) 265
Néstor Orpina (Col) 144
Nestos (Gre) 264
Netzahualcoyotl (Mex) 416
Neuende (Ger) 248
Neukrotimy (Rus) 546
Neuquen (Arg) 17
Neustadt (Ger) 250
Neustrashimy (Rus) 545
Neustrelitz (Ger) 249
Neuwerk (Ger) 247
Neva (Rus) 594
Nevada (USA) 759
New Orleans (USA) 794
New York City (USA) 762
Newcastle (Aust) 25
Newcastle (UK) 726
Newgagon (USA) 811
Newport News (USA) 762
Newton (UK) 745
Neyzeh (Iran) 308
Ngamia (Ken) 376
Ngurah Rai (Indo) 295
Niagara Falls (USA) 803
Niantic (USA) 811
Nibbio (Ita) 333
Nicholas (USA) 786
Nicholson (USA) 782, 783
Nicolas Suarez (Bol) 53
Nicolet (Can) 100
Niederösterreich (Aus) 34
Niedersachsen (Ger) 235
Niels Juel (Den) 157
Nienburg (Ger) 242
Nieugiety (Pol) 494
Night Hawk (Brz) 66†
Niijima (Jpn) 358
Nijigumo (Jpn) 369
Niki (Gre) 258
Nikola Martinovič (Yug) 851
Nikolai Chiker (Rus) 594
Nikolai Kolomeytsev (Rus) 577
Nikolai Yevgenov (Rus) 577
Nikolay Filchenkov (Rus) 561
Nikolay Matusevich (Rus) 572
Nikolay Sipyagin (Rus) 587
Nikolay Starshinov (Rus) 587
Nikolay Vilkov (Rus) 561
Nikolay Zubov (Rus) 572
Nikolayev (Rus) 541
Nilgiri (Ind) 282
Nils Strömcrona (Swe) 651
Nimble (UK) 746
Nimitz (USA) 766
Ningbo (CPR) 120
Ninoshima (Jpn) 358
Niovi (Gre) 262
Nipat (Ind) 284
Nipigon (Can) 86
Nirbhik (Ind) 284
Nirbhoy (Ban) 42
Nirdeshak (Ind) 288
Nireekshak (Ind) 288

866 INDEXES/Named Ships

Nirghat (Ind) ... 284
Nirupak (Ind) ... 288
Nishank (Ind) ... 284
Nisr (Egy) ... 182
Niteroi (Brz) ... 57
Nitro (USA) ... 804
Nitzhon (Isr) ... 318
Nivôse (Fra) ... 210
Niyodo (Jpn) ... 354
Njambuur (Sen) ... 606
Njord (Swe) ... 650
N'Madi (Mtn) ... 414
Noakhali (Ban) ... 43
Nobaru (Jpn) ... 368
Nodaway (USA) ... 818†
Nogales (USA) ... 811
Nogueira da Gama (Brz) ... 64
Noguera (Per) ... 482
Nojima (Jpn) ... 366
Nongsarai (Tld) ... 683
Noon (Bhr) ... 39
Norah (UK) ... 747
Norain (Bru) ... 69
Norby (Den) ... 160
Norderney (Ger) ... 247
Nordjylland (Den) ... 165
Nordkaperen (Den) ... 156
Nordkapp (Nor) ... 455
Nordkep (Nor) ... 452†
Nordsee (Ger) ... 251†
Nordsjøbas (Nor) ... 455
Nordsøen (Den) ... 165
Nordstrand (Ger) ... 248
Nordwind (Ger) ... 246
Norfolk (UK) ... 729
Norfolk (USA) ... 762, 763
Norge (Nor) ... 455
Norman McLeod Rogers (Can) ... 94
Normandy (USA) ... 776
Norna (UK) ... 751
Nornen (Nor) ... 456
Norrköping (Swe) ... 644
Norrtälje (Swe) ... 644
Norsten (Swe) ... 648
Northella (UK) ... 738, 740†
Northern Light (USA) ... 819†
Northern Samar (Plp) ... 487
Northland (USA) ... 824
Northumberland (UK) ... 729
Noshiro (Jpn) ... 354
Noto (Shiretoko class) (Jpn) ... 366
Noto (Yura class) (Jpn) ... 356
Nottingham (UK) ... 726
Novorossiysk (Rus) ... 534
Noyer (Fra) ... 226
NR 1 (USA) ... 761†, 822
Ntringui (Com) ... 145
Nube del Mar (DR) ... 169
Nuevo Rocafuerte (Ecu) ... 172
Numana (Ita) ... 331
Numancia (Spn) ... 621
Nung Ra (RoK) ... 388
Nunivak (USA) ... 828
Nunobiki (Jpn) ... 371
Nuoli 8, 10-13 (Fin) ... 191
Nurton (UK) ... 734
Nusa Telu (Indo) ... 302
Nusantara (Indo) ... 299
Nusrat (Pak) ... 469
Nusret (Tur) ... 162†, 703
Nuwajima (Jpn) ... 358
Nyayo (Ken) ... 375
Nynäshamn (Swe) ... 644
Nyong (Cam) ... 82†

O

Oak Ridge (USA) ... 808
Oakhill (USA) ... 796
Oakleaf (UK) ... 741
Ob (Rus) ... 583
O'Bannon (USA) ... 782
Oberst Brecht (Aus) ... 35
Obion (USA) ... 829
Obraztsovy (Rus) ... 544
O'Brien (Chi) ... 104
O'Brien (USA) ... 782, 783
Observation Island (USA) ... 813
Observer (Dom) ... 166
Óbuda (Hun) ... 274
Obuma (Nig) ... 444
Ocala (USA) ... 811
Ocean Surveyor (Swe) ... 651†
Oceanografico (Mex) ... 420
Oceanographer (USA) ... 832†
Ochakov (Rus) ... 541
Ocoa (DR) ... 169
Ocracoke (USA) ... 828
Odeleite (Por) ... 505
Oden (Swe) ... 650
Odenwald (Ger) ... 243
Oderbruch (Ger) ... 250
Odiel (Spn) ... 629
Odinn (Ice) ... 275
Odisseus (Gre) ... 264
Odivelas (Por) ... 505
Oeiras (Por) ... 505
Ofiom (Nig) ... 447
Ogden (USA) ... 795
Ogishima (Jpn) ... 358
Ogo (Fij) ... 188
Oguta (Nig) ... 445
Ohio (USA) ... 759
Ohue (Nig) ... 446
Ohyodo (Jpn) ... 353
Oil Mariner (UK) ... 740†
Oilbird (UK) ... 745
Oilman (UK) ... 745
Oilpress (UK) ... 745
Oilwell (UK) ... 745
Oirase (Jpn) ... 367
Ojibwa (Can) ... 83
Ojika (Miura class) (Jpn) ... 356
Ojika (Nojima class) (Jpn) ... 366
Ok Cheon (RoK) ... 387
Oka (Rus) ... 579
Okanagan (Can) ... 83
Okba (Mor) ... 425
Okean (Moma class) (Rus) ... 572
Okean (Passat class) (Rus) ... 575
Okeanos (Gre) ... 254
Oker (Ger) ... 244
Oki (Jpn) ... 366
Okinami (Jpn) ... 370
Okishio (Jpn) ... 344
Okitsu (Takami class) (Jpn) ... 358
Okitsu (Teshio class) (Jpn) ... 367
Oklahoma City (USA) ... 762
Okmulgee (USA) ... 811
Okrika (Nig) ... 446
Okrylenny (Rus) ... 543
Oksøy (Nor) ... 453
Oksywie (Pol) ... 494
Oland (Ger) ... 251†
Olaya (Per) ... 483
Olaya Herrera (Col) ... 144
Oldenburg (Ger) ... 251†
Oldendorf (USA) ... 782
Olekma (Rus) ... 581
Olfert Fischer (Den) ... 157
Olib (Cro) ... 149
Oliveira E Carmo (Por) ... 502
Oliver Hazard Perry (USA) ... 785†, 786
Oliver Twist (UK) ... 750
Olivier (Fra) ... 226
Oljevern 01, 02, 03, 04 (Nor) ... 456
Olmeda (UK) ... 741
Olna (UK) ... 741
Oltul (Rom) ... 514
Olwen (UK) ... 741
Olympia (USA) ... 762
Olympias (Gre) ... 263
Olympus (UK) ... 83†
Omaha (USA) ... 762
Ombrine (Alg) ... 8
Ommen (Nld) ... 433
Ona (Arg) ... 18
Ona (Chi) ... 113
Onaizah (SAr) ... 601
Onaran (Tur) ... 708
Öncü (Tur) ... 711
Onda (Rus) ... 586
Önder (Tur) ... 711
Ondine (Fra) ... 223
Onega (Rus) ... 587
Onjuku (Mex) ... 420
Onondaga (Can) ... 83
Onslow (Aust) ... 23
Ooi (Jpn) ... 360†
Oolah (Aust) ... 34
Ooshima (Jpn) ... 358
Oosumi (Jpn) ... 365
Opelika (USA) ... 811
Opossum (UK) ... 723
Opportune (USA) ... 806
Oqbah (SAr) ... 601
Orage (Fra) ... 215
Orangeleaf (UK) ... 741
Orca (USA) ... 809
Orcas (USA) ... 828
Orce Nikolov (Yug) ... 851
Ordóñez (Spn) ... 626
Oregon II (USA) ... 832†
Öregrund (Swe) ... 645
Orel (Rus) ... 546
Öresund (Swe) ... 647
Orfe (Ger) ... 239
Oriole (Can) ... 90
Oriole (USA) ... 800
Orion (Aust) ... 23
Orion (Brz) ... 63
Orion (DR) ... 168
Orion (Ecu) ... 173
Orion (Fra) ... 218
Orion (Gre) ... 264
Orion (Rus) ... 595
Orion (Swe) ... 651
Orion (Swi) ... 656
Orkan (Pol) ... 493
Orkla (Nor) ... 453
Orkney (UK) ... 738
Orla (Ire) ... 316
Ormi (Gre) ... 259
Ørn (Nor) ... 451
Orompello (Chi) ... 109
Orsa (Ita) ... 328
Orsha (Rus) ... 582
Örskaur (Swe) ... 646
Orson (Rus) ... 589
Ortolan (USA) ... 807, 822†
Orucreis (Tur) ... 699
Orwell (Pak) ... 470
Orwell (UK) ... 734
Oryx (Nam) ... 427†
Orzel (Pol) ... 491
OS 01-OS 03 (Jpn) ... 373
OS 572 (Rus) ... 572
OS-100, 138, 145, 225 (Rus) ... 588
Osage (USA) ... 829
Oscarsborg (Nor) ... 452†
Oshkosh (USA) ... 811
Osiris (Can) ... 83†
Oslo (Nor) ... 450
Osman (Ban) ... 40
Osman Gazi (Tur) ... 704
Osmotritelny (Rus) ... 543
Osorno (Chi) ... 112
Osprey (Can) ... 99
Osprey (UK) ... 751
Osprey (USA) ... 800
Oste (Ger) (Ger) ... 244
Östergötland (Swe) ... 641
Östhammar (Swe) ... 645
Oswald Pirow (SA) ... 614
Oswald Siahann (Indo) ... 294
Oswaldo Cruz (Brz) ... 65
Otama (Aust) ... 23
Otchyanny (Rus) ... 543
Otlichnny (Rus) ... 543
Otobo (Nig) ... 444
Otomi (Mex) ... 422
Otowa (Jpn) ... 371
Otra (Nor) ... 453
Otso (Fin) ... 193
Ottawa (Can) ... 85
Otter (Aust) ... 33
Otto Treplin (Ger) ... 251†
Ottumwa (USA) ... 811
Otway (Aust) ... 23
Ouachita (USA) ... 829
Ouessant (Fra) ... 203
Ouistreham (Fra) ... 218
Oulu (Fin) ... 190
Oumi (Jpn) ... 362
Ouragan (Cam) ... 82†
Ouragan (Fra) ... 215
Ouranos (Gre) ... 264
Ovens (Aust) ... 23
Owerri (Nig) ... 446
Oyashio (Jpn) ... 372
Ozelot (Ger) ... 237
Özgen (Tur) ... 711

P

P 1-P 23 (Fra) ... 226
P 03, 04 (StL) ... 598
P 07-11, 101-106 (Par) ... 475
P 15 (Eth) ... 186
P 23, P 27, P 29, P32, *et al* (Mlt) ... 412
P 24-P 27 (Bru) ... 69
P 25, P 26, P 30, P 31 (Mlt) ... 411
P 30, 35 (Gn) ... 268
P 30-33, 34-37, 101-105 (Bhm) ... 37
P 101-102, 124, 231-235 *et al* (Spn) ... 627
P 101-109, P 151-152 (Sri) ... 637
P 111-123, P 140-149 (Sri) ... 638
P 201, 214, 221, 231 *et al* (Sri) ... 637
P 203, 204, 206, 207 (Eth) ... 186
P 215-219, 227-232 (Nig) ... 445
P 233-238, P 239-42 (Nig) ... 446
P 301-P 304 (Pak) ... 468
P 311-P 313 (Spn) ... 627
P 401-P 403 (Sur) ... 639
P 463-468, 453-458, 473-475 (Sri) ... 636
P 551-P 568 (Pak) ... 471
P 700 series (Fra) ... 228
P 1551, P 1555 (SA) ... 616
P 8002-8003, 3004-3005 (Brz) .. 62
P Khlyustin (Rus) ... 579†
P Kudrevich (Rus) ... 579†
P Minyayev (Rus) ... 579†
P Pakhtusov (Rus) ... 593
P Pavlenko (Rus) ... 579†
P Rybaltovsky (Rus) ... 579†
P Shchyogolev (Rus) ... 579†
P Ukhov (Rus) ... 579†
P W Botha (SA) ... 614
P Yushchenko (Rus) ... 579†
PA 3 (Fin) ... 196†
Pabbatha (Sri) ... 638
Pabna (Ban) ... 43
Pacific Sentry (USA) ... 826
Pacocha (Per) ... 477†
Paderborn (Ger) ... 239
Padma (Ban) ... 43
Padre (USA) ... 828
Paducah (USA) ... 811
PAE KU series (RoK) ... 386
Paea II (NZ) ... 440†
Pahlawan (Mly) ... 409
Paita (Per) ... 481
Pakan Baru (Indo) ... 302
Palacios (Per) ... 479
Palang (Iran) ... 306
Palatka (USA) ... 811
Palawan (Plp) ... 490
Paletuvier (Fra) ... 226
Palikir (Mic) ... 423
Palinuro (Ita) ... 336
Pallada (Rus) ... 579
Palma (Ita) ... 331
Palmaria (Ita) ... 337
Paluma (Aust) ... 30
Pamir (Rus) ... 584
Pamlico (USA) ... 830
Pampano (Gua) ... 267
Pampanu (Gua) ... 267
Pampeiro (Brz) ... 62
Pamyat Merkuryia (Rus) ... 572
Pan Chao (RoC) ... 664
Panah (Mly) ... 406
Panan (Indo) ... 303
Pandbong (Indo) ... 298
Pandora (Gre) ... 264
Pandrosos (Gre) ... 264
Pangai (Ton) ... 689
Pangan (Tld) ... 684
Pangasinan (Plp) ... 486
Panonsko More (Yug) ... 853
Panquiaco (Pan) ... 472
Pansio (Fin) ... 192
Pantellaria (Ita) ... 334
Panther (Ger) ... 238
Panthère (Fra) ... 225
Panuco (Mex) ... 421
Pao Hsing (RoC) ... 673
Paolucci (Ita) ... 335
Papanikolis (Gre) ... 253
Papaw (USA) ... 829
Papayer (Fra) ... 226
Papudo (Chi) ... 109
Pará (Brz) ... 58
Paraguassu (Brz) ... 65
Paraguay (Par) ... 474
Paraíba (Brz) ... 58
Paraibano (Brz) ... 64
Parainen (Fin) ... 196
Paraná (Brz) ... 58
Parang (Indo) ... 303
Parati (Brz) ... 62
Parayan (Rus) ... 558
Parche (USA) ... 764
Pargo (USA) ... 764
Pari (Mly) ... 406
Parinas (Per) ... 482
Parizeau (Can) ... 101
Parker (Arg) ... 14
Parksville (Can) ... 92
Parnaiba (Brz) ... 61
Paros (Gre) ... 261
Parramatta (Aust) ... 27
Partisan (Den) ... 162
Partizan, Partizan II, III (Yug) ... 852
Partridge Island (Can) ... 97
Parvin (Iran) ... 309
Pasadena (USA) ... 762
Passat (Rus) ... 575
Passau (Ger) ... 240
Passereau (Fra) ... 226
Passopp (Swe) ... 653
Pastor Rouaix (Mex) ... 419
PAT 01-PAT 06 (Indo) ... 303
Pathfinder (USA) ... 816
Patoka (USA) ... 830
Patos (Alb) ... 3
Patria (Ven) ... 839
Patriot (USA) ... 799
Patriot State (USA) ... 819†
Patriote (Ben) ... 52
Patrioten (Den) ... 162
Patuakhali (Ban) ... 43
Patuxent (USA) ... 817
Paul Bogle (Jam) ... 270†, 341
Paul Buck (USA) ... 817
Paul F Foster (USA) ... 782
Paul Hamilton (USA) ... 784
Paulo Afonso (Brz) ... 67†
Paus (Mly) ... 406
Pavayacu (Per) ... 481†
Pavel Bashmakov (Rus) ... 577
Pavel Gordiyenko (Rus) ... 576
Pawhuska (USA) ... 811
Paysandu (Uru) ... 834
PB 23-PB 27 (Jpn) ... 355
PB 60-PB 74 (RoC) ... 667
PBC 3501-3526, 5501-5507 (RoC) ... 668
PBR 211-PBR 216 (Bur) ... 77
PC 32-51, 52-65 (Sin) ... 612
PC 211-216, 301-304, 306 (Yug) ... 852
PC 211-216 (Yug) ... 851
PC 501-503, 505-507 (RoK) ... 390
PC 1001-PC 1003 (RoK) ... 390
PCL 1-22 (RoC) ... 668
PD 41, PD 50 (Rus) ... 596
PDB 12-PDB 15 (Bru) ... 69
Pea Island (USA) ... 828
Peacock (UK) ... 739
Pechenga (Rus) ... 581
Pechora (Alesha class) (Rus) ... 559
Pechora (Partizan class) (Rus) ... 587
Pecos (USA) ... 817
Pedang (Indo) ... 303
Pedro de Heredia (Col) ... 141
Pedro Teixeira (Brz) ... 61
Pegas (Rus) ... 572
Pégase (Fra) ... 218
Pegasus (USA) ... 802
Peggy (USA) ... 799†
Pegnitz (Ger) ... 240
Pejuang (Bru) ... 68
Pekan (Mly) ... 409
Peleliu (USA) ... 793
Peleng (Rus) ... 569
Pelias (Gre) ... 265
Pelican (USA) ... 800
Pelikaan (Nld) ... 436
Pelikan (Ger) ... 238
Pelikan (Pol) ... 494
Pelikan (Tur) ... 701
Pelikanen (Swe) ... 652
Pelops (Gre) ... 265
Pemburu (Bru) ... 68
Pendant (USA) ... 831
Pendekar (Mly) ... 405
Penedo (Brz) ... 62
Penhors (Fra) ... 219†
Peninsula de Araya (Ven) ... 840
Peninsula de Paraguana (Ven) ... 840
Penjaga (Mly) ... 409
Pennsylvania (USA) ... 759
Penobscot Bay (USA) ... 827
Pensacola (USA) ... 796
Penyerang (Bru) ... 68
Penyu (Mly) ... 408
Peoria (USA) ... 797
Perak (Mly) ... 409
Perangan (Mly) ... 408
Perch (UK) ... 751
Perdana (Mly) ... 405
Perekop (Rus) ... 579
Peresvet (Rus) ... 593
Perkasa (Mly) ... 405
Perkun (Pol) ... 499
Perle (Fra) ... 202
Pernambuco (Brz) ... 58
Persée (Fra) ... 218
Perseo (Ita) ... 328
Perseus (Swi) ... 656
Persey (Rus) ... 572
Persistence (Sin) ... 611
Persistent (USA) ... 815
Pertanda (Mly) ... 409
Perth (Anzac class) (Aust) ... 27
Perth (mod DDG 2 class) (Aust) ... 24
Pertuisane (Fra) ... 228
Perwira (Bru) ... 68
Perwira (Mly) ... 409
Pescarusul (Rom) ... 511
Peshawar (Pak) ... 471
Petalesharo (USA) ... 811
Petar Drapšin (Yug) ... 851
Peter Bachmann (Ger) ... 246
Peter Tordenskiold (Den) ... 157
Petersburg (USA) ... 818†
Peterson (USA) ... 782
Petr Ilichev (Rus) ... 561
Petr Kotsov (Rus) ... 576
Petrel (Arg) ... 17
Petrel (HK) ... 272
Petrel (USA) ... 828
Petrel (Ven) ... 841
Petrohue (Chi) ... 113
Petropavlovsk (Rus) ... 541
Petula (Hon) ... 270
Peuplier (Fra) ... 226
Peyk (Tur) ... 700
PFC Dewayne T Williams (USA) ... 821
PFC Eugene A Obregon (USA) ... 820
PFC James Anderson Jr (USA) .. 820
PFC Willian B Baugh (USA) ... 820
PG 01, 02, 03 (Jpn) ... 356
PGM 401-406, 412-415 (Bur) ... 76
Pham Ngu Lao (Vtn) ... 843
Phetra (Tld) ... 685
Philadelphia (USA) ... 762
Philippine Sea (USA) ... 776
Philips van Almonde (Nld) ... 431
Phoebus (USA) ... 810†
Phoenix (USA) ... 762
Phosamton (Tld) ... 685
Phraongkamrop (Tld) ... 688
Phromyothee (Tld) ... 687
Phuket (Tld) ... 681
Pi An (RoK) ... 388
Piast (Pol) ... 498
Piave (Ita) ... 337
Picharnpholakit (Tld) ... 688
Picuá (DR) ... 169
Picua (Ven) ... 837†
Picuda (Gua) ... 267
Pierce (USA) ... 832†
Pierre Radisson (Can) ... 93
Piet Heyn (Nld) ... 431
Pieter Florisz (Nld) ... 431
Pietro Cavezzale (Ita) ... 334
Pigasos (Gre) ... 259
Pijao (Col) ... 139
Pilefs (Gre) ... 265
Pilen (Swe) ... 645
Pillan (Chi) ... 112
Piloto Alsina (Arg) ... 18
Piloto Pardo (Chi) ... 108, 109†
Pin Klao (Tld) ... 679
Pinar 1-Pinar 6 (Tur) ... 709
Pinega (Rus) ... 566
Ping Jin (RoC) ... 667
Pinguin (Ger) ... 238
Pingvinen (Swe) ... 652
Pingxiang (CPR) ... 119
Pinson (Fra) ... 226
Pintado (USA) ... 764
Pioneer (USA) ... 799
Pioneer Commander (USA) ... 819†
Pioneer Contractor (USA) ... 819†
Pioneer Crusader (USA) ... 819†
Pionera (Bol) ... 53
Pionir, Pionir II (Yug) ... 852
Pioppo (Ita) ... 333†, 333
Piorun (Pol) ... 493
Piqua (USA) ... 811
Piraim (Brz) ... 65
Pirajá (Brz) ... 62
Piratini (Brz) ... 62
Pirireis (Tur) ... 696
Pirpolitis (Gre) ... 258
Pisagua (Per) ... 477
Pisces IV (Can) ... 89†
Pisco (Per) ... 481
Pishin (Pak) ... 468
Piteå (Swe) ... 644
Pittsburgh (USA) ... 762
Pivert (Fra) ... 226
Piyale Pasca (Tur) ... 697
PK 151-189 series (RoK) ... 387
PKM 200 series (RoK) ... 387
PL 20-21, 22-32, 35-36, *et al* (HK) ... 273
PL 60-PL 68 (HK) ... 272
Plan de Iguala (Mex) ... 422
Planet (Ger) ... 245
Planeta (Pol) ... 497†
Planetree (USA) ... 829
Platane (Fra) ... 226
Platano (Ita) ... 332
Platte (USA) ... 804
PLC 1-4 (Mly) ... 409
Pledge (USA) ... 800
Pleias (Gre) ... 262
Plotarhis Blessas (Gre) ... 258
Plotze (Ger) ... 239
Plover (UK) ... 739
Plug (Rus) ... 593
Pluton (Fra) ... 218
Pluton (Rus) ... 572
Plymouth (TT) ... 690
PM series (Amur, Oskol classes) (Rus) ... 567
PM series (Malina class) (Rus) ... 566
PN 20, 21 (Yug) ... 855
PO 51 (Cro) ... 150
Po Hang (RoK) ... 385
Pochard (UK) ... 745
Pochetny (Rus) ... 595
Podchorazy (Pol) ... 496
Podgora (Yug) ... 853
Podor (Sen) ... 605
Pogo (Can) ... 92
Pogy (USA) ... 764
Pohjanmaa (Fin) ... 192
Pohorje (Yug) ... 852
Point Arena (USA) ... 828
Point Baker (USA) ... 828
Point Barnes (USA) ... 828
Point Batan (USA) ... 828
Point Bennett (USA) ... 828
Point Bonita (USA) ... 828
Point Bridge (USA) ... 828
Point Brower (USA) ... 828
Point Camden (USA) ... 828
Point Carrew (USA) ... 828
Point Chico (USA) ... 828
Point Countess (USA) ... 828
Point Divide (USA) ... 828
Point Doran (USA) ... 828
Point Estero (USA) ... 828
Point Evans (USA) ... 828
Point Francis (USA) ... 828
Point Franklin (USA) ... 828
Point Glass (USA) ... 828
Point Hannon (USA) ... 828
Point Henry (Can) ... 99
Point Heyer (USA) ... 828
Point Highland (USA) ... 828
Point Hobart (USA) ... 828
Point Huron (USA) ... 828
Point Jackson (USA) ... 828
Point Ledge (USA) ... 828
Point Lobos (USA) ... 828
Point Lookout (USA) ... 828
Point Martin (USA) ... 828
Point Monroe (USA) ... 828
Point Nowell (USA) ... 828
Point Race (Can) ... 99
Point Richmond (USA) ... 828
Point Sal (USA) ... 828
Point Spencer (USA) ... 828
Point Steele (USA) ... 828
Point Stuart (USA) ... 828
Point Swift (USA) ... 828
Point Turner (USA) ... 828
Point Warde (USA) ... 828
Point Wells (USA) ... 828
Point Whitehorn (USA) ... 828
Point Winslow (USA) ... 828
Pointer (UK) ... 747
Poisk (Rus) ... 576
Pokagon (USA) ... 811
Polar (Ang) ... 8

Polar (Por) 507
Polar Sea (USA) 827
Polar Star (USA) 827
Polaris (Mrt) 414
Polaris (Ven) 841
Polarstern (icebreaker) (Ger) .... 251†
Polarstern (research ship) (Ger) . 251
Polcino (Mex) 419
Polcuatro (Mex) 419
Poldos (Mex) 419
Polemetchik (Rus) 558
Polemistis (Gre) 258
Polifemo (Ita) 338
Polipo (Ita) 336
Pollux (Aust) 34
Pollux (Mrt) 414
Pollux (Spn) 630
Pollux (Swi) 656
Pollux (USA) 821
Polocho (Mex) 419
Polsiete (Mex) 419
Poltres (Mex) 419
Poluno (Mex) 419
Polux (Gua) 267
Polyus (Rus) 571
Ponce (USA) 795
Pondicherry (Ind) 288
Ponoi (Rus) 587
Ponton 1–Ponton 7 (Tur) 709
Pontos (Gre) 254
Ponza (Ita) 337
Poolster (Nld) 435
Popenguine (Sen) 605
Porbandar (Ind) 288
Porkkala (Fin) 192
Porpora (Ita) 336
Port Hardy (Can) 99
Port Mouton (Can) 99
Port Nelson (Bhm) 36
Port Royal (USA) 776
Porte Dauphine (Can) 91
Porte de la Reine (Can) 91
Porte Quebec (Can) 91
Porte St Jean (Can) 91
Porte St Louis (Can) 91
Portland (USA) 796
Porto Conte (Ita) 338
Porto Corsini (Ita) 338
Porto d'Ischia (Ita) 338
Porto Empedocle (Ita) 338
Porto Esperança (Brz) .... 61†
Porto Ferraio (Ita) 338
Porto Fossone (Ita) 338
Porto Pisano (Ita) 338
Porto Salvo (Ita) 338
Porto Torres (Ita) 338
Porto Venere (Ita) 338
Portsmouth (USA) 762
Porvoo (Fin) 190
Poryvisty (Rus) 546
Poseda (Bul) 70
Poséidon (Fra) 224
Poseidon (Ger) 251
Poseidón (Spn) 632
Poshak (Ind) 289
Posidon (Cypr) 155
Posydon (Gre) 254
Posyet (Rus) 586
Potengi (Brz) 65
Poti (Brz) 62
Potomac (USA) .... 818†, 820
Poughkeepsie (USA) 811
Powerful (Bmd) .... 52†
Powerful (UK) 746
Powhatan (USA) 818
Poyraz (Tur) 701
Poznan (Pol) 495
PP series (RoC) .... 673†
Ppiboy (Bul) 72
PR 01–PR 30 (Cam) 82
PR 36-39 (Yug) 855
Prab (Tld) 684
Prabal (Ind) 286
Prabparapak (Tld) 681
Prachand (Ind) 286
Pradhayak (Ind) 289
Prairial (Fra) 210
Pralaya (Ind) 286
Prasae (Tld) 678
Prat (Chi) 105
Pratap (Ind) 286
Prathong (Tld) 684
Predanny (Rus) 548
Prefecto Derbes (Arg) 19
Prefecto Pique (Arg) 19
Premier Maître l'Her (Fra) 212
Preserver (Can) 89
Preserver (HK) 272
President El Hadj Omar Bongo (Gab) 229
President Tito (Mlt) 411
Presidente Eloy Alfaro (Ecu) 171
Presidente Rivera (Uru) 836
Prespa (Gre) 265
Prestol (DR) 167
Prevail (USA) 815
Preveze (Tur) 695
Priboy (Rus) 575
Pride (USA) .... 819†
Prignitz (Ger) 250
Priliv (Nanuchka class) (Rus) 553
Priliv (Passat class) (Rus) 575
Primauguet (Fra) 207
Primerny (Rus) 548
Primo Longobardo (Ita) 322
Primorye (Primorye class) (Rus) . 568
Primorye (Sorum class) (Rus) 595
Primula (Bel) 48
Princeton (USA) 776
Principe de Asturias (Spn) .... 620, 675†
Pripyat (Rus) 559
Prisma (Fin) 196
Priwall (Ger) .... 251†
Priyadarsini (Ind) 291
Probstei (Ger) .... 251†
Procida (Ita) 337
Procion (DR) 168
Procyon (Gua) 267
Proet (Tld) 687
Professor Anichkov (Rus) .... 579†
Professor Bogorov (Rus) 577
Professor Fedyinsky (Rus) 576
Professor Gagarinsky (Rus) 576
Professor Golitsyn (Rus) 576
Professor Khromov (Rus) 576
Professor Kurentsov (Rus) 577
Professor Multanovsky (Rus) 576
Professor Pavel Molchanov (Rus) 576
Professor Polshkov (Rus) 576
Professor Shtokman (Rus) 577
Professor Vieze (Rus) 575
Professor Vodyanitsky (Rus) 577
Professor Zubov (Rus) 575
Progreso (Mex) 422
Progreso (Par) 476
Proleter (Yug) 852
Prometeo (Ita) 338
Proserpina (Spn) 633
Protea (SA) 615
Protecteur (Can) 89
Protector (Aust) 32
Protector (HK) 272
Protec (Ita) 336
Proteus (Gre) 254
Proud Seahorse (UK) .... 740†
Providence (USA) 762
Providencia (Col) 143
Provider (Can) .... 89, 89†
Provo Wallis (Can) 96
Provorny (Rus) 548
Prut (Rus) 581
Psara (Gre) 256
Psyché (Fra) 203
PT 1–PT 23 (Sin) 612
PT 15 (Jpn) 355
PT 82, 83, 86, 87 (Yug) 855
Pucallpa (Per) .... 483†
Puck (Pol) 494
Pudeto (Chi) 113
Puebla (Mex) 419
Puelo (Arg) 21
Puerto Cabello (Ven) 840
Puerto Deseado (Arg) 17
Puffer (USA) 764
Puffin (HK) 272
Puget Sound (USA) 803
Pula (Yug) 850
Pulai (Mly) 409
Pulau Rani (Indo) 300
Pulau Ratewo (Indo) 300
Pulau Rengat (Indo) 300
Pulau Rupat (Indo) 300
Pulkovo (Rus) 585
Puma (Ger) 237
Puncher (UK) 739
Puni (Bru) 68
Punjab (Pak) 468
Puno (Per) 483
Punta Ballena (Ven) 841
Punta Barima (Ven) 841
Punta Brava (Ven) 840
Punta Burica (CR) 147
Punta Cardon (Ven) 841
Punta Caxinas (Hon) 271
Punta Macoya (Ven) 841
Punta Macuro (Ven) 841
Punta Mariusa (Ven) 841
Punta Mastun (Mex) 419
Punta Moron (Ven) 841
Punta Morro (Mex) 419
Punta Mosquito (Ven) 841
Punta Mulatos (Ven) 841
Punta Perret (Ven) 841
Punta Playa (Ven) 841
Punta Unare (Ven) 841
Purak (Ind) 289
Puran (Ind) 289
Purga (Rus) 593
Pursuer (UK) 739
Purus (Brz) 61
Pusan 801-3, 805-6 (RoK) 389
Pushmataha (USA) 811
Pushpa (Ind) 289
Putsaari (Fin) 196
Putumayo (Ecu) 173
PV 10-12, 30-37 (HK) 273
PV 11, 104, 205, 306 *et al* (Fin) 198
Pvt Franklin J Phillips (USA) 820
PX 10–PX 33 (Sin) 612
Pyhauranta (Fin) 192
Pyi Daw Aye (Bur) 79
Pylky (Rus) 546
Pyotr Velikiy (Rus) 536
Pyro (USA) 804
Pytheas (Gre) 262
Pytlivy (Rus) 546, 547
PZHK series (Rus) 590
PZHS 64, 92, 96 *et al* (Rus) 584

Q

Q 2 (Omn) 458
Q 31–Q 36, Q 71–Q 95 (Qat) 508
Qa'am (Iran) .... 309†
Qadissiyat Saddam (Iraq) 315
Qaysan (Sud) 639
Qena (Egy) 180
Qionsha (CPR) .... 130†
Quartier Maître Anquetil (Fra) 212
Querandi (Arg) 18
Quest (Can) 91
Quetzalcoatl (Mex) 416
Quezon (Plp) 485
Qui Nonh (Vtn) 845
Quidora (Chi) 108
Quillen (Arg) 21
Quilotoa (Ecu) 174
Quindio (Col) 143
Quiñones (Per) 479
Quisquis (Ecu) 173
Quita Sueno (Col) 141
Quito (Ecu) 172
Quokka (Aust) 32
Quorn (UK) 734

R

R 1 (Omn) 459
R 2, R 4-7 (Par) 475
R 21, 23, 27, 29 (Cub) 154
R 327 (CPR) 131
R B Young (Can) 101
Raahe (Fin) 190
Rabha (Qat) .... 509†
Racine (USA) .... 797, 799†
Rad (Lby) 397
Rade Končar (Yug) 851
Radhwa 1-6, 12, 14-17 (SAr) 602
Radist (Rus) 558
Radoom (UAE) 715
Raduga (Rus) 553
Rafael del Castillo y Rada (Col) .. 141
Rafaqat (Pak) 469
Raffaele Rossetti (Ita) .... 334†, 334
Rahav (Isr) 317
Rahmat (Mly) 403
Raif Denktas (Tur) 712
Rainier (USA) .... 805, 832†
Rais Ali (Alg) 5
Rais Hamidou (Alg) 5
Rais Kellich (Alg) 5
Rais Korfou (Alg) 5
Raisio (Fin) 191
Rajah Humabon (Plp) 485
Rajah Jarom (Mly) 407
Rajah Lakandula (Plp) .... 485†
Rajaji (Ind) 290
Rajhans (Ind) 292
Rajkamal (Ind) 292
Rajkiran (Ind) 292
Rajput (Ind) 280
Rajshahi (Pak) 468
Rajshree (Ind) 292
Rajtarang (Ind) 292
Raju (Fin) 195
Rakata (Indo) 303
Rakshaka (Sri) 636
Ramadan (Egy) 178
Ramadan (Yem) 847
Ramadevi (Ind) 291
Ramage (USA) 784
Rambler (USA) 831
Raminthra (Tld) 688
Ramiz Sadiku (Yug) 851
Ramses (Egy) 182
Rana (Ind) 280
Ranagaja (Sri) 638
Ranakamee (Sri) 636
Ranarisi (Sri) 636
Ranasuru (Sri) 636
Ranawiru (Sri) 636
Rancagua (Chi) 109
Rance (Fra) 219
Rang (Tld) 687
Rangamati (Ban) 43
Range Sentinel (USA) 813
Ranger (UK) 739
Ranger I (StK) 597
Rani Jindan (Ind) 291
Ranjit (Ind) 280
Rankin (Aust) 23
Rano Kau (Chi) 112
Ranvijay (Ind) 280
Ranvir (Ind) 280
Rapel (Chi) 113
Raposo Tavares (Brz) 61
Rapp (Nor) 452
Rappahanock (USA) 817
Rari (Fra) .... 199†, 220
Ras Ajdir (Tun) 694
Ras Al Fulaija (Lby) 398
Ras Al Hamman (Lby) 398
Ras Al Hani (Lby) 398
Ras Al Madwar (Lby) 398
Ras Al Massad (Lby) 398
Ras Al Qula (Lby) 398
Ras El Blad (Tun) 694
Ras El Drek (Tun) 694
Ras El Helal (Lby) 400
Ras Maamoura (Tun) 694
Ras Tarsa (Alg) 7
Rask (Nor) 452
Rastoropny (Rus) 543
Ratcharit (Tld) 680
Ratnagiri (Ind) 288
Rattanakosin (Tld) 679
Rauma (Fin) 190
Rauma (Nor) 453
Raunen (Den) 159
Ravn (Nor) 451
Rawi (Tld) 685
Razia Sultana (Ind) 291
Razitelny (Rus) 546
Razumny (Rus) 546
Rbigah (Qat) 508
RCP 1–RCP 9 (Mly) 407
Reasoner (USA) .... 699†
Rebun (Jpn) 366
Recalde (Spn) 625
Reclaimer (USA) 806, 808
Recover (TT) 691
Recovery (USA) 806
Red Beech (USA) 829
Red Birch (USA) 829
Red Cedar (USA) 829
Red Oak (USA) 829
Red Wood (USA) 829
Redeem (TT) 691
Redpole (UK) 739
Redstone (USA) 814
Reduktor (Rus) 570
Redwing (USA) 811
Reeves (USA) 779
Reform (TT) 691
Regent (UK) .... 743†
Regge (Nld) 437
Regina (Can) 85
Regulus (USA) 821
Rehab (TT) 691
Rehmat (Pak) 469
Reid (USA) 786
Reiher (Ger) 238
Reina Sofiá (Spn) 621
Reinøysund (Nor) 453
Reiun (Jpn) 373
Relay (TT) 691
Relentless (USA) 815
Reliance (dry dock) (USA) 808
Reliance (Reliance class) (USA) . 825
Reluctant Lady (Aust) .... 33†
Remada (Tun) 693
Renchong (Mly) 406
Rencong (Indo) 297
Renown (UK) 720
Rentaka (Mly) 406
Rentz (USA) 786
Repiter (Rus) 570
Repulse (UK) 720
Requin (Alg) 8
Rescuer (HK) 272
Rescuer (Mrt) 415
Researcher (USA) .... 832†
Reshef (Isr) 318
Reshitelni (Bul) 71
Resitelny (Rus) 548
Resko (Pol) 495
Resolute (dry dock) (USA) 808
Resolute (Reliance class) (USA) . 825
Resolution (Sin) 611
Resolution (UK) 720
Resource (UK) 743
Resourceful (USA) 808
Restauracion (DR) 167
Restigouche (Can) 87
Retalhuleu (Gua) 267
Retivy (Rus) 546
Retriever (Mrt) 415
Rettin (Ger) 250
Reuben James (USA) 786
Revelle (USA) 815
Revenge (UK) .... 720†
Revi (Fra) .... 199†, 220
Review (TT) 691
Revnostny (Rus) 546
Reyes (Chi) .... 111†
Rezky (Rus) 546
Rezvy (Rus) 546
Rhein (Ger) 241
Rheinland-Pfalz (Ger) 235
Rhin (Fra) 219
Rhode Island (USA) 759
Rhön (Ger) 241
Rhon (Ger) 250
Rhône (Fra) 219
Rhoun (Ger) 241
Riachuelo (Brz) 54
Riazi (Iran) 310
Ribble (UK) 734
Ribeira Grande (Por) 506
Richard B Russell (USA) 764
Richard G Mathieson (USA) 817
Richland (USA) 808
Richmond (UK) 729
Richmond K Turner (USA) 779
Rift (Rus) 577
Rig Seismic (Aust) .... 30†
Rigel (Ecu) 172
Rigel (Mrt) 414
Rigel (Spn) 630
Rigel (Ven) 841
Rihtniemi (Fin) 191
Rimac (Per) .... 481†
Rimfaxe (Den) 163
Rimini (Ita) 331
Rin (Tld) 687
Ringen (Den) 161
Rio Altagracia (Ven) 841
Rio Apure II (Ven) 842
Rio Arauca II (Ven) 842
Rio Atrato (Col) 142
Rio Azangaro (Per) 481
Rio Babahoyo (Ecu) 175
Rio Bocono (Ven) 841
Rio Branco (Brz) 64
Rio Bueno (Chi) 113
Rio Cabriales (Ven) 842
Rio Capanaparo (Ven) 841
Rio Caparo (Ven) 841
Rio Caribe (Ven) 842
Rio Caroni (Ven) 841
Rio Catatumbo II (Ven) 842
Rio Cauca (Col) 142
Rio Caura (Ven) 841
Rio Chama (Ven) 842
Rio Chira (Per) 484
Rio Chone (Ecu) 175
Rio Chui (Brz) 67
Rio Cuyuni (Ven) 841
Rio Das Contas (Brz) 67
Rio Daule (Ecu) 175
Rio Deseado (Arg) 20
Rio Doce (Brz) .... 67†
Rio Escalante (Ven) 841
Rio Formoso (Brz) 67
Rio Grande do Norte (Brz) 56
Rio Grita (Ven) 841
Rio Guainia (Ven) 841
Rio Guanare (Ven) 841
Rio Guarico II (Ven) 842
Rio Huarmey (Per) 483
Rio Icabaru (Ven) 842
Rio Ilave (Per) 481
Rio Inambari (Per) 481
Rio de Janeiro (Brz) 60
Rio Limay (Arg) 21
Rio Limon (Ven) 841
Rio Locumba (Per) 483
Rio Lujan (Arg) 20
Rio Lurin (Per) 484
Rio Magdalena (Col) 142
Rio Majes (Per) 484
Rio Manu (Per) 481
Rio Manzanares (Ven) 841
Rio Matage (Ecu) 175
Rio Meta II (Ven) 842
Rio Minho (Por) 504
Rio Motatan (Ven) 841
Rio Negro (Arg) 17
Rio Negro (Brz) 67
Rio Negro (Uru) 834
Rio Negro II (Ven) 842
Rio Nepeña (Per) 483
Rio Neveri (Ven) 841
Rio Ocoña (Per) 483
Rio Oiapoque (Brz) 67
Rio Orinoco (Ven) 841
Rio Paraguay (Arg) 20
Rio Paraña (Arg) 20
Rio Pardo (Brz) 67
Rio Pativilca (Per) 483
Rio Piura (Per) 484
Rio de la Plata (Arg) 20
Rio Portuguesa II (Ven) 842
Rio Puyango (Ecu) 175
Rio Quequen (Arg) 20
Rio Ramis (Per) 481
Rio Real (Brz) 67
Rio Rinihue (Chi) 113
Rio San Jorge (Col) 142
Rio San Juan (Ven) 841
Rio Santa (Per) 484
Rio Sarare (Ven) 842
Rio Sinaruco (Ven) 842
Rio Sinu (Col) 142
Rio Tambo (Per) 483
Rio Tambopata (Per) 481
Rio Tocuyo (Ven) 841
Rio Torbes (Ven) 841
Rio Tumbes (Per) 484
Rio Turbio (Ven) 841
Rio Turvo (Brz) 67
Rio Tuy (Ven) 842
Rio Uribante (Ven) 842
Rio Uruguay (Arg) 20
Rio Venamo (Ven) 841
Rio Ventuari (Ven) 841
Rio Verde (Brz) 67
Rio Viru (Per) 484
Rio Yaracuy (Ven) 842
Rio Yuruan (Ven) 841
Rio Yuruari (Ven) 841
Rio Zaña (Per) 483
Rio Zarumilla (Ecu) 175
Riohacha (Col) 141
Rioni (Rus) 587
Rios (Per) 483
Riowele (EqG) 184
Rishiri (Jpn) 366
Ritsa (Rus) .... 566†, 587
Riva Trigoso (Ita) 338
Riverton (Can) 91
Rizal (Plp) 485
Roach (UK) 751
Roanoke (USA) 805
Roanoke Island (USA) 828
Robert Foulis (Can) 96
Robert G Bradley (USA) 786
Robin (USA) 800
Robinson (Arg) 14
Robles (Per) .... 483†
Robust (UK) 746
Roca (Arg) 21
Rödlöga (Swe) 648
Rodney M Davis (USA) 786
Rodos (Jason and 511 classes) (Gre) 260
Rodqm (UAE) 715
Rodrigo de Bastidas (Col) 141
Rodriguez Zamora (Col) .... 143†
Rodsteen (Den) 160
Roebuck (UK) 739
Rogin (Nor) .... 452†
Rollicker (UK) 746
Rolnik (Pol) 493
Romat (Isr) 318
Romauld Muklevitch (Rus) 571
Romblon (Plp) 490
Rommel (Ger) 234
Romø (Den) 160
Romsø (Den) 160
Rondônia (Brz) 61
Roraima (Brz) 61
Rosales (Arg) 14
Rosca Fina (Brz) 66
Rosenheim (Ger) 250
Rossiya (Rus) 592
Rossoch (Rus) 582
Rotsund (Nor) 453
Rotte (Nld) 437
Rottweil (Ger) 240
Rotvaer (Nor) 454
Rouget (Fra) 226
Rover I, II (StK) 597
Rovuma (Por) 503
Roysterer (UK) 746
Röytta (Fin) 191
RP series (Ita) 339
RPC 11–RPC 15 (Bur) 77
RPL 56, 57, 60, 61, 62, 63 (Sin) 611
RSC series (UK) 747
RT 84 (Cub) 153
Rubin (Rus) 548
Rubis (Fra) 202
Rude (USA) .... 832†
Ruissalo (Fin) 191
Rulevoy (Rus) 558
Rumb (Rus) 572
Rumbek (Sud) 639
Rush (USA) 824
Rushcutter (Aust) 28
Rushmore (USA) 796
Ruslan (Rus) 594
Russell (USA) 784
Ruwan Yaro (Nig) 447
Rüzgar (Tur) 701
RV 37-41, 142, 243 (Fin) 198
RV 40, RV 50 (Nld) 437
Ryanny (Rus) 546
Rybachi (Rus) 572
Rybitwa (Pol) 494
Rymättylä (Fin) 191
Rys (Pol) 498
Ryusei (Jpn) 371

S

S 24, 25, 26 (Bru) 69
S A Agulhas (SA) 617
Saale (Nor) .... 455†
Saarburg (Ger) 242
Saaristo (Fin) 196
Saba Al Bahr (Omn) 459
Sabahan (Mly) 408
Sabalan (Iran) 307
Sabalo (Ven) 837
Saban (Bur) 79
Sabaq el Bahr (Tun) .... 693†
Sabatøren (Den) 162
Sabola (Indo) 304
Sabqat (Pak) 469
Sabrata (Lby) 398
Sachishio (Jpn) 344
Sachtouris (Gre) 255
Saco (USA) 811
Sacramento (USA) 805
Sadarin (Indo) 304
Sadd (Pak) 471
Sadh (Omn) 457
Sadko (Rus) 593
Sado (Jpn) 367
Saelen (Den) .... 156, 449†
Saettia (Ita) .... 333†
Safaga (Egy) 181

868 INDEXES/Named Ships

Safeguard (UK) 752†
Safeguard (USA) 806
Safra 1, 2, 3 (Bhr) 39
Safwa (SAr) 602
Sagami (Bihoro class) (Jpn) 367
Sagami (Fleet Support) (Jpn) 361
Sagar (UAE) 715
Sagar Kanya (Ind) 288†
Sagar Sampada (Ind) 288†
Sagarawardene (Sri) 635
Saginaw (Newport class) (USA) 797
Saginaw (Pamlico class) (USA) 830
Sagittaire (Fra) 218
Sagittario (Ita) 328
Sagres (Por) 506
Sagu (Bur) 77
Saham 1, 2, 3 (Bhr) 39
Sahin (Tur) 701
Saibling (Ger) 239
Saiburi (Tld) 676
Saif (Pak) 466, 471
Saif 1–Saif 10 (Bhr) 39
Saikai (Jpn) 374
St Angus (UK) 740†
Saint Anthony (Can) 92
St Brandan (UK) 740†
Saint Charles (Can) 92
St John's (Can) 85
St Likoudis (Gre) 264
Saint Louis (Sen) 605
St Sylvestre (Cam) 82†
St Ursula (VI) 846
Saipan (USA) 793
Saire (Fra) 226
Sakarya (Tur) 695
Sakate (Jpn) 348, 361
Sakhalin (Sibir class) (Rus) 577
Sakhalin (Sorum class) (Rus) 595
Saku (Fij) 188
Sakushima (Jpn) 358
Salah Rais (Alg) 5
Salak (Sud) 639
Salamaua (PNG) 473
Salamis (Cypr) 154
Salamis (Gre) 256
Saldiray (Tur) 695
Salinas (DR) 169†
Salmaid (UK) 744
Salmaneti (Indo) 304
Salmaster (UK) 744
Salmoor (UK) 744
Salopa 1–Salopa 15 (Tur) 709
Salt Lake City (USA) 762
Salta (Arg) 11
Salto (Uru) 834
Saluki (UK) 747
Salvatore Pelosi (Ita) 322
Salvatore Todaro (Ita) 329
Salvatore V (Aust) 28†
Salvor (USA) 806
Salwa (SAr) 603
Sam Houston (USA) 760
Sam Kok (RoK) 387
Sam Rayburn (USA) 760†
Samadar (Indo) 304
Samadikun (Indo) 295
Samana (Bhm) 36
Samana (DR) 168
Samandira 1, 2 (Tur) 704
Şamandira Motoru 1-7 (Tur) 710
Samar (Ind) 291
Sambathra (Mad) 401
Sambro (Can) 99
Samed (Tld) 687
Samos (Gre) 260
Sams (Lat) 393
Samsø (Den) 160
Samson (Nor) 455
Samsun (Tur) 703
Samudra Manthan (Ind) 288†
Samudra Nidhi (Ind) 288†
Samudra Sandhari (Ind) 288†
Samudra Sarvekshak (Ind) 288†
Samuel L Cobb (USA) 817
Samuel B Roberts (USA) 786
Samuel Eliot Morison (USA) 785†, 786
Samuel Gompers (USA) 803
Samuel Risley (Can) 95
Samui (Tld) 687
San Andres (Col) 143
San Bernardino (USA) 797
San Diego (USA) 803
San Francisco (USA) 762
San Giorgio (Ita) 332, 336†
San Giusto (Ita) 332, 336†
San Jacinto (USA) 776
San Jose (USA) 803
San Jose (Van) 836
San Juan (Arg) 11
San Juan (USA) 762, 763
San Lorenzo (Per) 483
San Luis (Arg) 11
San Marco (Ita) 332
San Martin (Arg) 21
San Miguel (Pan) 472
San Onofre (USA) 808
San Rafael (Hon) 271†
San Salvador II (Bhm) 36
Sana'a (Yem) 848
Sanaga (Cam) 82†
Sanaviron (Arg) 16†, 18
Sancaktar (Tur) 703†, 705
Sanchez Carrillon (Per) 480
Sand Lance (USA) 764
Sandhamn (Swe) 645
Sandhayak (Ind) 288
Sandoval (Per) 483†
Sandown (UK) 735
Sangamon (USA) 829
Sangay (Ecu) 174
Sangitan (Mly) 408
Sangram (Ind) 291
Sangsetia (Mly) 409
Sanibel (USA) 828
Sanket (Ban) 45
Sans Souci (Hai) 269†
Sansón (Spn) 634
Santa Ana (USA) 819†
Santa Barbara (USA) 803
Santa Cruz (Arg) 11
Santa Cruz de la Sierra (Bol) 53
Santa Fé (Arg) 11
Santa Fe (USA) 762
Santa María (Spn) 621
Santal (Fra) 226
Santaquin (USA) 811
Santiago del Estero (Arg) 11
Santillana (Per) 480
Santisima Trinidad (Arg) 13
Santos Degollado (Mex) 418
Santos (USA) 819†
São Gabriel (Por) 506
São Miguel (Por) 506
Sapanca (Tur) 703
Sapelo (USA) 828
Sapfir (Rus) 548
Saphir (Fra) 202
Sapri (Ita) 331
Saqa (Fij) 188
Sarandi (Arg) 12
Sarang (Ind) 291
Saratoga (USA) 699†, 765†, 770, 771
Sarayu (Ind) 285
Sarbsko (Pol) 495
Sardelle (Ger) 239
Sardina (Gua) 267
Sardine (Ger) 239
Sargaco (Brz) 66
Sargento Aldea (Chi) 107, 110†
Sargento Borges (Brz) 67
Sarhad (Pak) 468
Sariyer (Tur) 703
Sarköy (Tur) 708
Sarobetsu (Jpn) 367
Saroma (Jpn) 368
Saros (Tur) 703
Sarpen (Nor) 454
Sarucabey (Tur) 703†, 705
Sasila (Indo) 304
Saskatchewan (Can) 86
Sassafras (USA) 829
Satakut (Tld) 684
Satsuma (Erimo class) (Jpn) 366
Satsuma (Miura class) (Jpn) 356
Sattahip (Tld) 681
Saturn (Den) 162
Saturn (Rom) 512
Saturn (Rus) 595
Saturn (Swi) 656
Saturn (USA) 813
Saturno (Ita) 338
Saudi Makkah (USA) 819†
Saudi Riyadh (USA) 819†
Saugus (USA) 811
Saule (Fra) 226
Sava (Yug) 849
Savannah (USA) 805
Savaştepe (Tur) 697
Savatar (Iran) 312
Save (Por) 503
Savea (Ton) 689
Savel (Por) 505
Savitri (Ind) 285
Savo (Sol) 613
Sawagiri (Jpn) 348
Sawakaze (Jpn) 350
Sawangi (Indo) 304
Sawayuki (Jpn) 349
Sayany (Rus) 583
Sazan (Alb) 4
SB 3, 4, 5, 10 (Arg) 21
SB 38, 43 (Rus) 585
SB 365, 521-524, 931 (Rus) 595
SB 406, 408, 921 (Rus) 584
Sbeitla (Tun) 694
Scan (USA) 819†
Scandica (Swe) 652
Scarab (UK) 744†, 749
Scarborough of Cerberus (Aust) 33†
Sceptre (UK) 722
Schalbe (Tan) 674
Scharhörn (Ger) 251†
Scharhörn (tug) (Ger) 248
Schedar (Gua) 267
Schelde (Nld) 437
Schenectady (USA) 797
Scheveningen (Nld) 433
Schiedam (Nld) 433
Schirnau (Ger) 243
Schlei (Ger) 239
Schleswig (Ger) 239
Schleswig-Holstein (Brandenburg class) (Ger) 236
Schleswig-Holstein (customs launch) (Ger) 251†
Schleswig-Holstein (Hamburg class) (Ger) 234
Schultz Xavier (Por) 507
Schwansen (Ger) 251†
Schwedeneck (Ger) 244
Schwimmdocks A, B, C (Ger) 231†, 245
Scioto (USA) 829
Scirocco (Ita) 327
Scorpius (Den) 162
Scotia (UK) 751†
Scott (USA) 781
Scout (USA) 799
Scranton (USA) 762
Scylla (UK) 728
SD 13 (Pol) 498
Sderzhanny (Rus) 544
SDL-1 (Can) 89†
Sea Cliff (USA) 822†, 822
Sea Dog (Gam) 230
Sea Dragon (Sin) 609
Sea Glory (HK) 273†
Sea Guardian (HK) 273†
Sea Hawk (Sin) 609
Sea Hawk (USA) 828
Sea Horse (HK) 272
Sea Horse One (Aust) 34
Sea Leader (HK) 273†
Sea Lion (Sin) 609
Sea Panther (HK) 272
Sea Quest (TC) 713
Sea Scorpion (Sin) 609
Sea Tiger (Sin) 609
Sea Widow (Aust) 33†
Sea Wolf (Sin) 609
Seabhac (Ire) 316†
Seafood (Guy) 269
Seagull (UK) 748
Seahorse (USA) 764
Seal (UK) 748
Sealift Antarctic (USA) 817
Sealift Arabian Sea (USA) 817
Sealift Arctic (USA) 817
Sealift Atlantic (USA) 817
Sealift Caribbean (USA) 817
Sealift China Sea (USA) 817
Sealift Indian Ocean (USA) 817
Sealift Mediterranean (USA) 817
Sealift Pacific (USA) 817
Sealyham (UK) 747
Searcher (UK) 752†
Seattle (USA) 805
Seawolf (USA) 761
Sebastian Lerdo de Tejada (Mex) 418
Sebastion de Belal Calzar (Col) 142
Sebha (Lby) 398
Sebo (Gha) 252
Sechelt (Can) 92
Second Maître le Bihan (Fra) 212
Seddulbahir (Tur) 703
Sedge (USA) 829
Seeadler (Ger) 238
Seeadler (PNG) 473
Seeb (Omn) 457
Seefalke (Ger) 250
Seehund 1-18 (Ger) 240
Seeker (UK) 752†
Sefid-Rud (Iran) 312
Segama (Mly) 408
Segeri (Col) 144
Sehested (Den) 160
Seima (Rus) 582
Seinda (Bur) 77
Seiun (Jpn) 373
Sekiun (Jpn) 373
Selar (Mly) 408
Selçuk (Tur) 703
Selendon (Per) 483
Selenga (Rus) 583
Seleuta (Tun) 694
Sellin (Ger) 249
Semani (Alb) 3
Sembilang (Indo) 297†
Semen Chelyuskin (Dobrynya Nikitich class) (Rus) 593
Semen Chelyuskin (Nikolay Zubov class) (Rus) 569
Semen Dezhnev (Dobrynya Nikitich class) (Rus) 593
Semen Dezhnev (Nicolay Zubov class) (Rus) 572
Semen Rosal (Rus) 559
Semko (Pol) 498
Sendai (Abukuma class) (Jpn) 353
Sendai (Teshio class) (Jpn) 367
Seneca (USA) 824
Sénégal II (Sen) 605
Senezh (Rus) 572
Senja (Nor) 455
Sentry (USA) 799
Seoul (RoK) 384
Separacion (DR) 167
Sepura (PNG) 473
Serampang (Mly) 406
Serande (Alb) 4
Serang (Mly) 405
Serangan Batu (Mly) 408
Serdar (Tur) 705
Sergey Krakov (Rus) 577
Sergey Lazo (Rus) 561
Sergey Sudetsky (Rus) 587
Sergipe (Brz) 56
Seri (Mex) 422
Serranilla (Col) 143
Service (Can) 92
Serviola (Spn) 623
Sesta (Fin) 196
Seteria (Bru) 68
Sethya (Bur) 79
Setogiri (Asagiri class) (Jpn) 348
Setogiri (Shimagiri class) (Jpn) 370
Setoshio (Iseshio class) (Jpn) 372
Setoshio (Yuushio class) (Jpn) 344
Setoyuki (Jpn) 349
Setter (UK) 747
Settsu (Jpn) 365
Setun (Rus) 580
Setyahat (Bur) 79
Sevan (Rus) 567
Sever (Rus) 572
Seyhan (Tur) 703
Seymen (Tur) 703
Sfinge (Ita) 329
SFP series (Rus) 589
SG 111-115 (Pol) 500
SG 141-152, SG 161-165 (Pol) 499
SG series (Tur) 712, 713
Sgt Matej Kocak (USA) 820
Sgt William R Button (USA) 821
Shabab Oman (Omn) 460
Shabaz (Pak) 471
Shabonee (USA) 811
Shabwa (Yem) 848
Shackle (USA) 831
Shafak (Lby) 397
Shahamanat (Ban) 45
Shahayak (Ban) 44
Shahbandar (Mly) 409
Shaheed Akhtaruddin (Ban) 43
Shaheed Daulat (Ban) 43
Shaheed Farid (Ban) 43
Shaheed Mohibullah (Ban) 43
Shaheed Ruhul Amin (Ban) 44
Shaheen (UAE) 715
Shahid Marjani (Iran) 311
Shahjalal (Ban) 44
Shahrokh (Iran) 310
Shakhter (Rus) 584
Shakti (Ind) 289
Shaldag (Isr) 318†
Shalki (Ind) 277
Shamrock (Mnt) 423
Shamsher (Pak) 465
Shamshir (Iran) 308
Shankul (Ind) 277
Shankush (Ind) 277
Shao Yang (RoC) 661
Shaoguan (CPR) 120
Shaoxing (CPR) 120
Shaqra (SAr) 601
Sharaba (Lby) 397
Sharabh (Ind) 287
Sharada (Ind) 285
Shardul (Ind) 287
Shasta (USA) 803
Shearwater (USA) 828
Sheean (Aust) 23
Sheepdog (UK) 747
Sheffield (UK) 730
Shehab (Lby) 397
Sheikan 639†
Sheksna (Rus) 582
Shen Yang (RoC) 662
Shenandoah (USA) 803
Shenjin (Alb) 4
Shepparton (Aust) 30
Sheraton (UK) 734
Sherman (USA) 824
Shetland (UK) 738
Shih Yen (CPR) 131
Shijian (CPR) 131
Shikinami (Jpn) 370
Shikine (Jpn) 366
Shikishima (Jpn) 364
Shiloh (USA) 776
Shimagiri (Jpn) 370
Shimakaze (Jpn) 345
Shimanami (Jpn) 369
Shimayuki (Jpn) 349
Shimokita (Jpn) 366
Shinano (Jpn) 367
Shinas (Omn) 457
Shinonome (Jpn) 369
Shippegan (Can) 99
Shippingport (USA) 808
Shiraito (Jpn) 371
Shirakami (Jpn) 367
Shiramine (Jpn) 369
Shirane (Jpn) 347
Shirasagi (Jpn) 374
Shirase (Jpn) 363
Shiratori (Jpn) 374
Shirayuki (Jpn) 349
Shiretoko (Jpn) 366
Shishumar (Ind) 277
Shizuki (Jpn) 368
Shkiper Gyek (Rus) 589
Shkval (Bul) 72
Shoalwater (Aust) 28
Shoryu (Jpn) 371
Shoshone (USA) 818†
Shou Shan (RoC) 665
Shouaiai (Lby) 397
Shoula (Lby) 397
Shoun (Jpn) 373
Shoyo (Jpn) 371, 372†
Shreveport (USA) 795
Shtorm (Bul) 72
Shuguang 1-3, 04-08 (CPR) 133
Shujaat (Pak) 468
Shushuk (Pak) 463
Shwepazun (Bur) 79
Shwethida (Bur) 77
Shyri (Ecu) 170
Siada (Indo) 298
Sibarau (Indo) 298
Sibenic (Cro) 148
Sibilla (Ita) 329
Sibir (Rus) 592
Sibiriyakov (Rus) 571
Sibirsky (Rus) 594
Siboney (Cub) 153
Sicandra (Por) 505
Sichang (Tld) 683
Siegburg (Ger) 240
Sierra (USA) 803
Sierra Madre (Plp) 487
Sigacik (Tur) 703
Sigalu (Indo) 298
Signalshik (Rus) 558
Sigrun (Swe) 653
Sigurot (Indo) 298
Sikanni (Can) 92
Sikuda (Indo) 298
Sil (Spn) 629
Silas Bent (USA) 816
Silba (Yug) 853
Silea (Indo) 298
Silifke (Tur) 703
Siliman (Indo) 298
Silmä (Fin) 197
Silny (Rus) 546
Silversides (USA) 764
Simcoe (Can) 96
Simeoforos Kavaloudis (Gre) 258
Simeoforos Simitzopoulos (Gre) 258
Simeoforos Starakis (Gre) 258
Simeoforos Xenos (Gre) 258
Simeto (Ita) 338
Simferopol (Rus) 542
Simon Bolivar (USA) 760
Simon Bolivar (Ven) 840
Simon Fraser (Can) 95
Simon Lake (USA) 807
Simorgh (Iran) 310
Simpson (Chi) 104
Simpson (USA) 786
Şimşek (Tur) 701
Sin Mi (RoK) 388
Sinai (Egy) 180
Sind (Pak) 468
Sindhu Durg (Ind) 285
Sindhudhvaj (Ind) 277
Sindhughosh (Ind) 277
Sindhukesari (Ind) 277
Sindhukirti (Ind) 277
Sindhuraj (Ind) 277
Sindhuratna (Ind) 277
Sindhuvijay (Ind) 277
Sindhuvir (Ind) 277
Sine-Saloum II (Sen) 605
Singa (Indo) 298
Sinmin (Bur) 77
Sinop (Tur) 703
Sioux (USA) 818
Siping (CPR) 120
Siput (Mly) 408
Siqqat (Pak) 466
Sir Bedivere (UK) 29†, 744
Sir Galahad (UK) 744
Sir Geraint (UK) 744
Sir Humphrey Gilbert (Can) 94†, 95
Sir James Douglas (Can) 96
Sir John Franklin (Can) 93
Sir Percivale (UK) 744
Sir Tristram (UK) 744
Sir Wilfred Grenfell (Can) 98
Sir Wilfrid Laurier (Can) 94
Sir William Alexander (Can) 94
Sir William Roe (UK) 747†, 750
Sir Zelman Cowan (Aust) 34†
Sira (Yem) 848
Sirène (Fra) 203
Siretul (Rom) 514
Siri (Nig) 445
Siribua (Indo) 298
Siries (Gua) 267
Sirik (Iran) 312
Sirius (Brz) 63
Sirius (Bul) 73
Sirius (Den) 162
Sirius (Ecu) 174
Sirius (Mrt) 414
Sirius (Swi) 656
Sirius (Uru) 836
Sirius (USA) 813
Sirjan (Iran) 311
Sirocco (Rus) 575
Sirocco (USA) 801
Siroco (Spn) 619
Siros (Gre) 260
Sirte (Lby) 398
Sisu (Fin) 193
Sitio Forte (Brz) 66
Sitkinak (USA) 828
Sittard (Nld) 433
Sivrihisar (Tur) 702
Sjaelland (Den) 162
Sjöbjörnen (Swe) 642
Sjöhästen (Swe) 642
Sjöhunden (Swe) 642
Sjölejonet (Swe) 642
Sjöormen (Swe) 642
Sjøtroll (Nor) 456
SKA 11–SKA 16 (Den) 165
Skaden (Den) 159
Skagul (Swe) 649
Skarv (Nor) 451
SKB 1, 2, 4 (Den) 165
Skeena (Can) 88
Skenandoa (USA) 811
Skenderbeu (Alb) 4
Skifteskaur (Swe) 646
Skinfaxe (Den) 163
Skjold (Nor) 451
Sklinna (Nor) 449
Skolpen (Nor) 449
Skorpios (Gre) 259
Skory (Rus) 544
Skramsösund (Swe) 647
Skredsvik (Swe) 652
Skua (Can) 99
Skua (HK) 272
Skua (UK) 751
Skudd (Nor) 451
Skuld (Swe) 649†, 653
Slamet Riyadi (Indo) 294
Slava (Bul) 70
Slava (Rus) 540
Slavutich (Rus) 578
Sledge (USA) 831
Sleipner (Den) 163
Sleipner (Swe) 649
Slimak (Pol) 497
Slite (Swe) 645
Smeli (Bul) 71
Smerch (Bul) 72
Smetlivy (Rus) 544
Smilax (USA) 831
Smiter (UK) 739
Smolny (Rus) 579
Smyge (Swe) 646
Smyshlenny (Rus) 544
Snapphanen (Swe) 645
Snar (Nor) 452
Snaypr (Rus) 558
Snögg (Nor) 452
Soares Dutra (Brz) 65
Sobat (Sud) 639
Sobenes (Chi) 111†
Soca (Yug) 850
Socorro (Col) 143
Södermanland (Swe) 641
Sögüt (Tur) 709
Sohag (Egy) 180
Sohai 201, 209 (DPRK) 380
Sok Cho (RoK) 385
Sokoto (Nig) 446
Sokullu Mehmet Pasca (Tur) 706
Solea (Ger) 250
Solimões (Brz) 61
Soloman Atu (Sol) 613
Soloman Kariqua (Sol) 613
Solta (Cro) 149
Somerset (UK) 729
Somme (Fra) 220
Söndüren (Tur) 711
Song Nam (RoK) 385
Song Rim-Ho (DPRK) 380†
Songkhla (Tld) 681
Sonne (Ger) 251
Sonthonax (Hai) 270
Soo Gun-Ho (DPRK) 380†
Sooke (Can) 92
Sooraya (Sri) 636
Sora (Can) 99
Sorachi (Jpn) 367
Sorocaima (Ven) 841
Sorong (Indo) 302
Sørøysund (Nor) 453
Sorrel (USA) 829
Sosva (Rus) 582
Sotong (Mly) 408
Soufa (Isr) 319
Sour (Leb) 394
Souris (Can) 99
Souru (Iran) 311
South Carolina (USA) 780
South Cotobato (Plp) 487
Southampton (UK) 726
Southern Cross (USA) 819†
Southland (NZ) 438-9
Souya (Jpn) 357
Sovereign (UK) 722
Sovereignty (Sin) 610
Sovetskiy Soyuz (Rus) 592
Sovietsky Pogranichnik (Rus) 583
Sovremenny (Rus) 543
Soya (Jpn) 365

Named Ships/INDEXES 869

Soyana (Rus) 582
SP 1 (Ger) 245
Spa (Bel) 50
Spadefish (USA) 764
Spaniel (UK) 747
Spar (USA) 829
Spartan (UK) 722
Spartanburg County (USA) 797
Spasilic (Cro) 150
Spassk (Rus) 577
Speditøren (Den) 161
Spejaren (Swe) 645
Spencer (USA) 824
Sperber (Ger) 238
Spessart (Ger) 241
Spetsai (Gre) 256
Spey (UK) 734
Speyside (TT) 691
Spica (Gua) 267
Spica (Ita) 330
Spica (USA) 813
Spica (Ven) 841
Spiekeroog (Ger) 247
Spiggen II (Swe) 641†
Spin (Bel) 51
Spiro (Arg) 14
Spitfire (UK) 748
Spjutet (Swe) 645
Splendid (UK) 722
Sposobny (Rus) 544
Spraungskaur (Swe) 646
Spravedlivy (Rus) 594
Spray (Can) 98
Spreewald (Ger) 250
Springeren (Den) 156
Springfield (USA) 762
Sprotte (Ger) 239
Spruance (USA) 782
Spulga (Lat) 393
Spume (Can) 98
Sqipetari (Alb) 4
Squall (USA) 801
Squalo (Ita) 331
SR 153 (Syr) 659
SR series (Pelym, Bereza classes) (Rus) 591
Sri Banggi (Mly) 407
Sri Gaya (Mly) 409
Sri Indera Sakti (Mly) 407
Sri Johor (Mly) 406
Sri Kelantan (Mly) 406
Sri Kudat (Mly) 409
Sri Melaka (Mly) 406
Sri Menanti (Mly) 409
Sri Negri Sembilan (Mly) 406
Sri Perlis (Mly) 406
Sri Sabah (Mly) 406
Sri Sarawak (Mly) 406
Sri Selangor (Mly) 406
Sri Tawau (Mly) 409
Sri Trengganu (Mly) 406
Srinakarin (Tld) 687
Sriyanont (Tld) 687
SRS 571-573, 583-4 *et al* (Por) 514
SS 01, 02, 04-35 (Jpn) 373
SS 21, 83 (Rus) 585
SS 30, 35, 40, 47 (Rus) 585
SSV 704 (Rus) 572
SSV series (Balzam, Vishnya classes) (Rus) 568
SSV series (Moma class) (Rus) 569
SSV-10 (Rus) 557
Stakhanovets (Rus) 594
Stålbas (Nor) 455
Stalwart (StK) 597
Standoff (Can) 91
Stark (USA) 786
Starkodder (Swe) 645
Starling (UK) 739
Starshkiy (Rus) 558
Staten Island (USA) 828
Stavanger (Nor) 450
Steadfast (floating dock) (USA) 808
Steadfast (Reliance class) (USA) 825
Stefan Malygin (Rus) 577
Stegg (Nor) 451
Steigerwald (Ger) 241
Steil (Nor) 451
Stella Maris (Gua) 267
Stella Polare (Ita) 336
Stephen W Groves (USA) 786
Steret (USA) 778
Sterne (Can) 99
Sterne (Fra) 217
Stethem (USA) 784
Stevan Filipović (Yug) 851
Stier (Ger) 240
Stiglich (Per) 482
Stihi (Rom) 514
Stikine (Can) 92
Stimfalia (Gre) 265
Stint (Ger) 239
Stockholm (Swe) 643
Stollergrund (Ger) 244
Stonewall Jackson (USA) 760
Stord (Nor) 449
Støren (Den) 159
Storione (Ita) 331
Storis (USA) 826
Storm (Nor) 451†
Storm (Rus) 553
Storozhevoy (Rus) 546
Stout (USA) 784
Stoyky (Rus) 543
Strabon (Gre) 263
Strelets (Rus) 572
Streljko (Cro) 148†
Strogij (Bul) 72
Stromboli (Ita) 333
Strömstad (Swe) 644
Strong Virginia (USA) 820
Stroptivy (Rus) 594
Strymon (Gre) 264
Stuart (Aust) 27
Stump (USA) 782
Sturgeon (USA) 764
Sturgeon Bay (USA) 827
STV 02 (UK) 745†
Stvor (Rus) 572
Styrbjörn (Swe) 645
Styx (Fra) 218
Su Won (RoK) 385
Su Yong (RoK) 388
Suarez Arana (Bol) 53
Subhadra (Ind) 285
Suboficial Oliveira (Brz) 64
Subteniente Usorio Saravia (Gua) 266
Success (Aust) 31
Suenson (Den) 160
Suffren (Fra) 209
Suganami (Jpn) 370
Sui Chiang (RoC) 667
Sui Hang Biao No.1 (CPR) 130†
Sui Hang CE Nos 1, 2 (CPR) 130†
Suiryu (Jpn) 371
Suitland (USA) 810†
Sujata (Ind) 285
Suk (Tld) 685
Sukanya (Ind) 285
Sukhothai (Tld) 679
Sukkur (Pak) 468
Sukrip (Tld) 681
Sulisker (UK) 751
Sultan Kudarat (Plp) 486
Sultan Venturer (UK) 749
Sultanhisar (Tur) 702
Sulzbach-Rosenberg (Ger) 240
Suma (Jpn) 362
Sumac (USA) 830
Sumner (USA) 816
Sun Chon (RoK) 385
Sundang (Mly) 406
Sundarban (Ban) 45†
Sundew (USA) 829
Sundsvall (Swe) 643
Sunfish (USA) 764
Superb (UK) 722
Suphairin (Tld) 681
Supply (USA) 805
Supporter (UK) 749
Sura (Indo) 298
Sura (Rus) 590
Surcouf (Fra) 213
Suribachi (USA) 804
Surin (Tld) 683
Suriya (Tld) 687
Surma (Ban) 43
Surmene (Tur) 703
Surriada (Por) 507
Suruga (Jpn) 366
Surveyor (USA) 832†
Susa (Lby) 398
Sustain (USA) 808
Sutherland (UK) 729
Sutlej (Ind) 288
Suval (Rus) 553
Suvarna (Ind) 285
Suvorovets (Rus) 594
Suwad (Bhr) 39
Suzuka (Jpn) 366
Svaerdfisken (Den) 159
Svanen (Den) 165†
Svärdet (Swe) 645
Svärten (Swe) 648
Svartlöga (Swe) 648
Svenner (Nor) 449
Sventa (Rus) 581
Sverdrup II (Nor) 456†
Svetkavitza (Bul) 72
Svir (Rus) 583
Svirepy (Rus) 546
Swan (Aust) 26
Sweetbriar (USA) 829
Sweetgum (USA) 829
Swift (Can) 99
Swift (UK) 752†
Swift Archer (Sin) 610
Swift Cavalier (Sin) 610
Swift Centurion (Sin) 610
Swift Challenger (Sin) 610
Swift Chieftain (Sin) 610
Swift Combatant (Sin) 610
Swift Conqueror (Sin) 610
Swift Knight (Sin) 610
Swift Lancer (Sin) 610
Swift Swordsman (Sin) 610
Swift Warlord (Sin) 610
Swift Warrior (Sin) 610
Swiftstream (HK) 272
Swiftsure (UK) 722†
Swinoujscie (Pol) 494
Swivel (USA) 831
Sycomore (Fra) 226
Sydney (Aust) 25
Sydney (Can) 91
Sylphe (Fra) 223
Sylt (Ger) 247, 251†
Sylvania (USA) 803
Syöksy (Fin) 195
Sysola (Rus) 582
Szaszhalombatta (Hun) 274
Szczecin (Pol) 499
Szkwal (Pol) 499

T

T 2, T 3 (Omn) 459
T 11-19, T 110 (Tld) 681
T 91-99, 213-230, 231 (Tld) 682
T 154, 711, 830, 867 *et al* (CPR) 138
T 80001 *et al* (Ger) 249
T F R Rios V (Bol) 53
T T Lewis (Bar) 46
Ta Han (RoC) 672
Ta Hu (RoC) 670
Ta Peng (RoC) 672
Ta Sueh (RoC) 672
Ta Teng (RoC) 672
Ta Tung (RoC) 672
Taabot Italia (USA) 819†
Taape (Fra) 199†, 221
Tabarca (Spn) 626
Tabark (Tun) 693
Tabarzin (Iran) 308
Tabasco (Mex) 419
Tabbouk (SAr) 604
Tabuk (Pak) 467
Tabuk (SAr) 600
Tachikaze (Jpn) 350
Tachin (Tld) 678
Tackle (USA) 831
Tactica (Bol) 53
Tae Pung Yang (RoK) 391
Taejon (RoK) 382
Tafelberg (SA) 615†, 615, 616†
Tagbanua (Plp) 489
Tagil (Rus) 591
Tagomago (Spn) 626
Taheri (Iran) 311
Tahoma (USA) 824
Tai Hu (RoC) 672
Tai Wu (RoC) 671
Tai Yuan (RoC) 665
Taicang (CPR) 136
Taif (SAr) 599
Taifun (Rus) 553
Tailor (Aust) 32
Tailte (Ire) 316†
Taimuang (Tld) 681
Taimur (Pak) 465
Taino (survey ship) (Cub) 153
Taino (training ship) (Cub) 153
Tajo (Spn) 629
Takachiho (Jpn) 368
Takanami (Jpn) 370
Takane (Jpn) 362
Takapu (NZ) 440
Takashima (Jpn) 358
Takashio (Iseshio class) (Jpn) 372
Takashio (Uzushio class) (Jpn) 345
Takatori (Jpn) 367
Takatsuki (Hidaka class) (Jpn) 368
Takatsuki (Takatsuki class) (Jpn) 350
Takbai (Tld) 681
Takelma (ex-) (Arg) 15†
Takeshio (Jpn) 344
Takip (Tur) 711
Taksin (Tld) 677
Takuyo (Jpn) 371
Talara (Per) 481
Talaud (Indo) 302
Talent (UK) 721
Talibong (Tld) 685
Talita II (Arg) 21
Tallashi (Ban) 44
Taman (Rus) 567
Tamanaco (Ven) 841
Tamanami (Jpn) 370
Tamaqua (USA) 811
Tamaroa (USA) 825
Tamaulipas (Mex) 419
Tambaú (Brz) 60
Tambora (Indo) 303
Tamengo (Bol) 53
Tammar (Aust) 32†, 32
Tamoio (Brz) 54
Tampa (USA) 824
Tamyr (Rus) 592
Tana (Nor) 453
Tanin (Isr) 317
Tanjung Oisina (Indo) 302
Tanjung Pandan (Indo) 302
Tanner (USA) 816
Tansin (Hon) 271†
Tanu (Can) 101
Tanveer (Ban) 43
Tapajos (Brz) 54†
Tapatai (Fra) 221†
Tapi (Tld) 678
Tapper (Swe) 644
Tapuina (Per) 483†
Tara Bai (Ind) 291
Taragiri (Ind) 282
Tarakan (Aust) 30
Tarangau (PNG) 473
Tarantola (Ita) 337
Tarapunga (NZ) 440
Tarasco (Mex) 421
Tarawa (USA) 793
Tareq (Iran) 305
Targe (UK) 750
Tarif (UAE) 715
Tarik (Mor) 427
Tariq (Egy) 177
Tariq (Pak) 465†
Tariq (Qat) 508
Tariq (SAr) 601
Tariq Ibn Ziad (Iraq) 312
Tariq Ibn Ziyad (Lby) 397
Tarmo (Fin) 193, 650†
Tarshish (Isr) 318
Tasaday (Plp) 489
Tashiro (Jpn) 361
Tashkent (Rus) 541
Taşkizak (Tur) 707
Tatsugumo (Jpn) 369
Tatubla II (Hai) 271
Taurus (Brz) 63
Taurus (Ecu) 173
Taurus (USA) 802
Tautog (USA) 764
Tautra (Nor) 454
Tauvo (Fin) 196
Tavda (Rus) 580
Tavolara (Ita) 337
Tawfiq (Ban) 43
Tawheed (Ban) 43
Tawjeed (Ban) 43
Tax (Nld) 436
Tayfun (Tur) 701
Tayga (Rus) 572
Taylor (USA) 786
Taymyr (Rus) 572
Tayrona (Col) 139
Tazarka (Tun) 693
TB 1 (Ger) 245
TB 8235–TB 8238 (Ban) 42
Te Kukupa (CI) 146
Te Yang (RoC) 662
Tecun Uman (Gua) 266
Tecza (Pol) 499
Tegernsee (Ger) 242
Tegualda (Chi) 108
Tegucigalpa (Hon) 270
Tehuelche (Arg) 18
Teide (Spn) 630†, 631†
Teist (Nor) 451
Tekirdag (Tur) 704
Telamanca (CR) 147
Telenn Mor (Fra) 223
Telopea (Aust) 33
Teluk Amboina (Indo) 299
Teluk Bajur (Indo) 299
Teluk Banten (Indo) 299
Teluk Bone (Indo) 299
Teluk Ende (Indo) 299
Teluk Kau (Indo) 299
Teluk Langsa (Indo) 299
Teluk Mandar (Indo) 299
Teluk Mentawai (Indo) 302
Teluk Penju (Indo) 299
Teluk Ratai (Indo) 299
Teluk Saleh (Indo) 299
Teluk Sampit (Indo) 299
Teluk Semangka (Indo) 299
Teluk Tomini (Indo) 299
Tembah (Can) 97
Temenggong (Mly) 409
Temerario (Uru) 834
Tempest (USA) 801
Tenace (Fra) 225
Tenace (Ita) 338
Tenacious (USA) 815
Tenente Boanerges (Brz) 64
Tenente Castelo (Brz) 64
Tenente Magalhães (Brz) 67
Teniente Farina (Par) 474
Teniente Herreros (Par) 476
Teniente José Azueta Abad (Mex) 417
Teniente Luis Bernal Baquero (Col) 143
Teniente Miguel Silva (Col) 144
Teniente Olivieri (Arg) 16
Teniente Sorzano (Col) 144
Tennessee (USA) 719†, 759
Tenyo (Jpn) 371
Teodolit (Rus) 570
Tepuruk (Mly) 408
Terek (Rus) 582
Terepaima (Ven) 841
Teriberka (Rus) 587
Terijah (Mly) 408
Teritup (Mly) 408
Terme (Tur) 704
Termoli (Ita) 331
Tern (HK) 272
Terne (Nor) 451
Terra Nova (Can) 87
Terry Fox (Can) 94
Teruzuki (Akizuki class) (Jpn) 359
Teruzuki (Murakumo class) (Jpn) 369
Teshio (Chikugo class) (Jpn) 354
Teshio (Teshio class) (Jpn) 367
Teuri (Jpn) 361
Texas (USA) 773
TF 1, 3, 5, 6 (Ger) 247
TF 107 (Tur) 711
Thach (USA) 786
Thalang (Tld) 683
Thalia (Gre) 262
Thar (Egy) 182
That Assuari (Qat) 508
Thayanchon (Tld) 680
The Luke (Aust) 33
Themistocles (Gre) 254
Theodore Roosevelt (USA) 766, 767
Thepha (Tld) 681
Thetis (Den) 158
Thétis (Fra) 222
Thetis (Gre) 264
Thetis (Nld) 436†, 436
Thetis (USA) 824
Thoaban (UAE) 714
Thomas C Hart (USA) 699†
Thomas G Thompson (USA) 815
Thomas S Gates (USA) 776, 777
Thompson (Arg) 19
Thomson (Chi) 104
Thong Kaeo (Tld) 684
Thong Lang (Tld) 684
Thor (Ger) 247†
Thorbjørn (Den) 164, 165†
Thorn (USA) 782
Thrace (Gre) 257
Thule (Swe) 650†
Thunder (Can) 91
Thunder Bay (USA) 827
Thunderbolt (USA) 801
Thurø (Den) 160
Thyra (Den) 165†
Tianée (Fra) 223
Tianshan (CPR) 120
Ticonderoga (USA) 776, 777
Tidestream (HK) 272
Tien Shan (RoC) 665
Tien Tan (RoC) 665
Tierra del Fuego (Arg) 17
Tiger (Ger) 238
Tigre (Fra) 225
Tiira (Fin) 198
Tijgerhaai (Nld) 429
Tiji (Bel) 51†
Timbira (Brz) 54
Tioman (Mly) 408
Tippecande (USA) 817
Tippu Sultan (Pak) 465
Tir (Ind) 289
Tirad Pass (Plp) 489
Tirebolu (Tur) 704
Tireless (UK) 721
Tirfing (Swe) 645
Tisa (Yug) 850
Tista (Ban) 42
Tista (Nor) 453
Titan (Gre) 265
Titan (USA) 815
Titano (Ita) 338
Titilupe (Ton) 690
Tiuna (Ven) 841
Tjaldrid (Fae) 187
Tjeld (Nor) 451
Tjerk Hiddes (Nld) 432
Tlaxcala (Mex) 422
TM 530, 531, 532 (Rom) 514
TNT 11, 27 (Rus) 583
Toba (Arg) 18
Tobermory (Can) 99
Tobol (Rus) 565
Tobruk (Aust) 29, 31†
Tobruk (Lby) 397†
Tocantins (Brz) 54†
Todak (Indo) 298
Todak (Mly) 406
Tofino (Can) 99
Tofiño (Spn) 630
Tohok (Indo) 297†
Tokachi (Chikugo class) (Jpn) 354
Tokachi (Teshio class) (Jpn) 367
Tokiwa (Jpn) 361
Tokuun (Jpn) 373
Toky (Mad) 401
Toledo (Blz) 51
Toledo (USA) 762
Toll (Arg) 20
Tolmi (Gre) 259
Tolú (Col) 143
Tom O'Malley (USA) 810†
Tomahawk (USA) 811
Tomb (Alb) 3
Tombak (Mly) 406
Tomonami (Jpn) 370
Tompazis (Gre) 255
Tomsky Komsomolets (Rus) 561
Tonb (Iran) 310
Tone (Abukuma class) (Jpn) 353
Tone (Bihoro class) (Jpn) 367
Tonelero (Brz) 54
Tongeren (Bel) 50
Tongkol (Indo) 297
Tongpliu (Tld) 681
Tonina (Arg) 20
Tonina (Spn) 618
Tontogany (USA) 811
Toowoomba (Aust) 27
Topaz (Sey) 607
Topcider (Yug) 852
Topeka (USA) 762
Tor (Swe) 650†, 650
Toralla (Spn) 626
Torbay (UK) 721
Torch (UK) 745
Tordön (Swe) 645
Toreador (UK) 745
Tori (Est) 185
Torishima (Jpn) 358
Tormentor (UK) 745
Tornade (Cam) 82†
Tornado (UK) 745
Toronto (Can) 85
Torpedista Hernández (Spn) 633
Torpen (Nor) 454
Torpito Tenderi (Tur) 711
Torrens (Aust) 26
Torrent (UK) 746
Torskaur (Swe) 646
Torsou (Fin) 195
Tortuga (USA) 796
Tortuguero (DR) 167
Torun (Pol) 495
Toucan (Fra) 226
Toumi (Jpn) 369
Toun (Jpn) 373
Tourmaline (Fra) 199†, 224
Tourville (Fra) 209
Tovarisch (Rus) 506†, 830†
Tovuto (Fij) 188
Towada (Jpn) 361
Towline (USA) 831
Townsend Cromwell (USA) 832†
Townsville (Aust) 28
Traxotis (Gre) 259
Trabzon (Tur) 704
Tracy (Can) 95
Trafalgar (UK) 721
Traful (Arg) 21
Tral (Rus) 558
Tramontana (Spn) 619
Träskö (Fin) 195
Travailleur (Fra) 226
Traverz (Rus) 570
Treberon (Fra) 223
Tremiti (Ita) 334
Trenchant (UK) 721
Trenton (USA) 795
Trepang (USA) 764
Tres de Noviembre (Pan) 471
Trevally (Aust) 32
Trichonis (Gre) 265
Trident (Bar) 6†, 46
Trident (Fra) 228
Tridente (Brz) 67
Trieste, Trieste II (USA) 822†
Triki (Mor) 425
Trindade (Brz) 66
Trinidad (Bol) 53
Tripoli (USA) 794
Trishul (Ind) 283
Tritão (Brz) 67
Triton (Den) 158
Triton (Fra) 222
Triton (Gre) 254
Triumph (UK) 721
Triumph (USA) 815
Triunfo (Brz) 67
Tromp (Nld) 430
Trompeteros (Per) 481†
Tronador (Chi) 112
Trondheim (Nor) 450
Tropik (Rus) 572
Truett (USA) 785†, 785
Trumpeter (UK) 739
Truxton (USA) 762†, 774
Trygg (Nor) 451
Trygg (Swe) 644
Tsesar Kunikov (Rus) 562
Tsna (Rus) 580
Tsugaru (Jpn) 365
Tsukishima (Jpn) 358
Tsukuba (Jpn) 368
Tsushima (AG) (Jpn) 372
Tsushima (Yaeyama class) (Jpn) 358
Tubarauo (Brz) 64†
Tübingen (Ger) 239
Tucha (Rus) 553
Tucson (USA) 762
Tufao (Por) 507
Tughril (Pak) 465
Tui (NZ) 441
Tuima (Fin) 191, 192†
Tuisku (Fin) 191
Tukan (Pol) 494
Tukoro (Van) 837
Tulagi (Sol) 613
Tulcan (Ecu) 172
Tuloma (Rus) 587
Tulugaq (Den) 160
Tumleren (Den) 156
Tumpat (Mly) 408
Tuna (Aust) 32
Tunas Samudera (Mly) 408
Tunda Satu (Mly) 408

870 INDEXES/Named Ships

Tungurahua (Ecu) ... 174
Tunis (Tun) ... 692
Tunny (USA) ... 764
Tupa (Fra) ... 223
Tupi (Brz) ... 54
Tupper (Can) ... 95
Turaif (SAr) ... 603
Turbinist (Rus) ... 558
Turbulent (UK) ... 721
Turgay (Rus) ... 587
Turgutreis (Tur) ... 699
Turia (Spn) ... 626
Turquoise (Fra) ... 202†
Tursas (Fin) ... 197, 654†
Turtle (Aust) ... 33
Turtle (USA) ... 822†, 822
Turunmaa (Fin) ... 189
Turva (Fin) ... 197
Tuscaloosa (USA) ... 797
Tuscumbia (USA) ... 811
Tuskegee (USA) ... 811
Tuuli (Fin) ... 191
Tuwaig (SAr) ... 602
Tvertsa (Rus) ... 587
Tybee (USA) ... 828
Tydeman (Nld) ... 434
Tyfon (Gre) ... 259
Typfoon (Bul) ... 72
Typhoon (USA) ... 801
Tyr (Ice) ... 275
Tyrrel Bay (Gra) ... 266
Tyrsky (Fin) ... 191
Tyulen (Rus) ... 595
Tzacol (Gua) ... 266
Tzu-I (RoC) ... 664

U

U 11, U 12 (Ger) ... 232
U 13–U 30 (Ger) ... 233
U 201-U 238 (Fin) ... 195
U 911 (CPR) ... 130
Überherrn (Ger) ... 240
Ucayali (Per) ... 481
Učka (Yug) ... 852
Uckermark (Ger) ... 242, 250
Udaloy (Rus) ... 542
Udaygiri (Ind) ... 282
Udomdet (Tld) ... 680
Uerkouane (Tun) ... 694
Ufa (Partizan class) (Rus) ... 587
Ufuli (Mld) ... 410†
Ugor (Yug) ... 855
Uisko (Fin) ... 197
Újpest (Hun) ... 274
Ukishima (Jpn) ... 358
Ul Rung (RoK) ... 388
Ula (Nor) ... 449
Ülkü (Tur) ... 707
Ulla (Spn) ... 626
Ulm (Ger) ... 239
Ulma (Rus) ... 587
Ulsan (RoK) ... 384
Ulua (Hon) ... 270
Ulubat (Tur) ... 709
Uluçalireis (Tur) ... 696
Ulusage (Sol) ... 613
Ulvön (Swe) ... 648
Ulyanovsk (Rus) ... 532†
Umar Farooq (Ban) ... 41
Umeå (Swe) ... 644
Umgeni (SA) ... 615
Umhloti (SA) ... 615
Umigiri (Asagiri class) (Jpn) ... 348
Umigiri (Murakumo class) (Jpn) . 369
Umka (Rus) ... 595
Umkomaas (SA) ... 615
Umlus (SAr) ... 602
Umoja (Ken) ... 375
Umur Bey (Tur) ... 707
Umzimkulu (SA) ... 615
Un Bong (RoK) ... 388
Una (Yug) ... 850
Unanue (Per) ... 482
Undaunted (USA) ... 808
Underwood (USA) ... 786
Undine (Ger) ... 240
União (Brz) ... 57
Unicorn (UK) ... 723
United States (USA) ... 766, 770†
Unseen (UK) ... 723
Unza (Rus) ... 587
Upholder (UK) ... 723
Uppland (Swe) ... 641
Uraba (Col) ... 143
Uraga (Jpn) ... 365
Uragan (Bul) ... 72
Uragan (Rus) ... 553
Ural (Arktika class) (Rus) ... 592
Ural (Kapusta class) (Rus) ... 578
Ural (Sorum class) (Rus) ... 595
Uranami (Jpn) ... 370
Urania (Ita) ... 329
Urania (Nld) ... 435
Uranus (Swi) ... 656
Urayuki (Jpn) ... 369
Urazuki (Jpn) ... 370
Urd (Swe) ... 653
Uredd (Nor) ... 449
Urf (Swe) ... 641†
Urho (Fin) ... 193
Uriah Heep (UK) ... 750
Uribe (Chi) ... 110
Urk (Nld) ... 433
Ursula (UK) ... 723
Uruguay (Uru) ... 833
Usel (Ita) ... 336†
Ushuaia (Arg) ... 20
Uskok (Yug) ... 849
Ussury (Rus) ... 587
Ustka (Pol) ... 494
Usumacinta (Mex) ... 416
Utatlan (Gua) ... 266
Uthaug (Nor) ... 449
Uthörn (Ger) ... 250
Utile (Fra) ... 226
Utique (Tun) ... 694
Utla (Nor) ... 453
Utö (Swe) ... 647
Utsira (Nor) ... 449
Utstein (Nor) ... 449
Utvaer (Nor) ... 449
Uusimaa (Fin) ... 192
Uwajima (Jpn) ... 358
Uzushio (Jpn) ... 372

V

V 2–V 21 (Ger) ... 246
V series (Ita) ... 339†
V 101–V 106 (Tun) ... 693
V 201 (CPR) ... 134
V A H Ugarteche (Bol) ... 53
V Adm Fomin (Rus) ... 587
V Admiral Vorontsov (Rus) ... 572
V Sukhotsky (Rus) ... 577
VA 2–VA 5 (Spn) ... 635
Vaarlahti (Fin) ... 194
Vauderskaur (Swe) ... 646
Vadim Popov (Rus) ... 576
Vaedderen (Den) ... 158
Vagir (Ind) ... 277
Vagli (Ind) ... 277
Vagsheer (Ind) ... 277
Vahakari (Fin) ... 194
Vai (Fiji) ... 188
Vajra (Ind) ... 291
Väktaren (Swe) ... 645
Vala (Rus) ... 583
Valas (Fin) ... 194
Valcke (Bel) ... 51
Valday (Rus) ... 585
Vale (Nor) ... 452
Vale (Swe) ... 645
Valente (Brz) ... 67
Valentin G Farias (Mex) ... 418
Valerian Albanov (Rus) ... 577
Valerian Uryvayev (Rus) ... 576
Valeureux (Fra) ... 226
Valiant (Sin) ... 609
Valiant (Customs) (UK) ... 752†
Valiant (Valiant class) (UK) ... 723
Valiant (UK) ... 719
Valiant (USA) ... 825
Valiente (Uru) ... 834
Valley Forge (USA) ... 776, 777
Valour (Sin) ... 609
Valpas (Fin) ... 197
Van (Tur) ... 709
Van Amstel (Nld) ... 432
Van Galen (Nld) ... 432
Van Nes (Nld) ... 432
Van Speijk (Karel Doorman class) (Nld) ... 432
Van Speijk (trials ship) (Nld) ... 436
Vancouver (Can) ... 85
Vandegrift (USA) ... 786
Vanguard (UK) ... 719
Vanguard (USA) ... 814
Vanguardia (Uru) ... 835
Vanidoro (Fij) ... 188
Vano (Fin) ... 194
Vaqar (Pak) ... 471
Var (Fra) ... 220
Varad (Ind) ... 291
Varaha (Ind) ... 291
Varberg (Swe) ... 644
Vardar (Yug) ... 850
Varma (Fin) ... 193
Varuna (sail training ship) (Ind) .. 290
Varuna (Vikram class) (Ind) ... 291
Varyag (Rus) ... 532
Vascao (Por) ... 507
Vasco da Gama (Ind) ... 287
Vasco da Gama (Por) ... 501
Vashon (USA) ... 828
Vasiliy Lominadze (Rus) ... 576
Vasily Chapayev (Rus) ... 538
Vasily Golovnin (Rus) ... 572
Vasily Poyarkov (Rus) ... 593
Västerås (Swe) ... 644
Västergötland (Swe) ... 641
Västervik (Swe) ... 644
Vaygach (Samara class) (Rus) ... 572
Vaygach (Tamyr class) (Rus) ... 592
VCA 36 (Spn) ... 629
VD 141–VD 165 (Rom) ... 513
Vector (Can) ... 101
Veer (Ind) ... 284
Veera (Ind) ... 291
Vega (Gua) ... 267
Vega (Ita) ... 330
Vega (Por) ... 507
Vega (USA) ... 816
Vehdat (Pak) ... 469
Veinticinco de Mayo (Arg) ... 12
Vejrø (Den) ... 160
Vektor (Rus) ... 576
Vela (Ind) ... 277
Velarde (Per) ... 480
Velasco (Spn) ... 628
Velimir Škorpik (Cro) ... 148
Vella Gulf (USA) ... 776
Ven (Swe) ... 648
Vencedora (Spn) ... 623
Vendaval (Brz) ... 66
Vendémiaire (Fra) ... 210
Vendres (Fra) ... 219†
Vengeance (Sin) ... 609
Venta (Rus) ... 566
Ventante (Por) ... 507
Ventôse (Fra) ... 210
Venturous (UK) ... 752†
Venturous (USA) ... 825
Venus (Rom) ... 512
Venus (Swi) ... 656
Veracruz (Mex) ... 419
Vernøy (Nor) ... 454
Vestkysten (Den) ... 165
Vesuvio (Ita) ... 333
Vetluga (Rus) ... 566
Vetra (Lit) ... 401
Viareggio (Ita) ... 331
Viben (Den) ... 159
Vibhuti (Ind) ... 284
Vicealmirante Othón P Blanco Nunez de Caceres (Mex) ... 417
Vicente Guerrero (Mex) ... 421
Vicksburg (USA) ... 776
Victor Cubillos (Col) ... 143†
Victor Denison (Rus) ... 587
Victor Kingsepp (Rus) ... 595
Victoria (Spn) ... 621
Victoria (Ven) ... 839
Victorious (UK) ... 719
Victorious (USA) ... 815
Victory (Sin) ... 609
Vidal Gormaz (Chi) ... 109
Vidar (Nor) ... 452
Vidar (Swe) ... 645
Viedma (Arg) ... 21
Vieste (Ita) ... 331
Vietnam Herioco (Cub) ... 153
Viggen (Swe) ... 648
Vigia (Spn) ... 623
Vigilance (Dom, Sin) ... 609
Vigilant II (StL) ... 598
Vigilant (Customs) (UK) ... 752†
Vigilant (fishery protection) (UK) ... 751
Vigilant (Vanguard class) (UK) ... 719
Vigilant (USA) ... 825
Vigilante (Gn) ... 268
Vigorous (USA) ... 825
Vigour (Sin) ... 609
Vigra (Nor) ... 454
Vigraha (Ind) ... 291
Vihuri (Fin) ... 195†
Viima (Fin) ... 197
Viiri (Fin) ... 195
Vijay Durg (Ind) ... 285
Vijaya (Ind) ... 291
Vikram (Ind) ... 291
Vikrant (Ind) ... 278†, 279
Viksten (Swe) ... 648
Viktor Bugayev (Rus) ... 575
Viktor Buinitskiy (Rus) ... 576
Villamil (Spn) ... 625
Villar (Per) ... 479
Villarrica (Chi) ... 112
Ville de Québec (Can) ... 85
Vilsund (Den) ... 163
Vilyuy (Rus) ... 566
Vinash (Ind) ... 284
Vincennes (USA) ... 776
Vincenzo Martellotta (Ita) ... 334
Vindhyagiri (Ind) ... 282
Vindicator (USA) ... 815
Vinga (Swe) ... 648
Vinha (Fin) ... 195
Vipul (Ind) ... 284
Viraat (Ind) ... 278
Virginia (USA) ... 773
Vis (Yug) ... 855
Visborg (Swe) ... 646
Vise (Bel) ... 50
Vise (USA) ... 831
Vishera (Rus) ... 582
Visud Sakorn (Tld) ... 687
Vitaskaur (Swe) ... 646
Viteazul (Rom) ... 514
Vitse-Admiral Kulakov (Rus) ... 542
Vittorio Veneto (Ita) ... 323†, 324
Vityaz (Rus) ... 574
Vivek (Ind) ... 291
Vizir (Rus) ... 572
Vizzari (Ita) ... 340
Vlaardingen (Nld) ... 433
Vladimir Kavraysky (Rus) ... 571
Vladimir Kolechitsky (Rus) ... 581
Vladimir Obruchev (Rus) ... 576
Vladimir Parshin (Rus) ... 576
Vladimir Rusanov (Rus) ... 593
Vladimir Trefolev (Rus) ... 585
Vladivostok (Kara class) (Rus) ... 541
Vladivostok (Moskva class) (Rus) ... 592
Vlado Bagat (Yug) ... 851
VM series (Rus) ... 590
VO 163 (Plp) ... 488
Voga Picada (Brz) ... 66
Vogelsand (Ger) ... 248
Vogtland (Ger) ... 242, 250
Voima (Fin) ... 194
Voinicul (Rom) ... 514
Volga (Ivan Susanin class) (Rus) ... 594
Volga (Ugra class) (Rus) ... 565
Volkan (Tur) ... 701
Volkhov (Rus) ... 582
Volklingen (Ger) ... 239
Volna (Rus) ... 575
Vologda (Rus) ... 588
Volstad Jr (Nor) ... 455
Von Steuben (USA) ... 760
Voronezhsky Komsomo ets (Rus) ... 561
Vorovsky (Rus) ... 546, 547
Vossbrook (Ger) ... 251†
Vostok (Rus) ... 572
Vsevolod Berezkin (Rus) ... 576
VTR 13, 15, 109, 124 (Rus) ... 588
VTR 73, VTR 74 (Rus) ... 587
VTR 294, VTR 295 (Rus) ... 587
VTR series (MP 4, Muna classes) (Rus) ... 587
Vučedol (Yug) ... 853
Vukov Klanac (Cro) ... 149
Vukovar (Cro) ... 148
Vulcain (Fra) ... 218
Vulcan (HK) ... 273
Vulkanolog (Rus) ... 576
Vung Tau (Vtn) ... 845
Vyacheslav Frolov (Rus) ... 576
Vyazma (Rus) ... 582
Vychegda (Rus) ... 559
Vytegra (Rus) ... 587
Vyuga (Rus) ... 593

W

W 2 (Pol) ... 499
W E Ricker (Can) ... 102
Waban-Aki (Can) ... 100
Wabash (USA) ... 805
Wadsworth (USA) ... 785†, 786
Wahag (Lby) ... 397
Waikato (NZ) ... 438-9
Wainwright (USA) ... 778
Waitangi (NZ) ... 441
Waitipu (Guy) ... 269
Wakagumo (Jpn) ... 370
Wakakura (NZ) ... 440
Wakanami (Jpn) ... 370
Wakasa (Futami class) (Jpn) ... 362
Wakasa (Shiretoko class) (Jpn) .. 366
Wakashio (Jpn) ... 344, 372
Walchensee (Ger) ... 242
Wallaby (Aust) ... 33
Wallaroo (Aust) ... 29
Waller (Aust) ... 23
Walney (UK) ... 735
Walrus (Aust) ... 33
Walrus (Nld) ... 429
Walter Körte (Ger) ... 251†
Walter S Diehl (USA) ... 817
Walther Herwig (Ger) ... 250
Walther von Ledebur (Ger) ... 244
Walvisbaai (SA) ... 615
Wan Shou (RoC) ... 672
Wanamassa (USA) ... 811
Wandelaar (Bel) ... 47
Wandenkolk (Brz) ... 67†
Wang Nai (Tld) ... 684
Wang Nok (Tld) ... 684
Wangerooge (Ger) ... 247
Wapakoneta (USA) ... 811
Wapato (USA) ... 811
Warana (Aust) ... 34
Warden (UK) ... 747
Warnemunde (Ger) ... 250
Warrigal (Aust) ... 33
Warrior (USA) ... 799
Warrnambool (Aust) ... 28
Warszawa (Pol) ... 492
Warumungu (Aust) ... 27
Warunta (Hon) ... 271†
Washington (USA) ... 828
Washtucna (USA) ... 811
Wasp (USA) ... 792
Waspada (Bru) ... 68
Wasserschutzpolizei 5 (Ger) ... 251†
Watercourse (UK) ... 746
Waterfall (UK) ... 746
Waterford (USA) ... 808
Waterfowl (UK) ... 746
Waterman (UK) ... 746
Waters (USA) ... 816
Waterspout (UK) ... 746
Wathena (USA) ... 811
Wattle (Aust) ... 33
Wauwatosa (USA) ... 811
Wave Rider (Aust) ... 28†
Waveney (UK) ... 734
Waxahatchie (USA) ... 811
Wedge (USA) ... 831
Wee Bong (RoK) ... 388
Weehawken (USA) ... 811
Weeraya (Sri) ... 636
Wega (Ger) ... 251
Wei Hsing (RoC) ... 673
Weiden (Ger) ... 240
Weihe (Ger) ... 238
Weilheim (Ger) ... 239
Welding (Nor) ... 452
Wellington (NZ) ... 438-9
Wellington (UK) ... 748
Wenatchee (USA) ... 811
Werra (Ger) ... 241
West Virginia (USA) ... 759
Westdiep (Bel) ... 47
Westensee (Ger) ... 242
Westerwald (Ger) ... 243
Westfort (Can) ... 99
Westgat (Nld) ... 436
Westhinder (Bel) ... 47
Westminster (UK) ... 729
Westport (Can) ... 99
Westra (UK) ... 751
Westralia (Aust) ... 31
Westwal (Nld) ... 437
Wetzlar (Ger) ... 239
Wewak (Aust) ... 30
Whale (USA) ... 764
Whidbey Island (USA) ... 796
Whirlwind (USA) ... 801
White Heath (USA) ... 829
White Holly (USA) ... 829
White Lupine (USA) ... 829
White Pine (USA) ... 829
White Plains (USA) ... 803
White Sage (USA) ... 829
White Sumac (USA) ... 829
Whiting (USA) ... 832†
Whyalla (Aust) ... 28
Wicko (Pol) ... 495
Wickrama (Sri) ... 635
Wielingen (Bel) ... 47
Wierbalg (Nld) ... 437
Wiesel (Ger) ... 237
Wigry (Pol) ... 495
Wildwood (Can) ... 93
Wilfred Templeman (Can) ... 102
Wilhelm Pieck (Ger) ... 496†
Wilhelm Pullwer (Ger) ... 245
Wilhelmus Zakarias Yohannes (Indo) ... 295
Wilk (Pol) ... 492
Wilkes (USA) ... 816
Willamette (USA) ... 804
Willem van der Zaan (Nld) ... 432
Willemoes (Den) ... 160
Willemstad (Nld) ... 433
William H Bates (USA) ... 764
William H Standley (USA) ... 778
Wilton (UK) ... 738
Windhoek (SA) ... 615
Windward Sentry (USA) ... 826
Winnemucca (USA) ... 811
Winnipeg (Can) ... 85
Wire (USA) ... 831
Wische (Ger) ... 242
Wisting (Nor) ... 454
Witte de With (Nld) ... 431
Wittensee (Ger) ... 242
Witthayakhom (Tld) ... 680
Wladyslawowo (Pol) ... 494
Wodnik (Pol) ... 496
Wol Mi (RoK) ... 388
Wolf (Ger) ... 238
Wolfsburg (Ger) ... 239
Wollongong (Aust) ... 28
Wombat (Aust) ... 33
Won Ju (RoK) ... 385
Woodrush (USA) ... 829
Worden (USA) ... 779
Worthy (USA) ... 815
Wrangell (USA) ... 828
Wright (USA) ... 821
Wrona (Pol) ... 498
WSP 1, 4 (Ger) ... 251†
Wu Hu (CPR) ... 121
Wu Kang (RoC) ... 671
Wu Yi (RoC) ... 671
Wustrow (Ger) ... 248
Wuxi (CPR) ... 120
Wyaconda (USA) ... 830
Wyman (USA) ... 816
Wyoming (USA) ... 759
Wytrwaly (Pol) ... 494
Wyulda (Aust) ... 33

X

X 573, 580, 606, 675, *et al* (CPR) ... 136
Xia (CPR) ... 115
Xiaguan (CPR) ... 119
Xiamen (CPR) ... 120
Xian (CPR) ... 118
Xiangtan (CPR) ... 120
Xiangyang Hong 01-16 (CPR) ... 132-3
Xichang (CPR) ... 119
Xing Fengshan (CPR) ... 132
Xining (CPR) ... 118

Y

Y 1, 2 (Arg) ... 18
Y 111 and series (Spn) ... 633
Y 116, Y 117 (Spn) ... 632
Y 231-237, Y 251-255 (Spn) ... 631
Y 271–Y 273 (Spn) ... 633
Y 301–Y 310 (Bur) ... 77
Y 352, Y 382-5, Y 441, Y 501 and series, Y 601 (Spn) ... 634
Y 361-362, 364-365, 611 (Spn) ... 631
Y 375, 376 (Den) ... 161
Y 433, 528, 529, 755, 771 (CPR) ... 135
Y 565 (Spn) ... 633
Y 753-55, Y 790-798 *et al* (Fra) ... 224
Y 831, 832, 833, *et al* (CPR) ... 127
Y 1501–Y 1530 (SA) ... 616
Y 8000 series (Nld) ... 436†
Y 8678, Y 8679 (Nld) ... 436
Yablonya (Rus) ... 577
Yadanabon (Bur) ... 79
Yaegumo (Jpn) ... 369
Yaeshio (Jpn) ... 345
Yaeyama (Kumashiri class) (Jpn) ... 367
Yaeyama (Yaeyama class) (Jpn) ... 358
Yaezuki (Jpn) ... 369
Yaffo (Isr) ... 318
Yagan (Chi) ... 113
Yaguar (Rus) ... 584†
Yahiko (Jpn) ... 366
Yakal (Plp) ... 488
Yakhroma (Rus) ... 582
Yakit (Tur) ... 709
Yakov Gakkel (Rus) ... 576
Yakov Smirnitsky (Rus) ... 577
Yakushima (Jpn) ... 358
Yamagiri (Asagiri class) (Jpn) ... 348
Yamagiri (Murakumo class) (Jpn) ... 369
Yamagumo (Jpn) ... 359
Yamakuni (Jpn) ... 367
Yamal (Rus) ... 567, 592
Yamayuki (Hatsuyuki class) (Jpn) ... 349
Yamayuki (Murakumo class) (Jpn) ... 369
Yan Berzin (Rus) ... 595
Yan Gyi Aung (Bur) ... 75
Yan Jiu (CPR) ... 137
Yan Khwin Aung (Bur) ... 76
Yan Lon Aung (Bur) ... 79
Yan Min Aung (Bur) ... 76
Yan Myat Aung (Bur) ... 76
Yan Nyein Aung (Bur) ... 76
Yan Sit Aung (Bur) ... 76
Yan Taing Aung (Bur) ... 75
Yan Ye Aung (Bur) ... 76
Yana (Rus) ... 580
Yaqui (Mex) ... 422
Yaracuy (Ven) ... 841
Yarhisar (Tur) ... 702
Yarmouk (SAr) ... 603
Yarmuk (Syr) ... 658
Yashima (Jpn) ... 365
Yauza (Rus) ... 586
Yavdezan (Alg) ... 7
Yavuz (Tur) ... 699
YD 200, 204, 205 (Plp) ... 489
YDT 6, 8, 9, 10, 11, 12 (Can) ... 92
Yee Ree (RoK) ... 385
Yegorlik (Rus) ... 581
Yehuin (Arg) ... 21
Yelcho (Chi) ... 110
Yellow Elder (Bhm) ... 36
Yellowstone (USA) ... 803
Yenisei (Rus) ... 583
Yenisey (Rus) ... 595
Yermak (Rus) ... 592
Yerofei Khabarov (Rus) ... 593
Yeruslan (Rus) ... 587
YF 2068-74, 2075, 2116 *et al* (Jpn) ... 357
YFD 54, 68, 69, 70, 83 (USA) ... 808
YFU 83, 91 (USA) ... 810
Yi Chon (RoK) ... 381
Yibin (CPR) ... 120
Yildiray (Tur) ... 695
Yildirim (Tur) ... 699
Yildiz (Tur) ... 701
Yinchuan (CPR) ... 118
Yingtan (CPR) ... 122
Yliki (Gre) ... 265
Ymer (Swe) ... 650
YO 47, 129, 203 *et al* (USA) ... 810
YO series (Jpn) ... 361†
Yo Su (RoK) ... 385
Yocona (USA) ... 826
Yodo (Jpn) ... 371
YOG 58, 78, 88, 196 (USA) ... 810
Yogaga (Gha) ... 252
Yojoa (Hon) ... 271
Yokose (Jpn) ... 361
Yola (Nig) ... 445

Yonakuni (Jpn) 366
Yong Dong (RoK) 387
Yong Ju (RoK) 385
Yong Mun (RoK) 389
Yongxingdao (CPR) 129
Yopito (Ven) 841
York (UK) 727
Yorktown (USA) 776
Yos Sudarso (Indo) 294
Yosemite (USA) 803
Yoshino (Bihoro class) (Jpn) 367
Yoshino (Chikugo class) (Jpn) 354
Yosuro (Hon) .... 271†
Young Endeavour (Aust) .... 33†
YP 676-705 (USA) 811
Ystad (Swe) 644
YT series (Jpn) 363, 364
YTL 9, 11, 12, 14 (RoC) 672
YTM 352 (Spn) 634
Yu (Mly) 406
Yu Chai (Tan) 674
Yu Shan (RoC) 665
Yu Tai (RoC) 671
Yuan Wang 1, 2, 3 (CPR) 131
Yubari (Teshio class) (Jpn) 367
Yubari (Yubari class) (Jpn) 353
Yubetsu (Jpn) 353
Yucatan (Mex) 419
Yücetepe (Tur) 697
Yueh Fei (RoC) 664
Yuen Feng (RoC) 671
Yugumo (Jpn) 351
Yukigumo (Jpn) 369

Yukishio (Iseshio class) (Jpn) 372
Yukishio (Yuushio class)
 (Jpn) 344
Yukon (Can) 86
Yukon (USA) .... 17†, 817
Yun Hsing (RoC) 673
Yun Tai (RoC) 672
Yun Yang (RoC) 662
Yunbou (SAr) 602
Yung An (RoC) 670
Yung Cheng (RoC) 546
Yung Chi (RoC) 670
Yung Chou (RoC) 670
Yung Hsin (RoC) 670
Yung Jen (RoC) 670
Yung Ju (RoC) 670
Yung Kang (RoC) 671
Yung Lo (RoC) 670
Yung Nien (RoC) 670
Yung Shan (RoC) 670
Yung Sui (RoC) 670
Yunus (Tur) 706
Yupiter (Rus) 569
Yura (Jpn) 356
Yurishima (Jpn) 358
Yury Lisyansky (Rus) 593
Yusotei-Ichi-Go (Jpn) 357
Yusotei-Ni-Go (Jpn) 357
Yuugiri (Jpn) 348
Yuushio (Jpn) 344
Yuzbasci Tolunay (Tur) 707
Yuzuki (Jpn) 369
YW series (Jpn) .... 361†

Z

Z 5, Z 6 (Pol) 497
Zabaykalye (Primorye class)
 (Rus) 568
Zabaykalye (Sorum class)
 (Rus) 595
Zacatecas (Mex) 422
Zadorny (Rus) 546
Zafer (Tur) 698
Zagreb (Yug) 850
Zahra 14, 15, 17, 18, 21
 (Omn) 461
Zahra 16, 20, 22, 27 (Omn) 462
Zahra 24 (Omn) .... 460†
Zaire (Por) 503
Zakarpatye (Rus) 568
Zambeze (Por) 503
Zamboanga del Sur (Plp) 487
Zambrano (Per) .... 483†
Zander (Ger) 239
Zangezur (Rus) 585
Zannefin (Bel) .... 51†
Zao (Jpn) 365
Zapal (Rus) 558
Zapolarye (Rus) 595
Zapolyarye (Rus) 572
Zaporozhye (Rus) 568
Zapoteco (Mex) 421
Zarnitsa (Rus) 553
Zaryad (Rus) 558

Zawziety (Pol) 494
Z'bar (Mtn) 414
Zborul (Rom) 511
Zbyszko (Pol) 499
Zeefakkel (Nld) 435
Zeehond (Nld) .... 429†
Zeeleeuw (Nld) 429
Zeemeeuw (Bel) 51
Zeffiro (Ita) 327
Zefir (Pol) 499
Zelengora (Yug) 852
Zeltin (Lby) .... 395†, 399
Zena (Dji) 166
Zenit (Rus) 572
Zenitchik (Rus) 558
Zenobe Gramme (Bel) 50
Zephyr (Rus) 575
Zephyr (USA) 801
Zeta (Yug) 850
Zeus (Gre) 264
Zeus (USA) 818
Zeya (Rus) 580
Zezere (Por) 507
Zhanjiang (CPR) 118
Zhaotong (CPR) 120
Zharky (Rus) 546
Zheleznyakov (Rus) 558
Zhemchug (Rus) 548
Zhenghe (CPR) 129
Zhenjiang (CPR) 120
Zhiguli (Rus) 585
Zhitomir (Rus) .... 582†
Zhongdong (CPR) 122

Zhoushan (CPR) 121
Zhuhai (CPR) 118
Zibar (Bul) 72
Zierikzee (Nld) 433
Žikica Jovanovič-Španac
 (Yug) 851
Zinnia (Bel) 49
Zinat Al Bihar (Omn) .... 460†
Zleitan (Lby) 398
Zobel (Ger) 237
Zodiak (Pol) .... 497†
Zodiak (Rus) 572
Zolotoy Rog (Rus) 581
Zond (Okean class) (Rus) 570
Zond (Valerian Uryvayev class)
 (Rus) 576
Zoroaster (Sey) 607
Zorritos (Per) 482
Zorza (Pol) 499
Zoubin (Iran) 308
Zreczny (Pol) 494
Zuiderkruis (Nld) ... 435†, 435, 630†
Zuidwal (Nld) 437
Zuiun (Jpn) 373
Zulfiquar (Pak) 465
Zum Zum (Pak) 471
Zunyi (CPR) 118
Zurara (UAE) 715
Zwaardvis (Nld) 429
Zwinny (Pol) 494
Zwrotny (Pol) 494
Zyb (Rus) 553
Zyklon (Rus) 553

Class Index

† denotes reference is in text or note.

2nd Lt John P Bobo (USA) 821
13.7m, 18m (Mly) 410
65 ft (USA) 831
65 ton (Fra) 226
81-Go (Jpn) 362
93 Ton (Fra) 226
105 Ton (Fra) 226
400, 500, 600, 700 (Ita) .... 339†
3812-VCF (Hai) 270

A

A 12, A 14 (Swe) 642
A 17, A 19 (Swe) 641
A 69 (Arg, Fra) 13, 212
A A Krylov (Rus) 573
A N Andreyev (Rus) 573
Abeking & Rasmussen (Nig) 445
Aberdovey (UK) .... 749†, 750
Abhay (Ind, Mrt) .... 284, 414†
Abkhaziya (Rus) 571
Abnaki (Mex, USA) .... 422, 818†
Abtao (Per) 477
Abukuma (Jpn) 353
Achelous (Indo, Plp, RoC) 301, 488, 671
Acme (USA) .... 799†, 801
Adept (UK) 746
Adjutant (Gre, Ita, Nor, Spn, RoC, Tur) .... 262, 332, 333†, 453, 626, 629, 670, 703
Admirable (Bur, DR, Mex, Plp, Vtn) 75, 167, 418, 420, 488, 843
Aerostat (USA) 826
Agat (Rus) .... 573†
Agave (Ita) .... 331, 333†, 336†
Agdlek (Den) 160
Aggressive (Bel, Fra, Ita, Spn, USA) 49, 218, 331, 629, 800
Agosta (Fra, Pak, Spn) .... 116†, 203, 463, 619
Aguinaldo (Plp) .... 487, 489†
Ailanthus (CPR) 134
Aist (Rus) 564
Ajax (Pak) 470
Ajr (Iran) 310
Akademik Boris Petrov (Rus) 576
Akademik Fedorov (Rus) 574
Akademik Fersman (Rus) 575
Akademik Krylov (Rus) 571, 571
Akademik Kurchatov (Rus) 575
Akademik M Keldysh (Rus) 574
Akademik Orbeli (Rus) .... 573†
Akademik Sergei Vavilov (Rus) 574
Akademik Shuleykin (Est, Rus) 185, 576
Akagi (Jpn) 368
Akashi (Jpn) 363, 372
Akizuki (Jpn) 359, 369
Akshay (Ban) 43
Akula (Rus) .... 515, 524, 524, 526†
AL8K (Uga) 713
Al-Shaali (Kwt) 392
Alamosa (Plp) 488
Albatros (Ger) 238
Albatros (Ita) .... 329†
Albatros (Rus) 548
Albatroz (Por) 504
Aleksandr Brykin (Rus) 566
Aleksey Maryshev (Rus) 576
Alesha (Rus) 559
Alfa (Alpha) (Rus) .... 524†, 526†, 526, 530†, 531†
Alfange (Ang) 9
Alfeite (GB) 269
Algerine (Tld) 685
Algol (USA) 821
Aliya (Isr) 318
Alkmaar (Kwt, Nld) 433
Allen M Sumner (RoC) 663
Allen M Sumner (Fram II) (Brz, Iran, RoK, RoC, Tur) 56, 306, 383, 663, 698
Alligator (Rus) .... 561, 638†
Almirante (Chi) 104
Almirante Clemente (Ven) 840
Almirante Guilhem (Brz) 67
Almirante Padilla (Col) 140
Aloe (Tur) .... 710†
Alpinist (Rus) 569
Alpinist (modified) (Rus) 577
Alpino (Ita) 326
Alta (Nor) 453
Altay (modified) (Rus) 581
Alvin, modified Alvin (USA) 822
Älvsborg (Swe) 646
Amatsukaze (Jpn) 352
Amazon (UK) 732
Amga (Rus) 566
Amguema (Rus) 575, 586
Amphion (Iran, RoC) 311, 671
Amsterdam (Nld) 435
Amur I, II (Rus) 567
AN-2 (Hun) 274
Anadyr (Rus) 586
Anaga (Spn) 626
Anami (Jpn) 368
Anchorage (USA) .... 796†, 796, 798†
Andizan (Rus) 586
Andizhan (modified) (Rus) .... 566, 571†
Andromeda (Por) 505
Andryusha (Rus) 559
Ane (Swe) .... 650†
Angara (Rus) 586
Angeln (Tur) 707
Anglo-French NG (Fra, UK) 208, 728
Animoso (Ita) 326
Annapolis (Can) 86
Antares (Mlw) 402
Antonio Zara (Ita) 340
Antonov (Rus) .... 515†, 587, 597†
Antyey (Rus) 520
Anvil (USA) 831
Anzac (Aust, NZ) 27, 439
AOR 90 (Spn) 630
AP.1-88/200/400 (Can) 100
Appleleaf (UK) 741
Aquarius (Swi) 656
Aragosta (Ita) .... 334†
Aratú (Brz) 62
Arauca (Col) 141
Archer (UK) .... 291†, 739
Arco (Con) 145
Arcoa 25 (Zai) 856
Arcor 25 (Alb) 3
Arcor 46 (Mor) 426
Arcor 53 (Mor) 427
Arcor Type (IC) 341
Arctic 22/24 ft (Bar, Bmd) .... 46†, 52†
ARD 12 (Ecu) 173
Argo (DR) 167
Argos (Ang, Por) .... 8†, 504
Argus (Brz) 63
Ariadne (Ger) .... 413†
Arkö (Swe) 647
Arkosund (Swe) 647
Arktika (Rus) 592
Arleigh Burke (Flights I & II) (USA) 784
Arleigh Burke (Flight IIA) (USA) .... 754†, 781
Arleigh Burke (improved) (Jpn) .... 346†
Arminza (Cub) 153
Artigliere (Ita) 328
Arun (UAE) .... 716†
Asagiri (Jpn) 348
Asagiri, modified (Jpn) 352
Asalto (Arg) .... 18†
Ase (Jpn) 363
Ashdod (Isr) 320
Asheville (Col, Gre, RoK, Tur, USA) .... 141, 259, 386†, 386, 702, 812
ASI 315 (HK) 272
Assad (Iraq, Lby, Mor) 312, 397, 424
Atlantik (Rus) .... 573†
Atle (Swe) .... 193†, 650
Atrek (Rus) .... 568†
Atsumi (Jpn) 356
Attack (Aust, Indo) 28, 298
Attacker (Leb) 394
Audace (Ita) 325
Auk (Mex, Plp, RoC, Uru) 418, 485, 667, 835
Austin (USA) .... 795, 798†
Austin (converted) (USA) 804
Avenger (USA) 799
Avon (UK) 751
Ayabane (Jpn) 373
Ayer Chawan (Sin) 611
Aztec (Leb) 394
Azteca (Mex) 419
Azuma (Jpn) 360

B

Babochka (Rus) .... 555, 556†
Baglietto 20 GC (Alg) 7
Baglietto GC 23 (UAE) 716
Bainbridge (USA) 774
Baklazhan (Rus) 594
Baleares (Spn) 622
Balsam (Plp, USA) 489, 829
Baltika (Rus) 559
Baltyk (Pol) 497
Balzam (Rus) 568
Bang Rachan (Tld) 683
Bango (Indo) .... 304†
Baptista de Andrade (Por) 502
Bar (Tur) 710
Baracuda I (Rus) 526
Baracuda II (Rus) 525
Baracuda 30 ft (UAE) .... 716†
Barbaros (Tur) 699
Barbel (USA) .... 837†
Barceló (Spn) .... 145†, 626
Barkat (CPR, Pak) .... 125†, 469
Barnegat (Ita, Plp, Vtn) 334, 485, 843
Barroso Pereira (Brz) 65
Baskunchak (Rus) .... 567†, 583, 597†
Bat Sheva (Isr) 320
Bataan (Plp) 488
Batoor (Rus) 565
Batral (Chi, Fra, Gab, IC, Mor) .... 109, 216, 229, 341, 401†, 413†, 426
Batram (Mad) 401
Battle (Iran) 306
Bavenit (Rus) .... 573†
Bay (Aust) 28
Bay (Can) 91
Bay (Jam) 341
Bay (USA) 827
Bayandor (Iran) .... 678†
Baycraft (Ecu) 175
Bazán 52 ft (GB) 269
Bazan Type T 26.5 (Ang) 8
Beleijan (CPR) 127
Belknap (USA) .... 773†, 774†, 778
Bellatrix (DR) 168
Beluga (Rus) .... 529†, 531
Benjamin Franklin (USA) 760
Bereza (Bul, Rus) 74, 591
Berezina (Rus) 580
Berk (Tur) 700
Bertram (Egy, Jor) 182, 374
BES-50 (Spn) 625
BH 2 (Fra) 219
BH.7 (Iran) 311
Bigliani (Ita) 340
Bihoro (Jpn) 367
Bima VIII (Indo) .... 303†
BINRS (Fra) 218
Bird (UK) 739
Biya (CpV, Cub, Rus) 102, 153, 573
Bizan (Jpn) 369
Bizerte (Tun) .... 605†
Black Swan (Egy) 177
Blohm & Voss Z-28 (Arg) 20
Blue Ridge (USA) 791
Bluebird (Den, Sin, Tld, Tur) 163, 612, 683, 708
Bodan (Ger) .... 248†, 249
Bodensee (Tur) .... 708†
Boeing Jetfoil (Indo) 298
Boghammar (Iran, UAE) .... 309, 716†
Bogomol (Gn, GB, Iran, Iraq) 267, 268, 309, 313
Bolster (USA) .... 806†, 806
Bolva 1, 2, 3 (Rus) 568
Bombarda (Por) 505
Boris Chilikin (Rus) 581
Boston Whaler (Bar, Bmd, Bol, Cam, CR, Dom, Gra, Iran, Jam, Pan, StK, StL) .... 46†, 52†, 53†, 82†, 147, 166†, 266, 309, 342, 471†, 597, 598
Botica (Yug) 852
Botved (large) (Den) 161
Bouchard (Par) 474
Bougainville (Fra) 216
Bowen (TT) 691
Braila (Rom) 514
Brandenburg (Ger) 236
Bravo (Rus) .... 529†, 531
Bredstedt (Ger) 249
Bremen (Ger) .... 235, 242†
Bremse (Ger, Jor, Mlt, Tun) 250, 375, 412, 694
Broadsword (Gua, Yem) 266, 847
Broadsword (UK) 730, 731
Brooke (Pak, USA) .... 465†, 467
Brooke Marine 29m (Mly) 408
Brooke Marine 33m (Ken, Nig, UK) .... 376, 445, 752†
Brooke Marine 37m (Ken, Omn) 375, 457
Brutar, Brutar II (Rom) .... 511†, 511
Bryza (Pol) 496
Buhler (StV) 598
Bukhansan (RoK) 390
Bulldog (UK) .... 446†, 630†, 740
Burevestnik (Rus) 546
Burya (Rus) 553
Buyskes (Nld) 434

C

C3-S-33a (converted) (USA) 816
Cabildo (Gre, RoC) 261, 669
Cacine (Por) 503
Çakabey (Tur) 705
California (USA) .... 773†, 780
Camcraft 40 ft (Tld) 689
Camcraft 65 ft, 77 ft (UAE) 716
Camcraft 100 ft (ElS) 183
Cannon (Plp, Tld) 485, 679
Capana (Ven) 838
Cape (Bhm, CR, Iran, Mex, MI, Mic, Tur, Uru) .... 36, 148, 308, 310, 413, 419, 423†, 423, 704, 834
Carlskrona (Swe) 646
Carpentaria (Bur, Indo, Sol) .... 77, 304†, 304, 613
Carpenter (Fram I) (Tur) 698
Cassard (Fra) 208
Cassiopea (Ita) 330
Castle (UK) 738
Castor (Spn) 630
Cat 900, 1000 (Kwt) .... 392†
CAT 900S (SL) 608
CDIC (Fra) .... 214, 216†
Centurion (USA) .... 761†
Cerberus (Nld) 436
CG 27 (Omn) 461
CG 29 (Omn) 460
CG 40 (TT) 690
CGC type (Bur) 77
Chaho (Iran, DPRK) .... 308, 379†, 379
Chakri Naruebet (Tld) 675
Chamois (Fra) .... 218†, 221
Chang Bogo (RoK) 381
Chanticleer (Tur, USA) 708, 807
Chao Phraya (Tld) 676
Charles de Gaulle (Fra) 204
Charles F Adams (Gre, USA) .... 24†, 56†, 254, 784†
Charles F Adams (modified) (Ger) 234
Charles Lawrence (Chi, Mex, RoC) .... 110†, 416, 665
Charleston (USA) 797
Charlie I (Rus) .... 277†, 520†, 523, 524†, 528†
Charlie II (Rus) .... 520†, 523, 524†
Cheng Kung (RoC) 664
Chengdu (CPR) 119
Cherokee (Arg, Chi, Col, DR, Ecu, Indo, Pak, Per, RoC, Tur, USA, Ven) .... 15, 107, 110, 141, 169, 174, 303, 470, 483, 672, 710, 818†, 825, 840
Cheverton 27 ft (Bhr, Omn, UAE, UK) .... 39, 459†, 715, 752†
Cheverton 50 ft (Bhr) 39
Cheverton 55 ft (Mld) 411
Cheverton Loadmaster (Bru, Iraq) 68, 314
Chikugo (Jpn) .... 354†, 354
Chiyoda (Jpn) 360
Chodo (DPRK) 379
Chon Buri (Tld) 681
Chong-Jin (DPRK) .... 379, 380†
Chong-Ju (DPRK) .... 376†, 379
Chui-E (Alg) 7
Chun Jee (RoK) 388
Cimarron (jumboised) (USA) 804
Circé (Fra) 218
Clamp (USA) 831
Claud Jones (Indo) .... 295, 700†
Clemenceau (Fra) .... 204†, 205
Clovelly (UK) 749
CME (Spn) .... 629, 703†
Cohoes (DR, Uru) 167, 835
Collins (Aust) .... 23, 32†
Colossus (Arg, Brz) 12, 55
Comandante João Belo (Por) 502
Comando (Arg) .... 18†
Combatboat 90H (Swe) 649
Combattante II (Gre, Iran, Lby) 259, 308, 397
Combattante III (Gre) 258
Combattante IIIB (Nig) 445
Combattante IIIM (Qat, Tun) 508, 692
Commandant Rivière (Fra, Uru) .... 211, 502†, 833
Compass Island (converted) (USA) 813
Conejera (Spn) 626
Constitución (Ven) 839
Coontz (USA) .... 780, 784†
Cormoran (Ang, Mor, Plp, Spn) .... 5†, 426, 486, 625
Corrubia (Ita) 340
Cosar (Rom) 513
Cosmos (USA) 831
Costa Sur (Arg) 17
Cougar (Kwt, Sri) 392, 637
County (Chi, Pak) 105, 464
Courtney (Col) 140
CP 100, 400, 5000, 6000 (Ita) .... 339†
Cpl Louis J Hauge, Jr (USA) 820
Crestitalia 16.5 metre (Pak) 471
Crestitalia 70 ft (Egy) 182
Croitor (Rom) 513
Crosley (Mex, RoC) 416, 665
CTM (Fra) 217
Cutlass (Gua) 266
Cyclone (USA) 801

D

D 59116 (Omn) 461
Da Dong (CPR) 129
Da Liang (CPR) 130
Dabur (Arg, Chi, Fij, Isr, Nic) .... 16, 109, 188, 316†, 320, 443
Dadao (CPR) 129
Dadie (CPR) 131
Dagger (Indo, TC) 297, 713
Daio (Jpn) 366
Dajiang (CPR) 129, 131
Dalang (CPR) 130
Dalarö (Swe) 645
Daldyn (Rus) 590
Damen tug (Egy) 182
Damen 85 ft (HK) 272, 273
Damen 540 (Mly) 407
Damen 1500 (Nig) 445
Damen (CPR) 135
Damen Mk III (HK) 272
Danlin (CPR) 135
Daphne (Den) .... 159†
Daphné (Fra, Pak, Por, SA, Spn) 203, 463, 501, 614, 618
Daring (Per) 479
Darss (Ger, Spn) .... 173†, 241†, 630
Dauntless (Jam) 342
Daxin (CPR) 129
Dayun (CPR) 135
Dazhi (CPR) 129
DC 35 Type (Egy) 182
DDG-2 (modified) (Aust) 24
De Cristofaro (Ita) 329
De Ruyter (Per) 478
De Soto County (Arg, Brz) .... 16†, 60
Deba (Pol) 496
Deepak, Mod Deepak (Ind) 289
Deirdre (Ire) 316
Delfin (Rus) 518
Delfin (Spn) 618
Delhi (Ind) 280
Delta I, II (Rus) .... 516†, 518†, 519
Delta III, IV (Rus) .... 516†, 518
Delta 80 (SA) 616
Delvar (Iran) 311
Dergach (Rus) 552
Descubierta (Egy, Spn) 177, 623
Descubierta (modified) (Mor) 424
Desna (Rus) 577
D'Estienne d'Orves (Fra) 212
DGK/300 (RoC) .... 660†
Dhafeer (UAE) .... 716†
Dilos (Gre) .... 260, 265†
Ding Hai (CPR) 134
Diver (RoC, RoK, Tur, USA) 389, 670, 708, 826
Dixie (Tur, USA) 706, 803
Djebel Chinoise (Alg) 5
Dmitry Ovstyn (Rus) 577
Dobrynya Nikitich (Rus) .... 591†, 593, 594†
Dobrynya Nikitich (modified) (Rus) 571
Dog (UK) 747
Dogan (Tur) 701
Dokkum (Nld) .... 433, 436†
Dolphin (Egy, Isr) .... 175†, 317
Dolphin (USA) 805
Dom Aleixo (Por) 504
Don (Rus) .... 513†, 565†, 565
Dong Fang Hong (CPR) .... 131†, 134
Dong Hae (RoK) 385
Dongxiu (CPR) 130
DS-01 (Sen) 606
DSM 501 (Cro, Yug) 149, 853
DTM 221 (Sud) 639
Dubna (Rus) 581
Duke (UK) 729
Dun (Can) 89
Duna (Alb) .... 4†
Durance (Aust, Fra) 31, 220
Durance (modified) (SAr) 602
Durango (Mex) 421
Dvora (Isr, Sri) .... 319, 636, 668†
Dzheyran (Rus) 564

E

E-71 (Bel) 47
Eagle (USA) 830
Echo I, II (Rus) .... 520†, 523
Edenton (USA) 807
Edic (Eth, Fra, Leb, Mad, Mor, Sen, Tur) .... 187, 214†, 216, 224†, 394, 401†, 401, 426, 606, 705
Edic 700 (Fra, Sen) 216, 606
Edsall (Mex, Tun) .... 417, 692†
EDVM 25 (Brz) 60
EDVP 400, 500 (Brz) 60
Eilat (Isr) 317
Eithne (Ire) 315
Ejdern (Swe) 648
El Tucayan (Nic) 443
Elbe (Ger) 241
Elbrus (Rus) 585
Elicura (Chi) 109
Emba I, II (Rus) 580
Emory S Land (USA) 806
Emsworth 52 ft (Omn) 461
Enforcer (Iran) 309
Enterprise (Bar, USA) 46, 772
Epitrop (Rom) 512
Éridan (Fra) 218, 469
Erimo (Jpn) 366
Esmeraldas (Ecu) 171
Espada (Ecu) 174
Etna (Ita) 333
Explorer (Aust) .... 30†

F

F 65 (Fra) 206
F 67 (Fra) 209
F 70 (Fra) 207, 208
F 70 (Spn) 622
F 100 (Spn) 621
F 2000S (SAr) 599
Fabius (Mex) 421
Falster (Den) .... 162, 703†
Famous Cutter (USA) 824
Fatahillah (Indo) 293
FBM Catamaran (UK) 749
FBM Marine 26m (UK) .... 752†
Felicity (UK) 747
Fennica (Fin) 193
FFG 7 (Aust) 25
Finik (Rus) 573
Finik 2 (modified) (Pol) 498
Fish (Aust) 32
Fleet (Aust) .... 33†
Fletcher (Mex, RoC) 415, 664
Floréal (Fra) 210
Flower (Bel) 48
Fluvial (Mex) 420
Flyvefisken (Den) 159
Forrest Sherman (USA) .... 780†, 809†
Forrestal (USA) .... 770, 771, 772†
Fort (Can) 90
Fort (Jam) 341
Fort Grange (UK) 742
Fort Victoria (UK) 742
Foudre (Fra) .... 214†, 215
Foxtrot (Cub, Ind, Lby, Pol, Rus, Syr) .... 151, 277, 395, 492, 529†, 530
FPB 22ft (UAE) .... 716†
FPB 42 (Sey) 607
Franco-Belge Type (IC) 340
Franco-British NG (Fra, UK) 208, 728
Frank S Besson (Plp, USA) 487, 798
Frankenthal (Ger) 240
Frauenlob (Ger) 240
Fremantle (Aust) 28
Friesland (Per) 479
Friponne (Rom) 514
Frosch I, II (Ang, Indo) .... 8†, 300, 302
FS 381 Type (Plp) 489
FS 1500 (Col, Mly) 140, 404
Fulin (CPR) 136
Fuqing (CPR, Pak) 136, 470
Furseal (RoK) 388
Furusund (Swe) 647
Fushun (CPR) 127
Futami (Jpn) 362
Fuzhi (CPR) .... 136†
Fuzhou (CPR) 135, 136

G

Gaeta (Ita) ... 331
Gagarin (Rus) ... 578
Galati (CPR) ... 135
Galeb (Cro, Yug) ... 149, 854
Galerna (Spn) ... 619
Ganzhu (CPR) ... 134
Garcia (Brz, Pak) ... 58, 465†, 466, 467†
Garian (Lby) ... 398
Garsøy (Nor) ... 454
GB 23 (Ger) ... 250
GDR 407 (Ger) ... 246
Gearing (Fram I) (Brz, Gre, Mex, Pak, RoK, RoC, Tur) ... 56, 255, 382, 416, 465, 468, 661, 662, 697
Gearing (Fram II) (RoK, RoC, Tur) ... 382, 661, 697
Georges Leygues (Fra) ... 207
Gepard (Ger) ... 237
Gepard (Rus) ... 515†, 545†, 549
Gillöga (Swe) ... 648
Girl (modified) (UK) ... 746
Girne (Tur) ... 702
Glavkos (Gre) ... 254
Glen (Can) ... 92
Glycine (Fra) ... 225
Godavari (Ind) ... 280†, 281
Golf (CPR, Rus) ... 114, 528†
Goliat (Pol) ... 498
Gorya (Rus) ... 558
Goryn (Rus) ... 595
Göteborg (Swe) ... 643
Gotland (Swe) ... 641
Granay (Rus) ... 529
Granit (Rus) ... 520, 521
Graúna (Brz) ... 61
Grèbe (Fra) ... 217
Griffon 1000 TD (Tld) ... 684
Grisha I, II, III, V (Geo, Lit, Rus) ... 230†, 400, 493†, 515†, 548, 597†
Gromovoy (CPR) ... 137
GRS Type (Ita) ... 335
Gåssten (Swe) ... 648
Guanajuato (Mex) ... 418
Guardian (Gra, Hon) ... 266, 270, 341†
Guardian II (Bar) ... 46
Guesette (Tun) ... 693
Gulf (Can) ... 93
Guppy 1A (Per) ... 477
Guppy II (RoC, Ven) ... 660, 837†
Guppy IIA, III (Gre, Tur) ... 253, 696
Gus (Rus) ... 564
Gustav Königs (Ger) ... 242
Gyre (USA) ... 814

H

H 800, H 900 (Pol) ... 498
Hai (CPR) ... 134
Hai Lung (RoC) ... 660
Hai Ou (RoC) ... 668
Hai Ping (RoC) ... 673
Hai Yang (CPR) ... 134
Hai Ying (CPR) ... 131
Haibing (CPR) ... 137
Haijui (CPR) ... 124
Hainan (Alg, Ban, Bur, CPR, Egy, DPRK, Pak) ... 7†, 42, 76, 124†, 125, 180, 378, 468
Hajar Dewantara (Indo) ... 296
Hakuun (Jpn) ... 373
Halcon (Arg, Mex) .. 19, 417†, 623†
Halifax (Can) ... 85†, 85, 432†
Halmatic 14 metre (Bhr) ... 39
Halmatic 20 metre (Bhr) ... 38
Halmatic 40 ft (SL) ... 608
Halmatic M 140 (VI) ... 846
Halmatic M 160 (Ana, Mnt, TC) ... 9, 423, 713
Halter 65 ft (Tld) ... 688
Halter 78 ft (Plp, RoC, SAr) ... 487, 601, 673
Ham (Cro, Ind, Yug) ... 149, 288, 336†, 853
Hamagiri (Jpn) ... 370
Hamashio (Jpn) ... 372
Hamburg (Ger) ... 234
Hämeenmaa (Fin) ... 192
Hamelin (Syr) ... 657†
Hameln (Ger) ... 240
Hameln 186 ft (Tld) ... 687
Hamilton (USA) ... 824
Han (CPR) ... 116, 463†
Han Kang (RoK) ... 390
Hanchon (DPRK) ... 380
Hang Fen (CPR) ... 134†
Hantae (DPRK) ... 380
Harpers Ferry (USA) ... 796
Haruna (Jpn) ... 347
Harushio, Improved Harushio (Jpn) ... 344†, 344
Haskell (converted) (USA) ... 813
Hatakaze (Jpn) ... 345
Hatsushima (Jpn) ... 358
Hatsuyuki (Jpn) ... 349
Hatteras (USA) ... 801
Hauk (Nor) ... 451, 645†
Hauki (Fin) ... 194
Hawk (Jor) ... 375
Hayanami (Jpn) ... 370
Hayase (Jpn) ... 357
Hayes (USA) ... 813
HDA 8000 (RoK) ... 388
Hecla (Indo, SA, UK) ... 300, 615†, 740
Hecla (improved) (UK) ... 740
Hegu (Ban, CPR, Egy, Iran, Pak) ... 42, 124, 179, 308, 468
Helgoland (Ger) ... 247
Hellenic 56 (Gre) ... 258
Helsinki (Fin) ... 190†, 190
Hema (CPR) ... 124
Hendijan (Iran) ... 312
Hengam (Iran) ... 310
Henry J Kaiser (USA) ... 817
Hercules (DR) ... 169
Heritage (USA) ... 828†
Hermes (Ind) ... 278
Hero (Jam, USA) ... 341, 824
Heroj (Yug) ... 849†, 849
Herstal (Bel) ... 50†
Hibiki (Jpn) ... 362
Hidaka (Jpn) ... 369
Hila (Fin) ... 195
Hiryu (Jpn) ... 371
Hisingen (Swe) ... 648
Hoku (CPR, Iran) ... 124, 308†
Hokuto (Jpn) ... 373
Hola (CPR) ... 124
Hollyhock (Hon) ... 271
Holzinger (Mex) ... 417
Hongqi (CPR) ... 135
Honours (UK) ... 747†
Hormuz 21, 24 (Iran) ... 310
Hotel (Rus) ... 523†, 528†
Houjian (CPR) ... 123
Houxin (CPR) ... 124†, 124
Hsun Hsing (RoC) ... 672
Huang (CPR) ... 123
Huangfen (Ban, CPR, DPRK, Pak) ... 42, 124, 378, 468
Huangpu (CPR) ... 126†, 126
Huchuan (Alb, Ban, CPR, Rom, Tan) ... 2, 42, 126, 512, 674
Hudung (CPR) ... 130
Hugin (Den) ... 164
Hugin (Swe) ... 644†, 645
Hujiu (CPR) ... 138
Huludao (CPR, Tun) ... 125, 692
Humaitá (Brz) ... 54
Humbolt (Mex) ... 420
Hungnam (DPRK) ... 380
Hunley (USA) ... 807
Hunt (UK) ... 734, 735†
Huxin (CPR) ... 126
Hvidbjørnen (modified) (Den) ... 157
Hydra (Gre) ... 256
Hysucat 18 (Tld) ... 682
Hyundai type (RoK) ... 390

I

IKL/Vickers 540 (Isr) ... 317
Ilo (Per) ... 481
Ilyusha (Rus) ... 560†, 561
Impeccable (USA) ... 815
Imperial Marinheiro (Brz) ... 61
India (Rus) ... 529†, 531
Ingul (Rus) ... 584
Inhaúma (Brz) ... 58
Insect (UK) ... 744†, 749
Interceptor (Qat, Sen) ... 509, 605
Intermarine 55 ft (Nig) ... 446
Invincible (UK) ... 724, 725
Iran Ajr (Iran) ... 310
Iran Hormuz 21, 24 (Iran) ... 310
Iroquois (Can) ... 84
Irtysh (Rus) ... 583
Iseshio (Jpn) ... 372
Ishikari (Jpn) ... 354
Iskra (Rus) ... 582†
Island (UK) ... 738
Island (USA) ... 828
Isuzu (Jpn) ... 360
Itaipú (Par) ... 474
Ital Thai Marine (Tld) ... 687, 688
Italian Type A (Ven) ... 841
Iva (Rus) ... 590
Ivan Rogov (Rus) .. 536†, 562, 564†
Ivan Susanin (Rus) ... 594, 597†
Iwo Jima (USA) ... 794
Izu (Jpn) ... 365

J

Jacob van Heemskerck (Nld) ... 431
Jägaren (Swe) ... 644
Jaguar (Gre, SAr, Tur) ... 259, 601, 701†, 702
James Madison (USA) ... 760
Jason (Gre) ... 260†, 260
Jerong (Mly) ... 406
Jiangdong (CPR) ... 120†, 122
Jianghu (CPR) ... 312†
Jianghu I (CPR, Ban, Egy) ... 40, 120, 176
Jianghu II (CPR) ... 120
Jianghu III and IV (CPR) ... 121
Jiangnan (CPR) ... 119
Jiangwei (CPR) ... 122
Jija Bai, Jija Bai Mod I (Ind) ... 291
Jin Jian Xun 05 (CPR) ... 138
Jingsah (CPR) ... 129
Jinyou (CPR) ... 136
João Coutinho (Por) ... 503, 623†
John F Kennedy (USA) ... 768, 769
John McDonnell (USA) ... 816
Juliett (Rus) ... 116†, 520†, 523
Juniper (USA) ... 829
Jura (Mtn) ... 414

K

K 8 (Nic, Rus, Vtn) ... 442, 561, 845
Kagitingan (Plp) ... 487
Kaiboban (CPR) ... 134
Kal Kangean (Indo) ... 298
Kala (Fin) ... 194
Kalinin (Rus) ... 586
Kaliningradneft (Rus) ... 582
Kalmar (Rus) ... 518, 564
Kaman (Indo) ... 308
Kamchatka (Rus) ... 578
Kamenka (Rus, Vtn) ... 573, 846
Kampela (Fin) ... 194
Kan (CPR) ... 132
Kangan (Iran) ... 311
Kano (Cmb) ... 80
Kansha (CPR) ... 130
Kaper (Pol) ... 499
Kapitan Belousov (Rus) ... 194†, 593
Kapitan Chechkin (Rus) ... 593
Kapitan Izmaylov (Rus) ... 594
Kapitan Sorokin (Rus) ... 593
Kapitan Yevdokimov (Rus) ... 593
Kapusta (Rus) ... 578
Kara (Rus) ... 536†, 540†, 541
Karel Doorman (Nld) ... 430†, 432
Kareliya (Rus) ... 590†
Karhu 2 (Fin) ... 193
Kartal (Tur) ... 701
Kashin (Rus) ... 544
Kashin (modified) (Pol, Rus) ... 492, 544
Kashin II (Ind) ... 280
Kashtan (Rus) ... 584
Kaszub (Pol) ... 493
Katun I, II (Rus) ... 584
Kazbek (modified) (Rus) ... 582
KBV 101, 171, 181 (Swe) ... 654
KBV 271, 281 (Swe) ... 655
KDX-2000 (RoK) ... 383
Kebir (Alg, Bar) ... 6, 7†, 46
Kedah (Mly) ... 406
Kefal I, II (Rus) ... 528
Kefal III (Rus) ... 527
Keith Nelson (Bhm, Qat, UAE) ... 36, 509, 714
Kellar (Por) ... 505
Keyla (Rus) ... 568†, 587
Keystone State (USA) ... 821
Khabarov (Rus) ... 588, 591, 597†
Khamronsin (Tld) ... 680, 687†
KHK 121 (Pol) ... 497
Khobi (Alb, Indo, Rus) ... 3, 302, 582
Khukri (Ind) ... 283
Kidd (USA) ... 773†, 781
Kiev (Rus) ... 534
Kiev (modified) (Rus) ... 532†, 535
Kiiski (Fin) ... 193
Kiisla (Fin) ... 197
Kilauea (USA) ... 803, 812
Killer (Sri) ... 636
Kilo (Alg, Ind, Indo, Pol, Rom, Rus, Syr) ... 4, 277, 305, 491, 509, 515†, 529†, 529, 656†
Kimjin (Nic, Tan, Uga) ... 376†, 442, 674, 714
King (Arg) ... 15
Kinugasa (Jpn) ... 374
Kirov (Rus) ... 515†, 536, 537
Kitty Hawk (USA) ... 768, 769
Klasma (Rus) ... 580
Knox (Gre, RoC, USA) ... 257, 622†, 666, 699†, 785
Knurrhaahn (Ger) ... 243
Kobben (Den, Nor) ... 156, 449
Kojima (Jpn) ... 365
Köln (Tur) ... 700
Kolomna (Rus) ... 574
Komandor (Rus) ... 589
Komar (DPRK, Egy, Iran, Pak, Syr) ... 178†, 179†, 308†, 378, 468†, 554†, 657
Končar (Cro, Yug) ... 148, 851
Končar (improved) (Lby) ... 397†
Konda (Rus) ... 582
Kondor I (Ger, GB, Mlt, Tun) ... 249, 268, 411, 639†, 694
Kondor II (Indo, Uru) ... 300, 834
Kongo (Jpn) ... 346
Koni (Bul, Cub, Lby, Yug) ... 71, 151, 396, 510†, 549†, 850†
Koni (Type II) (Alg) ... 5
Korall (Rus) ... 591
Kormoran (Pol) ... 497
Korolev (Rus) ... 578
Kortenaer (Gre, Nld) ... 235†, 256, 431
Koskelo (Est, Fin) ... 184, 197†
Kosmonaut Vladislav Volkov (Rus) ... 578
Kosmos (RoK) ... 381
Kotlin (Rus) ... 118†
Kotor (Yug) ... 850
Kovel (Rus) ... 571
Kowan (DPRK) ... 380†
Kralj (Cro) ... 148
Kraljevica (Ban, Indo) ... 42, 298
Kresta I (Rus) ... 538†, 539
Kresta II (Rus) ... 538, 542†, 543†
Kris (Mly) ... 406
Krivak I, II, III (Rus) ... 536†, 542†, 546, 547, 554†, 597†
Krögerwerft (SA) ... 616
Krogulec (Pol) ... 494
Kronshtadt (Alb, CPR, Indo, Rom) ... 2, 123†, 297†, 512†
KSS-1 Tolgorae (RoK, SAr) ... 381, 599†
KSV 90 (Ger) ... 241
Ku Song (DPRK) ... 379
Kuangzhou (CPR) ... 136†
Kuha (Fin) ... 192, 193†
Kunashiri (Jpn) ... 367
Kurihama (Jpn) ... 363
Kurobe (Jpn) ... 360
Kutter (Den) ... 161
Kuznetsov (Rus) ... 515†, 532, 533
KW 15 (Tur) ... 712
Kynda (Rus) ... 539†, 539

L

L Y Spear (USA) ... 803†, 806
La Fayette (Fra, RoC) ... 213, 666
La Fayette (Improved) (SAr) ... 600
Lago (Ven) ... 842
Lama (Rus) ... 567
Lance (Gam) ... 230
Landsort (Sin, Swe) ... 610, 648, 654†, 799†
Lang Hitam (Mly) ... 408
Lantana (EqG) ... 184
Lash (USA) ... 819
Launceston (Plp) ... 486
Lazaga (Mor, Spn) .. 425†, 425, 625
LCA Mk II, III (Nld) ... 434
LCG (Tld) ... 684
LCM 3 (Bur) ... 78
LCM 6 (Arg, Fra, RoC, SAr, Sen, Tld, Uru, USA) ... 16, 217, 602, 606, 669, 685, 799, 835
LCM 8 (Aust, Pan, Spn, RoK, Tur, USA) ... 33, 388, 472, 629, 706, 798
LCPL Mk 11, 12, 13 (USA) ... 799
LCT 3 Type (Ita) ... 337
LCU (Bur, Plp) ... 78, 488
LCU Mk 9 (UK) ... 737
LCU 501 (Gre, RoC, Par, Tld) ... 261, 476, 669, 685
LCU 1466 (RoC) ... 669
LCU 1466A (Col) ... 143
LCU 1600 (USA) ... 798
LCU 1610 (Brz, SAr) ... 60, 602
LCU 1610 (converted) (USA) ... 809†, 810†
LCU 2001 (USA) ... 798
LCVP (IC, Ita, Jpn, Tld) ... 335, 341, 357, 685
LCVP Mk 4 (UK) ... 737
LDM 100 (Por) ... 505
LDM 400 (Ang, Por) ... 8†, 505
LDP 200 (Ang) ... 8†
Le Redoutable (Fra) ... 201†
Le Triomphant (Fra) ... 201, 204†
Leaf (Aust) ... 31
Leahy (USA) ... 773†, 779
Leander (Chi, Ecu, Ind, NZ, Pak, UK) ... 106, 171, 282, 438, 439, 465†, 465, 728
Lebed (Rus) ... 564
Lebedev (Rus) ... 573†
Leizhou (CPR) ... 135, 137
Leningrad (Rus) ... 582
Leniwka (Pol) ... 495
Lentra (Rus) ... 571
Leopard (Ban) ... 41
Léopard (Fra) ... 225
Lerici (Ita, Mly, Nig) ... 331, 387†, 406, 446
Lida (Rus) ... 515†, 560
Lienyun (CPR, Vtn) ... 127, 845
Lima (Rus) ... 529†, 530
Lindau (Ger) ... 239
Lindormen (Den) ... 163
L'Inflexible (Fra) ... 201
Loadmaster 60 ft (Bhr) ... 39
Lohi (Fin) ... 195
Lokki (Fin) ... 198
Lon (Rus) ... 565
Long Beach (USA) ... 775
Loreto (Per) ... 481
Los Angeles (USA) ... 527†, 761†, 762, 763
Losos (Rus) ... 531
Loyal (UK) ... 749
LSIL 351 (Tld) ... 684
LSM 1 (Gre, Par, RoC, RoK, Tld) ... 260, 261†, 388, 475, 668, 684
LSM 1 (modified) (Tur) ... 703
LST 1-510 (Gre, RoC, RoK, Vtn) ... 260, 388, 669, 845
LST 1-511 (CPR, Indo, Plp) ... 127, 299, 487
LST 511-1152 (Gre, RoC, RoK, Mex, Mly, Sin, Tld, Vtn) ... 260, 388, 407, 421, 611, 669, 684, 845
LST 512-1152 (Ecu, Indo, Plp, Tur) ... 172, 299, 487, 705
Lubin (Yug) ... 855
Lublin (Pol) ... 495
Luchegorsk (Rus) ... 573†
Luda (CPR) ... 118†, 118
Luhu (CPR) ... 117
Lüneburg (Ger, Gre) ... 242, 263
Lung Chiang (RoC) ... 667
Lupo (Ita, Ven) ... 312†, 328, 838
Lupo (modified) (Per) ... 480
Lürrssen 28 metre (Indo) ... 304†, 304
Lürssen FPB 36 (Chi, Mtn) ... 108, 413
Lürssen FPB 38 (Bhr, UAE) ... 37, 715†
Lürssen FPB 45 (Bhr, Ecu, Gha, Ind, Mly, Sin) ... 38, 172, 252, 291†, 406†, 609
Lürssen FPB 62 (Bhr, UAE) ... 38, 714
Lürssen PB 57 (Gha, Indo, Kwt, Nig) ... 252, 297, 298, 392, 445, 625†
Luza (Rus) ... 583
LVI 85 S (Sen) ... 606
Lynch (Arg) ... 20
Lyness (USA) ... 813

M

M 15 (Swe) ... 649, 653†
M 40 (Rom) ... 511
M 117 (Yug) ... 852
M 301 (Yug) ... 853
M-Boot 80 (Aus) ... 35
M/V 100 (UAE) ... 715
Mab 12 (Cypr) ... 155†
Machete (Gua) ... 267
Mackenzie (Can) ... 86
Mackerel (USA) ... 477†
Mackinaw (USA) ... 827
Maestrale (Ita) ... 327
Magar (Ind) ... 287
Magnet (UK) ... 750
Majestic (Ind) ... 279
Makar (Ind) ... 288
Malaspina (Spn) ... 630, 840†
Malina (Rus) ... 566
Mamry (Pol) ... 495
Mangusta (Alg) ... 8
Manly (UK) ... 749
Mannheim 59 (Ger) ... 248
Manta (Ecu) ... 172
Manych (Rus) ... 591
Marañon (Per) ... 481
Marina Tsvetayeva (Rus) ... 586
Mark (RoC, USA) ... 671
Mars (USA) ... 803, 812
Marshal Nedelin (Rus) ... 577
Marsun (Tld) ... 688
Matka (Rus) ... 554, 555†
Matsunami (Jpn) ... 369
Matsuura (Jpn) ... 368
Maury (USA) ... 816
Mayak (Est, Rus) ... 185, 570†, 570, 587
Mayakovsky (modified) (Rus) ... 568†, 573†
Mayang (DPRK) ... 378
Mazinger (RoK) ... 390
MCB (Tur) ... 704
Meghna (Ban) ... 43, 61†
MEKO 140 (Arg) ... 11†, 14
MEKO 200 (Por, Tur) ... 501†, 699
MEKO 200 ANZ (Aust, NZ) ... 27†, 439†
MEKO 200 (modified) (Tur) ... 699
MEKO 200HN (Ger, Gre) ... 256, 432†
MEKO 360 (Arg, Nig) ... 12, 443
Melville (USA) ... 814
MEN 212, MEN 215 (Ita) ... 335
MEN 223 (Ita) ... 323†
Mercougar (EIS) ... 183
Mercy (USA) ... 817
Meriuisko (Fin) ... 195
Mettawge (CPR) ... 136†
MFPD-3 (Cro, Yug) ... 149, 853
MHV 20, 70, 80 (Den) ... 162
MHV 90, 800 (Den) ... 161
Micalvi (Chi) ... 108
Mihashi (Jpn) ... 368
Mike (Rus) ... 524†, 526†
Mikhail Kalinin (Rus) ... 575†
Mikhail Rudnitsky (Rus) ... 583
Minegumo (Jpn) ... 351
Miner (Rus) ... 558
Minerva (Ita) ... 329
Ming (CPR) ... 116
Minister (SA) ... 614†, 614
Mirna (Cro, Yug) ... 149, 852
Mission (Pak) ... 469
Mission (converted) (USA) ... 814
Miura (Jpn) ... 356, 357†
Mivtach (Isr) ... 319
Mizuho (Jpn) ... 364†, 365
Mizutori (Jpn) ... 362
Mk III PB (Col) ... 142
Moa (NZ) ... 440
Mol (Eth, Rus) ... 186, 847†
Molniya (Rus) ... 554
Moma (Bul, Cro, Pol, Rus) ... 73, 150, 497, 498†, 569, 572
Moma (modified) (Pol) ... 496
Moorhen (UK) ... 745
Moray (Nld) ... 429†
Mornar (Yug) ... 851
Moskit (Pol) ... 497
Moskva (Rus) ... 538, 541†, 592
Motyl (Pol) ... 498
MP 4 (Rus) ... 587
MP 6 (Rus) ... 588
Mrowka (Pol) ... 498
MSB 5 (Pan) ... 472
MSB 29 (Pan) ... 471
MSC 60 (Nor) ... 453
MSC 268 (Iran, RoK, RoC, Pak, Spn, Tur) ... 310, 387, 469, 629, 670, 703
MSC 289 (RoK) ... 387
MSC 292 (Iran) ... 310
MSC 294 (Gre, Tur) ... 262, 263†, 703
MSC 322 (SAr) ... 602
MTC 1011 (Ita) ... 334, 337†
MTM 217 (Ita) ... 335
MTP 96 (Ita) ... 335
Mubarraz (UAE) ... 715
Mudyug (Rus) ... 591
Muheet (Omn) ... 457
Mukha (Rus) ... 556†, 556
Muna (Rus) ... 587
Muntenia (Rom) ... 510
Murakumo (Jpn) ... 369
Muravey (Geo, Rus) ... 230†, 556†, 556, 597†
Musca (Rom) ... 513
MV-45 (Qat) ... 509
MWV 50 (RoC) ... 670

N

N 500 (Ita) ... 339†
Näcken (Swe) ... 642
Najin (DPRK) ... 377
Namacurra (Mlw, SA) ... 402, 616
Nampo (DPRK, Mad) ... 380, 401
Nana-Go (Jpn) ... 359
Nanuchka I, III, IV (Rus) ... 553
Nanuchka II (Alg, Ind, Lby) ... 5, 285, 397, 657†
Naresuan (Tld) ... 677
Narhvalen (Den) ... 156
Narvik (Fra) ... 218†
Narwhal (USA) ... 765
Nasty (Gre) ... 259
Natsugiri (Jpn) ... 370
Natya (Lby, Syr, Yem) ... 398, 658, 848
Natya I (Ind, Rus) ... 288, 515†, 558
Natya II (Rus) ... 558
Nawarat (Bur) ... 75
Neftegaz (Rus) ... 595
Neosho (USA) ... 804†
Nepa (Rus) ... 585
Neptun (Rus) ... 585
Neptune (USA) ... 818
Nercha (Rus) ... 582
Nestin (Hun, Iraq, Rom, Yug) ... 274, 314, 513†, 853
Neustadt (Ger, Mtn) ... 250, 414
Neustrashimy (Rus) ... 515†, 545, 554†
New Generation (Fra, UK) ... 208, 728
Newcon (USA) ... 827
Newport (USA) ... 797
NFR 90 (NATO) ... 428†
Niels Juel (Den) ... 157
Nikolay Zubov (Rus) ... 569, 572
Nimitz (USA) ... 766, 767, 772†
Nisr (Egy) ... 182
Niteroi, modified Niteroi (Brz) ... 57, 66
Nitro (USA) ... 804
NOAA (Mlt) ... 411
Nojima (Jpn) ... 366
Nordkapp (Nor) ... 455
Normed (Tld) ... 683
Norrköping (Swe) ... 644
Notek, Notek II (Pol) ... 495
November (Rus) ... 518†, 523†
Nunobiki (Jpn) ... 371
Nuoli (Fin) ... 191
Nurena, Nurena-M (Rus) ... 519
Nyayo (Ken) ... 375, 458†

874 INDEXES / Named Classes

Nyryat (Alg) 7
Nyryat-1 (Alb, Cuba, Egy, Rus) 4, 153, 181, 573, 589
Nyryat 2 (Rus) 573, 589

O

Ø (Den) 160
Oakleaf (UK) 741
Ob (Rus) 583
Oberon (Aust, Brz, Can, Chi, UK) 23, 54, 83, 104, 723
Obluze, modified (Pol) 494
Obluze (Pol) 499
Obuma (Nig) 444
October (Egy) 179
Oden (Swe) 650
Offshore Performance (Jam) 342
Ohio (USA) 759
Ohre (Ger) 242
Oilpress (UK) 745
Ojika (Jpn) 366
Okean (Rus) 570
Okhtensky (Egy, Rus) 181, 595, 597†
Oksøy (Nor) 453
OL (UK) 311†, 741
Olekma (Rus) 581
Oliver Hazard Perry (USA) 621†, 786, 787
Olivieri (Arg) 16
Olmeca II (Mex) 419
Olya (Bul, Rus) 73, 561
Ondatra (Rus, Yem) 563, 848
Onega (Rus) 589
Onjuku (Mex) 420
OPV 310 (Kwt) 391
Orel (Cub, Rus) 154, 585
Orlan (Orlenok) (Rus) 565
Osa I (Alg, Bul, CPR, Cro, Cub, Egy, DPRK, Iraq, Pol, Rom, Rus, Syr, Yug) 6, 42†, 72, 124, 148, 152, 179, 313, 378†, 378, 494, 499, 512, 554, 556†, 588, 657, 851
Osa II (Alg, Ang, Bul, Cub, Eth, Fin, Ind, Iran, Iraq, Lby, Rus, Syr, Vtn, Yem) 6, 8†, 72, 152, 186, 191†, 286, 308, 313†, 398, 554, 657, 843, 847
Oscar I, II (Rus) 515†, 520, 521
Oskol (Rus) 567†, 567
Oslo (Nor) 450
Osman Gazi (Tur) 704
Osprey (Bur) 75
Osprey (USA) 754†, 800
Osprey 55, Mod Osprey 55 (Gre) 258
Osprey 55 (improved) (Sen) 605
Osprey Mk II (Mor) 425
Oste (Ger) 244
Ouragan (Fra) 215
Outrage (Hon) 271

P

P series (Aust) 34
P 4 (Alb, CPR, DPRK) 2†, 123†, 377†
P 6 (CPR, Egy, DPRK, Rus, Syr) 125, 178†, 308†, 379†, 379, 401†, 588†, 657†
P 21 (Ire) 316
P 32 (Mor) 425, 426
P 41 (Ire) 316
P 48 (Sen, Tun) 605, 693
P 48S (Cam) 81
P 101 (Spn) 627
P 202 (Spn) 627
P 231 (Spn) 627
P 400 (Fra, Gab) 217, 229
P 802 (Alg) 8
P 1200 (Alg, Nig) 8, 447
P 1903 (Omn) 460
P 2000 (Omn) 461
P 6071 (Nor) 449
Pabna (Ban) 43
Pacific 38 (UK) 751†
Pacific Forum (Cl, Fij, Mic, Ml, PNG, Sol, Ton, Van, WS) 146, 188, 413, 423, 473, 613, 689, 837, 846
Paltus (Rus) 531
Paluma (Aust) 30
Pamir (Rus) 584
Pamir (modified) (Rus) 569
Pamlico (USA) 830
Pansio (Fin) 192
Pao Hsing (RoC) 673
Papa (Rus) 520†
Parchim I (Indo) 296
Parchim II (Rus) 530†, 549, 555†
Partizan (Rus) 587
Passat (Rus) 575
Pat (Indo) 303
Patapsco (Gre, RoC) 263, 672
Pathfinder (USA) 816
Patra (Fra, IC, Mtn) 217†, 228, 340, 413
Pauk I (Bul, Rus) 71, 515†, 554†, 555, 597†
Pauk II (Cub, Ind) 152, 284, 555†
Paul Revere (Spn) 629
PB 57 (Gha, Indo, Kwt, Nig) 252, 297, 298, 392, 445
PB 90 (Bur, Iraq) 76, 313
PB Mk III, Mk IV Series (USA) 801
PBC 3521, PBC 5501 (RoC) 668
PBI (Iran) 309
PBR Mk II (Cmb, Tld, USA) 80, 682, 802
PC 461 (Tld) 681
PC 1638 (Chi, Tur) 109, 702
PCE 827 (Bur, Plp) 75, 486
PCF 46, PCF 50, PCF 65 (Plp) 490
PCL Type (RoC) 668
Peacock (Ire, UK) 316, 739
Pedretti (Ita) 334
Pedro Teixeira (Brz) 61
Pegasus (SAr) 603
Pelikan (Rus) 559
Pelym (Cub, Rus) 153, 591
Pembanteras (Mly) 410
Penumpas (Mly) 410
Perdana (Mly) 405
Perwira (Bru) 68
Pescalonso (Spn) 626
Peterson Type (CpV) 102
Petrushka (Rus) 589
Petya I, I (modified) (Rus) 550
Petya II (Az, Eth, Ind, Rus, Vtn) 35, 185, 282, 283†, 550, 842
Petya II (modified) (Rus) 550
Petya III (Syr, Vtn) 657, 842
PF 103 (Iran, Tld) 307, 678
PFG-2 (RoC) 665
PGM (Bur) 76
PGM 39 (Plp) 490
PGM 53 (Eth) 186
PGM 71 (DR, Ecu, Iran, Per, Tld, Tur, Vtn) 168, 174, 309, 484, 681, 702, 844
PHM (USA) 802
Piast (Pol, Uru) 498, 835
Pigeon (USA) 807
Pilica (Pol) 494, 499
Pimentel (Per) 482
Pinega (Rus) 566
Pinnace 1300 (UK) 748
Pipa-Got (DPRK) 380
Pirana (Col) 142
Piraña (Con) 145
Piranha (EIS, Hon) 183, 271
Piratini (Brz) 62
Piyavka (Rus) 557, 597†
Plascoa (Dji) 166
Pluskwa (Pol) 498
PO 2 (Alb, Bul, Rus, Vtn) 2, 73, 74†, 589, 844
Po Hang (RoK) 385, 390†
PO Type (Cro) 150
Point (CR, Mex, Pan, USA, Ven) 146, 419, 471, 828, 841
Polar Star (USA) 827
Polimar (Mex) 419
Polnochny A (Bul, Egy, Rus, Yem) 73, 180, 558, 563, 848
Polnochny B (Alg, Ang, Cub, Eth, Rus, Syr, Vtn) 6, 8, 153, 186, 558, 563, 658, 845
Polnochny C (Ind, Pol) 287, 495
Polnocny D (Ind, Lby) 287, 399
Poluchat (Lby, Syr) 398, 659
Poluchat I (Alb, Alg, Ang, Cub, Egy, Iraq, Rus, Vtn) 4, 7, 8†, 153, 181, 313, 588, 844
Poluchat II, III (Rus) 588
Polycat 1450 (Qat) 508
Polyus (Rus) 571
Pomornik (Rus) 515†, 564
Ponza (Ita) 337
Poolster (Nld) 435
Porte (Can) 91
Poshak (Ind) 289
Posilipo (UAE) 716
Poti (Bul, Rom) 72, 511
Potok (Rus) 588
Powhatan (USA) 818
Pozharny I (Iraq, Rus) 315, 590
PR 48 (Cam, Mad) 81, 401
PR 72 (Mor) 425
PR 72M (Sen) 605
PR 72P (Per) 480
PR 360T (Ben) 52
Prabparapak (Tld) 681
Pradhayak (Ind) 289
Predator 1100 (Kwt) 392†
Primorye (Rus) 568
Protector 40 ft (EIS) 183
Protector 43 ft (Ven) 842
Protector 108 ft (Bhm, Chi) 36, 112
Province (Omn, Tld) 375†, 458, 680†
Prut (Rus) 585
PS 700 (Lby) 399
PT 71, PT 82 (Yug) 855
Puerto Deseado (Arg) 17
Pulkovsky Meridian (Rus) 573†
Punta (Ven) 841
Puyango (Ecu) 175
PX, Improved PX, PX 25 (Mly) 409
Pyranja (Rus) 531

Q

Qionsha (CPR) 127, 130†

R

R and Modified R (Can) 93, 94
R-2 Mala (Cro, Lby, Swe, Yug) 148†, 395, 641†, 849†, 850
Raj (Ind) 292
Raleigh (USA) 795†
Raleigh (converted) (USA) 804
Ramadan (Egy) 178
Rana (Sri) 636
Rapier (UK) 604
Ratcharit (Tld) 340†, 680
Rattanakosin (Tld) 679
Rauma (Fin) 190
Red (USA) 829
Redwing (Fij, Spn) 188, 629
Regent (UK) 743
Reinøysund (Nor) 453
Reliance (Swi) 656
Reliance (USA) 825
Reshef (Isr) 318, 625†
Resolution (UK) 720
Restigouche (improved) (Can) 87
Rhein (Ger, Tur) 241, 706
Rhin (Fra) 219
Ribnadzor-4 (Lat) 394
Riga (Bul) 70, 119†
Rihtniemi (Fin) 191
Rio (Col) 142†, 142
Rio 630 (Ita) 339†
Rio Doce (Brz) 67
Rio Minho (Por) 504
Rio Pardo (Brz) 67
River (Aust) 26
River (Ban) 43
River (DR) 167
River (SA) 615
River (UK) 734, 735†
Robert D Conrad (Brz, Chi, Mex, Tun, USA) 63, 109, 420, 505†, 693, 814
Rodman (Spn) 634
Roebuck (UK) 739
Romat (Isr) 318
Romeo (Alg, Bul, CPR, Egy, DPRK, Rus, Syr) 4†, 70, 117, 175, 376, 530†, 656
Romeo (modified) (CPR) 116
Ropuchka I, II (Rus) 562
Roraima (Brz) 61, 65†
Roslavl (CPR, Rom, Rus) 138, 514, 596
Rotork FPB 512 (Bru, UAE) 69, 716†
Rotork Sea Truck (Nig, Syr) 446, 659
Rotork Type 412 (12 m) (Col, Ecu, IC, Iran, Jor) 142, 172, 311, 341, 374
Rover (Indo, Por, UK) 302, 506, 742
Rover 663 (Mrt) 414†
RPC (Tld) 682
RPL (Sin) 611
RR 4000 (Fra) 220
Rubis (Fra) 202
Rudderow (RoC) 665
Ruissalo (Fin) 144†, 191
RV 1, 8, 9, 10, 30 (Fin) 198†

S

S 80 (Spn) 618†
S 90 (Ita) 322
S-143 (Ger) 625†
S 500 (Ita) 339†
S-NAC-2 (Brz) 54†
Saar 2 (Isr) 319
Saar 3 (Chi, Isr) 108, 319
Saar 4 (Chi, Isr) 108, 317†, 318, 614†
Saar 4.5 (Isr) 318
Saar 5 (Isr) 317
SAB 12 (Cypr, Ger) 155, 250
Sabah (Mly) 406
Sachsenwald (Ger) 241
Sacramento (USA) 805
Safeguard (USA) 806
Saint (Can) 92
St Laurent (Can) 88
Sal (UK) 744
Salisbury (Ban) 41
Salta (Arg) 11
Samar (Ind) 291
Samara (Rus) 572
Samuel Gompers (USA) 803, 806†
San Giorgio (Ita) 332, 356†
Sandhayak (Ind) 288
Sandown (SAr, UK) 601, 735
Sandown (modified) (Spn) 629
Santa Maria (Spn) 621
São Roque (Por) 506
SAR 33, SAR 35 (Tur) 712
Sariwon (DPRK) 376†, 378
Sarucabey (Tur) 704†, 705
Sassnitz (Ger, Pol) 249, 493, 554†
Sattahip (Tld) 681
Sauda (Nor) 453
Sauro, Improved Sauro (Ita) 322
Sav (Den) 163
Sava (Yug) 849
Savage (Tun, Vtn) 692, 842
Sawari (Iraq) 314
Schmel (Rus) 597†
Scholle (Rus) 596
Schoolboy (RoK) 387†
Schütze (Ger) 62†, 240, 615†
Schwedeneck (Ger) 244
Scorpene (Spn) 618†
SDB Mk 2 (Ind) 287, 288†, 292
SDB Mk 3 (Ind) 286
Sea Ark (Ven) 842
Sea Bird (USA) 828
Sea Dolphin (RoK) 387, 394†
Sea Dragon (RoK) 390
Sea Fox (RoK) 387
Sea Guard (SAr) 603
Sea Hawk (RoK) 387
Sea Wolf (RoK) 390
Seacraft (Blz) 52†
Seafox (Egy) 180
Seagull (RoK) 390
Seal (UK) 739, 748
Sealift (USA) 817
Seaspray (HK) 273
Seawolf (USA) 754†, 761†, 761
Sechura (Per) 482
Sekstan (Alb, Egy, RoC, Syr) 4, 181†, 591, 659
Selga (Lat) 393
Serviola (Spn) 623
Sewart 40 ft (Iran, Sud) 309, 639
Sewart 85 ft (Gua) 266
Sgt Matej Kocak (USA) 820
Shabwah (Yem) 848
Shalanda (Rus) 588†
Shalanda I (Alb) 4
Shan (CPR) 127
Shanghai (CPR, Rom) 125, 127†, 512
Shanghai II (Alb, Ban, Egy, Gam, DPRK, Pak, SL, Sri, Tan, Tun, Vtn, Zai) 2, 43, 179, 230, 379, 468, 608, 636†, 674, 692, 843†, 856
Shantou (CPR, EqG, GB, Vtn) 123†, 184, 269, 843†
Shark (RoK) 390
Shark 33 (UAE) 716†
Shark Cat (Aust, HK) 34, 273
Shelon (Rus) 588
Shengli (CPR) 136
Shershen (Ang, CpV, Cro, Egy, Vtn, Yug) 8†, 102, 148, 179, 843, 852
Shih Yen (CPR) 131
Shijian (CPR) 131
Shikinami (Jpn) 370
Shikishima (Jpn) 364
Shimagiri (Jpn) 370
Shirane (Jpn) 347
Shiretoko (Jpn) 366
Shmel (Cmb, Rus) 81, 557
Shuguang, Shuguang 04 (CPR) 133
Sibir (Rus) 577
Sibiriyakov (Rus) 571
Sidehole 1, 2 (Rus) 596
Sierra I, II (Rus) 515†, 524†, 525, 526, 527†
Silas Bent (USA) 816
Silba (Cro, Yug) 149, 853
Silmä (Fin) 197
Simmoneau 30, 36 (Cam) 81
Simmoneau 51 (SM 500) (Nig, SAr, Sri) 446, 601, 637
Simmoneau SM 465 (Mly) 409†
Simmoneau Standard 12 (Kwt) 392
Simon Lake (USA) 803†, 806†, 807
Sin Hung (DPRK, Nic) 376†, 379, 442†, 442
Sin Hung (modified) (DPRK) 379
Sinnam (DPRK) 379
Sinpo (DPRK) 379
Sir Lancelot (Sin, UK) 29†, 287†, 310†, 610, 744
Sirius (Brz) 63
Sirius (Cro) 149
Sirius (Sey) 607
Sirs (UK) 747†
Sivuch (Rus) 552
Sjöormen (Swe) 642
Skanor (Swe) 645†
Skanör (Swe) 645†, 645
Skat (Rus) 564
Skorpion (SAr) 603
SL (Vtn) 846
Slava (Rus) 540
Slingsby SAH 2200 (SAr) 604
Sliva (Rus) 584
Smit Lloyd (Chi) 112
Smolny (Rus) 579
Snögg (Nor) 451†, 452
SO 1 (DPRK, Iraq, Vtn, Yem) 125†, 313†, 377, 844, 847†
Sofya (Rus) 582
Soho (DPRK) 377
Sohung (DPRK) 378
Soju (DPRK) 378
Sokol (Rus) 555
Søløven (Den) 398†
Soman (DPRK) 379
Songjong (DPRK) 380
Sonya (Bul, Cub, Rus, Syr, Vtn, Yem) 72, 153, 515†, 560, 658, 845, 848
Sooraya (Sri) 636
Sorum (Rus) 595, 597†
Sorum (modified) (Rus) 515†, 572
Sotoyomo (Arg, Brz, DR, Hai, Per, RoC, RoK, Uru) 16, 67†, 169, 269, 389, 482, 672, 836
Souya (Jpn) 357
Sovremenny (Rus) 515†, 543
Soya (Jpn) 365
Sparviero (Ita, Jpn) 333, 356
Spasilac (Cro, Iraq, Lby) 150, 315, 399
Spear (Qat, StK, UAE, Yem) 508, 597, 716†, 849
Spica, Spica II (Swe) 160†, 643†, 644†, 690†, 851†
Spica-M (Mly) 405
Spitfire (UK) 747†, 748
Split (Yug) 850
Spruance (USA) 776†, 782, 783, 784†
SRN 6 (Can, Iran, Iraq, SAr) 100, 310, 314, 604
Stalwart (USA) 815, 832†
Steber 36 (Aust) 34
Stena (UK) 743
Stenka (Az, Cub, Geo, Rus) 35, 154, 230†, 556, 597†
Stenka (modified) (Cmb) 80
Stinger (Gn) 268
Stinger (USA) 802
Stockholm (Swe) 643
Stollergrund (Ger) 244
Storis (USA) 826
Storm (Nor) 451
Stromboli (Iraq, Ita) 314, 333
Stroptivy (Rus) 594
Sturgeon (USA) 764, 765†
Suffren (Fra) 209
Sukanya (Ind) 285
Suma (Jpn) 362
Sumidagawa (Tld) 687, 688
Sund (Den) 159†, 163
Super Dvora (Isr, Sri) 319, 636
Supply (USA) 754†, 805
Sura (Rus) 584†, 584
Suribachi (USA) 804
Susa (Lby) 398
Svetlyak (Rus) 515†, 555†, 556, 597†
SVK (Swe) 645
Swallow (Pak) 471
Swallow (RoK) 387
Swath (RoK) 387
Swift 36 ft, 42 ft (CR) 147
Swift 45 ft (Col, Ecu) 142, 174
Swift 50 ft (Mlt, Tld, Zai) 412, 680, 856
Swift 65 ft (Ant, Col, CR, Dom, EIS, Gn, Hon, Nig, Pan, StL) 9, 142†, 147, 166, 183, 268, 270, 446, 472, 598
Swift 74.5 ft (Sin) 610
Swift 77 ft (EIS, Gn) 183, 267
Swift 90 ft (Egy) 181
Swift 93 ft (Egy) 182
Swift 105 ft (Col, CR, Eth, Hon, SL) 141, 146, 186, 270, 608
Swift 110 ft (Col, DR, Egy, StK) 141, 168, 181, 597
Swift 120 ft (StV) 598
Swift FPB 20 (Bhr) 38
Swift Mk 1, Mk 2, Mk 3 (improved) (Plp, USA) 490, 801†
Swift PBR Mk II (Cmb) 81
Swift PGM (Bur) 76
Swiftsure (UK) 722
Sword (Bhr, TT) 39, 691
SX 756 (Ind, Pak) 277†, 463†
Szkwal (Pol) 500

T

T 4 (Ang, Cmb, Vtn, Yem) 8†, 80, 138†, 845, 847
T 5 (USA) 817
T 42 (Swe) 645†
T 43 (Alb, Alg, Bul, CPR, Egy, Indo, Rus, Syr) 3, 6, 74, 126, 133†, 136†, 180, 300, 559, 589, 658
T 58 (Gn) 267, 585†
T 58 PGF/PGR (Rus) 555
T 91 (Tld) 682
T 213 (Tld) 682
T 301 (Alb) 3
T-AGOS (USA) 754†
T-AVB 3 (USA) 821
Tachikaze (Jpn) 350
Tacoma 108 ft (Lbr) 394
Tacoma 270 ft (RoC) 673
Tacoma 304 ft (Tld) 678
Tacoma 328 ft (Indo) 299
Tacoma PSMM 5 (RoK) 386
Taechong I, II (DPRK) 378
Tai Hu (RoC) 672
Taiwan Type LCU (RoC) 670
Takami (Jpn) 358, 359†, 361, 362
Takatori (Jpn) 367
Takatsuki (Jpn) 350, 368
Talara (Per) 481
Tamyr (Rus) 592
Tang (Tur) 696
Tango (Rus) 529†, 529
Tanya (Rus) 560
Tapper (Swe) 644
Tarantul I (Ger, Ind, Pol, Rom, Rus, Yem) 284, 286†, 493, 511, 554, 847
Tarantul II, III (Bul, Rus) 71, 515†, 554, 555†
Tarawa (USA) 793, 798†
Tarmo (Fin) 193
TB 11PA, TB 40A (DPRK, Zai) 380, 856†
TCD 90 (Fra) 215
Technautic (Tld) 688
Tecimar (Dji) 166
Telnovsk (Rus) 587, 597†
Terrebonne Parish (Gre, Per, Spn, Tur, Ven) 260, 481, 629, 705, 839
Teshio (Jpn) 367
Tetal (Rom) 510
Thetis (Den) 158
Thetis (Gre) 258
Thomaston (Brz, USA) 60, 421†, 796†
Thong Kaeo (Tld) 684
Thornycroft 78 ft (Iraq) 313
Thornycroft type (Brz) 61
Ticonderoga (USA) 776, 777
Tiger (Bhr) 39
Tiger (Ger) 238
Tiger 40 (Sin) 611
Timsah (Egy) 181
Tir (Ind) 289
Tisza (Indo) 302
TNC 45 (Arg, Iraq, Kwt, UAE) 16, 313†, 392, 715
Tolgorae (RoK) 381
Tomba (Rus) 567
Ton (Arg, SA, UK) 17, 506†, 615, 704†, 734, 738†, 739†
Tonti (RoK) 389
Topaz (Rus) 559
Toplivo (Alb, Rus, Yem) 3, 583, 848
Toplivo 2 (Egy) 181
Toralla (Spn) 626
Tornado (UK) 745
Toti (Ita) 322
Tourville (Fra) 209
Towada (Jpn) 361
Town (Pak) 468
TR 40 (Rus) 557
TR 1700 (Arg) 11
Tracker 64 ft (Bhr, SA, Nig) 39, 447, 616
Tracker Mk 2 (Brz, Gam, Leb, Mld, Sen, Yem) 62, 230, 394, 410, 605, 849
Trafalgar (UK) 721
Tral (DPRK) 378
Tribal (Indo) 295
Trinity Marine (Ml) 413
Tripartite (Bel, Fra, Indo, Nld) 48, 218, 300, 433, 703†
Tritão (Brz) 67
Triton (UK) 747
Troika (Ger) 127†, 239, 240
Tromp (Nld) 430
Tropik (Rus) 573†
Truxtun (USA) 774
Tsaplya (Rus) 515†, 564
Tugur (Alb, Rus) 3, 596
Tuima (Fin) 191
Tumleren (Den) 156
Tupi (Brz) 54
Tursas (Fin) 197
Turunmaa (Fin) 189
Turya (Cmb, Cub, Geo, Lit, Rus, Sey, Vtn) 80, 152, 230†, 401, 555, 607, 844
Tuzhong (CPR) 138
Tydeman (Nld) 434
Tyler-Vortex 43 ft (Omn) 458
Type 01 (CPR) 119
Type 010 (CPR) 126
Type 11 (Yug) 854
Type 12 (Ind) 283
Type 15 (Sud, Yug) 639, 852
Type 16 (Yug) 852
Type 20 (Yug) 851
Type 20 GC (Alg) 7
Type 21, 22 (Cro, Yug) 150, 854
Type 021, 024 (Ban, CPR) 42, 124
Type 21 (UK) 465†, 732
Type 22 (UK) 730, 731
Type 23 (UK) 729
Type 025, 026 (CPR) 126
Type 25T (Tld) 677

Named Classes / INDEXES 875

Type 026 (Ban, CPR) 42
Type 033 (CPR) 117
Type 035 (CPR) 116
Type 037 (Bur, CPR) 76, 125
Type 039 (CPR) ..... 116†
Type 41 (Ban) 41
Type 41/61 (Mly) 404
Type 42 (Arg, UK) 13, 726, 727
Type 42 (RoC) 667
Type 051 (CPR) 118
Type 052 (CPR) 117
Type 053 (CPR) 120
Type 053 H1 (Ban) 40
Type 053 HT, 053 HT (H) (CPR, Tld) 122, 676
Type 053K (CPR) 122
Type 61 (Ban) 41
Type 61MP (Ind, Rus) 280, 544
Type 062 (CPR) 125
Type 065 (CPR) 119
Type 067 (CPR) 128
Type 068 (Ban) 45
Type 069 (Ban) 44
Type 072, 079 (CPR) 128
Type 80 (Swe) ..... 644†
Type 81MP (Pol) 492
Type 083 (CPR) 125
Type 83 (Omn) 457
Type 90 (Pol) 499
Type 092, 094 (CPR) ..... 115†, 115
Type 100 (Can) 99, 100
Type 101A (Ger) 234
Type 103B (Ger) ..... 231†, 234
Type 104K (Bul) 73
Type 122 (Ger) ..... 235, 236†
Type 123 (Ger) ..... 231†, 236
Type 124 (Ger) ..... 231†, 235†
Type 130 (Bul) 74
Type 131 (Mlt, Yug) 411, 852
Type 140 (Cro, Yug) 149, 852
Type 143, 143A, 143B (Ger) ..... 231†, 237, 238
Type 148 (Ger) 238
Type 151 (Pol) 493
Type 153 (Ger) 249
Type 180 (Jpn) 368
Type 200 (Can) 99
Type 201 (Cro, Yug) 148, 852
Type 205 (Alg, Bul, CPR *et al*) *see* Osa I
Type 205 (Ger) ..... 231†, 232, 449†
Type 206, 206A (Ger) 232
Type 206 (CPR, Tun) 125, 692
Type 206F (Pol) 494
Type 207 (Den, Nor) 156, 449
Type 207M (Pol) 495
Type 209 (Arg, Brz, Chi, Col, Ecu, Gre, Ind, Indo, Per, RoC, RoK, Tur, Ven) ..... 11, 54, 104, 139, 170, 175†, 254, 277, 293, 381, 477, 614†, 695, 837
Type 212 (Ger) ..... 231†, 233, 317†
Type 240 (Cro, Yug) 148, 851
Type 300 (Can) 99
Type 312 (CPR) ..... 127, 683†
Type 331 (Ger) 239
Type 332 (Ger) 240
Type 343 (Ger) 240
Type 350, 350-M2 (Jpn) 368
Type 350-M3, 350-M4 (Jpn) 367
Type 351 (Ger) 239
Type 369 (Ger) 247
Type 394 (Ger) 240
Type 400 (Can) 98, 99
Type 400 (Cro) 148
Type 401 (Ger) 241
Type 404 (Ger) 241
Type 410S (Pol) 495
Type 414 (Ger) 248
Type 423 (Ger) 244
Type 430A (Ger, Gre) 247, 264
Type 471 (Aust, Swe) ..... 23†
Type 500 (Can) 98
Type 500 (Pol) 497
Type 501 (Bul) 73
Type 520, 521 (Ger, Gre) 239, 261
Type 520 (CPR) 123
Type 540 (Isr) 317
Type 570 (Pol) 498
Type 600 (Can) ..... 96†, 98
Type 620 (Pol) 493
Type 641 (Cub, Ind, Lby, Pol, Rus, Syr) ..... 151, 277, 395, 492, 529†, 530
Type 667R (Pol) 498
Type 670 (Ger) 242
Type 700 (Can) 97, 98
Type 701 (Ger) 242
Type 701 (Par) 475
Type 702 (Ger) ..... 231†, 241†
Type 703 (Ger) 242
Type 704 (Ger) 241
Type 705 (Ger) 243
Type 711, 712, 715 (Ger) 245
Type 716 (Pol) 496
Type 718 (Ger) 243
Type 720 (Ger) 247
Type 722 (Ger) 247
Type 724 (Ger) 247, 248, 250
Type 725 (Ger) 248
Type 730 (Ger) 243
Type 732 (Ger) 240, 245
Type 737 (Ger) 243
Type 738 (Ger) 247
Type 740 (Ger) 241, 245, 246
Type 741 (Ger) 245
Type 742 (Ger) 244
Type 743, 744, 744A (Ger) 246
Type 745 (Ger) 244
Type 748 (Ger) ..... 231†, 244
Type 750 (Ger) 245
Type 751, 752 (Ger) ..... 231†, 244
Type 754 (Ger) 247
Type 760 (Ger) 243
Type 762 (Ger) 241
Type 763 (Ger) 242
Type 767 (Pol) 495
Type 770, 771, 773 (Rus *et al*) *see* Polnochny A, B, C
Type 773U (Lby) 399
Type 776 (Pol) 495
Type 800 (Can) 97
Type 861K (Pol) 497
Type 863 (Pol) 496
Type 864 (Rus) 568
Type 865 (Rus) 571
Type 872 (Rus) 573
Type 874 (Pol) 497
Type 877 (Alb) 5
Type 877E (Alg, Ind, Indo *et al*) *see* Kilo
Type 888 (Pol) 496
Type 900 (Can) 96
Type 905 (Ger) 247
Type 909 (Ger) 247
Type 910-915 (Ger) ..... 246†
Type 912 (Pol) 499
Type 912M (Pol) 494
Type 918 (Pol) 494, 499
Type 934 (Ger) 246
Type 945, 946 (Ger) 243
Type 956 (Ind) 291
Type 1000 (Can) 95
Type 1050 (Can) 95
Type 1075, 1081 (Ita) 322
Type 1100 (Can) 94
Type 1100 (Gre) 254
Type 1200, Type 1300 (Kwt) ..... 392†
Type 1200 (Arg, Col, Gre, Per, RoK, Tur) 11, 139, 254, 381, 477, 695
Type 1200/1300 (Can) ..... 94†, 94
Type 1241 (Ger, Ind, Pol *et al*) *see* Tarantul I
Type 1259 (Bul) 73
Type 1300 (Chi, Ecu, Indo, Ven) 104, 170, 293, 837
Type 1300 Ro-Ro (Nig) 447
Type 1400 (Brz, Tur) 54, 695
Type 1500 (Ind) 277
Type 1500 (Pol) 498
Type 2000 (Mly) 403
Type 2400 (UK) 723
Type B 23 (Rus) 562
Type B 88 (Rus) 575
Type B 93 (Rus) 575
Type B 98 (Rus, Syr) 590, 659
Type B 199 (Pol) 497
Type B 208 (Pol) 498
Type B 823 (Pol) 499
Type B 961 (Rus) 586
Type OS-1 (Pol) 496
Type P 957 (Ind) 291
Type R-30 (Pol) 498
Type S-12 (Pol) 500
Type SKS-40 (Pol) 499
Type T 26.5 (Ang) 8
Type T 2212 (SA) 616
Type ZP 1200 (Pol) 497
Typhoon (Rus) ..... 516†, 517, 566†

U

Uda (Rus) ..... 581†, 582
Udaloy, Udaloy II (Rus) ..... 515†, 542, 554†
Ugra (Ind, Rus) 289, 565
Ugra II (Rus) 579
Ula (Nor) 449
Ulsan (Ind, RoK) ..... 285†, 384
Una (Cro, Lby) ..... 148†, 395†
Una (Yug) ..... 849†, 850
Uniflite 10m (Pak) 471
Uniform (Rus) 530
Upholder (UK) 723
Urho (Fin) ..... 193, 650†
Uribe (Mex) 417
US 45 ft (Guy) 269
US Mk II, III (Iran) 309
Utenok (Rus) 564
Utka (Rus) 565
Uzushio (Jpn) 345

V

V 4 (Mex) 423
Vadim Popov (Rus) 576
Vala (Rus) 583
Valas (Fin) 194
Valday (Rus) ..... 555†, 585
Valerian Uryvayev (Lit, Rus) 401, 576
Valiant (UK) ..... 722†, 723
Valpas, improved Valpas (Fin) 197
Van Mill (EqG, Nig) 184, 445
Van Speijk (Indo) ..... 294, 295†
Van Straelen (Per) 482
Vanguard (UK) 719
Vanya (Bul, Rus, Syr) 72, 560, 658
Vanya (modified) (Rus) 560
Vasco da Gama (Por) ..... 256†, 501, 502†
Västergötland (Swe) 641
Veer (Ind) 284
Vegesack (Tur) 704
Veritas (Chi) 112
Victor I, II (Rus) ..... 524†, 528
Victor III, IV (Rus) ..... 524†, 526†, 527
Victorious (USA) 815
Victory (Sin) 609
Vidar (Nor) 452
Vigilance (Bru, Omn) ..... 68†, 457†
Vigilante (Uru) 834
Vihuri (Fin) 195
Vikhr (Rus, Syr) 590, 659
Vikram (Ind) 291
Ville (Can) 92
Vinograd (Rus) 573
Virginia (USA) 773
Vishnya (Rus) 568
Vita (Qat) 508
Vityaz (Rus) 574
Voda (Rus) 590
Voima (Fin) 194
Vosh (Rus) ..... 557, 597†
Vosper 25m (Omn) 457
Vosper 32m (Mly, Pan, Tun) 409, 472, 693
Vosper 33.5m (Per, Qat, UAE) 483, 508, 715
Vosper 62m (Tld) 687
Vosper Mk 5 (Iran) 307
Vosper QAF (UAE) 715
Vosper Thornycroft 34 ft (Nig) 447
Vosper Thornycroft 75 ft (Omn, StV, Tan) 461, 598, 674
Vosper Thornycroft 100 ft (Lby) 398
Vosper Thornycroft Mk 3, Mk 9 (Nig) 444
Vosper Thornycroft Mk 7 (Lby) 396
Vosper Type A, B (Sin) 609, 610
Vosper Type (Bhm) 36
Vostok (Rus) ..... 567†
Vukov Klanac (Yug) 853
Vulcan (USA) 806
Vydra (Bul, Egy, Rus) ..... 72†, 73, 180, 563, 638†
Vytegrales (Rus) ..... 567, 577†, 578†

W

Walchensee (Ger) 242
Walrus (Nld) 429
Wangerooge (Ger) 247
Warnow (Ger) 248
Wasp (USA) ..... 792, 798†
Wasp 11 metre (Bhr) 39
Wasp 17 metre (TT) 690, 691
Wasp 20 metre (Bhr, Blz, TT) 39, 51, 690
Wasp 30 metre (Bhr) 38
Waspada (Bru) 68
Water (Ecu, UK) 173, 746
Watercraft 45 ft (UAE) 716
Watercraft 46 ft (Omn) 461
Watercraft P 1200 (Qat) 509
Watercraft P-2000 (Nig) 446
Waters (USA) 816
Wellington (Iran) 311
Westerwald (Ger) 243
Westport (USA) 801
Whale (RoK) 390
Whidbey Island (USA) ..... 796, 798†
Whiskey (Alb, CPR, Cub, DPRK, Syr) ..... 2, 116, 151†, 376†, 656†
Whitby (Ind) 283
White Sumac (USA) 829
Wichita (USA) ..... 805†, 805
Wielingen (Bel) 47
Wild Duck (UK) 745
Wildcat (RoK) 387
Wilkes (USA) 816
Willemoes (Den) 160
Win (HK) 273
Winchester SRN6 *see* SRN6
Wisloka (Pol) 499
Wisting (Nor) 454
Wodnik (Pol) 496
Wodnik II (Rus) 579
Wood (Can) 92
Work Boats Mk II (UK) 751
Wosao (CPR) 127
Wu Chin I, II Conversions (RoC) 661
Wu Chin III Conversion (RoC) 662
Wu Kang (RoC) 671
Wulai (CPR) 134

X

X-Ray (Rus) ..... 523†, 531
Xia (CPR) 115
Xing Fengshan (CPR) 132

Y

Y 301, Y 301 (improved) (Bur) 77
Y type (Den) 161
Yaeyama (Jpn) 358
Yahagi (Jpn) 368
Yamagumo (Jpn) ..... 351†, 351, 359
Yamayuri (Com, Jpn) 145
Yan Jiu (CPR) 137
Yanha, modified Yanha (CPR) 137
Yankee I, II (Rus) ..... 516†, 519†, 519
Yankee (conversion) (Rus) ..... 516†, 520†, 523, 524†, 528†
Yankee Notch (Rus) 528
Yankee Pod, Yankee Stretch (Rus) 530
Yannan (CPR) 134
Yanxi (CPR) 134
Yarrow 308 ft (Mly) 403
Yarrow 320 ft (Tld) 677
Yavuz (Tur) 699
Yaz (Rus) ..... 557, 597†
Yellowstone (USA) 803
Yelva (Cub, Lby, Rus) 154, 400, 590
Yen Bai, Yen Kuan, Yen Tai (CPR) ..... 134†
Yen Fang (CPR) 135
Yen Hsi (CPR) 133
Yen Pai (CPR) 136
Yen Ting (CPR) 130
Yenka (CPR) 136
Yenlai (CPR) 133
Yenlun (CPR) 133
Yermak (Rus) 592
Yevgenya (Ang, Bul, Cub, Ind, Iraq, Moz, Nic, Rus, Syr, Vtn, Yem) ..... 8, 73, 152, 287, 314, 427, 442, 560†, 560, 658, 845, 848
Yildiz (Tur) 701
YMP (Tur) 703
YO 65 (Den) 163
YO 174 ft, 235 ft (RoK) 389
YOG/YO (Mex, Plp) 422, 488
Yokohama (Tld) 687
Yongdo (DPRK) ..... 376†
YP, YR (Ecu) 173
YP 654 (USA) 801
YSB (Egy) ..... 181†
YTB (SAr) 602
YTL (Par) 475
YTL 422 (Plp, Tld) 489, 687
Yubari (Jpn) 353
Yuch'In (Ban, CPR) 44, 45, 128
Yudao (CPR) 128
Yuen Feng (RoC) 671
Yug (Rus) 572
Yukan (CPR) 128, 135
Yukto I, II (DPRK) 380
Yuliang (CPR) 128
Yulin (Tan) 674
Yuling (CPR) 128
Yun Hsing (RoC) 673
Yung Gang (CPR) 137
Yunnan (CPR, Sri) ..... 128†, 128, 638
Yura (Jpn) 356
Yurka (Egy, Rus, Vtn) 180, 559, 845
Yusotei (Jpn) 357
Yuushio (Jpn) 344
YW Type (Ecu, Plp) 173, 488

Z

Z (Egy) 176
Z-28 (Arg) 20
Zafar (Iran) ..... 308†
Zarya (Rus) ..... 573†
Zbyszko (Pol) 499
Zenit (Rus) 595
Zeus (USA) 818
Zhuk (Ang, Ben, Bul, Cmb, CpV, Con, Cub, Est, Eth, Gn, Iraq, Moz, Mrt, Nic, Rus, Sey, Syr, Vtn, Yem) ..... 8†, 72, 80, 102, 145, 154, 186, 268, 313, 415, 427, 442, 515†, 556, 597†, 607, 657, 844, 847
Zodiac (Cmb) 80
Zuiderkruis (Spn) 630
Zuiun (Jpn) 373
Zwaardvis (Nld) ..... 429, 660†

Aircraft by Countries

Algeria 7
Angola 9
Argentina 14, 15
Australia 27, 28
Bahrain 38
Belgium 49
Belize 52
Bolivia 53
Brazil 59
Brunei 69
Bulgaria 71
Burma 78
Cameroon 82
Canada 90
Chile 107
China 123
Colombia 141
Cuba 152
Cyprus, Republic 155
Denmark 158
Dominican Republic 168
Ecuador 172
Egypt 178
Finland 198
France 213, 214
Gabon 229
Germany 236, 237
Ghana 252
Greece 257
Hong Kong 273
Iceland 275
India 285, 286
Indonesia 297
Iran 308
Ireland 316
Israel 320
Italy 330
Japan, MDF 355
Japan, MSA 366
Korea, South 386
Libya 397
Malaysia 405
Mauritania 414
Mauritius 415
Mexico 418
Netherlands 433
New Zealand 440
Nigeria 444
Norway 451
Pakistan 467
Panama 472
Papua New Guinea 473
Paraguay 475
Peru 480
Philippines 486
Poland 494
Portugal 503
Qatar 509
Romania 511
Russia and associated States 550, 551
Saudi Arabia 600
Senegal 606
Seychelles 608
Singapore 610
South Africa 615
Spain 624, 625
Sudan 639
Surinam 640
Sweden 644
Syria 657
Taiwan 667
Thailand 680
Turkey 701
United Arab Emirates 716
United Kingdom 732, 733
United States of America (Navy) 788, 789, 790
United States of America (Coast Guard) 826, 827
Uruguay 834
Venezuela 839
Vietnam 843
Yugoslavia 851

FLOREAL
Ocean Capable Patrol Vessel

6 units for the French Navy.

CHANTIERS DE L'ATLANTIQUE

CHANTIERS DE L'ATLANTIQUE / S.A.
38, Avenue Kléber / 75116 Paris / France
Tel. (33-1) 47 55 27 54 / Telex : 645 043 SHIPYAR / Fax : (33-1) 47 55 27 77